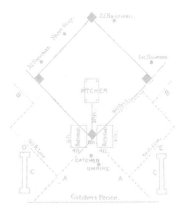

THE DICKSON
BASEBALL DICTIONARY

THIRD EDITION

ALSO BY PAUL DICKSON

Baseball's Greatest Quotations

Slang: The Topical Dictionary of Americanisms

The Mature Person's Guide to Kites, Yo-Yos, Frisbees and Other Childlike Diversions

Dickson's Word Treasury

Dickson's Joke Treasury

Baseball: The President's Game (with William B. Mead)

The Congress Dictionary: The Ways and Meanings of Capitol Hill (with Paul Clancy)

War Slang: American Fighting Words and Phrases from the Civil War to the Gulf War

The Worth Book of Softball

Sputnik: The Shock of the Century

The Hidden Language of Baseball

The Bonus Army: An American Epic (with Thomas B. Allen)

The Joy of Keeping Score

Family Words: A Dictionary of the Secret Language of Families

THE
DICKSON
BASEBALL
DICTIONARY

THIRD EDITION

PAUL DICKSON

*Edited and Augmented
by Skip McAfee*

W. W. NORTON & COMPANY

New York · London

For information about permission to reproduce selections from this book,
write to Permissions, W. W. Norton & Company, Inc.,
500 Fifth Avenue, New York, NY 10110

For information about special discounts for bulk purchases,
please contact W. W. Norton Special Sales at
specialsales@wwnorton.com or 800-233-4830

Manufacturing by RR Donnelley, Willard
Book design by Charlotte Staub Thomas
Production manager: Andrew Marasia

Library of Congress Cataloging-in-Publication Data

Dickson, Paul.
The Dickson baseball dictionary / Paul Dickson ; edited and augmented
by Skip McAfee.—3rd ed.
p. cm.
Includes bibliographical references.
ISBN 978-0-393-06681-4 (hardcover)
1. Baseball—United States—Dictionaries. I. McAfee, Skip. II. Title.
GV862.3.D53 2009
796.357—dc22

2008051238

W. W. Norton & Company, Inc.
500 Fifth Avenue, New York, N.Y. 10110
www.wwnorton.com

W. W. Norton & Company Ltd.
Castle House, 75/76 Wells Street, London W1T 3QT

1 2 3 4 5 6 7 8 9 0

TO ANDREW AND ALEX
who brought their old man back
to baseball, and
TO SKIP
who kept this project afloat
for so many years.

Also, Nancy rules.

CONTENTS

THE JARGON
OF THE DIAMOND

The diamond has a language all its own;
If a player makes an error, it's a "bone";
    If he attempts the "squeeze"
    And strikes out, it's a "breeze";
A play at which the fans belch forth a groan.

A safe drive to the field is called a "bingle";
If good for one base only, it's a "single";
    If the hurler throws a "cripple"
    And the batter clouts a "triple,"
The swat will put the nerves of fans a-tingle.

When a runner's left on base, 'tis said he "died."
If he goes out on a high fly, he has "skied";
    A one-hand stop's a "stab";
    The pitcher's mound, the "slab";
Successful plays are certainly "inside."

When a player's making good his work is "grand."
But let him boot just one and he's "panned";
    If he comes up in a "pinch"
    And he "whiffs" well, it's a cinch,
The fickle fans will yell, "He should be 'canned.'"

—*Baseball Magazine*, Oct. 1916

PREFACE
TO THE
THIRD EDITION

Before the ink had dried on the first edition of this book, which was published in the spring of 1989, good people—fans of baseball, and both professional and self-taught lovers of American words—began to call and write with their lists of omissions from what I had deemed to be a work that defined the national game one entry at a time. I had thought that the dictionary pushed the whole business of baseball terminology and slang to its logical conclusion.

I was wrong.

That first edition, immodestly titled *The Dickson Baseball Dictionary*, contained 5,000 entries. With the help of more than a hundred new recruits and volunteer lexicologists led by the indefatigable Robert "Skip" McAfee, who signed on as editor for the second edition, the *New Dickson Baseball Dictionary* was published exactly 10 years later in the spring of 1999 with nearly 7,000 entries, which seemed, at the time, to be fairly close to definitive at last.

Wrong again.

Ten more years have elapsed, and you are now looking at *The Dickson Baseball Dictionary, Third Edition*. It contains no fewer than 10,000 entries and more than 18,000 definitions; and more than 400 people have helped with the project. If someone had told me at the very beginning of this undertaking that there would be 10,000 terms to define, I would have said this was impossible. This accomplishment is not one to be credited to the author and his army of lexical irregulars, but rather one to be scored to the game itself, with an assist to that rich and flexible entity known as the English language.

I twice underestimated the size of this undertaking for several reasons.

1. The language of the game is, as a roster of readers pointed out, more varied, complex, and fraught with subtle distinctions than I had originally imagined—sort of like the game itself. This was manifested in the number of terms that had more than one meaning. There are 15 baseball meanings for *hook*, 13 for *slot*, 11 each for *break, jump,* and *cut*, 9 apiece for *crack, flip,* and *catch,* and 8 for *hole.*

2. The game outside the lines has continued to change, occasioning the need for terms like *wild card, realignment, Executive Council, interleague play,* and *contraction,* to say nothing of terms of self-abuse like *greenie* and *steroid.* The growth of *sabermetrics* and other attempts to better understand the game through statistical terms has mushroomed.

3. Old-school terms that had worked when I began collecting terms to define are being supplemented or even replaced. The late Shirley Povich, writing in *The Washington Post* in 1996, summed it up for the old-school vocabulary of the game: "Almost gone from the language is the 'curveball' that was such a staple for so many generations. It's the play-by-play orators who have substituted with the 'sidearm' and 'forkball.' The 'screwball,' too, has all but vanished from the lexicon of baseball. But the fastball has taken on multiple identities. Play-by-play men talk now of a 'four-seam fastball,' a 'two-seam fastball,' and 'a cut fastball,' whatever that is." Since Povich's passing, a new crop of pitching terms have come into play, including such verbal oddities as the *Bugs Bunny changeup* and the *gyroball,* the latter made instantly famous by Daisuke Matsuzaka in the spring of 2007.

So with 25 years—give or take a year—since I began writing down a list of terms to be defined, I can only now claim that this is as close as can be gotten to definitive; but given the nature of the game and the nature of the language, the collecting of information and the recruiting of new volunteers continues.

Paul Dickson
Garrett Park, Maryland

INTRODUCTION

Baseball needs a Webster and a standing–Revision Board to keep the dictionary of the game up to date. The sport is building its own language so steadily that, unless some step soon is taken to check the inventive young men who coin the words that attach themselves to the pastime, interpreters will have to be maintained in every grand stand to translate for the benefit of those who merely love the game and do not care to master it thoroughly.

—Hugh S. Fullerton, "The Baseball Primer,"
The American Magazine, June 1912

In the early part of the 20th century an odd movement started: Its purpose was to suppress baseball slang. Time has obscured some of the details, but what it amounted to was a movement toward linguistic purity and away from sports-page baseballese at a time when it was booming and those outside fandom were confused. Important voices—*Collier's Weekly* and the *New York Tribune*—were early leaders of the crusade.

In 1913 the *Chicago Record-American* began covering games two ways: one account in the slang of the time and, next to it, a description of the game in "less boisterous" terms. A Professor McClintock of the English department at the University of Chicago brought the matter to national attention when he suggested that the republic would be better served if baseball slang were dropped and if, for starters, the newspapers would start describing the sport in dictionary English.

The baseball slang of McClintock's day was prolific and inventive. In his three-volume *Dictionary of 1913 Baseball and Other Lingo* (2001–2003), based primarily on reporting in the *San Francisco Bulletin* for Feb.–May 1913, Gerald L. Cohen unearthed no fewer than 21 different terms for *pitcher*: box artist, boxman, curvist, flinger, gunner, heaver, hillman, hurler, hurlster/hurlester, hurlsmith, mound artist, moundsman, moundster, pitcher, slab artist, slabman, slabster, slinger, speedburner, tosser, and twirler.

McClintock's call came at a time when, for example, *The Washington Post*'s Joe Campbell ("the Chaucer of baseball") would write, "Amie Rusie made a Svengali pass in front of Charlie Reilly's lamps and he carved three nicks in the weather," as a way of saying that Rusie had gotten Reilly to strike out.

A few managers and players actually agreed with McClintock, but there was little sympathy expressed by the press, which whipped McClintock's notion into something big. "The question has assumed the importance of a national issue," said an editorial in the *Charleston News and Courier*. "It has received editorial discussion in the columns of the most influential newspapers, and it has aroused interest from end to end of this baseball-loving land." Calling the notion the "injury which is now proposed," the paper went on to say, "It is to be hoped, and it may reasonably be expected, that the movement will not accomplish the results which its more radical advocates desire. Baseball stories told in conventional English are dull reading indeed; and it is a pertinent fact that the decadence of cricket in England is attributed by many British newspapers to the failure of the press to put brightness or 'ginger' into the descriptions of the game."

The Washington Post chose to make fun of McClintock by describing play using dictionary English. Sample: "Johnson gave the batter a free pass to first" becomes "Mr. Johnson pitched four balls that in immediate sequence made a detour of the plate, which, according to the rules of the game, entitled the batter to go to first base, despite the fact that he had not even aimed his bat at the baseball in any one instance." After a thorough roasting, the *Post* concluded, "Much of the English used by Professor McClintock himself was once regarded as slang."

On the other hand, *The Nation* magazine saw the threat as a serious one and wrote about it as if it were a disease: "One of the most puzzling problems of this puzzling era is the effect wrought upon our native speech by contact with the national pastime."

Grantland Rice, then "Sporting Editor" of the *Nashville Tennessean*, wrote a poetic rebuttal in a ditty called "Knocking Slang" which ended with this stanza:

> *Nix on this slang; it's on the blink,*
> > *And my remarks are here emphatic.*
> *The geek who slings it through the ink*
> > *Has beetles in his bush league attic.*
> *Let's slip in the Big Revive.*
> > *For scholarly and classic diction.*
> *Come on you mutts now, with the dive*
> > *And do a Brodie at this fiction.*

All of this was, of course, a passing controversy that amounted to little; but it did serve to drive home the point that baseball had its own ever-changing language and that it was not to be meddled with by learned disciples of the King's English, no matter how many initials they had after their names.

Ironically, not too many years would pass before men and women with PhDs would be making names for themselves not by decrying slang but by collecting it—not only that of the diamond, but also of the carnival, the hobo jungle, the railroad yard, the soda fountain—and publishing it in *American Speech*, that superb journal devoted, then as now, to the riches of the American dialect.

Sometimes lost in all of this discussion of the propriety of slang is the fact that it provided for a remarkably rich and effective style of writing, one that allowed the drama of nine innings to be compressed into one socko, lung-straining sentence. Such sentences tended to retain their vitality for many years. An example from the *San Francisco Examiner* for April 13, 1932: "Greeting big George Earnshaw like a long lost 'cousin,' Babe Ruth and the New York Yankees fell upon the right-handed act of the Athletics this chilly afternoon, blasted him off the field in four innings and outslugged the American League champions 12 to 6."

If baseball is a game of slang, it is also a game of heaped-on modifiers. A word like *single* seldom stands naked. Listen, as one is described in a sentence by Richard Justice of *The Washington Post* (May 22, 1986): "[It was] the only California run scored after Davis had wild-pitched rookie Wally Joyner (three for four) into scoring position and then given up a broken-bat, opposite-field bloop single to Brian Downing."

The baseball prose of the daily press and later the broadcasters was a part of the entertainment. "What makes 'baseball slang' a joy is that it changes overnight and varies with the ingenuity of the reporter; today the Babe elevates the pill, tomorrow the Bambino clouts the sphere—and so *ad infinitum*" is how a pro-slang editorial in *The Outlook* put it on June 13, 1923.

A few other conclusions derived from the study of baseball language are in order.

1. The basic language of the game transcends eras.

In 1999, at the All-Star Game in Boston, Cal Ripken Jr. was honored as one of the 100 best players of the 20th century. After mingling with the likes of Ted Williams and Carlton Fisk, Ripken told Rich Thompson of the *Boston Herald* that what amazed him the most about meeting some of these players, whom he had only known as baseball cards when he was a kid, was the common language they shared. "I spent some time earlier in the afternoon with some of the great baseball players that were nominated and what was cool to me is that the language of baseball transcends different eras. We talked baseball with the same dimensions and strike zones."

2. Baseball is a metaphoric circus.

The game has a particular infatuation with what one critic of sportswriters termed "the incorrect use of correct words." There are hundreds of examples, but the point can be made by simply listing a selection of synonyms for the hard-hit ball or line drive. It is variously known as an *aspirin*, *BB*, *bolt*, *clothesline*, *frozen rope*, *pea*, *rocket*, and *seed*. A player's throwing arm seems to be called everything but an arm: *gun*, *hose*, *rifle*, *soupbone*, *whip*, and *wing*, to name just a few. The arm is not the only renamed body part. From top to bottom, players have *lamps* (eyes), a *pipe* (neck or throat), *hooks* (hands), *wheels* (legs), and *tires* (feet).

So many allusions are made to food and dining—such as pitches that seem to "fall off the table"—that a fairly well-balanced diet suggests itself in terms like *can of corn*, *cup of coffee*, *fish cakes*, *banana stalk*, *mustard*, *pretzel*, *rhubarb*, *green pea*, *juice*, *meat*, *grapefruit league*, and *tater*. Among the many terms for the ball itself are *apple*, *cantaloupe*, *egg*, *lemon*, *orange*, *pea*, *potato*, and *tomato*. Implements? There is the *plate* (also known as the *platter*, *pan*, and *dish*) and, of course, the *forkball*. Dessert? The red abrasion from a slide into base is a *strawberry*, and the fan's time-honored sound of disapproval is a *raspberry*.

The game proudly displays its rustic roots, and there is a tone to the language of the game that is remarkably pastoral. If any imagery dominates, it is that of rural America. Even under a dome, it is a game of *fields* and *fences*, where *ducks [sit] on the pond* and pitchers sit in the *catbird seat*. New players come out of the *farm system*, and a *farm hand* that pitches may get to work in the *bullpen*.

3. Basic ballyard slang comes back from obscurity.

Slang, we are always being told, is ephemeral. This is only somewhat borne out by baseball slang because, for every seemingly fleeting term or phrase, there seems to be one that hangs on for several generations. Many terms that began as slang have been so widely accepted and are used so routinely that they are no longer considered slang. This point was first made in an article in the *Saturday Review* in 1933 in which the author, Murray Godwin, pointed to the permanence of such "slang" as *sacrifice* and *wind up*. Compare this, for example, to the slang of popular music or high school, which seems to change constantly.

Etymologist Peter Tamony put it much more strongly. In his essay on the term "Dick Smith" (a name assigned to a loner in both baseball and horse racing slang), he wrote (*Newsletter and Wasp*, Sept. 15, 1939), "It is always amusing to be able to run down the history and origin of a real slang word. Real slang always laughs at the professors and others who hold that it is ephemeral. They mistake mere metaphor and simile for slang. To hold that slang is largely ephemeral is to say that dress is ephemeral because women's fashions change four times a year. A large part of our slang has a long, long history, but records of it are short. It is only since the advent of the modern sports page, about 1900, that this vital and human aspect, this color of our speech, has been properly recorded."

Baseball slang is in fact hard to kill, and specific terms have a way of asserting themselves after being written off as archaic. While researching this book, I encountered many articles that declared as dead terms that are still very much alive today. For example, a 1964 article in *Baseball Digest*, written by Tim Horgan of the *Boston Traveler*, tells us, "There are no more bleachers. They are now 'porches.'" The same article reported that "No pitcher today . . . throws a fastball or, as our forefathers knew it, 'a high hard one.'" In 1933, Damon Runyon described a hit that "used to be called" a "Texas Leaguer"; and in 1937, sportswriter Curley Grieve of the *San Francisco Examiner* told his readers, "A left-handed hurler is no longer a southpaw. He's a cock-eyed hurler."

Similarly, a 1982 article on baseball slang that appeared in the USAir inflight magazine listed the term *wheelhouse* (for the area of the batter's greatest hitting strength) as one of a number of bygone words that had "gone down swinging." If the term is dead, no one has bothered to tell the many writers and sportscasters who use it regularly.

Then there is the term *can of corn*, which 20 years ago was annually declared dead but comes back as surely as Opening Day. "One phrase that's out is can of corn," wrote Scott Ostler in the *Los Angeles Times* (1986): "Several players warned me to stay away from that one." New York Mets catcher Gary Carter deemed the term "ancient history" in an article in the *St. Petersburg Times* (1987) on the latest in baseball slang. But then it came back in a big way; it's presently everywhere, and nobody is forecasting its demise. In fact, according to an article in *USA Today* (March 30, 2007) entitled "Do foreign executives balk at sports jargon?," *can of corn* has become business jargon for "a decision or action that is a no-brainer; a product that sells itself."

On the other hand, consider another vegetable. Several writers have reported the term *pea* (for a ball batted or pitched so fast that it can hardly be seen) as an example of the very latest in baseball lingo, even though it can be traced back at least to 1910. To fill out the platter, there is *rhubarb*, which never seems to have gone out of vogue since it made its baseball debut in the late 1930s.

4. Baseballese tends to be low-key and light.

Although some of the terms for whacking the ball with the bat are strong (to *crush, smash, powder*) and *base stealing* is aptly named, other actions are described in absurdly mild terms. The most glaring example can be heard when the pitcher throws the ball at the batter in an attempt to intimidate him.

Terms associated with this act include *bean* and *beanball, dust* and *duster, brush* and *brushback, knockdown, shave,* and *barber.* It is sometimes called a *purpose pitch* or *chin music.* Such behavior may lead to a noisy and sometimes violent confrontation that is called a *rhubarb.*

Compare this to a headline run over a *Washington Post* interview with New York Giants linebacker Lawrence Taylor a few days before Super Bowl XXI: "Taylor: 'Kill Shots' Make the Game." Comedian George Carlin (*Brain Droppings,* 1997) has a routine in which he compares the pastoral game of baseball to football, which is played on a gridiron where there is blitzing, red-dogging, and drives into enemy territory, and where bombs are thrown. Baseball is played in a park, and the offensive plays include the free pass, homer, and sacrifice fly. In football you spear, march, and pile on; in baseball you walk, stretch, and run home. In an op-ed piece in *The New York Times* (Sept. 6, 1987), Steve Palay pointed out that the language of arms control is very close to that of football (throw weight, end run, hammering out an agreement, etc.), but that it would be better served if it were taken from baseball. "Arms control is not won," Palay concluded, "it is played. And going into 'extra innings' sounds so much better than 'sudden death.'"

"In baseball," wrote Ira Berkow (*The New York Times,* June 24, 1986), "there is a certain lightness of spirit that doesn't exist in football. What can you say about the 'blitzes' and 'bombs' in football other than try to avoid them? But not so baseball. On a Game-of-the-Week telecast, Vin Scully once noted that something was buzzing around the head of the batter, who then stepped out of the box to swat it. 'That,' said Scully, 'must be the dreaded infield fly.'"

All of this is not to say that baseball terminology lacks a dark side. A letter from Jim Land of Felton, Calif., published in *The Sporting News* (Oct. 5, 1987), made the point: "Baseball terminology, steeped in tradition, pays tribute to chicanery. For example, stealing bases, stealing signs, cheating toward the lines, robbing homers and hits, stabs, swipes, bluffs and suicide squeeze are all part of the game. There are hidden ball tricks, faked tags and in-the-vicinity plays."

5. Clubhouse chatter defies logic.

For reasons that are unclear, baseball seems driven to come up with its own terms for things that are used widely in other sports. Everywhere else, teams are piloted by head coaches; but baseball insists on *managers* (and with rare exception dresses them like players), and all the referees are called *umpires.* If other sports had to deal with discrimination and segregation, baseball dealt with the *color line.* Substitutes are good enough for most sports, but not for baseball, which insists on loading its *benches* and *bullpens* with *firemen, pinch hitters, pinch runners,* and *platoon players.* Baseball players never seem to turn, they always *pivot.* In realms as diverse as bowling and bombing, a *strike* is a hit; but in baseball alone it is a miss. Out of bounds works for everyone else, but baseball insists on *foul territory*. If the same facility is used for football on Sunday and baseball on Monday, it is transformed overnight from a *stadium* to a *ballpark*. And the *locker rooms* used by the football players become *clubhouses* for the baseball players.

6. The major influence on baseball language was Henry Chadwick.

If one person had to be singled out for having the most influence on the official language of the game, it would be a pioneering Englishman named Henry Chadwick, but this may be only because he came along so early that he was essentially given the opportunity to fill in blanks. He wrote the first rule book, created the first box score, and served as one of the game's first journalists. He also created many of the early instructional baseball manuals that were used during the latter half of the 19th century.

There have been several attempts to assign somebody else the title of Father of Baseballese. Among the contenders are a number of midwestern and western baseball writers who, writing in the late 19th century, had a great impact in building the vocabulary needed to describe the game. John Allen Krout, in his 1929 *Annals of American Sport*, gives some of their names: "Shortly after 1883 Leonard Washburn, Finley Peter Dunne, who earned national fame as the creator of Mr. Dooley, and Charles Seymour began to write their entertaining stories of Anson's White Stockings for the Chicago papers."

But all of this is somewhat misleading because so many people have had a continuing impact on the language of baseball. A very small and incomplete list would have to include Branch Rickey, Casey Stengel, Earl Weaver, Red Barber, Yogi Berra, Ring Lardner, Red Smith, Dizzy Dean, Jim Murray, Gaylord Perry, Theodore A. "TAD" Dorgan, Alexander Cartwright, Pierce Egan, Jim Brosnan, Satchel Paige, Willard Mullin, Leo Durocher, Babe Ruth, and Dennis Eckersley.

7. The influence of baseball on American English
   at large is stunning and strong.

In *The Old Ball Game* (1971), that great work on the lore of baseball, Tristram Potter Coffin wrote, "No other sport and few other occupations have introduced so many phrases, so many words, so many twists into our language as has baseball. The true test comes in the fact that old ladies who have never been to the ballpark, coquettes who don't know or care who's on first, men who think athletics begin and end with a pair of goal posts, still know and use a great deal of baseball-derived terminology. Perhaps other sports in their efforts to replace baseball as 'our national pastime' have two strikes on them before they come to bat."

Perhaps the best way to drive this home is to present a partial list of terms and phrases that started in baseball (or, at least, were given a major boost by it) but that have much wider application, to wit: A team, ace, Alibi Ike, Annie Oakley, back-to-back, ballpark figure, bat a thousand, batting average, bean, bench, benchwarmer, Black Sox, bleacher, bonehead, boner, box score, the breaks, breeze/breeze through, Bronx cheer, bunt, bush, bush league(r), butterfingers, charley horse, choke, circus catch, clutch, clutch hitter, curveball, doubleheader, double play, extra innings, fan, fouled out, gate money, get one's innings, get to first base, go to bat for, grandstander, grandstand play, ground rules, hardball, heads up, hit and run, "hit 'em where they ain't," hit the dirt, home run, hot stove league, hustler, in the ballpark, in a pinch, in there pitching, "it ain't over 'til it's over," "it's a (whole) new ball game," jinx, "keep your eye on the ball," Ladies' Day, Louisville Slugger, minor league, muff, "nice guys finish last," ninth inning rally, off base, on-deck, on the ball, on the bench, out in left field, out of my league, phenom, pinch hitter, play ball with, play the field, play-by-play, rain check, rhubarb, right off the bat, rookie, rooter, Ruthian, safe by a mile, "say it ain't so, Joe," screwball, seventh-inning stretch, showboat, shut out, smash hit, southpaw, spitball, squeeze play, Stengelese, step up to the plate, strawberry, strike out, sucker, switch hitter, team play, Tinker to Evers to Chance, touch all the bases, two strikes against him, "wait 'til next year," whitewash, "Who's on First?," windup, "you can't win 'em all," "you could look it up."

Elting E. Morison, writing in *American Heritage* (Aug.–Sept. 1986), asked, "Why is baseball terminology so dominant an influence in the language? Does it suggest that the situations that develop as the game is played are comparable to the patterns of our daily work? Does the sport imitate the fundamentals of the national life or is the national life shaped to an extent by the character of the sport? In any case, here is an opportunity to reflect on the meaning of what I think I heard Reggie Jackson say in his spot on a national network in the last World Series: 'The country is as American as baseball.'"

HOW TO USE
THE
DICTIONARY

Having long thought that I needed a baseball dictionary, I imagined what one would look and feel like well before the first word of the first edition was put down on paper. From the outset the idea was that it had to be useful to a nine-year-old looking for a clear definition of the infield fly rule, but it also had to be a book that would appeal to two of the toughest audiences for the printed word: the baseball fanatic and the lover of language.

First and foremost, this is a dictionary meant for these three users. But it is also a book for browsing, and for that reason there is flexibility in the presentation of entries. If, for example, a good story begs to be told as a digression, it gets told.

Nonetheless, a general format was adopted for the first edition and is used, with minor adjustments, in the third edition:

Entry. The term is entered in boldface, followed (if necessary) by part of speech (when there is more than one definition or when there could be confusion), followed by the definition, which may also include the historic background of the concept or object in question, as well as abbreviation, alternate spelling, example(s) of use, and variation. If there are two or more definitions for the term, the number of the definition is given in boldface. If the term is archaic or obsolete, the abbreviation *hist.* is given after the entry. Great restraint has been exercised in using the *hist.* label because, as I pointed out in the Introduction, certain terms have a way of making a comeback at the very moment they are deemed to be dead. (I had been convinced that *yakker* [for curveball] was archaic until I heard Jim Palmer use the term twice during a baseball telecast. I had already labeled *twirler* [for pitcher] as archaic when I read this line in the July 1, 1987, *Lewiston* [Maine] *Daily Sun* in an account of a game in Jay, Maine: "The Litchfield twirler had a shutout until the seventh inning.") A term is labeled *hist.* only when it refers to a rule, practice, or element of the game that is no longer a part of it and that seems unlikely ever to stage a comeback.

Cross-references. A term appearing in italic letters within a definition or at the end of a definition indicates a cross-reference and may be consulted as a separate entry. Cross-references include See also, Compare, and Synonym(s).

Illustration. When it appears useful to the reader, the definition may be accompanied by an illustration that clarifies or expands on the definition.

1st Use. A dated reference may accompany the definition. In most cases it is, of course, impossible to cite the very earliest example that appears in print, so this feature is really meant to give the reader a feel for the relative antiquity and early use of the term. Lest there be any question, the citation given will be the earliest found. Many of these citations are marked with the names of the researchers who found them, primarily Edward J. Nichols, Peter Tamony, David Shulman, Gerald Cohen, Peter Morris, Barry Popik, and Charles D. Poe. For reasons of space, not every "first use" includes the actual quotation. Most of those without the actual quote are from Nichols' 1939 Pennsylvania State College doctoral dissertation, *An Historical Dictionary of Baseball Terminology*. Nichols relied heavily on the A.G. Spalding collection of baseball material at the New York Public Library, which includes the scrapbooks of Henry Chadwick, and on the multivolumed records of the Knickerbocker Base Ball Club, maintained since 1845. These records contain rulings, discussions, and other material that have never been published, so a reference to the Knickerbocker Rules of 1845 (or any other year) pertains to these records.

Usage Note. There may be special context in which a term may be used—or in which, in the author's opinion, it should not be used.

Etymology. When possible, the history of the term is given. If there are several theories about the origin of a term, all will be given and often they will be followed by a discussion of their relative merit. Such explanations are not attempted when the term itself appears to suggest its origin, as is the case with *fly ball.* Some terms will have more than one etymology and these may be in conflict with one another. The principle at work in this dictionary is that *all* the claims should be presented. If there is a bias lurking in this book, it is that words and phrases can have a motley assortment of etymologies that have acted corroboratively to give the term momentum and popularity. One of them may, in fact, be the original, but that does not mean the others did not have important influence.

Extended Use. Examples may be given of use of the term in the English language at large. It is through these subentries that one gets to see the immense influence of baseball on the American language. Interestingly, there are many terms that no longer sound like baseball terms but which appear to have sprung first from the diamond, such as *jazz*.

NOTES

Abbreviations. The following abbreviations are used throughout this dictionary:

Abbrev.	Abbreviation	*OED*	*Oxford English Dictionary*
adj.	adjective	pron.	pronounced
adv.	adverb	specif.	specifically
Co.	Company	Syn.	Synonym
esp.	especially	Univ.	University
hist.	obsolete or archaic	*v.*	verb
n.	noun	Var.	Variation

Expert authority. In certain cases an expert has been asked to contribute a detailed definition of a term. In these cases the name of the individual is listed at the end of the definition.

Softball terms. It has long been assumed that the vocabulary of softball and that of baseball are identical or almost so. This assumption is wrong and commonly made by those who think of softball as a pale reflection of baseball. Folks who play the game and spend odd hours with their heads poked in rule books or the latest issue of *Balls and Strikes* know better. More than one hundred softball terms occur here, all of which are clearly marked [softball term]. These are terms unique to softball or are definitions of baseball terms with significantly different meanings.

Deanisms. Every attempt has been made to give the source of the quotes used in the book. However, quotes attributed to colorful Hall of Fame pitcher Dizzy Dean have proven elusive because they have appeared in several versions of often undated pamphlets and ballpark handouts named "Dizzy's Definitions," "Dizzy Dean's Dictionary," and the like.

Excluded terms. Countless terms were rejected because there was only a single citation attesting to their use. It appears that from time to time someone sits down and cranks out a list of terms native to the national game that may or may not have ever been uttered by an actual player. Terms that appear to last for only a moment and leave no evidence that they had application were rejected.

Ballparks. The dictionary includes entries for those ballpark names that have become iconic rather than attempting to list all names.

Names of ballplayers. Nicknames of specific ballplayers are not included.

Baseball teams. All current major-league teams, and many former major-league teams, as well as selected teams from the Negro leagues and a few minor leagues, are entered under their nicknames, not their geographic or city names.

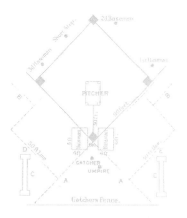

THE
DICTIONARY
A–Z

A

A 1. See *Class A*. **2.** Scoreboard abbrev. for *assist*, 2. **3.** Box score abbrev. for *attendance*, 2. The figure in parentheses after the attendance figure indicates park capacity.

AA 1. See *Class AA*. **2.** Abbrev. for *American Association*, 1. **3.** Abbrev. for *American Association*, 3.

AAA See *Class AAA*.

AAABA Abbrev. for *All-American Amateur Baseball Association*.

AABC Abbrev. for *American Amateur Baseball Congress*.

AABS Abbrev. for *aggressive at-bat stat.*

AAGPBL Abbrev. for *All-American Girls Professional Baseball League*.

AB 1. Scorecard and box score abbrev. for *at-bat*, 2. **2.** *n.* Syn. of *at-bat*, 1. "A time at bat is often referred to as 'an A.B.'" (*The New York Times*, June 2, 1929).

A-ball Minor-league baseball at the Class A level. "At this time last year, he [José Morban] was playing A-ball, but he's made vast improvements" (Mike Hargrove, quoted in *The Baltimore Sun*, July 11, 2003).

ABCA Abbrev. for *American Baseball Coaches Association*.

ABC ball A style of offensive baseball in which basic fundamentals are used to advance runners one or two bases at a time.

ABL Abbrev. for *Alaska Baseball League*.

Abner Doubleday Field The nearly 10,000-seat ballpark in Cooperstown, N.Y., that rests on the site of the former cow pasture where Civil War officer Abner Doubleday allegedly invented baseball in 1839. Owned and man-

Abner Doubleday Field. Alleged birthplace of baseball as it looked in 1919. *National Baseball Library and Archives, Cooperstown, N.Y.*

aged by the village of Cooperstown, the field is still used regularly; from 1940 through 2008, it has been the site for the annual *Hall of Fame Game*. The original brick portion of the park dates to 1939. Syn. *birthplace of baseball.*

aboard On base; e.g., "Smith hit a home run with two men aboard." The term is one of several long-standing nautical allusions in baseball terminology. IST USE. 1907 (*McClure's Magazine*, April; Edward J. Nichols).

above the hands Said of a high pitched ball. The term has come into common play since the 1990 World Series.

abroad Playing away from one's home field. A schedule card may have two columns: one for the team "at home" and the other for the team "abroad." "Each Club shall pay . . . all proper and necessary traveling expenses of Players while 'abroad,' or traveling with the Club in other cities, including board, and first-class jet air and hotel accommodations, if practicable" (2007–2011 Basic Agreement, Article VII-A). IST USE. 1870. "When the Red Stockings play a match game abroad, business . . . stops, and the whole population awaits with anxious solicitude its result" (*Chicago Tribune*, June 6; Peter Morris).

accept the offering To swing at the pitch.

accessories A collective term for pine-tar rag, bat weight, rosin bag, and other items used by players. "Accessories Give Players Extra Edge" (*Baseball Digest* article title, Sept. 1969).

accordion act Collapsing in a pennant race. "Anybody who's waiting for the New York Yankees to pull an accordion act and fold is in for both a surprise and a long wait" (Jim Henneman, *The Baltimore Sun*, June 1, 1994).

ace 1. *n./hist.* A run or score in the earliest era of baseball. An account of the game between the New York Ball Club and a Brooklyn club on Oct. 21, 1845, at Elysian Fields in Hoboken, N.J., indicated "Hunt made a single ace" and "four aces were made off a single hit" (*New York Morning News*, Oct. 22, 1845). Syn. *count,* 3. IST USE. 1845. "The game to consist of twenty-one counts, or aces; but at the conclusion an equal number of hands must be played" (Knickerbocker

Rules, Rule 8th, Sept. 23). **2.** *v./hist.* To score a run. "The Globes handled the bat first, but failed to ace the home-plate until the eighth inning" (*The Boston Daily Globe*, Aug. 11, 1880). **3.** *n.* A team's best pitcher, usually a starter; a stopper who keeps a couple of losses from turning into a losing streak. "There are only 28 staff aces, starters who are considered the rock of their rotation" (*USA Today Baseball Weekly*, Apr. 7–13, 1993). Wilson Alvarez signed with the Tampa Bay Devil Rays in Dec. 1997 to be the number-one starter: "That's every pitcher's dream—to be the ace. That's why I'm here" (*The Baltimore Sun*, Dec. 4, 1997). See also *number 1,* 2. IST USE. 1902. "The work of McCreedie has been watched closely too, and he gives promise of being an Ace" (*The Sporting News*, Nov. 15; Peter Tamony). ETYMOLOGY. Baseball lore and tradition have always attributed the origin of this term to one man. In 1869, pitcher Asa Brainard won 56 out of 57 games played by the Cincinnati Red Stockings, baseball's first professional team. From then on, according to lore, any pitcher with a dazzling string of wins was called an "Asa," which later became "ace." Although there were those who questioned this as a folk etymology, recent work by Peter Morris finds references to Brainard as "Acey" in game accounts (*Brooklyn Eagle*, Oct. 14, 1864, and July 23, 1870); also, the *New England Base Ballist* (Oct. 14, 1864) refers to "Ace Brainard." Lexicographer David Shulman has dated the term as applied to tennis—for a serve that is not touched by the receiver and that scores for the server— to 1885. The fact that the ace is the most valuable card in a deck of cards certainly helped the term evolve. Lexicographer Eric Partridge and others have traced the term "flying ace" (an outstanding fighter pilot of World War I) to cards. **4.** *n.* The "star" of any baseball team. **5.** *n.* A pitcher's best pitch; a low-percentage, tough-to-hit pitch used in a two-strike situation. "Eddie Rommel was the first man I know to develop a knuckle ball to the point where he really used it as his 'ace'" (George Herman Ruth, *Babe Ruth's Own Book of Baseball*, 1928, p.79; Peter Morris). **6.** *adj.* Best, or foremost; e.g., "Smith threw his ace fastball."

across the body 1. Said of a defensive play when a fielder either catches a ball by extending the gloved hand to the opposite side of his body or expeditiously throws the ball over his body rather than with his arm extended straight away from his body. 2. Said of a pitcher whose front foot is striding in a direction opposite to that of his throwing arm. To throw across the body is "to pitch in a manner where the arm must twist slightly to redirect the ball toward the plate, passing over the chest rather than being open and unimpeded" and "caused by, in the case of a right-hander, the lead foot landing about three inches too far to the right, leaving the arm having to compensate for the pitch to travel toward the target" (Alan Schwarz, Baseball America.com, Nov. 14, 2006). "[Darren] Dreifort used to step across his body in his delivery, but now he directs his follow-through toward home plate" (*Sports Illustrated*, March 31, 2003). "[Matt] Clement stopped throwing across his body, switching to a top-to-bottom motion" (*Sports Illustrated*, March 31, 2003).

across the letters Said of a pitched ball that passes across the batter's chest at the approximate location on the uniform of the letters spelling out the team's name.

across the shirt Said of a pitched ball that is close to the batter, chest high. IST USE. 1937 (*Pittsburgh Press*, Jan. 11; Edward J. Nichols).

action pitch The pitch thrown when the count is full (three balls and two strikes) with two outs and runners on first base, on first and second bases, or with the bases loaded. The situation calls for the baserunners to start running just before the ball is delivered. See also *all runners breaking*.

activate To return a player to the team's active roster after injury, illness, or suspension.

activator A sign that tells the player to proceed with the designated play. Syn. *green light*, 3.

active list A list of all players who are currently eligible to play in a championship season game for a major-league club. The list must be filed by the opening date of the season. The maximum number of players is 25 and the minimum number of players is 24 from Opening Day until midnight on Aug. 31 of the same season, at which time the number of players may be increased to 40. Players on the disabled list are not included on the active list. Compare *reserve list*; *inactive list*. Abbrev. *AL*, 2.

active player A player who is regularly and actively engaged in playing baseball; a player on the active list.

activity A relief pitcher or pitchers warming up; e.g., "There's activity in Detroit's bullpen."

add a foot To gain physical maturity and thus increase the velocity of one's fastball. "If a boy really added a foot to his fastball, it would be roughly equivalent to an extra 1.5 miles per hour. An 86 fastball, for example, would become 87.44. 'In that case,' one scout said, 'I can tell you that I've seen high-school pitchers add *five* feet to their fastball between junior and senior year'" (Kevin Kerrane, *Dollar Sign on the Muscle*, 1984, p.93).

add and subtract For a pitcher to change speeds. "[Zack Greinke] was showing the poise and pitchability of a veteran on the mound by adding and subtracting velocity from his 86–92 mph fastball" (*Baseball America*, July 7–20, 2003; Peter Morris).

addition by subtraction The art of improving a team's roster by removing or releasing a player not performing up to standards or one who is causing disharmony in the clubhouse. "Getting rid of [Sidney] Ponson looks like addition by subtraction [as] ... he entered last night's game with the third-highest ERA of any regular starting pitcher in the major leagues, so it's not as if John Maine or another young pitcher can't replace what he has done so far" (Peter Schmuck, *The Baltimore Sun*, July 24, 2005). "Trading [Gary] Sheffield creates a more serene clubhouse that results in addition by subtraction" (*St. Paul Pioneer Press*, March 31, 2002). The phrase was coined by baseball executive Branch Rickey. See also *Rickeyism*. Syn. *positive subtraction*.

adios *v.* To hit a home run; e.g., "Smith adiosed that one." The term is Spanish for "goodbye," and this bit of "Spanglish" is in keeping with the traditional penchant of sportscasters to say "goodbye" to the baseball as it is heading into home run territory.

Adirondack bat A bat made of northern white ash from the Adirondack Mountains of New York. It has been manufactured in Dolgeville, N.Y., since the mid-1940s, and became part of Rawlings in 1975. Players who popularized the bat include Bobby Thomson, Willie Mays, Reggie Jackson, and Roberto Clemente.

adjudged Said of a judgment decision made by the umpire.

adjusted Said of a statistic that has both been *normalized* to account for annual differences in performance and recomputed to account for intrinsic differences in run scoring among ballparks. Statistics that are often adjusted include batting average, on-base percentage, slugging percentage, and earned run average. Many "new" statistics (such as batting runs and pitching runs) are automatically adjusted as a consequence of the manner by which they are computed. Abbreviations for adjusted statistics include the letter "A" before the abbreviation for the original statistic or a plus sign following it; e.g., *Total Baseball* adjusts "production" and abbreviates it either as "APRO" or "PRO+." See also a set of terms beginning with the term "equivalent."

adjusted runs prevented A statistical index for pitchers that, unlike other adjusted indices, adjusts for baserunners allowed in incomplete innings rather than average performance variations across years and ballparks; specif., the number of runs (both earned and unearned) a pitcher allows per nine innings, plus the run potential for any innings in which the pitcher leaves with baserunners aboard, minus any inherited *runs prevented* for innings in which the pitcher enters with baserunners aboard. To use an example discussed by Baseball Prospectus (*Baseball Between the Numbers*, 2006), with runners on first and third and nobody out, 1.84 more runs are expected to score before the inning is over, which is 1.32 more than the 0.52 runs that occur in an average inning. If a starter is taken out at that point and a reliever who enters the game gives up only one run during that inning, the starter is charged with those extra 1.32 runs on top of any given up in previous innings. As the reliever only allowed one run, he is credited with saving 0.32 runs, which is subtracted from any runs given up in later innings. Abbrev. *ARP*.

adjustment 1. A batter's changing his approach in reaction to a pitching technique that is getting him out, or a pitcher's reacting to the success batters are having against him. Batters must work on their weaknesses and recognize pitching patterns; *Sports Illustrated* (May 29, 2006) noted "[David] Wright's ability to make adjustments, not only from at bat to at bat, but also from pitch to pitch." Johnny Sain (quoted in Roger Kahn, *The Head Game*, 2000, p.198; Peter Morris): "A good hitter adjusts. That's one reason he is a good hitter. He's learned that if I'm throwing as hard as I can and he's swinging as hard as he can, I'm going to beat him. He's going to make out. So he gives in. That's not surrender. Not at all. That's adjustment." Cleveland Indians pitching coach Mike Brown (quoted in *Baseball America*, Dec. 24, 2001–Jan. 6, 2002): "Pitchers are still developing once they get to the big league level. . . . In the minor leagues they call it development. In the major leagues it's called adjustments." Baltimore Orioles manager Sam Perlozzo (quoted in *The Baltimore Sun*, Apr. 11, 2006): "This game is a game of adjustments." **2.** The reaction of a player upon leaving the game of baseball, which he may have begun to play at the age of seven or eight. "He's made the Adjustment. He doesn't like it, but he's made the Adjustment" (Dock Ellis, quoted in Donald Hall & Dock Ellis, *Dock Ellis in the Country of Baseball*, 1976).

admire a third strike To be called out on strikes while watching the third one.

adorn To pitch; to be the pitcher in a game. "Jack [Lively] was practically invincible every time he adorned the mound" (*San Francisco Bulletin*, Feb. 8, 1913; Gerald L. Cohen).

advance 1. For a batter to move a baserunner ahead one or more bases because of a hit, groundout, or sacrifice. "When you get runners on base, you want to advance them. That's the way baseball works" (Will Clark, quoted in *The Baltimore Sun*, Apr. 4, 2000). **2.** To act as an advance scout. "The Yankees . . . have two full-time advance scouts and at least one other scout who occasionally will advance a team or two" (Mike Klis, *Baseball America*, Aug. 4–17, 2003; Peter Morris).

Advanced A Syn. of *high Single A.*

advance sale The number of tickets sold before the actual day of a baseball game.

advance scout A scout who looks for the strengths and weaknesses of the team that the scout's team will be playing next. ETYMOL-OGY. The origin of the term is unknown; however, "references to advance scouting in baseball history go back almost a hundred years, if not more, and are commonplace throughout the century" (Bill James, *The Bill James Guide to Baseball Managers from 1870 to Today*, 1997, p.206; Peter Morris). Christy Mathewson (*Pitching in a Pinch*, 1912) blamed the defeat of the New York Giants in the 1911 World Series to poor advance scouting. The claim by Tony Kubek (in George F. Will, *Men at Work*, 1990, p.16) that Casey Stengel invented advance scouting is, according to James, "so misguided as to be comical." Yet Peter Schmuck (*The Baltimore Sun*, May 22, 1994) wrote that the practice of advance scouting dates to the early 1950s, when the Brooklyn Dodgers began sending an advance man to the Polo Grounds or to Philadelphia to scout the teams on their way to Ebbets Field: "Former Dodgers executive Al Campanis claims some credit for the concept, which he said sprang from a conversation in 1950 with then general manager Buzzie Bavasi." Campanis told Bavasi that he had scouted for a college football team and thought that the practice could be extended to baseball. The Dodgers felt it was a success, and the Chicago Cubs were the next to adopt the practice.

adviser A euphemistic term to describe an agent when he is consulted by an amateur player. "Any family whose son expects to be drafted and will seriously consider signing should investigate using an agent to help with the process. . . . [It] is legal according to NCAA regulations—though it requires you use the euphemism 'adviser' until you actually sign" (*Baseball America*, June 23–July 6, 2003). Peter Morris noted that the euphemism is far from ~ng new to baseball: "Branch Rickey . . . discovered that [Tommy Thevenow] had an adviser, manager, or something. Great horrors, multiplied! When this intelligence was transmitted to [Sam] Breadon, the even-mannered chief executive of the [St. Louis] Cardinals fairly exploded" (*The Sporting News*, March 10, 1927).

affiliated club A minor-league club that has a working relationship with a major-league club. Syn. "affiliate."

affiliation The relationship between a major-league club and a minor-league franchise for the purpose of developing players.

affiliation shuffle The periodic and massive movement of minor-league clubs when working agreements with the major-league clubs expire. The Professional Baseball Agreement specifies that each major-league club must have a certain number of affiliated clubs at each level. "The commissioner's office kept its promise to deliver a non-complex short-season club to the [Kansas City] Royals a year after they lost out in the affiliation shuffle" (Will Kimmey, *Baseball America*, Oct. 13–26, 2003; Peter Morris). Syn. "affiliation musical chairs."

AFL Abbrev. for *Arizona Fall League.*

afterpiece *hist.* The second game of a doubleheader.

A game 1. The best effort exerted by a player or team. Minnesota Twins manager Tom Kelly (quoted in *The Baltimore Sun*, Aug. 14, 2001): "If we don't bring our A game with us, we don't have a chance. We have to bring our A game no matter who we're playing." Baltimore Orioles pitcher Sidney Ponson (quoted in *The Baltimore Sun*, June 29, 2005): "I always bring my A game against the Yankees. . . . You always want to beat the best and they always think they're better than us, so I try to prove a point." EXTENDED USE. The maximum effort in other sports or endeavors. When *Elle* magazine (Aug. 2004) asked tennis player Andy Roddick whether women should withhold sex on the first date, he replied: "Yes! You don't want to bring out your A game too fast." **2.** The baseball game that is telecast nationally to approximately

80 percent of the country, but not to the markets of the participating clubs. Compare *B game*, 2.

agate The baseball. The term may have derived from "marble," another name for the ball. Agates or aggies were popular forms of marbles. IST USE. 1913 (*The Sporting News*, Oct. 30; Peter Morris).

agent See *player agent*.

aggregation A baseball team. "The old White Stockings was a great aggregation, so were the Baltimore Orioles" (Cap Anson, quoted in *San Francisco Bulletin*, March 6, 1913; Gerald L. Cohen). IST USE. 1898 (*New York Tribune*, June 17; Edward J. Nichols).

aggressive 1. Said of a team or player who plays heads-up, all-out baseball. Peter Morris notes that the term originally had a negative connotation before competitiveness became more acceptable. For example, Henry Chadwick (*The Sporting Life*, June 9, 1894): "The 'aggressive hustling' method of play indulged in by League teams this season . . . is nothing but rowdy ball playing." Chadwick continued his assault (*The Sporting News*, March 23, 1895): "I have noticed . . . a tendency on the part of base ball scribes to advocate brutal and unfair methods in professional base ball under the guise of having teams play their game in what is called the 'hustling' and aggressive style of play so much in vogue among the League teams in 1894." Even Baltimore Orioles manager Earl Weaver had doubts about baseball's blather about the supposed advantages of "aggressiveness" (quoted in *The Washington Post*, Sept. 5, 1982): "Most of the time, you don't have to be aggressive in baseball. Do the sure things, play within yourself and you'll win." 2. Said of a pitcher who does not pitch tentatively, but attacks the strike zone or challenges the batter. "When we go after this guy [Barry Bonds], let's aggressively get after him" (Los Angeles Dodgers manager Jim Tracy, quoted in *The Baltimore Sun*, Apr. 16, 2002).

aggressive at-bat stat A measure of the determination of a Little League team's batters to hit the ball, computed by adding the number of times the batters put the ball in play (whether it results in a hit, error, or out) and the number of times a batter strikes out swinging, divided by the total number of plate appearances. The measure penalizes those batters who receive bases on balls or are hit by pitches. The statistic was introduced by Stephen Barr and Brian Opitz (*The New York Times*, June 5, 1999), who believe "the most important lesson you can teach young ballplayers is to make contact at the plate" and "even a strikeout swinging . . . [shows that] the kid goes down trying." Abbrev. *AABS*.

aggressive hitter A hitter who habitually swings at pitches delivered out of the strike zone. Mark Teixeira (quoted in *The Baltimore Sun*, July 16, 2006): "Most guys that play this game are aggressive hitters. . . . You see a ball up there; you want to crush it. . . . Everybody's aggressive, but at the same time, I need to be more selective and hit my pitch more often." Baltimore Orioles outfielder Nick Markakis was encouraged "to be more aggressive at the plate, rather than watching too many fastballs go by early in the count" (*The Baltimore Sun*, Aug. 5, 2006).

aggressive in the strike zone Said of a pitcher who throws quality pitches over the plate without trying to be too precise with the location of the pitches, esp. early in the count. St. Louis Cardinals pitcher Jason Marquis (quoted in *The Baltimore Sun*, Aug. 28, 2005): "When you go through a [seven-start losing] streak . . . you start doubting yourself. You start changing your game plan and start to be a little too tentative. You stop being aggressive in the strike zone. You start trying to make perfect pitches on the black and fall behind on the count." Baltimore Orioles pitcher Adam Loewen (quoted in *The Baltimore Sun*, June 3, 2006): "I just want to be aggressive in the strike zone, and good pitches will get just about any hitter out."

agreement 1. See *Tripartite Agreement*. 2. See *National Agreement*. 3. See *Basic Agreement*. 4. See *Major League Agreement*. 5. See *Professional Baseball Agreement*. 6. See *National Association Agreement*. 7. See *Cincinnati Agreement*. 8. See *gentlemen's agreement*.

ahead At an advantage; e.g., said of a team that is winning or of a pitcher with a count of more strikes than balls. Compare *behind*, 1.

ahead in the count **1.** Said of a pitcher when there are more strikes than balls on the batter. Compare *behind in the count*, 1. Syn. "ahead of the count"; "ahead on the count." **2.** Said of a batter with more balls than strikes. Compare *behind in the count*, 2. Syn. "ahead of the count"; "ahead on the count."

ahead of the pitch Said of an overanxious batter who hits a fat pitch before it even reaches the plate, thereby pulling it foul.

AIBS Abbrev. for *all-important box score.*

AILC Abbrev. *for all-important loss column.*

aim To try to pinpoint a pitch in the strike zone; to work too hard to put the ball over the strike zone. When a pitcher aims the ball, he may deviate from his natural motion. See also *guide*, 1.

"ain't the beer cold!" An expression used by Baltimore Orioles broadcaster Chuck Thompson for anything good that occurs on the field, such as a home run or the defeat of an opponent. Thompson picked up the expression from Robert R. Robertson, who spotted for Thompson at Baltimore Colts games sponsored by the National Brewing Co. See also *guide*, 1.

air ball *hist.* Syn. of *fly ball.* IST USE. 1862 (*New York Sunday Mercury*, July 13; Edward J. Nichols).

airhead A zany or spacey player; one with little brainpower.

air it out **1.** For a batter to unwind and hit the ball for a long distance. **2.** For a pitcher to give it all he has when throwing the ball, or to show his best effort. **3.** For a player to test his arm, coming off an injury. "Plans call for [disabled pitcher Rocky] Coppinger to air it out on Wednesday" (Baltimore Orioles pitching coach Ray Miller, quoted in *The Baltimore Sun*, April 7, 1997). **4.** For an outfielder throwing as hard as he can, usually from a deep position, to try to nail a runner attempting to advance an extra base.

airmail To throw the ball over another player's head. "A catcher who throws one into center field on an attempted steal air mails the second baseman" (Joe Falleta, quoted in *Baseball Digest*, Dec. 1983). President Ron-

ald Reagan airmailed his 1986 ceremonial Opening Day pitch. Asked how a team keeps its errors low, infielder Billy Ripken told *Washington City Paper* (June 12, 1992): "You try to eliminate plays like the two-hopper that you grab and airmail into the dugout." Also spelled "air mail."

air out **1.** To lecture (Orel Hershiser, *Out of the Blue*, 1989). **2.** See *air it out.*

air pocket A mythical air current that causes a fielder to drop or misjudge a fly ball. See also *"hit an air pocket."*

airtight Said of a great defense; e.g., an "airtight infield" rarely allows batted balls to get through. IST USE. 1910 (*Baseball Magazine*, September; Edward J. Nichols).

airway [softball term] The path that a ball goes through in underhand pitching.

AK Abbrev. for *ant-killer.*

AL **1.** Abbrev. for *American League*, 1. **2.** Abbrev. for *active list.*

alabaster blast Pittsburgh Pirates announcer Bob Prince's term for a ball hit sharply down in front of the batter and bouncing over the head of the pitcher and other infielders due to the extraordinarily hard infield at Forbes Field. See also *Baltimore chop*; *Pittsburgh chopper.* Syn. "alabaster blaster."

alabaster plaster The rock-hard infield surface of Forbes Field in Pittsburgh.

a la carte Said of fielding a ball with one hand. The term was sometimes corrupted to "aly carte" by Dizzy Dean. IST USE. 1933 (Edgar G. Brands, *The Sporting News*, Feb. 23; Peter Morris).

Alaska Baseball League A wood-bat league of high school and college players who play summer baseball to gain experience. Abbrev. *ABL.*

albatross contract A long-term contract that is so exorbitant as to make it virtually impossible to trade a player. "Because they could not give away [Albert] Belle with three years remaining on his albatross contract, the Orioles must contract a lineup around him" (Gerry Fraley, *Baseball America*, Oct. 2–15, 2000; Peter Morris).

Al Capone A double play ("twin killing").

ALCS Abbrev. for *American League Championship Series*.

ALDS Abbrev. for *American League Division Series*.

Alibi Ike A player who has an excuse for every fault and mistake. IST USE. 1915 (Ring W. Lardner, short story "Alibi Ike," *Saturday Evening Post*, July 31; Peter Morris). ETYMOLOGY. In the story, the nickname "Alibi Ike" is given to a baseball player. The introductory passage: "His right name was Frank X. Farrell, and I guess the X stood for 'Excuse me.' Because he never pulled a play, good or bad, on or off the field, without apologizin' for it." Traced back to 1743 when it first appeared in English, the word "alibi"—from the Latin word for "elsewhere"—took on new life with Lardner's characterization. The name itself gained further recognition in the 1932 film adaptation, *Alibi Ike* starring Joe E. Brown. EXTENDED USE. A fast talker who has an excuse for whatever went wrong, none of which is ever his fault or mistake. "Alibi Ikes Can be Cured" (*San Francisco Examiner*, March 19, 1966; Peter Tamony). John Ciardi (*Good Words to You*, 1987) noted that after Lardner created the term, "it became an established Am. slang idiom almost at once and remains so."

alive 1. Said of a fastball that seems to have its own animation; one that appears to speed

Alibi Ike. From the film *Alibi Ike* based on the short story of the same title. Joe E. Brown in the title role of the oafish Ike in the 1932 film, with leading lady Olivia de Havilland. *Museum of Modern Art Film Still Archives*

up and take a sudden hop or rise as it nears the plate. Such a ball is often said to "move." **2.** Said of an inning that is prolonged by timely hitting or baserunning. "Stan Javier disrupted [Marty] Barrett's attempted double-play pivot at second base, keeping the inning alive" (*Tampa Tribune*, Oct. 9, 1988). **3.** See *stay alive*.

All-American A high school or college player voted as the best player in the country in his position at his level. IST USE. 1888. "[There were] one or more representatives of each league club on the all-American team [that accompanied the Chicago White Stockings on A.G. Spalding's world tour after the 1888 season]" (*Los Angeles Times*, Sept. 22). This established the first use of the term in baseball, not in football, which lexicographer Barry Popik has verified as 1889. ETYMOLOGY. Spalding's "all-American team," which toured the world in 1889 to show the American game to its best advantage, was similar to the modern idea of an all-American team in name only. It was simply a barnstorming team selected for the players' willingness to participate, rather than for their skill level; two players were minor leaguers. Their name, according to Peter Morris, reflected the fact that they were representing their country on foreign soil and "is almost certainly derived from the all-England cricketers; Spalding was certainly well aware of the all-England cricketers, since they are mentioned in his account of his 1874 tour of England."

All-American Amateur Baseball Association An organization founded in 1944 and based in Johnstown, Pa., that helps advance, develop, and regulate baseball at the amateur level. It emphasizes "sports for sports' sake" and holds that sportsmanship is the "greatest lesson to be learned from athletic competition." Abbrev. *AAABA*.

All-American Girls Professional Baseball League A league that began playing in 1943 and ended in 1954. The brainchild of Chicago Cubs owner Philip K. Wrigley, the game originally was a hybrid of baseball and softball: the ball evolved from 12 inches to 9 inches in circumference, the basepaths from 65 feet to 85 feet, and pitching distance from 40 feet to 60 feet. Pitchers originally threw underhand, then sidearm, and, since 1948, overhand. The league had as many as 15 teams, all in the Midwest, and in 1948 it drew more than one million fans who paid 50 to 75 cents for admission. Teams played 120 games each season and player salaries ranged from $50 to $125 per week. Players endured charm school, dress codes, and curfews, and were answerable to female chaperones. The league was intended to serve as a substitute entertainment to baseball during World War II, but it survived the war and was probably a casualty of television. Some 556 women played in such places as Rockford, Ill. (the Peaches), Racine, Wis. (the Belles), Milwaukee (the Chicks), Fort Wayne, Ind. (the Daisies), and Kalamazoo, Mich. (the Lassies). The league was celebrated in the film *A League of Their Own* (1992). See Merrie A. Fidler, *The Origins and History of the All-American Girls Professional Baseball League*, 2006. Abbrev. *AAGPBL*. USAGE NOTE. The league began as the All-American Girls Softball League (AAGSBL) on Feb. 17, 1943. By Sept. 1943, the name was changed to All-American Girls Baseball League (AAGBBL). At the end of the 1945 season, the extra "B" was dropped, but later re-added for 1951–1954. Period nicknames for the league included All-American Girls Ball League (1944 and late 1940s) and the American Girls Baseball League (1954). During the 1980s, when the former players formed their players' association, they added the term "Professional" so that the All-American Girls Professional Baseball League became their name of choice. However, Merrie A. Fidler (*The Origins and History of the All-American Girls Professional Baseball League*, 2006) noted that at the conclusion of the 1943 season the league name was officially changed to the more descriptive All-American Girls Professional Ball League. This title was retained until the end of the 1945 season when All-American Girls Baseball League (AAGBL) was officially adopted.

All-American out A poor hitter.

All-American team An honorary team comprising the best players from the two major leagues. Based on his research, Edward J. Nichols (*An Historical Dictionary of Base-*ball Terminology, PhD dissertation, Jan. 1939, p.1) noted, "All-Star teams may actually play, whereas all-American teams are merely honorary selections." However, the first "all-American team" was assembled to compete with the Chicago White Stockings during A.G. Spalding's world tour following the 1888 season.

all-classification record A statistical accomplishment that is a record for both the major leagues and the minor leagues. "Lost in the shuffle of Barry Bonds' record-setting home run year is the fact that the Giants left fielder broke the all-classification record for homers in a season" (*Baseball America*, Oct. 29–Nov. 11, 2001; Peter Morris).

alley 1. One of the two areas between the outfielders in left-center field and in right-center field. "Rickey Henderson's average continues to dwindle as he swings for the fences instead of the alleys" (*St. Petersburg Times*, Apr. 3, 1987). See also *power alley*; *gap*, 1. IST USE. 1923. "[Travis] Jackson . . . lined a home run through the 'alley' between [center fielder Hy] Myers and [right fielder Max] Flack" (*St. Louis Post-Dispatch*, July 22; Peter Morris). **2.** The center or "heart" of home plate. See also *down the alley*; *slot*, 8. **3.** The place where a batter prefers the ball to be pitched. "The second . . . [homer] Terry [Moore] hit was right in his 'alley,' low and inside" (*Brooklyn Eagle*, July 27, 1940; Peter Morris). **4.** The *dirt path* between the pitcher's mound and home plate that was common to most ballparks in the late 19th century and the first half of the 20th century. This skinned area began disappearing from major-league ballparks in the late 1940s, but some recently built ballparks (esp. in the minor leagues) have installed the path. The reasons that it first appeared (perhaps inherited from cricket fields) and disappeared are both mysteries. Syn. *path*, 2; *pitcher's path*; *channel*; *keyhole*; *runway*, 2. **5.** The approximate middle space between first base and second base or between second base and third base. See also *slot*, 6.

alley hitter A hitter who drives the ball into the alleys between outfielders.

alley softball [softball term] An urban form of softball played in alleys. It has rigid rules, as described by Fred Ferretti (*The Great American Book of Games*, 1975): "[A] ball hit off the wires and caught is an out. A ball that hits or even grazes a house wall and is caught before hitting the ground is an out. A ball that lands atop any shed, house, or garage roof is an out. So is a ball landing in any yard. And what was safe, you ask? Any line drive to dead center (straight down the alley), so long as it isn't caught. Pull hitters shun alley softball."

alligator jacket A lightweight rubberized top worn under the baseball uniform shirt to keep the body warm (Bill Werber and C. Paul Rogers III, *Memories of a Ballplayer*, 2001, p.135).

alligator mouth Ballplayer slang for the mouth of a person who talks big but appears to lack courage (Jim Bouton, *Ball Four*, 1970).

all-important box score The newspaper box score that adds much to the fans' enjoyment of the game. Bob Brown (*Orioles Gazette*, July 30, 1993) used the initialism *AIBS*: "We live only 20 minutes from downtown but if the Orioles are playing at night a time zone away, the paper dropped in our driveway probably won't have that AIBS (all-important box score)."

all-important loss column The column in the league or division standings that records the number of losses incurred by a team in relation to the number of games played or to be played or games a team is ahead or behind another team. The term points to the fact that there is more to a club's standings than the column in which wins are counted, because standings are based on the number of wins and losses, not on the winning percentage. Also, because teams will have played different numbers of games at any given point, the true measure of a team's performance is the number of losses it has posted. The loss column is also "all-important" because the losses cannot be "made up" or overcome. Abbrev. *AILC*.

all-injured team A facetious and mythical team of players who, because of injuries, played the least but made the most money in a season.

all-money team A mythical team composed of players making the most money at each position.

all–New York Series A World Series between the New York Yankees and either the New York Giants, Brooklyn Dodgers, or New York Mets. IST USE. 1934. "There is an ancient tradition, or let me say axiom, in baseball that the team in the lead on July 4 is the team that will win the pennant. New York fans are sure that this situation is a true augury of an all-New York World Series" (*The Sporting News*, July 12; Barry Popik). See also *Subway Series*.

all-or-nothing 1. Said of a power hitter who generally strikes out when he doesn't hit a home run. "[Dean Palmer is] an all-or-nothing hitter who, for all his power, doesn't hit a lot of doubles" (STATS Inc., *The Scouting Notebook*, 2000; Peter Morris). 2. Said of a team that hits many home runs but does not score frequently. "Toronto had an all-or-nothing lineup last season. It led the AL with 244 home runs but finished eighth in scoring" (Gerry Fraley, *Baseball America*, Apr. 16–29, 2001).

all over the plate Said of a pitcher having difficulty in delivering the ball in the strike zone.

allow 1. To give up hits and/or runs; e.g., "Smith allowed five hits and three runs in the fifth." 2. To make an error; e.g., "Jones allowed the hot grounder to go between his legs."

all-rookie team A mythical team composed of the best rookie players at each position.

all runners breaking Said of baserunners on first base or first and second bases or bases loaded advancing to the next base during the pitcher's windup. It occurs when there are two outs and the count on the batter is three balls and two strikes. The baserunners break during the pitcher's windup because the pitch must result in a batted ball, walk, or the final out of the inning; i.e., there is no risk in sending the runners. See also *action pitch*.

all star A player selected at almost any level of baseball to a team comprising the best players from a league or geographic area. IST USE. 1894. "[Oscar Meyer] did not have nine stars by any means, but he made it very hot for some that thought they did have an 'all star' combination" (*The Sporting News*, Jan. 20; Peter Morris).

All Star A player chosen to play in the All-Star Game.

All-Star balloting The act of voting for players to appear in the All-Star Game. Various methods have been used: beginning in 1933 and 1934, fans voted for the players through ballots printed in the *Chicago Tribune*; from 1935 through 1946, the managers voted; from 1947 through 1957, fans voted; from 1958 to 1969, the players, managers, and coaches voted; and since 1970, the fans have voted the starting lineups, with the players, managers, and coaches selecting additional players, and finally the manager of each team filling out the roster. The last player for each team is chosen by online fan balloting, a kind of runoff with five players chosen from each league. At least one player must be selected from each major-league team. Each roster has 20 position players and 12 pitchers. The decision to turn the balloting over to the fans has, according to the critics of nonprofessional voting, turned selection of the game's starting players into more of a popularity contest than a true contest based on merit; e.g., in 1957, Cincinnati Reds fans stuffed the ballot "box" when seven of eight starters voted in were Reds players. Even with spaces for write-ins, the number of names on the ballot has risen regularly. Balloting has been an activity sponsored by a company willing to put up a million dollars a year for the privilege. The Gillette Safety Razor Co. conducted the voting from 1970 to 1986, and *USA Today* and its parent, Gannett Co. Inc., picked it up beginning in 1987.

All-Star berth A selection to play in the All-Star Game.

All-Star break The three-day, mid-July break in the schedule of major-league baseball to accommodate the All-Star Game and related festivities. It represents the unofficial midpoint of the season and is an important point of reference when charting a team's fortunes; e.g., a manager may say that his team will be in fine shape if it is within three games of first place by the time of the All-Star break. *Sport* (Oct. 1984, p.15) noted the All-Star break is a "trial" for sabermetrician Bill James, who lamented, "Three days without box scores. Jeez, that's tough." Syn. *break*, 10.

All-Star card A baseball card portraying a player who participated in the previous season's All-Star Game. The first All-Star cards appeared in the 1958 Topps baseball set.

All-Star Game 1. The annual interleague game played each July between players selected as the best at their positions in the American League and the National League. The starting players are selected by fan balloting. Beginning in 2003, Games 1, 2, 6, and 7 of the World Series have been scheduled in the city of the club whose league was the winner of that season's All-Star Game. The designated hitter is used when the game is played in an American League ballpark. The game is played under the supervision and control of the commissioner of baseball; the date and ballpark in which the game is played is determined by the Executive Council. The first All-Star Game was played on July 6, 1933, at Comiskey Park in Chicago. It was the brainchild of *Chicago Tribune* sports editor Arch Ward, who saw it as a one-shot "dream game" (or "game of the century") to go along with the 1933 Century of Progress Exposition going on in the city. Though opposed by some owners, the idea appealed to the presidents of the two leagues and commissioner Kenesaw Mountain Landis. A third-inning, two-run home run by Babe Ruth led the American League to a 4–2 win. Because of travel restrictions during World War II, the game was not played in 1945. There were two All-Star Games a year from 1959 through 1962, but this idea was scrapped as it became clear that two games lacked the luster of one. The only game to be postponed was the one scheduled for July 14, 1981, which was moved to Aug. 9 because of a players' strike. Syn. *dream game*; *Midseason Classic*; *Summer Classic*; *Midsummer Classic*; *summer spectacle*. ETYMOLOGY. Before 1933, there were several unofficial "all-star" exhibition games; e.g., a game between all-stars from Brooklyn and New York in 1858; and the game on July 24, 1911, to benefit the widow of Cleveland pitcher Addie Joss, in which the best of the American League defeated the Cleveland Indians, 5–3, and more than $13,000 was raised. F.C. Lane (*Baseball Magazine,* Dec. 1913) proposed "the All America Baseball Club" in which "the crack team of the American League contrasted with the crack team of the National." Later, *Baseball Magazine* (March 1916, pp. 48–52) proposed a midseason "All-Star Series" between selected teams consisting of the two best players from each team in the American League and the National League. **2.** Any similar contest at other levels of play and in softball.

All-Star team A team participating in an All-Star Game. "Choosing an all star team of baseball players is a fad with most fans" (F.C. Lane, *Baseball Magazine*, Dec. 1913). IST USE. 1905 (*The Sporting Life*, Sept. 2; Edward J. Nichols).

All-Star Week The week of festivities surrounding the All-Star Game. An editorial in *The Baltimore Sun* (July 15, 1993) entitled "An All-Star Week to Remember" discussed FanFest, an old-timers game, a tribute to black baseball players, the home run derby, an architectural forum on stadium architecture, and the game itself.

all-time **1.** Describing a player past or present who is considered the best or one of the best in baseball history. **2.** Describing the best ever of baseball, up to and including the present. **3.** Describing baseball records that are the best for any particular player, team, or league. **4.** Describing an outstanding event; e.g., "Whereas, sports fans everywhere are celebrating the outstanding accomplishment of [Boston Red Sox pitcher] Roger Clemens as one of the all-time great individual performances in the history of baseball" (Sen. Edward Kennedy [D-Mass.], U.S. Senate Resolution 393 commending Clemens for striking out a record 20 batters in a single, nine-inning game, *Congressional Record*, May 1, 1986).

all-time all-timer One of the greatest of the great baseball players.

all-timer One of the all-time great players of baseball.

all to the mustard In good physical condi-

tion. IST USE. 1907 (*New York Evening Journal*, Apr. 18; Edward J. Nichols).

all-wild-card World Series A World Series in which both teams are wild cards. "The first all-wild-card World Series [between the Anaheim Angels and the San Francisco Giants in 2002] has the makings of a seven-game stress test" (Tom Verducci, *Sports Illustrated*, Oct. 21, 2002).

Almendarista A follower of the blue-colored Almendares Alacranes (Scorpions) of the Cuban League. See also *Habanista*; *eternal rival*.

almohada Spanish for "base."

Alphonse and Gaston *adj./hist.* Said of an act, play, base hit, error, or fielding situation in which one or more players defer to one another, often allowing the ball to drop to the ground in the process. "[Red] Murray and [Billy] Gilbert gave an Alphonse-and-Gaston exhibition on [Frank] Chance's fly back of second, [Frank] Schulte scurrying home" (*The Sporting News*, June 4, 1908; Peter Morris). IST USE. 1902 (*The Sporting Life*, May 24; David Shulman). ETYMOLOGY. Alphonse and Gaston, two cartoon characters created by Frederick Burr Opper (hired by William Randolph Hearst in 1899), deferred to one another to the point where they were unable to get anything done: "After you, my dear Alphonse." "No, after you, my dear Gaston." This was often be repeated several times. The characters have become symbolic of exaggerated politeness.

altered bat [softball term] A bat whose physical structure has been changed by, for example, attaching a flare or cone grip to the bat

Alphonse and Gaston. The comic characters, created by Frederick Burr Opper, who became a metaphor for debilitating politeness. *Author's collection*

handle, replacing the handle of a metal bat with a wooden or other type of handle, inserting material inside the bat, applying excessive tape (more than two layers) to the bat grip, or painting a bat at the top or bottom for other than identification purposes. Compare *doctored bat*; *illegal bat*.

alternative pitch An illegal pitch of any sort. USAGE NOTE. The term is an obvious euphemism and tends to be used with tongue firmly in cheek.

aluminum bat A piece of tubular aluminum closed at both ends and shaped like a conventional wooden baseball bat. The relative lightness of an aluminum bat and its hollow core, stiff handle, and springy walls allow a batter to increase bat speed and propel the ball at a much greater velocity and for a greater distance than with a wood bat of similar proportion. The thin walls of an aluminum bat flex inward up to a quarter inch when hit by a ball and spring back, pushing the ball away faster and farther. Aluminum bats were approved for use in Little League in 1971, and have been used by college players since 1972 (they were approved by the National Collegiate Association of America in 1974) and at virtually all levels of amateur baseball, but not in the professional leagues, where they are prohibited. Aluminum bats are widely used in softball. Some aluminum bats have wood cores. Although initially more expensive than wood bats, aluminum bats break or become damaged with far less frequency; hence, they are appealing in terms of cost. Generally speaking, they are said to help weak hitters drive the ball farther and give an extra edge to sluggers. However, aluminum bats are opposed by the professional baseball establishment for several reasons, including their potentially devastating effect on batting records and fielders' safety and the fact that they ping rather than crack when coming in contact with a ball. The Massachusetts Interscholastic Athletic Association banned the use of aluminum bats beginning with the 2003 state baseball tournament. See also *graphite bat*.

aluminum-bat swing A batting stroke, developed by a player using an aluminum bat, that is too long or cannot cover the inside part of the plate, thereby affecting the player's ability to swing a wood bat effectively.

amateur draft Original name of *first-year player draft*. The formal name of the draft was changed in 1997 to preempt players from signing with an independent professional club and then claiming to be exempt from the draft.

amateur player Any player who is not a professional. Henry Chadwick (*The Game of Base Ball*, 1868, p.38) distinguished two classes of amateur players: those who play "for exercise and amusement only" and those "unskilled in playing the game, but who know more of it than the 'Muffins' do." USAGE NOTE. Peter Morris notes that there have always been debates as to what constitutes an amateur player. The secretary of the Chelsea Base Ball Club complained that "the Chelseas have been called gate money amateurs owing to the fact that most of their matches were on enclosed grounds" (*Brooklyn Eagle*, March 29, 1874). Similarly, the *Brooklyn Eagle* (Aug. 26, 1875) reported, "The amateur nines were not exactly amateurs in the strict sense of the word, for two-thirds of the so-called amateur nines of 1875, included players who were compensated for their services, if not by regular salaries—as in the professional organizations—at least by a share of gate receipts, or some other form of remuneration." And *The Sporting Life* (Apr. 14, 1917) noted sarcastically, "Johnny Leber . . . will not report. He says he can make more money playing 'amateur' ball in Cleveland."

Amateur Softball Association of America [softball term] The governing body of American softball, headquartered in Oklahoma City, Okla. It was founded in 1933 by Leo Fischer and Michael J. Pauley in conjunction with the Century of Progress Exposition in Chicago. Its purpose was to establish a standard set of rules for a game to be played at the exposition; subsequently, it adopted softball's first universally accepted rules of play. The association directs slow pitch, fast pitch, and modified pitch programs for male, female, and coed (co-recreational) leagues with players aged 9 through 70 and over. It includes 87 local associations, more than 250,000 teams, and a membership of more than four million. Abbrev. *ASA*.

Amazing Mets A description that has been used for the New York *Mets* from its beginning in 1962 to the present. Mets manager Casey Stengel exclaimed after watching the team win its first exhibition game: "They're amazing!" But before long, Stengel turned that sentiment into a lament: "They're amazing. Can't anybody here play this game?" *The New York Times* (May 2, 1962) quoted Stengel: "The amazing Mets are in an amazing slump." No matter how good or bad they have been in the intervening years, the Mets have remained amazing, albeit for different reasons. The term shows up in book titles, newspaper headlines, and even a record album, *The Amazing Mets*, made by members of the team in 1968 and featuring such selections as "We're Gonna Win" and "Green Grass of Shea." Also spelled "Amazin' Mets." See also *Amazin's*.

Amazin's A variation on *Amazing Mets* and the term that manager Casey Stengel himself often used to refer to the New York *Mets*. "The Amazin's amazed us so often that almost every one of the 2,175,373 fans who saw them at home this year . . . must be convinced that he was there on that one special afternoon or crucial evening when the Mets won *the* big game that fused them as contenders and future champions" (Roger Angell, *The Summer Game*, 1972; Charles D. Poe).

ambish Ambition on the part of a player or team. 1ST USE. 1908 (*New York Evening Journal*, Apr. 13; Edward J. Nichols).

amble to first To receive a base on balls.

American Amateur Baseball Congress An organization, founded in 1935 and headquartered in Battle Creek, Mich., that supports amateur baseball through programs of education, research, and service in the United States, Puerto Rico, and Canada, with affiliates in many foreign countries. It has seven divisions named for former major-league players: Roberto Clemente (8 & under), Willie Mays (10 & under), Pee Wee Reese (12 & under), Sandy Koufax (14 & under), Mickey Mantle (16 & under), Connie Mack (18 & under), and Stan Musial (unlimited age). Abbrev. *AABC*.

American Association 1. A major league that existed from 1882 to 1891 as a rival to the National League. It played ball on Sundays, sold beer at the park, charged only 25 cents for admission (half the National League rate), and had a permanent core of umpires. The Association floundered due to financial and leadership problems. Four of its teams (St. Louis, Baltimore, Washington, and Louisville) were absorbed by the National League. Full name: American Association of Professional Base Ball Clubs. Abbrev. *AA*, 2. Syn. *Association*; *Beer and Whiskey League*. 2. An abortive players' league (1894) with eight teams, 25-cent admission, a schedule that would not conflict with that of the National League, and no reserve clause. See Harold Seymour, *Baseball: The Early Years*, 1960, pp.271–73. 3. A minor league that existed from 1903 to 1997 (except for 1963–1968 when its member clubs were divided between the International League and the Pacific Coast League), with cities primarily in the midwestern United States. It was a Class A league from 1903 to 1907, a Class AA league from 1908 to 1945, and a Class AAA league from 1946 to 1962 and from 1969 to 1997. The league disbanded because it was easier to have a postseason series with two leagues instead of three. The clubs were again split between the International League and the Pacific Coast League. Abbrev. *AA*, 3. 4. An independent league organized in 2005 by the merger of two independent leagues (Northern League and Central League) and consisting of teams primarily in the midwestern United States. Official name: American Association of Independent Professional Baseball Leagues.

American Baseball Coaches Association An organization founded in 1945 and based in Hinsdale, Ill., with more than 5,000 members who coach at various levels of the game. It aims to correlate baseball with educational objectives. It originated the NCAA College World Series and holds national clinics. Abbrev. *ABCA*.

American Baseball Guild A players' union organized in 1946 by Robert Murphy, a Boston lawyer with the National Labor Relations Board, as a means of airing the players' grievances, which primarily concerned the lack of financial security. The Guild sought salary arbitration, a $6,500 minimum salary, and a requirement that players sold to another team receive 50 percent of the purchase price. Murphy called for a players' strike before a Pittsburgh–New York night game on June 7, 1946. With the stands full of fans, the players on the Pirates voted 20 to 16 in favor of the strike, but since a two-thirds vote was required, Murphy's strike request was turned down. The union quickly fell apart, but the owners were eager to block any further efforts by Murphy (and defections by players to the Mexican League) and made several concessions that included payment of spring training expenses (*Murphy money*), the first player pension plan, a minimum annual salary of $5,000, and a 25 percent limit on annual salary reductions.

American League 1. One of the two major leagues, originally a minor league (Western League) that was renamed the American League following the 1899 season and upgraded to a major league in 1901 by Byron Bancroft "Ban" Johnson to compete with the National League. The original teams were Boston, Baltimore, Chicago, Cleveland, Detroit, Milwaukee, Philadelphia, and Washington, D.C. Currently, the American League has 14 teams divided into three divisions: East (Baltimore Orioles, Boston Red Sox, New York Yankees, Tampa Bay Rays, Toronto Blue Jays); Central (Chicago White Sox, Cleveland Indians, Detroit Tigers, Kansas City Royals, Minnesota Twins); and West (Los Angeles Angels, Oakland A's, Seattle Mariners, Texas Rangers). Since it came into being after the National League, it has always been called the *junior circuit*. One of the immediate differences between the older league and the new was that Johnson gave the umpires stronger authority over the game; a current difference is the existence of the designated hitter in the American League. Abbrev. *AL*, 1. **2.** See *Negro American League*.

American League Central The Central Division of the American League, created in 1994, consisting of five teams grouped around midwestern cities (Chicago White Sox, Cleveland Indians, Kansas City Royals, Minnesota Twins, Milwaukee Brewers from 1994 to 1997, and Detroit Tigers beginning in 1998).

American League Championship Series The *Championship Series* in which the two American League teams that won divisional titles (and since 1995, the Division Series) play for the American League pennant and the right to play the National League champion in the World Series. Abbrev. *ALCS*.

American League Division Series The *Division Series* in which the three division winners and a wild card in the American League determine the two teams to play in the American League Championship Series. Abbrev. *ALDS*.

American League East The East Division of the American League, consisting of teams grouped around eastern cities, created in 1969 when the American League expanded from 10 to 12 teams. The division consisted of six teams from 1969 to 1976 (Baltimore Orioles, Boston Red Sox, Cleveland Indians, Detroit Tigers, Milwaukee Brewers from 1972 to 1976, New York Yankees, and Washington Senators from 1969 to 1971), seven teams from 1977 (with the addition of the Toronto Blue Jays) to 1993, and five teams since 1994 (Baltimore Orioles, Boston Red Sox, New York Yankees, Toronto Blue Jays, Detroit Tigers from 1994 to 1997, and Tampa Bay Rays beginning in 1998).

American League style The real and imagined style of play and officiating in the American League, accentuated since 1973 when the league adopted the designated hitter. Though it's never been statistically proven, the strike zone is supposedly higher in the American League; and there is said to be less emphasis on the running game and more emphasis on hitting home runs. Compare *National League style*.

American League West The West Division of the American League, consisting of teams grouped around western cities, created in

1969 when the American League expanded from 10 to 12 teams. The division consisted of six teams from 1969 to 1976 (California Angels, Chicago White Sox, Kansas City Royals, Minnesota Twins, Oakland A's, Seattle Pilots in 1969, Milwaukee Brewers from 1970 to 1971, and Texas Rangers from 1972 to 1976), seven teams from 1977 (with the addition of the Seattle Mariners) to 1993, and four teams since 1994 (California/Anaheim/Los Angeles Angels, Oakland A's, Seattle Mariners, and Texas Rangers).

American Legion Baseball A national program for 14- to 19-year-olds that culminates in an annual World Series tournament. Sponsored since 1925 by the American Legion, a national veterans service organization, it is the oldest and largest nationwide teenage baseball program in America and aims "to give players an opportunity to develop their skills, personal fitness, leadership qualities and to have fun."

American Women's Baseball Federation An amateur sports organization founded in 1992 "to organize and promote baseball as a mainstream and lifetime opportunity for women." It organizes tournaments, promotes youth activities, holds training camps, and helps the nation's women's baseball teams to network and conduct competitions. Abbrev. *AWBF.*

America's pastime The game of baseball, more commonly termed *national pastime.*

America's Team A name that the Atlanta Braves of the 1990s tried to give itself, presumably because so many people saw the team play on owner Ted Turner's cable channel TNT. The precedent for the name was the professional football Dallas Cowboys, which had been long known as America's Team.

amphetamine A synthetic racemic drug that stimulates the central nervous system and acts as an antidepressant. Baseball players began to use amphetamines during the 1940s to combat fatigue, sharpen focus, enhance performance, boost energy, promote a sense of well-being, and get through a long season; their use became widespread in the major and minor leagues, esp. among position players, with estimates that at least half of all

players took amphetamines before a game. Trainers made them easily available in the clubhouse, distributing pills that were often taken with coffee or highly caffeinated energy drinks. Because of their potentially damaging effects, including serious short- and long-term health and behavioral problems, amphetamines were made illegal without a prescription under the Controlled Substances Act of 1970. Major League Baseball banned amphetamines at the beginning of the 2006 season; the agreement with the Major League Baseball Players Association includes testing and penalties. Syn. *greenie*; *bean*, 3.

anchor 1. *v.* To be at the base of. Scott McGregor, Mike Flanagan, and Mike Boddicker "anchored a [Baltimore Orioles] rotation that averaged 41 complete games a season in 1982, 1983 and 1984" (Richard Justice, *The Washington Post*, Feb. 24, 1987). **2.** *n.* A solid starting pitcher. "They [San Diego Padres] know they can't win with Eric Show as the anchor of their staff" (*Tampa Tribune*, Dec. 4, 1988). **3.** *n.* A device that holds a base in place. "[Detroit groundskeeper Billy Houston has] introduced a double anchor at first" (*Detroit Free Press*, May 16, 1887; Peter Morris).

anchorage A base. IST USE. 1909. "[Dave Altizer] caught [Doc] Gessler off first after a fly catch on which the Red Sox captain ventured too far away from his proper anchorage" (*Chicago Tribune*, July 11; Peter Morris).

anchor man Syn. of *leadoff batter*, 1.

ancient mariner A poor infielder. ETYMOLOGY. The beginning of Samuel Taylor Coleridge's poem, "The Rime of the Ancient Mariner" (1798): "Like the Ancient Mariner, he stoppeth one of three. / By the long gray beard and glittering eye, / Now wherefore stopp'st thou me?" The Mariner detained one of three young men going to a wedding feast and mesmerized him with the story of his youthful experiences at sea. Art Hill (*I Don't Care If I Never Come Back*, 1980) wrote, "In recent years it has become fairly general to say of a poor infielder that he plays like the Ancient Mariner. That is, 'he stoppeth one of three.'" Bob Edwards (*Fridays with Red*, 1993, p.45) mentioned a letter from John Bunzel, who attributed the term to Red Barber: "One afternoon he described a game in which the shortstop kicked away two ground balls before making a good play on a third—at which Red declared, 'Like the Ancient Mariner, he stoppeth one of three!'" (Peter Morris)

anemic Weak. IST USE. 1902. "[Addie Joss] was forcing the Tigers to bat out anemic flies or weak-legged grounders" (*Detroit Free Press*, May 5; Peter Morris).

angel 1. A small, white cloud that comes to the aid of a fielder by blocking out the sun and therefore making it easier for him to catch a high fly ball. Syn. *guardian angel*. IST USE. 1909. "Pitilessly, the sun beats down from a sky, broken only by the fleecy-white clouds that the players call 'angels' because they afford so benevolent a background for the batted ball" (*Baseball Magazine*, August; David Shulman). 2. One who invests money in a team with scant hope of financial reward; a "starry-eyed owner who thinks baseball is a sport" (Bert Dunne, *Folger's Dictionary of Baseball*, 1958). This use of the term comes from the theatrical "angel" who backs a play financially.

Angels Nickname for the American League West Division expansion franchise in Anaheim, Calif. The franchise began playing in Los Angeles in 1961 and was known as the Los Angeles Angels until it relocated to Anaheim in 1965, when it was known as the California Angels. After the 1996 season, the club was renamed the Anaheim Angels. Beginning with the 2005 season, the club changed its name to Los Angeles Angels of Anaheim. Also known as Halos. ETYMOLOGY. Named for Los Angeles—which is Spanish for "the angels" and is known as the "City of Angels"— where the club was located in 1961. Also named for the Pacific Coast League entry, the Los Angeles Angels.

angler A player or his agent who "casts" about looking for testimonials, product endorsements, speaking engagements, and other off-field sources of income.

annex To win a game. "Bob Friend scattered nine hits to annex the opener" (*The Sporting News*, May 27, 1956). IST USE. 1913. "The Seals annexed a majority of the games of the series" (*San Francisco Bulletin*, Apr. 28; Gerald L. Cohen).

Annie See *Baseball Annie*.

Annie Oakley 1. A free pass to a baseball game. See also *machine-gun ticket*. 2. A *base on balls*; a "free pass" or "free ticket" to first base. "[Bob] Lemon's No-Hitter Lift to Tribe, Only Three Tigers Get On All Via Annie Oaklies" (*San Francisco News-Call Bulletin* headline, July 1, 1948; Peter Tamony). 3. A pitch designed for show rather than function. Umpire Ernie Stewart (quoted in Larry R. Gerlach, *The Men in Blue*, 1980, p.121): "Bobo Newsom . . . had a big old 'Annie Oakley' [slow] curveball that was nothing on earth but a crowd rouser. He never tried to make it a strike, and he never threw it unless he had a five-run lead or there were two out or two strikes. He threw it when he didn't want you to hit the ball."

ETYMOLOGY. Named for the legendary female star of Buffalo Bill's Wild West Show who used to show off her sharpshooting skills by putting bullets through the suit symbols of playing cards. Since free passes to baseball games have traditionally had holes punched

Annie Oakley. With rifle given to her by "Buffalo Bill" Cody. The female sharpshooter's name became part of baseball and theatrical slang. *George Grantham Bain Collection, Library of Congress*

in them, the jump to baseball was a natural one. While the inspiration for the term is easily traced to the famed sharpshooter, its transfer has been a matter for much conjecture. The most commonly repeated version appears in Courtney Ryley Cooper's 1927 biography *Annie Oakley, Woman at Arms*. The full Cooper account:

"And by one of her tricks, Annie Oakley achieved a form of notoriety which she did not expect. The feat was to place a playing card, the ace of hearts, as a target at a distance of twenty-five yards. Then, firing twenty-five shots in twenty-seven seconds, she would obliterate that ace of hearts in the center, leaving only bullet holes in its place. A card thus shot by Annie Oakley formed quite a souvenir in the Eighties.

"There came into being a baseball magnate who looked with some disfavor upon passes as all baseball managers look upon these avenues of free admission. It is the custom, that the doortender may know the ticket to be free, to punch a hole or two in the card, this saving a miscount when the proceeds of the day were checked. One day a card came through to the gate which had been thoroughly perforated. The magnate remarked laconically: 'Huh! Looks like Annie Oakley'd shot at it!'

"The remark was repeated and re-repeated. Soon along Broadway, a new name came into being for a free ticket of admission. It was an Annie Oakley, and passes remain Annie Oakleys to this date. The surprising thing being that Annie Oakley herself denied ever having had one of the things. 'I always pay my way,' she averred."

Oakley herself established that the baseball magnate was none other than Ban Johnson, longtime American League president. In an interview in *The World* for June 28, 1922—areproduced in *American Speech* (Feb. 1933) along with the letters mentioned below—she told of Johnson looking at a pass and suggested that "the man has been letting me use it as a target. Now the term is in use in Australia and England, as well as America."

Several readers of *The World* were not happy with this explanation and in the following days the newspaper published their letters. One man insisted that it came from Oakley's first appearance with the Barnum and Bailey Circus at Madison Square Garden when "a number of her pictures, ticket size, were scattered throughout the streets of the city. Finders were entitled to free admission to 'the greatest show on earth.' You can imagine the resultant eagerness of small boys and their equally boyish fathers, to find an 'Annie Oakley.'"

A second writer insisted that virtually all slang comes from the underworld and its fringes and that the term in question "originated among the hangers-on of circuses and street fairs and was, like so many bits of argot, an opprobrious word, usually accompanied with profanities and obscenities. If you have ever experienced the mood of circus people on a rainy day, when the paid admissions were few and passes many, you will understand how the expression in question came to be used."

A final letter insisted that the term originated when a man walked through the gates at Madison Square Garden and was asked to produce a ticket. "Don't need one," he said, "I'm Annie Oakley's brother." He was let in free and the next evening 37 of Miss Oakley's brothers showed up to see her act.

Roe Fowler from Fresno, Calif., in a letter to the *Smithsonian* magazine (Nov. 1990), wrote: "In 1912 or 1913 my father took me to see Annie Oakley's last touring show, 'The Young Buffalo Wild West,' in Herrin, Ill. In her final stunt her assistant, probably Frank Butler, tossed her loaded rifles with full magazines. She emptied each one at a sheet of tin, firing as fast as she could pull the trigger and recock the rifle, spelling out her name in bullet holes. While the audience applauded wildly, she took a bow, then grabbed the rifle and fired backward, dotting the 'i.' That brought down the house." Fowler wrote that it was this name-spelling act, not the playing-card shoot, that gave the name "Annie Oakleys" to complimentary tickets. The theater's name, spelled out in tiny perforations like the bullet holes Annie shot into the tin sheet, made counterfeiting of comps more difficult. He added: "As a reporter on the *Chicago Tribune* in the 1920s I got many an Annie Oakley from the theater critics, and all were perforated in that manner."

Despite these alternative theories, it is the

Ban Johnson version that seems to have the greatest credibility (probably because this is Oakley's own version). When Johnson died on March 28, 1931, the obituary carried in many newspapers noted that he had coined the term when he "likened a well-punched baseball pass to a discarded Annie Oakley target" (*San Francisco News*, March 30, 1931; Peter Tamony).

announced for A term used in a box score for a pinch hitter who was denied an opportunity to bat because he was removed for another pinch hitter.

answer the bell For a relief pitcher to be warmed up and ready to pitch when summoned by the manager. The bell alludes to the telephone connecting the dugout and the bullpen.

ant *hist.* A baseball fan. ETYMOLOGY. According to Patrick Ercolano (*Fungoes, Floaters and Fork Balls*, 1987, p.4), the term "dates from the early 1900s and stems from the observation that fans in the stands often appear as small as ants to the players (and, to some players, as insignificant as ants)."

ante-over A game of ball played by two groups of children, on opposite sides of a schoolhouse, over which the ball (often a tennis ball) is thrown. If a player on one side catches the ball, he/she runs to the other side and tries to tag or throw it at an opponent. Virginia Brown Bassler (*Columbia* [Md.] *Flier,* Jan. 6, 2000) reminisced, "After yelling, 'ante-over,' the ball would be thrown by a member of the team who was strong enough to get it over the roof. (It was a great accomplishment when I was finally strong enough to do that!)" There are many spelling variations, including "anti-over" and "anti-I-over."

antesala Spanish for "third base" (waiting room).

antesalista Spanish for "third baseman."

antitrust exemption The U.S. Supreme Court opinion (decided May 29, 1922) that removed baseball from the antitrust laws because, in the words of the Court, the sport "would not be called trade or commerce in the commonly accepted use of those words." Writing for the unanimous Court decision in *Federal Baseball Club of Baltimore* v. *National League of Professional Baseball Clubs* (259 U.S. 200), Justice Oliver Wendell Holmes Jr. held that baseball was immune from the antitrust laws not because it was sport rather than a business and not because it was a sacred national pastime, but because baseball was not engaged in interstate commerce and hence was beyond the scope of the Sherman Antitrust Act of 1890. The Court concluded that the crossing of state lines to play baseball was "a mere incident, not the essential thing" to the actual playing of the game. The "essential thing" was that an exhibition was being staged and taking place in one state, and "personal effort, not related to production, is not a subject of commerce." The interpretation of interstate commerce was narrowly defined at the time (it was greatly expanded by the Supreme Court during the New Deal era). There are those who consider this decision ridiculous after the Court held that vaudeville, boxing, and even professional football were deemed interstate commerce; yet, other businesses are so excused, such as agricultural co-ops and insurance companies, and are legally allowed to collude in sharing risk information and setting rates. The exemption issue was reconsidered in *Toolson* v. *New York Yankees* (1953) and *Flood* v. *Kuhn* (1972), and although the Supreme Court admitted that the 1922 decision was an "anomaly" and that baseball is clearly interstate commerce, it followed its precedent in upholding the exemption as an established aberration that has survived the expanding concept of interstate commerce, and arguing that the U.S. Congress has the opportunity to enact remedial legislation. The exemption covers team relocations, league expansion, broadcasting contracts, and protection of minor-league markets. The *Curt Flood Act* of 1998 revoked part of the exemption for labor relations.

ant-killer A hard-hit ground ball or one pounded into the dirt in front of home plate; one that appears to be hit so hard that it will kill insects in its path. Abbrev. *AK*. IST USE. 1874 (*Chicago Inter-Ocean*, July 7; Edward J. Nichols). Despite this early first appearance, the term is listed by the *Los Angeles Times* (May 15, 1994) as current "baseball lingo."

anvil chorus Critical fans. "Hank [Greenberg] was tortured by thoughts of the going-over the anvil chorus would give him when he muffed his first fly ball" (Stanley Frank, *Saturday Evening Post*, March 15, 1941). "The anvil chorus is after Buck [Weaver] . . . and he'll have to lead the world at his post it seems, to avoid the knockers" (George S. Robbins, sportswriter for the *Chicago Daily News*, writing about Weaver in Apr. 1916, quoted in Irving Stein, *The Ginger Kid*, 1992, p.76). More recently: "The chant of M-V-P is now heard with regularity at Dodger Stadium, an appropriate accompaniment to his [Adrian Beltre's] own anvil chorus in a breakout season of consistency, maturity and acknowledged leadership" (Jim Salisbury, *Philadelphia Inquirer*, Aug. 29, 2004). The term is not always limited to fans; e.g., "The ball players who are inclined to join the 'anvil chorus' from hammer valley, organized to discredit the Federals [Federal League], are certainly a bunch of sickly skates" (Charles A. Lamar, *Atlanta Constitution*, Feb. 1, 1914). ETYMOLOGY. The rousing "Anvil Chorus" from Giuseppe Verdi's 1853 opera *Il Trovatore*, depicting Spanish gypsies striking their anvils at dawn and singing the praises of hard work, good wine, and their gypsy women.

anybody's game Said of a baseball game whose outcome is very much in doubt. "Each contest was anybody's game until the last man was out" (*Brooklyn Eagle*, Sept. 6, 1892). IST USE. 1866. "The score was such as to make it 'anybody's game'" (*Brooklyn Eagle*, Aug. 27; Peter Morris).

A1 See *Class A1*.

apagafuego Spanish for "relief pitcher."

Aparicio double A walk and a stolen base. IST USE. 1959. "When larcenous Luis Aparicio, a .260 hitter, stole fifty bases in his first sixty-one tries, an 'Aparicio double' became renowned throughout the league as a walk and a stolen base" (*The New York Times Magazine*, Sept. 27; David Shulman).

APBA (pron. "app-bah") A tabletop baseball board game that combines the randomness of dice with the on-field performance of individual major-league players. It is mathematically calculated to express the individual strengths and weaknesses of each player. Created in 1931 by John Richard Seitz, it has been sold as a baseball simulation game since 1951, and is now popular as a computer game. Dwight D. Eisenhower's grandson David (quoted in an Associated Press article, July 22, 1984), once raved, "The beauty of APBA is it lets you participate in something you couldn't ordinarily participate in. There just couldn't be a better board game. In some ways, it's better than the game on the field." The term is a proper noun (a registered trade name), not an acronym, and derives from the original American Professional Baseball Association. "Never, no never, call it 'Ay, Pee, Bee, Ay!'" (APBA Game Co. "warning," quoted in Raymond Mungo, *Confessions from Left Field*, 1983, p.100).

APBPA Abbrev. for *Association of Professional Ball Players of America*.

appeal **1.** *n.* An official notice by the defensive team that a rule has been broken, or a request that a call be reexamined; specif. when a) the fielding team claims that a member of the batting team has violated a rule or that an umpire has made a decision that is in conflict with the rules; or b) the fielding team asks the plate umpire to seek the help of the umpires at first base or third base in determining if the batter took a full swing at the ball for a strike or only took half a swing (not a strike) for a ball (such an appeal is made after a pitch that was called a ball). **2.** *n.* An opportunity for a player who has been disciplined or suspended to present his side of the incident. After Major League Baseball hears from the umpires and reviews videotapes, a ruling is made. If the player challenges the ruling, the discipline is stayed pending a hearing; but if the appeal is dropped, the discipline starts immediately. Players can "abuse" the system by strategically withdrawing their appeals when the discipline (usually a suspension) will do the least harm. **3.** *v.* To make an appeal.

appeal play A play made in conjunction with and as a part of an appeal; e.g., if a baserunner neglects to touch a base when running, it is the responsibility of the defensive team, not the umpire, to claim the violation. To make an appeal play in a dead-ball situation, the pitcher must first put the ball back in play by stepping on the pitching rubber, then stepping off the rubber and throwing the ball to a teammate who tags the base in question. At this point the umpire decides if the runner is safe or out. The appeal play and the appeal must be made before the next pitch is delivered. If the ball is still in play at the time of the appeal, the ball may be thrown directly to the base.

appear To play in a baseball game.

appearance 1. Playing in a baseball game. 2. See *plate appearance.*

appearance clause A clause in a pitcher's contract that stipulates he is to be given a bonus if he appears in a stipulated number of games.

appearance game An exhibition game played to show the talents of certain stars or to pair two teams that do not play normally. "The All-Stars met little resistance from the Elite Giants. It was the Giants' second game of the day, an 'appearance' game as they called it, a game set up for the fans instead of the players" (William Brashler, *The Bingo Long Traveling All-Stars and Motor Kings*, 1973, p.51; Charles D. Poe).

apple The baseball. IST USE. 1918. "Manager [Lee] Fohl and the Cleveland players were persistently complaining that the apples the Fresno rain king [Dutch Leonard] were serving were spotted with licorice" (*The Boston Globe*, May 22; Peter Morris).

apple comes up Failure to accomplish a desired result in a key situation. The term is a reference to one's Adam's apple; to choke. See also *feel the apple.*

apple-knocker 1. A batter. IST USE. 1926. "Harry Heilmann, another apple-knocker of some distinction in the American League" (Joe Williams, *New York World-Telegram*, Dec. 27; Peter Morris). 2. A baseball player, esp. one from a rural area.

apple orchard A ballpark. IST USE. 1933 (Walter Winchell, *Havana Evening Telegram*, Apr. 11).

apple tree A verbal symbol for choking, and an allusion to the Adam's apple. When Dick Young wrote in the *New York Daily News* that "the tree that grows in Brooklyn is an apple tree" (in reference to the Dodgers losing the 1951 pennant to the New York Giants), he was using what George Vecsey (*The New York Times*, Sept. 2, 1987) later deemed "the ultimate sports phrase for choking in the clutch."

apply the whitewash To shut out; to keep the opponent from scoring. IST USE. 1888 (*Chicago Inter-Ocean*, July 3; Edward J. Nichols).

appreciation day 1. A celebration dedicated to a particular player, held in conjunction with a baseball game. "It is 'Gehrig Appreciation Day' at Yankee Stadium, July 4, 1939" (*Baseball Magazine*, June 1942; David Shulman). 2. Allowing fans to attend a baseball game without charging admission. "[Larry MacPhail] inaugurated a system of 'appreciation days,' on which thousands of unemployed fans were permitted to witness the games free of charge" (*The Sporting News*, Feb. 23, 1933; Peter Morris).

approximate value An informal index of a player's offensive performance in a given season, with 10 indicating an average performance by a regular and 20 indicating a Most Valuable Player–type season. The term is used to evaluate "quick and dirty" situations, such as which of two teams "won" a trade between them; e.g., the Lou Brock for Ernie Broglio trade during the 1964 season (Brock's subsequent approximate values summed to 162, and Broglio's to 6). The concept was introduced by Bill James in *Baseball Research Journal* (1978), first appeared in his self-published *Baseball Abstract* (1980), and was discussed in detail in his first conventionally published *Baseball Abstract* (1982). See also *value approximation method; trade value.*

apricot The baseball. "This [holding a baseball] is what we call the stitched potato, or the apricot" (Joe DiMaggio, to girlfriend Dorothy Arnold, quoted in Richard Ben Cramer, *Joe DiMaggio: The Hero's Life*, 2000, p.130).

April Cobb *hist.* A spring whirlwind; a rookie

who looks like the next Ty Cobb for a short period of time.

aqueous toss *hist.* A spitball. 1ST USE. 1920 (*The New York Times*, Oct. 7; Edward J. Nichols).

arbiter **1.** An *umpire*, 1. **2.** *hist.* Syn. of *referee* in early baseball. 1ST USE. 1859. In the first-ever intercollegiate game, between Amherst and Williams, "William R. Plunkett . . . was chosen arbiter or referee, and it is somewhat remarkable, that his services were required to decide every point, the Umpires not being able to agree upon any question proposed for their decision" (*Pittsfield* [Mass.] *Sun*, July 7).

arbitration **1.** An action taken by the commissioner of baseball to decide a dispute or controversy "related in any way to professional baseball" between major-league clubs or between a major-league club and any Major League Baseball entity, other than those whose resolutions are expressly provided by another process (Major League Constitution, Art. VI, Sect. 1). **2.** See *salary arbitration.* **3.** See *grievance arbitration.*

arbitrator **1.** An *umpire,* 1. In complaining that Ban Johnson should rotate the umpires more often, rather than leaving one in the same city for several weeks, one reporter wrote, "All hands enjoy seeing a change in the arbitrators just as much as they do in the teams" (*The Washington Post*, Aug. 25, 1904; Peter Morris). Famous umpire Bill Klem was known as the "Old Arbitrator." 1ST USE. 1904. "['Silk'] O'Loughlin is umpiring poorly in Cleveland. The arbitrator needs a rest" (*The Washington Post*, Aug. 5; Peter Morris). **2.** An individual who conducts arbitration.

árbitro Spanish for "umpire."

arc [softball term] The point at which the ball reaches its highest point in its trajectory from the pitcher's hand to the plate in slow pitch softball. It is measured in feet from the ground to that high point. The prescribed arc is between 6 feet and 12 feet in the Amateur Softball Association of America and between 3 feet from the release point and 10 feet from the ground in the United States Specialty Sports Association. See also *minimum arc*; *maximum arc*; *unlimited arc.*

arcade card Syn. of *exhibit card.*

Arch Ward Memorial Trophy The name for the trophy presented from 1962 to 1969 and from 1985 to 2001 to the most valuable player in the All-Star Game. It honors the sports editor of the *Chicago Tribune* who conceived of the All-Star Game concept. The trophy was renamed the *Commissioner's Trophy* from 1970 to 1984 and renamed the *Ted Williams Award* in 2003.

Area Code Games A *showcase* in which the players are placed on teams according to their area codes. The Area Code Games were the first attempt (by California businessman Bob Williams in 1987) to assemble high school players for scouting and recruiting purposes.

area scout A scout who looks for raw talent in a specific territory.

"aren't your hands bleeding yet?" Traditional taunt to a player spending too much time at the plate during batting practice.

argollada Spanish for "shutout" (noun).

argument bonus money Money collected by fans passing the hat to pay the fines of Carolina League players who were ejected from games during the 1930s. See R.G. Utley and Scott Verner (*The Independent Carolina Baseball League, 1936–1938*, 1999, p.55).

Arizona Fall League A six-team league featuring players who have less than one year of major-league service time and minor-league all-stars and who play from early October to late November at spring training venues in the Phoenix area. Formed in 1992, the league is owned and operated by Major League Baseball. All 30 major-league clubs must participate by sending six professional players. The league serves as an accelerated training ground and finishing school for prospects. "An invitation to play, in effect, is notice from your employer that they expect big things from you" (Tom Haudricourt, *Baseball America*, Nov. 26–Dec. 9, 2001; Peter Morris). Basketball superstar Michael Jordan played in the league in 1994. Not to be confused with the Arizona League, a rookie league. Abbrev. *AFL.*

Arlie Latham **1.** *hist.* An infielder who makes a futile attempt to field a ground ball; "a third

Arlie Latham. Posing for an 1888 "Old Judge" tobacco card. *National Baseball Library and Archives, Cooperstown, N.Y.*

baseman lifting a leg to avoid being struck on the shin by a hard-hit ball" (Frank Graham and Dick Hyman, 1960, *Baseball Wit and Wisdom*). ETYMOLOGY. Named for third baseman Walter Arlington "Arlie" Latham, a major leaguer in the 1880s and 1890s, who had a peculiar manner in dodging hard-hit balls. **2.** A "ball hit to infielder on [a] nice, easy hop" (Al Schacht, *Al Schacht Dope Book*, 1944). **3.** A player or coach who yells and gesticulates in the coach's box to distract the opposing pitcher. ETYMOLOGY. Named for Latham, whose coaching antics while a player for the St. Louis Browns in the 1880s and later with the New York Giants were animated. Fred Lieb (*Comedians and Pranksters of Baseball*, 1958) noted that Latham "amused New York fans by dancing jigs in the coaching box and performing other acrobatic gyrations."

Arlie Latham hit *hist.* A ground ball too fast for an infielder to stop. IST USE. 1907 (*New York Evening Journal*, Apr. 24; Edward J. Nichols). ETYMOLOGY. Named for third baseman Walter Arlington "Arlie" Latham, a

major leaguer in the 1880s and 1890s, who would dodge such hard-hit ground balls.

arm 1. A player's throwing or pitching arm. IST USE. 1863 (*New York Sunday Mercury*; Edward J. Nichols). **2.** Throwing ability, usually applied to a fielder who makes fast, accurate throws. **3.** A euphemism for a pitcher; e.g., "Any baseball team can use a good arm." **4.** A euphemism for a fielder with the ability to throw a baseball a long distance and with accuracy; e.g., "Smith is a good arm from right field to third base."

ARM Abbrev. for *average run equivalent method.*

arm action The movement of a pitcher's arm during the delivery of a pitch. It is the part of a pitcher's mechanics that scouts emphasize when evaluating a prospect because it is believed to be a good indicator of one's propensity to incur arm injuries. Scouts use adjectives such as "free," "easy," "smooth," "effortless," "clean," "quick," and "loose" to distinguish good arm action versus "stiff," "violent," and "ugly." Josh Boyd (*Baseball America*, Nov. 12–25, 2001) quotes a scout as saying, "To pick up arm action and delivery distinctions, we watch a pitcher from the opposite side of his throwing hand, to see balance, rhythm and where he lands, as well as the involvement of his legs in the delivery." Arm action is also important to a pitcher's ability to disguise a curveball or changeup; *Baseball America* (Dec. 10–23, 2001) evaluated Miguel Ascencio by noting that his "curveball is coming around, occasionally showing the tight spin of a quality pitch, but too often he telegraphs the pitch with his arm action." The term has particular significance to scouts because arm action is viewed as a characteristic that cannot be changed by good instruction; e.g., Cleveland Indians assistant general manager Mark Shapiro (quoted in *Baseball America*, June 11–24, 2001): "A lot of organizations don't like to draft high school pitchers because it's more of a projection. That's not as much of a factor to us as durability, poise, makeup, arm action—stuff like that. There are other things about a pitcher you can teach and change, but not those." (Peter Morris)

arm angle The orientation of the pitcher's

arm relative to his body at the release point. "[Kent] Mercker now varies his arm angle from pitch to pitch, though he gets more movement on his 91-mph fastball from the sidearm slot than he did throwing over the top" (*Sports Illustrated*, Apr. 22, 2002). USAGE NOTE. As used by pitchers and pitching coaches, the term refers to a position of the arm; e.g., a pitcher will "lower" his arm angle when changing from a three-quarters to a sidearm delivery, or a pitcher throwing straight over the top will refer to his "high" arm angle. The term is not used in reference to its geometric calculation expressed in degrees. Former major-league pitcher Dave Baldwin (personal communication, Dec. 14, 2005) describes the arm angle as two-dimensional: "Imagine a vertical line passing through the shoulder joint (the vertex) of the pitching arm. The arm angle refers to the angle formed, during delivery, by the vertical line and an imaginary line connecting the pitching hand to the vertex." See also *arm slot*.

arm behind the barn The undiscovered pitching phenom that early scouts were always in search of (Kevin Kerrane, *Dollar Sign on the Muscle*, 1984, p.23). The "barn" part of the phrase is the pronounced tendency of baseball language to emphasize the game's associations with pastoral and frontier imagery. See also *backwood scout*.

arm fake A deceptive defensive move in which the player with the ball simulates throwing the ball to one base in the hope of drawing a runner off another base. Compare *head fake*.

armor 1. Syn. of *catcher's equipment*. 2. See *body armor*.

arm path The route traveled by the pitcher's arm. "[Mike Hinckley] has an extremely good . . . delivery with a very short arm path" (*Baseball America*, Sept. 15–28, 2003; Peter Morris).

arm pitch A pitch, esp. a fastball, that lacks movement because it is thrown without making adequate use of the wrist. "Care should be exercised at all times that the fast ball does not become simply an 'arm pitch,' no matter how well it may work for a while" (Bob Feller, *Pitching to Win*, 1952).

arms A team's *pitching staff*. "Young arms have Rangers riding high in the AL West" (*USA Today* headline, May 30, 1986). "We have a lot of good young arms" (Baltimore Orioles manager Johnny Oates, quoted in *The Baltimore Sun*, Sept. 10, 1994).

arm slot The position of the pitcher's arm at a given *arm angle*; the track that the pitcher's arm takes to get to the release point. "[Baltimore Orioles pitching coach Mark] Wiley is stressing that [Sidney] Ponson stay in a good arm slot and not change angles" (*The Baltimore Sun*, March 5, 2002). Right-handed pitcher B.J. Ryan lowers his arm slot against left-handed batters to give them "a different look" (*The Baltimore Sun*, March 15, 2005).

arm speed The speed at which the pitcher's arm moves forward. "The last three innings I got more comfortable, more in sync. The arm speed got a little better" (Kevin Appier, quoted in *The Baltimore Sun*, Apr. 3, 1996).

arm thrower A fielder who fails to coordinate his stride or body momentum with arm motion in the act of throwing. An arm thrower is often said to have poor mechanics.

arm trouble Any physical problem with a pitcher's throwing arm, such as muscle soreness, elbow stiffness, or rotator cuff injuries. Although the term is usually applied to pitchers, any player can have arm trouble.

army ball [softball term] An early name for softball. The term probably derives from the fact that an early form of softball was played on army bases before, during, and after World War I.

around the horn 1. *adj.* Describing a force double play in which a ground ball is fielded by the third baseman who throws to the second baseman who then throws on to the first baseman; e.g., "The Seals pull a twin killing around the horn" (San Francisco Seals telecast, July 19, 1956; Peter Tamony). Many modern writers, however, drop the "a" in the word "around"; e.g., "[Ray] Knight started two 'round-the-horn double plays both of which required hard-nosed, low-bridge pivots by [Rick] Burleson with spikes aimed at his knees" (Thomas Boswell, *The Washington Post*, Apr. 7, 1987). Syn. *'round the horn*.

USAGE NOTE. This would appear to be the older and more traditional of two current meanings of the term (see below). **2.** *adv.* Pertaining to throwing the ball around the infield for practice and/or show, especially after a strikeout; said of the pattern in which the ball is thrown from catcher to third baseman to shortstop to second baseman to first baseman, after the first or second out has been made and nobody is on base. The custom of throwing the ball around the infield is an old one, perhaps dating to 1877 when the Chicago White Stockings were on tour. IST USE. 1884. "[Providence catcher Barney Gilligan] blocks the view of umpires [of third strikes] and throws it around the horn" (*The Sporting Life*, Sept. 3, p.7; Frank Vaccaro). **3.** *n./hist.* A "side-arm curve to batter when count is 3 and 2" (*The Sporting News Record Book*, 1937). "A pitcher's wide-breaking curve" (Edwin M. Rumill, *Christian Science Monitor*, Sept. 1, 1937).

ETYMOLOGY. The term is an old nautical one referring to the long voyage between the Atlantic Ocean and the Pacific Ocean, which, before the opening of the Panama Canal, required a vessel to go around the tip of South America at Cape Horn. It is suggested that the ball is going the long way around to get back to the pitcher instead of being tossed to the pitcher immediately after the out. Robert Hendrickson (*Salty Words*, 1984) noted, "Cape Horn, incidentally, isn't so named because it is shaped like a horn. Captain Schouten, the Dutch navigator who rounded it in 1616, named it after Hoorn, his birthplace in northern Holland."

EXTENDED USE. Said of a passing pattern in basketball. "If you're not good defenders individually, then you won't be a good defender in a zone, and we were trying to pass it around the horn and get good shots" (Washington Wizards forward Jerry Stackhouse, quoted in *The Baltimore Sun*, Dec. 29, 2002).

around the plate Said of a pitcher who consistently throws strikes or near strikes; said of a pitcher who is not wild. "Sidney [Ponson] has such great stuff that at times he can be around the plate too much. He needs to learn there are times when you need to throw strikes and other times when you need to throw balls" (Baltimore Orioles catcher Charles Johnson, quoted in *The Baltimore Sun*, May 12, 1999).

ARP Abbrev. for *adjusted runs prevented.*

arrived Said of a player who has started to play to his potential (Tom Meany, ed., *The Artful Dodgers*, 1966).

arsenal The full complement of pitches available to a pitcher, including other intangibles, such as control or lack thereof. "In those days [Bob] Feller's lack of control was an added weapon in his arsenal" (Arnold Hano, *A Day in the Bleachers*, 1955, p.107). "[Mark Buehrle] has a large arsenal, including a nasty sinker, an effective cut fastball and multiple curves" (*USA Today Sports Weekly*, Sept. 11–17, 2002). See also *repertoire.*

arson squad An effective group of relief pitchers who appears "to throw gasoline on a fire." The term was used to describe the California Angels bullpens of the 1980s.

article of ball *hist.* The quality of performance of a baseball player or team. Two illustrations from the *San Francisco Bulletin* (Gerald L. Cohen): "Gregory pitched a high-class article of ball for the Oaks" (Feb. 10, 1913) and "[The San Francisco] Seals will have to play a better article of ball from this time on" (Apr. 16, 1913).

artificial grass Syn. of *artificial turf.*

artificial turf A synthetic playing-field surface textured and colored to resemble grass. The first such surface was installed in the Houston Astrodome in 1966. It can be installed both indoors and outdoors. See also *Astroturf.* Syn. *turf; artificial grass; fake grass; carpet,* 3; *rug; synthetic turf;* "artificial surface." USAGE NOTE. Although the term is a perfectly good one, the material itself is not without its strong critics who will let you know what they think of it. Leonard Koppett (*The New York Times*, March 30, 1986): "Artificial turf spoils all the formulas and ruins the rhythms of the game, especially in the outfield." Even its supporters will grant the point that artificial turf changes the nature of the game. It is generally agreed that balls hit along artificial turf move faster and that the turf produces more injuries than its natural and more forgiving counterpart.

artillerist A pitcher. IST USE. 1910 (C.M.

Klump, *Who's Who and What's What in Baseball*).

artillery 1. A team's pitching staff. IST USE. 1907. "Heine Batch used his bat to good effect on the Pittsburg artillery" (*Brooklyn Daily Eagle*, July 14; Peter Morris). USAGE NOTE. The term "artillery fire" meant "pitching": "The hurlesters of the company engaged in a little light artillery fire" (*San Francisco Bulletin*, March 19, 1913; Gerald L. Cohen). 2. A team's most powerful hitters. IST USE. 1912 (*New York Tribune*, Sept. 6; Edward J. Nichols).

artist 1. An accomplished baseball player in the late 1800s and early 1900s. "The most experienced players of a nine come under this head, viz., such as are not only physically active and expert, but mentally quick, and shrewd in judgment of the 'points' in the game" (Henry Chadwick, *The Game of Base Ball*, 1868, p.38). "Had [Cap] Anson been grasping he would be a captain of industry today, but the great player was an artist and loved the game above the shekels" (*San Francisco Bulletin*, Feb. 28, 1913; Gerald L. Cohen). 2. A skilled pitcher. "[Tom] Glavine . . . again looked like an artist the way he painted the corners, even if he occasionally went outside the lines" (Roch Kubatko, *The Baltimore Sun*, July 16, 2000). See also *box artist*.

art of misdirection A pitcher's ability to throw strikes effectively by confusing batters with breaking balls of all types. Red Barber (National Public Radio, *Morning Edition*, Nov. 14, 1986) said that this was the quality that had enabled Mike Scott to win the 1986 National League Cy Young Award.

A's Short for *Athletics*, 1.

ASA [softball term] Abbrev. for *Amateur Softball Association of America*.

ascend *hist.* To become nervous or rattled; to lose self-control. IST USE. 1901 (Burt L. Standish, *Frank Merriwell's Marvel*; Edward J. Nichols).

ascension *hist.* Short for *balloon ascension*. "The fans . . . tried to make [Jack] Townsend believe that he was due for an ascension. He refused to ascend, however, pitching steadier than ever" (*The Washington Post*, Aug. 16, 1904; Peter Morris).

ash A baseball bat. Because of its resiliency and strength, most bats are made of northern white ash (*Fraxinus americana*), which grows in Pennsylvania, Canada, and the Adirondack Mountains of New York. IST USE. 1866. "As a batsman, too, his average each year shows him to be in the front rank in handling the ash" (*Frank Leslie's Illustrated Newspaper*, Nov. 3).

ash-handle A baseball bat. "It was never a bat, it was always something Tony Tracker called an 'ash-handle,' as in 'You ain't never goan hit that bawl if you don't choke up on the ash-handle, Horsefoot'" (Stephen King, *It*, 1986, p.526; Charles D. Poe).

ash heap *hist.* A derogatory term for a hard and rocky or rough infield. See also *contractor's back yard*; *Hogan's brickyard*; *home-brew field*. IST USE. 1897. "There is not a stronger team in the league on its 'own ash heap' than [Ned] Hanlon's warriors [Baltimore Orioles]" (Harry Weldon, *St. Louis Post-Dispatch*, Sept. 24; Peter Morris). ETYMOLOGY. The reference is to the hard, flinty residue of burned coal that is piled in ash heaps. Before World War II, bad infields and ash heaps were much more common sights.

aspirin Short for *aspirin tablet*. "[Allie Reynolds] could throw that ball . . . looked like an aspirin coming up there" (Al Gionfriddo, quoted in Rick Phalen, *A Bittersweet Journey*, 2000, p.22).

aspirin tablet The baseball; esp. the ball thrown by a fastball pitcher, in which the ball appears smaller than it really is. "[Don] Newcombe was throwing aspirin tablets" (Bill Rigney, quoted in Thomas Kiernan, *The Miracle at Coogan's Bluff*, 1975, p.133). Dizzy Dean referred to it as "a fast ball that shrank up to the size of a aspirin when it reached the plate" and Jim Brosnan called it "the best way for a pitcher to cure his manager's headache." Compare *balloon*, 1. Syn. *aspirin*.

assign *hist.* To sell a player's contract to another club. According to *The Sporting News* (Feb. 10, 1921; Peter Morris), the concept of selling players was originally controversial, hence the word "assign" was being used as a euphemism.

assigned to the bench Kept out of a baseball game.

assist 1. *n*. Any throw or deflection of the ball by one fielder to another contributing to a putout. Syn. *assistance*. IST USE. 1865 (Chadwick Scrapbooks; Edward J. Nichols). 2. *n*. A statistic that is credited to a fielder who throws or deflects (slows down or redirects) a batted or thrown ball and who contributes to a putout or would have contributed to a putout except for a subsequent error by another fielder. No assist is credited to a catcher (or anyone else) on a strikeout, unless the catcher drops the third strike and has to throw the batter out. A putout is credited to the catcher on all other strikeouts. Abbrev. *A*, 2. 3. *v*. To make the play in which an assist is registered.

assistance An early synonym for *assist*, 1. "Cassidy was ready for a right-field assistance" (*New York Clipper*, May 24, 1879; Peter Morris).

assist average An early fielding statistic, measured as assists per game. It was devised by Philadelphia baseball writer Al Wright in 1876 (John Thorn and Pete Palmer, *The Hidden Game of Baseball*, 1985).

Association Short for *American Association*, 1. USAGE NOTE. The term was often used in lower case; e.g., "The Philadelphia men will have a chance to recoup their losses in the American association" (W.L. Harris, *Bismarck* [N.D.] *Daily Tribune*, Dec. 25, 1890).

Association ball The rowdier style of baseball played in the American Association, a rival major league from 1882 to 1891, which distinguished itself from the National League with such populist items as cheaper admission and the sale of alcohol. "[Patsy] Tebeau's [Cleveland] team is playing what some persons have been pleased to call 'Association ball,' a style of play that was popular in thug towns along the 80s" (*The Sporting Life*, Oct. 7, 1893; Peter Morris).

Association of Professional Ball Players of America A nonprofit organization founded on Oct. 9, 1924, that provides financial assistance to handicapped, ill, or impoverished former major- and minor-league players, as well as umpires, managers, and coaches. Abbrev. *APBPA*.

assortment Syn. of *repertoire*; *stuff*, 1. IST USE. 1898 (*New York Tribune*, June 7; Edward J. Nichols).

asterisk 1. A figurative symbol that indicates a special achievement. In baseball record-keeping, the asterisk is used in conjunction with entering an event or achievement in the official baseball record. Because the record book merely portrays things in a numerical or statistical fashion, the historical context in which an event occurs or an achievement is accomplished can be lost. The inclusion of an asterisk, along with a verbal explanation to which it refers, is felt to be a way to note or retain the historical circumstances surrounding an item entered into the record book. "An asterisk should be placed on [Dwight] Gooden's start . . . since his removal was due to a rain delay" (*New York Daily News*, July 6, 1987). See also *Year of the Asterisk*.
  2. Specifically, the long-held and sometimes bitterly disputed asterisk that was thought to have been attached in the record book to an accomplishment by Roger Maris when he was with the New York Yankees. The asterisk was allegedly affixed by baseball commissioner Ford C. Frick when, in 1961, Maris topped Babe Ruth's single-season home run record. Because Maris broke the record during a 162-game schedule, giving him eight more games than the 154-game schedule in which Ruth set the record, some fans and sportswriters felt that Maris' achievement should only be entered in the record book with an asterisk, calling attention to these extra games. In fact, no asterisk was ever affixed to Maris' achievement. It was suggested at one point, but it never appeared in the official record. For eight years there were separate records kept for 154- and 162-game seasons.
  In 1968, the Special Baseball Rules Committee ruled that baseball would have one set of records and that "no asterisk or official sign shall be used to indicate the number of games scheduled." On Sept. 4, 1991, baseball's "statistical accuracy committee" led by commissioner Fay Vincent took it even further, listing Maris' 61 home runs in 1961 as the highest total recorded—or as Shirley Povich (*The Washington Post*, Sept. 7, 1991) put

it, "[The] unchallenged home run record belongs to Maris—no asterisk, no notations, no nothing."

Yet, the myth of Maris' asterisk persists. Tony Kubek (*USA Today*, July 2, 1986) was quoted as supporting the idea of putting asterisks next to the names of teams setting hitting records with designated hitters: "[If] Frick put an asterisk by Roger Maris' name, which was ridiculous, then you should do the same here." Frank Robinson (*The Baltimore Sun*, Apr. 30, 1996) once said of one of his hitting records being eclipsed, "You know what they say, put an asterisk by it. They did it when Maris broke Ruth's record."

In his autobiography, Ford C. Frick (*Games, Asterisks, and People*, 1973, p.155) noted that the asterisk was discussed at a 1961 press conference: "Oh, yes, during the conference the word 'asterisk' was mentioned; not by the commissioner but by Dick Young, one of the outstanding baseball writers of his time. Dick remarked kiddingly, 'Maybe you should use an asterisk on the new record. Everybody does that when there's a difference of opinion.' Dick and other writers have had a lot of fun with 'asterisk' stories through the years. But the honor is not mine. To Dick a low obeisance for a clever line, with or without an asterisk."

The HBO original film *61**, directed by Billy Crystal (2001), perpetuated the asterisk myth. Although the movie did not clarify that there never was an asterisk in the record book, "the asterisk in the title is warranted as a reminder of the extraordinary events of that year and as a mark of excellence for Billy Crystal's achievement" (Frank Ardolino, *NINE: A Journal of Baseball History and Culture*, Spring 2002, p.182).

Astrodome The home field of the Houston Astros from 1965 to 1999. The first domed sports arena, it was termed the *Eighth Wonder of the World* by its promoters. It introduced the concepts of easy parking, wide seats, "fun" scoreboards, luxury boxes, and artificial turf. Architectural historian Stephen Fox (quoted in *The New York Times*, Oct. 3, 1999): "It is one of the great monuments of American hubris in the 1960's in this kind of sense of no limits. It is not a tremendously refined work of architecture." IST USE. 1964.

"The 'rain or shine stadium,' also known as Houston's Big Bubble, but officially the Harris County Domed Stadium, will probably . . . be called Astrodome Stadium" (*The New York Times*, Dec. 6). ETYMOLOGY. Coined in tribute to the astronauts based at the National Aeronautics and Space Administration facility near Houston, the term was in the language from the World War II era as a name for the transparent dome on the top of the fuselage of an aircraft from within which astronomical observations could be made for purposes of navigation.

Astros Nickname for the National League Central Division expansion franchise that began playing in Houston, Tex., in 1962 as the Houston *Colt .45s*. When the club moved into the brand-new Astrodome in 1965, it sported a new name, the Astronauts, but this was quickly shortened to the Astros. Also known as *'Stros*.

Astroturf The brand name for one of the earliest and most popular forms of *artificial turf*. It received its name from the Astrodome, the home field of the Houston Astros, where it was first installed. Originally, transparent panels on the Astrodome's roof allowed adequate sunlight to grow real grass, but this made conditions too bright for the players, and two of the eight panels had to be painted to control the sun's glare. This killed the real grass, and by June 1966 the artificial turf had been laid. The first visiting team to play on the rug was the Philadelphia Phillies, whose third baseman that night was Dick Allen; he scoffed, "If cows don't eat it, I ain't playing on it." A later version (*Esquire*, March 28, 1978) had Allen saying, "If a horse won't eat it, I don't want to play on it." Astroturf is no longer used, as it proved to be hard on players, shortened careers, and was unappealing to fans. Sometimes spelled "AstroTurf."

at-bat *n.* 1. A turn in the batter's box, lasting from the time the batter takes his position until he is put out or becomes a baserunner; e.g., "Smith walked in his last at-bat" or "Jones had seven at-bats in the doubleheader." Syn. *time at bat*; *AB*, 2. EXTENDED USE. A performance. Baltimore Ravens safety Will Demps (quoted in *The Baltimore Sun*, Dec. 5, 2003): "I knew if my number was called, I had to be ready for the at-bat." **2.** An official statistic for the batter coming to the batter's box, excluding those appearances in which the batter walks, sacrifices, is hit by a pitched ball, or is interfered with by the catcher. Compare *plate appearance.* Abbrev. *AB,* 1. IST USE. 1861 (*New York Sunday Mercury*, Aug. 10; Edward J. Nichols).

at bat *adv.* Taking one's turn in the batter's box for the purpose of batting; e.g., "Smith was at bat with the bases loaded" or "Jones had another productive season at bat." Syn. *at the plate.* IST USE. 1866. "The Center Fielder . . . should always go to long field where a hard-hitter is at bat" (*Beadle's Dime Base-Ball Player*; Peter Morris). EXTENDED USE. Referring to a person "in the spotlight." A jazz reviewer commenting on the soloist in a big band concert wrote, "I can't tell which one is at bat" (*San Francisco News-Call Bulletin*, Sept. 24, 1960; Peter Tamony).

at bat, on deck, in the hold The sequence of terms traditionally used in reference to the current batter and the player scheduled to bat next, followed by the subsequent player in the lineup. In the modern era it is usually given as "at bat, on deck, in the *hole*," but this is a corruption of "in the hold," a reference to the interior of a ship, below decks.

ETYMOLOGY. Aside from "at bat," few borrowings from other lexicons are as evident as these from a ship: to be on deck is to be on the ship's main deck (or floor), and the hold is the area of the ship below the main deck. That these terms have obvious roots in nautical language is made clear by Joanna Carver Colcord (*Sea Language Comes Ashore*, 1945): "The newspaperman's dogwatch, the baseball player's on deck and in the hole (hold), the contractor's wrecking crew, the bus-driver's and the soda-fountain clerk's double-deckers, are also sea-borrowings."

According to one important source, the terms can be traced to an official scorer of a game played in Belfast, Maine, a town with both a rich baseball and nautical history. The source is a short, unsigned story that appeared in *The Sporting News* (March 24, 1938) and was based on a report sent to its offices by Robert Patterson Chase, a nonagenarian from Belfast. According to the report, the Boston

team was making a tour of Maine in 1872 and played, among others, The Pastimes of Belfast on August 7 of that year. The scorer for each team was called upon to announce the batters. The Boston scorer simply announced: "G. Wright at bat; Leonard and Barnes next." To quote from the original story: "But when the Belfast team had its turn, the Belfast scorer would say 'Moody at bat, Boardman on deck, Dinsmore in the hold,' using nautical terms which made such a hit with the Boston scorer that he carried them back to Boston, after which they became general." *The Sporting News* added that the final outcome of the game was Boston 35, Belfast 1: "So, all the Maine town got out of that contest was the distinction of being a contributor to the lexicon of the game."

Further investigation of this claim was made by the compiler of this dictionary on a visit to Belfast in Aug. 1987. The investigation revealed the following:

1. The game in question did occur, on the 6th (not the 7th) of Aug. 1872, according to *The Republican Journal*, in an article published on the 8th. It said in part: "The visit of the famous Boston Red Stocking Baseball Club to our city on Tuesday the 6th was an unusual treat to the lovers of the national game."

2. According to *The Republican Journal*, the pitcher for the Pastimes was named Chase. No other name or initial is given, but it suggests that the man who gave the report to *The Sporting News* may have been an actual participant in the game. He would have been 25 at the time, and was the only Chase in the local city directory who seemed to have been of playing age in 1872. Chase was a well-known and respected resident of Belfast who died when he was nearly 100.

3. Ironically, the story was known locally in Belfast, but had been largely forgotten until a Belfast reporter, on vacation in Houston in the mid-1980s, read about it in the scorecard at the Astrodome. Jay Davis, editor of the local *Waldo* (County) *Independent*, published in Belfast, says that his paper then reinvestigated the original events and while it could not prove them conclusively, it could not find anything to cause him to

doubt their authenticity. Subsequently, John G. Arrison (Stephen Phillips Memorial Library, Penobscot Marine Museum) discovered an article in *The Republican Journal* (Sept. 2, 1937) entitled "Local Baseball History Recalled by R.P. Chase—Novel Phraseology of Belfast Scorer Appeals to Bostonians" in which the aforementioned gives a detailed account of the game and the origin of the phrase. It is virtually the same as *The Sporting News* account but adds that Chase thought the term was forgotten until he was listening to the radio broadcast of a World Series game and "was startled by hearing the announcement in the old Belfast form." Chase wrote to George Wright, the last surviving member of the Red Stockings, affirming that he had in fact played against him in the 1872 game and reporting how pleased he had been to hear the phrase on the radio. "Mr. Wright replied immediately, stating that he well remembered the game here and the amusement the new form of announcement gave the players of the Boston team." The article had appeared in response to Wright's death on Aug. 21, 1937.

This is all well and good, but it belies one of the central premises of lexicography, which is that one needs citations to prove or disprove a theory on the origin of a term. In this case, David Shulman convincingly eliminates the Belfast story as the origin of the term "on deck"—although it was almost certainly used there and may, in fact, have sounded new to people at the game—with an earlier citation from *The Ball Players' Chronicle* (Sept. 26, 1867): "Well I went on deck and took up a bat." Meanwhile, the sequence "at bat, on deck, in the hold" did not show up in print until after the Belfast game.

A team A group composed of a club's top players by position. The term is used both figuratively, to refer to a club's best players (as in "he's potential A team material"), and literally, such as during spring training, when the assembled players are divided into an A team and a *B team* for the purpose of practice play. EXTENDED USE. Any elite grouping.

at 'em ball A hard-hit ball directed at a defensive player ("at him"), frequently the pitcher, often resulting in a double play because of the extra time it gives to make a second out. Var. *atom ball*.

athletic hose Syn. of *sanitary socks*.

Athletics 1. Nickname for the American League West Division franchise in Oakland, Calif. The franchise originated as the Philadelphia Athletics (1901–1954) and was then renamed the Kansas City Athletics (1955–1961), the Kansas City A's (1962–1967), the Oakland A's (1968–1986), and finally the Oakland Athletics in 1987. See also *Mackmen*; *White Elephants*. Syn. *A's*. ETYMOLOGY. From "Athletic," the name of an amateur club in Philadelphia in 1859. **2.** Popular nickname for major-league franchises in 19th-century Philadelphia: National Association (1871–1875), National League (1876), and American Association (1882–1891).

athletic supporter Syn. of *jockstrap*. An old Philadelphia gag (which lost its punch when the city's American League Athletics moved to Kansas City): "Are you a Phillies fan?" "No, I'm an Athletic supporter."

at home 1. Played at a team's home ballpark. "The Anthracite Club plays much better ball abroad than at home" (*The Sporting Life*, July 30, 1883). Compare *away*, 3. **2.** Said of a play at home plate; e.g., "Smith was out at home on Jones' strong throw from left."

Atlantic luck *hist.* Good fortune. The term referred to the Atlantic club of Brooklyn, one of the powerhouses of the 1860s, and the club that ended the Cincinnati Red Stockings' two-year unbeaten streak on June 14, 1870. IST USE. 1870 (*New York Herald*, June 1; Edward J. Nichols).

atom ball A punning variation of *at 'em ball*. San Francisco Giants manager Dusty Baker (quoted in *The Baltimore Sun*, Oct. 9, 2000): "[Bobby J. Jones] had the atom ball working pretty good. We hit some balls extremely hard . . . but we just couldn't find any holes." See also *nuclear fission ball*.

atomic balm A thick, gooey salve called Capsolin, derived from red-hot chili peppers grown in China, used by pitchers to mask arm pain. Most pitchers diluted it with cold cream or Vaseline, but Sandy Koufax used it straight, "gobs of it" (Jane Leavy, *Sports Illustrated*, Sept. 4, 2002).

Atlantic luck. The Atlantics of Brooklyn (bottom row) pose with the original Athletics of Philadelphia. The image is a wood engraving from a photograph that appeared in *Harper's Weekly*, Nov. 3, 1866. *Library of Congress*

atrapado robando Spanish for "caught stealing."

attaboy 1. An enthusiastic expression of encouragement. ETYMOLOGY. The term originated with Detroit Tigers manager Hughie Jennings in 1907. According to H.G. Salsinger (*Detroit News*, Jan. 10, 1926; Peter Morris), "[Jennings] coached the players in a number of plays that they had never used before. It was difficult work. . . . Jennings did not become discouraged. He used to stand in the field and direct the rehearsals. When one play went well he shouted, 'That's the Boy!' He began getting results and continued the yell as an expression of approval. When the season started . . . he had abbreviated the expression . . . shouting "'At's th' boy!' But even that was too long so he abbreviated it to 'Attaboy.' It gradually became popularized and has been one of [the] strictly American expressions for a number of years with no hint of wearing out." **2.** A congratulation given to a long reliever before a *hold*, 6, was awarded. Jim Henneman (*The Baltimore Sun*, July 22, 1994) commented, "After a good performance they got a pat on the back, accompanied by a congratulatory 'attaboy.' At the end of the season, the pitcher with the most 'attaboys' was long reliever of the year."

attack 1. Syn. of *go after*. "[Jonathan Papelbon] attacks the strike zone with mid-90s fastballs" (*Sports Illustrated*, Apr. 17, 2006). "All our pitchers need to attack the hitters more" (Detroit Tigers catcher Brad Ausmus, quoted in *The Baltimore Sun*, Apr. 23, 1999). **2.** For a batter to swing at a pitch without waiting too long. "I was just trying to be too fine, trying to wait and see the ball too long, letting balls get too deep on me instead of attacking the ball" (Jay Payton, quoted in *The Baltimore Sun*, Aug. 14, 2007).

attack point A point tallied for each total base and steal earned by a team in the Japanese Central League, used to determine the victor of a game that ends in a tie, with the team earning the most attack points being declared the victor (*The Washington Post*, Apr. 5, 1993).

attempt 1. *n.* An effort to steal a base; e.g., "Smith has 26 steals for 47 attempts." **2.** *v.* To try to steal a base.

attendance 1. The number of spectators actually present at a baseball game. The National League abandoned this practice of computing attendance figures following the 1992 season. See also *turnstile count.* **2.** The number of tickets actually sold (*paid attendance*) for a baseball game. The American League has long followed this practice, and the National League adopted it beginning with the 1993 season. Attendance figures are somewhat inflated because season-ticket holders who do not attend are counted. Abbrev. *A,* 3.

attendance clause A provision of some modern contracts promising a bonus to a player if the home attendance for a season goes above a certain number. The assumption here is that the player in question is a draw who will help the gate. Howard Smith (*Cleveland Plain Dealer,* Aug. 27, 1978) noted that Harry Caray, who then announced for the Chicago White Sox, had an attendance clause in his contract. Jerry Howarth (*Baseball Lite,* 1986) observed that while the word "attendance" was "formerly a noun of interest to major league owners, it is now an adjective for 'clause' when players negotiate salary bonuses."

at the bat Said of a team or player on the offense. "Cook made Harvard's only error, but he redeemed himself at the bat" (*Harper's Weekly,* June 11, 1892). "Casey at the Bat" (title of Ernest Lawrence Thayer's poem, *San Francisco Examiner,* June 3, 1888). "In the averages at the bat, George Wright, [Cal] McVey and [Charlie] Gould take the lead" (*Frank Leslie's Illustrated Newspaper,* July 17, 1869). Compare *in the field.* IST USE. 1867. "Williams followed at the bat, and sent a good grounder" (*Daily National Intelligencer* [Washington, D.C.], July 29). USAGE NOTE. Variation is "at their bats"; e.g., "The Olympics had the first innings, and quickly were at their bats" (*Syracuse Standard,* Sept. 29, 1859; Larry McCray).

at the plate Syn. of *at bat.*

audible signal base A base that emits sound when it is touched. The idea of such a base had been discussed for decades, but never attracted much interest. Consider this description by Lester L. Sargent (*Baseball Magazine,* March 1914, p.76): "A step toward the dawn of universal peace has been taken in the audible Signal-Base for Baseball Fields, which is the invention of Stephen H. Wills. Those terrible things that are said about the umpire will be said no more. Everybody will know for sure whether or not the runner reached the bag safe, for when he does touch base an electric bell will be rung by the base itself."

audition A trial given to a minor-league player when a major-league club uses regular-season games to make the kind of experiment generally reserved for spring training. "With another Brewers season going down the drain, the final weeks became an audition for next year" (Tom Haudricourt, *Baseball America,* Oct. 29–Nov. 11, 2001; Peter Morris).

Aunt Susie A curveball. David Halberstam (*The Summer of '49,* 1989) wrote that "Aunt Susie" was the name used by New York Yankees pitchers in the era (1947–1953) of Vic Raschi, who lacked one, and Allie Reynolds, who had one.

Australian wool A component of the supposedly livelier baseball in 1919. William Curran (*Big Sticks,* 1990, p.66) commented, "The response of those who cherished the idea of a conspiracy to corrupt the baseball was to turn the Australian-wool explanation into a running joke. . . . [By June 3, 1920] a New York reporter writes of a home run by Ping Bodie, 'Ping jarred the ball right where the Australian wool was the thickest.' . . . As late as the 1930s, baseball writers continued to make mocking references to Australian wool, and my impression is that anyone could convulse a 1920s speakeasy gathering merely by uttering the words."

authority An attribute of a hitter who swings the bat with power and purpose; e.g., "Smith hits with authority."

autographed ball A baseball with the signature of a player or players. A long-standing baseball tradition has been the autographing of baseballs by players. Autographs themselves have become a baseball commodity, with stars getting paid handsomely to sign their names.

automatic double A more accurate term for

Autographed ball. Goose Goslin of the Washington Senators obliges a fan at the 1925 World Series. *Library of Congress*

ground-rule double. See also *rule-book double.*

automatic out **1.** A batter who most likely will make an out at the plate or be retired. **2.** An out made by such a batter. USAGE NOTE. There are many, including the compiler of this dictionary, who believe that any out is a pitching feat and anything but automatic, and do not use the term.

automatic pitcher A *pitching machine*. Lee Allen (*The Hot Stove League*, 1955, p.114) reported that the first automatic pitcher was demonstrated by Princeton professor Charles E. Hinton at that institution's gymnasium on Dec. 15, 1896. It resembled a short, breech-loading cannon, mounted on a two-wheeled carriage. *The Boston Globe* (Apr. 16, 1896; Peter Morris): "Professor Hinton of Princeton has, it is said, invented a machine that will pitch balls automatically, and that will curve them also. The apparatus will deliver a ball every twenty seconds, but the time between balls can be changed. The speed of the balls can be regulated as well as the curves. The balls always go directly over the plate. It is said that . . . Princeton . . . will use this for batting practice next year."

automatic strike **1.** A pitch delivered when the count on the batter is three balls and no strikes. It is so called because, in the hope of receiving a base on balls, the batter may not swing at the next pitch; the manager of the batting team sometimes will order a batter to take the pitch. Knowing this tendency of batters and managers, pitchers are more likely to put the ball in the strike zone. Keith Hernandez (*Pure Baseball*, 1994, p.210) noted the use of the term "semiautomatic strike." IST USE. 1933. "The pitch when the count is three and nothing" (*Famous Sluggers and Their Records of 1932*). **2.** The penalty for a batter who refuses to take his position in the batter's box and (in the minor leagues) for a batter who intentionally leaves the batter's box and delays play. The umpire shall call a strike on the batter (the pitcher no longer is ordered to pitch the ball for the penalty to be called). The ball is dead during the penalty.

automatic switch Reversing the meaning of a sign or signs when it becomes apparent they are being stolen; e.g., when the catcher puts down the sign for a curve, the pitcher throws a fastball. A classic example of the automatic switch occurs when the catcher gives a normal sign but then places his bare hand on top of his mitt to call for the opposite.

automatic take Not swinging in an automatic strike situation. The batter is ordered to take the next pitch (i.e., not swing at it), hoping for a fourth ball and a base on balls.

automobile squint The theory when automobiles first became popular that driving one adversely affected a ballplayer's batting eye. "They said that the 'automobile squint' has got him [Tris Speaker] and that he can't see the ball as well as before he started piloting a big car. At any rate, Speaker's batting notch has fallen considerably and the automobile craze is blamed for it" (*St. Louis Post-Dispatch*, Aug. 21, 1910; Peter Morris).

Autumn Classic Syn. of *World Series*. "If the Autumn Classic is baseball's prime-time ode, opening day is when baseball's fans are born and reborn, when hope springs eternal for all teams" (*USA Today*, Apr. 7, 1987). Sometimes spelled "autumn classic." IST USE. 1933. "Coveted pasteboards for the autumnal classic—World series to you—are sold only in complete sets and at no reduction in price from the good old days" (*The New Yorker*, Sept. 30, p.27; Jonathan Jacobs).

AVE Abbrev. (used by Major League Baseball) for *batting average*.

average One of the general classes of statistics of baseball, usually defined as the ratio of a team's or player's successful performances (such as wins or hits) divided by total opportunities for successful performance (such as games or times at bat). The term is most often applied to *batting average*, but is also used for earned run average, fielding average, and slugging average.

average and over *hist.* The method for expressing averages during the late 1860s, used for *runs per game*, *hits per game*, *outs per game*, and *total bases per game*. It consists of a whole-number average plus a remainder. To use an example offered by John Thorn and Pete Palmer (*The Hidden Game of Baseball*, 1985), a batter with 23 hits in six games would be credited with a hits per game index of 3–5 (an average of 3 and a remainder of 5).

average bases allowed A pitcher's number of total bases allowed divided by his innings pitched. It was proposed as a measure of pitching effectiveness by Alfred P. Berry in 1951 and evaluated by John Thorn and Pete Palmer (*The Hidden Game of Baseball*, 1958).

average player A player who cares more about his individual statistics than the well-being of the team. Hugh Jennings (*Rounding Third*, 1925; Peter Morris): "There are any number of Pete Brownings in the major leagues today. The only thing they ever worry about is their batting averages. Because of this they are known professionally as 'average' players. As long as they get their hits they don't care what happens to the team."

average run equivalent method A method for evaluating an outfielder's throwing arm. It is calculated by comparing the number of bases advanced by runners on either first base or second base after singles to the number of these runners thrown out, with the result then transformed into an estimate of runs above or below the league average for which the outfielder's throwing is responsible in a given year. For the years 1959 to 1987, Juan Beniquez had the best performance (–12.4 runs in 1976) and Ron Swoboda had the worst (+7.8 runs in 1967). The method was proposed by Clem Comly (*By the Numbers*, Aug. 2000). Abbrev. *ARM*.

AVG Abbrev. for *batting average*.

avocado An inviting pitch hit for a home run. "[Don] McMahon probably didn't throw more than ten or 12 pitches the inning he worked, but one of them happened to be an avocado with two men on, and it sailed out of the park" (Oliver Kuechle, *The Sporting News*, July 20, 1960).

award bonus Payment to a player conditioned on the player having achieved a particular status in connection with a recognized or agreed-upon award or honor. Compare *performance bonus*.

award share A measure of the support a player receives for an annual award for which he is continuously eligible (such as the Most Valuable Player Award and the Cy Young Award). A player's award share for a given year is that player's number of votes for the award as a proportion of the highest possible number of votes. For example, in the 1941 American League Most Valuable Player (MVP) Award voting, Joe DiMaggio came in first with 291 of 336 possible votes, or 291/336 or .87 award shares, and Ted Williams finished second with 254 votes, or 254/336 or .76 award shares. The primary use of this measure is to represent overall voting results for a player across his career. In their careers, Williams received 6.42 MVP award shares and DiMaggio received 5.46. The measure was introduced by Bill James in his *Baseball Abstract* for 1985.

away 1. Syn. of *out*, 1; e.g., "two away" is two out. IST USE. 1881 (*New York Herald*, July 15; Edward J. Nichols). **2.** Said of a pitch thrown far from the batter or outside the strike zone. A strategy called "pitch him away, play him away" is one in which the pitcher consistently pitches a batter outside and the defense overshifts to the opposite field, where the batter is more likely to hit the ball. "The scouting report on [Vernon] Wells—*attack him away, work the outside corner*—got around, and pitchers made the adjustment" (Albert Chen, *Sports Illustrated*,

June 12, 2006). Compare *in*, 3. **3.** Played in another team's ballpark; e.g., "The Cubs played three games away." Compare *at home*, 1. IST USE. 1880. "Of the nine away-from-home games yet to play six are with Buffalo and Cincinnati" (*Chicago Tribune*, Aug. 8; Peter Morris).

away game A game played on the other team's field, as opposed to a *home game*. The 162-game major-league schedule comprises 81 away games and 81 home games. Syn. *road game*. EXTENDED USE. Foreign territory. "Since the War of 1812, all of our foreign wars have been 'away' games. We need forces we can get to the theater of war quickly" (Jack Kelly, *The Baltimore Sun*, Feb. 15, 2002).

away team Syn. of *visiting team*.

AWBF Abbrev. for *American Women's Baseball Federation*.

awful A *Texas Leaguer*, 2.

"aw nuts" An informal school of sportswriting that came to prominence in the early 20th century and brought a new and more detached, cynical approach to the craft. Many of the key figures were baseball writers, such as Ring Lardner, Charles Dryden, Westbrook Pegler, and W.O. McGeehan. They thought that sports were more often than not corrupt and that the public was gullible; their style was known for skepticism, irreverence, and needling. Jonathan Yardley (*Ring: A Biography of Ring Lardner*, 1977) noted that Lardner wrote "in a light-hearted, bantering tone that managed to make the point without offending the players themselves . . . a blend of dispassion and compassion." Lardner sought to demythologize ballplayers but not to debunk them. Compare *"gee whiz."* (Peter Morris)

AWOL Absent. The term is usually applied to a fielder who is not present when a fly ball or foul ball comes down in his territory. ETYMOLOGY. Time-honored military acronym for "absent without official leave," which has been in use since before the Civil War. Confederate soldiers caught while AWOL were made to walk about the camp carrying a sign bearing these letters. The term was brought back from World War II by players who had been in the armed forces.

ax A baseball bat.

B

B 1. See *Class B*. **2.** Abbrev. for *bunt*, 1. **3.** Abbrev. for a batter's handedness (left-handed, right-handed, or switch-hitting).

BA Abbrev. for *batting average*.

BAA Abbrev. for *batting average against*.

Babe 1. The most famous nickname in baseball, the one given to George Herman Ruth, the single most dominant figure in baseball. The 1933 edition of *Who's Who in Baseball* gave this explanation: "The nickname 'Babe' was originally applied to him when he joined the Baltimore Orioles in 1914. Coach Steinam, who was owner [Jack] Dunn's right-hand man, greeted the big fellow when he came into the ball yard, shouting to the other Baltimoreans: 'Boys, here's Jack's New Babe!'" In his autobiography *The Babe Ruth Story* (1948), Ruth pointed out that the "clincher" came a few days later when he was playing with the controls of a hotel ele-

Babe. The other Babe: Babe Herman (left) with Hack Wilson. *National Baseball Library and Archives, Cooperstown, NY*

vator. After almost decapitating himself, Ruth was chewed out by Dunn. One of the older players, taking pity on him, called him a "babe in the woods." "After that," wrote Ruth, "they all called me Babe." Ruth was not the only player to be called "Babe"; probably the most famous was Floyd C. "Babe" Herman, who was also known as "the other Babe." Ruth may have been able to claim a record for the most aliases in the history of baseball. Sportswriters competed to invent new titles with which to decorate the daily headlines: Bam, Bambino (Italian for "little baby"), Baron of Bam, Basha of Bingle, the Battering Bambino, Behemoth of Biff, Behemoth of Bust, Big Bam, Big Bambino, Caliph of Clout, Caliph of Crush, Colossus of Clout, Colossus of Club, Colossus of Sport, Duke of Wallop, Goliath of Grand Slam, Home Run King, Jidge, King of Clout, King of Klout, King of Slam, *King of Swat*, Maharajah of Mash, Mauling Mastodon, Monk, Monkey,

Babe. Babe Ruth as a spectator at the 1934 World Series. *Photograph by Joseph Baylor Roberts*

Prince of Pounders, Rajah of Rap, Rajah of Smack, Slambino, *Sultan of Swat*, Tarzan of Slam, Wai of Wallop, Wazir of Wham, and Wizard of Whack.
2. Any big, fat player. The term was used only after Babe Ruth began showing the effects of excessive drinking and eating. 3. A player with a youthful-looking appearance. The first prominent player with this nickname was Pittsburgh Pirates pitcher Charles "Babe" Adams: "A strikingly handsome man, Adams was tagged with the nickname Babe by female fans in Louisville, who crooned, 'Oh, you babe' when they saw him" (Dennis DeValeria and Jeanne Burke DeValeria, *Honus Wagner*, 1995, p.208). 4. An element of infield chatter, as in "humm-babe."

Babe Ruth A home run. Babe Ruth hit so many home runs that his name became synonymous with a home run. In the 1930s, his name was a common sports-page eponym (*Journalism Quarterly*, 1934).

Babe Ruth, the Ultimate compliment to a baseball player or any athlete, or any person of prominence; e.g., "Clay Carr [is] the Babe Ruth of rodeo riders" (*Sports Illustrated*, May 16, 1994), "Charley Eckman . . . was the Babe Ruth of basketball referees" (*The Baltimore Sun*, June 27, 1999), "Bill Tilden . . . the Babe Ruth of tennis" (*Sports Illustrated*, Aug. 25, 2003), "Johnny Unitas: The Babe Ruth of the NFL" (Babe Ruth Museum exhibit, Nov. 2003), "Willie Sutton . . . the Babe Ruth of bank robbers" (*Time* magazine), "Billy Haughton: The Babe Ruth of harness racing" (Andrew Postman and Larry Stone, *The Ultimate Book of Sports Lists*, 1990), and Josh Gibson as "the black Babe Ruth" and Sadaharu Oh as "the Babe Ruth of Japan." The importance of the name "Babe Ruth" was underscored in Eleanor Gehrig's book *My Luke and I* (1976) when she mentioned that her late husband, Lou Gehrig, was deemed "the Babe Ruth of the high schools" and the "college Babe Ruth."

Babe Ruth Award See *World Series Most Valuable Player Award*, 1.

Babe Ruth Curse Syn. of *Curse of the Bambino*. IST USE. 1986. "Babe Ruth Curse Strikes Again" (George Vecsey, *The New York Times* headline, Oct. 28).

Babe Ruther One who plays in the Babe Ruth League. "Knox [County] Babe Ruthers Place Third in State" (*Camden* [Maine] *Herald* headline, July 31, 1986).

"Babe Ruth is dead" Advice given to a pitcher who is nibbling the corners and getting behind every hitter. The full thought here is to remind the pitcher of an irrefutable historical fact: "Babe Ruth is dead; so throw strikes to this guy!"

Babe Ruth League A nonprofit, organized network of baseball (and, since 1984, softball) for boys and girls from ages 4 to 18. It was founded in 1951 by Marius D. Bonacci in Trenton, N.J. The League is structured in age-based divisions: Cal Ripken Baseball (ages 4–12), known as the Bambino Division until 1999; two Babe Ruth Baseball divisions (ages 13–15 and 16–18); three softball divisions for girls (ages 4–12, 13–16, and 17–18); and Bambino Buddy Ball (ages 5–20) for physically and mentally disabled players. The League administers annual World Series competitions for each of its divisions. Initially registered under the name Little Bigger League, the organization was renamed in 1954 after Claire Ruth (Babe Ruth's widow) endorsed the program. Also known as "Babe Ruth Baseball."

BABIP Abbrev. for *batting average on balls in play*.

baby act *hist.* A play considered "ungentlemanly" (that is, "weak") in the late 19th century, such as a bunt or an intentional base on balls.

baby ball *hist.* Syn. of *baby hit*. "[Glynn] struck a baby ball" (*Kalamazoo Telegraph*, Sept. 1, 1875; Peter Morris).

baby boomer A nickname for a strong, young power hitter of the mid-1980s. ETYMOLOGY. The term refers to a person born in the period after World War II, when the birth rate skyrocketed. In the 1980s the baby boomers were seen as coming into a time of great influence. The baseball baby boomers were born much later, but the term fit because they were young (babies) and could hit the long ball (boomers).

baby hit *hist.* A bunt for a base hit. "[Mike] McGeary got first on a baby hit" (*London*

[Ont.] *Free Press*, March 24, 1877; Peter Morris). "The fans hated the bunt, which they called the 'baby hit,' but apologists said the game never had been so scientifically conducted" (Lee Allen, *The Sporting News*, June 22, 1968). The *Brooklyn Daily Eagle* (July 23, 1873; Peter Morris) referred to Tommy Barlow of the Atlantics making six of "what [Washington's] Nick Young calls 'baby hits'" but then added: "As for sneering at it and calling it baby hitting, this is absurd . . . The real baby hits are those which give easy chances for fly catches." See also *baby play*. Syn. *baby ball*. IST USE. 1871. "White sent a 'baby' hit to Brainard and went out at first" (*The Cleveland Morning Herald*, May 22).

baby play *hist.* Bunting. Many 19th-century players scorned the baby play as a strategy that could potentially ruin the game. Cap Anson was particularly opposed to the practice and made the term popular. They viewed the bunt as a weak act that might be fine for infants and youngsters, but not for grown men. "The *Tribune* does not approve of any subterfuge, or baby play, to escape hitting the ball" (*Chicago Daily Tribune*, May 14, 1876; Greg Rhodes). See also *baby hit*.

Baby Ruth The name of a log-shaped candy bar made of caramel and peanuts, covered with chocolate, that many have long assumed was named after the baseball player Babe Ruth. The Curtiss Candy Co. introduced the candy bar in 1921 and priced it at five cents; it soon became one of the hottest-selling candy bars on the market. The company's "official" explanation was that the bar was named after "Baby" Ruth Cleveland, the first-born daughter of former President Grover Cleveland, despite the fact that Ruth had died of diphtheria at age 12 in 1904. The notion that a candy bar called "Baby Ruth" should appear on the market at the same time that Babe Ruth, the slugger, suddenly became the most famous ballplayer in America may just be a notable coincidence; another theory is that the candy company *did* name the bar after the baseball player, but hoped to avoid paying royalties. Robert Hendrickson (*The Facts on File Encyclopedia of Word and Phrase Origins*, 1987) shed additional light on the situation: "When another company got Babe Ruth to endorse Babe Ruth's Home Run Candy in 1926, Baby Ruth's manufacturer appealed to the Patent Office on the grounds of infringement and won, the Babe's candy bar never appearing." The candy bar is now manufactured by Nestlé. When the Irish dramatist George Bernard Shaw was exposed to baseball, he is said to have asked an American journalist (quoted by Tom Meany, *Babe Ruth*, 1947), "Who is this Baby Ruth? And what does she do?"

backcatcher 1. A playground term for the *catcher*, 1, in much of Canada and elsewhere in the United States. See also *hindcatcher*. Syn. *batcatcher*. ETYMOLOGY. Possibly a poorly informed description distinguishing one who catches pitches and fields behind the batter from one who is positioned in front of the batter. **2.** [softball] A synonym of "catcher."

backdoor curve A curveball thrown three to six inches outside the strike zone that suddenly breaks over the outside corner. "The tendency for the batter is to 'give up' on this pitch, figuring it's a ball outside. Surprise! The backdoor curve . . . thrown consistently for a strike in a great location is a very effective pitch because it never actually crosses the strike zone. It just nicks the zone in passing" (Keith Hernandez, *Pure Baseball*, 1994, p.34).

backdoor fastball Syn. of *two-seam fastball*.

backdoor slide A slide in which the runner touches a base or home plate with his hand as he slides beyond the bag with his body. Something of a rarity, this slide is performed when an advancing baserunner sees that he is about to be tagged out. He fakes a conventional slide, throws himself beyond the base, and reaches back to the bag with his hand. It is a desperation play that only works when it confuses the fielder.

backdoor slider A fast, sharp-breaking slider that starts outside the strike zone but at the last instant bends over the outside edge of the plate. Thrown by a right-handed pitcher to a left-handed batter, it looks like a fastball wide of the strike zone but curls back to nip the outside corner. Compare *backup slider*.

back end 1. The trailing runner in a double steal. With runners on second base and first base, the back end is the runner on first base. With runners on third base and first base, the back end is the runner on third base since he begins his attempt to steal after the runner on first base makes his attempt. "Garrett Jenkins scored on the back end of a double steal" (*Tampa Tribune*, Apr. 23, 1990). **2.** The second out of a double play. **3.** The second game of a doubleheader. **4.** The bottom of the order. **5.** See *back of the rotation*. **6.** See *back of the bullpen*.

back foot The batter's foot away from the pitcher. Compare *front foot*.

backfoot slider A slider that starts over the middle of the plate and breaks late, down and in, toward the back foot of the batter. It is thrown by a right-handed pitcher to a left-handed batter, and vice versa. Florida Marlins manager Joe Girardi, on Dontrelle Willis (quoted in *The Baltimore Sun*, Apr. 15, 2006): "When he's trying to put guys away, he's going to throw some back-foot sliders. Tonight he hit a couple of back feet." Arizona Diamondbacks manager Bob Brenly, on Randy Johnson (quoted in *ESPN The Magazine*, July 22, 2002): "Before the game, he'll say he's going to start this guy with a two-seam fastball. If he gets strike one, he'll throw a backfoot slider."

backhand **1.** *v.* To field a batted or thrown ball by extending the gloved hand across the body. **2.** *n.* The gloved hand extended across the body. "Backhands aren't easy, so in practice I take a lot of ground balls hit to my backhand" (infielder Lou Whitaker, quoted in Steve Fiffer, *How to Watch Baseball*, 1987, p.74).

back into To clinch a championship despite the team's poor play when the nearest contender mathematically eliminates itself by losing. "For awhile it seemed as if the Padres might back into the division title, losing seven of 11 games while the second-place Astros kept a similar pace" (*Tampa Tribune*, Sept. 29, 1989).

backlot A sandlot; an amateur or semipro baseball field. IST USE. 1908 (*Baseball Magazine*, December; Edward J. Nichols).

back number *hist.* A poor player, esp. one who has seen better days. "While Billy [Sul-

livan] has not taken a seat with the back numbers, still he is less active behind the bat than formerly" (*San Francisco Bulletin*, March 22, 1913; Gerald L. Cohen). "When a player no longer was effective he became a back number and resided in Hasbeen Valley" (Mike Sowell, *July 2, 1903*, 1992, p.4).

back off To pitch inside to a batter so that he moves away from the plate, thus giving the pitcher more room for his delivery.

back of Podunk Said of a team that is very low in the standings or is out of contention. Syn. "back of Squeedunk."

back of the bullpen The positions occupied by the setup man and the closer in a team's bullpen. Syn. *back end*, 6.

back of the rotation The position in a four-man starting rotation occupied by the fourth pitcher, or the positions in a five-man starting rotation occupied by the fourth and the fifth pitchers. "The team's primary need is . . . a No. 2 or No. 3 starter—not someone for the back of the rotation" (*The Baltimore Sun*, March 17, 2004). Compare *front of the rotation*; *middle of the rotation*. Syn. *back end*, 5; *bottom of the rotation*.

backspin **1.** A reverse rotation of a pitched ball (such as a fastball), which generates an upward force and makes it appear to the batter that the ball is rising. Compare *topspin*. **2.** A reverse rotation of a batted ball which causes it to rise and return to the field of play.

backspinner A pitch thrown with a backward, rotary motion so that the ball, when struck by the batter, will hit the ground and bounce backward, recoil, stop dead, or roll forward only a short distance.

backstop **1.** *n.* A screen behind and extending over the home plate area to keep the ball in the playing area and protect spectators from foul balls. In the major leagues, the backstop must be at least 60 feet from home plate. "Backstop . . . the name for a wooden shield which prevents the ball from rolling more than a certain distance back of home plate, if the catcher fails to hold it" (John B. Foster, in *Collier's New Dictionary of the English Language*, 1908). IST USE. 1870. "The [Washington] Olympic Club . . . [has] a fine club house, plenty of seats and a fine pagoda over the back stop" (*New York Clipper*, Feb. 19; Darryl Brock). **2.** *n.* Syn. for *catcher*, 1. IST USE. 1884. "[Rudolph Kemmler] looks like a back-stop when he wears the body protector" (*Columbus Dispatch*, May 21; Peter Morris). **3.** *n.* The Australian term for catcher. **4.** *v.* To be a catcher in a baseball game. "[Charles Johnson] backstopped the champion Florida Marlins in 1997" (*The Baltimore Sun*, Apr. 2, 2000).

backstopper Syn. for *catcher*, 1. IST USE. 1909. "The collision at the plate caused Hughey's new backstopper to give up his hold on the ball" (Ring W. Lardner, *Chicago Tribune*, May 4; Peter Morris).

backstopping *n.* Playing as the catcher. "[William Carrigan's] backstopping and throwing have left little to be desired" (Alfred H. Spink, *The National Game*, 2nd ed., 1911, p.98). IST USE. 1905 (*The Sporting Life*, Sept. 2; Edward J. Nichols).

backswing The return movement of the bat after a batter swings at a pitch.

back them up To hit a pitched ball hard enough to force the outfielders back to the fences to play the ball.

back through the box Said of a ball that is hit sharply through the pitcher's mound. Such hits often end up as hits to center field.

back-to-back Said of two events of the same kind, usually performed by the same individual on consecutive occasions; e.g., Johnny Vander Meer pitched back-to-back no-hitters on consecutive starting dates in 1938, and Mark McGwire in 1997 became the first player with back-to-back 50-homer seasons since Babe Ruth did it in 1927 and 1928. Two home runs, or any other hit, in a row are invariably described as "back-to-back." IST USE. About 1900. John Ciardi (*Good Words to You*, 1987) reported that this term started in baseball about the turn of the 20th century and long ago was generalized to the language at large. USAGE NOTE. Ciardi also noted that the term can become absurd in a sentence such as, "Remember when Reggie Jackson hit three back-to-back homers in one World Series Game?" Ciardi's answer: "I do, as a matter of fact, but after the third, what was

his position relative to the other two, and after the second, what was his position relative to the first and third? I hope this question will show the absurdity of this Am. idiom."

"back to the mines!" "A cry from disgruntled spectators to a player to take himself back to the job with pick and shovel that he held before disgracing his Club and themselves by playing ball" (C.M. Klump, *Who's Who and What's What in Baseball*, 1910). IST USE. 1902. "The National League magnates have been ordering back to the mines the men who were formerly employed by them" (*Detroit Free Press*, May 3; Peter Morris).

back to the woods Returning a player to the minors. Former manager Bill Joyce (quoted in *The Washington Post*, Sept. 25, 1904; Peter Morris): "There is nothing in the line of discipline for a good player that has the good effect of a trip to the minors. Managers are rapidly discovering the benefits of this system of rebuke, and 'back to the woods' for insubordinate players is becoming more frequent." IST USE. 1900. Describing the non-stop stream of chatter indulged in by Jack Dunn while pitching: "Here comes Del. I wonder what the . . . is going to do. Out, of course. Why, the . . . couldn't hit a balloon. Back to the woods with you and get a reputation" (*Brooklyn Eagle*, May 13; Peter Morris).

backup **1.** *n.* A player who fills in for a regularly assigned player when the latter is unable to play; a substitute. "Todd Pratt is an adequate backup with a sometimes dangerous bat" (*Sports Illustrated*, Oct. 18, 1999). **2.** *adj.* Said of a reserve or substitute player; e.g., a "backup catcher."

back up *v.* **1.** To play in such a way as to help another player in a difficult situation; e.g., to move into a supporting position to help the player who is fielding or receiving the ball in the event it is missed, dropped, or overthrown. The pitcher may get behind ("back up") the third baseman on a throw from the outfield, or behind the catcher on a throw to home plate. IST USE. 1864. "Jerome threw the ball over [Harry Brainard's] head: fortunately Fletcher was backing up well, and securing the ball, rapidly returned it to Harry at 2d base in time to cut Devyr off" (*Brooklyn Eagle*, Oct. 18; Peter Morris). **2.** For a pitcher to use movement on a pitch so that it appears to head straight toward the batter, but then sneaks into the strike zone. "[Texas Tech righthander Shane Wright] said he often throws his fastball at a lefthanded hitter's hip, then backs it up over the inside corner, Greg Maddux style" (John Manuel, *Baseball America*, Apr. 12–May 2, 1999; Peter Morris).

backup slider A slider that starts three to six inches inside but at the last instant breaks over the inside edge of the plate. It is often an accidental pitch—almost always a mistake. The catcher calls for a slider, but the pitcher releases the ball improperly, rolling his wrist or releasing the ball with a vertical, clockwise side spin. As there is no deflection (the spin axis of the ball is parallel to the ball's trajectory), the catcher is surprised; moving his glove in anticipation of the sliding movement, he must suddenly "back up" his glove to catch the ball. See also *cement mixer.* Compare *backdoor slider.*

backward See *pitch backward.*

backward runner A baserunner who, having advanced one or more bases, is forced to return to a previous base. If such a runner has tagged a new base while advancing, he must retouch that base before returning to the original one; e.g., a runner, leaving first base as a ball is hit to the outfield and thinking it will hit the ground, crosses second base and advances toward third, then realizes that the ball is caught and must return to first, making sure to retag second base on the way.

backwood scout A scout who specializes in searching for raw prospects. See also *arm behind the barn.*

backyard A team's home field. "It's going to be tough to beat us at home. A lot of teams have to come in our backyard and we feel good about that" (Darryl Strawberry, quoted in *USA Today Baseball Weekly*, Sept. 20–26, 1991).

backyarder A World Series played by two teams from the same geographic area; for instance, the 1989 Series between the Oakland Athletics and the San Francisco Giants.

bad actor A player who is difficult to deal with. "[St. Louis Cardinals manager Jack] Hendricks complained . . . that all season long [Rogers] Hornsby had been a 'bad actor'" (Charles Alexander, *Rogers Hornsby*, 1995, p.46).

bad ball A pitched ball thrown outside the strike zone in hopes of enticing the batter to swing. Syn. *bad pitch.* IST USE. 1896. "[Eddie] McFarland is what is called a 'crazy' hitter. That is, he hits at bad balls" (*St. Louis Post-Dispatch*, May 1; Peter Morris).

bad-ball hitter A hitter who willingly swings at pitches outside the strike zone. Such a practice is usually a deficiency because the hitter tends to swing and miss or hit fly balls, but some players have turned it into an asset. Roberto Clemente, Joe Medwick, Yogi Berra, Hank Aaron, Kirby Puckett, Manny Sanguillen, Matty Alou, and Tony Oliva were all considered excellent bad-ball hitters. "[Vladimir] Guerrero doesn't always wait for a good pitch—he's one of the best bad-ball hitters in the game" (*Sports Illustrated*, Apr. 5, 2004). Great bad-ball hitters are almost always either great contact hitters or exceptionally powerful pull hitters, and most of them receive few bases on balls.

bad birthday A birthday that falls just prior to Aug. 1. "Born on July 31, 1975, [Randy Flores] has what youth coaches refer to as a bad birthday. With everyone's cutoff date Aug. 1, he was guaranteed to be the youngest player at his playing age every season" (Sean Kernan, *Baseball America*, June 28–July 11, 1999; Peter Morris). See also Allan Simpson (*Baseball America*, Oct. 30, 1995).

bad bounce A batted ball that bounces and then unexpectedly deflects in a direction contrary to what the fielder anticipates; e.g., "The grounder took a bad bounce and hit Smith in the face." See also *bad hop*; *base on stones.*

bad call An umpire's decision that is felt to be an incorrect ruling on a play. The term is commonly used by the real or imagined victim and applied to a ball crossing the plate (was it a ball or a strike?) or a runner arriving at a base (safe or out?). EXTENDED USE. Any perceived misjudgment.

bad face The visage of a low-rated baseball prospect who lacks athleticism, drive, determination, or maturity. "You sometimes have to fight to get some scouts past a guy with a bad face. I thought it was crazy, but there's something to it. You see almost no one in the big leagues with a bad face" (Eddie Bane, quoted in Alan Schwarz, BaseballAmerica .com, Nov. 14, 2006). Compare *good face, the.*

bad hands 1. A player with poor fielding ability, especially one who has difficulty holding on to the ball; one who has trouble with short hops. 2. The hands of a poor infielder. "[Dick] Stuart knew he had bad hands and there was nothing he could do about it. . . . If you're going to shake hands with a guy who has bad hands you are supposed to say, 'Give me some steel, baby'" (Jim Bouton, *Ball Four*, 1970). Compare *good hands.* Syn. *hubcap hands*; "bad paws."

bad head 1. A player with an ugly face. 2. A player with a bad psyche.

bad hop A batted or thrown ball that suddenly changes direction because it hits an object or irregularity on the field. "[Terry] Steinbach bounced a single that took a bad hop over shortstop Kent Anderson's shoulder" (*Tampa Tribune-Times*, Aug. 13, 1989). Marian Edelman Borden (*The New York Times*, July 25, 1985) defined a bad hop as "any ball that comes toward your son and doesn't roll into his glove." See also *base on stones*; *bad bounce.* IST USE. 1915. "[Clyde] Milan beat out a hit to [Eddie] Collins, the ball taking a bad hop and hitting the Sox second sacker in the chest" (Stanley T. Milliken, *The Washington Post*, June 13; Peter Morris).

bad hose The poor throwing arm of a player.

bad lamps 1. The poor eyesight of a player. 2. The lighting of a poorly lit field.

bad news A player's contract with reduced salary. The term was used in the 1930s.

Bad News Bears The name of an unruly, motley Little League team in four movies: *The Bad News Bears* (1976), *The Bad News Bears in Breaking Training* (1977), *The Bad News Bears Go to Japan* (1978), and *Bad News Bears* (2005). The name has been used to characterize a club in decline or in the middle of a losing streak.

bad-pitch *v.* To throw a ball outside the strike zone with the hope of enticing the batter to swing. "You just can't bad-pitch around him [Ichiro Suzuki] . . . If you try to bad-pitch around him, he'll slap it through a hole" (Milwaukee Brewers manager Ned Yost, quoted in *The Baltimore Sun*, March 27, 2005).

bad pitch *n.* Syn. of *bad ball.*

bad wood Poor contact between the bat and ball.

bag 1. *n.* A square canvas sack filled with light material and used to mark first base, second base, and third base since the earliest days of baseball. IST USE. 1857. "The first, second, and third bases shall be canvas bags, painted white, and filled with sand or sawdust" (*Spirit of the Times*; David Shulman). 2. *n.* The *base*, 2. IST USE. 1876. "Compton made his first on a safe hit, advancing Tucker a bag" (*Daily Arkansas Gazette* [Little Rock], Sept. 3). 3. *n.* A *stolen base*. "Last year, my goal was to get 60–70 stolen bases. . . . I want to get about 70–80 bags this year" (Curtis Goodwin, quoted in *Orioles Gazette*, Apr. 22, 1994). 4. *v.* To win a game. IST USE. 1913 (*The Sporting Life*, Nov. 29). 5. *v./hist.* To bat a ball. IST USE. 1870 (*New York Herald*, June 14; Edward J. Nichols). 6. *v./hist.* To catch a batted ball.

bagel A mythical award given to a batter who goes hitless in five at-bats (Marvin Pave, *The Boston Globe*, Aug. 11, 1997).

bagger 1. *hist.* A one-base hit; a single. IST USE. 1880 (*Chicago Inter-Ocean*, June 3; Edward J. Nichols). 2. The extent of a hit; e.g., "two-bagger" for a double and "three-bagger" for a triple. EXTENDED USE. Craig Stock (*Chicago Tribune*, Oct. 21, 1994) commented that money manager Peter Lynch borrowed from baseball slang to describe how he tried to find "two-baggers" or "three-baggers," i.e., stocks that would quickly double or triple in price. Many have aped Lynch in this application. 3. A first baseman, second baseman, or third baseman, who would be a first bagger, second bagger, or third bagger, respectively.

Baggie The blue, flabby, plastic, canvas "fence" that rises 23 feet in right-center field at the Hubert H. Humphrey Metrodome in Minneapolis. It appears to have the characteristics of a mammoth trash-can liner. An outfielder playing the Baggie races directly to the fence so that he can be positioned underneath the ball when it strikes the canvas and drops straight down. Syn. *Hefty bag*; *trash bag*.

bagman *hist.* Syn. of *baseman.* IST USE. 1902 (*The Sporting Life*, Oct. 4; Edward J. Nichols).

bag of bones An extremely thin player.

bag of peanuts A broken or misshapen hand, like that of a veteran catcher. IST USE. 1963. "His hand looked like a bag of peanuts" (Leonard Shecter, *Baseball Digest*, June).

bag path *hist.* Syn. of *basepath.* IST USE. 1913. "Neither did he [San Francisco Seals second baseman Joe Wagner] err in fielding his position at the second station on the bag path" (*San Francisco Bulletin*, March 29; Gerald L. Cohen).

bag puncher *hist.* A term used in the National League for a player who talks too much (*American Speech*, Apr. 1930). Compare *barber*, 1.

bags clogged Syn. of *bases loaded.* IST USE. 1913 (*Harper's Weekly*, Sept. 6; Edward J. Nichols).

bags full Syn. of *bases loaded.* "I focus a little more when I go up there with the bags full" (Mo Vaughn, quoted in *Sports Illustrated*, June 21, 1999, p.51).

bail Short for *bail out*, 1. "[Kenny] Lofton 'bails' slightly against left-handers, so the Orioles fed him breaking balls down and away, then busted him inside" (*The Baltimore Sun*, Oct. 7, 1996).

bailiwick The base or territory that a fielder covers. "All, except Freddy Crane, who had nothing to attend to in his bailiwick, did brilliant play" (*Brooklyn Eagle*, June 29, 1869; Peter Morris). ETYMOLOGY. The district within which a bailiff has jurisdiction.

bail out 1. For a batter to step back or fall away from a pitch. This act is seldom voluntary and usually takes place when the ball is, or appears to be, coming at the batter. A batter commonly bails out when he is expecting a fastball and the pitcher serves him a breaking pitch. Some batters are said to "bail out slightly." Bob Gibson (*From Ghetto to Glory*, 1968, p.157) wrote, "[Willie] Mays has a habit of bailing out—pulling away from a pitch. That may look like a flaw, but it really isn't. Once the pitcher releases the ball, Willie comes back in and that's not bailing out at all. He's set to hit the pitch when it gets there." Syn. *bail.* **2.** To have a successful relief-pitching appearance. "Steve Kline bailed him [Dave Veres] out of a jam in the seventh, and Rick White bailed out Kline with two outs in the eighth" (*The Baltimore Sun*, Oct. 13, 2002).

bait 1. To lure the pitcher into throwing a good pitch; e.g., a good hitter who is often "semi-intentionally walked" may swing at two bad pitches to draw the pitcher into throwing a "half-good" pitch in hope of a strikeout. **2.** To lure the batter into swinging at a bad pitch by throwing the ball just outside the strike zone. **3.** To upset an umpire by making uncomplimentary remarks to him.

Baker *hist.* A home run. Before Babe Ruth came along, Frank "Home Run" Baker led the American League or tied for the lead in home runs for four straight years (1911–1914), and he earned the nickname "Home Run" for his two homers in the 1911 World Series. IST USE. 1912 (*New York Tribune*, Oct. 15; Edward J. Nichols).

Baker Bowl Home field of the Philadelphia Phillies from 1895 to 1938. It was known as Huntingdon Grounds until 1913, when William F. Baker became president of the Phillies. The park was described as a "bandbox" in the 1930s because its small dimensions made it an easier venue in which to hit home runs. It was nicknamed "Dump by the Hump" during the Depression, as its most distinctive feature was the "hump" in the outfield caused by the tracks of the Pennsylvania Railroad (Michael Gershman, *Diamonds*, 1993).

balance a box score Syn. of *prove a box score.*

balanced schedule A playing schedule in which teams play approximately the same number of games against all teams within their league. Compare *unbalanced schedule.*

balance point **1.** The stage in a pitcher's delivery between the windup and the release. "[Jeff] Allison has minor mechanical faults, sometimes rushing through his balance point in his delivery, causing his arm to drag" (Allan Simpson, *Baseball America*, June 9–22, 2003; Peter Morris). **2.** [softball term] The moment in the underhand pitching delivery in which the pitching hand is at its highest point above the head and the opposite foot is at its highest point above the ground.

balance the budget To tie the score. The term may have been introduced by Los Angeles Dodgers broadcaster Vin Scully during the 1989 All-Star Game.

balata ball The baseball used during the 1943 major-league baseball season when supplies of rubber were rationed during World War II. Balata was a material without strategic use, a rubberlike gum obtained from the milky juice or latex of a tropical American tree (*Manilkara bidentata*). Most commonly used for golfball covers, machinery belts, and telephone cable insulation, it was implemented by A.G. Spalding and Brothers as a binder in the manufacture of baseballs. Red and black layers of balata substituted for the traditional layer of rubber surrounding the cork center. The balata ball used ground cork instead of high-grade cork and the cover of the ball came from domestic horsehide. Initially, the balata ball was much less resilient than the traditional baseball (see *clunk ball*), making it difficult to hit (a hard swing would produce a weakly hit ball to the infield, and many games at the start of the 1943 season resulted in 1–0 and 2–1 scores); later in 1943, Spalding made balls containing rubber cement that remained soft and sticky. See Richard Goldstein (*Spartan Seasons: How Baseball Survived the Second World War*, 1980, pp.131–34).

balk **1.** *n.* Any illegal act or motion by the pitcher that the umpire deems to be an attempt to deceive a baserunner into making a move that may get him picked off base. When a balk is called, the ball becomes dead and all runners advance one base. Most balks are called as the pitcher shows a move that appears to be a delivery to the plate; specif.,

Balk. Postcard interpretation. *Andy Moresund Collection*

failure by a pitcher to complete the delivery of the ball to home plate once his foot has made contact with the rubber. It is a departure from the pitcher's regular delivery that is, ostensibly, designed to deceive the baserunner. A common balk occurs when the pitcher does not come to a stop after his stretch. Rule 8.05 of the *Official Baseball Rules* spells out 13 specific balk situations that may occur while the pitcher is in contact with the rubber; e.g., making any motion naturally associated with the pitch and failing to make the delivery, feinting a throw to first base and failing to complete the throw, or failing to step directly toward a base before throwing to that base. Even without a change in the balk rule, the degree to which balks are called tends to vary, depending on the strictness with which the rule is being interpreted. Scores of balks were called at the beginning of the 1988 season that probably would have been ignored the previous year. Bob Considine (*The Saturday Evening Post*, Apr. 9, 1938; Peter Tamony) once termed the balk "a misdemeanor which permits runners to advance a base under the protection of a temporary armistice." See also *foul balk.* Abbrev. *BK.*

Syn. *baulk.* IST USE. 1845. "A runner cannot be put out in making one base, when a balk is made by the pitcher" (Knickerbocker Rules, Rule 19th). USAGE NOTE. In 1978, a year in which the balk rule was being strongly enforced, Ira Miller (*San Francisco Chronicle*, May 16, 1978; Peter Tamony) wrote, "It is one of baseball's least understood rules. It even sounds funny. Say 'balk' and people hear 'ball.' It's pronounced 'bawk' as in the first syllable of 'awkward,' which is how umpires are making pitchers feel about it." ETYMOLOGY. From "balca," the Anglo-Saxon word for "beam." Balcas were put across the doors of huts in the days before locks and keys to thwart or stop intruders. Tracing the term through "baulk" for a "false shot or mistake," Peter Tamony concludes, "The sense of this word seems in general to be to stop short, to frustrate, to disappoint. In billiards, the balk-line is a line drawn a certain distance from the cushion, and used in connection with certain methods of playing billiards. In baseball, a feint or false motion made by the pitcher in the delivery of the ball to the batter, which is penalized."

2. *v.* To commit a balk. "Detroit's Jeff Robinson balked Jose Oquendo home with the winning run" (*St. Petersburg Times*, March 21, 1988). EXTENDED USE. To recoil; to fail to deliver, such as a politician "balking" on tax reform. **3.** *v./hist.* To interfere with a fielder. "When [Mike] Tiernan was on first and started to steal second, [Jack] Glasscock, who was at the plate, stuck his bat out and balked [catcher Jim] Keenan so he could not throw. Keenan's hand came in contact with the bat and his fingers were badly bruised" (*The World* [New York], July 1, 1890; Gerald L. Cohen). **4.** See *catcher's balk.*

balkamania The furor during the early weeks of the 1988 season when the balk rule was reinterpreted along stricter lines. During the first 11 days of the season, 88 balks had been called in the American League and 36 in the National League, a situation that caused *The Sporting News* (Apr. 25, 1988) to headline its article on the subject "Balkamania Unchecked."

balk move A pitcher's move that suggests a balk. USAGE NOTE. This is a highly subjective notion, as a "balk move" is something alleged by the team at bat. A pitcher charged with making a balk move to first base will insist that it is nothing more than his regular move.

ball 1. A pitch that is not swung at by the batter and that is judged to be outside the strike zone by the umpire. See also *called ball,* 1. IST USE. 1863. "Should a pitcher repeatedly fail to deliver to the striker fair balls, for the apparent purpose of delaying the game, or for any other cause, the umpire, after warning him, shall call one ball, and if the pitcher persists in such actions, two and three balls; when three balls have been called, the striker shall be entitled to the first base" (Constitution and By-Laws of the National Association of Base Ball Players, with the Rules and Regulations of the Game of Base Ball, 1864, Sec. 6; John Thorn, who notes that this pamphlet covered the meetings of Dec. 9, 1863). ETYMOLOGY. Probably a shortened version of the original *"ball to the bat."* **2.** The baseball itself. IST USE. 1845. "The ball must be pitched, and not thrown, for the bat" (Knickerbocker Rules, Rule 9th). However, this may be facetiously superseded by the following: "He will seize firm hold on you, and whirl you round and round, and throw you like a ball into a wide land; there you shall die" (Isaiah 22:17–18). ETYMOLOGY. The first known use of the word "ball" in English in the sense of a globular body that is played with (thrown, kicked, batted, etc.) was in 1205: "Summe heo driuen balles wide" (*Layamon's Brut, or Chronicle of Britain*; *OED*). **3.** The game of baseball. "Manager McKee has now a team that can play pretty good ball—and probably win—the championship of the Northwestern League" (*The Sporting Life*, July 30, 1883). In some childhood circles this term actually overwhelms the proper one. In his autobiography (*The Education of an American*, 1938), Mark Sullivan wrote, "We did not know our game as baseball but merely as 'ball,' and in other respects we failed to conform to the orthodox formula." **4.** A type of pitch; e.g., fastball, screwball, spitball, or curveball. **5.** A generic term commonly used in the late 18th and early 19th centuries for an uncertain recreation that involved a ball and may have included a bat. Thomas L. Altherr (*NINE*, Spring 2000) identified many diarists during this period who referred to having "played ball"; e.g., "We are oblige'd to walk 4 miles to day to find a place leavel enough to play ball" (Revolutionary War soldier Henry Dearborn, writing on April 17, 1779; Lloyd A. Brown & Howard H. Peckham, eds., *Revolutionary War Journals of Henry Dearborn 1775–1783*, 1939). In a letter to his nephew Peter Carr, urging him to take up hunting as recreation, Thomas Jefferson wrote on Aug. 19, 1785, "Games played with the ball and others of that nature, are too violent for the body and stamp no character on the mind" (Julian P. Bond, ed., *The Papers of Thomas Jefferson*, 1953).

ball-and-strike count The ratio of called balls to strikes accumulated by a batter during a single turn at bat. See also *balls and strikes*. Syn. *ball–strike count*.

ball-and-strike umpire The *plate umpire* who is responsible for judging whether a pitch was in or out of the strike zone. In cow-pasture games, schoolyard games, and in other fields not major or minor, the ball-and-strike umpire may stand behind the pitcher.

Ballantine Blast A home run. The term was made popular by Mel Allen, whose New York Yankees broadcasts were sponsored by Ballantine beer and ale. Allen was contractually required to call every Yankees home run a "Ballantine Blast."

ball boy A young man whose job is to retrieve and/or collect foul balls, or to carry out balls to the plate umpire. See also *ball girl*. Also spelled "ballboy."

ball club 1. *hist.* A baseball bat. "I have sent you to day by express a box of balls and ball-clubs for the boys . . . with my desire that they will have lots of fun out of them and also that they will take care of them and not lose either balls or clubs" (Michigan governor John J. Bagley, in a letter to the superintendent of the State Reform School in Lansing, quoted in *Grand Rapids Daily Eagle*, Apr. 13, 1874; Peter Morris). 2. A baseball team; an organization whose prime activity is the building up and support of a baseball team. See also *club*, 1. Sometimes spelled "ballclub." Syn. *baseball club*. IST USE. 1837. "This institution shall be denominated 'The Olympic Ball Club'" (Constitution of the Olympic Ball Club of Philadelphia, Art. I, Dec. 12; published privately in 1838).

ball dog Syn. of *ball hound*. Linguist Kelsie Harder (Potsdam College) reported (letter of Feb. 25, 1989), "I heard it used in Perry County, Tenn., where I used to play baseball hour after hour and never gained much ability. I remember hearing: 'Young boys dog them balls out there in them corn middles.'"

balldom The realm of baseball. The term was used by George L. Moreland in the title of his 1914 book *Balldom: "The Britannica of Baseball."* See also *baseballdom*. IST USE. 1902. "Notre Dame . . . gave Anson, Stahl and Powers to balldom" (Ren Mulford Jr., *The Sporting Life*, Sept. 6; Peter Morris).

ball exit speed ratio A measure of the liveliness of the collision between the bat and a pitched ball. When the speeds of the bat and the pitched ball are the same, the ratio equals to the speed of the ball just after it leaves the bat to the sum of the speed of the pitched ball just before it collides with the bat and the speed of the bat just before it collides with the ball. The certification process—as required by the National Collegiate Athletic Association (NCAA)—is accomplished by measuring the performance of a bat under controlled conditions and then assigning a number (the ball exit speed ratio) to it; the NCAA has set the maximum allowed ratio to be 0.728. Once that number is known, one can determine the ball exit speed when the bat speed and the pitch speed are specified; conversely, if one measures the bat speed, pitch speed, and the ball exit speed, then one can determine the ball exit speed ratio. Abbrev. *BESR*. See James Ashton-Miller et al. (*Baseball Research Journal*, 2004, p.12).

ball field An area for playing baseball. See also *baseball field*. Sometimes spelled "ballfield." IST USE. 1864 (*Brooklyn Daily Eagle*, Sept. 20; Edward J. Nichols).

ball-four A base on balls. "[Miguel] Tejada's eagerness to go yard turns too many ball-fours into ground balls" (*ESPN The Magazine*, May 27, 2002).

ball game **1.** A baseball game. See also *game*, 1. Sometimes spelled "ballgame." IST USE. 1848. "The boys suspend their ball game while he drives over the green" (*Knickerbocker*, XVIII, p.216; *OED*). **2.** The moment or event that determines the outcome of a game. The term is often used as an expression of a loss, as "there goes the old ball game." Earl Weaver on a key out (quoted in Thomas Boswell, *How Life Imitates the World Series*, 1982): "That one at-bat was the ball game." Baltimore Orioles pitcher Sidney Ponson, after a tough loss (quoted in *The Baltimore Sun*, Apr. 16, 2001): "I had to battle and battle, then I left a pitch out over the plate for [John] Flaherty and that's the ballgame." See also *new ball game*, 1; *whole new ball game*. EXTENDED USE. A coherent event or set of circumstances, a state of affairs, a continuing activity, such as the movement of a bill through Congress. "Duncan's only comment on the close vote yesterday was 'The ball game isn't over yet'" (*San Francisco Examiner*, May 30, 1968; Peter Tamony). During the Vietnam War, the term "ballgame" meant a military operation, according to Leonard B. Scott in the glossary to his novel about the war (*Charlie Mike*, 1985). **3.** A baseball player; e.g., Ted Williams referred to himself as "Teddy Ballgame."

ball game is at first, the The notion that if the runner on first base scores, his team will win the game. Similarly, "the ball game is at second" and "the ball game is at third" allude to the game-winning potential of runners at second and third bases, respectively.

ball girl A young woman whose job is to retrieve and/or collect foul balls, or to carry out balls to the plate umpire. Alessandra Stanley (*The New York Times*, July 5, 1991) noted that ball girls "must be pretty and perky as football cheerleaders, yet they don helmets, gloves, and the team uniform to perform a task that is far more difficult—and at times more dangerous—than waving a pompon." See also *ball boy*. Also spelled "ballgirl."

ball-goer *hist.* One who attends a baseball game. "There are a great many ball-goers in this country who will hesitate a long while before surrendering the extra quarter" (*The North American* [Philadelphia], Feb. 7, 1888).

ball ground An area where baseball is played. "Curtis Welch . . . made some of the most phenomenal and brilliant catches this year ever seen on a ball ground" (*Detroit Free Press*, Oct. 9, 1887). Syn. *ground*, 4. IST USE. 1856. "The Club presented their President with an elegant silver Pitcher, with a view of the ball ground carved out upon it" (*Spirit of the Times*, Dec. 13; *OED*).

ball hawk **1.** An especially fast and adept outfielder; one who covers a lot of ground. Willie Mays was always regarded as being in this elite group. Ducky Medwick was one of the first, if not the first, players to be linked to this honorific term. Harry Grayson (*They Played the Game*, 1944, p.80) described Turkey Mike Donlin: "He was a ball hawk in center field and a strong and accurate arm swung from his shoulder." See also *hawk*, 1; *flyhawk*. Sometimes spelled "ballhawk." IST USE. 1920 (*The New York Times*, Oct. 10; Edward J. Nichols). EXTENDED USE. A defensive back in football. "New Mexico has . . . a ball hawk in the secondary in Brandon Payne, who tops the nation in passes defensed and broken up" (*The Baltimore Sun*, Dec. 30, 2004). **2.** A person who collects as souvenirs balls that are hit outside a ballpark. Ball hawks are common at the smaller major- and minor-league parks and at those that are used for exhibition games during spring training because more balls land out of the park at such sites.

ball-hitter *hist.* A baseball bat. "Years ago . . . ball players were proud of their bats because of their elegant coats of paint and varnish, but now the professionals take pride in the plainness of their ball-hitters" (George Rawlings, quoted in *St. Paul Daily News*, Apr. 6, 1889).

ball hound One who will chase and return stray baseballs. Syn. *ball dog*. IST USE. 1935. "A couple of 'ball hounds,' youngsters not quite old enough for the team yet loyally interested in it, should be relied upon to rescue balls going out of the grounds" (Ralph H. Barbour, *How to Play Better Baseball*, 1935, p.147; David Shulman).

"ball in" A command to throw the practice ball(s) to the dugout at the start of a half inning.

ballin' Slang for playing baseball. "These kids [2003 Florida Marlins] don't see ghosts right now—they just go out there ballin'" (Marlins infielder Lenny Harris, quoted in *Sports Illustrated*, Oct. 27, 2003, p.52).

ballist *hist.* A 19th-century baseball player. Peter Morris reports that shortly after the *New England Base Ballist* began publication, the Aug. 27, 1868, issue noted that the *Boston Post* had written, "The title 'Ballist' is a verbal atrocity and bastard, and ought never to be uttered or printed." The *New England Base Ballist* snidely responded by reprinting a recent article from the *Boston Post* in which the word "drunkist" was used to describe an intoxicated man. See also *baseballist*.

ballite *hist.* A baseball fan. See also *baseballite*. Also spelled "ball-ite."

ball lot *hist.* The playing area for a baseball game. "[Dutch Reuther] bobbed into instant fame on the St. Ignatius ball lot during the visit of the White Sox" (*San Francisco Bulletin*, May 12, 1913; Gerald L. Cohen). IST USE. 1906 (*The Sporting Life*, March 10; Edward J. Nichols).

ballman A baseball player. "For the past two weeks joy has reigned supreme among the ballmen of the diamond-field sport of this city" (*The New York Times*, Oct. 19, 1889).

balloon **1.** *n.* A ball that looks big to the batter because it is moving slowly and gives the illusion of being oversized. Compare *aspirin tablet*. **2.** *n.* A fly ball. IST USE. 1920 (*The New York Times*, Oct. 6; Edward J. Nichols). **3.** *v.* To bat a ball high in the air; to hit a fly ball. IST USE. 1905. "Keane ballooned to Hoffman" (*The Washington Post*, May 4; Peter Morris). **4.** *n.* A wild throw. IST USE. 1892 (*Chicago Herald*, May 13; Edward J. Nichols). **5.** *v.* To overthrow. "[Third baseman Bill] Hague gave [batter Tom] York three bases by 'ballooning' his hit clear over [first baseman George] Latham's head" (*St. Louis Globe-Democrat*, July 21, 1877; Peter Morris). **6.** An umpire's inflated, portable *chest protector* worn outside the uniform. "Although 'the balloon' was difficult to mas-

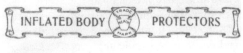

The Reach Inflated Umpire Body Protector

PATENTED NOVEMBER 24, 1903

No. 15 - - - - - Each $12.00

We have had numerous inquiries from umpires for a Body Protector that would thoroughly protect.

This led us to design one which we guarantee will protect the wearer from the hardest blows and at the same time not interfere with his movements.

It Protects Every Part of the Body That Needs Protection

Balloon. Advertisement in the 1907 *Reach Official American League Base Ball Guide* of an inflatable chest protector. This was a precursor to the modern balloon chest protector. *Library of Congress*

ter, it did provide more protection" (Ron Luciano, *Strike Two*, 1984, pp.165–66; Charles D. Poe). The balloons were abandoned by American League umpires in 1985. Syn. *bubble*, 1. ETYMOLOGY. The name is an allusion to the puffy, bloated look of the outside chest protector.

balloon ascension *hist.* An occurrence in which a pitcher suddenly loses his effectiveness or control. The term was commonly framed in terms of spectators witnessing a balloon ascending. Max Carey (quoted in F.C. Lane, *Batting*, 1925, p.88): "The more you worry the pitcher, the more likely he is to take a balloon ascension." See also *up in the air*; *rattles*. Syn. *ascension*. IST USE. 1904. "Faintheartedness and any tendency to what are termed . . . 'balloon ascensions' must be overcome at the outset, for nothing is more fatal to success" (Deacon Phillippe, quoted in *Syracuse Post Standard*, March 27; Peter Morris).

balloon ball A slowly thrown pitch that arches high in the air and drops precipitously as it passes through the strike zone. It is a rarely thrown pitch that can be effective when the odd trajectory is enough to throw the batter's timing off. See also *eephus*. IST USE. 1909. "Before Edgar Willetts could get his balloon ball working right, the Pirates scored two runs" (*New Haven Evening Leader*, Oct. 12; Peter Morris).

balloon fly *hist.* A high fly ball. "Connecting with a balloon fly—catching a high ball" (*The Atchison* [Kans.] *Daily Globe*, June 23, 1896). Var. "balloon flier."

ball orchard A ballpark. "That the Oakland fans like their new ball orchard was tolerably well indicated by the morning crowd" (*San Francisco Bulletin*, Apr. 14, 1913; Gerald L. Cohen). Syn. *orchard*, 2; *baseball orchard*. IST USE. 1907. "Ball orchards are the favorite breeding places of green-eyed monsters" (*The Washington Post*, March 31; Barry Popik).

ballpark An enclosed baseball field, including its seating areas and commercialized facilities; a stadium. It is a short form of *baseball park*. See also *park*, 1; *in the ballpark*; *out of the ballpark*. Also spelled "ball park." IST USE. 1899. "Billy Phyle . . . went out to the ball park" (*Chicago Daily News*, Aug. 4; *OED*). USAGE NOTE. The term is an honorific for a classic baseball venue. Roger Angell (*Five Seasons*, 1977, p.86) wrote, "[Chicago's] Wrigley Field is one of the few remaining enclosures that still merit the title of 'ball park'—a grassland enclosed by an ancient red brick wall and a gentle, curving, spacious sweep of stands." The home of the Texas Rangers in the late 1990s was aptly named The Ballpark in Arlington. ETYMOLOGY. The first such enclosed playing area was Union Grounds in Brooklyn, N.Y., which opened on May 15, 1862. The enclosure was invented and designed by William Cammeyer. EXTENDED USE. **1.** A given realm; a sphere of activity or influence. "Perhaps your mother-in-law 'took over' because she is an R.N. and the hospital is her ballpark" (*San Francisco Examiner*, Aug. 10, 1971; *OED*). **2.** A broad area of approximation; a range within which comparison is possible. "[The] Discoverer XIV capsule . . . came down some 200 miles from the center of its predicted impact area, but still within the designated 'ballpark' area 300 miles south-southwest of Oahu, Hawaii" (*San Francisco Examiner*, Aug. 21, 1960).

ballpark figure A rough estimate, within a reasonable or acceptable range. EXTENDED USE. The term has a decidedly odd connection to baseball, given that most figures having to do with the game (such as batting averages and earned run averages) are relentlessly precise. *The New York Times Magazine* (Aug. 3, 1973) reported, "*Ball-park figure*: In its meaning of 'rough estimate,' this comes from 'in the ball park,' a baseball reference reflecting a nostalgia for a once-national pastime now in decline. In the early sixties, this usage grew in government as the Air Force [and the National Aeronautics and Space Administration] used 'ball park' to describe satellite recovery areas—delimited spaces like ball parks. A 'ball-park figure' is usually followed by a demand for 'the bottom line' or 'net net,' accounting terms." From *The New York Times* (Dec. 9, 1965): "A report that the initial development and production order would be for about 200 aircraft was accepted in qualified quarters as an 'accurate ballpark figure'—jargon for a reasonable guess." IST USE. 1963. "As business heads like to say, these are good ballpark figures" (in reference to the costs for art as a percentage of the cost of an office or public building) (*Los Angeles Times*, July 4).

ballpark frank A *hot dog*, 2. Possibly the most beloved food sold by vendors at baseball stadiums, it is often said to taste better at a game than elsewhere. At some parks hot dogs are given local nicknames, such as the Fenway Frank (Boston) and the Dodger Dog (Los Angeles). On the other hand, not everyone is convinced that these franks are superior. "I ask you, is there anything in the world tastier than a ballpark frank?" writer Rick Horowitz asked himself in a *Washington Post* (Apr. 8, 1987) article on ballpark food. "Are you kidding?!" he answered. "Hot dogs steamed since the 1958 World Series? Buns carved out of broken bat handles?"

ballplayer 1. A professional baseball player. See also *baseballist*. Also spelled "ball player." Syn. *baseball player*, 1. IST USE. 1833. "The Olympic ball club was established by the union of two associations of town ballplayers in the year 1833" (Constitution and By-Laws of the Olympic Base Ball Club). USAGE NOTE. This term carries its own honor, denoting a player with an instinctual feel for the game. Smoky Joe Wood (quoted in Lawrence S. Ritter, *The Glory of Their Times*, 1966, p.159), commenting on his phenomenal 1912 season when he had a 34–5 pitching record and a batting average of .290: "Doggone it, I was a *ballplayer*, not just a pitcher." *The Boston Globe* (May 18, 1886; Peter Morris): "Joe Sullivan made his first run today, and took a new departure in his batting that won the game, and pleased those of his friends mightily who have all along asserted that Joe is a ball player." *Chicago Tribune* (Apr. 23, 1906; Peter Morris): "With one out [Joe] Tinker drew a base, and J. Evers, ball player, smashed the ball into the crowd in right for a triple." Evan Grant (*Baseball America*, Aug. 23–Sept. 5, 1999): "When the [Texas] Rangers used their top pick in the 1997 draft on Jason Romano, two things about him stood out. First, he was a ballplayer more than an athlete." Michael Lewis (*Moneyball*, 2003): "[Oakland] had drafted players dismissed by their own scouts as too short or too skinny or too fat or too slow. They had drafted pitchers who didn't throw hard enough for the scouts and hitters who hadn't enough power. . . . They had drafted ballplayers." **2.** Any individual who plays baseball. Syn. *baseball player*, 2.

ballplayer's ballplayer A player who is widely respected and admired by other players. "[Ryne] Sandberg was a ballplayer's ballplayer, the kind to whom a Carl Yastrzemski or a Cal Ripken or a Tony Gwynn could relate, a workman punching a clock, putting in a solid eight-hour shift and going home without causing his employers a single minute's distress" (Mike Downey, *The Baltimore Sun*, Jan. 6, 2005). See also *player's player.*

balls and strikes The count on a batter. See also *ball-and-strike count.* IST USE. 1871. "The umpiring . . . was perfectly fair and impartial, although a leniency towards both pitchers and batsmen, in calling balls and strikes, lengthened the game" (*The Cleveland Morning Herald*, May 22). EXTENDED USE. Decisions to be made. Maryland state senator Brian E. Frosh, outraged that the state's Public Service Commission failed to be a neutral arbiter between consumers and utility companies, was quoted in *The Baltimore Sun* (March 19, 2006): "The chairman of the Public Service Commission is supposed to be calling balls and strikes. And you can't be calling balls and strikes when you are plotting strategy with a member of the industry."

ball-shoe Syn. of *baseball shoe.* IST USE. 1909. "Most of all I'll want my glove and ball-shoes" (Zane Grey, *The Short-Stop*).

balls in play The number of at-bats minus both home runs and strikeouts. Abbrev. *BIP.*

balls-in-play average The probability that a batter will hit a ball in play, determined by subtracting home runs from hits and dividing that by the number of at-bats minus both home runs and strikeouts.

ballstock A "cousin" of *English base-ball* that was popular in Germany in the late 18th century and continued to be played into the 1900s, but is now virtually extinct. The game was described by Johann Christoph Gutsmuths (*Spiele zur Uebung und Erholung des Körpers und Geistes für die Jugend, ihre Erzieher und alle Freunde Unschuldiger Jugendfreuden*, 1796) as "das deutsche Ballspiel," or the *German ball game*, which was large in scale, required more strength in hitting and running, and was bound by fewer "small rules" than English base-ball. Gutsmuths used the term "ballstock" for "bat"; the game was given the name "ballstock" when it was described in several books on games published in England in the mid-19th century. According to David Block (*Baseball Before We Knew It*, 2005, p.182), "Gutsmuths's documentation of the game is an important contribution to baseball history, because it is the strongest surviving evidence of an ancient family of European ball games that may have influenced the inception of baseball in England."

ball–strike count Syn. of *ball-and-strike count.*

ball team Syn. of *team*, 2. IST USE. 1888. "The personnel of the average professional ball team . . . has improved" (*Outing*, July; *OED*).

ball tosser *hist.* **1.** A baseball player. "There isn't so much difference between a group of anarchists [Reds] and a bunch of Cincinnati [Reds] ball tossers" (*San Francisco Bulletin*, March 1, 1913; Gerald L. Cohen). "Stray hits and flies in right field territory will be entrusted to the tender mercies of [Joe] Visner, the Cleveland ball tosser" (*The Washington Post*, Feb. 4, 1891). See also *tosser*, 2. IST USE. 1876 (*Chicago Inter-Ocean*, May 1; Edward J. Nichols). **2.** A pitcher. "A lovely delegation [of Chicago White Sox sluggers] to send against a poor unsuspecting ball tosser like Mr. Pope [Oakland pitcher]" (*San Francisco Bulletin*, March 7, 1913; Gerald L. Cohen). See also *tosser*, 1.

"ball to the bat" *hist.* A warning given to the pitcher by the umpire in early baseball— before the advent of balls and strikes—for the first pitch delivered beyond the legitimate reach of the bat after the pitcher had been told where to pitch the ball (Henry Chadwick, *National Chronicle*, July 3, 1869). See also *ball*, 1.

ball town *hist.* A city that supports baseball, such as one that keeps a team in the black. Sam Thompson (quoted in *Detroit Free Press*, March 18, 1887): "When I played in Danville [Ind.] the population was about 500 and 400 people turned out for every ball game. The price of admission was fixed at fifteen cents, but a large proportion of the spectators dropped a quarter or a half into the hat. That's the kind of ball town I came from." *The Sporting Life* (July 22, 1883): "Detroit is one of the best playing ball-towns in the country." See also *baseball town*. IST USE. 1879. "Detroit will be known hereafter as a ball town" (Detroit manager W.M. Hollinger, letter to the *New York Clipper*, reprinted in the *Detroit Post and Tribune*, March 1; Peter Morris).

ballwick *hist.* A team's home field. "The Beaneaters are playing strong ball on their own ballwick" (*The Washington Post*, June 18, 1896). ETYMOLOGY. Probably a corruption of "bailiwick."

ball with eyes on it A weakly hit batted ball, usually a grounder, that barely gets past the outstretched gloves of two fielders. It is so described because it would seem to need "vision" to chart such an evasive course. See also *seeing-eye single*; *eyes on it*.

ballyard A ballpark. See also *yard*, 1. Also spelled "ball yard." IST USE. 1913. "[Two sportswriters on horseback] whirled into the ball yard to glimpse the morning work and then, emitting wild yells, went charging out of the lot" (Scoop Gleeson, *San Francisco Bulletin*, Feb. 28; Gerald L. Cohen). USAGE NOTE. The term is used by some sportswriters, but is far from universal. Dave Kindred (*The Washington Post*, Oct. 4, 1982) called Baltimore's Memorial Stadium a "ballyard"; Thomas Boswell (*The Washington Post*, Oct. 11, 1987), writing about San Francisco's Candlestick Park at the beginning of the 1987 National League Championship Series, wrote, "Oh, thou loveliest of ball yards, how you have been maligned."

Baltimore bounce Syn. of *Baltimore chop*.

Baltimore chop A batted ball that hits the ground close to home plate and then bounces high in the air, allowing the batter time to reach first base safely. "[Bill] Hinchman broke loose with a single that bounded over [Dave] Altizer's head. The revival of the ancient Baltimore chop was appreciated" (*The Washington Post*, July 20, 1907; Barry Popik). See also *chop*, 3; *chop hit*; *alabaster blast*; *butcher-boy stroke*; *Pittsburgh chopper*. Syn. *Baltimore bounce*. IST USE. 1905. "[Joe] Kelley netted a high bouncing bingle in old-fashioned Baltimore chop" (*Boston Daily*, June 16). USAGE NOTE. A Baltimore chop is occasionally described as a batted ball bounced deliberately off home plate; but Robert Smith (*The New York Times*, May 10, 1984) disagreed: "To slap a pitched ball onto so small a target is a feat beyond the skill of most batters. And a ball bounced off the plate is too often possessed of backspin that will spin it off into foul ground." ETYMOLOGY. The term got its name, by all accounts, in the 1890s when the tactic was perfected by Wee Willie Keeler of the old Baltimore Orioles. Two other Baltimore batsmen (John McGraw and Wilbert Robinson) also used it as a method to get on base. Evidence suggests that at the Orioles' field, the dirt near home plate was sun-baked or purposely hardened to make the ball bounce higher. A description of the tactic from an 1896 edition of the *Baltimore News* appears in Jordan A. Deutsch et al., *The Scrapbook History of Baseball* (1975, p.38): "A chopped ball generally goes for a hit. It requires great skill in placing to work this trick successfully, and it is done in this fashion: A middle-height ball is picked out and is attacked with a terrific swing on the upper side. The ball is made to strike the ground from five to ten feet away from the batsman, and, striking the ground with force bounds high over the head of the third or first baseman." Although Mike Whiteford (*How to Talk Baseball*, 1983, p.78) noted that "today's Baltimore chops . . . are almost always accidental," the term is very much alive as this kind of hit occurs frequently on artificial turf.

Baltimore dinger A cheap home run (Bill Mazeroski, *Bill Mazeroski's Baseball '89*, 1989).

Baltimore farewell The collective act by fans of waving handkerchiefs in a derogatory or unsympathetic fashion upon the departure of an opposing pitcher who has been removed from the game. "It's the subtlety of the thing which leaves visiting pitchers muttering to themselves" (*The Washington Post*, Sept. 6, 1957; Barry Popik). ETYMOLOGY. Murray Wieman (*Baltimore Evening Sun*, Apr. 12, 1955) revealed that the custom was spawned in Baltimore, back when the Orioles were a team in the Class AAA International League: "In spite of critics who called it 'small town' the farewell blossomed again last season [1954] as the Orioles went big league."

Bambi A meek or extremely mild-mannered player, manager, or coach, from the name of the fictional deer. "Though he [Cal Ripken Sr.] never kicked dirt on an umpire or turned his cap around to argue nose-to-nose as [Earl] Weaver is famous for, Ripken says he will be no Bambi with the umpires" (*USA Today*, Jan. 28, 1987).

banana 1. *n.* A good player; a prospect who makes the team. "There isn't a scout in the business who hasn't touted more lemons than bananas" (Dick Friendlich, *Relief Pitcher*, 1964, p.103; Charles D. Poe). **2.** *n.* A throw that sails off to one side and misses its intended target. **3.** *v.* To throw a ball that veers away from its intended target; e.g., "Smith's throw to second bananaed and pulled Jones off the bag."

banana boat A player who has played winter ball in Latin America. Joseph C. Goulden recalls that the designation was "a derisive name for minor leaguers who played Central American and Mexican baseball during the off-seasons in the late 1940s, employed chiefly by bench jockeys of opposing teams. This was the period when a three-year man in Class C baseball might earn upwards of $225 monthly during the regular season, so he went south for both the money and the experience. The next summer, however, he would hear the growl, 'banana boat, banana boat, TOOT TOOT TOOT!' from the other team's dugout."

banana oil A mythical solver of all problems on and off the field. IST USE. 1943. "But the old banana oil of psychology would be the right lubricant" (*Baseball Magazine*, January; David Shulman).

banana stalk A bat of inferior wood or low quality. "This banana stalk won't crack an aspirin" was an ad in an issue of *Time* magazine (Nov. 22, 1948; Peter Tamony) whose theme was baseball slang. See also *morning journal*. Syn. *banana stick*. IST USE. 1933. "A bat with poor wood in it" (*The Sporting News*, Feb. 23).

banana stick Syn. of *banana stalk*.

bandbox A ballpark whose small dimensions make it easier to hit home runs; e.g., Baker Bowl in Philadelphia in the early 1930s and Ebbets Field in Brooklyn in the 1950s. Today the term is most likely to attach itself to Boston's Fenway Park (which John Updike quoted in *Yankee* [June 1985], termed a "lyric little green bandbox"), Chicago's Wrigley Field (also known as the "friendly confines"), and Baltimore's Oriole Park at Camden Yards ("Is Camden Yards small? Small? It's a bandbox" said Wally Joyner, quoted in *The Baltimore Sun*, May 28, 1996). The term is sometimes used to suggest that a batter's numbers are less impressive because of the dimensions of his home field. See also *crackerbox*. Also spelled "band box." IST USE. 1899. "31 of Boston's 37 home runs were made in their bandbox at South End" (*Cincinnati Post*, reprinted in *The Sporting Life*, Nov. 11; Peter Morris). ETYMOLOGY. The term dates to the 17th century for a cylindrical box used to carry light, fragile items such as hats. It became a common piece of baggage in the 19th century and was often disparaged in print: "Of all the items in the travelling apparatus to the sex, none certainly can be a greater nuisance than the bandbox. It is the weakest, most insecure, and inconvenient baggage that ever married man was doomed to take care of" (*Daily National Journal*, Aug. 6, 1831).

bang 1. *n.* A base hit. "After [Buck] Weaver's scratch bang in the first inning, the Sox didn't get another hit until Ray Schalk cracked a single to left in the fifth" (*The New York Times*, Oct. 7, 1919). IST USE. 1916. "[Lee Magee] went to third on [Hugh] High's infield bang" (*The New York Times*, July 20). 2. *v.* To bat a ball unusually hard. IST USE. 1881. "[Fred] Goldsmith banged the ball over right-field fence for two-bagger" (*Chicago Tribune*, May 15; Peter Morris). 3. *v.* To eject from a game. St. Louis Cardinals manager Tony La Russa claimed that a pitcher deliberately throwing at a batter "would have been banged from the game" (William Safire, *The New York Times Magazine*, Oct. 16, 2005). 4. *v.* For an umpire to prematurely cancel, suspend, postpone, or terminate a baseball game due to inclement weather. Writer Bill Madden (*New York Daily News*), quoted by William Safire (*The New York Times Magazine*, Oct. 16, 2005): "[Umpire Durwood Merrill] banged the game before it even began. Turned out, the rain didn't start until after 10 p.m." ETYMOLOGY. Perhaps from the motion of a judge banging a gavel, an act of finality.

bang-bang play 1. An attempted tag or force play at a base when the runner and the ball arrive simultaneously. The events occur in quick succession, making it difficult for the umpire (and spectators) to determine whether the runner is safe or out. During the play, the umpire will watch for the runner's foot touch-

ing the bag while listening for the distinctive sound of the ball hitting the glove: the call is based on what the umpire hears or sees first. Umpire Ron Luciano (*The Umpire Strikes Back*, 1982; Charles D. Poe) wrote, "I blew a play at first base. I admit it. I was wrong. But I wasn't *that* wrong. It was a bang-bang play and I anticipated the throw arriving before it did and I called the runner out." Syn. *banger*, 2; *bing-banger*. 2. Any defensive play accomplished with precision and speed.

banger 1. A big hitter in the heart of a team's lineup. New York Yankees manager Joe Torre (quoted in *The Baltimore Sun*, Apr. 2, 2002), commenting on Jason Giambi: "This is what you want, your big banger up there with no place to put him." 2. An umpire's term for *bang-bang play*, 1.

bangqiu Baseball in China. "Chinese sports ministers have declared *bangqiu* an athletic priority" (L. Jon Wertheim, *Sports Illustrated*, June 14, 2004).

bang-up game A well-played, exciting baseball game. "The injury did not prevent Lalonge from getting into the afternoon game and playing a bang-up game" (*San Francisco Bulletin*, March 12, 1913; Gerald L. Cohen).

banish For an umpire to eject a player, coach, or manager from a game. IST USE. 1912 (*New York Tribune*, Apr. 21; Edward J. Nichols).

banjo Syn. of *Texas Leaguer*, 2. See also *banjo hit*, 2.

banjo eyes The wide-eyed look of a batter attempting to steal a sign from the catcher while at the plate. J.G. Taylor Spink attributes this term to Chicago Cubs second baseman Billy Herman (Fred Lieb, *Comedians and Pranksters of Baseball*, 1958).

banjo hit 1. A weak hit as the result of a poor swing or accidental contact with the ball, such as one made on a checked swing or by hitting the ball on the end of the bat. "A ball that sounds 'punk' when it hits the bat" (*New York Sun*, June 23, 1932). According to both Tim Considine (*The Language of Sport*, 1982) and Lee Allen (*The Hot Stove League*, 1955), the term was coined in 1924 by Jersey City second baseman Ray "Snooks" Dowd for the way the ball "plunks" off the bat. 2. A hit that falls between the infield and outfield;

a *Texas Leaguer* in the International League. See also *banjo*. 1st use. 1933 (*The Sporting News Record Book*).

banjo hitter A hitter who cannot hit the long ball. Todd Richissin (*The Baltimore Sun*, Apr. 3, 2000): "With enough banjo hitters in the lineup to field an impressive bluegrass festival, the [Cleveland] Indians of years past always had their critics laughing and generations of fans expecting the worst." When basketball legend Michael Jordan tried his hand at baseball in 1994, he was widely described as a banjo hitter. Upon his leaving, Dave Kindred (*The Sporting News*, March 20, 1995) wrote, "The woods are full of banjo hitters. But Jordan's leaving is important for what it says about baseball." See also *ukulele hitter*. 1st use. 1943. "A 'banjo hitter' is one who hits pop flies over the field" (*Baseball Magazine*, Jan. 1943; David Shulman). usage note. Although it underscores the inability to hit for distance, the term is not necessarily derogatory, as it can be applied to an effective place hitter. "As a baseball player, little Bert Campaneris dreams of powering the ball over distant fences such as Hank Aaron or Willie Mays, but he is happy at being a banjo hitter with a pair of speedy legs" (Associated Press dispatch, Oct. 17, 1973; Peter Tamony).

Bankers' League Nickname for *Negro National League* because many of the league's owners were numbers bankers (Neil J. Lanctot, *Negro League Baseball*, 2004, p.60). They controlled a form of lottery in which an individual bets on the appearance of a certain combination of digits from a regularly published source, such as the last three digits in the daily amount cleared by a Federal Reserve Bank. Largely illegal, these lotteries were known as "numbers," or the numbers game.

Banks' dictum The name given to Chicago Cubs Ernie Banks' famous line, "It's a great day for a ball game. Let's play two!" The line is quoted widely and often, and tends to be uttered when the weather is mild and the players are primed. To many, the line captures the spirit and joy of the game of baseball. 1st use. 1983. "The Ernie Banks dictum" (Peter Sharpe, *The New York Times*, July 23).

banner 1. Syn. of *pennant*, 2. 1st use. 1880 (*New York Herald*, Aug. 30; Edward J. Nichols). 2. A paper or cloth sheet emblazoned with a message from a fan or fans. A product of the television age (since TV cameras often focus on them), banners—before they became a national phenomenon—took on great importance during the early seasons of the New York Mets. A famous banner was displayed by Michael Sergio, who parachuted into Shea Stadium with a "Go Mets!" banner at the beginning of the sixth game of the 1986 World Series.

banner day A promotion in which fans are encouraged to display posters and banners at the ballpark. The idea evolved from the practice of fans bringing placards and bedsheets emblazoned with slogans proclaiming their feelings toward the teams and players on the field. The real impetus for banners came during the inaugural season (1962) of the New York Mets, when hapless fans carried signs emblazoned with mottos such as "We Don't Want To Set The World On Fire—We Just Want To Finish Ninth." At first the banners were confiscated, but later they became an accepted part of the game. A "banner night" is a promotion at a night game.

banner year A highly successful season enjoyed by a player, a team, or baseball itself. 1st use. 1904. "Baseball's Banner Year: National Game's Greatest Prosperity Seen in Present Season" (*The Boston Globe* headline, reprinted in *The Washington Post*, Sept. 18; Peter Morris).

banquet *hist.* A bonehead or sloppy play. "[Terry] danced gayly off the base and when Davis popped a fly to Ward he started for third thinking two were out. Ward caught the ball and drove it to Richardson, effecting a pretty but ridiculously easy double [play]. It was a chump play on Terry's part, and the New Yorkers gave him a round of hoots. This was the finest piece of 'banquet' work that the Brooklyns had as yet exhibited" (*The World* [New York], Oct. 26, 1889; Gerald L. Cohen).

banquet circuit The banquets and other social recognition given to the players in the off-season. Syn. "banquet trail."

Banshee Board Bill Veeck's *exploding scoreboard.*

baptism The act of removing the smooth, slippery surface of a new baseball before bringing it into play. This is usually performed prior to the start of a game by the home plate umpire, who uses a special rubbing mud.

barber 1. *hist.* A garrulous player; one who talks incessantly or engages in chatting and joking during a game, in the manner of an extroverted barber; a willing and eager conversationalist; the American League equivalent of *bag puncher* (*American Speech*, Apr. 1930). IST USE. 1927 (*New York Sun*, July 18; Edward J. Nichols). ETYMOLOGY. Hy Turkin maintained that the talkative Waite Hoyt coined the term when he was a pitcher with the New York Yankees. This meaning of the term was the only one that prevailed in baseball until about 1950 when the next two began to be heard. 2. A pitcher who throws pitches that come close to or "shaves" the batter's head. Sal Maglie was called "The Barber" because he did not hesitate to throw brushback pitches. 3. A pitcher with enough precision and control to "shave" the corners of the strike zone. Sal Maglie was also called "The Barber" for his pinpoint control: "I was shavin' the corners like a good Italian barber" (Maglie, quoted in Thomas Kiernan, *The Miracle at Coogan's Bluff*, 1975, p.191).

barbering Chatting, as one is likely to do in a barber's chair. Dizzy Dean defined the term as "conversing, chinning, or chewing the fat" in his booklet "Dizzy Daisies." Arthur Mann (*Baseball Confidential*, 1951, p.11): "[Leo Durocher's] eternal barbering, on and off the field, did not help matters. He popped off furiously about some of the shortcomings of the veterans." IST USE. 1928. "The boys were sitting around the clubhouse punching the bag and 'barbering' a little about what we might expect in the [1927 World Series]" (George Herman Ruth, *Babe Ruth's Own Book of Baseball*, p.20; Peter Morris).

Barberism A homespun phrase or instant epiphany made famous by broadcaster Red Barber, whose "style made tremendous use of literary nuance" (*USA Today Baseball Weekly*, Oct. 28–Nov. 2, 1992). Examples

Barberism. Red Barber in a 1955 *New York World-Telegram & Sun* photo by Al Ravenna. *Library of Congress*

include: "sittin' in the catbird seat"; "tearin' up the pea patch"; "slicker than oiled okra"; "one foot in the pickle vat"; and "Oooohhh Doctor!" (upon a sudden turn of events).

bare-handed Said of the act of fielding a batted or thrown ball without the use of a glove. Such plays are usually made on slowly hit balls and often result in quick, off-balance throws. A bunt will often take a third baseman by surprise, and his only hope of making the play at first base in time might be to field the ball bare-handed and whip it across the infield in the same motion. Also spelled "barehanded."

bargain-basement single A "cheap hit"; e.g., a ball that seems about t o roll foul (but then stays fair) while the third baseman looks on, or a ball that spins away from an infielder who would have had a sure double play (Walter K. Putney, *Baseball Stories*, Spring 1952).

bargain bill A *doubleheader*, so called because one gets to see two games for the price of one.

bargain day *hist.* A day on which a doubleheader is scheduled. "Johnson and Boehling will work in the bargain-day contests" (*The Washington Post*, Sept. 7, 1913; Peter Morris). IST USE. 1912 (*New York Tribune*, Sept. 5; Edward J. Nichols).

barker Syn. of *first base coach.* IST USE. 1918. "Otto Knabe, official barker of the Cubs" (*Boston American*, Sept. 7; Peter Morris). ETYMOLOGY. One who "barks," in the sense of a person who hawks at an entrance to a nightclub or carnival sideshow.

barn ball A forerunner of baseball that survived after baseball became popular. It was a game of two players, a ball, a bat (usually an ax handle or stick), and the side of a barn or other building. One player threw the ball against the barn for the other to hit with the bat. If the batter missed and the pitcher caught it, the batter was out and the pitcher was up. However, if the batter hit the ball, he had a chance to score a run by touching the barn and returning to his batting position before the pitcher could retrieve the ball and hit him with it. John Allen Krout (*The Annals of American Sport,* 1929) noted: "Here were the fundamentals of the game of baseball; the pitcher, the batter, the base hit and the run."

barnburner 1. An exciting baseball game. 2. An exciting baseball season. "Another incredible pennant race with the Giants, one as ferocious and exciting as the barnburner of 1951" (Bruce Chadwick, *The Dodgers,* 1993, p.100). 3. An exciting baseball player. "I've seen guys who are barnburners early in spring training and when the bell rings it didn't work" (Colorado Rockies pitching coach Frank Funk, quoted in *The Denver Post,* March 18, 1998).

barn door An easy pitch to hit; one that is slow and seems to be the size of a barn door. IST USE. 1912. "If I was pitchin' barn doors and you was battin', you'd swear every door I threw would be the size of a French pea" (*The Sporting Life,* May 18).

barnstorm To play exhibition games in small towns and cities, some of which may not have baseball teams of their own. ETYMOLOGY. The term was borrowed from the world theater of the early 1880s, when plays were performed in whatever venue was available, even if it was in a barn.

barnstormer A team or individual who barnstorms. IST USE. 1902 (*The Sporting Life,*

Barker. Barker at a sideshow at the Rutland Fair, Rutland, Vt. Jack Delano photograph, 1944. *Office of War Information. Overseas Picture Division. Washington Division, Library of Congress*

July 5; Edward J. Nichols). ETYMOLOGY. The term was borrowed from the world theater of the early 1880s in reference to traveling actors. Alfred H. Holt (*Phrase Origins,* 1936) wrote: "Since the War, 'barn-stormer' has also been applied to an aviator who parks his 'crate' (usually an old OX–5 with a Liberty motor) in a barn at some conveniently large and level pasture, and takes people joy-riding at a dollar or two a shot."

barnstorming team A professional or semi-pro baseball team, not affiliated with any league, that travels about the country, in season, challenging the best of local, home-grown teams. The 1992 New England Grey Sox included such former major-league players as Bob Stanley, George Foster, Tug McGraw, and Ferguson Jenkins.

barnstorming tour A series of exhibition games that at one time was played by major-league teams in various cities from spring training to Opening Day, or after the regular season had ended. A.G. Spalding wrote that baseball's first barnstorming tour took place in 1860 when the Excelsiors of Brooklyn played in several cities of central and western New York. Groups of individuals also engaged in off-season barnstorming tours, a practice that was generally frowned upon by major-league owners who did not want to see their best players hurt playing for pick-up "all-star" teams. "The players participated in a major vs. minor all-star game in Los Angeles on February 15, thus breaking the barn-storming rule which prohibits big leaguers playing for money later than thirty days after the World Series ends" (*San Francisco Examiner*, March 8, 1948; Peter Tamony). For the players, barnstorming tours were an important source of income: "We did it to make money [in the 1950s]" (Yogi Berra, quoted in *The New York Times*, Jan. 11, 1988). Syn. "barnstorming loop." IST USE. 1893. "The barnstorming tour of the Reds Successful" (*The Sporting Life* headline, Oct. 14; Peter Morris).

barrage Many hits and/or runs in close succession. "[Scott Erickson] left the Rangers' third [inning] shell-shocked by a six-run, seven-hit barrage" (*The Baltimore Sun*, Apr. 18, 1998). Syn. *unscheduled batting practice*.

barrel The top, thick, or heavy part of a baseball bat, often referred to as the *fat part of the bat* or *good wood*, 1. Syn. *butt*, 2.

barrel-hoop curve A sweeping curveball. IST USE. 1910. "The first curves pitched were of the variety now known as the 'barrel hoop.' It was a slow curve, pitched underhand, with the hand swung nearly to the level of the knee, fingers downward and hand held almost at right angles with the wrist. As the hand was swung the wrist was jerked sharply and the ball, sliding off the first finger, revolved rapidly . . . to move in a slow wide arc. All curves are developments of the 'barrel hoop'" (John J. Evers and Hugh S. Fullerton, *Touching Second: The Science of Baseball*, p.104; Peter Morris).

barry A bonehead play. "The biggest 'barry' pulled in base ball in years" (*St. Louis Post-Dispatch*, Sept. 29, 1913; Peter Morris).

bars A children's game in the early 14th century in England that consisted of running from one bar or barrier to another. According to Henry Chadwick (*The Ball Players' Chronicle*, July 18, 1867), the name of the game was subsequently corrupted to "base"; Shakespeare, in *Cymbeline* (first performed 1609–1610, published 1623), had one of his characters say, "He with two stripling lads more like to run / The country base, than to omit such slaughter." As late as 1770, Chadwick noted that the "celebrated game" was played in London: "To distinguish it from other games which had sprung out of it, it was called 'prisoners' base' . . . The skill in this game consisted simply of running with agility and swiftness, in such a way as not to be caught by the opposing party, from one 'bar' or 'base' to another." Chadwick surmised that the game later employed a ball, and "thus formed the game of 'rounders,' 'round ball,' or 'base ball.'" Chadwick admitted another plausible derivation: "The object of each side in the game of 'bars' was to keep the other party at bay, the places where they were so kept, that is the 'bases,' were styled 'bays,' of which 'base' is a corruption."

Bart Giamatti Award An annual award presented since 1991 to an individual associated with baseball who "best exemplifies the compassion" demonstrated by the late baseball commissioner. The award recognizes community and charitable work.

Bartman seat The seat down the left-field line at Wrigley Field in Chicago (aisle 4, row 8, seat 113) occupied by 26-year-old Cubs fan Steve Bartman who, on Oct. 14, 2003, during the top of the eighth inning of Game 6 of the National League Championship Series between the Cubs and the Florida Marlins, reached for and deflected a foul fly ball hit by Marlins second baseman Luis Castillo, thereby preventing Cubs left fielder Moises Alou from making the catch. Because the ball was clearly beyond the field of play, no interference was called. The Cubs led the series 3–2 and had a 3–0 lead in the game at the time; however, after Castillo drew a walk, the Marlins went on to score eight runs to win the game and eventually the series. Bartman has been reviled by Cubs fans because the team was five outs away from going to the World Series for the first time since 1945.

base 1. One of the four corners or points of the baseball diamond, each 90 feet from the next. Each base is an incremental unit used in reaching the fourth unit and scoring a run. Only one runner is allowed on any base at any one time. USAGE NOTE. "While technically correct, it is not the custom to speak of a 'home run with four on bases.' The batter is really on a base, but custom has decreed that the first, second and third bases are meant when 'bases' are mentioned" (*The Sporting News*, July 28, 1910; Peter Morris). EXTENDED USE. To "touch base" is to make contact, to "touch all the bases" is to be thorough, to be "off base" is to be wrong, and to be "off one's base" is to be out of one's mind. In the language of teenage sexuality, knowing your way "around the bases" is to know that first base is kissing, second base is petting above the waist, third base is petting below the waist, and fourth base (a home run) is sexual intercourse. *National Lampoon* (Apr. 1991) changed the disposition of the bases: first base was touching a girl's breast, second base was a blow job, third base was sexual intercourse, and home was "having a long conversation about the relationship." According to Jancee Dunn (*Rolling Stone*, Nov. 11, 1999; Peter Morris), "Guess what the bases are these days? 'First base is really not that bad; it's just, like, French kissing,' says one girl. 'Second base is really just, like, oh, God, feeling somebody or something. Over or under the clothes. It's really not that big of a deal. And then, um, third base is, like, the biggest one.' She collapses in giggles." Frank Deford (quoted in Ron Fimrite, ed., *Birth of a Fan*, 1993, p.74) noted, "What does it tell us about America that every kid in the U.S. who tries to get a little nookie thinks about it strictly in baseball terms?" **2.** A marker representing a base. The home base is a rubberized plate; the other three are canvas bags measuring 15 by 15 inches. See also *bag*, 2; *brick*, 4; *cushion*, 1; *hassock*; *hummock*; *jute rag*; *pillow*, 1; *pouch*; *precinct*, 2; *sack*, 1; *sandbag*; *satchel*; *station*. IST USE. 1845. "The base shall be from 'home' to second base, forty-two paces; from first to third base, forty-two paces, equidistant" (Knickerbocker Rules, Rule 4th, Sept. 23). **3.** Syn. of *stake*, 1. **4.** A term used by Robin Carver (*The Book of Sports*, 1834) to describe a game identified as baseball with four "stones or stakes" placed 12 to 20 yards "asunder" in a diamond-shaped configuration. Carver reprinted the rules for rounders first published by William Clarke (*The Boy's Own Book*, 2nd ed., 1828) in London, and changed the name of the game from "rounders" to "base": "This game is known under a variety of names. It is sometimes called 'round ball.'

But I believe that 'base' or 'goal ball' are the names generally adopted" in the United States. "The young men are expert in a variety of games at ball—such as cricket, base, cat, football, trap-ball" (Horatio Smith, *Festivals, Games and Amusements*, 1831; David Block). Syn. *goal ball*. IST USE. 1821. "The grounds of Kensington House are spacious, and well adapted to the playing the noble game of cricket, base, trap-ball, quoits and other amusements, and all the apparatus necessary for the above games will be furnished to clubs and parties" (*New-York Evening Post*, June 2; John Thorn). USAGE NOTE. George Ewing, a New Jersey ensign at Valley Forge, wrote in his diary for April 7, 1778: "Exersisd in the afternoon in the intervals playd at base" (see *The Military Journal of George Ewing [1754–1824], a Soldier of Valley Forge*, 1928, p.35). This may be the first written use of the term "base" in North America (Thomas L. Altherr, *NINE*, Spring 2000); but John Thorn (personal communication, Dec. 19, 2006) states that this "oft-cited Ewing reference to base is to an ancient game of tag, not involving a ball." Louisiana Purchase explorers Lewis and Clark attempted to teach the Nez Percé Indians to play the game of "base" in 1806. David Block (personal communication, June 2005) suggests, "The use of the term 'base' in 1830s New England must be viewed differently than its use in earlier periods, such as the Valley Forge and Lewis & Clark references, when the game prisoner's base was still widely popular. Without any accompanying indication that a ball was involved, these earlier references should not be assumed to be about baseball." **5.** *hist.* A base hit. "I caught one on the end of my bat and put it into right field for a base" (Ed Delahanty, quoted in *The Washington Post*, July 22, 1900). IST USE. 1876. "[Spalding] came home on Barnes' fine drive for a base" (*The Boston Globe*, Sept. 13).

base ball *hist.* An earlier spelling of "baseball" that is seldom used today but was dominant in the 19th century. "It was not very wonderful that Catherine [Morland], who had by nature nothing heroic about her, should prefer cricket, base ball, riding on horseback, and running about the country, at the age of fourteen, to books" (Jane Austen, *Northanger Abbey*, written in 1798 or 1799 but published Dec. 1817, dated 1818). Sidney Babcock, in a 24-page chapbook (*The Boy's Book of Sports: A Description of the Exercises and Pastimes of Youth*, 1835), updated the description of rounders by definitely calling the game "base ball" to reflect current practices, such as reversing the base-running direction from clockwise to counterclockwise (David Block, *Baseball Before We Knew It*, 2005). 1ST USE. 1755. "Went to Miss Seale's [Jeale's] to play at Base Ball, with her, the 3 Miss Whiteheads, Miss Billinghurst, Miss Molly Fluttor [Flutter], Mr. Chandler, Mr. Ford, & H. Parsons & Jolly [Jelly]" (English lawyer William Bray, diary entry, March 31; see David Block, *Base Ball: A Journal of the Early Game*, Fall 2007, pp. 6–8).

base-ball *hist.* An earlier spelling of "baseball." "Base-ball" was standard usage in England, and virtually all known 18th- and early 19th-century U.S. references to the game use the hyphenated form of the term (David Block, *Baseball Before We Knew It*, 2005). The 1896 rules and specifications of the U.S. Government Printing Office called for the term to be written with a hyphen. In a letter written on Nov. 14, 1748, Mary Lepel (known by her title, Lady Hervey), describing the activities of the family of the Prince of Wales, wrote, "In the winter, in a large room, they divert themselves at base-ball, a play all who are, or have been, schoolboys, are well acquainted with. The ladies, as well as gentlemen, join in this amusement" (*Letters of Mary Lepel, Lady Hervey*, 1821). Another early British use of the term "base-ball" was discovered by David Block (*Base Ball: A Journal of the Early Game*, Fall 2007, pp.9–10): "The younger Part of the Family . . . retired to an *interrupted* Party at *Base-Ball* (an *infant* Game, which as it advances in its *Teens*, improves into *Fives* [handball], and in its State of *Manhood*, is called *Tennis*)" (John Kidgell, *The Card*, 1755, p.9). 1ST USE. 1744. "B is for / Base-ball / The Ball once struck off, / Away flies the *Boy* / To the next destin'd Post, / And then Home with Joy" (John New-

bery's *A Little Pretty Pocket-Book, Intended for the Instruction and Amusement of Little Master Tommy and Pretty Miss Polly*, published in London in 1744, republished in the United States several times between 1762 and 1787); the British Library owns a single copy of the 1760, or 10th, edition, and no earlier copies are known to exist in institutional collections or in private hands. 1ST USE (in the United States). 1791. For the preservation of the windows in the new town-meeting house in Pittsfield, Mass., "no person or Inhabitant of said Town, shall be permitted to play at any game called Wicket, Cricket, Base-ball, Bat-ball, Foot-ball, Cats, Fives or any other games played with Ball, within the Distance of eighty yards from said Meeting House" (Pittsfield, Mass., town ordinance, Sept. 5; Berkshire Athenaeum document XVIII, A #10). See also J.E.A. Smith, *The History of Pittsfield . . . From the Year 1734 to the Year 1800*, 1869, pp.446–47, who incorrectly gave the date of 1793). (John Thorn)

baseball 1. The game itself, comprising a body of rules, records, and traditions and played at many skill levels, by everyone from young children to seasoned professionals. *Official Baseball Rules* (Rule 1.01): "Baseball is a game between two teams of nine players each, under the direction of a manager, played on an enclosed field in accordance with these rules, under jurisdiction of one or more umpires." The *Daily Evening Bulletin* (San Francisco) on Sept. 24, 1869 noted, "The National game of baseball, which has created such a *furore* in the East, bids fair for an exciting revival on this coast." Baseball has been defined many ways in many quarters, including this Freudian interpretation: "The pitcher-father tries to complete a throw into the mitt of his mate crouched over home plate. A series of sons step up and each in turn tries to intercept the throw. If any of them is successful, he can win 'home' and defeat the pitcher—if he is able first to complete a hazardous journey out of the adult world of the father's allies" (Thomas Gould, *The Ancient Quarrel Between Poetry and Philosophy*, quoted in *New York Times Magazine*, Sept. 11, 1983). Abbrev. *BB*, 4. 1ST USE (unambiguous). 1858. "From my window I can see boys playing hop-scotch, and baseball, and leap-frog, and also flying kites" (*Frank Leslie's Illustrated Newspaper*, Apr. 24). USAGE NOTE. There is no way to know whether the earliest instances of "baseball" as one word are intentional or are merely typographical errors. John Thorn noted that the draft version of the Pittsfield, Mass., town ordinance (1791) spelled the term as one word without a hyphen, but the version recorded in the town's book spelled it with a hyphen. An excerpt from Mary Russell Mitford (*Our Village*, 1828), third in a series of sketches of village scenes and characters, vividly drawn, published in *The Albion, A Journal of News, Politics and Literature* (Aug. 9, 1828), portrayed a three- or four-year-old girl "playing and rolling about, amongst grass or mud all day . . . her longing eyes fixed on a game of baseball at the corner of the green," before entering the schoolhouse, "looking as demure as a Nun, and as tidy; her thoughts fixed on button-holes, and spelling-books—those ensigns of promotion; despising dirt and baseball, and all their joys." David Block (personal communication, Apr. 23, 2006) cites the following from S.R. Calthrop's lecture on "Physical Development, and Its Relations to Mental and Spiritual Development," delivered at the 29th annual meeting of the American Institute of Instruction, in Norwich, Conn., Aug. 20, 1858 (published 1859): "This, then, is what cricket, and boating, battledore and archery, shinney and skating, fishing, hunting, shooting, and baseball mean, namely, that there is a joyous spontaneity in human beings; and thus Nature, by means of the sporting world." *The New York Times* converted "base-ball" (hyphenated) into "baseball" (one word) in 1884. As noted by Charlie Bevis (*The Baseball Research Journal*, No.35, 2007, p.15), separate words ("base ball") often evolve into hyphenated compounds ("base-ball") and later become solid compounds ("baseball"). **2.** The white, red-stitched, leather-covered ball (sheepskin before 1880, horsehide or cowhide since 1974) consisting of cork, rubber, and yarn used to play the game of baseball, being not less than 9 nor more than 9¼ inches in circumference and weighing between 5 and 5¼ ounces. **3.** The organized game in its entirety; the "industry." "Baseball has never answered any charges directed against it by anyone regarding the war records of its players" (George Weiss, quoted in *Springfield* [Mass.] *Union*, May 5, 1954). "Neither baseball nor the players union believes there is a reliable blood test for hGH [human growth hormone]" (*The Baltimore Sun*, June 20, 2006). **4.** The jargon that is specific to baseball. " 'Bean' is baseball for 'head'" (John J. Evers and Hugh S. Fullerton, *Touching Second: The Science of Baseball*, 1910). See also *baseballese*, 1. **5.** A civil religion. "At the center of baseball's symbolic power there resides a unique language of civil religion, proclaiming that the game can redeem America and serve as a light to all nations" (Christopher H. Evans, in Christopher H. Evans and William R. Herzog II, eds., *The Faith of Fifty Million*, 2002, p.15). A civil religion has "its own prophets and its own martyrs, its own sacred events and sacred places, its own solemn rituals and symbols" (Robert N. Bellah, in Donald G. Jones and Russell E. Richey, eds., *American Civil Religion*, 1974, pp.40–41). **6.** The adult version of rounders since 1892, currently played in the Liverpool region and in South Wales. Its misnomer in the United States is "Welsh baseball." **7.** [softball term] Women's fast pitch softball; specif., "baseball modified." It is of some significance that despite the title, in Viola Mitchell's *Softball for Girls* (1942), the terms "softball" and "baseball" were used interchangeably.

EXTENDED USE. **1.** A general metaphor for other organized activities relying on teamwork. "R. Sargent Shriver, Jr., director of the Peace Corps, said today the Corps will be operated like a baseball team, with the manager empowered to yank out a player before he ruins the game" (Associated Press dispatch, May 18, 1961; Peter Tamony). **2.** A method of wagering; e.g., daily-double play in which the bettor couples a horse in one race with all horses in the other race (Tom Ainslie, *Ainslie's Complete Guide to Thoroughbred Racing*, 1968). The term is also used in dog racing: "And the most popular method of selecting quinellas is called, by golly, a 'baseball.' Since there generally are eight greyhounds in each race, students of the sport have noticed there can be a problem in forecasting the two which will run best. So, in a 'baseball' you select three lean pooches, which means you're betting on three combinations. With this baseball though, there are more wild pitches than two-baggers" (Harry Jupiter, *San Francisco Examiner*, March 20, 1967; Peter Tamony). **3.** Any of several children's games that ape the scoring of baseball but that do not involve other elements of the game; specif., a mumblety-peg-like jackknife game played under flexible rules by two or more children who toss a pocketknife with two open blades and depending on how the knife sticks in the ground, the thrower is credited with a single, double, triple, or home run, or if the knife lands flat, the thrower is out (*The Dictionary of American Regional English*, under the heading for "baseball"). **4.** A baseball-shaped grenade, 2.5 inches in diameter, used during the Vietnam War. See also *baseball grenade*. **5.** A pocket billiards game in which players try to score "runs" by pocketing 21 consecutively numbered object balls, the number of runs scored corresponding to the total of the numbers on the balls pocketed. Each player has nine opportunities, or "innings," at the table, which he plays in succession until he misses (fails to score) or loses his turn as the result of a foul (*Encyclopaedia Britannica: Micropaedia*, v.1, 1984). **6.** A particle that is roughly a billion billion times more massive than the proton and neutron, which form the atomic nucleus (Walter Sullivan, *New York Times*, Feb. 13, 1979).

baseball age **1.** A baseball player's seasonal age, usually defined to be his age on July 1 of a given season. This standard is used for statistical purposes. **2.** A baseball player's age other than his real age, usually younger. Dave Anderson (*The New York Times*, Feb. 1, 1990): "Through the years, many baseball players have fibbed about their ages. Their 'baseball age' is always a year or two younger than their real age." Jim Bouton (*Ball Four*, 1970, p.117) wrote, "Most baseball people have two ages, real and baseball. The older they get, the greater the discrepancy between their numbers. Some of the players were clever enough to cheat by two or three years as soon as they signed and thus were more valuable throughout their careers." IST USE. 1901. "I was 39 according to my base ball age, when I quit, but I kept the date of my first birthday a secret" (Cap Anson, quoted in *The Sporting News*, Nov. 9; Peter Morris).

Baseball Alumni Team Original name of *Baseball Assistance Team.*

Baseball Annie A generic name for an unattached woman who favors the company of baseball players; a female camp-follower. The phrase was given prominence after Philadelphia Phillies first baseman Eddie Waitkus was shot without provocation on June 14, 1949: "He sat up in bed and tolerantly described Ruth [Steinhagen, a 19-year-old] as a 'Baseball Annie,' one of an army of hero-worshiping teen-age girls who follow the players around" (*Time* magazine, June 17, 1949; Peter Tamony). Although the term is not as commonly used as it once was, it is still used in special situations. "Margo Adams, who has filed a $6 million palimony suit against [Wade] Boggs, has been categorized by some as a Baseball Annie, a woman attracted to ballplayers" (Ira Berkow, *The New York Times*, Aug. 12, 1988). Other "Annies" include Anthem Annie, a nickname given to Donna Greenwald (Columbia, Md.), who has sung the national anthem at every major-league ballpark, and Annie Savoy, a muse of the religion of baseball who declared in Ron Shelton's movie *Bull Durham* (1988), "There's never been a ballplayer slept with me who didn't have the best year of his career," and "I'd never sleep with a player hitting under .250 . . . unless he had a lot of RBIs or was a great glove man up the middle." See also *Baseball Sadie; green fly.*

baseball arm A nonmedical term for a painful throwing arm that can take a pitcher out of the rotation or hamper a fielder; any sore arm produced from playing baseball. See also *baseball pitcher's arm*. EXTENDED USE. The term can be applied to players in other sports as well. "A baseball arm will be the long range football problem at Stanford during the interim until plans start for the next Big Game" (*San Francisco Call-Bulletin*, Nov. 24, 1952; Peter Tamony).

Baseball Assistance Team A charitable foundation established in 1986 that offers financial support to indigent and needy retired ballplayers and others associated with baseball. It is an arm of Major League Baseball, but funded by donations from major companies and individuals. Originally named *Baseball Alumni Team.* Abbrev. *BAT.*

baseball bat See *bat,* 1.

baseball bedroom A room in a boardinghouse without sink or toilet, so called because it featured "a pitcher on the dresser and a catcher underneath the bed" (Doug Clark, *How to Survive the Money Crash,* 1979, p.136).

baseball bet A bet on a baseball game. EXTENDED USE. A horse-racing bet involving a parlay on three or more horses.

baseball bride The wife of a baseball player. EXTENDED USE. One's ninth wife, after the fact that there are nine players on a baseball field. "Bandleader Charlie Barnett breezed into town last night with his 'baseball bride'" (*San Francisco News,* Aug. 18, 1955; Peter Tamony).

baseball bug *hist.* 1. Syn. of *baseball fever.* "Just as eagerly is the 'baseball bug' watched these days as the proverbial 'ground hog'" (*Daily Argus* [Mount Vernon, N.Y.], Jan. 16, 1911). A 1940s Bugs Bunny cartoon entitled "Baseball Bugs" may be a play on this term. **2.** Syn. of *bug,* 1.

baseball cage Syn. of *batting cage,* 2. IST USE. 1901. "The Badger's [*sic*] baseball management has some fifty candidates practicing every afternoon in the baseball cage" (*Milwaukee Journal,* March 8; Peter Morris)

baseball camp A commercial enterprise, usually operated by former major-league players and dedicated to teaching beginning and semi-experienced youths the fundamentals of baseball. The periods of instruction vary from camp to camp. Not to be confused with *fantasy baseball camp.* See also *baseball school.*

baseball cap The billed hat worn by baseball players. It shades a player's eyes from the sun during the day and from artificial lights at night. Its distinctive coloring and graphics help promote the team and make for a popular retail product. According to an exhibit at the National Baseball Hall of Fame and Museum,

Boston Baseball Series, No. 105. Copyright, 1909, by O. D. Williams, Boston

Hey! youse watch me swipe it.

Baseball cap. Postcard, 1910. *Andy Moresund Collection*

the Knickerbockers adopted the first official baseball cap on Apr. 24, 1849. The first caps were chip (or straw) hats; a few years later, the Knickerbockers switched to a cap made of merino wool that featured the two main characteristics of the modern-day baseball cap: a crown and a bill (or visor). It was once rigid custom for a player to doff or touch the peak of his cap when crossing home plate after hitting a home run. IST USE. 1889. "A base-ball cap free to every purchaser" (M.J. Flavin & Co., San Francisco, advertisement for "outing suits," *Daily Evening Bulletin* [San Francisco], June 10). EXTENDED USE. As baseball caps are now ubiquitous, the term is just as likely to show up in a news story as on the sports pages. An item in the *Gary* [Ind.] *Post Tribune* for Aug. 12, 1967, reported that "Two gunmen wearing black baseball caps escaped with an estimated $2,500 from the Gary Federal Savings and Loan." Jess Cagle (*Time* magazine, Jan. 8, 2001): "[Movie director Steven] Soderbergh is back to wear-

Baseball cap. Congressman Gerald Ford with an unidentified teammate at the annual congressional game, pitting Democrats against Republicans, on May 29, 1949. *Gerald Ford Presidential Library*

ing a baseball cap. It's a standard fashion accessory among those in his profession." A *Washington Post* editorial (Feb. 28, 1993) entitled "Hail to the Cap" noted, "The baseball cap, an item once worn almost exclusively by young boys . . . has come quite a distance in recent years. This week the President of the United States was wearing one on his travels, and he wasn't doing it in the consciously folksy way some past presidents have but rather as part of the standard all-

business garb of a chief executive: hard shoes, suit, tie, dignified topcoat . . . baseball cap." The item of clothing has even taken hold across the Atlantic, in ways that the sport itself has not: Bill Glauber (*The Baltimore Sun*, March 21, 2001) wrote: "A sartorial revolution has occurred in the land where bowler hats and cloth caps once were the national headwear for decades. Britons have fallen in love with baseball caps."

baseball card A small piece of cardboard depicting a baseball player, a group of players, or a team; a *trading card* with a baseball motif. Approximately the size of a playing card (the modern-day card was standardized by the Topps Company Inc. in 1957 as a 2½-by-3½-inch rectangle, although they have been produced in many shapes and sizes), most feature a portrait or action photograph of a baseball player, past or present, on one side and appropriate biographical data and career statistics on the other side. The first baseball cards were printed in 1887, on paper. They are collected and traded, and many are collectors' items. They have been used in games such as *flipping* and scaling against walls, and in wedging between bicycle spokes (1950s and 1960s). Baseball cards have been included as a premium with

Baseball card. A small photographic depiction of the 1865 Atlantic of Brooklyn, with an 1865 copyright. The original is the same size as a modern baseball card (2½ x 3½ inches). *Library of Congress*

tobacco and chewing gum as well as with such widely diverse products as soft drinks, bread, potato chips, candy, taffy, and breakfast cereals. Some baseball "cards" may be made with metal, leather, plastic, or wood. See also *bubble-gum card*; *cigar card*; *cigarette card*; *tobacco card*; *rookie card*. EXTENDED USE. A promotional card featuring an individual and a city. "In an effort to promote Hot Springs as the town where [Bill] Clinton spent much of his boyhood, advertising executives have cooked up a plan to put the ex-president on a baseball card," with one side featuring a portrait of Clinton playing golf and the back side displaying facts about his life in Hot Springs, "as well as a subtle promotion for the city" (*The Baltimore Sun*, Aug. 2, 2001).

baseball catcher A bizarre invention by James E. Bennett (patent number 755,209 acquired on March 22, 1904) that basically replaced the catcher's mitt with a rectangular wire cage reinforced by slotted walls of wood and placed on the catcher's chest. The object was to protect the catcher's hands. After the ball passed through the open front end, it dropped to the bottom and passed through an opening into a pocket where the catcher retrieved the ball. The device also included a wire mesh on the top to protect the catcher's face.

Baseball Chapel An international, evangelical, and nondenominational ministry spread through all levels of professional baseball, committed to spiritual guidance and development and promotion of the Christian gospel. It is recognized by the major leagues and minor leagues and is responsible for the appointment and oversight of team chapel leaders. The ministry is directed toward players, coaches, and managers and their wives, umpires, trainers, front office personnel, ballpark staff, and members of the media. Headquartered in Springfield, Pa., Baseball Chapel was founded in 1973 for players whose work kept them from making it to church on Sunday. Baseball commissioner Bowie Kuhn approved Detroit sportswriter Watson Spoelstra's proposal that a chapel program be organized for every major-league team; by the start of the 1975 season, every team conducted services at the ballpark. A minor-league program was established in 1978.

baseball club Syn. of *ball club*, 1. 1ST USE. 1855. "Atlantic Base Ball Club, Jamaica, N.Y" (title) (*Dictionary of American English*).

baseball code A set of *unwritten rules* that specify preordained behavior on and off the field; a set of instructions for the way the game is supposed to be played and for providing a form of peaceful co-existence, allowing a diverse group of men to survive a grueling 162-game schedule and possible postseason. Author Jeff Pearlman (quoted in *The Baltimore Sun*, Apr. 5, 2006): "In Major League Baseball, there is a code. *The Code.* Simply put, ballplayers do not rat out other ballplayers." Umpire Tom Gorman (*Three and Two!*, 1979) wrote, "If an opposing pitcher knocks down one of his teammates, a player expects his pitcher to get even and knock down the other pitcher, or one of the opposition players. It's part of the baseball code." Essentially, baseball code dictates that players do whatever they can to win without embarrassing opponents or overvaluing individual achievements. Tim Keown (*ESPN The Magazine*, June 25, 2001) discussed baseball code at length, explaining that the code's most stringent statutes deal with blowouts, "when the losing team is most susceptible to frustration, anger and embarrassment." A player adhering to the code should not, for example, swing at a 3–0 pitch, steal after the sixth inning, stretch singles into doubles, or exhibit excessive pride in his own accomplishments in a game his team leads by five or more runs. Keown noted that some aspects of baseball code have become obsolete, mainly through disuse, such as the way a player wears his uniform. Although the rules of the baseball code are unwritten, there is one rule that is posted in every clubhouse: "What you see here, what you hear here, what you say here, let it stay here when you leave here." It was the violation of this credo that led to such strong criticism of Jim Bouton's best-selling 1970 memoir *Ball Four.*

baseball coil An electromagnet wound so that the current-carrying wires trace a path resembling the characteristic shape of the stitches on a baseball, producing magnetic field lines that come in from two directions along one axis and exit in two perpendicular directions along another axis (John G. Cramer, *Analog Science Fiction and Fact Magazine*, Oct. 2001). The coil is used in magnetic-mirror geometries to produce a minimum-B configuration.

baseball column A newspaper report on baseball, created by *The Brooklyn Union* in 1869. Lexicographer Stuart Berg Flexner (quoted in William Safire, *I Stand Corrected*, 1984): "Such columns grew into the popular 'sporting column,' 'sporting page' and 'sporting section' (created primarily for baseball fans) in the 1890s, then became known as the 'sports page' or 'sports section' in the 1920s."

baseball daisy *hist.* A female fan who strategically dated pitchers of the opposing team. "The 'daisy' would take them out 'for a round of the cabarets' the night prior to their pitching assignment and thus impair their effectiveness" (Richard C. Crepeau, *Baseball: America's Diamond Mind, 1919–1941*, 1980, p.160).

baseball diamond See *diamond*.

baseball dice A tabletop baseball game in which the roll of a pair of dice determines the outcome of each at-bat; e.g., double-sixes is a home run, but a two and a three is an out. See also *dice baseball*. IST USE. 1947 (Frank G. Menke, *The New Encyclopedia of Sports*, p.367).

baseballdom The domain of baseball, especially professional baseball. See also *balldom*. IST USE. 1867. "All base ball-dom were gathered together on the Union grounds" (*The Ball Players' Chronicle*, Aug. 22; Peter Morris).

baseballeer *hist.* A rarely used term for a baseball player or fan in the earlier days of the 20th century. The most recent example of its use is by Frank G. Menke (*New Encyclopedia of Sports*, 1944, p.79): "The report was like some heaven sent gift which arrived for the harassed baseballeer."

baseballer A baseball player. "And Mr. Clarke sadly advises all golfers, cricketeers and baseballers that the moon, with its reduced gravitational pull, is no place to swat a ball" (*The New York Times Book Review*, Apr. 25, 1955). Although the term has a certain anachronistic whiff to it, citations are still made: "Equally sleek are the customers at Rusty's Restaurant, 1271 Third Ave., owned by baseballer Rusty Staub" (*Harper's Bazaar*, Feb. 1981). IST USE. 1881. "Truly, there is nothing half so sweet in life as the baseballer's dream" (*New York Clipper*, Feb. 19; Peter Morris). EXTENDED USE. One who freebases cocaine, smoking it as a pure powder through a water pipe. A comment about Hollywood: "There are a lot of 'baseballers' in those hills" (*Newsweek*, June 23, 1980).

baseballese 1. The overall language of baseball, comprising official terminology, slang, and jargon. Each setting in baseball, from the dugout to the front office and press box, has its own specialized language. "They liked his language—some of it authentic American baseballese, but most of it just plain Dizzy Dean" (Norman Cousins, *Saturday Review*, Aug. 2, 1946). "In baseballese, contending teams must be 'strong up the middle' and players must 'give 110 percent,' because 'it's a long season' played 'one game at a time,' and 'pennants aren't won on paper.' ... Remember, baseball is something like life. Baseballese is something like English" (John Leo, *Tampa Tribune*, Apr. 13, 1997). IST USE. 1912. "Some writers call it 'baseballese'; you call it either one you please" (Edmund Vance Cooke, *Baseballogy*). 2. The language of baseball players as distinguished from—and held as superior to—the language of those who write about the game. This distinction was made forcefully by William G. Brandt (*Baseball Magazine*, Oct. 1932, p.495) in the article "That Unrecognized Language—Baseballese." After giving some authentic

THE FIRST BASE.

"WAKE UP, WAKE UP, MY DUCK LEGGED MAN, AND STIR YOUR SOLID PEGS!"

Baseballese. From *Base Ball as Viewed by a Muffin*, published in 1867. *Library of Congress*

examples, Brandt wrote, "That's baseballese. [*You Know Me Al* author] Ring Lardner's half-wit bushers don't talk that way. Nor any of the sluggers in the baseball yarns you read in 'Flimsy Stories.' In fact you won't read baseballese anywhere. The boys who play ball for keeps don't need a special patois to express all their thoughts. . . . It is really remarkable that so few of the actual terms used in baseballese ever see the light of a printed page. Now and then they make the newspaper sporting pages, but the commendable modern journalistic trend away from the silly jabber of twenty years ago, when every strikeout was a 'breeze' and every homer a 'circuit clout,' has also militated against the popularization of dozens of words that have become full-standing baseballese by the prime standard of word-legitimization."

baseball farm A minor-league team. "The San Jose Bees, a very minor league team, almost won a championship in 1973, providing a semi-dramatic framework for a determinedly undramatic overview of life on the modern, mechanized baseball farm" (Robert Lipsyte, *The New York Times Book Review*, Apr. 6, 1975). See also *farm*, 1.

base-ball fashion A type of spelling bee using baseball analogies. "Sides are chosen as in base ball, with a catcher and a pitcher on each side. One side spells at a time. The pitcher on the first side 'takes up' and corrects a word when misspelled by the other. Every word that is spelled correctly is tallied for the side that spelled it, and every misspelled word is called out, if spelled correctly by the other side. Three out, all out. The scholars say it is lots of fun to spell this way" (*Woodstock* [Ont.] *Review*, March 30, 1877; Peter Morris). See also *baseball spelling bee*.

baseball fever Passion for the game of baseball. It usually starts with spring training and ends after the World Series. The motto of organized baseball in 1987 and in television ads in the early 1990s was "Baseball fever—catch it!" A humorous song in which baseball is described as a crazed fad, entitled "The Base Ball Fever" (words by H. Angelo and music by James W. Porter), was popular in 1867. Syn. *baseball bug*, 1. IST USE. 1860.

"Base Ball Fever Among the Printers" (*Rochester* [N.Y.] *Evening Express*, Sept. 27; Priscilla Astifan). USAGE NOTE. Peter Morris (*Baseball Fever*, 2003) noted that the term had long been used to convey "the boyish enthusiasm" engendered by baseball: "The first amateur clubs appeared in the 1850s and were often ridiculed for playing a child's game—'base ball fever' was then a term of mockery—but as they persevered and issued challenges to other teams from nearby towns, rivalries developed, rules began to conform, and a tradition started to take shape." The *Grand Rapids* [Mich.] *Daily Enquirer and Herald* (May 25, 1859) noted that "games and amusements, like diseases, are epidemic in their character." The comparison of the spread of baseball to an epidemic, according to Morris, "would prove an enduring one, with the phrase 'base ball fever' and similar metaphors quickly becoming popular." The *Chicago Tribune* (Aug. 24, 1867) editorialized: "The journalists initiated a rage for base ball in this city, and the fever is spreading throughout all circles of society. . . . It is base ball for breakfast, base ball for dinner, and base ball for supper." Morris quoted (pp.268–69) from *Harrisburg Topic* (reprinted in *Detroit Free Press*, June 27, 1870), which opined, "The base ball fever now amounts to a ridiculous display of petty vanities which claim to have a monopoly of our attention.

Baseball fever. Waiting in line for tickets for the opening game of the 1924 World Series, Griffith Stadium, Washington, D.C. This picture was taken by Herbert French, who notes on the image: "Picture snapped at 10 p.m. tonight October 3rd, twenty four hours before the tickets will be placed on sale." *National Photo Company Collection, Library of Congress*

American journalism is to blame for this cultivation of a national snobbishness, and it is about time that the telegraph were employed in furnishing newspapers with intelligence of a more useful character than that of reports of base ball contests."

baseball field The surface on which a baseball game is played, usually located in a park or stadium. "A baseball field is found on the edge of the settlement and baseball seems to be the favorite sport" (*Harper's Magazine*, June 1902, p.42). See also *ball field*. IST USE. 1874. "A base ball field" (Henry Chadwick, *Chadwick's Base Ball Manual*; *OED*).

baseball finger Digital syndrome defined as a "disruption of the tendon to the tip of a finger caused by the ball striking the finger" (*Annals of Western Medicine and Surgery*, 1952). IST USE. 1889. "Then, can you tell me what a 'base-ball finger' is?" "A WHAT?" "A base-ball finger! I heard an American lady use that term" (A.C. Gunter, *That Frenchman*; David Shulman).

baseball fingers "Thickened, distorted fingers caused by injuries received in excessive playing of baseball" (Erle Fiske Young, *The New Social Worker's Dictionary*, 1941). EXTENDED USE. The term also shows up as a generic name for distorted fingers. "Fingers distorted at the joints by accident are called 'baseball fingers,' and are frequently marks of identification" (*New York Daily Tribune*, Dec. 20, 1903).

baseball game Syn. of *ball game*, 1. IST USE. 1886. "Any respectable base ball game can attract from 2,000 to 7,000" (*Baltimore American*, quoted in *Boston Journal*, July 21; *OED*).

baseball grenade A nickname for a handheld explosive device that is baseball-shaped and meant to be thrown in the manner of a baseball. "Pieces of a 'baseball grenade' that sent half a dozen policemen scurrying from Taraval station will be turned over to Army ordnance experts" (*San Francisco News*, March 25, 1954; Peter Tamony). See also *baseball* (EXTENDED USE, 4).

baseball grip The general manner in which the bat is held firmly by a batter, with one's two fists touching but not linked. EXTENDED USE. A method for holding a golf club that was made popular by professional golfers Bob Rosberg and Art Wall in the late 1950s. It bears some resemblance to the grip used by a baseball player in holding a bat, although the bottom thumb is not tucked in but extends along the shaft.

baseball gum The thin piece of aromatic, pink bubble gum included in certain packages of baseball cards. The practice of pairing gum and baseball cards began in 1933 when the Goudey Gum Co. of Boston issued a set of cards depicting 239 famous players. Though paper and latex shortages during World War II brought production to a halt, some companies began issuing gum and cards as soon as the war ended. When the Topps Company Inc. began manufacturing its own cards in 1951, the collecting and trading of baseball cards became a fad. "Just chew it like baseball gum," wrote Hunter S. Thompson (*Fear and Loathing in Las Vegas*, 1971). See also *bubble-gum card*.

Baseball Hall of Fame See *National Baseball Hall of Fame*.

baseballia Materials concerning or characteristic of baseball and the culture of baseball; collectible baseball Americana.

baseballiana An assembly of items, or bibliography, representative of, or associated with, baseball.

baseballically Relating to the game of baseball. "The Babe [Ruth] was one of my children, you know, baseballically speaking. First Lou [Gehrig] and now the Babe" (Edward G. Barrow, retired Yankees president and the man who converted Babe Ruth from a pitcher to an outfielder, quoted at the time of Ruth's death, *Washington Star*, Aug. 17, 1948). "[Ted Williams] talks about how he thinks George Will knows a lot politically but not too much 'baseballically'" (Leigh Montville, *Sports Illustrated*, July 15–22, 2002). IST USE. 1893. "We are game to the death, if we don't get killed, baseballically, before we know it" (*The Daily Picayune* [New Orleans], May 14).

baseball immortal Any of the greatest and most influential players to play the game, an individual who presumably will never be forgotten. The title is totally subjective and seems to be bestowed on one who has had an effect on the very nature of the game. It is bestowed by common and repeated usage; e.g., if almost all of the nation's sportswriters call Ty Cobb a "baseball immortal," he is one. The caption for a *New Yorker* cartoon (Aug. 16, 1982) in which two angels eye a uniformed New York Yankees player with a halo and wings reads, "I don't care if he *is* a baseball immortal. He should wear a robe and carry a harp like the rest of us." Leo Durocher was quoted (*San Francisco Chronicle*, July 27, 1989; Peter Morris) as saying, "I don't want to achieve immortality by being inducted into baseball's Hall of Fame. I want to achieve immortality by not dying." See also *immortal*; *eleven immortals*; *Hall of Famer*.

Baseball Index, The A computerized catalog/database of "virtually everything" ever published about baseball. It is an ongoing project of the Bibliography Committee of the Society for American Baseball Research to catalog all books, pamphlets, magazine and feature newspaper articles, recordings, musical scores, dissertations, films, and television programs having to do with baseball. Abbrev. *TBI*.

baseballing Freebasing, or purifying, cocaine, using ether to "free" the alkaloid cocaine (or "base") from the additives and impurities that characterize drugs bought on the street.

baseballism An expression or custom peculiar to the game of baseball; e.g., the referring to as a team's locker room as a "clubhouse" or the practice in which the manager of a baseball team dresses in the team uniform (unlike the coaches in other sports, who wear street clothes). IST USE. 1887. "The solution of this 'Prisoner puzzle' of baseballism came in quite an unexpected manner" (*The Atchison* [Kans.] *Daily Globe*, March 2).

baseballist *hist.* One who plays or is in some other way closely associated with the game of baseball. "The Englishmen were not a little astonished at the wonderful celerity and dexterity displayed by the base-ballists in fielding" (Jacob Morse, *Sphere and Ash: History of Base Ball*, 1888, p.30). It was a term of honor, as can be heard in a speech by Rep. J.M. Glover of Missouri (*The Congressional Record*, Apr. 2, 1886): "[He is well known]

as a baseballist among constitutional lawyers, and a constitutional lawyer among baseballists." See also *ballist*; *ballplayer*, 1. Sometimes spelled "base ballist"; "base-ballist." IST USE. 1866. "That illustrious baseballist, Mr. Blindman, was appointed umpire" (*The Galaxy*, p.562; David Shulman). USAGE NOTE. The term was fairly common in the 19th century for a person who would be termed a "ballplayer" today. A weekly journal, *New England Base Ballist*, began publication in 1868. A headline in *The National Police Gazette* (Sept. 20, 1890): "Young Lady Baseballists."

baseballistic Pertaining to baseball. "My private opinion is that you are a set of political and base-ball-istic shysters" (George G. Small, *A Presidential Base-Ball Match*, 1872, p.25). "Baseballistic" (*Daily Arkansas Gazette* [Little Rock] headline, Oct. 12, 1875).

baseballistics Baseball statistics. The term was used by Bert Randolph Sugar for the title of his 1990 book.

baseballite *hist.* A baseball fan; a person with an enthusiasm for the sport. The term seems to have been in vogue in the 1930s and may have been a poke at the word "socialite." See also *ballite*.

baseballitis A mock-disease name for infatuation with the game of baseball. "Since early childhood I've been afflicted with a near-fatal illness known as diamond fever or, to call it by its medical term, baseballitis" (Frank Bar-

Baseballitis. After standing in line all night, Elsie Tydings gets the first tickets to Washington's first World Series, in 1924. *National Photo Company Collection, Library of Congress*

nicle, *Clearwater* [Fla.] *Times*, Apr. 4, 1986). *Baseball-itis* was the title of V.H. Smalley's one-act comedy in 1910. Actress Lillian Russell (quoted in *Baseball Magazine*, Jan. 1909), defined a "bug" as "A person of peculiar eccentricities, born of frenzy and expressed in wild, incoherent shrieks that develop a monomania called baseballitis." IST USE. 1909. "With the third inning faded into the dim and forgotten past, the fourth spasm in the afternoon's matinee of Dementia Baseballitis hopped into the glare of the calcium glim" (*Baseball Magazine*, September).

baseballization Making baseball happen. John Krich's *El Béisbol* (1989) "closes with a terrific fantasy of the baseballization of the Americas" (Tom Miller, *The New York Times Book Review*, June 4, 1989, p.9).

baseball jacket A jacket or coat used in the context of fashion to describe a garment patterned after a *warmup jacket*. "He [a rock star] wears a baseball jacket piped in red" (*The New York Times*, Nov. 1973).

base-ball law A term that developed in the late 19th century for the complex body of rules that regulated the relations among professional baseball clubs and leagues, and esp. players' eligibility to play for particular clubs. "The [reserve] rule is a special statute of 'base-ball law,' made for a special purpose" (John Montgomery Ward, *Lippincott's Magazine*, Aug. 1887). Ward further expounded (*Cosmopolitan*, Oct. 1888), "The general public may not know that there is a law in the land higher than any common law. 'Base-ball law' is a law unto itself, and so reckless have these legislators become, in the undisputed exercise of their powers, that they make but little pretense to conformation with the rules laid down by courts of law and equity." IST USE. 1879. "At the recent [National] League meeting a *Tribune* man was afforded an opportunity to see representatives from all the Clubs composing that organization, both when engaged in heated debate over some knotty point of base-ball law, and when under the more genial influences of after-dinner smoke" (*Chicago Tribune*, Apr. 20; David Ball).

Baseball League A major league proposed by real-estate entrepreneur Donald Trump in 1989. Plans for the league never materialized.

baseball leather The outer skin or cover of a baseball, made from fronts of horsehides until 1975 when cowhide was used. Sheepskin is used for inexpensive baseballs.

baseball lifer An individual whose lifetime income is derived solely from participating in professional baseball; one who begins his career as a player and spends the rest of his working life as a manager, coach, scout, or executive. Some examples of lifers might be Casey Stengel, Don Zimmer, John McGraw, Connie Mack, and Earl Weaver. Thomas Boswell (*The Washington Post*, Oct. 8, 1981): "That century-old species, the baseball lifer who sustains the game's sense of itself . . . Baseball lifers didn't measure each other by their dollars, but by their line in the record book, their style, savvy or courage on the field; the game measured its own by their qualities, not their wallet." Syn. *lifer.*

baseball man 1. A professional who knows, loves, and understands the game of baseball, be he an owner, manager, coach, scout, player, or trainer. Charles S. "Chub" Feeney was "the very definition of the vanishing species known as Baseball Men" (Ron Fimrite's obituary of Feeney, *Sports Illustrated*, Jan. 24, 1994). Frank Robinson told *The Baltimore Sun* (Feb. 22, 2002) that "My No. 1 priority is to be a baseball man. I want to contribute to this game. I'm a baseball man. It's in the blood." Rich Dubroff (*How Was the Game?*, 1994) described Cal Ripken Sr. as "a downright grouch. He was the epitome of an old-time 'baseball man.' His answers . . . were full of clichés, and he was sure to use the word 'baseball' in nearly every sentence." Syn. *baseball person.* IST USE. 1927. "[John McGraw] became the greatest manager and the greatest 'baseball man' the game has ever known" (John B. Sheridan, *The Sporting News*, Feb. 10; Peter Morris). USAGE NOTE. To be called a "baseball man" is a major compliment, and to be told that one is not is to be marked as an outsider to the game. "[Maine Guides owner Jordan] Kobritz is a good businessman, but no matter how much research he did and how many books he read he could not turn himself into a baseball man" (Steve Buckley, *Maine Sunday Telegram*, Aug. 31, 1986). 2. A baseball player.

"A Baseball Man's Error. . . . Commisky [*sic*], first-base of the St. Louis Club, will be united in marriage with Miss Annie Kelly" (*The Daily Republican-Sentinel* [Milwaukee], Sept. 29, 1882).

baseball martini A drink composed of four parts gin and one part cigar smoke, a staple of the winter banquet circuit, which, according to Arnold Hano (*Willie Mays*, 1966, p.114), "has never done anything to a player except make him fat and acquaint him with a baseball martini."

baseball mother A dedicated woman who, in the process of ferrying her children to baseball practice and games, becomes a dedicated supporter. "She is a baseball mother. So even though she was due at a class reunion one recent evening and perhaps should have been at home washing her hair or on her way to the Detroit airport to pick up her husband, Lou, there she was in the bleachers, watching her 14-year-old son Ken play in a Babe Ruth League game" (*The New York Times*, July 3, 1976).

baseball movie A feature film that includes baseball in a major portion of its fictional scenario with actors playing ballplayers; e.g., *The Natural* (1984), *Bull Durham* (1988), and *Field of Dreams* (1989). Such films are meant to entertain or be emotionally satisfying, but are not always accurate. "If an incompetent baseball movie seems worse than other bad movies, it's probably because the action on the screen reminds you that you could have gone to the ballpark instead" (Terrence Rafferty, *Gentlemen's Quarterly*, Oct. 2001, p.182). "If there are any rules for making memorable baseball movies, the most important one may be: Deliver something ESPN can't" (Michael Sragow, *The Baltimore Sun*, Apr. 1, 2007).

baseball mud Syn. of *rubbing mud*.

Baseball Network, The 1. An organization formed to find jobs for minorities in baseball. It was founded in the late 1980s by Frank Robinson when he was the only black manager in baseball. **2.** A short-lived (1994–1995) joint venture by ABC, NBC, and Major League Baseball to create regional television coverage for the last 12 weeks of the regular season and the first round of the playoffs by sharing network advertising revenues (in lieu of broadcast rights fees), production facilities and costs, and corporate sponsorship.

baseball nut A baseball fan who is unusually exuberant about the game.

baseballogy A term used by Edmund Vance Cooke for the title of a collection of baseball ballads (1912) incorporating the mention of prominent players.

baseball orchard Syn. of *ball orchard*.

baseball parachute A parachute used by the Navy during World War II for mine-laying and precision deliveries of delicate cargoes. "Unlike conventional chutes, which swing their loads in pendulum fashion, the baseball chute has a hemispheric canopy cut like a baseball cover and deposits its burden gently and vertically on the ground" (*Life* magazine, Jan. 7, 1946).

baseball park Syn. of *ballpark*. 1ST USE. 1885. "The same clubs will occupy the diamond at the Denver Base Ball park" (*Rocky Mountain News* [Denver], May 31).

baseball pass A one-handed, overhead basketball pass that requires making a motion similar to that of throwing a baseball. It is

Baseballology. *Ron Menchine Collection*

used to pass to a teammate cutting down court and is essential to the repertory of members of fast-breaking teams. "Jason Kidd caught the Sacramento Kings napping and fired a 70-foot baseball pass to Keith Van Horn for a layup" (*The Baltimore Sun*, Feb. 25, 2002).

baseball person Syn. of *baseball man*, 1.

baseball pitcher's arm A malady often caused by throwing a baseball; "a condition of sprain, with pain and soreness over the points of insertion of the muscles, occurring sometimes as a result of overuse by base-ball players" (*Century Dictionary*, 1909). See also *baseball arm*.

baseball pitcher's elbow A "fracture of bone or cartilage from the head of the radius at the elbow due to strenuous baseball pitching" (*Journal of the American Medical Association*, 1930, p.404).

baseball plant A tall, branching South African succulent shrub (*Euphorbia obesa* and *Euphorbia clava*) with leafy tips and that grows to four feet (Molly Price, *The New York Times*, Feb. 24, 1974).

baseball player 1. Syn. of *ballplayer*, 1. IST USE. 1857. The National Association of Base Ball Players convened in May 1857. USAGE NOTE. This term carries its own honor. Baltimore Orioles manager Ray Miller (quoted in *The Baltimore Sun*, March 30, 1999): "[Jesse Garcia is] a baseball player. That's the ultimate thing to become, a gamer. Sometimes people say, 'I don't know what to think about the guy. He's not real fast, he's not a real great hitter, he's not whatever. He's just a baseball player.' That's a pretty good compliment. That means he knows what the heck's going on." Tampa Bay Devil Rays scouting director Dan Jennings (quoted in *Baseball America*, July 8–21, 2002), commenting on draft pick Jason Pridie: "If you want a one- or two-word deal, this guy's a baseball player. Everything about him, he's just a baseball player. He's blue-collar. He's a throwback." 2. Syn. of *ballplayer*, 2.

baseball poker A form of seven-card stud. According to Albert A. Ostrow (*The Complete Card Player*, 1945, p.513), it varies from the conventional game of seven-card stud through these exceptions: a) a three of any suit dealt face up makes a player's hand dead, and he must drop out of play; b) a three of any suit dealt face down is wild; c) a four of any suit dealt face up entitles the player to have an extra card dealt face up; and d) all nines are wild. The fact that it is called "baseball poker" probably derives from the fact that a face card with a three on it is the rough equivalent of a three-strike count in baseball.

baseball pool An illegal lottery in which one wagers on the appearance of a certain set of winning numbers taken from the box scores of different baseball games. It is a form of gambling that has been popular since about 1900 and is a variation on the numbers game or numbers pool, which gets its winning number from horse racing or stock market totals. It has existed in many variations, including, it seems, crooked ones: "It's anybody's guess as to how much money fans have tossed into a bottomless well playing phony baseball pool" (*Easy Money* magazine, July 1936).

baseball principle The argument that watching a baseball game on television has no effect on the outcome of the game. Coined by Cornell Univ. physicist David Mermin (*Science* magazine, May 19, 1989), the principle has been applied to problems in quantum physics.

baseball rat A baseball player devoted to the game. Baltimore Orioles scout Ed Sprague, commenting on pitching prospect Matt Riley (quoted in *The Washington Post*, May 26, 1999): "He's coming fast. You've got to give him credit. He's a baseball rat. He loves the game. He's a sponge for information." Allan Simpson (*Baseball America*, June 9–22, 2003; Peter Morris) wrote that "[Shane] Costa is a baseball rat [who] plays the game hard" See also *rat*.

Baseball Reliquary A nonprofit, educational organization founded by Terry Cannon in 1996 in Monrovia, Calif., "dedicated to fostering an appreciation of American art and culture through the context of baseball history and to exploring the national pastime's unparalleled creative possibilities." It is supported in part by a grant from the Los Angeles County Arts Commission.

baseball-rounders A term used by J.M. Walker (*Rounders and Quoits*, 1892) for a largely forgotten hybrid game of American baseball and British rounders. David Block (personal communication, June 2005) comments that he has not seen any other references to this term.

baseball rule A legal concept that bars spectators who are injured by flying baseballs from suing teams for injury. A court in Milwaukee decreed that the Admirals hockey team was protected by the baseball rule even though the offending object was a hockey puck (*Milwaukee Journal Sentinel*, Sept. 24, 1997).

Baseball Sadie A woman whose weakness is ballplayers. See also *Baseball Annie*.

baseball's attic Nickname for *National Baseball Library and Archives* in Cooperstown, N.Y. "A Library Known as 'Baseball's Attic'" (*The New York Times* headline, July 31, 1984). The term was probably inspired by "nation's attic," the traditional nickname for the Smithsonian Institution.

baseball's Bible See *Bible of Baseball*.

baseball scholarship A scholarship given to an outstanding high school baseball player to play on a college team. Often, the recipient is optioned by a major-league club toward the end of his college years.

baseball school A school for aspiring ballplayers, providing an opportunity to work out with and play before the critical eyes of veteran major-league players or former players, who serve as instructors. James T. Farrell (*My Baseball Diary*, 1957, p.161) reported that Ray Doan started the first baseball school in Arkansas in the 1930s, and that Jersey Joe Stripp operated the first baseball school in Florida. See also *baseball camp*.

baseball score The outcome of a baseball game. EXTENDED USE. The term is used in football for game with a low score, such as 7–3 or 3–0.

baseball sense Instinct for making the correct move, whether it be in a play on the field or in an advantageous trade. George Sisler (*Sisler on Baseball*, 1954): "There is a significant term in the game known as 'baseball sense' ... [which is] applied to players who always do the right thing at the right time, always throw to the right base, and, in general, do what is necessary and correct at any time during the game to meet a particular situation." IST USE. 1911. "If all the baseball sense of the bleachers at any big league game could be centered in the brains of a baseball team I think that club would be the best thinking aggregation ever put together" (John J. Evers, *Baseball Magazine*, September; Peter Morris). USAGE NOTE. The term was used in 1887 in regard to arranging the National League schedule by disfranchising Kansas City: "The latter city is not a good one in a baseball sense of the word, and besides it is too long a jump for any club to make, especially with St. Louis out" (*The Atchison* [Kans.] *Daily Globe*, March 2, 1887).

baseball's Gettysburg Address Lou Gehrig's farewell speech delivered on July 4, 1939, at Yankee Stadium. The term was coined by Gehrig biographer Ray Robinson (*Sports Illustrated*, May 14, 2001).

baseball shoe A special shoe designed for and worn by baseball players that features cleats for traction and a full set of laces for support. Harold R. Quimby (*The Shoe Dictionary*, 1955): "A shoe built of leather for the sport indicated with sole having cleats or plugs to prevent slipping. Usually laced to the toe." The first official baseball shoe was invented and produced by Waldo M. Claflin of Philadelphia in 1882; it was a "high" shoe, laced well up around the ankle. Later, the "low" shoe made of kangaroo leather was universally adopted in the interest of speed. Syn. *ball-shoe*; *cleats*, 2; *spikes*, 2.

baseball shot An attempt to score in basketball by throwing the ball with a motion similar to that of throwing a baseball. Boston Celtics head coach Red Auerbach believed that this technique would have a major impact on the future of basketball (*The Sporting News*, Dec. 23, 1959): "It can't miss. Some kid with unusually big hands will come along and wind up like a baseball pitcher, or a football passer, and throw the ball in."

baseball shoulder A painful and debilitating shoulder of a player, usually a pitcher. The pain may be caused by calcific deposits and fraying of the tendons (*Journal of the American Medical Association*, Nov. 21, 1959).

baseball sleeve Short (usually ¾ length), cuffless sleeve common to the shirts worn under the short-sleeved uniform shirt. "[The baseball sleeve is] the important detail of jersey blouses worn under dresses, jackets and jumpers which have short sleeves of their own and a cutaway neckline which reveals turtle neck, cowl-drape or 2-inch band of the jersey neckline" (*Women's Wear Daily*, June 4, 1952).

baseball slide Falling to the ground by a National Football League quarterback to avoid being tackled. The action is similar to that of a baserunner sliding into a base. "[Charlie Batch] never mastered the baseball slide, which is why he has yet to stay healthy for a full season" (*ESPN The Magazine*, June 24, 2002).

Baseball's Mecca Syn. of *Cooperstown*, 1.

baseball spelling bee A spelling bee involving four "bases." Earl E. Dodge (personal communication, Nov. 13, 2002) explains, "I remember baseball spelling bees from grade school back in the 1940s. You would have to spell a word to get to first base (we had chairs set in a diamond representing home plate and the three bases) or were out if you misspelled it and so on around to home where you scored a run if you got the fourth one right."

"Baseball's Sad Lexicon" Title of a 1910 poem by Franklin P. Adams that appeared in the *New York Evening Mail* and featured the double-play combination of *Tinker to Evers to Chance*. The poem first appeared on July 12 under the heading "That Double Play Again." By July 14, parodies began to appear almost daily in the *New York Evening Mail*. On July 18 the poem appeared under the more familiar title, "Baseball's Sad Lexicon." Adams was in Chicago when the New York Giants faced the Chicago Cubs on July 11. Trailing 4–1 entering the top of the eighth inning, the Giants scored once and had runners on first and second with one out when Art Devlin grounded into a 6-4-3 double play. Adams wrote to Ernest Lanigan, director of the National Baseball Hall of Fame, on Nov. 24, 1946, "I wrote the double play thing . . .

because I wanted to get out to the game, and the foreman of the composing room at the *Mail* said I needed 8 lines to fill. And the next day T.E. Niles said that no matter what else I ever wrote, I would be known as the guy that wrote those 8 lines. And they weren't much good, at that." The eight-line poem as published on July 18: "These are the saddest of possible words: / 'Tinker to Evers to Chance.' / Trio of bear cubs, and fleeter than birds, / Tinker and Evers and Chance. / Ruthlessly pricking our gonfalon bubble, / Making a Giant hit into a double— / Words that are heavy with nothing but trouble: / 'Tinker to Evers to Chance.'"

baseball stitch A sewing stitch, worked under and over from the inside, for meeting the two edges of the leather cover being sewed on a baseball. The sewing technique makes two edges meet exactly, rather than overlap. No machine has yet been devised to sew baseballs, which are all produced by hand. EXTENDED USE. This sewing technique is often used when mending sails. It is also likely to show up in other areas, such as tent repair: "Better way still is to sew large tears with baseball stitch using greased thread" (Joe Godfrey Jr. and Frank Dufresne, *The Great Outdoors*, 1949).

baseball strike See *strike*, 6.

Baseball's Valhalla Syn. of *Cooperstown*, 1.

baseball swing A swing used in activities other than baseball, but resembling a batter's attempt to hit a pitched ball, such as a golfer's motion when driving the ball.

baseball team Syn. of *team*, 2.

baseball tee See *tee*, 1.

baseball throw A field event, now rare, in which individuals throw a baseball for distance. It was an event at the 1932 Olympics.

baseball time Time without arbitrary constraints, as opposed to the clock-controlled time periods found in other sports (football, basketball, and hockey, for example). Edgar Allen Beam (*Maine Times*, June 4, 1981) commented, "The traditional home run trot was a reminder of one of the sport's chief beauties: baseball time. Baseball takes its own sweet time and baseball time is often difficult for the non-fan to appreciate. . . .

The satisfying sight of a batted ball disappearing over a distant fence momentarily suspends time. The idea is to savor the moment in a triumphant circuit of the bases which, under any other circumstances, must be won with cunning and speed."

Baseball Tomorrow Fund A $10 million joint venture of Major League Baseball and the Major League Baseball Players Association to support youth baseball programs by constructing new fields and renovating old ones, providing equipment and uniforms, training new coaches, developing baseball and softball skills programs, and providing opportunities for young people to attend major-league games. The funds were committed in 1999.

baseball toss A contest to determine the ability to throw a baseball for distance and accuracy.

baseball town A city that appreciates, and has a passion for, its home team. Michael Olesker (*The Baltimore Sun*, Aug. 22, 2000) wrote, "[Baltimore] has been a remarkable baseball town for a long time now. Marquee value counts, but so does a sense that those guys on the field aren't simply going through the motions." Pedro Martinez (quoted in *The Baltimore Sun*, May 13, 2000): "I feel really happy to see that the people here [Baltimore] appreciate what's good. Not only are they rooting for their team, they're also rooting for the good things that happen in baseball. . . . I can tell now that this is a baseball town." See also *ball town*.

baseball wife A wife whose baseball-player husband is away from home often and for extended periods of time and who therefore often carries the burden of family life. Tom House (*The Jock's Itch*, 1989, p.54) noted that most players marry early ("almost always the prototypical homecoming queen/princess/cheerleader") and depend on their wives to do the laundry, cook, balance the checkbook ("ballplayers usually can't do any of the above") and to provide a support system ("the ego boost"): "It's her role as the wife of a ballplayer, and it might be one of the toughest jobs on the face of the earth."

baseballwise In a manner pertaining to base-ball. 1ST USE. An early use was recorded in the radio broadcast of the first game of the 1946 World Series (Oct. 6) when it was observed, "Baseballwise the day is perfect."

baseball with cards A game in which the various situations and events from the game of baseball are evoked by turning over playing cards from a shuffled deck.

baseball with dice A game in which the various situations and events from the game of baseball are evoked by throwing dice. The rules of the game (*Foster's Complete Hoyle*, 1928) are as follows: "Each side has 3 dice, to represent 3 strikes. Only aces count as runs, and as long as a side scores it continues to throw. Nine turns in a game."

Baseball Writers' Association of America An association of writers and beat reporters who cover a major-league team for an accredited news organization on a daily basis. It was founded in 1908 by two dozen disgruntled writers infuriated by their treatment during the pennant races and World Series: they demanded and received permanent press box facilities in all parks. It remonstrates with Major League Baseball, its leagues, and its clubs when limited access to players, managers, and coaches makes reporting on the game difficult. The Association provides official scorers, consults on rule changes, and participates in Hall of Fame elections and postseason awards by invitation. Abbrev. *BWAA* or *BBWAA*.

basebally Quintessentially baseball; characteristic of the game. Miss Manners (columnist Judith Martin) on spitting in baseball (*The Baltimore Sun*, Oct. 21, 1993): "If it's properly done [not aimed at anyone or anyone's shoes] it's part of the charm. It's a terribly basebally thing to do." Wilfrid Sheed (*My Life as a Fan*, 1993, p.13): "There is no way I can now extract the essence of them [my memories] for the basebally illiterate (or should it be basebally-challenged?) without encumbering these readers with a few baseball details."

baseball year Syn. of *major-league year*.

base-ballyhoo *hist.* Hyperbole and boosterism sometimes associated with the game of baseball; bunkum baseball-style.

basebrawl A fight among baseball players, triggered by an event such as a batter charging the mound after being hit by a pitched ball. Steve Wulf (*Sports Illustrated*, Aug. 16, 1993) characterized Nolan Ryan's pummeling of Robin Ventura as a "basebrawl," epitomizing "a baseball season marred by bench-clearing incidents."

base clogger A slow runner; e.g., a runner whose baserunning skills routinely keep him from advancing from first base to third base on a single. Mickey Mantle, on New York Yankees teammate Elston Howard (*The Mick*, 1985; Charles D. Poe): "We called him 'base clogger' because if you hit a double you had to stop at first and wait up for him."

base coach One of the two uniformed team members positioned in the coach's box at first base and third base to direct the batter and baserunners and to relay signs. Syn. *wigwagger*.

base-getter *hist.* One who achieves a base and advances with regularity. IST USE. 1911. "But Arthurs has made him into a great field captain and a base-getter of remarkable skill" (Zane Grey, *The Young Pitcher*; David Shulman).

basegirl A player in the All-American Girls Professional Baseball League.

base hit 1. A batted ball on which the batter advances safely to, but no farther than, first base; a single. IST USE. 1871. "Each nine made 13 first base hits" (*The Cleveland Morning Herald*, Aug. 14). 2. A batted ball that permits the batter to get on any base safely with no error being made and no baserunner being forced out on the play. See also *hit*, 1. Abbrev. *BH*. Syn. *base knock*. 3. A statistic credited to a batter who reaches base safely with no error being made and no baserunner being forced out on the play.

base jockey A runner who, when on first base, yells derisive comments to the opposing pitcher.

base knock Syn. of *base hit*, 2. See also *knock*, 3. IST USE. 1913. "The Californian [Ping Bodie] is crazy about his base knocks, which are only made up at the plate" (*San Francisco Bulletin*, May 15; Gerald L. Cohen).

baseline 1. One of four lines connecting the

bases; specif., the white chalk marking between home plate and first base and between home plate and third base, and the imaginary line between first base and second base and between second base and third base. Compare *basepath*. Also spelled "base line." IST USE. 1868. "The base lines are the lines running from base to base, intersecting at the center of each base when the bases are in position" (Henry Chadwick, *The Game of Base Ball*). 2. An imaginary straight line established by a baserunner when a tag attempt occurs, extending from the runner to the base he is attempting to reach safely.

baseman A defensive player assigned to cover first base, second base, or third base. Syn. *bagman*; *base player*, 1; *sacker*; *station keeper*. IST USE. 1864. "Their ... basemen being good men for the positions" (*New York Clipper*, Aug. 13; Peter Morris).

basement Syn. of *cellar*. IST USE. 1911 (*Baseball Magazine*, October; Edward J. Nichols).

base on balls An advance to first base awarded to a batter when the umpire has called four balls, either pitches outside the strike zone or penalties for infractions incurred by the pitcher. In 1889, it was ruled that, in the course of one at-bat, four balls would result in a walk. In the years preceding 1889, the rule changed with confusing regularity in the National League: before 1880 (nine balls for a walk); 1880 (eight balls); 1881–1883 (seven balls); 1884–1885 (six balls, but seven balls in the American Association, and seven balls in the Union Association for 1884); 1886 (seven balls, but six balls in the American Association); 1887–1888 (five balls); and 1889 to the present (four balls). In 1887 only, a base on balls was scored as a base hit. Abbrev. *BB*, 2. Syn. *walk*, 1; *Annie Oakley*, 2; *casualty pass*; *four wide ones*; *free check*; *free pass*; *free passage*; *free ride*; *free ticket*; *free transit*; *free transportation*; *free trip*; *furlough*; *gift*, 1; *handout*; *life*, 2; *pass*, 1; *promenade*; *saunter act*; *ticket to first*. IST USE. 1858 (Chadwick Scrapbooks; Edward J. Nichols). EXTENDED USE. To "wait for a base on balls" is to forgo action in the hope that something will happen or to assume a passive posture in an attempt to force one's opponent to make a false move. "People love a fighter but have no respect for a candidate who waits for a base on balls" (*San Francisco News*, Feb. 22, 1950, p.14; Peter Tamony).

base on stones A base hit in which a ground ball strikes a pebble or other impediment, causing it to bounce away from a fielder. Use of the term has declined in direct proportion to steady advances in groundskeeping and the use of artificial turf. See also *bad hop*; *bad bounce*. IST USE. 1932. "Base on stones—A ground ball that hits a pebble and takes a bad bounce away from the fielder for a base hit" (*New York Sun*, June 23).

base open Said of a base that is not occupied by a baserunner; esp. said of first base when second base and/or third base are occupied but first base is not.

base–out percentage A ratio between the number of bases a player gets for his team and the number of outs he makes. It equals (total bases + stolen bases + walks + hit by pitches + sacrifice flies + sacrifices) divided by (at bats – hits + caught stealing + grounded into double plays + sacrifices + sacrifice flies). Base–out percentage was proposed by Barry Codell (*Baseball Research Journal*, 1979). Babe Ruth's 1.428 is the highest lifetime figure. Sabermetric research has shown that base–out percentage is a fairly good predictor of offensive performance, but no better than some simpler measures, such as on-base plus slugging. Compare *total average*. Abbrev. *BOP*, 1.

base–out situation A label for the combination of baserunners and outs applicable to a given point in a game. For example, a plate appearance might occur with runners on second base and third base, and two outs. The base–out situation can change during a plate appearance due to events such as a stolen base, a runner caught stealing, a wild pitch, a passed ball, and a balk. As there are three outs in an inning and eight possible combinations of baserunners (bases empty, first base, second base, third base, first and second bases, first and third bases, second and third bases, and bases loaded), there are 24 possible base–out situations during an inning. Three outs and the resulting end of the inning is a 25th.

Data for either the number of runs that score on average (*run potential*) or the probability of scoring at least one run can be used for two purposes: to analyze the value of different strategic moves, and to measure offensive and pitching performances (see *value added approach* and *pitcher run average*). Several analyses of base–out situations have concluded that many of the conventions of percentage baseball are wrong. For example: sacrifice bunts usually cost the offensive team runs, although there are situations in which they increase the probability of scoring one run; intentional walks usually cost the defensive team runs; and stolen bases have little effect on run scoring. Analysis of this type was first performed by George R. Lindsey (*Operations Research*, July–Aug. 1963). The term was used by John Thorn and Pete Palmer in *The Hidden Game of Baseball* (1985).

basepath The six-foot-wide lane that connects the four bases and serves as the path along which the baserunner runs and which he cannot leave to avoid a tag. Compare *baseline*. Also spelled "base path." Syn. *path*, 1; *bag* path; *runway*, 1; *towpath*. IST USE. 1876. "Four pearls at each corner of the badge [presented to players of the Indianapolis team] represent the bases, and a line of blue enamel, running from pearl to pearl, makes a very pretty base path" (*St. Louis Globe-Democrat*, Apr. 25).

base play *hist.* Performing as a first baseman, second baseman, or third baseman. IST USE. 1869. "[First baseman] Van Velsor showed some very fine base play" (*Buffalo Courier*, reprinted in *Syracuse Journal*, July 30; Larry McCray).

base player *hist.* **1.** Syn. of *baseman*. "Radcliff and Force both infringing the rule which prohibits base players from preventing a base runner from reaching his base" (*Brooklyn Daily Eagle*, July 29, 1873; Peter Morris). IST USE. 1868. "Base Players.—The three fielders who attend to the first, second, and third bases" (Henry Chadwick, *The Game of Base Ball*, p.38). **2.** A ballplayer. "Last season an element of weakness . . . prevailed in the form of 'chin-music' and ill-natured 'chaffing,' in which baseplayers pretty generally took part" (*New York Clipper*, Jan. 31,

1875; Tom Shieber). Sometimes spelled "baseplayer."

base por bolas Spanish for "base on balls."

baser A single. IST USE. 1877. "[Jim] O'Rourke led off with a baser" (*The Boston Globe*, Apr. 16; Peter Morris).

base robada Spanish for "stolen base."

baserunner A player on the team at bat who occupies a base or is attempting to reach or return to a base. See also *runner*, 1; *batter-runner*. Also spelled "base runner." IST USE. 1868. "Base Runner.—The player on the batting side running the bases" (Henry Chadwick, *The Game of Base Ball*, p.38).

baserunner kill *hist.* An assist credited to an outfielder.

baserunning 1. *n.* The integral facet of the game by which one travels from one base to the next. It includes such skills as leading, sliding, and stealing. Also spelled "base running." **2.** *adj.* Pertaining to one's ability as a baserunner.

bases bulging Syn. of *bases loaded*.

bases choked Syn. of *bases loaded*.

bases-clearing Said of a hit that brings all baserunners home; e.g., "Smith hit a bases-clearing double."

bases crammed Syn. of *bases loaded*. "[Mickey] Mantle hit a home run with the bases crammed" (Billy Pierce, quoted in Bob Vanderberg, *Sox: From Lane and Fain to Zisk and Fisk*, 1982, p.139).

bases crowded Syn. of *bases loaded*. IST USE. 1912 (*New York Tribune*, Sept. 5; Edward J. Nichols).

bases drunk Syn. of *bases loaded*. "'Bases drunk' is Jimmie [*sic*] Dykes' favorite phrase for a 'full house' or three men aboard" (*Baseball Magazine*, January; David Shulman). IST USE. 1909. "But with the bases drunk—or loaded—Smith struck out" (*The Washington Post*, May 12; Peter Morris).

bases empty Said of a game situation in which there are no runners on base.

bases-empty home run A home run with no runners on base, which therefore scores no additional runs. Compare *bases-loaded home run*. Syn. *solo home run*.

bases full Syn. of *bases loaded*. IST USE. 1871. "Leonard and Brainard went to first on called balls, and the bases were now full" (*The Cleveland Morning Herald*, May 6).

bases jammed Syn. of *bases loaded*. IST USE. 1913. "Joe Engel was in the hole in the fifth when the bases were jammed" (Thomas Kirby, *The Washington Post*, May 10; Peter Morris).

bases juiced Syn. of *bases loaded*. "In this combustible 1999 baseball season, batters are going yard with the bases juiced almost as fast as you can say Creighton Gubanich" (Tim Crothers, *Sports Illustrated*, June 21, 1999, p.48).

bases loaded Said of a game situation in which there are runners on first base, second base, and third base. Syn. *bags clogged*; *bags full*; *full house*; *sacks full*; *sold out*, 1; and various words used with "bases," such as bulging, choked, crammed, crowded, drunk, full, jammed, juiced, tenanted, and waterlogged. IST USE. 1880. "Surely the man who hits safely when men are on base . . . is of far more value to his club than the man who earns a base for himself twice as often, and makes a weak hit or fouls or strikes out when the bases are loaded" (*Chicago Tribune*, July 11; Peter Morris).

bases-loaded home run A home run with runners on each base, resulting in four runs; a *grand slam*, 1. Many regard a bases-loaded home run to be the game's most spectacular offensive play. Compare *bases-empty home run*.

bases-loaded walk 1. A base on balls with the bases loaded. **2.** A base on balls that loads the bases.

bases on balls percentage The number of walks a player achieves per 100 at-bats plus bases on balls. The 2001 major-league average was 8.7. The career leader is Ted Williams with 20.76.

bases on balls per game The average number of walks a pitcher gives up in nine innings. It is calculated by multiplying the number of bases on balls given up by 9, then dividing by the number of innings pitched.

bases over plate appearances A measure of a batter's offensive performance, consisting of total bases plus walks divided by plate appearances. It is basically similar to indices such as on-base plus slugging, total average, and the basic version of runs created, and as such should be a relatively good predictor of offensive performance. It is used regularly by Allen St. John in his *Wall Street Journal* column entitled "By the Numbers." In an Apr. 29, 2005, column, St. John reported that the highest career index of .740 belongs to Babe Ruth. Abbrev. *BOP*, 2.

bases per plate appearance A ratio between the number of bases a player gets for his team and the player's number of plate appearances. It equals (total bases + walks + hit by pitches + stolen bases – caught stealing – grounded into double plays) divided by (at-bats + walks + hit by pitches + sacrifice flies). The ratio is used by Bill Gilbert in his annual reports of batting achievements. Abbrev. *BPA*.

base stealer A runner who advances from one base to the next without the aid of a hit, error, balk, passed ball, wild pitch, base on balls, hit by pitch, outfield throw to another base, or defensive indifference. Generally, a base stealer is a fast runner with an ability to judge the pitcher's attention and reflexes. Sometimes spelled "base-stealer." See also *stealer.* Syn. *burglar*, 2; *thief*, 1; *robber*, 3. IST USE. 1892 (*New York Press*, Aug. 7; Edward J. Nichols).

base stealing The act of a runner advancing a base without the aid of a base hit, putout, error, force out, fielder's choice, balk, passed ball, or wild pitch. Frederick Ivor-Campbell (personal communication, Nov. 13, 2001): "Perhaps from the beginning, [baserunners] ran the bases as freely as the delivery of the pitcher and the ability of the catcher would permit. None of the early rules addressed base stealing, pro or con, and the understanding of all rules makers is that whatever is not specifically prohibited will be done if it makes strategic or tactical sense." Syn. *larceny*; *petit larceny*; *robbery*, 2; *thievery*; *thieving.*

base-stealing runs The *linear weights* measure of the number of runs for which a player is personally responsible through base stealing. According to *The Baseball Encyclopedia* (2004, p.1693), it is calculated by multiply-

ing a player's number of stolen bases by .22 (an estimate of the number of runs a stolen base produces on average), multiplying the player's number of caught stealing by .38 (the estimated number of runs a caught steal costs on average), and then subtracting the latter from the former. Vince Coleman is the single-season leader with 24 in 1986; Rickey Henderson is the career leader with 182. Base-stealing runs was devised by Pete Palmer and originally described (with a now-obsolete formula) by John Thorn and Pete Palmer in *The Hidden Game of Baseball* (1985). Abbrev. *BSR*. Syn. *stolen base runs.*

base-stealing wins The linear weights measure of the number of wins for which a player's base stealing is directly responsible. It is computed by dividing a player's base-stealing runs by runs per win. It is defined so that the league average in a given year is zero. Base-stealing wins was devised by Pete Palmer and originally described by John Thorn and Pete Palmer in *The Hidden Game of Baseball* (1985). Abbrev. *BSW*. Syn. *stolen base wins.*

bases tenanted Syn. of *bases loaded.* IST USE. 1908 (*Baseball Magazine*, December; Edward J. Nichols).

base-sticker A baserunner who takes either a short lead off a base or no lead at all.

bases touched *hist.* Syn. of *total bases run.*

bases waterlogged Syn. of *bases loaded.* IST USE. 1910 (*New York Tribune*, July 10; Edward J. Nichols).

basetender *hist.* An infielder stationed near one of the three bases in the early days of baseball.

base-to-base Syn. of *station-to-station*, 1.

base umpire An umpire stationed at first base, second base, or third base. See also *field umpire*; *first base umpire*; *second base umpire*; *third base umpire.*

bash 1. To hit the ball with great power. "[Bruce Chen's] assorted off-speed pitches seemed to hang over the plate, waiting for Rangers to bash them" (*The Baltimore Sun*, May 5, 2006). **2.** To bump forearms with one who has just hit a home run.

bashball Baseball characterized by many

home runs and high scores. "Last season [the Seattle Mariners] broke the Orioles' year-old record for most home runs in a season. They remain wedded to bashball" (*The Baltimore Sun*, June 2, 1998).

basher A hitter with great power.

bashing The ritual of bumping forearms at home plate with a teammate who has just hit a home run. The practice began in the late 1980s with the Oakland Athletics' sluggers Mark McGwire and Jose Canseco, who compared forearms they had built up in the off-season and were often referred to as the Bash Brothers. See also *bash*, 2.

Basic Agreement The overarching labor contract between the owners of the 30 major-league clubs and the players (Major League Baseball Players Association) that contains virtually all conditions of employment. These include: determination of salary, pension plan, benefits plan, disabled lists, moving allowances, termination pay, minimum salary for major-league players, salary arbitration, assignment of player contracts, reservation rights, contract tenders to unsigned players, rules governing free agency, the first-year player draft, waivers, drug testing, luxury tax and revenue sharing, contraction, team debt, suspension of players, grievances, interleague play, redistribution of the commissioner's discretionary fund, licensing, medical care, injury rehabilitation, safety and health, and working conditions such as scheduling, discipline, spring training and expense allowances, and travel. It was attained as a result of the 1981 baseball players' strike and is renegotiable every four years. Syn. *collective bargaining agreement*.

basket catch A catch in which a defensive player cups his glove and bare hand together, close to his body and belt-high, to trap the ball. Catching balls at the waist means that the fielder does not have to bring the ball down and back up to let loose a throw (the ball is already down). Several prominent players (starting with Rabbit Maranville and including Willie Mays and Roberto Clemente) have used this technique, although Morris A. Shirts (*Warm Up for Little League Baseball*, 1976) did not advise it for youthful players. See also *vest-pocket catch*. Syn. *belt-*

buckle catch. ETYMOLOGY. A likely shortening of *breadbasket catch*.

basket glove A fielder's glove in which the ordinary lacing between the thumb and the forefinger is removed and the separation is made wider with lacing or string that is taped and extends over the top of the fingers. The glove (which was banned in 1939) was devised for Hank Greenberg, the Detroit Tigers star of the 1930s and 1940s, whose big hands made it difficult for him to wear the regulation-size glove. Syn. *orange crate*; *lobster trap*; *lobster net*.

bass-ball An early 19th-century colloquial spelling of "base-ball." "The undersigned, all residents of the new town of Hamden ... challenge an equal number of persons of any town in the county of Delaware, to meet them at any time at the house of *Edward B. Chace*, in said town, to play the game of BASS-BALL, for the sum of one dollar each per game" (*Delhi* [Hamden, N.Y.] *Gazette*, July 13, 1825).

bastard pitch An unhittable pitch. Don Baylor (*Don Baylor*, 1989, p.xxvii): "It was down and away and out of the strike zone, four or five inches off the plate. A pitcher's pitch in layman's terms, a bastard pitch in hitter's terms. Down and away, unhittable."

baste *hist.* To hit a ball hard. IST USE. 1891 (*Chicago Herald*, May 12; Edward J. Nichols).

baste ball A term used by Princeton College student John Rhea Smith (*Journal at Nassau Hall*, March 22, 1786, Princeton Library MSS, AM 12800) in his diary: "A fine day, play baste ball in the campus but am beaten for I miss both catching and striking the ball" (Varnum Lansing Collins, *Princeton*, 1914, p.207). Thomas L. Altherr (*NINE*, Spring 2000) commented, "Smith's use of 'baste' instead of 'base' is quite intriguing, suggesting a linguistic connection for striking the ball rather running to a base." According to William B. Mead and Paul Dickson (*Baseball: The President's Game*, 1993), "Princeton College banned 'baste ball,' a popular game among students, on grounds that it 'is in itself low and unbecoming gentlemen Students and ... is an exercise attended with great danger.'" David Block (personal communication, June 2005) considers "baste" to be a misspelling of "base."

bat 1. *n.* The sculpted wooden implement that is used to hit a pitched ball. There are different regulations for bats at various levels of organized baseball and softball, but the major leagues require that it be made of a single piece of wood, which cannot be longer than 42 inches, thicker than 2¾ inches in diameter at its thickest point, and 16/19th of an inch in diameter at its thinnest point; there is no maximum weight. The differential between a bat's length (in inches) and its weight (in ounces) shall not be greater than 3½ (2007–2011 Basic Agreement, attachment 29). The acceptable colors are natural, brown, black, and a two-tone stain. A regulation bat is usually made from northern white ash, maple, or willow, but was originally fashioned from hickory. Metal bats are increasingly used at lower levels of the game and almost exclusively in softball. IST USE. 1845. "The ball must be pitched, and not thrown, for the bat" (Knickerbocker Rules, Rule 9th, Sept. 23). 2. *v.* To take a turn as a batter. 3. *v.* To hit a pitched ball. IST USE. 1858. "Now, Charley, give me a good ball that I may bat it" (George F. Cooledge, *The Little One's Ladder, or First Steps in Spelling and Reading*; David Block). 4. *n.* One's hitting ability; e.g., "Ozzie Smith bulks up in hopes of improving his bat" (*St. Petersburg Times*, April 2, 1987) and "Off-season focus takes nothing from his [Eric Davis'] bat" (*The Baltimore Sun*, March 10, 1998). 5. *n.* A player seen in his role as a hitter. "We're looking for a left-handed bat" (Milwaukee Brewers manager Tom Trebelhorn, quoted in *St. Petersburg Times*, Feb. 29, 1988).

EXTENDED USE. This baseball term has long been borrowed by the greater language:

"Right off the bat": from the start, or immediately. "The producers got the verdict right off the bat, and they are wise enough to fold up and depart when the decision is thumbs down" (*National Police Gazette*, Jan. 14, 1928).

"To go to bat for": to take up someone else's cause or argument. "When Morgenthau went strongly to bat for [the new tax bill], Roosevelt turned on him sharply" (Drew Pearson, *San Francisco Chronicle*, May 23, 1939; Peter Tamony).

"To not get the bat off one's shoulder": not given a chance. On an attorney not being able to make his case: "Being well-known as a Wall Street attorney he didn't even get his bat off his shoulder" (*San Francisco News*, June 8, 1933; Peter Tamony).

"To bat two for three," "to bat three for four," etc.: to be successful but not altogether successful. "Mayor Bats Two for Three on the Washington Circuit" (*San Francisco News-Call Bulletin* headline, June 17, 1960; Peter Tamony).

BAT Abbrev. for *Baseball Assistance Team.*

bat and trap The modern name for *trap ball* in England.

bat-around *n.* The occasion upon which all nine batters in a team's lineup come to the plate in an inning, with the 10th batter coming up. IST USE. 1880 (*Chicago Inter-Ocean*, May 19; Edward J. Nichols).

bat around *v.* To have all nine batters in a team's lineup come to bat during an inning, with the 10th batter coming up.

bat a thousand Var. of *bat one thousand.*

batazo Spanish for "hit."

batazo podrido Spanish for *Texas Leaguer,* 2.

bat bag A canvas or leather duffel bag in which bats are carried. IST USE. 1889. "We carried our uniforms in a large trunk and bats in a large bat-bag" (Bob Leadley, quoted in *Detroit Free Press*, Feb. 10; Peter Morris).

bat-ball A generic term for an early bat-and-ball game. Bat ball was one of the games prohibited by the Pittsfield (Mass.) town ordinance of Sept. 5, 1791 (John Thorn). Ralph Waldo Emerson wrote in his journal (June 1, 1840; Wendy Knickerbocker): "In playing with bat-balls, perhaps . . . [a boy] is charmed with some recognition of the movement of the heavenly bodies, and a game of base or cricket is a course of experimental astronomy, and my young master tingles with a faint sense of being a tyrannical Jupiter driving spheres madly from their orbit." There is an early (1844) reference to "bat ball" in *The Hurrah Game: Baseball in Northampton, 1823–1953* (2002, p.3) by Brian Turner and John S. Bowman. The term was used in *Little Charley's Games and Sports* (published by C.G. Henderson in Philadelphia in 1852) in a description of trap ball (David Block, *Baseball Before We Knew It*, 2005, p.214).

batboy A young man employed by a team to take care of its players' personal equipment before, during, and after games. Traditionally, the most important responsibility of the job is to retrieve each player's bat from home plate where it has been dropped or tossed and put it back in its proper place in the bat rack. The bat boy is also responsible for keeping the home plate umpire supplied with baseballs. "The New York Yankees . . . forgot to vote World Series money to their batboys, but rectified the problem the other day by tapping the fine fund and sending each the grand sum of $100" (Melvin Durslag, *San Francisco Examiner*, Feb. 28, 1977). See Neil D. Isaacs, *Batboys and the World of Baseball*, 1995. Abbrev. *BB*, 3. Also spelled "bat boy." IST USE. 1906. "A little son of Second Baseman [Pug] Bennett acted as bat boy for the cardinals. He is four years old, was decked out in a regulation uniform, and made a particularly fetching figure as he walked out solemnly after each bat" (*Chicago Tribune*, May 11; Peter Morris). USAGE NOTE. The concept of batboys is older than 1906. The 1883 Philadelphia Athletics of the American Association had a "bat-carrier" (*Detroit Post and Tribune*, Feb. 1, 1886; Peter Morris).

batboy body The physique of a scrawny or skinny player.

batboy shot A home run of such clear and immediate magnitude that the batter is simply able to hand his bat to the batboy because he has the time for such a ritual. ETYMOLOGY. According to Joe Goddard (*The Sporting News*, March 6, 1982): "This is the brainchild of Yankee Oscar Gamble, who says he knows when he hits one well and it's out of the park. 'I don't even look at it,' Gamble says. 'I know it's gone. I just turn around and hand my bat to the batboy.'"

bat breaker 1. A batter who swings the bat with such tremendous force that it results in a broken bat. **2.** A pitcher who generates broken bats by throwing inside so that the batter hits the ball closer to the handle. **3.** A pitch that results in a broken bat.

bat-burning ceremony A mostly metaphoric ritual during which the useless bats of a baseball team are burned in a bonfire.

batcatcher A playground term that is probably a corruption of *backcatcher*, 1.

bat cleanup To bat in the cleanup position.

bat control The ability to use the bat as a tool. Good bat control involves getting a piece of the ball, executing the hit and run, fouling off pitches, hitting the ball where it is pitched, and rarely striking out.

bat day A promotion at which fans are given souvenir bats at a baseball game.

bat dodger A pitch that causes batters to swing and miss. The term was used by Satchel Paige to describe one of his pitches.

bate Spanish for "bat" (noun).

bateador Spanish for "batter" and "hitter."

bateador emergente Spanish for "pinch hitter."

bateo y corrido Spanish for "hit and run."

Bates *hist.* A worn-out or declining player; a veteran player who has seen his best days. Var. "Batesy."

batfest Short for *batting fest*. "Sox on Rampage Crush Yankees in 15 to 9 Batfest" (*Chicago Tribune* headline, Sept. 19, 1920; the White Sox pounded out 21 hits). IST USE. 1907. "[Harry] Steinfeldt's grounder ended the batfest" (I.E. Sanborn, *Chicago Tribune*, Aug. 22; Peter Morris).

batgirl A young woman engaged by a team to take care of the players' bats and other equipment during a game. Also spelled "bat girl." IST USE. 1942. "She's the only batgirl in major-league baseball" (*Baseball Magazine*, June).

bat grip A sleeve or coating that is placed over the bat handle to give the batter a firmer grip when swinging. It also protects the handle, the thinnest part of the bat, from chipping.

bat handle The narrow or slender end of the baseball bat.

bat head The thick end of the baseball bat. "If you have a right-handed batter and he fouls the ball over the first-base dugout, you know the bat head was way behind" (Ray Miller, quoted in William Zinsser, *Spring Training*, 1989, p.114). Syn. *head*, 1.

bat in To get a hit that scores one or more runners.

bat messer A 100-mph fastball. "Kyle Farnsworth . . . throws triple-digit fastballs the players call 'bat messers'" (Gene Wojciechowski, *ESPN The Magazine*, June 25, 2001, p.70). Syn. *lane changer.*

bat night A promotion at which fans are given souvenir bats at a night baseball game.

bat off the rubber *hist.* To remove a pitcher from the game because of the success of the opposing team (John B. Foster, in *Collier's New Dictionary of the English Language*, 1908).

"bat on ball" An Australian form of encouragement called out to a batter.

bat one thousand To be perfect at the plate. Because an average of 1.000 is a virtual impossibility after a dozen or so at-bats, the term finds greater application in baseball fiction (e.g., Bob Allison and Frank Ernest Hill, *The Kid Who Batted 1.000*, 1951) than in real life. Var. of *bat a thousand.* EXTENDED USE. To be absolutely correct; to perform flawlessly.

baton swinger *hist.* A batter. 1ST USE. 1915. "I use baseball terms . . . fanning the baton swinger" (Burt L. Standish, *Covering the Look-In Corner*, p.183; David Shulman).

bat performance factor [softball term] A measure of the coefficient of restitution of the bat–ball collision (i.e., the so-called trampoline or springboard effects, determined by shooting the ball at a mounted bat), divided by the coefficient of restitution of the ball. The standard bat performance factor is 1.20. Abbrev. *BPF.*

bat rack An open, slotted box located in front, or in a corner, of the dugout or hung from the dugout wall that holds a team's supply of bats during a game. Syn. *lumberyard*, 1. 1ST USE.

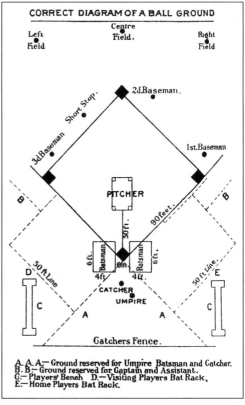

Bat rack. Placement of racks specified in this 1889 field diagram. *Author's collection*

1883. "Bats must be kept in the rack" (*Detroit Free Press*, Apr. 29; Peter Morris).

bat ring [softball term] A metal or plastic ring for measuring the diameter or circumference of a legal bat. If the head of the bat will not fit through the ring, the bat is deemed to be illegal and is disallowed for play.

bats both Said of a switch-hitter. Abbrev. *BB*, 5.

bat shy Said of a batter who is intimidated by inside pitching. "[Roger Bresnahan] was hit in the face with a pitched ball, and [John] McGraw worried while he was laid up, for fear that it would make him bat shy" (Christy Mathewson, *Pitching in a Pinch*, 1912). "The accident made [Jack] Burdock bat shy and he gave up playing baseball" (*The Sporting News*, Dec. 10, 1931; Peter Morris).

bats left Said of a left-handed batter. Abbrev. *BL.*

bat slinger A batter. "[Rowdy Elliott] 'kidded' those bat slingers from across the bay into striking out in the ninth and tenth" (*San Francisco Bulletin*, May 7, 1913; Gerald L. Cohen).

batsman Syn. of *batter*, 1. "Ted Williams . . . [is] one of the outstanding batsmen in the history of the major leagues" (Bob Burnes, *The Sporting News*, Aug. 17, 1960). The term was commonly used in the early days of baseball for "the striker at the bat." IST USE. 1856. "He who strikes it fairly must be a fine batsman" (*Porter's Spirit of the Times*, Dec. 6; Peter Morris).

batsmanship A player's ability as a batter.

batsmith Syn. of *batter*, 1. "The batsmiths began to tickle the pill" (*San Francisco Bulletin*, Apr. 4, 1913; Gerald L. Cohen).

bat speed The velocity of the bat as the batter swings at the pitch. The greater the bat speed, the greater the velocity of the batted ball and the longer a batter can wait on breaking pitches. In general, the lighter the bat, the greater the bat speed. It is generally regarded that, to be successful, a hitter must generate good bat speed; e.g., Ken Griffey Jr.'s bat speed is greater than 100 mph, and Jose Canseco was often described as having "awesome bat speed." Syn. *life*, 4.

bats right Said of a right-handed batter. Abbrev. *BR*, 1.

batted ball A ball that has been struck by the batter, as distinguished from a *thrown ball*, in interpreting the rules of baseball.

batter 1. *n.* An offensive player with a bat who is positioned in the batter's box and is attempting to hit a pitched ball. The main focal point of the game of baseball is the contest between the batter and the pitcher. Compare *hitter*, 1. Syn. *batsman*; *batsmith*; *sticker*, 1; *stickman*; *sticksmith*; *stickster*; *striker*. IST USE. 1869 (*DeWitt's Base-Ball Guide*, p.39; Edward J. Nichols). USAGE NOTE. Ty Cobb (quoted in F.C. Lane, *Batting*, 1925): "A batter is a man who can bunt, place his hits, beat out infield drives and slug when the occasion demands it, but he doesn't slug all the time." 2. *v.* To bat hard against the opposing pitcher; to defeat a team with many base hits. "Orioles batter Indians" (*The Baltimore Sun* headline, Apr. 20, 2006, describing an 18–9

Baltimore victory). IST USE. 1912 (*New York Tribune*, Sept. 15; Edward J. Nichols).

batter-fielder wins Syn. of *total player rating*. Abbrev. *BFW*.

batter park factor The park factor credited to a team's batters in the linear weights system.

batter-runner A *baserunner* who has just completed his time at bat, before he is put out or until the play on which he becomes a runner is completed. Syn. *player running bases*.

batter's box 1. One of the two rectangular six-foot-long by four-foot-wide areas in which the batter must stand. Each box is positioned six inches on either side of the plate, for right- and left-handed batters. Though the boundary for each box is lined with white lime before the game, batters have been known to scrape away the back line with their feet to distort the umpire's ability to determine if they have stepped out of the batter's box. "The batter's box is changed from a square of three by six feet to a square of four by six feet, . . . while the square is removed six inches from the home plate instead of twelve inches, as formerly was the case" (*The North American* [Philadelphia], March 4, 1886). The batter's box was introduced in 1874 as the "batter's position." 2. [softball term] One of the two rectangular seven-foot-long by four-foot-wide areas in which the batter must stand. Each box is positioned six inches on either side of the plate, for right- and left-handed batters. The front line of the box is four feet in front of a line drawn through the center of home plate. Prior to 2007, the batter's box was three feet wide.

batter's circle Syn. of *on-deck circle*.

batter's eye 1. The eye of a batter. Regarding the reconfiguration of the Coliseum in Los Angeles for baseball use, Jeane Hoffman (*Los Angeles Times*, Nov. 14, 1957) wrote, "The sun will be in the batter's eye by the second game of a double-header." Regarding a ball game played under the lights, *The Washington Post* (May 4, 1930) noted: "Artificial lighting does not affect batters' eyes." David Falkner (*The New York Times*, June 22, 1986): "Before the game was an inning old, it was interrupted because the setting sun from behind the center-field fence was shining too intensely in the batter's eyes." Compare *batting eye*. IST USE. 1890. "Wild Bill [Widner] takes his own time about delivering the ball. He generally poses a couple of minutes looking at the people in the grand stand through the batter's eye" (*Rocky Mountain News* [Denver], Sept. 3). **2.** A glare-free section of the outfield wall in straightaway center field, painted in a flat, dark color, or sometimes covered with greenery, that makes it easier for the batter to follow an incoming pitch as it leaves the pitcher's hand. Major-league recommendations call for minimum dimensions of 40 feet high and 80 feet wide. IST USE. 1964. "Structural steel work for the 'batter's eye' in center field has been completed [at Shea Stadium]. This will be covered with a screen of green nylon mesh that will serve the two-fold purpose of improving the batter's vision and hiding speakers for the public address system" (Harry V. Forgeron, *The New York Times*, March 1). ETYMOLOGY. Derived from the eyesight of the batter. Cecilia Tan (personal communication, July 1, 2005) found two 1906 uses of the term in regard to the painted backdrop. From the *Atlanta Constitution* (Apr. 27): "The large-sized sign on the back fence of Piedmont Park which has been troubling the players . . . will be blotted out tomorrow, according to Manager Smith. . . . When the signs were first placed on the fence, it was decided to leave a green space without any fancy work on the fence directly in front of the batter's eye. When the painter left the green space he made a miscue and put the space too far over to the right, and it doesn't help the players' peepers a bit." From a column by Hugh S. Fullerton (*Chicago Tribune*, Sept. 16): "The Orioles were not hitting. They could not find out why until one day Willie Keeler remarked that the ball when pitched from the pitcher's box was the same color as the center field fence and the ball was lost to them against the dark background [the balls being dark and dirty rather than white]. The players . . . figured that the reason they were not hitting was because there was a lack of relief in the color scheme of the grounds. . . . [Now] in center field is a panel of color to relieve the batter's eye and show the ball in relief against it." Washington outfielder/first baseman Charles Hickman (quoted in *The Washington Post*, Jan. 27, 1907) urged owners to color a 90-foot section of the center field fence dark to aid the batter: "What's the use of trying to hit pitchers like Harry White and 'Rube' Waddell with a big yellow sign often reflecting the rays of the sun in the batter's eyes?"

batters facing pitcher The total number of plate appearances by batters facing a specific pitcher. Abbrev. *BFP.*

batter's interference An act by a batter that impedes, hinders, or confuses any fielder attempting to make a play; e.g., when the batter's swinging bat interferes with the catcher's trying to throw out a baserunner attempting to steal. See also *interference*, 1.

batter's run average A batter's on-base percentage multiplied by his slugging percentage. The statistic was devised by Richard D. Cramer and presented in an essay co-written with Pete Palmer (*Baseball Research Journal*, 1974). Despite its simplicity, batter's run average is a relatively good predictor of offensive performance, comparable to *total average* and the basic version of *runs created*. A revised version is known as *batter win average*. Abbrev. *BRA.* Syn. *on-base times slugging*; *SLOB.*

batter's wheelhouse See *wheelhouse.*

"batter up!" Umpire's call to the batter that it is time to step into the batter's box and for play to start. Traditionally, the call is made at the beginning of the game, at the start of each half inning, and after a long time-out, such as that taken for a change of pitchers. Syn. *"striker to the line."* EXTENDED USE. A call to get military aircraft airborne.

batter win average A method for evaluating a player's offensive performance, computed by multiplying a batter's on-base percentage by his slugging percentage and again by a number representing composite offensive performance by the player's league. The term was presented by Richard D. Cramer (*Baseball Research Journal*, 1977). It is a revised version of *batter's run average.* Abbrev. *BWA.*

battery 1. The pitcher and catcher collec-

Battery. Pitcher Walter Johnson (right) and catcher Herold "Muddy" Ruel, Washington Senators, 1924. *National Photo Company Collection, Library of Congress*

tively. In Steve Kluger's novel *Changing Pitches* (1984), a successful battery is described as one in which the pitcher and catcher could switch brains and nobody would know the difference. IST USE. 1868 (Chadwick Scrapbooks; Edward J. Nichols). ETYMOLOGY. In 1881, John Montgomery Ward recruited pitcher Charlie Sweeney and catcher Sandy Nava for Providence during a coast-to-coast barnstorming trip. After they proved successful together in California, the press dubbed the 1884 Sweeney/Nava combination as "the California battery." In his book *Base-Ball: How to Become a Player* (1888, pp.46, 65), Ward used the analogy of the pitcher and catcher as the positive and negative poles, respectively, of an electric battery. The explanation offered by Richard G. Knowles and Richard Morton (*Baseball*, 1896) is that the term "has its origin in telegraphy, the pitcher being the transmitter, and the catcher the receiver." However, Henry Chadwick (*Technical Terms of Baseball*, 1897) clearly implies a military borrowing when he gives this definition: "This is the term applied to the pitcher and catcher of a team. It is the main attacking force of the little army of nine players in the field in a contest." Most later attempts to pin a history on the term have alluded to this comparison to a military artillery unit or battery, in which the "catcher" provides ammunition for a raised work or parapet ("battery") where guns are mounted and where the "pitcher" fires it. P.P. Rohrbaugh (Glen Rock, Pa.) provided the

following explanation (*The Sporting News*, Jan. 11, 1940): "The pitcher . . . is the gun and armed with a 'ball,' which is also a bullet and which he shoots at the batsman. . . . If the ball is missed by the batsman, it is returned by the catcher to be loaded into the gun, which happens to be the pitcher. Remember 'Bullet Joe Bush.' " The following week, *The Sporting News* (Jan. 18, 1940) printed Frank J. Reiter's (Kenmore, N.Y.) contrived attempt to explain the origin of the term: "General Abner Doubleday, the founder of baseball, being a military man, may have originated the phrase, or someone in the army so named it in honor of General Doubleday. As the word 'fire' is a military command, and as the pitcher literally 'fires' the ball to the plate much in the same manner as a field artillery battery fires a cannon, this may have prompted the name of a military unit to be applied to the pitcher and catcher." 2. *hist.* A term commonly used in the late 19th century for the pitcher alone. *The Ohio State Journal* (Apr. 1891; John Lewis) noted that Columbus had three good batteries, referring to the pitchers only.

battery error *hist.* An action by the pitcher or catcher, other than a fielding misplay, that enables the batter-runner to reach base or a baserunner to advance to another base; specif., a base on balls, a hit batsman, wild pitch, passed ball, or balk. Battery errors were lumped in with the player's fielding errors in the statistics of 1876 until 1887. See also *error.* "[The Brooklyns] gave a perfect exhibition of fielding, not even a battery error being charged against them" (*The North American* [Philadelphia], Aug. 4, 1886).

batterymate The pitcher or the catcher. Also spelled "battery mate." IST USE. 1909. "[Orval] Overall drove his battery mate home with his long smash over the right field fence" (Ring W. Lardner, *Chicago Tribune*, July 9; Peter Morris).

battery points *hist.* The pitcher and catcher. "The [players] are not extensively represented in the battery points, the only little ones of first caliber being [Jack] Warhop, the Yankee's [*sic*] pitcher, and Stevens [Jim Stephens], the St. Louis Browns' backstop" (*Mansfield* [Ohio] *News*, Oct. 21, 1911; Peter

Morris). Syn. *points*, 3. IST USE. 1899 (*The Sporting News*, Jan. 14; Peter Morris).

battery umpire *hist.* Syn. of *plate umpire.* "The battery umpire . . . hands down the decisions on balls and strikes" (National League president Nicholas E. Young, quoted in *The Washington Post*, Dec. 17, 1897).

bat the breeze To strike out (*Brooklyn Daily Eagle*, May 1, 1892, p.4).

batting 1. Attempting to hit a pitched ball; the act of coming to home plate with a bat in an attempt to become a baserunner. IST USE. 1861 (*New York Sunday Mercury*, Aug. 10; Edward J. Nichols). EXTENDED USE. Drafting a player in basketball. "We were batting fifth [in draft order] and weren't sure his boy [Stephon Marbury] was going to be around long enough for us to get a swing at him" (Minnesota Timberwolves official Kevin McHale, quoted in *Sports Illustrated*, Jan. 20, 1997, p.80). 2. A team's collective ability to hit. IST USE. 1856. "The playing on both sides was excellent, the Newark being a little better in the field, but the Columbia leading in the batting" (*Porter's Spirit of the Times*, Oct. 4; Frederick Ivor-Campbell).

batting apparel Syn. of *batting clothes.* "[The St. Louis Browns] had on their batting apparel" (*The North American* [Philadelphia], Aug. 4, 1886).

batting a thousand Said of a batter with a (mythical) perfect batting average.

batting average The standard and most popular numerical measure of hitting ability. It is the ratio determined by dividing the number of hits made by a batter by that batter's number of official at-bats. It is usually expressed in thousandths (three decimal places), although in exceptional cases it is carried beyond three places (e.g., to determine which of two batters with identical three-decimal-place batting averages has the higher of the two). The customary standard of excellence is an average of .300 or better in a given year, whereas .400 is viewed as indicative of truly superlative performance and has not been achieved since Ted Williams hit .406 in 1941. The player with the highest batting average wins the batting championship. However, variation in batting averages across seasons

has been great enough to revise the standard in seasonal context. At one extreme, the entire National League in 1930 recorded a combined batting average of .303, with more than 70 percent (44 of 62) of players with 300 or more official at-bats hitting .300 or better (Bill Terry achieving .401). At the other extreme, the entire American League in 1968 recorded a combined batting average of .230, with only one .300 hitter (Carl Yastrzemski at .301). As both Terry and Yastrzemski batted about 32 percent higher than their league's average, it can be argued that their achievements were, in actuality, similar. Despite the statistic's common usage, sabermetricians have found a team's batting average to be a relatively poor predictor of the team's ability to score runs. Further, batting average makes no distinction among the single, the double, the triple, and the home run (all hits are equal) and gives no indication of the value of a base hit to the team; it also neglects the offensive value of a base on balls. The batting average is used over time to determine the probability that a batter will get a hit in a given official at-bat. Abbrev. *BA*; *AVE*; *AVG*. Syn. *plate record*; *credit account*. IST USE. 1874. "The following players led the batting averages of first base hits" (*Brooklyn Eagle*, March 29; Peter Morris). USAGE NOTE. The batting average, in its current form, was first introduced by H.A. Dobson in *Beadle's Dime Base-Ball Player* of 1872 (for 1871 performances, expressed as average number of base hits per games played), and first computed "officially" in 1876 for the newly created National League. EXTENDED USE. Success or failure in other realms; e.g., "The only way to judge your wife is by her general batting average" (*Vanity Fair*, March 1919, p.30; Stuart Y. Silverstein), and "NBC's batting average for new comedies has been poor recently" (David Bauder, Associated Press, May 13, 2003). Success rate is often measured in terms of "batting a thousand" or "batting zero." An ad from an investment corporation (*Forbes*, Oct. 6, 1986) opens: "If the S&P is hitting .333, then our top two hitters are batting over .630."

batting average against The batting average of the players who have faced a given pitcher or team. Abbrev. *BAA.*

batting average on balls in play A batting average for batted balls that could have been fielded, computed by subtracting home runs from hits and then dividing this number by the number of at-bats minus both home runs and strikeouts. Allen St. John (*The Wall Street Journal*, Aug. 18, 2006) used the term "ball-in-play batting average" or "BPBA." Abbrev. *BABIP*. Syn. *hit rate*.

batting bee A succession of hits. IST USE. 1904. "After this batting bee [Al] Orth settled down" (*The Washington Post*, Sept. 11; Peter Morris).

batting cage 1. A portable, wire-enclosed framework, open on one side, that is wheeled behind home plate during batting practice to prevent foul balls from being hit into the stands and to stop balls behind home plate. Minimum dimensions for batting cages are 18 feet wide, 14 feet deep, and 9 feet high. A time-honored prank is to ask a rookie or batboy to go back to the clubhouse and pick up the "keys" to the batting cage. Syn. *cage*, 1. IST USE. 1906. "[Oscar] Knolls lambasted Joe Tinker in the side in the batting cage today, and Joe has an ugly bruise" (*Chicago Tribune*, March 23; Peter Morris). 2. An enclosed indoor framework used for batting practice and instruction. It can be used in bad weather, in the off-season, or when a hitting coach wants to work with a batter in private. See also *indoor cage*. Syn. *cage*, 2; *baseball cage*.

batting champion The player who wins the batting championship. Syn. *batting king*.

batting championship 1. The honor earned by the player in each major league with the highest batting average at the end of the regular season. Since 1957, a batter must have at least 3.1 official plate appearances per team's scheduled game (477 plate appearances for a 154-game schedule and 502 plate appearances for a 162-game schedule); the multiplier for the minor leagues is 2.7. In previous years, the qualifying minimums included playing in 100 games or having 400 at-bats. A player who does not have enough plate appearances can still win the batting championship if he has enough hits that he would still have the highest batting average after the additional plate appearances are added on as outs (this exception allowed Tony Gwynn to win the 1996 National League batting title). Syn. *batting crown*; *batting title*. 2. The race for the title of batting champion.

batting circle Syn. of *on-deck circle*.

batting clothes The clothes worn by a player who is hitting well. It is a figurative term used to describe a period of good hitting and does not refer to a special uniform (although batters have been known to wear the same uniform during a batting streak). "Heine Zimmermann left his batting clothes at home and fanned twice" (*San Francisco Bulletin*, Apr. 18, 1913; Gerald L. Cohen). Syn. *batting apparel*; *batting togs*. IST USE. 1884.

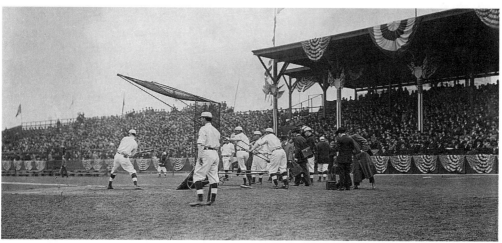

Batting cage. New York Highlanders batting practice at Hilltop Park, Apr. 21, 1911. *George Grantham Bain Collection, Library of Congress*

"The home nine had their batting clothes on" (*The Washington Post*, June 8; Peter Morris).

batting coach Syn. of *hitting coach*.

batting crown Syn. of *batting championship*, 1.

batting eye The visual judgment of a batter who can determine the location of a pitch in relation to the strike zone; the ability to distinguish between balls and strikes. Andy Seminick (on Rogers Hornsby, quoted in *Sports Illustrated*, June 24, 2002): "He was opposed to reading and going to the movies. He said they hurt your batting eye." Compare *batter's eye*, 1. IST USE. 1888. "Donahue ... is also regaining his batting eye" (*San Francisco Examiner*, Apr. 2; Peter Morris).

batting eye index A measure of a player's batting eye, computed by subtracting the number of strikeouts from the number of bases on balls and dividing by the number of games played. Ted Williams is both the single-season (.889 in 1954) and career (.572) leader. The statistic was contributed by Cappy Gagnon (*Baseball Research Journal*, 1988). Abbrev. *BEI*.

batting eye ratio A measure of a player's batting eye, computed by dividing the number of bases on balls by the number of strikeouts. A ratio greater than 1.00 most likely represents a .300 hitter; a ratio of less than 0.50 most likely represents a hitter with a low batting average.

batting fest A hitting spree, often celebrated at the expense of a single pitcher. Syn. *batfest*. IST USE. 1916. "After turning the enemy down in one, two, three order, High School proceeded to indulge in another batting-fest" (Christy Mathewson, *First Base Faulkner*, p.164; David Shulman).

batting glove A thin leather or vinyl glove worn by a batter to gain a better grip on the bat handle and to prevent blisters. Batters usually wear a batting glove on their bottom hands (left hand for a right-handed batter), although some batters wear gloves on both hands. It was introduced by Kansas City outfielder Ken Harrelson in 1964, and later popularized by Rusty Staub. Bobby Thomson of the New York Giants wore golf gloves in spring training and batting practice as early

as 1949, but he never wore them during the regular season. Two Brooklyn Dodgers hitters (Johnny Frederick and Lefty O'Doul) wore absorber-type material to protect hand injuries in 1932 (*The Sporting News*, May 12, 1932).

batting helmet A protective headgear made of hard, shatterproof plastic, worn by a player while he is at bat and on the bases. Designed to fit over a player's cloth baseball cap, the helmet includes a flap to cover the ear and the temple. Batting helmets are mandatory at all levels of organized baseball, including (since 1971) the major leagues. Beginning in 1983, major leaguers must wear a single ear-flap helmet (or at the player's option, a double ear-flap helmet). A light plastic liner was first adopted experimentally for a whole team by the 1941 Brooklyn Dodgers (see *Brooklyn safety cap*). Pittsburgh Pirates executive Charlie Muse helped create a plastic helmet that provided maximum protection above the ears; the 1953 Pirates were the first team to adopt permanent use of the helmet. However, individual batters, after being beaned, wore protective headgear much earlier: Roger Bresnahan wore a "pneumatic head protector," manufactured by the A.J. Reach Co., in 1907; Frank Chance adopted a device "stuffed with the very best quality of sponge" (*The Washington Post*, June 8, 1913); pitcher Joe Bosk of Utica wore headgear with a pad on one side (*Toronto Globe*, Apr. 27, 1914; Peter Morris); and Willie Wells of the Newark Eagles wore a modified construction worker's hard hat (*New York Age*, Aug. 26, 1937; Larry Lester). For many years, batting helmets were fiercely resisted by the players before they gained popularity. See also *ear flap*. Syn. *beanie*; *skuller*.

batting king Syn. of *batting champion*.

batting lineup The players composing the batting order.

batting list *hist.* Syn. of *batting order*. IST USE. 1877. "The men who opened the batting list for the home nine" (*Winona* [Minn.] *Republican*, August; Peter Morris).

batting order The official listing of the successive appearance in which each batter will come to the plate. The batting order must be submitted to the home plate umpire before the game begins and cannot be changed. Any substitute must be inserted in the batting order in the position of the player being replaced. See also *batting rotation*. Compare *lineup*. Syn. *striking order*; *batting list*. IST USE. 1878. "The batting order of the Indianapolis team will be . . ." (*Chicago Tribune*, March 17; Peter Morris).

batting out of order   The act of a player who appears at the plate out of the proper place in the batting order. On appeal by the defensive team, the proper batter is declared out by the umpire. "Before a game we triple-check to make sure the [lineup] card in the dugout matches the one we hand in [to the umpire]. A manager's worst fear is batting out of order" (Texas Rangers manager Buck Showalter, quoted in *Sports Illustrated*, Apr. 4, 2005). Syn. "batting out of turn."

batting practice   **1.** That period of pregame time set aside for hitters to improve the swings, speed, and timing of their batting habits. The batting practice period has its own rituals and traditions; e.g., it is customary for each batter to take the same number of practice pitches, and some teams have established cycles of batting, such as starting each practice plate appearance with a bunt. It is also a time for a batter to work on his timing and adjust for the wind, lights, and other environmental factors. Mark McGwire and Jose Canseco were two sluggers who attracted fans to batting practice because they put their power on display. Abbrev. *BP*. IST USE. 1894. "Members of the Boston baseball team are badly in need of a little batting practice. . . . Manager [Frank] Selee will suggest . . . the putting up of nets such as they use at the big colleges for batting practice" (Tim Murnane, *Boston Globe*, May 7; Peter Morris). **2.** The offensive production of a team having a field day against a particular team or pitcher. IST USE. 1872. "[Liberty's] pitcher is exceedingly swift, though somewhat wild in delivery, and afforded excellent batting practice for the Troys against their game with the Baltimores to-morrow" (*Chicago Tribune*, July 3).

batting-practice elbow   A discomfort in the

Batting practice. Frank "Home Run" Baker, Philadelphia Athletics, Oct. 8, 1913. *George Grantham Bain Collection, Library of Congress*

elbow endured esp. by pitchers who take batting practice to prepare for interleague play. Mike Hargrove (quoted in *The Washington Post*, June 2, 2000): "Everybody gets batting-practice elbow swinging a bat. But on a scale of 1 to 10, with 10 being your arm is ready to blow up, and a one being you're okay, BP elbow is about a 1½ ."

batting-practice fastball A thrown fastball whose speed is a little less than that of a normal fastball and thereby can be hit more easily; a fastball with "nothing on it." Sometimes the pitch is thrown down the middle of the plate on a 3–0 count just to get a strike called, as the batter is not likely to swing at it. The term can be used derogatorily. Knuckleballer Tim Wakefield "continually changes speeds and occasionally surprises hitters with a batting-practice fastball" (Albert Chen, *Sports Illustrated*, June 12, 2006).

batting-practice pitcher An individual who regularly pitches to the team during batting practice. There are no rules on who performs this chore, but it is commonly a member of the club staff who is not on the roster. A good batting-practice pitcher has a smooth delivery, pinpoint accuracy, and a toss that neither sails nor sinks, and can tailor pitches to a hitter's preferences within the strike zone.

batting-practice screen A protective screen placed in front of the batting-practice pitcher. It is seven feet high and eight feet wide with a four-feet-by-four-feet notch in the upper corner. Barry Landers (letter on file at the National Baseball Library and Archives, May 4, 1973) noted, "It is obvious as to why it [the screen] is there; however, back in 1927, there was no screen. An incident involving my father, who pitched batting practice for the New York Yankees in Spring training of that year, sparked the use of the screen. He was pitching to the immortal Babe Ruth, when 'the Babe' slapped a hard line drive back at him, striking him in the face and knocking out all his teeth in front. From that day to this, a screen is used to protect the batting-practice pitcher." Syn. *pitching screen*.

batting rotation The *batting order*, which may be changed from one game to the next.

batting runs The *linear weights* measure of a player's offensive performance, representing the number of runs for which a batter is personally responsible through batting. It is defined relative to the player's league, so that the league average in a given year is zero. It is calculated by multiplying the player's total for each of a set of offensive events, both positive (singles, doubles, triples, home runs, walks, hit by pitch) and negative (outs), by a weight associated with it, and then adding (or, in the case of negative events, subtracting) the products. The computation of the weights is based on the run potential from various base–out situations. The exact formula: [.33(BB+HBP) + .47(1B) + .38(2B) + .55(3B) + .93(HR)] divided by AB – H (*The Baseball Encyclopedia*, 2004, p.1693). Batting runs is a good predictor of offensive performance for all but the weakest and strongest hitters. Babe Ruth is both the single-season (119 in 1921 and 1923) and career (1322) leader. Batting runs was devised by Pete Palmer and originally described by John Thorn and Pete Palmer in *The Hidden Game of Baseball* (1985). Abbrev. *BR*, 2.

batting slump A period of at-bats during which a batter fails to get a hit or gets only a few hits. IST USE. 1908. "There is nothing more discouraging to a young player than to start the season with a batting slump" (J. Ed Grillo, *The Washington Post*, Apr. 26; Peter Morris). See also *hitting slump*.

batting stance The set position taken by the batter in the batter's box as the ball is about to be delivered by the pitcher. Not only do different batters have different stances, but the same batter may change stances during the course of a game. See also *closed stance*; *open stance*; *square stance*, 1; *straddle stance*.

batting station hist. Syn. of *home plate*. "[The mayor's] arm was not in good shape . . . and the gold ball crossed the batting station still a ball" (*San Francisco Bulletin*, Apr. 2, 1913; Gerald L. Cohen).

batting streak 1. See *hitting streak*. 2. hist. A period of hitting success by a team. "[The Tecumsehs of London were] taken with what is called in base ball circles 'a batting streak,' and hit the ball safely all over the field"

(*Detroit Post*, June 26, 1875; Peter Morris).

batting tee See *tee*, 1.

batting title Syn. of *batting championship*, 1.

batting togs Syn. of *batting clothes*. IST USE. 1890. "Tub Welch had his batting togs on, making three singles and one double" (*The Sporting News*, Apr. 12; Peter Morris).

batting wins The linear weights measure of the number of wins for which a player's batting is directly responsible. It is computed by dividing a player's batting runs by runs per win. It is defined so that the league average in a given year is zero. Babe Ruth is both the single-season (11.5) and career (127.5) leader. Batting wins was devised by Pete Palmer and originally described by John Thorn and Pete Palmer in *The Hidden Game of Baseball* (1985). Abbrev. *BW*.

battinses A procedure for selecting informal boys' baseball teams. An old-timer reminisced (*Grand Rapids* [Mich.] *Herald*, June 8, 1902; Peter Morris), "We'd go through a solemn little ceremony known as 'battinses' in order to choose sides . . . the two biggest boys, or one big boy and the kid that owned the ball, would go through this ceremony. One . . . [would] throw the . . . bat to the other, who would catch it around the middle. Then they'd each put a hand over the other's hand until the end of the bat was reached. The boy that clutched the last remaining handful had to throw the bat backward over his shoulder ten paces. If he successfully accomplished this he had the privilege of picking out the kids that he wanted to play on his side. If he didn't make good in throwing the bat backward the other boy had the first pick of the boys. This, of course, made up some pretty lop-sided scratch teams, but that never bothered any of us—the lop-sideder the better." See also *choose up*, 1.

Battle of Broadway The intense rivalry between the New York Giants and the New York Yankees in the 1920s.

battlin' backstop A tough, combative catcher. "[Thurman] Munson was a seeming throwback to the 'battlin' backstops' of old, establishing an identity as one of the toughest

catchers in the game" (Associated Press obituary for Munson, Aug. 3, 1979).

bat weight A metal or plastic doughnut-shaped ring that is slipped onto the barrel of a bat to make it feel heavier than normal. The purpose of the weight is to strengthen the batter's arm and wrists and to make the unadorned bat feel lighter in the batter's box. The bat weight is used by the on-deck batter while limbering up and replaces the method of swinging two bats simultaneously. See also *doughnut*.

bat-wielder A batter. "None of the bat-wielders who are reported to be after his [Ping Bodie's] job showed us anything" (*San Francisco Bulletin*, March 10, 1913; Gerald L. Cohen).

batwork A player's hitting ability. "Teaching batwork requires the highest order of patience, a quality my enemies have claimed I was without" (Ty Cobb, *My Life in Baseball*, 1961, p.208). IST USE. 1906 (*The Sporting Life*, March 3, p.7; Edward J. Nichols).

Bauer and Black player One who is always playing with a lot of bandage tape, from the name of a company that makes such tape. The term appears in Fred Lieb's *Comedians and Pranksters of Baseball* (1958) along with the traditional comment for such a player: "As long as the tape and baling wire hold up, you ought to have a hell of a year."

baulk Alternate spelling for *balk* that was common in early baseball.

Bay Bridge Series 1. Nickname for the 1989 World Series between the San Francisco Giants and the Oakland Athletics. See also *Earthquake Series*. 2. A series of interleague games between the San Francisco Giants and the Oakland Athletics.

bazooka 1. The strong throwing arm of a pitcher, catcher, or fielder. 2. See *fungo bazooka*.

BB 1. A ball thrown with such speed that it seems as small as a ball-bearing (BB) pellet when it crosses the plate: "Roger Clemens is still the Rocket, slinging BBs" (Jeff Passan, *The Baltimore Sun*, Apr. 27, 2005). 2. Box score abbrev. for *base on balls*. 3. Abbrev. for *batboy*. 4. Abbrev. for *baseball*, 1. 5. Abbrev. for *bats both*.

BBWAA Abbrev. for *Baseball Writers' Association of America*.

beachhead A batter who has reached first base to start an inning. ETYMOLOGY. A term brought back from World War II by players who had been in the armed forces.

Beacon Award An award inaugurated by Major League Baseball in 2007 to honor an individual for his or her efforts on behalf of civil rights throughout the world.

bean 1. *n./hist.* A player's head. "A 'bean' you ask? Why, bean is baseball language for head" (Frank Chance, *The Bride and the Pennant*, 1910). IST USE. 1909. "Ellis singled over [pitcher Ed Higginbotham's] bean in the fifth" (Ring W. Lardner, *Chicago Tribune*, July 5; Peter Morris). Peter Tamony noted that T.A. Dorgan used the term in a cartoon (*San Francisco Examiner*, June 19, 1910) in which a man is hit in the head with a ball, which causes another character to remark, "right on the bean." ETYMOLOGY. This explanation appeared in 1920 when the term was still novel: "The slang expression 'bean' was derived from descriptions of pitchers throwing the ball at the heads of batsmen. This was originally described as a 'bean ball' and from that the word 'bean' became synonymous with 'head'" (Sid Mercer, *San Francisco Call & Post*, July 2, 1920; Peter Tamony). EXTENDED USE. The brain (as in, "use your bean"). 2. *v.* To hit a batter in the head with a pitched ball. IST USE. 1910. "[Birdie Cree] was hitting about .400 early in the season until Walter Johnson happened to 'bean' him with one of his fastest shoots" (*The Sporting News*, Aug. 18; Peter Morris). EXTENDED USE. To hit someone in the head. 3. *n.* Syn. of *amphetamine*.

beanbag A term used to describe the ball adopted by the National League in 1931 in an attempt to decrease hitting. According to Thomas Holmes (*Brooklyn Daily Eagle*, Aug. 17, 1931; Peter Morris), the ball had raised seams to give the pitcher a better grip, and a slightly thickened horsehide cover to reduce the velocity of batted balls.

beanball A pitch thrown intentionally at a batter's head for the purpose of either moving the batter away from home plate or to punish him, his team, or another player for something he has done. Pitchers who throw beanballs are supposed to be ejected from the game, but it is usually difficult for the umpire to determine that the act was premeditated. John J. Evers and Hugh Fullerton (*St. Louis Post-Dispatch*, May 3, 1910): "One of the greatest and most effective balls pitched is the 'bean ball' . . . and pitching at the batter's head, not to hit it, but to drive him out of position and perhaps cause him to get panic-stricken and swing at the ball in self-defense is an art." The only player ever to be killed in a major-league game was Ray Chapman of the Cleveland Indians, who was hit in the head by a pitch thrown by Carl Mays of the New York Yankees on Aug. 16, 1920. But there have been other such fatalities at other levels of the game. A chilling headline (*San Francisco Call-Bulletin*, Sept. 23, 1947; Peter Tamony): " 'Bean Ball' Is Fatal To S.F. Sandlotter." Compare *brushback pitch*; *knockdown pitch*. Also spelled "bean ball." Syn. *beaner*; *duster*, 1; *Rawlings lobotomy*. IST USE. 1905. "While pitching, Mr. [Chief] Bender places much reliance on the bean ball" (Charles Dryden, *The Athletics of 1905*; David Shulman). EXTENDED USE. A direct shot meant to do damage, often verbal. "Henry Wallace is winding up another bean ball for President Truman's foreign policy and expects to pitch it in Paris" (Lyle C. Wilson, *San Francisco News*, Apr. 16, 1947).

beanballer One who throws a beanball. "[Larry] Jansen, a married, mild-mannered patriarch, hardly seemed the type to be a beanballer" (Harvey Rosenfeld, *The Great Chase*, 1992, p.20).

beanball war Games between two teams characterized by potentially lethal retaliatory pitches thrown at batters' heads and bodies, often spread over several days. "Baseball must act to defuse beanball wars" (*Christian Science Monitor* headline, Aug. 3, 1987). Compare *brushback war*. Syn. *beanbrawl*.

beanbrawl A *beanball war*. The July 20, 1987, cover for *Sports Illustrated*: "Beanbrawls: baseball's headhunting wars get ugly."

Beaneaters Common nickname for various baseball teams from Boston, Mass.; e.g., the National League franchise from 1883 to 1906 (the club was renamed the Boston *Braves* in 1912) and the Players' League franchise in 1890. IST USE. 1880 (*Chicago Inter-Ocean*, June 29; Edward J. Nichols).

Beane Diff The difference between a team's on-base percentage and the on-base percentage its pitchers allow. The statistic honors Oakland Athletics general manager Billy Beane, an enthusiastic adherent of such analysis (Allen St. John, *The Wall Street Journal*, Oct. 18, 2004).

beaner 1. Syn. of *beanball*. 2. One who throws the beanball. Carl Mays was described as a "beaner with little regard for the consequences of his actions" (Mike Sowell, *The Pitch That Killed*, 1989, p.20). IST USE. 1912. "Bing! Up comes another 'beaner'" (Christy Mathewson, *Pitching in a Pinch*, 1912; David Shulman).

beanie Syn. of *batting helmet*.

bean up To take a greenie (amphetamine). "Players 'bean up' to enhance focus and alertness and to give their tired and sore bodies a jolt of energy" (*Sports Illustrated*, Dec. 12, 2004). Players prone to erratic mood swings during and immediately after games are often referred to as "beaned up." IST USE. 2002. "It's not uncommon for players to bean up in the clubhouse proper, rather than back rooms and training rooms that are off-limits to the media" (Tom Verducci, *Sports Illustrated*, June 3).

beany Said of a player who is a bit off mentally, a condition attributed to being hit in the head by a ball. "The beany is [a] condition similar to 'The Dance,' a disease among prizefighters struck on the head often" (Hugh S. Fullerton, *American Magazine*, June 1912).

Bearded Wonders A generic name for a renegade team. See also *House of David*.

bear down To exert total concentration and maximum effort in any aspect of the game; often applied when a pitcher gives his all and uses his last ounce of energy. See also *get naked*. IST USE. 1928. "The moment a pitcher starts to strain—'bearing down' we call it in

baseball—he becomes wild" (George Herman Ruth, *Babe Ruth's Own Book of Baseball*, 1928, p.42).

bear's nest A shabby hotel. ETYMOLOGY. This term has long been a bit of slang common to the Los Angeles Dodgers: it is part of the baseball language that Dodgers rookies learn on arriving at the team's spring training camp at Vero Beach, Fla (Fresco Thompson, quoted in *Los Angeles Times*, July 8, 1961).

beat out To reach a base slightly ahead of the fielded ball thrown to that baseman. It is implied that the batter-runner was fast enough to beat the throw. See also *leg out*, 1. IST USE. 1892 (*Brooklyn Daily Eagle*, May 1, p.4).

beat reporter A journalist who writes about a particular subject on a daily basis; specif., a sportswriter who covers a major-league team on a daily basis. One must be a beat reporter to become a member of the Baseball Writers' Association of America.

beat the ball Syn. of *beat the throw*.

beat the breezes *hist.* To swing at and miss a pitched ball. IST USE. 1912 (*New York Tribune*, Sept. 21; Edward J. Nichols).

beat the bushes To look for baseball talent in the minor (or bush) leagues. IST USE. 1913. "In these days of bitter competition for playing talent the only way to get players of promise is to 'beat the bushes' for them" (*The Washington Post*, July 27; Peter Morris).

beat the tag To reach a base before being touched by the ball in the gloved or bare hand of the fielder covering that base.

beat the throw To reach a base ahead of the ball. Syn. *beat the ball*. IST USE. 1892 (*Brooklyn Daily Eagle*, July 27; Edward J. Nichols).

beauty 1. A star player. "His [John McGraw's] $11,000 beauty, 'Rube' Marquard, who last season won nineteen straight games" (C.H. Claudy, *Technical World Magazine*, July 1913; Marquard's salary was $11,000). IST USE. 1895 (*Spalding's Official Base Ball Guide*, p.84; Edward J. Nichols). 2. A called strike that should have been hit out of the park. 3. A spectacular act of skill on the baseball field. IST USE. 1866

Beauty. Brooklyn Dodgers pitcher Rube Marquard, 1917. *George Grantham Bain Collection, Library of Congress*

(Chadwick scrapbook, Sept. 16; Edward J. Nichols).

beauty parlor hitter A player in the All-American Girls Professional Baseball League who "talks a good game."

beaver-shooting Ogling women at the park or in a hotel, or glimpsing a colleague having sex. This crude term was first discussed at length by Jim Bouton (*Ball Four*, 1970, pp.36–38, 183). Bouton wrote: "Beaver-shooting . . . can be anything from peering over the top of the dugout to look up dresses to hanging from the fire escape on the twentieth floor of some hotel to look into a window. I've seen guys chin themselves on transoms, drill holes in doors, even shove a mirror under a door. . . . In baseball if you shoot a particularly good beaver you are a highly respected person, one might even say a folk hero of sorts. Indeed, if you are caught out late at night and tell the manager you've had a good run of beaver-shooting he'd probably let you off with a light fine."

be ball A neologism used by Satchel Paige for the "only type" of pitch he threw because "it be where I want it to be" (John B. Holway, *The Washington Post*, July 7, 1991).

Beckett Short for *The Baseball Card Price Guide* by Dr. James Beckett and Dennis W. Eckes, the leading and most reliable price guide in baseball card collecting since 1979. The name "Beckett" has become an important point of reference in pricing cards; e.g., one card that is particularly hot may sell for "50 percent over Beckett" while run-of-the-mill cards sell "under the Beckett price."

beef 1. *n.* A loud and prolonged protest or complaint, esp. in response to an umpire's decision. "The beef resulted from a called strike on [Bobby] Thomson" (Harvey Rosenfeld, *The Great Chase*, 1992, p.148). ETYMOLOGY. According to Hy Turkin (*Baseball Almanac*, 1955), the protest or complaint sounds "as if noises come from lowing [mooing] cattle or beef." **2.** *v.* To protest or complain; to have a dispute with. IST USE. 1904. "The Senators raised a howl because [umpire Charles] King allowed the play to go through . . . and the 'beefing' resulted in the crowd menacing King as he left the field" (*The Washington Post*, Aug. 21; Peter Morris).

bee-liner A batted ball that travels fast and straight, not far from the ground; a low *line drive*. IST USE. 1900. "Newell scored on a bee-liner by Hamilton" (*Idaho* [Boise] *Daily Statesman*, May 3; Peter Morris).

beep baseball A variation of baseball played by the blind, featuring a sound-emitting ball and bases that buzz. Each team is allowed six at-bats per inning, and the opposing fielders must prevent three batters from getting on to end the inning. The National Beep Baseball Association sponsors a "world series" each year.

Beer and Whiskey League A nickname for the *American Association*, a major league from 1882 to 1891. The term referred to the league's tolerance of alcohol in its parks; several of its prominent backers were connected to the beverage industry. See David Nemec, *The Beer and Whisky League*, 1994. Also called "Beer Ball League."

beer league A semipro or lower baseball

league where everyone goes out for beer after a game. "Stocky and strong, [Jay] Gibbons looks like a beer league hitter" (John Manuel, *Baseball America*, Dec. 11–24, 2000; Peter Morris).

Beer Night A promotional event in which beer is sold at a game at a greatly reduced price. On June 4, 1974, the Cleveland Indians let their fans drink all the beer they could hold for ten cents a cup at Municipal Stadium; predictably, the fans became intoxicated and unruly, fighting with each other, the police, and the players, and forcing umpire Nestor Chylak to forfeit the game to the Texas Rangers after Cleveland tied the score at 5 in the bottom of the ninth (the crowd of 25,134 quaffed an estimated 60,000 cups).

Bees Nickname for the National League franchise in Boston from 1936 to 1940. The club reverted to Boston *Braves* in 1941.

bees in the hands An expression for the stinging sensation a batter's hands feel when a pitch strikes the handle or end of the bat, usually on a cold day against a pitcher throwing fastballs. Keith Hernandez (*Pure Baseball*, 1994, p.104) wrote about pitchers like Tom Henke who threw "heavy" balls that one must hit "in the sweetest part of the sweet spot to get any results. Otherwise, it's 'bees in the hands.'" Syn. "bees in the bat."

be gone Ballplayers' slang addressed to a home run (*Athletics*, Sept. 2005).

behind 1. *adv.* At a disadvantage; e.g., said of a team that is losing or of a pitcher with a count of more balls than strikes. Compare *ahead*. 2. *prep.* Supporting. "If things are going badly for a defensive team, the pitcher may be singled out as the target of derision, even though it may not be totally his fault, as in the situation that his team is making a lot of errors 'behind him'" (Lawrence Frank, *Playing Hardball*, 1983, p.105). 3. *adv./hist.* Said of the position or location of the catcher in early baseball. Catchers were said to be "playing behind," referring to an area of the field where a defender may be stationed; e.g., "It was now the Nationals' turn to take the field, and for the first time during the tour they had the right men in the right places.

George Wright playing short, Parker at second, and Robinson at left, with Norton behind, and Berthrong in the field" (Henry Chadwick, *The Game of Base Ball*, 1868, p.96; Paul Hunkele). 4. *n.* A term sometimes used by vintage base ball players for the catcher; however, there is no clear documentation that the term was used as a noun in the 1850s and 1860s. John Thorn (personal communication, Dec. 17, 2005) notes that one of the positions in a New York Knickerbockers intramural match on Thanksgiving Day 1848 was listed as "behind" and that the Knickerbockers used "one behind" in a match with the Empire club on Aug. 30, 1856.

behind in the count 1. Said of a pitcher when there are more balls than strikes on the batter. Compare *ahead in the count*, 1. Syn. *down in the count*. 2. Said of a batter with more strikes than balls. Compare *ahead in the count*, 2.

behind the ball See *stay behind the ball*.

behind the bat Syn. of *behind the plate*. IST USE. 1876. "The Clippers out-played the Reds . . . behind the bat" (*Winona* [Minn.] *Republican*, Aug. 25; Peter Morris).

behind the log Said of the catcher's position ("log" = bat). "['Tub'] Spencer's work sparkled while he was doing duty behind the log" (*San Francisco Bulletin*, March 8, 1913; Gerald L. Cohen).

behind the plate Said of the area of operation for the catcher and the plate umpire. Syn. *behind the bat*.

BEI Abbrev. for *batting eye index*.

béisbol Spanish for "baseball." The term is often used when Latin baseball is discussed. "People of Cuba have serious case of 'béisbol' fever" (*USA Today* headline, Apr. 29, 1987). See Michael M. Oleksak and Mary Adams Oleksak, *Béisbol: Latin Americans and the Grand Old Game*, 1996. IST USE. 1926. "'Béisbol' doesn't look it, or sound it, but it's 'baseball.' 'Béisbol,' newly coined word, meets up demands of Latin pronunciation for the game" (*The New York Times*, Apr. 5; Barry Popik).

belabor a pitcher For a team to get several hits off a pitcher.

bell cow The leader of a pitching staff. "The

Yankees still don't have what managers sometimes describe as a 'bellcow,' a starter who is a stopper, as Catfish Hunter was" (Dave Anderson, *The New York Times*, Dec. 11, 1988). Sometimes spelled "bellcow." Syn. *bellwether*. ETYMOLOGY. The head cow of a herd, which had a bell attached to its collar so that the herd might be located easily.

bells on Said of a ball that has been hit hard. IST USE. 1908 (*New York Evening Journal*, June 19; Edward J. Nichols).

bellwether Syn. of *bellcow*.

belly The front of the body, esp. the stomach. Dave Dravecky (*Comeback*, 1990, p.163) wrote that the expression "everybody on their bellies" meant "don't let anything through the infield" or "dive for the ball."

belly slide Syn. of *headfirst slide*. IST USE. 1944. "Eddie [Mota] lost his footing and did a beautiful belly-slide across the infield" (*Waukesha* [Wis.] *Freeman*, Sept. 20; Peter Morris).

belly whopper A *headfirst slide*, characterized by a long, airborne dive into the base. Dizzy Dean's definition (*Dizzy's Definitions*): "Hittin' the dirt head first on your stummick. Pepper Martin was the last great belly-whopper."

belt 1. *v.* To hit a ball hard. "Darnell Coles belted a two-run homer" (*Tampa Tribune*, March 4, 1989). IST USE. 1891 (*Chicago Herald*, Aug. 25; Edward J. Nichols). **2.** *n.* A ball that has been hit hard. IST USE. 1907 (*Harper's Weekly*, Dec. 14; Edward J. Nichols). **3.** *n.* A home run. "Two belts tie Sosa, McGwire" (*The Baltimore Sun* headline, Sept. 26, 1998), describing the occasion upon which Sammy Sosa and Mark McGwire each hit his 66th home run on Sept. 25, 1998. **4.** *v.* To win a baseball game decisively; e.g. "The Tigers belted the Yankees, 14 to 1."

belt ball An early style of leather ball, used in town ball and the formative years of baseball (1850s to 1870s), consisting of two circular pieces and a long rectangular strip, the latter placed around the circumference of the ball and the ends stitched together, with the circular pieces sewed to the sides of the strip. The configuration of the stitches formed an "H" pattern, unique to the belt ball. Syn. *H-style ball*. (Robert Loeffler)

belt-buckle ball A pitched ball that has been scratched or cut on the pitcher's belt buckle. The defacing of the ball makes it curve unnaturally, putting the batter at an unfair disadvantage. The umpire, detecting such a pitch, can eject the pitcher from the game.

belt-buckle catch Syn. of *basket catch*.

belter A home run hitter.

belt high Said of the location of a called strike at the batter's belt.

bench 1. *n.* The seating area in the dugout for a team's players, substitutes, and coaching staff. IST USE. 1881. "A new rule was made, requiring the erection of a players' bench, with hat-rack at each end, on each club's grounds" (*St. Louis Globe-Democrat*, Dec. 9). **2.** *n.* Syn. of *dugout*. **3.** *n.* Collectively, the players a team holds in reserve. Even though they don't sit on the bench, pinch hitters are part of the "bench" in this metaphorical sense. EXTENDED USE. The figurative location of those who are not participating or have been taken out of participation. "Blonde Miss North Gets Off Bench for First of Monroe Roles" (*Life* magazine sub headline on Sheree North getting a Marilyn Monroe role, March 21, 1955). **4.** *v.* For a manager to remove a player from the lineup for one or more games; to demote a starting player to the role of a substitute player. IST USE. 1902 (*The Sporting Life*, July 12; Edward J. Nichols). EXTENDED USE. To get rid of or demote; to remove from active participation. "You would have heard from me before now if I hadn't been . . . writing dialogue for Twentieth Century-Fox's *Cleopatra* . . . [b]ut now that I'm benched I can write" (letter from Nunnally Johnson to Groucho Marx, Feb. 7, 1960, collected in *The Letters of Nunnally Johnson*, 1981, p.182; Stuart Y. Silverstein). **5.** *v.* For an umpire to eject a player or manager. "The Cincinnati players kicked until [Charlie] Irwin, for using parlor language, was benched" (Tim Murnane, *Boston Globe*, Sept. 7, 1900; Peter Morris).

bench blanket Syn. of *benchwarmer*.

bench-bound Said of a player who is unable to play because of having been removed earlier from the lineup; e.g., "Smith was benchbound when his spot came up in the ninth."

bench brigade The full roster of a baseball team.

bench clearing *n.* A quick emptying of the dugout, leaving an empty bench in its wake. It can be prompted by a brawl on the field or by the umpire, who can clear the bench to retain control over the game.

bench-clearing *adj.* Said of an incident (such as a melee or brawl) in which players of both teams come out of their dugouts. "Two of the four bench-clearing fights the Mets were involved in this summer were started by [Ray] Knight" (*The Washington Post*, Oct. 17, 1986).

bench coach A coach who assists or advises the manager from the bench. His duties include serving as a confidant or sounding board for the manager during games, suggesting specific plays or substitutions, acting as a liaison between the manager and the players, and running the team if the manager is absent or ejected. Such a coach is also often viewed as a "manager-in-waiting." Ted Williams is credited with creating the position when he was managing the Washington Senators (1969–1971), although the term did not begin to appear in print until later. "[Minnesota] Twins manager Tom Kelly cannot understand the . . . creation of 'bench coach.' Doesn't a bench coach do what a manager should be doing, Kelly has asked" (Gerry Fraley, *Baseball America*, Dec. 27, 1999–Jan. 9, 2000; Peter Morris). Syn. *dugout coach*. IST USE. 1985. "The New York Yankees announced the hiring of . . . Joe Altobelli as bench coach" (*The Washington Post*, Nov. 15).

bench jockey 1. One who verbally abuses or yells derisive comments at opposing players or umpires from the safety of the dugout. Bruce Catton (*American Heritage*, Apr. 1959) called such a player "the man who will say anything at all if he thinks it will upset an enemy's poise." Bench jockeys began to disappear in the late 1960s; the emergence of a strong players' union turned players into "brothers." Mark Kram (*Detroit Free Press*, Apr. 3, 1983): "The bench jockey has gone the way of the three-fingered glove. Etiquette disallows such conduct from the contemporary player, and in a way it is as if

something has been torn from the fabric of the game." See also *jockey*, 1. Syn. *dugout jockey*. 2. A substitute who rides the bench or seldom gets to play; a *benchwarmer*. IST USE. 1939. "The doctor's orders were soon grapevined around the league, and all the bench jockeys on the circuit were quickly counting ten [i.e., keeping quiet] on every pitch Lefty made" (Gordon S. "Mickey" Cochrane, *Baseball: The Fans' Game*, 1939; David Shulman).

bench manager A nonplaying manager. "Bench managers who, if wise, direct and counsel rather than order their men" (John J. Evers and Hugh S. Fullerton, *Touching Second: The Science of Baseball*, 1910). IST USE. 1904. "Ed Barrow is the first bench manager Montreal has had" (*The Washington Post*, Aug. 14; Peter Morris).

bench player A utility player who is always ready to replace a starting player who is injured or whose performance is faltering. "Bench players can keep a team flying high when injuries or batting slumps strike the regulars" (William Gildea, *The Washington Post*, Aug. 29, 1997).

bench polisher A substitute player whose constant presence on the bench is said to "polish" it.

bench strength An array of competent players on the bench who are available for play if and when needed. "In a trade to help their bench strength, the New York Mets obtained utilityman Pat Tabler from the Kansas City Royals" (*Tampa Tribune*, Aug. 31, 1990).

benchwarmer A substitute player whose constant presence sitting on the bench is said to "warm" it. "The days for 'bench warmers' with salaries are also past" (*Sporting Times*, Jan. 9, 1892). Sometimes spelled "bench warmer." Syn. *bench blanket*; *bench jockey*, 2; *rider of the lonesome pine*. IST USE. 1887. "Mr. Benchwarmer—Well, the base-ball season is nearly over. Mrs. Benchwarmer—Well, what of it?" (*Philadelphia Call*, quoted in *Chicago Daily Tribune*, Oct. 9). EXTENDED USE. 1. A judge (who also sits on a bench) is sometimes called a "benchwarmer." A book on judges by Joseph C. Goulden is entitled *The Benchwarmers* (1974). 2. A wallflower at a dance. "Every member of the championship team was there and there was not a benchwarmer among them, each taking a fair partner in the dance" (*The Boston Daily Globe*, Apr. 17, 1915).

benchwarming 1. *n.* Sitting in the dugout. "The most unplayed, but not unpaid, athlete of his time, Charlie [Silvera], as Yogi Berra's stand-in with the Yankees, collected over $50,000 in bonus pelf for six World Series, during which he did nothing but practice the gentle art of bench warming" (Jack McDonald, *San Francisco Call-Bulletin*, Sept. 23, 1960). Sometimes spelled "bench warming." IST USE. 1902. "Drill is as good for a recruit as Clarke is for a veteran, has hit for .281, and is excusable by reason of bench warming" (Paul W. Eaton, *The Sporting Life*, Aug. 30; Peter Morris). 2. *adj.* Said of a benchwarmer. Sometimes spelled "bench-warming." "[John] McGraw took the place of his unwilling bench-warming predecessor" (*New York Sun*, Apr. 21, 1903; Peter Morris).

bend 1. *n.* A curveball. IST USE. 1904. "Persons who have seen him [Nap Lajoie] warm up . . . say that they believe he could give many a slab artist points on the delivery of bends and shoots" (*The Washington Post*, Sept. 25; Peter Morris). 2. *v.* "[To] curve the ball" (*The Sporting News*, Oct. 30, 1913).

bender 1. A curveball. "[Rube Marquard] possesses great speed and a wonderful array of benders" (Alfred H. Spink, *The National Game*, 2nd ed., 1911, p.139). IST USE. 1899. "The [Kid] Nichols curve is none if your roundhouse benders, but a quick-breaking upward shoot that is harder to negotiate than it looks" (Buck Freeman, quoted in *The Washington Post*, Oct. 15; Peter Morris). USAGE NOTE. Parke Cummings (*The Dictionary of Baseball*, 1950) claimed that the term is "not often used in modern times"; however, STATS Inc. (*The Scouting Notebook*, 2000) described Andruw Jones as "a dead fastball hitter . . . [who] also laid off the steady diet of benders and offspeed pitches that came his way," and *Baseball America* (Dec. 24, 2001–Jan. 6, 2002) noted that Bobby Bradley's "best pitch is a curveball and he throws two different kinds, a big bender and one with a shorter break." 2. *hist.*

A curveball pitcher. Portland pitcher Bill James was described as "the long, lean bender of breaks" (*San Francisco Bulletin*, Apr. 11, 1913; Gerald L. Cohen).

benefit game An exhibition game, usually played to raise funds for the family of a deceased player or for some other worthy cause. Among the earliest benefit games were two played in New York City on July 26 and Aug. 7, 1870, for *New York Tribune* baseball reporter William Picott, who had died suddenly at age 31, leaving a widow and four children (Peter Morris).

Bengals Nickname for the Detroit *Tigers*. The term was commonly used before about 1950; its usage slipped after the Cincinnati Bengals joined the then-American Football League.

bent-leg slide A slide in which a runner bends both legs when approaching a base. Syn. *figure-4 slide*.

bereavement list A list of players who are unable to render services because of the serious or severe illness or death of a member of the player's immediate family (spouse, parent, grandparent, sibling, child, or grandchild). The bereavement policy was introduced beginning with the 2003 season. The minimum period of placement on the list is three consecutive days; the maximum period is seven consecutive days. During the period of placement, the club may replace the bereaved player on its roster. A player on the bereavement list is not counted on the club's active roster but is included on its reserve list; the player receives salary and service time while on the list.

berm The sloping grassy knolls that overlook the outfield fences in many ballparks. Dell Diamond in Round Rock, Tex., "currently has seating for . . . 3,500 more fans on the grass berm beyond the outfield" (*Baseball America*, July 7–20, 2003; Peter Morris).

Bermuda Triangle An area between the infield and outfield where batted balls are "lost" and become base hits. "[Tom Pagnozzi] dropped a Bermuda Triangle single among three defenders at the right-field line" (*St. Louis Post-Dispatch*, July 24, 1993). "The area in short right field [at the Seattle Kingdome] is still so notorious for lost pop flies that it is known as The Bermuda Triangle. Two foul balls have gone up but have never come down; both were ruled strikes" (Philip J. Lowry, *Green Cathedrals*, 1992, p.88; Peter Morris). ETYMOLOGY. The triangular area in the Atlantic Ocean, bounded by Bermuda, Puerto Rico, and Melbourne (Fla.), in which ships and aircraft have supposedly disappeared mysteriously.

Berraism Syn. of *Yogiism*.

berth 1. A player's position on a team. IST USE. 1908 (*Baseball Magazine*, September; Edward J. Nichols). 2. A team's position in the standings. "[The Orioles] may not even be that far from competing for a wild-card berth" (Peter Schmuck, *The Baltimore Sun*, July 26, 2006). IST USE. 1910 (*Baseball Magazine*, May; Edward J. Nichols). USAGE NOTE. Peter Morris suggests that the term originally designated a position in the standings in either the first division or the second division; e.g., "The White Sox . . . finished in the first division when they generally had been picked for a lower berth" (*Chicago Tribune*, Apr. 6, 1913) and "There did not appear to be a chance for anything but a second division berth . . . when the season opened" (Chandler Richter, *The Sporting Life*, Sept. 4, 1915). This meaning was derived from the various classes of tickets for travelers on ships and trains; it has particular pertinence to baseball in that veteran players usually obtained lower berths in the sleeping cars of their trains.

BESR Abbrev. for *ball exit speed ratio*.

best To defeat the opposing team. IST USE. 1912 (*New York Tribune*, Sept. 6; Edward J. Nichols).

best interests The legal empowerment that gives the commissioner of baseball the jurisdiction to act on any matter, transaction, or practice that involves the integrity of, or public confidence in, the game of baseball. Conduct not considered to be in the "best interests" of baseball includes instances in which players or others attempt to lose baseball games intentionally, fail to perform and compete at all times to the best of their abilities, bribe competing clubs or umpires, or gamble on baseball games. The term "best interests" appears in the Major League Constitution (Art. II, Sect. 2b), the National Association Agreement (Art. 18), and the Professional Baseball Agreement (Art. II[B]).

best-of-five Describing the means of determining the modern Division Series playoff format in which the first team to win three games advances to the Championship Series.

best-of-seven Describing the means of determining the modern League Championship Series playoff (since 1985) and World Series format in which the first team to win four games is the champion.

bēsubōru Japanese for "baseball." Baseball was introduced to Japan in 1872 by Horace Wilson. Starting in 1908, several U.S. professional teams made tours of Japan (one of these was Babe Ruth's 1934 tour) and played against amateur teams consisting mostly of university students. Two professional teams were established in 1920. Currently, Japanese professional baseball consists of two major leagues of six teams each—the *Central League* and the *Pacific League*, which form Nihon Professional Baseball—and two minor leagues (the Eastern League and the Western League). Beginning in 2007 the two major leagues schedule 144 regular-season games, with the winners of each league's playoffs meeting in the best-of-seven Japan (Nihon) Series to determine the champion. Interleague play began in 2005. Games may end in a tie after 12 innings. Compared with its American counterpart, Japanese baseball is more rigorous and disciplined and less aggressive, with fewer home runs, more sacrifice hits, a strike zone that is larger near the batter but smaller away from the batter, and a ball that is slightly smaller and wound tighter. Teams are usually named after their corporate owners/sponsors, rather than the cities in which they play, and are allowed to have up to four foreigners (gaijin) on the roster (two position players and two pitchers). Japanese baseball emphasizes effort, tradition, practice, and teamwork. Robert Whiting (*You Gotta Have Wa*, 1989, p.49) considered Japanese baseball "as clear an expression of the Japanese character as one could find, reflecting the real life and spirit of the people."

be-there play A play in which a fielder throws the ball to a place where a teammate will be when the ball arrives, such as a catcher throwing to second base with the knowledge that the second baseman or shortstop is on his way to cover the bag.

betsy A baseball bat. "[Al] Simmons generally swung a big brown betsy" (Bob Broeg, *The Sporting News*, June 26, 1971). See also *Black Betsy*.

between-innings commentator A baseball announcer who fills in with baseball talk and trivia between innings.

between the lines Syn. of *between the white lines*. "Ryne Sandberg was . . . a between-the-lines gamer who checked his personality . . . at the clubhouse door" (*Sports Illustrated*, June 20, 1994).

between the seams The location, on the surface of a pitched ball, of the spot most advantageous for the batter to hit. IST USE. 1910 (*American Magazine*, July; Edward J. Nichols).

between the white lines On the field of play; the location of the action of the game itself, as opposed to off-the-field activity. The "white lines" are the foul lines, which both physically and symbolically mark the realm of the actual game itself. Players have been known to say that what another player does off the field is his own business and that all that matters is what goes on "between the white lines." Television critic Ken Hoffman criticized Dodgers announcer Vin Scully by saying, "If it's not between the white lines, Scully pretends it doesn't exist" (*Houston Post*, June 27, 1987; Charles D. Poe). Chicago White Sox outfielder Albert Belle (quoted in *The Baltimore Sun*, Feb. 21, 1997): "Once I step between the white lines, I can't control what people think of me, but I can hit home runs, drive in some runs, steal a few bases and make a couple of spectacular catches. That's all I'm concerned about." Probably the most famous line using the phrase was uttered by pitcher Early Wynn: "That space between the white lines—that's my office. That's where I conduct my business." See also *white lines*. Syn. *between the lines*. USAGE NOTE. Implied in the term is

baseball isolationism. "At the conclusion of every baseball storm—be it a strike or a rash of drug busts or the latest contract hassle—players and executives fall back on that old bromide: 'All that really matters is what goes on between the white lines'" (*Sports Illustrated*, Feb. 27, 1984). EXTENDED USE. On the field of play in other sports. National Football League safety Will Demps (quoted in *The Baltimore Sun*, Aug. 12, 2006): "After you get that first hit in, it's just another football game, which is played between the white lines."

BFP Abbrev. for *batters facing pitcher.*

BFW Abbrev. for *batter-fielder wins.*

B game **1.** A game played by team aspirants during spring training. "B games are games that the clubs occasionally schedule so they can give some playing time to second-stringers and also get a look at rookies up from the minors for a tryout" (William Zinsser, *Spring Training*, 1989, pp.128–29). B games are also scheduled to give the pitchers some work since all teams have large staffs during spring training. **2.** The baseball game that is telecast in the home markets of the clubs participating in the *A game*; also, the backup game that is aired in the event the A game is rained out or delayed.

BH Abbrev. for *base hit*, 2.

biangular Spanish for "double."

Bible hitter A hitter who swings at the first pitch. Preacher Roe (quoted in Carl Erskine, *Tales from the Dodger Dugout*, 2000, p.110): "That feller is a dead first-ball hitter: Thou shall not pass."

Bible of Baseball Moniker for *The Sporting News*, a tabloid newspaper established in St. Louis in 1886 by Alfred Henry Spink to cover all sporting events and even some theater; it portrayed itself as "The Base Ball Paper of the World." The publication changed its focus in the early 20th century under the direction of Charles Spink (Alfred's brother) to cover primarily baseball. Syn. *baseball's Bible.*

biff **1.** *v./hist.* To bat a ball hard. "He has biffed triples" (*The World* [New York], June 26, 1889; Gerald L. Cohen). IST USE. 1888. "Biff, biff, biff" (*The World* [New York], June 7, 1888; Gerald L. Cohen). ETYMOLOGY.

Bible of Baseball. President John F. Kennedy is shown with Dave Powers, his unofficial "undersecretary for baseball," who is in the middle of the group consulting *The Sporting News*. To Powers' left is Senators general manager Ed Doherty. Behind JFK's right shoulder is White House aide Lawrence O'Brien. This was Kennedy's first opener and the last ever staged at Griffith Stadium. *John Fitzgerald Kennedy Presidential Library*

Coined by William T. Hall, a Chicago sports reporter, according to H.L. Mencken (*The American Language*, 1919). **2.** *n./hist.* A long base hit. "One gigantic biff and the ball went down through center" (Alfred H. Spink, *The National Game*, 2nd ed., 1911, p.248). **3.** *v.* To make an error. "[Alex Rodriguez] biffs a play" (Chris Ballard, *Sports Illustrated*, July 31, 2006, p.18).

biffer *hist.* A hard-hitting batter. IST USE. 1908 (*New York Evening Journal*, Feb. 24; Edward J. Nichols).

biff stick *hist.* A baseball bat. IST USE. 1908 (*New York Evening Journal*, March 16; Edward J. Nichols).

big arena *hist.* Syn. of *major leagues*. "If [Elliott] does not enter the big arena in 1914 it will only be because he does not take proper care of himself during the summer" (*San Francisco Bulletin*, Feb. 1, 1913; Gerald L. Cohen).

big as a balloon Said of a slowly pitched ball that is very easy to hit. IST USE. 1910 (*American Magazine*, June; Edward J. Nichols).

big ball **1.** Playing the game of baseball with an emphasis on home runs and extra-base hits. "Big-ball Yankees belt 2 more HRs, 118 for year" (*The Baltimore Sun*, June 26, 2002). Compare *little ball*, 1. **2.** [softball term] An early name for softball.

big bang theory The assumption that, in a majority of games, the winning team scores as many or more runs in one inning than the losing team scores in the whole game; the notion that baseball is a game of *big innings*. The name was applied to the theory by Thomas Boswell (*How Life Imitates the World Series*, 1982, p.71), and given impetus by Earl Weaver's hypothesis that pitching, defense, and three-run home runs win baseball games. Research by David W. Smith (*By the Numbers*, June 1992) has suggested that big bangs generally occur when the losing team scores only one or two runs and are, therefore, more a function of good pitching than of big innings.

big bat A club's leading hitter. "[Von Hayes] has become the big bat in [the] Philadelphia lineup after the retirement of Mike Schmidt" (*St. Petersburg Times*, March 24, 1990).

Big Bertha **1.** The *cleanup hitter*; the fourth

player in the batting order. **2.** A vastly oversized catcher's mitt that was designed by Baltimore Orioles manager Paul Richards to make it easier for Gus Triandos to handle Hoyt Wilhelm's most unpredictable knuckleball. The mitt (Wilson model #1050 CL) was 45 inches in circumference and would be illegal today because of a 1965 rule stipulating that no glove can have a circumference of more than 38 inches. **3.** A favorite bat. In 1927, Babe Ruth referred to his ash-blonde bat as "Big Bertha." **4.** A colossal base hit. When Babe Ruth became the first and only player ever to hit a home run into the old, wooden center-field bleachers at the Polo Grounds, *The New York Times* (June 14, 1921) wrote: "The Babe had had it upon his mind to perpetrate this Big Bertha shot for some time, but never seemed to get around to it." ETYMOLOGY. "Big Bertha" was the nickname for the German army's mammoth 420-millimeter gun of World War I. It was named for Bertha Krupp, the sole heir to the Krupp armament empire.

Big Bill 1. A slow-hopping ground ball that the batter-runner is able to beat out. Ty Cobb (*My Life in Baseball*, 1961, p.150) cited the 1890s Baltimore Orioles for perfecting the "Big Bill": "You chopped the ball into the ground deliberately—infielders were forced to charge the lazy bounders and throw on the run, or lose their man." ETYMOLOGY. Edward J. Nichols (*An Historical Dictionary of Baseball Terminology*, Jan. 1939, p.7) cited a letter from *The Sporting News* (Apr. 15, 1937) that asserted that the term was named for third baseman Bill Bradley (who played for several teams between 1899 and 1915), who hit many such bounders. **2.** The final hop of an easily fielded ground ball, so named because it bounces as high as the bill on a crouched infielder's cap.

big bounce Syn. of *bounder*.

big brush *hist.* Syn. of *major leagues*. "Duffy Lewis . . . knows that he will have a whole lot of running around to do before the season opens in the big brush" (*San Francisco Bulletin*, March 5, 1913; Gerald L. Cohen).

big circus *hist.* Syn. *major leagues*. "[Joe] Berger . . . is anxious to take another whirl into the big circus" (*San Francisco Bulletin*, Feb. 4, 1913; Gerald L. Cohen).

big classic Syn. of *World Series*. IST USE. 1915 (*Baseball Magazine*, December; Edward J. Nichols).

big club A major-league baseball club. "You have to picture Lou Gehrig as an awkward twenty year old the day he joined the 'big club'" (Eleanor Gehrig, *My Luke and I*, 1976, p.108; Charles D. Poe).

big company *hist.* Syn. of *major leagues*. IST USE. 1912 (*New York Tribune*, Sept. 22; Edward J. Nichols).

big cut A full swing for power, used when the batter may be trying to hit a home run.

big dance The *World Series*.

big E Short for *earned run average*.

big eater A hitter who will hit for power rather than slash balls down the line or into the gaps. The term is often used by scouts for corner infielders (Alan Schwarz, Baseball America.com, Nov. 14, 2006).

big fly A *home run*, especially in the 1980s and early 1990s. R.J. Reynolds (Scripps Howard News Service, Sept. 9, 1986), facetiously: "The home run. But . . . no one calls it by such an outdated term. That would be like saying someone was *cool* or *groovy*. Today, you hit *the big fly*." See also *go big fly*. Syn. *large fly*.

Big Four 1. Four star players (A.G. Spalding, Deacon White, Cal McVey, and Ross Barnes) on Boston's four-time championship team of the National Association of Professional Base Ball Players who covertly signed 1876 contracts with Chicago during the 1875 season. This led to the end of the National Association and the formation of the National League. **2.** Four star players (Deacon White, Dan Brouthers, Hardy Richardson, and Jack Rowe) whom Buffalo attempted to sell to the Detroit Wolverines. Although the transfer was temporarily blocked, it eventually went through after the 1885 season. The move led to the dissolution of the Buffalo team and propelled Detroit to the 1887 World's Championship.

biggies 1. The members of the front office of

a baseball team. "[The lone holdout] demands a pay hike, or salary boost . . . from baseball's biggies" (Frank Sullivan, "The Cliché Expert Testifies on Baseball" [short story], *The New Yorker*, Aug. 27, 1949; Peter Morris). **2.** Syn. of *major leagues*.

big gun 1. A team's best slugger. IST USE. 1902 (*The Sporting Life*, Sept. 27; Edward J. Nichols). **2.** A team's ace pitcher. IST USE. 1913. "One of the big guns of the American League is Vean Gregg, who . . . is going like a streak of Nebraska wind" (*San Francisco Bulletin*, Apr. 19, 1913; Gerald L. Cohen).

big hit 1. A key hit; a hit in the clutch. IST USE. 1877. "[Bennett] made the big hit of the game—a clean two-baser" (*Milwaukee Daily Sentinel*, May 14). **2.** A home run. IST USE. 1922 (*Spalding's Official Base Ball Guide*, p.40; Edward J. Nichols). **3.** A very popular player. "[Cy] Parkins is a big hit with the natives here and they go out of their way to extend him courtesies" (*San Francisco Bulletin*, March 3, 1913; Gerald L. Cohen).

big hop A batted ball that takes a high bounce and is easy to play, as it allows the fielder to watch the ball and predict where the bounce will take it.

big inning An inning in which at least three runs are scored by one team. "The [Red] Sox played for the big inning and a sensational victory. Stuffy [McInnis] blazed away at the ball, abhorring the sacrifice" (Burt Whitman, *Boston Herald and Journal*, Sept. 7, 1918; Peter Morris). The big inning often occurs as the result of home runs being hit with runners on base. Big innings are relatively rare. Research by David W. Smith (*By the Numbers*, June 1992) showed that during the period from 1984 through 1991, only 2.5 percent of innings in American League (AL) games and 2 percent of innings in National League (NL) games met the definition; or, big innings occurred about once every four AL games and once every five NL games during that interim. This finding implies that if a team achieves a big inning then it will probably win the game; in support of that implication, prior to the 1986 World Series, *USA Today* (Oct. 17, 1986) reported that teams that have had big innings during previ-ous World Series games had a 40-7 (.851) record. See also *big bang theory*. IST USE. 1880. " 'The end crowns the work' in most things, but in base ball it's the big-inning" (*Cincinnati Commercial*, reprinted in *The Galveston Daily News*, July 20). USAGE NOTE. The term comes into play in a well-worn baseball riddle: Where is baseball mentioned in the Bible? Answer: Genesis ("In the beginning [Big Inning] . . . ").

big knock A home run. "Relief pitcher Tom Niedenfeur, who gives up home runs by the bushel . . . is going to a place [ballpark] where big knocks are a way of life" (*Tampa Tribune*, Dec. 11, 1988).

big-league 1. *adj.* Syn. of *major-league*. "A pitcher who can stand up against their sallies is capable of doing the twirling for a 'big' league club" (*San Francisco Examiner*, Apr. 23, 1888; Peter Morris). EXTENDED USE. Said of the highest level in any given field; major, large, important; e.g., "a big-league appetite." "Tammany is a patriotic institution. If it had put forward a big league candidate the interest in the campaign might have diverted public attention from the war" (Franklin P. Adams, *New York Tribune*, Aug. 21, 1917, p.9; Stuart Y. Silverstein). **2.** *v.* To act superior based upon being, or having been, a major league baseball player. "Players try to own this game. But the players know they're not going to big-league me. . . . I'm the man here" (Chicago White Sox manager Ozzie Guillen, quoted in *Sports Illustrated*, Feb. 20, 2006). "He hasn't big-leagued it. Ruben [Rivera] has been very professional here, very humble" (Bowie Baysox manager Dave Trembley, quoted in *Baltimore Sun*, Aug. 18, 2003).

big league *n.* Syn. of *major league*, 1. IST USE. 1882. "The American Base Ball Association threatens to bark savagely at the big league [National League]. Players know on which side their bread is buttered" (*The Cleveland Herald*, Aug. 28). ETYMOLOGY. Under the heading "Baseball Language in the 1890s," Bill James (*Bill James Historical Baseball Abstract*, 1986) stated, "The term 'big league' apparently referred originally to the size of the one major league [National

League], which had twelve teams in it. But . . . 'big league' came to stand for . . . 'major league.'"

big league-itis A tendency toward arrogant or condescending behavior (such as not taking instructions) by a major-league player. "[Dontrelle Willis] seems refreshingly immune from big league-itis" (Jerry Crasnick, *Baseball America*, Aug. 4–17, 2003; Peter Morris).

big leaguer 1. Syn. of *major leaguer*. IST USE. 1908. "Major league teams . . . are frequently beaten in the spring by teams which do not class with them, because the big leaguers do not exert themselves" (*The Washington Post*, Apr. 1; Peter Morris). 2. A flashy player who calls attention to himself.

big leagues Syn. of *major leagues*. IST USE. 1889. "The [Lee Base Ball Club] is one of the foremost of amateur clubs, and during its existence has turned out many fine ball tossers, who are now members of the big leagues" (*Brooklyn Eagle*, Dec. 12; Peter Morris). USAGE NOTE. Peter Morris notes that the term fell into disuse in the 1890s when there was only one major league. It was revived after the American League gained recognition as a legitimate major league. EXTENDED USE. An area of greatest competition, achievement, or rewards. "The Baltimore Symphony Orchestra . . . is very definitely in the big leagues" (*Baltimore Sun*, Oct. 13, 2002). "NBC . . . tabbed [Greg] Kinnear [to host a late-night talk show], and he moved into the big leagues" (*People* magazine, Nov. 10, 2002).

Big Mac Affectionate nickname for the 10 editions (1969–1996) of *The Baseball Encyclopedia* published by the Macmillan Publishing Co. See also *Macmillan*. ETYMOLOGY. From the popular McDonald's hamburger.

big-market club Syn. of *large-market club*.

big mitt 1. Syn. of *catcher's mitt*. "[Oakland catcher] Hust . . . handles the big mitt dexterously for a new hand" (*San Francisco Bulletin*, Feb. 27, 1913). IST USE. 1905 (*The Sporting Life*, Oct. 7, p.18, as "big mit"; Edward J. Nichols). 2. Any oversized catcher's glove that was designed to reduce the frequency of passed balls. "Orioles catcher

Clint Courtney used the 'big mitt' for the first time [May 27, 1960] to catch knuckleball pitcher Hoyt Wilhelm" (*The Baltimore Sun*, May 27, 2004).

big one 1. A ball pitched to a batter after two strikes have been called on him. IST USE. 1907 (*New York Evening Journal*, n.d.; Edward J. Nichols). 2. A putout at first base. 3. The last out of an inning. 4. A home run. "[Frank Howard] did confide . . . this spring that he had set a new goal and thought he could hit 'at least 40 big ones'" (*The Washington Post*, Apr. 11, 1969).

big out A putout at an important or crucial time in a game. "There are always a couple of big outs in every game" (Baltimore Orioles pitcher Ben McDonald, quoted in *The Baltimore Sun*, May 6, 1996).

Big Red Machine Nickname for the Cincinnati Reds in the middle to late 1970s. The moniker was more commonly used when the team was playing well, such as when the Reds won back-to-back World Series in 1975 and 1976.

Bigs, the Syn. of *major leagues*. "Just think what Joe DiMaggio would have accomplished if he'd played more than 13 seasons in the Bigs" (*The Baltimore Sun*, March 9, 1999). Sometimes lowercased as "the bigs."

big series Syn. of *World Series*. IST USE. 1920 (*Baseball Magazine*, November; Edward J. Nichols).

big show 1. Syn. of *major leagues*. "Sid Smith of the St. Louis Americans . . . stated that he was glad to get back to Atlanta as he did not care about the big show, anyhow" (*The Sporting News*, March 11, 1909; Peter Morris). Sometimes spelled "Big Show." See also *Show, the*. IST USE. 1907 (*New York Evening Journal*, Apr. 8; Edward J. Nichols). EXTENDED USE. Highest level of competition in any endeavor. 2. Syn. of *World Series*. IST USE. 1911. "Since [Larry Cheney] is reporting before Sept. 1 he may qualify to participate in the big show if the Cubs win the National League pennant" (*Indianapolis Star*, Aug. 28; Peter Morris). EXTENDED USE. The Super Bowl of the National Football League.

big smoke *hist.* Syn. of *major leagues*. IST

USE. 1908 (*Baseball Magazine*, November; Edward J. Nichols)

big stick 1. A baseball bat. "Joe Jackson, they say, cannot write, but he is inscribing his name on the tablets of baseball fame with that big stick of his" (*San Francisco Bulletin*, May 31, 1913; Gerald L. Cohen). IST USE. 1908. "The Giants suddenly got out the 'big sticks' and swatted the ball with such continuity and vigor that they piled up an even dozen runs" (*New York Herald*, May 5; Peter Morris). ETYMOLOGY. The term probably entered baseball in the wake of Theodore Roosevelt's line delivered on Sept. 2, 1901, at the Minnesota State Fair: "Speak softly and carry a big stick." **2.** A heavy hitter; one given to hitting home runs and extra-base hits. "They [St. Louis Cardinals] desperately need a big stick in the middle of their lineup, someone who can serve as the cop on the block, so to speak, for [Whitey] Herzog's conga line of rabbits" (Joe Henderson, *Tampa Tribune*, Jan. 15, 1989).

big team The parent major-league club as viewed by a minor leaguer.

big tent Syn. of *major leagues.* "Hap Hogan sent two catchers last year into the big tent" (*San Francisco Bulletin*, May 7, 1913; Gerald L. Cohen). The term is an obvious reference to the circus. IST USE. 1908. "Every one of these earnest athletes should make good under the big tent" (*Frederick* [Md.] *News*, Aug. 8; *OED*).

big time Syn. of *major leagues.* "Manager [Lee] Fohl opines that both of these athletes will be ready for the 'big time' after a season with Milwaukee" (*The Sporting Life*, Jan. 20, 1917; Peter Morris). IST USE. 1914 (*New York Tribune*, Oct. 11; Edward J. Nichols).

Big Time A player who has a major impact on the game; a leader among ballplayers. "Kirk Gibson . . . [is] what players call 'Big Time.' Others play the game. He means to change it" (Thomas Boswell, *The Washington Post*, Oct. 11, 1988). Chicago Cubs manager Dusty Baker (quoted in *The Baltimore Sun*, Jan. 9, 2006) referred to Andre Dawson (who "played on sheer guts and bad knees") as a "big-time player."

big-timer Syn. of *major leaguer.*

big top *hist.* Syn. of *major leagues.* The term is an obvious reference to the circus. IST USE. 1927. "It wouldn't surprise me to hear of [umpire Bill Rudolph] calling balls and strikes under the 'big top' within a few years" (*The Sporting News*, Feb. 3; Peter Morris).

big W A victory, based on the abbreviation "W" for a win achieved by a team or a pitcher. Jim Bouton (*Ball Four*, 1970, p.155): "I ended up with my first big W, as we baseball players call it. It was my first major-league win earned with the knuckleball."

big yard *hist.* Syn. of *major leagues.* IST USE. 1913. "During his [Grover Cleveland Alexander] first season in the big yard he won 27 [*sic*] games and lost 13" (*San Francisco Bulletin*, Feb. 26; Gerald L. Cohen).

bill 1. *n.* A game in the schedule. IST USE. 1912 (*New York Tribune*, Sept. 8; Edward J. Nichols). **2.** *v./hist.* To schedule a game. IST USE. 1902 (*The Sporting Life*, July 12, p.5; Edward J. Nichols). **3.** *n.* The visor of a baseball cap. **4.** *n.* A .100 batting average. A player who is hitting .300 is said to be hitting "three bills."

billet A piece of wood that will be developed into a baseball bat.

Bill Hassemer bounce *hist.* A positive situation that turns out badly. Edward J. Nichols (*An Historical Dictionary of Baseball Terminology*, Jan. 1939, p.7) defines the term as "a batted ground ball that bounds high and squarely into a fielder's glove." *The Sporting News* (Feb. 24, 1910; Peter Morris) discussed various theories of the etymology of this term, noting the one that appeared "most authentic" to be that of sportswriter Charles Dryden, who coined the term by incorrectly referring to Bill "Hassemer" (the player's real name was spelled "Hassamaer"), who was with Louisville "when everything was going wrong—about 1899." *The Sporting News* explained, "He hit a ball that passed through the pitcher's hands to the second baseman, who also muffed it, allowing Hassemer to reach second. That same night Hassemer was released to Columbus, and the idea got around that even what appeared to be good fortune couldn't counterbalance Bill Hassemer's natural bad luck. Hence, a 'Bill Hassemer bounce' was applied to a seemingly 'easy-money' chance that, somehow, went wrong." While Hassamaer did not play for Louisville in 1899, he did play for both Louisville and Columbus during the 1896 season. His first game with Columbus took place on July 12.

billiard A batted ball that hits the ground in front of the plate and rolls back toward the batter, exhibiting the same kind of reverse spin produced by a billiard ball. IST USE. 1937 (*Pittsburgh Press*, Jan. 4; Edward J. Nichols).

Bill Klem Any person in baseball who avers that he is never wrong. ETYMOLOGY. An eponym for infallibility inspired by Hall of Fame umpire Bill Klem, who is credited with several statements in which he never admits a bad call; e.g., "It ain't nothin' till I call it" and "Gentlemen, he was out because I said he was out."

Bill Klem Award An award given for service as an "outstanding umpire." It was first presented in 1962 and honors one of baseball's greatest umpires.

Bill Slocum Memorial Award An award to honor a person who made a "high contribution to baseball over a long period" (or "long and meritorious service to baseball"). It was

Bill Klem. The Hall of Fame umpire (pictured here in 1914) who worked in 18 separate World Series. *George Grantham Bain Collection, Library of Congress*

created in 1929 by the Baseball Writers' Association of America and was first awarded (posthumously) to Miller Huggins. Al Schacht (the "Clown Prince of Baseball") received the 1946 award for his work with the USO during World War II.

Billy Ball The style of aggressive, alert, intimidating, and fan-pleasing baseball practiced by Alfred Manuel "Billy" Martin in his various terms as manager for five major-league teams; "old-fashioned baseball" (Billy Martin, quoted in *Houston Post*, May 10, 1987). Martin's baseball philosophy combined speed, daring, a manic style, and execution of the fundamentals (hit-and-run plays, double steals, suicide squeezes, bunting to reach base, sacrificing, hitting behind the runner) with a willingness to intimidate (including throwing at batters). Thomas Boswell (*Why Time Begins on Opening Day*, 1984, p.280) mentioned Martin's "outlaw gambits" and "guerilla warfare," such as "greaseballs, scuffballs, beanballs, high-spikes slides, obscene bench jockeying, field-filling brawls, corked bats, hotdogging and—the A's trademark—perpetual stylin' and stallin.'" "It was about establishing an aggressive and unpredictable approach to the game, throwing fear and uncertainty into the heads of opponents and into the minds of opposing managers" (David Falkner, *The Last Yankee*, 1992). Base stealer Rickey Henderson (quoted in *The New Yorker*, Sept. 12, 2005): "Billy was the publisher of Billy Ball, and I was the author." For all of its successes, Billy Ball has also been characterized by controversy and dissension: "Feuding Rips Away Facade of Billy Ball" (*San Francisco Examiner* headline, March 7, 1983). The term was introduced as one word ("Billyball") by *Oakland Tribune* sportswriter Ralph Wiley in 1981 when Martin was manager of the Oakland Athletics. See also Billy Martin, *Billyball*, 1987.

billy goat Syn. of *goat's beard*.

Billy Goat Curse An urban myth or scapegoat to explain why the Chicago Cubs have not appeared in a World Series since 1945 and have not won a World Series since 1908. IST USE. 2003. "A suppressed 'billy goat' curse that inspired the *Chicago Tribune* headline on Thursday [Oct. 16, 2003]: 'The Bleat Goes On'" (*The New York Times*, Oct. 17). "Chalk it up to the Billy Goat Curse or just the karma of being the Chicago Cubs. The lovable losers from the Second City found a way to cough it up again and add a dismal new chapter to their history of hopelessness" (Peter Schmuck, *The Baltimore Sun*, Oct. 16). ETYMOLOGY. The curse was created on Oct. 6, 1945, after Game 4 of the World Series when William (Vasili) Sianis, owner of a tavern (now the famous Billy Goat Tavern) near Wrigley Field in Chicago, brought his pet goat (Murphy or Sinovia) to occupy the box seat for which Sianis had a ticket. Owing to the animal's objectionable odor, the Cubs ejected Sianis and his goat. Outraged at the ejection, Sianis allegedly placed a curse upon the Cubs that they would never win another pennant or play in a World Series at Wrigley Field. The Cubs lost Game 4 to Detroit, 4–1, and eventually lost the Series; they have not returned to the Fall Classic since, nor have they won a National League pennant. See Steve Gatto, *Da Curse of the Billy Goat*, 2004. Syn. *Curse of the Billy Goat*.

Billy Martin Rule The practice by which umpires go out of their way to make calls against a certain individual. The term is facetious because the "rule" is seldom enforced, although certain players and managers sometimes are subject to extra scrutiny. Named after Billy Martin, a volatile manager for five teams between 1969 and 1988, who often abused umpires and disputed their calls. During the 1988 World Series, Martin hurled a fistful of dirt at umpire Dale Scott's chest; umpires were so incensed that they voted to "take strong measures to curb his temper" (Childs Walker, *The Baltimore Sun*, Sept. 14, 2007).

bing To hit a ball hard. An "onomatopoetic term" based on the sound of the bat solidly meeting the pitched ball. IST USE. 1909. "Bing one, Cap!" (Zane Grey, *The Short-Stop*, p.285; Edward J. Nichols).

bing-banger Syn. of *bang-bang play*, 1.

bingle **1.** *n. hist.* A base hit of any kind. "Bingle is synonymous with a base hit" (*The Washington Post*, July 22, 1900). Gerald L. Cohen cites two attestations from the *San Francisco Bulletin* for 1913: "The big fellow grabbed three bingles, . . . one of which was a smash over the fence that netted him a home run" (May 26) and "Jack [Killilay] . . . permitted eight bingles, three of which were triples" (May 31). "Ernie Lombardi has made more than 1,500 big league base hits and practically every one of them was an honest bingle. . . . Nobody can accuse Schnoz of beating out those infield grounders" (Arch Ward, *Chicago Daily Tribune*, June 20, 1945). See also *bingo*. IST USE. 1898. "In the third inning yesterday the first local batter up drew a bingle" (*Youngstown Vindicator*, July 29; Peter Morris). **2.** *n.* A single, usually a "clean" one. The term became restricted to one-base hits by the mid-20th century. **3.** *v.* To get a base hit. "A player who bingles, swats the ball safely to some part of the field where a biped in white flannel knickerbockers is not roaming at the immediate time" (*The Washington Post*, July 22, 1900). "Del Howard . . . bingled safely to center, scoring the run that won the game" (*San Francisco Bulletin*, May 30, 1913; Gerald L. Cohen). IST USE. 1899. "I was always the John L. Sullivan of baseball when I bingled 'em out" (Honus Wagner, quoting Pete Browning, *The Washington Post*, July 20).

ETYMOLOGY. David Shulman (*American Speech*, Feb. 1937) conjectured, "If it is not an erroneous reading of 'single,' perhaps it may be a blend of 'bang' or 'bing' with 'single.'" Responding to Shulman's suggestion, Peter Tamony did not doubt that the term was based "on the onomatopoetic 'bing,'" but posed an alternate theory (*American Speech*, Oct. 1937) by asking, "Was such a hit first called a 'bingo,' from the exclamation in use, and later blended with 'single'?"

bingler A batter who gets a hit. "In past seasons a swat such as this has always entitled the bingler to a $50 check" (*San Francisco Bulletin*, May 8, 1913; Gerald L. Cohen).

bingling The act of getting hits. "The Seals hit hard, too, the beauty of their bingling being that the hits were manufactured at the right moment" (*San Francisco Bulletin*, May 21, 1913; Gerald L. Cohen).

bingo *hist.* A base hit of any kind. "Truck Egan is showing his form of other seasons, playing a swell short and getting his timely bingoes as of yore" (*The Sporting News*, Nov. 15, 1902; Peter Tamony). "With the wall 368 feet away . . . bingo buffs over the barrier will not be so plenty" (*The Sporting Life*, March 11, 1911; Peter Morris). See also *bingle*, 1. 1ST USE. 1898. "Fred Cooke got his usual bingo" (*Youngstown Vindicator*, June 11; Peter Morris).

bingo hitter A hitter whose batting average is below .100. "Your Bingo Hitters—'N–34, G–52,' the wise guys call out from the opposing dugout when an acknowledged B.H. strides up with his lumber" (*Sports Illustrated*, Aug. 22, 1983).

bingo league A mythical league in which the hitters' batting average is below .100, as in "O-89."

BIP Abbrev. for *balls in play*.

birch *hist.* To hit the pitched ball. "[Bill Lange] has birched the ball in the vicinity of .400" (*San Francisco Bulletin*, March 11, 1913; Gerald L. Cohen). "[McCarl] laced out a double and a single. If he keeps up this sort of birching, McCarl will be the sensation of the league" (*San Francisco Bulletin*, March 15, 1913; Gerald L. Cohen).

bird cage *hist.* A slang nickname for *catcher's mask*, so called because of its resemblance to a small wire cage. 1ST USE. 1877. "The new 'catcher's mask,' which had never before been seen on the Chicago grounds. The crowd variously named it . . . 'the bird cage'" (*Chicago Tribune*, July 20; Peter Morris).

bird dog *n.* A friend or associate of a scout who tips him off to high schoolers and other young players with major-league potential; an assistant or part-time scout. A bird dog is not paid, but is occasionally given a small bonus if the player eventually becomes a major leaguer. Bird dogs are the first people one meets in Pat Jordan's *A False Spring* (1973): "The bird dogs came first. They just appeared one spring day in your sophomore year of high school as if drawn by the odor of freshly cut outfield grass. . . . They were called bird dogs because they sniffed out talent, although the name does not do justice to the men. The bird dogs were kindly old men in plaid shirts and string ties. They owned taverns and hard-

Bird cage. Catcher George Gibson of the Pittsburgh Pirates. *George Grantham Bain Collection, Library of Congress*

ware stores, and had even played ball with Kiki Cuyler and Georgie Cutshaw. Now in their last years, they measured out the weekday afternoons at an endless succession of high school baseball games." After the bird dogs, wrote Jordan, "came the full-time scouts." See also *commission scout*. 1ST USE. 1950 (Sam Nisenson, *Handy Illustrated Guide to Baseball*, p.157; David Shulman).

bird-dog *v.* To play close to a base in an attempt to catch a runner off that base; e.g., "Smith was bird-dogging Jones at third but Jones did not fall for it." ETYMOLOGY. A reference to the dog used by a hunter to hunt and retrieve birds. "To bird-dog" is also general slang for "to watch closely."

Bird Land Baltimore Orioles and the geographic area from Delaware and Pennsylvania through Virginia where the team has a broad fan base.

Birds Nickname for the Baltimore *Orioles*. For some reason the sobriquet has not worked for the other avian teams: the Toronto Blue Jays and the St. Louis Cardinals. 1ST USE.

1922. "The [Baltimore] Orioles visited Newark [in 1885] to play an exhibition game and . . . failed to get a man to first base. Sixteen of the Birds fanned" (Ernest J. Lanigan, *The Baseball Cyclopedia*, p.111; Peter Morris).

birthplace of baseball *Abner Doubleday Field* in Cooperstown, N.Y (Bo Smolka, *The Baltimore Sun*, June 15, 2003).

bite 1. *n.* The sharp downward break, late and fast, of a curveball or slider. **2.** *v.* For a breaking pitch to exhibit a sharp bite. "I threw him a breaking ball and it just didn't bite" (Jesse Orosco, quoted in *The Baltimore Sun*, July 28, 1995). **3.** v. To swing at a bad or unexpected ball, as a fish bites at a baited hook. The term has usually been applied to a hapless batter who cannot resist swinging at and missing the elusive slow curve. "The message 'he will bite' passed through the league among the players generally means the end of the usefulness of that player" (Hugh S. Fullerton, *American Magazine*, June 1912). IST USE. 1905 (*The Sporting Life*, Sept. 2, p.10; Edward J. Nichols). **4.** *v.* To hit a batter with a pitch, as if to take a "bite" out of him.

biter Syn. of *slider*, 1.

bite the dust 1. To slide. A player sliding is likely to send up a cloud of dusty soil. See also *hit the dirt*, 2. IST USE. 1910 (*New York Tribune*, July 9; Edward J. Nichols). **2.** To fall to the ground on a pitched ball. See also *hit the dirt*, 1. **3.** To suffer a defeat. "Oakland naturally bit the dust . . . thanks to the shutout article of pitching . . . and the kindly interference of the rain" (*San Francisco Bulletin*, May 9, 1913; Gerald L. Cohen). EXTENDED USE. Since approximately 1870 this term has been slang for dying or being killed violently.

bittle-battle An ancestral name for the game of stool-ball, suggested by folklorist Alice Bertha Gomme in the discussion of the traditional games of England, Scotland, and Ireland (*Dictionary of British Folk-Lore*, 1894). The term allegedly was mentioned in the *Doomsday Book* (1086), ordered by William the Conqueror to inventory what the Normans had conquered. According to Harold Peterson (*The Man Who Invented Baseball*,

1973, p.27), "bittle" is a Saxon word meaning "stick" or "bat."

BK Abbrev. for *balk*, 1.

BL Abbrev. for *bats left*.

black The so-called black border of home plate; the perceived inside and outside edges of the strike zone. Hal Lebovitz (*The Sporting News*, Sept. 17, 1984) wrote, "There was a time when the plate had a black border. The black isn't and wasn't part of home plate. But when a pitch comes that close, it would be difficult to argue with an umpire who assumed it also got a fraction of the white. . . . Most plates are now solid white, with no black border."

Black and Decker A player used for odd jobs, such as warming up bullpen pitchers. ETYMOLOGY. From the Black and Decker tool manufacturer. The term originated in Kansas City, where the Royals' bullpen applied this tag to bullpen catcher John Wathan and explained it to mean "A weak tool, less than human" (Dan Quisenberry, quoted in *The Sporting News*, March 6, 1982).

Black and Decker ball 1. A pitch that breaks a batter's bat, the implication being that the pitch figuratively saws the bat in half. **2.** Syn. of *emery ball*.

blackball Baseball as it was played in the Negro leagues. See John B. Holway (*Blackball Stars: Negro League Pioneers*, 1988). Also spelled "black ball." Syn. *black baseball*; *race baseball*.

black baseball Syn. of *blackball*.

Black Betsy A large, fearsome-looking baseball bat, usually painted black, first popularized by Shoeless Joe Jackson and used by other sluggers, including Babe Ruth. The name was originally given to the bat by its manufacturer, A.G. Spalding and Co. (*Spalding's Official Base Ball Guide*, 1922; Edward J. Nichols). Jackson's hickory bat was slightly and oddly curved, 34½ inches long, and about 48 ounces in weight. Donald Gropman (*Say It Ain't So, Joe!*, 1979, p.11) wrote, "But she was more than just a bat; she was Joe's talisman, his trademark, the handmade tool of his profession. She fit the grip of his big hands so perfectly and sliced through the air so smoothly when he cut loose at the plate that it seemed as if some of the sweeping power came from her, seemed as if Black Betsy was alive and eager to whack the baseball as it came whistling in over the plate." See also *betsy*. IST USE. 1917. "There should have been two easy outs on those pop flies and [Jack] Graney on first base when [Bobby] Roth trundled his 'Black Betsy' to the plate" (Ed Bang, *The Sporting Life*, May 26; Peter Morris).

blackboard *hist.* A "scoreboard" on which fans "watched" a game as the action was relayed via telegraph and posted. Specs Toporcer (quoted in Lawrence S. Ritter, *The Glory of Their Times*, new enlarged ed., 1984, p.261): "When I was 13 years old, I got a job posting scores [for the Giants] in an old-fashioned corner saloon . . . The scores would come in on a Western Union ticker tape, and I'd proudly write them on a large blackboard in the back room of the saloon." IST USE. 1881. Peter Morris found two citations of this term during the 1881 season (e.g., "people now began to cast affectionate glances at the blackboard").

blackcatcher An unscrupulous scout in the Dominican Republic who "could be rapacious: lying to parents and prospects alike, cheating them, in some cases sequestering them" (Alan M. Klein, *Sugarball*, 1991, p.42). The term was coined "facetiously" by Klein who reported that the scouts' "techniques were so reminiscent of those of the West African slave traders of three centuries earlier."

black cord fever A "boredom alleviator" engaged in by inebriated ballplayers who pick up the phone in their hotel rooms and start calling. Tom House (*The Jock's Itch*, 1989, p.70): "You don't realize until you go to check out of the room just how much you spent on black cord fever. I've seen guys who have had bills of four hundred or five hundred dollars for three days in one city. And they have no idea who they called."

black ink test An informal test of a player's domination of league statistics, performed by counting the number of times that the player led the league in a variety of "important" statistics. The name derives from the tradition of using boldface type to indicate league-leading figures in compilations of annual statistics such as *Total Baseball* and *The Baseball Encyclopedia*. The term was introduced by Bill James (*The Politics of Glory*, 1994, pp.65–67). See also *gray ink test*.

blackout *n.* The act of blocking the television broadcast of a game. When a Boston Red Sox game versus the New York Yankees was kept off a New England cable-TV system, *The Boston Globe* (June 27, 1986) ran an explanation under the headline "Light Shed on Blackout."

black out *v.* To keep a game off television or radio for any number of reasons, usually economic. A team may have an agreement with a local television station or cable system that a game cannot be shown unless a certain number of tickets are sold in advance of the game.

black seats Empty bleacher seats, such as those in dead center field in Yankee Stadium for which tickets are not sold. Reggie Jackson (*Reggie*, 1984, p.195) wrote: "[Charlie Hough] threw me a knuckler. Didn't knuckle. I crushed it nearly 500 feet into the black, those beautiful empty black seats in dead center."

Black Sox **1.** A derogatory name for the 1919 Chicago *White Sox* team on which certain players conspired and accepted bribes from gamblers to lose the World Series to the Cincinnati Reds. The Reds won the best-of-nine Series, five games to three, amidst swirling rumors that bribery had tainted one or several of their victories. The whole incident became known as the *Black Sox Scandal* and the 1921 trial of the players was known widely as the Black Sox trial. To bring respectability back to the sport and restore its "clean" image, the new commissioner of baseball, Judge Kenesaw Mountain Landis, was given extraordinary power. ETYMOLOGY. It has been suggested that the term originated before 1919 when the sportswriters and fans reacted to the dirty uniforms that the White Sox players wore because the owner, Charles Comiskey, refused to wash the uniforms more than once a week. However, this belief is not documented and may reflect an anti-Comiskey bias. "The term had less to do with laundry issues and more to do with the disgrace of the scandal—i.e., white is pristine, black is bad.

The anger and frustration fans felt at that time [1920] prompted the media to label [the club] the Black Sox" (Rich Lindberg, personal communication, June 29, 2007). **2.** A derogatory name for the eight 1919 Chicago White Sox players who were initially indicted for throwing the 1919 World Series. In W.P. Kinsella's novel *Shoeless Joe* (1982), the narrator muses, "Instead of nursery rhymes, I was raised on the story of the Black Sox Scandal, and instead of Tom Thumb or Rumpelstiltskin, I grew up hearing of the eight disgraced ballplayers: [Buck] Weaver, [Eddie] Cicotte, [Swede] Risberg, [Happy] Felsch, [Chick] Gandil, [Lefty] Williams, [Fred] McMullin, and, always, Shoeless Joe Jackson." **3.** Nickname for various Baltimore franchises in the Negro leagues between 1923 and 1934.

Black Sox Scandal The name given to the events beginning in Oct. 1919, when certain Chicago White Sox players conspired with gamblers to "fix" or throw the 1919 World Series to their opponent, the Cincinnati Reds, who won the best-of-nine Series, five games to three. On Sept. 28, 1920, Sox pitcher Eddie Cicotte testified to a Cook County (Chicago) grand jury (looking into issues involving baseball and gambling) that he had accepted $10,000 in bribe money, confirming that the fix was in; later that day, Sox outfielder Shoeless Joe Jackson admitted to the grand jury that he accepted money, although he denied that he played less than his best. The grand jury indicted eight White Sox players (who were immediately suspended), as well as other players and gamblers. Although the Black Sox trial in Summer 1921 found the players to be not guilty of conspiracy charges, the new commissioner of baseball, Judge Kenesaw Mountain Landis, banished the players from organized baseball. The tampering by gamblers in Oct. 1919 was not the first or last instance of game fixing, but the Black Sox Scandal became the most famous, and the harsh punishments did much to deter future bribery attempts, and to repair the image of baseball as a clean sport. See Gene Carney, *Burying the Black Sox*, 2006 (Gene Carney).

blank 1. *n.* An inning or game in which a team fails to score. "Relaxed [Dwight]

Gooden Throws Three Blanks" (*New York Daily News* headline, March 14, 1987). "The Resolutes drew a blank for their share of the innings" (*New York Clipper*, Aug. 6, 1864; Peter Morris). See also *blank score*; *blind*, 1; *skunk*, 2; *whitewash*, 3; *goose egg*, 1. IST USE. 1862 (*New York Sunday Mercury*, June 29; Edward J. Nichols). **2.** *v.* To allow no runs in an inning or game. The term is beloved of headline writers. "The A's blanked the Texas Rangers 5–0 . . . to win the AL West" (*Tampa Tribune*, Sept. 29, 1989). IST USE. 1870 (*New York Herald*, June 29; Edward J. Nichols).

blanket 1. A square (normally five to six inches) piece of felt or other fabric portraying a baseball player in the 1910s. The fabric came wrapped around a pack of cigarettes, and was sometimes sewn together to form a "blanket." **2.** Syn. of *sliding pad*.

blank score *hist.* The score when there are no runs in an inning or when the batter fails to score a run in a game (Henry Chadwick, *The Game of Base Ball*, 1868, p.39). See also *blank*, 1.

blanquear Spanish for "shut out" (verb).

blast 1. *v.* To hit a home run; to hit the ball with a hard blow. **2.** *n.* A hard-hit ball, usually a home run. **3.** *v.* To cause a pitcher to be removed from the game by making too many hits; e.g., "The Tigers blasted Smith out of the box in the second inning."

blaze To hit a ball hard. IST USE. 1912 (*New York Tribune*, Oct. 13; Edward J. Nichols).

blazer A fastball. "Fastball pitchers . . . throw 'blazers'" (Lowell Cohn, *San Francisco Chronicle*, June 4, 1980).

bleacher 1. A roofless section of unreserved benches for spectators at a baseball game. The term is usually given in the plural. See also *bleachers*, 1. IST USE. 1888. "The bleacher was loaded to its utmost capacity" (*Rocky Mountain News* [Denver], Oct. 29). **2.** A spectator sitting in the bleachers; a *bleacherite*. "To be a bleacher this year is more of a distinction than to be a grand standite" (*San Francisco Examiner*, March 23, 1891; Peter Morris). IST USE. 1889. " 'Tobogganed agin,' sententiously replied a mournful looking bleacher" (*The World* [New York], Aug. 28; Gerald L. Cohen).

bleacher bum One of a horde of boisterous, often shirtless fans who inhabit the bleachers. The Bleacher Bums of Wrigley Field in Chicago were formed in 1966 by ten bleacher fans wearing construction helmets. "With two out in the ninth inning and after almost six hours of raucous cheering, chanting and singing, a wave swept thru the overstuffed bleachers in Wrigley field and the wedged-in 'bleacher bums' rose to their feet, clapping" (George Langford, *Chicago Tribune*, July 29, 1968).

bleacher critic A critical fan sitting in the bleachers. EXTENDED USE. A critic who, to use another sport's terminology, sits on the sideline. "But Secretary of State Cordell Hull, speaking directly over the Columbia network, was performing primarily for the home folks answering bleacher critics of his foreign policy pitching" (*Newsweek*, Apr. 17, 1944, p.25).

bleacheries 1. Syn. of *bleachers*, 1. "The bleacheries were black with people and on the pathways surrounding these seats the people were jammed together in one immovable mass" (*Brooklyn Eagle*, Sept. 8, 1889; Dean A. Sullivan). **2.** Syn. of *bleachers*, 2. "The bleacheries sang 'Home, Sweet Home' to O'Day" (*The World* [New York], Sept. 17, 1889; Gerald L. Cohen).

bleacherite A spectator who sits in or frequents the bleachers. *The Washington Post* (Sept. 5, 1895) reported the arrest of "a turbulent bleacherite"; in fact, a bleacherite originally was considered coarse and given to swearing, "a collarless fellow whose trousers were last pressed when he bought them" (*The Washington Post*, May 30, 1915). A later example of the term appeared in the "Jocks" column of *People* magazine (June 24, 1974): "In Cincinnati, bleacherites poured beer on Houston outfielder Bob Watson as he lay stunned after running into the left field fence." When Hugh S. Fullerton (*American Magazine*, June 1912) defined the term, he gave it a certain nobility with lines like this: "The bleacherites usually are much better posted on the game than those patrons who occupy the grand stand boxes and seats and are much more dreaded by the players because of their caustic criticism." Indeed, as *The Washington Post* (May 30, 1915) later claimed, "Who made baseball the national pastime? The fans. And who are the genuine fans? The bleacherites. . . . And when it comes to knowing the game from A to Izzard the man in the sun is a hundred mental steps above his brother in the shade." Syn. *bleacher*, 2. IST USE. 1890 (*New York Press*, July 10; Edward J. Nichols).

bleacheritis The name of a mock disease for the deteriorated physical conditioning of those who have given up active participation in athletics and become spectators: "The active athlete of the teens succumbs to bleacheritis by 30 and is interested only because he has money on the Giants" (C.C. Furnas, *The Next Hundred Years*, 1936).

bleachers 1. The uncovered, unreserved, backless benches for spectators at a ballpark; currently, the most distant and inexpensive seats, which are beyond the outfield wall and may be covered, in the case of domed stadiums. "The grand stand and bleachers were well filled with something over 2,000 spectators" (*Chicago Tribune*, May 18, 1889; OED). The bleachers carry with them a certain rowdy, romantic image: "The democracy of the game is at its best on the bleachers and in the grandstand. There the wealthy banker, straight from downtown by the 'Wall Street subway special,' hobnobs with the office-boy for once, on terms of perfect equality" (*New York Evening Post*, Sept. 14, 1911). One appeal of the bleachers has always been their relative cheapness. *The Sporting News* (July 14, 1954) reported that "Ebbets Field prices will continue to be $3 for lower boxes, $2.50 upper boxes, $1.75 grandstand, and 50 cents bleachers." Another draw has been the party atmosphere that exists in some parks. Sean O'Sullivan, reporting from Fenway Park (*The Boston Globe*, June 25, 1986): "Beachballs are only the newest, and most visible, of the bleacher game-time activities. But while beer-spilling, Frisbee-throwing and marijuana-smoking are time-honored traditions in the cheap seats, this season seems to have brought, if anything, an improved situation." See also *bleacher*, 1. Syn. *bleacheries*, 1; *scorchers*. IST USE. 1888 (*New York Press*, June 5; Edward J. Nichols). ETYMOLOGY. Derived from *bleaching boards*. EXTENDED

Bleachers. Ebbets Field crowd. *George Grantham Bain Collection, Library of Congress*

USE. The term that originated in baseball is now applied to the cheaper backless seats in football stadiums, gymnasiums, and even nightclubs. Bleacher seats are offered for rock concerts and religious revival meetings. Every four years they become inaugural fixtures in Washington: "A mile of tiered board bleachers flanked Pennsylvania Avenue from the Treasury to Capitol Hill" (Nan Robertson, *The New York Times*, Jan. 19, 1969). Foreign affairs conducted in an aloof manner constitute "bleachers diplomacy": "In that part of the world [Southeast Asia] Washington seems to practice 'bleachers' diplomacy, as a non-participating spectator of events" (Blair Bolles, *Headline Series 78 of Foreign Policy Association*, Nov.-Dec. 1949, p.58).
2. The spectators in the bleachers. "The bleachers nursed their wrath until the game was over when they swarmed into the field and started to mob the offending official" (*The Sporting Life*, May 13, 1905; Peter Tamony). Syn. *bleacheries*, 2. IST USE. 1888. "Ryan and Hanlon do brilliant work in the field and cause the grand stand and bleachers

to rise and applaud" (*Rocky Mountain News* [Denver], Oct. 29). ETYMOLOGY. From sitting in the roofless section of the ballpark where the sun's rays would "bleach" the spectators; in contrast, the grandstand was a covered structure.

bleaching boards *hist.* The planks laid lengthwise as spectator seats at baseball games. The term evolved into *bleachers*, but also coexisted with it. "The attendance of ladies was so large that the overflow of the fair sex had to find seats on the bleaching boards" (*Brooklyn Eagle*, Sept. 8, 1889; Dean A. Sullivan). "The hornyhanded sons of toil made a brave show upon the bleaching boards, where they were jammed and crowded without a seat to spare, so that they overflowed the grounds and crowded in upon the players" (*The Illustrated American*, May 10, 1890). Thomas W. Lawson (*The Krank: His Language and What It Means*, 1888) defined the term as "the resting place for the kranks [fans] who are not acquainted with the doorkeeper of the grandstand." IST USE. 1877. "The bleaching-boards just north of the north pavilion now hold the cheap crowd which comes in at the end of the first inning on a discount" (O.P. Caylor, *Cincinnati Enquirer*, May 10; Peter Tamony).

bleeder 1. A batted ball that, as the result of an erratic roll, pop, bad bounce, or overall slowness, becomes a base hit. Dizzy Dean once described it as "a weak scratch hit that is just slow enuff so the runner can beat it out to first base." A typical bleeder is a ground ball that slows to a stop about halfway down the baseline, with a possible assist from the infield grass. IST USE. 1933. "Bleeder: A scratchy single" (Edgar G. Brands, *The Sporting News*, Feb. 23; Peter Morris). ETY-MOLOGY. Mike Whiteford (*How to Talk Base-ball*, 1987, p.82) stated, "The term is a sarcastic one, suggesting the ball was hit so hard that it's bleeding. Following such a hit, players often say, 'Wipe the blood off it.'" A tad more logical, perhaps, is Bert Dunne's (*Folger's Dictionary of Baseball*, 1958) explanation that the term grew out of the phrase "that hit had blood on it!" Dunne further noted that "while the ball was hit on the handle, the batter's fists were figuratively responsible, bled in the process, and left blood on the ball." Thomas P. McDonald (letter, Apr. 13, 1991) suggests that the term might also derive from the speed of the ball, in conjunction with the term *trickler*: "Blood trickles from a superficial cut, as opposed to gushing or spurting from a slashed artery, and I think the term 'bleeding' is usually associated more with the former. Thus the trickler is also a 'bleeder.'" **2.** *hist.* A sharply hit ball "threatening to split the first finger that's laid upon it" (William G. Brandt, *Base-ball Magazine*, Oct. 1932). This meaning appears to have been totally canceled out by the first. **3.** *hist.* An underpowered fly ball that drops unexpectedly. H.L. Mencken (*The American Language*, Suppl. II, 1948, p.737) and the *New York Sun* (June 23, 1932) list "bleeder" as a synonym of *Texas Leaguer*, 2.

blem A slang term used by scouts for a college senior. ETYMOLOGY. Short for "blemished." Mark Whicker (*The Orange County* [Calif.] *Register*, Oct. 25, 2005): "A college junior is eligible to be drafted by a major-league team. He can play the negotiating

game . . . [or] threaten to return to school if he doesn't get a check with two commas in it. . . . Three years of college baseball is enough. . . . A senior has that used-car smell. He has been in the showroom too long. If he were that good, he would be a pro already. . . . Seniors . . . are, by definition, blemished."

blind *hist.* **1.** *n.* A club's scoreless inning. *Ball Players' Chronicle* (June 20, 1867): "A blank score at Albany, N.Y., is called 'a blind.'" Henry Chadwick (*Technical Terms of Base Ball*, 1897) noted that the term, used primarily in the eastern United States, was already considered of historic interest only: "An old-time term used to indicate the retirement of a side in a game without their being able to score a single run." See also *blank*, 1. Syn. *blinder.* IST USE. 1864. "Harvard being credited with five blind innings" (*New York Clipper*, Aug. 13; Peter Morris). **2.** *v.* To prevent a team from scoring in an inning or a game; to shut out. "It was a hardly contested fight from the beginning to the end, so close that it was but necessary to blind the Unions in the ninth to make the game tie on that innings" (*Brooklyn Eagle*, Oct. 8, 1868; Peter Morris).

blinder *hist.* Syn. of *blind*, 1. "The provincial term in the Middle States for a blank score in a game" (Henry Chadwick, *The Game of Base Ball*, 1868, p.39).

blind mice A derogatory term for a group of umpires. See also *three blind mice.*

blind staggers Awkward maneuvering of a fielder positioning to catch a high windblown fly ball.

blind swing A swing when the batter takes his eye off the ball.

blind Tom An *umpire*, 1. The term refers to an umpire's faulty judgment because of poor eyesight. USAGE NOTE. Although the term is an affront, it can be used affectionately: "Bill Engeln [is] about to start his fourth season as a National League umpire and his twentieth as a blind tom" (Jack McDonald, *San Francisco Call-Bulletin*, Jan. 25, 1955; Peter Tamony). ETYMOLOGY. It is quite likely that the term originated with and was appropriated from Old Blind Tom, a popular black musical prodigy of the period just after the Civil War.

block 1. *n.* An action by a defensive player (usually the catcher) meant to prevent a runner from tagging a base, accomplished with the aid of the defensive player's body. A block can be ruled an obstruction if it occurs when the blocker does not have the ball or is not in the process of fielding it. 2. *v.* To stand in the basepath to prevent a runner from touching a base before the defensive player tags him. See also *block the plate*. IST USE. 1900. "[O'Brien] scored the winning run on another passed ball by Clarke. Dineen took the throw from Clarke and blocked off his man, but [umpire Hank] O'Day could only see Pittsburg and the run was allowed to count" (Timothy Murnane, *The Boston Globe*, Sept. 5; Peter Morris). 3. *n./hist.* Syn. of *blocked ball*. 4. *v.* For a catcher to prevent a pitch in the dirt from getting past him. 5. *n.* See *roll block*. 6. *n.* See *trading block*. 7. *v.* To make a minor-league prospect's advance to the major leagues more difficult because he plays the same position as that of an established star. "Chase Utley's road to the big leagues was effectively blocked by Scott Rolen last year, which necessitated a move to second base" (*Baseball America*, July 7–20, 2003; Peter Morris). 8. *v.* To claim a player on waivers to prevent him from being claimed by another club. 9. *v./hist.* To bunt. "[Kessler] was trying to 'block' a ball—that is, allowing a ball to strike the bat and fall nearly at his feet on fair ground" (*New York Clipper*, Jan. 17, 1880; Peter Morris).

block ball *hist.* Syn. of *blocked ball*. IST USE. 1881. "Balls stopped by anyone not engaged in the game are now termed 'block' balls, and on all such balls runners are at liberty to make all the bases they can while the ball is dead, which it is until returned to the pitcher and held by him while in position" (*New York Clipper*, Dec. 7; Peter Morris).

blocked ball A batted or thrown ball in play that is touched, stopped, or handled by a person not engaged in the game, or that touches any object that is not part of the official equipment or official playing area. Such an occurrence causes a dead ball. This was not so during the early 1880s; see *block ball*. Syn. *block*, 3. IST USE. 1891 (*Chicago Herald*, June 25; Edward J. Nichols).

blocker 1. A catcher or other defensive player who blocks either a base or home plate. See also *plate blocker*, 1. IST USE. 1905 (*The Sporting Life*, Sept. 2, p.11; Edward J. Nichols). 2. A baserunner who throws himself into ("takes out") the second baseman or shortstop to prevent a double play.

block pickoff A *pickoff play* in which the shortstop bluffs toward second base, then retreats; with the runner distracted, the second baseman makes a rush toward the base (O.H. Vogel, in *Ins and Outs of Baseball*, 1952; Peter Morris). Compare *jockey pickoff*.

block signal A signal that uses the coach's body as a map, with each of four sections or "blocks" having a different meaning; e.g., holding hands above the belt or below the belt constitutes two blocks.

block the ball off For a batter to throw the bat in front of the ball instead of taking a hefty swing, thereby often shooting it to the opposite field. The term was used by Ted Williams (Richard Hoffer, *Sports Illustrated*, Sept. 18, 1995, p.74).

block the bases To issue an intentional base on balls, which sets up a force play at second base and third base and "pave[s] the way for a double play" (George Herman Ruth, *Babe Ruth's Own Book of Baseball*, 1928, p.204; Peter Morris).

block the plate For a catcher (or a pitcher, if he is covering the plate) to stand in the way of the runner and use his body to prevent the runner from scoring while attempting to tag him out. It is only legal when the fielder has the ball or is in the process of fielding it. Catcher Charles Johnson (quoted in *The Baltimore Sun*, Apr. 2, 2000): "Blocking the plate isn't something that requires a lot of finesse. It's you against the runner. You have to split your vision. You see the guy coming, but you keep your eye on the ball. It's timing. If he's going to get there first, you can't tag him out. Step out of there. Otherwise he barrels into you and—no baseball. [If the ball arrives first] catch the ball first. Then set yourself up so he slides into your gear, not you." See also *block*, 2.

blood bounty Money paid for retaliatory action on the field. "Money irate manager offers to player who will drag ball down first, cause pitcher (who has been throwing at hitters) to cover, offering opportunity to 'run up his back' and spike pitcher" (Bert Dunne, *Folger's Dictionary of Baseball*, 1958).

bloodless hit Syn. of *phantom hit*.

blood rule [softball term] A rule that prohibits a player, coach, or umpire who is bleeding or who has blood on his/her uniform from participating further in the game until appropriate medical care or treatment can be administered.

bloomer 1. A player who looks good in spring training, but is a failure when the regular season starts. The term is probably a corruption of *early bloomer*. "Many a young ballplayer that looks like the flower of the flock on the spring training trip turns out a bloomer before May" (*San Francisco Bulletin*, Feb. 22, 1913; Gerald L. Cohen). 2. An erratic player who "blows hot and cold."

Bloomer Girls A generic name for women's baseball teams that barnstormed the United States, regionally and nationally, from the 1890s to 1934. There were no leagues and Bloomer Girls teams rarely played each other. They challenged local town, semipro,

and minor-league men's teams. Each roster had at least one male player (usually the pitcher, catcher, or shortstop), and future major leaguers Smoky Joe Wood and Rogers Hornsby got their starts on such squads; some clubs included young men disguised as women. The Bloomer Girls frequently won their games, playing solid competitive baseball. Many of the Bloomer Girls teams abandoned bloomers in favor of standard baseball uniforms. By the 1930s, public opinion held that they had inferior abilities when it came to sports, and women's professional baseball disappeared until the formation of the All-American Girls Professional Baseball League. ETYMOLOGY. From the loose-fitting, Turkish-style trousers advocated by suffragist Amelia Jenks Bloomer that made sports more practical for women athletes. The first "bloomer girls" were bicyclists: "The Summer girl has at last met her match. She has lowered her colors to her sister in bloomers. . . . The new queen completed her triumph . . . in the great parade of cyclists at the League of American Wheelman's national meet. She was there in her best pair of baggy trousers, her sweetest smile, and she pedaled before the thousands fringing

Bloomer Girls. The Boston Bloomers vs. the Boston Red Sox. *Andy Moresund Collection*

the route fortified with the assurance that unstinted praise would follow" (*The New York Times*, July 10, 1895).

bloop 1. *n.* A poorly hit ball that drops between the infielders and the outfielders for a hit; a *Texas Leaguer*, 2. The term is onomatopoetically named for the "bloop" sound that is suggested when the bat hits the ball, such as the sound "of a soft tomato struck by a broomstick" (Jim Brosnan, *The Long Season*, 1960). Syn. *blooper*, 1. 2. *v.* To hit a bloop. "I made a pretty good pitch, but that's how you hit .350. You hit one hard, then bloop one in" (pitcher Mike Flanagan, quoted in *The Washington Post*, Sept. 25, 1986).

bloop and a blast A bloop single followed by a home run. ETYMOLOGY. Battle cry of the Pittsburgh Pirates during announcer Bob Prince's heyday. The cry was used most often in the bottom of the ninth when the Pirates were one run down.

blooper 1. Syn. of *bloop*, 1; *Texas Leaguer*, 2; *flare*, 1. "A 'blooper' is a soggy fly to an unoccupied spot behind the backs of the infield" (*The New York Times*, Oct. 8, 1937). IST USE. 1937 (Bill Snypp, *Lima* [Ohio] *News*, Apr. 27; Peter Morris). 2. Syn. of *blooper ball*, 1. IST USE. 1967. "I went into a long, elaborate windup and sent him a slow, curving blooper, the kind a batter always wants to hit and always misses" (C. Potok, *Chosen*, p.35; OED). 3. An embarrassing play, often resulting in an error.

blooper ball 1. A pitch that is lobbed into a high arc, which, when thrown correctly, drops precipitously through the strike zone, tantalizing the batter in the process. It has also been termed a "glorified slow ball" thrown with a high arc. See also *eephus*; *folly floater*; *freaky floater*. Syn. *blooper*, 2. IST USE. 1946. "[Rip Sewell] made the mistake of tossing one of his blooper balls to [Ted] Williams with two on base" (*San Francisco Examiner*, June 27; OED). 2. A weak base hit. "Rod [Carew] remembers some of [his teammates] yelling, 'blooper ball!' whenever he got a hit that wasn't a solid line drive" (Bill Gutman, *Heavy Hitters*, 1980; Charles D. Poe).

bloop single A bloop that allows the batter to reach first base safely. "[Jackie] Gutierrez moved him to third with a bloop single to center" (*Boston Globe*, Aug. 11, 1984).

blow 1. *v.* To fail in any of several ways; e.g., lose a game, relinquish a lead, misplay a ball, lose a save opportunity, miss a sign, or make a bad umpiring call. 2. *n.* A base hit. The term is probably what Babe Ruth and his Yankee teammates called a "single" as it is the only alternative to single offered in *Babe Ruth's Own Book of Baseball* (1928). IST USE. 1913. "[Nap] Lajoie did not get a hit today. The nearest the Frenchman came to a blow was in the eighth inning when he sent a long fly to [Howard] Shanks" (*The Washington Post*, July 14; Peter Morris). 3. *n.* A clutch hit. "[Scott Garrelts] yielded four singles and two walks, the big blow being a two-run single by Ron Hassey" (*Tampa Tribune*, March 13, 1989). 4. *v.* To throw a fastball with such speed that it cannot be hit. "[Bartolo Colon] blew a third-strike fastball past Mo Vaughn" (Tom Verducci, *Sports Illustrated*, Oct. 12, 1998, p.45). 5. *n.* A respite, rest, or breather. After being taken out of a game for two innings, Cal Ripken Jr. told *The New York Times* (July 17, 1989), "It was an opportunity, with the heat and everything else, to get a two-inning blow."

blow a tire To pull a leg muscle (Phil Pepe, *Baseball Digest*, Nov. 1974, p.58).

blow away To strike out a batter. "[Paul] Byrd's inability to blow guys away (43 K's in 70⅓ IP) means Royals fielders earn their paychecks" (*ESPN The Magazine*, June 10, 2002).

blow-down pitch *hist.* A rarely used synonym of *brushback pitch*. "A pitched ball high and close to the batsman designed to drive him away from the plate" (Ralph H. Barbour, *How to Play Better Baseball*, 1935; David Shulman).

blower A fastball pitcher. "I'm not a blower who can throw it 95 miles per hour" (Damon Allen, quoted in *The Baltimore Sun*, March 20, 1994).

blown call A bad judgment or incorrect decision by an umpire. "He had another homer in the game, but it was ruled a double on a blown call by umpire Dan Morrison" (*Tampa*

Tribune, March 30, 1986). Memory for blown calls can survive long after the act: "[Bob] Feller Can't Forget Blown Call" (*USA Today* headline, Oct. 19, 1990) was an allusion to a pickoff play in the first game of the 1948 World Series.

blown save A statistic charged to a relief pitcher who enters the game with a *save opportunity* but departs with the save opportunity no longer in effect because he gave up the lead. The value of this statistic as a counterpart to *save* was noted when saves started to be recorded in the 1960s, and informal calculations of blown saves began shortly thereafter. The statistic was introduced by the makers of Rolaids antacid tablets in 1988 and included in the calculations for the Rolaids Relief Man Award. Compare *hold*, 6. Abbrev. *BS*. Syn. *squander*, 2.

blowout *n*. **1.** A leg or foot injury. The term is a play on "bad wheel." **2.** A one-sided game, such as one in which a team outscores its opponent by a wide margin. See also *laugher*.

blow out *v*. **1.** To defeat overwhelmingly. "They're not just getting beat, they're getting blown out" (George Steinbrenner on the 1987 New York Yankees, quoted in *Tampa Tribune*, Aug. 13, 1987). **2.** To injure oneself, esp. a pitcher who hurts his arm; e.g., "Smith blew his arm out by pitching a doubleheader."

blow smoke To throw a fastball.

blow the lid off "To open a season of games" (Maurice H. Weseen, *A Dictionary of American Slang*, 1938).

blow up To fail suddenly and utterly; to lose effectiveness quickly. "In the Spring" (a poem by Grantland Rice, *The Sporting Life*, Apr. 4, 1908; Stuart Y. Silverstein): "In the spring the bush league phenom trolls in from some rural station; / In the spring he blows up swiftly with a mighty detonation." The *San Francisco Bulletin* (Apr. 24, 1913; Gerald L. Cohen) declared, "Nothing can blow up quicker than a ball club." Calvin T. Ryan (*Word Study*, Feb. 1952) noted that the term "is one of those rare examples of slang which just about hits the nail on the head." IST USE. 1907. "The first game was closely fought for seven innings and then [Sam] Leever 'blew up'" (*Brooklyn Daily Eagle*, July 14; Peter Morris).

bludgeon **1.** *n*. A baseball bat. "Gallant Larry Lajoie and his bludgeon knouted and lashed the Mackman into submission" (anonymous writer, quoted in *Los Angeles Times*, Aug. 8, 1913). IST USE. 1889. "Into this dream of peace strode a gigantic figure in black [Roger Connor], with a bludgeon over his shoulder, like an executioner of the feudal ages" (*The World* [New York], June 14; Gerald L. Cohen). **2.** *v*. To hit the ball.

bludgeon wielder A batter, usually one who hits the ball hard. IST USE. 1913 (*Harper's Weekly*, Sept. 6; Edward J. Nichols).

blue An *umpire*, in reference to the color of the umpire's uniform. USAGE NOTE. The term may have been derogatory at one time, as if it referred not to the color of the umpire's uniform but to someone who "blew it." However, it is common to hear coaches, scorers, spectators, and players at Little League, high school, and college games use the term whenever they address the umpire, even on friendly terms, such as "What's the count, blue?"

Blue Book The administrative manual and directory of organized baseball, issued annually since 1909, and now published privately. Its contents have varied. It usually covers attendance reports, business updates, a product and service directory, league schedules, hotel and ballpark directions, major-league administration and support (parks statistics, team payrolls, free agent signings, club directories), information on minor leagues, independent leagues, foreign leagues, and fall and winter leagues, and rosters of personnel for baseball and field operations, scouts, amateur baseball, media, and umpires. It sometimes includes spring training camp directories and exhibition schedules, college baseball information, records, milestones, necrology, and player statistics and biographical information for all leagues. "There is no book published of more value to baseball officials and players than the Baseball Blue Book" (Alfred H. Spink, *The National Game*, 1911, p.405). See also *Green Book*; *Red Book*; *Orange Book*.

bluecoat An *umpire*, 1. "The ball game went on—fortunately, without any especially difficult calls to challenge the bush-league bluecoats" (Roger Angell, describing a game during an umpires' strike, *The Summer Game*, 1972, p.258; Charles D. Poe).

blue dart A hard, low *line drive*, often difficult to field. "I never saw a shortstop [Billy Hunter] make the play he did on Joe Astroth's blue dart. If that wasn't a hit, I never saw one" (Bobo Holloman, quoted in *San Francisco News*, May 7, 1953; Peter Tamony). See also *blue darter*. IST USE. 1932 (*New York Sun*, June 23).

blue darter A low *line drive* "that speeds viciously through the air, as though it were propelled by a blue gas flame" (Mike Whiteford, *How to Talk Baseball*, 1983, p.82). The term was used by Donald Gropman (*Say It Ain't So, Joe!*, 1979) for the line drives often hit by Shoeless Joe Jackson. "The specialty of the left-handed hitting [Sam] Rice was the blue-darter single that singed the pitchers' ears" (Shirley Povich, *The Washington Post*, Apr. 8, 1985). See also *blue dart*; *darter*. ETYMOLOGY. "Big blue darter" is another name for the Cooper's Hawk, a bird that "will dash into the farmyard like a bolt, passing within a few feet of individuals and carrying off a young chicken with incredible swiftness" (R.I. Brasher, in T. Gilbert Pearson, *Birds of America*, 1936, Part II, pp.67–68).

Blue Jays 1. Nickname for the American League East Division expansion franchise in Toronto, Ont., Canada, since 1977. The club took its name from Labatt Blue beer (Labatt, Canada's largest brewery, was an original owner of the club and often used a blue jay in its ads). Also known as *Jays*. 2. Nickname for the National League franchise in Philadelphia, Pa., in 1943 and 1944. The name was not accepted by the fans and newsmen, and the club reverted to *Phillies*.

blue shirt A fan who sits in the bleachers. "Rogers Hornsby, whose place even Frank Frisch may find difficult to fill to the satisfaction of the 'blue shirts' in the bleachers of Sportsman's Park" (*The Sporting News*, Jan. 6, 1927; Peter Morris). ETYMOLOGY. From "blue collar" worker.

bluff bunt Syn. of *fake bunt*. IST USE. 1910. "The 'bluff bunt,' aimed to pull defensive infielders out of position" (John J. Evers and

Hugh S. Fullerton, *Touching Second: The Science of Baseball*, 1910; Peter Morris).

blunder An error. IST USE. 1863 (*New York Sunday Mercury*, March 9; Edward J. Nichols).

board 1. *n./hist.* A flat and/or stiff glove or mitt from which balls are likely to bounce, as if it were a board or plank. The term is used less often today because modern gloves come with deep, preformed pockets and break in quickly. 2. *v.* To get on base. "[The Orioles] boarded two base runners" (*The Baltimore Sun*, Apr. 18, 1998). 3. *n.* Short for *scoreboard*, 1. "We got on the board early, and that was a key" (Erik Hanson, quoted in *The Baltimore Sun*, June 22, 1995). 4. *n./hist.* Syn. of *flat bat*.

boarding house The hotel where "big league clubs stop" (Al Schacht, *Al Schacht's Dope Book*, 1944).

boatload mentality The view that signing large numbers of Latin-American players for very little money will result in a handful of players making it to the major leagues. Marcos Bretón and José Luis Villegas (*Away Games: The Life and Times of a Latin Ball Player*, 1999) credit the term to Colorado Rockies vice president Dick Balderson, who was accounting for the extraordinary increase in the number of minor- and major-league ballplayers from Latin-American countries. Peter Morris notes that this view is the logical culmination of Branch Rickey's scouting dictum (quality out of quantity), but the term is a double-edged sword: while opportunities have greatly increased, so has exploitation.

boat race A blowout, when the ability of the winning team's starting pitcher cannot be evaluated properly. The term is used by scouts when a game is called early. ETYMOLOGY. Derives from America's Cup sailing competitions won by five or more miles (Alan Schwarz, BaseballAmerica.com, Nov. 14, 2006).

bob-and-weave The *knuckleball*, so called because of its erratic nature. "The bob-and-weave became [Al] Nipper's bread-and-butter pitch ... that sometimes dances, sometimes delights and sometimes disappoints" (*The Boston Globe*, June 21, 1987).

bobble 1. *v.* To mishandle, drop, or lose control of a batted or thrown ball, which often results in an error. See also *juggle*, 1. **2.** *n.* A ball that has been mishandled; an error. "Shortstop Zoilo Versalles made a career-high 39 errors [in 1965]; the first of three straight seasons in which he led American League shortstops in bobbles" (*Sports Illustrated*, June 12, 2000). See also *juggle*, 2. IST USE. 1909. Grantland Rice, in his poem "Modern Base Ball Lingo," defined "bobble" (*The Sporting Life*, Dec. 4; Stuart Y. Silverstein) as "A butter-fingered, rubber-mitted stab / In the booting of a bounder where the grabber doesn't grab." ETYMOLOGY. The term was first used in the early American West as slang for "mistake" or "blunder"; it is listed in 1893 in a "Texas Vocabulary" by F.K. Wister, which appears in the 1968 collection *Owen Wister Out West* (p.159; David Shulman). Also: "Sal, I'm mightily afeerd you'll make a bobble of it" (William C. Campbell, *A Colorado Colonel*, 1901, p.327; David Shulman).

bobblehead doll A doll reproduced with the identifiable facial features of a popular baseball player atop a pudgy, child-like, whimsical body, and whose oversized, spring-mounted head nods up and down when shaken. The dolls are popular giveaway items to induce attendance at baseball games; they also are drawing monetary value as collector's items, as are the older, less attractive ones produced in the 1960s. Once a staple of car dashboards, the dolls enjoyed a resurgence after the San Francisco Giants gave away 35,000 Willie Mays bobblehead dolls on May 9, 1999.

bobo A fan, usually of a manager. Followers of Los Angeles Dodgers manager Tommy Lasorda sat in an area known as "Bo-bo Row." Roger Bresnahan was known as New York Giants manager John McGraw's bobo (Bill James, *The Politics of Glory*, 1994). Also spelled "bo-bo." See also *little bo-bo*.

body armor Padded protective equipment worn by batters; e.g., shin guards and plastic elbow and arm covers. Such equipment makes batters less intimidated by inside pitches and promotes "diving" into pitches. Major League Baseball executive vice president Sandy Alderson (advocating reducing body protection, quoted in *The Baltimore Sun*, Nov. 8, 2000): "Body armor has become offensive, not defensive. Players should be able to protect themselves without a Roman shield."

body block Syn. of *roll block.* "The boys go in for football stuff to break up the double play, throwing body blocks on the second baseman or shortstop" (Ty Cobb, *My Life in Baseball*, 1961, p.168).

body check For a catcher to put his whole body in front of a pitch in the dirt so that it cannot get past him. Branch Rickey (*Branch Rickey's Little Blue Book*, 1995, pp.45–46): "With a runner on base anywhere, every dirt pitch should be body-checked. . . . Catchers who do not shift both feet on all pitches, or who do not body check on all direct pitches with a runner on base anywhere are defective fielding catchers."

body protector *hist.* An early synonym of *chest protector.* The 1884 preseason *Reach's Official American Association Base Ball Guide* carried an ad for Gray's Patent Body Protector. Peter Morris uncovered two 1884 citations: Washington catcher Ed McKenna "wore a body protector" (*Cincinnati Enquirer*, May 20) and Columbus catcher Rudy Kemmler "looks like a back-stop when he wears the body protector" (*Columbus Dispatch*, May 21).

Bogart A big game. The term was coined by Dennis Eckersley (*Athletics*, Sept. 2005).

boggle A near error. "Boggle is not exactly an error, but is closely allied to one. For example, a pitcher might . . . get his hand on the ball just enough, perhaps, to induce it to carom over toward third base, while the runner kept on his way to first base" (*The Washington Post*, July 22, 1900). Compare *bungle*, 1.

boiler The stomach of a player, manager, or coach, esp. when upset. A gastric ailment such as an ulcer or an upset stomach is known as a "bad boiler."

boiling-out place *hist.* A spring training camp, usually situated in a hot climate. IST USE. 1908 (*New York Evening Journal*, Feb. 11; Edward J. Nichols).

boing ball A facetious, onomatopoetic term used to describe baseball played on an artificial surface because of the tendency of the ball to bounce erratically and make odd synthetic noises. It apes the "boing" sound of animated cartoons.

bola Spanish for "ball."

bola de nudillos Spanish for "knuckleball." See also *mariposa*.

bola de tenedor Spanish for "forkball."

bola de tirabuzón Spanish for "screwball."

bola de velocidad Spanish for "fastball."

bola ensalivada Spanish for "spitball."

bola en territorio bueno Spanish for "fair ball."

bola en territorio malo Spanish for "foul ball."

bola rápida Spanish for "fastball."

bolshevik 1. *hist.* Slang for a *clubhouse lawyer*, 1 (Fresco Thompson, quoted in *Los Angeles Times*, July 8, 1961). 2. A player perceived by baseball club owners in the 1970s as a threat to their authority. "I'd want to . . . seek out an antiorganization man and see how baseball deals with what its ruling class calls 'bolsheviks'" (Roger Kahn, *A Season in the Sun*, 1977). ETYMOLOGY. A derogatory term for an extreme political radical.

Bolshevik League Nickname for *Players' League* of 1890. ETYMOLOGY. The term was applied after the fact because the Bolshevik party did not emerge until 1903 in Russia; it seized power in that country in Nov. 1917. In the United States, the term "Bolshevik" and its variations (including the slangy "Bolshie" or "Bolshy") were applied to that which was wild-eyed, radical, and anticapitalistic. The application of the term by conservative sportswriters to a group of baseball players was clearly meant to be derogatory (Charles D. Poe).

bolt 1. A *line drive*. 2. Players' slang for a pimple or boil: "get a wrench for that bolt" (Jim Bouton, *Ball Four*, 1970).

bomb 1. *v.* To surrender many hits during a finite period (e.g., an inning or game). "Bombed" is said of "pitchers whose pitches return from the plate traveling faster than they were going when they arrived" (Jim Brosnan, *The Long Season*, 1960). 2. *v.* To

defeat decisively with many hits; e.g., "The Reds bombed Smith with five extra-base hits." 3. *n.* Syn. of *home run*. When Ken Griffey Jr. decided to forgo his pursuit of Roger Maris' single-season home run record during the late stages of the 1997 season, he said (*The Washington Post*, Oct. 19, 1997), "I've got six bombs to go. There ain't no way I'm going to reach it."

bombard To get many hits off a pitcher. 1ST USE. 1905 (*The Sporting Life*, Sept. 2; Edward J. Nichols).

bombardment A rash of hits. "[Walter] Johnson was treated to a bombardment which netted them [St. Louis Browns] four runs" (*The Washington Post*, May 21, 1921).

bomber A home run hitter.

Bombers Short for *Bronx Bombers*.

bombo Spanish for "fly ball," "flyout," "pop fly," "popout," and "pop-up."

Bonds The black-and-cherry color combination of a *Sam Bat*. The term refers to Barry Bonds, one of the original players to use a Sam Bat.

bone 1. *v.* To rub repeatedly the maximum hitting point or "sweet spot" of one's bat, originally with an animal bone (such as a cow's femur) and later with a soda-pop bottle, to compress and "harden" the surface of the bat and to close the wood's pores. It is perfectly legal to bone a bat; but there is an element of voodoo about it, as the bat loses its elasticity and the velocity of the batted ball is decreased. Roy Hobbs, the tragic main character of Bernard Malamud's novel *The Natural* (1952), took care of his bat Wonderboy in such a fashion: "Hadn't used it much until I played semipro ball, but I always kept it oiled with sweet oil and boned it so it wouldn't chip." 1ST USE. 1928. " 'Boning' a bat consists in rubbing it with a bottle or bone or some hard smooth surface of that nature. The idea is that such constant rubbing smoothes the surface, fills in and contracts the wood pores on the surface and prevents breaking. I've seen fellows sit for hours at a time boning away at their favorite bats" (George Herman Ruth, *Babe Ruth's Own Book of Baseball*, pp.176–77; Peter Morris). 2. *n.* A heedless or foolish play. See also *pull* *a bone.* Syn. *boner*, 1. IST USE. 1912. "The 'bones' and 'boozles' that they [New York Giants] made gave Boston [Red Sox] the greatest of all base ball titles" (*The Sporting Life*, Oct. 26; Peter Morris). **3.** *n.* The fist-to-fist congratulatory gesture between a player and a teammate, sometimes coupled with a look of intimidating indifference. This celebratory ritual of the 1990s has replaced the *high five* of the 1980s. The origin of the gesture and term have been claimed by Jose Canseco and Mark McGwire (when they were Oakland A's teammates) and by Brady Anderson in 1989 (*Sports Illustrated*, Sept. 14, 1998).

bonehead 1. *n.* A dumb player. "A Newark paper quotes Manager [Bill] Murray as saying that next season he 'will have no boozers or bone-heads on the Philly team'" (*The Sporting Life*, Dec. 12, 1908; Peter Morris). IST USE. 1908 (*New York Evening Journal*, March 9; Edward J. Nichols). USAGE NOTE. The Japanese term for "bonehead" is "bon hedo" (Fred H. Miike, *Baseball Mad Japan*, 1974; Tim Wiles). EXTENDED USE. A stupid person or one who makes stupid comments. Actor Kevin Spacey (discussing Rev. Jerry Falwell's blaming gays and liberals for the Sept. 11, 2001, terrorist attacks, quoted in *W*, Nov. 2001): "What an absolute dunce! . . . You would think that maybe, at a moment like this, those kind of stupid, backward . . . right-wing ideological comments would not be needed. But then he's a bonehead, so how would he know?" **2.** *adj.* Said of a dumb play or dumb player. "[Bill] Abstein tried a 'bone-head' play a moment later and was caught at the plate" (*St. Louis Post-Dispatch*, Oct. 16, 1909; Peter Morris). IST USE. 1907. "The greatest of all 'bone-headed' plays was made by [John] Anderson when he tried to steal second with the bases full" (*The Sporting News*, Dec. 26; Peter Morris). EXTENDED USE. Stupid or foolish. "I don't like ta knock ya, but when ya pull a bonehead stunt like ya did yesterday, y're in love, or else y're getting balmy in the bean" (*Railroad Man's Magazine*, Aug. 1916; Peter Tamony). ETYMOLOGY. This "sweet word" we are told by lexicographer Gretchen Lee (*American Speech*, Apr. 1926) began in baseball as a

term of ridicule for a particularly unintelligent player or action. Many sources agree that the origin and certain initial popularity of both "bonehead" and "boner" stem from a single incident: *Merkle's boner.* Describing that 1908 event, Mark Sullivan (*Pre-War America*, volume III of *Our Times*, 1930) stated, "At the Polo Grounds, New York, a dispute historic in baseball, which enriched the language with two exceedingly forceful words, 'bonehead' and 'boner,' arose over whether Frederick Charles Merkle did or did not touch second base." As to the origin of "bonehead" and "boner" in their modern sense, Sullivan reported: "In their wrath at Merkle, an excellent player, the New York fans fixed upon a previously anemic and almost meaningless word, and gave to it a significance with which every reader is familiar. For more than twenty years, there has been rarely a game when from some part of the stands there did not arise from time to time, in shrill falsetto or hoarse bellow, the cry 'bonehead' directed at any player disapproved, not always justly, by a 'fan.'" The sad part of the story is that Merkle is remembered for this one play, but he had an otherwise respectable career playing for four teams from 1907 to 1926.

As Sullivan suggests, there is evidence to hint that "bonehead" (but not "boner") predates the Merkle play. Alfred H. Holt (*Phrase Origins*, 1936) reports that the term has been spotted in print as early as 1903 for a person who acts stupidly (presumably with bones where there should be brains) and that it was popularized by the 1908 incident. A specific point of origin was suggested by Hy Turkin when he noted that manager George Stallings first used the term to describe the "brainless play" of his 1898 Phillies; Lee Allen (*Hot Stove League*, 1955) agrees but insists that the term was applied mainly to Phillies owner Col. John I. Rogers, who released Stallings in 1898. Still one more piece of the puzzle: Norman Macht noted in the necrology section of the 1913 *Spalding's Official Base Ball Guide* that Edward Aschenbach, manager of teams in the New York State league, "coined the term 'bonehead.'" As is often the case with American slang, researchers are faced with conflicting claims that are long past the point of being sorted out; however, what is clear and conclusive in this case is that the term was a slang rarity until the 1908 incident.

boner 1. A dumb play, usually as the result of an error of judgment or lack of concentration as opposed to a mere physical mistake, such as a baserunner taking off on a catchable fly thinking that there are two outs when, in fact, there is only one; specif., *Merkle's boner*. Ron Fimrite (*Sports Illustrated*, Oct. 15, 1990) defined "boner" as "a mental blunder or fit of absentmindedness, a sudden blanking out, a momentary wandering that brings on dreadful consequences." Syn. *bone*, 2; *bull*; *Merkle*; *rock*, 1. 2. Any stupid move on or off the field. "Bill Sullivan the old White Sox catcher talked to me and told me not to pull no boner by refuseing [*sic*] to go where they sent me" (Ring W. Lardner, *The Saturday Evening Post*, May 23, 1914). USAGE NOTE. Historically, the term has not been used lightly in baseball and tends to be reserved for only the most serious gaffes. In its most extreme case (the infamous Merkle's boner) it hung on Fred Merkle for the rest of his life. "Fred Merkle, Of 'Boner' Fame, Dies" (Associated Press obituary headline, March 2, 1956; Peter Tamony). ETYMOLOGY. Gretchen Lee (*American Speech*, Apr. 1926) noted, "The sweet word 'Bone-head' began with ball players, and from it has sprung the useful term 'boner,' meaning an error in judgment." EXTENDED USE. A foolish mistake or obvious blunder; an error, but without the sting it carries in the context of baseball. The term has also specifically come to mean a hilarious classroom gaffe or howler.

boneyard 1. The imaginary dying grounds for washed-up pitchers (Al Schacht, *Al Schacht Dope Book*, 1944). 2. The figurative landing site of a deep home run ball.

bonk A lightly hit ball.

bonus 1. A cash incentive given to a draft choice for signing with a team; e.g., Gregg Olson received a $200,000 bonus from the Baltimore Orioles in 1988. See also *signing bonus*. 2. A special incentive or reward payment built into a player's contract, based on a particular aspect of that player's performance, such as innings pitched, games played, or selection to the All-Star team. See also *performance bonus*. 1ST USE. 1884. "Should the Louisvilles win the championship, the players of the team are each to receive a handsome cash bonus, and [Guy] Hecker will be given a house and a lot" (*Brooklyn Eagle*, Aug. 10; Peter Morris).

bonus baby A free-agent player signed under the bonus rule of 1953–1957. Such players were usually 18 or 19 years old, so full of promise and talent that they overshadowed their high school or college teammates and had professional teams scrambling to sign them; however, many bonus babies had failed careers as they were not ready for baseball at the major-league level and their talent rusted in idleness on the bench. The first bonus baby was Vic Janowicz, who signed out of Ohio State Univ. with the Pittsburgh Pirates for $25,000. Pat Jordan (*False Spring*, 1975) wrote, "The term 'bonus baby' is usually applied to any player receiving more than $10,000 upon signing a contract. Naturally, whenever a team invests such money in a player they treat him more tenderly than they would a player in whom they invested little money. A bonus baby had only to hint at improvement in order to advance in the minors. But a non-bonus baby had to fashion a record of unquestionable success before he advanced." See also *bonus rule*, 2. Syn. "bonus kid."

bonus player 1. A prospective player who is given a cash bonus as an extra incentive to sign with a major-league team. The first bonus player was pitcher Charlie Devens who signed with the New York Yankees for $20,000 in 1932. The first bonus player to capture popular attention was outfielder Dick Wakefield, who received $52,000 and a new car to sign with the Detroit Tigers upon his graduation from the Univ. of Michigan in 1941. Sportswriter Jimmy Cannon defined "bonus player" as one "who is paid a fortune to watch ballgames," as many such players fail to live up to expectations. The term did not attract attention as a new term until after World War II; "bonus player" is listed as new in 1947 in Kenneth Versand's *Polyglot's Lexicon 1943–1966* (1973). 2. A free agent with less than 90 days of professional experience who signs for more than $4,000 with a major-league club ($5,000 if the player is retained in the majors), $4,000 by minor-league clubs higher than Class B, and $3,000 by minor-league clubs in classes B, C, and D, under the *bonus rule* in effect from 1953 to 1957.

bonus rule 1. A rule in effect from 1947 to 1952 by which a player who was signed to a contract of more than $6,000 had to be placed on the major-league roster at the end of his professional season, could not be optioned to the minors, nor assigned outright to a minor-league club without passing through waivers. **2.** A rule in effect from 1953 to 1957 by which a player who signed a professional contract with a major-league team for more than $4,000 had to remain on the team's roster as an active player for a period of two full seasons, unless irrevocable waivers were asked for his unconditional release. A player given a bonus contract by a minor-league team had to go through an unrestricted draft before his contract could be assigned, sold, or traded to any other club. The rule was instituted at the Dec. 1952 winter meetings to discourage paying large amounts of money to untried players. See Brent Kelley, *Baseball's Biggest Blunder* (1996). See also *bonus baby*; *bonus player*, 2.

boob A fool; a dolt. "Cy Falkenberg, who was a boob in 1912, but a star in 1913, won his ninth straight game for the Naps yesterday" (*San Francisco Bulletin*, May 30, 1913; Gerald L. Cohen). ETYMOLOGY. David Shulman (*American Speech*, Feb. 1951) noted that the term is not baseballese, but seems to have originated with baseball players. The earliest use that Shulman could find was in Christy Mathewson's *Pitching in a Pinch* (1912): "There's a poor 'boob' in the hospital now that stopped one with his head." The term may have been inspired by the much older term "booby," for a fool.

boo bird A fan given to jeers, boos, and catcalls when the home team falters. "The boo birds in the Cleveland stands were in full voice. Even Earl Averill, a star for eight years and one of the great hitters of all time, came in for his share of sour notes from the fans" (Bob Feller, *Strikeout Story*, 1947; Charles D. Poe).

book 1. *n.* The official rules of the game of baseball. **2.** *n.* The information that a team has on the specific strengths and weaknesses of an opposing pitcher, batter, or manager; a scouting report. Clubhouse food, out-of-town restaurants, umpires, and practically any other variable may have a book. Ken Singleton (quoted in *The Sporting News*, June 13, 1981): "You keep a book on umpires the way you do with pitchers." Jim Henneman (*The Baltimore Sun*, June 7, 1994) wrote, "While constantly aware of his speed, the opponents' 'book' on [Brady] Anderson is that he no longer relies on the bunt as a primary offensive weapon." **3.** *n.* The record book or encyclopedia of baseball. The term is often used in the plural. Alan Newman (quoted in *Baseball America*, May 3–16, 1999; Peter Morris): "My goal when I started baseball was to get in the book; get in the *Baseball Encyclopedia*. If I got one pitch in, whatever it took to get there." Jose Lima, who allowed a National League record of 48 home runs in 2000 (quoted in *Sports Illustrated*, Oct. 9, 2000): "I have the National League record. So what? At least I'm in the book for something—and it's not for stealing drugs." **4.** *v.* To move very fast or with maximum speed; e.g., "Smith was really booking around the bases for a stand-up triple." **5.** *n.* See *Book, The*.

Book, The An unwritten compendium of conventional wisdom, strategic thought, intuitive impulses, and time-tested axioms that define how the game of baseball should be played; the collection of assumptions and percentages used to make on-field decisions; the accumulated baseball knowledge "of the ages." This set of unwritten but widely observed "rules" are followed by the game's managers, players, and fans; it has "served as silent mentor to every manager who ever decided to go for the win on the road or play for a tie at home" (Peter Schmuck, *The Baltimore Sun*, July 24, 2002). Perhaps the most often-cited example of a tenet of The Book is that left-handed batters face right-handed pitchers and vice versa. Other tenets include: never intentionally walk the potential winning run; don't make the first and third out at third base; never throw behind the runner; don't use the closer in a tie game; hit to the right side with a runner at first base; and don't play the infield in early in the game. A manager who makes an unconventional move is said to be "going against The Book"; but he is apt to respond by saying, "I never play by The Book because I never met the guy that wrote it," or "He who lives by The Book can also die by The Book." Sometimes spelled "the book."

book-crazed Being overly obsessed with baseball statistics.

bookends A pair of defensive players positioned on opposite sides of the playing field; specif., the left fielder and right fielder collectively, and the first baseman and third baseman collectively. The term was used in 1986 to describe first baseman Don Mattingly and third baseman Mike Pagliarulo of the New York Yankees.

boom **1.** *v.* To hit the ball hard. IST USE. 1909 (*Baseball Magazine*, July; Edward J. Nichols). **2.** *n.* A home run. New York Yankees manager Joe Torre (quoted in *The Baltimore Sun*, Oct. 18, 1999): "Darryl [Strawberry] gives you . . . the threat of a home run. And we might need a boom tonight."

boomerang ball A batted ball that comes back to the pitcher.

boost *hist.* **1.** *n.* A batted ball that results from the batter's hitting underneath the ball and pushing it into the air. IST USE. 1904. "[Joe] Cassidy's best stunt was his capture of [Tom] Jones' boost in the third" (*The Washington Post*, Aug. 7; Peter Morris). **2.** *v.* To hit the bottom half of the ball, causing it to pop up in the air. IST USE. 1908 (*New York Evening Journal*, Aug. 26; Edward J. Nichols).

boot **1.** *n.* An error, such as one made while handling a ground ball. Typically, the ball bounces off the fielder's glove, as if it were kicked or booted. Originally, a booted ball was (and still is on occasion) one that had actually been kicked ("booted") in error, but the term has long since been generalized to any fielding error. IST USE. 1904. "He can put his boots into more ground balls than any shortstop in the league" (*The Washington Post*, Aug. 19; Peter Morris). **2.** *v.* To commit a boot. "Why does he waste his efforts booting baseballs, when Yale is mourning the lack

of a punter?" (Hugh S. Fullerton, *American Magazine*, June 1912). See also *kick*, 3. IST USE. 1896. "[Jimmy] Bannon booting a grounder away from him in the greenest kind of style" (*Boston Globe*, Apr. 18; Peter Morris). EXTENDED USE. To err; to mishandle. **3.** *v.* To remove from a game; e.g., "The umpire booted Smith for kicking dirt on him."

booth The area in a ballpark where radio and television announcers work, usually from an elevated position behind home plate. "Booth" is a traditional baseball term that is often used when the work area bears no resemblance to a booth. "This spring, after dreaming of it for years, I finally entered 'the booth.' Actually, it's not a booth at all; it's more like a pen, open to the elements except for some light wire mesh designed to protect the announcers from irate fans" (J. Anthony Lucas, *The New York Times Magazine*, Sept. 12, 1971).

booze cage *hist.* An area in a ballpark where alcoholic beverages are served. "In view of the fact that we had a tailender here last year the booze cage was the only redeeming feature of the ball park. . . . The booze cage will be on hand again this year and so will the thirst that makes its presence necessary" (*San Francisco Bulletin*, Feb. 18, 1913; Gerald L. Cohen).

BOP **1.** Abbrev. for *base–out percentage*. **2.** Abbrev. for *bases over plate appearances*.

bopper A home run hitter. The term is often prefaced by the word "big": e.g., "a true No. 4 hitter is a guy who's going to hit 40 home runs, a big bopper in the middle of the lineup that everybody's afraid of" (Jeff Conine, quoted in *The Baltimore Sun*, March 20, 2003).

boring Descriptive of a pitch moving with heavy sink into the lower part of the strike zone. "Carlos Zambrano's sinker has incredible boring action, particularly down and in to righthanders" (Mike Arbuckle, quoted in Alan Schwarz, BaseballAmerica.com, Nov. 14, 2006).

Borough Hall *hist.* A sidearm pitch in Brooklyn during the period when that borough hosted the Dodgers (Al Schacht, *Al Schacht's Dope Book*, 1944).

Bosox Nickname for the Boston Red Sox.

bosque Spanish for "outfield."

Boston ball Syn. of *Massachusetts game*.

Boston game Syn. of *Massachusetts game*.

Boston Massacre 1. The widely used nickname for the 1978 fade by the Boston Red Sox, which culminated with Bucky Dent's home run that decided the one-game playoff in favor of the New York Yankees. "Red Sox rooters have known heartbreak. They haven't forgotten the Boston Massacre in 1978 and the 14½-game lead that vanished like an apparition" (Tom Pedulla, *The Gannett Westchester Newspapers*, June 25, 1986). Also recalled as "the Collapse," "the Fade," and "the Fold." 2. The four-game sweep of the Boston Red Sox by the New York Yankees at Fenway Park in Boston, Sept. 7–10, 1978, by scores of 15–3, 13–2, 7–0, and 7–4. The Yankees came to town four games behind and left town tied for first. 3. The five-game sweep of the Boston Red Sox by the New York Yankees at Fenway Park in Boston, Aug. 18–21, 2006, in which the Yankees outscored the Sox, 49–26, leaving the Sox 6½ games behind the first-place Yankees. "The hated New York Yankees came to town . . . the collective result of which has already been anointed 'The Boston Massacre'" (George Kimball, *Irish Times*, Aug. 24, 2006). 4. Any egregious defeat or series of defeats incurred by the Boston Red Sox at Fenway Park. For example: "The Boston Massacre, 1951 version, was enacted by a band of Cleveland Indians . . . who descended on the Red Sox and laid 'em waste, 15 to 2, in a gory spectacle before 23,321 Boston citizens" (*The Washington Post*, Sept. 20, 1951).
ETYMOLOGY. The name comes from the event that took place on March 5, 1770, when British soldiers fired on a crowd of colonists in Boston; five people died. The word of the Boston Massacre spread rapidly and served to strengthen the spirit of revolution.

bottle To contain an opponent. To "bottle a game" is to win it or make certain of winning it.

bottle bat 1. A baseball bat with an especially thick barrel, an abrupt taper, and very thin handle, which gives it a milk bottle–like appearance. The bat was made famous by Heinie Groh, who used it with great effectiveness from 1912 to 1921. Groh's bat had a barrel about 17 inches long, which necked down to a thin handle also about 17 inches long; he choked up to swing the 46-ounce bat. A bottle-shaped bat would be legal today as long as it was not more than 2¾ inches at its thickest and not more than 42 inches in length. Syn. *fat bat*. 2. Any thick-handled bat (Robert K. Adair, *The Physics of Baseball*, 1990, p.94).

bottom 1. The *second half* of an inning. The home team's scoring always appears on the bottom line of the scoreboard. 2. See *bottom of the order*.

bottom falls out Said of a pitched ball that drops sharply as it crosses the plate. Syn. "bottom drops out."

bottom half The *second half* of an inning.

bottom of the ninth The last half of the ninth inning. EXTENDED USE. Last chance to accomplish something. New York Giants quarterback Kerry Collins, commenting on the fourth quarter (quoted in *The Baltimore Sun*, Nov. 15, 2001): "We weren't quite to the bottom of the ninth. We had to start making plays."

bottom of the order The last three batters in the batting order, almost always a team's least effective or weaker hitters and, in the National League, including the pitcher. They are likely to get one less at-bat in a game than those at the top of the order. See also *top of the order*, 2; *middle of the order*. Syn. *weak end of the order*.

bottom of the rotation Syn. of *back of the rotation*. "The [Cleveland] Indians . . . have unproven youth and lack of consistency at the bottom of the rotation" (*Sports Illustrated*, Apr. 5, 2004).

bottom out For a pitcher not to come to a complete stop when pitching out of the stretch.

Boudreau shift Original name for the *Williams shift*. Ted Williams (quoted in *Sports Illustrated*, Aug. 21, 1967): "I remember when [Ty] Cobb criticized me for not trying to punch the ball to leftfield away from Boudreau's shift. Boy, I thought Cobb was an old crab, and here I am getting older, and I find *I'm* more critical."

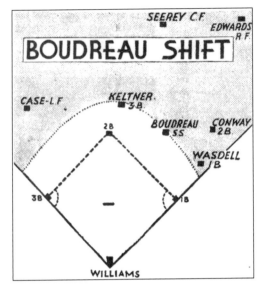

Boudreau shift. A newspaper diagram of the shift. *National Baseball Library and Archives, Cooperstown, N.Y.*

bounce 1. *n.* The rebounding of a baseball on the ground. **2.** *v.* To bat a ball so that it hits the ground before it reaches a fielder. **3.** *v.* Syn. of *eject*.

bounce a beauty To make a safe hit with a well-directed ground ball.

bounce back 1. To hit the ball so that it bounds back to the pitcher. **2.** To recover quickly; e.g., "After losing the first game of the doubleheader, the Giants bounced back to take the second game." **3.** Syn. of *recoil,* 1.

bounceout *n.* A batted ball that promptly starts to bounce and is fielded immediately for the out.

bounce out *v.* To hit the ball so that it bounces and is fielded for an easy out.

bouncer 1. A ground ball that takes a series of moderate bounces. **2.** An umpire who ejects players for arguing. "Silk" O'Loughlin was termed "a quick bouncer" for his tendency to eject players for even mildly disputing one of his calls (*The Washington Post,* Aug. 28, 1904; Peter Morris).

bounce target *hist.* Syn. of *cutoff man.* A "bounce target" is "provided by a player placing himself in line between the home base and an outfielder making a throw-in to indicate the length and direction of the throw and to intercept it if advisable" (Ralph H.

Barbour, *How to Play Better Baseball,* 1935, p.166; David Shulman).

bound 1. A bounce of a batted and thrown ball. **2.** *hist.* A base in the Massachusetts game. IST USE. 1858. "Four Bases or Bounds shall constitute a round [scoring of a run]" (Rules of the Massachusetts Game, Rule 3, May 13).

boundary belt A home run.

bound catch *hist.* A batted ball caught on the first bounce, thereby retiring the batter, in the *bound game.* It was officially abolished in 1864; however, the *foul bound* persisted until 1885. The term was used to distinguish it from a *fly catch.* IST USE. 1863. "In fielding we noted . . . a good bound catch by Ibbottson" (*Brooklyn Eagle,* Oct. 8; Peter Morris).

bounder A high-bouncing, easy-to-field ball. Syn. *big bounce.* IST USE. 1868. "This is the technical term for a bounding ball from the bat which strikes the ground within the lines of the in-field" (Henry Chadwick, *The Game of Base Ball,* p.39).

bound game *hist.* A game played in baseball's early years in which the *bound rule* was in effect. The Knickerbockers originally played the bound game, but switched to the "manlier" *fly game* in the late 1850s. In 1864, the fly game officially replaced the bound game, although the bound game persisted in some rural areas for many years. See also *bound catch; on the bound.*

bound rule *hist.* A rule in baseball's early years by which a batter was declared out if his batted ball was caught on the first bounce. By the late 1850s, the bound rule became a source of controversy. The Knickerbockers began seeking its elimination in 1857, having determined that the practice negatively affected the game; they viewed the rule as "a childish way to play the game and that men ought to have to catch the ball without it being cushioned by the ground" (Peter Morris, *Baseball Fever,* 2003). It was officially abolished at the National Association of Base Ball Players convention in Dec. 1864. However, before that date, many games were played under the *fly rule* when both clubs consented to its application. See also *bound game.*

bow-and-arrow 1. *n.* An umpire's technique in calling a third strike by punching one arm forward while jerking the elbow of the other arm backward, aping the movements of an archer (*Sports Illustrated*, Apr. 16, 1990). **2.** *adj.* Said of a pitching motion in which the pitcher pulls the ball out of the glove directly behind his ear, thereby creating deception (Alan Schwarz, BaseballAmerica.com, Nov. 14, 2006).

bowel-locker A sharp-breaking curveball (Dick Kaegel, *The Seattle Times*, Sept. 18, 1988).

Bowery, the Row of lockers reserved for players who are past their prime. ETYMOLOGY. The term dates from the middle 1930s and is a direct reference to the Bowery, a street running diagonally across the east side of lower Manhattan in New York City. The street and the area around it have long been associated with grim poverty and human dereliction. Metaphorically, it stands for the end of the road. The name comes from the Dutch word "bouwerji" for "farm."

bowled ball *hist.* A pitch in which the ball is rolled along the ground or "tossed in so as to touch the ground before reaching the [home] base" (Henry Chadwick, *The Game of Base Ball*, 1868, p.39). Such a pitch was ruled a called ball.

bowling ball A term used by pitcher Roger Clemens for an inside (or "heavy") fastball (Buster Olney, *The Last Night of the Yankee Dynasty*, 2004; and *The Sporting News*, March 25, 2005).

bow tie A brushback pitch thrown at the batter's throat or under his chin. The term was believed to have been coined by Satchel Paige. The phrase "put a bow tie on him" was used by Nolan Ryan for throwing a pitch up by the neck.

box 1. *n.* A designated area on the playing field within which a player or coach is obliged to stand; e.g., *batter's box*, *catcher's box*, *pitcher's box*, and *coach's box*. However, in the 19th century it was all but exclusively a reference to the pitcher's position (originally a box-shaped area) or, as one reference put it, "the little square in the middle of the diamond." IST USE. 1882. "[Pitcher George] McGinnis will take the box" (*St. Louis Post-Dispatch*, Aug. 26; Peter Morris). **2.** *n.* Short for *box seat*. **3.** *n.* Short for *box score*; e.g., "Give me a few minutes to read yesterday's boxes." **4.** *v.* To get in front of the ball to prevent it getting past; e.g., a catcher who blocks a pitch is said "to box it." **5.** *v.* To field a ground ball awkwardly. "[Melvin Mora] extended the seventh inning by boxing Scott Hatteberg's one-out double-play grounder for his 12th error" (*The Baltimore Sun*, Sept. 25, 2000).

box artist *hist.* A skilled pitcher. See also *artist*, 2. IST USE. 1902. "Neal Ball the redoubtable 'box artist' of the Holland independent team" (*Detroit Tribune*, Aug. 17; Peter Morris).

boxball Syn. of *box baseball*.

box baseball An urban form of baseball played with two contestants, a rubber ball, and no bat on a sidewalk, using as few as two or as many as five "boxes" (a sidewalk box usually being three feet on a side). A common version used three sidewalk boxes: one for the pitcher, who leans in to bounce an underhand lob (usually with a spin) into and across a middle neutral box to the hitter's box, where the "batter" slaps the ball with the palm of his open hand or with a fist into the pitcher's box and "hopefully far beyond on the subsequent bounce, with . . . the value of the hit determined by distance of the first bounce" (Stephen Jay Gould, *Triumph and Tragedy in Mudville*, 2003, p.45). Balls caught on the fly by the pitcher are outs. Some versions allow the hitter to throw the ball in the air and then hit it with his fist. In a two-box version, each player stands at the crack of the two boxes with a penny placed on the middle of the crack, the penny being awarded to the first player who hits it with the ball. Syn. *boxball*.

boxcar town *hist.* A small town; an "extra small town, usually for exhibition game" (Al Schacht, *Al Schacht's Dope Book*, 1944). In the derogatory talk of players, the term suggested a sleepy town whose main feature was a siding where the railroad stored boxcars.

boxman *hist.* A pitcher. "One of the Greatest Battles of Boxmen in Years to be Fought at

Fenway Park" (*The Boston Globe* headline, Sept. 6, 1912). IST USE. 1886. "Down South they are not pitchers nor twirlers; they are 'boxmen'" (*Official Base Ball Record*, June 12; Peter Morris).

box score A condensed statistical summary of a baseball game, traditionally a feature of newspaper sports sections. "The box score is the catechism of baseball, ready to surrender its truth to the knowing eye" (Stanley Cohen, *The Man in the Crowd*, 1981). "The box score is [getting] . . . longer, more tedious, more self-important every spring, and I say more power to it. Indeed, the standard box score is now a ludicrously complicated rectangle half a foot long" (Steve Rushin, *Sports Illustrated*, Apr. 19, 1999). For years it was believed that the first box score appeared in the *New York Clipper* (July 16, 1853). However, historian Melvin Adelman located a newspaper account of a baseball game in the *New York Herald* (Oct. 25, 1845), accompanied by a sort of proto-box score that qualifies as a "condensed statistical summary" of the game. Box scores did not appear with regularity until 1876 and the founding of the National League. Henry Chadwick is given credit for the creation of the shorthand ("phonographic") box score, although some have insisted that *New York Herald* writer Michael J. Kelly (in 1868) deserves the credit. Syn. *box*, 3. IST USE. 1908. "In the Spring the young fan's fancy turns to full box scores" (Grantland Rice, poem "In the Spring," *The Sporting Life*, Apr. 4, p.3; Stuart Y. Silverstein). ETYMOLOGY. According to Edward J. Nichols (*An Historical Dictionary of Baseball Terminology*, PhD dissertation, Jan. 1939, p.9), the term is derived "from the old newspaper custom of placing the data in a boxed-off section on the page." EXTENDED USE. The term has long been used for statistical summaries in other sports and as a metaphor for results in other areas. A headline in the *New York Herald Tribune* (Oct. 4, 1936) proclaimed "Republicans See Errors in 'Box Score' of New Deal"; the story under the headline read in part: "Arthur M. Curtis, assistant to the chairman of the Republican National Committee, Friday issued a statement calling attention to 'five errors' and one 'deliberate misplay' which belong in the 'box score' brought to the nation by President Roosevelt's Pittsburgh address." Roosevelt had talked of "the box score of the government of the United States" in his speech. This political use of the term continued: when Harry Truman became president he issued periodic "box scores" scoring congressional action on his legislative program. "Truman 'Box Score' Hits Congress Again" (*San Francisco Call-Bulletin* headline, Aug. 12, 1948; Peter Tamony). Another interesting extended use involves the U.S. National Aeronautics and Space Administration and the Goddard Flight Center's developing a box score to keep track of the number of objects in orbit by type (payload or debris) and by the nation or organization that owns them.

box seat A choice and most expensive seat at the ballpark, located near home plate, first base, or third base. According to Lee Allen (*The Hot Stove League*, 1955, p.114), the first box seats were introduced at the Union Grounds in Brooklyn in 1871. "[Mutuals president William H.] Cammeyer has erected a platform [at the Union Grounds in Brooklyn] in front of and above the dressing rooms of the Mutual Club to which persons who

Box seat. New York Yankees owner Frank J. Farrell's box seats at the Polo Grounds. *George Grantham Bain Collection, Library of Congress*

wish to be exclusive can obtain admission by the payment of an extra quarter" (*New York Clipper*, June 3, 1871). Syn. *box*, 2.

boxwork *hist.* Pitching. IST USE. 1888 (*New York Press*, Apr. 2; Edward J. Nichols).

box worker A pitcher. "Fans . . . marveled at the pitching of 'Big Ed' Walsh, Chicago's premier box worker" (*San Francisco Bulletin*, March 10, 1913; Gerald L. Cohen).

boy A scout's term for any amateur player. "Seattle would have first pick in the June draft and . . . they might make Ron Darling the number one boy in the country" (Kevin Kerrane, *Dollar Sign on the Muscle*, 1984).

boy blue An *umpire*, 1. ETYMOLOGY. Almost certainly inspired by the horn-blowing "Little Boy Blue" of nursery rhyme fame and a tie-in to the traditional blue umpire's uniform.

boy manager A manager who is not yet 30 years old. The Hall of Fame plaque for Fred Clarke states that he was "the first of the successful 'boy managers,' at twenty-four." Others known as boy managers were Bucky Harris (age 27) and Joe Cronin (age 26), both of whom managed the Washington Senators.

boys in blue The umpires. See also *men in blue*. IST USE. 1930. "Umpires have few friends, but Joe Cronin swears by the boys in blue" (Harold C. Burr, *Brooklyn Daily Eagle*, Sept. 8; Peter Morris). ETYMOLOGY. An obvious borrowing from the nickname of both the Union soldiers of the Civil War and police forces of modern times, who have both been recognized by their blue uniforms.

Boys in blue. Umpiring crew with Miller Huggins, manager, New York Yankees, 1923. *George Grantham Bain Collection, Library of Congress*

Boys of Summer 1. A retrospective nickname for the Brooklyn Dodgers of the 1950s, created by Roger Kahn in his 1972 book on the Brooklyn Dodgers, *The Boys of Summer*. The book, according to Kahn, was "not on sports but on time and what it does to all of us." ETYMOLOGY. The term itself comes from a line in a Dylan Thomas poem, "I see the boys of summer in their ruin," which Kahn quotes at the beginning of his book. 2. A term used by broadcasters and writers to connote all baseball players. An Opening Day story from *USA Today* (Apr. 7, 1987) begins, "The Boys of Summer are back—at last." There has been some play on the term; e.g., players in spring training are called the "Boys of Spring"; the 1989 Chicago Cubs managed by Don Zimmer were called the "Boys of Zimmer"; and popular broadcaster Jon Miller is called the "Voice of Summer" (*The Washington Post*, July 31, 1988).

BP Abbrev. for *batting practice*, 1.

BPA Abbrev. for *bases per plate appearance*.

BPF [softball term] Abbrev. for *bat performance factor.*

BR 1. Abbrev. for *bats right*. 2. Abbrev. for *batting runs.*

BRA Abbrev. for *batter's run average.*

Brabender's Law A facetious "law" of postseason play that states that "the wildest celebrants are players who have not enjoyed the catharsis of playing" (George Vecsey, *The New York Times*, Sept. 22, 1986). The law is named for Baltimore Orioles pitcher Gene Brabender, who drenched the clubhouse with champagne after spending all of his time in the bullpen as his team swept the Los Angeles Dodgers in the 1966 World Series. Although the term may not be used often, the concept survives. After the Toronto Blue Jays won their second straight World Series in 1993, Paul White (*USA Today Baseball Weekly*, Nov. 17–30, 1993; Peter Morris) wrote that little-used rookie Willie Canate "was easily the most active celebrant during the Blue Jays' various clinching parties" and that Canate "was wielding champagne bottles like fire hoses after the World Series."

brace of homers Two home runs, such as when a player hits two home runs during a game.

braille-man *hist.* A coach skilled at sending signs and hand signals to baserunners. Most signs involve use of the hands.

brain cramp A mental error, such as a fielder throwing to the wrong base, a pitcher failing to cover first base on a grounder to the right side, a player arguing with the umpire while holding the ball, or a baserunner failing to score from third base on a slow chopper to the infield. Miguel Tejada suffered "a brain cramp at shortstop yesterday—he held the ball too long before throwing late" (*The Baltimore Sun*, March 22, 2004). After walking to the mound and starting to speak Spanish to Japanese pitcher Hideo Nomo, Los Angeles Dodgers catcher Mike Piazza confessed to having had a "brain cramp" (*Sports Illustrated*, May 13, 1996). See also *vapor lock*. Syn. *brain lock*; *brain spasm*. ETYMOLOGY. Buster Olney (*San Diego Union-Tribune*, Apr. 4, 1994) wrote that if former San Diego Padres pitching coach Pat Dobson did not originate the term, "then he was responsible for popularizing its use."

brain lock Syn. of *brain cramp*.

brains 1. The manager of a baseball team. **2.** A cagey or tricky player.

brain spasm Syn. of *brain cramp*.

brain surgeon A facetious reference to a ballplayer. When Leonard Shecter (*Baseball Digest*, June 1963) asked what was easier to become than a successful ballplayer, a disgusted pitcher replied, "I think I'll take up something simple, like brain surgery."

Branch Rickey Award An annual award jointly sponsored by the Rotary Club of Denver and the Major League Baseball Players Alumni Association and presented to a currently active major-league player, manager, or executive who has demonstrated high standards and social concerns through contributions to the community. First given in 1992, the award is named for the Hall of Famer who served as player, manager, and executive.

brander *hist.* A hard-hit ball that burns or "brands" the ground. IST USE. 1869 (*New York Herald*, Sept. 16; Edward J. Nichols).

brannigan A brawl. The term (capitalized) was used frequently by Ty Cobb in his autobiography (*My Life in Baseball*, 1961); e.g., "Don't start a Brannigan. But if somebody else does, give 'em hell" (p.126). Not to be confused with *pull a Brenegan*.

brash Said of a pugnacious player. "[Gene Mauch] was almost always described as 'brash,' a baseball term that seems to mean pushier than your limited ability would normally allow for" (Maury Allen, *Bo: Pitching and Wooing*, 1973, p.312; Charles D. Poe).

brass A team's management, including the owner, general manager, and field manager. "[Dwight] Evans takes [verbal] shot at Red Sox brass" (Associated Press dispatch, July 4, 1987). IST USE. 1946. "Manager Frankie Frisch is the 'CO,' the 'Old Man,' or 'The Brass,' and he and his coaches have come to be known as 'GHQ'" (Chester L. Smith, *Baseball Digest*, May). ETYMOLOGY. The term came into common use during World War II and was a reference to the decorative gold braid on the bills of senior officers' hats, and was often used as "brass hat." It established itself as service-wide military slang for high-ranking officers as a class. It was brought back and reapplied by baseball players returning from wartime service.

bravery suit The protective gear worn by the plate umpire. "On occasion an umpire will forget to wear part of his 'bravery suit'" (Ron Luciano, *Strike Two*, 1984).

Braves Nickname for the National League East Division franchise in Atlanta, Ga. The franchise originated as the Boston Red Stockings in the National Association (1871–1875) and became the Boston Red Caps in the National League (1876–1882), was renamed the Boston Beaneaters (1883–1906), the Boston Doves (1907–1910), the Boston Rustlers (1911), and the Boston Braves (1912–1935 and 1941–1952), relocated to Milwaukee (1953–1965), and became the Atlanta Braves in 1966. See also *Beaneaters*; *Bees*; *Miracle Braves*. ETYMOLOGY. After James E. Gaffney, a contractor and Tammany Hall chieftain, bought the Rustlers, John Montgomery Ward, one of Gaffney's partners, suggested renaming the club owing to the fact that members of the Tammany machine were often referred to as "braves." The Tammany Society, which had been formed in New York

City in 1789, was named for a Delaware Indian chief (Tammany or Tamanend) known for his sagacity. Tammany Hall was the most famous of the big-city political machines and had a major influence (often corrupt, sometimes effective) in New York politics for about 100 years (roughly from the middle of the 19th century to the middle of the 20th century).

bread-and-butter pitch A pitcher's most effective pitch; the specific pitch by which the pitcher "earns a living." Bert Dunne (*Folger's Dictionary of Baseball*, 1958) noted, "When pitcher is denied right to dust off batter, he cries, 'You're taking away my bread and butter.'"

breadbasket catch A catch of a high fly ball with the glove held just above the waist as opposed to with one's arms over one's head. "Breadbasket" has been a slang word for "stomach" since the 16th century. See also *basket catch*.

breadwinner 1. A productive player who "brings home" the most in terms of wins, saves, or winning runs. **2.** A pitcher's throwing arm. "[Danny] Jackson, a left-hander, bats right-handed, thus exposing his breadwinner to a wild pitch" (Keith Hernandez, *Pure Baseball*, 1994, p.53).

break 1. *v.* To deviate along the trajectory of a pitched ball. "The deceptive feature of this delivery [spitball] is the fact that it is nothing but a straight ball until just as the batter swings at it, then it 'breaks' sharply" (*The Sporting Life*, May 13, 1905; Peter Tamony). IST USE. 1899. "[Jack] Katoll is spoken of as the possessor of a sizzling curve that comes up with a phenomenal burst of speed and breaks lightning fast" (*Chicago Daily News*, May 8; Peter Morris). **2.** *n.* The deviation in the trajectory of a pitched ball. "If it [the fastball] takes a sharp jump, due to the speed, we call that the 'break on his fast one'" (John J. McGraw, *My Thirty Years in Baseball*, 1923). IST USE. 1904. "Speed naturally gives a break to a fast ball" (Jimmy McAleer, quoted in *The Washington Post*, Sept. 11; Peter Morris). **3.** *n.* A runner's start toward the next base. **4.** *n.* A lucky or unlucky event; e.g., "to make your own breaks is to create your own luck." See also *breaks, the*. IST USE. 1906.

"Even the dubs of any league expect as good as an even break at home" (Hugh S. Fullerton, *Chicago Tribune*, May 27; Peter Morris). **5.** *n.* The turning point in a game; a crucial play—often a mistake—on which a team capitalizes. "Time and again these two have kept the score board clean as far as the sixth or 'lucky seventh' and then would come the break for which each team was working" (William Patten & J.W. McSpadden, *The Book of Baseball*, 1911; Peter Tamony). IST USE. 1905. "The Sox hung on like bulldogs, averting defeat by steady playing at times and by sensational or heady work at others, until a break came in the eighth, through which they pulled the game in a twinkling" (*Chicago Tribune*, June 1; Peter Morris). **6.** *v.* To end something; e.g., to "break" a hitting streak or to "break" another player's record. **7.** *n.* A prompt movement by a fielder to a batted ball; e.g., getting a "good break to the ball" involves knowing the pitcher's habits, the batter's manners, and the pitch being thrown. **8.** *v.* For a baserunner to make a sudden dash from one base toward another; e.g., "Smith breaks toward second as the ball was hit to right field." IST USE. 1887 (*Chicago Inter-Ocean*, Apr. 8; Edward J. Nichols). **9.** *v.* To run toward, or react promptly to, a batted ball; e.g., "Smith breaks to the ball as soon as it is hit." **10.** *n.* An interruption. The term is often used as a shortened form of *All-Star break*; e.g., "I've been throwing the ball well since the break" or "Orioles are 12–7 since the break." **11.** *n./hist.* A breaking ball. "The long, lean bender of breaks just smiled . . . from the first inning until the final frame" (*San Francisco Bulletin*, Apr. 11, 1913; Gerald L. Cohen).

break ball A possible precursor to *breaking ball*. "McClusky does not depend upon any one sort of ball, having them all, but his best is a 'break' ball that takes an unexpected angle just before reaching the plate" (*The Sporting Life*, May 17, 1902; Peter Morris). The term was also cited by Edward J. Nichols (*An Historical Dictionary of Baseball Terminology*, PhD dissertation, 1939, p.10) as appearing in *Collier's Magazine* (June 22, 1912).

breaker Syn. of *breaking ball*.

break his dishes To break a batter's bat handle; e.g., "The pitcher got in his kitchen [inside] and broke his dishes." Phil Pepe (in Zander Hollander, ed., *The Encyclopedia of Sports Talk*, 1976) reported: "The term has been refined as in, 'He got in his refrigerator and broke his eggs.'" See also *kitchen*, 1; *pots and pans.*

break in 1. To make good with a club; to make the team. See also *break into.* 2. To condition or soften a glove or mitt to fit a player's hand or for game use. IST USE. 1901. "Jimmie Burke is mourning the loss of his fielding glove. . . . 'I would not care so much,' said Jimmie, 'only I had just got it broke in'" (*Milwaukee Journal*, Apr. 15; Peter Morris).

breaking Deviating. Curveballs are variously described by the manner of their deviation; e.g., high-breaking, low-breaking, fast-breaking, slow-breaking.

breaking ball Any pitched ball (curveball, slider, sinker, knuckleball, screwball) that deviates from a relatively straight and natural trajectory; a catchall for any pitch that can't be identified. The generic nature of the term was underscored when announcer Brooks Robinson (telecast, Aug. 18, 1987) admitted that this was the term broadcasters used when they were not sure what kind of pitch had just been thrown. Robinson is not alone in this perception. Jerry Howarth (*Baseball Lite*, 1986) noted that it was a "term used by radio and television sportscasters who have difficulty detecting the difference between a slider and curve." See also *break ball.* Syn. *breaker; breaking pitch; break*, 11.

breaking pitch Syn. of *breaking ball.*

breaking stuff An assortment of breaking balls. Darrin Fletcher (quoted in *Sports Illustrated*, Apr. 8, 2002): "Usually he [Pedro Martinez] gets me out with breaking stuff. I'm wondering why he didn't throw me any today."

break into To make one's professional debut at a particular level of the game; e.g., to "break into" the minors or to "break into" the majors. See also *break in*, 1.

break one off To throw a breaking ball.

break on top To score first in a game.

break open 1. To get the first run(s) in a game. 2. To establish a commanding lead in a game. "The Phillies broke the game open with five runs in the seventh" (*The Baltimore Sun*, May 2, 2001).

break point The midpoint between the two figures in salary arbitration. "If they [the arbitrators] deem a player to be worth a penny more than the break point, he wins, and vice versa" (Stephen Cannella, *Sports Illustrated*, Feb. 4, 2002).

breaks, the Luck and good fortune, often created by another's mistake or miscue. "Bonesetter Reese is one gentleman who can always look forward to a successful season if he only gets the 'breaks'" (*San Francisco Bulletin*, March 20, 1913; Gerald L. Cohen who noted the irony). V. Samuels (*American Speech*, Feb. 1927) noted, "The player of the side favored by luck 'gets the breaks.'" The term appears to have been regarded as exclusive to baseball as late as 1943: Franklin Faskee (*Baseball Magazine*, Jan. 1943), in an article entitled "The Breaks," reported, "Some call it fate. The old-time player called it the jinx. And players and fans now call it 'the breaks.'" See also *break*, 4. IST USE. 1902 "All the breaks, including the four errors charged to them, were against McAleer's men, and except in the ninth, their hits were wasted" (*The Sporting News*, Aug. 23; Peter Morris). EXTENDED USE. The breaks and the breaks of the game are common ways of connoting luck in many realms of modern life.

break the wrists To bring the top hand over the bottom hand when taking a full swing at a pitched ball. The term and concept come into play when a batter starts to swing at a pitch and then attempts to stop. If, in the view of the umpire, the batter has turned or rolled ("broken") his wrists, the pitch will be called a strike; if not, the pitch will be judged on its own merits (as a ball or called strike) as if the bat had not moved at all.

break up 1. To score the game-winning run(s) with a hit or a flurry of hits. IST USE. 1904. "[Barry] McCormick broke up the game by scoring [Hunter] Hill on a beautiful hit to right field [in the bottom of the 10th inning]" (*The Washington Post*, Aug. 25; Peter Morris). 2. To get the first base hit in a potential no-hitter. **3.** To prevent a double play with a break-up slide. **4.** To dismantle a winning team by trading or releasing players. "Connie Mack broke up his great machine that had won four flags in five years" (Lee Allen, *The Sporting News*, Sept. 21, 1968).

break-up slide A slide that is made to prevent a double play or triple play. The baserunner who is about to be forced out attempts to slide into the infielder who is making the play so that he will not be able to relay the ball.

breast protector *hist.* An early synonym of *chest protector.* An 1884 preseason ad in *Spalding's Official Base Ball Guide* for a catcher's and umpire's "breast protector" noted, "It is made of chamois skin and canvas, well padded and quilted, and is used by nearly all Professional Catchers and Umpires." From the *Evansville Daily Journal* (Aug. 3, 1884): "A breast protector . . . saves a catcher many hard knocks."

breastworks *hist.* Home plate. The term was used in the phrase "behind the breastworks" for a catcher playing his position.

breeze **1.** *v.* To work with ease, whether it is to run the bases without interference or to win against easy competition; e.g., "Smith breezed through the lineup by retiring nine batters in a row." Washington Senators manager Clark Griffith (quoted in *San Francisco Bulletin*, Feb. 26, 1913): "If only I had one first-class left-hander, I'd breeze home with the American League flag in a canter." **2.** *n.* An easy victory; e.g., "Smith won it in a breeze." **3.** *v.* To throw the fastball. **4.** *n.* A strikeout. IST USE. 1910 (*Baseball Magazine*, September; Edward J. Nichols).

EXTENDED USE. Baseball's popular term of ease has been long applied to other easy conquests, such as "breezing" through an examination or "it was a breeze."

breezer A fastball.

Brenegan See *pull a Brenegan*. Not to be confused with *brannigan*.

Brew Crew Nickname for the Milwaukee *Brewers*, so named after its 13-game winning streak at the beginning of the 1987 season. "Bruised Brew Crew: Milwaukee last in Central, first in the trainer's room" (*The Baltimore Sun* headline, May 23, 1994).

Brewers Popular nickname for clubs based in Milwaukee, Wis.: the National League franchise in 1878; the Union Association franchise in 1884; the American Association franchise in 1891; the American League charter franchise in 1901 (it became the St. Louis Browns in 1902 and the Baltimore Orioles in 1954); and the minor-league American Association franchise from 1903 to 1952. It currently is the nickname for the National League Central Division franchise that entered the American League in 1970 when the Seattle Pilots, an expansion team in 1969, relocated to Milwaukee. The franchise joined the National League beginning with the 1998 season. The team is sometimes affectionately referred to as the *Brew Crew.* ETYMOLOGY. The nickname is natural for a city that has long regarded itself as America's beer capital.

brick **1.** An inexpensive ball; a rocklike ball. See also *nickelbrick.* **2.** A ball thrown by a pitcher or infielder that feels heavy to the fielder catching it. **3.** A lot of 50 or more baseball cards bought, sold, or traded as a unit and packed like a solid brick. A brick usually contains cards of one type or characteristic (e.g., a "Mariners brick") and does not normally include rarities. **4.** Syn. of *base,* 2. "[Chick] Gandil whipped a hard drive to left, cleaning the bricks" (*The Washington Post*, Aug. 3, 1913; Peter Morris). IST USE. 1910. "Twice the bricks were jammed with callers" (*Newark* [Ohio] *Advocate*, July 6; Peter Morris)

brickyard A rough and uneven infield. See also *Hogan's brickyard.*

Bridegrooms **1.** Nickname for the American Association franchise in Brooklyn, N.Y., in 1889, and renamed the Brooklyn Gladiators for 1890. So named because several players got married before the 1888 season, when the club was known as the *Trolley Dodgers* (*The The Sporting Life*, March 28, 1888; Clifford Blau). **2.** Nickname for the National League franchise in Brooklyn, N.Y., from 1890 to 1898, and renamed the Brooklyn Superbas in 1899 and the Brooklyn *Dodgers* in 1911.

bridge **1.** *v.* To give up a home run. "When a pitcher is 'bridged' he has allowed a home run" (*Sports Illustrated*, Sept. 13, 1982). **2.** *n.* A home run. The term was introduced by

Oakland A's pitcher Dennis Eckersley. **3.** *n.* Syn. of *setup man. Sports Illustrated* (Oct. 22, 2001) noted that Mike Stanton was a "valuable bridge to [Mariano] Rivera."

bridgemaster A pitcher who gives up a lot of home runs. The term was introduced by pitcher Dennis Eckersley.

bring along To expose a player to increasingly difficult learning situations. "The Yankees might bring third baseman [Hensley] Meulens along quickly, though he's more likely a future prospect" (George Vass, *Baseball Digest*, March 1989, p.30).

bring home Syn. of *bring in*, 1. IST USE. 1863. "Kleinfelder scored one run, obtained on a splendid centre field hit, which gave him his third base, from whence he was brought home by Moore" (*Brooklyn Eagle*, June 19; Peter Morris).

bring in **1.** To score a runner. IST USE. 1864. "[Wes] Fisler, who made a clean home run and brought a man in" (*New York Clipper*, Aug. 6; Peter Morris). Syn. *bring home.* **2.** To move the infielders and/or outfielders closer to home plate in an attempt to prevent the opposing team from scoring a run on a batted ball.

bring it To throw a pitch with great velocity; to throw a fastball. "As a young man of 30, Satch [Paige] could 'bring it,' at a velocity the big-leaguers did not regularly see in their splendid isolation" (Jack Mann, *Washington Times*, June 10, 1982). EXTENDED USE. To employ one's full resources. Baltimore Ravens linebacker Terrell Suggs (quoted in *The Baltimore Sun*, Dec. 11, 2005): "If we don't stop the run this game, they're [Denver Broncos] going to run us right out of the stadium. We are definitely going to have to bring it, or it's going to be pretty ugly."

bring up To promote a player from a minor-league team (usually a farm club). If such a player fails, it is often said that "he was brought up too soon." See also *call up.*

Broadway **1.** The middle of the plate. "[Lou] Whitaker missed the fastball down Broadway by a fraction" (Keith Hernandez, *Pure Baseball*, 1994, p.157). See also *right down Broadway.* Syn. *Main Street.* **2.** *hist.* "A flashy dresser, loud talker" (*The Sporting News Record Book*, 1937). "A flashily dressed athlete" (Edwin M. Rumill, *Christian Science Monitor*, Sept. 1, 1937). Once a popular baseball catchall nickname, it may have been last widely used to describe pitcher Charlie Wagner of the Boston Red Sox (1938–1942, 1946). Lyn Lary, whose major-league career extended from 1929 through 1940, served as the epitome of the player who attracted the name; today it is hard to find his name in print without an adjective like "dapper" or "snappy." When Lary and Leo Durocher, another snappy dresser, were both with the New York Yankees in 1929, Durocher got nicknamed "Fifth Avenue," presumably because he was a bit less flashy than Lary. EXTENDED USE. The term may have made a permanent transfer to football with the dubbing of "Broadway" Joe Namath of the New York Jets.

Brock system One of a number of computational methods, each consisting of a set of equations that provides an estimation of a player's final career statistics, based on the player's performance and age at the time of the estimation. It received its name because an examination of outfielder Lou Brock's career was integral to its original design. The system was created by Bill James, and an early version (Brock2) was described in detail in his *Baseball Abstract* (1983). The most well-known version (Brock6) was first mentioned in James' *Baseball Abstract* (1986).

broken-bat *adj.* Said of a hit (usually a single) achieved in spite of, or because of, a bat that breaks when it comes in contact with the ball. Milwaukee Brewers manager Phil Garner (quoted in *Milwaukee Journal Sentinel*, Sept. 10, 1993): "It's appropriate we should lose that game on a frickin' broken-bat bleeder up the middle."

broken play A play, such as a hit and run or a steal, that began but was stopped because the umpire called a time-out or the batter fouled a pitch, thereby revealing the strategy of the team at bat.

Bronx Bombers Nickname for the New York Yankees that first became popular in the 1930s when heavyweight boxing champion Joe Louis was known as the Brown Bomber. The term connotes a team that hits many home runs and is still in common use when referring to the Yankees. It displaced "Ruppert's Rifles" and "McCarthymen" as nicknames for the Yankees. Syn. *Bombers*. IST USE. 1936. "Bronx Bombers Gain Speed" (*The New York Post* headline, June 18, p.36; Barry Popik). USAGE NOTE. When the Yankees are not doing well, variations of the term have been used, such as "Bronx Bummers" (Mike Downey, *The Sporting News*, Sept. 12, 1988) and "Bronx Bunnies" (Roger Angell, *The Summer Game*, 1972). ETYMOLOGY. Although the term was popularized in the wake of Louis' Yankee Stadium prizefight against Max Schmeling in June 1936, the term was used six years earlier for a boxer: "Lightweight history repeated itself when Singer, the Bronx bomber, beat Mandell with the first punch" (*Gettysburg* [Pa.] *Times*, July 29, 1930). The term also referred to a baseball player who hailed from the Bronx (Hank Greenberg): "The six foot four inch, 210-pound Bronx Bomber points out that they [ballplayers] are great consumers" (NEA Service, Apr. 19, 1936; Barry Popik). The term was coined by *New York World-Telegram* writer Daniel M. Daniels in July 1936, after Louis' Yankee Stadium fight against Max Schmeling in June 1936 (Barry Popik).

Bronx cheer A contemptuous razzing sound made by sticking the tongue between the closed lips and expelling air; a *razzberry*. It has long been associated with New York baseball fans who have never been shy about criticizing players in disfavor. "The crowd gave the hero a Bronx cheer for the effort and razzed him frequently thereafter, with some justice, too, for [Babe] Ruth's actions were an insult to the intelligence of the people who had paid their good money to see him play baseball" (*The New York Times*, Apr. 10, 1924; Barry Popik). IST USE. 1923. "When Griffith, up again, flied to centre for the third out, the fans gave the Giants a hearty Bronx cheer" (*The New York Times*, May 4, 1923; Barry Popik). ETYMOLOGY. Although there is no direct evidence to support the connection, the term may have been created in reference to the Bronx-based New York Yankees. Barry Popik noted that the term appeared in *The New York Times* in a nonbaseball context as

early as Oct. 29, 1904: "Bronx Cheers for Herrick." Writer Arthur "Bugs" Baer claimed that he invented the term for that "clarion call of disgust" in reference to a Benny Leonard prizefight in Madison Square Garden in which the "tender-hearted Bronxites" were upset that the referee did not stop the fight in the right round (*San Francisco Examiner*, Apr. 6, 1956): "They let go with that accolade of tight-lipped criticism that sounded like tearing a yard of calico. I named this 'The Bronx Cheer.'" EXTENDED USE. The "cheer" has been evident in other sports. "The Bronx cheer has even invaded Forest Hills. During tight tennis matches there this last summer the gallery with increasing frequency undertook to line the matches" (*San Francisco News*, Dec. 31, 1931; Peter Tamony).

Bronx Zoo A derogatory nickname for the New York Yankees during the ownership of George Steinbrenner, taken from the name of the famous zoo of the same borough. The clear implication is that of a motley assortment of wild animals. "Not for nothing are the New York Yankees of George Steinbrenner known as the Bronx Zoo" (William Gildea, *The Washington Post*, Apr. 27, 1986). "The Boss [Steinbrenner] had taken on some of the biggest names in the game during his tumultuous tenure as curator of the Bronx Zoo" (Peter Schmuck, *The Baltimore Sun*, July 18, 1994). The term has also referred to the Yankees' clubhouse and to Yankee Stadium. IST USE. 1978. "[Billy] Martin's resignation had been the culmination of his long-standing disputes with Steinbrenner and [Reggie] Jackson. The feud, sometimes involving other Yankee players, had earned the club the nickname the 'Bronx Zoo' in the popular press" (*Facts on File World News Digest*, Aug. 11, 1978; Tom Dalzell). ETYMOLOGY. In 1979, Sparky Lyle and Peter Golenbock published an account of the Yankees' 1978 season called *The Bronx Zoo*. According to Golenbock's preface the title was the "masterstroke" of the book's editor, Larry Freundlich of Crown Books.

Brooklyn safety cap A *batting helmet* created by Johns Hopkins surgeons Dr. George E. Bennett and Dr. Walter Dandy for use by the Brooklyn Dodgers. "Zippered pockets are cut in each side of a regulation baseball cap. Into one of these pockets on the side he faces the pitcher, the batter will slip a plastic plate which is about a quarter of an inch thick . . . [and] about the width and length of a man's hand . . . [covering] the vulnerable area from the temple to about an inch behind the ear" (*Chicago Tribune*, March 9, 1941; Peter Morris).

Brooks Nickname for the Brooklyn Dodgers.

Brooksian Characterized by adroit fielding, esp. in play at third base, in the manner of Brooks Robinson of the Baltimore Orioles (1955–1977). "[Wade] Boggs has been semi-Brooksian at third base" (Tony Kornheiser, *The Washington Post*, Oct. 25, 1986). ETY-MOLOGY. Named for Brooks Robinson who won virtually every possible award and accolade for defensive play during his 23-year career. In 9,196 chances he made only 264 fielding errors. "Brooksian" is one of those rare cases in which a player has been honored with an eponymous adjective.

broom See *umpire's broom*.

brother act An occasion when two or more brothers of requisite ability play for the same team. "Over the years baseball has known a number of brother acts, prominent among them being Dizzy and Paul Dean, Paul and Lloyd Waner, Morton and Walker Cooper, and Wes and Rick Ferrell" (Douglas Wallop, *Baseball: An Informal History*, 1969, p.27).

Brotherhood of Professional Base Ball Players First union of professional athletes in the United States, organized by John Montgomery Ward and a few New York Giants teammates in Oct. 1885 to protect and promote the rights of players. It eventually created its own league, the *Players' League*, in 1890. The Brotherhood challenged the reserve clause and attempts to restrict players' salaries (see *Brush Classification Plan*); it promoted profit sharing with players and the abolition of unilateral contract transfers. The union was hailed as "the greatest move in the history of the National Game" (see *The Sporting News Centennial Issue*, Feb. 28, 1986). Usually referred to as "the Brotherhood."

brown *adj./hist.* Said of inept or inferior play. 1ST USE. 1889. "Some of the brownest work ever seen on a baseball field characterized the home team's play in the second. It was enough to drive a baseball man to drink. . . . It was one complete jumble of uncanny mistakes, high-salaried muffs and skyscraping throws. . . . People who can't play any better than they did here shouldn't be allowed to eat" (*The World* [New York], Aug. 18).

brown derby A crucial misplay.

Brownies Nickname for the St. Louis *Browns* of the American League (1902–1953). The term, which tended to be used to underscore the chronic ineptitude of the team, was a play on "brown" as a term for imperfection.

Brown rule A limited form of free agency granted by the National Commission in 1914 in an attempt to avert the challenge of the Federal League. "Ten-year major league veterans, in a change dubbed the 'Brown rule' in honor of the veteran pitcher [Mordecai 'Three-Finger' Brown], received the right of unconditional release" (Robert Burk, *Never Just a Game*, 1994; Peter Morris).

Browns 1. Nickname for the American Association franchise in St. Louis, Mo., from 1883 to 1891. 2. Nickname for the National League franchise in St. Louis, Mo., from 1892 to 1898. The franchise was known as the St. Louis Perfectos in 1899 and renamed the St. Louis Cardinals in 1900. 3. Nickname for the American League franchise in St. Louis, Mo., from 1902 to 1953. The franchise relocated from Milwaukee after the 1901 season and became the Baltimore Orioles in 1954. The team was named for the brown trim of the club uniform and was often referred to as the *Brownies*.

brown spitter A *spitball* moistened with chewing tobacco juice. Gaylord Perry (*Me and the Spitter*, 1974, p.42) admits that it was one of the few variations on the spitball that he did not throw: "I couldn't take to the tobacco."

Brown Stockings 1. Nickname for three franchises in St. Louis, Mo.: the National Association club in 1875; the National League club in 1876 and 1877; and the American Association club in 1882 that was renamed the St. Louis Browns in 1883. **2.** Nickname for the National League franchise in Worcester, Mass., from 1880 to 1882.

Bruins Nickname for the *Cubs*. ETYMOLOGY. "Bruin" is a synonym for "bear"; it originated in the character of Sir Bruin, a bear in the medieval German epic *Reynard the Fox*.

brush Syn. of *umpire's broom*.

Brush and Von der Ahe's rule Syn. of *trap ball rule*.

brushback *n.* Syn. of *brushback pitch.* "The intent of the brushback, which is simply a fastball inside, is to move back a batter who crowds the plate and looks for a breaking pitch on the outside" (Bob Gibson, quoted in *The New York Times*, July 13, 1986).

brush back *v.* To move a batter away from the plate with the aid of a *brushback pitch.* Syn. "brush aside"; *polish his buttons.*

brushback ball Syn. of *brushback pitch.*

brushback pitch A pitch that comes so close to the batter's body that he is forced to step backward and thereby is unable to dig in at the plate. When a batter crowds the plate, taking away some of the pitcher's target area, a pitcher may throw a pitch close to the batter's body to encourage him to move back. Or, as Jim Brosnan (*The Long Season*, 1960) put it, "To let the batter know the pitcher may, occasionally, lose control and to keep him from digging in at the plate with confidence." The brushback pitch is not to be confused with a *beanball*, which is intentionally thrown at the batter's head. Red Smith once wrote that the brushback pitch, coming after two strikes, was, "in the classic pattern, as rigidly formalized as the minuet" (Ira Berkow, *Red: A Biography of Red Smith*, 1986). Others are less understanding. Mike Royko (*Houston Chronicle*, Aug. 6, 1987; Charles D. Poe): "Some of the philosophers who broadcast baseball games [say] . . . 'the brushback pitch' is part of baseball. That is what they call a ball thrown 90 miles an hour in the general direction of someone's nose." Bob Gibson (*From Ghetto to Glory*, 1968, p.145) wrote, "One of the most valuable weapons at a pitcher's command is the brushback pitch. First let me clear something up. A brushback pitch is not to be confused with a deliberate knockdown. There is a difference. A world of difference." Compare *knockdown pitch.* Syn. *brushback*; *brushback ball*; *brush-ball*; *brush-off pitch*; *blow-down pitch.*

brushback pitcher A pitcher who uses the brushback pitch to keep the batter away from the plate. When Boston Red Sox manager Billy Herman was asked who was the best brushback pitcher in baseball, he replied, "Freddie Fitzsimmons is my man. He once hit me in the on-deck circle."

brushback war Baseball games in which opposing pitchers employ excessive brushback pitches. The Boston Red Sox and the Cleveland Indians "made headlines a couple of times . . . when a brushback war led to a pair of bench-clearing incidents at Fenway Park" (*The Baltimore Sun*, Oct. 5, 1999). Compare *beanball war.*

brush-ball Syn. of *brushback pitch.*

Brush Classification Plan A plan proposed by Indianapolis owner and president John T. Brush and approved by the National League in 1888 in which players would be placed into one of five salary classes based on the "habits, earnestness, and special qualifications" of the players' on-field performance and their off-field personal behavior. The plan established maximum salaries for each class: A ($2,500), B ($2,250), C ($2,000), D ($1,750), and E ($1,500). Most players did not make the maximum within each class. The plan was passed three days after John Montgomery Ward, head of the *Brotherhood of Professional Base Ball Players*, had left for Australia as part of an around-the-world tour; the unpopularity of the plan led directly to the formation of the Players' League in 1890.

brush-off pitch Syn. of *brushback pitch.*

Brush Resolution A 21-point behavior code for players, passed by the National League in 1898 at the behest of Cincinnati owner and president John T. Brush, to eliminate "filthy" or "obscene, indecent or vulgar" language and other rowdy conduct that was being blamed for declining attendance. The penalties authorized by the resolution (suspensions and "life-long expulsion") were too harsh, and no one was willing to report violations of it. It died of disuse after two seasons.

Brush Rules The basic set of rules for staging the *World Series*, established in 1905 by New York Giants owner and president John T. Brush. Many important features of these rules are still followed today, including the best-of-seven-games format. The Brush Rules also established the principle of a date after which no new players could be added to a team in anticipation of postseason play.

BS Abbrev. for *blown save.*

BSR Abbrev. for *base-stealing runs.*

BSW Abbrev. for *base-stealing wins.*

B team A second team created from a club's roster for the purpose of playing an *A team,* which is composed of the best players at each position. In the major leagues such teams are created to play each other in practice games and are a fixture of spring training, esp. during the first week or two. "John Morris homered . . . pacing the St. Louis Cardinals' 'B team' to an 8–1 intrasquad victory . . . over the squad's veterans" (*St. Petersburg Times,* March 7, 1986).

bubble 1. Syn. of *balloon,* 6. 2. Syn. of *knuckleball,* 1. 3. See *on the bubble.*

Brush Rules. John T. Brush, New York Giants owner, 1910. *George Grantham Bain Collection, Library of Congress*

bubble-gum ball A spitball moistened with chewing tobacco and bubble gum. The pitch was pioneered by Detroit Tigers pitcher Orlando Peña, who is quoted by Gaylord Perry (*Me and the Spitter,* 1974) as saying, "I mix tobacco with a piece of gum and chew it good. Tastes like sweet tobacco. When you blow a bubble with that mixture, anybody who sees it wants to throw up. I knew guys playing winter ball in Cuba who would put a spot of gum right on the ball. Every time the umpire found it, he would throw out the ball. But you could win a ball game in a tight spot with it."

bubble-gum card A *baseball card* sold with pieces of bubble gum since 1933. Bazooka, a subsidiary of Topps Confection Co., produced bubble-gum cards in 1959–1971 and 1988–1991. For many years the cards have become far more important than the gum, and in reality the gum is now the premium and the cards are the prime product being sold. "When someone asked Doug Rader what advice he would give a kid, he suggested that they eat bubble-gum cards. 'Not the gum,' he said, 'but the cards. They have a lot of good information on them'" (*Sports Collectors Digest,* Nov. 26, 1982). See also *baseball gum.*

bubble player A player who is about to be traded or sent back to the minor leagues, or who is either on the verge of being sent down or called up; a player "on the bubble."

Buccos Var. of *Bucs.*

buck A batting average of .100. A player who is hitting a "buck-ninety" has a batting average of .190. See also *dollar; Interstate.*

Buck Canel Award An annual award presented since 1980 by the Latin American Press Organization to the best Latin American major-league baseball player. It is named for a well-known New York broadcaster of baseball games to Latin America.

bucket 1. See *foot in the bucket.* 2. See *step in the bucket.*

buckethead A very ugly player. Bob Hertzel (*Baseball Digest,* Jan. 1987) noted that "scullion" is twice as ugly as a *mullion,* and "buckethead, well, forget it."

bucket hitter A hitter who often steps back from the pitch; one who "steps in the bucket."

buckler A knee-buckling curveball. "When it's right, [Josh Beckett's curveball is] a buckler" (Minor-league pitching coach Randy Hennis, quoted in *Baseball America*, July 9–22, 2001; Peter Morris).

Bucs Nickname for the Pittsburgh *Pirates*. The term is short for "Buccaneers," which is often used interchangeably with "Pirates." In 1986, the club came up with a new slogan: "The New Bucs: We Play Hardball." Syn. *Buccos.*

Bud Black market A punning term to describe the 1990–1991 free-agent market because of the $10 million contract that pitcher Bud Black signed with the San Francisco Giants. The contract, widely viewed as exorbitant for a 33-year-old pitcher with a career record of 83–82, raised the bar for what other free agents would demand and get that offseason (John Helyar, *Lords of the Realm*, 1994, p.486).

budder Syn. of *rookie*, 1.

buffalo To bluff or intimidate an opposing team or player. IST USE. 1905 (*The Sporting Life*, Sept. 2; Edward J. Nichols, who noted the term probably derived from a superstition connected with a three-horned buffalo).

bug 1. *hist.* A baseball enthusiast; a fan: "One who tears through the latest congressional investigations, Mexican war, Newport scandal, Wall-street flurry and Chinese murder in order to find out whether Tyrus Raymond Cobb is still lambasting the pill for .376" (*The Washington Post*, July 19, 1914). Actress Lillian Russell (*Baseball Magazine*, Jan. 1909): " 'Bug' as thus applied I find means a person of peculiar eccentricities, born of frenzy and expressed in wild, incoherent shrieks that develop a monomania called baseballitis." See also *diamond bug.* Syn. *baseball bug*, 2. IST USE. 1904. "A Brooklyn Bug near the Reds' bench became so violently insolent that one of the Redbirds . . . put his clenched fist into the countenance of the man who abused him" (*The Sporting Life*, Sept. 17; Peter Morris). USAGE NOTE. The term was in common use for "fan" from about 1904 to 1916, when the older term "fan" came back into use. "In baseball parlance there are three classes of persons who come under the observation of players in a professional way. These are baseball folk, 'bugs' and 'nuts.' A 'bug' is anyone of sound mentality who enthuses over and mixes up with those concerned in the game, but who neither plays it, writes it or finances it. . . . A 'nut'—well, he's just a 'bug' who's let it tell on his mind" (Joe S. Jackson, *Detroit Free Press*, March 14, 1909). 2. Syn. of *knuckleball*, 1.

bugaboo *hist.* Syn. of *sore arm.* IST USE. 1935. " 'Bugaboo' or sore arm, necessitates the application of dry heat" (Ralph H. Barbour, *How to Play Better Baseball*, p.159; David Shulman).

bug bruiser *hist.* A hard-hit ground ball. IST USE. 1874 (*Chicago Inter-Ocean*, July 7; Edward J. Nichols).

bug crawler 1. "A ball that when hit has a lot of over-spin, eliminating the usual hop" (Carol R. Gast, *Skill on the Diamond*, 1953). 2. Syn. of *swinging bunt.*

bugette A female bug (fan).

buggywhip 1. *n.* A light-weight bat. "I saw that buggywhip you've got for a bat. I saw you whip the ball over the fence in right field" (Chet Brewer, quoted in Tony Salin, *Baseball's Forgotten Heroes*, 1999). 2. A quick, slashing swing at a pitched ball. "[Ox Eckhardt is] almost on top of the plate, and when he swings he falls away from it. See how he holds his bat? He cuts at a ball—buggywhips it" (Casey Stengel, quoted in a 1936 *New York Post* article by Jerry Mitchell, in Tony Salin, *Baseball's Forgotten Heroes*, 1999; Peter Morris). 3. A pitcher's quick or sudden, whiplike, slinging motion, which often puts stress on the elbow.

bug on the rug 1. A ground ball that eludes one or more fielders and gets into the outfield, usually into one of the corners. The term has been around for decades, but became more popular with the advent of ruglike artificial playing surfaces, after which announcers tended to use the term to describe a ball bouncing on plastic grass. It has been attributed to Pittsburgh Pirates announcer Bob Prince, who supposedly introduced it about 1970, but it appears in much earlier listings of baseball slang. 2. A baserunner. A runner trying to two bases is a "bug loose on the rug."

Bugs Bunny changeup A slow changeup disguised as a fastball but which appears to stop in front of the plate. The ball is held firmly against the palm and is 10 to 20 miles per hour slower than a fastball. The pitch is thrown by Trevor Hoffman and Johan Santana. IST USE. 1997. "Catcher Jeff Reed calls the superb changeup by Philadelphia's Mark Portugal a 'Bugs Bunny changeup.' Why? 'Because it just stops right there,' Reed said" (John Henderson, *Denver Post*, May 5). ETYMOLOGY. From a 1946 Looney Tunes short ("Baseball Bugs") in which Bugs Bunny single-handedly defeats the Gas-House Gorillas by delivering a changeup so devastatingly slow that he is able to strike out the side with one pitch (Michael Greicius and Quinn Greicius, in William Safire, *The New York Times Magazine*, Nov. 6, 2005).

building block A player around whom a team is assembled.

bulb *hist.* The baseball. "Schirm kind of chokes his stick, but that in no way interferes with his ability to clout the bulb" (*San Francisco Bulletin*, Feb. 27, 1913; Gerald L. Cohen). IST USE. 1908 (*New York Evening Journal*, March 5; Edward J. Nichols).

bulge 1. *hist.* A slow curveball. IST USE. 1907 (*New York Evening Journal*, Apr. 25; Edward J. Nichols). 2. The advantage, or lead, in runs made or games won; e.g., "The Yankees have a five-game bulge over the Tigers."

bull *hist.* Syn. of *boner*, 1. IST USE. 1902 (*The Sporting Life*, July 5; Edward J. Nichols).

bulldog A tenacious pitcher; a tired pitcher who refuses to lose and finds something extra to win; a pitcher who is always ready to take the ball. An example was Orel Hershiser, whose nickname was "Bulldog."

Bull Durham See *bullpen* (ETYMOLOGY).

bullet 1. A hard-hit line drive. "A 'bullet' is a ball the batter hits 'on the nose' and into the hands of a waiting fielder" (*The New York Times*, June 2, 1929). 2. A strong throw. "[Mike Cameron] grabbed the ball and fired a bullet to cutoff man Bret Boone" (*Sports Illustrated*, May 14, 2001). 3. A fastball.

bullhead An umpire who favors the visiting club. John J. Evers and Hugh S. Fullerton (*Touching Second: The Science of Baseball*, 1910; Peter Morris): The "'bullhead' . . . gives all close decisions against the home club for fear he will be called a 'Homer.'"

bullpen 1. The area of a ballpark where the relief pitchers and warmup catcher are situated during the game. There are two bullpens, one for each team, located outside of fair territory, usually either at opposite ends of the outfield or along each foul line. The appointments differ, but all major-league bullpens contain mounds and home plates. The primary purpose of the bullpen is a place where relief pitchers can prepare and warm up for entry into the game. Joe Garagiola (*The Sporting News*, May 16, 1956) commented, "A bull pen is supposed to be a place for warming up pitchers. That's what it is a little bit of the time. Mostly it's a place for eating peanuts, trading insults with the fans, second-guessing the manager and picking all kinds of silly all-star teams, like the all-screwball team or the all-ugly team or the all-stack-blowing team." Sometimes spelled "bull pen"; "bull-pen." Syn. *pen*, 2; *bully*; *warming pan*. IST USE. 1913. "Ira Thomas is the skipper of the [Athletics] pitchers. He corrects the faults of the youthful trajectory hurlers and takes them to the 'bullpen' in the afternoon and keeps them warmed up" (*The Washington Post*, Aug. 17; Peter Morris). 2. The relief pitching staff of a team. "I believe a bullpen can win a postseason series more than it can lose one" (Boston Red Sox general manager, quoted in *Sports Illustrated*, Oct. 6, 2003). 3. Pitchers appearing in relief in a given game. "Bullpen Collapses after Ron's [Darling] Seven No-Hit Innings" (*New York Post* headline after a stunning Mets loss, June 29, 1987). 4. Short for *bullpen session*. Baltimore Orioles pitcher Juan Guzman (quoted in *The Baltimore Sun*, May 5, 1999): "I wanted to do a couple bullpens before my next start. Mechanically, I've been off a little bit. . . . My two bullpens corrected it." Milwaukee Brewers pitcher Jamie Wright (quoted in *Milwaukee Journal Sentinel*, Apr. 14, 2002; Robert F. Perkins): "Today was probably about the eighth time I've thrown a bullpen

Bullpen. Spectators draped over a mammoth Bull Durham Tobacco sign. This picture was taken on Aug. 9, 1911, at the old Huntington Avenue Baseball Grounds in Boston, when a record crowd of 33,904 came to see the Red Sox play the Detroit Tigers. *National Photo Company Collection, Library of Congress*

this winter, so I'm right on schedule." Catcher John Buck (quoted in *Baseball America*, Aug. 4–17, 2003): "I usually hate catching bullpens, but it's the closest thing to playing and I even volunteered to catch some."

USAGE NOTE. Currently, the bullpen is the realm of high-priced specialists rather than a place for pitchers who simply can't pitch for a full game or are out of favor, as it once was. The degree to which the situation has changed is underscored by the fact that as recently as 1966, Jack McDonald (*San Francisco Chronicle*) defined the bullpen as "a group of ex-starting pitchers in the manager's doghouse." David Shulman found three uses in Lester Chadwick's *Baseball Joe in the Big League* (1915); e.g., "He took a ball, and nodding to Rad, who was not playing, went out to the bullpen." Another early example shows up in the Tamony collection, which includes a line from T.A. Dorgan's "Indoor Sports" (*San Francisco Call & Post*, June 7, 1917): "I been out here in the bull pen all season warming up—I ain't been in one game yet."

ETYMOLOGY. The origin of the term has long been debated in baseball. Joseph Durso (*The New York Times*, March 10, 1967) provided two interesting theories. Writing during spring training, Durso quoted New York Mets manager Casey Stengel: "You could look it up and get 80 different answers, but we used to have pitchers who could pitch 50 or 60 games a year and the extra pitchers would just sit around shooting the bull, and no manager wanted all that gabbing on the bench. So he put them in this kind of pen in the outfield to warm up, it looked like a place to keep cows or bulls." Stengel's quote was followed by this contrasting opinion from Johnny Murphy, who spent 11 years in the bullpen for the New York Yankees: "It came from Bull Durham tobacco, I was always told. All the ball parks had advertising signs on the outfield fences and Bull Durham was always near the spot where the relief pitchers warmed up."

Murphy's explanation has been given various twists. Michael Gartner, in his nationally syndicated column on language (*Newsday*, Apr. 27, 1986), asserts that the bullpen–Bull

Durham connection originated in the days when all games were day games and when "pitchers warming up for relief duty often chose to limber up in the shade of those big signs." In the early days of the 20th century, the Bull Durham name was, indeed, closely associated with the ballpark. In fact, by 1910, the big bull-shaped signs were on the outfield fences of almost every park in the country. As part of its advertising campaign, Bull Durham drew minor- and major-league attention to the 40-foot-long, 25-foot-high signs by offering a reward to any batter who could hit a ball off one. Quoting from the 1911 edition of *The "Bull" Durham Base Ball Guide*: "Any player who hits the bull with a fairly-batted fly ball, during a regular scheduled league game on any of the grounds where these 'Bull' Durham signs are located on the field, will receive $50.00 in cash." In addition, any player hitting a home run in a park with a bull on the fence got a carton containing 72 packs of the tobacco.

In 1909, the first year of the *"hit the bull"* contest, there were 50 signs in place and 14 players won. The next year, with nearly 150 Bull Durham signs being hit 85 times, Blackwell's Durham Tobacco Co. gave out $4,250 in cash and more than 10,000 pounds of tobacco. According to *The "Bull" Durham Base Ball Guide*, the sign promotion scheme was expanded because "interest in the National Game was then waning in various parts of the country" and this was seen as a way to stimulate interest, which it apparently did.

While there is significant merit to the Bull Durham theory (particularly because the term hadn't been used in baseball until after the signs were in place), the term "bull pen" had long been used in the United States to denote either a log enclosure for holding cattle or a holding area for prisoners. A reader from Deer Trail (Colo.) wrote an unsigned letter to *The Sporting News* (Nov. 2, 1939) that sided with the jail theory: "The place in most jails where prisoners exercise is known as the bullpen. I just remembered when a young boy, I asked the policeman where he was going with two drunken men and he said to the bullpen and sober them up to be good

men." Lexicographer David Shulman (letter, 1997) attests to the fact that "bullpen" was criminal slang for a "prison yard" before it showed up applied to baseball.

This concept of the bullpen as an enclosure where, in the words of Shulman, "pitchers were confined . . . for warming up until called on to pitch" may have strongly influenced and helped corroborate the notion of the bullpen as an enclosure for pitchers. In fact, it was in use as early as 1877 for an area in foul territory beyond first base and third base where spectators could stand penned in like bulls. O.P. Caylor (*Cincinnati Enquirer*, May 10, 1877; Peter Tamony) wrote, "The bull-pen at the Cincinnati Grounds, with its 'three-for-a-quarter' crowd, has lost its usefulness." Tamony theorized that this use of the term came from the Civil War when soldiers on both sides used the term "bull pen" for a roped-off corral where prisoners of war were herded like cattle. Tamony believed that the Bull Durham signs reinforced and redefined the term "bull pen" in baseball. Early bullpens for pitchers were almost always placed along the outfield foul lines (as some still are), which would suggest how this term developed.

One other theory, which is published from time to time, likens the relief pitchers to the reserve bulls in bullfighting, who are penned near the arena should the starting bull be found to be lacking. There is a certain neatness to this idea, but it would appear to be pure conjecture.

Dan Schlossberg (*The Baseball Catalog*, 1989, p.235) commented that Milwaukee Brewers infielder Bill Friel, a former railroad employee, introduced the term in 1901: "There were shanties with benches at intervals along the roadbed and workers would sit and talk there during work-breaks. When Friel played, pitchers who weren't working sat on a similar bench, in right field foul territory. He referred to it as the bullpen because the railroad bench had the same name."

Finally, the *Oxford English Dictionary*, citing *Spirit of the Times* (Dec. 19, 1857), defines "bull-pen" as "a schoolboys' ball game, played by two groups, one group outlining the sides of a square enclosure, called the 'bull-pen,' within which are the opposing players." Richard Hershberger uncovered two subsequent citations: "Jim Phillips . . . could not throw well enough to make his mark in that famous Western game of bullpen" (Evert A. Duyckinck, in *Cyclopædia of American Literature*, 1875) and "[a fielder would sometimes] grab up the ball . . . knock a base-runner down with it, forgetful . . . that they were not engaged in the time-honored pastime of town ball or bull-pen" (*Atlanta Constitution*, May 27, 1888, in an article about the New York game).

EXTENDED USE. **1.** The term has many specialized meanings for defined spaces and enclosures outside baseball, which may or may not have been inspired by the baseball bullpen. These include the barracks in a lumber camp, a used-car lot, a cashier's cage in a bank, the box in some courtrooms where defendants sit during trials, a room for railroad crewmen, a work area in a large company, the sale ring at a horse auction, a smoking area for oil refinery workers, the penalty box in ice hockey, the area in a jazz club where a youngster can pay to sit without being bothered by a waiter, an area where prisoners are kept during a riot, an enclosure for prostitutes, and a flophouse for men only. **2.** Backup support. "Three or four big movies does not make for a record summer. You have to have a solid bullpen . . . to support the weight of those big blockbusters to build up the overall box office" (Paul Dergarabedian, Media By the Numbers president, quoted in Associated Press release, July 4, 2007).

bullpen boss A *bullpen coach*. "[Bucky Walters is the New York Giants] new bull pen boss" (*The Sporting News*, Nov. 30, 1955). "Birds' bullpen boss Elrod Hendricks claims his boys are into each pitch" (Melody Simmons, *The Washington Weekly*, June 21, 1985).

bullpen by committee A relief staff with no prominent member or closer. The term was used by manager Whitey Herzog for the 1985 St. Louis Cardinals bullpen staff in which he used everybody, but it is now applied widely to relief staffs from which different pitchers are used depending on the game situation. "How's this for a bullpen by committee? The last seven saves by the Rockies . . . were credited to six different pitchers" (*Sports*

Illustrated, June 28, 1993, p.53). See also *closer by committee*.

bullpen catcher A catcher assigned to duty in the bullpen to warm up relief pitchers.

bullpen coach A *pitching coach* who spends all or most of his time in the team's bullpen, advising and preparing the relief pitchers. Most major-league teams have such a coach. Syn. *bullpen boss*.

bullpenner A relief pitcher; a denizen of the bullpen. "[I] told him [Ted Lilly] he's a bullpenner" (New York Yankees manager Joe Torre, quoted in *The Baltimore Sun*, May 12, 2002). Syn. *'penner*.

bullpen session A workout for pitchers, held in the bullpen, sometimes between starts, for the purpose of correcting mechanical mistakes, developing a new pitch, or rehabilitating an injury; a pregame warmup routine held in the bullpen ("my bullpen will tell me how well I'll do in the game"). "David Cone threw all of his pitches during a bullpen session for the first time since going on the disabled list with right shoulder tendinitis" (*The Baltimore Sun*, Apr. 18, 2001). "Scott Erickson . . . [was] urged during a Tuesday bullpen session to dramatically slow his delivery" (*The Baltimore Sun*, July 1, 1999). See also *side session*. Syn. *bullpen*, 4. IST USE. 1999. "[Rick] Ankiel is so demanding of himself that he seethes when he doesn't throw well in bullpen sessions between starts" (Tom Verducci, *Sports Illustrated*, June 28, p.66).

bullshit See *shit*, 2.

bully Syn. of *bullpen*, 1. Player-turned-broadcaster John Lowenstein has used the term, which has infuriated some purist fans, but it shows no signs of growing. "Some things about John Lowenstein can be put down as mere idiosyncrasies, such as his habit of referring to the bullpen as 'the bully'" (Ray Frager, *The Baltimore Sun*, Aug. 11, 1989). The term was also used by Garret Mathews (*Can't Find a Dry Ball*, 2002).

bumblebee A player who should not be able to play as well as he does, in the same way that, according to folklore, a bumblebee is able to fly but defies the laws of aerodynamics. Charlie Metro applied this term to Pete Rose.

bump 1. *v.* To hit a ball lightly. "[Nap Lajoie] has none of the Willie Keeler method of holding the stick a foot from the end and simply bumping the ball" (*The Washington Post*, Sept. 25, 1904; Peter Morris). IST USE. 1897. "Davis bumped the pebble to left for two sacks" (*The New York Times*, July 20). **2.** *v.* To get hits off a pitcher "He was bumped for four or five hits, but they were scattered through as many innings" (*San Francisco Bulletin*, March 13, 1913; Gerald L. Cohen). IST USE. 1902 (*The Sporting Life*, July 5, p.6; Edward J. Nichols). **3.** *n.* A weak base hit. "[Case] Patten and [Jake] Stahl beat out slow rollers to the infield, the latter's short bump scoring [Joe] Cassidy" (*The Washington Post*, Aug. 14, 1904; Peter Morris). **4.** A home run. "I might be able to hit .280 or .290, but not with 35 bumps. I'm here for the bumps" (Gorman Thomas, quoted in Daniel Okrent, *Nine Innings*, 1985, p.122; James D. Szalontai). **5.** *n.* A fastball; e.g., "He has good bump tonight" (Relief pitcher Mark Davis, quoted in *San Diego Union-Tribune*, Apr. 11, 1994). **6.** *n./ hist.* An overwhelming defeat. "A pitcher gets his 'bumps' when his delivery is hit hard, a team 'gets its bumps' when it is badly beaten" (Hugh S. Fullerton, *American Magazine*, June 1912). IST USE. 1904. "All the speed, curves and skill in the world will not save you from getting your 'bumps' sometimes" (Deacon Phillippe, quoted in *Syracuse Post Standard*, March 27; Peter Morris).

bumper The thick pad attached to walls in modern ballparks. Many bumpers now carry advertising.

Bums An endearing nickname for the Brooklyn Dodgers, more commonly *Dem Bums*. ETYMOLOGY. According to Joe Williams (Scripps-Howard syndicated column, March 22, 1932; Peter Morris) the Dodgers were in search of a new nickname (since the current name, Robins, had honored the departed manager Wilbert Robinson); after being shut out by the lowly Boston Braves, "a large red-faced gent got up out of a box and came over to the press stand. 'If you fellows are still trying to dope out a name for the Brooklyns I can help you,' he raged. 'Call 'em the bums.'" A different version was supplied by Willard Mullin (*The Sporting News*, Dec. 3, 1958):

The character of the bum was inspired by his taxicab driver in 1937, who asked him, "How did our Bums come out?" after the Dodgers won the first game of a doubleheader, which put them in fourth place, then losing the second game, which sent them back into the second division.

bun *hist.* The baseball. One 1918 scrapbook clipping from a Detroit newspaper talks of Harry Heilmann "banging the bun in goodly fashion."

bunch To make a cluster of base hits in one inning. "The Phillies bunched four singles ... to break a 2–2 tie in the seventh" (*The Baltimore Sun*, Aug. 31, 2003). IST USE. 1880 (*New York Herald*, July 23; Edward J. Nichols).

bungle 1. *n.* An error or misplay. "A bungle is a most atrocious sort of play. It is one of those lamentably grievous errors where the small boy swallows his chewing gum, the man in the grand stand gets up dejectedly and walks to the first exit, and the topmost bleacherite, where the sun shines hottest, rises to his feet and bawls stentoriously, 'You soft-shelled lobster'" (*The Washington Post*, July 22, 1900). Compare *boggle*. IST USE. 1898 (*New York Tribune*, May 29; Edward J. Nichols). **2.** *v.* To make an error.

bunny ball Syn. of *rabbit ball*, 1.

bunt 1. *n.* A batted ball that is intentionally met with a loosely held bat and tapped softly

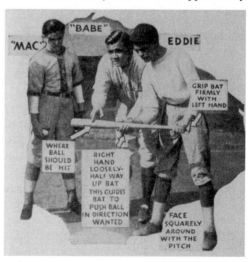

Bunt. The Babe shows how it is done in an instructional pamphlet. *Ron Menchine Collection*

into the infield. The purpose of a bunt is to advance a baserunner (sacrifice bunt) or get the batter to first base on the element of surprise. Its success depends to a large degree on the placement of the ball on the infield. An ideal bunt is one that proves difficult for infielders to reach. The bunt is performed as the batter loosens his grip, flexes his knees, and squares around to face the pitcher. The hands are separated along the handle of the bat and it is presented as if the batter wants the pitcher to read the bat label. The bat is not swung at the ball; rather, the ball is tapped with the bat. Credit for introducing the bunt goes to Dickey Pearce of the original Brooklyn Atlantics in 1866 (*Total Baseball*, 7th ed., 2001, gave the credit to Tom Barlow of the Atlantics, also in 1866), but the practice did not become common until after 1876 when Tim Murnane of the Boston Red Stockings started "butting" the ball with a special flat-sided bat. Gerald Secor Couzens (*A Baseball Album*, 1980) added: "The bunt was referred to as a freak play in accounts of 1888 and did not take on its importance in game strategy until much later." This is confirmed in a profile of Pearce written by Sam Crane (*New York Journal*, Dec. 20, 1911): "It was not known as a bunt at that time and Dickey himself had no idea that he was making baseball history." Tom Shieber cites a reporter for the *New York Clipper* (July 14, 1860) who described probably the first "unintentional" bunt: "Brown was at the bat, and . . . in bringing his bat down, Brown hit with the bat in a similar manner to that in which a cricketer blocks a straight ball; judgment was asked, and as the Umpire deemed it an accident, it was decided 'no hit,' but we think it should have been considered fair, for the reason, that had a player been on first base at the time, he could easily have made his second base before the pitcher could have fielded it, and the decision may lead to similar accidents on other occasions when such play would have a more important bearing on the game. If, in the act of striking, the ball be hit forward of home base, however light the touch, it ought to be considered a fair ball, otherwise accidents similar to the above will be of frequent occurrence." IST USE. 1876. "[A gentleman from St. Louis] proposes to change the lines from home to first

Bunt. Tommy McMillan, shortstop, Rochester, International League, assumes the bunting stance, 1911. *George Grantham Bain Collection, Library of Congress*

and home to third bases from straight lines into curves, with the bent inward toward the pitcher, so that when a 'bunt' or 'fool hit' was struck, it must go foul; and only 'the straight-out, decent, manly hits' be given to the player" (*Chicago Daily Tribune*, May 14; Greg Rhodes). Compare *swinging bunt*. Abbrev. *B*, 2. **2.** *n.* The act of bunting. **3.** *v.* To execute a bunt. Syn. *butt*, 1; *put the ball on the ground*. IST USE. 1875. "Fairchild 'bunted' the ball just over home plate and his legs got him there" (*Grand Rapids* [Mich.] *Morning Democrat*, Aug. 17; Peter Morris). EXTENDED USE. To set aside or give up; to avoid. "Kodak Conent to Bunt" was the headline for an article on Kodak's abandoning its leadership in controlling innovation "to create smaller technological advantages in a range of products and processes" (Peter Behr, *The Washington Post*, Sept. 11, 1986). **4.** *n.* [softball term] A legally tapped ball in fast pitch softball. It is not swung at, but intentionally met with the bat and tapped within the infield. It is, however, illegal in slow pitch softball: if it occurs, the batter is called out and all runners return to their bases.

USAGE NOTE. Knowing what a bunt is has long been a test of whether one knows anything about baseball. A character in a 1952 *Boy's Life* story is ridiculed for not knowing "a bunt from a Buffalo." A story by Jerome Beatty (*McClure's* magazine, March 1917) contains the following incident: "An' another thing I asks him. I used to be the greatest sacrifice hitter in baseball. So I asks him, 'Young man, can you bunt?' 'Mister Ryan,' says he-Jake fairly yelled his protest against such disgusting incompetence—'Mister Ryan, I don't like to brag about myself, but I can bunt farther than any other man on the team!' Them's his very words! Can you beat it?"

ETYMOLOGY. The term is a nasalized variation or corruption of the term "butt" (to strike or push), which comes from the batter's butting at the ball with his bat in the manner of a goat butting. Michael Gartner (*Newsday*, Apr. 27, 1986) suggested the original butt "quickly became known as a 'bunt,' probably because somebody misheard the word in Brooklyn." But *Merriam-Webster's Collegiate Dictionary* (10th ed., 1993) notes that "bunt" as an alternative term for "butt" can be dated back to 1584. The term itself may have come into baseball by rail. In railroading, to "bunt" was to "shove" a car onto a side trench or (and this may be even more to the point) to "nudge" an uncoupled freight car to get it moving.

bunt along To advance a baserunner by making a bunt.

bunt and run *hist.* Original name for *safety squeeze*. "On the bunt-and-run the runner at third takes a long lead but does not make a break for home until the ball is actually hit" (Gordon S. "Mickey" Cochrane, *Baseball: The Fan's Game*, 1939, p.117).

bunt-ball A variation of baseball played without an outfield. The infielders were required to stay behind the baselines until the batter made contact, and any ball that crossed the baselines on the fly was automatically out. The object was to reach base on a bunt or Baltimore chop, move up on sacrifices, steals, and errors, advance the runner, and take advantage of situational opportunities. The game demanded a high degree of offensive (making contact) and defensive skills (Merritt Clifton).

bunt hit A bunt for a base hit. It was invented by Tommy Barlow of the Hartford Blue Stockings in the early 1870s.

bunting 1. The art of making bunts. **2.** The flag or banner that represents winning a pennant; the *pennant*, 2, itself. "The first round in the fight for the little piece of bunting that represents so much to base ball teams and to baseball patrons is over" (*Cleveland Plain Dealer*, Oct. 18, 1892; Peter Morris). IST USE. 1887. "[Adrian] Anson showed his prophetic knowledge to advantage when he predicted that the Giants and Chicagos would have the fight for the bunting" (*The Washington Post*, July 31; Peter Morris, who notes that Detroit actually won).

Burger Blast A home run. The term was made popular by Waite Hoyt, whose Cincinnati Reds broadcasts were sponsored by Burger beer.

burglar 1. A quick-thinking player who takes advantage of the breaks; one who is said to "steal" opportunities. **2.** Syn. of *base stealer*.

burn *hist.* Syn. of *soak*, 2.

burn a hole To pitch or throw a ball with great velocity; e.g., "Smith's pitches burned a hole in Jones' mitt." IST USE. 1907 (Burt L. Standish, *Dick Merriwell's Magnetism*, p.206; Edward J. Nichols).

burn ball *hist.* A variant of baseball in which a baserunner can be put out ("burned") by being hit with a ball. See also *soak ball*. IST USE. 1888. "The boys used to play 'burn ball,' if you were hit by the ball before reaching the base, you were out" (Michael J. Kelly, *"Play Ball"*; David Shulman). ETYMOLOGY. The "burn" in burn ball is an overt reference to the fact that an object of the game was to inflict pain and leave bruises.

burner A very fast baserunner. "With one triple and seven steals in his career, [Jim] Leyritz is no burner" (STATS Inc., *The Scouting Notebook 1999*; Peter Morris).

burning *hist.* **1.** Syn. of *soaking*. **2.** In English base-ball, a method of retiring a baserunner who had overrun or neglected to touch a base by throwing the ball at the base, while simultaneously calling out the word "burned" (David Block, *Baseball Before We Knew It*, 2005, p.70).

burn off To run close behind another baserunner, thereby forcing (or "burning") him to advance or be put out.

burnout A game in which two players throw a baseball to each other at a given distance and then, advancing on each other, throw the ball as hard as they can until one of them backs away.

burn over To throw a hard fastball. "Tyler Christian . . . fairly burned them over the plate during his short sojourn on the mound" (*San Francisco Bulletin*, March 4, 1913; Gerald L. Cohen). IST USE. 1901 (Burt L. Standish, *Frank Merriwell's Marvel*, p.148; Edward J. Nichols).

burn up the circuit To win routinely and decisively on the road. The term is applied to teams, pitching staffs, individual pitchers, and, on rare occasions, to dominant hitters (such as one with a string of game-winning runs batted in). IST USE. 1926. "Mullen has been 'burning up' the International League" (*The Sporting News*, Aug. 26; Peter Morris).

bury To strike out or retire a batter.

buscón (pron. "boo-SCONE") A Latin American scout or bird dog. "The increased demand for foreign talent has created a cut-throat industry of street-level entrepreneurs dedicated to locating and grooming potential major leaguers. Known as 'buscones,' or 'finders,' the street agents often train the players from puberty. In many cases, the buscones . . . are above-board coaches who spend considerable time and resources to support athletes, but their growth has been accompanied by reports of over-charging, extortion and outright theft" (Steve Fainaru, *The Washington Post*, June 17, 2001). ETYMOLOGY. In the Dominican Republic, Spanish for a facilitator for legal or bureaucratic matters, such as a job recruiter for organizations in the United States.

bush 1. *adj.* Unprofessional, unsportsman-like, amateurish, unseasoned. The term is used to refer to both crude play on the field and poor behavior off the field. It can be applied at any level of the game; e.g., it is "bush" to talk too much on the field, wear your uniform incorrectly, show too much enthusiasm, or steal a base when your team is way ahead. Syn. *bushie, 3; bushy; bush-league.* USAGE NOTE. The label is scornful to the point that a player at any level of play strives to avoid it. EXTENDED USE. Amateurish or inferior, such as an actor who is accused of a "bush performance." **2.** *n.* Exile; a low rung of the minor leagues at the end of a baseball career. "The 'bush' with its sadness of cheap hotels, rancid food, and fetid dressing-rooms; of inferior craftsmanship and memories of gone glories" (William Patten and J.W. McSpadden, *The Book of Baseball*, 1911; Peter Tamony). Plural *bushes.* IST USE. 1905. "Manager [Bill] Armour has gone out into the bushes and signed two twirlers" (*The Sporting Life*, Sept. 2; David Shulman). **3.** *n.* A common term for a ballplayer who has yet to establish himself in the major leagues; esp. a college player. "You might have been an All-American with nine degrees, but if you weren't a big league baseball player they all called you 'Bush'" (Red Auerbach, commenting on Chicago White Sox pitcher Johnny Rigney's greeting, "How are you doing, Bush?" in *On and Off the Court*, 1985, p.8; Charles D. Poe). Sometimes spelled *Bush.* See also *Joe Bush.*

bushel basket An oversized fielder's glove with a deep pocket. Compare *pancake*, 2.

busher 1. A *rookie*, just up from the bush leagues. Hugh S. Fullerton (*Collier's*, Sept. 11, 1909): "In the major leagues there are three classes of players, designated in the picturesque language of the game as 'bushers,' 'bone-heads,' and 'topnotchers.' The 'busher' is the freshman, inexperienced but promising and derives its name from the fact that he recently graduated from the 'bush' or minor league." The term is frequently derogatory and associated with rural areas; e.g., "In baseball parlance the charge 'busher' embodies all that is evil, wicked and undesirable. A busher comes from a small town, and in baseball anything managerial that isn't snatched from the finishing schools of New York, Boston, Philadelphia, St. Louis or cities that can support two major league ball clubs and at least 3000 policemen is a total loss" (W.J. O'Connor, Jr., *St. Louis Post-Dispatch*, Apr. 6, 1915; Peter Morris). The term was given a boost with the publication of Ring Lardner's novel *You Know Me Al*

(1916), which is the tale of Jack Keefe: the term "busher" is key to the book (Keefe has a fight with one of his girlfriends because he thinks she called him one), and each of the six chapters has the word in its title (e.g., "A Busher's Letter Home," "The Busher Comes Back," and "The Busher's Honeymoon"). Syn. *bushie*, 1; *bush leaguer*, 1. IST USE. 1907. "Call them rank bushers, second section mutts / Tail enders of the punkiest degree?" (C.H. Zuber, poem "Edward Hanlon's Soliloquy," *The Sporting Life*, Apr. 6, 1907; Stuart Y. Silverstein). **2.** A player in the bush leagues. Syn. *bush leaguer*, 2; *bushie*, 2. **3.** Any professional baseball player who lacks class. Syn. *bush leaguer*, 3.

bushes Plural of *bush*, 2. Syn. *woods*.

bushie **1.** *n.* Syn. of *busher*, 1. **2.** *n.* A minor-league player. Syn. of *busher*, 2. **3.** *adj.* Syn. of *bush*, 1.

bush-league *adj.* Syn. of *bush*, 1. IST USE. 1907. "The Cubs did themselves and their city more harm with the bush league public by their protesting today than if the umpire had handed the enemy forty runs and a dozen victories" (*Chicago Tribune*, Apr. 1; Peter Morris). EXTENDED USE. Having to do with mediocrity or inferiority. "[The failure to renew the lease was] a bush-league thing, too amateurish for a company like The Rouse Co." (David Rakes, quoted in *Columbia* [Md.] *Flier*, Oct. 9, 2003). Compare *major-league*.

bush league *n.* A lesser minor league consisting of teams in small cities or towns, usually composed of players who are too old or lacking in experience or ability to compete in the major leagues. "Surplus players can be bought from other leagues for a short time in emergencies, even if it is necessary to go into the 'bush' leagues to get them" (*Chicago Tribune*, Apr. 1, 1906; Peter Morris). IST USE. 1902. "Sioux City will belong to the north tri-state league, composed of Rock Rapids, Sheldon, Le Mars, Iowa, Flandreau, Yankton and Sioux Falls, S.D., generally known as the 'bush leagues'" (*Lincoln* [Neb.] *Evening News*, Feb. 21; Bill Mullins). ETYMOLOGY. From the nickname for the lower levels of the minor leagues, which were traditionally typified as "out where the bushes grow" or where the land has not been cleared. "[The term 'bush'] probably originated as a condescending reference by the established players in the Major Leagues to the unkempt and overgrown nature of the playing fields of lesser leagues than the Major Leagues (the so-called 'Bush Leagues')" (Lawrence Frank, *Playing Hardball*, 1983, p.60). EXTENDED USE. Lacking in good taste or sense. "It's bush league to make sport of someone's physical characteristics" (Peter Schmuck, *The Baltimore Sun*, Sept. 30, 2004).

bush leaguer **1.** Syn. of *busher*, 1. "Consider the bush leaguer on the bench! He toils not" (L.F. Heacock, *The Sporting Life*, Feb. 10, 1906; Edward J. Nichols). IST USE. 1904. "Taffe is the 'bush leaguer' from Vandalia that Donnelly has taken on for a trial" (*Decatur* [Ill.] *Daily Review*, Sept. 4; Bill Mullins). **2.** Syn. of *busher*, 2. IST USE. 1903. "This versatile artist's floaters kept the Looloos so completely at sea thereafter that in the ninth Pete became brash and produced a local bush leaguer in young Bobbie Whalen" (*Los Angeles Times*, Sept. 25; Bill Mullins). **3.** Syn. of *busher*, 3.

bushness Inexperience. " 'Dobie, I hate to bug your ointment,' said Tommy, 'but there is a distinct chance your bushness is showing'" (Steve Kluger, *Changing Pitches*, 1984, p.110; Charles D. Poe).

bush shaker A baseball scout. "I was a bush shaker scouting for the Yankees and I still regret losing Herb Score and Frank Lary" (Spud Chandler, quoted in Don Warfield, *The Roaring Redhead*, 1987; Peter Morris).

bushwhacker A baseball scout. "The only way to get players of promise is to 'beat the bushes' for them, and be sure that the beating is done by experienced 'bushwhackers' who know their business" (*The Washington Post*, July 27, 1913; Peter Morris).

bushy Syn. of *bush*, 1. "I never had any further trouble with [Ed] Barrow so long as I remained in Boston. I imagine my notes to him sounded pretty bushy" (Babe Ruth, *The Babe Ruth Story*, 1948, p.70; Charles D. Poe).

businessman's special A weekday baseball

game, played in the mid- to late afternoon, that caters to a salaried, white-collar clientele that, presumably, can get out of work for a few hours or wants to entertain clients. As day games have become less common, there are fewer businessman's specials every year. St. Louis Cardinals manager Whitey Herzog (*Village Voice*, Sept. 2, 1986) stated that Chicago Cubs reliever Lee Smith had the biggest advantage in baseball because he gets to pitch "those damn three o'clock businessman specials" at Wrigley Field, adding, "it's hard enough to hit that guy in the daylight, much less the twilight."

bussie A players' nickname for the team bus driver. This term was popular among major leaguers before teams started traveling by plane. Today the term is used by players during spring training and in the minor leagues where bus travel is still common. According to an item in *Comedians and Pranksters of Baseball* (edited by Fred Lieb, 1958), the ritualistic joke is to ask the bussie if the regular driver is off. Jim Bouton (*Ball Four*, 1970) wrote that the way you tell a driver that he is going too slowly is to call out, "Hey, bussy, there's a dog pissing on your rear wheel." Also spelled "bussy." USAGE NOTE. The term has stayed alive through new incarnations. Leonard Shecter (*Baseball Digest*, June 1963) reported, "Once this meant simply bus driver. But times change and now it's applied to those in charge of vehicles of any sort, from bus driver to pilots of jet aircraft." Ballplayers address a cab driver as "bussie." Tim Horgan (*Baseball Digest*, June 1964) added that the term also applied to "the park employee who drives the relief pitcher in from the bullpen."

bust 1. To hit the ball hard. The term appeared frequently in Ty Cobb's *Busting 'Em and Other Big League Stories* (1914); e.g., "When a Big Leaguer is hitting the ball hard, the rest of his team says:—'That's busting 'em.'" IST USE. 1913. "Just let me hit one. I know I can bust a fence off [Rube] Marquard" (*San Francisco Bulletin*, March 13; Gerald L. Cohen). 2. To throw a fastball close to the batter's body in an effort to move the batter away from home plate. "[David Ortiz] has good gap-to-gap power . . . but righties can bust fastballs inside" (*Sports Illustrated*, Oct. 14, 2002). "[Kenny] Lofton 'bails' slightly against left-handers, so the Orioles fed him breaking balls down and away, then busted him inside" (*The Baltimore Sun*, Oct. 7, 1996). 3. To pitch the ball hard without aiming for anything tricky. "[Dallas Green] says there would be more hard throwers around if college coaches would let the kids develop their arms by 'just busting the ball,' instead of teaching them how to finger the ball, and cut it and ride it" (Dick Young, *The Sporting News*, June 6, 1983; Peter Morris).

busy cup of tea *hist.* A very active, energetic player who shows real spunk. "For nearly two weeks [Jim] Thorpe has been the busy cup of tea, working out with the Giants' young recruits. . . . If energy and grit will get a player anywhere, Thorpe may become a star some fine day" (*San Francisco Bulletin*, Feb. 28, 1913; Gerald L. Cohen).

butcher 1. *n.* A bad defensive player; one who has a difficult time holding on to the ball. 2. *v.* To fail to hold onto the ball.

butcher-boy *v.* To swing at a pitched ball with a downward chopping motion. "I know what Casey's [Stengel] telling him. He's telling him, 'Don't swing hard now. Just butcher-boy the ball. Just butcher-boy it'" (Phil Rizzuto, quoted in John Lardner, *The New Yorker*, July 18, 1959; Peter Tamony).

butcher-boy stroke A batter's downward chopping swing which ensures a high-bounding ground ball to protect the runner; a forceful bunt. In situations calling for a ground ball, Casey Stengel (who coined the term) told his players to use the butcher-boy stroke, likening the motion to that which a boy in a butcher shop would use when chopping meat. See also *Baltimore chop*.

butt *hist.* 1. *v.* Syn. of *bunt*, 3. "[Arlie] Latham has a great way of butting the ball out in front of the plate, and depending on his running to get to first" (*New York Sun*, May 23, 1896; Peter Morris). 2. *n.* Syn. of *barrel*.

butter To make an error. "The shortstop buttered the ball" (*The Washington Post*, March 22, 1914).

buttercup hitter A weak hitter, one without

power. IST USE. 1934 (*Akron* [Ohio] *Beacon Journal*).

butterfingers A derogatory term for a player who drops the ball; a clumsy, inept, error-prone player. "If we . . . should undertake to wield the bat-stick with some of yonder toddlers, the little blackguards would cry out 'butter-fingers!' and we should deserve the ignominy" (Philip Quilibet [George Edward Pond], *Galaxy*, July 1871; John Thorn). "The ancient 'butterfinger[ed]' plague is making itself a factor in the major league pennant races" (Howard Sigmand, *San Francisco Call-Bulletin*, Aug. 25, 1952). As late as Apr. 1927, *American Speech* reported the term as peculiar to baseball rather than the language at large. IST USE. 1836. "With a bound, see the ball go, / Now high in the air as hit it just so, / No catch is Jo.; oh, how he lingers, / He'll soon have the name of old butter fingers" (*Rose of Affection*, an 8-page chapbook published by Turner and Fisher; David Block). ETYMOLOGY. The term—used for someone who drops things or cannot hold on to anything, as if his fingers were coated with slippery butter—can be traced back to 1615 (J.F. Farmer and W.E. Henley, *Slang and Its Analogues*, 1890). It is old English slang that entered both cricket and baseball. Charles Dickens (*The Pickwick Papers*, 1837) employed the term to characterize a clumsy cricket player. EXTENDED USE. The term, which saw its early American popular use in baseball, has since been used for anyone who is clumsy and drops things.

butterfly *hist.* A *knuckleball* that seemingly floats on its way to the plate. "A particularly effective form of pitching delivery otherwise called the knuckleball" (Edwin M. Rumill, *Christian Science Monitor*, Sept. 1, 1937). Syn. "butterfly ball." ETYMOLOGY. The erratic flight of a knuckleball is similar to that of a butterfly.

butterfly curve Syn. of *screwball*, 2. "Carl Hubbell . . . [threw] his butterfly curve in the shadow of Coogan's Bluff" (J. Roy Stockton, *The Gashouse Gang*, 1945, p.66).

buzz **1.** To throw a pitch dangerously close to a batter's body or head. "[Troy] Glaus landed on his back when righthander Russ Ortiz buzzed another fastball under his chin" (Stephen Cannella, *Sports Illustrated*, Nov. 4, 2002). "[Roger] Clemens buzzed him and [Miguel] Cabrera snapped his neck back just in time to miss getting tagged in the helmet" (*The Baltimore Sun*, Oct. 23, 2003). "We buzzed his tower" (Todd Hundley, concerning pitching inside to Joey Hamilton, quoted in *The New York Times*, July 28, 1997). ETYMOLOGY. From the practice of playful pilots who use aircraft as instruments of expression. **2.** *hist.* To strike out.

buzzball A pitch thrown dangerously close to a batter.

buzz chick The term for "baseball" in Boontling, a deliberately contrived language developed in the upper Anderson Valley of Boonville, Calif., for secretive communication. The term is an imitation of the sound of the pitched ball followed by the sound of hitting the catcher's mitt.

buzzer A fastball that asserts itself by the noise it makes as it passes a batter's ear. It is presumably "louder" than a *hummer*, 1. IST USE. 1918. "[Jim Vaughn's] buzzer, the speedball, is a mighty breeze and is difficult to hit" (Burt Whitman, *Boston Herald and Journal*, Sept. 6; Peter Morris).

BW Abbrev. for *batting wins*.

BWA Abbrev. for *batter win average*.

BWAA Abbrev. for *Baseball Writers' Association of America*.

bye **1.** One of the four "bases" in early baseball. "The game called baseball by the country boys of twenty years ago . . . [included] the placing of the bases, or 'byes,' as they were then called [in a square]" (*Bismarck* [N.D.] *Daily Tribune*, Apr. 1, 1887). **2.** One of five "bases" in an early Canadian game resembling baseball. Dr. Adam E. Ford (letter to *The Sporting Life*, May 5, 1886; reprinted in Nancy B. Bouchier and Robert Knight Barney, *Journal of Sport History*, Spring 1988) described a game played on June 4, 1838, in Beachville, Upper Canada, in which there were five "byes," with the first bye placed a mere six yards from the "home bye." William Humber (*Diamonds of the North*, 1995, p.18) called the measurements in Ford's account "preposterous" and suggested that the entire account of the game be viewed skeptically.

"bye, bye, baby" Trademark home run call of New York/San Francisco Giants broadcaster Russ Hodges.

bye-bye ball A home run.

bye-ya A home run. ETYMOLOGY. From a Latin-American player who bid "farewell to a four-bagger" (*Sports Illustrated*, Apr. 18, 1983, p. 86; Barry Popik).

by way of Toledo Said of a baserunner who tags the base with the wrong foot, causing him to lose ground (Chicago Park District [Burnham Park], *Baseball*, 1938).

C

C **1.** See *Class C*. **2.** Abbrev. for *catcher*, 1. **3.** Abbrev. for *catcher*, 2.

cabbageball [softball term] The 16-inch softball, so called because it resembles a head of cabbage.

cabinet card An oversized baseball card printed on thick cardboard stock for display in a cabinet. Issued by cigarette manufacturers, cabinet cards were popular in the 19th and early 20th centuries and are highly valuable. To get a single card, one needed to send in coupons from several cigarette packs, which accounts for the general scarcity of cabinet cards today.

cackle clout A foul ball, a play on the homonym "fowl."

Cactus League Commonly used nickname for the major-league teams that conduct spring training and play exhibition games against each other in the southwestern United States. After teams began to train in 1947, Arizona-based teams were still referred to as part of the *Grapefruit League*. This changed in 1954 when Arizona had four teams training in the state for the first time. The terms "Cactus League" and "Cactus Loop" had begun appearing in newspaper articles two years earlier. The name seemed to solidify at the end of the 1954 spring training season when an American Legion post sponsored a trophy (immediately dubbed the Cactus Cup) for the team with the best training record in the Southwest. Cactus League clubs have included the Anaheim Angels, Chicago Cubs, Chicago White Sox, Cleveland Indians, Milwaukee Brewers, Oakland A's, San Diego Padres, San Francisco Giants, Colorado Rockies, Seattle Mariners, and Arizona Diamondbacks. IST USE. 1952. "Bobby Thomson . . . exploded his second home run of the Cactus League circuit" (*The New York Times*, March 26, 1952, p.37). ETYMOLOGY. The term comes from the cacti that are common to the southwestern area of the United States. The national board of arbitration of minor-league baseball leagues approved the application of the Cactus League of Texas, with headquarters in El Paso (*The New York Times*, Nov. 13, 1909). The name "Cactus League" was proposed for an Arizona minor league in the 1920s, but the name "Arizona State League" was chosen instead.

caddie **1.** A reserve player who generally is used as a substitute in the late innings of a game. "As a rule, the 'caddie' is younger, quicker, but has less experience and makes less money than the player for whom he is substituted" (Jim Brosnan, *The Long Season*, 1960). **2.** Alternate spelling of *caddy*.

caddy Syn. of *setup man*. "[Roberto] Hernandez has pitched four times in his new role as caddy for incumbent closer Rod Beck" (*Milwaukee Journal Sentinel*, Aug. 7, 1997). Also spelled *caddie*, 2.

Cadillacing Performing a *Cadillac trot* at "low throttle." During a June 1966 postgame interview of Los Angeles Dodgers catcher John Roseboro by radio broadcaster Vin Scully, Roseboro told Scully that, having thought he had hit a home run, "I was just Cadillacing along"; however, the ball did not go out of the park and Roseboro should not have been trotting around the bases. "[José Guillen] added further fuel to the feud by 'Cadillacing' around the bases after a game-turning home run" (Peter Schmuck, *The Baltimore Sun*, June 19, 2005).

Cadillac trot A *home run trot* by a high-salaried slugger, often staged to show up a high-priced pitcher or other opponent. During the 1986 National League Championship Series, CBS radio announcer Johnny Bench said that the term should now be called the "Mercedes trot." See also *Cadillacing*. ETYMOLOGY. The term certainly can be traced to a famous line uttered by slugger Ralph Kiner in the 1950s: "Hitters of home runs drive Cadillacs, single hitters jalopies" (Jack McDonald, *San Francisco News Call-Bulletin*, March 27, 1981, p.28). On another occasion Kiner told a reporter that he never choked up on the bat because the "Cadillacs are down at the end of the bat" (Joseph McBride, *High & Inside*, 1980, p.154).

cage 1. Syn. of *batting cage*, 1. 2. Syn. of *batting cage*, 2. IST USE. 1890. "Baseball was lively during the mild winter months at Princeton, more practice being had out of doors than in the cage" (*Outing*, April; Peter Morris). 3. Syn. of *catcher's mask*. IST USE. 1883. "[Fred] Thayer soon after visited the club room of the Boston nine . . . and spoke . . . about the new invention [catcher's mask]. Most of them laughed at the idea of a man going around with a cage on his head" (*Grand Rapids* [Mich.] *Morning Democrat*, Sept. 4; Peter Morris).

cake 1. Something done easily; e.g., a pitcher who tells a manager "it's cake" means he is fired up to retire the side. See also *piece of cake*. 2. *hist.* A player of little skill. The term appears in the third stanza of Ernest L. Thayer's 1888 poem "Casey at the Bat": "And the former [Flynn] was a lulu and the latter [Jimmy Blake] was a cake." According to Martin Gardner (*The Annotated Casey at the Bat*, 1967, p.179), "cake" was a slang word at the time for a "dude, dandy, or male homosexual," but Thayer "probably means no more than a handsome, vain ball player, much concerned about his personal appearance, but a weak player."

cake and coffee Low pay; a long-established player slang, usually used in reference to the salaries of minor-league players. Syn. *coffee and cake*. IST USE. 1934. "How would you feel if you'd been playing the cakes and coffee route for years and somebody suddenly dropped you in soft on the champagne and caviar circuit?" (Pat Robinson, *Fort Worth Star-Telegram*, Feb. 5). ETYMOLOGY. Presumably a reference to the fact that the player is getting something to eat and drink and little else.

cakewalk An easy, lopsided victory or season. "Mike Mussina's 8–0 cakewalk on Sunday" (*The Baltimore Sun*, Aug. 19, 2003). "With a first-class utility infielder and clever young pitcher it would be a cakewalk this year for Boston" (Tim Murnane, *The Boston Daily Globe*, June 27, 1898). ETYMOLOGY. From the dances and promenades (or walks) that were once staged as contests. The contest, which was popular among 19th-century African-Americans, often rewarded the winning couple with a cake—hence the name. The idea of being able to win with a set of fancy steps no doubt conveyed the idea of an easy win.

calcimine Syn. of *kalsomine*. "Your colorful descriptions such as 'wielded a calcimine brush' . . . are fun to read" (Brien K. Martin, *The Sporting News*, Aug. 17, 1987).

calentadero Spanish for "bullpen."

call 1. *n.* An umpire's stated or signaled ruling on a pitch (ball, strike, balk, foul ball, or hit batsman) or a play (safe or out). 2. *v.* To make an umpiring decision. IST USE. 1867. "It is the duty of the umpire to decide without any appeal whatever, such as calling baulks, balls and strikes" (*The Ball Players' Chronicle*, July 11; Peter Morris). 3. *n.* The catcher's signal for a specific pitch. 4. *v.* For a catcher to signal for a specific pitch. "There are days when I'll start to wind up before the catcher has even given me the sign because I know he's gonna call what I want to throw" (Walt Terrell, quoted in Steve Fiffer, *How to Watch Baseball*, 1987, p.29). 5. *n.* The manager's decision on a starting pitcher, or his signal to the bullpen for a relief pitcher or for a relief pitcher to begin warming up.

call a game 1. For an umpire to officiate or control a baseball game. An accolade for an umpire is that he "calls a good game." 2. For an umpire to signify that a game can begin. IST USE. 1870. "The game was called at 3 o'clock and Mart King struck an attitude over the home plate" (*Chicago Tribune*, July 6; Peter Morris). **3.** For an umpire to cancel, suspend, postpone, or terminate a baseball game due to bad weather or other problems. IST USE. 1866 (Henry Chadwick, *Base Ball Player's Book of Reference*, p.50; Edward J. Nichols). **4.** For a catcher to signal to the pitcher the pitches to be thrown to specific batters and to control the positioning of defensive players. Tom Fitzgerald (*Baseball Digest*, Nov. 1983, p.77): "Calling a good game may be the most obscure skill in baseball. You certainly can't detect it from the stands. Even some catchers downplay its importance. After all, pitchers have veto power." **5.** For a broadcaster to announce a game and describe what happens on the field. "Gentle man [Jack Buck] knew how to call a game" (*The Baltimore Sun*, June 21, 2002).

called ball **1.** A pitched ball delivered outside the strike zone and which is not swung at. It is deemed to be a ball by the umpire. The number of called balls required for a walk has varied from nine (1879) to four (1889). See also *ball*, 1. Compare *called strike*. Syn. *wide*, 2; *wide one*. IST USE. 1886. "Next the Chicagos came to bat, [Abner] Dalrymple reaching first on called balls" (*Chicago Tribune*, May 4; Peter Morris). **2.** *hist.* "The penalty inflicted on the pitcher for unfair delivery. Three called balls give a base" (Henry Chadwick, *The Game of Base Ball*, 1868, p.39). In the early days of baseball, the batter requested where the ball should be pitched. If the pitcher did not comply, he was warned that he was throwing unfairly, and a "ball" was called. The batter could not legally hit a called ball, nor could he be put out. IST USE. 1867. "King to bat, and off to first on called balls" (*Daily National Intelligencer* [Washington, D.C.], July 29). **3.** The penalty inflicted when, with the bases unoccupied, the pitcher does not deliver the ball to the batter within a specified time (20 seconds prior to 2007, 12 seconds since 2007) after the pitcher receives the ball and the batter is in the batter's box. The intent of the penalty is to avoid unnecessary delays.

called game A game that has been terminated, for any reason, by the umpire-in-chief, unless it becomes a *suspended game*. Games are most commonly called for rain, but they have also been called for fog, wind, sleet, snow, and darkness, and for going past a curfew time. If a game is called before the trailing team has batted in five innings, the game is replayed from the beginning. If the losing team has had its five innings and the game is called, it is recorded as a *shortened game*. IST USE. 1867. "The umpire called game on account of the rain coming down too muchly" (*Daily National Intelligencer* [Washington, D.C.], July 29).

called out looking To get a called strike for not swinging with two strikes on the batter.

called shot A hit, usually a home run, whose destination is predicted in advance. Hitters as early as 1881 (Paul Hines) and others, such as Joe Medwick, Hank Aaron, Graig Nettles, Greg Myers, Babe Ruth (in 1918), and even pitcher Bob Gibson have claimed to call their shots, and succeeded, but many others have boasted and failed, or their efforts have gone unreported. USAGE NOTE. Ty Cobb told reporter H.G. Salsinger in the presence of several other reporters (*Detroit News*, May 5, 1925; Peter Morris), "I would like you to pay particular attention today because for the first time in my career I will be deliberately going for home runs." Cobb homered in the first, second, and eighth innings, while going 6 for 6 and hitting two more homers the next day. Then he went back to spray hitting.

The most famous called shot was allegedly made by Ruth in Wrigley Field on Oct. 1, 1932, in the fifth inning of the third game of the World Series, when he hit a long home run some 430-plus feet against Charlie Root of the Chicago Cubs, a blast over the bleacher screen in deep right-center field at the base of the flagpole (just outside the playing field) to break a 4–4 tie. Participants in the game gave varying accounts of whether Ruth called his shot by pointing at pitcher Root, at the Cubs dugout (which had been riding him mercilessly), or toward center field. Ruth himself gave conflicting accounts, thereby fueling the legend as it grew over the years, but he became more convinced that he had called his shot.

Newspaper accounts published after the game claimed that Ruth did indeed call his shot: "Ruth Calls Shot as He Puts Homer No. 2 in Side Pocket" (Joe Williams, *New York World-Telegram*); "Babe notified the crowd that the nature of his retaliation would be a wallop right out [of] the confines of the park" (John Drebinger, *The New York Times*); "He pointed like a duelist to the spot where he expected to send his rapier home" (Paul Gallico, *New York Daily News*); and "Babe Calls His Shot" (Westbrook Pegler, *Chicago Sunday Tribune*). Quin Ryan, the Cubs broadcaster, told his radio audience, "That ball went out to almost the exact spot that Babe had been pointing to." Perhaps none of these accounts proves that Ruth pointed to center field to say "I'm hitting it there" and then did so; but that was the interpretation of some of the media who covered the game at the time. The *Reach Official American League Base Ball Guide* for 1933 and *Spalding's Official Base Ball Guide* for 1933 assumed that Ruth called his shot.

By the mid-1990s, 16-millimeter home movies taken by Harold Warp (a Chicago businessman) and Matt M. Kandle (a Chicago printing equipment inventor) surfaced, showing Ruth pointing. "Having seen a private, stop-action screening of the restored [Kandle] film, I would say Ruth clearly was pointing straight out, toward the pitcher (or the outfield), but definitely not the [Cubs] dugout" (Bill Deane, personal communication, June 7, 2006). Ruth may not have called his shot, but he made a brazen gesture toward his opponents and followed up with a long home run.

The issue of whether Ruth actually called his shot is still being argued. However, according to Bill Deane (*The Diamond*, Oct. 1993, p.19), the Court of Historic Review and Appeals in California concluded in its decision of June 11, 1986: "It is not important if the incidents referred to in . . . legends really did in fact happen. What is important is that a large segment of the people believe that they did occur, and it is for us as individuals to place whatever credence or value on these stories as we might desire. . . . It is the Court's opinion that the legend of Babe Ruth pointing to the center-field fence in the 1932 World Series shall remain intact for future generations of baseball fans and sportswriters to argue about. The petition before this Court to rule against the Babe Ruth legend is therefore denied."

called strike A pitched ball that a batter does not swing at, but which is judged to have passed through the strike zone by the umpire. Compare *called ball*, 1.

callejon de poder Spanish for "power alley."

call for the ball To yell a claim to a ball to prevent a misplay or a collision. When two fielders are headed for the same batted ball, one or the other, usually the one in the best position, takes command and claims it. See also *call off*. 1ST USE. 1888. "The necessity of 'calling' for a fly hit applies with particular force to the centre fielder. As soon as he has seen that he can get to a hit and has decided to take it, he calls out loudly so that every one must hear, 'I'll take it,' and all other fielders near him respond, 'Go ahead'" (John Montgomery Ward, *Base-Ball: How to Become a Player*, p.115).

call hitter *hist.* Syn. of *guess hitter*, 1.

call in To bring in a relief pitcher. "Willie Mains was called in to stop the slaughter and he did excellent work with his crossfire" (*The Boston Globe*, Apr. 19, 1896; Peter Morris).

calling card A pitch thrown intentionally close to a batter. Syn. *wakeup call*.

call off For a defensive player to alert a teammate not to approach a batted ball that the defensive player will handle. See also *call for the ball*.

call the turn *hist.* For the batter to guess what kind of pitch is about to be delivered. "Calling the turn is a style of batting [that] . . . while effective, is extremely dangerous for the batter, as to guess wrong is to court serious injury" (John J. Evers and Hugh S. Fullerton, *Touching Second: The Science of Baseball*, 1910; Peter Morris).

call time 1. For an umpire to create a temporary cessation of play; to take time out. 2. For a player to request a time-out from the umpire.

call-up *n.* 1. The act of bringing up a minor-league player to the majors. "[Corey] Patterson played better down the stretch and earned his first call-up to Chicago" (*The Baltimore Sun*, Feb. 28, 2006). Sometimes spelled "callup." 2. A player who has been called up.

"[Zach] Duke is one of a handful of recent call-ups who have given the Pirates hope" (*Sports Illustrated*, Aug. 15, 2005). Sometimes spelled "callup."

call up *v.* To bring to the major leagues a player from a minor-league club when the parent team needs his services during the season. See also *come up*, 1; *bring up*.

camarero Spanish for "second baseman."

cambio Spanish for "changeup."

camera day A promotional event at the ballpark in which fans are allowed on the field to take close-up photographs of the players.

camera eye A batter with a keen judgment of the strike zone who draws many bases on balls.

caminata Spanish for "base on balls."

camp 1. A team's spring training home. News from spring training is often reported in the newspapers under the headings "Around the Camps" or "News from the Camps." "[José] Leon made the Opening Day roster after batting .415 in camp" (*The Baltimore Sun*, Apr. 24, 2003). 2. See *baseball camp*. 3. See *fantasy baseball camp*.

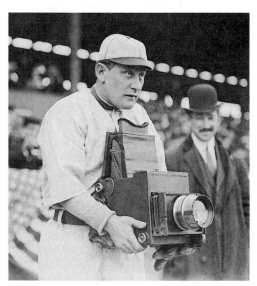

Camera day. Herman A. "Germany" Schaefer trying out the other side of the camera during the Washington Senators' visit to play the New York Highlanders in Apr. 1911. A versatile infielder and quick baserunner, he played most of his career with the Detroit Tigers and the Washington Senators. *George Grantham Bain Collection, Library of Congress*

campocorto Spanish for "shortstop."

camp under To position oneself underneath a fly ball and wait for it to drop into the fielder's glove. IST USE. 1914. "Williams hit it right straight up and Lord was camped under it" (Ring Lardner, *Saturday Evening Post*, March 7; Peter Morris).

can 1. *v.* To remove from service by an umpire or manager; to release or discharge a player from the team. IST USE. 1908 (*New York Evening Journal*, May 30; Edward J. Nichols). ETYMOLOGY. According to Ted Sullivan (quoted in *New York Evening Journal*, Nov. 12, 1908), after Kansas City (of the Union Association) catcher Bill Dugan allowed three passed balls that helped lose the game to Baltimore in late 1884, he telegraphed his wife: "Will be home in the morning; have my dinner can shined up—I'm going to work at my trade." Dugan told manager Sullivan, "I'm going back to my old trade, and I had better start now, so I'm going to 'can' myself." Wrote Sullivan, "So ever after that incident, when the players heard of any one being released, they said he had to 'shine up a dinner can.'" 2. *n.* Removal from the game or release from the team. "Tris Speaker Gets 'Can' Indefinitely" (*Boston Post* headline, Aug. 29, 1918; Peter Morris). In Harry Stein's novel *Hoopla* (1983), a character in the 1910s says, "He went ahead and issued five passes in a row, before the Tall Tactician finally figured it out to give him the can." 3. [softball term] *n.* The literal name (not slang) for home plate in Over the Line play.

cancel Christmas To have something bad happen; to acknowledge failure. "If you give him [Pedro Martinez] a big lead, you can cancel Christmas" (Mo Vaughn, quoted in *Baseball Digest*, Jan. 2001). "The Phillies traditionally give you one shot. If you're demoted after that, you might as well cancel Christmas" (Jimmy Rollins, quoted in *Sports Illustrated*, Sept. 18, 2006, p.64). ETYMOLOGY. The term was used by Roger Clemens: "cancel Christmas is when we send somebody to their room pretty quick at the batter's box" (*The Sporting News*, March 25, 2005).

Candlestick Park Home field of the San Francisco Giants from 1960 to 1999, known as 3Com Park at Candlestick Point from 1996 to 2001. It sets nestled into Morvey's Hill, overlooking San Francisco Bay. Candlestick Point, which overlooks the park, is named for the rocks and trees that poke up from the surrounding area like giant candles. The park was known for its inhospitable winds and chilliness: "It's the most beautiful ballpark in baseball—at 10:30 in the morning" (St. Louis Cardinals manager Whitey Herzog, quoted in *St. Petersburg Times*, Oct. 9, 1987). It was the site of the last Beatles concert (Aug. 29, 1966) and the home field for the San Francisco 49ers of the National Football League. Nicknames: *Stick, The*; *Icebox*.

cankle A pairing of an ankle and a calf that shows no distinguishing musculature features, as if it were one body part. "Guys with cankles are usually horrendous middle infielders—their first step is usually slow, so they're destined to be corner infielders" (Dan Jennings, quoted in Alan Schwarz, Baseball America.com, Nov. 14, 2006).

cannon 1. An exceptionally strong and accurate throwing arm. The term has been used for pitchers, catchers, infielders, and outfielders. 2. A defensive player with a cannon arm. 3. A hitter who hits the ball hard, often referred to as a "big cannon."

cannon ball A ball pitched or thrown with great velocity, as if it were fired out of a cannon. IST USE. 1877. "To catch [George] Bradley requires a man who can stop a cannon-ball, and very few are equal to the task" (H.W. Raymond, *The Boston Globe*, June 13; Peter Morris).

cannon shot An exceptionally long-hit ball. "The Astros have a squirt-gun offense in a ballpark which requires cannon shots for home runs" (Joe Henderson, *Tampa Tribune*, Dec. 25, 1988). "Mo Vaughn hit a cannon shot—off the Canon copier sign" (*The Baltimore Sun*, June 29, 2002).

cannon's mouth An infielder's location when positioned close to the batter during a probable bunt situation. Implied is the danger that the batter may unexpectedly take a full swing and imperil the fielder with a hard-hit ball.

can of corn An easily caught fly ball; a high, lazy fly ball that allows a defensive player time to stand under the ball and catch it eas-

ily. Var. "can o' corn." IST USE. 1930. "[Jesse Hill] leaped up to turn what looked like a sure double into just a can of corn, as the baseball boys call an out" (*Los Angeles Times*, June 19). USAGE NOTE. "We still have yet to hear even one player refer to . . . a 'can of corn' . . . a high, lazy fly to the infield" (*Baseball Magazine*, Jan. 1943). From time to time, the term is deemed to be an archaic bit of slang, but it is still used by sportscasters with regularity; e.g., "a big can of corn tonight" on a ball held up by the wind (Jerry Remy, New England Sports Network, June 11, 1990). ETYMOLOGY. It has long been assumed that the phrase comes from the old-time grocery store where the grocer used a pole or a mechanical grabber to tip an item, such as a can of corn, off a high shelf and let it tumble into his hands or his apron, which was held out in front like a fire net. An alternate theory was suggested by Mike Whiteford (*How to Talk Baseball*, 1983, p.85), who quoted Pittsburgh Pirates announcer Bob Prince as saying, "it's as easy as taking corn out of a can." Still another theory, suggested by Bert Dunne (*Folger's Dictionary of Baseball*, 1958), is that the "can of corn" ball is hit with a "kerplunk" sound, presumably that of a can being hit with a stick. Also suggested is that corn is a staple, hence a "sure thing," something to count on. Peter Tamony developed a separate theory that was published in the form of a letter appearing in Bucky Walter's "Mail Bag" (*San Francisco Examiner*, Aug. 24, 1977): "[The term] 'can of corn' no doubt developed out of the complex of usage surrounding 'cornball,' a confection made of pop corn and molasses, munched by the young for over a century. Popped corn flies wildly, of course, making a handy word association with a light pop-up to the outfield." Tamony, incidentally, determined that the term was in use in the early to mid-1920s, based on a series of interviews in 1953 with semiprofessional players.

EXTENDED USE. 1. An easy accomplishment or decision; a sure thing; a product that sells itself. The term also underscores the degree to which a bit of baseball slang can work its way into other realms; e.g., "a can of corn decision" in San Francisco that made the sponsor of a semiprofessional baseball team responsible for an injury to a bystander. In the case, a player for a team sponsored by the Double Play Tavern dropped an easily catchable fly ball (i.e., a can of corn) with two out and the bases loaded in the bottom of the ninth inning during a scoreless tie. The player who dropped the ball was so angry that he threw it across the street, accidentally hitting a woman at a gas station. The woman sued and won the case, which was reported in full under the headline, "Can of Corn Decision" (*San Francisco News*, May 12, 1959; Peter Tamony). **2.** An easygoing, good-humored personality. When Robin Williams accepted the best supporting actor Oscar in 1998 for his role in *Good Will Hunting*, he characterized the residents of South Boston (where much of the movie was set) as "a can of corn . . . You're the best." Janice Page (*The Boston Globe*, June 5, 2005) commented, "If you've ever wondered what the celebrities who come to Boston think of us . . . you might think Williams's borrowed colloquialism should tell you that they like us, really."

cantaloupe A pitched ball that looks big to the batter.

"can't anybody here play this game?" A lament and backhanded rallying cry, first uttered by Casey Stengel after taking over as manager of the inept 1962 New York Mets. The phrase became the title of a 1963 book by Jimmy Breslin.

can't buy a hit Said of a player or team having difficulty in getting out of a batting slump.

can't catch cold *hist.* Said of a poor defensive player who is unable to catch anything, from a baseball to a common cold. IST USE. 1915 (*Baseball Magazine*, December; Edward J. Nichols).

can't hit a balloon *hist.* Said of an inept hitter. IST USE. 1908 (*Baseball Magazine*, September; Edward J. Nichols).

can't-miss Said of a young player who appears headed for baseball success, whether to the majors or for stardom. "In 1983, that heaviest of burdens—'can't-miss' status—was conferred upon a dozen or so major-league rookies" (Bruce Lowitt, *St. Petersburg Times*, March 30, 1988). "Because he [Sean

Burroughs] was the son of the 1974 AL MVP, Jeff Burroughs, he was labeled a can't-miss prospect" (Tom Friend, *ESPN The Magazine*, May 13, 2002).

canto *hist.* Syn. of *inning*, 1. The term likens the divisions of a baseball game to one of the divisions of a long poem. "During the nine cantos just three Dodgers reached the initial hassock" (*Newark Evening News*, Apr. 16, 1915). See also *stanza*. IST USE. 1913 (*The Sporting News*, Oct. 30; Peter Morris).

can't pitch hay *hist.* Said of an ineffective pitcher. IST USE. 1915 (*Baseball Magazine*, December; Edward J. Nichols).

can't play Designation given to an amateur or college player who has no future in professional baseball. Abbrev. *KP.*

can't spit To show fear. "[A scout's] comment on a pitcher who is inclined to go into a panic in a tight situation. It derives from the fact that fear or excitement usually stops the flow of saliva" (Herbert Simons, *Baseball Magazine*, Jan. 1943).

can't teach that A flare that drops into the shallow outfield. ETYMOLOGY. David A. Markiewicz (*Fort Worth Star-Telegram*, March 26, 1998) quoted Texas Rangers manager Johnny Oates: "Last year, Mike Simms broke a bat on a little flare. He points to a spot near the right-field foul line about 15 yards from the edge of the infield. It dropped in for a hit and someone said, 'Can't teach that.'" Markiewicz added that the phrase has since become a staple of the Rangers' clubhouse.

cap 1. *n.* The visored hat that is a standard element of a player's uniform at all levels of baseball. It is usually decorated with the team's initials or insignia. See also *baseball cap.* **2.** *n.* The last play, of whatever kind, by a player or team in any baseball game, series, or season. **3.** *v.* To score a run to end an inning or game. "Ed Jurak's bases-loaded single capped a two-run, ninth-inning rally and lifted [the Giants] . . . to a victory over Chicago" (*Tampa Tribune*, March 16,1989).

capacity crowd Spectators who fill all seats in a ballpark.

cap day An event in which young fans come to the ballpark wearing, or to receive (free), the caps of the home team.

Cape Cod Baseball League An amateur, wooden-bat, no admission-charge summer league on the Cape Cod (Mass.) peninsula featuring college ballplayers. There are ten teams within 15 to 46 miles of each other. The league began play in 1885, and adopted wooden bats exclusively in 1985. One out of every six major-league players in 1999 was a graduate of the league (John Steadman, *The Baltimore Sun*, July 25, 1999). Graduates include such major leaguers as Carlton Fisk, Thurman Munson, Will Clark, Jeff Bagwell, Nomar Garciaparra, Todd Helton, Mo Vaughn, and Scott Erickson. See also Jim Collins, *The Last Best League*, 2004.

captain 1. An honorary title bestowed on a player to acknowledge leadership. Such an appointment is rare: "First baseman Eddie Murray, clearly the most respected man on the Orioles, was named the first captain in the history of the franchise by manager Earl Weaver yesterday during a team meeting" (Tim Kurkjian, *The Baltimore Sun*, Feb. 28, 1986). "Real captains aren't born or preordained, they're self-selected by their own ethic, then recognized because failure to do so would hurt the team" (Laura Vecsey, *The Baltimore Sun*, Dec. 27, 2004). Sometimes, but not always, the team captain will wear a small letter "c" on his uniform sleeve. 2. *hist.* A player in the early days of baseball who handled the functions currently assumed by the field manager. "[The Unions] only have one captain, whose name is law" (*Detroit Free Press*, Aug. 4, 1868; Peter Morris). Jean-Pierre Caillault noted that the Athletic Club Rules for 1883 specified the duties of the captain: "The Captain shall have absolute control in directing, placing and playing the men during the games and at practice, without interference from any one. . . . To him every player is required to render explicit obedience when directed while at play. He shall have the arrangement of the nine in every game, and shall be absolute in declaring what players shall or shall not play." IST USE. 1845. "The presiding officer shall designate two members as Captains, who shall retire and make the match to be played, observing at the same time that the players put opposite to each other should be as nearly

equal as possible" (Knickerbocker Rules, Rule 3d, Sept. 23). ETYMOLOGY. The constitution of the Olympic Ball Club of Philadelphia (a town ball club), published privately in 1838, specified that the "Recorder" shall be "the umpire between the captains on Club days" (Article VI, Section 3).

cap-tipper *hist.* A *showboat* in the 1930s.

card 1. Short for *drawing card*. IST USE. 1882. "[Bert] Dorr, the new pitcher, was the big card, and but for his appearance the crowd would have been very small" (*St. Louis Post-Dispatch*, Aug. 28; Peter Morris). 2. A colorful or eccentric ballplayer. "[John] McGraw . . . thought he saw in [Charles] Grant a ball player and a card" (Sol White, comp., *Sol White's History of Colored Base Ball*, 1907; Peter Morris). 3. See *baseball card*.

cardboard *hist.* An admission ticket to a baseball game. IST USE. 1912 (*New York Tribune*, Sept. 26; Edward J. Nichols).

Cardinals Nickname for the National League Central Division franchise in St. Louis, Mo., since 1900. The franchise was known as the St. Louis Browns (1892–1898) and the St. Louis Perfectos (1899). Also known as *Redbirds* and *Cards*. ETYMOLOGY. After the Perfectos changed their drab-brown uniforms to those featuring bright red trim, *St. Louis Republic* sportswriter William McHale reporter overheard a woman remark that the color was a "lovely shade of cardinal." This remark appeared in the paper along with the suggestion that the team adopt the name, which it did in 1900. The cardinal bird perched on a bat was adopted as a symbol for the team, and two cardinals perched on a bat was first used on the team uniforms in 1922.

cardinal sin of baseball 1. Gambling on baseball by baseball personnel. 2. Issuing a base on balls to the pitcher.

Cards Short for *Cardinals*.

career assessment Syn. of *favorite toy*. The term has been used by STATS Inc., publications since 2000.

career minor leaguer A player who has a long minor-league career, without any particular prospects of rising through the minors and becoming a major leaguer; a local player who has spent many years with the same minor-league team. Such players were common during the heyday of the minors from the 1920s to the 1950s, but there have been few of them since the "player development plan" was instituted in 1962. The term carries a bit of a stigma. Bruce Aven (quoted in *Baseball America*, Apr. 12–May 2, 1999): "I didn't want to be a career minor leaguer. If I didn't think I had a chance to make it to the major leagues, I wouldn't have come back."

career record 1. The statistical data accrued by a baseball player during his playing career. **2.** The achievement for the highest or best lifetime total in a particular category; e.g., Cy Young holds the "career record" for most games won (511).

career value The value of a player to his team over the course of his entire career; e.g., the argument that Willie Mays was a greater player than Mickey Mantle presumes that career value is the proper interpretation of "greater player." The term was introduced by Bill James in his *Baseball Abstract* (1985). Compare *peak value.*

career year The best season of a player's career; a season as statistically good as a particular player can expect to have during his playing years. Tom Verducci (*Sports Illustrated*, Sept. 9, 1996) noted that a career year occurs "when a player far exceeds his well-established statistical norms"; e.g., Norm Cash in 1961, Joe Charboneau in 1980, and George Brett in 1980.

caress *hist.* To hit the ball. 1ST USE. 1912 (*New York Tribune*, Sept. 7; Edward J. Nichols).

Caribbean Series A round-robin tournament held in February, featuring, since 1970, the winners of the winter leagues in Venezuela, Mexico, Puerto Rico, and the Dominican Republic. The Series began in 1949 when Cuba and Panama participated with Venezuela and Puerto Rico. The series was discontinued from 1961 to 1969.

Carmine Hose Nickname for the Boston Red Sox.

carnage A clobbering during which many runs are scored. "A one-sided game" (Maurice H. Weseen, *A Dictionary of American Slang*, 1934).

carom 1. *n.* A batted ball that bounces or ricochets off a wall or fence in the manner of a carom shot in billiards. **2.** *v.* To hit a pitched ball. "[Nap Lajoie] can carom a low ball off his socks" (*The Washington Post*, Sept. 25, 1898). The term is usually applied to hitting a ball that glances off a fielder's glove or part of his body. **3.** *n./hist.* A score. 1ST USE. 1891 (*Chicago Herald*, May 8; Edward J. Nichols).

carousel is spinning The sight of three baserunners, on a full count, taking off for the next base when the ball is pitched. The term has been used by New York Mets announcers (Brian O'Neill, *Roanoke* [N.C.] *Times & World-News*, June 25, 1982). See also *merry-go-round.*

carpet 1. The infield playing surface, including the basepaths. 1ST USE. 1902. "[Fred] Hartman astonished the multitude by making two hits yesterday. Both came at times when there was nothing on the carpet and went for naught" (*St. Louis Post-Dispatch*, July 16; Peter Morris). **2.** A baseball field. "Ask a television fan what was going on in Chicago in 1933 . . . and his thoughts will go back to the green Comiskey [Park] carpet and the mighty man named [Babe] Ruth" (Lee Allen, *The Sporting News*, July 13, 1960). **3.** Syn. of *artificial turf.*

carrera Spanish for "run."

carrera impulsada Spanish for "run batted in."

carrera limpia Spanish for "earned run." The literal translation is "clean run."

carrera sucia Spanish for "unearned run." The literal translation is "dirty run."

carry 1. *v.* For a batted ball to go a long distance. The term is used in the context of such atmospheric factors as humidity, fog, and wind. "Atlanta's muggy summer weather helps the ball to carry farther" (*St. Petersburg Times*, March 17, 1988). Jay Buhner commented on Safeco Field in Seattle (*Times Colonist*, July 1, 1999): "[The ball] carries decent, down the lines. But it doesn't carry very well to the gaps, and it doesn't carry to centre field at all." Jamie Moyer, describing Ryan Howard's home runs (quoted in *Sports Illustrated*, Sept. 18, 2006, p.64): "They start out like routine flies and carry and carry and carry until they land 30 rows back in the bleachers." **2.** *n.* The way a batted ball travels for distance. "It is very hard to judge the carry of the ball off the bat" (Cal Ripken Jr., quoted in *The Baltimore Sun*, Jan. 22, 2006). **3.** *n.* The way a thrown ball travels for distance. "He [Jerry Hairston Jr.] has real good carry to the ball when he throws it" (Jerry Hairston Sr., quoted in *The Baltimore Sun*, July 11, 1999). **4.** *n.* The distance that a batted or thrown ball travels beyond what was expected. "Anything hit in Safeco will have to move through Seattle's wet, thick, sea-level air, which means it'll lose 10 to 15 feet off the carry it got in the Kingdome, especially at night" (*Times Colonist*, July 1, 1999).

carry a club To be single-handedly able to hit and score enough to enable a team to play winning baseball. "When Jack Clark is hot, he can carry a club for three or four weeks at a time" (Kevin Horrigan, *St. Louis Post-Dispatch*, May 29, 1987). Syn. "carry a team."

carry a safe *hist.* To run slowly; to run as if weighed down by a heavy object.

carry my glove Said of an exceptional fielder. The term is usually used in the negative: "he can't carry my glove."

carry the mail 1. *hist.* To steal a base (*The New York Times*, June 2, 1929). **2.** To run swiftly. "He is a fellow who can 'carry the mail,' or get from here to there in a hurry" (Herbert Simons, *Baseball Magazine*, Apr. 1943). IST USE. 1931. "No ice wagon could have carried the mail sufficiently on that play, and [Glenn] Wright, running with long, smooth and powerful strides, was never in danger of being thrown out" (Thomas Holmes, *Brooklyn Daily Eagle*, Aug. 17; Peter Morris).

carte-de-visite An early baseball card, popular in the 1860s and 1870s, depicting photographs of studio-posed baseball players, or a baseball team, given away as a promotional item by tobacco and sporting-goods firms, photography studios, and civic organizations. The photos are usually black-and-white or sepia-toned and mounted on cards that measure 2½ by 4 inches. The "contrived elegance" of a carte-de-visite is "suggestive of a Victorian drawing room," and the players "look statuesque—almost stuffed—more like barristers than ballplayers" (*Sports Collectors Digest*, Nov. 11, 1988). Abbrev. *CdV.* See Mark Rucker, *Base Ball Cartes*, 1988. ETYMOLOGY. French for "visiting card," a paper photo print glued to a card mount, popular in France and England during the 1850s. It was the first widely available and affordable form of photography.

Cartwright myth The belief that Alexander Joy Cartwright (1820–1892) had more to do with the creation of baseball than is actually the case. John S. Bowman (letter, Sept. 18, 1989), who created the term (Joel Zoss and John S. Bowman, *Diamonds in the Rough*, 1989), challenged the belief that Cartwright "almost single-handedly organized the Knickerbockers, set down the rules of modern baseball, and then set about to convert many teams and individuals to 'his' game. Harold Peterson [*Sports Illustrated*, Apr. 14, 1964; *The Man Who Invented Baseball*, 1973]

Cartwright myth. Alexander Cartwright, a New York bank teller who helped organize the Knickerbocker Base Ball Club in 1845. *National Baseball Library and Archives, Cooperstown, N.Y.*

was greatly responsible for promoting this new myth, and it still permeates many articles and books. Well-informed people know that Cartwright doesn't deserve all this priority." John Thorn (*Total Baseball*, 8th ed., 2004) has shown that statements inscribed on Cartwright's Hall of Fame plaque (which deemed him "Father of Modern Base Ball")—namely that he set the bases 90 feet apart, established nine innings as a game and nine players as a team, organized the Knickerbocker Base Ball Club of New York in 1845, and carried baseball to the Pacific Northwest and Hawaii in pioneer days—are "demonstrably false" and lacking "evidence of truth." Further, recent research reveals that the claims that Cartwright laid out the game on a diamond rather than a square, introduced the concept of foul territory, and eliminated the practice of retiring baserunners by throwing the ball at them are also false. See also *Father of Baseball*, 2 (John Thorn, Sept. 2005).

carve the air *hist.* To swing at pitches without making contact. Syn. "carve nicks in the weather." IST USE. 1886. "Hatfield carved the air three times" (*The Boston Globe*, May 15; Peter Morris).

carving Allowing a pitch to get deep into the hitting zone and then slicing it between the third baseman and the shortstop. The term was used by Tony Gwynn (*Sports Illustrated*, June 2, 2003).

casaba A baseball.

Casey 1. *n.* A player who strikes out at the crucial moment in a game; one who fails in the manner of Casey, the figure in Ernest Lawrence Thayer's 1888 poem, "Casey at the Bat." Usually stated as *do a Casey* or *pull a Casey*. 2. *v.* To strike out.

Casey act A strikeout; esp. one occurring at a crucial moment in a game and in the manner of "Casey at the Bat." IST USE. 1912 (*New York Tribune*, Oct. 15; Edward J. Nichols).

"Casey at the Bat" A 13-stanza poem by Ernest Lawrence Thayer (1863–1940), written under the pen name of "Phin," that appeared in a humor column in the *San Francisco Examiner* on June 3, 1888, with the title "Casey at The Bat: A Ballad of The Republic." It gave epic quality to a single

strikeout and became a metaphor for failing in the clutch. Although the poem's sole purpose was to fill space (Thayer received $5 for his effort), it is probably the most popular poem ever written by an American; it is almost certainly the most recited and most parodied. It was termed "the nation's best known piece of comic verse" by Martin Gardner (*The Annotated Casey at the Bat*, 1967, a book that contains, among other things, 27 variations and updates in the style of the original). The poem was made many times into movies, cartoons, illustrated books, an opera, and a ballet; it has been featured in paintings and sculptures, and on postage stamps. The poem attracted little attention until it was recited for the first time by vaudevillian and comic actor William De Wolf Hopper (1858–1935) on Aug. 14, 1888, at Wallack's Theatre in New York City before an audience that included players from the New York Giants and Chicago White Stockings. Hopper (who also starred in Gilbert and Sullivan's comic operas) claimed to have recited the poem 10,000–15,000 times during his lifetime. Most famous is the poem's final stanza: "Oh, somewhere in this favored land the sun is shining bright; / The band is playing somewhere, and somewhere hearts are light, / And somewhere men are laughing, and somewhere children shout; / But there is no joy in Mudville—mighty Casey has struck out."

cashew An undisciplined, zany nonconformist; a "nutty" player. "The [Philadelphia Phillies] roster included such cashews as Richie Allen, who liked everything about a ball park except getting there" (Bob Uecker, *Catcher in the Wry*, 1982, p.68; Charles D. Poe).

cast For a pitcher to lead with his elbow while delivering a breaking ball, leaving the hand too far behind the arm and decreasing the potential to impart power spin (Alan Schwarz, BaseballAmerica.com, Nov. 14, 2006).

castoff A player who has been let go or dismissed by a team. Occasionally, a castoff from one team goes on to become successful with another. Syn. *discard.* IST USE. 1897. "None of the twirling cast-offs of the Orioles have cleaved a large field of congealed aqua, as the erudite savant, Dod Clarke, would put it" (*The Washington Post*, June 14).

casualty pass *hist.* Syn. of *base on balls.* 1ST USE. 1922 (Ernest J. Lanigan, *Baseball Cyclopedia*, p.90; Edward J. Nichols). ETYMOLOGY. This is almost certainly a reference to the pass given to a wounded soldier to allow him to retreat from the front lines to seek medical attention.

cat 1. A great fielding pitcher; one with feline agility, such as Harry "The Cat" Brecheen. **2.** A short object, either a piece of wood from four to eight inches long and one to two inches in diameter and tapered to a point at the ends, or a ball, struck by a bat in various cat games of Europe (tip-cat, cat and dog) and early America (old-cat games). According to Robert Smith (*Baseball's Hall of Fame*, 1965), "cat" was short for "catapult," defined as "a stick used to propel the ball out of a ring" in the game of cat-ball. **3.** Synonym of *cat-ball.* Cat was one of the games prohibited by the Pittsfield (Mass.) town ordinance of Sept. 5, 1791 (John Thorn).

cat and dog An early two-base version of the game of cat that was most commonly played in Scotland. According to Per Maigaard (*Genus*, Dec. 1941), the game calls for three players, two having a small club (called a "dog") and the third a wooden stick (called a "cat"), each defending a hole (base) in the ground. The player with the cat throws it at one of the batsmen who defends his hole with his dog. If the cat enters the hole, the defender has lost and becomes the thrower, and the thrower becomes a batsman; if the defender strikes the cat away, he changes holes with the other batsman, and the pitcher resumes throwing the cat. Cat and dog was the likely forerunner of the American game of *two-old-cat* (David Block, *Baseball Before We Knew It*, 2005, pp.130, 176, 195, and 269).

catapult See *cat*, 2. Thomas Altherr (*NINE*, Spring 2000) mentioned "catapult ball" as a "pre-baseball folk game" in Europe, but David Block (*Baseball Before We Knew It*, 2005) claimed that such a game did not exist.

cat-ball A simple game of ball, which, according to the number of batters available, was known as "one-old-cat," "two-old-cat," "three-old-cat," and "four-old-cat." The term was used by John Montgomery Ward (*Baseball: How to Become a Player*, 1888) for "the original American ball game," with two varieties: one-old-cat and two-old-cat. Charles A. Peverelly (*The Book of American Pastimes*, 1866, p.472) and Preston D. Orem [*Baseball (1845–1881) from the Newspaper Accounts*, 1961, p.4] note that in some parts of New England cat-ball was called "two-old-cat." Syn. *cat*, 3.

catbird seat A position of control and mastery, often stated as "sitting in the catbird seat." The term was popularized in the 1940s by Brooklyn Dodgers announcer Red Barber, who would use it, for example, to describe a batter with a count of three balls and no strikes, or a pitcher with a big lead. The term is often used to describe a team's first-place position in the standings; e.g., "Twins, Giants in Catbird Seat," as those two teams were on the verge of clinching playoff berths (*The Sporting News* headline, Oct. 5, 1987). Ty Cobb (*My Life in Baseball*, 1961, p.111) wrote, "[Frank] Navin paid me $20,000 per annum, then $35,000 and, finally, $50,000. From 1913 on, I was in the catbird seat when it came to money." USAGE NOTE. Bob Edwards (*Fridays with Red*, 1993, pp.48–49; Peter Morris) quoted Barber from his NPR talk show of Apr. 4, 1990: "When I came to New York and started using those expressions over the radio, James Thurber would listen. And then he got the idea of doing 'The Catbird Seat' for *The New Yorker* magazine. I had never met Mr. Thurber, and he never called and asked permission or anything else. And then a couple of years after that, I wanted to write a column for the *New York Journal American* . . . and I found out that I couldn't use the title 'The Catbird Seat.' And also I saw in *Variety* that they were going to make a motion picture out of 'The Catbird Seat,' and I sent word to Mr. Thurber that that was gettin' the goose a little far from the gander. I understand that he got furious." ETYMOLOGY. The term has long been attributed to Barber. Though he denied having created the term, he explained how he once "bought" it. In his biography (*Rhubarb in the Catbird Seat*, 1968), Barber tells the story of how, while playing penny ante poker in Cincinnati with friends, he sat for hours unable to win a hand. Then he related: "Finally, during a round of seven-card stud, I decided I was going to force the issue. I raised on the first bet, and I raised again on every card. At the end, when the showdown came, it was between a fellow named Frank Cope and me. Frank turned over his hole cards, showed a pair of aces, and won the pot. He said, 'Thank you, Red. I had those aces from the start. I was sitting in the catbird seat.' I didn't have to be told the meaning. And I had paid for it. It was mine." One question that has never been satisfactorily answered is, why the catbird? James Rogers (*The Dictionary of Clichés*, 1985) commented, "The catbird commands a good view from its lofty perch, but then, so do many birds. Why the catbird's vantage point was signaled out is beyond explaining." However, according to birder and writer Bill Young, catbirds "do not typically sing from lofty perches; they are generally seen at eye level or below."

EXTENDED USE. The term is used to describe anyone finding himself or herself in an advantageous situation: "[Israeli Foreign Minister Shimon] Peres in the Catbird Seat" (*Newsweek* headline, Sept. 29, 1986).

catch 1. *v.* To retrieve and control a thrown or batted ball, usually with the aid of a glove or mitt. The term is most commonly applied to a ball that has not hit the ground; however, in baseball's early years a batter was declared out if his batted ball was caught either on the fly or on the first bound. IST USE. 1883 (*The Sporting Life*, Apr. 22; Edward J. Nichols). **2.** *v.* To play the position of catcher. "Bo [Belinsky] is starting tomorrow and, Ron [Brand], you will catch him" (Grady Hatton, quoted in Maury Allen, *Bo: Pitching and Wooing*, 1973). **3.** *n.* The act of a fielder's receiving and controlling or securing firmly in his hand or glove a batted or thrown ball before it hits the ground. To make a valid catch, the fielder must hold the ball long enough to prove that he has complete control of the ball and that his release of the ball is voluntary. IST USE. 1862 (*New York Sunday Mercury*, June 29; Edward J. Nichols). **4.** *n.* A game in which two or more people throw a ball back and forth. IST USE. 1913. "Sand-lotters and men who played the game in their younger days are out on vacant lots or in their back yards or the alleys back of their homes tossing the ball and 'playing catch'" (*The Washington Post*, Feb. 23; Peter Morris). **5.** *v.* To rise in the standings and overtake a higher-ranked team. **6.** *v.* To hit a ball well. "I hit all my homers in batting practice. Every now and then I catch one in a game" (Lance Johnson, quoted in *Baltimore Sun*, Oct. 10, 1993). **7.** *n./hist.* Any player who catches the ball in early baseball; e.g., "be a sure catch, a good thrower . . . a reliable batter and a good runner" (Harry Wright correspondence, letter to Charles Tubbs) and "Dorgan is a sure catch" (*Detroit Free Press*, May 14, 1887) (Peter Morris). **8.** *n.* Short for *catcher*, 1. **9.** *n.* Short for *catcher*, 2. IST USE. 1867. "The Nationals made a change in their field, sending Berthrong to catch" (*Daily National Intelligencer* [Washington, D.C.], July 29).

Catch, The The over-the-left-shoulder catch in deep center field at the Polo Grounds made by Willie Mays of the New York Giants on Sept. 29, 1954, during the eighth inning of the first game of the World Series, off a long drive hit by Vic Wertz of the Cleveland Indians off pitcher Don Liddle. There were runners on first and second bases, and no outs. According to contemporary press reports and later analysis, the distance from home plate has been stated as 450 feet (Robert Kemp Adair, *The Physics of Baseball*, 1990, p.74), 460 feet (*The Sporting News*), and 470 feet (*Newsday*). Recent estimates based on park diagrams, photographs, and geometric calculations give a distance of 410 to 420 feet. "When baseball heads into the 22nd century, they'll still be talking about The Catch" (*Time* magazine, special advertising insert for the 1981 World Series). EXTENDED USE. The fourth-quarter touchdown catch at the back of the end zone by San Francisco 49ers receiver Dwight Clark, which set up the 28–27 victory over the Dallas Cowboys in the National Football Conference championship game on Jan. 10, 1982, at Candlestick Park. The desperate six-yard pass was thrown by quarterback Joe Montana with 51 seconds left to play.

catchability The competence or skill of a fielder. On scouting reports, the term is not very useful because it lacks detail and explanation (Alan Schwarz, BaseballAmerica.com, Nov. 14, 2006).

catch and carry [softball term] A legal catch that a defensive player carries into dead-ball territory. Any runners advance one base, unless the act was intentional, in which event runners advance two bases.

catch-and-throw 1. *n.* A continuous defensive play in which the fielder catches the ball and immediately throws it to a base. "[Jerry Hairston] saved at least one run with a running catch-and-throw from behind second base" (*The Baltimore Sun*, March 29, 2001). **2.** *adj.* Said of the defensive skills of a catcher. "From a catch-and-throw standpoint, [José] Diaz is as good as it gets" (Bill Ballew, *Baseball America*, Oct. 15–28, 2001; Peter Morris). **3.** *adj.* Said of a good defensive catcher, usually with the implication that his offense is lacking. "Brandon Inge is definitely the Tigers' best catch-and-throw guy behind the plate, but they want to send him down to learn how to swing the bat" (*Sports Illustrated*, March 25, 2002).

catcher 1. The player behind home plate to whose mitt the pitcher aims the ball. The role of the catcher is relatively complex and extends far beyond being a target for and receiver of pitched balls; e.g., the catcher orders (calls) the pitches to be thrown through the use of signals, backs up throws to first base, attempts to field pop fouls, blocks pitched balls in the dirt, sets defensive alignments, handles the pitching staff by knowing the strengths and weaknesses of the pitchers, attempts to tag out baserunners trying to score, and attempts to throw out would-be base stealers. Abbrev. *C*, 2. See also *backcatcher*; *hindcatcher*. Syn. *catch*, 8; *backstop*, 2; *backstopper*; *game-caller*; *grabber*; *hind snatcher*; *receiver*; *snatcher*; *stopper*, 3; *wind paddist*. IST USE. 1856. Researcher Frederick Ivor-Campbell (personal communication, Nov. 13, 2001) comments, "The evidence that I have seen shows that by 1856 catchers were called catchers." **2.** The position played by the catcher. Abbrev. *C*, 3. Syn. *catch*, 9. IST USE. 1854. A diagram in the published booklet of the Eagle (New York City) club's rules shows the catcher's position, labeled "catcher" (Frederick Ivor-Campbell).

catcher's balk A misnomer for a balk that is charged to the pitcher when the catcher is not entirely in the catcher's box while the pitcher is issuing an intentional base on balls. The catcher must stand with both feet within the lines of the catcher's box until the ball leaves the pitcher's hand; failure to do so results in a balk charged to the pitcher. The term has also been incorrectly used to describe *catcher's interference*.

catcher's box 1. The rectangular area extending eight feet from the tip of home plate in which the catcher must remain until the pitch is delivered. It is 43 inches wide. **2.** [softball term] The rectangular area extending 10 feet from the rear outside corners of the batter's boxes in which the catcher positions himself or herself. It is eight feet, five inches wide.

catcher's earned run average The earned run average of a team's pitchers with a given catcher. At times, its use leads to insights about a catcher's defensive performance that are unavailable using other statistics. Craig R. Wright and Tom House (*The Diamond Appraised*, 1989) helped popularize this statistic, but credited the Japanese with introducing the measurement: "When a pitcher is struggling in a game, the Japanese manager will sometimes change the whole battery, or perhaps leave the pitcher in and change catchers. And in their statistical records, many teams keep track of the number of runs allowed per nine innings caught for each of their catchers." Abbrev. *CERA*, 1.

catcher's equipment The protective gear worn by the catcher, consisting of a catcher's mask or helmet, catcher's mitt, chest protector, and shin guards. The equipment is designed to protect the catcher from being injured by the baseball (and to a much lesser extent, the bat). In baseball's early days, catchers stood well behind the plate and wore no equipment. As they began to move closer to the batter, some catchers began to don protective equipment, but there was considerable resistance to such "unmanly" garb. George Ellard, a nonprofessional catcher, protested the wearing of protective gear with the poem "The Red Stockings" (1880s), which contains these lines: "We used no mattress on our hands, / No cage upon our face; / We stood right up and caught the ball, / With courage and with grace." See also *tools of ignorance.* Syn. *paraphernalia; fernalia; armor,* 1.

catcher's interference An act by the catcher that hinders the batter (e.g., pushing the batter, touching the batter or his bat, or running in front of the batter to catch a pitched ball) or a baserunner (e.g., blocking home plate without holding or attempting to field the ball). The batter is awarded first base (he is not charged with an official at-bat), but the catcher is charged with an error. The baserunner is awarded the base to which he was advancing. If catcher's interference is called with a play in progress, the umpire will allow the play to continue; the offense may elect to accept the play rather than the penalty. See also *catcher's balk.*

catcher's mask A padded metal grate that protects the catcher's face from the baseball (such as errant pitches and foul tips) and the bat. Invented by Fred Winthrop Thayer, captain of the Harvard baseball club, the mask was first worn by Harvard catcher James Alexander Tyng in a game on April 12, 1877, against the Live Oaks, a semiprofessional team from Lynn, Mass. A tinsmith took a fencer's mask, ripped out the close-meshed wires, inserted a thicker, wide-spaced brass wiring, and attached shock-absorbing pads to rest on the forehead and the cheeks. Not only did the new invention protect the catcher's face from the ball and bat, it also allowed him to move closer to the plate and pay greater attention to the runners on base. However, the catcher's mask attracted quick criticism. An article on Thayer by John Hanlon (*Portland* [Maine] *Sunday Telegram,* June 1, 1896) recounted several critics, including a sportswriter who commented, "There is a great deal of beastly humbug in contrivances to protect men from things which do not happen. There is about as much sense in putting a lightning rod on a catcher as there is a mask." But as the demand for masks grew steadily, Thayer realized that he had come up with a good idea. On Jan. 15, 1878, he applied for a patent (no. 200,358), which was granted less than a month later. One of the three

Catcher's mask. Sailors at play, Brooklyn Navy Yard. *George Grantham Bain Collection, Library of Congress*

"original" models used in conjunction with the patent application has been silvered and is on display at the Harvard Varsity Club in Cambridge, Mass. See also *mask; goalie-style mask.* Syn. *cage,* 3; *bird cage; wire cage; face mask.* IST USE. 1877. "The new 'catcher's mask,' which had never before been seen on the Chicago grounds" (*Chicago Tribune,* July 20; Peter Morris).

catcher's mitt The large, rounded, padded leather glove worn by catchers since the 1890s. It has one internal section for the four fingers and another for the thumb. It may not be more than 38 inches in circumference, nor more than 15½ inches from top to bottom. Catchers were wearing gloves as early as 1870, and catcher's mitts began to evolve around 1877. In *The Sporting News* (Feb. 23, 1939), a claim was made that the "father of the catching glove" was Kansas City (Western League) catcher Joe Gunson, whose invention was prompted by an injury in 1888; he never realized any gains from his idea, as others soon devised similar aids for themselves. New York Giants catcher Buck Ewing introduced the catcher's mitt to the National League in 1888 (*New York Sun,* Apr. 27, 1890). On Aug. 8, 1889, Philadelphia catcher Harry Decker was granted the first patent for a padded catcher's mitt; it became so popular that it was referred to as a *Decker.* See also *one-handed glove.* Syn. *big mitt,* 1. EXTENDED USE. A figurative receptacle. "Universities across the country created graduate programs in homeland security, institutes on terrorism and counter-terrorism, all raising huge catcher's mitts into the air for the billions of dollars of grants and contracts just blowing in the wind" (Ian S. Lustick, *The Baltimore Sun*, Dec. 31, 2006).

catches missed *hist.* An early synonym for *error*, used in the *New York Sunday Mercury* for 1863 (Alan Schwarz, *The Numbers Game*, 2004).

catch leaning See *caught leaning*.

catch looking To fool or deceive a batter with a pitch that crosses the plate for a called third strike. See also *strike out looking*.

catch napping See *caught napping*.

catch on To become a member of a baseball club. "Old Cy Young is finding it no easy task to catch on as a big league scout" (*San Francisco Bulletin*, Feb. 23, 1913; Gerald L. Cohen). IST USE. 1902 (*The Sporting Life*, Sept. 20, p.5; Edward J. Nichols).

catch stealing See *caught stealing*.

catch up 1. To bring the bat around to hit the ball. The term is often used negatively; e.g., "[David Ortiz] couldn't catch up with good fastballs on his hands" (*Sports Illustrated*, June 19, 2006) or "Batters using the heavier bats are having trouble catching up with high and tight fastballs" (Tarik El-Bashir, *The Washington Post*, March 25, 2001). 2. To try to overtake a team higher in the standings.

catch-up game A game in which one team comes from behind to lead or win.

caught asleep Syn. of *caught napping*.

caught leaning Said of a baserunner who was picked off a base by the pitcher or catcher after trying to get a jump on the next base.

caught looking See *catch looking*.

caught napping Said of a less-than-alert baserunner who was picked off a base by a quick throw or suddenly caught between bases, or who was otherwise outwitted by the defense. A quaint but accurate early definition of "baseball napping": "When a player through carelessness or sleepy-headedness is caught off his base" (Mrs. John A. Logan, *Home Manual*, 1889). Syn. *caught asleep*. IST USE. 1860. "[Mattie O'Brien] kept his opponents well on the bases when they reached them. He caught [Frank] Pidgeon napping at first base in capital style" (*Brooklyn Eagle*, Oct. 30; Peter Morris).

caught stealing Tagged out while attempting to steal a base. The *Official Baseball Rules* (Rule 10.07[h]) provides that a runner shall be charged as "caught stealing" (an official statistic) when he a) tries unsuccessfully to steal a base, b) is picked off a base while trying to advance (any move toward the next base is considered an attempt to advance), or c) overslides while stealing. In 1982, when Rickey Henderson set the all-time single-season steal record of 130, he was also caught stealing a record 42 times. Abbrev. *CS*.

caulker *hist.* A hard-hit ball. "Ryan knocked a 'caulker,' which was finely stopped by Pinkham and fielded to first base" (*Brooklyn Eagle*, Sept. 12, 1866; Peter Morris).

CBA Abbrev. for *collective bargaining agreement*.

CdV Abbrev. for *carte-de-visite*.

ceiling Relative level for improvement; e.g., a "high ceiling" indicates opportunity for improvement. The term is usually applied to rookies. "[Jorge] Maduro has 'a very high ceiling,' meaning a lot of room for improvement, because he's a big kid . . . with a great batting ability" (*The Miami Herald*, July 19, 1998). "Ryan Garko has a low ceiling in terms of potential" (anonymous scout, quoted in *The Baltimore Sun*, May 6, 2007).

cellar The position in league or divisional standings held by the team with the worst won-lost record. "Frank Chance's Highlanders got out of the cellar position for a day or so, but some person carelessly left the cellar door open and they tumbled back in" (*San Francisco Bulletin*, May 17, 1913; Gerald L. Cohen). IST USE. 1907 (*Lajoie's Official Base Ball Guide*, p.166; Edward J. Nichols). Syn. *basement*; *pit*, 1.

cellar championship A facetious term for the efforts of two or more teams to determine which one will end up in last place in the final standings. IST USE. 1905. "With a team which never had a look-in for anything better than cellar championship . . . the club made money" (National Association of Professional Base Ball Leagues, *Official Guide—1905*; David Shulman).

cellar dweller A team with the worst won-lost record in the standings at any given moment during the season. Syn. "cellar tenant"; "cellar occupant."

cello pack A set of baseball cards packaged in transparent cellophane. The term is used by collectors to distinguish cellophane-packed cards (which collectors tend to prefer because the top and bottom cards in each pack are exposed) from those in a *wax pack*. A cello pack that has not been opened and has a major baseball star's card showing carries a premium over the price of the single card.

cement mixer A mediocre pitch. Roger Clemens used the term for a *backup slider* that spins badly (*The Sporting News*, March 25, 2005).

center 1. *n.* Short for *center field*. IST USE. 1864. "Joe Oliver playing at left field, P. O'Brien at centre, and Pearce at second base" (*New York Clipper*, Oct. 22; Peter Morris). USAGE NOTE. The spelling "centre" was dominant in the United States throughout the 19th century and remained common well into the 20th century; e.g., "[Fred] Dunlap then made a two-bagger through centre" (*Chicago Tribune*, May 4, 1886; Peter Morris). **2.** *v.* To hit the ball squarely. "[Nick Markakis has] a nice swing. He centers the ball consistently" (Baltimore Orioles scouting director Tony DeMacio, quoted in *Baseball America*, June 23–July 6, 2003).

center field 1. The area beyond second base, which is not regularly covered by either the right fielder or the left fielder; the center of the outfield. Sometimes spelled "centerfield." Syn. *center*, 1; *center garden*; *middle pasture*. EXTENDED USE. The central defensive area in other sports; e.g., that part of the field patrolled by the free safety in football or the middle of the court in basketball. "[Baltimore Ravens free safety Ed] Reed plays one great center field" (*The Baltimore Sun*, Aug. 8, 2004). "[Cleveland Cavaliers power forward Drew Gooden] tries to play centerfield too much, going for steals and coming off his man to try to block shots" (*Sports Illustrated*, Jan. 20, 2003). **2.** The position of the player who defends center field. Abbrev. *CF* or *cf*. Syn. *center*, 1; *middle field*.

center fielder The defensive player who is positioned in center field. Because of the size of the area the center fielder must patrol, the player in this position is usually quite fast and has a strong, accurate arm. "Oh, to be a center fielder, a center fielder—and nothing more!" (Philip Roth, *Portnoy's Complaint*, 1969, p.50). Abbrev. *CF* or *cf*. Sometimes spelled "centerfielder." Syn. *center gardener*; *middle gardener*; *midfielder* IST USE. 1866. "The Center Fielder should always be in readiness to back up the second base, and should always go to long field in cases where a hard-hitter is at bat" (Henry Chadwick, *The Base-Ball Player*; Peter Morris). EXTENDED USE. The free safety position in football. "Why else take out the free safety—the so-called center fielder—on obvious passing plays?" (Gerald Eskenazi, *The New York Times*, Aug. 1, 1999).

center garden *hist.* Syn. of *center field*, 1. IST USE. 1868. " 'Centre garden,' as the boys call the field" (*Brooklyn Eagle*, Aug. 15; Peter Morris).

center gardener *hist.* Syn. of *center fielder*. IST USE. 1897. "Walter Brodie, the center gardener of the Pirates" (*The Washington Post*, June 14).

centering A numerical reference regarding the alignment of the borders of a baseball card surrounding the photograph and how they measure to each other. A "perfectly centered" card is designated "50/50," indicating both side-to-side and top-to-bottom alignments are the same. It is an important factor in determining a card's grade or condition.

Central Division 1. See *American League Central*. **2.** See *National League Central*.

Central League One of Japan's two major professional baseball leagues (the other being the *Pacific League*), founded in 1949. It does not use the designated hitter. The league consists of six teams: Hanshin Tigers, Chunichi Dragons, Tokyo Yakult Swallows, Hiroshima Toyo Carp, Yokohama BayStars, and Yomiuri Giants. See also *bēsubōru*. Syn. *Se League*.

CERA 1. Abbrev. for *catcher's earned run average*. **2.** Abbrev. for *component ERA*.

ceremonial first pitch The traditional tossing of a baseball by an honored person to the catcher of the home team before the begin-

Ceremonial first pitch. President Warren G. Harding throwing out first ball, Apr. 26, 1923. The Philadelphia Athletics beat the Washington Senators 2–1. *National Photo Company Collection, Library of Congress*

ning of a game in the home team's ballpark, or for some other noteworthy event. It is most commonly associated with the first game of the season, as well as the All-Star Game and World Series games. Originally, the first pitch was thrown from the stands next to the home team's dugout, but more currently, the pitch is made from the mound or close to the mound. At its most spectacular, the president of the United States throws out the first ball on Opening Day to signal the beginning of another season; the first president to do so was William Howard Taft on Apr. 14, 1910, in Washington, D.C. Sometimes the symbolism is even greater than the actual event. When President Harry Truman threw the ceremonial first pitch in 1946 at Griffith Stadium, he was showing the nation that the war years were indeed over and that the president once again had time for such trivial pursuits as throwing out the first ball. According to *The Baltimore Sun* (Apr. 17, 2005), before the Washington Nationals played its first home game in 2005, manager Frank Robinson warned his players, "Always expect a bad throw. Be surprised when it is not." After catcher Brian Schneider caught President George W. Bush's ceremonial first pitch, he remarked, "I'm a lucky guy, and I'll always remember this day for the rest of my life." At a lower level, various people are asked to throw out balls as an honor, for reasons as simple as being the president of the company

sponsoring Seat Cushion Night. The first ceremonial first pitch was tossed by the governor of Delaware when Wilmington of the Atlantic Association opened its new park on Apr. 3, 1890, in an exhibition game against the American Association's Athletic club (Cliff Blau, personal communication, July 19, 2003). See also *throw out the first ball.* Syn. *first pitch,* 1; *first ball,* 2.

cerrador Spanish for "closer."

CF 1. Abbrev. for *center field,* 2. Sometimes *cf.* **2.** Abbrev. for *center fielder.* Sometimes *cf.*

CG Abbrev. for *complete game,* 1.

chaffing *hist.* Syn. of *chin music,* 2. "In those days, when the first professional association was just getting on its feet, there were no cast-iron regulations about where the players should sit or stand, and very often a whole team stood close around the batter, giving him points when they could, and spending the remainder of the time in 'chaffing' with the umpire or pitcher" (*Philadelphia Press,* Aug. 20, 1883). "There is a value in the rule of silence as far as 'chaffing' or 'chin-music,' as it is called, is concerned" (*New York Clipper,* Jan. 30, 1875; Tom Shieber). IST USE. 1863 (Chadwick Scrapbooks, Aug. 9; Edward J. Nichols).

chain gang The St. Louis Cardinals farm system of the 1920s and 1930s.

chain saw Syn. of *cut fastball.*

chain-store baseball *hist.* The system instituted by Branch Rickey of the St. Louis Cardinals soon after World War I by which a major-league club gathered a "chain" of minor-league teams of every classification (either owning them outright or having working agreements with them) and held the rights to players on those teams (players would "graduate" to larger circuits until they were ready for the major leagues). The system provided an unending source of "finished" young players developed by the major-league club. The system later was known as *farm system.* See *Saturday Evening Post* (March 9, 1935) for the origin and development of chain-store baseball. Syn. "chain baseball."

chair position "The right position for a catcher to catch the ball as the pitcher throws it; he looks almost as if he is sitting on the edge of a chair" (Morris A. Shirts, *Warm Up for Little League Baseball*, 1971).

chalk The white powder that is spread on the playing field to mark the foul lines, baselines, on-deck circles, coach's boxes, catcher's box, and batter's boxes. Lime is often used as a substitute for chalk.

chalker A hand-operated piece of equipment used to mark the white lines needed on a baseball field.

chalk line Any line drawn on a baseball field, although it usually refers to one of the foul lines.

chalk raiser A batted ball that is ruled fair because, in hitting the chalked foul line, it raises a corroborating puff of white-line dust.

chalk up **1.** To record a baseball feat or victory as if on a blackboard. "Ewell Blackwell . . . chalked up a no-hitter against the Braves" (Red Foley, *The Sporting News*, May 23, 1956, p.5). IST USE. 1905 (*The Sporting Life*, Oct. 7, p.11; Edward J. Nichols). **2.** To hit a ball off the end of the bat, in allusion to billiards, where the end of the cue is "chalked up." Players once commonly hollered "chalk up" when a batter hit the ball off the end of the bat.

challenge **1.** *v.* To pitch one's best pitch to a batter, daring him to hit it, usually expressed as "challenge the hitter"; to pitch to that area of the strike zone where the batter displays his greatest strength, as opposed to avoiding it. This is most likely to occur when the pitcher's strength seems to match that of the batter. Art Hill (*"Don't Let Baseball Die,"* 1978, p.124) commented, "When a pitcher 'challenges' a hitter, he throws him the pitch he's looking for *because it is also the pitcher's best pitch*; he pits strength against strength." Andre Dawson (concerning Nolan Ryan, quoted in *USA Today Baseball Weekly*, Sept. 29–Oct. 5, 1993): "Basically, he'll challenge you; you'll get a pitch to hit." See also *go after*. Syn. *come at*. **2.** *v.* For a runner to test the throwing capability of an outfielder by a runner who attempts to advance an extra base. "[Rickey] Henderson never broke stride rounding third and challenged center fielder Bernie Williams, whose throw bounced sev-

eral times in the infield" (*The Baltimore Sun*, July 7, 1994) **3.** *n.* A call to engage in an ostensibly amateur baseball competition in the 1860s. Peter Morris (personal communication, July 29, 2000): "A club holding or claiming a particular championship was obliged to accept a properly issued challenge. This system was obviously borrowed from chivalric tradition, but it was modified for baseball's peculiar needs." F.M. Delano (president of the Brother Jonathan Base Ball Club, quoted in *Detroit Free Press*, June 14, 1863): "A challenge to a game of baseball, as to anything else, gives the challenged party choice of time and place."

challenge fastball A fastball that figuratively says, "Here's my best, hit it if you can."

Chalmers Award An award presented from 1911 through 1914 to one player in the American League and one player in the National League who "should prove himself as the most important and useful player to his club and to the league at large in point of deportment and value of services rendered." The award was conceived by Hugh Chalmers, president and general manager of the Chalmers Motor Co. of Detroit. A commission of baseball writers (one writer from each of the 11 major-league cities) decided the winner of the award (officially known as the Chalmers Touring Car Award). The players selected for the award received a Chalmers "30" automobile (approximate value of $1,500). The Chalmers Award was a precursor to the Most Valuable Player Award. In 1910, a Chalmers automobile was presented to the batting champions in each league. According to the *San Francisco Bulletin* (Feb. 26, 1913; Gerald L. Cohen), the National Commission objected to the award because "the national game is being used to advertise a commodity, and . . . the contest created jealousy and ill feeling among prominent players."

champ Short for "champion." The earliest attestation of "champ" is in a baseball context: "The 'Champs' enjoyed themselves in various ways during the morning" (*New England Base Ballist*, Aug. 6, 1868; Peter Morris).

champagne celebration A postgame clubhouse ritual in which a victorious team cele-

Chalmers Award. Walter Johnson receiving the 1913 award. *National Photo Company Collection, Library of Congress*

brates by spraying and drinking champagne. It usually occurs when a team clinches its division or the pennant, or wins the World Series, but not exclusively—in 1950, the St. Louis Browns held a champagne celebration upon winning their 55th game, which (under the former 154-game schedule) meant that it was impossible for them to lose 100 games.

championship game A regular-season game that counts in the standings, as opposed to an exhibition game. It was very common in baseball's early days for major-league teams to play many exhibition games during the championship season; hence, the need to distinguish between games that counted toward a championship and those played as exhibitions.

Championship of the World Syn. of *World's Championship Series*, 2. The term was used to label the St. Louis scorecards for the 1926 and 1934 World Series.

championship season 1. The full schedule of 162 regular-season major-league games, to be completed over a period of no fewer than 178 days and no more than 183 days, during the course of which the divisional championships are established. It excludes preseason and postseason games. **2.** A specific season in which a particular team wins the championship.

Championship Series A set of playoff games (best four of seven games) between the two division (and since 1995, the *Division Series*) winners in each of the major leagues (National League and American League) to determine the two pennant winners to play in the World Series. The series was the best three of five games from 1969 to 1984. See also *League Championship Series*; *American League Championship Series*; *National League Championship Series*.

Champions of the World 1. The term used by *The Sporting Life* and *The Sporting News* for the victorious Providence Grays (champions of the National League) who defeated the New York Metropolitans (champions of the American Association) in the 1884 postseason series. The contests were referred to as the *World's Championship Series*, although the series had been touted as the "Championship of the United States" or the "United States Championship." The 1884 series was the first designated "World Series." Since there were no other nations playing high-caliber organized baseball at the time, it was not too pretentious to call the winners the "Champions of the World." IST USE. 1865. "Game 40 to 28, Atlantic ahead, and still the champions of the world" (*Brooklyn Eagle*, Aug. 15; Peter Morris). **2.** A resplendent title claimed annually by the winner of the World Series. Many have commented on this all-embracing title, including linguist

Peter Tamony (*News Letter and Wasp*, Oct. 13, 1939) who wrote, "That baseball . . . is played only in the United States, and that the game is not international is of little moment in the excitement attending the outcome of the series. Whichever team wins holds the Championship of the World, and is thus, in our scheme of things entitled to a place just to the right of that of the gods."

chance A reasonable opportunity for a defensive player to field a batted or thrown ball with the likelihood of making or assisting a putout or an error. Generally the first baseman accepts the most chances in a game since he ends most infield outs. A fielder's *total chances* are determined by adding putouts, assists, and errors. IST USE. 1867 (Chadwick Scrapbooks, Sept. 9; Edward J. Nichols).

chances accepted A fielder's putouts plus assists.

change 1. *adj./hist.* Said of a relief or substitute player or players; e.g., a "change pitcher" or a "change catcher." "The Athletics pitted their change battery against the amateur Hartville Club" (*The Sporting Life*, Apr. 15, 1883; David Shulman). IST USE. 1865. "Their nine [the Stars], however, needs two pitchers on it, no nine being complete without a change pitcher" (*New York Clipper*, June 10; Robert H. Schaefer). 2. *n.* Syn. of *changeup*.

change livery *hist.* To change teams.

change of base *hist.* Syn. of *change of scenery*. "[Mike Mitchell] has played long enough with the Reds and a change of base [to the Chicago Cubs] will freshen him up. Often a new pasture is the very best thing for a player" (*San Francisco Bulletin*, Feb. 14, 1913; Gerald L. Cohen).

change of pace *hist.* A once commonly used term for *changeup*. It is a slowly pitched ball, thrown in an effort to deceive the batter into thinking it is a fastball, thereby throwing off the batter's timing; "a slow ball throwed with a fast ball motion" (Dizzy Dean). Rogers Hornsby (*My Kind of Baseball*, 1953, p.143) wrote, "The change of pace can be achieved by dragging the back foot across the mound or by holding the ball deeper in the hand and gripping it tighter, and like the curve, the ball

should be kept low." Formerly, it was known simply as a *slow ball*. The term "change of pace" has gone out of style because of the tendency to use the term "changeup" to describe the same pitch. In an 1889 baseball glossary, the term defined the strategy of a pitcher who "alternates in his delivery between a slow and swiftly pitched ball." This would indicate that when "change of pace" was first used, it was applied to both fast and slow pitches. IST USE. 1867. "J. Williams, the Capital pitcher, would occasionally drop a ball short, but the change from swift to slow was too apparent to be effective. This style to work well must be done on the sly, the change of pace not being perceptible" (Henry Chadwick, *The Ball Players' Chronicle*, July 18; Peter Morris).

change of scenery The opportunity afforded a player to rejuvenate his career by being traded to another club. When it was reported that Los Angeles Dodgers pitcher Hideo Nomo had requested a trade, he said it was true that he "definitely needed a change of scenery, a change of environment" (*The Baltimore Sun*, June 2, 1998). After being traded from the Boston Red Sox to the Chicago Cubs, Nomar Garciaparra "came to appreciate the change of scenery, a fresh start, less pressure, different expectations" (Laura Vecsey, *The Baltimore Sun*, Apr. 22, 2005). "Not being in contention can wear on a guy mentally, and I think having a change of scenery, where he feels he can contribute, will give him something to play for" (Lance Berkman, quoted in *Sports Illustrated*, July 24, 2006, p.49). See also *new life*, 1. Syn. *change of base*. USAGE NOTE. The term "scenery" connotes one's club. Paul Lowry (*Los Angeles Times*, July 9, 1919) noted that Marty Krug, deposed as manager of the Los Angeles Angels in the Pacific Coast League, "might knock 'em over in new scenery."

changeup A modern term for *change of pace*; specif., a slow ball thrown after one or more fastballs, or a *letup pitch* thrown to look like a fastball to upset the batter's timing. It is thrown with the same windup, motion, hand position, arm angle, and arm speed of a fastball but with reduced velocity and the intention of deceiving the batter, making it, in the opinion of some, the most difficult pitch to master. To do so requires a different grip, usually either a "choke" hold (in which the ball is shoved back into the hand and the pitcher lifts his index finger or middle finger from its tight grip at the moment of delivery) or a "circle" configuration (see *circle change*). The changeup takes longer (15 to 20 mph slower than the fastball) to get to the plate, causing the batter to swing too early. Properly spotted, the changeup makes the fastball look that much faster. "The slow pitch that follows the fast breaking curve is the changeup off the curve ball" (Arthur Mann, *How to Play Winning Baseball*, 1953). See also *off-speed pitch*. Also spelled "change-up." Syn. *change*, 2. 1ST USE. 1948. "He's got everything—speed, curve, change-up and plenty of heart" (*Birmingham News*, May 7, p.46). USAGE NOTE. The term is still a pretentious way of saying "slow ball" to older ears. In his essay "The Grand Old Game," Jim Murray (*The Best of Jim Murray*, 1965) quotes veteran writer Jack Olsen: "Know what they call a 'slow ball' nowadays? A 'changeup'! Now, I ask you!" EXTENDED USE. A different direction. When CBS decided to introduce *Courting Alex* (starring Jenna Elfman) to buck the male sitcom trend, Ed Bark (*The Dallas Morning News*, Jan. 22, 2006) noted, "It's time to throw a changeup."

channel Syn. of *alley*, 4.

chapter *hist.* Syn. of *inning*, 1. 1ST USE. 1913. "Abbott smashed out a bingle and two scored. . . . One more was added in the second chapter" (*San Francisco Bulletin*, March 3; Gerald L. Cohen, who notes the term was used only by journalists).

charge 1. *n.* A player on a team. 2. *v.* See *charge the ball*. 3. *v.* See *charge the mound*.

"CHARGE!" *v.* A rallying cry bellowed in unison by fans after a bugle (usually tape-recorded) sounds the six-note cavalry charge. Such cries are often prompted by instructions appearing on electronic scoreboards. The cheer first appeared at baseball games when the Dodgers played in the Los Angeles Coliseum in 1958, after the trumpet trill had been played regularly at Univ. of Southern California Trojan football games for years, also in the Coliseum. The cheer was originated by lone fans who rose in the stands and blew their own bugles. Ron Henry (personal communication, Oct. 30, 2004) claims that the cavalry charge was played at football games at Southwest High School in Minneapolis as far back as 1949 and the Univ. of Minnesota in 1952. See also *"we want a hit!"*

charge the ball To rush forward to field a batted ball in an effort to reduce the time it takes to reach the ball and make a play. The time that is saved by charging a ball (often fractions of a second) may be crucial.

charge the mound For a batter to run to the mound after being hit or knocked down by a pitch and to start a fight with the pitcher. The batter is often ejected and suspended: in 1994, Reggie Sanders of the Cincinnati Reds received a five-game suspension for charging the mound. Montreal Expos manager Felipe Alou (quoted in *Sports Illustrated*, May 16, 1994, p.81): "If a hitter doesn't like it when someone pitches inside, he should retire. . . . Now guys charge the mound without even getting hit. It's cowardly."

charge the plate For a batter to stand off the plate, then stride toward the pitch, thereby sacrificing power but gaining considerable plate coverage.

charity hop A batted ball that bounces waist-high, making it easy to field; a gift to an infielder. See also *gravy hop*; *Hollywood hop*; *Sunday hop*.

charley horse A muscular cramp or pain, esp. one in the legs or quadriceps, usually produced as a result of physical exertion or a strain or bruise. Sportswriter Ren Mulford (*Bangor* [Maine] *Whig & Courier*, Apr. 30, 1898) defined the term: "Charley-horse is a complaint that selects shining marks for its victims. The fastest runners are prone to its attacks. Charley-Horse was never heard of until base ball was discovered. It is a strain of the rear muscles of the thigh." See also *"here comes Charley."* Syn. "Charlie horse." 1ST USE. 1886. "Several years ago, says the *Chicago Tribune*, Joe Quest, now of the Athletics, gave the name of 'Charlie horse' to a peculiar contraction and hardening of the muscles and tendons of the thigh, to which base ball players are especially liable from the sudden starting and stopping in chasing balls, as well as the frequent slides in base running. Pfeffer, Anson and Kelly are so badly troubled with 'Charley horse' there are times they can scarcely walk" (*The Boston Globe*, July 17). The term enjoyed wide use by 1887; e.g., "Dalrymple and Brown, of the Pittsburgs, are suffering with 'Charlie horse,' or lame legs" (*St. Louis Globe-Democrat*, Apr. 30); " 'Charlie horse' seems to be the complaint that has laid up a good many ball players this spring" (*The Sporting Life*, May 11; Barry Popik); and "This 'Charley Horse' is playing the very mischief with the ball players this season" (*The National Police Gazette*, July 30).

ETYMOLOGY. The term "charley horse" is one of those wonderful terms that has fascinated many, all of whom seem to have come up with a different theory of its origin. The term appeared in a poem entitled "Christmas Wants" (*The Congregationalist*, Dec. 16, 1875): "By a three-year-old baby. / A red wheel-barrow. / A tin bath-tub. / A train of tin cars. / A little boat. / A Charlie horse with a hair tail to it." Several stories, seemingly contradictory, contributed to give the term the momentum it needed to become popular. The earliest attempt to explain the term (*St. Louis Post-Dispatch*, July 15, 1887) was located by lexicographer Barry Popik: "The name is said to owe its origin to the fact that a player afflicted with it, when attempting to run, does so much after the fashion of a boy astride of a wooden horse, sometimes called a 'Charley horse.' "

H.L. Mencken (*The American Language*, Suppl. II, 1948) cited Bill "Boileryard" Clarke, an original Baltimore Oriole of the 1890s, who argued that the term had come "from the name of Charley Esper, a left-handed pitcher, who walked like a lame horse." This theory was discredited when it was learned that the term was already in use by the time Esper joined the Orioles in 1894. Another version involving members of the same Orioles team appeared in Forrest C. Allen's *My Basket-ball Bible* (1930) and was repeated in *American Notes and Queries* (Apr. 1947). One day at a local racetrack, several players put money on a horse called Charlie who, winning throughout the race, pulled up lame in the final stretch. The following day

a player pulled a tendon in his leg and was likened by one of the coaches to "our old Charley horse."

Hy Turkin (*The 1955 Baseball Almanac*, 1955) related a similar story with the Chicago White Stockings, asserting the term was "coined by either Billy Sunday or Joe Quest in the 1880s after a horse backed by the Chicago players had pulled up lame in the stretch." A note written by Peter Tamony in the Tamony collection, attributed to "Baseball Slang and Origins" (but not further identified), agreed with Turkin, but tapped Sunday as the one who coined the term. It read, "When George Gore hit what should have been an inside-the-park homer and strained a thigh muscle rounding second, so that he had to limp into third, Billy cried, 'Here comes the Charley horse.' "

Lee Allen (*The Sporting News*, May 2, 1962), on the other hand, insisted that it was Quest who coined the term in 1882. Allen reported, "Son of a blacksmith from New Castle, Pa., Quest noticed that players hobbling around with a peculiar muscle injury of the legs reminded him of an old white horse, Charlie, employed at his father's shop." Peter Morris found a much earlier and more detailed account of this version in the form of a note in the *Grand Rapids* (Mich.) *Daily Democrat* (June 28, 1889): "Years ago [when] Joe Quest was employed as an apprentice in the machine shop of Quest & Shaw in Newcastle [Pa.], his father, who was one of the proprietors of the firm, had an old white horse by the name of Charley. Doing usage in pulling heavy loads had stiffened the animal's legs so that he walked as if troubled with strained tendons. Afterwards, when Quest became a member of the Chicago club, he was troubled, with others, with a peculiar stiffness of the legs, which brought to his mind the ailment of the old white horse Charley. Joe said that the ball players troubled with the ailment hobbled exactly as did the old horse, and as no one seemed to know exactly what the trouble was, Quest dubbed it 'Charley horse.' The name has spread until today it has become part of the language of the national game."

Tim Considine (*The Language of Sport*, 1982) found an unreferenced explanation: "Often in the 1800s, old workhorses kept on the grounds of ballparks were called Charley. The movements of the injured, stiff-legged ballplayers were likened to the labored plodding of these old horses, and the injury itself eventually became known as a 'charley' or 'charley horse.'"

Gerald Secor Couzens (*A Baseball Album*, 1980) traced the term back to the Sioux City (Iowa) team of 1889 and an old white horse named Charley. Couzens attributed this version to a minor-league coach named Walter McCredie. This same story appeared in an unsigned article in *San Francisco Chronicle* (July 2, 1934), but the old white horse in this version inspired the coinage in 1890, not 1889.

EXTENDED USE. The leap from the slang of ballplayers to standard English is described by Tristram Potter Coffin (*The Old Ball Game*, 1971) as being so complete "that most people would have trouble describing the ailment if the phrase were taken [away] from them." In the *Journal of the American Medical Association* (Nov. 30, 1946, p.821), an article entitled "Treatment of Charley horse" described it as "injury to a muscle, usually the quadriceps femoris," and "consists first in a contusion to the muscle, which results in a hematoma . . . [that later] may organize into a myositis ossificans, forming soft bone in the muscle." Such usage indicates, according to Coffin, the term has been "a part of even the most formal American English for a quarter of a century."

Charlie A curveball. See *Uncle Charlie.*

chart 1. *v.* To keep a detailed record of each pitch in a game; to record pitches on a pitching chart. It is an old and widely observed custom in baseball that the next day's pitcher charts the game. **2.** *n.* See *pitching chart.* **3.** *n.* See *spray chart.*

chase 1. *v.* For an offense to force the removal of a pitcher by getting hits, literally chasing the pitcher out of the game. "The Red Sox have chased the opposing starter before the sixth inning in six of their past seven games" (*The Baltimore Sun*, Aug. 20, 2003). **2.** *v.* For an umpire to eject a participant from the game. Beans Reardon (quoted in Larry R. Gerlach, *The Men in Blue*, 1980, p.17): "I never chased very many ballplayers. I didn't

believe in chasing them." IST USE. 1904. "The umpire was justified in chasing [Bill] Clarke, but it does not seem that the Senators are getting their share of close decisions" (*The Washington Post*, Sept. 22; Peter Morris). **3.** *n.* The pursuit of first place in the standings. *The Great Chase: The Dodgers-Giants Pennant Race of 1951* is the title of a 1992 book by Harvey Rosenfeld. **4.** *v.* To swing at a pitch out of the strike zone. "Damon Buford . . . will chase fastballs up and sliders away" (*Sports Illustrated*, Oct. 18, 1999). Compare *lay off.* **5.** *v.* To pursue a batted ball. "Chase the Leather, or the Sphere—To run after the ball when batted to the field" (*Brooklyn Daily Eagle*, May 1, 1892, p.4). "Chase flies" is to play an outfield position (*The Sporting Life*, Feb. 10, 1905, p.7; Edward J. Nichols). **6.** *v.* To drive in a run. "Kelley stole second and [Buck] Ewing chased him home with the only home run of the day" (*Los Angeles Times*, Nov. 21, 1887).

chase card A baseball card that is so desirable or rare that people buy packs of baseball cards searching for them. Once occurring naturally and randomly, chase cards are now produced in more limited numbers and inserted sparingly, and have brought an element of lottery to the hobby. *Sports Illustrated* (July 29, 1996) reported that premium cards, often of exotic design, are inserted at a "ratio that varies from one card to every two boxes to one card to every case to stimulate interest."

chatter Lively, often meaningless, rhythmic, rapid-fire talk engaged in for team morale. Infield chatter is intended to keep everyone alert and on his toes and to encourage the pitcher, while chatter from the bench or dugout is meant to inspire the batter. Writer Courtland Milloy tried to capture some chatter from the Continental League of the District of Columbia (*The Washington Post*, May 26, 1987): " 'Dada boy. Dadda boy, baby,' the catcher yelled out to the pitcher's mound during a recent game. 'Make him think. Pick 'em up. Lay it on 'em, baby. . . . [Ball one, above the strike zone]. Too high, but no damage done. . . . [The next pitch, strike one]. Dada boy, baby. That's the one. Do it for me two mo' times.'" Chatter is rarely heard at the major-league level. Rick Reilly (*Sports

Illustrated, Apr. 12, 2004) wrote, "Before 1960 chatter was as common as clubhouse cigarettes, but then crowds got too big and noisy for players to hear it. Besides, opponents had the same agents and were swapping wives, and chatter just kind of keeled over and died." IST USE. 1928 (*The New York Times*, Oct. 7; Edward J. Nichols).

Chavez Ravine The location of Dodger Stadium in Los Angeles, Calif. The stadium was built into one side of the ravine, on a hill overlooking downtown. When the Angels played there from 1962 to 1965, it was only referred to as Dodger Stadium when the National League club was in residence. When the Angels were at home, it was called Chavez Ravine so as not to refer to the Dodgers.

chaw Chewing tobacco; a smokeless form of the weed that has long been common in baseball circles. Dizzy Dean: "A cud of tabaccer. Some pitchers can't even start warmin' up without at least one good chaw." An article on a campaign to battle smokeless tobacco among Little Leaguers contained this line on antichaw pitcher Nolan Ryan: "After his two sons began playing Little League baseball, Ryan said he saw youngsters as young as 10 years of age using dip [snuff] and chaw" (*The Houston Post*, Sept. 29, 1987; Charles D. Poe). In 1997, Sen. Frank Lautenberg (D.-N.J.) persuaded the players' union to make the All-Star Game tobacco-free. In 1993, tobacco was banned at all levels of the minor leagues.

cheap hit A ball that is batted into fair territory for a hit, but that lacks power and relies on an odd bounce, fortunate placement, or some other "lucky" factor; e.g., a hit made as the result of a poor swing, such as one that tips off the end of the bat and rolls too slowly to be fielded promptly. Syn. *dinky hit*; *dinker*.

cheap seats The bleachers and other areas distant from home plate. The term is not used to comment on the spectators or their chosen seats, but on the distance of a home run or deep foul ball; e.g., "Smith just put one in the cheap seats." The seats are cheap because they are far from most of the action. See also *nosebleeds*. IST USE. 1912 (*American Magazine*, August; Edward J. Nichols).

cheap win 1. A victory in which the winning team did nothing spectacular, but the losing team did even worse (had fewer hits or more errors). 2. A victory for a pitcher when his *game score* is less than 50. The statistic was introduced by Bill James in his *Baseball Abstract* (1988). Compare *tough loss*.

cheated Said of a batter who is retired without taking a good swing at the pitch. "[Jason Giambi] doesn't get cheated in his at bats" (Larry Rothschild, quoted in *Sports Illustrated*, Jan. 24, 2000).

cheater 1. An illegal bat, such as an aluminum bat used in batting practice (Roger Angell, *Late Innings*, 1982, p.339). 2. A cheap home run (Bill Mazeroski, *Bill Mazeroski's Baseball '89*, 1989). 3. A pitcher who tries to evade the rules. 4. A player who uses steroids.

cheaters Eyeglasses.

cheating 1. Any action of a fielder playing the percentages in regard to what he thinks the batter or baserunner will do; e.g., an infielder positioning himself closer to the base than normal so as to prevent a stolen base or to take part in a double play, or an outfielder shading himself slightly to the right or the left. 2. Fraudulent or deceitful activity that is contrary to the rules and regulations of baseball. Johnny Bench intoned on the subject (quoted in *The Baltimore Sun*, Oct. 28, 2006): "Cheating is putting Vaseline on the ball. That makes it go absolutely crazy. That's unhittable. That's not a level playing field. Cheating is putting cork in your bat. Cheating is stealing signs from second base. That's not acceptable. And of course, using steroids is cheating." 3. Striding and swinging too early in anticipation of a fastball, thereby leaving the batter unable to adjust to off-speed pitches. "You see hitters cheating when they don't have the bat speed to catch up to good fastballs" (Doug Carpenter, quoted in Alan Schwarz, BaseballAmerica.com, Nov. 14, 2006).

cheat up For a first baseman to move out with the baserunner as the latter takes his lead, "worrying him because [he is] . . . in such proximity while gaining greater fielding ground at the same time" (David Falkner,

Nine Sides of the Diamond, 1990, pp.51–52; Peter Morris).

check **1.** *v.* To hold a swing after it has begun. **2.** *n.* A *checked swing*. **3.** *v.* See *check the runner*. **4.** *v.* To stop a rally.

checked swing *n.* A half or partial swing of the bat; a swing stopped midpoint before the batter's wrists break or turn. The guidelines for umpires state that the decision on a checked swing depends entirely on the umpire's judgment as to whether the batter struck at the pitch; also, the call must be made loudly and clearly. If a ball is thrown outside the strike zone and the batter checks his swing, the pitch will be called a ball by the umpire. But if the batter swung the bat head across home plate, or, in the opinion of the umpire, intended to hit the ball, it would be called a strike. Often the plate umpire asks for help from the umpire at first base (for a right-handed batter) or the umpire at third base (for a left-handed batter) as to whether the batter swung. See also *half swing*. Sometimes called *check swing*. Syn. *check*, 2

checked-swing *adj.* Said of a batted ball created by a checked swing. "Cal Ripken hit a checked-swing grounder to second" (*The Baltimore Sun*, Aug. 5, 1994).

checker **1.** A batter who is able to keep his wrists from breaking and his bat from crossing the plate when a pitch is not to his liking. **2.** See *cross-checker*.

checklist **1.** A numerical or alphabetical list of baseball cards contained in a particular set or series. **2.** A book containing a number of checklists.

checklist card A baseball card that does not feature a player but rather lists the numbers and names of other cards in the set; e.g., all the Red Sox in a set may appear on a Boston Red Sox checklist card.

check swing Syn. of *checked swing*.

check the runner **1.** For a pitcher to glance at the baserunner to dissuade him from taking too long a lead. **2.** For an infielder or pitcher fielding a batted ball to glance at a baserunner to dissuade him from advancing before throwing to first base to retire the batter.

ched Short for *cheddar*. "Should I go out there and throw some ched? Or should I just . . . throw some stuff that moves all over?" (Zack Greinke, quoted in *Baseball America*, Aug. 4–17, 2002; Peter Morris).

cheddar A fastball in the upper 90-miles-per-hour range; a contemporary player's term for *cheese*. "Doc [Gooden] blew some big-league cheddar" (Lenny Dykstra, quoted in *Newsday*, March 1, 1988). Keith Hernandez discussed "the high, rising cheddar" in *Pure Baseball* (1994, p.180).

cheerleader The loudest bench jockey on a team.

cheese Syn. of *fastball*, 1. Bill "Spaceman" Lee (*The Wrong Stuff*, 1984) translates Dennis Eckersley's "cheese for your kitchen" as meaning "a fastball up and in" and added that Eckersley also called himself the "Cheese Master." See also *cheddar*; *easy cheese*; *good cheese*; *hard cheese*; *high cheese*. ETYMOLOGY. Even though the term is relatively new to baseball, it may have a much older basis. *London Guide* (1818) defined "cheese" as standing for "the best thing of its kind." The term appears in most 19th-century slang dictionaries as meaning anything first-rate in quality (as in "that's the cheese") and is usually traced to the word "chiz," which means "thing" in Hindustani and Anglo-Indian, rather than the food. James Rogers (*The Dictionary of Clichés*, 1985) traces the term "chiz" to an origin in Persian and Urdu and notes that it is also the source of "the big cheese."

chemistry A distinct sense of teamwork, cooperation, and friendship created by a mix of individuals on a team; instant support, morale, and esprit de corps of like-minded people on a team, often stated as "good chemistry." Keith Moreland (*Vineline*, Aug. 1987) offered this formula: "The makeup of an organization—the players, coaches and the fans. And the talent. The total ingredients that go into a team's makeup." The term has created its own set of clichés: e.g., "chemistry or lack thereof may be the problem"; "chemistry is attitude"; and "chemistry starts with the manager and coaches." Laura Vecsey (*The Baltimore Sun*, Oct. 15, 2002): "Bad chemistry is supposed to be the thing that prevents individual players from melding into a championship whole." The moral: good chemistry is good for a team.

cherry A pitch that a batter can hit well; an "unconvincing" pitch. New York Mets manager Davey Johnson (quoted in George F. Will, *Men at Work*, 1990): "If a guy is a first-ball, fastball, high-ball hitter, and you are a fastball pitcher, give him a first-ball fastball a little higher than he likes it and see if he'll bite on it rather than hook him and miss, hook him and miss, and then give a cherry fastball."

cherry pie A poor hitter; an easy out. An unflattering term created and used almost exclusively by Casey Stengel, it is probably a play on "easy as pie" applied to an easy out.

chestiness *hist.* Conceit by a player. Syn. "chesty." IST USE. 1909 (*New York Evening Journal*, July 14; Edward J. Nichols).

chest pad Syn. of *chest protector*.

chest protector A pad used by catchers and home-plate umpires to protect the body— from the shoulders to the waist—from pitched and fouled-off balls, esp. foul tips. Most are worn, but some umpires' models are held like a warrior's shield. Initially inflatable rubber vests, chest protectors gave way to leather and canvas pads filled with cotton felt, then with kapok, and eventually with foam (Peter Morris, *A Game of Inches*, 2006, p.438). See also *balloon*, 6; *West Vest*; *inside protector*. Syn. *protector*; *breast protector*; *body protector*; *liver protector*; *sheepskin*, 2; *pad*, 2; *chest pad*; *mattress*; *wind pad*. IST USE. 1883. "Heavy cork chest-protectors [worn by catchers]" (*Lapeer* [Mich.] *Democrat*, May 16; Peter Morris). ETYMOLOGY. The first documented use of chest protectors for catchers appeared in the *Detroit Free Press* (May 1, 1883; Peter Morris): "A heavy cork pad protects [Charlie] Bennett's chest from foul tips this season." Bennett later (*Detroit Free Press*, Aug. 2, 1914) said his wife designed the chest protector, assisted by Bennett's practical suggestions, by "sewing strips of cork of a good thickness in between heavy bedticking material." See also *Leslie's Illus-*

trated Weekly (Oct. 15, 1914) for "a woman's gift to baseball." The first documented use of chest protectors for umpires appeared in the *New York Sun* (Apr. 22, 1888; Peter Morris): John Gaffney wore a "breast and stomach protector" made of pasteboard sections "joined together with elastic, and made to fit tight around."

chewing the rag Syn. of *rag chewing*. "Patsy Tebeau and his men got sore on each other, and, in the elegant phraseology of the ball field, kept 'chewing the rag'" (*The World* [New York], Aug. 29, 1894; Peter Morris).

chewing tobacco See *chaw*.

CHI Abbrev. for *clutch hitting index*.

Chicago *hist.* 1. *v.* To *shut out* the opposing team; to have been shut out. To have been "Chicagoed" (or "Chicago'd") was to be shut out. Arthur "Bugs" Baer (*San Francisco Examiner*, Jan. 19, 1953; Peter Tamony) wrote a column on the term, which he opened with the line: "Baseball word you never hear any more is 'Chicagoed.'" IST USE. 1870. "Each party was 'Chicagoed'" (*Cleveland Leader*, July 30; Peter Morris). ETYMOLOGY. George L. Moreland (*Balldom*, 1914) concluded: "The word was coined by some wag when on July 23, 1870, the Mutuals of New York shut out the Chicago [White Stockings] team by a score of 9 to 0. Shutouts prior to that date had been few and far between, for previous to this game but five shutout games had ever been played." *De Witt's Base-Ball Guide* (1876) confirmed the 1870 game, adding, "From that time on all contests in which one side has failed to score a run have been known as Chicago defeats, the nine so beaten being said to have been 'Chicagoed.'" *The Sporting News* (May 10, 1886) noted that "Chicago," as a less derogatory term, replaced *skunk*, 1. Contrary theories that the term was based on the effectiveness of the Chicago White Stockings of the 1880s, or that it came from the 1876 Chicago team featuring their ace, Al Spalding, who pitched eight shutouts, are baseless. 2. *n.* An inning in which no runs are scored. "The game recorded thirteen Chicagos for the Atlantics and twelve for the Philadelphias" (*Elizabeth* [N.J.] *Daily Journal*, Sept. 13, 1873; Andy

Singer). IST USE. 1870. "The first two innings gave two 'Chicagos' for the Forest Citys" (*Cleveland Herald*, July 30; Peter Morris). EXTENDED USE. The term is applied to a shutout in card playing.

Chicago slide The original name for *hook slide*, which was invented and first employed by Mike "King" Kelly when he played for the Chicago White Stockings from 1880 to 1886. See also *"slide, Kelly, slide!"* Syn. *Kelly spread.* IST USE. 1906. "[Mike] Kelly invented the 'Chicago slide,' which was one of the greatest tricks ever pulled off. It was a combination slide, twist, and dodge. The runner went straight down the line at top speed and when nearing the base threw himself either inside or outside the line, doubled the left leg under him (if sliding inside, or the right, if sliding outside), slid on the doubled up leg and the hip, hooked the foot of the other leg around the base, and pivoted on it, stopping on the opposite side of the base. Every player of the old Chicago team practiced and perfected that slide and got away with hundreds of stolen bases when really they should have been touched out easily" (Hugh S. Fullerton, *Chicago Tribune*, May 20; Peter Morris and Joanne Hulbert).

Chicken on the Hill A home run hit by Pittsburgh Pirates slugger Willie Stargell at Three Rivers Stadium. Stargell owned a chicken restaurant in Pittsburgh's Hill District and whenever he homered, the person at the counter would receive free chicken.

chickenshit See *shit, 2.*

chicken winger A pitcher who leads with his elbow with limited extension, shortening his delivery into a more awkward and less fluid motion. The term is generally applied to left-handed pitchers who lack strong fastballs; e.g., John Tudor (Alan Schwarz, Baseball America.com, Nov. 14, 2006).

chief of staff Syn. of *umpire-in-chief.*

chief of umpires The administrator of umpires. When the ailing Harry Wright was fired as Philadelphia manager after the 1893 season, the position of chief of umpires was created for him in response to public outcry.

chill a bat For a hitter in a slump to discard his regular bat and borrow a bat from a player who is in the midst of a hitting streak; to take the "heat" out of a bat (H.G. Salsinger, *Baseball Digest*, Aug. 1945).

chinaware *hist.* A brittle player who is always getting injured.

Chinese blow A lucky hit; a *fluke hit.*

Chinese home run 1. A derogatory term for a home run hit over the portion of the outfield fence closest to home plate, often one that lands just inside (or hits) the foul pole in a ballpark with small dimensions. The most famous locale for Chinese homers was the Polo Grounds, which had 280- and 258-foot foul lines. "The Polo Grounds where a player might hoist an outfield fly close to the foul lines and watch it drop into the not-too-distant pews for a cheap (or Chinese) home run—but legal none the less" (Gay Talese, *The New York Times*, March 3, 1958). Syn. "Chinese homer"; *Pekinese poke.* IST USE. 1930. "[Harry Heilmann's homers] were real home runs. One of them went over the left field bleachers, and the other was hit high up. They were not Chinese home runs in that short bleacher in right [at the Polo Grounds]" (Cincinnati Reds manager Dan Howley, quoted by Brian Bell in *The Washington Post*, June 22). 2. A long foul ball, used mostly in sandlot baseball. In Stephen King's *Skeleton Crew* (1985), there is a story called "The Monkey," which contains this line: "Hal was too small to play, but he sat far out in foul territory, sucking his blueberry Popsicle and chasing what the big kids called 'Chinese home runs.'" This use may very well be limited to New England. A query to King about his use of the term brought this reply (Nov. 9, 1987): "I first heard the term 'Chinese home run' in Stratford, Conn., learning to play the game. When I moved back to Maine in 1958, the term was also used—in both cases, a Chinese home run was a foul ball, usually over the backstop." USAGE NOTE. The term is not to be taken lightly, as a letter from Phil Harmon (New York City) in *Sports Illustrated* (Aug. 21, 1971) attests: "Shame on you for calling [Aug. 9, 1971] Bobby Thomson's historic sudden-death home run against the Dodgers in the 1951 National League playoff a 'Chinese home run.' It is the first time I ever heard it characterized in such a demeaning way, and I can only conclude that the writer, Larry Keith, is an anguished Dodger fan who still doesn't believe it happened."

Common in the 1950s, the term has been used sparingly since the demolition of the Polo Grounds. It did come into play, however, when the Dodgers relocated to the Los Angeles Memorial Coliseum in 1958 and home runs began landing in the left-field seats, which were only 250 feet from the plate. Cartoonist Willard Mullin labeled the Coliseum "Flung Wong O'Malley's Little Joss House in Los Angeles."

A note in Herb Caen's column (*San Francisco Chronicle*, May 18, 1981; Peter Tamony) underscores why the use of the term is now an invitation to controversy and charges of racial insensitivity: "Bill King, the Oakland A's announcer, got off a racist line Thurs. night, but he'll learn. After describing Bobby Murcer's homer as 'not a Chinese home run'—meaning it was well hit—I'm sure he has heard from militant Oriental groups, all of which hit hard." This point was made obliquely by Jimmy Cannon (*Baseball Digest*, Apr. 1956) when he gave "Chinese home run" this definition: "A cheap homer which would be called something else if the Chinese had enough influence."

ETYMOLOGY. When pinch hitter Dusty Rhodes hit a three-run home run at the Polo Grounds that won the opening game of the 1954 World Series for the New York Giants, it was described as a "260-foot pop fly" or "Chinese home run." Joseph H. Sheehan (*The New York Times*, Oct. 1, 1954) attempted to trace the term: "According to Garry Schumacher of the Giants' front office, who in his baseball writing days was a noted phrase-coiner, 'Chinese homer' was one of the numerous Thomas Aloysius 'TAD' Dorgan contributions to the lexicon of American slang." Sheehan concluded that the connotation of a cheap homer came from the association in Dorgan's era of the name "Chinese" with coolies and cheap labor. "The term carried the added connotation of a homer of little account, in line with the cynical observation of a colorful political leader who reportedly once stated, 'Why should we care about the Chinese. There ain't a vote in a million in them.'"

The debate over the Chinese Exclusion Law in the 1910–1920 era served as the motivation for Dorgan's term for an insubstantial home run. David Shulman commented, "The idea was to express a cheap home run as Chinese then represented what was cheap, such as their labor." Dorgan used his cartoon "Indoor Sports" to introduce, or popularize, slang; his coinage fit in with a larger group of Chinese terms, such as a "Chinese Rolls-Royce," which is a Ford according to Abraham Roback (*Dictionary of International Slurs*, 1944), and probably was not intended to be especially disparaging. Sheehan noted that Dorgan was a "benign and gentle" satirist with two adopted sons of Chinese ancestry.

J.G. Taylor Spink (*The Sporting News*, May 7, 1958) did an exhaustive search for the origin of the term and came to the same conclusion that Sheehan did. However, the Spink article was reprinted in the *Los Angeles Times* and inspired several letters to the newspaper, including one from a retired San Francisco sportswriter named Travis McGregor. His thoughts appeared in *The Sporting News* (May 28, 1958) and are repeated here in part: "The use of the term 'Chinese homer' goes far beyond the answers given in Mr. Spink's article, and I think you will find it originated in San Francisco prior to World War I. There was a young China boy there at about 1912 or 1913, if my memory is correct, who had an unpronounceable name, keen sense of humor, a degree from Stanford and a great yen to be a newspaperman.... The typewriter jockeys gave up on spelling his name and renamed him Mike Murphy, and he was a one-man show at the ball games.... While Mike was educated beyond any trace of an accent his quips were all in Chinese dialect, and made with a perfectly straight face. 'Ow,' he would wail, 'look the way he bat. Wave at ball like Mandarin with fan.' The old Oakland park's short fence caught the most of it from Mike and his 'Mandarin fan' waving balls out of the park were knocked back to 'Chinese homers.'" Later in the letter, McGregor gets to Dorgan. "For two or three seasons Mike was a riot—an Oriental Fred Allen, and Tad Dorgan drew a number of cartoons featuring Mike's comments." McGregor adds that several writers picked up and used the term, including Ring Lardner and Damon Runyon, and he thought that the first writer to put it into print was either Ed Hughes or Harry Smith of the *San Francisco Chronicle*.

While not disputing the Dorgan story, Dan Schlossberg (*The Baseball Catalog*, 1989, p.236) notes that the term was used in the 1920s by *New York Tribune* sports editor Bill McGeehan to describe the right-field wall at the Polo Grounds, which looked "thick, low, and not very formidable—like the Great Wall of China." But this seems to be one of those terms that has attracted a fascinating collection of explanations. Russ Hodges, longtime Giants announcer, gave this explanation to the *San Francisco Call-Bulletin* (Apr. 21, 1958; Peter Tamony): "Years ago in the Polo Grounds, Chinese gamblers were wont to gather in the left-field stands at the foul line, a little over 250 feet. Any hit that went out at that point was followed by cries of: 'There goes one for the Chinese.'"

Other explanations, such as those that appeared in Joe Falls' *The Sporting News* column, which solicited etymologies from readers, seem to be purely conjectural: that a short homer is so named because the Chinese are a shorter people; that the outfield seats in the Polo Grounds used to stick out like a pagoda; and that it was inspired by the "short jump" of Chinese checkers. Without question, the wildest of all the theories was one suggested by Tom Becket (St. Louis), which, as far-fetched as it sounds, does offer an explanation—even as an elaborate pun—for the fact that, in New England, Chinese homer may refer to a long, foul ball. In this version, the term harks back to the turn of the 20th century and a game in Salem, Mass., between teams of Irish and Polish immigrants. The game lasted into the 17th inning, at which point there was only one ball left to use because the others had been lost. Becket explained, "A shortstop named Chaney fouled a fast ball into the high grass deep beyond the backstop. After 20 minutes of searching for the ball, the umpires declared the victory for the Irish. They ruled that the Polish team, which was the home team, had failed to furnish the necessary amount of baseballs to complete the game. So the cheer went up, 'Chaney's home run won the game.' From

then on, any foul ball clearing the backstop was heralded as another Chaney's home run. Various misunderstandings as to dialects eventually brought it to the now-familiar 'Chinese home run.'"

Chinese line drive *hist.* A pop fly. IST USE. 1930. "The sports writers call those little flies over the infield . . . 'chinese line drives'" (*Country Home*, August; David Shulman). USAGE NOTE. This term carries the same derogatory implications as "Chinese home run" and was probably inspired by it.

chink 1. *v.* To hit a ball weakly; to squeeze out a hit. USAGE NOTE. The term is widely used but subject to offensive interpretation; e.g., "steal bases, advance runners, chink in some hits" (New York Yankees manager Dallas Green, quoted in *Hartford Courant*, Apr. 5, 1989). Although it has been argued that this is the "chink" defined as "a short metallic sound," it was interpreted by Ralph Chin in an angry letter to the *Hartford Courant* (Apr. 8, 1989) "as a demeaning metaphor about people of Chinese extraction." 2. *n.* A single (Bill Mazeroski, *Bill Mazeroski's Baseball '89*, 1989).

chinker A lucky base hit; a *Texas Leaguer*, 2. "Randy Velarde's game-winner . . . was a chinker that happened to find an open space" (Jim Henneman, *The Baltimore Sun*, Aug. 10, 1994). Syn. *chink hit*, 2.

chink hit 1. A batted ball that is not hit squarely, the bat making a "chink" sound on contact. 2. Syn. of *chinker*.

chin music 1. A brushback or knockdown pitch that passes close to the batter's jaw, thrown so high and inside that the batter supposedly can hear it "buzz or sing." Scott Ostler (*Los Angeles Times*, March 31, 1978): "When a pitcher throws inside on a batter, causing breeze to whistle around his Adam's apple, baseball folks call it chin music. The other day . . . Nolan Ryan played an entire medly [*sic*] of his favorite inside tunes." 2. *hist.* Impudent talk from a player, coach, or umpire, taking the form of sarcastic allusions, irritating comments, complaints, joking, jockeying, fault-finding, arguing. "Last season an element of weakness . . . prevailed in the form of 'chin-music' . . . in which baseplayers pretty generally took part" (*New York Clipper*, Jan. 30, 1875; Tom Shieber). "The Clevelands have been hearing some chin music that sounded like the mother tongue to them. It was Schaffer's [George 'Orator' Shafer]" (*Detroit Free Press*, May 5, 1883; Peter Morris). "After seven innings of Mr. [Hughey] Jennings's profuse chin music [New York Yankees pitcher Ray] Keating got nervous and blew up like a firecracker" (*The New York Times*, May 15, 1914). See V. Samuels (*American Speech*, Feb. 1927). Syn. *chaffing*. IST USE. 1868. "[The Athletic club of Philadelphia] are active, muscular, and are disposed to indulge freely in 'chin music' towards one another, which does not help their game" (*Detroit Advertiser and Tribune*, June 23; Peter Morris). **3.** *hist.* Shouting from the grandstand or bleachers. "Nearly 10,000 people witnessed the game, each one of whom wasted an inordinate amount of chin-music in the general effort to brace the Giants up to victory or death" (*The World* [New York], Sept. 4, 1888; Gerald L. Cohen). Compare *pedal music*. IST USE. 1875. "The Kalamazoos wish us to say that 'chin music' from spectators is not wanted in the future" (*Kalamazoo* [Mich.] *Gazette*, Oct. 15; Peter Morris). **4.** *hist.* Informal talking with fans. "When we got back to the hotel . . . the place was still as loaded with yokels as before. . . . I had to make chin music with them, just like everything was peachy" (Harry Stein, *Hoopla*, 1983, p.276). ETYMOLOGY. Idle talk, unnecessary conversation, chatter, loquacity. "After endless chin music calculated to allay her trepidation" (S.J. Perelman, *The New Yorker*, Sept. 20, 1952). The term dates back to 1824: "Now all his castles sunk in night, / No object now remains but flight: / For now from gangways, wharves, and piers. / Such loud horse-laughter stuns his ears, / That Pat, so tir'd of their chin-music, / Thought he could not leave it too quick" (Ebenezer Mack, *The Cat-Fight: A Mock Heroic Poem*, 1824, no.153).

chip A calcium deposit, such as one that sometimes develops in a pitcher's elbow and that can be debilitating.

chipmunk A punning, self-deprecating name for a sportswriter who, in the words of Milton Gross (who described himself as the first chipmunk), is so called "because in the long run all we do is nibble around the edges" (quoted in Pat Jordan, *The Suitors of Spring*, 1973, p.85). A chipmunk takes an irreverent, amusing attitude toward sports; often writes for, and admires the stories of, other chipmunks rather than writing for his readers; drinks wine instead of whiskey; puts distance between himself and the players; and is younger and better educated than his predecessors, "definitely more iconoclastic, certainly more egocentric, and probably less grateful to be covering the great New York Yankees" (David Halberstam, *October 1964*, 1994, p.175). Other early chipmunks were Stan Isaacs, Leonard Shecter, and Maury Allen. ETYMOLOGY. The term was coined by sportswriter Jimmy Cannon in the early 1960s for a group of young sportswriters gathered in the press box who seemed to be chirping together; one of them had teeth that protruded. According to Cannon (quoted in Jerome Holtzman, ed., *No Cheering in the Press Box*, 1974, p.280; Peter Morris), "I was trying to write a piece in the Yankee Stadium press box and four guys are sitting next to me, jabbering away. I said, 'You sound like small, furry animals. You're making that kind of noise.' I said 'You sound like a God damn lot of chipmunks.' . . . My definition of a Chipmunk is a guy who wears a corduroy jacket and stands in the press boxes with other guys wearing corduroy jackets and they only discuss what they've written. The don't watch the game. They hate baseball. They hate the players. . . . The Chipmunks refuse to follow the techniques of the interview. They go up and challenge guys with rude questions. They think they're very big if they walk up to an athlete and insult him with a question. They regard this as a sort of bravery."

chirping Making complimentary remarks about an opposing player. The term "chirpy" is applied to a player whose mouth is constantly moving (Jane Gross, *The New York Times*, March 28, 1984). Ken Griffey Sr. described Eddie Murray as the "chirpiest" player he encountered during the 1983 season.

Chisox Nickname for the Chicago White Sox.

choke 1. *v.* To play badly in a crucial situation or lose one's resolve; to fail at the moment of maximum expectation. Players, managers, coaches, and umpires have all been accused of choking. IST USE. 1933. "He chokes in the clutch" refers to a player who is "not so good in a pinch" (*Famous Sluggers and Their Records of 1932*). 2. *n.* A bad showing, especially in a pinch. When in 1978 the Boston Red Sox blew a 14½-game division lead, it was labeled "The Great Choke" by Joe Henderson (*Tampa Tribune*, Sept. 20, 1989). USAGE NOTE. According to baseball tradition, the term is not to be used lightly, esp. when emotions are running high. "In fact, so strong is the feeling concerning the word 'choke' that a player needs only to hold his hand to his throat after an umpire's decision to get thrown out of the game" (Tristram Potter Coffin, *The Old Ball Game*, 1971). EXTENDED USE. The choke is a factor and a term in almost every sport and in situations outside baseball, from business to military conflict. 3. *v.* For a pitcher to grip the ball too tightly or too far back in the hand when throwing a curveball, causing the pitch to break less sharply, and therefore be easier to hit (Kevin Kerrane, *Dollar Sign on the Muscle*, 1984, p.92). 4. *v.* See *choke up*, 1.

choke bat A thick-handled bat favored by the scientific hitters in the first two decades of the 20th century.

choke grip A *grip* in which the bat is held several inches from the narrow end (handle). It is used by place hitters. Compare *modified grip*; *end grip*.

choke hitter A hitter who chokes up on his bat; one who uses the choke grip. A good choke hitter has "power in his forearms and wrists, with a great deal of wrist motion and a perfect follow-through . . . [and] will hit sharp line drives, hard grounders and 'bloopers' over the infield" (Carl Stockdale and Rogers Hornsby, *Athletic Journal*, March 1945). George Herman Ruth (*Babe Ruth's Own Book of Baseball*, 1928, pp.151–52) commented that choke hitters stand flatfooted and take a half swing: "They poke the ball, rather than hit it—and while they don't get as much distance as the swing hitters, they are much harder to fool." IST USE. 1920. "When

Miller Huggins was manager of the Cardinals he tried to make me a choke hitter, specializing in snappy singles, a la Willie Keeler, but he saw the change was not helpful and I went back to swinging" (Rogers Hornsby, quoted in *Brooklyn Daily Eagle*, June 10; Peter Morris).

choker One who fails in the clutch; one who chokes. "Phil Garner stopped short of calling his players chokers Sunday, but the Milwaukee Brewers' manager left little doubt that he is starting to question the intestinal fortitude of some members of his team" (Tom Haudricourt, *Milwaukee Journal Sentinel*, Sept. 15, 1997).

choke sign Grabbing or clutching the neck, or wrapping a towel around the throat, indicating that an umpire or player has lost his nerve or failed in a crucial situation.

choke the bat Syn. of *choke up*, 1. "Two years ago I tried choking the bat. I had it about in the middle and was hitting finely. Last year I tried the same thing with the very same bat, but it didn't work at all. I had to take it on the end. The bat has not changed a particle" (Sam Crawford, quoted in *Detroit News*, March 30, 1907; Peter Morris).

choke up 1. To grip the bat one or more inches above the customary lower end; to move one's hand up the handle of the bat to achieve greater control (but also reduce the power of the swing). Syn. *choke the bat*. IST USE. 1912 (*American Magazine*, June, p.205; Edward J. Nichols). ETYMOLOGY. From the impression that the bat is being grabbed by the neck and choked. 2. To become nervous in a tight situation; to choke. 3. For a batter to take a batting stance close to the plate. Pitcher Carl Mays (quoted in *Fort Wayne* [Ind.] *Sentinel*, July 27, 1916; Peter Morris): "Batsmen who are 'beaned' the most are the fellows who crowd the plate. . . . Some of them 'choke up' to within two inches of the plate instead of sticking within the six-inch boundary prescribed by the rules of the game."

choose up 1. *v.* To form sides for an informal game of baseball, softball, or their variations, selecting players on an alternating basis. The most common ritual involves designating two captains, one of whom tosses a bat, the other grabbing it with one hand below the trademark, with the captains then alternating placing their hands around the bat as they climb up the handle. The captain whose hand reaches the knob then grabs the top of the bat handle and rotates the bat around his head three times without losing his grip or dropping the bat. If successful, the captain is designated the winner and gets to choose the first player. Regional variations of the ritual include a) the captain grabbing the knob of the bat and tossing it over his shoulder and b) trying to kick the bat out of the hand of the captain who is spinning the bat around his head. David Block (personal communication, Dec. 8, 2005) notes that the hand-over-hand procedure "may not own a formal name, but it does go back a long way," quoting from an 1864 juvenile novel by Alfred Oldfellow, *Uncle Nat; or, the Good Time Which George and Frank Had*: "Jim tossed up the bat and Tom caught it. Then hand over hand, first one and then the other boy, till the end was in Jim's grip, just enough of it for him to feel with his thumb and fore-finger." The boys then argued about whether Jim would be able to swing the bat, and then "very carefully he did it, three times around the head fair! And so Jim had the first choice." The ritual was also used to determine *first ups*. See also *battinses*. **2.** *n.* An early form of baseball.

chop 1. *v.* To swing directly down toward the ground as the bat advances forward, a move that often results in a grounder. "Jay Knoblaugh chopped a grounder for an infield single" (*Tampa Tribune*, Aug. 28, 1989). **2.** *n.* The motion of swinging down on the ball. **3.** *n.* A ground ball resulting from a chopping motion: "[Billy] Hatcher scored on an infield chop by [Paul] O'Neill" (*Tampa Tribune*, Oct. 17, 1990). See also *Baltimore chop*. IST USE. 1905 (*The Sporting Life*, Oct. 7, p.9; Edward J. Nichols).

chop-down batter A batter who chops down on the ball. "We very often find batters [who chop down] . . . in the seven, eight and nine positions in the batting order" (Carl Stockdale and Rogers Hornsby, *Athletic Journal*, March 1945).

chop hit A hit resulting from the chopping action of the batter. "The Orioles are bouncing chop singles through and over the infield. These choppy hits are calculated to make the nerve ooze from the craw of . . . a weak-kneed twirler. Since his divorcement from the Orioles Jack Doyle's chop hits over the heads of the infield seem to have vanished from the Doyle system of batting" (*The Washington Post*, Sept. 25, 1898). See also *Baltimore chop*. IST USE. 1911 (*Baseball Magazine*, October, p.54; Edward J. Nichols).

chop one off the high limb To swing at a ball that is pitched above the strike zone.

chopper A batted ball hit with a chopped stroke. See also *high chopper*.

Choose up. *National Photo Company Collection, Library of Congress*

chopstick A baseball bat. IST USE. 1908 (*New York Evening Journal*, Apr. 25; Edward J. Nichols).

chuck 1. *v.* To pitch a baseball. IST USE. 1903. "When you pitch to [Ed] Delahanty, you just want to shut your eyes, say a prayer and chuck the ball" (anonymous pitcher, quoted in *Philadelphia Sporting Press*, July 13; Jerrold Casway). 2. *v.* To throw a baseball. IST USE. 1904. "[Joe] Cassidy scooped up [the ball] after passing second base and chucked the runner out" (*The Washington Post*, Aug. 20; Peter Morris). 3. *n.* A pitched or thrown ball. IST USE. 1897. "[Dummy Hoy] was nailed burglarizing a sack by [Ed] Doheney's [*sic*] quick chuck to Gleason" (*The World* [New York], May 14; Peter Morris).

chuck and duck 1. *adj.* Said of a pitcher or team that yields many home runs. "The Angels pitching staff will be hard-pressed to defend its 'chuck and duck' title, earned for allowing a major league high 202 homers last season" (Gerry Fraley, *Baseball America*, March 16–29, 1998; Peter Morris). The term is also applied to a pitcher who throws the ball over the plate and relies on his fielders to make outs, rather than trying to strike batters out: "[Paul] Byrd's success was strictly of the chuck-and-duck variety; he almost became the first American League pitcher ever to surrender more home runs (36) than walks (38)" (*Baseball Prospectus,* 2003; Peter Morris). 2. *n.* A line drive for a base hit. "Sometimes you hang a curveball. Then it becomes a chuck n' duck" (R.J. Reynolds, quoted in Bob Hertzel, *Baseball Digest*, Jan. 1987).

chucker 1. A pitcher, usually a fastballer. The term originally referred to a pitcher who threw only fastballs and no breaking balls. IST USE. 1915. "The Pirates' chuckers were the class of the league" (*St. Louis Post-Dispatch*, Apr. 9; Peter Morris). 2. A mediocre or unrefined pitcher. "I learned the art of pitching after my career was over. I was more of a chucker than a pitcher" (Vida Blue, quoted in *Baseball America*, Oct. 27–Nov. 9, 2003; Peter Morris). IST USE. 1937 (*New York Daily News*, Jan. 31; Edward J. Nichols). 3. Var. of *chukker.*

Chuckie A hanging curveball. ETYMOLOGY. From "Uncle Charlie," a synonym for a curveball.

chukker *hist.* Syn. of *inning,* 1. Var. *chucker,* 3. IST USE. 1915. " 'Me and Benny' was the combination that took the lead in the very next chukker" (*Brooklyn Daily Eagle*, July 16; Peter Morris). ETYMOLOGY. A borrowing from polo in which a chukker is a discrete period of play usually lasting for 7½ minutes.

chump A dupe or stupid person. David Shulman noted the term is not strictly a baseball term but because of its original context "seems to have been originated by ballplayers." IST USE. 1883. "Maybe Manager [Frank] Bancroft isn't regarded as a chump by baseball people" (*The Sporting Life*, May 27).

church ball [softball term] An early name for softball.

chute 1. The area over home plate where it is easiest for the batter to hit the ball; the middle of the strike zone. See also *down the chute*, 1. 2. The gap between outfielders. See also *down the chute*, 2. IST USE. 1895. "[Ad] Gumbert . . . pasted a two bagger into the left field chute" (*Brooklyn Eagle*, Aug. 6; Peter Morris). 3. See *up the chute.*

cigar box A small ballpark. "The Seals excelled last spring in four-base slams, thanks to the close proximity of fences around the cigar-box park at Paso Robles" (*San Francisco Bulletin*, Feb. 26, 1913; Gerald L. Cohen). IST USE. 1899 (*The Sporting News*, March 4; Peter Morris).

cigar card A *baseball card* produced and distributed by a tobacco company. See also *tobacco card.*

cigarette card A *baseball card* that came in a cigarette pack. The card was used to stiffen the soft packs and to promote sales. Eleanor Gehrig (*My Luke and I*, 1976, p.32; Charles D. Poe) wrote that her husband Lou, when he was a boy, saved and traded the cigarette cards that carried pictures of Ty Cobb, Zack Wheat, and Christy Mathewson.

cinch 1. *n.* A team that is certain to win a game or a pennant. "He [Art Fromme] thinks the Pirates are a cinch to cop the honors [win the National League pennant]" (*San Francisco Bulletin*, Feb. 14, 1913; Gerald L.

Cohen). IST USE. 1889. "If Brooklyn wins the Association championship New York will have a 'cinch'" (Pittsburg manager Ned Hanlon, quoted in *The World* [New York], Oct. 11; Gerald L. Cohen). **2.** *v.* To win a game or a pennant; to make certain of victory. IST USE. 1905. "This cinches the pennant for the White Sox" (*The Sporting Life*, Apr. 22; David Shulman). **3.** *v./hist.* To be put out at home (*The Sporting News*, Nov. 27, 1897).

Cincinnati Agreement A part of the reserve clause preventing a player from signing with another club after his club's season ends. It resulted from an 1899 case involving George Wrigley, who played the entire season with Syracuse of the Eastern League and, when that minor-league season ended, signed with the New York Giants of the National League for 30 days starting on Sept. 15. The reserve clause was clarified later to prevent the situation in which a player could play for another club in the same season (Jonathan Fraser Light, *The Cultural Encyclopedia of Baseball*, 1997, pp.612–13).

Cincinnati base hit *hist.* A base hit credited to a batter who reached first base when an infielder failed in an attempt to throw out a baserunner other than the batter. This scoring rule was in effect only during 1913. Although some scorers called the play a fielder's choice or a sacrifice, sportswriter Jack Ryder of the *Cincinnati Enquirer* was the most outspoken advocate for crediting the batter with a hit. The Baseball Writers' Association of America rejected the rule change by a mail vote in 1914. See Norman L. Macht (in Society for American Baseball Research, *Road Trips*, 2004, p.154). See also *life*, 5. Syn. "Cincy base hit." IST USE. 1913. "[Chick] Gandil laid down a perfect bunt, [Ray] Morgan scoring, and the first sacker being credited with a 'Cincinnati base hit'" (*The Washington Post*, July 20; Peter Morris).

Cincinnati Peace Treaty The agreement that brought peace between the National League and the American League, signed in Cincinnati on Jan. 10, 1903. The key figure in the agreement was August "Garry" Herrmann, the newly named president of the Cincinnati Reds, who gave up his claim on the services of Sam Crawford to the Detroit Tigers of the American League. The agreement recognized the reserved rights of every club (no more player raids), as well as its territorial rights, and adopted a standard set of playing rules. In anticipation of future cooperation, plans were made for establishing the National Commission to govern major-league baseball.

Cinderella A team that emerges from the lower level and becomes a contender in the manner of the Cinderella fairy tale. Cleveland Indians manager Charlie Manuel (quoted in *The Baltimore Sun*, May 6, 2001): "I'm getting tired of having the Cinderella story come out of the [American League] Central every year. Last year it was the Cinderella White Sox. Now it's the Cinderella Twins."

circle **1.** *v.* To run around the bases and reach home plate. "[George McCarl's hit] soared over 'Hap' Smith's head and rolled to the most distant corner of the ball park, permitting McCarl to circle the bases" (E.T. [Scoop] Gleeson, *San Francisco Bulletin*, March 3, 1913; Gerald L. Cohen). **2.** *n.* Short for *on-deck circle*. **3.** *v.* For an outfielder to track a fly ball in a meandering or indirect fashion.

circle baseball A game played by children of westward-moving pioneers in the late 19th century. A rag ball was tied on the end of a rope and sticks were used to hit the ball. "The winner is the first player to hit the ball five times. If a player hits the rope instead of the ball, he changes places with the person in the middle swinging the ball" (Alma Heaton, *Games Our Pioneers Played*, 1997).

circle change A *changeup* in which the pitcher uses his thumb and index finger to form a circle around one side of the ball, with the outside three fingers atop the ball (as if flashing the "OK" sign) sitting deep in his palm. The overhand motion causes the ball to tumble out of the circle, as if the pitcher's hand were pulling down a window shade, with the outside fingers propelling the ball loosely, rotating it in such a way that the ball runs down and in (when thrown by a right-handed pitcher to a right-handed batter). The purpose of the grip is to force the middle finger to exert more pressure on the ball at release, thereby giving the pitch more down-and-away movement; the tighter the grip, the slower the pitch. Paul Richards tried to popularize the pitch; Frank Viola, Greg Maddux, Tom Glavine, and Pedro Martinez threw it.

circle the wagons For a weak defensive player to be uncertain or tentative when fielding a pop fly. ETYMOLOGY. From the practice in the early American West of forming the wagons of a covered-wagon train into a circle for defense against an Indian attack.

circuit 1. *n.* A league; e.g., the National League is called the *senior circuit* and the American League is called the *junior circuit*. "The Las Vegas Convention and Tourist Bureau will try [to create] . . . a new spring training circuit in and around the gambling Mecca" (*The Baltimore Sun*, March 23, 2000). 1ST USE. 1880 (*Brooklyn Daily Eagle*, July 22; Edward J. Nichols). ETYMOLOGY. The term may stem from the theatrical reference to a group of theaters visited on a regular basis. 2. *n.* The four bases, collectively, such as those touched after hitting a home run. "The ball struck the top of the barrier and bounded outside, letting Frank [Smith] trot around the circuit" (*Chicago Tribune*, Apr. 30, 1905; Peter Morris). 1ST USE. 1871 (*New York Herald*, Sept. 23; Edward J. Nichols). 3. *adj.* A term used to modify other terms signifying a *home run*; e.g., "circuit belt," "circuit blow," "circuit clout," "circuit drive," "circuit slam," "circuit smash," "circuit tripper," and "circuit wallop." "No, the Colossus [Babe Ruth] didn't bust out one of his circuit drives" (H.W. Lanigan, *Boston American*, Aug. 19, 1918; Peter Morris). A "circuit slugger" is one who hits many home runs. 1ST USE. 1908 for "circuit clout" (*New York Evening Journal*, May 14; Edward J. Nichols). 4. *n.* The French word for a home run.

circuiter 1. One who scores a run. "Smith was the circuiter in the fourth" (W.A. Mason, *Marion* [Ohio] *Daily Star*, Sept. 10, 1907; Peter Morris). 2. A home run. "The grand slam man [Babe Ruth] hit his thirty-seventh circuiter in Chicago yesterday" (Copeland C. Burg, *Lincoln* [Neb.] *Star*, Aug. 25, 1931; Peter Morris).

circus catch A spectacular catch, suggesting the moves of a circus acrobat. Such a catch may involve a jump, dive, flip, roll, or combination thereof. "Circus Solly" Hofman (Chi-

cago Cubs outfielder, 1904–1912) was given his nickname because he was known for making acrobatic catches of fly balls. Thomas W. Lawson (*The Krank: His Language and What It Means*, 1888) defined the term as "catching the ball between the upper and under eyelid." See also *Jawn Titus*. Syn. *showboat catch*. 1ST USE. 1886. "Steve Brady made a circus catch and Hardie Henderson tried to get [Ed] Greer to swear out a warrant for him" (*The Sporting Life*, Apr. 28; Barry Popik). EXTENDED USE. The term has been applied to spectacular football catches for some time and is used metaphorically for any melodramatic feat.

circus play 1. An unusually excellent or spectacular play. 1ST USE. 1885 (*Chicago Inter-Ocean*, July 15; Edward J. Nichols). 2. A bungled play. "Melvin Mora drew a leadoff walk, and then Jerry Hairston singled to left field, starting a circus play for the [Texas] Rangers. Texas left fielder Kevin Mench bobbled the ball, allowing the runners to advance a base. Mench fired to third, but [Alex] Rodriguez cut off the ball and tried nabbing Hairston on his way to second. But the throw went into shallow right field, allowing Mora to score" (*The Baltimore Sun*, Aug. 28, 2002).

circus stop A spectacular catch at first base. "[Sam] Thompson worked most of the time at first base, where he made all manner of circus stops" (*Detroit Morning Times*, Apr. 12, 1888).

circus throw A spectacular throw. 1ST USE. 1891 (*Harper's Weekly*, May 9, p.351; Edward J. Nichols).

citrus circuit An early syn. for *Grapefruit League*. "Note to Don Heffner and Ralph Kress, St. Louis Browns holdouts, somewhere in California: They don't even mention you any more in the Browns' section of the citrus circuit" (*Brooklyn Eagle*, March 25, 1939; Peter Morris).

city series A series of postseason games between two teams in the same city and from different major leagues, often billed as the "championship" of the city, such as in Chicago (White Sox vs. Cubs between 1903 and 1942), St. Louis (Browns vs. Cardinals), New

York, Philadelphia, and Boston. The creation of the city series was meant to duplicate the success and excitement of the World Series, not conflict with it. See also *cross-town series*. See Jerry Lansche, *The Forgotten Championships: Postseason Baseball, 1882–1981*, 1989.

CL Abbrev. for *Continental League*, 2.

claim points A measure of player performance in a very specific skill, used in calculating the win shares for a given player. For example, for catchers, claim points are individually assigned for four indices: number of caught stealing, error percentage, passed balls, and sacrifice hits allowed.

clamshell A style of catching a line drive before players wore gloves in which the fielder put his wrists together and tried to stop the ball in his joined palms.

clang A bad fielder, presumably from the metaphoric noise made by his glove and skillet-hard hands. Syn. *clank*, 1.

clank 1. Syn. of *clang*. Outfielder/first baseman/catcher Curt Blefary was sometimes known as "Clank." 2. An error.

class One of the several levels at which professional baseball is played, with the major leagues at the top followed by the various rankings of the minor leagues. The class ranking system was originally set up on the basis of the population of the city or town in which the team played and was used to fix the salaries and prices of players.

Class A 1. The highest level of minor-league baseball from 1902 to 1907. Teams were limited to 18 players. Leagues included the Eastern League, the Western League, the American Association (joined 1903), the Pacific Coast League (joined 1904), and the Southern Association (joined 1905). 2. The second highest level of minor-league baseball, below Class AA, from 1908 to 1935. 3. The third highest level of minor-league baseball, below Class A1 from 1936 to 1945, and below Class AA from 1946 to 1962. 4. The lowest level of minor-league baseball, below Class AA but above *rookie league*, since 1963, when all Class B, Class C, and Class D leagues were moved to Class A. Minimum seating capacity for Class A ballparks is 4,000. See also *high Single A*; *low Single A*; *short A*. Syn. *Single A*.

Class AA 1. The highest level of minor-league baseball from 1908 to 1945. Leagues included the American Association, the Eastern League (forerunner of the International League), and the Pacific Coast League. 2. The second highest level of minor-league baseball, below Class AAA, since 1946. In 1963, all Class A and Class AA leagues were grouped in Class AA. Minimum seating capacity for Class AA ballparks is 6,000. Currently, there are three Class AA leagues: Eastern League, Southern League, and Texas League. Syn. *Double A*.

Class AAA The highest level of minor-league baseball, effectively established in 1946 when the three Class AA leagues of 1945 (the American Association, the International League, and the Pacific Coast League) moved up from Class AA. Minimum seating capacity for Class AAA ballparks is 10,000. Currently, there are three Class AAA leagues: International League, Pacific Coast League, and Mexican League. Syn. *Triple A*.

Class AAAA The level of play (one step above the minor leagues and a notch below the major leagues) of the *Senior Professional Baseball Association* (*Insight*, Feb. 26, 1990). See also *4-A*, 2.

Class A-Advanced Syn. of *high Single A*.

Class A1 A level of minor-league baseball, below Class AA and above Class A, from 1936 to 1945. The only leagues to have this classification were the Southern Association and the Texas League. In 1946, the Class A1 leagues joined Class AA.

Class B A level of minor-league baseball, below Class A, from 1902 to 1962. In 1963, all Class B leagues were moved to Class A, in favor of a new rookie league.

Class C A level of minor-league baseball, below Class B, from 1902 to 1962. In 1963, all Class C leagues were moved to Class A, in favor of a new rookie league.

Class D The lowest level of minor-league baseball, below Class C, from 1902 to 1962 (except in 1943, when Class E was in operation). In 1963, all Class D leagues were moved to Class A, in favor of a new rookie league.

Class E A minor-league classification established in 1937 and restricted to players with no professional experience in Class D or higher. The only Class E league to operate was the Twin Ports League in 1943, consisting of three teams in Duluth, Minn., and one in Superior, Wisc.; they played four games a week before disbanding on July 13. The players were primarily workers in war-related jobs along Lake Superior.

Class F *hist.* "A term of contempt used among players toward weak players, insinuating that they rank below all organized clubs" (Hugh S. Fullerton, *American Magazine*, June 1912). At that time, the minor leagues ranged from Class AA down to Class D.

Classic 1. The World Series; more commonly, *Fall Classic*. 2. The All-Star Game; more commonly, *Summer Classic*.

classification See *Brush Classification Plan*.

class man A player in semipro or low minor-league baseball who has had prior professional experience. R.G. Utley and Scott Verner (*The Independent Carolina Baseball League, 1936–1938*, 1999, p.47) noted that in the 1935 Carolina Textile League "each team could employ up to four class men, defined as players who had three or more years of experience at any level of organized professional baseball." *The Sporting News* (Robert Harper, Dec. 23, 1926; Peter Morris): "Richmond, during a certain period, had more than five 'class' men on the field." Syn. *class player.*

Class of . . . 1. A group of Hall of Famers who were inducted in the same year; e.g., the Cooperstown Class of 1999 included Nolan Ryan, George Brett, Robin Yount, and Carlton Fisk. 2. A group of rookies who came into the major leagues in the same year; e.g., the Class of 1924 included Al Simmons, Earle Combs, Charlie Gehringer, Red Ruffing, and Chick Hafey. 3. A group of players who were drafted in a given year. 4. A group of players from a given minor league who eventually played in the major leagues. 5. Expansion franchises that entered baseball together. Alan Schwarz (*Baseball America*, Apr. 2–15, 2001; Peter Morris) wrote about the Arizona Diamondbacks and Tampa Bay Devil Rays: "For a blue-print of two ways not to run a baseball team, look no further than the Class of '98."

class player Syn. of *class man.*

claw Pine-tar stick used to rub on bats to improve the batter's grip (*Newsweek*, July 15, 1991).

Claxton Shield The trophy awarded to the winning state in the Australian interstate series for the years 1934 to 1989 (except for 1940–1945). The Australian Baseball League superseded state competition in 1990. The International Baseball League of Australia revived the trophy in 2000 before the league failed. The trophy was donated by renowned South Australian sportsman Norm Claxton.

clean 1. *adj.* Said of a period in which a pitcher gives up no hits or walks; e.g., a "clean inning" or a "clean outing." 2. *v.* See *clean the bases.*

clean hit A safely batted ball that at no point looked as if it would be fielded for an out; a solid hit. "Sam Thompson opened the Detroit half of the second with a clean hit to right" (*Detroit Free Press*, Oct. 18, 1887). IST USE. 1869 (Henry Chadwick, *National Chronicle*, Jan. 30; Peter Morris).

clean home run *hist.* A home run in which "the batsman hits a ball far enough out of the reach of the out-fielders as to enable him to run round to home base before the ball can be returned in quick enough to put him out" (Henry Chadwick, *The Game of Base Ball*, 1868, p.39).

clean house To trade or release many players on a team, esp. when a new general manager or manager takes over.

clean score *hist.* Not being put out. "Flanders, of the Stars, made a clean score" (*Brooklyn Eagle*, July 13, 1866; Peter Morris).

clean swing A simple, easy swing with a good follow-through; a good "stroke."

clean the bases To get a hit, usually a home run, on which all baserunners score. Syn. *clear the bases.* IST USE. 1906. "[Dummy] Hoy started all the trouble in the fifth by cleaning up three crowded bases with a rattling two-base hit" (*The Washington Post*, June 3).

clean their clocks To defeat a team decisively.

cleanup **1.** *n.* Syn. of *cleanup position.* **2.** *adv.* Said of the cleanup position; e.g., "Smith is batting cleanup." **3.** *n.* Syn. of *cleanup hitter.* **4.** A batter whose hit drives in all base-runners. "The term 'Cleanup' has been applied to Young because he has a penchant for driving 'em all home with the wallops in the pinch" (*San Francisco Bulletin*, May 2, 1913; Gerald L. Cohen).

clean up *v.* **1.** To defeat thoroughly. "The Seals stand a good chance to clean up their rivals" (*San Francisco Bulletin*, May 10, 1913; Gerald L. Cohen). **2.** To drive in all baserunners. IST USE. 1910 (*Baseball Magazine*, September, p.9; Edward J. Nichols).

cleanup hitter The player who bats in the fourth position in the batting order, usually reserved for a player with a high batting average and the ability to drive in runs with extra-base hits. The assumption is that he is most likely to get a hit that will score any or all of the preceding players who have reached base, thus "cleaning" or "clearing" the bases of baserunners. "Lou Gehrig was the prototypical and most famous cleanup hitter, not only because of his uniform number, 4, but also because he cleaned the bases a record 23 times with grand slams" (Tom Verducci, *Sports Illustrated*, Apr. 4, 2005). Sometimes spelled "clean-up hitter." Syn. *cleanup*, 3; *cleanup man*; *Big Bertha*, 1; *number-four hitter*; *fourth-place hitter.* IST USE. 1907 (*New York Evening Journal*, Apr. 15; Edward J. Nichols). EXTENDED USE. **1.** The most dependable or most skillful person in any group, such as in a team of lawyers. **2.** A political candidate who can help effect reform or a sweeping change in policy. In supporting congressional candidate William S. Mailliard in 1952, an editorial in the *San Francisco Examiner* termed him a "clean-up hitter" who would help get rid of "the New Deal, the Square Deal, the Fair Deal and all the rotten deals we've had for the 20 long years" (Peter Tamony).

cleanup man Syn. of *cleanup hitter.* IST USE. 1910 (*Baseball Magazine*, September, p.8; Edward J. Nichols).

cleanup position The fourth position in the batting order. Sometimes spelled "clean-up position." Syn. *cleanup*, 1. IST USE. 1911.

"Hardy, who had been moved up into the 'clean-up' position, buzzed a line drive" (Charles E. Van Loan, *The Big League*, p.171; David Shulman).

clear the bases Syn. of *clean the bases.* IST USE. 1870. "Swandell's hit to centre field cleared the bases" (*Putnam's Magazine*, March; Richard Hershberger).

clear the bench **1.** For an umpire to order all the substitute players from the dugout to the clubhouse for objectionable conduct (such as violent disapproval of a call) when the offender(s) cannot be identified. A warning must first be given, but if the bench is cleared, all substitutes depart. Players can be recalled by the manager but only as needed for substitution in the game. Although the practice is a rarity in major-league baseball, on Sept. 27, 1951, umpire Frank Dascoli removed (but did not eject) 15 Brooklyn Dodgers (including basketball Hall of Famer Bill Sharman, who thus was removed from a major-league baseball game without ever playing in one). IST USE. 1910. "The new rule adopted this year empowering umpires to 'clear the bench' has emphasized the need of regulating the retirement of players" (*The Sporting News*, July 28; Peter Morris). **2.** For a manager to remove his substitute players from the bench (dugout) to keep them from being ejected by the umpire. "To keep his angry players from all being ordered to the showers, [Brooklyn Dodgers manager Charlie] Dressen himself cleared the bench" (Harvey Rosenfeld, *The Great Chase*, 1992, p.91). **3.** For a manager to send into the game all the substitute players when a team is leading or losing by a seemingly insurmountable margin.

clear the fences To hit a home run that goes out of the ballpark.

clear the pitcher's slot To reach base ahead of the pitcher with two outs.

clear waivers To not be claimed by another team when a player is placed on waivers.

cleats **1.** The projections on the bottoms of shoes, used to achieve greater traction on the field. They are made of rubber, plastic, or metal. See also *spikes*, 1. IST USE. 1935 (Ralph H. Barbour, *How to Play Better Baseball*; David Shulman). **2.** Syn. of *baseball shoe.*

clever *hist.* Said of a high-performing or skilled player. The term was used frequently to describe an effective player in the 19th century. Bryan Di Salvatore's 1999 biography of John Montgomery Ward is entitled *A Clever Baseballist.*

clicker **1.** A small handheld device used by a coach to count the number of pitches thrown. **2.** Syn. of *indicator*, 1.

click on all nine To possess good teamwork.

cliff-hanger A close, hotly contended contest whose outcome is decided late in the game.

climb the ladder **1.** To throw consecutively higher and higher pitches to induce the batter to swing at a pitch out of the strike zone. The strategy is a common way to approach a high-ball hitter. See also *stair-step*, 1; *up the ladder*, 1. **2.** To swing at a high fastball. **3.** To leap or jump high to snare a line drive or high bouncing ball. See also *up the ladder*, 2.

clinch **1.** To conclusively decide a particular position in the final standings. **2.** For a player to establish a spot on a team's roster or in its starting lineup.

clincher **1.** A game in which a title championship is, or is likely to be, won. "[Bobby] Ojeda Gets Call for Clincher" (*The New York Times* headline, Sept. 4, 1986). **2.** [softball term] A softball invented by Frederick deBeer and made of horsehide and kapok with a hidden seam. It is esp. suited for the streets and sidewalks of New York City and Chicago, where they are a major factor in the market.

clinic **1.** A magnificent play by a player or team; e.g., "[Alvaro] Espinoza Sparks Twins with Clinic on Fundamentals" (*Orlando Sentinel* headline, March 22, 1987) or "The Orioles held a clinic by their superb fielding." **2.** An instructional session in which players and/or coaches teach others (usually children) the finer points of baseball. Clearly implied by the term is that problems are brought to the clinic where solutions will be sought. ETYMOLOGY. The term, originally indicating a medical facility, appears to have made the leap to other realms in the 1930s and 1940s when, as H.L. Mencken (*The American Language*, Suppl. II, 1948) noted that "clinic" was being used for a beauty parlor. A letter from Atcheson L. Hench of the Univ. of Virginia (*American Speech*, Oct. 1949) cited 13 other nonmedical clinics dating as far back as a 1933 "Clothing Clinic," including several baseball clinics, the first of which was announced in *The Baltimore Sun* (Jan. 21, 1944): "The second meeting of the baseball clinic sponsored jointly . . . is scheduled for tonight." Another early baseball clinic noted by Hench also appeared in *The Baltimore Sun* (Dec. 27, 1946): "Eddie Stanky . . . announced he would open his second annual free baseball clinic for youngsters and oldsters here [Mobile, Ala.]."

clinker *hist.* **1.** An error. IST USE. 1934 (*Akron* [Ohio] *Beacon Journal*). **2.** A scratch hit. "Connor then sent Ewing to second with a clinker between second and third" (*The World* [New York], Aug. 30, 1889; Gerald L. Cohen). **3.** An outstanding player. "In the points, he [Mike Tiernan] also proved a 'clinker,' not a hit being made off his delivery" (*The World* [New York], June 16, 1887; Gerald L. Cohen).

clip **1.** To hit a ball sharply. IST USE. 1905 (*The Sporting Life*, p.7; Oct. 7; Edward J. Nichols). **2.** To pitch a ball that just passes inside one of the four corners of the strike zone; e.g., "to clip the corner." **3.** For a ball to hit a batter, baserunner, or the foul line.

clipper A base hit. "Ewing started the fun with a clipper to centre field, and took first" (*The World* [New York], July 18, 1889; Gerald L. Cohen).

clobber **1.** To hit a ball hard. **2.** To hit very well against a specific pitcher; to *pin his ears back.*

clock **1.** To hit a ball hard; e.g., "Smith clocked one over the wall." The term is used in reference to the precise timing required to hit a pitch squarely. IST USE. 1932 (*Baseball Magazine*, October, p.496; Edward J. Nichols). **2.** To measure the speed of a pitch.

close (pron. "klos") *adv.* **1.** Said of a runner kept near to his base (usually first base) when the pitcher throws over to the base; e.g., "Smith kept the runner close with his throws to first." **2.** Syn. of *shallow*, 2.

close (pron. "kloz") *v.* **1.** For a pitcher to end a game by retiring the last batter. **2.** To move the front foot closer to the plate in a batting stance.

close and late Said of a game situation in the seventh inning or later when the batting team is leading by one run or tied or has the potential tying run on base, at bat, or on deck. The term is used by STATS Inc. for statistical purposes. See also *late-inning pressure situation*. Syn. *late and close*.

close call An umpire's ruling on a split-second or bang-bang play. Because the distances between the bases seem so perfectly set, such calls are common. See also *close play*.

closed mouth A sign between the shortstop and second baseman to determine who will cover second base in the event a baserunner attempts a steal. The player signals by putting his glove in front of his face and turning his head toward his teammate. Normally, a closed mouth means the second baseman will cover (Paul Dickson, *The Hidden Language of Baseball* 2003). Compare *open mouth*.

closed shoulder 1. A batter's shoulder that has not yet turned out at the instant the bat meets the ball. 2. A pitcher's shoulder that is kept in its arm slot rather than flying open and the ball tailing away.

closed stance A *batting stance* in which the front or striding foot is closer to home plate than the rear foot. Compare *open stance*; *square stance*, 1.

close out 1. For a pitcher to get the last out in a game. "We're going to . . . do what we've done all year and close out games" (St. Louis Cardinals pitcher Ray King, quoted in *The Baltimore Sun*, Oct. 18, 2004). 2. For a pitcher to retire a batter.

close play A play in which a baserunner reaches a base a split second before or after the ball. He is either just safe or just out. See also *close call*. Syn. *close shave*, 2.

closer 1. A relief pitcher who tries to get the final out or outs in a game. A closer is the team's most reliable pitcher; he almost never pitches without a lead or for more than one inning. Closers generally are veteran pitchers: "No one is a closer until they've got 40 or 50 saves behind them" (Baltimore Orioles manager and former pitching coach Ray Miller, quoted in *The Baltimore Sun*, Feb. 15, 1998). The closer concept was invented by Chicago Cubs manager Herman Franks in 1977 when he used Bruce Sutter only when the Cubs had an eighth- or ninth-inning lead. Michael Bamberger (quoted in *Sports Illustrated*, March 24, 1997) commented, "The closer has become identified with certain traits. He has an oversized body. Or an outsized personality. Or, at the very least, the sinister face [i.e., with facial hair] of a 19th-century outlaw." Tom Verducci (*Sports Illustrated*, June 18, 2001): "Facial hair . . . is to closers what masks were to Greek thespians." Syn. *closing reliever*; *stopper*, 2; *game-ender*; *finisher*. 2. *hist.* A starting pitcher who often pitches complete games. 3. *hist.* A scout who was noted for his ability to get a prospect to sign a contract. The term was largely made obsolete by the advent of the amateur draft in 1965.

closer by committee A relief staff on which saves are distributed among several pitchers. The term has taken on added significance as it has become rare for a club not to have one pitcher designated as its closer. "In its first five games, the much-publicized closer-by-committee [of the Boston Red Sox] allowed 17 earned runs in 24 innings and was 0-for-3 in save opportunities" (Peter Gammons, *Baseball America*, Apr. 28–May 11, 2003; Peter Morris). See also *bullpen by committee*.

close shave 1. A ball that is pitched close to a batter's head, as if it were close enough to shave the whiskers on his face; a knockdown pitch. IST USE. 1914. "If you step back and fail to stand up to the plate on the next pitch after a close shave, all the twirlers in the league are soon on you" (Ty Cobb, *Busting 'Em and Other Big League Stories*; Peter Morris). 2. Syn. of *close play*.

close the door To pitch the final outs of a game. "[Closer] Jorge Julio tried closing the door, and it swung back and hit him" (*The Baltimore Sun*, March 12, 2004). See also *shut the door*.

close the gap To cut off batted balls to the outfield that might otherwise reach the left-center field or right-center field walls. "Devon White could really close the gap, because he had the speed, first-step quickness and angle management" (Jack Zduriencik, quoted in

Alan Schwarz, BaseballAmerica.com, Nov. 14, 2006).

close up For an outfielder to move closer to the infield for a particular batter. IST USE. 1864. "The fielders had got pretty well down for a long batter just before me, but when they saw that 'fellow from the country' take his 'posish,' they closed up pretty well" (*New York Clipper*, May 28; Peter Morris).

closing reliever Syn. of *closer*, 1. "The Atlanta Braves' closing reliever [Bruce Sutter] appeared to be his old dominating self in one perfect inning" (*USA Today*, March 12, 1986).

clothesline A low line drive whose flight to the outfield resembles a taut clothesline. It is rarely stopped by an infielder because it is normally too far (10 to 15 feet) off the ground. See also *hemp*; *frozen rope*; *hang a clothesline*. Syn. "clothesliner"; "clothesline drive." IST USE. 1937 (*Philadelphia Record*, Oct. 11; Edward J. Nichols).

cloud-buster A very high fly ball.

cloud-hunter *hist.* A ball batted high in the air. IST USE. 1874 (*Chicago Inter-Ocean*, July 9; Edward J. Nichols).

cloud-scraper *hist.* A ball batted high in the air. IST USE. 1891 (*Chicago Herald*, July 1; Edward J. Nichols).

cloud-searcher *hist.* A ball batted high in the air. IST USE. 1874 (*Chicago Inter-Ocean*, July 7; Edward J. Nichols).

clout 1. *v.* To hit the ball with power or harder than usual. IST USE. 1905. "[Jake Weimer's] delivery was an open book for the Phillies and they clouted him right and left" (*Chicago Tribune*, May 25; Peter Morris). 2. *n.* A ball hit for a long distance, usually a home run. IST USE. 1908 (*New York Evening Journal*, May 14; Edward J. Nichols).

clouter A power hitter; esp. one who is known for hitting long home runs. IST USE. 1908 (*Spalding's Official Base Ball Guide*, p.185; Edward J. Nichols).

clouting spree An impressive display of hitting by a team.

clout king A powerful and outstanding hitter regarded as tops in his league.

clown An individual who performs comically on the field before or after a game, or between innings. Clowns range from professionals who have clowned for a few to the players like catcher Rick Dempsey, who occasionally put on his own one-man show during rain delays at Memorial Stadium in Baltimore.

clowning An old baseball tradition in which an entertainer, often a former player, puts on a sideshow to go with the game. The clowning takes place before the game, between innings, or during the break between two games of a doubleheader.

clown prince An entertainer who performs comic baseball routines. One of the first was Germany Schaefer. The title "Clown Prince of Baseball" was first taken by Al Schacht after his playing days (pitcher for the Washington Senators, 1919–1921) were over and he became baseball's most famous clown; his routines centered on the foibles and eccentricities of the national pastime. The next man to adopt the title was Max Patkin.

club 1. *n.* A baseball organization that assembles the players and supporting staff for a *team*, provides a playing field, and represents the team in league affairs and the public in general. See also *ball club*, 1. IST USE. 1837. "This institution shall be denominated 'The Olympic Ball Club'" (Constitution of the Olympic Ball Club of Philadelphia, Art. I, Dec. 12; published privately in 1838). USAGE NOTE. Benjamin G. Rader (*Baseball: A History of America's Game*, 1992) wrote, "In contemporary sports, the words 'club' and 'team' are used interchangeably. The main, if not the exclusive, purpose of such organizations is to play games against other teams and sometimes to make money. To the Knickerbockers, however, the term 'club' meant far more than simply a team of baseball players bent on victory or monetary remuneration. The Knickerbocker club, like many of the other pioneering baseball clubs, was both an athletic and a social association. While providing opportunities for playing baseball, it also scheduled suppers, formal balls, and other festive occasions in the off-season. Individuals could acquire membership only by election; the club consciously tried to keep out those who had a 'quarrelsome disposition' or who did not fit well into the group for other reasons. The Knickerbockers

Clown prince. "Clown Prince of Baseball" Al Schacht (left) with Nick Altrock, Oct. 4, 1924. *National Photo Company Collection, Library of Congress*

drew up bylaws, elected officers, and even fined members who breached the organization's code of dress and behavior." Albert G. Spalding (*America's National Game*, 1911) wrote that the founders of the National League (1876) proposed "a sharp line of distinction" between the two terms: "Heretofore Base Ball Clubs had won and lost games, matches, tournaments, trophies. Henceforth this would be changed. The function of Base Ball Clubs in the future would be to manage Base Ball Teams. Clubs would form leagues, secure grounds, erect grandstands, lease and own property, make schedules, fix dates, pay salaries, assess fines, discipline players, make contracts, [and] control the sport in all its relations to the public." *The Sporting News* (Jan. 27, 1894; Peter Morris) observed the distinction between "club" and "team": "Though slight, the difference is marked and should be observed closely. The club is that body of benevolent gentlemen associated together for the sole purpose of 'coughing up' enough of the 'long green' to provide the necessities of life (and other incidentals) for the poorly paid, over worked, underfed, easily deluded, unsuspecting and downtrodden ball players of this unhappy land of ours. Whereas the 'team' is but nine of the miserable mortals above enu-

merated. In other words the 'club' means the business men at its head and the 'team' is the ball players who work for them."
2. *n.* A baseball *team*. **3.** *n.* A baseball bat. See also *ball club*, 1. **4.** *v.* To hit a baseball. "Kirby Puckett clubbed a solo home run" (*Tampa Tribune*, June 27, 1989). **5.** *v.* To defeat a team decisively.

club ball A mythical medieval game that, according to Joseph Strutt (*The Sports and Pastimes of the People of England*, 1801), was the ancestor of cricket and other bat-and-ball games. Strutt extracted the term from a 14th-century Latin proclamation, but there is no evidence that a particular game of that name ever existed. Some modern historians consider the club-ball theory "a disingenuous attempt by Strutt to address the origins of bat-and-ball games for which he had no other satisfactory explanation" (David Block, *Baseball Before We Knew It*, 2005, pp.183–84).

clubber *hist.* A batter. "[Hod] Eller knew that . . . two of the most dangerous clubbers in the American League were all set to riddle his shine ball" (*The New York Times*, Oct. 7, 1919)

clubbie Nickname for *clubhouse man.* "Players are closer to the clubbies than they are to the manager. The clubbie takes care of every whim the player has" (Nick Cafardo, *The Baltimore Sun*, Apr. 30, 2007).

clubby Nickname for *clubhouse man.* "[Wayne Hardaway] spent most of his five decades in baseball as a Twins minor league clubhouse attendant—a clubby" (Steve Rushin, *Sports Illustrated*, Oct. 16, 2006, p.15).

clubhouse The area at a ballpark comprising a team's locker room, showers, lounge, and the manager's office. Many modern clubhouses offer hydrotherapy pools, doctor's offices, batting cages, sauna, kitchen, and rooms for laundry, weight-training, videos, and meetings, and even the services of a barber. Every park has two clubhouses: one for the home team and one for the visiting team. *Sports Illustrated* (July 7, 2003) admired the fact that "Tropicana Field's visitors' clubhouse features four hanging TVs, three couches, three recliners and the big leagues' most extensive candy collection." Mark Kramer (*The New York Times Magazine*, Sept. 11, 1983) wrote: "Many ballplayers seem caught in adolescence, their development perhaps arrested by long enclosure, early wealth, and their teammates' high spirits and scrutiny. They call their locker rooms 'the clubhouse.'" Jerry Howarth (*Baseball Lite*, 1986) described the clubhouse as "a ballplayer's private domain to eat, sleep, shower, shave, play cards, check the mail, listen to music, roughhouse, tease, autograph baseballs and generally relax while awaiting what they are paid to do." See also *dressing room*, 1; *locker room*, 1. Syn. *house*, 3. IST USE. 1864. "At the close of play the parties adjourned to the club house and there received the usual hospitalities extended to their guests by the Eurekas" (*New York Clipper*, Aug. 13; Peter Morris). USAGE NOTE. Peter Morris comments, "The term 'clubhouse' is an example of a term still in common use that offers reminders of the debt that baseball owes to the social club. The building described in the 1864 citation above would have had little resemblance to the functional shower and dressing rooms that bore this name for most of the 20th century. In recent years, however, baseball clubhouses have become far more luxurious and thus much closer to the earliest meaning of the term."

clubhouse attendant Syn. of *clubhouse man.*

clubhouse boy Syn. of *clubhouse man.* "Clubhouse boys [are] combination valet, equipment expert, loan company, buffer and the personification of the three famous monkeys" (Joe Garagiola, *Baseball Is a Funny Game*, 1960, p.10).

clubhouse lawyer 1. An outspoken player given to complaining and talking of reform and "rights"; "a player who airs bolshevik views in the clubhouse" (*The Sporting News Record Book*, 1937). With the unionization of players through the Major League Baseball Players Association, clubhouse lawyers are less common than they once were. "Bob Farley ... denied today that he is hard to manage or a clubhouse lawyer, as tagged by Chicago White Sox pilot Al Lopez when traded to Detroit the other day" (*San Francisco News-Call Bulletin*, June 28, 1962; Peter Tamony). Joe Garagiola (*Sport*, Apr. 1962) commented, "A clubhouse lawyer is a .210 hitter who isn't playing. He gripes about everything. His locker is too near the dryer. His shoes aren't ever shined right. His undershirt isn't dry. His bats don't have the good knots in them that the stars' bats have. He's not playing because the manager is dumb. When he does play he says, 'Well, what do you expect? I ain't played in two weeks.' And he's a perpetual second guesser." See also *lawyer*, 1. Syn. *bolshevik*, 1. IST USE. 1929. "He [Del Pratt] was the greatest clubhouse lawyer baseball ever knew" (John Kiernan, *The New York Times*, June 17; Steve Steinberg). **2.** A player who advises other players on contract matters.

clubhouse man A person who performs many of the menial tasks around the clubhouse, including packing and unpacking players' equipment and personal property, laundering and mending uniforms and hanging them in the lockers, polishing shoes, organizing the media room, helping players answer fan mail, running errands, supplying the clubhouse with everything from mouthwash to Twinkies, and arranging for pregame and postgame snacks or meals. Tom House

(*The Jock's Itch*, 1989, pp.83–84): "The unsung hero, the clubhouse man. Without this guy, I believe, baseball as we know it would cease to exist. I doubt any ball club could field a full team without the clubhouse man to get them there." House noted that the clubhouse men "become like mothers for players who aren't married and like wives for players who are." See also *equipment manager*. Syn. *clubhouse boy*; *clubhouse attendant*; *clubhouse manager*; *clubbie*; *clubby*.

clubhouse manager Syn. of *clubhouse man*.

clubhouse meeting A gathering of team members, either before or after a game, in which players receive important messages from the team's management. Managers try to keep such meetings to a minimum. "The Phillies lost nine of the first 10 games on the trip and were swept in a big four-game series in Montreal, which prompted [manager Larry] Bowa to call his first clubhouse meeting of the year" (*The Baltimore Sun*, Sept. 10, 2003). Syn. *team meeting*.

club nine A baseball team consisting of exactly nine members and supported by a 19th-century gentlemen's club.

club record The highest or best achievement attained by a baseball club or by a player while performing for a baseball club. It is the prerogative of each club to choose which records to claim as its own; in the major leagues, the general practice has been for records to remain with their franchises even if the franchises relocate (e.g., the Giants, the Dodgers, and the Braves). However, the Baltimore Orioles did not claim any records of the St. Louis Browns when the latter moved to Baltimore in 1954. "The records are there. It's up to each team how to use them, and it's basically a public relations decision" (National Baseball Hall of Fame and Museum library director Jim Gates, quoted by Barry Shrug, *The Washington Post*, Aug. 31, 2006).

clunk ball The *balata ball* that was used at the start of the 1943 season, characterized by a hardening of the ball when the rubber cement, made from a poor grade of reclaimed rubber, seeped into the wool and dried (Associated Press dispatch, May 5, 1943; Peter Morris). An improved, livelier version was introduced on May 8.

cluster For a team to get a series of hits or runs in quick succession.

clutch Any difficult, tense, or critical situation, often one in which the outcome of a game hinges on the success or failure of a team or individual player. There have been various attempts to define a clutch situation, such as runners in scoring position in the late innings of a close game. "When a batter produces a safe 'blow' at an opportune moment, his fellow-players say that he has hit . . . 'in the clutch'" (*The New York Times*, June 2, 1929). See also *pinch*, 1; *late-inning pressure situation*. Syn. *saddle*, 1. IST USE. 1925. "Twice thereafter he delivered in the clutch and finally [Tris] Speaker put him in right field" (*The Sporting News*, May 14; Benjamin Zimmer). ETYMOLOGY. The origin of the term is suggested in the 1954 *Gillette World Series Record Book* (edited by Hy Turkin): "When a clutch is engaged in any machinery, parts are made to move, and any defect in the clutch will cause faulty operation or danger." EXTENDED USE. A key situation or moment in any endeavor.

clutch hitter A player with a reputation for getting hits in key situations and/or with runners in scoring position. "When a batter is called a 'good clutch hitter' it means that he is dangerous when he comes to bat with the tying or winning run on the bases" (H.G. Salsinger, *Baseball Digest*, Aug. 1945). Players characterized as clutch hitters included Tommy "Old Reliable" Henrich, Hank Aaron, Pete Rose, and David Ortiz. The idea implies that there are hitters who consistently raise their performance in clutch situations throughout all or much of their careers. However, the best sabermetric evidence strongly suggests that there is little consistency in a player's clutch hitting from one season to the next, and that most players with this reputation are in fact good hitters in all circumstances. Syn. *gamer*, 2. EXTENDED USE. Anyone who can come through when it counts the most.

clutch hitting index The ratio between a player's runs batted in and *expected runs batted in*, adjusted for league average and slot in the batting order, rounded to two decimal places, and multiplied by 100. It is intended to measure the extent to which a batter drives in runs at the rate predicted by his overall offensive performance. League-average performance is 100. Cap Anson is both the single-season (178 in 1880) and career (132) leader. The term was defined by John Thorn et al. (*Total Baseball*, 6th ed., 1999, pp.2529–30). Abbrev. *CHI.*

clutchiness A measure of clutch hitting performance in a given season. It is computed by subtracting a measure of the number of wins a player would be expected to contribute to his team, based on his slugging percentage and on-base percentage, from his actual contributions, as calculated by win probability added or an analogous measure. A positive number implies that the player performed better in high leverage situations than in low, whereas a negative number implies the opposite.

clutch pitching index The ratio between a pitcher's *expected runs allowed* and actual runs allowed, rounded to two decimal places and multiplied by 100. It is intended to measure the extent to which a pitcher prevents runs at the rate predicted by his overall pitching performance. League-average performance is 100. The lifetime leader is Bob Rhoads with 117; the single-season leader is Doc White with 152.8 in 1904. The term was defined by John Thorn et al. (*Total Baseball*, 6th ed., 1999, p.2530). Abbrev. *CPI.*

clutch series A series of games played between two contending teams when the outcome will have a bearing on team standings.

Clydesdale A slow runner. "Jason Thompson had no wheels or was a Clydesdale" (Bob Hertzel, *Baseball Digest*, Jan. 1987). ETYMOLOGY. A reference to the Scottish breed of strong, hardy draft horses.

coach 1. *n.* An assistant to the manager in professional baseball. A coach is a team member in uniform and performs several jobs before, during, and between games. A major-league club usually has a pitching coach, a hitting coach, a bullpen coach, a first base coach, a third base coach, and a bench coach. The first full-time major-league coach was Arlie Latham of the Cincinnati Reds in 1900 (Peter Morris, *A Game of Inches: The Game on the Field*, 2006, p.360). **2.** *n.* A person in charge of a collegiate or scholastic baseball team, similar to a manager in professional baseball; an individual who oversees and teaches playing techniques and practices. IST USE. 1882. In a description of an exhibition game between the Detroit Wolverines of the National League and the Univ. of Michigan, which the professionals won easily, it was said of the collegiates: "Their great lack is a 'coach.' It is entirely unnecessary for the pitcher, second baseman or short stop to all back up first base, leaving the second wholly uncovered" (*Detroit Free Press*, Apr. 29; Peter Morris). **3.** *v.* To serve as a coach; to instruct or direct a baseball player. IST USE. 1875 (*Hartford Courant*; David Arcidiacono).

coacher *hist.* **1.** An early term for the first base coach or the third base coach. Hugh S. Fullerton (*American Magazine*, June 1912): "The duties of the coachers were to play clown, make noise and strive to excite or anger opposing players. The coacher in the modern game usually is quiet, studying the movements of the opposing pitcher and catcher and assisting base runners." IST USE. 1879. "Michael Scanlon, of Washington, the 'coacher' and acting manager of the Nationals, is earning a fame in this respect greater than that of Harry Wright" (*Chicago Tribune*, July 6; Peter Morris). ETYMOLOGY/USAGE NOTE. Peter Morris explains, "The earliest sense of the word 'coach' was the one meaning a carriage, and its name derived from a Hungarian town named Kocs where early coaches were built. The word was Anglicized in the 16th century and was almost immediately followed by 'coacher,' meaning the driver of a coach. The function of directing a baserunner home made it natural to borrow the term for baseball. It is worth noting that it makes more sense to compare a base coach to a coacher (who directs and spurs the horses on) rather than to a coach (which merely carries the traveler). And indeed 'coacher' appears to have preceded 'coach' into the baseball lexicon. 'Coacher' remained more common during the 19th century and precise writers, such as Christy Mathewson (*Pitch-*

ing in a Pinch, 1912), continued to use 'coacher' well into the 20th century; e.g., Harry 'Steamboat' Johnson (*Standing the Gaff*, 1935, p.142) wrote, 'I would not call the runner out if he hit the ball clear out of the park, if the coacher touched him at third base.' Eventually, however, the shorter term entirely superseded the original and more logical version and it is now 'coacher' that sounds strange to the ear." **2.** A catcher who was a valuable aid to a pitcher. "Holbert, though a trifle old, is a great coacher to any pitcher" (*Canton* [Ohio] *Repository*, Apr. 13, 1888; Peter Morris).

coacher's box *hist.* Syn. of *coach's box*, 1. IST USE. 1896 (Richard G. Knowles and Richard Morton, *Base Ball*; Edward J. Nichols).

coaches Plural of *coach*.

coaching line The outline of the coach's box. Syn. "coach line"; "coacher's line." IST USE. 1887. "The Chicago people have seen [George] Van Haltren play ball, but they never saw him work along the coaching line" (*San Francisco Examiner*, July 18; Peter Morris).

coach-pitch league A league for very young children in which the coaches do the pitching so that there is some hitting. "At 4, [Joe] Mauer was asked to leave his tee-ball league because he hit the ball too hard for the other players. So he moved up to a coach-pitch league" (Will Kimmey, *Baseball America*, Sept. 29–Oct. 12, 2003; Peter Morris). Despite the name, pitches sometimes are delivered by a pitching machine.

coach's box 1. One of two designated areas on a baseball field where the first base coach and the third base coach must remain while the ball is in play. The rectangular box is 10 feet wide and 20 feet long, marked off with chalk or lime and situated 15 feet in foul territory from and along the baseline. Syn. *coacher's box*. **2.** [softball term] One of two designated areas on a softball field where the first base coach and the third base coach must remain while the ball is in play. The rectangular box is 3 feet wide and 15 feet long, and situated 8 feet in foul territory from and along the baseline.

coach's interference A call by an umpire

Coach's box. *Photograph by Joseph Baylor Roberts*

when a base coach touches, grabs, or gets in the way of a baserunner in an attempt to stop the runner. In such cases the runner is called out. A thrown ball that hits a base coach is not considered interference. See also *interference*, 1.

coal-hole cover A slang term for home plate. "Cunny couldn't find the coal-hole cover" (*The New York Times*, July 20, 1897).

coaster A player in the Pacific Coast League. "It is surprising the number of coasters playing in the major leagues now" (*San Francisco Bulletin*, May 21, 1913; Gerald L. Cohen). Sometimes spelled "Coaster." IST USE. 1909 (*Baseball Magazine*, September, p.42; Edward J. Nichols).

Coast League Shortened version of *Pacific Coast League*.

coat-and-tie decision A policy decision made by the owner and/or executives of a baseball organization.

coax a pass For a batter to earn a base on balls by being patient, fouling off pitches, not swinging at pitches out of the strike zone, making the pitcher throw many pitches, or coming back after being behind in the count. See also *work the count*. Syn. *work a pass*. IST USE. 1910 (*New York Tribune*, July 18; Edward J. Nichols).

coaxer A pitch designed to try to make the batter reach outside the strike zone. IST USE. 1869. "The first ball was very tempting, and [George Zettlein] struck at it without hitting it. . . . Martin grinned and sent another coaxer, and Zettlin [*sic*] struck out" (*Brooklyn Eagle*, Sept. 7; Peter Morris).

Cobb's Lake The area of dirt in front of home

plate at Navin Field in Detroit, which the groundskeepers soaked with water to slow down Ty Cobb's bunts and keep them in fair territory, and which caused infielders to slip as they tried to field them. See also *doctoring*, 4.

Cobb-Wagner grip A batting grip characterized by space between the hands along the bat, as used by Ty Cobb and Honus Wagner.

cob-fence route *hist.* The circuit of small, rural towns visited by teams in the low minor leagues. "The regulars followed the cob-fence route, playing exhibition games each afternoon with minor-league clubs" (Burt L. Standish, *Courtney of the Center Garden*, 1915; David Shulman).

cock **1.** *n.* The preparatory action of the arm and wrist prior to the forward movement of a throw. **2.** *v.* To draw the arm backward in preparation for throwing a ball. **3.** *n.* The slant or cant of the bat as held by the batter. **4.** *v.* To position the bat and arms, slightly tensed and pulled back, in preparation to swing at a pitch; to move the wrists slightly backward to start the batter's swing.

cockeye *hist.* A left-handed baseball player, esp. a pitcher. IST USE. 1934 (*Akron* [Ohio] *Beacon Journal*).

coconut A player's head (Bob Hertzel, *Baseball Digest*, Jan. 1987).

coconut snatching Switching a player to a new position. The term was used by Branch Rickey for moving players from one position to another, as in the case of a pitcher who might thrive in the outfield or perform better as a hitter and base stealer. ETYMOLOGY. "On the islands, he [Rickey] used to say, it would take two fellows to gather coconuts from a palm tree. There was the coconut catcher, who stood safely on the ground, and the coconut snatcher, who climbed the tree and threw the coconuts down to the coconut catcher. Eventually, if the coconut snatcher was smart enough, he would be able to talk the coconut catcher into trading positions. So, in the Dodger organization, moving from one position to another became known as coconut snatching" (Tommy Lasorda, *The Artful Dodger*, 1985, p.209; Charles D. Poe).

code See *baseball code*.

coed softball [softball term] An official form of softball played by two teams, each composed of five men and five women who are positioned so that two men and two women are in the outfield, two men and two women are in the infield, and one man and one woman pitch and catch.

coefficient of restitution The ratio of the velocity of a baseball or softball rebounding from the surface of a hard, immovable object to the incoming velocity. It is equal to the square root of the proportion of the energy dissipated in the collision. The coefficient of restitution is a measure of the liveliness or "bounciness" of the ball: the higher the coefficient, the livelier the ball. The test sanctioned by the major leagues involves shooting the baseball from an air cannon at a velocity of 85 feet/second (58 miles/hour) against 2½-inch-thick solid northern white ash board mounted on a concrete column 9½ feet away; incident and rebound speeds of the ball are measured with light screens. Specifications stipulate that the baseball must register on rebound 54.6 percent of the original velocity, plus or minus 3.2 percent (or a coefficient of restitution between 0.514 and 0.578); in addition, the ball must hold its shape within 0.08 of an inch after being subjected to 65 pounds of pressure. Coefficients of restitution for softballs are commonly 0.44, 0.47, and 0.50. Abbrev. *COR*.

coffee **1.** See *cup of coffee*. **2.** See *players' coffee*.

coffee and cake Syn. of *cake and coffee*. EXTENDED USE. Peter Tamony found the term used in jazz circles as early as 1936 for a very poor paying job, one that might only pay carfare, and in boxing, where coffee-and-cakes fighters were willing to enter the ring for little pay.

coffin corner Syn. of *third base*, 1. It is so called because a ball batted to the third baseman usually results in an out.

coffin-corner hit A base hit in which the ball lands in the coffin corner (inside the 10-yard line) on a field where football is also played.

coked up Said of a player on fire, ready for anything. ETYMOLOGY. The term was used by Casey Stengel in an allusion to the heat and fire of the carbon fuel, as opposed to cocaine or Coca-Cola.

cold bat 1. The bat of a player in a hitting slump. Compare *hot bat*, 1. **2.** A player who is wielding a cold bat.

collar 1. *n.* A figurative term for the cause or result of a player going hitless during a game; e.g., "he's got a collar" or "he wears the collar" or "he took the collar." See also *horse collar*, 1. Syn. *Van Heusen*. IST USE. 1932 (*Baseball Magazine*, October; Edward J. Nichols). ETYMOLOGY. A literal "zero" from the round shape of a collar (Harwell E. West, *The Baseball Scrap Book*, 1938). **2.** *v.* To have failed to get a hit during a game; e.g., "[Nomar] Garciaparra is Collared" (*The Boston Globe* headline, as Garciaparra's consecutive-game hitting streak ended at 30, Aug. 31, 1997). **3.** *v.* To catch a baseball. "Challis put a liner to short and Renwick 'collared it'" (*Grand Rapids* [Mich.] *Morning Democrat*, Aug. 17, 1875; Peter Morris).

collect To score; to get a hit (Maurice H. Weseen, *A Dictionary of American Slang*, 1934). "[Eddie] Murray is one of only three players in major-league history to collect 3,000 hits and 500 home runs" (Tom Haudricourt, *Milwaukee Journal Sentinel*, Aug. 15, 1997).

collective bargaining agreement A generic term for *Basic Agreement*. Abbrev. *CBA*.

college of coaches An experiment initiated by Chicago Cubs owner Philip K. Wrigley in which the team had no manager during the 1961 and 1962 seasons, but was instead led by a group of coaches, who rotated responsibilities every few weeks. Included in the rotation was the role of "head coach," as the "manager" was called; serving in that capacity were Vedie Himsl, Harry Craft, Elvin Tappe, Lou Klein, and Charlie Metro. Minor-league managers were also rotated. This management innovation (referred to by Wrigley as a "management team") was born out of frustration, but eventually failed because of lack of leadership, dissension among the coaches, and players' difficulties in adjusting to different coaches. The "college" introduced computerization and developed a more uniform approach to player development. The experiment ended when Bob Kennedy

was appointed as permanent "head coach" for 1963, prompting the *Chicago Tribune* headline (Feb. 21, 1963), "Cubs Coaching Staff Stops Revolving."

college swing A swing in which the batter hits the ball near the handle of the bat. This approach works well with the aluminum bats used in college baseball, but tends to break the wood bats of professional baseball. "Every time [A.J. Hinch would] . . . inside-out a pitch or break his bat, his manager at Class A Modesto, former big leaguer Jeffrey Leonard, would gibe from the dugout: 'College swing! That doesn't work in pro ball'" (Alan Schwarz, *Baseball America*, March 16–29, 1998; Peter Morris).

college try See *old college try*.

College World Series An elimination series of games to determine the best Division I college baseball team. It is sponsored by the National Collegiate Association of America and is held each June in Omaha, Neb. Abbrev. *CWS*.

collision A scornful term for a player fresh out of college. IST USE. 1933 (Edgar G. Brands, *The Sporting News*, Feb. 23; Peter Morris). ETYMOLOGY. Corruption of the term "collegian."

collusion A secret agreement or arrangement; specif., the agreement among team owners to forgo the purchase of high-priced, first-rate free-agent players (such as Kirk Gibson and Carlton Fisk) after the 1985–1987 seasons. The owners settled collusion claims for $280 million in 1990 after arbitrators ruled they had worked together to hold down the salaries of free agents; they also agreed to triple damages for future collusion. The agreement allowed the Major League Baseball Players Association to distribute the settlement monies among the players after arbitrators determined who was entitled to shares. USAGE NOTE. According to Alan Schwarz (*Baseball America*, Oct. 2–15, 2000), "Baseball's collusion rules apply only to major league free agents. Clubs are free to set a common strategy with respect to the draft."

Colonels 1. Nickname for the American Association franchise in Louisville, Ky., that began playing as the Louisville Eclipse (1882–1884) and was renamed the Louisville

Colonels (1885–1889 and 1891) and the Louisville Cyclones (1890). **2.** Nickname for the National League franchise in Louisville, Ky., from 1892 to 1899. **3.** Nickname for the American Association (1902–1962) and the International League (1968–1972) minor league franchises located in Louisville, Ky.

color bar Syn. of *color line*.

color barrier Syn. of *color line*.

color line The unwritten rule that prohibited African-American players from playing in organized baseball. It was broken on Apr. 18, 1946, when Jackie Robinson played for the Montreal Royals of the International League in preparation for a career with the Brooklyn Dodgers. In the major leagues, the color line was broken on Apr. 15, 1947, when Robinson donned a Dodgers uniform. At its convention in Philadelphia in Dec. 1867, the National Association of Base Ball Players had resolved: "No club composed of persons of color, or having in its membership persons of color, shall be admitted into the National Association" (*Milwaukee Daily Sentinel*, Dec. 19, 1867). The National Association dropped the rule in subsequent years. "These men [several top African-American players] would prove a boon to some of the weak clubs of the league and association, but if there is one thing the white ball player insists on doing it is drawing the color line very rigidly" (*Detroit Free Press*, Dec. 4, 1887; Peter

Color line. The *USS Maine* baseball team. All of the members of the team except one were killed when the ship was blown up in Havana harbor in 1898. This is a fascinating image because it depicts an African-American player on an otherwise white team, a rarity then and for the next 49 years. *Library of Congress*

Morris). See also *gentleman's agreement*, 1. Syn. *color bar; color barrier*. IST USE. 1887. "The *Philadelphia Times* will say to-morrow that for the first time in the history of baseball the color line has been drawn, and that the 'world's champions,' the St. Louis Browns, are the men who have established the precedent that white players must not play with colored men" (*The New York Times*, Sept. 12). USAGE NOTE. Although the term and its synonyms were known in the National Football League between 1933 and 1946, they were particularly applied to baseball. The term was applied to Jack Johnson's efforts to arrange boxing matches; e.g., "Whenever a match with Johnson is mentioned . . . the old excuse, the color line, is hustily pressed into service" (*The National Police Gazette*, Dec. 8, 1906).

color man A radio or television broadcaster, often a former player or manager, who delivers background information, anecdotes, sidelights, and/or his own thoughts and analysis of the game to supplement the talk of the play-by-play announcer. Pittsburgh sportscaster Bill Currie (*The Sporting News*, Aug. 16, 1975) described a color man as "a guy paid to talk while everybody goes to the bathroom."

colors A colored uniform that distinguishes one as a member of a team; specif., two or more colors by which a team is identified and known. When Charles O. Finley owned the Oakland A's, he insisted that his team's colors were Kelly Green, Fort Knox Gold, and Wedding Gown White. IST USE. 1915. "The bleachers . . . appreciated spectacular play, no matter what colors the player wore" (*The Washington Post*, May 30).

colt *hist.* A young 19th-century player who has come to the major leagues. "The three 'colts,' [Mike] Slattery, [Mike] Tiernan and [Elmer] Foster, covered the outfield [for the New York Giants]" (*The World* [New York], Apr. 18, 1888; Gerald L. Cohen). When the Chicago White Stockings had a large number of young players, they became known as the Colts. IST USE. 1869 (*New York Herald*. July 13; Edward J. Nichols).

Colt .45s Nickname for the National League expansion franchise that played in Houston, Tex., from 1962 to 1964. The club was so named to recognize the revolver, "the gun that won the West." When the Colt Firearms Co. objected to the use of its emblem on team souvenirs and others were bothered by the violent notion of a club named for a handgun, the club was renamed the Houston *Astros* upon moving into the new Astrodome in 1965. Despite the firearms name, almost everybody referred to the team as the Colts.

comb **1.** To hit the ball straight up the middle of the field, usually coming close to hitting the pitcher; e.g., "Smith's hit back through the box combed the pitcher's hair." ɪsᴛ ᴜsᴇ. 1912 (New York *Tribune*, Sept. 7; Edward J. Nichols). **2.** To hit the ball; e.g., "Jones combed the pitcher's curves."

combatant A player determined by an umpire to have had the greater degree of participation in a brawl and who will accordingly receive a more severe punishment. "The umpiring crew listed all [24 Missoula] Osprey players as 'combatants,' a designation that calls for both a fine and a suspension" (*Baseball America*, Sept. 18–Oct. 1, 2000; Peter Morris).

combination **1.** Syn. of *combination play*. ɪsᴛ ᴜsᴇ. 1889. "League Stars: How They Play Combinations" (Tim Murnane, *The Boston Globe* headline, March 10; Peter Morris). **2.** See *double-play combination*.

combination ball *hist.* A pitch that combines elements of two or more pitches, such as a sinking fastball or a knuckle curve. "By using his combination ball Merriwell succeeded in fanning Strothers" (Burt L. Standish, *Dick Merriwell's Salvation*, 1907; David Shulman). ɪsᴛ ᴜsᴇ. 1888. "A common ball with those pitchers who use the drop ball is the combination down and out shoot, which is very deceptive when coupled with good speed. . . . Some men have claimed to have a combination in-and-out curve, but such a ball never existed" (*Cleveland Plain Dealer*, Apr. 29, reprinted from *St. Louis Globe-Democrat*; Peter Morris).

combination card A baseball card that depicts two or more players.

combination play Any play that relies on teamwork between two or more players; e.g., a pickoff play, a rundown play, and a relay.

Syn. *combination*, 1. ɪsᴛ ᴜsᴇ. 1898. "Tom McCarthy is booked to originate a few new combination plays for the Harvard boys" (*The Boston Globe*, March 13; Peter Morris).

combination signal Two or more motions tied together to represent one sign. For example, "skin and skin"—touching the face and then the chin—might be the real sign, whereas "skin, color, and skin"—touching the face, touching uniform lettering, and touching the chin—would be nothing more than three decoys. More complicated than most signs, they are missed more easily than flash signs and are more likely to be stolen.

combine To join with one or more other pitchers in establishing a win or loss, such as four pitchers combining on a three-hitter.

combined no-hitter A game in which neither the starting pitcher nor one or more relief pitchers yield a base hit; e.g., the Baltimore Orioles defeated the Oakland A's 2–0 on July 13, 1991, when starter Bob Milacki and relievers Mike Flanagan, Mark Williamson, and Gregg Olson yielded no hits. See also *no-hitter*, 1.

come around **1.** To score a run. "Pokey Reese singled, stole second and came around on Jason LaRue's soft single" (*The Baltimore Sun*, Apr. 6, 2001). **2.** To perform better. "[Mark Koenig] played good ball for me last year and I'm confident he'll come around all right" (New York Yankees manager Miller Huggins, quoted in *The New York Times*, Apr. 27, 1927). **3.** To get into shape; to recover from an injury. "Litschi's smashed digit, which has caused his absence from the line-up this week, is coming around nicely, and he expects to get back into the game within the next few days" (*San Francisco Bulletin*, May 10, 1913; Gerald L. Cohen).

come at Syn. of *challenge*, 1. "[Randy Johnson] was coming right at the Yankees' hitters and challenging them to make contact with his fastball" (*The Baltimore Sun*, Oct. 29, 2001).

comeback **1.** *n.* A rally by a team behind in the score or the standings. The term can be applied to an individual game or to several games over the course of a season or to post-season play. Teams that have rebounded from two-game deficits (2–0, 3–1) to win the World Series are considered to have made comebacks. **2.** *n.* A good season by a team, manager, or player, following a poor or mediocre one. "Eastern writers predict that the Athletics are due for a comeback stunt this season" (*San Francisco Bulletin*, Apr. 19, 1913; Gerald L. Cohen). IST USE. 1905 (*The Sporting Life*, Sept. 9, p.19; Edward J. Nichols). **3.** *n.* Syn. of *comebacker*, 1. **4.** *adj.* Said of an inside pitch that moves over the plate at the final moment. "Greg Maddux has a comeback fastball—lefthanded hitters flinch at it because it starts right at them but it breaks back over the plate" (Deric Ladnier, quoted in Alan Schwarz, BaseballAmerica.com, Nov. 14, 2006).

comebacker 1. A ball that is hit directly back to the pitcher. "[Roger Clemens] injured his right hand trying to field a comebacker" (*The Baltimore Sun*, Apr. 16, 2002). Sometimes spelled "come-backer." Syn. *comeback*, 3. **2.** A game in which a team, losing at one point, scores enough runs to tie or take the lead.

"come back, little Sheba" A hallmark phrase used by sportscaster Red Barber for a batted ball that bounced back to the mound. ETYMOLOGY. The term is the name of a William Inge play, which was made into a popular 1952 film that won an Oscar for actress Shirley Booth. It is an apparent play on the term "comebacker."

Comeback Player of the Year Award One of various annual awards presented to one player in each major league who made a dramatic reversal from a season or more of decline and poor play, or who rebounded from a year or more lost to or ruined by a serious injury. Major League Baseball officially sanctioned the award in 2005; it is presented by Viagra as the result of fan balloting on Major League Baseball's Web site (MLB .com). Representatives of Major League Baseball and the editorial staff at its Web site select six nominees from each league. Other versions of the award have been given by *The Sporting News* (since 1965, selected by the editorial staff), the Associated Press, the Baseball Writers' Association of America, United Press International, ESPN, and the Major League Baseball Players Association

(*Players Choice Award* in 1992 and since 1997).

come from ahead 1. To win or be winning in a game after losing a lead and reclaiming it. **2.** To lose or be losing in a game after having a lead; e.g., "The Cubs came from ahead [3–1] to suffer a 4–3, extra-inning loss to the Astros" (*The Baltimore Sun*, Sept. 28, 1998).

come from behind To be losing in a game before scoring enough runs to tie or take the lead.

come home To score.

come home dry To fail to take advantage of a scoring opportunity.

come in 1. To pitch the ball so it moves toward the batter. "When a catcher knows the pitcher has great control and can 'come in there' with the ball whenever necessary, he uses the pitch-out a great deal" (George Herman Ruth, *Babe Ruth's Own Book of Baseball*, 1928, p.137; Peter Morris). **2.** To throw a strike after falling behind in the count. **3.** For a fielder to run rapidly toward an advancing ground ball.

come inside To pitch close to the batter. "Todd Stottlemyre came inside to Rickey Henderson on the second pitch of the game, causing both benches and bullpen to empty" (*Tampa Tribune*, May 22, 1990).

come off 1. To have played a particular kind of game or series or finished a particular kind of season; e.g., it is sometimes said that a player is "coming off" a good (or bad) spring training season. **2.** For a batter to pull the ball too much. "A nagging injury to his right big toe two years ago had caused [Bobby Higginson] . . . to come off the ball and pull it too much" (*Sports Illustrated*, March 26, 2001).

comer 1. A promising player. IST USE. 1889. "[Emmett] Rogers, the catcher, is a 'comer'" (*The Sporting News*, Aug. 17; Peter Morris). **2.** A team that is a contender in waiting. IST USE. 1889. "The Aetna's considered the Cass club hardly in their class, but a long tie game between the two changed matters, and they recognized that the Cass were comers" (*Detroit Free Press*, Feb. 24; Peter Morris).

come through 1. To be successful; to win. St.

Louis Cardinals first baseman Albert Pujols, after hitting a game-winning home run (quoted in *The Baltimore Sun*, May 30, 2006): "I got another chance, and I came through. That's what it's all about, stay focused and get a good pitch to hit, and hopefully come through. I concentrate on coming through and winning some games." IST USE. 1927. "[Mark] Koenig Comes Through" (*The New York Times* headline, Apr. 27). **2.** For a ball to pain a fielder's hand when the glove does not provide adequate cushion. "[First baseman George] Stovall armed himself with a specially designed mitt. . . . It is long and resembles the business part of a shovel, but even that did not prevent the bad throws from 'coming through,' as the ball players say when a ball stings them through the glove" (Harry Neily, *The Sporting Life*, Sept. 6, 1913; Peter Morris).

come to eat Said of a fastball or slider that moves in on the batter and is likely to take a "bite" out of the batter.

come up 1. To join a major-league team from the minor leagues. See also *call up.* **2.** To step up to the plate to hit.

come up throwing To field a ground ball or catch a fly ball and get it to the appropriate base with immediacy. "Going into the hole at deep short, where you've got to master coming up throwing" (Rogers Hornsby, *My Kind of Baseball*, 1953, p.149).

comfortable Describing a pitching success that does not involve making the batter look bad or being intimidated. Randy Johnson's three strikeouts of Frank Thomas occasioned this remark from Thomas: "It was a real comfortable o-fer tonight" (Associated Press dispatch, Aug. 9, 1997).

comfort zone 1. That part of the strike zone best adapted to a batter's ability to get a hit; e.g., Warren Spahn was a master at keeping the ball away from the batter's "comfort zone." **2.** A speed on a fastball that a pitcher can attain on a regular basis, without undue effort. "[Macay McBride] was timed as high as 95 [mph] in high school, has found a comfort zone around 90–91 mph" (*Baseball America*, July 21–Aug. 3, 2003; Peter Morris).

"coming down" The traditional call made by the catcher to alert the second baseman or shortstop that he is about to throw the ball to second base at the end of the pitcher's warmup between innings.

Comiskey *hist.* A player or person affiliated with the Chicago White Sox. "The White Sox . . . monopolized the individual hitting department. There were three Comiskeys among the league's top five hitters" (Edgar Munzel, *The Sporting News*, May 2, 1951). Syn. "Comiskeyite." ETYMOLOGY. Derived from long-time (1901–1931) White Sox owner Charles A. Comiskey.

command 1. *n.* The ability of a pitcher to take charge in a game, using an assortment of pitches; esp., the confidence of a pitcher to throw any pitch, or a series of pitches, for a strike, regardless of the game situation, the score, or the count, and to make the pitch arrive at the precise spot and with the exact velocity he desires, while making the ball go in any direction, such as up, down, in, or out. The term does not necessarily mean *control*, which is the ability to throw the ball over the plate (throwing strikes), as "command" of a pitch is getting the ball over the plate plus getting it to do something. Curt Schilling (quoted in *Baseball America*, July 5–21, 2002): "Control is the ability to throw strikes, command is the ability to throw quality strikes." The term is used in such phrases as "command of the ball," "command of the strike zone," and "command of the game." The term became popular in the 1990s, but it was commonly used in the 19th century as well; e.g., "Command is another feature in the pitcher's work, and this is a technical word for placing the ball at will" (*The Sporting Life*, Dec. 12, 1883; Peter Morris), and "Unless he [the pitcher] has perfect command he will never be a winning pitcher" (John Montgomery Ward, *Base-Ball: How to Become a Player*, 1888, p.52). Cy Young (quoted in Alfred H. Spink, *The National Game*, 2nd ed., 1911, p.391): "Command of the ball is the first essential to success in pitching." IST USE. 1862. "[Jim] Creighton, of the Excelsiors, being celebrated for his great speed and the perfect command of the ball in delivery, that he possesses" (*Brooklyn Eagle*, July 28; Peter Morris). **2.** *v.* For a pitcher to exert command of his pitches in the strike zone. Baltimore Orioles manager Mike Hargrove (quoted in *The Baltimore Sun*, Apr. 3, 2001): "The art of pitching isn't necessarily throwing the ball by people or getting people to miss the ball. It's commanding your pitches, putting it in the spot you want at the speed you want and keeping it off the fat part of the bat." IST USE. 1888. "[Charlie] Buffinton has one of the best drop balls ever seen and when he can command it is almost invulnerable" (*Cincinnati Commercial-Gazette*, Jan. 19). **3.** *n.* The ability and patience of a batter to reduce the strike zone to a finite area (for Barry Bonds, it's about the size of a quarter) and never swing at a bad pitch. "[Elijah Dukes at bat displays] exceptional command of the strike zone" (Albert Chen, *Sports Illustrated*, March 19, 2007). **4.** *v.* For a batter to exert command in the strike zone. "Commanding the strike zone for hitters . . . is our organizational philosophy, and, yes, it's obviously the Ted Williams philosophy" (Oakland Athletics general manager Billy Beane, quoted in *The Boston Globe*, July 22, 2002).

commando A livelier type of baseball used in the Mexican League beginning in 1984.

command ratio A measure of a pitcher's raw ability to pitch the ball over the plate, computed by dividing strikeouts by bases on balls. Ron Shandler (*Ron Shandler's Baseball Forecaster*, 2006) noted, "Baseball's upper echelon of command pitchers will have ratios in excess of 3.0. Pitchers with ratios under 1.0 . . . have virtually no potential for long term success."

commish Slang for *commissioner*.

Commission See *National Commission*.

commissioner The individual elected by major-league owners for a three-year term to formulate and administer the overall policies of the game and to exercise executive supervision of all the activities of major- and minor-league baseball; the chief executive officer of Major League Baseball. A commissioner was in place from 1920, when Judge Kenesaw Mountain Landis was selected in the wake of the Black Sox Scandal in an effort to restore public confidence in the

Commissioner. Judge Kenesaw Mountain Landis, who as the first Major League Baseball commissioner was granted absolute power over the game in the wake of the Black Sox Scandal. He exercised his authority over the game until his death in 1944. *George Grantham Bain Collection, Library of Congress*

game, to 1992, when Fay Vincent, who was selected to fill out the remainder of the term of A. Bartlett Giamatti, was forced to resign. The position was held by a commissioner pro tem, Bud Selig, from Sept. 1992 to July 1998, at which point Selig was voted into the position officially. The duties of the commissioner include: a) supervising the World Series and the All-Star Game; b) settling grievances of players, teams, or leagues that cannot be settled at lower levels; c) acting as the final judicial authority on all matters of appeal; d) making decisions regarding on-field discipline, playing-rule interpretations, and game protests; e) ensuring an appropriate level of long-term competitive balance among the major-league clubs; f) negotiating baseball's labor contract; and g) investigating and resolving acts that may be detrimental to, or not in the best interests of, the game. See also *Czar.* Syn. *commish.*

commissioneritis A mock disease in which the commissioner of baseball decides to take an expansive view of the duties of his position. St. Louis Cardinals president Fred Kuhlmann (quoted in John Helyar, *Lords of the Realm*, 1994, p.473): "I call it 'commissioneritis.' Almost invariably, the degree of it grows while they're in office." Peter Gammons (*Baseball America*, Dec. 13–26, 1993; Peter Morris): "Owners [are reluctant to hire a new commissioner because] they fear . . . commissioneritis. When Peter Ueberroth took over in October 1984, his first move was to grandstand for the media and intervene in the umpires' playoff strike, for which baseball paid dearly the next nine seasons."

Commissioner's Games The *World Series*, so called because the commissioner has supreme authority over the games. Critics say that the commissioner has relinquished some of that authority to the television networks, which are influential as to the hour at which the games begin.

Commissioner's Historic Achievement Award An award presented to a player or former player who made an historic impact on the game of baseball. It has been awarded in recognition of a "prolific career" (Tony Gwynn), an "unprecedented season" (Barry Bonds in 2001), a "remarkable record" (Cal Ripken Jr.), and a "record-setting season" (Seattle Mariners in 2001).

Commissioner's Trophy 1. The official name for the trophy presented to the winner of the World Series. It was originally created by Major League Baseball in 1967. In 2000, Tiffany & Co. unveiled a new trophy, consisting of a cylindrical array of miniature poles with tiny pennants, one for each team, all standing on a stadium-like base. **2.** The name for the trophy presented during the period of 1970 to 1984 to the most valuable player in the All-Star Game. It was renamed the *Arch Ward Memorial Trophy* in 1985.

commission scout A *bird dog* who receives a small stipend when a prospect he has found is signed.

commit oneself To make a half swing in which the wrists break. If the umpire determines that the batter has "committed himself," a strike is called.

common card One of the vast majority of baseball cards that is not rare and that depicts an average player who is not a star or particularly notable for any reason; the least expensive card in a manufacturer's basic set. Having no premium value, all common cards from a given year may bring a standard price. Syn. "common."

commuter A baseball player who is being shifted between major-league and minor-league teams.

comp A free ticket to a baseball game. Short for "complimentary ticket." IST USE. 1898. "No 'Comps' for Ladies . . . Last year 'comps' were scattered, broadcast among the gentler sex and resulted in complaints from many who failed to receive tickets, as well as a financial loss to the club" (*Milwaukee Journal*, Apr. 19; Peter Morris). EXTENDED USE. A free ticket to any event for which there is a paid admission charge.

compact Said of a batter's swing or a pitcher's motion that is efficient, with no wasted movement.

company *hist.* Professional baseball. Texas League president J. Doak Roberts (quoted in the *Los Angeles Times*, Jan. 25, 1921): "Emmett Rogers, Scrappy Bill Joyce and Arthur Sunday . . . were the first Texas Leaguers ever sold to higher company." The terms "fast company," "big company," and "high company" refer to the major leagues.

compensation free-agent draft The selection of players as compensation for teams that lost Type A free agents in the *free-agent reentry draft*.

compensation pick 1. A draft pick received by a club if one of its free agents, to whom it has offered salary arbitration, signs with another club. Up until 2002, the practice was as follows: For Type A free agents, the compensation was the signing team's first-round draft pick in the succeeding summer's first-year player draft (if the signing team finished in the top half of the standings) or its second-round draft pick (if it finished in the bottom half of the standings), plus a *sandwich pick* between the first and second rounds of the first-year player draft. For Type B free agents, the compensation was the signing team's first- or second-round pick (as per Type A compensation), but no sandwich pick. For Type C free agents, the compensation was a sandwich pick after the second round, but before the third round, in the first-year player draft. Draft-pick compensation for losing Types A, B, and C free agents was eliminated in the 2002–2006 Basic Agreement between the owners and the players. **2.** A draft pick in the first-year player draft received by a club that failed to sign its draft pick from the preceding year. If a club fails to sign its first- or second-round pick, it will receive a compensation pick in the next year's draft that is one spot behind the pick that was lost (e.g., if the fifth pick fails to sign, the club will receive a sixth pick in the next year's draft). See also *sandwich pick.*

compensation pool Players up for consideration in the compensation free-agent draft. It resulted from the 1981 strike settlement and was eliminated with the 1985 strike settlement.

competitive balance 1. Equal distribution of potential success among the clubs in a league. "Public confidence [in baseball] shall include . . . the public perception . . . that there is an appropriate level of long-term competitive balance among the Clubs" (Major League Constitution, Art. II, Sec. 4). Sportswriter Peter Schmuck (*The Baltimore Sun*, Apr. 3, 2005) noted, "The National League . . . has something called competitive balance. There has been a different NL team in the World Series each of the past seven years." **2.** See *law of competitive balance.*

competitive-balance tax A term used by major-league baseball owners for what is popularly known as the *luxury tax.*

complete game 1. An official statistic credited to a pitcher who pitches an entire game without relief, regardless of the number of innings pitched. Since 1900, the average number of complete games has gone from almost 117 a team to as few as three (the 1991 New York Yankees). Abbrev. *CG.* **2.** A baseball game that is not postponed, called, or otherwise delayed.

Complete game. Walter Johnson, who pitched 38 complete-game 1–0 victories for the Washington Senators from 1907 through 1927. *Photograph by Joseph Baylor Roberts*

complete-game victory A complete game in which the pitcher is credited with a win. A fascinating complete-game record belongs to Walter Johnson, who pitched 38 complete-game 1–0 victories during his career with the Washington Senators (1907–1927).

complete package Syn. of *complete player.* "Eddie Murray . . . was a Gold Glove first baseman. He could switch-hit for both average and power. He was what baseball people call, 'a complete package'" (Ronald M. Shapiro and Mark A. Jankowski, *The Power of Nice*, 1998, p.210).

complete player A player who has speed and a strong arm, excels in fielding, is a consistent hitter, and hits for power; a player (such as Hank Aaron) who is fundamentally sound in every aspect of the game. See also *five-tool player.* Syn. *complete package.*

complex league A *rookie league* in which the youngest or least experienced players participate in games played in the spring training complex of a major-league team; e.g., the Gulf Coast League and the Arizona League. Compare *short-season league.* See also *instructional leag*ue.

complimentary runner [softball term] A substitute baserunner who by the mutual consent of the opposing managers does not prevent the original runner from staying in the game.

component ERA An estimate of what a pitcher's earned run average "should have been" in a given season, based only on the number of hits, home runs, walks, hit by pitches, batters faced, and innings pitched for which he is responsible. The statistic tends to be a better predictor of a pitcher's earned run average for the next season than that pitcher's actual earned run average. The statistic appeared in STATS Inc.'s annual *Major League Handbook* beginning in 1999. Abbrev. *CERA*, 2; *ERC*.

composite bat **1.** A bat composed of two or more pieces of wood glued or laminated together and layered on the outside with plastic, designed to duplicate the effect of wood but not to break or bend under normal use. Composite bats are stronger and more durable than wooden bats, and perform better. Syn. "composite wood bat." **2.** [softball term] A bat consisting of carbon fiber layered with resin or Kevlar, designed to perform like a wooden bat but with greater durability and longevity.

compression [softball term] A measure of the pounds of force required to squeeze a softball 0.25 inches. A softball with a 375-lb. compression indicates that the testing facility had to apply 375 pounds of force to compress the diameter of the ball by a total of 0.25 inches. A higher value indicates that the ball will compress less when hit, and bats will have a higher performance. Reductions in softball compression have a greater effect than reductions in the coefficient of restitution in decreasing overall bat and ball performance in the field. There is a direct correlation between ball compression and pitcher-response times: the harder the ball, the less time the pitcher has to react to the ball.

computer baseball A system whereby a manager feeds his own and the opposing team's statistics into a computer and, from the results obtained, forms decisions on how to use his players and manage his team.

concealed ball trick *hist.* Syn. of *hidden-ball trick*, 1. "The old concealed ball trick is having a new lease on life" (*Detroit Free Press*, May 6, 1902; Peter Morris).

concentration The edge or advantage a pitcher must possess to succeed. It was once known as *rhythm*. "The pitchers with the good concentration, those are the guys that

can overcome adversity when they're 60 to 70 percent effective" (Steve Stone, quoted in Steve Fiffer, *How to Watch Baseball*, 1987, p.27). USAGE NOTE. This is a tricky term because it does not relate to "concentration" in the traditional sense as much as to the concept of effectiveness on the mound. In fact, a seemingly distracted pitcher throwing a no-hitter might be described as having "concentration." Phil Pepe (*Baseball Digest*, Nov. 1974, p.58) wrote, "When a veteran pitcher recently explained an early KO by saying, 'I lost my concentration,' my first thought was, 'What else does he have to concentrate on for two and a half hours?' Then it occurred to me that this was just another change in the jargon of ballplayers."

Concepcion play A method of playing on artificial turf, named for Cincinnati Reds shortstop Davey Concepcion, who quickly discovered that sharply hit balls did not slow down when hit through the infield. Concepcion started playing much deeper, almost in shallow left field. Since his throws were longer, he began making them lower so they would reach the first baseman on one true hop (*USA Today Baseball Weekly*, July 19–25, 1991).

concrete ashtray Syn. of *cookie cutter*.

concrete donut Syn. of *cookie cutter*.

Confederate soldier A visiting player in his gray uniform, as opposed to a home-team player in his traditional white uniform.

conference **1.** *n.* See *mound conference*. IST USE. 1939. "The umpires [in the Southern Association] . . . are urged to cut down on the number of conferences between managers and pitchers" (*The Sporting News*, June 8; Peter Morris). **2.** *v.* To meet on the pitcher's mound. "The Orioles conference on the mound" (announcer Jon Miller, radio broadcast, May 10, 1987).

confrere *hist.* A teammate. "Willie [McCorry] thinks he is a better all around man than his tall confrere [Seals teammate Phil Douglass]" (*San Francisco Bulletin*, May 14, 1913; Gerald L. Cohen).

connect **1.** To hit the ball successfully, squarely, and solidly. IST USE. 1905 (*The Sporting Life*, Sept. 2, p.14; Edward J. Nichols). **2.** To hit a home run. "[Bobby] Jones connected in the fifth inning . . . for his first homer in 297 at-bats" (*The Baltimore Sun*, Apr. 13, 1999).

connectamundo A home run.

consecutive-game hitting streak A series of successive games in which a player has produced at least one hit per game. The streak is not terminated if all the batter's plate appearances (one or more) result in a base on balls, hit batter, catcher's interference, obstruction, or sacrifice bunt; however, a sacrifice fly or no hit will terminate the streak. The streak is determined by the consecutive games in which the player appears, not by his team's games. Joe DiMaggio of the New York Yankees holds the major-league record: 56 games in 1941. (*Official Baseball Rules*, Rule 10.23[b])

consecutive-game playing streak A series of successive games in which a player has appeared in his team's games. The *Official Baseball Rules* (Rule 10.23[c]) states that the streak shall be extended if a player plays one half-inning on defense, completes a time at bat by reaching base or being put out, or is ejected from a game by an umpire before he can comply with the requirements of this rule; however, a pinch-running appearance only shall not extend the streak. Cal Ripken Jr. of the Baltimore Orioles holds the major-league record: 2,632 games, from 1982 to 1998. Syn. "consecutive game streak."

consecutive hitting streak A series of successive base hits produced by a hitter. The streak is not terminated if the plate appearance results in a base on balls, hit batter, catcher's interference, obstruction, or sacrifice bunt; however, a sacrifice fly will terminate the streak. (*Official Baseball Rules*, Rule 10.24[a])

contact The point at which the bat meets the baseball. "[Rafael Palmeiro] always makes good contact" (Rick Down, quoted in *The Baltimore Sun*, March 8, 1996).

"contact down, we're going" A coach's instruction to a runner on third base that if the ball is on the ground anywhere he is to go home.

contact hitter A hitter known for his ability to get hits by squarely meeting the ball with the bat; a hitter who rarely strikes out. Contact hitters are more likely to hit singles than extra-base hits; e.g., Tony Gwynn. *Sports Collectors Digest* (Apr. 15, 1983) commented: "When you talk about contact hitters the discussion must begin and end with Joe Sewell. He almost never struck out." *The Baltimore Sun* (Oct. 8, 1996) called Wade Boggs "one of the greatest contact hitters in the history of the game." *Sports Illustrated* (Apr. 4, 2005) described David Eckstein as "a quintessential contact hitter (first among AL hitters in lowest percentage of swings that missed)." Compare *power hitter*. USAGE NOTE. The term is not universally loved. In a column on overworked sports terminology, sportswriter Jim Murray (*Los Angeles Times*, Jan. 3, 1983) put "contact hitter" at the top of his list with this comment: "If a guy isn't a good 'contact' hitter, what kind of 'hitter' is he? There's no such thing as a 'non-contact hitter.' Every hit is 'contact,' isn't it?"

contact play An offensive play in which the baserunner advances on any contact made by the batter; e.g., a play in which the runner on third base advances to the plate when the batter hits the ball.

contend To be in the race for the championship. "[Earl] Weaver Confident that O's Will Contend" (*The Baltimore Sun* headline, Apr. 2, 1982).

contender Any baseball team that is capable of winning a championship. IST USE. 1904. "[Jimmy Collins] says that if they [Boston Americans] can recover the batting eye in time and Cy Young can pitch in winning form again, their chances are better than those of the other contenders" (*The Washington Post*, Aug. 23; Peter Morris).

contest A baseball game.

Continental League 1. A league chartered in Dec. 1920 to represent states rather than cities. The brainchild of Boston-based Andy Lawson, the league postponed its scheduled Apr. 1921 commencement and then disappeared. One of its distinguishing features was the consideration of using African-American players (Jonathan Fraser Light, *The Cultural Encyclopedia of Baseball*, 1997, p.188). **2.** A proposed third major league officially formed on July 27, 1959, after the New York Giants and the Brooklyn Dodgers fled west. It was to include New York, Houston, Toronto, Denver, Minneapolis–St. Paul, Atlanta, Dallas–Fort Worth, and Buffalo; its president was Branch Rickey, who advocated that a third major league was preferable to piecemeal expansion. The league was a threat to the existing order, and the cities were promised teams in the existing leagues if the Continental League did not become a reality. Although the league never materialized, the promise resulted in the creation of the New York Mets and eventually all of the other cities, except for Buffalo, were given teams. Abbrev. *CL.*

contract A written agreement between a player and his club, in which the terms of employment are set forth. IST USE. 1872. "The Forest City Base Ball Association has cancelled its contracts with the players, and a compromise made between the officers of the association and the players, the difficulty growing out of the refusal of the association to keep the club on their hands without playing" (*Cleveland Leader*, Aug. 5; Peter Morris).

contraction The reduction of the number of franchises in a league; e.g., the folding of a financially weak franchise to ease the economic strain it places on the rest of the baseball industry. The concept was discussed in 2001 when Major League Baseball planned to eliminate two franchises; critics suggested that contraction was a bargaining ploy to influence negotiations with the players' union. Baseball commissioner Bud Selig (quoted in *The Baltimore Sun*, Nov. 7, 2001): "It makes no sense for Major League Baseball to be in markets that generate insufficient local revenues to justify the investment in the franchise." The Basic Agreement (2002–2006) between the owners and players specified that there be no contraction through 2006, and the players' union agreed not to contest the move if the owners decided to contract in 2007. Contraction was discussed in 1994 during labor negotiations, but it was not seriously considered. IST USE. 1969. "Gentlemen of baseball—practical men, as you think yourselves: Not in the name of sentiment, but in the name of absolute, hard-nosed, hardheaded pragmatism, the man you need may be Henry David Thoreau, and what you need may be, not expansion but contraction, not speed but the nourishment of old roots, not closer fences or lowered scoreboards but a renewed connection between the game and its essential followers" (Mark Harris, *The New York Times Magazine*, May 4, p.74).

contract-jumper A player who breaks his contract with one team to play with another team. The term got much play when members of the union known as the Brotherhood of Professional Base Ball Players formed their own Players' League in 1890 and several players quit their existing teams and joined new ones. When the new league folded, the contract-jumpers were allowed to rejoin their old teams without penalty. There have been other contract-jumpers in the 20th century, including the handful of players who joined the "outlaw" Mexican League in 1946. See also *jump*, 6; *jumper.* IST USE. 1891. "[A better course] would be the adoption of a rule by all base ball organizations refusing to recognize the contract of any club with a contract jumper. The sooner contract jumpers are weeded out of base ball the better it will be" (*St. Paul Daily News*, March 30).

contractor's back yard The bumpy or uneven surface of a poorly kept infield, used before the advent of modern groundskeeping techniques. See also *ash heap*; *Hogan's brickyard*; *home-brew field.*

contract year The period of a player's contract, from Dec. 12 of one year through and including Dec. 11 of the following year.

control The ability of a pitcher to throw strikes on a consistent basis to get ahead in the count or to keep from walking the batter; the pitcher's accuracy. The term also refers to a pitcher's ability to throw enough strikes to get batters to swing at balls out of the strike zone. Good control is "the pitcher's principal stock in trade" (Hugh S. Fullerton, *American Magazine*, June 1912). A good pitcher should be able to throw 70 percent of his pitches for strikes and to throw breaking pitches for strikes when behind in the count. See also *command*, 1; *location.* Syn. *placement.* IST USE. 1879. "[John Lynch] has complete control of the ball, with all the curves and various paces in delivery" (*New York Clipper*, Nov. 15; Peter Morris).

control artist Syn. of *control pitcher*.

controlled velocity The changing speed of a fastball in which the pitcher sometimes throws harder, then lets up a little, to enhance the pitcher's command.

control pitcher A pitcher known for his ability to issue few bases on balls; e.g., Greg Maddux. Bill James (*Baseball Abstract*, 1984) noted that pure control pitchers are those with low strikeout and low walk totals. Syn. *control artist*.

controman A modern name for an individual in baseball who always seems to get in trouble when talking to the press; a player who "creates controversy with his quotes" (*The Sporting News*, March 6, 1982).

Coogan's Bluff The name of the 115-foot-high craggy ridge or cliff behind the Polo Grounds in New York City, under which the backstop and seats behind home plate were situated. It was located on the fringe of Manhattan Island, bordering on the Harlem River at 157th Street and Eighth Avenue, where goats formerly grazed. Once synonymous with the name of the ballpark, it was sometimes also known as "Coogan's Hollow." ETYMOLOGY. Named for James Coogan, a prominent merchant and Manhattan's first borough president in 1899.

cookie 1. A pitch that is easy to hit; one that is easy to "get your teeth into." "If you fall behind [in the count], you have to give them [the batters] a cookie" (Baltimore Orioles pitcher José Mercedes, quoted in *The Baltimore Sun*, Aug. 25, 2000). "Hitters who feasted on thigh-high fastballs all summer won't see those cookies in the playoffs" (*ESPN The Magazine*, Sept. 23, 2003). **2.** Syn. of *run batted in* (Tom Verducci, *Sports Illustrated*, June 15, 1998).

cookie cutter A generic term for a circular, symmetrical, concrete, and bland ballpark built in the 1960s and 1970s and characterized by artificial surface, massive parking lots, a large capacity, and multipurpose functions (football games, rock concerts, evangelical crusades, truck rallies, etc.). Cookie cutters were antiseptic and not located in surrounding neighborhoods or urban settings but next to highway on-ramps; they were, however, great revenue producers. Broadcaster Ernie Harwell (quoted in *The Washington Post*, Aug. 9, 1984) observed, "They have no personality, like drugstores and shopping malls." Examples include Atlanta–Fulton County Stadium (Atlanta), Busch Stadium (St. Louis), Riverfront Stadium (Cincinnati), Three Rivers Stadium (Pittsburgh), and Vet-

Coogan's Bluff. The Polo Grounds as seen from Coogan's Bluff, 1909. *George Grantham Bain Collection, Library of Congress*

erans Stadium (Philadelphia). Mark Bowden (*Sports Illustrated*, March 15, 2004) wrote of Veterans Stadium, "It wasn't a ballpark, it was a venue, and as a venue it sort of worked." Michael Farber (*Sports Illustrated*, Nov. 28, 1996) characterized the cookie cutters as "the structural equivalent of the Nehru jacket." Compare *retropark*. Syn. *donut*, 3; *concrete donut*; *concrete ashtray*.

cookie jar 1. The location of the bat after a checked swing that is called a strike; e.g., "Smith's bat was in the cookie jar." 2. The supply of amphetamines controlled by the trainer. Tom House (*The Jock's Itch*, 1989, p.95): "I remember one player, a pitcher, who was greened up on a regular basis. He was always in the cookie jar."

coop Syn. of *dugout*. IST USE. 1908. "Player's bench or coop, the quarters provided for the players when they are not actively engaged on the field" (John B. Foster, in *Collier's New Dictionary of the English Language*).

co-op club 1. A minor-league club that agreed to develop players from several different major-league organizations rather than to serve as a farm club for a single major-league team. "As a co-op club, they're dependent on last-minute deals with major league teams who don't have room for all their signees on their Class A squads" (Ben Brown, *USA Today*, June 17, 1986). The Professional Baseball Agreement ratified after the 1996 season ended co-op clubs by guaranteeing every minor-league club a player development contract. Minor-league baseball's last co-op club was the Bakersfield Blaze of the California League in 1996. 2. *hist.* A club in the National Association of Professional Base Ball Players that split its share of gate revenues among other clubs. Peter Morris comments, "The co-op clubs were an unmitigated disaster for the National Association, being neither competitive nor financially viable, and almost always disbanding quickly. Some never played a single road game, simply arranging a few home games with established clubs, pocketing some money and disbanding. The established clubs were willing to do this because it meant an easy win, but the co-op clubs

seriously undermined the financial viability of the National Association."

Cooperstown 1. The town in New York State that is the traditional home of baseball and the location of the National Baseball Hall of Fame and Museum and of the National Baseball Library and Archives. The town was established in 1786 by Judge William Cooper, father of author James Fenimore Cooper. Syn. *Baseball's Valhalla*; *Baseball's Mecca*. 2. A synonym for the *National Baseball Hall of Fame and Museum*; e.g., "If he stays healthy, Dwight's [Gooden] on his way to Cooperstown" (Gary Carter, quoted in *Newsweek*, Sept. 2, 1985); "[Mike Piazza's] career statistics . . . put him on a path to Cooperstown" (*The Baltimore Sun*, May 23, 1998); and "The A's latest victory [19th in a row] was historic enough that Cooperstown noticed [by requesting manager Art Howe's lineup card]" (*The Baltimore Sun*, Sept. 3, 2002). EXTENDED USE. A great collection. "The size of the [International Piano Archives] is staggering. . . . Think of this as a Cooperstown for classical piano fans" (*The Baltimore Sun*, Dec. 7,1998).

Cooperstowner Syn. of *Hall of Famer.*

Cooperstown myth Syn. of *Doubleday myth.*

Cooperstown stuff Outstanding baseball-playing ability and statistics that are needed to be considered for election to the National Baseball Hall of Fame.

cop To win a game or a pennant. "Though the New York Highlanders have both a Chance and a Chase in their lineup, it does not appear that they have a 'Chance' to cop the American League bunting or much of a show to give any of the other clubs a 'Chase' for it" (*San Francisco Bulletin*, May 17, 1913; Gerald L. Cohen). IST USE. 1907 (*Lajoie's Official Baseball Guide*, p.13; Edward J. Nichols).

co-plan The practice of Negro league clubs during the Depression by which management received 25 to 30 percent of the net profits of a game and the remainder was allotted to the players. Taking players off fixed salaries caused player income to become increasingly unstable: "players on co-plan teams might earn $100–$125 a month, although they were also responsible for their own room and board" (Neil J. Lanctot, *Negro League Baseball*, 2004, p.16; Peter Morris).

cop off *hist.* To get a hit. "Elmer Zacher . . . copped off three safe drives" (*San Francisco Bulletin*, March 21, 1913; Gerald L. Cohen).

COR Abbrev. for *coefficient of restitution.*

corecreational Describing a team or league in which both sexes participate. *Syn.* "corec."

cork **1.** *n.* A team's most effective relief pitcher; a stopper. "The expression became popular with Ted Wilks, who choked off many rallies as a relief pitcher for the St. Louis Cardinals in the 1940s" (Zander Hollander, *Baseball Lingo*, 1967). **2.** *v.* To doctor a bat with cork. See also *corking.* **3.** *v.* To hit a ball hard; e.g., "O'Day corked the ball to right, for a base" (*The World* [New York], Sept. 5, 1889; Gerald L. Cohen). IST USE. 1870. "The Actives took hold of Sanders' pitching from the start, and, when Whittemore and Sawyer put in the 'droppers,' they 'corked' the ball harder than ever" (*Chicago Tribune*, July 30; Peter Morris).

corkball **1.** A variation of baseball that has been played in the St. Louis, Mo., area since the early 1900s. The ball is cork-centered, weighs 1¼ ounces, and is 6¼ inches in circumference. The bat cannot be any longer than 38 inches and its diameter cannot be thicker than that of the ball. Corkball is normally played inside a cage that is about 75 feet long and about 20 feet wide. Teams usually have five players, but can have as few as two—a pitcher and a catcher. Two strikes constitute an out, five balls is a walk, and a hit is any ball landing in fair territory. Four walks, four hits, or a combination thereof constitute a run (there is no baserunning). Each additional walk or hit in the same inning adds a run. There are five innings in a game and three outs to an inning. A batter is out if he hits a foul ball, or hits a fair ball that is caught before hitting the ground or the cage. There are several corkball leagues in and around St. Louis and Memphis. Announcer Tim McCarver (*Oh, Baby, I Love It!*, 1987), a former major-league catcher, noted that when he was a youngster in Memphis, "I got an early start on my announcing career while playing corkball, imitating Harry Caray on the play-by-play." **2.** A similar game played in the Olympia mill village of Columbia, S.C. According to John Ruoff (personal communication, Jan. 24, 2002), the game is played with a broomstick for a bat and a bottle cork wrapped in adhesive tape for a ball (the original "cork" may have been a wooden bobbin from the textile mill). A team consists of a pitcher (throwing underhand) and a catcher. The batter hits from the opposite of his normal handedness. Outs are recorded when a ball hit in the air is caught by the pitcher or if the batter swings and misses and the ball is caught by the catcher. There are two outs to an inning. A hit is anything hit past the pitcher and a run is anything hit over the fence. The team with the most runs and hits after three innings is the winner. **3.** A similar game played in the midwestern United States. According to Tim Wiles (personal communication, Jan. 23, 2002), the game is played with a tennis ball, a pitcher and one or more fielders, and a batter. If the batter swings and misses, or if the pitch hits a strike zone spray-painted on a brick wall, it is a strike. A grounder fielded cleanly is an out, as is a liner or fly caught in the air. A grounder past the pitcher is a single. Doubles, triples, and home runs have to travel in the air past specified points. After an out, the fielder becomes the pitcher, the pitcher becomes the batter, and the batter becomes the fielder. See also *wallball.*

cork center Ground-up cork with a heavy covering of pure India rubber upon which strands of yarn are wound, replacing the baseball's previous solid rubber-centered core. Invented and patented by Benjamin F. Shibe on June 15, 1909 (patent number 924,696; a second patent—932,911—for a variant was granted on Aug. 31, 1909), the cork-centered ball was more rigid and durable than the rubber-centered ball, with greater elasticity and resiliency as the outer layers of yarn were wound under greater tension. It was introduced in the 1910 season and used in the 1910 World Series, and became official for the 1911 season. The livelier ball appreciably increased the batting averages in both major leagues by some 20 points. The first ad for the cork-centered ball appeared in *The Sporting News* (May 12, 1910; Robert H. Schaefer): "Big Improvement Made in Base Balls. A.J. Reach Company Patents a Cork Core, supplanting the rubber center, and producing the finest ball ever known. More rigid and durable, will absolutely keep its shape." *The Sporting News* (July 28, 1910; Peter Morris) reported, "This season the manufacturers have proof of the assertion that of 280 clubs over the country using the cork-center ball, not one has been returned from losing its shape." Hugh Jennings (quoted in *The Sporting News*, May 25, 1911; Robert H. Schaefer): "These lively [cork center] balls come at infielders like rifle shots." See also *cushioned cork center.* IST USE. 1910. "Manufacturers of the American League official baseball have announced that this year's ball has a cork instead of a rubber center. . . . The makers say the cork center has resulted in a much livelier baseball" (*Los Angeles Times*, May 8; Peter Morris). ETYMOLOGY. According to a 1987 press release from Rawlings, the idea of a cork center can be traced back to 1863 when an Englishman named Weeks patented a cork-center ball for cricket. The cork center was used in baseballs circa 1900, but without a buffering layer of rubber, the wool yarn would swell after the ball was made.

corked bat A *doctored bat* that has been partially drilled axially at the barrel end to create a hole that is filled with cork, rubber, or any of several other substances for the purpose of giving the batter an added advantage over the pitcher. A corked bat is lighter (by one or two ounces, depending on the dimensions of the hole and the density of the filling substances) and easier to swing with more control as the center of gravity of the bat moves closer to the hands; however, a corked bat transfers less energy to the ball, thereby taking speed and distance off the hit. Physicist Robert K. Adair contends that a corked bat may reduce by about three feet what would have been a 375-foot drive with a conventional wooden bat: "there's probably more superstition involved" (quoted in *The Baltimore Sun*, June 5, 2003). A study at the Baseball Research Center at the Univ. of Massachusetts–Lowell found the speed of corked bats increased just

more than one mile per hour or about one percent. Norm Cash, who won the 1961 American League batting title (.361 average), later admitted he used such a bat. See also *corking*, 1.

corker 1. One who corks a bat. **2.** A hard-hit ball. "Sam Thompson had three corkers in addition to his triple, which were captured by fine fielding" (*Detroit Free Press*, March 25, 1887). IST USE. 1861. "A 'corker' to right field" (*New York Clipper*, Aug. 3; Peter Morris). **3.** *hist.* An excellent or remarkable play, player, or team. "Slattery's catch was a corker" (*The World* [New York], Aug. 17, 1890; Gerald L. Cohen). St. Louis Cardinals manager John McCloskey, commenting on the Pittsburgh Pirates (*Pittsburgh Post*, June 30, 1908): "Fred Clarke's family must have our goat. His club is a corker." IST USE. 1867 (*New York Herald*, Aug. 27; Edward J. Nichols).

corking 1. *n. Doctoring* a bat with cork to make the bat lighter and increase bat speed. Corking involves drilling a hole up to one inch in diameter and 6 to 12 inches deep in the head or barrel of the bat, filling the hole with ground-up cork, rubber balls, sawdust, or other lightweight material, inserting a dowel in the hole to compress the substances, replacing the top section (matching the grain) with a plug of wood shavings and glue, sanding it down, and painting, staining, or dyeing it to remove evidence of tampering. Some corked bats have voids in the drilled hole. There are two theories as to the benefits of corking a bat: 1) the nature of the cork acts as a springboard, allowing the batter to hit the ball farther; and 2) the reduction in weight (about 2 ounces) in the barrel of the bat allows the batter the advantage of a faster swing. As with doctoring a ball, any such bat tampering is expressly illegal, but not uncommon. The practice of corking a bat goes back a long way: "In 1865 and 1866 a perfect frenzy of ball-playing swept over the United States. . . . [One] team bore vast round beams of bass-wood as large as a man's thigh, bored out and charged with cork to make them light" (*New York Evening Post*, reprinted in the *Detroit Free Press*, May 23, 1883; Peter Morris). Owing to Babe Ruth's success with massive bats, very little corking was done from the 1920s to the 1950s; but when batters believed that bat speed generated more force than bat weight, corking was revitalized. See also *corked bat.* **2.** *adj.* Excellent. "[Chicago White Sox manager Nixey] Callahan believes he has a corking team this year" (*San Francisco Bulletin*, March 1, 1913; Gerald L. Cohen). IST USE. 1905. "The Cleveland team has a corking good infield" (*Louisville Courier Journal*, quoted in *The Washington Post*, Apr. 9).

cork popper Syn. of *Opening Day.*

corkscrew arm A left-handed baseball player.

corkscrew ball Syn. of *screwball,* 2.

corkscrew delivery A pitcher's delivery in which he turns his back to the batter and swings his body completely around before throwing with a sidearm motion. Addie Joss employed such a delivery.

corkscrew-er *hist.* A tricky curveball. "And how did you like that corkscrew-er?" (Arthur E. McFarlane, *Redney McGaw*, 1909; Peter Tamony).

corkscrew twist A curveball that changes or appears to change direction more than once. IST USE. 1891 (*Chicago Herald*, May 8; Edward J. Nichols).

corner 1. One of the two parallel sides of home plate that provides the umpire with a visual basis for determining the inside and outside edges of the strike zone. To be successful, a pitcher must keep his pitches "on the corner" where they are more difficult for the batter to hit. Syn. *edge,* 4. IST USE. 1901 (Burt L. Standish, *Frank Merriwell's School Days*, p.242; Edward J. Nichols). **2.** The point where a foul line meets the outfield fence or wall. **3.** Left field or right field. **4.** First base or third base. **5.** *hist.* Any base. "[Pinky] Lindsay's slash to right for two corners" (*Chicago Tribune*, May 4, 1906; Peter Morris). IST USE. 1891 (*Chicago Herald*, May 5; Edward J. Nichols).

corner clipper A pitch that crosses over the edge of home plate. Syn. "corner cutter." IST USE. 1913 (*Harper's Weekly*, Sept. 6, p.20; Edward J. Nichols).

corner infielder The first baseman or the third baseman.

cornerman 1. The first baseman or the third baseman. **2.** The umpire at first base or at third base.

corner outfielder The right fielder or the left fielder. Syn. *wing outfielder.*

corps See *mound corps.* IST USE. 1902 (*The Sporting Life*, Apr. 26, p.9; Edward J. Nichols).

corral 1. To catch or field a ball. IST USE. 1908. "Corralled, colloquialism for catching the ball accurately, fielding it accurately" (John B. Foster, in *Collier's New Dictionary of the English Language*). **2.** To collect accomplishments. IST USE. 1908. "Corralled ... to note the number of plays gained by a player during a contest" (John B. Foster, in *Collier's New Dictionary of the English Language*).

correction A term used by baseball executives for the fall of attendance and general interest in the game following a strike or work stoppage. Milwaukee Brewers manager of television operations Tim Van Wagoner termed the strike that ended in 1995 "our industry correction" (*Milwaukee Journal Sentinel*, Sept. 19, 1997).

corredor Spanish for "runner."

corredor emergente Spanish for "pinch runner."

Corsairs Nickname for the Pittsburgh *Pirates.* IST USE. 1913 (*The Sporting Life*, Sept. 6; Peter Morris).

cotton ball Wiffle ball played with a cloth practice golf ball.

couldn't hit . . . The beginning of any of several highly exaggerated taunts to typify a player who does not do well at the plate; e.g., "he couldn't hit the inside of a barn" or "he couldn't hit a bull in the ass with a shovel." On an Oct. 9, 1982, telecast, Tommy Lasorda said Willie Miranda "couldn't hit water if he fell out of a boat." Harry J. Casey (*Baseball Magazine*, Feb. 1912; Peter Morris): "No line of caste or class prevents the gilded youth from assenting gravely when the ragged Mickey declares, 'Dat guy dere couldn't hit it with a broom.'" A variation is "he couldn't knock skin off rice pudding." Similar taunts and insults are used in other realms, from prizefighting ("couldn't punch his way out of a paper bag") to selling ("couldn't sell ice water in hell") and are not a baseball exclusive. IST USE. 1900. Describing the nonstop stream of chatter indulged in by Jack Dunn while pitching: "Here comes Del. . . . The [expletive deleted] couldn't hit a balloon. Back to the woods with you and get a reputation" (*Brooklyn Eagle*, May 13; Peter Morris).

count 1. *n.* The tally of balls and strikes charged to a batter at any given moment. It is always given with the number of balls followed by the number of strikes; e.g., "three balls and two strikes" or "3 and 2." The count is determined and kept track of by the home plate umpire. IST USE. 1913. Describing the strategy of the runner on third base breaking for the plate with the bases loaded and three balls on the batter: "This would trick any except a foxy pitcher into forgetting the count and playing for that runner by pitching where the catcher could tag him" (*The Washington Post*, Sept. 7; Peter Morris). **2.** *n.* The paid attendance at the ballpark. **3.** *n./hist.* Syn. of *ace*, 1. IST USE. 1845. "The game to consist of twenty-one counts, or aces; but at the conclusion an equal number of hands must be played" (Knickerbocker Rules, Rule 8th, Sept. 23). **4.** *n.* The score of a baseball game. "[Chicago pulled] out victory in the third game of the local series by a count of 3 to 2" (*Chicago Tribune*, Aug. 1, 1905; Peter Morris). **5.** *v.* To score a run. "[Jim] Fogarty made a hit and went to third on a single by [Arthur] Irwin, both counting on a two-base hit by [Ed] Dailey [*sic*, spelled Daily]" (*The North American* [Philadelphia], Aug. 4, 1886).

counter 1. *hist.* A run. "A pair of counters came through on two hits and a classy exhibition of base running" (*The Washington Post*, May 21, 1921). IST USE. 1917. "The hit that drove over the counter against [Babe] Ruth was a fluke" (*The Sporting Life*, May 19; Peter Morris). **2.** Syn. of *indicator*, 1. **3.** [softball term] A scored run; one that counts. Because home runs over a certain limit are

now counted in some forms of softball, this term has relevance.

counting house *hist.* Syn. of *home plate*. IST USE. 1910 (*Baseball Magazine*, April; Edward J. Nichols).

counting pan *hist.* Syn. of *home plate*. IST USE. 1904 (*The Washington Post*, Aug. 16; Peter Morris).

counting station *hist.* Syn. of *home plate*. IST USE. 1904. "[Ed] McFarland's one-base blow sent [George] Davis to the counting station" (*The Washington Post*; Sept. 3; Peter Morris).

"counting your money?" Once a common belittling remark hollered at a runner picked off base.

country Solid or powerful; e.g., Hank Greenberg was "a good country hitter" (*Time* magazine, Nov. 20, 1950; Peter Tamony). A team devoid of finesse and dominated by power is said to play "country hardball."

country club 1. A derogatory term for a team that has little discipline or has members playing for themselves rather than the team; a team with "great skill but without the normal barbed humor and collective wisdom that winning teams must have" (George Vecsey, *The New York Times*, Oct. 28, 1986). The Boston Red Sox prior to the "Impossible Dream" year in 1967 was regarded as a country-club team. "The years 1961–66 . . . was the peak of 'Boston Country Club' years, when spoiled, pampered players devoured managers . . . and finished sixth, eighth, seventh, eighth, ninth, and ninth while leading the league in closing times honored and signs missed" (Bob Ryan, *The Boston Globe*, Dec. 22, 1999). **2.** *hist.* A club in the 1860s, and often subsequently, usually from a small rural area, that would have no chance competing against one from a big city. William J. Ryczek (*When Johnny Came Sliding Home*, 1998): "The term 'country club' was a derisive one used principally by the top New York teams and the press to refer to those clubs arising in small, remote hamlets rather than traditional baseball centers such as New York, Philadelphia, and Washington. Teams from the city were not supposed to lose to 'country clubs.'" *The Atchison* [Kans.] *Daily Globe* (March 2, 1887) noted that Californian pitcher George Van Haltren will find that National League clubs "will hit him harder than the country clubs of California." IST USE. 1864. "The Atlantics then began their second innings, and having got the range of Clyde's pitching, the way they went in to astonish both natives and foreigners was a caution to ye country clubs" (*New York Clipper*, Oct. 1; Peter Morris).

country mile The long distance traveled by a batted ball. "He is the answer to a scout's prayer. He can throw a baseball into a barrel at 100 yards, is a ten-second sprint man and can hit a ball a country mile" (*Saturday Evening Post*, March 9, 1935; Peter Tamony). EXTENDED USE. A good distance for anything, from a golf ball to a thrown football.

country sinker A spitball. "That new-old pitch, the 'country sinker,' which you and I know as the spitball" (Arnold Hano, *Roberto Clemente: Batting King*, 1968, p.10).

count the stitches 1. To look at a slowly pitched ball as it drifts to the plate. ETYMOLOGY. The term is based on an exaggerated notion because it would be impossible to see the individual stitches on any pitched ball, no matter how slow. As a matter of fact, there are 216 stitches on a regulation baseball. **2.** To pitch a ball so slowly that one is said to be able to count the stitches as the ball approaches the plate. IST USE. 1909 (Zane Grey, *The Short-Stop*, p.89; Edward J. Nichols).

county-fair player A player who shows off; a grandstand player. IST USE. 1933 (Walter Winchell, *Havana Evening Telegram*, Apr. 11).

courtesy runner 1. A substitute who is allowed to run for an injured player without removing that player from the game. Courtesy runners were allowed, if the opposing manager consented, in the major leagues until 1950. **2.** [softball term] A player who runs for a baserunner without a charged substitution. A player may be a courtesy runner only once per inning. A courtesy runner whose turn at bat comes while he or she is on base will be declared out and removed from the base, but can come to bat.

courtesy trot The perfunctory jog toward the wall by an outfielder on a long home run. The outfielder "spares his pitcher some embarrassment by making it look like there was a chance to catch the ball" (Zack Hample, *Watching Baseball Smarter*, 2007, p.203).

cousin 1. A particular pitcher whom a hitter consistently finds easy to hit; a hitter's favorite pitcher. "To [Fred] Lynn, [Jim] Slaton is like a favorite cousin who just doesn't get to town often enough" (Tom Marr, WFBR broadcast, May 22, 1986, following a Lynn home run off Slaton). See also *coz*; *lamb*, 2. IST USE. 1928. "Yeah they was all callin' him 'Cousin Dick'" (said of a pitcher who had just been yanked, in T.A. "TAD" Dorgan's column "Outdoor Sports," *San Francisco Call & Post*, Aug. 23; Peter Tamony). The term also appears in *Babe Ruth's Own Book of Baseball* (1928), with Ruth stating that pitcher Paul Zahniser "was a 'cousin' of mine . . . every time he pitched against us I knew I would get two or three hits and so did he." ETYMOLOGY. The term has been widely attributed to New York Yankees pitcher Waite Hoyt, who likened certain batters who faced him to cooperative family members. It was apparently a term more commonly used by players than writers in its early days. William G. Brandt (*Baseball Magazine*, Oct. 1932) listed it as one of the terms "unfamiliar to the public"; in making it "public" Brandt wrote, "Every batter has a list of 'cousins,' pitchers whose deliveries he finds comparatively easy to slap upon the nostrils." **2.** A hitter whom a pitcher finds easy to strike out. **3.** A team that another team consistently defeats, such as the Kansas City Royals who were cousins to the Baltimore Orioles in a period between May 1969 and Aug. 1970, when the Royals were beaten 23 times in a row. "The Boston Red Sox were what baseball men call 'cousins' to the winning Senators, dropping seventeen and capturing only four" (*San Francisco Chronicle*, Sept. 22, 1933). EXTENDED USE. An easy opponent in other sports. An article on how basketball player Bob Lanier commonly scored many points when he played against the Portland Trail Blazers was headlined "Piston Center Finds Cousins" (*San Francisco Examiner*, Nov. 29, 1972; Peter Tamony).

cover 1. *v.* To protect a base from an advancing runner by positioning oneself on or near it. "As a good infielder, you must . . . be ever alert to cover a base when the play calls for it" (Joe Gargan, *Athletic Journal*, May 1944). IST USE. 1861 (*New York Sunday Mercury*, Aug. 10; Edward J. Nichols). **2.** *v.* To protect efficiently a section of the playing area; e.g., great outfielders are known for their ability to "cover" a large part of the outfield. "Beals Becker . . . will cover right field for the Rhinelanders this season" (*San Francisco Bulletin*, March 22, 1913; Gerald L. Cohen). The ultimate compliment of this nature may have been issued by Ralph Kiner, who once said, "The earth is two-thirds covered by water, and the other one-third is covered by Garry Maddox." See also *cover ground*. **3.** *v.* For a pitcher to hide the ball that is about to be pitched so that the grip cannot be spotted and interpreted by the opposition. Some gloves have a tightly woven, basket-style webbing to help hide the ball. **4.** *n.* The leather material that fits snugly over the innards of a baseball. Sheepskin, horsehide, and cowhide have been used. **5.** *v.* To hit a long ball. "[The batter] covered the whole ball with the bat" (Dick Kaegel, *The Seattle Times*, Sept. 18, 1988).

cover ground To run across a large amount of the field. See also *cover*, 2. IST USE. 1870. "Jimmy Wood . . . covered as much ground as three ordinary players" (*Chicago Tribune*, July 15; Peter Morris).

covering up *hist.* The practice by which a major-league club purchased a player from a minor-league club before the *drafting season* opened, held the player until the following spring, and then sold the player back to the original club without giving the player a trial on the field. The National Commission adopted rules in March 1906 to prevent covering up and established a scale of fines. IST USE. 1898. "It is ludicrous to hear a howl from Indianapolis regarding 'covering up' of minor leaguers. This offense is charged against Connie Mack by the Brushville management [John T. Brush owned both Indianapolis and Cincinnati, and used Indianapolis as a farm club for Cincinnati]. It would come with better grace from any other baseball

town in the country" (*Milwaukee Journal*, Apr. 19; Peter Morris).

cover man The second baseman or the shortstop who will cover second base when the ball is hit or thrown to that location. Before the pitch, the players agree as to who should be the cover man.

coward's model A large, fat baseball bat.

"cowboy up" Boston Red Sox first baseman Kevin Millar's cocky motto for the resilient 2003 Red Sox. The phrase, which originated in the world of rodeo, was adopted by the team and its fans after the Texas-born Millar told reporters, "I want to see somebody cowboy up and stand behind this team and quit worrying about all the negative stuff" (*The Boston Globe*, Sept. 24, 2003).

cow-catcher home run A home run into the triangular net in left field at Braves Field in Boston (Walter K. Putney, *Baseball Stories*, Spring 1952).

cowhide 1. The baseball. **2.** The covering of the baseball. Horsehide was the official cover material from 1880 until baseball commissioner Bowie Kuhn authorized the use of cowhide in 1974. See also *horsehide*, 2.

cowhide joyride A home run.

cow pasture A derogatory term for a field that is in poor playing condition.

cow pasture league A derogatory term for a semipro or very low minor league. IST USE. 1917. "Ben Lawrence, recently secured from a cow pasture league in Minnesota" (*Mansfield* [Ohio] *News*, Feb. 13; Peter Morris).

cow's horn A curveball.

cowtail To take a cowtail swing. "No poet, however great, could describe my sensation when I cowtailed a pitch for my third single of the day—the game-breaking hit" (Ty Cobb, *My Life in Baseball*, 1961).

cowtailer A batter who takes a cowtail swing.

cowtail swing A long swing of a bat held at the very end of the handle, resembling the looping motion of a cow swishing its tail.

coz Short for *cousin*, 1. A batter facing his favorite pitcher may greet him with "Hello, Coz" (*Saturday Review of Literature*, Aug. 26, 1933).

cozy roller *hist.* A slowly batted ground ball. IST USE. 1907 (*New York Evening Journal*, June 5; Edward J. Nichols).

cp and nc Scouting report shorthand for "can't play and no chance." "Bad even in wartime baseball . . . cp and nc" (Frank Cashen, of his mid-'40s run as a second baseman for Loyola College in his native Baltimore, quoted in Ken Denlinger, *The Washington Post*, Oct. 7, 1986).

CPI Abbrev. for *clutch pitching index.*

crab 1. A player who finds fault with others; a complainer; a grouch. Johnny Evers' nickname, "The Crab," was originally bestowed due to his unorthodox manner of sidling over to ground balls before gathering them, but it also referred to his temperament: "Evers developed a reputation as a troublemaker by squabbling regularly with teammates, opponents, and especially umpires" (David Shiner, in SABR, *Deadball Stars of the National League*, 2004). See also *human crab.* USAGE NOTE. Although this slang meaning of "crab" predates baseball, it was so commonly used in baseball circles in the early 20th century that it was considered to be a baseball term. "Many of the worst 'crabs' in baseball are the pleasantest and most genial when off the field, their crabbedness evidently being the result of the nervous strain of playing" (Hugh S. Fullerton, *American Magazine*, June 1912). **2.** A competitive ballplayer. "A crab, in baseball vernacular, is one who is fighting so hard all the time to win that he refuses to see anything good on the opposing team or in any play that does not work out to the advantage of his side. In other words, he's out there with the determination to win so thoroughly imbued in him that he never, never whistles in the clubhouse after losing a game" (*Indianapolis Star*, March 28, 1916; Peter Morris). IST USE. 1877. "Ten years ago I was a big crab on the field; shortstop, you know" (*Milwaukee Daily Sentinel*, Oct. 30). USAGE NOTE. The term "crab" (indicating a complainer) gradually assumed positive connotations as competitiveness became a more valued trait both in baseball and in American society.

crack 1. *n.* See *crack of the bat.* **2.** *n.* A baseball bat that has a crack in it. **3.** *n.* A time at bat. "The old boy never hesitated to grab a stick and face the opposing pitcher for the one and deciding crack" (*San Francisco Bulletin*, March 18, 1913; Gerald L. Cohen). **4.** *n.* A swing at a pitched ball. "Everybody in the Wolves' lineup took a crack at the horsehide" (*San Francisco Bulletin*, Apr. 30, 1913; Gerald L. Cohen). **5.** *n.* A batted ball. "[Harry] Wolverton followed with a crack toward [Joe] Kelley" (*Boston Daily*, June 16, 1905). IST USE. 1901 (Burt L. Standish, *Frank Merriwell's Marvel*, p.215; Edward J. Nichols). **6.** *v.* To get a solid hit. "Coy cracked one of Stroud's pitches out of the lot" (*San Francisco Bulletin*, May 30, 1913; Gerald L. Cohen). IST USE. 1905 (*The Sporting Life*, Sept. 2, p.12; Edward J. Nichols). **7.** *adj.* Exhibiting excellence. "During his career as a player [John] McGraw was a crack third baseman" (*San Francisco Bulletin*, Apr. 7, 1913; Gerald L. Cohen). See also *cracking.* IST USE. 1861 (*New York Sunday Mercury*, Aug. 10; Edward J. Nichols). **8.** *n.* An excellent player. "[San Francisco fans] believe if California couldn't have players as skillful as the Eastern cracks, that the game shouldn't be supported" (*The Washington Post*, July 8, 1896). **9.** *v.* To weaken or decline in playing ability, esp. pitching (Maurice H. Weseen, *A Dictionary of American Slang*, 1934). IST USE. 1911 (*Baseball Magazine*, October, p.46; Edward J. Nichols).

crackerbox A small, old ballpark. Writer Charles Einstein (letter, March 5, 1990) compares "crackerbox" to *bandbox*: "It connotes the same small area as bandbox, but where bandbox also has the feel of the neat and immaculate, crackerbox denotes the exact opposite—the dilapidated, crumbling state, often beyond repair, that so often characterized the small-town or old-time stadium and led to its eventual replacement."

crackerjack A first-rate or spectacular player or team. "Shannon is putting up a beautiful game at second base. He is the cracker-jack of the association, all points considered" (*New York Sporting Times*, July 11, 1891, p.5; Barry Popik). "Good players of all kinds are wanted by every manager, but a 'crackerjack' third baseman has a strangle hold on his job as long as he bats .200 or better" (S. DeWitt

Clough, *Letters From a Baseball Fan to His Son*, 1910). Sometimes spelled "crack-a-jack" in early usages. IST USE. 1888. "Gov. Hill will be among those who will attend the opening game at the Polo Grounds to-morrow. . . . The Governor thinks Danny Richardson is a 'Cracker Jack' and Dan thinks the Governor is the greatest man in the country" (*The World* [New York], Apr. 24; Gerald L. Cohen). ETYMOLOGY. The term was in use for many years as slang for a sailor's biscuit using salted meat or anything first-rate or excellent. It was applied in horse racing: "Tom Stevens brings two cracker-jack two-year-olds from Mobile, so the touts say, in Wary and Poteen" (*Spirit of the Times*, May 1, 1886; Peter Tamony). The term did not come into its own until 1896, when the firm of F.W. Rueckheim and Brother of Chicago started selling a confection of caramel-coated popcorn and peanuts under the name and trademark "Cracker Jack." (It had been sold as early as the Columbian Exposition in Chicago in 1893, but without the name.) Before long, it was a baseball park staple (along with peanuts and popcorn) and became embedded in the national psyche in the song "Take Me Out to the Ball Game" (1908). In *Mr. Dooley's Opinions* (1910) by Finley Peter Dunne, we read: "A good seat on th' bleachers, a bottle hand f'r a neefaryous decision at first base an' a bag iv' crackerjack was a far as iver I got tow're bein' a sportin' character an' look at me now!"

cracking Exhibiting excellence. "Elmer Meredith was a cracking good pitcher" (*San Francisco Bulletin*, May 16, 1913; Gerald L. Cohen). See also *crack*, 7.

crack of the bat The sound made when the bat contacts a pitched ball. "[Joe Tobin] speeded across the field with the crack of the bat and captured a seemingly safe drive to deep left" (*San Francisco Bulletin*, March 26, 1913; Gerald L. Cohen).

cradle 1. *n.* A training device built of long, cupped wooden slats used to sharpen the reflexes of infielders. It is shaped like a large cradle, and balls are thrown into it so they will carom off at odd and unpredictable angles. 2. *v.* To use the arms and chest to field

a ball, as a mother cradles a baby in her arms. "You'll see him [Cal Ripken Jr.] cradle the ball a lot" (*Baseball Digest*, Dec. 1983).

cradle-snatcher A scout or bird dog who trails extremely young prospects.

crafty Said of certain skillful and cunning left-handed pitchers of small stature, such as Whitey Ford and Bobby Shantz. "[Rick] Krivda pitched superbly, in the classic style of a crafty left-hander: off-speed stuff away to get the hitters reaching over the plate, and fastballs inside" (*The Baltimore Sun*, Sept. 26, 1996).

crank 1. *n./hist.* A baseball fan in the late 19th century. "There is living in Camden, N.J., a crank named Farnham, who . . . imagines that he invented the national game and should receive a royalty on every game played. He seems rational on all other points" (*The Sporting Life*, Jan. 23, 1884; Peter Morris). "The real, simon-pure baseball crank . . . thinks baseball, talks baseball, dreams base-

THE BASE BALL CRANK
He's a howling megaphone, a human idiot,
When will he cease to talk unmitigated rot,
When will he stop his senseless howl
Of strike and base and home and foul.
He talks of nothing else but ball,
That is he does not talk, he can only bawl.

Crank. Postcard. *Ron Menchine Collection*

ball and, in fact, does all but play it. It is generally a fact that the real baseball crank cannot play right-field in even a 'scrub nine'" (*Milwaukee Sentinel*, Oct. 12, 1884). In his work on baseball slang used in *The World* (New York) in the 1880s, Gerald L. Cohen (*Studies in Slang*, part 2, 1989) reported, "At least from 1887 through 1890 the standard term in NYC [New York City] for a baseball fan was a 'crank,' short for 'baseball crank.' During this span I recall seeing only one unambiguous attestation of 'fan.'" IST USE. 1882. Cohen found other references to the term from 1882 to at least 1913; e.g., "Let the cranks rejoice, the small boys yell, and the girls look happy, for the Giants have won a ball game" (*The World* [New York], May 11, 1890). USAGE NOTE. The term has been commonly, but inaccurately, invoked vintage baseball clubs for matches using rules from the 1860s and 1870s. ETYMOLOGY. Derived from the German "krank" for "sick," as well as 16th-century English for "crook" or "bend" and British dialect for "lively" or "high-spirited." The term was popularized in Dec. 1881 during the trial of Charles J. Guiteau, the crazed assassin of President James A. Garfield; it immediately spread to one obsessed with baseball. See also *crankess*; *crankism*; *krank*. **2.** *n.* A ballplayer with peculiarities. "Nearly every ball player in the profession has his little hobbies and eccentricities, and they are playfully called 'cranks' by their fellow-players" (*The Sporting Life*, July 18, 1891; Peter Morris). **3.** *v.* To pitch. "Max Surkont cranked his sixteenth victory of the . . . season tonight" (*San Francisco News*, Aug. 5, 1950; Peter Tamony). **4.** *v.* To hit the ball for a long distance, usually a home run. "On Sept. 6, [1996, Eddie] Murray cranked homer No. 500" (*The Baltimore Sun*, Aug. 2, 2003).

crankess *hist.* A female *crank*. Gerald L. Cohen (*Studies in Slang*, part 2, 1989) labeled the term a "humorous and artificial creation" and gave this example from *The World* (New York) (May 24, 1890): "It was 'ladies' day' at the grounds, and . . . about five hundred crankesses took advantage of the Giants' invitation to see the game."

crankism *hist.* Eccentric behavior by a baseball fan, based on adherence to an obsession that is often delusional. "The man with the brilliant idea [suggesting to Detroit players that the team use their pitchers as catchers and vice versa] skipped with celerity, remarking . . . that people who spurned valuable suggestions would never get along in the world. He was the most severe case of base ball crankism ever met with" (*Detroit Free Press*, Apr. 26, 1902; Peter Morris). "The surprisingly good work by the New York team has finally put to rest all adverse criticism, and even those persons who are soaked and sodden with crankism are at last losing sight of their *ignis fatuus* in the broad glow of hope which the Giants are shedding" (*The World* [New York], Aug. 5, 1888; Gerald L. Cohen).

crank it up To pitch better than normal. "It looked like he really cranked it up" (New York Yankees manager Joe Torre, commenting after Hideki Irabu struck out a career-high 12 batters in pitching a complete game, quoted in *The New York Times*, Aug. 1, 1999; Peter Morris). See also *crank up*, 1.

crank up **1.** To wind up to deliver a pitch. See also *crank it up*. **2.** To hit the ball. "I don't want him [Kenny Lofton] to start cranking up and thinking he's a big power hitter" (Cleveland Indians manager Charlie Manuel, quoted in *The Baltimore Sun*, Apr. 4, 2000).

crash **1.** *v.* To hit a ball very hard. "[Kirk Gibson] crashed a towering home run over the right-field fence to win the game" (Bruce Chadwick, *The Dodgers*, 1993, p.142). **2.** *v./hist.* For a team to make successive hits. Hugh S. Fullerton (*American Magazine*, June 1912) wrote, "Verb used in baseball, not to signify a single sound, but a series of hard hits. A team 'starts crashing,' when three or four batters in succession make hits." Today, the term would suggest a team that was falling apart. **3.** *n./hist.* A hard batted ball. IST USE. 1912 (*Outing Magazine*, June, p.360; Edward J. Nichols).

Crawfords Nickname for an African-American franchise in Pittsburgh, Pa., originally formed as an independent club (1931–1932) and later a member of the Negro National League (1933–1938). The 1935 team is generally regarded as the greatest black team of all time. Star players included

Cool Papa Bell, Oscar Charleston, Josh Gibson, Judy Johnson, and Satchel Paige. The franchise moved to the Negro American League in Toledo, Ohio (1939), and Indianapolis (1940). Named for a bathhouse in Pittsburgh.

cream To hit a ball hard.

cream puff An easy ball to hit, such as one thrown by a batting-practice pitcher. Joseph "Stretch" Suba, a batting-practice pitcher, served up "big, fat, medium fast cream puffs for the All-Star hitters to feast on" (Mickey Herskowitz, *Houston Post*, July 15, 1986; Charles D. Poe). See also *Cuban sandwich*.

cream-puff hitter A weak hitter, one who is not a power hitter.

crease An obvious paper wrinkle on a baseball card, usually caused by bending the card. Creases are a key factor in determining a card's grade and value.

credit account Syn. of *batting average*. "Cartwright isn't far behind with a mark of .297 and Jimmy Johnston comes next with a credit account of .267" (*San Francisco Bulletin*, May 6, 1913; Gerald L. Cohen).

creeping La Russaism The trend toward micromanaging. The evocative term was coined by Boston sportswriter Bob Ryan in reference to St. Louis Cardinals manager Tony La Russa.

crest *hist.* Syn. of *mound*, 1 (*The Sporting News*, Oct. 30, 1913).

crew 1. The group of umpires working a particular game. 2. See *ground crew*. 3. A baseball team (Maurice H. Weseen, *A Dictionary of American Slang*, 1934).

crew chief The umpire in charge of an umpiring crew. He supervises the work of the umpires assigned to his team. When he works behind the plate, he assumes the duties of the *umpire-in-chief.*

cricket An English game, similar to baseball in some respects, popular in certain U.S. cities between 1800 and 1860, frequently requiring two to three days to complete. Traced back to 1597, the game is played with a ball and bat by two teams of usually 11 players each on a large field having two wickets 22 yards (20 meters) apart, each defended by a batsman. The object of the game is to score runs by batting the ball far enough so that one can "exchange" wickets with the batsman defending the opposite wicket before the ball is recovered. By 1840, there were several organized cricket clubs in the United States, with particular concentration in New York and Philadelphia; many early baseball players were accomplished cricketers. Cricket has retained a loyal following, esp. in the Philadelphia area, where it is still played today.

crickets "The sound heard when someone's opening draft bid on a player [in fantasy baseball] is also the only bid" (Ron Shandler, *Ron Shandler's Baseball Forecaster*, 2006).

Crimson Hose A nickname for the Boston Red Sox.

cripple 1. *n.* A pitch thrown when the count is against the pitcher (3–0, 2–0, or 3–1) and he must sacrifice speed for accuracy to ensure that the ball is in the strike zone. The pitch is so named because it is usually easy to hit. "Balls that are pitched with little or no curve and require no great effort to meet solidly are called 'cripples'" (*The New York Times*, June 2, 1929). Ted Williams would "jump on the cripple" (Chicago White Sox pitcher Thornton Lee, quoted in Edwin Howsam, *Baseball Graffiti*, 1995). Syn. *cripple pitch*; *pay ball*, 1. 1ST USE. 1914 (*New York Tribune*, Oct. 13; Edward J. Nichols). 2. *v.* To put the pitcher in a position where he must throw a cripple. 3. *n.* A weak team; a team often defeated (Maurice H. Weseen, *A Dictionary of American Slang*, 1934).

cripple count A count of 3–0, 2–0, or 3–1. "To be successful you have to throw something other than a fastball in a so-called cripple count" (Tom Glavine, quoted in *Sports Illustrated*, Oct. 22, 2001).

cripple hitter A hitter who does well when the pitcher makes a mistake or is behind in the count; e.g., Frank Howard, Dave Kingman, Ozzie Smith, and Pete Incaviglia. See also *mistake hitter*. Syn. *cripple shooter.*

cripple pitch Syn. of *cripple*, 1.

cripple shooter Syn. of *cripple hitter.*

croaker *hist.* A critical baseball fan. "A croaker is a person who always expects our team to win, and is never satisfied with any game however excellent the work may be" (*Evansville* [Ind.] *Journal*, Apr. 21, 1889; Peter Morris). IST USE. 1881. "Now the croaker will wonder why the management didn't have [George] Bradley pitch two months ago" (*Cleveland Herald*, Sept. 7; Peter Morris).

crockery limb A pitcher's arm that has stopped functioning. See also *glass arm*, 1.

crocus sack An impending victory. The term became part of broadcaster Red Barber's baseball language; e.g., he would say that a game was "all tied up in a crocus sack" if it were almost won.

crook *hist.* A curveball. "Parkins was the only pitcher in the lot who curved the ball, and he had a few of the boys performing contortionist tricks trying to follow the course of his crooks" (*San Francisco Bulletin*, Feb. 27, 1913; Gerald L. Cohen). IST USE. 1908 (*New York Evening Journal*, May 7; Edward J. Nichols).

crooked arm An uncomplimentary reference to a left-handed pitcher. IST USE. 1932 (*Baseball Magazine*, October, p.495; Edward J. Nichols).

crooked number Any number greater than 1 and less than 10, in reference to the lack of straight lines for numerals 2 through 9. A high-scoring game is one with crooked numbers. A 1–0 game is one in which neither team was able to post a crooked number. IST USE. 1993. "All this profligate hitting and high scoring [in the 1993 World Series] (what Tony La Russa calls 'crooked numbers') by the two teams" (Roger Angell, *The New Yorker*, Nov. 22, 1993, p.92).

crooked pitch The curveball. The term was used by Martin Quigley to title his history (1984) of the curveball.

crooky Dizzy Dean's term for the curveball (Robert Smith, *Baseball's Hall of Fame*, 1965, p.141).

cross 1. To outguess an opposing player or team. "With Juan [Ivy] Olson playing near second base, expecting to hold [Jack] Smith to that cushion and anticipating a bunt from [Jack] Miller, Jack 'crossed' the Brooklyn infield by crashing a base knock through the

spot that Olson should have been covering" (*St. Louis Post-Dispatch*, June 17, 1919; Peter Morris). IST USE. 1909 (*American Magazine*, June, p.403; Edward J. Nichols). 2. See *cross the plate*. 3. Syn. of *cross up*. "[Lefty] Williams . . . kept on crossing [Ray] Schalk in the second game" (*New York Evening Telegram*, Sept. 29, 1920).

cross bats *hist.* To engage another team in a baseball game. "More than seventy-five teams crossed bats in and around San Francisco" (*San Francisco Bulletin*, May 8, 1913; Gerald L. Cohen). Syn. *measure bats.* IST USE. 1874. "For the first time in five years the Athletics, of Philadelphia, and the Yales crossed bats" (*Forest and Stream*, June 25; Peter Morris). ETYMOLOGY. Analogy with the military term "cross swords."

cross-checker A scout who looks at specific players, verifying previous assessments of other scouts; a scout who is responsible for a large region and is better able to measure a player's abilities versus other top talent in the surrounding area. "[Jim McLaughlin] pioneered the use of the 'cross-checker,' a second scout brought in to test the opinion of the first scout" (*The Baltimore Sun*, Feb. 9, 2004). See also *national cross-checker.* Compare *special assignment scout.* Also spelled "crosschecker."

crossfire A sidearm delivery in which the pitch appears to cross the strike zone on the diagonal. It is accomplished when the pitcher steps toward the baseline rather than taking the usual step toward home plate; e.g., a right-handed pitcher works from the extreme right edge of the rubber and steps toward third base before releasing the ball. It gives the impression that the ball will hit the batter before it goes over the outside part of the plate. Lefty Eddie Plank of the Philadelphia Athletics (1901–1914) was known for this style of delivery, which once was quite popular. IST USE. 1896. "Willie Mains was called in to stop the slaughter and he did excellent work with his crossfire" (*The Boston Globe*, Apr. 19; Peter Morris).

cross-firing Throwing a sequence of pitches: "sending the ball first over one side of the plate then the other and then right over centre" (Lester Chadwick, *Baseball Joe of the Silver Stars*, 1912; David Shulman).

cross-foot For a baseman to shift his foot when expecting a throw. From *Athletic Journal* (May 1945, p.41; Robert F. Perkins): "In the case of shifting the feet when taking a throw, it is best not to 'cross-foot.' In other words, he should run to a spot directly in front of the bag and get set for the throw. As the throw comes in he should touch the base with one foot. Which foot touches the bag depends upon where the throw is."

cross hairs The middle of the strike zone.

cross-handed Said of an "incorrect" grip or hold on the bat in which the batter's hands are crossed; e.g., left hand on top of the right hand for a right-handed batter or right hand on top of the left hand for a left-handed batter. "[Hank] Aaron started as a cross-handed hitting softball player" (United Press International dispatch, Aug. 1, 1982). IST USE. 1885. "[Jack] Clements of the Philadelphias bats cross-handed" (*Detroit Post*, May 16; Peter Morris).

cross-over pivot The *pivot* when attempting to turn a double play often required of a second baseman who, after receiving the ball from the shortstop, touches second base with his left foot and relays the ball to first base as he swings his right foot over the bag and plants it.

cross-over step The footwork of a base stealer accomplished by a quick pivot on the right foot, followed by crossing the left leg (the one closest to the base) over and around the right leg. "The cross-over step is the fastest and most effective start . . . in stealing bases" (John W. "Jack" Coombs, *Baseball: Individual Play and Team Strategy*, 1938; Peter Morris).

cross-seamer Syn. of *four-seam fastball*.

cross-seam fastball Syn. of *four-seam fastball*.

cross signal A sign that is opposite from what is expected. As explained by Branch Rickey (*Branch Rickey's Little Blue Book*, 1995, p.51; Peter Morris): "Suppose you have a signal for a sacrifice bunt and you signal the batter to bunt on the first pitch, but only if it is a strike. The pitch is high and outside—a ball—and now you want him to hit free because the first and third basemen have left their positions before the pitch was delivered. Don't give him the 'hit free' signal, give him the 'cross' signal, which tells the batter to do the opposite of what you last wanted him to do. This confuses the opposition. They are looking for you to give either the bunt or the 'hit free' signal. Even if they see the 'cross' signal they won't know for certain what it is you want the batter to do."

cross the plate To score a run.

cross-town series A series of games between two teams in the same city, such as the White Sox vs. the Cubs in Chicago. See also *city series*.

cross up To fool or mislead a player on one's own team. The term is commonly used when a pitcher delivers an unexpected pitch to the catcher, such as a breaking ball when a fastball is anticipated. Maurice H. Weseen (*A Dictionary of American Slang*, 1934) defined the term as "to deceive, especially a batter." Syn. *cross*, 3.

crotch 1. The space between the thumb section and the fingers section of a catcher's mitt and first baseman's mitt. 2. The space or area between the thumb and first finger of a fielder's glove; it may be filled with flexible leather webbing.

crouch 1. *n.* The catcher's playing position: balanced on the balls of his feet with his weight on his haunches. 2. *v.* To assume the catcher's crouch. 3. *n.* A low batting stance. "The 'Elberfeld crouch' is the latest thing in Metropolitan base ball. The kid's position in trying to work the pitcher for a base on balls is what earned the new name" (*The Sporting Life*, Aug. 8, 1903; Peter Morris). USAGE NOTE. Peter Morris notes that the term "crouching position" appeared earlier: "[Thayer] Torreyson at the bat is a study. He takes a crouching position, lunges fiercely at the first one pitched" (*Youngstown* [Ohio] *Vindicator*, reprinted in *Grand Rapids* [Mich.] *Evening Press*, May 2, 1898). 4. *v.* To take a low batting stance.

crowd 1. *n.* The spectators as a collective

body at a baseball game. **2.** *v.* See *crowd the plate.*

crowd the corners To fill the bases with runners.

crowd the plate To take a batting stance close to home plate; to hover close to the strike zone; to crouch on the inner edge of the batter's box as close to the plate as possible. "Alfonso Soriano . . . crowds the plate to reach the corner, but jams himself inside" (*ESPN The Magazine*, Sept. 23, 2003). IST USE. 1901 (Burt L. Standish, *Frank Merriwell's Marvel*, p.154; Edward J. Nichols).

crow hop 1. A small jump-step used by a fielder to gain momentum before throwing the ball. See also *hop-step.* **2.** An extra little step at the end of a pitcher's motion. USAGE NOTE. Is this term an antique? Tristram Potter Coffin (*The Old Ball Game*, 1971) reported, "In the spring of 1969, pitcher Jerry Johnson was interviewed on the radio. He told how he had rid his pitching motion of a little 'crow hop' . . . during winter ball. Two weeks later members of the Houston Astros . . . denied the phrase was still in use." **3.** [softball term] "The act of a pitcher [in fast pitch softball] who steps, hops, or drags off the front of the pitcher's plate, replants the pivot foot, thereby establishing a second impetus (or starting point), pushes off from the newly established starting point and completes the delivery" (Amateur Softball Association of America, *Official Rules of Softball*, Rule 1, 2006).

crown 1. *n.* An honor figuratively worn by a player or team that comes in first place, either in the standings or in the statistical accounting of some aspect of performance; e.g., the "batting crown" goes to the player who has the highest batting average in his league. **2.** *v.* To hit the ball (*The Sporting Life*, Nov. 29, 1913).

cruise 1. To win a game easily; e.g., "The Mariners cruised past the Twins, 8–2." **2.** To pitch effectively; e.g., "[Kevin Tapani] cruised until the seventh, when the Angels staged a two-out rally" (*Tampa Tribune*, July 31, 1990).

crunch A difficult position; a *jam,* 1.

crush 1. To hit a pitched ball with great strength. "[Paul Molitor] crushed his home run into the second deck in left field" (*The Baltimore Sun*, Oct. 24, 1993). **2.** To defeat a team overwhelmingly.

crusher A base hit that decides or clinches a ball game. "The crusher was delivered by Tommy Henrich in the fifth when he leaped upon a [Whit] Wyatt fastball and sent it over the right field wall for a home run" (*New York Post*, Oct. 6, 1941; Raymond V. Curiale).

crush zone The point or area where the batter is most likely to hit the ball; the batter's *wheelhouse.* "A pitch thrown right in the crush zone, I mean, when it leaves the pitcher's hand the ball is right in a place where the batter was swinging—and he got all of it" (Keith Moreland, *Vineline*, Aug. 1987).

crutch *hist.* A baseball bat. "[Perry Werden] made a tolerable showing with his 'crutch'" (*The Sporting Life*, Dec. 9, 1893; Peter Morris).

crybaby 1. A derogatory name for a player with a reputation for arguing with umpires. **2.** A player who criticizes his manager. The Cleveland Indians of 1940 were nicknamed the "Crybaby Indians" for their moaning to the front office and media about manager Ossie Vitt, whom the players reviled.

CS Box score and scorecard abbrev. for *caught stealing.*

cuadrangular Spanish for "home run."

cuadro Spanish for "infield."

cub *hist.* A recruit or rookie. The term's popularity at the beginning of the 20th century probably influenced the naming of the youthful Chicago Cubs. IST USE. 1906 (*The Sporting Life*, March 10, p.5; Edward J. Nichols).

Cuban A name for a black American ballplayer in the days before many Latin Americans were in the major leagues and well before the color line was broken. The first club of African-American professionals was called the Cuban Giants, an amalgam of three black clubs, one of which had toured Cuba. Franklin P. Huddle (*American Speech*, Apr. 1943) noted, "Since Negroes have, by devious means, been kept out of major league baseball, their evasion is to sometimes call themselves Cubans. Thus, Cuban All-Stars is a frequent name of a Negro team."

Cuban forkball A spitball. The term received a boost through an often-repeated comment by relief pitcher John Wyatt who played during the 1960s: "I use a Cuban forkball. I learned to use it while I was swimming in the Mediterranean Sea." The term also was used by Orlando Peña when he staged a comeback and returned to the major leagues in 1973 and, according to Gaylord Perry (*Me and the Spitter*, 1974, p.44; Charles D. Poe), "it is not a dry pitch."

Cuban League A collective term for a series of winter professional baseball leagues in Cuba, which, though under different names and terms of conditions and with some interruptions, retained an essential continuity from 1878 until 1961.

Cuban palmball A spitball. "A prime suspect in those days was Pedro Ramos, who resembled [Gaylord] Perry by touching his cap and shirt frequently before pitching his 'Cuban palmball.' The ball did so many tricks en route to the plate that the umpire once made Ramos go into the clubhouse and change his shirt three times" (Joseph Durso, *The New York Times*, Aug. 31, 1982).

Cuban sandwich An especially tantalizing pitch thrown by a batting-practice pitcher, such as those thrown by Minnesota Twins hitting instructor Tony Oliva, who said: "The Cuban sandwich is a confidence builder. If you cannot hit a long ball off a Cuban sandwich, you are in trouble" (Patrick Reusse, *The Sporting News*, 1986). See also *cream puff*.

Cubbies An affectionate nickname for the Chicago *Cubs*, making it a nickname for a nickname. Joey Johnston (*Tampa Tribune*, Oct. 6, 1984) wrote, "The Cubbies? Other teams aren't called the Metsies or the Soxies. But the Chicago Cubs are different. They are not just a team, but a shared experience that has been passed through the generations."

Cubness The special quality of being a member or fan of the Chicago Cubs despite their many seasons of futility (having never won the World Series since 1908). Cubs broadcaster Jack Brickhouse (quoted in Ron Berler, *The Boston Herald*, Oct. 15, 1981):

"Cubness is a way of life—something that's handed down from player to player, from veteran to rookie, from one baseball generation to the next." But Berler claimed that the term "is synonymous with the rankest sort of abject failure, and is a condition chronic among all Cubs, past and present."

Cubs Nickname for the National League Central Division franchise in Chicago, Ill. The club was founded as the White Stockings (1876–1889), and was also known as the Colts (1890–1897) and the Orphans (1898–1901) after manager Cap Anson, the team's "father," departed following the 1897 season. Reflecting on the number of young players on the team, Fred Hayner (*Chicago Daily News*, March 27, 1902) suggested the team be called the Cubs, which became the official team name in 1907. See also *Cubbies*; *Bruins*. Also known as *North Siders*.

cudgel 1. *n.* A baseball bat. 1ST USE. 1904. "[Frank Huelsman] is a power at the bat, and all teams dread the moment he takes up his cudgel, for the fences are none too far for him to reach" (*The Washington Post*, Sept. 5; Peter Morris). 2. *v.* To hit a pitched ball. "Buck Weaver . . . cudgeled a three bagger to the deepest corner between the right and centre terraces" (*The New York Times*, Oct. 7, 1919).

cue ball shot A fluke base hit achieved when the ball is hit off the end of the bat, suggesting a cue stick striking a billiard ball. Such a hit is sometimes said to have been "cued up." Syn. "cue shot."

cuff 1. To get hits against a pitcher. "[Mule] Watson lasted six innings yesterday and was cuffed for seven hits and four runs" (Sid Mercer, *New York Globe and Commercial Advertiser*, Sept. 27, 1916). 2. To make an error. "Frank Frisch cuffed a few grounders around" (John Kieran, *The New York Times*, Oct. 12, 1930).

cull A mediocre ballplayer. "[Ned] Hanlon was to take the best [players] for Brooklyn [in 1899] and the 'culls,' as we called the mediocre or slipping players then, were to go to Baltimore" (John J. McGraw, *My Thirty Years in Baseball*, 1923, p.117). "Say, cull, don't it hurt to have them eyeballs rubbing together?" (*The Sporting Life*, Oct. 7, 1893). FIRST USE/ETYMOLOGY. 1878. "In picking over farm articles the few which are refused by all buyers and by the farmer himself are called 'culls.' Let us, then, have the honor to propose as the name of the new St. Louis team, 'The Culls'" (*Chicago Tribune*, Apr. 14; Peter Morris).

cunny thumb **1.** A pitcher who throws slow balls. See also *cutty-thumb*. Sometimes spelled "cunnythumb." Syn. *cunny thumber*, 1; "cunny-thumb pitcher"; "cunning thumb." IST USE. 1937 (*New York Daily News*, Jan. 17; Edward J. Nichols). **2.** A curveball thrown by holding the thumb parallel to the first two fingers in contrast to placing the thumb on the opposite side of the ball; it is a sharp curve because the pitcher gets more spin on the ball when it has no resistance from the thumb (Stan Baumgartner, *The Sporting News*, 1952). **3.** An awkward player who is "all hands, in fielding ball" (Al Schacht, *Al Schacht's Dope Book*, 1944).

cunny thumber **1.** Syn. of *cunny thumb*, 1. See also *thumber*, 2. **2.** A player with a poor throwing arm; a player who throws "like a woman"; an awkward player. ETYMOLOGY. This is an old term used in marbles played by children on both sides of the Atlantic Ocean. In marbles it refers to a shooter using the "female manner"; i.e., from a closed fist with the thumb tucked under the first three fingers. Eric Partridge (*Dictionary of Slang and Unconventional English*, 1984) noted that "cunny" is a reference to female genitalia (*pudendum muliebre*) dating back to the 17th century. Despite this clearly sexual reference, there seems to have been no taboo about its use in baseball (or in marbles for that matter) as it shows up in such places as Dizzy Dean's various glossaries. Its decline in use as a baseball term has paralleled the decline in marbles as a childhood pastime.

cup A small, hard, metal or plastic device commonly worn by players to protect their genitals. Jim Bouton (*Ball Four*, 1970, p.325; Charles D. Poe) wrote, "What baseball players do to each other is punch each other in the groin and say 'cup check.'"

cup of coffee A brief trial in the major leagues by a minor-league player. "Billy Williams'

cup of major league coffee cooled in just 10 days" (United Press International story, *San Francisco Chronicle*, Aug. 29, 1969; Peter Tamony). These trials often take place during the month of September, when teams are allowed to expand their rosters to 40 players and take a glimpse at new talent. IST USE. 1908. "It isn't often that Hank O'Day is caught napping, but a young player just getting his 'cup of coffee' in the league put one over on Hank and Mr. Klem yesterday" (*New York Globe*, June 11; Peter Morris). ETYMOLOGY. The phrase seems to have derived from the observation that a young player's first taste of the major leagues is usually quite short, figuratively just long enough to drink a cup of coffee. EXTENDED USE. The term has been applied to quick trial periods in other sports. An example from professional football: "[Henry] Schichtle had a cup of coffee last season with the New York Giants and was picked up by the new Atlanta Falcons and put on waivers there before the 49ers took a look at him" (*San Francisco Chronicle*, Aug. 2, 1966; Peter Tamony).

cupped barrel The barrel of a cupped bat with a teacup end.

cupped bat A baseball bat whose top end has been scooped out to form a *teacup end*. A Japanese innovation, cupped bats have been legal in the major leagues since 1971. The indentation in the end of the bat must be curved with no foreign substance added and may be no deeper than one inch, no wider than two inches, and no less than one inch in diameter (*Official Baseball Rules*, Rule 1.10[b]). The concave shape allows the bat weight to be shaved by an ounce or so over the same bat with a convex (rounded) end. Some believe that the cup creates a vacuum, which allows the batter to obtain extra speed in his swing; but the Official Playing Rules Committee disputed this notion when it legalized the bat with the conclusion that "the driving power is not accentuated, and batter does not have an advantage." Syn. *cupped-end bat*; *hollow-end bat*.

cupped-end bat Syn. of *cupped bat*.

curb ball A variation of baseball played without a bat, usually one to a side. A rubber ball is thrown against a street curb by the player on offense, while the defense tries to catch the ball on the fly as it comes off the curb. A ball caught on the fly is an out. Hits and runs are registered by the number of bounces the ball takes or by the distance it flies; some versions allow running the bases. Michael Olesker (*The Baltimore Sun*, July 15, 1999) described curb ball in Baltimore: "One of the old city games, squeezed into any available space, squeezed between houses, squeezed onto narrow streets, squeezed between cars driving through. One guy throws a ball at a street curb, and tries to hit the point at the top to make it fly over the heads of fielders positioned in the street, and over parked cars, and runs to each of four street corners, each one a base." Compare *stoopball.*

curfew **1.** The time of the day that players must be in quarters according to rules established by the manager. **2.** The hour that a game must end in accordance with a league curfew rule or local regulations. "Suspension of Saturday's game after eight innings because of the league's 1 a.m. curfew was the first at Memorial Stadium since July 31, 1978" (*USA Today*, June 22, 1987).

curfew rule A municipal or league regulation stipulating the hour at which a game must be terminated or suspended; e.g., in the American League all night games since 1968 must be called at 1 a.m. local time, but if an inning is started prior to that time, the inning can be completed.

Curse of the Bambino The expression of the misfortune that the Boston Red Sox had not won a World Series for 86 years because the team sold the great Babe Ruth (sometimes called "The Bambino") to the New York Yankees on Dec. 26, 1919 (made public on Jan. 5, 1920). The Red Sox (behind Ruth's pitching) won a World Series in 1918 and were not able to repeat that feat until they defeated the St. Louis Cardinals in the 2004 World Series. While the Yankees enjoyed unparalleled success in the decades following their acquisition of Ruth, the Red Sox appeared in four World Series and lost all of them, each in seven games. The Curse has been applied (retroactively) to Red Sox failures in 1946 (Enos Slaughter's "mad dash"), 1948 (losing a playoff game to Cleveland), 1949 (losing

Curse of the Bambino. Theatrical producer and Boston Red Sox owner Harry H. Frazee, the man who sold Babe Ruth to the New York Yankees for $125,000 and a $300,000 loan with Fenway Park as collateral. *George Grantham Bain Collection, Library of Congress*

the pennant to the Yankees), 1967 and 1975 (losing the World Series), 1978 (Bucky Dent's home run winning the pennant for the Yankees), and 1986 (within, literally, one strike of winning the World Series, the New York Mets prevail with help from a fielding error by Bill Buckner). Julia Ruth Stevens, the daughter of Babe Ruth, when asked about the Curse, replied (*The New York Times*, Oct. 19, 1999), "Well, mostly, I think it's a myth." Stefan Fatsis (*The Wall Street Journal*, Oct. 15, 2004) noted that the Curse is "good business, even if the official Red Sox line is it doesn't exist"; Fatsis quoted club president Larry Lucchino: "We don't believe in those stinking curses. We believe in rationality, preparation, hitting, pitching, things like that." Stephen King (*The Boston Globe*, Oct. 2, 1995) wrote, "There is no Curse of the Bambino. I, who was writing about curses and supernatural vengeance . . . tell you that it's so. . . . The Red Sox have been victims of

Curse of the Bambino. Babe Ruth in Red Sox uniform, 1916. *George Grantham Bain Collection, Library of Congress*

an extraordinary run of ill luck, that's all." Syn. *Babe Ruth Curse.* ETYMOLOGY. *The Boston Globe* writer Dan Shaughnessy used the term as the title of his 1990 book. Shaughnessy cited (p.19) John McKeon (Amesbury, Mass.) who, after the 1986 World Series, printed a thousand 16-page booklets detailing lowlights from 68 years of "anguish" and sold them outside Fenway Park on Opening Day in 1987; said McKeon, "We'll never win, we'll never be free of this warped, evil cycle. This is the Curse of the Bambino. Once a fan accepts this fate and understands the cycle, he can make peace with himself and accept any loss, any disappointment, because *he knows* it is coming." Shaughnessy also quoted (p.22) former Red Sox pitcher Bill "Spaceman" Lee: "My theory is that it [the sale of Ruth to the hated Yankees] happened because of a curse by an orphan child from Baltimore. I remember the day I first said that. I gave a speech and said, 'Until they exhume the body of Babe Ruth and publicly apologize for selling him to New York, . . . the city of Boston will never win a major baseball championship.'" USAGE NOTE. During and after the 1986 World Series, George Vecsey, in his column "Sports of the Times"

in *The New York Times,* used the terms "Curse of Babe Ruth" (Oct. 27) and "Babe Ruth Curse" (Oct. 28). The latter column was titled "Babe Ruth Curse Strikes Again" and detailed past "accidents, calamities, disasters, bad luck, flops and failures" affecting the Red Sox. "The players don't deal with concepts like The Curse of Babe Ruth, but who is to say the whiff of failure has not settled into the steel, the earth, the wood and the very ozone of Fenway Park?"

Curse of the Billy Goat See *Billy Goat Curse.*

curtain call The practice of a player coming out of the dugout to acknowledge the fans. The call usually starts in the form of a chant of the player's name ("Rusty-Rusty-Rusty" or "Ed-die-Ed-die-Ed-die") to honor the player for a home run, personal milestone, crucial hit, or, in the case of a pitcher, a number of strikeouts. The first curtain call may have occurred on May 28, 1956, when Pittsburgh Pirates slugger Dale Long hit a home run off Brooklyn Dodgers pitcher Carl Erskine, thereby becoming the first player to hit a home run in eight consecutive games. The Forbes Field crowd gave him a three-minute standing ovation and demanded that Long come out of the dugout to take a bow. Dave Anderson (*The New York Times,* July 20, 1987) quoted Long: "Branch Rickey told me it was the first curtain call he'd ever seen in baseball." Roger Maris, upon hitting his 61st home run on Oct. 1, 1961, was forced/pushed out of the dugout by his teammates. George Vecsey (*The New York Times,* Aug. 15, 1982), recalling the notoriously ornery temperaments of pitchers Early Wynn and Bob Gibson, asked, "Can you imagine what Early Wynn would have done to the next batter after somebody took a bow for hitting a home run? There is reason to believe the current practice of curtain calls did not begin until Bob Gibson was safely retired after 1975." During his last at-bat in Fenway Park in 1960, Ted Williams hit a home run; John Updike (*The New Yorker,* Oct. 22, 1960) remembered, "Though we thumped, wept, and chanted 'We want Ted' for minutes after he hid in the dugout, he did not come back." Updike later learned that both the players and the umpires had begged Williams to come out and acknowledge the crowd. Compare this to Carl Yastrzemski's final at-bat in Fenway Park in 1983. He popped out to the second baseman, and then, as described by Stephen Williams (*Inside Sports*, Jan. 1984): "The fans clamored for Yaz and he came out and lifted his hat, and then he came out again, and later that night, when he was supposed to be attending a cocktail party in his honor, he stood on a street in the Back Bay and signed autographs for an hour."

curtain raiser The first game of the season, a series, or a doubleheader. 1ST USE. 1909. "[Frank] Chance ran in and covered the plate when they were running [Honus] Wagner to death in the first inning of the curtain raiser" (*Chicago Tribune*, May 3; Peter Morris).

Curt Flood Act A 1998 law that repealed that part of baseball's *antitrust exemption* dealing with labor relations. It clarified that major-league players and owners have the same legal rights, and are subject to the same restrictions, under the antitrust laws as the players and owners in other professional sports leagues; e.g., if baseball enacts rules that restrict player movement or compensation, the sport would be subject to antitrust laws. It marked the first time the U.S. Congress addressed the antitrust exemption by repealing a small part of the exemption, but expressly disclaimed any effect on any other aspects of baseball's antitrust status, such as codifying baseball's immunity on issues related to expansion, franchise relocation, the amateur draft, and the minor leagues. The Act is named for the outfielder who challenged the reserve clause in court after he retired following the 1969 season to protest being traded by the St. Louis Cardinals to the Philadelphia Phillies.

curve **1.** *v.* To pitch a curveball. 1ST USE. 1856. "Many [believe] a slow ball curving near the bat, to be the most effective" (*Porter's Spirit of the Times*, Dec. 6; Peter Morris). **2.** *n.* Syn. of *curveball*. "The curve is in common use" (*Chicago Tribune*, Aug. 26, 1877). 1ST USE. 1874 (*New York Herald*, July 7; Edward J. Nichols). **3.** *n.* The course of a curveball.

EXTENDED USE. **1.** *n.* A surprise; e.g., "Russians Throw Curve Into Suez Parley" (*San Francisco News* headline, Aug. 10, 1956; Peter Tamony). **2.** *n.* A tough, tricky question, such as one that shows up in an examination. A character in a Steve Canyon comic strip says, "That's an unfair curve to throw at a newspaperman" (*San Francisco Examiner*, July 17, 1956; Peter Tamony). **3.** *n.* Distracting. A kidnapper's instructions to captive's relatives not to reduce the amount of extortion demanded, nor to inform police of negotiations, warned, "Don't pitch any fancy curves" (A.J. Pollock, *The Underworld Speaks*, 1935).

curveball A pitch that is thrown with a forceful, downward spin and snap of the wrist, causing it to drop or break and veer to the side as it nears home plate. A good curveball will break both laterally and downward about two feet. A right-handed pitcher's curveball tends to veer to the left (down and away to right-handed batters and down and in to left-handed batters), while that thrown by a left-handed pitcher veers to the right. The curveball is gripped with the index and middle fingers slightly separated across the seams on top of the ball and the thumb underneath; the wrist is cocked to the left (for a right-handed pitcher) and snapped forward on release, giving the ball the topspin (which

Curtain raiser. With coattails flying, President Lyndon B. Johnson tosses the first ball on Opening Day, 1964. *Lyndon B. Johnson Presidential Library*

Curveball. Lyman Briggs (right), Director of the National Bureau of Standards, and Ossie Bluege, comptroller of the Washington Senators and, formerly, the club's third baseman and manager, at Griffith Stadium in 1959. Briggs demonstrated how to measure the spin of a pitched ball with the aid of a flat measuring tape affixed to the ball. Other Senators who assisted Briggs were pitchers Camilio Pascual and Pedro Ramos, catcher Ed Fitz Gerald, and manager Cookie Lavagetto. *National Institute of Standards and Technology*

means the top of the ball rotates in the direction of flight) it needs to dart downward as it approaches the plate. Although few now doubt that the ball actually curves, there have been those who always maintained that it was an illusion. Several experiments determined that the curve was real: in a well-publicized experiment, physicist Lyman J. Briggs (director emeritus of the U.S. National Bureau of Standards) determined that a curveball does in fact curve and that the absolute maximum curve (or break) from the line of trajectory was 17.5 inches over the distance of 60.5 feet from the mound to the plate (reported in *San Francisco Chronicle*, March 30, 1959). See Martin Quigley (*The Crooked Pitch*, 1984) for a history of the curveball in American baseball. Also spelled "curve ball." There are many synonyms, including: *curve*, 2; *deuce*, 1; *Uncle Charlie*; *yakker*, 1; *yellow hammer*; *number 2*. IST USE. 1877. "A curve ball is one which starts to come over the plate and then curves away from it, or starts away from it and then changes its course and comes over the plate" (*Chicago Tribune*, Aug. 26). Although 1877 is the earliest citation for the term, the curveball became widespread during the years 1872 to 1875. ETYMOLOGY. The pitch has been credited to W. Arthur "Candy"

Cummings of Brooklyn, who first began working on it in 1864 at boarding school. He later said he came upon the idea in 1863 while throwing clamshells, which naturally curved. In 1867, he first applied it in a game while playing for the Excelsiors of Brooklyn. But there are many other claims. See Peter Morris (*A Game of Inches*, 2006, pp.118–36) for a full discussion of the origin of the curveball. EXTENDED USE. Deception; a misleading trick. Andy Breckman, executive producer and creator of USA Network's television series *Monk*, discussing the challenge of developing stories for Monk, the obsessive-compulsive detective played by actor Tony Shalhoub (quoted in *The Baltimore Sun*, July 6, 2006): "What we love doing is throwing Tony Shalhoub curveballs and seeing if he can hit them. And he can."

curveballer A pitcher who relies chiefly on his curveball. EXTENDED USE. A person with questionable ethics. "In a business [prize-fighting] full of curve ballers, Fran threw right down the middle" (*San Francisco Chronicle*, March 2, 1968; Peter Tamony).

curver 1. A curveball. 2. A curveball pitcher. 3. A device used by pitchers to develop a curveball, consisting of a piece of rubber, one end of which was looped and slipped over the index finger or middle finger and the other end of which was held in the palm of the hand. The "baseball curver" was described in *Baseball Magazine* (March 1914, pp.76–77): "The curver is formed of a yielding or elastic material . . . and provided with a vacuum cup which takes hold of the ball and a ring portion attached to or formed integrally with the cup which is slipped over two or more of the fingers. The cup may be shifted to any desired position relative to the fingers, so that great and small curves and curves of various kinds may be pitched with comparative ease."

curvist A curveball pitcher. "[Oakland] was opposed by Frank Arellanes, the Santa Cruz curvist" (*San Francisco Bulletin*, May 30, 1913; Gerald L. Cohen). ETYMOLOGY. Apparently from "curve" + "(art) ist."

cushion 1. *n.* Syn. of *base*, 2. IST USE. 1887. "[Jerry] Denny got one safely to center, which planted [Jack] Glasscock on [Fred] Dunlap's cushion [second base]" (*Detroit*

Tribune, Sept. 28; Peter Morris). **2.** *n.* A comfortable lead in a game, a series of games, or the overall standings. **3.** *v.* To field a ball in such a relaxed way that it settles easily into the glove, ready to be transferred smoothly to the throwing hand. "When a guy cushions the ball, he's fielding it lovingly—it implies a confidence with what he's doing" (Deacon Jones, quoted in Alan Schwarz, Baseball America.com, Nov. 14, 2006).

cushioned cork center A small sphere of composition cork that is molded to layers of rubber and applied to the outside of the center core of the baseball. The first layer of black rubber consists of two hemispheric shells; the two openings where the shells meet are sealed with a cushion of red rubber, and a layer of red rubber surrounds the entire center. Patented by Milton Reach in 1924, it was introduced in 1925 and replaced the *cork center*. IST USE. 1925. "The center of the Reach cushioned cork center ball is made of a lathe-turned perfect sphere of live cork, surrounded by black semi-vulcanized rubber, which is vulcanized by another cover of red rubber" (*Port Arthur* [Texas] *News*, Oct. 25; Peter Morris).

Cushion Night A promotion at a night baseball game in which seat cushions are given away to fans. More often than not, it seems, many fans forgo sitting on the cushions for throwing them on the field. "For the second straight year, the Chicago White Sox 'Cushion Night' resulted in a delay of play Friday night" (*Des Moines Register*, May 31, 1987).

cuspidor ball *hist.* A spitball. IST USE. 1907 (*Chicago Tribune*, Apr. 3; Peter Morris).

cuspidor curve *hist.* A spitball.

cut 1. *n.* A batter's swing. "Lord, he has a wicked cut" (Dennis "Oil Can" Boyd, on first pitching to Jose Canseco, quoted in *USA Today*, May 16, 1986). IST USE. 1918. "The burly slugger [Babe Ruth] took one of his famous 'cuts' and the pill landed high and dry on the embankment in centre field" (*Boston Post*, July 11; Peter Morris). **2.** *n.* An opportunity to swing the bat, either in a game or in batting practice. Often used in the plural; e.g., "I need to get my cuts." **3.** *n.* The release of a player from the team; e.g.,

"Smith could not survive the cut and was returned to the farm." **4.** *v.* To release a player. **5.** *n.* A *cut fastball*. "Since he's [lefthander Jamie Moyer] developed a cut, he has become a lot more effective vs. right-handed hitters" (New York Yankees manager Buck Showalter, quoted in *The Baltimore Sun*, Aug. 10, 1995). **6.** *n.* The tailing or late darting action of a cut fastball. "[Pat Rapp said] he didn't have much cut on his fastball" (*The Baltimore Sun*, March 24, 2000). **7.** *v.* For a pitcher to turn his wrist and pull down on the pitch when throwing a cut fastball. "The pitch . . . was delivered with a driving, downward flick of [Bob] Gibson's long forefinger and middle finger (what pitchers call 'cutting the ball'), very much resembling an inhumanly fast slider" (Roger Angell, *Late Innings*, 1982; Charles D. Poe). **8.** *v.* To hit, drive, or throw a baseball so that it spins or is deflected. **9.** *imp.* An instruction yelled by a player to another to cut off a thrown ball. **10.** *v.* See *cut a base*. **11.** *v.* To pitch a ball to a precise part of the strike zone. See *cut the corner*; *cut the plate*.

cut a base To fail to touch a base while running or advancing. "Under the present rules the umpire does not call a runner out for 'cutting' a base and can not do so until the ball is fielded to an opponent standing on the bag cut before the player returns to it" (*The Sporting News*, July 28, 1910; Peter Morris).

cut ball A ball that is cut, slit, or deeply scratched so that when thrown it will create an irregular airflow, which will cause it to break unnaturally. "Mike Scott throws the best one. It's scraped on one side of the ball. If you hold it in the middle to throw it the ball will break in the opposite direction of where you cut it" (Keith Moreland, *Vineline*, Aug. 1987).

cut changeup A pitch that moves like a decelerated slider. "[Pat] Strange began the summer session using . . . a unique cut changeup" (*Baseball America*, Nov. 12–25, 2001; Peter Morris).

cut down To throw out a runner, especially when an extra base or stolen base is being attempted. IST USE. 1912 (*New York Tribune*, Sept. 5; Edward J. Nichols).

cut-down day The date on which a major-league team must reduce its roster to the maximum number of players allowed (currently 25). The surplus players must be traded, sold, or sent to minor-league teams by the deadline. Jim Brosnan (*Pennant Race*, 1962) remarked, "Cut-down day is a time of man-sized tears and tribulations. . . . Any game on cut-down day has the elements of a last-chance drama."

cut fastball A "tame" variation of the slider, thrown with one's top two fingers held slightly off to the side and the wrist given a flick (as if one were cutting cheese) instead of a complete turn; a semislider that moves from the middle of the plate to the corner because the pitcher "cuts" his delivery, turning his wrist a bit to pull down through the ball when releasing it. When thrown by a right-handed pitcher, a cut fastball suddenly tails down and away from a right-handed batter, but moves in on a left-handed batter; for a southpaw, the movements are opposite. The cut fastball has been described as a flat, hard slider with a smaller, sharper horizontal break (the pitcher places slight pressure on his middle finger upon release) as it nears the plate and as a cross between a slider and a fastball; it usually lacks the red dot that the batter sees on a slider. Keith Hernandez (*Pure Baseball*, 1994, p.10) writes, "The cut fastball breaks the least of all the pitches that break at all, but that little bit is enough to be effective if located properly." Relief pitcher Mariano Rivera is known for his "wicked" cut fastball (*Sports Illustrated*, Nov. 12, 2001). See also *little cutter; sailer.* Syn. *cut*, 5; *cutter; poorman's slider; chain saw.* USAGE NOTE. The term probably originated in the early 1980s, although the pitch itself has been around at least since the 1930s. Ethan Allen (*Major League Baseball: Technique and Tactics*, 1938, p.29), discussing Johnny Allen's fastball, noted, "[It] is unique because it slides or breaks like a curve. He throws it much as a curve but keeps the fingers and wrist stiff when the ball is released." See Rob Neyer, in Bill James and Rob Neyer, *The Neyer/James Guide to Pitchers*, 2004, pp.12–13.

cutie A pitcher who specializes in throwing curveballs and slow stuff on the corners. "Traded to Detroit, [Don Mossi] became a cutie, saving his fast one" (Eddie Lopat, quoted in *The Sporting News*, Apr. 6, 1960; Peter Morris).

cut in To intercept a catcher's throw to second base on a double-steal attempt and return the throw immediately to the catcher should the runner on third base start for home. This technique was described by John J. Evers and Hugh S. Fullerton (*Touching Second: The Science of Baseball*, 1910).

cut loose 1. To pitch hard and with authority after warming up. IST USE. 1904. "I begin active training by merely going through the motions, adding a little more effort each day, but never 'cutting loose' until the opening game" (Deacon Phillippe, quoted in *Syracuse Post Standard*, March 27; Peter Morris). **2.** For an outfielder throwing as hard as he can to try to nail a runner attempting to advance an extra base. **3.** To discharge a player from the team.

cutoff *n.* The interception of a throw coming in from the outfield on its way to home plate or another base.

cut off *v.* **1.** To intercept a throw coming in from the outfield on its way to home plate or another base. **2.** For an outfielder to field a batted ball before it gets by him. **3.** *hist.* To throw out a runner. "George Wright . . . cut Waterman off at second" (*The Cleveland Morning Herald*, May 6, 1871). IST USE. 1863 (Chadwick Scrapbooks clipping, Aug. 9; Edward J. Nichols).

cut off extension To deliver a pitch without the elbow too close to the body, thereby impeding the proper exertion of force and follow-through. "When you cut off extension you don't have your arm in the right place to deliver the ball" (Doug Carpenter, quoted in Alan Schwarz, BaseballAmerica.com, Nov. 14, 2006).

cutoff man The player (usually an infielder and sometimes the pitcher) who intercepts or intends to intercept a throw from the outfield and then decides whether to relay the ball to the plate or another base or to hold the ball. "With a runner on second and a hit to center field, it is vital to hit the cutoff man. That can be one of the toughest plays in baseball" (Toronto Blue Jays outfielder Lloyd Moseby, quoted in *USA Today*, Apr. 6, 1987). Failure to hit the cutoff man often allows the runner to advance an additional base. Syn. *bounce target*.

cutoff play A play in which the ball, hit to the outfield with one or more runners on base, is thrown toward home plate and intercepted by another player (usually an infielder) who then must decide to try to retire the lead runner, who may be attempting to score; to throw the ball to another base in an effort to prevent another runner from advancing; or to hold the ball. The unpredictable outcome of the cutoff play based on the fielder's split-second decision makes it an exciting play for the spectator. The cutoff play was invented in the mid-1890s either by Brooklyn (Bill James, *The Bill James Historical Baseball Abstract*, 1985, p.45) or the Baltimore Orioles (George Herman Ruth, *Babe Ruth's Own Book of Baseball*, 1928, p.143); it was also used by the Boston Beaneaters (*Atlanta Constitution*, May 3, 1895; Peter Morris).

cutoff position The point on the field at which a throw from the outfield can be intercepted.

cutoff sign A simple instruction from the third baseman, who is watching a fielded ball come in from the outfield, to the shortstop to either "cut if off" or "let it go." The message is either signaled by voice or with a simple hand sign.

cutout 1. The dirt area immediately around a base on a field with artificial turf. "The [Tampa Bay Devil Rays are] researching the benefits and costs of all-dirt basepaths or cutouts around the infield at the Thunder-Dome" (*Baseball America*, Apr. 29–May 12, 1996; Peter Morris). **2.** The heel and toe area of a player's outer or team socks that have been left out of the socks to create a stirrup and allow some of the white sanitary socks to show. Roger Angell (*The Summer Game*, 1972) noted that Frank Robinson "wears the highest cutouts in the American League."

cutter 1. A batter who swings at many pitches

outside the strike zone. **2.** Syn. of *cut fastball*. **3.** See *grass cutter* and *daisy cutter*.

cut the corner 1. To pitch a ball across the inside or outside edge of the plate. IST USE. 1908 (*Spalding's Official Base Ball Guide*; Edward J. Nichols). **2.** For a runner to barely touch the edge of a base while rounding it.

cut the pie To play baseball with flamboyance.

cut the plate To pitch a ball over the center of home plate, as if to cut it in half. "Umpire Levy called a strike on a ball that cut the plate at the proper height" (*San Francisco Bulletin*, May 24, 1913; Gerald L. Cohen). Syn. "cut the heart of the plate." IST USE. 1901 (Burt L. Standish, *Frank Merriwell's School Days*, p.241; Edward J. Nichols).

cutty-thumb Said of a slow-ball or junk-ball pitcher. David Halberstam (*Summer of '49*, 1989) quoted Joe Page referring pejoratively to Eddie Lopat as a "cutty-thumb" pitcher. See also *cunny thumb*, 1.

cut up To swing at a ball with an upward motion of the bat. "[Babe Ruth] cuts up at nine of ten balls. This would be a defect in most batters" (John Bassler, quoted in F.C. Lane, *Batting*, 1925). See also *uppercut*, 2.

cut way to base *hist.* To slide into a base feet first with one's spikes up. IST USE. 1911 (*American Magazine*, May; Edward J. Nichols).

CWS Abbrev. for *College World Series*.

Cy A recipient of the Cy Young Award. "[Pedro] Martinez, the three-time Cy Young Award winner . . . saluted [Pat] Hentgen, a one-time Cy himself" (*The Baltimore Sun*, Apr. 3, 2001). See also *Cy Young*, 2.

cycle 1. A single, double, triple, and home run (not necessarily in that order) hit by a player in the same game. See also *hit for the cycle*. IST USE. 1933. "Jimmy [*sic*] Foxx, Athletic's [*sic*] slugger, is one of only six players in all major league history to 'hit for the cycle,' that is, get a single, double, triple and homer in four times at bat in one game" (*The Washington Post*, Sept. 27; Barry Popik). **2.** See *natural cycle*. **3.** See *home run cycle*.

cyclone *hist.* A hard-hit ball (*The Sporting News*, Nov. 27, 1897). IST USE. 1896. "Unchaining a cyclone . . . [is] to bat a ball which moves off very swiftly, pursuing a course near the earth" (*The Atchison* [Kans.] *Daily Globe*, June 23).

cyclone pitcher A pitcher who delivers the ball with great speed. It is because of this trait that Denton True Young became known as "Cy." "Up-and-coming 'cyclone' pitchers [in 1893] such as Pink Hawley, Bill Hutchinson, and Jack Stivetts were throwing with exceptional speed, and were all too often wild" (Tom Shieber, in *Total Baseball*, 4th ed., 1995, p.118). IST USE. 1889. "Hunolt, Stockton's 'cyclone' pitcher . . . pitches a straight ball over the plate with a speed that is terrific and of which he has perfect control" (*San Francisco Examiner*, Apr. 14; Peter Morris). USAGE NOTE. The names "Cy-clone" or "Cy Clone" have been used to describe some young pitchers of the modern era because of their resemblance to previous winners of the Cy Young Award. Storm Davis' nickname was "Cy Clone" because he was "being systematically and deliberately cloned from bits and pieces of all the Orioles' perennial Cy Young Award candidates" (Thomas Boswell, *The Washington Post*, June 12, 1983).

Cyclops *hist.* A player who wears glasses (Frank Graham and Dick Hyman, *Baseball Wit and Wisdom*, 1962, p.210).

Cy Old A former Cy Young Award winner who is pitching against a younger Cy Young Award winner. "This last game was a battle of 'Cy Young versus Cy Old,' the 24-year-old [Barry] Zito, last year's American League Cy Young award winner, against the 40-year-old [Roger] Clemens, winner of six Cy Young awards" (Murray Chass, *The New York Times*, May 5, 2003). ETYMOLOGY. In 1983, Baltimore Orioles pitcher Mike Flanagan, winner of the 1979 American League Cy Young Award, referred to himself as "Cy Young" and his older teammate, Jim Palmer, three-time winner of the award, as "Cy Old."

Cy Young 1. Short for *Cy Young Award*. "[Roger] Clemens won the Cy Young in each of his two years in Toronto" (*Sports Illustrated*, March 1, 1999). **2.** A recipient of the Cy Young Award. "[Curt Schilling] was everything today, no question. That's why he's a Cy Young. He was unbelievable"

(Sammy Sosa, quoted in *The Baltimore Sun*, Aug. 17, 2002). See also *Cy*.

Cy Young Award An annual award presented by the Baseball Writers' Association of America to the outstanding pitcher in the major leagues from 1956 to 1966 and to the outstanding pitcher in each major league since 1967. Selections are made by two writers from each league city. Since 1970, writers name three pitchers, with five points allotted for each first-place vote, three points for each second-place vote, and one point for each third-place vote. The award is named for Denton True "Cy" Young, who won 511 games from 1890 to 1911. Officially known as "Cy Young Memorial Award." Syn. *Cy Young*, 1.

Cy Younger A recipient of the Cy Young Award.

Cy Young jinx Apparent bad luck that afflicts a Cy Young Award winner the following year. The idea took root in the 1980s when Steve Stone, Pete Vuckovich, LaMarr Hoyt, Orel Hershiser, Frank Viola, and Guillermo Hernandez won the Cy Young Award and then fell on hard times. Jerry Howarth (*Baseball Lite*, 1986) defines the Cy Young Award as "the kiss of death, often followed by an arm injury, surgery or simply an off year." Robert Wood (personal communication, Sept. 24, 2001): "Pitchers who win the Cy Young are apt to pitch heavy workloads in that season, pitch better than expected, receive better than expected offensive support (especially since Cy Young voters relied heavily on won-lost records), all things that can lead to significantly worse seasons the year after."

Czar A name associated with the *commissioner* of baseball because of his great personal power when dealing with issues having to do with the best interests of the game. Before there was a commissioner, the term was applied to the presidents of the two major leagues (esp. Ban Johnson of the American League). It is hardly a misnomer, as the commissioner has absolute power in a few critical areas. When, in the wake of the 1919 Black Sox Scandal, Judge Kenesaw Mountain Landis was appointed the commissioner, he was often referred to as "Czar" Landis in the newspapers. Besides the other commis-

Czar. Judge Kenesaw Mountain Landis. *George Grantham Bain Collection, Library of Congress*

sioners following Landis, the title has been bestowed on other powerful baseball figures; e.g., a United Press International story on Los Angeles Dodgers owner Walter O'Malley was titled "Baseball Czar" (*San Francisco Chronicle*, Jan. 29, 1969; Peter Tamony). IST USE. 1912 (*Hampton Magazine*, May, p.284; Edward J. Nichols). ETYMOLOGY. Originally the title of the powerful Russian emperors, the term was applied to railroad magnates and political bosses, among others, before it came to baseball. "Czar is what they call me in the papers when they do not call me 'rogue'" (Alfred Henry Lewis, *The Boss, and How He Came to New York*, 1902). It was also used as a nickname for T.B. Rein during the years (late 19th century) he was speaker of the House of Representatives and ran that body with rigid, rigorous adherence to the parliamentary rules. Since the title was pinned on Landis it has been used liberally for people given extraordinary powers.

D

D 1. See *Class D*. 2. Syn. of *defense*, 2. "I've played pretty good 'D,' but offensively I just haven't gotten my swing back yet" (Jeff Reboulet, quoted in *The Baltimore Sun*, March 25, 2003). 3. Abbrev. for *double*, 1. 4. *hist.* Abbrev. for a ball caught "on the bound." ETYMOLOGY. From the last letter in the word "bound."

dabber A *finesse pitcher*. "Randy Jones . . . was promptly dubbed a 'dabber' by [Cincinnati] Reds manager Sparky Anderson. A dabber, in baseball terminology, is a pitcher who nibbles at the corners of the plate rather than throw a good fastball, usually because he doesn't have one." (*Mansfield* [Ohio] *News Journal*, July 10, 1975; Peter Morris).

Da Bums Var. of *Dem Bums*.

daffiness The madcap or clownishly inept behavior of a player or team. In the 1920s and early 1930s the hapless Brooklyn Dodgers were dubbed the "Daffiness Boys" by Westbrook Pegler for their lovable incompetence and pixilated reputation, such as having three baserunners on one base. "No manager ever had more woes than [Casey] Stengel in the days when he piloted the 'daffiness boys' of the Brooklyn Dodgers and later the equally inept Boston Braves" (*San Francisco News*, June 21, 1956; Peter Tamony). The "daffiness" label seems to have a special place in baseball, where it can stick with a team or player for years; e.g., Babe Herman, who brought "the Brooklyn Dodgers and Brooklyn itself a national reputation for irrepressible daffiness" (Martin Weil, *The Washington Post*, Nov. 30, 1987). The collective nickname "Daffiness Boys" was also applied to Jay Hanna "Dizzy" Dean and Paul Dee "Daffy" Dean, brothers from Arkansas

Daffiness. The "Daffiness Boys": Jay Hanna "Dizzy" Dean (left) and Paul Dee "Daffy" Dean of the St. Louis Cardinals.

who were first-rate pitchers in the 1930s for the St. Louis Cardinals, a team that captured the public fancy as a repository for cutups and pranksters.

daily win A team meeting held before each game (Al Schacht, *Al Schacht's Dope Book*, 1944).

daisies The outfield; e.g., "Jones patrols the daisies."

daisy clipper Syn. of *daisy cutter*, 1. IST USE. 1888. A ball bouncing through a meadow as "the sphere in the act of parting a Kranklet from her bonnet" (Thomas W. Lawson, *The Krank: His Language and What It Means*).

daisy cutter 1. A sharply hit ground ball along the surface of the ground without rebounding, presumably removing any daisies in its path. Henry Chadwick (*The Game of Base Ball*, 1868, p.39) noted that the daisy cutter is "very difficult to field, and, consequently, shows good batting." See also *grass cutter*; *skimmer*; *scooter*. Syn. *daisy clipper*; *daisy dipper*; *daisy kisser*; *daisy mower*; *daisy scorcher*; *timothy trimmer*. IST USE. 1866 (*New York Herald*, Sept. 20; Edward J. Nichols). 2. A low, fast pitch or underhanded pitch. IST USE. 1857. "The umpires called play, Grange being again on the defensive to the under-hand 'daisy cutters' of Sadler" (*Bell's Life*, Nov. 1).

ETYMOLOGY. From as early as 1809 (*OED*), "a horse that keeps his feet near the ground in trotting or running [and therefore cuts the heads off daisies]" (*New York Clipper Almanac*, 1881; Peter Tamony).

EXTENDED USE. 1. A small World War II rocket or anti-personnel bomb, not much larger than a grenade, that spreads out and "cuts daisies" in all directions. "Marines promptly nicknamed the skipping, hell-raising rocket shells 'Daisy Cutters'" (*Time* magazine, Feb. 7, 1944). It was also the official nickname for a larger bomb in the Vietnam War and first Gulf War. 2. A 14,994-pound bomb (formally known as the BLU–82) that creates a fireball, used in the war against terrorists in Afghanistan. It detonates about three feet above ground, releasing a cloud of gas that ignites, vacuuming air from caves and burning occupants. "[It is] extremely useful against troops that are in light defensive positions" (Gen. Peter Pace, vice chairman of the Joint Chiefs of Staff, quoted in *The Baltimore Sun*, Nov. 7, 2001).

daisy dipper Syn. of *daisy cutter*, 1. IST USE. 1874 (*Chicago Inter-Ocean*, July 7; Edward J. Nichols).

daisy kisser Syn. of *daisy cutter*, 1. "[Oakland first baseman] Jack Ness . . . speared a daisy kisser from Tennant's bat with his gloved hand" (*San Francisco Bulletin*, May 30, 1913; Gerald L. Cohen).

daisy mower Syn. of *daisy cutter*, 1. "Small boys [shall convey] . . . bouquets from the enthusiastic spectators to each participant who shall distinguish himself by catching a 'Daisy Mower' . . . in his hat" (*Flint* [Mich.]

Wolverine Citizen, Aug. 31, 1867; Peter Morris).

daisy scorcher Syn. of *daisy cutter*, 1. IST USE. 1910. "Hagner bumped a daisy scorcher to Joe" (Christy Mathewson, *Won in the Ninth*; David Shulman).

damaged goods A player who has been injured and whose career is in jeopardy (George Gmelch, *Inside Pitch*, 2001, p.59).

damp sling *hist.* A spitball. IST USE. 1907 (*New York Evening Journal*, May 1; Edward J. Nichols)

dancer A *knuckleball*.

D&M model glove *hist.* The type of glove presumably worn by a fielder who has committed an error. Such a player was once taunted by his teammates: "What are you using, the D&M [dropping and moaning] model?" The initials stand for Draper & Maynard, a legitimate brand name.

dandy 1. *n.* A first-rate ballplayer or play. "Mickey Welch is a dandy and the king-pin of them all" (*The World* [New York], Aug. 26, 1887; Gerald L. Cohen). "Johnny Ward opened the game . . . with a home run, and it was a dandy" (*The World* [New York], July 12, 1890; Gerald L. Cohen). 2. *adj.* Said of a first-rate ballplayer or play. "Cincinnati has acquired a dandy shortstop [Joe Tinker]" (*San Francisco Bulletin*, Feb. 17, 1913; Gerald L. Cohen). "Darby brought Caruthers home with a dandy sacrifice hit" (*The World* [New York], Oct. 20, 1889; Gerald L. Cohen).

dangle The looseness of a pitcher's arm action, "the well-lubricated unhinging of the limbs and body" (Tom Verducci, *Sports Illustrated*, July 7, 2008).

Daniel Webster A player who is good at taunting umpires and possesses other verbal skills; a player who looks or acts wise. The term refers to the oratorical skills of the 19th-century statesman Daniel Webster.

Danny Thompson Award An annual award given by Baseball Chapel for "exemplary Christian spirit in baseball." It honors Thompson, an infielder for the Minnesota Twins in the 1970s, who died of leukemia in 1976.

dark one A fastball. "The dark one. Lights out. The pitch that finishes off a batter" (Pete

Fromm, *How This All Stands*, 2000, p.176; Steve Milman).

Darren Baker Rule An age requirement of 14 for batboys. During Game 5 of the 2002 World Series, Baker, the three-year-old batboy and son of San Francisco Giants manager Dusty Baker, wandered into the action in the area of home plate. "Darren, excited to retrieve the bat of his favorite player, Kenny Lofton, nearly got himself hurt and almost interfered with the ensuing play. J.T. Snow, who had scored, scooped up Darren before David Bell came charging across the plate. . . . Because of Darren's innocent actions, major league baseball implemented . . . the 'Darren Baker Rule'" (Rich Marazzi, *Baseball Digest*, July 2003, p.86).

dart A fastball. "John Smoltz . . . [was] throwing unhittable 97-mph darts" (Tom Verducci, *Sports Illustrated*, May 5, 2003).

darter A line drive. See also *blue darter*.

darting hummer A fastball with an erratic flight.

dart thrower A pitcher who aims the ball excessively, implying some hesitancy or timidity (Alan Schwarz, BaseballAmerica.com, Nov. 14, 2006).

dash off with the pennant To win the league championship.

Dauvray Cup A trophy made by Tiffany & Co. and awarded between 1887 and 1890 to the winner of the postseason series between the champions of the National League and the American Association—and to the Boston Beaneaters in 1893 after winning the National League titles in 1891, 1892, and 1893. The cup was commissioned by the famous New York actress Helen Dauvray in 1887, shortly after her marriage to John Montgomery Ward, and carried, at Dauvray's behest, the stipulation that the first team to win the cup for three years (not necessarily in succession) would get to keep it. The cup is now lost. It was succeeded by the *Temple Cup*.

Davenport translations A method designed by Clay Davenport (*Baseball Prospectus*) for estimating batters' *equivalent average* across years and across leagues. For example, Ryan Howard's 2005 minor-league batting data "Davenport translated" to an equivalent aver-

age of .341, which was 20 points above any other minor leaguer's that year, foreshadowing his major-league performance. Abbrev. *DTs*.

Day 1. A ceremony or celebration to commemorate a player, manager, coach, or other baseball individual, given before or after a game or between games of a doubleheader. Gifts often are given to the person being honored. Days can be set for players about to retire or retiring, or after retirement. 2. A promotional event at a baseball game. Examples include: Cap Day, Bat Day, Poster Day, Hot Pants Day, Camera Day, Senior Citizens Day, and Fan Appreciation Day. See also *Night*.

day ball Baseball played during the daylight hours, as opposed to *night ball*; specif., baseball as played at Wrigley Field in Chicago, where there were no lights for night games until 1988. "Everybody wants to say we [the Chicago Cubs] lost in '69 because of day ball" (catcher Randy Hundley, quoted in *Sport*, Oct. 1984). Syn. *day baseball*.

day baseball Syn. of *day ball*. "Day baseball . . . gave me more of a semblance of a normal life. Home games in Chicago meant being at home with the family at night" (Bobby Thomson, *"The Giants Win the Pennant! The Giants Win the Pennant!,"* 1991, p.211). USAGE NOTE. The term is a retronym: once night baseball became popular, the need for "day baseball" became as plain as day (so to speak).

day game A game played in natural light. It is a distinction that came about with the advent of artificial lights and the *night game*.

daylight play A defensive maneuver performed by an infielder and the pitcher in an effort to pick off a baserunner. While the runner takes his lead, the infielder quietly slips back to the base; simultaneously the pitcher steps off the rubber and spins around toward that base. If the pitcher feels there is a chance to pick off the runner (if he sees "daylight" between the runner and the base), he throws the ball to the infielder for the attempted pickoff. If the pitcher does not see daylight, he simply holds the ball, having at least moved the runner back to the base.

day-night doubleheader A *doubleheader* wherein the second (night) game starts several hours later than the first and for which there are separate admissions. See also *separate-admission doubleheader.*

day-tripper A home run.

D-Backs Short for *Diamondbacks.* Syn. "D'backs."

dead *hist.* Syn. of *out,* 1; e.g., "three hands dead" meant that the side was retired.

dead arm The fatigued or overworked throwing arm of a pitcher. The term sounds worse than what it means; the arm is not injured. Colorado Rockies pitching coach Frank Funk referred to dead arm (*Sports Illustrated,* Aug. 24, 1998) as "a case of asking your arm to do more than it has ever done before, and it goes through a stage where it gets fatigued, but it's not sore. It just feels weak. You try to throw the ball just as hard as you ever did. It just doesn't go that hard." USAGE NOTE. Historically, the term referred to a more serious arm condition. "Freddie Federico, the [Milwaukee] Brewers' trainer, said he had seen scores of torn [rotator] cuffs over his lengthy career. 'But until recently,' he said, 'we just called it a dead arm'" (Daniel Okrent, *Nine Innings,* 1985, p.69; Peter Morris).

dead-arm period An interval of time (from a few days to about two weeks), common during spring training, during which a pitcher's throwing arm feels weak, affecting his velocity and command. The "cure" is rest. Mike Mussina, going through a dead-arm period, explained (*The Baltimore Sun,* Sept. 21, 1996), "Sometimes it comes back quickly and sometimes you have [a dead arm] and it comes and goes. . . . Sometimes it's more gradual. I may feel very good [today] or I may feel sluggish. You just have to keep working. I know it will go away sooner or later." See also *dead spot.*

dead as a doornail Said of baserunner who is thrown out easily while attempting to steal a base.

dead ball 1. A ball that is not in play because of a legally created, temporary suspension of play. The ball may be deemed "dead" if it has hit a batter, been handled by a spectator, come in contact with an umpire or baserunner, or been thrown out of play. Other dead-ball situations include a pitcher's balk, interference by a baserunner, an uncaught foul ball, and time-out called by an umpire. If an area of the field is deemed dangerous for play, a ball hit to that area is ruled dead. The ball becomes live again when the umpire allows the pitcher to take the ball and step on the pitching rubber. Compare *live ball,* 1. See also *delayed dead ball.* "A ball is said to be 'dead' when no player can be legally put out by a fielder, as in the case of a called or balked ball hit by the batsman, or when a ball is stopped by outsiders" (Henry Chadwick, *The Game of Base Ball,* 1868, p.39). IST USE. 1866. "Any ball delivered by the pitcher on which a ball or a balk has been called, shall be a dead ball and not considered in play until it is settled in the hands of the pitcher, and he be within the lines of his position" (amended rule of the National Association of Base Ball Players, quoted in *Milwaukee Daily Sentinel,* Dec. 20). **2.** A baseball that, due to certain properties of its component materials, deadens the impact when hit with a bat; specif., a baseball used before 1920 without a resilient core. Since the balls used during 19th-century games were provided by the home team, a good fielding team preferred to use dead balls (less than one ounce of rubber as its core) while an offensive team preferred the livelier ball (with more rubber). Compare *lively ball,* 1. IST USE. 1870. "The balls known [as] Atlantic or Bounding Rock, may now be deemed 'dead'" (Chadwick Scrapbooks; John Freyer). **3.** The style or strategy of baseball known as inside baseball. **4.** A hit batsman in Cuba. "[Cubans] say 'dead ball' when the pitcher hits a batter, and they carry it that way in the boxscores" (*The Washington Post,* Apr. 25, 1954; Peter Morris).

dead-ball era The period ending with the 1919 season when the game was played with an apparently much less lively baseball, one that lacked resiliency. The term is a misnomer, as most baseball historians agree that the era ended in 1920 with rule changes (banning the spitball and other trick pitches and freak deliveries, replacing discolored and scuffed balls with shiny new ones) and use of better-quality materials, not with the change in the ball. The era was characterized by the use of the hit and run, the stolen base, the sacrifice, and the bunt; batters choked up on the bat and were loath to take hard swings; runs were at a premium; and ballparks had huge dimensions. The era ended when Babe Ruth began swinging for the fences. Compare *lively ball era*. USAGE NOTE. In Feb. 2000, the Society for American Baseball Research formed the "Deadball Era Committee," which specifies the years 1901 to 1919 for the era, spells "deadball" without a hyphen, and uses uppercase when referring to the era.

dead batter A batter who approaches the plate without a bat. Bert Dunne (*Folger's Dictionary of Baseball*, 1958) added, "Dugout legalists claim there is no rule in the book that forces batter to use a bat at the plate, and that umpire must proceed in normal fashion, calling balls and strikes."

dead body 1. A bench jockey's description of a nonchalant or low-key player. 2. A scout's term for a player with "slow reflexes, heavy feet, or bad hands" (Kevin Kerrane, *Dollar Sign on the Muscle*, 1984, p.90).

dead duck A baserunner caught in a rundown.

deaden To bunt the ball in such a manner that it slows quickly after it hits the ground; e.g., "to deaden the ball" is to bunt effectively.

dead fish 1. A slowly pitched ball; a *nothing ball*. "A 'dead fish' in the ball players' lexicon is a pitch with nothing on it" (Charles P. Ward, *Detroit Free Press*, June 6, 1939; Peter Morris). Syn. *dead mackerel*; *herring*. IST USE. 1937. "Dead Fish—a slow ball" (Jimmy Powers, *New York Daily News*, Jan. 10). 2. An unorthodox pitch of any kind. Ron Guidry called his new screwball the "dead fish" (*The Washington Post*, Apr. 14, 1986). Houston Astros outfielder Terry Puhl, commenting on Bruce Sutter's forkball (*The Sporting News*, Sept. 23, 1978): "It starts out like a fast ball and winds up like a dead fish." 3. A bunted ball that scurries a short distance and then stops ("dies") in the grass. Such a hit rarely occurs on artificial turf. "[Nellie Fox] worked on bunting, the 'dead-fish' kind" (Paul Richards, quoted in *The Baltimore Sun*, March 2, 1997).

dead foul ball *hist.* "Any ball sent to the bat from the pitcher's position, which shall accidentally hit the striker's bat, shall be declared a 'dead foul ball,' and no base shall be run or player be put out on such a ball" (National Association of Professional Base Ball Players Rules, Rule II, Sec. 7, 1872; Peter Morris).

dead from the neck up Said of a physically gifted player who is intellectually challenged (Joe Morgan, *Baseball for Dummies*, 1998, p.354).

dead hands The hands of a batter who keeps them locked in a rigid position while swinging, rather than rolling his wrists.

deadhead 1. *v./hist.* To get a base on balls; to get a "free ride." IST USE. 1912. "Deadhead to first" (*New York Tribune*, Oct. 6; Edward J. Nichols). 2. *n./hist.* A base on balls in Philadelphia was known as a "dead head" (*The Sporting Life*, July 7, 1906; Peter Morris). 3. *n.* A spectator admitted to a baseball game on a complimentary ticket. ETYMOLOGY. "Persons who drink at a bar, ride in an omnibus, or railroad car, travel in steamboats, or visit the theatre without charge, are called 'deadheads'" (*Bartlett's Dictionary of Americanisms*, 1848).

dead mackerel Syn. of *dead fish*, 1. "Dead mackerel. A slow ball. 'He kept feeding me the dead mackerel and what could I do?'" (H.G. Salsinger, *Baseball Digest*, Aug. 1945). Compare *mackerel*. ETYMOLOGY. From the old saying "dead as a mackerel," which is how the slowly pitched ball appears when compared to the fastball.

dead-pull hitter A hitter who always pulls the ball to his field of maximum power.

dead-red 1. Said of a batter anticipating or waiting for a fastball. When the batter is ahead in the count and the pitcher is likely to throw the fastball, the batter is said to be "sitting or looking dead-red." ETYMOLOGY. The apparent color of a spinning fastball as it approaches the plate. The color comes from the interplay of seams and cowhide as the ball spins. 2. *hist.* Said of a red-colored dead ball used in the 1870s. It was thought that a ball colored a restful red would be easier on a player's eyes than the white (highly

Deanism. Dizzy Dean's many bylined guides and dictionaries carried his own version of baseballese. *Author's collection*

reflective) ball hovering in a bright sky. Ball manufacturers offered a "Dead Red" baseball in their advertisements (Robert H. Schaefer).

Dead Sox A derogatory nickname for the Boston Red Sox. In Stephen King's *Different Seasons* (1982; Charles D. Poe), a character's mood is elevated when the 1967 Red Sox win the pennant: "There was a goofy sort of feeling that if the Dead Sox could come to life, then maybe *anybody* could."

dead spot A period of ineffective pitching. "Pitchers go through a dead spot in the spring where they try to throw something good and nothing comes out. Your arm feels good and your delivery is good, but it's just not there" (Toronto Blue Jays manager Jimy Williams, quoted in *St. Petersburg Times*, March 21, 1986). See also *dead-arm period*.

dead zone A signal given to let the recipient know that the next sign—normally a legitimate indicator—is a fake. It is intended to foil sign stealers.

deal 1. *v.* To trade a player or players. To say that a team will not "deal" a certain player is to say he will not be traded. 2. *n.* A trade. IST USE. 1886. "The indications are before many days there will be another base ball deal . . . with a view of exchanging players" (*The Bos-*

ton *Globe*, June 4; Peter Morris). 3. *v.* To defeat a team or pitcher. "The Boston Red Sox dealt him [Jered Weaver] his first major league loss" (*The Baltimore Sun*, Sept. 5, 2006). 4. *v.* For a pitcher to deliver a pitch.

deal from the bottom To pitch underhand. Syn. "deal off the bottom"; "deal from the bottom of the deck." IST USE. 1937 (*The Sporting News Record Book*, p.64; Edward J. Nichols). ETYMOLOGY. From the unfair or "underhand" passing out of cards in poker.

Deanism Any one of scores of words, phrases, and statements coined by pitcher and announcer Jay Hanna "Dizzy" Dean. Though many were grammatically incorrect, they often were quite inventive and descriptive. In his own vernacular, for instance: players always "slud" into a base; he "throwed" him out at first; players returned to their "respectable bases"; Stan Musial stood "confidentially" at the plate; "the doctors X-rayed my head and found nothing" (after he was hit in the head by a thrown ball in the 1934 World Series); "don't fail to miss tomorrow's game"; and "a lot of people that ain't sayin' 'ain't' ain't eatin.'" Jerry Howarth (*Baseball*

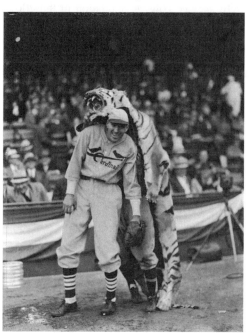

Deanism. Dizzy Dean clowning with Detroit Tigers mascot at 1934 World Series. *Photograph by Joseph Baylor Roberts*

Lite, 1986) insisted that Dean helped to establish the popularity of the live television *Game of the Week* when, on the air, he referred to an act of courage as "testicle fortitude."

death march A series of losses. "It's a death march" is what manager Phil Garner said of the Milwaukee Brewers' fourth straight loss (*Milwaukee Journal Sentinel*, Aug. 11, 1997).

death valley 1. A particularly deep outfield area in a given ballpark. Because of the deep dimensions, it is more difficult to hit home runs, and fly balls are almost certain outs. Well-known "death valleys" are left-center field (and original center field) in Yankee Stadium and center field in Tiger Stadium. **2.** The central swath of home plate, excluding the inside and outside portions, where a batter can easily drive the ball (Thomas P. McDonald).

debt equity rule A requirement that prohibits a major-league club from carrying debt that is more than roughly 60 percent of the revenues and market value of the franchise. The rule has been on the books, but largely ignored, for years. Compare *60–40 rule*.

debt service rule A regulation in the 2007–2011 Basic Agreement between the owners and the players that stipulates that a club may not have more total outstanding debt (calculated as an average over the course of each fiscal year) than 10 times EBITDA (earnings before interest, taxes, depreciation, and amortization) over the most recent two or three years, except that any club that incurs (or has incurred within the last 10 years) stadium-related debt to finance construction of a new ballpark or major renovation of an existing ballpark may not have more debt than 15 times EBITDA. The rule restricts the amount clubs can spend on back-loading player contracts. Compare *60–40 rule*.

deceiver *hist.* **1.** The pitcher. "The latest terms to indicate the pitcher and catcher are 'deceiver' and 'retriever'" (*The Boston Globe*, Apr. 25, 1894; Peter Morris). **2.** A deceptive pitch. "Cy [Parkins] was in good humor and he jollied the crowd along as he doled out deceivers to the batters" (*San Francisco Bulletin*, March 3, 1913; Gerald L. Cohen).

decent wood Syn. of *good wood*, 1.

decision 1. The scoring outcome of a game; e.g., "The Cubs won by a 3–2 decision." **2.** A win or a loss by a pitcher or a team. **3.** A ruling by an umpire. IST USE. 1861 (Chadwick Scrapbooks; Edward J. Nichols).

decision pitch Syn. of *payoff pitch*.

deck 1. *n.* The location or position of the player next in line to hit after the present batter. See also *on deck; on-deck circle*. **2.** *n.* A layer or tier of seats in a ballpark. IST USE. 1909. "John Moran, director of public safety, . . . appeared in the middle of the diamond and looked bashfully up at the third deck of the box seats" (Ring W. Lardner, *Chicago Tribune*, July 1; Peter Morris). **3.** *v.* Syn. of *knock down*.

Decker The pillow-like, padded *catcher's mitt* patented by catcher Harry Decker in 1889. It was stitched to the back of a round pad that covered the palm of the hand, almost literally resembling a flat pillow. The mitt was so popular that for several years catcher's mitts were referred to as "Deckers."

decking The act of knocking down a batter with a pitch, or being knocked down by a pitch.

decoy 1. To run in such a manner as to deceive a defensive player; e.g., a batter singles and acts as if he will stop at first base to trick the fielder into thinking the play is ending, at which point he breaks for second base. **2.** To deceiver a baserunner. Examples include: luring the runner off his base with the hidden-ball trick; fielding a ball as though it will be misplayed; feinting the motions for a double play (when the batter hits a fly ball) in the hope that the runner will be decoyed into sliding or hesitating; confusing a runner to return to a base; and standing at a base as though no throw is coming in, hoping the runner will slow up or not slide and then can be tagged out. A rarer example would be for the second baseman to act in such a way as to entice the runner on first to try and steal. Syn. *deek*, 1; *deke*, 1. **3.** To lead a batter to guess incorrectly the type or location of the next pitch.

decoy sign A meaningless sign from the catcher, dugout, or coach's box that misleads and confuses those trying to steal the sign.

deek 1. Short for *decoy*, 2. **2.** To mislead with a decoy sign.

deep 1. *adv.* Far from home plate; e.g., both infielders and outfielders may "play deep," while the batter may hope to hit the ball deep or "go deep." A batter planning to touch up a pitcher might say "I'm going to take him deep." Compare *shallow*, 2. **2.** *adj.* Said of that part of the field that is the greatest distance from home plate; e.g., "deep center" or "deep short." Compare *shallow*, 1. **3.** *adj.* Rich in talent; e.g., a "deep bench" or a "deep bullpen." Earl Weaver's term for having much talent in reserve was *deep depth*. **4.** *adj.* See *deep in the count*. **5.** *adv.* Said of a starting pitcher working into the late innings. "The [Milwaukee] Brewers needed [Jamey] Wright to pitch deep due to injuries and their thin bullpen" (*Milwaukee Journal Sentinel*, June 10, 2002; Robert F. Perkins). "With starters being limited in how many pitches they can throw, they don't throw as deep into games as they used to" (Baltimore Orioles closer Chris Ray, quoted in *The Baltimore Sun*, Aug. 27, 2006). **6.** *adv.* Said of a pitch that a patient batter with exceptional plate coverage waits for as long as possible. "Let's begin with the swing. . . . The head stays down and the hands stay back, so [the batter] sees the ball 'deeper,' as the hitting coaches put it" (Charles P. Pierce, *Sports Illustrated*, July 5, 2004). "I trust that I can hit a fastball. . . . I don't have to go get it. I can let it travel and get deep, deep to the plate" (Albert Pujols, quoted in *Sports Illustrated*, May 22, 2006). **7.** *adj.* [softball term] Said of a pitch that falls past the batter in slow pitch softball, analogous to "high" in baseball or fast pitch softball; the pitch is called a ball. Compare *short*, 4.

deep count A tally against the batter of either two balls and two strikes (2 and 2) or three balls and two strikes (3 and 2). "[Jeremy Accardo] can be a deep-count pitcher" (anonymous scout, quoted in *The Baltimore Sun*, Aug. 19, 2007).

deep depth The situation when a team has much talent in reserve. The term was used by Baltimore Orioles manager Earl Weaver. "Weaver's uncanny ability to make use of spare parts and one-trick artists led the organization to focus on its bench more than

most. And the Orioles' 'deep depth' became a trademark of the Weaver era" (Childs Walker, *The Baltimore Sun*, Aug. 6, 2005). See also *depth*, 1.

deep in the bleach Said of a long home run hit into the bleachers.

deep in the count Said of a balls-and-strikes situation in which many pitches have been thrown. "We're going deep in the count and causing a lot of pitching changes" (New York Yankees manager Joe Torre, quoted in *Sports Illustrated*, March 29, 1999). "You want to know what the best hitters can do? They can hit deep in the count" (Seattle Mariners manager Lou Piniella, quoted in *Sports Illustrated*, March 25, 2002). Compare *early in the count*.

deep in the hole Said of the area toward the outfield between the shortstop and third base.

deep-pocketed club A baseball organization with much money to spend on players.

deep short The area in shallow outfield that is some distance further back than the shortstop's normal playing position.

deer A fast runner; a player who can "high-tail it."

deerfoot A fast runner. Clyde Milan, who stole 495 bases in his career, was nicknamed "Deerfoot."

deface To mar the surface of the ball by rubbing it with soil, rosin, paraffin, licorice, sandpaper, emery, or other foreign substance. A pitcher who intentionally defaces the ball is ejected from the game and receives an automatic 10-game suspension.

defense 1. The team, or any player on that team, in the field. **2.** The total strategy of the team in the field, involving such variables as the positioning of fielders, pickoff plays, and pitchouts. The purpose of the defense is to get three outs per inning without allowing the offense to score a run. Syn. *D*, 2.

defense independent pitching statistics Home runs, strikeouts, bases on balls, and the number of hit batsmen. Voros McCracken claimed that, with the exception of home runs, pitchers have no control over the number of hits on batted balls that they give up, such that the responsibility for hits given up per inning belongs to the fielders and plain luck. As a consequence, pitchers should only be evaluated on the three statistics they do control: home runs, strikeouts, and bases on balls. Sabermetric research has shown that pitchers do have some control over the number of hits on batted balls they give up, but not nearly as much as previously supposed. The concept was first mentioned by Clifford Blau (*By the Numbers*, May 2000). Abbrev. *DIPS*.

defensive average An estimate of a player's fielding efficiency, comparing the number of plays a fielder makes to the number of balls hit into the area he patrols. The raw data is gathered by slicing the playing field into a set of zones and assigning each zone to one or more players who are within reach of balls hit into that zone. Although in practice fraught with measurement problems, it is in principle the most accurate and most important indicator of a player's performance at fielding batted balls. The first analysis of defensive average was performed by Pete DeCoursey using data gathered by Project Scoresheet and published in *Philadelphia Baseball File* (March 1989). See also *zone rating*, a variation devised by STATS Inc.

defensive batting average An informal statistic representing a combination of a fielder's zone rating, fielding percentage, proportion of successful double plays made (for second basemen), and proportion of extra bases taken by baserunners on hits (for outfielders). The statistic is defined in STATS Inc.'s *Baseball Scoreboard*.

defensive efficiency record A measure of a team's defensive performance, indicated by the percentage of times that a batted ball in play (i.e., neither foul, strike, nor home run) is turned into an out by a team's defense. For example, the 1982 San Diego Padres had a defensive efficiency record of .719, whereas the New York Mets had a record of .691; the difference between the two (.028) is approximately equivalent to a .025 difference in team batting average, which is substantial. The measure was devised by Bill James and described in his self-published *Baseball Abstract* (1978); a discussion can be found in

his first conventionally published *Baseball Abstract* (1982). See also *park-adjusted defensive efficiency*. Abbrev. *DER*.

defensive indifference Allowing a runner to advance a base without attempting to stop him; e.g., when the first baseman does not hold the runner at first base, second base is open, and the catcher makes no attempt to throw. To rule defensive indifference, the *Official Baseball Rules* (Rule 10.07[g]) states that the official scorer shall consider "the totality of the circumstances," including the inning and score of the game and whether a) the defensive team held the runner on base, b) the pitcher had made pickoff attempts, c) the fielder expected to cover the base to which the runner advanced or made a move to do so, and d) the defensive team had a legitimate strategic motive not to contest the runner's advance. The situation often occurs in the ninth inning when the defensive team is ahead by two or more runs and the runner on first base is not the tying or go-ahead run. It can also occur in the bottom of the ninth or extra innings with runners on first base and third base and two outs. No stolen base is awarded when a runner advances solely because of the defensive team's indifference to his advance; it is scored as a fielder's choice. The ruling was introduced in 1920 and clarified in 2007.

defensive innings The number of innings in which a fielder appears at a given position. The number is particularly useful when evaluating the defensive performance of players who tend to be used as late-inning defensive replacements or who are often pinch-hit for, and as a consequence do not characteristically play full games. See *range factor* for an example of its application.

defensive misplay An objectively observable event that has a negative cost to the defense. Bill James (personal communication, Dec. 12, 2007) gives as examples a fielder going back on a ball that lands in front of him and an outfielder running toward a ball that bounces over his head.

defensive replacement A player sent late into a game by the team in the lead to replace a player who can hit better than he can field.

defensive spectrum A listing of the relative demands that different defensive positions place on a player. The most demanding position is shortstop, followed in order by second base, center field, third base, right field, left field, first base, and designated hitter, the least demanding "position." Catchers and pitchers are not included, due to the special talents demanded by those positions that make them not comparable to the rest. Implications of the defensive spectrum include the following: 1) as players age, they move from more to less demanding positions; 2) the more demanding a player's position, the greater the odds that poor hitting will be tolerated; and 3) there is usually more available talent toward the less demanding side of the spectrum. The model was proposed by Bill James in his self-published *Baseball Abstract* (1981); a description is found in his first conventionally published *Baseball Abstract* (1982).

defensive winning percentage Syn. of *defensive won-lost percentage*.

defensive won-lost percentage An informal index of a player's defensive performance, computed by assigning points for factors such as a player's range factor, fielding percentage, and number of double plays in a given season. It is designed on a scale of 0 to 1, so that the average defensive player records a .5. The statistic was devised by Bill James and described in detail in his first conventionally published *Baseball Abstract* (1982). Syn. *defensive winning percentage*.

defensive won-lost record An informal index of a player's defensive performance in a given season, based on the player's defensive won-lost percentage, the position he plays, and the number of games he has played in that season. The statistic was devised by Bill James in his *Baseball Abstract* (1983).

deke 1. Short for *decoy*, 2. ETYMOLOGY. The term is long established in hockey for pulling the goaltender out of position. It also has a long football application. It began to find wide baseball application by around 1990. 2. To mislead with a decoy sign.

Delahanty bunt A home run by a "mere mortal batter," in comparison to one hit for a great distance by powerful outfielder Ed Delahanty (Mike Sowell, *July 2, 1903*, 1992, p.5).

delay An official suspension of play before or during a game. "After an [*sic*] 36-minute pregame sun delay, an 86-minute delay due to power failure, and 10 innings of baseball, the [Pittsfield] Cubs and [Albany-Colonie] Yankees finished in a 4–4 tie in a game suspended by an Eastern League curfew rule" (*Berkshire Eagle*, July 5, 1985).

delayed dead ball A *dead ball* resulting from an infraction that occurs before a play is completed; e.g., interference by a batter during an attempted putout on a runner, obstruction of the batter by the catcher, obstruction of a baserunner by a fielder, interference by an umpire with the catcher attempting to throw, or intentionally throwing a fielder's glove at a batted or thrown ball.

delayed double steal A *double steal* attempted when there are baserunners at first base and third base. The play begins when the runner at first moves toward second on an apparent steal attempt. Before the catcher, who has the

Delay. Postcard, ca. 1910. *Andy Moresund Collection*

ball, makes the throw to second, the runner stops as if to return to first. If the catcher relaxes, the runner then starts again for second at top speed to induce the catcher's throw. As the ball is thrown, the runner on third breaks for home.

delayed squeeze Syn. of *safety squeeze*.

delayed steal A stolen base on which the runner advances to the next base after the pitch; e.g., when the catcher throws the ball back to the pitcher. The success of the maneuver hinges on the extent to which the element of surprise has caught a fielder unaware or out of proper defensive position, as, e.g., when the second baseman and shortstop are playing well back and neither makes a break to cover second base. Lee Allen (*The Hot Stove League*, 1955, p.115) noted that the maneuver was "apparently first employed by Miller Huggins . . . in 1903." John J. Evers and Hugh S. Fullerton (*Touching Second: The Science of Baseball*, 1910; Peter Morris): "Frank Chance, in 1906, commenced to work the 'delayed steal' persistently and was proclaimed the discoverer of the play. Yet [Mike] Kelly, [Billy] Hamilton, [Bill] Lange, [Tip] O'Neill, [Charles] Comiskey, [Hugh] Duffy and many others used the play, and 'Sadie' Houck stole in that way with much success." IST USE. 1906. H.G. Merrill (*The Sporting News*, Dec. 22, 1906; Peter Morris) wrote that Kid Elberfeld was "said to have developed the 'delayed steal' last year" but claimed that a minor leaguer named Bill O'Hara had employed the play regularly in 1905.

delill *hist.* **1.** *n.* A short bat, 18 to 24 inches long, shaped like a miniature baseball bat, used in town ball games. According to Alfred Rochefort (*Healthful Sports for Boys*, 1910, p.23) and Irving A. Leitner (*Baseball: Diamond in the Rough*, 1972, p.32), it was held in one hand by the striker, who, instead of swinging at the ball, allowed the pitch to be deflected off the bat at a given angle, directing the ball to whatever area of the playing field he chose. ETYMOLOGY. Unknown. **2.** *v.* To use a delill.

deliver **1.** To pitch; to complete one's delivery. IST USE. 1866 (Constitution and By-Laws of the Olympic Ball Club of Philadelphia, p.28; Edward J. Nichols). **2.** To come through in a pinch; to get a hit in a clutch situation. IST USE. 1913. "Dode Birmingham . . . acted as substitute batter for Vean Gregg in the eighth, but failed to deliver" (*The Washington Post*, Aug. 23; Peter Morris). **3.** To succeed; to show results. "I don't intend to take any and all players that the major league clubs want to pawn off on me, but men that I know will deliver the goods" (Del Howard, quoted in *San Francisco Bulletin*, March 11, 1913; Gerald L. Cohen). **4.** To bat in a runner. "Jim Leyritz delivered the first run on a groundout" (*The Baltimore Sun*, Oct. 15, 1998).

delivery **1.** The complete combination of pitcher movements in executing a pitch, from windup to the release of the ball. IST USE. 1864. "Umpires must remember, in deciding on this movement of the feet, that no one can lift his foot in delivering a ball until the ball leaves his hand, the lifting of the hind foot being the result of this delivery, as it is from the pressure of the foot on the ground that he derives the power to impel the ball with speed" (*New York Clipper*, May 7; Peter Morris). **2.** A pitched ball. "The goal of getting outs earlier in the count by inducing hitters to put those deliveries into play" (*Sports Illustrated*, Apr. 8, 2002).

delivery speed The amount of time that elapses between the pitcher's first move in the windup and the moment the ball hits the catcher's glove. A delivery speed of 1.3 seconds is considered difficult to steal against.

Dem Bums Traditional affectionate nickname for the Brooklyn Dodgers, established and characterized by a bewhiskered, cigar-chomping cartoon tramp drawn by Willard Mullin. See also *Bums*. Var. of *Da Bums*. IST USE. 1940. Mullin's cartoon, titled "Dem Bums," showed the Brooklyn caricature dressed as a drum major leading the National League (*New York World-Telegram*, Apr. 20; Barry Popik).

demolition derby A *grand slam*, 1.

dent the ball To hit the ball hard.

dent the ozone *hist.* To swing and miss. See also *ozone*, 2. IST USE. 1909 (*Baseball Magazine*, December, p.53; Edward J. Nichols).

dent the plate To score a run.

department A position on a baseball team. 1ST USE. 1861. "On the part of the Newark club we noticed that the pitching and catching departments were well attended to" (*Brooklyn Eagle*, Aug. 23; Peter Morris).

deposit the pill To hit the ball a long distance; e.g., to hit a home run is sometimes stated as "to deposit the pill in the seats."

depth 1. The situation in which a team has two or more qualified players who can fit in at any playing position (except the pitcher); the bench strength of a baseball team. Earl Weaver referred to a superior bench as *deep depth*. **2.** Scouting jargon related to the break on a breaking pitch. "[Brandon Claussen's] knockout pitch is a quality slider with excellent two-plane depth" (*Baseball America*, Jan. 21–Feb. 3, 2002; Peter Morris).

depth chart A listing by position of an organization's players ranked in order of major-league readiness. "[Craig] Counsell will open spring training fourth on the depth chart at utility infielder, behind Jason Bates, Jeff Huson and rookie Neifi Perez" (Mike Klis, *Baseball America*, Feb. 17–March 2, 1997; Peter Morris, who notes that Counsell was a World Series hero that year for the Florida Marlins). ETYMOLOGY. Probably borrowed from football, where the practice is more prevalent.

DER Abbrev. for *defensive efficiency record.*

derby 1. A competition for a position on a club in which there is no incumbent or clear-cut front runner. "Tony Womack emerged as the winner of the [Pittsburgh Pirates'] second-base derby with fellow rookies Lou Collier and Brandon Cromer" (John Perrotto, *Baseball America*, Apr. 14–27, 1997; Peter Morris). **2.** See *home run derby*, 1–3.

derrick To remove a pitcher from a game; to "lift" a pitcher from a game. See also *hook*, 8; *yank*, 1; *lift*, 1. 1ST USE. 1912. "In the eighth Manager [Jake] Stahl derricked [Buck] O'Brien and sent [Hugh] Bedient to the hill" (*Los Angeles Evening Herald*, Oct. 10; Peter Morris).

derrotado Spanish for "losing pitcher."

designated for assignment Said of a player whose team opens a roster spot while waiting for the player to clear waivers. The team must trade or release him within ten days or reassign him (if he accepts) to a minor-league team within seven days. Since there are certain situations in which a team needs a player's permission either to trade him or send him to the minors, the designation allows the player some time to make a decision. Occasionally, a club will designate a player for assignment while it is trying to trade him.

designated hitter A hitter in the American League, listed in the starting lineup and assigned to bat for the starting pitcher and all subsequent pitchers in the game. The designated hitter may be used defensively, continuing to bat in the same position in the batting order, but the pitcher must then bat in the place of the substituted defensive player. The designated hitter has been in effect since the beginning of the 1973 season and is used throughout baseball in the minor leagues, colleges, and elsewhere, except in the National League. During the World Series, both teams can use a designated hitter in games played in the American League ballpark, but neither team can use it in the National League ballpark. Between 1976 and 1986, before this World Series plan went into effect, the rule had been to use the designated hitter in alternating years. The idea of a designated hitter was not a new one when it was adopted by the American League. It was first proposed in the 1890s (Bill James, *The Bill James Historical Baseball Abstract*, 1986, p.47), suggested by National League president John H. Heydler in 1928, and discussed at various times during the 1930s. In 1906, Philadelphia Athletics manager Connie Mack suggested that the pitcher be denied a chance to bat, and a substitute player sent up for him every time: "He argues that a pitcher is such a poor hitter that his time at bat is a farce, and the game would be helped by eliminating him in favor of a better hitter" (*Philadelphia North American*, reprinted in *The Sporting Life*, Feb. 3, 1906; Bill Deane). The Pacific Coast League was denied permission to use a designated hitter in 1961. Several minor leagues (including the International League) experimented with the designated hitter in 1969. The first designated hitter was Paul Flesner of Dallas–Fort Worth in a loss to visiting Amarillo in a Texas League game on Apr. 11, 1969. The first major-league designated hitter was Ron Blomberg of the New York Yankees; he drew a walk against Luis Tiant of the Boston Red Sox on Apr. 6, 1973. "The designated hitter obliterated what used to be one of the crisis points in the game. Would the manager lift the pitcher for a pinch-hitter? Will he or won't he? Now, no more manager-on-the-spot. No more fan-surmise or speculation or second-guessing. The pitcher won't bat. He's now a eunuch in the batting order. The DH will hit. That's it, the manager's refuge. Dullsville" (Shirley Povich, *The Washington Post,* March 20, 1996). See also *designated pinch hitter; option batter; wild card pinch hitter.* Abbrev. *DH,* 2. Syn. *DH,* 3; *tenth man,* 5. EXTENDED USE. A stand-in. "Embryonic stem-cell research has become the stand-in, the designated hitter, if you will, for the struggle between science and ideology, moderates and extremists" (Ellen Goodman, *The Baltimore Sun,* Aug. 9, 2004). Also, the wording may have been directly appropriated in the term "designated driver" for a person who agrees not to consume alcohol at a social event so as to drive others home.

designated pinch hitter *hist.* An early term for *designated hitter,* but seldom used since its adoption by the American League in 1973.

designated player 1. A player *designated for assignment.* The player is not eligible to participate in a game after having been so designated until he is released or assigned to another club. 2. [softball term] A player in fast pitch softball who may be substituted for any player in a game but who must stay in the same position in the batting order while remaining in the game. The player is designated before the game and may reenter once only if the reentry is into the same position in the batting order. The designated player can play defense, or the player whose bat has been taken over by the designated player can stay in the game defensively. See also *flex.* Compare *extra player.* Abbrev. *DP,* 2.

designated runner A player whose only role is to enter the game as a substitute baserunner. The term was created for Herb Washington, a world-class sprinter hired in 1974–1975 to pinch run for the Oakland A's.

Washington scored 33 runs without ever once appearing at the plate.

designated sitter A designated hitter during a World Series when the designated hitter is not used; e.g., Don Baylor of the Boston Red Sox during the 1986 World Series.

desk contract The contract signed by an amateur ballplayer and kept on a tentative basis until the player proves that he is worth keeping. This ethically dubious tactic was practiced by Branch Rickey. "Operating in a buyer's market, [Joe] Cambria was able to tie up many prospects with desk contracts . . . until the players proved themselves worthy of a real commitment" (Kevin Kerrane, *Dollar Sign on the Muscle,* 1984, p.31; Peter Morris).

deslizamiento Spanish for "slide" (noun).

deuce 1. Syn. of *curveball.* Baltimore Orioles pitcher Rick Krivda had "I believe in the deuce" inscribed on the bill of his cap (*Orioles Gazette,* July 6, 1992). ETYMOLOGY. A borrowing from the most basic level of sandlot baseball where the catcher has two signals: one finger for the fastball and two for the curveball. 2. A double play. "They're going to turn the deuce—[Eddie] Murray to [Cal] Ripken and back to Murray" (Tom Marr, broadcast of Baltimore Orioles vs. Milwaukee Brewers game, June 30, 1986).

deuces wild A situation in a baseball game in which there are two outs, the count is two balls and two strikes on the batter, and, perhaps, two runners are on base and/or two runs have been scored. Popularized by broadcasters Vin Scully and Joe Garagiola on NBC-TV's *Game of the Week,* this term is occasionally used to describe such situations by radio and television announcers.

Devil Rays Former nickname of Tampa Bay *Rays* from 1998 to 2007. Also known as *D-Rays.*

dewdrop 1. A slow curveball. "The pitcher went through his preliminary gymnastics. This time it was a little dewdrop that didn't reach the plate" (*New York Sun,* reprinted in *The Washington Post,* Oct. 30, 1904). IST USE. 1898. "It's a lovely thing for a pitcher with a reputation to get away with nothing but horseshoe curves and dewdrop benders" (Jack

Doyle, quoted in *Fort Wayne* [Ind.] *Sentinel*, June 13; Peter Morris). **2.** A softly hit ball. "Hogan tossed Redman out at first on Harry's dewdrop in front of the plate" (W.A. Mason, *Marion* [Ohio] *Daily Star*, Sept. 10, 1907). IST USE. 1900. "Ward scored on Rhea's dewdrop to left field" (*Idaho Daily Statesman*, May 3; Peter Morris). **3.** *hist.* A foul ball.

dexter meadow Syn. of *right field*, 1.

DFE Abbrev. for *draft, follow, and evaluate*.

DH 1. Abbrev. for *doubleheader*. **2.** Abbrev. for *designated hitter*. Also "dh." **3.** *n.* Syn. of *designated hitter*. "The DH was introduced into the American League to get the bats out of pitchers' hands and get more offense" (Don Baylor, *Don Baylor*, 1989, pp.83–84). **4.** *v.* To perform as a designated hitter; e.g., "You DH a guy as kind of a semi-day off" (Mike Hargrove, quoted in *The Baltimore Sun*, Apr. 30, 2000).

DH-ing Acting as the designated hitter; batting but not fielding. "I'd rather be DH-ing, and that's God's truth" (Reggie Jackson, quoted in *The Washington Post*, May 18, 1986). Also spelled "DHing."

dial 8 To hit a home run. The term refers to the former practice of dialing the number 8 on a hotel phone before a long-distance call could be made. Syn. *dial long distance*. IST USE. 1984. "To 'dial 8' means to hit a home run" (George F. Will, *The Washington Post*, March 29). ETYMOLOGY. The phrase is credited to Thom Diehle of Washington, D.C. (E.J. Dionne Jr., *The Washington Post*, Oct. 19, 1997).

dial long distance Syn. of *dial 8*. "When Greg Gross, who had forgotten to hit a home run since 1978, suddenly remembers how to dial long distance, shouldn't we send the ball bag in for a complete physical?" (Thomas Boswell, *San Francisco Chronicle*, June 5, 1987). When a pitcher serves up a home run, the hitter's teammates may yell, "Dial long distance, and charge it to the pitcher."

dial 9 To hit a home run. The term refers to dialing the number 9 on an interoffice phone to get an outside line.

diamond 1. *n.* The enclosed square, resembling a diamond-shaped figure, formed by home plate, first base, second base, and third base; the infield of a baseball field. The term is a misnomer (a true diamond has two acute angles and two obtuse angles, but a square has four 90-degree angles, which define the infield), but the enclosed space appears diamond-shaped when viewed from any corner or from the grandstand. IST USE. 1877. "The pitching of Salisbury proving too immense for them to strike sufficiently to get the ball out of the diamond" (*Winona* [Minn.] *Republican*, June 15; Peter Morris). USAGE NOTE. David Block (*Baseball Before We Knew It*, 2005, p.198) noted that the 1835 booklet *The Boy's Book of Sports; a Description of the Exercises and Pastimes of Youth*, published by S. Babcock, introduced the first known application of the term "diamond" to the game of baseball. ETYMOLOGY. According to Dan Schlossberg (*The Baseball Catalog*, 1989, p.236), "Baseball's use of the term . . . stems from the urban planning of the nineteenth century. Towns were generally built around a square, featuring public buildings. In the east, that square was called a diamond." **2.** *n.* The entire playing surface on which the game of baseball is played. Bill Reddy (quoted in Peter Golenbock, *Bums*, 1984): "You looked down, and there was the diamond. It glistened. The grass was green. I've been to Ireland, and they have the greenest grass I've ever seen since, and still it wasn't as green as the grass at Ebbets Field." IST USE. 1875. "A nine of the Wisconsin Marine Fire Insurance Company's Bank met a nine of the First National Bank on the diamond" (*Milwaukee Daily Sentinel*, Aug. 19). **3.** *adj.* Pertaining to the game of baseball; e.g., "The Diamond Sport's Flaws" (*Christian Science Monitor* editorial title, Apr. 3, 1987).

diamond artist *hist.* A term used during the 1930s for a ballplayer.

Diamondbacks Nickname for the National League West Division expansion franchise that began playing in Phoenix, Ariz., in 1998 as the Arizona Diamondbacks. Also known as *D-Backs* and *Snakes*. ETYMOLOGY. The poisonous diamondback rattlesnake is among the most common snakes found in Arizona and easy to spot, with diamond-shaped markings on its back, outlined with a narrow, light-colored border.

diamond ball [softball term] A forerunner of modern softball. The term came into use as a replacement for *kitten ball* in 1916 by the Minneapolis Park Board. The first group that tried to organize softball on a national scale was the National Diamond Ball Association, which was founded in 1925 and continued until the formation of the Amateur Softball Association of America in 1933.

diamond bug *n./hist.* A term used during the 1930s for a baseball fan. See also *bug*, 1.

diamond classic Syn. of *World Series.* IST USE. 1918. "The crowd of 19,274 spectators—the smallest that has witnessed the diamond classic in many years" (*The New York Times*, Sept. 6, in reference to the first game of the 1918 World Series).

Diamond Dick *hist.* "An ancient term for baseball umpire" (*Houston Post*, Oct. 31, 1992).

diamondeer *hist.* A term used during the 1930s for a ballplayer.

diamond in the rough An unpolished but talented player found in an outlying or unexpected locale. *Diamonds in the Rough* is the title of David V. Hanneman's 1989 biography of legendary scout Tony Lucadello; but the term's antecedents date back to the earliest days of scouting: "Everybody in the crowd was impressed with the idea that in [Charlie] DeArmond the Reds had picked up a jewel—one of those diamonds in the rough that you read about" (Ren Mulford Jr., *The Sporting Life*, Oct. 3, 1903; Peter Morris).

dice baseball A tabletop baseball game, such as *baseball dice*, Strat-O-Matic, and APBA.

Dick Baney Effect The theory that good-looking baseball uniforms breed confidence but bad-looking uniforms erode it. Named for the Seattle Pilots pitcher who said (quoted in *Village Voice*, Oct. 7, 1986), "I looked down at myself and I looked like a clown. I figured if I looked like a clown, I must be pitching like a clown, and so I did." As noted by *Village Voice*, the Pilots' uniform had gold braid sewn on the cap, bogus gold braid printed on the sleeves, and a logo consisting of a ship's wheel with little wings surrounding a baseball.

Dick Howser Trophy A trophy given annually to the best Division I college baseball player in the United States. It is awarded by the National Collegiate Baseball Writers Association to promote baseball excellence and scholastic achievement. The St. Petersburg (Fla.) Area Chamber of Commerce is the founder and owner of the trophy. Howser was a popular American League shortstop and manager who died of cancer in 1987.

Dick Smith A loner; a player who is unfriendly, won't be one of the boys, keeps to himself, and seldom ever treats. Tom Laird (*Collier's*, March 22, 1940; Peter Tamony), writing about the DiMaggio brothers, asked Joe if his younger brother Dom would be "a Dick Smith"; Joe replied, "Not if I can help it. That was one of my big mistakes—being a lone wolf. I was afraid to talk about anything, not only to the newspapermen but to my teammates as well, and I got to be known as a Dick Smith." Peter Tamony (*Newsletter and Wasp*, Sept. 15, 1939) noted that the term was virtually unknown to fans, but common among players: "He [the generalized 'Dick Smith'] is the man who has never been known to say 'Here's how' to anyone. If he is treated he does not return the favor, and if in company he is the chap who never picks up the check."

ETYMOLOGY. Dick Smith does not appear to be the name of an old ballplayer, as has often been asserted. Tamony wrote that Dick Smith "must have been a well known character before baseball became the national pastime," for he is mentioned in the *Congressional Record* (June 29, 1876) and his name is there used as a synonym for "sponging." The term came up in the context of the custom of the House of Representatives to provide lemonade and iced tea for its members in the warm months. The drinks were paid for out of the House contingency fund until the practice was halted by Rep. "Blue-Jean" Smith (Ind.). Members then had the choice of running to the Senate for drinks or drinking "iced Potomac" (river water, which apparently caused its share of illness and intestinal distress). In supporting a bill to rectify this, Rep. Conger (Mich.) proposed that the House enable itself "to supply the necessary wants of its members, without either playing 'Dick Smith' on the Senate or leaving so many of its members confined to their rooms by sickness resulting from drinking iced Potomac."

Tamony examined the *Dictionary of American Biography* and found that there was, in fact, a well-known person whose reputation was such that it could have become an eponym for sponging. Richard Penn Smith (1799–1854) fit the bill. Tamony wrote: "In 1821 he published a series of moral and literary essays under the title of 'The Plagiary.' Between 1825 and 1833 he wrote twenty plays, of which fifteen were performed. Some of these plays were of extreme and lasting popularity, and Smith is given much space in the histories of the drama in America. But Smith was a practical playwright. For his dramas he depended mainly on foreign writers for his inspiration. Did this plagiarism, this dependence on others for ideas and inspiration, make Smith's name a synonym for sponging? It is very likely that it did."

EXTENDED USE. According to H.L. Mencken (*The American Language*, Suppl. II, 1948), the term is also used on the racetrack. Tamony found it as a logger's term for a drink of liquor consumed privately and a bar term for a lone drinker. Columnists from Damon Runyon to Charles McCabe have used the term in the context of bar culture: "One proprietor I know has a great fancy for Irish bartenders, and for a peculiar reason. He knows they are addicted to Dick Smithing and other weaknesses" (Charles McCabe, *San Francisco Chronicle*, Dec. 17, 1974; Peter Tamony).

die 1. To be left on base at the end of an inning. IST USE. 1873. "[The Mutuals of Jackson] would get the bases all full, and then the reds [the Red Stockings of Boston] would let them die there" (*Adrian* [Mich.] *Press*, Aug. 22; Peter Morris). 2. To be put out; to be "retired." IST USE. 1871. "[White] died at third while trying to make more bases than his hit was worth" (*The Cleveland Morning Herald*, May 22). 3. For a well-hit ball to be caught because it did not carry as far as expected due to heavy air conditions or incoming winds. "Jorge Posada's fly to right died at the wall" (*The New York Times*, Oct. 20, 2004). 4. To have failed; to have had a bad day at the ballpark. 5. To be released

from the team. "Ballplayers often refer to a player who has just been released as having 'died'" (Rick Wolff, *The New York Times*, Apr. 23, 1989).

diesel A large, strong player (Garret Mathews, *Can't Find a Dry Ball*, 2002).

differentials Dizzy Dean's term for "credentials" when he was in broadcasting.

difficult corner Syn. of *third base*, 1. It is so called because of the skill required by the third baseman. IST USE. 1885. "[Jim] Fogarty, of the Philadelphia League Club, guarded the 'difficult corner' for the Stars" (*The Sporting Life*, Dec. 30; Peter Morris, who notes that the term may be the antecedent of *hot corner*).

difficult station Syn. of *third base*, 1. "The Seal guard [Walter Cartwright] at the difficult station is all at sea when it comes to running in on a slow-hit ball" (*San Francisco Bulletin*, Apr. 5, 1913; Gerald L. Cohen)

dig 1. *n.* The movement on a breaking ball. Univ. of Denver physicist Tom Stephen (undated press release from the Univ. of Denver) observed that Denver's air (17 percent thinner than that at sea level) "offers less resistance to a ball in flight, and gives less of a 'dig' ... [and] a 14-inch curveball at sea level will curve only 11 inches in Denver." 2. *v.* To run hard.

dig down To apply oneself vigorously; to reach for something extra. "[Babe] Ruth dug down to first at top speed and reached the bag a half step ahead of [Terry] Turner's throw" (H.W. Lanigan, *Boston American*, Aug. 19, 1918; Peter Morris). "You want to go 1–2–3, obviously, but to watch the way he [relief pitcher B.J. Ryan] came back and dug down deep, that's the sign of a closer" (Baltimore Orioles manager Lee Mazzilli, quoted in *The Baltimore Sun*, Sept. 26, 2004).

dig in 1. To twist one's spikes into the dirt of the batter's box, esp. with the back foot, to gain better traction for swinging the bat; to anchor oneself in the batter's box. 2. To focus one's concentration on a key play or situation.

dig in his spurs To be a particularly active jockey, or player, who "rides" the opposition (*The New York Times*, June 2, 1929).

dig out 1. To field successfully a poorly thrown ball that bounces in the dirt. "[First baseman Candy LaChance] saves his infielders many an error by his remarkable skill in digging the balls out of the dirt" (Jacob C. Morse, *The Sporting Life*, Sept. 10, 1904; Peter Morris). IST USE. 1901. "Dig out of the dirt" (Burt L. Standish, *Frank Merriwell's School Days*, p.254; Edward J. Nichols). **2.** To retrieve a batted ball in a corner of the outfield.

digs An inning in Australia.

dilly *hist.* **1.** A spectacular play. **2.** A great player. "Pittsburgh may be a one-man team, but that man [Honus Wagner] is a 'dilly'" (New York Giants pitcher Hooks Wiltse, quoted in *New York American*, Aug. 9, 1908; Peter Morris). **3.** A "silly player" (Al Schacht, *Al Schacht Dope Book*, 1944).

dime 1. *n.* A tight-spinning slider. Compare *quarter.* **2.** *n.* The *red dot* (about the size of a dime) seen on a fast-spinning pitch with a large break. Compare *nickel*, 2. **3.** *v.* See *play on a dime.*

dime ball An inexpensive baseball (costing 10 cents) of better quality than a *nickel ball.* Compare *quarter ball.*

dime hit Syn. of *scratch hit.* IST USE. 1907 (*New York Evening Journal*, May 8; Edward J. Nichols).

dimensions The particular measurements of a given ballpark, both in terms of overall size and of the playing field itself. By extension, the term also serves to underscore the differences among ballparks.

dime player An infielder who lacks hustle and spirit; one who cannot or will not "get off the dime." See also *play on a dime.*

dime ya For a pitcher to display exceptional control. When speaking of a particularly capable pitcher, Casey Stengel was known to say: "He can dime ya."

ding To get a base hit or score a run. "The Expos dinged him [Jimmy Key] for single runs in the second and third innings" (*The Baltimore Sun*, March 3, 1998).

"ding-dong" A cry yelled from the dugout when the catcher takes a foul tip off his protective metal cup.

dinger A *home run.* "Home runs . . . are now 'Dingers,' as in blasts that ring a bell . . . Ding!" (Phil Pepe, *Baseball Digest*, Nov. 1974, p.58). "Bang, there goes another one. It seems every day in baseball is dinger day" (Ben Brown and Mel Antonen, *USA Today*, June 30, 1987). ETYMOLOGY. Probably from "humdinger," an action of remarkable excellence.

dink 1. *v.* To hit a slow ground ball; e.g., "Smith dinked a grounder to the pitcher." **2.** *v.* To pitch a slow ball. IST USE. 1916. "Dinking up" is "pitching balls easy to hit" (*American Magazine*, August, p.8; Edward J. Nichols). **3.** *adj.* Said of a cheap hit. "He [Travis Driskill] gave up . . . a couple of dink hits" (Baltimore Orioles pitching coach Mark Wiley, quoted in *The Baltimore Sun*, July 25, 2002). See also *dinky hit.*

dinker Syn. of *cheap hit.* "You had two . . . dinkers to rightfield" (Jason Giambi, addressing Alex Rodriguez, quoted in *Sports Illustrated*, Sept. 25, 2006, p.40).

dinky curve *hist.* Syn. of *slider*, 1.

dinky dink *hist.* Betrayal or jilting. The term was used frequently in the sports pages of the early 1890s: "To prevent the 'dinky-dink' . . . each club had to hand over a majority of its stock to the [American] Association president" (Harold Seymour, *Baseball: The Early Years*, 1960, p.257; Charles D. Poe). Albert L. Johnson, president of the 1890 Cleveland franchise in the Players' League and the 1891 Cincinnati franchise in the American Association, once claimed that he had "received the 'dinky dink,' which, by the way, is the latest baseball slang, invented, it is said, by [Cincinnati manager] Mike Kelly, and means, as Johnson defines it, 'when a man is thrown down so hard that you can hear him strike the ground two blocks away'" (W.L. Harris, *Bismarck* [N.D.] *Daily Tribune*, Dec. 25, 1890). "When that time comes, and then only, will the national game in New York be in safe hands and freed from the 'dinky dink' of the ruthless Goths and vandals" (*The Sporting Times*, Nov. 14, 1891; David Shulman).

dinky-doo Syn. of *dipsy-doodle.*

dinky fly A batted ball that goes neither high nor far and is easily caught. "Any time [a batter] . . . popped out a dinky fly . . . said batter felt like committing murder when he returned to the bench to meditate" (*San Francisco Bulletin*, Feb. 13, 1913; Gerald L. Cohen).

dinky hit Syn. of *cheap hit*. "Just one dinky hit and we win" (*San Francisco Bulletin*, Apr. 1, 1913; Gerald L. Cohen). See also *dink*, 3.

dinner tong *hist.* A player's hand. "['Blondy' Moeller] allowed the ball to ooze through his dinner tongs" (Edward M. Thierry, *Baseball Magazine*, Sept. 1909). Syn. *lunch hook*.

dip 1. *n.* The sudden downward motion of a breaking ball or spitball. "[Frank] Corridon had a slow ball with a big dip to it, of which he was somewhat fond and proud" (*The Washington Post*, Apr. 27, 1913; Peter Morris). **2.** *n.* Chewing tobacco, so called because the act of getting it out of its container is called "dipping" (Lawrence Frank, *Playing Hardball*, 1983, p.118). **3.** *v.* To chew tobacco.

DIPS Abbrev. for *defense independent pitching statistics*.

DIPS ERA An earned run average computed solely from the defense independent pitching statistics: strikeouts, walks allowed, hit batsmen, and home runs (Baseball Prospectus, *Baseball Between the Numbers*, 2006).

dipsy-doodle 1. Any odd-breaking pitch, such as a slow, tantalizing curveball, a suspected spitball, or a screwball. "Say, that's a regular dipsy doodle you got there! How do you do it, Professor?" (Valentine Davies, *It Happens Every Spring*, 1949; Charles D. Poe). Also spelled "dipsy doodle." IST USE (as "dipsy-dew") 1932 (*Baseball Magazine*, October; Edward J. Nichols). USAGE NOTE. Variations of the term include "dipsey-doodle," "dipsey-dow," "dipso-do," "dipsy-dew," "dipsy-do," "dipsy-doo," *dypsydo*, and *dinky-doo*. Edward J. Nichols (*An Historical Dictionary of Baseball Terminology*, PhD dissertation, Jan. 1939) commented, "This initial uncertainty as to spelling [of 'dipsy-dew'] is typical of new terms invented by the players rather than the sports reporters." **2.** A swinging strikeout. Pittsburgh Pirates sportscaster Rosey Rowswell called such an out "the old dipsey doodle" (*The Sporting News*, Apr. 5, 1969).

ETYMOLOGY. An act or movement to confuse or distract an opponent; e.g., a quick, sliding motion of the body, such as that made by a ball carrier to evade tacklers in football. EXTENDED USE. In 1937, the Tommy Dorsey Orchestra recorded "The Dipsy Doodle," a tune that became a hit, by Larry Clinton, who recalled (quoted in George T. Simon, *The Big Band Songbook*, 1975; Douglas D. Connah Jr.), "[The melody] was sort of a wacky-sounding thing, and it needed a wacky-sounding title. Then I remembered Carl Hubbell of the Giants and the screwball pitch he used to throw. They called it the dipsy doodle pitch, so that's what I called my new tune."

dipsy-doodler A pitcher who throws a dipsy-doodle. Gayle Talbot (Associated Press dispatch, Oct. 3, 1952) characterized Ed Lopat as "the greatest of the dipsy-doodlers."

director-general *hist.* The manager of a baseball team. "Harry Wolverton, director-general of the Sacramento team and one of the best informed personages at present actively connected with the great sport of baseball" (*San Francisco Bulletin*, May 30, 1913; Gerald L. Cohen).

director of player development The member of the front office of a major-league club who is responsible for providing experience and instruction for minor-league players. See also *player development*.

dirt The ground around home plate and the basepaths; e.g., "the ball is in the dirt" indicates a low pitch. See also *hit the dirt*.

dirtbag Syn. of *dirt ball*, 3. "[Grady Sizemore] plays the game the right way and he gives your team energy every day. He's a dirtbag. He'll do whatever he can to beat you" (Toronto Blue Jays manager John Gibbons, quoted in *Sports Illustrated*, May 14, 2007, p.60).

dirtball 1. Hard-nosed baseball. "The addition of Paul Lo Duca and Marquis Grissom and the development of intense competitors like Mark Grudzielanek have transformed the Dodgers from the Hollywoods to a respected, dirtball team battling against adversity" (Peter Gammons, *Baseball America*, Oct. 15–28, 2001; Peter Morris, who notes that the term is likely borrowed from or influenced by the common description of clay-court tennis as "dirtball"). **2.** Var. of *dirt ball*, 1.

dirt ball 1. A pitched ball that lands in the dirt, usually just in front of or alongside the plate, and that is difficult to handle. Var. *dirtball*, 2. 2. A ball that has been defaced with dirt. Umpire Tom Gorman (*Three and Two!*, 1979; Peter Morris) wrote, "They tell me [Ferguson] Jenkins is now throwing what the players call a 'dirt ball,' that is, he scrubs dirt into the seams and the ball drops straight down, like a spitter." 3. A player who often dirties his uniform with intense, hustling play. Michael Farber (*Sports Illustrated*, Aug. 14, 2006, p.44) wrote: "Players who dirty their uniforms every game are referred to as dirt balls. . . . [Chase] Utley is *SI*'s [*Sports Illustrated*'s] choice as the game's dirtiest player. In the best possible way." Syn. *dirt dog*; *dirtbag*. 4. A game played by reporters in the press box in which there is betting on the number of times the ball lands and stays on the dirt pitching mound at the end of every half inning. As explained by Martin O'Malley and Sean O'Malley (*Game Day*, 1994; Peter Morris), "Usually the first baseman or catcher or infielder rolls the ball toward the mound after the third out, and sometimes the ball stays on the dirt and sometimes it rolls off. Sometimes the umpire accepts the ball from an outfielder, then drops the ball on the mound, where it either stays or rolls off. Usually it rolls off, or never reaches the mound, so if you bet on it staying on the mound dirt you get odds."

dirt dog Syn. of *dirt ball*, 3.

dirter 1. A term used by Casey Stengel for a ground ball. 2. *hist.* A base hit (*San Francisco Bulletin*, March 15, 1913; Gerald L. Cohen).

dirt path Syn. of *alley*, 4. "There is a dirt path between the pitcher's mound and home plate, reminiscent of the paths seen in very early pictures of the game" (Bank One Ballpark [Ariz.] brochure, 2003). Syn. "dirt pathway."

dirt save A save credited to a catcher when he deflects a legally pitched ball that goes in the dirt prohibiting, in the official scorer's judgment, any and all baserunners from advancing. The term was introduced in 1988 and included on the scorecard of Memphis State Univ.'s baseball games for three seasons.

dirty Syn. of *nasty*, 1 (Garret Mathews, *Can't Find a Dry Ball*, 2002).

dirty ball Dishonest or unsportsmanlike play. IST USE. 1888. "One day in 1886, when the St. Louis Maroons were playing in Philadelphia, Manager Wright of the Phillies and Jack Glasscock of the Maroons were seated side by side on the Phillies' bench talking about the merits and demerits of 'dirty' ball playing" (*St. Louis Post-Dispatch*, Aug. 31; Peter Morris).

disabled list A list of players who have been removed from the team's active list for a specified period owing to injury, illness, or ailment. A player must be certified as disabled by a physician. The period of inactivity has varied over the years, including stints of 10, 15, 21, 30, and 60 days. The National League created the first disabled list in July 1915. In 1990, two disabled lists were established: a *15-day disabled list* and a *60-day disabled list*. Players can be disabled retroactively, up to a maximum of 10 days, beginning with the day after the last day they played. Players may be assigned to a minor-league club for injury rehabilitation for a maximum of 20 days (30 days for pitchers). There is no limit on the number of players who can be placed on the disabled list. Former syn. *injured reserve list*. Abbrev. and syn. *DL*. IST USE. 1887. "Jerry Reardon the St. Louis boy who fractured his right leg while running bases here is still on the disabled list" (*The Sporting News*, June 11; Peter Morris). USAGE NOTE. The term "disabled list" was used informally, no doubt influenced by "sick list," long before it emerged with a formal meaning. Lyle Spatz (personal communication, July 16, 2003): "When the term first came into use, being disabled was not necessarily considered a permanent condition; it was more a baseball synonym for 'sidelined.'" Peter Morris (personal communication, May 7, 2004) surmises that the term survived a number of other lists, such as "salary list," "sick list," and "hospital list"; e.g., "[Ross] Barnes . . . has been unable to hit anything since the season opened, having been on the sick list all the time" (*The Boston Globe*, June 13, 1877) and "Chicago's hospital list was increased by the pop bottle nuisance" (*Chicago Tribune*, Aug. 10, 1905).

discard Syn. of *castoff*. IST USE. 1908 (*Baseball Magazine*, August; Edward J. Nichols).

discernible stop The pause at the belt by a pitcher in the set position following his stretch and before he releases the ball toward the plate or throws it to a base. Failure to come to such a stop results in a balk; however, no stop is required if there are no runners on base. See also *stop position*.

Disco Demolition Night A promotional event held on July 12, 1979, by the Chicago White Sox at Comiskey Park that drew more than 50,000 fans, many of whom were teenage rock fans. The main attraction (aside from baseball) was a gigantic bonfire, scheduled to be lit between games of a doubleheader, in which thousands of disco records would be burned. It resulted in the White Sox forfeiting the second game to the Detroit Tigers as about 6,000 fans poured onto the field, drinking beer, ripping up the turf, and setting fires. Thirty-seven fans were arrested. The event was devised by Mike Veeck (the son of White Sox owner Bill Veeck) and radio executive Jeff Schwartz.

dish Syn. of *home plate*, an obvious play on the word "plate." See also *platter*. IST USE. 1897. "[Bid] McPhee didn't connect with three beauts that cut the dish" (*The World* [New York], May 14; Peter Morris).

dish up To pitch. "Particularly gratifying was the work dished up by Pitcher 'Flame' Delhi yesterday" (*San Francisco Bulletin*, March 10, 1913; Gerald L. Cohen).

dislodged base [softball term] A base that is displaced from its proper position. A baserunner is not penalized for a dislodged base, nor is the runner expected to tag a base that is far out of its proper position.

disputed Applied to an umpire's call or to an entire game whose outcome is being questioned by one of the teams.

disqualified list A list of players who violate their contracts or fail to render their services to the club, or who knowingly play with or against a club which during the current season has had a connection with an ineligible player or person. A player on the disqualified list receives no pay or service time, is not eligible for free agency, and is not eligible to play with any major- or minor-league club. Compare *ineligible list*; *restricted list*; *suspended list*.

distance See *go the distance*.

dive 1. To slide into a base headfirst. 2. To reach over or across the plate to hit an outside pitch; to lean into the plate to hit a pitch to the opposite field. Pittsburgh Pirates pitching coach Ray Miller (quoted in *Sports Illustrated*, Aug. 16, 1993): "Nowadays you've got so many hitters standing over the plate, diving for that outside pitch." Batters are less intimidated by inside pitches than they once were because body armor promotes diving into pitches.

dive hitter A hitter who takes a big stride toward the plate to reach a pitch on the outer half of the strike zone. Syn. "diver."

divide a pair To split a doubleheader.

diving catch An acrobatic catch in which a fielder throws himself headfirst to the ground to reach the ball. It is one of the more dramatic ways a player shows off his fielding skills. Dan Sperling (*A Spectator's Guide to Baseball*, 1983) notes, "Diving catches made at the 'hot corner' are perhaps the most remarkable of all, because third basemen usually have only a split-second in which to react." IST USE. 1907. "Hofman also endeavored to show the Bostonians where he gained the alias 'Circus Solly' by an attempted diving catch, but he hit the ground so hard he jarred the ball out of his mit" (I.E. Sanborn, *Chicago Tribune*, Aug. 23; Peter Morris).

division One of two informal classifications determined by the standings of the American League (eight teams in 1901–1960, ten teams in 1961–1968) and the National League (eight teams in 1900–1961, ten teams in 1962–1968). A team that finished among the top four (later, five) was in the *first division* and one that finished among the bottom four (later, five) was in the *second division*.

Division One of the three classifications (East, Central, and West) of the teams in the American League and in the National League, each having its own standings throughout the regular season.

Division Series One of two sets of playoff games (best three of five) among the three

Division winners and a wild card in each of the major leagues (National League and American League) to determine the two teams in each league to play in the *Championship Series*. The series began in 1995 when the third Division and the wild card were first introduced. The team with the best winning percentage plays the wild card (so long as those two teams are not in the same Division) or plays one of the other two Division champions that has the lower winning percentage (if the wild card is from the same Division). Many argue that a best-of-seven format is a better way to test the clubs involved. See also *League Division Series*; *American League Division Series*; *National League Division Series*.

Dixie Highway The figurative destination of a player who has been released or fired from the team; e.g., "hit the Dixie Highway," "take the Dixie Highway," or "walk the Dixie Highway."

Dixie Series The best-of-seven series pitting the playoff champions of the Southern Association and the Texas League from 1920 to 1958. It was revived for one year (1967) when the Southern League champ (Birmingham A's) defeated the Texas League champ (Albuquerque Dodgers).

Dixie Youth Baseball A program founded in 1955 when 61 leagues from South Carolina withdrew from Little League because they refused to play in a district tournament with an all-black team from Charleston. Originally known as Little Boys League, Dixie Youth Baseball has been integrated since the early 1960s and has leagues in 11 Southern states.

DL 1. Abbrev. for *disabled list*. 2. *n.* Syn. of *disabled list*. "Chan Ho Park . . . had been on the DL with a pulled right hamstring" (*The Washington Post*, May 13, 2002). 3. *v.* To put on the disabled list. Baltimore Orioles manager Mike Hargrove (quoted in *The Baltimore Sun*, Aug. 19, 2000): "You can't just DL a guy, especially as talented as Brady [Anderson] is, and then he's ready to go seven days into the [15-day] period."

DNF Abbrev. for *draft-and-follow*, 2.

DNP Abbrev. for "did not play."

do a Casey To fail in the manner of Casey, the figure in Ernest Lawrence Thayer's 1888 poem "Casey at the Bat"; specif., to strike out. Syn. *pull a Casey*. IST USE. 1926. "To fan out, to fail to make a hit" (Clement Wood, *A Dictionary of American Slang*, p.61; David Shulman).

doble matanza Spanish for "double play."

Doc 1. A nickname given to a relief pitcher ("a doctor to cure sick games"); e.g., Otis "Doc" Crandall. 2. A nickname given to a player who has a connection to healing (such as a medical or dental student); e.g., George "Doc" Medich. 3. A nickname given to an exceptional pitcher; e.g., Dwight "Doc" Gooden. 4. A nickname given to a player reputed to be "wise"; e.g., "Doc" Moskiman, who "gave far more analysis to his pitching than most other pitchers" (Gerald L. Cohen, *Dictionary of 1913 Baseball and Other Lingo*, Vol.1, 2001).

dock *hist.* Syn. of *home plate* (*The Sporting News*, Oct. 30, 1913; Peter Morris).

doctor 1. *v.* To engage in *doctoring*. The term was applied to baseball high jinks long after establishing itself elsewhere as a term for secret product adulteration. 2. *n.* A temporary nickname for someone caught or suspected of the act of doctoring. 3. *v.* To falsify. "It is impossible to convince a Pittsburger that [Jake] Beckley did not lead with the stick. They will tell you that [Cap] Anson's percentage was doctored by the Chicago official scorers. The figures were: Anson, .343; Beckley, .342" (*Bismarck* [N.D.] *Daily Tribune*, May 4, 1889).

doctored ball A baseball that has been altered purposely to affect its flight when pitched. See also *doctoring*, 1; *marked ball*. IST USE. 1917. "The natural surface of even a new baseball is rather rough and the friction would be less on the surface made shiny by the application of talcum powder or licorice. This tends to pile up the air on the side of the ball which has not been 'doctored' and slow up the speed of that side" (Paul Purman, *Fort Wayne* [Ind.] *Sentinel*, July 5; Peter Morris).

doctored bat A baseball bat that has been altered illegally. A batter bringing such a bat into the batter's box shall be called out and ejected from the game, and may be subject to additional penalties. Compare *altered bat*. See also *doctoring*, 2; *corked bat*; *illegal bat*.

doctored grounds A playing area that has been modified to improve the performance of the home team. See also *doctoring*, 4.

doctoring 1. Gaining an edge illegally by making the ball move erratically after it has been pitched. This may involve the use of a substance or damage to the ball. Any list of agents that have been used to doctor balls would include: BB shot, bottle cap, dirt, emery paper, licorice, nutmeg grater, oil, paraffin, phonograph needle, pine tar, resin, slippery elm, spikes, spit, talcum powder, K-Y jelly, and Vaseline. Most doctoring is difficult to detect; real or imagined doctoring has led to some of the most heated and prolonged debates in baseball. See also *doctored ball*. Syn. *tampering*, 3. **2.** Altering a baseball bat in such a way as to enhance the bat's distance factor and/or cause an unusual reaction of the bat surface against the surface of the ball; e.g., putting nails in the bat, honing one side of the bat to make it flat and thus increase the hitting surface, filling a grooved bat with wax, using excessive pine tar, and corking a bat. See also *corking*, 1; *doctored bat*. Syn. *tampering*, 4. **3.** Modifying a baseball glove. "Most players were using gloves that were illegal under a strict definition of the rules, and the practice of 'doctoring' gloves, particularly the webbing, was growing" (*The Sporting News*, June 15, 1939; Peter Morris). **4.** Modifying the home field or its boundaries to give the home team an advantage; e.g., keeping a spot near first base wet or soft to deter an especially good base stealer, tapering the foul lines to make bunts roll foul or building up the ground outside the foul lines to make bunts stay fair, packing the path to first base slightly downhill to help a speedy batter-runner, varying the thickness of the infield grass at various positions, mixing clay with dirt to develop a hard-surfaced infield, manipulating vents in a domed stadium to produce tailwinds when the home team is batting, and raising, lowering, or tilting the pitching mound in the visitor's bullpen to confuse pitchers who warm up on an unconventional mound but then perform on a conventional one. "I'm not accusing the Yankees of doctoring the infield but it's very thick-sodded and that's certainly a great help to their infield" (Detroit Tigers manager Jack Tighe, quoted in an Associated Press dispatch, May 1, 1958; Peter Tamony). See also *doctored grounds*; *Cobb's Lake*. Syn. *tampering*, 5.

Dr. Long Ball A home run. "[Baltimore Orioles manager Earl Weaver says] his team needs Dr. Long Ball to make a house call to his dressing room to cure a Baltimore slump" (Terry Pluto, *Cleveland Plain Dealer*, Sept. 20, 1982). Not to be confused with *Long Ball*. See also *long ball*, 1.

do damage To score one or more runs.

Dodger blue The color of the Los Angeles Dodgers. The term is used in reference to the uniform or the team; former manager Tommy Lasorda's Hall of Fame plaque states that he claimed to "bleed Dodger blue." "[Lasorda spread] the gospel of Dodger Blue—the elixir, he has often said, that runs through his veins" (*Los Angeles Magazine*, Apr. 2002, p.50).

Dodger Dog The 10-inch knockoff of the foot-long Nathan's Famous hot dog provided by Arthur Food Services, the concessionaire at Dodger Stadium from 1962 to 1991. About 50,000 Dodger Dogs were sold at each game. "Besides peanuts and Cracker Jack, it's probably the most famous delicacy in baseball" (Los Angeles Dodgers team historian Mark Langill, quoted in Associated Press article, June 28, 2006).

Dodger double A term used by Los Angeles Dodgers fans when Maury Wills singled and stole second base.

Dodgers Nickname for the National League West Division franchise in Los Angeles, Calif. The franchise, which originated as the Brooklyn *Bridegrooms* (1890–1898), was renamed the Brooklyn *Superbas* (1899–1910), was renamed the Brooklyn Dodgers (1911–1913), the Brooklyn *Robins* (1914–1931), the Brooklyn Dodgers (1932–1957), and finally the Los Angeles Dodgers in 1958. The name "Dodgers" was officially adopted in 1932. ETYMOLOGY. See *Trolley Dodgers*.

Dodgertown A 450-acre complex in Vero Beach, Fla., where the Brooklyn/Los Angeles Dodgers held spring training from 1948 to 2008. Dodgers president and general manager Branch Rickey converted the former naval air base into the most progressive and well-equipped of the spring camps. Arthur Daley (*The New York Times*, March 18, 1956) described Dodgertown: "It is a factory that rolls ball players off an assembly line with the steady surge of Fords popping out of the River Rouge plant." It features two golf courses, tennis courts, a conference center, and villas for the players. Streets are named for former players. Roofless dugouts at Holman Stadium allowed fans to feel closer to the players.

dodge the bullet To get out of a threatening situation; esp. appropriate to pitchers. ETYMOLOGY. Bert Dunne (*Folger's Dictionary of Baseball*, 1958) suggested that the term is a literal and graphic reference to the infielder who "lifts his leg" to get out of the way of a hard-hit ground ball.

dodgy *hist.* Said of a pitcher or pitcher's delivery in which the ball appears to be thrown at the batter. "Last season, McKever's pitching . . . was made effective by his skill in what is called 'dodgy delivery,' that is, the balls he pitched, though apparently for the striker, were not such as he would strike at with any chance of hitting fairly" (*New York Clipper*, July 9, 1864; Peter Morris). "[John] Curren caught well in the face of [Larry] Corcoran's dodgy delivery—first slow and then fast, regular strategic pitching" (*New York Clipper*, March 16, 1878; Peter Morris). According to Edward J. Nichols (*An Historical Dictionary of Baseball Terminology*, PhD dissertation, Jan. 1939, p.21), a "dodgy pitcher" is one who "throws beanballs" (citing an 1867 clipping from Chadwick Scrapbooks).

do-fer pitch A term used by pitcher Tommy John for a pitch that will work ("do-fer awhile") until the pitcher gets something else working (*Tampa Tribune*, July 21, 1987).

dog **1.** A player who lacks fighting spirit or does not give his best at all times. **2.** A player's foot. Syn. *pup*.

dog days The late summer or September of a baseball season. "The time of year when the weather is hot, the body tired and, for the handful of teams that aren't close to the wild card, the games meaningless" (Stephen Cannella, *Sports Illustrated*, Aug. 20, 2001, p.61).

doghouse A figurative place of exile for a player who has displeased the manager. "[Curtis Goodwin] is still deep in [Phil] Regan's doghouse after twice missing a bunt sign last week in the same at-bat" (*The Baltimore* Sun, Oct. 1, 1995). Most managers claim that they do not have, own, or believe in doghouses.

doghouse fiddle *hist.* To attempt a double steal (*Baseball Magazine*, Oct. 1916, p.26; Bill Mullins).

dog it **1.** To malinger; to slow down for a minor ache or pain. "[Houston Astros pitcher J.R. Richard] had been complaining of injuries all season, and his teammates had thought he was 'dogging' it" (Edwin Silberstang, *Playboy's Guide to Baseball Betting*, 1982; Charles D. Poe). **2.** To fail to play one's best or make a sufficient effort; to play lazily. The term is often applied to a batter-runner who does not try to beat the ball to first base or to a fielder who backs away from a sharply hit ball. IST USE. 1911. "I've seen plenty of his kind before; he'll dog it, I tell you" (Charles E. Van Loan, *The Big League*, p.140; David Shulman).

dog kennel The dugout (George Gipe, *The Great American Sports Book*, 1978, p.90).

dog meat A utility player.

dog-piling The distinctive and particularly exuberant method of celebrating a big win in which players jump on their recumbent teammates, usually on or near the pitcher's mound. The practice is esp. common in college baseball, where it has come to be metaphoric for a championship. When the Texas A&M baseball team won the Big 12 Championship in 2007, the winning pitcher said, "Tonight was amazing. We have come a long way from last season to dog-piling" (Web-based press release from Texas A&M).

dog robber A derisive name for an umpire in reference to his integrity (Joseph McBride, *High and Inside*, 1980, p.35).

dollar One hundred points of a batting average; e.g., "Smith is hitting below the two-dollar [.200] mark." One dollar (.100) is equivalent to a *buck*.

dollar sign on the muscle A money code expressing an ultimate evaluation of a ballplayer. The term was used as the title of Kevin Kerrane's book *Dollar Sign on the Muscle* (1984). Kerrane found the term in the Philadelphia Phillies 1981 scouting manual: "A new column titled 'Dollar Evaluation' has been added to your prospect-summary sheet. Your dollar evaluation should be the highest figure you would go in order to sign a player if he were on the open market. The figure would be based solely on the player's ability. Other factors, such as what the player is asking for, or what you think you can sign him for, would not be considered when determining a dollar evaluation. . . . Boiled down, it is the 'dollar sign on the muscle' and no more." The dollar amount was an "investment-analysis" figure by which the scout rates a ballplayer beyond the number grades for his tools, projected skills, and makeup. USAGE NOTE. Branch Rickey (*The American Diamond*, 1965) noted, "it is indeed a risky business to put the dollar mark on the individual muscle." From *Branch Rickey's Little Blue Book* (edited by John J. Monteleone, 1995, pp.58–59): "A scout may know that, from certain characteristics of a prospect, he will not go far and he acts upon that fact and doesn't recommend the player. Now, knowing that is important to me and our organization, and those facts help to better arm the organization and anybody in it who must put a dollar mark on muscle. And that's the important thing in this business." Brooklyn Dodgers secretary-historian Harold Parrott, marveling at Rickey's uncanny ability to evaluate baseball prospects (quoted in Joseph McBride, *High & Inside*, 1980, p.184): "Nobody could match his knack for putting a dollar sign on a muscle."

dome An enclosed ballpark, which may have a retractable roof, used for baseball and other sports; e.g., Metrodome (Minneapolis), SkyDome (now named Rogers Centre) (Toronto), Kingdome (Seattle), Olympic Stadium (Montreal), Tropicana Field (St. Petersburg, Fla.), and Astrodome (Houston), the original enclosed ballpark, which opened Apr. 9, 1965.

domeball Baseball played in a domed ballpark. The term is used to emphasize the differences between indoor and outdoor baseball, as baseball played under a dome is also played on artificial turf ("Inside Information: The Mysteries of Domeball," *SPORT* magazine, Apr. 1984).

dome dong Syn. of *dome run*. IST USE. 1987. "[A dome dong is] a home run in a domed stadium, a phrase first applied to homers in Seattle's Kingdome" (Mike Whiteford, *How to Talk Baseball*, p.92).

dome-field advantage The real or imagined edge held by a team playing in a domed ballpark, due to fan support and familiarity with the dimensions and physical features under the dome. The term is a play on the concept of *home-field advantage*.

dome run A home run hit in a domed ballpark, such as the "cheap" home runs hit in Seattle's Kingdome, whose configuration and controlled atmosphere can be kind to powerful hitters who find it easier to hit home runs under a dome. Clearly implied is that the dome run would not have been a home run if hit in a traditional open-air ballpark. Syn. *dome dong*. ETYMOLOGY. "Since . . . it's not quite fair for a Kingdome home run to count as much as a real one . . . I propose a new statistical category in baseball records, that of the Dome Run, or 'domer,' the DR" (Raymond Mungo, *Confessions from Left Field*, 1983, p.113).

domestand A homestand in a domed ballpark.

dong A home run. "[Brady Anderson's] got 15 dongs and leading the league" (Billy Ripken, quoted in *The Boston Globe*, May 6, 1996).

donkey 1. A rookie or a minor-league player up for a tryout with a major-league team. "A rookie was a yannigan, unless he happened to make an ass of himself, in which case he became a donkey" (Mike Sowell, *July 2, 1903*, 1992, p.4). 2. A player whose faulty play led to the team's defeat. "If you screw up and you lose, well, no one likes to be the donkey" (Bobby Thomson, *"The Giants Win the Pennant! The Giants Win the Pennant!,"* 1991, p.119).

donkey baseball 1. A baseball game in which all the players (except for the pitcher, catcher, and batter) are mounted on donkeys. When the ball is hit, the batter jumps on a waiting donkey and attempts to circle the bases as the ball is chased by mounted fielders. The game became a very popular amusement in the Great Depression and reached its peak in 1934 when it was launched in Florida spring training and played from coast to coast. It was adopted by the House of David's bearded barnstormers, then managed by Grover Cleveland Alexander (*Chicago Tribune*, June 27, 1924, p.20); American Legion Post #453 staged a five-day tournament in Los Angeles (*Los Angeles Times*, June 29, 1934, p.A10). The game has survived to this day. It is often staged for charity fund-raising with "well-groomed" donkeys provided by the Buckeye Donkey Ball Co., an outfit founded in 1934. IST USE. 1934. "Nay, Nay, Say Dean Brothers, Beaten at Donkey Baseball" (*The Washington Post*, Feb. 4; this article described a game in which the Boston Red Sox defeated the St. Louis Cardinals "four grunts to two" and asserted that "donkey baseball is now the rage in the Florida cities among the big league Spring Grapefruit League"). **2.** A short-lived game in which the team with the lowest score won the contest. The gist of the game was to highlight defensive play by crediting each run scored to one's opponent. The game probably would have been forgotten save for the fact that it was carried on in newspaper sports pages as a trivia question well into the 20th century. USAGE NOTE. Peter Morris noted that "donkey" was used in a metaphorical sense for a baseball game in Brooklyn in 1861 (*Brooklyn Eagle*, Nov. 16): "Yesterday afternoon a very amusing, and perhaps the most novel match ever played, took place . . . it being on the plan of a 'Donkey Race' . . . The conditions of the game were, the nine making the LEAST runs should gain the victory and the player scoring the MOST runs to get the ball." Commented the *New York Clipper* (Nov. 30, 1861): "The individual who arranged the details of the game, christened it the 'Donkey Match,' but why it should have been so denominated we have not yet been able to learn."

donnybrook 1. A high-scoring game. **2.** An inordinately wild fight among baseball players.

don the spikes To take part in a baseball game.

"don't lose the glove" A traditional barb yelled by the opposition to a player who is a good fielder but not much of a hitter.

donut 1. Syn. of *doughnut*. **2.** A rubber circle that some batters wear on their thumbs while batting to cut down on the painful reverberation of the bat. **3.** Syn. of *cookie cutter*.

do one's chores To perform well in a game.

do-or-die squeeze Syn. of *suicide squeeze*. IST USE. 1938 (John W. "Jack" Coombs, *Baseball*; Peter Morris).

doorkeeper Syn. of *first baseman*. Harry Grayson (*They Played the Game*, 1944, p.115) on Hal Chase: "No doorkeeper played as deep and far from the bag."

doormat The team in last place in a league or division.

doozie maroony An extra-base hit. The term was coined by pioneer Pittsburgh Pirates broadcaster Rosey Rowswell. Var. "doozie marooney"; "doozy marooney"; "doozy maroony."

dope 1. *n.* Inside or advance information; prediction or opinion. "The dope will prove that a care-free player will do better than one who carries his troubles on the diamond" (S. DeWitt Clough, *Letters from a Baseball Fan to His Son*, 1910). "There is a great deal in the dope that [Walter] Johnson has something on a club before he starts" (*San Francisco Bulletin*, Feb. 10, 1913; Gerald L. Cohen). IST USE. 1902. "[Frank] Selee's Men Now Meet Eastern Teams Which New York Holds Safe on Record to Date, So Second Place Seems Assured Unless 'Dope' Goes Wrong" (*Chicago Tribune* headline, May 11; Peter Morris). ETYMOLOGY. Alfred H. Holt (*Phrase Origins*, 1936) wrote, "Though cursed with a multiplicity of uses in American slang, the little word seems to be traceable in almost every sense to the Dutch 'doop' (pronounced 'dope'), a thick liquid or sauce." Holt observed that one form of dope is any drug used to stimulate a horse in a race. To have knowledge of this may have led to the idea of inside or secret information as "dope." **2.** *v.* To figure out or predict the outcome of a baseball game, series, or season by using available information and tips. An exhibit at the National Baseball Hall of Fame and Museum noted that sportswriter Hugh S. Fullerton "boosted doping from status of a questionable journalistic ploy" to a "scientific" experiment. "You can't dope out anything in baseball" (W.A. Phelon, *The Sporting Life*, May 27, 1905). "The Athletic leader [Connie Mack] dopes the Tigers to finish second, the Nationals third and the champion Red Sox fourth" (*San Francisco Bulletin*, Feb. 26, 1913; Gerald L. Cohen). **3.** *n.* The records and data concerning the game of baseball (Edward J. Nichols, *An Historical Dictionary of Baseball Terminology*, PhD dissertation, Jan. 1939, p.21). IST USE. 1897. "We [Philadelphia Phillies] had a likely youngster, a pitcher, named [Jack] Fifield, who had won thirty games . . . according to [George] Stallings' dope" (St. Louis manager Billy Hallman, quoted in *The Washington Post*, June 14, 1897). **4.** *n.* A slowly pitched ball (*The New York Times*, June 2, 1929). "Luther Taylor had his dope box with him yesterday when he went up against the Superbas; and when he opened up his goods every ball was a hashee jag that sped angularly through the atmosphere to the tune of nothing doing at all. . . . Every Giant was glad that Taylor's dope was right" (*New York Evening Call*, July 1, 1908). **5.** *n.* [softball term] A substance other than rosin that a pitcher puts on his or her hands.

dope book A reference book that contains baseball records and statistics. "If the dope book shows that a player hit but .250 that does not mean he is no hitter" (Harry Wolverton, quoted in *San Francisco Bulletin*, Feb. 12, 1913; Gerald L. Cohen). IST USE. 1902. "Barney Dreyfuss . . . is frequently made the target for jokes because he keeps a dope book on all the minor league players" (*Grand Rapids* [Mich.] *Herald*, June 22; Peter Morris). ETYMOLOGY. Peter Tamony noted that a "dope-book" in the earlier context of horse racing is a book containing a chart of previous performances of racehorses.

dopemaker Syn. of *dopester*. "The two Chicago teams . . . are scheduled to play a post-season series for the local championship. Already the Windy City dopemakers are fig-

uring the winner" (*The Washington Post*, July 22, 1900).

dopester One who compiles and analyzes baseball statistics and records and thereby predicts the performances of players and teams. "To the 'dopesters' the Seals' showing helped to confirm their opinions" (*San Francisco Bulletin*, Apr. 2, 1913; Gerald L. Cohen). Syn. *dopemaker.* IST USE. 1911. "Will some wise baseball dopester explain how a pitcher could prevent the hits from being scattered?" (*Trenton* [N.J.] *Evening Times*, Apr. 26; Peter Morris).

doryoku Japanese for unflagging effort, a prime virtue in Japanese baseball. "I'm going to do my best, *doryoku*, to keep my pitch count low and be able to pitch into the later innings" (Daisuke Matsuzaka, quoted in *Sports Illustrated*, March 26, 2007, p.65).

double 1. *n.* A hit on which the batter reaches second base safely. Abbrev. *D*, 3; *2B*, 4. Syn. *two-baser; two-base hit; two-sacker; two-bagger; two-cushion shot; two-master; double bagger; double baser; second-base hit; keystone hit; dub piece.* IST USE. 1880 (*Brooklyn Daily Eagle*, Aug. 27; Edward J. Nichols). **2.** *v.* To hit a double; e.g., "Smith doubled twice in the same game." **3.** *n.* A *double play.* The term appears in the 1910 poem "Baseball's Sad Lexicon" by Franklin P. Adams: "Making a Giant hit into a double" (from Tinker to Evers to Chance). IST USE. 1871. "There was some very fine play on both sides, including five 'doubles'— three by the Olympics and two by the Forest City" (*The Cleveland Morning Herald*, May 22). **4.** *v.* To complete a double play; e.g., "White doubled Brown at first." **5.** *n.* A *doubleheader.* To "split a double" is "to win one of a two-game series played on the same day" (Maurice H. Weseen, *A Dictionary of American Slang*, 1934).

Double A Syn. of *Class AA*, 2.

double bagger Syn. of *double*, 1. IST USE. 1878. "Peters hit for a base, second on Goodman's out, and home on Foley's double bagger" (*Milwaukee Sentinel*, June 28; Peter Morris).

double-barreled matinee Syn. of *doubleheader.* "The first double-barreled matinee of the championship season was played by the Pirates and der Browns" (*The Washington Post*, Apr. 29, 1898).

double baser Syn. of *double*, 1. IST USE. 1878. "Two double basers by Manning" (*New York Clipper*, Sept. 14; Peter Morris)

double bill Syn. of *doubleheader*. IST USE. 1907. "Today's double bill disposed of two postponed games left over from the spring trip here" (*Chicago Tribune*, Aug. 31; Peter Morris).

double clutch A motion made by a fielder in which he starts to throw and then stops because he does not have a good grip on the ball, or sees that he had more time than he thought to retire the runner, or because the fielder receiving the ball was late in covering his base, or because of indecision. Syn. *double pump*, 2.

double cover ball A baseball in which two hourglass shapes cut from hides are stitched together. The ball originally (1872) contained no rubber, but in 1877 the National League adopted as "official" a double cover ball with a center of one ounce of molded vulcanized rubber. According to the *Cleveland Plain Dealer* (Apr. 1, 1888; Peter Morris), the rubber was "wrapped with woolen yarn very tightly until it was about two-thirds the size of the ball required, this was then covered with horse hide; this ball was then again wrapped with yarn, but not so tightly until of the requisite size and again covered with horse hide." The ball was manufactured by L.H. Mahn (Jamaica Plains, Mass.) with the Spalding label, and remained the standard for the National League until 1884.

double curve The fanciful pitch that breaks twice on its way to the plate, such as that thrown by the fictional Dan Manly (George C. Jenks, *Double Curve Dan, the Pitcher Detective*, 1888); "an ocular delusion" (O.P. Caylor, *Outing, an Illustrated Monthly Magazine of Recreation*, Aug. 1891). "From the Cincinnati camp comes the wonderful tale of a new curve which [Christy] Mathewson has discovered. It has always been the ambition of a pitcher to master the legendary 'double curve,' a ball which will curve one way and then suddenly twist another way, like a billiardist sometimes

manipulates an ivory ball. Ivy Wingo and Tom Clarke, the two Red catchers, say that the snake-like ball which Matty has discovered jumps two ways in the most black magic fashion. They state that it takes a decided outward hop and then shoots in again" (*The New York Times*, March 18, 1917; Brock Helander). See also *double shoot*. Syn. *snake ball*, 2; *zigzag curve*; *spiral curve*. IST USE. 1877. "It is easy to find out that he [Bobby Mitchell] is young, an amateur, a 'second Nolan,' left-handed, has a 'double curve,' and is 'the coming pitcher,' but who is he?" (*Chicago Tribune*, Apr. 29; Peter Morris).

Doubleday Baseball The tattered, misshapen relic discovered in an attic trunk in 1935 by a farmer living in Fly Creek, N.Y., a crossroads village near Cooperstown. The ball is purported to have belonged to Abner Graves (an ancestor of the farmer), who claimed he was present when Abner Doubleday invented baseball. It symbolizes the legendary first baseball game, although there is no evidence to that effect. IST USE. 1935. The ball was labeled the "Doubleday Baseball" (Walter Littell, *Freeman's Journal* [Cooperstown, N.Y.], April; Bill Deane).

Doubleday Field See *Abner Doubleday Field*.

Doubleday myth The controversial claim that Civil War Union officer Abner Doubleday invented baseball in 1839 in Cooperstown, N.Y. Though Doubleday never claimed to have invented the game, credit was given to him after his death by Albert G. Spalding and the Mills Commission formed to prove that baseball was a purely American creation. Since then, its debunkers have become legion. "The Doubleday myth, however, is as much a part of our culture as George Washington's chopped-down cherry tree" (Bill Tames, *Kansas City Star*, Aug. 21, 1986). Harold Peterson (*The Man Who Invented Baseball*, 1973) wrote: "Abner Doubleday didn't invent baseball. Baseball invented Abner Doubleday." Syn. *Cooperstown myth*. IST USE. 1939. "The Myth of Doubleday" (Joe Williams, *New York World-Telegram*, June 13; Barry Popik).

double-decker A grandstand with an upper deck. IST USE. 1887. "Work upon the new

Doubleday myth. Abner Doubleday and wife. He was a Union officer stationed at Fort Sumter, S.C. His long-alleged involvement with the creation of baseball has been debunked. Civil War glass plate negative. *Library of Congress*

grand stand—a 'double-decker'—is progressing very rapidly" (*Indianapolis Sentinel*, March 25; Peter Morris).

doubledip Syn. of *doubleheader*. "We lost a doubleheader (doubledip) to the Mets yesterday" (Hoke Norris, "Voo and Doo," *The Georgia Review*, Summer 1968).

double duty The work of a player who, within a single season or over the course of a career, handles two assignments; e.g., a pitcher used both as a starter and as a reliever (Dennis Eckersley, John Smoltz, Woodie Fryman, and Jack Quinn) or a player (such as Ted Radcliffe of the Negro leagues) who pitched one game of a doubleheader and caught the other game (thus earning Radcliffe the nickname "Double Duty").

double elimination A tournament format by which a team must be defeated twice before it is eliminated from play. It ensures that a top team will not be eliminated too early in the tournament and that the weaker teams have two chances. It was used until 1987 in the College World Series for its eight finalists. Compare *round-robin*; *single elimination*.

double error Two errors charged to a fielder during the course of one play; e.g., fumbling a ground ball to allow the batter-runner to reach first base, then throwing the ball away to allow the batter-runner to advance.

double figures Any baseball statistic (runs, hits, steals, etc.) between 10 and 99.

doubleheader A set of two games played in succession on the same day between the same two teams and to which spectators are admitted for the price of a single game. Traditionally, there is a 20-minute break between games. Some doubleheaders (such as the *day-night doubleheader*) have separate admissions. Historically, there have been two reasons for doubleheaders: postponements of previously scheduled games and games scheduled in advance as a means of attracting fans. The first time two major teams played each other twice on the same day seems to have been on July 4, 1873 (Resolutes of Elizabeth [N.J.] at Boston), with one game in the morning and a second game in the afternoon. Doubleheaders were scheduled as regular events until the early 1980s; they are becoming rarer in the major leagues with most now being played later in the season to make up postponed games: "Like movie double features, the baseball doubleheader is on the verge of extinction" (*Forbes*, March 9, 1987). See also *twi-night doubleheader*; *separate-admission doubleheader*. Abbrev. *DH*, 1. Formerly spelled "double header"; "double-header." Syn. *double,* 5; *double bill*; *doubledip*; *double-barreled matinee*; *twin bill*; *bargain bill*. 1ST USE. 1890. "Rain and wet grounds prevented yesterday's local games. . . . The Athletic and Baltimore Clubs will have a double-header, the first beginning at two o'clock" (*The North American* [Philadelphia], Sept. 16). ETYMOLOGY. The term was first used to describe a form of firework with two rockets. Most early citations of double-headers were accident reports suggesting a dangerous form of pyrotechnics. "[A] little boy about eight . . . lost one of his eyes in Madison street by being struck with a 'double-header'" (*National Intelligencer*, July 8, 1840). The term was next applied to shipbuilding. "The desire, long expressed by the public, to see a *fast* vessel in our navy is about to be realized in the *Wampanoag*. The *Peoria*, one of the 'double-headers,' is rapidly fitting for sea" (*The New York Times*, Dec. 29, 1863). The term was then used in railroading as early as 1878 for a train with two engines or two trains traveling so close together that they move as one. "The two extras were bowling along merrily when they struck this grade; and although there is a time card rule that says that trains will be kept ten minutes apart, they were right together, helping each other over the grade. In fact, it was one train with two engines, something of a double header with the second engine in the middle" (Jasper Ewing Brady, *Tales of the Telegraph: The Story of a Telegrapher's Life and Adventures in Railroad, Commercial and Military Work*, 1900). Because railroad doubleheaders could be used to economize on labor they became an issue in the railroad strikes of 1877. Finally, the term was used to describe bigamists, and in 1875 to describe creatures born (or stillborn) with two heads. EXTENDED USE. Two paired or consecutive events; e.g., "A doubleheader at the big prison is the simultaneous execution of two inmates in the state's pale green gas chamber" (*San Francisco Examiner*, July 4, 1967; Peter Tamony). In his book *The Scotch* (1964), John Kenneth Galbraith wrote about two back-to-back one-hour sermons which he termed "a devotional doubleheader."

double hit The rare situation in which the batter's bat actually hits the ball twice. It usually occurs on a lightly hit ball when a batter accidentally lets go of the bat. Moving faster than the rolling ball, the bat catches up to it and hits it again. The batter who accomplishes this feat is declared out by the plate umpire.

double killing Syn. of *double play*.

double-name job The locker of a rookie in an overcrowded spring-training camp. Leonard Shecter (*Baseball Digest*, June 1963) explained: "This is rookie talk. When spring training camps are crowded with players from all over the system there aren't enough individual lockers to go around. The rookies are asked to double up. That means there are two names hung over the locker, both with astronomically high uniform numbers, like

73 and 94. That's the kind of number you get when you're in one of those double-name jobs."

double no-hitter A game in which both pitchers allowed no hits. Fred Toney of the Cincinnati Reds and Hippo Vaughn of the Chicago Cubs pitched a double no-hitter for nine innings on May 2, 1917 (the Reds won, 1–0, in the 10th inning).

double off To be caught off base and put out before tagging up after the batter has flied or lined out, resulting in a double play. "[Carl] Yastrzemski made a diving, rolling catch of [Reggie] Jackson's drive at the foot of the wall in left, and the relay doubled [Thurman] Munson off first base" (Roger Angell, *The New Yorker*, Oct. 1978).

double play A defensive play in which two players are put out as a result of continuous action, providing that no error is committed between putouts. Both outs must occur between the time the ball leaves the pitcher's hand and the point at which it is returned to him on the pitcher's mound. Speaking for many fans, reporter Alistair Cooke once said, "Next to a triple play, baseball's double play is the most exciting and graceful thing in sports." Shortstop George Wright has been credited with having made the first double play while playing for the Cincinnati Red Stockings; he supposedly used the hidden-ball trick. However, Edward J. Nichols found a published reference to the double play before the Red Stockings came into being in 1866. Alfred H. Spink (*The National Game*, 2nd ed., 1911, p.220) claimed that Dickey Pearce of the Atlantics of Brooklyn turned the first double play in 1869 by dropping a fly ball and then forcing the runner out. Abbrev. *DP*. Syn. *double*, 3; *doublet*; *double killing*; *twin killing*; *pitcher's best friend*. 1ST USE. 1858 (Chadwick Scrapbooks; Edward J. Nichols). EXTENDED USE. Two accomplishments made at the same time.

double-play ball A ground ball hit to a fielder at a speed and location ideal for turning an easy double play.

double-play combination The shortstop and the second baseman collectively, because the most common double play involves a pre-

Double play. Washington fielder tags second base ahead of sliding baserunner and turns to throw ball to first base to complete double play. *Photograph by Joseph Baylor Roberts*

cisely timed maneuver between these two players. The shortstop or second baseman fields the ball and tosses it to his teammate who steps on second base to force the runner coming from first and then throws on to that base to retire the batter. "The day when he [second baseman Billy Ripken] forms a double-play combination with his brother Cal may not be that far away" (*Washington Times*, Feb. 26, 1987). Syn. *second base combination*; *keystone combination*.

double-play depth The positions taken by the shortstop and second baseman to enhance the possibility of turning a double play. The positions are taken when there are less than two outs and first base is occupied.

double-play pivot See *pivot*.

double-play support The average number of double plays turned behind a particular pitcher per game. It is an indicator of a pitcher's performance in inducing batters to hit into double plays. The term first appeared in Bill James' self-published *Baseball Abstract* (1978), and can be found in his first conventionally published *Baseball Abstract* (1982).

double-plus Syn. of *plus-plus*.

double pump 1. The part of a pitcher's windup when he throws his arms back over his head twice before delivering the ball. See also *pump*, 1. **2.** Syn. of *double clutch*. **3.** A motion made by a batter to restart his swing.

double shoot The fanciful curveball that veers in two different directions on its way to the plate, such as that thrown by the fictional Frank Merriwell (Burt L. Standish, *Frank Merriwell's Danger*, 1897). "A few years ago there was a story afloat that some exponent of the pitcher's art had invented a 'double shoot,' a ball which so defied the laws of gravitation that it would curve twice in its course, first in and then out, or combining a drop and an up curve" (*The Washington Post*, Sept. 4, 1904; Peter Morris). See also *double curve*; *shoot*, 1; *inner-outer*.

double squeeze A *squeeze play* that enables runners to score from third base and second base while the ball is being thrown to first base in an attempt to retire the batter. Peter Morris (*A Game of Inches: The Game on the Field*, 2006, p.288) reported that the play may have originated as early as 1890, that it was used in the Pacific Coast League in 1904, and that its first known occurrence in a major-league game took place when the Chicago Cubs executed it against Brooklyn on July 15, 1905. The play was refined by the Philadelphia Athletics in 1913 with Jack Barry as the bunter: "The Mackmen, when they were at their best in 1913, were thought to have discovered a new mode of attack, since they were experts at getting two runs on one bunt" (*New York Sun*, March 3, 1918; Steve Steinberg). However, by 1933, sportswriter James M. Gould (*The Sporting News*,

Jan. 19, 1933; Peter Morris) described the double squeeze as "a play which, in these modern days, never is seen." Syn. "double squeeze play." IST USE. 1907. "To add more interest to the uncertainty of the 'squeeze' play's birthplace 'Kid' Elberfeld and 'Hal' Chase have invented the 'double squeeze' and it is even more spectacular than its sensational predecessor" (*The Sporting News*, May 4; Peter Morris).

double steal A strategic baserunning maneuver in which two baserunners advance to the next base without the aid of a hit, error, balk, base on balls, or hit batter. Usually employed when first base and second base are occupied, it is a risky play that is not easy to execute, hence it is something of a rarity. See also *delayed double steal*. IST USE. 1895. "A double steal was effected, . . . [Tom Daly] running to second while [Candy] LaChance sprinted home" (*Brooklyn Eagle*, Sept. 6; Peter Morris).

double switch Entering two players in the lineup as defensive replacements and not replacing each one in the batting order with a player who plays the same position. The lineup shuffle is usually done in the late innings of a close game to get a good hitter into the pitcher's place in the batting order while bringing in a relief pitcher, in the National League or at any other level of the game where there is no designated hitter. Knowing that the pitcher's turn in the batting order is coming up in the next offensive inning, the manager brings in the reliever as well as a second new defensive player. The new player (who is not the pitcher and presumably is a good hitter) is inserted into the pitcher's spot and the new pitcher is put in the spot from which the original player has been removed.

doublet *hist.* Syn. of *double play*. "There were a number of fine plays and doublets made by both clubs" (*Syracuse Journal*, Oct. 4, 1867; Larry McCray).

double up To retire or be retired by a double play. The term is usually applied to the second player to be put out; e.g., "Jones is out, Smith is doubled up" or "The shortstop tagged Jones and doubled up Smith by throwing to first." IST USE. 1871. "Brainard sent a poor little fly to [first baseman] Carleton who captured it and doubled up by stepping on first and putting out Leonard who had started to run" (*The Cleveland Morning Herald*, May 22).

doughnut A common name for the heavy, circular *bat weight* used by batters warming up in the on-deck circle. It is a modern alternative to the earlier practice of warming up by swinging two bats at once. Invented by Bergenfield (N.J.) construction worker Frank Hamilton, it was introduced by New York Yankees catcher Elston Howard in the early 1960s and, according to the *The Sporting News*, was in use in most spring-training camps by 1968. Marketed originally as "Elston Howard's On-Deck Bat-Weight," it was immediately dubbed the "doughnut" or *iron doughnut* by those who used it. "The purpose of the weight is to help a batter in such areas as speeding up his swing and developing stronger wrists and forearms," said Howard (*The Sporting News*, Apr. 27, 1968), who added that it also loosened shoulders, would fit over the bat actually used during a game, and could be removed by simply tapping the bat handle against the ground. Syn. *donut*, 1.

Dowd Report The 225-page report prepared by Washington, D.C., attorney John M. Dowd and submitted to baseball commissioner A. Bartlett Giamatti on May 9, 1989, that detailed the incriminating evidence of Pete Rose's gambling on baseball when he was manager of the Cincinnati Reds during the 1985, 1986, and 1987 seasons. Dowd and his investigative staff spent four months gathering damning evidence that Rose violated Major League Rule 21 by placing more than 400 bets on major-league games, including 52 Reds games (there was no conclusive evidence that Rose bet against the Reds). As a result of the report, Giamatti declared Rose "permanently ineligible" and placed him on the ineligible list. Rose's lifetime banishment from baseball prevented him from being considered for induction into the National Baseball Hall of Fame.

down 1. *adj.* Syn. of *out*, 1; e.g., "two down" is two out. IST USE. 1888 (*Chicago Inter-Ocean*, July 12; Edward J. Nichols).

EXTENDED USE. Tim Considine (*The Language of Sport*, 1982) stated that when one says "two down, one to go," that person is borrowing from baseball. **2.** *adj.* Defeated by or trailing the opposing team. **3.** *adv.* Toward second base from home plate. An item in *American Speech* (Dec. 1956) commented on the confusing terminology of directional words: "The pitcher who stands on a mound to deliver the ball, throws his pitches up to the plate; whereas the catcher . . . pegs the ball down to second. Oddly enough, the same pitcher while in the process of warming up is described as throwing down to his receiver, and none of the fielders is said to throw up to the plate." **4.** *adv.* Toward home plate from the mound. **5.** *adj.* Said of a pitch that is low; e.g., "Smith threw the pitch down and away." **6.** *v.* To defeat in a baseball game; e.g., "The Giants downed the Dodgers last night." **7.** *adv.* Said of the number of games a team is behind in the standings. Compare *up*, 5.

down and away Syn. of *low and outside*. "[Atlanta Braves pitching coach] Leo Mazzone's first commandment: Master the down-and-away fastball" (Tim Verducci, *Sports Illustrated*, Feb. 17, 2003).

down and in Syn. of *low and inside*.

down and out Syn. of *low and outside*.

down-and-up slide *hist.* Syn. of *pop-up slide*. "I used . . . the down-and-up slide, in which you hit the dirt and bound up running" (Ty Cobb, *My Life in Baseball*, 1961, p.168).

down-curve A curveball that drops down; a *down-shoot*. Although it is a 19th-century term, it was used by Arnold Hano (*A Day in the Bleachers*, 1955, p.140) to describe Bob Lemon's pitch: "The down-curve was breaking around the knees, picking up the outside corner." Also spelled "down curve." IST USE. 1883. "Many people . . . believe in an 'up' curve and a 'down' curve" (*Philadelphia Press*, Aug. 20; Peter Morris).

downer An overhand curveball that drops close to the batter's ankles; a *drop ball*, 1, or *overhand curve*. Syn. *sinker,* 2.

downhill Pertaining to a style of pitching in which the ball is thrown from the highest release point possible, thereby applying a steeper angle to the pitch, and giving the impression of extra downward movement (Alan Schwarz, BaseballAmerica.com, Nov. 14, 2006). The arm usually, but not always, comes over the top, the hand on top of the ball, the opposite arm pointing down toward the target, and the pitching arm coming down with the body. It results in greater velocity on the ball, which stays low in the strike zone. The term is usually applied in relation to tall pitchers. "I work downhill. Stay tall. Stay back. Work downhill" (Roger Clemens, quoted in *Sports Illustrated*, June 2, 2003). "[Jimmy Gobble] throws on a good downhill plane but is still inconsistent with his location" (Will Lingo, *Baseball America*, Oct. 13–26, 2003; Peter Morris). "Adam Harben doesn't overpower batters at 6 feet 5, 210 pounds. But his height makes him tough, allowing him to, in baseball jargon, 'pitch downhill'" (Tom Puleo, *The Hartford Courant*, Apr. 22, 2006). Compare *uphill*.

down in the count Syn. of *behind in the count*, 1.

down Main Street Syn. of *down the middle*, 2.

down shoot *hist.* A 19th-century term for a curveball that drops precipitously as it nears the plate. "The amateur Baltimore Club . . . [introduced] the overhand curve, or the 'down-shoot' then becoming the vogue with the three-quarter motion now allowed in the major leagues" (*Dorchester* [Md.] *Democrat-News*, July 7, 1883; Martin Payne). John Clarkson (*Cincinnati Commercial-Gazette*, Jan. 19, 1888) and Tim Keefe (*The Illustrated American*, May 10, 1890) were described as throwing the down shoot. "Ed Delahanty was telling me that he stood up to the plate, and gave [Cy Seymour's] downshoot the nod as it whisked over the plate. 'It was the most dangerous curve that I ever saw,' said Del" (Arthur Irwin, quoted in *The Sporting News*, Jan. 21, 1899; Peter Morris). Compare *upshoot*, 1. See also *down-curve*; *shoot,* 1; *drop ball*, 1. Also spelled "down-shoot"; "downshoot." IST USE. 1880. "He is a fine pitcher, has any amount of curve, a fine down shoot ball and good command of it" (*The Washington Post*, June 30; Barry Popik).

downstairs The location of a ball that is pitched low. Compare *upstairs*, 2.

down the alley Syn. of *down the middle*, 2. Said of a "perfect strike" (Al Schacht, *Al Schacht Dope Book*, 1944). "The pitcher who pitches down the groove—'Down his alley' the boys say sometimes—is inviting trouble" (George Herman Ruth, *Babe Ruth's Own Book of Baseball*, 1928, p.48; Peter Morris). See also *alley*, 2. IST USE. 1912 (*American Magazine*, June, p.199; Edward J. Nichols).

down the chute 1. Syn. of *down the middle*, 2. "He threw Rick nothing but fastballs down the chute, and Manning got two base hits" (Bill Lee, *The Wrong Stuff*, 1984; Charles D. Poe). See also *chute*, 1. 2. Said of a ball hit into the gap between outfielders. IST USE. 1896. "Jones shot the ball down the chute in left field for three bases" (*Brooklyn Eagle*, Aug. 1; Peter Morris). See also *chute*, 2.

down the cock Syn. of *down the middle*, 2.

down the line 1. *adv.* Said of a batted ball that closely follows a foul line, esp. a base hit along the side of either foul line. 2. *n.* A home run hit at Yankee Stadium because of a shorter-than-most distance for the ball to travel.

down the middle 1. Said of the four defensive players positioned along the imaginary center line of the field from home plate to center field and who are said to anchor the defense: catcher, second baseman, shortstop, and center fielder. "There is little Roy Weatherly, brisk center fielder who stars . . . afield and completes the amazing new 'down-the-middle' combine with [Rollie] Helmsley, catcher, and the brilliant infield pair, [Lou] Boudreau and [Ray] Mack" (Cy Peterman, *Philadelphia Inquirer*, July 15, 1940; Peter Morris). IST USE. 1939. "They [several veteran observers] base their calculations [of who will win the pennant] on the strength of a club 'down the middle,' or on a line from the catcher's box through pitcher and the second-base sector through center field" (Jimmy Wood, *Brooklyn Eagle*, March 25; Peter Morris). USAGE NOTE. In what seems contradictory, in baseball parlance, a synonym for "down the middle" is *up the middle*, 2. 2. Said of a pitch, usually a fastball, that is delivered straight through or splits the center or middle of the strike zone, thereby becoming an inviting pitch to hit. Such a

pitch, if taken by the batter, is said to be an "automatic" strike. Syn. *down the alley*; *down the chute*, 1; *down the cock*; *down the pike*; *down the pipe*; *down the slot*; *right down the middle*; *right down Broadway*; *down Main Street*. IST USE. 1928. "In all the innings Alex [Grover Cleveland Alexander] pitched against the Yankees in the [1926] world series I don't believe he threw two balls 'down the middle.' And when he did the batter was so surprised that he couldn't swing" (George Herman Ruth, *Babe Ruth's Own Book of Baseball*, p.51; Peter Morris). EXTENDED USE. Said of an easy situation. Baltimore defense attorney A. Dwight Pettit, concerning state's attorney Patricia C. Jessamy's "defensive" handling of the Michael Austin case (quoted in *The Baltimore Sun*, Jan. 15, 2002): "To me the Austin case was a fast ball down the middle, and she was supposed to hit it out of the ballpark."

down the pike Syn. of *down the middle*, 2.

down the pipe Syn. of *down the middle*, 2. See also *pipe*, 3.

down the river Said of a trade or sale that sends a player to the minor leagues or a team that is lower in the standings.

down the slot Syn. of *down the middle*, 2. "However, a third fast ball down the slot seemed to find him unprepared, for again he was late swinging and got underneath the pitch, raising a pop fly that climbed in front of the plate" (Dick Friendlich, *Relief Pitcher*, 1964; Charles D. Poe).

down the stretch Said of the last four to five weeks of the regular season.

down the wire Said of a game or season whose final outcome is not known until the last play or game, respectively.

downtown 1. *n.* The figurative landing site of a deep home run ball. See also *go downtown*. Compare *suburbs*, 1. ETYMOLOGY. Peter Tamony suggested that the term had an early association with outfielder Ollie Lee Brown. It started in 1964 when he was a member of the minor-league team in Fresno, Calif., that played on the outskirts of town. According to Tamony's notes, the fans came up with the cheer, "Hit it downtown, Ollie." However, writer Charles Einstein (letter, March 5,

1990) clarifies, "When he [Brown] later came up to the San Francisco Giants, he did pick up the nickname 'Downtown' Brown, at least partially for the euphony, and he may have had it at Fresno. But the term was in use before that. I myself was using it in 1961 while covering the Giants at spring training, as a generic to describe balls disappearing far over the left field wall—with inordinate frequency, in that dry, thin air—in the direction of downtown Phoenix, which was only a few blocks north of the crackerbox old park at Central and Mohave, where the club trained in those days." Lawrence Frank (*Playing Hardball*, 1983, pp.94–95) noted that in some ballparks, such as Wrigley Field in Chicago, "a ball hit over the outfield fence will very often land on the city streets outside of the stadium." **2.** *v.* To hit a long home run. "Come on, Lefty, downtown one and gag those bench jockeys" (Edward R. Walsh, USAir in-flight magazine, Sept. 1982).

downtowner A *home run.* "[Reggie Jackson's] startling production of downtowners (forty to date) may bring him within range of Roger Maris's record by mid-September" (Roger Angell, *The Summer Game*, 1972, p.218; Charles D. Poe).

DP 1. Box score and scorecard abbrev. for *double play.* **2.** [softball term] Abbrev. for *designated player*, 2.

draft 1. *n.* A yearly, established system by which teams acquire new players from a choice group so that each team receives some of the most promising players. In 1892 the National League instituted a draft whereby a club exercised its right to purchase a player from a minor league that had signed the National Agreement. See also *first-year player draft*; *Rule 5 draft*; *minor-league draft*; *expansion draft*; *free-agent reentry draft.* **2.** *v.* To acquire a player in the draft. IST USE. 1893. "Baltimore has notified the Atlanta management that [it] has drafted [Jack] Wadsworth, and that he will play in that city this coming season" (*Atlanta Constitution*, Feb. 19; Peter Morris). **3.** *n.* A notice, filed with the commissioner of baseball and the president of the National Association of Professional Baseball Leagues, of the intention of a major-league club to

acquire the territory of, or to compensate, an affiliated minor-league club. The notice includes a precise description of the territory the major-league club intends to include in its territorial definition.

draft-and-follow 1. *adj.* Said of a high school or first-year junior-college player who was selected in the first-year player draft but not immediately signed as the club watched the player's coming amateur season before deciding to offer a contract the following May. Clubs had 51 weeks to sign draft-and-follow players; if the player did not sign before the closed period began, he went back into the draft pool. A club also lost its rights to a draft-and-follow player if he decided to attend a four-year college. The draft-and-follow rule was eliminated in the 2007 Basic Agreement. **2.** *n.* A draft-and-follow player. "About 60 or 70 draft-and-follows are signed each year" (*Baseball America*, June 11–24, 2001; Peter Morris). Abbrev. *DNF.* Syn. *draft, follow, and evaluate.*

draft, follow, and evaluate *n.* Syn. of *draft-and-follow*, 2. "Major league teams can hold the rights to a DFE [draft, follow, and evaluate] . . . without signing him for up to a week before the following year's [first-year player] draft, as long as he doesn't attend a four-year college" (Brian Cazeneuve, *Sports Illustrated*, Aug. 9, 1999). Abbrev. *DFE.*

drafting season *hist.* The period (in the early 20th century) between Oct. 1 and Feb. 1 when major-league clubs could draft a minor-league player for a specified price. Many shenanigans took place as the drafting season approached. "One of the tricks of baseball is for major league clubs to 'buy' stars of the minor organizations before the drafting season opens, and hold the players until the following spring, when they are turned back to their original owners" (*The Washington Post*, Aug. 25, 1904; Peter Morris). See also *covering up.* Syn. "draft season."

draftitis An affliction that hurts a player's draft status in the period leading up to the draft whereby the player withers under scouts' scrutiny and fails to display his skills. Jim Callis (*Baseball America*, June 8–22, 2003; Peter Morris): "[David Purcey] seems to have draftitis as a draft-eligible sophomore. He tried to overthrow at the start of the season, then tried to aim his pitches when his command evaporated."

draft pick A player selected by virtue of the draft.

drag 1. *v.* To execute a drag bunt. IST USE. 1925. "Before the ball even gets to the plate, you start full speed for first. As the ball crosses the plate, you hook the bat around it and drag it past the pitcher. You hold the bat precisely as if you were going to hit the ball through the infielders. If you execute the play properly, you will have a grand lead to first base" (John Tobin, quoted in F.C. Lane, *Batting*, 1925, p.85). 2. *n.* Short for *drag bunt*. 3. *v.* To pull a leveling device over the dirt surface of the infield to smooth the surface irregularities caused by the players' spiked shoes.

drag a piano To run slowly. A plodding baserunner is one who is "dragging a piano."

drag bunt A bunt purposely hit away from the pitcher down the first base line by a left-handed batter. The ball trickles along so slowly down the line that the batter is able to beat it to first base. The bunt gets its name from the appearance that the batter is "dragging" the ball as he sprints to first base. With the drag bunt, the batter is bunting for a base hit as opposed to a *sacrifice bunt*, where the batter's primary goal is to advance a runner already on base. Proficient drag bunters have included Mickey Mantle, Rod Carew, and Maury Wills. Syn. *drag*, 2; *drag play.* IST USE. 1928. "Balls pushed toward first base we call 'drag bunts'" (George Herman Ruth, *Babe Ruth's Own Book of Baseball*, 1928, p.192).

drag play Syn. of *drag bunt.* "I like a slow ball best of all for the 'drag play'" (Carson Bigbee, quoted in F.C. Lane, *Batting*, 1925, p.86).

drain To be exhausted as a starting pitcher; e.g., "Smith was drained by the ninth inning."

draw The number of people in attendance at a game.

draw a blank To fail to score. IST USE. 1864. "The Resolutes drew a blank for their share of the innings" (*New York Clipper*, Aug. 6; Peter Morris).

draw a pass To be issued a base on balls. IST

USE. 1900. "[Kid] Nichols drew a pass" (*The Boston Globe*, Sept. 1; Peter Morris).

draw a throw To make a fielder throw to a base; e.g., a runner at first base takes a large lead so that he can study the move of a pitcher with whom he is not familiar, or a baserunner pretends to advance to another base, forcing the pitcher to make a throw. The gist of this strategy is to give the fielder the impression that he can get the runner out. IST USE. 1901 (Burt L. Standish, *Frank Merriwell's School Days*; Edward J. Nichols).

draw a walk To be issued a base on balls.

draw in To bring the infielders in closer to the plate in anticipation of a bunt or a play at the plate.

drawing card A player who attracts paying customers. "[Ty] Cobb is the greatest star the baseball game has ever known, and probably its greatest drawing card" (*San Francisco Bulletin*, Apr. 12, 1913; Gerald L. Cohen). Babe Ruth's Hall of Fame plaque states that he was the "greatest drawing card in history of baseball." Syn. *card*, 1. IST USE. 1879. "[Ross Barnes] is certainly worth more money to the team than [Will] Foley as a playing or drawing card" (*Chicago Tribune*, June 8; Peter Morris).

drawn game *hist.* A game that ends with each team having the same number of runs after each has come to bat in the same number of innings. "A *tie game* becomes a drawn game whenever the score is a tie—after five innings have been played—and the game be called or terminated either from rain, or the approach of darkness, or from a mutual agreement to call it a drawn game" (Henry Chadwick, *The Game of Base Ball*, 1868, p.46). IST USE. 1867 (*New York Herald*, July 4; Edward J. Nichols).

drawn-in infield A defense in which the infielders are positioned closer to home plate to give them a better chance to throw out a runner at the plate if the batter hits a ground ball. "The infield played back even with the bases full, preferring to spot the Phillies that one run that was on third base in order to play for the double play . . . rather than take a chance on Gavvy [Cravath] slamming a hot drive through the drawn-in infield" (Jim Nasium, *The Sporting News*, Dec. 2, 1926).

IST USE. 1909. "[Lord] soaked a single through the close drawn infield" (I.E. Sanborn, *Chicago Tribune*, July 5; Peter Morris). Syn. *drawn-up infield*.

drawn-in outfield A defense in which the outfielders are positioned closer than normal to the infield when the potential winning run is at third base with less than two outs. "Henry Rodriguez . . . singled with the bases loaded over the drawn-in Minnesota outfield with no outs to win the game" (*The Baltimore Sun*, July 17, 1999).

drawn-up infield Syn. of *drawn-in infield*.

D-Rays Short for *Devil Rays*.

dreamer A player who is not alert on the field.

dreamer's month The month of March, because the regular season usually does not get under way until early April and the only games being played are spring-training exhibition games. At this point in the baseball year, anything seems possible for any team. "They call it Dreamer's Month. In March, on paper, every team looks stronger than it did a year ago, and they are counting heavily on a player they got in a trade with a team that no longer wanted him" (Bob Uecker, *Catcher in the Wry*, 1982; Charles D. Poe).

dream game Syn. of *All-Star Game*, 1. The term was used by the press when the Game was first being planned as an event for the Century of Progress Exposition in Chicago in 1933. Although the first game was successful and exciting (Babe Ruth won it with a two-run homer), it was not until the second All-Star Game in 1934 that the "dream game" description seemed to fit. An article by Kenneth B. Byrd (*Baseball Magazine*, Sept. 1934), entitled "Carl Hubbell and the Dream Game," ends, "But we will wager that twenty or thirty years from now the score will be forgotten. All that will be remembered of the classic is the phenomenal pitching performance of Carl Hubbell. He has assured the permanency of the 'dream game' by making it for [Babe] Ruth, [Lou] Gehrig, [Jimmie] Foxx, [Al] Simmons, and [Joe] Cronin a nightmare."

dream week A session of a *fantasy baseball camp* in which adults pay to train, work out, and play baseball with ex-players.

dress Syn. of *suit* up.

dressing room 1. An area of a ballpark where the players dress. The term is sometimes used interchangeably with *clubhouse*, but in the early days of baseball or in the minor leagues, often there were no clubhouses, only a room for players to dress and sometimes shower. "I'll never forget old Dizzy [Dean] hugging Paul [Dean] in the dressing room after the game, wrestling him and yelping" (Frankie Frisch, quoted in John P. Carmichael, *My Greatest Day in Baseball*, 1968, p.55). See also *locker room*, 1. 2. An area at a ballpark where the umpires don and doff their clothing and equipment. "I requested that a resolution be passed making it mandatory for all clubs to provide adequate dressing-room facilities for the umpires just as they are required to do for the visiting players" (letter from National League president Harry Pulliam to all club presidents, March 3, 1908). Syn. *locker room*, 2.

dribble 1. *v.* To hit a ball weakly. "Mark Jones broke up the no-hitter in the eighth, dribbling a 1–2 inside fastball past the mound" (*Tampa Tribune*, July 26, 1989). 2. *n.* A weakly batted ground ball. IST USE. 1912 (*New York Tribune*, Sept. 17; Edward J. Nichols).

dribbler A slow-rolling ground ball or one that bounces in short hops, often hit off the end of the bat or close to the handle. See also *squibber*. IST USE. 1915. "The batter hit the next one for a dribbler, and just managed to reach first" (Lester Chadwick, *Baseball Joe in the Big League*).

drill 1. *v.* To hit a ball hard, on a straight line and well-placed; to hit a line drive. "[Kenny Lofton] drilled a first-pitch, line-drive single to right" (*The Baltimore Sun*, Oct. 15, 2002). 2. *v.* To be hit hard or hurt. The term is applied when a player is hit by a thrown, pitched, or batted ball, or by a bat, or when he collides with another player. "One of the worst feelings in baseball is seeing someone get drilled like that" (Alan Ashby, on Dickie Thon's severe beaning, quoted in *The Washington Post*, Oct. 14, 1986). 3. *v.* To hit a batter with a pitched ball or a runner with a thrown ball. When Bob Sebra hit Tracy Jones with a ball in 1990, he bragged, "I drilled him, I hit him on purpose. . . . I wasn't trying to hit him in the head but I was trying to drill him" (*Tampa Tribune*, July 2, 1990). **4.** *v.* To train players in the basics of baseball. **5.** *n.* A physical conditioning exercise or routine. IST USE. 1866. A description of the Continentals of Kalamazoo as an experienced club noted that the players "gave evidence of discipline and drill, the different players yielding implicit obedience to every suggestion of their captain" (*Niles* [Mich.] *Weekly Times*, May 24; Peter Morris).

drinker A fielder in the Negro leagues who was "so good that he seemed to drink in every ball hit to him" (David Halberstam, *October 1964*, 1994, p.149).

drive **1.** *n.* A hard-hit ball. See also *line drive*. IST USE. 1871. "Birdsall, by a hard drive to center field, made three bases" (*The Cleveland Morning Herald*, May 6). **2.** *n.* A base hit. **3.** *v.* To hit the ball hard; specif., to hit a ball with strength and quickness to a deep part of the outfield or between the outfielders. "I want him [Brady Anderson] to drive the ball, but not lift the ball" (Baltimore Orioles manager Davey Johnson, quoted in *The Baltimore Sun*, March 17, 1996). "[Mark McLemore] is back driving the ball into the alleys" (*The Baltimore Sun*, June 22, 1994). "[Roberto Alomar acknowledged] he wanted to drive the ball . . . rather than line it somewhere" (*The Baltimore Sun*, Aug. 12, 1996). IST USE. 1860. "Flanley followed and drove the ball to the right field" (*New York Clipper*, Sept. 1; Peter Morris). **4.** *v./hist.* To throw the ball. "Ward caught the ball and drove it to Richardson, effecting a pretty but ridiculously easy double [play]" (*The World* [New York], Oct. 26, 1889). **5.** *n.* A campaign; e.g., a "pennant drive."

drive ball A game described in *The Boy's Book of Sports* (published by Sidney Babcock in New Haven, Conn., 1835) in which two boys with bats face each other, taking turns hitting fungoes to each other. David Block (*Baseball Before We Knew It*, 2005, pp.48, 198) explained the game: "When one boy hits the ball, the other has to retrieve it as quickly as he can, then fungo it back from the spot he picked it up. The idea was to advance forward by a combination of hitting the ball as far as possible past your opponent and also retrieving the opponent's ball before it could get too far behind you."

drive from the hill To force a pitcher from the game by getting base hits.

drive in To score a baserunner by way of a hit, sacrifice, sacrifice fly, groundout, walk, or other means.

drive the yellow bus To pitch with great effectiveness. The term is applied to pitchers of the magnitude of Randy Johnson, who takes large numbers of batters "to school" or "schools" them. The yellow bus refers to the traditional American school bus.

drive to the showers To get so many hits off a pitcher that his manager removes him from the game.

driveway The path of a pitched baseball; e.g., "Smith watched the curve come down the driveway."

drizzler A weakly hit ground ball. IST USE. 1912. "[He] pounded out a little drizzler that Sam quickly gathered in and threw to first" (Lester Chadwick, *Baseball Joe of the Silver Stars*; David Shulman).

drooler *hist.* A spitball.

drooper *hist.* A *Texas Leaguer* in the Western League. IST USE. 1932 (*Baseball Magazine*, October; Edward J. Nichols).

drop **1.** *n.* A pitch that suddenly sinks as it nears the plate. Although the term is still in use, it is now more likely to be called a *sinker*, 1. See also *drop ball*, 1. IST USE. 1866 (*New York Herald*, July 8; Edward J. Nichols). **2.** *n.* The sudden downward path of a curveball. **3.** *n.* A misplay by a fielder who loses control of the ball, usually resulting in an error. "So many games without a boot, a bobble, an overthrow or a drop—especially for a shortstop [Mike Bordick]" (Dave Sheinin, *The Washington* Post, Sept. 17, 2002). **4.** *v.* To mishandle a ball in play, usually resulting in an error. **5.** *v.* To lose a baseball game; e.g., "The Braves dropped the next five games to go into fourth place."

drop a bunt To lay down a bunt. Syn. *drop one*.

drop-and-drive Said of a compact pitching motion or delivery in which the pitcher, as he strides toward the plate, plants his lead leg and flexes his back leg at the knee, with the knee nearly touching the ground, and pushes hard off the rubber; by getting his trunk very low to the ground and using his strong legs, the pitcher propels his entire body behind the pitch and toward the plate. The term is used most commonly to describe the motions of fastball pitchers such as Tom Seaver, Nolan Ryan, and Roger Clemens. The term is used less positively today because drop-and-drive pitchers often have difficulty staying on top of the ball. Compare *stay tall and fall.*

drop ball **1.** *hist.* A pitch that suddenly sinks just before reaching the batter and passes home plate lower than its general line of flight seemed to indicate; a curveball that breaks straight down rather than horizontally. The term was popular in the 19th century; its modern equivalent is *overhand curve.* "[Matt] Kilroy is said to have developed a most amazing drop ball. The ball is pitched to the batsman shoulder high and drops to the knee" (*St. Louis Post-Dispatch*, July 31, 1886). Thomas Bond is credited with originating the pitch in 1876. See also *drop*, 1; *down shoot; sinker*, 1. Syn. *drop curve; dropper*, 2; *downer.* IST USE. 1883. " 'Drop' balls, or balls which apparently shoot or curve downwards, are all deceptive work, and are thrown from the highest start the rules allow" (Bobby Mathews, quoted in *Philadelphia Press*, Aug. 20; Peter Morris). **2.** *hist.* An early term for a spitball. In discussing the newly developed spitball, *The Washington Post* (Nov. 1, 1903) observed, "Californians tell of pitchers . . . [who] mix it up with a few bad ones so wide of the plate that the average batter can't reach them. Then comes the new drop ball like a falling, slanting chunk of lead, and the batter is sewed up neatly." **3.** [softball term] A ball thrown in fast pitch softball with a straight downward spin, the ball dropping as it comes to the plate, forcing the batter to take a golf-like swing. Pitchers use it when they want the batter to hit a ground ball, and top pitchers use it to get a strike. It has been likened to the "sinker" in baseball but drops more abruptly and graphically. Syn. *drop pitch*, 2.

drop curve *hist.* Syn. of *drop ball*, 1. "The term 'drop curve' was frequently used before World War II, and not so frequently afterward" (Rob Neyer, in Bill James and Rob Neyer, *The Neyer/James Guide to Pitchers*,

2004, p.13). The modern equivalent is *over-hand curve.* IST USE. 1886. "He possesses a drop curve that proves a puzzler" (*The Sporting News*, May 17; David Shulman).

drop down To pitch with a lower arm angle; to pitch sidearm or underhanded. "Rusty Staub's the last left-handed batter I ever dropped down on . . . and he ripped a pea. . . . I've never dropped down since and won't" (Bob Ojeda, quoted in *USA Today*, June 6, 1986).

drop-in A pitch that fools the batter by appearing to be too high, before dropping into the strike zone at the last moment. "[Jeremy Griffiths] threw that drop-in curveball when he wanted to for strikes" (Pawtucket Red Sox manager Buddy Bailey, quoted in *Baseball America*, May 26–June 8, 2003). IST USE. 1884. "The ambitious but unsuccessful Association players were nonplussed, and . . . looked like boys when trying to bat [Dan Casey's] 'drop-ins'" (*The Sporting Life*, Aug. 6; Peter Morris).

drop off the table See *off the table.*

drop one Syn. of *drop a bunt.*

dropped ball A batted ball that is handled by a fielder but not held long enough to constitute a catch (Henry Chadwick, *The Game of Base Ball*, 1868, p.40).

dropped third strike An error charged to the catcher when the third strike on a batter is not caught, providing first base is unoccupied or first base is occupied with two out, and that allows the batter to advance safely to first base. If the batter is not in the process of running to first base, he shall be declared out once he leaves the dirt circle surrounding home plate. The pitcher is credited with a strikeout even if the batter reaches first base on a dropped third strike. The rationale for requiring the catcher to catch the third strike comes from the principle that the defense has to make a proper fielding play to record an out.

dropper **1.** A fly ball that falls in for a hit. IST USE. 1876. "[Deacon] White's contribution was a dropper into left field, on which he reached second, while [Cal] McVey scored" (Spalding Scrapbooks, vol. 3; David Shulman). **2.** Syn. of *drop ball*, 1. "The Actives took hold of Sanders' pitching from the start, and, when Whittemore and Sawyer put in the 'droppers,' they 'corked' the ball harder than ever" (*Chicago Tribune*, July 30, 1870; Peter Morris).

drop pitch 1. A breaking ball that drops sharply as it nears the plate. 2. [softball term] Syn. of *drop ball*, 3.

drop-step stance The set position by which an outfielder faces the batter, placing the toe of one foot even with the heel of the front foot, as the ball is delivered by the pitcher. The expected direction of the batted ball determines which foot is dropped back. "This position enables the player to get a quicker jump on the ball" (Ken Dugan, *How to Organize and Coach Winning Baseball*, 1971). Compare *square stance*, 2.

drop-the-bat *hist.* A now-illegal ploy in which the batter would drop his bat during the pitcher's windup to cause a halt in the delivery and a balk. It was once practiced on inexperienced pitchers with runners on second or third.

drop the hammer To throw a curveball.

drop the pace *hist.* For a pitcher to throw slower pitches than before (Henry Chadwick, *The Game of Base Ball*, 1868, p.39).

drought An extended period of futility for a hitter, pitcher, or the whole team: "[Manny Ramirez] is in a 2-for-22 drought" (*The Baltimore Sun*, Apr. 16, 2006); "[Sidney] Ponson is winless in his past eight starts, the longest drought of his . . . career" (*The Baltimore Sun*, Aug. 20, 2001); and "The Mets ended an 18-inning scoring drought with a first-inning run" (*Tampa Tribune*, May 17, 1987). Baseball's longest drought is currently being experienced by the Chicago Cubs, who last won the World Series in 1908. See also *slump*, 1; *dry spell*.

drub To defeat decisively. IST USE. 1883 (*Chicago Inter-Ocean*, May 24; Edward J. Nichols).

drubbing A decisive or humiliating defeat. "While they were suffering their nightly drubbings, the unspoken message of the Baltimore Orioles in 1987 was: Our kid pitchers are in accelerated classes, and we'll have to be patient" (Richard Justice, *The Washington Post*, Feb. 23, 1988). IST USE. 1871. "We learn that the Forest City Club of Rockford,

Illinois, will be here Wednesday next and give our boys a 'drubbing'" (*The Cleveland Morning Herald*, May 22).

drugstore bat A cheap bat. Once the majority of major leaguers began using Louisville Slugger bats, Shirley Povich (*The Washington Post*, June 15, 1937; Peter Morris) reported that "with some derision, ball players call any other kind of bat a drug-store bat."

drugstore drop *hist.* A term used by pitcher Burleigh Grimes for his spitball.

drunk Said of the bases when each is occupied by a runner. *Newsweek* (May 15, 1987) cited the term "sacks are drunk" as baseball slang for the bases being loaded, and noted the old barroom boast: "The bases were loaded and so was I."

dry-dock To bench a player. "Joe Sambito is the big brother in the bullpen, temporarily dry-docked with an arm injury" (George White, *Baseball Digest*, Dec. 1983, p.66). ETYMOLOGY. A borrowing from the dry-docking of ships which are brought out of the sea into an enclosed and drained dock so that repairs can be made below the water line.

dry spell 1. A period of no specific duration during which a player remains hitless and/or does not get on base, drive in any runs, or do anything productive for the team. See also *slump*, 1; *drought*. 2. A period of time during which a starting pitcher is not able to pitch complete games nor win any. See also *drought*. 3. A period during which a team does not win a pennant or a World Series. See also *drought*.

dry spitter 1. One of various pitches that behaves like a spitball (not much spin combined with a sharp downward break) but is unmoistened. The term has been applied to the *knuckleball* thrown by Eddie Cicotte, Ed Summers, and Fred Fitzsimmons (John J. Ward, *Baseball Magazine*, Feb. 1927), the *emery ball* thrown by Russell Ford (Westbrook Pegler, *San Francisco Call-Bulletin*, Sept. 27, 1956), the *forkball* thrown by Big Jim Weaver (F.C. Lane, *Baseball Magazine*, June 1936), and the shine ball. USAGE NOTE. After the spitball revolutionized the game from 1905 on, there were many claims that a pitcher had replicated its movement without the saliva. For example, *The Sporting Life* (Apr. 18, 1908; Peter Morris): "A topic of much discussion among the Giants . . . is the 'dry spitter,' a new pitching delivery of which Chris Mathewson claims to be the originator. Matty calls his freak ball the 'spitless spitter,' for he does not moisten the ball, yet it breaks like a spitter. . . . The 'dry spitter' differs radically from the common spitball not only because the ball is not moistened, but because it is a slow instead of a fast ball." **2.** A baseball that has been unintentionally doctored by the dust on the pitcher's hand.

dry ups **1.** Dry heaves suffered by a pitcher who gets too nervous before a game. **2.** The times that a relief pitcher warms up without getting into a game.

DTs Abbrev. for *Davenport translations.*

dub *hist.* **1.** *n.* A weak or poor player; an inexperienced or disappointing player or manager. "A good team can make a manager look like a world-beater, and a bunch of dubs can make a manager look like a dub" (Del Howard, quoted in *San Francisco Bulletin*, Feb. 28, 1913; Gerald L. Cohen). IST USE. 1884. "[Lew Simmons] will make, . . . in the expressive slang of the day, a 'dub' of a manager" (Harry Stovey, quoted in *The Sporting Life*, Dec. 3; Peter Morris). **2.** *n.* A weak team. "Even the dubs of any league expect as good as an even break at home" (Hugh S. Fullerton, *Chicago Tribune*, May 27, 1906; Peter Morris). "Pennants are won by beating the dub teams" (*Chicago Tribune*, Apr. 23, 1906; Peter Morris). **3.** *v.* To hit a ball feebly. "[Bub] McAtee dubbed an easy bounder to the pitcher, and resumed his seat" (*Chicago Tribune*, July 27, 1870; Peter Morris). **4.** *adj.* Said of a poor fielding play. "Ewing had made a dub throw" (*The World* [New York], Oct. 20, 1889; Gerald L. Cohen).

dub piece Syn. of *double*, 1.

duck egg *hist.* A scoreless inning. "The Mutuals were now obliged to accept a 'duck egg' from their opponents" (*Brooklyn Eagle*, Sept. 23, 1862; Peter Morris). See also *goose egg*, 1. IST USE. 1861. "Hardy['s] . . . entrance into the game broke the series of duck eggs that were being laid by the Exercise players" (*Brooklyn Eagle*, Sept. 17; Peter Morris).

ETYMOLOGY. Borrowed from cricket. "In cricket 'lingo' . . . a player who scores a blank gets a 'duck egg'" (*Forest and Stream*, Dec. 25, 1873; Peter Morris).

duck fart A bloop single. The term was coined by Chicago White Sox announcer Ken Harrelson because the sound made by the ball coming off the bat is presumably similar to that made by a duck farting (rather than a solid "crack"). See also *duck snort.*

duck snort A more acceptable synonym of *duck fart* coined by Chicago White Sox announcer Ken Harrelson. "I'd like to see him [Carlton Fisk] hit a little duck snort to right" (Ken Harrelson, quoted in Steve Fiffer, *How to Watch Baseball*, 1987, p.160).

ducks on the pond Runners on the bases (as if they are bobbing about) waiting for a hit to send them home. IST USE. 1939. "[Joe DiMaggio's] runs batted in record would indicate he doesn't hit when there's 'ducks on the pond'" (*San Francisco News*, Aug. 5, 1939, p.13; Peter Tamony). ETYMOLOGY. Coined, or at least brought to baseball, by Washington Senators broadcaster Arch McDonald. EXTENDED USE. A situation that has a good chance to succeed.

dues collector A baseball bat, in the candid vernacular of Reggie Jackson. In 1974, Jackson wrote 'Dues Collector' on the sweet spot of his bat.

duffer *hist.* A clumsy ballplayer. "I'll give you something to chase, you little duffer" (anonymous batter to an outfielder, quoted in *The World* [New York], July 16, 1890; Gerald L. Cohen). IST USE. 1884. "No matter how fine a game the home club may have played, or under what disadvantages the players might have labored, when they do not win he [the 'excitable' spectator] pronounces them 'duffers,' and with crushing irony wonders why they don't go back to farming or drive a team" (*Milwaukee Sentinel*, Oct. 12).

Duffy's Cliff A five- to six-foot-high mound that formed a steep incline in front of the left field wall in Boston's Fenway Park, from the opening of the park in 1912 until 1933. It was greatly reduced, but not eliminated, in 1934. The feature stretched from the left field foul pole to the flagpole in center field and began its incline about 25 feet from the wall. It was frequently and inaccurately reported as 10 feet in height. The mound received its name from Red Sox left fielder Duffy Lewis, who excelled at playing on and around the incline from 1912 to 1917. The original purpose of the mound was as a picnic area for fans who preferred lawn seats. Smead Jolley once complained that they taught him how to run up the cliff but not how to run down it.

dugout An enclosure for the seating facilities reserved for players (when they are not in the field), team members in uniform (manager, coaches), and the trainer. Major-league rules state that the dugout must be roofed and closed at the back and at either end. It gets its name because it is traditionally dug into the ground, with the bench below the playing field, so that spectators can see over it while players are prevented from talking to fans and vice versa. Despite the name, many dugouts are built on top of the ground, especially in parks where amateurs play. There is no requirement that the home team have its dugout on a particular side of the field. Syn. *coop*; *bench*, 2; *hole*, 4; *pit*, 2. 1ST USE. 1908. "The dugouts of the new-fangled players' benches have been put into good shape" (*Brooklyn Eagle*, Apr. 13; Peter Morris). EXTENDED USE. Realm of nonparticipation. When California passed on the first ballot at the 1960 Democratic Convention in which John F. Kennedy was nominated, the *San Francisco Examiner* (July 14, 1960; Peter Tamony) ran the headline: "State Stayed in the Dugout."

dugout coach Syn. of *bench coach*.

dugout diplomacy The use of baseball to support foreign policy. The term was used in reference to the 1999 spring training series between the Baltimore Orioles and a Cuban team, as part of the relaxation of U.S. policy toward Cuba.

dugoutese The inside slang of ballplayers. 1ST USE. 1943. "In fact, even many of the accepted terms usually are sidestepped by most writers . . . everyday dugoutese" (*Baseball Magazine*, January; David Shulman).

dugout jockey Syn. of *bench jockey.*

dummy sign A sign from the catcher, dugout, or coach's box that is meaningless and meant only to mislead and confuse those trying to steal the sign.

dump 1. To bunt the ball. Syn. "dump one." 1ST USE. 1898. " 'Dumping the ball,' as bunting is termed in base ball parlance, does more to break up a pitcher's effectiveness than any other method . . . of batting" (*Brooklyn Eagle*, June 13; Peter Morris). **2.** To bloop a single to the outfield. "Craig Reynolds dumped a curveball into right for the single that loaded the bases" (Richard Justice, *The Washington Post*, Oct. 10, 1986). **3.** To win a baseball game; e.g., "The Giants dumped the

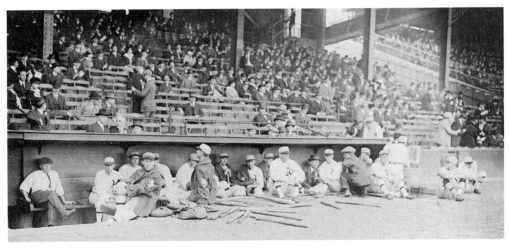

Dugout. Philadelphia Athletics dugout at Shibe Park prior to start of the first game of the 1914 World Series. *George Grantham Bain Collection, Library of Congress*

Dodgers, 7–3." **4.** To throw or lose a game deliberately. **5.** For an umpire to eject a participant from the game. **6.** To remove a pitcher from the game; e.g., "The manager dumped Smith for Jones in the fourth inning." **7.** To release or trade a player because his salary does not fit the club's budget. "Florida looks to dump salaries in deal with L.A" (*Miami Herald* headline, May 16, 1998).

dumper A player who works to throw or lose a game; a traitor. In discussing the barring of Louisville players in 1877, Leonard Shecter (*The Jocks*, 1969, p.190) wrote, "[Louisville] collapsed because . . . it collected the dumbest group of dumpers the baseball world has ever known."

dump list A list of players who are available for trading or releasing, or who are not protected in an expansion draft.

dungeon The last place in the standings.

dunk To hit a ball that drops quickly.

dunker A batted ball that pops up over the infield; a *Texas Leaguer*, 2. IST USE. 1933 (*Famous Sluggers and Their Records of 1932*)

Dunlap *hist.* A spectacular catch. IST USE. 1893. "A volley of cheers followed the drive and doubled in volume when Long was seen to make what the players called a 'Dunlap' or grand-stand catch" (*Donahoe's Magazine*, Aug. 27; David Shulman). ETYMOLOGY. Most likely named for Fred Dunlap, considered the game's greatest second baseman (1880–1891) by his contemporaries.

Duracell rule An unwritten rule that "if there is a close play in right field at Yankee Stadium, never, ever rule against the home team for fear of getting a concussion from a shower of batteries" (Thom Loverro, *Washington Times*, Oct. 10, 1996).

duro seam [softball term] A softball that has concealed stitches.

dust **1.** To pitch a ball deliberately close to the batter. "The Yankees retaliated when Brad Halsey dusted Dave Roberts with his first pitch of the bottom of the eighth" (*The New York Times*, Sept. 27, 2004). See also *dust off*. **2.** To strike out the batter. The term is used in Australia, as in "dust him!" or "one more to dust!"

dust bowl A particularly dusty field; one that has not been watered down before play begins.

duster **1.** *hist.* A *beanball* to drive the batter away from the plate. "The deliberate aiming of a ball at the batsman is, of course, strictly forbidden, but 'dusters' are often used in the first two or three innings [as] the psychological effect on the batsman for the rest of the game is often potent" (*The New York Times*, June 2, 1929). See also *ear duster.* IST USE. 1916. "Ban Johnson favors a two-base passport to every batsman who is a victim of the 'duster'" (*Fort Wayne* [Ind.] *Sentinel*, July 27; Peter Morris). **2.** A pitch thrown far inside to drive the batter back and away from the plate. J. Roy Stockton (*The Gashouse Gang*, 1945, p.146): "An age-old pitching custom has been to push a batter back from the plate with what the trade calls a duster. It loosens up the hitter and prepares him for a curve through the outside corner." Although the distinction is often lost on the batter when one comes his way, a duster is no longer considered a beanball because it is not aimed at his head. "Danger in Dusters" (*The Sporting News* headline, June 20, 1970).

dusting bee A game characterized by dusters; a pitching "war" fought with dusters.

dust off To pitch a duster, either a beanball or a brushback pitch. See also *dust*, 1. IST USE. 1916. "Do pitchers intentionally disable dangerous hitters by 'dusting them off' or 'putting them in the dirt'?" (*Fort Wayne* [Ind.] *Sentinel*, July 27; Peter Morris). USAGE NOTE. The term originally referred to throwing a pitch at the batter's head. "Dusting them off" is a phrase used "to describe balls aimed at or close to the batsman's head, the idea being to drive him away from the plate and make him panicky" (*The New York Times*, June 2, 1929). Later, the term referred to driving away a batter who had become too comfortable at the plate; e.g., "to deliver a pitch so close to the batsman as to imaginably brush his uniform" (Ralph H. Barbour, *How to Play Better Baseball*, 1935, p.168; David Shulman). ETYMOLOGY. There are two schools of thought as to the phrase's origin: 1) making the batter "hit the dust"; e.g., George Herman Ruth (*Babe*

Ruth's Own Book of Baseball, 1928; David Shulman) defined "dusting off" as "making the hitter drop to the ground by pitching at him"; 2) moving the batter off the plate; e.g., Ty Cobb (*Memories of Twenty Years in Baseball*, 1925; Peter Morris) noted the expression originated from "a cry from the bench" that the pitcher "dust him off," meaning "come so close with the ball as to knock the dust out of his clothes."

dust sprayer A player who slides frequently.

dust the jewel For the umpire to clean off home plate.

dustup Syn. of *rhubarb*.

DX Abbrev. for *scoring index*, 1.

dying quail A pop fly that drops suddenly and unexpectedly, like a bird that has been shot on the wing. It often falls between fielders for a base hit. A wind blowing in from the outfield may be an important factor. Ira Berkow (*The New York Times*, Oct. 6, 1988): "The hit is often referred to in baseball . . . as a dying quail. And never did one of them look more like it was on its last flap than that . . . broken-bat bingle . . . which was struck by Gary Carter . . . to drive in two runs." Brooks Robinson (WMAR telecast, May 29, 1986): "[That was] a dying quail single that will look like a line drive in the paper tomorrow." See also *dying seagull*; *wounded duck*. Syn. *quail*; *dying swan*. IST USE. 1954. "[Mickey Mantle] dropped [Roy] Campanella's 'dying quail' looper in the first" (Joseph M. Sheehan, *The New York Times*, Apr. 11).

dying seagull A *dying quail* in a coastal region. Peter Tamony surmised: "This figure of speech would probably not be familiar to inlanders."

dying swan Syn. of *dying quail*. "Gil McDougald pumped a dying swan over second base that no one could reach" (Mickey Mantle, *The Mick*, 1985, p.80; Charles D. Poe).

dynamite bat A bat wielded by a strong, powerful hitter.

dynasty A team able to come up with a cluster of championship seasons; a team that maintains almost uninterrupted winning traditions. A team that wins three or more pennants in a decade is generally considered a dynasty; e.g., the New York Yankees (1949–1953), the Philadelphia Athletics (1910s), and the Brooklyn Dodgers (1950s). USAGE NOTE. For reasons unclear, baseball never has empires or eras but only dynasties. ETYMOLOGY. From the dynasty established by a string of rulers from the same family or group; e.g., the Ming Dynasty in China.

dypsydo Syn. of *dipsy-doodle*, 1.

Dust sprayer. Joe Harris, of the Washington Senators, sliding into third base. *National Photo Company Collection, Library of Congress*

E

E 1. Common box score and scorecard abbrev. for *error*. "[Graig Nettles] still stencils 'E–5' (the scorekeeper's shorthand for 'error–third baseman') on his glove to remind him 'to be humble'" (*The New York Times*, Aug. 29, 1982). In the ballpark, "E" takes on special meaning as it is flashed on the scoreboard when the official scorer decides that a player has committed an error. (If the official scorer rules a tough chance by a fielder to be a base hit, "H" is flashed on the scoreboard.) One of the more ingenious, if commercial, systems for showing "E" and "H" appeared in Ebbets Field after World War II: it was a huge sign for Schaefer Beer, whose "H" or one "E" lit up when the scorer made his ruling. **2.** Syn. of *error*. **3.** See *Class E*.

eagle claw *hist.* A well-shaped fielder's glove.

eagle eye Unusually sharp visual power for judging pitched balls.

ear bender A stranger who talks with players in hotels.

ear duster A pitch thrown at or close to the batter's head. See also *duster*, 1.

ear flap An enlargement of the standard *batting helmet* that covers the batter's ear on the side facing the pitcher. It began as a Little League safety precaution and made its major-league debut on May 2, 1960, when Washington Senators outfielder Jim Lemon wore the new protective helmet (*The Washington Post*, May 3, 1960; Peter Morris). According to Frederic Kelly (*The Baltimore Sun Magazine*, Apr. 5, 1981), "the ear flap . . . worked its way into the big leagues when Baltimore's Brooks Robinson adopted it." The ear-flap

helmets were made mandatory in the major leagues in 1983.

early bloomer A rookie who looks particularly good in spring training or the early days of the regular season, but who fades quickly and must be dropped from the team. See also *bloomer*, 1; *morning glory*; *phenom.*

early innings The first, second, and third innings of a baseball game.

early in the count Said of a balls-and-strikes situation in which very few pitches have been thrown. "[Charles Nagy] got behind hitters and didn't throw enough pitches over for strikes early in the count" (Cleveland Indians manager Mike Hargrove, quoted in *Milwaukee Journal Sentinel*, Oct. 9, 1997). Compare *deep in the count.*

early man A player who takes his batting practice before the players who are in the starting lineup that day. "The 'early men' were those not in the day's lineup, or who needed extra batting practice. The starters monopolized the batting cage once the formal practice began" (Dick Friendlich, *Relief Pitcher*, 1964, p.109; Charles D. Poe).

early reliever A relief pitcher who is brought into the game in the early innings, usually before the third.

early shower 1. The figurative destination of a player ejected from the game by an umpire. **2.** The figurative destination of a starting pitcher who is relieved early in the game.

early swing A swing at a pitch that is far out in front of the plate. The ball is usually missed altogether or, at best, hit into foul territory.

earned bases *hist.* Syn. of *total bases.* IST USE. 1887. "The home nine made fifteen clean hits, of which four were doubles, two triple baggers and one home run, giving them a total of twenty-six earned bases" (*The Washington Post*, May 18).

earned run A run that is scored without the aid of an error, passed ball, obstruction, or catcher's interference, and that is charged to the pitcher. In some instances, a run charged as earned against a relief pitcher can be considered unearned against the team. According to Jules Tygiel (*Past Time*, 2000, p.25), the distinction between earned run and *unearned run* was pioneered by Henry Chadwick in 1859. Abbrev. *ER.* Syn. *earnie.* IST USE. 1867. "Two runs only were earned" (*The Ball Players' Chronicle*, June 6; Peter Morris). USAGE NOTE. Clifford Blau (personal communication, Oct. 2, 2000): "Earned runs was originally an offensive concept. Runs were considered to be earned only if they scored exclusively as a result of hits. If there was a walk or stolen base, even if the run would have scored without them, the run was considered to be unearned." Morris noted the following statement in *The Washington Post* (June 22, 1913): "This year the two major leagues have cut away from this archaic system [won-lost records], and will substitute for it a method of rating pitchers according to their efficiency. The new rating will be based on a modification of the old 'earned run,' the difference being that the modern 'earned run' will include all tallies for which a pitcher is responsible, either by being hit safely or by giving base on balls or wild pitches. Stolen bases also will figure in 'earned runs' on the theory that a considerable percentage of steals are due to the pitcher's inability to hold the runners to their bases, thereby making it practically impossible for catchers to throw them out."

earned run average A pitcher's statistic representing the average number of runs legitimately scored from his deliveries for a full nine-inning game (27 outs). The figure is usually carried to two decimal points. It is calculated by multiplying the number of earned runs by 9, which is then divided by the number of innings (including fractions of an inning) pitched ($9ER/IP$); e.g., if a pitcher has worked 20 innings and has given up seven earned runs, his earned run average is 9 times 7 or 63, divided by 20, equaling 3.15. Along with the won-lost record, this statistic is generally a good indicator of a pitcher's efficiency over the course of a season, particularly in the case of starting pitchers. Traditionally, an earned run average of less than 3.00 is considered excellent. However, variation in earned run averages across seasons has been great enough that this standard should be considered in seasonal context. At one extreme, American League pitchers as a group recorded an earned run average of 2.98 in 1968, with exactly half (25 of 50) of the pitchers who started 15 or more games recording less than 3.00, the leader being Luis Tiant at 1.60. At the other extreme, National League pitchers as a group recorded an earned run average of 4.97 in 1930, with only one less than 3.00 (Dazzy Vance at 2.61). Whereas Vance's earned run average was 52 percent below his league's average and Tiant's was 54 percent below his league's average, it could be argued that their achievements were similar. "This season, in facing some of the strongest batting teams of the National championship arena . . . the average of earned runs made off [Thomas Poorman's] pitching has not exceeded two" (*New York Clipper*, Aug. 30, 1879; Peter Morris). Earned run average became an official statistic in 1912. Abbrev. *ERA.* Syn. *big E.* IST USE. 1876. One of the original statistics compiled during the first year of the National League (John Thorn and Pete Palmer, *The Hidden Game of Baseball*, 1985).

earned run average championship The title given to a pitcher with the lowest earned run average in a given league. To qualify for the title, a pitcher must have a minimum of 162 innings pitched.

earned runs prevented A pitcher's statistic that accounts for the number of earned runs below or above the league average collected by a given pitcher. The statistic was introduced by *The New York Times* in 1984.

earnie Short for *earned run.*

ear syphilis A condition in which an umpire is overly sensitive to comments from players and fans and allows his performance to be affected. Bill McKinley (quoted in Larry R. Gerlach, *The Men in Blue*, 1980, p.160): "That happened to (Nicholas) Red Jones. Red was a good umpire, but he had what we called ear syphilis. He heard *everything*. It took his concentration off the game. It bothered him so much that they finally had to fire him after six years."

Earthquake Series Nickname for the 1989 World Series between the San Francisco Giants and the Oakland Athletics during which the 7.1 Loma Prieta earthquake rocked the region before the start of Game 3 on Oct. 17. The earthquake killed 65 people and delayed the Series for 10 days. See also *Bay Bridge Series*, 1.

East Division 1. See *American League East*. 2. See *National League East*.

Eastern Colored League A *Negro league* formed in 1923 by Ed Bolden (owner of the Philadelphia Hilldales). Other teams included the Bacharach Giants (Atlantic City), Brooklyn Royal Giants, New York Lincoln Giants, Baltimore Black Sox, and eastern Cuban Stars. The league met the western Negro National League in a world series from 1924 to 1927, the west winning three of them. The league was weakened when the Brooklyn Royal Giants refused to adhere to the league schedule; it disbanded in 1928. A successor eastern league, the American Negro League, operated for the 1929 season. Abbrev. *ECL*. (John Holway and Lawrence D. Hogan)

Eastern League 1. A minor league founded in 1884 (Class A from 1902 to 1907 and Class AA from 1908 to 1911), predecessor of the *International League*. 2. A minor league founded in 1923 (Class B from 1923 to 1932, Class A from 1933 to 1962, and Class AA since 1963), operating primarily in the northeastern United States. It was founded as the New York–Pennsylvania League and renamed the Eastern League in 1938. 3. One of two minor leagues in Japan.

Eastern Shuttle Series Nickname for the 1986 World Series between the New York Mets and the Boston Red Sox. Despite the best efforts of Pan American, which had just initiated a shuttle service between the two cities (situated 210 miles apart), the name of the long-established but now defunct Eastern Air Lines air bus between the two cities is the one that stuck.

easy Vulnerable; quickly dispatched. Neither a batter nor a pitcher would like to be known as "easy." IST USE. 1897 (*New York Tribune*, July 14; Edward J. Nichols).

easy cheese A fastball (*cheese*) thrown with an apparent effortless delivery. "[Curt Schilling's] smooth delivery belies the power of his 97-mph fastball—'easy cheese,' in the vernacular" (Tom Verducci, *Sports Illustrated*, Nov. 3, 2003).

easy money *hist.* An opponent who is weak. IST USE. 1907 (*New York Evening Journal*, Apr. 17; Edward J. Nichols).

easy out 1. A hitter who poses no substantial threat. The term is often applied to a pitcher when he comes to bat. A pitcher will often complain that there are no "easy outs" in an opponent's lineup. See also *sure out*, 2. EXTENDED USE. Anyone who can be dealt with easily. 2. An out in which the defense displays little skill, such as a one-hopper to an infielder, or the offense gives up an out, such as a sacrifice bunt. IST USE. 1917. "There should have been two easy outs on those pop flies" (*The Sporting Life*, May 26; Peter Morris). EXTENDED USE. Anything that can be dealt with easily. 3. A common cliché chanted at the amateur level of the game, used to rattle the batter who may, in fact, be a good hitter.

easy save A *save* (as defined by STATS Inc.) that requires an inning or less of work and in which the first batter does not represent the tying run. Compare *tough save*; *regular save*.

eat himself out of the league Common expression told to a player who likes food, consumes more than he should, and becomes ineffective as a result of being overweight. "Elmer Flick literally 'ate himself out of the league'" (Hugh Jennings, *Rounding Third*, 1925).

eat the ball 1. For a player to field a ground ball but not make a throw; e.g., the shortstop holds a cleanly fielded ball because the speedy batter-runner is already at first base, or the first baseman holds the ball because the pitcher did not cover first base. "[Bill Hall] gets to balls other shortstops don't, but he has to learn when to eat the ball and when to attempt a fabulous play" (*Baseball America*, Dec. 24, 2001–Jan. 6, 2002; Peter Morris). **2.** For an outfielder to catch a ball easily. "Williamson hit to right field, and although it was the kind of a high fly that Mike usually 'eats,' he kept up the order of things by making a muff of it" (*The World* [New York], Aug. 27, 1887; Gerald L. Cohen).

eat up 1. To field a ground ball or catch a fly ball skillfully. 1ST USE. 1886. "When [Alex] McKinnon came in from the field yesterday after his phenomenal catch he was congratulated by the spectators. 'Oh! I eat 'em up out there,' replied Mac" (*St. Louis Post-Dispatch*, July 14; Peter Morris). **2.** To cause a player to fail. A ground ball that a fielder cannot handle is said to "eat him up." "The Cubs' power guys [pitchers] can run the ball in on him [Mike Lowell] and eat him up" (anonymous scouting report, *Sports Illustrated*, Oct. 13, 2003).

Ebbets Field Home field of the Brooklyn Dodgers in Brooklyn, N.Y., from 1913 to 1957. Named for Charles H. Ebbets, the man who had it built, the park was squeezed into one city block and had limited parking and cramped seats. It was demolished in 1960, and a housing development is now located on the park's former site. "But more than the scenery has changed—a sign on the apartment building says: 'No Ball Playing'" (*USA Today,* June 24, 1993).

ebony hunter An *ivory hunter* who searches for African-American players. "In the early 1950s . . . scouts whose organizations allowed them to look actively for black players were sometimes called 'ebony hunters' by unfriendly rivals" (Kevin Kerrane, *Dollar Sign on the Muscle*, 1984, p.31).

E-card A candy or gum baseball card (as opposed to one given out with tobacco) issued before 1930. Compare *R-card.*

Eck-ese Distinctive baseball slang dispensed by pitcher Dennis Eckersley; e.g., a home run is a "bridge," off-speed stuff is a "salad," a slider is a "slide piece," and the long walk off the mound taken by the pitcher who gives up a game-winning run is a "walk-off."

Eckstein A player, often undersized, who has

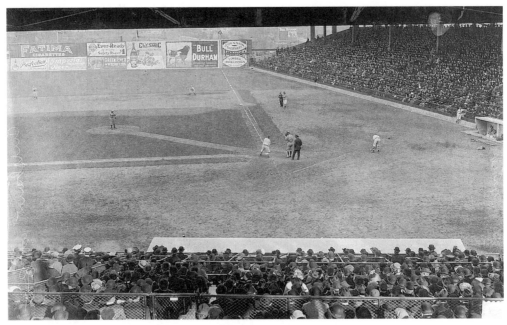

Ebbets Field. New York Yankees pitcher Ray Caldwell, in an exhibition game, the first game played at Ebbets Field, Apr. 5, 1913. *George Grantham Bain Collection, Library of Congress*

seemingly little physical ability but shows enough desire and hustle to remain a prospect, or once reaching the major leagues, is a surprisingly tough out. "Placido Polanco is an Eckstein—a pain-in-the-ass player who keeps coming at you, a get-dirty-type guy" (Deacon Jones, quoted in Alan Schwarz, Baseball America.com, Nov. 14, 2006). ETYMOLOGY. David Eckstein, the 5' 6½" shortstop.

ECL Abbrev. for *Eastern Colored League.*

ecological fastball A fastball that seldom exceeds 55 miles per hour. ETYMOLOGY. Attributed to San Francisco Giants pitcher Allen Ripley (*Sports Illustrated*, Sept. 29, 1980) and inspired by the 55-miles-per-hour speed limit in effect after the oil embargo imposed in the 1970s by the Organization of Petroleum Exporting Countries (OPEC).

edge **1.** *v.* To win a game by one run; e.g., "The Giants edged the Dodgers, 4–3." **2.** *n.* The balance in favor of one team over another, or one player over another; an advantage. Pitchers gain an edge by selecting their pitches and by (illegally) doctoring the ball; baserunners gain an edge with long leads and stolen bases; and batters can gain an edge by (illegally) doctoring their bats. "We have the edge now and should get the next three games" (Philadelphia Athletics manager Connie Mack, quoted in *New York Tribune*, Sept. 2, 1914, p.6; Stuart Y. Silverstein). "I don't know why we can't turn playing in Candlestick into the biggest homefield edge in baseball" (San Francisco Giants manager Roger Craig, quoted in *USA Today*, March 4, 1986). IST USE. 1910 (*American Magazine*, April, p.782; Edward J. Nichols). **3.** *n.* The bite on a pitched ball. **4.** *n.* A *corner* of home plate. **5.** See *on edge.*

edge off To take a lead from a base in small, incremental steps; e.g., "The potential tying run was edging off third."

Edge-U-Cated Heel A closing flex at the outer heel of a fielder's glove, formed by extending the lacing along the thumb and little finger to form a U-shaped heel. This allows the sides of the glove to follow more closely the contours and action of the hand and wrist, permitting a snugger, more flexible fit while the hand controls a much larger glove. Previously, gloves had a big, wide-open heel such that a line drive could spin the glove around or tear it off the hand. Introduced in 1959 by Rawlings, the Edge-U-Cated Heel made the one-handed catch more reliable.

Edison *hist.* A pitcher who is always experimenting with new pitches. The term refers to Thomas Alva Edison, the great American inventor. Syn. *Thomas Edison.* IST USE. 1943. "An 'Edison' is a pitcher who is experimenting all the time" (*Baseball Magazine*, January).

Edna *hist.* A generic name for the wife of a baseball player who, according to Bert Dunne (*Folger's Dictionary of Baseball*, 1958), is "married to a genius," namely the player in question. ETYMOLOGY. Possibly from the temporarily famous line, "How'm I doin', Edna?" blurted out by 1934 Detroit Tigers pitcher Schoolboy Rowe to his sweetheart during a radio interview. "All the next season, when Schoolboy pitched against us we shouted after about every pitch, 'How'm I doin', Edna? How'm I doin', Edna?'" (Bill Werber and C. Paul Rogers III, *Memories of a Ballplayer*, 2000, p.156).

eel ball *hist.* A spitball. ETYMOLOGY. "The players have evolved another name for the spit ball, less offensive than the expressive but inelegant title by which it was christened. They call it the 'eel' ball now, because it has all the characteristics of that aquatic article and is harder to handle generally. They don't expect to hit it any oftener under the new name, but believe it will be more acceptable to the public" (*Chicago Tribune*, Apr. 26, 1905; Peter Morris).

eephus (pron. "EE-fuss") A slowly thrown, high-arcing pitch likely to reach an apex of 25 feet above the ground between the mound and the plate. The ball is thrown overhand and aimed upward in the hope that it will, at its most effective, drop from the top to the bottom of the strike zone as it crosses the plate. The pitch will forever be associated with Pittsburgh Pirates pitcher Truett "Rip" Sewell, who described it to Donald Honig (*Baseball When the Grass Was Real*, 1975, p.254): "It's got to be thrown straight overhand. I was able to get a terrific backspin on the ball by holding onto the seams and flipping it off of three fingers. The backspin held it on its line of flight to the plate. So that ball was going slow but spinning fast. Fun to watch, easy to catch, but tough to hit. It helped me win 21 games in '43 and again in '44." In the 1946 All-Star Game at Fenway Park, Sewell threw three straight eephus pitches to Ted Williams; anticipating the third one after taking the first and fouling off the second, Williams ran up a few feet toward the mound and drove the ball over the right-field fence. "Eephus" is one of several names for this unorthodox pitch, which is also known as *blooper ball*, 1; *gondola*; *parachute*; *balloon ball*; *rainbow pitch*; *Leephus*; and *La Lob*. However, "eephus" seems to be reserved for the bloopers of the most outlandish trajectory. Syn. "eephus pitch"; "eephus ball."

USAGE NOTE. Since Sewell's retirement the term has held on, but seems to be used mostly in humorous situations. When Sewell died in 1989, the term received wide exposure in his obituaries; e.g., " 'Eephus' pitcher dies at age 82" (*USA Today*, Sept. 5, 1989). When Minnesota Twins pitcher Bob Tewksbury adopted the eephus to deal with Mark McGwire in two at-bats yielding a groundout and a pop fly, the *Pittsburgh Post-Gazette* (July 5, 1998) noted that the "rarely used eephus pitch works in Major Leagues." When Alex Rodriguez yanked a blooper ball over the fence, the *Seattle Times* headline (Aug. 27, 2002) announced: "Eephus gets a Seat in Bleachers."

ETYMOLOGY. The pitch was first thrown by Sewell in a 1942 exhibition game against the Detroit Tigers in Muncie, Ind. Catcher Al Lopez called for a changeup with a 3–2 count on Dick Wakefield, and Sewell threw the blooper. Sewell (quoted by Ray Fitzgerald, *The Boston Globe*, July 12, 1981) described what happened next: "Wakefield started to swing, then he stopped, and then he swung again and almost fell down when he missed. After the game, when everybody stopped laughing, [Pirates manager Frankie] Frisch wanted to know what I called the pitch, and Maurice Van Robays, an outfielder, said 'that's an eephus ball.' 'What's an eephus?' I asked him. 'Eephus ain't nuthin.' So it was always eephus after that." Sewell also told Fitzgerald that he had developed the pitch as a result of a hunting accident that left 14

pieces of buckshot in his foot. After the accident, he was unable to pivot as before and adopted a straight, overhand motion, "something like an Australian crawl." The eephus came out of this and was thrown "by holding the ball in the palm of his hand with the fingers on top and delivered much in the manner of a shot-putter." Articles in *The Washington Post* (Apr. 17, 1944, and March 24, 1945; Frank Vaccaro) place the Wakefield incident as occurring during a late 1941 spring training game and mention that Sewell struck out Chicago Cubs outfielder Dom Dallessandro with the eephus during the 1941 season.

Before the term was used by Sewell, "ephus," "e-phus," and "ephus ophus" were used as slang for dependable information, the lowdown, or the right "dope." Peter Tamony noted its use in both underworld and political contexts before and after Sewell's time in the major leagues; e.g., "The ephus is that by delaying things this long, Governor Olson has quietly knocked the election into a cocked-ballot" (*San Francisco News*, June 19, 1939). According to Dan Schlossberg (*The Baseball Catalog*, 1989, p.236), the term was originated by New York Yankees pitcher Lefty Gomez who described "eephus" as that certain something that marked fine pitching from poor: "Eephus is that little extry you have on your good days," said Gomez.

"ee-yah!" The ear-splitting yell or shout made famous by Detroit Tigers manager and third base coach Hughie Jennings before World War I. The call unnerved opposing teams and was accompanied by dance-like gyrations (raising of the right leg with bent knee and flinging into the air two fistfuls of plucked infield grass). ETYMOLOGY. Jennings began using the yell during Detroit's spring games in Macon, Ga., before the 1907 season (*Detroit News*, Dec. 12, 1907): "I just started saying 'that's the way.' Those Tigers played so fast I had to keep yelling fast to keep up with them. Finally 'that's the way' was just one word, 'way-ah' then it became 'wee-ah.'" H.G. Salsinger (*Detroit News*, Jan. 10, 1926; Peter Morris) gave a similar version: "[Jennings] would jump about the coaching

"Ee-yah!" Detroit Tigers manager and third base coach Hughie Jennings, in full shout, ca. 1910. *George Grantham Bain Collection, Library of Congress*

box at first or third and yell: 'That's the way.' Later he drew it out into a long 'That's the way-ah.' Then it became 'That's swaya.' After a time he abbreviated it to 'Swaaa-ah.' And then 'Wee-ah.' But there came still another change. It was slight, but it converted the phrase into 'Eeyah' or 'Ee-yah.'" *The Sporting Life* (June 9, 1886; Peter Morris) reported that Arlie Latham's new coaching yell was "that's the way"; since Latham was the game's best-known base coach, it seems likely that Jennings' version may have evolved from Latham's coaching call. Two other claims concerning the origin of the term are suspect: 1) when Jennings was a youth, he worked as a mule driver in the coal mines and, to speed the mules on their way so he could get to the baseball field, he would yell "wee-up now!" with the phrase gradually evolving to "ee-yah" (Jennings confirmed or denied that the term originated as a mule-driving command, nor did he deny that

he was conveying secret signals); and 2) Jennings learned the term from Hawaiian pitcher Jimmy Williams, who pitched for the Tigers in 1914, the term deriving from the Hawaiian phrase "weeki-weeki," meaning "watch out" or "look out" (but Jennings was shouting the yell many years before 1914). The yell became so well known that American infantrymen, going "over the top" of trenches in World War I assaults, let out the trademark Jennings yell as a rallying cry. See Jack Smiles, *"Ee-Yah": The Life and Times of Hughie Jennings, Baseball Hall of Famer*, 2005, pp.111–15.

efectividad Spanish for "earned run average."

egg The baseball.

egg feast A low-scoring game; one with many "goose eggs" on the scoreboard. IST USE. 1891 (*Chicago Herald*, June 8; Edward J. Nichols).

8 The scorekeeper's designation for the center fielder.

eighth **1.** *n.* The eighth inning. **2.** *adv.* Said of the eighth position in the batting order; e.g., "Smith is batting eighth."

800 number A home run.

Eighth Wonder of the World The *Astrodome* in Houston, so called by Houston Astros president Roy Hofheinz when it opened in 1965 as baseball's first indoor stadium.

86 fastball The average major-league fastball, as clocked in miles per hour by the radar gun (Kevin Kerrane, *Dollar Sign on the Muscle*, 1984, p.93).

eject For an umpire to remove a participant from the playing area. Syn. *bounce*, 3.

ejection The banishment from a game of a player, coach, manager, other team member, or a spectator who, in an umpire's judgment, has violated a given rule, argued balls and strikes or other calls, or behaved in an unsportsmanlike manner. Several managers have been so contentious that they normally get ejected more than once during a season; Bobby Cox holds the career record for most ejections of a manager. On May 2, 1995, a fan was ejected from Wrigley Field for heeding his father's last request by dumping his father's ashes over the left-field wall from the bleachers during the seventh-inning stretch of a Chicago Cubs game.

elastic ball *hist.* Syn. of *lively ball*, 1. *The New York Times* (July 30, 1870; Richard Hershberger) reported a game in which the Atlantics of Brooklyn easily defeated the Pastimes of Baltimore who "unwisely present[ed] an elastic ball for the match, instead of a dead ball." IST USE. 1870. "The Atlantic Club of Brooklyn, use what has only lately been termed an 'elastic' ball, and which is no more nor less than a Ross or Van Horn ball, both being very lively" (Chadwick Scrapbooks; John Freyer). ETYMOLOGY. Nineteenth-century balls containing three to five ounces of rubber as the core bounced so well they were referred to as "elastic" in the sense of recovering size and shape after deformation. They presented a hazard to bare-handed fielders of the 19th century: "Two young people have been killed outright from being struck on the head with one of these elastic rubber balls" (*New York Clipper*, July 9, 1870; Robert H. Schaefer).

elbow bender A pitcher. IST USE. 1937 (*Philadelphia Record*, Aug. 22; Edward J. Nichols).

elbowing Pitching.

el derecho Spanish for "righty."

electric Said of a pitcher's repertoire, or of a given pitch, with so much late-breaking movement as to be nearly unhittable, as if the ball leaps out of the pitcher's hand; also said of a pitcher with nearly unhittable stuff. "There's a new term going around—electric, like 'This guy has electric stuff'" (Toronto Blue Jays scout Gordon Lakey, quoted in *Boston Sunday Globe*, May 10, 1998). "Mariano Rivera's stuff is electric again" (*Sports Illustrated*, Oct. 13, 2003). "The kid's [Chris Ray] got an electric arm" (Baltimore Orioles pitching coach Ray Miller, quoted in *The Baltimore Sun*, July 6, 2005). "[Gavin Floyd] showed a lot of composure and poise, and really had an electric curveball" (Philadelphia Phillies pitching coach Joe Kerrigan, quoted in *The Baltimore Sun*, Sept. 4, 2004). See also *filthy*, 1; *nasty*, 1.

electronic pitcher A pitcher outfitted with a transistorized radio device, which is used to receive instructions from the dugout. This idea has been experimented with in the minor leagues (e.g., Atlanta of the International League in 1964). However, the bench-to-mound radio has never gathered much long-term interest.

electronic scoreboard A scoreboard developed through the application of electronics. IST USE. 1902. "The St. Louis grounds are adorned by a score board that will be of considerable value when the electronic apparatus that goes with it is put in working order" (*Detroit Free Press*, May 1; Peter Morris).

elephant jockey A big, cumbersome player (Chicago Park District [Burnham Park], *Baseball*, 1938).

elevator shaft The figurative destination of a high pop-up hit directly over the batter in the batter's box. The term is a play on the notion that the ball is shot up into an elevator shaft.

eleven immortals The select group of living inductees who were present at the National Baseball Hall of Fame when it was dedicated in 1939: Babe Ruth, Ty Cobb, Walter Johnson, George Sisler, Nap Lajoie, Connie Mack, Cy Young, Honus Wagner, Grover Cleveland Alexander, Eddie Collins, and Tris Speaker. See also *immortal*; *baseball immortal*.

El Foldo A collapse or failure. IST USE. 1938. "Getting back to the class of the National League's favored clubs, there has been a lot of comments on the 'El Foldo' acts being staged by the Pirates, Giants, Cubs, and Reds" (Charles J. Doyle, *The Sporting News*, Sept. 1; Barry Popik).

Elias scale A set of statistics compiled by the Elias Sports Bureau to rank, by playing position, all major-league players who are eligible to be free agents. This ranking determines if a team will be compensated should a player sign with a new team. The use of the Elias scale is one consequence of the 1981 players' strike and is described in detail in the memorandum of agreement between players and owners that settled the strike. An informal discussion of the procedure was offered by Jerome Holtzman (*Baseball Digest*, Feb. 1982). Sabermetric research has found several fundamental flaws in the Elias scale that invalidate its use as an evaluation procedure, most notably through the inclusion of highly correlated and thus duplicative measures (e.g., games started and innings pitched for starting pitchers, batting average and on-base percentage for position players) and a bias toward ranking players based on their playing time. The first player to be given a perfect ranking score of 1.000 was New York Yankees first baseman Don Mattingly in 1987.

Elias Sports Bureau A New York–based company, founded by Al Elias and Walter Elias in 1913, that specializes in analysis of sports statistics. It is the official statistician for the major leagues. From 1985 to 1993, it published an annual book of statistics and commentary entitled *Baseball Analyst* (which is not to be confused with a newsletter of sabermetric research with the same title published by Bill James between 1982 and 1989).

elimination number The *magic number* used by Major League Baseball. It is equal to 163 minus the sum of losses and division leader's wins. Syn. *E number.*

El Series A theoretical World Series between the White Sox and the Cubs in Chicago. Fans could take the elevated train between ballparks without the need of a transfer.

Elysian Fields A quasi-public, rural retreat developed by John Stevens III on a promontory in Hoboken, N.J., with a commanding view of the Hudson River. The 100-acre park was one of the earliest in the United States developed in the English landscape garden style and served as a popular recreation spot in the New York metropolitan area during the first half of the 19th century. It was readily accessible by ferry from Manhattan. Elysian Fields was the site for the first match games of baseball: the New York Ball Club defeated a Brooklyn club 24–4 on Oct. 21, 1845 (*New York Morning News*, Oct. 22, 1845; Dean A. Sullivan); and the New York Nine defeated the Knickerbocker Base Ball Club of New York 23–1 in four innings on June 19, 1846, in the first game played under the Knickerbocker Rules of 1845. The Elysian Fields was a popular venue for baseball and cricket matches in the 1850s and 1860s. The park also hosted musical concerts, ox roasts, box-ing matches, hot-air balloon demonstrations, and oratory competitions, and featured ice-skating ponds, a mile-long riverside promenade, and a deer park. Part of the park is now occupied by the Stevens Institute of Technology. See William A. Mann, "The Elysian Fields of Hoboken, New Jersey," *Base Ball: A Journal of the Early Game*, Spring 2007, pp.78–95. ETYMOLOGY. Derived from Greek mythology for "Elysion," the name for the "Isles of the Blessed," the realm to which those given immortality by divine favor were spirited after death. The name "Elysian Fields" came to mean paradise, or any place or state of perfect happiness.

embezzle 1. To steal a base. IST USE. 1887. "[Sam] Thompson embezzled second" (*Detroit Free Press*, Apr. 30; Peter Morris). 2. *hist.* To employ strategy. "Embezzling the plate describes a case where strategy temporarily takes the place of leg talent" (*The Atchison* [Kans.] *Daily Globe*, June 23, 1896).

emblem 1. Syn. of *pennant*, 3. "The emblem of the Professional Base Ball Championship of the World shall be a pennant, to be presented to the victorious club each year" (*Spalding's Official Base Ball Guide*, 1905, pp.333–35; Dean A. Sullivan). 2. A button, medal, or medallion presented to each player on the team that won the World Series in the early part of the 20th century. "The emblem of the Professional Base Ball Championship of the World shall be . . . an appropriate memento, in the form of a button, to be presented to each player of the victorious club . . . and the players thereof shall be permitted to wear the memento or button as long as they please" (*Spalding's Official Base Ball Guide*, 1905, pp.333–35; Dean A. Sullivan).

Emerald Age A span of time from the late 19th century to the early 20th century during which second-generation Irish-American youths were baseball's dominant ethnic group (sometimes totaling as much as 40 percent of major-league rosters) and popularized a heady, daring, spirited, and spontaneous style of play. The term was introduced by Jerrold Casway (*Ed Delahanty in the Emerald Age of Baseball*, 2004), who wrote, "Baseball for [Irish kids] had an acculturating flavor and nonelitist pretensions, a kind of sporting crucible for boys . . . a shortcut to the American dream. . . . [Their] competitiveness was an expression of their survival instincts, a search for advantages and one-upmanship against society and its prevailing norms." Casway (personal communication, June 11, 2007) gives 1885 to 1914 as the boundaries for the Emerald Age.

emergency disabled list Syn. of *60-day disabled list*.

emergency hitter An early syn. of *pinch hitter*, 1. "The position of 'emergency hitter' is about the hardest and most thankless on a team. The particular batsman who is called upon to produce a wallop at the psychological moment hasn't had the opportunity of getting wise to the movements of the pitcher he is suddenly called upon to face" (*Cincinnati Times Star*, reprinted in *The Sporting News*, July 8, 1909; Peter Morris).

emergency pitcher A pitcher thrust into a starting role due to circumstances that require immediate action, such as an injury to the scheduled starter. IST USE. 1886. "Jim White is said to be pulling the wires to have Brother Will signed by the Detroits as emergency pitcher" (*The Boston Globe*, May 17; Peter Morris).

emergency swing A defensive swing taken by a batter when he belatedly realizes that a pitch may be in the strike zone.

emery ball A pitched ball that has been roughed up with emery cloth, sandpaper, or other abrasive agent. When such a ball is pitched, the scuffed side is more resistant to the force of air, causing it to move erratically as it nears the plate. See also *scuffed ball*. Syn. *dry spitter*, 1; *Black and Decker ball*, 2. IST USE. 1914 (*New York Tribune*, Sept. 20; Edward J. Nichols). ETYMOLOGY. The pitch was invented by Russ Ford in 1908 and introduced to the major leagues in 1910; it became the first pitch specif. banned in 1915. Ford secreted a piece of sandpaper inside his glove and scuffed up one side of the ball with it. According to Ford (quoted in *The Sporting News*, Apr. 25, 1935; Peter Morris), "I took the emery paper from the outside of my glove and sewed it on the web between the thumb and fourth finger.

Emery ball. Russ Ford in action, 1912. *George Grantham Bain Collection, Library of Congress*

Later, I placed a disc of emery paper, one inch in diameter, on a ring which I wore and cut out the center of my pitching glove." The emery secret got out in 1914 and other pitchers threw the pitch, but not with the success that Ford had; this was also the year that the term began to appear in print: "A pitcher not familiar with the proper way to throw the emery ball is at a big disadvantage when using a ball that has been roughened" (Billy Evans, *Atlanta Constitution*, Nov. 8, 1914; Peter Morris). In 1987, when knuckleballer Joe Niekro was caught with a verboten emery board in his pocket, he explained that he just liked to work on his nails between innings.

émigré A player who moves from one team to another.

empty base 1. A base that is not occupied by a baserunner. 2. A base that is not covered by a defensive player; e.g., when both the first baseman and the third baseman charge in to field a bunt down the third base line and the throw sails over the unattended first base.

end grip A *grip* in which the bottom hand is close to or touching the knob of the bat. It is used mainly by power hitters. Compare *modified grip*; *choke grip*.

end of the line The pitch when the count is two balls and two strikes (2–2) because pitchers do not want to go to 3-2. Thomas Boswell (*Why Time Begins on Opening Day*, 1984, p.296): "*Never* take a nap on a 2-2 pitch. That's when you're most likely to find out the pitcher's true opinion of both his strength and the batter's weakness."

endorsement A practice pioneered by baseball players as they found they could earn a few extra dollars by lending their names and faces to a product or service. Modern players sometimes make millions of dollars through endorsements.

English 1. *n.* A spinning motion of a batted or pitched ball with just enough rotation to cause it to veer from its natural course. Sometimes lower-cased as "english." IST USE. 1910. "[The spitball] whirls rapidly for a short distance, until the heavy friction begins to overcome the natural rotary motion of the ball, when it stops rotating, as if a struggle between the two forces was going on, then the thumb 'English' gains control and the ball darts just as it would have done if curved naturally, shooting in the direction the heaviest friction was applied" (John J. Evers and Hugh S. Fullerton, *Touching Second: The Science of Baseball*; Peter Morris). ETYMOLOGY. From the slang of billiards and pool for spin applied to the cue ball when one strikes it away from the center, which causes it to curve. It appears to have been next adopted by cricket and then baseball. 2. *v.* To bunt or bat a ball that acts oddly due to a spinning motion. Ted Shane (*Saturday Evening Post*, July 27, 1940; Peter Tamony) wrote, "Some [Negro league players] are positive magicians at bunting, being able to English it so that it either stops dead as a fielder reaches for it, or corkscrews back around a catcher as he tries to pounce on it." Sometimes lower-cased as "english." IST USE. 1915. "[Casey] Stengel tapped a mild two-bagger over third, the second bag being due to the ball englishing toward the stand after it hit the foul line" (Thomas S. Rice, *Brooklyn Daily Eagle*, July 25; Peter Morris).

English base-ball A forerunner of American baseball played in England before 1750 until well after 1800 as a popular children's pastime. It was described in 1796 by a German physical education pioneer, Johann Christoph Gutsmuths, in *Spiele zur Uebung und Erholung des Körpers und Geistes für die Jugend, ihre Erzieher und alle Freunde Unschuldiger Jugendfreuden* (*Games for the Exercise and Recreation of Body and Spirit for the Youth, His Educator and All Friends of Innocent Joys of Youth*), as "englische Base-ball" or "ball with free station." The game used a short bat, two feet long with a four-inch flat face at the hitting end. The number of bases varied with the number of players and were irregularly spaced 10 to 15 paces apart. The batting team was entitled to only one out before the side was retired. A pitcher, standing only five or six steps from the batter, lobbed the ball in an arc to the batter who had three attempts to put the ball in play and who, if successful, ran counterclockwise from base to base as far as possible without being put out, the objective being to return to a home base (an area rather than a specific spot) where all players from the hitting team gathered, not just the player who was batting. Outs were obtained by catching the ball on the fly, or touching or hitting the runner with the ball, or throwing to a base (David Block, *Baseball Before We Knew It*, 2005, pp.67–68). Compare *ballstock*. See also *rounders, 1*.

enshrine To be inducted into the National Baseball Hall of Fame.

entrada Spanish for "inning."

entrepreneurial player A player who takes the assets he has and puts them to especially good use. To be referred to as an entrepreneurial player is a compliment of the first order. "[Carl Yastrzemski] was the best and last great entrepreneurial player. He took modest assets (coordination, strength), invested heavily (time, toughness, heart, lots of extra batting practice), and got down to business" (Susan Orlean, *The Boston Globe*, June 1, 1986).

E number Syn. of *elimination number.*

envio Spanish for a "pitch" (noun). ETYMOLOGY. Spanish for "shipment."

EP [softball term] Abbrev. for *extra player.*

Epworth League *hist.* A figurative repository for players outside the game. To be sent to the Epworth League is "to be dropped outside of organized baseball" (Franklin P. Huddle, *American Speech*, Apr. 1943).

EqA Abbrev. for *equivalent average.*

EqBA Abbrev. for *equivalent batting average.*

EqBB9 Abbrev. for *equivalent walks allowed per 9 innings.*

EqERA Abbrev. for *equivalent earned run average.*

EqH9 Abbrev. for *equivalent hits allowed per 9 innings.*

EqHR9 Abbrev. for *equivalent home runs allowed per 9 innings.*

EqK9 Abbrev. for *equivalent strikeouts allowed per 9 innings.*

EqMLVr Abbrev. for *equivalent marginal lineup value.*

EqOBP Abbrev. for *equivalent on-base percentage.*

EqR Abbrev. for *equivalent runs.*

EqRA Abbrev. for *equivalent runs allowed.*

EqSLG Abbrev. for *equivalent slugging percentage.*

EqSO9 Abbrev. for *equivalent strikeouts allowed per 9 innings.*

equalizer 1. The curveball. 2. A run that ties a game, esp. late in the game.

equipment 1. A team's game paraphernalia, including such items as bats, gloves, and the catcher's protective gear. 1ST USE. 1877. "The near future may bring about many other improvements in the equipments of a base ball player" (*Providence Dispatch*, reprinted in *Boston Globe*, May 19, discussing the new catcher's mask; Peter Morris). 2. A pitcher's *stuff*, 1.

equipment manager The club official responsible for obtaining, maintaining, and transporting the team's equipment. See also *clubhouse man.*

equivalent average A measure of a player's offensive performance, based on the player's *raw equivalent average* and calibrated to the scale of a batting average, with .260 as the average figure, to assist interpretation. The statistic is used for major-league players and for estimating a minor-league player's performance if he is playing in the major leagues. The statistic was designed by Clay Davenport and used in *Baseball Prospectus* until 2002. See also *Davenport translations.* Abbrev. *EqA.*

equivalent batting average An *adjusted* bat-ting average, featured in *Baseball Prospectus* since 2003. Abbrev. *EqBA.*

equivalent earned run average An *adjusted* earned run average, featured in *Baseball Prospectus* since 2003. Abbrev. *EqERA.*

equivalent hits allowed per 9 innings An *adjusted* rate measure for pitchers, featured in *Baseball Prospectus* since 2003. Abbrev. *EqH9.*

equivalent home runs allowed per 9 innings An *adjusted* rate measure for pitchers, featured in *Baseball Prospectus* since 2003. Abbrev. *EqHR9.*

equivalent marginal lineup value An *adjusted* version of *marginal lineup value*, reported as a rate per game measure and featured in *Baseball Prospectus* since 2003. Abbrev. *EqMLVr.*

equivalent on-base percentage An *adjusted* on-base percentage, featured in *Baseball Prospectus* since 2003. Abbrev. *EqOBP.*

equivalent runs An estimate of runs for which a player is responsible through his offensive performance, based on his equivalent average. The statistic was designed by Clay Davenport and used in *Baseball Prospectus* since 2002. Abbrev. *EqR.*

equivalent runs allowed An estimate of the number of runs allowed for which a pitcher is responsible, based on the equivalent average of opponent batters. Abbrev. *EqRA.*

equivalent slugging percentage An *adjusted* slugging percentage, featured in *Baseball Prospectus* since 2003. Abbrev. *EqSLG.*

equivalent strikeouts allowed per 9 innings An *adjusted* rate measure for pitchers, featured in *Baseball Prospectus* since 2003. Abbrev. *EqSO9*; *EqK9.*

equivalent walks allowed per 9 innings An *adjusted* rate measure for pitchers, featured in *Baseball Prospectus* since 2003. Abbrev. *EqBB9.*

ER Abbrev. for *earned run.*

ERA Abbrev. for *earned run average*, which is always stated as an initialism rather than as a word.

ERA+ Abbrev. for *relative ERA.*

erase 1. To put out a baserunner. "Lenny Harris . . . was erased on a double play" (*The Baltimore Sun*, July 22, 2000). **2.** To retire a batter, esp. to strike out a batter; e.g., "Smith erased Jones on three pitches."

eraser rate A statistic marking a team's success at catching opposing base stealers. Listed as a percentage, it is computed by dividing the number of opponents caught stealing by the number of their attempted steals. For a period in the early 1980s, Eraser Rate Awards were presented to the team with the best record in each league. The awards were sponsored by Major League Baseball and Erasermate, a pen produced by Paper Mate.

ERC Abbrev. for *component ERA*.

ERP Abbrev. for *estimated runs produced*.

error **1.** A misplay on the part of the defensive team that prolongs the time at bat of a batter or the life of a baserunner, or permits a baserunner to advance one or more bases. An error occurs when a batted ball is missed or dropped, when a wild throw is made, or when a putout is missed because the ball is mishandled. An error can also occur when a ground ball goes through a fielder's legs untouched or a pop fly falls untouched when the fielder could have handled the ball with ordinary effort. An error can also occur when a fielder's throw strikes a baserunner. Mental mistakes or misjudgments are not scored as errors. Errors are determined by the subjective judgment of the official scorer and are given to a specific player and his team. They are recorded in the most basic accounting of a game, which calls for giving each team's tally in terms of "hits, runs, and errors." See also *battery error*. Abbrev. *E.* Syn. *E*; *catches missed*. IST USE. 1858 (Chadwick Scrapbooks clipping; Edward J. Nichols). **2.** A statistic charged against a fielder whose action has assisted the offensive team.

error card A baseball card with erroneous information, spelling, or depiction on either side of the card; e.g., a wrong player photograph, inaccurate biographic information, or incorrect statistical data. An example was the 1957 Topps "reversed negative" depiction of Hank Aaron in his opposite batting stance.

errorless Having completed a game, a series

of games, or a string of consecutive innings without committing an error. The term is applied to individuals, parts of a team (such as a collective infield), and teams as a whole.

error of omission Syn. of *mental error.*

error percentage One minus fielding percentage. The statistic reveals differences in fielding percentages more clearly than the standard measure; e.g., the discrepancy between two players with fielding percentages of .995 and .990 is not as obvious as the same discrepancy expressed as .005 and .010 (the second is twice the first). The statistic is used by Bill James and Jim Hentzler in *Win Shares* (2002).

esláider Spanish for "slide" (verb).

established performance level A number representing a specific player's "normal" performance for a given statistical measure. For example, to determine a player's "established hit level," take the sum of three quantities (the player's hits for the last season multiplied by 3, the player's hits for the season before last multiplied by 2, and the player's hits for two seasons before) and divide by 6. The statistic is critical in performing a *favorite toy* analysis. An early version of the concept was first proposed by Bill James in his self-published *Baseball Abstract* (1980) under the title "established value"; the current name first appeared in *Baseball Abstract* (1981), and the final version was described in James' first conventionally published *Baseball Abstract* (1982). See also *major-league equivalency.*

estafar Spanish for "steal" (verb).

estimated runs produced A method for estimating the number of team runs that would result from a player's offensive contributions in a given year, based (most simply) on the number of bases for which a batter is responsible minus the number of outs a player makes, with weights attached to some of the formula components. The method was proposed by Paul Johnson and is found in Bill James' *Baseball Abstract* (1985). It provides slightly more accurate estimates than James' runs created, particularly in the case of batters having particularly good offensive seasons. Abbrev. *ERP.*

eternal rival One of two clubs—the Almendares Alacranes (Scorpions) and the Habana Leones (Lions)—whose rivalry dominated the Cuban League because they were the only constants in the league, and in some years the only two clubs. See also *Almendarista*; *Habanista*.

ethyl chloride A chemical spray that is used as a local anesthetic to "freeze" a painful area so that a player may stay in the game. It is often used after a batter has been hit by a pitch.

even count A count of one ball and one strike, or of two balls and two strikes.

even innings *hist.* The equal number of innings that have been played by both teams. "When a game is called, on account of darkness or rain, the victory is decided by the score of the last 'even innings' played, provided five on each side have been completed" (Henry Chadwick, *The Game of Baseball*, 1868, p.40).

even stance Syn. of *square stance*, 1.

even the count To make the ball-and-strike count even (the same number of balls and strikes) by the batter or by the pitcher.

even with the bag Said of a first baseman or third baseman playing adjacent to, and in line with, the base.

Everlast The glove of a poor defensive player. ETYMOLOGY. Everlast is a brand of gloves worn by boxers.

everyday player A player who appears regularly in the starting lineup. Cal Ripken Jr. (quoted in *The Baltimore Sun*, Oct. 1, 2001): "I've been pretty good during my career at keeping the engine running pretty level. I think that was the key of being an everyday player." Compare *part-time player.* IST USE. 1892. "Seven of [Mobile's] every-day players are left-handed batters" (*Atlanta Constitution*, May 3; Peter Morris). USAGE NOTE. "Every-day catcher" was a term of approval for a catcher who rarely missed games in the days when catchers wore little equipment. "[Albert Strueve] in base ball parlance is known as an 'every day catcher'" (*Evansville* [Ind.] *Journal*, July 27, 1884).

Evil Empire The New York Yankees. The term was coined by Boston Red Sox president Larry Lucchino, in a playful reference to the name given to the Soviet Union by President Ronald Reagan, when the Yankees and its "unlimited budget" beat out the Red Sox in signing Cuban defector pitcher José Contreras: "The evil empire extends its tentacles even into Latin America" (*The New York Times*, Dec. 25, 2002). ETYMOLOGY. The term was used by Reagan in 1983 to describe the former Soviet Union in the context of his announcing his Star Wars antimissile initiative.

ex- A prefix indicating "former"; e.g., "ex-player," the last (and 18th) stage in the life cycle of a player, according to Frank Deford (*Sports Illustrated*, July 27, 1981, p.53).

ex-Cub factor theory A theory created by writer and long-suffering Chicago Cubs fan Ron Berler (*The Boston Herald*, Oct. 15, 1981) which held that a) the greater the number of former Chicago Cubs players on a team, the worse that team will be, and b) no team with more than three ex-Cubs on it can win the World Series, or the team with the most ex-Cubs on it will lose the World Series. Berler noted that since the 1981 New York Yankees had five ex-Cubs on their roster, they were doomed to lose the World Series; he was right—they lost to the Los Angeles Dodgers in six games. All World Series teams since 1945 with three or more ex-Cubs have lost the Series, except for the 1960 Pittsburgh Pirates and the 2001 Arizona Diamondbacks. In the 1986 World Series, the New York Mets, with no former Cubs on its roster, defeated the Boston Red Sox, whose first baseman, ex-Cub Bill Buckner, committed a critical error in Game 6. USAGE NOTE. The basis for the theory is the fact that the Cubs have gone the longest (since 1908) of any team without winning a World Series.

excuse-me hit A base hit, most commonly a single, resulting from an excuse-me swing. The hit is such a fluke that the batter is expected to "excuse" himself.

excuse-me swing A checked swing in which the batter unintentionally makes contact with the pitch.

execute To make a play or carry out a specific

action dictated by a situation in the game. IST USE. 1912 (*New York Tribune*, Sept. 5; Edward J. Nichols).

Executive Council The nine-member governing body whose functions are to advise the commissioner of baseball, protect the interests of the clubs and their players, recommend changes in rules and regulations, approve the budget for financing the commissioner's office, and exercise the powers and duties of the commissioner during any vacancy in the office of the commissioner; the commissioner's "cabinet" of owner-advisors. It is composed of eight club members (four from each league) and the commissioner, who serves as chair. The Executive Council was organized in 1921 as baseball's ruling body, originally consisting of the two league presidents, one club owner from each league, one player from each league, and the commissioner. It operated Major League Baseball in the absence of an official commissioner from 1992 to 1998.

Executive of the Year Award **1.** One of two awards presented annually by *The Sporting News* for the best executive in the major leagues (since 1936) and the best executive in the minor leagues. Currently, two executives from each major-league club vote for the major-league award. **2.** One of two awards presented annually by *Baseball America* for the best executive in the major leagues (since 1998) and the best executive in the minor leagues. Both are selected by the editorial-board staff based on the executive's overall record and reputation in the industry and what the executive has accomplished in a given year or season.

exhibit card A thick-stock, postcard-sized baseball card with a single color picture on the front, commonly sold from vending machines in amusement park "penny arcades" from the 1920s to the 1960s. Syn. *arcade card*. ETYMOLOGY. From the Exhibit Supply Co., Chicago, the principal manufacturer of exhibit cards.

exhibition game An unofficial game that does not count in the standings; esp., a spring-training game. Exhibition games often are scheduled between teams that do not meet during the regular season or between a major-

Exhibition game. Babe Ruth (left) and Jack Bentley in New York Giants uniforms for Oct. 1923 exhibition game, flanking Baltimore Orioles manager Jack Dunn. *George Grantham Bain Collection, Library of Congress*

league team and one of its farm clubs. The annual All-Star Game is a special example of an exhibition game. No major-league club can schedule or play any exhibition game during the championship season without the prior approval of the commissioner. IST USE. 1868. "On Wednesday next an exhibition game will be played on the Excelsior Grounds on State Street, between the Excelsiors and a picked nine" (*Chicago Tribune*, Aug. 16; Peter Morris).

expand the strike zone **1.** For an umpire to allow a pitcher to throw successive strikes further outside the strike zone. "Terry Tata will call the balls and strikes . . . and he may allow [Greg] Maddux to expand the strike zone" (*The Baltimore Sun*, Oct. 21, 1996). **2.** For a batter to swing at pitches outside the strike zone. "Pitchers started feeding him [Alfonso Soriano] breaking balls away . . . [that] he became so concerned with getting to those pitches that he expanded his strike zone, and the more he reached for those outside offerings the farther off the plate the pitchers went" (*Sports Illustrated*, Apr. 5, 2004).

expansion The addition of one or more new franchises to the major leagues. A special draft is held at such times to enable the new teams to select players from existing teams. Between 1901 and 1960 there was no expansion, but new teams have since been added in 1961 (Los Angeles Angels and expansion Washington Senators), 1962 (Houston Colt .45s and New York Mets), 1969 (Seattle Pilots, Montreal Expos, San Diego Padres, and Kansas City Royals), 1977 (Seattle Mariners and Toronto Blue Jays), 1993 (Florida Marlins and Colorado Rockies), and 1998 (Tampa Bay Devil Rays and Arizona Diamondbacks). Because of expansion, the regular-season schedule was increased from 154 to 162 games in 1961 (American League) and 1962 (National League).

expansion draft A special *draft* of players when an expansion team is created; existing teams are required to make available a group of players from which the new team builds its roster, but are also allowed to exclude (protect) a specified number of players. The selection rules for each expansion since 1961 have varied. In the Nov. 1997 draft, teams were allowed to protect 15 players, and Arizona and Tampa Bay were allowed to select 70 nonprotected players. A prototype of the modern expansion draft was used as early as 1881 when Detroit entered the National League and the seven existing clubs were allowed to protect five players each.

expansion team A team that has been created through expansion and that is often referred to as such for many years after its entry into a league; e.g., the Florida Marlins, a Cinderella story in expansion, having gone from its inaugural season in 1993 to a World Series victory in 1997.

expectations The signing bonus that a potential draft pick is likely to demand. The term is a code word used by scouts and other members of the front office: "What is delicately known in the draft room as 'expectations'" (Michael Lewis, *Moneyball*, 2003). "Expectations are a heavy burden when you continually come up short" (Rick Maese, *The Baltimore Sun*, Apr. 18, 2006).

expected remaining future value Syn. of *trade value.*

expected runs Syn. of *run potential.*

expected runs allowed An estimate of a pitcher's runs given up based on his performance. It is used in calculating *clutch pitching index.* The term was defined by John Thorn et al. (*Total Baseball*, 6th ed., 1999).

expected runs batted in An estimate of a batter's number of runs batted in based on his batting performance and normal batting order position. It is used in calculating *clutch hitting index.* The term was defined by John Thorn et al. (*Total Baseball*, 6th ed., 1999).

expectoration exhibitor *hist.* A flamboyant name for a spitball pitcher. IST USE. 1907 (*New York Evening Journal*, June 7; Edward J. Nichols).

expectoration pellet *hist.* A spitball.

experts league A *fantasy baseball league* comprising professional fantasy writers from various publications and Web sites. Many fantasy owners use the prices from experts-league auctions as guideposts for their own player purchases.

explode 1. To get maximum energy behind a swing. One criticism of basketball superstar Michael Jordan as a baseball player was that he had no "explosiveness" in his hands: "You have to be able to recognize a breaking ball, wait and explode on it" (Detroit Tigers scout Dave Roberts, quoted in *The Baltimore Sun*, Nov. 18, 1994). 2. For a fastball to appear to jump during the last six or eight feet of its trajectory to the plate. A ball pitched so fast that the batter's eye cannot follow its approach is said to "explode" rather than grow larger upon arriving so quickly. 3. To unleash a barrage of hits or score many runs. The term is usually applied to a team; e.g., "The Twins exploded for 10 runs in the fifth."

exploded box score A box score with detailed statistics and extra information.

exploding scoreboard A scoreboard configured to make a flashy and noisy display when the home team hits a home run or accomplishes some other feat. See also *Banshee Board*; *Monster, The*, 1. ETYMOLOGY. The term and the concept came from the fertile mind of Chicago White Sox owner Bill Veeck, who introduced the first exploding scoreboard in the original Comiskey Park in Chicago in 1960. Replete with mortars for Roman candles, smoke, and strobe lights, the scoreboard, as Veeck later reported in his autobiography *Veeck . . . as in Wreck* (1962), was inspired by a pinball machine that hits the jackpot at the finale of William Saroyan's play, *The Time of Your Life* (1939).

Expos Nickname for the National League East Division expansion franchise in Montreal, Quebec, Canada, from 1969 to 2004. It was the first major-league team to be located in Canada. The franchise moved to Washington, D.C., in 2005 to become the Washington Nationals. ETYMOLOGY. The team was named for the popular World's Fair, Expo '67, hosted by Montreal. Also known as *'Spos.*

express A fastball. The term was used by Roy Campanella. Compare *local.* See also *redball express*; *Ryan's Express.*

extended spring training A period during which a player remains in spring-training camp for a few extra weeks to recover from an injury or to remedy some other specific problem before reporting to a minor-league club or to the major-league club. "The Cardinals' extended spring-training camp, where low-level minor leaguers work on their fundamentals before starting an abbreviated season" (*The New York Times*, June 12, 2001).

extension 1. The ability of a pitcher to stretch his body and be relaxed; e.g., the more "extension" a pitcher has, the better he is able to deliver pitches with a lot of stuff. **2.** The practice whereby a batter puts his arms over the plate so that his swing will give maximum velocity to the bat.

extra base An additional base gained on a base hit, such as when a hitter stretches a single into a double. See also *take the extra base.*

extra-base club A team that relies on power hitting. "The Yanks in those days, as now, were what the players call an extra-base club" (*The Sporting News*, Nov. 10, 1938; Peter Morris).

extra-base hit A double, triple, or home run; a hit on which the batter advances safely past first base. Abbrev. *XBH*. Syn. *long hit.*

extra inning Any additional inning of play beyond a game's regulation nine-inning length.

extra-innings game Any game that goes beyond the regular nine innings. In the event of a tie after nine innings of play, play continues until one team has scored more runs than the other at the end of a complete inning or when the home team scores the tie-breaking run. IST USE. 1885 (*Spalding's Official Base Ball Guide*, p.19; Edward J. Nichols).

extra pitch A pitch that pitchers are encouraged to develop when they are not successful with their particular repertoire.

extra player [softball term] An optional 11th player in slow pitch softball or the 11th and 12th in co-recreational slow pitch softball. The extra player remains in the same position in the batting order for the entire game and does not play defense (equivalent to the designated hitter in baseball). Compare *designated player*, 2. Abbrev. *EP*.

extrapolated runs A method for measuring a player's offensive performance, calculated by multiplying the player's total for each of a set of offensive events, both positive (walks, singles, stolen bases, etc.) and negative (caught stealing, grounded into double plays, etc.), by a weight associated with it, and then adding (or, in the case of the negative events, subtracting) the products. It was designed by Jim Furtado and appeared for the first time in the *Big Bad Baseball Annual* (1999). Abbrev. *XR*.

extrapolated wins An estimate of the number of runs for which a player is responsible through his offensive performance, based on his equivalent average. It represents the number of games an otherwise average team would win with that player in the lineup rather than with a player at the replacement level for his position. The estimate, based on the earlier *offensive wins above replacement*, was designed by G. Jay Walker and Jim Furtado and appeared for the first time in the *Big Bad Baseball Annual* (1999). Abbrev. *XW*.

eye 1. See *batting eye.* **2.** See *batter's eye*, 1.

eyeballing A situation in which an umpire and a manager or player disagree vociferously, their noses almost touching and their eyes glaring.

eye in the sky A strategic observer—such as a coach positioning the defense, a scout, or other individual, in a press box or other elevated position—who communicates with the dugout. "[Houston Astros general manager] Dick Wagner does not permit opposing teams to use an eye-in-the-sky" (*San Francisco Chronicle*, June 6, 1987). Charlie Metro claimed that he was the first eye in the sky with the Los Angeles Dodgers in the 1970s (Thomas L. Altherr, personal communication, Aug. 28, 1997). Syn. *spy in the sky.*

eye on the ball Watching the ball carefully. "As the pitcher steps on the pitching . . . rubber ready to start his wind-up it becomes increasingly important [for the batter] to keep 'eyes on the ball'" (James Smilgoff, *Athletic Journal*, Apr. 1946). "[Ping Bodie] had his eye on the ball, slamming a double, a single and a couple of hard grounders at the infielders" (*San Francisco Bulletin*, March 31, 1913; Gerald L. Cohen). See also *"keep your eye on the ball."*

eyes on it Said of a batted ball that seems to find its way past fielders. See also *ball with eyes on it.*

F

F **1.** Abbrev. for *fly*, 1. **2.** Abbrev. for *flyout*. **3.** Abbrev. for *foul fly*.

FA Abbrev. of *fielding average*, 2.

face **1.** To come to bat; e.g., "Smith always struck out when he faced a fireballer." IST USE. 1874 (*New York Sun*, July 31; Edward J. Nichols). **2.** To pitch to a batter; e.g., "Jones faced only 29 batters." **3.** See *facing for position*.

facelift Renovations, esp. improvements, to a baseball park. "Cozy Bowen Field, built in 1939, went through a $500,000 facelift in 1989 with public money" (John Manuel, *Baseball America*, Dec. 23, 1996–Jan. 5, 1997; Peter Morris).

face mask Syn. of *catcher's mask*.

facing for position *hist.* "Standing in such a manner as to ensure the bat's meeting the ball so as to have it go to the right, the centre or the left, just as you stand to ensure such a hit" (*Spalding's Official Base Ball Guide*, 1902, p.90). Henry Chadwick earlier defined "facing for a hit" (*The Game of Base Ball*, 1868, p.40): "This is done when the batsman takes his stand, facing the position in the field he desires to send the ball. Thus, if he intends hitting a ball to third base, he faces the short-stop; if to the center field, he faces the pitcher, and if to the right field he faces the first base man."

factory set A complete set of baseball cards assembled and collated by the manufacturer rather than by a dealer or collector. It is sold directly to a dealer or card-shop owner, and is not available through the usual retail outlets. The set usually includes a distinct box with a security seal or inner packing to secure the cards.

fadeaway **1.** *hist.* An off-speed pitch that, when thrown by a right-hander, breaks down and away from a left-handed batter or down and in toward a right-handed batter; an antecedent of the *screwball*. The pitch was made famous by Christy Mathewson, who is credited with its invention and its naming circa 1908. Syn. *fader*; *fallaway*, 2. IST USE. 1908 (*New York Evening Journal*, March 5; Edward J. Nichols). ETYMOLOGY. The term apparently derives either from the fact that the pitcher seems to fall off the mound after he has delivered the ball or that the ball loses speed suddenly as it approaches the batter and falls, or "fades," away at an unnatural angle. **2.** Short for *fadeaway slide*.

fadeaway slide A *hook slide*. "Third base coach Sam Perlozzo gambled successfully by waving [Jeff] Reboulet, who beat the relay with a fadeaway slide around catcher John Flaherty" (*The Baltimore Sun*, Aug. 12, 1999). Syn. *fadeaway*, 2. IST USE. 1911. "Runners have perfected numerous slides designed to outwit the player at the second base end; the fadeaway slide being the most used" (Buck Herzog, quoted in *Baseball Magazine*, September; Peter Morris).

fader Syn. of *fadeaway*, 1. "Yet before [Christy] Mathewson learned the trick of pitching his 'fader,' there was one who pitched the same ball in even more wonderful style" (John J. Evers and Hugh S. Fullerton, *Touching Second: The Science of Baseball*, 1910; Peter Morris).

fagot *hist.* A 19th-century nickname for a baseball bat. IST USE. 1891 (*Chicago Herald*, May 21; Edward J. Nichols). ETYMOLOGY. From the word for a bundle of sticks.

fair In fair territory, and therefore playable.

fair ball **1.** A ball in play; a batted ball that lands in fair territory (between the foul lines). A ball is fair if it meets one of the following criteria: it is touched by a fielder while in fair territory; it lands in fair territory beyond first base or third base; after hitting the ground is still in fair territory when it passes first base or third base or stops; it goes over the outfield fence between the foul poles; or it hits the foul pole. Compare *foul ball.* IST USE. 1845. "Three balls being struck at and missed and the last one caught, is a hand out; if not caught is considered fair, and the striker bound to run" (Knickerbocker Rules, Rule 11th). **2.** *hist.* A pitch that passes over home plate, at the height (high or low) requested by the batter, in early baseball. Before formal strike zones existed, a pitch that the umpire expected a batter to swing at was known as a "fair ball," and the umpire called "fair ball" (not counted as a ball or strike) by way of warning the batter (*National Chronicle*, Apr. 24, 1869). The "fair ball" warning commenced in 1866; beginning in 1879, the warning pitch came only after two strikes (all other pitches had to be either balls or strikes). The two-strike warning was eliminated in 1881. Compare *unfair ball.*

fair foul *hist.* **1.** A foul ball that was allowed as fair if it struck the ground in fair territory before reaching first base or third base. Compare *foul-fair.* IST USE. 1869. "[McMahon] hit a fair-foul ball, which, under ordinary circumstances, would have earned him a base" (*New York Clipper*, June 26; Dean A. Sullivan). **2.** Syn. of *fair-foul hit.* IST USE. 1872. "After waiting for a ball that suited him, he [Ross Barnes] hit one of his favorite fair fouls, for which he is getting an enviable reputation, ... as the ball traveled out toward left field" (*Boston Evening Journal*, July 3).

fair-foul hit *hist.* A base hit, allowable under early rules, in which the batter deliberately hits the ball with tremendous backspin so that after hitting in fair territory, the ball immediately spins into foul territory beyond the reach of the fielders. The technique was mastered by several hitters, esp. Ross Barnes and Dickey Pearce, but was banned after the 1876 season. Henry Chadwick claimed he had suggested the concept of fair-foul hitting in 1864 (Robert H. Schaefer, "The Lost Art of Fair-Foul Hitting," *The National Pastime*, No.20, 2000). According to William M. Rankin (*The New York Clipper*, Oct. 22, 1908), Pearce discovered the fair-foul hit when trying to draw a bunt away from the third baseman. Syn. *fair foul*, 2.

fair ground Syn. of *fair territory.*

fair hit A base hit resulting from a ball batted onto fair territory.

fair pole A term popular among sportscasters for *foul pole* because a ball that strikes the pole is considered a fair ball.

fair run average A pitcher's adjusted runs prevented per nine innings. Abbrev. *FRA.*

fair side The infield edge of first base and of third base.

fair territory The playing area within and including the foul lines, from home plate to the bottom of the playing field fence and perpendicularly upward. Compare *foul territory.* Syn. *fair ground.*

fair-weather fan A fan who roots for or supports a team only when it is doing well or challenging for the pennant. "[A] fair-weather fan ... gives up on his team when things are going badly and switches the TV or radio to the enemy's games" (Barry Petchesky, *The Baltimore Sun*, July 7, 2005).

faithful, the Baseball fans. IST USE. 1867. Detroit hotels were filling up with "congregations of the faithful—in base ball—all eager and anxious" for that city's grand baseball tournament to begin (*Detroit Free Press*, Aug. 13; Peter Morris).

fake bunt A bluff, in which the batter assumes the bunting stance without attempting to bunt the ball. It is used to draw the infielders in close and away from their bases. Syn. *bluff bunt.*

fake grass Syn. of *artificial turf.* The term is used without affection.

fake steal play A play in which, with runners on first base and third base, the runner on first acts as though he is trying to steal, but has the real intention of becoming caught in a rundown that will allow the runner on third to score. "The Senators are rusty on the fake steal play, and let one slip by them" (*The Washington Post*, Aug. 20, 1904; Peter Morris).

fake tag A form of obstruction (in softball and high school baseball) by a fielder pretending to make a tag but who neither has the ball nor is about to receive the ball; this motion impedes the progress of a runner (by slowing him down or forcing him to slide) who is either advancing or returning to a base. The umpire shall award the obstructed runner and each other runner affected by the obstruction of the bases they would have, in his opinion, reached had there been no fake tag.

fallaway *hist.* **1.** A curveball that drops slowly toward the ground as it nears the plate. "Tim Keefe . . . had a fall-away ball, a slow ball delivered with a fast motion. The ball looks as if it were going to hit you in the side, then it falls away from you across the plate" (Ned Hanlon, quoted in *The Washington Post*, Aug. 28, 1904). **2.** The original name of Christy Mathewson's *fadeaway* (Harold Seymour, *Baseball: The Golden Age*, 1971, p.147).

fallaway slide A slide featuring a sudden, evasive drop to the ground before one reaches the base; specif., a *hook slide*. Ty Cobb (*My Life in Baseball*, 1961, p.167) described his fallaway slide: "I'd come straight in, then collapse right or left while throwing in a body feint. Sometimes I'd deliberately slide wide, go right past the bag, then reach back and hook the outside corner with my trailing toe." IST USE. 1910 (*Baseball Magazine*, May, p.72; Edward J. Nichols).

fall behind For a pitcher to throw more balls than strikes to a given batter.

Fall Classic Syn. of *World Series*. The term is one of baseball's oldest clichés, fully expressed in the notion of "titans clashing in the Fall Classic." Sometimes lower-cased as "fall classic."

fall-down range The range of a corner infielder whose lateral mobility is so limited that "the only way to reach a ground ball would be to fall on top of it" (Alan Schwarz, BaseballAmerica.com, Nov. 14, 2006).

fall from ahead To blow a lead in a game.

fall-in *n.* A fly ball that falls in.

fall in *v.* For a ball to land in the outfield without being caught. "[We] feel like we're swinging the bats OK. We're just not getting them to fall in" (Chipper Jones, quoted in *The Baltimore Sun*, Oct. 10, 2004).

fall league An instructional league that plays during the fall; e.g., the Arizona Fall League.

fall off the table See *off the table.*

fall on a pitcher To get many hits off a pitcher during an inning or over the course of a game. "Hits and runs were fully as scarce to the Oaks until the eleventh, when they fell on [pitcher George] Mogridge with a small and sickly thud" (*San Francisco Bulletin*, March 21, 1913; Gerald L. Cohen).

false rise Syn. of *sinker*, 1. "[Addie Joss] often threw his fastball as a ground-ball producing sinker, which was then sometimes called a 'false rise'" (Scott Longert, *Addie Joss: King of the Pitchers*, 1998, p.76).

falsie An extra-thick sliding pad.

Family, The Nickname for the 1979 Pittsburgh *Pirates*, which won the World Series. The name came from the popular 1979 disco anthem "We Are Family," written by Nile Rogers and Bernard Edwards and sung by Sister Sledge, and was given to the team by Willie Stargell, its dynamic leader on the field and a fatherly, yet forceful, presence off it. "We won, we lived and we enjoyed as one" (Stargell, quoted in *The Baltimore Sun*, Apr. 10, 2001).

Family Day A promotional event at a ball game in which a) families get a special rate

Fall Classic. Washington Senators manager Bucky Harris, in the grandstand, presenting to President Calvin Coolidge the ball that will be used to open the 1924 World Series. *Library of Congress*

on tickets or b) the players are brought onto the field before the game with their families. Such an event held in conjunction with a night game is a "Family Night."

fan (spectator) **1.** *n.* An enthusiastic follower of the game of baseball; a devotee. This meaning was reflected in an article entitled "Fellow-Fans" (*Outlook* magazine, June 13, 1923): "Now the fan may be a rooter, but the rooter is not always a fan. The rooter is out to see his side, or college, or city, win; the fan is out to see the game." **2.** *n.* A fanatic who can be rowdy and obnoxious at the ballpark; a term of derision. *The Sporting News* (Nov. 2, 1889) noted that "the 'fan' has a mouth and a tongue" and that every town is "afflicted" with such fans. The *San Francisco Evening Bulletin* (Aug. 12, 1889) observed that such fans "abuse the umpire even when he is in the right." IST USE. 1889. "As Stockton is noted for possessing the worst 'fans' in the country this section promised to be a scene of pandemonium from the time the umpire calls 'play ball' until the last man is put out" (*San Francisco Evening Bulletin*, March 23). **3.** *n.* Any spectator at a baseball game; one who follows the game of baseball. According to *Gallup Poll News Service* (Apr. 6, 2007), 43 percent of Americans identify themselves as baseball fans: "That is low by recent standards, as an average of 49 percent of Americans have said they were fans of the sport since Gallup started tracking this measure in 1993" (the high point came in 1998, when Sammy Sosa and Mark McGwire pursued the single-season home run record, at which time 56 percent of Americans considered themselves baseball fans). "A sigh of relief has gone up from the heart of many a baseball fan owing to the fact that the cowboys left for the east last night" (*St. Louis Globe-Democrat*, July 20, 1886). IST USE. 1886. "The Boston fans explain the poor playing of their nine so far by saying that [Old Hoss] Radbourn does not get effective until June" (*The Sporting News*, May 31; Fred R. Shapiro). USAGE NOTE. In his studies of *The World* (New York), Gerald L. Cohen found the first use on July 12, 1890: " 'Give us more batting in professional games' has been the cry of 'fans' for years." Cohen added (*Studies*

Fan. Baseball fans, including women, waiting in line for gates to open, Oct. 5, 1920. *George Grantham Bain Collection, Library of Congress*

in Slang, part 2, 1989), "This attestation of 'fan(s)' is the only unambiguous one I have noticed in the 1887–1890 columns of *The World* and significantly, it was not written by a NY sportswriter but is reprinted from another city's newspaper. . . . In New York City the only word for 'fan' at that time was 'crank.' "

ETYMOLOGY. There are three explanations for the origin of the term "fan"—each with significant evidence behind it. None of the three "win" as the answer, which is not uncommon when dealing with something as ephemeral as the moment when a word or phrase comes into being. The very real possibility is that, to use the phrase coined by lexicographer Peter Tamony, what is at work here are collaborative etymologies that have over time reinforced each other.

1. "Fan" comes from the word "fanatic." It is commonly assumed and quite often stated that the term is a back formation or clipping of "fanatic." The *Oxford English Dictionary* lists "fan" along with "fann" and "phan" as a clipped form of "fanatic" and cites uses dating to 1682: "The Loyal Phans to Abuse"

and "To be here Nurs'd up. Loyal Fanns to defame" (both from *New News from Bedlam*). The Loyal Phans in question are from the time of Charles II and were, according to an etymological note in *The Times* (London) entitled "Fans and Phans" (May 12, 1934), always seeming to be abused. In reaction to the claim that "fan" is an Americanism, *The Times* concluded: "There is nothing new under the sun, not even the phan"—to which could be added, "and the phans are still loyal."

The link to the concept of the enthusiast is affirmed by meaning as well as by the word "fanatick," defined in Samuel Johnson's *A Dictionary of the English Language* (1798 edition) as both a noun ("An enthusiast; a man mad with wild notions") and an adjective ("enthusiastic; superstitious"). Johnson noted that "fanatic" came directly from the Latin "fanaticus."

As for baseball, according to Gerald Secor Couzens (*A Baseball Album*, 1980), the re-clipper of "fanatic" was Timothy P. "Ted" Sullivan, manager and scout in the early 1880s. Others claim the word was shortened by Chris Von der Ahe, owner of the St. Louis Browns in the 1880s, who supposedly had trouble pronouncing the word "fanatic" with his thick German accent. Tamony did much research on the term and sided with the Sullivan theory, which he spelled out in a letter to Jim Brosnan (Dec. 9, 1963). The crucial paragraph: "A much better claim to origination is made by . . . Sullivan, one of the real founders of the modern game, in his book, *Humorous Stories of the Ball Field: A Complete History of the Game and Its Exponents* (1903). Sullivan wrote that Charles Comiskey called an enthusiast who visited the clubhouse in St. Louis a 'fanatic' and that he [Sullivan] clipped the word to 'fan.' He sets the date as 1883: he was then building the St. Louis team which was later to be taken over by Comiskey."

The strongest case for "fanatic" as the origin of "fan" was mounted by Barry Popik and Gerald L. Cohen (*Comments on Etymology*, Oct. 1996), who concluded that "it is already recognized that 'fan' probably derives from 'fanatic' and is attested at least

Fan. Chris Von der Ahe, baseball card issued by Goodwin & Company. *Library of Congress*

by 1889": "Their work on the diamond is a revelation to local 'fans'" (*Breeder and Sportsman*, Dec. 7; Peter Tamony), and "Kansas City baseball fans are glad they're through with Dave Rowe as a ball club manager" (*Kansas City Star & Times*, March 26; Peter Tamony). Here is their overview as it appeared in the article, quoted directly:

"Sports 'fan' very probably arose in St. Louis, ca. 1883, and its origin most likely involves baseball maven Ted Sullivan. In a January 18, 1896, account in *The Sporting Life*, Sullivan credits Chris Von der Ahe with coining the term in conversation with him, and Sullivan immediately picked up the term and spread it ('The expression was a hit with me. Comiskey and the players took it up, and then the newspapers'). In 1898 Sullivan claimed sole credit for originating the term, but there seems no reason to remove credence from the earlier version involving both Von der Ahe and Sullivan."

Fan. Crowd in the Polo Grounds grandstand, final game of the 1908 World Series. *George Grantham Bain Collection, Library of Congress*

Popik and Cohen add, "Barry Popik has spotted two attestations from 1887—two years earlier than the previously noticed first attestation—and, most importantly, with the first one in a St. Louis publication (*The Sporting News*). From Missouri, sports 'fan' spread first to Philadelphia, and the second 1887 quote appears in a Philadelphia publication (*The Sporting Life*). . . . The third attestation thus far noticed . . . is from March 26, 1889 in the *Kansas City Star & Times*, a Missouri publication. This attestation, together with the first 1887 one, help point to Missouri as the birthplace of sports 'fan.'"

All of this is quite compelling, but then there is this:

2. "Fan" comes from the word "fancy." William Henry Nugent (*American Mercury*, March 1929) showed how many common sports terms used in North America are not Americanisms but rather much older transplants from the British Isles. Nugent traced several terms back to the writings of Pierce Egan, whom he calls "the father of newspaper sports slang." Egan, who published many books and articles on sports in the 1820s, used much of the "flash and cant" of the boxing ring and racetrack in his accounts of events, while others writing on the same subjects left them out. This was not just the slang of the sportsman but, as Nugent pointed out, "words that he had picked up from the speech of vagabonds, jail-birds, bartenders, soldiers and actors." Nugent's evidence on "fan" comes in part from a lexicon that Egan compiled in 1823, entitled

Francis Grose's Dictionary of the Vulgar Tongue as Revised and Corrected by Pierce Egan (the third edition of the work, which was first issued by Grose in 1785). The book contains the following entry: "The Fancy: one of the fancy is a sporting character that is either attached to pigeons, dog-fighting, boxing, etc. Also, any particular article universally admired for its beauty; or which the owners set particular store by, is termed a fancy article, as a fancy clout, a favorite handkerchief, etc; also, a woman, who is the particular favourite of any man, is termed his fancy woman and vice versa." Nugent concluded, "The 'fancy' was long a class name in England and America for followers of boxing. Baseball borrowed it and shortened it to 'the fance,' 'fans,' and 'fan.' I do not agree with Ted Sullivan . . . that he originated it ['fan'] as an abbreviation of 'fanatic.'"

An even earlier use of "fancy" can, in fact, be found in Egan's *Boxiana* (1818): "The various gradations of the fancy hither resort to discuss matters incidental to pugilism." In Egan's *Real Life in London Or, The Rambles and Adventures of Bob Tallyho, Esq. and His Cousin, The Hon. Tom Dashall, Through the Metropolis; Exhibiting a Living Picture Of Fashionable Characters, Manners, and Amusements in High and Low Life* (1821), there are many allusions to "the Fancy," who are not defined per se but described as "the young lads of the Fancy" and are well-bred and wealthy but have a clear penchant for boxing and pleasures of the night. In one poem in the book, "The Joys of a Mill, or a Toddle to a Fight," boxers are on notice to put up a good fight "to please the Fancy, make opponents know it well."

The term "fancy" was firmly established and, for example, appeared in J.S. Farmer and W.E. Henley's monumental *Slang and Its Analogues* (published in several volumes between 1890 and 1904) where it is defined as "The fraternity of pugilists: prize-fighting being once regarded as THE FANCY *par excellence*. Hence, by implication, people who cultivate a special hobby or taste." Farmer and Henley also point to "fancy-bloke," a sporting man, as a variation.

"Fancy" appeared in print in America as early as 1824 in an article in the *National Advocate*, reprinted in the *Providence Patriot* (Oct. 23): "Some of the fancy have been here for a length of time desirous of treating the good people of this country with a real English fight." By 1858, the Fancy (with a capital "F") was out in "full force" and willing to pay a dollar to witness a sparring match (*New York Herald*, Nov. 9). The *St. Louis Globe-Democrat* carried a column entitled "Facts for the Fancy" as early as Aug. 3, 1876, when referring primarily to baseball, along with other sports, such as horse racing, boxing, rowing, and sharpshooting; also, there were references to "base ball fanciers."

3. There is another explanation that has to do with the behavior of the spectator who has little more than "a mouth and a tongue"—one who creates wind like a fan. Research into the etymology of "fan" for earlier editions of this dictionary uncovered occasional restatements of the claim made by Connie Mack that "fan" was first created to describe spectators who fanned themselves to keep cool. Peter Morris fans (so to speak) the embers of this theory: "It certainly doesn't prove anything, but I found a very suggestive note from 1879 indicating that scorecards now had handles attached so they could be used as fans. The avid fans would have been the ones who purchased scorecards, so their association with the word 'fans' would make sense."

But Morris took this a step further in a paper delivered at the 2003 convention of the Society for American Baseball Research, entitled "What It Means to Be a Fan." Morris reviewed the various accounts of the Sullivan/Von der Ahe story and then dropped what he called a "bombshell" by alluding to an earlier explanation by Sullivan. Five years before his 1896 account in *The Sporting Life*, Sullivan gave another version that appeared in *The Sporting News* (Sept. 12, 1891). According to Morris: "This account resembles the 1898 version [in which Sullivan claimed sole credit] but has many important differences. This time, Sullivan and Comiskey are talking when

they are joined by two or three men who 'commenced to talk base ball.' After they had bored Ted considerably they left. Addressing Comiskey, Ted asked what name in the dictionary would fit the men that had addressed them. Comiskey said the dictionary was unequal to this occasion. 'Then,' said Ted, 'I will coin a name of my own; I pronounce them "fan."'"

Morris continued, "So in this earliest version, the word 'fan' has no relationship to fanatic; instead Ted is 'coin[ing] a name of [his] own.' Now by coining, he obviously did not mean that he was making up a word. If he had, he would have called the men something like 'friggles' and there would be no doubt. Clearly this is instead a metaphorical coining. While this is conjecture on my part . . . the most likely scenario is that Sullivan thought to himself that the men were 'windbags,' asked himself what else just blows wind around, and settled upon a fan."

Morris also addressed the question of why the term's origins have been shrouded in mystification and obfuscations. "The answer seems to me to be that 'fan' was originally a term of derision intended to designate, not all spectators, but only the most loud-mouthed and ignorant ones. Baseball men used it amongst themselves, but understandably wished to keep it from the game's supporters, something they did successfully for several years. Its unexpected appropriation by fans made it desirable to suppress its origins and that may even have been why Sullivan changed his story."

fan (strikeout) **1.** *v.* To strike out a batter; to be put out on strikes. "[Rube Marquard] fanned [Hans] Lobert—whiff! whiff! whiff!—like that" (Christy Mathewson, *Pitching in a Pinch*, 1912, p.30). IST USE. 1903. "[Rube Waddell] 'fanned' twelve of the St. Louis Browns" (*Chicago Tribune*, July 19; Peter Morris). **2.** *v.* To swing and miss; to strike out. Edward J. Nichols (*An Historical Dictionary of Baseball Terminology*, PhD dissertation, Jan. 1939) collected several constructions (1888 to 1908) based on this meaning, including: "fan the air," "fan the climate," "fan ether" (air), and "fan ozone." IST USE. 1882. "[Pud Galvin] persists in getting about a mile away from the right spot [home plate] and as a consequence fans air quite often" (*The Cleveland Herald*, July 31, p.5). USAGE NOTE. Peter Morris notes that the term's usage in reference to a pitcher developed later than in reference to a batter, "suggesting that a strikeout was originally viewed as a failure by a batter rather than a success by a pitcher." **3.** *n.* A strikeout. "[David Hudson] struck out 18 batters and nearly tied a 24-year-old state record for fans in a game" (*Columbia* [Md.] *Flier*, Apr. 21, 1994).

fanalytics The serious, scientific approach to fantasy baseball analysis. "A contraction of 'fantasy' and 'analytics,' fanalytic gaming might be considered a mode of play that requires a more strategic and quantitative approach to player analysis and game decisions" (Ron Shandler, *Ron Shandler's Baseball Forecaster*, 2006).

Fan Appreciation Day A promotion to thank the fans for supporting the team. Prizes are sometimes given away, such as the throwing out of the first pitch. The Oakland Athletics had an annual promotion during which a new car was given away to a fan.

fan club A club devoted to a particular player or team. Members of a fan club may enjoy certain benefits, such as discounted tickets, souvenirs, and a membership card. IST USE. 1908. "But what good does it do a fellow to join the Fan Club?" (*Baseball Magazine*, December, p.51; Bill Mullins).

Fancy Dan *hist.* **1.** A player who works to make every play seem spectacular; a player who poses and puts on airs. "A player who would rather make a one-handed catch than use two hands" (Bill Snypp, *Lima* [Ohio] *News*, Apr. 27, 1937; Peter Morris). IST USE. 1927 (*The Sporting News Record Book*, p.64; Edward J. Nichols). **2.** A skilled fielder. "[Fred] Tenney was an excellent fielder— what ball players would call a 'Fancy Dan' around first base" (Harold Seymour, *Baseball: The Early Years*, 1960; Charles D. Poe).

fandango A strikeout.

fandom Baseball fans collectively; the realm of the fan. "Fandom . . . means agony, and one agony in being an Orioles fan is that the only seats they'll sell you for games with the

Red Sox, Yankees, Indians, Blue Jays, Tigers and Brewers are so high above the field that acrophobia can make you hysterical" (Russell Baker, *The New York Times Magazine*, 1980). IST USE. 1893. "If both [umpires] should be of that all-too-common variety known in the parlance of fandom as 'rotten'" (Ren Mulford, *The Sporting News*, Dec. 9; Peter Morris).

fanesse A female baseball fan. "One of the social fads of the day in Atlanta is the learning of all baseball slang, so that the fair fanesses and gay beaux will have all the words of the baseball vocabulary ready and at their tongues' end for the game Saturday" (*Atlanta Constitution*, May 22, 1903).

FanFest **1.** An interactive exhibit and card-memorabilia show that is held at the site of the All-Star Game each year. **2.** A daylong celebration of baseball conducted by a major-league club during the off-season. It may include such features as appearances by current and former players, clinics, video batting cages, question-and-answer sessions, exhibits, trivia quizzes, memorabilia dealers, live music, and even national-anthem tryouts. Team members sign autographs, pose for photos, and talk baseball with fans.

fan-friendly Said of attempts to make going to the ball game a more pleasurable experience; e.g., alcohol-free "family" sections, pay-as-you-go "fun zones" for kids, outfield restaurants, and deployment of security guards.

fan interference Syn. of *spectator interference*.

fannette A female baseball fan. Alternate spelling: "fanette." IST USE. 1911. "Yesterday was Ladies' Day and a fair crowd of the fannettes was out to see the game" (*Newark* [Ohio] *Advocate*, Sept. 2; Peter Morris).

fanning bee **1.** An artful display of pitching in which swinging strikes are plentiful. IST USE. 1910. "On this occasion there was always a 'fanning bee,' as the boys call it" (Christy Mathewson, *Won in the Ninth*; David Shulman). **2.** A gathering of fans and/or players to discuss baseball. "A new baseball spirit was born in Sacramento last night, when almost 1000 fans gathered at Serra Hall for the big fanning bee and [to] do honor to the new manager, Harry Wolverton" (*San Francisco Bulletin*, Feb. 20, 1913; Gerald L. Cohen). See also *hot stove league*. IST USE. 1896. "There is a certain team . . . whose players all go to bed at the same time after they adjourn their fanning bees. Each man is afraid the other will talk about him, and to avoid knocking they all quit together" (*The Washington Post*, June 18). USAGE NOTE. Martin Gardner (*Annotated Casey at the Bat*, 1967, p.186) was incorrect when he defined the term as a tryout or "practice baseball game."

fanny A player in the All-American Girls Professional Baseball League who strikes out often.

fantasy baseball camp A mock training camp in which ordinary fans can, for a hefty fee, practice and play baseball with retired major leaguers and get a feel for the life of a professional ballplayer. An ad for "The Mickey Mantle–Whitey Ford Fantasy Baseball Camp" carried the line, "Play ball with your Yankee Heroes" (*The Wall Street Journal*, Aug. 19, 1986). Jules Tygiel (*Past Time*, 200, p.205) wrote: "The training junkets became popular gifts from wives on their husband's fortieth birthdays. Acquisitive child-men carted home baubles and souvenirs: camp T-shirts, replica big league contracts, videotaped highlights of the week's play, group camp photos, personalized bats, baseball trading cards with their photos and personal information, and uniforms bearing their names." Not to be confused with *baseball camp*. See also *dream week*. Syn. "fantasy camp." ETYMOLOGY / IST USE. 1983. The first fantasy baseball camp took place in Jan. 1983 in Scottsdale, Ariz., featuring players from the 1969 Chicago Cubs and organized by former Cubs catcher Randy Hundley. The word "fantasy" was quickly attached to the camps: "Baseball fantasy to be fulfilled" (Associated Press story on the Dodgers camp, *Oneonta* [N.Y.] *Star*, Feb. 3, 1983) and "Fantasy Island in the desert" (story on the Cubs camp, *The Washington Post*, Jan. 23, 1983). Tygiel observed (p.206) that the "most satisfying fantasy" was "the chance to fraternize with real baseball players, with whom, observed a pair of sociologists, the campers

had 'sustained imaginary social relations since adolescence.'"

fantasy baseball league A simulated baseball game in which the statistical performances of real major-league players are used to determine the relative performances of make-believe baseball teams. It fosters attachment to, and investment in, the performance of players who belong only to a team of one's own device. Teams are stocked via auction (money need not be "real") or draft (no money involved). Most leagues use Internet-based services to keep statistics and manage roster moves. Fantasy baseball leagues are allowed to use player names and statistics without licensing agreements because they are not the intellectual property of Major League Baseball or of individual players. The model for fantasy baseball league is *Rotisserie League Baseball*. "I'm involved, romantically or not, in a fantasy baseball league" (*USA Today*, July 16, 1991). See also *experts league*.

fantasy-camper One who pays to come to a fantasy baseball camp. "Luis Tiant hurls a pitch to a fantasy-camper Sunday afternoon in Winter Haven" (*St. Petersburg Times* photo caption, Feb. 8, 1988).

fantasy game A game in which two teams clash on paper, in a computer, or by some other artificial means. Fantasy games were popular during the baseball strike of 1981 when some radio stations took to broadcasting them.

fan the atmosphere *hist.* To strike out. "[Sam] Thompson fanned the atmosphere in the second" (*Detroit Free Press*, Oct. 11, 1887).

far corner *hist.* Syn. of *third base*, 1. IST USE. 1913. "[Walter] Cartwright is always the finished ball player but it cannot be denied that a stronger man at the far corner would make the infield that much more impregnable" (*San Francisco Bulletin*, March 11; Gerald L. Cohen).

farm 1. *n.* A *farm club*. "[New York Yankees manager] Frank Chance has threatened to retard the growth of Rochester, N.Y. He has made it known that he may remove the 'farm' of the New Yorks from that city to Jersey

City, N.J" (*San Francisco Bulletin*, Feb. 26, 1913; Gerald L. Cohen). See also *baseball farm*. IST USE. 1897. "It is evident that Thornton . . . is in need of further seasoning in minor league company, and Uncle may send him to join the Chicago farm hands on one of the farms in the Western League" (*The Washington Post*, June 14). **2.** *v.* To send a player to a lower-level team for development. See also *farm out*. IST USE. 1895. "Hogan has . . . been 'farmed' to Indianapolis" (*Chicago Daily Tribune*, May 4). **3.** *n./hist.* The playing field with connotations of the game's rural connections. "[Oscar] Bielaski made two most magnificent catches, taken at extreme points of his 'farm' [the outfield], from the bats of Pierce [Dickey Pearce] and [Lipman] Pike" (*St. Louis Post-Dispatch*, May 20, 1875; Peter Morris).

farm club A minor-league baseball club owned by or having an agreement with a major-league team for the purposes of developing young or inexperienced players and retaining veteran players in reserve when a call-up is needed due to injury. Syn. *farm*, 1; *farm team*; *farming ground*. IST USE. 1896. "[Dick] Padden, who has been playing with the Pittsburg farm club in the eastern league, has been called back" (*The Boston Globe*, July 15; Peter Morris).

farm director The executive of a major-league club who is in charge of minor-league operations.

farm hand A minor-league player assigned to a farm club; a player who labors in the farm system. Also spelled "farmhand." IST USE. 1896. "Frank Eustace, our Louisville farm hand" (*The Sporting News*, Aug. 22; Peter Morris). ETYMOLOGY. From the name for a hired man in agriculture (farm hand, hired hand, ranch hand).

farming ground *hist.* Syn. of *farm club*. "Providence, which is the farming ground for Detroit" (*San Francisco Bulletin*, March 18, 1913; Gerald L. Cohen). IST USE. 1910 (*Baseball Magazine*, April, p.8; Edward J. Nichols).

farm out To assign a player to a minor-league club; to return a player to the minor leagues for further training and experience; to send a player back to the farm. Before there was a farm system as such, teams would place players on minor-league teams to let them gain experience. It was regarded by some as an abuse by which the richer teams were able to reserve younger players and recall them at will. See also *farm*, 2. IST USE. 1887. "A strong fight is being made against the new scheme of league clubs 'farming' out surplus players to minor association clubs" (*Detroit Free Press*, May 18; Peter Morris). EXTENDED USE. To reassign; e.g., "I'd like to farm out some of this work."

farm system A major-league club's network of affiliated minor-league teams. A club in the farm system may be owned by the parent club or may be independently owned and operated. In the case of independent ownership, the minor-league club contracts with the major-league club on an exclusive basis to manage and develop players. Although the concept of a farm system was developed by Harry Wright in the 1880s and later by major-league clubs reassigning major-league players to friendly "subsidiary" clubs in the minors in the 1890s, the first modern farm system was the brainchild of Branch Rickey, who developed it for the St. Louis Cardinals and later the Brooklyn Dodgers. He came up with the idea "by necessity" upon becoming manager of the Cardinals in 1919, as the team had finished the previous season in last place. As he later told a congressional subcommittee on monopoly power that was looking into organized baseball in May 1952, he needed a way to compete with the richer clubs by ensuring himself a steady supply of players. He started by buying a half-interest in a Class D team in Arkansas for "a pittance." Using borrowed money, he bought half-interests in the Houston and Syracuse teams in the Texas and International leagues, respectively. Thus, the Cardinals cultivated their own talent. Previously, players had been optioned to minor-league teams on an individual basis. See also *chain-store baseball*. Syn. *vertical trust*. IST USE. 1926. "Regarding this 'farm system,' [Charley] Barrett says" (*The Sporting News*, Dec. 30; Peter Morris). EXTENDED USE. Up-and-coming politicians in a political party. "It is becoming obvious that the local party has no depth in its lineup. It is devoid of a farm system that grooms aspiring bright young people who share its views for elected office" (Norris West, *The Baltimore Sun*, Oct. 5, 1997).

farm team Syn. of *farm club*. IST USE. 1896. "The Pittsburg 'farm' team, the Toronto club of the Eastern League, will commence playing Sunday games" (*The Washington Post*, June 22; Peter Morris).

far station *hist.* Syn. of *third base*, 1. IST USE. 1913. "The boy . . . drove the ball to the clubhouse for a triple. As he came up standing at the far station his teammates threw bats and gloves in the air" (*San Francisco Bulletin*, Apr. 3; Gerald L. Cohen).

far turn *hist.* Syn. of *third base*, 1. IST USE. 1912 (*New York Tribune*, Sept. 8; Edward J. Nichols)

fashion a hit To hit safely. IST USE. 1928 (*The New York Times*, Oct. 7; Edward J. Nichols).

fast *hist.* Said of a promising or up-and-coming young player, team, or league; capable of playing professional baseball. "Miller Huggins [is] a very fast player" (*Detroit Free Press*, March 3, 1907; Peter Morris). "Those players are not reckoned fast enough for the big circus" (*San Francisco Bulletin*, Feb. 11, 1913; Gerald L. Cohen). Compare *slow*, 2.

fastback The hole for one's forefinger in a fielder's glove, giving it a snugger fit, greater extension, and overall control.

fastball 1. A pitch thrown at top speed and with great power. It has a relatively even trajectory but usually has a backward spin, with the bottom of the ball rotating in the direction of flight, which can cause it to hop when it reaches the plate. A fastball falls more slowly than expected, which causes it to appear to rise. When thrown by a right-handed pitcher, a fastball tails in to a right-handed batter and tails away from a left-handed batter. It is the most common pitch in baseball. An anonymous scout observed: "The first thing a scout looks for is a fastball with good velocity and movement. A fastball should sink, rise, slide, or tail. A major-league fastball is in the high 80s [miles per hour]." Also spelled "fast ball." There are many synonyms for "fastball," including: *cheese*; *gas*; *hard one*, 1; *heat*, 2;

number 1. IST USE. 1905 (*The Sporting Life*, Sept. 2; Edward J. Nichols). ETYMOLOGY. Because overhand pitching was not allowed until 1884, the fastball as we know it did not come along until then. Before then fastballs existed, but came from the waist or below. EXTENDED USE. 1. Energy, spirit. "ABC's Keith Jackson, the official voice of college football, is still bringing his best fastball" (Milton Kent, *The Baltimore Sun*, Aug. 22, 1997). To "lose something off one's fastball" is to slow down; e.g., noting that announcer Pat Summerall made some noticeable mistakes during a football broadcast, *The Baltimore Sun* (Jan. 21, 2000) commented, "Now come the whispers that perhaps Summerall has lost a few miles off his fastball." 2. Any fast-moving object or idea. "To be born black in Okolona, Miss., in 1935 was to have two strikes against you and a fastball coming at your head" (Cal Thomas, concerning syndicated columnist William Raspberry, quoted in *The Baltimore Sun*, Jan. 4, 2006). "With [quarterback] Brett Favre firing fastballs again, Green Bay can't be taken lightly" (Peter King, *Sports Illustrated*, Jan. 21, 2002).
2. [softball term] The game of fast pitch softball in Canada. 3. [softball term] A pitch that comes off the fingers with a straight but slightly downward spin in fast pitch softball. It drops slightly as it comes to the plate and is most effective when thrown to the corners of the strike zone.

fastball count A count with more balls than strikes, when it is expected that the pitcher will throw a fastball since it is the easiest pitch to control. "The Tribe also adjusted to the steady diet of off-speed stuff they were seeing from opponents, even on fastball counts" (Stephen Cannella, *Sports Illustrated*, May 22, 2000). See also *hitter's count*.

fastballer A pitcher who relies chiefly on his fastball; e.g., Nolan Ryan, whose pitch has been clocked at 100.9 miles per hour.

fastball motion The pitcher's motion which simulates a fastball but delivers an off-speed pitch.

fast-breaking curve A pitch that early in its flight breaks into a curveball.

fast company *hist.* Syn. of *major leagues.* "As a member of the Detroit Tigers he [Al Klawitter] is now back in fast company for another trial" (*San Francisco Bulletin*, March 21, 1913; Gerald L. Cohen). In 1929, Paramount Pictures produced *Fast Company*, the first talkie baseball film. Compare *slow company.* IST USE. 1896. "It was thought that [Bert] Cunningham was on his last legs . . . and was no longer fit for fast company" (*The Washington Post*, July 8). ETYMOLOGY. The term may have originated in horse racing. "There is talk of a big two-year-old match being arranged [between] . . . Harry White . . . and Tyrant. . . . Both have proved themselves good companions in fast company" (*The New York Times*, Feb. 4, 1884).

fast curve Syn. of *short curve.*

faster company *hist.* Syn. of *major leagues.* "The players taken from the New England League to play in faster company are making good with a vengeance" (*The Sporting Life*, May 27, 1905).

fastest company *hist.* Syn. of *major leagues.* "[Deacon] McGuire was a member of the Detroit baseball team of 1885, and has never been out of the fastest company since" (*The Washington Post*, Nov. 1, 1903).

Fast Food Fall Classic Nickname for the 1984 World Series, which pitted the Detroit Tigers (owned by Tom Monaghan of Domino's Pizza) and the San Diego Padres (controlled by the heirs to McDonald's).

fast hook The removal of a pitcher at the first sign of trouble.

fast infield A hard infield on which ground balls pick up speed and get through quickly.

fast pellet A nickname for the apparently livelier ball introduced in 1920.

fast pitch softball [softball term] An official and once dominant form of softball played by teams of nine players, in which the underhand pitch is delivered to the batter with great speed and, depending on the skill of the pitcher, a varying element of deception. Compare *slow pitch softball.* Also called "fast pitch." Syn. *original softball.*

fast society *hist.* **1.** Syn. of *major leagues.* "Nothing would suit us better than to get Oscar Vitt back from [the] Detroit [Tigers] to play third base for [the] San Francisco [Seals], but the Detroit management . . . wouldn't think of letting a man like Vitt escape from fast society" (*San Francisco Bulletin*, March 1, 1913; Gerald L. Cohen). **2.** Professional baseball. "There are three good pitchers wandering around without a job, any one of whom ought to get by in fast society" (*San Francisco Bulletin*, May 10, 1913; Gerald L. Cohen).

fast start A given number of games characterizing a successful beginning of the season for a player or a team; e.g., the 1984 Detroit Tigers had a fast start when the team won 35 of its first 40 games. The term also can be applied to such feats as the number of at-bats before a player dips below a .500 batting average, a high batting average at the end of April, or the most innings before a pitcher's earned run average exceeds 1.00.

fast surface Artificial turf on which a bouncing ball appears to pick up speed.

fat Said of a high earned run average. "Allen Anderson won 17 games last year but had a fat 3.80 ERA" (*Tampa Tribune-Times*, Nov. 26, 1989).

fat bat Syn. of *bottle bat*, 1.

fat cat syndrome The pattern of a team that falls apart the season after winning a championship. It implies a certain level of collective self-satisfaction seasoned with a dash of winter dissipation.

father Chadwick *hist.* A player who is past his prime and has outlived his usefulness, in reference to the venerable sportswriter Henry Chadwick. "Of one thing the Evansville fans may be assured should [Angus] Grant take the team next season, there will be no signing of very-past-masters of the game. The 'father Chadwicks' will have to munch hay if their living depends on jobs with Grant" (*Grand Rapids* [Mich.] *Herald*, Sept. 4, 1904; Peter Morris). ETYMOLOGY. Chadwick became something of a scold in his later years. The term appeared in the headline for a story (*Galveston Daily News*, June 6, 1897) in which he berated the use of "trash slang" among certain writers (e.g., "swiped a bag" for stole a base).

Father of Baseball 1. Honorific assigned to writer Henry Chadwick (1824–1908), the nation's first modern sportswriter and baseball's first publicist. "A cloud was cast upon the opening of the season by the death on April 20 of Henry Chadwick, 'the Father of Baseball'. 'Father Chadwick' . . . had been a baseball enthusiast for more than half a century" (*Collier's*, May 2, 1908). Chadwick, who was born in England, advanced the theory that baseball had evolved from the British game of rounders. He expanded the box score, developed a scoring system, insisted on uniform standards, prepared numerous guides on how to play the game, and served on early rules committees. Chadwick introduced quantitative reporting and measurements to chronicle and popularize baseball.
2. Honorific sometimes applied to baseball missionary Alexander Joy Cartwright (1820–1892), a bank teller and bookseller, who helped organize the Knickerbocker Base Ball Club of New York in 1845, transforming a children's game into an adult sport by formalizing a game already growing in popularity. Cartwright has been incorrectly credited with several of the sport's innovations. See *Cartwright myth*. 3. Honorific sometimes assigned to Dr. Daniel Lucius "Doc" Adams (1814–1899), a physician and member of the Knickerbocker Base Ball Club of New York, who in 1857 set the bases at 90 feet apart and established nine players as a team, fixed the pitching distance at 45 feet, and advocated tirelessly for the fly game (seeking to eliminate the rule that outs be registered with catches on the first bounce). Adams added the position of shortstop to relay throws from the outfield and later to become a part of the infield. "Dr. D.L. Adams; Memoirs of the Father of Base Ball; He Resides in New Haven and Retains an Interest in the Game" (*The Sporting News*, Feb. 29, 1896 headline). "For his role in making baseball the success it is, Doc Adams may be counted as first among the Fathers of Baseball" (John Thorn, *Total Baseball*, 8th ed., 2004). See also John Thorn, *Elysian Fields Quarterly*, Winter 1992. 4. Sobriquet sometimes applied to several baseball pioneers, including: William Rufus Wheaton (1814–1888), a lawyer and member of the Knickerbocker Base Ball Club

Father of Baseball. Henry Chadwick. *National Baseball Library and Archives, Cooperstown, N.Y.*

of New York, who helped codify the rules of the New York game; Louis Fenn Wadsworth (1825–1908), an attorney and member of the Knickerbocker Base Ball Club of New York, who (according to Duncan F. Curry in 1877 and, despite later doubts, affirmed by John Thorn's research) presented a diagram of the ball field laid out substantially as it is today and introduced nine innings as a game; Duncan F. Curry (1812–1894), first president of the Knickerbocker Base Ball Club of New York, on whose tombstone is written "Father of Baseball"; Albert Goodwill Spalding (1850–1915), a tireless player, magnate, and tour promoter; William A. Hulbert (1832–1882), founder of the National League; and W. Harry Wright (1835–1895), who brought baseball its legitimacy and popularity by assembling and managing the first openly professional game and establishing innovative strategies and standards for "smart baseball" (see Christopher Devine, *Harry Wright: Father of Professional Base Ball*, 2003).

fat one A home run pitch; a pitch that is delivered down the middle of the strike zone and easy to hit. "Mariners Go Far, 5–1, On [Ken] Dixon's Fat Ones" (*The Washington Post* headline, June 5, 1986).

fat part of the bat The *barrel* end of the bat. 1ST USE. 1918. "Ping Bodie . . . caught the ball with the fat part of his bat, lining it to right field" (Burt Whitman, *Boston Herald and Journal*, Apr. 21; Peter Morris).

fat pitch A pitch that is slow and easy to hit; a pitch that is so hittable, it appears larger to the batter. "A fat, 3-and-0 pitch can be a terrible mistake even . . . against a struggling 1-for-13 hitter" (*Tampa Tribune*, March 12, 1989).

fatted calf *hist.* A player who is not in good physical condition. IST USE. 1937. "A player out of condition" (Bill McCullough, *Brooklyn Eagle*, Sept. 5).

fatten the average To increase the percentage of safe hits, thereby increasing a player's or a team's batting average. IST USE. 1897 (*New York Tribune*, June 2; Edward J. Nichols).

favorite toy A method for estimating the probability that a player will achieve a particular milestone, such as 500 home runs or 3,000 hits. It is based on a player's *established performance level* for the relevant index, along with an age-based estimate of how many years the player has left in his career. The method was created by Bill James and first appeared in his self-published *Baseball Abstract* (1981); a description appears in James' first conventionally published *Baseball Abstract* (1982). Syn. *career assessment.*

FC Scorecard abbrev. for *fielder's choice*, 2.

FDR pitch Lew Burdette's term for a wild pitch: it stands for *fire, duck,* and *run* (Joe Garagiola, *Baseball Is a Funny Game*, 1960, p.144).

feathering Flipping a sidearm throw. The term was used by infielder Cal Ripken Jr. when he had to lead the first baseman to the bag, "which required a little touch on the throw" (*The Baltimore Sun*, Jan. 22, 2006).

feathers The figurative surface of a scuffed ball. Ty Cobb (*Memoirs of Twenty Years in Baseball*, 1925): "Ray Chapman was killed by a ball that took a quick jump. Carl Mays had not intended using a trick ball but the ball had got 'feathers,' that is roughed up by contact with the hard dirt."

Federal Express A home run.

Federal League 1. An outlaw professional baseball league formed in 1913 with teams in six cities (Chicago, Cleveland, Indianapolis,

Federal League. Brooklyn Tip-Tops manager Lee Magee, in 1915. *George Grantham Bain Collection, Library of Congress*

Pittsburgh, St. Louis, and Covington, Ky., whose team later transferred to Kansas City, Mo.) using highly touted semiprofessionals from local leagues, marginal minor leaguers, and former major-league players. **2.** An outlaw major league that fielded eight teams in 1914 and 1915 (Indianapolis Hoosiers [1914 only], Newark Peppers [1915 only], Chicago Whales, Baltimore Terrapins, Buffalo Blues, Brooklyn Tip-Tops, Kansas City Packers, Pittsburgh Rebels, and St. Louis Terriers) using many players that jumped from the American League and the National League. The league challenged the antitrust nature of organized baseball's reserve clause, but presiding judge Kenesaw Mountain Landis' reluctance to hand down an immediate decision clouded the league's future. The league foundered due to generous player contracts, legal fees for injunctions and court rulings over player contracts, and capital investments in new ballparks. The Federal League was the last serious attempt to establish a third league of professional baseball at a major-league level. See Marc Okkonen, *The Federal League of 1914–1915* (1989). Abbrev. *FL.* Syn. *Feds*; "Federals."

Feds Short for *Federal League*, 2.

feeder **1.** A simplified, informal version of rounders played on a diamond-shaped field in English metropolises and in New England in the early 1800s (William Clarke, *The Boy's Own Book*, 2nd ed., 1828). As described by J.L. Williams (*The Every Boy's Book*; *a Compendium of All the Sports and Recreations of Youth*, 1841), the game was characterized by having only one player (the feeder) positioned in the field at any given moment; he stayed on the field until he retired a batter by catching a ball on the fly, or by causing the batter to miss striking the ball three times, or by striking him by a thrown ball while running between bases, at which point the feeder joined the batting party and the player who had been put out became the new feeder. The batter, upon striking the ball, ran in a clockwise direction (David Block, *Baseball Before We Knew It*, 2005, pp.77, 139). **2.** The pitcher in the game of feeder. Syn.: *pecker*. **3.** A player or coach who stands behind the mound during batting practice and supplies the pitcher with balls.

feel the apple To choke under the pressure of expectations. The term is a reference to one's Adam's apple. See also *apple comes up*. Var. "feel the apple in his throat." Syn. *take the apple*.

feet-first slide A slide in which the runner bends one of his legs and tucks it under the other, the lead leg remaining straight and aimed at the base; e.g., a hook slide. It was introduced in the 1880s when runners aimed to spike an African-American covering second base: "To give the frequent spiking of the darkey an appearance of accident the 'feet first' slide was practiced" (Ed Williamson, quoted in *The Sporting Life*, Oct. 24, 1891; Peter Morris). IST USE. 1890. "The Toledo men are dirty ball players. They slide feet first. It is contemptible work, and should be called down" (*Columbus* [Ohio] *Post*, Apr. 19; Peter Morris).

fence **1.** Any boundary surrounding the field of play. "When you go into the fence, you use the fence to come back throwing. Don't let the fence use you" (Willie Mays, quoted in *The New York Times*, March 3, 1986). When he owned the Cleveland Indians, Bill Veeck

(quoted in *The New York Times*, Oct. 4, 1982) employed a "remarkably mobile" fence, moving it "closer or further away from the plate depending . . . on the hitting habits of the visiting team," noting that "the fence always seemed easier to relocate in moonlight." **2.** That portion of the field's boundary over which home runs are hit. IST USE. 1861. "He sent a whizzer away 'over the fence'" (*New York Mercury*, Oct. 16; David Shulman).

fence ball An informal game with two, three, or four players. Howard Garson (personal communication, Jan. 22, 2002) describes the game: "The batter would stand at second base and hit the ball at the backstop. Anything caught was an out, and foul balls, singles, doubles, etc. depended on where it hit the fence. Over the fence was an out."

fence buster **1.** A long-ball hitter; esp., a slugger who hits home runs. "[Shoeless Joe] Jackson and [Happy] Felsch, famous in their day as fence busters" (*The New York Times*, Oct. 7, 1919). IST USE. 1907 (*New York Evening Journal*, Apr. 8; Edward J. Nichols). Syn. "fence breaker." **2.** A home run.

fence-shy Said of a cautious outfielder or corner infielder who has the tendency to give up on a fly ball or foul ball at the wall for fear of a collision (Alan Schwarz, BaseballAmerica .com, Nov. 14, 2006).

Fenway Park Home field of the Boston Red Sox since 1912 and renovated in 1934. Located in Boston, Mass., it is one of the last of the old-time ballparks and is much admired for its cozy atmosphere and odd dimensions, which were dictated by the path of railroad tracks rather than the ingenuity of architects. It is the smallest ballpark in the major leagues and is dominated by a gigantic left-field wall known as the *Green Monster*. The park was named by former owner John I. Taylor for the fact that it was in the Fenway section of Boston. "I love this park. I think Fenway is the essence of baseball" (Tom Seaver, quoted in *The Boston Globe*, July 1, 1986). ETYMOLOGY. A fen is an area of low marshland, which described the Back Bay section of Boston until it was filled in during the late 1800s. However, part of the area was maintained in its original state as a park and the road between downtown Boston and the Back

Fenway Park. The ballpark as it looked in 1914, two years after it opened. *George Grantham Bain Collection, Library of Congress*

Bay fen was named "The Fenway." The name attached itself to the neighborhood surrounding the site of the ballpark.

fernalia Syn. of *catcher's equipment*. ETYMOLOGY. "Obviously, a corruption of the word 'paraphernalia.' Some catcher couldn't pronounce it and gave up" (Frank Gibbons, *Baseball Digest*, May 1959).

Fernandomania Wild enthusiasm for Mexican screwball pitcher Fernando Valenzuela, who had a sensational rookie season for the Los Angeles Dodgers in 1981, leading the National League in strikeouts (180), innings pitched (192.1), shutouts (8), and complete games (11), winning both the Rookie of the Year and Cy Young awards. The left-hander's success swept the large Mexican-American community in Los Angeles and sent Dodgers ticket sales soaring.

fetcher *hist.* An early baseball term for "fielder."

fiddle *hist.* To steal a base (*Baseball Magazine*, Oct. 1916, p.26; Bill Mullins).

fiddle hitcher A pitcher who uses delaying tactics. Dizzy Dean explained (1943): "Usually a pitcher who's been up there a long time and has lost his stuff, so he takes to fiddle hitchin' to get them batters out. He's a guy what fiddles around—hitchin' his trousers, fixin' his cap, kicken' around in the dirt—so's the opposin' batter will get riled up and blew up."

field 1. *n.* The playing area; the baseball field itself. IST USE. 1845. "A ball knocked out of the field . . . is foul" (Knickerbocker Rules, Rule 10th, Sept. 23). **2.** *n.* A ballpark; e.g., Ebbets Field and Wrigley Field. **3.** *n.* The outfield of a baseball park. **4.** *n.* The active players on a baseball team. **5.** *n.* The defensive team; the players who are in the field. **6.** *v.* To stop, catch, or throw a baseball in play. IST USE. 1855. "The general play of the Gothams was loose, with the exception of Cudlip and Sheridan, who fielded excellently, as usual" (*Spirit of the Times*, Sept. 22; Peter Morris). **7.** *v.* To play as a fielder; to have players on the field; to deploy defensively, as in "to field" an infield. **8.** *n./hist.* An outfielder. "Darby, field" (box score, *New York Atlas*, Sept. 12, 1858).

field base A precursor of baseball in the 1830s and 1840s (Peter Morris, *Baseball Fever*, 2003, pp.6–7).

field box A seat in an area of the ballpark that rims the outfield at field level.

field day A form of exhibition, very popular in the early 20th century, featuring competition among baseball players in baseball-related skills and usually followed by a game. Cincinnati Reds president Garry Herrmann (quoted in *The Sporting Life*, May 9, 1908; Peter Morris): "Field days should be held annually by all means. The public wants to see which of the players excel in certain parts of the game and the players are anxious to participate in the contests."

fielder A player in any defensive position (although the term is seldom applied to the pitcher or catcher). See also *infielder*; *outfielder*. IST USE. 1859. "At each of the bases is stationed one man to watch the runner, and the fielders [the outfielders and the short fielder], who are outside throw the ball to him in order that he may touch the runner with it before he reaches the base" (*New York Herald*, Oct. 16; Peter Morris).

fielder's choice 1. The act of a defensive player who fields a batted ball and attempts to put out a baserunner (who was not forced to advance) rather than retire the batter-runner; i.e., the fielder has chosen to allow the batter-runner to take first base so that a preceding runner can be put out. Whether there has been a fielder's choice is determined by the official scorer. When one is ruled, the batter is charged with a turn at bat, but he is not credited with a base hit, even though he reached base. A fielder's choice can also apply to an infield play in which no one was retired, but a hit was not awarded. Compare *force play*. Syn. *fielder's option*. IST USE. 1889. "Murphy in the second and Farmer in the third got first on what, in genteel baseball parlance is known as a 'fielder's choice.' In plain, every day lingo, three men went after the ball and none of them got it where any one of them should have caught it" (*Milwaukee Sentinel*, May 20; Peter Morris). USAGE NOTE. The term "fielder's choice" has sometimes been used incorrectly for a "force play." 2. A term used by the official scorer to account for a) a batter who reaches base safely when the defense attempts to put out a runner farther along the basepath, b) a baserunner who advances a base while the attempt is made to put out another runner, and c) a baserunner who makes an undefended steal of a base. Abbrev. *FC*.

fielder's glove See *glove*, 1.

fielder's option Syn. of *fielder's choice*, 1. IST USE. 1912 (*New York Tribune*, Sept. 29; Edward J. Nichols).

field general A team's manager as opposed to the general manager. IST USE. 1910. "Fielder Jones, manager of the Chicago White Stockings, and one of the best field generals in the world" (John J. Evers and Hugh S. Fullerton, *Touching Second: The Science of Baseball*; Peter Morris).

field goal Kicking the ball, similar to a football player kicking a field goal. During the fifth inning of the third game of the 1951 World Series, New York Giants second baseman Eddie Stanky kicked the ball out of the hands of New York Yankees shortstop Phil Rizzuto while sliding into second base on an attempted steal. The ball went into center field as Stanky reached third base. "Stanky's Famous Field Goal in Classic" (*The Sporting News*, Jan. 2, 1952).

field hand A baseball player.

fielding 1. The defensive act of catching, stopping, controlling, and throwing batted and thrown balls. Syn. *field work*. 2. A team's collective ability to play defense. IST USE. 1845. "The fielding of the Brooklyn players was, for the most part, beautiful" (*New York Morning News*, Oct. 22; Frederick Ivor-Campbell).

fielding average 1. *hist.* An early fielding statistic, calculated by dividing putouts plus assists by games played, devised by Philadelphia baseball writer Al Wright in 1875 (John Thorn and Pete Palmer, *The Hidden Game of Baseball*, 1985). It is identical to *range factor*. "The men having the best and poorest fielding average in the various positions were as follows" (*Chicago Tribune*, July 11, 1880; Peter Morris). 2. Syn. of *fielding percentage*. Abbrev. *FA*.

fielding championship The best fielding percentage for a player at a given position. To qualify, a player must have appeared in a minimum of two-thirds of his team's games (for an infielder or an outfielder) or one-half of his team's games (for a catcher). A pitcher must have pitched at least as many innings as the number of games scheduled, but if another pitcher has a fielding percentage as high or higher and has handled more total chances in fewer innings, he shall be the fielding champion.

fielding glove See *glove*, 1.

fielding percentage A statistic that is used to evaluate a fielder's sure-handedness, computed by dividing a player's total number of putouts and assists by the sum of his chances (putouts, assists, and errors). A player with 670 putouts and assists in 687 chances has a fielding percentage of .975. Sabermetricians consider fielding percentage a poor overall index of fielding performance because it ignores the fielder's range. Syn. *fielding average*, 2. Abbrev. *FP*.

fielding practice Pregame warmup, or a special defensive session, which usually involves a coach hitting balls with a fungo bat. IST USE. 1890. "The fielding practice consists of the throwing and batting of grounders" (*Yenowine's News* [Milwaukee], June 1).

fielding range Syn. of *range factor*.

fielding runs The *linear weights* measure of runs saved by a player's defensive performance. It is defined relative to the player's league, so that the league average in a given year is zero. The specific formula for calculating fielding runs is dependent on the particular demands of the player's position. See *The Baseball Encyclopedia* (2004, pp.1693–94) for the exact formulas. Glenn Hubbard is the single-season leader with 61.8 in 1985; Napoleon Lajoie is the career leader with 367. Fielding runs was devised by Pete Palmer and originally described by John Thorn and Pete Palmer in *The Hidden Game of Baseball* (1985). Abbrev. *FR*.

fielding runs above average The number of runs a fielder has saved his team relative to that of the average player at the same position in the same year. Abbrev. *FRAA*.

fielding runs above replacement The number of runs a fielder has saved his team relative to that of a replacement-level player at the same position in the same year. Abbrev. *FRAR*.

fielding wins The linear weights measure of the number of wins for which a player's fielding is directly responsible. It is computed by dividing the player's fielding runs by runs per win. It is defined so that the league average in a given year is zero. Glenn Hubbard is the single-season leader with 6.5 in 1985; Bill Mazeroski and Napoleon Lajoie are the career leaders with 37.7. Fielding wins was devised by Pete Palmer and originally described by John Thorn and Pete Palmer in *The Hidden Game of Baseball* (1985). Abbrev. *FW*.

field manager The individual who oversees the actual playing activities of a baseball team.

field of dreams Baseball as a metaphor of hopes and mythology. The term came into general use after the movie *Field of Dreams*, based on W.P. Kinsella's novel *Shoeless Joe* (1982), was released in 1989. "The term 'Field of Dreams' has almost become generic now. It turns up on the sports page every day, and that's fun to see" (W.P. Kinsella, quoted in Mike Shannon, *BASEBALL—The Writers' Game*, 1992, p.187). EXTENDED USE. 1. An out-of-the-ordinary accomplishment. "Soccer enthusiasts can build their field of dreams, a Howard County [Md.] board decided last night, approving plans for the largest privately owned soccer complex in Maryland" (Jamie Smith Hopkins, *The Baltimore Sun*, Jan. 9, 2002). 2. An athletic endeavor that includes several world-class athletes, such as a marathon with champions from various races.

field umpire An umpire stationed anywhere but behind home plate. The field umpire may take any position on the playing field that he thinks is best suited to make impending decisions on the bases. See also *base umpire*.

field work *hist.* Syn. of *fielding*. "The hard hitting must be taken into account in judging of the field work done by each team, for many of the errors made were excusable ones" (*The Daily Inter Ocean* [Chicago], Aug. 24, 1881).

fiend *hist.* 1. An enthusiastic ballplayer. Dr. Daniel Adams, longtime member of the Knickerbockers of New York, reminisced (*The Sporting News*, Feb. 29, 1896; Dean A. Sullivan), "James W. Davis, a broker, and secretary of our club . . . ought to go down to history as the first base ball fiend. Indeed, we used to call him a fiend in the old days because of his enthusiasm. He was an outfielder." **2.** A diehard baseball fan. The *San Francisco Bulletin* reported (May 16, 1913; Gerald L. Cohen), "One of the largest crowds of San Francisco people to cross the bay to a Thursday afternoon game went over . . . to see the Seals repeat their performance of the day before. Two boats going each way were crowded to the gunwales with the baseball fiends, there being little room left for anyone else." IST USE. 1858. "The Knickerbocker's 'fiend,' you know, he always goes it strong; / On America's game of base ball he will shout his loud acclaim" (from the song " 'Ball Days' in the Year A.D. 1858," sung at the Knickerbockers supper given for the Excelsiors, Aug. 20, 1858, quoted in Henry Chadwick, *The Game of Base Ball*, 1868, p.180).

15-day disabled list A *disabled list* established in 1990 in which the player remains on the roster, but the team is permitted to add a substitute player during the time the disabled player is out of action. A player on the 15-day disabled list may be shifted to the *60-day disabled list* at any time. There are no limits on the number of players who can be placed on the list.

fifth **1.** *n.* The fifth inning. **2.** *adv.* Said of the fifth position in the batting order; e.g., "Smith is batting fifth."

fifth infielder **1.** A role that belongs to but is not always assumed by the pitcher. The term is used by coaches and managers to emphasize the importance of a pitcher being ready to field a ball after it has been delivered. "Most balls hit through the box go for base hits, which is why the pitcher should be the fifth infielder" (New York Yankees pitcher Vic Raschi, quoted in *San Francisco News*, July 6, 1949; Peter Tamony). **2.** An outfielder who plays in the infield. This move occurs in a bunt situation, or when the bases are loaded and there are less than two outs in the bottom of the ninth inning or an extra inning when a well-hit ball to the outfield will end the game. See also *five-man infield.*

50-50 club A mythical group of players who have achieved 50 accomplishments in two statistical categories in a single season, such as 50 extra-base hits and 50 stolen bases (accomplished by Lou Brock and several other players) or 50 home runs and 50 stolen bases (not yet accomplished by any player). Compare *20-20 club; 30-30 club; 40-40 club.*

fifty-five A player whom a scout believes will be a major-league player. Michael Lewis (*Moneyball*, 2003, p.32): "The scouts put numbers on players. . . . A player who receives a '55' is a player they think will one day be a regular big league player."

55-footer A bad pitch that bounces in the dirt before reaching home plate. The term is facetious because the actual distance from the pitcher's rubber to the plate is 60 feet, 6 inches. Var. "55-foot breaking ball"; "55-foot fastball." USAGE NOTE. There are variations of the term depending on the distance. "Sometimes you try to make the perfect pitch and you throw a 58-footer" (Los Angeles Dodgers pitcher Derek Lowe, on throwing a wild pitch, quoted in *The Washington Post*, May 8, 2005).

fifty percent color line An informal restriction that some journalists believed existed in the early 1950s against clubs fielding a lineup with a majority of African-Americans. Roger Kahn (*The Boys of Summer*, 1972): "There existed in 1953 what John Lardner called the 50 percent color line; that is, it was permissible for a major league team to play only four black men out of nine. The ratio, five whites to four blacks, substantiated white supremacy. But to have five blacks playing with four whites supposedly threatened the old order."

figger filbert Var. of *figure filbert*. The obituary of statistician Al Munro Elias (*Brooklyn Daily Eagle*, Aug. 2, 1939; Peter Morris) reported that Elias was "commonly referred to as a 'figger filbert,' but that term carried a connotation which Al did not relish." Fred Lieb (*The Sporting News*, Jan. 5, 1939) credited Damon Runyon with giving this nickname to Elias.

fight off **1.** To be a persistent batter who fouls off pitches until getting the pitch wanted or drawing a walk. "Luke Appling was one of the greatest hitters to fight off the pitch to get what he wanted to hit, which was generally the curveball" (Thornton Lee, quoted in

Edwin Howsam, *Baseball Graffiti*, 1995, p.91). Typically, a batter with a two-strike count will foul off a pitch that would be difficult to hit but that would be a called third strike if he did not attempt to hit it. **2.** To hit an inside pitch, such as one near the batter's fists. "The fastball is right there, jamming [Kirk] Gibson at the belt, but he fights it off for a foul" (Keith Hernandez, *Pure Baseball*, 1994, p.186).

fight the ball For a fielder to reach out for the ball before it reaches him, therefore fumbling it; to become overly anxious in fielding a ball. "[Buck Weaver's] tendency to make every play as fast as possible has kept him 'fighting the ball' thereby making for himself a lot of hard chances which he could handle easier" (Irving Sanborn, *Chicago Tribune*, Apr. 1914). A catcher who "fights the ball" is trying to catch it before it reaches his hands. IST USE. 1894. "[Mike Grady's] habit of 'fighting' the ball, that is trying to get the ball before it reaches him, has been in part overcome, but it shows up as plain as ever when a man attempts to steal a base. His over-anxiety to make the play causes him to throw wild" (*The Sporting News*, June 16; Peter Morris).

figure eight 1. The cover design of a baseball in which two pieces of leather, each shaped in the form of an "8," are stitched together. A complete cover is obtained by bending one piece one way and the other piece in the opposite direction. There are several claims (as early as 1858) as to who invented the figure-eight design, which is still used today. **2.** [softball term] A delivery in fast pitch softball in which the arm is swung in a figure eight, combining some of each of the *slingshot* and *windmill* deliveries. The ball is moved back quickly, but not shot forward as in the slingshot; rather, it follows a figure-eight pattern as it heads toward the batter. It is more difficult to master than the other two deliveries.

figure filbert One who loves numbers; a statistics nut. A filbert is a type of nut. Syn. *figger filbert*.

figure-4 slide Syn. of *bent-leg slide*.

filbert A baseball fan. "[Charles Dryden says] Pierce is president of the 'Nut' family. His first name is Filbert" (*The Sporting Life*, Aug. 30, 1913; Peter Morris).

fill in To substitute for a regular player on a short-term basis.

fill the bases To put runners at first base, second base, and third base. IST USE. 1884 (*De Witt's Base-Ball Guide*, p.47; Edward J. Nichols).

filthy 1. Said of a pitch that features a combination of speed, movement, and location that makes it unhittable; e.g., Mariano Rivera's cut fastball, thrown so hard that its movement is explosive, very late and very sharp. "[Carlos] Zambrano['s] . . . arsenal features a filthy sinking fastball" (*Sports Illustrated*, Apr. 4, 2005). According to TV announcer Joe Morgan (Oct. 11, 1998), a "filthy" pitch is more "effective" than a "nasty" pitch. See also *nasty*, 1; *electric*. **2.** Said of a pitcher with filthy stuff. Craig Biggio (discussing Roy Oswalt, quoted in *Sports Illustrated*, Feb. 27, 2006): "He started doing his homework, studying reports and tendencies. Since then, he's been filthy." See also *nasty*, 2.

final count 1. The last run scored in a baseball game. "McArdle banged out a clean safety that sent Hughes over the line with the final count" (*San Francisco Bulletin*, Apr. 3, 1913; Gerald L. Cohen). **2.** The final score of a baseball game.

find *n.* A newly discovered player who shows excellent promise. "Most ballplayers who are considered big 'finds' in March are frequently considered small 'losses' in May or June, and sometimes before that" (*San Francisco Bulletin*, March 26, 1913; Gerald L. Cohen). IST USE. 1907 (*New York Evening Journal*, Apr. 20; Edward J. Nichols).

find a pitcher To begin to hit effectively against a pitcher after "finding" his secret or weakness. "[The Seals] couldn't 'find' Mr. Tozer's offerings to any alarming extent" (*San Francisco Bulletin*, Apr. 24, 1913; Gerald L. Cohen). IST USE. 1888 (*Chicago Inter-Ocean*, July 7; Edward J. Nichols).

find the handle 1. For a fielder to control or keep a firm grip on a batted or thrown ball. See also *handle*, 3. **2.** A command shouted to a fielder who has just dropped or juggled the ball, or made a glaring error.

find the plate For a pitcher to throw strikes consistently. "Monte Kennedy . . . could throw hard, but always had trouble finding the plate" (Bobby Thomson, *"The Giants Win the Pennant! The Giants Win the Pennant!,"* 1991, p.67).

fine 1. *n.* A monetary penalty imposed on an individual for behavior deemed detrimental to the club, the league, or baseball in general. Fines can be imposed by the manager, the club owner, and the commissioner. In the early days of baseball, fines were handed out by umpires; e.g., "All fines incurred for violation of Sections 9, 10 and 11 must be paid to the umpire, before leaving the field" (Constitution and By-Laws, Excelsior Base Ball Club, Brooklyn, 1860; Peter Morris). **2.** *adv.* Precise or exacting. "I stopped trying to be so fine with every pitch and just threw the ball" (Baltimore Orioles pitcher Eric Bell, quoted in *The Washington Post*, July 24, 1987).

finesse pitcher A pitcher who relies on placement, deception, touch, change of speed, intellect, and guile rather than velocity and power. "[Jamie] Moyer is a finesse pitcher, mixing and matching his average fastball with his off-speed stuff. When he is going well, it's because he's spotting his pitches well, not because he's blowing away hitters" (*The Baltimore Sun*, June 27, 1995). Compare *power pitcher*. Syn. "finesser"; *dabber*.

fingering The "mysterious science" used by pitchers to obtain the proper grip on the ball, depending on the desired pitch. It is accomplished by employing a combination of finger position and pressure on the ball. An important element of fingering is how the pitcher's fingers are positioned in regard to the seams of the ball.

fingernail ball 1. An illegal pitch in which the ball is cut by the fingernail. According to *The Sporting News* (1952): "Dave [Danforth] dampened the seams of the ball and then, when wet, cut them with a sharp finger nail. When the seams dried, Dave made the ball bob like a cork on a lake in a storm." 1ST USE. 1916. "[During the 1915 season] hardly a game passed by in any league without some manager making accusations against the opposing pitcher . . . [e.g., there was] the 'fingernail ball'" (Billy Evans, *Atlanta Constitu-*

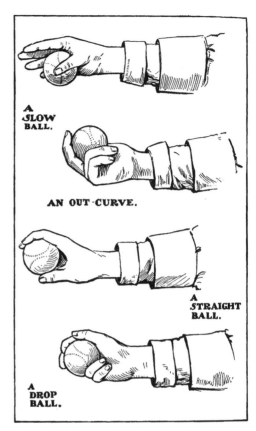

Fingering. Pitches, ca. 1900. *Ron Menchine Collection*

tion, Jan. 16; Peter Morris). **2.** Syn. of *fingertip ball*.

finger system The system of communication by which the catcher signals a suggested pitch to the pitcher by flashing the fingers on his bare hand. From the crouched position, the catcher gives the finger signals between his legs to keep the batter from seeing them. Some catchers put white adhesive tape on their fingers so they can be better seen from the mound. Traditionally, one finger is given for a fastball, two fingers for a curveball, and three fingers for an offspeed pitch. Compare *pump system*.

fingertip ball A *knuckleball* thrown by gripping the ball with one's fingertips. Syn. *fingernail ball*, 2. USAGE NOTE. Early in the history of the knuckleball, pitchers experimented with several different grips, yet when the fingertip grip became the grip of choice, the pitch was known as a "knuckleball." Pitcher Gene Bearden (*Baseball Register*,

1948): "My knuckler probably should be called a fingertip ball. I file my nails down and grasp the ball with my thumb and little finger, resting the tips of my three other fingers on the ball."

finisher Syn. of *closer*, 1. IST USE. 1910. "Strangely enough, [Doc] Crandall, while a good finisher, is a fizzle as a starter" (*The Sporting News*, Aug. 18; Peter Morris).

finishing coach A coach capable of putting the "finishing" touch on pitchers who already have a good assortment of pitches. The term was used by Kansas City Royals general manager Allard Baird (*Kansas City Star*, March 31, 2002).

finish off 1. For a pitcher to take the final step in retiring a batter. "[Mike Mussina threw] first-pitch strikes and two-strike curveballs, as he tried finishing off hitters" (*The Baltimore Sun*, Apr. 8, 1996). 2. For a team to eliminate another team in the postseason.

Finnish baseball Syn. of *pesäpallo*.

fire 1. *v.* To throw the ball with power and force, such as a pitcher throwing a fastball or an infielder throwing to first base to retire a speedy hitter. 2. *n.* An exceptional fastball. "[Ryne Duren] simply overpowered hitters; he threw fire" (Edwin Howsam, *Baseball Graffiti*, 1995, p.105). 3. *n.* A rally or threat to score. Relief pitchers are brought in to "put out fires." "Bill Dawley and Frank DiPino . . . are as adept at dousing late-inning fires as any bullpen tandem in baseball" (George White, *Baseball Digest*, Dec. 1983, p.65).

fire and fall back To swing the bat with such force that one falls backward. The term is a play on the recoil that results from firing a powerful firearm.

fireball A fastball. IST USE. 1931 (*The World* [New York], Feb. 26; Edward J. Nichols).

fireballer A pitcher whose primary pitch is an overpowering fastball.

fire brigade That part of a pitching staff consisting of relief pitchers. "Orioles Owe Medals to Their Fire Brigade" (*The Washington Post* headline, June 22, 1989).

firecracker league Syn. of *Fourth of July league*. "The 'outlaw' league [Federal League], which is a firecracker proposition

which will probably explode on the Fourth of July if it is so fortunate as to survive that long" (Thomas Kirby, *The Washington Post*, May 11, 1913; Peter Morris).

fireman 1. A relief pitcher; one who comes in "to put out a fire" (a rally by the opposition). "Mace 'Fireman' Brown . . . failed to put out the conflagration and Chicago added three more runs" (*The Washington Post*, Aug. 13, 1948; Barry Popik). Syn. *hoser*. IST USE. 1939. "Johnny Murphy, grand old fireman of the Yankees, today had his first defeat of 1939" (*New York World-Telegram*, June 15; Barry Popik). USAGE NOTE. In a letter (June 12, 1960) to Jack McDonald of the *San Francisco News-Call Bulletin*, Peter Tamony pointed out that the term had been in use colloquially in the 1920s (based on his interviews with players of the period), that it was showing up in print by 1940, and by the end of the 1950s it was "the name . . . of a new era in baseball." ETYMOLOGY. Peter Morris notes that the term is "the logical culmination of the metaphorical references to relief pitchers as rescuers." The first player whose name was broadly associated with the term was New York Yankees relief pitcher Johnny Murphy, who was nicknamed "Fireman." Peter Tamony (letter to *San Francisco Chronicle*, Feb. 26, 1979) wrote, "As he doused rallies, Johnny Murphy . . . evoked the term 'fireman.'" In the late 1940s, New York Yankees relief pitcher Joe Page was nicknamed "Fireman" and, in fact, posed for publicity photographs in a fire chief's hat. 2. *hist.* A player who showers and dresses quickly after a game, in the manner of a fireman departing quickly to fight a fire. IST USE. 1937. "Fireman— player who showers and dresses quickly" (Jimmy Powers, *New York Daily News*, Jan. 10). USAGE NOTE. An interesting distinction was made when both meanings of the term coexisted in Herbert Simons' article on baseball language (*Baseball Magazine*, Jan. 1943): "A 'fireman' in baseball writers' parlance, usually is a relief pitcher who rushes in to quench the conflagration, but to the player, he's the teammate who showers and dresses the fastest after a game."

Fireman of the Year Award An annual award

presented by *The Sporting News* from 1960 to 2000 originally to the relief pitcher in each major league with the highest combined total of wins and saves. The winner is now chosen by a consensus of *The Sporting News* editors, and the award was renamed *Reliever of the Year Award* in 2001.

fireplug A short, stocky player.

firepower The offense of a baseball team. "With a dropoff in firepower, this Tribe won't be lighting up in the postseason" (*Sports Illustrated*, March 25, 2002).

fire sale Large-scale sale or trading of players to reduce payroll and increase revenue; e.g., "the Great San Diego Fire Sale" of 1993 when the Padres traded Gary Sheffield and Fred McGriff, signaling to the sports world that "the great corporate fad of the 1990s—downsizing—had finally come to major-league baseball" (Kevin Baker, *Harper's Magazine*, Apr. 1994). "The world champion [Florida] Marlins' fire sale [1997–1998] is nothing new to baseball" (Keith Olbermann, *Sports Illustrated*, May 25, 1998). Syn. *garage sale*. IST USE. 1896. " 'Firesale' Friedman is the way Mr. Robison of the Clevelands refers to the New York President [Andrew Freedman]. He is a sort of markdown, sacrifice magnate" (*St. Louis Post-Dispatch*, March 15; Peter Morris).

Firestone A zero on the scoreboard. During a telecast of a Minnesota Twins game on Aug. 25, 1989, broadcaster Jim Kaat declared, "Keep hanging up those Firestones." Kaat, a former player, explained the term was "an old one" that was often heard in dugouts. The allusion is to Firestone tires, which resemble zeros.

fireworks 1. An impressive offensive display, usually including a rapid succession of extra-base hits. "The Yankees hit three home runs off [Bruce] Chen to build a 6–0 lead . . . The fireworks came early. Chen certainly was lit up" (*The Baltimore Sun*, July 5, 2005). IST USE. 1893. "Tommy Hernon opened the fireworks for Oakland in the last half with a double to left" (*The Sporting News*, Oct. 21; Peter Morris). **2.** A spectacular defensive play. "[Knowles'] fielding of the position . . . was fine, three of the stops he made being of

the fireworks order" (*Atlanta Constitution*, Apr. 30, 1895; Peter Morris).

firing line Syn. of *rubber*, 1. The term jibes nicely with "battery." IST USE. 1901. "[Deacon] Phillippe's clever work on the firing line enabled Pittsburg to make it three straight over Boston" (*Decatur* [Ill.] *Review*, Sept. 4; Peter Morris).

first 1. *n.* Short for *first base*, 1. IST USE. 1864 (*Brooklyn Daily Eagle*, Sept. 20; Edward J. Nichols). **2.** *n.* Short for *first base*, 2. **3.** *n.* The first inning. **4.** *adv.* Said of the first position in the batting order; e.g., "Smith is batting first." **5.** *n.* That which is new to the game. Baseball is usually fascinated by "firsts." An exception was pointed out in a *Life* magazine editorial (Aug. 13, 1971) on the 1971 All-Star Game: "They [the announcers] didn't allude to an All-Star 'first'—for the first time both starting pitchers were black." Lee Allen ("Cooperstown Corner," *The Sporting News*, Apr. 6, 1968) cautioned that the word "first" is "a very dangerous word to employ in writing baseball history" owing to ongoing research that turns up earlier "firsts." Two examples of "firsts": the first woman to receive a World Series share was Edna Jameson, who worked for the Cleveland Indians in 1920; and the first major-league club to travel by airplane was the Boston Red Sox, which flew from St. Louis to Chicago on July 30, 1936. See also Lloyd Johnson, *Baseball's Book of Firsts* (2005), a guided tour of more than 150 of the game's defining moments on and off the field.

first and fifteenth player A player who thinks only of paydays, such as the first and fifteenth days of the month (Al Schacht, *Al Schacht Dope Book*, 1944).

first bagger Syn. of *first baseman*. IST USE. 1914. "Hal Chase, Comiskey's first bagger . . . had pulled the ten-day reverse notice on the White Sox" (William A. Phelon, *Baseball Magazine*, August; Peter Morris).

first ball 1. The *first pitch* thrown to a batter. **2.** See *ceremonial first pitch*.

first-ball hitter A hitter who routinely swings at the first pitch; e.g., Chicago White Sox shortstop Ozzie Guillen. "[Nomar Garciaparra is] a first-ball, fastball hitter. If you get ahead, he really expands his zone" (anonymous scout, quoted in *Sports Illustrated*, Oct. 13, 2003). IST USE. 1910. "A few years ago the Chicago club purchased a player late in the season ... yet [Frank] Chance released him without even bringing him to Chicago ... Someone asked Chance why the man was released. 'First ball hitter,' explained Chance loquaciously" (John J. Evers and Hugh S. Fullerton, *Touching Second: The Science of Baseball*; Peter Morris).

first-ball itch A compulsion to swing at the first pitch.

first base **1.** The base located to the right side of and 90 feet from home plate, which is one quarter of the way around the bases on the way to scoring a run; the base to be touched first by a baserunner. See also *initial*, 1. Abbrev. *1B*, 1. Syn. *first*, 1; *first corner*; *first position*; *first sack*; *first station*; *initial*, 2; *gateway*; *getaway bag*. IST USE. 1845. "The bases shall be ... from first to third base, forty-two paces, equidistant" (Knickerbocker Rules, Rule 4th, Sept. 23). **2.** The defensive position played by the first baseman. Abbrev. *1B*, 2. Syn. *first*, 2. EXTENDED USE. **1.** Initial success. A resident opposed to a high school site in Maryland, upon learning that the judge would hold a hearing, wrote, "It looks like we have at least gotten to first base" (*The Baltimore Sun*, Oct. 16, 2003). The term is often phrased in the negative; e.g., "I never got to first base." **2.** In teenage slang, at various times since the 1930s, first base has meant kissing.

first base coach A member of the managerial staff who stands in the coach's box adjacent to first base. His primary job is to instruct the baserunner at first base on whether it is safe to advance. He may also relay signals from the manager to the batter or to a runner on second base, as well as attempt to steal the opponent's signs. Don Buford (quoted in *The Baltimore Sun*, May 19, 1994): "He helps the runner get back safely on pickoff attempts. He reminds the runner where the outfielders are playing, where the infielders are playing, helps him get a better jump. He reminds players to extend their leads so they can be aggressive on the bases. I remind them how many outs there are." Syn. *barker*.

first base line The line extending from home plate to first base. See also *right field line*.

first baseman The defensive player stationed at first base. Abbrev. *1B*, 3. Syn. *first bagger*; *first sacker*; *doorkeeper*. IST USE. 1860. "The 'Detroit' club had two practiced pitchers, while the 'Risers' had to fill that post by their first base man, thus disarranging the whole field, their regular pitcher being unavoidably absent" (*Detroit Advertiser*, Oct. 1; Peter Morris).

first baseman's mitt A special, scooplike, thinly padded leather glove that enables the first baseman to more easily catch thrown balls. It may not be more than 12 inches long from top to bottom, nor more than 8 inches wide across the palm; it may be of any weight. See also *open-face mitt*; *snare mitt*.

first base slot The ideal position for the first base umpire to make a call, "at about a forty-five degree angle, and approximately two feet behind and to the right of the bag" (Lee Gutkind, *The Best Seat in Baseball, But You Have to Stand!*, 1975, p.13).

first base umpire The *base umpire* at first base.

first bound The first bounce of a batted ball, after which, if the ball was caught (in baseball's early years), the batter was declared out. See also *bound game*.

first corner Syn. of *first base*, 1. Ist Use. 1896. "The Pirates are weak at the first corner" (*The Washington Post*, Oct. 4).

first division *hist.* The top half of a league's standings at any given time (the first four teams in an eight-team league or the first five teams in a ten-team league) before 1969, when each of the two major leagues was broken into two divisions. Compare *second division*. IST USE. 1892 (*Chicago Herald*, Apr. 13; Edward J. Nichols).

first half **1.** That part of the baseball season before the All-Star break in mid-July. Compare *second half*, 1. **2.** That part of the inning when the visiting team gets its turn at bat. Compare *second half*, 2. Syn. *top*, 1; *top half*; *upper half*, 1.

first-letter system A system of communication by which the first letter of an object, which is touched, is the same as the first letter of the name of the play to be executed; e.g., a touch of the hat activates a hit-and-run play, of the belt calls for a bunt, and of the shirt indicates a steal attempt.

first lieutenant A player close to the manager.

first nine *hist.* The nine players who, when available, represented a baseball club in a match game. Compare *second nine*.

first on balls Reaching first base on a base on balls. "[Dan] Brouthers was sent to first on balls . . . and [Charlie] Bennett was given first on balls" (*The North American* [Philadelphia], Aug. 4, 1886).

first on error An official batting statistic collected by the National League for certain seasons in the 1910s that counted the number of times an error allowed a batter to reach first base. The total for the National League in 1912 was 1196. See also *reached on error.* Abbrev. *FOE.* (Ron Selter)

first-order measure A team's projected winning percentage based on its actual runs and actual runs allowed as measured by the Pythagenport method. If a team's actual winning percentage is considerably better, then the team has been particularly lucky and/or has a particularly well-performing bullpen. The measure was proposed by *Baseball Prospectus.* Compare *second-order measure*; *third-order measure.*

first pitch 1. See *ceremonial first pitch.* **2.** The *first ball* pitched to a batter in a game or starting an inning. EXTENDED USE. The first attempt at solving a problem or considering a change. When Douglas M. Godine was named general manager of Columbia, Md., in 2006, he said he did not have any specific ideas about how to transform the area, explaining, "I'm just throwing the first pitch out in the first inning" (*The Baltimore Sun*, Apr. 2, 2006).

first-pitch strike A first pitch to a batter that results in a called strike, swinging strike, foul ball, or ball put into play. "The strike-one count changes the complexion of an at bat tremendously. It's only one pitch, but the hitter is behind in the count, and you can do a lot more things with your second pitch. You

can expand the [strike] zone" (New York Yankees pitching coach Mel Stottlemyre, quoted in *Sports Illustrated*, June 4, 2001, pp.50–51). Abbrev. *FPS.*

first position Syn. of *first base*, 1.

first sack Syn. of *first base*, 1.

first sacker Syn. of *first baseman.* IST USE. 1905 (*The Sporting Life*, Oct. 2; Edward J. Nichols).

first station Syn. of *first base*, 1. IST USE. 1908 (*Baseball Magazine*, September; Edward J. Nichols).

first string The collection of players on a team who are best at their positions and who are chosen for regular play. Compare *second string.* IST USE. 1912 (*New York Tribune*, Apr. 15; Edward J. Nichols). ETYMOLOGY. See *second string.*

first stringer A player in the starting lineup. "Cady was a young pitcher . . . even though he had not been accepted as a first stringer" (Burt L. Standish, *The Man on First*, 1920; David Shulman). IST USE. 1920 (*New York Tribune*, Oct. 10; Edward J. Nichols).

first ups The team to come to the plate at the very beginning of the game. In organized baseball, the visiting team always has first ups. "We used to choose up sides by palming our hands on a bat and the guy whose fist last closed around it got 'first ups'" (Jim Murray, *The Best of Jim Murray*, 1965). See also *choose up*, 1. Compare *last ups*.

first-year player Any player who has never before signed a professional baseball contract.

first-year player draft A *draft* in which players completing their senior year of high school or junior year of college are selected by major-league teams in reverse order of their percentages of games won at the close of the previous championship season. It was adopted for U.S. residents in 1965 to end the bidding wars for bonus babies who were then having to be kept on major-league rosters, thereby stunting their professional development. There are 50 selection rounds, conducted each year in June. The signing deadline for draftees (other than college seniors) is Aug. 15. A player who is selected but returns to school without signing a contract is subject to selection in the next year's draft. If a club fails to sign its first- or second-round pick, it will receive a compensation pick in the next year's draft that is one spot behind the pick that was lost (e.g., if the fifth pick fails to sign, the club will receive a sixth pick in the next year's draft). A player eligible for selection, but who is not selected, may be signed by any major- or minor-league club. A selected player cannot be traded for at least one year after he has signed a contract; and a team cannot trade its exclusive right to negotiate with a player it has drafted but not signed. Players from Canada, Puerto Rico, the Virgin Islands, and other U.S. territories, and foreign players attending American schools, are now subject to the draft. A defector from Cuba is not subject to the draft if he establishes residency in a foreign country. The first player drafted in the first draft (1965) was Rick Monday, a 19-year-old Arizona State Univ. sophomore who was selected by the Kansas City A's and spent 19 years in the major leagues. Arthur Daley (*The New York Times*, June 11, 1965) commented on the new draft: "It's a new device, born of desperation, and is supposed to protect the owners from their own greed and selfishness. It eliminates the offering of wild and outlandish bonuses to outstanding prospects by dumping all future players into a pool." See also *Nieves rule*; *Incaviglia rule*. Syn. *amateur draft*; *free-agent draft*; *Rule 4 draft*.

fish 1. *v.* To swing at a pitch outside the strike zone. "He wasn't trying to throw me a strike, he was trying to make me fish" (Larry Owen, quoted in *Tampa Tribune*, July 12, 1987). IST USE. 1910. "[Mordecai] Brown pitched low curves outside the plate and low fast straight balls inside during the game, and the new man 'fished,' i.e., swung at balls he could not reach" (John J. Evers and Hugh S. Fullerton, *Touching Second: The Science of Baseball*, excerpted in *St. Louis Post-Dispatch*, May 3, 1910; Peter Morris). See also *go fishing*. 2. *n.* A batter who refuses the lure of swinging at pitches outside the strike zone; e.g., "This fish ain't biting."

Fish Nickname for the Florida *Marlins*. The club has also been called "Flying Fish," as well as "Little Fish," in deference to the Miami Dolphins ("Big Fish") of the National Football League.

fish cakes *hist.* Low pay, particularly that which is paid in the minor leagues. The term appears to have been popular in the 1930s.

fisherman A batter who chases ("casts for") pitches outside the strike zone (Bill McCullough, *Brooklyn Eagle*, Sept. 5, 1937).

fish hook A curveball (Jimmy Powers, *New York Daily News*, Jan. 10, 1937).

fishing trip A swing at a pitch outside the strike zone. "A player who goes on 'a fishing trip' hasn't been away on a vacation. He merely took a swing at a bad ball" (*Baseball Magazine*, January, 1943; David Shulman). IST USE. 1932. "Fishing Trip—Taking a swing at a bad ball" (*New York Sun*, June 23).

Fisk Pole The left field foul pole at Fenway Park, renamed in memory of Boston Red Sox catcher Carlton Fisk's game-winning home run off the pole in the 12th inning of Game 6 of the 1975 World Series against the Cincinnati Reds. Compare *Pesky's Pole*.

fist 1. To hit a pitch with the part of the bat just above the batter's hands. "You can throw him inside as much as you want, and he [Derek Jeter] can still fist the ball off" (Jesse Orosco, quoted in *Sports Illustrated*, June 21, 1999). 2. To jam the batter; to throw the ball in at his fists; e.g., "The pitcher fisted him with a slider inside."

fister A bloop hit over the infield resulting from hitting a pitch near the batter's hands. "I'd get a lot of leggers and fisters" (Boston Red Sox infielder Billy Klaus, quoted in *The New York Times*, March 29, 1956; Peter Morris).

fitness of the ground Field conditions as they are affected by the weather, groundskeeping, and other uses (such as a football game) of the playing surface.

5 The scorekeeper's designation for the third baseman.

five and fly A five-inning pitching performance in which the starting pitcher gets credit for the win after the bullpen pitches the final four innings. "Pitchers who make a living off five-inning victories are only slightly more respected than convicted felons" (Joel Bierig, *Chicago Sun-Times*, March 25, 1990; Grant Barrett). ETYMOLOGY. Quitting the military after the required five years of service.

five by five A variant of *Rotisseries League Baseball* that adds runs scored and strikeouts to the standard four offensive and four pitching categories respectively. Demonstrated to be slightly less likely to emulate the major-league standings than the original eight categories, it is believed by adherents to create more realistic salary structures on Rotisserie-type fantasy teams by reducing the effect of steals and saves. Also spelled "5×5." (F.X. Flinn)

five-cent curve Syn. of *nickel curve*.

five-dollar ride in a Yellow Cab A long home run (Jim Nash, *The Sporting News*, Apr. 1, 1972).

five eyes A training tip for batters that reminds them to keep the following on the pitcher: two eyes, front shoulder, front hip, and front ankle.

5.5 hole The area between the third baseman (5) and the shortstop (6). Syn. *five-point-five hole*. ETYMOLOGY. The term was popularized by Tony Gwynn, a left-handed batter who got many hits through the hole. Peter Morris speculates that the term may also reflect the influence of the common hockey term "5 hole," for the space between a goaltender's legs, which is based on diagrams of the five places a shooter can beat a goalie.

5–4–3 The scorekeeper's notation for a common double play in which the ball goes from the third baseman (5) to the second baseman (4) to the first baseman (3).

five hundred A playground game in which a batter self-tosses and hits fungoes to fielders arranged in a loosely crowded group. A ball caught in the air is worth 100 points, on one bounce worth 75 points, and on two bounces worth 50 points; grounders fielded on three or more bounces (or as the ball is still moving) are worth 25 points. The first fielder to accumulate 500 points becomes the next batter. Variations include a pitcher lobbing the ball to the batter, 10 "pity" points awarded for retrieving a ball that had stopped rolling, and points deducted for misplays. Also spelled "500."

.500 baseball The performance of a team that wins as often as it loses. Syn. ".500 ball."

500-500 club A mythical group of players who have 500 career home runs and 500 career stolen bases. Charter (and only) member: Barry Bonds.

500 home run club A mythical group of players who have 500 career home runs. Hitting 500 home runs has been a benchmark for automatic enshrinement in the National Baseball Hall of Fame. "Why do people want to change what 500 means? Five hundred is like 2,130 or 56. It's still magic" (New York Mets coach Don Baylor, quoted in *Sports Illustrated*, Apr. 14, 2003).

five-man infield An infield that includes an outfielder in a bunt situation or in a game-ending situation when the home team has the potential winning run at third base with less than two outs in the ninth or an extra inning. It was first unveiled by Brooklyn Dodgers president Branch Rickey during spring training of 1950 (*The Sporting News*, Feb. 1, 1950; Peter Morris). See also *fifth infielder, 2; six-man infield*.

five-man rotation A rotation of five starting pitchers in which each works every fifth game (with at least four days of rest). The late–1960s New York Mets expanded their rotation from four to five to accommodate a large group of talented young pitchers. The mass switch to five-man rotations began in the 1970s, when baseball turned to full-scale specialization in the bullpen and there was enough quality pitching, and was completed by 1990. See also *four-man rotation*.

five men rule The *reserve rule* when the National League introduced it in 1879, permitting each club to designate five players who could not be signed by any other league club. "[Ned Williamson] blames the five men reserve rule for the unevenness of things, and hopes to see the day when there will be no players reserved" (*St. Louis Globe-Democrat*, March 26, 1882).

five-o'clock hitter A hitter who shows tremendous power in batting practice but "turns meek once the game starts" (*Sports Illustrated*, May 11, 1998). See also: *10-o'clock hitter*; *12-o'clock hitter*; *one-o'clock hitter*; *two-o'clock hitter*; *six-o'clock hitter*; *seven-o'clock hitter*.

five-o'clock lightning *hist.* The scoring of runs late in the game. The term was used when baseball was played exclusively during the day, with most games beginning around three o'clock, and was applied most often to the New York Yankees teams from the 1920s to the 1950s. "They used to call it '5 o'clock lightning,' because we always seemed to strike late in the game to get as many runs as we needed" (New York Yankees shortstop Phil Rizzuto, quoted in *The Washington Post*, March 31, 1986). ETYMOLOGY. New York Yankees pitcher Waite Hoyt claimed to have coined the expression to describe the Yankees' late-inning victories in the late 1920s: "The eighth inning generally came at about a quarter to five . . . [and] we used to win a lot of games around that time of day" (quoted in Eugene Murdock, *Baseball Between the Wars*, 1992).

five-point-five hole Syn. of *5.5 hole*.

five-run home run The unreachable goal of a batter who tries to hit a home run when his team is losing by four or more runs (Zack Hample, *Watching Baseball Smarter*, 2007, p.208).

five-tooler Syn. of *five-tool player*.

five-tool player A gifted position player who excels at the five major baseball skills: hit for average, hit for power, run, field (catch), and throw. *Sports Illustrated* (Nov. 24, 2003) called Willie Mays "the prototypical five-tool player." See also *tools*, 1; *complete player*. Syn. *five-tooler*; *tools player*; *tool shed*, 1.

Fizz Kids Nickname for the 1964 Philadelphia Phillies, which led the National League by 6½ games with 12 games to play, then proceeded to lose 10 straight games to finish in a tie for second place. The term is a play on the nickname *Whiz Kids* for the 1950 Phillies.

fizzle 1. A stupid play (George Gipe, *The Great American Sports Book*, 1978, p.90). **2.** A player or team that starts fast and then fades.

FL Abbrev. for *Federal League*, 2.

flag 1. *n.* The *pennant*, 1. "Connie Mack broke up his great machine that had won four flags in five years after the unexpected loss to the Braves [in 1914]" (Lee Allen, *The Sporting News*, Sept. 21, 1968). IST USE. 1883 (*The Sporting Life*, Aug. 13; Edward J. Nichols). **2.** *v.* To signal a runner as he approaches a base. **3.** *v.* To catch or stop a batted ball; e.g., "Jones flagged Smith's line drive." The term probably was derived from the railroad term for stopping a train with a red flag. IST USE. 1920 (*The New York Times*, Oct. 10; Edward J. Nichols). **4.** *v.* To throw out a baserunner. IST USE. 1905. "The base runner will be enabled to take a fast start without the pitcher being able to flag him" (*The Washington Post*, March 16; Peter Morris).

flag chase Syn. of *pennant race*.

flag down To catch a pitched or batted baseball; e.g., "The catcher could not flag down Smith's knuckleball" or "The outfielder flagged down the long fly ball."

flagman Syn. of *third base coach*.

flail A baseball bat. "[Babe Ruth] handles a long, heavy bat that would break the back of the average player. It takes a man with Babe's great strength to get that flail up and around in time to meet the ball" (Burt Whitman, *Boston Herald and Journal*, May 15, 1918; Peter Morris).

flake An odd or eccentric player; a kidder or comic; a kook. Famous baseball flakes include Jackie Brandt (the "original" flake), Phil Linz, Denny McLain, Bill "Spaceman" Lee, Mark Fidrych, Al "The Mad Hungarian" Hrabosky, Ross Grimsley, and Jay Johnstone. Charles P. Pierce (*Sports Illustrated*, July 5, 2004) wrote, "[Baseball] is not kind to its gnostics, players so consumed by the study of their individual abilities that they've lost sight of the game's fundamental rituals, like marshaling their postgame clichés or listening to bad country music on the clubhouse sound system. Baseball's orthodox theologians call these people 'flakes,' and they are always on the lookout for them, lest the game find itself unduly plagued with unusual ideas or alternative rock." USAGE NOTE. The term carries a certain element of endearment and tends to be applied to likable, but not always reliable, characters. ETYMOLOGY. By the late 1950s, the term "flakey" began to replace the beatnik term "kook" for an oddball character. According to Joseph McBride (*High & Inside*, 1980), a San Francisco Giants teammate in 1957 gave offbeat outfielder Jackie Brandt the nickname "Flakey" because "things seem to flake off his mind and disappear." The adjective became a noun ("flake") by the early 1960s. Maury Allen (*Bo: Pitching and Wooing*, 1973) claimed that Brandt's St. Louis Cardinals teammate Wally Moon created the term in 1956: "Moon suggested that Brandt was so wild his brains were falling out of his head, flaking off his body, hence, a flake." The term, however, had earlier slang meanings. It has referred to a small packet of cocaine since the 1920s. In another earlier incarnation, Walter Winchell (*San Francisco Call-Bulletin*, Feb. 8, 1935; Peter Tamony) noted in an article on Harlem slang that it was one of several nicknames (along with "ofay," "pink," and "keltch") for a white person.

flaky Strange, eccentric, a bit off; said of a player who behaves oddly. *The New York Times* (Apr. 26, 1964) reported, "The term 'flake' needs explanation. It's an insider's word, used throughout baseball, usually as an adjective; someone is considered 'flaky.' It does not mean anything so crude as 'crazy,' but it's well beyond 'screwball' and far off to the side of 'eccentric.'" Texas Rangers relief pitcher Jim Kern, on the subject of "floating with life" (*San Francisco Examiner*, Nov. 30, 1979; Peter Tamony): "I found it's much easier to have a flaky front and do as you wish underneath, rather than present a straight intellectual front. Then when you do something flaky, they say, 'Oh, my gosh, look at this one.' Now they come to expect it and you do something weird and they say, 'Yeah, that's him.'" Also spelled "flakey." ETYMOLOGY. See *flake*. Eric Partridge (*Dictionary of the Underworld*, 1949) noted that "flaky" has been a term for cocaine addiction since the 1920s. EXTENDED USE. The term is used widely in other realms, such as when President Ronald Reagan said that Col. Mu'ammar al-Gadhafi of Libya was "flaky," thereby implying that the Libyan strongman was strange and possibly not sane. Ann Landers said in a 1962 column: "This man is as flaky as mother's apple-pie crust."

flameball A high-velocity fastball.

flamethrower A fastball pitcher; e.g., Nolan Ryan and Roger Clemens. "Flamethrowers are supposed to break down, lose their fast ball; they try to adapt, retire. Not Ryan" (Ron Givens, *Newsweek*, Aug. 28, 1989, p.65).

flame-throwing Possessing a superior fastball.

flannels A player's clothes worn on the field. A flannel is a soft wool or cotton fabric used to make jerseys and trousers. "Frequently profane and always loud . . . [Ted] Williams, who never wore a necktie, dominated his stage like a John Wayne in flannels" (Gordon Edes, *The Boston Globe*, July 6, 2002). IST USE. 1875. "One of our number . . . put on his white flannels and colored stockings and star-bedecked cap" (*St. Louis Globe-Democrat*, Aug. 22).

flap 1. The activator in a pitcher-catcher signal system that is given after a number of fingers have been flashed. For example, if the "flap" is four, the real sign comes after a total of four fingers have been thrown, so that 1–2–1–2–1, or 4–2–2–3, or 3–1–2–1–2 would be a curveball (2). 2. See *ear flap*.

flare 1. *n.* A looping fly ball likely to fall in between the infield and outfield and that is usually hit to the opposite field. Since the 1970s, the term has been another synonym for *Texas Leaguer*, 2, or *blooper*, 1. "Against a right-hander like [Mike] Boddicker the left-handers have to get on [base]. You can't expect a right-hander to hit defensively against him and get a flare to right" (Mike Schmidt, quoted in *New York Post*, Oct. 13, 1983). USAGE NOTE. Announcer Vin Scully said during a World Series broadcast (Oct. 21, 1986) that the modern player preferred "flare" to "Texas Leaguer." 2. *v.* To hit a flare. "[Paul] Lo Duca flared the ball to right field for a two-run double" (*The Baltimore Sun*, Apr. 11, 2005).

flash 1. *v.* To give a sign or signs quickly in the hope that one's opponents cannot steal them. 2. *n.* A sign given only once and quickly, such as a tug of the belt.

flash leather To make a great defensive play.

flat Said of a pitch that has a straight trajectory and no deceptive movements and is usually easy to hit. Compare *live* (adj.).

flat bat A bat with a flat side, legal in the major leagues from 1885 to 1893. Up to one-half inch of a bat's diameter was removed to eliminate the precise roundness of the bat. The flat bat was used primarily for bunting; however, the original intent of the flat bat was to "do away with so many foul tips and high fly balls, and in a measure improve batting" (*The New York Times*, Nov. 21, 1884; Tom Shieber). Tim Murnane first used a flat bat in the late 1870s. See also *soft bat.* Syn. *board,* 4.

Flatbushers Nickname for the Brooklyn Dodgers. Ebbets Field, the home of the Dodgers, was built in the Flatbush section of Brooklyn, about three miles south by southeast down Flatbush Avenue from the Manhattan Bridge.

flat-footed 1. Unprepared, inattentive, asleep, not on one's toes; said of a player caught napping. "[Patsy] Flaherty returned the ball and the runner was caught flat footed and made to look foolish" (Christy Mathewson, *Pitching in a Pinch*, 1912, p.273; Stuart Y. Silverstein). 2. Said of a baserunner who runs on his heels rather than the balls of his feet. 3. Said of a batting stance in which both feet are flat on the ground as opposed to one in which the batter rests on the balls of his feet; said of a batter who does not stride. The flat-footed position is considered to be the optimum one for hitting a sacrifice fly.

flea box A very small ballpark (Al Schacht, *Al Schacht Dope Book*, 1944).

fleeceball A childhood game played indoors with a ball that was soft (perhaps filled with some fleece). Rules of baseball applied, except that fielding the ball off a wall was an out. According to Thomas L. Altherr (letter, Aug. 28, 1997), the game was played in western New York in the 1950s.

flew Past tense of "fly." "Wallace flew to Lush for the third out" (*St. Louis Post-Dispatch*, July 4, 1904; *OED*). "Johnny Damon flew to center on a two-strike pitch" (*The Baltimore Sun*, Aug. 13, 2000). See *fly,* 2.

flew out Past tense of "fly out." "[Joe] Carter flew out on the next pitch" (*The Baltimore Sun*, March 17, 1998). IST USE. 1874. "Schaffer flew out to Hines" (*The Boston Daily Globe*, June 27). See *fly out,* 1.

flex [softball term] A player in fast pitch softball who is initially listed in the 10th place on the lineup card, may play any defensive position, and may enter the game on offense only in the *designated player*'s batting position. Syn. *flexible player.*

flexible player [softball term] Syn. of *flex.*

flies and grounders A childhood game in which a batter tosses the ball up and hits it in sequence to other players who must cleanly field a certain number of fly balls and grounders before becoming the batter. Each fielder's total does not reset to zero when a new batter starts, so one's turn at bat can be very short (becoming the batter does reset the totals to zero). There has been controversy over what constitutes cleanly fielding a grounder. Syn (in Texas) "flies and skinners."

fling To pitch a baseball. IST USE. 1907. "[Harry Tonkin] flung the rest of the inning" (Charles Dryden, *Chicago Tribune*, Aug. 17; Peter Morris).

flinger A pitcher. IST USE. 1904. "[Bill] Wolfe has not measured up to the standard of excellence possessed by the Chicago flinger [Frank Smith]" (*The Washington Post*, Sept. 2; Peter Morris). USAGE NOTE. The term is often used in a context with a clear derogatory edge, long paired with "alleged," which makes it an outright insult.

flip 1. *n.* A pitch thrown in the direction of the batter's body. "A good 'flip' may require that the pitcher throw the ball at a spot where the batter would be if he didn't know the pitch was obviously meant just for him, and duck" (Jim Brosnan, *The Long Season*, 1960, p.vi). 2. *v.* To throw a pitch in the direction of a batter's body; to cause a batter to hit the dirt. 3. *n.* A light, underhand toss that goes only a short distance. 4. *v.* To toss the ball underhand without much velocity, as when the second baseman "flips" the ball to the first baseman. 5. *v.* To propel a fielded ball with a snap of the wrist. 6. *n./hist.* Syn. of *flipper,* 2. IST USE. 1869 (*New York Herald*, Aug. 15; Edward J. Nichols). 7. *v.* To use one's fingers to change the meaning of a sign to confuse sign stealers and, perhaps, draw batters into harm's way. **8.** *n.* The change of a sign; e.g., if two fingers is the call for a curveball, after the flip, two fingers signifies a fastball. **9.** *n.* Syn. of *flip game.*

flip game A variation of *pepper* played by baseball players in which a ball is batted gently on the ground at a distance of about 20 feet to the first of a line of five or six players, who flip the ball to each other with their gloves until all the players have touched the ball once—and only once—before the final player catches the ball. The object of the game for the fielders is to avoid making any fielding mistakes. "It's a good game, passes the time, and probably adds to your manual dexterity" (Jim Bouton, *I'm Glad You Didn't Take It Personally*, 1971, p.59). Syn. *flip*, 9.

flipper **1.** A pitcher. **2.** A player's throwing arm. "[Bill 'Spaceman' Lee] showed that there still was some zip in the ol' flipper by opening 1978 with seven consecutive victories" (Allen Abel, *The Globe and Mail* [Toronto], Dec. 16, 1978). Syn. *flip*, 6. IST USE. 1888 (*New York Press*, Apr. 2; Edward J. Nichols)

flipping A game played with *baseball cards.* Cullen P. Vane (San Jose, Calif.) describes the version he played as a child: "The game involved two players who would turn over a stack of cards and start 'flipping' them over with each player alternating. If I flipped over a Yankee and my opponent flipped a Yankee on top of it, then he would get the whole pile of cards that had built up. This is similar to War, which is played with a regular deck of cards. I can remember playing this game for hours during recess with hundreds of cards being exchanged. Of course it was always important to take out your favorite player's cards before starting." See also *pitching baseball cards.*

flippy Syn. of *loopy.*

flivver *hist.* A player who fails to use or show his ability. IST USE. 1915 (*Baseball Magazine*, December, p.75; Edward J. Nichols). ETYMOLOGY. Slang for something or someone of unsatisfactory quality. "He can't deliver . . . the fellow is a flivver!" (Franklin P.

Adams, "It's Really Disheartening," *In Other Words*, 1912, p.7; Stuart Y. Silverstein).

floater **1.** A slowly pitched ball with very little spin or twist, intended to catch the batter off balance; a pitch that seems as if it "floats" its way toward home plate. The pitch was first made popular by Bill Phillips of Indianapolis in 1904. "Jake Stahl caught one of the floaters fair on the nose for a three-bagger" (*The Washington Post*, Aug. 14, 1904; Peter Morris). See also *folly floater*; *freaky floater.* IST USE. 1902. "Every batter has a different position of the feet when he expects a fast one or a floater, a high or a low ball" (Clark Griffith, quoted in *The Sporting Life*, May 31; Peter Morris, who suggests that the term was originally generic rather than specific). **2.** Syn. of *knuckleball*, 1. "Two of Cleveland's runs were unearned because [Josh] Bard couldn't corral floaters by [Tim] Wakefield" (*The Baltimore Sun*, Apr. 27, 2006).

Flock Nickname for the Brooklyn Dodgers. ETYMOLOGY. The Dodgers were known as the Robins when they were managed by Wilbert Robinson (1914–1931); consequently, the team was often referred to as the Flock (conjuring up the image of a group of robins gathering as a flock).

floop To hit weakly, but safely; to bat poorly, but successfully. The term is perhaps a blend of "flub" plus "bloop," or "fluke" plus "bloop." IST USE. 1937 (*The New York Tribune*, Oct. 10; Edward J. Nichols).

flopper A spectator who pays off an usher to get a better seat. The practice evolved into a tightly organized and accepted ritual at Shea Stadium, home of the New York Mets, as reported by H. Eric Semler (*The New York Times*, June 26, 1989): "Aware that many season-ticket holders will not show up at games, at least a dozen ushers in the field-level and loge sections, the two lowest levels, openly and aggressively try to sell the empty seats to wandering spectators, sometimes called 'floppers.'"

Florence Nightingale A sacrifice hitter in the All-American Girls Professional Baseball League.

Florida water Dugout water used by players

to sponge their faces and remove the sweat from their hands (Bill Werber and C. Paul Rogers III, *Memories of a Ballplayer*, 2001, p.93).

flub 1. *n.* An error. 2. *v.* To make an error.

fluffballer A pitcher who throws off-speed pitches.

fluffie-duffie A ball popped over the infield in the All-American Girls Professional Baseball League.

fluffy duff A player who is easily hurt. The term was used by Dizzy Dean and may have been coined by him.

fluid hitter A hitter whose swing is smooth and easy, not intermittent.

fluke A play or score made by chance, accident, or luck. "Two flukes in the opener assayed a pair of tallies for the champs" (*Chicago Tribune*, Aug. 17, 1907; Peter Morris). 1ST USE. 1887. "The New Yorks won on the worst kind of a fluke.... [Catcher] Stockwell in returning the ball to [pitcher] Duryea threw it low and Duryea allowed it to pass, and [Roger] Connor stole home" (*Los Angeles Times*, Nov. 21).

fluke hit A hit that should have resulted in an out but by a fluke, the batter having reached base safely; e.g., a bloop, hit by a slugger where the outfield is playing deep. See also *Chinese blow*. 1ST USE. 1901. "[Ray] Nelson's little infield fluke hit gave New York two runs, which, with another fluke single and two nice hits, evened up the score" (*The New York Times*, June 17).

flutterball Syn. of *knuckleball*, 1.

fluttering cuff The loose, ragged sleeve of pitcher Dazzy Vance, which so distracted batters that a rule was established that prohibited pitching with ragged or slit sleeves.

fly 1. *n.* Short for *fly ball*. Abbrev. *F*, 1. 1ST USE. 1860. "Holder was caught out on a fly by the short stop" (*New York Herald*, Aug. 24). 2. *v.* To bat a ball high into the air, which is caught by a fielder before touching the ground. Past tense: "flied" or sometimes *flew*. "Baker then flied to center" (*Durant* [Okla.] *Daily Democrat*, July 2, 1948; *OED*). 1ST USE. 1908 (*Brooklyn Daily Eagle*, May 28; Edward J. Nichols). 3. *n.* A pest; a persistent fan or

sportswriter who will not leave a player alone. "Another fund-raiser is electing the leading 'fly' at the end of each road trip, the guy who had the worst trip for bugging people, being a pest, just flying them. The man elected is charged a dollar" (Jim Bouton, *Ball Four*, 1970). See also *green fly*. 4. *v.* To run fast. "He [Nook Logan] covers as much ground as anyone I've ever seen. He can fly" (Jay Gibbons, quoted in *The Baltimore Sun*, May 30, 2005).

fly away To be put out by hitting a fly ball that is fielded before hitting the ground; e.g., "Smith flied away to the center fielder." Syn. *fly out*, 1.

fly ball A batted ball that rises high into the air before it drops, as opposed to one batted on the ground. A traditional rule of thumb is that to be called a fly ball, the ball should reach a height of around 15–20 feet before dropping. A fly ball that is caught before touching the ground is an out. Sometimes spelled "flyball." Syn. *fly*, 1; *air ball*. 1ST USE. 1864. "Rogers taking fly balls in style" (*Brooklyn Eagle*, Sept. 14; Peter Morris). EXTENDED USE. 1. Someone who is goofy, semi-nutty, or an oddball. 2. A dog steeplechase in which dogs catch tennis balls and then soar over a series of hurdles (Abigail Tucker, *The Baltimore Sun*, Apr. 10, 2006).

fly-ball pitcher A pitcher who entices batters to hit fly balls rather than ground balls but is also vulnerable to home runs. A fastball pitcher often causes the batter to hit the bottom of the ball, thereby producing fly balls. "[Rick Helling is] a fly-ball pitcher who will be challenged working at hitter-friendly Camden Yards" (*The Baltimore Sun*, Feb. 11, 2003). Compare *ground-ball pitcher*.

fly catch *hist.* The fielding of a fly ball before it touches the ground, which thereby retires the batter, in the *fly game*. The term was used to distinguish it from *bound catch*. 1ST USE. 1862 (Chadwick Scrapbooks, Aug. 24; Edward J. Nichols).

flycatcher An outfielder. Also spelled "fly catcher." 1ST USE. 1887. "If the ladies were asked to choose the cutest little center flycatcher, Johnson would get all the votes" (*San Francisco Examiner*, Aug. 14; Peter Morris). ETYMOLOGY. From the name of a class of birds that all contain the word "fly-catcher" in their names; e.g., the Least Fly-catcher, the Scissor-tailed Flycatcher, and the Great Crested Flycatcher, the last being known for its prodigious appetite for weevils, beetles, and other insects that feed on crops.

flychaser An outfielder. "Carl Crawford, Rocco Baldelli and Jose Cruz Jr. . . . give the [Tampa Bay] Devil Rays three centerfield-quality fly chasers" (Tom Verducci, *Sports Illustrated*, June 28, 2004). Also spelled "fly chaser." IST USE. 1912. "[Otis Crandall] turned out to be a very good fly chaser" (Christy Mathewson, *Pitching in a Pinch*; Peter Morris). USAGE NOTE. Ty Cobb (*My Life in Baseball*, 1961, p.225) observed, "The term 'fly-chaser,' often applied to outfielders, is one of baseball's most glaring misnomers. Outfielding should be as much a specialty as playing shortstop or second base. An out-fielder is called upon to field as many ground balls as he is flies, and the improper fielding of them causes more errors and allows more runs than missed fly balls."

flyer 1. A fast runner. 2. *hist.* A fly-ball base hit. "Brainerd sent a flyer to the centre field, [and] got to his first base" (*New York Herald*, Aug. 24, 1860).

fly game *hist.* A game played in baseball's early years in which the *fly rule* was in effect. See also *fly catch*; *on the fly*. Compare *bound game*.

flyhawk An outfielder. See also *hawk*, 1; *ball hawk*, 1. IST USE. 1927. "[Tris Speaker] can still make catches which it is believed no other flyhawk could negotiate, and throw strikes from the center field fence" (Paul W. Eaton, *The Sporting News*, Feb. 10; Peter Morris).

fly open 1. For a pitcher to pull his front side (arm and shoulder) sideways before releasing the ball, thereby allowing the hitter to see the ball longer. For a right-hander, the left shoulder is turned too far too soon and the torso is out in front of the arm, leaving the arm to do too much of the work in flinging the ball across the body, unassisted by the position of his frame; this causes the pitcher's throws to be harder and flatter than they should be as well as higher in the strike zone. "[Ben McDonald's] front shoulder, which he needs to keep tucked down as he begins his delivery was flying open, and he couldn't control his fastball" (*The Baltimore Sun*, May 22, 1995). See also *open up*, 1. Syn. *fly out*, 3. **2.** For a batter to allow his head and front shoulder to pull away from the plate as he swings. "Even before the ball was to the catcher, my shoulder was [flying] open, which made every pitch I saw almost unhittable" (Javy Lopez, quoted in *Sports Illustrated*, Sept. 1, 2003). See also *open up*, 2; *pull off the ball*.

flyout *n.* A fly ball batted in either fair or foul territory that is caught before it touches the ground; a fly-ball out. "Robin Ventura hit a game-ending flyout" (*The Baltimore Sun*, Oct. 1, 1999). Sometimes spelled *fly out*, 2; "fly-out." Abbrev. *F*, 2.

fly out 1. *v.* To hit a fly ball that is caught for an out before it hits the ground. "Cuthbert flied out to Harry Wright" (*Boston Globe*, June 13, 1872). Syn. *fly away*. IST USE. 1870 (*New York Herald*, May 8; Edward J. Nichols). USAGE NOTE. Although the past tense of this verb is sometimes stated as *flew out*, it is now customary to say or write "flied out." The verb "to fly out" is not derived from the verb "to fly" but from the noun "fly." When a noun ("fly") based on an irregular verb ("to fly out") is backformed into a verb, it ends up with a regular conjugation ("flied out"). *The Literary Digest* (Nov. 4, 1911), commenting on a reader's observation that no dictionary allowed the usage "flied out," noted that the "baseball 'fan'" is the arbiter: "No grammatical ruling or lack of dictionary authority affects his love for these pithy, expressive phrases that constitute the vernacular of baseball; so 'flied out' will continue to be current, secure in the position accorded it by widespread usage." William Safire (*On Language*, 1980, p.96) noted, "When a batter has hit a fly ball which is then caught, the past tense of his action is 'flied out.' The only time 'flew out' would be correct is if the batter dropped his bat, flapped his arms, and soared out of the stadium, thereby earning himself the frothiest head in the *Guinness Book of World Records*." It has not always been so. "Flew out" and "flied out" were both regularly used in the past tense of "fly out" during the 19th century. Peter Morris senses that the terms had about equal currency, "but I have not made any effort to determine whether choice was affected by any specific factors." **2.** *n.* Syn. of *flyout.* IST USE. 1881. "[Kelly] scored on Williamson's fly out to Hanlon" (*The Daily Inter Ocean* [Chicago], Aug. 24). **3.** *v.* Syn. of *fly open,* 1. "[Mike Mussina], trying to throw the ball a little harder, would burst out in his delivery, his front side flying out ahead of his arm. It affected his control" (*The Baltimore Sun,* June 15, 1996).

fly-retriever *hist.* An outfielder. "There were several fly-retrievers who laid claim to the championship [title of the premier outfielder]" (*San Francisco Bulletin,* March 8, 1913; Gerald L. Cohen).

fly rule *hist.* A rule in baseball's early years by which a batter was declared out if his fly ball was caught before it touched the ground. To make the game "more manly and scientific," J.W. Davis of the Knickerbocker Base Ball Club of New York proposed the rule on March 7, 1857; it was adopted by the Knickerbockers but only in matches for which both clubs consented to its application. The fly rule was officially adopted by the National Association of Base Ball Players in 1863. See also *fly game.* Compare *bound rule.*

fly the flag To win the league championship; to win the pennant.

fly tip *hist.* Syn. of *foul tip.* "Fly tip.—This is a foul ball, just tipped by the bat, and held by the catcher sharp from the bat" (Henry Chadwick, *The Game of Base Ball,* 1868, p.40).

FO Abbrev. for *force out,* 1.

FOB 1. *hist.* An initialism from the days of the Brooklyn Dodgers for bases that were "full of Brooklyns" or "full of Bums." The term was coined by Dodgers broadcaster Red Barber. **2.** An initialism used in Pittsburgh for bases that were "full of Bucs." The term was used by Pirates announcer Rosey Rowswell. **3.** An initialism used by Baltimore Orioles announcers for bases "full of Birds."

FOE Abbrev. for *first on error.*

fog 1. *v.* To throw a baseball with great force; e.g., "the center fielder fogged the ball to third" or "the pitcher fogged it in." See also

fog it through. **2.** *n.* A fastball. IST USE. 1937 (Bill McCullough, *Brooklyn Eagle,* Sept. 5).

fogger 1. A fastball pitcher. "He's a fogger with a fast one that's fast" (John R. Tunis, *The Kid from Tomkinsville,* 1940, p.172). IST USE. 1937 (*New York Daily News,* Jan. 31; Edward J. Nichols). **2.** A baseball thrown with great force.

fog it through To throw a fastball past a batter. The phrase was created by Dizzy Dean and associated with his delivery, but applied to others as well. See also *fog,* 1. ETYMOLOGY. Dean explained that when he reached back for that something extra for his fastball, it appeared so quickly that it seemed to be coming out of a fog (Joseph McBride, *High & Inside,* 1980, p.51).

fold 1. *v.* To fall from a strong position in a game or in the standings. "I think every time we were about to fold, we came back to win" (Greg Maddux, quoted in *Tampa Tribune,* Sept. 27, 1989). **2.** *n.* The point at which a team fails. "[The California Angels were] pulling a fold in its biggest series of the year [after] the Royals had taken the first two games of the series 10–1 and 10–0" (*Tampa Tribune,* Sept. 21, 1984).

follow through *v.* To complete a throwing or batting motion. To "follow through" guarantees that everything the thrower or batter does prior to release of, or contact with, the ball is done correctly. IST USE. 1906. "Possibly batters could improve their hitting by learning to 'follow through,' as the golfer and billiardist do, but if batters stopped to follow through their batting swing the chances are they would be thrown out on what would be otherwise base hits" (George M. Graham, *The Sporting Life,* Jan. 6; Peter Morris).

follow-through *n.* **1.** The continuation of the arm and body in the direction of a pitch or throw; the final stage of a pitcher's motion. J.E. Gargan (*Athletic Journal,* Apr. 1944): "Now as the throw is being made, bring your leg on the throwing aside around and forward . . . and transfer your weight to it as the ball is released. This will give you the follow-through with your body and add power to your throw." IST USE. 1909 (*Baseball Magazine,* June;

Edward J. Nichols). **2.** The continuation of the swing by the batter after the ball has been hit or missed, bringing the bat all the way around for maximum power. Rogers Hornsby (*My Kind of Baseball*, 1953) discussed a "free follow-through so essential to good hitting." James Smilgoff (*Athletic Journal*, Apr. 1946): "The follow-through should be in balance . . . with the weight over the front, or stride foot, and well forward. A good follow-through gives added impetus to the ball, and maintains body balance for a good break-away from the plate toward first base. There must be good rotation in the hips to maintain body balance in the follow-through."

folly floater A *blooper ball* thrown from a hesitation motion by New York Yankees pitcher Steve Hamilton. Although Hamilton described the pitch as a "gag" or novelty, he actually did use it in games. See also *floater*; *hesitation hummer*.

foot in the bucket **1.** The position of a batter who pulls away from the plate as he swings at the ball. It may come as a result of fear of being hit by the ball. It is an awkward move that suggests that the batter's back foot is stuck in an imaginary bucket. More commonly, however, it seems to result from the batter's being fooled by the speed or delivery of a pitch, causing a premature swing and shift of weight. This causes the front foot to come forward. "Take your foot out of the water-bucket, Mister Conley" (C.E. Van Loan, *Score by Innings*, 1919, copyrighted 1913, p.335; David Shulman). "He [Hughie Jennings] had the bad habit of pulling away with his forward foot when swinging at the ball. In baseball we call that putting one's foot in the water bucket, the idea being that a player will pull so far away as to step to the bench" (John McGraw, *My Thirty Years in Baseball*, 1923). See also *step in the bucket*. IST USE. 1912 (*American Magazine*, June, p.205; David Shulman). ETYMOLOGY. The concept appeared earlier than 1912. Peter Morris notes a Napoleon Lajoie quote (*Dallas Morning News*, May 14, 1905): "Whenever you see one of these fellows reaching for the water bucket with his front hoof you can put it down he is a mark for the man in the box." Evidence from the first metaphoric use of "water bucket," discovered by Morris, suggests it derives from another then-common term as illustrated in this quotation from the *New York American* (Oct. 3, 1908): "[Pitcher George McQuillan] has sent many a Giant back hitless to the water bucket in days gone by." Thus, Morris concludes the term "foot in the bucket" implied that the batter would soon be headed back to the bench. Reinforcing the etymology, Christy Mathewson (*Pitching in a Pinch*, 1912; Peter Morris) cited a typical catcher talking to an intimidated young batter: "Yer almost had your foot in the water-pail over by the bench that time." EXTENDED USE. To have one's "foot in the bucket" is to act timidly. "Secretary-General Thant of the United Nations shows signs of having his foot in the bucket in getting ready to duck a formal request by the South Vietnamese Government for U.N. observers at the September elections" (*San Francisco Examiner*, June 7, 1966; Peter Tamony).

2. An unorthodox batting stance in which the batter's front foot is pulled back toward the foul line rather than pointed out toward the pitcher. Dizzy Dean's description: "Sort of a sprattle-legged stance at the plate. The batter looks like he has got a pain in the hip." Although such a stance might be interpreted as a sign of timidity in a batter, it is actually an effective, respected stance, used by such successful hitters as Arky Vaughan, Roy Campanella, Al Simmons, and Vern Stephens. So closely was Simmons associated with this stance that when he died on May 26, 1956, his Associated Press obituary noted that his "odd 'foot in the bucket' stance earned him a niche in baseball's Hall of Fame." Syn. *foot in the dugout*. ETYMOLOGY. Phil Pepe (in Zander Hollander, ed., *The Encyclopedia of Sports Talk*, 1976) stated that the stance took its name from the front foot, which is withdrawn toward the foul line, "toward the old water bucket in the dugout."

foot in the dugout Syn. of *foot in the bucket*, 2.

footwork The movement and positioning of the feet of a catcher about to make a play or a throw. A catcher with "quick" feet aligns himself to make a throw in less than a second to attempt to retire a baserunner. The term is also applied to the movement of a first baseman's feet.

foozle 1. *n.* A play that is weakly or imperfectly performed; a bungled play. "[Goldblatt] scoring on Shaneman's foozle of Sullivan's fly" (*Dartmouth Alumni Magazine*, 1922; David Shulman). 2. For a fielder to fumble a batted ball. IST USE. 1905 (*The Sporting Life*, Sept. 9, p.15; Edward J. Nichols). 3. For a batter to make an out. "Kelley and Keeler foozled and Matty's troubles were over momentarily" (*Brooklyn Eagle*, July 24, 1901).

foozler A lucky base hit (Walter K. Putney, *Baseball Stories*, Spring 1952).

for a cent *hist.* A cheap base hit. "Reynolds followed with a little bat 'for a cent' towards first base, but it proved to be safe for the first baseman dare not, and the pitcher could not get it in time to keep him from the base" (*Adrian* [Mich.] *Daily Press*, July 20, 1874; Peter Morris). ETYMOLOGY. A general slang term for something unostentatious.

force 1. *n.* Syn. of *force play*. IST USE. 1905 (*The Sporting Life*, Oct. 7, p.9; Edward J. Nichols). 2. *v.* To cause a baserunner to be put out in a force play. IST USE. 1869 (*DeWitt's Base-Ball Guide*, p.85; Edward J. Nichols). 3. *v.* To cause a baserunner to attempt to advance a base when a ground ball is hit. Henry Chadwick (*The Game of Base Ball*, 1868, p.40): "Players running bases can only be forced to leave them when all are occupied, and a fair ball is struck, or, when the first base is occupied and a fair ball is hit." 4. *v.* To cause a baserunner to advance a base without liability to be put out when the batter or another runner is awarded a base; e.g., preceding runners are "forced" to advance by the award of bases as the penalty for obstruction, or a runner on first base is "forced" to advance to second base upon the batter being hit by the pitch. See also *force in*. 5. *v.* For a tired pitcher to throw the ball with difficulty; e.g., "Smith forced the ball to the plate."

force bunt Syn. of *push bunt*. IST USE. 1910. "The 'force bunt' was brought into prominence by little Butler, of Columbus" (John J. Evers and Hugh S. Fullerton, *Touching Second: The Science of Baseball*; Peter Morris).

force double play A fielding play in which two putouts are made on a force play. Typically, with a runner on first base, the batter hits a ground ball that is thrown to the fielder covering second base, who touches the bag for a force out, and then throws the ball to first base to retire the batter. The fielder at second base is the key to this play because he must touch the base and throw the ball to first base while avoiding the sliding runner. Dan Sperling (*A Spectator's Guide to Baseball*, 1983, p.55) wrote, "Although it's a fairly common baseball occurrence, a force double-play involving the batter, a base runner, and three fielders is a thing of beauty to behold because of the clockwork precision with which it is executed." Compare *reverse force double play*.

force in To cause the baserunner on third base to score a run by walking the batter with the bases loaded. See also *force*, 4.

force off 1. *n.* Any play that forces a runner to leave a base. The term was used frequently in written rules of the early 1880s to signify instances in which a fielder deliberately dropped an infield fly or a catcher dropped a third strike with the bases loaded and turned it into a triple play. *Spalding's Official Base Ball Guide* (1885; Peter Morris): "There is comparatively but little doubt as to the character of a catch, or of the nature of a failure to hold the ball sufficiently as to constitute a legal catch under the rule, under the varying circumstances of a game, except in the case of a 'force off,' that is, when it becomes a point of skillful play to purposely drop a fly ball or miss a catch in order to force a base runner to leave a base." It is easy to see how efforts to discourage deliberate "force offs" eventually gave way to the infield fly rule and no dropped third strikes with first base occupied and less than two outs. 2. *v.* To cause a baserunner to leave his base on a ground ball or a dropped fly ball. IST USE. 1864. "[Henry Burroughs] missed the catch, thereby allowing the striker to make his base, by which the others were forced off theirs, and the ball being passed rapidly to third and second and held well on each base, both the players

Force out. Postcard. *Andy Moresund Collection*

forced off their bases were put out" (*New York Clipper*, June 25; Peter Morris).

force out 1. *n.* The putout of an advancing baserunner who is forced to move to the next base. Abbrev. *FO*. Also spelled "force-out"; "forceout." IST USE. 1870 (*New York Herald*, May 8; Edward J. Nichols). **2.** *v.* To put a runner out by touching the base in a force play. IST USE. 1877. "[Jim] White, after reaching on a muff by [Paul] Hines, was forced out at third base by [Jim] O'Rourke" (*The Boston Globe*, June 19; Peter Morris).

force play A play in which a baserunner legally loses his right to occupy a base when the batter becomes a runner. The defensive action results in the retiring of a baserunner by touching the base to which he is headed, and must (is "forced" to) occupy, because there is an advancing runner behind him. In such plays, a fair ball (other than one caught on the fly) with a runner on first base forces the runner to advance to second base. In a force play, the

runner does not have to be tagged. Compare *fielder's choice*, 1. Syn. *force*, 1.

Ford C. Frick Award An annual award established in 1978 to honor members of the broadcasting profession who have made "major contributions" to baseball. It is given to an active or retired broadcaster with a minimum of 10 years of continuous major-league broadcast service with a ball club, network, or combination of the two. Winners of the award are selected by all living Frick Award winners plus a six-member panel of baseball executives and media personnel appointed by the National Baseball Hall of Fame; an online fan-vote component (to select three of the 10 names on the final ballot) was launched in 2003. Award winners are honored during the annual Hall of Fame induction ceremonies; but contrary to public opinion and newspaper accounts, they are not inducted into a "broadcasting wing" of the Hall of Fame (the list of honorees is displayed in an exhibit in the National Baseball Museum in Cooperstown, N.Y.). The award is named in memory of the former sportswriter, radio broadcaster, National League president (1934–1951), and commissioner of baseball (1951–1965), whose death on Apr. 8, 1978, precipitated the award. Syn. *Frick Award*.

foreign substance A generic term used in the rules of baseball for illegal materials, such as pine tar, petroleum jelly, and hair dressing, applied to the ball to give the pitcher an advantage, or pine tar or other substance applied to the bat more than 18 inches from the bat-handle end. The one substance that is officially allowed is rosin.

forfeit 1. *v.* To lose a forfeited game. **2.** *n.* Syn. of *forfeited game*.

forfeited game A game in which a victory is awarded to a team by the umpire-in-chief because the opposition acted in violation of the rules of baseball. A team can be forced to forfeit a game if it refuses to play, delays the game, fails to remove an ejected player, or fails to place nine players on the field. A game may also be forfeited to the visiting team in the case of unruly behavior on the part of the hometown fans, or when the field becomes unplayable through negligence of the home team. The official score of a forfeited game is 9–0 because many early forfeited games occurred when one team could not field nine players; however, according to Frank Vaccaro (personal communication, March 31, 2005), the 9–0 score was adopted in the late 1860s to combat gamblers who booked bets on games and bets on which team would win "certain innings" or "most innings in which a score was made." *Official Baseball Rules* (Rule 10.03[e]): "The official scorer shall not consider that, by rule, the score of a forfeited game is 9 to 0, notwithstanding the results on the field at the point the game is forfeited." See also *Beer Night*; *Disco Demolition Night*. Syn. *forfeit*, 2.

"forget it!" An exclamation used by some sportscasters to describe a long, powerful hit that is obviously a home run. The term is uttered after the outcome of such a hit is never in doubt. Also stated as "you can forget about that one."

forkball **1.** A pitch that is gripped between the index and middle fingers—which are spread as far apart as possible, suggesting a two-pronged fork—and that breaks suddenly downward as it approaches the plate. The grip limits the spin of the ball and causes it to drop or sink sharply as it reaches the plate. The forkball is thrown with the motion of a fastball, comes in with the speed of a changeup, and drops at the last moment like a spitball; it is similar to a knuckleball in that it is unpredictable and difficult to control. Pitchers with long and lean fingers throw the ball with a strong wrist snap. The first pitcher to become known for his forkball was Joe Bush. It is associated with Ernie Bonham and was popularized by Elroy Face. The forkball is similar to the *split-fingered fastball*: while both are held between the index and middle fingers and break downward with a tumbling motion, the forkball is held toward the base of the fin-

Forkball.

gers (deeper in the palm of the hand) and "choked" or thrown with less velocity, while the split-fingered fastball is held toward the end of the fingers and thrown harder. Sometimes spelled "fork ball." See also *dry spitter*, 1. Syn. *forked ball*, 1. IST USE. 1913. "It does look as if the broken finger which he [Oakland southpaw Harry Ables] sustained is still stiffened up, but we have seen him throw his fork ball and he looked to have as much stuff as ever" (*San Francisco Bulletin*, May 27; Gerald L. Cohen). USAGE NOTE. John Thorn and John B. Holway (*The Pitcher*, 1987, p.158) claim that Bert Hall of the Tacoma Tigers first employed the forkball on Sept. 8, 1908, and assert that "that day the pitch—and the name *forkball*—were both born." J.W. Foley (*St. Louis Post-Dispatch*, Apr. 2, 1915; Peter Morris): "[Pete] Standridge . . . has a delivery called the 'fork ball' . . . This freak ball is held between the middle and index fingers and is what is sometimes called a 'dry spitter.'" **2.** Euphemistic name for a "spitball." A profile by Joel Schwarz of pitcher Gaylord Perry (*American Way*, Sept. 1982) noted, "He also acquired another pitch for his repertoire, a pitch he sometimes calls a 'spitter' but most frequently refers to as a 'forkball.' . . . Fred Lynn [adds:] . . . 'There ain't a forkball alive that does what that pitch does.'" **3.** A ball pitched by a forkhander (left-handed pitcher).

forkballer A pitcher who throws the forkball. "[The Boston Braves] bought the Cardinals' temperamental fork-baller Morton Cooper" (*Time* magazine, June 4, 1945).

forked ball **1.** Syn. of *forkball*, 1. **2.** A characterization of a knuckleball (*The New York Times*, June 2, 1929).

forkhander A *left-handed pitcher*. IST USE. 1920. "A hectic heave by the young forkhander" (J.V. Fitz Gerald, *The Washington Post*, Apr. 27). ETYMOLOGY. In one method of eating with knife, fork, and spoon, the fork is used by the left hand alone. More commonly, the fork is set on the left side of the plate.

forkle A term used by pitcher Rod Nichols for a pitch which is held like a forkball but is said to react like a knuckleball (*The Baltimore Sun*, July 21, 1991).

fork side The left side. "Such veteran infielders as Bill Werber . . . Dick Bartell and Joe Orengo, looked on from the sidelines and began to wonder, after watching Danna at short, whether it wouldn't be better if they threw from the fork side instead of being right-handed" (Harry Cross, *New York Herald Tribune*, Feb. 23, 1942; James D. Szalontai).

for the first time in history A phrase that, when written or spoken, indicates the occurrence of an event in baseball that has never happened before. Because such events are rare, the words have taken on a special significance. "Next time somebody suggests you leave early to beat the traffic, remember: that could be the game when you finally hear the true fan's favorite words, 'For the first time in the history of baseball'" (Thomas Boswell, *The Washington Post*, Aug. 8, 1986).

45-foot lane A designated area that the batter-runner must stay within when running to first base. Three feet wide, the lane begins halfway down the baseline from home plate and extends 45 feet to first base. The lane is designed to keep the batter-runner from going inside the diamond and interfering with the throw to first. A batter-runner ruled to have left the lane in a deliberate attempt to interfere with the defensive play is called out by the umpire. The batter-runner must stay within the double lines except when getting into position to round first base on his way to second base. See also *three-foot line*. Syn. *runner's box*.

40-40 club A mythical group of players who have hit 40 or more home runs and stolen 40 or more bases in a single season. It came into prominence at the end of the 1988 season as explained by Eric Brady (*USA Today*, Oct. 4, 1988): "[Jose] Canseco hit 42 home runs and stole 40 bases. Baseball records go back 112 years, but you can count the 40-40 club members on one finger. Canseco. Period. End of list." However, Barry Bonds joined the 40-40 club in 1996, Alex Rodriguez in 1998, and Alfonso Soriano in 2006. Compare *20-20 club*; *30-30 club*; *50-50 club*.

40-man roster The reserve list of players on a major-league club. Rosters may include 40 players until Opening Day, when the number must be reduced to 25. The number increases back to 40 on Sept. 1. Clubs expand their rosters to provide bench depth in a pennant race, to reward a productive minor leaguer, or to gauge the development of a player. Compare *25-man roster.*

foshball A pitch that combines the properties of a straight changeup and an off-speed split-fingered fastball, with a sharp sinking motion. It is thrown off the seams (the fingers are spread slightly apart) with a looser grip than the split-fingered fastball, but moves more than a changeup; it has a sharp sinking motion, but does not "fall off the table" when it reaches the plate. As thrown by a right-handed pitcher, it breaks away from a left-handed batters. The pitch is attributed to Mike Boddicker and was used by David Nied and Chuck Smith. Syn. "fosh"; "fosh change"; *fush ball*. ETYMOLOGY. According to Rob Neyer (Bill James and Rob Neyer, *The Neyer/James Guide to Pitchers*, 2004, p.15), Earl Weaver thought the pitch appeared to be a cross between a fastball and a dead fish. Al Nipper suggested that "fosh" was an acronym "for the feelings the batters had when the pitch sailed past them for a strike: 'F' for 'full,' 'O' for 'of,' and 'SH' for . . . " (Jimmy Golen, Associated Press dispatch, March 10, 1996). Nied (quoted in *USA Today Baseball Weekly*, Dec. 30, 1992–Jan. 12, 1993) suggested that "fosh sounded like the perfect word for the movement of the pitch."

foul 1. *n.* Syn. of *foul ball.* **2.** *v.* To hit a ball into foul territory. **3.** *n.* Syn. of *foul territory.* **4.** *adj.* In foul territory.

foul away Syn. of *foul out.*

foul back To hit a ball backward into foul territory; e.g., "Smith fouled one back to the screen."

foul balk *hist.* A term used in early rule books that evolved simply into *balk*, 1. "The old foul balk rule was scratched. The regular balk was substituted" (*St. Louis Globe-Democrat*, March 13, 1883).

foul ball A legally batted ball that settles in foul territory before reaching first base or third base, or first touches the ground in foul territory beyond first base or third base, or while in or over foul territory, touches an umpire, player, or any foreign object. A batted ball that hits the pitcher's rubber and rebounds into foul territory between home plate and either first base or third base is a foul ball. A foul ball counts against the batter as a strike, unless it is caught on the fly, which then counts as an out. A batter cannot strike out on a foul ball, however, unless he bunts the ball foul with two strikes. Jerry Howarth (*Baseball Lite*, 1986) defined foul balls as "head-hunting white blurs coveted by fans who risk life and limb and often times beer trying to catch them." Syn. *foul*, 1. IST USE. 1845. "A ball knocked out [of] the field, or outside the range of the first or third base, is foul" (Knickerbocker Rules, Rule 10th, Sept. 23). EXTENDED USE. A bad or ignorant person. There is much evidence to suggest that cartoonist/writer T.A. Dorgan was the first to apply the term to an individual. Peter Tamony collected several examples from Dorgan's work, including one in which one of his characters says in reference to a boasting athlete: "Oh, he's just a foul ball" (*San Francisco Call & Post*, July 1, 1925).

foul ball indicator A device that determines if a long ball has passed the foul pole in fair or foul territory. Several such devices have been developed over the years, but none has yet established itself in the game. One system that received much press attention in 1949 was based on a foul pole with free-swinging rods attached: if the ball touched one of the rods on the foul side a red light went on, while a green light was lit if it passed on the fair side. It was granted U.S. patent 2,461,936.

foul bound *hist.* A foul ball caught after taking one bounce. Under baseball's early rules, a foul bound was an out. Although the *bound catch* was officially eliminated in 1864, the foul-bound catch persisted for several years. In 1883, the National League mandated that a foul ball had to be caught on the fly to be an out. The American Association ended foul-bound catches in the middle of the 1885 season. Abbrev. *LD.* IST USE. 1866. "Thompson was then caught out by Phelps on a foul bound" (*Detroit Advertiser and Tribune*, June 28; Peter Morris).

foul bunt A bunt that lands in foul territory. If a batter bunts foul after two strikes, it is counted as a third strike.

foul-fair *hist.* A fair ball that hits in foul territory and then bounds or rolls into fair territory before passing first base or third base. The *Chicago Tribune* (Apr. 29, 1877) pointed out that the legislation that abolished the *fair foul* in 1876 had created a new breed of hits: "By the rule of this year a ball which strikes foul ground first, and then bounds into fair ground before passing first or third base, is a fair ball. Inasmuch as it struck foul ground first, it must be called a 'foul-fair,' following the custom of last year." The concept remains, but the term never caught on.

foul fly A foul ball that rises high into the air. Henry Chadwick (*The Game of Base Ball*, 1868, p.40) defined "foul fly" as "a high foul ball caught on the fly." Abbrev. *F*, 3.

foul ground Syn. of *foul territory*.

foul hit *hist.* "A ball hit . . . so that it goes outside the foul lines; that is, back of the diamond, or the extension of its lines to first and third bases" (Jessie H. Bancroft and William Dean Pulvermacher, *Handbook of Athletic Games*, 1916).

foul league A mythical league for batters who hit "numerous drives off the third or first base lines" (*The New York Times*, June 2, 1929).

foul line One of the two white boundary markings that extend from home plate to the left-field foul pole and from home plate to the right-field foul pole, forming a 90-degree angle at home plate. A. Bartlett Giamatti (*Take Time for Paradise*, 1989) noted that "these perpendicular lines theoretically extend to infinity." IST USE. 1865. "Foul lines were distinctly drawn and whitened" (*Brooklyn Eagle*, Aug. 15; Peter Morris).

foul-off *n.* A pitched ball that is hit foul. EXTENDED USE. Something that was screwed up. "I have seen a buffoon platoon become the company pride in eight weeks, and I have seen a foul-off gun crew develop into a crack outfit in three weeks" (Robert C. Ruark, on the new military draft, *San Francisco News*, Aug. 6, 1948; Peter Tamony).

foul off *v.* To hit a pitched ball foul. IST USE.

1893. "The proposed amendment, by which the unskilled will be charged with a strike for 'fouling off' whether through intention or inexpertness" (*The Sporting News*, Dec. 23; Peter Morris).

foul-out *n.* A ball that is caught for an out in foul territory. Also spelled "foulout."

foul out *v.* To hit a ball that is caught for an out in foul territory. Syn. *foul away*. IST USE. 1870. "Start fouled out" (*New York Herald*, July 5; Peter Morris).

foul pole Either of two vertical posts erected at the intersection of the outfield fence and the foul line. It aids the umpires to determine if a ball that is hit over the fence is fair or foul. A batted ball that hits the foul pole on the fly is a home run. The foul poles in major-league ballparks must be at least 30 feet tall (45 feet is recommended) with a screen to the fair side of the pole. No white signs are allowed on or immediately adjacent to each side of the pole. See also *fair pole*. Syn. *foul post*. IST USE. 1904. "[Deacon] McGuire did better with a double to the left foul pole" (*The Washington Post*, Sept. 21; Peter Morris). USAGE NOTE. Some consider the term a misnomer. "When a fair ball that looks foul hits the foul pole it becomes a fair ball, and since the foul pole is fair it should be called a fair pole" (Jerry Howarth, *Baseball Lite*, 1986).

foul post *hist.* Syn. of *foul pole*. "The foul posts . . . shall be located at the boundary of the field and within the range of home and first base, and home and third base" (*De Witt's Base-Ball Guide*, 1878; Peter Morris). IST USE. 1868. "Chapman now hit a splendid ball to left field, near the foul ball post" (*Brooklyn Eagle*, Aug. 18; Peter Morris).

foul screecher An untutored spectator who cheers foul balls not knowing that they are not hits. According to Dizzy Dean: "A ladies' day fan who screams on every pop foul."

foul strike The proper term for a foul ball, batted with less than two strikes, that is not caught on the fly. Originally, a ball batted foul was not counted as a strike, allowing batters such as Roy Thomas, Honus Wagner, and Willie Keeler to deliberately foul off pitches in the strike zone, thereby tiring pitchers, causing delays in the game, and boring the fans. The rule was changed (in 1901 in the National League and 1903 in the American League) to count fouls as strikes unless there were already two strikes on the batter. IST USE. 1845. "No ace or base can be made on a foul strike" (Knickerbocker Rules, Rule 18th, Sept. 23).

foul territory That part of the playing field outside the lines of the 90° angle formed by the foul lines, extended to the fence and perpendicularly upward. A fly ball is playable within foul territory unless it is in an area that has been deemed to be out of play. Compare *fair territory*. Syn. *foul*, 3; *foul ground*. IST USE. 1908 (*Brooklyn Daily Eagle*, May 21; Edward J. Nichols).

foul tick *hist.* A foul ball in pre–Civil War baseball (John Grossman, *Sports Illustrated*, June 27, 1994). See also *tick*, 2.

foul-tip *v.* To hit a foul tip.

foul tip *n.* A ball that glances off the bat directly into the catcher's hands and is legally caught. It counts as a regular swinging strike rather than as a foul ball; thus, the batter is out if he foul-tips a ball with two strikes against him and the ball is in play. A tipped ball is not counted as a foul tip if it is not caught (it becomes a foul ball) or if it hits any part of the catcher's body before landing in his hands. Syn. *fly tip*; *tip-foul*; *tick*, 2. IST USE. 1861 (*Beadle's Dime Base-Ball Player*; Edward J. Nichols).

4 The scorekeeper's designation for the second baseman.

four A colloquial reference to home plate in Australian baseball; e.g., a third base coach yelling "four!" to a baserunner running full speed into third base.

4-A **1.** Said of a player who is overqualified for Class AAA minor leagues but not quite talented enough for the major leagues (*USA Today*, May 19, 1998). Also spelled "Four-A." Syn. *Quadruple-A*. **2.** Said of a fictitious league in which the teams are playing below major-league standards but are too good for the minor leagues. "The [Detroit] Tigers are in a league of their own—the 4-A league" (Pat Caputo, *Baseball America*, Nov. 26–Dec. 9, 2001; Peter Morris). See also *Class AAAA*. **3.** Said of Japanese baseball, a level below Major League Baseball. "[Bobby] Valentine realizes he must . . . legitimize Japanese baseball, which Americans have long thought of as 'Four A' ball" (Chris Ballard, *Sports Illustrated*, Apr. 30, 2007, p.70).

four aces *hist.* A grand slam. An account of a game in Hoboken, N.J., at the Elysian Fields mentioned "four aces" were scored off a single hit (Fox Butterfield, *The New York Times*, Oct. 4, 1990). IST USE. 1845 (*New York Morning News*, Oct. 21).

4B Abbrev. for *home run*.

four-bagger Syn. of *home run*. "The Dodgers came back with a . . . four-bagger by [Pee Wee] Reese" (Harvey Rosenfeld, *The Great Chase*, 1992, p.26). IST USE. 1883 (*Chicago Inter-Ocean*, June 9; Edward J. Nichols).

four-base hit A home run. Variations include "four-base drive," "four-base knock," and "four-base slam." IST USE. 1883 (*The Sporting Life*, June 3; Edward J. Nichols).

four-baser A home run. IST USE. 1880 (*Chicago Inter-Ocean*, June 2; Edward J. Nichols).

four-cornered hit A home run. IST USE. 1915 (*Baseball Magazine*, December; Edward J. Nichols).

four-cushion shot A home run. "In the fifth [Buck Freeman] tore off a four-cushion shot on a fly drive to the center field fence" (*The Washington Post*, Aug. 22, 1899).

four-day rider A term used by Satchel Paige for a three-quarters or sidearm curveball (John B. Holway, *The Washington Post*, July 7, 1991).

four-days rest The normal amount of time between games for a starting pitcher.

4H club A philosophy that acknowledges that scouting is a very speculative profession. Boston Red Sox scout Joe Stephenson (quoted in Allan Simpson, comp. and ed., *The Baseball Draft*, 1990, p.19; Peter Morris): "We belong to the 4H club. You hope you find a prospect. You hope you get him in the draft. You hope you can sign him. And you hope he can play."

400-400 club A mythical club created in 1998 when Barry Bonds became the first player to hit 400 home runs and steal 400 bases in a career.

.400 hitter A hitter who has achieved a benchmark season's batting average of .400 or higher. The feat was last accomplished by Ted Williams when he batted .406 in 1941. Ever since Williams' achievement, a perennial question is asked: Will there ever be another .400 hitter? Rod Carew, George Brett, Tony Gwynn, and Wade Boggs have flirted with the number for parts of seasons but all have come up short. Should another one come along, his manager would do well to listen to skipper Joe McCarthy's decades-old comment on the subject (*The Sporting News*, 1948): "A manager who cannot get along with a .400 hitter ought to have his head examined." EXTENDED USE. One who has achieved greatness or performed at high standards. A headline in the *Bangor* [Maine] *Daily News* (July 18, 1987), on the performance of Maine's senators in the Iran-Contra hearings: ".400 Hitters on a Mediocre Team."

four-man rotation A rotation of four starting pitchers in which each works every fourth game (with at least three days of rest). In the present era, teams with such a rotation are often looking for a fifth starter. The last major-league team to use a four-man rotation for an entire season was the 1984 Toronto Blue Jays. See also *five-man rotation*.

four-master A home run.

four o'cat Syn. of *four-old-cat*.

four-old-cat A variant of *old-cat* with eight or more players, four of whom serve as throwers and alternate as catchers and four of whom serve as batsmen stationed at four bases on a square field. Individual scores are credited to the batsman making the hit and running from one corner (base) to the next. The game was described by Albert G. Spalding (*Spalding's Official Base Ball Guide*, 1905) as an "old colonial" American game that he believed was a forerunner of baseball. Syn. *four o'cat*.

Four-seam fastball.

four-ply Said of a *home run*; e.g., "four-ply shot" (*New York Tribune*, Oct. 16, 1912; Edward J. Nichols), "four-ply blow," "four-ply wallop" (*Orioles Gazette*, July 6, 1992), and "four-ply swat."

four-ribeye steak Syn. of *grand slam*, 1.

four-sacker A home run. IST USE. 1905 (*The Sporting Life*, Sept. 9; Edward J. Nichols).

four-seam To throw a four-seam fastball.

four-seam changeup A changeup thrown with the middle and ring fingers held across two seams. See also *two-seam changeup*.

four-seamer 1. A home run hit on a fat pitch, as described by Joe Goddard (*The Sporting News*, March 6, 1982): "The ball doesn't move at all. It goes straight down the middle, about thigh-high, and the hitter gets all four seams. The result makes the fans go 'ooh-ah.'" Compare *two-seamer*, 1. 2. Syn. of *four-seam fastball*.

four-seam fastball A power fastball in which the ball is gripped across (not with) the four seams so that as it comes rotating out of the hand the four seams (instead of just two) are spinning into the air, giving maximum motion to the ball, which will appear to rise with a hop to it. It is straighter and faster than the *two-seam fastball*. The pitch is favored by power pitchers, such as Roger Clemens and Randy Johnson. See also *riding fastball*; *rising fastball*. Syn. *four-seamer*, 2; *cross-seamer*; *cross-seam fastball*.

4-6-3 The scorekeeper's notation for a double play in which the ball goes from the second baseman (4) to the shortstop (6) covering second base to the first baseman (3). Compare *6-4-3*.

fourth 1. *n.* The fourth inning. 2. *adv.* Said of the fourth position in the batting order; e.g., "Smith is batting fourth."

Fourth of July The date, roughly halfway through the regular season, that is a standard landmark for measuring a team's success. It is an old cliché or prophecy in baseball that the teams in first place on the Fourth of July will win their divisions, but this actually happens less than half the time. "Old Mr. McGillicuddy's diligent young men are in the spot customarily occupied by pennant winners on Independence Day" (Frank Getty, *The Washington Post*, July 5, 1929; Peter Morris). Syn. *July 4th*.

Fourth of July league An early minor league that disbanded immediately after the July 4th holiday. Since the Independence Day holiday was a tremendous revenue generator, leagues whose demise was inevitable would stick it out until the holiday, and then fold. "Any number of 'Fourth-of-July' leagues did business until about the middle of the season, and then passed peacefully out of existence" (National Commission chairman August "Garry" Herrmann, quoted in *The Sporting News*, Jan. 9, 1908; Peter Morris). Syn. *firecracker league*; *shoestring league*. IST USE. 1897. "[Disappointed] Columbus patrons . . . bought season books for Fourth of July leagues" (*Detroit Free Press*, May 2; Peter Morris).

fourth out An out recorded as a result of a successful appeal on a baserunner who crossed the plate before the third out. An example of a fourth out occurs when, with runners on second base and third base and one out, a fly ball is caught for the second out, the runner from second base is tagged out trying to reach third base for the third out, and the runner from third base—who had broken for home and crossed the plate—is declared out on appeal (before the defensive team left the field) for leaving the base before the catch was made, thereby negating the run (an appealed out takes precedence in determining an out). See also *quadruple play*.

fourth-place hitter Syn. of *cleanup hitter*.

four-timer *hist.* A home run. IST USE. 1891

(*Chicago Inter-Ocean*, May 5; Edward J. Nichols).

four-wheel drive A home run.

four wide ones Syn. of *base on balls*. IST USE. 1904. "[Jimmy] Williams side-stepped four wide ones" (*The Washington Post*, Sept. 22; Peter Morris).

foxhole slide Syn. of *headfirst slide*. The term was introduced by U.S. Marines in the Southwest Pacific (*Christian Science Monitor*, Feb. 18, 1944).

fozzle *hist.* To make an error. "[Gregory] spilled the beans by fozzling Wells' easy tap" (*San Francisco Bulletin*, Feb. 28, 1913; Gerald L. Cohen).

FP Abbrev. for *fielding percentage*.

FPS Abbrev. for *first-pitch strike*.

FR Abbrev. for *fielding runs*.

FRA Abbrev. for *fair run average*.

FRAA Abbrev. for *fielding runs above average*.

fracas **1.** An on-field fight: syn. of *rhubarb*. "The National League president [Ford C. Frick] had watched the [Sal] Maglie-[Jackie] Robinson fracas . . . and threatened to curb the action of the Dodger star" (Harvey Rosenfeld, *The Great Chase*, 1992, p.19). **2.** *hist.* A baseball game. "The Angels . . . after trimming the Oaks by a score of 2 to 1 in 12 innings in the morning fracas, came back at their rivals in the afternoon and swept them off the map" (*San Francisco Bulletin*, May 26, 1913; Gerald L. Cohen).

frame Syn. of *inning*, 1. IST USE. 1910 (*New York Tribune*, July 13; Edward J. Nichols). ETYMOLOGY. Edward J. Nichols (*An Historical Dictionary of Baseball Terminology*, Jan. 1939, p.28) concluded that the term was taken from bowling as "both 'inning' and 'frame' [constituted] divisions of play in their respective games."

frame the pitch For a catcher to keep his glove in the strike zone, or as close to it as possible, when receiving a borderline pitch, or to bring the ball into the strike zone with a subtle move of his mitt, thereby giving the plate umpire the impression that the pitch is in the strike zone, even if it is not. Keith Hernandez (*Pure Baseball*, 1994, p.13) com-

mented, "Gary Carter was terrific at framing the pitch for his pitchers and getting more than his share of strike calls on the close ones. If a pitch was called a ball and Gary agreed, he tossed it right back to the pitcher. But if he thought it was a strike, he'd hold the ball perfectly still for a couple of seconds, a polite way to say to the ump, 'Look again. I think you missed that one.'" Other catchers proficient at framing the pitch were Bob Boone, Carlton Fisk, and Rick Dempsey. See also *pull a pitch*. Syn. *jerk*, 5.

franchise **1.** The formal agreement or grant that establishes the existence and ownership of a baseball club. It amounts to a license, which can only be legally granted by Major League Baseball and either the American League or National League. When a club moves from one city to another, the franchise or license remains in force but has been relocated. IST USE. 1900. "The owner of the Manhattan franchise [Andrew Freedman], however, is said to be a rich man, so that he could afford the rather dubious luxury he enjoyed. Other franchise owners attach themselves to the game for the money there is in it" (*Brooklyn Eagle*, Apr. 19; Peter Morris). **2.** A baseball club. Thomas Boswell (*The Washington Post*, Sept. 30, 1986) on the Boston Red Sox: "Talent produced mediocrity— the franchise's history in a nutshell." **3.** Syn. of *franchise player*. According to Peter Tamony, the term was not used in the sense of its application to a player until after World War II, and it may not have come into its own until it began to be attached to Willie Mays. Curley Grieve (*San Francisco Examiner*, Sept. 29, 1957; Peter Tamony) pointed out that Mays was "the franchise" just as Carl Hubbell was "the meal ticket." Grieve added that the Mays partisans emphasized, "Hubbell showed once every four days. Willie you can see every day. That's why he's the franchise and not merely a meal ticket." *Time* magazine (June 27, 1977) headlined its article on Tom Seaver's trade from the New York Mets to the Cincinnati Reds: "How the Franchise Went West."

franchise player A superior player, usually young, around whom a successful team can be built; a player who gives significant added

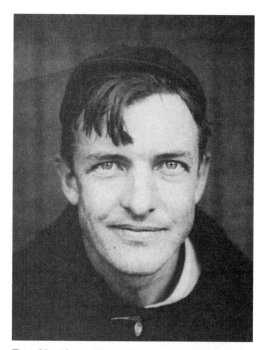

Franchise player. Christy Mathewson in the 1910 photograph by Paul Thompson that was used as the basis of a rare Mathewson baseball card. Mathewson epitomized the term before it was coined. *George Grantham Bain Collection, Library of Congress*

value to the franchise. "He [Cal Ripken Jr.] is what baseball men covet beyond all else, a franchise player. The pilings on which pennant-winners rest. A neophyte Mike Schmidt or Johnny Bench" (Phil Musick, *USA Today*, March 16, 1983). Franchise players have included Lou Brock (St. Louis Cardinals), Mickey Mantle (New York Yankees), Willie Mays (New York/San Francisco Giants), and Tom Seaver (New York Mets). Syn. *franchise*, 3. EXTENDED USE. The term has gained a much more specific use in the National Football League, where a team can designate a player as a "franchise player" and thereby limit his access to free agency.

frank *hist.* To be given a base on balls. 1ST USE. 1904. "[Billy] Wolfe was franked to first by [Clark] Griffith in the fifth" (*The Washington Post*, Sept. 18; Peter Morris). ETYMOLOGY. Since the early 19th century, the verb has been used to allow a person or thing free passage. The most common use then and now is to mark a piece of mail with an official notation permitting the sender free mailing. Members of Congress and federal agencies retain the privilege.

Frank Merriwell finish A dramatic and successful ending to a baseball game in the manner of Burt L. Standish's (pseudonym for Gilbert Patten) fictitious character Frank Merriwell, who triumphed each week in spectacular fashion by performing unmatchable feats of last-minute derring-do. Merriwell's exploits as a scholar sportsman (at Fardale Academy and Yale College) captured the imagination of millions from 1896 to 1914 in *Tip Top Weekly*, a pulp-fiction magazine for boys. "[Frank Merriwell] stood for fair play, sensitive masculinity and what was called 'muscular Christianity'" (Frank Deford, *Sports Illustrated*, Aug. 25, 2003). Compare *Garrison finish*, 1.

FRAR Abbrev. for *fielding runs above replacement*.

fraternity *hist.* Ballplayers as a group. "Certain evils have followed in the train of professional ball-playing, which, if not checked in their progress, will ultimately so damage the reputation of the fraternity as to materially interfere with the future welfare of the game" (*The New York Times*, Nov. 27, 1870; Peter Morris).

Fraternity of Professional Baseball Players of America Formal name for *Players Fraternity*.

fraternization Conversation between players of opposing teams on the field of play. Such behavior is prohibited: "Players of opposing teams shall not fraternize at any time while in uniform" (*Official Baseball Rules*, Rule 3.09). The prohibition, however, is seldom enforced. The term was used frequently during the 1950s when it was argued that the practice would somehow reduce the intensity of performance. Steve Fiffer (*How to Watch Baseball*, 1987) pointed out that different managers have different policies on fraternization; e.g., New York Mets manager Davey Johnson was quoted: "I don't believe in fraternization. I frown on my players talking to guys on the other team, but I don't have a rule." See also *Stargell Rule*.

freak An unconventional pitch or pitching delivery, usually designed to fool the batter.

The term is sometimes applied to an illegal pitch, such as the emery ball, but also to a pitch that is legal but idiosyncratic, such as the screwball. Eddie Cicotte (*Baseball Magazine*, July 1918) described the emery ball as "a freak pure and simple." Hod Eller, an exponent of freak deliveries, complained (quoted in *Baseball Magazine*, Sept. 1921, p.439), "I am not going to defend freak deliveries, although it certainly hit me hard when they abolished them, but I am sure of one thing, they will have to do something before long to help out the pitcher."

freak show stat A baseball statistic that is cute or entertaining but of little real value; e.g., players' double-figure totals in doubles, triples, and home runs. The *Baseball Analyst* newsletter featured a regular column entitled "Dan Greenia's Freak Show" in which, for one example, Greenia "discovered" that the number of column inches devoted to a player in the annual *Baseball Register* is probably a good predictor of the player's odds of enshrinement in the National Baseball Hall of Fame (*Baseball Analyst*, Apr. 1984).

freaky floater A *blooper ball*, 1. Wayne Minshew, describing a Phil Niekro pitch (*The Sporting News*, Aug. 28, 1971): "The pitch is off-speed but slower than the normal change-up. It floats to a height of about 10 to 15 feet, but not as high as the blooper [eephus] Rip Sewell threw a few years ago." See also *floater.*

Fred Hutchinson Memorial Award An annual award presented since 1965 to a major-league player for dedication to team, community, and family, for competitive spirit, and for overcoming physical adversity with courage, honor, and dignity. It honors the memory of Fred Hutchinson, Detroit Tigers pitcher and manager of three teams, who died of cancer in 1964. The award was created by friends of Hutchinson and is administered by the Seattle Mariners in conjunction with the *Seattle Post-Intelligencer* and the Fred Hutchinson Cancer Center in Seattle. Voting is done by a panel of baseball writers and broadcasters. A sister award (scholarship) is given to a young medical student involved in cancer research. Syn. *Hutch Award.*

free agency 1. The state of being a free agent. 2. The system under which free agents operate. It allows a player with at least six years of major-league experience to sign with the club of his choice after his current contract expires (players with less than six years of experience are bound to their clubs by the reserve clause). A player has 15 days from the first day after the World Series to file for free agency. Modern free agency came to Major League Baseball as a result of a dispute involving pitchers Andy Messersmith and Dave McNally, who, after the 1975 season, persuaded arbitrator Peter Seitz that the standard major-league players contract gave a club only a one-year option on its player's services, not the perpetual option claimed by the clubs. Rules governing free agency were first formalized in the 1976 Basic Agreement. Ten years later, Murray Chass (*The New York Times*, Dec. 22, 1985) wrote, "After Seitz created free agency, free agency created millionaires, agents and unhappiness among owners, but it also produced unprecedented popularity for baseball."

free agent 1. A professional baseball player who has no contractual obligation to play for one team and is free to negotiate directly with any team, including the one he was playing for when the contract expired. One can also become a free agent when his club releases him or fails to tender or renew his contract. IST USE. 1907. "President [Ban] Johnson of the American League received word from Chairman [Garry] Herrmann of the national commission that 'Sandow' Mertes, the outfielder, whose case was acted upon recently, was an absolute free agent, as all National League clubs had waived claim to him" (*Chicago Tribune*, Apr. 14; Peter Morris). 2. A player with six or more full seasons of major-league experience who is without a contract for the following season. He may play for any team that meets his salary demands. Formerly, if a free agent was not signed by Jan. 8, his former team could not re-sign him until May 1; these deadlines were eliminated in the 2007–2011 Basic Agreement. See also *Type A free agent*; *Type B free agent*; *Type C free agent*; *minor-league free agent*. 3. A player who has been discharged or is unemployed.

This euphemistic application of the term is significantly different from its true meaning.

free-agent draft Syn. of *first-year player draft.*

free-agent reentry draft A *draft* in which veteran players who played out their options and chose to be free agents were selected. Selection in this draft only gave a club the right to negotiate with a player. Thirteen clubs (including the player's original team) could draft a player, thereby limiting the field of competition for a player's services. The draft, used in the 1970s and 1980s, was eliminated in 1985. See also *compensation free-agent draft.*

free-agent year Syn. of *walk year.*

free baseball A Southern term for extra innings.

free check *hist.* Syn. of *base on balls.* IST USE. 1902 (*The Sporting Life*, July 12; Edward J. Nichols).

free foot Syn. of *stepping foot.*

free hitter *hist.* A batter who is successful at taking a hard, full swing with a follow-through; e.g., Pete Browning and Napoleon Lajoie. See also *free swinger,* 1. IST USE. 1895. "Speer is an old player and a natural free hitter" (Walter Camp, *Harper's Weekly,* reprinted in *Stevens Point* [Wisc.] *Gazette,* May 22; Peter Morris).

free-look free agency Syn. of *new-look free agency.*

free pass Syn. of *base on balls.* IST USE. 1897. "Anderson received a free pass to first" (*Brooklyn Eagle,* May 7; Peter Morris).

free passage Syn. of *base on balls.* IST USE. 1917 (*The New York Times,* Oct. 8; Edward J. Nichols).

free ride Syn. of *base on balls.* IST USE. 1908 (*Brooklyn Daily Eagle,* May 24; Edward J. Nichols).

free swinger **1.** A batter who takes a full, powerful swing. "In the history of baseball there have not been more than fifteen or twenty free swingers altogether, and they are the real natural hitters of the game, the men with the eyes nice enough and accurate enough to take a long wallop at the ball" (Christy Mathewson, *Pitching in a Pinch,*

1912). "The free swinger in baseball, the man who takes a healthy cut" (*The Sporting News,* Jan. 5, 1922; Peter Morris). "Like all heavy hitters, [Napoleon Lajoie] takes a free swing at the ball, and a pitcher can never entice him into pulling away from the ball" (*The New York Times,* July 3, 1904). See also *swinger,* 1; *free hitter.* IST USE. 1909 (*Baseball Magazine,* November, p.6; Edward J. Nichols). **2.** An impatient batter who tends to swing at pitches out of the strike zone; one who will swing at almost any ball pitched to him. Free swingers seldom draw walks. "[Benito Santiago] is renowned for his ability to swing at any pitch within a time zone at home plate, a living definition of the term 'free-swinger'" (Buster Olney, *The Baltimore Sun,* Oct. 12, 1995). See also *swinger,* 2.

free ticket Syn. of *base on balls.* IST USE. 1896. "[Fred] Tenney was given a free ticket to first by King" (*The Boston Globe,* July 2; Peter Morris). USAGE NOTE. A free ticket is seldom simply thrown or delivered but issued: "[Wade] Boggs was issued a free ticket in the second inning" (*The Boston Globe,* Aug. 10, 1986).

free transit Syn. of *base on balls.* IST USE. 1917 (*The New York Times,* Oct. 7; Edward J. Nichols).

free transportation **1.** Syn. of *base on balls.* IST USE. 1901. "In the sixth and seventh, the first man up got free transportation" (*Brooklyn Eagle,* July 24; Peter Morris). **2.** An awarded base given to a batter who has been hit by a pitched ball.

free trip Syn. of *base on balls.*

Freeway Series A series of interleague games between the Los Angeles Dodgers and the Los Angeles Angels of Anaheim.

freeze **1.** For a pitcher to throw a strike on a pitch the batter did not expect. "[Jim Bibby] froze him with a looping curve ball on the outside corner of the plate" (*Tampa Tribune,* Nov. 2, 1989). **2.** For a batter to take a pitch he did not expect and simply stared at. "[Livan Hernandez] struck out . . . John Olerud . . . who froze on a curve" (*The Baltimore Sun,* March 11, 1996). **3.** For a fielder to fail to attempt to make a throw or move to complete a play. "[Ron Coomer] fielded the ball cleanly, but froze without throwing to first" (*Milwaukee Journal Sentinel*, July 7, 2001; Robert F. Perkins). **4.** *hist.* For a fielder to field a batted ball unerringly or with assurance. IST USE. 1868 (*New York Herald*, Aug. 14; Edward J. Nichols). **5.** To cause a baserunner to hold his lead; e.g., "Jones froze the runner with his quick move to first." **6.** To dampen a ball's life by keeping it in a freezer or refrigerator in an attempt to help the pitcher. The practice and the belief that a warm ball goes farther than a cold one goes back many years. Frederick G. Lieb (*The Pittsburgh Pirates*, 1948; Charles D. Poe) wrote, "There used to be an icebox in the Pittsburgh Club's offices, and Connie [Mack] conceived the idea of stuffing boxes of baseballs into the icebox, and freezing them overnight. The practice supposedly froze the life out of baseballs." Roy Campanella (*It's Good to Be Alive*, 1959, pp.82–83; Charles D. Poe) wrote, "Freezing the balls was supposed to deaden them and help to keep those heavy-hitting Homestead Grays down to size. It never stopped Josh [Gibson]."

freight delivery *hist.* Slow pitching. IST USE. 1892 (*Chicago Herald*, May 4; Edward J. Nichols).

freight-train base ball *hist.* Throwing baseballs to each other while atop a moving freight train. *The Boston Globe* (June 7, 1886, reprinted from *Chicago Herald*; Peter Morris) carried the following story: "Freight train base ball. . . . It's great fun, too. We don't do any batting, but we're great on fielding. The head brakeman stands on the front car, the rear brakeman in the middle of the train, and the conductor gets aboard the caboose. The we play pitch, with the fireman for referee. There ain't many errors . . . An error means a lost ball, and the man that lets it get away from him has to buy a new one. . . . The craze has run so high that I'll bet there ain't a dozen cars running out of Chicago that don't carry a stack of base balls along in their caboose. . . . If you want fun, and want to have the blood run pretty lively in your veins, just take a hand in a game on top of a freight train going twenty to twenty-five miles an hour."

French baseball A schoolyard game played

in Toronto with four or five players to a side in which one side of the field is not in play and the bases are run backward in reverse order (normal third base becomes first base). As explained by David McDonald (personal communication, Jan. 24, 2002), since most of the players bat right-handed, any ball hit to right field is an automatic out. The offensive team provides the pitcher. Why "French"? "I guess, to us growing up in Toronto, it was different but in a familiarly different way," concludes McDonald.

fresh leaguer *hist.* A "new-comer" to the American Association (1882–1891) (*The Sporting Life*, Jan. 14, 1885; Barry Popik). Compare *old leaguer*, 1.

Frick Award Short for *Ford C. Frick Award*.

Friday starter The best starting pitcher on a college team. College marquee games usually take place on Fridays and rotations are arranged around that day. "[Univ. of Mississippi pitcher Pete Montrenes is] a Friday starter with something to prove in his pressure-filled junior year, his draft year" (John Manuel, *Baseball America*, March 19–Apr. 1, 2001; Peter Morris).

friendly confines A home ballpark; specif., the particularly cozy quarters of *Wrigley Field*, the home ballpark of the Chicago Cubs. The term was first used in Chicago by Cubs announcer Jack Brickhouse in the early 1950s, but the term had been applied earlier to other ballparks, such as Sportsman's Park in St. Louis, Fenway Park in Boston, Yankee Stadium in New York, and Wrigley Field in Los Angeles. The Cubs trademarked the phrase "The Friendly Confines" in 1988, but abandoned the mark a year later. IST USE. 1922. "It was only the second victory for the Brooklyn players since leaving the friendly confines of Ebbets Field some ten days ago" (*The New York Times*, May 19).

friendly match *hist.* A game in early baseball not designated as a *match game*; e.g., a practice game or an exhibition game. "A friendly match was played on the 28th ult." (*Spirit of the Times*, July 7, 1855; Peter Morris).

fringe player A player who has just enough ability to get by; a mediocre player who soon will be returned to the minor leagues.

fringe prospect A marginal minor-league player; one who is on the borderline of being promoted to the major leagues. "The [White Sox] pitching coaches informed [Chad Bradford] that he'd been officially classified as a 'fringe prospect.' [Bradford recalled,] 'They said, "If you have a good season, you can stay around. If not, you're on your way out."'" (Michael Lewis (*Moneyball*, 2003).

Frisbee curve A slider that is reminiscent of the distinctive sideways and downward slide at the end of a typical toss with a Frisbee; also, a slow curveball. Named for the trademark for a plastic concave disk sailed between two or more players and thrown with a flick of the wrist.

frisk *hist.* To win (*The Sporting Life*, Nov. 29, 1913).

frock A woman's baseball uniform in the All-American Girls Professional Baseball League.

front-and-backer *hist.* A "perfect strike through the plate, which was one of Kid Gleason's favorite expressions" (Herbert Simons, *Baseball Magazine*, 1943).

front-door Said of a cut fastball or slider that comes at the batter's rib cage, then breaks late over the inside corner of the plate at the batter's hands. The pitch is effective against aggressive dive hitters.

front end of the rotation Syn. of *front of the rotation*.

front foot The batter's foot nearest the pitcher. Compare *back foot*.

front-foot hitter A hitter who swings with his weight on his front foot.

front-footing The practice of a batter transferring his weight to the front foot, with the back foot nearly off the ground. It commits the batter to swing sooner, thereby decreasing his power, producing ground balls, and (against curveballs) resulting in strikeouts.

front office The business and financial side of a baseball club; the realm of a club's general manager and his staff. The front office is responsible for obtaining, contracting for, and trading players. "More than 250 baseball executives gathered here today for a unique five day 'school' on front office matters" (*San Francisco Call-Bulletin*, Jan. 19, 1948; Peter Tamony). IST USE. 1936. "Frequently you hear of ball clubs having difficulties because the 'front office' interferes too much with the players and managers trying to run their end" (*Charlotte Observer*, July 23; Peter Morris). ETYMOLOGY. The term has a long history as an underworld term for police headquarters, an interrogation room, or the warden's office in a prison.

front of the rotation The position in a starting rotation occupied by the first and second pitchers. "There's been no clear No. 1 front-of-the-rotation kind of guy [on the market]" (Mike Flanagan, quoted in *The Baltimore Sun*, Dec. 28, 2004). Compare *middle of the rotation*; *back of the rotation*; *top of the rotation*. Syn. *front end of the rotation*.

front-runner 1. An individual who only favors a successful team. "He's no front runner; he was here when they were struggling" (John Lowenstein on Boston Red Sox fan and once Speaker of the House Thomas P. "Tip" O'Neill, Home Team Sports telecast, Sept. 10, 1986). "I hate front-runners, people who are with you when you're up and against you when you're down" (Ted Williams, *My Turn at Bat*, 1969). 2. A player who only performs well when his team is winning.

frostie [softball term] A pitch in slow pitch softball that is above 12 feet in arc. The term alludes facetiously to the frost that appears at higher altitudes.

frozen 1. Said of a minor-league player whose

Front office. Rickwood Field, Birmingham, Alabama. Business office at bottom left. *Historic American Buildings Survey, Library of Congress*

playing ability is such that there is very little hope he will ever be called up to the major leagues. **2.** Said of a major-league player whose playing ability is such that he can play only one position; e.g., "Smith was frozen at first base by his lack of throwing ability." **3.** Said of a batter who did not swing because the pitcher threw a pitch that the batter did not expect. "[Derek] Jeter was frozen on a called strike three" (*The Baltimore Sun*, Oct. 26, 2003). **4.** Said of a baserunner held in place by the actions of the pitcher.

frozen arm The throwing arm of a pitcher who is unable to throw the ball. "I'd heard old pitchers talk about a 'frozen arm,' but . . . I'd never known what they meant. I literally couldn't throw the ball to the plate" (David Cone, quoted in Roger Angell, *A Pitcher's Story*, 2001, p.49).

frozen rope A hard-hit *line drive*, so called because of the rigid, low, and straight path it takes, with hardly an arc, seemingly to defy gravity. "You can almost see the icicles dripping off it," wrote Leonard Shecter in defining the term (*Baseball Digest*, June 1963). Because it is so much hyperbole, the image is often embellished with something on the order of broadcaster Red Rush's "you could hang a week's wash on it and not have to worry." See also *rope*, 1; *hemp*; *clothesline*. EXTENDED USE. A term used in military intelligence for a very important message that has been intercepted by a third party. "A 'frozen rope' was the current NSA [National Security Agency] nickname for a very important signal intercept" (Tom Clancy, *Clear and Present Danger*, 1989).

fudge An informal pick-up game played by a few players who periodically switch positions. "Sometimes enough boys were present to permit a game of what they called 'fudge,' each taking his turn at fielding, playing first base, pitching, catching and batting" (Christy Mathewson, *Pitcher Pollock*, 1914; David Shulman).

full count Three balls and two strikes on a batter. Syn. *long count*; *three-two count*. IST USE. 1937 (Tom Manning, NBC Radio World Series broadcast, Oct. 6; Edward J. Nichols). ETYMOLOGY. A boxing term for when a

downed pugilist takes the maximum count of ten before standing up.

full gorilla Aggressively, or with the utmost force. "He was always the type of pitcher who went full-gorilla all the time. . . . He was always aggressive and went right after us" (*Houston Chronicle*, July 4, 1994; Grant Barrett): "[Jarrod Washburn] threw off a bullpen mound and said he felt only slight discomfort while going 'full gorilla'" (Elliott Teaford, *Daily Breeze* [Torrance, Calif.], Aug. 5, 2005; Grant Barrett).

full house Syn. of *bases loaded*. IST USE. 1909. "A pass to [George] Browne made a full house" (*The Washington Post*, May 17; Peter Morris). ETYMOLOGY. A clear borrowing from the game of poker.

full right A left-handed catcher's glove (Paul Gallico, *The Washington Post*, March 20, 1935).

full route All of the game; nine innings (or more in the event of an extra-inning game). A pitcher who has gone the "full route" has pitched a complete game. IST USE. 1910. "Eight days before the date for opening the season the manager sends one pitcher 'the full route'—nine innings—and studies carefully the condition of the man" (John J. Evers and Hugh S. Fullerton, *Touching Second: The Science of Baseball*; Peter Morris).

full-season A Syn. of *low Single A*.

full Seitz Free agency after a one-year option on a player's services as ruled by arbitrator Peter Seitz, whose Dec. 1975 decision stated that major-league clubs did not have a perpetual option. However, the 1976 Basic Agreement granted a club full control over a player for six major-league seasons.

full swing **1.** A swing at a pitch with the full reach or extension of the batter's arms. **2.** Syn. of *full windup*. "By practicing I got so I could shoot the ball faster to first base with wrist and forearm than I could pitch it to the plate with a full swing" (Matt Kilroy, quoted in John J. Evers and Hugh S. Fullerton, *Touching Second: The Science of Baseball*, 1910; Peter Morris).

full windup A complete, legal delivery that begins with the pitcher swinging his arms above his head as he steps back with one foot. It is usually taken when the bases are empty or, often, when there is a runner on third base only. A full windup takes more time and allows baserunners to take longer leads. Syn. *full swing.* IST USE. 1914. "Sallee was so sore he kind o' forgot himself and took pretty near his full wind-up pitchin' to Tommy" (Ring W. Lardner, "My Roomy," *The Saturday Evening Post*, May 9; Peter Morris).

fumble **1.** *v.* To make an error. IST USE. 1870. "[Al] Pratt got his first and [Jim] White third on a grounder fumbled over by [Charley] Hodes" (*Chicago Tribune*, June 4; Peter Morris). **2.** *n.* An error. IST USE. 1876. "Gillian went to bat and got first by a fumble from Gillespie" (*Jackson* [Mich.] *Weekly Citizen*, June 27; Peter Morris).

fundamentals The basic elements of winning baseball, such as throwing to the right base, moving runners up, and executing rundowns, cutoff plays, and pickoff plays. Fundamentals may be boring, but they win games. Bill Starr (*Clearing the Bases*, 1989, p.100) amplifies: "When a manager talks about fundamentals, he is generally talking about three aspects of baseball: the hit and run; hitting a ground ball behind a runner on second base with no one out, so as to advance the runner to third; and for outfielders, to hit the cutoff man on throws to the plate or third base." A baseball fundamental is "any baseball act that is so simple that the man in the stands thinks, 'I could do that. Why can't those big leaguers?'" (Ken Singleton, quoted in Thomas Boswell, *How Life Imitates the World Series*, 1982, p.60). Compare *tools,* 1.

fungo **1.** *n.* A fly ball hit to a player during fielding practice in which the batter (often a coach) tosses the ball into the air and hits it as it descends with a long and narrow bat. "Then him and Carey was together in left field, catchin' fungoes" (Ring W. Lardner, *Saturday Evening Post*, July 16, 1915). Plural "fungoes." **2.** *n.* A training exercise in which fungoes are hit to fielders. The primary purpose is to give fielders practice in catching fly balls. **3.** *n.* A base hit in which the ball is hit softly but enables the batter to reach first base safely because of where it is hit; a scratch hit.

"The only time in the game when a batter can count with some show of reason of making a sacrifice hit—a fungo over the infielders' heads" (*Perry* [Iowa] *Chief*, Sept. 6, 1889; *OED*). "[Cap Anson] scored on Earle's 'fungo' single to right field" (*The World* [New York], July 13, 1890; Gerald L. Cohen). See also *fungo hit.* **4.** *v.* To hit a fungo during fielding practice or during a game. "[Nick] Levya fungoes a grounder to the right of the mound" (*St. Petersburg Times*, Feb. 25, 1987). See also *fungo bat,* 2. **5.** *n.* Syn. of *fungo bat,* 1. "You couldn't have hit a ball through there with a fungo" (Richard Ford, *Inside Sports*, July 31, 1981). **6.** *n.* A playground game in which a batter hits fungoes and the first fielder to catch a given number of fly balls becomes the batter (Stewart Culin, *American Folk-Lore*, 1891, p.232). **7.** *n.* A pre- or postgame hitting contest between individuals staged as an exhibition (as part of a "field day," along with contests for ball throwing for distance and for bunting and running). **8.** *n.* A skinny player on the opposing team, who might elicit the question, "Who dressed the fungo?" (*Kalamazoo* [Mich.] *Gazette*, July 11, 2004).

IST USE. 1867. "Fungoes.—A preliminary practice game in which one player takes the bat and tossing the ball up hits it as it falls, and if the ball is caught in the field on the fly, the player catching it takes the bat. It is useless as practice in batting, but good for taking fly balls" (Henry Chadwick, *Base Ball Player's Book of Reference*, p.138). David Shulman was able to date the use of "fungo" back to *The Sporting Life* (March 3, 1886): "While watching some of our freshmen practicing 'fungo' batting the other afternoon it occurred to me that it was about the worst kind of practice a batsman could imagine in training his eye in batting." Gerald L. Cohen found the earliest use of "fungo" as a verb (*The World* [New York], July 19, 1889): "Outside of the first inning the visitors fanned and fungoed in a delirious way."

ETYMOLOGY. The etymology of "fungo" is generally regarded as unknown (as labeled in the *Merriam-Webster Collegiate* and the *American Heritage* dictionaries) or uncertain (as labeled in the *Oxford English Dictionary,* which adds that it may be from the Scots "fung," to pitch, toss, fling). John Ciardi (*Good Words to You,* 1987) wrote, "*Fungo* in baseball has never been explained. I have seen efforts to derive it from L[atin] *fungo,* I do, I undertake to discharge an obligation. Having noted the suggestion, I undertake to believe the form remains unexplained." This allows for plenty of good theories, and a certain amount of lexical frustration.

There are five theories (six if Ciardi's suggestion is included), summarized below:

1. "The 'Fun/Go' Theory." David Shulman (*American Speech,* Feb. 1937) guessed that "fungo" may be explained through the elements of a compound word, "fun" and "go." Bill Bryson Sr. (quoted in *The Sporting News,* May 23, 1981) reported that the chant, "One goes, two goes" etc., comes from a street game in which a player catching a certain number of fly balls was qualified to replace the batter. Henry Miller (cited in a letter to *The Sunday Times* [London], July 17, 1994) noted that 1916 he hit a ball 438 feet and 2 inches using a fungo bat, so called because it was the bat for having a "fun" go rather than a "serious" go. A variation on this theory was discussed by Patrick Ercolano (*Fungoes, Floaters and Fork Balls,* 1987, p.75): "Still others believe that the word has its derivation in a rhyme recited during early versions of fungo, a rhyme consisting of the words 'run and go.'" Hy Turkin (*The 1955 Baseball Almanac,* 1955, p.207) suggested "an old game in which the man using this style of hitting would yell, 'One go, two goes, fun goes.'" Still another variation on this theory was discussed by William Safire (*What's the Good Word?,* 1982), who noted no fewer than 13 theories (genuine and tongue-in-cheek) that were originally sent to him in response to a query in his *New York Times* language column. A letter from Frederick L. Smith (Short Hills, N.J.) claimed that in a substantial amount of English literature, especially some humorous pieces by P.G. Wodehouse, there is reference to "the warm-up for cricket matches involving 'fun goes,' i.e., practice strokes before the game began

in earnest. I have always taken it as a fact of life that 'fungo' represents a shortening of this English usage."

2. "The Fungible Theory." As stated by Zander Hollander (*Baseball Lingo,* 1967): "The word 'fungible' means something that can be substituted for another and it is thought that in baseball the thin fungo stick got its name because it replaces the conventional bat."

3. "The Fungus Theory." A letter published in *The New York Times* (Apr. 11, 1936) and signed M.R.M. argued that the term does not come from the manner of hitting the ball but rather asked, "Would it not be plausible to state that the word 'fungo,' instead is applied to the bat itself, one of such resiliency that it causes the ball to travel further than does the ordinary bat; in other words, a bat of spongier, softer wood? Hence fungus, fungeous, fungus." According to a note made by Peter Tamony, the matter was discussed on KLX radio in San Francisco on Apr. 10, 1956. Bert Dunne, radio-TV director of the San Francisco Seals and a student of baseball terminology, attributed the term to an unnamed Princeton professor who claimed the bat hitting the ball sounded like fungus wood. Dunne added that the early fungo bats were regular bats that had been split in two and then bound with tape. Tamony himself had written (*American Speech,* Oct. 1937, p.243) that the word "refers to the lightness of the instrument." Several others believed the term came from the feel rather than the sound of fungus; e.g., Joseph McBride (*High and Inside,* 1980, p.53) explained that "the bats, with very narrow handles and extra-thick heads, were so soft that they seemed to be made of fungus"; and Graham Masterton (letter published in *The Sunday Times* [London], July 17, 1994) noted that "the wood used to make . . . [fungo] bats was so soft that it felt like fungus." Another fungus variation appeared in the Safire collection of letters (see above): Stephen V. Fulkerson (Santa Paula, Calif.) wrote that he first heard the term in the early 1930s as a synonym for "nongenuine" or "not bona fide," such as a fungo that is not a

real fly ball. He related this to fungus in the sense that rural people regard a fungus as lacking the character of a real plant, which puts its roots in the ground.

4. "The Fang-en Theory." Gerald L. Cohen (*Studies in Slang*, Part 2, 1989) wrote, "Perhaps its origin is to be sought in German *fang-en* 'to catch'; we now think of fungoing a ball as hitting it, but the early quotes . . . show clearly that the emphasis of a fungo game was on the ball's being caught." Cohen cited the following from *The World* (New York) (Oct. 26, 1889): "[John Montgomery] Ward's fungo was simply poussecafé for [Pop] Corkhill, and he swallowed it smoothly."

5. "The Fung Theory." Another letter in the Safire collection (see above) is from Joan H. Hall, associate editor for the *Dictionary of American Regional English*. She asserted, in accordance with the *Oxford English Dictionary*, that it is from a Scottish verb, "fung": "According to *The Scottish National Dictionary*, the verb 'fung,' meaning 'to pitch, toss, fling,' was in use in Aberdeen as early as 1804: 'Ye witches, warlocks, fairies, fien's! Daft fungin 'fiery pears an' stanes.'" She noted that the connection with ball playing is that the ball is flung into the air before it is hit and that the "-o" ending is common in other games (bingo, beano, bunco, and keno).

EXTENDED USE. 1. The act of striking or clubbing with a bat or stick. "I'm sure that if most Americans should walk through the crowded wards [of wounded] they would grab baseball bats and hit a few fungoes the next time the Communists assemble in Union Square" (Jimmy Cannon, on a Communist rally in New York, quoted in *Time* magazine, Aug. 28, 1950; Peter Tamony). 2. An estimate of distance. "Mesa, Arizona, the new spring training quarters of the Chicago Cubs, is only a short fungo drive from Phoenix" (Milton Richman, *Baseball Magazine*, March 1952).

fungo bat 1. *n.* A bat used for pregame fielding practice; a bat designed to hit fungoes. It is usually longer, lighter in weight, and thinner than a regular bat, and often with an enlarged end. "A fungo bat looks to be a cross between a baseball bat and a broomstick" (David Allison, *Country Journal*, June 1978, p.30). Syn. *fungo*, 5; *fungo stick.* 2. *v.* To hit a fly ball with a fungo bat. See also *fungo*, 4. IST USE. 1915. "He used to come out sometimes on Saturdays and fungo bat for the players" (Burt L. Standish, *Covering the Look-In Corner*, p.158; David Shulman).

fungo bazooka A mechanical device that uses air pressure to propel fly balls and line drives for fielding practice. George Plimpton (in Ron Fimrite, ed., *Birth of a Fan*, 1993, p.164) would have banished such a machine: "It is unthinkable aesthetically to have a snout-nosed machine, trailing a long electric cord, wheeled out to the fungo circle to perform this time-honored function [hitting fungoes]."

fungo circle One of two circular patches of dirt located on either side of home plate in foul territory. They are used by fungo batters and average about seven feet in diameter.

fungo hit *hist.* A high fly ball or pop fly; a ball that appears to have been hit with a fungo bat. "Of the twenty-four put outs credited to Cincinnati, all but three were on flies, or fungo hits" (*Brooklyn Eagle*, June 6, 1896; Peter Morris). See also *fungo*, 3. IST USE. 1889. "In the sixth inning fungo hits to the outfield disposed of the first two batsmen" (*Brooklyn Eagle*, Sept. 8; Peter Morris).

fungo hitter A player or coach known to be skilled at hitting fungoes. "Arthur Neff [Nehf], the pitcher, is the longest fungo hitter of the crowd" (*The New York Times*, March 11, 1920; OED). Other famous fungo hitters include Kid Gleason, Hank Gowdy, Arthur Fletcher, Chuck Dressen, and Jimmy Reese.

fungo hitting The act or practice of hitting fungoes. "Walter Johnson broke the world's record for fungo hitting . . . driving the ball high in the air a distance of 481 feet 8 inches" (*San Francisco Bulletin*, March 28, 1913; Gerald L. Cohen). IST USE. 1871. "This is not skillful batting—it is little else than 'fungo' hitting" (*Brooklyn Eagle*, May 31; Peter Morris). USAGE NOTE. The term was closely associated with Henry Chadwick, who believed that fungo hitting was "death" to good batting. "The weakest batting is shown when the batsman indulges in fungo hitting" (Henry Chadwick, *Technical Terms of Baseball*, 1897, p.16; David Shulman).

fungo stick Syn. of *fungo bat*, 1. "It is a fungo stick, in reality, but when Hub is swinging it . . . it looks more like a redwood tree" (*The Washington Post*, July 14, 1914; *OED*).

furlough *hist.* Syn. of *base on balls*. ETYMOLOGY. Leave of absence traditionally as applied to a member of the armed forces but which has been extended to general use, including when prisoners are given time off for good behavior. The term has been attested to in English since 1625 (*OED*) and derives from the German "verlof" for "leave." It appears to have entered baseball during World War II by players who had been in the armed forces. Chester L. Smith (*Baseball Digest*, May 1946) included the term in his article entitled "Diamond Slang Goes G.I."

fush ball Syn. of *foshball*. 1ST USE. 1983. "[Mike] Boddicker calls it a fork ball, but since he pushes it from between his fingers with a sidespin that produces a screwball, his pitching coach, Ray Miller, has named it the 'fush ball'" (Thomas Boswell, *The Washington Post*, July 17, 1983). ETYMOLOGY. A blend of "fork" plus "push."

futility player A player who plays many positions, none of them well. The term was coined by Bill James (*Baseball Abstract*, 1983).

future Hall of Famer An active player whose career statistics and accomplishments in the game all but assure his being voted into the National Baseball Hall of Fame. "Future Hall of Famer Reggie Jackson returned to play for the Oakland Athletics" (*USA Today*, Apr. 17, 1987).

Futures Game An annual all-star game of top minor-league prospects from all classifications, held at a major-league park since 1999. Conceived by Executive Vice President of Baseball Jimmie Lee Solomon, the Futures Game pits American-born players versus foreign-born players. It is scheduled as part of the major-leagues' All-Star Game festivities.

fuzzy concrete Artificial turf. The term is used by players who prefer real grass. "Is it still necessary to cover the playing fields with what has been less than affectionately called 'fuzzy concrete'?" (Rick Lawes, *USA Today Baseball Weekly*, July 19–25, 1991).

FW Abbrev. for *fielding wins*.

G

G Abbrev. for game, 3.

gab-circuit Off-season baseball talk (chatter, conjecture, speechifying, etc.) beloved of fans. See also *hot stove league*.

gaijin Foreign players in the Japanese professional baseball leagues. Teams are allowed to have up to four gaijin on the roster (two position players and two pitchers). ETYMOLOGY. Japanese for "outsiders."

game **1.** A contest between two teams that is the basic unit of baseball competition. A game usually consists of either eight-and-a-half or nine innings (when the home team is ahead after eight-and-a-half innings have been played, the last half inning is not played). Games are also deemed complete if play is suspended for rain or any other reason after the team that is losing has been at bat at least five times. A game is won by the team with the most runs, which means that extra innings must be played if the two teams are tied at the end of the ninth inning. See also *ball game*, 1. USAGE NOTE. In recent years it has become customary in both the electronic and print media to refer to games in the Division Series, the League Championship Series, and the World Series as Game 1, Game 2, etc. When used in this context, the word "game" is always capitalized. **2.** A unit of measurement used to determine a team's exact position in the standings. This unit is expressed in terms of full and half games out of first place or *games behind*. See also *length*. **3.** A unit of measurement used to determine the extent of participation by a player or a team; e.g., Pete Rose played in 3,562 games, more than any other player in major-league history. Abbrev. *G*. **4.** The call made by the umpire to signify the end of a contest. **5.** The sport and business of baseball itself. "Committee to Draft a Code of Laws on the Game of Base Ball" (*The New York Herald*, Jan. 23, 1857). **6.** The overall baseball ability of an individual player. Mike Hargrove, discussing Kenny Lofton (quoted in *The Baltimore Sun*, Apr. 16, 2002): "When Kenny's on his game, he's as good as there is. . . . Kenny's game is using the whole field, getting on base, stealing and scoring runs."

game ball **1.** A ball that has actually been in play as opposed to a souvenir ball; specif., the first ball used in a game. **2.** The ball in play at the end of a game, given to the most deserving player, often the pitcher.

game-caller Syn. of *catcher*, 1.

game-day staff The employees of a baseball club who work only on days when a home game is scheduled, as opposed to the full-time employees; e.g., ushers, security personnel, food vendors, and mascots.

game-ender Syn. of *closer*, 1.

game face The look or manner that indicates the high level of concentration of an athlete before and during competition. The term implies more than an expression; it's also a focus or frame of mind, a mental preparation for the game, and a physical sense. New York Yankees manager Joe Torre, commenting on pitcher Roger Clemens (*The Baltimore Sun*, July 3, 2000): "You could just see he was stalking and just seemed very focused. He had his game face on and it just looked like he was anxious to get out there." Pitcher Dave Stewart used his game face to intimidate batters: "He stares at batters with a glare that just dares them to hit his pitch" (Hal Bodley, *USA Today*, Oct. 17, 1990). ETYMOLOGY. The

Game face. Beals Becker, New York Giants, 1905. The face came first, the term came later. During his career Becker gained a reputation for being sensitive to fan criticism and played markedly better on the road than at home. *George Grantham Bain Collection, Library of Congress*

term first appeared in football: "It's a different Gale Sayers when the game is near ... then he puts on his game face" (*The Washington Post*, Oct. 31, 1965).

game of inches Euphemism for the game of baseball because there are so many close plays decided by inches or fractions thereof. This time-honored phrase encompasses several givens about the game; for example, a matter of inches often determines whether a batter-runner is safe or out at first base, a batted ball is either fair or foul, a pitch is either a ball or a strike, or a player stealing a base is safe or out. "Baseball is a game of inches" (Branch Rickey, *Quote* magazine, July 31, 1966). "Baseball is, after all, a game of inches and even fractions" (Shirley Povich, *The Washington Post*, Oct. 21, 1986). IST USE. 1957. "It was a game of inches in many cases. For instance, Jim Lemon, who hit his sixth homer of the spring in the sixth, narrowly missed another in the ninth with two on. That would have won the game" (Bob Addie, *The Washington Post*, Apr. 1). EXTENDED USE. The term has been applied to other sports where success is measured precisely. Tennes-

see Titans cornerback DeRon Jenkins, explaining why the receiver he was covering was able to catch a pass (*The Baltimore Sun*, Oct. 8, 2001): "Half a step, that's all it was. I was there, but when I turned and looked for the ball, I stumbled a little bit. It's a game of inches, and that's all that it was." In golf: "As they say, it's a game of inches. . . . On the 120-yard, par 3 fifth hole, the pro [John Ruedi] . . . dropped his tee shot just 2½ inches from the cage" (*The Washington Post*, March 4, 1960).

Game of the Week A regular-season baseball game selected to be televised nationally each week, traditionally on Saturday afternoons, and aired by ABC (1953–1954), CBS (1955–1965, 1990–1992), and NBC (1966–1989). The game usually depicted league leaders, or large-market franchises that could draw the largest audience. It was a fixture until 1992 when irregular scheduling killed the ratings. "The other morning, I was telling some of our young players here how I used to wait all week for Saturday when I was a kid, to watch the old 'Game of the Week' on television. They couldn't get over that: '*One game*—get out of here!' They couldn't believe it" (Oakland A's pitcher Ron Darling, quoted by Roger Angell, *The New Yorker*, May 3, 1993).

game plan Pregame preparation and study by a player (esp. a pitcher) or a team regarding their approach to playing a specific game. The idea is to adhere to the plan by executing it. "He's the most prepared pitcher I've ever played with. Nobody has a game plan and then executes it as well as Curt [Schilling] does" (Mark Grace, quoted in *Sports Illustrated*, Oct. 22, 2001). "I thought our game plan was excellent. We wanted to make him throw a lot of pitches and get him out of the game early" (Philadelphia Phillies manager Jim Fregosi, quoted in *The Baltimore Sun*, Oct. 17, 1993). "[Ichiro Suzuki is] able to go to the plate with the same game plan against all types of pitchers. Most guys have a game plan for a hard thrower: Be quick. A game plan for a guy with a great change or breaking ball: Wait on the ball. This guy never has to alter his approach" (Desi Relaford, quoted in *ESPN The Magazine*, May 27, 2002).

EXTENDED USE. A planned approach in other endeavors. "It's important that you remain focused on your game plan. Good financial plans define not only your goals, but also an acceptable level of risk" (letter to investors, Pioneer Investment Management, Apr. 2001).

gamer **1.** A player who approaches the game with tenacity and spirit, thrives in pressure situations, and continues to play even when hurt; a competitor, willing to do whatever it takes to win; a player who doesn't make excuses. The term is a compliment, most esp. when it comes from another player. "In dugouts, one accolade ranks higher than all others: 'He's a gamer.' . . . Nobody in recent times has been summarized more often with that one phrase—'he's a gamer'—than George Brett" (Thomas Boswell, quoted in Walter Iooss Jr. and Thomas Boswell, *Diamond Dreams*, 1995). "I hope people will remember me as a gamer—a true compliment in my mind. A gamer comes to the ballpark ready to meet the challenges of the day, no matter how difficult they are" (Cal Ripken Jr., quoted in *Sports Illustrated*, Oct. 20, 2003). ETYMOLOGY. From the idea of a player who is "game." EXTENDED USE. Anyone who is willing to carry on in the face of adversity. **2.** A player who delivers in big games; a *clutch hitter*. **3.** *hist.* Any player in a game. **4.** A favorite glove; one's regular glove used in a game. "Most major leaguers work with at least three gloves—a workhorse for practice, a backup for emergencies and the prized 'gamer,' which is so valued that on team flights most players keep them in their carry-on bags rather than stow them with team equipment" (Bruce Selcraig, *Baseball America*, May 28–June 10, 2001). **5.** A favorite bat. Most players are averse to lending their gamer to a teammate. **6.** The winning run. "Reggie Jackson singled home the gamer" (*New York Post*, Aug. 21, 1980; David Shulman).

-gamer A suffix indicating a series of games. "Milwaukee lost its eighth straight game, its longest losing streak since an 11-gamer last July" (*The Baltimore Sun*, July 23, 2002).

game-saving Said of an outstanding fielding play that allows a lead to be maintained or prevents a team from giving up the winning run.

games back Syn. of *games behind*.

games behind The number of games by which a team in a division or league is out of first place or behind any given team in the standings. It is expressed as a combination of whole and half numbers, with each victory or loss counting as a half of a game. To compute the number of games a team is ahead or behind, add the difference in the number of wins and the difference in the number of losses and divide by 2. Another way to view games behind is the number of times a trailing team would have to defeat a leading team to have the same won-lost difference in the standings. The term is usually used in comparison to the first-place team, but can be used to compare any two teams in the same division. See also *game*, 2; *half game*. Abbrev. *GB*, 1. Syn. *games back*.

game score An informal statistic for quantifying a starting pitcher's performance in a given game. It is calibrated so that a score of 50 indicates an average performance, a score of 90 represents an outstanding performance, and a score under 10 denotes a disastrous outing. The statistic was proposed by Bill James in his *Baseball Abstract* (1988): start with 50 points, add 1 point for each out recorded (so 3 points for every complete inning pitched), add 2 points for each inning completed after the fourth, add 1 point for each strikeout, subtract 2 points for each hit allowed, subtract 4 points for each earned run allowed, subtract 2 points for each unearned run allowed, and subtract 1 point for each walk. Park factor and the pitcher's batting statistics are not counted. The top game score ever for a nine-inning game was Chicago Cubs pitcher Kerry Wood's 105 for his performance (one hit, no walks, 20 strikeouts) against the Houston Astros on May 6, 1998. See also *cheap win*; *tough loss*. Abbrev. *GS*.

Game 7 The last and deciding game of a best-of-seven League Championship Series or World Series. Luis Gonzalez, whose bloop single off New York Yankees relief pitcher Mariano Rivera won the 2001 World Series for the Arizona Diamondbacks (quoted in *Sports Illustrated*, May 24, 2004): "I wish I could bottle that Game 7 feeling. Because there's nothing like it." Tim Povtak (*Orlando*

Sentinel, June 23, 2005): "When it comes to drama, tension and anticipation, Game 7 is the most fitting way to crown a champion, separating the best from the very best, and doing it all under a winner-take-all format. It's the purest thing in sports." EXTENDED USE. The ultimate, do-or-die, conclusive performance. Figure skating coach Doug Leigh (quoted in *The Baltimore Sun*, Feb. 17, 1994): "My guy [Elvis Stojko] skates 'em out all the time. We're getting ready for Game 7."

games finished The number of games in which a relief pitcher was the last pitcher. Abbrev. *GF*.

game situation The "turning point" in a game (Keith Hernandez, *Pure Baseball*, 1994, p.97).

Game 6 The sixth game of a best-of-seven League Championship Series or World Series. Steve Rushin (*Sports Illustrated*, March 20, 2006): "I once asked [Kirby] Puckett to name the single thing he'd be remembered for, and he instantly answered, 'Game 6,'" referring to his 11th-inning home run on Oct. 26 to propel the Minnesota Twins over the Atlanta Braves, 4–3, in the 1991 World Series, won by the Twins. The term is often associated with the Boston Red Sox, who have been involved in two classic Game 6's: 1) Carlton Fisk's dramatic 12th-inning home run on Oct. 21 to defeat the Cincinnati Reds 7–6 in the 1975 World Series; and 2) the New York Mets 6–5 victory on Oct. 25 when a wild pitch by Bob Stanley and an error by first baseman Bill Buckner (a ground ball rolled through his legs) extended the 1986 World Series to a seventh game, won by the Mets. EXTENDED USE. Esp. in New England, a mention of Game 6 (e.g., "It's Game 6 all over again") is a reference to a run of bad luck.

games started The number of games in which a given pitcher was the starter. Abbrev. *GS*.

game time 1. The time of day that a game is scheduled to begin. 2. Syn. of *time of game*.

game winner 1. The pitcher credited with winning a game. 2. The run that results in a victory.

game-winning RBI The run batted in that gives the winning team the lead it never relin-quishes. The game-winning RBI was an officially kept statistic from 1980 to 1988, and it appeared in the box scores of games. It was dropped because it proved to be meaningless in lopsided games, particularly when the winning run was scored in the first inning of an 11–1 laugher. Although it has not been kept as an official statistic since 1989, broadcasters and fans still allude to it. Abbrev. *GWRBI*.

ganador Spanish for "winning pitcher."

gap 1. *n.* The space between outfielders. Because only three players cover the entire outfield, wide stretches of uncovered field exist. The size of the gaps (between the center fielder and the left fielder and between the center fielder and the right fielder) is determined by the defensive position of the outfielders. In ballparks where advertising is allowed on the outfield wall, ads for The Gap clothing chain began to appear in the spaces between outfielders in the late 1990s. See also *alley*, 1. Compare *hole*, 1, which is the space between infielders, although "gap" has also referred to such a space; e.g., "On reaching first base, he [the runner] forces the baseman to remain on the bag, and widens the right field gap by six feet at least" (John J. Evers and Hugh S. Fullerton, *Touching Second: The Science of Baseball*, 1910). 2. *v.* To hit a ball in the gap. 3. *v.* To force the batter to bend at the waist when an inside fastball, thrown off the plate, tails into the strike zone. "Gapping the batter" occurs when a right-handed pitcher faces a left-handed batter, or a left-handed pitcher faces a right-handed batter (Jerry Weinstein and Tom Alston, *Baseball Coach's Survival Guide*, 1998).

gap hitter A hitter (such as Tony Gwynn) who hits the ball between the outfielders.

gapper A batted ball that goes into the gap. If such a ball falls safely, it usually rolls to the wall and goes for an extra-base hit. "The gapper hit the hard dirt of the warning track and bounded into the bleachers" (*Wisconsin State Journal*, Aug. 1, 1997). See also *tweener*, 1. Syn. *gap shot*.

gap power The strength to drive balls between outfielders; the ability to get extra-base hits to the middle of the field but not over the fence. "[Ray Lankford] has gap power: hit 16 triples and 26 doubles" (*Baseball Digest*, March 1989).

gap shot Syn. of *gapper*.

gap-to-gap Having the tendency to hit doubles and triples to left-center field and/or right-center field, rather than shoot balls down the lines. The term implies limited power as much as good speed. "Craig Biggio had some power in his prime, but he was more of a gap-to-gap hitter—and a good one" (Mike Arbuckle, quoted in Alan Schwarz, BaseballAmerica.com, Nov. 14, 2006). Compare *pole-to-pole*.

garage sale Syn. of *fire sale*. "Wayne Huizenga's garage sale of his 1997 World Series champion [Florida Marlins began] with the trade of outfielder Moises Alou to the Astros for three minor league righthanders" (David Rawnsley, *Baseball America*, Dec. 27, 1999–Jan. 9, 2000; Peter Morris).

garden 1. The outfield; short for *outer garden*. The term was used in the early days of baseball; more recently, Roy Blount, Jr. (*Sports Illustrated*, Sept. 29, 2003) observed that "in the rightfield corner" Trot Nixon "patrols that garden for the Red Sox." IST USE. 1869 (*New York Herald*, Sept. 14; Edward J. Nichols). ETYMOLOGY. "The outfield is 'the garden' because flowers grew wild in the fields where early games were held" (Joseph Pereira, *The Wall Street Journal*, Oct. 22, 2005). 2. *hist.* A baseball field. "The entire field" (*Brooklyn Daily Eagle*, May 1, 1892, p.4). IST USE. 1868. "Centre 'garden,' as the boys call the field" (*Brooklyn Eagle*, Aug. 15; Peter Morris).

gardener *hist.* 1. A fielder; specif., an *outfielder*. "Flower beds were once features in right and center fields at the Polo Grounds, but [John] McGraw had them uprooted to give his gardeners more range" (Will Wedge, *The Sporting News*, May 21, 1936). IST USE. 1893. "[Walton] trotted in on Davey's fly that came down midway between the dazed man on third and the breathless left gardener" (*San Francisco Examiner*, Apr. 9; Peter Morris). 2. A *groundskeeper*. "In previous years, Groundkeeper [John] Murphy of the New York Polo grounds [*sic*] has been conceded

the world's championship among baseball landscape gardeners" (*The Washington Post*, Sept. 14, 1913; Peter Morris).

gardening Smoothing the dirt on a baseball field, such as by a pitcher around the mound or by a batter preparing the batter's box before stepping in to bat.

garner 1. To achieve a hit safely; e.g., "Smith garnered four hits today." IST USE. 1892 (*Chicago Herald*, June 13; Edward J. Nichols). 2. For a team to win a game.

Garrison finish *hist.* 1. A game in which a team, initially almost hopelessly behind, comes through to win the game. It has been said that a true Garrison finish requires the winning team to have been down by five runs with two outs in its last at-bat (*The Sporting News*, July 16, 1984). Compare *Frank Merriwell finish*. IST USE. 1896. "With the score 5 to 1 against them, the colts [*sic*] started in for a 'garrison finish' and batted out a victory" (*The Boston Globe*, July 23; Peter Morris). 2. A dramatic finish to a pennant race. "In the last week of the [New York League's] season the Uticas made a Garrison finish, winning seven straight and passing under the wire by a nose" (*Reach's Official Base Ball Guide*, 1901; Peter Morris). ETYMOLOGY. From the legendary ability of the 19th-century jockey Snapper Garrison to win horse races at the wire.

gas 1. Syn. of *fastball*, 1. 2. Fastball pitching. "[Roger Clemens] just came in throwing gas" (Marty Barrett, quoted in *The Boston Globe*, Aug. 4, 1986).

Gashouse Gang Nickname given to the 1934–1937 St. Louis Cardinals, but most strongly associated with the scrappy 1934 world champions. They were a rowdy, gritty, hard-playing, fun-loving crew, on and off the field, that included Dizzy Dean, Pepper Martin, Ducky Medwick, Ripper Collins, Leo Durocher, and manager Frankie Frisch. Their "trademark" was a dirty uniform. Also spelled "Gas House Gang." IST USE. 1934. "[The] *gas house gang* playing the nice boys from the right side of the tracks" (Dan Daniel, *New York World-Telegram*, Oct. 9). Earlier, Joe Williams (*New York World-Telegram*, Oct. 4) wrote, "I picked the Tigers but the Cardinals have got me worried. They looked like a bunch of boys from the gas house district who had crossed the railroad tracks for a game of ball with the nice kids." Peter Morris cites Robert Gregory's 1992 biography of Dizzy Dean (*Diz: Dizzy Dean and Baseball During the Great Depression*) for the source of these two quotations. USAGE NOTE. Morris suggests that the nickname probably was being used orally in the press box in 1934, and that the *New York World-Telegram* writers were the first to put it in print. However, the nickname itself did not take hold until the 1935 season. The term first appeared in a sports context in football. Penn State director of athletics Hugo Bezdek (quoted in *Chicago Daily Tribune*, Dec. 11, 1932): "They used to talk about the gashouse gang that played for [the Univ. of] Illinois, but I don't know whether they really were a gashouse gang or not. They may have been genuine Illinois students."

ETYMOLOGY. Originally, the Gashouse District was an area on the Lower East Side of Manhattan that once housed several large gas tanks. It was a rough neighborhood described in part by Frank Moss (*The American Metropolis*, 1897): "Perhaps the most unique of all vicious drinking places is a 'dead house' on 18th Street in what is called the 'gas-house district,' a 'Mecca' for vagrants and 'bums' of New York, Brooklyn and New Jersey." But the seedy neighborhood was best known for a vicious band of thugs known as the Gashouse Gang. The term "gashouse" implied "the wrong side of the tracks, underdogs, survival with wits and fists—concepts with which many victims of the Great Depression could identify" (Joseph Lawler, *Sports History*, March 1988).

There are several versions of how the moniker was applied to the Cardinals. One version has the St. Louis team coming into New York from Boston, where they had just played in the rain. The players' uniforms were particularly dirty because they were a "sliding" team, and the equipment man did not have time to have them cleaned. When they appeared on the field at the Polo Grounds, one shocked reporter commented that they looked like "the gang from around the gas house." This version was given by Frisch (*The Saturday Evening Post*, July 18, 1959) and in a radio interview (May 11, 1963) in which he acknowledged that his was not the only version of the story. Frisch added that he thought the reporter was Frank Lamb of the *New York Evening Journal*. But in his biography of Dizzy Dean (*Ol' Diz*, 1992), Vince Staten questioned this version because May 20 and July 23 were the only two days during the 1934 season that the Cardinals played in New York a day after a game in Boston—and both of those games in Boston were played under clear skies with no hint of rain.

More commonly heard is the story of a conversation between Frank Graham (*New York Sun*) and Durocher. Graham said that the Cards were so good that they could play in the American League, then regarded as superior to the National League. Durocher replied, "They wouldn't let us play in the American League. They'd say we were just a lot of gashouse players." From then on Graham called the team the Gashouse Gang. The very same story has been told and published with Pepper Martin in Durocher's place (Lee Allen, *The Hot Stove League*, 1955, p.98).

In his autobiography (*Nice Guys Finish Last*, 1975), Durocher told of the team arriving dirty and unkempt for the confrontation with the Giants. "The next day I saw a cartoon in the *World-Telegram* by Willard Mullin. It showed two big gas tanks on the wrong side of the railroad track, and some ballplayers crossing over to the good part of town carrying clubs over their shoulders instead of bats. And the title read: 'The Gas House Gang.'" But the Mullin cartoon, and a reference to the "Gas House Gang" by Tom Meany in the *New York World-Telegram*, appeared on May 14, 1935, some seven months after the introduction of the nickname.

Dean biographer Staten looked for clarity in *Frank Frisch, the Fordham Flash* (1962), the autobiography of Frisch (written with J. Roy Stockton). Frisch, who was not only the manager but also the second baseman on the Gashouse Gang, credited Warren Brown of the *Chicago Herald-Examiner* with using the phrase in print in July 1935. Frisch wrote: "[Brown] climbed aboard the Cubs' train, New York bound. Curtains were drawn. All the little and big Cubs apparently had turned in for the night. 'What's the matter?' Brown wanted to know in a loud voice. 'Are you boys afraid that Pepper Martin is on the train? You had all better stay on your side of the tracks, or the Gas House Gang will get you.'"

Gregory (pp.237–38) noted that the coinage of the nickname was first attributed by *The Sporting News* to George C. Carrens (*Boston Transcript*); also, Ed Bang (*Cleveland Press*) was said to deserve the credit. "But all the credit should go to those who never seemed to ask for it—Williams, Daniel, Meany, and Mullin." In addition, Graham and Brown, as well as Bill Corum (*New York Herald American*), helped to popularize the nickname.

Gashouser A member of the Gashouse Gang. "[Don Gutteridge] broke in with the Gashousers in 1936" (*Sports Illustrated*, Aug. 26, 2002).

gate 1. The total number of persons who pay for admission to a baseball game. IST USE. 1888. "There is a 'big gate' awaiting the championship should they decide on making the trip" (*The Sporting Life*, Nov. 21; David Shulman). **2.** Short for *gate receipts*. "Let it be said that the mere announcement that [Rube] Marquard or [Walter] Johnson is to pitch in an important game will bring in at the 'gate' more than the $11,000 that Marquard cost the Giants" (C.H. Claudy, *Technical World Magazine*, July 1913. **3.** A strikeout; e.g., "Jones gave Smith the gate." **4.** An ejection. IST USE. 1918. "Umpire [Billy] Evans thought Harry got too abusive, however, and gave him the gate" (*Detroit Free Press*, July 5; Barry Popik).

gate crasher An individual who gains admission to an important event, such as the World Series, without paying admission. The practice became something of a fad in the 1920s when the newspapers covered several daring gate crashers who seemed able to get in everywhere. "The original reference to sporting events has passed from the language for lack of practitioners" (John Ciardi, *Good Words to You*, 1987).

gate money The money that is collected at the turnstiles. See also *gate receipts*. IST USE. 1869 (*De Witt's Base-Ball Guide*, p.67; Edward J. Nichols).

gate receipts The total amount of money received in admission prices to a baseball game. Fifteen percent of the gate receipts from all World Series games are paid to the office of the commissioner, 60 percent of the total gate receipts from the first four World Series games are contributed to the players' pool (of which 36 percent is given to the team winning the World Series), and the balance is equally divided between the two participating clubs. See also *gate money*; *paid attendance receipts*. Syn. *gate*, 2. IST USE. 1870. "In 1869 the Red Stockings . . . became so famous that their gate-receipts were very large" (*Lakeside Monthly* [Chicago]; David Shulman).

gateway Syn. of *first base*. It is so called because first base is the threshold to the other bases and the opportunity of scoring. The term is flamboyant baseballese.

gather in To field a batted ball. IST USE. 1874 (*Chicago Inter-Ocean*, July 30; Edward J. Nichols).

gazoonie *hist*. A *rookie*, 1. " 'Gazoonies' is probably the most modern nickname for recruits, who through the years have come to be known as 'rookies'" (Herbert Simons, *Baseball Magazine*, Jan. 1943). IST USE. 1942. "Jake (Cub) Mooty's 'gazoonies' for second-stringers" (Herbert Simons, *Baseball Digest*, October).

GB 1. Abbrev. for *games behind*. **2.** Abbrev. for *ground ball*. **3.** Abbrev. for *grand bounce*.

GDP Abbrev. for *grounded into double play*.

"gee whiz" An informal school of sportswriting characterized by the sensational or emotional approach to the craft. Practitioners included Grantland Rice, Paul Gallico, and Heywood Broun. According to Charles Fountain (*Sportswriter: The Life and Times of Grantland Rice*, 1993), they were "optimist[s], anticipating heroics and triumph, yet somehow able to be both heart-broken and exhilarated in defeat." Gallico (*Farewell to Sport*, 1938) commented, "The sportswriter has few if any heroes. We create many because it is our business to do so, but we do not believe in them. We know them too well." Compare *"aw nuts."* (Peter Morris)

Gehrig Award Short for *Lou Gehrig Memorial Award.*

Gehrig's disease Syn. of *Lou Gehrig's disease.* The term "Gehrig's disease" had come into use even before Lou Gehrig succumbed to it. One of its first uses in print came in an Associated Press story by Harold C. McKinley on the day (June 4, 1941) of Gehrig's funeral. That story, which ran in the *Washington Evening Star* of that date under the headline "Science Helpless Treating It, Is Ignorant Even of Cause of 'Gehrig's Disease,'" noted that "no virus has been found in cases of 'Gehrig's disease' as the affliction has become popularly termed."

general admission **1.** A catchall term that refers to the areas of the ballpark where seats are not reserved and are filled on a first-come, first-served basis. The term commonly applies to seating in the bleachers in portions of the upper deck. General admission tickets carry a common price, although there are sometimes special prices for children and/or senior citizens. IST USE. 1882. "The Mohawk Ball Club of St. Louis . . . will play the Spauldings of Chicago to-day at the ball park. Admittance to the grand stand will be 50 cents; general admission 25 cents" (*The Daily Inter Ocean* [Chicago], June 17). **2.** The price for an unreserved seat in the grandstand.

general manager The director of a club's baseball matters and personnel. The role of general manager has changed from an all-encompassing position of authority to a more specific baseball operations post. Duties include signing and trading players, evaluating talent, balancing the budget, navigating waivers, and managing the front office. According to Lou Piniella (*Sweet Lou*, 1986): "The definition of a good general manager is a guy who can call up another GM at three o'clock in the morning and have the guy help him out with a player, instead of screaming at him for the early wake-up call." Abbrev. *GM.* IST USE. 1916. "Branch Rickey's official title with the St. Louis Browns is 'vice president and general manager'" (*The Sporting News*, Feb. 10; Peter Morris). Bill James (*The Bill James Historical Baseball Abstract*, 1986, p.132) noted, "The term 'General Manager'

was first applied to William Evans . . . who became General Manager of the Cleveland Indians in 1927." USAGE NOTE. In the 19th century and well into the 20th century, the individual now known as the general manager was often referred to as the business manager or financial manager, or simply the manager; e.g., the *Chicago Tribune* (May 11, 1879; Peter Morris) noted that Jim White had brought in his brother-in-law to be the "General Financial Manager and Official Scorer" of the Cincinnati club.

gentleman's agreement **1.** The *unwritten rule* on racial exclusion in organized baseball, in effect from the late 1880s until 1946. *The Sporting Life* (June 29, 1895; Greg Bond) reported, "During the twenty years that the National league has been in existence there have been few, if any, colored men that donned a uniform to play in one of its teams. . . . Nothing is ever said or written about drawing the color line in the League. It appears to be generally understood that none but white shall make up the League teams, and so it goes." See also *color line.* **2.** An understanding among clubs to bypass the spirit of the waiver rules; specif., the "unwritten law" that "if you waive claim on my players, I'll waive claim on yours" (Jim Nasium, *The Sporting News*, Dec. 30, 1926). Nasium (pen name for Edgar F. Wolfe) wrote, "Through the application of this unspoken word, which is an invisible club that each big league team holds over every other big league team, the waiver rule is rendered inoperative and each year big league teams send back to the minor leagues many players who would strengthen a lot of other teams in the big leagues." IST USE. 1908. "A 'gentleman's agreement' will be entered into between major and minor league magnates, by which the former, after securing waivers, will sell the player outright to the latter, accepting the word of the minor league club-owner that the farmed player should be released to it under a pretended purchase in time to escape the dangers of the draft" (*The Sporting News*, Feb. 6; Peter Morris).

George factor The real or imagined influence of wealthy principal owner George Steinbrenner on his New York Yankees. "One thing we don't have is the George factor. That's good for two or three losses down the road" (Toronto Blue Jays outfielder Joe Carter, quoted in *USA Today Baseball Weekly*, May 25, 1994).

George Stallings pitcher "A 3-and–2 pitcher; one who gets behind every batter; a wild hurler" (Gordon S. "Mickey" Cochrane, *Baseball: The Fan's Game*, 1939). ETYMOLOGY. Named for manager George Stallings, whose presumably last words as he emerged from a coma to address his doctor, who asked about the cause of his sickness, were, "Bases on balls, you fathead, was the cause of it all" (Rabbit Maranville, *Run, Rabbit, Run*, 1991).

German ball game Syn. of *ballstock*.

get 1. To retire an opposing player; to put out; e.g., "Smith got Jones by catching his pop fly." **2.** To deceive another player; to trick an opponent. Walter Camp (*Century*, Apr. 1910) gave several examples, including one in which Boston Red Sox catcher Lou Criger "got" Cleveland's Napoleon Lajoie: "There were two strikes and three balls on Lajoie. Criger had returned the ball to the pitcher, but had his mask off and was pretending to fasten a buckle on it, saying to Lajoie, 'We'll get you this time.' Lajoie turned slightly, and, seeing Criger with his mask off, said, 'You will, will you?' when the pitcher shot the ball over the plate, catching Lajoie entirely unprepared as he heard the umpire say, 'Strike three, and out!'" **3.** For a manager to remove a pitcher from the game. **4.** To obtain a player in a trade or by other means.

get across 1. To score a run; e.g., "The Giants got four runs across in the sixth." **2.** To put a pitch over the plate. "[Carl] Zamloch has dished up an assortment of stuff that would require 60 pages to catalogue. It will go great if it gets across" (*San Francisco Bulletin*, March 31, 1913; Gerald L. Cohen).

get ahead For a pitcher to throw more strikes than balls. "I was able to throw strikes and get ahead of the hitters" (Fernando Valenzuela, quoted in *Tampa Tribune-Times*, Aug. 13, 1989).

get a hold of it For a batter to hit the ball squarely, on the thick end of the bat. "When they tossed her in there fast, and you got a

George Stallings pitcher. Stallings as manager of the 1914 Miracle Boston Braves. *George Grantham Bain Collection, Library of Congress*

hold of it, she was gone" (Goose Goslin, quoted in Lawrence S. Ritter, *The Glory of Their Times* [booklet], 1998, p.29). See also *get hold of it*.

get a jump 1. For a baserunner to make a quick break toward the next base as the pitcher begins his motion toward the plate. **2.** For a fielder to begin instinctively to move before, or just as, the ball is hit toward the point on the field where the ball can be caught or fielded. Getting a jump on the ball is "knowing the pitchers, total concentration and being able to react" (Jerry Remy, quoted in *Baseball Digest*, Nov. 1983, p.82).

get all of it To hit the ball solidly and with power, usually for a home run, but at least extra bases. "I hit the ball on the sweet spot of the bat and got all of it" (Yokohama BayStars left fielder Hitoshi Tamura, quoted in *The Baltimore Sun*, March 5, 2006). Syn. *get it all*.

get a piece of the ball For a batter barely to make contact with the ball, usually resulting in a foul ball. Batting with two strikes, a player will try to "get a piece of the ball" to keep from striking out.

get around To swing the bat fast enough to hit the pitch. "If he [Ichiro Suzuki] can get around on an inside pitch, he has surprising pop for a player listed at 5' 9" and 160 pounds" (Mark Bechtel, *Sports Illustrated*, Apr. 23, 2001, p.40). Softball pitcher Lisa Fernandez' fastball is said to be so fast that "hitting greats Sammy Sosa and Barry Bonds would have trouble getting around on her" (*Parade* magazine, Aug. 8, 2004).

"get at 'em!" The war cry of the 1890s Baltimore Orioles.

get a ticket To receive a base on balls.

get away **1.** For a pitch to be wild and beyond the reach of the catcher. "I failed to snap my wrist sufficiently and my hook got away from me in majestic style—sailing far over . . . [the batters'] heads to the wire screen behind home plate" (George Plimpton, *Out of My League*, 1961, p.97). **2.** For a throw to elude an infielder, such as one in the dirt.

getaway **1.** The frequency with which baseball games are won at the beginning of the season. "It was hitting that was winning for the White Sox, who startled the rest of the league with their fast getaway" (Edgar Munzel, *The Sporting News*, May 2, 1951). **2.** The quickness with which the batter gets out of the batter's box after hitting the ball, or the baserunner starts for another base. "I have practiced the quick get-away so much that I start full speed for first base before I even meet the ball" (Ross Youngs, quoted in F.C. Lane, *Batting*, 1925, p.84). Also spelled "getaway." IST USE. 1912. "A man starts for the base, times his get-away just right, and slides into the bag" (Christy Mathewson, *Pitching in a Pinch*). ETYMOLOGY. Borrowed from track. "Ability to make a quick get-away, as a track man would term it, is the main qualification of a good base stealer" (John W. "Jack" Coombs, *Baseball*, 1938; Peter Morris).

getaway bag *hist.* Syn. of *first base*, 1. IST USE. 1907 (*Lajoie's Official Base Ball Guide*, p.110; Edward J. Nichols).

getaway day **1.** The last day of a homestand for a team; the day the club gets away for a road trip. IST USE. 1904. "Today was getaway day for the [Philadelphia] Athletics, and they signalized the occasion by putting up about the worst game of the season" (*The Washington Post*, Sept. 17; Peter Morris). **2.** The last day of a series between two teams,

on which one or both of the teams leaves for another city. Both teams have a getaway day when the visitors leave and the home team ends its homestand.

getaway game A game on getaway day.

get down To slide.

get healthy To hit successfully, individually or as a team, against a pitcher or group of pitchers, esp. for an individual or team that has not been hitting well. In a game in which the Boston Red Sox defeated the Baltimore Orioles 15–4, Jack Wiers (WTOP radio, June 10, 1987) said, "A lot of Red Sox got healthy tonight."

get him over To advance a baserunner with a bunt, sacrifice, or groundout.

get hold of it For a batter to connect solidly with the pitch. See also *get a hold of it*. Syn. "get hold of a ball." IST USE. 1913. "Any time that [Jim] Thorpe gets hold of a ball he makes it travel, but he is liable to have trouble with curve balls" (*San Francisco Bulletin*, March 6; Gerald L. Cohen).

get in one's kitchen To throw an inside pitch. See also *kitchen*.

get into the bullpen To cause an opposing team to use its relief pitchers.

get it all Syn. of *get all of it*. Commenting on Brad Wilkerson's towering home run that became the first in Washington Nationals history to reach the upper deck at RFK Stadium, Nationals manager Frank Robinson said (quoted in *The Baltimore Sun*, Apr. 27, 2005), "I was impressed. He got it all, no doubt about it."

get it down To bunt the ball. Discussing his successful suicide-squeeze bunt, Jerry Hairston Jr. recalled (quoted in *The Baltimore Sun*, Aug. 27, 2000), "All I want is to get it down because [the runner on third base] was coming. If I get it down, we score."

get it started **1.** For a batter to begin his swing. "It's the lightest bat I've ever used. When I was with the Giants I swung at least 35 ounces and used a bat with a thicker barrel. This bat feels like a toothpick in comparison, but I can get it started quicker" (Jack Clark, quoted in *Philadelphia Daily News*, June 25, 1987). **2.** To get the hit that begins a rally.

get jocked To be overpowered; to lose in spectacular fashion. "[Marty] Pattin started . . . against Detroit [and] he got jocked, surrendering eight runs in three and two-thirds innings" (Bill "Spaceman" Lee, *The Wrong Stuff*, 1984, p.101).

get loose For a relief pitcher to warm up and get ready in the bullpen.

get naked For a pitcher to *bear down*. "A coach might yell to a pitcher who seems to be losing his concentration: 'Hey, get naked out there'" (Leonard Shecter, *Baseball Digest*, June 1963).

get on 1. To advance to one of the bases; specif., to get to first base. "[George Burns] leads the batting order and . . . is 'getting on' and scoring a lot of runs" (*New York Globe and Commercial Advertiser*, Sept. 27, 1916). IST USE. 1908 (*Baseball Magazine*, July, p.38; Edward J. Nichols). 2. For a batted ball to reach quickly and close to the body of a fielder.

get one's goat To anger or frustrate one's opponent. American League umpire Billy Evans (quoted in *Indianapolis Star*, Dec. 18, 1919; Joanne Hulbert): "In 1914 the Boston Braves made the Philadelphia Athletics look foolish in the world series . . . Since then it has been common talk that the Braves won because they, to use the slang of the ball field, 'got the goats' of the Philadelphia players from the start, and thereby to a great extent ruined their effectiveness." See also *goat*.

get one's innings Syn. of *have one's innings*, 1.

get-over pitch A pitch that a pitcher can rely upon when he needs to throw a strike.

get-small-quick ball A home run, so named because of the way the ball appears to get smaller and smaller as it travels into the stands or out of the ballpark. Shirley Povich quoted Washington Senators pitcher Walter Johnson: "The balls [Babe] Ruth hit got smaller quicker than anyone's" (Gordon Beard, *Orioles Gazette*, Aug. 13, 1993).

get the bats going To increase offensive production. Cleveland Indians manager Charlie Manuel, commenting on every Indians starter getting at least one hit (quoted in *The Baltimore Sun*, Apr. 23, 2001): "That's the first time this year we got our bats going. . . . Everybody got in the flow."

get the bounce To be lucky; e.g., a hard-to-field ball is either fielded or goes for a hit, depending on which team "gets the bounce."

get the call 1. To be chosen to play; often applied to a relief pitcher when he gets the signal to come into the game. IST USE. 1920 (*The New York Times*, Oct. 4; Edward J. Nichols). 2. To receive the umpire's benefit of doubt on a close play or a pitch on the border of the strike zone.

get the corners For a catcher to successfully expand the strike zone of his pitcher by means of skillful interaction with the umpire. John J. Evers and Hugh S. Fullerton (*Touching Second: The Science of Baseball*, 1910; Peter Morris): "The importance of 'getting the corners' is realized by all players, and the catcher who gets this advantage is invaluable to his club. . . . The best tactics . . . are those employed by the catchers who seldom kick, and who win the friendship and confidence of the officials."

get the gate To be removed from a game during its progress; esp., to be ejected by the umpire.

get the range of *hist.* Syn. of *solve*. "The Atlantics then began their second innings, and having got the range of Clyde's pitching, the way they went in to astonish both natives and foreigners was a caution to ye country clubs" (*New York Clipper*, Oct. 1, 1864; Peter Morris).

"get the spring out" A comment said to a fielder who looks in his glove after committing an error.

get the thumb To be ejected from the game.

get to To hit successfully, individually or as a team, against a particular pitcher; e.g., "The Cubs got to Smith with five consecutive doubles." IST USE. 1905 (*The Sporting Life*, Sept. 2, p.5; Edward J. Nichols).

get to first base To make an offensive start by putting a runner on first base by means of a hit, base on balls, or hit batsman. EXTENDED USE. To achieve the first step in a procedure or activity.

"get two" 1. To turn a double play. 2. A cry of encouragement to the infielders when there is a runner at first base with less than two outs.

get under the ball **1.** For a pitcher to rush his delivery whereby the body moves forward faster than the arm, the elbow under and leading the hand/wrist, resulting in the ball staying high in the strike zone. Compare *stay back*, 2. **2.** For a batter to swing upward, hitting the bottom part of the ball, resulting in a pop-up or a long fly ball. "After tweaking his batting stance—crouching lower and keeping his weight back in order to get under the ball more—he [Mike Piazza] turned around his season" (*Sports Illustrated*, Aug. 14, 2006). Compare *stay on top of the ball*, 1. **3.** For a fielder to position himself in preparation to catch a ball hit high in the air; e.g., "Jones moved several paces to his left to get under the ball." IST USE. 1905 (*The Sporting Life*, Oct. 7, p.11; Edward J. Nichols).

get up with the pitch For a runner on first base to face the catcher, begin to glide sideways toward second base, and then turn smoothly and sprint off the glide as the ball is put in play (George F. Will, *Men at Work*, 1990).

geyser ball A spitball. "Seals New Pitcher Phil Douglass Spitball Artist . . . discarded his fast one and his curve when he hit upon the discovery of the 'geyser ball'" (*San Francisco Bulletin*, Apr. 4, 1913; Gerald L. Cohen).

GF Abbrev. for *games finished*.

ghost Syn. of *non-roster invitee*. "Ghosts trying to scare up roster spots" (Mike Cunniff, *Morris* [Ill.] *Daily Herald*, Feb. 24, 2006; Grant Barrett).

ghostball Syn. of *knuckleball*, 1.

ghost runner Not a real baserunner, employed in playground baseball and variations of softball, when there is an insufficient number of players or when it is a baserunner's turn to bat again. The ghost runner could only advance as many bases as the batter attained. Syn. *invisible man*, 2; *imaginary runner*.

Giants **1.** Nickname for the National League West Division franchise in San Francisco. The franchise originated as the Troy Trojans (1879–1882), relocated to New York City as the *Gothams* (1883–1884), was renamed the New York Giants in 1885, and became the San Francisco Giants in 1958. See also *McGrawmen*. IST USE. 1885. According to research by Peter Mancuso, *The World* (New

Giants. John McGraw, manager, New York Giants, in 1923 with Giants manager James J. Mutrie (1885–1891). *George Grantham Bain Collection, Library of Congress*

York) on Apr. 14 reported on a preseason game the preceding day between the New York Gothams and the Jersey City team of the Eastern League. The report, presumably written by P.J. Donahue, referred to the New York team as the "Gotham Giants" and "Mutrie's giants," and stated that the team's "new nickname" was "Giants," but did not specify the origin of the name. The nickname "Giants" rapidly came into wide use within several days. *The Boston Globe* (Apr. 24, 1885; Paul Browne) stated that "the New Yorks have been titled the Giants"; and *Rocky Mountain News* (June 8, 1885) reported that "the people pin their faith . . . in the East [to] the marooned stockinged [New York] giants." By the beginning of June 1885, *The New York Times* made the transition to "Giants." ETYMOLOGY. Baseball folklore has long held that New York manager Jim Mutrie, after a particularly outstanding play or after a rousing extra-innings victory, bounded from the dugout and exclaimed: "My big fellows! My giants!" The team did have some players of large stature; however, according to research by Mancuso and others, there is no contemporary or even 19th-century account that described Mutrie's

Giants. New York Female Giants in 1913. *George Grantham Bain Collection, Library of Congress*

making such a statement. Mancuso comments, "The strongest independent evidence that Mutrie nicknamed the team 'Giants' is not articulated until the mid-1930s when John B. Foster, former editor of *Spalding's Official Base Ball Guide*, made a statement during an interview to *The Sporting News* that he investigated the matter of how the Giants were named 20 years earlier. He claims that he received then (1915) approx. 20 letters from former players and others that Mutrie did indeed name the team 'Giants' because of their size. *Spalding's Guide* of 1915 contained Foster's editorial, but only stated that the Giants were so named because of their size, with no other substantive details." **2.** A popular nickname for teams in the Negro leagues; e.g., Cuban Giants (first professional black team, 1885–1899); Chicago American Giants (charter franchise in the Negro National League, 1920–1931, and charter franchise in the Negro American League, 1937–1948 and 1950); Baltimore Elite Giants (Negro National League, 1938–1948, and Negro American League, 1949–1950); Bacharach Giants (charter franchise in the Eastern Colored League, 1923–1928, located in Atlantic City, N.J.); and Brooklyn Royal Giants (charter franchise in the Eastern Colored League, 1923–1927). **3.** Nickname for the Players' League franchise in New York City in 1890. **4.** Nickname for the Yomiuri (Tokyo) team in the Japanese Central League. **5.** An informal nickname bandied about in the sporting press and applied to various clubs in the 1870s and 1880s before it became attached to the New York National League club in 1885. The name was often used as a nickname to refer to a team's national stature. Clubs so named included the Chicago White Stockings of the National Association (1874) and the National League (1876 through 1885); and the Louisville Grays of the National League (1876). "It is said that Chicago 'giants' contemplate a tour through the south, to awaken more interest in the national game" (*Arkansas Gazette* [Little Rock], Aug. 27, 1876). The nickname was even applied to the New York Gothams in 1883: "The Giants of the New York Team Obliged to Acknowledge Their Superiors" (*Chicago Daily Tribune* subheadline, Aug. 3; Richard Hershberger).

giddyup The late speed of a pitcher's fastball, which appears to ascend as it crosses the plate. The illusion often is caused by a smooth delivery that hides how fast the pitch will be (Alan Schwarz, BaseballAmerica.com, Nov. 14, 2006). "[Grant] Roberts still has what scouts call 'giddyup' on his fastball. His pitches pop the catcher's mitt" (Marty Noble, *Baseball America*, March 29–Apr. 11, 1999). "His fastball looks like it hits a grease spot on the way to home plate. It's got some giddyup" (Kansas City Royals scout Gerald Turner, concerning top draft pick Colt Griffin, quoted in *The Baltimore Sun*, Aug. 9, 2001). See also *late life.*

GIDP (pron. "gidap") An acronym for *grounded into double play.* The term is used in referring to the statistic that accounts for "times grounded into double plays."

gift 1. Syn. of *base on balls.* IST USE. 1886. "[John] Morrill also was tendered a gift of first on balls" (*The Boston Globe*, June 1; Peter Morris). 2. Anything given up by the defense because of bad play or inattention; e.g., a single that went for a "double" because the fielder failed to get to the ball quickly. 3. An error or misplay that puts a batter on base or allows a baserunner to advance. IST USE. 1879 (*Spirit of the Times*, Aug. 28; Edward J. Nichols).

Gillette A pitch thrown in the direction of a batter's head; a brushback pitch that is likely to come close to (in the manner of a Gillette razor) but not hit the batter. The term is an obvious play on the idea of a "close shave." IST USE. 1937 (*New York Daily News*, Jan. 17; Edward J. Nichols).

gilt-edge *hist.* Said of excellent ballplaying. The term was in constant use in the late 19th and early 20th centuries. "Jack Killilay . . . showed superb form. He pitched gilt-edge ball" (*San Francisco Bulletin*, Apr. 11, 1913; Gerald L. Cohen). "The veteran shortstop 'Truck' Eagan now playing gilt-edge ball" (*Los Angeles Times*, May 28, 1905).

gimme A favorable situation, such as a belt-high fastball or a short fence that invites a cheap home run. Regarding the Houston Astros home field, *Sports Illustrated* (May 22, 2000) noted that "architects made left-field [315 feet down the line] a gimme for hitters." ETYMOLOGY. From "give me"; e.g., "Give me an easy ball to clobber."

ginger The zest, pep, vigor, or fighting spirit of a player; e.g., Chicago White Sox infielder Buck Weaver was called "The Ginger Kid" because of his enthusiastic play. "Shorty Fuller is full of ginger. He seldom stops to watch the course of a batted or thrown ball, but immediately shows a disposition to 'git up and git' for it" (*St. Louis Post-Dispatch*, Apr. 11, 1889; Peter Morris, who suggests that hustle is the main characteristic of ginger). IST USE. 1889. "The ginger will have left his bones ere he will have a like opportunity again" (Frank C. Payne, quoted in *The Daily Inter Ocean* [Chicago], March 1). ETYMOLOGY. A pungent, spicy plant. "[The term] 'full of ginger' is an expression that was sprung upon the base ball public by the irrepressible Arlie Latham . . . [for] a lively, hustling band of players" (*The Sporting News*, July 6, 1889; Peter Morris).

gink *hist.* A baseball fan. "He'll ramp and stamp and whoop and yell; he'll tear his lungs plumb out; / He'll dislocate his voice to boot, but still the gink'll shout" (Louis Schneider, "Bugs," *Baseball Magazine*, Dec. 1908, p.62; Bill Mullins).

give him the gate For an umpire to eject a participant from the playing area. "Umpire [Billy] Evans thought Harry [Heilmann] got too abusive . . . and gave him the gate" (*Detroit Free Press*, July 5, 1918).

give him the player To direct the first baseman and the third baseman to play away from the foul lines. Syn. *give up the line.*

give in For a pitcher to capitulate to the batter by throwing him a pitch that he likes to hit. The term is usually stated in the negative. Gaylord Perry (quoted in *American Way*, Sept. 1982): "Most of the opposing players know I'm only trying to win. They know I'm not going to give in on anything, and I do mean anything." Jason Johnson (quoted in *The Baltimore Sun*, June 24, 2002): "I went after the hitters like I wanted to. I wasn't going to give in to anybody." Tommy John (quoted in *The Washington Post*, Sept. 5, 1982): "You should *never* give in to the batter, not even if the bases are loaded and there are three balls on the hitter." Compare *go after.*

give oneself up 1. To hit the ball behind a

teammate on base in an effort to bring him home or advance him to scoring position. **2.** To hit a sacrifice bunt.

giver *hist.* The pitcher.

give the nod **1.** For a manager to indicate that a player, usually a starting or relief pitcher, has been selected to play. The term commonly is used to indicate which pitcher has been chosen to come in from the bullpen. **2.** To get a favorable decision from the umpire. ETYMOLOGY. From the nod of approval. Harold Wentworth and Stuart Berg Flexner (*Dictionary of American Slang*, 1960) stated that the term has been a common sports expression since about 1920 and was first used to describe a boxer who won a prizefight ("got the nod") because of the referee's or judge's decision rather than a knockout.

give up To allow the opposition an advantage whether it be a walk, hit, or run; e.g., "Smith gave up six hits and three runs in four innings."

give up the line Syn. of *give him the player*.

glancing blow A slight impact when the ball strikes a batter or fielder and bounces away, usually with no injury to the player.

glass arm **1.** A sore or weak throwing or pitching arm. "For a back number with a 'glass' arm, George Hanley seems to be holding up his own end in [keeping] the San Jose team in great shape" (*The Sporting Times*, June 13, 1891; David Shulman). Shulman also noted that the following issue of *Sporting Times* (June 20) reported that the term "glass arm" was becoming obsolete and replaced by *crockery limb*. Peter Tamony noted that the glass metaphor is not limited to baseball and serves as a reference to fragility in other sports, such as when a boxer has a "glass jaw." IST USE. 1891. "Then [Tim] Keefe develops a 'glass' arm" (*The North American* [Philadelphia], May 7). ETYMOLOGY. H.L. Mencken (*The American Language*, Suppl. II, 1948) thanked Adm. C.S. Butler (letter, Nov. 30, 1943), who noted that a "glass arm" was usually myositis (inflammation) of the long tendon of the biceps muscle: "Its action is three- or four-fold and its relations to synovial sheaths, bursas and joints complicated. Damage of these structures often produces a stiffness and rigidity

accompanied by loss of the power to supinate the forearm. . . . The arm feels rigid, and as if likely to break like glass." EXTENDED USE. The term has been applied to stiff or weak arms in other realms. An article on shortwave radio (*American Speech*, Oct. 1929) reported its use as a synonym for "telegrapher's cramp." **2.** A player with a chronically weak or sore arm.

gliding A flaw in a pitcher's delivery in which, instead of pushing toward home plate with the pitch, the pitcher drifts away and throws across his body.

global draft A proposed international draft to cover all amateur players. Only players residing in the United States, Canada, Puerto Rico, the Virgin Islands, and other U.S. territories, and foreign players attending American schools, are subject to the first-year player draft.

Global League An ill-fated "third" major league founded in the late 1960s by Walter J. Dilbeck to place teams in Latin America, Japan, and the United States. It collapsed in May 1969.

globe *hist.* The baseball. IST USE. 1872. "There lay the ball snugly hidden under it [his cap]. You see his cap had fallen off and over the little globe" (George G. Small, *A Presidential Base-Ball Match*, p.24).

globule The baseball. "Moore and Maggart . . . hammered the globule over the right-center wall" (*San Francisco Bulletin*, Apr. 23, 1913; Gerald L. Cohen). IST USE. 1908 (*Brooklyn Daily Eagle*, May 22; Edward J. Nichols).

glorieta A shaded pavilion that is an important architectural feature of Cuban baseball stadiums, somewhat akin to modern luxury boxes. Roberto González Echevarría (*The Pride of Havana*, 1999) described the glorieta as "a sort of large gazebo from which women and other spectators watched games protected from the sun and in which dances, dinners and literary soirees were held."

glorious uncertainty *hist.* Unpredictability of a baseball game. Peter Morris notes that the term was commonly used in reports of early baseball. "In looking for the cause of so overwhelming a defeat, we are somewhat puzzled, and can attribute it to nothing else than that 'glorious uncertainty,' without which these admirable athletic contests would lose half their interest" (*New York Clipper*, Aug. 7, 1858). "Were it not for the 'glorious uncertainty' of base ball, that pastime would never have been chosen as the National game of America" (*St. Louis Globe-Democrat*, Apr. 26, 1876). ETYMOLOGY. From cricket. "The 'glorious uncertainty' of cricket seems to have attached itself to this great kindred sport" (*New York Clipper*, July 17, 1858; Peter Morris).

glory circle *hist.* Baseball's elite; the unofficial hall of fame before there was a National Baseball Hall of Fame. IST USE. 1908 (*Spalding's Official Base Ball Guide*, p.279; Edward J. Nichols).

glory time A period late in a game during which a relief pitcher can earn a potential save (Peter Pascarelli, *Sport*, Aug. 1984).

glove **1.** *n.* A covering of padded leather worn on a fielder's hand used to protect the hand and help catch and retain a batted or thrown ball. A glove originally was intended solely as a means of protecting a player's hand by softening the impact of handling balls, but it soon began to evolve as a means to better fielding. Gloves were being used as early as 1867; however, because they conflicted with ideals of manliness, they were usually fingerless, offered only minimal cushioning, and were flesh-colored. Accordingly, nobody was anxious to claim being the first to use them (much as there was a stigma attached to the first ice hockey players to don goalie masks and helmets), but once introduced, they quickly spread into general use in the late 1870s. In the major leagues, a glove shall not measure more than 12 inches in length and 7¾ inches in width. Compare *mitt*, 1 and 2. Syn. *fielder's glove*; *fielding glove*. **2.** *n.* Fielding ability. An exceptional defensive player is said to have a "good glove." Wil Cordero "can't hide glove: former infielder tries the outfield" (*Sports Illustrated*, March 31, 1997). USAGE NOTE. The term "glove" alone means the same as "good glove." Tim Horgan (*Baseball Digest*, June 1964) wrote, "If you chance to overhear Player A say to Player B, 'Don't lose your glove,' it doesn't mean there's a sneak thief in the house. It means Player B can't hit his weight and the only thing that keeps him in

the lineup is his fielding prowess." **3.** *n.* A fielder, usually a skilled one. "Billy, you were the best damn glove I ever saw" (Roger Kahn, concerning third baseman Billy Cox, quoted in Rick Phalen, *A Bittersweet Journey*, 2000, p.124). **4.** *v.* To catch and control a ball; to field a ball with a glove. "Lenny Harris dove to his left and gloved Tom Herr's smash" (*Tampa Tribune*, July 5, 1989). **5.** *n.* See *batting glove*. **6.** *n.* See *sliding glove*.

glove action The fielding skill of a player. "[Cal Ripken Jr.] has the best glove action I've seen" (Mark Belanger, quoted in *Baseball Digest*, Dec. 1983).

glove and a prayer The assets of an ineffective pitcher. See also *prayer ball*; *nothing but his glove*. IST USE. 1912. "All he has when he goes to the box is a glove and a prayer" (*The Sporting Life*, May 18).

glove-and-throw Said of a fielding play in which the ball was fielded and quickly thrown to the appropriate teammate; e.g., "It was a fine glove-and-throw assist by the second baseman."

glove doctor An individual (sometimes a trainer) who helps players customize their gloves.

glove hand The catching hand on which the glove is worn. A fielder who throws with his right hand wears the glove on his left hand.

gloveman **1.** A good defensive player. The term is applied sparingly to identify excellent fielders such as Marty Marion, Brooks Robinson, and Ozzie Smith. Also spelled "glove man." Syn. *leatherman*. **2.** A weak hitter whose defensive ability keeps him on the team. Joseph McBride (*High and Inside*, 1980) noted that the term is used as a "backhanded insult." Compare *woodman*.

glove-to-glove drill An exercise where catchers are timed in how quickly they can catch a pitch and deliver a throw to second base. "Anything under 2.0 seconds is outstanding" (*Baseball America*, Feb. 3–16, 1997).

glovework Defensive ability; the art of fielding baseballs. "Name an active player picked for the All-Star team in recent years in either league because of his glovework. Ozzie Smith, the St. Louis Cardinals' graceful shortstop, is one. Can you think of anybody else?" (Steve Fiffer, *How to Watch Baseball*, 1987, p.71). Sometimes spelled "glove work."

glue to the bag To keep a baserunner close to the base. IST USE. 1910 (*New York Tribune*, July 12; Edward J. Nichols).

GM Abbrev. for *general manager*.

go 1. To pitch. 2. To try to advance to the next base.

go after For a pitcher determined to retire the batter and not to capitulate to him; to pitch a batter aggressively; to *challenge* a batter. Jeff Francis (quoted in *Sports Illustrated*, June 6, 2005): "Go right after guys, try and get them to hit the ball." Keith Hernandez (*Pure Baseball*, 1994, p.96): "Some managers do like to hear that the pitcher wants to go after this batter. Damn the consequences; full speed ahead. Show no respect." Garrett Stephenson (quoted in *The Baltimore Sun*, July 27, 1996): "I have to be aggressive. I have to go after hitters and pitch inside." Troy Percival (quoted in *The Baltimore Sun*, Oct. 19, 2002): "We're going to go right after people. We're not nibbling." Compare *give in*. Syn. *go at*; *attack*, 1.

go against the book To violate the conventional wisdom of baseball strategy, such as when a pitcher walks the potential winning run to get at a lesser batter.

go-ahead inning The inning in which the team that is losing or tied scores enough runs to take the lead.

go-ahead run The run that puts a team in the lead. The term is often used to describe a runner on base; e.g., "The tying run is at second, the go-ahead run is on first." It is sometimes but not always the game-winning run.

goal An early term for a marker representing a base. "Nat . . . sent the ball at first bat, over the heads of all, so far that he had time to run round the whole circle of goals, turning a somerset as he came in" (William M. Thayer, *The Bobbin Boy*, 1860).

goal ball Syn. of *base*, 4 (Robin Carver, *The Book of Sports*, 1834).

goalie-style mask A *catcher's mask* based on the mask worn by hockey goaltenders, but designed to offer greater vision and protection. It was introduced on Sept. 13, 1996, by Toronto Blue Jays catcher Charlie O'Brien. The mask is also worn by home-plate umpires. Syn. *hockey-style mask*.

go all the way 1. To pitch a complete game. 2. To win a division or league title or the World Series.

goal tender A batter who patiently waits for good pitches at which to swing. IST USE. 1933. "Goal tender—Good waiter at the plate, who offers at no bad balls" (Edgar G. Brands, *The Sporting News*, Feb. 23; Peter Morris).

go around To swing through a pitch; to take a half swing that carries the bat across the plate.

go at Syn. of *go after*. "[Bob] Gibson . . . didn't fool around . . . He went right at the hitters" (Murray Chass, *The New York Times*, Oct. 29, 2001). "Once we got a two-run lead, I knew I could go right at them" (Roy Oswalt, quoted in *The Baltimore Sun*, Oct. 20, 2005).

goat A derisive name for a player who is singled out for a serious lapse in performance; one who loses (or appears to lose) a game for his team. Because of the severity of the term, it is more likely to come into play after the loss of an important regular season game or during the playoffs or World Series. It is correctly known as a "postgame sobriquet." "Mickey 'Goat' as Sox Win" was the headline for an article on a game in which Mickey Mantle allowed a run to score because he had collided with another player (*San Francisco Call-Bulletin*, May 22, 1957; Peter Tamony). The term and the concept are regarded with some seriousness; in the back of every player's mind is the hope not to be the goat. On occasion the term is applied to a manager or an umpire. "Often the player seeks to cover up his own blunder by making the umpire the 'goat'" (Billy Evans, *Pearson's Magazine*, Sept. 1912). See also *get one's goat*. IST USE. 1909. "Catcher [Charles] Schmidt, who had been the 'goat' of the first game [of the World Series], redeemed himself at this time" (*St. Louis Post-Dispatch*, Oct. 10; Peter Morris). ETYMOLOGY. Most references to this term note that it is a derivative or "clipped" form of "scapegoat" and applied to a player whose error is being blamed for a team's defeat. Gerald L. Cohen (*Comments on Etymology*, Dec. 1, 1985) insisted that there is a major "discrepancy" in this theory: "A scapegoat is innocent, whereas the goat is not; he has blundered, usually at a crucial moment. And the standard etymology of 'goat' as a shortening of 'scapegoat' is therefore almost certainly in error." Cohen cited the 1889 sports pages of *The World* (New York), where an article on the New York Giants noted "the meek and lowly goat, whose job it is to haul the peanut wagon up and down the board walk." Cohen's theory is that "the original 'goats' were players severely humbled by their errant play."

goat horns The figurative bony growth on the head of a player whose inept play caused the team to lose (Tom Meany, ed., *The Artful Dodgers*, 1953, p.62).

goatland The mythic resting place for baseball's famous goats. IST USE. 1920 (*Spalding's Official Base Ball Guide*, p.11; Edward J. Nichols).

goat's beard A plastic or leather flap hinged at the bottom of a catcher's or umpire's mask that protects the throat from foul tips and flying bats. It was introduced in 1976 by Los Angeles Dodgers catcher Steve Yeager after a teammate's bat shattered and lodged splinters in his throat while he was in the on-deck circle. The greater protection afforded by the goalie-style masks introduced in 1996 allowed catchers to shed the goat's beard. In 1888, A.G. Spalding & Brothers marketed a neck-protecting mask with a dog-skin extension filled with goat hair at the bottom of the mask. Syn. *throat guard*; *throat protector*; *billy goat*; *Stevie*.

go back 1. To hit a ball out of the ballpark. "A batter with power can hit a ball out of the ball yard. . . . He can go back, go massive or go yard. As in, 'Lotta guys on this team can go back'" (Dick Kaegel, *The Seattle Times*, Sept. 18, 1988). 2. For an outfielder to cover the field behind him.

gobble To field or catch a thrown or batted ball, often stated as "gobble the ball" or "gobble up." IST USE. 1867. "Addy out on a fly,

gobbled up by Wright" (*Daily National Intelligencer* [Washington, D.C.], July 29).

go big fly To hit a home run. "They [1990 Toronto Blue Jays] have a lot of guys who can go 'big fly'" (Tom Yantz, *Hartford Courant*, June 25, 1990). Keith Hernandez, on his thoughts on going to the plate with the idea of hitting a home run (quoted in Davey Johnson and Peter Golenbock, *Bats*, 1986): "I'm looking in. I'm looking in. If I get it, I'm going big fly." See also *big fly*.

go deep 1. To hit a home run. "[Javy] Lopez became the 11th player to go deep in his first All-Star at-bat" (*Milwaukee Journal Sentinel*, 1997). See also *take deep*. 2. To hit a ball for a long distance, resulting in an out or a hit. "Late in the game, I play deeper, because they're trying to go deep" (Dave Winfield, quoted in Steve Fiffer, *How to Watch Baseball*, 1987, p.77). 3. For a pitcher or batter to go to a 2–2 or 3–2 count. "[Kevin Appier] walked only one despite going deep into a lot of counts" (*The Baltimore Sun*, Apr. 3, 1996). 4. For a starting pitcher to pitch into the late innings. "The inability of Orioles starters to go deep into games . . . [was] putting undue strain on the relievers" (*The Baltimore Sun*, May 5, 2006). 5. For a team to use many relief pitchers in a game. "The Nationals had to go deep into their bullpen, using five relievers" (*The Baltimore Sun*, Apr. 26, 2006).

go down and get it For a batter to hit a low pitch solidly and with power. B.J. Ryan, on giving up a home run to Erubiel Durazo (quoted in *The Baltimore Sun*, Aug. 19, 2004): "He fought off some tough pitches. I tried to go down and away and he just went down and got it." Reggie Jackson (*Reggie*, 1984): "Reggie Cleveland threw me a fastball down. I mean, *down*. . . . I went down and got it like a golfer hitting a sand shot and hit it about 430 feet into the bleachers." Compare *go out and get it*. Syn. *reach down and get it*.

go down looking Syn. of *strike out looking*.

go down on strikes To strike out.

go down swinging Syn. of *strike out swinging*.

go down the line To order the batter to wait the pitcher out when the count is three balls and no strikes or one strike. Syn. *play the string* (Chicago Park District [Burnham Park], *Baseball*, 1938).

go downtown To hit a home run. See also *downtown*, 1.

go fishing To be lured into swinging at a ball thrown (usually low) just outside the strike zone. See also *fish*, 1.

go for a long one "Try an extra base on a hit" (*New York Sun*, June 23, 1932).

go for the downs To try to hit a home run.

go for the fences To try to hit a home run.

go for the pump To try to hit a home run.

go get 'em To be a good fielder. "Sports writers speak of players as being 'good, sensational, fair, mediocre or poor fielders,' but the players themselves sum it up as 'he can go get 'em,' or 'he can't go get 'em'" (*The New York Times*, June 2, 1929).

Go-Go Sox Nickname for the Chicago *White Sox* in the 1950s (esp. 1959) when they were stealing many bases.

"going!" A call by a fielder to alert others that a baserunner is attempting to steal a base.

"going, going ... gone" 1. A popular and dramatic description of a home run ball in flight. The phrase was popularized by New York Yankees announcer Mel Allen, who used it to describe balls heading into the outer reaches of Yankee Stadium. Sometimes the "gone" was omitted from the phrase if the ball was caught at the wall. This serves to heighten the drama for those moments when the announcer pauses after saying "going, going ... " ETYMOLOGY. Allen did not invent the phrase and probably was not the first to apply it to baseball. Patrick Ercolano (*Floaters, Fungoes and Fork Balls*, 1987, p.79) claimed it was coined by Cincinnati Reds announcer Harry Hartman in 1929. It is, after all, an echo from the early 1800s auction houses where the same words were first used to signal a sale. It was also an advertising slogan used for a bottled hair-remover known as Newbro's Herpicide. 2. Description for any-

thing that is departed. "GOING, GOING, GONE; Payroll Purge: Marlins to Dump Stars, Salaries" (*Miami Herald* headline, May 16, 1998). In reference to the ball that Michael Tucker hit for the first home run at Turner Field in Atlanta, Beth Warren wrote (*The Atlanta Journal-Constitution*, Apr. 22, 2006), "this hard-hit ball is 'going ... going ... GONE'" when the Atlanta History Center, which lists "conserving historic assets" as one of its duties, reported that the ball was missing.

gold coast *hist.* The group of clubhouse lockers reserved for bonus babies.

Golden Age 1. A period when baseball seems to have been played to near perfection. Determining such a period is based more on nostalgia and reverence (given that legendary ballparks and heroic figures are often mistily recalled, with a sense of innocence) than on history, as each individual has his/her own definition. For example: "Each man's 'Golden Age' is the era his nostalgia is most loyal to—when his sensibilities were being intensely formed, and the world was new, radiant, significant" (Marvin Cohen, *Baseball the Beautiful*, 1974, p.14). Lawrence Ritter's perspective (*USA Today*, Apr. 26, 1983): "From an emotional standpoint, I think each individual fan has his own 'Golden Age.' It's the period when that fan was between 8 and 16 years old. That's when baseball first captured the imagination; when players had appeal beyond human bounds." Likewise, Leonard Koppett (*The New York Times Magazine*, March 30, 1986): "Every fan has a personal Golden Age, coinciding roughly with the first decade of that person's interest in baseball, whether it starts at the age of 6 or 26. That era, for that individual, sets the norm to which everything afterward is related. For me, that was the decade of the 1930s." The term is often assigned to a time when the number of major-league teams was low and the ratio of excellent ballplayers to average ones was high; hence, the term is sometimes applied to the 1920s (a time of optimism and Ruthian achievements) or to the post–World War II period when New York City teams were dominant. Most people speak of the Golden Age as having already passed; others may disagree. "This is the golden age for ball players," said Cap Anson (quoted in *The Washington Post*, May 2, 1909; Peter Morris). Jon Miller (*Confessions of a Baseball Purist*, 1998) argued that the golden age of baseball is "right now." But Tom Verducci (*Sports Illustrated*, Nov. 18, 2002) opined that those in the baseball populace who "snicker" at sabermetrics believe "that the golden age refers to the Paleozoic." A selective list of "Golden Ages": 1919–1941, or the years between the two world wars (Richard C. Crepeau, *Baseball: America's Diamond Mind*, 1980); 1920–1929 (Peter L. de Rosa, Bridgewater [Mass.] State College baseball history course, 1999); 1940s–1950s (Gene Fehler, *Tales from Baseball's Golden Age*, 2000); 1941–1964 (Bill Gutman, *The Golden Age of Baseball*, 1989); 1922–1941 (Leonard Koppett, *Leonard Koppett's Concise History of Major League Baseball*, 2004); 1904–1942 (Neal and Constance McCabe, *Baseball's Golden Age: The Photographs of Charles M. Conlon*, 1993); 1946–1960 (J. Ronald Oakley, *Baseball's Last Golden Age*, 1994); 1903–1930 (Harold Seymour, *Baseball: The Golden Age*, 1971); and 1947–1957 (Jules Tygiel, *Past Time*, 2000). Syn. *Golden Era*. **2.** A similar period associated with a specific team or league. Peter Williams (*When the Giants Were Giants*, 1994) subtitled his book "Bill Terry and the Golden Age of New York Baseball" (1920s to 1930s). Harvey Frommer refers to the 1947-to-1957 period in his 1980 book *New York City Baseball: The Last Golden Age*; Richard Bak (*Yankees Baseball: The Golden Age*, 2000) cites the 1920-to-1961 period. Roberto González Echevarria (*The Pride of Havana*, 1999) gives 1898–1930 as the Golden Age for Cuban baseball.

Golden Era Syn. of *Golden Age*, 1. Baseball commissioner Bud Selig (Major League Baseball press release, Aug. 23, 2004): "This is the Golden Era of the sport; it has never been more so." Frank Smith pitched during what many call the major-leagues' "golden era" and loved every minute of it (*Watertown* [N.Y.] *Daily Times*, June 16, 2002): "The '50s was so good to us, thank God I played

in that era. It was right after World War II and people didn't have much to complain about." Rick Phalen (*A Bittersweet Journey: America's Fascination with Baseball*, 2000) noted that many viewed "baseball during the 'Golden Era' of 1946 to 1960." *Total Baseball* (8th ed., 2004) has a chapter on the Golden Era of 1946 to 1968. Brent Kelley is the author of *Baseball Stars of the 1950s: Interviews with All-Stars of the Game's Golden Era* (1993). And, finally, Eddie Gold and Pat Ahrens refer to the period 1878 to 1940 in their 1985 book *The Golden Era Cubs*.

golden sombrero A mythical award given to a batter who strikes out four times in a game. See also *hat trick*; *platinum sombrero*; *Horn*. Syn. *silver sombrero*. IST USE. 1984. "I almost got the Golden Sombrero. That's when you strike out four times, see. I only got the regular sombrero [hat trick]" (Chicago Cubs first baseman Leon Durham, quoted in *Chicago Tribune*, Apr. 14).

Golden Spikes Award An annual award presented since 1978 by USA Baseball (formerly the United States Baseball Federation) to the top amateur baseball player in the United States who exhibits "exceptional athletic ability and exemplary sportsmanship." It is sponsored by the Major League Baseball Players Association, underscoring the commitment of major-league players to the grassroots development of baseball programs, particularly for youth.

golden spine High-paid players comprising the "spine" of the defense: catcher, second baseman, shortstop, and center fielder.

Gold Glove Award An annual award for "superior fielding performance" sponsored by the Rawlings Sporting Goods Co., St. Louis, since 1957, given to a player at each position in the American League and the National League, as voted (since 1965) by major-league managers and coaches late in the regular season (they may not select players on their own teams and they vote only for players in their own leagues). In 1961, the method for selecting outfielders was changed from choosing a left fielder, a center fielder, and a right fielder to three outfielders regardless of position. Recipients originally were chosen by sportswriters (1957) and then by players (1958 through 1964). Defensive excellence includes such factors as range, throwing arm, general glove work, ability to make tough plays, and minimum errors. The award is a Rawlings custom-built glove or mitt hand-crafted of special metallic gold-finished leather, mounted on a hardwood stand bearing an engraved plate. See Bill Deane, in *Total Baseball*, 8th ed., 2004, pp.727–28.

Gold Glover A recipient of the Gold Glove Award.

golf To bat a low pitched ball, lifting it up as if it were a golf shot. "[Len Dykstra] golfed the ball into right field for a home run" (*USA Today*, Oct. 16, 1986). IST USE. 1917 (*The New York Times*, Oct. 9; Edward J. Nichols).

golf ball A ball that is batted in an upward fashion in the manner of a golf swing. Golf balls usually result in fly balls.

golf hitter A hitter given to swinging at low pitches.

GOM An initialism for *Grand Old Man*, often applied to Connie Mack, manager of the Philadelphia Athletics for 50 years (1901–1950). William Safire (*Political Dictionary*, 1978) noted that British statesman William Gladstone was also known as "the GOM."

go massive To hit a ball out of the ballpark. "A batter with power can hit a ball out of the ball yard. . . . He can go back, go massive or go yard" (Dick Kaegel, *The Seattle Times*, Sept. 18, 1988).

gondola Syn. of *eephus*.

gone 1. Syn. of *out*, 1; e.g., "Two gone in the bottom of the fifth" means there are two outs. IST USE. 1899 (Burt L. Standish, *Frank Merriwell's Double Shot*, p.70; Edward J. Nichols). 2. Ejected from a game. 3. Said of a ball hit for a home run. See also *"going, going . . . gone."*

goner A home run.

gonfalon Syn. of *pennant*, 2. A heading and subheading from *The Sporting News* (May 2, 1951): " 'Break Up Dodgers' Chant Gets Muffler; String of Setbacks Allays Rivals' Apprehension Over Possible Brooklyn Waltz to '51 Gonfalon." IST USE. 1910. "Trio of bear cubs [Tinker, Evers, and Chance] . . . ruthlessly pricking our gonfalon bubble, making a Giant hit into a double" (Franklin P. Adams, "That Double Play Again," *New York Evening Mail*, July 12). ETYMOLOGY. A banner suspended from a crossbar, often with several streamers or tails, esp. as used by various Italian republics. The Italian word for "flag" is "gonfalone."

gonfalonia interruptus A facetious, pseudo-medical term for the struggles of a team bogged down in its quest for the pennant (gonfalon). "The type of pitcher he [Tom Seaver] is and the type of person he is may cure that ancient regional affliction of *gonfalonia interruptus*" (*The Boston Globe*, July 1, 1986).

go nine To pitch a complete game (nine innings). "You've got to have a big man in the bullpen to win. Starters don't go nine any more" (Hal McRae, quoted in *Baseball Digest*, Oct. 1983).

go north with the team For a player to join a major-league team after spring training. "[Bill Caudill] needs to beat people out to go north with the team" (Dave Perkins, *Toronto Star*, Feb. 25, 1987; Grant Barrett). IST USE. 1903. "Pitcher Eul, the Peoria man who has been dickering with McFarland, got in in time to go north with the team and John Mertens was left at home" (*Decatur* [Ill.] *Review*, June 2; Grant Barrett).

good Excellent, in the context of baseball. This understatement is present in many baseball usages, from "good arm" to "good wood," or "he pitched good" to "I'm swinging pretty good."

good arm 1. A fielder with the ability to throw the ball accurately and for distance. 2. A pitcher with a strong delivery and a good fastball.

good ball 1. A pitch in the strike zone. Ted Williams (quoted in William Safire and Leonard Safir, eds., *Words of Wisdom*, 1989): "Rogers Hornsby told me . . . 'Get a good ball to hit.' . . . It means a ball that does not fool you, a ball that is not in a tough spot for you." 2. *hist.* A base hit. "[Hamilton sent] a good ball to the left field [and] got to second base" (*The New York Herald*, Aug. 24, 1860).

goodbye, Dolly Gray Snatching defeat from the jaws of victory. According to Paul Hallaman (personal communication, May 20, 2001), Gray (a pitcher for the Washington Senators, 1909–1911) once blew a one-hitter by walking seven straight batters on 3–2 counts before being relieved. The term was used by Casey Stengel.

good cheese A blurring fastball (*cheese*).

"good cut!" An exclamation said to a batter who takes a mighty swing at the ball and misses. Marian Edelman Borden (*The New York Times*, undated) pointed out that in Little League the phrase is "yelled to the batter who has swung with a great deal of force at the ball over the umpire's head."

good express A blurring fastball.

good eye Exceptional visual acuity by a batter. "[Buck Ewing's] good eye is shown in the fact that he did not strike out once in the exhibition games" (*The Boston Globe*, Apr. 12, 1892; Peter Morris)

"good eye!" An exclamation said to a batter who does not swing at a pitch out of the strike zone.

good face, the The visage of a highly rated baseball prospect, implying athleticism or a hard-nosed attitude. Kevin Kerrane (*Dollar Sign on the Muscle*, 1984, p.101) described the almost mystical allegiance of many older scouts to the idea that it is possible to discern a great prospect by looking at his face. Kerrane quoted Los Angeles Dodgers general manager Al Campanis: "You ever hear of 'the good face'? Well, I never used to sign a boy unless I could look in his face and see what I wanted to see: drive, determination, maturity, whatever. . . . Some scout would give me a report on a boy, and I'd say . . . 'Does he have the good face?'" Michael Lewis (*Moneyball*, 2003, p.7) wrote, "Some of the scouts still believed they could tell by the structure of a young man's face not only his character but his future in pro ball. They had a phrase they used: 'the Good Face.' Billy [Beane] had the Good Face." Compare *bad face*.

good field, no hit The classic description of the exceptional defensive player who is not a good hitter. "Fittingly, it was good-field-no-hit Marty Castillo who got one of the night's few fat pitches—a high fastball" (*Newsweek*, Oct. 22, 1984). ETYMOLOGY. All accounts trace the phrase back to Cuban-born Miguel "Mike" Gonzalez, whose command of English was less than perfect. Upon catcher Moe Berg's retirement in 1941, one week after the Japanese attack on Pearl Harbor (Berg became a spy for the U.S. government), Tom Meany wrote in *P.M.*, "It is ironic that the suave and polished Berg should have been the subject of baseball's most illiterate message: 'Good field, no hit.' But it was so." In 1924, Berg was a young shortstop with the Brooklyn Dodgers at its Clearwater, Fla., spring training site. Mike Kelley of Minneapolis wanted to purchase Berg's contract and wired Gonzalez, a catcher for the St. Louis Cardinals, for his opinion, which resulted in Gonzalez' famous four-word telegraphic message. Berg batted .186 in 49 games with Brooklyn in 1923. The *Brooklyn Eagle* (June 26, 1926; Peter Morris) suggested that the prospect may have instead been shortstop Ray French (career batting average of .193 in 82 games).

good-guy award An award given by a city's baseball writers' chapter to a player who is particularly cooperative (Peter Morris).

good hands 1. The asset of a good defensive player. "Closer to the hitter than any other infielder, a third baseman needs good hands and must be able to react immediately to the batted ball" (Steve Fiffer, *How to Watch Baseball*, 1987, p.74). See also *soft hands*. Compare *bad hands*, 2. **2.** The hands of a capable hitter.

"good idea" A statement said to a batter who tried to do something worthwhile. See also *"have an idea."*

good stuff The repertoire of a pitcher who has command of his pitches and uses them effectively. To be told that one has "good stuff" is to be paid a major compliment. The term can be applied to a particular pitching performance or to a pitcher's overall ability.

good town An enjoyable city for a player to visit on a road trip. *The Sporting News* (July 1, 1978) noted that "good town" is as much a part of the baseball vernacular as "line drive" and stated that "Montreal is perhaps the best, but San Diego and Chicago are not far behind in the opinion of the Braves, who were asked to rate National League cities."

good wood **1.** The *barrel*, or thickest part, of the bat, where the ball is hit with the greatest power. To "put good wood on the ball" is to hit the ball solidly. "As the best relief pitcher in baseball in the late 1950s Elroy Face rarely allowed hitters to get good wood on the ball" (Stephen Cannella, *Sports Illustrated*, Aug. 18, 2003). See also *wood*, 1. Syn. *decent wood*. **2.** An outstanding baseball bat. "Ball players are always trading bats. Goose Goslin never comes to New York that he doesn't come over to our dugout and look over all the bats. Wallie Schang is another one who is always looking for 'good wood'" (George Herman Ruth, *Babe Ruth's Own Book of Baseball*, 1928, p.174).

go on the pitch To try to steal a base at the moment the pitcher goes into his motion.

gooseberry A bruise from sliding. See also *strawberry*. "When I make up my mind to hit the dirt, I never change it, and I go down traveling at full speed. . . . The worst you can get as a result of this system are some sliding 'gooseberries' and, maybe, a spike wound" (Ty Cobb, *Busting 'Em and Other Big League Stories*, 1914; Peter Morris).

goose egg **1.** *n.* A zero on the scoreboard, in allusion to the shared oval shape of a goose egg. "After 25 innings, it's still all goose eggs; Texas teams resume scoreless battle today" announced *The Boston Herald* (July 16, 1988) in describing a Jackson Mets and San Antonio Missions Double-A Texas League game. "Goose-Egg Diet Plunges Seals into Basement" (*San Francisco News* headline, June 27, 1952; Peter Tamony); the story that followed claimed that the "[San Francisco] Seals recently have accumulated enough goose-eggs to open a market." See also *duck egg*; *blank*, 1; *lay an egg*. Syn. *hen fruit*. IST USE. 1866. "The 'children' were 'about three times' put out for another 'goose egg'" (*Brooklyn Eagle*, Sept. 12; Peter Morris). EXTENDED USE. Charles Earle Funk (*A Hog on Ice and Other Curious Expressions*, 1948) pointed out that the egg in the expression, "to lay an egg," is derived from the

goose egg of the scoreboard and "has no bearing whatsoever on the output of a hen." Goose egg stands for the zero cipher in other sports; e.g., "[Washington Capitals goalie] racks up some goose eggs" (*The Washington Post*, Feb. 22, 1988). To "crack" or "break an egg" is to begin to score in cricket (just as not scoring is to "lay an egg"), and the zero-term in tennis, "love," derives from "l'oeuf," which is French for "egg." Both "goose egg" and "lay an egg" have generalized to any realm in which one fails to score. **2.** *v.* To fail to score in an inning. "The Senators squeezed in a run in their half of the fourth, were goose-egged in the fifth and in the sixth" (*The Washington Post*, Apr. 13, 1901; Peter Morris).

go out For a batter to make an out. "The best method of pitching to him is to pitch natural and take a chance of his going out" (Cincinnati Reds pitcher Art Fromme, quoted in *San Francisco Bulletin*, Feb. 14, 1913; Gerald L. Cohen). IST USE. 1863 (Chadwick Scrapbooks, Aug. 9; Edward J. Nichols).

go out and get it For a batter to swing at an outside pitch and hit it solidly. "That third pitch . . . was outside, but you went out and got it, and hit it right through the middle" (Ted Williams, quoted in Bobby Thomson, *"The Giants Win the Pennant! The Giants Win the Pennant!,"* 1991, pp.15–16). Compare *go down and get it*.

gopher ball **1.** A pitch that is destined to be hit for a home run; one that will "go for" extra bases. Jim Brosnan (*The Long Season*, 1960) defined the term: "Similar to the ordinary, legal-size baseball, but dangerous for pitchers to handle . . . should be avoided." Syn. "gopher." IST USE. 1930. "What's a gopher ball? . . . Every time I pitched it I heard the fellows on the other team yelling, 'Go for two! Go for three!'" (St. Louis Browns pitcher Dock Coffman, quoted in *The Washington Post*, March 22; Barry Popik). **2.** A *home run* given up by a pitcher. USAGE NOTE. The term is now used without a hint of its punnish origin: "Any informed student of the game knows that no pitcher wants to go down in the record books as having been the pitcher who served up a record-breaking gopher ball; thus careful pitching is the order of the day" (Tom Mitchel, letter to

International Herald Tribune, Sept. 22, 1986).

ETYMOLOGY. In some earlier explanations of the term it is said that it is a contraction of "go far," but usage suggests it is the "go fer" as in "go for a double, triple, or home run." Lawrence Frank (*Playing Hardball: The Dynamics of Baseball Folk Speech*, 1983, p.108) suggests the term "presumably originated in the early days of baseball when there were no fences (or fences that were far from home plate) and a fielder had to 'go for' a ball that was hit past him." Hy Turkin (*Baseball Almanac*, 1955) reports that the term was coined by Lefty Gomez when he pitched for the New York Yankees (1930–1942). Neal McCabe and Constance McCabe (*Baseball's Golden Age*, 1993, p.50) quote Gomez: "I throw the ball, and then the batter swings—and then it will go for three or four bases." Gomez explained that base coaches of opposing teams invariably bellowed to the batter-runner, "go-fer three" (*The Washington Post*, Apr. 14, 1931; Barry Popik). Although there have been many published explanations of this term's being a play on "go fer," opinion is not unanimous. Parke Cummings (*Dictionary of Baseball*, 1950) reports: "Like the gopher, which vanishes into its hole, the ball quickly vanishes into the stands or out of the park." Along those same lines, Ray Corio (*The New York Times*, Feb. 8, 1988) adds, "But there's also the line of thought that the expression reflects how a pitcher feels as he watches his pitch soar over a fence: like digging a hole and crawling into it, gopher style."

gopher hunter *hist.* A sharply batted ground ball (*Chicago Inter-Ocean*, Aug. 9, 1874; Edward J. Nichols).

gopheritis A mock disease in which a pitcher is unable to keep the ball in the ballpark. "Pitchers with gopheritis have a fly ball rate of at least 40%" (Ron Shandler, *Ron Shandler's Baseball Forecaster*, 2006).

gorilla ball An offense based on home runs. The term, coined by former Louisiana State Univ. baseball coach Skip Bertman, is closely associated with college baseball, where aluminum bats have placed a great emphasis on power hitting. "This year's Col-lege World Series proved, for once and for all, that 'Gorilla Ball' is dead. Pitching now means everything in college baseball" (Brian David, *Bryan–College Station Eagle*, June 28, 2005).

gorker A cheap hit. "You hate to take a guy out after two gorkers" (Baltimore Orioles manager Earl Weaver, quoted in *The Washington Post*, June 12, 1983).

go signal A verbal signal given by a base coach to a baserunner to steal, advance to the next base, or tag up after a fly ball is caught. The coach must time this perfectly to send the runner at the precise moment. Syn. "go sign." EXTENDED USE. Metaphorical conversion of the nation from a wartime to a civilian economy at the end of World War II. "Truman Flashes 'Go' Signal on Reconversion" (*San Francisco Examiner* headline, Aug. 15, 1945).

go south **1.** To depart for a Southern spring-training camp. IST USE. 1906 (*The Sporting Life*, Feb. 10, p.5; Edward J. Nichols). **2.** To lose a game. IST USE. 1915 (*Baseball Magazine*, December, p.22; Edward J. Nichols). **3.** For a player or team that was doing well to struggle badly.

got a big one left Said of a batter with two strikes against him.

Gothams Original nickname of the National League New York franchise when it replaced the Troy Trojans after the 1882 season. The club was renamed the New York *Giants* in 1885. ETYMOLOGY. Gotham is the traditional name for New York City dating back to the writings of Washington Irving and earlier. The nickname of the Gotham Base Ball Club founded in the early 1850s was "Gothams."

go the distance To pitch a complete game. Syn. *go the route*. ETYMOLOGY. Lawrence Frank (*Playing Hardball*, 1983, p.103) noted that the similarity of this term to one in boxing, in which "going the distance" means the boxer finishes the fight, is "indeterminable, but would not be surprising in light of the intense struggle for power between the pitcher and the hitter." EXTENDED USE. To win an election. "N.H. Democrats wonder if [Vice President Al] Gore can go the distance" (*The Baltimore Sun* headline, Sept. 29, 1999).

go the other way To hit to the opposite field; i.e., for a right-handed batter to hit the ball to right field or for a left-handed batter to hit the ball to left field. "[Going] the other way, that's my swing" (Chris Hoiles, quoted in *The Baltimore Sun*, July 19, 1996).

go the route Syn. of *go the distance*.

"got him!" A broadcaster's terse comment that a batter has been struck out or otherwise retired. "It's a joy to hear him [announcer Vin Scully] say, 'Got him!' time and time again— a simple salute to the strikeout" (*The Washington Post*, Oct. 24, 1986). USAGE NOTE. "'Get him, get him,' shouted Manager Hanlon to Kennedy in the eighth when Roaring Bill had two strikes on Cross with two men out. In base ball parlance this means that the batter must be retired" (*Brooklyn Eagle*, May 17, 1899; Peter Morris).

go to bat for To pinch hit. EXTENDED USE. To support or defend someone or something. "Part of feeling at home in America meant that Jews could go to bat for their co-religionists elsewhere" (Tony Carnes, *The Wall Street Journal*, Sept. 9, 2005).

go to grass *hist.* To lose; to be defeated. 1ST USE. 1889. "The cow-eyed daisies which charm the susceptible Benedicts in centre field held up their ruffled heads and saw the champions go to grass again" (*The World* [New York], July 24; Gerald L. Cohen).

go-to guy 1. A dependable player, esp. a relief pitcher. "In the playoffs a three-game losing streak sends you home. So you're more likely to go to your go-to guys quicker and more often" (Mike Hargrove, quoted in *Sports Illustrated*, Oct. 6, 2003). "He's going to be an everyday player, but I don't think he is a go-to guy" (anonymous scout, regarding Oakland A's outfielder Travis Buck, quoted in *The Baltimore Sun*, May 27, 2007). 2. A player who is always accessible to reporters after a game, win or lose, and speaks honestly and intelligently; e.g., Kansas City Royals first baseman Mike Sweeney (Joe Posnanski, *Kansas City Star*, March 30, 2003).

go-to pitch A pitcher's best pitch.

go to school To learn from another player through experience.

go to the hat For a pitcher to touch, tug, or otherwise fuss with his cap while on the mound. It is an affectation that can come in handy if one has hidden an illegal substance on the cap and is "loading up" for an illegal pitch, or, as Gaylord Perry has been known to do, touch a clean cap to encourage the batter to think that he is fueling up for an illegal pitch.

go to the mouth To touch the lips or mouth. This action is illegal if it is made by a pitcher while on the mound. An automatic ball is called for this infraction, and the pitcher can be ejected if cheating is suspected. The move is illegal because it suggests that the pitcher may be preparing to throw a spitball or other illegal pitch. If a pitcher needs to touch his mouth, he must step down from the mound. On a particularly cold day, a pitcher can ask for and receive from the plate umpire permission to blow on his hand without stepping off the mound.

go to the wire To be decided at the end of a game or season; e.g., characterizing a game whose outcome is not known until the ninth inning or a team's season whose final standing is not known until the final day. ETYMOLOGY. The term originated in horse racing for a close race. "Wire" is long-established track slang for the finish line.

"go to war, Miss Agnes!" An expression used by Baltimore Orioles broadcaster Chuck Thompson to emphasize something big and exciting on the ballfield, such as a home run. Thompson picked up the expression from golfer Bob Sharman, who, instead of swearing, used it to express frustration in situations such as missing a putt. Thompson stopped using the expression as the Vietnam War dragged on.

got too much Said of a pitcher when he has an excess of deceitful motion (curve, slide, etc.) on the ball and therefore cannot control his delivery.

go up For a player to move to a higher level of minor-league play or to break into the major leagues. 1ST USE. 1909 (*Baseball Magazine*, October, p.26; Edward J. Nichols).

go up top To hit a home run.

go with the pitch To hit the ball to the side of

the plate where it is pitched rather than to try to pull or "overpower" it; e.g., a right-handed batter would hit an outside pitch to right field and an inside pitch to left field, whereas a left-handed batter would hit an outside pitch to left field and an inside pitch to right field. "[I was] trying to do too much. . . . I was going for the fences instead of going with the pitch" (Rob Ducey, quoted in *Tampa Tribune-Times*, March 5, 1989).

go yard To hit a ball over the fence; e.g., hitting a home run is "going yard." "[Mark McGwire] went yard for the 16th time" (*Sports Illustrated*, June 1, 1998). See also *leave the yard*. ETYMOLOGY. Believed to have been invented at Baltimore's Oriole Park at Camden Yards (*Athletics* [Oakland A's magazine], Sept. 2005), or to have become more popular after construction of Oriole Park. "A batter with power can hit a ball out of the ball yard. . . . He can go back, go massive or go yard" (Dick Kaegel, *The Seattle Times*, Sept. 18, 1988).

grab hist. 1. To get a base hit. "Buddy Ryan grabbed three nice fat hits for himself, one being a triple" (*San Francisco Bulletin*, May 30, 1913; Gerald L. Cohen). 2. To win (*The Sporting Life*, Nov. 29, 1913).

grabber hist. Syn. of *catcher*, 1.

grab off hist. To get a base hit. "The Honolulu twirler held the Oaks to six hits, while his teammates grabbed nine off 'Buffalo Bill' [Malarkey]" (*San Francisco Bulletin*, May 30, 1913; Gerald L. Cohen).

"grab some bench" To taunt a batter who has struck out to take a seat in the dugout. Syn. "grab some pine."

graded card A baseball card whose physical condition has been assessed by an independent source, such as a price guide, and given a ranking or grade ranging from gem-mint (ranking of 10) to near-mint, excellent, good, fair, and poor. Physical condition includes centering all around, sharpness and wear of corners, evenness of borders, smoothness of edges, registration and focus of photographs, intensity of color, visible imperfections, presence of foreign material, and signs of misuse. The card is then placed in a hermetically sealed plastic holder, with the grade designation. Grant Sand-

ground, senior price editor for Beckett Grading Services (quoted in *Spirit*, publication of Southwest Airlines, Dec. 2000, p.116): "The cool thing about graded cards is that you can buy and sell, sight unseen, and feel confident. You don't need to worry about the seller being biased or overgrading his stuff."

grand average hist. Syn. of *slugging percentage*. The term was used in *The Boston Traveler* (July 11, 1914; Andrew Milner).

grand bounce hist. Ejection from the game. The term was used frequently in the 1880s and 1890s. Abbrev. *GB*, 3.

grand larceny A terrific fielding play that takes a potential base hit away from the batter. Compare *larceny*.

grandmother A woman whose fictional funeral traditionally figures into excuses for people to get out of work for an afternoon at the ballpark. The death rate among grandmothers has decreased in direct proportion to the decrease in day games played during the workweek. R.E. Sherwood (*Baseball Magazine*, Sept. 1913) defined the term: "An elderly female in high favor with office boys in general. Her death often forms an excuse among them for leave of absence. If the home team is on the road, the excuse goes; if at home, the office boys GOES—to look for another job." An earlier and more disarming reference appeared in the *Atlantic Monthly* (Aug. 1908, p.229) in the form of this immortal stanza by Rollin Lynde Hartt: "Lives there a man with soul so dead / But he unto himself has said, / 'My grandmother shall die to-day / And I'll go see the Giants play'?" The *Cleveland Plain Dealer* (Apr. 15, 1908; Cait Murphy) noted that the Spalding sporting goods store posted the following notice: "Closed for the day on account of grandmother's illness. Employees of this store can be found at the Cleveland ball park." Mary Cantwell (in Ron Fimrite, ed., *Birth of a Fan*, 1993, p.43) wrote, "My colleagues are mostly males, and on opening day a few of them don't show up at the office. Later they say they had to go to their grandmother's funeral, and then there are great bursts of laughter and an all-around jabbing of elbows." IST USE. 1890. "A boy who has asked his employer for the afternoon off to attend his grandmother's burial is told,

'This is the eighth grandmother you have buried since the base ball season opened.' The boy replies: 'I know it sir; I came of a very old family, and my ancestors can't stand the excitement of two leagues. They're dying off fast'" (*Terre Haute* [Ind.] *Express*, July 29; Peter Morris).

grand old game The game of baseball. "The lively ball naturally has changed the hitting. . . . But it's still baseball—a grand old game" (Honus Wagner, *Baseball Grins*, 1933, p.29).

Grand Old Man Honorific title for an elderly baseball man with great experience and respect. The title has been applied to Connie Mack, Cap Anson, and Cy Young, among others. "Zip Collins: A Grand Old Man of Baseball" was the title of an article by Bob O'Donnell (*Washington Times Magazine*, Feb. 24, 1983) regarding the 90-year-old former ballplayer. Mike Bianchi (*The Baltimore Sun*, May 20, 2007) honored 76-year-old Don Zimmer as "the grand old man of the grand old game" for his 59 years of service in baseball. See also *GOM*. IST USE. 1886. "I don't believe the 'grand old man' [Henry] Chadwick would join in such a combination" (*The Sporting Life*, May 26; Barry Popik).

grand salami Syn. of *grand slam*, 1.

grand slam 1. A home run hit with the bases loaded. Abbrev. *GS*, 2. Syn. *grand slammer*; *grand salami*; *salami*; *grannie*; *slam*, 3; *slammer*; *jackpot*; *bases-loaded home run*; *demolition derby*; *four-ribeye steak*. IST USE. 1929. "The game's most remarkable feature was the stark fact that each manager, in his turn, picked a pinch-hitter who delivered a home run with the bases filled. One pinch-hitter thus producing what is known in baseball as a grand slam is enough to make a ball game momentous. When two managers inside of a half-inning thus score a tie on each other in picking grand-slam pinch-hitters the game becomes one for the ages" (William E. Brandt, *The New York Times*, May 27, p.31). USAGE NOTE. The term had earlier, but different, usages in baseball: it could describe a hard-hit ball, scoring a lot of runs, or any home run. "Bill Killifer set his teeth tightly and took one last grand slam at the ball and shot a high ballooner between right and cen-

tre fields" (*The New York Times*, Sept. 6, 1918). "With one grand slam, the Cincinnati Reds fell upon the White Sox in the sixth inning . . . with a violent concentrated attack [scoring four runs]" (*The New York Times*, Oct. 7, 1919). ETYMOLOGY. The term, which is now used in many other sports, was first used in the game of contract bridge, where it applies to the taking of all 13 tricks. EXTENDED USE. Anything extraordinary and/or powerful. It would appear that the term first moved to golf in 1930 when it was widely applied to Bobby Jones' feat of winning all of golf's four major championships (the British and U.S. Opens and the British and U.S. Amateurs). It was first used as a tennis expression in 1938 to describe Don Budge's unprecedented feat of winning all four major tournaments (Wimbledon, and the French, Australian, and U.S. Opens). The term is also applied to a diversity of things and events outside sports. Peter Tamony collected several, including these two headlines: "A Grand Slam for Culture" (when two new theaters opened in Los Angeles) and "Grand Slam Driver Held" (he ran into four other cars). The term was the name of a powerful British bomb used during World War II; in fact, when the first atomic bomb was dropped on Japan in 1945, it was said to have 2,000 times the power of the British "grand slam" bomb, the largest previously used. The term is also the name of a cocktail (made by mixing ½ jigger of blended whiskey, ¼ jigger of vermouth, ⅛ jigger of curaçao, and ⅛ jigger of lime juice). **2.** A sweep of all four games of a series. "Grand Slam Gives Yankees 24 Wins in 27 Series Games" (*The Sporting News* headline, Oct. 13, 1938) after the New York Yankees defeated the Chicago Cubs in the World Series, four games to none. See also *slam*, 4; *sweep*, 3.

grand slammer Syn. of *grand slam*, 1. IST USE. 1940. "Jim Tabor smashed out a 'grand slammer' against Johnny Humphries in the fourth inning" (*San Francisco News*, Aug. 20, 1940; Peter Tamony).

grandstand **1.** *n.* The location of the main seating area at a ballpark, traditionally behind the box seats. The grandstand is usually covered and contains reserved seats, which are

Grandstand. Charles City, Iowa. *Andy Moresund Collection*

priced between the cheap (bleachers) and the expensive (box) seats. See also *stands*. IST USE. 1870. "The immense audience disposed for the most part, on the seats of the 'grand stand'" (*Lakeside Monthly*, 4; David Shulman). **2.** *n.* The spectators in the grandstand. IST USE. 1888. "Ryan and Hanlon do brilliant work in the field and cause the grand stand and bleachers to rise and applaud" (*Rocky Mountain News* [Denver], Oct. 29). **3.** *v.* To play for the admiration and applause of the crowd; to show off. R.E. Sherwood (*Baseball Magazine*, Sept. 1913) defined "grandstanding" as "the custom prevalent among players of taking a drink of water in front of the grandstand after making a home run." See also *play to the grandstand*. IST USE. 1889. "On the New York team there is always a temptation to individual 'grand-stand' or theatrical play" (Chadwick Scrapbooks; David Shulman). EXTENDED USE. To show off in other realms. "Some members of the [congressional investigating] committee relished the chance to grandstand in front of the TV cameras" (Bill Kearns, letter to *The Baltimore Sun*, Feb. 21, 2002). Peter Morris notes an interesting example in a quote from Peter Gammons (*Baseball America*, Dec. 13–26, 1993): "When Peter Ueberroth took over [as baseball commissioner] in October 1984, his first move was to grandstand for the media and intervene in the umpires' playoff strike, for which baseball paid dearly the next nine seasons."

grandstander 1. Syn. of *grandstand player*. IST USE. 1911. "He had never been a grandstander" (Charles Van Loan, *The Big League*, p.164; David Shulman). EXTENDED USE. One who is given to pretentious display. When Atlanta Braves pitcher John Smoltz blasted an Atlanta clergyman for demanding that the Braves trade their problem pitcher, John Rocker, *The Baltimore Sun* (March 5, 2000) commented, "It's about time someone had the courage to challenge the hypocrisy of some of the grandstanders who are using Rocker's comments to get time on television." **2.** A person sitting in the grandstand. Also spelled "grand-stander." IST USE. 1891. "During the four New York games there were never less than 2,200 people at a game, and 50 per cent of the patrons here were 'grand-standers'" (*Sporting Times*, May 23; David Shulman).

grandstand manager A spectator who second-guesses the manager and tends to be quite vocal about it. "Grandstand managers, some of them with horns, have sprouted up all over since Lefty O'Doul sent outfielder Joe Brovia to Portland" (*San Francisco Call-Bulletin*, March 4, 1949; Peter Tamony). IST USE. 1920. "[Miller Huggins'] club has been going downward instead of upward this season and as a result the grand stand managers are on his back" (J.V. Fitz Gerald, *The Washington Post*, Apr. 29; Peter Morris).

grandstand play Any play that is staged to elicit applause or impress the fans. The play may be a simple one, but it is embellished and made to look difficult and even heroic. "When necessary, bench a man for each attempt at grandstand play. Most coaches need a little courage in this respect" (Coleman R. Griffith, *The Psychology of Coaching*, 1926). See also *play to the grandstand*. IST USE. 1883. "Little [William] Hunter of Saginaw worked the grand stand almost to death yesterday, and several others were guilty of the same piece of foolishness! Grand stand plays are monotonous . . . Every other ball pitched Hunter would execute a combined acrobatic song and dance, fall on his side (each move a picture), and the spectators would applaud" (*Grand Rapids* [Mich.] *Eagle*, Aug. 10; Peter Morris). EXTENDED USE. **1.** A showy move or style that is usually both spectacular and ineffective. "They spent so much time in arguin' and makin' grandstand play, that the interests of the city were forgotten" (William L. Riordan, *Plunkitt of Tammany Hall*, 1905; Peter Tamony). **2.** An unexpected and dramatic move in the courtroom. "Defense attorneys in the Nick De John murder trial demanded perjury charges yesterday against Mrs. Anita Rocchia Venza, and were met by snorts from the prosecution of 'grandstand play'" (*San Francisco Examiner*, Feb. 26, 1949; Peter Tamony).

grandstand player A player who seeks the adulation of the crowd by routinely making easy plays look difficult. "It's little things of this sort which makes the 'grand stand player.' They make impossible catches, and when they get the ball they roll all over the field" (Mike J. Kelly, *"Play Ball,"* 1888; David Shulman). Syn. *grandstander*, 1; *Hollywood player*; *jumping jack*; *tumble bug*, 2. IST USE. 1886. "[Kid] Baldwin of the Cincinnatis has the credit of being the greatest grandstand

player" (*The Sporting News*, May 24; David Shulman). USAGE NOTE. Although a grandstand play here and there is tolerated and even appreciated, a player does not want to become known as a grandstand player. Alfred H. Spink wrote of Charles Comiskey (*The National Game*, 2nd ed., 1911, p.177): "He had no use for the grandstand player who could hit the ball over the fence when the bases were clear and his side a mile ahead, but he loved the man who could hit the ball right on the nose when a run was needed and a good clout meant the game."

grand tour A home run. IST USE. 1912 (*New York Tribune*, Oct. 7; Edward J. Nichols).

grannie Syn. of *grand slam*, 1. The term began to be heard during the 1997 season. "Even grand slams, the rarest of taters, are losing luster. The rate of grannies has nearly doubled in just the past eight years" (*Sports Illustrated*, July 17, 2000). Also spelled "granny."

grapefruit **1.** The baseball as viewed by a batter who is hitting well or by the catcher when the pitcher has nothing on the ball. IST USE. 1943 (*Baseball Magazine*, January; David Shulman). **2.** A dead or cheap baseball (Chicago Park District [Burnham Park], *Baseball*, 1938).

grapefruit game A spring exhibition game played in Florida. IST USE. 1961. "Last year 306,000 attended 143 grapefruit games in Florida" (*The New York Times*, Feb. 19; David Shulman).

Grapefruit League The name for the major-league teams that conduct spring training and play exhibition games against each other in Florida. "Florida's so-called Grapefruit League baseball season began today in earnest, with four of the ten major league clubs training in the State engaged in exhibition play" (*The New York Times*, March 8, 1928, p.18). See also *Limestone League*. Compare *Cactus League*. Syn. *citrus circuit*; "Grapefruit Circuit"; "Grapefruit Loop." IST USE. 1924. "[Donie Bush retained] the leadership that he enjoys at the head of the grapefruit league" (N.W. Baxter, *The Washington Post*, March 26).

graphite bat A baseball bat made from a lightweight, virtually unbreakable combination of graphite, fiberglass, and polyester resin. Although graphite bats are in use in softball and at various levels of baseball, their only plate appearance in major-league baseball has been in spring-training experiments. Unlike the *aluminum bat*, which gives off a "ping" sound, graphite sounds more like wood when the ball is hit.

grass 1. Traditional vegetation that is grown as the surface for a baseball field and that covers everything except the pitcher's mound, basepaths, and other specific areas, which are covered with dirt. 2. A specific grassy area of the playing field, esp. the infield; e.g., "Jones is in the grass" indicates an infielder who, for defensive reasons, has come in close to the plate and out of the basepath. An infielder can also play on the outfield grass when defending against a pull hitter.

grass burner Syn. of *grass cutter.*

grass clipper Syn. of *grass cutter.* IST USE. 1868. "Wright goes to first on his short grass clipper to center field" (Chadwick Scrapbooks; David Shulman).

grass cutter A sharply hit grounder that skims quickly along the grass or hugs the ground and does not hop. See also *lawn mower; skimmer; daisy cutter,* 1. Syn. *grass burner; grass clipper; grass trimmer.* IST USE. 1870. "Parsell got 1st on hit, and home by the assistance of Decker, who made his 3d on a grass cutter to l.f." (*Flint* [Mich.] *Wolverine Citizen,* Sept. 3; Peter Morris).

grasser A sharply hit ground ball. "The average fan, watching the speed and certainty with which Hans [Wagner] goes after the grassers" (*The Sporting News,* March 3, 1906). IST USE. 1902. "A flaming grasser which would have made a projectile from a 13-inch gun look like a bean bag tossed from one baby to another" (*Yale Record,* reprinted in *Grand Valley* [Moab, Utah] *Times,* Jan. 24; Peter Morris).

grasshopper A bouncing ground ball. IST USE. 1887. "[Jerry] Denny drove a grasshopper at [Jack] Rowe and a double play was the result" (*Detroit Free Press,* Apr. 29; Peter Morris).

grass puller A first base coach, or third base coach in the early part of the 20th century whose method of transmitting signs was to pull grass. Hughie Jennings and Arlie Latham were two coaches who turned grass pulling into an element of a coaching sideshow. IST USE. 1908 (*Baseball Magazine,* July, p.49; Edward J. Nichols).

grass trimmer Syn. of *grass cutter.* IST USE. 1867. "Barnes to first on a grass-trimmer" (*Daily National Intelligencer* [Washington, D.C.], July 29).

graveyard The deep part of the outfield where solidly hit balls are caught.

gravy hop A ground ball that takes a high, easy-to-field bounce. See also *charity hop; Hollywood hop; Sunday hop.*

gray ink test An informal test of a player's domination of league statistics, performed by counting the number of times that the player appeared in the top ten of a league in a statistic. The term was coined by Bill James. See also *black ink test.*

grays See *road grays.*

Grays 1. Nickname for the National League franchise in Providence, R.I. The franchise was originally named the Rhode Islanders (1878) and renamed the Grays (1879–1885). 2. Nickname for an African-American franchise known as the Homestead Grays, formed in 1912 as an independent club and later a member of the Negro National League (1935–1948), before disbanding after the 1950 season. Named for a steel-mill town near Pittsburgh, the Grays played most of their games at Forbes Field in Pittsburgh; during the 1940s, they played at Griffith Stadium in Washington, D.C. The Grays won nine consecutive Negro National League championships (1937–1945) and featured such stars as Josh Gibson and Buck Leonard.

grazer An outfielder.

greaseball An illegal pitch that has been doctored with a secret dollop of hair dressing, petroleum jelly, lard, or similar sticky substance to give the ball an unpredictable trajectory. "Today, people still talk about the spitter, but the spitter is dead. Nowadays, it's a grease ball the pitchers are throwing" (Gaylord Perry, *Me and the Spitter*, 1974, p.30; Charles D. Poe). Also spelled "grease ball." Syn. *greaser*; *jellyball*.

greaser Syn. of *greaseball*.

great A baseball player whose feats have become legendary; e.g., "Babe Ruth is among the greats of baseball."

Great American game The game of baseball (Maurice H. Weseen, *A Dictionary of American Slang*, 1934).

greater fool theory The principle that the only way to make money on a baseball franchise is to find someone to pay even more for it (Will Lingo, *Baseball America*, Apr. 13–26, 1998). The theory was popular during the 1960s and 1970s when the economics of minor-league baseball was very bleak. Commissioner Bud Selig and many owners often refer to this theory regarding major-league franchises. In testimony before the U.S. Senate Judiciary Committee (Nov. 21, 2000), Selig said the time had ended in which owners made tremendous profits on the sale of small- and middle-market franchises: "We used to call it the 'greater-fool theory.' The problem, Senator, is we've run out of greater fools. The appreciation of these franchises is over." Jerry Crasnick (*Baseball America*, Jan. 7–20, 2002) asked, "Is [prospective owner Donald] Watkins a savior, a publicity seeker or the latest example of what owners commonly refer to as the 'greater fool' theory?" Peter Morris wonders "whether [the owners] are aware of the implication that they themselves are the biggest set of fools available."

Greater New Yorks Nickname for the New York entry in the American League from 1903 through 1906. The club was officially nicknamed the *Yankees* in 1913.

Greatest Living Player Title bestowed on Joe DiMaggio in 1969 by an unofficial vote of baseball writers during the celebration of baseball's centennial. For the next 30 years until his death in 1999, DiMaggio insisted on being introduced at public functions as "baseball's greatest living player." Willie Mays assumed the title in 1999.

Great Experiment The breaking of baseball's color line by Jackie Robinson, initiated when Brooklyn Dodgers general manager Branch Rickey signed a contract with Robinson on Oct. 23, 1945, thereby starting the successful integration of African-Americans in baseball. Such integration came before the civil rights movement and before the historic *Brown vs. the Board of Education* ruling by the U.S. Supreme court (1954). Jules Tygiel (*Baseball's Great Experiment: Jackie Robinson and His Legacy*, 1983, p.206) wrote that Robinson's first season (1947) in the major leagues was "a tale of courage, heroics, and triumph": "It remains a drama which thrills and fascinates, combining the central themes of the illusive Great American Novel: the undertones of Horatio Alger, the interracial comradery [*sic*] of nineteenth-century fiction, the sage advisor and his youthful apprentice, and the rugged and righteous individual confronting the angry mob." ETYMOLOGY. Long-established metaphor for America and its constitutional form of government, with attestation dating to 1803, when the *National Intelligencer* (Jan. 17) reported on the discussion of states having separate penal codes as an issue "that would, in a few years test this great experiment." In regard to the color line, according to Tygiel, the terms "great experiment" and *noble experiment* were used by Rickey, but Tygiel's publisher (Oxford Univ. Press) preferred "great" because "noble" referred to Prohibition.

Greenberg Gardens The 30-foot area between the former and new left-field fences of Forbes Field when Hank Greenberg joined the Pittsburgh Pirates in 1947. To encourage more home runs from the slugger, the fence was moved in from 365 feet to 335 feet. From 1948 to 1953, after Greenberg retired, when Ralph Kiner remained the team's great slugger, the same happy hunting ground became known as *Kiner's Korner*. IST USE. 1947. "The 'Greenberg Gardens' plot in the Forbes Field . . . has sprouted a flourishing crop of home runs—nine in four games" (*San Francisco Examiner*, Apr. 21; Peter Tamony).

Green Book The annual administrative manual and directory for the National League. Its contents include: history, office information, committees, and administrative rules for the League; franchise histories, directory of club officials, rosters, and logos for each team; prior year's standings, player statistics, and awards, and postseason results; All-Star Game information; attendance figures; and information on beat writers and broadcasters. See also *Red Book*; *Blue Book*; *Orange Book*.

green cathedral A baseball park, field, or stadium. The term was popularized by Philip J. Lowry for the title of his book *Green Cathedrals* (1986) and is now commonly used to refer reverentially to a specific baseball park. In the introduction to the revised edition (1992) of *Green Cathedrals*, Lowry hoped the title of the book would a) convey the "quiet spiritual reverence" for the ballpark, which "holds treasured memories and serves as a sanctuary for the spirit, a haven where the ghosts of ... greats from the past can continue to roam among their modern-day counterparts," and b) celebrate "the mystical appeal of the hundreds of ballparks, past and present, where the soul of the game of baseball resides." ETYMOLOGY. The term was used in the 19th century for a forest bower used for spiritual contemplation. A writer from *Frank Leslie's Illustrated Newspaper* (Nov. 13, 1858, p.378) wrote about a place in the woods where philosophers gathered: "Ralph Waldo Emerson shakes me by the hand, and invites me, looking upwards, to admire the dome. We look up and find ourselves standing under a clump of hoary pines with large naked trunks and spreading green tops forming a lofty green cathedral."

green fly A derisive modern name for a non-baseball person (such as a *Baseball Annie* or a devoted baseball fan) who is a nuisance to a ballplayer, hovers around players' entrances and hotel lobbies, constantly looks for free tickets, souvenirs, or autographs, or works to be in the company of professional players; the baseball equivalent of the rock groupie. "When a green fly comes around, you may hear someone yell, 'Get the swatter'" (Mike Gonring, *Baseball Digest*, June 1979). A quote from *The Boston Globe*, which was reprinted in *The Atlantic Monthly* (June 1987), noted that "[players] speak disparagingly of this pesky breed as '*greenflies*,' refer-

ring to the species that is soft-bodied, pear-shaped and gathers in colonies." Tom House (*The Jock's Itch*, 1989, p.23) wrote, "Baseball people know the second ... a 'green fly' ... walks into a clubhouse. It just affects the flow, the feel, the communication processes, the eye contact." The term first appeared in professional baseball players' vernacular during the 1970s, and is esp. used to deride baseball reporters at the major-league level. See also *fly*, 3. Also spelled "greenfly." ETYMOLOGY. Named for the most persistent and obnoxious kind of insect. The greenfly (*Coloradoa rufomaculata*), an aphid, is an important pest of chrysanthemums. The green peach aphid, bluebottle fly, and blow-fly have all attracted this name.

greenie A green-colored *amphetamine* pill used by baseball players to enhance performance. "Greenies are pep pills ... and a lot of baseball players couldn't function without them" (Jim Bouton, *Ball Four*, 1970).

green light 1. A coach's sign flashed to a batter allowing him to swing. It is most commonly given on a 3–0 count. See also *hit sign*. **2.** A sign given to a baserunner to take an extra base or attempt to steal; also, the permission granted by the manager to a baserunner to steal at his discretion. Keith Hernandez (*Pure Baseball*, 1994) wrote,

Green light. President Franklin D. Roosevelt, who loved action-packed games ("I get the biggest kick out of the biggest score"), but his pleasure was limited by his infirmity. He was embarrassed to have the fans see his paralyzed legs and once told Clark Griffith, "If I didn't have to hobble up those steps in front of all those people, I'd be out at the park every day." *Photograph by Joseph Baylor Roberts*

"Speed has changed all the old thinking about base stealing. The quick guys have a permanent green light. When they get a jump, they can go." Compare *stop sign*; *red light*. **3.** Syn. of *activator*. **4.** The nickname given to President Franklin D. Roosevelt's personal letter of Jan. 15, 1942, permitting commissioner Kenesaw Mountain Landis to continue scheduling baseball during World War II. The president wrote in response to Landis' offer to cancel baseball: "I honestly feel that it would be best for the country to keep baseball going. . . . If 300 teams use 5,000 or 6,000 players, these players are a definite recreational asset to at least 20,000,000 of their fellow citizens— and that in my judgment is thoroughly worthwhile."
ETYMOLOGY. An obvious borrowing from the green light of traffic control.

Green Monster The imposing 37.17-foot-tall left-field wall, 231 feet in length, at Fenway Park in Boston, marked (since 1995) as 310 feet from home plate. Before it was painted green in 1947, it was covered with advertisements. It has been blamed and credited for events ranging from turning line-drive home runs into sliding doubles as they bounce off the wall and converting high fly balls into home runs when such balls are lofted over it. The wall has been an attractive target for right-handed pull hitters and an object of despair for left-handed pitchers. In 2003, three rows with 274 pale-green barstool seats were installed atop the wall, replacing a 23.3-foot screen that had served as the last barrier between home runs and the windows on Lansdowne Street; space was also allotted for more than 100 standing-room-only fans. From 1934 through 1994, the wall was marked as 315 feet from home plate. Dan Shaughnessy (*The Boston Globe*, Apr. 25, 1995) insisted, "It's 309 feet 3 inches. I know. I measured it myself." The original 1912 Osborn Engineering Co. blueprints documented the distance as 308 feet. Syn. *Wall, The*.

green pea A *rookie*, esp. one with little experience; a real novice. IST USE. 1912. This was Casey Stengel's favorite term for a young and inexperienced player and one that was eventually regarded as an element of Stengelese. The term shows up in a 1912 *The Sporting Life* article on player slang: "You're the green pea of the American League." By the 1920s, it appears to have been common slang. EXTENDED USE. A novice in other areas. "The delegation which arrived here [at the Democratic National Convention] last Saturday, for the most part 'green peas' in national convention work, are now veterans" (*San Francisco News*, July 26, 1952).

greensward 1. Ground on which grass is grown; specif. used to describe the grass areas of a baseball field. The term was commonly used during the first decade of the 20th century. IST USE. 1887. "[Detroit groundskeeper Billy Houston's] eyes brightened as he looked at the beautiful expanse of green sward" (*Detroit Free Press*, May 16; Peter Morris). **2.** A baseball field. "The Elites are carded for the first of a three-game series with the Cleveland Buckeyes on the Bugle Field greensward on Friday night" (*The Afro American*, Sept. 16, 1944, p.18; Bob Luke).

green weenie 1. A plastic, gag-store hot dog painted green, which was first brought into play by the Pittsburgh Pirates in 1960. Trainer Danny Whelan noted that when it was pointed at an opposing pitcher—when he was given "the green weenie"—the Pirates started hitting, but when it was pointed at a Pirates pitcher, strikeouts materialized. They went into mass production and were sold as souvenirs in 1966. When the green weenie was waved or shaken en masse by Pirates fans, a curse supposedly fell upon visiting teams. One was wielded by sportscaster Bob Prince in the booth to put hexes and jinxes on opponents of the Pirates on its way to the 1971 National League pennant. **2.** A pitch that a batter does not like. Jim Brosnan (*The Long Season*, 1960) referred to "slipping the green weenie past" Ernie Banks.

greet For a batter to face the pitcher and hit the ball. "Pete Incaviglia greeted Al Leiter with a sacrifice fly and the Phillies had the lead" (*The Baltimore Sun*, Oct. 24, 1993).

grenade A bloop hit. "I knew I could just drop a little grenade down the leftfield line" (Tony Gwynn, quoted in *Sports Illustrated*, June 15, 1998). See also *hand grenade*, 2.

Greyhound squad The daily list of players cut from a major-league club's spring-training roster, who then presumably leave for their minor-league assignments on Greyhound buses (Bob Uecker, *Catcher in the Wry*, 1983, p.16; Charles D. Poe).

grievance A complaint that involves the existence or interpretation of, or compliance with, any agreement, or any provision of any agreement, between the Major League Baseball Players Association and the major-league clubs (collectively or individually), or between a player and a club (except for disputes relating to the players' benefit plan) (2007–2011 Basic Agreement, Art. XI-A).

grievance arbitration A mechanism for an impartial third party, such as a judge, to determine the resolution of charged violations of the Basic Agreement.

Griffmen 1. Nickname for the Washington *Nationals* (Senators) while Clark C. Griffith was manager (1912–1920) and later under the stewardship (1920–1960) of owners Clark C. Griffith and Calvin R. Griffith. Syn. "Griffs." 2. Nickname for the New York entry in the American League while Clark C. Grif-

Griffmen. Clark C. Griffith, 1920. *George Grantham Bain Collection, Library of Congress*

fith was manager (1903–1908). The club was officially nicknamed the *Yankees* in 1913.

grille Slang for mouth. "That grounder took a bad hop and hit him in the grille" (Garret Mathews, *Can't Find a Dry Ball*, 2002).

grinder A tough, intense, and consistent player with an unmatched work ethic who comes to play every day. Three-hundred-game winner Don Sutton characterized himself (*The Sporting News*, June 30, 1986) as "an unspectacular grinder, a mechanic." Bob Ryan (*The Boston Globe*, Dec. 22, 1999) labeled Carl Yastrzemski "the Ultimate Grinder" because "he was not afraid of work" and noted that "the game never came easy for him, but he had the combined body and will . . . to simply Be There, day-in, day-out." Chris Ballard (*Sports Illustrated*, May 8, 2006) wrote that Texas Rangers shortstop Michael Young is a " 'grinder,' vernacular for a player who works his butt off . . . [because] he can't survive on his talent alone."

grip 1. The exact manner in which a batter holds the bat at the plate. The grip will vary considerably depending on whether a batter is swinging away or bunting. Batters use batting gloves and pine tar to keep their grips from slipping. See also *choke grip*; *modified grip*; *end grip*. 2. The exact manner in which a pitcher holds the ball as he prepares to deliver it. The grip taken for a given pitch usually determines the type of pitch to be thrown.

grooming The preparation and maintenance of the playing field by the ground crew.

groove 1. *n.* The path a pitch takes down the middle of the strike zone, at the height where a batter can most easily hit the pitch. See also *in the groove*, 1. 1ST USE. 1908. "[Glenn] Liebhardt then went in to pitch and so far forgot himself as to put the ball in the groove for Sam Crawford [who] . . . slammed the ball into the bleachers for a home run" (Ed F. Bang, *The Sporting Life*, May 9; Peter Morris). 2. *v.* To throw a nonbreaking pitch down the middle of the strike zone where it is most hittable for the batter. "[Ugueth] Urbina grooved the pitch, belt-high, over the inner half of the plate, and [Ruben] Sierra drilled it down the left-field line" (*The Baltimore*

Grip. Frank "Home Run" Baker's batting grip, ca. 1912. *George Grantham Bain Collection, Library of Congress*

Sun, Oct. 23, 2003). It is sometimes done deliberately to help the batter achieve something special; e.g., when New York Yankees Mike Kekich grooved a fastball to Frank Howard, who hit a home run during the last game of the Washington Senators at RFK Stadium, Sept. 30, 1971. IST USE. 1911. "He 'grooved' the first ball" (Charles E. Van Loan, *The Big League*, p.170; David Shulman). **3.** *n.* A period when one performs at one's absolute best or in a consistently high form; e.g., when a batter is hitting well over a period of games, he is said to be "in a groove," where everything feels right, and the ball appears to be as large as a beach ball. "If I get into my groove, I'm gonna play every day" (Don Baylor, *Don Baylor*, 1989, p.47). See also *in a groove*, 2. **4.** *n./hist.* A batter's weakness. "Big Leaguers know their own 'grooves' and are naturally trying to cover them up. . . . [Joe Tinker's] 'groove' was a slow curve over the outside corner, and I fed him slow curves over that very outside corner with great regularity" (Christy Mathewson, *Pitching in a Pinch*, 1912, pp.1–2, 46). **5.** *n./hist.* A gap between fielders. "Every ball player knows there are five 'infield grooves' and four 'outfield grooves,' spaces between fielders where any ball hit with moderate force will be 'safe' unless a moderate stop intervenes" (John J. Evers and Hugh S. Fullerton, *Touching Second: The Science of Baseball*, 1910; Peter Morris).

groove ball A pitch thrown down the middle of the plate. "Hartzell soaked a groove ball into right for two bases" (I.E. Sanborn, *Chicago Tribune*, July 9, 1909; Peter Morris).

groove hitter Syn. of *mistake hitter.* "[Sam Crawford] was what we call a groove hitter. If a pitcher ever let his delivery slip so as to put a ball in Crawford's groove he would kill it" (Ty Cobb, *Memoirs of Twenty Years in Baseball*, 1925; Peter Morris).

groover A nonbreaking pitch delivered to the heart of the strike zone; an easy pitch to hit. IST USE. 1909. "Might have known the first ball would be a groover" (Charles E. Van Loan, *Outing*, September; Peter Morris).

ground **1.** *v.* To hit a ground ball. "The Giants chose to play the infield in, and [Mike] Scioscia foiled the strategy by grounding a two-run single up the middle" (*Tampa Tribune*, Sept. 26, 1989). **2.** *v.* To be thrown out as a result of hitting a ground ball; e.g., "Smith grounded to third." Syn. *ground out.* **3.** *v.* To win by a shutout; e.g., "The Yanks grounded the Royals, 4–0." **4.** *n.* Short for *ball ground.* See also *grounds*, 1. IST USE. 1860. "In selecting a suitable ground, there are many points to be taken into consideration. The ground should be level, and the surface free from all irregularities, and, if possible, covered with fine turf" (*Beadle's Dime Base Ball Player*). **5.** *n.* Part of the baseball field covered by an outfielder. "[Corey Patterson] covers a lot of ground in the outfield" (*The Baltimore Sun*, Jan. 8, 2008).

ground ball A batted ball that hits the ground as it comes off the bat and then rolls or bounces along the ground. Abbrev. *GB*, 2. Also spelled "groundball." Syn. *grounder.* IST USE. 1860 (*Beadle's Dime Base-Ball Player*, p.23; Edward J. Nichols).

ground-ball percentage The proportion of batted balls against a pitcher that are hit on the ground rather than in the air. The statistic has been featured in *Baseball Prospectus* since 2006.

ground-ball pitcher A pitcher who entices batters to hit ground balls rather than fly balls; e.g., sinkerballer Scott Erickson. A pitcher with a sharp-breaking curveball causes many batters to hit the top of the ball, thereby producing ground balls. "[Mariano Rivera] evolved from a strikeout pitcher into a ground-ball pitcher [1.6 ground balls to every fly ball in 1998]" (*The New York Times*, Feb. 28, 1999). Compare *fly-ball pitcher*.

ground coverer A defensive player who is able to field successfully balls that are hit to a wide range of the field. IST USE. 1902 (*The Sporting Life*, July 12, p.3; Edward J. Nichols).

ground crew A group of workers who, under direction of the groundskeeper, prepare and maintain the condition of the playing field. The crew's duties include protecting the field from rain, dragging the basepaths, and chalking the various lines and boxes on the field. Syn. *grounds crew*.

grounded into double play A statistic recorded since 1939 for the number of times a player grounded into a double play. The statistic counts double plays where both outs were made on runners forced to advance, as well as reverse force double plays. Abbrev. *GDP*. Acronym *GIDP*.

grounder Syn. of *ground ball*. IST USE. 1857. "Powers gives a twisting ball, th' fielders get a 'grounder'" (Everett L. Baker, "Impromptu," *Buffalo Courier*, Sept. 27; Priscilla Astifan). USAGE NOTE. Despite early use, the term was on the road to obscurity until Casey Stengel began to use it constantly: "Only he [Stengel] referred to ground balls as 'grounders'" (Jack Mann, *Newsday*, Oct. 10, 1960). EXTENDED

Ground crew. Pregame activities at home plate involving managers, umpires, and ground crew, 1913. *George Grantham Bain Collection, Library of Congress*

USE. A case that is handled easily, like a soft ground ball. "Most of the homicides I catch are grounders; the rest are either drug related or mob hits" (William J. Caunitz, *One Police Plaza*, 1984, p.92; Charles D. Poe).

ground hog *hist.* **1.** A member of the ground crew. **2.** Syn. of *groundskeeper*.

groundkeeper *hist.* Early variation of *groundskeeper*. "A uniformed groundkeeper was treading the top of this wall, picking batting-practice home runs out of the screen" (John Updike, *The New Yorker*, Oct. 22, 1960). IST USE. 1873. "Mr. Hunt, the worthy ground keeper, arranged things so as to insure a clear field for the contest" (*Brooklyn Eagle*, Aug. 28; Peter Morris).

groundout *n.* An out resulting from a ball being hit on the ground.

ground out *v.* To be thrown out as the result of hitting a ground ball; e.g., "Smith grounded out to third." See also *ground*, 2.

ground-rent man *hist.* A player given by a major-league team to a minor-league team as payment for allowing the major-league team to use the minor-league team's field during spring training. "At the close of the [1907] season he [Tris Speaker] was purchased by Boston and turned over to Little Rock the following spring as ground-rent man, the Red Sox having trained on the Little Rock grounds" (*San Francisco Bulletin*, Apr. 4, 1913; Gerald L. Cohen).

ground-rule double A two-base hit awarded by the umpire that results from hitting into a special situation outlined in the ground rules. USAGE NOTE. The term is commonly used when a batted ball bounces in fair territory and goes over the fence or into the stands; however, this is a general baseball rule (*Official Baseball Rules*, Rule 6.09[e]) and the proper term is *rule-book double*. The term "ground-rule double" dates back to when many parks had roped areas in the outfield, and individual parks had different ground rules for handling them. The term's use has not kept pace with the changing rules, although the meticulous announcer Jon Miller always makes a point of calling this hit an *automatic double*, a far more accurate term. Previous to 1930 in the American

League and 1931 in the National League, a ball that bounced over the fence was considered a home run. See also *roof-rule double*.

ground rules A set of special rules unique to the specific conditions and dimensions of a given ballpark. The rules are made by the home team and must be understood by both teams before play begins. Many of the rules address whether a ball is in play if it hits an obstacle, such as a rolled tarp; e.g., a batted ball that is not judged a home run and strikes a catwalk in fair territory at Tropicana Field (home field for the Tampa Bay Rays) is judged fair or foul in relation to where it strikes the ground or is touched by a fielder, or a fly ball hitting the roof of the ground-crew shed in right field and bouncing back onto the field at Oriole Park at Camden Yards is a home run. One of the odder ground rules ever established was during the first game of the 1965 World Series, which was attended by then Vice President Hubert H. Humphrey. It was decided that even if a ball hit the Secret Service man sitting on the field in front of Humphrey, the ball would remain in play. IST USE. 1879. "Home clubs [have the] power to enforce its ground rules against visiting clubs" (*The Galveston Daily News*, Dec. 6). USAGE NOTE. The basic concept of a ground rule was introduced earlier than 1879; e.g., "Balls batted into an adjacent corn field should only carry the batter to his first base" (*Adrian* [Mich.] *Times and Expositor*, July 6, 1871; Peter Morris). EXTENDED USE. A basic set of rules and procedures that is set out in advance, whether it be for an election debate or a pie-eating contest.

ground-rule triple A three-base hit awarded by the umpire that results from hitting into a special situation outlined in the ground rules. The rule was in force during the 1903 World Series when batted balls bounded into overflow crowds that were allowed to stand in the far reaches of the outfield. The *St. Louis Star* (June 14, 1927; Wayne Townsend) commented regarding Sportsman's Park: "A change has been made in the rule which allowed a batter a home run if he hit a ball behind the projecting wire screen, which guards the bleacher and pavilion wall. Hereafter, it will be a three-base hit in Cardinal games as in the American League games."

grounds 1. The area in which baseball is played, including both the field and the stands. Early use of the term referred to an area without boundaries, fences, or entrances. See also *ground*, 4. IST USE. 1845 (*Brooklyn Daily Star*, Oct. 23; Edward J. Nichols). 2. A ballpark; e.g., the Polo Grounds in New York City.

grounds crew Syn. of *ground crew*.

groundskeep To serve as a groundskeeper; to prepare and maintain the condition of the playing field.

groundskeeper The chief of the ground crew. Because the way in which the grounds are kept can give the home team small advantages, the position can have a certain strategic importance; or, as Bill Veeck (*The New York Times*, June 21, 1982) once put it, "A good groundskeeper can be as valuable as a .300 hitter." For instance, such factors as the length of the infield grass, the moistness of the basepaths, and the subtle slope of the ground around the foul lines are variables in the hands of the groundskeeper. Milt Richman (*Baseball Digest*, May 1947) identified the groundskeeper as "the guy who smoothens every position except your own." Originally spelled *groundkeeper*. Syn. *ground hog*, 2; *manicurist*; *gardener*, 2.

groundskeeper single A single that occurs when the batted ball strikes a pebble (*San Francisco News*, Dec. 8, 1953).

ground-to-fly ratio A statistic that helps to

Ground rules. Discussing the ground rules for the 1915 World Series at Baker Bowl in Philadelphia. The 1915 Fall Classic was notable mostly for the debut of a young twenty-year-old lefty named George Herman Ruth.

categorize a batter or a pitcher as a ground-ball or fly-ball specialist; e.g., in 2002, Boston Red Sox sinkerballer Derek Lowe's ratio of 3.46 to 1 indicated that batters were 3.46 times more likely to hit the ball on the ground than in the air when facing him, whereas Florida Marlins speedster Luis Castillo's ratio of 3.39 to 1 indicated that if he hit the ball, it would most likely be on the ground (*Boston Herald*, March 30, 2003).

GS **1.** Abbrev. for *games started*. **2.** Abbrev. for *grand slam*, 1 (a home run). It tends to be used in headlines; e.g., "[Mike] Greenwell GS Powers Red Sox Past Rangers" (*Bangor* [Maine] *Daily News*, Aug. 3, 1988). **3.** Abbrev. for *game score*.

guante Spanish for "glove."

guarantee system In early baseball, a system used to pay the visiting club a share of the gate receipts in which the visitors received a set amount, which could be very costly to the home team if attendance was low, or lucrative if attendance was high. Compare *percentage system*.

guardabosque Spanish for "outfielder." ETYMOLOGY. Spanish for "forest ranger."

guardian *hist*. A fielder at one of the bases. IST USE. 1903. "[Herman] Long is still an able guardian of second base" (*The Washington Post*, Nov. 1).

guardian angel Syn. of *angel*, 1.

guard the bag For a fielder to play close to a base.

guard the line To position the first baseman close to the first base line or the third baseman close to the third base line to prevent an extra-base hit down the line. It is a popular defensive strategy if the potential tying or winning run is on base or at the plate in the seventh inning or later. Syn. *protect the line*.

guard the plate Syn. of *protect the plate*, 1.

guesser *hist*. **1.** An umpire. IST USE. 1933 (*Ironwood* [Mich.] *Daily Globe*, Apr. 14; Peter Morris). **2.** A creative-thinking manager or player. "[Pitcher] 'Vic' Willis, one of the best 'guessers' in the business" (John J. Evers and Hugh S. Fullerton, *Touching Second: The Science of Baseball*, 1910; Peter Morris). USAGE NOTE. Morris notes that,

while one might consider the use of the term "guesser" to describe a strategic decision-maker to be somewhat derisive, it is simply an acknowledgment that "when two accomplished strategists match wits, luck will play a major factor in the success or failure of a particular stratagem."

guess hitter **1.** A hitter who goes to the plate looking for a particular pitch and is willing to wait for it; a hitter who tries to anticipate a pitch or outguess the pitcher based on the situation at hand (bases loaded, 3–2 count, etc.). Frank Deford (*Sports Illustrated*, March 19, 2001) wrote concerning Lou Piniella: "He credits much of his success as a batter to being a 'guess hitter,' which means not so much guessing as having studied the pitcher's past performance . . . and, more often, of the catchers who called the pitches—survey how the defense arrayed itself and then bet his swing." Shirley Povich (*The Washington Post*, Sept. 9, 1986) quoted Hank Greenberg on being labeled a "guess hitter": "Guess hitter, bull. We're all guess hitters, if everybody would only tell the truth." Syn. *call hitter*. IST USE. 1928. "No 'guess' hitter ever makes a good hitter" (George Herman Ruth, *Babe Ruth's Own Book of Baseball*, 1928, p.213; Peter Morris). **2.** An indecisive hitter who often swings at any pitch.

guide **1.** For a pitcher to pinpoint a pitch; e.g., "Smith guides the ball to the outside part of the plate." See also *aim*. **2.** For a hitter to place the ball where he wants it to go; e.g., "Smith guided the ball to left."

gully jumper *hist*. A railroad train.

gumshoe man A scout. "Arthur Irwin, the highly talked of scout of the New York Americans . . . is still one of the gumshoe men" (*San Francisco Bulletin*, Feb. 11, 1913; Gerald L. Cohen).

gum the bases To run slowly along the basepath. "In spite of . . . his habit of gumming the bases when in transit, the Cap was the most popular player" (Charles E. Van Loan, *The Lucky Seventh*, 1913, p.247; David Shulman).

gun **1.** *n*. A strong throwing arm, usually that of an outfielder or catcher. "The Rangers rarely pitched out because [catcher] Ivan Rodriguez has the best gun in the game"

(*ESPN The Magazine*, May 13, 2002). See also *rifle*, 1; *shotgun*, 1. IST USE. 1929. "[A] 'good gun' means that the possessor has a strong arm" (*The New York Times*, June 2, 1929). **2.** *n.* A pitcher's arm. **3.** *n.* A pitcher. "The young guns combined for 239 K's in 240 Triple-A innings" (*ESPN The Magazine*, March 17, 2003). **4.** *v.* To throw hard and accurately; e.g., "Smith gunned the ball to first base." See also *rifle*, 2. **5.** *n.* Short for *radar gun*. "The Brewers gun caught the knuckleballer [Dennis Springer] throwing four pitches at 47 mph" (*Wisconsin State Journal*, Aug. 16, 1997).

gun down To throw out a baserunner with a strong throw.

gunner *hist.* A pitcher. "Big Ed Walsh was the only gunner that could locate the plate" (*San Francisco Bulletin*, Feb. 6, 1913; Gerald L. Cohen). IST USE. 1907. "The [St. Louis] Browns began to hit hard, and became terrors to opposing gunners" (*The Washington Post*, Jan. 27).

gunning corps *hist.* A pitching staff. "Walter Johnson [is] the 'Big Swede' of Clark Griffith's gunning corps" (*San Francisco Bulletin*, May 13, 1913; Gerald L. Cohen).

gun pitcher A pitcher whose fastball appears faster on radar than it does to the batter; e.g., Kevin Tapani (*Sports Illustrated*, Aug. 7, 1989).

gun-shy Said of a player who is afraid of the ball, esp. after having been hit or injured by a pitched or batted ball.

guy *v./hist.* To jeer at; to rib or kid. "The cranks have assaulted the umpire, they roast him in the press, they guy the life out of him on the field" (*The Daily Picayune* [New Orleans], May 14, 1893). Gerald L. Cohen (*Studies in Slang*, part 2, 1989) concluded, "It is now clear from *The World* [New York] that the term was entrenched in baseball speech of the late 19th century, and the only question is why it later died out." An example from *The World* (Aug. 17, 1890): "[Cap] Anson guyed [Arlie] Latham unmercifully when he dropped [Jerry] Harrington's splendid throw in the second inning." IST USE. 1884. "[The small boy] 'guys' the visitors unmercifully, and if they show the slightest

indication of remonstrating with the umpire he yells derisively until the audacious objector subsides" (*Milwaukee Sentinel*, Oct. 12). ETYMOLOGY. Theater slang.

GWRBI Scorecard and box score abbrev. for *game-winning RBI*.

gyroball A theoretical pitch in which the ball stays on a nearly flat plane while spinning about an axis parallel to the direction of motion, much like a spiral pass in football or a rifle bullet, then suddenly changes course, breaking straight down, supposedly as much as three feet before entering the strike zone. Designed on a computer by Japanese physicist Ryutaro Himeno to reduce stress on the pitcher's arm, the "miracle" or "mythical" pitch supposedly harnesses complex physical forces and is rumored to be unhittable. According to Doug Cantor (*Esquire*, Oct. 2006, p.174), the pitch takes advantage of "double-spin mechanics," a "complicated balance of hip and upper-arm movement combined with precise pronation of a pitcher's wrist just after release that produces an unusual bulletlike sideways spin on the baseball." This alignment prevents any deflection of the pitch (except that due to gravity), and the hard spin stabilizes the axis (like a gyroscope); the angle between the spin axis and the direction of spin is zero. The upper arm rotates at the end of the delivery such that the palm faces outward and the arm is twisted downward away from the body, as opposed to directly across the body. Thrown with a curveball grip, the pitch behaves like a cut fastball: when thrown by a right-handed pitcher to a right-handed batter, the gyroball, in mathematical models, breaks severely down and away. It is supposedly thrown by Daisuke Matsuzaka. Batters facing Matsuzaka claim the pitch has a clockwise (reverse) spin and a movement that is faster than a changeup but slower than the split-fingered fastball. Dave Baldwin (personal communication, Apr. 9, 2007) believes "the gyroball is the same as the backup slider American pitchers throw accidentally—except the gyroball is pitched deliberately, and batters can be set up for it." Alan Nathan and Dave Baldwin (*Baseball Research Journal*, No.36, 2007, p.80) studied the gyroball mechanics and concluded, "The gyroball is not the miracle pitch that the media has hyped it to be, but it could be an effective pitch if used with discretion. Because the gyroball's spin is perpendicular to the pitch's trajectory . . . the pitch will have no spin-induced deflection." ETYMOLOGY. Japanese baseball coach Kazushi Tezuka claims to have created the gyroball in 1995 when he was given a toy known as X-Zylo Ultra (a flying gyroscope), which, when thrown as a spiral, could travel as far as 600 feet. According to Lee Jenkins (*International Herald Tribune*, Feb. 22, 2007),

Tezuka, using a fastball grip, turned the inside of his throwing arm away from his body and released the ball as if it were a football, making it spiral toward home plate. "The pitch started on the same course as a changeup, but it barely dipped. It looked like a slider, but it did not break. The gyroball, despite its zany name, is supposed to stay perfectly straight." R. Himeno and K. Tezuka (*Makyuu no Shoutai*, 2001) first described the spin and behavior of the gyroball, as well as the mechanics used in delivering the pitch.

H

H **1.** Scorecard and box score abbrev. for *hit*, 1 (hits made or hits allowed). **2.** Box score abbrev. for *hold*, 6.

Habanista A follower of the red-colored Habana Leones (Lions) of the Cuban League. See also *Almendarista*; *eternal rival*.

hack **1.** *n.* An opportunity to bat, such as during batting practice. "Albert Belle has been in one of those grooves when a hitter is dying to go to the park every day just so he can get in his hacks" (*The Baltimore Sun*, Oct. 10, 1995). **2.** *v.* To swing at a pitched ball. Chuckie Carr rejected a 2–0 take sign and later explained, "Chuckie don't play that game. Chuckie hacks on 2–0" (*Milwaukee Journal Sentinel*, Sept. 2, 1997). **3.** *v.* To swing a bat without form or grace, or without patience. **4.** *n.* A poor or clumsy swing at a pitch out of the strike zone. **5.** *n.* An aggressive or hard swing at a pitched ball. "[Steve] Avery did not have his good stuff early . . . His slider slid high, his fastball was imprecise, and the Indians were taking some healthy hacks" (*The Baltimore Sun*, Oct. 26, 1995). **6.** *n.* An attempted place hit; e.g., "Smith took a hack at right field, but fouled it off."

hacker A batter with poor form at the plate or one who regularly takes reckless or undisciplined swings at pitches outside the strike zone. "I'm still a hacker. I'll go up there and swing at anything I like, on any count" (Jay Gibbons, quoted in *The Baltimore Sun*, Apr. 24, 2002).

hair Velocity as applied to a moving ball, whether it be a pitch or a line drive. The Cincinnati Reds pitchers during the mid-1960s measured their fastballs by how much "hair" they had: "the faster the pitcher, the more

hair he had on the ball" (Joe Morgan, *Baseball for Dummies*, 1998, p.357).

Hairs vs. Squares Nickname for the 1972 World Series that pitted the hirsute Oakland A's ("The Mustache Gang") versus the clean-shaven, short-haired Cincinnati Reds.

half **1.** Syn. of *half inning*. IST USE. 1895. "[Ad] Gumbert had two strikes and three balls on [Yale] Murphy in New York's half when the little fellow pasted a two bagger into the left field chute" (*Brooklyn Eagle*, Aug. 6; Peter Morris). **2.** One game of a doubleheader. **3.** One of two parts of a baseball season, before or after the All-Star break in July.

halfball A variation of baseball played in Philadelphia streets or schoolyards, using a hollow rubber ball cut in half and a baseball bat sawed lengthwise in half (the handle remained whole). The pitcher flicks the spinning, diving ball underhand and the batter's hit is determined by the distance of the hit. There is no baserunning. If a grounder is stopped, even if not cleanly, it is an out; fielders are more like goalies than catchers. Some games are played from one street curb to another; the softness of the ball keeps it in play (no balls hit over the roof of a building). See also *half-rubber*.

half gainer **1.** A headfirst dive for a catch. ETYMOLOGY. From the name of a common dive in aquatic sports. **2.** Syn. of *headfirst slide*.

half game A mathematical expression of the difference in the division or league standings between two teams when one team has played an even number of games and the other team has played an odd number of games. In reality, there is no "half game" played. The figure is a construct to determine the number of *games behind* based on the number of games played, not based on the percentage of wins. "Brooklyn crawled up on the Phillies yesterday, and is now only a half game behind. 'Half a game' sounds funny to the uninitiated, but in base ball the percentage counts, and the one thousandth part of a percentage decides the championship or the position of any club in the race" (*Philadelphia Public Ledger*, Aug. 2, 1890; David Ball).

half inning One of two equal portions of a full inning, when one team is at bat and the other team is in the field. The visiting team bats during the first (top) half and the home team bats during the second (bottom) half. When the fielding team records three outs, the teams switch positions and begin a new half inning. Syn. *half*, 1.

half-liner Syn. of *Texas Leaguer*, 2.

half-rubber A schoolyard variation of baseball played with a sponge-rubber ball that has been cut in half and a thin bat, which is likely to have been fashioned from a broomstick. Its appeal comes from the fact that it allows for several odd, sidearm, breaking pitches and makes it difficult to get hits. There are two players on each team and no baserunning; rather, bases are reached by imaginary men and earned when the ball is hit beyond a designated line. The game is discussed in detail by Hugh M. Thomason (*Western Folklore*, Jan. 1975), who describes the game as he played it in rural southeastern Georgia in the mid-1930s. Lowry Axley (*American Speech*, Aug. 1927) claims that the game and its name were invented in Savannah, Ga., where, according to one player, it was originated "some eight or ten years ago by two boys who got the idea when they were hitting pop-bottle caps with broom handles." See also *halfball*. Also spelled "halfrubber."

half swing 1. *n.* A swing that is stopped before going past the front of the batter's body, usually resulting in a called strike. See also *checked swing*. 2. *v.* To start a swing and then stop.

halfway 1. Said of the position taken by a baserunner between bases when a fly ball is hit so that he will have time to retreat to the original base if the ball is caught. "When the player goes halfway (he really should go as far as he can go and still be able to get back safely once the catch is made), he is thinking, 'I can't tag up here and make it to second so I'm going to put myself in the best position to advance in the event the ball is dropped, lost in the sun or the lights, or there is a miscommunication between outfielders'" (Cal Ripken Jr., *The Baltimore Sun*, Jan. 22, 2006). **2.** Said of the defensive position often taken by the infield when there is a slow runner on third base and less than two outs. The position puts the fielder in a spot midway between regular depth and the "in" position. It sets up an opportunity for a play at the plate without fully compromising the defensive positioning.

halfway mark *hist.* Syn. of *second base*, 1.

halfway station *hist.* Syn. of *second base*, 1.

Hall of Excellence The title assigned to the Little League's "hall of fame." Michael Cammarata, a New York City firefighter who died in the World Trade Center collapse on Sept. 11, 2001, was the first former player inducted posthumously.

Hall of Fame 1. See *National Baseball Hall of Fame*. Abbrev. *HOF.* IST USE. 1903 "[National League] President [Harry] Pulliam proposes to establish a base ball 'Hall of Fame' at League quarters in New York" (*The Sporting Life*, March 21; Peter Morris, who notes that the connotation here was literal rather than figurative). USAGE NOTE. Subsequent references to a baseball "hall of fame" became a figurative way to acknowledge anyone who achieved a great accomplishment, such as pitching a no-hitter or achieving 200 hits in a season: "Hall of Fame [is] an honor roll of pitchers who have pitched full games without allowing opposing teams to hit safely" (*Baseball Magazine*, Nov. 1908; Edward J. Nichols), and "Those Athletics . . . have brought forward a new candidate for the batting hall of fame" (Joe S. Jackson, *The Washington Post*, Sept. 10, 1911; Peter Morris). *Baseball Magazine* (Jan. 1911) proposed "The Hall of Fame for the Immortals of Baseball, Comprising the Greatest Players in the History of the Game"; it was to be "a lasting tribute to our most illustrious players, based upon the judgments of the leading authorities of the nation's grandest sport." In succeeding issues, the editors selected three players per month into their Hall. Consequently, *The Sporting News* (May 18, 1911; Robert H. Schaefer): "Joe Jackson continues the hitting sensation and Cleveland fans have already placed him in the Hall of Fame." The term was also connected with the Chalmers Award, which also employed the term: "Members of the Philadelphia Athletics are of the opinion that the hall of fame committee which awards two autos . . ." (*Syracuse* [N.Y.] *Herald*, Sept. 25, 1911; Benjamin Zimmer), and "The Chalmers trophy idea, which was conceived . . . for the purpose of forming a baseball Hall of Fame" (*San Francisco Bulletin*, Feb. 26, 1913; Gerald L. Cohen). "It was suggested that he [Harry Heilmann] had a good chance to make another place for himself in baseball's hall of fame" (Brian Bell, *The Washington Post*, June 22, 1930). There are other baseball halls of fame besides the one in Cooperstown, N.Y., such as: the Negro Leagues Hall of Fame in Kansas City, Mo.; the Maryland Oldtimers Baseball Association Hall of Fame in Baltimore; the St. Louis Cardinals with their own hall of fame; and those in other countries, including Cuba, Japan, Canada, and Mexico with their own baseball halls of fame. ETYMOLOGY. The Hall of Fame in Cooperstown, though the most famous, was not the first American example of such an institution. The prototype American institution is the Hall of Fame for Great Americans, created on a New York Univ. campus in 1901 to honor American men and women who achieved greatness in any of 16 categories. The concept of a Hall of Fame was seen as a counterpart to Westminster Abbey in London by its architect Stanford White. In other sports, there are now hundreds of halls of fame, including the National Jockeys Hall of Fame, the Lacrosse Hall of Fame and Museum, and the U.S. Croquet Hall of Fame. **2.** The group of individuals who have been elected to the National Baseball Hall of Fame. **3.** The shortened name of the *National Baseball Hall of Fame and Museum* in Cooperstown, N.Y. The term has been used to designate the building as well as the museum; e.g., "Sammy Sosa donated the bat he used for his 500th home run to the Hall of Fame" (*The Baltimore Sun*, Apr. 14, 2003).

Hall of Fame assessment system An informal method for evaluating a player's chances for induction into the National Baseball Hall of Fame, based on both seasonal and career accomplishments in statistical categories and other achievements (such as Most Valuable Player Awards and All-Star Games). It is calibrated such that players with 130 or more points are almost certain to be inducted, players with less than 70 points are almost certain to be left out (unless they have accomplishments in other areas, such as managing), and players with 100 points have a 50/50 chance of induction. The method was proposed by Bill James in his self-published *Baseball Abstract* (1980); a discussion can be found in his *Baseball Abstract* (1986). Syn. *Hall of Fame monitor.*

Hall of Fame career standards test An informal method for evaluating a player's chances for induction into the National Baseball Hall of Fame, based on statistical achievements. It is calibrated with a maximum of 100 points (with the exception of Babe Ruth, who acquired points in both hitting and pitching) and with 50 points indicating an "average" Hall of Famer. The method was proposed by Bill James and defined in his *The Politics of Glory* (1994).

Hall of Fame Game An annual exhibition game played at *Abner Doubleday Field* in Cooperstown, N.Y. from 1940 to 2008, between two major-league teams (selected by the commissioner) under the auspices of the National Baseball Hall of Fame and Museum. It was originally played in conjunction with the annual Hall of Fame induction ceremonies. The game often featured minor-league prospects of the two teams involved.

Hall of Fame honoree An individual who receives the J.G. Spink Award or the Ford C. Frick award (although the awardees are not members of the National Baseball Hall of Fame).

Hall of Fame monitor Syn. of *Hall of Fame assessment system.*

Hall of Famer An individual inducted into the National Baseball Hall of Fame; a *base-*

Hall of Famer. Ty Cobb (left) visits Christy Mathewson of the New York Giants during the 1911 World Series. *George Grantham Bain Collection, Library of Congress*

ball immortal. Abbrev. *HOFer.* Syn. *Cooperstowner.*

Hall of Fame season A term used by Bill James (*Baseball Abstract*, 1998) to describe a year in which a player achieves the triple milestones of a .300 batting average, 30 home runs, and 100 runs batted in.

hall of shame A list, book, article, or other place where poor performances, error rates, and other negatives are collected. The term is, of course, a play on "Hall of Fame." Authors Bruce Nash and Allan Zullo have turned the idea into a series of books, but they seem to be running out of material. Does Mike Schmidt really belong in The Baseball Hall of Shame because he once forgot to buckle his pants and walked onto the playing field?

Halos Nickname for the Angels.

ham A ballplayer's hand.

ham-and-cheese A desirable pitch from the batter's standpoint. "Tonight, he [Frank Castillo] just threw me a ham-and-cheese over the plate, and I hit it for a three-run triple" (Henry Rodriguez, quoted in *Milwaukee Journal Sentinel*, June 10, 1997).

ham-and-eggs Said of an ordinary player or league. A relief pitcher brought in after the game has already been decided may be "reliable but nondescript, like a meal of ham and eggs" (Patrick Ercolano, *Fungoes, Floaters and Fork Balls*, 1987, p.85). "[Pitcher] Bob Ewing's work in one of these Ham and Eggs League contests attracted the attention of the Cincinnati club" (*The Sporting Life*, Oct. 26, 1907).

hamburger league A minor league, so called because the players can only afford hamburgers for dinner, as opposed to the steaks consumed by major leaguers.

hamfatter *hist.* A vociferous baseball fan. "The Brooklyn cranks howled. They had never seen a liner caught before and regarded it as a marvel. 'Who struck out?' queried the Williamsburg hamfatters" (*The World* [New York], Oct. 20, 1889; Gerald L. Cohen). ETYMOLOGY. The term was applied "sneeringly" to variety and minstrel blackface comedians, dancers, and singers following the Civil War (*New York Sun*, May 6, 1929).

ham hitter *hist.* An inferior hitter.

hammer **1.** *v.* To hit the ball with great power. 1ST USE. 1887. "Samuel Thompson had expressed doubt as to his ability to hit a high ball. The manner in which he hammered the leather dissipated his doubts" (*Detroit Free Press*, March 9, 1887). **2.** *v.* To hit well against a pitcher in a particular game. "Daniel Cabrera was hammered for seven runs by Boston in his 2006 debut" (*The Baltimore Sun*, Apr. 28, 2006). 1ST USE. 1869 (*New York Herald*, Sept. 7; Edward J. Nichols). **3.** *n.* A player who hits pitches with hammerlike blows; e.g., Henry Aaron was known as "Hammerin' Hank" and his autobiography is entitled *I Had a Hammer* (1991). **4.** *n.* An effective pitcher. "They [Minnesota Twins] have begun to retool by adding some good young arms . . . but they lack the big hammer they had in Frank Viola" (*Tampa Tribune-Times*, Nov. 26, 1989). **5.** *n.* A great overhand curveball. "[Andrew Miller's] 12-to-6 hammer breaking ball is a second plus pitch" (Josh Boyd, *Baseball America*, March 31–Apr. 13, 2003; Peter Morris). See also *yellow hammer.*

hand *hist.* **1.** A turn at bat during the earliest days of baseball. Robert Smith (*Baseball*, 1947) observed that the early game of baseball was a gambling vehicle and made this point: "The very language of early baseball, as evolved by the Knickerbockers, was that of the gaming table: a turn at bat was a 'hand' and a run was an 'ace.'" IST USE. 1845. "The game to consist of twenty-one counts, or aces; but at the conclusion an equal number of hands must be played" (Knickerbocker Rules, Rule 8th, Sept. 23). **2.** A player, esp. the player at bat, in early baseball. IST USE. 1845. "Three hands out, all out" (Knickerbocker Rules, Rule 15th, Sept. 23; Frederick Ivor-Campbell).

handcuff 1. *v.* To hit or throw a ball so hard that a fielder cannot stop or catch it cleanly. "Bobby Abreu led off with a hard grounder that handcuffed second baseman Jose Vidro for an infield hit" (*The Baltimore Sun*, June 11, 2006). "[Manny Ramirez] uncorked a poor throw . . . that handcuffed second baseman Tony Fernandez" (*Wisconsin State Journal*, July 17, 1997). IST USE. 1920. "Groh handcuffed Shannon for a single" (J.V. Fitz Gerald, *The Washington Post*, Apr. 12; Peter Morris). **2.** *n.* The glove hand of a fielder when he cannot get it on a batted or thrown ball (as if he were wearing handcuffs). The situation is more likely to occur with hard-hit balls. **3.** *v.* For a pitcher to hold the opposition to very few hits (as if the batters were handcuffed). "The right-hander [Shawn Hill] had enough to handcuff the Philadelphia Phillies for seven innings" (*The Baltimore Sun*, June 12, 2006). See also *shackle*. IST USE. 1934. "Handcuff—To defeat; to hold an opposing team to few hits and a low score" (Maurice H. Weseen, *A Dictionary of American Slang*). **4.** *v.* For a pitcher to overwhelm a batter. "[Carl Pavano has] a slider that handcuffs righthanded batters" (*Sports Illustrated*, March 25, 2002). IST USE. 1945. "Pitchers handcuff batters when they have so much on the ball they throw it past them" (H.G. Salsinger, *Baseball Digest*, August). **5.** *n.* The figurative restraint that prevents a batter from hitting freely or swinging away. The phrase, "take the handcuffs off," is to give the batter the green light.
ETYMOLOGY. The term may have had its first sports application in boxing, where it referred to a fighter who was not using his hands to full advantage. When writer Stuart Bell of the *Cleveland Press* discovered a fight to be a fake, the *San Francisco News* (May 4, 1933; Peter Tamony) reported, "Bell had every reason to believe that one of the fighters was wearing handcuffs. Not only did the referee toss the middleweights from the ring, but the fans did some rioting."

hand down *hist.* Syn. of *hand out.*

hand grenade 1. The baseball. **2.** A hit lobbed over the infield. "[Kevin Higgins] dumped a pop fly just over the outstretched hands of third baseman Todd Zeile. In baseball terminology it was a hand grenade" (Kevin Kernan, *San Diego Union-Tribune*, May 30, 1993). See also *grenade.*

hand grenader *hist.* A pitcher.

handle 1. *n.* The narrow end of the baseball bat, where it is grasped or held by the hands. IST USE. 1870. "Kelley's extra white ash bat . . . 1¼ inches at the handle" (Chadwick Scrapbooks; John Freyer). **2.** *v.* To field successfully a batted or thrown ball. IST USE. 1862 (Chadwick Scrapbooks, Sept. 21; Edward J. Nichols). **3.** *n.* The nonexistent part of a batted or thrown ball that must be grasped for it to be fielded successfully. "[The ball] was rolling foul . . . but it came back fair and I tried to rush it and couldn't get a handle on it" (Sid Fernandez, quoted in *The Baltimore Sun*, July 24, 1994). See also *find the handle*, 1. **4.** *n.* A ground ball that takes a high, easy hop for the fielder. **5.** *v.* For a batter to hit a pitch successfully. "I had a good at-bat, fouled off some tough pitches and finally got a pitch I could handle" (Jerry Hairston Jr., quoted in *The Baltimore Sun*, Aug. 2, 2004). **6.** *v.* See *handle a pitcher.* **7.** *v.* See *handle the bat.*

handle a pitcher For a catcher to play an effective role for a particular pitcher. Edward J. Nichols (*An Historical Dictionary of Baseball Terminology*, PhD dissertation, Jan. 1939, p.32) noted that the term "usually refers to the ability of the catcher to obtain effective cooperation from a pitcher." To handle a pitcher also involves giving him good direction in the form of signals and being able to keep the pitcher calm when he is having difficulties. IST USE. 1894 (Spalding's Official Base Ball Guide; Edward J. Nichols).

hand left *hist.* Syn. of *hand out.* ETYMOLOGY. A cricket term signifying an out.

handle hit A batted ball that is hit off the handle of the bat, often a ground ball that dribbles down the line. It may or may not be a base hit. IST USE. 1912. "[Marty O'Toole] has the knack of keeping the ball so close to the batsman that most of the grounders and flies that are sent out are 'handle hits' . . . and only a small percentage of the balls so hit go safe" (*The Sporting Life*, Apr. 27; Peter Morris).

handle the bat To bat well; to be able to make contact and to control where the ball is hit. The term has been applied to the batter hitting second in the order—"You want someone who can handle the bat and . . . get on base" (Lee Mazzilli, quoted in *The Baltimore Sun*, March 5, 2004)—and to a batter hitting further down in the order—"Down in the bottom of the order, the job description is handling the bat" (Merv Rettenmund, quoted in Roger Angell, *The New Yorker*, May 3, 1993, p.47). "I've got to show them I can handle the bat at the major-league level" (Charlie Greene, quoted in *The Baltimore Sun*, Feb. 23, 1998). IST USE. 1870. "There is probably nothing as troublesome to the ball player as the matter of selecting a bat, which he can handle with confidence and certainty" (Chadwick Scrapbooks; John Freyer).

hand lost *hist.* Syn. of *hand out.* "Hands lost . . . is the old way of recording the outs in a match. Whenever a player is put out, a 'hand is lost,' and an 'out' is recorded in the score books" (Henry Chadwick, *The Game of Base Ball*, 1868, p.41). Abbrev. *HL.*

hand out *hist.* A player declared out; a putout. A hand out was charged to a batter directly put out either at bat or on the bases, such that a runner retired on a force out would be charged rather than the batter. The term appeared in the earliest box scores in 1845 and as late as 1872. Abbrev. *HO.* Syn. *hand lost*; *hand left*; *hand down.* IST USE. 1845. "Three balls being struck at and missed and the last one caught, is a hand out" (Knickerbocker Rules, Rule 11th, Sept. 23).

handout Syn. of *base on balls.*

hand over hand The method of determining which club bats first by the captains' alternating hands on a baseball bat. "In [Candy] Cummings' days ball clubs at the start of the game tossed up for their raps. Both teams wanted to be on the offensive right off the reel [before the ball became dilapidated], but Mr. Cummings has it that he was usually lucky on the 'hand over hand' on the bat and won out" (*The Sporting News*, Dec. 29, 1921; Peter Morris). IST USE. 1866. "The two recognized leaders had tossed the bat and were putting hand over hand. One, gripping the scarcely protruding end of the bat with his very nails, managed to whirl it round his head three times and toss it off its own length, or failed to do so, and sides were chosen" (*Galaxy*, July 15; Richard Hershberger).

hand protector *hist.* The two-fingerless fielder's glove worn by players in the late 1870s.

hands 1. Fielding ability. An infielder has *good hands* or *bad hands.* "Dave Kingman has feet for hands" (Glen Waggoner and Robert Sklars, *Rotisserie League Baseball*, 1987). See also *soft hands.* 2. Hitting ability. A capable hitter is said to have *good hands.* "A player who hits singles has baby hands. A player in a slump, well, his hands went on vacation" (Glen Waggoner and Robert Sklars, *Rotisserie League Baseball*, 1987).

hands lost *hist.* Plural of *hand lost.*

hands made of stone The hands of an inept fielder.

hands out *hist.* Plural of *hand out.*

handyman A player who can play several positions as well as bat; a "handy" man to have around. An article by Michael Vega on Rick Cerone (*The Boston Globe*, May 22, 1988) was headlined "Designated Handyman," alluding to the fact that he had been used for short periods at more than one position, including an inning each in two different games as a pitcher for the 1987 New York Yankees.

hang 1. To throw a pitch (such as a curveball or slider) that does not break, or breaks slowly and slightly, and therefore "hangs" over the plate, usually up and in the middle of the strike zone. According to Keith Hernandez (*Pure Baseball*, 1994, p.38), the pitch "doesn't have enough spin because the pitcher's hand snaps the ball too early in the release . . . [hence] the pitch doesn't break as much as normal, or at all, and 'hangs' right over the plate a little below belt-high." Without the speed or movement of the fastball, the pitch will be sitting high in the strike zone, almost as if on a tee waiting for the batter to hit it out of the park. "For a pitcher, a mortal sin. He who hangs too many curves, soon hangs up his glove forever" (Jim Brosnan, *The Long Season*, 1960). IST USE. 1937. Edward J. Nichols (*An Historical Dictionary of Baseball Terminology*, PhD dissertation, Sept. 1939, p.32) traced the term to an interview he conducted with Boston Braves pitcher William "Roy" Weir. **2.** Syn. of *strand*, 2.

hang a clothesline To hit a line drive, which, in flight, resembles a white *clothesline*. Syn. *hang out the clothes*; *hang out the hemp*; *hang out the wash*; *hang out a rope*. IST USE. 1932 (*Baseball Magazine*, October, p.496; Edward J. Nichols).

hanger Any breaking pitch that stays up in the strike zone and should be hit out of the park; specif., a *hanging curve*.

hang in Syn. of *hang tough*.

hanging curve A high curveball that "hangs," breaking slightly and giving the batter an easy target. It is the bane of pitchers and the delight of batters. Syn. *hanger*.

hanging slider A high slider that "hangs" over the plate.

hang out a rope Syn. of *hang a clothesline*. "A line drive is a rope and to hang out a rope is to hit a line drive" (Phil Pepe, *Baseball Digest*, Nov. 1974, p.58).

hang out the clothes Syn. of *hang a clothesline*.

hang out the hemp Syn. of *hang a clothesline*.

hang out the wash Syn. of *hang a clothesline*.

hang out to dry To pick off a baserunner.

hang them up Syn. of *hang up one's spikes*.

hang time The length of time it takes a fly ball to descend from its peak in flight to being fielded.

hang tough For a batter to foul off pitches,

working the count to his favor, and not capitulating to the pitcher. Syn. *hang in*.

hang up **1.** To catch a runner between bases. **2.** To be caught in a rundown. **3.** *hist*. To score a run. **4.** To set a record. "Now there is a good nine in Washington, and he [Walter Johnson] is going to hang up a great record" (*San Francisco Bulletin*, Feb. 10, 1913; Gerald L. Cohen).

hang up one's spikes To retire from playing professional baseball. New York Mets third baseman David Wright (quoted in *Sports Illustrated*, May 29, 2006): "As soon as baseball becomes a job, as soon as I stop caring, as soon as the smile goes away, I'll hang up my spikes and do something else." Syn. *hang them up*.

Hank Aaron Award An annual award given to the most outstanding offensive player in each major league. It was first presented in 1999 to the hitter with the most hits, home runs, and runs batted in; the winner is now determined by a panel of fans at MLB.com (30 percent) and play-by-play broadcasters and color analysts for each club's radio and television rightsholders (70 percent). Points are awarded on a 5–3–1 basis. The award honors baseball's former career home run king.

happy feet The moving feet of a batter who starts toward first base while making contact with the pitch, often too early to remain in proper batting position. "Ichiro [Suzuki] is one of the few hitters who has the hand–eye coordination to get away with having happy feet" (Deric Ladnier, quoted in Alan Schwarz, BaseballAmerica.com, Nov. 14, 2006).

Happy Haitian Theory A theory, attributed to broadcaster Tony Kubek, to explain the unusual frequency of home runs in 1987. According to George F. Will (*Bunts*, 1998, p.245): "Baseballs were then manufactured in Haiti and the theory was that the fall of the Duvalier regime so inspirited Haitians that they worked with more pep, pulling the stitching tighter, thereby flattening the seams—and flattening curveballs. The smoother balls [which made it difficult for pitchers to get a good grip] had less wind resistance to give them movement when pitched, or to slow their subsequent flight over outfielders."

happy zone That part of the strike zone where

a batter most enjoys seeing a pitch; the area "where a hitter's average jumps by 100 points" (*The Baltimore Sun*, May 2, 1994). For example, Ted Williams' happy zone, where he felt he could hit .400, was down the middle, between the belt and the letters. Syn. *hitting zone*. IST USE. 1969. "If I'm a real dangerous hitter and they're pitching me cute, a little outside, a little low, a hair inside, I'm not going to get that ball I can really hit, I'll have to bite at stuff that is out of my happy zone" (Ted Williams, *My Turn at Bat*, 1969, p.124).

hard With velocity and power; fast. "[Sidney Ponson's] fastball moves. It's harder than you think" (Mark McGwire, quoted in *The Baltimore Sun*, March 22, 2000). Compare *soft*, 1.

hardball A term that seemingly refers to baseball—the game as well as the ball. When the term is used in the context of baseball it refers to a tough style of play; e.g., " 'Billy' Campaign Adds Major Hard Sell to A's Hard-Ball Style," a headline (*San Francisco Examiner*, March 25, 1981; Peter Tamony) for a story on Oakland A's manager Billy Martin and the efforts of the A's front office to promote his style of management at the gate. IST USE. 1883. "He must now learn to cut jackets, play hard-ball, choose partners for cat and chermany, be kept in" (G.W. Bagby, *Selected Miscellaneous Writings* [1885], vol. II, p.19; *OED*). USAGE NOTE. The term does not sit well with baseball purists who see it as a misnomer. Red Smith (*The New York Times*, July 1, 1981) commented that it is a "misbegotten term" that has been given "an unappetizing usage, signifying nothing"; Smith was quick to point out, "There is a game called softball; in fact, there are two—slow-pitch and fast-pitch softball. There is no game called hardball. Nobody plays hardball." ETYMOLOGY. It is commonly assumed that "hardball" came into being as a way to distinguish baseball from softball; e.g., "He played softball in junior high, and hardball for an American Legion team" (*The Baltimore Sun*, Apr. 24, 1941; *OED*). However, Peter Tamony discovered an item in a club newsletter (Olympic Club's *Olympian*, March–Apr. 1945) that discussed the club's changeover from a "soft

ball" (a tennis ball) to a "hard ball" (black-rubber Irish handball). EXTENDED USE. Currently, the term seems to be used most commonly to refer to a tough, relentless adversary or adversarial situation; esp., political rough stuff. Presumably, no soft balls are thrown when hardball is being played. "More Hardball Over Big Government" (*The Washington Post* headline, Jan. 6, 1987). An article on Jim Bunning, a new congressman and a former major-league pitcher, was headlined: "Bunning Ready to Play Some Hardball in D.C." (*USA Today*, Oct. 6, 1986). The first extended use occurred in a discussion of the highly competitive newspaper business in Chicago (*Time* magazine, Oct. 30, 1944; Peter Tamony): "Last week a man with a winning streak stepped into what he called this 'hard-ball league.'" The term has a specific use among drug addicts: "Mixing cocaine with heroin is called speedballing or hardballing" (*San Francisco Examiner*, on the death of John Belushi, March 12, 1982; Peter Tamony).

hard ball A fastball (*The New York Times*, June 2, 1929).

hard cheese An exceptional fastball (*cheese*). "[Nolan Ryan] threw some good hard cheese up there" (Wally Backman, quoted in *St. Petersburg Times*, March 5, 1987).

hard curve A slider. "The term . . . has been used over the years to describe many pitches, and in the 1950s and 1960s was often used interchangeably with 'slider'" (Rob Neyer, in Bill James and Rob Neyer, *The Neyer/James Guide to Pitchers*, 2004, p.15).

hard-hit *adj.* Said of a ball that was struck forcefully.

hard-hitting Said of a hitter or team that gets many extra-base hits. The term does not necessarily connote home run or line-drive hitters, and it does not apply to singles hitters. IST USE. 1891. "According to the latest slate hard-hitting outfielders will be found among the Nationals this year" (*The Washington Post*, Feb. 4).

hard knuckleball A fast knuckleball. "[Jared Fernandez] puts his knuckles, not fingertips, on the ball, enabling him to throw a 'hard knuckleball'" (*Baseball Prospectus*, 2003).

Peter Morris (Oct. 2, 2003) comments, "This is intriguing because the earliest knuckleballers actually used their knuckles rather than their fingertips, but within a couple of years the fingertips became the dominant way to launch the ball. But that approach is now so rare that a new term has had to be invented for what was originally—and more logically—called a knuckleball."

hard-nosed Said of a player (such as Ty Cobb, Pete Rose, and Lenny Dykstra) whose style of play is tough and tenacious.

hard one 1. Syn. of *fastball*, 1. See also *high, hard one.* **2.** A hard-hit ball. "Sprague hit a 'hard 'un' to centre field" (*Brooklyn Eagle*, Aug. 15, 1865; Peter Morris).

hard out A player who is difficult to retire; a batter with a good eye for balls outside the strike zone.

hard slider A fast slider that breaks slightly and late. Umpire Eric Gregg (*Working the Plate*, 1990, p.170) wrote that J.R. Richard "threw the hardest slider I ever saw."

harness 1. *hist.* The uniform and equipment of a player, esp. those of a catcher. IST USE. 1902 (*The Sporting Life*, July 5; Edward J. Nichols). **2.** See *in harness.*

Harry Wright rule *hist.* A rule in place from 1879 to 1891 that prevented nonplaying managers from appearing on the field. Named for the Boston manager who would stand on the sidelines shouting instructions to his players.

Harvey's Wallbangers Nickname for the hard-hitting 1982 Milwaukee Brewers after Harvey Kuenn became manager in June. According to *Newsweek* (Aug. 2, 1982), Kuenn told his players, "Look, you guys can flat-out hit. So just go out there and have some fun." The name was a play on the name of a mixed drink called a Harvey Wallbanger. According to Daniel Okrent (*Nine Innings*, 1985, p.56), Brewers marketing vice president Dick Hackett moved to protect the name legally, "working with the importers of Galliano, the liqueur used in the similarly named cocktail."

hasn't got it Said of a pitcher with little stuff.

hassock *hist.* Syn. of *base*, 2. See also *hazzard.* IST USE. 1902. "The initial hassock"

(*Yale Record*, reprinted in *Grand Valley* [Moab, Utah] *Times*, Jan. 24; Peter Morris).

hat trick A mythical award given to a player who strikes out three times in a game. See also *golden sombrero; platinum sombrero; Horn.* IST USE. 1989. "If he strikes out three times, it's a 'hat trick'" (Bill Mazeroski, *Bill Mazeroski's Baseball '89*). USAGE NOTE. The term has been used in baseball for other three-fold feats: a batter hitting into three double plays in a game, a batter hitting three home runs in a game, a pitcher stopping three team losing streaks, a team winning three consecutive player-of-the-week awards, and a player getting his first hit, first home run, and first complete game in the same game. ETYMOLOGY. The term comes from cricket; it was created in the 19th century for the practice of presenting to a bowler a new hat when he took or knocked down three wickets on three consecutive balls. *The Oxford English Dictionary* listed the term in use as early as 1877 in this context: "Having on one occasion taken six wickets in seven balls, thus performing the hat-trick successfully" (J. Lillywhite, *Cricketers' Companion*, p.181). Peter Morris notes that the term "hat feat" preceded "hat trick" in cricket in 1873. It has also been stated that the term is Canadian and that it was created to describe spectators collecting money in a hat for a hockey player who had just scored three goals. This practice may well have been common, but the application of the term to hockey clearly postdates its appearance in cricket by many years. The term has been applied to a mythical award for accomplishing three of anything in other sports; e.g., in soccer for a player who has scored three goals in one game, in horse racing for a jockey who wins three races in a row, and in basketball for a team that wins three consecutive National Basketball Association championships.

haul it in To catch a batted or thrown ball.

have a ball To issue a challenge in very early baseball, when the stakes for a match game was usually a new ball (Peter Morris).

"have an idea" To think. "When a pitcher seems to be losing his cool a coach might shout at him, 'Have an idea out there'" (Jim Bouton, *Ball Four*, 1970). See also *"good idea."*

have one's innings **1.** To accumulate sufficient playing time. Syn. *get one's innings*. EXTENDED USE. To have had a chance; e.g., "Jones had his innings when he was given the opportunity to present his proposal." **2.** To have one's proper turns at bat.

Hawaiian runner A slow baserunner, one who takes at least 5.0 seconds from home plate to first base (the average player gets to first base in 4.2 or 4.3 seconds) (Angus Lind, *The New Orleans Times-Picayune*, Apr. 27, 1994). ETYMOLOGY. From *Hawaii Five-O*, a televised police drama that was popular on CBS from 1968 to 1980.

hawk **1.** *n.* An outfielder who covers his territory with speed and skill. See also *ball hawk*, 1; *flyhawk*. **2.** *v.* To be an adept outfielder. "[Don Mueller] used to call me Hawk, because, he said, I could really hawk the ball" (Bobby Thomson, *"The Giants Win the Pennant! The Giants Win the Pennant!,"* 1991, p.98).

hay pounder *hist.* A baseball player from a rural area.

hay shaker *hist.* **1.** A baseball player from a rural area. **2.** A rookie player.

hazzard A base, in the parlance of Dizzy Dean, who was giving his own twist to *hassock*.

HB Abbrev. for *hit batter*.

HBP **1.** Scorecard and box score abbrev. for *hit by pitch*, 2. **2.** Abbrev. for *hit by pitcher*.

head **1.** Short for *bat head*. **2.** One's physical appearance, usually used in a negative context. "Men who are considered to have 'the bad head' include Rocky Bridges, Don Mossi, and Yogi Berra" (Leonard Shecter, *Baseball Digest*, June 1963).

head case A temperamental player.

head fake A deceptive tactic by which the player with the ball looks at a baserunner in the hope that the glance will be enough to get the runner to stop or return to a base, allowing the player with the ball to throw to another base. Compare *arm fake*.

headfirst slide A slide characterized by a dive with arms outstretched to reach or return to a base. Most players lean forward and land on their hands and knees before sliding on their bellies; others (such as Roberto Alomar) dive

Headfirst slide. *Photograph by Joseph Baylor Roberts*

at full speed, land on their stomachs, hit the dirt with their palms, and reach for the base with one hand. It is uncertain whether the headfirst slide gets the runner to the base faster. The slide is a risky move (head, neck, fingers, hands, arms, and shoulders are vulnerable), hence it is used as a measure of a player's mettle. Ned Cuthbert (a member of the Keystone Club of Philadelphia) is credited with making the first headfirst slide in 1865; other practitioners included Pete Rose and Rickey Henderson. See also *belly whopper*. Syn. *belly slide*; *half gainer*, 2; *foxhole slide*.

headhunter A pitcher who throws beanballs; one who aims for the head. "To Mets fans, . . . [Roger] Clemens is the ultimate headhunter—an unrepentant intimidator who would throw at his grandmother if the last piece of apple pie were on the line" (Peter Schmuck, *The Baltimore Sun*, 2002). IST USE. 1962. "Don Drysdale, reportedly the most vicious headhunter baseball has seen since Sal Maglie's pitching days" (Zane Chastain, *Lima* [Ohio] *News*, May 30; Peter Morris). Also spelled "head hunter."

head in the locker The figurative condition of a player with little or nothing to say to anyone, including his teammates.

heads-up *adj.* Alert and quick-thinking; taking advantage of an opportunity. Leo Durocher (*Nice Guys Finish Last*, 1975, p.3) wrote, "If a man is sliding into second base and the ball goes into center field, what's the matter with falling on him accidentally so that he can't get up and go to third? . . . I don't call that cheating; I call that heads-up baseball."

"heads up!" *interject.* A command to stay alert. "If the coach sees either infielder edge in toward the base he should call 'heads up,' warning the runner that a pick-off may be attempted" (O.H. Vogel, *Ins and Outs of Baseball*, 1952; Peter Morris). "As we all know, 'Heads up!' on a ball field means 'Heads *down!*' and I quickly cringed away and received a glancing blow on the back of my right shoulder—a line foul from the batting cage, hit by Ted Sizemore" (Roger Angell, *Late Innings*, 1982, p.38).

head-to-head **1.** In direct personal opposition; e.g., batter vs. pitcher. **2.** A form of fantasy baseball in which two teams are pitted against each other over a specified period of time (such as a week), during which they accumulate points for various achievements (walk, stolen base, RBI) but lose points for certain failures (caught stealing, strikeout, grounding into a double play). The team scoring the most points in the specified time period is credited with a victory.

head-work *hist.* The thinking of a player using good judgment in his work. This term was common in the late 19th century and early 20th century. According to Henry Chadwick (*The Game of Base Ball*, 1868, p.41), "This is a term specially applied to the pitcher who is noted for his tact and judgment in bothering his batting opponents by his pitching. A pitcher who . . . uses head-work in pitching tries to discover his adversary's weak points, and to tempt him to hit at balls, either out of his reach or pitched purposely for him to hit to a particular part of the field." Alfred H. Spink (*The National Game*, 2nd ed., 1911, p.58) discussed Dickey Pearce by observing, "His judgment was sound and his knowledge of strategy was up to the highest point. He was generally considered a model representative of ball playing skill in what is technically known as head-work." Ty Cobb (*My Life in Baseball*, 1961, p.163) reminisced, "Headwork . . . enabled us old-timers to pull off unassisted triple plays and consecutive steals and hit-'em-where-they-ain't base hits that make lyrical reading today and often sound downright impossible." Also spelled "headwork."

head-worker *hist.* A player who exemplifies head-work. "[Wilson] is an accurate thrower as well as being what is termed a head-worker" (*San Francisco Examiner*, Apr. 29, 1889; Peter Morris).

healthy *n./hist.* A batter's swing at a pitched ball. "Elliott takes his third healthy and runs through the field down to the clubhouse" (Ring W. Lardner, *The Saturday Evening Post*, May 9, 1914; Peter Morris).

healthy average A good percentage, usually applied to a batting average.

hear the bell ringing To open the season. "Maybe the Cincinnati Reds hear the bell ringing. That's old baseball talk meaning the start of the season" (Jim Selman, *Tampa Tribune*, Apr. 4, 1986).

hearth stone Syn. of *home plate*.

heart of the game Pitching, so called by those who see it as the key to the sport. "Wanted: Pitchers of All Kinds. 'Heart of the Game' Is in Great Demand" (*The New York Times* headline, Apr. 3, 1988).

heart of the hide A fine-grade leather, usually from Black Angus steers raised in the upper Midwest that have no cattle brands, tick marks, or barbed-wire scratches, used for making fielder's gloves. The heart of the hide consists of the side of one animal from shoulder to butt. Abbrev. *HOH.*

heart of the order That part of the batting order with the best hitters, commonly the third, fourth, and fifth positions. Pitchers test their mettle going through the "heart of the order." "The next three hitters . . . all struck out swinging. If the Orioles had a heart of the order, it had stopped beating" (*The Baltimore Sun*, Aug. 10, 2003). See also *middle of the order*; *meat of the order.*

heart of the plate The center or middle of the plate, as opposed to the corners. IST USE. 1897. "I'm going to shove it plump over the heart of the plate" (pitcher John Clarkson, quoted in *The Sporting Life*, Oct. 30).

heat **1.** *hist.* Syn. of *inning*, 1. The term was borrowed from horse racing. **2.** A *fastball* of high quality. See also *high heat*. Syn. *heater.*

EXTENDED USE. A hard shot in hockey. "[Petr Nedved's] got that high heat in close. He can shoot with the best of them" (New York Rangers coach, quoted in *The Baltimore Sun*, Dec. 24, 2001). **3.** The ability to throw the fastball. "A fast ball is heat and when a pitcher is throwing hard he's bringing heat to the plate" (Phil Pepe, *Baseball Digest*, Nov. 1974, p.58).

heater Syn. of *heat*, 2. "[Mike Boddicker's] fastball, once a true heater, was chilled by elbow tendinitis" (Phil Hersh, *Baseball Digest*, Jan. 1984, p.42).

heatface "A guy who throws heat is Heatface" (R.J. Reynolds, quoted by Scripps Howard News Service, Sept. 17, 1986).

heat up 1. For a relief pitcher to *warm up*. "Relievers 'heat up' in the bullpen" (Lowell Cohn, *San Francisco Chronicle*, June 4, 1980). **2.** For a team to begin to win games.

heave 1. *v.* To pitch or throw. IST USE. 1913. "Bill Burns . . . heaved the spheroid across the plate" (*San Francisco Bulletin*, Feb. 7; Gerald L. Cohen). **2.** *n.* A thrown or pitched ball. IST USE. 1907 (*Harper's Weekly*, Dec. 14, p.1828; Edward J. Nichols). **3.** *v./hist.* To throw a game. "How to 'Heave' a Game . . . certain charges made against Wm. Wansley—the catcher of the Mutual club—of 'selling' or 'heaving' the game, as it is technically termed" (*New York Clipper*, Nov. 11, 1865; Peter Morris, who notes that the article also quoted a letter [Oct. 25, 1865] from Mutuals shortstop Thomas Devyr that "We are going to 'heave' this game."

heave-ho Ejection of a player from the game; e.g., "Smith got the old heave-ho for arguing too strenuously."

heaver *hist.* A pitcher. IST USE. 1911. "Now that the offside heaver, Harry Krause, seems to have struck his stride, Connie [Mack] has a splendid lot of pitching talent" (*Sandusky* [Ohio] *Star Journal*, July 8; Peter Morris).

heaving Pitching. "Koestner did the heaving for the southerners" (*San Francisco Bulletin*, Apr. 10, 1913; Gerald L. Cohen).

heavy Said of a talented baseball player; having the basic ability to play professional baseball. "Harkin is not heavy enough to make a Class AA twirler" (*San Francisco Bulletin*, March 3, 1913; Gerald L. Cohen).

heavy air Atmosphere that creates resistance and shortens a ball's flight, supposedly due to damp weather or high humidity (an erroneous assumption made by ballplayers because water vapor is lighter than air).

heavy ball 1. A ball that feels weighty or hard to a catcher or infielder because of the way it is thrown. An odd or eccentric spin on the ball is often the cause. It brings an extra sting to the hands of the receiver. First baseman Jeff Conine (quoted in *The Baltimore Sun*, Apr. 20, 2003): "[Jose Morban] throws a heavy ball. It feels like you're catching a ball that weighs a couple ounces more than a normal baseball because he has such great carry through it." IST USE. 1897. "Infielders who have caught these sizzling throws of Jim's [McGuire] have told me that the ball feels as heavy as a lump of lead when it lands in their mitt" (Earl Wagner, quoted in *The Washington Post*, June 14). **2.** A pitch that, due to its spin and sinking movement, is hit by the batter off the end of the bat, causing the batter's hands to sting, as if he had hit a rock. **3.** A sinking pitch that drops sharply as it nears the plate, causing the batter to hit ground balls. In 1997, Scott Erickson was credited as having the "heaviest ball" in the American League (*The Baltimore Sun*, Sept. 6, 1997). "I had a very good sinker. . . . I didn't grip the seams of the ball, I just let it slip out. It was tougher to control, but it was very heavy and it didn't have rotation on it, so it would sink" (Thornton Lee, quoted in Edwin Howsam, *Baseball Graffiti*, 1995, p.88). Syn. *heavy sinker*; *heavy pitch.* **4.** A ball saturated with water.

heavy hitter A hitter who hits the ball hard; one who hits home runs and extra-base hits; a slugger. "The class of batsmen known as 'heavy hitters,' men who think that a home run hit—a chance hit at best—is the ne plus ultra of batting" (Henry Chadwick, quoted in *St. Louis Globe-Democrat*, Jan. 30, 1887). IST USE. 1870 (*Cleveland Leader*, July 30; Peter Morris). EXTENDED USE. An individual to be reckoned with; someone important. "Stephen King's apparent desire to be a literary heavy hitter weighs down his already elephantine new novel [*It*]" (*Newsweek*, Sept. 1, 1986).

heavy-legged Said of a player (often a catcher) who runs with a laboring stride and effort. "[It] has less to do with weight or musculature of legs than the lack of grace or efficiency a runner exhibits" (Alan Schwarz, BaseballAmerica.com, Nov. 14, 2006).

heavy pitch Syn. of *heavy ball*, 3.

heavy sinker Syn. of *heavy ball*, 3.

heel The part of a fielder's glove covering the bottom of the palm, adjacent to the wrist; the bottom edge of a fielder's glove.

heeler *hist.* A spectator in early baseball who showed partisanship or other unacceptable conduct, such as insolent, aggravating, or profane language meant to provoke a player or umpire. "The disreputable club 'heelers,' who form the noisy and bullying element of base ball assemblages at professional contests . . . [that have] been marked by cowardly personal assaults on umpires in the field, scenes of disgraceful rows by club 'heelers' hissing and insulting remarks by partisans in grand stand assemblages" (*Brooklyn Eagle*, Aug. 17, 1884; Peter Morris). ɪsᴛ ᴜsᴇ. 1871. "There is no crowd that follows a club more partisan than are the Star 'heelers'" (*Brooklyn Eagle*, May 31; Peter Morris).

Hefty bag Syn. of *Baggie*.

heifer step A unit of measurement used by broadcaster Dizzy Dean to describe the distance a runner was short of a base. The term lacked a certain precision, however, because he defined it as 2½ feet in "Dizzy Daisies" and "about 36 inches" in *Dizzy's Definitions*.

helicopter 1. *n.* A high, breaking pitch with nothing on it. "[Mark] Leiter's first pitch is indeed the curve, but with nothing on it, a helicopter curve, as we say . . . right over the middle of the plate" (Keith Hernandez, *Pure Baseball*, 1994, p.174). ɪsᴛ ᴜsᴇ. 1987. "Look out for that helicopter" (*St. Petersburg Times*, March 5). 2. *n.* The bat, or part of a broken bat, as it turns like the rotor blades of a helicopter when accidentally sent flying after the batter swings and hits or misses the pitch. 3.

v. For a batter to swing and accidentally send the bat, or part of the bat, flying like the rotor blades of a helicopter. "A hitter broke his bat and the barrel segment came helicoptering toward the mound" (*The Baltimore Sun*, March 28, 1999).

helmet See *batting helmet*.

help out For a batter to try to obstruct or hinder the throw of the catcher who is trying to stop an advancing runner. ɪsᴛ ᴜsᴇ. 1911 (*American Magazine*, May, p.15; Edward J. Nichols).

"help yourself" An encouragement directed to the pitcher when he comes to bat.

hemp A hard-hit line drive. "[Larry] Hisle was laying out some hemp," (*Baseball Digest*, June 1979). The term is a play off other terms with the same meaning: *clothesline* and *frozen rope*.

hen fruit Syn. of *goose egg*, 1. ɪsᴛ ᴜsᴇ. 1891 (*Chicago Herald*, June 24; Edward J. Nichols).

hen-house hoist A foul ball.

"here comes Charley" *hist.* A greeting for a limping player presumed to be suffering from a *charley horse*.

herky-jerky Said of the motion of a pitcher with an esp. awkward delivery. Bruce Sutter (quoted in *Sports Illustrated*, July 17, 2006, p.24): "I was . . . herky-jerky with my motion, and sometimes you couldn't tell how fast the ball was coming. It looked like I was throwing it harder than I was."

Hernandez Rule Allowing the first baseman to position himself with one foot in foul ground when holding runners. The practice is illegal, but not enforced in the National League. Named for St. Louis Cardinals and New York Mets first baseman Keith Hernandez.

herring Syn. of *dead fish*, 1.

hesitation [softball term] A false or deceptive move or bluff legally allowed in 16-inch slow pitch softball to throw off the timing of the batter. Each real pitch of the ball can be accompanied by two hesitations.

hesitation hummer A pitch developed by New York Yankees pitcher Steve Hamilton that started with the slow delivery of the *folly floater* but then "hummed" in as a fastball.

hesitation pitch A pitch that is delivered with a pause, or hitch, between the windup and the throw. Such an abnormality can cause problems for the batter in timing his swing. The pitch was developed by Satchel Paige in the Negro leagues.

HGH Abbrev. of *human growth hormone*. Sometimes written as "hGH."

H glove A glove that allows the fielder to look through the webbing as he shields his eyes when trying to catch a fly ball. The name is derived from the leather in the webbing, which forms the letter "H."

hiccup A small difficulty or minor setback; e.g., a relief pitcher who earns a save after giving up one or more runs is sometimes accused of a "momentary hiccup." Detroit Tigers shortstop Carlos Guillen was batting .432 with seven extra-base hits through Detroit's first 10 postseason games in 2006 "despite a 3-for-16 hiccup in the Tigers' sweep of the A's in the AL Championship Series" (Albert Chen, *Sports Illustrated*, Oct. 30, 2006, p.45).

hickory *hist.* A baseball bat. During the early days of baseball, it was assumed that a heavy wood like hickory would be most effective for hitting, but this assumption was soon revised. IST USE. 1857. "The Atlantic's [*sic*] now tried their hands at the hickory" (*New York Clipper*, Sept. 12; Peter Morris).

hidden-ball trick **1.** A time-honored legal ruse in which a defensive player (usually an infielder) conceals the ball and hopes that the baserunner believes it has been returned to the pitcher. When the runner steps off the base, he is summarily tagged out with the hidden ball. The play was popular in the late 19th century; however, antipathy to the trick was a widely shared sentiment and there were attempts to eliminate it. According to *The Sporting Life* (May 20, 1905, reprinted from *Boston Journal*), "It was the late Harry Wright who insisted that the trick was unprofessional and he would not allow his players to attempt it on opponents. Mr. Wright argued that the spectators were entitled to see how each man went out, and could not be expected

to follow the ball when it was juggled by the players." The success rate of the trick declined with the appearance of base coaches. Syn. *concealed ball trick.* IST USE. 1896. "Masterly work in the field resulted in team work for the Senators that made the Orioles appear as a lot of the veriest amateurs, the hidden ball trick . . . being among the clever points gained" (*The Washington Post*, Apr. 29; Barry Popik). USAGE NOTE. The play predates the term. According to Bill Deane, the trick made its big-league debut on May 25, 1876, when Chicago White Stockings legend Cap Anson was duped and caught off third base (*Sports Illustrated*, July 15–22, 2002); however, newspaper accounts describe the play as early as 1873. **2.** An illegal play in which a hidden second ball is brought into play. The trick is occasionally performed and rarely detected. An Associated Press story (June 26, 1964) of a Class A New York–Pennsylvania League game at Binghamton, N.Y., described the trick: "As a high fly hit by Dan Napoleon soared toward the fence last night, evidently bound for home run territory, it was suddenly snared from the air in a spectacular catch—or so it appeared. But later, [Binghamton outfielder] John May . . . admitted he didn't catch the ball after all. He said he went through the gestures, but actually substituted a ball from his pocket for the one that was hit out of the park." The story goes on to say that Napoleon was credited with a home run and that Binghamton lost the game. **3.** A pitcher's ability to keep the ball hidden from the batter's view until it is delivered. Because the pitcher's grip on the ball determines the type of delivery, a pitcher will try to hide the ball until the last moment. When Chicago Cubs pitcher Don Cardwell no-hit the St. Louis Cardinals on May 15, 1960, because he "hid the ball . . . in his glove until delivery," the headline in the *San Francisco Call-Bulletin* (May 17, 1960; Peter Tamony) read: " 'Hidden Ball Trick' Gave Cardwell $2000 'Bonus.' "

EXTENDED USE. There is a hidden-ball trick in football, which dates back to the 19th century and, according to Peter Tamony, was first employed by Vanderbilt in a game with Auburn in 1895. Variations of the term are used for deceptive moves in other areas, esp.

politics. In a comment on the House of Representatives' "quick fixes" for problems, Thomas L. Stokes wrote, "Those are 'hidden ball' plays—now you see it, now you don't" (*San Francisco News*, Aug. 9, 1948; Peter Tamony).

hide 1. See *horsehide*. IST USE. 1904. "Anderson walloped the hide to center for two bases" (*The Washington Post*, Sept. 22; Peter Morris). 2. See *cowhide*.

high Toward the top of, or above, the strike zone.

high A Syn. of *high Single A*.

high and away Syn. of *high and outside*.

high and inside Said of a pitch that is high and close to the batter and that may or may not be in the strike zone. Syn. *high and tight*; *up and in*. EXTENDED USE. Describing something that is difficult to handle; thorny. "Mayor Elmer Robinson wound up and pitched a fast one high and inside today to Supervisor Edward T. Mancuso" (*San Francisco Call-Bulletin*, Dec. 8, 1953; Peter Tamony).

high and low Syn. of *high-low*.

high and outside Said of a pitch that is high and far from the batter and that may or may not be in the strike zone. Syn. *high and away*; *up and away*.

high and tight Syn. of *high and inside*. IST USE. 1939. "[Vince DiMaggio] waits for his pitches and no longer bites at the 'high and tight' throws that made him an easy mark for National League pitchers during two long years" (Parke Carroll, *The Sporting News*, June 15; Peter Morris).

high ball 1. Syn. of *high pitch*. "A high ball is 'one around the neck' or 'one around the ears'" (*The New York Times*, June 2, 1929). Compare *low ball*, 1. 2. *hist.* In the early days of baseball, a "fair ball" that passed over home plate between the batter's waist and his shoulders (1871–1876), or between the batter's belt and his shoulders (1877–1886). Compare *low ball*, 2. 3. A ball hit high in the air. "[Long high balls are] favorable for a fielder to catch . . . [and] thought a great deal of by the spectators at a match, but with a good captain and sharp fielders every such

ball ought to be caught" (Henry Chadwick, *The Game of Base Ball*, 1868, p.41). IST USE. 1867. "Hunt sent a high ball to left" (*Daily National Intelligencer*, Aug. 27).

high-ball hitter A hitter with a reputation for swinging at balls that come in above his belt. Compare *low-ball hitter*.

high cheese A fastball (*cheese*) delivered high in the strike zone.

high chopper A batted ball that bounces high. The cliché is that infielders wait "an eternity" for high choppers to come down. "Jeff King . . . hit a high chopper . . . and beat the pitcher's throw to first" (*Tampa Tribune*, Sept. 11, 1990). See also *chopper*.

high company *hist.* Syn. of *major leagues*.

high-drop mound A pitcher's mound that appears to be higher than normal. Compare *low-drop mound*.

high five Celebratory hand-slapping that takes place with one's arms extended high over one's head. It began to show up in baseball as a way of welcoming a player at the plate after hitting a home run. It is one of several slaps, clasps, and other congratulatory gestures that have been popular. Compare *bone*, 3. ETYMOLOGY. The origin of the gesture and the term is a subject of dispute. Some reports trace the gesture to Los Angeles Dodgers outfielder Glenn Burke's celebration of Dusty Baker's grand slam on Oct. 5 during the 1977 National League Championship Series, although it is unclear if Baker slapped Burke's raised hand. What is not disputed is that beginning in 1978 the Dodgers did a lot of high-fiving (*Sports Illustrated*, Sept. 23, 1996, p.8). Other reports claim that Derek Smith of the Univ. of Louisville basketball team, which won the NCAA championship for the 1979–1980 season, created the high five during preseason practice and introduced it to the nation in 1979 as the team made numerous TV appearances.

high-flier *hist.* Syn. of *high fly*. IST USE. 1867. "Smith sent a high-flier toward the right field, but King took it in nicely" (Chadwick Scrapbooks, October; David Shulman).

high fly A batted ball that is hit high in the air. Syn. *high-flier*. IST USE. 1871. "Bass sent up a high fly and while Glenn and Hall were

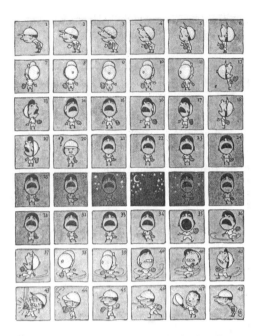

High fly. From *Life*, Sept. 17, 1914. *Author's collection*

making up their minds which should go for it, it came down bewteen them and Bass swam to second" (*The Cleveland Morning Herald*, May 22).

high, hard one A powerful fastball that comes in high in the strike zone. The term is the title of a 1967 book by former pitcher Kirby Higbe. IST USE. 1928 (*The New York Times*, Oct. 7; Edward J. Nichols).

high heat A fastball of extra-high velocity. See also *heat*, 2.

Highlanders Nickname for the New York entry in the American League from 1903 to 1912. The name derived from Hilltop Park in Washington Heights, one of the highest elevations in Manhattan, where the team played during those years. Donald Dewey and Nicholas Acocella (*The Ball Clubs*, 1996, p.367) noted that the club was so named "partly because of the romantic connotations of Gordon's Highlanders, a prominent British military unit." The club was officially renamed the *Yankees* in 1913; however, sportswriters occasionally referred to the team as the Highlanders as late as 1921.

high-low A warm-up drill for fielders in which the ball is deliberately thrown high and low for added difficulty. John J. Evers

and Hugh S. Fullerton (*Touching Second: The Science of Baseball*, 1910) described the exercise: "High-low isn't a game, properly speaking; it is a torture. ... [It] consists in throwing the ball short distances either just too high, just too low, or just too far to the right or left for the victim to reach it without a sudden movement, leap or dive. Half a dozen men play at once, and the principal skill lies in looking at the top of Jones' head and throwing the ball at Smith's feet. It looks easy, but outsiders who attempt to stay in the circle fall exhausted in five minutes trying to hold the pace." See also *pepper*, 2. Syn. *high and low*; *high-on-low*.

high maintenance Preferred treatment given to a difficult or demanding player; catering to a moody or fragile player: for example, Barry Bonds' being granted carte blanche access for his personal trainer. "Baseball people routinely describe him [Roberto Alomar] as 'high maintenance'" (Ken Rosenthal, *The Baltimore Sun*, May 12, 1999).

high mass *hist.* A Sunday doubleheader.

high-neck-in pitch A term used by Dizzy Dean for a *knockdown pitch*.

high number 1. A number assigned to a baseball card issued late in the baseball season, when there is less interest in baseball cards. It is printed and distributed in significantly decreased amounts than the lower-numbered cards and therefore creates a scarcity factor. 2. The last series of baseball cards distributed for a set in a given year, often released after the baseball season, when interest in baseball is waning.

high-on-low Syn. of *high-low*.

high pitch A pitch that is above the strike zone. Unless swung at by the batter, a high pitch should be called a ball by the plate umpire. Compare *low pitch*. Syn. *high ball*, 1.

highpockets A name for a tall, skinny player with long legs; e.g., 1920s New York Giants first baseman George "Highpockets" Kelly, who was 6' 4" and weighed only 190 pounds.

high pop A pop fly that rises high in the air.

high-revenue club See *large-market club*.

high school *adj.* Said of an amateur or bush-league player.

high school hop A big, high bounce of a batted ball that is easy to field.

high school rule A rule adopted by Major League Baseball in the early 1950s prohibiting a team from even discussing a professional career with a promising player who still had high school eligibility remaining. The rule came about because teams had signed and sent high school players to the minor leagues before they had graduated and completed their eligibility. After the 1951 season, an amendment to the rule allowed clubs to talk to a high school student about a professional career and to discuss the terms of a contract, but forbade signing the player to a contract.

high Single A A *Class A* level of minor-league baseball, above *low Single A* but below Class AA; e.g., the Florida State League, the Carolina League, and the California League. No more than two players may have six or more years of prior minor-league experience on a high Single A team. Syn. *high A*; *Advanced A*; *Class A-Advanced.*

high sky A cloudless, bright blue sky under which it is difficult to judge fly balls. "That terror of all ball players—a high sky—is a term in the vernacular of the profession the meaning of which is clear to the initiated only. It refers to a clear blue sky unbroken by the white, fleecy clouds that are generally seen in fair weather. With these clouds as a foundation for the eyes of the players it is an easy job to judge a ball. Without the clouds it is very difficult" (*The Sporting Life*, July 24, 1897; Peter Morris). IST USE. 1892. "The sun shone down from what, in base-ball parlance, would be called a high sky, as if through a lens, scorching everything in its focus" (*Chicago Daily Inter-Ocean*, May 31; Peter Morris).

high strike A pitch thrown high in the strike zone that umpires sometimes call a ball. Although the *Official Baseball Rules* define the upper limit of the strike zone as the horizontal line at the midpoint between the top of the batter's shoulders and the top of his uniform pants, umpires beginning in the mid-1980s through the 1990s called such a pitch a ball. Tim Kurkjian (*Sports Illustrated*, June 12, 1995) observed, "It's not unusual to see a pitch that is thrown an inch above the belt called a ball." Before the American League adopted the inside chest protector in 1977, umpires tended to call the high strike since the balloon protectors compelled them to adopt a more upright stance directly behind the catcher. Compare *low strike.*

hightail it To move quickly. IST USE. 1939. "On throws from right or center field, with no play at the plate suggested, the pitcher should hightail it over behind the third baseman" (Gordon S. "Mickey" Cochrane, *Baseball: The Fan's Game*; David Shulman).

highway robbery A spectacular fielding play that prevents a potential base hit. IST USE. 1910 (*Baseball Magazine*, December, p.34; Edward J. Nichols).

high wine *hist.* Rubbing alcohol (white corn whisky) for a pitcher's arm (Damon Runyon, *The Railroad and Current Mechanics*, Nov. 1913, p.237; Steve Milman).

hill Syn. of *mound*, 1. "[Joe] Benz . . . with the wicked spit ball, opened on the hill for the White Sox" (*San Francisco Bulletin*, March 7, 1913; Gerald L. Cohen). Var. *hillock*; *hilltop*, 1. IST USE. 1908 (*New York Evening Journal*, March 11; Edward J. Nichols).

hillman *hist.* A pitcher. "I know but little of the other hillmen in the National League" (Connie Mack, quoted in *San Francisco Bulletin*, Feb. 12, 1913; Gerald L. Cohen).

hillock Var. of *hill.*

hill staff The pitching staff of a team.

hilltop 1. Var. of *hill.* "They continued to play well, but not well enough to beat a team like the Hawks—not with Powder Hurley on the hilltop" (Burt L. Standish, *The Man on First*, 1920; David Shulman). 2. Home field. "The Ducks have been hard to beat on their own hilltop" (*San Francisco Bulletin*, Apr. 24, 1913; Gerald L. Cohen).

Hilltoppers Nickname for the New York entry in the American League from 1903 to 1912. The name derived from Hilltop Park where the team played during those years. The club was officially nicknamed the *Yankees* in 1913.

hindcatcher 1. A playground term for the *catcher*, 1, in various parts of the southern

United States. Roy Blount Jr. wrote (in Ron Fimrite, ed., *Birth of a Fan*, 1993, p.34) that growing up in Georgia "my position is what we called 'hindcatcher.'" See also *backcatcher*, 1. **2.** The position played by the hindcatcher. **3.** A player who stands behind the catcher to retrieve passed balls. See also *pig tail*.

hind snatcher *hist.* Syn. of *catcher*, 1 (*Famous Sluggers and Their Records of 1932*, 1933).

Hindu Doing a play over again; a "do-over."

hipper-dipper *hist.* A curveball with a sharp break in its trajectory; a "sneaky curveball" (Al Schacht, *Al Schacht Dope Book*, 1944, p.40).

hippodrome *hist.* **1.** A fraudulent baseball game in which the winner is determined beforehand; a rigged contest. IST USE. 1865. "'Hippodrome' Tactics in Base Ball: How to 'Heave' a Game; the first and last instance of selling a game of ball" (*New York Clipper* headline, Nov. 11; Dean A. Sullivan). **2.** A stunt or attention-getting feat performed on the field to enliven a game. "[Arlie] Latham, the clown, who always caused unlimited mer-riment by his antics and hippodromes, did not begin his funny tricks until the sixth inning. . . . [He] made the spectators laugh at his witty sayings and repartee" (*Brooklyn Eagle*, Sept. 8, 1889; Dean A. Sullivan). As noted by Peter Morris (personal communication, March 31, 2003), the term resurfaced in baseball in the 1930s in relation to the debate over night baseball; Pittsburgh Pirates owner Barney Dreyfuss said (*Baseball Magazine*, Oct. 1930) that night baseball made "a hippodrome of the game by assuming the guise of circus stuff under the lights." ETYMOLOGY. From the name of ancient structures and arenas used for equestrian shows and other spectacles, including chariot races held in ancient Greece and Rome. More to the point was the Hippodrome in New York City, an immense showcase for vaudeville acts and spectaculars.

hippodroming *hist.* **1.** Presenting the game of baseball as a competition but actually having a predetermined outcome; more specif., losing a game deliberately to build up a close but fraudulent rivalry or to cash a bet at good

Hippodrome. The New York City vaudeville palace. *Author's collection*

odds. The practice was prevalent during the late 1860s and the 1870s when gamblers bribed players to throw games. "The clubs . . . who indulged in the 'hippodroming' and knavery connected with pool rooms destroyed all the public desire to see the clubs play" (*Brooklyn Eagle*, Feb. 3, 1878; Peter Morris). The practice was not limited to baseball, and hippodroming schemes were played out in foot racing, wrestling, and boxing, to name a few. IST USE. 1869. "Not content with lowering the national game to the level of the hippodroming of the turf, they [professional clubs] aim to get control of the National Association [of Base Ball Players], and especially of its Committee of Rules" (*New York Clipper*, Dec. 18; Dean A. Sullivan). **2.** The practice of promoting baseball with stunts, such as hiring a woman player or using prizefighters John L. Sullivan and Jim Jeffries as umpires. "When he got to the big leagues . . . [Ed] Barrow eschewed all such hippodroming for he felt baseball by itself was all the entertainment a man needed" (Robert Smith, *Baseball's Hall of Fame*, 1965; Charles D. Poe).

historic base ball Syn. of *vintage base ball*.

his umps *hist.* A mock title of royalty conferred on an umpire, a play on "his honor" or "his highness." "Del approached his umps and declared emphatically he was safe. His umps said nary a word" (*San Francisco Bulletin*, Apr. 17, 1913; Gerald L. Cohen). Also spelled "His Umps"; "his ump." See also *umps.* IST USE. 1908 (*Baseball Magazine*, July, p.56; Edward J. Nichols).

hit **1.** *n.* A batted ball that moves in fair territory and allows the batter to reach a base safely before the ball and without the help of an error and without the ball being caught on the fly. Although most are obvious and automatic, the official scorer may have to decide whether a given batted ball is to be credited as a hit or an error. The ability to get 200 hits in a season is regarded as an exceptional feat. See also *base hit*, 2. Abbrev. *H*, 1. IST USE. 1860. "By a well directed hit the batter [Russell] got away to the first base, and by a subsequent hit of Flanly's he succeeded in getting home" (*The New York Herald*, Aug. 24). **2.** *n.* Any batted ball. **3.** *v.* To bat a ball; e.g., "Smith hit a ground ball to third." **4.** *v.*

To bat a ball and get on base safely; e.g., "Jones hit a double." IST USE. 1866 (*New York Sunday Mercury*, Sept. 16; Edward J. Nichols). **5.** *v.* To take a turn at the plate. **6.** *v.* For a pitcher to strike a batter with a pitched ball; e.g., "[Jaret Wright] walked four batters and hit two" (*The Baltimore Sun*, May 22, 1998).

hit air To swing and miss. IST USE. 1908 (*Baseball Magazine*, July, p.63; Edward J. Nichols).

"hit an air pocket" The common excuse or alibi of a fielder who has misjudged or dropped a fly ball. See also *air pocket.*

hit and run **1.** *n.* Syn. of *hit-and-run play.* Sometimes spelled "hit-and-run." IST USE. 1896. "[The Duffyites] did a little of the 'hit and run' business" (*The Boston Globe*, July 1; Peter Morris). **2.** *v.* To attempt or execute the hit-and-run play. "You would never hit-and-run with two outs" (Keith Hernandez, *Pure Baseball*, 1994, p.24).
EXTENDED USE. **1.** The term "hit and run" began showing up as a description for automobile accidents in which injury is done and the driver of the car leaves the scene. "Mother Jailed in Hit-and-Run Injury of Boys" (*New York Herald Tribune* headline, Dec. 6, 1936; Edward J. Nichols). Peter Tamony found examples dating as far back as 1929. **2.** Anything that strikes quickly. A letter to "Dear Abby" opened, "There is a cheap little flirt who is a freshman at school and she is the hit and run type. She likes to go after a boy who is going with another girl just to see if she can get him. After she breaks them up, she drops the boy and finds somebody else to break up" (*San Francisco Chronicle*, Oct. 18, 1968; Peter Tamony). *Time* magazine (Nov. 20, 1950) described certain strike techniques used against American Telephone and Telegraph as " 'hit and run' picketing": to create maximum effect, the pickets would show at one locale, where fellow workers would refuse to cross picket lines, and then abruptly move to another site.

hit-and-run game Use of the *hit-and-run play* as part of a team's offense. "The hit-and-run game and the base stealing game are still the methods by which teams seek to win" (Grand Rapids manager Frank Torreyson, quoted in *Grand Rapids* [Mich.] *Evening Press*, May 21, 1898; Peter Morris). IST USE. 1896. "The hit-and-run game is worked to perfection" (*The Sporting News*, Apr. 25; Peter Morris).

hit-and-run play A prearranged offensive play, usually executed with no outs, in which, to get a head start, a baserunner starts to run to the next base as soon as the pitcher delivers the ball to the batter, who must try to hit it to protect the runner. The play is usually undertaken with a runner on first base only: as he heads to second base, either the shortstop or the second baseman moves to cover the bag, giving the batter a gap in the infield defense through which to hit the ball. If the batter gets a hit, the baserunner usually is able to advance to third base. If the ball is hit to an infielder, the baserunner's head start reduces the defense's chance of turning a double play. However, if the batter swings and misses, the runner may be thrown out, and if the ball is hit for a pop fly or line drive, the runner is likely to become part of a double play. The play is geared toward the batter, who must swing at the pitch. Broadcaster Ralph Kiner and others have observed that "hit-and-run play" is a misnomer; it should really be "run-and-hit play" because the runner runs before the ball is hit. Compare *run-and-hit play*. See also *hit-and-run game*; *steal and slam*. Syn. *hit and run*, 1. ETYMOLOGY. Bill James (*The Bill James Historical Baseball Abstract*, 1986, pp.47–48) discussed the origin of the play: "The best evidence is that Tommy McCarthy [Boston Beaneaters] invented the hit and run play. Monte Ward [New York Giants manager] picked up on it [in 1893] and taught it to Willie Keeler, and Keeler brought it to Baltimore." John McGraw and the Orioles popularized the play in the 1890s. Other claimants cited by early baseball historians have included Cap Anson, Mike "King" Kelly, and Harry Wright. Lave Cross (quoted in *Detroit Tribune*, March 16, 1905) suggested that Pete Browning accidentally originated the play in the 1880s as a result of a missed signal. The *Chicago Daily Tribune* (July 1, 1877; Timothy Prosser) carried the following story: "Some chap stated the following conundrum,

Hit-and-run play. Willie Keeler (left) and John McGraw standing with Joe Kelley (left) and Hughie Jennings seated. *National Baseball Library and Archives, Cooperstown, N.Y.*

professing not to understand it: 'Why do batsmen strike a ball when a base-runner is half-way to second base on a clever steal?' The answer was found in Thursday's game, when McVey started to second, and Anson hit the ball in the exact spot where McGeary had been standing before he ran to his base to catch McVey. It is really a clever batting trick to hit to right field when it lies all open." It appears that the play preceded the introduction of the term.

hit around For a team to rough up ("push around") a pitcher. "You can tolerate a guy not having his good stuff on a given day and getting hit around. But when you don't give the fielders behind you a chance, that's when the frustration starts to set in" (Baltimore Orioles pitching coach Mike Flanagan, quoted in *The Baltimore Sun*, June 9, 1995).

hit a ton 1. To be on a hitting streak. 2. To hit a baseball with great force.

hit away To take a full swing at the pitch; e.g, when the take sign is not active. The term is normally used to describe a situation in which one might assume that the batter would not take a full cut at the ball; e.g., when the count on the batter is 3–0 or when a bunt seems appropriate. See also *swing away*.

hit back to the box To hit the ball back to the pitcher.

hit batsman Syn. of *hit batter*.

hit batter A batter hit by a pitched ball. See also *hit by pitch*, 2. Abbrev. *HB*. Syn. *hit batsman*.

hit-batter pitch A pitch intended to hit a batter's body but not to hit him in the head. Regarding his hit-batter pitch, Bob Gibson explained (*The New York Times*, July 13, 1986), "Note that I didn't say 'beanball' pitch. Nobody in his right mind throws a rock 90-plus miles an hour at a guy's head."

hit behind the runner To hit the ball down the first base side of the field to help a baserunner advance to the next base. This is a common element in successful hit-and-run plays in which the ball is hit into right field. One of the earliest and strongest advocates of hitting behind the runner was John McGraw. "Batting from the left side, [Darrell] Evans this season has excelled at hitting behind the runner" (*Baseball Digest*, Oct. 1983, p.76). USAGE NOTE. It would be difficult to overemphasize the degree to which this phrase and the advice behind it has become an element of the game. Arthur Mann (*American Mercury*, March 1933; Peter Tamony) noted the conventional wisdom on this matter: "The biggest problem found among young players is presented by the chronic left-field hitter. No matter how good a young batter may be, he must be taught to 'hit behind the runner,' or into right field when a man is on base, for this placement facilitates the runner's trip around the base paths."

hit by pitch **1.** *v.* To be struck by a pitched ball while in the batter's box. **2.** *n.* Awarding first base to a batter who has been hit by a pitch. If the batter makes a reasonable effort to get out of the way of the pitch and does not swing at the ball, he is awarded first base. If the batter leans in and is struck by the ball in the strike zone or he clearly makes no effort to avoid being touched by the ball, the batter is not awarded first base. If the umpire deems that a pitcher has intentionally hit a batter, the pitcher will be ejected from the game. The rule first came into play in 1884 in response to Cincinnati pitcher Will White,

who made a practice of hitting batters to keep them away from the plate. The American Association introduced the award of first base, at the umpire's option, for the 1884 season, and made the award nearly automatic in 1885 (the National League adopted the rule and made its enforcement nearly automatic in 1887). Peter Morris (personal communication, July 29, 2000) found two sources (*St. Louis Post-Dispatch*, Apr. 10, 1889, and Apr. 17, 1904) that credit Tony Mullane's habit of "polishing" batters' buttons (to "get even" with players who hit him freely) with the adoption of the rule. See also *hit batter*; *Welch Amendment*. Abbrev. *HBP*, 1. Syn. *hit by pitcher*; *hit by pitched ball*.

hit by pitched ball Syn. of *hit by pitch*, 2. Abbrev. *HPB*.

hit by pitcher Syn. of *hit by pitch*, 2. Abbrev. *HBP*, 2; *HP*. IST USE. 1892 (*Brooklyn Daily Eagle*, May 1, p.4).

hitch **1.** A hesitation, extra motion, or other abnormality a batter makes with the bat before starting his swing to meet the pitch and that usually affects his timing. A hitch requires the batter to assume, at the last possible moment, some new position. Two common hitches occur when the batter drops his hands just before the pitch is delivered, thereby keeping him from starting his swing properly, and when he draws the bat backward just before starting his swing. Depending on the context in which it appears, the term may refer to a flaw or a strength, but it tends to be used more often in pointing to a defect. "If a hitter's bat goes back farther before it starts forward you can lay a coin or two out of my pocket that this batter has something simulating a hitch" (Branch Rickey, *Branch Rickey's Little Blue Book*, 1995, p.22). The term can be used in a positive way: "One of the things the Orioles liked about [Jim] Traber this spring is that he has enough of a hitch in his swing to spray the ball to all parts of the field" (Richard Justice, *The Washington Post*, July 23, 1986). Babe Ruth, Walker Cooper, Jimmie Foxx, Rudy York, Hank Aaron, Willie Mays, and Jeff Bagwell were all noted for the hitch in their swings. IST USE. 1939. "[Vince] DiMaggio had a pronounced hitch in his swing when he reported for spring training" (Parke Carroll, *The Sporting News*, June 15; Peter Morris). ETYMOLOGY. The term may be nautical in origin, coming from a hitch in a rope, a jam that prevents it from running smoothly through a block. **2.** A pause in a pitcher's windup intended to throw off the batter's timing; the key element in a hesitation pitch.

hitchy-koo *hist.* Fidgeting in the batter's box by a nervous batter. IST USE. 1933 (Edgar G. Brands, *The Sporting News*, Feb. 23).

"hit 'em where they ain't" The rallying cry for batters through the decades since 1897 when William "Wee Willie" Keeler hit .424. He was asked by a reporter how a man of his size (5' 4½", 140 lbs.) could put together such an average: "Simple. I keep my eyes clear and I hit 'em where they ain't." Although the line was undisputedly Keeler's, the idea behind it was hardly new. "For the Mutuals, Hunt sent a very safe one to center, where 'nobody was'" (*New York Clipper*, Sept. 7, 1867; Peter Tamony). The phrase is one of baseball's hoariest axioms and shows up in various contexts. In the 1920s, Arthur "Bugs" Baer wrote, "Willie Keeler hits them where

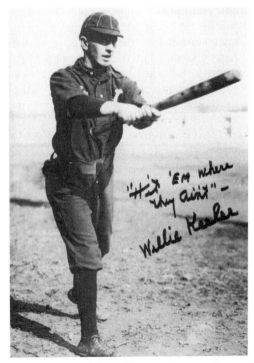

Hit 'em where they ain't. "Wee Willie" Keeler. *National Baseball Library and Archives, Cooperstown, N.Y.*

they ain't. Babe Ruth hits 'em where they're never going to be."

hit famine A hitting slump for a team or individual.

hitfest A game in which many hits are made and hence many runs are scored.

hit for average To hit in a way that will improve or maintain a player's batting average; specif., to concentrate on hitting safely rather than on hitting the long ball.

hit for distance To concentrate on hitting the long ball.

hit for the cycle To hit a single, double, triple, and home run (not necessarily in that order) within the course of a single game. It is a rarity that many top hitters (such as Willie Keeler, Ty Cobb, Babe Ruth, and Willie Mays) never accomplished in a career. Only two players have done it three times: Babe Herman and Bob Meusel. Compare *homer for the cycle*; *throw for the cycle*, 1; *run for the cycle*. IST USE. 1933. "[Jimmie Foxx] is one of only six players in all major league history to 'hit for the cycle,' that is, get a single, double, triple and homer in four times at bat in one game" (*The Washington Post*, Sept. 27; Barry Popik). USAGE NOTE. The emphasis on this feat has increased in recent years; many old-timers may never have heard of it during their playing years. Dave Kingman drove this home when he hit for the cycle as a rookie in 1972: "When Chris Speier mentioned it to me in the dugout, I didn't know what it meant. I had never done it, and I had never even heard of it" (*San Francisco Examiner*, Apr. 17, 1972; Peter Tamony).

hit in a pinch *hist.* **1.** *n.* A base hit at the right moment with runners on base. **2.** *v.* To hit the ball safely at a crucial moment.

hit in the slats To be hit by a pitched ball in the upper torso. "Slats" were defined as "ribs" in the early 1900s (Robert L. Chapman, *New Dictionary of American Slang*, 1986).

hit it out To hit a home run. See also *out of the ballpark*. EXTENDED USE. Success. Evan Thomas (*Inside Washington* television show, Jan. 29, 2000) said Presidential candidate John McCain "hit it out of the park" when discussing abortion.

hit king **1.** An unofficial title for the player who has the most hits or the highest batting average in the league by the end of the season. "Men in masks [catchers] vying to become hit kings" (*Sports Illustrated* headline, Aug. 28, 2006, p.77). **2.** The player with the most career hits; i.e., all-time hits leader Pete Rose. "As long as I can always write, 'Pete Rose, Hit King,' that means something" (Pete Rose, quoted in *The Wall Street Journal*, Apr. 15, 2005). Often spelled "Hit King."

hitless **1.** Said of a team or player without a base hit in a given number of at-bats or games. **2.** Having given up no hits; e.g., "Smith pitched five hitless innings." **3.** Said of a team with a poor batting average; specif., the *Hitless Wonders*.

Hitless Wonders Nickname given to the early 20th-century Chicago *White Sox* for their ability to win games with light hitting. The name got special play in 1906 when the team won the American League pennant with a team batting average of .230 (the lowest in the league) and won the World Series with an average of only .198. The key was the team's pitching staff, which, among other accomplishments, recorded 32 shutouts during the season. Gustav W. Axelson (*"Commy": The Life of Charles A. Comiskey*, 1919) wrote, "In hitting the [White Sox] had, year after year, gradually dropped from .275 [actually .276] in 1901 to .237 in 1905. They had already acquired the title of 'hitless wonders,' but they were rapidly becoming more hitless without being wonders." IST USE. 1905 (*The Sporting Life*, Oct. 7, p.13; Edward J. Nichols).

hit-me pitch A pitch that is easy to hit; e.g., a middle-of-the-plate fastball

hit metal For a batted ball to be misplayed by a fielder who presumably is playing with an iron glove (*Sports Illustrated*, Sept. 13, 1982).

hit off the fists To hit an inside pitch off the handle of the bat near the fists. The hands will sting and the ball, most likely, will be a bloop hit.

Hitless Wonders. The 1906 Chicago White Sox. *National Baseball Library and Archives, Cooperstown, N.Y.*

hit one's weight To hit poorly; to have a low batting average. The phrase is usually used negatively, as in "he's not even hitting his weight." The phrase links a player's three-digit weight with a three-digit batting average and, because most players weigh less than 225 pounds, a player not hitting his weight would not have a very good average.

hit over one's head To hit better than expected; to hit greater than one's average for an earlier period, such as the previous season.

hit rate Syn. of *batting average on balls in play.*

hit safely To hit the ball so that it cannot be fielded for an out.

hit sign A sign given to the batter permitting him to swing at the next pitch or series of pitches. See also *green light,* 1.

"Hit Sign, Win Suit" The words on a sign installed on the right-center field wall in Ebbets Field in 1931 by clothier, politician, and Brooklyn Dodgers fan Abe Stark. The sign—three feet high and 30 feet wide, 318 to 344 feet from home plate, at the concrete base of the scoreboard—advertised Stark's family clothing store at 1514 Pitkin Ave. in the Brownsville section of Brooklyn and was a pledge that any player hitting the sign on the fly would be given a free suit from the store. The sign stayed in place until 1958 when the Dodgers moved to Los Angeles. The first two balls to hit the sign were hit by Mel Ott of the rival New York Giants.

hitsman *hist.* Syn. of *hitter,* 1.

hitsmith *hist.* A good hitter. IST USE. 1907 (*New York Evening Journal,* Apr. 5; Edward J. Nichols).

hits per game *hist.* A statistical measure of player performance recorded by pioneer baseball writer Henry Chadwick beginning in 1867, expressed in *average and over* format; the precursor to batting average (see John Thorn and Pete Palmer, *The Hidden Game of Baseball,* 1985).

hits, runs, and errors The scoreboard line that records a team's offensive prowess and defensive shortcomings. EXTENDED USE. A method of tallying one's success in almost any endeavor, including war. "I have had to

lay off tellin' about the battle till my next, Joe, because they ain't added up the hits, runs, and errors yet" (H.C. Witwer, *A Smile a Minute,* 1919; David Shulman).

hittability The competence or skill of a hitter. On scouting reports, the term is not very useful because it lacks detail and explanation (Alan Schwarz, BaseballAmerica.com, Nov. 14, 2006).

hittable **1.** Said of a pitcher who is relatively easy to hit against. **2.** Said of a pitch that is relatively easy to hit.

hitter **1.** A *batter;* esp., one who hits the ball. Syn. *hitsman.* IST USE. 1883 (*The Sporting Life,* Apr. 15; Edward J. Nichols). **2.** A batter who gets many hits; e.g., *Hitter,* the title of Edd Linn's 1993 biography of Ted Williams.

-hitter A suffix to describe a pitching performance or game in terms of the number of hits allowed; e.g., "no-hitter," "one-hitter," "two-hitter," and "12-hitter."

hitter-friendly Said of a hitter's park. "How tough is it for any pitcher . . . to fashion a 3.21 ERA for Texas, whose home park is known to be hitter-friendly?" (*Sports Illustrated,* July 4, 2005).

hitterish Said of a player or team in the midst of a hitting streak. The term was used by broadcaster Dizzy Dean.

hitter's count A count with more balls than strikes: 1–0, 2–0, 2–1, 3–0, and 3–1. "[Mark Prior] had enough confidence in his curve to throw it consistently in hitter's counts" (*Sports Illustrated,* Oct. 13, 2003). "The pitcher's next pitch is a fastball off the plate. Ball two. It's 2–1: a hitter's count" (Michael Lewis, *Moneyball,* 2003, p.285). See also *fastball count.*

hitter's park A ballpark in which it is relatively easy to score runs; a ballpark with relatively small dimensions that appeals to hitters. Examples include Wrigley Field (Chicago) with the wind blowing out during the summer months, Fenway Park (Boston), Ebbets Field (Brooklyn), Crosley Field (Cincinnati), Baker Bowl (Philadelphia), and Coors Field (Denver). See also *homer-friendly park.* Compare *pitcher's park.*

hit the air To swing at and miss a pitched

ball. IST USE. 1906 (*The Sporting Life*, March 3, p.7; Edward J. Nichols).

hit the bat Syn. of *Indian ball,* 1.

hit the black To throw a pitch that crosses the inside or outside edges of the plate for a strike.

"hit the bull" A frequent exhortation in the days when Bull Durham signs were on outfield fences. The phrase was associated with a scheme, hatched by the makers of Bull Durham tobacco prior to World War I, that awarded a player $50 for hitting their sign. The signs were cut out in the shape of a bull and placed on the outfield fences of as many as 150 major-league and minor-league parks. See also *bullpen* for further discussion. IST USE. 1909 (*Baseball Magazine*, June, p.60; Edward J. Nichols).

hit the corner To throw a pitch that passes just inside or outside the edge of the strike zone.

hit the cutoff man For an outfielder to throw the ball so that the cutoff man (usually an infielder) can intercept it and decide whether to relay or hold the ball.

hit the dirt **1.** For a batter to drop to the ground to avoid getting hit by a pitched ball, usually thrown in the vicinity of the batter's head. See also *bite the dust,* 2. **2.** For a baserunner to begin his slide into a base. See also *bite the dust,* 1. IST USE. 1908 (*New York Evening Journal,* Apr. 16; Edward J. Nichols). **3.** For a baserunner to dive back toward the base he occupied to avoid being picked off.

hitting candy *hist.* Amassing three or four base hits in a game (*The New York Times,* June 2, 1929).

hitting coach An offensive team coach responsible for the welfare and success of the team's hitters. Syn. *batting coach.*

hitting instructor A coach who visits the various minor-league affiliates of a major-league team to provide hitting instruction wherever needed.

hitting machine **1.** A player who consistently gets base hits. "[Edgar] Martinez is a hitting machine" (*Milwaukee Journal Sentinel,* Oct. 1, 1997). See also *machine,* 2. **2.** A device that measures the exit velocity of a ball struck by a bat. The Baum Hitting Machine, invented by Steve Baum of Traverse City, Mich., is used by Major League Baseball to test balls believed to be juiced (*Sports Illustrated,* March 25, 2002).

hitting shoes The figurative shoes of the hitters on a team that is batting around.

hitting slump A period of poor performance by a hitter, such as two hits in 27 at-bats. See also *batting slump.*

hitting streak **1.** See *consecutive hitting streak.* **2.** See *consecutive-game hitting streak.*

hitting tee See *tee,* 1.

hitting zone Syn. of *happy zone.*

hit to all fields For a batter to be able to hit a pitch to any given part of the field. "Ty [Cobb] could hit any ball that he could reach, pulling to right field, slicing to left, or driving it through the middle as the case might be. Because of this ability to hit to all fields, defensive players could not station themselves with any degree of certainty in spots where he was most likely to drive the ball" (E.A. Batchelor, quoted in Ty Cobb, *My Life in Baseball,* 1961, p.11).

HL Abbrev. for *hand lost.*

HO Abbrev. for *hand out.*

Hobbsian In the heroic manner of outfielder and slugger Roy Hobbs, portrayed by Robert Redford in the 1984 movie *The Natural,* in which Hobbs tears the cover off the ball with his magical bat and later hits the climactic, game-winning home run that knocks out the stadium lights. The movie was based on Bernard Malamud's 1952 novel *The Natural,* in which Hobbs strikes out rather than hitting a home run.

hockey-style mask Syn. of *goalie-style mask.*

"hoe her down" *hist.* An encouragement yelled to a baserunner to run fast. "[Buck] Ewing stood on the coaching lines with his hat in his hand and his hair standing straight on end. 'Go it, John [Montgomery Ward],' he yelled. 'Hoe her down.' John was 'hoeing her down' for all he was worth" (*The World* [New York], Aug. 13, 1889; Gerald Cohen). ETYMOLOGY. A derivation from "hoedown," a community dancing party.

HOF Abbrev. for *Hall of Fame,* 1.

HOFer Abbrev. for *Hall of Famer.*

Hogan's brickyard *hist.* A rough, uneven, or stony baseball field; a lumpy diamond. See also *brickyard.* ETYMOLOGY. According to Joseph McBride (*High and Inside*, 1980, pp.56–57), the Irish surname "Hogan" was a widely used slang expression for a building contractor who kept his bricks and other supplies "in rough, bumpy yards, which ballplayers compared to unkempt minor-league parks." See also *ash heap; contractor's back yard; home-brew field.* Syn. "Hogan's back yard."

hog tie To keep the opposition from scoring.

hog wild runner *hist.* A determined baserunner who often ignores the coach's signs or is intent on reaching the next base. "On nearly every ball club, there are some players who are known in the frank parlance of the profession as 'hog wild runners.' The expression means that these players are bitten by a sort of 'bug' which causes them to lose their heads when once they get on the bases. They cannot be stopped, oftentimes fighting with a coacher to go on to the next base, when it is easy to see that if the attempt is made, the runner is doomed" (Christy Mathewson, *Pitching in a Pinch*, 1912; Peter Morris).

HOH Abbrev. of *heart of the hide.*

hoist 1. To hit a fly ball "[Joe] Jackson hoisted a fly to the infield, which [Heinie] Groh gathered in" (*The New York Times*, Oct. 7, 1919). IST USE. 1912 (*New York Tribune*, Sept. 8; Edward J. Nichols). 2. To hit a home run over the fence. "[Bertrand Coy] hoisted an ordinary fly over the short right-field fence" (*San Francisco Bulletin*, May 29, 1913; Gerald L. Cohen).

hold 1. *v.* See *hold a runner.* 2. *n.* The act of the pitcher who holds the ball for an inordinately long time, hoping the baserunner will tip his hand. 3. *v.* For a runner to remain at a base when the ball is pitched or hit. 4. *v.* To prevent a hitter from taking an extra base; e.g., "The outfielder cut the ball off and held the hitter to a single." 5. *n.* Syn. of *hole*, 3. 6. *n.* An unofficial statistic credited to a relief pitcher who enters a game with a *save opportunity* and maintains the lead until replaced by another pitcher. The term and statistic were created to reward relief pitchers who

are often overworked and underappreciated. Various media and statistical organizations have developed their own definitions of a hold, which may include not giving up any runs (earned or unearned), pitching a minimum of one inning or recording at least one out, and not receiving credit for a win, loss, or save. Although the value of a hold had been recognized much earlier, holds were first compiled by STATS Inc. in 1987; the publication credits a hold to a pitcher who "enters the game in a save situation, records at least one out, and leaves the game having never relinquished the lead" (*STATS Player Profiles*, 2002). A pitcher cannot receive credit for both a hold and either a win, save, or game finished. See also *attaboy*, 2. Compare *blown save*. Abbrev. *H*, 2. 7. *v.* For a relief pitcher to enter a game in a save situation and to leave without giving up the lead. 8. *n.* Good contact with a batted ball. "When they tossed her in there fast, and you got a hold of it, she was gone" (Goose Goslin, quoted in Lawrence S. Ritter, *The Glory of Their Times* [booklet], 1998, p.29). 9. *v./hist.* To catch effectively the deliveries of a pitcher. IST USE. 1901 (Burt L. Standish, *Frank Merriwell's School Days*, p.229; Edward J. Nichols).

hold a runner 1. For the pitcher, the catcher, or an infielder (esp. the first baseman) to keep a runner on base from taking a large lead. Infielders do their part by staying close to the base awaiting a possible pickoff throw from the pitcher. The pitcher keeps his eye on the runner and occasionally throws to the base in question. Syn. *hold on.* IST USE. 1909. "Neither [Charley] Schmidt nor [Oscar] Stanage could compare with [George] Gibson in 'holding' runners" (*The Sporting News*, Oct. 21; Peter Morris). 2. For a fielder to prevent a baserunner, who is not forced to run, from advancing to the next base during a play. This is usually accomplished by the fielder with the ball either faking a throw toward the runner being held or just looking in his direction. 3. For the third base coach to signal (usually by holding the arms up) the baserunner to stop at second or third base and not advance further, or for the first base coach to stop the batter-runner from trying for a double. "Orioles coach Mike Ferraro took some abuse from the crowd when he held runners at third base two different times in the fifth inning" (*The Baltimore Sun*, Sept. 27, 1993). Syn. *hold up*, 1.

hold down 1. For a pitcher to restrict the opposing batters to a few hits. IST USE. 1891 (*Harper's Weekly*, May 23; Edward J. Nichols). 2. To play a position. "Willie Hogan held down third base for Oakland" (*San Francisco Bulletin*, March 11, 1913; Gerald L. Cohen).

holder A relief pitcher credited with a hold. The term was proposed by Buster Olney (*The Baltimore Sun*, May 26, 1996).

holding sign A sign that is activated when it is held longer (sometimes for several seconds) than all the other signs. It can be as simple as doffing one's cap for a few seconds or bending an elbow. It the simplest sign to receive because it is held long enough for the message "to sink in"; therefore, the sign is esp. suited for less-experienced players or for players who need to look more than once to expel any doubt about the sign.

hold on Syn. of *hold a runner*, 1.

holdout *n.* 1. An act or instance of holding out. *The Washington Post* headline (Apr. 5, 1987): "[Roger] Clemens Ends 29-Day Holdout." 2. A player who has not come to terms with his team and misses part or all of spring training and, in a few cases, some of the regular season. In an extreme case, Edd Roush of the New York Giants sat out the entire 1930 season because his team wanted him to take a pay cut after coming off a .324 season. Traditionally, a player becomes a holdout when he returns his unsigned contract to the team's front office. Babe Ruth was a holdout on several occasions. IST USE. 1888 (*New York Press*, Apr. 19; Edward J. Nichols). USAGE NOTE. The practice may have predated the term. Lee Allen (*The Hot Stove League*, 1955, p.115) noted that Charlie Sweasy, second baseman for the Cincinnati Red Stockings, was the first professional holdout: paid $800 in 1869, he held out for $1,000 for 1870 and did not report until he was paid that sum.

hold out *v.* To decline to accept and sign a tendered player's contract, usually for more money or better terms. "[Rube] Marquard claimed that the reason he was holding out was because [John] McGraw neglected to send him a fatter contract after the had done the great things which he did for the Giants in 1912" (*San Francisco Bulletin*, March 11, 1913; Gerald L. Cohen).

"hold the grain up" Syn. of *"keep the Spalding up."*

hold up 1. Syn. of *hold a runner*, 3. 2. For the batter to stop his swing.

hole 1. The space between any two infielders; commonly, the area between the third baseman and the shortstop, near the outfield grass. "Chet Lemon . . . reached after a weak throw by shortstop Rafael Santana on a grounder into the hole" (*Tampa Tribune*, Sept. 9, 1988). Compare *gap*, 1, which is the space between outfielders; tradition dictates this distinction, although "hole" is occasionally applied to the space between outfielders. See also *third base hole*; *slot*, 7. 2. A position in the batting order. "The lineup is going to be exciting from the leadoff guy to the guy in the nine hole" (Larry Bigbie, quoted in *The Baltimore Sun*, March 4, 2005). 3. The position of the batter in the dugout following the hitter in the on-deck circle; the position of the third batter in the batting order at any given point in a game. See also *at bat, on deck, in the hole*. Syn. *hold*, 5. IST USE. 1937 (Red Barber, NBC World Series broadcast, Oct. 10; Edward J. Nichols). ETYMOLOGY. From the nautical "hold" (cargo space in the hull of a vessel), which, according to Joanna Carver Colcord (*Sea Language Comes Ashore*, 1945, p.102), was originally "hole" and became "hold" through what she terms "a mistaken etymology." Baseball turned it back to "hole," although the common nautical pronunciation of "hold" is "hole." 4. Syn. of *dugout*. 5. A difficult position during a game, such as for a pitcher with runners on base and heavy hitters coming to bat or for a batter or pitcher behind in the count; a distinct disadvantage during a game, such as trailing by five runs in the sixth inning. "[Mordecai Brown's] curves never broke sharper and his control never seemed better, the batsmen nearly always finding themselves 'in the hole' as baseball parlance goes—i.e.; with two strikes recorded against them and facing the necessity of hitting at every possible good ball or fanning" (*Chicago Tribune*, Oct. 5, 1908). "It is a very good plan to keep your batter in the hole, or at least not get where you must put every ball over the plate" (Cy Young, quoted in Alfred H. Spink, *The National Game*, 2nd ed., 1911, p.391). IST USE. 1886. "[Detroit manager Bill] Watkins said that his pitchers were 'kept in the hole' continually by [umpire] Connelly, who, he says, is afraid to call a strike on [Cap] Anson" (*St. Louis Post-Dispatch*, July 15; Peter Morris). **6.** A losing position; e.g., "The Yankees dropped the next two games and went in the hole by seven games." **7.** A hitter's weakness. Tino Martinez (quoted in *Sports Illustrated*, June 30, 2003): "Lefthander, righthander, soft thrower, power guy, fastballs away, fastballs in—he [Albert Pujols] doesn't have any holes." But Michael Lewis (*Moneyball*, 2003, p.145) stated that "every hitter has a hole": "[Jason] Giambi's hole was waist-high, on the inside corner of the plate. It was about the size of a pint of milk, two baseballs in height and one baseball in width." IST USE. 1913. "What ball should be pitched to such heavy sluggers of the Cobb, Crawford, Lajoie, Jackson type. Have they . . . a so-called 'hole' where it is impossible for them to hit, or would it be better for the pitcher to stick them over and trust to luck to have them hit the ball at some of the fielders?" (*The Washington Post*, Apr. 6; Peter Morris). See also *hole in his swing*. **8.** A deficiency in a player's game. Baltimore Orioles director of minor-league operations Doc Rodgers (quoted in *The Baltimore Sun*, Aug. 18, 2003): "It's the same Ruben [Rivera], a Gold Glove center fielder with some holes in his offensive game. And those holes are things that, as long as he plays, he'll continue to work on."

hole in his bat A facetious excuse for a swing and a miss, as if the ball went right through the bat. IST USE. 1886. "Hackett has a hole in his bat that even the big bouquet he got yesterday couldn't fill" (*The Boston Globe*, June 6; Peter Morris).

hole in his swing A hitter's weakness, where he doesn't make contact. Shawn Estes (quoted in *Sports Illustrated*, March 4, 2002): "[Paul Lo Duca is] the kind of hitter that

pitchers hate to face, because he doesn't have any holes in his swing and puts the ball in play." Jane Leavy (*Squeeze Play*, 1990): "They say that every great slugger has a hole in his swing, a vulnerable place in the arc of presumed contact" See also *hole*, 7.

hole in the air A swing that misses a pitched ball. IST USE. 1909 (Zane Grey, *The Short-Stop*, p.42; Edward J. Nichols).

hole in the glove A facetious excuse for a ball that is totally missed by a fielder, as if it went right through a hole in the glove. IST USE. 1903 (*Hackensack* [N.J.] *Weekly*, scrapbook clippings; Edward J. Nichols).

holiday *hist.* A doubleheader.

holler guy A coach or player known for his constant chatter and shouts of encouragement; baseball's version of a uniformed cheerleader. The cliché is that every good team needs a holler guy. Asked the importance of a holler guy, Robin Roberts (quoted in *The Baltimore Sun*, June 2, 1995) said, "It seems to me that most of those are guys who can't hit or field."

hollow-end bat Syn. of *cupped bat*.

Hollywood hop A batted ball that takes an easy bounce into a fielder's glove, which presumably makes him look good enough for the movies. See also *charity hop*; *gravy hop*; *Sunday hop*.

Hollywood player Syn. of *grandstand player*.

"holy cow!" Signature phrase of broadcasters Harry Caray, Phil Rizzuto, and Halsey Hall. Caray developed the phrase during a semipro baseball tournament in Battle Creek, Mich. (Harry Caray, *Holy Cow!*, 1989). When Lisa Winston (*USA Today*, Dec. 25, 1994) looked into the origin of the phrase in a baseball context, she concluded that it was heard on the radio as early as the 1930s, when Jack Holiday of WTPS in New Orleans used it frequently during broadcasts of games of the New Orleans Pelicans of the Southern Association. The phrase achieved a certain notoriety when Rizzuto repeated it several times on Oct. 2, 1978, after New York Yankees shortstop Bucky Dent hit the game-winning home run in the division playoff against the Boston Red Sox. On Phil Rizzuto Day at Yankee Stadium, the venerable

"Holy cow!" President Ronald Reagan joins Cubs announcer Harry Caray in the broadcast booth at Chicago's Wrigley Field on Sept. 30, 1988, during a political swing. Reagan called an inning and a half of action. "You know, in a few months I'm going to be out of work and I thought I might as well audition," the president said. "You could tell he was an old radio guy," Caray said. "He never once looked at the television monitor." *Ronald Reagan Presidential Library*

Yankee shortstop and announcer was presented with a live cow furnished with a gleaming halo. ETYMOLOGY. Slang used to express surprise or astonishment. "O, holy cow! I'm sick of bacon and tired of eggs" (J.P. McEnvoy, "The Potters," *The Washington Post*, March 11, 1923; Barry Popik).

home 1. *n.* Short for *home plate*. IST USE. 1845. "The bases shall be from 'home' to second base, forty-two paces" (Knickerbocker Rules, Rule 4th, Sept. 23). USAGE NOTE. The term was used by William Clarke (*The Boy's Own Book*, 2nd ed., 1828) in describing rounders: "As they get home . . . they play at the ball in rotation, until they all get out." 2. *adv.* To, at, or toward home plate; e.g. "A hit may bring Smith home." 3. *n.* Short for *home field*. 4. *adj.* Said of a game played on one's home field. 5. *n.* Short for *home team*, 1.

home-and-home *hist.* Said of a match or series in early baseball competition in which the scheduled games of the two teams alternated between the respective locations of their grounds; esp. when the third game was played at a neutral site. "According to the usages of the National Association the first game in a home-and-home series is played upon the grounds of the challenging club" (*Detroit Advertiser and Tribune*, Oct. 10, 1866; Peter Morris). IST USE. 1863. "The first game of a home-and-home match for the championship of the State . . . was played on the grounds of the Peninsular Cricket Club" (*Detroit Advertiser and Tribune*, Aug. 7; Peter Morris).

home-bagger A *home run*. "When I was playing for the Dodgers . . . I hit a really long drive for a home-bagger" (Frank Howard, quoted in *The Washington Post*, Apr. 11, 1969).

home base Syn. of *home plate*. The term is seldom used today. "The home base . . . to be

... marked by a flat circular iron plate, painted or enameled white" (*Porter's Spirit of the Times*, March 7, 1857). IST USE. 1856. "[Gelston] was headed off and put out on the home base" (*Porter's Spirit of the Times*, Oct. 4). EXTENDED USE. A person's individual place of operation, not to be shared with anyone else (*American Speech*, Winter 1997, p.409). "His 'home base' is now the same kind of 8-by-10-foot low-walled desk that his executive assistants and staff have" (*San Francisco Chronicle*, Dec. 30, 1996).

home-brew field A rough, pebble-strewn playing surface; one on which a ground ball takes many unexpected hops. This is a play on "hops" as an ingredient of beer. See also *ash heap*; *contractor's back yard*; *Hogan's brickyard*. IST USE. 1937 (*The Sporting News Record Book*, p.65; Edward J. Nichols).

home depot *hist.* Syn. of *home plate*. "[The pitch] rushes up to the home depot, inviting you to take a nice healthy swing at it" (*San Francisco Bulletin*, Feb. 10, 1913; Gerald L. Cohen).

home field The ballpark where the home team plays. Syn. *home*, 3; *home grounds*; *home orchard*; *home pasture*.

home-field advantage The tendency for home teams to win a greater proportion of games than visiting teams. Research has shown the home-field advantage in major-league baseball to be about 54 percent, which is low for a team sport (basketball's "home-court" advantage is about 67 percent). The combination of factors that gives the home team presumed extra help includes knowledge and familiarity with the nuances of the ballpark, the enthusiasm and support of the home crowd, the wearying effect of travel for the visiting team, and the ability "to sleep in one's own bed" (rather than live out of a hotel); research has not been successful in determining which of these are actually involved. Bruce Chen (quoted in *The Baltimore Sun*, Apr. 9, 2005): "Obviously, the people here [New York City] know baseball. They love the Yankees, and the team definitely has a home-field advantage." Other examples of home-field advantage include adjusting the height of grass to slow down or speed up infield balls, and wetting down infield clay to thwart speedy runners. See also *dome-field advantage*. Syn. "home-field edge."

home free Said of a team that has a large lead and is certain to win the game; e.g., "A 10-run lead in the last of the eighth assured the Brewers they would be home free." See also *on ice*.

home game A contest that a team plays at its own ballpark. Compare *away game*.

home grounds Syn. of *home field*. IST USE. 1884. "The Bostons play twenty games in May and twelve in June on their home grounds before going West" (*The Washington Post*, March 16).

home guard Syn. of *home team*, 1. "We may have the pleasure of seeing the home guard up in the first division" (*San Francisco Bulletin*, Apr. 12, 1913; Gerald L. Cohen).

home half The *second half* of an inning when the home team gets its turn at bat.

homeling A member of the home team. "The Baltimore Elite Giants saw their advantage dissipated in a three-run Cuban rally. But the homelings came back to match the output and retain the one-run lead" (*The Afro-American*, June 9, 1949, p.3; Bob Luke).

home orchard *hist.* Syn. of *home field*.

home pasture *hist.* Syn. of *home field*. "In the three games on the home pasture George McCarl ... astounded the followers of baseball by his finished work at first base" (*San Francisco Bulletin*, March 11, 1913; Gerald L. Cohen). See also *pasture*, 2.

home plate The base over which the pitcher is required to throw the ball, at which the batter stands to hit the ball, and which the baserunner must touch to score a run; the focal point of the game. Since 1900, home plate has been a five-sided slab of whitened rubber, 4 inches thick with beveled edges, 17 inches wide at the end facing the pitcher, 17 inches deep, 8½ inches along the parallel sides, and 12 inches along the diagonals (coinciding with the first and third base lines) leading to the point facing the catcher. It weighs 20 pounds and is securely anchored and flush with the ground at the intersection of the foul lines, its rear end forming a right

Home plate. Toothpick box cover. *Author's collection*

angle, which determines the direction of the foul lines. The width of home plate determines the horizontal extent of the strike zone (the one-inch strip of black around the border is not part of the strike zone). Home plate has evolved since 1845 from a circular, flat iron plate, painted or enameled white, and believed to be a foot in diameter, although any object (dish, piece of wood, stone, white marble) could be used. In 1869, a 12-inch square was introduced, one point oriented toward the pitcher and one toward the catcher. In 1872, a white square marble or stone was fixed in the ground even with the surface. The white rubber square was introduced in 1885 (American Association) and 1887 (National League) to reduce injuries to sliding baserunners. The modern plate eliminated two corners of the square and made the sides parallel, thereby giving the pitcher a larger target and the umpire a better view of the strike zone. "Home plate . . . has a peculiar significance for it is the goal of both teams, [where] . . . everyone wants to arrive at the same place, which is where they start" (Bart Giamatti, *Take Time for Paradise*, 1989, p.87). Abbrev. *HP*, 2. Syn. *home*, 1; *home base*; *home depot*; *home turkey*; *turkey*; *dish*; *platter*; *plate*, 1; *pan*; *batting station*; *counting house*; *counting pan*; *counting station*; *knocker's stone*; *pay station*; *receiving station*; *registering station*; *registry station*; *rubber*, 2; *saucepan*; *saucer*; *scoring iron*; *slab*, 3; *hearth stone*; *pentagon*; *dock*; *white*. IST USE. 1867 (*New York Herald*, Sept. 26; Edward J. Nichols). EXTENDED USE. **1.** The

nickname for a carrier in U.S. Navy jargon. **2.** The home airfield in U.S. Air Force jargon. **3.** The apex (foot spot) of the pyramid of racked balls where the 1-ball is placed in the pocket billiards game of baseball.

home plate is jumping around The condition that describes a pitcher's location when he constantly misses the strike zone with pitches on the corners; e.g., the outside corner pitch is too far outside and the inside corner pitch is too far inside. See also *plate jumping*.

home plate umpire Syn. of *plate umpire*.

home player *hist.* **1.** A player on the home team. "In eight innings . . . two home players reached second base" (I.E. Sanborn, *Chicago Daily Tribune*, Sept. 2, 1911). **2.** A player playing in his home town. "The talented home player, Mr. Paul Hines [a Washingtonian, playing for Providence in a game in Washington]" (*The Washington Post*, Aug. 22, 1878; David Ball).

homer **1.** *n.* A *home run*. IST USE. 1875. "By [Lipman] Pike's error a first-base hit was changed to a 'homer'" (*New York Clipper*, July 24; Peter Morris). EXTENDED USE. A common metaphor for an action that has been a clear success. A headline in *The Baltimore Sun* (May 20, 2005) for an article on a uniform drug testing policy for U.S. professional sports declared, "Congress hits homer on doping." **2.** *v.* To hit a home run. "We may be tolerant of 'homer' as a substitute for 'home-run' on the sports pages, yet we may well draw the line when the already contracted word is suddenly forced to do duty as a verb and appears in a headline: 'Jones Homers Again'" (Robert E. Garst and Theodore M. Bernstein, *Headlines and Deadlines*, 1940, p.143; Stuart Y. Silverstein). **3.** *n.* A broadcaster or sportswriter who shows obvious bias for the home team. "He was loud. He was obnoxious. He was the worst homer in the history of baseball broadcasting" (Ken Fuson on Harry Caray, *The Baltimore Sun*, Feb. 20, 1998). **4.** *n.* An umpire whose decisions seem consistently to favor the home team. Larry R. Gerlach (*Men in Blue*, 1980, p.100) quoted umpire Ernie Stewart, who said that a homer is a "gutless umpire" and proudly proclaimed, "I never was called a homer." Syn. *home umpire*; *homie*. IST USE. 1888 (*New York Press*, June 3; Edward J. Nichols). EXTENDED USE. The term is used for officials in all major sports and is just as likely to show up in football where it may have come into use earlier. For instance, Peter Tamony found this quote from a football coach (*San Francisco News*, Nov. 13, 1932): "Referee Arthur Badenock is an out and out 'homer.' He cost Stanford a game and did his best to take the UCLA game away from the Gaels."

homer ball 1. Syn. of *home run ball*. **2.** A schoolyard game played in Ontario with a pitcher, a batter, and two or three outfielders and a fenced field. The object is for the batter to hit as many balls over the fence (homers) before popping or lining out to one of the fielders (including the pitcher). The batter does not necessarily always hit the soft pitches in the same place; also, most of the hits are in the air since the batter has to loft the ball to get it over the fence. Whoever catches a pop fly or line drive becomes the next batter and the former batter becomes the pitcher. (Mike P. Moffatt)

homerfest A season in which there are many home runs, including home runs hit by players not normally known for their power. "No one seriously expected to see a power display comparable to last year's unprecedented homerfest, but the power surge continues" (*The Baltimore Sun*, July 15, 1999).

homer for the cycle To hit a solo homer, a two-run homer, a three-run homer, and a grand slam in one game. The feat has been accomplished only once in professional baseball: Tyrone Horne (Arkansas Travelers) homered for the cycle against the San Antonio Missions on July 27, 1998. See also *home run cycle*. Compare *hit for the cycle*.

homer-friendly park A ballpark in which noticeably more home runs were hit than in the average league park for a given era; e.g., Baker Bowl (Philadelphia) and the Polo Grounds (New York City) in the 1930s. See also *hitter's park*.

homer hankie An imprinted, souvenir, handkerchief-sized square of white cloth held and waved by Minnesota Twins fans in 1987 during the American League pennant drive and

World Series. Homer hankies were sold as a promotional stunt by the local newspaper, the *Star Tribune*, whose name was on each hankie along with the words "Twins 1987" inscribed above a red baseball, and "Championship Drive" inscribed below the ball. Minnesota Twins fans have since waggled homer hankies in subsequent postseasons. Also spelled "Homer Hankie"; "homer hanky."

Homeric clout A home run.

Homer in the Gloamin' A dramatic home run hit on Sept. 28, 1938, under darkening skies at lightless Wrigley Field by Chicago Cubs player-manager Gabby Hartnett off Pittsburgh Pirates pitcher Mace Brown in the bottom of the ninth inning. Hartnett's home run won the game, 6–5, propelling the Cubs into first place ahead of the Pirates and eventually to the National League pennant.

home run A four-base hit on which the batter scores. It is usually accomplished by driving the ball out of the playing area but into fair territory. The batter and his team are awarded a run when he has touched all four bases. A ball that does not leave the park but allows the batter to score without the help of an error is an *inside-the-park home run*. A home run causes all the runners on base to score, and provides baseball with much of its excitement and drama. Home runs routinely change the course of a game and are instrumental in putting fans in the seats. The ability to hit the home run has been at the core of the star quality of many great enduring hitters, including Babe Ruth, Mickey Mantle, Willie Mays, and Hank Aaron. There are many slang synonyms for the home run, including: *homer*, 1; *big fly*; *bomb*, 3; *dinger*; *downtowner*; *four-bagger*; *gopher ball*, 2; *home-bagger*; *jack*, 1; *master fly*; *moon shot*, 1; *rainbow drop*; *round-tripper*; *scud*; *tater*; *tonk*. See also *circuit*, 3; *four-ply*. Abbrev. *HR*; *4B*. IST USE. 1856. "On the Eagle Club taking the bat they soon place 4 [runs] to their credit, and would have done better, but for an injudicious attempt on the part of Mr. Gelston to get a home run, when he was headed off and put out on the home base by Mr. Burns" (*Porter's Spirit of the Times*, Oct. 4; Frederick Ivor-Campbell). USAGE NOTE. An early clarification of the meaning of a home run: "A striker

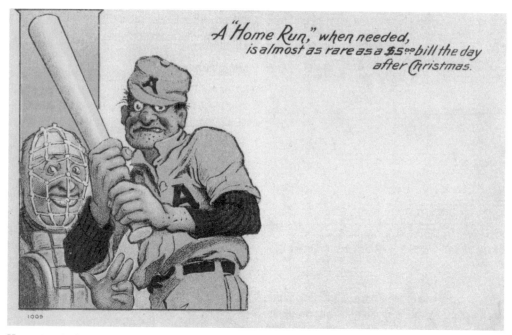

A "Home Run," when needed, is almost as rare as a $5.00 bill the day after Christmas.

Home run. *Andy Moresund Collection*

makes a home run whenever he succeeds in going round from base to base without stopping at either of them, no matter where the ball may have been hit, or what the character of the hit may be; 'a clear home run,' however, is only made when the batsman reaches home before the ball is returned to the in field" (*New York Clipper*, Aug. 6, 1864; Peter Morris). Morris notes a possibly idiosyncratic use of the term for just scoring a run: "[Tom] Letcher's home run hit was the longest ever seen on the Chattanooga grounds. It was made, too, when [Dan] Lally was on the base, and was productive of two home runs" (*Atlanta Constitution*, Apr. 30, 1893).

ETYMOLOGY. The term was used in American horse racing as a synonym for "home stretch" as early as 1833 (*American Turf Register and Sporting Magazine*, October, p.84): "The home run is a trying and deeply interesting part of the race. If a horse is clear of his adversary, he has a right to choose his track; but, having done this, his right of choice ends, and in the run home, he has not any right to cross to right or left, making another selection: he must abide by the track he had chosen." The literature contains dozens of examples from horse racing before the term transferred to baseball. These appear in the sporting press

as well as general newspapers, such as this from the *Brooklyn Daily Eagle* (June 6, 1851): "The noble grey, steady and true, kept her distance, and finally came in upon the home run nearly a distance in the lead."

EXTENDED USE. **1.** A big scoring play in other sports. A long forward pass for a spectacular touchdown in football or a three-point play in basketball may be called a "home run." It may even apply to a boxing punch: "He [Ingemar Johansson] earned it the way a real champ should by blasting home runs with a lethal right that caused many to compare it with the blockbusters Rocky Marciano used to fell challengers" (*San Francisco Examiner*, June 30, 1959). **2.** A major accomplishment; an action that has been a clear success. An article that questions the ability of a major corporation to come up with a dramatically new product is headlined: "Does Kodak Have Any Home-Run Hitters?" (*The Washington Post*, Sept. 11, 1986). When Dan Rather defended in court an investigative report on insurance fraud that had appeared on *60 Minutes*, he declared the segment "a home run" (Associated Press, May 31, 1983). "The Italian tenor [Carlo Bergonzi] hit his share of artistic home runs as a top Verdi tenor for five decades" (*The Baltimore Sun*,

Home run. Frank "Home Run" Baker, Philadelphia Athletics. *George Grantham Bain Collection, Library of Congress*

May 3, 2000). A "home run film" is one that will capture the largest possible audience (*American Speech*, Winter 1997, p.409). **3.** A large capital gain in a stock in a short period of time, according to a 1989 equity trading glossary produced by Goldman Sachs. **4.** Intermittent teenage slang for sexual intercourse, on a scale of physical involvement that starts at first base. A letter from a teenage girl to "Dear Abby" (published in her column on Dec. 31, 1967) concluded, "So far I've gone to 'second and third base.' I'm afraid I can't stop myself. Is there something wrong with me?" Abby's answer, in part: "If, at age 14, you've gone to 'second and third base' you had better get out of that league or you'll be known as the 'Home-Run Queen' by the time you're 16."

home run ball A pitch that is hit for a home run. Syn. *homer ball*, 1; *home run pitch*. IST USE. 1937 (*Philadelphia Record*; Sept. 28; Edward J. Nichols).

home run call **1.** A broadcaster's description of a home run. Examples include: "Going, going ... gone!" (Mel Allen), "Open the window, Aunt Minnie, here she comes!" (Rosey Rowswell), "Kiss it goodbye!" (Bob Prince), "Tell it goodbye" (Lon Simmons), "Bye, bye, baby" (Russ Hodges), "It might be, it could be, it is a home run" (Harry Caray), and "It is high, it is fair, it is gone" (John Sterling). **2.** An umpire's designation of a home run. "Change to Camden Yards

foul poles could end confusion by giving umps better view of ball on close home run calls" (*The Baltimore Sun*, Apr. 3, 2006).

home run cut Syn. of *home run swing*.

home run cycle A solo homer, a two-run homer, a three-run homer, and a grand slam hit by a player in one game. See also *homer for the cycle*.

home run derby **1.** A game in which many home runs are hit by one or both teams. "A crowd of 55,144 saw Boston open the four-game set . . . with a day of home run derby" (*The Baltimore Sun*, July 5, 2003). **2.** An exhibition in which a few sluggers compete to see how many home runs they can hit or how far they can hit them. In such contests, anything short of a home run is considered an out. The home run derby at the All-Star break began in 1985. **3.** A race to determine who will hit the most home runs. John Eisenberg (*The Baltimore Sun*, Sept. 28, 1998): "For the longest time, a dead heat between Mark McGwire and Sammy Sosa seemed the perfect ending to baseball's home run derby [of 1998]. Neither slugger deserved to run second." McGwire hit 70 home runs and Sosa hit 66 home runs, both breaking the 1961 record of 61 home runs hit by Roger Maris. **4.** A playground game in which the batter tries to hit the ball over the fence for a home run; failure to do so results in an out.

home run factor A measure of a ballpark's home-run-hitting tendencies relative to other ballparks, currently calibrated so that an average ballpark has a rating of 100. The measure is described by John Thorn et al. (*Total Baseball*, 6th ed., 1999). Abbrev. *HRF*.

home run getter *hist.* A home run hitter. "[Sam] Thompson has supplanted [George] Wood as the Phillies' home run getter" (*The Sporting Life*, July 28, 1889). See also *run-getter*.

home run in an elevator shaft A pop fly that is hit straight up and esp. high and comes straight down and that is usually caught near home plate.

homerunist A batter who often hits a home run (Maurice H. Weseen, *A Dictionary of American Slang*, 1934).

Home run king. A button commemorating Aaron's record. *Author's collection*

home run king **1.** An unofficial title for the player who has hit the most home runs in the league by the end of the season. Often capitalized as "Home Run King." IST USE. 1921. "No Bush League batter was ever more thoroughly or hopelessly discomfited than the powerful home run king [Babe Ruth] on that occasion [when St. Louis Browns pitcher Urban Shocker waved in his outfielders when Ruth came to bat in July 1920]" (F.C. Lane, *Baseball Magazine*, January, p.381; Steve L. Steinberg). **2.** The player with the most home runs in the history of the game; the current title-holder is Barry Bonds. "I realize there are going to be a lot of cynics . . . during [Barry Bonds'] attempt to become Major League Baseball's all-time home run king" (Peter Schmuck, *The Baltimore Sun*, March 3, 2006). Often capitalized as "Home Run King."

home run percentage A statistic that accounts for the number of home runs hit per 100 times at bat. It is computed by dividing the number of home runs by the number of at-bats and multiplying by 100. Mark McGwire's home run percentage of 9.4 is the best in major-league history. Barry Bonds holds the highest single-season percentage with 15.34 in 2001. Compare *home run ratio*.

home run pitch Syn. of *home run ball*.

home run ratio The number of at-bats per home run. Compare *home run percentage*.

home run rule [softball term] A restriction on the number of home runs allowed in a slow pitch softball game. Excess home runs are counted as fouls or outs.

home run swing A very powerful swing in which the batter is obviously trying to hit a home run. It is often cautioned against by managers and batting instructors who see it as an ineffective way to get a home run and an effective way to increase strikeouts. Syn. *home run cut*.

home run trot The jog of a batter touching the bases after hitting a home run; "one of the last truly American joys" (Rick Reilly, *Sports Illustrated*, May 11, 1998). Home run trots have included Babe Ruth's little mincing steps, Mickey Mantle's running head down as if in shame, Jimmy Piersall's going around backward on his 100th home run, Rickey Henderson's stutter-stepping in slow motion, and Jeffrey Leonard's "one flap down" (left arm hanging limp while leaning toward the pitcher as he ran). See also *Cadillac trot*. IST USE. 1950. "[Hank Greenberg] caught a fat pitch on the big end of his bat one day, and knew he had hit it well. Hank started giving it that old home run trot toward first base. When he neared second he looked up just in time to see the left fielder making the catch behind shortstop. That's the Comiskey Park wind for you" (Jimmy Dykes, quoted in *The Washington Post*, Dec. 12; Peter Morris).

homestand A series of two or more consecutive games played at a team's home field against one or more visiting teams. "Philadelphia capped an 8–1 homestand by beating Arizona" (*The Washington Post*, May 13, 2002). Also spelled "home stand." IST USE. 1902 (*The Sporting Life*, July 5, p.6; Edward J. Nichols).

homestretch **1.** Approximately the last month of the regular season when teams vie for their places in the final standings. Sometimes spelled "home stretch." Syn. *stretch*, 5. ETYMOLOGY. The term is borrowed from horse racing, where the homestretch is the straight part of the racetrack from the last turn to the finish line. **2.** The ninth inning of a given game. IST USE. 1881 (*New York Herald*, Aug. 10; Edward J. Nichols). **3.** The basepath between third base and home plate.

home sweet home team *hist.* A team that plays well at home but poorly on the road.

home team **1.** The team that hosts a visiting team on its own field. By tradition (and since 1950 by the rules), the home team always bats in the bottom, or second, half of each inning, which gives it the final chance to score. If a game is played on neutral grounds, the home team is designated by mutual agreement. Compare *visiting team.* Syn. *home*, 5; *home guard*; *host team.* IST USE. 1878. "The home team responded with one run, made on two safe hits and a sacrifice" (*Cincinnati Commercial*, May 22; Peter Morris). EXTENDED USE. Hometown. Reporting on the premature relocation of John Wiley & Sons from New York City to Baltimore, Brad McDearman (*The Baltimore Sun*, Aug. 31, 1999) noted, "The home team . . . has a great advantage in this type of battle. And the earlier New York knows about it, the better organized its effort will be." **2.** *hist.* A team that does disproportionately well at home. "The Athletics have always been especially noted as a 'home team'" (Joe S. Jackson, *The Sporting News*, July 28, 1910; Peter Morris). Compare *road team.*

home territory The specific geographic area within which a major- or minor-league club operates and plays its home games. A home territory is defined by the boundary lines of an entire county or counties (or parish or Canadian division or district); e.g., the Cincinnati Reds' home territory includes: Butler, Warren, Clermont, and Hamilton counties in Ohio; Boone, Kenton, and Campbell counties in Kentucky; and Dearborn and Franklin counties in Indiana. Generally, the home territory of each major-league club must have boundaries that are no closer than 15 miles from the boundaries of all other (major- and minor-league) clubs' home territories. See also *territorial rights.*

hometown series A World Series played by two teams from the same metropolitan area; e.g., the 1941, 1947, 1949, 1952, 1953, 1955, and 1956 World Series between the New York Yankees and the Brooklyn Dodgers.

home turkey *hist.* Syn. of *home plate.* "The moment the ball was caught [George] Gore started for the home turkey and [Buck] Ewing pulled for third" (*The World* [New York], Aug. 10, 1889). Gerald L. Cohen (*Studies in Slang*, Pt.2, 1989) speculated that the 19th-century home plate was likened in shape to a turkey plate; thus, a blend of "home plate" and "turkey." See also *turkey.*

home umpire *hist.* Syn. of *homer*, 4. According to the *Detroit Free Press* (July 1, 1888; Peter Morris), National League president Nick Young specifically instructed umpire John Kelly to give the benefit of the doubt to the home team, explaining that "to carry out this idea it is not necessary to be 'a home umpire,' but where an honest doubt exists the home club should not be the sufferer." Umpire Billy Evans (*Pearson's Magazine*, Sept. 1912; Peter Tamony): "They [the players] at once seek to discover if he is a home umpire. Woe unto him if the players see he has a penchant for favoring the home team." IST USE. 1886. "Johnny Egan must be doing some pretty square umpiring. The New Yorkers are fond of 'home umpires.' Evidently John does not belong to that class" (*The Boston Globe*, May 10; Peter Morris).

home whites The traditional uniform worn by a team on its home field. Home teams have worn white uniforms since 1911. Compare *road grays.*

homie Syn. of *homer*, 4. "Alexander Pompez

Home whites. New York Giants, 1909. *George Grantham Bain Collection, Library of Congress*

has told umpires 'that they must not be "homies," that his visitors must be given an even break'" (Dr. W. Rollo Wilson, *Pittsburgh Courier*, June 25, 1927).

honkbal Baseball in the Netherlands.

Honor Rolls of Baseball A second level of honor instituted by the National Baseball Hall of Fame in 1946 to recognize five managers, 11 umpires, 11 executives, and 12 sportswriters who made nonplaying contributions to baseball. Eight of the 39 honorees were later inducted into the Hall of Fame. The Honor Rolls appeared to be less of an honor than they were intended to be, and soon died of neglect. The Honor Rolls themselves never took physical form. Sometimes called "Honor Roll of Baseball." See David L. Fleitz, *Baseball Research Journal*, no.34, 2005.

hoodoo 1. *n.* An object, sign, player, or anything else about which a player, coach, or manager is superstitious; e.g., a cross-eyed newsboy. "It looks right now as if the Seals are going to remove every hoodoo which different pitchers have placed on them in the past" (*San Francisco Bulletin*, May 21, 1913; Gerald L. Cohen). Dizzy Dean defined the term as "what ol' Diz used to have on all them batters in the National League when I was the world champion player." IST USE. 1883 (*Chicago Inter-Ocean*, June 26; Edward J. Nichols). USAGE NOTE. Although synonymous with *jinx*, "hoodoo" seems to have a close association with the game of baseball in particular, and one is much less likely to hear it applied in other areas. Under the heading "Jinxes and Hoodoos," *The SABR Bulletin* (Oct. 1986) gave a sampling that included spilling coffee, cutting oneself while shaving, picking up the wrong bat, stepping on a baseline, seeing a dog on the diamond, having the entire team on the bench at once, and chewing gum in the outfield. 2. *n.* An object, animal, or person used to bring bad luck to the opposition; the opposite of a *mascot*, 2. In one report a manager was viewed as going from the status of "being a 'mascot' and becoming a 'hoodoo' for the team he is managing" (*San Francisco Evening Bulletin*, June 19, 1889). See also *whammy*. 3. *v.* To create bad luck. "[Buck Ewing's dog] sat on the players' bench yesterday and hoodooed the

Hoosiers" (*The World* [New York], July 19, 1889; Gerald L. Cohen). "Most of them think a change in hotels would surely 'jinx' or hoodoo them" (*Literary Digest*, May 9, 1914). IST USE. 1887. "There is a black cat however, in the vicinity that comes into the park once in a while to hoodoo the visiting team" (*St. Louis Globe-Democrat*, June 19).

ETYMOLOGY. It is widely assumed that "hoodoo" is a play on the word "voodoo," but that may not necessarily be the case. Canadian writer and etymologist Bill Casselman has explored the origin of both terms (Billcasselman.com): "There is a thin strand of semantic connection only. In the eighteenth and nineteenth centuries, black slaves of Hausa origin brought with them to their enslavement in the American south a distinct magic practice called 'hoodoo.' The word comes directly from the Hausa language where the verb 'hu'du'ba' means 'to arouse resentment, produce retribution.' Voodoo is a different word and quite a different concept. The word 'voodoo' comes from another African language called Ewe where 'vodu' is the name of a specific demon or tutelary deity. Voodoo passed into American English by way of Louisiana Creole 'voudou.' Very early in America, hoodoo came to mean 'jinx' or 'cast a spell on' as a noun and a verb: 'Something hoodooed me out in the swamp last night. I think it was my ex-husband.'" In the 19th century, a hoodoo could have supernatural aspects; e.g., from an article entitled "Why the Brooklyn Base Ball Team Is Winning": "A shadowy figure with wings that spread out at least twelve feet flew in the window. . . . It was the hoodoo beginning his deadly work. . . . The red-haired girl . . . and the white horse . . . are the mascots purchased two weeks ago by Manager [Charlie] Byrne immediately after the terrible series of disasters. . . . Everything has now prospered and the terrible hoodoo has fled" (*Brooklyn Eagle*, Aug. 11, 1887, p.4).

hook 1. *n.* Any curveball, because of its hook-like trajectory. IST USE. 1910. "[Mordecai] Brown's 'hook' curve is the highest present development of the fast overhand curve pitch which breaks sharply down and outward" (John J. Evers and Hugh S. Fullerton, *Touch-*

ing Second: The Science of Baseball; Peter Morris). **2.** *v.* To throw a curveball. "I usually hook him [Dave Henderson] a lot, and I threw him a fastball, and I think it surprised him" (Lee Smith, quoted in *The Baltimore Sun*, Apr. 5, 1994). IST USE. 1908 (*New York Evening Journal*, March 5; Edward J. Nichols). **3.** *n.* A batted ball that curves away to the left when hit by a right-handed batter or to the right when hit by a left-handed batter; e.g., "Smith's hook went down the left-field line." **4.** *n.* The path of a batted ball that curves away to the left when hit by a right-handed batter or to the right when hit by a left-handed batter; e.g., "That ball had a lot of hook on it." **5.** *v.* To hit a ball that veers off in one direction. "They hooked a couple of balls down the line" (Pat Dobson, quoted in *The Baltimore Sun*, May 9, 1996). **6.** *n.* The removal of a pitcher who is getting into trouble, usually used in the phrase "to get the hook." "In case the Mets get hot, they'll go for the hook" (broadcaster Vin Scully, Game 2 of the 1986 World Series, Oct. 19). See also *slow hook*; *quick hook*, 1. ETYMOLOGY. From the theatrical image of an actor or performer who is so bad that he or she is pulled off the stage by a theater manager wielding a long pole with a hook on its end. This was reportedly a custom practiced on amateur nights during the age of vaudeville and became a staple sight gag in movie cartoons. **7.** *n.* The tendency of a manager to remove a pitcher from the game. A manager may have a *quick hook*, 2 (tendency to remove a pitcher at the first sign of trouble), or, if he does it enough, may be called "Captain Hook" (e.g., Sparky Anderson when he managed the Cincinnati Reds) or "Dr. Hook." **8.** *v.* To replace or be replaced by a relief pitcher. "He [Rocky Coppinger] was one hitter away from getting hooked" (Baltimore Orioles manager Davey Johnson, quoted in *The Baltimore Sun*, June 12, 1996). See also *derrick*. **9.** *n.* Syn. of *jam*, 1. See also *off the hook*; *on the hook*. **10.** *n.* The ejection by an umpire of a player, manager, or coach. "Late in the game, when things have kind of built up and people have been yakking back and forth, sometimes they'll get a quick hook" (Mike Hargrove, quoted in *The Baltimore Sun*, Apr. 30, 2000). **11.** *n.* A pitcher's pitching arm (Maurice H. Weseen, *A Dic-*

tionary of American Slang, 1934). **12.** *v.* To go into a base with a hook slide. "Schmidt has the art of hooking a base down to a fine point" (*San Francisco Bulletin*, March 11, 1913; Gerald L. Cohen). **13.** *n.* The release of a player from his contract. "With a little wising up in the fielding end of the game [Hughes] . . . ought to sidestep the hook" (*San Francisco Bulletin*, March 8, 1913; Gerald L. Cohen). **14.** *v.* To obtain a position in the major leagues. "It seems that about every player that went up [from the Pacific Coast League] hooked a steady job" (*San Francisco Bulletin*, May 21, 1913; Gerald L. Cohen). **15.** *n.* See *hooks*.

hook arm **1.** A *left-handed pitcher*. **2.** The pitching arm of a pitcher.

hookie A left-handed batter in Australia.

hooks **1.** The hands of an adept fielder; e.g., George Wiltse was known as "Hooks" for his fielding prowess. **2.** The clumsy hands of a fielder, in allusion to the hook of Captain James Hook, the villain of J.M. Barrie's play *Peter Pan* (1904) and novel *Peter and Wendy* (1911); e.g., "Congalton . . . missed a fly with both hooks, thereby adding some to the gayety of the pastime" (Charles Dryden, quoted in *Chicago Tribune*, Aug. 16, 1907). Clifford Jordan (letter, Aug. 5, 1989) recalls how the term was used in his younger days: "We would gleefully call out 'hooks' when an opposing player made a noticeably clumsy error. That is, rather than 'hooks' meaning he could hook into anything, 'hooks' meant he owned awkward metal prongs, not soft, capable hands."

hook slide A feet-first slide during which the runner tucks one leg bent under his body and uses the other to catch, or "hook," the side or one corner of the base or home plate as he passes it. The hook slide is used to avoid being tagged by giving the defensive player a smaller target; the runner does not slide directly at the base, but away from the defensive player, angling his body so that only his toe can reach the corner of the base. One of the most famous hook slides was Jackie Robinson's steal of home against the New York Yankees in the eighth inning of the first game of the 1955 World Series. Syn. *Chicago slide*; *fadeaway slide*; *fallaway slide*; *straddle slide*. IST USE. 1906 (*The Independent*; Edward J.

Hook slide. Sliding home to score against the Washington Senators in Griffith Stadium. *Photograph by Joseph Baylor Roberts*

Nichols). ETYMOLOGY. It is generally agreed that the hook slide was first perfected by Mike "King" Kelly of the Chicago White Stockings, who taught it to other members of his team; thus, it became known as the "Chicago slide." However, Lee Allen (*The Hot Stove League*, 1955, p.115) noted that it was first used by William S. Gummere (later to become Chief Justice of the Supreme Court of New Jersey) while playing for Princeton in a game against the Athletics of Philadelphia in the late 1860s: "He slid and buried his face in his right arm, the style later adopted by Ty Cobb."

hookworm league *hist.* A derisive nickname for spring training played in the southeastern United States, a region with a prevalence for the hookworm parasite. IST USE. 1917 (*American Magazine*, July, p.42; Edward J. Nichols).

hoopdy scoop A curveball.

hootenanny throw An overthrown ball that sails over the head of the intended fielder and out of play.

hooter A particularly noisy fan. "Each night, Chicago broadcaster Don Drysdale has his camera crew scan the stadium looking for 'The Hooter,' the rumpled old man whose howl could be heard all over Comiskey [Park] when the White Sox were hitting" (*USA Today*, May 13, 1986).

Hoover 1. A highly adept infielder who appears to sweep or suck up batted balls in the manner of a Hoover *vacuum cleaner*. "Heretofore uncelebrated as a fielder, [Wade] Boggs has been semi-Brooksian at third base: if not a Hoover, at least a Dust Buster" (Tony Kornheiser, *The Washington Post*, Oct. 25, 1986). Sometimes lowercased as "hoover." USAGE NOTE. Pittsburgh Pirates broadcaster Bob Prince would often use the expression "we need a Hoover" or "give me the Hoover" when the opposition had runners on the bases and a double play was needed to "clean" the bases. Mel Durslag (*TV Guide*, May 17, 1975) reported, "The station Prince works for was unhappy. They figured this was a commercial reference Hoover wasn't paying for. Prince started observing, instead, 'We need a J. Edgar.'" **2.** A batter adept at hitting successfully with men on base; one who cleans the bases.

hop **1.** A bounce of a thrown or batted ball. A ball that bounces erratically takes what is commonly called a *bad hop*, while a bounce that makes it easy for a fielder is called a *gravy hop*. IST USE. 1908 (*New York Evening Journal*, March 19; Edward J. Nichols). **2.** The apparent jumping or vertical rise of an extremely fast pitch; the slight, sudden change in elevation of a fastball. "It is well known that the backspin applied to the overhand fast ball causes the ball to rise—or hop. . . . Though the hop is not likely to be much greater than 4 inches, this is more than enough to trouble the batter swinging" (Robert Kemp Adair, *The Physics of Baseball*, 1990, p.31). IST USE. 1912. "[Rube] Marquard had 'the hop' on the ball and eighteen Red Sox batsmen went out on flies" (*The Sporting Life*, Oct. 19; Peter Morris).

hop-ball The fictional pitch in the book by Shirley W. Smith and Valentine Davies and the 1949 movie *It Happens Every Spring*, in which a chemistry professor discovers a mixture that makes baseballs repellent to wood (i.e., baseball bats). The ball hops like "Barnum's flea."

hope A baseball player of whom much is expected. "If the fans will remember, the Seal 'hopes' were wonderful batters last year" (*San Francisco Bulletin*, Feb. 28, 1913; Gerald L. Cohen).

hopper **1.** A batted ball that bounces on the ground, often modified as a "high hopper," "lazy hopper," "two-hopper," etc. Syn. *rabbit ball*, 2. IST USE. 1904. "[Monte] Beville, sent a hopper past [Jack] Townsend" (*The Washington Post*, Aug. 20; Peter Morris). **2.** A fastball that has a hop on it.

hopping Said of a fastball with such velocity that it appears to jump slightly before it reaches the plate.

hop-step "An instantaneous movement of hopping toward first base [when fielding a ground ball]" (George "Specs" Toporcer,

Baseball: From Back Yard to Big League, 1954, p.157). See also *crow hop*, 1.

Horn A mythical award given to a batter who strikes out six times in a game. See also *hat trick*; *golden sombrero*; *platinum sombrero*. ETYMOLOGY. The eponymous term was coined by Mike Flanagan (*Sports Illustrated*, July 29, 1991) to "honor" Baltimore Orioles slugger Sam Horn, who was the first nonpitcher to accomplish the feat in a game against the Milwaukee Brewers on July 17, 1991.

horse **1.** *n.* A reliable, durable, or tireless player, esp. a pitcher. Minnesota Twins catcher A.J. Pierzynski (quoted in *The Baltimore Sun*, Aug. 7, 2002): "[Pitcher Eric Milton has] been our horse, and we've ridden him for a while." ETYMOLOGY. Probably a clipped form of *workhorse*, 1. **2.** *v.* To get a charley horse. "When you see a player make a long slide which appears unnecessary, the reason is that he would rather rip six inches of skin off his thigh than stop standing up and take chances of 'horsing' himself" (John J. Evers and Hugh S. Fullerton, *Touching Second: The Science of Baseball*, 1910; Peter Morris). **3.** See *on his horse*.

horse-and-buggy league A minor league in which the teams travel by bus rather than by air or, when the phrase first came into use, by rail. IST USE. 1909. "It is common jest for major leaguers, after they are so safely established that they do not fear return to the minors, to speak of the Class C and D organizations as 'horse and buggy leagues'" (Joe S. Jackson, *Detroit Free Press*, March 11; Peter Morris).

horse collar **1.** *n.* A score of zero. The term is most commonly used for a batter going hitless during a game. "No more fitting term could be applied to a hitless effort than a horse-collar" (Curley Grieve, *San Francisco Examiner*, March 11, 1937). George Herman Ruth (*Babe Ruth's Own Book of Baseball*, 1928) defined the term as "a zero in the box score hit column." See also *collar*, 1. Sometimes spelled "horsecollar." IST USE. 1907 (*New York Evening Journal*, Apr. 25; Edward J. Nichols). ETYMOLOGY. From the shape of the box-score cipher (0), which resembles the big, bulky stuffed collar over the back of the neck of a workhorse. **2.** *v.* For a pitcher to prevent the opposing team or batter from scoring or making a base hit, respectively. "Addie Joss . . . horse-collared [the Chicago White Sox] on October 2, 1908, and . . . later held them hitless again on April 30, 1912" (Jim Ellis, *The Sporting News*, May 22, 1959).

horsehide 1. The baseball. IST USE. 1886. "[Guy Hecker] has been knocking the horse hide for the past two days" (*St. Louis Post-Dispatch*, Aug. 9; Peter Morris). **2.** The covering of the baseball. Horsehide had been the traditional cover for baseballs since 1880, but a shortage of quality horsehide in the early 1970s prompted the rules committee to allow cowhide covers along with horsehide. Cowhide balls began showing up in the major leagues in 1974, and the horsehide balls were dropped in 1975 by manufacturers. See also *cowhide*, 2.

horsehider A baseball player. "My brother Leo was a crackerjack horsehider at Fairleigh Dickinson" (Brendan Boyd, *Blue Ruin*, 1991, p.238).

horseshit See *shit*, 2.

horseshoe Syn. of *knuckleball*, 1.

horseshoe drive A lucky hit (Maurice H. Weseen, *A Dictionary of American Slang*, 1934).

horseshoes 1. *hist.* A lucky play (catch or stop) or lucky player. IST USE. 1914. "I've heard of ballplayers calling each other that ['Horseshoes'], and Lucky Stiff, and Four-leaf Clover, ever since I was a foot high" (Ring W. Lardner, narrator in short story "Horseshoes," *The Saturday Evening Post*, Aug. 15; Peter Morris). USAGE NOTE. The term relates to the long-established superstition that horseshoes bring good luck. "Hundreds thought [Pat Flaherty] was lucky and when the Reds began to pound the ball on the youth here one week ago shouts of 'Where is your horseshoe, Pat?' came from many parts of the stand" (A.R. Cratty, *The Sporting Life*, Sept. 17, 1904; Peter Morris). Also: "The Naps would not have been able to score but for Bill Hinchman and his horseshoes" (Ring W. Lardner, *Chicago Tribune*, May 5, 1909; Peter Morris). **2.** A row of scoreless innings

(Edwin M. Rumill, *Christian Science Monitor*, Sept. 1, 1937).

hose 1. *n.* A player's throwing arm. "No pitch ever has been thrown with an arm because that term does not exist in baseball. A guy who throws 'heat' does so with a 'good hose'" (Bob Hertzel, *Baseball Digest*, Jan. 1987). **2.** *n.* Socks; e.g., the Chicago White Sox are nicknamed the "Pale Hose," and the Boston Red Sox are nicknamed the "Carmine Hose." **3.** *v.* To defeat emphatically.

hoseball A Philadelphia street game that was a cross between stickball and halfball and used a piece of old hose (3 to 6 inches long) as the "ball." See also *tireball*.

hoser Syn. of *fireman*, 1.

hospital list See *disabled list*.

hospital throw A throw by an infielder to another that leaves the latter exposed to injury by a sliding or charging baserunner.

hostilities Play; competition. The term is likely to be used during a particularly hard-fought series of games.

host team Syn. of *home team*, 1.

hot 1. Said of a swiftly batted or thrown ball that is difficult to handle. "Schmidt drove out a hot one at Kernan, and on that gentleman's error in handling it, Schmidt was safe" (*San Francisco Bulletin*, March 22, 1913; Gerald L. Cohen). **2.** Said of a player or team performing effectively or at one's (its) best. "He's [Will Clark] so hot he could fire a gun up into the air and kill a fish" (San Francisco Giants outfielder Candy Maldonado, heard by Tom Gill on a Giants broadcast, Aug. 10, 1987). "[The Angels] have been one of the hottest teams in the majors, with nine victories in their past 11 games" (*The Baltimore Sun*, Aug. 8, 1997). IST USE. 1899 (Burt L. Standish, *Frank Merriwell's Double Shot*, p.250; Edward J. Nichols).

hot ball 1. A baseball that is thrown or batted with such great speed that it is difficult to catch; a "lightning-like shot thrown or hit to the infielders" (Mrs. John A. Logan, *Home Manual*, 1889). IST USE. 1867. "Millholland taking lots of 'hot' balls from the bat" (*Detroit Advertiser and Tribune*, July 3;

Peter Morris). **2.** *hist.* A fastball. "Boyle was plunked in the side by a hot ball in the sixth and sent to first" (*The World* [New York], July 12, 1890; Gerald L. Cohen). The poem "Base Ball," by an anonymous author, was published in *The New England Base Ballist* (Aug. 20, 1868, p.1; John Thorn): " 'Oh, drop that bat!' the maiden said, / 'And make a long "home run" instead,' / A 'hot ball' hit him in the eye, / But still he answered with a sigh, 'Base ball!' "

hot bat 1. The bat of a player who is hitting well or is on a hitting streak. "Don Mueller had a hot bat for two days, walloping those five homers" (Bobby Thomson, *"The Giants Win the Pennant! The Giants Win the Pennant!,"* 1991, p.179). Compare *cold bat,* 1. See also *live bat.* **2.** A player who is wielding a hot bat.

hot box 1. The location of a runner caught between two bases and two infielders who are trying to tag him out. **2.** An infielding or baserunning drill in which a runner travels back and forth between two bases trying to beat the tag. Also spelled "hotbox." See also *running bases*; *pickle,* 3.

hot-bread belt The Southern spring-training area, so named from the association of Southern training regions with hot bread. IST USE. 1910 (*American Magazine*, April, p.796; Edward J. Nichols).

hot corner Syn. of *third base,* 1. "I liked the whiplash grace of a third baseman's throw from the 'hot corner' " (Ted Berkman, *Christian Science Monitor*, May 10, 1983). See also *difficult corner.* IST USE. 1889. "The Brooklyns had Old Hick [Carpenter] on the hot corner all afternoon and it's a miracle he wasn't murdered" (Ren Mulford, no source; Hy Turkin, editor of *The 1955 Baseball Almanac*, wrote [p.207] that the phrase was "coined by writer Ren Mulford in the 1880's after a game in which Cincinnati third baseman Hick Carpenter fielded seven sharp drives that almost tore him apart"). ETYMOLOGY. It is commonly assumed that the term came about because of the hot shots aimed at the third baseman, but the explanation is not universally accepted. "Third base was so named about 40 years ago when most of the star sluggers were right-handed. Nowa-

days, however, with so many hardhitting left-handers, first base is equally 'hot' " (*Fan and Family*, Oct. 1935). EXTENDED USE. **1.** Any particularly tough or tight spot. **2.** A defensive position in basketball. "[Satch] Sanders labored in the hot corner for the Celtics. . . . It was Sanders' slavish duty to keep rival beasts . . . from scoring more than 25 points" (Coles Phinizy, *Sports Illustrated*, March 4, 1974, p.28).

hot dog 1. A player who calls attention to himself with theatrics or plays to the crowd and/or the television camera; a player who grandstands or "exaggerates his place in the mortal scheme of things" (Jim Brosnan, *The Long Season*, 1960). Defenders of hot dog players have puckishly suggested the term came from the fact that they play the game "with relish." Baseball did not originate this use of "hot dog," which, incidentally, became widespread when surfers began to show off in the 1960s. Syn. *Mr. Mustard*; *mustard man.*

2. A traditional sandwich sold at ballparks, consisting of a frankfurter in a split roll, often with various condiments. See also *ballpark frank.* IST USE. 1895. "How they contentedly munched hot dogs during the whole service" (*The Yale Record*, Oct. 19; Barry Popik). ETYMOLOGY. Popik, following the guidance of *OED* consultant David Shulman to seek the origin of "hot dog" in college slang, traced the term to Yale students, noting that

Hot dog. Concessionnaire Harry Stevens (left) and August "Garry" Herrmann, president of the Cincinnati Reds and the National Commission. *George Grantham Bain Collection, Library of Congress*

the New Haven (Conn.) eatery of that era, The Kennel Club, sold hot frankfurters and that Yale students referred to the lunch wagons that sold frankfurters as "dog wagons." The term spread to other college humor publications, such as Cornell's *The Widow* (Oct. 1, 1896) and Harvard's *The Harvard Lampoon* (May 8, 1901), and then into general usage. Local historian Dennis Means showed that the term was in use already in 1898 at Nantasket Beach (Mass.), well before Coney Island (N.Y.) officially accepted the term and before frankfurters were sold at baseball games. The book *Origin of the Term "Hot Dog"* (2004) by Barry A. Popik, Gerald Leonard Cohen, and David Shulman showed that "hot dog" (or "hot sausage") derived from the 19th-century popular belief that dog meat could turn up in sausages and from the combination of keen wit plus occasional bad taste exhibited by college students. Popik et al. convincingly rejected the oft-told story that hot dogs as a food and a term originated in baseball around 1900 at the Polo Grounds, home of the New York Giants. According to that story, a) concessionaire Harry Stevens was having a difficult time selling ice cream and soda on a chilly day in April and so he decided to offer small hot wursts, commonly known as "dachshund sausages" (but Popik noted they were not called that until the term "hot dog" originated), and b) cartoonist T.A. "TAD" Dorgan, needing a cartoon for the next day, drew little sausages with dachshund legs running around and therefore coined the term "hot dog." But the Dorgan/Polo Grounds "hot dog" cartoon doesn't exist, and Dorgan did not move from San Francisco to New York until 1903. His first two "hot dog" cartoons are from the Dec. 12 and 13, 1906, editions of the *New York Evening Journal* and pertain to a six-day bicycle race at Madison Square Garden. In an interview conducted by Fred Lieb (*The Sporting News,* Nov. 18, 1926), Stevens recounted, "I have been given credit for introducing the hot dog in America. Well, I don't deserve it. In fact, at first I couldn't see the idea. It was my son, Frank, who first got the idea, and wanted to try it on one of the early [1906] six-day bicycle crowds at Madison Square Garden. 'Pop, we can sell those people frankfurters

and they'll welcome them for a change,' Frank told me. At the time we had been selling mostly beer and sandwiches, and I told Frank that the bike fans preferred ham and cheese. He insisted that we try it out for a few days, and at last I consented. His insistence has all America eating hot dogs" (Gerald L. Cohen).

hot-dogging Playing the game in the manner of a hot dog, such as when a batter stands, stares, or struts at the sight of his home run. "Damaso Garcia . . . hot-dogged past the mound after grounding out" (Bob Hertzel, *Baseball Digest,* Dec. 1983). When asked about his antics on the mound by Richard Justice (*The Washington Post,* July 23, 1986), Dennis "Oil Can" Boyd replied, "That ain't hot-doggin'. That's the way we pitch back home." See also *styling.* Sometimes spelled "hot dogging" or "hotdogging." ETYMOLOGY. The term is used in other sports and activities and may first have been applied to acrobatic skiing. John Ciardi (*Second Browser's Dictionary,* 1983) defined the term as "a recently popular form of suicide on skis"; he added that it was "perhaps so called by association with festive exuberance; perhaps because the skier is likely enough to end up as dog meat."

hot grounder A ground ball hit with great speed. 1ST USE. 1887. "Sutcliffe retired on a hot grounder to Caruthers" (*Detroit Free Press,* Oct. 27).

hot-handed Said of a pitcher who has lots of great stuff.

hot one A hard-batted ball. "Schmidt drove out a hot one at Kernan" (*San Francisco Bulletin,* March 22, 1913; Gerald L. Cohen). 1ST USE. 1871. "Glenn sent a hot one to Kimball" (*The Cleveland Morning Herald,* May 22).

hot rock A fastball.

hot shot 1. A hard-hit ball. 1ST USE. 1884. "Base ball contests nowadays seem more like battles and even the phraseology of the game assumes a war-like aspect, when we speak of 'batteries,' 'firing the ball in,' 'hot shots,' etc" (*The Sporting Life,* June 4; Barry Popik). 2. A fastball. "Buck Ewing created a sensation by wearing an immense glove on his left hand while taking Tim Keefe's hot shot behind the bat" (*New York Sun*, Apr. 27, 1890; Peter Morris). **3.** A cocky player.

hot sign The actual "live" sign when embedded in decoys and following an activator or indicator.

hot stove league The gab, gossip, and debate that take place during the winter months when baseball is not being played. These discussions replaying the past season and anticipating the next occurred at such gathering places as saloons, poolrooms, general stores, barbershops, and drugstores where there was a coal- or wood-burning, potbellied stove at the center of the conversational group. The term was given added popularity with the publication of Lee Allen's book, *The Hot Stove League* (1955). See also *fanning bee*, 2; *gab-circuit*. Syn. *stove league*; *winter league*, 3. IST USE. 1908. "This situation [that the New York Giants will win] . . . will give the 'fans' something to talk about when the Hot Stove League opens its season" (*The Sporting Life*, Sept. 19, p.3; Stuart Y. Silverstein).

ETYMOLOGY. From Allen's book (p.v): "No one knows when baseball followers first began to gather in winter around the hot stove of a barber shop or country store. Obviously, there has been talk about baseball as long as the game has existed. The phrase, 'hot stove league,' is of uncertain origin. Ernest J. Lanigan . . . thinks it was almost certainly coined by a sports writer around the turn of the century, perhaps by Ren Mulford, who covered baseball in Cincinnati and wrote long winter columns about the sport. A glossary of baseball terms published in 1897 does not include it."

However, Peter Tamony assembled information showing that the term predates 1900, when it was used to describe the off-season in horse racing. A dispatch from Knoxboro, N.Y (*Spirit of the Times*, March 20, 1886), contained this line: "The sleighing has gone, and most of the trotting is done around the hot stove at present." An even earlier report (*Spirit of the Times*, March 17, 1877) contained a reference to "stove speed" ascribed to a trotter: it would seem to be a clear reference to a speed imagined during a gathering of the hot stove league.

The general idea is even older. Tamony discovered this quotation from P.T. Barnum's *Struggles and Triumphs* (1927) under "hot stove league": "In nearly every New England village, at the time of which I write [in the 1820s], there could be found from six to twenty social, jolly, story-telling, joke-playing wags and wits, regular originals, who would get together at the tavern or store, and spend their evenings and stormy afternoons in relating anecdotes, describing their various adventures, playing of practical jokes upon each other, and engaging in every project out of which a little fun could be extracted by village wits whose ideas were usually sharpened at brief intervals by a 'treat,' otherwise known as a glass of Santa Cruz rum, old Holland gin or Jamaica spirits."

Barry Popik offered the following from *The Sporting News* (Dec. 29, 1939), putting the idea in a baseball context back into the 19th century: "In Selma [Ohio] . . . exists one of the oldest Hot Stove leagues in the country. It was founded 45 years ago in Clark's general store and post-office, where it still holds its sessions, and while some of the original members have passed on, the same old stove still crackles and the surroundings generally are much the same as they were in the mid-nineties."

EXTENDED USE. Devotees of any endeavor who meet or discuss past or future developments. "Welcome to the Hot Stove League season of politics. The future is a blank page, so hypotheses abound. The past, however, has a box score. The most fascinating fact it reveals is the disconnection between the pinnacle and the base of national politics—the presidency and the House of Representatives" (George F. Will, *Newsweek*, Jan. 20, 1986).

hot-stover A follower of the game who is given to off-season talk of baseball; a member of the hot stove league. "Metropolitan hot-stovers believe that Sergeant Joe DiMaggio was on the verge of getting a medical discharge from the Army Air Force because of threatened stomach ulcers, just when the European war situation became grave" (*San Francisco News*, Dec. 25, 1944; Peter Tamony).

hot-stove season The winter for those who play or are fans of baseball. "The best time to sell a baseball serial used to be during the winter months, called the Hot-Stove season" (Christy Walsh, *Adios to Ghosts!*, 1937; David Shulman). IST USE. 1911. "A Western League scribe . . . recently pulled the prize dream of the hot stove season" (*St. Joseph* [Mo.] *News-Press*, reprinted in *Lincoln* [Neb.] *Evening News*, Jan. 20; Peter Morris).

hot stoving Rehashing plays, decisions, calls, trades, etc. The term is analogous to "Monday morning quarterbacking" in professional football.

hot-weather pitcher An older pitcher whose arm has been strained by overwork (*Baseball History Bulletin*, 2001).

Houdini A pitcher with a repertoire of trick pitches and deceptive deliveries, who, like the famous escape artist—Hungarian-born magician Harry Houdini (1874–1926)—is able to get out of tight spots.

house 1. A ballpark; e.g., The House That Ruth Built. Chicago Cubs manager Dusty Baker, commenting on a postseason series (*The Baltimore Sun*, Oct. 11, 2003): "We certainly want this game. It's the first game in their house, which no matter what, guarantees that you're going back to your house." 2. A team's home city. "I am always going to be happy in Baltimore. It's my house, and I am always going to be happy in my house" (Miguel Tejada, quoted in *The Baltimore Sun*, Aug. 19, 2005). 3. Short for *clubhouse*. 4. The dugout. "That's [strikeout of Joe Randa] a lot of guys he's [Roger Clemens] sent back to the house" (David Justice, quoted in *The Baltimore Sun*, Apr. 3, 2001). 5. Home plate. EXTENDED USE. A figurative "home" in a sporting event, resulting in a score; esp., the end zone in football. Andy Knobel (*The Baltimore Sun*, Jan. 27, 2002): "Where is the house? You know, the house with all the footballs in it. The house we hear about time after 1,000th time when someone with the football Took It To The House. It's a pretty good-sized house evidently." 6. A league. Regarding Jose Vidro's participation in the World Baseball Classic, Washington Nationals general manager Jim Bowden said

(*The Baltimore Sun*, Feb. 21, 2006), "If he were to be injured, we'd rather see it happen in our house and not somebody else's." 7. Retirement. Buster Olney (*The Washington Post*, June 2000): "[Chuck] Knoblach said . . . he had two possible career paths. Either he would solve his throwing problems, or he would 'take it to the house'—as in quit baseball."

house at the side of the road Announcer Ernie Harwell's phrase, likening a batter at home plate who has been called out on strikes to the "house at the side of the road."

house dick A player "who spends most of his off-the-field time sitting around the hotel lobby" (*Baseball Magazine*, Jan. 1943; David Shulman). ETYMOLOGY. This is a clear allusion to the hotel detective, who has long been known as a "house dick" in American slang and who also hangs around the hotel. The presumption at work here is that the hotel-bound player might be mistaken for the hotel's detective.

house man A sportscaster who is unequivocally and relentlessly loyal to the home team; "one who blindly and obediently expresses what he hopes is management's point of view" (Leonard Shecter, *The Jocks*, 1969, p.94; Charles D. Poe). After losing his job as a pregame/postgame show host on a Chicago White Sox cable television program, Jimmy Piersall was quoted: "I called it the way I saw it and that's the reason I'm losing my job. I wouldn't be able to get up and shave my face in the morning without cutting my throat if I became a house man" (*The Washington Post*, Apr. 7, 1983).

House of . . . A term used to give a ballpark an apt nickname. Joe Henderson (*Tampa Tribune*, Dec. 11, 1988) wrote, "If the Astrodome is the House of Pain, San Diego's Jack Murphy Stadium is the House of Chablis. Boxseats there should come equipped with hot tubs."

House of David A nickname given to several barnstorming or nonleague traveling teams whose distinguishing characteristic was that all the players wore long beards. Franklin P. Huddle (*American Speech*, Apr. 1943) explained, "These are, quite often, pretty disreputable outfits, since they are likely to be made up of men who have been thrown out of organized baseball. Many of these gentry grow beards and call themselves (in imitation of the real thing) House of David teams . . . The beards serve the twin purpose of advertising and disguise." The teams were also known as the *Bearded Wonders*. "No one seemed to mind that King Ben [Purnell] recruited his wig and false-beard-wearing talent from that category of player which . . . was on extended leave from the major leagues" (Arthur Orrmont, *Love Cults and Faith Healers*, 1961, p.105). Grover Cleveland Alexander pitched for a House of David team during the Great Depression; he was the only player granted permission not to wear a beard. A character (Lionel) in William Brashler's *The Bingo Long Traveling All-Stars and Motor Kings* (1973) told Bingo, "You got to watch out for the other barnstormers like Max Helverton's Hooley Speedballers and

House of David. Poster for Aug. 24, 1936. *Wisconsin State Historical Society*

them white teams from Michigan, them House of David boys with the beards." ETYMOLOGY. The term is derived from a religious organization founded in 1903 and dedicated to reassembling the 12 tribes of Israel.

house pet A management favorite; a "player who sits in manager's lap" (Bert Dunne, *Folger's Dictionary of Baseball*, 1958).

House That Ruth Built, The Nickname for Yankee Stadium, so called, in most accounts, because of the fame Babe Ruth brought to the New York Yankees and its ballpark. Ruth's exploits of 1920–1922, which led the Yankees to their first two pennants and doubled attendance, brought in enough money to enable the Yankees to build their own stadium (completed in 1923) rather than to continue to share the Polo Grounds with the New York Giants, who were beginning to feel like guests in their own park and therefore did not renew the Yankees' lease. The term is a play on the nursery rhyme title, "The House That Jack Built." IST USE. 1923. "Upwards of 50,000 persons were sweltering in the huge concrete cistern, otherwise known as the house that Ruth Built" (*Canandaigua [N.Y.] Daily Messenger*, May 12; Barry Popik). USAGE NOTE. Michael Gershman (*Diamonds: The Evolution of the Ballpark*, 1993) claimed that "reporter Fred Lieb named Yankee Stadium after Ruth when he homered to beat the Red Sox on the day it opened, April 18, 1923"; however, no primary citation prior to 1926 has been found. EXTENDED USE. Variations of the term occur when a new ballpark is being built; e.g., Safeco Field in Seattle was called "the house that Junior built," referring to the Mariners star Ken Griffey Jr. (*The Oregonian*, July 10, 1999). When new executive director Ruth Eger of the Joseph Richey House, a Baltimore hospice, led the charge to expand its home-care service, she began "its transition into the House that Ruth will build" (*City Paper* [Baltimore], March 8–15, 1995).

"how about that!" A comment that followed a home run or other exciting, dramatic, or unexpected occurrence when Mel Allen was in the broadcast booth.

how-do-you-do An awkward situation that inhibits a player. "When one ball player talks about giving a hit the 'how-do-you-do,' he

House That Ruth Built. Left to right: New York Yankees president Jacob Ruppert, Commissioner Kenesaw Mountain Landis, Yankees co-owner Tillinghast Huston, Boston Red Sox owner Harry H. Frazee, and a man named Flynn, at the opening of Yankee Stadium, Apr. 18, 1923. *George Grantham Bain Collection, Library of Congress*

means that it comes so fast he has no relish for getting in front of it and that it is really too warm to handle" (Ty Cobb, *Busting 'Em and Other Big League Stories*, 1914; Peter Morris).

"how's that?" A common interjection used by early baseball players to request a ruling from an umpire or to try to elicit a ruling in their favor. The term retained some currency long after umpires routinely announced their rulings. "[Hal] Chase made a bluff run down the line [trying to force a balk] and the instant [Frank] Lange pitched exclaimed 'How's that?' to the umpire" (*New York Sun*, May 22, 1912; Peter Morris). IST USE. 1867. "The constant cry of 'judgment on that,' 'how's that,' & c., in reference to unfair balls by the pitcher, or refusal to strike at fair balls by the batsman, has become almost a nuisance" (*The Ball Players' Chronicle*, July 11; Peter Morris).

HP 1. Abbrev. for *hit by pitcher*. 2. Abbrev. for *home plate*.

HPB Abbrev. for *hit by pitched ball*.

HR Abbrev. for *home run*.

HRF Abbrev. for *home run factor.*

H-style ball Syn. of *belt ball*.

hubcap hands Syn. of *bad hands*, 2. So called because the ball bounces off the hands as if they were metal.

huckleberry Syn. of *rookie*, 1.

huddle rule *hist.* A rule in the Southern Association that forbade more than four players, including the manager, to gather at the mound for a conference (*The Sporting News*, June 8, 1939; Peter Morris).

Hudson Harness An elastic strip worn in practice as an aid in training pitchers to develop a faster spin and greater break of the curveball. It is designed to hold the thumb behind the ball rather than roll it over the top. The harness was designed by Washington Senators pitching coach Sid Hudson during the 1960s (Dave Baldwin and others, *The Baseball Research Journal*, no.35, 2007, pp.26–27).

hug 1. For a first baseman or third baseman to position himself close to a foul line. 2. For a baserunner to stay close to a base. IST USE. 1869 (*DeWitt's Base-Ball Guide*, p.40; Edward J. Nichols). 3. For a batter to stand close to the plate. 4. For a batted ball to stay close to the ground or the foul line. "On hard-hit ground balls that hug the ground, an infielder may set by dropping to one knee" (O.H. Vogel, *Ins and Out of Baseball*, 1952; Peter Morris).

hugger A ground ball that stays inside the foul line.

hum To throw a ball with great force or speed. "Even during warmups, he [Barry Larkin] was humming the ball" (*St. Petersburg Times*, March 31, 1990).

human crab A very disagreeable person. "Bill is looked upon as the 'human crab' in baseball, but he is a mighty good fellow when you get close to him" (*San Francisco Bulletin*, March 1, 1913; Gerald L. Cohen). See also *crab*, 1.

human growth hormone A synthetic substance that replicates a hormone (somatotropin) secreted by the anterior pituitary gland and that is used to stimulate growth and cell reproduction and to increase bone thickness. Some ballplayers were accused in the Mitchell Report (Dec. 2007) of using the substance to enhance their performance and energy levels, to increase their muscle mass, to strengthen or repair connective tissue (thereby presumably speeding recovery from injury or fatigue), and to serve as a substitute for anabolic steroids. The substance has been available since the 1980s, and possession is illegal without a prescription. Although it was banned by Major League Baseball in Jan. 2005, it is undetectable through urine testing (the substance clears the system quickly, making detection during testing difficult). Blood testing, which is prohibited by the Basic Agreement, is not widely accessible and is in the developmental stage. Abbrev. *HGH*.

human rain delay A batter who takes considerable time preparing to receive each pitch by warming up, swinging the bat, pounding his spikes, moving in and out of the batter's box, adjusting his helmet or batting gloves, calling time, etc. The term was applied specif. to Mike Hargrove and Carlton Fisk. See also *rain delay*.

human whiff machine A hitter with a very low batting average.

humidity dispenser *hist.* A particularly waggish term for a spitball pitcher IST USE. 1912 (*New York Tribune*, Sept. 22; Edward J. Nichols).

humidor An environmentally controlled chamber that can store baseballs to prevent them from becoming overly dry and shrinking below specifications. The humidor used by the Colorado Rockies since 2002 in the low humidity, mile-high mountain air at Coors Field in Denver can store about 400 dozen baseballs at 70°F and 50 percent humidity. The purpose of the humidor is to make balls easier for pitchers to grip and more difficult for batters to hit out of the park. The humidor generated questions from opposing managers who wondered if the Rockies were benefiting from its use: "The thing that concerns me is, which balls came from the humidor and which ones came from the microwave and which ones came from the freezer? If the balls all look the same, how do you know?" (Arizona Diamondbacks manager Bob Brenly, quoted in *The New York Times*, May 19, 2002).

"humm-babe" A unit of chatter that permeates every level of the game from the school yard to the major leagues. San Francisco Giants manager Roger Craig used it so much that during the 1986 season *Sports Illustrated* (Aug. 4, 1986) termed it "a cult phrase in San Francisco." USAGE NOTE. Ira Berkow (*The New York Times*, June 24, 1986) observed, "If you get close to the field, you'll hear the fielders speaking only to the pitcher. 'Humma, humma, baby, c'mon, humma.' Or sentiments to that effect. It's a kind of lullaby." ETYMOLOGY. The phrase probably evolved from more articulate chatter along the lines of encouraging the pitcher to "hum that ball," or "throw the hummer," or "come on babe."

hummer **1.** A fastball, named for the whizzing sound it seems to make as it comes across the plate. "At age 59, if that's what he was, Satch [Paige] had lost the hummer" (Jack Mann, *Washington Times*, June 10, 1982). See also *buzzer*. **2.** *hist.* A hard-batted ball. IST USE. 1876. "He succeeded in getting in a 'hummer,' which was 'nipped' in time to get him out at first" (*Adrian* [Mich.] *Morning Press*, May 1; Peter Morris). **3.** An outstanding ballplayer.

"A third baseman from the South wants to play here and if he comes down in his price we will get a 'hummer'" (*The Sporting Life*, Feb. 15, 1896; Peter Morris).

hummock *hist.* Syn. of *base*, 2 (*The Sporting Life*, Nov. 29, 1913).

humpback liner A batted ball that travels like a line drive, then sinks precipitously; a cross between a line drive and a pop fly; a *Texas Leaguer* in the Southern Association. Also spelled "humped-back liner"; "hump-backed liner"; "hump-backed liner." IST USE. 1933 (*The Sporting News Record Book*).

humpty-dump A type of music played by ballpark organists at odd times during a game, which many fans find disconcerting and annoying.

humpty-dumpty 1. A player, often unskilled, who is unpopular or unproven with his teammates. "[Ron] Hansen, who had been named American League Rookie of the Year in 1960 and wasn't a humpty-dumpty, was not about to be awed by the Chicago [White Sox] shortstop tradition" (Bob Vanderberg, *Sox: From Lane and Fain to Zisk and Fisk*, 1982, p.247). Dizzy Dean ("Dizzy Daisies") used the term for "a person held in contempt." 2. A substitute player. Leo Durocher (*Nice Guys Finish Last*, 1975) stated, "The way it has always been in baseball, the humpty-dumpties, the substitutes, come out early to take their batting and fielding practice, and then the bell rings and the hitting cage belongs to the regulars." Umpire Tom Gorman (*Three and Two!*, 1979) claimed, "It's the humpty-dumpty hitters, the guys with the .210 average, who do 90 percent of the beefing."

hump up For a pitcher to rear back and throw his best fastball; to exert extra effort. "If I get two strikes and it looks like he doesn't want heat, then I will hump up on one or two" (Zack Greinke, quoted in *Baseball America*, Aug. 4–17, 2003; Peter Morris).

Hundred Thousand Dollar Infield See *One Hundred Thousand Dollar Infield*.

hungry Said of a player or team wanting to do well because of previous failures; said of a player eager to make a name for himself.

hunky *hist.* Said of a player who is familiar and comfortable with his position in the field. "[Charlie Smith] is an excellent general player; but the moment he sets foot on third base he is what the boys call 'hunky,' that is, 'he's at home'" (Henry Chadwick, *The Game of Base Ball*, 1868, p.36).

hunter *hist.* An outfielder who plays far afield (Chicago Park District [Burnham Park], *Baseball*, 1938).

hunt leather *hist.* 1. To try to field a ball. "The game was . . . a one-sided affair from the start . . . our boys keeping their hosts busy 'hunting leather' all the time" (*St. Louis Post-Dispatch*, Apr. 20, 1875). See also *leather-hunting*, 1. 2. To try to hit a pitched ball (*Chicago Inter-Ocean*, May 3, 1885; Edward J. Nichols). See also *leather-hunting*, 2.

hurl 1. To deliver the ball from the pitcher's mound; to pitch. IST USE. 1911 (William Patten and J. Walker McSpadden, *The Book of Baseball*, p.158). 2. To throw a baseball.

hurler Syn. of *pitcher*, 1. IST USE. 1906. "Poor Bell! It's the old story about the pitcher going to the well once too often. But the big hurler was not in the least disturbed" (*Altoona* [Pa.] *Mirror*, Aug. 21; Sam Clements). USAGE NOTE. The term was used earlier (*Los Angeles Times*, May 28, 1905), apparently to describe a hitter: "Peerless among the home-run hurlers of the West, the veteran shortstop 'Truck' Eagan now playing gilt-edge ball . . . has carved out with his clout club a unique place for himself." The term has been commonly but inaccurately used by vintage base ball clubs when in fact it is a 20th-century term.

hurlester *hist.* A pitcher. "In the afternoon the hurlesters of the company engaged in a little light artillery fire [pitching]" (*San Francisco Bulletin*, March 19, 1913; Gerald L. Cohen).

hurlsmith *hist.* A pitcher. "Henry Krause, the boy hurlsmith of the Philadelphia Athletics" (Alfred H. Spink, *The National Game*, 2nd ed., 1911, p.136).

hurlster *hist.* A pitcher. "Only one of last year's crew of hurlsters is with the company this year" (*San Francisco Bulletin*, March 27, 1913; Gerald L. Cohen).

hurry the throw For an infielder, pitcher, or

catcher to get rid of the ball as quickly as possible, esp. when trying to turn a slow roller, bunt, or bobbled ball into an out.

hurt To destroy an opponent's chances of winning by being effective at the plate or on the mound.

hustle 1. *v.* To play aggressively, quickly, and alertly. Henry Chadwick (*The Sporting News*, March 23, 1895; Peter Morris) complained that the "base ball definition" of "hustling" was "simply to endeavor to win a game either by fair means or foul," such as yelling like "a mad bull on the coaching lines" or "willfully colliding" with opponents or performing "under the generic term of 'dirty ball playing.'" 2. *n.* Playing baseball in an alert, energetic, and aggressive manner. IST USE. 1884. "The Baltimore Club will this year make the best of the Association clubs 'hustle' to win a ball" (*The Sporting Life*, Apr. 23; Peter Morris). USAGE NOTE. A noted modern player who performed in an aggressive manner was Pete Rose, who attracted the nickname "Charlie Hustle." Ira Berkow (*The New York Times*, Sept. 12, 1985) noted that it was a derisive nickname at first, but Rose wore it as a "badge of distinction": "He made believers out of many who at first had deprecatory thoughts about this brash young rookie who ran to first on walks, who slid headfirst into bases, who sometimes taunted the opposition and barreled into them when they were in the way." ETYMOLOGY. Although the term has often been described as an Americanism, Peter Tamony showed that it was, in fact, "employed by English pickpockets from about 1750 on." In a paper he delivered (Oct. 19, 1962) to the International Society for General Semantics, he summarized his findings: " 'Hustle,' the English word, has cognates in Dutch and Low and High German, and the import in these languages is 'to shake together, to toss.' In the early 19th century,

these older terms came to mean 'to push forward, to impel, to urge, to move hastily, to hurry, to bustle . . . to work busily.' As hustle and bustle characterized American life and seemed so characteristic of Americans, hustle was upgraded or ameliorated, and became an admired American trait. . . . The meaning has persisted in criminal slang, and indicates almost anyone who seems to be getting by without visible means of support—someone with a racket. It has been closely connected with prostitution and pimps and, of course, all kinds of gambling and games of chance."

hustle blister Syn. of *strawberry*.

hustle bump One of the "marks and bruises on a player's body" (Fresco Thompson, *Los Angeles Times*, July 8, 1961).

hustle double "A fairly ordinary hit that the batter turns into a double by running full speed right out of the batter's box" (Zack Hample, *Watching Baseball Smarter*, 2007, p.214).

hustler 1. *hist.* A manager in the late 19th century who promoted his team very aggressively. "No more enthusiastic and industrious manager than Mr. [Horace] Phillips has ever handled a base ball club. His untiring energy has earned him the sobriquet 'Hustler' Phillips, and if Pittsburg does not have a strong nine it will be because there is no more good material lying around loose" (*The Sporting News*, Dec. 11, 1886; Peter Morris). IST USE. 1886. Phillips' nickname, "Hustler," first appeared in the *New York Mail and Express*, reprinted in *St. Louis Globe-Democrat* (Oct. 7). 2. A highly energetic and enthusiastic ballplayer. IST USE. 1887. "[Frank Ringo] is working the trade with cigars. He is a hustler both as a drummer [traveling salesman] and a ball player" (*The Sporting News*, June 18; Peter Morris).

Hutch Award Short for *Fred Hutchinson Memorial Award*.

I

I Abbrev. for *interference*, 1.

IA Abbrev. for *International Association.*

IBA Abbrev. for *International Baseball Association*, 1.

IBAF Abbrev. for *International Baseball Federation.*

IBB Abbrev. for *intentional base on balls.*

ice To all but assure the final outcome of a game through a hit or defensive play; e.g., "Smith's grand slam iced the game."

icebox *hist.* The bullpen. "When the season opens such twists as the 'spit ball,' 'snake twist,' and the 'grasshopper shoot' will be relegated to the icebox" (Cy Young, quoted in *Chicago Tribune*, Apr. 16, 1905; Peter Morris).

Icebox Nickname for *Candlestick Park.*

ice cart *hist.* Syn. of *ice wagon.* "Cleveland's men can field and bat, but as 'ice carts' on the bases they lay over the old Mets" (*The World* [New York], Apr. 19, 1888; Gerald L. Cohen).

ice-cream cone **1.** A ball that is caught in the top of the webbing of a fielder's glove, so called because the ball sticks up out of the glove like a scoop of ice cream. **2.** A catch in which the ball is lodged in the top of the webbing of a fielder's glove. See also *snow cone.*

ice down To use ice or some other cooling agent to soothe and reduce swelling or inflammation; e.g., to "ice down" a pitcher's throwing arm after the game. When asked if he did this during his years as a major-league pitcher, Warren Spahn answered, "Ice is for mixed drinks" (*The Boston Globe*, May 21, 1988).

ice hit The base hit that assures the final outcome of a game; the hit that puts the game on ice (Walter K. Putney, *Baseball Stories*, Spring 1952).

ice man A relief pitcher; one who is able to "freeze" an opposing team's rally. Interestingly, this term and "fireman" are synonyms.

ice wagon A player who runs slowly, resembling the labored movement of an ice wagon. "The Giants are still running bases with the airy sprightliness of a caravan of ice-wagons" (*Puck's Library*, vol. 1, 1887; Richard Miller). Syn. *ice cart.* IST USE. 1886. "Of the nine Detroiters who played yesterday five moved around like so many ice wagons" (*The North American* [Philadelphia], Aug. 4).

icing Syn. of *insurance*, 1. "[Carlos] Baerga hit a two-run homer . . . in the sixth for some icing" (*The Baltimore Sun*, Aug. 27, 1990).

icon player Syn. of *special player.*

IF **1.** Abbrev. for *infield*, 2. **2.** Abbrev. for *infielder.* **3.** Abbrev. for *infield fly*, 1.

if necessary Said of a game or games in a playoff schedule that may not be played if one team wins the playoff before all games are played. "Come the postseason . . . baseball rediscovers the beauty of the . . . urgent effort required by the brevity of a schedule blessed with those two magic words—*if necessary*" (Tom Verducci, *Sports Illustrated*, Oct. 20, 2003).

IGF Abbrev. for *Industry Growth Fund.*

igniter The player who starts a rally. See also *spark plug.*

"I got it" A fielder's expression to teammates that he will catch a fly ball.

IL Abbrev. for *International League.*

illegal Contrary to the rules of baseball. "[Baseball] is remarkable for the way in which the penalizing of illegal play is woven into the game" (Jessie H. Bancroft and William Dean Pulvermacher, *Handbook of Athletic Games*, 1916, p.81).

illegal bat **1.** A bat that has been altered or tampered with to improve the distance that a batted ball will travel, or to cause an otherwise unusual reaction to the ball; e.g., a bat that has been corked, flat-surfaced, nailed, or grooved, or covered with a substance such as wax. A batter bringing an illegal bat to the batter's box shall be called out and ejected from the game, and may be subject to additional penalties. See also *doctored bat.* **2.** [softball term] A bat that does not meet the requirements stated in the rules of the Amateur Softball Association of America or other body and is not marked by the words "OFFICIAL SOFTBALL" by the manufacturer; e.g., a bat listed on a banned-bat list, or a bat consisting of visible cracks. Compare *altered bat.*

illegally batted ball A ball hit with either of the batter's feet entirely outside the batter's box. In such cases, the ball is dead and the batter is out. The same is true for a ball that is hit twice, such as one that is popped up in front of the batter and hit again as it comes down. A ball hit with a bat that has been doctored is also deemed to be illegally batted.

illegally caught ball A ball stopped or caught with a cap, glove, or any other part of the player's uniform or equipment that is detached from its proper place; one example would be the throwing of a glove to stop the progress of a ball. Such action for a batted ball results in an automatic triple being awarded to the batter, and for a thrown ball results in two bases being awarded to the runner.

illegal pitch A pitch that violates the rules; specif., a) a pitch delivered to the batter when the pitcher's pivot foot is not in contact with the rubber, and b) a *quick return pitch,* 1. When ruled, an illegal pitch is a balk with runner(s) on base and a ball if there are no runners on base, provided that the batter does not swing at the pitch. If a batter reaches first base on an illegal pitch, the play counts.

illegal pitcher [softball term] A player who is legally in the game but who may not pitch as a result of being removed from the pitching position by the umpire; said removal may be prompted by the occurrences of two charged conferences in one inning or pitching with excessive speed (in slow pitch softball) after a warning.

illegal player [softball term] A player who has entered the game without reporting. When the infraction is brought to the plate umpire's attention by the offended team after the first legal or illegal pitch—and before the team in violation informs the umpire—the player is ejected from the game.

imaginary runner Syn. of *ghost runner.*

immortal A player or other individual elected to the National Baseball Hall of Fame. Election has invoked the notion of baseball immortality. A modicum of reality was imposed at the moment Dizzy Dean was told that he had been elected and he responded, "Well, I guess now I'm 'mongst them mortals." See also *eleven immortals*; *baseball immortal.*

impact player A player who has an effect on the team's ability to win ball games. "Frank Cashen ... believes [Keith] Miller has an opportunity to be an 'impact player,' the ultimate tribute to any prospect" (Dave Anderson, *The New York Times*, Dec. 11, 1988).

imparable Spanish for "base hit."

import **1.** *hist.* A player on a town club in early baseball, brought in from elsewhere, usually with financial inducements. **2.** A player on a team from another country. "The Korean Baseball Organization reduced the number of imports per team to two per its agreement with the Korean Pro Baseball Player's Association" (*Baseball America*, Apr. 14–27, 2003; Peter Morris). Syn. "imported player." **3.** A player's wife or girlfriend brought on a road trip or flown in to a city. See also *road beef.*

Impossible Dream The 1967 season when the Boston Red Sox battled three other teams to win the American League pennant after finishing in ninth place the previous year. The team was led by Triple Crown winner Carl Yastrzemski and American League Cy Young Award winner Jim Lonborg. The term refers to the hit song from the popular musical *Man* *of La Mancha.* See Bill Nowlin and Dan Desrochers, eds., *The 1967 Impossible Dream Red Sox* (2007).

improper batter A batter who bats out of order and completes a time at bat in the place of the *proper batter.*

improved bat An improvement in a player's ability to get timely hits.

in 1. *adv.* Toward home plate, such as an infield that is playing close in anticipation of a bunt or a play at home plate, or an outfield playing shallow. Syn. *up,* 4. **2.** *adv.* Toward the batter, such as a pitch thrown inside or close to the batter; e.g., "Smith's pitch was up and in." Compare *out,* 4. 1ST USE. 1887 (*Harper's Weekly,* Sept. 10, p.647; Edward J. Nichols). **3.** *adv.* Said of a pitch thrown close to the batter or between the batter and the strike zone. Compare *away,* 2. **4.** *adv.* Across home plate; e.g., "The run is in to tie the score." **5.** *adv.* Participating in a game; e.g., "Jones is in, replacing Brown." Compare *out,* 5. **6.** *n.* The side at bat (John B. Foster, in *Collier's New Dictionary of the English Language,* 1908).

inactive list A list of players not on the *active list*; specif., the disabled list, bereavement list, suspended list, voluntarily retired list, restricted list, disqualified list, and ineligible list.

in a hole See various definitions of *hole.*

in-and-out 1. Said of a game or sequence of innings characterized by a quick succession of outs. **2.** Said of inconsistent or erratic play. "[Pitching] is one of the main reasons for the club's in-and-out performances of the last six weeks" (*San Francisco Bulletin,* May 31, 1913; Gerald L. Cohen).

in-and-outer *hist.* A pitcher who pitched some good games, but who also had games where he was ineffective (*Baseball History Bulletin,* 2001).

in-between 1. Said of a ball fielded on the short hop. **2.** Said of a batter who is "behind the fastball and out in front of the curve" (Baltimore Orioles manager Mike Hargrove, quoted in *The Baltimore Sun,* Apr. 30, 2001).

in-betweener A base hit that falls between an infielder and an outfielder. Compare *tweener,* 1.

Incaviglia rule A rule that a player selected in the *first-year player draft* cannot be traded within a year of being drafted. The rule was adopted after Pete Incaviglia was drafted by the Montreal Expos in 1985 and refused to sign, forcing the team to trade him.

incentive clause That part of a player's contract that promises a bonus for achieving certain playing-time goals (such as plate appearances or games started) and/or honors (such as placing fifth in Most Valuable Player voting) during the season. Such clauses cannot be based on performance or skill (such as batting average, home runs, runs batted in, or games won) nor contingent on the standing of the signing club at the conclusion of the season. A common incentive stipulates that a player will be given a cash bonus if he makes the All-Star team. "Once upon a time, general managers tossed incentive clauses into contracts because a) they wanted to get an obnoxious agent out of their office, b) they thought giving incentives instead of higher base salaries would keep payrolls lower, or c) they figured the incentives wouldn't be met" (Richard Justice, *The Washington Post,* Aug. 24, 1986). Incentives can be many and varied. According to Murray Chass (*The New York Times,* Jan. 11, 1987), in Reggie Jackson's 1987 contract with the Oakland A's, Jackson was given the following: a) $1,000 per plate appearance from his 476th through the 600th; b) 15 cents for each home admission from 1.6 to 1.7 million, 20 cents for each home admission from 1.7 to 1.8 million, and 30 cents for each admission greater than 1.8 million; and c) $250,000 if he was named the league's Most Valuable Player, $125,000 for finishing second through fifth in voting, and $50,000 for finishing sixth through 10th.

incomplete game A game of less than five complete innings.

in contention Said of a team that is competing for a championship.

in-curve *hist.* **1.** A 19th-century term for a pitch thrown by a right-handed pitcher that curved in toward a right-handed batter or one thrown by a left-handed pitcher that curved in toward a left-handed batter. The pitch is now known as a *screwball.* The *St. Louis Post-Dispatch* (Aug. 12, 1894; Peter Morris) explained how to "produce" the in-curve: "Grasp the ball firmly between the thumb and first two fingers, the remaining fingers being doubled in the hand. Throw the ball at a height equal to the shoulder. At the instant of releasing it from the hand twist the fingers sharply toward the body, allowing the ball to roll off their ends." According to O.P. Caylor (*Outing, an Illustrated Monthly Magazine of Recreation*, Aug. 1891), "What was formerly believed to be an 'in curve,' as it was then called, is now known as an 'in shoot.' It is a very swift, straight ball which goes very close to the batter's body." Also spelled "incurve," "in curve." Syn. "incurver." See also *inshoot*; *indrop*. Compare *outcurve*. IST USE. 1878. "Harry Wright says pitchers with the 'in curve' are in great demand" (*St. Louis Post-Dispatch*, March 16; Peter Morris). **2.** An early 20th-century term for a fastball. According to John McGraw (*My Thirty Years in Baseball*, 1923), "To [the professional player] there is no such thing as an incurve. That is what we call a fast ball. Of course, I am assuming that the pitcher is right-handed. A so-called incurve is nothing more than a ball thrown in a natural way with great force. A ball thus thrown will naturally curve inward, to a certain extent. If it takes a sharp jump, due to the speed, we call that the 'break on his fast one.' In other words, the inshoot is the natural course of a ball. A curve is unnatural, due to a reverse twist being put on it."

independent league A minor league that is formed and developed without the sanction of Major League Baseball, but respects the contracts of those leagues within organized baseball; e.g., the California State League (1928–1936). The Northern League (1993, name changed to Northeast League in 2002) and the Texas-Louisiana League (1994) were the first of the modern independent leagues. Compare *outlaw league*. Syn. *wild-cat league*.

independent putout Any putout by a catcher on a play that is not a strikeout, such as a tag and force at home or other bases, or a caught pop fly. It was described by Bill James and Jim Henzler (*Win Shares*, 2002).

independent team A minor-league team that is not owned by, nor has a player development contract with, a major-league team.

Indian ball **1.** A playground game in which a batter self-tosses the ball and hits fungoes to any number of fielders: if the ball is caught on the fly, the fielder becomes the batter; if the ball is fielded on the bounce, the batter places the bat lengthwise, perpendicular to the fielder, who throws or rolls the ball back, trying to hit the bat, and becomes the batter if successful. If the batter catches the ball after it hits the bat and before it hits the ground, he remains as the batter. Syn. *roll to the bat*; *hit the bat*; "Indian baseball"; "Indian hit the bat." **2.** A playground game with as few as four players (batter, pitcher, infielder, and outfielder), with fair territory greatly reduced (e.g., a right-handed batter hitting to right field would be declared out). As described by D. Bruce Brown (personal communication, Jan. 26, 2002) who played the game in Utah: "Your teammate pitched to you. You only got two pitches. . . . The offense was recorded as follows: ball caught anywhere on the fly (out), grounder fielded cleanly in the infield (out), grounder that reached the outfield grass (single), ball hit over the head of the infielder (double), grounder that gets past the outfielder (triple), and ball hit over the head of the outfielder (home run)."

Indians Nickname for the American League Central Division franchise in Cleveland, Ohio, since 1915. The team mascot is a cartoon Indian named "Chief Wahoo." The club went through a series of name changes before becoming the Indians: Bluebirds (or Blues) (1901), Broncos (or Bronchos) (1902), *Naps* (1903–1911), and Molly McGuires (1912–1914). Baseball folklore long held that a newspaper ran a contest among fans who selected "Indians" in honor of Louis Sockalexis, a Penobscot from Old Town, Maine, and member (1897–1899) of the Cleveland *Spiders* of the National League, who died in 1913. Yet there is no evidence that a newspaper ran such a contest, nor that the team was named after Sockalexis. The Indians corrected the myth in its 2000 media guide. The nickname was the choice of owner Charles W. Somers after he received suggestions from newspapermen. An interesting note appeared in *The Sporting Life* (March 27, 1897; Bill Deane) shortly after Sockalexis joined the

Spiders: "There is no feature of the signing of Sockalexis more gratifying than the fact that his presence on the team will result in relegating to obscurity the title of 'Spiders,' by which the team has been handicapped for several season [*sic*], to give place to the more significant name 'Indians.'" However, the name "Spiders" lasted until the team disbanded after the 1899 season.

Indian sign A jinx or hoodoo. IST USE. 1908 (*Baseball Magazine*, June, p.28; Edward J. Nichols).

indicator 1. A card or a small handheld mechanical device used by an umpire to keep track of balls, strikes, outs, and innings. Some modern indicators have the capacity to display runs scored as well. "Steve Zabriskie and Ralph Kiner are second-guessing umpires so much, I am going to give them indicators" (Tom Gorman, supervisor of National League umpires, quoted in *Newsday*, June 30, 1986). See also *umpire's assistant*; *tally machine*. Syn. *clicker*, 2; *counter*, 2; *Ouija board*; *register*, 3. IST USE. 1885. "Spalding's Automatic Umpire Indicator" (advertisement; Dan Gutman letter, March 31, 1993). 2. A sign, given by the manager or a coach, that is embedded in a sea of meaningless gestures and precedes the real sign; e.g., an indicator might be tapping the belt or standing in a specific place in the coach's box, after which the next sign is the operative one. Compare *wipe-off sign*. Syn. *key*, 1.

indicator handler *hist.* An umpire. "Touching on umpires reminds me of my career as an indicator handler" (National League president Nicholas E. Young, quoted in *The Washington Post*, Dec. 17, 1897).

indicator holder *hist.* An umpire. "The popular indicator holder ["Bull" Perrine] is suffering from a severe attack of locomotor ataxia" (*San Francisco Bulletin*, Feb. 6, 1913; Gerald L. Cohen).

indicator man *hist.* An umpire. "The indicator man who uses burly tones, throws out his chest and sasses the crowd can't expect much mercy in a real baseball league" (*San Francisco Bulletin*, March 22, 1913; Gerald L. Cohen).

indifference See *defensive indifference*.

individual offensive bunt A bunt to get the batter on base rather than one whose purpose is to advance runner(s) already on base.

individual sign A sign sent to one player and not the others, such as looking at or away from, or walking toward or away from, the batter to whom the sign is being given.

indoor baseball 1. [softball term] The original name for the game from which modern *softball* derived. Its rules were written by George W. Hancock, a young reporter for the Chicago Board of Trade, who was one of the group of young men who created the game—using a boxing glove for a ball and a broom handle for a bat—while waiting at the Farragut Boat Club for the telegraphed results of the Harvard-Yale football game on Thanksgiving Day, 1887. Thus, softball in its first incarnation was baseball played inside a gymnasium. See also *indoor-outdoor*; *playground baseball*. 2. A facetious term for baseball played in domed ballparks. 3. Baseball adapted for playing indoors. IST USE. 1889. "A meeting of the Mid-Winter Indoor Base-Ball League was held at the Carleton club-house" (*The Daily Inter Ocean* [Chicago], Oct. 27).

indoor cage An indoor *batting cage* that uses a tee.

indoor-outdoor [softball term] *Indoor baseball* adapted for playing outdoors. Less than a year after indoor baseball was invented, it had caught on to such an extent that by the summer of 1888 it was being played outdoors, and some preferred to call it "indoor-outdoor."

indoor team Any team that plays its home games in a domed or enclosed ballpark.

indrop *hist.* A 19th-century term for an *incurve* that drops down as it approaches the batter. "To throw this curve grasp and throw the ball in the same manner as for regular 'in-curve' except that as the ball leaves the hand the palm should be turned half upward and to the left [for a right-handed pitcher], instead of squarely to the left as in 'in-curve'" (Edward J. Prindle, *Baseball, and How to Play It*, 1896, 1902, 1906). Also spelled "in-drop"; "in drop." Compare *outdrop*.

industrial league A generic name for a baseball or softball league that is sponsored by

Indoor baseball. Earliest known image of the game that became softball, from 1897. *Library of Congress*

and named after an industrial or commercial enterprise. Syn. *shop league.*

industrial softball [softball term] Softball in which industrial or commercial enterprises sponsor teams for their employees. For many years softball has been a popular sport for both sexes in the recreation programs sponsored by such firms. One company (Avco Lycoming) spoke for many when it stated that its reasons for an active softball program were that interdepartmental softball competition a) promotes job efficiency, morale, and a strong sense of company loyalty; b) functions as a social "leveler" by affording friendly contact among employees at all personnel levels; c) promotes the physical and mental well-being of employees; and d) promotes an excellent medium for observing the potential leadership abilities of employees (*Balls and Strikes*, Apr. 1967).

industrial team A baseball or softball team in an industrial league.

Industry Growth Fund A fund established under the 1997 Basic Agreement and operated jointly by the Major League Baseball Players Association and the 30 major-league clubs to promote the growth of baseball in the United States, Canada, and throughout the world by enhancing fan interest, increasing baseball's popularity, and ensuring industry growth in the 21st century. Activities include licensing and marketing products, promoting player tours, supporting baseball federations, developing new media technology, and encouraging community service. Abbrev. *IGF.*

ineligible list A list of major-league players or others found guilty of misconduct (attempting to throw games, bribe players or umpires, or bet on games) or convicted of crimes involving moral turpitude. Players on the ineligible list are not eligible to play or associate with any major- or minor-league club. Compare *suspended list*; *restricted list*; *disqualified list.*

infield 1. The area on the playing field bounded by the four baselines; the diamond. IST USE. 1858 (Chadwick Scrapbooks; Edward J. Nichols). **2.** The area on the playing field bounded by the "outside edges" of the basepaths. This definition applies because there is no official definition of where the infield actually ends and the outfield begins. Abbrev. *IF*, 1. ETYMOLOGY. "Infield" was a

Scottish farming term for the land near or around the farmhouse or homestead, or arable land that was regularly tilled and fertilized (attested to in 1733 in the *Oxford English Dictionary*). Its meaning was reflected in the practice of early baseball clubs, which put considerable time into grading and sodding the infield, and much less into the outfield. EXTENDED USE. The area enclosed by a racetrack laid out for horse racing or automobile racing. "[We] walked across the infield and then across the smooth thick turf of the course to the paddock" (Ernest Hemingway, *Farewell to Arms*, 1929, p.138). Also, in cricket, the part of the playing area near the wicket (*OED*, 1898). **3.** The defensive positions comprising first base, second base, third base, and shortstop, taken collectively. **4.** The infielders (first baseman, second baseman, third baseman, and shortstop) considered as a group. Technically, the pitcher and catcher are infielders but generally are not being referred to when a team's infield is being discussed. 1ST USE. 1864. "The out-fielders were not troubled much, as the heavy work was done by the in-field" (*New York Clipper*, Aug. 20; Peter Morris). **5.** Short for *infield practice*. "A steady rain . . . [wiped] out pre-game batting practice and infield for both teams" (*The Baltimore Sun*, Oct. 4, 1995). **6.** Pregame fielding practice in which infielders and outfielders throw to bases (Tom Verducci, *Sports Illustrated*, March 27, 2006).

infield back Said of the infield playing at its normal depth. Compare *infield in*.

infield chatter See *chatter*.

infielder A defensive player positioned in the infield; specif., the first baseman, second baseman, third baseman, or shortstop, and sometimes the pitcher and catcher. Henry Chadwick (*The Game of Base Ball*, 1868) included the pitcher and catcher among the six infielders. Abbrev. *IF*, 2. 1ST USE. 1865 (*New York Herald*, July 1; Edward J. Nichols).

infielder's glove A glove that is generally designed to be broken in with the fingers curled down, toward the pocket (Daniel Okrent, *Nine Innings*, 1985, p.48). Compare *outfielder's glove*.

infield fly 1. A batted ball popped up over the infield. Abbrev. *IF*, 3. **2.** A declaration by the umpire that the infield fly rule is in effect. **3.** Short for *infield fly rule*. David Nemec (*The Rules of Baseball*, 1994, p.29) claimed that "the term 'infield fly' did not first appear in the rulebook until 1895."

infield fly rule A special rule to protect the baserunners, in which the batter is declared automatically out by the umpire when, in his judgment, a fair fly ball (not including a line drive nor an attempted bunt) can be caught with ordinary effort by an infielder (and the pitcher, the catcher, or an outfielder who stations himself in or near the infield) facing the infield, when first and second bases are occupied, or when the bases are loaded and there are less than two outs. The fielder does not need to catch the ball. The umpire declares the rule is in effect by saying "infield fly" and signals it by raising a clenched fist straight overhead. If the ball is near the baselines, the umpire yells "infield fly, if fair." If the fly becomes a foul ball, it is treated the same as any foul. The umpire's judgment governs the rule: in no sense is it considered an appeal play. The rationale for the infield fly rule is to prevent the fielder from intentionally dropping the ball, picking it up quickly, and forcing the offensive team into a double play; i.e., the rule removes the force situation which would cause two runners to be doubled up after an intentional drop. The ball is live and all baserunners may advance at the risk of the ball being caught, or retouch and advance after the ball is touched by the fielder (the fielder is required to tag the runner). If a runner is off base and hit by the ball, both the runner and the batter are out; however, if the runner is on the base and is hit by the ball, only the batter is out. In either case, the ball is dead. The infield fly rule was preceded by the *trap ball rule*. Although the infield fly rule was instituted in 1901, the name of the rule was first used eight years later. Syn. *infield fly*, 3. 1ST USE. 1909 (*American Magazine*, May, p.39; Edward J. Nichols).

infield hit Any hit that does not escape the infield but allows the batter time to reach first base safely. Such hits must be either hit slowly enough or placed well enough to allow the batter to outrun a throw to first base. "With his blazing speed from home to first . . . Ichiro [Suzuki] leads the majors in infield hits" (*Sports Illustrated*, June 10, 2002). IST USE. 1895 (*New York Press*, Aug. 3; Edward J. Nichols).

infield in Said of an infield playing closer to home in anticipation of a bunt or a play at the plate. The infield often plays in when there is a runner on third base and less than two outs. Colorado Rockies manager Don Baylor said it is always "automatic" to play his infield in at Coors Field whether Colorado is leading or not (*Sports Illustrated*, May 13, 1996, p.53). Compare *infield back*. Syn. *infield up*.

infielding Infield defensive play. IST USE. 1913 (*Harper's Weekly*, Sept. 13, p.21; Edward J. Nichols).

infield out An out made on a ball hit within the infield or recorded by an infielder.

infield practice That period of pregame activity set aside for infielders to improve their fielding (catching and throwing) skills; the action or process of infield practice. Syn. *infield*, 5.

infield roller A slow ground ball that is batted onto the infield.

infield up Syn. of *infield in*.

ínfil flái Spanish for "infield fly."

infinite regression A situation in a ball game in which managers try to outthink each other. One game saw Atlanta Braves manager Bobby Cox "standing in his dugout thinking that [Philadelphia Phillies manager Jim] Fregosi knows that I know that he knows . . . what we ballplayers call an infinite regression" (Keith Hernandez, *Pure Baseball*, 1994, p.87).

in flight Said of a batted, thrown, or pitched ball that has not yet hit the ground or been touched by a fielder or other object.

in harness Engaged as a ballplayer. "Kid Nichols is still in harness and pitching as well as ever" (*The Washington Post*, Nov. 1, 1903).

inherited runner A baserunner at the time a relief pitcher enters the game. In 1992, box scores began to note the number of inherited runners and how many of them scored off each reliever.

inherited runs prevented A measure of a relief pitcher's performance, based on a comparison of the number of inherited runners the reliever allows to score during that inning with the run potential of the base–out situation in which the pitcher enters (Baseball Prospectus, *Baseball Between the Numbers*, 2006).

in his kitchen See *kitchen*.

inicialista Spanish for "first baseman."

I-95 A batting average of .195, a play on the north-south Interstate Highway 95. A player who cannot get his average off I–95 is one who cannot break .200.

I-95 Series Nickname for the 1983 World Series between the Philadelphia Phillies and the Baltimore Orioles, their two cities linked by Interstate Highway 95.

initial **1.** *adj.* Describing *first base*, 1. Terms popular from 1880 until about 1915 included "initial bag," "initial base," "initial corner," "initial cushion," "initial hassock," "initial sack," and "initial station." "Mundy Mundorff . . . openly pilfered everything in sight after getting his feet on the initial cushion" (*San Francisco Bulletin*, Apr. 26, 1913; Gerald L. Cohen). IST USE. 1880. "Initial bag" (*Chicago Inter-Ocean*, June 25; Edward J. Nichols). **2.** *n.* Syn. of *first base*, 1. IST USE. 1887 "Pitchers have always experienced some difficulty in preventing a batter from reaching the initial on six balls" (*San Francisco Examiner*, Feb. 7; Peter Morris).

in jeopardy Said of the state of an offensive player who, while the ball is in play, is in a position to be put out.

injured reserve list *hist.* Former syn. of *disabled list*. The term is used in fantasy baseball leagues.

injury list See *disabled list*.

injury rehabilitation assignment Sending a major-league player recovering from an injury or illness to a minor-league team for the purpose of getting him back into playing shape before resuming his place on the major-league roster. The assignment is accomplished with the concurrence of the player coming off the disabled list and can last no more than 20 days (30 days for pitchers). It is not counted as an optional assignment. A player so assigned continues to receive the player's major-league salary and major-league service time, although he is not counted against the active list limit of either the major- or minor-league club. According to the Basic Agreement (2007–2011) between the players and the owners, players with fewer than five years of major-league service can be sent to a club's spring training facility for rehabilitation; however, each day starting with the 11th counts toward the maximum length for rehabilitation assignments (30 days for pitchers, 20 days for others).

ink 1. *v.* To put one's signature to, as on a contract or other legal document. "Kansas City inked [Jose] Lima, sight unseen, for the major league minimum" (*Sports Illustrated*, Aug. 4, 2003). **2.** *n.* Media recognition. "I'm getting more ink about not getting ink than most people do who always get ink" (Joe Rudi, in 1974, quoted in *Sports Illustrated*, Sept. 6, 1999, p.80). USAGE NOTE. The term is self-conscious sports talk, beloved of sportswriters. It originally referred to printed media, but now encompasses all media.

in motion Said of a baserunner who begins a movement toward a steal of the next base. "The fast runner is often sent in motion on 3–1" (Keith Hernandez, *Pure Baseball*, 1994, p.23).

inner game The strategy and tactics of baseball as it relates to such matters as batting order, defensive positioning, and the use of pinch hitters. See also *inside baseball*.

inner garden *hist.* The infield. Compare *outer garden.* IST USE. 1907 (*New York Evening Journal*, May 24; Edward J. Nichols).

inner gardener *hist.* An infielder.

inner-outer A pitch thrown by Burt L. Standish's fictional character Frank Merriwell, which curved twice on its flight to the plate. See also *double shoot.* Compare *upperdowner.*

inner works *hist.* **1.** The area in which the infielders play. Compare *outer works*, 1. IST USE. 1912 (*New York Tribune*, Apr. 15; Edward J. Nichols). **2.** The infielders as a working unit. Compare *outer works*, 2. IST USE. 1908. "The inner works held together

well" (John B. Foster, in *Collier's New Dictionary of the English Language*).

inning 1. That part of a game within which the two teams alternate on defense and offense and during which there are three putouts for each team. Syn. *canto*; *chapter*; *chukker*; *stanza*; *frame*; *heat*, 1; *period*; *verse*; *loop*, 4; *round*, 1; *session*, 1; *spasm.* IST USE. 1854. "Players must take their strike in regular rotation; and after the first inning is played the turn commences at the player who stands on the list next to the one who lost the third hand" (Knickerbocker Rules, Rule 13, Apr. 1). ETYMOLOGY. The term "inning" came directly from cricket, a sport in which the team at bat is "in" and the one on the field is "out"; a time at bat (an at-bat) is an "innings." See also *innings*, 1. EXTENDED USE. A period of play in other sports and games; e.g., a bowling frame (one bowler's turn), or one of nine opportunities for a player to play at the table in the pocket billiards game of baseball, is called an "inning." Peter Morris (personal communication, Aug. 3, 1997) discovered that when the Univ. of Michigan played its first intercollegiate football game against Racine College in 1879, each half was referred to as an "inning." **2.** One unit of a pitcher's statistic referring to the opposition's times at bat; every three outs recorded by a pitcher. See also *innings pitched.*

innings 1. *hist.* A term used in early baseball to denote a single *inning.* Henry Chadwick (*The Game of Base Ball*, 1868, p.41): "An innings, in base ball, is played when three men on the batting side have been put out. The moment the third hand is out the innings terminates." IST USE. 1845. "[Brooklyn] decided in favor of giving their antagonists the first innings" (*New York Morning News*, Oct. 22; Dean A. Sullivan). ETYMOLOGY. A unit of play in cricket, in which each team's or individual player's turn at bat is called an "innings." USAGE NOTE. The term "inning" eventually replaced the British term "innings." A *Detroit Free Press* writer tried to make a distinction (reprinted in *Cleveland Plain Dealer*, May 12, 1889; Peter Morris): "Base ball authorities have long held that 'inning' referred to a time at bat for one side, and 'innings' to a time at bat for both sides." But this distinction was not consistently followed by sportswriters for many years. David Block (*Baseball Before We Knew It*, 2005, pp.197–98) noted that the 1835 book *The Boy's Book of Sports; a Description of the Exercises and Pastimes of Youth* (published by S. Babcock of New Haven, Conn.) introduced the first known application of the term "innings" to the game of baseball. **2.** The work of a pitcher in preparing for a game; e.g., "Smith got his innings in today for the game on Tuesday." **3.** The work of a player during a game; e.g., "Jones will see some innings at shortstop tomorrow." "If he [Doug Drabek] keeps the ball down, he's going to give you innings" (Ray Miller, quoted in *The Baltimore Sun*, Feb. 26, 1998). EXTENDED USE. An opportunity or chances. "[Actor Liam Neeson], who's in the film for maybe 10 minutes, gets his innings in" (*Gangs of New York* screenwriter Jay Cocks, quoted in *The Baltimore Sun*, Jan. 1, 2003). Logan Pearsall Smith (*Words and Idioms*, 1925) listed "to have one's innings" as a borrowing from cricket. **4.** Plural of *inning*.

innings eater A starting pitcher who can be relied upon to pitch a lot of innings with respectable, but generally unspectacular, results. Such a pitcher will throw more than 200 innings a year, may have some complete games, and be known as a "workhorse." "[Josh Pearce] gives his team confidence he'll go six or seven innings every time out . . . and projects as a middle-of-the-rotation innings-eater" (*Baseball America*, Dec. 24, 2001–Jan. 6, 2002; Peter Morris). Syn. *innings monster; innings guy.*

innings guy Syn. of *innings eater*. Jim Armstrong (*Denver Post*, Apr. 20, 1993): "Bryn Smith was your basic innings guy, more essential than quintessential. He never was going to win any Cy Young Awards, but he always grabbed the ball and headed for the mound. Every fifth day of every summer of every year. . . . He wasn't fancy or anything, but he always started."

innings monster Syn. of *innings eater*. The term has been applied to Scott Erickson, "an innings monster who is used to going full throttle" (*The Baltimore Sun*, March 12, 2001). "Every time I write Scott Erickson's name down . . . I feel like he's going to give me nine innings" (Baltimore Orioles manager Ray Miller, quoted in *The Washington Post*, July 23, 1999).

innings pitched A pitcher's statistic referring to the opposition's times at bat, expressed in fractions, with each out counting as one-third of an inning; e.g., a starting pitcher removed with one out in the seventh inning is credited with 6⅓ "innings pitched." See also *inning*, 2. Abbrev. *IP*.

in order **1.** Referring to the retirement of the first three batters in an inning. "[Sid Fernandez] did strike out the side in order in the first" (*The Baltimore Sun*, Aug. 9, 1994). **2.** Referring to three consecutive outs in one inning without a hit or a runner reaching first base; e.g., "Smith retired the next three batters in order." **3.** Referring to an uninterrupted string of retired batters; for example, "Jones retired the first nine batters in order."

in play **1.** Regarding that period in which the game is being played as opposed to a period in which plays cannot begin or continue. Compare *out of play*, 1. **2.** Describing a ball that is live, when runners can advance or be put out and runs can score. The ball is in play until it is ruled dead by the umpire or a third out is made. A ball is put back in play only after it is in the hands of the pitcher in position and the plate umpire has called "Play!" Compare *out of play*, 2. **3.** Said of a fair ball hit by a batter who is able to make contact; e.g., "Smith put the ball in play with the nubber." See also *put the ball in play*, 1.

in relief Said of a relief pitcher in a game; e.g., "Smith was in relief for three innings."

insert A special baseball card randomly included in, but not a part of, a set of cards to help increase sales. Almost every new set of cards contains at least one type of insert. Many modern inserts are sequentially numbered and rarer than the card sets into which they are inserted.

in-shoot **1.** *hist.* Alternate spelling of *inshoot*. 1ST USE. 1881 (*New York Herald*, July 29; Edward J. Nichols). **2.** [softball term] An underhand pitch in fast pitch softball that curves toward the batter.

inshoot *hist.* A 19th-century term for a pitch

that breaks, or otherwise has a pronounced movement, toward the batter, but not as sharp as a curve. "[Right-hander Fred Goldsmith] discovered the 'inshoot,' that is, he was able to deliver a swift ball with a distinct swerve toward a right-handed batter" (*Grand Rapids* [Mich.] *Herald*, May 17, 1903; Peter Morris). Old Hoss Radbourn, Gus Weyhing, and Bob Caruthers had great inshoots. See also *in-curve*, 1; *shoot*, 1. Compare *outshoot*. Also spelled "in shoot"; *in-shoot*, 1. 1ST USE. 1887. "The pitcher had a little ball and it was white as snow, and where the striker thought it was, that ball it wouldn't go. It had a sudden inshoot curve, it had a fearful drop, and when the striker wildly struck, that ball it didn't stop" (*St. Louis Globe-Democrat*, July 29).

inside Said of a pitch that comes between the batter and the strike zone. During the 1986 World Series, broadcaster Vin Scully said (Oct. 18) that the best story to come out of that year's spring training involved a pitching coach telling a rookie pitcher that he would have to learn "to pitch inside"; the pitcher's response: "Have I been traded to Houston?" Compare *outside*. 1ST USE. "[Bill] Dahlen is a dangerous hitter 'inside'—which means when the ball is pitched between him and the plate" (John J. Evers and Hugh S. Fullerton, *Touching Second: The Science of Baseball*, 1910; Peter Morris).

inside ball Syn. of *inside baseball*. 1ST USE. 1898. "Jake Beckley is now looked on as one of those players willing to turn a trick at any time. 'Inside ball' is Beckley's motto" (Tim Murnane, *Boston Daily Globe*, June 27).

inside baseball An alert, unrelenting style of play that placed a premium on strategy, tactics, guile, cunning, teamwork, speed, and quick-thinking players. It was characterized by playing for one run at a time through techniques such as the hidden-ball trick, sacrifice bunt, squeeze play, bunting for a hit, double steal, Baltimore chop, cutoff play, hit-and-run play, hitting behind the runner, outfielders backing each other up, pitchers covering first base, and place hitting. Inside baseball emphasized getting on base by any means necessary (drawing a base on balls, getting hit by the pitch, hitting to all fields, being patient at the plate), gaining an edge by dissecting opponents' moves and weaknesses, being daring and aggressive on the basepaths, unnerving opponents (such as by sharpening spikes in the dugout before a game) and umpires, capitalizing on game situations, keeping the opposing team guessing, doctoring the home grounds, and scrapping for every run. It was the gospel of 1890s Baltimore Orioles manager Ned Hanlon, who perfected the style, and early 1900s New York Giants manager John McGraw, who embraced it. John B. Foster (in *Collier's New Dictionary of the English Language*, 1908) noted the term is "a much abused expression to denote clever team work much of which is the result of a vivid imagination." See also *inner game*; *scientific baseball*; *little ball*, 1. Syn. *inside ball*; *inside game*; *inside work*; *smart baseball*. 1ST USE. 1898 (Tim Murnane, *The Boston Daily Globe*, June 27). EXTENDED USE. The inner circle. William Safire (*The New York Times*, June 19, 1988) explored the term's new "political or professional denotation," which he defined as "minutiae savored by the cognoscenti, delicious details, nuances discussed and dissected by aficionados." Safire gave several examples of the term in use outside of baseball, including this line from Richard Weiner, chairman of the Michigan Democratic Party: "The people in my state are interested in jobs, the economy and education. The rest is *inside baseball*." The earliest example mentioned by Safire was in 1978 by Sen. Edward M. Kennedy (D.-Mass.) in a letter quoted by Myra MacPherson of *The Washington Post*, in which Kennedy spoke of a legislator who "chairs endlessly boring hearings ... then cuts through testimony with *inside baseball* jokes that no visitors understand but laugh at anyway."

inside corner The side corner of home plate that is closest to the batter. Compare *outside corner*. 1ST USE. 1901 (Burt L. Standish, *Frank Merriwell's School Days*, p.243; Edward J. Nichols).

inside game Syn. of *inside baseball*. 1ST USE. 1906 (*Lajoie's Official Base Ball Guide*, p.13; Edward J. Nichols).

inside hitter A batter who is adept at hitting pitches thrown close to him. 1ST USE. 1932

(*Baseball Magazine*, October, p.496; Edward J. Nichols).

inside-out 1. *v.* To sweep the bat through the strike zone at a slight angle, from the back inside portion of the plate toward the outside front portion, resulting in the ball's being hit to the opposite field. "[Left-handed hitter Will Clark] was doggedly trying to inside-out the ball: keep his bat level and hit the pitch off his fists into left field" (Roger Angell, *The New Yorker*, May 3, 1993, p.52). **2.** *adj.* Said of a batter who tries to inside-out the pitch. Jeff Conine (quoted in *The Baltimore Sun*, Apr. 25, 2004): "[Miguel Cabrera is] more of an inside-out hitter. His real power is to right center and right field."

inside-out swing A swing in which the batter's hands move ahead of the barrel of the bat so that when contact is made with an inside pitch the ball tends to head toward the opposite field; it involves using a short stride and a quick stroke. "The inside-out swing is a means to delay the head of the bat through the strike zone so that the bat hits the ball above, not in front of, the plate" (Keith Hernandez, *Pure Baseball*, 1994, p.48). Wade Boggs and Tony Gwynn were known for their prowess with this swing. "When [left-handed hitter Mo] Vaughn was in Boston, he was known for using an inside-out swing to poke pitches in on his hands off the Green Monster in leftfield" (*Sports Illustrated*, June 24, 2002).

inside pivot A *pivot* in which the shortstop or second baseman receives the ball and then tags second base on the infield side before throwing to first base in an attempt to turn a double play. Compare *outside pivot*.

inside protector An umpire's *chest protector* worn beneath his shirt. National League umpire Bill Klem (*The Sporting News*, Jan. 30, 1913; Peter Morris) claimed to have invented an "aluminum rib protector" worn inside the coat. For much of the 20th century, National League umpires wore inside protectors. The American League adopted the inside protector for all new umpires in 1977.

inside signal A catcher's sign given from inside his thigh. Compare *outside signal*.

inside the ball See *stay inside the ball*.

inside-the-parker Syn. of *inside-the-park home run*.

inside-the-park home run A *home run* in which the ball does not leave the field of play and allows the batter to score without the help of an error. It usually occurs when a fleet-footed batter hits a ball that bounces away from an outfielder. Abbrev. *IPHR*. Syn. *inside-the-parker.*

inside work Syn. of *inside baseball*. IST USE. 1908 (*Baseball Magazine*, July, p.41; Edward J. Nichols).

inspect the ball For an umpire to examine the ball to determine if it is fit for continued play. The inspection commonly is done after a batted ball is returned to the pitcher or if a ball is thrown or batted in the dirt. If the ball is nicked or badly scuffed or has pulled stitches, it is removed from play. A ball may also be inspected if there is suspicion that it has been doctored.

instructional league A special league sponsored by major-league teams to give the youngest and least-experienced professional players further training; a "finishing school" where prospects receive intensive instruction focusing on specific deficiencies. See also *winter instructional league*; *complex league*.

insurance 1. The addition of runs to an existing lead which the opposition is not likely to surmount. Generally, anything up to four runs is considered insurance, as the tying run cannot come to the plate. Syn. *icing*. **2.** The availability of a nonstarting player who can be called on to do a capable job of filling in for a regular. "I want to keep him [infielder Kelly Gruber]. I think it's good insurance" (Baltimore Orioles manager Davey Johnson, quoted in *The Baltimore Sun*, March 29, 1997). **3.** A nonstarting player who can be called on to do a capable job of filling in for a regular. "The Pirates got themselves some insurance by signing Wally Backman" (*St. Petersburg Times*, March 24, 1990). **4.** A pool of capable reserve players.

insurance man A relief pitcher who can put down a rally and turn around what seems to be a losing game.

insurance policy 1. A player who can play more than one position effectively. **2.** A backup player at a given position. When Texas Rangers catcher Bill Haselman became an everyday player after starter Ivan Rodriguez was out for the year, manager Johnny Oates remarked (*The Baltimore Sun*, July 26, 2000), "We signed him as an insurance policy. The premiums are paid and now we have to cash in that policy."

insurance run Any run that is made by a team already ahead late in a game; most often the run that adds to a team's one-run lead.

intangible An unknown, indefinite, or elusive aspect of baseball that is not initially perceived. John Leo (*Charleston Daily Mail*, Apr. 10, 1997) mused, "[It's] mandatory to talk about the mystical aspects of the game known as 'intangibles.' As Oriole[s] scout Jim Russo once mystically observed, 'You play 162 games and a lot of intangibles come to the surface.'"

intensity Concentration and/or determination possessed by a player or a team. "This year, I'm feeling good. I have that intensity again and that hunger" (Tom Herr, quoted in *St. Petersburg Times*, March 27, 1987).

intentional base on balls A base on balls in which the pitcher deliberately throws the fourth ball outside the strike zone and to the catcher outside the catcher's box. This action, almost always a decision made by the manager, is usually taken to a) avoid pitching to a particularly good or hot hitter, b) get to a right-handed batter if the pitcher is right-handed or get to a left-handed batter if the pitcher is left-handed, c) fill first base if it is unoccupied and there are runners on second base and/or third base, thereby setting up a force situation and/or enhancing the chance for a double play, and d) (in the National League) walk the number eight hitter because the pitcher is a much weaker hitter, with the added advantage (sometimes) of forcing the opposing manager to remove a pitcher for a pinch hitter. The catcher must remain in the catcher's box until the pitch is delivered. A batter cannot legally hit a ball if he is outside the batter's box, so there is no chance of one of these pitches being hit unless the pitcher accidentally throws it in or close to the strike zone. Francis X. Clines (*The New York Times*, Oct. 27, 1986) reported this bewildering definition given by a British fan after the 1986 World Series, which had been telecast on Britain's Channel 4: "That means he's deliberately given unplayable to force him to settle for a first-base advance." Compare *unintentional intentional base on balls*. Abbrev. *IBB*. Syn. *intentional walk*; *intentional pass*. ɪsт usᴇ. 1893. "An intentional base on balls to Ewing filled the corners" (*Brooklyn Eagle*, July 6; Peter Morris). ᴜsᴀɢᴇ NOTE. The tactic of issuing an intentional base on balls preceded the introduction of the term by more than 20 years. Greg Rhodes found the following newspaper account of a June 27, 1870, game between the Red Stockings of Cincinnati and the Olympics of Washington: "The pitcher of the Olympics did his best to let George Wright take his first every time on called balls, as he preferred that to George's style of hitting." Peter Morris (*A Game of Inches: The Game on the Field*, 2006, pp.334–40) showed that the intentional base on balls was rare in the 1870s and 1880s, but rose to prominence in the 1890s when offenses began to feature one-run strategies and inside baseball techniques. The early 20th century saw various attempts to ban or hinder the intentional base on balls, such as allowing the batter to take second base.

intentional pass Syn. of *intentional base on balls*. ɪsт usᴇ. 1898 (*New York Tribune*, Apr. 24; Edward J. Nichols).

intentional walk Syn. of *intentional base on balls*. Abbrev. *IW*.

intercept To cut off a throw coming in from the outfield on its way to home plate

interference 1. An act by the team at bat that impedes, hinders, or confuses any fielder attempting to make a play. Examples include: intentionally deflecting the course of a batted or thrown ball; leaving the baseline for the obvious purpose of crashing into the pivot man on a double play; stepping out of the batter's box to hinder a catcher's throw; and failing to avoid a fielder who is attempting to field a batted ball. A specific case of interference at first base occurs when the batter-runner collides with the first baseman receiving the throw in fair territory (if the collision occurs in foul territory, however, the runner is given first base). See also *runner's interference*;

batter's interference; *coach's interference.* Compare *obstruction.* Abbrev. *I.* **2.** An act by a fielder that hinders or prevents a batter from hitting a pitch; e.g., *catcher's interference.* **3.** See *umpire's interference.* **4.** See *spectator interference.*

interim manager An individual picked to fill a team's managerial position on a short-term basis while a long-term, permanent manager is being sought. An interim manager is usually hired from the ranks of a team's coaching staff when the manager is fired during the course of a season.

interleague play Games between teams in different leagues; specif., games between teams in the American League and the National League. Each major-league club may be scheduled to play up to 18 interleague games during a championship season. For generations, interleague play at the major-league level was restricted to exhibition games, the All-Star Game, and the World Series; but this came to an end on June 12, 1997, when the San Francisco Giants and Texas Rangers began the first regular-season interleague game at the Ballpark in Arlington, Arlington, Tex. The appeal of interleague play is based on the appearance of the game's most popular players in otherwise inaccessible markets, the addition of attractive regular-season matchups, and the promotion of local rivalries such as the Mets vs. the Yankees. Negatives include removing some of the grandeur of the World Series, compromising the integrity of the regular-season schedule, and offending traditionalists. Home-team rules apply (use of the designated hitter in American League ballparks; pitchers batting in the National League ballparks). Commissioner Bud Selig (quoted in *The Baltimore Sun*, June 2, 2000): "[Interleague play] is everything I thought it would be from the time Hank Greenberg and Bill Veeck talked about it back in 1948. I think it's really wonderful. I really do." Interleague play in the minor leagues has been part of the Texas League and Mexican League (1959–1961) and the American Association and International League (1988–1991).

intermission The period (usually 20 minutes) between games of a doubleheader.

International Association A professional "trade association" that operated from 1877 to 1880 and posed a threat to the newly organized National League. It was not intended to be a "league," whether major or minor. It originally consisted of seven teams, including two from Canada, and grew to fifteen teams in 1878. After the 1878 season, the association lost its Canadian members and changed its name to the *National Association.* By the 1880 season, the association had only three teams. The National League destroyed the association by signing its players and absorbing entire teams, seducing them to abandon the association in exchange for the benefits of monopoly; from 1879 to 1882, one-half of the National League teams were transplanted from the association. The association charged 25 cents admission, offered speedy sidearm pitching, conducted the first complete season schedule for all teams, had the earliest pitching rotations, and gave cash awards for teams finishing from first to third places (*New York Clipper*, May 11, 1878; Frank Vaccaro). Abbrev. *IA.* Original full name: *International Baseball Association,* 2.

International Baseball Association **1.** Former name (1976–2000) of the *International Baseball Federation.* Abbrev. *IBA.* **2.** *hist.* Original full name of *International Association.*

International Baseball Federation The worldwide governing body for baseball, founded in 1938 and based in Lausanne, Switzerland, that sanctions play between teams sponsored by the national baseball federations of 112 member countries through competition tournaments, including the World Cup of Baseball, the World Baseball Classic (in conjunction with Major League Baseball), and the Olympic baseball tournament (in conjunction with the International Olympic Committee). Formerly known as the *International Baseball Association.* Abbrev. *IBAF.*

International League A minor league (Class AA from 1912 to 1945 and Class AAA since 1946) with franchises primarily in the eastern parts of the United States and Canada (there were teams in Havana, Cuba, from 1954 to 1960 and San Juan, Puerto Rico, in 1961). It was the successor to the *Eastern League*, 1. Abbrev. *IL.*

international play Any game or series of games played by a major-league club or clubs (or a group or groups of major-league players, such as an all-star squad) outside the United States and Canada, or within or without the United States and Canada against a foreign club or clubs.

International Softball Federation [softball term] The worldwide governing body of softball since 1952, headquartered in Plant City, Fla. It organizes and conducts world championship competition in fast pitch (women's and men's), slow pitch (women's, men's, and coed), and modified pitch (men's). National softball associations are members of the federation, which qualifies teams for the Olympics. Abbrev. *ISF.*

Interstate A batting average between .100 and .199 (or a "*buck* and change"), so called in reference to the U.S. Interstate Highway system with numbers less than 100; e.g., I–95 = .195. "It feels good to get off that Interstate" (New York Yankees outfielder Jesse Barfield, who was batting .238, quoted in *The New York Times*, June 18, 1989). Sometimes spelled "interstate."

intestinal fortitude Courage. The term was created around 1937 as a gentle way of saying "guts." This euphemism may not have started in baseball, but it commonly has been used to describe individual action in baseball.

in the bag Safely won.

in the ballpark Said of an action within the confines of the ballpark. EXTENDED USE. Something (a cost estimate, a plan, etc.) that is plausibly accurate and within the realm of consideration. John Ciardi (*Good Words to You*, 1987, p.23): "The image is of a fly ball landing somewhere within the broad expanse of the baseball playing field (i.e., not over the fence and out of reach), hence within a negotiable area." William Safire (*I Stand Corrected*, 1984) noted that the term originated in the early 1960s, where "the ballpark was used as a microcosm: To be 'in the ballpark' (even if out in left field) was to be 'in this world.'" *The Wall Street Journal* (June 19,

1962; *OED*): "Its speed, range, and over-the-weather altitude put it in the same ballpark with the big airline jets." *San Francisco Examiner* (Oct. 8, 1968): "The figures I have indicate this pay-out 'is in the ball park.'" Compare *out of the ballpark.*

in the black Said of a pitch thrown over one of the two lateral edges of home plate. "[Orel] Hershiser never gives you anything right down the middle; he's always *in the black*" (*Los Angeles Times*, May 15, 1994). See also *on the black.*

in the dirt Said of a pitch that hits the ground.

in the field Said of a team or player on the defense. Compare *at the bat.* 1ST USE. 1860 (Constitution and By-Laws of the Excelsior Base Ball Club, p.15; Edward J. Nichols).

in the game Said of a player who is focused on what is occurring on the field. Florida Marlins hitting coach Bill Robinson (quoted in *Sports Illustrated*, May 27, 2002) commented that Mike Lowell has "a tremendous work ethic" and that "his head is in the game."

in the groove **1.** Said of a pitch through the center of the strike zone or one that is easy to hit. "Parkin stuck the ball right in the groove most of the time" (*San Francisco Bulletin*, May 14, 1913; Gerald L. Cohen). See also *groove*, 1. **2.** Describing a player who is consistently performing well. "[Mark Eichhorn] may have been in the finest groove of his pro career" (*The Baltimore Sun*, June 19, 1994). See also *groove*, 3. **3.** Describing a team that is winning a high percentage of its games.

in the hole See various definitions of *hole.*

in the jug *hist.* Said of a baserunner caught in a rundown. "It is discouraging to see the amount of time taken and the number of throws back and forth used by an inexperienced team to retire a runner, 'in the jug'" (George Sisler, *Sisler on Baseball*, 1954; Peter Morris).

in the neighborhood Said of a fielder who is close enough to touch a base in a *neighborhood play*. Rudy Martzke (*USA Today*, Oct. 15, 1986) explained, "A shortstop or second baseman is 'in the neighborhood'—but doesn't touch—second base, because he's avoiding an incoming slide. An out, at umpire's discretion."

in there 1. Said of a pitch in the strike zone. "[Some hitters] can't seem to withstand the temptation to swing at the first one if it's 'in there'" (George Herman Ruth, *Babe Ruth's Own Book of Baseball*, 1928, p.197; Peter Morris). 2. Said of a batted ball that falls in for a hit.

in the slot 1. Syn. of *on deck*. 2. Said of the position of the plate umpire looking over the catcher's shoulder nearest the batter. 3. Said of a pitch that cuts the heart of the plate. See also *through the slot*.

in the soup In trouble; at a disadvantage. "'Brooklyn's in the soup! Brooklyn's in the soup!' yelled the New York cranks as the Association men [the Brooklyn team] marched in from the field" (*The World* [New York], Oct. 30, 1889; Gerald L. Cohen). IST USE. 1889. "Lost in the Soup. No Record Yesterday for the Denver Base Ball Nine—It Probably Rained in Des Moines" (*Rocky Mountain News* [Denver] headline, June 3).

in the tank Said of a contending team that goes into a losing streak.

in-the-vicinity play Syn. of *neighborhood play*.

in the well Said of a fly ball hit to an adept or steady outfielder.

into the stands Said of a ball that is hit into the spectators' seating area and, depending on where it falls, is either a foul ball or a home run.

intrasquad game A game played between members of the same team, commonly during the early days of spring training.

invisible man 1. *hist.* A sportswriter when things are going well for the home team and nothing negative is being written. 2. Syn. of *ghost runner*.

IP Box score abbrev. for *innings pitched*.

IPHR Abbrev. for *inside-the-park home run*.

Irish baseball The style of baseball played by the 1890s Baltimore Orioles, whose manager (Ned Hanlon) and more than half of the team were of Irish extraction.

iron Ballplayer's slang for money.

iron arm The arm of a pitcher who is able to pitch effectively for long periods of time.

iron-armed pitcher Syn. of *Iron Mike*.

iron bat The bat of a player who is able to hit the ball consistently for distance.

iron doughnut See *doughnut*.

iron glove 1. A sloppy fielder, one who is prone to making errors. Jim Bouton (*Ball Four*, 1970) noted that the proper form of address for a player so gifted is: "Give me some steel, baby." *USA Today* headline (June 6, 1986) for a list of leading error-makers: "All-Iron Glove Team." 2. The figurative glove of a player who is not a good fielder. Charlie Hough was quoted on Texas Rangers teammate Pete Incaviglia: "He has a glove contract with U.S. Steel." See also *lead glove*.

iron hand A fielder who plays as though his hands were made of iron. See also *metal*.

iron man 1. A pitcher who works without seeming to tire or lose concentration; a work-horse. The "iron" refers to the durability of a pitcher who can pitch as often as the needs of the team dictate. IST USE. 1900. "Had it not been for [Joe] McGinnity, who has truly proven his title to be called the 'Iron Man,' there would have been a worse tale to tell. But he went in on successive days and pulled out a draw and a victory" (*The Sporting News*, Sept. 15; Barry Popik). USAGE NOTE. It has been popular legend that New York Giant's pitcher Joe McGinnity's nickname was "Iron Man" because he would pitch two complete games back to back: on three occasions in one month during the 1903 season he won both games of a doubleheader. But Noel Hynd (*The Giants of the Polo Grounds*, 1988, p.115) noted that McGinnity did not obtain his nickname through the durability of his arm: "Rather, when he first came to pitch in New York he already had the nickname. It was a relic of his minor league days with Kansas City, where a sportswriter had asked him what he did in the off-season. 'I work in a foundry,' McGinnity had replied. 'I'm an iron man.'" 2. Any player who is tough, not easily injured, and seldom, if ever, misses a game. "The Iron Man" was Lou Gehrig's nickname earned while playing 2,130 consecutive games (1925–1939). The most

MCGINNITY, NEWARK

Iron man. Joe McGinnity's baseball card, issued by the American Tobacco Company. *Library of Congress*

recent "Iron Man" is Cal Ripken Jr. who earned the title by playing in 2,632 consecutive games (1982–1998). **3.** *hist.* The price of admission to a ball game. ETYMOLOGY. Joseph McBride (*High & Inside*, 1980, p.59) noted, "Silver dollars were once called 'iron men,' and $1 was formerly a common price for a general-admission ticket." The term showed up often in T.A. "TAD" Dorgan's cartoons: "You know papa left me two million iron men and I must spend it some way" (*San Francisco Examiner*, Aug. 22, 1911; Peter Tamony).

Iron Mike A generic name for a mechanical *pitching machine* that threw only overhand fastballs. Sometimes called "Warren Spahns" (after the pitcher with a great overhand delivery), Iron Mikes were popular in the 1950s.

Although mechanical pitching machines had been in existence since the late 19th century, it was not until the Brooklyn Dodgers used one in their spring-training camp just after World War II that they became accepted. *The New York Times Magazine* (March 18, 1956) described how the mechanism worked: "An attendant feeds . . . baseballs into a trough. A belt conveyor feeds them one at a time to Iron Mike. His mechanized arm swings back and then sweeps directly overhand, slinging the ball toward the plate." *Time* magazine (Apr. 17, 1950) reported on a highly publicized game between Wake Forest College (which called its apparatus "Iron Mike") and North Carolina State Univ. in which both teams batted against the machine. Syn. *iron-armed pitcher.*

irregular 1. A player who is normally found on the bench; one who is not a regular starter. IST USE. 1908. "One by one the Detroit irregulars are drawing their assignments" (*Detroit Free Press*, March 4; Peter Morris). **2.** A player for a ragtag team of amateur baseball or softball players put together to face a team that regularly plays together. Irregulars are often given special compensatory opportunities to score. An item in the company newsletter (Sept. 1972) of the Foster Manufacturing Co., Wilton, Maine, told of a formula for irregular scoring that allowed "7 runs for each one scored by a player over 35 years of age, and 7½ runs for each run scored by a player 35 years old who is also overweight 35 or more pounds."

irregular regular An off-and-on type of player.

irrevocable waivers A form of *waivers* in which the club placing the player on waivers cannot withdraw the waiver request if another team claims the player. If the player is claimed by another club, the player's former team receives no compensation. Compare *revocable waivers.* Syn. *outright waivers; special waivers.*

I–70 Series Nickname for the 1985 all-Missouri World Series between the St. Louis Cardinals and the Kansas City Royals, whose cities are linked by Interstate Highway 70. See also *Show-Me Series.*

ISF [softball term] Abbrev. for *International Softball Federation.*

ISO Abbrev. for *isolated power.*

isolated power A measure of a player's performance in hitting for extra bases. One method for computing isolated power is to subtract a player's number of hits from his number of total bases, and then divide by his number of official at-bats. Another method is to subtract a player's batting average from his slugging percentage. In some extremes, Babe Ruth's career isolated power was .348, whereas Roy Thomas' was .099. Isolated power is a better indicator of raw power than *slugging percentage* because it is not affected by the batter's ability to get hits. As a consequence, a low-average slugger may have a mediocre slugging percentage but very good isolated power. The term and concept were devised by Allan Roth and Branch Rickey and introduced in Rickey's sabermetric classic "Goodby to Some Old Baseball Ideas" (*Life* magazine, Aug. 2, 1954). Compare *power factor.* Abbrev. *ISO.*

issue To walk a batter. IST USE. 1902. "[Case Patten] rarely issues passes" (*The Sporting Life,* Aug. 9; Peter Morris).

"it ain't over 'til it's over" An aphorism that summarizes baseball's ability to go down to the last moment of play, until the last man is out. It is also one of Yogi Berra's most famous lines, which has become a baseball axiom. "Yogi's line gets better and better," was the reaction of John McNamara to the late-inning heroics on display during the 1986 American League Championship Series (*Cleveland Plain Dealer,* Oct. 16, 1986). EXTENDED USE. Widely applied to the world at large.

"it only takes one" A familiar cry to a batter to get a hit to score a run. According to Lee Allen (*The Hot Stove League,* 1955, pp.115–16), the *Kansas City Star* in 1900 attributed the line "it only takes one to hit it!" to short-stop Herman Long, who claimed that he first uttered it while playing for Kansas City of the American Association in 1889.

"it's only a game" The ritualized reassurance given to those (esp. youngsters) who have lost a game that it is, in fact, not the end of the world. It is deemed a "famous speech by [Little League] parents in a station wagon on the way home" (Marian Edelman Borden, *The New York Times,* undated). "Don't forget: it's only a game, not a sacrament" (Bryan Di Salvatore, "Baseball," *Elysian Fields Quarterly,* Fall 2006, p.30).

ivory **1.** One or more skilled ballplayers who are considered a valuable commodity. "Cuba, which long has developed 'ivory' for the American market, has splendid representatives in Conrado Marrero, Sandy Consuegra, and Minnie Minoso" (Fred G. Lieb, *Baseball Magazine,* Aug. 1953). "[Ivory is] a natural growth found in the bush league jungle, and polished up in the major league" (R.E. Sherwood, *Baseball Magazine,* Sept. 1913). USAGE NOTE. The link between the hard, white matter (a variety of dentine) and baseball players is that both are valuable commodities. **2.** A high-priced rookie. **3.** One or more dumb players. "Chick Gandil . . . was such a valuable addition to the ivory collection when he first tried to break into the big leagues that President [Frank J.] Navin of the [Detroit] Tigers turned him down when he had a chance to get him. Navin thought that such a thick-skulled player as Gandil evidently was could never develop into a major leaguer" (*Detroit Times,* reprinted in *San Francisco Bulletin,* May 1, 1913).

ivory-headed Dumb. Martin Rothan (*New Baseball Rules and Decisions,* 1947) explained that an ivory-headed player is one "who doesn't act quick, makes the wrong play, does not use his brains." USAGE NOTE. Thomas P. McDonald (letter, Apr. 13, 1991) notes that "bone-headed" is a common expression for dumbness: "Perhaps 'ivory-headed' derives in some convoluted way from the common misconception that ivory is bone, although as far as I know, either term could have been derived from the other. But there are certainly instances in which ivory and bone are used in synonymous fashion (e.g., piano keys, which are called both bones and ivories)." Tris Speaker was quoted by Donald Gropman (*Say It Ain't So, Joe!,* 1979): "I pulled an ivory play, a boner pure and simple." Note the contrary use of "ivory" as signifying both a dumb player and a skillful player (see *ivory*).

ivory hunter A scout who searches for young, talented players; one who "seeks diamond phenoms" (*The Sporting News*, Oct. 13, 1913). "The baseball scouts, who call themselves ivory hunters, met the other night . . . to honor John J. 'Patty' Cottrell, voted Pro Scout of the Year" (Art Rosenbaum, *San Francisco Chronicle*, Feb. 15, 1974; Peter Tamony). See also *ebony hunter.* IST USE. 1913. "Batting out of place and winning a game while the St. Louis players looked on, Frank Chance proved conclusively that ivory hunters are wasting time in Africa with St. Louis, Mo., U.S.A. on the Rand-McNally" (*San Francisco Bulletin*, May 31; Gerald L. Cohen). ETYMOLOGY. The term "ivory" connoted a dumb player; hence, an ivory hunter was one who observed bonehead players, as noted in *The Washington Post* (July 27, 1913; Peter Morris): "Baseball scouts have been dubbed 'ivory hunters,' because of the great quantity of thick-headed players turned out under the old system. It has been considered a term of opprobrium by some to be called a scout." EXTENDED USE. Student slang for a corporate recruiter who visits college campuses.

ivory-nut A minor-league player available for the major leagues. "Fruit of the 'bush' leagues 'palmed' off on the managers of the 'big time' clubs, thereby proving that the said manager often 'falls' for the 'nut' game; hence the phrase, 'he takes the palm'" (R.E. Sherwood, *Baseball Magazine*, Sept. 1913). ETYMOLOGY. The seed of the palm tree.

IW Scorecard abbrev. for *intentional walk.*

J

jab 1. To hit the ball for a short distance. 1ST USE. 1920 (*Spalding's Official Base Ball Guide*, p.65; Edward J. Nichols). 2. For a catcher to catch a ball in a jerky manner. "[Colorado Rockies coach Fred Kendall is] cutting my body movement down behind the plate so I don't distract the pitcher, and keeping me relaxed so I'm not jabbing at pitches" (catcher Ben Petrick, quoted in *Baseball America*, May 29–June 11, 2000; Peter Morris). 3. For an infielder to stab at a ground ball.

jabber An infielder who stabs at ground balls. Examples include Ryne Sandberg, Jackie Robinson, and Chase Utley (*Sports Illustrated*, Aug. 14, 2006).

jack 1. *n.* A home run. "I won't ever bunt again. I'm hitting jacks now" (Jason Kendall, quoted in *The Baltimore Sun*, Nov. 6, 1999). 2. *v.* To hit a home run. "A year ago he [Junior Spivey] probably would have tried to jack that ball into the seats" (Bob Brenly, quoted in *ESPN The Magazine*, July 8, 2002). 3. *v.* To remove a pitcher from the game. Syn. *jerk*, 2. 1ST USE. 1931 (*The World* [New York], Feb. 25; Edward J. Nichols).

Jackie Robinson Award Since 1987, the official name for the *Rookie of the Year Award*, 1, named for the player who was the first Rookie of the Year in 1947.

Jackie Robinson Day April 15, celebrated by all major-league clubs, in recognition of Robinson's breaking the color line on that date in 1947, when he debuted with the Brooklyn Dodgers.

jackpot Syn. of *grand slam*, 1.

jackrabbit 1. Syn. of *rabbit*, 1. "I was watching the game on TV the other day and it was amazing the way the Cardinal outfielders were running around out there. Jackrabbits. Jackrabbits all over the place" (Atlanta Braves general manager Bobby Cox, quoted in *New York Post*, June 29, 1987). 2. Syn. of *jackrabbit ball*. 3. The quality in a jackrabbit ball that, when hit, makes it travel a long distance. "There was no jackrabbit in the ball throughout his [Owen "Chief" Wilson's] career" (Roy Blount Jr., *Sports Illustrated*, Aug. 9, 1993). See also *rabbit*, 4.

jackrabbit ball A baseball that seems to carry farther than most regular balls. "Today, playing deep, against the jack-rabbit ball, the garden men make many a 'sensational' catch" (Ty Cobb, *My Life in Baseball*, 1961, p.229). "The next year [1930] we had the so-called jackrabbit ball. . . . I don't know whether it was a jackrabbit ball or not. I don't believe in that too much. It's the same old story: If a guy's hitting a lot of home runs, they rap the baseball" (National League umpire Beans Reardon, quoted in Larry R. Gerlach, *The Men in Blue*, 1980, p.14). See also *rabbit ball*, 1. Syn. *jackrabbit*, 2. 1ST USE. 1912 (*New York Tribune*, Sept. 11; Edward J. Nichols).

jake 1. *v.* To loaf or to stall; to refuse to play because of a real or imagined injury. New York Yankees manager Lou Piniella accused Rickey Henderson of "jaking it" and asked to have him traded (*Tampa Tribune*, Aug. 12, 1987). 2. *n.* A player who is often out of the lineup because of a real or imagined ailment, or a feigned injury; a player who will not exert himself or give his best at all times, a player who is given to loafing or stalling. Before Houston Astros pitcher J.R. Richard was found to have a potentially fatal blood

Jake. Jake Stahl, 1912. *Andy Moresund Collection*

clot, "they were saying that he was 'jaking,' that he could have played but didn't want to, that he was letting down his teammates" (Art Spander, *San Francisco Examiner*, Aug. 1, 1980; Peter Tamony). Syn. *jaker.* IST USE. 1927. According to Frank Graham (*New York Sun*, July 18), the term "jake," meaning one who stalls, was applied by Earle Combs to New York Yankees teammate Tony Lazzeri. Combs remarked, "I never thought you'd be a jake." Lazzeri replied, "I'm not a jake. Hug [Yankees manager Miller Huggins] just told me [Mark] Koenig was going to play short-stop and [Ray] Morehart second base. What could I do?" ETYMOLOGY. There is universal agreement that the term derived from Garland "Jake" Stahl, an American League first baseman in the early part of the 20th century; but there is some dispute as to why. One theory, favored by *The Sporting News*, Hy Turkin, and others, says that Stahl was an aggressive player with a lot of hustle whose trip to eponymity came about because his

name was pronounced "stall." Thomas P. Shea (*Baseball Nicknames*, 1946) insisted that when Stahl played for the Boston Red Sox he refused to play first base because of a bad foot, and that is where the loafing connection was made. Alfred H. Spink (*The National Game*, 2nd ed., 1911, p.186) observed, "If Stahl could get a case of swelled head and begin to think he is really as good as he is, he would be the greatest of them all. Modesty has held him back and I have feared he would finish his career without finding out how good he is."

jaker Syn. of *jake*, 2.

jam 1. *n.* A difficult situation during a game. Usually it is said that a pitcher is in a "jam" when the opposing team is in a position to score, such as when the bases are loaded with no outs. "[Randy Johnson] escaped a bases-loaded jam with only one run scoring" (*The New York Times*, Oct. 23, 2001). See also *crunch*. Syn. *hook*, 9. **2.** *v.* See *jam the batter*. **3.** *v.* To load the bases. IST USE. 1920 (*New York Times*, October; Edward J. Nichols). **4.** *n./hist.* A rally. "When 'the jam is on' a rally is under way" (H.G. Salsinger, *Baseball Digest*, Aug. 1945). **5.** *v.* To hit the ball (*The Sporting Life*, Nov. 29, 1913).

jamball A ball pitched inside in such a way that it is difficult for a batter to hit it solidly or get good wood on it.

jammer A fastball on the fists; a fastball or slider that moves in on the batter.

jam sandwich Throwing a pitch near the batter's fists with a fastball (John Maffei, *Padres Magazine*, 1993, p.21).

jam shot 1. A base hit blooped over the infield on an inside pitch or one off the fists. "We've given up a ton of jam-shot hits where we were trying to pitch in" (Ray Miller, quoted in *The Baltimore Sun*, Apr. 21, 1999). **2.** A brushback pitch or a knockdown pitch.

jam the batter To throw the ball close to the batter and near his hands, making it difficult for him to hit successfully and keeping him off balance; to throw inside. The intention is not to hit the batter, but rather to make him a lot less effective by forcing him to hit with the lower end of his bat. "[Right-handed pitcher Scott Erickson] has jammed left-handed hitters more often with fastballs" (*The Baltimore Sun*, Oct. 13, 1996).

January 8 Eight Free agents who tested the owners' resolve in the collusion-wracked 1986–1987 off-season by refusing to re-sign with their previous clubs. Allowing the January 8 deadline to pass meant that the players could not return to their previous teams until at least May 1, a considerable risk since they were receiving no offers from other clubs. "[Bob] Horner, [Rich] Gedman, [Bob] Boone, [Tim] Raines, and four other players would become known as the 'January 8 Eight': players who went beyond the signing deadline and into the teeth of collusion" (John Helyar, *Lords of the Realm*, 1994; Peter Morris). The players met with varied fates. Raines, for example, agreed to a three-year contract with the Montreal Expos, but Horner rejected San Diego's offer and did not sign.

Japanese baseball See *bēsubōru*.

Japanese liner *hist.* A *Texas Leaguer* in the Pacific Coast League.

jar To bat a ball hard. To "jar the pitcher" is to bat the ball freely (John B. Foster, in *Collier's New Dictionary of the English Language*, 1908).

jardín Spanish for "outfield."

jardín central Spanish for "center field."

jardín derecho Spanish for "right field."

jardín izquierdo Spanish for "left field."

jardinero Spanish for "outfielder."

jaw To argue with, or complain to, the umpire. IST USE. 1891. "There are a great many base ball players who can wield the pen as skillfully as they can 'jaw' the umpire" (*The Sporting News*, June 20; Peter Morris).

Jawn Titus *hist.* A spectacular catch; a *circus catch.* IST USE. 1917 (*American Magazine*, July, p.43; Edward J. Nichols). ETYMOLOGY. Nichols noted that the derivation is uncertain, but "may refer to a player named [John] Titus [Philadelphia Phillies outfielder, 1903–1912] . . . who may have been known for making sensational catches"; see *Spalding's Official Base Ball Guide*, 1908, p.280.

jay *hist.* An inexperienced player. From *The Sporting News* (Oct. 25, 1890; Peter Morris): "Miller, Wilson and Cain are jay ball players. Miller is left handed, has no speed, no control of the ball, and was hammered by every club he faced, as was also Wilson." IST USE. 1887. "Fritz Pfeffer seemed amazed when called out for obstructing the batted ball. The Louisville German thought he had jays to deal with" (*The World* [New York], Aug. 26; Gerald L. Cohen). ETYMOLOGY. According to Cohen (*Studies in Slang*, part 2, 1989), this derogatory term derived from the bird that draws special attention because of its beautiful plumage. By transference, a jay was a gaudily dressed person, esp. a gullible or unsophisticated country person who dressed in the city in garish clothing; hence, a greenhorn or person lacking experience in city ways.

Jays Short for *Blue Jays*, 1.

jazz Pep, energy, fighting spirit, vim, vigor. "The poor old [San Francisco] Seals have lost their 'jazz' and don't know where to find it. It's a fact . . . that the 'jazz,' the pepper, the old life, has been either lost or stolen, and that the San Francisco club of today is made up of 'jazzless' Seals" (E.T. "Scoop" Gleeson, *San Francisco Bulletin*, March 29, 1913). Umpire Steve Palermo (quoted in *Sports Illustrated*, Feb. 27, 1995): "There's a thing called the jazz. At 7:35, when you hear the national anthem and you know you have 40,000 people coming to your office, it's just an incredible adrenaline rush. That's the jazz of it all."

USAGE NOTE. According to Gerald L. Cohen's detailed treatment of the term "jazz" (*Comments on Etymology*, Oct.–Nov. 2005), the story of this term began in a baseball context in San Francisco in 1913 at a time when no attestations of the term existed in reference to music. Jazz music was already being played, of course, but it was not yet so named by early 1913. In its baseball context, the term "jazz" existed for several years in California; ongoing research will clarify whether this baseball term spread beyond California's borders, but in any case, baseball "jazz" (pep, fighting spirit, etc.) was soon crowded out in popular consciousness by the musical term "jazz." During 1913 spring training of the Class AA San Francisco Seals, sportswriter Gleeson adopted the term, which he acquired from fellow San Francisco journalist Spike Slattery. Slattery had told Gleeson of a crap-shooting game he had witnessed in which one player issued the incantation to lady luck, "Come on, the old jazz!" Gleeson first used the term in a derogatory sense (roughly, "hot air" or "baloney"): "[George] McCarl has been heralded all along the line as a 'busher' but now it develops that this dope is very much to the 'jazz'" (*San Francisco Bulletin*, March 3, 1913). Three days later, Gleeson had a complete change of heart and began to use the term in a favorable way, observing that the Seals might have lacked talent, but they had pep and fighting spirit—i.e., the "jazz"—and this jazz would give them a fighting chance for the pennant: "What is the 'jazz'? Why, it's a little of that 'old life,' the 'gin-i-ker,' the 'pep,' otherwise known as the enthusiasm. A grain of 'jazz' and you feel like going out and eating your way through Twin Peaks. It's that spirit which makes ordinary ball players step around the Lajoies and Cobbs. The Seals have it and we venture to say that everybody in the big town who has ever stopped to 'pan' the San Francisco club in the past several months will be inoculated with it by the time the coming string of games is over" (*San Francisco Bulletin*, March 6, 1913). Ernest J. Hopkins praised the "futurist word" (*San Francisco Bulletin*, Apr. 5, 1913): "This remarkable and satisfactory-sounding word . . . means something like life, vigor, energy, effervescence of spirit, joy, pep, magnetism, verve, virility, ebulliency, courage, happiness—oh, what's the use?—JAZZ. . . . 'Jazz' is at home in bar or ballroom; it is a true American." The term evidently was intended to serve as a lexical rabbit's foot for the Seals.

Cohen noted an earlier attestation of the term, discovered by George Thompson, in the *Los Angeles Times* (Apr. 2, 1912), in which Portland Beavers pitcher Ben Henderson was quoted: "I got a new curve this year and I'm goin' to pitch one or two of them tomorrow. I call it the Jazz ball because it wobbles and you simply can't do anything with it." On Apr. 3, the *Los Angeles Times* referred to Henderson's "'jass' ball." Cohen believes the 1912 attestations are "insignificant, being distinguished by their isolation; thus far no other attestations have surfaced in 1912. . . . Most likely Henderson's 'jazz ball' . . . was not really a new pitch but represented a bit of high-spirited malarkey for Opening Day of the 1912 season. . . . My own guess is that Henderson's allegedly wobbling 'jazz' pitch is connected with jags (bouts of intoxication). . . . Henderson was plagued by alcoholism (hence perhaps his having the term 'jags' very much on his mind)."

Cohen, following in the footsteps of Peter Tamony (*Jazz, the Word, and Its Extension to Music: A Reprise*, 1968) and Dick Holbrook (*Storyville*, Dec. 1973–Jan. 1974, pp.46–58), traced the use of the term from its San Francisco baseball context in 1913 to its first known musical attestation on July 11, 1915, in the *Chicago Daily Tribune*. The term was applied to the syncopated rag played by Art Hickman (an entertainer who was present at the Seals 1913 training camp) and his band in San Francisco. Musician Bert Kelly, who was with Hickman in 1914, claimed to have brought the term that year to Chicago, and thence to national and international recognition. Cohen credits David Shulman for conclusively showing the *Oxford English Dictionary*'s (2nd ed., 1989) 1909 attestation for the origin of the term to be invalid; and he cites Barry Popik who noted that the treatment of the term "jazz" by Geoffrey C. Ward and Ken Burns (*Jazz: A History of America's Music*, 2000) was "thoroughly erroneous." (Gerald L. Cohen)

jeep *hist.* A small, fast player in the immediate post–World War II era.

jellyball Syn. of *greaseball*.

jelly bean *hist.* A new, inexperienced player; a *rookie*, 1.

jelly-legs A batter whose knees buckle when he is fooled by an inside breaking ball.

jerk 1. *v.* To pull a high, inside pitch for an extra-base hit or home run. "He'll [Robin Yount] spray one down the rightfield line, he'll gap one to right center, then he'll jerk one to left" (Don Sutton, quoted in *Sports Illustrated*, Sept. 27, 1982). 2. *v.* Syn. of *jack*, 3. 1ST USE. 1912 (*New York Tribune*, Apr. 21; Edward J. Nichols). 3. *v./hist.* For a pitcher to deliver a ball with a motion in which the arm touches the side of the body, thereby catapulting the ball toward the batter. "A 'jerked' ball is a ball delivered swiftly from the hand by the arm first touching the side of the pitcher; if the arm does not touch his side the ball is not 'jerked'" (Henry Chadwick, *Ball Player's Chronicle*, July 18, 1867; Peter Morris). Jerking the ball originally resulted in a balk, but became legal in 1872. Presumably, the advantage in jerking the ball was to make it difficult for the batter to pick up the pitch by looking at the pitcher's hand. IST USE. 1860. "The ball must be pitched, not jerked nor thrown to the bat" (National Association of Base Ball Players, Rules and Regulations, Sec. 6). **4.** *n./hist.* The touching of the body by the pitcher's arm when he swings it forward in delivering the ball. "A jerk, in the ordinary sense of the term, is made when the elbow of the arm holding the ball, touches the side of the person so delivering it" (*New York Clipper*, June 3, 1865; Robert H. Schaefer). **5.** *v.* To *frame the pitch*.

jerker *hist.* A pitcher who jerked the ball.

jersey A long-sleeved pullover that may be worn under a player's uniform shirt.

Jesse James An *umpire*, 1. It is a players' term because the umpire "robs" from them. Before there were three umpires for each game, it was common to refer to the two umps as "Jesse and Frank" or "the James Brothers."

Jesse James single A base hit that is allowed when a batted ball strikes an umpire.

jewel *hist.* A good ballplayer. IST USE. 1888 (*New York Press*, June 3; Edward J. Nichols).

J.G. Taylor Spink Award An annual award established in 1962 for "meritorious contributions to baseball writing." It is voted on by a committee of Baseball Writers' Association of America members. Award winners are honored during the annual National Baseball Hall of Fame induction ceremonies; but contrary to public opinion and newspaper accounts, they are not inducted into a "writers' wing" of the Hall of Fame. (The list of honorees is displayed in an exhibit in the National Baseball Museum in Cooperstown,

N.Y.) The award is named for the longtime publisher of *The Sporting News*, whose death on Dec. 7, 1962, precipitated the award. Syn. *Spink Award.*

Jim Dandy An admirable person, thing, or feat; a prime example; something of superior quality or excellence. "He responded to the deep and heartfelt 'rooting' of the 3,500 spectators with a hit that in baseball parlance can only be designated as a Jim Dandy" (*The World* [New York], Aug. 7, 1888; Gerald L. Cohen). IST USE. 1887. "The Giants gave the local patrons of the game a couple of surprises during the past week, and whereas on Wednesday night they were proclaimed 'Jim Dandy' players, they were on Thursday declared to be 'no good'" (*The World* [New York], June 19; Gerald L. Cohen). USAGE NOTE. The term, which the *Oxford English Dictionary* traced in a nonbaseball context to 1887, shows up quickly in baseball writing. In fact, Cohen (*Studies in Slang*, part 2, 1989) wrote that his work on the baseball columns of *The World* (New York) "provides the startling indication that 'jim-dandy' either arose in baseball speech or was spread into standard English by it."

jimjam *hist.* A 19th-century term for a *wild pitch*.

jineger *hist.* Vigor or energy. The term may have derived from "ginger," "vinegar," or a combination of the two. Also spelled "jinnegar"; "jinniger."

Jints A colloquialism for the Giants when they were in New York City. To call the Giants "the Jints" was to use a friendly nickname.

jinx **1.** *n.* A person or influence that brings bad luck; a run of bad luck. "The Portland catcher reached for the ball, but the jinx knocked it out of his hand" (*San Francisco Bulletin*, Apr. 14, 1913; Gerald L. Cohen). See also *hoodoo*, 1; *whammy*; *sophomore jinx*. IST USE. 1908. John B. Foster (in *Collier's New Dictionary of the English Language*, p.1008) defined "jinx" as "another name for a ball player's superstitious ideas." **2.** *v.* To create bad luck. "Most of them think a change in hotels would surely 'jinx' or hoodoo them" (*Literary Digest*, May 9, 1914; Peter Tamony).

USAGE NOTE. "Jinx" is a 20th-century word that was so strongly associated with the game of baseball that it appeared as baseball slang rather than general slang as late as 1927 (so identified by V. Samuels, *American Speech*, Feb. 1927). Baseball reporters and cartoonists popularized the term during the 1910 and 1911 seasons. "Nearly all base ball players are superstitious and many of them fear a 'jinks'" (*The Sporting News*, June 23, 1910; Peter Morris). Gabriel Schechter (*Victory Faust*, 2000, p.39, 108, 115) cited three 1911 instances (Sid Mercer in the *New York Globe*, headline in the *New York American*, and Damon Runyon). The term is still used: *USA Today Baseball Weekly* (Sept. 27–Oct. 3, 1991) referred to the "Blue Jays' jinx" (noting Toronto's failures in the 1985, 1987, and 1989 seasons); and the term is applied to those doomed souls who appear on the covers of *Sports Illustrated* (Chicago White Sox pitcher Wilbur Wood was 13–3 when he made a 1973 cover appearance, then lost eight of his next nine decisions).

ETYMOLOGY. Barry A. Popik and Gerald L. Cohen (*Comments on Etymology*, Oct. 2001, p.242) cited an 1859 poem "More Copy" in which a newspaper clerk named Jinks "drives a colleague to near distraction by repeatedly insisting that the editor wants him to provide more copy"; but since there is no story to be had, Jinks' continuing insistence causes him to be referred to as "our devil" and his name generalized to denote bad luck. Alfred H. Holt (*Phrase and Word Origins*, 1936) linked the use of the term in baseball (the *Oxford English Dictionary* cited a 1912 usage by Christy Mathewson) for "a hoodoo of some sort" with the wrynecked woodpecker or "jynx," which was associated with charms and spells; according to Holt, "that particular bird was sometimes used to cast charms." Webb Garrison (*Why You Say It*, 1954) wrote of the bird: "Medieval scholars considered it to have special links with occult forces. So jynx feathers were widely used in making 'philtres, allurements, baits and enticements' for the lovelorn. Jumping the Atlantic, the name of the wizard's bird [of preference]

became linked with voodoo and other forms of black magic hence, any symbol of bad luck is known as a jinx."

EXTENDED USE. Bad luck in all realms.

jit (pron. "heet") Spanish for "base hit."

J. Louis Comiskey Memorial Award The official name of the *Rookie of the Year Award* presented by the Chicago chapter of the Baseball Writers' Association of America (BBWAA) for 1944 through 1947. The J. Louis Comiskey Memorial Award was resurrected in 1950 with new criteria, honoring "long and meritorious service to baseball" in the tradition of Comiskey, president/treasurer of the Chicago White Sox from 1932 to 1939.

job lot *hist.* One of a group of diverse or sundry players. From *The World* (New York) (July 25, 1890; Gerald L. Cohen): "For indomitable pluck and earnest work no team in either League can compare with Capt. Ward's Brooklyn Club. At the beginning of the season the players were called 'job lots,' and other pet names. To-day they stand second in the Players' League race and have won game after game which other teams would have abandoned in despair." USAGE NOTE. The Chicago Park District (Burnham Park) (*Baseball*, 1938) defined "job lots" as "a Jewish player." ETYMOLOGY. A parcel of assorted goods sold as a single transaction; a miscellaneous quantity of odds and ends.

jock 1. An athlete. ETYMOLOGY. From "jockstrap." 2. *n.* Short for *jockstrap.* IST USE. 1916. "Ask your dealer, and if he will not supply you with Mizpah Jock No. 44, send us 75¢" (classified advertisement, *Baseball Magazine*, August, p.120; *OED*). 3. See *get jocked.*

jockey 1. *n.* A player who bedevils or "rides" the opposition; sometimes called a *bench jockey* because the heckler often comes from the dugout where he also "rides" the bench or the pine. Defined by William Morris (*It's Easy to Increase Your Vocabulary*, 1957) as "A loud voiced, often sharp-witted player who continuously ridicules the opposing players with well-timed references to their real or supposed inadequacies of antecedents." IST USE. 1927. "A 'jockey' . . . is a bench-warming player whose chief duty . . .

is to 'ride' opposing players. And they do some tall riding . . . ply[ing] the verbal whip and from the first pitch to the last putout" (John Kieran, *The New York Times*, May 26). ETYMOLOGY. An obvious and neat play on the word "ride." **2.** *v.* To heckle the opposition and/or the umpires; "to reveal an opponent's private life—but loudly, and sarcastically when possible" (Gordon S. "Mickey" Cochrane, *Baseball: The Fan's Game*, 1939, p.189).

jockeying 1. Taunting or yelling derisive comments at opposing players and umpires. Mark Kram (*Detroit Free Press*, Apr. 3, 1983): "Jockeying was considered accepted behavior, a component of attack. Often crude, viciously personal—for example, you were a natural target if you were of strong ethnic origin or your wife just ran off with the insurance agent—jockeying was intended to throw you off your game, dig at your concentration and thus gain for the successful practitioner a narrow, if not decided, psychological edge." IST USE. 1928. "Players rag each other a lot. 'Jockeying' we call it in baseball" (George Herman Ruth, *Babe Ruth's Own Book of Baseball*, p.296; Peter Morris). **2.** *hist.* The practice of professional players in the early days of baseball who traveled about to play for money (*New York Herald*, July 11, 1869; Edward J. Nichols).

jockey pickoff A *pickoff play* in which the shortstop bluffs toward second base, then starts back toward his position, and then makes another break toward the base (O.H. Vogel, in *Ins and Outs of Baseball*, 1952; Peter Morris). Compare *block pickoff*.

jockey silks A derisive name for the bright uniform colors worn by American Association (1882–1891) players (Jonathan Fraser Light, *The Cultural Encyclopedia of Baseball*, 1997).

jock's itch Nickname for "terminal adolescent syndrome" among professional ballplayers. The term was introduced by Tom House (*The Jock's Itch: The Fast-Track Private World of the Professional Ballplayer*, 1989), a former major-league pitcher with a PhD in psychology: "Have you ever had an itch you couldn't scratch? Athletes have one for life, a 'jock's itch' that a ton of Tinactin won't cure.

It's a malady that leads to infidelity, drug abuse, alcoholism, bankruptcy, and most of the other fashionable disasters you hear about today. It's a condition that causes thirty-year-old men to act the same way they did when they were thirteen. . . . A burning itch to have it all, right now, before the quarter runs out and the ride is over."

jockstrap An elastic undergarment worn to protect the male genitals in active sport and to hold the protective cup in place. Syn. *jock*, 2; *athletic supporter*. IST USE. 1919. "You can enjoy perfect comfort and freedom. Schnoter's Suspensories and Jock Straps have gained their widespread popularity by quality, wear, fit and low price" (*The Billboard* [Cincinnati], Dec. 20; Peter Tamony). ETYMOLOGY. John Thorn (personal communication, Oct. 5, 2006) suggests the term derived from Jacques Strop, a supporting character in the French plays *L'Auberge des Adrets* (1823) by Benjamin Antier and *Robert Macaire* (1834) by Frederick Lemaître.

jockstrap sniffing A derogatory term for a sportswriter's quest for a story or good quote on an otherwise slow day. Leonard Shecter (*The Jocks*, 1969, p.55; Charles D. Poe) observed that the term refers to the fact that sportswriters "must go to the clubhouse and elicit clever quotes from dull men." Tom House (*The Jock's Itch*, 1989) remarked that "many players look at writers as obnoxious, overweight jock-sniffers."

Jody The name of the man that Negro league players feared was romancing their wives or girlfriends while they were on the road. "He's the man at home, the one comes in the back door when you go out the front" (Jim Bland, quoted in Alan J. Pollock, *Barnstorming to Heaven*, 2006, p.64; Peter Morris). Pollock commented, "All black teams knew Jody and discussed him regularly."

Joe Bush A college ballplayer, esp. one who shows his lack of experience. See also *bush*, 3.

Joe College An individual who typifies the enthusiasm of collegiate athletics. ETYMOLOGY. J.L. Kuethe (*American Speech*, June 1932), writing on college slang, reported that "Joe" was a "term used to designate anyone whose real name is unknown" and "when used with a place or profession 'Joe' indicates a perfect example of the type connected with that place or profession." Thus, "Joe College" is the perfect specimen of "the college man."

Joe Cronin Award An annual award presented by the American League to a player who has made a "significant achievement." It is named for the former American League president and Hall of Fame shortstop.

Joe Gum A player who makes costly mistakes (Chicago Park District [Burnham Park], *Baseball*, 1938).

Joe Orsulak An unorthodox or "God-awful looking" swing, one where the batter is fooled by the pitch and "lunges, spins and nearly falls down," in the manner of Pittsburgh Pirates outfielder Joe Orsulak (Bob Hertzel, *Baseball Digest*, Jan. 1987). The term was coined by Pirates outfielder R.J. Reynolds in 1986.

Joe Quote A player who talks a lot, esp. to the press; a *motormouth*.

John Anderson play The particular boner committed when a runner attempts to steal an occupied base. The term is named for the outfielder/first baseman who, while playing for the St. Louis Browns against the New York Highlanders on Sept. 24, 1903, supposedly tried to steal second base with the bases loaded, and was thrown out. However, press accounts (e.g., *New York Sun*, Sept. 25; Peter Morris) indicate that Anderson, having taking an aggressive lead, was picked off by the catcher throwing the ball to first base. In the end, Anderson's nonattempted steal became his most famous play.

John Fan *hist.* A typical male enthusiast. IST USE. 1927. "When John Fan goes out to see his favorite game in 1927, he will have such infinite variety that his eyes will be bewildered at first as he looks about him" (*The Sporting News*, Feb. 17; Peter Morris).

Johnny Ward *hist.* A ballplayer who reports late to practice. The act was performed frequently by John Montgomery Ward (Mike Sowell, *July 2, 1903*, 1992, p.79).

Johnny Wholestaff The collective group of a team's pitchers who are available for the decisive game of a postseason series (Al Leiter,

Fox telecast of the National League Championship Series, Oct. 15, 2003; Peter Morris).

Johnson An all-purpose slang term for penis used in the clubhouse and applied to mean almost anything; e.g., "mammoth Johnson" (bat), "four-run Johnson" (grand slam), and "slider-Johnson" (nasty slider) (Dick Kaegel, *The Seattle Times*, Sept. 18, 1988).

Johnson & Johnson 1. A player who is accident prone or easily injured. IST USE. 1937 (Bill McCullough, *Brooklyn Eagle*, Sept. 5). ETYMOLOGY. Named for the manufacturer of bandages and surgical dressings. 2. A player who commonly has adhesive tape showing.

Johnson effect The principle that when a team wins substantially more (or fewer) games than predicted by the Pythagorean method in a given year, it will probably win fewer (or more) games the next year. It was proposed by Toronto journalist Bryan Johnson (*The Globe and Mail* [Toronto], Oct. 14, 1982) and discussed by Bill James in his *Baseball Abstract* (1983, p.106).

joint exhibit A list of players' salaries, as prepared by Major League Baseball and the Major League Baseball Players Association.

jolt To hit the ball (*The Sporting Life*, Nov. 29, 1913).

Jonah *hist.* 1. *n.* A person or thing that brings bad luck; e.g., a beautiful woman who rattles the players on the field. "[New York Giants manager Jim Mutrie] says that the Washingtons have always been Jonahs for the Giants" (*The World* [New York], Apr. 22, 1888; Gerald L. Cohen). "The *Cleveland Herald* says that tobacco chewing is the Jonah of many a pitcher, and if less of the weed was used there would not be so many dulled perceptions or even stiff arms" (*The Washington Post*, May 11, 1884; Peter Morris). IST USE. 1876. "Dan Boynton, an old member of the club, expects to get home on half-fare, but Spalding has stabbed his plan and wishes something unpleasant if that Jonah, to whom he ascribes the loss of the game, can ride on the same train with the club" (*St. Louis Globe-Democrat*, May 7). 2. *n.* A player or team who suffers bad luck. After the Philadelphia Phillies began the 1883 season with a losing streak over two weeks, *The Baltimore Sun* (May 16, 1883) noted, "The Philadelphia

Jonahs created additional astonishment . . . by winning a game from the Detroits." **3.** *v.* To bring bad luck. "It is a well-known fact that a cross-eyed man will Jonah the squarest ball-game that was ever played" (*The World* [New York], Aug. 28, 1888; Gerald L. Cohen).

USAGE NOTE. According to Gerald L. Cohen (*Comments on Etymology*, Apr. 1, 1986), the term had great significance in the baseball world of the 1880s and 1890s. ETYMOLOGY. The term is a reference to the Jonah of the Bible who, before he was thrown to the whale that devoured him, had brought the wrath of God down on his ship. The term has had a long history in nautical talk. Robert Hendrickson (*Salty Words*, 1984) explained, "A 'Jonah' still means a bringer of bad luck who spoils the plans of others. The phrase is so popular that it has even become a verb, 'Don't jonah me!'"

Jones Rule Evidence of any kind that confirms that a pitched ball struck the batter; e.g., blood on the batter's hands (Ron Luciano, *The Umpire Strikes Back*, 1982, p.99). ETYMOLOGY. Named for Milwaukee Braves pinch hitter Nippy Jones, who, in the 10th inning of Game 4 of the 1957 World Series, proved he had been hit in the foot by a pitch from New York Yankees pitcher Tommy Byrne by showing that there was shoe polish on the baseball. Similarly, New York Mets outfielder Cleon Jones proved he was nicked on his left shoe by a pitch from Baltimore Orioles pitcher Dave McNally in the sixth inning of Game 5 of the 1969 World Series by revealing shoe polish on the baseball.

jonrón (pron. "hoan-roan") Spanish for "home run."

journey *hist.* A baseball game.

journeyman A veteran ballplayer who is reliable but not a star; esp. one who has played for several teams. *The Boston Globe* (July 12, 1981) referred to Clyde Vollmer as a "journeyman outfielder . . . a spare who could back up all three outfield positions." ETYMOLOGY. The traditional position of a tradesman between apprentice and master; one who has served his apprenticeship but still works for someone else.

joy spot Syn. of *sweet spot*, 2.

joy zone Syn. of *sweet spot*, 2.

J. Pluvius *hist.* Syn. of *Jupe Pluvius*. "The Oaks and Sox slushed away for five rounds . . . when old J. Pluvius turned on all his guns and then it was to the clubhouse quick" (*San Francisco Bulletin*, March 24, 1913; Gerald L. Cohen). 1ST USE. 1902 (*The Sporting Life*, July 12, p.5; Edward J. Nichols).

judge of play *hist.* The umpire.

judgment *hist.* A request made of the umpire in the very early days of baseball to make a decision. The umpire was primarily an onlooker, who made rulings only when one of the teams called out "judgment" after a close play. "[Ned] Hanlon called for judgment on [pitcher John Clarkson's delivery] and [umpire] Hengle ruled that it was a balk" (*Chicago Tribune*, reprinted in *Detroit Free Press*, May 14, 1887; Peter Morris).

judgment call **1.** Any one of the hundreds of decisions rendered by the umpire during a game that is primarily based on the perception of the umpire rather than interpretation of the rule book. Examples include whether a ball is in the strike zone, or whether the ball beat the runner to the base, or whether a ball landed in fair or foul territory. If the umpire makes a judgment call, even if it was incorrect, the play is not subject to appeal. **2.** A ruling by an umpire for a situation that is not specifically covered in the rule book; e.g., when Dave Kingman sent a towering fly through the Metrodome roof, the umpire ruled it a ground-rule double.

Judy Syn. of *Punch-and-Judy hitter*. "A singles hitter is a Judy, drawn from a punch and judy hitter" (Phil Pepe, *Baseball Digest*, Nov. 1974, p.58).

Judy hitter Syn. of *Punch-and-Judy hitter*.

juego Spanish for "game."

juego sin hits Spanish for "no-hitter."

jugada de cuña Spanish for "squeeze play."

jugador Spanish for "ballplayer."

jugador de cuadro Spanish for "infielder."

juggle **1.** *v.* To mishandle a batted or thrown ball. While a fielder may juggle a ball without dropping it, the act may consume enough time to allow a runner to be safe who otherwise would have been put out. See also *bobble*, 1. **2.** *n.* A ball that has been mishandled;

an error. See also *bobble*, 2. IST USE. 1905. "It took [Fred] Raymer's juggle on the heels of [Bill] Hinchman's walk and steal to make the 10th [run]" (*Boston Daily*, Sept. 27).

jughandle A curveball with a sharp break or broad arc that bends like the handle of a jug. Pittsburgh Pirates pitcher John Morrison was nicknamed "Jughandle Johnny" in the 1920s because of his sharp-breaking curveball. See also *rainbow*, 1; *roundhouse curve*. Also spelled "jug handle"; "jug-handle." Syn. "jughandle curve."

JUGS gun A *radar gun* used to measure the velocity of a pitched ball between three to five feet after it leaves the pitcher's hand. The early reading eliminates variables, ensuring consistency, and generally registers a speed three or four miles per hour faster than a reading taken with the *Ra-gun*. The average major-league fastball registers 88 to 90 mph on the JUGS gun. It is available from JKP Sports, Tualatin, Ore. Sometimes spelled "jugs gun"; "Jugs gun." Syn. "JUGS."

juice 1. *v.* To hit the ball with great power for distance; to crush the ball. Commenting on contemporary, high-salaried players, Maury Wills observed (*The New York Times*, Aug. 17, 2003), "They don't want to bunt. They want to juice the ball. That's what's fashionable." 2. *n.* Hitting power. "The kid [Baltimore Orioles first-round draft pick Brandon Snyder] swings the bat, he's got juice" (Orioles manager Lee Mazzilli, quoted in *The Baltimore Sun*, June 14, 2005). 3. *n./hist.* Pitching ability. "There is no way of telling, except by the eye, which pitcher had the greatest juice" (Connie Mack, quoted in *San Francisco Bulletin*, Feb. 12, 1913; Gerald L. Cohen). 4. *v.* To make the baseball more lively. 5. *v.* To alter a baseball so that its flight pattern will not be normal; e.g., "Smith juiced up the ball so that it would swerve." 6. *n.* Steroids. "Evidence of testing for performance-enhancing drugs is more anecdotal than it is empirical, because who knows for certain which players got off the juice?" (Tom Verducci, *Sports Illustrated*, May 30, 2005). "In the wake of the steroid scandal, this will be a favorite pastime of baseball fans: deciding which players are on the juice—and which ones *were* on the juice when all those

home run records were set" (Kevin Cowherd, *The Baltimore Sun*, Apr. 4, 2005). 7. *v.* To strenghten one's body with steroids. Howard Bryant's 2005 history of steroid use in baseball is entitled *Juicing the Game: Drugs, Power, and the Fight for the Soul of Major League Baseball*. The term is often used in the past tense; e.g., *Juiced: Wild Times, Rampant 'Roids, Smash Hits, and How Baseball Got Big* is the title of Jose Canseco's 2005 book.

juiced ball A baseball with extra carrying power; a more lively ball. The juiced-ball theory crops up every time there is a big offensive upsurge: the 1987, 1993, and 1994 baseballs were believed by some to have been juiced, but others disagree: "Every guy who hits the ball in the right spot, it's going to go. It doesn't matter if it's juiced or not" (Chicago Cubs outfielder Sammy Sosa, quoted in *USA Today*, May 10, 1994). Syn. "juice ball"; "juiced-up ball."

Juiced Era Syn. of *Steroid Era*.

juicer A ballplayer who uses steroids. "According to the juicers' First Amendment, an athlete is presumed innocent until the pee changes color, even when his head has expanded to the size of one of those Mardi Gras goblins" (Bill Conlin, *Philadelphia Daily News*, March 8, 2006).

July 4th Syn. of *Fourth of July*.

jump 1. *n.* The first step of a baserunner to leave a base quickly when the ball is pitched. A good jump involves the distance taken by the runner and his timing of the pitcher's motion. Ty Cobb (*Memoirs of Twenty Years in Baseball*, 1925; Peter Morris) on contemplating a steal of second base: "I knew he [the pitcher] was feeling me out to see when I intended to start. Two or three times I would take the jump on the second ball pitched, for example, whether I had any hopes of making it or not." IST USE. 1912. "[Fred] Snodgrass had the jump, and probably would have made the base had he kept on going" (Christy Mathewson, *Pitching in a Pinch*; Peter Morris). 2. *n.* The move that a fielder makes toward the ball as soon as it is hit. "Getting a jump on a ball is instinct, and instinct is the residue of concentration applied over a long period of time" (Gene Mauch, quoted in *Baseball Digest*, Nov. 1983). IST USE. 1925. "I couldn't get that important first jump in going for a fly ball" (Ty Cobb, *Memoirs of Twenty Years in Baseball*; Peter Morris). **3.** *v.* For a batted ball to take off with an extra spurt. "I know the way the ball can jump off my bat. Seems like one at-bat I'll have it, and the next two or three it might be gone" (Jack Clark, quoted in *St. Louis Post-Dispatch*, May 29, 1987). **4.** *n.* The hopping motion on a good fastball as it crosses the plate. Hugh S. Fullerton (*American Magazine*, June 1912) explained, "Sometimes pitchers throw much faster than at others, and on such days they 'have the jump on the fast one' which means that the ball, revolving rapidly, piles up a mound of compressed air and actually jumps over it, rising sometimes, it seems, an inch or two during its sudden leap before resuming its way to the plate." IST USE. 1899 (Burt L. Standish, *Frank Merriwell's Double Shot*, p.13; Edward J. Nichols). **5.** *v.* For a pitched ball to rise. John J. Evers and Hugh S. Fullerton (*Touching Second: The Science of Baseball*, 1910; Peter Morris): "If the ball is gripped tightly with the finger tips at the moment it is released from the hand its speed piles up a billow of air in front of it, and at some point before crossing the plate, the air resistance becomes so great that the ball 'jumps' an inch or more upward in the direction the greatest amount of pressure of the fingers was applied." **6.** *v.* To leave a baseball team without permission; esp., to break one's contract with a baseball team. See also *contract jumper.* IST USE. 1885. "A.J. Mullane . . . made himself notorious early in the season of 1884 by 'jumping' his contract with the St. Louis Union Club, and leaving its service to play [for] the Louisville team of 1884" (*Spalding's Official Base Ball Guide*, p.99; Peter Morris). **7.** *n.* An early lead in a game; e.g., "The Yankees got the jump on the Orioles by scoring three runs in the first inning." **8.** *v.* To lunge at a pitch, as though swinging for the fences or anticipating a different type of pitch. Tom Verducci (*Sports Illustrated*, June 7, 2004) wrote that "[Derek Jeter's] anxiety had him 'jumping at the ball.' Rather than waiting for a pitch to get to him, especially an outside pitch, Jeter would lean forward in his haste to hit it, jerking his head instead of keeping it steady." **9.** *n.* A promotion from the minor leagues to the major leagues. "Daniel Cabrera and John Maine . . . made the jump from Single-A to the Orioles' rotation in one year" (*The Baltimore Sun*, Sept. 12, 2004). **10.** *n.* Travel between two cities as part of a road trip. St. Louis Browns secretary Sidney J. Mercer (quoted in *St. Louis Post-Dispatch*, Apr. 17, 1904; Peter Morris): "The longest jump that the Browns make during the coming season is from St. Louis to Boston, a distance of 1308 miles," and "On jumps between Detroit and Cleveland lake steamers are used." IST USE. 1895. "In making the schedule for the season it was found that the jumps required could not be made in time to put the teams all over the association on the field in time for work" (*Atlanta Constitution*, May 2; Peter Morris). **11.** See also *jump on.*

jump around See *home plate is jumping around.*

jump ball A fastball with a late hopping action. The pitch was thrown by Joe McGinnity (who called it *Old Sal*) and Kid Nichols. Cy Young (quoted in Alfred H. Spink, *The National Game*, 2nd ed., 1911, p.391): "When in good shape I use a jump ball considerably [as] it comes with extra speed and if worked well into the batsman is perhaps the most difficult ball to hit safe." IST USE. 1889. "Sanders sent in a 'jump ball.' The bat connected with the ball's underside, and away she sped up into the rain" (*The World* [New York], Sept. 21; Gerald L. Cohen).

jumper A player who has left a team, without permission, to play elsewhere or engage in another line of work; a player who has broken his contract with a team. After Sal Maglie left the New York Giants to play in the outlaw Mexican League, he returned to the Giants; commenting on Maglie's return, Giants manager Leo Durocher wrote (*Nice Guys Finish Last*, 1975; Charles D. Poe), "I'll play an elephant if he can do the job, so why shouldn't I play a jumper?" See also *contract jumper.*

jump game The first (and most "important") game in a World Series (Grantland Rice, *The Boston Globe*, Oct. 3, 1916).

jumping jack A player who shows off; a *grandstand player*. IST USE. 1932 (*Baseball Magazine*, October; Edward J. Nichols).

jump on 1. For a baserunner or fielder to move quickly on the sound of the ball making contact with the bat; e.g., "Outfielder Smith jumped on the ball when he heard the crack of the bat." **2.** For a batter to hit the pitch he was looking for and to hit it hard. "[Travis] Driskill left another splitter up in the strike zone, and [Kevin] Millar jumped on it for his 19th home run" (*The Baltimore Sun*, Aug. 10, 2003). **3.** For a team to take control of a baseball game; e.g., "The Giants jumped on the Dodgers with eight runs in the first inning."

June bug A rookie who is sent back down to the minor leagues by early summer. IST USE. 1945. "June Bug [is a] recruit who is on his way back to the minor leagues by June" (H.G. Salsinger, *Baseball Digest*, August).

June Swoon The falling apart after Memorial Day of a team that got off to a good start in April and May. Frank Deford (*Sports Illustrated*, Aug. 22, 1983, p.76) wrote, "It is no mere coincidence that a lot of mediocre clubs regularly come a cropper with a June Swoon. That's when the best breaking pitches finally start to break consistently, and more sharply. June is National Off-Speed Month." While it's been applied to several teams, the term has been most closely associated with the San Francisco Giants ever since the franchise moved there from New York in 1958. Tom Weir (*USA Today*, May 29, 1986) noted that since moving to San Francisco the team had a composite record of 373–405 in the month of June (not good, not awful); he added: "If the Giants of the Mays-McCovey-Marichal era hadn't always been so hot in April and May—387–256 from 1958–71, the supposed Swoon never would have been coined." IST USE/ETYMOLOGY. Sportswriter Art Rosenbaum, who popularized the phrase in the late 1950s and early 1960s when the Giants seemed destined for an annual fall from the top of the National League standings after quick starts, wrote (*San Francisco Chronicle*, June 22, 1989), "It just slipped into my typewriter, and it became an annual story. The songs of those days rhymed with June as in swoon, moon, tune and the Giants were accommodating to the phrase. They would fall dead in that month every year. It's one of those things you write about and not think about until later." Rosenbaum first used "June Swoon" in the summer of 1959, but according to researchers at the Tamony Collection at the Univ. of Missouri, the first printed use of the term came in *Time* magazine (June 17, 1957). A nonbyline story on Nellie Fox and the Chicago White Sox made just a passing reference: "The White Sox get off to a fast start, then fall into a 'June Swoon.'" Over the years Rosenbaum has written several articles claiming to have started the Swoon craze, although he acknowledged that Bob Stevens, the *Chronicle*'s baseball writer at the time, may have actually coined the term.

junior circuit The *American League*, because it came into being when the National League was 25 years old. The term is still used but much less commonly than it was before World War II. Compare *senior circuit*.

junior club *hist.* A club in the early days of baseball made up of players under the age of 18. IST USE. 1858 (*New York Clipper*, Oct. 16; Peter Morris).

Junior World Series 1. The annual minor-league postseason playoff games featuring the top teams in the American Association and the International League beginning in 1931. The series was formerly known as *Little World Series* (1904–1930). The series continued through 1975 (with no series in 1935 or from 1963 to 1969). From 1998 to 2000, the Triple-A World Series pitted the International League and the Pacific Coast League champions. USAGE NOTE. Referring to the series as the minor-league "World Series" was somewhat pretentious, as it did not include the Pacific Coast League, the third Triple-A league. **2.** A term sometimes used to refer to the Little League World Series.

junk The assortment of slower and softer pitches characterized by erratic and deceptive movement, as opposed to the standard fastballs and curveballs. Bert Dunne (*Folger's Dictionary of Baseball*, 1958) defined the term as "slowly-thrown balls for which hitter must supply his own power." Something of a misnomer, junk can be as effective as the faster stuff. "An old Cuban named Conrado Marrero has buried American League under a load of 'junk'" (*Life* magazine, June 11, 1951; Peter Tamony). IST USE. 1949. "[Mickey] Haefner, noted for his knuckle ball, said he didn't use much 'junk'" (Associated Press dispatch on a one-hitter thrown by Washington Senators pitcher Haefner, May 11; Peter Tamony).

junkball An unorthodox, tricky, or abnormal pitch. IST USE. 1944. "His variety of pitches, and his frequent reliance on 'junk balls' serves to set up his pitches" (*Baseball Magazine*, December; David Shulman).

junkballer A pitcher who relies on off-speed pitches and trickery rather than the fastball or curveball. Syn. *junkman*; "junk pitcher"; *slopper*. USAGE NOTE. Despite how it sounds, the term carries with it a certain admiration. Hoyt Wilhelm, Eddie Lopat, Doyle Alexander, and Stu Miller were noted junkballers. It was said of Miller that he had three speeds: slow, slower, and slowest.

junkman Syn of *junkballer*. "[Don] Mossi interests me very much because he now pitches a lot the way I used to in my junkman days" (Eddie Lopat, quoted in *The Sporting News*, Apr. 6, 1960; Peter Morris).

Jupe Pluvius *hist.* Rain that interrupts or postpones a game. Syn. *J. Pluvius*; "Jupiter Pluvius"; "Jupe Pluve"; *Pluvius*; *Old Pluvy*. IST USE. 1868 (*New York Herald*, Aug. 13; Edward J. Nichols). ETYMOLOGY. From the ancient incantation to Jupiter Pluvius, with "Pluvius" being an ancient epithet for Jupiter as rainmaker.

jute rag *hist.* Syn. of *base*, 2. "[Edwards] let an easy fly sift through his hands, which muff put two runners on the jute rags" (*San Francisco Bulletin*, March 11, 1913; Gerald L. Cohen).

K

K **1.** The symbol for *strikeout*, 2. The "K" has long been a staple of headlines for the simple reason that it takes up much less space than the word "strikeout": "[Bob] Feller Setting 'K' Record" (*San Francisco Call-Bulletin*, June 5, 1946; Peter Tamony). Fans sometimes keep track of the number of strikeouts a pitcher has thrown by hanging signs that read "K" over the ballpark railings. "It's undeniable that Dr. K is a great moniker for Dwight Gooden, and so are the K banners that unfurl from the cheap seats in Shea Stadium every time he puts the Kibosh on an opposing batter" (Michael Olmert, *The Washington Post*, May 4, 1986). ETYMOLOGY. When Henry Chadwick explained his scoring system (*New York Clipper*, March 23, 1861), he developed a series of letter symbols. He selected "K" for "struck out" and later explained the decision (*Outing*, July 1888; Peter Morris): "The letter K in struck is easier to remember in connection with the word than S." An alternate version that the symbol was created in 1861 by M.J. Kelly, later a baseball writer for the *New York Herald*, has not been documented. The symbol was given new prominence with the nicknaming of strikeout pitcher Dwight Gooden as "Dr. K." **2.** *n.* Syn. of *strikeout*, 2. Roger Clemens was called "The King of K's" by *Sports Illustrated* (July 3–10, 2006, p.95) for striking out a record 20 Seattle batters in 1986. **3.** *v.* To *strike out*, 1. "[Laynce Nix] K'd every 3.5 ABs last season" (*ESPN The Magazine*, Feb. 16, 2004). **4.** *v.* To *strike out*, 2. "[Randy] Myers K's side in 9th" (*The Baltimore Sun* headline, Apr. 6, 1996).

Я (backwards K) Scorecard symbol for a strikeout on a called third strike. Syn. *KC*.

kalsomine *hist.* A shutout. "Christy's [Mathewson] kalsomine and control records stand forth as brilliant as ever" (Alfred H. Spink, *The National Game*, 1911, 2nd ed., p.142). IST USE. 1870. "A coat of kalsomine on the Peninsulars" (*Grand Rapids* [Mich.] *Daily Eagle*, July 9; Peter Morris). USAGE NOTE. The term has an adjectival form: "The kalsomining process to which Cleveland was subjected fully made up for the defeats which Detroit has sustained in the two preceding days" (*Detroit Free Press*, reprinted in *The Cleveland Herald*, Aug. 20, 1881). ETYMOLOGY. Var. of *calcimine*. Patrick Ercolano (*Fungoes, Floaters and Fork Balls*, 1987, p.103) explained that the term was so called "because calcimine—which some creative misspeller long ago turned into 'kalsomine'—is a type of whitewash, and 'whitewash' is a synonym for 'shut out.'"

kangaroo **1.** *n.* A runner who leaps or takes high strides. **2.** *v.* To run the bases by leaps and bounds. IST USE. 1896. "Kangarooed to second" (*The Atchison* [Kans.] *Daily Globe*, June 23). **3.** *v.* To bounce over. "That ball almost kangarooed over Davis' head" (Vin Scully, All-Star Game broadcast, July 11, 1989).

kangaroo ball A lively baseball. "Salt Lake was using a kangaroo ball and the theory was soberly propounded that singles went for homers because the air was thin" (Westbrook Pegler, *San Francisco Call-Bulletin*, May 14, 1958; Peter Tamony). See also *rabbit ball*, 1.

kangaroo cave *hist.* A section of the grandstand reserved for sportswriters. IST USE. 1908 (*New York Evening Journal*, Aug. 21; Edward J. Nichols).

kangaroo court A clubhouse session during which a senior player assesses guilt and small fines for errors and omissions on the field or other minor infractions, such as missing a sign, a bunt, or the cutoff man, failing to run out a pop-up or to move a runner up, commenting to the press while the game was in progress, or wearing an ugly suit. Brian McCann and Jeff Francoeur each ran afoul of the Atlanta Braves kangaroo court for living at his parents' home while playing in the majors (they were fined $20 each). Broadcasters have been assessed fines for announcing players' birthdays. Frank Robinson was the first great clubhouse jurist when he appointed himself judge of the Baltimore Orioles Kangaroo Court of the late 1960s: he would don a mop as a headdress before games to conduct trials and impose fines, which were put aside for postseason parties. Said Robinson (quoted in *USA Weekend*, Apr. 2–4, 1993, p.5): "If you goofed up in the game, your teammates got on you instead of the manager. We could stay loose but still learn from our mistakes." Teams establish kangaroo courts to create team unity and greater discipline. ETYMOLOGY. The term has a long history as an irregular or mock court, such as one convened by prisoners in a jail. They are characterized by a disregard of normal court procedures. Darryl Lyman (*The Animal Things We Say*, 1983) states that the expression apparently stems from the jumping of the kangaroo and the fact that "the principles of law and justice are disregarded or perverted (that is, 'jumped' over)" in such a court. Charles Earle Funk (*A Hog on Ice*, 1948) guessed that the term may refer to the idea that the earliest kangaroo courts, established around the time of the 1849 Gold Rush, were convened to try "jumpers" (those who stole the mining claims of others).

kangaroo hop 1. A routine batted ball that suddenly takes a big bounce in front of the fielder and goes over his head. 2. An Australian term for a lead from first base (*Sports Illustrated*, July 27, 1981). Syn. *'roo hop*.

kangaroo out *hist.* To break one's contract with his team to play for another. "[John] McGraw had jumped—'kangarooed out,' it was called in those more lyrical times—to the Giants from the Orioles in July 1902" (Frank Deford, *Sports Illustrated*, Aug. 25, 2003).

KC Scorecard symbol for a strikeout on a called third strike. Syn. Ɔ.

keep alive To prolong a rally; e.g., "Smith and Jones kept the inning alive by hitting back-to-back doubles."

"keep both hands on the ball" [softball term] An instruction given to softball pitchers who legally must have both hands in front of the body and on the ball before delivering it.

keeper league A fantasy baseball league in which some players can be retained by their owners from year to year.

"keep him honest" 1. An instruction given to the pitcher to throw strikes, the idea being that if the batter is to reach base, he should earn it with a hit rather than a walk. "[Mike Trombley's] fastball has been used more this season to get ahead of hitters and 'keep them honest at the plate'" (Roch Kubatko, *The Baltimore Sun*, May 11, 2001). 2. An instruction given to the pitcher to make the batter afraid. "The pitcher may want to throw the ball very close to the batter to 'loosen him up' and 'keep him honest' (keep him guessing as to what pitch will be thrown next, and where); in short, make him afraid" (Lawrence Frank, *Playing Hardball: The Dynamics of Baseball Folk Speech*, 1983, p.106). 3. An instruction given to the pitcher to ensure that a baserunner not get too big a lead off a base, either by throwing to the base or by at least keeping an eye on him.

keep one's head in the locker To have little or nothing to say; to lack the ability to communicate (H.G. Salsinger, *Baseball Digest*, Aug. 1945).

keep score To record the game's action by using specific symbols and abbreviations.

keep the position warm Said of a player, usually a free-agent signee, who plays a position for a year while the club waits for a prospect to be ready to take over. "Whoever handles the [Atlanta Braves third base] job in 2004 will be keeping the position warm while [Andy] Marte hones his skills" (Bill Ballew, *Baseball America*, Sept. 15–28, 2003; Peter Morris).

"keep the Spalding up" Advice given to the batter to grip the bat (manufactured by the A.G. Spalding Co.) so that its *trademark* is facing upward. It was feared that if the batter hit the pitch on the trademark, the bat would break. Syn. *"hold the grain up."*

keep the team in the game For a starting pitcher to keep the score close even though his team may not be leading. Typically, a pitcher leaving the game in the sixth inning with a 1–0 deficit would be congratulated for "keeping the team in the game." "I did my job as a starter, kept the team in the game, and gave the club six or seven innings every time out" (Tim Wakefield, quoted in *The Baltimore Sun*, Oct. 5, 1995).

"keep your eye on the ball" An instruction to be alert on the baseball field. It can be a reminder given to a batter to watch the pitch carefully as it is delivered: "A batter should watch the ball all the way, from the start of the pitcher's wind-up to the release of the ball, and until the bat meets the ball, or until the ball crosses the plate" (James Smilgoff, *Athletic Journal*, Apr. 1946). However, A. Terry Bahill, an engineering professor at the Univ. of Arizona, conducted experiments to show that a big-league fastball moves too fast for the eye to follow: by trying to keep his eye on the ball, even a keen-eyed batter will lose sight of it by the time it gets within five feet from the plate. According to Bahill (*Sports Illustrated*, Sept. 12, 1983, and *The New York Times*, June 12, 1984), better batters train themselves to lose the ball somewhere in midflight, then make a quick guess as to where it's going and a corrective eye movement to pick it up again. Additionally, a "general instruction" to umpires is: "Keep your eye everlastingly on the ball while it is in play. It is more vital to know just where a fly ball fell, or a thrown ball finished up, than whether or not a runner missed a base" (*Official Baseball Rules*, Rule 9.05). See also *on the ball*; *eye on the ball*. 1ST USE. 1907. "We were forever being told 'Keep your eye on the ball'" (*Screen Book*; *OED*).

keep your skirt down To stay close to the ground to field a ground ball. Kenneth Forehand (letter, Apr. 29, 1994) explained its significance: "This may be one of the most used terms in baseball instruction in reference to a fielder (usually an infielder) who raises up on a ground ball and allows it to go between his legs." See also *skirt*.

Kelly spread *hist.* Syn. of *Chicago slide*. "Most runners [in the 1880s] used the 'Kelly spread,' a contemporary version of the modern hook slide" (Harold Seymour, *Baseball: The Early Years*, 1960, p.181; Peter Morris).

Kenesaw Mountain Landis Award The official name, since 1944, of the *Most Valuable Player Award*, bearing the name of baseball's first commissioner.

Kentucky wonder *hist.* A pitch thrown close to the batter. "Such a pitch is known as a 'bean ball,' 'Kentucky wonder,' or 'duster'" (Franklin P. Huddle, *American Speech*, Apr. 1943).

key 1. *n.* Syn. of *indicator*, 2. Don Zimmer (quoted in Steve Fiffer, *How to Watch Baseball*, 1987, p.148): "I can go through all kinds of signs—most of it is decoy anyway—but nothing is really on until I hit the key." 2. *v.* To be instrumental in starting or continuing a rally. "Frank Thomas keyed a seventh-inning comeback with a two-run single" (*Tampa Tribune*, Sept. 30, 1990).

key hit A timely hit that turns the game around or determines its outcome; e.g., "Smith's key hit in the ninth brought in the winning run."

keyhole Syn. of *alley*, 4.

keyhole fastball A fastball thrown with great precision, as if it could be thrown through a keyhole.

keystone 1. *adj.* Describing *second base*, 1. Terms include "keystone bag," "keystone corner," "keystone cushion," "keystone hassock," "keystone sack," and "keystone station." 1ST USE. 1906. "[Jake] Stahl on first and [Lave] Cross on third . . . will brace up the youngsters around the keystone bag" (*Chicago Tribune*, Apr. 8; Peter Morris). USAGE NOTE. These terms were long regarded as synonyms by sportswriters tired of repeating the term "second base." "Keystone sack," for example, was "a term used by baseball writers who are paid by the word, to designate second base [which was] generally believed to be stone from the number of runners who limp after sliding into it" (R.E.

Sherwood, *Baseball Magazine*, Sept. 1913). **2.** *n.* Syn. of *second base*, 1. IST USE. 1913. "[Second baseman Dick Egan] had nobody to work with him around the keystone in 1912, but with [Joe] Tinker at short Cincinnati's infield will be a horse of another color" (*San Francisco Bulletin*, Feb. 17; Gerald L. Cohen). **3.** *adj.* Describing defense or fielding up the middle of the infield. "Yeah, kid— you're the keystone tenant. But holding onto it depends on how well you do" (Ed Conrow, *Ellery Queen's Mystery Magazine*, Oct. 1986). "At this time there were remarkable second basemen. It seemed to be the age of great keystone sackers" (*San Francisco Bulletin*, March 20, 1913; Gerald L. Cohen). ETYMOLOGY. It is often claimed that the term is a play on the fact that many important, or "key," defensive plays involve second base. Hy Turkin (*Baseball Almanac*, 1955) posited a minority opinion: "Viewed from the plate, second base seems to be the middle of the arch formed by the basepaths. In architecture, a keystone is the tapering stone at the crown of an arch." Since these two explanations are complementary, they may both have been a factor in the creation of the term.

keystone combination Syn. of *double-play combination*.

keystone hit Syn. of *double*, 1.

keystoner Syn. of *second baseman*. IST USE. 1917. "[Nap Lajoie is] the king of the keystoners" (*The Sporting Life*, March 10; Peter Morris).

kick **1.** *n.* An element of the pitcher's windup that occurs when he lowers his arms, raises his nonpivot leg, and strides toward home plate. Runners know that they have a better chance of stealing a base from a pitcher with a big kick. "Jesse Orosco, with his high leg kick, was responsible for two [steals] in the eighth inning" (*The Baltimore Sun*, Apr. 24, 1996). See also *leg kick*, 1. **2.** *v.* For a pitcher to raise his nonpivot leg and stride toward the plate before delivering the pitch. **3.** *v.* To mishandle a ground ball; to commit an error. See also *boot*, 2. IST USE. 1906. "Bounder after bounder went towards short and Robby [Yank Robinson] kicked every one of them" (Hugh S. Fullerton, *Chicago Tribune*, Apr. 8; Peter Morris). ETYMOLOGY. A play on the error that

occurs when the fielder boots the ball as he tries to field it. **4.** *n.* An error. **5.** *v./hist.* To protest the decision of the umpire; to complain. "[Cap] Anson, true to his word, did not kick again while [umpire John] Kelly was rendering decisions" (*San Francisco Bulletin*, Feb. 10, 1913; Gerald L. Cohen). See also *kicking*. IST USE. 1871. "They [Forest City of Cleveland] kicked against the umpire and threw up the game" (*The Cleveland Morning Herald*, Aug. 14). **6.** *n./hist.* A protest or complaint. "The contest was marked by numerous 'kicks' by the players against the decisions of Powers, who, however, was fair" (*The World* [New York], June 14, 1887). IST USE. 1886. "Umpire [John] Eagan declared [Charlie] Sweeney had made a balk and that [Sid] Farrar was entitled to second base. This drew forth a mammoth kick from the home team, who finally gave in, however, and proceeded to play" (*The Sporting Life*, May 26). **7.** *v.* For an umpire to make a bad or wrong decision; to blow a call or play. "Asked if he [Doug Harvey] miscalled many pitches—'kicked 'em,' in umpires' parlance—he says that no ump ever had a perfect game" (*Sports Illustrated*, Oct. 19, 1998). Umpire Shag Crawford (quoted in Larry R. Gerlach, *The Men in Blue*, 1980, p.209): "If you kick it [a play], you just handle whatever arises from your error of judgment and go on with the game." **8.** *v.* See *kick out*. **9.** *n.* See *leg kick*, 2.

kick at the can A chance to win. A team that is behind by a few runs has a last "kick at the can" in the ninth inning. ETYMOLOGY. The term probably derives from the childhood game of kick the can, in which the child who is "It" guards an empty tin can (mounted on a rock or sitting on a manhole cover), closes his eyes, counts to 100, and begins searching for the other players who have run and hidden. If "It" finds someone, both race to the can: if "It" arrives first, he taps the other "out"; if the other arrives first, he kicks the can and "It" has to retrieve it, while all others who have been "out" are free to run and hide again.

kick away *hist.* To lose a game through ineptitude and blundering. IST USE. 1918 (*Spalding's Official Base Ball Guide*, p.81; Edward J. Nichols).

kickball A variation of baseball, popular during elementary school recess, but also played by adults, using a large, soft-rubber ball (approximately 10 inches in diameter). The pitcher rolls the ball toward the kicker, who "bats" it with his foot. Outs are made when a runner is tagged or hit with a thrown ball; however, throwing a kickball "is about as easy . . . [as throwing] a wide-screen television" (*The Baltimore Sun*, March 21, 2004). The World Adult Kickball Association, which hails the sport as "The New American Pastime," plays with 11 fielders, 5 innings, no "head shots" (hitting a runner with the ball above the shoulder is not allowed), and no ghost runners.

kicker *hist.* One who argues; a complainer. "The Boston players are the wildest and wooliest lot of kickers that ever played on a Cleveland diamond" (*Cleveland Plain Dealer*, Oct. 18, 1892; Dean A. Sullivan). IST USE. 1871. "As kickers, the Clevelands have no equals. They will kick at anything, and if no other objective point appeared they would kick the dust off the bones of their grandfathers" (*The Cleveland Morning Herald*, Aug. 14).

kicking *hist.* Protesting the decision of the umpire; complaining. Mike "King" Kelly (*Play Ball: Stories of the Diamond*, 1888): "The people who go to ball games want good playing, with just enough kicking to make things interesting thrown in." In 1896, Baltimore Orioles manager Ned Hanlon argued vehemently against a proposal to ban kicking (reprinted in *The Baltimore Sun*, July 8, 1996): "Had the Orioles had less of that aggressiveness, we would never have won any pennants. Players are only human, and when they are compelled to suppress all noise and excitement, their hearts will go down in their boots, they will become indifferent, the game will go glimmering and the public will leave in disgust." See also *kick*, 5. IST USE. 1871. "There was considerable 'kicking' done, but it was nearly all by the White Stockings, who are known and acknowledged as without their peers in the mulish art" (*The Cleveland Morning Herald*, Aug. 14).

kick it out For a fielder to kick a ball rolling on the foul side of the first base line or third base line, thus ensuring that the ball stays foul and does not become fair by rolling into fair territory.

kick out For an umpire to eject a participant. When umpire Joe West ejected St. Louis Cardinals pitcher Julian Tavarez for having pine tar on his cap, West said (*The Baltimore Sun*, Aug. 21, 2004), "By rule, I have to kick him out of the game."

kicks Spikes or cleats; a ballplayer's term for shoes.

kid *hist.* A rookie in the National League. "Irrespective of a man's real age during his first year in the major organization he is called a 'kid'" (*Bismarck* [N.D.] *Daily Tribune*, May 4, 1889).

Kid **1.** An affectionate nickname for a young, promising player; specif., Ted Williams, who was known as "The Kid." Boston Red Sox rookie shortstop Nomar Garciaparra assumed the nickname when *The Boston Globe* (Aug. 31, 1997) noted, "The Kid kicked at the first base bag in frustration." **2.** A nickname to denote a player shorter than average, such as William "Kid" Gleason and Norman "Kid" Elberfeld, both 5' 7". "'Kid' Fear, the Omaha catcher, was behind the bat. As indicated by his professional name, he is small of stature" (*Grand Rapids* [Mich.] *Democrat*, Apr. 11, 1895; Peter Morris). **3.** *hist.* A nickname to denote a player who is a kidder (James H. Bready, *Baseball in Baltimore*, 1998, p.62). **4.** (pron. "keed") Babe Ruth's universal nickname for those he greeted ("hiya, Kid"), esp. younger teammates; the name was used often because of Ruth's legendary inability to recall names.

kill *hist.* **1.** *v.* To put out; e.g., "The Cubs killed Smith attempting to score." **2.** *n.* A putout.

killer instinct The desire or inclination to defeat or finish off an opponent when the latter is struggling. Atlanta Braves pitcher Tom Glavine (quoted in *Milwaukee Journal Sentinel*, Oct. 2, 1997): "I hope we have the killer instinct. In any series, you want to get it over with as soon as possible. You don't want to give the other team any confidence."

killer pitcher A pitcher who is extraordinarily effective against a given team over a period of time, "usually with a percentage of .600 or better" (Zita Carno, *Baseball Research Journal*, no.30, 2001, p.32).

killing A putout. IST USE. 1920. "[Val] Picinich led off . . . with a single . . . and was doubled up, [Joe] Judge lining into the twin killing" (*The Washington Post*, Apr. 10; Peter Morris).

kill the ball To swing at a pitch with great ferocity. The term is usually used facetiously since "killing" the ball often leaves the batter off balance and the ball untouched. One of the commonest bits of advice given to youngsters learning the game is: "Don't try to kill the ball." But to Rogers Hornsby (quoted in F.C. Lane, *Batting*, 1925, p.64), such advice sounded like, "Don't try to be a good batter." IST USE. 1901 (Burt L. Standish, *Frank Merriwell's School Days*, p.240; Edward J. Nichols).

kill the rally To end a scoring opportunity, such as by making the third out with the bases loaded.

"kill the umpire" The ritualistic response to a perceived bad call by the umpire. In the early days of baseball, umpires were often the targets of rocks, pop bottles, and tomatoes, and were frequently assaulted on and off the field by players and fans; by one account, "At the conclusion of the game the police were compelled to draw their revolvers to keep the crowd from doing Mr. Ellick (the umpire) bodily harm" (*The New York Times*, Aug. 1, 1886). Several minor-league umpires did indeed lose their lives because of close calls. The phrase was recorded in Ernest L. Thayer's 1888 poem "Casey at the Bat." IST USE. 1876. The *Cincinnati Star* (June 23; Peter Morris) remarked that the fans who yelled "Kill him" at the umpire were guilty of bad taste.

kill zone The area of the strike zone in which a batter or pitcher enjoys particular success; the *wheelhouse* of a batter.

kimono pitch A pitch delivered from behind the pitcher's back. From a set position, the pitcher would take his arm back normally and, while striding forward, continue the backward swing before delivering the ball from behind his back. The pitch, which would surprise the batter despite having little velocity and only a slight drop, was invented by New York Yankees southpaw Tommy Byrne in 1955 while on a postseason exhibition tour

BASE BALL

A peaceful man he claims to be,
And justice to admire;
Yet at the game he is the first
To mob the poor umpire.

COPYRIGHT 1908 BY H. M. ROSE

"Kill the umpire." Postcard. *Andy Moresund Collection*

of Japan; it was banned by the American League shortly thereafter (Martin Quigley, *The Crooked Pitch*, 1984, pp.143–44).

kindergartner *hist.* Syn. of *rookie*, 1. IST USE. 1917 (*The New York Times*, Oct. 4; Edward J. Nichols).

kindling A team's bats rendered "useless" by a pitcher recording strikeouts and broken bats. Greg Maddux has been associated with creating splintered wood that is useful only to start fires: "The late movement on his pitches caused so many futile swings and broken bats that the Indians lost count of the kindling" (Tom Verducci, *Sports Illustrated*, Oct. 30, 1995, p.38).

Kiner's Korner The name of the left-field area at Forbes Field in Pittsburgh from 1948 to 1953. Originally named *Greenberg Gardens*, it was created to increase home run production. After a chicken-wire fence was erected inside the scoreboard as a new wall, home run balls did not have to be hit as far. Greenberg Gardens was renamed in 1948 for Ralph Kiner, Pittsburgh's prodigious home run hitter.

King and His Court, The [softball term] A barnstorming softball team of four players led by Eddie Feigner, a hard-throwing pitcher who founded the team in 1946 and pitched in more than 10,000 games. The other three players were a catcher, a first baseman, and a shortstop.

King of Swat A nickname applied to sluggers; specif., Ed Delahanty and Babe Ruth.

kiss To hit a ball exceptionally hard. Edward J. Nichols (*An Historical Dictionary of Baseball Terminology*, PhD dissertation, Jan. 1939) noted the association of the term with "smack." IST USE. 1911. "[Gabby Street] kissed center field fence with a mighty drive" (Joe S. Jackson, *The Washington Post*, Sept. 10; Peter Morris).

Kissing Bandit A woman named Morganna Roberts who, beginning in 1971, periodically bounded onto the diamond to plant chaste kisses on ballplayers, including Pete Rose, Cal Ripken Jr., Johnny Bench, George Brett, and Steve Garvey, among others. "She got her nickname from a Cincinnati sportswriter, but in fact there was no banditry about her,

for few athletes resisted her heavily lipsticked advances" (Steve Rushin, *Sports Illustrated*, June 30, 2003).

"kiss it goodbye!" A salutation for a home run made famous by Pittsburgh Pirates announcer Bob Prince and also adopted by Washington Senators broadcaster Shelby Whitfield, whose book about the history of the franchise was entitled *Kiss It Goodbye*. A variation of the term was used in a baseball sense as early as 1908: "[Glenn] Liebhardt then went in to pitch and so far forgot himself as to put the ball in the groove for Sam Crawford. It was then a case of 'kiss yourself goodby,' for the mighty Crawford slammed the ball into the bleachers for a home run" (Ed F. Bang, *The Sporting Life*, May 9; Peter Morris).

kit-cat A 17th-century English forerunner of the American game of *three-old-cat*, featuring a triangular base layout and three batsmen (David Block, *Baseball Before We Knew It*, 2005, p.130).

kitchen 1. The area of a batter's torso inside or at the edge of the high and inside portion of the strike zone. A fastball coming into this area—"pitchin' in the kitchen," "getting in his kitchen," "cheese for your kitchen," etc.—is esp. tough, if not impossible, to hit. The term is often used in more elaborate metaphors; e.g., "he got in his kitchen and rattled a few pots and pans" or "he could get in your kitchen and saw your bat off." The term may also be father to others of a culinary nature, such as "he comes to eat" for a ball that moves in on a batter. See also *pots and pans*; *break his dishes*. 2. The stomach or strike area where most home run hitters generate the bulk of their power. 3. A pitcher's vulnerability. Lawrence Frank (*Playing Hardball: The Dynamics of Baseball Folk Speech*, 1983, p.104) wrote, "As the primary defender of the home territory, the pitcher is often subject to taunts that incorporate elements of home life. A team that is threatening to score on the pitcher may yell 'We're in your kitchen!' This statement ... stresses the fact that the other team is in control of the pitcher's home territory and implies they have assumed control of the major possessions of the pitcher: his house, his food, and possibly his wife or girl friend."

kitten ball [softball term] An early form of softball that used an outdoor version of the indoor game that was played in Chicago. It was introduced in Minneapolis in 1895 by Lt. Lewis Rober Sr. of Fire Dept. Company #11 as a form of exercise. Rober later transferred to another station and started another team, dubbed the Kittens; by 1900 leagues had been formed in Minneapolis. The bases were 45 feet apart. See also *diamond ball*. Also spelled "kittenball." Syn. *kitty-ball*. ETYMOLOGY. Rober named his team the Kittens after seeing a cat playing with a string of yarn. Minneapolis Fire Dept. captain George Kehoe coined the term "kitten ball" to honor Rober as the game's founder.

kitty-ball [softball term] Syn. of *kitten ball*.

Kitty League Nickname for the Kentucky-Illinois-Tennessee League, a Class D minor league that operated at various times between 1903 and 1955.

Klem's line The line drawn in the dirt by National League umpire Bill Klem during an altercation. He would say, "Don't cross the Rio Grande." Any player or manager who crossed that line was ejected from the game. "Klem's line is a symbol applicable not only to player-umpire relationships, but to player-fan and player-player relationships as well. For an umpire or another player will take a surprising amount of abuse if the proper clichés are used and the matter doesn't drag on too long" (Tristram Potter Coffin, *The Old Ball Game*, 1971).

Klutz World Series Nickname for the 1945 World Series between the Detroit Tigers and the Chicago Cubs which was played by unseasoned kids and retreads taking the place of regular players serving in the armed forces.

knee-buckling Said of an inside breaking ball (curveball or slider) that causes the batter to freeze or flinch in the belief that the pitch is about to hit him, and to bend his knees before bailing out. It occurs when a right-handed pitcher faces a right-handed batter, or a left-handed pitcher faces a left-handed batter. "Vicente Padilla, whose stuff is as knee-buckling as an all-night tequila session" (Michael Farber, *Sports Illustrated*, Apr. 4, 2005).

knee knocker A low pitch intended to hit or come extremely close to a batter's legs.

knee saver A piece of equipment consisting of wedge-shaped foam pads that catchers strap on behind their shin guards to support the knees and reduce strain (*The New York Times*, Apr. 2, 2000; Peter Morris).

Knickerbockers A gentlemen's social club that codified the first set of written rules for baseball competition. The club played informal, intramural baseball games as early as 1842. Consisting of young clerks, tradesmen, professionals, and assorted "gentlemen" in New York City, the club adopted a constitution and bylaws and a set of 20 rules on Sept. 23, 1845. The rules (later amended in 1848 and on Apr. 1, 1854) described an early version of the New York game and clarified aspects of baseball that were not standardized at the time (Tom Shieber, in David Block, *Baseball Before We Knew It*, 2005, p.92); e.g., 21 runs constituted a game, the ball had to be pitched (tossed underhand) and not thrown (overhand) to the batter, baserunners could not be retired by having the ball thrown at them, three outs were required to retire the side, a batted ball caught on the first bound was an out, and various other rules regarding offensive interference, pitcher's balks, and foul balls. The bylaws included fines for breaching the club's code of dress and behavior. The club rented a field and dressing rooms at the Elysian Fields in Hoboken, N.J. (readily accessible by ferry from Manhattan). It took a genteel approach to the game, allowing its members to play for fun while getting limited exercise away from work in an activity that traditionally had been child's play. The club also scheduled suppers, formal balls, and other festive occasions. It disbanded in the early 1880s. Full name: Knickerbocker Base Ball Club of New York.

knight of the keyboard A term used derisively and scornfully by Ted Williams for a sportswriter. On being elected to the National Baseball Hall of Fame, Williams declared (quoted in *Sports Illustrated*, Aug. 21, 1967),

"I thought a couple of the knights of the keyboard might try to keep me dangling awhile." The term is usually used in the plural, and sometimes capitalized.

knob 1. The rounded projection at the end of the bat handle that helps keep the bat from slipping out of the batter's hands. 2. The pitcher's mound (*The Sporting Life*, Nov. 29, 1913).

knock 1. *v.* To hit the ball. "Ivan Howard . . . has been known to knock home runs while batting right handed" (*San Francisco Bulletin*, May 20, 1913; Gerald L. Cohen). IST USE. 1835. "One of them stands ready to toss the ball—one to knock it, and two to run after it, if they fail to catch it" (description beneath a woodcut of boys playing ball, in a miniature chapbook *Sports of Youth*; *a Book of Plays*, published by S. Babcock of New Haven, Conn.; David Block). 2. *n.* A batted ball. IST USE. 1867. "McMillan by a short knock was unable to reach the first base" (*Detroit Advertiser and Tribune*, June 17; Peter Morris). 3. *n.* A batted ball for a base hit; specif., a *base knock*. "Thomas . . . was soused for four safe knocks and two runs before settling down" (*San Francisco Bulletin*, March 15, 1913; Gerald L. Cohen). IST USE. 1867. "Spaulding got in a terrible knock, brought home King and Stearns, and made his second [base]" (*Daily National Intelligencer* [Washington, D.C.], July 29). 4. *n./hist.* A turn at bat. "Players must take their knocks in the order in which they are numbered" (Rules of the Massachusetts Game, Rule 10, May 13, 1858). 5. *n./hist.* A foul tip that was not caught in the Massachusetts game. "If the Ball is not caught after being struck at three times, it shall be considered a knock, and the Striker obliged to run" (Rules of the Massachusetts Game, Rule 11, May 13, 1858). 6. *v.* To bat hard against a pitcher. IST USE. 1874 (*New York Herald*, July 31; Edward J. Nichols). 7. *v.* To be removed from a game; e.g., "Smith was knocked for baiting the umpire" or "Jones was knocked for a pinch hitter."

knockdown *n.* Syn. of *knockdown pitch*. "A deliberate knockdown is when you throw a ball at a hitter's head. You want to knock him down, maybe even hit him. It's a pouting gesture" (Bob Gibson, *From Ghetto to Glory*, 1968, p.145; Charles D. Poe).

knock down *v.* To force a batter to drop to the ground with a pitch that either intimidates or directly hits the batter. Syn. *deck*, 3; *put down*, 2.

knockdown pitch A vicious pitch that forces the batter to drop to the ground to avoid getting hit. It is often aimed at the batter's head. Bill Starr (*Clearing the Bases*, 1989, pp.92–94) wrote, "Brushback pitches do no harm. It's the knockdown pitch, a pitch at the batter's shoulders, that is dangerous. It's the rare pitcher who will use the batter's shoulders for a target. . . . In the [1920s to the 1950s] . . . a high inside pitch, a knockdown pitch, was automatically delivered following a home run. The target was the next hitter, who, of course, was innocent." Compare *beanball*; *brushback pitch*. Syn. *knockdown*; *high-neck-in pitch*; *throat cutter*. IST USE. 1962. "There's the brushback, and there's the knockdown pitch" (*The Saturday Evening Post*, June 30; David Shulman).

knockdown rule A rule stipulating that if in the umpire's judgment a pitch was thrown intentionally at a batter, the umpire may: a) expel the pitcher, or the pitcher and the manager, from the game; or b) warn the pitcher and managers of both teams that another such pitch will result in the immediate expulsion of that pitcher (or his replacement) and the manager (*Official Baseball Rules*, Rule 8.02[d]). The rule effectively has reduced knockdown pitches back to a maximum of one per game.

knocker 1. *hist.* A batter or striker in early baseball. IST USE. 1883. "At the bat the knocker couldn't knock at all" (*St. Louis Globe-Democrat*, Nov. 5). 2. A critical baseball fan; one who criticizes. "[Henley] has won three straight out of his five starts, although it is only a few weeks ago that the knockers were demanding his scalp" (*San Francisco Bulletin*, Apr. 25, 1913; Gerald L. Cohen). IST USE. 1900. "There is a well-founded rumor abroad that the veteran scribe, Tim Murnane, has his weather eye fixed on the presidency of the National League. Members of the knocker club will certainly get busy when this rumor has traveled through the circuit" (*The Washington Post*, July 22).

knocker's stone *hist.* Syn. of *home plate*.

knock in To bat in a run.

knock on the door For a minor leaguer to perform in such a manner that he is ready to join a major-league team.

knock out To cause a pitcher to be removed from the game, usually because of timely hitting. "The Phillies scored two more runs, knocking out losing pitcher Zane Smith" (*Tampa Tribune*, July 1, 1989). Syn. *knock out of the box*; *send to the showers*. IST USE. 1883 (*The Sporting Life*, May 20, p.2; Edward J. Nichols). ETYMOLOGY. Obvious antecedent in prizefighting. EXTENDED USE. To defeat or diminish.

knockout comer A young player who has the potential to be an outstanding player.

knock out of the box Syn. of *knock out*. IST USE. 1883. "The curve delivery in base ball pitching was the greatest change ever introduced into the game; and in these days, when an old-time straight pitcher would be knocked out of the box in an inning, there are a good many claimants for the credit of originating it" (*Philadelphia Press*, Aug. 20). USAGE NOTE. The term persists although the "pitcher's box" was eliminated after the 1892 season. "The old expression 'The pitcher was knocked out of the box,' must be amended under the new rules. 'He was knocked off the rubber slab,' might do" (*The Sporting Life*, June 3, 1893; Peter Morris).

knockout pitch A pitch that a pitcher relies on for strikeouts or outs. "[Brandon Claussen's] knockout pitch is a quality slider with excellent two-plane depth" (*Baseball America*, Jan. 21–Feb. 3, 2002; Peter Morris).

knock the ball out of the park To hit a home run. EXTENDED USE. To have success. "How about Carol Burnett knocking the ball out of the park in her little CBS outing . . . when she gathered her old gang together, tugged her ear, answered audience questions and showed us clips of 'bloopers' from her show" (Liz Smith, *Baltimore Sun*, Nov. 30, 2001).

knock the ball over the fence To hit a home run. EXTENDED USE. A metaphor for success in other fields. In 1967, President Lyndon B. Johnson said, "They booed Ted Williams, too, remember? They'll say about me I knocked the ball over the fence but they don't like the way that he stands at the plate" (*The New York Times*, May 30, 1968).

knock the bat out of his hands To retire the batter easily. "You can knock the bat out of his hands with fastballs" (anonymous scout, concerning Darren Lewis, quoted in *Sports Illustrated*, Oct. 18, 1999). "You thought you could knock the bat out of his hands because he looked so frail, and he'd kill you" (Carlton Fisk, on Brooks Robinson, quoted in Steve Fiffer, *How to Watch Baseball*, 1987, p.190).

knock the cover off the ball To hit the ball with such great force that the ball unravels. It is largely a figurative phrase, since such a feat is virtually impossible. "Even the little fellows are up there trying to knock the cover off the ball" (Branch Rickey, quoted in *The Sporting News*, June 1, 1963). Roy Hobbs, Bernard Malamud's hero in *The Natural* (1952), was told by his manager to "knock the cover off the ball," and he did so (literally). Other "knock" phrases include: "knock the blood out of it," "knock the juice out of it," "knock the stuffing out of the ball," and "knock the cover loose." Syn. *tear the cover off the ball*. IST USE. 1873 (*New York Herald*, Aug. 10; Edward J. Nichols). USAGE NOTE. There are variations of the term; e.g., "[Deacon Jim White] is pounding the cover off the ball as has ever been his custom" (*Milwaukee Sentinel*, May 7, 1885).

knoll Syn. of *mound*, 1. "[Bucky Walters] attached no particular significance to his work on the knoll" (Art Morrow, *The Sporting News*, Nov. 30, 1955).

knot 1. *v.* To even the score or a count; e.g., "an RBI single that knotted the game at 5 in the eighth" or "Smith took a strike to knot the count at 2 and 2." IST USE. 1915 (*Baseball Magazine*, December, p.71; Edward J. Nichols). 2. *n.* A tie score. IST USE. 1905. "Tom Jones walloped a safe one into center, which scored two runs and tied the game up in a knot" (*Chicago Tribune*, Apr. 16; Peter Morris).

knothole club 1. *hist.* A group of young fans

who try to see a baseball game without paying admission. **2.** A group of young fans formed by a major-league team as a promotional effort. Typically, youngsters received a card that enabled them to receive discounted or free tickets to games and the right to attend special clinics; the youngsters were also expected not to miss school and to refrain from smoking and swearing. The club nurtured the interest of young fans who, in later years, would develop into loyal fans paying full-ticket prices. It is generally agreed that the St. Louis Cardinals under Branch Rickey in 1917 was the first team to organize a knothole club, initially conceived by James C. Jones Jr., a St. Louis attorney. The Brooklyn Dodgers shepherded 2,256,000 youngsters into Ebbets Field on free Knothole Club passes between 1940 and 1957. See also *knothole gang*. ETYMOLOGY. From the image, favored by cartoonists and illustrators, of youngsters watching the game through knotholes in the tight wooden outfield fence.

knothole customer A spectator who found a way to see a baseball game without paying admission. Under the heading, "Curing a Knot-Hole Customer," *The Sporting News* (Aug. 1, 1929) told of an adult, watching a Laurel (Miss.) game through a knothole, who received a broken nose when an outfielder slammed into the fence.

knothole day A day, usually a Saturday, when the knothole club was able to get into the ballpark free or at a reduced rate.

knothole gang Syn. of *knothole club*. Marshall K. McClelland (*Pacific Stars and Stripes*, undated) reported that early in 1889, Abner Powell, the innovative owner of the New Orleans Pelicans, gathered together the youngsters of New Orleans and organized the first "Knot Hole Gang": "As long as the kids observed strict rules of personal behavior both inside and outside the park, Abner permitted them to see a free game or two each week the Pelicans were at home." In the 1930s, the Boston Braves had a Knothole Gang in which gang members, ages 14 and under, "bought knotted wood pieces for 50 cents; the wood served as a season-long ticket to the left field stands" (*The Boston Globe*, June 27, 1993).

Knothole gang. *Andy Moresund Collection*

When the Dodgers were still in Brooklyn, there was a television show before each game hosted by Happy Felton called "The Knot-Hole Gang" on which three sandlot players appeared. As Mel Allen (*It Takes Heart*, 1959; Charles D. Poe) explained, "The boys were asked to pitch or field grounders and fly balls, and the one judged the best was allowed to return to the show on the following day and interview the Brooklyn player of his choice."

knotholer A member of a knothole club or gang. "Wrigley Field . . . still has the concept of knotholers—people watching across the street" (Dewayne Staats, quoted in Curt Smith, *The Storytellers*, 1995).

knothole rate Free admission to a game (Maurice H. Weseen, *A Dictionary of American Slang*, 1934).

knubber A lucky hit that squirts through the infield; a scratch hit. See also *nubber*, 1. IST USE. 1937 (*New York Daily News*, Jan. 17; Edward J. Nichols).

knuck Said of the knuckleball or a knuckleball pitcher. "'Knuck' Star Started Jinx in No-Hitter" (*The Sporting News* headline, May 22, 1959).

knuckle 1. *n./hist.* Abbreviated version of *knuckleball*, 1. "There was 'the hook,' 'the knuckle' ... and so many others that there seemed to be no end to them" (J.W. Duffield, *Bert Wilson's Fadeaway Ball*, 1913; David Shulman). **2.** *v.* To show the various movements of the knuckleball. "When a knuckleball doesn't knuckle it's not a knuckleball, it's a piece of cake, pound cake" (Jim Bouton, *I'm Glad You Didn't Take It Personally*, 1971, p.62; Charles D. Poe). **3.** *v.* For a line drive to break late in flight when it encounters a wind current.

knuckleball 1. A slowly pitched ball that is gripped with the fingertips, fingernails, or knuckles of the middle two or three fingers pressed against the ball and thrown or "pushed" with little or no spin so that it will dance, float, flutter, dart, bob, weave, wobble, sail, or dip in a totally unpredictable manner; "a curveball that doesn't give a damn" (Jimmy Cannon). Because the ball does not rotate and is moving slowly (usually less than 80 miles per hour, often only 50 mph), it is more directly affected by air currents and breezes. The ball's behavior is as erratic as the flight of a hummingbird (Pat Jordan, *A False Spring*, 1975, pp.75–76). The ball may move up, down, or sideways as much as 11 inches (*Newsweek*, July 27, 1992). Most knuckleball pitchers hold the ball with the fingertips, not the knuckles, and throw it without twisting the hand or wrist. The pitch

Knuckleball.

can be devilishly difficult to hit and not at all easy to catch (hence, not a great pitch to use when runners are in scoring position). Bob Uecker said that the best way for a catcher to handle the pitch was "to wait until the ball stops rolling and then pick it up" (quoted in *Science 83*). The best evidence suggests that Eddie Cicotte and Eddie Summers developed the knuckleball when both were pitching for Indianapolis (a Detroit Tigers farm club) in 1906, although the pitch may have been thrown as early as the 1880s. Other pitchers who perfected the pitch include Emil "Dutch" Leonard, Hoyt Wilhelm, Phil Niekro, and Charlie Hough. See also *fingertip ball*; *spinner*, 2; *dry spitter*, 1. Also spelled "knuckle ball." Syn. *knuckle*, 1; *knuckler*, 1; *bob-and-weave*; *bug*, 2; *butterfly*; *floater*, 2; *flutterball*; *dancer*; *mariposa*; *moth*; *bubble*, 2; *ghostball*; *horseshoe*; *rabbit*, 2; *raw-raw*; *tumbler*. 1ST USE. 1908 (*New York Evening Journal*, March 24; Edward J. Nichols). **2.** A hard-hit ball that changes direction during its flight. **3.** [softball term] A ball that breaks suddenly with little rotation in fast pitch softball. The ball is pushed out of the hand rather than rolling off the fingers.

EXTENDED USE. An unpredictable or uncertain situation. "It is an astonishing knuckleball of history that the president [George W. Bush] who abhors mess is presiding over a spectacularly messy conflict" (Maureen Dowd, *The Baltimore Sun*, Oct. 26, 2001). Concerning a football punt, Washington Redskins coach Steve Spurrier said (*The Baltimore Sun*, Dec. 24, 2002), "So if it's a short knuckleball, we're not going to touch it. Just let it hit and get out of the way."

knuckleballer A pitcher whose main pitch is the knuckleball. "They say you don't want to have a knuckleballer pitching for you or

Knuckleball. Cleveland Indians pitcher Eddie Fisher demonstrates the traditional fingering, 1968. *Courtesy of the Cleveland Indians*

against you" (Los Angeles Dodgers manager Tommy Lasorda, quoted in *Milwaukee Journal Sentinel*, Aug. 4, 1997). Syn. *knuckler*, 2; *knuckles*. IST USE. 1909. "It was all right for [Detroit Tigers manager Hughie Jennings] to try [Ed] Summers again on a clear day, but after the knuckle baller had shown poor form . . . the wise manager would in such an important series, when one game meant so much, have yanked him out" (*The Sporting News*, Oct. 21; Peter Morris).

knuckle curve A curveball thrown from a knuckleball grip, which causes the ball to drop sharply just before it reaches the batter. A blend of knuckleball and curveball, it seems to cause the ball to drop into the catcher's mitt, like a coin into a slot machine. The pitch, as thrown by Mike Mussina, is a regular curveball but with the index finger dug into the ball to provide leverage. Syn. *spike curve*. IST USE. 1907. "Pitcher Morgan of the Philadelphia club has a new curve that he calls a 'knuckle curve'" (*Lansing* [Mich.] *Journal*, June 5; Peter Morris).

knuckle duster A pitch thrown close to the batter's knuckles.

knuckler 1. Syn. of *knuckleball*, 1. IST USE. 1913. "It was [Eddie] Cicotte who brought the knuckler into the spotlight of the national game" (*Williamsport* [Pa.] *Gazette and Bulletin*, March 17; Peter Morris). 2. Syn. of *knuckleballer.*

knuckles Syn. of *knuckleballer.* Eddie Cicotte, who reportedly developed the knuckleball, was nicknamed "Knuckles."

Koppett's Law Poor fielding will lose many more games than good hitting will win games: "You can score only one run and still win, but you must get 27 outs" (George F. Will, *Newsweek*, March 22, 1999). Named for baseball writer Leonard Koppett, who propounded the importance of fielding in his book *A Thinking Man's Guide to Baseball* (1967).

Koufaxian In the manner of Brooklyn/Los Angeles Dodgers left-handed pitcher Sandy Koufax (1955–1966); said of masterful pitching technique. "Ken Dixon, who might need a Koufaxian final three weeks to oust any of the top four starters, has looked sharp" (*The Baltimore Sun*, March 16, 1986).

KP Abbrev. for *can't play.*

KP duty Assignment to the bullpen. ETYMOLOGY. A term ("kitchen police") brought back from World War II by players who had been in the armed forces.

krank *hist.* Var. of *crank*, 1. The term appears in the title of Thomas W. Lawson's 1888 book on baseball slang: *The Krank: His Language and What It Means.* See also *kranklet.* USAGE NOTE. Peter Morris notes that the term was virtually unheard of in the 19th century except for the title of Lawson's book; it may have been the author's idiosyncratic spelling. Unfortunately, "krank" has been overused in recent years by historians who seek a period feel without doing much research.

kranklet A female *krank.* "The 'krank' . . . was said to have achieved a high degree of cultivation, whereas the female of the species, the 'kranklet,' was only partially developed" (Harold Seymour, *Baseball: The Early Years*, 1960, p.329).

KS 1. Scorecard symbol for a strikeout when the third strike is a swing and a miss. 2. A cheer, chanted "kay ess, kay ess," when a pitcher strikes out a batter.

K 2–3 Scorecard notation for a strikeout in which the catcher drops the third strike and must throw the ball to first base to retire the batter.

kudo A term used by pitcher Dennis Eckersley for the bow a batter takes when he bails out or falls away from a pitch (*Sports Illustrated*, Dec. 12, 1988).

KY A strikeout attributed to pitches with balls doctored with K-Y lubricant. "Gaylord Perry, a nonentity at twenty-seven, discovered Vaseline, K-Y vaginal jelly, and hitter hydrophobia (spitter on the brain), and has won 296 games (so far)" (Thomas Boswell, *How Life Imitates the World Series*, 1982).

K-Y ball A variation on the illegal spitball in which K-Y vaginal lubricant (Gaylord Perry's favorite substance) is used to doctor the ball.

kyuyo Japanese for "rest and recuperate." A unique custom in Japanese baseball occurs when the manager of a floundering team is told by his club to take a break or leave of absence, which may last from a few days to a few seasons. As explained by *Baseball America* (Oct. 13–26, 2003; Peter Morris): "The theory is that the club would improve when the players, embarrassed by the maneuver, work harder in order to start winning again and get their manager back. A kyuyo usually results in the manager never returning, however, so as a practical matter it's a low-key firing."

K zone Syn. of *strike zone*, 1.

L

L **1.** Abbrev. for *loss*, 1. **2.** Abbrev. for *loss*, 2. **3.** Box score abbrev. for *losing pitcher*. **4.** Abbrev. for *line drive*. **5.** *hist.* Abbrev. for a foul ball. ETYMOLOGY. From the last letter in the word "foul."

label **1.** *n.* The printed or branded portion of the head of a baseball bat that contains the manufacturer's name. **2.** *v./hist.* To bat a ball; to "mark" the ball for a base hit. IST USE. 1908 (*New York Evening Journal*, Apr. 25; Edward J. Nichols).

label for four To hit a home run (Maurice H. Weseen, *A Dictionary of American Slang*, 1934).

lace To hit the ball hard. "In the second inning [Claude] Ritchey laced a single out in left field" (*The New York Times*, Apr. 28, 1908; Barry Popik). "[Barry Bonds] promptly laced a pitch just over the fence" (*The Baltimore Sun*, Apr. 6, 2004). IST USE. 1888. "Lace it out" (a caption in Thomas W. Lawson, *The Krank: His Language and What It Means*; David Shulman).

ladder **1.** See *climb the ladder*. **2.** See *up the ladder*. **3.** See *up-and-down the ladder*.

Ladies' Day A promotional event offering women free or reduced admission to the ballpark on certain days. The practice of admitting women free was adopted to ensure better behavior from male spectators as well as to encourage women to become regular cash customers. IST USE. 1883. "Every Thursday, while the [Athletics are] in town, will be set aside for 'ladies' day'" (*New York Clipper*, Apr. 7; Peter Morris). USAGE NOTE. It is difficult to pinpoint the first Ladies' Day, since admitting women free was a common practice from the earliest efforts to collect admission at baseball games. Various clubs experimented with the idea as early as 1866. In the 1870s, women were often admitted free if accompanied by a male escort. Games began to be specifically advertised as Ladies' Days in the 1880s. In 1883, the Philadelphia Athletics and Baltimore Orioles separately sponsored the first "official" Ladies' Day in the major leagues, in an attempt to "encourage American women to come out to the park, free of charge, [and] to look in on the game that had stolen the hearts of their men folk" (Catherine Rondina and Joseph Romain, *Ladies Day: One Woman's Guide to Pro Baseball*, 1997, p.i). In 1884, the Union Association management inaugurated "the idea of ladies' day, when the ladies are cordially invited to accept

Ladies' Day. Bucky Harris autographing scorecards on dugout steps on Ladies' Day. *George Grantham Bain Collection, Library of Congress*

the freedom of the grounds and grand stand" and designated each Thursday during the season "to be set apart and known as ladies' day" (*The Washington Post*, Apr. 17, 1884). New Orleans Pelicans owner Abner Powell introduced Ladies' Day in New Orleans in 1887. Barry Popik found a line from *The Sporting Life* (Aug. 25, 1886) stating "'Ladies' Day' is now six years of age." The building of women's bathroom facilities made Ladies' Days more feasible. But the custom is said to have truly taken hold with the Cincinnati Red Stockings in the latter part of the 1880s. Club owner Aaron Stern noted that the number of women in the stands increased significantly when a handsome pitcher named Tony "Count" Mullane was on the mound. Early in 1889, Stern announced that Mullane would pitch each Monday and all women would be admitted free providing they were accompanied by a paying male escort. This became a regular attraction and soon spread to other clubs; but when crowds of women often waited outside the ballpark or at the box office for men to take them through the turnstiles, the practice stopped. The custom was given a boost in the days after World War II when owners used Ladies' Days to attract customers. Ladies' Days disappeared in the early 1970s when legal proceedings forced courts to ban preferential treatment on grounds of discrimination against men. Women's groups protested Ladies' Day as an antiquated practice from the days when women and men were not on an equal footing in society. ETYMOLOGY. Stuart Berg Flexner (*Listening to America*, 1982) discovered that the term predated baseball and was used to designate a day when men could bring women to their clubs. He found it used as early as 1787: "George Washington recorded the term in his diary that year, noting that a club at which he dined had a 'ladies' day' every other Saturday."

ladle To hit a ball hard.

Lady Godiva pitch A pitch with nothing on it. "Eddie Siever pitched for us and his 'Lady Godiva ball' (nothing on it) was hammered for a 5–1 Chicago win" (Ty Cobb, *My Life in Baseball*, 1961, p.74). Syn. *nudist pitch*.

lallapalooza A spectacular play. Var. "lallapaloosa." IST USE. 1905. "Van had got into the game with a lallapaloosa to center" (*The Sporting Life*, Apr. 22; David Shulman). ETYMOLOGY. Var. of *lollapalooza*.

La Lob A trick pitch, invented and named by New York Yankees (1981–1983) pitcher Dave LaRoche, that slowly floats toward home plate with a high-arcing trajectory. Frederick C. Klein (*The Wall Street Journal*, Oct. 5, 1982) described it as "the sort of pitch you throw to your seven-year-old son in your backyard." Klein was recalling two La Lob confrontations between LaRoche and Milwaukee Brewers slugger Gorman Thomas. Late in the 1981 season, Thomas struck out swinging at the pitch. The two players met again on June 30, 1982, and LaRoche threw seven consecutive La Lobs. Five were fouled off, one was taken for a ball, and the last one was slapped into left field for a hit. When Thomas reached first base, he raised his fists over his head, Rocky style. See also *eephus*.

lam To bat a ball hard. "[Hickman] did lam the ball with great force, but failed to place one safe until the ninth" (Charles Dryden, *Chicago Tribune*, Aug. 30, 1907). IST USE. 1900. "[Paxton] lammed a cuckoo in the direction of the setting sun" (*Idaho* [Boise] *Daily Statesman*, May 2; Peter Morris).

lamb 1. A young ballplayer; a rookie. According to Herbert Simons (*Baseball Magazine*, Apr. 1943), Ted Williams used the term so frequently that he became known as "The Lamb." IST USE. 1933. "'Lamb' is a newcomer or a youngster" (Walter Winchell, *Havana Evening Telegram*, May 3). 2. A pitcher who is easy to hit; a *cousin*, 1. 3. A player with a low batting average.

lambaste To bat a ball hard. "Many a National League pitcher will tell you of trying to 'waste' a pitch, only to have Joe [Medwick] reach up or down or out and lambaste it into the seats" (J. Roy Stockton, *The Gashouse Gang*, 1945, p.139). IST USE. 1907. "Such a lambasting as the eel ball got in the ninth will not be forgotten before the Cubs come back here in 1908" (I.E. Sanborn, *Chicago Tribune*, Aug. 30; Peter Morris).

laminate To hit the ball extremely hard. IST USE. 1914. "Murder it, Ted, old man! Laminate it!" (Burt L. Standish, *Lefty O' the Blue Stockings*; David Shulman).

lamp **1.** *v.* To scout a player. "Barnett told me they wasn't nobody else on neither club worth lampin'" (Ring Lardner, *The Saturday Evening Post*, July 25, 1914; Peter Morris). **2.** *v.* To look at attractive female spectators. "Lamp the girl in row 22" (John Hall, *Baseball Digest*, Dec. 1973). IST USE. 1914. "In one o' the boxes . . . was the prettiest girl I ever looked at. . . . She was sittin' where we could lamp her from our bench and all the boys had give her the oncet over before the game ever started" (Ring Lardner, *The Saturday Evening Post*, July 25; Peter Morris). **3.** *n.* The eye of a batter. Usually used in the plural.

lamps Eyes. "[Bill Klem] said he didn't miss any [calls] in his heart, but he didn't say anything about his lamps" (umpire Shag Crawford, quoted in Larry R. Gerlach, *The Men in Blue*, 1980, p.209). "Jesse Burkett's batting lamps are beginning to burn brighter, and they will develop an X ray glint before the season has reached the half" (*The Washington Post*, June 14, 1897).

land **1.** To get a base hit. "Van landed it for a clean homer" (*The Sporting Life*, Oct. 21, 1893; Peter Morris). **2.** To win (*The Sporting Life*, Nov. 29, 1913).

landing *hist.* A base. "[Bill] Gilbert, who will handle the second landing" (*Milwaukee Journal*, Apr. 17, 1901; Peter Morris).

landing gear The arms and front of the body as applied to a player sliding into a base. Broadcaster Vin Scully used the term to describe Bo Jackson dropping down to slide in the All-Star Game, July 11, 1989.

Landis-Eastman Line The geographic line in the eastern United States, west or south of which no major-league team (except for the St. Louis Cardinals) could hold spring training from 1942 to 1945 because of government-imposed travel restrictions during World War II. Teams were forced to train north of the Ohio and Potomac rivers and east of the Mississippi River. The Line (spoofing the Mason-Dixon Line) was drawn by baseball commissioner Kenesaw Mountain Landis and enforced by Joseph B. Eastman, head of the Office of Defense Transportation.

land on **1.** To bat a ball hard. IST USE. 1896. "The batters of both sides seemed to have little trouble in landing on the ball whenever they pleased" (*The Boston Globe*, July 18; Peter Morris). **2.** To hit a pitcher hard. "[Dutch Schwering] landed on Sinclair, the Emeryville twirler for four safeties, one being a homer" (*San Francisco Bulletin*, March 3, 1913; Gerald L. Cohen).

lane changer Syn. of *bat messer.*

lanzador Spanish for "pitcher."

lanzador relevista Spanish for "relief pitcher."

lanzamiento Spanish for "pitch" (noun).

lanzamiento descontrolado Spanish for "wild pitch."

lanzamiento franco Spanish for "pitchout."

lanzamiento rompiente Spanish for "curveball."

lanzar Spanish for "pitch" (verb).

lap-sitter A manager's "yes" man (Jimmy Powers, *New York Daily News*, Jan. 10, 1937).

lapta (pron. "lahp-TA") An ancient bat-and-ball folk game played in Russian villages and from which the Russians claim the American game of baseball was stolen. Sergei Shachin (*Izvestia*, July 4, 1987), citing cultural historians, insisted that baseball was descended from lapta, which had been brought to what was to become California by Russian émigrés in the late 18th century. According to *The New York Times* (Sept. 16, 1952), the Russian magazine *Smena* described lapta as follows: "At opposite ends of a broad square there are marked 'cities.' The players are divided into two teams. The players in turn with a blow of a round stick knock a ball up and ahead, and during its flight run around to the 'city' of the opposing team and back. The latter tries to catch the ball and strike the runner with it." The *Smena* article, a particularly interesting example of Cold War rhetoric, claimed that the evils of capitalism had transformed lapta into a "beastly battle," marred by violence, betting, and crass exploitation of workers. See also Bill Keller ("In Baseball, the Russians Steal All the Bases," *The New York Times*, July 20, 1987) and John Leo ("Evil Umpires? Not in Soviet Baseball," *Time* magazine, Aug. 10, 1987, p.56).

larceny Syn. of *base stealing*. On Ping Bodie's inability to steal second base in 1917, columnist Bugs Baer wrote, "He had larceny in his heart [head], but his feet were honest." The line so amused press baron William Randolph Hearst that he hired Baer to write for his *New York American*. Compare *grand larceny*. IST USE. 1910 (*Baseball Magazine*, December, p.36; Edward J. Nichols).

Laredo See *throw Laredo*.

large fly Syn. of *big fly*.

large-market club A major-league club in a heavily populated metropolitan area, such as New York, Los Angeles, or Chicago, which tends to have higher attendance and supplements ticket sales with more revenue than other clubs for the television, cable, and radio rights to their games. The term now more properly refers to a *high-revenue club* (thanks in part to income from luxury boxes in new ballparks), regardless of its market size. Large market clubs include the New York Yankees, New York Mets, Los Angeles Dodgers, and Chicago Cubs. Compare *small-market club*; *medium-market club*. Syn. *big-market club*. USAGE NOTE. The term "large-market club" has much less to do with market forces than the philosophy of the club's ownership. There are many examples of clubs that rapidly go from so-called large market to small market, or vice versa. *Baseball Prospectus* (2000; Peter Morris) observed, "The incessant yammering over large and small markets is at best a waste of time, and at worst a controversy based on falsehoods promoted by Major League Baseball and team owners. . . . Even the terms 'small market' and 'large market' are misused so badly that, until some effort is made to define and use them accurately, serious debate will be doomed."

larrup 1. To hit a baseball with force. One of Lou Gehrig's many nicknames was "Larrupin' Lou." IST USE. 1886. "Deacon White larruped the sphere away down the right foul line for three excellent bases" (*Chicago Tribune*, July 6; Peter Morris). ETYMOLOGY. A colloquialism among the Irish dating back to at least the early 19th century. It means "to beat, thrash, or flog" and is said to be a corruption of the nautical term "lee rope." The earliest example listed in the *Oxford English Dictionary* dates to 1823. 2. To defeat a team convincingly. "A's Larrup [Joel] Horlen, Rout Chisox, 12–2" (*The Washington Post* headline, May 24, 1970).

larruper A powerful hitter. IST USE. 1908 (*New York Evening Journal*, Aug. 26; Edward J. Nichols).

Larry Slang term for *losing pitcher*.

laser Syn. of *line drive*.

lash To hit a ball hard. IST USE. 1905. "Lajoie lashed out a single" (*Chicago Tribune*, June 2; Peter Morris).

Lasker Plan A plan formulated in 1920 by Albert D. Lasker, a prominent Chicago businessman and a stockholder in the Chicago Cubs, to restructure organized baseball in the wake of the Black Sox Scandal. Its basic premise was that the club owners were "incapable of governing their own business, in view of their interminable politicking, their public squabbles, and the growing whisperings about game throwing" (Harold Seymour, *Baseball: The Golden Age*, 1971). The plan provided for a triumvirate composed of eminent persons without financial interest in baseball who would be invested with "unreviewable authority," including power to reprimand or fine owners and players and even to declare a franchise forfeited. The plan was supported by the National League and three American League clubs (Boston, New York, and Chicago), but was abandoned when all 16 major-league clubs endorsed Judge Kenesaw Mountain Landis as baseball's first commissioner.

last For a pitcher to remain in the game for a given length of time; e.g., "Smith lasted for six innings." IST USE. 1902 (*The Sporting Life*, July 5, p.8; Edward J. Nichols).

last bullet [softball term] The upcoming third out in the last inning for the losing team.

last ditch Last place in the standings. "Cleveland [Spiders] had become the occupant of the last ditch as early as the opening month of the season, and did its best months' work in May, after which it failed to make any effort to get out of its tail-end position" (*Spalding's Official Base Ball Guide*, 1900, p.14; Peter Morris, who wondered if this is where the phrase "last-ditch effort" came from).

last half The *second half* of an inning.

last licks The home team's opportunity to bat in the second half of the last inning of a game.

last man 1. The player (batter or baserunner) who makes the final out in a game. Grantland Rice (*The Sporting Life*, Jan. 5, 1907) observed, "The game's never lost till the last man is out." 2. The last player on a team to enter a game. "I was down to my last man . . . but that's why you have a bigger roster in September" (San Francisco Giants manager Dusty Baker, quoted in *Milwaukee Journal Sentinel*, Sept. 11, 1997).

last ups The team to come to the plate in the bottom half of the last inning of the game. In organized baseball, the home team always has last ups. "This was one of those games where it seemed like last ups was going to come away with it" (Scott Hatteberg, quoted in *The Baltimore Sun*, May 11, 2006). Compare *first ups*.

late and close Syn. of *close and late*.

late foot A winning or hitting streak toward the end of the season; e.g., "The White Sox are showing late foot."

late hitter Syn. of *opposite-field hitter* (John W. "Jack" Coombs, *Baseball*, 1938).

late-inning *adj.* Toward the end of the game. EXTENDED USE. Late in any realm. "Late-Inning Hardball in the House" (*The Washington Post* headline, Dec. 28, 1987).

late-inning defensive replacement A good defensive player inserted into the lineup toward the end of the game, generally to help protect a lead.

late-inning pressure situation "Any plate appearance occurring in the seventh inning or later with the score tied or with the batter's team trailing by one, two, or three runs (or four with the bases loaded)" (Elias Sports Bureau, *Baseball Analyst*, 1985). Player performance in late-inning pressure situations was included in all nine of the published *Baseball Analysts*. See also *clutch*; *close and late*. Abbrev. *LIPS*.

late innings The seventh, eighth, and ninth innings of a baseball game. EXTENDED USE. Late stages of a project.

late life Movement on a fastball right before it reaches home plate. "[Jonathan Papelbon's] fastball doesn't sink as much as most fastballs in the last five feet to the plate but instead creates the illusion of 'hopping,' or what hitters call 'late life'" (Tom Verducci, *Sports Illustrated*, Oct. 1, 2007). See also *life*, 3; *giddyup*.

late pitcher *hist.* A warm-weather pitcher. "It is said that [Harley] Payne is a late pitcher, which means in base ball parlance, that he is at his best when the warm weather sets in" (*Brooklyn Eagle*, May 1, 1896; Peter Morris).

late reliever A relief pitcher brought into a game in the late innings.

late-season pickup A player signed or acquired after the All-Star break, often seen as valuable to a pennant drive. Syn. "late-season acquisition."

latest line A gambling tool featuring a list of odds favoring or disfavoring teams before a given day's games. Latest lines are published in many newspapers and their prime function is to aid betting.

lather To hit. "Bobby Adams, Connie Ryan, and Johnny Pramesa lathered the always-reliable Sal Maglie for homers" (Harvey Rosenfeld, *The Great Chase*, 1992, p.67). IST USE. 1934 (*Journalism Quarterly*; David Shulman).

laugher A game with a lopsided score; a rout; an easy win. Ralph Andreano (*No Joy in Mudville*, 1965, p.24) wrote that the term is used "to indicate that a game is reasonably beyond winning (or losing) because a team is so far ahead (or behind) in the number of runs scored." Baltimore Orioles manager Earl Weaver (quoted in *USA Today*, June 9, 1986): "When Lee Lacy hits three home runs and drives in six runs, you figure the game is going to be a laugher. But at one point, it sure wasn't." See also *blowout*, 2; *romp*.

launch 1. *v.* To hit a home run. "[Jay] Payton one-upped him to a degree by launching a shot to dead center that struck the wall in front of the black seats" (Bob Ryan, *The Boston Globe*, May 29, 2005). 2. *n.* A home run. "When [Barry] Bonds hit his second, a 407-foot launch to centerfield, the Giants were behind 8–4" (Jeff Pearlman, *Sports Illustrated*, Oct. 15, 2001).

launching pad **1.** A ballpark in which home runs are hit with great frequency. After the Baltimore Orioles set a single-month home run hitting record in May 1987, coach Frank Robinson said of Memorial Stadium: "It's a launching pad" (UPI dispatch, June 2, 1987). Atlanta–Fulton County Stadium long enjoyed the nickname "The Launching Pad." The term has also been applied to Wrigley Field in Chicago and Coors Field in Denver. **2.** A not-so-endearing syn. of *mound*, 1.

laundering The early efforts by major-league clubs to avoid the restrictions in the 1903 National Agreement on sending players to a minor-league team by repeatedly selling and repurchasing a player to a minor-league club with which they held a cozy but unofficial relationship.

lawn *hist.* A baseball field. "[Happy Felsch] misjudged the ball . . . and he only touched it as it flittered down to the lawn" (*The New York Times*, Oct. 7, 1919).

lawn mower A hard-hit ground ball. See also *grass cutter*. IST USE. 1876. "Simonds took first on lawn-mower badly handled by Lunt" (*Milwaukee Daily Sentinel*, June 12).

law of competitive balance The tendency for a team whose won-loss record goes up (or down) one year to go down (or up) the next year. It is partly a result of random variation (similar tendencies occur in many other contexts, which statisticians refer to as "regression toward the mean") and of changes in a team's talent base across seasons. The term was introduced by Bill James (*Baseball Abstract*, 1983): "There exists in the world a negative momentum, which acts constantly to reduce the differences between strong teams and weak teams, teams which are ahead and teams which are behind, or good players and poor players. . . . The balance of strategies always favors the team which is behind [and] psychology tends to pull the winners down and push the losers upwards." Syn. *plexiglas principle*.

law of retaliation An unwritten understanding among players that if a pitcher on team A throws at a batter on team B, the pitcher on team B will throw at a batter on team A. This thinking has resulted in many bench-clearing incidents that have been detrimental to baseball in general.

lawyer **1.** A player who talks or complains a lot; a "player who airs radical views in the clubhouse and dugout" (Edwin M. Rumill, *Christian Science Monitor*, Sept. 1, 1937). See also *clubhouse lawyer*. **2.** A player, coach, or manager who tends to contest the decisions of umpires.

lay an egg To fail to score. "[Miles Wolff] thought it would be cute if a giant wooden goose perched on the outfield scoreboard laid an egg every time the opposition failed to score a run in an inning, goose egg being baseball slang for a zero" (Stefan Fatsis, *The Wall Street Journal*, July 23, 1999).

lay back **1.** For a batter to wait for his pitch. **2.** To play baseball in a nonaggressive manner.

lay down **1.** To execute a bunt. Syn. *lay one down*; "lay it down." IST USE. 1905. "[Johnny] Kling, instead of laying the ball down, sent a long fly to left" (*Chicago Tribune*, May 4; Peter Morris). **2.** To stop trying one's best in a game. IST USE. 1911 (*American Magazine*, May, p.183; Edward J. Nichols).

"lay it in there" An encouragement to a pitcher to throw a strike or to give the batter something to hit.

layoff *n.* A period of inactivity for either a player or a team. "After a four-day layoff because of rainouts and off days, the Pirates couldn't wait to lay it on the Atlanta Braves" (*The Washington Post*, May 11, 1989). Sometimes spelled "lay-off." IST USE. 1912 (*New York Tribune*, Oct. 7; Edward J. Nichols).

lay off *v.* To refrain from swinging at a borderline pitch or a pitch out of the strike zone; e.g., many batters cannot "lay off" swinging at a rising fastball at the top edge of the strike zone. "[Ryan Minor] has to learn to lay off the pitcher's pitch and look for his pitch" (Don Buford, quoted in *The Baltimore Sun*, Feb. 4, 2000). Compare *chase*, 4.

lay on To bat a ball hard. IST USE. 1880 (*Chicago Inter-Ocean*, May 8; Edward J. Nichols).

lay one down Syn. of *lay down*, 1.

lay one in To throw a pitch that is easy to hit.

lay the ball over the plate To throw a pitch precisely over the plate. "[Chief Bender] can lay the ball over the plate almost to the eighth of an inch when he is 'right'" (Connie Mack, quoted in *San Francisco Bulletin*, Feb. 12, 1913; Gerald L. Cohen).

lay the bat on the ball For a batter to make contact. "[Gorman] Thomas spread his stance and cut down his swing, just looking to lay his bat on the ball" (Steve Wulf, *Sports Illustrated*, Oct. 25, 1982, p.37). Tony Gwynn described the process (*Sunday Oregonian*, June 23, 1991): "I don't swing real hard. I just get the bat through the zone. I don't kill the ball. Tap it. Lay the bat on the ball. I hit it hard enough to get it through the infield, but soft enough to get it out, way out in the outfield."

lay the wood To hit the ball hard; e.g., "Smith laid the wood to the ball." IST USE. 1908 (*Baseball Magazine*, June, p.25; Edward J. Nichols).

layup incentive An achievement noted in a player's contract that is as easy to make as a layup in basketball; e.g., 25 starts or 150 innings pitched for a healthy starting pitcher.

lazy Describing a ball without great velocity. IST USE. 1907. "[Ed] Reulbach drew a base on balls and was out at second on [Kid] Durbin's lazy grounder" (*Chicago Tribune*, Apr. 7; Peter Morris).

lazy hit Syn. of *Texas Leaguer*, 2. IST USE. 1932 (*Baseball Magazine*, October, p.496; Edward J. Nichols).

LCI Abbrev. for *level of competition index*.

LCS Abbrev. for *League Championship Series*.

LD *hist.* Abbrev. for *foul bound* (*Chicago Tribune*, July 22, 1870). ETYMOLOGY. Peter Morris surmised that since Henry Chadwick used "L" for "foul" (using the last letter of the word), then "D" may have been chosen for "bound" according to the same logic.

LDS Abbrev. for *League Division Series*.

lead [pron. "leed"] **1.** *n.* The distance a baserunner stands from the base he occupies in the direction of the next base when the ball is pitched. The runner tries to take a lead that gives him an advantage in reaching the next base safely while still allowing him the option of getting back to the original base before the pitcher or catcher can pick him off. Syn.

leadoff, 3. IST USE. 1901 (Burt L. Standish, *Frank Merriwell's School Days*, p.260; Edward J. Nichols). EXTENDED USE. An advantage. Avoiding comparison with Marilyn Monroe, blonde movie hopeful Sheree North said, "Let's say she takes a bigger lead off first than I do" (*Life* magazine, March 21, 1955, p.65; Peter Tamony). **2.** *n.* The advantage in runs scored by one team over another. **3.** *v.* To have scored more runs than the opposing team at any given time during a game. **4.** *v.* To be ahead in a particular statistical category; e.g., a team in first place "leads" other teams in the standings or the player with the most home runs "leads" in the chase for the home run crown.

lead bat A bat that has been weighted down with lead or other metal. It is swung in the on-deck circle to make one's regular bat seem lighter and easier to swing.

leaded coffee Syn. of *players' coffee*.

leader card A baseball card that depicts one or more players who led their respective league in a particular statistical category during the previous season.

lead glove The figurative glove employed by an inept fielder or one with "hands made of stone." See also *iron glove*, 2.

leading lady **1.** Syn. of *lead runner*. **2.** The first batter up in an inning.

leadoff **1.** *adj.* Said of the first in an inning or game; e.g., "leadoff double," "leadoff run," or "leadoff walk." "[Brady] Anderson had batted leadoff in all 15 of his starts" (*The Baltimore Sun*, May 12, 1998). Also spelled "lead-off." **2.** *n.* Syn. of *leadoff batter*, 1. Also spelled "lead-off." IST USE. 1906. "[Bill] O'Neill looks like a good lead off, being left handed, fast, and a good waiter" (*Chicago Tribune*, March 26; Peter Morris). **3.** *n.* Syn. of *lead*, 1. "A big leadoff does not ensure a successful steal" (Steve Fiffer, *How to Watch Baseball*, 1987, p.105).

lead off *v.* **1.** To be the first batter in the batting order or in an inning. IST USE. 1860. "Smith led off [the third inning]" (*The New York Herald*, Aug. 24). **2.** For a baserunner to take a lead. "I make them practice leading off and getting back to the base with their eyes closed" (coach Dave Nelson, quoted in Steve Fiffer, *How to Watch Baseball*, 1987, p.104).

leadoff batter 1. The player who is first in the batting order. Because this batter comes to bat more than any other player on the team, the position is normally reserved for a player with a high on-base percentage, plate discipline, bat control, good speed, and the ability to steal bases. Exceptional leadoff batters include Tim Raines, Maury Wills, Lou Brock, and Rickey Henderson. Also spelled "lead-off batter." Syn. *leadoff*, 2; *leadoff hitter*; *leadoff man*; *number-one hitter*; *anchor man*. 2. The player who is the first to bat for a team in an inning.

leadoff hitter Syn. of *leadoff batter*, 1.

leadoff man Syn. of *leadoff batter*, 1. 1ST USE. 1910 (*Baseball Magazine*, April, p.64; Edward J. Nichols).

leadoff runner The first player to get on base in an inning or a game.

lead runner The baserunner farthest along the basepath. Syn. *leading lady*, 1.

league A group of teams or clubs who play each other in a prearranged schedule over an extended period of time to decide on a championship from among its members, and who are governed by a common set of rules and regulations. The National League of 1876 introduced the concepts of a numerically limited group of members (with new entrants selected by the current members) and a minimum city size for its members. The National League appears to be the model for the use of the term "league" in a sporting sense, although the term was used earlier for military or economic alliances (e.g., the Hanseatic League, a medieval trade network of northern European towns). The term (sometimes capitalized) was commonly used in the 19th century to refer to the National League; e.g., "[Wally Walker] was given a trial behind the plate for the Detroit league team" (Bob Leadley, quoted in the *Detroit Free Press*, Feb. 10, 1889; Peter Morris).

League Alliance An attempt by the National League (1877 to 1882) to organize the various professional clubs that were not in the league. The main purpose was to regulate various issues between clubs, including the protection of players' contracts. Clubs included the Nationals of Washington (1880), the Metropolitans of New York (1881–1882), and the Athletics of Philadelphia (1882). The Alliance was formally removed from the National League constitution following the 1882 season as it failed to organize professional baseball as a whole.

League Award The forerunner of the present Most Valuable Player Award. Beginning in 1922 and through 1928, the American League (AL) awarded a trophy to the player "who is of greatest all-around service to his club and credit to the sport" and "to recognize and reward uncommon skill and ability." The AL award lost its credibility because it limited nominees to one per team and excluded player-managers and previous winners, and because award-winners parlayed their honors into substantial pay raises. The National League instituted a cash award for its winners beginning in 1924 and through 1929, and without the restrictions of the AL award. See Bill Deane, in *Total Baseball*, 8th ed., 2004, pp.708–9.

League Championship Series The *Championship Series* in either the American League or the National League; specif., the *American League Championship Series* and the *National League Championship Series*. Abbrev. *LCS*.

League Division Series The *Division Series* in either the American League or the National League; specif., the *American League Division Series* and the *National League Division Series*. Abbrev. *LDS*.

league president The official charged with the responsibility for the day-to-day activities of the teams in a given professional league. The *Official Baseball Rules* specified that the league president should enforce the rules of the game, resolve rules disputes, determine the resolution of any protested games, and impose fines and suspend players, coaches, managers, and umpires for violations of the rules. In 1999, the presidencies of the American League and the National League were eliminated, and in Jan. 2000 Major League Baseball dissolved the offices of the two leagues, thereby centralizing authority in the commissioner's office; the functions of the league president are now carried out by designees of the commissioner.

leaguer An individual identified with a particular league; e.g., "major leaguer," "Negro leaguer," and "Little Leaguer." IST USE. 1887. "Andy Groth is playing ball like an old 'leaguer'" (*San Francisco Examiner*, Sept. 5; Peter Morris). USAGE NOTE. The term was used earlier to distinguish between players in the American Association (1882–1891); e.g., "The new-comers to the American Association arena were known as 'fresh leaguers,' to distinguish them from the vets, or 'old leaguers'" (*The Sporting Life*, Jan. 14, 1885; Barry Popik). The term's popularity increased greatly during the 1890 season when the Players' League challenged the established National League and American Association and offered direct rivals in most National League cities. To distinguish between the various clubs, it was common to refer to the National League's clubs and players, respectively, as "league" and "leaguers"; e.g., "The Pittsburg leaguers have lost everything but hope" (*Brooklyn Eagle*, June 22, 1890; Peter Morris). When used alone to refer to the National League, the term was often capitalized.

leak For a pitcher's rear end to leave the rubber before his arm is ready to pitch, causing the ball to be up in the strike zone.

lean To take a lead toward the next base; "to take an exceptionally long lead, preparatory to a steal" (George Herman Ruth, *Babe Ruth's Own Book of Baseball*, 1928). To be picked off while taking such a lead is to be caught "leaning the wrong way."

lean against To bat a ball especially hard. IST USE. 1907 (*New York Evening Journal*, Apr. 25; Edward J. Nichols).

lean on To hit a pitch. "[Hod] Eller leaned on the ball with all his might and whacked a stunning two-bagger" (*The New York Times*, Oct. 7, 1919).

leaping Lena Syn. of *Texas Leaguer*, 2.

learn the hitter To study the habits of a hitter to understand the pitches he will hit and the direction in which such hits will go. "[Shortstop Dickie Thon is] learning the hitters, and he'll learn more as he plays" (Houston Astros coach Denis Menke, quoted in *Baseball Digest*, Oct. 1983, p.62).

learn the pitcher To study the habits of a pitcher to better understand the giveaway motions that will indicate the type of ball he intends to deliver as well as his pickoff move.

leather 1. *n.* A fielder's glove or gloves. "We told [Tim] Teufel, 'Way to get leather on it.' He just got the wrong leather" (New York Mets manager Davey Johnson, on Teufel's error during the 1986 World Series, quoted in *The Washington Post*, Oct. 25, 1986). 2. *n.* A general expression for fielding. A game with several stellar defensive plays is said to be "full of leather." "[Greg Maddux] flashed enough leather to cushion every seat in the house, making two spectacular plays among his five chances" (*The Baltimore Sun*, Oct. 13, 1999). 3. *n.* A defensive player. *Sports Illustrated* (March 25, 2002) rated defensive players as "Golden Glover, Good Leather, and Iron Hands." 4. *v.* To play flawless defense. "They [Baltimore Orioles] just leathered everything. We put the ball in play, but they caught everything" (Seattle Mariners outfielder Jay Buhner, quoted in *Milwaukee Journal Sentinel*, Oct. 7, 1997). 5. *v./hist.* To hit the ball; e.g., "Smith leathered one to center." IST USE. 1932 (*Baseball Magazine*, October, p.496; Edward J. Nichols). 6. *n./hist.* The baseball, in a reference to its horsehide cover. "[Harry Davis] places the willow against the leather in a very healthy manner" (Alfred H. Spink, *The National Game*, 2nd ed., 1911, p.180). ETYMOLOGY. Borrowed from cricket. "In cricket 'lingo' the ball is not the ball but the 'leather'" (*Forest and Stream*, Dec. 25, 1873; Peter Morris).

leather-beater *hist.* A baseball bat. IST USE. 1889. "Two baggers are not strangers to his leather-beater" (*The World* [New York], June 26; Gerald L. Cohen).

leather-hunting *hist.* 1. Trying to field a ball. "Callahan threw very wild to [Billy] Barnie, and while the latter was 'leather-hunting' [Phil] Powers scored amidst applause" (*London* [Ont.] *Free Press*, July 2, 1877; Peter Morris). See also *hunt leather*, 1. 2. Trying to hit a pitched ball (*The Sporting Life*, Apr. 29, 1883, p.3; Edward J. Nichols). See also *hunt leather*, 2.

leather lungs A loud, critical fan who can be heard throughout the ballpark.

leatherman Syn. of *gloveman*, 1.

leather player A good defensive player but a weak hitter; one who is likely to be known for his fielding rather than hitting prowess. Compare *wood player*. IST USE. 1937 (*New York Daily News*, Jan. 21; Edward J. Nichols).

leather-slapper A good fielder.

leave on base To end an inning with one or more baserunners unable to score.

leave the ball over the plate To throw a pitch, usually a mistake, that is easy to hit. "Pitchers typically are reluctant to throw off-speed pitches inside, because mistakes—left up or over the plate—are easily crushed" (Tom Verducci, *Sports Illustrated*, June 17, 2002). "[Jake] Peavy left a full-count cut fastball over the plate and [Albert] Pujols drove it an estimated 422 feet into the Padres' bullpen beyond" (*The Baltimore Sun*, Oct. 11, 2006).

leave the ball up To throw a pitch up in the strike zone, usually a mistake, that is easy to hit. "[Pat Burrell is] a power hitter. I left the ball up and he hit it out" (Livan Hernandez, quoted in *The Baltimore Sun*, June 11, 2006). "I wasn't throwing good pitches. I left the ball up and I feel like I let my team down" (Baltimore Orioles pitcher Bruce Chen, quoted in *The Baltimore Sun*, May 5, 2006).

leave the bench swinging For a batter to come to the plate ready to swing the bat; esp. for a batter who will swing freely at whatever pitch is delivered, rather than working the count.

leave the yard To hit a home run. "It was a beautiful sound, and I knew the ball would be leaving the yard" (Philadelphia Phillies shortstop Jimmy Rollins, commenting on teammate Ryan Howard's home run, quoted in *Sports Illustrated*, Sept. 18, 2006, p.64). See also *go yard*. IST USE. 1986. "Today, [when hitting a home run] you go to the suburbs, just go deep or leave the yard" (R.J. Reynolds, quoted by Bob Hertzel, Scripps Howard News Service, Sept. 17).

Leephus Pitcher Bill "Spaceman" Lee's blooper pitch, a play on Rip Sewell's *eephus*. Syn. *space ball*.

left Short for *left field*. IST USE. 1867. "The nine will be as follows: ... Waterman, left ..." (*The Ball Players' Chronicle*, Aug. 8; Peter Morris).

left center The area of the playing field between center field and left field. Syn. "left-center field."

left field 1. The left side of the outfield as viewed from home plate. Sometimes spelled "leftfield." Syn. *left*; *left garden*. 2. The position of the player who defends left field. Abbrev. *LF* or *lf*. Syn. *left*. IST USE. 1864. "Joe Oliver playing at left field" (*New York Clipper*, Oct. 22; Peter Morris). EXTENDED USE. 1. Things that are unusual, unexpected, or irrational are deemed to have come out of, or from, left field. An investigator working on efforts to determine the cause of the explosion of TWA Flight 800 observed (quoted in *The Baltimore Sun*, Aug. 17, 1996), "You think things are starting to look like they've got a pattern, and all of a sudden there's something that comes ... from left field." See also *out in left field*. 2. The political left. "Canadian businessmen last week were playing host to two more trade missions out of far left field. In Canada searching for business were one team of sales-minded Russians and another of inscrutable Hong Kong traders acting as agents for their neighbors, the Communist Chinese" (*Time* magazine, Jan. 20, 1961). 3. A bad seat in a restaurant or arena. "Unless a name is in the Register, he is given a seat in left field" (Jack Lait and Lee Mortimer, *New York Confidential*, 1948).

left fielder The defensive player who is positioned in left field. Abbrev. *LF* or *lf*. Sometimes spelled "leftfielder." Syn. *left gardener*. IST USE. 1864. "The good looking left fielder of the Eurekas will have to drop the ornamental style and adopt the useful in fly catching if he desires to keep up his past reputation" (*New York Clipper*, Aug. 13; Peter Morris).

left field foul line The line extending from home plate to the fence in deep left field that delineates foul from fair playing areas. Since June 1, 1958, the line must extend at least 325 feet. Syn. *left field line*.

left field line The *third base line* extended beyond the infield; the *left field foul line*.

left garden *hist.* Syn. of *left field*, 1. IST USE. 1891. "Starting with Martin Sullivan, of Boston, in the left garden" (*The Washington Post*, Feb. 4).

left gardener *hist.* Syn. of *left fielder.* IST USE. 1893. "Davey's fly . . . came down midway between the dazed man on third and the breathless left gardener" (*San Francisco Examiner*, Apr. 9; Peter Morris).

left-handed Said of a player who favors the left hand or the left side of the body. Compare *right-handed.* Also spelled "lefthanded."

left-handed batter A batter who swings from the left and faces the pitcher with the right side of his body as he stands on the right (first base) side of home plate. A left-handed batter has a natural, one-step headstart on the basepath when he completes his swing. Since batters tend to have an advantage over pitchers throwing from the opposite side of the body, left-handed batters tend to have an advantage because there are many more right-handed pitchers. Because of these advantages, many batters have learned to bat left-handed while still throwing with their right hand. Abbrev. *LHB.*

left-handed pitcher A pitcher who throws with his left arm. Abbrev. *LHP.* Syn. *southpaw*, 1; *forkhander*; *hook arm*, 1.

left-hander A left-handed player; esp., a pitcher who throws with his left arm. There are many left-handed pitchers, but second basemen, third basemen, shortstops, and catchers typically do not throw left-handed. Traditionally, the left-handed player has had to overcome a certain amount of prejudice. E.V. Durling (*San Francisco Examiner*, Sept. 17, 1956; Peter Tamony) actually wrote, "Right handers are steadier than left handers. They steady an infield. The southpaws are usually temperamental and easily rattled. They are also inclined to fancy 'show off' playing such as overdoing the one hand catch." When Arizona Diamondbacks southpaw pitcher Brian Anderson cut his finger on a cologne bottle, burned his cheek testing an iron, and locked himself out of a hotel room stark naked, Peter Schmuck (*The Baltimore Sun*, Apr. 1, 2001) wrote, "The guy is definitely a left-hander." On the other hand (no pun intended), pitcher Tom Glavine was quoted in *The New York Times* (March 25,

2001): "You think of left-handers, you think of guys who sink the ball, change speeds and locate." The term is also used for a left-handed batter. Compare *right-hander.* Also spelled "left hander"; "lefthander." IST USE. 1879 (*Spirit of the Times*, Aug. 23, p.59; Edward J. Nichols).

leftie Var. of *lefty.*

left on Describing a runner remaining on base when the third out is made. Abbrev. *LO*, 1.

left on base 1. *adj.* Said of the situation in which one or more runners are on base when the third out is made in a half inning. "Being left on a base generally shows poor batting on the part of one or other of the batsmen succeeding a base runner" (Henry Chadwick, *The Game of Base Ball*, 1868, p.42). Syn. *stranded.* IST USE. 1864. "Pascal and McWhinne being well put out at first base by Sprague and J. Wilson on a tip bound, Midgely being left on the base" (*New York Clipper*, Oct. 1; Peter Morris). 2. *n.* The number of runners remaining on base at the end of a half inning. As a statistic, the collective number of runners left on base during a game or a number of games is a barometer of a team's overall inability to score. Abbrev. *LOB.*

left out A common nickname for the left fielder at the amateur level. It refers to the fact that the ball is seldom hit to left field at the non-professional level, where batters tend to push the ball to the right.

left patrol *hist.* Left field or left fielder (Maurice H. Weseen, *A Dictionary of American Slang*, 1934).

left-side hit and run A tactic employed by the Baltimore Orioles of the International League in the early 1920s, as recounted by Merwin Jacobson in a 1976 interview (reprinted in James H. Bready, *Baseball in Baltimore*, 1998; Peter Morris): "[Fritz] Maisel, leading off, would get aboard; [Otis] Lawry would sacrifice; I was up next, the heavy hitter, and I'd bunt, toward third. Maisel, off with the pitch, would round third, never slowing. While the third baseman was running in after the ball and trying to throw me out, Maisel would score, most often standing."

lefty A left-handed player; one who throws with the left arm or bats from the right side of home plate as he faces the pitcher. Var. *leftie*. IST USE. 1886. "In last Wednesday's game Nashville presented her left-handed battery . . . to offset our 'lefty' battery" (*The Sporting Life*, Apr. 7, 1886; David Shulman). EXTENDED USE. Slang for a leftist, especially during the 1950s. "In your June 2 editorial re the Oppenheimer case, you describe Dr. Albert Einstein as a 'dedicated international lefty'" (*San Francisco News*, letter to the editors, June 7, 1954; Peter Tamony).

lefty one out guy A left-handed relief pitcher brought in to face just one batter (Alan Schwarz, *The New York Times*, Oct. 2, 2005). Syn. *loogy*.

legal That which is in accord with the official rules of the game.

legal game A game that lasts five innings (or 4½ innings with the home team in the lead) before being officially called by the umpire because of rain, darkness, or other condition that warrants the halt of play.

legger 1. Syn. of *leg hitter*. IST USE. 1937 (*New York Daily News*, Sept. 5; Edward J. Nichols). 2. An infield hit by a leg hitter; a *leg hit*. "I'd get a lot of leggers and fisters" (Boston Red Sox infielder Billy Klaus, quoted in *The New York Times*, March 29, 1956; Peter Morris).

leg guard Protective material for a ballplayer's legs. See also *shin guard*. IST USE. 1888. "They can't spike you if you use Rawlings' Leg Guards. . . . Prevents Spiking, Prevents Bruising, Prevents Breaking. To be worn under or over the stocking" (Rawlings ad, *The Sporting News*, June 16, p.8; David Arcidiacono).

leg hit An infield single accomplished by the speed of the batter-runner. A key ingredient of a leg hit is that, while the ball has been properly fielded without error, the batter-runner outruns the ball to the base. Pittsburgh Pirates outfielder Lloyd "Little Poison" Waner set a record for singles (198 in 1927) because of his many leg hits. Syn. *legger*, 2.

leg hitter A fast player who is adept at beating out infield hits and bunts. The player's speed can, to some degree, compensate for weak hitting. "The National League decided to make official the practice of rolling infields after five innings. . . . It brought no joy to leg hitters who sometimes beat out . . . balls which strike errant pebbles" (*San Francisco News*, Dec. 8, 1953). Syn. *legger*, 1. IST USE. 1933 (*Famous Sluggers and Their Records of 1932*, 1933).

leg-in-the-face Said of a pitcher's high leg kick.

"leg it!" *hist.* A common 19th-century call from the grandstand, urging a player to "run!"

leg it out See *leg out*.

leg kick 1. The element in a pitcher's delivery in which he raises his nonpivot leg. Base stealers take advantage of a pitcher with a high leg kick: "There are some pitchers you know you can run on, because they have such a big leg kick" (Steve Sax, quoted in *Baseball Digest*, Jan. 1984, p.45). See also *kick*, 1. 2. An element of a batter's stride in which he raises his front foot off the ground before committing to a swing. Mel Ott and Sadaharu Oh had high leg kicks that helped them to hold their weight back and thereby increase their power. A leg kick enabled the batter to

Leg hitter. Lloyd "Little Poison" Waner. *National Baseball Library and Archives, Cooperstown, N.Y.*

turn on inside pitches but inhibited his ability to reach and hit balls low and away.

leg out 1. For a batter or runner to arrive safely at a base ahead of the ball. "[Ty Cobb] got a lot of safe hits by 'legging out' slow grounders" (E.A. Batchelor, quoted in Ty Cobb, *My Life in Baseball*, 1961, p.11). See also *beat out*. **2.** To chase down a ground-ball hit; e.g., "Smith legged it out to reach the ball in the gap."

legs cut out from under it Description of a well-hit ball that falls short of its destination because it has been hampered by the wind.

lemon 1. *hist.* A player of poor ability, esp. one of whom much was expected. "A lemon in the grapefruit belt" is a "high-priced rookie who flops in the spring training camp" (H.G. Salsinger, *Baseball Digest*, Aug. 1945). Syn. *onion*, 2. IST USE. 1908. "When Manager John McGraw strayed out to Springfield, Ill., to pick a peach from the Three-Eye baseball orchard, he evidently took a bridle path instead of the highway, and wound up in a lemon grove. He is reported to have paid something like $4,000 for the privilege of plucking a particular fruit named [Larry] Doyle" (*St. Louis Post-Dispatch*, May 21; Peter Morris). **2.** The baseball. "[Lou Gehrig] would come up and bust the lemon out of the country" (Paul Gallico, *Lou Gehrig, Pride of the Yankees*, 1942).

lemon peel ball A center-wound homemade baseball covered with one piece of leather that was cut into a "lemon peel" shape with three to five "peels," which were then stitched together to form the cover. It was the most common style of baseball used in town ball and early baseball games from the early 1800s through the 1870s.

Lena Blackburne Baseball Rubbing Mud See *rubbing mud*.

length A unit of measurement (number of games) used to determine a team's exact position in the standings; e.g., "The Tigers were 15 lengths ahead of the Orioles." The expression is borrowed from horse racing. See also *game*, 2.

Lester Plan A proposal by *Philadelphia Record* sports editor W.R. Lester in 1893 to correct the growing imbalance between pitcher and hitter by lengthening the baselines from 90 to 93 feet and stationing the pitcher 65 feet, 7 inches from home plate in the geometrical center of the diamond. Although the proposal failed, the pitching distance was changed from 55 feet, 6 inches to 60 feet, 6 inches (Mike Sowell, *July 2, 1903*, 1992, pp.98–99).

let down To defeat an opposing team. "[Bob Harmon] let the Giants down yesterday with two hits and beat Matty Mathewson 8 to 1" (*San Francisco Bulletin*, May 21, 1913; Gerald L. Cohen). IST USE. 1905 (*The Sporting Life*, Sept. 2, p.21; Edward J. Nichols).

"let him know you're out there" An exhortation to the pitcher to throw close to a batter's body.

"let's play two" The exuberant exhortation of Ernie Banks, former Chicago Cubs infielder (1953–1971), who professed an infectious enthusiasm for the game of baseball. See also *Banks' dictum*.

letter-high Said of a pitched ball that comes in across the chest at the level of the letters on the batter's jersey spelling out the name or initials of his team. IST USE. 1927 (Hal Totten, WMAQ-Chicago broadcast, June 17; Edward J. Nichols).

letter mailer A term used by Casey Stengel for a player who stayed out late at night. The term presumably stems from the time-honored excuse of curfew breakers who have been caught returning at a later hour: "Gee, I only went out to mail a letter."

letters The name of the team as written across the batter's jersey, indicating the approximate top of the strike zone. See also *numbers*, 3.

let the ball play him For a fielder to wait on a ground ball without moving, instead of taking a step either forward or back, leading to an awkward hop that could result in a bobbled catch or wild throw. Buck Herzog (quoted in *Baseball Magazine*, Sept. 1911):

Lemon peel ball.

"It is my advice to those who contemplate playing shortstop to make the play on a slow hit ball always on a dead run. You gain nothing by slowing up, for the ball will then 'play you.' Always take a chance and play the ball fast."

lettuce and tomato hitter A weak hitter with no power (Bill Snypp, *Lima* [Ohio] *News*, Apr. 27, 1937; Peter Morris).

lettuce ball Syn. of *rabbit ball*, 1. The term is so called because it "eats lettuce for breakfast" (*The Sporting News*, May 17, 1969).

letup *n.* Syn. of *letup pitch*.

let up *v.* To throw a slow ball after a fast one, using the same motion.

letup pitch A pitch that is used to confuse the batter because it comes after a fastball and has less speed. See also *changeup*. Syn. *letup*; "letup ball."

level To even up a ball-and-strike count; e.g., "The count levels at 2 and 2."

level of competition index A measure of the quality of players across eras, derived by dividing the number of major-league players at a given time (number of teams times 25) by the number of United States males (in millions) aged 20 to 39 years; the lower the index, the better the competition. According to Bill Deane (in John Thorn, ed., *The National Pastime*, 1987, p.150), who introduced the index, the measure "indicates the relative degree of difficulty of a man making it to the major leagues at a given time and, simultaneously, reflects the depth of talent in the majors." The index has dropped steadily from 31.2 in 1901 to 16.3 in 1985. Abbrev. *LCI*.

level playing field A metaphor for fairness, esp. when discussing baseball's economics (e.g., the large range of team budgets) or the prevalence of steroid use by some players and not by others. An example of an unlevel playing field is the alignment of divisions in the major leagues: one division (American League West) has four teams, one (National League Central) has six teams, and all the others have five teams.

level swing A swing that cuts across a flat plane as opposed to one in which the batter chops at or uppercuts the ball. Although a level swing is prized by hitting coaches, Ted Williams disagreed: "You've got to swing a little bit *up*" (quoted by Shirley Povich, *The Washington Post*, Sept. 8, 1995).

leverage A measure of the importance of a given point in a baseball game, based on the probability that the team at bat will win the game considering the inning, the base–out situation, and the difference between the two teams' runs scored at that point in the game; specif., the ratio between how much a single run scored at that point in the game increases the probability of the team at bat winning the game and how much a single run scored at the beginning of the game increases that probability. For example, if a run at the beginning of the game increased the odds of a team winning by 5 percent and a run at a given point in the game increased those odds by 10 percent, then that point in the game would receive a leverage of 2. The term was introduced by Keith Woolner in *Baseball Prospectus* for 2005.

leveraging The practice by which managers routinely adjust their pitching rotations to match their best starting pitchers against their top rival teams (Chris Jaffe, 37th SABR Annual Convention Program, July 28, 2007, p.49).

LF 1. Abbrev. for *left field*, 2. Sometimes *lf.* 2. Abbrev. for *left fielder*. Sometimes *lf.* 3. *hist.* Abbrev. for a foul ball caught "on the fly."

LHB Abbrev. for *left-handed batter*.

LHP Abbrev. for *left-handed pitcher*.

lick 1. *n.* A time or turn at bat. "The New Yorks . . . failed to score when next they had a 'lick'" (*The World* [New York], Aug. 26, 1887; Gerald L. Cohen). IST USE. 1883 (*The Sporting Life*, May 6, p.1; Edward J. Nichols). 2. *n.* A big swing. Henry Chadwick (*New York Clipper*, Jan. 21, 1871; Peter Morris) criticized batters who took 'big licks' instead of sticking with a safer style of hitting. 3. *n./hist.* A safe hit. "In the sixth and last inning, the Mutuals got off some of their 'biggest licks'" (*New York Sunday Mercury*, Oct. 16, 1861; David Shulman). IST USE. 1860 (Chadwick Scrapbooks; Edward J. Nichols). 4. *v.* To beat decisively.

licorice *hist.* Vigor or energy. IST USE. 1907

(*New York Evening Journal*, Apr. 12; Edward J. Nichols).

licorice ball A pitched ball that has been doctored with licorice. Pitchers used the sticky substance to get a better grip on the ball. "[Bill] Armour was throwing out balls smeared with licorice—an antidote for pitching the spit ball" (*New York Evening Telegram*, July 13, 1905; David W. Smith). The pitch was made illegal on Feb. 9, 1920.

lid *hist.* Ballplayer's slang for hat. "Coy, Rohrer, Ness and Mundorff will be presented with lids when the hatter gets around to the day of awards" (*San Francisco Bulletin*, Apr. 18, 1913; Gerald L. Cohen).

lid is off The beginning of a baseball season.

lidlifter 1. An Opening Day game. 2. The first game of a doubleheader.

life 1. Another chance for the batter or the batting team, such as when a catchable foul fly ball is dropped. "Howe had a life given him by Schaffer muffing his fly in right field" (Chadwick Scrapbooks, 1868; David Shulman). See also *new life*, 2. IST USE. 1867. "Here would have been three out and no run but for errors of play . . . some very good play at the bat being shown after the lives had been given them" (*Ball Players' Chronicle*, Aug. 1; Dean A. Sullivan). 2. Syn. of *base on balls*. "Umpire [Jackson] Brady . . . gave [Ned] Williamson a life after he had been struck out" (*The World* [New York], Aug. 26, 1887; Gerald L. Cohen). IST USE. 1874 (*Chicago Inter-Ocean*, July 6; Edward J. Nichols). 3. Movement on a fastball, usually right before it reaches home plate. "The biggest concern would be having real good life on your fastball and not being able to harness it in the strike zone" (pitcher Pat Hentgen, quoted in *The Baltimore Sun*, Oct. 16, 2000). David Hernandez' fastball "definitely has a little extra life on it: it gets up on people a little quicker than they expect" (Delmarva Shorebirds pitching coach Kennie Steenstra, quoted in *The Baltimore Sun*, May 15, 2006). See also *late life*. 4. Syn. of *bat speed*. "He's [Javier Lopez] got no life in his bat" (anonymous scout, quoted in *Sports Illustrated*, Aug. 14, 2006). 5. *hist.* A play in which a fielder attempts to retire a lead runner when

he could get the batter-runner out at first base and both are declared safe. Such a play is now scored as a fielder's choice. "If a man is on either first, second or third and the batter hits an intentional tap to the infield, and neither the batter nor the base runner are retired, providing the play was made on the runner but too late to get him and both are safe, that is a 'life'" (George L. Moreland, *Balldom*, 1914, p.237; Peter Morris). See also *Cincinnati base hit*.

lifer Short for *baseball lifer*. "He's [Jack McKeon] a lifer, and when the game is in your blood, it never leaves" (Joe Torre, quoted in *Sports Illustrated*, Oct. 27, 2003).

lift 1. *v.* To remove a player (especially a pitcher) from the game. See also *derrick*. IST USE. 1908. "Lifted from the game, a player who is suspended by the umpire or who is retired by the captain because of inefficiency" (John B. Foster, in *Collier's New Dictionary of the English Language*). 2. *v.* To hit a ball high in the air; e.g., "Hogg lifted a pop fly back of first base" (*Chicago Tribune*, June 11, 1905; Peter Morris). IST USE. 1868 (Chadwick Scrapbooks; Edward J. Nichols). 3. *n.* The height of a well-hit ball that has consistent loft and therefore distance. "[Nick Swisher] has good bat speed and he's getting some lift that he never had before" (anonymous scout, quoted in *The Baltimore Sun*, July 16, 2006). 4. *v.* To win a baseball game; e.g., "[Kirby] Puckett's HR in 10th Lifts Twins" (*Tampa Tribune* headline, June 27, 1989).

light ball A ball that is thrown with such a slow spin that it feels light in weight to the catcher.

light bat A player who is not a power hitter.

lighted frolic *hist.* A night game under the lights in the 1930s and 1940s, when such games were still a novelty (Maurice H. Weseen, *A Dictionary of American Slang*, 1934).

light-hitting 1. Said of a team that lacks power hitters. 2. Said of a player who is not a power hitter.

lightning ball [softball term] An early name for softball.

lightning pitcher *hist.* A pitcher with a great fastball. "Base ball has never been a rage in the Valley City since our lightning pitcher, Lew Farmer, took the position of local editor for the *Boston Journal*" (*Grand Rapids* [Mich.] *Daily Morning Democrat*, May 10, 1874; Peter Morris).

lights Artificial illumination provided for night games.

light tower power piece A towering home run; "a truly awesome blast" (Bill Mazeroski, *Bill Mazeroski's Baseball '89*, 1989).

light up To get several hits off a pitcher; e.g., "The Orioles lit up Smith for ten hits in two innings." John Maffei (*Baseball Digest*, May 1986) defined "lit up" as "what happens to a pitcher when he doesn't have a good yakker, isn't throwing aspirin and can't pull the string."

limber up To flex and bend the body or arm before a game. See also *warm up*. IST USE. 1871. "[Asa Brainard] went through some vigorous gymnastics to 'limber up' his arms, which amused the spectators" (*The Cleveland Morning Herald*, May 22).

Limestone League The substitute name for the *Grapefruit League* when six major-league clubs held spring training in Indiana in 1943.

limit 1. See *player limit*. 2. See *pitch limit*.

Limit Agreement A stipulation in the 1885 National Agreement that called for a salary cap of $2,000. The salary limit so angered John Montgomery Ward that the Brotherhood of Professional Base Ball Players was formed in Oct. 1885. The Limit Agreement failed to curb escalating salaries.

Linda Ronstadt A fastball. Dave Scheiber (*St. Petersburg Times*, March 5, 1987) reported, "Good fastballs enjoy an updated alias as well. They're called a Linda Ronstadt. No, the sultry singer was never known for her pitching prowess, but she did record the tune 'Blue Bayou' in 1977. And baseball linguists soon turned that into 'blew by you' as in what that sizzling fastball just did." See also *Louisiana*.

line 1. *v.* To hit a ball along a straight path; to hit a line drive. IST USE. 1892 (*Brooklyn Daily Eagle*, Aug. 1; Edward J. Nichols). 2. *v.* Syn. of *line out*, 1. 3. *n./hist.* Syn. of *line drive*. "[Spencer] did succeed in driving two

lines to the fence" (*San Francisco Bulletin*, May 1, 1913; Gerald L. Cohen). 4. *v.* To mark the foul lines on the field. 5. *n.* One of the various boundary marks on and around the playing field; e.g., a foul line or a baseline. IST USE. 1866 (Constitution and By-Laws of the Olympic Ball Club of Philadelphia, p.28; Edward J. Nichols).

línea recta Spanish for "line drive."

linear weights A system for predicting team run scoring based on hitting, base stealing, fielding, and pitching contributions of its players. Adjusted for such variables as the ballpark in which the player performs, it expresses a player's effectiveness in terms of either runs or wins that he contributes to (or costs) his team in comparison with an average player at his position. The formula: LW = .46(1B) + .8(2B) + 1.02(3B) + 1.4(HR) + .33(BB) + .3(SB) − .6(CS) − [(AB−H)(normalizing factor)]. The normalizing factor (representing the value of an out) varies by league and from one year to the next, and is usually somewhere around .26. The system was devised by Pete Palmer and described in John Thorn and Pete Palmer, *The Hidden Game of Baseball* (1985). See also *batting runs*; *pitching runs*; *fielding runs*; *base-stealing runs*. Abbrev. *LW*.

line ball *hist.* 1. A batted ball that travels a straight line for some distance. IST USE. 1864. "McMahon batting a swift line ball towards second base, which Harry Brainard held in old Excelsior style" (*Brooklyn Eagle*, Aug. 18; Peter Morris). 2. "[A ball] thrown by a fielder on a line with the fielder to whom the ball is . . . thrown" (Henry Chadwick, *The Game of Base Ball*, 1868, p.42).

line drive A solidly batted ball, usually a base hit, that approximately parallels the ground during its flight rather than arcing in the manner of a fly ball. See also *blue dart*; *blue darter*; *bee-liner*; *frozen rope*; *rifle shot*, 2. Abbrev. *L*, 4. Syn. *line*, 3; *liner*; *line shot*; *line hit*; *bolt*, 1; *laser*; *trolley line*. IST USE. 1888. "Sam Thompson made a running catch of [Cap] Anson's vicious line drive" (*Detroit Free Press*, May 27). EXTENDED USE. A solidly hit ball in other sports. "[Football] fans are in for an array of [kickoff] kicks, everything from high bloopers . . . to line drives"

(Sandra McKee, *The Baltimore Sun*, Aug. 23, 2007).

line drive in the box score A facetious synonym for a bloop or scratch hit, since box scores do not differentiate between such hits and scorching line-drive hits.

line drive to the catcher A swinging strikeout. "He'll relate later that he hit a 'line drive to the catcher' for his missed third strike" (*Baseball Magazine*, Jan. 1943). IST USE. 1932. "Line drive to the catcher—Missing the third strike" (*New York Sun*, June 23).

line hit Syn. of *line drive*. "Jack Strobe cleaned the bases with a long line-hit" (Christy Mathewson, *First Base Faulkner*, 1916, p.164; David Shulman). IST USE. 1880 (*New York Herald*, Aug. 20; Edward J. Nichols).

line hitter A hitter who hits line drives. IST USE. 1928. "[Lou Gehrig is] what we call a 'line hitter'" (George Herman Ruth, *Babe Ruth's Own Book of Baseball*, p.155; Peter Morris).

line-hugger A batted ball that follows the first base line or the third base line.

lineout *n.* A line drive that is caught for an out.

line out *v.* **1.** To hit a line drive that is caught for an out. Syn. *line*, 2. **2.** To hit a line drive for a hit. IST USE. 1907 (*Lajoie's Official Base Ball Guide*, p.13; Edward J. Nichols).

liner **1.** Syn. of *line drive*. IST USE. 1872 (*Beadle's Dime Base-Ball Player*, p.26; Tom Shieber). **2.** A ball thrown with great force. "Malarkey threw a liner at his [Rodgers'] head, which if it hit him would, without a doubt, [have] ended Mr. Rodgers' days on the diamond. Rodgers promptly ducked" (*San Francisco Bulletin*, Apr. 10, 1913; Gerald L. Cohen). **3.** A warmup exercise in which a player runs on the warning track from one foul line to the other.

lines **1.** See *between the lines*. **2.** See *white lines*.

line score An inning-by-inning account of the runs scored in a game, commonly displayed on scoreboards in the ballpark; also, game statistics that include total runs, hits, and errors. The statistics appeared in early newspapers under the heading *synopsis of innings* (e.g., *New York Clipper*, July 31, 1858; Peter Morris). ETYMOLOGY. Jules Tygiel (*Past Time*, 2000, p.25) credited Henry Chadwick with introducing the line score in 1859.

line shot Syn. of *line drive*. IST USE. 1880 (*New York Herald*, Aug. 20; Edward J. Nichols).

lineup The players composing the *batting order* and the defense at any given moment during a game. It is always presented at the beginning of the game and updated with substitutions during the game. Sometimes spelled "line-up." IST USE. 1905 (*The Sporting Life*, Oct. 7, p.3; Edward J. Nichols). EXTENDED USE. Any listing of events or participants. "Even today, businesses pitch to clients, television networks design lineups, and people trying to reach first base with the opposite sex dread striking out" (*Houston Post*, Aug. 30, 1987).

lineup card A card that lists the starting players in their proper batting order and by position and that is presented to the home plate umpire by a representative of each team at the beginning of each game. Five other copies of the lineup card are deployed: one posted in the clubhouse, one posted in the dugout, one given to the opposing team, one held by the bullpen coach, and one kept by the manager. "Only the one in the dugout is created on a standard-issue form supplied by Major League Baseball—the better for possible resale value, of course" (Tom Verducci, *Sports Illustrated*, Apr. 4, 2005).

liniment *hist.* The worst; anything that is very bad or very poor (Maurice H. Weseen, *A Dictionary of American Slang*, 1934).

lip The part of the playing field where the infield dirt area meets the grass in the infield or the grass behind the infield.

lip pass An automatic base on balls when the pitcher licks his fingers four times while on the rubber. In 1968, the umpires were ordered to enforce more strictly the anti-spitball rule that a pitcher cannot go to his mouth on the rubber. When Chicago Cubs manager Leo Durocher instructed pitcher Jim Ellis in a spring training game to issue two intentional walks by licking his fingers, the rules committee suggested that Durocher would be

Lineup card. Charles Gehringer of the Detroit Tigers hands over the lineup card to the umpire during the 1935 World Series. *Photograph by Joseph Baylor Roberts*

fined $1,000 if another "lip pass" occurred. Durocher did not repeat the lip pass, but the umpires were instructed to be less vigilant about enforcing the rule.

lipper A ball that is hit off the edge or lip of the infield grass.

LIPS Abbrev. for *late-inning pressure situation*.

liquid shit A fastball that appears to pick up speed as it enters the strike zone. The illusion is created by the backspin on the ball and often fools hitters.

list *hist.* To blacklist. "Phil Knell, who was 'listed' for the same offense—jumping his contract" (*San Francisco Examiner*, March 4, 1889; Peter Morris).

little ball **1.** A style of offensive play that relies less on home runs than on execution of basic fundamentals such as sacrifice hits, squeeze bunts, hit-and-run plays, advancing or hitting behind the runner, pickoffs, double steals, infield hits, taking advantage of walks and errors, and putting the ball in play. It involves playing for one run and often playing over one's heads. The term may have originated with Gene Mauch when he was manager of the California Angels in the 1980s. "Gene Mauch used the squeeze bunt—'little ball' is his expression for it—earlier in the season because the Angels were not scoring many runs" (*The New York Times*, Oct. 18, 1982). "The Japanese play a radical form of Gene Mauch baseball—'little ball' to the extreme, nearly always playing for one run, bunting, hitting behind runners, and hitting to the opposite field" (Rich Dubroff, *How Was the Game?*, 1994, p.126). "Gene Mauch . . . did not take chances. He played it safe, played 'little ball'—sacrificing, not running the bases" (Don Baylor, *Don Baylor*, 1989). "[The Minnesota Twins] play a modest style of baseball, little ball, in which little things are done properly and every base hit counts" (Michael Bamberger, *Sports Illustrated*, Apr. 30, 2001). See also *inside baseball*. Compare *big ball*, 1. Syn. *small ball*, 1. **2.** A fastball that is difficult to see as it comes in toward the batter. "Johnny

Allen is also throwing the little ball, as the athletes say" (*The San Francisco News*, Aug. 13, 1940). See also *small baseball*.

little bo-bo *hist.* A manager's favorite player. See also *bobo*.

little cutter A *cut fastball* that is "thrown like a straight fastball but with a little pressure on one side of the ball, which makes it move" (Roger Angell, quoted in *The Washington Post*, Oct. 19, 1997).

Little Eva A player who performs well even though he is obviously tired and suffering from a hangover. IST USE. 1937. "Little Eva—A player who dissipates but delivers on the diamond" (Bill McCullough, *Brooklyn Eagle*, Sept. 5). ETYMOLOGY. The term comes from the innocent Little Eva of *Uncle Tom's Cabin*, who is the exact opposite of the dissipated ballplayer dragging himself onto the field and showing the effects of the previous night's revelry. "Little Eva" was also the nickname of Bill Lange, a prominent 19th-century player.

little league A minor league, to distinguish it from a big league. "George Whiteman, grizzled veteran of many big and little league campaigns" (*Boston Herald and Journal*, Sept. 6, 1918; Peter Morris).

Little League 1. An organized international network of baseball (and softball since 2001) for boys and girls from ages 6 to 18 in more than 100 countries. The world's largest youth sports organization, it was started in 1939 by tax collector Carl E. Stotz (1910–1992) of Williamsport, Pa. Although it was created for boys only, a 1974 court order included girls in the Little League program for the first time. Participation peaked at three million children and one million volunteers in 1996. Little League is highly structured in age-based divisions: baseball divisions include Tee Ball (ages 6–8), Little League (ages 9–12), Junior League (age 13), Senior League (ages 13–15), and Big League (ages 16–18); softball divisions (for girls) include Little League (ages 9–12), Senior League (ages 13–15), and Big League (ages 16–18); and Challenger Division for kids with physical or emotional disabilities. Several major-league players first played in Little League, the first of whom was Joey Jay, who pitched for the Milwaukee Braves and the Cincinnati Reds (1953–1966). Abbrev. *LL.* **2.** A generic name for baseball at the preteen level.

Little League elbow A childhood injury that can result from the stress of continually trying to throw a baseball hard. A similar injury is "Little League shoulder."

Little League home run 1. A run when a batter does not hit the ball a particularly impressive distance, but circles the bases on a series of overthrows and misplays by the fielders. **2.** A home run in which the entire team is waiting at home plate to congratulate the batter even though his team is still losing. Wade Boggs expressed this sentiment after he made his 3,000th career hit a home run on Aug. 7, 1999 (Peter Morris).

Little League pledge "I trust in God. I love my country and will respect its laws. I will play fair and strive to win, but win or lose I will always do my best."

Little Leaguer An individual who plays on a Little League team.

Little League World Series An annual round-robin tournament for 11- and 12-year-olds, held each August since 1947 in South Williamsport, Pa., involving 16 Little League teams (eight regional qualifiers from the United States plus eight international champions). Although the rules are basically the same as those observed by adult organizations, the physical dimensions of the field are smaller: two-thirds the size of a major-league field and 60 feet (rather than 90 feet) between the bases. Williamsport mayor Michael Rafferty (quoted in *Sports Illustrated*, Aug. 25, 2003): "When people think of Pennsylvania, they probably think of the Philadelphia Eagles or the Pittsburgh Philharmonic. But there aren't many other things in the state that draw this kind of international focus on an annual basis. It's like a mini-Olympics." There are World Series tournaments for other Little League divisions held in various parts of the United States. Abbrev. *LLWS*.

Little Miracle of Coogan's Bluff The miraculous finish to the New York Giants 1954 season, in which the team took the pennant and then swept the Cleveland Indians in the World Series. Not to be confused with *Miracle of Coogan's Bluff*.

Little Show Syn. of *minor leagues*. The term is not intended to be a slur. Mike Blake (*The Minor Leagues: A Celebration of the Little Show*, 1991) commented, "The way the game has evolved on the grass-roots level of the Bushes, there's nothing very little about this show; it is big, and it is America. It is a link to a naive, young, easily excited and entertained, if a bit unsophisticated, America that knew how to have a good time without all the trappings and hype of the 1990s."

Little Tom Satchel Paige's term for his "medium" fastball. Compare *Long Tom*.

Little World Series 1. The minor-league postseason playoff games featuring the top teams in the American Association and the International League from 1904 to 1930. The name of the series was changed to *Junior World Series* in 1931. 2. A late-season series between two teams contending for the pennant. The term was applied by New York City newspapers to the New York Yankees/Cleveland Indians series (Sept. 23–26) in 1921 and the New York Yankees/St. Louis Browns series (Sept. 16–18) in 1922. "The little world's series is on at the Polo Grounds with an all-star cast and perfect stage settings" (Sid Mercer, *New York Evening Journal*, Sept. 23, 1921; Steve Steinberg). "Hugmen Lead St. Louis by Half a Game as 'Little World Series' Opens" (Harry Harlow, *New York Evening Mail* headline, Sept. 16, 1922; Steve Steinberg).

live (pron. "lyve") *adj.* Said of a pitch that hops, jumps, dances, sails, floats, or otherwise deviates from a straight trajectory. Compare *flat*.

live (pron. "liv") *v.* To pitch to that part of the strike zone where the pitcher is most effective; to pitch to one's strength. "[Sandy] Koufax lived on fastballs on the outside corner" (Tom Verducci, *Sports Illustrated*, July 12, 1999, p.98). "I can't live up [in the zone]. I don't throw hard enough" (Bruce Chen, quoted in *The Baltimore Sun*, June 21, 2005). "[Andy Pettitte] needs to live

around the knees" (New York Yankees manager Joe Torre, quoted in *The Baltimore Sun*, May 14, 2000).

live arm An attribute of a pitcher who has a fastball that pops or a curveball that snaps. The term often appears in the scouting report on a pitcher with strength.

live ball 1. A ball that is in play. Compare *dead ball*, 1. 2. A baseball that is, or is believed to be, inherently livelier and therefore will go farther when hit. " 'Live' balls were used, that is, balls which had a good bit of rubber in them" (*Outing Magazine*, Jan., 1914, p.122; David Shulman). "Actually, the terms 'live' and 'dead' have been applied to baseballs for more than 100 years" (Rawlings executive M. Scott Smith, quoted in *USA Weekend*, July 10–12, 1987).

live bat The bat of a hitter who is in the midst of a hot streak. See also *hot bat*, 1.

live hitting Hitting in a real game situation as opposed to hitting in a simulated game. The term is used in reference to a pitcher getting ready during a rehabilitation assignment or extended spring training.

live in a mustard jar To act like a "hot dog" player; to show off.

lively ball 1. A baseball that appears to have more zip and distance in it than others because of the way it has been produced. Manufacturers could increase the liveliness of machine-wounded balls (without increasing the quantity of rubber in the core) by adjusting the tension settings and thereby tuning the ball's elasticity. The lively ball is often described as one that seems to jump right off the bat on its way to a long voyage. Compare *dead ball*, 2. Syn. *elastic ball*. IST USE. 1870. "The balls known [as] Atlantic or Bounding Rock, may now be deemed 'dead'; that is, they are not so lively—will not bound so high—as the Ross or Van Horn, although they are made according to the requirements of the association" (Chadwick Scrapbooks; John Freyer). 2. A baseball used during specific seasons in which many players, managers, and coaches insisted that the balls had more "life" to them; e.g., the Union Association ball of 1884, the Players' League ball of

1890, the cork-centered ball of 1911, the Reach ball of 1920, and the ball of 1988 when baseballs were first manufactured in Costa Rica. Christy Mathewson (*Spalding's Official Base Ball Guide*, 1923), addressing the 1922 season when batting averages hit an all-time high, remarked, "All this talk of a lively ball appears to be alibi stuff. The players are using long-handled bats trying for home runs because it is so popular. The bat is changed . . . so that the batter can get a full grip." See also *rabbit ball*, 1.

lively ball era The period beginning with the 1920 season when baseballs were manufactured with improved yarn, tighter winding, and resilient cores, ushering in a 20-year period of robust batting averages. Norman L. Macht (personal communication, Aug. 7, 1997) suggests an earlier date: "I believe the so-called lively ball era really began with the cork-centered ball in 1910. American League batting averages jumped in 1911; the National League's did so in 1912. But the style of the game did not change, and the prolonged use of dark, discolored, mushy balls did not change. The big change that began in 1920 came from banning the doctoring of the ball, the tighter windings of the yarn, and the use of superior materials, combined with Babe Ruth's swinging for the fences. It would be more appropriate to call it the 'clean ball era.'" Compare *dead-ball era*.

live pitching Pitching in a real game situation as opposed to pitching in a simulated game or during batting practice. The term is used in reference to a batter's recovering from an injury or layoff.

liver pad *hist.* An early form of chest protector that was inflated and applied around the liver. "The catcher will wear no liver pad" (*The Penny Press* [Minneapolis], Apr. 28, 1896). IST USE. 1890. "Judge Alexander . . . will wear a huge protector and an inflated liver pad" (*Rocky Mountain News* [Denver], July 30). ETYMOLOGY. A commercial medical device claiming to "cure by absorption, acting on the liver and stomach immediately, taking from the system every particle of Malaria and Billous poison" (classified ad for "Holman's fever and ague and liver

pad," *Daily Arkansas Gazette* [Little Rock], March 4, 1876).

liver protector *hist.* Syn. of *chest protector* (*Yale Record*, reprinted in *Grand Valley* [Moab, Utah] *Times*, Jan. 24, 1902; Peter Morris).

LL Abbrev. for *Little League*, 1.

LLWS Abbrev. for *Little League World Series*.

LO 1. Abbrev. for *left on*. 2. Box score abbrev. used by *USA Today* for the number of runners that a batter did not advance.

load 1. *v.* To apply an illegal foreign substance to a baseball; e.g., "Smith loaded the ball with slippery elm." See also *load up*. 2. *n.* A hesitation in a windup in which the pitcher stays back over the rubber before he starts his full delivery. It often helps the pitcher maintain consistent mechanics and release point (Alan Schwarz, BaseballAmerica.com, Nov. 14, 2006). 3. *v.* See *load the bases*.

load of coal A slow, soft pitch; a changeup. Syn. "load of garbage."

load the bases 1. For the team at bat to put runners on first base, second base, and third base. 2. For the team in the field to allow runners to occupy first base, second base, and third base.

load up To doctor the baseball by adding a foreign substance such as saliva or hair oil. "Pitchers will load up by putting stuff on their eyebrows, in their hair, on the hair on their chest, on their wrists, all over" (Billy Martin, *Billyball*, 1987). See also *load*, 1.

loaf season *hist.* A sarcastic term for the offseason. "John Lobert, who is spending the loaf season in Philadelphia" (*The Sporting Life*, March 4, 1916; Peter Morris).

lob 1. *n.* A soft throw or toss, such as by one fielder to another who is relatively close, or by a pitcher throwing with little or no speed. IST USE. 1877. "The Red Men [London Tecumsehs] scored 5, mainly through the pitching of 'lobs' by Bradley, enabling them to get several base hits" (*London* [Ont.] *Free Press*, July 2; Peter Morris). 2. *v.* To throw or pitch a lob. IST USE. 1886. "[John Hofford] is said to have lost all of last year's speed, and now only lobbs [*sic*] the ball to the plate" (*St. Louis Post-Dispatch*, May 28;

Peter Morris). **3.** *v.* To hit a ball into a slow, high arc.

LOB Scorecard and box score abbrev. for *left on base*, 2.

lobby sitter A player who hangs out in hotel lobbies between games on road trips.

lobster net Syn. of *basket glove*.

lobster trap Syn. of *basket glove*.

local A curveball or changeup; an off-speed pitch. The term was used by Roy Campanella. Compare *express*.

local World Series A World Series involving teams from the same city (such as New York Yankees vs. New York Giants in 1936 and 1937, St. Louis Browns vs. St. Louis Cardinals in 1944, and Chicago White Sox vs. Chicago Cubs in 1906) or from the same general area (such as Kansas City vs. St. Louis in 1985 and San Francisco Giants vs. Oakland A's in 1989).

locate **1.** For a pitcher to throw the ball where he wants it. "What makes him [Bret Saberhagen] so tough is that he can locate the ball anywhere in the strike zone on any pitch" (Travis Fryman, quoted in *Sports Illustrated*, May 4, 1998). "A loss of control [means] the pitcher cannot locate the plate" (*Cincinnati Commercial Tribune*, reprinted in *The Sporting Life*, May 17, 1902; Peter Morris). IST USE. 1899 (Burt L. Standish, *Frank Merriwell's Double Shot*, p.238; Edward J. Nichols). **2.** To get hits off a pitcher (Maurice H. Weseen, *A Dictionary of American Slang*, 1934).

location A pitcher's ability to place the ball where he wants it: inside, outside, up or down, in the strike zone, or intentionally wasted out of the strike zone. Pitching coach Sammy Ellis, discussing Jason Johnson (quoted in *The Baltimore Sun*, June 18, 2000): "Sometimes he tries to throw as . . . hard a fastball as he can throw, instead of thinking of location, which is what major-league pitching is all about." Russell Baker (*The New York Times*, Oct. 9, 1979) recalled a line he heard on television: "[Nolan] Ryan has good velocity and excellent location." After noting that the line sounded like something that happened in a physics lab, he translated it into traditional baseballese: "Ryan is throwing smoke and nicking the corners." See also *control*. USAGE NOTE. Joe Goddard (*The Sporting News*, March 6, 1982) reported that "location" seems to have replaced "control": "It's because some real estate agent became a pitcher," speculated Kansas City Royals relief pitcher Dan Quisenberry. Rick Horowitz opined (*Chicago Tribune*, June 5, 1986), "'Location' is whether it gets there; you used to call it 'control.'"

lock **1.** *n.* A certainty; a sure bet. "St. Louis manager Whitey Herzog figures the Cardinals are a lock to steal 200 bases for the seventh year in a row" (*St. Petersburg Times*, March 6, 1988). IST USE. 1958. "We haven't had a 20-game winner since [Ewell] Blackwell in '47 and this guy [Bob Purkey] looks like a lock now" (A. Murray, *New York Post*, June 11). ETYMOLOGY. Harold Wentworth and Stuart Berg Flexner (*Dictionary of American Slang*, 1960) traced the term to the wrestling term "mortal lock" for a deadly hold that cannot be broken. **2.** *v.* For a batter to become focused and to concentrate on the pitch to be delivered. "[Leo Gomez is] on every pitch right now. He's not getting fooled. He's not swinging at bad pitches. He's hitting everything hard. He's locked, as we like to call it" (Rafael Palmeiro, quoted in *The Baltimore Sun*, June 7, 1994). See also *lock in*.

locker room **1.** The specific area of a *clubhouse* where lockers are located and where players dress. Joe Garagiola (*Baseball Is a Funny Game*, 1960, p.9): "The Giant clubhouse at the Polo Grounds was a contemporary style, split level. Walk down a flight of stairs and you were on the level with the card tables, and off to the side was the manager's office. Down another flight and you were in the locker room. From there, steps led up to the shower room, on still a third level." See also *dressing room*, 1. USAGE NOTE. The term "locker room" is frequently used interchangeably with "clubhouse"; e.g., "The locker room is like a gated community, subject to the zoning laws of sport" (Michael Farber, *Sports Illustrated*, Jan. 14, 2002). **2.** Syn. of *dressing room*, 2.

Locker Room Leonard A male groupie in the All-American Girls Professional Baseball

League. "[Faye Dancer] handled the . . . Locker Room Leonards, like easy pop flies" (*The New York Times*, June 9, 2002).

lock in For a player to concentrate and be focused, such as a pitcher whose mechanics are working smoothly or a batter whose swing is so directed as to hit the pitch hard and into a desired area consistently. "When you're locked in, the ball seems to be coming at you in slow motion and you see it so clearly" (Alex Rodriguez, quoted in *Sports Illustrated*, March 15, 2002). After Carlos Beltran hit eight home runs in the 2004 postseason, Houston Astros manager Phil Garner remarked (quoted in *The Baltimore Sun*, Oct. 18, 2004), "I've got to tell you, this kid is some kind of locked in. Went up there with a single-minded purpose and got the job done." Tim McCarver (Fox TV broadcast, Oct. 14, 2002) noted that the term was used primarily for hitters, but is now also applied to pitchers. "He's [Tom Glavine] been locked in all year" (Atlanta Braves manager Bobby Cox, quoted in *Sports Illustrated*, June 17, 2002). See also *lock*, 2.

lock up To be a sure winner; e.g., "The Yankees have locked up the World Series by winning the first three games."

locust hitter *hist.* A weak hitter, so called because of the poor quality of locust wood; i.e., the hitter is so weak that it seems as if he is using a bat of locust. IST USE. 1907 (*Lajoie's Official Base Ball Guide*, p.110; Edward J. Nichols).

loft To hit a high fly ball; e.g., "Smith lofted one to center." IST USE. 1908. "Lofted the ball, batted it high into the air" (John B. Foster, in *Collier's New Dictionary of the English Language*).

log A baseball bat. "[Catcher Tub] Spencer's work sparkled while he was doing duty behind the log [i.e., behind the bat]" (*San Francisco Bulletin*, March 8, 1913; Gerald L. Cohen).

loge A luxury seating accommodation prominent in stadiums constructed in the 1960s; a forerunner of the skybox. Dale Swearingen (from foreword to Philip J. Lowry, *Green Cathedrals*, 1992, pp.xiv–xv) recalled, "Comfort was indeed the word for these second generation stadia, and that word was spelled L-O-G-E. These modern contrivances accomplished two significant things: First, they helped foster a caste system with respect to spectators and second, they wreaked havoc with upper deck seating geometries." Swearingen noted that the greater the amount of private funding for a stadium, the greater the number of loges, which, because optimum viewing was a priority, were often hung from beneath the upper deck in as many as three tiers.

loitering The practice of reporters waiting idly in the clubhouse "for players to emerge from hiding" (Tom Verducci, *Sports Illustrated*, May 17, 1993, p.49). Players view loitering as eavesdropping. The New York Mets posted a sign: "Notice to Media—No Loitering" and noted that the clubhouse "is not a lounge, reading room or a place for social exchange with other members of the media."

lollapalooza See *lallapalooza*.

lollipop 1. A soft pitch or weak throw. The term is usually used to describe a pitch that is extremely easy to hit, like a lollipop held out in front of the batter. "He hasn't got the fastball anymore; he throws lollipops" (Russ Hodges, San Francisco Giants broadcast, Sept. 15, 1963; Peter Tamony). At the annual home run derby staged before the All-Star Game, the pitcher's job is to serve lollipops to baseball's leading sluggers. Also spelled *lollypop*. 2. Syn. of *Texas Leaguer*, 2.

lollipop arm A weak throwing arm. "Why so many 'lollipop' arms among outfielders?" asked Bob Broeg (*Baseball Digest*, July 1984, p.61).

lollypop Australian term for a slow, usually unintentional, easy-to-hit descending pitch; Australian spelling of *lollipop*, 1.

lomita Spanish for "mound."

Lonborg Rule The stipulation that a team can retain a player injured away from the ballpark by placing him on the inactive list without pay. The rule was adopted by the club owners in 1968 after Boston Red Sox pitcher Jim Lonborg broke his leg in a skiing accident in the offseason.

long-armer A pitcher who extends his hand almost fully behind him as he cocks his arm, rather than bending the arm at the elbow as he draws his arm back.

long ball **1.** A home run. See also *Dr. Long Ball.* **2.** A batted ball that travels a considerable distance, usually deep into the outfield; a ball that will require an extraordinary catch or result in an extra-base hit. IST USE. 1868. "Long balls . . . is the name of balls hit to the outer field. When they are sent bounding along the ground they are telling hits, but when sent high they ought to be caught, and are not, therefore, included as good hits" (Henry Chadwick, *The Game of Base Ball,* p.42). **3.** A style of play characterized by power hitting. "The [Chicago] Cubs played long ball to seize control of the game" (*Tampa Tribune,* Aug. 9, 1989). **4.** A childhood variation of baseball in which there is only one base ("long base," corresponding to second base) toward which the batter-runner runs directly. A runner already on the base does not have to run home; any number of players may assemble on the long base and wait their chance to run, but if all the players occupy the long base at once, the side is out. The batter is out on a caught fly ball, a third strike, or when he is hit by, or touched with, the ball in passing to or from the long base. There are no foul balls. Three outs retire the side. See Henry S. Curtis, *Play and Recreation for the Open Country,* 1914. Syn. *long base,* 2; *long town.*

longball A term used by Per Maigaard ("A History of Battingball Games," *Genus,* Dec. 1941) for a family of children's bat-and-ball games that was played for centuries across northern Europe, characterized by two "homes" (bases), and served as the ancestor to rounders, cricket, and baseball.

Long Ball A term that is "often used as a nickname for catchers who signal for too many bad pitches" (Jim Brosnan, *The Long Season,* 1960). Not to be confused with *Dr. Long Ball.*

longballer Syn. of *long-ball hitter.*

long-ball hitter A home run hitter. "If he [the batter] takes a long step, brings his shoulders around with their weight behind the bat, has a good wrist motion and a perfect follow-through, we are up against a long-ball hitter" (Carl Stockdale and Rogers Hornsby, *Athletic Journal,* March 1945). Syn. *longballer.* EXTENDED USE. A powerful or dramatic performer. "The fact that he [boxer Rocky Marciano] is a long-ball hitter gives him

extraordinary and exciting appeal" (Joe Williams, *The San Francisco News,* Sept. 25, 1952; Peter Tamony).

long base **1.** The base (corresponding to second base in baseball) in the childhood game of long ball. **2.** Syn. of *long ball,* 4.

long bat *hist.* A hitting streak. "A 'jag' lasting a week. Very popular among ball players a decade ago, but now taboo" (R.E. Sherwood, *Baseball Magazine,* Sept. 1913).

long bench A superior collection of substitute players. The term appears to have started in football and jumped to baseball: "Like they say in football, the [San Francisco] Seals have the 'long bench'" (Bucky Walters, *The San Francisco News,* March 8, 1956).

long catch An exercise used by pitchers to strengthen their arms in which the ball is thrown a much greater distance than that between the pitcher's mound and home plate. New York Yankees pitcher Ron Guidry "increased his activity of playing long catch in the outfield from 130 to about 150 feet" (*Newsday,* March 27, 1988). See also *long toss,* 3.

long count Syn. of *full count.*

long distance orator *hist.* A player who argues from long or safe range, rather than fighting (Al Schacht, *Al Schacht Dope Book,* 1944, p.41).

long Dutchman An early bat-and-ball game (*Bismarck* [N.D.] *Daily Tribune,* Apr. 1, 1887).

long hit Syn. of *extra-base hit.* IST USE. 1900. "Stahl has passed Freeman for long hits" (*The Boston Globe,* Sept. 3; Peter Morris).

long man Syn. of *long reliever.*

long out A putout in which the ball comes close to being a home run but is caught on the fly deep in the outfield.

long potato A home run. The term was used in the Class A California League in 1966 (Ron Bergman, *Mustache Gang,* 1973, p.62; Charles D. Poe). See also *potato,* 3; *tater; long tater.*

long relief **1.** The replacement of a pitcher early in the game. **2.** A period of relief pitching, usually three innings or more, early in the game.

long reliever A relief pitcher who works in long relief. He often enters the game during the first three innings and may either finish the game or be replaced by another relief pitcher; he often pitches in mop-up duty or blowout situations. Compare *middle reliever*; *short reliever*. Syn. *long man*.

long shot A ball hit for a long distance; e.g., "Smith drove a long shot out of the park."

long side The left side of the infield (as viewed by the batter) from which throws to first base are the longest.

long stride The *stride* of a pitcher whose front foot lands on the heel, preventing him from following through on the pitch. Compare *short stride*.

long strike A foul ball that goes a long distance. IST USE. 1932 (*New York Sun*, June 23).

long summer The seemingly never-ending season for a team low in the standings. Typically, a sloppy early-season loss will occasion the line, "This could be a long summer."

long swing A batter's swing in which the barrel of the bat takes an extended arc to the ball.

long tater A well-hit home run. See also *tater*. ETYMOLOGY. Supposedly a Negro leagues expression for *long potato*.

Long Tom Satchel Paige's term for his "really fast" fastball. Compare *Little Tom*.

long toss 1. A ball thrown for a long distance, as from deep center to shortstop. Compare *short toss*, 1. 2. A high, arcing throw a player makes while warming up or recovering from an injury; e.g., a throw by a pitcher to a point some 20 feet behind home plate. See also *soft toss*, 1. 3. An arm-strengthening exercise or drill of high, arcing tosses by a player, usually a pitcher, recovering from arm problems. "We played long toss, where you stand far apart in the outfield and make long, arcing, outfielder's throws" (Dave Dravecky, *Comeback*, 1990, p.153). "[Curt Schilling] passed another test yesterday by extending his long-toss workout from 180 to 210 feet" (*The Baltimore Sun*, March 14, 2000). "Kevin Brown . . . played long toss yesterday and has regained much flexibility in the [right index finger] joint" (*The Baltimore Sun*, June 30, 1995). "Long toss is the best

way to develop arm strength. It is simply a game of catch with a great distance in between. . . . Play long toss on a football field and use the yard markers to help you keep track of your improved distances" (Cal Ripken Jr., *The Baltimore Sun*, Dec. 11, 2005). See also *long catch*. Compare *short toss*, 2. Syn. *long tossing*.

long tossing Syn. of *long toss*, 3. "I definitely notice a difference in what I can do now. I've been long tossing every day. I can notice a progression from week to week" (Baltimore Orioles catcher Chris Hoiles, quoted in *The Baltimore Sun*, March 13, 1996). "Long-tossing forces you to throw the ball naturally" (Tampa Bay Devil Rays manager Larry Rothschild, quoted in *Sports Illustrated*, July 16, 2001). See also *soft tossing*. Sometimes spelled "long-tossing."

long town Syn. of *long ball*, 4.

long winter The off-season following a disappointing year. After the Cleveland Indians eliminated the New York Yankees in the 1997 American League Division Series, Yankees catcher Joe Girardi said (*USA Today*, Oct. 7, 1997), "As much fun as we had this year, this season is really empty. . . . It will be a long winter."

loogy Acronym for *lefty one out guy*.

look 1. *n.* A glance made at a baserunner by the pitcher before delivering the ball. 2. *v.* For a pitcher to glance or stare at a baserunner before delivering the ball; e.g., "Smith looked the runner back to deter him from taking too long a lead." 3. *v.* For a fielder with the ball to hold a baserunner during a play by glancing in his direction rather than throwing the ball to the base. "[Scott Klingenbeck] gloved a one-hopper . . . looked [Chuck] Knoblauch back to third and threw to first" (*The Baltimore Sun*, July 5, 1995). 4. *v.* For the batter to allow a pitched ball to go by without swinging at it; to take a pitch; e.g., "Smith looked at the curveball just off the outside corner."

look-back rule [softball term] A rule in fast pitch softball that, when a runner is legitimately off the base after a pitch, or as a result of a batter's completing his or her turn at bat, and is stationary when the pitcher has possession and control of the ball within the eight-foot pitcher's circle, the runner will be declared out unless he or she immediately attempts to advance to the next base or immediately returns to the original base.

looker 1. A batter who patiently waits for the right pitch to hit. 2. A batter who is not aggressive enough at the plate, who prefers to draw a walk rather than expose his batting weakness.

look for To come to the plate anticipating a certain pitch or sequence of pitches; e.g., to "look for" a walk is to anticipate called balls. "All veteran hitters look for certain pitches or for a certain zone—inside or outside—or both in certain situations" (Keith Hernandez, *Pure Baseball*, 1994, p.117). To look for certain pitches requires the batter to have the discipline to take a strike.

look home For a fielder to refrain from throwing the ball to home plate but be ready to do so. "Cal Ripken . . . looked home then threw . . . to first on a sixth-inning grounder" (*The Baltimore Sun*, Apr. 14, 2000).

looking 1. Waiting for a pitch that suits the batter. "If I'm looking inside, the pitch could be about to hit me and I'll still swing at it" (Derek Jeter, quoted in *Sports Illustrated*, June 7, 2004). 2. See *catch looking*. 3. See *strike out looking*.

look them over 1. For a batter to wait for a good ball to hit even if it means taking a pitch for a strike. IST USE. 1937 (*The Sporting News Record Book*, p.65; Edward J. Nichols). 2. An instruction shouted to the batter to encourage patience.

loony Joe A left-handed pitcher.

loop 1. *n.* A baseball league or conference. IST USE. 1917. "You certainly have to hand it to the 'Magguts' in this loop for being, as the lawyers say, 'Sui Generis'" (George B. Barrett, *The Sporting Life*, March 10; Peter Morris). 2. *v.* To bat a ball in a short but fairly high arc. IST USE. 1914 (*New York Tribune*, Oct. 11; Edward J. Nichols). 3. *n.* A poorly hit pop fly. 4. *n./hist.* Syn. of *inning*, 1.

looper A fly ball that carries just beyond the infield for a hit; a *Texas Leaguer* in the American Association (minor league). In print, one often finds that a looper has been "plopped":

"Boston's first run was a cheapie, Jose Canseco plopping a looper down the right-field line" (*The Baltimore Sun*, May 11, 1995). IST USE. 1934. "Looper—A fly hit" (Maurice H. Weseen, *A Dictionary of American Slang*).

loophole free agent A player who becomes a free agent when the club that drafted him does not tender a contract within 15 days of the draft. "Bobby Seay and . . . Matt White, both 'loophole' free agents in 1996" (Lisa Winston, *USA Today Baseball Weekly*, Apr. 5–11, 2000).

loopy Said of a breaking ball that lacks bite and sharpness, implying a soft, predictable arc. Syn. *flippy* (Alan Schwarz, Baseball America.com, Nov. 14, 2006).

loose 1. *adj.* Said of a ball that is not under the control of a defensive player or said of an infield characterized by poor fielding. The term underscores a paradox of baseball talk: it is good for hitters to be "loose," but fielders should be "tight." Compare *tight*, 2. IST USE. 1861 (*New York Sunday Mercury*, Oct. 2; Edward J. Nichols). 2. *adj.* Descriptive of a fluid, easy swing of the bat. "One of the loosest and most productive swings in the Pacific Coast League belongs to San Diego's swivel-jointed outfielder, Harry Simpson" (*San Francisco Call-Bulletin*, Aug. 17, 1950; Peter Tamony). 3. *adj.* Descriptive of a generally good attitude and easy approach toward the game. A team that is winning is often described as "loose." A player who remains relaxed or lacks tension before a game or between innings is said to be "staying loose." Compare *wound tight*, 3. 4. *adv.* Said of a pitcher warming up in the bullpen; e.g., "Smith is getting loose and ready to relieve Jones." 5. *v.* To bat a ball safely. IST USE. 1917 (*The New York Times*, Oct. 4; Edward J. Nichols).

loose as a goose Syn. of *loosey-goosey*.

loose as ashes Said of a loose-jointed player.

loosener A pitch thrown close to a batter's head. IST USE. 1932 (*Baseball Magazine*, October, p.496; Edward J. Nichols).

loosen up 1. To begin hitting freely against a pitcher; e.g., "The Giants began to loosen up Smith." IST USE. 1928 (*The New York Times*,

Oct. 6; Edward J. Nichols). **2.** To throw a brushback pitch, a knockdown pitch, or a beanball, presumably to move the batter away from the plate. "*Loosen him up*, meaning that if enough baseballs are thrown close to a hitter, he'll fall down easily" (Jim Bouton, *Ball Four*, 1970). IST USE. 1932. "Loosen Him Up—Throw a bean ball" (*New York Sun*, June 23). **3.** For a pitcher to warm up and get ready to enter the game. "By the end of the game, you're already loosened up" (Baltimore Orioles pitcher Sidney Ponson, quoted in *The Baltimore Sun*, June 17, 1999). **4.** To mentally relax teammates by being funny. "A player who is funny can not only lift his teammates spirits, but can do it at the expense of the opposition and thus become of strategic importance to his team" (Lawrence Frank, *Playing Hardball: The Dynamics of Baseball Folk Speech*, 1983, p.22).

loosey-goosey Said of a player who is completely relaxed on the field, or whose moves are easy, graceful, and seemingly effortless. Al Pilarcik, describing outfielder Jackie Brandt (*The Baltimore Sun*, Aug. 31, 2004): "He was as loosey-goosey as they come. Jackie was so carefree, I'm surprised he didn't fall asleep out there." Syn. *loose as a goose*.

Lord Charles An appreciative name for a superb curveball, which elevates an *Uncle Charlie* to a regal level. "It doesn't merely break, it dives and is as fast as most pitchers' sliders" (Joe Morgan, *Baseball for Dummies*, 1998, p.358). See also *Sir Charles*. ETYMOLOGY. The term was created to describe Dwight Gooden's exceptional curveball. New York Mets pitcher Ed Lynch (quoted in *Sports Illustrated*, July 2, 1984): "You know how the curve is called an Uncle Charlie? Dwight's is so good we call it a Lord Charles."

Lords of Baseball The owners of major-league baseball teams. The term was created by the late sportswriter Dick Young (quoted by Milton Kent, *The Baltimore Sun*, Jan. 31, 1996): "The message has gone out to the Lords of Baseball that the game needs to broaden its appeal and take in more youth." Two books have given the term added currency: Harold Parrott's *The Lords of Baseball* (1976) and John Helyar's *Lords of the Realm* (1994). The term is sometimes used derogatively: Parrott refers to most owners as "little boys with big wallets" who do not grasp the nature of the business of baseball.

lose **1.** To have scored fewer runs than one's opponent at the completion of a baseball game. **2.** For a pitcher to issue a base on balls, usually after being ahead in the count; e.g., "I was ahead of him 0-2, but I lost him." **3.** To allow a weak hitter to hit safely (H.G. Salsinger, *Baseball Digest*, Aug. 1945).

lose a ball To hit a home run out of the ballpark. "Pete Rose has just lost a baseball in Philadelphia" (Cleveland Indians radio broadcaster Herb Score, Sept. 18, 1982). Var. "lose one." IST USE. 1887. "Roger Connor lost the ball over the roof of a house on Pearl street" (*Los Angeles Times*, Nov. 21).

lose a fly To misjudge or lose sight of a fly ball, such as a ball that is lost in the sun or in the lights. IST USE. 1902 (*The Sporting Life*, July 5, p.13; Edward J. Nichols).

lose a step To slow down as one gets older. "Other players give [Graig] Nettles his due, but suggest that he has, at 38, lost a step or two" (Mark Goodman, *The New York Times Magazine*, Aug. 29, 1982).

lose his athlete For a player to suffer a decline in quickness and agility while physically maturing, as opposed to being lazy. "It's always disappointing when a great high school shortstop loses his athlete and has to wind up at first base" (Logan White, quoted in Alan Schwarz, BaseballAmerica.com, Nov. 14, 2006).

loser **1.** Syn. of *losing pitcher*. **2.** The team that does not win a game.

losing pitcher The pitcher who is charged by the official scorer with the loss of a game because he is responsible for the baserunner who scores the opposition's winning run. No matter how many pitchers are involved in a losing effort, only one pitcher can be charged with responsibility for the other team's winning run. Compare *winning pitcher*. Abbrev. *LP*. Box score abbrev. *L*, 3. Syn. *loser*, 1; *Larry*.

losing streak Two or more games lost in succession by either a pitcher or a team. Syn. "losing spin." IST USE. 1886. "What's the matter with the Browns? Have they struck a losing streak?" (*St. Louis Post-Dispatch*, June 10; Peter Morris).

loss **1.** A defeat. Abbrev. *L*, 1. **2.** That which is credited against a losing pitcher and is counted both in his single-season and career records. In giving this statistic, the losses always appear after the number of wins; e.g., a season record of 18–8 means 18 wins and 8 losses. Abbrev. *L*, 2.

loss column The column in the league or division standings that records the number of losses incurred by a team in relation to the number of games played or to be played or games a team is ahead or behind another team. Compare *win column.*

loss points A statistic charged to a player if his performance during any plate appearance decreases the probability that his team will win the game. It is used in determining *player win average.* Compare *win points.*

lost art An aspect of baseball that is no longer heavily practiced or perfected, such as bunting. Gordon S. "Mickey" Cochrane (*Baseball: The Fan's Game*, 1939, p.45; Peter Morris) described a good pickoff move by a pitcher as "this seemingly lost art of the game."

lot **1.** A ballpark. "[Ed Delahanty hit] a terrific drive, which, had its elevation been correct, would have landed the ball somewhere out of the lot" (*Chicago Daily Tribune*, Aug. 12, 1900). IST USE. 1866 (Constitution and By-Laws of the Olympic Base Ball Club of Philadelphia; Edward J. Nichols). **2.** Short for *sandlot*, 1. IST USE. 1885. "One of the players engaged for next season [by Brooklyn] said the Metropolitans were nothing but a lot of 'scrubs' from the lots" (*The Sporting Life*, Feb. 11; Peter Morris). **3.** A baseball diamond, regardless of its size or location.

lotter Short for *sandlotter.* IST USE. 1909. "Billy Zimmerman [is] another lotter I picked up" (Larry Sutton, quoted in *The Sporting News*, Nov. 18; Peter Morris).

lottery The draft by major-league clubs of minor leaguers in the earliest 20th century. Which club obtained a player was determined randomly. "The West, though not winning as many stars in the annual lottery, came through

with a number of beauties" (J.C. Kofoed, *Baseball Magazine*, July 1916; Peter Morris).

Lou Brock Award An annual award presented since 1978 to the stolen-base leader in the National League. It honors the St. Louis Cardinals outfielder who set the season record of 118 stolen bases in 1974. Brock was the first active player to have an award named after him.

loud average A batting average that includes many extra-base hits. "[Fordham coach] Dan Gallagher . . . says [Mike] Marchiano is hitting a 'loud .500,' as evidenced by his 1.054 slugging percentage" (John Manuel, *Baseball America*, May 26–June 8, 1997; Peter Morris).

loud foul A foul ball, other than a foul tip; esp., a foul ball hit for a long distance, usually close to the foul pole. "Well, every time Mike [Donlin] got a hit he would look in my direction and start boasting. We went into the last game of the series with Mike leading me by a few points. Well, that day I got five straight hits and Donlin didn't even make a loud foul" (Honus Wagner, *Baseball Grins*, 1933).

loud out An out that results when a solidly hit ball is caught, usually directly at a fielder. "The home run of today is the cheapest of all hits . . . [as] all but a hundred would be nothing but loud outs were it not for the encroaching fences . . . that prevent the outfielders from demonstrating their maximum range" (Richard Maney, *The New York Times*, Sept. 10, 1950).

Lou Gehrig Memorial Award An annual award presented to a major-league player "who both on and off the field best exemplifies the character of Lou Gehrig." The award was established in 1955 by Phi Delta Theta, Gehrig's fraternity at Columbia University, and is administered by the fraternity's headquarters in Oxford, Ohio. Syn. *Gehrig Award.*

Lou Gehrig's disease The popular name for amyotrophic lateral sclerosis (ALS), the fatal paralytic disease that claimed the life of Hall of Famer Lou Gehrig in 1941 at age 37. It is a rapidly progressive, fatal neurological disease that attacks the nerve cells responsible

Lou Gehrig Memorial Award. Images of the photogenic Lou Gehrig. *National Baseball Library and Archives, Cooperstown, N.Y.*

for controlling voluntary muscles; its cause is unknown. The term has long been applied to all sufferers of the disease, and has done much to increase public awareness of the affliction. Hall of Fame pitcher Catfish Hunter died of ALS in 1999. Syn. *Gehrig's disease.* IST USE. 1953. "Lou Gehrig disease study started on Guam" (*Science News Letter*, Sept. 19; *OED*).

Louisiana A *Linda Ronstadt*, in reference to Ronstadt's remake of Roy Orbison's hit record, "Blue Bayou" (Scott Ostler, *Los Angeles Times*, 1986). Bayous, which are small streams or creeks that are offshoots of larger bodies of water, are most frequently associated with Louisiana.

Louisville *v.* To hit the ball hard, as with a Louisville Slugger. IST USE. 1942. "The good-looking kid . . . Louisville'd for .343 in his first season" (*Baseball Magazine*, August; David Shulman).

Louisville Slugger 1. A heavy baseball bat. It was once the trade name of a heavy bat manufactured by the Hillerich and Bradsby Co., originally of Louisville, Ky., but now based in nearby Jeffersonville, Ind. The bat was named in honor of Pete Browning, an outfielder and three-time batting champion for the Louisville Colonels, whose nickname was "the Louisville Slugger" and whose own bat in the 1884 season measured 37 inches and weighed nearly 48 ounces. Syn. *slugger,* 3. **2.** The name used by the Hillerich & Bradsby Co. of Louisville, Ky., for its full line of sports equipment ranging from baseball bats to golf clubs. The company attaches the "Louisville Slugger" name to other things as a sponsor, including the Louisville Slugger Museum and Louisville Slugger Field, which are both in downtown Louisville.

Louisville Slugger Award One of several awards, such as those given (since 1971) to new Hall of Fame inductees who were batting stars, to the top hitters in professional baseball (including the minor leagues), and to college coaches (not necessarily baseball) for "excellence in coaching."

lounge hitter A player who cruises the bar scene late at night (Kevin Kerrane, *Dollar Sign on the Muscle,* 1984, p.96).

low Toward the bottom of, or below, the strike zone.

low A Syn. of *low Single A.*

low and away Syn. of *low and outside.* "[Tom] Glavine and [Greg] Maddux established their low-and-away strikes with such precision throughout the 1990s that they became the pitchers most identified with the squashing of the strike zone—it became shorter and wider (wider, many said, than the plate)" (Tom Verducci, *Sports Illustrated*, June 17, 2002).

low and inside Said of a pitch that is low and close to the batter and that may or may not be in the strike zone. Syn. *down and in*.

low and outside Said of a pitch that is low and far from the batter and that may or may not be in the strike zone. Pitching coach Leo Mazzone taught his pitchers to work low and outside. Syn. *down and away*; *low and away*; *down and out*.

low ball 1. Syn. of *low pitch*. "A very low ball is termed 'one around his dogs' [feet]" (*The New York Times*, June 2, 1929). Compare *high ball*, 1. 2. *hist*. In the early days of baseball, a "fair ball" that passed over home plate between the batter's waist and his knees (1871) between the batter's waist and one foot off the ground (1872–1876), and between the batter's belt and his knees (1877–1886). Henry Chadwick (*The Game of Base Ball*, 1868, p.42) defined "low balls" as "balls pitched low over the home base and balow [*sic*] the knee of the batsman," commenting that "the striker has no right to demand a ball lower than a foot high from the ground, as balls lower than this cannot be delivered by the pitcher without his continually running the risk of sending in bowled balls." Compare *high ball*, 2. IST USE. 1867 (*New York Herald*, July 3; Edward J. Nichols).

low-ball hitter A hitter with a reputation for swinging at balls that come in below his knees. Compare *high-ball hitter*.

low bridge 1. *v*. To brush the batter back from the plate, causing him to bend back as if he were going under a low bridge. "Once in a while they 'low bridge' you, but no real shooting" (Philadelphia Athletics first baseman Ferris Fain, quoted in *San Francisco Examiner*, Aug. 3, 1949; Peter Tamony). 2. *n*. "The position assumed by a batter who is stooping to avoid being hit by a high or wide pitch" (Edward J. Nichols, *An Historical Dictionary of Baseball Terminology*, PhD dissertation, Jan. 1939). "The next time I came up, the low bridge went down and it

was a good one—bat one way, cap another, and me down" (Joe Garagiola, *Baseball Is a Funny Game*, 1960, p.45). IST USE. 1937 (Red Barber, NBC World Series broadcast, Oct. 6; Edward J. Nichols). 3. *v*. To knock a runner down. For shortstops and second basemen, throwing sidearm to low bridge aggressive runners forces the latter to slide quickly for self-preservation. "Bert Campaneris started a brawl using a relay throw to low-bridge the baserunner" (Don Baylor, *Don Baylor*, 1989, p.135).

ETYMOLOGY. The term originated in the days of the canal boat. According to W.E. Woodward (*The Way Our People Lived*, 1944; Peter Tamony), "The boat moved so slowly that the passengers had fairly long conversations with people walking along the canal bank. Now and then the boat would pass under a bridge. If it were dangerously low the captain or helmsman would yell 'Low Bridge' and the passengers would duck their heads." The term is also alluded to in the refrain of the popular American folk song "The Erie Canal" (Carl Sandburg, *The American Songbag*, 1927): "Low bridge, ev'ry body down! / Low bridge, for we're going through a town, / And you'll always know your neighbor, / You'll always know your pal, / If you ever navigated on the Erie Canal." The term was a universal way of telling someone to duck his head, even in a baseball sense: "[Batter] Newell needed a pot of glue [as] he threw his bat almost to third and the rooters cried, 'Low bridge'" (*Idaho* [Boise] *Daily Statesman*, May 3, 1900; Peter Morris).

Lowdermilk *hist*. A pitcher given to wildness. Named for Grover Cleveland Lowdermilk, whose lackluster pitching (career record of 23–39 between 1909 and 1920, with 296 strikeouts and 376 bases on balls) was characterized by legendary bases on balls and wild pitches. Lowdermilk attracted some new attention in the mid-1980s when the value of his 1912 baseball card hit $1,200.

low-drop mound A pitcher's mound that appears to be lower than normal. Compare *high-drop mound*.

lower deck The ground-level seating in a ballpark with more than one deck.

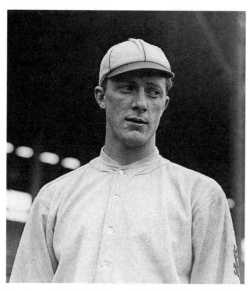

Lowdermilk. Pitcher Grover Cleveland Lowdermilk as a St. Louis Cardinal. *George Grantham Bain Collection, Library of Congress*

lower half 1. The *second half* of an inning. 2. The personal or mental *makeup* of a baseball player: what he is like inside, how he lives, and what he believes in. Baltimore Orioles scout Jim Russo (quoted in *The Baltimore Sun*, Feb. 9, 2004): "The lower half was guts, competitiveness, work ethic, integrity." Compare *upper half*, 2.

low-hit game A game in which a team gets very few hits (usually one or two).

low-impact ball A baseball used in some youth programs that acts like a regular ball but causes less damage if a child is hit with one. See also *reduced injury factor ball*.

low lead A good fastball.

low minors Professional baseball at the entry level; "a world of 'prospects,' 'suspects' and 'roster fillers' playing 140 games in 143 days for around $200 a week" (Robert Schmuhl, *Chicago Tribune*, Aug. 19, 1990).

low pitch A pitch that is below the strike zone. Unless swung at by the batter, a low pitch should be called a ball by the plate umpire. Compare *high pitch*. Syn. *low ball*, 1. EXTENDED USE. A crooked deal. "The major sure swings at low pitches! . . . He'll trust a stranger with a face that would set off a bank alarm!" ("Our Boarding House" cartoon, *San Francisco News*, June 13, 1956; Peter Tamony).

low Single A A *Class A* level of minor-league baseball, above *short-season league* but below *high Single A*; e.g., the South Atlantic League and the Midwest League. No more than two players may have five or more years of prior minor-league experience on a low Single A team. Syn. *low A*; *full-season A*.

low strike A pitch thrown low in the strike zone that umpires sometimes call a ball. Umpires who wore the inside chest protector were positioned over the catcher's shoulder and could see the low strike much better. Compare *high strike*.

LP Abbrev. for *losing pitcher*.

lucky seventh *hist.* The second (bottom or home) half of the seventh inning, which was once regarded as lucky for the home team. "Tiernan ended the inning with a fly, which Pinkney captured. The New Yorkers groaned in anguish, while the Gowanus jays smiled. 'Why, the New Yorks are not in it,' they yelled. 'Rats!' howled the New Yorkers. 'Wait till the lucky seventh'" (*The World* [New York], Oct. 24, 1889; Gerald L. Cohen). ETYMOLOGY. Edward J. Nichols (*An Historical Dictionary of Baseball Terminology*, PhD dissertation, Jan. 1939, p.44) suggested that the term was "probably named from the idea of the Lucky 'seven' as known in the game of dice." Sporting people have long associated good fortune with the number 7. However, A.H. Tarvin (*Baseball Digest*, Nov. 1944, pp.57–58) reported that the term can be traced back to 1886, when Chicago White Stockings pitcher John Clarkson used it to rally the team in a game against Boston. Tim Murnane, a reporter for *The Boston Globe*, overheard Clarkson's remark, and, after examining the scores of every game played by Chicago from 1876 to 1886, discovered that more runs were scored in the seventh inning than in any other. Lee Allen (*The Hot Stove League*, 1955, p.103) noted that *Cincinnati Enquirer* writer O.P. Caylor frequently referred to the "lucky seventh" in 1876.

lug the bunting To win the pennant (Maurice

H. Weseen, *A Dictionary of American Slang*, 1934).

Luis Tiant windup The twisty windup used by pitcher Luis Tiant, who would face out to center field before delivering the pitch.

lulu A remarkable or outstanding player. "Say, he's [Denny Lyons] a lulu wid de stick. There's no man in de Brotherhood who can beat him" (Pete Browning, quoted in the *Philadelphia Press*, reprinted in *The World* [New York], July 12, 1890). The term appears in the third stanza of Ernest L. Thayer's 1888 poem "Casey at the Bat": "And the former [Flynn] was a lulu and the latter [Jimmy Blake] was a cake." According to Martin Gardner (*The Annotated Casey at the Bat*, 1967, p.179), "lulu" is "something extraordinary, a humdinger," but was used by Thayer in a "derisive sense."

lumber **1.** *n.* A baseball bat or bats. "Ready with their 'lumber' preparatory to opening a big five-game series against the Giants tomorrow . . . are the 'big three' sluggers of the Pittsburgh Pirates" (*San Francisco Call-Bulletin* photo caption, May 3, 1958). 1ST USE. 1913. "Harry's [Krause] helpmates proceeded to show what will happen when lumber is admitted free [i.e., when a team has all

Lumber. Ty Cobb (left) and Shoeless Joe Jackson during the 1913 season. *Library of Congress*

the bats it needs] by giving an exhibition of pretty stickwork throughout the game" (*San Francisco Bulletin*, Apr. 9; Gerald L. Cohen). **2.** *n.* A lineup or a portion of a lineup filled with good hitters, such as the Pittsburgh Pirates "Lumber Company" of the late 1970s, composed of Dave Parker, Willie Stargell, Al Oliver, and Manny Sanguillen. **3.** *n.* The bench in the dugout. "Ping Bodie says he is becoming tired of warming the lumber in the rathskeller" (*San Francisco Bulletin*, May 15, 1913; Gerald L. Cohen). **4.** *v.* To run ponderously.

lumberjack A player who can hit reasonably consistent long balls and home runs.

lumber legs The legs of a slow-running player; e.g., "Smith's lumber legs seemed to be made of wood."

lumber man A player who is primarily a hitter; one who is likely to be known for his hitting rather than fielding prowess. See also *wood player*.

lumberyard **1.** Syn. of *bat rack*. **2.** Figurative source of talented hitters. "You can shake a tree and a thousand guys who can field will drop out. But it's harder to find guys from the lumber yard. Dave Winfield doesn't make $1.5 million because he's a good defensive outfielder" (Kansas City Royals designated hitter Hal McRae, quoted in *San Francisco Examiner*, May 22, 1981; Peter Tamony). Also spelled "lumber yard."

lumps Hard hitting against a pitcher. A pitcher getting back into the rotation after an injury will often remark that he will "take my lumps" until he is in the groove again: "I'm going to get my lumps here and there until I get fine-tuned" (Roger Clemens, Associated Press dispatch, Apr. 12, 1987). 1ST USE. 1937 (*The New York Times*, Oct. 8; Edward J. Nichols).

lunch Getting hit very hard; e.g., "The pitcher had his lunch handed to him after the barrage of hits."

lunch hook Syn. of *dinner tong*. 1ST USE. 1900. "[Heinie] Peitz held the ball concealed in his right 'lunch hook'" (*Cincinnati Enquirer*, July 10; Peter Morris).

lunge An erratic move made by a batter trying to get at a ball in front of the plate. It is usually the result of the batter's misjudging the speed or trajectory of the pitch.

luxury box Syn. of *skybox.*

luxury tax An assessment on a major-league club's player payroll (including earned bonuses), designed to limit the rate of increase in player salaries and slow the spending of high-revenue clubs; a financial penalty on a team that exceeds a mandated payroll limit. According to the Basic Agreement (2007–2011) between the players and the owners, teams whose payrolls exceed set thresholds will be taxed on portions above the thresholds. In 2007, the threshold was $148 million and the tax rate was 40 percent for clubs above the threshold and 22.5 percent for all other clubs. The tax rate differs depending on the number of years a specific club exceeds the threshold. The threshold increases 4.7 percent annually before topping out at $178 million for 2011, after which the luxury tax will disappear. Under the method of accounting used for the tax, payrolls (as of Dec. 12) are based on the average annual values of all contracts, regardless of the actual payout in a specific year, for players on the 40-man rosters; each payroll includes funds for benefits, such as pensions and health insurance, as well as spring training allowances, meal and tip money, travel and moving expenses, postseason pay, and college scholarships. Money from the luxury tax is to be used for player benefit plans, the Industry Growth Fund, or player development in countries lacking organized high school baseball. Syn. *competitive-balance tax.*

LW Abbrev. for *linear weights.*

M

mab To hit a home run off the M.A.B. Paints sign that hung from the facing of the second deck in Veterans Stadium in Philadelphia. The term was coined by Phillies players Doug Glanville and Desi Relaford.

mace *hist.* **1.** *n.* A baseball bat. "Babe Ruth and His 50-Ounce Mace" (*The Lima* [Ohio] *News* illustration caption, March 1, 1922). IST USE. 1877. "[In the window of an] auction-house is exposed a magnificent mahogany mace, tipped with elaborately worked silver" (*Milwaukee Daily Sentinel*, Oct. 30). **2.** *v.* To bat or to be batted. IST USE. 1920. "Jones was maced for a run in the fifth, two hits turning the trick" (J.V. Fitz Gerald, *The Washington Post*, Apr. 24; Peter Morris).

machine **1.** A baseball team; specif., one that works smoothly, precisely, and with good teamwork, such as the "Big Red Machine" of the Cincinnati Reds in the 1970s. "Your modern baseball fan will tell you that the [Chicago] 'Cubs' were the greatest baseball machine of all times" (*San Francisco Bulletin*, Feb. 21, 1913; Gerald L. Cohen). IST USE. 1908 (*Baseball Magazine*, November, p.1; Edward J. Nichols). **2.** An outstanding player. "[McCarl] is a perfect machine, handling ground balls, nasty hops and poor throws with equal precision" (*San Francisco Bulletin*, March 12, 1913; Gerald L. Cohen). Jose Vidro's teammates sometimes call him "Machine," as in *hitting machine* (*Sports Illustrated*, June 24, 2002).

machine-gun ticket A complimentary ticket to a baseball game, esp. in the 1930s. See also *Annie Oakley*, 1.

mackerel A curveball. IST USE. 1932. "A Mackerel or Swerve—A curve ball" (*New York Sun*, June 23). Compare *dead mackerel*.

Mackmen. Connie Mack was considered one of the greatest managers in baseball history. *Harrison and Ewing Collection, Library of Congress*

Mackmen Nickname for the Philadelphia *Athletics* during the years (1901–1950) when Connie Mack was the manager.

Macmillan A baseball encyclopedia; specif., *The Baseball Encyclopedia* published by Macmillan in 10 editions beginning in 1969 (the 10th edition was published in 1996). See also *Big Mac*.

Mad Dash The baserunning of St. Louis Cardinals outfielder Enos Slaughter, who scored the deciding run from first base on Harry Walker's double to left-center field in the eighth inning of Game 7 of the 1946 World Series. With two outs, Slaughter was attempting to steal second base and was off with the pitch. Third base coach Mike Gonzalez signaled Slaughter to stop but he ran through the sign, sliding home with what proved to be the winning run. It is alleged that Boston Red Sox shortstop Johnny Pesky hesitated ("held the ball") before throwing the ball to the plate; Pesky agreed: "I just couldn't seem to make myself throw quickly enough, and when finally I did get rid of it, I knew I couldn't hit him with a .22" (*The Sporting News*, Oct. 23, 1946, p.4). Some observers contended that Walker's hit was a single and that he advanced to second on the throw to the plate. Bob Broeg (*Bob Broeg: Memories of a Hall of Fame Sportswriter*, 1995, pp.162–63) countered, "I always resented that arbitrarily, unfairly and unromantically, the official scorers called Walker's game-winning hit a double. Harry, hoping to distract a throw as he watched Slaughter round third under full steam, did reach second. But, as he agreed, it was a single, not a double, as I insisted to the official scorers. They didn't listen. Too bad." The "Mad Dash" is commemorated by a bronze statue depicting Slaughter sliding home.

Maddux A relatively short, right-handed pitcher who succeeds with an ordinary fastball, control, and intelligence. The term, used by scouts when evaluating pitchers, is named for Greg Maddux (Alan Schwarz, Baseball America.com, Nov. 14, 2006).

maestro *hist.* A baseball manager. The term is usually applied to one who insists on running the team right down to minor details.

maggot *hist.* An owner of a baseball club. "It is plainly evident that the St. Louis sporting writers, after 3 or 4 years' trying to drive [Chris] Von der Ahe out of business, are falling into line with the boss 'maggot'" (*The Sporting Life*, Jan. 18, 1896; Peter Morris, who surmised that the term may have originated as a term of derision for the unpopular St. Louis owner). ETYMOLOGY. H.L. Mencken (*The American Language*, Suppl. II, 1948) lists the term as a piece of baseball slang, an apparent play on the word "*magnate*."

magic number The combination of wins and losses that add up to a championship for a first-place team or a team leading the wild-card race; specif., the total number of games that the leading team in a division, league, or wild-card race must win and/or the closest opponent must lose to clinch the championship for the leader. If, for example, Team A's magic number is six with Team B in second place, any combination of Team A wins and Team B losses adding up to six gives the championship to Team A. To determine the magic number, take the number of games to be played, add one, then subtract the number of games that the leading team is ahead in the loss column of the closest opponent. If more than two teams are in contention, each has a magic number against every other club and must attain it against each team. The magic number comes into play at the end of a season to dramatize the end of the pennant race and is often featured in headlines; e.g., "Red Sox Win, 2–0; Cut Magic Number to One" (*Buffalo News* headline, Sept. 28, 1986). When a team is eliminated, the term is sometimes used facetiously: "'Magic Number' for S.F. is 1961" (*San Francisco Chronicle* headline, Sept. 13, 1960; Peter Tamony). See also *elimination number*; *tragic number*, 1. 1ST USE. 1947. "[The Yankees] reduced the magic number to four. That is the combination of games the Yanks must win or the Red Sox must lose in order to insure the flag for the Yankees" (*The Washington Post*, Sept. 12).

magic wand *hist.* The bat of a player who is getting several lucky hits.

magic word A word or phrase that, when uttered to an umpire, almost certainly provokes the speaker's ejection from the game; specif., the word "motherfucker." Jim Bouton (*Ball Four*, 1970, p.176) has a detailed discussion of the word itself. Umpire Jim Evans (quoted in Bob Luke, *Dean of Umpires*, 2005, p.126): "If a player says to me 'you motherfucker,' or 'you cocksucker' . . . he's just thrown himself out of the game. It's so clear-cut it makes my job easy, as is the case when a player bumps me or kicks dirt at me." Class AA Texas League umpire Jeff Macias (quoted in *The New York Times*, July 27, 2005; Joseph Goulden): "Anything preceded by the pronoun 'you' that doesn't have something positive attached to it is [an] automatic [ejection]."

magnate An owner or dominant stockholder of a baseball team. The term has been in common use since the 1870s when it came into play for an individual as well as a collective reference to the owners acting in concert. See also *mogul*; *maggot*. IST USE. 1878. "Having Bull-Dozed All Hands, the Base Ball Magnates Adjourn" (*St. Louis Globe-Democrat* headline, Dec. 6). USAGE NOTE. The term is often used and defined sardonically to imply ruthlessness and insensitivity to the ballplayers in the owners' employ. "In the eyes of the base-ball 'magnate' the player has become a mere chattel" (John Montgomery Ward, quoted in *Lippincott's Magazine*, Aug. 1887; Peter Morris). "By 1913 [Charles] Comiskey, [Connie] Mack, and [Clark] Griffith proudly bore the lofty mantle of 'magnate,' the pretentious designation by which major league owners identified themselves" (Jules Tygiel, *Past Time*, 2000, p.35). *Baseball Magazine* (Jan. 1915, p.70) defined "magnate" as "a pirate making $22,000,000 a year out of us poor slaves that's gotta work for him." ETYMOLOGY. From ca. 1439 (*OED*), for a great man, noble, man of wealth, from Latin "magnus," for "great."

mailbox baseball An act of vandalism in which rural and suburban roadside mailboxes are struck from a moving car by a person swinging a baseball bat. It is a federal offense. A scene in the film *Stand By Me* (1986), in which the game is played from the open window of a 1949 Ford convertible, may have given the practice ill-deserved publicity.

mail in To give less than one's best on the field; to "go through the motions." The term usually refers to a team that is hopelessly out of contention. "The cellar-dwelling [Texas] Rangers mailed it in down the stretch [in 2000]" (Stephen Cannella, *Sports Illustrated*, Sept. 10, 2001).

Main Street Syn. of *Broadway*, 1. "Sometimes, you're not starting out trying to walk him [Barry Bonds], but if you start 2–0, you don't want to throw it down Main Street" (New York Yankees manager Joe Torre, quoted in *The Baltimore Sun*, Apr. 16, 2002).

major company *hist.* Syn. of *major leagues*. IST USE. 1902 (*The Sporting Life*, July 12; Edward J. Nichols).

major-league *adj.* Referring to a level of play, behavior, or scale that is at the level of the major leagues; e.g., a college or minor-league player may be said to have "major-league aspirations." "[Jason Johnson] looked like he threw pretty good. . . . He showed us . . . some major-league stuff" (Ray Miller, quoted in *The Baltimore Sun*, May 21, 1999). Syn. *big-league*, 1. IST USE. 1891. "[Joe

Magnate. National League owners meet on Feb. 11, 1913. The woman in the picture is Helene Robison Britton, who held the controlling interest in the St. Louis Cardinals between 1911 and 1918. *George Grantham Bain Collection, Library of Congress*

Knight] only dropped two flies last season. . . . There is something of a first year major League experience to think about" (*Cincinnati Enquirer*, Jan. 9; David Ball). EXTENDED USE. Anything imposing and of the highest level, whether it be a "major-league client" or a "major-league headache." Actress Barbara Stanwyck, in the film *Ball of Fire* (1941), on being presented with an engagement ring with a large diamond, called it a "major-league ring." Compare *bush-league.*

major league *n.* **1.** A league at the highest level of organized or professional baseball; specif., one of the two leagues (National League since 1876 and American League since 1901) that currently constitute the major leagues. Previous major leagues included the American Association (1882–1891), Union Association (1884), Players' League (1890), and Federal League (1914–1915). The Special Baseball Records Committee in 1968 decided that these six leagues would be considered "major league" for purposes of the official record. Many baseball historians consider the National Association (1871–1875) to be the first professional league in the major-league category, but the Committee cited the Association's "erratic schedule and procedures" as reason enough for exclusion. Factors that characterize a major league include a consistent schedule, high quality of competition, teams located in heavily populated cities, signing of star players, charging a premium for admission, and self-announcement as such. Syn. *big league.* IST USE. 1890. "John Reilly, Tom Loftus and Lefty Marr of the Reds were discussing the current baseball trade war and an anonymous questioner asked, 'Do you think there will be two major leagues next season?'" (*Chicago Inter-Ocean*, Sept. 16; David Ball). **2.** The highest level of professional baseball in other countries, such as Taiwan and Japan.

Major League Agreement The document, originally adopted on Jan. 12, 1921, and subsequently amended, that creates and defines the office of the commissioner and constitutes an agreement among the major-league clubs. It sets the rules of procedure for voting on such items as expansion, contraction, realignment of divisions, and termination of a club; it also specifies territorial rights of the clubs, conduct of the championship season and postseason, a "central fund" for All-Star Game revenues and broadcasting royalties, the fiscal responsibility of the clubs, and indemnification of baseball officials. The commissioner has sweeping authority to discipline club officials under the terms of the Major League Agreement, but his ability to discipline players is restricted by the Basic Agreement with the Major League Baseball Players Association. The Major League Agreement is embodied in the Major League Constitution.

major-league arm The arm of a pitcher with great potential. "[Bo Belinsky] had what they call in the trade 'a major-league arm.' That is, he could throw hard and his ball moved" (Phil Pepe, *No-Hitter*, 1968).

Major League Baseball The organizational entity that comprises the business and sport of the major leagues; the business name of the office of the commissioner of baseball having as its components the major-league baseball clubs. Abbrev. *MLB.*

Major League Baseball International An organization sponsored by Major League Baseball to promote baseball "in every corner of the globe."

Major League Baseball Players Alumni Association A nonprofit association of former major-league baseball players, founded in 1982 and incorporated in 1988, and headquartered in Colorado Springs, Colo. It sponsors golf tournaments and other charitable events, maintains biographical information on former players, assists players with drug and alcohol rehabilitation, conducts youth clinics, and "promotes a passion" for the game. The membership also includes widows and spouses, current major leaguers, former minor-league players, managers, coaches, scouts, umpires, sports media, trainers, front-office personnel, and fans. Abbrev. *MLBPAA.*

Major League Baseball Players Association The labor union of major-league baseball players—arguably the most powerful union in professional sports—formed in 1954 to represent the players in disputes with the owners. It was a loosely knit organization dominated by the owners until 1966, when top labor economist and negotiator Marvin Miller became its executive director. The union is concerned with base salaries, pension funds, licensing rights and revenues, free-agency rights, grievance procedures, and the rights of players to bargain collectively. Its members include managers, coaches, and trainers. Also known as *Players Association*. Abbrev. *MLBPA*.

Major League Baseball Properties The licensing arm of the major leagues that works to protect the trademarks of teams. Abbrev. *MLBP*.

Major League Baseball Umpires Association A former association of major-league umpires formed in 1968 to represent the umpires in disputes with the owners or players. It was decertified in 2000 and replaced by the *World Umpires Association*.

major-league contract A contract requiring a player to be kept on a major-league club's 40-man roster.

major-league draft Syn. of *Rule 5 draft*.

major-league equivalency An estimate of what a minor-league player's seasonal statistics would be if the player had played that season for the major-league team that controls his contract. The estimate is not a projection, but a conversion of current performance. Research has shown that this estimate is as accurate as estimates of a player's statistics for a given season based on his *established performance level*; it works best with Class AAA statistics. The concept was proposed by Bill James (*Baseball Abstract*, 1985); at the time, James considered this "by far the most important research that I have ever done." Abbrev. *MLE*.

major-league player A professional baseball player on the reserve list of a major-league club.

major-league pop-up Any pop fly hit very high in the air.

major leaguer A major-league baseball player. Syn. *big leaguer*, 1. *big-timer*. IST USE. 1908 (*Baseball Magazine*, September; Edward J. Nichols).

Major League Regulations A set of bulletins and directives adopted by the commissioner of baseball and binding on major-league clubs relating to games, ballparks, uniforms, and other facets of the administration of the game of baseball.

Major League Rules A document that includes 57 rules (three are reserved, so that Major League Rule 60 is the last) that govern off-the-field matters pertaining to the major leagues (not to be confused with the *Official Baseball Rules*, which pertains to on-the-field play). Major League Rules were formerly published in the Blue Book. Among the topics included in the Major League Rules are: drafts, waivers, options, roster limits, discipline and misconduct, conflict of interest, player contracts and salaries, umpires and official scorers, gate receipts, schedules, postseason (qualifications, scheduling, admissions, and division of gate receipts), territorial rights, regulation of minor-league franchises and playing facilities, standard player development contracts, and expansion, contraction, and relocation of franchises. The rules governing transactions can be convoluted and sometimes described in excruciating detail, which prompted Rob Neyer (on ESPN.com, Sept. 8, 1999) to observe, "General managers don't know them, agents don't know them, players don't know them, writers don't know them, and fans don't know them."

major leagues The highest level of professional baseball, consisting of the National League and the American League. Each of these two leagues is subdivided into East, Central, and West divisions. Abbrev. *ML*. Sometimes spelled "Major Leagues." Syn. *majors*; *major company*; *major society*; *big arena*; *big leagues*; *big brush*; *big circus*; *big company*; *big show*, 1; *big smoke*; *big tent*; *big time*; *big top*; *big yard*; *biggies*, 2; *Bigs, the*; *fast company*; *faster company*; *fastest company*; *fast society*, 1; *high company*; *Show, the*.

Major League Scouting Bureau A central scouting combine, formed in 1974 and headquartered in Lake Forest, Calif., that gathers, evaluates, and makes available reports on prospective baseball players for use by all major-league clubs.

major-league waivers A form of *waivers* that is required if a player is to be included in a deal after the July 31 trading deadline and up until the day following the close of the season. If the player is not claimed by another team within two business days after waivers have been requested, the player has "cleared waivers," and the team has secured waivers for the remainder of the waiver period. The team can then send the player to the minors, trade him to another team, or do nothing. If the player does not clear waivers (i.e., he is claimed by another team or teams), the club requesting waivers may withdraw the waiver request; the player then no longer can be traded during the season. If the club does not withdraw the waiver request, the player's contract is assigned to the club with the lowest percentage of games won in the league of the requesting club, or, if all the claims are from clubs in the other league, assignment is to the club in the other league with the lowest winning percentage. The waiver price, paid by the acquiring team to the player's original team, is $20,000.

major-league year A full year of service in the major leagues, constituting 172 days, from Opening Day until the last day of the regular season. See also *service time.* Syn. *baseball year.*

majors Syn. of *major leagues.* IST USE. 1911 (*Baseball Magazine*, October; Edward J. Nichols). EXTENDED USE. The top level of competition. "I made the majors" (singer Garth Brooks, quoted in *Parade Magazine*, Dec. 16, 2001).

major society *hist.* Syn. of *major leagues.* "The season . . . is almost upon us and we don't know whether we are going to use the Goldsmith ball or the kind they use in the major society" (*San Francisco Bulletin*, Feb. 18, 1913; Gerald L. Cohen).

make a living For a major-league player, esp. a pitcher, to perform what he does best or what he must do to continue his career. "[Kirk Rueter] makes a living on the outer reaches of the plate, relentlessly spotting that middling fastball on or just off the outside corner and coming inside only occasionally" (*Sports Illustrated*, May 13, 2002).

make a right turn Good fielding. The term refers to a retired batter-runner who turns right at first base on his way back to the dugout.

"make it be good" *hist.* A once-common encouragement to a batter to wait for a good pitch. IST USE. 1912. "The war cry of coaches and the order of managers to the batter when the opposing pitcher shows signs of wildness, the meaning being that the batter is not to hit the ball unless it is a perfect strike, whether or not he hits" (Hugh S. Fullerton, *American Magazine*, June, p.204; Edward J. Nichols).

make it look easy To make a difficult play appear to be simple. The term is usually applied to those of consummate skill or great ability.

make it look harder than it is To make a routine play look spectacular, sometimes stemming from ineptness or the urge to show off.

make it too good 1. To throw a pitch that is easy for the batter to hit; e.g., when a pitcher has to throw the ball in the strike zone on a 3–0 count. 2. To pitch with too much precision.

make-or-break season That baseball season late in a player's career during which he must either produce or retire from active participation in the game.

make the cut To be selected to remain on a team's roster after it is reduced to 25 players following spring training.

make the team To be placed on a team's roster as a regular major-league player.

makeup 1. The intangible qualities of a baseball player, such as his attitude, poise, focus, integrity, leadership, and the ability to withstand adversity; a player's character and personality. An anonymous scout listed the following traits: a strong desire to succeed, coachability, maturity, temperament, improvement, drive, hunger, consistency, knowledge of the game, and competitiveness. Cleveland Indians area scout Paul Cogan, discussing pitcher C.C. Sabathia (*Sports Illustrated*, July 23, 2001): "As good as he is, the grades I gave him for makeup and character were higher than his talent grades." Michael Lewis (*Moneyball*,

2003, p.25) noted that "bad makeup" is "a death sentence," meaning that "this kid's got problems we can't afford to solve," such as "anything from jail time to drinking problems to severe personality disorders." See also *lower half*, 2. IST USE. 1913. "Look at the way he [Duffy Lewis] steps around and his cocksure method of playing a ball. He knows just what to do with the pill when he gets it and has the natural makeup, speed, plenty of pep and a good arm required of a first-class man" (*San Francisco Bulletin*, March 1; Gerald L. Cohen). 2. Syn. of *make-up game*.

make-up call A decision by an umpire that favors the team that suffered an earlier adverse call. "No umpire in his right mind would make a make-up call because you try to get them all right every time" (Terry Cooney, quoted in John C. Skipper, *Umpires: Classic Baseball Stories from the Men Who Make the Calls*, 1997). Syn. *Revlon call*.

make-up date The date set to play a make-up game.

make-up game A game that has been rescheduled or a previously scheduled game that has been rained out or postponed. Many make-up games are scheduled as parts of doubleheaders. Syn. *makeup*, 2.

man, the The manager of a baseball team.

manage To act as a manager. IST USE. 1866. "With such energetic leaders as Charley Commerford to manage the affairs of the [Waterbury, Ct.] club, and to give tone and character to its members, our national game would soon be seen flourishing" (*Frank Leslie's Illustrated Newspaper*, Aug. 25).

management The decision-makers on a baseball club. IST USE. 1860. "I am instructed by the management of the Detroit Base Ball Club to challenge any first class base ball club in the State . . . to play a match game of base ball in this city" (letter from Detroit Base Ball Club secretary J.J. Dumon, June 1, published in *Detroit Daily Tribune*, June 1; Peter Morris).

manager 1. The uniformed individual appointed by the club to run the team on the field. Traditionally, the manager determines the lineup and batting order, makes substitutions, plans the game strategy, and represents the team in communications with the umpires and the opposing team. *Baseball Magazine* (Jan. 1915, p.70) defined "manager" as "bonehead pet of the magnate, whose fool ideas keep us from winning that old flag in a canter." Abbrev. *MGR*. **2.** *hist.* The individual responsible (from as early as 1870 until the mid-1880s) for hiring, signing, and disciplining the club's personnel, arranging the club's finances, and handling travel and lodging accommodations. In this sense, the manager was the equivalent of the modern general manager. The in-game, on-field maneuvers and strategy were the duties of the team's captain. IST USE. 1870. "The Forest City team start tonight for Baltimore and leave behind them very pleasant recollections of their quiet and gentlemanly conduct when here, and will be a very great pity if they get into disrepute through their present manager, whose regard for his pledged engagement is not sufficient to bear the test of an offer of five percent extra gate money" (*Cleveland Herald*, Aug. 26).

Manager of the Year Award 1. An annual award presented by *The Sporting News* to the best manager in major-league baseball (1936–1965) and, since 1966, to the best manager in each major league. **2.** An annual award presented since 1983 by the Baseball Writers' Association of America to the best manager in each major league, as voted by sportswriters. Each first-place vote is worth five points, second place is worth three points, and third place is worth one point. Although newer than the award presented by *The Sporting News*, it has come to be regarded as the more prestigious version.

manager's spot Syn. of *sweet spot*, 1.

M&M Boys Home run hitters Roger Maris and Mickey Mantle when they were members (1960–1966) of the New York Yankees. ETYMOLOGY. The term was inspired by the name of the popular M&M chocolate candy.

man from outer space A player whose feats are extraordinary.

manicurist Syn. of *groundskeeper*.

man in blue An *umpire*, 1.

man in the middle A baserunner caught in a rundown on the basepath.

manliness The quality or behavior of the grown working man in mid-19th century America. The term and concept played a critical role in the early history of baseball by separating the "national game," as a legitimate and serious activity requiring "manly" behavior and self-control, from its simple and primitive origins in children's or "boyish" games. Manliness "had more to do with decorum and bearing than with plebeian notions of bravery, such as being soaked with the ball and not whimpering" (John Thorn, *The Boston Sunday Globe*, July 10, 2005). And given that baseball "required the possession of muscular strength, great agility, quickness of eye, readiness of hand, and many other faculties of mind and body that mark a man of nerve. . . . Suffice it to say that it is a recreation that anyone may be proud to excel in, as in order to do so, he must possess the characteristics of true manhood to a considerable degree" (Henry Chadwick, ed., *Beadle's Dime Base-Ball Player*, 1860, p.6). In its new incarnation, baseball "took manliness beyond a mere demonstration of physical prowess and linked it to virtues such as courage, fortitude, discipline, and so on. The argument concluded that if ball games called these virtues into play . . . then ball playing was obviously one way of demonstrating manhood" (Melvin L. Adelman, *A Sporting Time*, 1986, p.106). By the end of the 19th century, the term came to signify less the opposite of childishness than the opposite of femininity.

Man of the Year Award See *Marvin Miller Man of the Year Award*.

man on the firing line The pitcher.

man overboard A runner who has run or slid past a base. ETYMOLOGY. A term brought back from World War II by players who had been in the armed forces.

Manuel rule A rule adopted by the American League in 1908 to give a victory to a pitcher whose team went ahead during the inning for which the pitcher was pinch-hit. The ruling by American League president Ban Johnson came about in a June 14 game in Chicago when, with the New York Yankees ahead 4–2, White Sox pitcher Moxie Manuel relieved in the fifth inning and shut out the Yankees through the eighth inning; after Ed Hahn batted for Manuel, the White Sox took the lead, 5–4, and won the game after Doc White and Ed Walsh shut out New York in the ninth. See Eugene C. Murdock (*Ban Johnson*, 1982, pp.90–91).

manufacture To score runs by stringing together singles, bunts, stolen bases, sacrifices, walks, errors, and hitting behind the runner, without the benefit of extra-base hits; to score runs by employing the basic fundamentals of baseball and taking advantage of the slightest opportunities. "[Len Dykstra] manufactured the only run that really mattered. He led off the first with a walk, stole second and went to third on a throwing error . . . before coming home on a ground out" (*The Baltimore Sun*, Oct. 22, 1993). IST USE. 1900. "Each side had three good opportunities for manufacturing runs" (*Chicago Daily Tribune*, Aug. 12). EXTENDED USE. To succeed by working hard, such as growing sales without a major product.

maple bat A durable, thin-barreled baseball bat made from sugar maple, a hard wood whose tightly knit grain prevents denting, cracking, and chipping and allows the bat to be used for a long period of time. Maple is denser, heavier, and stronger than the more springy northern white ash used in making traditional baseball bats. A maple bat can be swung faster and has a larger sweet spot. It was certified for major-league use in 1998. See also *Sam Bat*.

marathon A long, extra-inning baseball game.

marble 1. *hist.* The baseball. 2. *hist.* Home plate. Before it was replaced by rubber in 1885 (American Association) and 1887 (National League), home plate was commonly a marble slab. IST USE. 1875. "[Dick Higham] attempted to get home . . . but was neatly put out at the 'marble'" (*St. Louis Post-Dispatch*, May 7; Peter Morris).

marginal lineup value A measure of a player's batting performance, consisting of the difference in runs scored between a lineup of nine average players and a lineup of eight average players plus the given player. The statistic measures offensive performance using batting average, on-base percentage, slugging percentage, and plate appearances. An average hitter will have a marginal lineup value of zero. In 2006, Albert Pujols had a marginal lineup value of 79.8. The statistic has been featured in *Baseball Prospectus* since 2003. See also *equivalent marginal lineup value*. Abbrev. *MLV*.

marginal lineup value rate A player's marginal lineup value expressed as runs per game. Abbrev. *MLVr*.

marginal payroll/marginal wins A measure of the efficiency of a team's front office in terms of its winning percentage relative to its payroll. It is based on a formula that compares a team's record and payroll to that of a team of replacement-level players all earning the major-league minimum, the team being assumed to play .300 ball. The result can be interpreted as the amount of money the team spent on payroll for each win above 48.6 (0.3 of 162 games). The measure was devised by Doug Pappas and described in *Baseball Prospectus* (2004). Abbrev. *MP/MW*.

marginal value over replacement player A measure of how much a player ought to be paid based on his performance, computed by turning *value over replacement player* into a dollar figure in the context of present-day salary norms. One can compare the measure to a player's actual salary to evaluate whether he is earning his salary; one can also project the measure for subsequent seasons (with an 8 percent annual inflation adjustment to reflect the normal rise in salaries) to evaluate whether a player is likely to perform well enough to justify a long-term contract. The measure was introduced by *Baseball Prospectus*. Abbrev. *MORP*.

Mariners Nickname for the American League West Division expansion franchise in Seattle, Wash., since 1977. The name, suggested in a newspaper contest, recognizes "the natural association between the sea and Seattle and her people." The team is often referred to as the *M's*.

mariposa A *knuckleball*. See also *bola de nudillos*. ETYMOLOGY. Spanish for "butterfly."

marked ball A ball that has been scratched, cut, or scuffed to make it move erratically when pitched. See also *doctored ball*.

marker *hist.* A run. 1ST USE. 1913. "Leach, in center field for the Cubs, registered his team's only marker" (*The Washington Post*, Aug. 23; Peter Morris).

marlin A tale about a prospect that is hard to believe; a fish story. "[Art Stewart will] always say, 'Right after you left, the kid hit two homers, one of them 600 feet!' You just sit back and smile and go, 'marlin'" (Eddie Bane, quoted in Alan Schwarz, Baseball America.com, Nov. 14, 2006).

Marlins Nickname for the National League East Division expansion franchise that began playing in Miami, Fla., in 1993 as the Florida Marlins. The club was world champions by 1997 and again in 2003. Also known as *Fish*. ETYMOLOGY. The club was designated by state rather than city to increase its appeal to all Floridians. The marlin was chosen because the fish is "a fierce fighter and an adversary that tests your mettle" (Florida Marlins media guide, 1998).

marquee name A popular player. "[The Oakland A's] no longer seemed to have any offensive punch with the departure of their biggest marquee names [the traded Jose Canseco and the injured Mark McGwire]" (Michael Vega, *The Boston Globe*, July 23, 1993). ETYMOLOGY. From the large signboards atop theaters where star actors find their "names up in lights."

Marvin Miller For a fielder to allow a ground ball to roll under his glove. ETYMOLOGY. When a fielder "Marvin Millered a ball" it meant that, because of his "short" arm, he could not extend his glove all the way down to the ground. Miller, the former executive director of the players' union, had one arm that was shorter than the other. The term was used by Pittsburgh Pirates outfielder Andy Van Slyke.

Marvin Miller Man of the Year Award An annul *Players Choice Award* presented since 1997 to a major-league baseball player who exhibits leadership by his on-field performance and contributions to the community. The award is based on balloting conducted by the Major League Baseball Players Association. The award honors the former executive director of the Association.

mascot 1. An individual, most frequently a youngster and often the batboy, who takes care of the equipment, does odd chores, and is commonly felt to bring luck to the team. "Little Nick is the luckiest man in the country, and is certainly the Browns' mascott" (*The Sporting Life*, Apr. 21, 1886; Barry Popik). Many team photos from the late 19th century show a uniformed boy identified as the mascot. Ira L. Smith and H. Allen Smith (*Low and Inside*, 1949) explained the traditional linking of mascots and batboys in baseball: "The mascot has generally been utilitarian—it's all right to have him around for good luck, but the little twerp oughta do some work too." Some mascots were important figures. Frederick G. Lieb (*Connie Mack: Grand Old Man of Baseball*, 1945; Peter Tamony) wrote, "Sharing honors with Mack in bringing three world's titles to Philadelphia in four years was the little hunchbacked

Mascot. Eddie Bennett, New York Yankee mascot and batboy beginning in 1921, when this photograph was taken. He remained in that dual role for almost twelve years and saw the Yankees capture seven pennants and four World Series titles. *George Grantham Bain Collection, Library of Congress*

mascot, Louis Van Zelst. A kindly, good-natured boy, he had come to Mack in 1909 and said he was lucky and indeed he was. Nothing but good luck followed in his wake." IST USE. 1883. "The Anthracites have a Mascotte in 'Chic,' a little lad who carries bats, runs errands and makes himself generally useful. He is a bright boy and the players pin their faith to his luck-bringing qualities" (*The Sporting Life*, July 30, p.7). IST USE (spelled "mascot"). 1886. "[Charlie Gallagher] is said to have been born with teeth, and is guaranteed to possess all the magic charms of a genuine mascot" (*The New York Times*, June 20). **2.** An animal or costumed figure used to characterize and bring luck to a team. Such mascots are almost always given names. It has been written on several occasions that the custom of the animal mascot in America may have started in college football. "The first football mascot, so far as anyone can now recall, was Handsome Dan, a bulldog who belonged to a member of the Yale class of 1892" (*Sports Illustrated*, Nov. 5, 1956). But Gerald L. Cohen (*Comments on Etymology*, Feb. 1, 1987) found the following, earlier baseball reference from *The World* (New York) (May 25, 1887): "It was Pittsburgh's first victory from the Giants, and the ever-happy [Pud] Galvin's smile increased in magnitude. The Skye-terrier mascot was left at the hotel." The current Baltimore Orioles adopted the Bird as a costumed mascot, though he has nothing to do with baseball: "He now clearly exists to take the customers' minds off the game, to give them entertainment and distraction" (Jonathan Yardley, *The Washington Post*, Sept. 15, 1986). See also *hoodoo*, 2. IST USE. 1887. "Fred Carroll has purchased a monkey to do the mascot business for Washington" (*Detroit Free Press*, March 18). **3.** A good-luck charm. "Sam Crane played with the Nationals, and he proved a veritable mascot" (*The Washington Post*, May 17, 1887; Peter Morris).

ETYMOLOGY. The direct American origin of the term came in 1880 with the importation of the French comic opera *La Mascotte*. Prior to that date there are two theories for the derivation of the term: 1) from a Provençal word "masco" for "sorceress," and 2)

Mascot. Mascots for the Boston Red Sox and the Brooklyn Robins, 1916. *George Grantham Bain Collection, Library of Congress*

from "masqué," for "one who is covered or concealed," applied in provincial France to a child born with a caul, which was believed to bring luck. From whatever source, the notion of the mascot was quickly accepted in some quarters. According to *Illustrated American Magazine* (May 24, 1890; Peter Tamony): "Firm believers in both mascots and hoodoos are to be found among sporting men, and also among theatrical people. 'Getting a hunch' is an alternative expression for 'getting a tip' and it springs from the fact that hunchbacks, if properly approached, are a sure source of luck."

mash To hit a ball hard. "[Chris Shelton] can flat-out mash" (Tom Verducci, *Sports Illustrated*, Aug. 8, 2005).

masher A power hitter. "His lineup . . . lacked the mashers who provide instant offense with prodigious blasts" (*The Baltimore Sun*, Aug. 25, 2002). "[Ted Williams was] a masher of baseballs" (Bob Ryan, *The Boston Globe*, July 6, 2002).

mask Protective facial gear worn by the catcher and the home plate umpire; specif., the *catcher's mask.* "A new accompaniment of the game is to be introduced this year in the shape of a 'mask,' which is to be used for the protection of the catcher's face" (*New York Clipper*, Apr. 14, 1877; Peter Morris). Eight days after the debut of the catcher's mask, the *Harvard Crimson* (Apr. 20, 1877) declared, "The new mask proved a complete success, since it entirely protected the face and head and adds greatly to the confidence of the catcher, who need not feel that he is every moment in danger of a life-long injury." IST USE. 1877. "Mr. [Fred] Thayer of the Harvard College Club . . . invented a steel mask for protecting the face of the catcher of the nine. . . . It has proved a valuable protection to the face, and is in daily use at the gymnasium" (*New York Clipper*, Jan. 27; Peter Morris).

mask and mitten *hist.* The position of catcher. Syn. "mask and mit work." IST USE. 1908 (*Baseball Magazine*, November, p.22; Edward J. Nichols).

masked man The catcher.

masker *hist.* The catcher. IST USE. 1914. "A kid masker or two may perch upon the [Boston Red Sox] bench" (W.A. Phelon, *Baseball Magazine*, August; Peter Morris).

maskman The catcher. IST USE. 1902. "[William Sullivan] was generally considered the best maskman in the service of the American League" (*Reach's Official American League Base Ball Guide*; Peter Morris).

mask work The catcher's duties. IST USE. 1911. "[Fred Tenney] was erratic in his throws, and his all around mask work was anything but what a big league man should show" (Alfred H. Spink, *The National Game*, 2nd ed., 1911, p.187).

Massachusetts game An early variation of baseball, played in New England from the early 1800s and esp. popular in the Boston area in the 1850s. It employed a box-shaped (rather than a diamond-shaped) field and four 4-feet-high wooden stakes as bases placed 60 feet apart. The striker stood inside a space of four feet in diameter, at equal distance between the first and fourth bases; he would attempt to hit a ball thrown overhand from

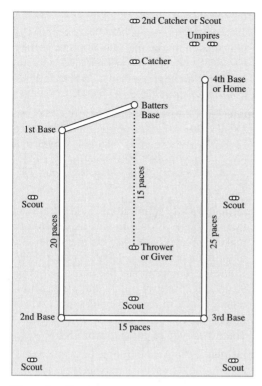

Massachusetts game.

the midpoint of the square, a distance of 30 feet. There was no "foul" territory. The game allowed for runners to be retired when hit with the ball thrown by a defensive player. A catch for an out had to be made on the fly, not on the first bound. A side might number 10 to 14 players, though 11 was most common. The Massachusetts Association of Base Ball Players (10 original clubs in and around Boston) met in Dedham, Mass., on May 13, 1858 to fix a set of 21 rules; Rule 16 stipulated that there be only one out per side. The Massachusetts game used a small, light, and softer ball. It was played throughout the Civil War in various settings, but rapidly lost ground to the *New York game* following the war. John Thorn (*The Boston Sunday Globe*, July 10, 2005) suggested that "its failure . . . may be chalked up to the game's unabashedly rural quality at a time of increasing urbanization, and in some measure may reflect the increasing dominance of New York among American cities." Still, at the height of its popularity the *New York Tribune* (Oct. 1, 1859; Priscilla

Astifan) was moved to report, "The only genuine game is what is known as the 'Massachusetts Game.'" See also *town ball*, 1. Syn. *Boston game*; *Boston ball*; *New England game*. IST USE. 1859 (*The Base Ball Player's Pocket Companion: Containing Rules and Regulations for Forming Clubs, Directions for the "Massachusetts Game," and the "New York Game," from Official Reports*, published by Mayhew and Baker, Boston; John Thorn).

massage To bat a ball. IST USE. 1932 (*Baseball Magazine*, October, p.496; Edward J. Nichols).

mass hits *hist.* For a team to collect many hits within a short period, usually an inning. IST USE. 1915 (*Baseball Magazine*, December, p.80; Edward J. Nichols).

mass migration The annual shifting of players from one club to another.

master One adept at a certain practice. Frank Viola was a "paint master" because he had excellent control of his pitches (Bill Mazeroski, *Bill Mazeroski's Baseball '89*, 1989). The term was coined by pitcher Dennis Eckersley.

master fly A *home run*. "Wow, that sure was some master fly" (*St. Petersburg Times*, March 5, 1987).

mastermind The manager of a baseball team. The term is sometimes applied with a hint of cynicism, such as in this definition: "Manager who wants to do the thinking for the entire team" (Harwell E. West, *The Baseball Scrap Book*, 1938). The term was often applied to longtime New York Giants manager John McGraw. IST USE. 1920 (*The New York Times*, Oct. 5; Edward J. Nichols).

masterpiece A well-pitched game. "[Greg Maddux] pitched a 100-pitch masterpiece that included one outfield putout, four strikeouts and 20 ground-ball outs" (*The Baltimore Sun*, June 8, 1998).

matador A timid infielder; specif., one who positions his body like a bullfighter to avoid being hit by the ball when fielding it.

match **1.** A baseball game. IST USE. 1845. "If there should not be a sufficient number of members of the Club present at the time agreed upon to commence exercise, gentlemen not members may be chosen in to make up the match" (Knickerbocker Rules, Rule 6th, Sept. 23). **2.** A series of baseball games, such as home-and-home.

match game A game in early baseball played between two organized clubs that resulted from a formal challenge and was played for a specific stake (usually a new ball), often on a best two-of-three basis. The term was used to distinguish such contests from a *friendly match*, a game between members of the same club, and a game that featured a picked nine. A letter from Detroit Base Ball Club secretary J.J. Dumon, published in *Detroit Daily Tribune* (June 1, 1860; Peter Morris): "I am instructed by the management of the Detroit Base Ball Club to challenge any first class base ball club in the State who are governed by the rules and regulations of the National Association of base ball players, to play a match game of base ball in this city." See also *stump match*. Compare *practice game*. IST USE. 1855. "The first match game of the season will be played between the Knickerbockers and Gothams, at the Red House, Harlem, on Friday, June 1st, play to commence about 3 o'clock" (*Spirit of the Times*, June 2; Dean A. Sullivan). USAGE NOTE. The first match game (although not then called as such) occurred between the Knickerbocker and New York clubs on Elysian Fields in Hoboken, N.J., on June 19, 1846.

matching A baseball-card flipping game in which a player drops a card and a second player must match it to keep both cards. If the first player's card lands with the photo side up ("heads"), the second player must flip heads also or lose both cards. The printed back of the card in this game is regarded as "tails."

matchup 1. The two starting pitchers in a baseball game. "[Pedro Martinez] burnished his reputation as a premier big-game pitcher by out dueling Barry Zito, 4–3, in the 13th postseason matchup of Cy Young Award winners" (Tom Verducci, *Sports Illustrated*, Oct. 13, 2003). "[Umpire Terry] Cooney was looking forward to that night's pitching matchup, [Dave] Righetti and [Fernando] Valenzuela, only the fourth time in World Series history that two rookies were the start-

ing pitchers" (John C. Skipper, *Umpires*, 1997). **2.** Hitter vs. pitcher. "Managers like to play matchups in the late innings, pitting lefthanded pitchers against lefthanded hitters and righthanders against righthanders" (*Sports Illustrated*, Oct. 6, 2003).

material Players, especially recruits. IST USE. 1866. "The Athletics are a junior club and contain some excellent material, which will only require practice to develop first class players" (*Detroit Advertiser and Tribune*, June 6).

mathematically eliminated Said of a team that no longer is able to win its division or make the playoffs because the magic number of the team or teams ahead of it is zero. Frank Robinson (quoted in *The Baltimore Sun*, Aug. 9, 1995): "Are we mathematically eliminated? No. I'm from the old school where unless you're mathematically eliminated . . . you expect you're going to win." Symbol: *z*.

matinee *hist.* An afternoon baseball game; specif., the afternoon game that was once traditionally played on the same day as a morning game. Such games were once common on holidays such as July 4th and Labor Day. Although there were no hard and fast rules for matinees, same-day games were not usually regarded as doubleheaders and one had to pay separate admissions to each game. IST USE. 1898 (*New York Tribune*, June 19; Edward J. Nichols).

mattress Syn. of *chest protector*. "[Umpires who] are not considered good enough to work with mattresses on their chest . . . have been favored with weak assignments on the bases" (Jimmy Powers, *New York Daily News*, July 30, 1931; Richard Carletti). IST USE. 1908 (*Baseball Magazine*, July, p.34; Edward J. Nichols).

Matty Alou A .300 hitter who lacks power and drives in few runs (Tom Verducci, *Sports Illustrated*, June 15, 1998). Named for Alou, who had a .307 career batting average, but only 427 runs batted in to go with his 1,777 career hits. In 1966, Alou led the National League with a .342 average but drove in only 27 runs.

maul 1. To get many hits off a pitcher. **2.** To bat a ball hard. IST USE. 1910 (*American*

Magazine, July, p.393; Edward J. Nichols).
3. To win a game (*The Sporting Life*, Nov. 29, 1913).

maximum arc [softball term] The highest point a legally pitched ball in slow pitch softball may reach in its trajectory from the pitcher's release of the ball to the plate. It is measured in feet from the ground: 12 feet in Amateur Softball Association of America rules and 10 feet in United States Specialty Sports Association rules. See also *minimum arc*; *unlimited arc*.

maximum-effort pitcher A pitcher who appears to throw all-out on every pitch; one who labors and exhibits grunts and other signs of exertion, often more than would seemingly be necessary. The term is common in scouting circles, but has negative connotations that are less apparent; e.g., 1) the pitcher is likely to be more injury-prone than one who is said to have a "loose" arm action; 2) the pitcher has less potential to improve his speed as his body fills out; 3) the pitcher is a "thrower" rather than a "pitcher"; and 4) the pitcher may have trouble fielding his position. "While [Richie Lentz] is physically mature with a powerful lower half, scouts see a maximum-effort pitcher with a low ceiling" (Allan Simpson, *Baseball America*, June 9–22, 2003; Peter Morris). Syn. "max-effort pitcher."

McCovey Cove An old shipping channel or inlet of San Francisco Bay just beyond the 25-foot-high, right-field brick wall of AT&T Park in San Francisco that serves as a splash landing for home run balls. Barry Bonds became the first player to hit a home run into the water. Boaters and kayakers use nets to retrieve the balls. Named for San Francisco Giants celebrated first baseman and Hall of Famer Willie McCovey.

McGrawism An aggressive action (such as rowdyism) or tactics (such as the hit-and-run play) characterized by rough, anything-goes baseball, suggested by the play and managerial style of New York Giants manager (1902–1932) John J. McGraw. IST USE. 1908. "McGrawism, to coin a word, seems effective if objectionable" (*St. Louis Post-Dispatch*, July 20).

McGrawmen Nickname for the New York

Giants during the years (primarily the 1920s) when John J. McGraw was the manager.

McKay Medal *hist.* A gold medal awarded in the late 1870s to the National League player who had "the best combined average in batting and fielding during the season" (*Chicago Tribune*, Apr. 6, 1879; Peter Morris). Confusingly, the *New York Clipper* (Dec. 6, 1879; Peter Morris) noted that the medal, awarded to Paul Hines in 1879, was earned by "the batsman securing the largest number of base-hits in [National] League championship games." Alfred H. Spink (*The National Game*, 2nd ed., 1911, p.262) wrote that Hines won the medal in 1879 as "the leading batsman" in the National League. It was offered by James W. McKay of Buffalo, N.Y.

McRae Rule An informal rule adopted in 1978 to discourage a baserunner from being overly aggressive toward the pivot man on an attempt to break up a double play. It mandated sliding and staying within the basepaths. Named for Hal McRae, who regularly wiped out infielders with rolling, football-style cross-body blocks. The rule change went into effect for the 1978 season largely because of McRae's nearly dismembering Willie Randolph during the 1977 American League Championship Series (David Falkner, *Nine Sides of the Diamond*, 1990, pp.87–88).

McGrawism. John McGraw, New York Giants, at Polo Grounds, 1914. *George Grantham Bain Collection, Library of Congress*

McGrawism. Babe Ruth (dressed as a Giant for an exhibition game) with John McGraw, Oct. 23, 1922. *George Grantham Bain Collection, Library of Congress*

meadow **1.** The outfield. "When [Brady] Anderson hears or reads suggestions that the position [center field] has passed him by, even in Camden Yards' smallish meadow, he becomes irritated" (*The Baltimore Sun*, March 12, 2000). **2.** *hist.* A ballpark. "Wandering through a 'meadow,' or a big league park" (Edwin M. Rumill, *Christian Science Monitor*, Sept. 1, 1937).

meal ticket A player of great importance and reliability to his team; specif., a team's winningest and most effective or dependable pitcher. Dizzy Dean once called St. Louis Browns pitcher Ned Garver a "meal ticket" because "he keeps 'em eatin' regular." The player most closely tied to the term was New York Giants southpaw Carl Hubbell, who was known as "The Meal Ticket" not only because he kept the groceries on his manager's table, but also because of his reliability between 1933 and 1937, when he won 115 games. "[San Francisco Giants manager Dusty Baker] used [Barry] Bonds as the decoy, moving Jeff Kent up to bat in front of the meal ticket, rather than behind" (*St. Louis Post-Dispatch*, Oct. 1, 2002). IST USE. 1905

(*The Sporting Life*, p.21; Oct. 7; Edward J. Nichols). ETYMOLOGY. The term had several slang meanings before it attached itself to Hubbell. However, all of the meanings—ranging from a hobo who carries another hobo's food or food money, to a woman supporting a panderer or pimp—refer to a valued asset. Another common application is to a prizefighter who is his manager's meal ticket: "A meal ticket is a valuable asset, but one punch can make it null and void" (*San Francisco Call*, March 14, 1914; Peter Tamony). EXTENDED USE. Any person or object that brings success.

mean Difficult to cope with; e.g., "Smith threw a mean curve to strike out Jones" or "The Yankees played a mean game of baseball."

meander *hist.* To proceed slowly on the basepaths; e.g., taking a base on balls, or "not compelled to hurry to score a run" (John B. Foster, *Collier's New Dictionary of the English Language*, 1908).

measure bats *hist.* Syn. of *cross bats*. IST USE. 1880 (*New York Herald*, July 26; Edward J. Nichols).

meat **1.** The thickest part of a baseball bat. "[Barry Bonds] gets the meat of the bat on everything, and he never misses" (Alan Embree, quoted in *Sports Illustrated*, Apr. 15, 2002). **2.** The limbs and body of a batter; e.g., to "take one on the meat" is to be hit by a pitched ball. **3.** A baseball player. A familiar greeting among players is, "How ya doing, meat?" (John Maffei, *Baseball Digest*, May 1986). **4.** A batter who is easy to retire. "[Germany] Schaefer got his knack of meeting the ball out in front. Pitchers who had found him their 'meat' suddenly discovered him to be their poison at bat"

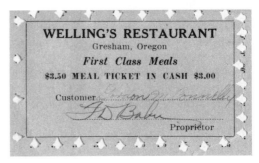

Meal ticket. *Author's collection*

(Hugh Jennings, *Rounding Third*, 1925; Peter Morris). **5.** An ineffective pitcher (Lawrence Frank, *Playing Hardball: The Dynamics of Baseball Folk Speech*, 1983, p.103). **6.** Short for *meatball*. "A pitch that a batter thought was easy to hit is also described as meat, as in 'It was meat'" (Lawrence Frank, *Playing Hardball: The Dynamics of Baseball Folk Speech*, 1983, p.103). **7.** See *meat of the order.*

meatball An easy-to-hit pitch that comes right down the middle of the plate; a pitch that is properly met with the bat for a hit. The term is a refashioning of "meet the ball," as in the plaintive cry of the Little League coach: "Just meet the ball." Syn. *meat*, 6. IST USE. 1912. "Two doubles and a single off our meatball expert, Joe Benz, coined a pair of runs" (Harold O. Johnson, *Chicago Record-Herald*, Aug. 17; Peter Morris).

meat hand **1.** A fielder's gloveless throwing hand, esp. that of the catcher; the hand with which players are loath to field hard-hit balls, so called because a ball caught in this hand hits flesh rather than leather. Connie Mack (*The Saturday Evening Post*, Apr. 4, 1936; Peter Tamony) recalled, "When I was sixteen . . . we chipped in and bought a glove for two dollars. It was made of buckskin and had no fingers. It was used in turn by one player after another, since it was common property. Up to that time we had played with our 'meat' hands, and the catcher caught the pitcher's offerings on the first bounce." Syn. *meat hook*. IST USE. 1912 (*American Magazine*, June, p.204; Edward J. Nichols). **2.** The hand closest to the knob of the bat when the batter grips the bat.

meat hook Syn. of *meat hand*, 1.

meat of the order The strongest hitters in the middle of the lineup. "If we can get through the eighth, 1–2–3, we're not looking at the meat of the order in the ninth" (Baltimore Orioles manager Mike Hargrove, quoted in *The Baltimore Sun*, July 4, 2003). See also *heart of the order*; *middle of the order.*

mechanics **1.** The technical elements and basic skills required by a pitcher to be effective; specif., the various aspects of a pitcher's stretch, windup, stride toward home plate, arm motion, and delivery that maximize the movement, velocity, location, and control of each pitch. Mechanics are often described by their flaws, which include: throwing with the pitcher's weight too far forward, forcing him to drag his arm across his body; initiating a delivery by dropping the arm position; twisting the upper body during delivery; failing to get the lower body to drive toward the plate; throwing too much over the top; drifting toward first base or third base rather than moving one's weight forward during delivery; turning one's back to the plate and failing to lift up the front leg; failing to keep the arm angle perpendicular to the ground, thereby causing more stress on the elbow; gliding into the delivery and turning the leg too soon; slumping down when throwing a curve, causing the ball to hit the dirt before it crosses the plate; shortening the stride, thereby causing the pitches to elevate and straighten; and rushing the arm motion to get over the top before the front foot hits the ground. "Mechanics . . . is nothing more than muscle memory, doing the same thing the same way enough times it comes naturally" (pitcher Ben McDonald, quoted in *The Baltimore Sun*, June 30, 1994). **2.** The technical elements and basic skills required by a hitter to be effective; specif., the various aspects of a batter's stance and swing that maximize his ability to see the ball and meet it solidly on contact. Examples of mechanics include: reducing extra movements in the swing, keeping the front shoulder in and down, bringing the bat through the strike zone, spreading the feet, and flattening the swing to eliminate a loop. "You have to be disciplined in your mechanics because you can't waste any at-bats" (Terry Crowley, quoted in *The Baltimore Sun*, June 23, 1994). **3.** The technical elements and basic skills required by a fielder to be effective; specif., the positioning of the hands, feet, and body to maximize a fielder's ability to catch, field, and throw the ball, such as extending the arm through the throwing motion rather than "pushing" the ball. Baltimore Orioles catcher Chris Hoiles "adjusted his mechanics to get his arm in position to throw more quickly" (*The Baltimore Sun*, Sept. 30, 1997); a separate account elaborated that Hoiles "is keeping his throwing hand inside his leg instead of below it so he can get to the ball faster, is on the balls of his feet rather than being flat-footed, and has his legs more off-center rather than squared up" (*The Baltimore Sun*, Apr. 12, 1998). **4.** The positioning, field movement, and hand and arm signaling required by an umpire to make a decision on a pitch or play.

EXTENDED USE. The basic techniques required to perform specialized skills in other sports. "Shooting a basketball isn't like hitting a baseball: if you start worrying about the mechanics of the shot and making ad hoc adjustments, you're on a slippery slope" (Bill Bradley, quoted in *The New York Times*, Dec. 18, 1994). "The aim [of a football minicamp]: retool [quarterback Dave] Klingler's poor mechanics, including footwork, arm–head action and release point" (*USA Today*, July 27, 1993).

media guide A highly detailed and richly statistical annual guidebook to a club and its individual players, prepared by the club and released in the spring for the use of the working press during the course of the season. Media guides are also sold to the public. Because they contain so many numbers and statistics, media guides often include minor errors, which are occasionally brought to light. "Media Guide Gaffs Keep Game Light" (*USA Today*, May 13, 1986) was the headline for a story on players who suddenly gain 100 pounds or a foot in height with the publication of the guide.

medium-market club A major-league club that is not among the top 10 in payroll. Compare *large-market club*; *small-market club*. Syn. *mid-market club*.

meeting 1. See *clubhouse meeting*. Meetings can be convened by the manager or the players. "[If] their [the players'] little meeting . . . ignited [them], I'm glad. If it took my meeting for them to have a meeting, I'm glad. I just wonder why it took them so long to have a meeting" (Philadelphia Phillies manager Larry Bowa, quoted in *Sports Illustrated*, Sept. 15, 2003). **2.** A baseball game. "This was the fourth time the A's beat the Rangers in five meetings since the All-Star break" (*The Baltimore Sun*, July 22, 2005).

meet the ball To swing the bat while the ball is still out in front of the plate so that the two objects meet at a point that is likely to result in contact; to take less than a full swing. "[Willie] Keeler says that the secret of successful batting is to 'meet the ball on the nose,' which means to hit it dead center. Force and a full swing don't count in comparison with planting the bat against the ball accurately, according to Keeler, who should know" (*The Washington Post*, May 1, 1905; Peter Morris). "[Charley] Comiskey's instructions to a batter, especially when there is a runner on third, always are: 'Just meet the ball, and it will go far enough. Don't hit like you were trying to knock it out of the lot'" (*St. Louis Post-Dispatch*, Sept. 6, 1888; Peter Morris). 1ST USE. 1887. "The natural swing of his [the batter's] arms bringing the bat forward to meet the ball" (*St. Louis Globe-Democrat*, Jan. 30). EXTENDED USE. "Life's magic elixir, the key to happiness and wisdom, meet new girls, live forever, be rich and famous by 'just meeting the ball'" (unsourced clipping, Apr. 10, 1985).

Meikyukai The Golden Players Club, a special honor for Japanese players who have reached 2,000 hits, 200 wins, or 250 saves, in Japanese or other leagues. The honor is automatic, not elective. Members receive a dark-blue jacket with Pegasus logos.

melee Syn. of *rhubarb*.

melon ball [softball term] An early name for softball.

Mel Ott Award An annual award presented to the National League home run champion. Named after the New York Giants outfielder who won six National League home run titles.

Mendoza Line The figurative boundary in the batting averages between those batters hitting above and below .200. It is named for shortstop Mario Mendoza, whose career (1974–1982) batting average for the Pittsburgh Pirates, Seattle Mariners, and Texas Rangers was .215. "When a struggling hitter pulls his average above .200, he has crossed the Mendoza Line" (*Sports Illustrated*, Sept. 13, 1982, p.52). "[Reggie Jackson] slipped below the Mendoza line (.200) in 1983, hitting .194" (Steve Daley, *Chicago Tribune*,

Mendoza Line. Mario Mendoza, eponymous hitter. *Texas Rangers publicity photo*

Apr. 26, 1984). See Al Pepper, *Mendoza's Heroes: Fifty Batters Below .200* (2002). IST USE. 1982. "Dave Revering has a lot of nerve demanding to play full-time. He can't even reach the famed Mendoza Line (.200)" (Al Strachan, *The Globe and Mail* [Toronto], July 28). USAGE NOTE. On rare occasion the term has been used to signify an average of .215, in reference to Mendoza's career average, but the overwhelming majority of citations (*Sports Illustrated*, *Baseball Digest*, *The New York Times*, etc.) allude to the .200 average. The term has also been used for low levels of other statistical categories in baseball. ETYMOLOGY. Popularization of the term has been credited to Kansas City Royals third baseman George Brett, who said, "The first thing I look for in the Sunday papers is who is below the Mendoza line" (Glen Waggoner and Robert Sklars, *Rotisserie League Baseball*, 1987). According to *Sports Illustrated* (July 2–9, 2007, p.116), the term was first coined by Mendoza's Seattle teammates—either Tom Paciorek or Bruce Bochte—in 1979, and Brett later picked up on it. Mendoza himself recalled, "At the beginning of the 1980 season Brett was struggling and made a comment about being around the Mendoza Line." Bill Deane (personal communication, Sept. 21, 2006) suggests that

Brett (or Paciorek or Bochte) were not thinking of .200 specifically when they coined the term, but whatever Mendoza's batting average happened to be at any given time. There have been several false claims that the Line was named for Minnie Mendoza, a .188 hitter for the Minnesota Twins in 1970. EXTENDED USE. A below-normal number; a minimum acceptable standard; a break-even level. The term has been used in discussing standards for automobile oil pressure, measuring IQs of death-row inmates, examining minimal grade-point averages, and referring to average minor-league hockey attendance below 2,000. A politician whose public approval rating is 20 percent is said to be hovering around the Mendoza Line. "With 32 bowl games this season, only nine bowl-eligible teams (all 6–6) didn't receive bids [as they] . . . all landed at college football's Mendoza line" (Jay Heater, *The Baltimore Sun*, Dec. 19, 2006). Alexander Wolff (*Sports Illustrated*, July 2–9, 2007, p.116) noted the "Kordoza Line" in the National Football League, named after Kordell Stewart's career passer rating of approximately 70, "another minimally acceptable mark."

men in blue The umpires. The term was used as the title of a 1980 book by Larry R. Gerlach. See also *boys in blue*.

mental error A mistake made when a player is preoccupied, forgetful, or distracted. A classic mental error occurs when, with a runner on first, an infielder throws to first base for a putout when he should have thrown to second base for the force and a possible double play. Syn. *error of omission*.

mercurochrome ball A baseball with "increased speed and carrying power" (Maurice H. Weseen, *A Dictionary of American Slang*, 1934).

mercy rule Syn. of *slaughter rule*. IST USE. 1971. "The [Midget League] victory over South Zanesville Monday was halted at the end of six innings on the mercy rule" (*Coshocton* [Ohio] *Tribune*, Aug. 11; Peter Morris).

Merkle 1. *n.* Syn. of *boner*, 1. "His most horrendous boner, a real Merkle, was perpetrated in Boston one night" (Earl Wilson, *Let 'Em Eat Cheesecake*, 1949; David Shulman). The term refers to New York Giants first baseman Fred Merkle. See *Merkle's boner.* Sometimes spelled "merkle." **2.** *v.* To commit a misplay on the scale of Merkle's boner. His mishap "has added a new verb to the dictionary, for in these days when a man performs some bonehead action, it is not termed that way. The recounters of the incident simply state that 'Smith merkled,' which is description enough" (*The Washington Post*, July 26, 1914). Sometimes spelled "merkle." EXTENDED USE. To make a mistake. "The verb 'to merkle' entered the American lexicon for many years, meaning 'to not arrive'" (Noel Hynd, *The Giants of the Polo Grounds*, 1988, pp.150-51).

Merkle's boner The baserunning mishap by first baseman Fred Merkle that cost the New York Giants the National League pennant in 1908. The incident occurred Sept. 23 at the Polo Grounds under the most dramatic of circumstances. It was the last half of the ninth inning in a 1–1 game between the Giants and Chicago Cubs. As the two teams were tied for first place, the winner of the game would take the lead in the National League. New York had two outs, with Moose McCormick on third and Merkle on first. Al Bridwell singled to center field, and McCormick crossed the plate with what appeared to be the winning run. The play, however, would not be complete until Merkle touched second base ahead of the ball. If Merkle did not touch second, he could still be retired by a force at the base—since, when there are two outs, no runs can score until a possible force play has been completed. Although there were claims to the contrary on the part of Merkle and others (including 8,000 fans who signed a petition that said they had seen him touch the bag), Merkle apparently veered right toward the clubhouse in center field before touching second. He presumed the game was over when McCormick crossed the plate, causing him to stop short of the bag. At this point, Cubs second baseman Johnny Evers signaled for the center fielder to throw him the ball so he could tag second. Jubilant with their apparent victory, fans and Giants players rushed onto the field, creating mass confusion. Before Evers could retrieve the ball and record the out at second base, a spectator grabbed the ball and threw it into the stands. The Giants pushed Merkle back to the base, as the ball, recovered by a Chicago fan, was tossed back to Evers. But all this took place after the umpires had left the field. Despite the fact that the New York papers credited the Giants with the win, it was decided by National League President Harry C. Pulliam that the game be recorded as a tie. The drawn game was replayed on October 8, a day after the season ended, and Chicago won both the game and the pennant. See also *boner,* 1.

merry circle The trip around the bases.

merry-go-round The situation when, with two outs, the bases loaded, and a full count on the batter, all the runners take off on the pitch. See also *carousel is spinning.*

message pitch A pitch thrown close to the batter, intended to convey the message: "Don't crowd the plate." See also *purpose pitch,* 1.

metal The figurative hand of a fielder who makes an error; e.g., a ball that "hits metal" has been misplayed by a fielder (*Sports Illustrated*, Sept. 13, 1982). The term is an extended metaphor for bad fielding, implying that one's hands, instead of being soft and pliable, are made of iron or become iron skillets off which balls bounce. See also *iron hand.*

metal bat A hollow, lightweight, strong bat made of aluminum, titanium, or another exotic alloy. Some youth leagues have banned metal bats under the theory that they produce hits with greater velocity and raise the risk of injury because of players' shorter reaction time.

Metness Fevered fondness for the New York Mets, perhaps a blend of "Mets" and "madness." "Wonder of Metness: Day at Shea" (*The New York Times* headline, Apr. 10, 1990).

Metropolitans Nickname for the American Association franchise in New York City from 1883 to 1887. Syn. *Mets,* 2.

Mets 1. Nickname for the National League East Division expansion franchise in New York City since 1962. The new team got off to a shaky start, but won the World Series in 1969. This occasioned sportswriter Jack

Lang's famous line: "They said man would walk on the moon before the Mets won a championship. Man barely won the race." See also *Amazing Mets*; *Amazin's*. ETYMOLOGY. The nickname was chosen by owner Joan Payson because its brevity met public and press acceptance, it was related to the club's corporate name (Metropolitan Baseball Club Inc.) and was descriptive of the New York metropolitan area, and it had a nostalgic link with the 19th-century New York Metropolitans of the American Association. **2.** Short for *Metropolitans*.

Mets theory A theory positing that when the New York Mets win, the stock market falls, and when they lose, the stock market goes up. The Mets theory is one of many tongue-in-cheek barometers, including the length of women's hemlines and the winner of the Super Bowl, that tie success or failure of the stock market to events and trends in popular culture. Explained in full in *Forbes* (Sept. 23, 1985), the theory was severely damaged in 1986 when the Mets and the Dow Jones average were both in top form.

Mexican jumping bean A major-league player who played in the outlaw Mexican League in 1946–1947. ETYMOLOGY. From the seed of certain Mexican plants of the spurge family in which the movements of a moth larva inside the seed cause it to jerk sporadically, or "jump."

Mexican League A Class AAA minor league consisting of teams playing in Mexico and regarded as that country's major league. Founded in 1925, the outlaw league for many years drew top players from the Negro leagues and Cuba. In 1946, multimillionaire liquor distributor Jorge Pasquel and his four brothers began to lure 23 big-league players (including Max Lanier, Mickey Owen, and Sal Maglie) to Mexico City with lavish salaries. The major leagues assessed five-year suspensions to those who crossed the border, but, threatened by two antitrust suits brought by disgruntled players, they eventually settled out of court, rescinded the blacklist, and issued amnesties to all fugitive players in 1949. By 1955, the Mexican League was fading. New owners helped to make the league a part of organized baseball as a Class AA

minor league (1955–1966); in 1967, the league was granted Class AAA status.

Mexican standoff A contest or confrontation with no result, but from which one escapes, such as when a pitcher comes out of a game with no decision; a tie, such as the splitting of a doubleheader. IST USE. 1891. "[Monk] Cline, who got a Mexican stand-off from Dave Rowe, has signed with Louisville" (*Sporting Times*, Sept. 19, 1891; David Shulman). ETYMOLOGY. Ramon F. Adams (*Western Words: A Dictionary of the Range, Cow Camp and Trail*, 1948) defines the term: "Getting away alive from any serious difficulty. The Mexican has never had the reputation, among the cowboys, for being a sticker in a fight. They claim that, if he does not win quickly in a gun battle or if he finds much opposition, he leaves in a hurry."

MGR Abbrev. for *manager*, 1.

Michael Jackson A batted ball that bounces off the wall. *Off the Wall* is the title of the 1979 album by the pop singer (Dick Kaegel, *The Seattle Times*, Sept. 18, 1988).

Michelangelo A superlative pitcher; one who is able to "paint a masterpiece" from the mound. Chicago Cubs pitcher Kerry Wood "hung his 20-strikeout Michelangelo on the Houston Astros" (Rich Reilly, *Sports Illustrated*, June 1, 1998).

Mickey Finn *hist.* A printed schedule of league games for a season. "Named for a former news reporter who became the first expert modern schedule maker" (Edward J. Nichols, *An Historical Dictionary of Baseball Terminology*, PhD dissertation, Jan. 1939, p.46). IST USE. 1906 (*The Sporting Life*, March 10, p.6; Edward J. Nichols).

micro league Computer-played baseball.

middle 1. The center of the plate, as opposed to the corners. **2.** The central part of the playing field; specif., the area between the second baseman and the shortstop. **3.** The collective positions of catcher, pitcher, second base, shortstop, and center field. See also *middle defense*. **4.** That period between the first (top) half and the second (bottom) half of an inning.

middle bag Syn. of *second base*, 1.

middle baseman Syn. of *second baseman*.

"I'll take Eddie Collins, hands-down, as my All-Time, All-Star middle baseman" (Ty Cobb, *My Life in Baseball*, 1961, p.262).

middle cushion Syn. of *second base*, 1.

middle defense A team's catcher, shortstop, second baseman, and center fielder, collectively. Syn. *spine*.

middle field Syn. of *center field*, 2.

middle gardener *hist.* Syn. of *center fielder*.

middle infield Second base and shortstop.

middle infielder The second baseman or the shortstop.

middle innings The fourth, fifth, and sixth innings of a baseball game. EXTENDED USE. Part way through an endeavor or proposal. Michael Tanner of the Cato Institute, commenting on the difficulties facing President George W. Bush's proposal to privatize Social Security accounts (quoted in *The Baltimore Sun*, Apr. 29, 2005): "I think the president is clearly down a couple of runs, but it's still the middle innings."

middle line of knuckles [softball term] A batting-grip alignment in which the second knuckle of each finger of each hand is in a straight line.

middle man 1. Syn. of *middle reliever*. **2.** The second baseman or the shortstop. **3.** One of the defensive players who patrol the middle of the diamond: catcher, second baseman, shortstop, or center fielder.

middle of the bullpen The position occupied by the middle reliever in a team's bullpen. "Aquilino Lopez . . . doesn't have a closer's stuff. He should pitch out of the middle of the bullpen" (*Sports Illustrated*, Apr. 5, 2004).

middle of the order The fourth, fifth, and sixth batters in the batting order. See also *top of the order*, 2; *bottom of the order*; *heart of the order*; *meat of the order*.

middle of the plate deviation theory A "theory" proposed by Jim Palmer for a pitcher (such as Arthur Rhodes) who aims the ball for the middle of the plate knowing that the ball rarely ends up in that area. "The need for pinpoint control diminishes drastically . . . [when] the ball misses the target more than 90 percent of the time" (Jim Henneman, *The Baltimore Sun*, Aug. 3, 1994).

middle of the rotation The position in a starting rotation occupied by the third pitcher. "[Matt Riley] has come back from arm surgery to re-establish himself as a legitimate . . . prospect who clearly has the ability to become a solid middle-of-the-rotation guy" (*Baltimore Sun*, Apr. 11, 2004). Compare *front of the rotation*; *back of the rotation*.

middle pasture *hist.* Syn. of *center field*, 1.

middle relief 1. The replacement of a pitcher in the middle of the game. **2.** A period of relief pitching in the middle of the game, generally the fifth, sixth, or seventh innings. "The soft underbelly of major league pitching—the middle relief" (Buster Olney, *The Last Night of the Yankee Dynasty*, 2004). IST USE. 1952. "Credit for the triumph went to the rookie knuckle-baller [Hoyt Wilhelm] for his five-and-one-third-inning middle relief, during which he allowed six hits and two runs" (Joseph M. Sheehan, *The New York Times*, Oct. 24).

middle reliever A relief pitcher who works in middle relief. A middle reliever usually replaces the starting pitcher and is replaced by the *short reliever*, the setup man, or the closer. Compare *long reliever*. Syn. *middle man*, 1. IST USE. 1961. "[Jim Coates] could be a starter . . . but for the present I think he'll help us more as a middle reliever" (*The New York Times*, Apr. 7).

middle sack Syn. of *second base*, 1.

middle station Syn. of *second base*, 1. "[Spencer] . . . nabbed three runners at the middle station" (*San Francisco Bulletin*, Apr. 2, 1913; Gerald L. Cohen). IST USE. 1910 (*Baseball Magazine*, April, p.25; Edward J. Nichols).

midfielder *hist.* Syn. of *center fielder*.

mid-market club Syn. of *medium-market club*.

midnight creeper Pitcher Satchel Paige's term for a fastball. Syn. "midnight rider."

Midseason Classic Syn. of *All-Star Game*, 1. Sometimes lower-cased as "midseason classic."

Midsummer Classic Syn. of *All-Star Game*, 1. Sometimes lower-cased as "midsummer classic."

midway Syn. of *second base*, 1. IST USE.

1906 (*The Sporting Life*, March 10, p.4; Edward J. Nichols).

midway station Syn. of *second base*, 1. IST USE. 1907 (*New York Evening Journal*, Aug. 20; Edward J. Nichols).

Mike Andrews Rule The stipulation that an injured player cannot be replaced on the roster once the World Series begins. The rule was instituted in the 1973 World Series when Oakland A's owner Charles O. Finley tried to replace infielder Andrews under the guise that he was injured, when in reality Finley was upset at Andrews' poor play.

MiLB Abbrev. for *Minor League Baseball.*

mileage Miles per hour of a pitch. "I don't care the mileage that he throws . . . because if today we didn't have the radar gun . . . and I get behind the plate, I say, 'I think that boy's right on,' and no questions asked" (scout Reggie Otero, quoted in Kevin Kerrane, *Dollar Sign on the Muscle*, 1984, p.98).

mile wide Describing a wild pitch or throw.

military list A list of players who have received definite orders to report for military service. A player on the military list does not count against his club's active list or reserve list.

Millennium Plan A radical plan, advanced by Francis C. Richter (editor in chief of *The Sporting Life*, Philadelphia) and originally published in *The Sporting Life* (Dec. 7, 1887), to rid professional baseball of labor unrest, escalating salaries, and other problems and that would result in 1,000 years of peace and harmony. The main feature of the plan called for the equalization of playing strength among the clubs in any professional league by pooling players and distributing them "impartially." It had many other points, including salary limits and equal salaries for players of equal merit, confederation of all leagues (major and minor), reservation of players by leagues rather than clubs, and a reserve corps of extra players to be used by teams as they were needed during the season. It stirred much interest at the time and was discussed for several years, but it never seriously engaged the players or the club owners.

millionaires club A group of players whose annual salaries reach seven figures. There were 73 players in the club on 1988 Opening Day rosters and disabled lists (*St. Petersburg Times*, Apr. 1, 1988).

million-ticket year A milestone during the course of a season that occurs when a club sells its one-millionth ticket. The ability to sell more than a million tickets was once considered a sign of a healthy franchise. Several clubs (e.g., Toronto Blue Jays and Colorado Rockies) have sold more than four million tickets in a season.

Mills Commission Common name for the Special Base Ball Commission appointed by Albert G. Spalding in 1905 to determine the origins of baseball. Rather than conducting research, the commission relied on recollections of old-timers scattered across the nation. The commission's report (dated Dec. 30, 1907, and released to the public on March 20, 1908) concluded that "base ball" had its origin in the United States and that the "first scheme for playing it . . . was devised by Abner Doubleday at Cooperstown, N.Y. in 1839." Spalding controlled the commission, his true intent being not to determine the origins of baseball, but to prove that baseball was a wholly American

Millionaires club. Pitcher Catfish Hunter in a stunt delivery in an armored car after signing a $3.75 million contract, March 14, 1975. *Andy Moresund Collection*

Millionaires club. Postcard. *Ron Menchine Collection*

creation. The commission's secretary was James E. Sullivan, secretary of the Amateur Athletic Union and president of Spalding's own American Sports Publishing Co. The commission members were Arthur Pue Gorman (U.S. Senator from Maryland, who died before the commission made its report), former players Alfred J. Reach and George Wright, and former National League presidents Morgan G. Bulkeley, Nicholas E. Young, and Abraham G. Mills. Mills has been recognized incorrectly as "chairman" because he was the only member of the body to respond to Sullivan's summation of the evidence and he wrote the final report, which was subsequently signed by other commission members. The commission's report was published in the 1908 edition of *Spalding's Official Base Ball Guide*. Syn. *Spalding Commission*.

mini A baseball card that is smaller than the traditional 3½ by 2½ inches.

minicamp A short training period that is not part of the team's normal spring training.

minimum arc [softball term] The lowest apogee a legally pitched ball in slow pitch softball may reach in its trajectory from the pitcher's release of the ball to the plate. It is measured in feet from the ground: six feet in Amateur Softball Association of America rules and three feet in United States Specialty Sports Association rules, which allow the pitcher to release the ball from as low as he or she wants, meaning that a ball released at ground level need only be three feet from the ground. See also *maximum arc*; *unlimited arc*.

minnion A ballplayer who is uglier than a *mullion* (Scott Ostler, *Los Angeles Times*, May 1986).

minor association *hist.* A minor league. The term may have predated its synonym ("minor league"); e.g., "Minor Base Ball Association." (*De Witt's Base-Ball Guide*, 1884; Edward J. Nichols). In its plural form, the term may have predated its synonym ("minor leagues"); e.g., "To the thoughtful it must seem a serious mistake for so many young players from the minor associations to be linking their business with the older clubs" (O.P. Caylor, *Cincinnati Commercial Gazette*, Oct. 31, 1886; David Ball).

minor company Syn. of *minor leagues.*

minor league *n.* Any professional baseball league other than the two major leagues; specif., any such domestic or foreign league (other than a winter league) that is party to an agreement with the major leagues and that recognizes the authority of the commissioner. IST USE. 1887 (*Reach's Official American Association Base Ball Guide*; David Ball).

minor-league *adj.* Referring to a level of play, behavior, or scale that is below the level of the major leagues; e.g., a "minor-league camp." EXTENDED USE. Second-rate, or anything not at the highest level, such as a "minor-league actor." "Getting millions of people to rely on pensions that are not going to be there is corrupting government on a scale that makes bribing a few congressmen look like minor-league stuff" (Thomas Sowell, *The Baltimore Sun*, Jan. 26, 2006)

minor-league association Any association of minor-league clubs and/or minor leagues that is party to an agreement with the major leagues and that recognizes the authority of the commissioner (Major League Rules, Rule 60[d]).

Minor League Baseball The business name for the *National Association of Professional Baseball Leagues* since 1999. Abbrev. *MiLB*.

minor-league contract A contract between a player on a minor-league club's reserve list and either a major- or minor-league club by which the player agrees to render services in seven separate minor-league playing seasons.

minor-league draft A *draft* in which major-league teams select players from other teams' farm clubs, subject to certain restrictions. A form of this draft has existed since the 1892 National Agreement, when the National League offered cooperating minor league clubs and leagues protection from player raids by major-league clubs in exchange for the right to draft minor-league players at artificially low prices between seasons.

minor-league free agent A minor-league player on Oct. 15 of the last year of his minor-league contract, unless the player's major- or minor-league club has remaining options to renew the contract. A minor-league free agent may negotiate a contract with any major- or minor-league club. See also *six-year minor-league free agent*.

minor-league player Any professional baseball player who is on a minor-league reserve list of a major-league club or on the reserve list of a minor-league club.

minor leaguer A minor-league baseball player. IST USE. 1897. "In New York these base ball terrors became, for the most part, class D minor leaguers" (*The Sporting News*, March 27).

minor leagues The level of professional baseball below that of the major leagues. They are the training ground for the major leagues and are sponsored, controlled, heavily subsidized, and sometimes owned by major-league teams. The minor leagues are classified on the basis of general ability and experience of the players. Since 1963 there have been four levels: AAA (highest level), AA, A, and rookie (lowest level). There were

as many as 59 minor leagues in 1949 (448 teams and nearly 42 million attendance). Syn. *minors*; *minor company*; *slow company*; *Little Show.* IST USE. 1887. "I am sorry that I ever put my name to an [American] Association contract. I would much rather play in one of the minor Leagues. There is but very little difference in the salary, and it is much pleasanter to be in a small city" (George Tebeau, quoted in *Cincinnati Commercial Gazette*, Nov. 13; David Ball).

Minor League Umpires Association An association formed in 2000 to help minor-league umpires receive better pay and compensation.

minors Syn. of *minor leagues*. IST USE. 1898 (*New York Tribune*, June 7; Edward J. Nichols). USAGE NOTE. The term has ruffled some feathers over the years. For example: "The chief complaint of the rebels seems to be that they are designated under the general term of 'minors,' which, in their minds, puts them on a level before the public with the trolley and other bush leagues. It might solve the whole difficulty if everybody concerned would agree to adopt the term 'mediors,' as applied to the American Association and Eastern League." (*The Sporting Life*, Dec. 12, 1908; Peter Morris). EXTENDED USE. A lower level of endeavor. "Comic Kathy Griffin got sent back down to the minors for joking about a 10-year-old actress going into rehab" (Patt Morrison, *The Baltimore Sun*, March 3, 2006).

Miracle Braves The 1914 Boston *Braves*, so called because the team won the National League pennant by 10½ games after falling 15 games behind the New York Giants on July 5 and coming from last place as late as July 19 (winning 61 of its last 77 games). The miracle was complete when the Braves, managed by George Stallings, swept the Philadelphia Athletics in the World Series.

miracle man A manager who achieves success with a reputedly poor team. George Stallings, manager of the 1914 Miracle Braves, who came from last place on July 19 to win the National League pennant and the World Series, was nicknamed "The Miracle Man." IST USE. 1914 (*New York Tribune*, Sept. 30; Edward J. Nichols).

Miracle Mets Nickname of the 1969 New York Mets, who won the National League pennant and the World Series. Previously, the team had never finished higher than ninth place. IST USE. 1969 (*The New York Times*, Oct. 17, p.60; Barry Popik).

Miracle of Coogan's Bluff The 1951 New York Giants pennant drive, which began on Aug. 11 when they were 13½ games behind and which ended with Bobby Thomson's pennant-clinching *Shot Heard 'Round the World*—arguably the most famous home run in the history of the game. The home run won a best-of-three playoff series for the National League pennant after the regular season had ended in a tie between the Giants and the Brooklyn Dodgers. Sometimes referred to as "Miracle at Coogan's Bluff" (the title of Thomas Kiernan's 1975 book). Not to be confused with *Little Miracle of Coogan's Bluff*. IST USE. 1951 (title of Red Smith's article in the *New York Herald Tribune*, Oct. 4).

Miranda Line "The sarcastic baseball term for barely hitting .200, named after good-field-no-hit 1950s shortstop Willie Miranda" (Thomas Boswell, *The Heart of the Order*, 1989, p.14). Miranda's lifetime average was .221. Boswell may have confused Miranda with Mario Mendoza of the Mendoza Line.

miscatch A fly ball dropped by a fielder in early baseball. "A muff of Pike's and a mis-catch of Birdsall helped the Brooklynites to three runs" (*Brooklyn Eagle*, Aug. 9, 1867; Peter Morris).

miscue An error. IST USE. 1902 (*The Sporting Life*, July 5, p.13; Edward J. Nichols). ETYMOLOGY. From the game of billiards, in which a cue stick and cue ball figure prominently.

misjudge For a fielder to end up too far in front, behind, or to the side of a fly ball, owing to miscalculation of the speed and height of the ball.

misplay 1. *v.* To handle the ball badly. 2. *n.* An error. IST USE. 1866 (*New York Herald*, July 7; Edward J. Nichols).

miss 1. *v.* To swing at a pitch and fail to hit it; e.g., "Smith swung and missed the ball." 2. *n.* A failure to hit the ball; e.g., "A swing and a miss." 3. *v.* For a pitcher to throw a called ball; e.g., "Jones missed the plate with a pitch low and outside." 4. *v.* For a runner to advance past a base without touching it; e.g., "Brown missed the bag while rounding second." 5. *n./hist.* An error. IST USE. 1883 (*The Sporting Life*, June 3, p.1; Edward J. Nichols).

Miss America A prima donna in the All-American Girls Professional Baseball League.

missed sign A sign that is incorrectly or not received.

missing Australian syn. of *out*, 1; e.g., "Two missing, get this one and we bat."

mistake A badly thrown pitch, such as a hanging curve. "Pitchers typically are reluctant to throw off-speed pitches inside, because mistakes—left up or over the plate—are easily crushed" (Tom Verducci, *Sports Illustrated*, June 17, 2002). See also *mistake pitch*.

Mistake by the Lake Nickname for the cavernous Cleveland Stadium (formerly known as Municipal Stadium), the home field of the Cleveland Indians (1932–1933 and 1947–1993), on the shore of Lake Erie. Its capacity reached 76,977 in 1968, and the center-field distance from home plate has ranged from 400 feet (1970) to 470 feet (1932). The term has also been applied to the city of Cleveland, Ohio, and to the perennially under-achieving Cleveland Indians of the 1960s through the 1980s.

mistake hitter A hitter who takes advantage of a pitcher's mistake. Many sluggers who strike out a lot are mistake hitters. "I'm not a guess hitter. I'm a mistake hitter. Mostly, I look for the fastball and hope he'll make a mistake and throw one I can hit" (Dale Murphy, quoted in *The New York Times*, May 7, 1986). Other mistake hitters include Steve Balboni, Ryne Sandberg, Mike Piazza, and Jorge Posada. See also *cripple hitter*. Syn. *groove hitter*.

mistake pitch A pitch thrown to a mistake hitter. "He gave me a slider that was up. It was a mistake pitch" (Trot Nixon, quoted in *The Baltimore Sun*, Sept. 2, 2003). See also *mistake*.

Mr. Baseball A title given to one who has devoted his life to baseball. "We will always believe, even though Judge [Kenesaw Mountain] Landis resented it . . . that the title belonged properly and without question to [*The Sporting News* publisher] J.G. Taylor Spink" (Robert L. Burnes, *The Sporting News*, Dec. 22, 1962). It was the long-time nickname for Connie Mack, manager of the Philadelphia Athletics from 1901 to 1950. In recent years the name has been used in a self-deprecating manner by broadcaster Bob Uecker.

Mr. Cub Nickname for Ernie Banks, Chicago Cubs infielder (1953–1971) and "franchise player," who had an infectious enthusiasm for the game of baseball.

Mr. Guess An *umpire*, 1.

Mr. Kodak "A hitter who takes his time getting into the box, allowing photographers time to focus on him" (Joe Goddard, *The Sporting News*, March 6, 1982).

Mr. March A spring-training sensation; a player who is great in March and then fails when the season begins.

Mr. Mustard Syn. of *hot dog*, 1.

Mr. October A nickname for a player who excels in the postseason. It was first applied to Reggie Jackson for his playoff and World Series homer heroics in the 1970s. Jackson hit 18 home runs in 77 postseason games, including three successive home runs in Game 6 (Oct. 18) of the 1977 World Series. In 1997, when John Smoltz' postseason pitching record for the Atlanta Braves reached 10–2, the name was applied to him; after Smoltz defeated the Houston Astros, Paul Newberry (Associated Press, Oct. 4, 1997) opened his story on Smoltz' three-hitter with this line: "Meet the new Mr. October, John Smoltz." In the 2004 postseason, the nickname was applied to Houston Astros outfielder Carlos Beltran, who hit .435 with eight home runs.

mit *hist.* A variant spelling of *mitt*. "A backstop, rigged out in a big mit, mask and chest protector" (*San Francisco Bulletin*, May 29, 1913; Gerald L. Cohen). IST USE. 1895. "The catcher and first baseman are permitted to wear a glove or mit (any size, shape or weight)" (National League rules change, quoted in *Rocky Mountain News* [Denver], Feb. 28).

Mitchell Report A 409-page review of baseball's performance-enhancing drug scandal, prepared by former U.S. Senator from Maine George J. Mitchell, which was released Dec. 13, 2007, after a comprehensive 20-month investigation. Authorized by baseball commissioner Bud Selig in March 2006, the report linked 89 former and current major-league baseball players with widespread and illegal use of anabolic steroids, human growth hormone, and other performance-enhancement drugs. It painted a picture of a rampant and accepted drug culture that was prevalent in clubhouses, outlined the history of steroids in major-league baseball (1990s to early 2000s), and plotted a course for the immediate future, including transparent and independent testing and an improved player education program. The investigation proceeded without subpoena power and relied substantially on hearsay evidence provided by four suppliers of illegal substances. The Major League Baseball Association and union members refused to cooperate in the preparation of the report, which had lasting impact on how the sport was perceived by the public and the media. "Baseball so ignored its responsibility to maintain the integrity of the game that it created a pervasive culture of drug use that has cast suspicion on all accomplishments, sullied the legitimacy of even honest achievement, and broken the sanctity of statistical comparison that has been the game's glue binding one generation to the next" (Raymond Daniel Burke, *The Baltimore Sun*, Dec. 17, 2007).

mitt 1. A padded, fingerless glove; specif., *catcher's mitt* and *first baseman's mitt*. It has long been said that the term stems from the mittenlike shape of both gloves, which have two sections: one for the thumb and one for the other four fingers. There was once a clear distinction between a mitt (worn by the catcher or first baseman) and a *glove*, which had fingers (worn at the other positions). IST USE. 1898. "If the ball was not thrown directly into his 'mitt,' the other fellow got the error, never the logy first baseman" (*Grand Rapids* [Mich.] *Evening Press*, May 7; Peter Morris). **2.** Any fielder's *glove*. USAGE NOTE. There may be an element of localism involved in calling baseball gloves "mitts." In the author's boyhood neighborhood in Yonkers, N.Y., everything was a mitt, while gloves were for boxing and sledding. However, some simply use "mitt" interchangeably with "glove," as this headline and subheadline from the *Miami Herald* (Apr. 5, 1986) would attest: "Mizuno Mitts Make Their Mark: Japanese gloves become popular with major leaguers." **3.** The hand. "[Umpire] Bush is also very dexterous with his mitts and can swing a haymaker with either hand" (*San Francisco Bulletin*, Feb. 7, 1913; Gerald L. Cohen).

mixed ball A fastball that breaks in (*The New York Times*, June 2, 1929).

mixed doubleheader A doubleheader in which the home team plays the first game against one team and the second game against another team.

mixer A "half-speed" pitch (*The New York Times*, June 2, 1929).

mix up To throw an assortment of pitches at various speeds to various locations in and around the strike zone to confuse and deceive the batter and disrupt his rhythm. Noting that nine of 10 Yankees hits against him came off fastballs, Baltimore Orioles pitcher Ben McDonald said, "Maybe I should've mixed it up a little bit more" (*The Baltimore Sun*, May 22, 1995. "What is known as 'change of pace,' or as the players themselves call it, 'mixing them up'" (*Ottumwa* [Iowa] *Courier*, March 16, 1903; Peter Morris). IST USE. 1895 (*New York Press*, July 11; Edward J. Nichols).

mix-up pitcher A pitcher who is about equally proficient with his fastball and curveball and relies on neither. George Herman Ruth (*Babe Ruth's Own Book of Baseball*, 1928, pp.83–84) noted, "There are what the boys call 'mix-up pitchers.' These are fellows who mix up a curve with a fast one. 'Change of pace' pitchers I guess you might call them."

ML Abbrev. for *major leagues*.

MLB Abbrev. for *Major League Baseball*.

MLBP Abbrev. for *Major League Baseball Properties*.

MLBPA Abbrev. for *Major League Baseball Players Association*.

MLBPAA Abbrev. for *Major League Baseball Players Alumni Association*.

MLE Abbrev. for *major-league equivalency*.

MLV Abbrev. for *marginal lineup value*.

MLVr Abbrev. for *marginal lineup value rate per game*.

mnemonic sign A sign consisting of a simple set of words whose first letters stand for each instruction; e.g., "Thomas Baker High School" stands for take, bunt, hit and run, and steal. In this case, flashing the number three would indicate that the player should follow the construction of the third word— "High," for "hit and run."

Mo Short for *momentum*. "Big Mo is here and he has a Yankees uniform on" (Atlanta Braves third baseman Chipper Jones, quoted in *USA Today*, Oct. 26, 1999).

model franchise A club that devises a new method of succeeding, usually in response to changing circumstances, and is imitated by others, changing the way clubs do business. For example, the Cleveland Indians combated free agency in the 1990s by signing their best young players to long-term contracts: "Other teams see the success and want to copy it. The Indians . . . have become the game's model franchise" (*Baseball America*, Apr. 29–May 12, 1996). Peter Morris notes that the term has been applied to a minor-league club's financial success (*Baseball America*, Oct. 15–28, 2001): "West Michigan has been a model franchise. The Whitecaps broke a 45-year-old attendance record for Class A by drawing 475,212 in their inaugural season in 1994. They pushed that number to 507,989 the next season, and 547,401 the season after that."

model game *hist.* A low-scoring game in the 1870s, with few hits or errors. "Not a single 'model game' was played [on Saturday], the fielding being poor in a majority of instances" (*Brooklyn Eagle*, June 28, 1875). The term was closely associated with Henry Chadwick: "The person who invented 'model games' has been sorely put to it of late to keep his theories abreast of the facts as they come up" (*Chicago Tribune*, May 20, 1877; Peter Morris).

modern era Baseball after 1900. The term is used to make a distinction between the 19th century and the 20th century. Robert W. Creamer (in Daniel Okrent and Harris Lewine, eds., *The Ultimate Baseball Book*, 1979, p.31) noted that 1901 was the "dawn of civilization" and the beginning of the "modern era" of baseball, "when the American League came into existence as a full-fledged rival of the older National League." Steve Hirdt (*ESPN The Magazine*, Sept. 23, 2003) wrote, "It's true that baseball's record books include the 'since 1900' designation to separate achievements that have come since the start of the game's 'modern era.' But even that distinction has become watered down, if it ever meant anything at all." USAGE NOTE. The term is controversial, as the year 1900 corresponds to no important change in the way the game was played; some researchers suggest the term is used to deny credit to the pioneers of baseball. The *SABR Baseball List & Record Book* (2007) chose 1893 as the start of the 'modern era' because it was the year that the current pitching distance was established and therefore a reasonable dividing line for compiling lists for a few categories.

modified grip A *grip* in which the bat is held a few inches from the narrow end (handle); it furnishes better bat control and still produces power (Ken Dugan, *How to Organize and Coach Winning Baseball*, 1971; Peter Morris). Compare *choke grip*; *end grip*.

modified pitch [softball term] A form of softball that puts the batter back in the game by prohibiting the fastest and most difficult-to-hit deliveries (the slingshot and the windmill) in fast pitch softball. Syn. "modified."

mogul The owner of a baseball club. "Notable baseball moguls and writers are panning the Federals with caustic pens" (Charles A. Lamar, *Atlanta Constitution*, Feb. 1, 1914). "The game's moguls sniffed a source of expanded revenue in destroying baseball's unique emphasis on a regular season" (Ste-

phen Jay Gould, *Triumph and Tragedy in Mudville*, 2003, p.308). See also *magnate*. IST USE. 1887. "[Detroit] President [Frederick K.] Stearns . . . had been frying a kettle of fish that will open the eyes of [A.G.] Spalding and the other league moguls when the operation is concluded" (*Detroit Free Press*, May 2; Peter Morris).

moist ball A spitball. Also spelled "moistball." IST USE. 1912. "Back in the bristling days of 1904 Jack Chesbro, moist-ball marvel, hurled fourteen straight victories" (Harold O. Johnson, *Chicago Record-Herald*, Aug. 17; Peter Morris).

moist curve *hist.* A spitball. IST USE. 1907 (*Chicago Tribune*, Apr. 1; Peter Morris)

moisture ball *hist.* A spitball. IST USE. 1905. "[George Winter] started off great for us with the 'spit ball,' but you saw what Detroit did to his moisture ball" (Cy Young, quoted in *The Sporting Life*, June 3).

mojo Magic; the art of casting spells. In Seattle's Safeco Field, "Unleash the Mojo" placards were everywhere: "It's the team's rallying cry. 'Mojo' is slang, Mariner-ese for magic" (Jack Wilkinson, *Atlanta Journal-Constitution*, Oct. 16, 2000). "The [Florida] Marlins definitely have some mojo to go with a solid young pitching staff" (Peter Schmuck, *The Baltimore Sun*, Sept. 30, 2003). "[Babe Ruth] has powerful mojo working, even from beyond the grave . . . [and] it can sap the life out of Red Sox fans" (Kevin Cowherd, *The Baltimore Sun*, Oct. 19, 2003).

Molly Putz A name for a player who performs badly on the field. Jim Bouton (*Ball Four*, 1970; Charles D. Poe) wrote that in response to a poor field performance, "a lot of managers say their players look like Molly Putz out there."

momentum A winning streak; the course of events that keeps a team winning. A baseball axiom states that momentum is the next day's starting pitcher: " 'momentum' is good pitching every day" (Dick Howser, quoted in Steve Fiffer, *How to Watch Baseball*, 1987, p.122), and "momentum in baseball is all about the starting pitching performance . . . [because] it doesn't take more than a good start to regain the momentum" (Boston Red Sox general manager Theo Epstein, quoted in *The Baltimore Sun*, Oct. 18, 2004). Some managers and writers claim there is no such thing as momentum. Dusty Baker (quoted in *The Baltimore Sun*, Oct. 13, 2003): "Momentum in baseball really isn't that big a deal . . . because the control is basically in the hands of the pitcher." Terry Pluto (*Cleveland Plain Dealer*, Sept. 20, 1982): "Ain't no such thing as momentum. You think you got it because you won five in a row and then you go out there and Tommy John shuts you out. So what happened to all that great momentum?" Kevin Baker (*Sometimes You See It Coming*, 1993, p.283): "There's no such thing as momentum in baseball. It's just one batter at a time against the pitcher." Syn. *Mo.* USAGE NOTE. The term is irksome to physicists. Dr. Albert G. Hill, a retired professor of physics at the Massachusetts Institute of Technology, told *The New York Times* (Apr. 6, 1982), "There's a lot of very good physics in baseball. But the use of the word 'momentum' is not one of them. We physicists invent a good word of our own and the sportscasters wreak havoc with it. We mean mass times velocity. They mean hot streak. It's tragic and it gets on my nerves."

Monarchs Nickname for an African-American franchise in Kansas City, Mo. It was at various times a charter member of the Negro National League (1920–1931), an independent club (1932–1936), and a charter member of the Negro American League (1937–1959).

money arm Syn. of *salary arm.*

moneybags Any highly paid player, esp. one who makes more than most of his teammates.

moneyball 1. The business of baseball in which skill and fans seem secondary to money, and in which clubs, hoping to secure winning seasons and the resulting broadcasting and merchandising incomes, negotiate expensive contracts with desirable players. Bradford Doolittle (*Kansas City Star*, July 6, 2004; Grant Barrett) wrote, "The word, moneyball, has pried itself into the baseball lexicon. There are moneyball players and moneyball teams. As with any kind of contrived language, the use of the term carries with it the stigma of stereotype." Also spelled *money ball*, 2. USAGE NOTE. The term was first used by Gerald Strine (*The Washington Post*, Apr. 12, 1977; Grant Barrett) in regard to the Baltimore Bullets of the National Basketball Association: "It remains to be seen whether coach Dick Motta, having put together a stronger bench, can get consistently superior efforts from Elvin Hayes and Phil Chenier now that the name of the game is Money Ball." In regard to baseball, New York Yankees owner George Steinbrenner was quoted (*The Globe and Mail* [Toronto], Oct. 9, 1978; Grant Barrett): "I didn't think we'd catch Boston. I knew we'd make a run at them, but the distance was too great. I didn't think we could win it. Ahh, but they're just money ball players." The term was brought into general use by David Guterson's cover story, "Moneyball! On the Relentless Promotion of Pro Sports" (*Harper's Magazine*, Sept. 1994). 2. The philosophy that eschews traditional baseball culture and qualitative judgments in favor of analyzing newer statistical measures and exploiting undervalued market trends to build an economical and successful baseball team; the theory that computer-driven statistical data are more reliable than human intuition and scouting reports in predicting performance and gauging the way baseball games are actually won. Moneyball precepts include the beliefs that talent should be acquired and developed at a discount to its true value; inefficiencies in the marketplace may be exploited even with limited resources available; college statistics are better predictors of success than high school statistics when drafting players; hitting ability contributes more to success than defense and baserunning; on-base percentage is the single most important offensive indicator and correlates closely to the number of runs a team scores; and closers are overpriced and rarely worth the investment of a large contract. The term was used by Michael Lewis in his 2003 book *Moneyball*, which chronicled Oakland A's general manager Billy Beane's attempts to build a successful baseball club with limited available resources by attacking baseball's customs, rituals, and unscientific culture.

money ball 1. A pitch that is hit for a home run. 2. Alternate spelling of *moneyball*, 1.

money hitter A hitter with a high batting average.

money line Baseball betting system in which the gambler bets that either the underdog or the favorite in a given game will win, following odds set by bookmakers. Because baseball games generally have low scores, there is no room to create a "point spread"; the number of runs by which a team wins is immaterial. The money line system, which seeks to enliven the bet without use of a point spread, works as follows: The favorite team is assigned a negative number, the underdog a positive number, both dictated largely by who is pitching. Each scenario is based on a $100 bet. A gambler betting on a +120 underdog would bet $100 to make $220 ($100 bet + $120 profit), whereas a gambler betting on a −130 favorite would bet $130 to make $230 ($130 bet + $100 profit). The money line is also used in hockey, which produces similarly low scores. See also *runs line*; *over or under.*

money pitch 1. A pitcher's most effective pitch. "[Bob Gibson's] money pitch was always the fast one, which sometimes rose and sometimes sank. You never knew which was coming" (Bob Uecker, *Catcher in the Wry*, 1982). See also *out pitch*, 1. 2. A pitch thrown for a strikeout in a key situation in a game.

money player 1. A player who is at his best when the most is at stake, such as one who shines when the team is making a drive for the pennant; a player who delivers in the clutch; one given to winning games; one who "earns" his salary. "[A player's] workmanship, both on the offense and defense, may be spectacular and brilliant, but if he cracks in the critical pinch plays he doesn't qualify for a money ball player" (Dean Snyder, *Iowa City Daily Press*, Sept. 27, 1920; Grant Barrett). IST USE. 1914. "[Josh] Devore was a good money player, a man who could rise to meet the occasion when a critical situation presented itself" (Ty Cobb, *Busting 'Em and Other Big League Stories*; Peter Morris). 2. A player who makes a great deal of money. Joseph McBride (*High and Inside*, 1980, p.64) noted, "The term was frequently used in the 1970s to refer to Reggie Jackson and

his fellow Yankees, a collection of prima donnas known as 'The Best Team Money Could Buy.'" 3. A player whose ability or reputation attracts many fans.

money wing Syn. of *salary arm.*

monkey *hist.* A poor hitter, so called because he "makes a monkey" of himself in a futile attempt to get a hit. IST USE. 1888 (*New York Press*, June 3; Edward J. Nichols).

monkey hat A baseball cap. "[Bill] Terry nudged the bill of his monkey hat briefly in response as he crossed the plate" (Joe Williams, Scripps-Howard syndicated column, July 18, 1934; Peter Morris).

monkey suit A baseball uniform. IST USE. 1914. "After a week's experience on the ground in a monkey suit . . . I have reached the conclusion that these spring trips are anything but joy parties" (Chicago Cubs fan Florance W. Crowley, quoted in *Lima* [Ohio] *Daily News*, March 11; Benjamin Zimmer).

Monster, The 1. Bill Veeck's *exploding scoreboard*. 2. See *Green Monster.*

monster shot A home run of major proportions; a tremendous home run, high into the upper stands or out of the ballpark.

moon shot 1. A *home run*, esp. one hit for a long distance. "[Mark] McGwire *really* uppercuts the ball, resulting in some tremendous moon shots" (physics professor Peter Brancazio, quoted in *The Baltimore Sun*, July 26, 1998). "[Mike] Piazza followed with a moon shot that ended up in the parking lot behind left field" (*The Baltimore Sun*, June 8, 2000). The term came into popular use in the wake of the National Aeronautics and Space Administration's Apollo missions to the moon. See also *Moon shot*, 1. Also spelled *moonshot.* IST USE. 1977. "The Federal Government's space program may be in limbo, but the earthlings who play major league baseball seem to have inaugurated their own moon shots" (*The New York Times*, May 15). 2. A base hit under a full moon. "Schmidt hits full-fledged moon shots. There appear to be heavy lunar influences on the hitting of Mike Schmidt . . . and not just because some of his home runs seem headed for outer space" (*USA Today*, Aug. 21, 1986). After five full-moon games in 1986, Schmidt was hitting 11-for-19 with 4 home runs and 12 runs batted in. **3.** Any high fly ball hit into the outfield that takes a long time to descend (Albert Kilchesty).

Moon shot **1.** A home run hit by Los Angeles Dodgers left-handed-hitting outfielder Wally Moon over the 42-foot-high screen that was a mere 251 feet down the left field line when Moon played with the Dodgers (1959–1961) in the Los Angeles Memorial Coliseum. Fourteen of Moon's 19 home runs in 1959 were hit over the screen. See also *moon shot*, 1. ETYMOLOGY/IST USE. 1959. The term appears to have made its public debut in a broadcast hosted by Vin Scully and Jerry Doggett. In a radio reminisce published on the Web by Randy S. Kraft entitled "First Dodgers," Kraft recalls Doggett saying, "Wally is getting a reputation for hitting balls off the screen so often, more than any other Dodger, and some people are calling them 'Moon Shots.'" Scully later announces, "Wally Moon does it again, a high fly ball that cleared the top of the left-field screen by INCHES. Hmm-Hmm! A real Moon shot for sure." **2.** Wally Moon's special swing: an uppercut slice to propel the ball over the left field screen in the Los Angeles Memorial Coliseum. "[Moon] developed a swing, called the Moonshot, which is a little bit of a golf shot, and which enables him to hit the ball to left field with power instead of pulling it to right field, as most left-handed hitters do" (*Sports Illustrated*, May 1, 1961).

mop up **1.** To enter the game as a relief pitcher when the game is hopelessly lost. The term is a play on the idea of "mopping up" the mess created by the earlier pitcher or pitchers. IST USE. 1937 (*Philadelphia Record*, Aug. 28; Edward J. Nichols). **2.** To clear the bases with a home run or base hit (Tom Meany, *The Artful Dodgers*, 1953, p.189).

mop-up duty Pitching in relief when the game is hopelessly lost. "[Baltimore Orioles manager Ray] Miller has gradually lost confidence in [Norm] Charlton and now uses him in mop-up duty" (*The Baltimore Sun*, May 12, 1998).

mop-up man A relief pitcher who commonly enters a game when the outcome is no longer in doubt, usually when the pitcher's team is

far behind. A team's top relief pitcher is seldom if ever used as a mop-up man.

Moriarty *hist.* A blind or wild swing at a pitch. The term is named for George Moriarty, an infielder (1903–1916) who was widely known for swinging without looking at the ball. IST USE. 1914. "I tried to slip the fast one over on him and he shut his eyes and took a Moriarty at it" (*Collier's*, Aug. 1, 1914; David Shulman).

morning glory A hitter who shines early in the season but then cools off; a spring hitter. The term is commonly applied to a rookie off to a hot start. Jim Nasium (*The Sporting News*, Feb. 10, 1927; Peter Morris) wrote, "The training camp is the natural habitat of the 'morning glory.' There he thrives and glows in the full effulgence of his glory, getting all the press notices and arousing the fans at home to the fullest pitch of enthusiasm over his feats in the daily exhibition games—only to flop when the real stars return to their pristine fury." Joseph McBride (*High and Inside*, 1980, p.65) noted, "The classic morning glory was the mythical rookie who wrote his mother from Florida, 'I'll be home soon, Ma. They've started throwing curves.'" See also *early bloomer.* IST USE. 1911. "[Tom] Lovett of Brooklyn carried off the honors in 1891 and Jack Stivetts captured them while with Boston in 1892. They were morning glories, disappearing soon from the center of the baseball stage" (Alfred H. Spink, *The National Game*, 2nd ed., p.119). ETYMOLOGY. The folk name for a flowering garden vine that opens its flowers only in the morning and then closes in the heat of the day. John Ciardi (*Good Words to You*, 1987) observed that the term began showing up in the 19th century as American sports slang for an athlete who begins brilliantly but grows lackluster when he tires. EXTENDED USE. Anyone whose performance lags over time. Ciardi's example: "The official flower for the fiftieth wedding anniversary should be the morning glory."

morning journal A baseball bat made of inferior wood, often said to have the effectiveness of a rolled-up newspaper. See also *banana stalk.* ETYMOLOGY. Joseph McBride (*High and Inside*, 1980, p.65): "Baseball

Florida Blues ∴ *Swing Time in Spring Time*

Morning glory. Prospect sending a telegram from spring training: "I'll be home soon, Mom. They started throwing curves today." *National Baseball Library and Archives, Cooperstown, N.Y.*

players are notorious hotel lobby-sitters, and one of the few things to do in a hotel lobby is to read the morning newspaper. Since newspapers are printed on a cheap kind of wood pulp, 'morning journal' became baseball slang for a bat with poor wood."

morning pitcher *hist.* A pitcher who throws well during morning practice but poorly during the game. "Charles Dryden calls the Phillies' pitchers 'the morning pitchers' because they pitch great ball in the morning practice and get the socks knocked off them in the afternoon game" (*The Washington Post*, Aug. 13, 1904; Peter Morris).

MORP Abbrev. for *marginal value over replacement player.*

moss A ballplayer's term for hair.

moss agate 1. A superior player. "Hunting for 'moss-agate' pitchers is one of the ills that baseball managerial flesh is heir to, and many a magnate in the various leagues has grown gray-haired in a single night while searching for a phenomenon" (*The World* [New York], Aug. 14, 1887; Gerald L. Cohen). 2. An inferior player. "Ned Crane's curves were pounded in a vigorous manner by the Senators yesterday. This, however, does not indicate that he is a 'moss agate.' More celebrated twirlers have had to suffer a severe drubbing" (*The World* [New York], Apr. 22, 1888; Gerald L. Cohen).

Most Valuable Player 1. The player selected by the Baseball Writers' Association of America to receive the *Most Valuable Player Award*. There is an ongoing debate as to whether the "most valuable player" is the best player on a pennant- or division-winner or whether it's the player who has the most impressive performance, regardless of his team's finish; e.g., "[Alex Rodriguez] was probably the best player in the [American] League, but I have always believed most valuable applied, when possible, to winning and impact in the pennant race" (Peter Gammons, *Baseball America*, Oct. 29–Nov. 11, 2001; Peter Morris). "Most Valuable Player? It's . . . use-your-own-criteria. . . . There's no absolute precedent, no true blueprint to follow. The trend changes yearly. . . . The ideal formula is to look at everything—a player's offensive and defensive stats, his team's record, and, yes, his direct impact on that standing" (Dan Connolly, *The Baltimore Sun*, Oct. 2, 2005). Abbrev. *MVP.* IST USE. 1875. Jim "Deacon" White was presented, by an ardent Boston Red Stockings admirer, with a silver tray, water pitcher, and loving cup inscribed "Won by Jim White as most valuable player to Boston team, 1875" (Bill Deane, in *Total Baseball*, 8th ed., 2004, p.707). 2. An honor voted to an outstanding player at any given time, such as during a specified period (week or month) or in a given venue (e.g., the World Series Most Valuable Player and the All-Star Game Most Valuable Player). EXTENDED USE. A key performer in any field. "Former Dallas Cowboys defensive end Harvey Martin, once a Super Bowl Most Valuable Player, has died of pancreatic cancer" (*The Baltimore Sun*, Dec. 28, 2001).

Most Valuable Player Award An annual award presented since 1931 by the Baseball Writers' Association of America (BBWAA) to the outstanding player in each major league. Selections have been made by one writer from each league city (1931–1937), three writers from each league city (1938–1960), and two writers from each league city (since 1961). Since 1938, each writer votes for 10 players in descending order, with each first-place vote being worth 14 points, each second-place vote 9 points, and each subsequent ranking given one less point down to 10th place, which is worth one point. Since 1944, the official name of the award is the *Kenesaw Mountain Landis Award*, in honor of baseball's first commissioner. A plaque engraved with the names of the winners hangs in the National Baseball Library in Cooperstown, N.Y. *The Sporting News* made its own selections from 1929 to 1937 before agreeing to unify the award by abiding with BBWAA balloting. See Bill Deane, in *Total Baseball*, 8th ed., 2004, p.709.

moth Syn. of *knuckleball*, 1.

motion 1. The pitcher's movement during his delivery to home plate. Bert Dunne (*Folger's Dictionary of Baseball*, 1958) noted that "hitting at a pitcher's 'motion' means batter was bewildered by arm action and swung at 'motion' instead of ball." 2. See *in motion*.

motion picture pitcher *hist.* A pitcher with a smooth delivery. "Sam [Jones] is what we used to call 'a motion picture pitcher.' His delivery is smooth, easy and graceful and he doesn't vary a bit in anything he throws" (George Herman Ruth, *Babe Ruth's Own Book of Baseball*, 1928, p.55).

motor 1. *v.* To run at top speed. 2. *n.* A player who can run fast (John Maffei, *Baseball Digest*, May 1986).

motorman's glove *hist.* A long, narrow fielder's glove. "[Bruno] Haas used . . . a glove players back then [1915] called a 'motor-man's glove'" (Tony Salin, *Baseball's Forgotten Heroes*, 1999; Peter Morris).

motormouth A player who talks all the time. See also *Joe Quote*.

mound 1. *n.* The elevated circle of dirt, 10 inches above the level of home plate and 18 feet in diameter, the center of which is 59 feet from the back of home plate toward second base, where the pitcher is situated and from which the ball is delivered to batters. The front edge of the rubber is set in the ground 18 inches behind the center of the mound and 60 feet, six inches from the back point of home plate. When the first official rules for the elevated pitcher's position were introduced in 1903, they called for the rubber to be no more than 15 inches higher than the baselines and home plate, and the slope toward the baselines and home plate to be "gradual." Since the rule dictated only the maximum height, mounds were allowed to vary in height from park to park. The lack of standard elevations caused problems: pitchers had difficulty adjusting, higher mounds deflected ground balls and tripped up infielders, and varying elevations allowed for "trickery." In 1950, the mound's height was standardized at 15 inches; it was lowered to 10 inches after the 1968 season in response to the pitching dominance of the late 1960s. Mounds evolved as a matter of groundskeeping practice: a slope provided better drainage and water absorption. After overhand pitching was legislated in 1884, pitchers found the mounds to be an advantage because throwing a ball "downhill" is easier than throwing on a level, and the extra momentum provided by the slope allowed the pitcher to generate increased velocity. Nineteenth-century pitcher John Montgomery Ward supposedly took credit in later years for the innovation of the mound. Syn. *pitcher's mound*; *pitching mound*; *hill*; *launching pad*, 2; *parapet*; *peak*; *turtle back*, 2; *turret*; *crest*; *knoll*. IST USE. 1907 (*New York Evening Journal*, May 4; Edward J. Nichols). The first use of the term "mound" in the *Official Baseball Rules* did not appear until the revised rules of 1950. **2.** *adj.* A synonym for "pitching," as in "mound artist," "mound assignment," "mound duty,"

"mound statesman," "mound mainstay," "mound strength," and, as applied to a relief pitcher in the *Orlando Sentinel* (Feb. 26, 1988), "mound savior." USAGE NOTE. The extent to which the word "mound" has become part of the patter of baseballese was driven home in Frank Sullivan's "The Cliché Expert Testifies on Baseball" (*The New Yorker*, Aug. 27, 1949). After explaining "moundsman" and "mound assignment," the expert is asked what the pitcher on the other team is called. He replies: "mound adversary," or "mound opponent," or "mound nominee." The pitchers have a "mound duel"; the winner is the "mound victor," and as a result he is a "mound ace" or an "ace moundsman" of the "mound corps." (Tom Shieber)

mound conference A meeting on the mound during a game between the pitcher and the manager or pitching coach, and often including one or more players, esp. the catcher, to discuss pitching strategy, "settle" the pitcher down, or call for a relief pitcher. A second visit by the manager or coach to the same pitcher in the same inning causes the automatic removal of the pitcher from the game. What actually goes on during these meetings? New York Yankees pitcher Vic Raschi revealed (*San Francisco News*, July 6, 1949; Peter Tamony) that most conferences were either held to slow down a pitcher who was working too fast or to relieve tension: "Once in a World Series game, the immortal first baseman, Lou Gehrig, walked over to the great Red Ruffing and asked him what town he was in."

mound corps Syn. of *pitching staff.*

mound duel Syn. of *pitchers' duel*, 1.

moundman *hist.* Var. of *moundsman.* "[Fitzgerald] has one of his beady eyes fastened on the moundman and the other on the third baseman" (*San Francisco Bulletin*, Apr. 12, 1913; Gerald L. Cohen).

mound presence The ability of a pitcher to project a sense of poise, confidence, or self-assurance. Baltimore Orioles pitching coach Mark Wiley, discussing pitcher Jorge Julio (*The Baltimore Sun*, Aug. 25, 2002): "He's shown a really good temperament and mound presence, and those things are hard to teach, especially at this level."

moundsman A pitcher. Var. *moundman*. IST USE. 1913. "So many promising moundsmen are grabbed up by the scouts of outside clubs while only a few are ever given trials at home" (*San Francisco Bulletin*, Feb. 11; Gerald L. Cohen).

moundsmanship Pitching skill. "Superb moundsmanship from rookies Francisco Liriano, Justin Verlander, Jered Weaver and Jonathan Papelbon" (Comcast, *Channel Guide Magazine*, Oct. 2006, p.16).

moundster *hist.* A pitcher.

mount 1. To ride or jockey an opponent. **2.** To pitch. "It will be four or five weeks before he [Dutch Ruether] gets a chance to mount the hill again" (*San Francisco Bulletin*, May 12, 1913; Gerald L. Cohen).

move 1. *n.* The action, speed, and deception of a pitcher when throwing to first base from a set position. "He [Whitey Ford] never showed him [Maury Wills] the move, never once threw to first base, and thus prevented him from measuring how big a lead to take" (Steve Fiffer, *How to Watch Baseball*, 1987, p.166). IST USE. 1935. "Practically every pitcher's 'move' is a technical violation of the balk rule but how often do you see an umpire call a balk?" (New York Yankees manager Joe McCarthy, quoted in *Brooklyn Daily Eagle*, March 19; Peter Morris). **2.** *v.* See *move the runner*. **3.** *v.* To advance to the next base. "Bruce Benedict lined out to shortstop . . . with runners on first and second moving on the pitch" (*Tampa Tribune*, June 29, 1989). **4.** *v.* To change a defensive player from one position to another; e.g., "The manager moved Jones from shortstop to center field." **5.** *v.* To trade a player or to send a player to the minor leagues. "Orioles officials said [Rafael] Palmeiro would not be moved against his wishes this season" (*The Baltimore Sun*, July 31, 2004). **6.** *n.* Making a trade or sending a player to the minor leagues. "[Cleveland] Indians made more moves than anyone in off-season" (*St. Petersburg Times*, March 24, 1990). **7.** *v.* See *move the ball around*. **8.** *v.* See *move off the plate*.

move-around fielder A fielder with a wide range who covers more than the average amount of territory (H.G. Salsinger, *Baseball Digest*, Aug. 1945).

move around the box For a batter to employ several different stances during one plate appearance.

move in the fences To reconfigure a ballpark to make it easier for batters to hit home runs.

move list A list of players who are available for trading or sale.

movement The characteristic of a pitched ball that deviates vertically or horizontally as it approaches and crosses the plate; a measure of deception. "[Walter] Johnson had a tremendous fastball and tremendous movement on it" (Thornton Lee, quoted in Edwin Howsam, *Baseball Graffiti*, 1995, p.85). "Unless a fastball has movement—that is, it rises or falls or tails in or out as it approaches the plate—the best batters will eventually be able to hit it" (Steve Fiffer, *How to Watch Baseball*, 1987, p.22). USAGE NOTE. *Sports Illustrated* (Aug. 2, 1993, p.11) determined that this term was a "new and worse" replacement for the "old and terse" term "stuff"; but two years later (May 1, 1995, p.117) the magazine used the term when it quoted Tony Gwynn on Greg Maddux: "The difference in him the last three years is that everything he throws has great movement."

move off the plate To pitch inside in an attempt to prevent the batter from digging in or leaning over the plate. Tom Seaver (quoted in *The Baltimore Sun*, Aug. 8, 2002): "Years ago, pitchers had the leeway to move hitters off the plate. Some guys . . . took the bruises and were not intimidated, but hitters weren't as comfortable at the plate as they are now."

move the ball around 1. To throw a series of pitches to various parts of the strike zone. "I just really wanted to move the ball around, not show two pitches in a row exactly the same" (Andy Pettitte, quoted in *The New York Times*, Oct. 18, 2001). **2.** For a batter or team to hit the ball successfully to various parts of the field. Baltimore Orioles manager Sam Perlozzo (quoted in *The Baltimore Sun*, Aug. 25, 2006): "They [Minnesota Twins] go with the pitch. They move the ball around the field. They're pesky and they take what you give them and make it tough."

move the runner To cause a baserunner to advance one or more bases by a hit, bunt, sacrifice, walk, hit by pitch, error, fielder's choice, groundout, or flyout. "Alan Trammell . . . moved a runner to third with a grounder to the right side, a classic give-yourself-up play in the late innings of a close game" (Tom Verducci, *Sports Illustrated*, May 13, 1996).

move-up *n.* Syn. of *work-up.*

move up **1.** To advance a base. IST USE. 1888. "[Charlie] Ganzel bunted the ball safely toward third and Capt. [Ned] Hanlon moved up a base" (*Detroit Free Press*, June 16; Peter Morris). **2.** To hit a ball that advances a baserunner. "Dave Parker moved [Carney] Lansford up with a grounder to first" (*Tampa Tribune*, Oct. 5, 1989).

moving lead Syn. of *walking lead.*

mow down For a pitcher to retire many batters or a series of batters. IST USE. 1889 "Even now the contending batteries are getting in shape to puzzle and mow down the would-be sluggers" (*Decatur* [Ill.] *Republican*, May 24; Peter Morris).

moxie **1.** Nerve and skill used in playing baseball; "a player's guts or know-how shown in a game" (Frank Graham and Dick Hyman, *Baseball Wit and Wisdom*, 1962). The term is usually couched in phrases such as "lots of moxie" or "the old moxie." **2.** General pluck and mettle on or off the field. "Love him or hate him—as club owners did . . . in refusing to renew [commissioner] Bowie Kuhn's contract—but no one can help admiring the moxie of the guy" (*Gloucester County* [N.J.] *Times*, Nov. 3, 1982). **3.** The power that makes a good and hard fastball. A catcher would say to a pitcher: "Put some Moxie on it!" (Edmund A. MacDonald, *Lewiston* [Maine] *Daily Sun*, July 12, 1986). ETYMOLOGY. The term comes from a concentrated liquid that was concocted and named in 1876 by Dr. Augustin Thompson of Lowell, Mass., and marketed as a "nerve tonic" or "nerve food" for a source of "pep" and "vigor" and sold as a patent medicine. Taken by the spoonful immediately before

meals, it was said to aid digestion and guaranteed to make one eat, sleep, and feel better. It was first produced as a carbonated beverage in 1884. Passage of the Pure Food and Drug Act in 1906 put an end to its medicinal claims; it was then sold as a soft drink. It was popular in New England and reputed to be Calvin Coolidge's favorite drink, but its popularity waned when Coca-Cola took over the market. The link between Moxie and one's nerves led to the obvious "nerve and skill" meaning of the word. William Morris and Mary Morris (*Morris Dictionary of Word and Phrase Origins*, 1977) wrote, "One theory is that the original 'Moxie' was so bitter that you had to have plenty of courage to drink the stuff." Frank N. Potter (*The Book of Moxie*, 1987) disputed this claim, insisting that the meaning was simply drawn from the word "nerve" in Moxie Nerve Food: "How do I know that I'm right about the derivation of 'moxie'? Well, before World War I, when I was a kid in Massachusetts, we always said, 'You're full of Moxie' never 'You've got moxie.' It's as simple as that." But Potter did not dispute the power of the early formula. He has written that the early tonic "got up into your nose like horse radish and made you snort."

The question is, how did "moxie" move to baseball? Several possible explanations present themselves. Potter (letter, Dec. 12, 1986) responded, "Moxie's being peddled in ball parks, especially in Boston, could have had something to do with the matter." Q. David Bowers, author of the 760-page *Moxie Ency-*

Moxie. Ad in *Baseball Magazine*, May 1908. *Author's collection* *clopedia* (1985), offered these thoughts (letter, Nov. 25, 1986): "In general, the word 'moxie' in a generic sense apparently began in a big way in the 1920s. The Moxie Co. scrapbooks contain a number of news articles with sports (in particular) references to use of the term at that time. Moxie was used to describe an athlete who had a combination of skill, energy, and enthusiasm—and this is the way it is still used today. The generic word 'moxie' seems to imply a special spirit or quality. Interestingly, the Moxie Co. encouraged the generic use of the name. They issued a number of advertisements and even large metal signs bearing the inscription THE DRINK THAT MADE THE NAME FAMOUS—a reference to Moxie, the beverage, making 'moxie,' the generic word, well known." Significantly, there is an ad for Moxie in the very first issue (May 1908) of *Baseball Magazine*.

As for the roots of the original term as it was applied to the drink, there are several theories. These were mentioned in an article entitled "The Moxie Man" by Ambra Watkins, which appeared in the program for the 5th Annual Moxie Festival held in Lisbon Falls, Maine, on July 8–9, 1988. The article was about Frank "Mr. Moxie" Anicetti, the creator of the festival and a leading collector of Moxiana, and it reported that he had been researching the origin of the term. The possibilities suggested by Anicetti include: 1) it comes from an Indian word meaning "dark water" (the color of the drink is almost black); 2) it was taken from a Moxie Lake north of the Rangeley Mountains in Maine; and 3) it began with a man named Captain Moonsey or a Maine Indian chief named Moxus. A simpler solution may rest in a report on local games played the previous day reported in the *Galveston Daily News* (July 18, 1887), which stated, "The Moxie Nerve Food Baseball club defeated the Athletics yesterday by a score of 5–3." The next score told of a match between the Diamond Stars and the Knights of Labor Club, suggesting that these clubs may have had sponsors.

MP/MW Abbrev. for *marginal payroll/marginal wins*.

M's Short for *Mariners*.

mud See *rubbing mud*.

mud ball A pitched ball that has been doctored by rubbing mud into its seams so that it will behave unnaturally; a pitched ball with an exaggerated break because of a bit of dirt stuck to one side of the ball that has been wetted with saliva. "Whitey [Ford] got away with throwing a mud ball that was positively evil. . . . Ford could make a mud ball drop, sail, break in, break out and sing 'When Irish Eyes Are Smiling'" (Jim Bouton, *Ball Four*, 1970, p.200). Such a ball is not to be confused with the balls legally rubbed up with mud by the umpires before a game. Also spelled "mudball." Syn. *mudder*. IST USE. 1916. "[During the 1915 season] hardly a game passed by in any league without some manager making accusations against the opposing pitcher . . . [e.g.,] there was the 'mud ball'" (Billy Evans, *Atlanta Constitution*, Jan. 16; Peter Morris). EXTENDED USE. A dirty allegation. Texas governor candidate Beauford Jester, after hearing a last-minute charge by Homer Price Rainey that he had Ku Klux Klan backing, said, "He [Rainey] has lost his fast ball, he has lost his curve ball. All he's got left is a mud ball" (*Time* magazine, Sept. 2, 1946; Peter Tamony).

mudder Syn. of *mud ball*.

mud field The playing field after a rain.

mudhen Ballplayer's slang for an ugly woman (Bob Hertzel, *Baseball Digest*, Jan. 1987).

Mudville 1. The mythical town represented by Casey and his teammates in Ernest L. Thayer's 1888 poem, "Casey at the Bat." By extension, "Mudville" has become the name for any town whose team comes up short. When the 1986 World Series ended, *The Boston Globe* (Oct. 28, 1986) ran this headline: "The Mets Take It, 8–5 . . . and Boston is Mudville Once Again." 2. The world of baseball, especially professional baseball referred to in a pejorative sense; e.g., the title of Stephen Jay Gould's 2003 book, *Triumph and Tragedy in Mudville*. "Seeking Joy (and Crowds) in Mudville Inc." was the title of a story in *The New York Times* (Apr. 24, 1995), which said in part: "After an eight-month absence, major league baseball returns this week, hoping all is forgiven. But just in case it isn't, the 28 teams are offering mea culpa, cut-rate tickets, free yearbooks, snappy slogans, car giveaways and European vacations." EXTENDED USE. The professional world of any activity. "There hasn't been much joy in Mudville (CBS News) since the late unpleasantness over the Dan Rather story" (Liz Smith, Tribune Media Services, Feb. 1, 2005).

muff **1.** *v.* To drop a grounder or fly ball; to miss a catch or bungle a play; to make an error. "A fielder is said to 'muff' a ball when he fails to pick it up neatly, or to hold it long enough to make it a fair catch" (Henry Chadwick, *The Game of Base Ball*, 1868, p.42). IST USE. 1867. "[Jack] Hinchman 'muffed' a fly-ball high in the air" (*Detroit Advertiser and Tribune*, June 17; Peter Morris). ETYMOLOGY. J. Louis Kuethe (*American Speech*, Dec. 1937) discussed the baseball glossary that appeared in Mrs. John A. Logan's *The Home Manual: Everybody's Guide in Social, Domestic, and Business Life* (1889, pp.102–3) and noted that a "possible explanation of the verb 'to muff' appears from the spelling of the noun form ['muffin'] of the word" as given in Logan's *Manual*, which refers the reader to "drop it like a hot cake." EXTENDED USE. To make any kind of error. "Too often cops bring in good cases only to have district attorneys muff them in court" (David Black, *Murder at the Met*, 1984; Charles D. Poe). The term also seems to apply in the case of intentional errors or missed shots. In Nicholas Pileggi's *Wise Guy: Life in a Mafia Family* (1985; Charles D. Poe), a fixer tells how schemes are mounted to make a basketball game pay off: "For instance, if the bookmakers or the Vegas odds-makers said the line was Boston by ten, our players had to muff enough shots to make sure they won by less than the bookies' ten points. That way they'd win their games and we'd win the bets." **2.** *n.* Any error. IST USE. 1860. "The fielding on both sides [Union of Morrisania and Excelsior of South Brooklyn] was of the very highest order . . . the muffs being almost entirely confined to the bases" (*The New York Times*, Sept. 8). Syn. *muffin*, 2. **3.** *n.* Short for *muffin*, 1. IST USE. 1860. "If we said of a ball-player noted

Muff. A 1907 postcard. *Ron Menchine Collection*

for catching anything but the *ball* that he was a '*muff*' we would be clearly known to express a rather poor opinion of the player by the significant but rather inelegant expression" (*Brooklyn Eagle*, Aug. 22; Tom Shieber).

muffed ball An error. Henry Chadwick (*The Game of Base Ball*, 1868, p.42) noted that "muffed balls are rated as errors of fielding and count against a batsman when he makes bases on them."

muffer **1.** One who "muffs" the ball. **2.** Syn. of *muffin*. IST USE. 1865. "The game of base ball between the 'Muffers' of Utica and of Syracuse took place on Saturday afternoon" (*Syracuse Journal*, July 3; Larry McCray).

muffery Bad or sloppy defensive play. IST USE. 1883. "The last inning was commenced and the Athletics got another streak of muffery" (*The Sporting Life*, Apr. 15; David Shulman).

muffin *hist.* **1.** An unskilled or ineffective player; baseball's equivalent of golf's "duffer." "This match [Knickerbockers vs. Empire], played between the third nines, facetiously termed 'muffins'" (*New York Clipper*, Oct. 16, 1858; Peter Morris). Here is how "muffins" were defined by Henry Chadwick (*The Game of Base Ball*, 1868, p.42): "This is the title of a class of ball players who are both practically and theoretically unacquainted with the game. Some 'muffins,' however, know something about how the game should be played, but cannot practically exemplify their theory. 'Muffins' rank the lowest in the grade of the nines of a club, the list including first and second nine players, amateurs, and, lastly 'muffins.'" Syn. *muff*, 3; *muffer*, 2. IST USE. 1857. "Ketchum gained a gay old 'muffin,' losing the foul fly" (Everett L. Baker, "Impromptu," *Buffalo Courier*, Sept. 27; Priscilla Astifan). **2.** Syn. of *muff*, 2. "Leggett then went to the bat, and by a 'muffin' on the part of one of the fielders got to his first base in safety" (*New York Herald*, Aug. 24, 1860).

muffin game *hist.* An immensely popular, light-hearted baseball game in the 1870s contested between the weakest members of baseball clubs or community members with no claim to athletic prowess and so named because of the numerous errors and misplays that characterized the fielding. Peter Morris (*Baseball Fever*, 2003, p.180) noted that such games served several functions: they conferred a special distinction on unskilled or inexperienced players; reminded spectators and players of the sheer fun of playing baseball; showed that society no longer frowned on displays of "unalloyed pleasure"; reminded spectators of the skill levels of the best players who routinely made difficult plays; allowed groups based on occupation, hobbies, and marital status to experience ballplaying; and provided reporters "an opportunity to unleash their creative powers." Muffin games attempted to return baseball to its roots since it had quickly become quite competitive and professional.

muffinism Bad ballplaying. IST USE. 1863. "The Keystone and Athletic Ball Clubs of Philadelphia, played a second nine match for the championship of muffinism" (*New York Clipper*, Nov. 7; Peter Morris)

mug a ball To make a fielding misplay. IST USE. 1874 (*Chicago Inter-Ocean*, July 16; Edward J. Nichols).

mulligan A second chance. Making a comeback at age 31 in 1996, pitcher Joe Magrane said (quoted in *The Baltimore Sun*, March 31, 1996), "It's not often a player gets a mulligan in his career." ETYMOLOGY. From "mulligan," the golf custom employed by duffers to allow each player one "do over" of a drive per round of golf.

mullion An ugly or unattractive person, male or female, but more often than not a player. Mike Gonring (*Baseball Digest*, June 1979) termed "mullion" the "most famous" word in baseball, adding that a mullion might also be overweight ("having tonnage") or old ("having mileage"). Scott Ostler (*Los Angeles Times*, May 4, 1986) seemed to concur: "Ballplayers might sit around the dugout or bullpen and select their major league all-mullion team. . . . One player told me that he once had a teammate named Buckethead, who was also a mullion, and thus was referred to as Muckethead." See also *scullion*; *minnion*; *buckethead*. Syn. *mulyan*. USAGE NOTE. The term is also used with affection. The legendary Jimmie Reese (California Angels coach, 1973–1994), who started his started as a batboy in 1917, called Jim Abbott his "pet mullion," used the term routinely when addressing Bo Jackson, and loved to say to rookies, "Hey, Mullion, who ever said you were a ballplayer?" ETYMOLOGY. Bastardization of the Italian word for "eggplant," used in a derogatory manner to refer to African-American players, as their skin color was similar to that of an eggplant's. Jim Brosnan (*The Long Season*, 1960, pp.247–48) noted the affectionate use of the term among African-American players, citing pitcher Brooks Lawrence who defined it as: "Not pretty. Not a queen. You know. Ugly, you might say."

multiple delivery A pitching style with a variety of pitches.

mulyan Var. of *mullion*. Pitcher Rod Beck noted the term is peculiar to baseball (*Chicago Tribune*, Aug. 19, 2004).

munshets An English antecedent to the American game of *one-old-cat*, 1. It features two players, one of whom wields a stick about three feet long and defends a small hole in the ground, and the other of whom throws a smaller stick in the direction of the hole. The batsman strikes at the smaller stick and, if successful, runs to a prescribed mark and back to the hole without being caught or touched with the stick by the thrower. The batsman can also be "out" if the fielder throws his stick as near to the hole as to be within the length or measure of that stick. Once the batter is out, the players exchange positions. (David Block, *Baseball Before We Knew It*, 2005, pp.130–31)

murder To get the better of an opposing team; to get many hits off a pitcher (Maurice H. Weseen, *A Dictionary of American Slang*, 1934).

murderers' row Any cluster of powerful hitters on a team, batting in succession, who are "murder" on opposing pitchers. "That brought up Willie Mays, to be followed by Willie McCovey and Orlando Cepeda—the heart of the order, a new black Murderers' Row" (David Halberstam, *October 1964*, 1994, p.189; Barry Popik). The term has been applied to various New York Yankees teams since 1918; e.g., "Joe [Bush] fanned 10 of the Yankees but the remnants of 'Murderers' Row', [Frank] Baker, [Del] Pratt and [Frank] Gilhooley, swatted the ball" (*The Boston Globe*, Aug. 11, 1918; Peter Morris). The nickname is most often assigned to the middle of the 1927 Yankees batting order, which included Babe Ruth (60 home runs, .356), Lou Gehrig (47 home runs, .373), Bob Meusel (.337), and Tony Lazzeri (18 home runs, .309). IST USE. 1905. "Yale's hitting in the last few years has been a cross between a crime and a joke, but this year the cry is loud for hitters and [Billy] Lush, a member of 'Murderers' Row,' as pitchers call the first six batters on the Cleveland list, is there to teach the team the art" (*The Washington Post*, Apr. 24; Barry Popik). Edward J. Nichols (*An Historical Dictionary of Baseball Terminology*, 1939, p.47) referred to an occurrence of the term (for "a group of powerful hitters on a team") in an 1858 clipping from Chadwick's Scrapbooks, a citation that was repeated by Bill Bryson (*Baseball Digest*, Apr. 1948); but

this occurrence has yet to be confirmed. ETYMOLOGY. According to Charles A. Hemstreet (*Nooks and Crannies of Old New York*, 1899; John Thorn), long before the Civil War, Murderers' Row was an alley in a New York City neighborhood later known as Darktown (now part of the fashionable Soho district). Checking an 1827 listing of street names, Thorn found the location matched a street name, Otter's Alley, which ran from Thompson to Sullivan Streets between Grand and Broome Streets. The term was later applied to the infamous Tombs prison (opened in 1838, now long demolished) in New York City for the row of cells in which condemned murderers and other violent or dangerous criminals were isolated. "The cells on the second floor contain those charged with murder . . . and is [*sic*] therefore called 'Murderers' Row'" (*Dark Side N.Y. Life*, 1873, p.731; Barry Popik). EXTENDED USE. The term has long been applied to other elite or notorious groups. "[Eisenhower] should be told he has taken under his wing a 'murderers' row' of reactionaries" (*San Francisco Chronicle*, Oct. 5, 1952; Peter Tamony). "Coke, Pepsi, Philip Morris and Procter & Gamble. That's a murderers' row in terms of marketing ability" (*The New York Times*, Sept. 22, 1983; Barry Popik).

murder smart stuff To hit a pitcher's trick pitch; to hit "the one he depends upon to fool the batters" (H.G. Salsinger, *Baseball Digest*, Aug. 1945).

Murphy money Spring-training spending money and/or money given to players for meals while on the road. "The clubhouse boy hands Ted [Williams] an envelope containing his Murphy money—that $25 weekly expense allotment each player receives in spring training" (*Chicago Daily Tribune*, Apr. 2, 1956). ETYMOLOGY. The term was discussed in Art Rosenbaum's column (*San Francisco Chronicle*, Apr. 12, 1972) from information gathered by Peter Tamony. In 1946, Boston lawyer Robert Murphy organized a players' union, called the *American Baseball Guild*. He advocated a pension plan for players, minimum salaries, and expense money. When a players' strike failed, the union quickly fell apart; but the owners made several concessions, including $25 per week for expenses on the road and for the period of spring training, an amount subsequently dubbed "Murphy money."

muscle 1. *n.* The strength and playing ability of a baseball team; e.g., "Ruth and Gehrig added muscle to the Yankees lineup." **2.** *v.* To force or use extra exertion; esp., to overpower a bad pitch into a hit. "Monte [Irvin] was so strong that as a batter he could take a ball that would nearly hit him on the fist and muscle it over the infield for a single" (Bobby Thomson, *"The Giants Win the Pennant! The Giants Win the Pennant!,"* 1991, p.98).

muscle man Syn. of *slugger,* 1 (H.G. Salsinger, *Baseball Digest,* Aug. 1945).

muscle heat A fastball pitched with great strength and speed.

muscle up For a batter to use his strength to hit the ball. "He [Paul Lo Duca] doesn't overswing, yet he can still muscle up and take you out of the ballpark" (Shawn Estes, quoted in *Sports Illustrated,* March 4, 2002).

muscular Christianity The religious belief, primarily in the 1850s and 1860s, that baseball could overcome a negative attitude toward recreational sports. Religious leaders invoked the vigorous physical activity of baseball as a source of moral instruction. Priscilla Astifan (*Rochester History,* Spring 2000, p.15) wrote, "Sometimes referred to as 'muscular Christianity,' baseball continued to gain favor for promoting physical strength and endurance and for encouraging good moral character by providing a favorable outlet for the excessive energies of youth. Although it had the ability to encourage selfish pride, dishonesty, greed and corruption, it also promoted team cooperation, respect for rules and authority, success with humility, defeat with grace, and a strong sense of community spirit."

mush bag An old, worn baseball used in batting practice.

mush ball 1. A dead ball. "[Ed Nolan] handles a 'mush' ball much more effectively than he does a hard ball" (*Cincinnati Enquirer,* May 31, 1878; Peter Morris). **2.** [softball term] The 16-inch softball, as distinguished from the smaller, 12-inch version. In some

Mush ball. Pitcher Calvin Ammons at a 16-inch tournament in Racine, Wisc., 1962. *Photograph by Russell Mott*

circles before World War II, the softball came to be known as the "mush ball pill." Also spelled "mushball." Syn. *pillow ball,* 1; *mushmelon,* 1. **3.** [softball term] The game of softball, using the 16-inch mush ball. Also spelled "mushball." Syn. *pillow ball,* 2; *mushmelon,* 2.

mushmelon [softball term] **1.** Syn. of *mush ball,* 2. **2.** Syn. of *mush ball,* 3.

musket *hist.* A baseball bat (Bill McCullough, *Brooklyn Eagle,* Sept. 5, 1937).

mussy ball *hist.* A blunder-filled game; a sloppy contest.

mustard 1. A fastball. **2.** High velocity of a thrown ball; e.g., a good fastball is one with a lot of "mustard."

mustard man Syn. of *hot dog,* 1.

Mush ball. Indoor baseball player Jimmy Baxter, leaning forward. *Library of Congress*

must have hit an air pocket A common excuse for a misjudged fly ball.

must win A game that is essential to staying alive in a season or a series, esp. in postseason play. The term is often applied to lesser games, sometimes even in a key series in July. Game 7 of the World Series is a "must win" for both teams. "This club [Baltimore Orioles] hasn't really been in a must win, in a big game [in five years]" (Orioles manager Davey Johnson, quoted in *The Baltimore Sun*, Sept. 25, 1996).

musty *hist.* A fastball. "Hugging a musty [is] catching a swift ball" (*The Sporting News*, Nov. 27, 1897).

MVP Abbrev. for *Most Valuable Player*, 1. "[Roger] Clemens Is MVP in AL" (*The Washington Post* headline, Nov. 19, 1986). IST USE. 1942. "A year ago we felt that [Ted] Williams had been robbed of the MVP award" (*Berkshire* [Pittsfield, Mass.] *Evening Eagle*, Nov. 5; Benjamin Zimmer). EXTENDED USE. Abbrev. for a key performer in any field. "State's Stock MVP is Under Armour" was the headline referring to a Baltimore sports apparel company that was the best-performing Maryland stock of the year (*The Baltimore Sun*, Dec. 31, 2005).

my pitch A batter's favorite pitch; the one he hits most effectively.

mystifier *hist.* A curveball. IST USE. 1910 (*Baseball Magazine*, April, p.27; Edward J. Nichols).

N

NA **1.** Abbrev. for *National Association of Professional Base Ball Players.* **2.** Abbrev. for *National Association of Professional Baseball Leagues.*

nab To throw or tag a runner out, esp. when he is trying for extra bases. IST USE. 1866. "Hatfield got to second base and was left there by the 'nabbing' of Martin at first base" (*Brooklyn Eagle*, Oct. 18; Peter Morris).

NABA Abbrev. for *National Adult Baseball Association.*

NABBP Abbrev. for *National Association of Base Ball Players.*

NABF Abbrev. for *National Amateur Baseball Federation.*

NACBC Abbrev. for *National Association of Colored Baseball Clubs of the United States and Cuba.*

nail **1.** *v.* To throw a runner out, esp. when he is attempting to steal or try for an extra base on a play. **2.** *v.* To be thrown out at a base. IST USE. 1865. "Pratt was nailed at first base" (*Brooklyn Eagle*, Nov. 28; Peter Morris). **3.** *n.* A good throw; one that "nails" the runner. **4.** *v.* To hit the ball with force. IST USE. 1889. "Every one of the boys [the New York Giants] nailed the pigskin for one or more hits" (*The World* [New York], May 30; Gerald L. Cohen). **5.** *n.* A forceful hit. **6.** *n.* The temporary status of a rookie or other player. Leonard Shecter (*Baseball Digest*, June 1963) explained that "they gave me a nail" is often the complaint of a rookie who has just joined a team: "There aren't enough lockers so he's asked to hang his clothes on a nail. It also means the clubhouse man doesn't expect him to be around long." **7.** *v.* To hit the batter with a pitched ball. "[Kirk] Saarloos nailed [Miguel]

Tejada in the back" (*The Baltimore Sun*, Apr. 7, 2005). **8.** *v.* To be hit by a pitched ball; e.g., "Smith was nailed twice by Jones." **9.** *hist.* To win (*The Sporting Life*, Nov. 29, 1913).

nail-biter A close, tense game in which both spectators and players are tense and on edge. It has been said of a poor relief pitcher that he can turn seemingly safe leads into nail-biters. "[Andy Pettite] doesn't know what a 'nail-biter' is. . . . When others are in a frenzy, he seems to send out calming vibes" (Thomas Boswell, *The Washington Post*, Oct. 18, 1999).

nail down To secure a victory, as when the closer finishes off the game.

nails **1.** A gritty player who is successful. Boston Red Sox relief pitcher Mike Timlin "was nails, limiting righthanders to a .198 batting average" (Daniel G. Habib, *Sports Illustrated*, Apr. 5, 2004). A scrappy player who will do anything to win (bunt, dive, run into walls) is "tough as nails" and often nicknamed "Nails": "Len Dykstra. Nails, the Mets call him. . . . It has been said that no Mets game is official until Dykstra gets his uniform dirty" (John Feinstein, *The Washington Post*, Oct. 12, 1986). **2.** A team that plays and usually wins tough, close games. "The Seattle Mariners have been nails in late innings because of a strong bullpen and rallying ability" (*San Francisco Examiner*, June 3, 1982).

naked **1.** See *play naked.* **2.** See *get naked.*

NAL Abbrev. for *Negro American League.*

"na na na na" The chant by Chicago White Sox fans when opposing pitchers were relieved or when the Sox hit a home run or had clearly won the game. It is derived from the lengthy, repetitive, fade-out chorus of the 1969 song of farewell titled "Na Na Hey Hey Kiss Him Goodbye," written by Gary DeCarlo and sung by the rock group Steam. The tune was picked up by Comiskey Park organist Nancy Faust in 1977. It has since been heard at arenas and stadiums throughout the United States and around the world.

NAPBL Abbrev. for *National Association of Professional Baseball Leagues.*

napping See *caught napping.*

Naps Nickname of the American League franchise in Cleveland, Ohio, from 1903 to 1911. A local newspaper in 1903 asked its readers to rename the team (known as the Broncos); as a result of the contest, they became the Naps in honor of Napoleon Lajoie, their star second baseman. In 1915, the club was renamed the Cleveland *Indians.*

nasty 1. Said of a pitch that combines speed and either break or movement, making it almost unhittable; e.g., a pitch that a batter knows is coming but still cannot hit, such as Mariano Rivera's cut fastball, John Smoltz' slider or split-fingered fastball, or Pedro Martinez' curveball. "So nasty is [Randy] Johnson's slider that . . . Barry Larkin . . . swung at one that whizzed between his legs" (Tom Verducci, *Sports Illustrated*, May 8, 2000). "[Kevin] Brown . . . with the nastiest moving fastball in baseball, stopped the Braves" (*The Baltimore Sun*, Oct. 9, 1998). Peter Morris uncovered a much earlier citation with a somewhat similar meaning (*Chicago Tribune*, Apr. 30, 1905): "The suggestion of Captain [Tommy] Corcoran of the Cincinnati team that the 'nasty' spit ball be referred to the national board of health doubtless will receive the approbation of the White Sox and Cleveland teams." See also *filthy*, 1; *electric.* Syn. *dirty.* ETYMOLOGY. The term may be related to the "Nasty Boys" (Rob Dibble, Randy Myers, and Norm Charlton) who manned the Cincinnati Reds bullpen in the early 1990s. **2.** Said of a pitcher with a nasty pitch or pitches. San Diego Padres pitching coach Dave Stewart (discussing Andy Ashby, quoted in *The Baltimore Sun*, June 5, 1998): "His sinker is so devastating that from time to time I don't know the sinker from the forkball, to be honest. He was nasty today." See also *filthy*, 2.

nation The loyal fans of a given team. The term may be defined geographically (see *Red Sox Nation*) or in general; e.g., when the St. Louis Cardinals won the 2006 World Series, "a celebration within rocking Busch Stadium . . . quickly spread throughout St. Louis, the state of Missouri and other Redbird Nation outposts" (Dan Connolly, *The Baltimore Sun*, Oct. 29, 2006).

National Adult Baseball Association An association of amateur baseball leagues, headquartered in Lakewood, Colo., organized into divisions by age (18 to over 60) and classes by talent or experience (AAA for players with several years of college and/or professional experience, AA for players with high school or some college experience, and A for players whose "love of the game perhaps exceeds their level of experience"). Abbrev. *NABA.*

National Agreement Short for "National Agreement of Professional Base Ball Associations" that came into effect for the 1884 season and succeeded the *Tripartite Agreement.* The name change was necessitated when the Eastern League (a minor league) added itself to the agreement; many provisions were also rewritten, but its purport, mutual recognition and regulation of players' contracts, remained the same. Subsequent versions of the National Agreement were enacted in 1885, 1891, 1892, 1901, 1903, and 1911. The 1885 agreement called for an annual salary cap of $2,000, an annual minimum salary of $1,000, and for clubs to reserve no more than 12 players. The National Agreement has been referred to as "baseball's constitution." It was defined most directly and given historical perspective by Hugh S. Fullerton (*American Magazine*, June 1912): "The contract entered into by the American and National leagues and later subscribed to by the minor leagues, numbering about forty, to insure peace, protect property rights and assign territory as well as to prevent competitive bidding for the services of players."

National Amateur Baseball Federation The oldest continually operated national baseball organization in the United States. Established in Louisville, Ky., in 1914, it promotes non-commercialized baseball, hosting more than 50 regional tournaments and eight national championship tournaments in eight age groups competing in affiliated leagues: rookie (10 and under), freshman (12 and under), sophomore (14 and under), junior (16 and under), high school (17 and under), senior (18 and under), college (22 and under), and major (unlimited age). Abbrev. *NABF.*

national anthem Francis Scott Key's "The Star-Spangled Banner," composed on Sept. 13, 1814, and almost immediately set to the music of "To Anacreon in Heaven," a popular British drinking song. Key's piece became the official national anthem on March 3, 1931. The patriotic song has been played before all major-league games since just before World War II. In fact, renditions had been heard at baseball games as early as May 15, 1862, at Union Grounds in Brooklyn (*Brooklyn Eagle*, May 16, 1862), with newspaper reports (1902, 1903, 1904, 1910, 1911, 1916, 1917, and during Game 1 of the 1918 World Series in Chicago) that described the playing of the song on Opening Day and other special occasions (such as holidays) when a band was present.

National Association 1. See *National Association of Professional Base Ball Players.* 2. See *National Association of Professional Baseball Leagues.* 3. See *National Association of Base Ball Players.* 4. See *International Association.*

National Association Agreement The document, adopted on Sept. 6, 1901, with amendments subsequently approved, that defines the structure of the minor leagues affiliated with the National Association of Professional Baseball Leagues.

National Association game The *New York game*, as adopted by the National Association of Base Ball Players. "The Massachusetts game dominated New England baseball until the early 1860s, when a number of older clubs switched their allegiances and new clubs were formed to play what had become known by then as the 'National Association game'" (Warren Goldstein, *Playing for Keeps*, 1989, p.13). IST USE. 1859. "The Clubs who have formed what they choose to call the 'National Association,' play a bastard game, worthy only of boys of ten years of age. The only genuine game is what is known as the 'Massachusetts Game,' and if the Englishmen [visiting cricket players] desire to be fairly matched, they must not permit themselves to be deluded by any men playing the small potato game recognized by the 'National Association'" (*New York Tribune*, Oct. 18; George A. Thompson).

National Association of Amateur Base Ball Players An association of amateur baseball players that met in March 1871 to withdraw

National anthem. President Woodrow Wilson at Army-Navy baseball game, 1919. *National Photo Company Collection, Library of Congress*

from, and replace, the National Association of Base Ball Players. The rules of the group were essentially those of the previous association with the exception of added strictures against professionalism, although clubs were allowed to charge admission. The new association aimed to "restore" baseball from its "vice-ridden" counterpart (National Association of Professional Base Ball Players). According to Warren Goldstein (*Playing for Keeps*, 1989, p.129): "In the process, they infused their cause with class snobbery and concentrated on the exploits of college baseball clubs ... for without them the amateur organization would have folded even earlier than it did. As it was, the association met only infrequently and died from lack of interest within a few years."

National Association of Ball Players An incorrect reference to *National Association of Base Ball Players*. The term was used by, among others, Jacob Morse (*Sphere and Ash*, 1888, p.8) and Preston D. Orem (*Baseball [1845–1881]*, 1961, p.17).

National Association of Base Ball Players An association of amateur baseball players that convened in May 1857 to establish a permanent code of rules by which all 16 clubs should be governed. At the second convention on March 10 and 24, 1858, the clubs (25 by then) created a constitution and bylaws and declared the convention a "permanent organization" under the name "National Association of Base Ball Players." Most of the clubs were from the state of New York, causing the *New York Clipper* (Apr. 3, 1858; Peter Morris) to call the association "a misnomer ... for the convention seems to be rather sectional and selfish in its proceedings ... there having been no invitations sent to clubs in other States. ... National, indeed!" The Association, nevertheless, became the central administrative body for baseball through 1870. Professional teams were allowed to compete following the 1868 season. The Association introduced a uniform code of rules (such as nine-inning games) and ethics. When the Association was unable to control gambling or enforce its rules, and bowed to pressure to include professionals on team rosters, the amateurs walked out to

form the National Association of Amateur Base Ball Players and left the professionals to form the National Association of Professional Base Ball Players. Abbrev. *NABBP*. See Marshall D. Wright, *The National Association of Base Ball Players, 1857–1870*, 2000. Syn. *National Association*, 3.

National Association of Colored Baseball Clubs of the United States and Cuba A governing body formed in 1906 in Brooklyn to safeguard "the property rights" of those engaged in black baseball "without sacrificing the spirit of competition in the conduct of the game" (i.e., preventing players from jumping to new teams). Abbrev. *NACBC*.

National Association of Professional Baseball Leagues The governing body of the affiliated minor leagues as a unit, founded in 1901, and headquartered in St. Petersburg, Fla. It was formed to thwart attempts by the major leagues to raid minor-league rosters and to be the voice of minor-league baseball with Major League Baseball. The Association operated independently of the major leagues until it subordinated itself by signing the National Agreement in 1903. The Association's business name since 1999 has been *Minor League Baseball*. Abbrev. *NA*, 2; *NAPBL*. Syn. *National Association*, 2.

National Association of Professional Baseball Leagues. One of baseball's oldest traditions was the annual presentation of a season pass to the president. Here's the first one, presented to President Theodore Roosevelt on May 16, 1907.

National Association of Professional Base Ball Players An association of baseball players that oversaw the first professional baseball league, commonly known as the *National Association*, which began play in April 1871. The Association governed professional players, not their clubs. It lasted only until 1875 and was marred by drinking, gambling, rowdiness, lack of leadership, players switching teams, lack of uniformity in scheduling, and insolvency of clubs (there were 25 teams during the Association's five-year history). Any club could join by paying a $10 entry fee. The inability of the weaker clubs to attract investors or spectators contributed to the demise of the Association. Only three teams lasted the entire period: Philadelphia Athletics, Boston Red Stockings, and New York Mutuals. The Special Baseball Records Committee in 1968 declined to designate the Association a "major league" because of its "erratic schedule and procedures." However, there are baseball historians, as well as Retrosheet and several committees of the Society for American Baseball Research, who agree that the Association deserves "major league" recognition. Abbrev. *NA*, 1. See William J. Ryczek, *Blackguards and Red Stockings*, 1992.

National Baseball Congress An organization, founded by Wichita sporting goods dealer and former newspaperman Raymond "Hap" Dumont in 1931, that originally sponsored semipro baseball but now consists of leagues with college and amateur players. Abbrev. *NBC*.

National Baseball Hall of Fame The gallery within the National Baseball Hall of Fame and Museum in Cooperstown, N.Y., reserved for bronze plaques that depict and honor those who have been elected and inducted into the pantheon of the game's most illustrious individuals. The idea for the Hall was proposed by Ford C. Frick in 1935 soon after he became president of the National League. Eligible candidates include players, managers, umpires, pioneers, and executive who have contributed to the game. Players are elected by the Baseball Writers' Association of America (BBWAA) and in some cases by the Veterans Committee, and nonplaying personnel are elected by the Veterans Committee. Players must have played in 10 major-league seasons during a period beginning 20 years before and ending five years prior to election; they are identified by a screening committee. The secret-ballot election is conducted by polling active and honorary members of the BBWAA who have been active baseball writers for at least 10 years. To be elected, a player must be named on at least 75 percent of the ballots cast. A player can remain on the ballot for 15 years if he continues to receive at least 5 percent of the vote each year. Voting is based on "the player's record, playing ability, integrity, sportsmanship, character, and contributions to the team(s) on which the player played." The building housing the Hall was dedicated in 1939, but the first players were elected in 1936: Ty Cobb, Walter Johnson, Christy Mathewson, Babe Ruth, and Honus Wagner. Tom Verducci (*Sports Illustrated*, July 28, 2003): "America may be without royalty, but we do have the [National] Baseball Hall of Fame for the bestowal of rank and nobility. In this country, to be inducted into the Hall (the only one in sports with real gravitas) is as close as one comes to being knighted." For a discussion of the usage and etymology of the term "Hall of Fame," see *Hall of Fame*, 1. See also *Veterans Committee*. Syn. *Baseball Hall of Fame*; *Pantheon*.

National Baseball Hall of Fame and Museum The legal corporate name of the official museum of baseball located in Cooperstown, N.Y., which was conceived in 1935, opened in 1938, and dedicated in 1939. It includes the National Baseball Library and Archives. Syn. *Shrine, the*; *national shrine*; *Cooperstown*, 2.

National Baseball Library and Archives The baseball research library within the National Baseball Hall of Fame and Museum complex in Cooperstown, N.Y. Syn. *baseball's attic*.

National Baseball Players Association A short-lived (1922–1923) players union led by Ray Cannon, the attorney who represented some of the Black Sox players. Its demand that it have a vote in the governmental structure of organized baseball was rejected as "preposterous." Although the Association claimed a membership of 225, the players lost interest, and the union soon collapsed.

National Baseball Trust A controversial plan, proposed by New York Giants owner Andrew Freedman in July 1901, by which the National League would be transformed into a holding company for the league's eight franchises (*New York Sun*, Dec. 11, 1901; Peter Morris). Each owner would receive a specified share of the whole league, thus expanding the unpopular practice of syndicalism, and jeopardizing the concept of competition by assigning players to teams. The plan was doomed to failure when Freedman assigned himself 30 percent of the stock, more than twice as much as any other owner.

National Commission Baseball's governing body from Sept. 1903, when the National League and the American League came to terms with each other, until Nov. 1920, when Kenesaw Mountain Landis was named the first baseball commissioner. The National Commission served as a judicial body to resolve disputes between teams and leagues that had signed the National Agreement. It consisted of three members: the president of the American League (B. Bancroft Johnson), the president of the National League (various individuals), and a chairman (August "Garry" Herrmann, president of the Cincinnati Reds) chosen by the two league presidents. Hugh S. Fullerton (*American Magazine*, June 1912) described the National Commission's vast scope of major- and minor-league domain as "about 42 leagues, composed of about 338 clubs, and over 10,000 players." R.E. Sherwood (*Baseball Magazine*, Sept. 1913) referred to the National Commission as "the 'big noise' in baseball, and court of last resort which satisfactorily 'adjusts' the differences between player and club." Also referred to as *Commission*.

national cross-checker A scout who compares the players recommended by regional scouts and *cross-checkers*.

national game The name given to baseball in the 1850s when it began to emerge as a sport that reflected and expressed the character of the United States and its people. Frederick Ivor-Campbell (*Nineteenth Century Notes*, the newsletter of the SABR Nineteenth Century Committee, Apr. 1992, pp.5–6) cited the minutes of the Aug. 22, 1855, meeting of the Knickerbocker Base Ball Club of New York in which club secretary James Whyte Davis alluded to "maintaining our respectability and pleasure in the national game of Base Ball." Ivor-Campbell suggested that the term was applied to baseball not because the game was the most widespread or most popular American sport, but because it was seen as "characteristically American." In the 1850s and 1860s, baseball as a national game was expressly contrasted with cricket, the "national game" of the English. See also *national pastime*. Sometimes capitalized as "National Game." IST USE. 1855. "[Base ball clubs are encouraged to participate in] a similar interchange of civilities . . . productive of the best results to all interested in this truly National game" (*New-York Daily Tribune*, Aug. 7; Tom Shieber).

USAGE NOTE. George B. Kirsch (*The Creation of American Team Sports*, 1989, p.92) observed that "national game" in America quickly began acquiring an exclusive application to baseball and quoted the *New York Clipper* (Aug. 16, 1856) that baseball "had its origin on this Continent, and is now thoroughly established as an American game, equal, to a certain extent, to the English game of Cricket." Four months later, the *New York Clipper* (Dec. 13, 1856) announced that "the game of Base Ball is generally considered the National game amongst Americans; and right well does it deserve that appellation." By 1859, *Harper's Weekly* (Oct. 15) would claim: "Our people, or 'that pure and reformed part of them' (as one of the old Episcopal collects says) which advocates athletic exercises, excuse the general neglect of cricket in this country by saying that baseball is our national game." Yet, the term did not always mean "nationwide"; *Porter's Spirit of the Times* (Nov. 15, 1856) viewed "the continued prevalence of Base Ball as the National game of the region of the Manhattanese." To be sure, baseball continued for a time to be regarded by many writers as but one among numerous actual or potential American "national" sports and games. A June 1857 editorial in *The New York Times* nominated pilot boat racing, and an opinion

National game. This 1860 Currier and Ives cartoon shows Abraham Lincoln in a baseball setting, getting the better of rivals for the presidency John Bell, Stephen Douglas, and John Breckinridge. Lincoln was known to be a baseball fan. *Library of Congress*

from the *New York Clipper* (July 24, 1858; Robert H. Schaefer) championed "the game of cricket": "We are happy to be able to say that within the last three years Young America has taken this matter [playing cricket] into such serious consideration, that ere long it will be ranked as a NATIONAL GAME—and why should it not?"

A fascinating use of "national game" appeared on the editorial page of *The New York Times* in 1881: "There is really reason to believe that baseball is gradually dying out in this country. It has been openly announced by an athletic authority that what was once called the national game is being steadily superseded by cricket. . . . Our experience with the national game of baseball has been sufficiently thorough to convince us that it was in the beginning a sport unworthy of men and that it is now, in its fully developed state, unworthy of gentlemen" (The full version of this premature obituary for baseball appeared

in Ira L. Smith and H. Allen Smith, *Low and Inside*, 1949, p.136, 140.) An equally misdirected claim appeared in *Century* magazine in 1872: "During these years the quiet and social home game of croquet has been steadily gaining ground, and to-day its devotees, not without justice, claim for it the distinction of the true and only 'National Game' of America." (Frederick Ivor-Campbell)

National Girls Baseball League [softball term] A fast pitch softball (despite its name) league of women players that operated from 1944 to 1955 with teams throughout the Chicago area. It competed with the All-American Girls Professional Baseball League for players and fans, but was less concerned with rules of dress, behavior, and deportment. Some of its games were televised on ABC. Abbrev. *NGBL*.

National League 1. One of the two major leagues, founded on Feb. 2, 1876, under the leadership of Chicago businessman William A. Hulbert, to replace the National Association of Professional Base Ball Players. The charter member teams were Boston, Chicago, Cincinnati, Hartford, Louisville, New York, Philadelphia, and St. Louis. The original league represented four western and four eastern cities and was set up with clear rules and policies, including standard player contracts, a code of conduct, and a prohibition on the sale of intoxicants in parks under the league's jurisdiction. It introduced the concepts of selection of members and minimum city size. Currently, the National League has 16 teams divided into three divisions: East (Atlanta Braves, Florida Marlins, New York Mets, Philadelphia Phillies, Washington Nationals); Central (Chicago Cubs, Cincinnati Reds, Houston Astros, Milwaukee Brewers, Pittsburgh Pirates, St. Louis Cardinals); and West (Arizona Diamondbacks, Colorado Rockies, Los Angeles Dodgers, San Diego Padres, San Francisco Giants). Abbrev. *NL*, 1. Syn. *senior circuit*. 2. See *Negro National League*.

National League Central The Central Division of the National League, consisting of teams grouped around midwestern cities, created in 1994. The division has consisted of five teams from 1994 to 1997 (Chicago Cubs, Cincinnati Reds, Houston Astros, Pittsburgh Pirates, and St. Louis Cardinals) and six teams since 1998 (with the addition of the Milwaukee Brewers).

National League Championship Series The *Championship Series* in which the two National League teams that won divisional titles (and since 1995, the Division Series) play for the National League pennant and the right to play the American League champion in the World Series. Abbrev. *NLCS*.

National League Division Series The *Division Series* in which the three division winners and a wild card in the National League determine the two teams to play in the National League Championship Series. Abbrev. *NLDS*.

National League East The East Division of the National League, consisting of teams grouped around eastern and midwestern cities, created in 1969 when the National League expanded from 10 to 12 teams. The division was made up of six teams from 1969 to 1992 (Chicago Cubs, Montreal Expos, New York Mets, Philadelphia Phillies, Pittsburgh Pirates, and St. Louis Cardinals), seven teams in 1993 (with the addition of the Florida Marlins), and has consisted of five teams since 1994 (Atlanta Braves, Florida Marlins, New York Mets, Philadelphia Phillies, and Washington Nationals [formerly Montreal Expos]).

National League style The real and imagined style of play and officiating in the National League, commonly portrayed as emphasizing the running game (sacrifice bunts, squeeze plays, hit-and-run plays, stealing bases), pinch hitting, and defense. The strike zone is supposedly lower in the National League. Baltimore Orioles manager Mike Hargrove believed the National League game offered a welcome relief (quoted in *The Baltimore Sun*, June 3, 2000): "You essentially have seven hitters in the lineup you've got to get out. . . . You pitch around the eighth hitter to get to the pitcher and then get him out. You bunt more. You use your bench more. Your bullpen comes into play more often." Compare *American League style*.

National League West The West Division of the National League, consisting of teams grouped primarily around western cities, created in 1969 when the National League expanded from 10 to 12 teams. The division has consisted of six teams from 1969 to 1992 (Atlanta Braves, Cincinnati Reds, Houston Astros, Los Angeles Dodgers, San Diego Padres, and San Francisco Giants), seven teams in 1993 (with the addition of the Colorado Rockies), four teams from 1994 to 1997 (Dodgers, Giants, Padres, and Rockies), and five teams since 1998 (with the addition of the Arizona Diamondbacks).

national pastime A term commonly applied to baseball in the United States. First used in 1856, it eventually overshadowed other names such as *national game* and "national sport." In a letter to the editor of the *Sunday Mercury* (New York) for Dec. 5, 1856, "a base ball lover" from Williamsburgh referred to the game of baseball as "the National Pastime." An article from *Porter's Spirit of the*

Times (Nov. 15, 1856) referred to cricket, "base ball," "foot ball," and "racket" as "sports and pastimes" that "we hope may become national throughout the U.S. of America." An article from *The New York Herald* (Jan. 23, 1857) noted, "Base ball has been known in the Northern States as far back as the memory of the oldest inhabitant reacheth, and must be regarded as a national pastime, the same as cricket is by the English." Syn. *America's pastime*. (Frederick Ivor-Campbell)

Nationals 1. Nickname for the National League East Division franchise in Washington, D.C. The franchise originated as the Montreal Expos in 1969 and relocated in 2005. **2.** Official nickname for the American League franchise in Washington, D.C., from 1905 to 1956. "By popular vote in Washington this spring the name 'Nationals' was adopted for the Washingtons in place of 'Senators'" (*The Sporting Life*, May 20, 1905). The name did not capture the public imagination and the newspapers continued to refer to the team as the *Senators*, the official name of the club from 1901 to 1904 and from 1957 to 1960, before it became the Minnesota Twins in 1961. Also known as *Nats* and *Griffmen*, 1. **3.** Frequent nickname for Washington, D.C., clubs in the late 19th century; e.g., those in the National Association (1872 and 1875), the Union Association (1884), and the American Association (1884, before it became the Richmond Virginians in mid-1884).

national shrine Syn. of *National Baseball Hall of Fame and Museum*.

Nats Short for *Nationals*, 2.

natural 1. A player who seems to have been born with, rather than having acquired, the ability to excel effortlessly at the game of baseball. The term has been applied to such players as Roger Bresnahan, Shoeless Joe Jackson, Roy Hobbs (the hero of Bernard Malamud's 1952 novel *The Natural*), and even Jose Canseco ("Canseco's 'The Natural,'" *Boston Herald* headline, Sept. 3, 1986). "[Dizzy Dean] is a 'natural,' pitching by instinct and not by design" (official program, 1934 World Series; Peter Morris). Syn. *natural ballplayer*. **2.** A situation in which signs are not needed. George Herman Ruth (*Babe Ruth's Own Book of Baseball*, 1928, p.102;

Peter Morris) explained, "Sometimes of course signs are not necessary. With a man on first base and a natural right field hitter up, the second baseman naturally plays over and the shortstop covers up. On a left field hitter the play is exactly the opposite. Those are what we call 'naturals.'" **3.** A fastball with natural movement. George Herman Ruth (*Babe Ruth's Own Book of Baseball*, 1928, p.137; Peter Morris) wrote, "[Wilcy Moore's] fast one is always a sinker. It's a 'natural,' as the boys say."

natural ballplayer Syn. of *natural*, 1. "I wasn't a 'natural' ballplayer, like Babe Ruth or Willie Mays" (Hank Greenberg, quoted in Lawrence S. Ritter, *The Glory of Their Times*, 1966). IST USE. 1871. "The fact is, [Deacon] White is what [Jim] Creighton was—a natural ball player" (Henry Chadwick, *New York Clipper*, Jan. 21; Peter Morris).

natural cycle A single, double, triple, and home run, hit in that order, by a player in the same game. On June 24, 2003, Montreal Expos outfielder Brad Wilkerson bunted for a single in the second inning, doubled in the fifth inning, tripled in the sixth inning, and homered in the seventh inning. Syn. *progressive cycle*.

natural hitter 1. A hitter whose innate ability (great hand–eye coordination, eyesight, size, swing) makes him a great hitter. Compare *pure hitter*. **2.** A free-swinging hitter; a slugger. Hugh Jennings (*Rounding Third*, 1925; Peter Morris) described Cap Anson: "[He] was the first of the great sluggers. He was what the old school called a natural hitter. He was slow on his feet and . . . had to get his hits clean, so he stood up and slugged the ball. . . . [He] can not use finesse; [he has] to swing." IST USE. 1893. "Base ball lost its most natural hitter, when big Dave [Orr] retired" (William M. Rankin, *The Sporting News*, Dec. 23; Peter Morris).

natural stuff A pitcher's hopping fastball and sharp curveball as opposed to such trick pitches as the screwball and knuckleball.

Navaho baseball A bat-and-ball game (aqejólyedi, or "run around ball") played by Navaho Indians in the 19th century. It featured a square infield, with the batter standing in the middle of the ground between two pitchers. The ball could be struck in any direction and the batter ran in a clockwise direction; if the baserunner was struck by or touched with the ball, his team was out. See Stewart Culin, *Twenty-fourth Annual Report of the Bureau of American Ethnology*, 1902–1903. (David Block, *Baseball Before We Knew It*, 2005, pp.267, 289)

Navy Yard home run *hist.* A strikeout. "The phrase was coined from the fact that at the Navy Yard the men quit work at three strikes of the bell" (*Philadelphia Inquirer*, Sept. 22, 1904). IST USE. 1903 (*The Washington Post*, Sept. 16; Peter Morris).

NBC Abbrev. for *National Baseball Congress*.

ND Abbrev. for *no-decision*.

NDFA Abbrev. for *non-drafted free agent*. "Another NDFA who has surfaced suddenly, Ricky Bottalico" (Alan Schwarz, *Baseball America*, Dec. 13–26, 1993; Peter Morris).

near beer pitcher A pitcher who commonly works himself into a three-balls-and-two-strikes (3–2) count. ETYMOLOGY. Patrick Ercolano (*Fungoes, Floaters and Fork Balls*, 1987) noted the term was coined by New York Yankees catcher Aaron Robinson in the 1940s: "The term alludes to near beer, a weakened type of brew that contains only 3.2 percent alcohol and is sometimes also called '3.2 beer.'" Robert F. Perkins (personal communication, May 8, 2000) disputes Robinson's interpretation: "Near beer is any of various malt liquors considered nonalcoholic because they contain less than a specified percentage [normally 0.5] of alcohol. When Prohibition was repealed, the first beer with an alcoholic content was a beverage with 3.2 content and it was referred to as '3.2' rather than beer."

near no-hitter The work of a pitcher who has either pitched a one-hitter or taken a no-hitter into the late innings.

neat's-foot oil A pale-yellow fatty oil made esp. by boiling the feet and shin bones of cattle, used chiefly as a dressing for leather, such as baseball fielding gloves.

necessities A word given a special baseball context on Apr. 6, 1987, when it was used to summarize what blacks were accused of lacking and why they were not being given jobs as managers and general managers. It was given this context by Los Angeles Dodgers vice president of player personnel Al Campanis when he was asked by newsman Ted Koppel on ABC-TV's *Nightline* if there was a prejudice against blacks in managerial positions. Campanis' reply: "No, I don't believe it's prejudice. I truly believe that they may not have some of the necessities to be, let's say, a field manager or perhaps a general manager." The word "necessities" became an immediate verbal symbol for prejudice and racism within baseball. Campanis apologized, the Dodgers asked him to resign, and, for a time at least, the issue of blacks in baseball management was brought into focus. "Not only did he embarrass baseball, he focused massive amounts of attention on an old, mostly ignored problem and appears to have shaken the sport to it conservative roots" (Richard Justice, *The Washington Post*, Apr. 12, 1987).

neck ball A ball thrown inside, in the vicinity of the batter's neck. "It's not necessarily meant as a malicious pitch, but . . . any game I've played in and they've hit back-to-back homers and [the next pitch] is a neck ball, it's a warning" (Baltimore Orioles manager Davey Johnson, on a pitch thrown at Cal Ripken Jr., quoted in *The Baltimore Sun*, Aug. 27, 1996). Syn. *necktie ball*.

necktie ball Syn. of *neck ball*. Satchel Paige (quoted in Dan Schlossberg, *The Baseball Catalog*, 1989): "Know how I'd pitch to you [Ernie Banks]? I'd throw the old necktie ball. You can't hit on your back."

Ned A name used by Casey Stengel for a dumb player; e.g., "Ned in the third reader" or "Ned standin' up in class" (to describe a dumb player ruining a play).

need a basket To field a batted or thrown ball poorly; e.g., does the player "need a basket" to stop a ball? IST USE. 1907 (*New York Evening Journal*, Apr. 27; Edward J. Nichols).

needle ball Ballplayers' slang for a "new baseball with its greater carrying quality" (Maurice H. Weseen, *A Dictionary of American Slang*, 1934).

negative scouting Focusing on a player's faults rather than his talent. "But negative scouting can kill you, because you'll write off some boys who are *gonna* be great. . . . Skills can be taught, talents can't" (Kevin Kerrane, *Dollar Sign on the Muscle*, 1984, p.91).

Negro American League A *Negro league* formed in 1937 with teams located in the Midwest and the South, including Kansas City, Chicago, Birmingham, and St. Louis. The league met the Negro National League in a world series from 1942 to 1948. After the demise of the Negro National League in 1948, the Negro American League absorbed some of the surviving franchises and separated into two divisions in an effort to revive black baseball. It lasted in a truncated form into the early 1960s. Abbrev. *NAL.* (John Holway and Lawrence D. Hogan)

Negro leaguer A player or official in the Negro leagues.

Negro leagues A generic term for baseball played by African-Americans and dark-skinned Latin Americans from 1885—when the first professional black team, the Cuban Giants (the players were actually North American), was formed as a product of the racial segregation established by the major and minor leagues in the 1880s—until the mid-1960s, when the progress of the integration of organized baseball resulted in the disappearance of the last of the black teams (Kansas City Monarchs, Birmingham Black Barons, and Detroit Stars). The Indianapolis Clowns remained as an independent barnstorming team through the mid-1980s.

Several leagues of black ballplayers operated across the history of Negro professional baseball, with some historians arguing for major-league designation for a Southern Negro League through scattered years in the 1920s and early 1930s. The first true Negro league, the *Negro National League*, was formed in 1920, with teams from the Midwest filling out its ranks. Its counterpart in the East, the *Eastern Colored League*, operated from 1923 through the 1927 season. The Negro National League went into demise during the Depression years, to be revived in 1933 as a largely eastern circuit, lasting through the 1948 season. The *Negro American League*, composed of midwestern teams, came into operation in 1937, and

Negro leagues. The New York Black Yankees played in Yankee Stadium. *Author's collection*

lasted in a truncated form through the early 1960s. The Negro leagues were loosely organized; seasons varied from 40 to 90 games, supplemented by barnstorming tours. The Negro leagues played annual all-star games beginning in 1933 and conducted several world series (1924–1927 and 1942–1948). During World War II, the Negro leagues grew into a $2 million-a-year business and was probably the single biggest black-dominated enterprise.

The Negro leagues presented an exciting brand of baseball and pioneered night baseball, shin guards, and batting helmets. They also produced some of the greatest players in the country: 35 players and administrators have been enshrined in the National Baseball Hall of Fame through 2006, including the Hall's first woman, Effa Manley (owner of the Newark Eagles). Negro leaguers played games against such white stars as Babe Ruth, Ty Cobb, Christy Mathewson, Lefty Grove, and Bob Feller, and won three games for every two they lost.

The breaking of the major league's color bar in 1947 hastened the demise of the Negro leagues, as the major leagues began to raid the black teams of their best players. "It's like coming into a man's store and stealing the goods right off the shelves," complained black owner Cum Posey of the Homestead Grays. Such major-league stars as Satchel Paige, Monte Irvin, Jackie Robinson, Roy

Campanella, Willie Mays, Larry Doby, Ernie Banks, and Hank Aaron began their professional careers in the Negro leagues. "The Negro leagues were designed to provide opportunity where opportunity was denied and to offer vibrant proof that there was no legitimate basis for the major leagues' unwritten rule. Their death was their ultimate victory" (Phil Dixon, *The Negro Baseball Leagues*, 1992). Abbrev. *NL*, 2. (John Holway and Lawrence D. Hogan)

Negro National League A *Negro league* formed in 1920 under the leadership of Andrew "Rube" Foster (founder/owner/manager of the Chicago American Giants) and C.I. Taylor (owner of the Indianapolis ABCs), consisting of eight (later six) teams in the Midwest, including the Chicago American Giants, Indianapolis ABCs, Kansas City Monarchs, St. Louis Giants (later Stars), Detroit Stars, Dayton Marcos (later Cleveland Buckeyes), and western (Cincinnati) Cuban Stars. The league collapsed in 1930, a victim of the Depression and the death of Foster. A new Negro National League was formed in 1933, largely as an eastern circuit, primarily through the efforts of Gus Greenlee (owner of the newly formed Pittsburgh Crawfords), with teams in Baltimore, Chicago, Cleveland, Columbus (Ohio), Nashville (Tenn.), and Pittsburgh (the Crawfords are considered by some to have been the best team in black baseball history, with such stars as Satchel Paige, Oscar Charleston, Cool Papa Bell, and Josh Gibson). Later teams included the Brooklyn/Newark Eagles, New York Cubans, Philadelphia Stars, and Homestead Grays (which operated out of Pittsburgh and later Washington, D.C., and set a world record of nine straight pennants from 1937 to 1945). The league disbanded in 1948. Abbrev. *NNL*. Syn. *Bankers' League*. (John Holway and Lawrence D. Hogan)

neighborhood call A called strike because the pitch was "merely in the neighborhood of (i.e., near) the plate" (Lawrence Frank, *Playing Hardball: The Dynamics of Baseball Folk Speech*, 1983, p.73).

neighborhood play A force play in which a sliding baserunner is called out because the defensive player, with a clearly caught ball that is on target, is close enough to touch the base. Umpires use their discretion to avoid injuries; however, if the defensive player obviously fails to touch the base, the umpire will not call the runner out. "Ordinarily the neighborhood play comes while the defensive team is making a double play, and most umpires will give a foot or so margin for error when the second baseman or shortstop tags second before making his relay to first" (Bill Hunter, *Burlington* [N.C.] *Times News*, July 3, 1969; Peter Morris). See also *in the neighborhood*; *phantom double play*, 1. Syn. *in-the-vicinity play*; *vicinity play*.

Nellie hitter A hitter who hits to left center and to right center (Bill Skowron, in Bob Vanderberg, *Sox: From Lane and Fain to Zisk and Fisk*, 1982; Charles D. Poe).

neoclassical park Syn. of *retropark*.

neutral win/loss An estimate of a pitcher's won-lost record if that pitcher were given league-average run support.

New American Base-Ball Association The formal name for an attempt to revive the American Association as a major-league rival to the National League for the 1900 season. The organizers included such notables as Al Spink, Cap Anson, Chris Von der Ahe, and John McGraw, with franchises to be located in Chicago, St. Louis, Milwaukee, Louisville, Boston, Baltimore, Philadelphia, and one other eastern city. However, the defection of the Philadelphia backers led McGraw to withdraw his proposed Baltimore franchise as well. This decimated the league's eastern half, and the league never played a game. Several of its organizers played a role in the American League's becoming a major league. (Peter Morris)

new ball game 1. A situation in which a game turns around quickly; e.g., when one team suddenly overtakes the other by scoring a lot of runs. The term underscores the point that no game can be taken for granted. "It must also be remembered that baseball not only gave to the language the phrase 'It's a new ball game,' but implements it every day" (Shirley Povich, *The Washington Post*, Oct. 10, 1986). See also *ball game*, 2; *whole new ball game*. EXTENDED USE. Any new start.

"As the trite saying goes, the Mark V made the use of buckshot a new ball game" (*Outdoor Life*, March 1969; *OED*). **2.** A tie game, thereby creating the situation as though the game was just starting over with a 0–0 score.

New Breed, The The name used by *New York Daily News* sportswriter Dick Young to describe the rabid, anti-authoritarian New York Mets fans during the franchise's early years (1960s). Roger Angell (*The Summer Game*, 1972, p.110) noted that their "perverse loyalty" was in part "engendered by a hatred for the kind of cold-blooded success typified by Mr. [Walter] O'Malley [of the Los Angeles Dodgers] and by the owners of the New York Yankees."

New England game Syn. of *Massachusetts game.* IST USE. 1865. "The chief club practicing the New England game, the Tri-Mountain Club" (*New York Clipper*, Feb. 18; Peter Morris).

new life 1. An opportunity afforded a player to redeem himself by playing for a different team. See also *change of scenery.* **2.** Another chance afforded a batter after the defense fails to retire him, as, for example, after a dropped foul pop fly. See also *life, 1.*

new-look free agency Free agency for players whose efforts to become free agents were thwarted when major-league owners were determined in 1990 to have colluded to depress the free agency market in 1986–1988. Owing to a $280 million collusion agreement/settlement between the owners and the Major League Baseball Players Association, free agents were given time to sign with new teams or remain with their current teams. Syn. *free-look free agency*; *second-look free agency.*

New York game An early variation of baseball played in and around New York City since 1840 and codified in the Knickerbocker Rules of 1845. It began to expand outside the New York metropolitan area in 1857, and most major cities had their first New York game by 1860. The New York game adopted foul lines radiating outward, a diamond configuration, nine innings, three outs per side, a harder ball, and no plugging of baserunners; until 1864, a catch for an out could be made on the first bound. It contrasted with the *Massachusetts game*, which it outstripped and supplanted as the game of choice after the Civil War. "It would be no more honor for the English Eleven to beat the best nine that could be selected, playing the New York game, than it would be to beat at cricket the best Eleven they could pick from any ordinary school in England. . . . The Englishmen may be assured that to whip any nine playing the New York baby game will never be recognized as a national triumph" (*Buffalo Morning Express*, Oct. 20, 1859, quoting an earlier 1859 issue of the *New York Tribune*; Priscilla Astifan). See also *National Association game.* IST USE. 1859 (*The Base Ball Player's Pocket Companion: Containing Rules and Regulations for Forming Clubs, Directions for the "Massachusetts Game," and the "New York Game," from Official Reports*, published by Mayhew and Baker, Boston; John Thorn).

next batter's box Syn. of *on-deck circle* (*Official Baseball Rules*, Rule 1.04).

next stop Peoria Said of a player who is in a slump, committing several errors, or otherwise on the skids. Peoria (Ill.) had a Class B minor-league team in the *Three-I League* during the first half of the 20th century, and was referred to as baseball's equivalent of Podunk.

NGBL Abbrev. for *National Girls Baseball League.*

nibbler 1. A weak ground ball. **2.** A pitcher who consistently hits the corners of the plate; one who paints the black. **3.** A pitcher who does not throw strikes, trying to get the batter to chase a bad pitch, and therefore gets behind in the count.

"nice guys finish last" The famous quote, essentially espousing victory at any price, attributed to Leo Durocher on July 5, 1946, when he was managing the Brooklyn Dodgers. In his autobiography *Nice Guys Finish Last* (1975), Durocher stated that he directed the remark against the New York Giants in front of several newsmen: "Walker Cooper, Mize, Marshall, Kerr, Gordon, Thomson. Take a look at them. All nice guys. They'll finish last. Nice Guys. Finish last." But some baseball researchers claim that Durocher misquoted himself. Ray Robinson (*The Home Run Heard 'Round the World*, 1991, pp.47–48) maintained that Durocher, who was being needled by broadcaster Red Barber for not being a "nice guy," retorted, "Nice guy? Who wants to be a nice guy? Look over there in that Giant dugout. Look at [manager Mel] Ott. He's a nice guy. Why, those Giants are the nicest guys in the world. But where the hell are they? In last place!" USAGE NOTE. Durocher was proud of the fact that the phrase had gotten him into *Bartlett's Familiar Quotations*—between John Betjeman and Dilys Laing—which cited his 1975 autobiography. EXTENDED USE. Impressive, but not truly engaging, people. Clare McHugh, reviewing a collection of short stories (*The Baltimore Sun*, Sept. 18, 2005), headlined her review "Nice guys invariably finish last, in T.C. Boyle's relentless world" and labeled Boyle's characters as those "you admire but don't really enjoy spending time with."

nick 1. To get hits off a pitcher; e.g., "The Cubs nicked Smith three times in the seventh." IST USE. 1912 (*New York Tribune*, Sept. 29; Edward J. Nichols). 2. To pitch a ball so that it just passes over a corner of the plate yet remains in the strike zone; e.g., "Smith's offering to Jones nicked the corner for a called strike."

nickel 1. Syn. of *nickel curve*. IST USE. 1932 (*Baseball Magazine*, October, p.496; Edward J. Nichols). 2. The red, circular spin pattern (about the size of a nickel) seen on a slowly spinning pitch with inferior deflection. Compare *dime*, 2.

nickel ball An inexpensive baseball (costing 5 cents) that often split when hit hard. See also *nickelbrick*. Compare *dime ball*.

nickelbrick An extremely cheap baseball of the type once commonly found in five-and-dime stores. Originally, it sold for a nickel at a time when a regulation ball might cost a dollar or more. L. Pacini (*San Francisco Examiner & Chronicle*, Aug. 20, 1978) wrote, "In my era, however, they went for twenty-five to thirty-five cents, and if you got a rare fifty-center you were kicked out of the neighborhood for showboating." He noted that the ball lacked a certain quality ("it was the only ball ever invented that windows broke") and

when hit hard would not unravel, but actually disintegrate. See also *brick*, 1; *nickel ball*. Syn. *nickel rock*.

nickel curve An early name for the *slider*, 1; disparaging term for a slow curveball. Frank Frisch (*Frank Frisch: The Fordham Flash*, 1962) called the slider a "nickel curve" to support his contention that baseball was not as good as it had been in his day. Leo Durocher (*Nice Guys Finish Last*, 1975) noted that Hugh Casey "had a slider (called a nickel-curve in those days) which he used only to show the batter that he could throw something else." Jim Bouton (*Ball Four*, 1970) said that the nickel curve is what the slider was called by old-time ballplayers "who didn't have to hit against it." Syn. *nickel*, 1; *five-cent curve*. IST USE. 1945. "Keep throwing that nickel curve" (*Council Bluffs* [Iowa] *Nonpareil*, Sept. 9; Merritt Clifton).

nickel nose A player or umpire with a large nose.

nickel rock Syn. of *nickelbrick*.

Nickel Series A nickname for a World Series between New York City teams in the days when it cost five cents to ride the subway.

Nieves rule A rule adopted in 1985 that non-residents of the United States would be eligible for the *first-year player draft* if they were currently attending school in the United States. Previously, amateurs were only eligible for the draft if they were permanent residents of the United States (excluding Puerto Rico and other territories). The rule was changed after Puerto Rican Juan Nieves attended a Connecticut university and received a large bonus after a bidding war that resulted because he was not draft-eligible.

Night A promotional event held during a night game; e.g., Whoopee Cushion Night. See also *Day*, 2.

night ball 1. Baseball played at night. "[Phil] Wrigley still holds to the conviction that baseball is a daylight pastime and declares that from an attendance standpoint, night ball is 'like a drug,' the effect of which soon wears off" (*The Sporting News*, March 19, 1952). Compare *day ball*. Syn. *night baseball*. 2. [softball term] An early name for softball.

night baseball Syn. of *night ball*.

nightcap 1. The second game of a double-header, so called because it is usually played late in the afternoon or early in the evening. IST USE. 1910. "The nightcap exhibition was one of the greatest pitchers' battles of the year" (*The Washington Post*, Aug. 10; Benjamin Zimmer). ETYMOLOGY. Originating in the early 19th century, the term is the name for the last drink of the night before retiring. **2.** *hist.* The ninth inning (Maurice H. Weseen, *A Dictionary of American Slang*, 1934).

night club tan The pale or washed-out appearance of a ballplayer (*Baseball Digest*, 1959).

night game A baseball game played under bright artificial lights in the evening, starting after 5 p.m. (formerly 6 p.m.) The night game was once a novelty of the electric age, but now most major-league games are played "under the lights." All major-league ballparks are equipped for night games. Baseball's transformation to a nighttime sport reached a critical milestone on Oct. 13, 1971, when the Pittsburgh Pirates defeated the Baltimore Orioles, 4–3, in the very first World Series night game ever played. Kansas City and St. Louis engaged in the first all-night World Series in 1985. The last major-league ballpark to become equipped for night baseball was Wrigley Field in Chicago, which hosted its first night game against the Philadelphia Phillies on Aug. 9, 1988. Compare *day game*.

The first night game took place on the Sea Foam House lawn at Oceanside Park on Nantasket Bay in Hull, Mass., on Sept. 2, 1880, less than a year after Thomas Alva Edison invented the light bulb. The game was a demonstration put on by the Northern Electric Light Co. Amateur players from two Boston department stores—Jordan Marsh & Co. and R.H. White & Co.—took the ferry boat from the mainland and played a nine-inning game ending in a 16–16 tie before 300 fans. The lighting provided by 36 carbon arc lamps, generating 30,000 candlepower, was poor (the players complained that the light was "too much like moonlight") and many errors were made; reporters believed the idea to be impractical.

The first major-league night game was played at Crosley Field in Cincinnati on May 24, 1935, when the Reds defeated the Philadelphia Phillies, 2–1. President Franklin D. Roosevelt, seated in the White House, pushed a button that turned on a light on a table on the field manned by Reds general manager Larry MacPhail, who then flipped a switch to flood the field with 1,090,000 watts of electric power from 632 lamps.

Nile Valley league *hist.* A mythical realm where the most spectacular or legendary feats in the game of baseball were performed. Hugh S. Fullerton (*American Magazine*, June 1912, p.204): "Whenever a player tells some extraordinary yarn concerning a play the other players instantly inquire if it happened in the Nile Valley league."

nine A baseball *team*. The term was coined because there are nine players in the starting lineup. Warren Goldstein (*Playing for Keeps*, 1989, p.158) noted that the term was clearly influenced by cricket's "eleven." IST USE. 1860 (minutes of the Knickerbocker Base Ball Club; Edward J. Nichols). USAGE NOTE. Despite the fact that there are actually 10 players on teams using a designated hitter, they are still referred to as nines.

Nine. Team from Atlanta, ca. 1899. Photo gathered for use in the American Negro Exhibit at the Paris Exposition of 1900. *Library of Congress*

Nine. This tobacco wrapper was the "First Nine" to refer to the original Cincinnati Red Stockings, the team that went undefeated in 1869. *Library of Congress*

9 The scorekeeper's designation for the right fielder.

nine guys named Robinson A mythical, but remarkable, all-star team fielded by players named Robinson: e.g., Don (pitcher), Wilbert (catcher), Eddie (1b), Jackie (2b), Brooks (3b), Craig (ss), Bill (of), Floyd (of), and Frank (of). The phrase originated with Earl Weaver's response to a question about the challenge of managing (quoted in Thomas Boswell, *The Washington Post Magazine*, March 28, 1982): "I don't welcome any challenge. I'd rather have nine guys named Robinson."

nine innings The standard duration of a game unless the score is tied at the end of the ninth inning.

nine-miler A home run (Phil Pepe, *Baseball Digest*, Nov. 1974, p.58).

nine miles A dugout exaggeration for the distance traveled by a long ball.

90 feet away Said of a runner on third base, who needs 90 feet (the distance between bases) to score a run. The term is commonly used in critical or tight situations when the runner on third represents the lead or tying run.

Nintendo slider A pitch that breaks unexpectedly over the plate, as if remotely controlled. "In baseball parlance, a 'Nintendo slider' is one that breaks as if controlled by a joystick" (Jim Souhan, *Minneapolis Star Tribune*, Oct. 5, 2004; Grant Barrett). ETYMOLOGY. Nintendo is a Japanese manufacturer of video game consoles.

ninth 1. *n.* The ninth inning. **2.** *adv.* Said of the ninth position in the batting order; e.g., "Smith is batting ninth."

ninth inning The last inning of a baseball game unless the score is tied. EXTENDED USE. Anything that is about to be over; the end game; the final chance. "President [George H.W.] Bush's proposed capital gains tax has entered the ninth inning" (*USA Today*, July 24, 1989).

ninth-inning rally A stirring finale in which one team stages a major effort to win the game in the last inning. "Many 'ninth inning rallies' by which spectacular games are won, are the results of the waiting of the batters who struck out during the early innings" (John J. Evers and Hugh S. Fullerton, *Touching Second: The Science of Baseball*, 1910; Peter Morris).

nip 1. To retire a baserunner on a close play. IST USE. 1868 (Chadwick Scrapbooks; Edward J. Nichols). **2.** To win a baseball game, usually by one run; e.g., "The Giants nipped the Dodgers, 4–3." **3.** *hist.* To field a batted ball, usually a fly ball. IST USE. 1869 (*New York Herald*, July 13; Edward J. Nichols).

NL 1. Abbrev. for *National League*, 1. **2.** Abbrev. for *Negro leagues*.

NLCS Abbrev. for *National League Championship Series*.

NLDS Abbrev. for *National League Division Series*.

NNL Abbrev. for *Negro National League*.

NNOF Abbrev. for *no name on front*.

"no batter" A chant or taunt used to tell the batter that he will not get a hit and to encourage the pitcher not to fear the batter.

noble experiment See *Great Experiment*. "When historians look at the racial integration of America, they often cite professional baseball's 'noble experiment,' when Branch Rickey signed Jackie Robinson" (Fred Glennon, in Christopher H. Evans and William R. Herzog II, eds., *The Faith of Fifty Million*, 2002, p.145).

no book Lack of information on the habits and weaknesses of a particular player, manager, or team.

"no catch" The plate umpire's call when the pitch is in the dirt on strike three.

nod The manager's decision to start a particular pitcher or bring in a particular relief pitcher. The term implies some deliberation on the part of the manager, such as when it is reported that a pitcher "got the nod" for Opening Day. ETYMOLOGY. From the head gesture for "yes."

no-decision A statistic for a starting pitcher who is not credited with a win or loss. Abbrev. *ND*.

no game A game that does not complete the 4½ or 5 innings to be a regulation game and must be rescheduled and played from the beginning.

no-hit 1. *adj.* Said of a game or a part of a game during which the pitcher gives up no hits. 2. *v.* To not allow a hit. "Yankees' [Dwight] Gooden No-Hits Seattle" (*The Washington Post* headline, May 15, 1996).

no-hit game Syn. of *no-hitter*, 1. IST USE. 1898. "Several no-hit games have been pitched this season" (*Fort Wayne* [Ind.] *News*, June 11; Benjamin Zimmer).

no-hit, no-run Descriptive of a game in which the pitcher allows no hits and no runs scored. The term is used to distinguish such a performance from one in which there are no hits but in which one or more runs score without the benefit of a hit (such as when four batters are walked in an inning). IST USE. 1904. "Mack, of Paterson, the youngest twirler in the [Hudson River League], had the honor of pitching the first 'no hit no run' game this season" (*The Sporting Life*, Sept. 24; Peter Morris).

no hits, no runs, no errors 1. A description of a *perfect game*, assuming a strong defense and no walks or hit batters. 2. A common summary of an inning of baseball play. EXTENDED USE. Lackluster; faultless but futile. "The once-popular comic epitaph for an old maid: 'Lived a virgin, died a virgin. No hits, no runs, no errors'" (John Ciardi, *Good Words to You*, 1987).

no-hitter 1. A game in which a team fails to get a base hit. A "statistical accuracy" committee appointed by commissioner Fay Vincent ruled on Sept. 4, 1991, that, to get credit for an "official" no-hitter, the starting pitcher must pitch at least nine innings, finish the game without giving up a base hit (even in extra innings), and be declared the winning pitcher. This decision erased more than 50 previously recognized no-hitters, including Harvey Haddix' 12-inning perfect game in 1959 (he gave up a base hit in the 13th inning), David Palmer's five-inning no-hitter in 1984, and Andy Hawkins' losing effort in 1990. See also *perfect game*; *combined no-hitter*. Syn. *no-hit game*; *no-no*. IST USE. 1911 (*Lincoln* [Neb.] *Evening News*, Aug. 31; Benjamin Zimmer). EXTENDED USE. Perfection. Steve Chapman (*The Baltimore Sun*, Sept. 13, 2006), regarding President George W. Bush's policies regarding terrorism: "Even the most competent administration couldn't hope to pitch a no-hitter." 2. A player who has a batting average of .000. An example given by Jerry Howarth (*Baseball Lite*, 1986) was pitcher Bob Buhl, who went 0 for 70 at the plate during the 1962 season.

no-hitter jinx An old superstition that if one speaks of a no-hit game while it is in progress, it will come to an end; i.e., an opposing player will get a hit. It became standard practice in baseball not to mention a no-hitter to the pitcher after five innings. It seems that Red Barber was the first to defy the jinx from the broadcast booth. Barber wrote (*Christian Science Monitor*, Oct. 31, 1988), "My first major league broadcast was opening day 1934, Chicago Cubs at Cincinnati. Lon Warneke of the Cubs didn't give up a hit until one man was out in the ninth inning. I had never heard of the fifth-inning jinx, so I broadcast Warneke's mastery as he performed it. From my first encounter with the jinx I never respected it."

no-man's land **1.** The basepath when a runner is a certain out. "[Pitcher Kenny] Rogers knocked the ball down and found [Jeffrey] Hammonds in no man's land. After hesitating, Hammonds took off for third base and was easily beaten" (*The Baltimore Sun*, May 25, 1998). **2.** The area behind third base, because "that's where every bad hop in the world will find you" (Davey Johnson, quoted in *The Baltimore Sun*, June 11, 1997). **3.** The area of the field between the infield and the outfield where fielders need to know by prearrangement who will be expected to catch a fly ball (Connie Mack, *Connie Mack's Baseball Book*, 1950, p.162). **4.** That part of the deep outfield difficult for an outfielder to cover.

nominal hit Syn. of *phantom hit.*

Nomomania Wild enthusiasm for Japanese pitcher Hideo Nomo, who had a sensational rookie season for the Los Angeles Dodgers in 1995, leading the National League in strikeouts (236) and winning both Rookie of the Year Awards. Nomo was hounded by the media as he was the first Japanese player in 31 years to debut in the major leagues.

non-affiliated club A minor-league club that is not tied to a major-league sponsor.

no name on front Descriptive of a baseball card mistakenly printed without the player's name on the front of the card; e.g., the 1990 Topps Frank Thomas rookie card, whose variation showed increased value. Abbrev. *NNOF.*

nonchalant *v.* **1.** To play with indifference or casually. Harvey Rosenfeld (*The Great Chase*, 1992, p.90) wrote, "Pirate pitcher Mel Queen smacked what looked like a line drive single to right in the third inning. Pleased with his hitting prowess, Queen nonchalanted it down to first. Carl Furillo rushed in quickly and rifled it to Gil Hodges to nip the disbelieving runner." **2.** To field with apparent ease or little effort. "Comment by Rookie Leo Wells of the White Sox after his first glimpse of Dom DiMaggio's fielding smoothness: 'Gosh, he certainly nonchalants them'" (*Baseball Digest*, Oct. 1942).

nonchalot *v.* To make a play with great ease or indifference. The term was a creative corruption by Dizzy Dean of the word "nonchalant," recast as a verb.

non-drafted free agent A player who was not selected in the first-year player draft. Abbrev. *NDFA.*

nonfan An individual who does not follow the game of baseball. 1ST USE. 1913. "And if you, a nonfan, ask *why* . . . you need go no further than a fundamental of American character to understand" (*Technical World*, issue 19; David Shulman).

no-no Syn. of *no-hitter*, 1. 1ST USE. 1969. "[Jim] Palmer's No-No was Bad Word Only for A's" (Doug Brown, *The Sporting News* headline, Aug. 30).

non-pitcher A *position player*; esp., one who has been given a relief-pitching assignment in a game that is a complete blowout.

non-roster invitee A player who is invited for a tryout in spring training without being placed on the team's official roster. "One of the most popular trends among major league-clubs in this era of payroll cutbacks is signing veteran players to minor league contracts and then inviting them to spring training as non-roster invitees" (*USA Today Baseball Weekly*, Feb. 23–March 1, 1994). Abbrev. *NRI.* Syn. *ghost.*

non-tender To decline to offer salary arbitration to a player whose contract is up and is arbitration-eligible but not yet an unrestricted free agent. A player who is non-tendered becomes an unrestricted free agent without compensation.

non-waiver trading deadline 4:00 EDT on July 31. After that date, players can be traded if they first clear waivers.

noon-to-cocktail-hour curve Syn. of *12-to-6 curve.* "[Barry Zito's] noon-to-cocktail-hour curve—scouts [*sic*] slang for a pitch that breaks downward like hands on a clock moving from 12 to 6—gave the Dodgers fits" (Steve Henson, *Los Angeles Times*, June 17, 2006).

noon-to-6 curve Syn. of *12-to-6 curve.*

"no pepper games" Common sign prohibiting fast-paced pregame bunting and fielding drills in major- and minor-league ballparks. Many ballparks have "No Pepper" or "No Pepper Games Allowed" signs stenciled on the dugout and ballpark walls in the home-plate area. Because these prohibitory signs have been visible on television for many years, the term is known to many who have never seen the drill performed. The ban, dating back to the late 1940s, stemmed from the fact that the field was sometimes damaged from pepper play and that it constituted a possible danger of injury to fans in the box seats if batted balls entered the stands. See also *pepper*, 2.

"no pitch" A call by an umpire to negate a pitch because time had been called. The situation may occur when an umpire was unable to stop play before the pitch was delivered.

no play Fielding a ball but being unable to make a throw. "[Mark] McGwire beat out an infield single—shortstop Jody Reed gloved it deep in the hole, but had no play" (*Tampa Tribune*, Oct. 9, 1998).

no prospect A scout's term for a player who will not reach the major leagues. "Because I didn't throw really hard, the Cubs organization labeled me no prospect" (Q.V. Lowe, quoted in George Gmelch and J.J. Weiner, *In the Ballpark*, 1998). Abbrev. *NP*, 2.

normalized Said of a statistic that has been altered to account for annual differences in performance by comparing it to the league average for that statistic. For example, a normalized batting average can be computed by assigning the number 100 to a league's mean batting average for a given year and then crediting each player in the league with a number based on the comparison, in percentage terms, between his batting average and the league mean. This alteration allows for comparisons across leagues and across seasons. Both Carl Yastrzemski's American League-leading .301 batting average in 1968 and Bill Terry's National League-leading .401 batting average in 1930 were about 32 percent higher than their respective league's mean batting average; therefore, a normalization for league mean would result in similar normalized batting averages (approximately 132) for the two.

northern spell A composite name applied in the 19th century to an ancient English pas-time very similar to *trap ball*, but played in more rustic or isolated parts of England and using a ball carved of wood (David Block, *Baseball Before We Knew It*, 2005, p.126).

northpaw *hist.* **1.** A right-handed pitcher. "The Reds' northpaw [Fred Toney] pitched hitless ball against the Cubs" (Ernest J. Lanigan, *Baseball Cyclopedia*; 1922, p.85; Edward J. Nichols). 1ST USE. 1909. "The enemy hit [Rube] Kroh's left-handed hooks some harder than the Cubs could slap offerings of Griff's [Clark Griffith] two sou'paws and one nor'paw" (I.E. Sanborn, *Chicago Tribune*, May 7, 1909; Peter Morris). ETYMOLOGY. A companion term with *southpaw*, a left-handed pitcher. **2.** The right hand of a right-handed pitcher. "[Robert Werner] utilizes his north paw in his twirling and is said to have considerable smoke" (*The Sporting Life*, Feb. 24, 1917; Peter Morris).

North Siders The Chicago *Cubs*. Wrigley Field is located in the North Side of Chicago. Compare *South Siders*.

nosebleeds The *cheap seats* high up in the stands.

nose out To win a game by one run. 1ST USE. 1913. "Little did the White Sox think that they would have to extend themselves to nose out a college team like St. Ignatius" (*San Francisco Bulletin*, March 11; Gerald L. Cohen).

nose-to-toes curve Syn. of *12-to-6 curve*.

no sweat Requiring little effort; accomplished with ease. "No Sweat as [Billy] Pierce Nabs 6–3 Win" (*San Francisco News-Call Bulletin* headline, May 16, 1962; Peter Tamony). ETYMOLOGY. Military slang for a sure or easy task, originating during the Korean War. "Our own Air Force, or flyboys, are credited with 'no sweat,' meaning no trouble at all" (*The New York Times Magazine*, June 5, 1955).

notch 1. To win a game. "[Frank] Viola notches 21st win" (*Tampa Tribune* headline, Sept. 6, 1988). "Lewiston notched a 9–6 come-from-behind Pine Tree League baseball win over Sabattus" (*Lewiston* [Maine] *Sun*, July 3, 1987). **2.** To score a run; esp. to hit a home run. "[Terry Kennedy] didn't notch his tenth home run in 1983 until mid-August" (*Baseball Digest*, Nov. 1983).

note-book pitcher *hist.* A pitcher who keeps records of batters and the most effective pitches to throw against them. IST USE. 1922 (Ernest J. Lanigan, *Baseball Cyclopedia*; Edward J. Nichols).

"not going!" Warning yelled by a defensive player to alert a teammate that a baserunner is not trying to advance on a batted ball.

not having a strike zone Said of a batter's ability to either slice or pull a tight pitch; e.g., a left-handed batter slicing a tight pitch into left field or pulling it down the right-field line.

nothing Something that is without quality or quantity. "To hear one of the visiting players tell it, [Jack] Dunn has nothing, which in baseball parlance means that he has neither speed, curves, nor any of the other elements that go to make up a successful pitcher" (*Brooklyn Eagle*, May 13, 1900; Peter Morris).

nothing across Said of a half inning in which there were no runs, no hits, no errors, and no runners left on base.

nothing ball A pitch without speed, spin, or curve; one without anything "on it." "[Rip Sewell and Jim Tobin], baseball's two most famous exponents of 'delayed action' slow balls . . . tantalized opposing batters with their assortment of nothing ball pitches" (*San Francisco News*, May 25, 1944, p.17). See also *dead fish*, 1. Syn. *nuthin' ball*. IST USE. 1931. "[Bill Sherdel] handed the Bruins the same old nothing ball until their backs bent" (*Decatur* [Ill.] *Review*, June 16; Peter Morris).

nothing but his glove Descriptive of an ineffective pitcher, unable to throw a curveball or otherwise present a deceptive motion. The term implies that the only advantage the pitcher has is his glove. "These young pitchers along the string bean circuit, who are supposed not to have anything but the glove and a return ticket, bother the [White] Sox more than do hurlers who have a rep" (Charles Dryden, *Chicago Tribune*, Apr. 5, 1907; Peter Morris). "Honest Al if this guy had of had anything at all I would of hit 1 out of the park, but he did not even have a glove. And how can a man hit pitching which is not no pitching at all but just slopping them up?"

(Ring Lardner, *Saturday Evening Post*, Sept. 12, 1914; Peter Morris). See also *nothing but the stitches*; *glove and a prayer*.

nothing but the stitches Descriptive of an ineffective pitcher. "Named from the idea that only the stitches on the seams of the ball are in evidence, the pitcher himself applying no skill to this throwing" (Edward J. Nichols, *An Historical Dictionary of Baseball Terminology*, PhD dissertation, 1939). See also *nothing but his glove*. IST USE. 1912 (*New York Tribune*, Sept. 5; Edward J. Nichols).

nothing on the ball **1.** Said of a pitcher who is pitching ineffectively. See also *not much on the ball*. Compare *on the ball*. IST USE. 1912 (*New York Tribune*, Oct. 10; Edward J. Nichols). EXTENDED USE. Said of a dull or incompetent person who is not bright or alert. **2.** Said of a pitch that has no special "stuff" on it and is therefore easy to hit.

not in it **1.** Said of a team that is not in contention in the pennant race. **2.** Said of a team that is down by several runs after the first few innings. "In common parlance, the Cincinnatis, after the first inning of the game, 'were not in it'" (*Brooklyn Eagle*, June 13, 1891; Peter Morris). EXTENDED USE. Said of a person who has been excluded from something. "Baseball vernacular has invaded the church. The crank who created a sensation in the N.Y. Cathedral last Sunday morning by shouting to Archbishop Corrigan: 'Out of my way, Pontius Pilate! I am the Lord's annointed [*sic*] and you are not in it with me' has evidently been feeding on the slop" (*The Sporting News*, Oct. 3, 1891; David Shulman).

not much on the ball Said of a pitcher possessing little effectiveness. See also *nothing on the ball*, 1. IST USE. 1912 (*New York Tribune*, Sept. 28; Edward J. Nichols). EXTENDED USE. Said of a person who is not very bright.

no-trade clause A clause in a player's contract that permits him to be traded only with his consent. The clause limits the club's right to assign the player's contract to no more than 16 clubs designated by the player. "[Rafael] Palmeiro had a no-trade clause in his last contract with the Texas Rangers and rejected a deal to the Chicago Cubs last season" (*The Baltimore Sun*, July 31, 2004).

no-windup delivery An abbreviated delivery by a pitcher in which the *windup* is abandoned. It is utilized to help prevent a baserunner from stealing. Don Larsen used the no-windup delivery to pitch his perfect game against the Brooklyn Dodgers in the 1956 World Series. See also *pitch from the stretch*.

NP **1.** Box score abbrev. for *number of pitches* thrown by a pitcher. **2.** Abbrev. for *no prospect*.

NRI Abbrev. for *non-roster invitee*.

nub **1.** *v.* To hit a slow bouncing ball that stays in the infield. **2.** *n.* A sore or crushed finger from a batted or thrown ball. IST USE. 1937 (*The Sporting News Record Book*, p.65; Edward J. Nichols).

nubber **1.** A weak hit that bounces into the infield; a hit that behaves like a bunt, commonly hit back to the mound or in the basepaths. "Gil Coan's first-inning nubber was the only safety the Senators could drum up off [Willie] Ramsdell's tantalizing knuckler" (*The New York Times*, Apr. 9, 1951). "Darnell Coles led off the 10th with a nubber that was booted by pitcher Steve Frey" (*The Baltimore Sun*, May 19, 1995). See also *knubber*. **2.** Syn. of *Texas Leaguer*, 2.

nuclear fission ball A ball that is hit powerfully and directly at a fielder or the pitcher. It is an exaggerated extension of *atom ball*.

nudist pitch Syn. of *Lady Godiva pitch*.

nuf ced Adequate or sufficient. "[Manager Harry Wolverton] said that Stroud, Munsell and Druck were the men on whom he counted to bring the club through the season into some positions well towards the top. Nuf ced" (*San Francisco Bulletin*, May 3, 1913; Gerald L. Cohen). Also spelled "nuff ced"; "nuf said"; "nuf sed." ETYMOLOGY. Corruption of "enough said." Michael T. McGreevey, owner of the Third Base saloon in Boston, earned his nickname "Nuf Ced" from the way he kept peace in his bar; when he grew frustrated with arguments concerning the Red Sox, he would pound his hand on the counter and declare, with certitude, "Nuf Ced."

nugget The baseball.

number-eight hitter The player who bats in the eighth position in the batting order; the position is often assigned to a young hitter to reduce expectations on him. In the National League, the eighth hitter sometimes is issued a base on balls to bring up the weak-hitting pitcher. Phil Garner (quoted in *Sports Illustrated*, Apr. 4, 2005): "Hitting eighth in front of the pitcher, you're going to have to expand your strike zone, so you're going to look bad sometimes. You need a guy who's willing to accept that." Syn. *second cleanup hitter.*

number 5 The fifth-best starting pitcher in a team's rotation.

number-five hitter The player who bats in the fifth position in the batting order, typically a power hitter.

number 4 The fourth-best starting pitcher in a team's rotation.

number-four hitter Syn. of *cleanup hitter*. Also spelled "No. 4 hitter." "A true No. 4 hitter is a guy who's going to hit 40 home runs, a big bopper in the middle of the lineup that everybody's afraid of" (Jeff Conine, quoted in *The Baltimore Sun*, March 20, 2003). EXTENDED USE. The best or most dependable player on an athletic team, such as in hockey: "We'd always had a No. 4 hitter, a home run hitter in Peter [Bondra]" (Washington Capitals assistant coach Tom Army, quoted in *The Baltimore Sun*, Oct. 6, 2001).

numbering System of using numbers to identify players on the field. The numbers are put on the backs of the players' uniforms and sometimes on the front. Although not required by the rules, the practice became universal among major-league teams in 1937. Some players are superstitious about their numbers; others are downright possessive. A great honor is bestowed on a player when his number is retired at the end of his career. ETYMOLOGY. According to Will Wedge (*The Sporting News*, May 21, 1936), the idea of wearing numbers was traced to the numbering of football players, which was in turn traced to the numbering of hockey players in Canada. The first baseball team to feature numbers on the backs of its players' jerseys

Numbering. Play at the plate at a time before players wore numbers and identification was difficult for the fans. *National Photo Company Collection, Library of Congress*

was the 1929 Cleveland Indians. The first team to number its players permanently was the 1929 New York Yankees; the numbers corresponded to each player's usual spot in the batting order: thus, Earle Combs wore 1, Babe Ruth wore 3, Lou Gehrig wore 4, and the catchers wore 8 and 9. Teams that previously experimented with numbering (using numbers attached to the sleeve) included the 1916 Cleveland Indians and the 1923 St. Louis Cardinals; the idea was dropped because the players were embarrassed, the fans did not take it seriously, and the press denounced the practice as "silly" and unnecessary.

number-nine hitter The player who bats in the ninth position in the batting order. He is the pitcher in the National League and often serves as a second leadoff batter in the American League.

number of pitches A box score statistic for the number of pitches thrown by each pitcher in a game. "Baseball's equivalent of Avogadro's number, according to popular wisdom, is 120—i.e., all major league pitchers have the same number of pitches in their arm before risking injury" (Tom Verducci, *Sports Illustrated*, March 31, 2003). See also *pitch count*. Abbrev. *NP*, 1.

number 1 1. The *fastball*, so called because the catcher's traditional signal for the pitch is a single finger pointed down. "The name of the game for [Roger] Clemens is good old No. 1, the heater" (*The Baltimore Sun*, May 18, 1994). **2.** A team's best pitcher; an *ace*, 3. "Every pitcher wants to be the No. 1 starter, the ace" (Jason Johnson, quoted in *The Baltimore Sun*, Jan. 28, 2004).

number-one hitter Syn. of *leadoff batter*. In selecting a number-one hitter, managers "should never compromise on-base percentage, because the number 1 hitter gets the most plate appearances over a season and must create RBI chances for the sluggers behind him" (Tom Verducci, *Sports Illustrated*, Apr. 4, 2005).

numbers 1. A player's statistical record. "You've got to prove yourself every day you're in a uniform. You have to go out and put up some numbers" (Baltimore Orioles manager Ray Miller, quoted in *The Baltimore Sun*, March 11, 1998). **2.** A situation in which several players are competing for a position on a team; e.g., "Smith was cut because the numbers were against him." **3.** The part of a player's body covered by the jersey with his uniform number; e.g., "The ball hit Smith in the numbers." See also *letters*.

number-seven hitter The player who bats in the seventh position in the batting order.

number-six hitter The player who bats in the sixth position in the batting order.

number 3 1. The catcher's signal to the pitcher with three fingers pointing down. William G. Brandt (*Baseball Magazine*, Oct. 1932) wrote that this signal could be "almost anything, screwball, fork-ball, knuckleball, slop-ball, squib, dipsy-dew." **2.** The third-best starting pitcher in a team's rotation.

number-three hitter The player who bats in the third position in the batting order, traditionally the best hitter on the team.

number 2 1. The *curveball*, so called because the catcher's traditional signal for the pitch is two fingers pointed down. **2.** The second-best starting pitcher in a team's rotation.

number-two hitter 1. The player who bats in the second position in the batting order, traditionally a batter with good bat control (able to bunt or hit the ball to right field to advance the leadoff batter-runner to third base), a vestige of the days when teams played for one run. **2.** Slang for a complementary player (Tom Verducci, *Sports Illustrated*, Sept. 25, 2006, p.41).

nuthin' ball Syn. of *nothing ball*.

O

O 1. The letter "O," which is used instead of the word "zero" in baseball expressions such as, "Smith was O for four at the plate today" (i.e., he had no hits in four at-bats). **2.** Syn. of *offense*, 2. "The book on [Toby Hall] before this year may have been all O and no D" (Richmond manager Carlos Tosca, quoted in *Baseball America*, Oct. 15–28, 2001; Peter Morris). **3.** Short for "ovation"; e.g., "The fans gave Smith a standing O."

oak A baseball bat. IST USE. 1875. "The way the Reds handled the oak in the seventh inning set all doubts at rest as to the result" (*Brooklyn Eagle*, Sept. 9; Peter Morris).

OAV Abbrev. for *opponents' batting average*.

Oavg Abbrev. for *opponents' batting average*.

OB Abbrev. for *organized baseball*. "They laughed when [Branch] Rickey and [William] Shea sat down to play the Continental, and Organized Baseball's trained seals barked that the Old Mahatma was in his dotage. But OB had to dance to the expansion tune, willy-nilly" (*New York Journal-American*, Nov. 16, 1965). IST USE. 1915. "[Michigan] will not be represented next year in any minor league that bears the O. B. brand" (Joe S. Jackson, *The Sporting Life*, Nov. 20; Peter Morris).

OBA 1. Abbrev. for *on-base average*. **2.** Abbrev. for *opponents' batting average*.

OBP Abbrev. for *on-base percentage*.

obs Abbrev. for *obstruction*.

obstruction The act of a defensive player who impedes the progress of a baserunner; specif., such an act when the fielder is not in possession of, or fielding, a thrown or batted ball. If the umpire determines that the runner would have been safe at the next base with-out the obstruction, the runner is awarded that base. A runner caught in a rundown is awarded the next base if obstruction is called. Compare *interference*, 1. Abbrev. *obs*.

obverse The front side of a baseball card displaying the face or picture. Compare *reverse*.

o'cat Syn. of *old-cat*.

odd corner Syn. of *third base*, 1. IST USE. 1913. "[Walter] Cartwright plays the game mechanically and at best can only be called a fair man at the odd corner" (*San Francisco Bulletin*, March 27; Gerald L. Cohen).

odd-even system A system of signs used by the catcher (esp. when a runner is on second base and presumably looking for a specific sign) in which three signs are flashed for each pitch; e.g., if the fingers flashed add up to an even number, a fastball (traditionally represented by one finger) is called for; if they add up to an odd number, a curveball (traditionally two fingers) is called for; and if the fingers are cupped at the end of the sequence, an off-speed pitch may be ordered.

odd side The left side. "In the [Sacramento] lineup there will be only three left-handed batters—Van Buren, Lewis and Dressen. [Manager] Wolverton bats from the odd side, but he will come to bat only in the pinch" (*San Francisco Bulletin*, Feb. 12, 1913; Gerald L. Cohen).

OERA Abbrev. for *offensive earned run average*.

OF 1. Abbrev. for *outfield*, 1. **2.** Abbrev. for *outfielder*.

OFB Abbrev. for *off-base percentage*.

O-fer Descriptive of a batter who fails to get a hit in any number of at-bats in a game or series of games. "Bob Buhl owns the worst O-fer in major league history—0 for 88 over two seasons" (*Sports Illustrated*, June 7, 2004). Davey Johnson, commenting on Rafael Palmeiro (quoted in *The Baltimore Sun*, Aug. 28, 1997): "If he goes O-fer, he's going to get down on himself." Sometimes spelled "ofer." Syn. *O-for*; *oh-for*; *oh-fer*, 1; *0-fer*. ETYMOLOGY. The term is created from "o [the letter, as a stand-in for zero] for," as one would say when speaking of an "0 for 3" game.

0-fer Syn. of *O-fer*.

off 1. Ineffective, or not in good playing form; e.g., "Smith was off his game because he was carousing the previous night." Compare *on*, 2. 1ST USE. 1876. "The Archers, who must have had an 'off' day in the field" (*Winona* [Minn.] *Republican*, July 28; Peter Morris). **2.** At the expense of the pitcher; e.g., "The Red Sox scored two runs off Smith in the third inning."

off and running Said of a baserunner who makes a quick getaway for the next base when a hit is made or on a hit-and-run play.

off balance Said of a batter who is guessing what pitch to expect. "I get outs by surprising batters, by keeping them off balance, and by putting the ball within an inch or two of where I intend it" (Dave Dravecky, *Comeback*, 1990, pp.21–22).

off base *adv.* Said of a baserunner who is taking a lead or is in a position to be put out. 1ST USE. 1872. "The Atlantics . . . would have made another [run] had not Thake got caught off his base" (*Brooklyn Daily Eagle*, July 30; *OED*). EXTENDED USE. **1.** Out of line; working from the wrong premise; disrespectful; mistaken. "He [unionist George Meany] doesn't, in his mind's eye, see a union or the labor movement as an impersonal entity or as an institution. He sees it as a bunch of people. And as long as he keeps seeing it that way, he won't get too far off base" (Merlyn S. Pitzele, *Saturday Evening Post*, Nov. 20, 1943; Peter Tamony). Not to be confused with *off one's base*, which refers to a person who is mentally unbalanced. **2.** Said of one who was unawares or caught by surprise. "There are more men caught off base at cocktail parties than ball games" (*Daily Ardmore-*

ite [Ardmore, Okla.], May 26, 1948; *OED*). **3.** Away from a military base. "They were captured merely through being off base at a time when the opposition chose to make a quick thrust" (*The New York Times*, July 6, 1942; *OED*).

off-base percentage A measure of the effectiveness of a relief pitcher, determined by the number of outs he records divided by the number of batters he faces (Allen St. John, *The Wall Street Journal*, Sept. 5, 2003). Abbrev. *OFB*.

off-color *hist.* **1.** Said of an inaccurate throw. "[Catcher Tub] Spencer's peg was a little off color . . . and two of the Oaks managed to get down to the second bag on him" (*San Francisco Bulletin*, Apr. 21, 1913; Gerald L. Cohen). **2.** Said of sloppy or uninspired playing. "One or two of the performers . . . played real ball, but the other members were entirely off color" (*San Francisco Bulletin*, March 29, 1913; Gerald L. Cohen).

off day Day when no game is scheduled or when a player or team does not practice.

offense 1. The team, or any player on that team, at bat. **2.** The array of tactics used by the team at bat. Such maneuvers as the use of pinch hitters, pinch runners, bunts, and hit-and-run plays are part of the team's offense. Syn. *O*, 2.

offensive earned run average A method for evaluating a player's offensive performance by estimating how many runs would be scored in a game if that player could record every at-bat. It is based on a batter's official at-bats, singles, doubles, triples, home runs, and bases on balls. The use of official at-bats rather than plate appearances is an obvious flaw, biasing the method in favor of players who receive many bases on balls; as a consequence, Ted Williams (13.20) and Babe Ruth (13.19) are the career leaders. The method was proposed by Thomas M. Cover and Carroll W. Keilers (*Operations Research*, Oct. 1977). See also *runs created per 27 outs* for an analogous method. Abbrev. *OERA*.

offensive losses The number of losses that a "team" consisting of a given player occupying all nine lineup positions would be expected to suffer in a given 162-game season, based on that player's runs created. See also *offensive winning percentage.*

offensive performance average A measure of a player's offensive performance, calculated by multiplying the player's total for singles, doubles, triples, home runs, bases on balls, hit by pitches, and stolen bases by a weight associated with each, adding these products, and then dividing by number of plate appearances. The computation of the weights is based on the run potential for each of these types of hits. The measure was proposed by Mark Pankin (*Operations Research,* July–Aug. 1978). Abbrev. *OPA.*

offensive sign A sign given to the batter or baserunner; e.g., a sign to take, bunt, hit and run, steal, squeeze, or no steal (the six conventional signs employed by third base coaches).

offensive winning percentage A measure of a player's offensive performance, represented by the won-lost percentage of an imaginary team consisting of that player occupying all nine lineup positions in every game, assuming average pitching and defense. It is computed by squaring the player's runs created per 27 outs, and then dividing by the sum of the player's runs created per 27 outs squared, plus the league average of runs scored by teams per game squared. The measure bears a purposeful similarity to the Pythagorean method. It was proposed by Bill James in his self-published *Baseball Abstract* (1981), and described in his first conventionally published *Baseball Abstract* (1982). See also *offensive wins; offensive losses.* Abbrev. *OWP.*

offensive wins The number of wins that a "team" consisting of a given player occupying all nine lineup positions would be expected to achieve in a given 162-game season, based on that player's runs created. See also *offensive winning percentage.*

offensive wins above replacement A measure of the number of wins for which a player's batting is directly responsible. It represents the number of games an otherwise average team would win with that player in the lineup rather than a player at the *replacement level* for his position. The measure was used in early issues of *Big Bad Baseball Annual.* See also *extrapolated wins.* Abbrev. *OWAR.*

offer **1.** To swing at a pitched ball; to attempt to bunt a pitch. IST USE. 1901 (Burt L. Standish, *Frank Merriwell's School Days,* p.244; Edward J. Nichols). **2.** To pitch a baseball. **3.** To make a player available for trade.

offering A pitched ball. IST USE. 1907. "So hard did Chance's men sting [Lew] Moren's offerings toward the end of his term on the slab that [Johnny] Kling nearly broke [Eddie] Grant's throwing hand with a terrific liner" (I.E. Sanborn, *Chicago Tribune,* Aug. 16; Peter Morris).

off field Syn. of *opposite field.*

official at-bat An at-bat that is entered in the official record of the game and used as the basis for batting statistics. Four types of plate appearances are not counted as official at-bats: when the batter is awarded a base on balls, is hit by a pitched ball, is awarded first base because of catcher's interference, or hits a sacrifice bunt or sacrifice fly.

Official Baseball Rules See *official playing rules.*

official distance Any field measurement stipulated by the official rules of the game; e.g., the distance between the bases (90 feet) and between the front edge of the pitcher's rubber and the back point of home plate (60 feet, 6 inches).

official game Any non-tied game that completes four-and-a-half innings with the home team in the lead or five innings with the visitors leading. The concept comes into play when a game is stopped for rain, darkness, or other reason. If a game is not an official game, it must be played over from the start or, in the case of a curfew or light failure, from the point at which play was suspended.

official playing rules The written code of on-field rules that govern the playing of baseball games by professional teams, and that are published annually as Sections 1 through 9 of the *Official Baseball Rules.* The rules were recodified, amended, and adopted on Dec. 21, 1949, and thereafter amended by the nine-member (Official) *Playing Rules Committee.* See also *official scoring rules.* Syn. *uniform playing rules.*

official scorer An individual whose responsibility is to observe the game, interpret the action taking place, and, using the *Official Baseball Rules*, prepare a report of the game, which is forwarded to the league's office (or statistician) "as soon as practicable" after the game ends. The official scorer also makes judgment calls, including whether a particular play should be recorded as a base hit or an error, and determines official times at bat, assists, passed balls, wild pitches, stolen bases, earned runs, sacrifice hits, the winning and losing pitchers, and who, if anyone, is credited with a save. The rulings of the official scorer have no bearing on the score or outcome of the game. In the major leagues, the official scorer (formerly a local reporter) is appointed by the commissioner of baseball and observes the game from a position in the press box. It is common for a group of official scorers to work on an alternating basis. During the World Series, there are three official scorers. "On the sports pages what the official scorer says is eternal truth" (Elmer Davis, *The New Yorker*, June 5, 1926). See also *scorer*. Abbrev. *OS*. 1ST USE. 1875. "The base ball reporter of the *Republican* and the official scorer of the St. Louis Base Ball Club are one and the same person" (*St. Louis Globe-Democrat*, June 26).

official scoring rules A set of "rules of scoring" (Section 10 of the *Official Baseball Rules*) by which the official scorer makes decisions concerning judgment calls on the field and ensures that records of championship games achieve uniformity. See also *official playing rules*.

official visit One of five invitations (as allowed by the National Collegiate Athletic Association) proffered by a college or university to a prospective student/athlete who is interested in attending that institution. It is an opportunity for the high school student to see the campus, sample campus life, meet the baseball coaches and scholastic advisor, and attend social events with a current player or student as a host. The visit can occur any time after July 1 up to the eight-day period that begins on the second Wednesday of November, during which the student can sign a national letter of intent to attend a particular institution. The institution can pay the player's airfare or gas mileage, meals and lodging for the player and his parents, and admission to campus events. The player and his family may not receive any benefit, inducement, or arrangement, such as cash, clothing, cars, gifts, or loans. The institution may invite only 25 players each year. (Ben Harrison, *Official Visit*, 2002)

officiate *hist.* To participate in a baseball game as a catcher or a pitcher. "[Deacon] McGuire still holds the record for continuous catching, having officiated in every one of the games played by the old Washington National League club during one of its seasons" (*The Washington Post*, Nov. 1, 1903). "Elmer Emerson, the speed king . . . will officiate as pitcher for Watsonville this season" (*San Francisco Bulletin*, May 1, 1913; Gerald L. Cohen).

off one's base Said of a baserunner who is taking a lead or is in a position to be put out. EXTENDED USE. Said of a person who is mentally unbalanced. While *off base* and "off one's base" are synonymous in the context of the game of baseball, they part company as general metaphors. "Off base" refers to someone who is out of line or incorrect, whereas "off one's base" refers to someone who is mentally unbalanced or crazy. Charles Earle Funk found the latter term in use as far back as 1883 when it appeared in George W. Peck's *His Pa*: "The boy knew the failing, and made up his mind to demonstrate to the old man that he was rapidly getting off his base."

off one's fists Said of hitting a ball with the handle of the bat, near the batter's hands.

off-season **1.** The time of year when baseball is not played (from the day after the last game of the World Series in October to the first day of spring training in February); or that time characterized by an "interminable cultural drought" (George F. Will, *The Washington Post*, March 29, 1984). It may be a misnomer to refer to the winter days as the off-season for the front office: "In many ways it is busier in the off-season than when we're playing" (Baltimore Orioles president Larry Lucchino, quoted in *Orioles Gazette*, Feb. 19, 1993). **2.** An unsatisfactory season for a player or a

Off-season. Nap Lajoie, between seasons, holding hen, ca. 1914. *George Grantham Bain Collection, Library of Congress*

team. IST USE. 1886. "The men [Dave Orr and Chief Roseman] are having that great dread of all ball-tossers, their 'off season'" (*The Sporting News*, May 17; Peter Morris).

off-season baseball Professional baseball played outside the continental United States during the winter months. Some major- and minor-league players from the United States play off-season baseball for conditioning and experience.

offside Said of a left-handed pitcher. "[Southpaw Jess Petty's] offside soupbone was extremely effective" (*The Washington Post*, March 26, 1924). IST USE. 1911. "The offside heaver, [left-handed] Harry Krause, seems to have struck his stride" (*Sandusky* [Ohio] *Star Journal*, July 8; Peter Morris).

off-speed 1. Said of pitching characterized by slow pitches; e.g., "Early on I was throwing a lot of off-speed stuff" (Pat Hentgen, quoted in *The Baltimore Sun*, July 27, 2003). 2. Said of a player who enlivens the game by marching to the beat of a different drummer; e.g., Bo Belinsky, Mark Fidrych, Bill "Spaceman" Lee, and Mickey Rivers (Jerry Howarth, *Baseball Lite*, 1986).

off-speed hitter A hitter who prefers off-speed pitches. "[Jim] Gentile was a good off-speed hitter who would wait well on that slow slop" (Dick Hall, quoted in *The Baltimore Sun*, May 25, 1995).

off-speed pitch An all-purpose term for any pitch (slider, curveball, knuckleball, forkball, and their many variations) that is thrown at less than full velocity. See also *changeup*.

off-stride 1. Said of a batter who steps into the ball before it reaches the plate. An off-stride batter is often overly anxious to swing. 2. Said of a pitcher who alters his pitching motion to accommodate an injury or to prevent adding to a strain. "As [Christy Mathewson] threw he swung 'off his stride,' and instead of planting his left foot straight in front he swung it into the hole to the left" (John J. Evers and Hugh S. Fullerton, *Touching Second: The Science of Baseball*, 1910; Peter Morris).

off the hook Out of a jam; e.g., a pitcher who gives up five runs in the first inning is said to be "off the hook" when his team scores six runs in the second inning, or a pitcher who has been taken out of the game with his team behind is said to be "off the hook" when his team rallies and saves him from being credited with a loss. "So many times this season their pitchers have gotten in trouble and we let them off the hook" (Chipper Jones, quoted in *Milwaukee Journal Sentinel*, Oct. 9, 1995). Compare *on the hook*.

off the schneid Said of a team or player coming out of a slump or a hitless or winless streak. "I'd like to see him [Dan Wilson] get off this schneid that he's on [he was 0 for 42 before blooping a single]!" (Seattle Mariners manager Lou Piniella, quoted in *The Baltimore Sun*, Oct. 18, 2000). See also *schneid*; *on the schneid*.

off the table Said of a curveball, sinker, or other sharp-breaking pitch that suddenly drops precipitously, as though it fell off the end of a table, before reaching the plate. "Some days, when the wind is blowing in your face . . . I'll have a great sinker—it'll just fall off the table" (pitcher Paul Byrd, quoted in *Kansas City Star*, March 31, 2002). Syd Russell (*San Francisco Examiner*, Feb.

26, 1961) described Frank Bertaina's curveball as one that "breaks off the table . . . just like a round object rolling off the edge of a flat surface."

off the wall Said of the rebound of a batted ball that strikes the outfield fence. The term is often used to describe a rebound off the Green Monster at Fenway Park in Boston. EXTENDED USE. Said of an eccentric or bizarre person or event.

off year An unsatisfactory year for a player or a team.

O-for Syn. of *O-fer.*

OFP Abbrev. for *overall future potential.*

oh-fer **1.** *adj.* Syn. of *O-fer.* **2.** *n.* A second-rate player. "The players in the pinstripes didn't look like Yankees. They looked like the AAA farm club of the Kansas City Athletics. A bunch of oh-fers" (*San Francisco Examiner,* Aug. 1, 1966; Peter Tamony).

oh-for Syn. of *O-fer.*

"oh, for the long one!" Broadcaster Harry Caray's pet call when he encouraged a player to hit a home run.

oil A term coined by Dennis Eckersley for liquor (Bill Mazeroski, *Bill Mazeroski's Baseball '89*).

old An adjective upon which baseball dotes in common phrases such as "the old ball game," "the old ballpark," "the old college try," and "the old clutch." This affectionate use of the word was noted by Frank Graham (*New York Sun,* July 18, 1927): "The fondness for the word 'old' on the part of men who in most cases are so young is as strange as it is pronounced. Invariably, it is the 'old army game,' the 'old life,' the 'old pepper,' and the 'old ball game.'" H.G. Salsinger (*Baseball Digest,* Aug. 1945) observed that players generally prefix their favorite nickname for the ball ("apple," "pill," "marble," etc.) with the adjective "old." "[Ping Bodie] brought joy to the South Side fans by repeatedly stepping in and pounding the old sphere in the pinch" (*San Francisco Bulletin,* March 22, 1913; Gerald L. Cohen).

old army game **1.** A style of offense based on the bunt and scientific hitting. "Brandon thought so much of the old army game he

sacrificed with one down" (H.G. Copeland, *Indianapolis Star,* Apr. 22, 1912; Peter Morris). "College teams all play the old army game. They can play that best, all being able to bunt" (Hugh Jennings, *Rounding Third,* 1925). "[The 1959 Chicago] White Sox have revived what was fondly called the 'old Army game'—single, sacrifice, single. They employ the hit-and-run. . . . Many fans have yearned for the 'good old days' when a club fought for one run and won with it. The White Sox are supplying that type of ball" (*The Sporting News,* Aug. 5, 1959). **2.** A style of offense based on eschewing the bunt and scientific hitting. "There was nothing left for the Griffmen to do but play the old army game, 'hit the ball where the enemy ain't.' Inside baseball was thrown to the wind" (Stanley T. Milliken, *The Washington Post,* June 15, 1914; Peter Morris). "In baseball, the 'old army game' signifies baseball of the most elemental kind in which each man takes care of himself. It is, in a phrase, baseball with team play eliminated" (*Fort Wayne* {Ind.} *Weekly Sentinel,* Dec. 22, 1915; Peter Morris). "The 'old army game' as we call it, the style adopted by a team of sluggers that go up to the bat relying upon their batting strength to win out, will never win a pennant nowadays" (Hugh Jennings, *The Sporting Life,* May 9, 1908; Peter Morris). IST USE. 1903. "In the fifth inning the 'old army game' was played by the Chicago men" (*The Sporting Life,* June 27; Peter Morris). ETYMOLOGY. The etymology of the term is confusing. Peter Morris has shown that its use by baseball reporters is wildly contradictory, as seen by the two opposite meanings above. Morris noted that the first sense was in use a bit earlier and is more centered in the Midwest, but there are exceptions. The term is also confusing because it has a contrary meaning in slang outside of baseball. Harold Wentworth and Stuart Berg Flexner (*Dictionary of American Slang,* 1960) defined the term: "Any swindle; any unfair or crooked gambling game or bet."

old ball game A sentimental expression for describing a baseball game or the game of baseball; e.g., Tristram Potter Coffin's *The Old Ball Game* (1971); Frank Deford's *The*

Old Ball Game (2005); and the last line ("At the old ball game") of the chorus of "Take Me Out to the Ball Game." Var. "ol' ball game."

old-cat A family of early American games that featured batting, fielding, throwing, and baserunning and used a ball or "cat" (a piece of wood from four to eight inches long). Variations of old-cat made it possible for more batsmen to participate and to add to the number of bases used. David Block (*Baseball Before We Knew It*, 2005, p.133) averred: "There is no evidence that 'old-cat' either preceded baseball in America or materially influenced its evolution." See also: *one-old-cat*, 1; *two-old-cat*; *three-old-cat*; *four-old-cat*. Syn: *o'cat.*

old college try A wild and desperate attempt to make a play. Sometimes the term carries a hint of showboating. George Herman Ruth (*Babe Ruth's Own Book of Baseball*, 1928) defined "giving it the old college try" as "playing to the grandstand or making strenuous effort to field a ball that obviously cannot be handled." In a column that appeared in the *Columbus* (Ohio) *Citizen* (Nov. 26, 1927) and was quoted in *American Speech* (Apr. 1930), Billy Evans wrote that "I gave it the old college try" was a phrase "often used in big league baseball, when some player keeps on going after a fly ball, usually in foul territory, with the odds about ten to one he would never reach it. Teammates of such a player often beat him to it by shouting in unison with the thought of humor uppermost: 'Well, kid, you certainly gave it the old college try,' as he falls short of making the catch." Evans continued, "When some player does something that a professional player might not ordinarily attempt, such as colliding with a fielder who had the ball ready to touch him out, in the hope that he might make him drop the ball, regardless of the danger he was courting, someone is sure to say, often ironically, if the speaker happens to be one of the players in the field: 'That's the old college spirit.'" IST USE. 1919. "[Frankie] Frisch was taking a long hold on his club and the old college try at the ball" (Christy Mathewson, *The New York Times*, Oct. 19, p.S5; Barry Popik). EXTENDED USE. The term was quickly

applied to any effort with limited chances of success.

older game [softball term] The game of baseball, as contrasted with softball, which is the *younger game.*

older than baseball An expression conveying age, on a par with "older than dirt." Contributer Bob Skole heard a woman comment that the safety deposit boxes in a Portland (Maine) bank were "older than baseball."

old fashion A game somewhat resembling rounders played by members of native communities in northern New England and the Canadian Maritimes and described by Colin D. Howell (*Northern Sandlots: A Social History of Maritime Baseball*, 1995, p.185–89; Peter Morris).

old folks The traditional nickname for the oldest player on a team.

Old League *hist.* The National League, particularly in reference to the American Association (1882–1891). "The Rivalry Between the Old League and Association Led to Post-Season Series of Which the Temple Cup Contests Were the Logical Successors" (*The Sporting Life* subhead, Oct. 30, 1897).

old leaguer *hist.* 1. A veteran player in the American Association (1882–1891) (*The Sporting Life*, Jan. 14, 1885; Barry Popik). Compare *fresh leaguer.* 2. A member of the National League. "The old leaguers were falling over each other to get to [Ban] Johnson" (Cy Sanborn, quoted in Mike Sowell, *July 2, 1903*, 1992, p.167). 3. *hist.* A player who has played in the National League for at least three years. "Irrespective of a man's real age . . . it is not until his third year that he is considered an old leaguer" (*Bismarck* [N.D.] *Daily Tribune*, May 4, 1889).

Old Man The manager of a baseball team. IST USE. 1946. "Manager Frankie Frisch is the 'CO,' the 'Old Man' or 'The Brass,' and he and his coaches have come to be known as 'GHQ'" (*Baseball Digest*, May).

old Oriole A feisty, hard-nosed player who stays in the game despite injuries. The term derives from the reputation for toughness and relentlessness of the Baltimore Orioles of the 1890s. "Baseball resists change and the old Oriole tradition that a player should show no fear, just as he should try to conceal an injury, still holds on" (Hugh Bradley, *New York Evening Post*, reprinted in *The Sporting News*, May 2, 1938; Peter Morris). "If he gets spiked or hit on the head or upset by a base-runner and laughs it off, he's an 'Oldoriole'" (William G. Brandt, *Baseball Magazine*, Oct. 1934). "The old-timers would watch somebody hustle to smother a grounder, or hang tough with a runner bearing down, and invariably remark: 'He plays like an old Oriole'" (Michael Olesker, *The Baltimore Sun*, Oct. 7, 2001). Var. "Oldoriole." IST USE. 1932 (*Baseball Magazine*, October, p.496; Edward J. Nichols).

Old Pluvy *hist.* Syn. of *Jupe Pluvius*.

Old Sal The name used by Joe McGinnity for his *jump ball*. IST USE. 1908 (*New York Evening Journal*, March 5; Edward J. Nichols). ETYMOLOGY. Short for "Old Sally."

old school Advocates of established practices and conventions; those who adhere to the unwritten rules of baseball. "Jim Leyland is as old school as they come, a baseball traditionalist who wears his spikes all day" (Chris Ballard, *Sports Illustrated*, Aug. 21, 2006). The term implies maturity, leadership, aggressiveness, intensity, lack of foolishness, a no-nonsense style. "[Benny Kauff] seems to belong to the old school players who did not know what a padded mitt was for" (*The Sporting Life*, May 19, 1917; Peter Morris). John Eisenberg, on Baltimore Orioles director of minor-league operations Doc Rodgers (*The Baltimore Sun*, Apr. 2, 2003): "Baseball fashion has moved toward a baggy, pajama-style look with no socks showing in recent years, and Rodgers, a self-described traditionalist, thought high socks would underline his old-school principles." See George Castle, *Throwbacks: Old-School Baseball Players in Today's Game*, 2003. IST USE. 1866. "[Charley] Commerford is well-known to the New York ball-players of the old school as the noted short stop of the original Gotham nine" (*Frank Leslie's Illustrated Newspaper*, Aug. 25). USAGE NOTE. The term has become a late 20th-century buzzword for tradition and throwbacks, popularized by a series of commercials for the ESPN Classic network.

old soldier's favorite A ground ball that "hops perfectly" (Bill Snypp, *Lima* [Ohio] *News*, Apr. 27, 1937; Peter Morris).

old styler *hist.* An *old timer* in the 19th century. IST USE. 1862 (*New York Sunday Mercury*, July 13; Edward J. Nichols).

old timer **1.** A retired ballplayer; a player from a previous baseball generation. Sometimes spelled "old-timer." Syn. *old styler*. IST USE. 1879. "Base Ball as it Was—An Old Timer's Reminiscences" (*Lowell* [Mass.] *Daily Citizen* headline, Nov. 28). **2.** A veteran player. "Clubs will engage cheaper players, leave the high-priced old-timers out in the cold" (*Chicago Tribune*, Aug. 26, 1877). Also spelled "old-timer." **3.** *hist.* A long hit, so named because it became rare after the deadening of the ball in 1870s. "Gifford followed with one of his 'old timers'" (*Detroit Free Press*, July 27, 1876; Peter Morris).

Old timer. Early convocation of baseball pioneers in Boston. *Library of Congress*

Old-Timers' Day A promotional ceremony at which retired players are honored and play a short game before the regularly scheduled game. New York Yankees general manager George Weiss established the first Old-Timers' Day in the early 1940s. "The idea evolved from the practice, which went as far back as the early 1900s, of asking a retired star to play all or part of an actual game as a promotional gimmick" (Patrick Ercolano, *Fungoes, Floaters and Fork Balls*, 1987, p.130). IST USE. 1908. "They were privileged, indeed, who attended the Old Timers' Day at Paddock's Island in Boston Harbor [on Aug. 12, 1908]" (*Baseball Magazine*, November; John Thorn).

old-timers' game A game played by retired players on Old-Timers' Day.

ole (pron. "o-lay") For a fielder to allow a batted ball to pass, similar to a bullfighter allowing the bull to pass; e.g., "Smith oles the ground ball."

olive in his throat Descriptive of a player feeling pressure in a crucial situation. "When men go to bat with 'olives' in their throats, you know pennant pressure is as omnipresent as the crisp fall air" (Ray Robinson, *The Home Run Heard 'Round the World*, 1991).

ol' rubber belly A common nickname for a veteran player with a bulging waistline. Syn. "ol' barrel." IST USE. 1933 (*Famous Sluggers and Their Records of 1932*).

Olympic rings Syn. of *platinum sombrero*. The term was coined by pitcher Bill Scherrer and refers to the five interlocking rings that make up the Olympic emblem (Peter Schmuck, *The Baltimore Sun*, Apr. 28, 1991).

O'Malley's Pleasure Dome Facetious name for the roofed stadium that Brooklyn Dodgers president Walter O'Malley discussed building in Brooklyn in the 1950s. A model stood in the foyer of the Dodgers offices.

on 1. Occupying a base or bases. "[Jesse Orosco] took over with two on in the seventh inning" (*The Baltimore Sun*, July 29, 1996). IST USE. 1907 (*New York Evening Journal*, Apr. 30; Edward J. Nichols). **2.** Effective, or in good playing form. "When he's [Neil Allen] on he can get the curveball up and still

get it over" (Ken Harrelson, quoted in Steve Fiffer, *How to Watch Baseball*, 1987, p.161). Compare *off*, 1. **3.** Operating or occurring; e.g., "The Cubs have a play on (such as a steal attempt)."

on a line Said of a ball, batted or thrown through the air, having a path that is approximately straight from the moment of impact or delivery; e.g., "Smith hit the pitch on a line over the infield" or "Jones threw the ball on a line from right field."

on base Said of one or more baserunners who have reached or are occupying one or more bases; e.g., "Smith got on base by singling to center."

on-base average Syn. of *on-base percentage*, 1. The correct term is "on-base percentage" because the statistic is an actual percentage, not an average. Abbrev. *OBA*, 1.

on-base percentage 1. A statistic used to illustrate a batter's overall effectiveness at getting on base, computed by dividing the number of times the batter reaches base (via hit, walk, or hit by pitch, but not including fielding error, fielder's choice, or dropped third strike, and ignoring being awarded first base on interference or obstruction) by his number of at-bats, walks, hit by pitches, and sacrifice flies (but not sacrifice bunts), and carrying the quotient to three decimal places. Because sacrifice flies were not included as an "official" statistic for much of the first half of the 20th century, some sources do not include sacrifice flies in the denominator. The statistic is a distinctly better index of a batter's performance at getting on base than the batter's batting average. A player may have a higher batting average than on-base percentage because sacrifice flies are not counted in the denominator for batting average. The statistic is particularly important in determining the effectiveness of a leadoff batter, whose job it is (more than any other player) to get on base; in current baseball, a leadoff batter with an on-base percentage of less than .360 is not performing competently. A high on-base percentage is the mark of a hitter who does not swing at many balls outside the strike zone. The idea that batters can be evaluated by their performance at getting on base goes back to 1879 (see *reached first base*), but the present-day statistic only began to appear regularly in the 1950s, and became an official statistic in 1984. The concept was brought back to life by Allan Roth and Branch Rickey, and appeared in Rickey's sabermetric classic "Goodby to Some Old Baseball Ideas" (*Life* magazine, Aug. 2, 1954), defined without sacrifice flies in the denominator. Abbrev. *OBP*. Syn. *on-base average*. **2.** The percentage of batters reaching base (via hit, walk, and hit by pitch) against a specific pitcher.

on-base percentage plus slugging percentage Syn. of *on-base plus slugging*.

on-base plus slugging The sum of a batter's on-base percentage and slugging percentage. Despite its simplicity, and the fact that it combines proportions based on different denominators, the statistic is a relatively good predictor of runs scored, comparable to *total average* and the basic version of *runs created*. The current league average is around .750, with a range from .600 for the weakest hitters to 1.000 for the strongest. The highest single-season on-base plus slugging is 1.422 (Barry Bonds in 2004); the career leader is Babe Ruth with 1.164. "A good shorthand method for measuring offensive production is to simply add slugging average to on-base percentage" (Geoffrey Himes, *Washington Weekly*, Apr. 12, 1985). The statistic was devised by Pete Palmer and originally described by John Thorn and Pete Palmer (*The Hidden Game of Baseball*, 1985). Abbrev. *OPS*. Syn. *production*; *on-base percentage plus slugging percentage*.

on-base times slugging Syn. of *batter's run average*. Abbrev. *OTS*.

on board Said of a batter who has reached a base. "[Les Lancaster] was just trying to throw one down the middle, since the count was 3–0 and he didn't want to put [Robby] Thompson, the go-ahead run, on board with a walk" (*Tampa Tribune*, Oct. 9, 1989).

on deck Said of a batter ready to take his turn at bat following the batter at the plate. Syn. *in the slot*, 1. IST USE. 1867 (*Hastings* [Mich.] *Banner*, Sept. 4; Peter Morris). ETYMOLOGY. See *at bat, on deck, in the hold* for full discussion of the etymology of this sequence. EXTENDED USE. Said of the next person to have a turn; e.g., a barber might say that a customer next in line for a haircut is "on deck." Despite the nautical origin of "deck," the use of "on deck" for "next" originated in baseball. Peter Morris (personal communication, Aug. 3, 1997) found an interesting 1875 extension of the term, listing upcoming games.

on-deck circle One of two circular spaces, each five feet in diameter, set in foul territory in front of each team's dugout where the batter following the player at bat stands or kneels to wait his turn. It provides a space for the on-deck batter to take practice swings. The on-deck batter must be in the on-deck circle and not waiting in the dugout, a stipulation meant to speed up the game. Syn. *next batter's box*; *batter's circle*; *batting circle*; *circle*, 2; *slot*, 11. EXTENDED USE. A metaphorical place that is next in line. "[Financial elites] use deregulation as a club to "privatize" electric power, airlines, telecommunications, postal services and prisons, with Social Security and Medicare in the on-deck circle" (Glenn C. Altschuler, *The Baltimore Sun*, Dec. 2, 2007).

1 The scorekeeper's designation for the pitcher.

one-armed man A fielder who makes one-handed catches.

one away One out.

1B 1. Abbrev. for *first base*, 1. **2.** Abbrev. for *first base*, 2. **3.** Abbrev. for *first baseman*. **4.** Abbrev. for *single*, 1.

one-bagger Syn. of *single*, 1.

one-ball hitter A hitter who is at his best or, at least not bothered, when there are two strikes against him.

one base at a time A style of play, whether intended or not, in which no baserunner is able to gain more than a base on any play. See also *station-to-station*, 1.

one-base hit Syn. of *single*, 1. IST USE. 1874 (*New York Sun*, July 31; Edward J. Nichols).

one-baser Syn. of *single*, 1. IST USE. 1875 (*New York Herald*, July 14; Edward J. Nichols)

one-cornered cat Syn. of *one-old-cat*, 1.

one-cushion shot A line drive that caroms off the wall, like a billiard or pool ball, usually for extra bases, and that is often difficult for an outfielder to field.

on edge *hist.* In top form; in good playing shape. "Nearly everyone in the Seal line-up is in good condition and only light work is necessary to keep them on edge" (*San Francisco Bulletin*, March 12, 1913; Gerald L. Cohen).

one-dimensional player 1. A player whose talents are limited, usually to slugging. "All I kept hearing was that I was a one-dimensional ballplayer. I couldn't do this, I couldn't do that" (Jack Clark, quoted in *Tampa Tribune*, Jan. 7, 1988). 2. A player who consistently hits to the same general area of the ballpark.

one down One out.

one down and two to go One out with two outs remaining.

one-eyed cat A playground variant of baseball with only home plate and first base. According to Royse M. Parr (personal communication, Dec. 11, 2005), "The best player combinations are two batters opposing a pitcher and a fielder, but more can play. The batter [tried] to hit the ball hard past the pitcher, run about 45 feet to first base and back to home plate before the fielder could throw the ball back to the pitcher covering home plate. A caught fly ball or over the fence is out. Runs counted for successful ventures to first base and back to home."

One Eye Jim Bats A variation of baseball. James S. Hanna (*What Life Was Like When I Was a Kid*, 1973, p.45; Charles D. Poe) described how the game was played in his Galveston (Tex.) neighborhood: "If there were not enough to make up two full teams we played a variation . . . called One Eye Jim Bats. This might well have been called progressive baseball, for each prospective player shouted the position he wanted to start at, the number one spot, of course, being 'batter' which was usually won by the biggest and loudest boy, with 'catch,' 'pitch,' 'first,' 'second,' etc. following in rapid order. If the batter succeeded in making a base hit, all players advanced to the next highest position, the catcher now becoming the batter, the pitcher becoming the catcher, and so on. If the batter

made a home run he was privileged to bat again; if he were put out, all players advanced and the ex-batter started at the bottom at third base. It was a good game and afforded everyone some experience in playing all positions." See also *work-up*; *one-old-cat*, 3.

one for the book An odd or freakish play that deserves to be noted. IST USE. 1932 (*Baseball Magazine*, October, p.496; Edward J. Nichols).

one game at a time A cliché applied to the effort of focusing solely on today's game, esp. when a team is trying to catch the leader in a pennant or divisional race. Florida Marlins pitcher Dontrelle Willis (quoted in *Sports Illustrated*, June 30, 2003): "I'm trying not to get ahead of myself. I'm just taking it one game at a time."

one gone One out.

one-handed catch A catch in which the fielder uses one hand only. IST USE. 1865 (Chadwick Scrapbooks; Edward J. Nichols).

one-handed catcher A catcher who keeps his throwing hand behind his back when receiving the pitch to protect it from foul tips and backswings. Bruce Edwards was the first to catch with one hand. Jerome Holtzman (*Chicago Tribune*, Aug. 9–10, 1986) wrote, "In [Al] Lopez's day [1930s], all catchers caught with two hands. . . . The two-handed catcher is better defensively because he can shift his feet for the low, outside pitch. The one-handed receivers are comparatively stationary. To shift, they must cross one leg in front of the other. So instead of shifting, they backhand the outside pitch."

one-handed glove A flexible, lightweight *catcher's mitt* with a built-in central hinge that follows the lateral line of the catcher's palm. The glove will fold itself around and hold a thrown ball in the pocket, thereby extending the natural catching motion of the hand. Introduced in the 1960s, the glove was first used by Randy Hundley and Johnny Bench.

one-hitter A game in which a team is held to one base hit. IST USE. 1918. "[Lefty Gregg] pitched a one-hitter against St. Louis" (*Lincoln* [Neb.] *Evening State Journal*, June 4, p.9; Benjamin Zimmer).

one-hole-cat Syn. of *one-old-cat*, 1. "One hold cat was . . . played with one 'hole'—a spot for grounding the bat, like the crease in cricket" (Robert Smith, *Baseball's Hall of Fame*, 1965). The game originally used holes in the ground for the "bases"; the term "hole" eventually became "ol' "; hence "one-ol'-cat" and later "one-o'cat."

one-hopper A batted ball that takes one bounce before reaching a fielder.

154-game schedule A team's complete schedule of regular season games in the major leagues from 1904 to 1917 and from 1920 to 1960 in the American League and 1920 to 1961 in the National League. Each team played every other team in its eight-team league a total of 22 games per season.

162-game schedule The schedule of games each team plays per season in the major leagues; a team's complete schedule of regular season games. The 162-game schedule began with expansion in the American League in 1961 and was instituted in the National League in 1962.

One Hundred Thousand Dollar Infield The Philadelphia Athletics infield from 1911 to 1914, consisting of first basemen Stuffy McInnis, second baseman Eddie Collins, shortstop Jack Barry, and third baseman Frank "Home Run" Baker. The infield was named for its alleged value (according to manager Connie Mack) and not for the players' collective salaries. Also expressed in lower case and as "$100,000 infield." Syn. *Hundred Thousand Dollar Infield.* IST USE. 1911 (*The North American* [Philadelphia], Aug. 21; Norman L. Macht).

one-liner A variation of the two-seam fastball in which the pitcher's fingers slip a little toward the white area of the ball and his forefinger presses down on the ball. The pitch is so named because the batter sees "a single dart of red stitches on the side of the ball as it arrives" (Roger Angell, *A Pitcher's Story*, 2001, p.95). The pitch was thrown by Don Drysdale.

one-name guy A player who is known by his first name or nickname alone; baseball's equivalent to a household name. Tony Kornheiser (*The Washington Post*, Oct. 23, 1987) wrote, "When I think of a World Series, the kind of names that come to my mind are Catfish [Hunter], Yogi [Berra], Brooks [Robinson] and Reggie [Jackson]. One-name guys."

one-o-cat An informal children's game played in Brooklyn in the late 1930s and early 1940s. According to Neil Massa (personal communication, Dec. 10, 2005), "The game was played when there were not enough players available to field two teams. There was a batter, a pitcher, a catcher, and as many infielders and outfielders as there were people available. The object was for the batter to get a hit. If he did, he became the first baseman and the first baseman batted. If the batter hit a fly ball which was caught, the catcher of the fly batted and the batter took the position of the catcher of the fly. If the batter grounded out he moved to right field, the pitcher batted, and the rest of the players rotated from right field to center field, etc., and through the infield and battery. The first baseman and batter could keep hitting as long as they got hits." Joe Pepitone (*Joe, You Coulda Made Us Proud*, 1975, p.48) recalled his youth: "We'd shag flies, hit grounders to one another, play one-a-cat [*sic*] where you batted until you made three outs." See also *one-old-cat*, 3.

one o'cat Syn. of *one-old-cat*, 1.

one-o'clock hitter A player who hits well in batting practice and poorly during the game. The term dates back to when games started at two o'clock and batting practice began at one o'clock. See also *10-o'clock hitter*; *12-o'clock hitter*; *two-o'clock hitter*; *five-o'clock hitter*; *six-o'clock hitter*; *seven-o'clock hitter*.

one-old-cat 1. An informal children's game that is the basic variation of *old-cat* with a batter, a pitcher, and two bases. The batter hit from one base, ran to the other base, and then returned to the original base; he was retired when the batted ball was caught on the fly or on one bounce. Once the batter was out, the players exchanged positions. David Block (*Baseball Before We Knew It*, 2005, pp.201–2) noted that the first reference to "one-old-cat" was 1837, even though the game was reputedly popular during the first decades of the 19th century, and it might have been played in America as early as the colonial era. Some references to one-old-cat mention more than two players. See also *munshets.* Syn. *one-hole-cat*; *one o'cat*; *one-cornered cat.* IST USE. 1837. "Just then, two of his playmates coming along with a ball, Dick . . . went to join them in a game of 'one-old-cat'" (Edward Gallaudet, *The Jewel, or, Token of Friendship*; David Block). **2.** An informal game that is usually played by three children. Rules vary depending on circumstances but a typical game has one base with one player at the plate, one pitching, and one in the field. Outs occur when a ball is caught on the fly or there are three strikes. The batter can score on a hit, which enables him to run to the base and return before being put out. The players rotate and each keeps his own score. **3.** A game played by the pitchers on a major-league club. As explained by Dodgers manager Walter Alston (*The New York Times Magazine*, March 18, 1956), "A pitcher remains at bat as long as he can make a hit. . . . Then when he goes out, he moves into right field as everyone moves up a position, the rotation going from right to center to left to third base to shortstop to second to first, to pitch and back to bat again. We don't use a catcher. It gives the pitchers a certain familiarity with every position and they have fun as well." See also *one-o-cat*; *One Eye Jim Bats*; *work-up.*

one-pitch [softball term] A form of slow pitch softball in which the batter begins his or her at-bat with a count of three balls, two strikes, and one foul. It is a fast game to play.

one player away Said of a team when it feels that it can get into postseason play with the addition of one key player. Michael Bauman (*Milwaukee Journal Sentinel*, Aug. 4, 1997) wrote, "And the reality is, the [Milwaukee] Brewers appear to be more than the proverbial 'one player away' from pennant-winning status, anyway."

one-run game A contest in which there is a difference of only one run separating the scores of the two teams.

one-sacker Syn. of *single*, 1. IST USE. 1908. "[It was a] timely one-sacker" (*Atlantic Monthly*, January; David Shulman).

one-time Said of a former player; e.g., "Smith was a one-time shortstop."

one-two-three *adj.* Said of an inning or batting order in which the first three batters are retired in succession. "The New-Yorks disposed of them in one-two-three order" (*The New York Times*, May 4, 1883). "Troy Percival worked a 1-2-3 ninth for his 18th save" (*The Baltimore Sun*, July 5, 2003). "[Mike Mussina] had only one one-two-three inning" (*The Baltimore Sun*, July 24, 1994). Var. "1-2-3." IST USE. 1862 (*New York Sunday Mercury*, Aug. 13; Edward J. Nichols).

one, two, three *n.* A practice game in which there are fewer than six fielders on a side. Henry Chadwick (*The Game of Base Ball*, 1868, p.43) described the game as follows: "When the batsman is put out—unless the ball is caught on the fly, in which case the fielder catching it changes place with the batsman—he takes his position at right field, the catcher takes the bat, the pitcher goes in to catch, and the first baseman takes the pitcher's position, and each of the other fielders advance one step towards the in-field positions. There should be at least four players on the batting side." See also *work-up.*

one-way contract A player's contract in which the player gets paid even if he is sent to the minor leagues (Richard Tellis, *Once Around the Bases*, 1998, p.299; Peter Morris).

one-way lead **1.** A lead taken off a base when the runner has determined that, regardless of the pitcher's move, he will return to the base. As explained by Branch Rickey (John J. Monteleone, ed., *Branch Rickey's Little Blue Book*, 1995, pp.41–42): "The reason for a one-way lead, sometimes, is to get acquainted with the pitcher's move; or it could conceivably be used to cause the catcher to call for a pitch-out, thinking that the runner is likely to go. Or it could well be used occasionally to draw a throw and thus break up the pitcher's concentration on his next pitch. No manager recommends it as a part of general practice." **2.** A gambling, aggressive lead in which the baserunner's whole being (weight and mind) is focused on the next base, rather than on returning to the base he is already on (*The Washington Post*, Sept. 5, 1982).

on his horse Said of an outfielder sprinting after a fly ball.

on ice Said of a team that has assured success. See also *home free*. IST USE. 1913. "Enough clouts were secured by the gray-clad swatters to put the game on ice" (*San Francisco Bulletin*, Apr. 28; Gerald L. Cohen).

onion 1. *hist*. The baseball. "When they ain't pasting the onion they're in a slump" (W.R. Hoefer, *Baseball Magazine*, July 1918, p.287; Bill Mullins). IST USE. 1917 (*American Magazine*, July, p.42; Edward J. Nichols). 2. *hist*. Syn. of *lemon*, 1. "The Yankees traded [Hal] Chase to Chicago for a bunion [Rollie Zeider] and an onion [Babe Borton]. . . . An 'onion' was a 'lemon'" (Mark Roth, quoted in Frederick G. Lieb, *Baseball As I Have Known It*, 1977). 3. *hist*. A stupid or obnoxious player. "Charley Dryden, the Chicago sage, has written [Frank] Chance . . . suggesting that if he finds a few 'onions' among his phenoms it would be an act of Christian charity to leave them in Bermuda, where their odor will not be noticed" (*San Francisco Bulletin*, March 12, 1913; Gerald L. Cohen). 4. A player's head.

onion picker *hist*. "An antiquated baseball term for a third baseman or an outfielder" (*The Baltimore Sun*, July 20, 2000).

on paper Said of a team that should perform well, without injuries and slumps, judging by the names listed on its roster. "On paper, I think we're better, but if it works on paper and doesn't work on the field, that doesn't do you any good" (Cleveland Indians manager Mike Hargrove, quoted in *The Baltimore Sun*, March 26, 1996). "[They should] put down a layer of paper in Candlestick Park [because] . . . the Giants always look good on paper" (*Sports Illustrated*, July 9, 1984). See also *paper team*. IST USE. 1893. "On paper the Atlanta team, as it now stands, is about as good as any team in the league" (*Atlanta Constitution*, Feb. 19; Peter Morris).

on schedule to What will happen if the present ratio is maintained; e.g., "At their present rate, the Angels are on schedule to win 96 games" (Tom Seaver, NBC "Game of the Week," Aug. 12, 1989).

on the ball Said of a pitcher who is working effectively, using speed, location, and movement. A good pitcher with the ability to deceive batters is said to have a lot "on the ball." "Gilligan has plenty of stuff on the ball, and with a good team behind him he will be a hard pitcher to beat" (*San Francisco Bulletin*, Feb. 15, 1913; Gerald L. Cohen). See also *"keep your eyes on the ball"*; *put something on the ball*. Compare *nothing on the ball*. EXTENDED USE. 1. At one's best; competent. "The lass has much on the ball" (*Mademoiselle*, Sept. 1961; *OED*). 2. Bright and alert; showing energy. The term often appears in the negative; e.g., "He's got nothing on the ball—nothing at all" for someone who is dull (*Collier's*, Apr. 13, 1912; *OED*).

on the bench Inactive, not playing; said of a utility player. IST USE. 1905 (*The Sporting Life*, Sept. 2, p.10; Edward J. Nichols).

on the black Said of a pitch thrown over one of the two lateral edges of home plate. See also *in the black*.

on the block Said of a player who is available for sale or trade. "Nick Esasky is, as always, on the block and Atlanta isn't even disguising its interest in him" (*Tampa Tribune*, Dec. 4, 1988). ETYMOLOGY. From the notion of being on the auction block.

on the bound *hist*. Pertaining to a putout in the *bound game*. Compare *on the fly*. IST USE. 1859. "Leggett had previously been put out by an easy catch on the bound by Russell" (*Wilkes' Spirit of the Times*, Sept. 24; Peter Morris).

on the bubble Said of a player who is about to be traded or sent back to the minor leagues, or who is either on the verge of being sent down or called up; one whose "bubble" is about "to burst." "Out of options and with a surplus of left-handed bats and outfielders on the roster, [David] Dellucci found himself on the bubble" (*The Baltimore Sun*, Apr. 11, 2001).

on the fists Said of an inside pitch that comes close to the batter's hands. Such a pitch is hit off the bat handle, the part of the bat closest to the batter's hands.

on the fly *hist*. Pertaining to a putout in the *fly game*. "The catcher will call to that fielder who he thinks will best take a ball on the fly" (*Beadle's Dime Base-Ball Player*, 1860, p.26). Even in bound games, fielders had a choice of trying to accomplish the more "manly" and difficult act of catching a fly ball on the fly rather than letting it bounce and making a very easy "boy-like" bound catch. Compare *on the bound*. IST USE. 1858. "Other players received their share of applause, particularly . . . Wright and P. O'Brien for catches on the fly in the long fields" (*Spirit of the Times*, July 24; Dean A. Sullivan). EXTENDED USE. Hurriedly; without pause; on the spur of the moment. Lowell Edwin Folsom (*Iowa Review*, Spring–Summer 1980, p.76) wrote, "[Walt Whitman] refers to his own writing techniques in terms of baseball, telling [Horace] Traubel, for example, 'That has mainly been my method: I have caught much on the fly: things as they come and go—on the spur of the moment.' And Traubel uses the same image to evoke some of his more fragmented conversations with Whitman: 'Two or three things I caught from W. on the fly, as I busied about the room.' At that time [1880s], 'on the fly' was an important new baseball term, since the original Knickerbocker rules in 1845 allowed for an out if the ball was caught 'on the first bound.' Only gradually did this rule change; for years, teams would stipulate whether or not the games they played would be 'on the fly' or 'on the bound.' If players chose to play on the fly, they had to be especially awake and alert, awaiting the unexpected. So Whitman probably did not mean to imply, with the figure of speech, casualness about his poetic methods so much as alertness combined with an element of surprise: his method was to be awake for every opportunity that came his way, to 'catch much on the fly.'"

on the full Said of a batted or thrown ball that is in the air or did not hit the ground in Australian baseball; e.g., "The center fielder threw the runner out at home with a perfect throw on the full to the catcher."

on the hip *hist.* Said of a pitcher who has the opposing batters under control. IST USE. 1905 (*The Sporting Life*, Sept. 2, p.13; Edward J. Nichols).

on the hook Said of a pitcher who has left the game with his team losing, or is slated to be the losing pitcher unless his team at least ties the score. Compare *off the hook*.

on the label Syn. of *on the trademark*.

on the line **1.** Said of batted ball that strikes a foul line. **2.** Said of a game at a moment when it is about to be decided.

on the meat Said of a player's being hit by a pitched ball; e.g., "Smith took one on the meat."

on the mound Said of a pitcher who is currently pitching.

on the nose Squarely or directly; e.g., hitting a ball "on the nose" is to connect with it solidly. Syn. *on the pick*. IST USE. 1883 (*The Sporting Life*, May 20, p.1; Edward J. Nichols).

on the pick *hist.* Syn. of *on the nose*. "I hit that ball right on the pick and it went past the shortstop so fast that he didn't even have time to wave at it" (Ring W. Lardner, *The Saturday Evening Post*, March 9, 1918; Peter Morris).

on the road Away from home. "The Tigers fell to 20–57 on the road, the worst mark in the majors" (*Tampa Tribune*, Sept. 20, 1989).

on the schneid Said of a hitless or winless period for a player or a team. See also *schneid*; *off the schneid*.

on the screws Said of a hard-hit ball, esp. one that is batted solidly and squarely. The term was used by broadcaster Bob Uecker.

on the shelf Said of a player who is temporarily inactive, usually because of an injury. IST USE. 1905 (*The Sporting Life*, Sept. 9, p.7; Edward J. Nichols).

on the trademark Said of the part of the baseball bat where the manufacturer's insignia is inscribed. See also *trademark*. Syn. *on the label*. IST USE. 1896. "Lange caught a swift ball squarely on the trade mark and drove it clear to the clubhouse in center field" (*The Boston Globe*, July 23; Peter Morris). USAGE NOTE. Hitting the ball on the trademark during the dead-ball era was considered desirable, at least in comparison to the handle or the end of the bat. However, batters are now advised to hold the trademark up when swinging the bat forward to avoid the risk of breaking the bat.

on top of the ball See *stay on top of the ball.*

OOB 1. Abbrev. for *opponents' on-base percentage.* 2. Abbrev. for *outs on base.*

ooze through the infield *n.* "A soft hit that is just out of reach of any infielder" (Walter K. Putney, *Baseball Stories*, Spring 1952).

OPA Abbrev. for *offensive performance average.*

open base A base not occupied by a runner. Sometimes, with less than two outs and a runner on second base or a runner on third base, or runners on second base and third base, a batter will be walked intentionally to fill first base to improve the chances of a force out or double play.

open classification A level of minor-league baseball one step above Class AAA, established in 1952 exclusively to help the *Pacific Coast League* build itself into a major league. When the National League moved into Los Angeles and San Francisco in 1958, the major-league hopes of the Pacific Coast League died and it returned to Class AAA.

opener The first game in a season, series, or doubleheader. IST USE. 1907. "Two flukes in the opener assayed a pair of tallies for the champs" (Charles Dryden, *Chicago Tribune*, Aug. 17; Peter Morris).

open-face mitt A *first baseman's mitt* in which the thumb is laced to the palm with leather to form a web (O.H. Vogel, *Ins and Outs of Baseball*, 1952; Peter Morris). Compare *snare mitt.*

open game An easy game to umpire. Umpire Tom Gorman (*Three and Two!*, 1979) wrote, "It was one of those games where nothing happened—what we call an open game. Everything was safe and out. No close plays. No conflict."

Opening Day The day on which the regular season begins, or the day on which a team begins its season, or the day on which a team plays its first home game. Cal Ripken Jr. on his Opening Day experiences (quoted in *The Baltimore Sun*, Apr. 2, 2001): "I still get the butterflies. I still get nervous. You always want to get off to a good start. There's a lot of excitement. You look forward to getting past it, but you also look forward to it." Roger Angell (quoted in *The New York Times*, Apr. 3, 1983) noted that, for the fans, the meanings of Opening Day are "psychic and profound": "Fans throng to their home parks in

Opening Day. The teams march onto the field behind a brass band at Griffith Stadium, Washington, D.C., 1934. *Photograph by Joseph Baylor Roberts*

very large numbers for these chilly inaugurals, because Opening Day represents so much to them. It is a ceremony of renewal and welcome—a celebration of the simultaneous return to springtime and baseball time, a brief moment of pure hope, and a noisy, cheerful restoration of the bonds of loyalty and affection that bind the fans to their home club, and vice versa." Syn. *cork popper*. IST USE. 1864. "[The Star Club] voted to have their opening-day for the season on Saturday week next, April 9th" (*Brooklyn Eagle*, Apr. 2; Peter Morris). USAGE NOTE. The term is usually capitalized; e.g., "They call it Opening Day, but The Day is more like it" (Jonathan Yardley, *The Washington Post*, Apr. 8, 1985).

opening inning The first inning.

Opening Night The night on which a team begins its season, or the night on which a team plays its first home game. "The Mariners, celebrating their 20th anniversary, are 12-8 on Opening Nights of seasons in which the team was owned by extortionist businessmen seeking unreasonable concessions from local taxpayers" (Ron C. Judd, *Seattle Times*, March 26, 1997).

open-lotter *hist.* A sandlotter who played on one of a city's vacant lots. "The Brooklyn players kicked like open-lotters" (*The World* [New York], Oct. 19, 1889; Gerald L. Cohen).

open market The availability of free-agent players seeking new connections.

open mouth A sign between the shortstop and second baseman to determine who will cover second base in the event a baserunner attempts a steal. The player signals by putting his glove in front of his face and turning his head toward his teammate. Normally, an open mouth means the shortstop will cover (Paul Dickson, *The Hidden Language of Baseball* 2003). Compare *closed mouth*.

open spaces Those parts of a ballpark usually not defended and where batted balls are difficult to field.

open stance A *batting stance* in which the front or striding foot is farther from the plate than the back foot. The front foot is pointed toward third base for a right-handed batter or toward first base for a left-handed batter. Compare *closed stance*; *square stance*, 1.

open the door To make an error or otherwise grant the opposition an opportunity to score; e.g., walking two batters with two outs would "open the door" for the team at bat.

open the floodgates 1. For a fielder to bring his glove up too quickly, allowing the ball to skid under the glove and between the fielder's legs. 2. For a player to make an error that leads to an opponent's big inning.

"open the window, Aunt Minnie, here she comes!" Pittsburgh Pirates radio sportscaster Rosey Rowswell's trademark salutation for a home run by a Pirate at Forbes Field, a small ballpark situated near a residential area. Players' agent Tom Reich (quoted by David A. Kaplan, *The National Law Journal*, May 4, 1987) noted a variation from 1947: "[Hank] Greenberg or [Ralph] Kiner would connect and Rosey would say, 'Get upstairs, Aunt Minnie, and raise the windows!' And that would be followed by the sound of shattering glass. Rosey would say, 'She never made it.'" Syn. *"raise the window, Aunt Minnie, here she comes!"*; "'open the window, Aunt Minnie, here it comes!'"

open up 1. For a pitcher to turn his shoulder too much toward third base (for a right-hander) or first base (for a left-hander). Catcher Lance Parrish (quoted in Steve Fiffer, *How to Watch Baseball*, 1987, p.32): "If the pitcher is rushing, he's probably opening up his front shoulder too quickly. If you watch closely, you'll see that this leads to dipping the throwing elbow, which leads to keeping the ball up in the strike zone or hanging a lot of breaking balls." See also *fly open*, 1. 2. For a batter to turn his front shoulder (closest to the pitcher) and hips ahead of the arrival of the pitch, causing him to be "out in front" (front shoulder turns to right for a left-handed batter, to left for a right-handed batter), often resulting in hooking the ball foul; to turn the front shoulder out too soon. "[Hideki Matsui has] been opening up his front side, and when you bail like that, it's hard to drive the ball" (anonymous New York Yankees hitting coach, quoted in *Sports Illustrated*, June 2, 2003). See also *fly open*, 2; *pull off the ball*.

oppo Ballplayer's slang for *opposite field*.

opponents' batting average The composite batting average of opposition players when facing a particular pitcher or team. Abbrev. *OAV*; *Oavg*; *OBA*, 2. See also *pitching average*, 2. 1ST USE. 1876. One of the original statistics compiled during the first year of the National League (John Thorn and Pete Palmer, *The Hidden Game of Baseball*, 1985).

opponents' caught stealing The number of times opposition players are caught stealing when facing a particular pitcher or team.

opponents' on-base percentage The composite on-base percentage of opposition players when facing a particular pitcher or team. The best pitchers have percentages less than .300, while the worst pitchers have levels greater than .375. Abbrev. *OOB*, 1.

opponents' slugging percentage The composite slugging percentage of opposition players when facing a particular pitcher or team. Abbrev. *OSP.*

opportunity A team's turn at bat.

opposite field The side of the playing field that is opposite the side of home plate from which a batter bats; e.g., right field is the "opposite field" for a right-handed batter, who bats from the left side of home plate. It is called "opposite" because it is the opposite of the direction in which a batter would naturally pull the ball (a right-handed batter naturally pulls to the left and a left-handed batter naturally pulls to the right). Syn. *off field*; *wrong field*; *oppo*. 1ST USE. 1949. "[Left-handed hitter] Cliff Mapes, who has tremendous power to opposite field, sliced a ball into the left field corner for a double" (*Nevada State Journal*, Oct. 9; Peter Morris).

opposite-field hitter A hitter who often hits to the side of the field opposite to that from which he bats. An opposite-field hitter takes a shortened swing, swings late, or swings at outside pitches. Syn. *late hitter; slice hitter*.

opposite-field home run A home run hit to the side of the field opposite to that from which a batter hits. Because it is more difficult to hit with power to the opposite field, it is enough of an oddity to merit the lead sentence in a report on a game: "Ernest Riles hit an opposite-field home run to cap a four-run,

ninth-inning comeback" (Associated Press dispatch, Apr. 11, 1986).

opposite way Syn. of *other way*.

opposition stolen bases The number of stolen bases recorded against a catcher in a given year. When divided by the number of games played, the resulting average is of some value for evaluating a catcher's or pitcher's performance at controlling the running game, particularly when noting that it is difficult for either to have a good average if the other's is poor. The statistic was described by Bill James in his self-published *Baseball Abstract* (1977) and his first conventionally published *Baseball Abstract* (1982). Abbrev. *OSB*.

OPS Syn. of *on-base plus slugging*.

option 1. *n.* The right of a major-league team to send a player to the minor leagues without putting him on waivers. Under such an arrangement the player is still under contract with the major-league team and can be recalled. See *optional assignment.* 2. *v.* To return a player (or be returned) to the minor leagues on the condition that he may be reclaimed by the major-league club at any time. Compare *outright*, 2. Syn. *option out*. 3. *n.* The right of a player to stay with his present team at the end of his contract or to sign with another. 4. *n.* A claim on the future services of a player. "Jeff Kent and the team [Los Angeles Dodgers] agreed to an $11.5 million, one-year contract extension through 2007. . . . The deal contains a $9 million team option for 2008 with a $500,000 buyout, and the option would become guaranteed if he has 550 plate appearances in 2007" (*The Baltimore Sun*, March 30, 2006). 5. *v.* To sign a new or prospective player to play with a given team at some future date. 6. *n.* See *fielder's option*.

optional assignment Sending a player on the 40-man roster of a major-league club to the minor leagues with the right to recall the player on or before Oct. 1 and without another club claiming that player through the waiver process. Players have three option years and may be sent up and down as many times as the club chooses within those seasons, but will be charged with only one option per season (a fourth option may be granted if the player signed his first major-league contract with less than five years of professional experience). After three years as a professional, a player must be exposed to waivers before he is sent to the minors, or he can be eligible for the Rule 5 draft if he is not protected on the team's 40-man roster. The minimum length of an optional assignment is 10 days (unless the player is assigned to another major-league club or the player's major-league club replaces another player on the disabled list). A player who is sent down for less than 20 days total in one season is not charged with an option. Optional assignments were officially recognized as part of the National Agreement in 1903.

optional sign A sign suggesting to a batter or baserunner that a possibility exists.; e.g., a bunt sign given by the third base coach who feels that the third baseman is playing too deep and the batter has the option of bunting.

option batter *hist.* An early name for the *designated hitter*. The idea had been proposed in the early 1960s and on several other occasions. "Rules Committee Bars Option Batter for PCL" (*Washington Star* headline for an article on a proposal to test the idea in the Pacific Coast League, Apr. 1, 1961). The term became immediately obsolete when the "designated hitter" concept and term were adopted.

option clause A provision in a player's contract that allows the club to invoke the terms of an expired contract for an additional season.

option out Syn. of *option*, 2.

orange The baseball.

orange alert A term used by Oakland A's president Charles O. Finley for *orange baseball*.

orange baseball A fluorescent orange-colored baseball suggested by Oakland A's president Charles O. Finley and used experimentally in an exhibition game between the A's and the Cleveland Indians on March 29, 1973; the effort was intended to make the ball more easily seen at night and on television screens. Pitchers found the orange base-

ball slick and hitters said they could not pick up the spin because the seams could not be seen. An orange baseball had also been suggested by Chicago Cubs president William L. Veeck Sr. in the 1920s when male fans wore white shirts and made a difficult background for the hitters. Compare *yellow baseball*. Syn. *orange alert*.

Orange Book The annual administrative manual and directory for the National Association of Professional Baseball Leagues, published since 1985, and now known as *Information Guide*. See also *Blue Book*; *Red Book*; *Green Book*.

orange crate Syn. of *basket glove*. "Hank Greenberg . . . may have pioneered the modern orange crate" (Joe Williams, *San Francisco News*, June 4, 1953; Peter Tamony).

orb The baseball. "The little white orb jumped off the bat and rocketed across the blue Florida sky" (Laura Vecsey, *The Baltimore Sun*, Feb. 24, 2005).

orchard **1.** The outfield. **2.** Short for *ball orchard*. "The series in the local orchard this week . . . should be productive of some good baseball" (*San Francisco Bulletin*, May 20, 1913; Gerald L. Cohen).

orchardman Syn. of *outfielder*.

order **1.** See *batting order*. 2. See *in order*.

order of position *hist.* "The regular order of positions of a base ball nine is as follows: Catcher, Pitcher, First Base, Second Base, Third Base, Short-stop, and Left, Center, and Right Fields" (Henry Chadwick, *The Game of Base Ball*, 1868, p.43).

order of the bat and ball *hist.* The game of baseball. "Everybody who is a fan and every one who does not belong to but is deeply in sympathy with this high and noble order of the bat and ball will go out to Piedmont park Saturday afternoon to see this heated contest between the 'Hen-Peckeds' and the 'Blessed Singles'" (*Atlanta Constitution*, May 22, 1903).

order of the can **1.** A mock honor accorded to a player who has been released ("canned") from a team. IST USE. 1904. "Catcher [Branch] Rickey . . . is so conscientious about Sabbath observance he would not even carry his mask on Sunday from the train at Cincinnati. Manager [Joe] Kelley thought him too good to be playing ball, so Rickey was decorated with the Order of the Can the next day" (*The Washington Post*, Sept. 7; Peter Morris). **2.** An ejection from a game. "[Cincinnati Reds first base coach Jimmy Wilson] was the first member of that team to draw the 'order of the can' from an umpire in the league this year" (*The Sporting News*, May 18, 1939; Peter Morris).

ordinary effort A criterion used by official scorers in determining whether a fielding play should have been made. The *Official Baseball Rules* for 2007 (Rule 2.00) defines it as follows: "The effort that a fielder of average skill at a position in that league or classification of leagues should exhibit on a play, with due consideration given to the condition of the field and weather conditions. . . . [This] is an objective standard in regard to any particular fielder. In other words, even if a fielder makes his best effort, if that effort falls short of what an average fielder at that position in that league would have made in a situation, the official scorer should charge that fielder with an error." The term is at the heart of many scoring controversies as each official scorer has a different perception of what constitutes "ordinary" effort.

Oregon boot *hist.* The figurative shoe of a slow runner. ETYMOLOGY. "In the penitentiaries of Oregon there is an appliance known as the 'Oregon boot.' It consists of a leaden shoe, which takes the place of the traditional ball and chain in preventing convicts getting up sufficient speed to make a good get-away" (*The Washington Post*, March 30, 1913; Peter Morris).

organization A baseball franchise in its entirety; a major-league ball club and its minor-league affiliates. IST USE. 1866. "Most, if not all, of the leading base ball organizations have their nines consolidated and in working order" (*Brooklyn Eagle*, Aug. 27; Peter Morris).

organizational player A minor-league player who has a job, not because he is a prospect, but because he fills out the roster so that the real prospects have games to play. George

King (*Baseball America*, May 3–16, 1999; Peter Morris) wrote, "After 10 years in the minor leagues, Clay Bellinger wore the dreaded organizational player label. Able to play multiple positions, Bellinger was the guy used to fill holes and was never mentioned as a prospect."

organized baseball Professional baseball, including the major leagues, the minor leagues, and the offices that administer them. The term does not include the independent leagues, and did not include the Negro leagues. Abbrev. *OB*. Also capitalized as "Organized Baseball." IST USE. 1906. "Clay, the strong Louisville outfielder, has refused the club's terms, and may put himself out of organized baseball" (*Chicago Tribune*, Apr. 8; Peter Morris).

oriflamme *hist.* The *pennant*, 2. IST USE. 1915 (*Baseball Magazine*, December, p.78; Edward J. Nichols). ETYMOLOGY. The word, borrowed from the French, has become a standard term for a "banner" or "emblem" in English. It refers to the red banner of St. Denis used as a military flag for the early kings of France. It undoubtedly entered baseball as part of the quest for new synonyms for "pennant."

original A unique ballplayer, often a flaky one; e.g., Boston Red Sox pitcher Bill "Spaceman" Lee was called an "original."

original softball [softball term] Syn. of *fast pitch softball*.

Orioles 1. Nickname for the American League East Division franchise in Baltimore, Md., since 1954. The franchise originated as the Milwaukee Brewers (1901) and became the St. Louis Browns (1902–1953). Also known as *O's* and *Birds*. **2.** Nickname for the American League franchise in Baltimore, Md., in 1901 and 1902. It became the New York entry in the American League in 1903. **3.** Nickname for the National League franchise in Baltimore, Md., from 1892 to 1899. **4.** Nickname for the American Association franchises in Baltimore, Md., from 1883 to 1889 (the franchise was known as the Lord Baltimores in 1892) and from 1890 to 1891. ETYMOLOGY. The black-and-orange Baltimore Oriole (*Icterus galbula*) is the Maryland state bird and has always been linked to the city because of its name. According to legend, the bird was named by Cecilius Calvert, the second Lord Baltimore.

Oriole way A system or philosophy of fundamentals, practice, discipline, and teaching procedures devised by Baltimore Orioles manager Paul Richards in the late 1950s, and later advanced by manager Earl Weaver and coach Cal Ripken Sr., for the proper method of teaching and playing baseball throughout the organization, from the lowest minors to the major leagues. The system included a meticulously planned·spring training and emphasis on every nuance of the game, such as cutoff plays, relays, throwing to bases, rundowns, baserunning, pitcher's fielding drills, signs, and defending against the bunt and stolen base. The Oriole way also included a tradition of good play, sportsmanship, and dignity (such as not throwing at batters), and a sense of order, moderation, tolerance, decency, professionalism, and respect for the game. The Oriole way meant that when minor leaguers became Orioles, they already knew an established method for handling game situations. Joe Strauss (*The Baltimore Sun*, May 31, 1998) noted that the Oriole way is "an organizational Old Testament containing the codified method of character, dress, instruction, and attitude . . . that transcended major and minor leagues." *The Baltimore Sun* editorialized (March 27, 1999) on the Oriole way: "Most Baltimore fans couldn't define the term exactly, but they liked that it implied reverence for the sport and the skills needed to play it well." EXTENDED USE. By analogy, used to describe any club that is perceived as an exemplar of player development. "It's a little early to dub 'The Phillies Way' baseball's model" (Alan Schwarz, *Baseball America*, Aug. 20–Sept. 2, 2001; Peter Morris).

Ortiz shift A strategic defensive alignment to deal with the pull-hitting strength of Boston Red Sox left-handed slugger David Ortiz. The shift was introduced in 2006 by Tampa Bay Devil Rays manager Joe Maddon, who noticed that the majority of Ortiz' balls to the right side were fly balls to the outfield. In Maddon's strategy, the second baseman played deep in the hole between first base and second base but closer to first base, the

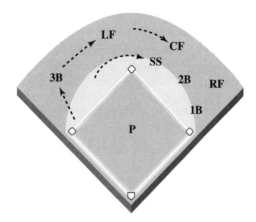

Ortiz shift.

shortstop played on the shallow outfield grass between second base and the second baseman, the left fielder went to left center and the center fielder to right center, the right fielder guarded the foul line, and the third baseman moved to left field. The shift emptied the left side of the infield and created a four- or six-man outfield; it did not go into effect when Ortiz batted with no out and with less than two strikes, and a variation of the shift occurred when there were runners on base. Other teams used a less-severe version, keeping the third baseman in the infield. See Albert Chen, *Sports Illustrated*, June 19, 2006, pp.44–45. Syn. *34 shift*.

OS Abbrev. for *official scorer*.

O's Short for *Orioles*, Its use is underscored when the national anthem is sung at home and the crowd bellows "Ohhhh!" on the line "Oh say does that star-spangled banner yet wave." The nickname took on a new significance at the beginning of the 1988 season when the "O" became a reference to zero as the club opened with a record-setting losing streak of 21 games.

OSB Abbrev. for *opposition stolen bases*.

Oscar A player deserving an award for his feats on the field; esp., a player faking something (putting on a act), such as sustaining an injury, being hit by a pitched ball, catching a ball that was actually trapped, or decoying a baserunner. The term derives from the nickname for the Academy of Motion Picture Arts and Sciences Awards statuette.

OSP Abbrev. for *opponents' slugging percentage.*

O'Sullivan sleeper *hist.* Misnomer for *Sullivan sleeper,* a railroad day coach on which there are no sleeping accommodations. "One phrase obsolete in the majors likely will be in vogue again this coming season. That's the 'O'Sullivan sleeper,' the old-timers slang for a day coach" (Herbert Simons, *Baseball Magazine,* Jan. 1943).

other pitches Pitches other than fastballs, such as a variety of screwballs and an assortment of changeups.

other thing A pitcher's second-best pitch. "Vance's sobriquet 'Dazzy' is said to be derived from his own pet name for his 'other thing' used as a co-weapon with his fast ball" (William G. Brandt, *Baseball Magazine,* Oct. 1932). "I was using off-speed pitches for outs, throwing other things in fastball counts" (Mike Mussina, quoted in *The Baltimore Sun,* March 11, 1998).

other way To the opposite field. Mike Mussina (quoted in *Orioles Gazette,* June 4, 1993): "Hitters that are selective give me a difficult time. . . . They have the ability to wait on a pitch. They can hit the ball deep and the other way with power. They can wait on the curve ball." Syn. *opposite way.*

OTL [softball term] Abbrev. for *Over the Line.*

0-to-3 player A player with less than three years of major-league service and not yet eligible for salary arbitration.

OTS Abbrev. for *on-base times slugging.*

Ouija board *hist.* The umpire's *indicator.* "Check the batteries in your Ouija board" was once a common line from a bench jockey on a bad call. ETYMOLOGY. From the popular Ouija board that employed a pointer to devine the future or communicate with the dead at a seance. The boards were first sold by the Kennard Novelty Co (Baltimore) in 1890. The origin of the name has been traditionally explained as a blend of the French and German words for "yes" ("oui" + "ja").

out **1.** *adj.* Not successful in getting on base or advancing to the next base; said of a batter or baserunner who has been retired by the defense. Perhaps the best definition of "out" appeared in Zander Hollander's *Baseball Lingo* (1967): "What the game is never over until the last man is." Compare *safe,* 1. Syn. *away,* 1; *down,* 1; *gone,* 1; *dead*; *missing.* 1ST USE. 1845. "Three hands out, all out" (Knickerbocker Rules, Rule 15th, Sept. 23). ETYMOLOGY. David Block (personal communication, Oct. 9, 2002) comments, "I believe 'out' descended from the medieval bat-and-ball game 'hand-in and hand-out,' which was similar to the game 'cat and dog,' which, in turn, was the predecessor of two-old-cat." **2.** *n.* A *putout.* **3.** *n.* One of the three required retirements that define the length of the half inning when the offensive team is at bat. **4.** *adv.* Away from the batter, such as a pitch thrown outside the strike zone; e.g., "Smith's pitch was down and out." Compare *in,* 2. **5.** *adv.* Not participating in a game; e.g., "Jones is out because of an injury." Compare *in,* 5. **6.** *adj.* Short for *out of play,* 2. **7.** *n./hist.* The team in the field. "Dowagiac won the toss and chose the outs" (*Detroit Advertiser and Tribune,* Sept. 15, 1866; Peter Morris).

outage Short for *power outage.* "The current outage at the plate didn't shake [Arizona Diamondbacks manager Bob] Brenly's faith in [Matt] Williams, one of the game's most feared sluggers" (*The Baltimore Sun,* Nov. 3, 2001).

out ball *hist.* Syn. of *out pitch,* 1. "[Tony Mullane] has an out ball which seems to ride the air, the batter usually striking under it" (*Cincinnati Commercial-Gazette,* Jan. 19, 1888).

out by a mile **1.** Said of a tag play in which the runner is clearly out. **2.** Exaggerated insistence that a player was out on a close call. When an umpire deems a runner safe at first on a close play, those who disagree are, by baseball tradition, required to say that he was "out by a mile." 1ST USE. 1926. "When he finally made up his mind and hastened to third, he was out by a mile as he slid in on his chest and got his uniform all dirty" (*The New York Times,* Oct. 3; Barry Popik).

outcurve *hist.* Syn. of *outshoot.* Rob Neyer (in Bill James and Rob Neyer, *The Neyer/ James Guide to Pitchers,* 2004, p.16): "Basically, a fancy name for a curveball that's not thrown overhand. That is, if a right-handed pitcher throws a curveball with a three-quarters delivery to a right-handed batter, the ball will curve away—out—from the batter." Also spelled "out curve." See also *outdrop*. Compare *in-curve*, 1. IST USE. 1865 (Chadwick Scrapbooks; Edward J. Nichols).

outdrop *hist.* A 19th-century term for an *out-curve* that drops down as it approaches the batter. "To throw this very easy curve it is only necessary to turn the hand a little over to the left [for a right-handed pitcher] so that the palm and first two fingers are turned half upward and to the left as the ball is released" (Edward J. Prindle, *Baseball, and How To Play It*, 1896, 1902, 1906). Also spelled "out-drop"; "out drop." Compare *indrop*. IST USE. 1893 (*Harper's Weekly*, July 8; Edward J. Nichols).

outduel To pitch a better game than the pitcher(s) on the opposing team; to *outpitch*. The term is usually applied to close games. "[Sid] Fernandez Outduels Dodgers" (*The Washington Post* headline, May 30, 1986).

outer field *hist.* An early synonym for "out-field." IST USE. 1861. "On the part of the Newark club we noticed that . . . the players in the outer field were active and efficient" (*Brooklyn Eagle*, Aug. 23; Peter Morris).

outerfielder *hist.* An early synonym for "out-fielder." IST USE. 1864. "A strict adherence to these new rules must perforce result in . . . the transfer of the interest of a match from the pitchers to the basemen and outerfield-ers" (*New York Clipper*, May 7; Peter Morris). USAGE NOTE. Morris comments: "In early baseball, the distinction between infielders and outfielders was regarded differently. The first, second, and third base-men were usually collectively described as the 'basemen,' while the shortstop (or short fielder) and outfielders were referred to collectively as 'fielders.' By the 1880s, short-stops had begun to assume more of the responsibilities for covering second base. The terms 'infielder' and 'outfielder' came into use to reflect the fact that it no longer made sense to classify the shortstop with the outfielders. One vague remnant of this early practice is the use of the number '5' to designate the third baseman and the number '6'

to designate the shortstop, when the reverse seems more logical to those who are only familiar with the modern positioning of these players."

outer garden *hist.* The outfield. Compare *inner garden*. Syn. *garden*, 1. IST USE. 1896. "[Fred] Tenney was on duty in the outer garden" (*The Boston Globe*, July 2; Peter Morris).

outer gardener *hist.* An outfielder. IST USE. 1898. "Walter Wilmot, the former outer gardener of Uncle Anson's Giants, was in Washington last week" (*The Washington Post*, Sept. 25).

outer patrol *hist.* One or more outfielders. "Harry (Young Dixie) Walker is up for another Cardinal trial, leaving Tex Marshall and Augie Bergamo from last season's outer patrol" (*The Sporting News*, Feb. 1942).

outer works *hist.* 1. The outfield. Compare *inner works*, 1. IST USE. 1911. "W.L. Schweitzer . . . was used in the outer works, being played in right, left and center at times" (Alfred H. Spink, *The National Game*, 2nd. ed., p.277). 2. The outfielders as a working unit. Compare *inner works*, 2. IST USE. 1908. "Outer works, another term for the outfield-ers" (John B. Foster, in *Collier's New Dictionary of the English Language*).

outfield 1. The area of the playing field most distant from home plate; specif., the playing area beyond the infield perimeter or diamond and within the foul lines. Walls or grandstand fences usually set the outside boundaries of the outfield. There is no strictly defined line dividing the infield from the outfield. For any major-league ballpark built after June 1, 1958, the right-field wall and the left-field wall must be at least 325 feet from home plate and the center-field wall must be at least 400 feet from home plate (although some newer parks have received exemptions due to economic or spatial reasons). Abbrev. *OF*, 1. IST USE. 1865 (*New York Herald*, July 11; Edward J. Nichols). ETYMOLOGY. "Outfield" was a Scottish farming term for the land further from the farmhouse or homestead that was cropped but not tilled or fertilized, or was used for pasture, usually on higher ground and often consisting of moorland. EXTENDED USE. In cricket, the part of the field furthest from the wicket (*OED*, 1895). **2.** The defensive positions comprising left field, center field, and right field, taken collectively. **3.** The outfielders (left fielder, center fielder, and right fielder), considered as a group. IST USE. 1888 (*Harper's Weekly*, July 28; Edward J. Nichols).

outfielder A defensive player positioned in the outfield; specif., the left fielder, the center fielder, or the right fielder. Abbrev. *OF*, 2. Syn. *gardener*, 1; *orchardman*. IST USE. 1864. "Their pitcher and basemen being good men for the positions, as are two of their outfielders and short stop" (*New York Clipper*, Aug. 13; Peter Morris).

outfielder's glove A glove that is broken in with its pocket running diagonally from webbing to heel; it is usually larger and less flexible than an *infielder's glove* (Daniel Okrent, *Nine Innings*, 1985, p.48).

outfield in Said of an outfield playing closer to home when the potential winning run is on third base with less than two outs.

outfielding Outfield defensive play. "Their out-fielding especially being tip-top" (*New York Clipper*, July 30, 1864; Peter Morris). IST USE. 1862 (*New York Sunday Mercury*; Edward J. Nichols)

outfield throw A ball thrown to an infielder or catcher by an outfielder in an attempt to throw out a runner. Dan Sperling (*A Spectator's Guide to Baseball*, 1983) wrote, "Among baseball's most thrilling plays and impressive sights is an outfielder's throw to a teammate who tags out a runner sliding into base. . . . Such a play is baseball theater at its best, as the ball and the runner converge on the base at nearly the same dusty instant, culminating in the umpire's dramatic one-armed gesture signifying 'Out!'"

outfit A baseball team. IST USE. 1905 (*The Sporting Life*, Sept. 2, p.3; Edward J. Nichols).

outhit To produce more hits than the opposition.

out in front Descriptive of a batter who swings too early, such as a pull hitter fooled by a changeup or curveball when he was expecting a fastball. "[Harold Baines'] bat has slowed down so much he compensates

by trying to get out in front, and ends up rolling his hands over and grounding out weakly to the right side" (*ESPN The Magazine*, June 25, 2001). IST USE. 1928. "Most batters who have trouble with slow ball pitching are 'pull' hitters. That is, they are meeting the ball 'out front'" (George Herman Ruth, *Babe Ruth's Own Book of Baseball*, p.164; Peter Morris).

outing **1.** A given appearance by a player in a game. The term tends to be applied more often to pitchers rather than players who are in the lineup day after day: "If his last two outings are any indication, [pitcher] Dave Steib is back" (Mike Payne, *St. Petersburg Times*, March 15, 1988). An outing can be long or short: "[Dwight] Gooden pitched two-plus innings—the shortest outing of his career" (*Tampa Tribune*, July 2, 1989). **2.** A given appearance of a team on the field; e.g., "The White Sox and the Red Sox had an outing at Comiskey Field."

out in left field Odd; out of it; a bit off; eccentric. The term was used originally to indicate something that occurred in left field; e.g., "Willard's three-bagger out in left field" (*The Boston Daily Globe*, June 9, 1887).

ETYMOLOGY. How left field got to be the metaphoric location for oddness has been the subject of no end of speculation. Several have suggested that it comes from the remoteness of left field; but right field is just as remote and, at the lower levels of the game at least, more likely to be populated by an odd player. As Ron Fimrite (*San Francisco Chronicle*, Apr. 28, 1969; Peter Tamony) wrote in an essay on right field: "There was but one position to which the clods, the kids with glasses, the little guys, the sissies, the ones that got good grades, the kids who played with girls, were exiled. That would be right field, the Siberia of my youth. . . . Right field was the back of the bus, the slow-learners class, the children's department, a sideshow. Anyone directed to play right field would have given anything to 'be out in left field.'"

One major theory postulates that the phrase was an insult heaped on kids who were stupid enough to buy left-field seats in Yankee Stadium, which for many years would have put them far away from a right fielder named

Babe Ruth. This theory was suggested by David Shulman in a letter quoted by William Safire (*I Stand Corrected*, 1984): "When I was in my teens, living in the Bronx, we kids were always most anxious to get our seats in the right field where we would be closest to Babe Ruth, so I suppose anybody in the left field was far out."

A second major theory suggests that the phrase was a reference to the mental hospital, the Neuropsychiatric Institute, in back of left field in the old West Side Park in Chicago. The most specific description of this theory appears in a letter from physician Gerald M. Eisenberg of Chicago, also quoted in Safire's *I Stand Corrected* (1984): "In Chicago, when someone said that one was 'out in left field,' the implication was that one was behaving like the occupants of the Neuropsychiatric Institute, which was literally out in left field." This has been corroborated by researcher Richard L. Miller of Cincinnati, who has been doing research on the Chicago ballparks.

Other theories, probably discounted, include: 1) left field is "deeper" than right field because the bench for most home teams was generally along the first base line—the preferred location for home team fans—and therefore coming in from left field was coming in from a "far out" region; 2) right field was often the sun field, hence more difficult to play, thus good-hitting but poor-fielding players were put in left field, where one could expect almost anything to happen when the ball was hit there; 3) due to a preponderance of right-handed pull hitters, balls were hit harder to left field, and the left fielder played farther back than the other outfielders; 4) due to a preponderance of right-handed pitchers, those with big sidearm deliveries made it look to right-handed batters as though the ball had come "out of left field"; and 5) the term has roots in quasi-political labels, with "right" suggesting correctness and dexterity and "left" connoting minority, sinisterness, radicalism, screwball pitchers, and being "left behind" (pun intended).

It should also be noted that the phrase "way out in left field without a glove" was used in the 1930s. According to a United Press International dispatch (Apr. 18, 1937; Peter Tamony), which carried George Kirksey's byline, the phrase was not meant to describe a player who is out of it: "Lefty Gomez is 'way out in left field without a glove' [because] . . . he is as proficient at whipping over a smart crack as a sizzling strike."

EXTENDED USE. A phrase applied broadly to describe odd, eccentric, unexpected, or exceptionally misguided or mistaken people and ideas in all walks of life. Three examples from *The New York Times* (supplied by Barry Popik): "What I mean is simply that our subcommittee has no intention of getting caught out in left field when the next batter may swing from the other side of the plate" (March 15, 1953); "The Pennsylvania delegation's seats in the Los Angeles Coliseum were described as 'stuck far out in left field'" (Nov. 9, 1960); and "The nation's new chief Communist-hunter was way out in left field today" (May 10, 1954). "It's worth noting that ['Out in Left Field'] used to be the title of the sports column in the old Communist newspaper [*Daily World*]" (E.J. Dionne Jr., *The Washington Post*, Oct. 19, 1997). See also *left field* (extended use, 1). Syn. *out of left field*. IST USE. 1936. "This naturally leaves us kibitzers out in left field" (in regard to a bridge hand) (*The Washington Post*, June 11).

out in order Said of a situation in which the first three batters coming to the plate in an inning are retired without one of them reaching first base. IST USE. 1877. "Eggler, Shezline [*sic*] and Reach went out in order" (*The Boston Globe*, May 29; Peter Morris).

outlaw *hist.* A player banned from organized baseball. Hugh S. Fullerton (*American Magazine*, June 1912) showed how the term was once used widely: "The club, league or player who offends against baseball law is punished by being 'outlawed' or blacklisted. . . . There are several hundred players on the blacklist at present who cannot play in any clubs belonging to the National Agreement until reinstated by the [National] Commission." IST USE. 1906 (*The Sporting Life*, Feb. 10; Edward J. Nichols).

outlaw curve An extremely effective curveball, so good it should be "outlawed." "One National League scouting director . . . said he saw Brownlie touching 96–97 mph with an outlaw curve early in the season" (*Baseball America*, Feb. 3–16, 2003; Steve Milman).

outlaw league A league that plays outside the rules and control of organized baseball, and does not respect the contracts of those clubs and leagues within organized baseball; e.g., the Players' League in 1890, the Pacific Coast League in 1903, the Federal League in 1914–1915, and the Carolina League in 1936–1938. The term is generally used to designate a minor league that did not elect to take the protection offered by the National Agreement, a distinction that was particularly important in the 1890s and first decade of the 20th century. Players who performed in outlaw leagues were often serving out suspensions from organized baseball, or had jumped their organized baseball contracts, or were running from the law (e.g., paternity suits). Compare *independent league*. IST USE. 1905. "The league of which Salt Lake City is a member is an 'outlaw' organization, but only because it has been refused protection by the national commission" (*Chicago Tribune*, Apr. 2; Peter Morris).

out looking Retired on a called third strike. Compare *out swinging*.

out man A weak hitter who is a good bet to make an out; an easy out. Pitchers are often out men.

out of here Said of a home run hit out of the ballpark. Syn. "outta here."

out of his hip pocket Said of the apparent source of the ball as the pitcher goes into his windup, turns his back to the batter, and delivers the ball.

out of left field EXTENDED USE. Syn. of *out in left field* (extended use). Dallas Cowboys quarterback, commenting on Washington Redskins associate head coach Gregg Williams' defense (quoted in *The Baltimore Sun*, Sept. 15, 2006): "The thing that makes it hard is that they play a lot of [man-to-man] coverage, and then all of a sudden here comes some exotic ... double-corner blitz. At times he's trying to lull you to sleep and then all of a sudden here comes this fastball out of left field."

out of line Outside the baselines.

out of options Said of a player who has been

on the 40-man roster of a major-league club during at least three different seasons and in his fourth professional season or later must clear irrevocable waivers before being sent to the minor leagues.

out of order See *batting out of order*.

out of play **1.** Regarding that period when the game is not being played as opposed to a period when plays can begin or continue. Compare *in play*, 1. **2.** Describing a ball that is dead, when runners cannot advance or be put out and runs cannot score. Compare *in play*, 2. Syn. *out*, 6.

out of reach Practically unwinnable, such as a game in which the score is 9–0 in the eighth inning.

out of the ballpark Said of a ball that is hit hard enough to leave the ballpark. See also *hit it out*. Syn. *out of the park*. USAGE NOTE. A possible precursor: "In response to cries from the bleachers 'to send her out of the lot' the great short stop [John Montgomery Ward] hit the ball foul over the grand stand and a new one was brought into play" (*Brooklyn Eagle*, Sept. 3, 1890; Peter Morris). EXTENDED USE. Something that is beyond negotiable limits; something that is "totally out of play" (William Safire, *I Stand Corrected*, 1984). "Treasury Secretary Dillon was nearly hooted out of the ball park for suggesting that a stock that sells for 15 times its yearly earnings might be reasonably priced" (*San Francisco Chronicle*, June 19, 1962). Compare *in the ballpark*.

out of the chute From the beginning; e.g., teams want to be winning right "out of the chute" at the start of the season or of a series. Syn. *out of the gate*.

out of the gate Syn. of *out of the chute*.

out of the inning Said of a pitcher who has survived a jam, often thanks to a double play that ends the inning.

out of the park Syn. of *out of the ballpark*. EXTENDED USE. Something beyond negotiable limits. "When you dangle one of these [witty one-liners] in front of an actor with Dame Judi's [Dench] formidable technique, the question is not whether she'll knock it out of the park, but how far" (*Newsweek*, Dec. 19, 2005).

out of turn See *batting out of order.*

out of uniform **1.** Said of a player who is not on the roster because of an injury or other reason. **2.** Said of a player who is not suited up at game time; e.g., being "out of uniform" can result in a suspension or fine at the manager's discretion.

outpitch *v.* To pitch a better game than the opposing pitcher. "He [Erik Bedard] had his A game today and he outpitched me. I tried to limit the damage as much as possible" (Boston Red Sox pitcher Tim Wakefield, quoted in *The Baltimore Sun*, May 18, 2006). Syn. *outduel.*

out pitch *n.* **1.** The pitch that pitchers depend on to get an out; a pitcher's best or special pitch used in a tight spot when an out is required. "Good catchers think in multi-pitch sequences, using different pitches thrown at varying speeds to set up a hitter for a specific pitch, the 'out' pitch" (Ron Luciano, *The Umpire Strikes Back*, 1982, p.161). See also *money pitch*, 1. Syn. *out ball.* **2.** A pitch that results in a strikeout.

outplay To perform better than one's opponent. IST USE. 1876. "The Clippers out-played the Reds at every point. They out-batted them, out-fielded them, out-generaled them in running bases, out-played them behind the bat and, in fact, in every point" (*Winona* [Minn.] *Republican*, Aug. 25; Peter Morris).

outpost The outfield. IST USE. 1902 (*The Sporting Life*, July 5, p.13; Edward J. Nichols).

outright **1.** *adj.* Said of a transaction between two teams in which a player is obtained for cash alone rather than in a trade or a trade plus cash. **2.** *v.* To send a player to the minors after severing all his contractual ties with the major-league team, or to release a player to another club without any conditions; e.g., "Mets outright struggling [Hideo] Nomo to minors" (*The Baltimore Sun* headline, March 25, 1999) and "[The Pittsburgh Pirates] outrighted catcher Dann Bilardello to their Class AAA Buffalo farm club" (*Tampa Tribune*, July 5, 1989). Compare *option*, 2.

outright waivers Syn. of *irrevocable waivers.*

outshoot *hist.* A 19th-century term for a pitch that breaks, or otherwise has a pronounced movement, away from the batter. "[Charlie Ferguson has] terrific speed and one of the widest outshoots of any pitcher on the diamond" (*Cincinnati Commercial-Gazette*, Jan. 19, 1888). See also *shoot*, 1. Compare *inshoot.* Syn. *outcurve.* IST USE. 1881 (*New York Herald*, July 29; Edward J. Nichols)

outside Said of a pitch that is delivered away from the batter on the far side of or beyond the strike zone. One of the reasons that pitchers like it when batters stand away from the plate is that they can throw an outside pitch for a strike that the batter cannot reach. Compare *inside.* IST USE. 1908 (*Spalding's Official Base Ball Guide*, p.85; Edward J. Nichols).

outside corner The side of home plate that is away from the batter. Compare *inside corner.* IST USE. 1901 (Burt L. Standish, *Frank Merriwell's Marvel*, p.206; Edward J. Nichols).

outside pivot A *pivot* in which the shortstop brushes second base on the outfield side before throwing to first base in the attempt to turn a double play. Compare *inside pivot.*

outside signal A catcher's sign given from outside his thigh, such as touching his mask or shin guard or picking up dirt. Compare *inside signal.*

outslug To get more runs than the opposition in a high-scoring game.

outs on base The number of outs during a game for which plays on baserunners are responsible, most notably on runners caught stealing or retired as part of a double play. Force outs and fielder's choices are not considered outs on base. Of the 27 outs in a nine-inning game, approximately one-and-a-half will be made on base. Abbrev. *OOB*, 2.

outs per game *hist.* A statistical measure of player performance recorded by pioneer baseball writer Henry Chadwick beginning in 1865, expressed in *average and over* format, in which outs recorded was divided by games played (see John Thorn and Pete Palmer, *The Hidden Game of Baseball*, 1985). See also *putout average.*

outstation *hist.* A position in the outfield (Maurice H. Weseen, *A Dictionary of American Slang*, 1934).

out swinging Retired on a swing and a miss for the third strike. Compare *out looking.*

oval The baseball. IST USE. 1905 (*The Sporting Life*, Sept. 9, p.1; Edward J. Nichols).

over Said of a pitch that is in the strike zone; e.g., "The pitch was over the plate" or "Get the pitch over!"

overall future performance Syn. of *overall future potential*.

overall future potential The final grade that a scout assigns to any prospect being evaluated, representing the composite of the grades on the *scouting scale* of 20 (poor) to 80 (excellent). A grade of 50 is major-league average; players drafted in the first round usually have grades of 60 to 65. Abbrev. *OFP*. Syn. *overall future performance*.

overall player runs The linear weights measure of a position player's total performance. It is the sum of the player's batting runs, base-stealing runs, and fielding runs, along with a positional adjustment. The term was introduced by Pete Palmer (*Sport*, Apr. 1984) and discussed by John Thorn and others (*The Hidden Game of Baseball*, rev. ed., 1985, p.239). Syn. *ultimate baseball statistic*.

overdog A team that goes from the role of underdog to powerhouse; e.g., the 1969 New York Mets. "Isn't there a certain cachet in tilting at windmills, trying on glass slippers, cheering for lovable losers? . . . the Mets will be dragging their fans into the World Series this Saturday as overdogs" (*The New York Times*, Oct. 7, 1969).

overdue Said of a player in a slump. George F. Will wrote an essay (March 20, 1975, reprinted in his 1998 book *Bunts*, pp.25–28) noting that the term "overdue" is often a signal that a player is just plain not very good, but is relative to the ability of the player: "Stan Musial batting .249 was overdue for a hot streak. [Roy] Smalley batting .249 was doing his best."

overhand Said of a pitch, throw, or delivery in which the hand is raised straight above the shoulder. As *underhand* and *sidearm* pitches are uncommon, most baseball pitches are overhand pitches. Overhand pitching was legalized in the National League for the 1884 season. IST USE. 1884. "The great mistake made by the League in doing away entirely with all restrictions in regard to the delivery of the ball by the pitcher, thus allowing him to throw overhand, underhand, round-arm, or even jerk the ball" (*St. Louis Post-Dispatch*, Jan. 2; Peter Morris).

overhand curve A curveball thrown with an overhand delivery that breaks straight down, rather than horizontally. Rob Neyer (in Bill James and Rob Neyer, *The Neyer/James Guide to Pitchers*, 2004, pp.16–17) stated, "Not to make a value judgment or anything, but the overhand curveball is the best curveball. . . . Generally, it takes great arm strength to throw a great overhand curveball and it's not an easy pitch to control . . . so not many pitchers have great ones, or even good ones." Compare *roundhouse curve*. Syn. *overhand drop*; *drop curve*; *drop ball*, 1; *downer*; *12-to-6 curve*. USAGE NOTE. The term "overhand drop" as well as the terms "drop ball" and "drop curve" were originally used for this pitch. In the late 1940s, the term "overhand curve" became popular, only to be replaced in the late 1990s by the visually vivid term "12-to-6 curve."

overhand drop *hist.* Syn. of *overhand curve*.

overmanage For a manager to hamper his team by employing more strategy than is called for or by using excessive teaching methods. The term is commonly used when a team gets into trouble after its manager has called on too many relief pitchers. IST USE. 1914. "[Philadlephia first baseman Harry] Davis went to Cleveland as a manager and was a rank failure. The explanation of this is that he endeavored to apply the [Connie] Mack methods to a lot of tough old birds . . . who had no notion of treating Davis like a father and who resented the constant bossing. . . . Davis attempted to make old-timers like [Nap] Lajoie and the rest accept the same doctrine instanter. Davis over-managed and the club was all torn up into factions" (Ty Cobb, *Busting 'Em and Other Big League Stories*; Peter Morris).

over or under Baseball betting based on the total number of runs scored in a given game. See also *money line*; *runs line*. Syn. *over/under*.

over-pitch *hist.* A pitched ball thrown past the catcher and formerly entered into the record of a game as such. Henry Chadwick

(*The Game of Base Ball*, 1868, pp.42–43) wrote, "The pitcher commits this error whenever he pitches a ball over the heads of the batsman and catcher. It is a mark of wild pitching resulting from too great an effort to pitch swiftly." IST USE. 1862 (*New York Sunday Mercury*, July 13; Edward J. Nichols).

overplay To use players at positions where they normally would not play. The practice occurs when there are roster shortages.

overpower To swing or pitch with excessive force.

overrun 1. For a runner to touch a base but then run or slide beyond it such that he may be tagged out. The batter-runner is allowed to overrun first base "if he returns immediately to the base" (*Official Baseball Rules*, Rule 7.08[c]), but if he breaks toward second base, he is liable to be tagged out. IST USE. 1870. "[William] Craver's eagerness led him to overrun the base, and [Everett] Mills, having recovered the ball, secured him after all" (*Chicago Tribune*, July 24; Peter Morris). 2. To misjudge the course of a batted ball that falls safely behind an onrushing fielder. "Another [run] scored when Kirk Gibson over-ran the ball for an error" (*Tampa Tribune*, July 10, 1989). 3. For an outfielder to chase a ball that has been batted into the corner or that is bouncing off the wall.

overshift A defensive adjustment that is so extreme that it creates open spaces, which batters can exploit. "[Ernie] Whitt took advantage of an overshift by Minnesota, laying down a one-out bunt single to an almost totally vacant left side of the infield" (*Tampa Tribune-Times*, Sept. 3, 1989). IST USE. 1947. "The Nationals . . . didn't bother to use the famed 'overshift defense' against [Ted] Williams in the first inning [of the All-Star Game]" (John Drebinger, *The New York Times*, July 9; Peter Morris).

overslide For a runner to slide into a base with such momentum that he slides past or loses contact with the base and is liable to be tagged out. IST USE. 1908 (*Brooklyn Daily Eagle*, May 29; Edward J. Nichols).

overstride To take too large a step toward the pitcher when swinging the bat; to lunge at the ball.

overswing 1. For a batter not to be selective of the pitches offered; to swing at pitches that normally cannot be hit on the outside chance one might get a hit; to be too aggressive at the plate. 2. To swing in the belief that the pitcher is throwing harder than he really is.

over the fence Said of a ball that is hit out of the ballpark for a home run. "The 'Phillies' made three runs in the sixth . . . including over-the-fence drives by [George] Wood and [Sam] Thompson" (*Philadelphia Record*, July 25, 1889). Syn. *over the garden wall*. IST USE. 1861 (*New York Sunday Mercury*, Aug. 10; Edward J. Nichols).

over-the-fence home run rule [softball term] One of a series of rules created to limit the number of home runs at various levels of slow pitch softball. A ball hit over the fence in a game by a team in excess of the prescribed limit is ruled an out. When the batter is ruled out because of the rule, the ball is dead and no runners can score.

over the garden wall Syn. of *over the fence* (*Famous Sluggers and Their Records of 1932*, 1933).

over-the-line 1. A playground variant of baseball played in Arizona with two teams of three, four, or five players on a side. According to James Vail (personal communication, Dec. 10, 2005), "There was some marker—a fence, but often just a tree, or even a mitt or baseball cap placed in the outfield—designating that any ball hit beyond it on the fly (i.e., 'over the line') was a home run. Any grounder caught by the pitcher or infielder was an out, as was any fly caught by the outfielder and any ball hit to the right side of second base. Grounders that went through

Over the Line. The pitch. San Diego tournament. *Photograph by Russell Mott*

the infield were singles. Safe hits to the out-field that were fielded by the outfielder after the first bounce were singles. Multiple-bounce drives to the outfielder were doubles. Balls that got past the outfielder without going over the line on a fly were triples. The batters did not run bases; instead, 'baserun-ners' advanced the same number of bases that the current batter accrued in his at-bat." **2.** A playground variant of baseball played in northeastern United States with as few as four players. According to Merritt Clifton (personal communication, Dec. 10, 2005), "The pitcher is on the batting team, and play-ers alternate between pitching and batting. The fielders play left and left-center against a right-handed hitter. Against a lefty, every-one moves over, to right and right-center. The 'line' is either the edge of the skinned infield or a line drawn from base to base. Anything that doesn't clear the line on the fly is out. Anything that clears the line but drops in front of the fielders is a single. Any-thing that bounces or rolls between them is a double. Anything that goes past them on the fly is a home run. There are no triples. Run-ners advance the same number of bases as the hit. [With more players,] the game moves to full-field."

Over the Line [softball term] A variation of softball created on the beaches of San Diego in 1954 by a group killing time waiting for a volleyball court. It is a beach game, but is also played on traditional softball fields. Each team is composed of three players and each team pitches to its own batters. Kneeling next to the plate, the pitcher gently tosses a heavy

Over the Line. The field of play. San Diego tourna-ment. *Photograph by Russell Mott*

foam ball into the air for the batter to swing at and drive the ball uncaught "over the line," which is usually 55 feet away and 60 feet long. Any ball hit short of the line is consid-ered a foul ball. Each hit (other than a home run) advances the batter and each ghost run-ner one base. Games are four innings and use regulation softball bats. Annual tournaments are still played in San Diego. Over the Line is "more than beer, babes and bats on the beach" (Old Mission Beach Athletic Club Web site [ombac.org]). Abbrev. *OTL*.

over the plate Said of a pitch in, under, or over the strike zone. EXTENDED USE. Said of something that is obvious.

over the roof Said of a home run that is hit over the top of the stands, a feat that is hardly possible in the modern ballparks.

over the top Describing an overhand pitching delivery or throwing motion. "When [Armando] Benitez throws over the top, his control is bet-ter, his slider is sharper and his mechanics are less of a health hazard" (*The Baltimore Sun*, May 5, 1995). "A backhand grab [at third base] necessitated an over-the-top throw" (*The Balti-more Sun*, March 24, 2000).

overthrow 1. *n.* A thrown ball that is too high or too wide of its intended target and that fre-quently lands out of play. In instances when the ball is thrown out of play, each baserun-ner (at the time of the throw) is given the base he was heading toward plus one additional base. IST USE. 1862 (*New York Sunday Mer-cury*, July 13; Edward J. Nichols). **2.** *v.* To throw a ball that is too high or wide or cannot be fielded by the intended receiver. "People who all along have insisted that [Sam] Thompson could not throw far were surprised to see him overthrow third base from deep right field" (*Philadelphia Record*, Aug. 28, 1889). IST USE. 1868. "Better hold a ball than over-throw it to a base" (Henry Chadwick, *The Game of Base Ball*, p.42). **3.** *v.* For a pitcher to throw too hard or to try to compen-sate; e.g., "the classic instance of a pitcher 'overthrowing,' trying to make too good a pitch" (Keith Hernandez, *Pure Baseball*, 1994, p.43). Andy Pettitte (quoted in *The Baltimore Sun*, Oct. 26, 1999): "Sometimes the juices get flowing a little bit too much.

That's one thing I can't let happen because my ball gets up in the zone a little bit when I try to overthrow."

overtime Any inning after the ninth. The term is borrowed from those sports whose finale is determined by a clock or timer and in which extra periods are played in the event of a tie at the end of the final period. IST USE. 1913. "The two teams would most likely have gone into an overtime contest with one run each" (Stanley T. Milliken, *The Washington Post*, Aug. 26; Peter Morris).

over/under Syn. of *over or under.*

OWAR Abbrev. for *offensive wins above replacement.*

own 1. For a batter to hit successfully against a given pitcher over a period of time; e.g., Sam McDowell said Frank Howard "owned" him, and Eric Milton admitted that Jason Giambi "pretty much owns me" (*The Baltimore Sun*, Sept. 14, 2000). Tim McCarver (*Oh, Baby I Love It!*, 1987) noted that Ty Cobb "owned" pitcher Walter Johnson: Cobb knew that Johnson would not use his blazing fastball to intimidate the batter, so Cobb would crowd the plate knowing that he would get a good pitch. **2.** For a pitcher to dominate a batter by getting him out on a regular basis. **3.** For a pitcher to throw a well-placed fastball to let the batter know that he should not get too comfortable at the plate. "Pedro Martinez has been known to throw his share

directly at the enemy, sending the message: 'I own that plate'" (Dan Connolly, *The Baltimore Sun*, Apr. 13, 2006).

owner One who possesses the title or majority shares of, or has some other form of control over, a professional baseball team.

OWP Abbrev. for *offensive winning percentage.*

Ozarkism An aphoristic line attributed to Philadelphia Phillies manager Danny Ozark (1973–1979), who had a particular ability to fracture the English language; e.g., "Even Napoleon had his Watergate" (quoted by Dick Young, *The Sporting News*, June 17, 1978), "I have always had a wonderful repertoire with my players," and "It is beyond my apprehension."

ozone *hist.* **1.** *v.* To strike out. "The mighty Corbett ozoned" (*Stanwood* [Wash.] *Tidings*, Sept. 1, 1905; David M. Larson). IST USE. 1905. "[Joe] Tinker led off for the Cubs and ozoned" (*Kanas City Journal*, reprinted in *The Washington Post*, May 3). **2.** *n.* The atmosphere. The term was used in the phrase *dent the ozone* and in a nickname for Smoky Joe Wood "for the air cleaved by the hapless batters who faced him" (Roger Angell, *Late Innings*, 1982, p.375; Charles D. Poe).

Ozzie Flip A gymnastic move by St. Louis Cardinals shortstop Ozzie Smith, who would run onto the infield and do a cartwheel into a back flip as he reached his position.

P

P 1. Abbrev. for *pitcher*, 1. **2.** Abbrev. for *pitcher*, 3.

PA Abbrev. for *plate appearance*.

pace 1. *n.* An illusion of speed in the pitching delivery, as in pitching a slow ball with the same arm movement as a faster pitch. See also *change of pace*. IST USE. 1865 (*New York Herald*, June 29; Edward J. Nichols). **2.** *n.* The rate of speed at which a pitcher works or a game progresses. ETYMOLOGY. The term is borrowed from horse racing. **3.** *v.* To lead; to perform in a manner that other players want to emulate; e.g., "Smith paced the Yankees to a 6–4 win." **4.** *v.* To field a ball without taking an unnecessary step (H.G. Salsinger, *Baseball Digest*, Aug. 1945).

pacer 1. A pitcher who works quickly. "The pacer [James] Whitney . . . was too costly in wearing out catchers last season. His great pace is his only point. He knows nothing of strategic play" (*Brooklyn Eagle*, Dec. 6, 1885; Peter Morris). **2.** A fast pitch. "The swift 'pacers' James White sent them being the main cause of their signal defeat" (*New York Clipper*, Aug. 27, 1870; Peter Morris).

pacesetter 1. The leading team in a league or division. **2.** The league or division leader in an individual batting or pitching category.

Pacific Coast League A Class AAA minor league (1946–1951 and since 1958) with teams in the western parts of the United States and Canada. Established in 1903 as an outgrowth of the California League that began operations in 1898, it was formerly a Class A (1904–1907) and Class AA (1908–1945) minor league. The League thrived in the early part of the 20th century, developing an increasingly special status, distinct from

the other Class AAA leagues, because of its geographic isolation and the inclusion of the best California markets. From 1952 to 1957 it was granted *open classification*, a step above Class AAA, with the idea that it would become a major league; but the notion and classification ended when the Brooklyn Dodgers and the New York Giants moved to Los Angeles and San Francisco (respectively) for the 1958 season. Attendance dropped, and franchises did not generate capital. Originally known as *Coast League*. Abbrev. *PCL*.

Pacific League One of Japan's two major professional baseball leagues (the other being the *Central League*), founded as the Taiheiyo Baseball Union in 1949. It uses the designated hitter. The league consists of six teams: Seibu Lions, Orix Buffaloes, Fukuoka Soft-Bank Hawks, Chiba Lotte Marines, Hokkaido Nippon Ham Fighters, and Tohoku Rakuten Golden Eagles. See also *bēsubōru*. Syn. *Pa League*.

pack A group of baseball cards that are sealed by the manufacturer for retail sale.

package A trade that involves more than one player or a player and money.

pack a punch To hit the ball with power.

pad 1. *n.* A padded mitt or glove. See also *pud*. IST USE. 1906 (*The Sporting Life*, Feb. 10, p.2; Edward J. Nichols). **2.** *n.* A catcher's *chest protector*. "It is a shame to bury a brilliant, fast young man as [Billy Maloney] in the catchers [*sic*] pad and mask" (*St. Louis Post-Dispatch*, Apr. 30, 1902; Peter Morris). **3.** *n.* A base. "[Cal Ripken Jr.] ranged to his right . . . but his throw pulled Mickey Tettleton off the pad at first" (*The Baltimore Sun*, Sept. 2, 1990). **4.** *v.* To score additional runs when in the lead; e.g., "The Cubs padded their lead with two runs in the eighth."

paddist The catcher. "Bill Goff has been signed to take care of part of the pitching burden while wires are out in all directions to land a capable paddist" (*Appleton* [Wisc.] *Post Crescent*, Apr. 10, 1928; Peter Morris). A caption in *The Sporting News* (May 31, 1947) refers to Jimmie Wilson as a "top paddist." See also *wind paddist*.

PADE Abbrev. for *park-adjusted defensive efficiency*.

Padres Nickname for the National League West Division expansion franchise in San Diego, Calif., since 1969. The club took the Padres nickname from the city's Pacific Coast League (1936–1968) franchise. Padres (Spanish for "priests") established many early Catholic missions that helped shape the history of the area. Also known as *Pads*.

Pads Short for the *Padres*.

paid attendance The number of tickets actually sold for a baseball game. Both major leagues have based their attendance figures on this practice since 1993. Attendance figures are somewhat inflated because season-ticket holders who do not attend are counted.

paid attendance receipts The total sum of gross receipts from tickets sold to a baseball game, less any admission, sales, or use taxes. See also *gate receipts*.

Paige's Rules A set of guidelines created by Satchel Paige (*Collier's*, June 13, 1953), baseball's "ageless wonder," for how to stay young and explaining his longevity as a pitcher: "1) Avoid fried meats which angry up the blood. 2) If your stomach disputes you, lie down and pacify it with cool thoughts. 3) Keep the juices flowing by jangling around gently as you move. 4) Go very lightly on the vices, such as carrying on in society; the social ramble ain't restful. 5) Avoid running at all times. 6) Don't look back, something might be gaining on you."

pain game A technique for relieving bullpen boredom: "They pull hairs out of each other's noses and try to see whose eyes water the most" (San Francisco Giants reliever Rod Beck, quoted in *Milwaukee Journal Sentinel*, Aug. 7, 1997).

paint To throw pitches over the inside or outside corners of home plate. "[Jack] McDowell painted both edges of the plate with fastballs" (*The Baltimore Sun*, Aug. 8, 1995). Syn. *paint the black*; "paint the corner."

paint brush A pitch that crosses the corner or edge of home plate. "He [California Angels pitcher Kirk McCaskill] had his paint brush out tonight" (Mark McGwire, quoted in *San Francisco Chronicle*, July 26, 1988).

paint master A pitcher who "paints the black" or pinpoints his pitches. The term was coined by pitcher Dennis Eckersley.

paint the black To *paint* the perceived edges of home plate, which may appear to be dark because of the contrast between the white plate and the surrounding dirt.

palant A bat-and-ball game occasionally played in Poland. David Block (*Baseball Before We Knew It*, 2005, pp.101–2) cited a Polish settler who played the game in colonial Jamestown in 1609 before an audience that included "delighted" Native Americans.

Pa League Syn. of *Pacific League*.

Pale Hose Nickname for the Chicago White Sox.

palm ball An off-speed pitch in which the ball is gripped between the pitcher's thumb and little finger and held near the base of the three middle fingers (the palm) that lie slightly curved around the ball. It is released with a fastball motion by "pushing" the ball as it floats out of the hand, making it break in an unpredictable manner with little or no spin. The pitch was originally described as a *slow ball* and was popular for a long time (Jim Konstanty and Dave Giusti threw it), but has been superseded by the circle change and split-fingered fastball. See also *slip pitch*. Also spelled "palmball." Syn. *wiggle ball*. IST USE. 1948. "[Ewell Blackwell demonstrates] how he holds his new pitch, the 'Palm Ball,' which he has added to his repertoire this year" (*Baseball Magazine*, June).

palocracy The informal network of close friends who ran organized baseball for decades. George F. Will (*Men at Work*, 1990, p.29) defined the term as "baseball's contribution to government" or "government by old pals" and noted that "a palocracy can make for kinder, gentler governance, but it also can make the world safe for mediocrity." According to Will (*Houston Chronicle*, Sept. 25, 1987), the term was coined by writer Thomas Boswell.

pan *hist.* Syn. of *home plate*. IST USE. 1891. "These three men make the pitchers put them over the pan day in and day out" (*Sporting Times*, May 23; David Shulman).

pancake **1.** An old, worn, and generally lifeless fielder's glove. **2.** A thinly padded glove preferred by some infielders (mostly shortstops and second basemen) who believe it allows them to handle and release the ball more quickly than would be possible with the more thickly padded *bushel basket*.

Pantheon Syn. of *National Baseball Hall of Fame*. "If a man was a great umpire or an outstanding writer, he should be elected to the diamond Pantheon, and not placed in an annex of that edifice, so to speak" (*The Sporting News*, May 2, 1946).

panty waist [softball term] An early name for softball.

PAP Abbrev. for *pitcher abuse points*.

paper See *on paper*.

paper team A team whose potential is greater than its actual performance; a team that looks

Pancake. New York Yankees pitcher Ray Keating wearing flat glove of yore, 1913. *George Grantham Bain Collection, Library of Congress*

good *on paper* but not in the field. "Throughout the late forties, the Red Sox were the best paper team in baseball, yet they had little three-dimensional to show for it, and if this was a tragedy, [Ted] Williams was Hamlet" (John Updike, *The New Yorker*, Oct. 22, 1960). IST USE. 1911 (*Baseball Magazine*, October, p.39; Edward J. Nichols).

papier mache A player who is easily injured. See also *tissue-paper player*. IST USE. 1934 (*Akron* [Ohio] *Beacon Journal*). ETYMOLOGY. Papier-mâché, a light and moldable pulpy paper.

parachute **1.** *n.* A softly hit pop fly that descends slowly between the infield and outfield; a *Texas Leaguer*, 2. **2.** *n.* A slow pitch; a changeup. "Before [Trevor] Hoffman struck out Ryne Sandberg with a changeup, manager Bruce Bochy stood in the dugout, imploring his closer to 'throw a parachute.' That's the lingo for Hoffman's slow ball. 'Halfway through, pull the rip-cord—it floats in,' [pitching coach Dan] Warthen said, smiling" (*San Diego Union-Tribune*, Apr. 4, 1996). **3.** *n.* Syn. of *eephus*. **4.** *v.* To float toward a target, as in the case of an outfield throw without enough oomph behind it, or a changeup that falls out of the strike zone (Alan Schwarz, BaseballAmerica.com, Nov. 14, 2006). **5.** A symbolic brake to cause a runner to slow down. Montreal Expos manager Jeff Torborg (quoted in *Milwaukee Journal Sentinel*, Aug. 13, 2001; Robert F. Perkins): "The parachute went out coming around third. . . . He was puffing a little bit. Nice slide. I don't know if that was a crash landing or a slide."

parachute hitter Syn. of *singles hitter*.

parade *hist.* To draw a base on balls.

parador corto Spanish for "shortstop."

paraffin ball A ball doctored with wax. "There was the paraffin artist. He'd melt paraffin on the side of his glove, then rub the ball's seams over it until they were slick. A paraffin ball could do everything but cook" (Jack McDonald, *San Francisco Call-Bulletin*, June 11, 1964).

parallel stance Syn. of *square stance*, 1.

parapet Syn. of *mound*, 1. "The opposing moundsmen get shelled from the parapet" (*The Sporting News*, Aug. 17, 1987).

paraphernalia Syn. of *catcher's equipment.*

parent club **1.** The club that holds a player's contract. **2.** The major-league affiliate of a given minor-league team.

park **1.** *n.* A baseball field; short for *ballpark.* "You know, you take your worries to the park and you leave them there" (Humphrey Bogart, in a 1950s promotional ad for baseball). **2.** *v.* To hit a home run; e.g., he "parked one" in the street. "[Rich Aurilia] had been trying to park every pitch in the bleachers" (Franz Lidz, *Sports Illustrated*, July 23, 2001). IST USE. 1927. "A short right field fence . . . has made it easy for left-hand hitting sluggers to park the ball outside" (Lou M. Kennedy, *The Sporting News*, Feb. 17; Peter Morris).

park-adjusted defensive efficiency A measure of a team's defensive performance (*defensive efficiency record*) that includes adjustments for how different ballparks affect average performance, such as the amount of foul territory that affects an infielder's range and the distance to the fences that affects an outfielder's performance. The term was introduced by *Baseball Prospectus* (*Sports Illustrated*, Feb. 25, 2008, p.34). Abbrev. *PADE.*

park effect Syn. of *park factor.*

park factor A measure of a ballpark's run-scoring tendencies relative to the "average" ballpark. These tendencies result in some parks yielding between 5 and 10 percent more (e.g., in Denver or Arlington, Tex.) or fewer (e.g., in San Diego or Seattle) runs over the course of a year than the average, owing to factors including park size, altitude, prevailing wind patterns, temperature and humidity, distance of outfield fences, amount of foul territory, grass vs. turf, groundskeeping practices, quality of field lighting, and hitting backgrounds. Different analysts use varied scales to represent park factor. The first important version, devised by Pete Palmer and described in detail by John Thorn and Pete Palmer (*The Hidden Game of Baseball*, 1985), was calibrated so that an average ballpark received a rating of 100, with above-average ballparks rating more than 100 and below-average ballparks rating less than 100. In contrast, *Baseball Prospectus* employs

1,000 as the average. Park factors are integral to calculating adjusted statistical indices, although the adjustment is calculated differently for batters than it is for pitchers. Researchers generally use one, three, or five years of data. Abbrev. *PF.* Syn. *park effect*; *park index.*

park illusion The distortion of offensive or defensive abilities as reflected in statistics due to the characteristics of a given ballpark. It is most evident in the inflated batting and pitching statistics for Colorado Rockies players, leading to an overestimation of the performance of the team's hitters and corresponding underestimation of the performance of the team's pitchers when based on statistics that have not been adjusted. The term was defined by Bill James in his *Baseball Abstract* (1985).

park index Syn. of *park factor.* The measure was used by STATS Inc. and defined in its *Major League Handbook* and *Baseball Scoreboard* for a ballpark's run-scoring (and also home run) tendencies relative to other ballparks.

part-time player A player who does not appear in the lineup on a regular basis. Compare *everyday player.*

pasaporte Spanish for "base on balls."

pásbol Spanish for "passed ball."

pass **1.** *n.* Syn. of *base on balls.* IST USE. 1897. "Anderson received a free pass to first" (*Brooklyn Eagle*, May 7; Peter Morris). **2.** *v.* To issue a walk to a batter. IST USE. 1910 (*Baseball Magazine*, December; Edward J. Nichols). **3.** *v.* To be issued a base on balls. IST USE. 1900. "Irwin was passed to first, filling the bases" (Timothy Murnane, *Boston Globe*, Sept. 8; Peter Morris). **4.** *n.* A free admission to a baseball game. **5.** *v.* For a baserunner to illegally pass another runner on the basepath. When this occurs, the runner passing his teammate is ruled out.

pass ball **1.** Syn. of *passed ball.* **2.** A pitch that does not cross the strike zone.

passed ball A legally pitched ball that the catcher fails to hold or control with ordinary effort, thereby allowing one or more baserunners to advance. It differs from a *wild pitch* in that the official scorer rules that the catcher should have stopped it. If a passed ball occurs on the third strike, it is treated as a dropped third strike and the batter may advance to first base. A passed ball is not registered as an error to the catcher and cannot be charged if there are no runners on base. Abbrev. *PB*. Syn. *pass ball*, 1. IST USE. 1858. Peter Morris notes that box scores in the *New York Clipper* (July 31) and the *Brooklyn Eagle* (Aug. 28) listed "balls passed catcher" and "balls passing the catcher," respectively. USAGE NOTE. Peter Morris observes, "There were no wild pitches in early baseball and any ball that eluded the catcher was considered a passed ball. Illustrating that the catcher was not necessarily to blame for a passed ball in early baseball: '[Al] Pratt failed to pitch as accurately as usual, hence the number of passed balls on which bases and runs were secured'" (*New York Clipper*, Sept. 12, 1863).

paste **1.** To bat a ball hard; e.g., "Smith pasted one in the sixth." IST USE. 1876 (*Chicago Inter-Ocean*, May 6; Edward J. Nichols). **2.** To get many hits off a pitcher or pitchers. "[Ralph] Branca tired and Brave batters pasted his successors" (Harvey Rosenfeld, *The Great Chase*, 1992, p.64).

pasteboard *hist.* An admission ticket to a baseball game. IST USE. 1887. "Did you see Max deal out the pasteboards and rake in the shining silver cartwheels?" (*Detroit Free Press*, May 12; Peter Morris).

pastime **1.** *n.* A baseball game. "In the morning pastime between the Pitchers and the Regulars he smacked out a couple of three-baggers" (*San Francisco Bulletin*, March 12, 1913; Gerald L. Cohen). **2.** *n.* See *national pastime*. **3.** *v./hist.* To play baseball. "[Bill Reiterman] has pastimed with the San Rafael, Olympic and Boyes Springs clubs" (*San Francisco Bulletin*, May 28, 1913; Gerald L. Cohen).

pastimer A baseball player. "A better pair of pastimers [outfielder George Van Haltren and minor-league third baseman Fred Lange] never represented the Golden State" (*San Francisco Bulletin*, Feb. 1, 1913; Gerald L. Cohen).

pasture **1.** The outfield. "[Center field was Willie Mays'] private pasture and he doesn't like any loose horsehide shrapnel falling around him" (Bob Hunter, quoted in *Sports Illustrated*, July 14–21, 2003). IST USE. 1891 (*Chicago Inter-Ocean*, May 5; Edward J. Nichols). **2.** A ballpark. "Their pitchers did not stand up under fire and the Angels hammered their offerings all over the pasture" (*San Francisco Bulletin*, May 6, 1913; Gerald L. Cohen). "The pasture that baseball takes place in is imaginatively transportable; the pastoral myth remains intact whether the viewer is in Wrigley, Fenway, Riverfront, SkyDome, or, perhaps most important, at home watching on TV. That pasture leads to many pleasant images of a lost America, of places yet unspoiled by pollution or crime or free agency" (David McGimpsey, *Imagining Baseball*, 2000, p.64). See also *home pasture*. **3.** A baseball team. "Cincinnati made the right move when it disposed of Mike Mitchell to the Cubs. . . . Often a new pasture is the very best thing for a player" (*San Francisco Bulletin*, Feb. 14, 1913; Gerald L. Cohen).

pastureman *hist.* An outfielder.

pastureworker *hist.* An outfielder.

patch *hist.* Syn. of *soak*, 2. "We still wanted to patch a man and some way we could not get used to this new way of putting a man out" (*Kalamazoo Gazette*, Feb. 11, 1906; Peter Morris).

patch ball *hist.* An early variation of baseball "with a flexible number of players in which a runner was out if he was 'patched' (hit with a thrown ball)" (Peter Morris, *Baseball Fever*, 2003, p.46).

path **1.** Short for *basepath*. IST USE. 1909. "Eddie Hahn and Frank Isbell were caught on the paths, the former on a snap throw . . . and the latter on a trick" (Ring W. Lardner, *Chicago Tribune*, May 3; Peter Morris). **2.** Syn. of *alley*, 4. "The path from the pitcher's point to the backstop, being 135 feet, has been cut out and filled in with clay" (*Chicago Tribune*, Apr. 14, 1878; Peter Morris).

patrol **1.** *v.* To play an outfield position. "It's up to [Juan] Encarnacion to prove that he deserves to patrol those grounds [left field] every day" (*Sports Illustrated*, June 28, 1999, p.74). **2.** *v.* For a base coach to direct baserunners. **3.** *n./hist.* The outfielders as a unit. See *outer patrol*; *left patrol*; *right patrol*.

Patsy Flaherty A pitching delivery without a

windup, such as that used by Don Larsen in the 1956 World Series. ETYMOLOGY. Pete Howe (*San Francisco Examiner*, May 26, 1957; Peter Tamony) wrote, "Patsy Flaherty was an old-time pitcher [early 1900s] in the National League who used the no-wind-up delivery so much it came to be called the 'Patsy Flaherty.' Casey Stengel batted against him and has described his pitching this way: 'Patsy picked up the ball and umpire hollered strike!'"

payback pitch A ball thrown by a pitcher to harm or intimidate a batter in revenge for a real or imagined transgression by the batter's team.

pay ball 1. Syn. of *cripple*, 1. 2. Syn. of *payoff pitch*. IST USE. 1937 (*New York Daily News*, May 2; Edward J. Nichols).

pay dirt Home plate. "You hit a triple . . . dusting off, taking a lead, jigging around 90 feet away from pay dirt" (Roy Blount Jr., *Sports Illustrated*, Sept. 29, 2003).

pay dues To advance step by step up the ladder of professional baseball by diligent effort without having had any special breaks or treatment.

payoff hit The base hit that wins the game on the final inning (Walter K. Putney, *Baseball Stories*, Spring 1952).

payoff pitch The pitch delivered when the count is full (three balls and two strikes). It is the "payoff" because, barring a foul, the batter must hit the ball, be walked, or strike out. Syn. *pay ball*, 2; *decision pitch*.

pay station Syn. of *home plate*. IST USE. 1937 (*New York Daily News*, Jan. 31; Edward J. Nichols).

pay wing Syn. of *salary arm*.

PB Scorecard and box score abbrev. for *passed ball*.

PBA Abbrev. for *Professional Baseball Agreement*.

PBP Abbrev. for *play-by-play*.

PCL Abbrev. for *Pacific Coast League*.

PDC Abbrev. for *player development contract*.

pea 1. A pitched, thrown, or batted ball that is moving so fast that it appears smaller than it actually is. "[I] made a pretty good catch

when Willie Crawford hit a pea against the fence" (Rusty Staub, quoted in *The New York Times*, July 13, 1986). See also *seed*. 2. The baseball. IST USE. 1910 (*Baseball Magazine*, April, p.28; Edward J. Nichols).

peacherino *hist.* A sensational play or player. The term is an elaboration of the word "peach." IST USE. 1908 (*New York Evening Journal*, Feb. 27; Edward J. Nichols).

peacocking Pinching the front of one's jersey and plucking it several inches from the chest. David Grann (*The New Yorker*, Sept. 12, 2005) noted that Rickey Henderson had performed this pregame ritual since he was a rookie in 1979.

peak *hist.* Syn. of *mound*, 1. IST USE. 1913 (*The Sporting News*, Oct. 30).

peak value The value of a player to his team at his highest clearly established level of performance; e.g., the argument that Mickey Mantle was a greater player than Willie Mays presumes that peak value is the proper interpretation of "greater player." The term was introduced by Bill James in his *Baseball Abstract* (1985). Compare *career value*.

peanut The pennant. "We went into New York, needing 14 out of the remaining 16 games to grab the 'peanut'—as the pennant was called" (Ty Cobb, *My Life in Baseball*, 1961, p.62).

pea patch The ballpark. Broadcaster Red Barber introduced the term in such phrases as "tearin' up the pea patch" for a hitter on a hot streak.

pearl The baseball; specif., a used baseball that is in excellent condition, such as a perfect batting-practice ball that is not blemished or stained.

pea shooter A small baseball bat. Tony Gwynn referred to his bat (32½ inches and 31 ounces) as a pea shooter (*Sunday Oregonian*, June 23, 1991).

pebble The baseball. IST USE. 1897. "Davis bumped the pebble to left for two sacks" (*The New York Times*, July 28, p.6).

pebble hit A base hit made when a rock, pebble, stone, or other field irregularity causes the ball to bounce away from the fielder. "In the old days, that would have been called a 'pebble hit,' but there are no pebbles on infields now" (World Series announcer, Oct. 4, 1952; Peter Tamony). See also *Pebble Play*.

pebble hunter A defensive player, usually an infielder, who picks up real or imaginary pebbles on which to blame his errors. He will allege that a ball took a bad hop because it struck a pebble. Syn. *pebble picker*. IST USE. 1912 (Hugh S. Fullerton, *American Magazine*, June, p.204; Edward J. Nichols). ETYMOLOGY. Fullerton (see above) wrote, "The term arises from the fact that one old-time player was caught carrying pebbles in his pocket to drop on the ground after he fumbled, and then find, claiming each time that the ball struck a pebble and bounded wrong."

pebble picker Syn. of *pebble hunter.*

Pebble Play An incident that occurred on Oct. 10, 1924, in the 12th inning of the seventh game of the World Series between the New York Giants and the Washington Senators, in which Earl McNeely's hit hopped over Giants third baseman Freddie Lindstrom's head leading to a run that gave the championship to the Senators. It was claimed and verified by members of the Giants that the ball did indeed hit a pebble. See also *pebble hit.*

Pecatonica An Illinois town that became synonymous with embarrassingly bad play on the baseball diamond after its club was beaten 49–1 at a major tournament held in Rockford, Ill., in 1866 (Peter Morris, *Baseball Fever*, 2003, pp.111–12). "The loss of a man by sickness or other cause at a critical time may transform a well disciplined and effective nine into a gang of muffers that would disgrace Pecatonica" (*Chicago Tribune*, Apr. 13, 1879; Peter Morris).

pecker Syn. of *feeder*, 2.

PECOTA A method for estimating player performance in future seasons, based on the player's performance in previous seasons and the career records of similar former players. For example, to project the future of a major-league player, the program may look at the statistics of the player's past three seasons (with extra weight given to the most recent) as well as the player's age, service time, defensive position, speed, and body type, and

Pebble Play. Freddie Lindstrom during 1924 World Series. *George Grantham Bain Collection, Library of Congress*

develop a list of as many as 100 statistically comparable former players since World War II, to return a range of probable outcomes. The method was devised by Nate Silver and described in *Baseball Prospectus* (2003). ETYMOLOGY. Acronym for Player Empirical Comparison and Optimization Test Algorithm, which "joyfully boils down to the last name of Bill Pecota," a former major-league utility man (Alan Schwarz, *The New York Times*, Nov. 13, 2005).

pedal music *hist.* **1.** The stamping of enthusiastic fans. **2.** The noise made by a player bringing his foot down forcibly. Compare *chin music*, 3. "The rattle and crash of O'Rourke's pedal music as he came across the turkey [home plate] made the spectators howl" (*The World* [New York], July 20, 1889; Gerald L. Cohen).

peddle To trade or sell a player's contract. "The Red Sox peddled Johnny Schmitz to Baltimore" (*The Sporting News*, May 23, 1956). IST USE. 1889. "Even the disbandment and retirement of a club did not free the players from the octopus clutch, for they were then peddled around to the highest bidder" ("Manifesto" of the Brotherhood of Professional Base Ball Players, Nov. 4; see Elwood Roff, *Base Ball and Base Ball Players*, 1912, pp.86–87).

peddle Peruna *hist.* To be boastful; to advertise oneself (Maurice H. Weseen, *A Dictionary of American Slang*, 1934). ETYMOLOGY. Peruna was a patent medicine heavily advertised at the turn of the 20th century. Many gave testimonials in its behalf. In Mark Sullivan's *Our Times* (1926–1935), a senator from Mississippi gives his testimonial: "For some time I have been a sufferer from catarrh in its most incipient stage. So much so that I became alarmed as to my general health. But hearing of Peruna as a good remedy, I gave it a fair trial, and soon began to improve. I take pleasure in recommending your great natural catarrh cure. Peruna is the best I have ever tried." The medicine was driven from the market by pure-food advocates who faulted it for being loaded with whiskey.

peeker **1.** A "pitcher who, with men on, can't resist turning head to watch runners as he is in act of delivery, takes eyes off catcher's target and invariably has bad control" (Bert Dunne, *Folger's Dictionary of Baseball*, 1958). **2.** A batter in the batter's box who turns his head back to attempt to see the catcher's signs and/or where he is positioning himself or holding his mitt as a target. The tactic of peeking is not against any written rule, but as an unwritten rule, it ranks among the highest.

peel off To hit the ball safely. IST USE. 1913 (*The Sporting News*, Oct. 30).

peewee A baseball that is smaller than usual. "A true peewee is treasured by hurlers, and its departure from the premises, by fair means or foul, is secretly mourned" (Roger Angell, *Five Seasons*, 1972, p.9).

Pee Wee Baseball A program of play and instruction for boys and girls who are six and seven years old.

peg **1.** *n.* A powerful and esp. accurate throw, traditionally from the outfield to the infield; but also a strong throw from the shortstop deep in the hole or from the catcher trying to nail a base stealer. **2.** *v.* To make a peg. IST USE. 1862. "Peter then pegged the ball in

good old style, but this time raised it too high" (*New York Sunday Mercury*, July 13; OED). **3.** *n./hist.* A base. "[Clyde] Milan then advanced a peg when [Sam] Rice grounded to Lee" (*The Washington Post*, May 21, 1921). IST USE. 1896. "Tiernan's sacrifice moved them up a peg each" (*Brooklyn Eagle*, Aug. 1; Peter Morris). ETYMOLOGY. From rounders. "Four other stations are marked with pegs stuck into the ground, topped with a piece of paper, so as to be readily seen" (Charles Peverelly, *The Book of American Pastimes*, 1866; Peter Morris).

pegger A player with a strong throwing arm; specif., the catcher. "Lalonge is . . . a first-class pegger" (*San Francisco Bulletin*, Apr. 22, 1913; Gerald L. Cohen).

Peggy Lee fastball A fastball that travels more slowly than expected, or has nothing on it. ETYMOLOGY. The term is used in connection with batters who see the pitch and are reminded of Lee's 1969 sad song, "Is That All There Is?" (words by Jerry Leiber and music by Mike Stoller). The move to baseball is attributed widely to pitcher Tug McGraw, who specialized in the pitch (his regular fastball minus about 10 miles per hour); but *The Sporting News* cites Dan Quisenberry as father of the term.

Pekinese poke Syn. of *Chinese home run*, 1. "16 of First 29 HR's in L.A. Labeled 'Pekinese Pokes'" (*The Sporting News* headline, May 7, 1958; Peter Tamony).

pellet The baseball. "[Cartwright] has demonstrated possibilities as a batsman, clicking the old pellet to the far corners of the field" (*San Francisco Bulletin*, March 4, 1913; Gerald L. Cohen). IST USE. 1904. "O'Neill then got next to Pelty for a pellet down right field" (*The Washington Post*, Aug. 31; Peter Morris).

pelota The baseball. "The old pelota went through Leon's [Durham] legs like, well, 'a knife through butter'" (*The Sporting News*, Oct. 15, 1984). ETYMOLOGY. Spanish for "ball."

pelotero Spanish for "ballplayer."

pen **1.** *n.* "A row of seats fenced in on all sides in the extreme front of the grandstand" (Thomas W. Lawson, *The Krank: His Language and What It Means*, 1888). **2.** *n.* Short for *bullpen*, 1. "After three days in the pen, [Ed] Whitson's back in the rotation" (Gannett Westchester Newspapers headline, June 13, 1986). Sometimes spelled "'pen." **3.** *n.* Relief pitching. "Everybody thought our pen wasn't any good. We didn't think that way" (Boston Red Sox relief pitcher Bob Stanley, quoted in *The Washington Post*, Oct. 21, 1986). **4.** *v.* To win a bullpen duel; e.g., "Pirates Pen SD [San Diego] in 15" (*Boston Herald* headline, July 13, 1990).

penalty The application (by the umpire) of the *Official Baseball Rules* following an illegal act; e.g., the umpire will call a ball (the penalty) on the pitcher if his pitching hand comes in contact with his mouth or lips while he is standing on the mound.

pencil A baseball bat; e.g., "Smith wrote out a hit with his pencil."

pencil in To enter a player's name in the starting lineup or during the course of a game. "On July 1, 1982, [Baltimore Orioles manager Earl] Weaver made a decision. He penciled [Cal] Ripken in at shortstop" (Bob Hertzel, *Baseball Digest*, Dec. 1983).

pennant **1.** The title achieved by the team that wins its division or league championship. Syn. *flag*, 1. **2.** The large triangular commemorative *banner* given to the team that wins its division or league. See also *bunting*, 2; *gonfalon*; *oriflamme*; *rag*, 3. 1st use. 1874. "The Bostons, who have the right to fly the pennant as champions" (*The Field* [London], July 11; Dean A. Sullivan). **3.** The *emblem* of the World Series championship, as selected by the commissioner.

pennanteer A pennant winner. "Oaks Play More Like Bushers than Haughty Champions: If they play as they did yesterday the Pennanteers will continue to slide until they have hit the bottom with the Wolves and Beavers" (*San Francisco Bulletin*, May 9, 1913; Gerald L. Cohen).

pennant fever The rabid enthusiasm of the fans when it appears the home team might win a division pennant. "Nothing says 'pennant fever' like howling mobs of beered-up fans from two teams going at each other like the very fate of the nation is at stake" (Kevin Cowherd, *The Baltimore Sun*, Apr. 4, 2005).

pennant insurance A player (esp. a pitcher) added to a pennant-contending team during the late stages of the season.

pennant porch The grandstand area created by a short outfield fence for home run hitters; specif., the 296-foot right-field walls in Municipal Stadium in Kansas City (erected and dismantled in 1964) and in Yankee Stadium.

pennant race The competition for the league or division championship, esp. toward the end of the season when several teams are in contention. Bob Costas (*Fair Ball*, 2000, p.127) intoned, "A pennant race is not the same thing as the mere act of qualifying for the playoffs. A pennant race has specific competitive and dramatic characteristics. A pennant race pos-

Pennant. Raising New York Giants 1917 National League pennant, June 14, 1918. *George Grantham Bain Collection, Library of Congress*

sesses a certain remorseless justice—a kind of unforgiving insistence on excellence—that is unique and central to its appeal. All of those characteristics are destroyed or diminished by the wild-card system." Syn. *flag chase*. IST USE. 1876. "For the first time since May last the Hartford have been obliged to take third place in the pennant race" (*Brooklyn Eagle*, July 24; Peter Morris).

pennant voyage A baseball season.

'penner Short for *bullpenner*. "Nothing, [Earl] Weaver fears, is beyond the reach of his 'penners'" (Thomas Boswell, *The Washington Post*, June 5, 1986).

Pennsy pinkie A *spaldeen*-type ball manufactured in Pennsylvania (Rich Dubroff, *How Was the Game?*, 1994, p.38).

pentagon Syn. of the five-sided *home plate*.

pep Energy, zest, determination, fighting spirit exhibited on the playing field (*The Sporting News*, Oct. 30, 1913). "[Del Howard is] the guy who put the 'pep' in pepper. Whatever life and fighting strength has been manifested by the Seals in the games with the White Sox was brought out by Howard" (*San Francisco Bulletin*, March 18, 1913; Gerald L. Cohen). IST USE. 1910 (*Baseball Magazine*, September; Edward J. Nichols).

pepper 1. *n.* Vigor and energy. "Some person must have sprinkled a box of pepper all over the ball field, judging from the noise and commotion caused by the players in their workout" (*San Francisco Bulletin*, March 11, 1913; Gerald L. Cohen). IST USE. 1895 (*New York Press*, July 8; Edward J. Nichols). **2.** *n.* A fast-paced pregame bunting and fielding drill played at close range (10 to 20 feet) among small clusters of players. It is designed as a hand-eye exercise to improve reflexes. One player chops or half swings at the ball with a brisk, bunt-like stroke. The batted ball is pitched quickly back to the batter by one of the fielders. The ball is continually thrown, batted, and fielded in rapid succession. Keith Moreland (*Vineline*, 1987) wrote, "Greatest game in the world for a hitter. Short pepper is when a batter tries to hit one-hoppers back to the guy throwing to him in pregame practice." Players sometimes play pepper to kill time before games or during rain delays, but

players of an earlier era played for fun, food, and/or money. Formerly, pepper games were played in the home-plate area (not on the outfield grass) during batting practice. Since the late 1940s, many ballparks have banned pepper to avoid damaging the field or wearing out the grass, and to prevent batted balls from entering the stands and endangering spectators. The game was known as *high-low* and perhaps by other names before it became "pepper." See also *flip game*; *"no pepper games."* IST USE. 1933. "Over at the left of the third-base line pepper games are in progress. Six or eight players, glove in hand, line up a yard apart. Thirty feet away stands a batter. He hits the ball with amazing precision. . . . Whoever grabs it returns it to the batter as quickly as he can get it out of his hands, only to have it batted back again double quick. This simple game is very popular among training players" (Arthur Mann, *American Mercury*, March; Peter Tamony). **3.** *n.* The ritual of briskly throwing the ball around the infield after a putout. **4.** *v.* To throw a baseball hard and fast; e.g., "Smith peppered the ball to first." **5.** *v.* For a team to hit a lot of hard balls into the same area of the ballpark. "[Miguel] Cabrera started peppering the bleachers [with three home runs]" (*The Baltimore Sun*, Oct. 16, 2003). IST USE. 1892. "Foutz, Burns, Daly and Shindle almost flattened the ball in peppering the score board with hits" (*Brooklyn Eagle*, July 5; Peter Morris).

ETYMOLOGY. The term would appear to derive from "pep" as well as the "peppy" or "peppery" nature of the drill, which in turn seem to come from the word "pepper," giving the term a circular etymology. The adjective "peppery" was fairly common in ballpark expressions before World War II; e.g., "peppery grasser" (a hit ball that is low and swift) and "peppery pilot" (a lively, aggressive manager of a team) (Maurice H. Weseen, *Dictionary of American Slang*, 1934).

pepper practice A period of pepper play before the game. IST USE. 1935. "We can suggest nothing more helpful to the young batter than 'pepper practice' in large doses" (Ralph H. Barbour, *How to Play Better Baseball*; David Shulman).

PERA Abbrev. for *peripheral earned run average*.

percentage An advantage. Ty Cobb (*Busting 'Em and Other Big League Stories*, 1914; Peter Morris) explained, "Most of the boys in the select 'three hundred' class [batting average of .300 or higher] are using their heads all the time they are at the plate to outguess the fielders and the opposing pitcher and stand them all on their heads. This style of hitting gives a player what we call the 'percentage,' or the edge, and every man who is to bat up over three hundred needs this 'percentage.'"

percentage baseball A strategy in which the game is played using conventional beliefs about the odds that various strategies will work to the team's advantage; e.g., waiting for hits to bring in baserunners rather than taking chances on the basepaths. Sabermetric research has shown that some strategies labeled as "percentage baseball" actually work against a team; e.g., walking a batter to create a force situation. IST USE. 1932 (*Baseball Magazine,* October, p.496; Edward J. Nichols).

percentage hit A fluke hit that nevertheless helps one's batting average; a *Texas Leaguer*, 2.

percentage manager A manager who makes decisions based on established form, statistics, and odds.

percentage of team wins An informal measure of a pitcher's contribution to his team's won-lost percentage, determined by dividing the pitcher's number of wins by the team's number of wins. The highest 20th-century mark belongs to Steve Carlton in 1972, when he was credited with 45.8 percent of the Philadelphia Phillies' wins (27 of 59).

percentage Patsy A player who plays to enhance his individual statistics rather than for the good of the team as a whole. IST USE. 1937. "One who plays for individual average" (Jimmy Powers, *New York Daily News*, Jan. 10).

percentage pitch A pitcher's best pitch, thrown over the plate. "Nine times out of ten, [Joe] Beggs says, the hitter will be hanging on your first offer because he figures it will be a 'percentage pitch'—that you will come right in there with it" (*Oelwein* [Iowa] *Daily Register*, Apr. 22, 1941; Peter Morris).

percentage point **1.** A unit in a player's batting average, equal to 0.001; e.g., "Smith added 18 percentage points to his batting average (from .282 to .300) in the two weeks following the All-Star Game." **2.** A unit in the won-loss average of a team, equal to 0.001.

percentage system In early baseball, a system used to pay the visiting club a share of the gate receipts. The visitors received a specific percentage of attendance revenues. Compare *guarantee system*.

perch A team's place in the standings.

perfect game A *no-hitter* in which all 27 opposing batters fail to reach first base, either by a base hit, base on balls, hit batter, fielding error, or any other means. As of this writing, there have been only 17 perfect games in the major leagues, with the most famous being the one pitched by New York Yankees hurler Don Larsen against the Brooklyn Dodgers in Game 5 of the 1956 World Series. The first perfect game was pitched on June 12, 1880, by J. Lee Richmond of the Worcester Brown Stockings against the Cleveland Forest Citys. Syn. *perfecto*. IST USE. 1909. "[Ed] Walsh congratulated Addie Joss on the latter's feat of pitching a perfect game [on Oct. 2, 1908]" (*The Washington Post*, Jan. 10).

perfecto Syn. of *perfect game*. "David Wells Perfecto" (*Sports Illustrated* headline, May 25, 1998), regarding the 15th perfect game in major-league history as the New York Yankees pitcher blanked the Minnesota Twins on May 17, 1998. IST USE. 1967. "[Stan] Bahnsen Hurls Perfecto" (unknown source headline, July 29).

perfect offensive player An award given annually since 1996 by the Fred Gunkle Fan Club (an association of Cleveland-based fans honoring Gunkle, who played one game for the Cleveland Forest Citys in 1879) to major leaguers who finish the season with a batting average better than .300, an on-base percentage better than .400, and a slugging percentage better than .500 (*Sports Illustrated*, July 5, 1999). Abbrev. *POP*, 2.

perfect pillow A catcher's mitt in the 1890s,

made of Plymouth buckskin. "A continuous roll or cushion, tightly packed with curled hair, is firmly stitched around the palm, forming a deep hollow, and the thumb of the glove is a sufficient bulwark to make it impossible for a foul tip, fly, or hand-thrown ball to put the human thumb out of joint" (*New York Sun*, Apr. 27, 1890; Peter Morris). See also *pillow*, 2.

performance bonus Payment to a player conditioned on the player having achieved certain specified levels of activity. See also *bonus*, 2. Compare *award bonus*.

performance scouting Scouting ballplayers based on their statistics: a young player is not what he looks like or might become, but what he has accomplished. Legendary scout Tony Lucadello (quoted in Mark Winegardner, *Prophet of the Sandlots*, 1990): "[Performance scouts are] guys who go on the basis of what the kid did. If he hit a home run or made a good play, why, they go strictly on that." Michael Lewis (*Moneyball*, 2003, p.38) noted that "performance scouting" is an "insult" in traditional scouting circles: "It directly contradicts the baseball man's view that a young player is what you can see him doing in your mind's eye."

period Syn. of *inning*, 1 (*The Sporting News*, Oct. 30, 1913).

period base ball Syn. of *vintage base ball*. In Apr. 1994, the Ohio Historical Society in Columbus planned a monthly publication to be "sent to all players of period base ball."

peripheral earned run average An estimate of what a pitcher's earned run average "should have been" in a given season, based on the number of hits, walks, strikeouts, and home runs for which he is responsible. The estimate is featured in *Baseball Prospectus*. Abbrev. *PERA*.

person Any part of the body, clothing, or equipment of a ballplayer or umpire.

perspiration pellet *hist.* A spitball. IST USE. 1907 (*New York Evening Journal*, June 7; Edward J. Nichols).

pesäpallo (pron. "pe-sap-o-low") A variety of baseball played in Finland since Lauri Pihkala invented it in 1922. The bases are arranged in a Z-shape fashion, the basepaths

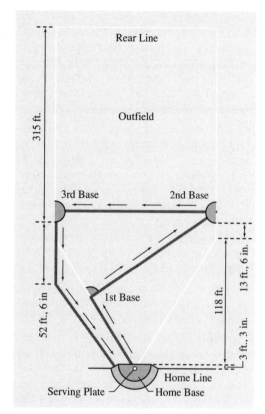

Pesäpallo.

get progressively longer, and the outfield is rectangular. The pitcher and the batter face each other on either side of home plate (which is round and sits about two inches off the ground). The pitcher lobs the ball vertically into the air about three feet above the batter's head, making the ball as challenging to hit as in slow pitch softball. After hitting the ball, the batter runs in a zigzag pattern: first base is to the batter's left, second base is at an angle across the field to the batter's right, and third base is back across the field again, slightly behind first base. A ball hit beyond the outfield boundary is an out. By eliminating the pitcher-batter duel, the ball is kept in play more often and the game is speeded up. There are nine innings, nine players on a side, and three outs (called "deads") in an inning. Syn. *Finnish baseball*. ETYMOLOGY. Finnish for "nest-ball."

Pesky's Pole The right field foul pole at Fenway Park, officially named in honor of Boston Red Sox infielder and coach Johnny

Pesky, most of whose six home runs in the park were hit near or around the pole or down the short (302 feet) right field line. According to Bill Nowlin and Jim Prime (*Mr. Red Sox: The Johnny Pesky Story*, 2004), Pesky claimed that Red Sox pitcher Mel Parnell originated the name. Compare *Fisk Pole*.

pest A persistent fan who always wants something, such as an autographed ball. Pests are nothing new, as the following definition by R.E. Sherwood (*Baseball Magazine*, Sept. 1913) attested: "A grave-yard comedian as funny as a crutch, equipped with a megaphone, a pass, and a .44 caliber voice, who tries to address the players by their maiden names. Generally loses both 'goat' and voice in the first inning."

pest hitter A batter whose hits are difficult to catch or retrieve (Maurice H. Weseen, *A Dictionary of American Slang*, 1934).

Pete Rose Rule The stipulation that any player on baseball's ineligible list shall not be an eligible candidate for the National Baseball Hall of Fame. The rule was passed by the board of directors of the Hall of Fame in 1991, just prior to the election in which Rose would have been eligible for the Hall of Fame for the first time. At the time, Rose was banned from baseball for gambling on baseball games.

petit larceny (pron. "petty larceny") Syn. of *base stealing*.

petticoat ball A strike at the knees in the All-American Girls Professional Baseball League.

PF Abbrev. for *park factor*.

PFP Abbrev for *pitcher fielding practice*.

PGP Abbrev. for *player game percentage*.

PH Abbrev. for *pinch hitter*, 1.

phantom 1. An item in baseball memorabilia collecting that was created for an event that did not take place, such as playoff tickets for a team that did not make the playoffs. 2. A player listed in baseball encyclopedias who did not actually play in the major leagues, usually the result of an ancient typographical error in a box score. Lee Allen (*The Sporting News*, Apr. 6, 1968) wrote that Ernie Lanigan introduced the term, and gave an example:

"There was no Deniens. He was a phantom all right, a misprint for . . . Clemens . . . It was apparent that a telegrapher, in tapping out the box score, had misread the 'Cl' for a 'D' and the 'm' for 'ni.'" 3. Short for *phantom hit*.

phantom double play 1. A double play in which the out at second base is an illusion because the fielder crosses the bag without touching it, or touches the base without possessing the ball, or takes a step away from the base when pivoting for the throw to first base. Despite the rule stating that the bag must be touched by the fielder possessing the ball, many umpires (to keep players from getting hurt in collisions) ignore the violation if the ball clearly beats the runner to second base. See also *neighborhood play*. 2. A double play in which the batter hits an easy fly ball on a hit-and-run play and the middle infielder fakes receiving a throw at second base, thereby deceiving a sliding baserunner, who is subsequently called out for not getting back in time. According to umpire Ron Luciano (*The Umpire Strikes Back*, 1982, p.174), this play was used effectively by the Kansas City Royals double-play combination of shortstop Freddie Patek and second baseman Cookie Rojas.

phantom hit *hist.* A base on balls. The term was used only in 1887 when a walk was counted as a hit, a rule that was denigrated by sportswriters. IST USE. 1887. "The Eastern term for a hit by a base on balls is 'a phantom hit'" (*San Francisco Examiner*, May 16; Peter Morris). Syn. *phantom*; *bloodless hit*; *nominal hit*.

phantom infield A crowd-pleasing pregame drill in which the infield goes through the rigors of infield practice without the benefit of a ball.

phantom tag A missed tag or a tag from a glove without the ball in it, either one of which is mistakenly credited as a legal tag. Some infielders discreetly remove the ball from the glove just before the tag to prevent the ball from being jarred loose as the play is made.

pheenom Var. of *phenom*. ETYMOLOGY. The term was coined by writer and New York Giants public relations director Garry Schumacher in the spring of 1947 to describe outfielder Clint Hartung, a player of questionable ability but with a reputation for versatility and indescribable power. The term, applied to a highly touted rookie who quickly fades, "has had a skeptical connotation" (Zander Hollander, ed., *Baseball Lingo*, 1967, p.95).

phenom A highly touted rookie; a rookie who gets off to a spectacular start at the beginning of the season or during spring training; an *early bloomer*. "Too often phenoms are soon-to-be-has-beens, players who come out of nowhere, hit a lot of home runs or strike out a lot of batters in a short time and then disappear" (Stephen Cannella and Jeff Pearlman, *Sports Illustrated*, June 21, 1999, p.82). The term "phenom" is "a compliment when you're talking about someone—an insult when you say it to his face" (Steve Kluger, *Changing Pitches*, 1984, p.89). "Bob Barr, Washington's phenom of last year, will probably pitch for Oswego this season [because] that's the way phenoms generally turn out" (*Detroit Free Press*, March 8, 1887). A.G. Spalding (*Base Ball: America's National Game*, 1911) tied the term to a rule change: "The removal of the straight-arm pitching restrictions by the amendment of the rules in 1884 was responsible for the evolution of the 'Phenom.' He came into the game from Keokuk, Kankakee, Kokomo and Kalamazoo. He was heralded always as a 'discovery.' His achievements were 'simply phenomenal.' Once in a great while he 'made good.' Usually he proved to be a flat and unmitigated failure." Yet not all phenoms fail. Grantland Rice (*The Tumult and the Shouting*, 1954, p.18) recounted the following from a news tipster in 1904: "Tyrus Raymond Cobb ... has just started spring training with Anniston. He is a terrific hitter and faster than a deer. At the age of 18 he is undoubtedly a phenom." Var. *pheenom*. IST USE. 1881. "[James] Whitney the Boston phenom" (*Detroit Free Press*, July 17; Peter Morris). USAGE NOTE. "Phenom" in its more common form of "phenomenal" or "phenomenon" was prevalent in the 19th century. "Ryan and Weaver changed places in the seventh inning, and this new 'phenomenal' [Ryan as pitcher] was too much for the blue stockings" (*The Boston Globe*, May 30, 1877; Peter Morris). Pitcher John

Francis Smith's nickname was "Phenomenal": "Heavy batting and the fine pitching of Phenomenal Smith won the game for Baltimore to-day" (*The World* [New York], July 13, 1887; Gerald L. Cohen). "The Clevelands tried a 'phenomenon' named Kelley ... at the ball park Thursday morning" (*The Sporting Life*, July 30, 1883, p.7). "[Harry] Wright has not been quite so previous with his phenomenons" (*The Washington Post*, March 16, 1884). "Phenomenal is a much abused word. It appears so often in the description of ordinary plays that it means little" (*The Sporting News*, Aug. 18, 1900; Peter Morris). ETYMOLOGY. Shortened form of "phenomenon" or "phenomenal player." The word "phenomenon" has had a long and distinguished history as a title for a boxer or racehorse. Peter Tamony unearthed references to other phenomenons dating back to 1807, when a prizefighter nicknamed the "Israelite Phenomenon" won a 34-round bout in England. In the United States, Tamony unearthed references to a bay gelding named Awful who had a spectacular season in 1838; his backers nicknamed him "The Phenomenon." Although the shortened form "phenom" has been used for boxers and other athletes, its early use and primary application has been to baseball players. EXTENDED USE. Now used for fast-starters in any field. The title of an article on young CEOs was "Pity the Poor Phenoms" (*Forbes*, Apr. 8, 1985).

phenomenon See *phenom*.

Philadelphia triple *hist.* Three consecutive fly-ball outs in an inning (Bugs Baer, *San Francisco Examiner*, July 27, 1946, p.9).

Phillies Nickname for the National League East Division franchise in Philadelphia, Pa., since 1883. The franchise replaced the Worcester Brown Stockings. The nickname is derived from the name of the city and was in use as early as 1874 (sometimes spelled "Fillies") for a Philadelphia team. The club was known as the *Blue Jays* in 1943 and 1944, although "Phillies" was still used by fans and declared the official team name in 1950. Also known as *Phils*; *Quakers*.

Phillips 99 ball A tightly wound, hopped-up baseball that carried far when hit.

Phils Short for *Phillies*.

phonographic needle pitch An illegal pitch given its odd trajectory by the surreptitious insertion of a 78-rpm stylus in the seam of the ball. The pitch was thrown by Urban Shocker (Jack McDonald, *San Francisco Call-Bulletin*, June 11, 1964) and is described in detail by Martin Quigley (*The Crooked Pitch*, 1984).

pianola *hist.* An easy win; a laugher. ETY-MOLOGY. Pianola was the trademarked name of a player piano that was easy to play compared to a regular piano.

piano legs The legs of a stocky player. "Piano legs are defined as a surplus of weight and muscular tissue on the lower limbs" (*The Sporting Life*, May 25, 1907, p.24; Steve Steinberg).

piano mover A slow runner.

Picasso A pitcher who "paints the black."

pick 1. *v.* To successfully field a ground ball, esp. one that is hard to handle. The term is often used as part of a compliment by one team member to another for a first-rate defensive play: "way to pick it" or "you really picked 'em." See also *pick it*. IST USE. 1925. "[Honus] Wagner pounced on ground hit balls and smothered them, rather than picked them cleanly" (Hugh Jennings, *Rounding Third*; Peter Morris). 2. *n.* A successfully fielded ground ball, esp. one that is hard to handle; e.g., "Smith made a good pick on that sharply hit grounder." 3. *v.* To catch a ball in the dirt. "Hatty [converted first baseman Scott Hatteberg] picked a throw out of the dirt—a play most first basemen made with their eyes closed" (Michael Lewis, *Moneyball*, 2003, p.168). 4. *n.* See *draft pick*.

picked nine *hist.* 1. Any team that did not play a regular schedule and whose players accordingly were under no obligation to play exclusively for that team. The looseness of the definition is implied in the following note from the *Detroit Free Press* (May 1, 1881; Peter Morris): "The Buffalos in their practice game have batted heavily and fielded well, but they have played against a 'picked nine,' and that term has a wide range of meaning, anywhere from a lot of muffers to a semi-professional club." The term dates from the 1850s and originally referred to an "all-star"

team. Picked nines were typically the best players from the teams in a single city, who played picked nines from other cities. The professional era of the 1870s essentially ended the practice of picked nines. 2. A professional club that exhibited little teamwork. "Lest our great 'individual' or 'picked' nine, as [the White Stockings] have been called throughout the country, should prove unequal, through lack of discipline, organization, practice, harmony, or whatever cause, when pitted against a club of the well-known strength and efficiency of the Forest City Club of Cleveland" (*Chicago Tribune*, June 4, 1870; Peter Morris).

picked off To be thrown out on a pickoff play.

pick 'em up and put 'em down Said of a baserunner who can run fast.

picker A scout who concentrates on a player's weaknesses. "A picker will pounce on a minor detail, something that possibly could be corrected with a little work, and overlook the things a ballplayer may do well" (Tony Lucadello, quoted in David V. Hanneman, *Diamonds in the Rough*, 1989, p.116).

picket 1. An outfielder. 2. *hist.* A run chalked up on the scoreboard. Several runs so chalked up gave the rough appearance of a picket fence. "In the seventh they put over another tally, following it with two more in the eighth, which gave them the grand total of six pickets" (*San Francisco Bulletin*, May 16, 1913; Gerald L. Cohen).

picket line The three outfielders, who are not only arrayed like fence pickets but can presumably "pick it."

pick it To play the infield well. "'Pick it' is this year's 'in' baseball phrase.... Ken Reitz, the Cardinal third baseman, can really pick it" (Roger Angell, *Five Seasons*, 1972). See also *pick*, 1.

pickle 1. *v.* To bat a ball very hard. "Jacques Fournier ... hits a ball an awful wallop. He pickled a couple yesterday, one clearing the right field fence and dropping over a roof" (*San Francisco Bulletin*, March 31, 1913; Gerald Cohen). IST USE. 1908 (*New York Evening Journal*, Aug. 20; Edward J. Nichols). ETYMOLOGY. "Named from the idea of 'pickling' in the sense of 'to salt away'" (Edward J. Nichols, *An Historical Dictionary of Baseball Terminology*, PhD dissertation, Jan. 1939). **2.** *n.* A play in which a baserunner is caught in a rundown between bases. Short for "in a pickle." **3.** *n.* A playground drill or game in which two youngsters stand at bases and throw the ball back and forth, trying to tag out a runner attempting to steal the base he was not occupying. See also *running bases*; *hot box*, 2.

pickle brine A salty solution given a role in baseball after pitcher Nolan Ryan started the custom of soaking his hands in it to toughen his skin and prevent blisters.

pickoff *n.* Syn. of *pickoff play*.

pick off *v.* **1.** To throw out a baserunner who has moved too far away from the base he is occupying. IST USE. 1888 (*New York Press*, Apr. 21; Edward J. Nichols). **2.** *hist.* To get a hit. "Justin Fitzgerald . . . picked off three nice bingles out of four times at bat" (*San Francisco Bulletin*, Apr. 9, 1913; Gerald L. Cohen).

pickoff move The motion made by a pitcher to pick off a baserunner.

pickoff play A play in which either the pitcher or the catcher makes a sudden toss of the ball to an infielder, with the intent of catching a runner off base by surprise and tagging him out. The play requires careful coordination between the players who are setting up the play. See also *time pickoff*; *block pickoff*; *jockey pickoff*. Syn. *pickoff*.

pickoff sign A sign that a pickoff play is about to be attempted. For example, for a pickoff attempt at first base, the catcher might knead the back of his mitt and the first baseman might tug his belt to acknowledge the sign and let the catcher know that he will arrive at the base when the ball is thrown.

pickoff throw A throw intended to catch a runner off base. IST USE. 1948. "First baseman Ed Robinson takes catcher Jim Hegan's attempted pickoff throw" (*Indiana* [Pa.] *Evening Gazette* photo caption, Oct. 9; Peter Morris).

pick of the club *hist.* A player-development scheme in which a major-league club signs more prospects than it could possibly use and

offers a minor-league club several of the players in exchange for the "pick of the club" at season's end. This practice was the ultimate embodiment of Branch Rickey's "quality out of quantity" philosophy. John B. Sheridan (*The Sporting News*, Feb. 5, 1920; Peter Morris) observed, "Branch Rickey did not devise the 'pick of the club' scheme of trading between major and minor league teams. But he worked it to his finest development." IST USE. 1909. "The indications are that practically the whole Wilkes-Barre team will be taken this fall through the privileges afforded through the systems known as 'pick of the team,' 'the draft,' the option and purchase privileges" (H.G. Merrill, *The Sporting News*, Sept. 2; Peter Morris).

pickpocket **1.** One who steals the signs of an opponent. **2.** A quick-handed infielder who "steals" potential base hits and turns them into outs.

pick the ball up **1.** For a batter to get a good look at the ball as it is pitched. See also *pick up*, 1. **2.** For a baserunner attempting to steal a base to locate the ball to determine whether he should slide into the base or go in standing up (which puts him in a much better position to advance an extra base on a base hit or an errant throw). **3.** For an outfielder to locate the ball in the air. Syn. *pick up*, 2.

pickup *n.* **1.** The act of fielding a ball immediately after it strikes the ground; e.g., a first baseman often makes "pickups" on low throws in the dirt. "[Brady Anderson] committed an error by not making a clean pickup of a Carlos Baerga single" (*The Baltimore Sun*, March 25, 1998). IST USE. 1875 (*New York Herald*, Aug. 7; Edward J. Nichols). **2.** A player who has been acquired by a club. "Bobby Bonilla was a good pickup for them [St. Louis Cardinals]: He can play first, third and the corner outfield spots" (*Sports Illustrated*, March 26, 2001, p.135).

pick up *v.* **1.** For a batter to get a good look at the ball as it is pitched. "[Dontrelle Willis'] windup and his motion . . . make him tough to pick up" (Washington Nationals manager Frank Robinson, quoted in *The Baltimore Sun*, Sept. 8, 2005). See also *pick the ball up*, 1. **2.** Syn. of *pick the ball up*, 3. **3.** For an infielder to field a ground ball. **4.** For a batter to drive in one or more baserunners; e.g., "Smith picked up the two runners by doubling to right." **5.** For a player or team to be successful after another player on the team has not done well; e.g., "Brown's single picked up Jones after he failed to sacrifice" or "We have to pick each other up and do the little things to win" or "Smith kept the ball down and picked us up big time." Oakland A's pitcher Dan Haren (quoted in *The Baltimore Sun*, Aug. 8, 2005): "There was a stretch there where I wasn't pitching that well and the offense picked me up every time." **6.** To acquire; e.g., "The Cubs picked up Jones to bolster their bullpen."

pick-up game An informal playground or schoolyard game in which players are divided into two teams just before it begins. "[Tris Speaker] had acquired enough mastery of the southpaw delivery to be in demand again for pick-up games" (*The Washington Post*, Aug. 24, 1913; Peter Morris). The term is now almost exclusively a basketball term.

pickup-point The split second (¹⁵/₁₀₀ of a second according to one estimate) at which the batter can see the pitched ball and decide whether to swing at it. Before reaching this point, the ball is an indistinct blur.

pickups A fundamental conditioning drill for pitchers to develop coordination, agility, and endurance, in which a stationary player or coach 10 feet away rolls 25 ground balls to the pitcher, alternating from the pitcher's left side to his right side, in an arc of about 12 feet, the pitcher picking up each ball with both hands and returning it with an underhand toss. The coach may change ball speeds while increasing the angle between the pitcher and the ball to relieve the monotony of the drill.

pie *hist.* Easy to handle or defeat. "Those who imagined that the Wolverines would be pie for the pennant-winners yesterday were sadly disappointed" (*The World* [New York], Sept. 29, 1888; Gerald L. Cohen). IST USE. 1887. "Hammill was pretty clever for the Commercial League, but he is pie for the amateurs at the Haight-street park" (*San Francisco Examiner*, Aug. 21; Peter Morris). ETYMOLOGY. Apparently from "easy as pie."

pie belt *hist.* A nickname for the major-league clubs and cities of the Middle West. IST USE. 1914 (*New York Tribune*, Sept. 19; Edward J. Nichols).

piece of cake An easy play by a defensive player, even if the ball is hit hard; an easy out. See also *cake,* 1.

piece of iron 1. A baseball bat made of extra-good wood (Al Schacht, *Al Schacht Dope Book,* 1944, p.43). **2.** *hist.* A baseball bat illegally plugged with nails, screws, or hardware.

piece of the ball See *get a piece of the ball.*

pier six 1. A rough-and-tumble situation, such as a brawl between opposing sides. "The Reno Silver Sox clobbered Visalia, 10–4 . . . last night but apparently gained only a draw in a pier six free-for-all with the Cubs" (*San Francisco News,* Aug. 31, 1955). ETYMOLOGY. Uncertain, but the use of the term may have been aided by a 1955 movie entitled *Riot on Pier Six,* regarding an honest stevedores' union versus a racketeer operating a smuggling business on the New Orleans docks. **2.** A one-sided game; a laugher or blowout. **3.** A game in which the lead keeps changing.

pie-thrower A pitcher who holds his palm too far under the ball rather than having his fingers on top of it, as if throwing a pie, putting stress on the elbow and shoulder. "If you're a pie-thrower, you tend to end up in the [strike] zone a lot with your pitches flattening out" (Mike Arbuckle, quoted in Alan Schwarz, BaseballAmerica.com, Nov. 14, 2006).

pigskin The baseball. "Every one of the boys [the New York Giants] nailed the pigskin for one or more hits" (*The World* [New York], May 30, 1889; Gerald L. Cohen). ETYMOLOGY. Borrowed from football.

pig tail *hist.* A player stationed behind the catcher to help keep the ball in play. "Gorman c" and "Madigan pig tail" were included in a list of 14-and-under players for the Randolph Stars (*St. Louis Post-Dispatch,* May 5, 1888; Peter Morris). See also *hindcatcher,* 3.

pike The middle of the strike zone. See also *down the pike.*

pile into a ball To hit a ball with great force.

pilfer To steal a base. IST USE. 1887. "As a

team, [St. Louis] stole bases much more freely. [Arlie] Latham captured half of those pilfered by St. Louis" (*Detroit Free Press*, Oct. 27).

pill 1. The baseball. "[Spence] zipped that old pill around the infield" (*San Francisco Bulletin*, March 8, 1913; Gerald L. Cohen). "Uncle Nick's little base ball pills [are] sure cure for the blues [in the] business world" (*The Sporting Life* cartoon showing an ailing Uncle Sam consuming a baseball, or pill, served on a spoon, May 15, 1897; Barry Popik). IST USE. 1892. "The druggists of Brooklyn are rejoicing on account of the victory of the Brooklyn college of pharmacy team over the marines at the navy yard. . . . The college boys are learning to handle the big pill as neatly as they do the small ones" (*Brooklyn Eagle*, July 31; Peter Morris). ETYMOLOGY. Perhaps derived from the pill-sized appearance of the baseball as it approaches the batter. **2.** The rubber-covered, cushioned or compressed cork center of the baseball. The pill is enveloped within two balanced rubber coverings and its cemented surface receives a series of one cotton and three wool windings of yarn.

pillow 1. Syn. of *base*, 2. "An accident to Frank Motz, the regular first baseman sent Isbel [Frank Isbell] to the initial pillow and he has stayed there ever since" (*Reach's Official American League Base Ball Guide*, 1902; Peter Morris). IST USE. 1890. "Jack Brady will rest the corns on his feet on the second base pillow" (*Rocky Mountain News* [Denver], July 30). **2.** A large, padded glove designed to cushion the hand against the force of the ball. In the 1890s, the term was generally used derisively: "It has come to such a pass that the infielder who wears a big glove depends entirely upon his pillow to stop a ball with" (Tim Hurst, *St. Louis Post-Dispatch*, July 3, 1894; Peter Morris). Later, the term was applied solely to catcher's mitts. See also *perfect pillow*.

pillow ball [softball term] **1.** Syn. of *mush ball*, 2. **2.** Syn. of *mush ball*, 3.

pill slinger *hist.* The pitcher. IST USE. 1914. "Of course, he's some pill slinger" (Burt L. Standish, *Brick King, Backstop*, p.50; David Shulman).

pilot 1. *n.* The manager of a baseball team, so called because he is at the controls. IST USE. 1906 (*The Sporting Life*, Feb. 10, p.6; Edward J. Nichols). **2.** *v.* To manage a baseball team. IST USE. 1888. "Charlie Comiskey, who for several years has successfully piloted the St. Louis Browns to victory" (Ren Mulford, *St. Louis Post-Dispatch*, Aug. 23; Peter Morris).

Pilots Nickname of the American League expansion franchise in Seattle, Wash., in 1969. So named because of the aerospace industry in Seattle. It slid into quick bankruptcy and in 1970 moved to Milwaukee, where it survives as the Brewers.

pimp it For a batter to stand at home plate and enjoy his long home run too much to suit the opposition (Garret Mathews, *Can't Find a Dry Ball*, 2002).

pimple ball A rubber ball, softer than a tennis ball, with tiny upraised bumps on its surface, used in streetball games such as punchball, box baseball, and stickball.

pinball baseball 1. Baseball as played on artificial turf where balls speed through the infield and take high bounces. "The National League . . . plays pinball 'baseball' on plastic rugs spread on concrete in cavernous, antiseptic new stadiums" (George F. Will, *The Washington Post*, Oct. 23, 1986). **2.** A game played on a pinball-style table in which a flipper bar and a metal ball are used to score singles, doubles, triples, and home runs.

pinch 1. *n.* A difficult or crucial situation in a game, such as losing by a run with only one out to go. "The St. Louis Americans . . . used the portly one [Tub Spencer] any number of times in a pinch and he always responded" (*San Francisco Bulletin*, Feb. 13, 1913; Gerald L. Cohen). Christy Mathewson's *Pitching in a Pinch* (1912) gave "pinch" an added boost as a baseball term. See also *clutch*. IST USE. 1902 (*The Sporting Life*, July 12, p.3; Edward J. Nichols). **2.** *adj.* Pertaining to a substitute; e.g., "Smith hit a pinch homer when he batted for Jones and sent the game into extra innings." **3.** *v.* For the plate umpire to call pitches that are disputed by the pitcher; e.g., "Jones accused the umpire of pinching him by calling the payoff pitch a ball." See also *squeeze*, 3. **4.** *v./hist.* To catch a runner off a base.

pinch hit **1.** *v.* To come to the plate and bat in place of the scheduled batter who must then automatically leave the game. EXTENDED USE. To substitute or take over for a regular performer. "Silvey has been pinch-hitting as an assistant director on the F.W. lot" (*Variety*, July 13, 1927). **2.** *n.* A hit made by a pinch hitter. **3.** *n./hist.* A hit made during a crucial or tight situation in a game. "Two men were out before Kruger [Otto Krueger] finally did his 'pinch hit' turn [i.e., getting a clutch hit]" (*St. Louis Post-Dispatch*, Apr. 14, 1902; Peter Morris). The *Chicago Tribune* informed its readers (Oct. 28, 1906) that "pinch" was "the term applied to a hit which scores runs after two men are out in an inning," but Morris notes that such a narrow definition did not last long.

pinch hitter **1.** A replacement sent in during the course of a game to bat for the scheduled batter who must then leave the game. Technically, the pinch hitter can only bat once; if his team bats around and he comes to the plate a second time, he is batting for himself. If he stays in the game to field as well as bat, however, he is no longer a pinch hitter but rather a substitute. The idea goes beyond mere substitution: the pinch hitter is put in expressly because he is more likely to get a hit. Abbrev. *PH*. Syn. *emergency hitter.* IST USE. 1902 (*The Sporting Life*, Apr. 26, p.8; Edward J. Nichols). ETYMOLOGY. The identity of the first pinch hitter long has been a matter of dispute. Claims go back to the 1870s when an injured player was replaced by a substitute who essentially functioned as a pinch hitter. Players given the designation as the first pinch hitter include Jim Devlin (1873), Bobby Clack (1876), Mickey Welch (1889), Ralph Johnson (1891), Charles Reilly (1892), and Jack Doyle (1892). But it was New York Giants manager John McGraw in 1905 who became a main proponent of pinch hitting when he engaged Sammy Strang as a pinch-hitting specialist. EXTENDED USE. **1.** A substitute; an understudy. "We should like to make Mrs. [William Randolph] Hearst an offer as pinch-hitter for Dulcinea, but we doubt whether she'd accept it" (Franklin P. Adams, *New York Tribune*, July 2, 1914; Stuart Y. Silverstein). "Esther Walker went on one night as a 'pinch hitter' at a Winter Garden show in New York and brought down the house" (*Victor Record Catalog*, 1920; Peter Tamony). **2.** A specialist. An article in *Sport Life* (July 1924; Peter Morris) described kickers as the "pinch hitters" of football because they similarly filled a narrow role rather than being all-around players.

2. *hist.* A clutch hitter; one who delivers a timely hit in a pinch. *The Washington Post* (Aug. 20, 1904; Peter Morris) noted that "pinch hitter" Mal Kittridge, who was Washington's catcher in the game, was purposely walked twice with Barry McCormick on second because "they are learning the fact that Kittredge [*sic*] is something of a hitter in the pinch." As observed by Morris, the current meaning of "pinch hitter" evolved from the idea that a player with a reputation for clutch hitting would be the best man for what is now known as a pinch-hitting opportunity. Syn. *substitute batter.*

pinch-hitting specialist A pinch hitter in some minor leagues who is allowed two trips to the plate without the removal of a player from the lineup.

pinch pitching *hist.* The clutch pitching of a relief pitcher who gets his team out of a jam (Gordon S. "Mickey" Cochrane, *Baseball: The Fan's Game*, 1939, p.151). Christy Mathewson (*Pitching in a Pinch*, 1912) described how relief pitcher Otis Crandall "has turned out to be one of the most valuable men on the club, because he is there in a pinch."

pinch run To enter the game as a substitute for a baserunner who must then automatically leave the game.

pinch runner A substitute runner sent in for a player who has reached base, usually in a situation requiring a much faster runner or if the runner on base was injured during the play. The original runner cannot continue to play in the game. IST USE. 1911. "Pinch Runner Nipped by Hidden Ball Play, Breaking up Late Rally" (*Chicago Daily Tribune* subheadline, Sept. 2). Abbrev. *PR*, 1.

pine The bench. To be told to "grab some pine" is to be told to sit on the bench. The legendary Johnny Pesky on Nomar Garciaparra (*The Boston Globe*, Aug. 25, 1997): "The best-looking shortstop we've ever had around here. . . . He has good baseball instincts. I'm telling you, if he'd come along in my era, I'd be sitting on the pine."

pineapple A rookie who sits quietly on the bench (pine).

pine-barren Said of a team lacking in good hitters.

pine tar A thick, sticky, blackish-brown liquid, obtained by destructive distillation of pine wood, but also available in a synthetic version, that is rubbed on a batter's hands or bat to create a better grip. It is usually applied by means of a cloth or towel that has been saturated with the substance. Pitchers use pine tar (illegally) to get a better grip on the ball.

pine tar ball An illegal pitch in which the ball has been rubbed with pine tar so that it is easier to grip and control. The pine tar is usually placed on the pitcher's glove before transfer to the ball. During the third game of the 1988 National League Championship Series, Los Angeles Dodgers pitcher Jay Howell was ejected from the game and suspended for three days after pine tar was found in his glove.

pine tar bat A baseball bat that has been rubbed with a pine tar rag to give the batter a better grip.

Pine Tar Game The game at Yankee Stadium on July 24, 1983, in which, with two outs in the ninth inning, Kansas City Royals slugger George Brett hit a two-run home run off Goose Gossage to give the Royals the lead, 5–4. On protest by Yankees manager Billy Martin, plate umpire Tim McClelland ruled that the pine tar on Brett's bat extended beyond the legal limit of 18 inches up the bat handle, nullified the home run, and called Brett out to end the game, giving the Yankees the win, 4–3. The Royals lodged a protest with American League president Lee MacPhail, who eventually ruled in Kansas City's favor, saying the "spirit of the rules" did not provide for a batter to be called out for excessive pine tar on his bat and that "games should be won and lost on the playing field—not through technicalities of the rules." The home run was restored and the game was resumed on Aug. 18, 1983, with Kansas City ahead with two outs in the top of the ninth. The Royals won the game 5–4. Also referred to as "Pine Tar Incident."

pine tar rag A pine tar-soaked cloth or towel that batters rub on their bat handles to provide a firmer grip.

pine tar rule The rule that stipulates that no material or substance to improve the grip on the bat may be applied more than 18 inches from the end of the bat handle (*Official Baseball Rules*, Rule 1.10[c]). Any such material or substance so found shall cause the bat to be removed from the game, but shall not be grounds for declaring the batter out or ejected from the game.

pingball A two-man variety of baseball, played with table-tennis balls, using imaginary players and specific areas of the field to designate base hits. The pitcher stood 33 feet from a home plate 12 inches square. The game was played in Shaker Heights, Ohio in the 1940s (Robert Boynton).

ping effect The distinctive, echoing sound when a ball is hit by an aluminum bat and the (commonly negative) reaction to it. "The sound of a ball struck by an aluminum bat is different to different ears, but no one could confuse it with the distinctive crack of an ash bat. In the bat business, that is called the ping effect" (Phil Patton, *Smithsonian* magazine, Oct. 1984).

ping hitter A hitter whose swing does not connect with any force or power; one who does not drive the ball with authority. The term does not necessarily imply a hitter using an aluminum bat (Alan Schwarz, Baseball America.com, Nov. 14, 2006).

pin his ears back To amass numerous hits against an opposing pitcher. See also *clobber*, 2.

pinpoint control Precise accuracy by a pitcher.

pinpointer A pitcher with precise control.

Pinstriper A member of the New York Yankees. A profile of Yankees coach and former player Clete Boyer in the *St. Petersburg Times* (Feb. 16, 1988) was simply titled "Pinstriper."

pinstripes A uniform decoration comprising

Pinstripes. New York Yankees baseball team, posed Oct. 19, 1926. *George Grantham Bain Collection, Library of Congress*

rows of thin vertical stripes. In a baseball context, the term is almost always used to refer to the pinstriped home uniforms of the New York Yankees. This is true despite the fact that other teams (including the Detroit Tigers, Philadelphia Phillies, and Chicago Cubs) have worn pinstripes. The first team to wear pinstripes was the Chicago Cubs during the 1907 World Series (Marc Okkonen, *Baseball Uniforms of the 20th Century*, 1991). The Yankees first wore pinstripes on Apr. 11, 1912, but did not adopt them permanently until 1915. Pinstripes have come to represent power. They have also created their own mythology. According to *USA Today* (March 12, 1987), the Yankees pinstripes came about as a result of Babe Ruth's excessive eating and drinking: "In 1929, Yankees management wanted the slugger to look thinner, so they added pinstripes to the white uniforms to hide his girth." EXTENDED USE. A metaphor for active organizational loyalty. *The Baltimore Sun* (Aug. 19, 1996) noted that United Nations secretary-general Boutros Boutros-Ghali, 73, "refuses to hang up his pinstripes." *The Baltimore Sun* (July 29, 2001) also noted that after Meyer Lansky's death in 1983, UPI reported that the business brains of the underworld "took the Mob from convict stripes to pinstripes."

Pinstripes Nickname for the New York Yankees.

pinwheel For the batter to twirl the bat as he gets ready in the batter's box.

pipe 1. *n.* Throat. A "hot pipe" is a sore throat.

2. *n.* A strong throw across the diamond to get the runner at first base (Garret Mathews, 2002, *Can't Find a Dry Ball*). **3.** *v.* To throw a ball across the heart of the plate. Kris Foster (quoted in *The Baltimore Sun*, Aug. 13, 2001): "I've hung a few sliders and piped a few fastballs down the middle." See also *down the pipe*.

Pipp *v.* To be replaced due to injury or illness and never regain one's position, as when Wally Pipp was replaced by Lou Gehrig. Bruce Anderson (*Sports Illustrated*, June 29, 1987, p.82): "Pipp has transcended mere trivia and become a metaphor. His very name conjures up a picture of a player sitting on the bench and watching his replacement sparkle. At the ball yard, nearly everyone knows what it is to be Pipped." Jonathan Eig (*Luckiest Man: The Life and Death of Lou Gehrig*, 2005, pp.64–65): "Take a day off and you'll suffer for it. The boss will find someone better to do your job. Wally Pipp reminds us that we're all easily replaced, like old technology. He lives on today as a verb (don't get Pipped!), as an eponym, as a warning." Sometimes spelled "pipp." ETYMOLOGY. See *Wally Pipp*.

Pirates Nickname for the National League Central Division franchise that began playing in Pittsburgh, Pa., in 1887 as the Pittsburgh Alleghenies and later as the Pittsburgh Innocents (1890). See also *Family, The*. Also known as *Bucs*; *Corsairs*. ETYMOLOGY. The club was dubbed Pirates in 1891 when it signed second baseman Lou Bierbauer away from the Philadelphia Athletics of the American Association, which protested the signing as "piratical."

pisser and a moaner, a One who whines and complains. "[Roger] Maris arrived at the [New York] Yankees with a somewhat seedy but well-earned reputation as a pisser and a moaner, in baseball parlance, a complainer, a griper. Something terrible was always happening to poor Roger" (Leonard Shecter, *The Jocks*, 1969, p.28; Charles D. Poe).

piss home run A cheap home run. "When he [Joe DiMaggio] hit a home run to right field, he would complain about his 'piss home run.' He'd say, 'Anybody could hit a piss home run to right'" (Billy Martin and Peter Golenbock, *Number 1*, 1980, p.159; Charles D. Poe).

Pipp. Wally Pipp. *George Grantham Bain Collection, Library of Congress*

piss-rod A line drive (Garret Mathews, *Can't Find a Dry Ball*, 2002).

pista de advertencia Spanish for "warning track."

pit 1. The lowest point in the standings; the *cellar*. **2.** *hist.* Syn. of *dugout*. IST USE. 1917 (*American Magazine*, April; Edward J. Nichols). **3.** See *sliding pit*.

pitch 1. *n.* The delivery of the ball to the batter by the pitcher. The pitch is only one element of the act of pitching; e.g., "Here's the windup, the stride, the pitch, and the ball nicks the inside corner of the plate." IST USE. 1861 (*New York Sunday Mercury*, Aug. 10; Edward J. Nichols). EXTENDED USE. A presentation, such as a "sales pitch." **2.** *n.* The ball delivered to the batter by the pitcher; e.g., a fastball or a curveball. **3.** *v.* To deliver the ball from the pitcher's mound to the batter. IST USE. 1845. "The ball must be pitched, not thrown, for the bat" (Knickerbocker Rules, Rule 9th, Sept. 23). USAGE NOTE. "Pitched" here referred to tossing the ball below the hip with an unbent elbow, the arm swinging straight and parallel to the pitcher's body, without a snap of the wrist, as in horseshoes. As pitchers increasingly began to use a covert wrist snap and bent-elbow delivery, the rule defining a legal delivery was relaxed in response; by 1884, all restrictions on the delivery were removed, as the ball was in fact thrown rather than pitched. The term "pitch" as used today is a survivor of a practice long since abandoned. The modern unrestricted delivery would be considered a "throw" in the original Knickerbocker Rules. EXTENDED USE. To become active; to be part of the action; to present. "Some observers opine that Yankee doughboys will be in there pitching for democracy within the next four weeks" (*San Francisco Examiner*, Sept. 21, 1939, quoting the Tokyo newspaper *Nichi Nichi*; Peter Tamony). Also applies in the sense of "to pitch woo" (for "to neck" or "to court" another) or to "pitch" a new product. **4.** *v.* To deliver the ball in a particular way; e.g., "Smith pitched Jones low and inside." **5.** *v.* To play in a game as a pitcher, or to fill the position of pitcher in a game; e.g., "Smith pitched a good game." EXTENDED USE. To play a game in another sport. "The [Baltimore] Ravens' defense pitched a shutout and held the [Cleveland] Browns to 211 yards of total offense" (Mike Preston, *The Baltimore Sun*, Dec. 22, 2003).

pitchability The competence or skill of a pitcher; the ability of a pitcher to throw strikes consistently and to command several pitches. "[Zack Greinke] was showing the poise and pitchability of a veteran on the mound" (*Baseball America*, July 7–20, 2003).

pitch and catch To throw a baseball back and forth between two or more players.

pitch around 1. To risk a base on balls by not throwing good pitches to a good hitter, often when first base is not occupied or when the next batter is a weak hitter. "You can't always pitch around him [Frank Thomas], because the guy [Julio Franco] behind him isn't too shabby either. You just try to keep the ball away from him and if you get him out, fine, and if you don't get him out, that's fine too" (Sid Fernandez, quoted in *The Baltimore Sun*, May 30, 1994). **2.** To try to get a free swinger out on pitches that are out of the strike zone. "He's [Vladimir Guerrero] impossible to pitch around. He can hit any pitch, and I would never, ever throw him the same pitch twice in a row" (Chicago Cubs pitcher Kevin Tapani, quoted in *Sports Illustrated*, May 1, 2001).

pitch backward To pitch the opposite of what is expected; e.g., to throw a changeup instead of a fastball in a hitter's count or throw a fastball when ahead in the count. "[Cory Scott is] so good with it [curveball] that he often pitches backward, using the curve to set up a fastball as an out pitch" (John Royster, *Baseball America*, May 29–June 11, 2000; Peter Morris).

pitch count A running tabulation of the *number of pitches* a pitcher has thrown in a game. The manager and pitching coach watch the pitch count to keep a pitcher from exhausting himself or injuring his arm. Excluded in the pitch count are the eight warmup tosses before innings and the dozens thrown in the bullpen before or during the game. Some teams do not count intentional walks and pitchouts on their pitch counts. "[New York Mets manager] Davey Johnson said he would've ended Ron Darling's no-hit bid if his pitch-count approached 160" (*New York Post*, June 29, 1987). Little League holds pitchers to daily pitch counts: 75 pitches for ages 9 and 10, 85 pitches for ages 11 and 12, 95 pitches for ages 13 to 15, and 105 pitches for ages 16 to 18.

pitched ball A ball delivered by the pitcher to the batter.

pitcher 1. The defensive player who starts the game and puts the ball back in play during the game by delivering the ball from the pitcher's mound to the batter. The primary objective of the pitcher is to put out batters. Abbrev. *P*, 1. Syn. *hurler*. IST USE. 1845. "When a balk is made by the pitcher" (Knickerbocker Rules, Rule 19th, Sept. 23; Frederick Ivor-Campbell). EXTENDED USE. One who presents ("pitches") ideas and policy. Eugene McCarthy used to call Richard Nixon "the same old pitcher" (*San Francisco Chronicle*, Aug. 28, 1968; Peter Tamony). 2. A term of distinction for a pitcher with great control, finesse, deceptive moves, and knowledge of the hitters, as opposed to a pitcher who depends solely on speed or power. "Bob

Feller, the former great baseball pitcher, has been quoted as saying that the California Angels Nolan Ryan was a thrower, not a pitcher" (*San Francisco Chronicle*, June 28, 1975; Peter Tamony). Compare *thrower*, 1. EXTENDED USE. The 9-ball, placed near the center of the pyramid of racked balls in the pocket billiards game of baseball. 3. The position played by the pitcher. Abbrev. *P*, 2.

pitcher abuse points A measure of the hypothetical effect the number of pitches thrown in a game has on the arm of a given starting pitcher. It is computed by cubing the number of pitches greater than 100; e.g., 120 pitches thrown would receive 20 cubed, or a total of 8,000 pitcher abuse points. Research has shown that individual games with larger numbers of pitcher abuse points (i.e., pitches thrown) are associated with ineffectiveness in subsequent starts, and that a consistent pattern of games with large numbers of pitcher abuse points is associated with subsequent arm injury, premature ineffectiveness, and shorter careers for starting pitchers. The reasoning behind the measure is based on evidence that pitcher abuse begins at about 100 pitches and increases at about a cubic rate as pitch totals increase thereafter. Originally introduced by Rany Jazayerli (*Baseball Prospectus*, 1999) in a more informal form, the current version was unveiled in *Baseball Prospectus* for 2001. Abbrev. *PAP.*

pitcher covering first A common defensive play that occurs when the first baseman moves off the bag to field a batted ball and tosses to the pitcher running to first base for the putout.

pitcher fielding practice A set of drills to sharpen a pitcher's skills in handling comebackers, covering first base, and executing other fielding plays. Abbrev. *PFP.*

pitcher-friendly 1. Said of a pitcher's park. "Starting pitching, the traditional [Los Angeles] Dodgers' strength in a pitcher-friendly home park [Dodger Stadium]" (Tom Verducci, *Sports Illustrated*, March 26, 2007, p.133). 2. Said of an umpire with a generous strike zone.

pitcher of record The pitcher who is charged with a win or loss, even if he has been removed from the game. A pitcher who has been removed as the pitcher of record remains so until the score becomes tied or a new lead is established, at which point a new pitcher of record is established.

Pitcher of the Year Award An annual award presented in 1944 and from 1948 onward by *The Sporting News* to the best pitcher in each major league, as judged by baseball "experts" to have had the most outstanding season. A similar award has been presented since 1994 by *Baseball Digest.*

pitcher park factor The park factor credited to a team's pitchers in the linear weights system.

pitcher reader A batter who recognizes the upcoming pitch by identifying the pitcher's grip or motion (H.G. Salsinger, *Baseball Digest*, Aug. 1945).

pitcher run average A method for evaluating the performance of a pitcher, computed by finding the difference in run potential from the *base–out situation* in which a pitcher enters and that for when he departs the game, and subtracting any runs scored for which he is charged. The method was introduced by Doug Bennion (*Baseball Analyst*, Dec. 1988). See also *runs prevented.* Abbrev. *PRA.*

pitcher run support See *run support.*

pitchers and catchers report The metaphoric message that spring has arrived, spring training will start, and the season is on its way. Pitchers and catchers invited to spring training workouts must report no earlier than 45 days prior to the start of the season. "Come November, passionate baseball fans begin counting the days to that glorious February morning when pitchers and catchers report" (Childs Walker, *The Baltimore Sun*, Feb. 14, 2006). "The first true sign of spring always has been the day pitchers and catchers report for spring training" (Matt Villano, *Newsweek*, March 21, 2005). The practice of pitchers and catchers reporting to spring training a few days earlier than their teammates began in 1903 by Connie Mack, whose object "of the early visit to the south is to try out the pitchers and get them in good condition for the preliminary games" (*Fort Wayne News*, Feb. 25, 1903; Peter Morris). Pitchers needed

to be in shape to throw batting practice and pitch spring training games, hence their head start and hence the need for catchers. Joe S. Jackson (*The Washington Post*, Jan. 21, 1911; Peter Morris) wrote that the practice became "a general custom" by 1911, noting that Frank Chance planned to take his battery members "South two weeks in advance of the team itself, so that he can start them as early as possible." IST USE. 1927. "The Phils did announce their spring training plans— pitchers and catchers will report at the Bradenton camp in Florida, a week earlier than the infielders and outfielders, which will be in late February" (*The Sporting News*, Jan. 13; Peter Morris).

pitchers' battle *hist.* Syn. of *pitchers' duel*, 1. IST USE. 1880 (*New York Press*, June 2, which used the term "pitcher's battle"; Edward J. Nichols).

pitcher's best friend The *double play.* "The double play is the pitcher's best friend, because you get two outs on one pitch" (Cleveland Indians pitcher Dave Burba, quoted in *Sports Illustrated*, March 26, 2001).

pitcher's box *hist.* The rectangular area from which the pitcher delivered the ball in the 19th century. It existed from 1863 (when two parallel lines, one yard apart and four yards long, were drawn at right angles to a line from home plate to second base) through 1892. It was defined by the *pitcher's points*, and its dimensions changed frequently during the 19th century: six feet wide and four feet deep (1867); six feet square (1869); four feet wide and six feet long (1879); four feet wide and seven feet long (1886); and four feet wide and five and a half feet long (1887). See also *pitcher's square.* Syn. *pitching box*; *rifle pit.* USAGE NOTE. Although the full term is no longer used, "box" survives in expressions such as "knocked out of the box" or "a shot through the box" (Tom Shieber).

pitchers' duel 1. A low-scoring game in which the quality of the pitching is quite clearly better than that of the hitting; a game dominated by good pitching. Often incorrectly spelled "pitcher's duel." Syn. *pitching duel*; *pitchers' battle*; *mound duel.* IST USE. 1900. "The game lacked in interest, as most pitcher's duels do" (*Chicago Daily Tribune*,

Aug. 12). **2.** A contest, usually at the sandlot level, in which two pitchers throw to the plate without a batter. The pitcher with the least number of walks wins.

pitcher's elbow A generic name for ailments that affect the pitching arm due to stress and strain put on tendons, ligaments, muscles, and nerves.

pitchers' game 1. A style of play "in which the brunt of the work of the attack in a contest falls upon the pitcher and catcher, while the majority of the fielders stand idly by as mere lookers on" (*Brooklyn Eagle*, Nov. 8, 1885). IST USE. 1884. "Everybody knows that what are called 'pitchers' games,' in which but a few scattered hits are made and where a couple of runs on either side hopelessly settle the game, are monotonous and becoming unpopular" (*The Sporting Life*, Feb. 27; Peter Morris). **2.** [softball term] A sobriquet since the 1930s for fast pitch softball dominated by the pitcher. The argument has always been stated that this form of the game was not a *team game*.

pitcher's glove The glove worn by the pitcher in professional baseball. It may be multicolored but cannot be distracting, in the opinion of the umpire; and, exclusive of piping, it may not be white or gray. The glove also may not have any attached foreign material of a color different from that of the glove.

pitcher's hand A putout in playground baseball in which the pitcher also serves as the first baseman; e.g., a batter is retired when an infielder throws a ground ball to the pitcher on the mound before the batter reaches first base.

pitcher's mound Syn. of *mound*, 1. Early Wynn was once asked if he ever threw the ball at a batter's head and he replied (quoted by George F. Will, *The Washington Post*, Aug. 11, 1986), "The pitcher's mound is my office and I don't like my office messed up with a lot of blood."

pitcher's paradise A large ballpark in which it is difficult to hit home runs. The term seems to have been initially applied to Cleveland's Municipal Stadium in the 1940s.

pitcher's park 1. A ballpark in which it is relatively difficult to score runs. Compare *hitter's park*. **2.** A ballpark with large outfield dimensions, such as Griffith Stadium (Washington, D.C.), or in which it is difficult to hit home runs, such as Shea Stadium (Flushing Meadows, Queens).

pitcher's path Syn. of *alley*, 4. "A little dinky roller down the pitcher's path robbed Carl Mays [from pitching a no-hitter] . . . at Fenway Park" (*Boston Herald and Journal*, June 22, 1918; Peter Morris).

pitcher's plate *hist.* A flat, circular, white iron plate from which the pitcher delivered the ball. The plate was introduced in 1857, but the term appeared later. The pitcher's plate was replaced by a rectangular slab of whitened rubber in 1893. See also *rubber*, 1; *pitcher's points*. Syn. *plate*, 4. IST USE. 1865. "The circle around the bases had been moistened and rolled, and the home and pitcher's plates, bases and foul lines were distinctly drawn and whitened" (*Brooklyn Eagle*, Aug. 15; Peter Morris).

pitcher's points *hist.* The markers that defined the *pitcher's box* in the 19th century. In 1857, a single pitcher's point designated the *pitcher's plate* from which the pitcher delivered the ball. A rear point was introduced in 1863. In 1872, two extra points were introduced, and rearranged in 1874 to be at the corners of a square. Originally circular, pitcher's points became square in 1868, before reverting to circles (six inches in diameter) in 1890. The placement and composition (originally iron, later stone, then rubber in 1890) of the pitcher's points changed frequently during the 19th century. Henry Chadwick (*The Game of Base Ball*, 1868, p.44) originally defined "pitcher's points" as "two iron quoits placed on the two lines of the pitcher's position on a line from home to second base." Syn. *points*, 2. IST USE. 1866 (Constitution and By-Laws of Olympic Club of Philadelphia, p.28; Edward J. Nichols). (Tom Shieber).

pitcher's rubber Syn. of *rubber*, 1.

pitcher's square *hist.* The *pitcher's box* when its length and width were both six feet (1869–1878). "He is strongest inside of the pitcher's square" (*Louisville Courier-Journal*, July 15, 1877; Peter Morris).

pitcher's strike A pitched ball that gets a pitcher out of a jam. A pitch that results in a pop fly with the bases loaded and two outs is regarded as a pitcher's strike.

pitcher's Triple Crown See *Triple Crown*, 2.

pitch from the stretch To pitch with a *no-windup delivery*, even without runners on base. Kid Nichols introduced the style in the 1890s, and it was popularized by Bob Turley and Don Larsen in the 1950s.

PITCHf/x A system that uses two sensor cameras to measure the position, speed, and acceleration of a pitched baseball, thereby revealing the break of a pitch from the time it is 40 feet from home plate to the time it crosses the plate. It can measure the position of the ball to better than ½ inch to the exact location of the ball. The system was developed by Sportvision and introduced to major-league baseball during the 2006 playoffs.

pitching 1. The art and science of systematically throwing the ball to batters with the intent to confuse and deceive them. 2. The collective pitchers on a team.

pitching average 1. The ratio obtained by dividing the number of pitching decisions into the number of games won; e.g., the pitching average of a pitcher with a 10–6 record is ¹⁰⁄₁₆, or .625. 2. The batting average of a set of players versus a specific pitcher. "Since Pitching Averages are the mirror of Batting Averages, and just as important, this makes Nolan Ryan the Ty Cobb of pitching" (John Holway, *Baseball Digest*, May 1984, p.28). See also *opponents' batting average*.

pitching baseball cards A childhood game in which contestants flip or scale baseball cards, with the player whose card comes closest to a wall or stoop being declared the winner. The practice came to a virtual halt with the advent of price guides and the commodification of the cards. See also *flipping*.

pitching box Syn. of *pitcher's box*.

pitching chart A complete pitch-by-pitch account of a team's pitches in a game, including the type, location, and velocity of the pitches and the results of batted balls. It is used to spot flaws in pitching strategy and technique. Tradition has it that the chart is kept by the pitcher who is scheduled to pitch the next day. See also *chart*; *spray chart*.

pitching coach A coach who works with the team's pitchers to help them improve their skills and strategy and who advises the manager on pitching changes during a game. The first pitching coach in the major leagues may have been Jack Coombs for the Detroit Tigers in 1920, although the term "pitching coach" was not used. Detroit manager Hughie Jennings (quoted in *Philadelphia Evening Bulletin*, May 18, 1920; David W. Smith) explained, "So I turned the whole thing over to Jack. . . . Here's one department I take my hands entirely off of. It's up to Jack. He says who pitches, how long he pitches, when does he come out and who goes in next." See also *bullpen coach*.

pitching corps Syn. of *pitching staff*. 1ST USE. 1898. "Rodman and [Nick] Altrock of the local pitching corps were left behind when the team left on the trip last night" (*Grand Rapids* [Mich.] *Evening Press*, Apr. 25; Peter Morris).

pitching duel Syn. of *pitchers' duel*, 1.

pitching gun An early *pitching machine*, 1. "Ted [Kennedy] set to work to devise a pitching gun which would serve up any kind of a curve, at any given height, at any rate of speed desired. He could mix a high inshoot with a low drop, a straight fast one with a slow floater—in short, anything" (Eddie Wray, *St. Louis Post-Dispatch*, Aug. 19, 1910; Peter Morris).

pitching in A standardized version of *stickball* in which the pitcher bounces the ball to the batter (Jay Feldman, *Sports Illustrated*, Sept. 11, 1989).

pitching machine 1. A device used to throw balls for batting practice. The original pitching machines were mechanical devices; by the mid-1930s, most major-league teams had such devices, which were called "Ol' Pete" (after pitcher Grover Cleveland "Pete" Alexander). Current pitching machines are more sophisticated and computerized, duplicating the speed, spin, and break of the curveball of the opponent's pitchers, as well as throwing pinpoint fastballs, sliders, screwballs, and changeups at random. See also *Iron Mike*; *automatic pitcher*; *pitching gun*. **2.** An exceptional and durable pitcher. IST USE. 1905. In the burgeoning industrial America of the early 19th century, New York Giants manager John McGraw described Christy Mathewson's stellar performance in the 1905 World Series (pitching three complete-game shutouts in six days against the Philadelphia Athletics) as "pretty much the perfect type of pitching machine" (quoted in Christopher H. Evans and William R. Herzog II, eds., *The Faith of Fifty Million*, 2002, pp.228–29).

pitching mound Syn. of *mound*, 1.

pitching rotation Syn. of *rotation*, 1.

pitching rubber Syn. of *rubber*, 1.

pitching runs The *linear weights* measure of a pitcher's performance. It represents the number of runs for which the pitcher is responsible compared to the league average, defined so that the league average in a given year is zero. See *The Baseball Encyclopedia* (2004, p.1695) for the exact formula. Cy Young is both the single-season leader for 20th-century pitchers, with 84.1 in 1901, and the career leader with 753. Pitching runs was devised by Pete Palmer and originally described by John Thorn and Pete Palmer in *The Hidden Game of Baseball* (1985). Abbrev. *PR*, 2.

pitching runs above average The number of runs a pitcher has saved his team relative to the average pitcher in the same number of innings in the same year. Abbrev. *PRAA*.

pitching runs above replacement The number of runs a pitcher has saved his team relative to a replacement level pitcher in the same number of innings in the same year. Abbrev. *PRAR*.

pitching screen Syn. of *batting-practice screen*.

pitching sequence The mix of pitches that a pitcher throws. Batters try to determine if there is a set sequence so that they can anticipate the pitches to come.

pitching staff The aggregate of starting and relief pitchers on a club's roster. Syn. *arms*; *mound corps*; *pitching corps*. IST USE. 1894. "The Phillies' pitching staff is in very bad shape" (*The North American* [Philadelphia], June 9).

pitching to the strings An innovative technique introduced by Branch Rickey whereby pitchers learn to create a visible strike zone in their minds by throwing to a movable structure consisting of two parallel horizontal strings about 36 inches apart (one shoulder high, the other knee high) attached to two six-foot poles 15 feet apart, and two vertical strings attached to the top lateral string 17 inches (width of home plate) apart, with the strings' bottom extensions wound around the lower lateral string. The strings attached to the poles are moved up and down to simulate the batters' various strike zones. Quoting Rickey: "Pitching to the strings will accelerate the mastery of control, and pitchers, particularly the younger ones, shall be given ample opportunity to use them" (*Branch Rickey's Little Blue Book*, 1995, p.68); and "The important job is to hit the strings. Anybody can put a ball through the rectangle, but when you hit the strings, you have caught the edge of the plate" (Arthur Mann, *Baseball Confidential*, 1951, p.79).

pitching wins The linear weights measure of the number of wins for which a pitcher is directly responsible. It is computed by dividing a player's pitching runs by runs per win. It is defined so that the league average in a given year is zero. Walter Johnson is both the single-season leader for 20th-century pitchers, with 7.9 in 1912, and the career leader with 73.2. Pitching wins was devised by Pete Palmer and originally described by John Thorn and Pete Palmer in *The Hidden Game of Baseball* (1985). Abbrev. *PW*.

pitch limit A predetermined number of pitches that a manager will not allow a pitcher to exceed in a game. A young pitcher in professional baseball "should expect pitch limits of 110–115" (David Rawnsley, *Baseball America*, Apr. 13–26, 1998; Peter Morris).

pitch of the 1980s Syn. of *split-fingered fastball*.

pitchometer A device that measures the

speed of balls thrown through two beams of light a foot apart, setting off an electric timer. Bob Feller was timed at 98.6 miles per hour on I.M. Levitt's (Fels Planetarium, Philadelphia) pitchometer in 1946 (Lee Allen, *The Hot Stove League*, 1955, p.140).

pitch on top To pitch winning baseball; e.g., "Smith says he will pitch the best he can because he feels like he can pitch on top."

pitchout *n.* A defensive move made with a runner on base, in which the pitcher deliberately throws a fastball high and wide of the strike zone so that the catcher can easily catch the ball and throw it to a base that a runner may be attempting to steal. The pitch is thrown wide to keep the batter from swinging at the ball and to give the catcher the best positioning. Used when a steal, squeeze, or a hit-and-run play is expected, it is a play that must be coordinated carefully among the pitcher, catcher, and infielder involved. In most cases, either the catcher or the manager calls for the play. Originally spelled "pitch out." Sometimes spelled "pitch-out." IST USE. 1903. "Pitch out is the sign for a wide ball when the backstop wants to throw to a base" (*Decatur* [Ill.] *Review*, Aug. 24; *OED*). ETYMOLOGY. Notes in the Peter Tamony collection describe two logical etymologies: a) a pitch "outside" the plate; and b) a pitch calculated to catch the man "out" at second. EXTENDED USE. In football, a short lateral pass behind the line of scrimmage, thrown by one back to another. The term may or may not have been adopted from baseball, but it did come into use many years after the term was common in baseball. IST USE (football). 1946. "Davis took a pitch-out pass from Tucker" (*The New York Times*, Dec. 1; *OED*).

pitch out *v.* To throw a pitchout. IST USE. 1910. "If the signal is caught, the catcher instantly orders the ball 'pitched out' high and fast in the best position for making a fast hard throw" (John J. Evers and Hugh S. Fullerton, *Touching Second: The Science of Baseball*, 1910; Peter Morris).

pitch recognition The ability of a batter to identify the type and location of a pitch almost immediately when the ball leaves the pitcher's hand. "Albert Pujols has great pitch recognition because he has a balanced stride with his weight back, and he swings easy. He knows when a pitch isn't a strike and won't be fooled" (Doug Carpenter, quoted in Alan Schwarz, BaseballAmerica.com, Nov. 14, 2006).

pitch to contact To allow a batter to hit a pitch to a teammate.

pitch to spots To pitch to specific areas of the strike zone, such as the corners; to mix the locations of pitches purposefully in an attempt to deceive the batter.

piten A form of *ten-man baseball* that became the norm in Cuba throughout the 19th century (Roberto González Echevarria, *The Pride of Havana*, 1999, p.110; Peter Morris).

Pittsburgh chopper A batted ball that becomes a hit because it bounces over a fielder's head. Its success depends on a downward-chopping swing and a hard infield. Named by and for the 1960 world champion Pittsburgh Pirates, who specialized in such hits. See also *Baltimore chop*; *alabaster blast*.

pivot The maneuver in which a defensive player (usually the second baseman) touches second base with one foot and whirls about to throw the ball to first base in an attempt to turn a double play. See also *inside pivot*; *outside pivot*; *cross-over pivot*.

pivot foot 1. The foot used by an infielder when touching second base and whirling about to throw to first base in an attempt to turn a double play. 2. The foot used by the pitcher to push off the rubber as he delivers the ball. The pivot foot must remain in contact with the rubber until the ball is released. The pitcher supports himself with the pivot foot as he strides forward with the *stepping foot*. A pitcher's pivot foot is always on the same side of the body as the arm he pitches with (a right-handed pitcher's pivot foot is always the right one). Since 2007, the pitcher may have only a portion of his pivot foot (rather than the entire foot) in contact with the rubber.

pivot man The second baseman who serves as the relay player at second base during an attempt to turn a double play. Second baseman Joe Gordon once put this term in perspective (quoted in *San Francisco News*, June 29, 1949; Peter Tamony): "Without a good pivotman a double play cannot be made.

Without double plays a club will win few close games." Jackie Robinson (quoted in *Mutual Baseball Almanac*, 1954) discussed the role of the pivot man: "If a second baseman doesn't pivot right, he won't pivot often. He'll be belted, spiked and stepped on, and he won't make double plays. On the double play that starts at shortstop, the second baseman can play two roles. He can be the pivot man. He can be the sitting duck. Myself, I preferred being a pivot man." Also spelled "pivotman."

PL Abbrev. for *Players' League*.

place 1. *v.* To hit a ball to a predetermined area on the field. "[Sudhoff] managed to place the ball in the right place for a few timely 'bingles' that sent runs over the plate" (Timothy Murnane, *The Boston Globe*, Sept. 12, 1900; Peter Morris). Syn. *place hit*, 2. IST USE. 1880 (*Brooklyn Daily Eagle*, Aug. 22; Edward J. Nichols). 2. *n.* A slot in the batting order; e.g., "fourth-place hitter" is the cleanup hitter.

place hit 1. *n.* A base hit in which the ball is batted to a predetermined area on the field. IST USE. 1889. "[Jack] Hayes pushed him home on a pretty place hit to short left" (*San Francisco Examiner*, Apr. 28; Peter Morris). 2. *v.* Syn. of *place*, 1.

place hitter A hitter with the proven ability to hit the ball to a desired location on the field. See also *sharpshooter*, 1. IST USE. 1928. "The place hitter is the chap who can take a ball which ordinarily he would hit to right, and hit it to left, or vice versa" (George Herman Ruth, *Babe Ruth's Own Book of Baseball*, 1928; David Shulman).

place hitting The ability to direct a batted ball to a predetermined area on the field, out of reach of a fielder. "Willie Keeler did some rare [i.e., very fine] place hitting yesterday, all four of his drives taking a different direction" (*Brooklyn Daily Eagle*, Sept. 12, 1901; Peter Morris). Ferdinand Cole Lane (*Batting*, 1925, p.72) characterized it as "this most difficult of batting arts." IST USE. 1888. "Harry Wright's opinion of scientific or 'place' hitting" (*The North American* [Philadelphia], Feb. 7).

placement Syn. of *control*. Pitcher Tommy

John (quoted in *The New York Times*, Sept. 11, 1983) discussed the concept by explaining, "Your tools—let's break that out. You have speed, movement, placement. I never had speed. I have movement and placement."

plank 1. To hit the ball hard, as if whacking with a plank. 2. To drive in a run; e.g., "Smith planked Jones with a double to right."

plant 1. *n.* The placement of the pitcher's front (stepping) foot on the ground before he releases the ball. 2. *v.* To place the pitcher's front (stepping) foot on the ground before he releases the ball. 3. *v.* To bat a ball; e.g., "Smith planted one down the line." IST USE. 1908 (*Brooklyn Daily Eagle*, May 22; Edward J. Nichols). 4. *v.* For a major-league club to place a player with a farm club (note the metaphorical play on farming). "Two of last year's tryout squad, 'planted' with a friendly minor league club, have been recalled" (John J. Evers and Hugh S. Fullerton, *Touching Second: The Science of Baseball*, 1910; Peter Morris). 5. *n./hist.* A ballpark. "[Pittsburgh] president Dreyfuss has plans all made to open his new million dollar plant on June 30" (I.E. Sanborn, *Chicago Tribune*, May 2, 1909; Peter Morris).

plaster 1. *v.* To defeat badly. 2. To hit a ball hard. "[Hod] Eller beat the Giants . . . by plastering the ball into the left field bleachers" (*The New York Times*, Oct. 7, 1919). IST USE. 1910 (*Baseball Magazine*, December, p.35; Edward J. Nichols). 3. *n./hist.* A fine imposed on a player by his club for an infraction of rules or neglect in play. IST USE. 1911 (*Baseball Magazine*, October, p.11; Edward J. Nichols).

plate 1. *n.* Short for *home plate*. IST USE. 1857. "The home base . . . to be . . . marked by a flat circular iron plate, painted or enameled white" (*Porter's Spirit of the Times*, March 7; Chip Atkison). 2. *adj.* Relating to home plate. 3. *v.* To score; to drive in a run; e.g., "[Nick] Markakis then plated two runs with a single" (*The Baltimore Sun*, June 13, 2006). 4. *n.* Short for *pitcher's plate*. IST USE. 1857. "The pitcher's position shall be designated . . . at a fixed iron plate placed at a point fifteen yards distant from the home base" (*Porter's Spirit of the Times*, March 7; Chip Atkison).

plate appearance An official statistic for the

batter coming to the batter's box, including those times when the batter walks, sacrifices, is hit by a pitched ball, or is interfered with by the catcher. See also *turn at bat*, 1. Compare *at-bat*, 2. Abbrev. *PA*. Syn. *trip to the plate*.

plate blocker 1. A catcher who tenaciously holds his position in front of home plate during close plays with a baserunner who is trying to score. See also *blocker*, 1. **2.** A catcher with the ability to prevent potential wild pitches.

plate coverage The ability of a batter to stay close enough to the plate to reach all pitches thrown in the strike zone. Daniel G. Habib (*Sports Illustrated*, May 22, 2006) wrote that Albert Pujols has "exceptional" plate coverage because of his "uncommon patience" to let the pitch get "deep to the plate" and his ability to drive the ball to the opposite field.

plate discipline The ability of a batter to have good awareness of the strike zone, work deep into counts, be selective regarding what pitch to hit, exert patience, and draw walks. Batters with good plate discipline refrain from swinging at pitches out of the strike zone, or pitches that are less hittable than those that might follow; they tend to have high on-base percentages.

plate jumping The mock complaint by a wild pitcher that the plate (i.e., the strike zone) will not stand still. See also *home plate is jumping around*.

plate man Syn. of *plate umpire*. "The plate man usually sets the tone in the locker room. . . . When I'm the plate man, I take time to review in my mind the pitchers" (umpire Durwood Merrill, quoted in George Gmelch and J.J. Weiner, *In the Ballpark: The Working Lives of Baseball People*, 1998, p.140).

plate record *hist.* Syn. of *batting average* (Maurice H. Weseen, *A Dictionary of American Slang*, 1934).

plate shy Said of a batter who is afraid to stand close to the plate. IST USE. 1912. "For a long time, 'Josh' Devore . . . was 'plate shy' with left-handers—that is, he stepped away— and all the pitchers in the League soon learned of this" (Christy Mathewson, *Pitching in a Pinch*; Peter Morris).

plate umpire The *umpire* stationed behind the catcher at home plate. See also *umpire-in-chief*; *ball-and-strike umpire*. Syn. *home-plate umpire*; *plate man*; *battery umpire*.

platinum sombrero A mythical award given to a batter who strikes out five times in a game. See also *hat trick*; *golden sombrero*; *Horn*. Syn. *Olympic rings*.

platoon 1. *v.* To use two or more players, on an alternating basis, for the same defensive position or designated hitter, thereby taking advantage of each player's offensive and defensive strengths. "The [New York] Mets even have a bench this year, at last permitting manager [Gil] Hodges to do some useful platooning" (Roger Angell, *The Summer Game*, 1972; Charles D. Poe). **2.** *n.* A group of players who alternate with each other; e.g., a three-player platoon in left field. Platoons usually involve a right-handed batter who plays against left-handed pitchers and a left-handed batter who plays against right-handed pitchers.

platoon advantage The circumstance in which a team's batters have the platoon differential in their favor.

platoon differential The tendency for a batter to hit better when facing a pitcher of the opposite handedness.

platoon player A player who is alternated with another at one defensive position. Platoon players are not usually among the stars or outstanding players on a team and would prefer to work themselves out of that role: "[Andy] Van Slyke Making Effort to Shed Platoon Player Label" (*St. Petersburg Times* subheadline, March 29, 1987). But Baltimore Orioles catcher Rick Dempsey (quoted in *Newsweek*, Oct. 24, 1983, after the Orioles won the 1983 World Series) embraced the label: "We're honest-to-God platoon players, and that means you'll never hear us bitchin' and complaining. We just come in, punch the clock and do what the manager says."

platoon system A management style in which players are moved in and out of the lineup depending on the circumstances. New York Yankees manager Casey Stengel was the first to employ the system on a large scale in 1949: "Where Casey relied heavily on the platoon system, Ralph [Houk] went for the set lineup" (Mickey Mantle, *The Mick*, 1986; Charles D. Poe). Boston Braves manager George Stallings brought the platooning tactic to prominence with his use of outfielders on the Miracle Braves of 1914.

platter Syn. of *home plate*. The term is a play on the word and image of "plate" as tableware and, without pushing too far, in the serving of a pitch. See also *dish*. IST USE. 1908. "Platter, another term for home base" (John B. Foster, in *Collier's New Dictionary of the English Language*).

play 1. *n.* Any specific act, event, maneuver, or point in a baseball game, such as a double play, a pickoff play, a hit-and-run play, or any action (such as an error, putout, or stolen base) that occurs between pitches; e.g., "Smith makes all the plays required of a shortstop." IST USE. 1858 (*Brooklyn Daily Times*, June 18; Edward J. Nichols). 2. *v.* To participate in a game. 3. *v.* To assume the duties of a particular position; e.g., to "play third base." 4. *v.* To catch or position oneself for catching a ball; e.g., "Smith played the ball off the wall." 5. *v.* To place oneself on the defense where one's knowledge and experience indicate where the batter most likely will hit the ball. "[Dickie] Thon had an alarming tendency to wander from the spot scouting reports suggested he should play a hitter" (Harry Shattuck, *Baseball Digest*, Oct. 1983, p.62). 6. *v.* To perform, as in "play to the grandstand." 7. *imper.* Short for *play ball!* To commence or resume action, the plate umpire points at the pitcher or the plate with the right hand and calls "play" (*Official Baseball Rules*, Rule 5.01). IST USE. 1857. "'Play' was called" (*New York Clipper*, July 18; Peter Morris). 8. *v.* To describe a player's basic skills (tools) that can or have been converted into tangible results. "The defensive part isn't a factor because the bat will always play" (Philadelphia Phillies assistant general manager Mike Arbuckle, quoted in *Baseball America*, July 21–Aug. 3, 2003; Peter Morris).

playable 1. Said of any ball that is live or in play. 2. Said of a below-average player who is adequate enough to play in the major leagues. "David Eckstein doesn't have a strong arm at shortstop, but it's playable because of his quickness and instincts" (Doug Mapson, quoted in Alan Schwarz, Baseball America.com, Nov. 14, 2006).

play at any base Any play involving a potential putout when the bases are loaded.

play at the plate Any play involving a fielder (usually the catcher) covering home plate and a baserunner attempting to score. "When the infield is drawn in for a play at the plate, the first and third basemen take a position right on the edge of the infield grass" (*Athletic Journal*, May 1945). USAGE NOTE. Because such plays tend to be exciting ones at key moments of the game, the phrase carries with it an extra amount of emotion.

play ball 1. Emblematic phrase for the start of any baseball game, from Opening Day to the opener of the World Series. Baseball commissioner Peter Ueberroth (quoted in *USA Today*, Apr. 4, 1986): "The best words—most fun words—in our language are 'play ball.' Those words conjure up home runs and strikeouts, extra innings and double plays. . . . 'Play ball' is what baseball is all about—its call to arms—and there isn't a baseball fan . . . who isn't a little excited over the beginning of a new season." IST USE. 1905. "When the season opens such twists as the 'spit ball,' 'snake twist,' and the 'grasshopper shoot' will be relegated to the icebox [bullpen], and it will be a case of play ball" (Cy Young, quoted in *Chicago Tribune*, Apr. 16; Peter Morris). EXTENDED USE. To cooperate or participate: e.g., "If the union will play ball with us on this one, I think we can make the deadline." At the 1987 Washington summit meeting, President Ronald Reagan took the occasion "to tell his guest [Mikhail S. Gorbachev] that the two leaders should 'play ball' with each other" (*The New York Times*, Dec. 15, 1987). 2. To engage in an uncertain late 18th- and early 19th-century recreation that involved a ball and may have included a bat. Thomas L. Altherr (*NINE*, Spring 2000) identified many diarists during this period who referred to having "played ball"; e.g., "We are oblige'd to walk 4 miles to day to find a place leavel enough to play ball" (Revolutionary War soldier Henry Dearborn, writing on April 17, 1779; Lloyd A. Brown & Howard H. Peckham, eds., *Revolutionary War Journals of Henry Dearborn 1775–1783*,

Play at the plate. Washington Senators catcher Herold Dominic "Muddy" Ruel in action. *Photograph by Joseph Baylor Roberts*

1939). **3.** *hist.* To pitch when the batter has two or three balls and no strikes (Bill Snypp, *Lima* [Ohio] *News*, Apr. 27, 1937; Peter Morris).

"play ball!" The command issued by the plate umpire to start a game or to resume action. It is sometimes abbreviated to a simple order of "play!" "With features rigid as a block of stone, / He cries, 'Play ball!'" ("The Umpire," *Detroit Free Press*, reprinted in *The Atchison* [Kans.] *Daily Globe*, July 27, 1893). 1ST USE. 1886. "McKeever held a long discussion with Pitcher Harmon about signs. The crowd got impatient; one man yelled 'Get a telephone!' while the umpire ordered them to 'play ball'" (*The Boston Globe*, May 13; Peter Morris).

play-by-play A running description of a game, with all the details. The term is usually applied to a broadcaster's commentary of a game on radio and television, although technically it only applies to printed accounts, now rare, in which each play of the game and the outcome of each plate appearance is reported. Abbrev. *PBP.* 1ST USE. 1912 (*New York Tribune*, Oct. 15; Edward J. Nichols).

EXTENDED USE. Any detailed verbal account: e.g., "I had to sit there and listen to his play-by-play of the whole argument."

play by the book To play baseball in accord with the conventional wisdom of the game. 1ST USE. 1911 (William Patten and J. W. McSpadden, *The Book of Base Ball*; Edward J. Nichols).

play catch To throw a ball back and forth with another person. Donald Hall's book of essays on baseball (1985) was entitled *Fathers Playing Catch with Sons*. "Sand-lotters and men who played the game in their younger days are out on vacant lots or in their back yards or the alleys back of their homes tossing the ball and 'playing catch'" (*The Washington Post*, Feb. 23, 1913; Peter Morris). 1ST USE. 1869. "White is a fine catcher and, moreover, one of the easiest and most graceful throwers who ever tossed a ball. He sends the ball down to the second with as little exertion as if he were 'playing catch'" (*Syracuse Journal*, July 30; Larry McCray).

play deep and cut across To position the outfielders when the defense anticipates balls being hit deep; "Advice [given] to outfielders from a pitcher who doesn't feel well and expects to be shelled off the mound during the game" (Jim Brosnan, *The Long Season*, 1960).

player **1.** One who plays baseball; a ballplayer. IST USE. 1845. "[The Captains] shall retire and make the match to be played, observing at the same time that the players put opposite to each other should be as nearly equal as possible" (Knickerbocker Rules, Rule 3d., Sept. 23). **2.** One who is admired by teammates and opponents as a ballplayer. "If he [Cal Ripken Jr.] isn't a player, then I don't know where you'll find one" (former minorleague manager Cal Ermer, quoted in *The Baltimore Sun*, Sept. 2, 1995).

player agent **1.** An individual who is certified by the Major League Baseball Players Association and authorized to conduct, or assist in, the negotiation of a player's salary with a professional baseball club, and may also make other business arrangements in the player's interest, such as commercial endorsements. It was not until 1970 that the team owners agreed to let agents represent players in contract negotiations. USAGE NOTE. David Arcidiacono discovered the following advertisement in *The Sporting News* (Jan. 10, 1891, p.5), following the dissolution of the Players' League: "Base Ball Agency: For Ball Players and Managers wanting engagements and players. Will handle business for players who wish a transfer from one club to another. Would like to hear from all disengaged players. W.R. Harrington, Chicago." **2.** *hist.* An employee of a ball club who was responsible for hiring new players. "Henry Fauchtwanger is the player agent of the Pittsburgs now" (*The Sporting Life*, June 6, 1903; Peter Morris).

player development Providing experience and instruction for minor-league players. In response to a dangerous decline in minorleague attendance that threatened the future of the minors, the major leagues adopted a "player development plan" on May 18, 1962. The majors increased funding of the minors in return for authority over personnel issues. This transformed the minors into being primarily developers of talent for the majors, and the "career" minor leaguer became effec-tively extinct, replaced by younger prospects. The plan also abolished classes B, C, and D, and replaced them with the rookie league. "IBM calls it R&D [research and development]. The Dodgers call it 'player development'" (*Forbes*, Apr. 12, 1982). See also *director of player development*.

player development contract An agreement between the major leagues and the minor leagues to cover areas subsidized by the majors in their working agreements with minor-league affiliates; also, an agreement between a major-league club and its minorleague affiliate. Major-league clubs provide an active roster of players, managers, coaches, trainers, and instructors, and their salaries and benefits, as well as expenses for spring training, medical supplies, and travel and hotels. Minor-league clubs provide the playing facility. This standard contract applies to all major- and minor-league clubs (including rookie-league clubs) regardless of their current contractual status (Major League Rules, Rule 56a). Abbrev. *PDC*.

player game percentage A method for evaluating the contributions to victories or losses made by a player in a season, based on data describing the probability that a team will win a game from various base–out situations. Each plate appearance changes the probability; and the players responsible for the change, usually the batter and pitcher, are given a number of credits associated with that change if the outcome favors their team, and the same number of debits if the outcome disfavors their team. A player's player game percentage is his number of credits minus his number of debits, divided by the number of games played for the entire season. The method was proposed by Jay M. Bennett and John A. Flueck in the 1992 *Proceedings* of the Section on Statistics in Sports of the American Statistical Association. See *player win average*; *win expectancy*; and *win probability added* for analogous methods. Abbrev. *PGP*.

player limit The maximum number of players that a team may have on its roster at a given time. A major-league club can reserve 40 players on its roster, only 25 of whom can be on the active list between Opening Day and midnight on Aug. 31. Syn. *roster limit*.

player-manager A manager who is also an active player on the team. Those who fill this position (such as Pete Rose with the Cincinnati Reds in 1984) tend to be senior players who concentrate more on managing than playing as they phase themselves out of the regular lineup. Player-managers are no longer as prevalent as they once were in pre–World War II baseball. Other notable player-managers were John McGraw, Connie Mack, Mickey Cochrane, Lou Boudreau, and Frank Robinson. Not to be confused with *player's manager.* Syn. *playing manager.* IST USE. 1898. "The chances are that Ollie Beard will be signed as player-manager [of Detroit]" (*Grand Rapids* [Mich.] *Evening Press*, May 12; Peter Morris).

Player of the Year Award 1. An annual award presented since 1988 by the Associated Press to the best major-league baseball player, based on balloting by sportswriters and broadcasters. The award was formerly presented by Seagram's Distillers and based on fan voting. Also known as "Major League Player of the Year Award" and "Major League Baseball Player of the Year Award."

Player-manager. Clifford "Cap" Clarke, Pittsburgh Pirates, 1910. *George Grantham Bain Collection, Library of Congress*

2. An annual award presented since 1936 by *The Sporting News* to the best major-league baseball player as judged by baseball "experts" and, since 1992, by a vote of the players. Also known as "Major League Player of the Year Award" and "Major League Baseball Player of the Year Award." **3.** An annual *Players Choice Award* presented since 1998 to the best major-league baseball player, based on balloting conducted by the Major League Baseball Players Association. **4.** One of several annual awards presented to the best baseball player by organizations such as *Baseball Digest* (since 1969), the American Legion, and *Baseball America* (for collegiate baseball's national player of the year since 1984, college summer player of the year since 1986, and minor-league player of the year—limited to prospects, rather than older players—since 1981.

player representative The member of a major-league team who has been elected by his teammates as their delegate to the Major League Baseball Players Association and who serves as the liaison for the team on all player-management issues. Syn. *rep*, 2; "player rep."

player running bases *hist.* Syn. of *batter-runner.* "The moment the striker has hit a fair ball he ceases to be 'the striker' and becomes 'a player running the bases'" (Henry Chadwick, *The Game of Base Ball*, 1868, p.43).

Players Association Short for *Major League Baseball Players Association.*

Players Choice Award One of 10 annual awards sponsored by the Major League Baseball Players Association and voted upon by members of the association: *Player of the Year Award* (since 1998); *Marvin Miller Man of the Year Award* (since 1997); and, for each major league, Outstanding Player Award (since 1993), Outstanding Pitcher Award (since 1994), Outstanding Rookie Award (since 1994), and *Comeback Player of the Year Award* (1992 and since 1997).

players' coffee Coffee or a highly caffeinated energy drink laden with amphetamines. Syn. *leaded coffee.*

Players Fraternity An early union of baseball players, founded in 1912 and led by former player-turned-attorney David L. Fultz, which was officially recognized by the National Commission in 1914 when the Federal League emerged to challenge the American League and the National League. The owners agreed to pay for uniforms, require green outfield fences (for better visibility and reduced injuries), supply written reasons for player suspensions, and give 10-year veterans the right to unconditional release from their contracts; the concessions kept players loyal to their teams (the Federal League disbanded in 1915 in part because it was unable to recruit established players). The Fraternity focused primarily on reforms in the minor leagues, where most of its membership was based. Fultz called a general strike in 1917 over improvements in the minors, but he overestimated the support of the American Federation of Labor and major-league players, and the strike never materialized. The Fraternity could not recover momentum and dissolved late in 1917. Formal name: Fraternity of Professional Baseball Players of America.

Players' League An outlaw major league created by members of the *Brotherhood of Professional Base Ball Players* who were frustrated by salary ceilings, fines, the reserve clause, and other realities of the existing major leagues. "[The Players' League] was a co-operative, where players were investors in their clubs, player trades were by consent, and the 'capitalists' (not owners) were to divide the profits equally with all the players" (Ethan Lewis, *"A Structure to Last Forever": The Players' League and the Brotherhood War of 1890*, Princeton Univ. master's thesis, 1995). It had but one season (1890); lack of money and organization put the league out of business before Opening Day 1891. The league included the Boston Beaneaters (Reds), Brooklyn Wonders, New York Giants, Chicago Pirates, Philadelphia Quakers, Pittsburgh Burghers, Cleveland Infants, and Buffalo Bisons. Full name: Players' National League of Professional Base Ball Clubs. Abbrev. *PL*. Also known retrospectively as *Bolshevik League*.

player's manager A team manager who commands special respect from players; a manager who can communicate with and relate to the modern player (often a former player himself, such as Ozzie Guillen and Joe Torre). The term originally carried the suggestion of softness: e.g., Ray Knight (quoted in *The Baltimore Sun*, Oct. 31, 1995): "Anybody that's labeled a player's manager is generally too soft because you allow them to do anything. . . . I believe in discipline . . . and doing things correctly. I don't want to be known as a player's manager. I don't care if they like me or don't like me." Conversely, Davey Johnson was known as a player's manager because he set down few rules (show up on time, play hard) and then let the players play. Don Baylor (*Don Baylor*, 1989) commented on Billy Martin as a player's manager: "He was known to be fair, making decisions on ability and not based on skin color." Not to be confused with *player-manager*. Sometimes spelled "players' manager."

player's player A player with widespread respect and admiration from other players. "In the clubhouse, he [Don Baylor] was a legendary force, the player's player" (*USA Weekend*, Apr. 2–4, 1993). See also *ballplayer's ballplayer*. EXTENDED USE. A respected individual in a given profession. Guitar virtuoso Michael Hedges "was a player's player . . . [who] had an intensity and drive that earned him a lot of respect with rock players" (*Guitar World* senior editor Chris Gill, quoted in *The Baltimore Sun*, Dec. 5, 1997).

players' pool The amount of money awarded to players from postseason play, calculated as 60 percent of the total gate receipts from a) the first four World Series games, b) the first four League Championship Series games, and c) the first three Division Series games, with the distribution being 36 percent to the World Series winner, 24 percent to the World Series and the League Championship Series losers, 12 percent to the Division Series losers, and 4 percent to non-wild card second-place teams. The division of the players' pool is made by a vote of the players. Non-uniform personnel of a club are not eligible to receive a percentage share of the pool, but are eligible to receive cash awards of defined dollar value, provided that no cash award shall exceed the value of a full share.

Players' Protective Association An early union of baseball players, founded in 1900 when discontented National League players united with former player-turned-lawyer Harry Taylor as advisor and Charles Zimmer as president. It demanded higher salaries, injury pay, an end to trading or selling player contracts without prior consent or compensation, a ban on unreasonable pay cuts and fines, and changes to the reserve clause (limiting players' reservation to three years). However, the leadership could not persuade players to resist the tempting salaries from the American League, and the union collapsed when the National Agreement ended the trade war between the major leagues and the minor leagues in 1903. Full name: Protective Association of Professional Base Ball Players. Abbrev. *PPA*. Commonly known as *Protective Association.*

player to be named later An unnamed player to be delivered at some future date to a team in order to complete a trade. The assignment must be completed within six months from the date of the agreement, which permits a stated cash consideration in lieu of the assignment. The player must not have been on the active list of any major-league club between the date of the agreement and the date of assignment; hence, the player to be named later is almost always a minor leaguer. Sometimes, the player has already been determined, but cannot be named because of the rule prohibiting a player from being traded within a year of being drafted. At other times, the two clubs have agreed on a short list of players, and the team receiving the unnamed player has a set length of time to choose one player from that list. On July 5, 2002, in a three-way deal, the Detroit Tigers traded Jeff Weaver to the New York Yankees; the Yankees sent three players to the Oakland Athletics; and the Athletics, in turn, sent Carlos Peña, Franklyn German, and a player to be named later (Jeremy Bonderman on Aug. 22, 2002) to the Tigers. Abbrev. *PTBNL*; *PTNL*. USAGE NOTE. Although the wording does not exactly match the modern usage, the concept was in use as far back as 1915: "The Baltimore Club has traded Bill Bailey, the southpaw pitcher, to Chicago for pitcher Dave Black and a pitcher yet to be named" (*The Sporting Life*, Sept. 25, 1915; Peter Morris). EXTENDED USE. Jocular usage in "[fill-in-the-blank] to be named later"; e.g., "I'll bet you dinner in a restaurant to be named later that Smith will defeat Jones." ABC broadcaster Dick Schaap (quoted in *The Baltimore Sun*, Jan. 11, 2001): "When David Brinkley left NBC for ABC, Jim McKay was the player to be named later."

player transfer sheet A daily report that indicates whether players have passed through waivers. A club can place a maximum of seven players per day on the sheet.

player value ranking A method used by *Sports Illustrated* to rank 450 position players and 350 pitchers in the major leagues, based on projections of their statistical production for the coming season. Statistics for position players include batting average, home runs, runs batted in, and stolen bases. Statistics for pitchers include wins, saves, earned run average, and walks plus hits per inning pitched (WHIP). Also considered are each player's career statistics, role on his team, prospects for improving or declining, injury history, and physical condition. *Sports Illustrated* associate editor David Sabino noted (*Sports Illustrated*, March 31, 2003) that determining a player's ranking goes beyond mere number crunching: "It's more an art than a science. And it's not saying who the best players are—it's saying who's going to put up the best numbers." Abbrev. *PVR*.

player win average A method for evaluating the contributions to victories or losses made by a player in a season, based on data describing the probability that a team will win a game from each of about 8,000 base–out situations for each inning (top and bottom) in a game and various combinations of runs scored (tie game, home team ahead by one, home team behind by one, etc.). Each plate appearance changes the probability, and the players responsible for the change, usually the batter and pitcher, are given a number of *win points* associated with that change if the outcome favors their team and the same number of *loss points* if the outcome disfavors their team. A player's player win average is his number of win points minus loss points for the entire season. The method was devised by Eldon G. Mills and Harlan D. Mills (*Player Win Averages*, 1970). See *player game percentage*; *win expectancy*; and *win probability added* for analogous methods. Abbrev. *PWA*.

play for one run An offensive strategy that argues against swinging for the fences and for moving a runner along one base at a time and staying out of double plays. "There is nothing more impressive in sports than a demonstration of the National League's type of tight, play-for-a-run baseball—when it works" (*Brooklyn Daily Eagle*, July 7, 1938; Peter Morris). Minnesota Twins manager Tom Kelly expressed surprise (*Sports Illustrated*, May 13, 1996) to see opposing teams play for one run "when I thought there would be more than that one run needed to win."

play for the grandstand Var. of *play to the grandstand*. IST USE. 1886. "He plays now for his side rather than for the grand stand" (*The Sporting News*, May 10; David Shulman).

playground A ballpark. IST USE. 1868. "We are pleased to know that the C.C. Club have taken measures to prevent the gathering of the young roughs in the trees in the immediate vicinity of the playground" (*Syracuse Journal*, July 28; Larry McCray).

playground average A high batting average, such as one that could be achieved in a playground league where a strong hitter can overwhelm young pitchers.

playground ball [softball term] An early name for softball.

playground baseball [softball term] A name given to an early version of softball in 1908 by the National Amateur Playground Ball Association. It was the linear descendent of *indoor baseball*, 1.

play hard To do everything physically needed to win a baseball game so long as the rules are not violated. "If you play hard every day and play good, hard baseball every day, you have a chance to win more games than most teams, because most teams I've found won't play hard every day" (Chicago Cubs manager Dusty Baker, quoted in *The Baltimore Sun*, Oct. 13, 2003).

play hurt To play baseball even when one is not feeling well or nursing an injury. Asked if a pitcher with a pulled groin should play hurt, Ken Harrelson (quoted in Steve Fiffer, *How to Watch Baseball*, 1987, p.162) said, "No. You can't fight through that kind of injury. You should only stay in if it's something that can't get any worse."

playing for a release *hist.* Said of a player who deliberately played badly hoping he would be released. In the 1880s, a player could be reserved indefinitely by a club, but could be released with ten days' notice. Accordingly, if a player's performance dropped off, it was common for the newspapers to speculate that the player believed he could earn more elsewhere if he were released from his current contract. IST USE. 1884. "A few errors and a little falling off at the bat by three players of the Baltimores have given rise to rumors that certain ones of the team were 'playing for a release'" (*The Sporting Life*, May 7; Peter Morris).

playing grounds A ballpark.

playing manager Syn. of *player-manager*.

playing rules See *official playing rules*.

Playing Rules Committee A nine-member committee that revises, repeals, or adopts the *official playing rules*. It consists of two members representing the American League, two members representing the National League, and four at-large members, all appointed by the commissioner; and one member representing the minor leagues. Syn. "Official Playing Rules Committee."

playing streak See *consecutive-game playing streak*.

playing the points *hist.* Said of a club in very early baseball that tried to win by using tactics that violated the spirit of the game. "The Nassaus did not adopt the 'waiting game' style of play in this match as they did in the Excelsior game. We would suggest to them to repudiate it altogether, leaving such style of play to those clubs who prefer 'playing the points,' as it is called, instead of doing 'the fair and square thing' with their opponents" (*New York Clipper*, Oct. 31, 1863).

play it off the wall To field a fly ball just before it hits an outfield wall, or to field the ball after it bounces off the wall and before it hits the ground.

play naked To perform on the baseball field without taking stimulants, such as caffeine tablets and esp. amphetamine capsules known as greenies. "You hear it all the time from teammates, 'You're not going to play naked, are you?'" (Ken Caminiti, quoted in *Sports Illustrated*, June 3, 2002).

playoff 1. *n.* A series of games between the leading teams in a league to determine a championship; specif., Division Series and League Championship Series. **2.** *n.* The playing of an extra game or games to break a tie in the standings at the end of the regular season. The first playoff occurred in 1946, when the St. Louis Cardinals defeated the Brooklyn Dodgers in two games to decide the National League championship. The most famous playoff occurred in 1951, when the New York Giants, on Bobby Thomson's dramatic ninth-inning three-run home run, defeated the Dodgers in two of three games to decide the National League championship. **3.** *n./hist.* The replaying of a game that originally resulted in a tie. Also spelled "play-off." IST USE. 1880 (*Chicago Inter-Ocean*, June 7; Edward J. Nichols). **4.** *adj.* Of or pertaining to a playoff game or series; e.g., "playoff hopes" or "playoff hero."

play on a dime Said of a fielder who fails to cover much ground. An Englishman observed (quoted in *New York Sun*, Oct. 9, 1929), "One of the fielders moved about very little and I heard a man sneer at him, saying: 'That guy plays on a dime.' Now, of course, that is simply impossible. No baseball player could stand upon a dime and hope to be of the slightest use to his team. It's all a bit too much for me." See also *dime player.*

play one's head off Syn. of *play over one's head.* "There I played my head off, as we say in baseball" (Ty Cobb, *Memoirs of Twenty Years in Baseball*, 1925; Peter Morris).

play out the string 1. For a player to put in his time at the end of his career. **2.** For a team to continue to play although it is not in contention. IST USE. 1912 (*New York Tribune*, Sept. 15; Edward J. Nichols).

play over one's head To perform better than usual or better than expected; to have greater success than warranted by one's ability. St. Louis Cardinals outfielder Ray Lankford (quoted in *The Baltimore Sun*, Apr. 1, 2001): "He [Jose Lima] was playing over his head. There is no way he can pitch the way he was pitching a year ago, and he came back to reality." Syn. *play one's head off.*

play scoreboard 1. For players to watch the scoreboard during a game to see how other teams are faring. Brooklyn Dodgers pitcher Don Newcombe (quoted in Bobby Thomson, *"The Giants Win the Pennant! The Giants Win the Pennant!,"* 1991, p.180): "When they [New York Giants] won those 16 straight games we began to notice them and become aware of what they were doing. We began to play scoreboard and we'd see the way they were pulling games out in the ninth inning, coming from behind so many times. Whenever a team plays scoreboard they're in trouble." **2.** For a player to know, at all times, the number of outs, the number of balls and strikes, which bases are occupied, and the score of the game. Duke Sims (quoted in Steve Fiffer, *How to Watch Baseball*, 1987, p.172): "Most of the time the scoreboard dictates what you can do, whether you're behind one or two runs, or up one or two."

play the percentages To manage with an eye on previous performance; e.g., if a pitcher is slow to pick off leading runners, the percentages suggest that runners should try to steal against him.

play the string Syn. of *go down the line.*

play the sun To face the sun in the outfield. IST USE. 1902 (*The Sporting Life*, Oct. 4, p.7; Edward J. Nichols).

play to the grandstand To show off; to perform. "To make fancy catches or stops on easy plays" (John B. Foster, in *Collier's New Dictionary of the English Language*, 1908). See also *grandstand, 2; grandstand play;*

play for the grandstand. 1ST USE. 1888. "Playing to the Grand-Stand. To accomplish this it is only necessary to smile, strike an attitude, and strike out" (Thomas W. Lawson, *The Krank: His Language and What It Means*; David Shulman). ETYMOLOGY. Charles Earle Funk (*Heavens to Betsy!*, 1955) asserted that the expression was related to the earlier "play to the gallery." Funk explained, "Originally, it had reference to those actors, especially in an English theater, who, going over the heads of the near-by, and frequently inattentive, occupants of orchestra seats or stalls, deliberately overacted their roles in seeking to gain the approval of the larger populace in the gallery."

play under protest To continue to play a game even though the manager of one team has indicated he intends to file a protest.

play up to the handle *hist.* To play excellently; to play up to expectations. "Brooklyn's boys have not been doing any great work of late. . . . [Manager Charlie Byrne] is not happy unless the men play up to the handle, and as a matter of fact no one can blame him" (*The World* [New York], June 26, 1887; Gerald L. Cohen).

play with anybody To win with confidence and consistency, regardless of the quality of the opposition.

plenty of wood Said of a team that has several power hitters. 1ST USE. 1910 (*American Magazine*, July, p.400; Edward J. Nichols).

plexiglas principle Syn. of *law of competitive balance*.

plowhorse A player who grinds out solid performances after others would have expected him to let up (Alan Schwarz, BaseballAmerica.com, Nov. 14, 2006).

plow-jockey *hist.* A country boy, from a time when many players entered baseball directly from the farm.

plug 1. *hist.* To bat a ball hard. 1ST USE. 1910 (*Baseball Magazine*, May, p.68; Edward J. Nichols). 2. *hist.* To put out a runner in town ball, the Massachusetts game, and other early variations of baseball by throwing the ball at and hitting him. Syn. of *soak*, 2. 3. To doctor a baseball bat by inserting illegal substances, such as cork.

plugger 1. A fan who roots for his or her team. 2. *hist.* A dumb play.

plugging 1. *hist.* Syn. of *soaking*. 2. The action by which a baseball bat is plugged.

plum A desirable home date, esp. a holiday. "I do not propose to discuss here the question as to which side has the right to the dates generally known in the east as 'plums' in baseball parlance" (W.I. Harris, *Bismarck* [N.D.] *Daily Tribune*, June 10, 1890; Peter Morris).

plunger Syn. of *stabber*, 1.

plunk 1. *v.* To hit a batter with a pitched ball. "Just because a guy hits a home run off you, you don't automatically plunk him the next day" (Boston Red Sox pitcher Derek Lowe, quoted in *Boston Herald*, July 23, 2002). 2. *n.* A batter hit by a pitch. 3. *n./hist.* A base hit. See also *plunket*. ETYMOLOGY. Gerald L. Cohen (*Studies in Slang*, Part 2, 1989) noted that the term has an onomatopoeic origin: "the ball lands plunk on the ground." Cohen found several examples from 1889 in *The World* (New York), including this one (Oct. 19): "In a puree of silence that was painful, the Brooklyns came in from the field on the players' bench with nine subdued 'plunks.'" 4. *v.* To hit the ball. 1ST USE. 1887. "[Jerry Denny] plunked the ball to the right field fence for three sacks" (*Detroit Free Press*, Apr. 30; Peter Morris).

plunker 1. *hist.* A base hit. " 'Plunkers' is now the proper caper in referring to base hits" (*Detroit Free Press*, Apr. 18, 1887; Peter Morris). 2. A *Texas Leaguer* in the Texas League. USAGE NOTE. Herbert Simons (*Baseball Magazine*, Jan. 1943) has an interesting note on this term: "Curiously, there aren't any Texas Leaguers ever hit in the Texas League. There, low flies that drop safely in the short outfield, too far for the infielders to reach and yet too near for the outfielders to get to, are known as 'plunkers.'" 1ST USE. 1933 (*The Sporting News Record Book*).

plunket Diminutive of *plunk*, 3.

plus 1. Said of a player or of a player's attribute or skill that is above the average at the major-league level; e.g., a "plus pitch" is one that rates a 60 on the 20-to-80 scouting scale. A pitcher may have a "plus arm," "plus stuff," or a "plus fastball"; a batter may have "plus power," a baserunner may have "plus speed," an infielder may have "plus arm strength," and a player may have "plus tools." "Bobby Higginson is a plus player defensively" (*Sports Illustrated*, March 25, 2002). An anonymous scout commenting on Baltimore Orioles draft pick Billy Rowell (quoted in *The Baltimore Sun*, June 11, 2006): "Billy has a chance to have plus tools all across the board. He has an above-average arm, above-average power. He is a plus runner." **2.** Said of the number of innings thrown by a starting pitcher who began an inning but was removed without having retired a batter; e.g., if the pitcher starts the fifth inning but is removed without having retired a batter, he is said to have pitched "four-plus innings."

plus-plus Said of a player or of a player's attribute or skill that is far above the average at the major-league level; e.g., a "plus-plus pitch" is one that rates a 70 on the 20-to-80 scouting scale. "I don't think anyone's got better stuff than the closer, Billy Koch. He's got plus-plus velocity and a real nasty curveball" (anonymous scout, quoted in *Sports Illustrated*, March 27, 2000, p.91). Syn. *double-plus*.

Pluvius *hist.* Short for *Jupe Pluvius*.

pneumonia ball A Walter Johnson fastball that supposedly passed the batter with such speed that he caught a cold from the breeze that was stirred up. IST USE. 1932. "Walter Johnson's 'high swift' was admiringly dubbed the pneumonia ball by sluggers who caught cold from the steady draught across their throats and chests" (William G. Brandt, *Baseball Magazine*, October, p.496).

PO Abbrev. for *putout*.

pocket The formed hollow or deepest part of a fielder's glove or mitt, around the center of the palm between the thumb and index finger, into which most balls can be caught and securely held. Although all gloves come with a pocket, a traditional part of the glove breaking-in process has been to reshape and deepen the pocket.

point **1.** An element of high skill and sophistication. Henry Chadwick (*The Game of Base Ball*, 1868, p.43) wrote about the "special

points of play in the game which occur most generally in first class matches"; i.e., those "points" alluded to when someone talks of the "finer points of the game." Peter Morris (*Baseball Fever*, 2003, p.123) noted that in "friendly games" the participants did not expect to win but hoped to "learn some of the 'points of the game'" (*Detroit Post*, Sept. 10, 1866). IST USE. 1864. "The technical phrase 'point' covers a number of actions in a match which it would not be consistent to term honorable" (*Brooklyn Eagle*, Sept. 21; Peter Morris). **2.** *hist.* A run. "Syracuse kept their balls from the bat closer to the ground, making 15 runs, and carrying the game by 6 points" (*Syracuse Standard*, Aug. 19, 1859; Larry McCray). **3.** See *percentage point*.

points *hist.* **1.** Syn. of *pitcher's points*. "[Tim] Keefe, who was in the points for New York, pitched a good game after the first inning" (*The World* [New York], May 4, 1888; Gerald L. Cohen). **2.** Syn. of *battery points*. "[Pitcher Cannonball] Titcomb and [catcher Pat] Murphy were in the points for New York yesterday and the Giants won. The Jersey battery is in luck."(*The World* [New York], May 9, 1888; Gerald L. Cohen).

poisoned ball An early 19th-century game played in France on a diamond-shaped field whose four points (bases) must be touched by runners in succession. Batters, who used their bare hands (not a bat) to propel the ball, were retired if the struck ball was caught on the fly. Runners were retired by being touched with the ball or struck with a thrown (or "poisoned") ball. A team was allowed only one out per at-bat. The batting team, after being retired, could retain its at-bats by retrieving the ball and then striking one of the fielding team players before they had left the field (similar to a rule in English baseball). Poisoned ball (la balle empoisonée) is described in a book of boys' games published in Paris about 1815, entitled *Les Jeux des jeunes garçons, représentés par un grand nombre d'estampes* (4th ed.), and is still played occasionally today. The game had several known variants (David Block, *Baseball Before We Knew It*, 2005, pp.150–51, 186–87, 217).

poisoned bat *hist.* The bat held by a hard hitter (Maurice H. Weseen, *A Dictionary of American Slang*, 1934).

poison pen A player's term for a sportswriter or other newspaperman (*The Sporting News*, Apr. 1, 1972).

poke 1. *v.* To bat the ball; to get a hit. IST USE. 1867. "Barker poked a ball to his feet, and before [shortstop] Norton could pick it up was at his post [first base]" (*Daily National Intelligencer* [Washington, D.C.], July 29). 2. *n.* A base hit, esp. a home run. IST USE. 1908 (*Brooklyn Daily Eagle*, May 25; Edward J. Nichols).

poke hitter A hitter whose specialty is placing or pushing balls through holes in the infield. "A ball player like Mikes had to be able to run, for he was a poke hitter, a man who pushed singles and doubles where he could get them" (William Brashler, *The Bingo Long Traveling All-Stars and Motor Kings*, 1973; Charles D. Poe).

poke off A well-hit ball that goes a long distance, usually a home run.

Polaroid A player caught looking at a third strike, in the candid vernacular of Reggie Jackson.

pole 1. *n.* A baseball bat. "Sean Burroughs can flat out swing the pole" (*Sports Illustrated*, March 25, 2002). USAGE NOTE. The term frequently connotes a long bat. Christy Mathewson (*Pitching in a Pinch*, 1912), describing Joe Tinker's switch to a longer bat: "Ever since he adopted the 'pole' he has been a thorn in my side and has broken up many a game." 2. *v.* To hit with power. "[Happy] Felsch tried his best to pole the ball out of the lot, but his calculations went badly astray" (*The New York Times*, Oct. 7, 1919). IST USE. 1884. "He bats from the shoulder and rather 'slaps' than 'poles' the ball" (*The Sporting Life*, Aug. 6; Peter Morris). USAGE NOTE. The term frequently connotes the use of the bat's length in hitting the ball. "[Rube Ellis] used a long bat and held it down near the end and 'poled 'em'" (Christy Mathewson, *Pitching in a Pinch*, 1912; Peter Morris). 3. *n.* One of the two foul poles. Garret Mathews (*Can't Find a Dry Ball*, 2002) noted, "In pregame workouts, pitchers run from the right field foul pole to the one in left. The pitching

coach varies the distance from day to day, but it is always measured in poles."

poleax To hit the ball with a swinging-down motion, as if wielding a poleax. "[Robby] Thompson poleaxed a fat 2–0 fastball from [Les] Lancaster for a two-run homer" (*Tampa Tribune*, Oct. 4, 1989).

pole bender A home run when the ball curls around the foul pole. Umpire Jeff Nelson (quoted in *The Baltimore Sun*, Sept. 2, 2003): "That's the thing with a pole bender. You have to take your eye off it when you turn around, and it's very tough to see when it goes into the crowd."

pole-to-pole Having the ability to hit with power throughout all 90 degrees of fair territory. Compare *gap-to-gap*.

pole vault For a pitcher to throw over a stiff front leg (David Rawnsley, *Baseball America*, Aug. 9–22, 1999).

police the parade grounds *hist.* To maintain a baseball field; to groundskeep. ETYMOLOGY. A term brought back from World War II by players who had been in the armed forces.

polished Said of a young player whose talents are refined beyond his years. "[Ryan] Anderson is a much more polished pitcher than [Randy] Johnson was at age 17" (Tom Gage, *Baseball America*, March 17–30, 1997; Peter Morris). Compare *raw*.

polished deception The use of style and grace by a pitcher to mask his mechanical weaknesses.

polish his buttons Syn. of *brush back*. Chris Von der Ahe (quoted in *St. Louis Post-Dispatch*, Apr. 17, 1904; Peter Morris): "[Tony Mullane] was a great hand at frightening the batters. 'Watch me polish his buttons,' he would frequently say as a good batter faced him. He would throw the ball right at the batter sometimes, particularly if he was a strong batter."

polish off To defeat an opposing team or retire an opposing batter. IST USE. 1871 (*New York Herald*, July 29; Edward J. Nichols).

Polo Grounds The name for four different ballparks in New York City, none of which exist currently. The first two were adjoining parks used for the Metropolitans (1883–

1885) and the Gothams (1883–1888). The third was used by the Giants in 1889 and 1890. The final park was used not only by the New York Giants (1891–1957), but also by the New York Giants of the Players' League (1890), the New York Yankees (1913–1922), and the fledgling New York Mets (1962–1963); it was rebuilt after it was largely destroyed by fire on Apr. 14–15, 1911. The original Polo Grounds was a polo field used by the Westchester Polo Association.

polota The baseball (Chicago Park District [Burnham Park], *Baseball*, 1938).

ponche Spanish for "strikeout." ETYMOLOGY. Spanish for "punch" (beverage).

poner afuera Spanish for "to put out."

pony Said of games in Chicago in the 1870s involving clubs of players aged 14 and under. 1ST USE. "Mr. Kelly states positively that every member of the [base ball club] is of the 'pony' age" (*Chicago Tribune*, Oct. 17, 1869; Peter Morris).

PONY Baseball An advanced international baseball program founded in 1950 for youths aged 5 to 18 in which the complete game of baseball (leading off, stealing bases, pitching from the stretch, etc.) and other baseball techniques and fundamentals are taught to children. The program has the following "leagues": Shetland (ages 5 and 6), Pinto (ages 7 and 8), Mustang (ages 9 and 10), Bronco (ages 11 and 12), PONY or Pony (ages 13 and 14), Colt (ages 15 and 16), and Palomino (ages 17 and 18). It is headquartered in Washington, Pa., and has divisions for girls slow pitch and fast pitch softball. "PONY" is an acronyn for "Protect Our Nation's (originally, Neighborhood) Youth." Full name of the program is PONY Baseball and Softball.

PONY League 1. The nickname for the Pennsylvania–Ontario–New York Class D minor league from 1939 to 1956. 2. A league for 13- and 14-year-old boys in PONY Baseball.

pool See *players' pool*.

pool cue shot A batted ball that comes off the end of the bat like a pool or billiard ball being hit by a cue.

pooling *hist.* The practice of shifting players from one franchise to an ailing franchise when both are owned by the same person or group, as in 1899 when the Robison brothers created a strong St. Louis club and a poor Cleveland club, and when Ned Hanlon took the better players in Baltimore and created a superior team in Brooklyn.

pool table A smooth infield. 1ST USE. 1937 (*New York Daily News*, Jan. 21; Edward J. Nichols).

pooper A *Texas Leaguer*, 2.

poor-man's slider Syn. of *cut fastball*.

pop 1. *n.* The extra speed, hop, and sound of the most effective fastball. "[Ryne Duren was] warming up in the bullpen and . . . the pop from the catcher's glove could be heard all over the stadium" (Edwin Howsam, *Baseball Graffiti*, 1995, p.105). "Brad Radke . . . is getting hit because he's lost pop off his fastball" (*Sports Illustrated*, June 6, 2003). 2. *v.* To throw a fastball; to throw hard. "Ron Guidry had begun popping the ball" (Roger Angell, *The New Yorker*, Aug. 15, 1983, p.60). The term refers to the sound made when a fastball hits the catcher's mitt; e.g., "It's good to hear that mitt popping" (*USA Today*, Feb. 24, 1987). 3. *n.* A hitter's power. "[Hideki Matsui] suddenly showed some pop in his bat" (*Sports Illustrated*, July 7, 2003). 4. *v.* To hit a ball hard. "I'm able to stand in the box, feel good and pop the ball" (Cal Ripken Jr., quoted in *The Baltimore Sun*, June 13, 2000). 5. *v.* Syn. of *pop up*. 1ST USE. 1884 (*De Witt's Base-Ball Guide*, p.47; Edward J. Nichols). 6. *n.* A *pop fly*, 1. 1ST USE. 1895. "We've got a strong infield—one that can handle the pops and grounders they are sure to get when Kirk is in the box" (Herbert Bellwood, *The Rivals of Riverwood*; David Shulman). 7. *v.* To select a player in the first-year player draft, often somewhat unexpectedly. "It's hard to believe now, but when I popped Manny Ramirez in the first round in 1991, people were really surprised" (Mickey White, quoted in Alan Schwarz, BaseballAmerica .com, Nov. 14, 2006).

POP 1. Abbrev. for *probability of performance*. 2. Abbrev. for *perfect offensive player*.

popcorn **1.** *n.* An easily caught fly ball. **2.** *n.* A fastball, in reference to high microwave "heat." **3.** *adj.* Said of a weak throwing arm. "I had a first baseman's arm, a popcorn arm" (Cecil Cooper, quoted in Daniel Okrent, *Nine Innings*, 1985, p.175; Peter Morris). See also *popgun*, 2.

popeye **1.** *v.* To elicit suspicion that a player is taking steroids or other illegal performance-enhancing substances. "It's not really hard to look at a player and see that he's popeye-ing you" (Alan Schwarz, BaseballAmerica .com, Nov. 14, 2006). **2.** *n.* A player suspected of using illegal performance-enhancing substances.

pop fly **1.** A high, but short, fly ball that usually comes down in, or just behind, the infield and is usually (or should be) caught by an infielder or an outfielder playing shallow; a batted ball that rises higher than it travels and allows the fielder plenty of time to get under and catch. "Professional ball players hate to be embarrassed by a simple pop fly, but in the crazy pattern of Candlestick's cross currents they can't do anything else but suffer and curse under their breath" (*San Francisco Examiner*, Apr. 14, 1966; Peter Tamony). Syn. *pop*, 6; *popper*; *pop-up*; *pot-fly*. IST USE. 1870 (*New York Herald*, June 29; Edward J. Nichols). **2.** *hist.* Syn. of *Texas Leaguer*, 2. "A 'Texas Leaguer' . . . is dubbed a 'pop fly' by players" (*The New York Times*, June 2, 1929).

pop foul A pop fly batted into foul territory.

popgun **1.** Said of a weak offense. "The [Atlanta] Braves' most glaring weakness—a popgun offense that last season scored fewer runs than all but three teams in the league" (Stephen Cannella, *Sports Illustrated*, Jan. 28, 2002). **2.** Said of a weak throwing arm. See also *popcorn*, 3.

pop-off **1.** A player with a mean spirit and a short temper; one who baits an umpire. Syn. *rebel*. IST USE. 1939 (Gordon S. "Mickey" Cochrane, *Baseball: The Fan's Game*). **2.** A vociferous or arrogant player; a braggart.

popout *n.* A pop fly that is caught for an out. Also spelled "pop-out."

pop out *v.* To be retired on a pop fly. IST USE. 1913. "[Eddie] Foster and [Clyde] Milan popped out" (*The Washington Post*, Aug. 25;

Oh! You pop fly

Pop fly. 1909 postcard. *Andy Moresund Collection*

Peter Morris).

popper Syn. of *pop fly*, 1.

poppycock season *hist.* Spring training.

pop the ball **1.** See *pop*, 2. **2.** See *pop*, 4.

pop time The elapsed time (in seconds) between the moment a pitch hits the catcher's glove and when his throw hits the glove of a middle infielder on a stolen-base attempt. The typical pop time for major-league catchers is two seconds flat (Alan Schwarz, BaseballAmerica.com, Nov. 14, 2006).

populated Said of a bases-loaded situation. "Heinie [Zimmerman] is always due for a hit when the sacks are populated" (*San Francisco Bulletin*, May 10, 1913; Gerald L. Cohen).

pop-up *n.* Syn. of *pop fly*, 1. Also spelled "popup." IST USE. 1874 (*New York Sun*, July 31; Edward J. Nichols). USAGE NOTE. Columnist Jeanne Brooks (*The Greenville* [S.C.] *News*, Sept. 12, 2004): "There was a crack, and the ball shot straight up like a rocket. . . . From the seats below, gasps (Mine). My husband managed to remain calm. 'Pop-up,' he said mildly. Which could lead one to instant doubts about the adequacy of the English language or at the least baseball terminology. NASA should have pop-ups like that. We'd be on Jupiter by now. This is the sort of revelation that comes to one sitting in a baseball stadium versus sitting in front of a television screen on which height and depth have been compressed to flatness."

pop up *v.* To bat the ball high into the air over the infield. "[They kept] popping up balls among the infielders which dropped into their hands most naturally and gracefully" (*Detroit Advertiser and Tribune*, July 27, 1872; Peter Morris). Syn. *pop*, 5. IST USE. 1867 (*New York Herald*, Aug. 10; Edward J. Nichols).

pop-up slide A short slide in which the baserunner comes into the base feet first and, in the same fluid movement, immediately pushes himself back up onto his feet to a standing position. The runner attempts the slide when he feels that he may have the opportunity to take another base on the play. Syn. *down-and-up slide*; *stand-up slide*; *scuttlefish slide*.

porcelain decorations Teeth; "what an infielder leaves on the field when he's hit in the teeth by a bad-hop grounder" (*Padres Magazine*, 1993, p.21).

porch An outfield bleacher, grandstand, or wall that is not far from home plate. See also *short porch*; *pennant porch*.

Porkopolis An early nickname for baseball cities with meatpacking industries; specif., Cincinnati. IST USE. 1876. "From the following special from 'Porkopolis,' it will be seen that the Cincinnati management make serious charges against one of the Louisville players" (*St. Louis Globe-Democrat*, May 7).

Porkopolitans An early nickname given the baseball teams of Cincinnati. IST USE. 1869. "If the Red Stockings keep on and hold their own, they will be the champion club before the summer is ended. Hurrah for the Porkopolitans" (*Harper's Weekly*, July 3).

Port Arthur A seaport in southeast Texas, from where figuratively a pitcher throws side-arm (see also *throw Laredo*), or a batter takes a hard, full swing at the pitch (Jimmy Powers, *New York Daily News*, Jan. 10, 1937).

portsider A left-hander, usually a pitcher. Variations using the term "port" seem limitless and include "portpaw" (a confusing synonym for "southpaw"), "portside thrower," "portside slinger," and "port flinger." IST USE. 1899. "[Frank] Selee's port sider, Harvey Bailey, one of the best left-handed pitchers ever raised in Indiana" (*The Washington Post*, Aug. 11; *OED*). ETYMOLOGY. The term "port" is the left side of a naval vessel when facing forward.

posish Slang for *position*, 1. IST USE. 1864. "The fielders had got pretty well down for a long batter just before me, but when they saw that 'fellow from the country' take his 'posish,' they closed up pretty well" (*New York Clipper*, May 28; Peter Morris).

position 1. *n.* A player's assigned place on a team, both in the field and in the batting order. Syn. *posish*. IST USE. 1858 (*Brooklyn Daily Times*, June 18; Edward J. Nichols). 2. *n.* The condition with reference to the pitcher standing on the mound and facing the batter. See also *windup position*; *set position*. 3. *v.* To station oneself at a particular spot defensively; e.g., "The manager positioned the outfielders near the wall with Smith coming to bat."

positional adjustment A method for assigning players a certain amount of credit when evaluating their performance depending on the demands of their position. It is used in the linear weights set when determining total player rating.

position player One of the defensive fielders other than the pitcher. It is the 16 position players that the fans elect in the All-Star Game voting, not the pitchers or reserves who are picked by the two managers. "[Jose Canseco] may be the best looking position player in the league, but he's got a lot of growing up to do" (Northwest League Medford A's manager Dennis Rogers, quoted in *Baseball America*, Aug. 15, 1983). See also *non-pitcher*.

positive subtraction Syn. of *addition by subtraction*.

post 1. To list the name of a player whom a Japanese club is willing to make available in the posting system during the period from Nov.

1 to March 2. **2.** To record a baseball statistic. "The rally enabled [Mike] Scott to post his 12th victory at the earliest time in his career" (*Tampa Tribune Times*, June 25, 1989).

postage-stamp outfielder *hist.* A slow-footed outfielder who barely covered any ground. The term was popular in the 1930s and 1940s.

posting system An agreement forged in Dec. 1998 between Major League Baseball and Nippon Professional Baseball under which exclusive negotiating rights for a Japanese player (made available by a Japanese club) can be sold to the major-league team submitting the highest sealed (blind) bid. The Japanese club can accept or reject the bid. The team that wins the auction has 30 days to sign the player; otherwise, the player is returned to his Japanese team for a year, after which he automatically becomes a free agent. The posting fee is not paid until the player signs a major-league contract; the fee is not counted against the luxury tax. The system was devised by Shigeyoshi "Steve" Ino, then general manager of the Orix BlueWave. It allows Japanese clubs to sell players before they become free agents after nine seasons. "The posting system was obviously designed to benefit the Japanese team owners; it allowed them to maintain the integrity of their game for the time being and to control the flow of players to the U.S., and was in keeping with the long tradition . . . whereby the front office wielded power over their players like feudal lords over their vassals" (Robert Whiting, *The Meaning of Ichiro*, 2004, p.146).

postponement The act of rescheduling a game on the same day or on a future day. Games are postponed because of bad weather or technical problems. With the exception of games played late in the season, after first place in the standings has been determined, major-league games are never canceled.

postseason 1. *n.* The period after the end of the regular *season* when the division playoffs, league championships, and World Series are staged. **2.** *adj.* Said of a game or series played in the postseason. "New York Mets, Dodgers and Boston Red Sox all failed in their bids to return to postseason play" (*Tampa Tribune*, Sept. 28, 1989).

pot To hit a pitched ball.

potato 1. The baseball. "[Lou] Gehrig clouting the potato out of the ballyard" (Paul Gallico, *Lou Gehrig, Pride of the Yankees*, 1942). See also *stitched potato*. IST USE. 1934 (Maurice H. Weseen, *A Dictionary of American Slang*). **2.** A player brought up from a farm club; e.g., "Every one of us potatoes came out of the Cardinal farm" (Johnny Hopp, quoted in *Baseball Digest*, Dec. 1983). **3.** A home run. See also *tater*; *long potato*.

potential Latent ability that may or may not be developed. The baseball meaning of the term is the same as that found in a standard dictionary, but it carries with it a certain negative connotation. "Baseball lifers like to say potential is a French word for, 'I ain't got it yet'" (Tom Keegan, *The Baltimore Sun*, May 5, 1994). "Potential can be a dirty word when you're struggling" (Rick Maese, *The Baltimore Sun*, Apr. 18, 2006). Pittsburgh Pirates manager Lloyd McClendon (quoted in *The New York Times*, May 25, 2003): "This game isn't based on potential; it's based on results. There comes a time when you've got to go out and get it done." Jim Henneman (*The Baltimore Sun*, May 28, 1995) commented, "In baseball, that's a nasty word that too often translates into 'could've, would've, should've.' A lot of managers have lost jobs waiting for potential to develop. And some have found the unemployment line because they weren't patient enough to allow it to happen."

potential tying run A batter or runner who, if he succeeds in scoring, will tie the game.

potential winning run A batter or runner who, if he succeeds in scoring, will win the game.

pot-fly *hist.* Syn. of *pop fly*, 1. "It looked like an easy pot-fly as it gracefully sailed up to me" (Thomas W. Lawson, *The Krank: His Language and What It Means*, 1888; David Shulman). ETYMOLOGY. Possibly a corruption of "pop fly."

pot holder A first baseman's glove in the All-American Girls Professional Baseball League.

pots and pans The part of the batter's *kitchen* where a jamball is thrown; e.g., "Smith threw an inside pitch and rattled the batter's pots and pans." See also *break his dishes*.

pouch *hist.* Syn. of *base*, 2. IST USE. 1891 (*Chicago Herald*, May 19; Edward J. Nichols).

pound 1. To get many hits off a single pitcher. "The Giants pounded out 12 hits off Chicago fireballer Bob Rush" (Harvey Rosenfeld, *The Great Chase*, 1992, p.93). IST USE. 1882. "The Troys presented Egan in the pitcher's box to-day, and he was very badly pounded throughout the game" (*The Daily Inter Ocean* [Chicago], June 17). 2. To hit a pitched baseball hard. "Pedro Martinez . . . served a fastball that Javy Lopez pounded for a home run" (*The Baltimore Sun*, Apr. 5, 2004). IST USE. 1873 (*New York Herald*, Aug. 10; Edward J. Nichols). 3. To throw a pitched ball hard and inside. "Most teams try to pound Ichiro [Suzuki] inside, hoping to back him off the plate" (Stephen Cannella, *Sports Illustrated*, June 10, 2002). "To get him [Tim Salmon] out you have to pound him inside with power stuff" (anonymous scout, quoted in *Sports Illustrated*, Oct. 14, 2002). USAGE NOTE. The term has also been used for throwing a pitch away from the plate. "[Kevin Millwood] pounded that fastball on the outside of the plate and he didn't seem to miss" (Baltimore Orioles manager Sam Perlozzo, quoted in *The Baltimore Sun*, July 15, 2006). EXTENDED USE. To throw a basketball into the pivot or to a player beneath the basket. "[Univ. of Maryland basketball coach Gary Williams likes to] pound the ball inside to his big men on offense" (*The Baltimore Sun*, March 20, 2004). 4. To throw strikes with great consistency. "It's unusual for a pitcher still in his teens to be able to pound the strike zone the way [Fausto] Carmona does" (Jim Ingraham, *Baseball America*, June 9–22, 2003; Peter Morris).

pound the atmosphere *hist.* To swing at and miss a pitched ball; to strike out. Syn. "pound the air"; "pound wind." IST USE. 1886. "[Sam] Thompson pounded the atmosphere" (*Detroit Free Press*, June 4).

pour the pine To hit a good ball solidly (Edgar G. Brands, *The Sporting News*, Feb. 23, 1933).

powder 1. *v.* To hit a pitched ball so hard that it travels at a high rate of speed; e.g., "Smith powdered the ball so hard that the shortstop did not see it." 2. *n.* The speed with which a pitcher delivers the ball from the mound. IST USE. 1932. "They like to refer to an excessive amount of speed as 'powder.' Maybe this is a derivative of the term 'fireball'" (William G. Brandt, *Baseball Magazine*, October). See also *smoke*, 1. 3. *n.* A fastball.

powder-puff ball Syn. of *puff ball*.

Powder River An explosive fastball. "Most good bullpen men are Powder River boys. Rear back and let 'er go" (Joe Garagiola, *Baseball Is a Funny Game*, 1960). IST USE. 1937. "Powder River—a fast ball" (Jimmy Powers, *New York Daily News*, Jan. 10). ETYMOLOGY. Uncertain. There is a Powder River in Montana and Wyoming, and Powder River County is located in southeast Montana.

power 1. *n.* The ability to hit the long ball. 2. *v.* To hit a pitched baseball with force. "[Kirk] Gibson powered a [Bret] Saberhagen fastball 430 feet over the center-field fence" (*The Sporting News*, Oct. 15, 1984). 3. *n.* The ability to pitch fastballs or to throw hard. 4. *v.* To pitch or throw the ball with force; e.g., "Brown powered the ball past the batter." 5. *adj.* Said of a breaking pitch thrown with a traditional grip but with fastball-like speed. Such a pitch tends to begin in the strike zone and then tails down and away. "[Donnie Bridges] complements [his 94–95 mph fastball] with a devastating 80–82 mph power curve that gets good spin and bite" (*Baseball America 2001 Prospect Handbook*; Peter Morris). 6. *v.* To play winning baseball. "Bobby Bonilla's two-run homer . . . powered Pittsburgh past Los Angeles" (*Tampa Tribune*, July 4, 1989).

power alley One of the two areas between the outfielders in left-center field and in right-center field. Since most powerful hitters naturally tend to drive the ball to the power alleys, home run balls more often travel through these corridors than to straightaway right, center, or left fields. Jim Bouton (*Ball Four*, 1970) defined the term as the place "where the sluggers put away knuckleballs that don't knuckle." John Pastier (personal communication, March 5, 2006) expands: "There's no agreement on where power alleys are situated, and there's no consistency among clubs as to where they place them, if they do at all. Two logical choices would be: 22.5 degrees off the lines (midway between the lines and center field) or 30 degrees off the lines (in the gaps). But logical choices do not necessarily square with empirical results. A hitter tends to have an individual 'power alley'; i.e., a sector of the field where he tends to hit the ball hardest and deepest. It could be in center field, or even slightly to the opposite field. The term is therefore misleading since it suggests a universal, narrowly defined zone that grows out of the mechanics of hitting a baseball. There seems to be no such place as a standard power alley that corresponds to all batters' hitting strengths. The suggested locations are more of a bookkeeping device to bring comparability to the listings of outfield dimensions. All things considered, 'power alley' is a snappy and comforting phrase that promises scientific precision, but is in fact vague, misleading, and one of baseball's greatest misnomers. Power alleys are not really tangible places, but rather figures of speech and states of mind." Philip J. Lowry (*Green Cathedrals*, 2006, p.xvi) defined the left field and right field power alleys as 22.5 degrees in from the foul line. See also *alley*, 1.

Powerball '98 The 1998 major-league baseball season in which a long-standing home run record was broken. "Can one or more of the Powerball '98 musclemen—Mark McGwire, Sammy Sosa, Ken Griffey Jr., Greg Vaughn—displace and erase Roger Maris and 61, baseball's magical number?" (Lyle Spencer, *Riverside* [Calif.] *Press-Enterprise*, Aug. 7, 1998).

power factor A measure of the extent to which a batter gets extra bases out of hits, computed by dividing the player's number of total bases by his number of hits. The measure was presented by Earnshaw Cook in *Percentage Baseball* (1964) and *Percentage Baseball and the Computer* (1971). Compare *isolated power*.

power/finesse rating A statistic that measures the level by which a pitcher allows balls to be put into play and helps relate a pitcher's success to his team's level of defensive ability. It is computed by dividing the sum of bases on balls and strikeout by the number of innings pitched. According to Ron Shandler (*Ron Shandler's Baseball Forecaster*, 2006), "A level of 1.13 or greater describes the extreme power pitchers, or more aptly described as pure throwers. A level of .93 or lower describes an extreme finesse style, or a high contact pitcher."

power game Offensive play characterized by sluggers who swing for home runs. "[Babe] Ruth's natural power was responsible for making baseball what it has been ever since—a power game" (Red Barber, *Christian Science Monitor*, May 23, 1984).

power hitter A hitter known for his home run hitting ability; a hitter who drives the ball for a long distance, often swinging from the heels; a slugger. Jimmy Cannon's definition: "A muscular player who strikes out a lot." Compare *contact hitter*. Syn. *powerhouse*, 1.

powerhouse 1. Syn. of *power hitter*. IST USE. 1933. " 'Powerhouse'—a distance hitter" (Walter Winchell, *Havana Evening Telegram*, May 3). 2. A great baseball team, usually with several home run hitters. The term has also been applied to a team with great pitching: "If you study the history of the Dodgers in the late Seventies and 1980s . . . it's been the pitching that's made them a powerhouse" (Gary Carter, quoted in Bruce Chadwick, *The Dodgers*, 1993, p.134).

power outage A lack of home runs or extra-base hits by a player or team over a protracted period. "Through five games, the Yankees have yet to hit a home run, their longest power outage since 1975 when they didn't homer until the seventh game" (*St. Petersburg Times*, Apr. 18, 1990). See also *outage*; *power shortage*.

power pitcher A pitcher who throws hard and strikes out many batters; e.g., Roger Clemens. Mel Stottlemyre Sr. (*Sports Illustrated*, June 2, 2003) observed that much of Clemens' power "comes through his great lower-body strength and pushing off properly." Ron Givens (*Newsweek*, Aug. 28, 1989) referred to Nolan Ryan as "the greatest power pitcher in the history of baseball." Compare *finesse pitcher*.

power shortage A deficiency, often temporary, of offensive production by a team's power hitters. "It's been a power shortage all year. . . . It's the longest offensive slumber by a group of good hitters that I can remember" (Philadelphia Phillies general manager Lee Thomas, quoted in *The Baltimore Sun*, July 17, 1995). See also *power outage*.

power/speed number An informal measure designed to highlight the achievements of players who are both fast and powerful, computed by multiplying home runs by stolen bases, multiplying that product by 2, then dividing by the sum of home runs and stolen bases. The highest power/speed number in a season is Alex Rodriguez' 43.9 in 1998, on 42 home runs and 46 stolen bases; the highest career number belongs to Barry Bonds (first to exceed 600). The measure was created by Bill James in his self-published *Baseball Abstract* (1981); a description can be found in his first conventionally published *Baseball Abstract* (1982). Abbrev. *PSN*.

power zone That area of the strike zone from which a power hitter generates long balls.

pow wow A meeting on the playing field, usually involving several players and a coach or manager; e.g., a meeting on the pitcher's mound to discuss strategy or a gathering at the scene of a disputed play.

PPA Abbrev. for *Players' Protective Association*.

PQS Abbrev. for *pure quality start*.

PR 1. Abbrev. for *pinch runner*. **2.** Abbrev. for *pitching runs*.

PRA Abbrev. for *pitcher run average*.

PRAA Abbrev. for *pitching runs above average*.

practice game *hist.* An early term for an exhibition game, as opposed to a *match game*. "When the Red Stockings play a practice game at home, business stops, and old men and young men, with their female adjuncts, go to see it" (*Chicago Tribune*, June 6, 1870; Peter Morris).

prairie A large playing area. IST USE. 1937 (*New York Daily News*, Jan. 21; Edward J. Nichols).

PRAR Abbrev. for *pitching runs above replacement*.

prayer ball A pitch with nothing on it; one

which the pitcher "prays" will not be hit. There are many variations of the term, including *glove and a prayer*. One of the odder examples appeared in a 1912 article on player slang, which contained the line: "Christian Science stuff is the only thing you ever get on the ball" (*The Sporting Life*, May 18, 1912).

precinct *hist.* **1.** That part of the outfield where an outfielder is positioned. "[Sy] Sutcliffe was put out into [Sam] Thompson's precinct and the game was resumed" (*Detroit Morning Times*, May 5, 1888). **2.** Syn. of *base*, 2 (*The Sporting News*, Oct. 30, 1913).

predicted ERA An estimate of what a pitcher's earned run average "should have been" in a given season, computed by multiplying opponents' on-base percentage by opponents' slugging percentage by 31. The reason for the 31 is unknown, other than that it works. The estimate was proposed by Mat Olkin (*By the Numbers*, June 1995).

predraft deal A nonbinding agreement on a bonus figure between a player and a major-league club prior to the first-year player draft. Major League Baseball rules forbid teams negotiating with players before the draft, but every team does it anyway (Michael Lewis, *Moneyball*, 2003, pp.99–100).

pre-rookie card A baseball card of a player issued while he is still in the minor leagues, before his rookie card is issued.

preseason That period of time before the opening of a regular baseball *season*. See also *spring training*, 2.

present the ball [softball term] For the pitcher to stand with both feet on the pitcher's rubber and ground with the ball in both hands just prior to beginning the pitching motion.

press box An area within the ballpark reserved for sportswriters and broadcasters. Press boxes have evolved from boxed-off wooden areas to plush, electronics-heavy quarters that in most major-league parks are located on the mezzanine level behind home plate. R.E. Sherwood (*Baseball Magazine*, Sept. 1913) defined "press box" as "a space in the stand reserved for baseball writers and 'scribblers,' located in rear of the home plate, and separated from the playing field by a lot of

Press box. Roosevelt Stadium, Jersey City, N.J. 1957. *Historic American Buildings Survey, Library of Congress*

holes tied together with wire." The lack of adequate facilities for reporters in Detroit at the 1908 World Series led to the foundation of the Baseball Writers' Association of America, whose main demand was the installation of permanent press boxes at all ballparks. IST USE. 1889. "Bob Ferguson . . . came on from Baltimore, where he was scheduled to judge yesterday's Cincinnati-Baltimore game. He sat in the press box and was an interested spectator of the contest" (*Brooklyn Eagle*, Sept. 8; Dean A. Sullivan). USAGE NOTE. Earlier terms for an area reserved for the press included "reporters' stand" (1871), "press stand" (1877), *reporters' box* (1883), and "press enclosure" (1886).

press pin A colorful identifying pin given to a member of the working press during the World Series and other major baseball events. Dating back to the 1911 World Series, press pins are quite attractive and eagerly sought as collector's items.

pretty 1. *n./hist.* An easily injured player (Edgar G. Brands, *The Sporting News*, Feb. 23, 1933). **2.** *adj.* Said of an excellent player. "He was a real pretty ball player" (*American Speech*, 1938; *OED*).

pretzel A curveball. Syn. "pretzel curve"; "pretzel bender." IST USE. 1887. "Getz [Charlie Getzien] was the twirler for the Wolverines, and he gave further proof that pretzel curves are at a premium" (*Detroit Free Press*, May 6; Peter Morris). ETYMOLOGY. Peter Morris suggests that Getzien may have been responsible for the term, as it seemed to have

been applied exclusively to him for some time, possibly referring to his German roots. Morris cites O.P. Caylor (*Outing*, Aug. 1891), who wrote: "The belief in the double curve still exists among the more ignorant ball players. As an instance of it we have the nickname of 'the Pretzel Pitcher,' given to Getzein [*sic*] by players who imagine the ball from his hands comes at them with the curves of a pretzel." Tim Considine (*The Language of Sport*, 1982) gave two derivations for the term: "one from the curved shape of a pretzel, and the other from the fact that a curveball can 'tie a batter up in a knot' like a pretzel."

price guide A third-party book listing the estimated values of baseball cards according to the current market. The first major sports collectibles price guide was *The 1979 Sport Americana Baseball Card Price Guide*, issued by James Beckett and Dennis W. Eckes.

prima donna 1. *n.* A temperamental player; one who thinks well of himself. **2.** *v.* To assume adulation and privileged treatment as a right. "Ty Cobb is making more trouble for the powers that be by prima donning through Georgia with a barnstorm nine playing any team that will meet his aggregation. . . . Why should Cobb be the pampered pet?" (*San Francisco Bulletin*, March 18, 1913; Gerald L. Cohen).

principal owner The title used by George M. Steinbrenner to describe his role with the New York Yankees. "What was left to talk about except the ways in which the principal owner had degraded the great American game?" (Lewis H. Lapham, *The Washington Post*, Apr. 21, 1984).

priority reliever A relief pitcher given consistent innings to hasten his development. Cleveland Indians director of player development Neal Huntington (quoted in *Baseball America*, Oct. 29–Nov. 11, 2001; Peter Morris): "A priority reliever for us is someone we like to get two to three innings of work every three days. We want to make sure they get more than just eight pitches and one inning." Morris adds, "Minor-league relievers are frequently pitchers who are not considered top prospects. This label is thus significant as a way of ensuring that not all minor-league relievers are thus typecast."

privilege man *hist.* One who operates a concession at a 19th-century ballpark. "Harry Stevens, the privilege man, is spending a few days in this city" (*The Washington Post*, Oct. 26, 1892; Bill Wagner).

pro 1. *n.* A professional ballplayer who plays and behaves accordingly. The term carries the clear connotation of a player who is highly experienced and capable, likely to pull through in a pinch. **2.** *adj.* Professional as opposed to amateur; e.g., "pro ball." ETYMOLOGY. Short for "professional."

PRO Abbrev. for *production*

probability of performance A measure of the extremity of an outstanding statistical achievement in a given year, based on the probability that an average player in the relevant league would have matched that achievement in that year given the same opportunity (e.g., the same number of at-bats), with the less probable performance the more outstanding. It is calibrated logarithmically, such that a probability of performance of 1 has a 10 percent likelihood of the average player matching that achievement, a probability of performance of 2 has a 1 percent chance, and a probability of performance of 3 has a one-tenth of a percent chance. Babe Ruth's 54 home runs in 1920 translate to a probability of performance of 44.88. The measure was introduced by Michael Sluss (*Baseball Research Journal*, 1999). Abbrev. *POP*, 1.

probable pitcher The pitcher who is expected to start the next game.

pro baseball Professional baseball as played in the major leagues and minor leagues.

production Syn. of *on-base plus slugging*. Abbrev. *PRO*.

productive out An out that results in a runner's advancing a base or a run scoring; specif., an out that occurs when a fly ball, grounder, or bunt advances a runner with nobody out, when the pitcher bunts to advance a runner with one out (thereby maximizing the effectiveness of the pitcher's at-bat), or when a grounder or fly ball scores a run with one out. The term was developed by *ESPN The Magazine* and the Elias Sports Bureau, but some sabermetricians doubt its usefulness or significance.

Professional Baseball Agreement The contract that governs the relationship between the major leagues and the affiliated minor leagues; the document that specifies the agreement between the commissioner of baseball (on behalf of the major-league baseball clubs) and the National Association of Professional Baseball Leagues (on behalf of its member leagues and member clubs). The agreement states that each major-league club must support at least one Class AAA club and one Class AA club. Other items covered include: uniform playing rules, player development contracts, adequate affiliations for major-league clubs, umpire development, compensation for drafted territories, statistics, All-Star and exhibition games, telecast rights, and marketing cooperation. Abbrev. *PBA*.

professor Ballplayer slang for an uneducated player.

profile *v.* To indicate that an amateur player may have a better chance to be successful in professional baseball at a position other than the one he is currently playing. "Georgia's Doc Brooks profiles more as a first baseman/ DH than as a catcher" (Jim Callis, *Baseball America*, Apr. 16–29, 2001; Peter Morris).

profiling system A scouting system that is designed to weight a player's tools according to his fielding position. See also *Yankee Profile*.

progressive cycle Syn. of *natural cycle*.

project (pron. "pró-ject") *n.* A player with raw skills who needs instruction and experience. "In his first six years of pro ball, he [Kenny Lofton] vaulted from crude project to major league star" (*Sports Illustrated*, May 1, 1995, p.98).

project (pron. "pro-ject") *v.* For a scout to evaluate a young player based on future potential. Legendary scout Tony Lucadello (quoted in David V. Hanneman, *Diamonds in the Rough*, 1989, pp.115–16): "When I see a young ballplayer, I try to project what he can be. . . . I can't just look at what a young man has done; I have to visualize what he can do." For pitchers, projecting involves improvements that occur over more than one year, based on factors that include "age, size, arm speed, leverage, arm action, delivery, makeup and breaking ball velocity" (Josh Boyd, *Baseball America*, Sept. 1–14, 2003; Peter Morris).

projectable Said of a young player whose skills are being evaluated at least partially on potential, because he is either still developing or is still learning his craft. "[Jason Isringhausen] has a very projectable pitcher's body and should add more speed as he fills out" (Jim Callis, *Baseball America*, Dec. 13–26, 1993; Peter Morris).

projection signing The signing of a prospective player to a contract on the basis of a scout's report that he will mature into a qualified player.

Project Scoresheet A volunteer effort to make scoresheets of all major-league games available to the public (Bill James, *Baseball Abstract*, 1985). It lasted from 1984 to 1990, resulted in two books entitled *The Great American Baseball Statbook* (1987 and 1988), and was instrumental in breaking the monopoly over raw baseball data previously held by Major League Baseball and the Elias Sports Bureau. See also *Retrosheet.*

promedio de embasarse Spanish for "on-base percentage."

promedio de slugging Spanish for "slugging percentage."

promenade *hist.* Syn. of *base on balls.* IST USE. 1905. "[Fred] Clarke led off with a promenade" (*Chicago Tribune*, May 6; Peter Morris).

promised land Syn. of *World Series.* "I'm not sure he's a guy that takes you to the promised land" (anonymous scout, on Toronto Blue Jays rookie pitcher Jesse Litsch, quoted in *The Baltimore Sun*, Aug. 12, 2007).

promoter An owner or club official who stages events, stunts, and other sideshow attractions and/or gives away free souvenirs to draw crowds. The most famous and flamboyant of the game's promoters was William L. "Bill" Veeck Jr., who at different points in his career owned the St. Louis Browns, Cleveland Indians, and Chicago White Sox. Veeck's most famous promotional stunt was using 3' 7" midget Eddie Gaedel to pinch hit

Promotion. Players in alternative uniforms as a promotion. *Ron Menchine Collection*

in a 1951 Browns–Detroit Tigers game. Veeck also pioneered promotional notions ranging from exploding scoreboards to free baby-sitting.

promotion An event used to attract people to the ballpark; e.g., Bat Day, Old-Timers' Day, Seat Cushion Night, Fan Appreciation Day, Knothole Day, Senior Citizens' Day, Cap Day, Hot Pants Day, Poster Day, and Wet T-Shirt Night. Some more innovative promotions have included Labor Day (pregnant women admitted free), Lawyers' Night (attorneys pay double), Mime-O-Vision Night (mimes re-create game action atop dugouts), and Call In Sick Day (fans cut work, team faxes excuses to their bosses). Minor-league club owner and marketing consultant Mike Veeck's philosophy (*Sports Illustrated*, Nov. 25, 2002): "Make 75 percent of the crowd laugh, annoy 15 percent, and who cares about the other 10 percent."

promotions schedule A schedule distributed by teams that lists the special events and giveaways offered during the season. For instance, the Baltimore Orioles 1987 promotion schedule listed no fewer than 24 special days and nights, including three on which bags were to be given out (Toyota Travel Bag Day, Chase Bank of Maryland Sports Bag Night, and Chevron School Tote Bag Day). Clubs generally try to arrange their promotions schedules around games that otherwise would have the least appeal to fans, specif. against weaker clubs or those that are not traditional rivals; as in the case in which "The Pirates and Brewers will continue to provide important giveaway scheduling dates for the Cardinals' marketing department" (*Baseball Prospectus*, 2003; Peter Morris). The oddest promotions schedules are posted by the minor leagues; e.g., the 1990 Triple-A Calgary Cannons 200-foot ice-cream sundae and the Single-A Clearwater Phillies "Dynamite Lady" Blows Herself Up. A planned June 7, 1997, free vasectomy drawing in honor of Father's Day offered by the Charleston River Dogs, a Class-A farm team of the Tampa Bay Devil Rays, was canceled due to fan disapproval.

proper batter A batter who comes to the plate in his turn in the batting order. A proper batter shall be called out, on appeal, when he fails to bat in his proper turn and another batter (*improper batter*) completes a time at bat in his place.

prospect A minor-league player who appears to have enough potential and youth to eventually establish a productive major-league career. The term has been used so widely that it is regarded with some skepticism, such that the term "legitimate prospect" appears redundant. In the pecking order of the minor leagues, the next rung down the ladder for a faltering young player from "prospect" is *suspect*. IST USE. 1912. "Cliff Curtis . . . has never been anything more than a prospect" (*The Sporting Life*, July 20; Peter Morris).

protect 1. To place a good hitter into the lineup so that the batter before him (usually also a good hitter) will see good pitches to hit and not be walked; e.g., Barry Bonds, a great hitter in the San Francisco Giants lineup, drew many walks because the Giants did not have a competent hitter immediately following him in the lineup. The issue of protection applies only to great hitters batting third or fourth in the lineup; however, there is little statistical proof that any hitter has offered great protection for another. **2.** For a pitcher to throw at (or hit) a batter after the opposing pitcher has hit a batter on the pitcher's team. "Not all pitchers will throw at batters. If you are a batter, you want *your* pitchers to throw at *their* hitters, to protect *you*" (Dock Ellis, *Dock Ellis in the Country of Baseball*, 1976). Pitcher Lou Grasmick (quoted in *The Baltimore Sun*, May 14, 2000): "If you didn't throw a knockdown, you were going to have a problem with your teammates. You were expected to protect them. If the other pitcher threw at one of your players, then you had to square the account. It was the way the game was played." **3.** To keep an allotted number of players out of the expansion draft when new teams draft players from existing rosters. The number protected in the 1992 and

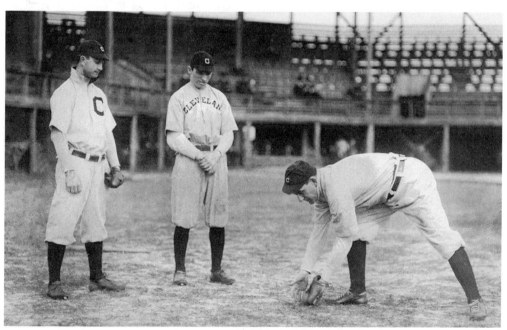

Prospect. Prospects watch Nap Lajoie. *George Grantham Bain Collection, Library of Congress*

1997 drafts was 15. **4.** To pitch effectively when the pitcher's team is winning; to "protect the lead." **5.** See *protect the runner.* **6.** See *protect the line.* **7.** See *protect the plate.*

protection year The year in which a minor leaguer must be added to the major-league club's 40-man roster if the club does not wish to risk losing the player in the Rule 5 draft.

Protective Association Short for *Players' Protective Association.*

protector Short for *chest protector.*

protect the line Syn. of *guard the line.*

protect the plate **1.** To swing at a pitched ball with the intention of fouling it off. It usually occurs when, with two strikes in the count, a batter will foul off a pitch that appears headed for the strike zone but not good enough to hit. The batter will cut down on his swing to avoid striking out. Jimmy Cannon (*Baseball Digest*, Nov.–Dec. 1956) insisted that such protecting was actually "a series of foul tips by a completely fooled batter who intends to hit every one out of the park." Syn. *guard the plate.* **2.** For a catcher to stand fast and effectively block home plate in anticipation of a close play with a runner trying to score.

protect the runner To swing at a given pitch to prevent a runner, who is attempting to steal a base or initiate a hit-and-run play, from being thrown out by the catcher. At a minimum the batter is trying to distract the catcher and hamper him from throwing out the runner.

protest **1.** *n.* An official complaint filed with the league office by the manager of a team who claims that an umpire's decision is a violation or misapplication of the rules. A protest will not be recognized on the field unless the umpires are notified at the time the play under protest occurs and before the next pitch, play, or attempted play. If a protest is upheld, the umpire's call is declared invalid and the game may be replayed from the point at which the call was made (the game may not be replayed if the violation did not adversely affect the protesting team's chance of winning the game). No protest is permitted on judgment decisions by the umpire (*Official Baseball Rules*, Rule 4.19). **2.** *v.* To lodge a formal protest.

protoball Games that were ancestral to mod-ern baseball, from ancient Egypt to 1870. Project Protoball (organized by Larry McCray of Lexington, Mass.) provides a wide range of primary and secondary information sources on the evolution of baseball. See also *safe-haven game.*

prove a box score To balance a box score by verifying that the total of the team's times at bat, bases on balls received, hit batters, sacrifice bunts, sacrifice flies, and batters awarded first base because of catcher's interference or obstruction equals the total of that team's runs, players left on base, and the opposing team's putouts (*Official Baseball Rules*, Rule 10.03[c]). Syn. *balance a box score.* USAGE NOTE. Clem Comly (personal communication, Feb. 17, 2005) notes, "Only certain parts of a box score balance. Even in recent years, pickoffs, appeals, attempted advances on almost wild pitches, and outs trying for extra bases on batted balls are not recorded in any way on the box score."

prune To trim a team's roster to meet the player limit.

prune picker A common nickname (ca. 1950) for a player from California.

pry off the lid To open the baseball season. "The New Orleans Eagles will pry off the lid in Birmingham against the Birmingham Black Barons" (*The Chicago Defender*, Feb. 24, 1951, p.18; Bob Luke).

PSN Abbrev. for *power/speed number.*

psycho An easily rattled or disturbed player.

psych out To gain a real or imagined psychological edge over another player or team; e.g., "Smith psyched out Jones by his intimidating presence on the mound." The term appeared in many sports around 1920. Syn. "psyche out."

psych up To ready oneself or become readied for a game; e.g., "Smith psyched himself up by reliving last week's victory." The term appeared in many sports around 1920. Syn. "psyche up."

PTBNL Abbrev. for *player to be named later.*

PTNL Abbrev. for *player to be named later.*

public enemy number one The curveball.

pud A padded mitt or glove (Bob Hertzel,

Baseball Digest, Jan. 1987). ETYMOLOGY. The term is likely a variation of *pad*, 1.

puff ball An illegal pitch in which the ball is covered with resin powder extracted from the rosin bag by the pitcher. It is a doctored ball that distracts the batter because it arrives at the plate trailing a cloud of white dust. As with other similar innovations, the creation of this pitch has been widely credited to Gaylord Perry. See also *resin ball.* Syn. *powderpuff ball.*

puff hitter A weak hitter, without power. IST USE. 1909 (Zane Grey, *The Short-Stop*, p.60; Edward J. Nichols).

pugball [softball term] A form of softball played on a small diamond.

pugger [softball term] One who plays pugball.

pull **1.** *v.* To hit the ball early in the swing for greater power. A right-handed batter will pull the ball toward left field; a left-handed batter will pull the ball toward right field. Pulling is the opposite of hitting to the opposite field. Compare *slice*, 1. IST USE. 1908 (*American Magazine*, May, p.29; Edward J. Nichols). **2.** *n.* The act or instance of pulling a pitched ball. **3.** *v.* To cause a baseman to remove his foot from a base. **4.** *v.* To remove a player (esp. a pitcher) from the game. IST USE. 1891 (*Chicago Herald*, May 10; Edward J. Nichols).

pull a bone To err; to commit a boner or *bone*. Syn. *pull a rock*. IST USE. 1914. "He goes to the water cooler first for his drink, as any ball player does after he fans or pulls a 'bone'" (Ty Cobb, *Busting 'Em and Other Big League Stories*; Peter Morris).

pull a Brenegan **1.** To get hit hard in the hand by the ball. **2.** To embarrass oneself in a debut. ETYMOLOGY. From Pittsburgh Pirates catcher Olaf Selmer "Sam" Brenegan, who played in his one and only game on Apr. 24, 1914, with no official at-bats. In the sixth inning against the St. Louis Cardinals, Brenegan allowed a runner on first base to advance to third base when he loafed after a wild pitch. In the seventh inning, he allowed a runner on first base to advance to third base on a passed ball that split his finger and was slowly pursued as he groaned in pain. For reasons unclear, Brenegan, whose time in the majors

was counted in minutes, was remembered via this phrase for years to come. Not to be confused with *brannigan*.

pull a Casey Syn. of *do a Casey*.

pull a pitch For a catcher to *frame the pitch* by moving his mitt quickly after catching the ball to give the illusion that the ball was actually received in the strike zone. Ron Luciano (*The Umpire Strikes Back*, 1982, p.167) noted that "This is something umpires really dislike."

pull a rock Syn. of *pull a bone*. "Any time you do something the manager knows you shouldn't, you pull a 'rock'" (Jim Brosnan, *Pennant Race*, 1962). IST USE. 1936 (*New York Herald Tribune*, May 21; Edward J. Nichols).

pull away For a batter to alter his stance for fear of being hit by a pitch. Christy Mathewson (*Pitching in a Pinch*, 1912; Peter Morris): "The catcher signs for the pitcher to throw the next one at the young batter's head. If he pulls away, an unapproachable sin in baseball, the dose is repeated." Syn. *pull back.*

pull back Syn. of *pull away*. "To pitch . . . at the big league level, you've got to be able to read the bat pretty well, whether a guy's diving or pulling back" (Ray Miller, quoted in *The Baltimore Sun*, March 15, 2005).

pull-down-the-window-shade change A changeup in which the pitcher, as he releases the ball, pulls down hard, as with a stubborn window shade. As noted by Roger Kahn (*The Head Game*, 2000), the motion "takes speed off the pitch, but makes the baseball spin rapidly [such that] the batter, seeing the furious spinning, thinks he is looking at a fast ball." The pitch was advocated by Branch Rickey.

pulled hamstring A common baseball injury in which the tendons attached to the hollow of the knee are damaged and the back of the thigh is affected.

pulled-in infield An infield in which the fielders play closer to home plate in an attempt to throw out a baserunner on third base who would otherwise score on a routine ground ball.

pulled-in outfield An outfield in which the

fielders play closer to home in an attempt to throw out the potential winning run on third base with less than two outs.

puller Syn. of *pull hitter.*

pull for To root for; to support a team. "I'm kind of exhausted from pulling so hard for San Francisco to lose, then playing our games" (San Diego Padres outfielder Tony Gwynn, quoted in *Tampa Tribune-Times*, Sept. 24, 1989). IST USE. 1889. "Anse didn't have much confidence in John's ability . . . and told John to sit on the bench and 'pull' for victory" (*The World* [New York], Aug. 8; Gerald L. Cohen).

pull hitter A hitter who mainly hits to the same side of the field on which he stands; one who habitually hits a bit early or "ahead" of the ball. A right-handed batter naturally pulls toward left field and a left-handed batter naturally pulls toward right field. Sometimes spelled "pull-hitter." Syn. *puller.* IST USE. 1928. "Most batters who have trouble with slow ball pitching are 'pull' hitters. That is, they are meeting the ball 'out front'" (George Herman Ruth, *Babe Ruth's Own Book of Baseball*, 1928, p.164; Peter Morris).

pull off the bag 1. To cause a baseman to leave the base to catch another fielder's wild throw. 2. To legally lure a runner off the base he occupies. John B. Foster (in *Collier's New Dictionary of the English Language*, 1908) defined "pulled off base" as "deceiving throw to induce a runner to leave base."

pull off the ball For a batter to open his stance and turn his head and front shoulder away from the plate (toward third base for a right-handed batter), creating a hitting position that is too inside-oriented to reach an outside pitch, often resulting in a weak ground ball, a pop fly, a swinging strike, or a hook foul. Power hitters who want to pull the ball may often pull off the ball. "When you pull off the ball, you pull your head off, you can't go the other way and you can't keep your hands in. It's a matter of concentration" (Chris Hoiles, quoted in *The Baltimore Sun*, June 15, 1997). "When you are pulling off the ball, you don't hit the ball on the good part of the bat. You're not seeing the ball well and you won't cover the plate" (Mike Devereaux, quoted in *The*

Baltimore Sun, June 10, 1994). See also *fly open*, 2; *open up*, 2. IST USE. (Var.) 1898. "[Kostal] has a nasty habit of pulling away from the plate on every ball and swinging high and wide" (*Grand Rapids* [Mich.] *Evening Press*, May 13; Peter Morris).

pull out of the fire To win a game that appeared to have been lost.

pull the string To throw a changeup, causing the batter, expecting a fastball, to swing too soon. IST USE. 1933. "Pull the string—throw a slow ball" (*Famous Sluggers and Their Records of 1932*). ETYMOLOGY. Although the term would seem to derive from the idea of a string used to restrain or hold back the ball, Bert Dunne (*Folger's Dictionary of Baseball*, 1958) stated that it is derived from a trick featuring "a trapped badger" in a box overhead. The rookie releases the "badger" by pulling the string, and, wrote Dunne, "down come refuse and worse."

pull the switch To substitute a batter or pitcher for one that bats or pitches from the other side, such as switching a right-handed pitcher for a left-hander.

pull the trigger To decide to swing at the pitch. According to Robert Kemp Adair (*The Physics of Baseball*, 1990), it takes a batter roughly 0.15 seconds to mentally "pull the trigger" and another 0.2 seconds to actually physically wield the bat. A batter who is geared for a fastball but fails to adjust to an off-speed pitch is one who was not able to "pull the trigger."

pull up To reach a base after making a hit. IST USE. 1913. "The runner pulled up at second" (Stanley T. Milliken, *The Washington Post*, Aug. 25; Peter Morris).

pulverize To hit a ball hard. "Others who are slender can pulverize the ball" (Bobby Veach, quoted in F.C. Lane, *Batting*, 1925, p.66; Peter Morris).

pummel 1. To hit a ball hard. IST USE. 1922 (*The New York Times*, June 5; Edward J. Nichols). 2. To bat hard against a pitcher. IST USE. 1912 (*New York Tribune*, Oct. 7; Edward J. Nichols).

pump 1. *n.* The part of a pitcher's windup in which he swings his arms back and forward over his head. See also *double pump*, 1. 2. *v.*

For a pitcher to swing his arms back and forward at the beginning of the windup. **3.** *v.* To have made mental preparation for an upcoming game; e.g., "Smith spent the evening getting pumped for the first game of the series the next day." **4.** *v.* To bat a ball. "Gil McDougald pumped a dying swan over second base that no one could reach" (Mickey Mantle, *The Mick*, 1985, p.80; Charles D. Poe). IST USE. 1920 (*The New York Times*, Oct. 7; Edward J. Nichols). **5.** *v.* To prepare to throw a ball; to fake a throw. **6.** *v.* For an umpire to call a third strike. **7.** *v.* To throw a fastball with intensity. "When the crowd is on its feet and he [Armando Benitez] gets too caught up, he just pumps fastballs and he gets hit" (*Sports Illustrated*, March 25, 2002). **8.** *n.* The celebratory arm motion, consisting of a clenched fist and a quick pull of the arm back to the body, favored by home run hitters in the 1990s. **9.** *v.* For a catcher, coach, or manager to give a signal by moving his hand or fingers. See *pump system*. **10.** *n.* A signal given in the *pump system*. **11.** *v.* See *pump out hits*.

pumpkin ball [softball term] An early name for softball.

pumpkin wood Inferior wood for a baseball bat. Ted Williams (*My Turn at Bat*, 1969, p.45) commenting on Stan Spence's lightweight bat: "There were imprints all over it where the ball had been hit, which showed it was lousy wood. Real pumpkin wood."

pump man A home run hitter. "[Lee] May was, as he likes to call home run hitters, 'a pump man'" (*The Baltimore Sun*, Oct. 21, 1994).

pump out hits To get many hits.

pump pellet *hist.* A spitball. IST USE. 1907 (*New York Evening Journal*, June 7; Edward J. Nichols).

pump system A method of signaling in which the number of times the signal is given is the signal. For a catcher, it is the number of times he moves ("pumps") his fingers, and not the fingers that are given. For a coach or manager, one sign may be for a bunt, two signs for the hit-and-run play, three signs for taking a pitch, and four signs for no sign (a decoy). New York Giants manager Leo Durocher pioneered a variation: count only the pumps given with the right hand and disregard those given with the left hand. Compare *finger system*.

pump up To infuse with enthusiasm, spirit, and inspiration. Jeff Reardon (quoted in Steve Fiffer, *How to Watch Baseball*, 1987, p.42): "Somebody like Jack Clark up with runners on base. I'll get more pumped up with him than, say, a pinch hitter that isn't a home run threat."

punch 1. *n.* Batting power. A team that produces a lot of hits is said to have "punch" in its lineup. IST USE. 1912 (*New York Tribune*, Sept. 6; Edward J. Nichols). **2.** *n.* A less-than-full swing at a pitched ball, causing the ball to fall in front of the outfielders. **3.** *v.* To hit a pitched ball without a full swing. **4.** *n./hist.* A swing at a pitched ball. IST USE. 1867. "Parker got to first base by a vigorous 'punch' at the ball in the true blue style" (*Flint* [Mich.] *Wolverine Citizen*, Sept. 14; Peter Morris). **5.** *v./hist.* To bat a ball, esp. a long ball. IST USE. 1895 (*New York Press*, Aug. 10; Edward J. Nichols. **6.** *n.* Pitching power.

Punch-and-Judy hitter A batter who tends to hit well-placed but weakly hit balls for singles; one who chokes up and punches or slaps at the ball rather than taking a full swing. "[Robin] Ventura was a Punch-and-Judy hitter, always trying to go to the opposite field" (*Tampa Tribune*, Jan. 4, 1989). Syn. *punch hitter*; *Judy*; *Judy hitter*; *push hitter.* IST USE. 1951. "First sacker Gordon Goldsberry, a .240 Punch-and-Judy hitter, rapped out four singles" (*The Daily Review* [Hayward, Calif.], Sept. 12; Merritt Clifton). ETYMOLOGY. An embellishment of "punch" using the image of the slapstick "Punch and Judy" puppet show from English fairgrounds. The puppets were a grotesque-looking husband and wife who hit each other with sticks in mock fights.

punchball An urban form of baseball popular in New York City, often played in the street or on concrete pavement, in which the "batter" tosses or bounces a rubber ball or beat-up tennis ball over his head, swings down overhand (as if serving a tennis ball) or swings underhand, and punches the ball with his closed fist toward the fielders of the opposing team. There is no pitcher or catcher, but otherwise regular baseball rules apply.

Stephen Jay Gould (*Triumph and Tragedy in Mudville*, 2003, pp.41–42) called punchball "the canonical 'recess' game . . . [because] you could often get in a three- to five-inning game during a full half hour of recess time."

punch drunk *hist.* Said of a player who has become overconfident or arrogant as the result of a string of hits. ETYMOLOGY. A direct borrowing from prizefighting for a boxer who appears stunned or "drunk" from too many punches; slap happy.

punch hitter Syn. of *Punch-and-Judy hitter*. "At bat he [Ty Cobb] had the exact posture of the punch hitter that he was" (Ted Williams, *My Turn at Bat*, 1969, p.92; Charles D. Poe).

punchless Said of a team without offensive power.

punchout *n.* Syn. of *strikeout*, 2. Sometimes spelled "punch-out."

punch out *v.* **1.** Syn. of *strike out*, 1. "I know I punched out twice, but I really didn't feel that bad after those two at-bats" (Todd Hollandsworth, quoted in *The Baltimore Sun*, Apr. 16, 2001). **2.** Syn. of *strike out*, 2. "Pitchers used to 'fan' or 'whiff' batters. Now, when a pitcher strikes out a hitter, he will say: 'I punched him out'" (Phil Pepe, *Baseball Digest*, Nov. 1974, p.58). **3.** For an umpire to call a third strike on a batter.

punch the bag To gossip; to "chew the fat"; to chat (Al Schacht, *Al Schacht Dope Book*, 1944, p.43).

punish **1.** To hit a pitcher hard. Henry Chadwick (*New York Clipper*, Feb. 18, 1871; Peter Morris) considered this term to have a very specific meaning: "The pitcher is 'punished' when the balls he pitches to the bat are easily hit to the field in such a manner as to prevent them from being fielded to put either the batsmen or a base runner out." However, according to Chadwick (*The Game of Base Ball*, 1868, p.44), a pitcher is not "punished" when his pitches are hit hard but caught. IST USE. 1867 (*New York Sunday Mercury*, Sept. 7; Edward J. Nichols). **2.** To hit the ball very hard. "Spencer was handy with the stick. He could punish the ball when it was necessary" (*San Francisco Bulletin*, Feb. 13, 1913; Gerald L. Cohen).

punk **1.** *n.* Syn. of *punk hit*. **2.** *v.* To meet the pitched ball and direct it to a certain place, esp. on a hit-and-run play. "Only once has the [hit-and-run game] . . . failed to work for us and that was when the batter failed to punk the ball" (Grand Rapids manager Frank Torreyson, quoted in *Grand Rapids* [Mich.] *Evening Press*, May 21, 1898; Peter Morris). **3.** *n.* An inferior or "worthless" player. "All his past fame was forgotten—he was now a hopeless punk" (Martin Gardner, *The Annotated Casey at the Bat*, 1967).

punk ball **1.** A ball that defies being hit solidly; one that is soft and flabby. "Fellows with unusually strong grips have been able to loosen the cover . . . and thus toss a 'punk' ball" (*San Francisco News* article on illegal deliveries, July 7, 1938; Peter Tamony). **2.** Poorly played baseball. "We know the Seals have played some mighty punk ball" (*San Francisco Bulletin*, May 26, 1913; Gerald L. Cohen).

punker A *Texas Leaguer*, 2.

punk hit A weakly hit ball that drops to the ground for a base hit. Syn. *punk*, 1. IST USE. 1888. "The hardest hit will sometimes go directly into the waiting hands of a fielder, while a little 'punk' hit from the handle or extreme end of the bat may drop lazily into some unguarded spot" (John Montgomery Ward, *Base-Ball: How to Become a Player*, p.119; Peter Morris).

punkin **1.** A baseball that has seen much use. ETYMOLOGY. From the word "pumpkin" and an apparent reference to a pumpkin's less-than-perfect roundness. **2.** A pitched ball that is easy to hit (Maurice H. Weseen, *A Dictionary of American Slang*, 1934).

punky Said of a punk hit. Three of Cleveland first baseman Charlie Carr's hits were "punky ones" (*The Washington Post*, Aug. 27, 1904; Peter Morris).

pup Syn. of *dog*, 2.

pure hitter An excellent hitter who combines innate ability with hard work and considerable batting practice; e.g., Ted Williams. The term implies that the player is more interested in hitting than fielding. Don Baylor (*Don Baylor*, 1989) said of Lyman Bostock, "Lyman was a pure hitter. He knew that, we all knew it. But he started out trying to earn every cent of his contract on each swing." Compare *natural hitter*, 1.

pure quality start A statistic credited to a starting pitcher who has 1) pitched a minimum of six innings (which measures stamina), 2) allowed no more than an equal number of hits to the number of innings pitched (which measures hit prevention), 3) struck out no fewer than two less than the number of his innings pitched (which measures dominance), 4) struck out at least twice as many batters as he has walked (which measures command), and 5) allowed no more than one home run (which measures ability to keep the ball in the ballpark) (Ron Shandler, *Ron Shandler's Baseball Forecaster*, 2006). For each criterion, a pitcher earns one point; any pitcher who averages three or more points over the course of the season is "probably performing admirably." The statistic does not consider earned runs (which is a function also of the bullpen and the defense), but rather emphasizes a pitcher's base skills. Compare *quality start*. Abbrev. *PQS*.

purloin To steal a base. IST USE. 1887. "Johnny Ward . . . is the king of base runners, leading the league in the number of cushions purloined" (*San Francisco Examiner*, Oct. 24; Peter Morris).

purpose pitch 1. A pitch thrown close to the batter to get him to back away from the plate. It is usually a high inside fastball that can act as a knockdown pitch. There are several "purposes" of a purpose pitch: to intimidate a hot hitter, to retaliate for having had a teammate hit by a pitch, to scare a batter after the previous batter has hit a home run, or to "modify" the batter's behavior for showboating or hotdogging. Umpire Ron Luciano (*The Umpire Strikes Back*, 1982) noted that the purpose of the purpose pitch was "to remind the batter that the pitched ball is a weapon." See also *message pitch*. ETYMOLOGY. Sportscaster Bob Uecker (*Catcher in the Wry*, 1983) and Joe Garagiola (*Baseball Is a Funny Game*, 1960, p.61) claimed that the term was created by Branch Rickey. According to Garagiola, it may have originated in the context of Rickey's observation that the intent of a purpose pitch was "to separate the [batter's] head from the shoulders." 2. A pitch that is not

meant to be hit but rather to set up another pitch (George F. Will, *Men at Work*, 1990).

purse A figurative baseball bat when the ball is hit barely over the infield. Players say the batter "hit it with his purse" when he gets a bloop hit (Garret Mathews, *Can't Find a Dry Ball*, 2002).

push 1. *v.* To hit the ball to the opposite field. 2. *v.* To hit a ball softly past the pitcher. "[Butler] pushed the ball slowly down the infield, striving to make it roll fast enough to pass the pitcher either to his right or his left, yet so slowly that the short stop or second baseman, playing deep, would have to take it while sprinting forward at top speed and make a perfect throw" (John J. Evers and Hugh S. Fullerton, *Touching Second: The Science of Baseball*, 1910; Peter Morris). IST USE. 1905 (*The Sporting Life*, Sept. 9, p.1; Edward J. Nichols). 3. *v.* To execute a push bunt. 4. *n.* Short for *push bunt*. "Chuck [Deal] twice fouled and with two strikes could not chance a sacrificial push" (Burt Whitman, *Boston Herald and Journal*, Sept. 7, 1918; Peter Morris). 5. *n.* The forward move made by the pitcher just before the ball is delivered. 6. *v.* For a pitcher (usually with a shoulder problem) to fail to rotate his arm upward, thereby losing his ability to snap the fastball.

push bunt A bunt, usually for a base hit, in which a right-handed batter tries to place (or "push") the ball past the pitcher and toward first base. Syn. *push*, 4; *force bunt*. IST USE. 1910. "Many plays, such as the 'push bunt' . . . have been 'discovered' about once a decade, and then neglected, if not forgotten, until some other genius brought them into action" (John J. Evers and Hugh S. Fullerton, *Touching Second: The Science of Baseball*; Peter Morris).

push-button manager A manager who, with a great collection of players, "had only to push a button to get the home run or outstanding defensive play needed to win" (Frank Graham Jr., *Casey Stengel*, 1958). IST USE. 1945. "Jimmy Dykes impishly referred to Joe McCarthy last year as the 'push button manager,' thereby riling Marse Joe no end" (Arthur Daley, *The New York Times*, Jan. 18). USAGE NOTE. Dykes, manager of the Chicago White Sox, had used the derisive term "push button" in 1944 when referring to McCarthy's tenure as manager of the New York Yankees in the 1930s: "Joe McCarthy will really have to go to work this season. He won't be able to sit back as in other years and simply push buttons to win pennants" (Arthur Daley, *The New York Times*, Apr. 13, 1944; Alan H. Levy).

push hitter Syn. of *Punch-and-Judy hitter*.

push home To drive in a run. IST USE. 1889. "[Jack] Hayes pushed him home on a pretty place hit to short left" (*San Francisco Examiner*, Apr. 28; Peter Morris).

push off For a pitcher to move forward off the rubber just before the ball is delivered.

"put a new handle on it" Time-tested advice given to a player who has just broken his bat.

put away 1. Syn. of *put out*. An outfielder making a catch is said to "put the batter away." Pitcher Jason Johnson (quoted in *The Baltimore Sun*, June 15, 2002): "I got ahead of hitters with my fastball and I put them away with my curveball." IST USE. 1881 (*New York Herald*, July 15; Edward J. Nichols). 2. For a team to go on an offensive run to seal the outcome before the game's conclusion. 3. To throw a strikeout pitch.

put-away pitch A strikeout pitch. "[Matt Riley's] curveball . . . has its sharp bite back, giving him two put-away pitches" (*Baseball America*, Aug. 18–31, 2003).

put down 1. To move a runner from first base to second base on a sacrifice. The word "down" indicates an advance from one base to another. IST USE. 1937 (*The Sporting News Record Book*, p.66; Edward J. Nichols). 2. Syn. of *knock down*.

put fannies in the seats Syn. of *put the meat in the seats*.

"put it over" A command to the pitcher to throw the ball in the strike zone. The command can come from the opposition who wants the batter to get a good ball to hit or from one of the pitcher's teammates encouraging him to stop throwing bad pitches. Washington pitcher Tom Hughes (quoted in *Detroit Times*, Aug. 21, 1906; Peter Morris): "No fielder can come in and tell a pitcher how to play ball; all they can say is 'steady down,' 'put it over' and a similar line of talk. That doesn't help a pitcher; it rather makes him mad." IST USE. 1889. "With only four balls, the pitcher will have to put them over the plate" (*San Francisco Examiner*, March 4; Peter Morris).

put mustard on the pretzel To throw a fastball (mustard) immediately after a curveball (pretzel).

put on To walk a batter.

put on the train To trade a player.

putout *n.* The retirement of a batter or baserunner by a defensive player; also, a statistic credited to a fielder whose action causes the out of a batter-runner or baserunner. The putout is credited to the fielder who actually retires the runner by catching a fly ball or line drive, tagging the runner, or touching a base while in possession of the ball. A strikeout is credited to the pitcher, but the catcher receives credit for the putout. There are rare situations in which a fielder gets credited with a putout without touching the ball, as when a batted ball strikes a baserunner. Rarely spelled "put-out." Abbrev. *PO*. Syn. *out*, 2. IST USE. 1869 (*New York Herald*, July 14; Edward J. Nichols).

put out *v.* To cause an opponent to be retired from play or removed from an opportunity to reach a base or score. Syn. *put away*, 1. IST USE. 1860 (*Beadle's Dime Base-Ball Player*, p.32; Edward J. Nichols).

putout average *hist.* An early fielding statistic, measured by putouts divided by games played, devised by Philadelphia baseball writer Al Wright in 1876 (John Thorn and Pete Palmer, *The Hidden Game of Baseball*, 1985). See also *outs per game*.

put out the fire For a relief pitcher to enter the game and stop an offensive rally; e.g., "With no out and two on, Smith put out the fire by retiring the next three batters."

"put some grass in your hat" Advice to an outfielder having trouble catching the ball.

put some mustard on it To reach back for a little extra velocity on a fastball.

put something on the ball To pitch a ball that will curve, break, float, or otherwise behave unnaturally; to throw harder "I know as well as the fans that I couldn't put anything on the ball last season" (Flame Delhi, quoted in *San Francisco Bulletin*, March 6, 1913). The term may have first referred to "saliva on a spitball" (Gerald L. Cohen, *Dictionary of 1913 Baseball and Other Lingo*, vol.2, p.233): "The pitchers are putting something more than hope on the ball" (*San Francisco Bulletin*, March 1, 1913; Gerald L. Cohen). See also *on the ball*.

put the ball in his pocket For a defensive player, esp. a catcher, to determine that he cannot make a play on a baserunner and refrains from throwing the ball. "If he [Ichiro Suzuki] hits a two- or three-bouncer to short, the guy [shortstop] might as well put the ball in his pocket" (anonymous scout, quoted in *Sports Illustrated*, March 25, 2002).

put the ball in play 1. For a batter to avoid striking out by hitting the ball fair in hopes of driving in a run or getting a hit. "[Eddie Murray was] trying to make contact, put the ball in play and drive in the run" (*The Baltimore Sun*, Sept. 12, 1996). See also *in play*, 3. EXTENDED USE. To get a program or activity started. "If there was one person who put the ball in play for us and changed the rules, it was Richard [Pryor]. There is no question that he is The Man" (Peter Kaminsky, said of Pryor receiving the first Mark Twain Prize for contributions to American humor, in reference to Pryor's influence in expanding the horizons of what could be laughed at, quoted in *The Baltimore Sun*, Oct. 22, 1998). 2. For a pitcher to coax the batter to hit the ball assuming that the defense will be able to make outs. "We have a good defense, so let them put the ball in play" (Chicago White Sox pitcher Mark Buehrle, quoted in *The Baltimore Sun*, Apr. 5, 2003).

put the ball on the ground To *bunt*, 3. "It has been noted that [Brady] Anderson has . . . 'put the ball on the ground' more than he has in the past two years. He hasn't been overly successful, but the Orioles continue to encourage him not to abandon the bunt as an offensive [weapon]" (Jim Henneman, *The Baltimore Sun*, June 7, 1994).

put the ball on the runner To apply a tag on a baserunner, esp. one who is an elusive slider. George Herman Ruth (*Babe Ruth's Own Book of Baseball*, 1928, p.103): "Tagging a man properly is an art. I've seen some great looking kids come up to the big leagues, kids who seemed to have everything. But they didn't stick, because they couldn't 'put the ball on the runner.'"

put the bat on the ball To hit the ball; to make contact with a pitched ball. The term implies an ability to handle a bat: "I have that much confidence that he [Mark Grace] will put the bat on the ball and find a hole" (Arizona Diamondbacks manager Bob Brenly, quoted in *Sports Illustrated*, June 18, 2001). The term also suggests a defensive approach by the batter. "[Lee Smith] threw two nasty pitches to me to get ahead. I just tried to put the bat on the ball" (Mark McGwire, quoted in *The Baltimore Sun*, July 11, 1994). Syn. *put wood on the ball*.

put the game away To close out a victory.

put the game on ice To lead a game definitively; to remove any chance of victory by the opposing team. "Enough clouts were secured by the gray-clad swatters to put the game on ice" (*San Francisco Bulletin*, Apr. 28, 1913; Gerald L. Cohen). Syn. "put the game in the ice box"; "put the game on cold storage."

put the game out of reach To have such a big lead that it is unlikely that the opposing team will catch up.

put the meat in the seats To be able to attract paying spectators. "[Ken Griffey Jr.] isn't just another guy in the clubhouse. He's the guy in Cincinnati who puts the meat in the seats" (Peter Schmuck, *The Baltimore Sun*, Feb. 24, 2002). The term was often used boastfully by Reggie Jackson. Syn. *put fannies in the seats*.

put the wood to it To hit the ball solidly. IST USE. 1909 (Zane Grey, *The Short-Stop*, p.96; Edward J. Nichols).

putty An injury-prone player.

putty arm A bad, weak, or sore throwing arm. IST USE. 1933 (*Famous Sluggers and Their Records of 1932*).

put wood on the ball Syn. of *put the bat on the ball*.

puzzler A deceptively pitched ball. IST USE.

1880 (*Chicago Inter-Ocean*, June 25; Edward J. Nichols).

PVR Abbrev. for *player value ranking.*

PW Abbrev. for *pitching wins.*

PWA Abbrev. for *player win average.*

Pythagenpat method An improvement to the *Pythagenport method* that calculates the exponent to be used in the *Pythagorean method* by using a simple and more accurate formula. The exponent is the sum of a team's runs scored and runs allowed per game, raised to the power 0.287. The method was developed by the sabermetricians David Smyth and "Patriot" in 2000.

Pythagenport method An improvement to the *Pythagorean method* that replaces the fixed exponent with a value that depends on runs scored and runs allowed per game. It was developed by Clay Davenport of *Baseball Prospectus* in 1999 and has now been replaced by the *Pythagenpat method.*

Pythagorean method A formula for predicting the expected winning percentage for a team in a given season, based on the number of runs scored and runs allowed. It is computed by squaring the number of runs the team scores, and then dividing by the sum of the number of runs the team scores squared plus the number of runs the team gives up squared. The inclusion of the squares compensates for the fact that most very good teams win, and most very poor teams lose, a substantial number of games by wide margins. Any team with a won-lost percentage substantially different than this prediction has been either particularly lucky or unlucky over the course of the season. A team that outscores its opponents by 100 runs is

expected to win about 91 games; a team that wins at least 100 games is likely to outscore its opponents by more than 200 runs. The legendary 1962 New York Mets scored 617 runs and gave up 948 runs, which leads to a predicted winning percentage of .298; their actual percentage was .250, indicating that besides being bad, they suffered bad luck. In contrast, the 1969 Miracle Mets scored 632 runs and gave up 541 runs, which translates to a predicted winning percentage of .577; their actual percentage of .617 was indeed a "miracle" in part. The term is a play on the Pythagorean theorem and the analogous reliance on squared numbers. The concept was devised by Bill James and first described in his self-published *Baseball Abstract* (1980); the term first appeared in the 1981 *Baseball Abstract*. A description can be found in James' first conventionally published *Baseball Abstract* (1982). See also *Pythagenpat method; Pythagenport method.* Syn. *Pythagorean winning percentage.*

Pythagorean theory The principle that the winning percentage of a team corresponds closely to the difference between runs scored and runs allowed.

Pythagorean winning percentage Syn. of *Pythagorean method.*

Pythians An African-American baseball team operating out of Philadelphia from 1866 to 1871. It applied for membership in the Pennsylvania Association of Amateur Base Ball Players in 1867 but was rejected in a ruling that banned all black clubs and players. The team disbanded when its leader, Octavius Catto, was murdered. See Jerrold Casway, *The National Pastime*, no.15, 1995, pp.120–23.

Q

QERA Abbrev. for *quikERA*.

QS Abbrev. for *quality start*.

"quack, quack" Time-honored call made by players to get the attention of the trainer. It is a puckish play on the notion that his healing skills and nostrums are based in quackery.

Quadruple-A Syn. of *4-A*, 1.

quadruple double Attaining double figures in doubles, triples, home runs, and stolen bases during a season. Compare *triple double*, 1. ETYMOLOGY. From basketball, when a player records double figures in points, rebounds, assists, and blocked shots or steals in a single game.

quadrupleheader A set of four games played in succession on the same day between the same two teams.

quadruple play A defensive play in which four players are put out as a result of continuous action, providing there are no errors committed between putouts. Ray Corio (*The New York Times*, Oct. 20, 1980) gave an example of a quadruple play: With the bases loaded and no outs, a fly ball is caught for the first out, the runners from first base and second base (running on the assumption that the ball was not catchable) are tagged out trying to return to their bases, and the runner on third base is declared out on appeal (before the defensive team left the field) for leaving the base before the catch was made, thereby negating the run (an appealed out takes precedence in determining an out). See also *fourth out*.

quail Syn. of *dying quail*. "I've never seen that many quails fall in one inning" (Baltimore Orioles catcher Sal Fasano, quoted in *The Baltimore Sun*, July 5, 2005).

quail-high hit A base hit that sails over the infield at the height that a quail flies when flushed (Walter K. Putney, *Baseball Stories*, Spring 1952).

Quakers 1. Nickname for the Philadelphia *Phillies*, esp. during its formative years (1883–1889). **2.** Nickname for the Players' League franchise in Philadelphia in 1890.

quality out of quantity The art of improving a team by signing or purchasing a lot of players with raw basic talent, and developing some of them into stars by teaching them baseball skills. The term was coined by baseball executive Branch Rickey. "Rickey's fundamental principle, 'quality out of quantity,' had direct implications for scouting. . . . The system depended on teaching" (Kevin Kerrane, *Dollar Sign on the Muscle*, 1984, p.24). See also *Rickeyism*. Syn. *quantitative quality*.

quality pitch A precisely thrown pitch with something on it, esp. one thrown in a difficult situation or at a crucial time. "Any time you can throw three quality pitches over the plate, you're going to be successful" (Baltimore Orioles catcher Chris Hoiles, quoted in *The Baltimore Sun*, Apr. 27, 1995). See also *quality strike*.

quality start A statistic credited to a starting pitcher who pitches at least six innings and allows three or fewer earned runs. Compare *pure quality start*. Abbrev. *QS*. ETYMOLOGY. The term was proposed by sportswriter John Lowe (*Philadelphia Inquirer*, Dec. 26, 1985): "The foremost attribute of this statistic is that it shows exactly how many times a man has done exactly what his job is—pitch well enough for his team to have a chance to win."

By the mid-1980s, relief pitching specialization was escalating and a starting pitcher was considered to have done his job if he pitched six innings and kept his team in the game.

quality strike A strike thrown to the precise spot and with the exact velocity desired. Baltimore Orioles pitcher Ben McDonald, discussing pitcher Arthur Rhodes (quoted in *The Baltimore Sun*, May 22, 1994): "He has to . . . not only throw strikes, but quality strikes. Instead of throwing the ball to the middle of the plate, he's got to hit the outer third and the inner third." Curt Schilling (quoted in *Baseball America*, July 5–21, 2002) defined "command" as "the ability to throw quality strikes." See also *quality pitch*.

quantitative quality Syn. of *quality out of quantity*.

quarry A rough infield (Bill McCullough, *Brooklyn Eagle*, Sept. 5, 1937).

quarter A loose-spinning slider. Compare *dime*, 1.

quarterback drill A pregame warm-up exercise in which players jog along in a line, throwing and catching the ball over their shoulders. Pitchers commonly use it to sharpen their reflexes.

quarter ball An inexpensive baseball (costing 25 cents) of better quality than a *dime ball*. When the cover ripped, exposing tightly wound yarn, it was wrapped in black friction tape and kept in use.

QuesTec A digital media company in Deer Park, N.Y., that was contracted by Major League Baseball in 2001 to install, operate, and maintain the controversial Umpire Information System (UIS) consisting of four video cameras (one at each dugout, one in center field, and one above the field) and computers that monitor, measure, and analyze the strike zone for each individual batter, pitch, and at-bat in 10 selected ballparks. The purpose of UIS is to evaluate the plate umpire's calls of balls and strikes and to train umpires to have a consistent strike zone. Computer software generates a compact disc that the umpire and his supervisor can review. Umpires whose calls do not match QuesTec's measurements at least 90 percent of the time are judged as "not meeting standards." The strike zone is set based on each batter's approach to hitting the ball, and is accurate to 0.5 inch. Umpires' concerns about QuesTec include inconsistently placed cameras in the various ballparks, difficulty in tracking certain types of breaking pitches, and inconsistency as where operators draw the top and bottom lines of the strike zone.

questionable pitch A pitched ball that is neither a clear ball nor a clear strike and may be ruled as either by the umpire.

question mark **1.** A player whose immediate future is uncertain because of injury, illness, or any of several other problems. **2.** A rookie or player from another team who is new and untested. "We have new guys in the lineup and a lot of question marks" (Atlanta Braves left fielder Chipper Jones, quoted in *Sports Illustrated*, March 31, 2003).

Quickball **1.** A truncated, fast-paced version of baseball intended to introduce newcomers to the sport, characterized by a compact diamond, a plastic ball, and no fielding gloves. It is a popular intramural game on university campuses; e.g., at Oklahoma State University, a team consists of four players, and there are two outs per inning and maximum of 10 runs per team per inning. **2.** The hard, durable, plastic ball used in Quickball, characterized by raised seams and asymmetrically positioned holes. It comes in various sizes.

quick bat **1.** An attribute of a batter with fast reflexes who can swing quickly and not be intimidated by a fastball. **2.** A batter with a quick bat. "The two quickest bats of this era have been [Gary] Sheffield and [Barry] Bonds" (Tom Verducci, *Sports Illustrated*, May 1, 2006).

quick belly button The hip action needed to hit line drives. The expression was used by Paul Waner.

quick exit The removal of a starting pitcher after a very short appearance (usually less than an inning) (*The Washington Post*, Oct. 7, 1989).

quick hands The hands of an adept fielder who can handle bad hops or relay the ball on a double play. New York Yankees scout Gene Michael (quoted in *Sports Illustrated*, March 26, 2001, pp.56–57) admired the hands of

Bill Mazeroski ("he was so quick"), who, when turning a double play, allowed the ball to hit the pad of his glove where the left index finger meets the palm and "bounce off, rather than going deep into the pocket."

quick hook 1. A term used by Bill James for the removal of a starting pitcher (*hook*, 6) before he has pitched six innings or given up four runs. Compare *slow hook*. 2. A manager's tendency to remove a pitcher (*hook*, 7) from a game at the first sign of trouble. "I should've hooked him [Kent Mercker] in the second inning. I mean, if that's a quick hook, that's the farthest thing from my mind. That's 11 people on base in three innings" (Davey Johnson, quoted in *The Baltimore Sun*, June 15, 1996).

quick look An opportunity afforded a minor-league player to get the feel of major-league baseball.

quickness 1. The ability of a defensive player to take an immediate first step toward a ground ball or fly ball. 2. The ability of a base stealer to reach top speed toward the next base (Alan Schwarz, BaseballAmerica.com, Nov. 14, 2006).

quick pitch 1. *n.* Syn. of *quick return pitch*, 1. 2. *n.* A legal pitch thrown quicker than usual between pitches. "As used by [Clyde] King, the quick pitch is thrown legally, but suddenly, without a windup; the idea is to catch the batter unprepared and ruin his timing" (Harvey Rosenfeld, *The Great Chase*, 1992, p.142). 3. *v.* To try to pitch to a batter when he is not yet ready to bat. Whitey Ford (*Slick*, 1987, p.210) confessed, "Occasionally, I would quick-pitch a hitter, catch him between practice swings or when he wasn't ready. That was easy. All I did was speed up my motion or instead of going into my big, full windup, I would just get the ball, pump, and throw, and the hitter wouldn't be ready for it."

quick release The speed and effectiveness by which a catcher relays a ball to a baseman on an attempted steal.

quick return pitch 1. An illegal pitch, by which the pitcher hurries his throw with the obvious intent of catching the batter off balance. It is thrown before the batter takes his position and becomes reasonably set (in the judgment of the umpire) in the batter's box. When detected by the umpire, it is treated as a ball (with no runners on base) or a balk (with runners on base). Syn. *quick pitch*, 1; "quick return." 2. [softball term] A pitch thrown with the obvious attempt to catch the batter off balance. This would be before the batter takes his desired position in the batter's box or while he is still off balance as a result of the previous pitch. When a quick return pitch is attempted, the umpire is expected to declare that "no pitch" has been made; however, in many cases it is not called and some pitchers have learned to use it effectively.

quiet bat 1. A bat that does not move while the batter waits for the pitch. "The big end of his bat is completely quiet when the ball leaves the pitcher's hand" (1956 scouting report on Roberto Clemente, in Branch Rickey, *Branch Rickey's Little Blue Book*, 1995, p.59). Rickey taught his scouts to look for "a bat you could set a quarter on and not have it fall off while the hitter waited for the pitch" (Howie Haak, quoted in Kevin Kerrane, *Dollar Sign on the Muscle*, 1984, p.98; Peter Morris). 2. The bat of a player who is in a batting slump. "It's the Orioles' quiet bats . . . that are spiking everyone's blood pressure" (John Eisenberg, *The Baltimore Sun*, Apr. 17, 2001). Syn. *sleeping bat*.

quikball A four-inning, Wiffle-ball-based variation of baseball that uses a small bat and dimensions of 85 feet down the lines and 100 feet to straightaway center field. It is played by students in the intramural program at New York Univ.

quikERA A measure of a pitcher's expected earned run average based on the proportion of plate appearances in which he records a strikeout, the proportion in which he gives up a walk, and his ground-ball percentage. The measure was proposed by Nate Silver of *Baseball Prospectus*. Abbrev. *QERA*.

quiver ball A "corkscrew floater" thrown by Christy Mathewson in 1911 that had a peculiar and deceiving "double break" after he wet his fingers (R.J. Lesch).

R

R Box score abbrev. for *run*, 2 (run scored or run allowed).

RA 1. Abbrev. for *red ass*. 2. Abbrev. for *run average*.

rabbit 1. A player with great speed. "Such rabbits as Clyde Milan, Maury Wills and Lou Brock" (Christopher Lehmann-Haupt, *The New York Times*, July 13, 1981). Syn. *jackrabbit*, 1. 2. Syn. of *knuckleball*; 1. Stu Miller had a "hippity-hopping" knuckleball. 3. Syn. of *rabbit ball*, 1. Baseball manufacturer Edward Hubbert Sr. (quoted in *The Sporting News*, July 1947): "I'm not surprised that the Giants are leading the National League in home runs. This baseball is a rabbit. It is the fastest, liveliest ball made, and if records aren't broken, it will be because there are no Ruths, Gehrigs or Foxxes around." IST USE. 1915. "The 'rabbit' was a baseball similar in appearance to the ordinary league ball; under its horsehide cover, however, it was remarkably different" (Zane Grey, *The Redheaded Outfield and Other Baseball Stories*, p.162; David Shulman). 4. The quality in a baseball that, when the baseball is hit, makes it travel a long distance. "Has the 1948 horsehide got a rabbit in it?" asked Jack McDonald (*San Francisco Call-Bulletin*, Apr. 28, 1948; Peter Tamony). "The pitchers need help—less rabbit in the ball" (Art Morrow, *The Sporting News*, Nov. 30, 1955). "Some of the balls, instead of having one rabbit have three or four rabbits" (Minnesota Twins pitcher Bert Blyleven, who gave up 50 home runs in 1986, quoted in *The New York Times*, May 10, 1987). Testing of balls in 1987 "robb[ed] conspiracy theorists of a smoking gun . . . there ain't no rabbit in those balls" (Ben Brown, *USA Today*, July 20, 1987). See also *jackrabbit*, 3.

rabbit ball 1. A baseball that appears to be livelier than an ordinary ball; one that jumps like a rabbit and can be hit for distance. The term appears in news stories whenever there is a sudden increase in home runs. As Peter Morris remarked (*A Game of Inches: The Game on the Field*, 2006, p.405), "Sometimes there is at least some basis for speculation, but often it seems to have been entirely fueled by paranoia." Although the term can be used for a single ball or a small number of them, it is usually applied to the ball in use throughout a particular season. These range from the ball of 1911, which was the first officially to have a cork center, to the 1987 ball, which was widely alleged to be "juiced up": "Bugs Bunny Would Enjoy 1987 'Rabbit Ball'" (*The Sporting News*, May 25, 1987). A few of the other alleged rabbit-ball years include 1925, 1930, 1950, 1956, 1961, 1969, 1977, and 1996. Over the years players and managers have found many ways of expressing their belief that a ball is a rabbit ball. For instance, in 1969, the International League used a ball from the MacGregor-Brunswick Corp. known as the 97; an unnamed player was quoted in *The Sporting News* (May 17, 1969) as saying, "The 97 is the only ball that eats lettuce for breakfast." See also *jackrabbit ball*; *kangaroo ball*; *lively ball*, 2. Syn. *bunny ball*; *lettuce ball*; *rabbit*, 3. IST USE. 1907. "The Cleveland camp followers, when Macon won on Wednesday, went to the old family chest and brushed the moth powder off the 'rabbit' ball story that was sprung a dozen times during the championship series a year ago" (Joe S. Jackson, *Detroit Free Press*, March 31; Peter Morris). 2. Syn. of *hopper*, 1.

rabbit ears 1. An attribute of a player or umpire who hears everything or is easily distracted by noise. The implication is that the player or umpire reacts to everything he hears. "A physical phenomena that enables a ballplayer or umpire standing in a ball park before a crowd of 50,000 noisy fans to hear his name whispered in the opponent's dugout twenty-five yards away" (Jim Brosnan, *The Long Season*, 1960). IST USE. 1943. "Those who have or apparently hear everything said about them by [bench] jockeys are said to have 'rabbit ears'" (*Baseball Magazine*, January; David Shulman). **2.** An overly sensitive player or umpire who is especially ready to hear everything said about him and to respond to comments and taunts; one who is easily ridden. IST USE. 1933 (Edgar G. Brands, *The Sporting News*, Feb. 23).

rabbitize To enliven a ball. "If Coast League baseballs aren't rabbitized, as Red Kennealy, the Wilson's man, claims they are not, let us at least say they have been traveling with rare vivacity" (Jack McDonald, *San Francisco Call-Bulletin*, June 6, 1956; Peter Tamony).

RABS Abbrev. for *runs per at-bat.*

race See *pennant race.* "We have to be professionals. We know we are out of the race, but we have to ... play hard" (Miguel Tejada, quoted in *The Baltimore Sun*, Sept. 18, 2006).

race baseball Syn. of *blackball.*

race to the bag A play in which a fielder with the ball is trying to beat the runner to a base for the force out.

rack pack Three packs of baseball cards, either wrapped in wax or without a wrapper, designed to hang from store displays and sold in supermarkets, major toy chains, and drugstores in the 1970s and 1980s.

radar gun An electronic device used to measure the velocity of a pitched ball in miles per hour. The "fast" radar gun (*JUGS gun*) measures the speed of the ball as it leaves the pitcher's hand; the "slow" radar gun (*Ra-Gun*) measures the speed of the ball as it crosses home plate. The velocity gap between the two readings diminishes the higher the ball is released, probably because the more downward trajectory reduces the decelerating force that gravity would place on an object moving horizontally. Pitching coach Charlie Puleo (*Orioles Gazette*, July 8, 1993) noted, "So many baseball people rely only on the radar gun and for a guy who doesn't throw 90 [mph], it can be a challenge to make a mark for yourself." Syn. *gun,* 5; *speed gun.*

radical realignment A 1997 proposal that would have scrapped the traditional major leagues and their divisions and started over.

radio ball A fastball thrown with such speed that the batter claims he can hear it but (supposedly) not see it. Syn. *radio pitch.* ETYMOLOGY. Joseph McBride (*High & Inside*, 1980, p.52) attributed the term to batters who faced Walter Johnson's fastball, noting the phrase of Washington Senators catcher Cliff Blankenship, "You can't hit what you can't see." The term also has been attributed in the 1950s to Roy Sievers regarding Herb Score's fastball (Herman L. Masin, *Baseball Laughs*, 1964) and George "Catfish" Metkovich regarding Max Surkont's fastball (Joe Garagiola, *Baseball Is a Funny Game*, 1960).

radio pitch Syn. of *radio ball.*

radish The baseball.

raftman A slow outfielder who appears to be poling a raft rather than running. The images used to describe slowness on the diamond are often nautical. An example from a 1912 collection of baseball slang: "He couldn't beat a towboat that was tied to the bank" (*The Sporting Life*, May 18, 1912).

rag 1. *v.* To ride, jeer, or heckle; to jockey. "Much laughter, too, and not a little ragging of the Indians" (Christy Mathewson, *Catcher Craig*, 1915). Two examples of ragging from an industrial-league game in Montgomery County, Md.: "Number 20—off your knees" (to a short player); and "Hey 12, get the piano off your back" (to a slow runner). **2.** *n.* A fielder's glove. **3.** *n./hist.* The *pennant,* 2. "Chicago has had the pennant so often that it will be sad to part with the 'rag'" (*San Francisco Examiner*, Sept. 26, 1887; Peter Morris). IST USE. 1887. "The Mets, Baltimores, Louisvilles and Clevelands all have admirers who believe that their favorites will 'carry away the rag'" (*The World* [New York], Apr. 16; Gerald L. Cohen).

rag arm **1.** A pitcher whose pitches lack speed and deception; one who pitches with nothing on the ball. The term is used disparagingly. **2.** A loose arm. The 10th commandment in Herb Pennock's "10 Commandments of Pitching" (*The Sporting News*, Apr. 24, 1971): "Work for what is called a rag arm. A loose arm can pitch overhanded, side-arm, three-quarter, underhanded—any old way—to suit the situation at hand."

rag chewing Arguing or complaining. "The Senators raised a howl because [umpire Charles] King allowed the play to go through, and the rag-chewing aroused the ire of the fanatic, who shared the hostilities against the umpire" (*The Washington Post*, Aug. 21, 1904; Peter Morris). Syn. *chewing the rag.*

ragged fielding Loose and unreliable defensive play. IST USE. 1885 (*Chicago Inter-Ocean,* June 3; Edward J. Nichols).

rag man A pitcher whose pitching-arm sleeve is frayed or loose. No player is allowed to wear ragged, frayed, or slit sleeves because they may distract one's vision (*Official Baseball Rules*, Rule 1.11[c][2]).

Ra-Gun A *radar gun* used to measure the velocity of a pitched ball as it crosses home plate. The later reading (after the ball has lost some of its speed—the reading is about three or four miles per hour slower than that of the *JUGS gun*) is considered more important because home plate is where the issue is settled. The average major-league fastball registers 84 to 86 mph on the Ra-Gun.

rainbow **1.** *n.* A wide, sweeping curveball with a rainbowlike arc; a *roundhouse curve.* "[Calvin] Schiraldi breaks off a rainbow" (Vin Scully, NBC telecast, May 9, 1987). "Amos Rusie's slow, rakish rainbow of a curve hath charms for the sluggers of Fred Clarke's team of Colonels" (*The Washington Post*, Sept. 25, 1898). See also *jughandle.* Syn. *rainbow curve.* **2.** *n.* A high arcing fly ball, esp. a home run. **3.** *n.* A long, high throw, usually from an outfielder, resembling the arc of a rainbow. **4.** *v.* To throw a rainbow. "[Catcher Bill] Carrigan appears to 'rainbow' the ball down to second, but manages to have it there ahead of the runner or thereabouts just the same" (*Detroit Free Press*, May 13, 1913; Peter Morris).

rainbow curve Syn. of *rainbow,* 1. "[Felix] Hernandez attacks hitters with . . . a rainbow curve" (Albert Chen, *Sports Illustrated*, Aug. 22, 2005). IST USE. 1891 (*Chicago Herald,* May 25; Edward J. Nichols).

rainbow drop Slang syn. of *home run.*

rainbow pitch Syn. of *eephus.*

rainbow play A trick play meant to deceive a baserunner attempting to steal a base in which the catcher lobs a high-arcing throw to an infielder while his teammates on the field and the bench scream "pop fly" and point to the sky, causing the baserunner to hesitate and get caught in a rundown (*Sports Illustrated*, June 11, 2007).

rain bringer A high fly ball. IST USE. 1932 (*Baseball Magazine*, October, p.496; Edward J. Nichols). Syn. *rainstorm.*

rain check The detachable part of a ticket to a baseball game, which can be used to gain admission to a future game if the game in question is called because of inclement weather before it becomes a regulation game (4½ or 5 innings, depending on the score). The custom of giving the ticket holder a rain check was institutionalized in 1890 in the National League constitution. It has long been claimed and often published that the first detachable rain check was issued in 1888 in New Orleans by team owner Abner Powell of the minor-league Pelicans. *Joe Reichler's Book of Baseball Records* (1957) quotes Powell on the discovery, noting that many people were getting into Sportsman's Park, where the Pelicans played, for free. When there was rain in that era of reusable tickets, the spectators lined up to pick up a ticket for the next day, reclaiming those that had already been turned in. "Usually," said Powell, "there were more fans in line than there were tickets in the box. All those free riders

Rain check. *Author's collection*

and fence jumpers joined the line, too. The situation became so acute that, despite week-day crowds of 5,000 and Sunday throngs of 10,000, we were losing money." Powell thought about this for several days in 1889 (according to this account—not 1887 or 1888, as is stated elsewhere) and came up with the rain-check idea. This claim was heavily publicized in 1953 when Powell died at age 92 in New Orleans and many newspapers carried his obituary. The Associated Press story said the first Powell rain check was issued in 1887, a year earlier than most other accounts and two years earlier than Reichler's claim. The discrepancy may not be all that important because linguistic research conducted by David Shulman points conclusively to earlier use of the term; e.g., "Rain checks given out on the St. Louis grounds are good for any succeeding championship game" (Spalding Scrapbooks, vol. IV, July 5, 1884; David Shulman), and "When clubs issue rain checks they shall not be required to pay the $63 guarantee to visiting clubs" (*The Washington Post*, Dec. 12, 1884). Sometimes spelled "raincheck." IST USE. 1883. "The crowd insisted that they should get back either money or rain-checks, but [St. Louis Browns] President Von der Ahe refused to do either" (*St. Louis Post-Dispatch*, June 21; Peter Morris, who suggests that the concept of rain checks was firmly established before they were used in baseball).

EXTENDED USE. **1.** A postponed or deferred acceptance. To ask for a rain check is to decline while asking to be reinvited later. "Sorry we can't make dinner, but we'd love to take a rain check on the invitation." **2.** A coupon guaranteeing a customer the sales price for a future purchase of a sales item that is out of stock. **3.** A parole, in criminal slang.

rain dance Delaying tactics used when it starts to rain. It is used both by managers losing a game that is not yet official (and that will have to be replayed if it is rained out) and by managers winning a game in which the required number of innings have been played (and which the team will win if the game is called for rain). "You don't think [Los Angeles Dodgers manager Tommy] Lasorda's about to go into his rain dance, do you?"

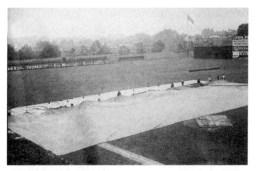

Rain delay. Covering the field with a tarp, Griffith Stadium, 1921. *National Photo Company Collection, Library of Congress*

(Harry Caray, WGN telecast, May 6, 1986, with the Dodgers leading the Chicago Cubs).

rain date The new date for a game that was rained out.

rain delay The official interruption of a game on account of rain. During such a period play is suspended in the hope that the rain will subside and the game can be resumed. Despite the fact that games played in domed stadiums are not supposed to suffer such delays, they are not immune. In April 1986, a game was delayed as water poured through a tear in the roof of the Hubert H. Humphrey Metrodome in Minneapolis. See also *human rain delay.*

rainmaker **1.** A towering home run; one that seems capable of rupturing a cloud and bringing rain. **2.** A very high pop fly, usually in the infield.

rainout *n.* A baseball game that is postponed or suspended because of rain or other inclement weather. Sometimes spelled "rain-out." Syn. *washout.*

rain out *v.* To cause, by sufficient amounts of rain, the postponement of a baseball game. The term is usually used in the passive; e.g., "The Friday night game was rained out." EXTENDED USE. **1.** To rain on any event hard enough to cause its postponement or cancellation. **2.** To fail because of some external event or condition.

rain rippler *hist.* A spitball. IST USE. 1907 (*New York Evening Journal*, June 7; Edward J. Nichols).

rain-shortened game A shortened game that is called after five innings because of rain.

rainstorm Syn. of *rain bringer* (Bill McCullough, *Brooklyn Eagle*, Sept. 5, 1937).

raise ball *hist.* A pitched ball that is delivered from below the waist and veers upward as it approaches the batter. As explained by the *Saginaw* [Mich.] *Evening Express* (May 24, 1884; Peter Morris), "What is called a 'raise ball' . . . is the most difficult to hit . . . as it is several feet higher from the time it leaves the pitcher's hand until it crosses the plate, and allowance must be made for the distance that it will rise. The difficulty comes in right here, for the ball does not go to the same height every time, cannot be judged with certainty, and if not hit squarely, continues to rise from the bat or go lightly to the ground." Joe McGinnity's raise ball was an underhand fastball delivered "from any angle in the vicinity of the knee" (James B. Foster, *How to Pitch*, 1908). John Clarkson threw a deceptive raise ball. The pitch became uncommon after overhand pitching was made legal. See also *upshoot*, 1.

"raise the window, Aunt Minnie, here she comes!" Syn. of "'*open the window, Aunt Minnie, here she comes!*'"

raisin' game An impromptu rural baseball game played on land recently cleared for roof-raisings. Peter Morris (*Baseball Fever*, 2003) noted that the game was "played purely for fun by any number of participants, with myriad local variations" in Michigan in the 1830s and 1840s. "The raising of a framed house or barn was an event that called together the entire neighborhood . . . [and] was looked forward to by the boys . . . with great satisfaction, as it gave them a half holiday from the labors of the farm and enabled them to enjoy a game of base ball after the building had been raised" (Melville McGee, *Michigan Pioneer and Historical Collections*, 1892; Peter Morris).

rake **1.** *v.* To get base hits by hitting the ball well; to get many hits, esp. off a given pitcher. "To no-hit a team that can flat-out rake the ball is pretty unbelievable" (Jim Street, commenting on Dwight Gooden's no-hitter, *Seattle Post-Intelligencer*, May 15, 1996). "A DH is usually a bigger person, usually a little slower, guys at the end of their career who can just rake (hit)" (Keith Lockhart, quoted in *Atlanta Journal-Constitution*, July 2, 1997;

Scott McClellan). "[Joe] Randa has raked me all season" (Mark Mulder, quoted in *The Baltimore Sun*, Oct. 7, 2005). IST USE. 1990. "[Cecil Fielder] rakes pitches . . . because he's a low-ball hitter" (Larry Whiteside, *The Boston Globe*, May 29). ETYMOLOGY. Probably related to sweeping or traversing a length of a position or body of troops with gunfire, and influenced by winning at gambling. **2.** *n.* A base hit. "I had a great day at the plate. Got me three rakes" (Garret Mathews, *Can't Find a Dry Ball*, 2002).

rake in To field a batted ball. IST USE. 1912 (*New York Tribune*, Oct. 13; Edward J. Nichols).

rally **1.** *n.* Several runs scored together or in rapid succession; a scoring surge. IST USE. 1858 (Chadwick Scrapbooks; Edward J. Nichols). **2.** *n.* A run-scoring surge during a half inning for the offensive team that causes it to tie or go ahead. **3.** *v.* To get several hits and runs in one inning; to make a rally. **4.** *v.* To make a comeback in a game, or within a season. **5.** *n.* A round of applause or cheers. "The crowd liked his [Harry Wolverton's] aggressiveness and at the end of each closing inning gave him a rally as he rambled to the bench" (*San Francisco Bulletin*, May 29, 1913; Gerald L. Cohen).

rally cap A baseball cap that has been turned inside out, put on backwards, or otherwise oddly displayed by the players on the bench and/or in the bullpen to invoke a rally. The superstitious notion began with the Texas Rangers in 1977–1979 and the Univ. of Texas in the late 1970s, and became popular during the 1986 season as the New York Mets, Houston Astros, and Boston Red Sox, among others, each came up with their own version. The Mets version had the caps worn backwards with the brims turned up, and the Astros simply turned their hats inside out. The Red Sox ritual, according to *USA Today* (Oct. 15, 1986), worked this way: "When the count reaches 2–2 with two out on a Red Sox hitter, the players in the bullpen take their hats off and hold them out, upside down."

rally-killing Said of that which forestalls or ends a rally, such as a double play, a timely strikeout, or an effective relief pitcher.

ram To hit a pitched baseball hard. IST USE. 1913. "The guy to ram out the hit that broke up the scramble was our old and esteemed friend Gas [for gasoline] Hetling" (*San Francisco Bulletin*, March 21; Gerald L. Cohen).

ramicack To hit a baseball (Maurice H. Weseen, *A Dictionary of American Slang*, 1934). ETYMOLOGY. Origin unknown, but the term seems to come with its own suggestions; e.g., "ram" and "crack."

range **1.** The ability of a fielder (esp. an infielder) to reach batted balls by moving quickly to his right or his left. A player with good range has great body control and first-step quickness to field balls in front or behind, or to either side of his starting position on the field when the ball is hit. **2.** The distance a fielder can be expected to cover in fielding a ball. "Range isn't just getting to balls. Range is where you can throw them out from" (infielder Mark McLemore, quoted in *The Baltimore Sun*, June 29, 1994). IST USE. 1856. "Wells, as second base, is excellent, and any balls that come in his range are bound to be caught" (*Spirit of the Times*, Dec. 20; Peter Morris).

range factor The average number of plays per game successfully made by a fielder (excluding first basemen and catchers), compiled by adding assists and putouts and then dividing by the number of games played. A more exact method requires the division by one-ninth of the fielder's *defensive innings*. Generally, shortstops and second basemen have a range factor between 4 and 5. The statistic was proposed by Bill James (*Baseball Digest*, March 1976) and described in depth in his *Baseball Abstract* (1982). As a statistical measure of defensive performance, it is a substantial advance over the standard fielding percentage, and many consider this to be James' most important contribution to baseball research. For an earlier version of range factor, see *fielding average*, 1. Compare *zone rating*; *range index*. Abbrev. *RF*, 3. Syn. *fielding range*.

range index A variation of *range factor* that employs an estimate of the number of successful defensive plays made by a fielder relative to the league average for its divisor. It was proposed by Bill James during the 1980s.

ranger A fielder who covers much ground.

Rangers Nickname for the American League West Division franchise that began playing in Arlington, Tex., in 1972 as the Texas Rangers. The franchise originated as the expansion Washington Senators (1961–1971) before moving to Texas where it was named for the law-enforcement agency whose men roamed Texas in the 1800s.

ransu-hyo A specially numbered code sheet worn on the wrist by Japanese players for determining what the pitch is going to be. "The commissioner of Japanese baseball eventually outlawed the ransu-hyo because they slowed the already turtlelike pace of the game" (Robert Whiting, *You Gotta Have Wa*, 1989, p.321).

rap **1.** *v.* To hit a ball sharply. "When he [Jack Ness] raps a ball on the trademark it generally rolls up against a fence" (*San Francisco Bulletin*, May 15, 1913; Gerald L. Cohen). IST USE. 1883. "The ball was rapped to short" (*St. Louis Globe-Democrat*, Nov. 5). **2.** *n.* A batted ball. IST USE. 1876. "[Joe] Start's rap to short left field" (*Detroit Free Press*, June 20; Peter Morris). **3.** *n.* Hitting power. "I developed some kind of rap that I don't think I had last year" (Kim Bartee, quoted in *The Baltimore Sun*, Aug. 9, 1995).

rapid-fire A drill for infielders to orient themselves with the bases so that they can throw quickly and accurately without wasting time. The infielder fields, and throws to a base, eight balls in rapid-fire order, each ball being hit before the infielder has time to get set (Ken Dugan, *How to Organize and Coach Winning Baseball*, 1971; Peter Morris).

raps *hist.* A turn at bat for a player or a team. IST USE. 1898 (*New York Tribune*, May 5; Edward J. Nichols). Syn. *tibs*.

RAR Abbrev. for *runs above replacement*.

raspberry **1.** A bruise or scraped skin, such as one incurred from sliding. **2.** Alternate spelling of *razzberry*.

rat A devoted baseball player or manager. A "batting-cage rat" is one who shows his eagerness to improve by spending extra time in batting practice. Alan Schwarz (*Baseball America*, Sept. 3–16, 2001; Peter Morris): "Kids devoted to basketball are called gym rats. Baseball has field rats." The term is used among umpires for a baseball player (*American Speech*, Summer 2000, p.187). See also *baseball rat*.

ratio Original name for *walks plus hits per inning*.

rattle 1. *v.* To disconcert or confuse an opponent; esp., for a batter to distract or disorient the pitcher by moving close to the plate, changing his batting stance, taking time outs, assuming the bunt position, talking to or kidding the pitcher, or simply getting base hits. IST USE. 1877. "Three or four of them assembled outside the foul line, in violation of the rules of the game, to 'rattle' Valentine" (*Winona* [Minn.] *Republican*, Aug. 20; Peter Morris). 2. *n.* A series of base hits in an inning. "This was a burlesque inning, which opened with a rattle of base hits and closed with the clanging of the gong in the enemy's favor" (*San Francisco Bulletin*, May 9, 1913; Gerald L. Cohen). 3. *v.* To hit a ball off the fence or wall, often with a sharp sound. "Howard gained the distinction of being the first man to rattle the boards on the Oakland grounds . . . and Page rattled the left-field fence with a drive over Johnston's head" (*San Francisco Bulletin*, Apr. 25, 1913; Gerald L. Cohen).

rattle of tinware *hist.* The rumored or threatened release of a player from a club. IST USE. 1915 (*Baseball Magazine*, December; Edward J. Nichols, who noted that the term is named from the association with the phrase "to tie the can on him").

rattles *hist.* Nervousness in a player or a team, resulting in ineffectiveness. "Faint-heartedness and any tendency to what are termed 'rattles' . . . must be overcome at the outset, for nothing is more fatal to success" (Deacon Phillippe, quoted in *Syracuse Post Standard*, March 27, 1904; Peter Morris). See also *balloon ascension*. IST USE. 1887. "The muff and the subsequent 'case of rattles' which the young player had, caused the loss for New York" (*The World* [New York], unknown date; Gerald L. Cohen).

rattling *hist.* Said of an excellent ballplayer or of a well-played baseball game. "There is no telling when, or where, a ball club will surprise even itself and play a rattling game"

(*San Francisco Bulletin*, March 21, 1913; Gerald L. Cohen).

raw Said of a young player whose talents have not been developed or harnessed; e.g., "The rookie shows signs of raw power." Compare *polished*.

raw equivalent average A measure of a player's offensive performance, designed by Clay Davenport and used in *Baseball Prospectus* since 1996. The statistic is a preliminary step in calculating *equivalent* average. It is conceptually similar to on-base plus slugging, along with a stolen base component, although Davenport has changed the details of the formula over the years. The 2008 version consisted of a player's sum of hits, total bases, sacrifice hits, and sacrifice flies, plus the sum of his bases on balls, hit by pitches, and stolen bases multiplied by 1.5, all divided by the sum of the player's at-bats, bases on balls, hit by pitches, caught stealing, sacrifice hits, sacrifice flies, and stolen bases. The measure is a relatively good predictor of runs scored. Abbrev. *REQA*.

rawhide The baseball.

Rawlings lobotomy A *beanball*; a pitch figuratively meant to remove part of a player's brain. The term is so labeled because Rawlings manufactures the ball and prints its company logo on each one.

raw-raw *hist.* A *knuckleball* in the early 20th century (*The Sporting News*, July 13, 1955; Norman L. Macht).

Rays Nickname for the American League East Division expansion franchise that played in St. Petersburg, Fla., as the Tampa Bay *Devil Rays* from 1998 to 2007. The club officially shortened its nickname to Rays in Nov. 2007.

razz 1. *v.* To nag or heckle a player or umpire. EXTENDED USE. To tease or nag in any realm. 2. *n.* Short for *razzberry*. "Some plaudits got, while others got the razz" (*New York Tribune*, Sept. 26, 1919, p.9; Stuart Y. Silverstein).

razzberry The sound made by sticking one's tongue between one's pressed lips and blowing loudly. The flatulent sound expresses unequivocal contempt. See also *Bronx cheer*. Sometimes spelled *raspberry*. Syn. *razz*, 2. ETYMOLOGY. Commonly believed to be a play on the rasping start of the word "raspberry" or the sound of a metal rasp. Charles Earle Funk (*Hog on Ice*, 1948) gave an alternative etymology after rejecting the notion that it comes from the metal rasp: "I think that the word should be written 'razzberry,' that it was a humorous extension developed from the slang, 'to razz,' to mock at or make fun of; and that the latter term was originally a contraction of 'to razzle-dazzle,' meaning bamboozle, banter or deceive." Funk noted that the first razzle-dazzle was an amusement-park ride on which one went in circles merry-go-round style while undulating up and down. Citing argot dictionaries, author Lawrence Block (personal communication, June 28, 1989) suggests that the term is Cockney rhyming slang: "razzberry" = "razzberry tart" = "fart." Tracy Dalton (personal communication, May 22, 1996) notes that the British expression "blow your raspberries" is also derived from rhyming slang, i.e., "raspberry tart" rhymes with "fart." EXTENDED USE. The very same sound and meaning when heard outside the ballpark.

RBI **1.** Box score abbrev. for *run batted in*. See also *ribbie*. USAGE NOTE. Charles D. Poe noted from his research (June 28, 1989): "There is not, apparently, any standardization concerning the abbreviation for the term 'runs batted in.'" Poe found it written RBIs, RBI, rbi's, RBI's, R.B.I., R.B.I.'s, and rbi. Conventions for pluralizing initialisms are confusing, but most sources use "RBI" for singular and plural, and/or "RBIs" for plural. "To refer to RBIs is redundant, strictly speaking. Yet those who decline to pluralize it ('He has 120 RBI') sound a little strange, as if they were talking about a currency" (E.J. Dionne Jr., *The Washington Post*, Oct. 19, 1997). Logically, the plural of "RBI" is "RsBI" but the convention of creating a new noun ("RBI") in the form of an initialism allows the formation of the plural in the usual way: "s" at the end (similar to "POWs" for "prisoners of war"). **2.** Abbrev. for *Reviving Baseball in Inner Cities*.

RBI importance That portion of a player's runs batted in that are counted as *victory-important RBI*.

RBI man A batter with the reputation of getting hits with teammates on base. The term implies that there are players who consistently raise their performances with baserunners aboard throughout all or much of their careers. Sabermetric research finds little evidence supporting the validity of this implication. Players with the label of "RBI men" are characteristically good hitters who bat behind hitters with high on-base percentages, and as a consequence go to the plate with more runners aboard than does the typical batter.

RBI opportunities The number of runs batted in a batter would accumulate if he hit a home run at every plate appearance. It was tracked as an official statistic by the American League for the first three weeks of 1918, and resurrected during the 1990s in STATS Inc.'s *Baseball Scoreboard*.

RBI situation That time in a game when one or more players are in a scoring position.

RBI value An informal method for rating the extent to which a run batted in increased or decreased a team's lead during a game. It was proposed by Tim Mulligan in Bill James' *Baseball Abstract* (1985).

RC **1.** Abbrev. for *runs created*. **2.** Abbrev. for *rookie card*, 1.

RCAA Abbrev. for *runs created above average*.

RCAP Abbrev. for *runs created above position*.

R-card A candy or gum baseball card issued after 1930, the beginning of the "modern" era in baseball cards. Compare *E-card*.

RC/G Abbrev. for *runs created per game*.

RC/25 Abbrev. for *runs created per 25 outs*.

RC/27 Abbrev. for *runs created per 27 outs*.

reach **1.** *n.* The distance a baseman can stretch his arm without losing contact with the base he is covering. See also *stretch*, 3. 1ST USE. 1902 (*The Sporting Life*, July 12, p.5; Edward J. Nichols). **2.** *v.* To get hits and runs off a pitcher;. "[Joe] Magrane . . . was reached for five runs" (*Tampa Tribune*, Sept. 13, 1988). **3.** *v.* For a batter to get on base. "Eleven of last 16 batters against him [Scott Erickson] reached" (*The Baltimore Sun*, March 7, 1998). **4.** *v.* To try to hit an outside pitch.

reach back For a pitcher able to summon extra speed or deception to get a strike or an out. "My location is much better, and when I need to reach back and turn it up a notch, I can" (Randy Johnson, quoted in *Sports Illustrated*, May 8, 2000). "I can still reach back and hump it up there in the upper 90s whenever I want to" (Roger Clemens, quoted in *Sports Illustrated*, March 27, 2000, p.87).

reach down and get it Syn. of *go down and get it*.

reached first base *hist.* An official statistic, adopted by the National League in 1879 only, computed by summing hits, walks, and times reached on error. It did not include being hit by a pitch. The 1879 leader was Paul Hines with 193. The statistic was a precursor to *on-base percentage*, 1.

reached on error An informal statistic for the number of times a batter was safe because of an error by the defense. Batters with speed can pressure fielders into making errors. See also *first on error.*

reaction position Syn. of *third base*, 2.

read 1. *v.* To decipher a pitcher's movements so closely that a batter can detect what pitch is about to be delivered or a baserunner can decide when to attempt to steal; also, to decipher the movement and direction of a batted ball. Milwaukee Brewers manager Phil Garner, commenting on Kenny Lofton (quoted in *Sports Illustrated*, May 1, 1995, p.98): "He always had speed, but he got lousy jumps and didn't run the bases well. He didn't read the ball well off the bat, and he didn't read pitchers well. But once he got it all down, he just took off." 2. *n.* An act or instance of reading a pitcher by a batter or baserunner, or reading the ball off the bat. "He has excellent base-running instincts. Good jumps, good reads" (Frederick Keys manager Mike O'Berry commenting on Harry Berrios, quoted in *The Baltimore Sun*, Aug. 10, 1994). "Marlon Anderson . . . has bad hands and slow feet and gets a terrible read off the bat" (*Sports Illustrated*, March 26, 2001, p.131).

real estate 1. A ballpark with large dimensions. When asked how he liked Oriole Park at Camden Yards, with its relatively small dimensions, relief pitcher Lee Smith said, "I like it, but like most pitchers, I like real estate" (*Orioles Gazette*, July 30, 1993). 2. An open area on a ball field. 3. The outfield. When Mike Cameron was chasing a Carlos Beltran drive that went for a home run, he said, "I just ran out of real estate" (quoted in *The Baltimore Sun*, July 21, 2003).

realignment A restructuring of the game, esp. of the makeup of leagues and divisions; e.g., the establishment in 1994 of three divisions (East, Central, and West) in each league and a new system for creating league championships, which included the use of wild cards, or the switch in 1998 of the Milwaukee Brewers to a 16-team National League. A 1992 realignment in the National League proposed by commissioner Fay Vincent, but not implemented, would have had the Chicago Cubs and St. Louis Cardinals moving to the National League West Division and the Cincinnati Reds and Atlanta Braves moving to the East Division beginning with the 1993 season.

ream A clownery or buffoonery routine engaged in by touring black teams to attract an audience. "There was an ambiguity in these . . . 'reams' . . . for if they played to white stereotypes, they also exalted the smooth and slick style that black players brought to the game" (Colin D. Howell, *Northern Sandlots: A Social History of Maritime Baseball*, 1995, p.173; Peter Morris).

rebel Syn. of *pop-off*, 1 (Gordon S. "Mickey" Cochrane, *Baseball: The Fan's Game*, 1939).

rebound 1. *n.* The bounce of the ball off a wall or fence. To catch a ball after such a bounce is to field it "on the rebound." 2. *v.* For a ball to bounce off a wall or fence.

recall 1. *n.* The process of assigning a major-league player to a minor-league club. It is normally understood that the player who is on recall status may be brought back to the parent club on short notice (such as 24 hours). 2. *v.* To bring back to a major-league club a player previously optioned to a minor-league club.

receiver Syn. of *catcher*, 1. IST USE. 1885. "Creegan, as 'receiver,' for [Billy] Incell, was more than good" (*The Sporting Life*, March 11; Peter Morris).

receiving station Syn. of *home plate*. "[Joe Dugan] sent five of the Mack runs to the receiving station, getting three hits" (J.V. Fitz Gerald, *The Washington Post*, May 1, 1920; Peter Morris).

receptor Spanish for "catcher."

reclamation project Signing a player released by another club in the hope that he can revert to previous, more proficient form. "The Brewers decided it's time to take on somebody else's reclamation project for a change" (Tom Haudricourt, *Baseball America*, May 3–16, 1999; Peter Morris).

recoil 1. *v.* To pull one's pitching arm back toward the body, often violently, after delivering the ball. "When pitchers recoil they think they're getting more velocity, but they're really not. Guys who recoil are usually maximum-effort guys—they're not that smooth" (Eddie Bane, quoted in Alan Schwarz, BaseballAmerica.com, Nov. 14, 2006). Syn. *bounce back*, 3. **2.** *n.* The movement imparted while recoiling.

reconciliation The new beginning required to attract fans back to the game after the players' strike that saw a canceled 1994 World Series and a delayed start to the 1995 season.

record 1. *n.* Virtually anything for which a claim can be made. "Records, the timeless array of revered numbers under constant challenge, are the hard coin of major league baseball realm" (Bill Conlin, *The Baltimore Sun*, Jan. 1, 2007). The Baseball Records Committee of the Society for American Baseball Research uses the term "record" in the sense that "some player, or some team, has the most or least of something for an inning, or a game, or a season, etc" (Annual Report of the Committee, 2001). USAGE NOTE. Peter Morris observes that academic sports historians place great emphasis on the term "record" when attempting to define the difference between premodern and modern sports. Allen Guttmann (*Sports Spectators*, 1986) described the emergence of modern sports in the mid-19th century as being "marked by an unprecedented mania for the modern sports record, that is, for the exactly measured unsurpassed achievement, the mark to be bettered if improvement upon the achievement is humanly possible." Guttmann claimed that this meaning for the word "record" occurred

in the 1880s, "and the concept itself probably antedates the usage by no more than a few decades." **2.** *n.* The standing of a team or player with respect to actions or achievements; e.g., games won and lost, hits made, or an earned run average. The Baseball Records Committee of the Society for American Baseball Research uses this sense of the term "record" for "a player's [or team's] game-by-game, season-by-season and lifetime accomplishments" (Annual Report of the Committee, 2001). **3.** *v.* To attain or add to one's record; e.g., "Smith recorded his 20th victory."

record book 1. The official document in which all numbers and statistics of players, clubs, and leagues are kept. The term is often used in the plural. **2.** A mythical document containing such records.

record player *hist.* A player who was more concerned about personal statistics than winning. "A record player is one who never attempts to stop a batted ball unless it comes very near him, for fear of making an error and having it charged against him. . . . A record player generally appears well in the score book and also on the diamond for he can pretend to attempt to stop a ball yet he is always very careful not to touch it with his hand and thus make an error" (*Evansville* [Ind.] *Journal*, Apr. 26, 1889; Peter Morris). IST USE. 1885. "One half of the New York team are said to be record players" (*Williamsport* [Pa.] *Sunday Grit*, July 12; Peter Morris).

recovery The retrieval of a ball after it has been momentarily fumbled. IST USE. 1880 (*Chicago Inter-Ocean*, June 28; Edward J. Nichols).

recreated game A broadcast of a baseball game based on Western Union telegraphers at the ballpark sending Morse Code signals to an announcer in a studio at home who, drawing on his knowledge of the players and their idiosyncrasies, would weave a coherent account of the game (J.A. Lucas, *The New York Times Magazine*, Sept. 12, 1971). Some announcers would create illusions, such as piping in crowd noises and simulating the crack of the bat. Recreated games were popular in the 1930s and 1940s when announcers rarely traveled with their teams on the road.

recreation ball [softball term] An early name for softball.

recruit 1. *n.* A new player on a ball club; specif., a *rookie*, 1. "A .484 batter in Oshkosh, an .084 performer in Gotham" (*The Washington Post*, July 19, 1914). IST USE. 1897. "Henry Ashcroft, although a recent recruit to the team, has covered several positions, but left field is regarded as his permanent station" (*Brooklyn Eagle*, Oct. 24; Peter Morris). USAGE NOTE. This term is now very common in college football and college basketball, yet baseball may have been the first sport in which it was used. **2.** *v.* To solicit new players. Discussing the effects of a new 35-man limit on roster sizes, A.J. Flanner (*The Sporting News*, July 21, 1910; Peter Morris) wrote, "In recruiting for 1911, the big league manager must consider the quality and quantity of members of his team during the present race, as well as the number and ability, present and prospective, of players on whom he has option, before he can intelligently start to secure minor league stars either by purchase or draft."

recta Spanish for "fastball."

recta de dedos separados Spanish for "split-fingered fastball."

recycled manager 1. A manager who has served a baseball team on more than one occasion; e.g., Billy Martin, who managed the New York Yankees five separate times (1975–1978, 1979, 1983, 1985, and 1988). **2.** A manager who has managed several teams; e.g., John McNamara, who managed the A's, Padres, Reds, Angels, Red Sox, and Indians between 1969 and 1991.

Red Nickname for a short-tempered player; a hothead.

red ass A tough, angry, intense player; a player who plays hard; a raging competitor who hates to lose. Bill Starr (*Clearing the Bases*, 1989, p.87) noted that Earl Whitehill was a "firebrand" when pitching in the 1920s and 1930s, "aptly described in the terminology of those days as a 'red-ass.'" The term can be complimentary when describing the competitive zeal of a Lou Piniella or Paul O'Neill, but it has also been applied to one who whines and argues with umpires. Abbrev. *RA*, 1. Also spelled "red-ass."

red-ball express A fastball. ETYMOLOGY. In railroad and trucking jargon, "red ball" describes a fast-moving vehicle that is on schedule. Traditionally, red balls are given priority over slower-moving units.

Redbirds Nickname for the St. Louis Cardinals.

Red Book The annual administrative manual and directory for the American League. Its contents include: history, office information, committees, and administrative rules for the League; franchise histories, directory of club officials, rosters, and logos for each team; prior year's standings, player statistics, and awards, and postseason results; All-Star Game information; attendance figures; and information on beat writers and broadcasters. See also *Green Book*; *Blue Book*; *Orange Book*.

Red Cross walk Awarding first base to a batter after he has been hit by a pitched ball, from the obvious association of the Red Cross and injuries suffered from being struck. IST USE. 1922 (Ernest J. Lanigan, *Baseball Cyclopedia*, p.56; Edward J. Nichols).

red dot The aspect or visual feature of a pitch as seen by the batter when a pole of the *spin axis* is located directly on the red seam of the ball. The red dot appears because the pole spins much more slowly than the rest of the ball. The location of the dot on the face of the ball indicates the angle of the spin axis relative to the direction of the forward motion (or trajectory) of the ball. The angle determines the direction of the deflection of the pitch. If the red dot is in the upper right quadrant for a pitch thrown by a right-handed pitcher, the pitch will slide away from a right-handed batter; if the red dot is in the upper left quadrant, the pitch will move toward the batter; and if the red dot is in the center of the face of the ball, the angle between the spin axis and the trajectory is zero and there is no deflection. If the pole is some distance from the seam, the pattern formed is a reddish circle or band. See also *dime*, 2 (David Baldwin).

red-hot ball A ball that is hit hard. IST USE. 1867 (*New York Sunday Mercury*, Sept. 7; Edward J. Nichols).

Redlegs Nickname for the Cincinnati *Reds* in 1944, 1945, and from 1954 to 1960, when the nickname "Reds" might have implied some association with Communism.

red light A sign given to a player that he should not attempt to steal, score, or swing away. Compare *green light*, 2.

red-light player A player who performs well when the red light of the network television camera is on and he is being watched by a large audience. "Lenny [Dykstra] is a red-light player" (Philadelphia Phillies manager Jim Fregosi, quoted in *Sports Illustrated*, Oct. 18, 1993, p.43).

redraft A player drafted in the first-year player draft who had been drafted in a previous year but not signed.

Reds 1. Nickname for the National League Central Division franchise in Cincinnati, Ohio, since 1890. When a justice of the Pennsylvania Supreme Court admonished the team for its unpatriotic nickname in 1961, *Cincinnati Enquirer* sports editor Lou Smith responded, "Let the Russians change. We had it first." See also *Redlegs*. **2.** Alternate nickname for the Cincinnati Red Stockings in the National League from 1876 to 1880. **3.** Common name for various baseball teams from Boston, Mass.; e.g., the Union Association franchise in 1884; and the alternate name for the Boston Beaneaters of the National League in 1890 and 1891.

red seats A section in Cincinnati's Riverfront Stadium where only the most spectacular home runs land. The term was applied elsewhere, even in spring training: "Red seats" was the description attached to Dave Parker's home run against the Pittsburgh Pirates in Bradenton (*Tampa Tribune-Times*, March 30, 1986).

Red Sox Nickname for the American League East Division franchise in Boston, Mass. The franchise entered the American League in 1901 and used several nicknames before adopting "Red Sox" in 1907; these included Americans, Somersets (in honor of owner and American League vice president Charles W. Somers), Puritans, Speed Boys, Plymouth Rocks, and Pilgrims (1903–1906). Also known as Bosox, Carmine Hose, and Rouge

Hose. ETYMOLOGY. The nickname originated in Ohio with the Cincinnati Red Stockings, baseball's first professional team. When the Red Stockings broke up following the 1870 season, many team members headed to Boston to form a new National Association team in 1871, and they carried with them both the name and the red stockings for which they were famous. Several Boston teams wore red stockings in the late 19th century. When the rival Boston Beaneaters of the National League abandoned its red stockings following the 1906 season, the American League team named itself "Red Sox" in 1907 and donned red stockings in 1908.

Red Sox Nation New England north and east of New Haven and east of the Connecticut River, including Hartford. The term refers to the loyal fans of the Boston Red Sox, and can exceed its geographic boundaries: "Baseball exists on a plane of high melodrama in Red Sox Nation, a state of mind in which citizenship requires only passion and an inhuman pain threshold" (Steve Marantz, *The Sporting News*, July 24, 1996). IST USE. 1993. "Citizens of Red Sox Nation" (Dan Shaughnessy, *The Boston Globe*, Sept. 4, 1993).

red-stitch [softball term] Syn. of *restricted flight*.

Red Stockings 1. Nickname for the first openly professional baseball club, located in Cincinnati, Ohio. Formed in 1869, the club was named for the color of its hose. Because of financial problems, the club reverted to non-pro status after the 1870 season. In 1871, the team became the Boston Red Stockings in the National Association. **2.** Nickname for the National Association franchise in Boston from 1871 to 1875. The club had relocated from Cincinnati, and became the Boston Red Caps in the National League in 1876. **3.** Nickname for the National League franchise in Cincinnati from 1876 to 1880 and the American Association charter franchise in Cincinnati from 1882 to 1889. It became the Cincinnati Reds in the National League in 1890.

reduced injury factor ball A *low-impact ball* made with a core of polyurethane that reduces the risk of serious head injury. It has the same weight and dimensions as a conventional baseball, but has a softer interior (i.e., lower compression) that significantly reduces the force delivered upon impact. The ball has increasing levels of softness for teens to tots. It was designed in 1985 by the Worth Sports Co., Tullahoma, Tenn. Syn. *RIF ball.*

reentry draft See *free-agent reentry draft.*

reentry rule [softball term] A rule in Amateur Softball Association of America that stipulates that any of the starting players may be substituted or replaced and reentered once, provided players occupy the original batting positions whenever in the lineup. Nonstarting players may not reenter; starting players may not reenter a second time. The starting player and that player's substitute may not be in the lineup at the same time. The rule encourages coaches to replace first-string players with second-string players during a game since the rule permits a player to reenter the game if his or her skill is later needed. Under United States Specialty Sports Association rules, the reentry rule is applicable only in women's softball.

referee *hist.* An official at an 1850s baseball game who made rulings on the field when the umpires did not agree. In early baseball, three men usually officiated at baseball games: two of these (known as umpires) were members of the respective clubs, while the third (the referee) was impartial and overruled any disagreements between the umpires. Illustrating the arrangement is a quotation from the *New York Clipper* (Sept. 19, 1857; Peter Morris): "At the desk are the umpires, watching the game, and noting its progress. The referee, solitary and alone, is seated between the batsman and the marquee, taking an impartial survey of the proceedings, and ready to mete out justice to all when appealed to." Referees disappeared from the game when the switch to one umpire was made in 1858. In the Massachusetts game, all three officials were referred to as referees. See also *umpire,* 1. Syn. *arbiter,* 2. IST USE. 1855 (*Spirit of the Times,* July 7; Peter Morris).

REff% Abbrev. for *reliever efficiency percent.*

refuse the ball For a pitcher to take himself out of the rotation or turn down a relief assignment. Tippy Martinez, on his overuse as a reliever for the Baltimore Orioles (quoted in *The Washington Post,* Feb. 22, 1987): "I could have refused the ball any one of those days. They would never have pressured me if I'd said, 'I can't go today.'" New York Mets manager Jeff Torborg (quoted in *The New York Times,* Feb. 28, 1993): "He [Anthony Young] never refused the ball [during his 14-game losing streak]. . . . You see players who are hyperventilating late in the game. They don't want the ball. You ask them how they feel and they say, 'Well, I've got a little tenderness.' A.Y. never complained." Compare *want the ball.*

regiment A baseball team (Maurice H. Weseen, *A Dictionary of American Slang,* 1934).

regional franchise A baseball club that draws from a larger area than its name alone suggests; e.g., the Boston Red Sox long ago established itself as a New England team.

register **1.** *v./hist.* To score a run. "[Joe] Judge doubled to right and registered on [Clyde] Milan's two-base swat to left" (*The Washington Post,* May 21, 1921). IST USE. 1905. "[Frank] Isbell and [Ducky] Holmes registered" (*Chicago Tribune,* June 2; Peter Morris). **2.** *v.* To record a reading on a radar gun. "[Kris] Honel's free and easy arm action allowed his fastball to register 86–89 mph" (*Baseball America,* July 21–Aug. 3, 2003; Peter Morris). **3.** *n./hist.* Syn. of *indicator,* 1. "A.G. Spalding has sent registers to each of the League umpires. The register is about the shape and size of a pocket match box and made of ivory" (*Indianapolis Sentinel,* March 27, 1887; Peter Morris).

registering station *hist.* Syn. of *home plate* (where balls, strikes, and runs are "registered"). IST USE. 1904. "[Patsy] Donovan, by a great head-first slide, was safe at the registering station" (*The Washington Post,* Aug. 9; Peter Morris).

registry station *hist.* Syn. of *home plate.* IST USE. 1915. "Instead of coming accurately, as usual, into the hands of the catcher waiting at the registry station, the ball struck the dirt a dozen feet from the pan" (Burt L. Standish, *Covering the Look-in Corner;* David Shulman).

regroup To attempt to bring a struggling team into line. Milwaukee Brewers manager

George Bamberger's definition of the verb was quoted in the *The New York Times* (June 18, 1985): "You do that by getting more runs and getting better pitching."

regular A player who routinely starts at the same position. "When [John] McGraw won the pennant in 1911, he did it with a club of youngsters, many of them playing through their first whole season as regulars in the company" (Christy Mathewson, *Pitching in a Pinch*, 1912, p.106; Stuart Y. Silverstein).

regular player A player who starts in most of a team's games. IST USE. 1866 (Chadwick Scrapbooks, Sept. 16; Edward J. Nichols).

regular save A *save* (as defined by STATS Inc.) that is neither an *easy save* nor a *tough save*.

regular season The period of time during which a championship of the division or league is determined. In the major leagues today, the term refers to 162 games played to determine the six divisional champions and two wild cards.

regulation ball *hist.* Any baseball that satisfied the physical dimensions of 1872 (weight of 5 to 5¼ ounces and circumference of 9 to 9¼ inches), irrespective of the type or quality of material used as its core. "[John] Van Horn's celebrated regulation ball, acknowledged by Clubs all over the country to be the best in use" (advertisement for the Van Horn ball, 1867; Robert H. Schaefer).

regulation base ball *hist.* A generic term used in the 1860s to denote the rules introduced by the Knickerbocker Base Ball Club and modified by the National Association of Base Ball Players (Peter Morris, *Baseball Fever*, 2003, pp.13–14).

regulation game A game played to official completion. A regulation game consists of nine innings, unless extended because of a tie score, or shortened because a) the home team does not need any of its half of the ninth inning or only a fraction of it, or b) the umpire calls the game, in which event a regulation game consists of at least five or more equal innings (4½ if the team batting at the bottom of the inning is in the lead). If the score is tied after nine completed innings, play continues until the visiting team has scored more runs than the home team at the end of a completed inning or the home team has scored the winning run in an uncompleted inning. In the minor leagues, a regulation game may consist of seven innings for one or both games of a doubleheader. Once a game is declared to be regulation ("official"), individual player performances become part of the record and the rain checks become invalid. A game that does not last for the required 4½ or 5 innings is declared "no game" and must be rescheduled and played from the beginning.

reg-yan Said of a preseason game between the regular players and the yannigans (rookies). "Angels Engage in a Bitter Reg-Yan Battle at Washington Park" (*Los Angeles Times* subheadline, Apr. 2, 1916; Peter Morris).

rehabilitation assignment See *injury rehabilitation assignment*. Syn. "rehab assignment."

reinstatement 1. Returning a player to the active list. Players on the voluntarily retired, restricted, disqualified, and ineligible lists may be reinstated upon application to the commissioner. For a player on the ineligible list, no application may be made until after the lapse of one year from the date of placement on the list. 2. Reestablishing the status of a player who has been banned from the game, even after his playing days are over.

relative batting average The ratio of a player's batting average to his league's batting average. League-leading batting averages usually range from 1.3 to 1.5. The ratio was proposed by David Shoebotham (*Baseball Research Journal*, 1976).

relative ERA A measure of how a pitcher's earned run average (ERA) in a season compares to that of the average pitcher in his league. The league's ERA is adjusted for the pitcher's home field and then divided by the pitcher's ERA. A relative ERA greater than 100 indicates a better pitcher performance than the league average. The greatest single-season relative ERA is Pedro Martinez' 285 in 2000 (comparing his 1.75 ERA with the league average of 4.91). Abbrev. *ERA+*.

relativity index A normalized version of runs created per 27 outs.

relay 1. *n.* A throwing maneuver in which the

ball is taken by a fielder and thrown to another fielder who acts as an intermediary thrower —or relay—for the ball on its way to its final destination; e.g., a throw from a cutoff man or from the middle man in a double play, or a ball caught in deep right field that is thrown to the second baseman in hopes of getting the ball to third base for a play. "Tim [Jordan] was caught going to second on a great relay from [Goat] Anderson to [Honus] Wagner to Batty [Ed Abbaticchio]" (*Brooklyn Daily Eagle*, July 14, 1907; Peter Morris). IST USE. 1902. "[Harry Steinfeldt] beat Jack Farrell's relay at least a dozen feet, but the Texan found the way to home plate full of knees, legs and shoes" (Ren Mulford, *The Sporting Life*, Aug. 2; Peter Morris). **2.** *v.* To catch a ball thrown by one player and then throw it to a third player. IST USE. 1905. "Before it had been relayed in [Homer] Smoot had crossed the plate" (*Chicago Tribune*, Apr. 16; Peter Morris).

relay position The point from which a ball sent in from the outfield can be relayed to a third player.

relay throw A throw made from the relay position. IST USE. 1912. "[Art Wilson] allowed [Tris] Speaker to score the final tieing run on a muff of [Tillie] Shafer's relay-throw" (*The Sporting Life*, Oct. 19; Peter Morris).

release 1. *v.* To cut or drop a player from a team's roster rather than trade or sell his contract or demote him to a minor-league farm team. IST USE. 1880 (*Chicago Inter-Ocean*, May 31; Edward J. Nichols). **2.** *n.* The discharge of a player from his contract, thereby making the player a free agent. A release for most players is a crossroads because it is unlikely that they will ever play at the major-league level again. IST USE. 1880 (*New York Herald*, July 5; Edward J. Nichols). **3.** *n.* The final position of a motion as the ball leaves the hand of a pitcher or fielder. **4.** *n.* The transition that is made by a first baseman who is holding a baserunner close to the base when the pitcher throws the ball to the plate. David Falkner (*Nine Sides of the Diamond*, 1990, p.53): "The release is a standard maneuver that a first baseman makes from a holding position to a fielding position lateral to the bag. A left-handed first baseman, facing home plate, will normally move out into a

fielding stance with a little preliminary step with his right foot followed by a couple of quick, skipping crossover steps."

release point The arm position at which the pitcher lets go of the ball. If the ball is released too early, it will be high; if released too late, it will be low.

release sign A sign that allows a player to look away from the one giving the sign. The purpose of a release sign is to assure that the receiver does not look away the moment the activator is given, hence giving it away. A common practice is to hold the receiver's attention while decoy signs are being sent until the sender signs off with a clap of the hands.

release time 1. The time that elapses from the instant the pitcher, in the stretch position, begins his move to the plate (the instant the "discernible stop" at the belt ends) to the moment the ball hits the catcher's mitt. It averages 1.35 to 1.4 seconds. **2.** The time that elapses from the instant a pitched ball hits the catcher's mitt to the instant his throw lands into the glove of a fielder covering the base that a runner is attempting to steal. It averages 2 seconds (to second base).

relief 1. The replacement of a pitcher during a ball game, usually because of ineffectiveness. IST USE. 1887. "[Larry] Corcoran was batted out of the box in the seventh inning and [John] Cahill came to the relief" (*The Washington Post*, May 18). **2.** A period of work by a substitute pitcher. IST USE. 1886. "[Dave] Foutz and [Bob] Caruthers, keep right on alternating day in and day out, with occasional relief from [Nat] Hudson" (*St. Louis Post-Dispatch*, July 31).

relief corps The entire relief pitching staff of a team.

relief duty The work of one or more relief pitchers. Syn. *rescue service.* IST USE. 1909 (*Reach Official American League Base Ball Guide*, p.63; Edward J. Nichols).

reliefer *hist.* Syn. of *relief pitcher,* 1. IST USE. 1937 (*Philadelphia Record*, Oct. 6; Edward J. Nichols).

relief man Syn. of relief *pitcher,* 1. IST USE. 1912 (*The New York Times*, Oct. 16; Edward J. Nichols).

relief pitcher **1.** A substitute pitcher who enters the game, often in a critical situation, to take over for the starting pitcher or another relief pitcher. One of the most dramatic developments in baseball during the 20th century has been the evolution of a typical pitching staff, from no regular relief pitchers early in the century to the first few relief pitchers of the 1920s to the relief staff of today, consisting of as many as six pitchers in a bullpen replete with its own awards, specialties (such as middle reliever and closer), conventional wisdom, and body of quotations; e.g., Dan Quisenberry (quoted in *Sports Illustrated*, Sept. 13, 1982): "You can't be thinking about too many things. Relief pitchers have to get into a zone of their own. I just hope I'm stupid enough." Abbrev. *RP.* Syn. *relief man*; *relief worker*; *reliever*; *reliefer.* IST USE. 1885. "We [the Raleigh club] have a new relief pitcher in Mr. Housman" (*The Sporting Life*, June 17; Peter Morris). EXTENDED USE. A backup quarterback in football. "[Baltimore Ravens quarterback] Eric Zeier is a capable relief pitcher who hasn't shown he can win as a No. 1" (*The Baltimore Sun*, Oct. 27, 1998). **2.** A pitcher who regularly fills the role of relief pitcher on a team and who seldom, if ever, starts a game.

relief points A scoring system used by Rolaids to determine the effectiveness of a relief pitcher. Four points are credited for a tough save, 3 points for a traditional save, and 2 points for a win; but 2 points each are subtracted for a loss or a blown save. See also *Rolaids Relief Man Award.*

relief truck The car, golf cart, or other vehicle that formerly ferried relief pitchers in from the bullpen. "That really got me pumped, when I came down the sideline in the 'relief truck'—that's what I call it—and heard the ['Ed-DEEE!'] chant" (Ed Whitson, quoted in *USA Today*, Apr. 28, 1986).

relief worker Syn. of *relief pitcher*, 1. IST USE. 1945 (*Baseball Magazine*, July; David Shulman).

relieve To act in the role of a relief pitcher. IST USE. 1861 (*New York Sunday Mercury*, Aug. 10; Edward J. Nichols).

reliever Syn. of *relief pitcher*, 1. IST USE. 1925. "Wizner and Huntzinger, his relievers, were no-hit, no-run performers" (*The New York Times*, Aug. 17; Fred R. Shapiro).

reliever efficiency percent A measure of how often a relief pitcher contributes positively to the outcome of a game; it is computed by dividing the sum of wins, saves, and holds by the sum of wins, losses, save opportunities, and holds, and multiplying by 100. Competent relief pitchers have a minimum reliever efficiency percent of 80. Abbrev. *REff% (Ron Shandler's Baseball Forecaster*, 2006).

Reliever of the Year Award An annual award presented by *The Sporting News* to the best relief pitcher in each major league. It was formerly the *Fireman of the Year Award*, but was broadened and renamed in 2001. See also *Rolaids Relief Man Award.*

relocation Moving a major-league club out of its assigned operating territory to another. The vote of three-fourths of the major-league clubs is required to approve the relocation of any major-league club.

remember Wally Pipp See *Wally Pipp.*

remove the force For a fielder to elect to retire a trailing runner first, meaning that more advanced runners now have to be tagged, and can retreat to their original bases if they wish. For example: with a runner on first and less than two outs, a ground ball is fielded by the first baseman who can either throw to second base for the force out and hope that a return throw will be in time to double up the batter-runner, or he can touch first, retiring the batter-runner and removing the force, and throw to second, where the runner now has to be tagged.

rent a player To obtain a key player for the balance of the season. It describes the practice by which a team involved in a pennant race trades for a player in the last year of his contract, after which he may become a free agent; thus, the team is "renting" him for the balance of the season in the hope that he will make the difference between a championship and mere contention. An example is the Toronto Blue Jays trade for pitcher David Cone on Aug. 27, 1992.

rep 1. A player's ability. Short for "reputation." IST USE. 1907. "These young pitchers . . . who are supposed not to have anything but the glove and a return ticket, bother the [White] Sox more than do hurlers who have a rep" (Charles Dryden, *Chicago Tribune*, Apr. 5; Peter Morris). 2. Short for *player representative*.

repeater A player who spends more than one year in a minor league (esp. a low minor league). Although repeating a league is not a positive development, it does not doom a prospect: "Improvements [by repeaters] are real, and, except at the lowest levels, there should be no stigma attached to such breakthroughs" (Clay Davenport, *Baseball Prospectus*, 2002; Peter Morris).

repeater rights A clause in the Basic Agreement whereby a player cannot file for free agency twice within five years of major-league service, and a club can retain the player's services if it offers the player salary arbitration within five business days after the end of the World Series. The clause was eliminated in the 1997 Basic Agreement.

repeat sign A separate sign to repeat the call on back-to-back offensive plays or pitches.

repertoire The mixture of different pitches that a pitcher throws during a given outing; a pitcher's *stuff*, 1. Boston Red Sox manager Jimy Williams, discussing Pedro Martinez (quoted in *The Baltimore Sun*, Oct. 17, 1999): "He used different pitches to start hitters off and to finish them off. He used his whole repertoire." See also *arsenal*. Syn. *assortment*. IST USE. 1910 (*American Magazine*, June; Edward J. Nichols).

replacement Syn. of *replacement player*.

replacement baseball Games played by replacement players during the early days of the 1995 spring-training season when the 1994–1995 players' strike was still on. It began on March 1, 1995, when the California Angels played Arizona State Univ. before about 1,300 fans in Tempe, Ariz.

replacement level The required level of offensive performance at which a position player is, in principle, usually able to maintain a regular position; e.g., the expected level of performance when a team's best available player substitutes for a suddenly unavailable starting player at the same position and with minimum expenditure of team resources. The replacement level seems to be about 80 percent of the average offensive performance for the position, although players with the reputation of being very good fielders often maintain their positions with performances below replacement level. The concept was first proposed by Bill James in his self-published *Baseball Abstract* (1979); a description can be found in his *Baseball Abstract* (1985). See *offensive wins above replacement* for another use of the concept.

replacement player 1. A player performing at replacement level; i.e., barely adequate to maintain a regular position. A substitute serves as a replacement player until the regular player returns. 2. A player who signed a contract to play in the major leagues when the players' strike of 1994–1995 was in effect. Replacement players participated in 1995 spring-training games, but were released before the start of the season. The term did not include a player who was in camp under a minor-league contract, although the Major League Baseball Players Association did consider minor-league players who played with replacements to be strikebreakers. *The Sporting News* (March 20, 1995) ran a guide on "how to spot a replacement player," with five distinctions, including "good periphery work habits: in contrast to the striking players, replacements typically will do menial chores historically left up to coaches and equipment people." *The Sporting News* piece included a line from Pat Jordan's diary: "I saw one White Sox player who saw a helmet sitting halfway between first base and the dugout during batting practice. Somebody could have tripped over it, so he ran out and picked it up. That's the kind of basic ethics you learn in youth ball that you see with the replacements now." Syn. *replacement*.

reporters' box An early syn. of *press box*. IST USE. 1883. "The reporters' box will be behind the catcher" (*Detroit Free Press*, May 9; Peter Morris).

REQA Abbrev. for *raw equivalent average*.

rescue service *hist.* Syn. of *relief duty*. IST USE. 1909 (*Reach Official American League Base Ball Guide*, p.31; Edward J. Nichols).

reserve clause A traditional provision in a player's contract that claimed (or "reserved") the player's services for the following season. Introduced in 1887, it gave the club the right to invoke the expired contract for an additional year even if the player and the team had not come to terms on a new contract by a specific date. It amounted to a "perpetual contract" under which the player was the property of the club, which could elect to keep, trade, or sell his contract. Team owners long insisted that this was needed to keep the leagues from being wrecked in bidding wars. The reserve clause was twice upheld by the Supreme Court (1922 and 1971).

Until the 1970s, owners and players alike behaved as though the reserve clause gave a club perpetual rights to all players it had under contract. After the 1975 season, pitchers Dave McNally and Andy Messersmith, who had never signed contracts for 1975, argued before arbitrator Peter Seitz that the reserve clause gave teams only the right to renew their contracts for one season, after which the club lost its exclusive rights to their services and they were free to negotiate with any club. Seitz agreed on Dec. 23, 1975. The reserve clause was finally overturned by a series of court decisions at lower levels. Its destruction ushered in the free-agent era in baseball. In subsequent Basic Agreements, the players agreed to reinstate the reserve clause, but in a more limited form, which now allows all players with six years of major-league experience to become free agents when their contracts expire. See also *reserve rule.* (Doug Pappas)

reserved seats Seating accommodations immediately behind the box seats in a ballpark. These seats are reserved in the sense that the spectator buys a specific seat, defined by row and seat number, and can buy or reserve it in advance of the day that the game in question is played. This is in contrast to general admission or bleacher seats, which are filled on the day of the game by the first person to occupy the seat.

reserve list A list of all players who have signed a major-league uniform player contract (unless such players have been assigned outright to a minor-league club) or who have been tendered a major-league uniform player contract by Dec. 20 for the following championship season. A major-league club may place a maximum number of 40 players on its major-league reserve list. A major-league club also must file a separate minor-league reserve list for each minor-league classification in which it desires to reserve minor-league players. A player on the disabled list is removed from the 40-man reserve list. Compare *active list.*

reserve player A player, usually with a minor-league club, who is not on a major-league club's regular roster of players but who stands ready to be so used on short notice.

reserve rule The rule that bound a player to his club from year to year. It was introduced in 1879 as a means of limiting player salaries. Each team was allowed to reserve a number of players on its roster, with all other clubs agreeing not to offer contracts to reserved players. A player under reserve could no longer sign with the highest bidder for his services, but only for the club that had reserved him. At first, the reserve list was limited to five players per team, but it grew to include all players (1883) on each major-league roster, and later all players in each club's minor-league farm system. The reserve rule was subsequently incorporated (1887) into player contracts as the reserve clause. See also *five men rule.* (Doug Pappas)

reservoir estimation technique An informal method for estimating a team's talent resources by computing the trade value of each of the team's players. The technique was defined by Bill James in his *Baseball Abstract* (1985).

resin bag Syn. of *rosin bag.*

resin ball An illegal pitch that breaks sharply because of resin powder on the ball and/or the pitcher's hand. See also *puff ball.* 1ST USE. 1925 (*The New York Times*, Dec. 20; Edward J. Nichols).

resin sack Syn. of *rosin bag.*

restricted flight [softball term] Said of a softball that has a softer core than that of a regular softball and does not travel as far when hit. The restricted flight balls approved by the

Amateur Softball Association of America have a coefficient of restitution of .44 or less and a maximum compression of 375 pounds or less. Abbrev. *RF*, 4. Syn. *red stitch.*

restricted list A list of players who, without permission from the player's club, fail to report to, or sign a contract with, the club within 10 days after the start of the regular season. The list allows a team to retain a player without his counting against the team's major-league roster. A player on the restricted list is not eligible to play with any major- or minor-league club. Compare *ineligible list*; *disqualified list*; *suspended list.*

resultado Spanish for "score" (noun).

retaining line Syn. of *three-foot line.*

retaliation rule A rule in English base-ball (and a recurring feature in several of baseball's early European relatives) whereby the batting team could retain its at-bat even after making out. As described by David Block (*Baseball Before We Knew It*, 2005, pp.71–72), "all they [the batting team] had to do was run onto the field, grab the ball, and then either tag or throw the ball at a straggling member of the fielding team before he was able to get off the playing field. In response, the defenders then had the opportunity to return the favor to the batting team before they made it back to the home plate area, and so on.... Over time the colorful practice faded quietly into oblivion, quite possibly, baseball's critics might argue, to the detriment of our modern game." ETYMOLOGY. The term was coined by Block as a shortened way of referring to the rule.

retire 1. To put out a batter or baserunner. "Allison hit light to Mills and retired" (*The Cleveland Morning Herald*, May 22, 1871). See also *retire in order*; *retire the side.* ETYMOLOGY. The term is used in both cricket and rounders, from which it appears to have been borrowed. 2. To quit professional baseball as a playing career. IST USE. 1867. "The loss of their catcher, Buckley, who had to retire, was also felt" (*Daily National Intelligencer* [Washington, D.C.], Sept. 20). USAGE NOTE. Morris notes that the term originally was a passive verb, with an "ignoble" connotation: e.g., "Glenn of the Pittsburg club is to

be retired" and "Daily, the one-armed pitcher of the Washington Club, has been retired" (*New York Sun*, May 30, 1886). Also: "Next season many of the old-timers will be 'retired'; that is, their services will not be in demand" (*The Sporting Life*, Aug. 5, 1893). The term transformed to an active ("noble") verb in the 1890s, and now implies not just the end of a career, but the end of a distinguished career. 3. *v.* To be removed from a game. "Allison had his thumb split and was obliged to retire" (*The Cleveland Morning Herald*, May 6, 1871).

retired number A uniform number no longer available for active players on a given team because it has been taken out of circulation to honor a key former player or manager who once wore it. The Boston Red Sox have specific criteria for retiring numbers: the player must be inducted into the National Baseball Hall of Fame, play 10 seasons with Boston, and finish his career with the Red Sox.

retire in order To put out successively three batters faced in an inning. IST USE. 1892. "Griffin singled, but the next three batters retired in order" (*Brooklyn Eagle*, July 5; Peter Morris).

retire the side Concluding the opposition's turn at bat for its half inning by attaining three putouts. IST USE. 1874 (*Chicago Inter-Ocean*, July 6; Edward J. Nichols).

retouch 1. *n.* The act of a runner's returning to a base, which he must do after a fly ball has been caught. 2. *v.* To return to a base to make contact with it.

retread A player whose career seems to be nearing its end, but who is given a chance with a new team; a major-league player who has been sent back to the minor leagues and then brought back to the majors. The term is a direct borrowing from automotive retreads, which are old tires that are given new life when wrapped in a new tread.

retriever *hist.* The catcher. "The latest terms to indicate the pitcher and catcher are 'deceiver' and 'retriever'" (*The Boston Globe*, Apr. 25, 1894; Peter Morris). USAGE NOTE. Don Baylor (*Don Baylor*, 1989) used "retriever" (as opposed to "receiver") for a catcher who "kept having to retrieve the ball from the backstop because he just could not catch a thing."

retropark A generic term for a baseball-only park reminiscent of the older parks built in the first half of the 20th century as a reaction to the *cookie cutter* parks built during the last half of the century. They are characterized by lower capacity, natural grass, intimate or cozy surroundings, an asymmetrical shape, exposed steel and brick exteriors, wider seats, scoreboards on the outfield walls, luxury and corporate suites, amenities such as cup holders and children's areas, and promenades featuring food and shops. They are built in the city proper or inner city and incorporate or blend in with other buildings in the existing urban landscape, providing the city skyline as a backdrop. They are not called "stadiums," and the playing field is below ground level so that spectators descend rather than climb to their seats. Retroparks often spur renewal of the team both in attendance and performance. Examples include Oriole Park at Camden Yards (Baltimore) which started the trend in 1992, Jacobs Field (Cleveland), Coors Field (Denver), Turner Field (Atlanta), Comerica Park (Detroit), Great American Ballpark (Cincinnati), Rangers Ballpark in Arlington (Texas), and Citizens Bank Park (Philadelphia). Syn. "retro ballpark"; *neoclassical park.*

Retrosheet 1. *n.* An all-volunteer, nonprofit organization formed in 1989 to collect, computerize, and distribute play-by-play accounts of as many major-league baseball games as possible, along with accompanying statistical data. Accounts are obtained from teams, sportswriters, fans, and newspapers. Detailed game accounts provide the basis for sophisticated analyses of baseball strategy as well as a variety of books and simulation games. Major-league teams, the National Baseball Hall of Fame and Museum, and sportswriters also use Retrosheet. All eras of baseball history are represented and new accounts continue to be accumulated, with the total numbering 140,000 (as of 2008). Retrosheet information is made freely available on its Web site, Retrosheet.org. See also *Project Scoresheet.* ETYMOLOGY. From "retro," meaning "old," plus "scoresheet"

(David W. Smith). 2. *v.* To use the Retrosheet Web site.

return A throw into the infield from an outfielder who has caught or picked up a batted ball. IST USE. 1912 (*New York Tribune*, Sept. 21; Edward J. Nichols).

return game The second game of the home-and-home matches that were an integral part of early baseball. Syn. *return match.* IST USE. 1855. "The return game between the above clubs" (*Spirit of the Times*, Oct. 20; Peter Morris).

return match Syn. of *return game.* IST USE. 1845. "The return match between the New York Base Ball Club and the Brooklyn players, came off yesterday on the ground of the Brooklyn Star Club" (*New York Morning News*, Oct. 25; Dean A. Sullivan).

Reuben's Rule The legal decision that allowed fans to keep foul balls, thereby changing the policy of major-league clubs that demanded that foul balls gathered by fans must be returned to the field of play. ETYMOLOGY. From Reuben Berman, a New York Giants fan who, on May 16, 1921, refused to give back a foul ball and was removed from the Polo Grounds. Berman sued the Giants for mental and physical distress and won the court case plus $100.

revenue sharing 1. The formula by which the home and visiting teams share the gate receipts generated by their game. 2. The collective term for proposals to reduce the disparity between large-market clubs and small-market clubs. According to the Basic Agreement (2007–2011) between the players and owners, each team contributes 31 percent of its net local revenue (gate receipts, broadcasting rights, concessions), after deductions for ballpark expenses, to a pool that is redistributed equally to all 30 teams. More than $320 million was split by the clubs in 2006. The Basic Agreement also created a central fund in which the average revenue for the 30 teams is determined, and money is paid by the rich teams and distributed to the poor teams in proportion to how much they exceed or trail the average. Clubs receiving revenue-sharing payments are supposed to reinvest them "to improve [their] performance on the field"; however, the Basic Agreement does not define this standard and states only that the commissioner "has the authority to enforce this provision."

reverse The back side of a baseball card depicting narrative or statistical information. Compare *obverse*.

reverse curve A pitch that breaks in the opposite direction from most curveballs; esp. a *screwball*, but also sometimes a knuckleball. "A reverse curve, or inshoot, was thrown by several early pitchers, including [Charlie] Sweeney and [Charles] Radbourn of the 1884 Providence champions" (John Thorn and John B. Holway, *The Pitcher*, 1987, p.155).

reverse force double play A double play in which the first out is a force play while the second out is on a runner for whom the force was removed by reason of the first out and who must be tagged out. Compare *force double play*.

Reviving Baseball in Inner Cities A program sponsored by Major League Baseball in partnership with Boys and Girls Clubs of America to give urban teenagers an opportunity to play baseball (boys) and softball (girls). The program also aims to increase the self-esteem of disadvantaged children and to encourage kids to stay in school and off the streets. Founded in 1989 by John Young, a former major-league scout, it gained full support from Major League Baseball in 1991. By 2006, it had attracted 120,000 participants in 203 cities worldwide. Abbrev. *RBI*, 2.

Revlon call Syn. of *make-up call*.

revocable waivers A form of waivers in which the club placing the player on waivers has the option of pulling the player back after he is claimed. Compare *irrevocable waivers*.

revolver *hist.* A player who practiced revolving. Syn. *rounder*, 1; *shooting star*. IST USE. 1870. "While in many respects [professionalism] is an excellent thing for the game, it has brought into being a class of players known as revolvers who are bringing contempt upon themselves and the game. A revolver is a player who changes from club to club for any reason" (*Brooklyn Eagle*, March 11; Peter Morris).

revolving *hist.* Moving from one league or team to another without regard to one's contract or club agreement, in search of better positions, better salaries, better teams, or changes of scenery. The practice was most popular in the late 1860s and 1870s, when many players yielded to the temptations of larger offers and repudiated their earlier agreements, often spurred by under-the-table inducements. The National Association of Base Ball Players tried to prevent revolving with a rule that a player had to be a member of a club for 30 days before playing for it, but the rule was frequently ignored (Peter Morris). Morris noted that the practice was prevalent among cricket players as early as 1861 (*New York Clipper*, July 13).

RF 1. Abbrev. for *right field*, 2. Sometimes *rf*. 2. Abbrev. for *right fielder*. Sometimes *rf*. 3. Abbrev. for *range factor*. 4. [softball term] Abbrev. for *restricted flight*.

RHB Abbrev. for *right-handed batter*.

Rhinelanders Nickname for the Cincinnati Reds.

RHP Abbrev. for *right-handed pitcher*.

rhubarb A ruckus with the umpire(s); a confused situation; a fight between players or between the players and fans; a stew; a noisy argument; a heated dispute. "Mr. 'Red' Barber . . . has used the term 'rhubarb' to describe an argument, or a mix-up, on the field of play" (*New York Herald Tribune*, July 13, 1943; *OED*). Dizzy Dean's definition adds: "Most of the fightin' is done with their mouths." The most complete definition and explanation of the term appears in H. Allen Smith's comic novel *Rhubarb* (1946). The title character is a cat, introduced while clawing its way out of a packing crate. "'Look at the son of a bitch go!' 'That's what I call tearin' up the pea patch! Look at that rhubarb!'" Smith continued: "Then and there the cat got his name—perhaps the only printable name he ever had—derived from a colloquialism insinuated into the Yankee vernacular by Red Barber, the baseball broadcaster. Mr. Barber in turn picked it up from the prose writings of Garry Schumacher and spread it to the far-wandering winds. In Mr. Barber's lexicon, a rhubarb was a noisy altercation, a broil, a violent emotional upheaval brought on by epical dispute such as whether

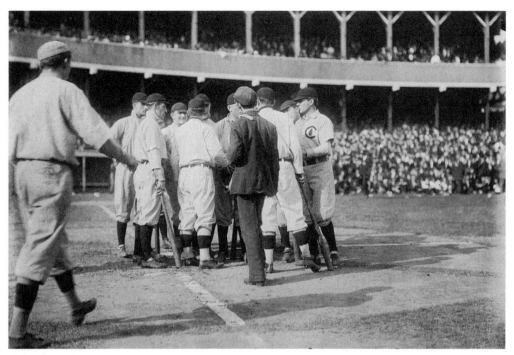

Rhubarb. Final game of the 1908 World Series. *George Grantham Bain Collection, Library of Congress*

one grown man had touched another grown man on the body with a ball the size of a smallish orange." Barber (*Rhubarb in the Catbird Seat*, 1968) added that Schumacher got the term from Tom Meany, the New York sportswriter. Syn. *dustup*; *fracas*, 1; *melee*; *rumble*. IST USE. 1943. " 'A rhubarb,' which has become Brooklynese for a heated verbal run-in, especially between players and umpires" (*Baseball Magazine*, January; David Shulman). Schumacher recalled having first used the term in 1938 at a Brooklyn Dodgers game in Cincinnati, where he was overheard by Barber, who used it on the radio. Red Smith later quoted Schumacher in his column (*New York Herald Tribune*, May 21, 1959) as saying that the word fit because it "suggested an untidy mess, a disheveled tangle of loose ends like the fibers of stewed rhubarb."

ETYMOLOGY. Although there is widespread agreement that Schumacher and Barber first made the term popular in the late 1930s and the 1940s, there is no such agreement as to why "rhubarb" made the leap from the farm-yard (a rhubarb being a tart vegetable belonging to the genus *Rheum*) to the ball-park. The term was employed in the early days of radio from the method a director used to create the impression of a menacing, argumentative crowd. To this end, he got a small group of actors to stand together and murmur "rhubarb-rhubarb-rhubarb." The *Oxford English Dictionary* attested to this point as it is referenced as far back as 1934, in A.P. Herbert's *Holy Deadlock*: "The chorus excitedly rushed about and muttered 'Rhubarb!' " A citation from *Radio Times* (Oct. 17, 1952): "The unemployed actors had a wonderful time. We'd huddle together in a corner and repeat 'Rhubarb, rhubarb, rhubarb'—or 'My fiddle, my fiddle, fiddle' —and it sounded like a big scene from some mammouth production."

An earlier and complementary variation on this idea, which does tie it, conjecturally, to a person, appeared in the letters column of *The Sporting News* (Jan. 21, 1967). James P. Cruger suggested that the term could have come from a German-born baseball man, perhaps Chris Von der Ahe, legendary owner of the St. Louis Browns (1882–1891), who recalled an old stage trick from his homeland: German crowd noises were created by actors repeating the word "Rhabarber." John Ciardi (*Good Words to You*, 1987) agreed in principle, noting that it probably arose from "theatrical practice in Brit. use since Shakespeare's time, in which the crowd noises are based on the sound of rhu-bar-bar." An equally speculative notion is that the term came from the old circus cry of "Hey, rube!," which circus hands supposedly used when there was a fire or when they were being attacked by local toughs.

EXTENDED USE. 1. Any noisy and/or heated argument. "The citizen waiting for a streetcar yesterday was of several minds about the 'rhubarb' between the Virginia Transit Company and its drivers" (*Richmond* [Va.] *Times-Dispatch*, Jan. 17, 1949; *OED*). Red Barber noted that the term was popularized during World War II, when Brooklyn had a presence in every part of the armed forces. The link to Brooklyn, however, took a long time to break. A UPI report on a brawl in Havana on Oct. 28, 1957, identified it as "a Brooklyn-style rhubarb" (Peter Tamony). 2. Nonsense or worthless stuff. "Peking opera . . . employed . . . a huge repertoire consisting almost entirely of rhubarb" (*Times Literary Supplement*, June 3, 1977; *OED*).

rhubarbs *hist.* A rural district. IST USE. 1915. "Until I came to Hillsboro I never imagined what the game meant as it's played out in the rhubarbs" (Burt L. Standish, *Covering the Look-in Corner*, p.291; David Shulman).

rhythm Good tempo, form, and consistency in pitching. See also *concentration*.

rhythm pitcher A pitcher who usually takes two or three innings to reach his peak effectiveness.

ribbie An acronym for *RBI*, the abbrev. for *run batted in*. Also spelled "ribby," "ribbee." Var. *rib-eye*. USAGE NOTE. The term tends to be spoken rather than written, but does show up in print on occasion; e.g., "[Steve Kemp's] pre-injury stats project to only 14 homers and 57 ribbies" (*The Village Voice*, Oct. 11, 1983). Willie McCovey was one of the first players to be quoted using the term. When it first began to show up in the mid-1950s, it fell roughly on some ears. Leonard Shecter called it an "unimaginative word" and "inane."

rib-eye Var. of *ribbie*. Syn. *steak*.

rib roaster A pitch aimed at the batter's ribs. "Sam Wise of the Bostons leans over the plate . . . [and] depends on his quick sight and agility to avoid inshoots but occasionally gets a rib-roaster" (*The World* [New York], Apr. 29, 1888; Gerald L. Cohen).

Rickeyism A term or aphoristic definition created by Branch Rickey, one of the most influential baseball executives of all time, who, among other things, created the farm system while with the St. Louis Cardinals and broke the color line with the Brooklyn Dodgers. He authored the line "luck is the residue of design" to describe his success with farm teams. Other examples: "leisure is the handmaiden of the devil" and "time proves all things." See also *addition by subtraction*; *quality out of quantity*.

ride 1. *v.* To heckle, deride, or bait a player, team, or umpire; to act like a bench jockey. "Any time a new umpire comes to a league, the players—that is, the trouble makers—try to ride him" (Pacific Coast League president Allan T. Baum, quoted in *San Francisco Bulletin*, March 28, 1913; Peter Tamony). "Used

Rickeyism. Branch Rickey, St. Louis Browns, 1913. *George Grantham Bain Collection, Library of Congress*

Rickeyism. Branch Rickey (1881–1965), the baseball executive who integrated Major League Baseball and created the framework for the modern minor-league farm system. *National Baseball Library and Archives, Cooperstown, N.Y.*

to be a guy would ride you, you would ride him back. Nobody rides anybody anymore" (Detroit Tigers manager Sparky Anderson, quoted in *Detroit Free Press*, Apr. 3, 1983). IST USE. 1912 (*New York Tribune*, Oct. 13; Edward J. Nichols). ETYMOLOGY. The conventional explanation is that the term comes from the idea of "riding one's back" and may also be associated with "horsing," from "horse-play." **2.** *v.* See *ride the bench.* **3.** *v.* To hit a home run. "Lou [Gehrig] rode one out of the park" (Paul Gallico, *Lou Gehrig, Pride of the Yankees*, 1942). **4.** *n.* The flight of a home run; e.g., "Smith gave that ball a ride." **5.** *n.* The upward movement of a fastball. "He's [Cal Eldred] got a lot of ride on his fastball" (Brady Anderson, quoted in *The Baltimore Sun*, Apr. 25, 2000). **6.** *v.* To throw a riding fastball. "[Darryl Kile is] very tough when he rides his fastball up in the zone" (*Sports Illustrated*, March 26, 2001, p.135). **7.** *v./hist.* To run while a batted ball is in the air. "A popular term among players in reference to the hitting of a ball is riding it" (*The New York Times*, June 2, 1929). **8.** *v.* For a manager to lead his team to the pennant. "This stretch drive of the Cardinals, 'ridden' by [Frankie] Frisch, must be accepted as one of the noteworthy performances of modern baseball" (1934 World Series official program; Peter Morris). ETYMOLOGY. Borrowed from horse racing, with

the manager as the figurative jockey in the metaphor of a stretch drive.

ride blindbaggage *hist.* To advance from one base to another through the aid of a teammate's batted ball. IST USE. 1920 (*The New York Times*, Oct. 8; Edward J. Nichols). ETYMOLOGY. It is an old railroad term for a free ride.

rider Syn. of *riding fastball.* "[Mike Hampton] throws . . . a 92–94 mph hard rider" (STATS Inc., *The Scouting Handbook 2000*; Peter Morris).

rider of the lonesome pine A *benchwarmer*; one who seldom gets in the game.

ride the bench To sit and wait for one's chance to come into the game as a substitute. Syn. "ride the pine"; *wear out the wood.*

riding fastball A fastball that is thrown up in the strike zone. Thrown across the seams by a right-handed pitcher, the ball moves in on a left-handed batter or away from a right-handed batter. See also *four-seam fastball.* Syn. *rider*; *sailing fastball.*

RIF ball Syn. of *reduced injury factor ball.*

riffle 1. *n.* A hearty swing at a pitched ball, whether or not the ball is hit. "The boys prefer to take 'riffles' this year instead of cuts" (William G. Brandt, *Baseball Magazine*, May 1932). IST USE. 1906 (*The Sporting Life*, Feb. 10; Edward J. Nichols). **2.** *v.* To hit the ball hard (Maurice H. Weseen, *A Dictionary of American Slang*, 1934).

rifle 1. *n.* An exceptionally strong throwing arm, usually that of an outfielder or a catcher. For example, 1950s Brooklyn Dodgers outfielder Carl Furillo was known as the "Reading Rifle." See also *gun*, 1; *shotgun*, 1. **2.** *v.* To throw the ball quickly and accurately. "He rifles it across the diamond" (*USA Today*, March 18, 1987). See also *gun*, 4. **3.** *n.* A player with a strong throwing arm. **4.** *v.* To hit a ball extremely hard and straight. "I liked . . . the sharp crack of a line drive rifled into the outfield" (Ted Berkman, *Christian Science Monitor*, May 10, 1983). IST USE. 1913. "There was a resounding smack and the ball fairly shot from home plate, rifled over the head of the shortstop" (*San Francisco Bulletin*, May 23; Gerald L. Cohen).

rifle arm 1. A powerful and accurate throwing arm, esp. of an outfielder. **2.** A player with a rifle arm.

rifle pit Syn. of *pitcher's box.*

rifle shot **1.** A swiftly thrown ball. "Forty times he [Frank Chance] has been knocked unconscious by the rifle shots of an opposing pitcher" (*The Washington Post*, June 8, 1913). IST USE. 1881 (*New York Herald*, July 26; Edward J. Nichols). **2.** A ball that is hit hard; a *line drive.* IST USE. 1890 (*New York Post*, May 10; Edward J. Nichols).

rig *hist.* A baseball uniform. The term came directly from cricket. IST USE. 1867 (*Philadelphia Sunday Mercury*; Edward J. Nichols).

right Short for *right field.* IST USE. 1867. "The nine will be as follows: . . . Peters, right" (*The Ball Players' Chronicle*, Aug. 8; Peter Morris).

right base The correct base toward which an outfielder returns a batted ball. The term occurs in the phrase "throw to the right base"; e.g., with a runner on first base and a single hit to the outfield, the outfielder needs to decide whether to throw to third base to try to put out the runner advancing from second base, or to throw to second base to prevent the batter-runner from taking an extra base on a throw to third base. Compare *wrong base.*

right center The area of the playing field between right field and center field. Syn. "right-center field."

right down Broadway Syn. of *down the middle*, 2. The term was coined by WJSV sportscaster Arch McDonald of Washington, D.C. See also *Broadway*, 1.

right down the middle Syn. of *down the middle*, 2. Commenting on a Bobby Abreu home run, Washington Nationals pitcher Tony Armas Jr. said, "It was a bad pitch. It was right down the middle" (*The Baltimore Sun*, May 31, 2006).

right field **1.** The right side of the outfield as viewed from home plate. Sometimes spelled "rightfield." Syn. *right*; *right garden*; *dexter meadow.* **2.** The position of the player who defends right field. Abbrev. *RF* or *rf.* Syn. *right.*

right field base hit *hist.* A base hit credited to a batter who deliberately hits a fly ball to right field that advances a runner. A few scorers advocated such a hit before scoring rules began to be standardized in 1880 (John H. Gruber, *The Sporting News*, Apr. 6, 1916; Peter Morris).

right fielder The defensive player who is positioned in right field. The right fielder often has a strong throwing arm: "the ability to stop runners at first from advancing two bases on a single is the quality to look for in a right fielder, [Texas Rangers manager Bobby] Valentine said" (*USA Today*, Apr. 6, 1997). Abbrev. *RF* or *rf.* Sometimes spelled "rightfielder." Syn. *right gardener.* IST USE. 1865. "The Atlantics . . . were minus the services of . . . Sid Smith, their . . . right fielder" (*The New York Times*, Aug. 24; Fred R. Shapiro).

right field foul line The line extending from home plate to the fence in deep right field that delineates foul from fair playing areas. Since June 1, 1958, the line must extend at least 325 feet. Syn. *right field line.*

right field line The *first base line* extended beyond the infield; the *right field foul line.*

right garden *hist.* Syn. of *right field*, 1. IST USE. 1890 (*New York Press*, July 13; Edward J. Nichols).

right gardener *hist.* Syn. of *right fielder.* IST USE. 1898. "Walter Wilmot will be the permanent right gardener for the Giants" (*The Washington Post*, Apr. 29).

right-handed Said of a player who favors the right hand or the right side of the body. Compare *left-handed.* Also spelled "righthanded."

right-handed batter A batter who swings from the right and faces the pitcher with the left side of his body as he stands on the left (third base) side of home plate. Abbrev. *RHB.*

right-handed pitcher A pitcher who throws with his right arm. Abbrev. *RHP.*

right-hander A right-handed player; esp., a pitcher who throws with his right arm. The term is also used for a right-handed batter. Compare *left-hander.* Also spelled "right hander"; "righthander."

rightie Var. of *righty.*

right in there pitching Said of a pitcher who is working hard from the mound; a compliment. In this phrase the word "pitching" means pitching with intensity or pitching well. EXTENDED USE. Said of one who is putting forth one's best effort (*American Speech*, Apr. 1943).

right of first refusal The principle that allows a player's former club to match the highest offer made to that player.

right off the bat Immediately; without ado; understanding quickly; from the very beginning. The term is an extended metaphor from the speed with which a ball flies off a bat. Del Howard (quoted in *San Francisco Bulletin*, Apr. 3, 1913; Gerald L. Cohen): "Unfortunately we are not so situated that we can carry a number of young players and develop them. We must have a winner right off the bat." Pitcher Tony Saunders, coming off a serious arm injury (quoted in *The Baltimore Sun*, March 3, 2005): "The thing that I was happy with was I executed the pitch. It was exactly where we wanted it to go. You're always happy when you do that, and for me to do it right off the bat, it was a good little building block for me." A 1911 book of baseball ballads from the *New York Evening Journal*, written by William F. Kirk, is titled *Right Off the Bat*. IST USE. 1888. The *Davenport Morning Tribune* (Dec. 2; Peter Morris) included an article about a conversation between a couple in which the husband complains bitterly about their son's using too much slang. In the process the husband makes such comments as, "He is altogether too fly, that boy, and if I catch him with those boys again he'll make a home run of the liveliest kind," and "You are entirely off your base, my dear," and "Let me hear that kid use slang again and I'll give it to him right off the bat." EXTENDED USE. From the start; immediately. "If the Wisconsin supreme court proposes to keep up the legislature of that State it will have to learn to take the gerrymanders right off the bat" (*The Washington Post*, Oct. 13, 1892; Peter Morris). "The bottom line was the way we started: we didn't shoot well and that put us in a predicament right off the bat" (Navy women's basketball coach Joe Sanchez, quoted in *The Baltimore Sun*, March 4, 2000). "Right off the bat last night, he [President George W. Bush] hailed the recent elections [in Iraq], as cheering Republicans saluted him with index fingers dipped in ink" (State of the Union speech, *The Baltimore Sun*, Feb. 3, 2005).

right of way The part of the basepath that a baserunner must yield to infielders attempting to make a play. A runner who fails to avoid an infielder can be called out for interference.

right patrol *hist.* Right field or right fielder (Maurice H. Weseen, *A Dictionary of American Slang*, 1934).

right short *hist.* **1.** The position between first base and second base for a 10th player, proposed by Henry Chadwick (*The Game of Base Ball*, 1868, p.44) and implemented for the 1874 season but abandoned after a few games. Chadwick argued that the position would free the first baseman and the third baseman to range into foul territory to chase elusive fair-foul hits. In effect, the position is now played by the second baseman. Syn. "right shortstop." **2.** The player who plays the right short position. See also *ten-man baseball*. Syn. *tenth man*, 6; *rover*, 1; "right shortstop."

right turn at first base The route taken by a batter who is out on a ground ball or fly. "So for the fourth time, [Dave] Winfield makes a right turn at first base" (Chuck Thompson, Yankees-Orioles telecast, Sept. 6, 1982).

righty A right-handed player; one who throws with the right arm or bats from the left side of home plate as he faces the pitcher. Var. *rightie*.

ring **1.** See *World Series ring*. **2.** "A party of men [who] conspire together to effect their object in a dishonorable manner" (Henry Chadwick, *The Game of Base Ball*, 1868, p.45). Chadwick described a "betting ring" as "a set of men connected with a club [who] join together and bribe players to sell games in order to win bets." He considered these rings as "the worst evil that the game is troubled with, as from them has sprung all the swindling and fraud which has made base ball disreputable in the opinion of so many people."

ringer A professional ballplayer who passes himself off as a nonprofessional to give his team an unfair advantage; one who plays baseball under false pretenses by keeping secret his identity and past performances. "The word went round that the collegians had a ringer and Joe was shown up in his true colors" (*San Francisco Bulletin*, Feb. 12, 1913; Gerald L. Cohen). IST USE. 1886. "Look out for 'ringers'" (*The Sporting Life*, Apr. 28; Barry Popik).

ring the bat [softball term] For an umpire to check the size of a softball bat by passing it through a bat ring to ensure that it is the officially permitted size.

ring up 1. To strike out a batter. **2.** For an umpire to call a strike, esp. a third strike. **3.** To record or gain a victory. **4.** To score a run. "Oakland managed to ring up a couple of tallies and make a twelve-inning tie of it" (*San Francisco Bulletin*, Apr. 14, 1913; Gerald L. Cohen).

rinky-dink 1. *n.* A player who does not get to play the game very often; a second-string player. **2.** *adj.* Descriptive of inferior playing, or unorganized amateur baseball (Maurice H. Weseen, *A Dictionary of American Slang*, 1934).

rip 1. *v.* To hit the ball hard; e.g., "Smith ripped one back through the box." **2.** *n.* An opportunity to swing the bat. "It was hard for power hitters to get a good rip when [Sal] Maglie ... [let] that big curve dance right under their chins" (Bobby Thomson, *"The Giants Win the Pennant! The Giants Win the Pennant!,"* 1991, p.238). The term is often used in the plural: "Ewell ('Reb') Russell and Eddie Cicotte await their turns to enter the cage and have their rips" (Donald Honig, *Shadows of Summer*, 1994, p.91). **3.** *n.* A base hit.

ripe *hist.* Said of a player who is ready to perform at the major-league level. IST USE. 1905 (*The Sporting Life*, Sept. 9, p.18; Edward J. Nichols).

Ripken Way A teaching method for youth baseball that embodies four principles: keep it simple, explain the why, celebrate the individual (in other words, everyone does things a little differently, and there isn't just one way to have success), and make it fun. Named for former major-leaguer Cal Ripken Jr., who runs the Ripken Youth Baseball Academy in Aberdeen, Md.

rise The apparent upward movement of a fastball as it approaches the batter. IST USE. 1901 (Burt L. Standish, *Frank Merriwell's School Days*, p.255; Edward J. Nichols).

rise ball [softball term] A pitch that rises as it approaches the plate; specif., a fastball that tends to hop as it gets to the plate. "The rise ball is really the pitch that provides the softball pitcher with a great advantage over the hitter. ... Even when the hitter times the rise ball accurately, he usually hits under the ball and pops it up" (Loren Walsh, *Inside Softball*, 1977). Syn. *riser*, 2; *upshoot*, 3.

rise-curve [softball term] A pitch that combines the rise of the fastball with the curve. "Many pitchers use the rise-curve as their best strikeout pitch" (Loren Walsh, *Inside Softball*, 1977).

riser 1. Syn. of *rising fastball*. **2.** [softball term] Syn. of *rise ball*.

rising ball A pitch thrown from a low release point in the early days of baseball, when a batter could request a high ball. The batter would initially feel that the ball would be out of the specified range, slowing his reaction time. Celebrated curveball pitcher Bobby Mathews (quoted in *Grand Rapids* [Mich.] *Morning Democrat*, Sept. 2, 1883, reprinted from the *Philadelphia Press*; Peter Morris): "Rising balls [start] ... from as near the ground as possible and pitched upward."

rising fastball A fastball that appears to rise in flight to the batter, who will usually swing under it. It is generally gripped across two of the wide seams of the ball. Unless thrown underhand, a fastball cannot "rise"; but thrown overhand with enough force, it will appear to rise because "it's not dropping as much as the batter's brain thinks it should" (Rob Neyer, in Bill James and Rob Neyer, *The Neyer/James Guide to Pitchers*, 2004, p.18). See also *four-seam fastball*. Syn. *riser*, 1.

RISP Abbrev. for *runner in scoring position*.

rite of spring Spring-training activities and their assorted hoopla. "[The] annual rite of spring, when major league teams pack their bags and baseballs and head south for the sun, has become big business in Florida" (*Tampa Tribune*, Feb. 27, 1989).

RO The letters (for "Rawlings Official") identifying the model baseball supplied to the major leagues under contract by Rawlings Sporting Goods.

road 1. *n.* The locale of any game not played on a team's home field. 2. *adj.* Away; not at home.

road beef A female whom a player meets while traveling (on the road) and goes to bed with (Jose Canseco, *Juiced*, 2005). See also *import*, 3.

road draw The ability of a team to sell tickets in other teams' home ballparks.

road game Syn. of *away game*.

road grays The uniform that a team wears for its away games. It is often gray and usually drabber than the *home whites*.

road record The statistics of a baseball team for games played away from its home field.

roadrunner A fleet-footed outfielder. "Billy North 'roams' the outfield with the 'grace of a gazelle' . . . a 'roadrunner,' blessed with 'Mercury-feet'" (Lowell Cohn, *San Francisco Chronicle*, June 4, 1980).

road schedule The schedule of baseball games to be played by a team away from home.

road secretary Syn. of *traveling secretary*.

road team 1. Syn. of *visiting team*. 2. *hist.* A team that plays well away from its home field yet performs poorly at home. Compare *home team*, 2. IST USE. 1905 (*The Sporting Life*, Sept. 9, p.18; Edward J. Nichols).

road trip A series of games played away from a team's home field.

roamer A fielder, usually an outfielder, who covers a lot of territory.

rob 1. To deprive a batter of a safe hit through skillful or spectacular fielding. IST USE. 1905. "[Nixey] Callahan robbed [Elmer] Flick of a clean triple in the fifth by a grand catch . . . spearing the ball close to his shoetops while at top speed" (*Chicago Tribune*, May 4; Peter Morris). 2. For the umpire to make what appears to be a bad call against a player or team. "The decision was the worst of several, and robbed the Sox of a run" (*Chicago Tri-*

Road grays. New York Giants pitcher Walt Dickson, wearing 1910 road uniform. *George Grantham Bain Collection, Library of Congress*

bune, May 13, 1905; Peter Morris). IST USE. 1900. "The 'robbed-by-the-umpire' . . . stories carted from West to East by the Eastern teams bid fair to make the present Eastern series one of the hottest of the season" (*The Washington Post*, July 22). 3. To steal a base.

robber 1. A fielder skillful in making defensive plays that deprive the batter of a hit. 2. An umpire, esp. one who appears to favor one team over the other. The term is derogatory. American League umpire Bill McGowan (*Liberty Magazine*, Sept. 11, 1937, p.43): "I like my job. I've liked it ever since the first wild-eyed fans down on the lots started to call me 'robber.'" IST USE. 1899 (Burt L. Standish, *Frank Merriwell's Double Shot*, p.10; Edward J. Nichols). 3. Syn. of *base stealer*. "The major league master robbers can all be identified, too, stolen bases having been introduced into the summaries of the box scores and into the averages during the season of 1886" (Ernest J. Lanigan, *The Baseball Cyclopedia*, 1922, p.47).

robbery 1. Sensational fielding that deprives a batter of a hit. IST USE. 1897 (*New York Tribune*, June 4; Edward J. Nichols). 2. Syn. of *base stealing.* "[Harry] Stovey perpetrated 143 robberies [in 1887]" (Ernest J. Lanigan, *The Baseball Cyclopedia*, 1922, p.47).

Roberto Clemente Award 1. An annual award given to a player who best exemplifies baseball on and off the field, with consideration given to sportsmanship, community involvement, and contribution to his team and to the game. Each major-league team nominates a player, and the award winner is selected by a panel of baseball executives and media personnel. Termed baseball's most prestigious off-the-field honor, it was created by the commissioner's office in 1971 as the Commissioner's Award and renamed on March 12, 1973, to honor Pittsburgh Pirates outfielder Roberto Clemente, who died on Dec. 31, 1972, in the crash of a plane taking relief supplies to victims of an earthquake in Managua, Nicaragua. **2.** An annual memorial award given by the Pittsburgh chapter of the Baseball Writers' Association of America to the year's most outstanding Pittsburgh Pirates player. **3.** A humanitarian award given by the city of Hialeah, Fla., to a private citizen in that community who best exemplifies Roberto Clemente's humanitarian virtues. **4.** An award given to the top Latin-American player in the major leagues.

Robert O. Fishel Award An annual award given by Major League Baseball for excellence in public relations. First presented in 1981, the award is named in honor of the former American League secretary and assistant to the president.

Robin Hood league An outlaw league, such as the Players' League of 1890. IST USE. 1922 (Ernest J. Lanigan, *Baseball Cyclopedia*; Edward J. Nichols).

Robins Nickname for the National League franchise in Brooklyn, N.Y., from 1914 to 1931, and renamed the Brooklyn *Dodgers* in 1932. So named in honor of manager Wilbert Robinson.

rock 1. *n.* A dumb play. Syn. of *boner*, 1. "Old ballplayers . . . called a bonehead play a rock" (Al Cartwright, quoted in *Orioles Gazette*, Dec. 1992). "['Rocks'] are blunders executed by a slow-thinking player" (Edwin M. Rumill, *Christian Science Monitor*, Sept.

1, 1937). **2.** *n.* The backward motion of a pitcher as he prepares to deliver the ball. **3.** *v.* To make several hits off a pitcher; e.g., "The Braves rocked Smith for five straight hits before being relieved." **4.** *n.* The baseball. "Nobody in his right mind throws a rock 90-plus miles an hour at a guy's head" (Bob Gibson, quoted in *The New York Times*, July 13, 1986).

rocker step The shifting, sideways motion used by a catcher to get positioned for pitches that are low and outside or by a pitcher to trigger his delivery.

rocket 1. A hard-hit, fast-moving line drive. "Jose Guillen lined a rocket right at Orioles first baseman Jeff Conine" (*The Baltimore Sun*, Aug. 28, 2003). "[Tom Brunansky sent] a three-run rocket . . . over the Green Monster" (*Tampa Tribune*, Sept. 30, 1990). See also *sky-rocket.* IST USE. 1857. "He sends a 'rocket' thro' the air, and 'dropping,' gains his base" (Everett L. Baker, poem "Impromptu," *Buffalo Courier*, Sept. 27; Priscilla Astifan). **2.** A fastball. **3.** A dead or cheap baseball.

rockhead A player who misses signs (Bill McCullough, *Brooklyn Eagle*, Sept. 3, 1937).

Rockies Nickname for the National League West Division expansion franchise that began playing in Denver in 1993 as the Colorado Rockies. Ownership chose the more inclusive "Colorado"—as opposed to "Denver"—to acknowledge the incredible number of season-ticket deposits received from across the region.

rocking chair *n.* **1.** The figurative position of the umpire at third base, presumably because he has so little to do. "Working the rocking chair: third-base duty, usually a dull assignment because so few runners reach third" (Jeff Strickler, *Minneapolis Star Tribune*, June 16). **2.** The figurative position of a catcher who does not need to move much, often because the pitcher has excellent control. "[Jack] Warner and [Rooney] Sweeny [*sic*] were great catchers of their time and it used to be said that either could sit in a rocking chair and catch the speediest pitching" (Alfred H. Spink, *The National Game*, 2nd ed., 1911, p.62; Peter Morris). **3.** A hip motion used by pitcher Nick Altrock to throw the ball to first base before he stepped. Ty Cobb (quoted in Bert Dunne, *Play Ball!*, 1951; Peter Morris): "Nick developed a peculiar rocking-chair motion with his hips—without moving his hips at all. . . . The rocking-chair is a hip motion and is not a balk, although it is intended to deceive the runner. It is not regarded as a balk because Nick did it every time and it was accepted as part of the pitching motion."

rocking-chair *adj.* **1.** Said of a pitch or game that was so easy for the umpire to call that he did not need to be in position. Larry R. Gerlach (*The Men in Blue*, 1980; Peter Morris) quoted umpires Ernie Stewart ("So help me, it was right there—oh, a rocking-chair pitch.") and Ed Sudol (describing his first professional game as an umpire: "I was scared, believe me. Fortunately, it was a rocking-chair game."). **2.** Said of a pitcher with excellent control. "[Christy Mathewson, Jack Coombs, and Herb Pennock] are what catchers call 'rocking chair pitchers.' Which means that their control is so good that you could sit in a rocking chair and catch them" (George Herman Ruth, *Babe Ruth's Own Book of Baseball*, 1928, p.40; Peter Morris). **3.** Said of a fielder who does not move much. "Don't be a stationary first baseman, a 'rocking chair' fielder with a perfect average" (George Sisler, *Sisler on Baseball*, 1954).

rockpile **1.** A rough infield, esp. one with more than its share of pebbles, or one that is rock hard. A teammate said to Jim Brosnan (*The Long Season*, 1960), "This infield is better than that rockpile in Pittsburgh." **2.** A stadium with a particularly rough infield. War Memorial Stadium in Buffalo, N.Y., immortalized in the movie *The Natural* (1984), was known as the "Old Rockpile."

Rocktober The time of the year that the Colorado Rockies were in the 2007 playoffs and World Series. ETYMOLOGY. The term had previously been used by radio stations as well as the makers of the 1984 film *Rocktober Blood* (*Sports Illustrated*, Oct. 29, 2007).

roid Short for *steroid*.

Rolaids Relief Man Award An annual award given since 1976 to one relief pitcher in each

major league by Warner-Lambert Inc., makers of Rolaids antacid tablets ("How do you spell relief?"). Unlike the many awards given on the basis of a vote, this one is determined on a scoring system: 4 points (beginning in 2000) for a *tough save* (in which the reliever comes in with the tying run anywhere on base), 3 points for a traditional save, 2 points for a win in relief, −2 points for a loss, and −2 points for a blown save. See also *relief points*; *Reliever of the Year Award*.

role player A nonstarting player who is used during certain specific situations; a player who performs a special function for a team, such as pinch running or playing a defensive position. See also *utility player*.

roletazo Spanish for "ground ball."

roll **1.** *n.* A slowly hit ground ball. IST USE. 1897. "Gleason's roll to second forced [Joyce]" (*The World* [New York], May 14; Peter Morris). **2.** *v.* To bat a ball easily on the ground. IST USE. 1908. "Roll one" (*Brooklyn Daily Eagle*, May 22; Edward J. Nichols). **3.** *v.* To score; e.g., "roll home" (Maurice H. Weseen, *A Dictionary of American Slang*, 1934).

roll block *n.* The maneuver by a baserunner who tries to disrupt the play of the pivot man at second base by tumbling into the player when a double play is being attempted. The roll block is akin to the similar play in football. Syn. "rolling block"; *body block*.

roll-block *v.* To try to break up a double play by rolling into and blocking the pivot man. "[Jim] Gantner suffered a torn medial collateral ligament in his left knee . . . when [Marcus] Lawton roll-blocked him trying to break up a double play" (*Tampa Tribune*, Aug. 17, 1989).

roller A slow grounder, such as one that trickles across the field. "B.J. Surhoff tied the game on a roller too slow for the Braves' middle infield to turn into a double play" (*The Baltimore Sun*, July 14, 2000). IST USE. 1871. "Schafer then sent another roller along the field, giving him three bases" (*The Cleveland Morning Herald*, May 6).

rolling curveball A curveball with a slow break, not sharp or hard.

roll over **1.** For a batter to turn his hands, causing him to pull outside pitches weakly. **2.**

To make a score (Maurice H. Weseen, *A Dictionary of American Slang*, 1934).

roll slide A slide in which the runner goes past the base or home plate (as if he missed his target), then rolls on his backside and sweeps a hand backward over the corner of the base or home plate. Ty Cobb (*My Life in Baseball*, 1961, p.167), describing the roll slide: "Five fingers isn't much to give a defensive man who has to catch the ball and put it on you in the same motion."

roll to the bat Syn. of *Indian ball*, 1.

romp An easy victory; a *laugher*. IST USE. 1907 (*New York Evening Journal*, May 2; Edward J. Nichols).

romp home To score (Maurice H. Weseen, *A Dictionary of American Slang*, 1934).

roofkeeping Manipulating the currents in the air-conditioning system in an enclosed stadium to benefit the home team. During the Houston Astrodome's inaugural season (1965), groundskeepers were accused of roofkeeping by the New York Mets during a streak in which the Astros won nine straight games at home.

roof-rule double A *ground-rule double* awarded a batter when the ball is batted onto the roof of a ballpark, into the ceiling material of a roofed ballpark, or through a drainage hole in the roof of a domed ballpark. Syn. *roof-top double*.

roofscraper A towering home run hit in a domed ballpark.

roof shot A batted ball (usually a home run) that leaves the playing field in fair territory and lands on or over the roof of a ballpark (such as Tiger Stadium in Detroit). Syn. *rooftopper*.

roof-top double Syn. of *roof-rule double*.

rooftopper Syn. of *roof shot*.

'roo hop Short for *kangaroo hop*, 2.

rook Short for *rookie*, 1. IST USE. 1917. "A well-recommended 'rook'" (*The Sporting Life*, Apr. 14; Peter Morris)

rookie 1. *n.* A player in his first season; a first-year player. See also *busher*, 1; *gazoonie*; *green pea*; *jelly bean*; *recruit*, 1; *yannigan*. Syn. *rook*; *rooky*; *huckleberry*; *kindergart-*

Rookie. Art Bues, infielder prospect in spring training, with the New York Giants, 1912. His rookie year was 1913 with the Boston Braves, but he played in only two games with one at-bat. *George Grantham Bain Collection, Library of Congress*

ner; *budder*. IST USE. 1908. "Glancing down the roster we still perceive that the extra choice rookies touted to shunt the ancient and honorable members from their jobs are as lonesome as the strawberry on the roof of the shortcake" (*The Washington Post*, Apr. 20; Peter Morris). 2. *n.* The official status (since 1971) of a player eligible for the Rookie of the Year Award; specif., a pitcher who has appeared in less than 50 major-league innings during the previous season(s), or a non-pitcher who has accumulated less than 130 at-bats during the previous season(s), or a player who has accumulated less than 45 days on the active roster of a major-league club or clubs during the period of 25-player limit (i.e., before Sept. 1) of the previous season, excluding time in the military service or on the disabled list. The formal guidelines were first established in 1957: a player could not have accumulated more than 75 at-bats or 45 innings pitched, or have been on a major-league roster between May 15 and Sept. 1 of any previous season(s). These were changed in Dec. 1957 to 90 at-bats, 45 innings pitched, or 45 days on a major-league roster before

Sept. 1. **3.** *n.* A player in his first year of eligibility for Hall of Fame voting. Before a player can become eligible he must have been out of baseball for at least five years. "One of the largest rookie crops in years—a total of 24 first-time candidates—helps swell the 1988 Hall of Fame ballot to 45 nominees" (*The Sporting News*, Dec. 7, 1987). **4.** *adj.* Relating to the first season, such as a "rookie manager" or a "rookie owner"; e.g., "They expressed themselves . . . as willing to trade . . . for the rookie outfielder" (*Chicago Daily News*, Oct. 21, 1944).

ETYMOLOGY. The term appears to be a corruption of the word "recruit" and may have originated as a derisive term for a fresh recruit in the Army, but this is far from certain. It was listed in the 1903 supplement to *Webster's New International Dictionary of the English Language* as soldier's slang for "recruit" with the notation that Rudyard Kipling had used the word and that its etymology was uncertain. By the time of World War I, it was in common use. In a review of war slang, *Literary Digest* (March 10, 1917) reported, "*Rookie* is soldiers' slang for a raw recruit. The origin of this meaning has been attributed to the name 'rookery,' given, in former military slang, to the quarters occupied by subalterns in barracks." Philip Howard (*A Word in Your Ear*, 1983) noted that the Falklands War of 1982 revived this term in the United Kingdom and that the British had to be reminded that it was not an Americanism but, in fact, made its first literary appearance in Kipling's *Barrack-Room Ballads* (1892) in the line, "So 'ark an' 'eed, you rookies, which is always grumblin' sore." Others have suggested: a) a jump from chess where the rook is often the last piece to be used when the game opens, and b) a play on the very old slang word "rook," to cheat, which was applied to new soldiers on the assumption that they would be easily cheated by con men.

EXTENDED USE. Although "rookie" probably existed in military slang first, its American popularity comes from baseball, from which it spread to other realms. The citations on the word collected by Merriam-Webster include, among others, rookie cook, rookie Senator, rookie cop, CIA rookie, rookie guard (basketball), rookie goalie, rookie priest,

rookie astronaut, rookie fireman, rookie starter, rookie year, rookie actor, rookie quarterback, and rookie artist; e.g., "Don't Pair Rookie Pilots, Warns FAA" (*USA Today* headline, Jan. 22, 1988).

rookie card 1. The first *baseball card* from a particular issuer that depicts a given player at the major-league level; a player's first year of cards, whether or not it is his rookie season. Usually only superstar players are associated with the term; e.g., the 1951 Bowman no.253 and the 1952 Topps no.311 are considered rookie cards of Mickey Mantle. In recent years the rookie cards of stars have risen in value much faster than second- and third-year cards, and must be considered the baseball collecting equivalent of a first edition in book collecting. "Don Mattingly seemed amused when told a 3-year-old baseball card picturing him as a rookie was selling for $95. But amusement turned to amazement when he learned people were buying it" (*St. Petersburg Times*, March 14, 1987). Abbrev. *RC*, 2. **2.** A baseball card that portrays one or more players with the notation on the card that these players are rookies.

rookie league A minor league, below the level of *Class A*, that features the more advanced high school or international players; e.g., the Appalachian League and the Pioneer League are classified as "rookie-advanced" leagues; and the Arizona League, the Gulf Coast League, the Dominican Summer League, and the Venezuelan Summer League are classified as "rookie leagues." Established in 1963, rookie leagues aim to assess and develop the talent of primarily first-year players. Rookie-league teams must have at least 10 pitchers as of July 1 each year. Minimum seating capacity for rookie league ballparks is 2,500. See also *complex league*. Compare *short-season league*.

Rookie of the Year The player selected to receive the Rookie of the Year Award. Abbrev. *ROY.* IST USE. 1941. "Catcher Walker Cooper, Card 'Rookie of the Year' Entry" (*The Sporting News* headline, Apr. 24; Peter Morris).

Rookie of the Year Award 1. An annual award presented by the Baseball Writers' Association of America to the outstanding rookie in the major leagues in 1947 and 1948, and to the outstanding rookie in each major league since 1949. Selections originally were made by three writers from each league city, but since 1961 have been made by two writers from each league city. Since 1980, writers have named three rookies, with five points allotted for each first-place vote, three points for each second-place vote, and one point for each third-place vote. In 1971, the current formal guidelines were established for determining rookie status: 130 at-bats, 50 innings pitched, or 45 days on a major-league roster. Since 1987, the award has been officially known as the *Jackie Robinson Award*, to honor the first recipient of the award in 1947. See Bill Deane, in *Total Baseball*, 8th ed., 2004, pp.721–22. EXTENDED USE. Other sports now have Rookie of the Year Awards; e.g., National Hockey League players who have played in "no more than 20 games in the preceding season" are eligible for honors in that sport. **2.** An award established in 1946 by *The Sporting News* for the top rookie. A single award for all of major-league baseball was given in 1947, 1948, and 1950; in 1949 and since 1951, *The Sporting News* has given an award to a player from each league. From 1963 through 2003, *The Sporting News* split the award into two separate categories: Rookie Player of the Year and Rookie Pitcher of the Year. In 2004, these two awards were discontinued in favor of the unified award. **3.** An award established in 1941 by the Chicago chapter of the Baseball Writers' Association of America to recognize the major leagues' top rookie from 1940 through 1947. The honor was named the *J. Louis Comiskey Memorial Award* in 1944.

rooky Alternate spelling of *rookie*, 1 (Maurice H. Weseen, *A Dictionary of American Slang*, 1934).

roomie Short for "roommate."

Rooms A common generic name for a player's roommate on the road.

room-service 1. Said of a batted ball or hop that comes right to the fielder who does not have to move to catch it. **2.** Said of a pitch (usually a fastball) that is so easy to hit that the batter may as well have ordered it; e.g., a "room-service cheeseburger" is a fastball right down the middle, a juicy offering (*The*

Washington Post, May 12, 1986). "[Mark] Redman delivered a room-service fastball that [Hideki] Matsui belted over the center-field wall" (Tom Verducci, *Sports Illustrated*, Oct. 27, 2003). ETYMOLOGY. The term is a play on the fact that hotel room service will bring food and drink directly to one's room.

root To encourage a player or team by cheering and applauding. IST USE. 1886. "The 'large' delegation which, according to *The World* [New York], accompanied the giants to Philadelphia to 'root for victory' . . . Perhaps if all hands 'root' a little harder the giants will win today. By the way, what does 'root' mean?" (*The Boston Globe*, May 4; Peter Morris). ETYMOLOGY. Although it has been stated often that the term comes from the notion of a fan who is so close to his or her team that he or she is "rooted" to it, Gerald L. Cohen (*Studies in Slang*, part 2, 1989) proposed another theory: "The basic meaning of 'root' is clearly 'to dig,' and rooting can be subdivided into the categories of feet-stamping ('pedal-music'), shouting ('chin-music'), and hand-clapping. I believe that 'pedal music' may be the key here; we may deal with the imagery of stamping so hard that one is visualized as digging a hole."

rooter An individual who cheers for a team or player; an exuberant fan. IST USE. 1889. "Cleveland has the most scientific crowd of 'rooters' in the country" (*The World* [New York], Aug. 14; Gerald L. Cohen).

rope 1. *n.* A line drive. "There would be no catching the rope off of [Robin] Ventura's bat, a just-fair 398-foot home run to right" (*The Baltimore Sun*, June 4, 1994). See also *frozen rope*; *screaming rope*. **2.** *v.* To hit a line drive. "For nearly all his adult life, since he was roping fastballs . . . at Auburn, [Frank] Thomas has been a hitting prodigy" (William Nack, *Sports Illustrated*, March 13, 2000).

rope arm The arm of a pitcher who does not bend his elbow, and thus slings the pitch.

rosin A translucent, amber-colored, friable resin obtained by chemical means from the dead wood of pine trees and used in making varnishes and printing inks, rubbing on bows of string instruments as the violin, and filling rosin bags.

rosin bag A small, finely meshed, sealed

cloth sack containing and covered with sticky rosin that is kept at the back of the pitcher's mound. Pitchers are legally permitted to rub rosin from the bag to dry their hands and improve their grip on the ball. It is illegal to dust the ball or a player's uniform with the rosin bag, or to apply rosin from the bag to a player's glove. If the ball hits the rosin bag, it is in play. Rosin bags were first introduced before the 1926 season. The rosin bag is used dramatically by some pitchers: Jerry Howarth (*Baseball Lite*, 1986) described it as "constantly picked up and dropped during the game while occasionally being slammed, kicked, hurled and spat at by angry bilingual pitchers speaking English and Profanity." Syn. *resin bag*; *resin sack*.

roster The active list of players on a team at any given moment. The length of the roster is set by league rules and changes during the course of the regular season. See also *25-man roster*; *40-man roster*. IST USE. 1888. "The following is the roster of the team which will represent Philadelphia" (*The North American* [Philadelphia], Feb. 7).

roster filler A minor leaguer who is not regarded as a prospect. The term is unflattering and "politically incorrect" (Marty Noble, *Baseball America*, Aug. 20–Sept. 2, 2001).

roster limit Syn. of *player limit*.

Rotary Smith Award College baseball's player of the year award from 1988 to 2003 as voted on by college baseball's publicists (sports information directors), former winners of the award, and coaches of those former winners. It was founded by the Greater Houston Sports Association; in 1996, the Rotary Club of Houston joined the award committee. The award paid tribute to R.E. "Bob" Smith of the Houston Astros. The award was succeeded in 2004 by the Roger Clemens Award, honoring the most outstanding college baseball pitcher.

rotation 1. The regular order in which a manager will field his starting pitchers. A modern manager wants to leave spring training with his rotation set for, at least, the early weeks of the season. An aspiring starter will try to work his way into the rotation. Commonly, a team has four or five starters in its rotation. Syn. *pitching rotation*; *starting rotation*. IST USE. 1911. " 'Rotation' is the keynote of a new system of handling the pitching staff which has been adopted by the management of the New York Americans for the coming

Rooter. Boston Red Sox rooters, 1915. *George Grantham Bain Collection, Library of Congress*

season. Six pitchers, Ford, Quinn, Vaughn, Fisher, Caldwell and Warhop, are relied on to carry the team throughout the summer, and they are to be worked in turn with clock-like regularity" (*The Sporting News*, Feb. 2; Peter Morris). **2.** Syn. of *wheel*, 1. **3.** The rotary movement of a four-man umpire crew such that the closest umpire is in position to call a play; e.g., on a fly ball down the left field line, the third base umpire runs down the line to determine if the ball is fair or foul or legally caught, the home plate umpire comes up the third base line for a possible play on the runner tagging up from second, and the first base umpire moves in to home plate in the event a runner tries to score. **4.** See *batting rotation*. **5.** The spin on a pitched ball. **6.** A simple version of baseball in which the players are not divided into sides: one player bats until he is retired, and then another takes his place. "Already you can see boys playing . . . 'rotation' in every school yard and vacant lot" (*Cincinnati Meddler*, reprinted in *The Sporting Life*, Apr. 11, 1908; Peter Morris).

rotator A baseball player, esp. a pitcher, who is used sparingly (Maurice H. Weseen, *A Dictionary of American Slang*, 1934).

rotator cuff A tendon structure that encircles, stabilizes, supports, and strengthens the shoulder joint, formed by four muscles attached to the joint capsule. It connects the upper arm bone (humerus) to the shoulder blade (scapula). When these muscles contract, they pull on the tendons, allowing the shoulder to move in many directions. The most common injuries occur when the muscles are overused and become inflamed. A player may strain or tear his rotator cuff while pitching or throwing, an injury that can have a significant effect on a pitcher's career. Torn rotator cuffs were not diagnosed until 1985; before the term came into general use, it was said that a pitcher so injured had blown or blown out his arm. A rotator cuff injury used to mean certain retirement, but advances in materials, technology, and technique can return a pitcher to the mound. "[Steve] Carlton, 41, is coming back from an 1-8 record and a strained rotator cuff last year" (*St. Petersburg Times*, March 7, 1986). Strength exercises can help prevent the injury.

rotiball league Syn. of *Rotisserie League Baseball*.

Rotisserie League Baseball A popular *fantasy baseball league* game in which participants draft real players for imaginary teams. Teams typically each receive $260 to draft 23 players from either the American League, the National League, or both, filling slots by position. Players are picked through an open auction. Each team's performance is based on the cumulative statistics of its players in four offensive categories (batting average, runs batted in, home runs, and stolen bases) and four pitching categories (earned run average, walks, saves, and the ratio of walks plus hits to innings pitched), though various other categories may be substituted or added on a league-by-league basis. Trades are permissible. See Glen Waggoner, ed., *Rotisserie League Baseball*, 1984. See also *five by five*. Syn. *Roto*; *rotiball league*. ETYMOLOGY. The idea of a statistical baseball league was first suggested by writer and editor Daniel Okrent and five other baseball enthusiasts when they met in January 1980 at a now-defunct French bistro in New York City called La Rotisserie Française. Okrent (quoted in *The Orlando Sentinel*, March 26, 2000) called La Rotisserie a "lousy restaurant . . . the place meant nothing to us. We never went back there."

Roto Short for *Rotisserie League Baseball*.

Rouge Hose Nickname for the Boston Red Sox.

rough up To score against a pitcher, or for a pitcher to have runs scored against him. "[Ron] Guidry was roughed up for six runs in the first inning" (*New York Post*, Aug. 13, 1987).

round *hist.* **1.** Syn. of *inning*, 1. "There were three or four good plays in the eighth inning and a half of play, but they were not the kind to start you talking after the curtain had fallen on round nine" (*San Francisco Bulletin*, Apr. 30, 1913; Gerald L. Cohen). IST USE. 1859. "Amherst had the first innings, and 25 rounds were played and recorded" (*Pittsfield* [Mass.] *Sun*, July 7; Dean A. Sullivan). ETYMOLOGY. A term borrowed from boxing. **2.** The scoring of a run. IST USE. 1858. "Four Bases . . . shall constitute a round" (Rules of the Massachusetts Game, Rule 3, May 13).

round a base To run across and touch a base in such a manner that the distance and time to reach the next base are minimized.

round-arm delivery Syn. of *three-quarters delivery*. USAGE NOTE. John B. Foster (in *Collier's New Dictionary of the English Language*, 1908) defined the term as "an over the shoulder delivery somewhat similar to that of the cricket bowler." But the *Brooklyn Eagle* (Jan. 27, 1878; Peter Morris) noted that "no overhand throw can be made, nor can any ball be delivered, as in the case of round arm bowling in cricket." Morris concludes that "since the delivery is not synonymous with overhand, but is clearly above the waist, it must have been about three-quarters delivery."

round ball 1. A term most commonly applied to early baseball played in New England, such as the Massachusetts game. Robin Carver (*The Book of Sports*, 1834) equated the term with "base" or "goal ball." The term "round ball" was offered in the many letters submitted by New England old-timers to the Mills Commission; in describing the brand of early baseball that they and their forefathers played in their youth, most of these correspondents referred to the game as "round ball" (David Block, personal communication, Oct. 20, 2002). For example (in a letter from Henry Sargent of Grafton, Mass., to the Mills Commission, May 23, 1905): "Mr. [George H.] Upton [Upton, Mass.] believes Round Ball was played by his father in 1820, and has the tradition from his father that two generations before, i.e., directly after the revolutionary war, it was played and was not then a novelty" (John Thorn). A match of "round ball" was played on Wadleigh Field, near Bangor, Maine, between two neighborhood teams in 1844 (Preston D. Orem, *Baseball [1845–1881] from the Newspaper Accounts*, 1961). ETYMOLOGY. The term derives from the circular field of play (John Thorn, *The Boston Sunday Globe*, July 10, 2005). 2. The game of baseball (facetiously) as opposed to football. 3. A nickname for basketball, a game that now lays claim to the term almost universally.

rounder 1. Syn. of *revolver*. 2. An opportunity for a potential score in the English game of rounders when all members of a side but one have been called out. The remaining player may "call for the rounder" by getting three opportunities to strike the ball so far that he can circle the bases before the other team can return the ball (i.e., the batter hits a "home run"). If he is successful, the inning is prolonged and the whole side gets to bat again. In some instances, the "taking of the rounder" can occur when all but two players have been retired. This distinctive feature of rounders may have given the game its name.

rounders 1. A regional (western England) pseudonym for *English base-ball*. David Block (*Baseball Before We Knew It*, 2005, pp.22–31) showed that the term first appeared in William Clarke's *The Boy's Own Book: A Complete Encyclopedia of All the Diversions, Athletic, Scientific, and Recreative, of Boyhood and Youth* (2nd ed., 1828; first American ed., 1829) to describe English base-ball. It was the first description of a baseball-like game to appear in English, and introduced the diamond-shaped layout with four bases, although runners ran in a clockwise direction. 2. An English game characterized by a short one-handed bat and a five-base infield, the fifth base sometimes positioned as part of a disjointed square and sometimes as part of a pentagon configuration. The game was described by J.L. Williams in *The Every Boy's Book* (1841). If a batter strikes at and misses three pitches, he is out. If a runner is struck by a thrown ball while between bases, he is out. If a batter is caught out, his whole team is out, as well. The batters run counterclockwise around the bases, gradually losing men who have been put out, until no one is left in the batter's box, at which time the opposing team comes to bat. Yet the fielding team must rush to the batter's box as quickly as possible because if a player on the batting team seizes the ball and throws it at, and hits, an opposing player, the batting team remains at bat. The last batter may "call for the rounder" and circle the bases before the struck ball is returned, thereby allowing the whole side to bat again. During the 1840s and 1850s, rounders became distinct from English base-ball, and by the early 1870s rounders and baseball had diverged into two separate sports. However, the adult version of rounders in Great Britain changed its name to "base ball" in 1892 to differentiate it from the schoolyard version. The adult version features a diamond with larger dimensions, forcing or tagging runners at a base, a two-handed bat, no foul territory, and eleven players to a side. The original game is still played by clubs in the Liverpool region and in South Wales, and is known under the misnomer *Welsh baseball* in the United States. The children's version of rounders retained the name "rounders" and is currently a popular organized activity in many parts of the United Kingdom. According to David Block *(Baseball Before We Knew It*, 2005, p.161), there is no historical evidence in England or the United States that the term "rounders" was ever applied to a bat-and-ball game before its appearance in 1828 (William Clarke, *The Boy's Own Book*). Other than American reprints of Clarke's book, there are no records of the term "rounders" being used in the United States during the long era of baseball's advent and maturation. "Given that the name 'base-ball' predated 'rounders' in England by nearly a hundred years," wrote Block, "it is time to finally put to rest the tired old axiom that baseball descended from that 'ancient' English pastime."

round heel *hist.* A poor player (Al Schacht, *Al Schacht Dope Book*, 1944, p.43).

roundhouse curve A big, sweeping or looping curveball; one that leaves no doubt that it is arcing. Though impressive to watch, such a pitch has a trajectory that experienced batters can often spot, enabling them to hit the ball. Thrown by a right-handed pitcher, the roundhouse curve starts high and inside to a right-handed batter and finishes low and outside. "[During spring training the] big league sluggers, who hit any kind of pitching in the season, swing wildly at the garden variety of 'round house curve'" (John J. Evers and Hugh S. Fullerton, *Touching Second: The Science of Baseball*, 1910; Peter Morris). See also *jughandle*; *rainbow*, 1. Compare *overhand curve*. Syn. "roundhouse." IST USE. 1899. "The [Kid] Nichols curve is none of your roundhouse benders" (Buck Freeman, quoted in *The Washington Post*, Oct. 15; Peter Morris). ETYMOLOGY. Probably suggested by the

name and shape of the circular railroad structure known as a "roundhouse." Other slang roundhouses include the lavatory on a ship and the full, nothing-held-back swing of the prizefighter. An Associated Press story (Sept. 27, 1938) from London, collected by Peter Tamony, begs to be repeated here in part: "Jack Doyle, handsome Irish heavy weight, knocked himself out tonight in the second round of his fight with Eddie Phillips. Letting go with a 'roundhouse right,' 'the Irish thrush' missed an opponent, fell between the ropes and struck his head on the edge of the ring. He still was prone on the floor outside the ropes when the referee finished the count of ten."

roundhouse swing A wild swing by a batter. "[Rogers Hornsby] is especially powerful in the shoulders and arms. He swings freely but not with a 'round-house' swing, most of the force coming from well above the hips" (Thomas S. Rice, *Brooklyn Daily Eagle*, June 10, 1920; Peter Morris).

round-robin A tournament format in which each team plays every other team at least once. A loss does not necessarily mean elimination. The winner of such a tournament is the team that wins the highest percentage of its games. Compare *single elimination*; *double elimination*.

round the bases To trot around the bases, touching each one, after hitting a home run, triple, or double.

'round the horn See *around the horn*, 1.

round town A schoolboys' game, a version of late 19th-century *town ball*, played primarily in isolated and rural settings in the central Appalachian area (southwestern Virginia and northeastern Kentucky), in which the ball was struck by a paddle held in one hand and soaking of baserunners was allowed, and which featured "four bases in a circle" (Dennis Reedy, *School and Community History of Dickenson County, Virginia*, 1992). The game is little attested, and most references occur in reminiscences of childhood. Compare *straight town*. (David Ball)

round trip A home run. "They call a home run a 'round trip' in the West" (*Brooklyn Eagle*, May 13, 1900; Peter Morris). See also *round-tripper*. IST USE. 1899. "De big Dutchman [Honus Wagner] just bent one wid a round trip ticket" (Wright A. Patterson, *Jackson* [Mich.] *Citizen*, June 16; Peter Morris).

round-tripper Syn. of *home run*. IST USE. 1939. "[Bill] Dickey cracked his round-tripper over Rip Radcliff's reaching glove" (*The New York Times*, Sept. 22; David Shulman). See also *round trip*. ETYMOLOGY. From the rail or air ticket that takes one to a destination and then returns one to the point of origin. The wordplay at work here is a trip from home and then back to home.

rout 1. *n.* A defeat, usually a dramatic one. 2. *v.* To defeat handily or convincingly; e.g., to hit a pitcher hard and drive him from the game.

route An entire baseball game. The term is commonly applied to a pitcher when he pitches a complete game and is said to have "gone the route."

Route 66 A winding course taken by an outfielder unsure of the direction and speed of a batted ball. ETYMOLOGY. U.S. Highway 66 was an historic road between Los Angeles (later Santa Monica, Calif.) and Chicago from 1926 to 1985, until it was replaced by the Interstate Highway System. The road was a major path for migrants who traveled west, esp. during the Dust Bowl years of the 1930s.

rover 1. *hist.* Syn. of *right short*, 2. "Most sources point out that the 'rover' was actually a fifth infielder rather than a fourth outfielder. Other sources are more specific in noting that the rover was used only as an additional infielder between first and second base or as an additional catcher" (Jonathan Fraser Light, *The Cultural Encyclopedia of Baseball*, 1997, p.626). 2. Syn. of *roving instructor*. 3. [softball term] The 10th player in slow pitch softball who plays at various positions in the field depending on the circumstances; specif., the *short fielder*, 2. Syn. *roving fielder*.

roving fielder [softball term] The proper name for *rover*, 3.

roving instructor A coach who visits the various minor-league affiliates of a major-league team to provide instruction wherever needed. Syn. *rover*, 2.

rowdyism A style of play characterized by lively, scrappy, and aggressive tactics as exemplified by the Baltimore Orioles of the 1890s and the Gashouse Gang (St. Louis Cardinals) of the 1930s. John McGraw typified the bullying, belligerent manner of the Orioles, including fights, threats, and noisy behavior. Orioles manager Ned Hanlon attributed "rowdyism on the ball field [as] . . . largely the fault of the umpires, who allowed the players to go too far" (*The Sporting Life*, Oct. 30, 1897). Rowdyism also included unruly fan behavior: "There is reason to demand from the club owners that they turn some of their attention from eliminating 'rowdyism' from the diamond and direct it vigorously toward protecting the player from rowdies in the stands" (*St. Louis Post-Dispatch*, July 15, 1907; Peter Morris).

ROY Abbrev. for *Rookie of the Year.*

Royal Rooters A group of boisterous and raucous Boston Red Sox fans from 1901 to 1916. The group (100 to 300 members), which sat in the left field stands, was headed by mayor John "Honey Fitz" Fitzgerald, accompanied by brass bands incessantly singing its favorite song ("Tessie: You Are the Only, Only, Only," the words adapted for taunting opponents), and well fortified by pregame meetings at Michael "Nuf Ced" McGreevey's Third Base saloon at the corner of Ruggles and Tremont in Roxbury, Mass. USAGE NOTE. The term has also been applied to fans of the Boston Braves in the late 1890s and in 1914.

Royals 1. Nickname for the American League Central Division expansion franchise located in Kansas City, Mo., since 1969. ETYMOLOGY. The "royal" in the team's name is an allusion to the American Royal Association, which sponsors an annual parade, livestock show, horse show, rodeo, and barbecue. The name was selected from 17,000 entries submitted in a 1968 contest held among the fans. 2. Nickname for the International League franchise located in Montreal from 1928 to 1960.

RP Abbrev. for *relief pitcher*, 1.

RPA 1. Abbrev. for *run producing average*. 2. Abbrev. for *run productivity average*.

RRF 1. Abbrev. for *runs responsible for*, 1. 2. Abbrev. for *runs responsible for*, 2. 3. Abbrev. for *runs responsible for*, 3.

RSAA Abbrev. for *runs saved above average.*

RSI Abbrev. for *run support index.*

rubber **1.** The rectangular slab of whitened rubber, 24 inches long and 6 inches wide, set into and atop the pitcher's mound so that the distance from the front edge of the rubber to the back point of home plate is 60 feet, 6 inches. It was introduced in 1893, with its size altered to its current dimensions for the 1895 season. The pitcher must come in contact with the rubber while delivering the ball to the batter. The ball is not in play until the pitcher, with the ball in his hand, steps on the rubber. The rubber is the same size at most levels of baseball, although the Little League rubber is 18 inches long and 4 inches wide. Rubber was used earlier than 1893; e.g., "Many ways may be devised for detecting any encroachment of the pitcher beyond the front line of the box, such . . . as a strip of thin rubber, several inches high, painted white, placed longitudinally along the front line" (*The Sporting Life*, Nov. 5, 1884; Peter Morris). See also *pitcher's plate.* Syn. *pitcher's rubber; pitching rubber; slab,* 1; *firing line.* **2.** *hist.* Syn. of *home plate.* "[E.C. Foster] played in 148 games . . . [and] crossed the rubber fifty times" (Alfred H. Spink, *The National Game,* 2nd ed., 1911, p.226). IST USE. 1884 (*De Witt's Base-Ball Guide,* p.20; Edward J. Nichols). **3.** *hist.* A trainer. "The need of a trainer, or a rubber, is now keenly felt by manager [Frank] Selee" (*The Boston Globe,* Apr. 2, 1900; Peter Morris). **4.** *hist.* A mouth guard used by catchers. "The catcher's rubber . . . protected the teeth and mouth only" (*Grand Rapids* [Mich.] *Morning Democrat,* Sept. 4, 1883; Peter Morris). **5.** Short for *rubber game.*

rubber arm **1.** A flexible, resilient, and durable pitching arm, frequently applied to that of a relief pitcher who can work often. IST USE. 1932. "George Connally has been good in relief, with his rubber arm and all" (Cleveland Indians manager Roger Peckinpaugh, quoted in *Brooklyn Daily Eagle,* May 16; Peter Morris). **2.** A pitcher with a rubber arm; a player whose arm never seems to tire. IST USE. 1933. "Name given to a pitcher who can work often" (*Famous Sluggers and Their Records of 1932*).

rubber band A pitcher with a weak arm.

rubber bat A lucky bat used by a player who gets more than his share of fluke hits. The term derives from the fanciful notion of a bat that bends and stretches to make contact with the ball. IST USE. 1933 (Edgar G. Brands, *The Sporting News,* Feb. 23).

rubber belly See "ol' rubber belly."

rubber chicken circuit The winter banquet circuit, sarcastically renamed for the poor quality of its mass-produced main courses. Under the headline "He'll Duck Rubber Chicken Circuit," Casey Stengel told *The Sporting News* (Oct. 18, 1950): "I'm 60 years old. I'm too old for that banquet stuff. You get no rest."

rubber-coated baseball A special ball designed for indoor drills and play.

rubber game The last and deciding game of a series when the previous games have been split; e.g., the seventh game of the World Series. Syn. *rubber,* 5. IST USE. 1855. "The rubber game between these two clubs was played on Wednesday last" (*Spirit of the Times,* Oct. 20; Peter Morris). ETYMOLOGY. When each side wins one of the first two games in the card game of contract bridge, the third and deciding game is called the "rubber game." The transfer to baseball makes sense as most regular-season series consist of three games.

rubbing mud A mildly abrasive soil that is smeared on baseballs (by an umpire, normally the home-plate umpire, or by the umpires' attendant) before the game to soften the seams and to remove the "factory gloss" or shine without discoloring the balls or damaging their covers, therefore making them easier to grip and throw. This procedure dates back many years to a time when tobacco juice or a wad of dirt from the playing field was used. Today both major leagues use a special commercial product known as Lena Blackburne Baseball Rubbing Mud, named for the Philadelphia Athletics coach who, in 1938, discovered a mud with just the right qualities at a still-secret site near Pennsauken Creek, a tributary of the Delaware River in Palmyra, Burlington County, N.J. The mud contains about 90 per-

Rubbing mud. Lena Blackburne in 1929. *National Baseball Library and Archives, Cooperstown, N.Y.*

cent ultrafine quartz grains, and very little clay; it resembles thick pea soup or chocolate mousse, looks like chocolate pudding, feels as smooth as cold cream, and when applied to the ball does not make the cover mushy. A secret organic ingredient is added to the mud to give it a fine grit. According to Princeton Univ. geologist Kenneth S. Deffeyes (*The New York Times*, Apr. 6. 1982), the mud was probably ground up by the Wisconsinian ice that covered the area during the last ice age in the Pleistocene Epoch more than 10,000 years ago. The mud was introduced to the American League in the late 1930s by Connie Mack and was adopted by the National League in the 1950s. Each major-league team receives at least six pounds per season; most minor-league teams and many college teams use the mud. Syn. *baseball mud.*

rube *hist.* A player from, or who appears to be from, the country. It was once a very common nickname; more than 25 major-league players have been known as Rube, including Edward "Rube" Waddell, George "Rube" Walberg, Richard "Rube" Marquard, and Ray "Rube" Bressler. ETYMOLOGY. General slang for a farmer or country man, which appears to derive from "Reuben," a name long associated with country bumpkins.

rubelet *hist.* A base hit obtained from the pitching delivery of Rube Waddell (1897–1910). 1ST USE. 1907 (*New York Evening Journal*, Apr. 18; Edward J. Nichols).

rubinoff *hist.* A player in need of a haircut (Edwin M. Rumill, *Christian Science Monitor*, Sept. 1, 1937).

rub-off sign Syn. of *wipe-off sign.*

rub up For a pitcher to move his hands with a rotary motion, and some ritualistic intensity, over the baseball to obtain a firmer grip before pitching it.

rug Syn. of *artifical turf.* "The [Cincinnati] Reds play on a rug, and while the game requires both bat and ball, it isn't the same game" (George V. Higgins, *The Progress of the Seasons*, 1989, p.38).

rugball A tongue-in-cheek term for baseball played on artificial turf.

rug rat A small, but intense, player. New York Mets coach Bill Robinson (quoted in *USA Today*, Aug. 14, 1986): "I call them [Lenny Dykstra and Wally Backman] little rug rats. They scurry around, getting on, stealing bases. They're mean and aggressive and they're never satisfied. Little guys are like that." ETYMOLOGY. From the slang expression for "infant."

rule-book double The proper term for a *ground-rule double* in which a batted ball bounces in fair territory and goes over the fence and into the stands. The term has been used by Chicago Cubs announcer Chip Caray. See also *automatic double.*

Rule 5 draft A *draft* of unprotected minor-league players, in which major-league clubs select in reverse order of their winning percentages at the close of the preceding championship season, with teams from each league choosing alternately. A player not on a major-league 40-man roster is eligible to be drafted if a) he was 18 or younger when he first signed a pro contract, and this is the fourth Rule 5 draft since he signed, or b) he was 19 or older when he first signed a pro contract, and this is the third Rule 5 draft since he signed. A selected player must remain on the 25-man major-league roster (or disability list) for the entire season or be offered back to the original club for half of the $50,000 draft price (prior to 1987, the draft price was $25,000). Since a returned Rule 5 player must first be placed on outright waivers, a third club could claim the player (that club would have to keep the player in the major leagues all season, or offer him back to his original club). There is also a minor-league phase of the Rule 5 draft: Class AAA teams can draft players for $12,000, and Class AA teams can draft players for $4,000. Players selected in the minor-league phase do not have to be offered back to their original clubs. Incorrectly spelled "Rule V draft." Syn. *major-league draft.* ETYMOLOGY. From Rule 5 of the Major League Rules.

Rule 4 draft Syn. of *first-year player draft.* ETYMOLOGY. From Rule 4 of the Major League Rules.

rules 1. See *official playing rules.* 2. See *official scoring rules.* 3. See *ground rules.* 4. See *Major League Rules.*

rumble Syn. of *rhubarb.*

run 1. *n.* A complete circuit of the bases, from first to second to third to home, in that order. 2. *n.* The score made by an offensive player. A run is credited to the team and the individual player after he (or his pinch runner) has touched all bases in order and arrives home safely before the third out in the offense's half inning. It is baseball's only unit of scoring. Abbrev. *R.* IST USE. 1845. Although the term "run" was not chosen in Rule 8 of the original rules of the Knickerbocker Base Ball Club (the terms "count" and "ace" were so chosen to identify a score), the term did appear on the club's preprinted score sheets (David Block, *Baseball Before We Knew It,* 2005, p.82) and in the *New York Morning News* report of the game (Oct. 22, 1845) between the New York Ball Club and Brooklyn held Oct. 21, 1845, at the Elysian Fields in Hoboken, N.J. ETYMOLOGY. The term was borrowed from cricket. 3. *v.* To act as a baserunner. IST USE. 1845. "Three balls being struck at and missed and the last one caught, is a hand out; if not caught is considered fair, and the striker bound to run" (Knickerbocker Rules, Rule 11th, Sept. 23). 4. *v.* To manage a baseball team. 5. *n.* The path or act of a pitch as it moves laterally across the plate or through the strike zone, or out of the strike

zone. 6. *v.* For a pitch to move in or out of the strike zone. "[Tom Glavine's] fastball sinks and runs with above average movement [and his] changeup runs away from righties" (*Sports Illustrated,* Oct. 12, 1998, p.51). "[Mark Buehrle was] using both sides of the plate, running the ball in on you" (Bret Boone, quoted in *ESPN The Magazine,* June 24, 2002). "Richie [Sexson] dives across the plate a lot, and the ball ran back in [and hit him]" (Baltimore Orioles manager Mike Hargrove, quoted in *The Baltimore Sun,* June 15, 2003). 7. *v.* For an umpire to eject a player, manager, or coach from the game. "[Boston Red Sox manager Joe Morgan] suffered his first big-league ejection when umpire Dale Scott ran him in the eighth inning" (*Tampa Tribune,* Aug. 7, 1988).

run and hit 1. *n.* Syn. of *run-and-hit play.* Sometimes spelled "run-and-hit." 2. *v.* To attempt or execute the run-and-hit play.

run-and-hit game Use of the *run-and-hit play* as part of a team's offense. "The run-and-hit game can be worked successfully with a team of fast players" (Connie Mack, quoted in *The Washington Post,* Apr. 24, 1904; Peter Morris).

run-and-hit play An offensive tactic in which a baserunner is given the green light to steal and the batter has the option of swinging at the pitch. As the runner starts with the pitch, the batter eyes the ball in hopes that it is one he can hit. The runner forces the middle infielder to cover second base, thereby opening a hole for the batter to hit into. If the ball is hit safely, the runner will be able to claim, at least, an extra base. If the ball is not swung at or is swung at and missed, the runner finds himself in the midst of a steal, which he may or may not accomplish depending on his speed and the skill of the catcher. The run-and-hit play differs from the *hit-and-run play* in that the batter chooses whether to swing; i.e., he does not have to protect the runner. See also *run-and-hit game.*

run average The total number of runs (whether earned or unearned) allowed by a pitcher per nine innings. Given that earned run average does not fairly assign responsibility to pitchers for runs scored when errors are involved, run average is in many ways a better measure of pitcher effectiveness. Abbrev. *RA*, 2.

runaway game A game in which scoring binges of great magnitude put the game out of reach for the losing team. Some youth leagues have rules concerning the limitation on runaway games; e.g., once the team at bat scores 10 runs in its half of an inning, the sides change regardless of the number of outs at the time.

run batted in A run that is caused by a particular batter and that is officially credited to him as part of his record. A run batted in is credited when a runner scores as the result of a base hit, sacrifice or sacrifice fly, hit by pitch, base on balls, infield out (other than a double play), fielder's choice, catcher's interference, or obstruction. The batter himself is counted when he hits a home run. The number of runs batted in that a batter accumulates in a season is an important conventional measure of that player's offensive performance; however, sabermetricians have shown that a batter's number of runs batted in is influenced by his batting order position and, in particular, how many players tend to be on base when he bats. See also *ribbie*. Abbrev. *RBI*, 1. Syn. *cookie*, 2. 1ST USE. 1879. John Thorn and Pete Palmer (*The Hidden Game of Baseball*, 1985, p.20) have stated that the term was used by "a Buffalo newspaper in 1879." USAGE NOTE. The *Chicago Tribune* invented the run batted in statistic and first published RBI totals for Chicago players in 1880: "The column of 'runs batted in' is computed upon the basis of results, but not of clean hits alone; that is to say, each batsman is credited with the result of his batting in the matter of bringing in runs, and no account is made of the fielding errors on the side of the opposing team" (*Chicago Tribune*, July 11, 1880; Peter Morris). When readers complained that the statistic discriminated against batters at the top of the order, the *Tribune* apologized and stopped publishing the statistic. In 1891, the National League rules committee rejected Henry Chadwick's suggestion that the run batted in be recognized in official records and box scores. John Lewis (personal communication, Oct. 22, 2002) notes that *The Ohio State Journal* in Apr. 1891 observed,

"The scorers are not paying any attention to Mr. Chadwick's rule about keeping a record of runs batted in by each player. The idea does not appear to go. It is doubtful even if Nick Young's mandate would make the official scorers pay attention to it. The scoring is complicated enough now without adding any more labor to it." In 1920, the run batted in gained official status (it was first recorded in the *Reach Official American League Base Ball Guide*), but most newspaper box scores did not show runs batted in for another 10 years, when Hack Wilson's season record (191 in 1930) gained widespread acceptance of the RBI in box scores.

run differential Runs scored minus runs allowed. A team's run differential for a season can be correlated with its winning percentage, although not as well as a computation on the Pythagorean method.

rundown *n.* 1. The act of the defense in an attempt to tag out a runner between bases. It often requires the fielders to throw the ball back and forth several times as the runner tries to avoid being tagged out. Syn. *run up,* 2; *run-out*. 2. Syn. of *running bases*.

run down *v.* 1. To tag out a runner who has been caught between two bases. See also *run up,* 1. 1ST USE. 1877. "[John] Morrill, in attempting to run down [Joe] Gerhardt between first and second, allowed [Orator] Schaffer [*sic*] to score" (*The Boston Globe*, June 29; Peter Morris). 2. To catch a fly ball after a long run; e.g., "Smith ran down the fly after a hard sprint."

rundown play A strategic move in which the offensive team allows one runner to get trapped in a rundown while another runner uses the opportunity to steal home. See also *run-up play*. 1ST USE. 1908 (*Spalding's Official Base Ball Guide*, p.69; Edward J. Nichols).

run for the cycle For a player to be retired at first base, second base, third base, and home (not necessarily in that order) during a game. Ron Luciano (*The Umpire Strikes Back*, 1982) erred when he claimed that Kansas City Royals outfielder Lou Piniella accomplished this feat ("He ran for the cycle. In a single game he managed to get himself

Rundown. When it is time to run backwards. Griffith Stadium, Washington, D.C. *Photograph by Joseph Baylor Roberts*

thrown out at every base"). But Thomas J. Ruane (personal communication, Aug. 25, 2000) has documented at least 22 instances of players getting thrown out at all four bases in games between 1963 and 2000; e.g., Minnesota Twins designated hitter Marty Cordova was thrown out at first base, forced at second base, caught stealing third base, and forced out at home in a game on June 4, 1999. Compare *hit for the cycle*.

run-getter *hist.* A batter whose primary function is to score runs, as opposed to driving them in. Alfred H. Spink (*The National Game*, 2nd ed., 1911) referred to Ty Cobb as a "run-getter par excellence" (p.242) and Briscoe Lord as a "very fair run-getter" (p.249). "The value of run-getters on a ball team has not always been appreciated by the management" (*The Sporting Life*, July 18, 1891; Peter Morris). See also *home run getter*. IST USE. 1869. "Treacey was the other run getter" (*Brooklyn Eagle*, Sept. 7; Peter Morris).

run-getting Scoring runs. "Los Angeles began run-getting in the first inning" (*Los Angeles Times*, Nov. 21, 1887).

"run hard" An instruction by a base coach to a runner who is approaching the base. "If the play is going to be close, the coach advises the runner to 'run hard,' at the same time circling the arm hard" (O.H. Vogel, *Ins and Outs of Baseball*, 1952; Peter Morris).

run his ankles hot To move swiftly.

run in **1.** *v.* To pitch close to the batter's body; e.g., "Smith's pitch ran in on the hands of the batter." "On the first pitch, he [Calvin Schiraldi] ran the ball in on me" (Ray Knight, quoted in *The Washington Post*, Oct. 26, 1986). **2.** *v.* To score a run. **3.** *n.* A run that has scored.

run into the box [softball term] An illegal movement in which the pitcher delivers the ball while running toward the plate.

run it out See *run out*, 1. IST USE. 1910. "The manager cannot keep the players from hitting [during spring training], so he turns their batting to his own purposes, and whenever they hit a fair ball he orders them to 'run it out' hard to first and jog all the way around the bases" (John J. Evers and Hugh S. Fullerton, *Touching Second; The Science of Baseball*; Peter Morris).

runner **1.** An offensive player who is advancing toward, touching, or returning to any base; a *baserunner*. IST USE. 1845. "A player running the bases shall be out, if the ball is in the hands of an adversary on the base, or the runner is touched with it before he makes his base" (Knickerbocker Rules, Rule 13th, Sept. 23). **2.** A pitch moving laterally. "A right-handed runner breaks right-handed bats, because it runs in hitters' hands while they try to shorten their swing" (Dan Jennings, quoted in Alan Schwarz, BaseballAmerica.com, Nov. 14, 2006).

runner in motion A baserunner who starts to run to the next base as the pitcher delivers the ball on a 3–2 count with two outs.

runner in scoring position A runner on second base or on third base. The term is often used in the plural when computing a player's batting average or slugging percentage when runners are in scoring position. See also *scoring position*. Abbrev. *RISP*.

runners at the corners Runners at first base and third base.

runner's box Syn. of *45-foot lane*.

runner's fielder's choice An attempted advance to another base by a runner, such as on a wild pitch or passed ball. The term has been used by ESPN.

runner's interference An act by a baserunner that impedes, hinders, or confuses any fielder attempting to make a play; e.g., leaving the baseline for the obvious purpose of crashing into the pivot man on an attempted double play, or intentionally deflecting the course of a batted or thrown ball. See also *interference*, 1.

runners left The number of baserunners stranded on base at the end of an inning.

runners left in scoring position **1.** The number of runners on second base and third base stranded by a given batter or team at the end of an inning during a game. **2.** The number of runners on second base and third base stranded by a given batter or team during a game, regardless of the number of outs.

runners moved up A statistic in modern box scores to indicate the number of runners advanced to another base by the efforts of the batter, who made an out.

running bases A playground game in which two fielders stand near their bases and toss a ball back and forth, trying to tag out a runner attempting to steal the base he is not occupying. A runner tagged out three times becomes a fielder. The game works best when an agile runner is willing to slide, and fielding misplays are common enough to give the runner a chance. The game is also played with multiple runners. See also *pickle,* 3; *hot box,* 2. Syn. *rundown,* 2.

running catch A defensive play in which a batted ball is caught on the fly by a swiftly moving fielder. IST USE. 1858 (Chadwick Scrapbooks; Edward J. Nichols).

running game **1.** An offensive strategy that stresses speed, hit-and-run plays, and stealing. "Their inability to stop Oakland's running game is killing the [Toronto] Blue Jays" (*Tampa Tribune*, Oct. 6, 1989). **2.** A baseball game characterized by many baserunners and attempted steals.

run on **1.** To attempt to stretch a hit into extra bases. **2.** To attempt to steal on a pitcher or catcher.

"run on anything" A command given to a baserunner with two out to run as soon as the ball is hit.

run-out *n./hist.* Syn. of *rundown*, 1. "An assist should be given to each player who handles the ball in a run-out or other play of the kind" (*Reach's Official American Association Base Ball Guide*, 1883, p.44; Peter Morris).

run out *v.* **1.** To run toward first base at maximum speed regardless of where or how the ball has been batted. "[Baltimore Orioles manager Sam Perlozzo] was displeased with specific patterns of sloppy behavior, such as not running out ground balls" (*The Baltimore Sun*, March 28, 2006). The reward for running out a fly ball comes on those occasions when the ball is dropped or missed and the runner gets to take one or more bases. See also *run it out*. **2.** *hist.* Said of a runner when he is tagged out between the bases in a rundown. "A player is said to be run out when he is touched between the bases in trying to get back to the base he left" (Henry Chadwick, *The Game of Base Ball*, 1868, p.44). IST USE. 1862. "Run out between bases—Reach by John Oliver" (*Brooklyn Eagle* box score note, July 22; Peter Morris). **3.** To put a player in the game. "I appreciated him [Baltimore Orioles manager Johnny Oates] running me out there game after game" (Jeffrey Hammonds, quoted in *The Baltimore Sun*, July 9, 1994).

run out the string For the batter to work the count to three balls and two strikes; to wait out the pitcher in the hope of getting a base on balls. Syn. *run the count*.

run potential The average number of runs scored in a given *base–out situation*. The first estimates of run potential were published by George R. Lindsey (*Operations Research*, July–Aug. 1963). Syn. *expected runs*.

run producing average A method for evaluating a player's offensive performance, calculated by multiplying the player's total for singles, doubles, triples, and home runs by a weight associated with each, adding these products, and then dividing by the number of at-bats. The computation of the weights is based on the run potential for each of these types of hits. Primarily due to the absence of the base on balls in the formula, the method is only a mediocre predictor of offensive performance. The method was proposed by George R. Lindsey (*Operations Research*, July–Aug. 1963); the name was used for the first time in an essay by Lindsey in Shaul P. Ladany and Robert E. Machel, eds (*Optimal Strategies in Sports*, 1977). Abbrev. *RPA*, 1.

run production Scoring.

run productivity average A method for evaluating a player's offensive performance, computed by multiplying the player's total for each of the ways he can get on base (walks, singles, doubles, etc.) by the runs produced (runs scored and runs batted in, minus home runs) associated with it, and then adding the products. As the components of runs produced are seriously biased toward indicators of a batter's offensive performance, run productivity average has been found to be only a mediocre predictor of offensive performance. The method was devised by Steve Mann in 1977. Abbrev. *RPA*, 2.

runs above replacement The number of runs created for a batter above that expected by a replacement-level player at the player's position. Abbrev. *RAR*.

run-sauntered-in *hist.* A run that scores on a wild pitch or passed ball. "To avoid acci-

dents, arguments, and 'runs-sauntered-in,' the best advice a young catcher ever got was to expect every pitch to be a wild pitch" (Gordon S. "Mickey" Cochrane, *Baseball: The Fan's Game*, 1939, p.41; Peter Morris).

runs created An estimate of the number of team runs that would result from a player's offensive contributions, as derived from one of several formulas. To compute runs created by the most basic formula, multiply the number of times that a player gets on base by the player's number of total bases, and then divide by the player's number of plate appearances. More technical versions include stolen bases, caught stealing, grounding into double plays, sacrifices, and sacrifice flies. To give an example of its range, the 1982 Montreal Expos included the National League leader (Al Oliver, with 124) and the league's lowest among regular players (Doug Flynn, with 29). Babe Ruth is the single-season (238 in 1921) and career (2,847) leader. The basic version of runs created is a good predictor of offensive performance, roughly comparable to *on-base plus slugging*, *batter's run average*, and total average; the technical versions are very good predictors except for extremely good and poor hitters. The measure was created by Bill James and first described in his self-published *Baseball Abstract* (1978) under the term "runs contributed," with the current term first used in his *Baseball Abstract* (1979). It is described in James' first conventionally published *Baseball Abstract* (1982). Abbrev. *RC*, 1.

runs created above average A normalized version of runs created formulated by Lee Sinins for his *Sabermetric Baseball Encyclopedia*: "It's the difference between a player's runs created total and the total for an average player who used the same amount of his team's outs." It is park adjusted. Abbrev. *RCAA*.

runs created above position A normalized version of runs created considering the average performance at a given player's regular position. The measure was formulated by Lee Sinins for his *Sabermetric Baseball Encyclopedia*. Abbrev. *RCAP*.

runs created per game Syn. of *runs created per 27 outs*. Abbrev. *RC/G*.

runs created per 25 outs See *runs created per 27 outs*. Abbrev. *RC/25*.

runs created per 27 outs A method for evaluating a player's offensive performance by estimating how many runs would be scored in a game if that player could record every plate appearance. The name is misleading because the number of outs that a team usually records in a nine-inning game is approximately 25 rather than 27, primarily due to outs on base. As a consequence, it is sometimes referred to as *runs created per 25 outs*. The measure is calculated by multiplying the player's runs created in a season by 25, and then dividing by the number of outs for which the player was responsible during that season. The measure was created by Bill James and appears without a title in his first conventionally published *Baseball Abstract* (1982) and as *runs created per game* in his *Baseball Abstract* (1983). See *offensive earned run average* for an analogous method. Abbrev. *RC/27*.

runs line Baseball betting based on the run differential between the two teams (analogous to a point spread in other sports). Gamblers betting on the favorite give a certain number of runs, or those betting on the underdog receive a given number of runs, rather than lay money. See also *money line*; *over or under*.

runs per at-bat The average number of at-bats it takes a player to score a run. The best lifetime figure is Babe Ruth's 3.87; the best single-season number is Billy Hamilton's 2.85 in 1894. The measure was developed by Richard Zitrin and Jules Tygiel, and evaluated by Bill James in his *Baseball Abstract* (1987). Abbrev. *RABS*.

runs per game *hist.* A statistical measure of player performance recorded by pioneer baseball writer Henry Chadwick beginning in 1865, expressed in *average and over* format, in which runs scored was divided by games played (see John Thorn and Pete Palmer, *The Hidden Game of Baseball*, 1985).

runs per win The number of additional runs a team would need to score in a given season to win one more game during that season. Although it varies from season to season depending on the average number of runs that teams are scoring in a game, it is usually around 10 runs per win. It is assumed that the extra 10 runs are distributed randomly across the entire season's games, and that on average one of these 10 runs will occur in a game in which the run will help turn a defeat into a victory (e.g., turning a loss into a tie which is eventually won in extra innings).

runs prevented A term used by STATS Inc. in *Baseball Scoreboard* for *pitcher run average*, esp. when applied to relief pitchers. See also *adjusted runs prevented*.

runs produced An informal statistical measurement that equals runs scored plus runs batted in, minus home runs. Of unknown origin, the measure was evaluated by Bill James (*Baseball Abstract*, 1987).

runs responsible for **1.** A player performance statistic that includes all runs scored following a batter's action, whether or not the batter was credited with a run batted in. It includes runs scored on ground-ball double plays and errors on batted balls. The statistic was defined by Elias Sports Bureau in *Baseball Analyst* (1985), and player performance in late-inning pressure situations was included in *Baseball Analyst* (1985 through 1988). Abbrev. *RRF*, 1. **2.** The official major-league statistic for runs batted in from 1920 through 1927. Abbrev. *RRF*, 2. **3.** The label for earned runs used in the Pacific Coast League in 1918 (Carlos Bauer, *The Statistical Record of the Early Coast League, 1903 through 1957*, vol. 1, 2004). Abbrev. *RRF*, 3.

runs saved above average A normalized measure of the average number of runs a pitcher gives up per inning. It was formulated by Lee Sinins for his *Sabermetric Baseball Encyclopedia*. Abbrev. *RSAA*.

run support The average number of runs that a team scores for a given starting pitcher in a given year. Pitchers with unusually high run support will tend to have a good won-lost percentage even with a poor earned run average; analogously, pitchers with unusually low run support will tend to have a poor won-lost percentage even with a good earned run average. There are several methods of calculating run support: runs scored multiplied by 9 and divided by number of innings pitched;

runs per game (regardless of the number of innings pitched); runs per inning (for the innings that the pitcher was in the game); and runs scored while the pitcher was the pitcher of record, divided by the number of starts. The measure was described by Bill James in his self-published *Baseball Abstract* (1977) and in his first conventionally published *Baseball Abstract* (1982). Syn. *pitcher run support.* EXTENDED USE. Scoring goals to help a hockey goaltender win a game. Columbus Blue Jackets goalie Marc Denis (quoted in *The Baltimore Sun*, Dec. 11, 2001) after his team defeated the New Jersey Devils, 3–1: "You go from three shutouts in a row to three goals against the Stanley Cup finalists. You'll never hear me complain about that. Definitely, I got some run support."

run support index An adjusted measure of a pitcher's average run support, proposed by Chris Jaffe at a research presentation during the 34th national convention of the Society for American Baseball Research, July 2004. Abbrev. *RSI.*

run the count Syn. of *run out the string.*

run through the bag For the batter-runner to run at full speed and stride until passing first base. After hitting a routine grounder to shortstop and beating the throw to first base, Marty Castillo commented (quoted in *The Sporting News*, Oct. 15, 1984), "I just put my head down and ran through the bag. The adreneline [sic] flows a little more in this type of game and you give more of yourself."

run up 1. *v.* To *run down* a runner on the basepath. IST USE. 1893. " 'Pete' Lohman performed the artistic work of the day . . . in 'running up' three men at once between bases" (*San Francisco Examiner*, Apr. 23; Peter Morris). 2. *n.* Syn. of *rundown,* 1. "Don't dodge with an opponent caught in a run up. Make him run hard, before you throw, so that he can't stop quickly and turn back" (Kid Nichols, quoted in *St. Louis Post-Dispatch*, Apr. 7, 1904). 3. *v.* To pitch a ball up and in; e.g., "I threw a 2–1 fastball in and he swung at it, so I tried it again and it ran up and in" (Andy Benes, quoted in *The Baltimore Sun*, Aug. 11, 1994). 4. *v.* To score more runs than necessary. 5. *v.* For a batter to move his hands on the bat before bunting (Zack Hample, *Watching Baseball Smarter*, 2007, p.225).

run-up play A defensive play in which a limited number of throws should be made to tag out a trapped baserunner. The general principle is to drive the runner back toward the base from which he started. The defensive player with the ball should run directly at the runner, holding the ball, until he forces the runner to make his break (*Athletic Journal*, May 1945). See also *rundown play.*

runway 1. The *basepath.* IST USE. 1879. "Run ways are to be filled in with clay and pressed" (*Detroit Post and Tribune*, Apr. 22; Peter Morris). 2. Syn. of *alley,* 4. 3. "The corridor that connects the dugout to the concourse beneath the stands" (Zack Hample, *Watching Baseball Smarter*, 2007, p.226).

run with the ball For an outfielder to take a couple of steps after catching a fly ball and before being in proper position to throw it. A 1956 scouting report on Roberto Clemente (quoted in Branch Rickey, *Branch Rickey's Little Blue Book*, 1995, p.59) noted, "He has a beautiful throwing arm. However, he runs with the ball almost every time he makes a throw, and that's bad."

ruptured duck 1. A line drive that drops suddenly and precipitously. 2. Nickname for the eagle insignia patch worn by players returning from World War II military service and authorized by Major League Baseball. The patch was worn in 1945, but many players chose not to wear it, not wanting to call attention to their war years. By 1946, no players were wearing the patch.

Ruptured duck.

rush seat An unreserved general admission or bleacher seat. ETYMOLOGY. The term, rarely used today, originated in the 19th century, when such seats were suddenly opened to the onslaught (or "rush") of the crowd as it poured through the gate before a game.

rusty gate See *swing like a rusty gate*.

Ruthian Colossal, dramatic, prodigious, magnificent; with great power. The term derives from the hitting style and lusty demeanor of Babe Ruth. The term has been applied to several nouns, such as: Ruthian clout, Ruthian drive, Ruthian quality, Ruthian smack, Ruthian smash, Ruthian swat, Ruthian swing, Ruthian proportions, and Ruthian appetite. It sometimes shows up as "Babe Ruthian"; e.g., "a fine Babe Ruthian cameo by Joe Don Baker as the Whammer" (*Newsweek*, review of the movie *The Natural*, May 28, 1984). Texas Rangers pitching coach Tom House, on pitcher Nolan Ryan (quoted in *Sports Illustrated*, Oct. 4, 1993, p.46): "He's Ruthian. A tier above superstars today." Bruce Lowitt (*St. Petersburg Times*, Apr. 15, 1999): "Ruthian is baseballese for awesome power. Babe Ruth is in the dictionary, but cobb is just a salad." IST USE. 1920. "A mighty Ruthian clout by Jacobson . . . tied the score in the ninth" (*The New York Times*, June 8). EXTENDED USE. Extraordinarily great in size or extent in any endeavor. Mike Capuzzo (*Sports Illustrated*, Dec. 7, 1992): "Babe Ruth's myth is so great that he has entered the American vernacular (Ruthian: larger than life)." John Watters (*Sports Illustrated*, May 2, 1994, p.60): "[West Indian cricket batsman Brian] Lara's 375 runs against England last week was, well, Ruthian." Computer writer Mike Himowitz (*The Baltimore Sun*, Feb. 28, 2002): "Say a publisher with a million customers releases a new version of a program that installs successfully 99 percent of the time. That would be a Ruthian slugging percentage." When asked if his passing feats had a "Ruthian quality," Miami Dolphins quarterback Dan Marino responded (*The Baltimore Sun*, Nov. 26, 1995), "Ruthian? You mean the candy bar?"

Ryanesque In the manner of pitcher Nolan Ryan; specif., said of a pitcher's sheer speed and overwhelming power over an extended period of time. Twenty-year-old pitcher Terrell Wade was "a walk-on who went from raw recruit to Nolan Ryanesque fastballer" (*USA Today*, July 19, 1993).

Ryan Express Both the nickname for and the baseball career of pitcher Nolan Ryan (1966–1993). "With the suddenness of a crackling fastball, the Ryan Express came to the end of the line" (Mike Dodd, *USA Today*, Sept. 24, 1993).

Ryanitis A mock disease that "mysteriously struck hitters on the day they were scheduled to face all-time strikeout leader Nolan Ryan" (Tom Weir, *USA Today*, March 6, 1987). The symptoms vary, but the result is that batters tried to get out of the lineup rather than face Ryan.

Ryan's Express Nolan Ryan's fastball. The term is a play on the 1965 movie *Von Ryan's Express*, based on David Westheimer's book of the same name about an American soldier in World War II leading fellow prisoners of war on a daring escape from the Germans in Italy.

Ruthian. Babe Ruth at White House, Dec. 7, 1921. *George Grantham Bain Collection, Library of Congress*

S

S **1.** Scorecard and box score abbrev. for *sacrifice*, 1. **2.** Abbrev. for *save*, 2. **3.** Abbrev. for successful *steal* of a base.

SA Abbrev. for *slugging average*.

sabermetrician One who engages in sabermetrics. A letter soliciting subscribers for *Sabermetric Review* begins with the salutation "Dear Sabermetrician." *Time* magazine (Sept. 5, 1983) referred to sabermetricians as "a small numbers-crunching band of men who call themselves baseball scientists."

sabermetrics The study and mathematical analysis of baseball statistics and records, with the goal of discovering objective knowledge about the basic principles that underlie the game. Examples of areas of study include the formulation and testing of methods for evaluating player or team performance, and the analysis of the value of strategic moves such as attempted stolen bases and sacrifice bunts during games. The term is often incorrectly applied to uses of baseball statistics for other goals, such as the evaluation of a specific player's or team's capabilities. *Insight* magazine (Apr. 7, 1986) noted, "It is a fascinating conglomeration of statistical breakdowns—some basic, others so bizarre and arcane that they almost defy explanation—of baseball's teams and players." The term was coined from the acronym "SABR" by Bill James and used in the introduction of his self-published *Baseball Abstract* (1980) and first conventionally published *Baseball Abstract* (1982). In *The Bill James Historical Baseball Abstract* (1986), James wrote, "Sabermetrics is not numbers; sabermetrics is the search for better evidence." That the term stuck is somewhat misleading, as not all "baseball scientists" are members of the Society for American Baseball Research, and most SABR researchers specialize in historical or biographical (rather than statistical) research. Said James (quoted in Scott Gray, *The Mind of Bill James*, 2006, p.39), "I would never have invented that word if I had realized how successful I was going to be. I never intended to help characterize SABR as a bunch of numbers freaks." Incorrect spelling: "sabrmetrics."

sabernomics Economic analysis applied to baseball.

SABR (pron. "saber") Abbrev. and acronym for *Society for American Baseball Research*.

SABRite A member of the Society for American Baseball Research (George F. Will, *Newsweek*, Apr. 14, 1986).

sac Abbrev. for *sacrifice*, 1.

sac fly Short for *sacrifice fly*, 1.

sack **1.** *n.* Any *base*, 2, save for home plate, from the fact that it is a filled canvas bag that resembles a stuffed sack. IST USE. 1891 (*Chicago Herald*, May 5; Edward J. Nichols). **2.** *n.* Home plate. "Barbour walked to the sack. His Honor [Northampton Mayor Calvin Coolidge] threw a ball that would have required stilts to reach, but Barbour made a pass at it" (*Northampton* [Mass.] *Daily Herald*, April 30, 1910; Brian Turner). **3.** *v.* To lay down a successful sacrifice bunt. "[Jack] Tobin walked, was 'sacked' to second" (*St. Louis Post-Dispatch*, Apr. 14, 1915; Peter Morris).

sacker *hist.* A *baseman*; e.g., "first sacker." IST USE. 1911 (*Baseball Magazine*, October, p.43; Edward J. Nichols).

sacking Playing a baseman's position (Maurice H. Weseen, *A Dictionary of American Slang*, 1934).

sacks full Syn. of *bases loaded*.

sacrifice 1. *n.* A *sacrifice hit*. Abbrev. *S*, 1; *sac*. IST USE. 1878. "The home team responded with one run, made on two safe hits and a sacrifice" (*Cincinnati Commercial*, May 22; Peter Morris). 2. *v.* To make a sacrifice hit; to advance a baserunner by means of a sacrifice hit. ETYMOLOGY. From the concept of a batter giving himself up for the good of the team by advancing or scoring a teammate.

sacrifice bunt A *sacrifice hit* in which a ball bunted with less than two outs advances one or more baserunners and the batter is put out at first base, or would have been put out except for a fielder's error. The batter is not credited with an official at-bat and may be credited with a run batted in if a baserunner scores. A sacrifice bunt is not credited to the batter if any runner is put out attempting to advance one base or if, in the judgment of the official scorer, the batter is bunting primarily for a base hit. Compare *drag bunt*. IST USE. 1935. "A sacrifice bunt is a bunted ball laid down for a like purpose" (Ralph H. Barbour, *How to Play Better Baseball*, p.173; David Shulman). ETYMOLOGY. The sacrifice bunt was "invented" by John Montgomery Ward in the 1880s (John Thorn, personal communication, June 13, 2004).

sacrifice fly 1. A *sacrifice hit* in which a fly ball or line drive, fair or foul, with less than two outs, is caught but hit deep enough for an outfielder (or an infielder running in the outfield) to handle and to allow one or more baserunners to tag up and score. It has been typified as a "bunt with muscles." The batter is not credited with an official at-bat, but is credited with a run batted in. The sacrifice fly was formally introduced in 1908, and until 1925 the batter was credited with a sacrifice fly only when a runner scored after a fair fly ball was caught. From 1926 to 1930, a sacrifice fly was awarded on any advance on a fly ball (not just a runner scoring). From 1931 to 1953 (with the exception of 1939), a batter who hit a sacrifice fly was charged with an official at-bat; and from 1931 to 1938, a batter was not credited with a run batted in when a runner scored on his flyout. The at-bat ruling was changed in 1954 to help create a few more .300 batters. It was assumed that the rule was worth seven to 10 points to a power hitter's batting average. Occasionally two runs score on a sacrifice fly; e.g., on Aug. 8, 1993, Albert Belle's fly to right field was caught over the fence, thereby allowing runners to score from second base and third base. Abbrev. *SF*, 1. Syn. *sac fly*. IST USE. 1885. "[Cap] Anson's long sacrifice fly to [Paul] Hines allowed [George] Gore to cross the plate, thus giving the Chicagos the lead" (*Providence Evening Bulletin*, July 30; Fred Ivor-Campbell). USAGE NOTE. When New York Yankees coach Joe Altobelli arrived at his Milwaukee hotel in 1986, he opened his suitcase and a large bug popped out; Altobelli reached for a magazine and clobbered the insect. Declared Moss Klein in *The Sporting News* (May 5), "Credit him with a sacrifice fly." 2. An informal game in which a catchable ball is batted or thrown to another player on the fly, after which a runner from third base tries to score after the ball is caught.

sacrifice game An offense based on bunting, as opposed to the hit-and-run game. "Boston stuck to the same old stereotyped 'sacrifice game' that has proved a dead letter for several moons, unless some special play calls for it" (Timothy Murnane, *The Boston Globe*, Sept. 6, 1900; Peter Morris). IST USE. 1896. "The Baltimore players are locked to neither the sacrifice game, nor the hit-and-run game. . . . If they fall off in their hitting, then they go to bunting" (Billy Earle, quoted in *The Boston Globe*, July 28; Peter Morris).

sacrifice hit A batted ball that advances a baserunner at the expense of the batter being put out; specif., *sacrifice bunt* and *sacrifice fly*, 1. "[Ross Barnes] was among the first to practically introduce the now well-known 'sacrifice hits,' which were written up in baseball books of 1869–70" (*New York Clipper*, May 3, 1879; Peter Morris). Abbrev. *SH*. Syn. *sacrifice*, 1; *sacrifice play*. IST USE. 1878 (*Detroit Post and Tribune*, Apr. 20; Peter Morris).

sacrifice hitter A hitter who makes a sacrifice bunt or a sacrifice fly. IST USE. 1888. "The sacrifice hitters . . . hold one hand close to the end of the bat and the other several inches further up on the stick" (*St. Louis*

Sacrifice hit. Postcard. *Andy Moresund Collection*

Post-Dispatch, Sept. 6; Peter Morris). EXTENDED USE. The term has seen limited use in politics for a candidate who runs for the good of the party and other candidates, but who is likely to lose. "With a 'sacrifice hitter'—another candidate involved—they can get the 'right to work' monkey off their backs by supporting him" (*San Francisco Call-Bulletin*, Dec. 17, 1957; Peter Tamony).

sacrifice play Syn. of *sacrifice hit*. "Alike in the field and at bat, a man may do the most effective work in that branch of baseball technically called 'sacrifice play' and yet not receive a word of credit for it at the hands of many of the reporters" (*The Sporting Life*, March 3, 1886; David Shulman).

sacrifice position The second slot in the lineup, so called because (at one time) that batter was frequently called on to bunt. "Second place in the batting order is looked upon as the 'sacrifice' position" (George Herman

Ruth, *Babe Ruth's Own Book of Baseball*, 1928, p.218).

saddle 1. *n.* Syn. of *clutch*. "When a batter produces a safe 'blow' at an opportune moment, his fellow-players say that he has hit 'in the saddle,' or 'in the clutch'" (*The New York Times*, June 2, 1929). **2.** *v.* To be burdened. "[Doug] Johns wasn't hit hard, but almost was saddled with the loss after giving up two runs and four hits in two-thirds of an inning" (*The Baltimore Sun*, March 22, 1998).

safe 1. Successful in getting on base or advancing to the next base. Compare *out*, 1. IST USE. 1862 (*New York Sunday Mercury*, July 13; Edward J. Nichols). **2.** The declaration by the umpire that a batter-runner or baserunner is entitled to the base to which he was advancing. The umpire signals the safe sign by holding his hands out to his side with the palms facing and parallel to the ground.

safe blow A base hit. "A hit is a 'blow' or a 'safe blow'" (*The New York Times*, June 2, 1929).

safe carrier A slow runner, one who seems as if he is running with a safe on his back.

safe-haven game A game that includes the presence of a base or bases where a runner has sanctuary; e.g., cricket, baseball, rounders, and their predecessors (such as stoolball). The term is used by Project Protoball in the study of the evolution of baseball to distinguish such games from "bat and ball" games (e.g., tennis, golf, and hockey). See also *protoball*.

safe hit A base hit. IST USE. 1865 (Chadwick Scrapbooks; Edward J. Nichols).

safe in the ice box Said of a game that is out of reach and won. IST USE. 1915. "Occasionally Joe went in as relief pitcher, when the game was safe in the 'ice box'" (Lester Chadwick, *Baseball Joe in the Big League*; David Shulman).

safe out Syn. of *sure out*, 1. "There was a force at second, but I took the safe out [throwing to first base]" (Cal Ripken Jr., quoted in *The Baltimore Sun*, March 25, 2001).

safety 1. A base hit; specif., a single. IST USE. 1902. "[Hughey Ahearn] walloped the

Safe. Dramatic play at the plate, Griffith Stadium, Washington, D.C. *Photograph by Joseph Baylor Roberts*

ball good and hard, but could only gather one safety" (*Brooklyn Daily Eagle*, July 7; Peter Morris). **2.** A reserve player. Baltimore Orioles outfielder Tony Tarasco (quoted in *The Baltimore Sun*, Apr. 8, 1997): "I'm trying to figure out how I went from playing every day in Montreal [in 1995], trying to bloom, to being a bench player they are keeping around for a safety. I'm not 30 years old. I'm not a safety."

safety ball *hist.* A baseball strategically hidden in the outfield grass, to be used (instead of the live ball) to prevent the batter-runner or baserunner from advancing another base. Baltimore Orioles outfielders in the 1890s would hide several safety balls near their positions, "a pluralized version of the hidden-ball trick" (Bill Mazer, *Bill Mazer's Amazin' Baseball Book*, 1990; Peter Morris).

safety set A set of baseball cards given out by police and fire departments to promote safety. Almost without exception, each card contained the image of a player and a safety tip.

safety squeeze A *squeeze play* in which the batter bunts and the runner on third base starts or breaks for home if, and only if, it looks like a good bunt. Compare *suicide squeeze*. Syn. *delayed squeeze*; *bunt and run*.

sailer A pitch that takes off horizontally as if it had a sail attached to it rather than dropping; an early name for *slider*, 1. The term has been used to describe more than one pitch, including the *cut fastball*. Ethan Allen (*Baseball Techniques Illustrated*, 1951) noted that it is "gripped with the fingers along the seams and released with pressure on the middle finger." Tommy Holmes (*Brooklyn Daily Eagle*, Aug. 21, 1934; Peter Morris) described right-handed pitcher Johnny Babich's fastball: "His 'sailer' had plenty of zip. . . . A fast ball that acts something like a curve in that instead of hopping it slides in toward a left-handed hitter." Rob Neyer (in Bill James and Rob Neyer, *The Neyer/James Guide to Pitchers*, 2004, p.18): "Granted, the term 'sailer' was also used to describe the pitch that became known as the slider, but 1) I believe it was more often used to describe the cut fastball, and 2) anyway, I think what people called a 'slider' in the 1930s and '40s was often, and perhaps usually, more like the cut fastball than anything else." Compare *sailor*.

sailing fastball Syn. of *riding fastball*.

sailor A scuffed-up pitch used by Eddie Cicotte; apparently different from a *sailer.* Ty Cobb (*Memoirs of Twenty Years in Baseball*, 1925) wrote, "This ball would start like an ordinary pitch and then would sail much in the manner of a flat stone thrown by a small boy." Cobb was convinced that Cicotte used some illegal tactic to achieve this effect, noting that Cicotte asked that the ball be rolled to him on the ground: "With a brand new ball that had not touched the dirt he couldn't deliver the sailor" (Peter Morris).

salad A term coined by pitcher Dennis Eckersley for an off-speed or easy-to-hit pitch.

salami Syn. of *grand slam*, 1. "[Jimmy] Key's streak of 2,512 innings without serving up a salami was the longest among active pitchers" (*Milwaukee Journal Sentinel*, Sept. 29, 1997). ETYMOLOGY. A pure play on the word "slam," which turns it into "s(a)lam(i)."

salary arbitration A mechanism, employed since 1974 as part of the first collective bargaining agreement between the Major League Baseball Players Association (MLBPA) and Major League Baseball, to settle salary disputes between a player and his club owner by which an independent third party selects the player's salary for the upcoming season. The action is requested by the player and represents an opportunity for the player to obtain a salary approximately equal to what he would earn without a reserve clause in his contract. In 2000, the third party was increased from one arbitrator to a panel of three arbitrators, who are not expected to be baseball experts, but are members of the National Academy of Arbitrators.

Salary arbitration is available to players after their third year and prior to their sixth year of major-league service while they are still under the reserve system. Originally, arbitration was available after two years of service (changed to three years in 1986); however, since 1990, a player in the top 17 percent of players (based on total service time) with two years of service and at least 86 days of service in the immediately preceding season are also eligible (see also *Super Two*). To retain a player, a club is required to tender a contract by Dec. 12. If the player and club are unable to negotiate a salary by Jan. 18, each party files a salary figure to be used in the arbitration process. The player and club may continue attempts to reach a salary agreement (and most of them do) prior to the hearings, which are scheduled in the first three weeks of February.

Salary arbitration is also available to certain players who are eligible for free agency. These players must be offered arbitration on or before Dec. 1 and must accept arbitration by Dec. 7. If a player accepts arbitration, he is considered signed for the next season. If a player rejects arbitration, or is not offered arbitration, he becomes a free agent. If a club fails to offer arbitration to an eligible free agent, the club cannot receive a compensation in next year's first-year player (amateur) draft; but if a club offers arbitration and the player chooses to sign with another club, the former club may receive a draft pick from the signing club, as well as a compensation pick between the first and second rounds.

If the player and the club are unable to reach a salary agreement, the issue is settled at a hearing. The player (or his agent) presents his case for one hour, after which the club presents its case for one hour. Each party receives one-half hour for rebuttal, sometimes presented by the MLBPA and the Major League Labor Relations Dept. The decision is made by the panel within 24 hours of the hearing. The criteria used by the arbitration panel in reaching its decision include: the quality of the player's contribution to the club during the past season (including overall performance, special qualities of leadership, and public appeal); the length and consistency of the player's career contributions; the record of the player's past compensation; the comparative salaries of players within a class of years; the existence of any physical or mental defects of the player; and the recent performance of the club in the league standings and attendance figures. Criteria not considered admissible by the panel include: financial position of the player or the club, press comments, testimonials (except for annual awards), offers made by the player or club prior to arbitration, the cost to the parties of their representatives, salaries in other sports or occupations, and evidence related to the luxury tax. The panel selects the salary it feels is more appropriate for the upcoming season; it does not select a compromise salary between those submitted. The judgment is binding and not subject to further appeal. (William C. Gilbert and Tal Smith)

salary arm A pitcher's throwing arm, so called because a pitcher earns his salary on the strength and effectiveness of his arm. "[Clem] Labine sometimes gets a knot on the inside of his salary arm, just below the elbow, caused by the strain in snapping off his curve" (Stan Baumgartner, *The Sporting News*, 1952). Syn. *salary wing*; *salary whip*; *salary member*; *money arm*; *money wing*; *pay wing*. IST USE. 1892 (*New York Press*, Aug. 11; Edward J. Nichols).

salary cap A ceiling below which major-league club owners proposed to spend no more than a specified amount on player payrolls. The payrolls were to include salaries, signing bonuses, pension and benefit plans, meal money, and spring training allowances. In the 1994 labor negotiations with the players, the owners first demanded a hard salary cap (one with no exceptions), then settled for a form of luxury tax.

salary drive A period of good performance and/or behavior, seemingly staged for the benefit of the player's paycheck rather than the benefit of the club. It is commonly mounted during the last month of the season so as to improve the player's statistics for salary negotiations and added leverage in arbitration. Broadcaster and former pitcher Jim Palmer (Home Team Sports, Oct. 1986) defined the term as "a great performance before free agency." IST USE. 1961. "Salary Drive: A player's hustle last month of the season" (Fresco Thompson, quoted in *Los Angeles Times*, July 8).

salary dump Releasing or trading a player because his salary does not fit the club's budget.

salary member *hist.* Syn. of *salary arm*. "Del Howard lays the dislocating of Jess Baker's salary member at the door of 'Scotty' Finlay, trainer of the Los Angeles club" (*San Francisco Bulletin*, May 13, 1913; Gerald L. Cohen).

salary whip Syn. of *salary arm*. "Carl Cashion

. . . has been nursing a torn muscle in his salary whip" (Stanley T. Milliken, *The Washington Post*, Sept. 7, 1913; Peter Morris).

salary wing Syn. of *salary arm*. Christy Mathewson termed his right arm "my salary wing" (Frank Deford, *Sports Illustrated*, Aug. 25, 2003). IST USE. 1901. "While you [a young pitcher] can stand hard work in the early spring and cold weather much better than the veteran can do it, still your salary wing is not infallible" (George E. Stackhouse, *Marion* [Ohio] *Star*, June 7; Peter Morris).

saliva heave *hist.* A spitball. "The big fellow [Ed Walsh] . . . bended them in true summer style, and used the saliva heave with great effect" (*Chicago Tribune*, March 26, 1906; Peter Morris).

saliva jive The loading of a spitball.

saliva toss *hist.* A spitball. IST USE. 1920 (*The New York Times*, Oct. 10; Edward J. Nichols).

saliva twist *hist.* A spitball. " 'Big Ed' Walsh will probably . . . distribute a few 'saliva twists' for the edification of the Seal batters" (*San Francisco Bulletin*, March 8, 1913; Gerald L. Cohen).

Sally League 1. Nickname for the South Atlantic League, founded in 1904 as a Class C minor league, which became the *Southern League* in 1964. IST USE. 1911 (*Spalding's Official Base Ball Guide*, p.265; Edward J. Nichols). **2.** Nickname for the South Atlantic League, founded in 1980 as a Class A minor league, a successor of the Western Carolinas League.

salt and pepper league A low minor league, where a young player goes for more "seasoning."

salvado Spanish for "save" (noun).

salvage corps A team's relief pitchers. IST USE. 1912 (*New York Tribune*, Sept. 13; Edward J. Nichols).

Sam Bat A kiln-dried, custom-made *maple bat* originally manufactured by Sam Holman, a carpenter and theater-set builder at the National Arts Centre in Ottawa and founder of the Original Maple Bat Co. The rock maple wood is logged out of Quebec and New York. Joe Carter was the first major leaguer to use (illegally) a Sam Bat in a game in 1997. Sam Bats have become very popular with major leaguers. See also *Bonds*.

Sammy Vick *hist.* A ballplayer who overeats. Vick (a New York Yankees outfielder from 1917 to 1920) was "noted for possessing one of the most voracious appetites in the big leagues" (George Herman Ruth, *Babe Ruth's Own Book of Baseball*, 1928). To "do a Sammy Vick" was to overeat.

SAN Abbrev. for *steroid-adjusted number.*

sand *hist.* Courage, stamina, grit, pluck, "guts." "[Tim] Keefe not only twirled a wonderfully effective game and showed his 'sand' by his cheerfully given consent to [Buck] Ewing's request that he pitch the second game" (*The World* [New York], Sept. 21, 1889). "[The Philadelphia club] has the best players in the business and ought to win the pennant right along, but they haven't the sand to stick up for themselves" (Boston Beaneaters first baseman Tommy Tucker, quoted in *Philadelphia Evening Item*, July 18, 1894). IST USE. 1875. "[The *Kalamazoo Gazette*] fanned the flames by attributing their [the Mutuals] departure to a lack of 'sand'" (*Kalamazoo Gazette*, Oct. 18; Peter Morris).

sandbag Syn. of *base*, 2. IST USE. 1870. "The 'sandbags' were also attended to in a manner highly creditable" (*Chicago Tribune*, June 6; Peter Morris).

sandblower A small ballplayer with little power. "It always seemed like the good players never played well, and all the sandblowers (little guys) would hit the ball out of the yard" (Edwin Howsam, *Baseball Graffiti*, 1995, p.11).

San Diego Chicken An individual outfitted as a chicken who entertained San Diego Padres fans as the first human mascot for a professional team. Ted Giannoulas, who portrayed the original Chicken, commented on his prospects of entering the National Baseball Hall of Fame (*The Baltimore Sun*, July 3, 1993): "Who knows? I mean, they have a broadcasters wing. They have a players wing. Maybe one day they'll have a chicken wing."

sandlot 1. *n.* A vacant lot, playground, pasture, yard, or other such location where youngsters and amateurs play baseball. Robert Smith

Sandlot. Cartoonist Gene Carr captures the spirit of the sandlot. *Postcard from Andy Moresund Collection*

(*Baseball in America*, 1961), writing on the growth of baseball in the 19th century, captured the spirit of the sandlot: "This was through the seventies and eighties, when boys began to play the game on the outskirts of every major city, in country pastures, and in public parks. The great dump of Manhattan's West Side, the prairies on the edges of fire-gutted Chicago, the filled land on Boston's Back Bay, the wide meadows on Philadelphia's outskirts, the vacant lots in Indianapolis, in Buffalo, in Paterson, the prairies around St. Louis, the back pastures of New England, the flatlands of New Jersey, the windy reaches of Iowa, even the back yards of San Francisco's Telegraph Hill saw baseball diamonds of every size scratched out where boys would play the new game." Sometimes spelled "sand lot." Syn. *lot*, 2. IST USE. 1887. "A team called the Joe Gerhardt's of which comedian Pete Daily is pitcher, will tackle the City Island team on the sand lots to-morrow. They will play for a basket of clams" (*The World* [New York], July 3; Gerald L. Cohen). **2.** *adj.* Relating to a class of amateur players, teams, and leagues whose games are played on sandlots. The term is generic and seldom specifically applies to a "sand lot," but rather to a lack of sophistication and organization. It has been said that college baseball, American Legion Baseball, Little League Baseball, and other organized programs had, by the mid-1960s, all but made sandlot baseball obsolete. Yet some sandlot leagues have survived. John Kelliher (*The Boston Globe*, May 22, 1988), manager of one of the clubs in the Boston Park League, declared, "You might say that our league's longevity [beginning its 59th season] is a modern miracle, one of sandlot baseball's very few survivors." Before about 1960, however, it was rare to pick up a baseball player's biography that did not contain a line on the dust jacket concerning "his rise from sandlot baseball to the big leagues." For several years, the Hearst newspapers sponsored its own "sandlot program"; in 1965, newspapers in the chain noted that seven graduates of the program were appearing in the major-leagues All-Star Game. In 1993, the movie *The Sandlot* brought the term back to a new generation.

ETYMOLOGY. Peter Tamony did extensive research on the term, culminating in his article "Sandlot Baseball" (*Western Folklore*, Nov. 1968). He traced the term back to 1850 in San Francisco when a cemetery was created from a "triangular piece of land crested by a hill of sand," which is now the site of the Civic Center. Some 5,000 people were interred at the spot from 1850 to 1860, when the board of supervisors ordered the dead moved, had the hill leveled, and opened the 17 acres as a park. In 1870, the city demanded the spot for a new City Hall. While the building was going up, the demagogue Dennis Kearney led his attacks on Chinese labor there, and the name "Sand Lot" was "cabled all over the English-speaking world." Tamony cited several examples in which the term jumped from the name for a specific city lot to a general and extended usage. Tamony found that the term clearly relates to baseball in the "Base Ball Supplement" to *Breeder and Sportsman* (June 7, 1890): "Why such players are overlooked . . . and 'skates' and 'wafters' are kept in the team simply because at one time they were alleged good players by some sand lot critic."

EXTENDED USE. Rough and untutored in other sports and other walks of life. "NFC Salvages Pro Bowl Triumph with 'Sandlot Plays'" (*San Francisco Examiner* headline, Feb. 7, 1983; Peter Tamony).

Sand Lot Kid The name of a bronze sculpture by Victor Salvatore depicting a barefooted farm boy that stands outside the gates to Abner Doubleday Field in Cooperstown, N.Y. Since it was put in place in 1939, it has become one of the true icons of the game.

sandlotter *hist.* A sandlot or amateur player; a graduate of the lower realms of the game. Syn. *lotter.* IST USE. 1904. "Can't always tell how good these sand-lotters are until they get a chance to show themselves" (*The Washington Post*, Aug. 18; Peter Morris).

sandpaper ball An illegally pitched ball that has been defaced with sandpaper. In 1987, the National League suspended Philadelphia Phillies pitcher Kevin Gross for 10 days for having sandpaper glued to his glove. IST USE. 1914 (*New York Tribune*, Sept. 23; Edward J. Nichols).

sandwich pick A supplemental *compensation pick* added between two rounds of a draft; specif., a draft pick between the first and second rounds of the first-year player draft when a club has lost a Type A free agent to another club or when a club has failed to sign its first-round draft pick of the first-year player draft from the preceding year; or a draft pick between the second and third rounds of the first-year player draft when a club has lost a Type C free agent to another club or when a club has failed to sign its second-round draft pick of the first-year player draft from the preceding year. Syn. *supplemental pick.*

sanitaries Short for *sanitary socks.* "Underneath you wear long white socks that are called sanitaries. Over those go the colored socks with the stirrups under the feet" (Jim Bouton, *Ball Four*, 1970; Charles D. Poe).

sanitary hose Syn. of *sanitary socks.* IST USE. 1927. Ad for Morehouse & Wells Co. (*Decatur* [Ill.] *Review*, Apr. 3; Peter Morris).

sanitary socks The long, white cotton socks worn under the outer colored stirrup socks to prevent blood poisoning in the event that a player is spiked. "[Willie McGee's] long, white sanitary socks had to be just so. Then it was time for his cardinal-red stirrup socks to be pulled high and taut" (Don Banks, *St. Petersburg Times*, March 28, 1987). Players began to wear sanitary socks in 1905 after Nap Lajoie was spiked badly and the dye in his stockings contributed to a case of blood poisoning (Dan Gutman, *Banana Bats and Ding-Dong Balls*, 1995, p.224). Syn. *sanitaries*; *sannies*; *sanitary hose*; *athletic hose*; *undersocks.* USAGE NOTE. In 1966, the Kansas

City A's introduced the first-ever colored sanitary socks: gold socks that complimented the uniform's gold highlights. Other clubs have donned colored sanitaries at times: blue (Chicago White Sox), gold (San Diego Padres), yellow (Milwaukee Brewers), and orange (San Francisco Giants). While seemingly an oxymoron, colored sanitary socks were "quite safe, as the dyed stockings were colorfast and thus were not hazardous to the player" (National Baseball Hall of Fame and Museum exhibit). ETYMOLOGY. The term is a direct reference to the fact that the white socks are not dyed, like one's outer socks, and that they would provide a cleaner and more sanitary dressing in the event of a spiking infection.

sannies Syn. of *sanitary socks*.

sap To hit the ball hard. "[Kid] Gleason's men hit Mitze's pitches terrifically. . . . Every Sox sapped the ball" (*San Francisco Bulletin*, March 31, 1913; Gerald L. Cohen).

satchel *hist.* Syn. of *base*, 2. IST USE. 1932 (*Baseball Magazine*, October; Edward J. Nichols).

satchelfoot A player with large feet requiring large brogans. The term reportedly was the source of Leroy "Satchel" Paige's nickname, which began as "Satchelfoots" in deference to his size–12 shoes (*Time* magazine, June 3, 1940).

saturated curve *hist.* A spitball. "One of [Harry] Howell's saturated curves" (*Chicago Tribune*, Apr. 18, 1905; Peter Morris).

saucepan *hist.* Syn. of *home plate*. IST USE. 1892 (*Chicago Herald*, July 19; Edward J. Nichols).

saucer *hist.* Syn. of *home plate*.

saunter act *hist.* Syn. of *base on balls*. IST USE. 1907 (*New York Evening Journal*, Apr. 17; Edward J. Nichols).

sausage sizzle The universal fund-raising and social focus in Australian amateur baseball in which a hot plate of butcher's sausages and onions is smothered in tomato sauce and served on buttered white bread.

save 1. *v.* For a relief pitcher to preserve a victory. "Three times in the late season [Chicago White Sox manager Fielder Jones] summoned [Ed] Walsh to pitch just one ball, and two of the games he saved" (John J. Evers and Hugh S. Fullerton, *Touching Second: The Science of Baseball*, 1910; Peter Morris). "I don't believe there was ever a pitcher who could go in to save a game in a pinch and do the job so completely as Big Ed Walsh" (Ty Cobb, *Memoirs of Twenty Years in Baseball*, 1915). "[Dolf] Luque won his first half dozen games and saved games for two of his colleagues" (Brian Bell, *The Washington Post*, June 22, 1930). IST USE. 1907. "[When a young pitcher is] called in to replace a pitcher who is being hit . . . it is natural that he should want to save the game" (Sol White, comp., *Sol White's History of Colored Base Ball*; Peter Morris).

2. *n.* The credit given to one relief pitcher for ensuring his team's victory by protecting the lead in a given game. To receive a save the pitcher cannot be taken from the game and must finish it. Even though the starting or other relief pitcher receives credit for the win, the save is the formal recognition of the closer's role in the victory. Only one save can be credited in a game. To be credited with a save, a pitcher must meet all four of the following conditions (*Official Baseball Rules*, Rule 10.19): 1) he is the finishing pitcher in a game won by his team; 2) he is not the winning pitcher; 3) he is credited with at least one-third of an inning pitched; and 4) he qualifies under one of the following conditions: a) he enters the game with a lead of no more than three runs and pitches for at least one inning, b) he enters the game with the potential tying run either on base, at bat, or on deck, or c) he pitches for at least three innings. See also *blown save*; *regular save*; *tough save*; *easy save*. Abbrev. *SV*; *S*, 2. ETYMOLOGY. According to *Sports Illustrated* (June 8, 1992), the save concept was invented by Chicago baseball writer Jerome Holtzman in 1960 to credit a relief pitcher who enters the game with the tying or go-ahead run on base or at the plate and finishes the game with the lead. Holtzman believed Chicago Cubs relief pitchers Don Elston and Bill Henry were constantly protecting leads but no one knew about it. However, Jack Lang (executive secretary, Baseball Writers' Association of America, personal communication, Jan. 4, 2000) states that Brooklyn Dodgers statistician Allan Roth introduced the save concept in

1952. Holtzman (personal communication to Bill Deane) acknowledged the efforts of Roth and others (Irving Kaze in Pittsburgh and Jim Toomey in St. Louis), but, "by their criteria, all a pitcher had to do was finish a winning game; what I did was develop a formula," or a systematic set of rules. *The Sporting News* popularized the save rule by listing save leaders during the 1960s. The save was officially adopted in 1969, but the reliever had to protect a lead until the end of the game or until he was lifted for a pinch hitter or pinch runner; if more than one pitcher qualified, the official scorer judged which of the pitchers was more effective. After the 1973 season, the reliever had to pitch three "effective" innings or enter the game with the potential tying or winning run on base or at the plate. The current rule was adopted beginning with the 1975 season.

save opportunity An unofficial statistic for a relief pitching appearance in which the pitcher has the chance to be credited with a save. The pitcher can convert the save opportunity (with either a save or a *hold*, 6) or lose the lead and be given a *blown save*. If the save opportunity still exists when the pitcher leaves the game, he is not charged with a save opportunity. The statistic is used to give perspective to the save statistic in that two pitchers with 12 saves may have had vastly different save opportunities (e.g., 14 vs. 24). Syn. *save situation.*

save percentage A statistical method for evaluating relief pitching, computed by dividing the pitcher's number of saves by his number of save opportunities, and multiplying by 100. A save percentage of greater than 90 is exemplary; one of less than 75 is poor.

save set-up A term created by the Elias Sports Bureau in 1986 for *hold*, 6. "We believe the set-up guy has become so important to the ninth-inning closer that he should be credited with a save set-up" (Seymour Siwoff, quoted in *Hartford Courant*, Apr. 13, 1986).

save situation Syn. of *save opportunity.*

sawed-off bat **1.** A baseball bat shaved flat on the end to reduce air resistance. **2.** A bat broken by an inside pitch.

saw off To pitch to the inside of the plate, causing the batter to hit the ball with the bat handle, figuratively "sawing off" the barrel of the bat, which often results in a broken bat or a weak grounder or infield fly.

saw the air *hist.* To swing at and miss a pitched ball. "[Jeremiah Reardon] succeeded in making every one of the Prickly Ash players saw the air with the exception of Bien" (*The Sporting News*, May 31, 1886; Peter Morris). Syn. *saw the wind.* 1ST USE. 1880 (*Chicago Inter-Ocean*, May 19; Edward J. Nichols).

saw the wind *hist.* Syn. of *saw the air.* 1ST USE. 1878. "[William] Sergeant would pitch them one that would make them 'saw the wind'" (*South Haven* [Mich.] *Sentinel*, June 1; Peter Morris).

"say hello to my li'l friend" Home run call by *SportsCenter* anchor Steve Berthiaume. It is a quote from machine-gunning Tony Montana, the character played by Al Pacino in the 1983 cult-classic movie *Scarface.*

"say hey!" The verbal trademark of Hall of Fame outfielder Willie Mays, the "Say Hey Kid." When Mays joined the New York Giants in 1951, he had trouble remembering names; when he wanted to speak to somebody, he would just call out, "Say hey."

"say it ain't so, Joe!" The oft-heard lament that came to represent the 1919 Black Sox scandal in which the World Series was "fixed" to accommodate gamblers. On Sept. 28, 1920, Shoeless Joe Jackson (the most famous Chicago White Sox player accused in the case) left the Criminal Courts Building in Chicago in custody of a sheriff after telling his story to the grand jury. According to the *New York Evening Telegram* (Sept. 29, 1920): "[Jackson] found several hundred youngsters, ranging in age from six to sixteen, waiting for a glimpse of their former idol. One little urchin stepped up to the outfielder and grabbing his coat sleeve, said:—'It ain't true, is it, Joe?' 'Yes, kid, I'm afraid it is,' Jackson replied." As with other elements of baseball lore, there is reason to question the veracity of the quotation and the response to it. David Shulman (*New York Daily News Sunday Magazine*, May 1, 1988) wrote, "To his dying day, Jackson never admitted guilt in the Black Sox scandal and denied saying anything after he left the Grand Jury room. It is dubious that

THE CHANGING WORLD

[Copyright: 1920: By The Chicago Tribune.]

Our national sport as it has been regarded.

It now joins the "Black Eye club."

"Say it ain't so, Joe!" As depicted in a 1920 *Chicago Tribune* cartoon. *Author's collection*

any newsboy could have approached him then, as he was carefully guarded." Responding to the claim of eyewitnesses, Shulman added that they were all reporters and "it is a fact that sometimes reporters contrive their own stories." Jackson was quoted in Harvey Frommer's *Shoeless Joe and Ragtime Baseball* (1992): "No such word 'Say it ain't so' was ever said. The fellow [Hugh S. Fullerton] who wrote that just wanted something to say. When I came out of the courthouse that day, nobody said anything to me. The only one who spoke was a guy who yelled at his friend 'I told you the big son of a bitch wore shoes.' I walked right out of there and stepped into my car and drove off." EXTENDED USE. Used broadly as an expression of disbelief or hoped-for denial. It was given a brief and specific workout when Senator Joseph Biden of Delaware dropped out of the race for the Democratic nomination for the presidency in 1987. Biden was alleged to have plagiarized the speeches of another politician. In 1988, the line came into play again when Ben Johnson, the Canadian runner, was stripped of his Olympic gold medal for testing positively for steroid use. This time the cry was, "Say it ain't so, Ben."

sayonara home run A home run that ends a game in Japanese baseball.

SB Scorecard and box score abbrev. for *stolen base*.

SBA Abbrev. for *stolen base average*.

SBR Abbrev. for *stolen base runs*.

SBW Abbrev. for *stolen base wins*.

scald To hit a ball very hard. "The first four Mets scalded the ball" (*The Baltimore Sun*, March 16, 2002).

scalped field A playing surface with little or no turf.

scantling *hist.* A baseball bat. "[Shaw] was reached for eleven hits. All of them rang clean from the scantlings of the visitors" (J.V. Fitz Gerald, *The Washington Post*, May 2, 1920; Peter Morris).

scatter For a pitcher to spread the small number of hits given up over several innings throughout a game so that few or no runs are scored. IST USE. 1887. "Only five hits being made off him, and they were badly scattered" (*The Washington Post*, June 19; Peter Morris).

scatter arm 1. A fielder or pitcher who habitually throws wildly; a player with an inaccurate throwing arm. IST USE. 1933 (*Ironwood* [Mich.] *Daily Globe*, Apr. 14; Peter Morris). **2.** The throwing arm of a player given to wild throws; e.g., Buck Weaver had a scatter arm when he was a rookie.

scatter hitter A hitter whose hits follow no apparent pattern.

scattershot Descriptive of wild and inaccurate throwing. "Everyone . . . wondered when [pitcher Bobby] Witt would conquer his scattershot control problems" (Joey Johnston, *Tampa Tribune*, March 15, 1989). "[John

"Say it ain't so, Joe!" Shoeless Joe Jackson. *Society for American Baseball Research*

McGraw] had what was known as a 'scatter-shot' arm . . . [meaning] that his throws aimed at first base often landed somewhere else" (Noel Hynd, *The Giants of the Polo Grounds*, 1988, p.102).

schedule The list of games that a team will play during a season. Normally, the schedule specifies each game's date, location, and the time of day at which it will be played. Each major-league team plays 162 regular season games, of which 81 are away and 81 are at home. The commissioner of baseball issues the official schedule for the following season by no later than Nov. 15. The maximum number of games per club shall be 140 in classes AAA, AA, and A leagues, 76 in short-season Class A leagues, and 60 in rookie leagues. IST USE. 1879. "Any league club may play clubs outside of the league previous to the opening of the league schedule games" (*Stevens Point* [Wisc.] *Journal*, Dec. 13; Peter Morris).

schneid A game, series of games, or period during which a team has been shut out or a batter has gone hitless. See also *schneider*; *off the schneid*; *on the schneid*.

schneider To shut out. See also *schneid*. ETYMOLOGY. According to Harold Wentworth and Stuart Berg Flexner (*Dictionary of American Slang*, 1960), the term came originally from the German and Yiddish "schneider" for one who cuts cloth, or a tailor. On its way to baseball, it appears to have become a gin rummy term for preventing an opponent from scoring a point in a game or match.

schoolboy A rookie or new player.

science The collective body of strategy and techniques accruing to the sport of baseball.

scientific baseball A style of play incorporating any technique that was an improvement over the earlier days of baseball. Sol White (*Sol White's History of Colored Ball*, 1907): "[Managers] should aim to blend the team into a highly polished and magnificent machine. The play itself is a science, if that term may be applied to sport. Compared to town ball or other old fashioned games, it suggests the present day harvesting engine and its prototype, the scythe." The term was associated with Ned Hanlon, manager of the Baltimore Orioles (1892–1898), who perfected the aggressive, brainy style of play that revolutionized how the game was played; in this sense, the term is synonymous with *inside baseball*. For example, Whitey Herzog (*You're Missin' a Great Game*, 1999) referred to "a style that goes back a hundred years in baseball history, to . . . the old Baltimore Orioles," noting that "hustle, scaring up runs, sliding hard—what [John] McGraw called scientific baseball— goes to the heart of the game." Also, the subtitle of the 1910 book *Touching Second* by John J. Evers and Hugh S. Fullerton is "The Science of Baseball." Peter Morris (*Baseball Fever*, 2003, p.96) noted that the terms "science" and "scientific" in baseball go back to the 1860s: "Baseball derived additional credibility by becoming associated with the growing belief in science. In the 1860s and 1870s, scientific breakthroughs provided Americans with a tremendous number of labor-saving devices, and *science* became a magic word to Americans. This new faith in science crept into baseball terminology." For example: "The American game of base ball, as played by clubs in nearly all the cities of the north, is quite a scientific, as it is a very popular game, for summer amusement" (*Monroe* [Mich.] *Commercial*, May 1, 1862; Peter Morris). Also: "[Dickey] Pearce demonstrated the difference between wild hits to the field and scientific batting" (*Chicago Tribune*, July 6, 1870; Peter Morris). As pitching techniques and fielding skills improved, the resulting lower-scoring games were described as "scientific." "In an era where science was making the lives of Americans vastly easier, ['scientific'] was a magic word . . . [and] association with science was the equivalent of an endorsement from an unassailable source" (Peter Morris, *A Game of Inches: The Game on the Field*, 2006, p.143). IST USE (of the term "scientific" in baseball). 1857. "Those that witnessed the game considered the Massapoags [of Sharon, Mass.] the most skillful and scientific players" (*New York Clipper*, Nov.7; Peter Morris).

scissors A positioning technique in which the plate umpire (esp. in the National League) spreads his legs as if he is ready to start a race. Compare *slot*, 1.

scissors slide A slide in which both legs clamp the bag. "The infielder dropped his hand on a one-handed tag and [Jo-Jo] White lashed out with his scissors slide and kicked the ball into left field" (Gordon S. "Mickey" Cochrane, *Baseball: The Fan's Game*, 1939, p.41; Peter Morris). Syn. "scissors glide."

scoop 1. *v.* To dig down to field a low batted or thrown ball. IST USE. 1870. "[Al] Martin's grounder was scooped up by [Levi] Meyerle and sent to first in ample time to retire him" (*Chicago Tribune*, July 24; Peter Morris). **2.** *n.* A catch of a low batted ball. IST USE. 1876. "Myers fouled out on a capital 'run and scoop' by Brown" (*Detroit Free Press*, July 30; Peter Morris). **3.** *n.* Fielding and tossing a ball in one motion. "[Shortstop] Stickney has that fancy 'scoop' whereby the ball goes to the second baseman without being picked up by the shortstop at all, being simply changed

in its direction" (*San Francisco Examiner*, Apr. 8, 1889; Peter Morris).

scooter A sharply hit ground ball that skims along the grass. See also *daisy cutter*, 1.

scorch 1. To pitch a hard fastball; e.g., "Smith scorched one over for a called strike." **2.** To hit a ball very hard. "The pitchers cut loose with plenty of speed, just enough, in fact, for the ball to go scorching off the bat like a shot out of a cannon" (*San Francisco Bulletin*, Feb. 27, 1913; Gerald L. Cohen).

scorcher 1. A hard-hit, low line drive. IST USE. 1867. "Wright, by a 'scorcher' to left field, which Jewett 'could'nt [*sic*] see,' made his second base" (*Daily National Intelligencer* [Washington, D.C.], Aug. 27). **2.** A hard fastball.

scorchers *hist.* Syn. of *bleachers*, 1. IST USE. 1931. "The term 'scorchers' applies to the bleachers where the fans sit and burn in the sun" (W. Clifford Harvey, *Baseball Magazine*, January).

score 1. *v.* To touch home plate for a run; e.g., "Smith scored the fifth run." IST USE. 1858 (Walt Whitman, *Brooklyn Daily Times*, June 18; Edward J. Nichols). **2.** *v.* To bring a baserunner safely to home; e.g., "Jones scored Brown with a double to left." **3.** *n.* The tally at any given moment in a game, expressed exclusively in runs. "The score of a game is the simple record of outs and runs, either of the game or of a player" (Henry Chadwick, *The Game of Base Ball*, 1868, p.45). IST USE. 1853 "The game was commenced on Friday the 1st, but owing to the storm had to be postponed, the Knickerbockers making nine aces to the two of the Gotham, the following is the score for both days" (*Spirit of the Times*, July 9; John Thorn). **4.** *n.* A run in a baseball game. **5.** *v.* To create a record of a baseball game, including runs, hits, errors, and other events. **6.** *v.* For the official scorer to make a judgment call; e.g., "The ground ball was scored as a hit by the official scorer."

scoreathon A game in which both teams score many runs.

scoreboard 1. A signboard erected at the ballpark for the benefit of the spectators that, at a minimum, shows each team's inning-by-inning scoring as well as the total number of

It's going to be a good game. | Ha! What did I tell you. | Ah ha! Got them on the run | Well, I'll be _____ !!!! | That's a little better. | Ha, ha, ha! That's going some. | Hip! Hip! Hurrah! All over but the shouting. | What the ??!!!?x--!?! | They always were a lot of dubs.

Scoreboard. Postcard, ca. 1915. *Andy Moresund Collection*

hits, runs, and errors credited to each team. Most scoreboards give other relevant details of the game, such as the lineups, ball-strike count, and scores of other games being played concurrently. Scoreboards appear at every level of the game and range from manually operated wooden structures to elaborate electronic screens replete with special effects and moving images. Today, scoreboards show video displays, deliver greetings, ask trivia questions, prompt fans to cheer, and advertise products. Syn. *board*, 3. IST USE. 1887. "Donovan took up the bat and sent the ball in the neighborhood of the score board" (*San Francisco Examiner*, May 23; Peter Morris). **2.** *hist.* A large electrical or mechanical board erected in a communal gathering place, such as a town square, city intersection, opera house, theater, or armory, or outside a newspaper office, that allowed fans to witness a pitch-by-pitch visual recreation of a ball game (esp. a World Series game) via instantaneous telegraph transmissions. The scoreboards were popular during the late 19th and early 20th centuries before radio broadcasts. Colored electric lights portrayed strikes, balls, outs, and runners on base. The newspaper score-

board was invented by *The World* (New York) editorial writer Edward Van Zile in 1888.

scorebook A bound collection of scorecards. IST USE. 1872 (*The Boston Daily Globe*, March 27, 1872; Peter Morris).

scorecard **1.** A card, chart, or sheet of paper on which the offensive and defensive plays of a game are noted using the special shorthand of the game. Sometimes spelled "score card." IST USE. 1866. "Parker's Improved Score Cards" were used at a game played in Hoboken, N.J., on Oct. 29 (Frederick Ivor-Campbell, *Nineteenth Century Notes*, the newsletter of the SABR Nineteenth Century Committee, Winter 1995). The word "Improved" implies that the term had been used earlier. **2.** A magazine-style program sold at the ballpark, containing ads, articles, and other information about the home team, including a scoresheet bound in the middle as its center spread. It also contains the rosters of both teams with each player's position and number. The vendors who sell them often have a one-line sales pitch that they shout repeatedly. Ken Abrahams at Al Lang Stadium in St. Petersburg, Fla., sold St. Louis Cardinals and New York Mets Grapefruit

League scorecards with this simple line (*St. Petersburg Times*, March 9, 1986): "Get the names and numbers of all the millionaires, just 50 cents." EXTENDED USE. A figurative document for identifying persons, such as in a novel with many characters.

scorekeeper An official who keeps a record of the score of a game; technically, the umpire-in-chief who conducts the game. Not to be confused with *scorer*.

scoreless tie A game or part of a game in which neither team has scored a run.

scorer An individual who is given the job of ruling on the plays in a baseball game; specif., *official scorer*. Not to be confused with *scorekeeper*. IST USE. 1860. Part of a box score (*Detroit Free Press*, Aug. 7; Peter Morris).

scoresheet A play-by-play account of a baseball game, kept by using a standard form such as one found in a scorecard (program) at the ballpark. Although ballpark scorecards usually list instructions on how to record the events of a game, individuals often have highly personalized systems for doing so. (David W. Smith)

scoring A system of recording the events of a game, usually marked on a scoresheet. It uses its own shorthand; e.g., every defensive player has a number (1 for pitcher, 2 for catcher, 3 for first baseman, 4 for second baseman, 5 for third baseman, 6 for shortstop, 7 for left fielder, 8 for center fielder, and 9 for right fielder). An out is noted by listing all the numbers of the players who touch the ball. A ground ball that is hit to the shortstop who throws it to first base for an out is noted as 6–3. Fly balls are noted by the player who catches the ball. A strikeout is a K, but if the batter is called out looking the K is reversed. Base hits are 1B (single), 2B (double), 3B (triple), and HR (home run). There are many variations on standard scoring, both public and private. Writing about a system he developed, Kenneth Ikenberry (*The Washington Post*, Aug. 7, 1982) noted that he tried to record every nuance of the game up to and including whether the pitcher was thinking about his stock portfolio when he threw the hanging curve. "I buy scorebooks of such ancient lineage that they spell baseball as two words on the cover, and I fill them with tiny symbolic letters, arrows, chevrons, circles, stars—the stuff of the cabala. When they are full I throw them in the back of the car."

scoring index **1.** A method for evaluating the offensive performance of a batter in a season, based on a term representing on-base percentage with extra-base hits subtracted, multiplied by a term representing total bases plus stolen bases. It was introduced by Earnshaw Cook in *Percentage Baseball* (1964) and *Percentage Baseball and the Computer* (1971), and has been found to be a good predictor of offensive performance. Abbrev. *DX*. **2.** A method for evaluating offensive performance of a batter in a season, based on estimating how many runs would be scored in an inning if that player could record every plate appearance. It was devised by statisticians Donato A. D'Esopo and Benjamin Lefkowitz in 1960, but remained unpublished until *Optimal Strategies in Sports* (1977). There is a difference of opinion concerning the success of this scoring index as a predictor of offensive performance; John Thorn and Pete Palmer (*The Hidden Game of Baseball*, 1985) found mediocre results, but Jim Albert and Jay Bennett (*Curve Ball*, 2001) encountered fairly good accuracy.

scoring iron *hist.* Syn. of *home plate* (*The Sporting News*, Oct. 30, 1913).

scoring position Second base and third base when occupied by a baserunner who should be able to score on a single to the outfield. A runner who attempts to steal second base is trying to get into scoring position. Having a runner or runners in scoring position is what puts a pitcher in a jam. See also *runner in scoring position*. IST USE. 1908. "With two strikes called, Abby [Ed Abbaticchio] drove one into the right field crowd and he and Honus [Wagner] took second and third, respectively, placing them in scoring position" (Harvey Woodruff, *Chicago Tribune*, Oct. 5; Bill James). USAGE NOTE. Bill James (personal communication, Sept. 23, 2006) notes that the term "exploded" in baseball in the 1920s and was used commonly in the first half of the 20th century in other sports, including football, soccer, rugby, polo, horse racing, lacrosse, curling, and tennis.

scoring rules See *official scoring rules.*

scout 1. *n.* An individual who evaluates and recommends or signs players at lower levels of the game; an individual who observes and reports on existing talent at any level of the game. IST USE. 1891. "Ted Sullivan, the base ball scout, is in Chicago in the interests of the Baltimore Club after Jack Pickett and has offered him $3,000 with $400 advance, for next season" (*The Sporting News*, Nov. 21; Peter Morris). **2.** *n.* An individual who observes a team's future opponent and reports on its potential strengths and weaknesses. **3.** *v.* To act as a scout. IST USE. 1909. "[Roger Bresnahan] jumped out Monday night for his home in Toledo to scout around Ohio for ball players who might make his club more formidable" (Ring W. Lardner, *Chicago Tribune*, July 7; Peter Morris). **4.** *n./hist.* A second catcher in the Massachusetts game who played far to the rear of the regular catcher, grabbed passed balls and wild pitches, and fielded batted balls that landed nearby ("foul balls" were then unknown and batters could run on hits behind the plate as well as in front of it) (Dan Schlossberg, *The Baseball Catalog*, 1975). **5.** *n./hist.* A fielder in the Massachusetts game and in rounders. "One of these swiftly-delivered balls, when stopped by a skillful batsman, is sure to give the outmost scout employment" (*Spirit of the Times*, Dec. 27, 1856; Peter Morris). "The scouts should seldom aim at the runners from a distance, but throw the ball up to the feeder or to some one near" (Charles Peverelly, *The Book of American Pastimes*, 1866; Peter Morris).

scouting report A detailed written evaluation of a player of potential worth to the scout's club or an evaluation of a team's future opponent.

scouting scale A standard scale used by scouts to attempt to bring uniformity and objective measurement to the inescapably subjective process of player evaluation. Scouts grade a player's present performance (measured against major-league players) as well as his future or projected performance if he reaches his potential. Criteria for judging position players include the five tools (hitting, hitting for power, running, arm strength, and fielding). The scale allows 20 points maximum for each of the five tools. Total scores: 80 (excellent or outstanding, a blue-chip major leaguer), 70 (very good), 60 (good or above average), 50 (major-league average), 40 (fair below average), 30 (well below average), and 20 (poor). Another scale uses the figures 2 to 8. Criteria for judging pitchers include the level of his fastball, curveball, slider, another pitch, control, mound presence, and aggressiveness. For easily measured attributes, such as the speed of a pitcher's fastball or the time of a runner in the 60-yard dash, the scout follows a chart for determining a prospect's score. The scale also includes a grade for the player's makeup (intangible qualities). See also *overall future potential.* Syn. *20-to-80 scale.*

scout seat One of the seats directly behind home plate that are reserved for scouts and other talent evaluators, so that their radar guns can be used most effectively. Scout seats are an important indication of the prestige of a game, particularly at a showcase event. "More than two weeks before the [2002 Futures Game], Major League Baseball had received requests for 40 scout seats" (Will Lingo, *Baseball America*, July 8–21, 2002; Peter Morris). Interestingly, legendary scout Tony Lucadello (quoted in Mark Winegardner, *Prophet of the Sandlots*, 1990) revealed, "Ninety-nine percent of all scouts sit behind home plate. That's about the worst place to be."

scout's player A player who tantalizes a scout with his potential (e.g., exhibiting power during batting practice), but whose athleticism and talent do not translate into production (Tom Verducci, *Sports Illustrated*, March 26, 2001, p.32).

scraper Short for *skyscraper.* "Larruped a scraper—batted a high ball" (*The Sporting News*, Nov. 27, 1897).

scrappy Said of player whose feisty and competitive nature helps him to overcome a physical disadvantage. The term frequently implies small; e.g., "[5' 7"] Craig] Grebeck's entire career is based on scrappy play in all phases of the game" (STATS Inc., *The Scouting Notebook 2001*; Peter Morris). John Leo (*Charleston Daily Mail*, Apr. 10, 1997) defined "scrappy" as "a baseball term meaning mediocre but extremely active and likable."

scratch 1. *v.* To score runs with a series of plays, such as singles, walks, steals, and sacrifices, instead of scoring runs with power, such as home runs. 2. *v.* To have difficulty in scoring or hitting; e.g., "One husky individual . . . had just scratched out a hit and made the first bag in safety" (*San Francisco Bulletin*, May 3, 1913; Gerald L. Cohen). IST USE. 1887. "In the fourth, [Sam] Thompson scratched a hit close by [pitcher Bob] Caruthers" (*Detroit Morning Times*, Oct. 11). 3. *n.* Syn. of *scratch hit*. "[Tip O'Neill] got a clean single to right and [Charlie] Comiskey secured a scratch to left" (*Detroit Free Press*, Oct. 16, 1887). IST USE. 1876 (*Chicago Inter-Ocean*, May 1; Edward J. Nichols). 4. *v.* To remove a player from the lineup or pitching rotation. 5. *n.* A player removed from the lineup or pitching rotation. 6. *n./hist.* Home plate. "Buck Ewing, bat in hand, walked up to the scratch and faced [Charlie] Buffington [*sic*], the premier pitcher of the Quakers" (*The World* [New York], Aug. 3, 1889; Gerald L. Cohen). IST USE. 1872. "Matt Carpenter next went to the scratch" (George G. Small, *A Presidential Base-Ball Match*, p.10). USAGE NOTE. The term "toe the scratch" first appeared in the *New York Herald* (Aug. 20, 1881) for a batter taking his position at home plate, facing the pitcher (Edward J. Nichols, *An Historical Dictionary of Baseball Terminology*, PhD dissertation, 1939, p.80). 7. *hist.* One run. "Brooklyn Wins by a Scratch" (*Brooklyn Eagle* headline, June 29, 1870; Peter Morris, who suggests that the term derives from the practice in early baseball of keeping the score of a game by making notches on sticks).

scratch hit A ball that is not hit solidly but that results, nevertheless, in a hit; a lucky or fluke hit, often an infield grounder. See also *scratch single*; *sea gull*. Syn. *scratch*, 3; *dime hit*. IST USE. 1879. "[A ball that falls between several fielders] would generally be considered a base-hit, providing none of the players touched the ball, although it would be of the kind known as a 'scratch hit' " (*Chicago Tribune*, July 20; Peter Morris).

scratch nine A team consisting of newly recruited or untried players. IST USE. 1880 (*Brooklyn Daily Eagle*, Aug. 25; Edward J. Nichols).

scratch run A run scored because of a scratch hit.

scratch single A one-base *scratch hit*. IST USE. 1887. "Rainey then got a scratch single" (*The World* [New York], Aug. 28; Gerald L. Cohen).

scratch the diamond For the ground crew to smooth the basepaths. Frank Gibbons (*Baseball Digest*, May 1959) wrote, "This is an oldie, brought around by Joe Sewell and it means drag the field."

scratchy In the nature of scratch hits. IST USE. 1905. "[Dave] Zearfoss' 'hit' in the second inning was extremely scratchy" (*Chicago Tribune*, May 7; Peter Morris).

screamer A hard-hit ball; a line drive. "[Willie] McCovey then struck a low screamer toward right—a sure championship blow but for the fact that the ball flew directly into the glove of Bobby Richardson, at second" (Roger Angell, *The Summer Game*, 1972, p.94; Charles D. Poe). IST USE. 1875. "[Ned Cuthbert] led off with a screamer to left field" (*St. Louis Post-Dispatch*, May 7; Peter Morris).

screaming meemie A vicious, low line drive that seems to "scream," probably due to a high rate of spin on the ball. Syn. "screaming mimi." ETYMOLOGY. The term is a bit of slang that has been applied to a variety of things. Peter Tamony noted that the "screaming mimis" were the jitters (as in the 1942 film *Balls of Fire*, starring Gary Cooper and Barbara Stanwyck). During World War II, it was used as slang for German artillery shells.

screaming rope An extraordinarily hard-hit line drive. See also *rope*, 1.

screecher A hard-hit line drive. "A screecher straight into Bradley's glove" (*The Washington Post*, May 17, 1909; Peter Morris). IST USE. 1891 (*Chicago Herald*, July 5; Edward J. Nichols).

screen 1. A wire or net barrier erected in front of spectators to protect them from batted balls (esp. behind home plate). According to David Nemec (*The Great Encyclopedia of*

19th Century Major League Baseball, 1997, p.125), Messer Park in Providence was the first to install a protective screen in 1879 "to save spectators in the 'Slaughter Pens' behind home plate from being skulled by foul balls." IST USE. 1879. "It is intended to put up a wire screen behind the catcher instead of the unsightly boards generally used" (*Detroit Post and Tribune*, Apr. 28; Peter Morris). **2.** A protective device employed during batting practice and situated at first base, second base, and the pitcher's mound (see *batting-practice screen*). **3.** A baserunner who gets between the ball and the fielder.

screw arm The left arm.

screw armer A left-handed pitcher.

screwball 1. A zany player (Hy Turkin, ed., *1954 Gillette World Series Record Book*). "Baseball boners pulled by bushers all over the country are pinned to the old Athletics' inimitable screwball, Rube Waddell" (Bennett Cerf, *Saturday Review of Literature*, Dec. 31, 1949). IST USE. 1944. "Screwball—Term often applied to a lefty given to eccentricities or to other player who does odd things" (Al Schacht, *Al Schacht Dope Book*, p.44).

2. A pitched ball that breaks in the opposite direction of a curveball. It is held the same as a fastball or curveball but is thrown with an inward rotation of the hand and arm. It is spun out of the hand between the middle finger and the fourth and fifth fingers with the middle finger and wrist providing the spin. Unlike with the curveball, the wrist is snapped a quarter turn inward and the ball breaks less, and with less speed. When thrown by a right-handed pitcher, the screwball breaks down and in to a right-handed batter and down and away to a left-handed batter. Because it is difficult to master, the screwball is not a popular pitch: the pitcher has to twist his arm with an inside-out motion, thereby making the elbow susceptible to injury. The pitch was first made famous by Christy Mathewson, who called it the *fadeaway*, and later revived by Carl Hubbell as the "screwball." Hubbell developed three speeds for the pitch. According to Frank Graham (*McGraw of the Giants*, 1944), Ty Cobb did not sign Hubbell because he thought the screwball would ruin Hub-

Screwball.

bell's arm, to which New York Giants manager John McGraw snorted, "That's a joke. Screw ball! When Matty was pitching it, they called it a fadeaway and it never hurt his arm." Also spelled "screw ball." Syn. *reverse curve; scroogie,* 1; *screwgie; corkscrew ball; butterfly curve; in-curve,* 1. IST USE. 1921. "[Dixie] Davis had an innovation in the pitching line in the shape of a screw ball that enabled him to stand [George] McBride's hirelings on their heads" (John A. Dugan, *The Washington Post*, May 21). ETYMOLOGY. A ball bowled in cricket with a "screw" or spin is a "screw ball"; e.g., "A 'screw' ball, which in slow bowling would describe the arc of a circle from the pitch to the wicket, becomes in fast bowling a sharp angle" (Capt. Crawley, *Cricket*, 1866, p.35; *OED*). George Vecsey interviewed Carl Hubbell (*The New York Times*, July 9, 1984), and after establishing the fact that Hubbell first threw the pitch in the minor leagues, Vecsey concluded, "If the pitch was thrown before Hubbell, it certainly had no mystique until a catcher in Oklahoma City—Hubbell says his name was Earl Walgamot—warmed him up before a game and said: 'That's the screwiest thing I ever saw.'" David Block (*Baseball Before We Knew It*, 2005, pp.207–8) uncovered an interesting passage from *The Knickerbocker* (Nov. 1845, v.26, pp.426–27), which bemoaned that the wearing of a "tournure" (a type of bustle worn in the rear beneath a skirt) distorted the grace and beauty of a woman's stride: "The motion very much resembles that of one who, in playing 'base,' screws his ball, as the expression is among boys; or of a man rolling what is known among the players of ten pins as a 'screw ball.'" Commented Block, "Notwithstanding the obnoxiousness of the source, this may be the earliest allusion to the practice of curving a baseball pitch." The term later showed up in *Galaxy* magazine (July 15, 1866; Richard Hershberger) in an unsigned section "Nebulae" by "the Editor": "This was the way in which we played base-ball . . . up to all the tricks of the field; of the fellows who knocked far balls, and low balls, and screw balls; and that most puzzling fellow of all, who, when you least expected it, knocked the ball with the pitch." It also appeared in the *Troy* [N.Y.] *Times* (reprinted in *Syracuse Journal*, June 18, 1868; Larry McCray) regarding pitcher Rua of the Union-Haymakers: "That 'screw' ball of his that twists and speeds as if shot from a rifle, was really artistic."

EXTENDED USE. **1.** *n.* Since the 1930s, an eccentric or madman. "The spirit of the screwball is neither national nor mortal but transcends time itself, and, like love's fragrant essence, is everywhere" (Nunnally Johnson, introduction to Stanley Walker, *Mrs. Astor's Horse*, 1935; Peter Tamony). **2.** *adj.* Eccentric, zany, or insane; e.g., "screwball comedy," a form of fast-moving, irreverent, romantic comedy film that thrived between 1929 and 1948 and featured madcap plots, odd pranks, and slapstick. "[MGM] has popped up with another of those screwball comedies—this one called *Three Loves Has Nancy*" (*The New York Times*, Sept. 2, 1938; *OED*). **3.** *adj.* Said of fast jazz improvisation or crazy, wide-open swing music. "The music of hot bands . . . is referred to as 'swing' or 'jive' of which in turn there are several kinds. Accepted meanings vary according to locale, and the terms overlap, but, roughly, the most-used designations, in order of their increasing hotness are 'gutbucket,' 'screwball,' and 'whacky,' the last being the wildest, most unbridled kind of swing" (Benny Goodman, *The New Yorker*, Apr. 17, 1937).

screwballer One who throws the screwball pitch. "The prime screwballer of our time is Fernando Valenzuela" (Roger Angell, *The New Yorker*, May 4, 1987, p.117).

screwbeenie Var. of *scrubini*.

screwgie Syn. of *screwball*, 2. "Without the benefit of a tape measure, my ego will not permit me to believe that there is any way

Luis [Aparicio] could hit my screwgie 315 feet on a line" (Bill [Spaceman] Lee, *The Wrong Stuff*, 1984, p.44). See also *scroogie*.

screwjack *hist.* **1.** A player who is notoriously wacky. **2.** A player who is notoriously lucky (Al Schacht, *Al Schacht Dope Book*, 1944, p.44).

screws See *on the screws*.

scribe A sportswriter. George Herman Ruth (*Babe Ruth's Own Book of Baseball*, 1928) noted that scribes are not just any writers but "the newspaper men who accompany a big league ball club on the road." IST USE. 1887 (*Base Ball Tribune*, May 23; Edward J. Nichols).

scrimmage **1.** *n.* An informal intra- or intersquad game. The term seems to have been borrowed from football and applied only at the amateur level. From a report on a high-school team: "The Whalers' first scrimmage of the season will take place at the high school field Saturday when they'll play a doubleheader against a team from Montville, Connecticut" (Steve Sheppard, *Nantucket* [Conn.] *Inquirer and Mirror*, Apr. 2, 1987). **2.** *v.* To conduct a scrimmage.

scroogie **1.** Syn. of *screwball*, 2. This slang term is also spelled, less commonly, as *screwgie*, and Charles D. Poe notes that "since the root word is 'screw' and not 'Scrooge,' it seems to me that 'screwgie' should be the preferred spelling. 'Scroogie' has a misleading Dickensian flavor to it." IST USE. 1953. "Mickey Mantle coined a new word to describe the pitch he hit for [a] home run—'It was some sort of a scroogie.' [Preacher] Roe confirmed Mantle's description: 'It was a changeup screwball'" (Associated Press, Oct. 2; Harold Wentworth & Stuart Berg Flexner, *Dictionary of American Slang*, 1960). **2.** A screwball pitcher (Harold Seymour, *Baseball: The Golden Age*, 1971, p.147).

scrotum ball Syn. of *submarine ball*. ETYMOLOGY. The term was introduced by Bill Heward (*Some Are Called Clowns*, 1974, p.41; Charles D. Poe) "as a more definitive label since the pitch, when released from below that point on the pitcher's anatomy and crossing the plate below that same mark on the batter's frame, is very effective."

scrub 1. An informal bat-and-ball game; e.g., a form of baseball played in New England "when there are too few players to have opposing sides" (*Dialect Notes*, 1892; *OED*). An exhibit at the National Baseball Hall of Fame and Museum notes that there is one batter and others in the field in this "forerunner of baseball." Bill Kirwin (editor of *NINE: A Journal of Baseball History and Culture*) remarks that scrub was a game played by children in the United States and Canada: "I remember playing this game until enough kids appeared to constitute a real game. The version we usually played used just one base with two batters and any number of fielders. We would then expand the game to two bases (first and third using three batters) and finally to all bases, although this rarely happened." Al Yellon (personal communication, Dec. 11, 2005) recalled playing "scrub," a game similar to *work-up*, in the Chicago suburbs in the 1960s. 2. An "old game" that "lies between Cat Ball and Base Ball, though whether it precedes or followed the game of Base Ball in point of time no man can say" (John Montgomery Ward, letter to Albert G. Spalding, June 19, 1907, published in *Spalding's Official Base Ball Guide*, 1908). 3. A substitute or member of the B or second team; a backup player on the bench. The term tends to be used in a derogatory manner. See also *scrubini*. Syn. *scrubbie*. IST USE. 1885. "One of the players engaged for next season [by Brooklyn] said the Metropolitans were nothing but a lot of 'scrubs' from the lots" (*The Sporting Life*, Feb. 11; Peter Morris).

scrubbie Syn. of *scrub*, 3.

scrubbini Var. of *scrubini*.

scrubeenie Var. of *scrubini*. "All the scrubeenies pray for extra innings in the spring. Or at least they should" (Jim Bouton, *Ball Four*, 1970). "Hell, I wasn't even a regular with the Yankees, I was just a 'scrubeenie,' as Phil Linz and Johnny Blanchard and the rest of us substitutes called ourselves" (Joe Pepitone, *Joe, You Coulda Made Us Proud*, 1975; Charles D. Poe). IST USE. 1954 (Kenneth Versand, *Polyglot's Lexicon 1943–1966*, 1973).

scrub game An informal baseball game between members of the same club (in which the players choose sides and no records are kept) or between two clubs. Syn. *scrub match*. IST USE. 1862. "[The Eckfords] have already commenced practicing and have had a scrub game with the Favorites" (*Brooklyn Eagle*, Apr. 7).

scrubinee Var. of *scrubini*. "Whether your name was Brooks Robinson or a 'scrubinee' like me, he treated all of us with the same respect and recognition" (utility infielder Bob Johnson, concerning Orioles public relations/publicity director Bob Brown, quoted in *The Baltimore Sun*, Apr. 30, 2000).

scrubini A modern variation on *scrub*, 3, which seems a touch more affectionate than the original. "The first year the Braves were in Milwaukee, the team was always getting some kind of award or presents, which usually did not include the 'scrubinis' and the bullpen crew" (Joe Garagiola, *Baseball Is a Funny Game*, 1960; Charles D. Poe). Var. *scrubbini*; *scrubeenie*; *scrubinee*; *screwbeenie*.

scrub match Syn. of *scrub game*. IST USE. 1855. "The Gotham and Baltic at the Red House, Harlem, and the Pioneer and Excelsior, of New Jersey, made up a scrub match among themselves" (*Spirit of the Times*, Dec. 8; Peter Morris).

scrub nine A team of rookies and/or substitutes. IST USE. 1868 (*New York Herald*, Aug. 11; Edward J. Nichols).

scrub team A team composed of scrub players. IST USE. 1877. "At Lynn, the 'scrub team,' known as the Worcesters, defeated the Live Oaks by 6 to 4" (*London* [Ont.] *Free Press*, May 20; Peter Morris).

scrubwoman A cleanup hitter in the All-American Girls Professional Baseball League.

scud Slang syn. of *home run* (George Gmelch, *Inside Pitch*, 2001, p.59).

scuff 1. *v.* To doctor a baseball by roughening its surface. 2. *v.* To rub shiny white baseballs with mud to remove their gloss. 3. *n.* A rough spot or mark on the ball, which causes it to break when pitched. "Each ball had a quarter-sized scuff mark in approximately the same spot, a scuff just big enough to give pitches an odd, violent movement" (Richard Justice, *The Washington Post*, Oct. 15, 1986).

scuffball Syn. of *scuffed ball*. "[The New York Mets] complained only about Mike Scott's supposed scuffball" (*USA Today*, Oct. 15, 1986).

scuffed ball A ball that has been illegally marked or roughed up to give it an unnatural trajectory. A scuffed ball, when pitched, offers more resistance to the natural airflow and therefore acts erratically, as air will not flow uniformly over it. The pitcher holds the ball with the rough side opposite to the direction he wants it to break (to make the pitch curve to the right, the scuff is put on the left side of the ball, and the ball is thrown like a Wiffle ball). Pitcher Mike Flanagan (quoted by Thomas Boswell, *How Life Imitates the World Series*, 1982): "It takes no talent whatsoever. You just throw it like a mediocre fastball. The scuff gives the break." See also *emery ball*. Syn. *scuffer*, 1; *scuffball*.

scuffer 1. Syn. of *scuffed ball*. 2. One who throws a scuffed ball.

scuffgate A controversy involving scuffed balls; specif., the discussion surrounding the alleged illegal pitching technique of Houston Astros hurler Mike Scott during the 1986 National League Championship Series against the New York Mets, who claimed that Scott put marks on the ball that were the size of 25-cent pieces. ETYMOLOGY. The term is one of many that play off the Watergate scandal of the 1970s by using the suffix "-gate."

scuffing 1. Roughing up, defacing, or marking a ball prior to pitching it. 2. The act of making a ball grippable without changing its natural flight.

scuffle 1. *v.* To fail to perform up to standard; to be ineffective or in a slump. "[Javier] Lopez scuffled for most of the spring, batting .128 with one home run, while trying to adjust to playing first base" (*The Baltimore Sun*, Apr. 3, 2006). "You've got nine guys in the lineup. You don't expect nine to scuffle" (Baltimore Orioles manager Sam Perlozzo, quoted in *The Baltimore Sun*, Aug. 25, 2005). See also *struggle*, 1. USAGE NOTE. According to John Marshall (*Seattle Post-Intelligencer*, July 8, 2003), the term gained prominence among the Seattle Mariners (esp. Bret Boone) during the 2003 season, but John Hickey (*Seattle Post-Intelligencer* beat writer for the Mariners) reports having heard the term used for two decades and says that it was long a "pet word" of manager Tony La Russa during his Oakland years. Boston Red Sox pitcher Dennis Eckersley used the term "scuffling" in 1980 (Jan Freeman, *The Boston Globe*, May 2, 2004). The term is often used in its participle form ("scuffling"), and in the late 19th century meant "struggling" or "eking out one's bare living"; later it blossomed as part of America's jazz vocabulary, and had transferred to the sports world by at least the 1970s: "In Oakland there will be a rematch of the 11th Super Bowl teams, with both scuffling to make the playoffs this year" (Dave Brady, *The Washington Post*, Dec. 11, 1977). 2. *n.* A mild, disorganized fight or tussle. "There were six ejections in the seventh inning following a sequence of inside pitches and two bench-clearing scuffles" (*The Baltimore Sun*, Apr. 25, 2005). USAGE NOTE. John Thorn (personal communication, July 8, 2004) notes that Cap Anson's 1871 contract with the Forest City Base Ball Club of Rockford, Ill., stipulated that he "abstain from profane language, scuffling and light conduct."

scuffling 1. *v.* Being in a slump. "Batting slumps spread through the Orioles' dugout like a virus until every hitter seemed to be scuffling at the same time" (*The Baltimore Sun*, May 5, 2005). 2. *adj.* Said of a player or team in a slump. "The sight of Atlanta's potent offense . . . covering for a scuffling starting staff produces a striking frisson of unfamiliarity" (*Sports Illustrated*, Sept. 1, 2003).

scull A free ticket of admission to a ball game. 1ST USE. 1907 (*New York Evening Journal*, Apr. 11; Edward J. Nichols).

scullion A very ugly player (John Maffei, *Baseball Digest*, May 1986). "A scullion is twice as bad as a mullion" (Bob Hertzel, *Baseball Digest*, Jan. 1987). See also *mullion*.

scuttlefish slide Syn. of *pop-up slide*. "An example of Negro League style later adopted by the majors was the so-called scuttlefish slide: a runner goes into a base feet first and horizontal, but in the same motion bounces up, to end standing on the bag" (James H. Bready, *Baseball in Baltimore*, 1998, p.182; Peter Morris).

seagull *hist.* A *scratch hit* in which the bat is broken.

Seagull Incident An incident that occurred in Exhibition Stadium in Toronto on Aug. 5, 1983, when New York Yankees outfielder Dave Winfield killed a seagull by tossing a warmup ball toward the bullpen. Winfield was charged with cruelty to animals; the charges were later dropped.

sea level 1. A won-lost mark of .500. A team can be said to be above or below sea level. "Red Sox find 'sea level,' but playoffs ocean away. . . . The Red Sox were last above sea level when they were 14–13 after 27 games on May 3" (*The Baltimore Sun*, Aug. 24, 1997). **2.** A batting average of .500. "[Ivan Rodriguez] batted .500 in June (43-for-86) to become the first Tiger with more than 70 at-bats ever to bat sea level for an entire month" (Peter Schmuck, *The Baltimore Sun*, July 4, 2004).

seam The curved line formed by the heavy, raised red stitching of the baseball. Although the two pieces of leather covering the ball are actually held together by one continuous seam, the stitching is almost always referred to in the plural. The seams are used by pitchers to gain added control over the ball; e.g., a pitcher will grip the ball across the seams to help his fastball rise, while a sidearm pitcher will grip a ball along the seams to help his fastball sink.

seamer A pitch thrown by gripping the ball either along the seams (see *two-seamer*) or across the seams (see *four-seamer*).

seamhead A dedicated baseball fan. "It's critical to note . . . with baseball's playoffs

Seam. Curved line of stitches on ball gripped by the pitcher, 1912. *George Grantham Bain Collection, Library of Congress*

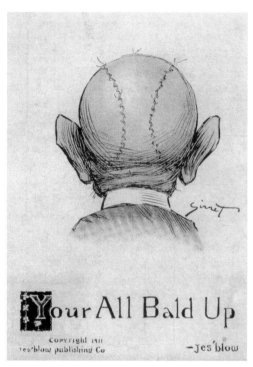

Seamhead. As depicted in a comic postcard, ca. 1912. *Andy Moresund Collection*

and World Series almost upon us, and its insufferable romantics (I prefer the far more derisive term 'seamheads') preparing to leave our sports pages all ooey and gooey with so much elitist, fluffy, poetic bunk about how baseball's championship chase ought to be the sole priority of autumn" (Bryan Burwell, *USA Today*, Oct. 1, 1993). "To appeal to the few remaining seamheads in Siberia-on-the-St. Lawrence, the [Montreal] Expos will offer two turn-back-the-clock promotions (old-style uniforms and concessions prices)" (Michael Farber, *Sports Illustrated*, March 18, 2002). Compare *stathead*. IST USE. 1989. "In other words, no baseball, at record prices. Not much trading to satisfy the seamheads who still believe the Hot Stove League is more fun than dinner and dancing with Jamie Lee Curtis" (Ray Ratto, *San Francisco Chronicle*, Dec. 7, 1989).

season A period of the year marked by the playing of baseball; specif., the days from early April (although sometimes the end of March) to early October when major-league teams play out their regularly scheduled

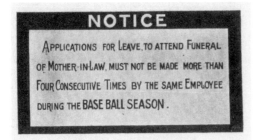

NOTICE

Applications for Leave, to attend Funeral of Mother-in-Law, must not be made more than Four Consecutive Times by the same Employee during the Base Ball Season.

Season. Postcard version of the classic workplace admonition. *Ron Menchine Collection.*

games. "The regular Ball season is considered to close with Thanksgiving, though many games will doubtless be played through the winter when the weather will permit" (*New Bedford* [Mass.] *Evening Standard*, Nov. 26, 1858; Kyle DeCicco-Carey). The term excludes *preseason* and *postseason* play. IST USE. 1845. "Two more Base clubs are already formed in our sister city [Brooklyn], and the coming season may witness some extra sport" (*New York Morning News*, Oct. 22).

seasonal notation A method for representing a player's career statistical record as if it applied to one season, for the purpose of providing a common framework for the interpretation of the player's career records. It is calculated by dividing career at-bats by 162, resulting in the number of 162-game "seasons" played, and then dividing career statistics by that number of seasons. To use an example from its originator, Bill James (*Baseball Abstract*, 1983): at the end of the 1982 season, George Hendrick had amassed 5290 at-bats and 214 home runs; dividing 5290 by 162 yields 9.03 162-game "seasons"; and dividing 214 by 9.03 results in 23.7 home runs per "season." The method first appeared in James' self-published *Baseball Abstract* (1977).

seasoning The process by which a minor-league player develops the skills to advance to the major leagues. IST USE. 1906 (*The Sporting Life*, Feb. 10, p.5; Edward J. Nichols).

season ticket A ticket, usually for a box seat, bought at a reduced rate by an individual or corporation for every home game. The ticket is only valid for the regular season, but it usually entitles its owner to an option to buy that seat or one like it for postseason play should the home team make it to the playoffs. According to Lee Allen (*The Hot Stove League*, 1955, p.116), season tickets were first sold in the National League by the Hartford club in 1876. IST USE. 1870. "There are one hundred and fifty honorary members, who ... get a season ticket" (*Lakeside Monthly*; David Shulman).

seat The place on the field where the feeder stands to toss the ball to the batter in the game of rounders (*The Ball Players' Chronicle*, July 18, 1867; Dean A. Sullivan).

seat-boomer Slang for a home run.

seating capacity The maximum number of spectators occupying the seats at a ballpark. "Colonel Jacob Ruppert, the Yankees' owner, yesterday announced that plans have been completed for increasing the seating capacity of the stadium to 84,000 for baseball" (*The New York Times*, Feb. 5, 1936). The seating capacity of Ebbets Field in Brooklyn went from 18,000 in 1913 to 31,903 in 1957.

seats The part of the ballpark where spectators sit; e.g., "Swing for the seats."

second 1. n. Short for *second base*, 1. IST USE. 1862 (Chadwick Scrapbooks clipping, Aug. 3; Edward J. Nichols). 2. n. Short for *second base*, 2. 3. n. The second inning. 4. adv. Said of the second position in the batting order; e.g., "Smith is batting second."

secondary average A metric invented by Bill James (*Baseball Abstract*, 1986) to measure components of offensive production other than batting average, computed by dividing *secondary bases* by official at-bats.

secondary bases The number of bases gained by a player independent of his batting average, computed by adding total bases, walks, and stolen bases, then subtracting hits and times caught stealing from that sum. The term was introduced by Bill James. See also *secondary average*.

secondary lead The distance a baserunner strays from the base after the pitch is thrown when he is not attempting to steal. The aim of the secondary lead is for the runner to get as far as possible off the base in the event the ball is hit, while still being able to return safely to the base if the ball is not hit.

second bagger Syn. of *second baseman.*

second base **1.** The base located 90 feet from first base on the opposite corner of the infield diamond from home plate; the halfway point on the trip around the bases. Abbrev. *2B,* 1. See also *keystone,* 1. Syn. *second,* 1; *halfway mark; halfway station; keystone,* 2; *middle bag; middle cushion; middle sack; middle station; midway; midway station; second corner; second sack; second station.* IST USE. 1845. "The bases shall be from 'home' to second base, forty-two paces" (Knickerbocker Rules, Rule 4th, Sept. 23). **2.** The defensive position given to the player who normally stands to the first base side of second base. Abbrev. *2B,* 2. Syn. *second,* 2. IST USE. 1856. "Wells, as second base, is excellent, and any balls that come in his range are bound to be caught" (*Spirit of the Times,* Dec. 20; Peter Morris). EXTENDED USE. In teenage slang, at various times since the 1930s, second base has meant petting above the waist.

second base combination Syn. of *double-play combination.* "With Chico Carrasquel alongside him [Nelson Fox], I believe we have as good a second base combination as there is in the league" (Chicago White Sox manager Paul Richards, quoted in *The Sporting News,* May 2, 1951).

second-base hit *hist.* Syn. of *double,* 1. "Kimball made a fine second-base hit" (*The Cleveland Morning Herald,* May 22, 1871).

second baseman The defensive player occupying the position between first and second base; one of two defensive infield players (the other being the shortstop) who cover second base. As seen from the plate, the second baseman is normally positioned to the right of the shortstop and to the left of the first baseman. He normally covers first base on a bunt and is likely to be involved when a ball is being relayed in from the outfield. Abbrev. *2B,* 3. Syn. *second bagger; second sacker; keystoner; middle baseman.* IST USE. 1864. "Oliver of the Atlantic was as famil-

iarly recognized one time as the 'second base man of the Atlantics' as by his own name" (*Brooklyn Eagle,* March 21; Peter Morris).

second base umpire The *base umpire* at second base.

second cleanup hitter Syn. of *number-eight hitter.*

second corner Syn. of *second base,* 1. IST USE. 1888. "As Sam [Thompson] jumped on the bag, the poor thing burst with grief, its contents being scattered all around the second corner" (*Detroit Free Press,* May 20)

second division *hist.* The bottom half of a league's standings at any given time (the last four teams in an eight-team league or the last five teams in a ten-team league) before 1969, when each of the two major leagues was broken into two divisions. Compare *first division.* IST USE. 1895. "The Baltimores, the winners of the flag last year, are not playing the ball they played last year, and the team is now down in the second division" (*Atlanta Constitution,* May 3; Peter Morris).

second guess **1.** *n.* Hindsight in criticizing the manager or players, either generally or in regard to specific decisions or plays. "No self-respecting sports writer should permit a mere baseball manager to dictate, because it is, and always should be, the inalienable right of the writers to run the ball club. There's no telling what might happen if the 'second-guess' gang in the press box lost its grip" (W.J. O'Connor, *St. Louis Post-Dispatch,* Apr. 7, 1915; Peter Morris). "Playing it over with the second guess is a favorite stunt in baseball" (*Atlanta Constitution,* Jan. 2, 1916; Benjamin Zimmer). "Second guesses are always right" (*The New York Times,* July 19, 1916; Benjamin Zimmer). IST USE. 1912. "Not criticizing the leaders, because second guess always is best, but in both cases it looked as if a bunt was the play" (*The New York Times,* Oct. 12; Benjamin Zimmer). **2.** *v.* To use critical hindsight. "I want to say right now that I have never second-guessed on any Cub player, nor have I ever had a thought of so doing" (Chicago Cubs manager Rogers Hornsby, quoted in *Decatur* [Ill.] *Daily Review,* Sept. 22, 1930; Benjamin Zimmer). Also spelled "second-guess." IST USE. 1922. "Second guessing is the natural born right of the baseball fan" (*Syracuse Herald*, June 9; Benjamin Zimmer).

second guesser One who habitually criticizes the players and their manager for specific actions; e.g., a fan or sportswriter who uses hindsight to question a manager's decision or strategy. "The second guessers can always make the best guess" (Ty Cobb, *Busting 'Em and Other Big League Stories*, 1914; Peter Morris). IST USE. 1914. "The baseball world is full of second guessers, a lot of whom believe they know more about the game than any manager or player living" (*Oshkosh* [Wisc.] *Daily Northwestern*, Jan. 3; Benjamin Zimmer).

second half 1. That part of a regular baseball season following the All-Star break in mid-July. Some pitchers are known as "second-half pitchers" because they do better in the second half of the season. Compare *first half*, 1. 2. That part of the inning when the home team gets its turn at bat. Compare *first half*, 2. Syn. *bottom*, 1; *bottom half*; *home half*; *last half*; *lower half*, 1.

second infield Infield practice before the game, after the starting infielders have practiced.

second-look free agency Syn. of *new-look free agency*.

second nine *hist.* A team in an early baseball club made up of players not quite good enough for the *first nine*. Members of the second nine would fill in for absent members of the first nine, but second nines also often issued their own challenges to either the first nine or second nine of another club. IST USE. 1858 (*New York Clipper*, June 19; Peter Morris).

second-order measure A team's projected winning percentage based on its equivalent runs and equivalent runs allowed as measured by the Pythagenport method. If a team's actual winning percentage is considerably better, then the team has been particularly lucky and/or has a particularly well-performing bullpen. The measure was proposed by *Baseball Prospectus*. Compare *first-order measure*; *third-order measure*.

second sack Syn. of *second base*, 1. IST USE. 1897. "Maryland would contribute Dumpling

Childs for the second sack" (*The Washington Post*, June 14)

second sacker Syn. of *second baseman*. IST USE. 1907. "The new second sacker had but one chance, and he accepted that cleanly" (Charles Dryden, *Chicago Tribune*, Aug. 30; Peter Morris).

Second Season The last two months of the 1981 season, which was bifurcated by a 50-day players' strike. It was a short season (48 to 54 games, depending on each team's remaining schedule) that began on Aug. 10. The term was applied laughingly by some.

second station Syn. of *second base*, 1. "['Tub'] Spencer allowed nine of the opposition to pilfer the second station" (*San Francisco Bulletin*, May 1, 1913; Gerald L. Cohen).

second-story act A stolen base. IST USE. 1907 (*New York Evening Journal*, Apr. 30; Edward J. Nichols).

second-story drive A home run. "Hap Felsch blasted a second-story drive and we went home with a 2–1 triumph" (Harry Stein, *Hoopla*, 1983, p.234).

second string The collection of players on a team who are not regularly given playing assignments but are available to replace or relieve those who start the game. Compare *first string*. IST USE. 1912 (*New York Tribune*, Sept. 16; Edward J. Nichols). ETYMOLOGY. Borrowed from the realm of the bow and arrow. Alfred H. Holt (*Phrase and Word Origins*, 1961) discussed this term under the entry for "two strings to his bow." Holt wrote, "The Elizabethans were very fond of this old archery figure for having something in reserve in case of accident. It is not so often heard today, but its two children, first-string and second-string, are well known on every athletic field, though almost nobody thinks to pay homage to their sturdy old father."

secret sauce The three ingredients that most reliably predict postseason success: a high strikeout rate for the pitching staff, adjusted for a team's league and ballpark (EqSO9); quality of defense, such as fielding runs above average (FRAA); and a reliable closer as measured by wins expected above replacement and adjusted for lineup faced (WXRL). Thus, a team that prevents the ball from going into play, catches it when it does, and preserves late-inning leads is likely to excel in the playoffs. The concept was introduced by *Baseball Prospectus*.

secure To get a base hit. "[Ping Bodie] secured one of the Sox's seven hits off Vean Gregg" (*San Francisco Bulletin*, Apr. 12, 1913; Gerald L. Cohen). IST USE. 1867. "Wheeler secured his first [base]" (*Daily National Intelligencer* [Washington, D.C.], July 29).

seed A pitched or batted ball that is moving so fast that it appears smaller than it actually is; it is said to look like a seed. See also *pea*, 1.

seeing-eye bat The figurative bat of a hitter in a streak when seemingly routine grounders become hits; a bat that for a period seems to be able to connect with every pitched ball for a hit. IST USE. 1952. "I got a seeing-eye bat, one of those Murine jobs" (*San Francisco Examiner*, July 17; Peter Tamony). ETYMOLOGY. From "Seeing Eye," the trademark used by trainers of guide dogs for the blind—the implication being that the bat is being guided, as if by a Seeing Eye dog.

seeing-eye single A slow or softly struck ground ball that eludes the infielders, as if it had the power of vision. "Among their 27 hits were the requisite number of seeing-eye singles, to be sure" (*The Boston Globe*, May 29, 2005). See also *ball with eyes on it*. ETYMOLOGY. See *seeing-eye bat*.

seesaw game A game in which runs are scored alternately by the two teams so that first one team, then the other, is ahead. IST USE. 1892 (*Chicago Herald*, May 21; Edward J. Nichols).

seesaw play A pickoff play executed against a runner on second base. "The see-saw play is sometimes well worked by short and second, the runner being caught by a sharp throw by the pitcher to one of the fielders mentioned when the runner's attention is diverted by the movements of the other" (Dudley Dean, *Atlanta Constitution*, June 5, 1892; Peter Morris). As employed by the Harvard club team, the play was described in the *New York Sun* (Apr. 26, 1889; Peter Morris): "The player who has succeeded in reaching second base, on seeing that baseman step back to his usual position, about ten feet back of the base line, steals several feet down the path toward third. When he is about in front of the short stop that player makes a dash toward second base, which causes the runner to dart in that direction also, but the short stop's run is only a feint, and the runner, on seeing the short stop stop, also stops before reaching second, and the pitcher throws the ball to the second baseman, who is on the base, and whom the runner has entirely forgotten, and the runner is out."

see the ball To concentrate and take a good swing at a pitch because the ball looks bigger than normal. Seattle Mariners manager Lou Piniella (quoted in *Orioles Gazette*, Aug. 13, 1993): "Seeing the ball means picking up the ball leaving the pitcher's hand, following the flight of the ball until it gets to the hitting zone . . . [where] it looks like a great big watermelon. You're not getting fooled. Your mechanics are good. You're focused, and most important of all, you're confident. And when you're confident, you're seeing the ball better." Harold Baines (quoted in *Baltimore Sun*, July 22, 1999): "The longer you see the ball, the more chance you have to hit it. When I'm seeing the ball well, I can track it all the way into the catcher's mitt."

see the barrels To experience an omen of good luck (*Baseball Magazine*, Oct. 1911, p.71). ETYMOLOGY. According to Joseph McBride (*High and Inside*, 1980, p.73), "'Turkey Mike' Donlin of the New York Giants arrived for a game at the Polo Grounds in the early 1900s and noted a wagon load of empty barrels going by. On that day, he got three hits but on the following day he went hitless and blamed this on the fact that he had not seen any barrels before the game. His manager, the crafty John McGraw, hired a wagon loaded with barrels to circle the grounds every day and Donlin went on a hitting spree."

seeya A home run. ETYMOLOGY. Asked about this term, Atlanta Braves pitcher Jim Nash (*The Sporting News*, Apr. 1, 1972) replied: "Yep, that's what you say as it goes out of the park. Seeya."

Se League Syn. of *Central League*.

sell 1. To get a batter to go after a pitch; e.g., a pitcher may be said to be having a difficult time "selling" his curveball. 2. For an umpire to convince the players of a close call by making his decision in an emphatic manner, with flair and authority. Gesture, body language, and voice contribute to selling the call, as does each umpire's personal sense of rhythm and style.

sellout *n.* A ball game in which all available seats are sold and some fans may be standing.

sell out *v.* 1. To throw a game. IST USE. 1874 (*Chicago Inter-Ocean*, July 4; Edward J. Nichols). 2. To sell all available seats for a game.

semi-pro 1. *adj.* Said of a player, team, or league engaged in the playing of baseball for pay but on a part-time basis. A semi-pro player is paid to play the game, but must depend on another occupation to make a living. Semi-pro teams in the early part of the 20th century and through World War II were formed by firehouses, police departments, towns (the town's merchants supported teams), industrial leagues (players worked for the same company they played for), independent players (they played for whoever would pay), barnstorming teams (under contract), and professional Negro leagues (which were called "semi-pro" in the 1930s and 1940s). More currently, semi-pro leagues consist of players who have serious aspirations and the required talent to advance beyond local adult amateur leagues. Also spelled "semipro." IST USE. 1908. "The 'Semi-Pro' League Ball; regulation size and weight. . . . Price, $1.00" (*Spalding's Official Base Ball Guide*, p.368; *OED*). ETYMOLOGY. Short for *semi-professional*. 2. *n.* A semi-pro ballplayer. IST USE. 1910. "The despised semi-pros were drawing big crowds" (*Baseball Magazine*, April; *OED*).

semi-professional Syn. of *semi-pro*, 1. IST USE. 1877. "Below are the tabulated announcements for games to be played by League and semi-professional clubs in the West" (*London* [Ont.] *Free Press*, Apr. 25; Peter Morris).

Senators 1. Nickname for the National League franchises in Washington, D.C., from 1886 to 1889 (also known as the Washington Statesmen) and from 1892 to 1899. 2. Official nickname for the American League franchise in Washington, D.C., from 1901 to 1904 and from 1957 to 1960, before it became the Minnesota Twins in 1961. The franchise was officially known as the Washington *Nationals* from 1905 to 1956. The Senators were the target of the old line on Washington: "First in war, first in peace, and last in the American League." 3. Nickname for the American League expansion franchise in Washington, D.C., from 1961 to 1971, before it became the Texas Rangers in 1972.

sencillo Spanish for "single."

send 1. To signal a runner to try to advance to the next base. 2. To bat a ball, usually hard; e.g., "Smith sent one down to third." IST USE. 1899 (Burt L. Standish, *Frank Merriwell's Double Shot*, p.69; Edward J. Nichols).

send a message To pitch close to the batter; to throw a message pitch.

send down 1. To assign a major-league player to a minor-league team for further training and experience. Paul Wilborn (*Tampa Tribune*, March 26, 1989) wrote, "[Getting] 'sent down' means back to Indianapolis, or Albuquerque or Jacksonville. It means another year of buses, tight budgets and no permanent address." Syn. *send out*. 2. To defeat. "The Angels found little or no difficulty in sending the 'Haps' down the line" (*San Francisco Bulletin*, Apr. 8, 1913; Gerald L. Cohen).

send in 1. To replace a player in the lineup; e.g., "Smith sent Jones in to bat for Brown." 2. To instruct a baserunner on third to go home; e.g., "The third base coach sent Wilson in."

send out Syn. of *send down*, 1.

send to base *hist.* For a pitcher to walk or hit a batter.

send to the rubber To put a relief pitcher into the game.

send to the shelf To strike out. The term comes from the notion of the batter going back to place his batting helmet on the shelf in the dugout.

Send to the shelf. Postcard, 1908. *Andy Moresund Collection*

send to the showers To remove a player (esp. a pitcher) during the game, usually because of ineffectiveness. The player presumably heads for the clubhouse and a hot shower. See also *knock out*. Syn. *shower*. 1ST USE. 1912. "His teammates had given [Ray Caldwell] a two run lead and were threatening to send [Ed] Summers to the shower baths" (*New York Sun*, June 2; Peter Morris). EXTENDED USE. To remove from any activity. An early example alluding to World War I: "No doubt Pershing and Foch has got the game sewed up tight or they would never take a chance and send me to the showers whilst they was more innin's to play" (H.C. Witwer, *A Smile a Minute*, 1919; David Shulman).

senior circuit Traditional nickname for the *National League* because it is 25 years older than the American League. Compare *junior circuit*.

Senior Professional Baseball Association A short-lived (1989–1990), eight-team Florida league of former major leaguers at least 35 years old (32 for catchers). See Jay Walker, *The Senior League Encyclopedia*, 1998. See also *Class AAAA*. Abbrev. *SPBA*.

senior softball [softball term] Softball played by those who are 60 (in some places, 55) years or older, characterized by an 11th player in the field, courtesy runners for the batter, an alternate home plate, and other safety features.

sensational Said of a particularly great or outstanding fielding play. "Today, playing deep, against the jack-rabbit ball, the garden men make many a 'sensational' catch" (Ty Cobb, *My Life in Baseball*, 1961, p.229). The term was used frequently in the 1950s.

separate-admission doubleheader A *doubleheader* in which the ballpark is cleared after the first game to collect, several hours later, new admission tickets for the second game; e.g., the first game is played in the morning and the second game in the afternoon. Separate-admission doubleheaders were more common than single-admission doubleheaders prior to the 1930s (and esp. in the first decade of the 20th century). When attendance declined during the Depression, teams began to schedule doubleheaders, hoping to lure more fans; this practice remained common at least into the 1970s. When attendance began to rise, single-admission doubleheaders were not economical and teams reverted to the earlier practice. See also *day-night doubleheader*. Syn. *split doubleheader*; *split-admission doubleheader*.

September call-up A minor-league player brought up to a major-league club in September when his season is over and the major-league roster expands from 25 to 40.

series 1. A scheduled set of games between two teams. The term can refer to a regular group of games (e.g., three games in Cleveland, or the games in a season), a postseason playoff, or the World Series itself. IST USE. 1866 (*New York Herald*, June 17; Edward J. Nichols). 2. The entire set of baseball cards issued by a particular manufacturer in a given year; e.g., the 1933 Goudey series. 3. A group of consecutively numbered baseball cards within a given set, printed at the same time, but deliberately split by the manufacturer to distribute at different times during the year; e.g., the first series of the 1951 Bowman issue (numbers 1–36). Until the 1970s, many card manufacturers issued cards in several series, which were released throughout the season.

Series, the Short for *World Series*.

Serio Mundial Spanish for "World Series."

serpentina Spanish for "curveball."

serpentinero Spanish for "hurler."

serve 1. *v.* To pitch. The term implies that the pitcher presents the ball to the batter in the manner of a waiter serving a meal or a drink; e.g., an easily hit pitch is one that is "served on a platter." "[Ken] Dixon Serves 3 Homers [to the Yankees]" (*The Washington Post* headline, Apr. 5, 1987). IST USE. 1913 (*Spalding's Official Base Ball Guide*, p.75; Edward J. Nichols). ETYMOLOGY. Nichols identified the term as borrowed from tennis. 2. *n.* A pitch. "Billy Cox took [Dave] Koslo's serve to left center field . . . [for] one of the longest singles ever to win a game" (Harvey Rosenfeld, *The Great Chase*, 1992, p.34).

server *hist.* The pitcher. "Cleveland club put the Reds 'way back' by the clever work of the servers" (*The Washington Post*, Oct. 18, 1903).

serve us ball [softball term] An early name for softball.

service time The amount of time a ballplayer spends in the major leagues (excluding preseason and postseason games). See also *major-league year*.

service time clock Recording the amount of time a ballplayer spends in the major leagues. "Starting [Josh Karp's] service time clock before he's ready . . . won't help anyone except Karp's accountant" (*Baseball Prospectus*, 2003; Peter C. Morris). Morris (personal communication, Dec. 13, 2003) observes that the concept of the service time clock conveys "that an organization has some very good reasons for not allowing a promising young prospect to make his major-league debut any sooner than necessary, since the debut initiates a countdown for the player's eligibility for arbitration and free agency. The club is the most obvious loser when a player prematurely becomes eligible for these goodies, since the club will either have to pay much more to keep him or lose him to free agency. However, the player is often a loser as well, since the club may feel the need to rush him, rather than allowing him to develop at his own pace."

session 1. *hist.* Syn. of *inning*, 1. IST USE. 1902. "The rout was completed in the next session" (*Chicago Daily*, Sept. 15). 2. *hist.* A baseball game. "Joe Wagner surprised a lot of skeptics by gathering two hits during the session" (*San Francisco Bulletin*, March 29, 1913; Gerald L. Cohen). 3. See *bullpen session*. 4. See *side session*. 5. See *spring session*.

set 1. The motionless position taken by a pitcher before beginning his delivery. A pitcher who holds his arms high above his head is said to have a "high set." 2. An entire run of baseball cards from a given issue, produced by a particular manufacturer during a single year. "If the same type card is printed over a period of years, a set refers to the span of years; e.g., a 1976 Topps set (nos. 1–660) or the T–206 set (524 different cards printed between 1909 and 1911" (James Beckett and Dennis W. Eckes, *The 1979 Sport Americana Baseball Card Price Guide*, p.218).

set down To retire one or more batters. "[Greg

Swindell] set down the next 19 hitters" (*Tampa Tribune*, July 30, 1988). IST USE. 1912 (*New York Tribune*, Oct. 17; Edward J. Nichols).

set one down 1. To retire a single batter. 2. To strike out a batter.

set oneself For a fielder to get in position to throw the ball after fielding it. IST USE. 1909. "[Bob] Bescher's throw home after catching [Del] Howard's fly in the third would have been a tough job for a right-handed gardener, as he was in motion toward center field and had no chance to set himself before the catch" (*Chicago Tribune*, May 8; Peter Morris).

set point The slight pause between a pitcher's stretch or windup and the delivery of the ball. "I told my pitching coach to watch certain keys [to my] mechanics. One was my set point. When I go into my windup, raising my arms and kicking up my leg, there's a momentary pause just before driving off my left foot toward the plate" (Dave Dravecky, *Comeback*, 1990, p.162).

set position One of two legal pitching positions, taken when the pitcher attempts to hold a runner on base. The pitcher faces the batter with his pivot foot or portion of his pivot foot in contact with the rubber and his stepping foot in front of the rubber, and holds the ball with both hands in front of his body and comes to a complete stop (A complete stop is not necessary with no runners on base.) From this position, the pitcher may deliver the ball to the batter, throw to a base, or step back and off the rubber with his pivot foot. After assuming the set position, any natural motion associated with the delivery commits the pitcher to pitch without alteration or interruption. Should the pitcher fail to come to a complete stop in the set position, a balk is called. Compare *windup position*. Syn. *stretch position*.

set tag A tag in which the fielder holds his glove with the ball in it on the ground in front of the base and waits for the runner to slide into it for an out.

set the table 1. To get on base to start an inning offensively. "B.J. Surhoff led off the inning with a single and stole second base to set the table for [Cal] Ripken, who slapped a line drive into right field" (*The Baltimore Sun*, Sept. 11, 1999). 2. To get a baserunner in scoring position. "[Shane Halter] consistently set the table for his teammates by getting on base or advancing a runner" (*Orioles Gazette*, Sept. 10, 1993, p.22). See also *table-setter*, 1. 3. To serve as a setup man; e.g., "[Norm Charlton's] main job will be to set the table for [closer] Armando Benitez" (*Sports Illustrated*, March 23, 1998).

settle down For a pitcher to regain control after several bad pitches. Often, the catcher will stroll out to the mound to "settle the pitcher down" by urging him to concentrate or take more time between pitches. "[Pitching coach Ray Miller] told me to settle down but it really took me three innings to get myself under control" (Denny Neagle, quoted in *The Baltimore Sun*, May 26, 1996). IST USE. 1895. "Moran settled down in the remaining four innings and the home team was blanked" (*Brooklyn Eagle*, Sept. 6; Peter Morris).

settle under For a fielder to get ready to catch a fly ball or pop-up. IST USE. 1879. "Jim [White] dashed his cap to the ground, and settled himself under the ball" (*Brooklyn Eagle*, July 9; Peter Morris).

set up 1. To insert a setup man before the closer; to get to a point in a game at which the setup man can enter. 2. To lead a batter into thinking that there is a pattern to the pitches he is seeing and then deliver an unexpected pitch. "If you're the man with the ball, you are trying to 'set up' the man with the bat, meaning you set up his expectations or his thinking and then try to take advantage of any preconception he has" (Tom Seaver, quoted in *The New York Times*, May 7, 1986). "[Jimmy] Key must have command of his changeup, which he uses to finish off hitters after setting them up with his fastball and breaking ball. If he throws bad changeups, they'll get whacked" (*The Baltimore Sun*, Oct. 21, 1996). 3. To increase the chance to turn a double play by intentionally walking the batter with first base open and a runner on second base and/or third base. Jim Murray (*Los Angeles Times*, Jan. 3, 1983) observed, "Overlooked is the fact that this also sets up the three-run homer."

setup man A relief pitcher who tries to hold

the lead, usually in the seventh or eighth innings, before turning the game over to the closer. Compare *short reliever*. Syn. *caddy*; *bridge*, 3; *table-setter*, 2.

setup pitching A rigid philosophy of pitching that the pitcher must throw a fastball inside followed by a curveball outside, or vice versa. George Sisler (*Sisler on Baseball*, 1954) did not care for such a theory: "This might work against poor or inexperienced hitters, but I do not believe it is very effective against good hitters. . . . Batters are just as smart as pitchers and can do a little thinking themselves, and it is foolish to think they can't."

7 The scorekeeper's designation for the left fielder.

seven-inning pitcher A starting pitcher who does not go the distance; one who regularly requires relief help after about seven innings of work. IST USE. 1895. "A singular fatality attends [Charley] Esper in the eighth and ninth innings of games in which he pitches. He really seems to be only a seven-inning pitcher" (*Fort Wayne* [Ind.] *Sentinel*, May 3; Peter Morris).

seven-o'clock hitter A player who hits well in batting practice and poorly during the game. See also *10-o'clock hitter*; *12-o'clock hitter*; *one-o'clock hitter*; *two-o'clock hitter*; *five-o'clock hitter*; *six-o'clock hitter*. ETYMOLOGY. From the fact that batting practice is likely to be in full swing at seven o'clock for a night game beginning at eight o'clock.

seventh 1. *n*. The seventh inning. 2. *adv*. Said of the seventh position in the batting order; e.g., "Smith is batting seventh."

seventh-inning stretch A time-honored baseball custom in which the fans ritualistically stand and stretch before their team comes to bat in the seventh inning. This is done not only to relieve muscles that have begun to stiffen, but also to bring luck to one's team (perhaps from the association of the number 7 with good luck). The simple ritual has different meanings to different people. Charles Einstein (*The New York Times*, Apr. 21, 1985) described his experience: "My own initial contact with it came in the seventh inning of the first game I ever saw, as a 6-year-old

taken to Fenway Park in Boston by my father. 'Did you know I was a magician?' he said. 'Stand up.' I stood up. So did all the other spectators, to the farthest cranny of the bleachers. Two minutes later, his voice even softer than before, my father said, 'Sit down.' Everybody sat." Einstein added that his grandfather had done this to his father and that, a generation later, he had done it to his own son. Herman L. Masin (*Baseball Digest*, June 1959) defined "seventh-inning stretch" as "girdle-adjustment time on Ladies Day." IST USE. 1910. "Ford cut short the seventh inning stretch by lamming a hot one to left" (*The New York Times*, May 26; Peter Morris). USAGE NOTE. "In most of the large cities, there is a peculiar practice in vogue at base ball games. At the end of every few innings some tired spectator, who has been wrestling with the hard side of a rough board seat, gets up and yells 'Stretch!' A second after, the entire crowd will be going through all the movements of a stretch" (*The Sporting Life*, July 22, 1883; Craig R. Wright). "The spectators stood up, men, women, and children, and took the seventh inning yawn and stretch" (*The New York Times*, Apr. 17, 1910; Tim Wiles).

ETYMOLOGY. The origin of the custom has probably been lost in the earliest days of the game. Baseball historian Dan Daniel is quoted by Zander Hollander (*Baseball Lingo*, 1967): "It probably originated as an expression of fatigue and tedium, which seems to explain why the stretch comes late in the game instead of at the halfway point." The earliest reference that has surfaced appears in an 1869 letter from Harry Wright of the Cincinnati Red Stockings to a friend (Howard Ferris, a Cincinnati resident): "The spectators all arise between halves of the seventh, extend their legs and arms, and sometimes walk about. In so doing they enjoy the relief afforded by relaxation from a long posture on the hard benches." David Shulman found this example by Christy Mathewson (*Won in the Ninth*, 1910): "In the stand-up session (Oh yes! seventh inning), however, the tonsorial artists made the Lowell hair stand up."

The most popular story of the practice's origin is much more colorful: It was created in 1910 when President William Howard Taft, on a visit to Pittsburgh, went to a baseball game and stood up to stretch during the seventh inning. The crowd, thinking the president was about to leave, stood up out of respect for the office.

Another story has been published several times, that of an incident that occurred in June 1882 at Manhattan College in New York City, during a game between the college and a semi-pro club called the New York Metropolitans. According to a Manhattan College press release on file at the National Baseball Library and Archives in Cooperstown, N.Y., the inventor of the ritual was Brother Jasper Brennan, the school's first "moderator of athletics" and source of the Manhattan "Jaspers" nickname. Quoting from the college's news release:

"Whenever there was a home game, the entire student body marched to the field and stayed in a section of the stands. Brother Jasper, since he was both the coach and the Prefect of Discipline, had to watch both the players on the field and the students in the stands. Before each game, he sharply admonished the students not to leave their seats or move about until the game was over and they were ready to return to the college for the evening meal. Then, the good Brother went down to the bench to direct the play of the team. . . . On a hot, sticky day in the spring of 1882, Manhattan was playing the Metropolitans. . . . The game, it turned out, was a long, drawn-out affair. As the game passed the mid-way mark, Brother Jasper noticed the youngsters in the stands were getting restless and unruly. So as the team came to bat in the seventh inning, he went over to the stands and told his charges to stand, stretch and move about for a minute or two. This eased the tension and unrest, and so Brother Jasper repeated it in the next few games. Soon the student body made it a practice 'to give it the old seventh inning stretch.' Since Manhattan played many of its games in the old Polo Grounds, the seventh inning stretch passed along to the Giant fans and eventually throughout the world of baseball, the unintentional invention of Brother Jasper."

sew up To finish a game successfully; e.g., to score the winning run, or to retire the side in the last inning.

SF 1. Scorecard and box score abbrev. for *sacrifice fly*, 1. **2.** Abbrev. for *short field*, 1.

SH Scorecard and box score abbrev. for *sacrifice hit*.

shackle To pitch effectively; to keep opposing batters from making hits; to *handcuff*, 3.

shade 1. For an outfielder to move slightly toward the part of the field where the batter is expected to hit the ball. "The Dodgers had been shading [Jeff] Blauser to right all day" (*Milwaukee Journal Sentinel*, July 22, 1997). **2.** For the shortstop to move a little closer to third base or second base, or the second baseman to move a little closer to first base or second base, in anticipation of where the batter is expected to hit the ball. "[Lance Johnson's] more of a pull hitter when he's ahead in the count, so I shaded him more up the middle" (shortstop Cal Ripken Jr., quoted in *The Baltimore Sun*, July 7, 1995). **3.** To win by one run. "The Sox shaded the peppery Seals [by a score of 3 to 2]" (*San Francisco Bulletin*, March 15, 1913; Gerald L. Cohen).

shadow 1. *v.* To remain close to a base for defensive reasons; e.g., "Smith shadowed the bag to remain close to the baserunner." **2.** *n./hist.* A manager's chief aide (Al Schacht, *Al Schacht Dope Book*, 1944, p.44).

shadow ball 1. A crowd-pleasing pantomime stunt in which a team played without the benefit of a ball. It called for a lot of action, including brilliant leaping catches, as players tossed an imaginary ball around the infield. Shadow ball was often performed by Negro leaguers before their games. **2.** A metaphor for the Negro leagues and the exclusion of African-Americans from organized baseball; "a metaphor for the black baseball that shadowed the segregated major leagues" (Steve Wulf, *Sports Illustrated*, Sept. 29, 1994, p.150). Ken Burns underscored the term by subtitling the "Fifth Inning" of *Baseball* (PBS television series, 1994) "Shadow Ball."

shadowing *hist.* A technique used by a pitcher to make it more difficult for the batter to pick up the pitch by hiding it in his windup. "Shadowing consists of the pitcher sidestepping and placing his body on the line of the batter's vision, so that the ball has no background except the pitcher's body and the batter cannot see it plainly until the ball almost is upon him" (John J. Evers and Hugh S. Fullerton, *Touching Second: The Science of Baseball*, 1910; Peter Morris). Practitioners included Bert Cunningham, Matt Kilry, Clark Griffith, and Ed Reulbach.

shag To chase and catch fly balls as a part of batting practice; to retrieve foul balls. "Dipsy Ruggles, our first baseman, wore sneakers instead of cleats and was able to shag foul balls over the ledge with the grace of a mountain sheep" (John Gould, *Christian Science Monitor*, Apr. 26, 1985). IST USE. 1911. "I was allowed to stand behind the catcher when the Factoryville team was playing, and 'shag' foul balls" (Carl H. Claudy, *St. Nicholas Magazine*, Apr.–Oct.; David Shulman). ETYMOLOGY. The term appears to have begun as "shack," a variation on "shake" (as in, to "shake it"), which became "shag." EXTENDED USE. To chase and retrieve, such as shagging golf or tennis balls.

shagger 1. One who shags fly balls in batting practice. IST USE. 1913. "[Jesse Becker] gave the 'Shaggers' a merry run for their money while he was at bat" (*San Francisco Bulletin*, Feb. 27; Gerald L. Cohen). 2. [softball term] A youngster who is hired to retrieve over-the-fence home runs in slow pitch softball tournaments and bring them back for reuse.

shake-off *n.* The act of indicating a refusal from a pitcher to a catcher who has called for a specific pitch. "Shake-offs . . . show a difference in approach between the pitcher and his catcher, and if a pattern sets in, these shake-offs allow you to judge whether the pitcher or the catcher seems to be calling the more aggressive game" (Keith Hernandez, *Pure Baseball*, 1994, p.153).

shake off *v.* For a pitcher to indicate his refusal to deliver the type of pitch called for by the catcher; to veto a pitch. The term is so called because the pitcher commonly shakes his head from side to side to indicate clearly that he will not throw the pitch called for and that he wants a new signal. Some pitchers shake off a sign with another gesture, such as a move of the glove, rather than the head. Syn. *throw off*. IST USE.

1928. "Frequently the pitcher will 'shake off' the catcher's sign. That is, he will change the catcher's signal for one of his own" (George Herman Ruth, *Babe Ruth's Own Book of Baseball*, 1928, p.122; Peter Morris). USAGE NOTE. The practice was in place in the 19th century. "Now it is almost the universal practice for the catcher to give it [the sign] to the pitcher, and if the latter doesn't want to pitch the ball asked for he changes the sign by a shake of the head" (John Montgomery Ward, *Base-Ball: How to Become a Player*, 1888; Peter Morris). EXTENDED USE. To get rid of; to elude. "Bud shakes off strike sign" (*Boston Herald* headline, July 23, 2002), referring to baseball commissioner Bud Selig's downplaying the possibility of a players' strike.

shake the catcher around For a pitcher to shake off all the signs and return to the original sign. Joe Garagiola (*Baseball Is a Funny Game*, 1960) explained, "A pitcher does that to confuse the hitter as to what the pitcher is going to throw." Mariano Rivera has been known to accept the pitch and then shake his head several times to confuse the batter.

shake the jinx To win a game after several defeats (Maurice H. Weseen, *A Dictionary of American Slang*, 1934).

shakeup A rearrangement of team personnel to obtain improved play. IST USE. 1902 (*The Sporting Life*, Apr. 26, p.7; Edward J. Nichols).

shaky start A bad beginning for a pitcher.

shallow 1. *adj.* Said of that part of the outfield closest to the infield; e.g., Dom DiMaggio played a "shallow center field" or "Smith hit a pop fly into shallow right." Compare *deep*, 2. 2. *adv.* Close to home plate; e.g., the infield is playing "shallow" to cut off a run on a ground ball. Compare *deep*, 1. Syn. *close*, 2.

Shandler Short for the annual *Ron Shandler's Baseball Forecaster*, the publication for baseball analysts and fantasy leaguers since 1986. "In my most serious league . . . [the] owners show up to our auction toting the *Forecaster*, the phrase 'Can I borrow your Shandler?' is as common that day as 'Pass the chips'" (Childs Walker, *The Baltimore Sun*, Dec. 14, 2006).

shank 1. *v.* To hit the ball off the handle of the bat. 2. *n.* A ball hit off the handle of the bat.

share the ball For a pitcher to allow the batters to hit the ball rather than to rely on strikeouts. "The hardest thing for any young pitcher is to realize he has to share the ball" (Seattle Mariners minor-league pitching coordinator Pat Rice, quoted in *Baseball America*, Dec. 10–23, 2001; Peter Morris). ETYMOLOGY. Likely derived from basketball, where a good point guard is said to be sharing the ball by positioning his teammates to score.

sharpen one's spikes To strongly imply that one is preparing to injure another player with the aid of spikes. The term can also be defined in the same manner as did Hugh S. Fullerton (*American Magazine*, June 1912): "The pretense of a player to sharpen the triangular toe and heel plates he wears on his shoes, is a threat to 'cut his way around,' or spike certain antagonists if they attempt to stop or touch him. Chiefly a form of braggadocio, and seldom carried into effect." Legend has it that Ty Cobb was a spike sharpener, but he claimed otherwise. He insisted that it was two other players ("neither of them regulars") who sharpened their spikes to unnerve the New York Yankees. Prescott Sullivan (*San Francisco Examiner*, June 12, 1958; Peter Tamony) quoted Cobb: "These two fellows decided to practice some amateur psychology. So . . . as the Yankees came on the field, the two sat on the bench filing their spikes. Neither of them played in the game. But the press had to have a 'name' to go with the story, so they chose 'Cobb.'" See also *spikes high*.

sharpshooter 1. An effective *place hitter*; a hitter who can put the ball where he wants it to go. IST USE. 1912 (*New York Tribune*, Sept. 21; Edward J. Nichols). 2. A pitcher with good control.

Shaughnessy Playoff A four-team postseason playoff plan in the minor leagues in which the teams that finished first and fourth in a league would play each other, the teams that finished second and third would play each other, and the winners of each matchup would play for the league championship and represent the league in further postseason play. The plan was devised in 1933 by Montreal Royals general manager Frank Shaughnessy and first adopted by the International League. The Texas League (1933) and the Pacific Coast League (1936) also adopted the plan, which boosted attendance and kept interest alive late in the season. Shaughnessy borrowed the idea from ice hockey.

shave 1. *v.* To pitch to the edges of the strike zone; e.g., "Smith shaved the corners with his breaking pitches." 2. *v.* To pitch high and inside; to brush a batter back as if the ball were being used to shave the batter's face. 3. *n.* A ball that is pitched close to a batter's face. "[Nini] Tornay walked several steps towards the mound and verbally challenged the statuesque Oakland righthander [Al Gettel] when he was treated to a 'shave' in the ninth inning" (*San Francisco News*, July 31, 1953; Peter Tamony).

she 1. An injured player, esp. one who may be favoring himself. USAGE NOTE. The term is a derogatory remark that somehow equates being or playing injured with femininity, or hints that someone who cannot tolerate pain is effeminate. 2. A pitcher's arm (Garret Mathews, *Can't Find a Dry Ball*, 2002).

sheepherder An *umpire*, 1.

sheepskin *hist.* 1. The baseball. The balls of the 1860s were covered with sheepskin; but the material proved to be too fragile, and by 1880 the shift had been made to the much more durable horsehide. The term survived for the ball itself, at least until 1885: "In Chicago the umpire starts into the game with a couple of extra balls in his pocket and when a foul tip sends the sheepskin over the fence he madly rolls one of the 'extras' to the pitcher and goes right on with the game" (*The Sporting Life*, July 15, 1885; Peter Morris). 2. An early synonym of *chest protector.* "The catcher's breast-protector, or the 'sheepskin' as it is often contemptuously referred to, is neither neat nor gaudy, but, like a trick mule in a kicking match, it gets there just the same" (*The Sporting News*, Nov. 1, 1890; Peter Morris). "Jack Clements . . . appeared on the field that year [1884] in a protector, and jeering sports writers referred to it as a 'sheepskin'" (Lee Allen, *The Sporting News*, Apr. 6, 1968).

shell 1. To hit a pitcher hard and often, as if

he had been attacked ("shelled") by a barrage of hard-hit baseballs; e.g., "The Marlins shelled Smith in his last two outings" or "The Cubs shelled Jones for nine runs and seven hits in less than two innings." **2.** To be hit hard and often. "Pete Harnisch . . . was shelled for seven runs" (*Milwaukee Journal Sentinel*, Sept. 8, 1997). **3.** To defeat a team by many runs; e.g., "The Braves shelled the Reds, 14–0."

shellac **1.** To defeat soundly; to trounce. **2.** To hit a pitched ball hard.

shelling The act of getting many hits and runs. *Sports Illustrated* (July 23, 2001) defined an "early shelling" as "a start in which the pitcher had surrendered five or more runs in five or fewer innings."

shelve To take a player out of action; to put a player on the disabled list. "White Sox shelve [Neil] Allen . . . after an examination of his right pitching arm that indicated an overdeveloped triceps muscle" (*The Washington Post*, Apr. 22, 1987).

shepherd *hist.* The manager of a baseball team.

shibbety hip Dugout chatter. The term (the spelling and actual definition of which are uncertain) was coined by Oakland Athletics players "to get the team going" (*Athletics* [Oakland A's magazine], Sept. 2005).

shift **1.** *v.* To change fielding position; to move defensive players from their traditional positions in the field to compensate for a batter's proclivities and/or to be in a better position for a double play. Fielders generally shift to their left for left-handed batters (because they tend to hit in that direction) and vice versa. **2.** *n.* The act of moving players for defensive reasons, often phrased as "the shift is on," usually accomplished by moving fielders to areas where a hitter is apt to hit the ball. Occasionally, a radical shift is named for the player the shift is created to defend against, such as the *Williams shift*, employed to stop Ted Williams. A more recent example: "The Boggs Shift Works" (*The Boston Globe* headline, July 30, 1988), in which the Milwaukee Brewers brought center fielder Robin Yount into the infield to defend against Wade Boggs— then hitting .359—with two runners on base

(Boggs then struck out). **3.** *v.* For the catcher to move in front of the path of a pitched ball so that he will be able to maintain his balance for catching and throwing. Bob Bennett (*On the Receiving End: The Catcher's Guidebook*, 1982) wrote, "In shifting, the basic idea is to step into the path of the ball. If the ball is thrown to the left, the step should be to the left with the left foot. If the ball is to the right, a step to the right should be taken with the right foot." Syn. *slide*, 4.

shifter A manager of a baseball team. 1ST USE. 1908. "Manager [John] McGraw, always a quick shifter, yanked him at once and substituted Leon Ames" (*Cincinnati Enquirer*, May 17, 1908; Peter Morris).

shillalah Var. of *shillelagh*. USAGE NOTE. The term has been used as a verb. "[Pat Martin] lasted only three innings, but it was quite long enough for the Nationals to put the game on ice. They shillalahed with abandon and bumping him for six hits, including a double and home run, jumped away with a five-run lead" (J.V. Fitz Gerald, *The Washington Post*, Apr. 21, 1920; Peter Morris).

shillelagh The baseball bat as an instrument of power. Syn. *shillalah*. 1ST USE. 1937 (*Philadelphia Record*, Oct. 11; Edward J. Nichols). ETYMOLOGY. From the Irish fighting club or cudgel.

shinburger **1.** A leg bruise that is commonly inflicted by a bad hop; a barked shin. **2.** A ball batted through the pitcher's box that ricochets off his shins (*The Sporting News*, Apr. 1, 1972). **3.** A borderline low strike, so called by the umpire (Eric Gregg, *Working the Plate*, 1990, p.95).

shine ball **1.** A ball that the pitcher renders esp. smooth on one side by rubbing it hard on his glove or clothing, or doctoring it with a foreign substance (such as transparent paraffin or talcum powder) on his uniform. Such shining or polishing helps the ball curve, as it slips from the fingers more easily when thrown with speed; rotating quickly, a shine ball baffles batters by showing the white or shiny side only at split-second intervals. The pitch has been illegal since 1920. Eddie Cicotte is said to have developed the shine ball in 1915 when he discovered that the ball did funny things after he darkened or scuffed one side of the ball and rubbed the other side to a shine on his trousers. Hod Eller was known as a "shine-ball pitcher." Syn. *shiner.* IST USE. 1917. "The shineball is only effective when the shiny spot is on one of the poles of rotation" (Paul Purman, *Fort Wayne* [Ind.] *Sentinel,* July 5; Peter Morris). ETYMOLOGY. Gerald Secor Couzens (*A Baseball Album,* 1980) reported that the pitch was "probably invented by Dave Danforth in 1915 while pitching for Louisville in the American Association. Oil was used on the field to control the dust problem, and the innovative Danforth discovered that by rubbing the oil-and-dirt-covered ball on his trouser leg the ball became smooth and shiny and hopped when he pitched it." **2.** A ball with a patch of factory gloss that has not been rubbed off completely. As explained by Lee Gutkind (*The Best Seat in Baseball, But You Have to Stand!,* 1999, p.45; Peter Morris): "That patch will glint off the sun or the lights, giving the batter a distorted picture of where the ball really is. When a pitcher throws this ball, the batter will turn to the umpire and ask, 'Shine ball'? If so, the umpire will throw a new ball in."

shiner Syn. of *shine ball,* 1.

shin guard A piece of protective (leather or molded plastic) equipment, often padded, strapped to the leg, worn by catchers, plate umpires, and some batters to prevent injury from foul tips and pitches in the dirt; it is also worn by some infielders. The guard protects the shin and sometimes the knee. See also *leg guard.* IST USE. 1897. "Infielder [Harry] Steinfeldt, of the Detroits [Western League], wears a pair of shin guards during play. He is the only man who plays the game who follows this precaution" (*The Sporting News,* July 31; Tom Shieber). ETYMOLOGY. Shin guards (strips of felt or wooden slats) were worn by infielders in the late 19th century; e.g., in 1887, second baseman Bud Fowler of the International League Binghamton Bingos played with the lower part of his legs encased in wooden guards after he was spiked repeatedly by vindictive white players. A.R. Cratty (*The Sporting Life,* Oct. 15, 1904; Peter Morris) noted that Boston catcher Tom Needham went to Philadelphia "where a metal shin guard was made for him." Philadelphia Phillies catcher Charley "Red" Dooin (*The Sporting News,* March 5, 1936) claimed he was the first catcher to use shin guards, under his stockings, in 1906: after first trying out rattan, he switched to papier-mâché. New York Giants catcher Roger Bresnahan, who donned a pair of shin guards modeled after a cricketer's leg pads on Apr. 11, 1907, was the first to

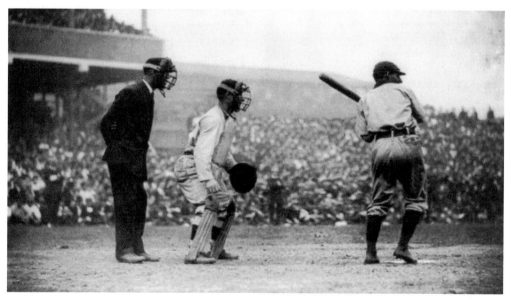

Shin guard. New York Giants catcher Roger Bresnahan wearing his shin guards outside his stockings. *George Grantham Bain Collection, Library of Congress*

wear the protective equipment outside the stockings, and thereby popularized their use.

shinola play Awarding first base to a batter who was hit by a pitch that nicked his polished shoe. Vernal "Nippy" Jones (fourth game of the 1957 World Series) and Cleon Jones (fifth game of the 1969 World Series) both verified that they had been so hit by showing the umpire a black spot of shoe polish on the ball.

shin-skimmer A hard-hit ground ball. IST USE. 1908 (*New York Evening Journal*, Aug. 21; Edward J. Nichols).

ship To trade a player, or to send a player to a minor-league team; e.g., "The Padres shipped Ozzie Smith to St. Louis for Garry Templeton."

shit 1. Slang for a breaking pitch. 2. Slang for an expression of exaggeration, disappointment, disparagement, or pretense. Lawrence Frank (*Playing Hardball: The Dynamics of Baseball Folk Speech*, 1983, pp.57–58) considered the points of difference among "bullshit," "horseshit," and "chickenshit" as defined in the realm of baseball folk speech: "The basic distinctions are that 'bullshit' means 'not true', 'horseshit' means 'bad' or 'low class', and 'chickenshit' means 'gutless' (i.e., afraid). Further, 'bullshit' is often used as a retort, or as an immediate reaction to an event. It is of a slightly stronger sense than the other two and thus often said in a harsher tone. 'Horseshit' is of a lesser degree accusative and often simply descriptive. Hence it is applicable in many more circumstances than 'bullshit'. 'Chickenshit' is the most specific of the three terms and is thus applicable in fewer situations." Kevin Kerrane (*Dollar Sign on the Muscle*, 1984, pp.90–91) noted that "horseshit" is a "handy label" among scouts for "anything deserving a low grade." Detroit Tigers manager Jim Leyland told his team after a player embarrassed his third base coach (as quoted in *Sports Illustrated*, Oct. 23, 2006, p.44): "If you ever do anything like that again . . . I'll quit. Because I don't want anything to do with that kind of horses——."

shit-can For a pitcher to eliminate a pitch that does not seem to be effective.

ShO Scorecard and box score abbrev. for *shutout*, 1.

shoemaker *hist.* A player who makes frequent errors; i.e., he "boots" the ball. IST USE. 1907 (*New York Evening Journal*, May 2; Edward J. Nichols).

shoe plate A metal plate worn by a pitcher to protect the shoe of the pivot foot when the ball is thrown. See also *toe plate*.

shoe shiner A pitch well below the knee.

shoestring catch A running catch made by a fielder just before the ball hits the ground. It is caught in the vicinity of the player's feet (or shoe tops) and can be quite spectacular to witness. IST USE. 1904. "[Danny] Green came up with a shoestring catch of [Mal] Kittredge's low fly" (*Chicago Tribune*, June 4; Peter Morris). EXTENDED USE. A similar catch in other games, such as football.

shoestring league Syn. of *Fourth of July league*. "[Shoestring leagues] were loosely funded and organized and would often fold just after the Fourth of July" (David Pietrusza, *Minor Miracles*, 1995; Peter Morris).

shoot 1. *n./hist.* A type of a sharp-breaking pitch. The term was popular in the 19th century and early 20th century for a curveball or one of its variants, because the pitch tended to dart, veer, or sail (i.e., "shoot") in a certain direction. The *Brooklyn Daily Eagle* (May 1, 1892) defined "shoot" as "the delivery of the ball to the batsman by the pitcher so that it flies up, down or to either side, when near the plate, from a straight course, according to the desire and ability of the pitcher." The term was often used in connection with curves, drops, slants, twists, and benders; e.g., "[The pitcher] was prepared to serve to the New York batsmen a choice selection of curves, shoots, and drops" (*The World* [New York], July 20, 1890; Gerald L. Cohen). Indeed, Bobby Mathews, an early master of the curveball, made this subtle, yet clear, distinction (quoted in *Philadelphia Press*, Aug. 20, 1883; Peter Morris): "Good, straight pitching . . . a good out 'curve,' and a good in 'shoot' are what the great pitchers are working with to-day." Morris infers that by "shoot" Mathews meant a type of breaking pitch that involves the sharpness and direction of the break, whereas a curveball is a pitch that when thrown by a right-handed pitcher breaks away from a right-handed batter. Morris notes that the distinction between different breaking pitches is often small, even to the practitioner, making lexical purity in their description elusive. Pittsburgh Pirates pitcher Deacon Phillippe was quoted (*Syracuse Post Standard*, March 27, 1904; Peter Morris): "Control and the ability to make curves and shoots break at the right point are obtained only by constant practice." The term was sometimes linked with a spitball or otherwise disfigured ball because the defects and imperfections caused the ball to sail (or "shoot"); 19th-century pitcher Al Maul (*The Sporting Life*, Dec. 1922) recalled that when a new ball was put in play, "we were allowed to saturate it with tobacco juice, rub it in the dirt and roughen it up a bit. . . . Yes, sir, the batters in those days used to see some funny shoots breaking over the corners of the plate." See also the many variations of "shoot": *inshoot*; *outshoot*; *upshoot,* 1; *down shoot*; *double shoot.* IST USE. 1883. "There are many people who believe in an 'up' curve and a 'down' curve, an 'in' curve and an 'out' curve, a zig zag and a 'double' curve, and 'shoots' and 'jumps,' and fast and slow balls to match" (*Philadelphia Press*, Aug. 20; Peter Morris). USAGE NOTE. The term appears to have assumed additional meanings in the late 19th century and the early 20th century, at which point the original meaning became obsolete. Gerald L. Cohen suggests that the term may have referred to a fastball; e.g., "['Cactus'] Henley pitched himself out of the hole. One runner was forced at the plate . . . another batter popped [out] . . . and the third succumbed to the speedy shoots of 'Cactus'" (*San Francisco Bulletin*, Apr. 2, 1913). Rob Neyer (in Bill James and Rob Neyer, *The Neyer/James Guide to Pitchers*, 2004, p.16) observed, "It would be nice if 'curves' and 'shoots' . . . were clearly differentiated, but they're not. That said, we suspect that the term 'shoot' generally referred to some variety of fastball." Morris suggests that a shoot differed from a curveball by more closely resembling a fastball, but breaking late; also, "shoot" started to refer to throws made by players other than the pitcher. Frederick Ivor-

Campbell (personal communication, Dec. 4, 2001) suspects that 19th-century writers "differed in their understanding of the word's meaning, and that 'shoot' was not a term with a consistent definition—in the 19th century anyway."
2. *n.* The sailing or hopping action of a breaking ball that has defects or has been tampered with. "All umpires, we may assume, know that certain balls will 'sail' or 'shoot,' not because of illegal handling, but because of structural defects or imperfections" (John B. Sheridan, quoted in *The Sporting News*, Feb. 26, 1920; Peter Morris). Connie Mack (*The Sporting Life*, June 1924; Peter Morris) referred to "the spit ball, the emery ball, the knuckle ball, and all sorts of trick pitches which caused the ball to take surprising and unexpected shoots." **3.** *n.* A quick bound by a batted ball to one side of a fielder (John B. Foster, in *Collier's New Dictionary of the English Language*, 1908; Gerald L. Cohen). **4.** *n.* A hard, nonbreaking throw by an infielder. "Kisinger hit to Hall, who lost Brew on a shoot to Killifer at home" (*New York Press*, June 25, 1911; Gerald L. Cohen). **5.** *v.* To throw a baseball hard. "A fellow who cannot shoot the balls across the full length of the diamond without effort would probably meet with more success elsewhere than at third [base]" (Dudley Dean, *Atlanta Constitution*, June 5, 1892; Peter Morris). **6.** *v.* See *shoot the ball.*

shooting star Syn. of *revolver.* IST USE. 1869. "'Revolving players' or 'shooting stars,' as ex-President Sands happily termed them" (*National Chronicle*, Jan. 16; Peter Morris).

shoot out For an umpire to call a player out by pointing to him as if he were being shot with a revolver. This unorthodox signal became the trademark of umpire Ron Luciano, who came upon it accidentally during the 1972 season. Luciano (*The Umpire Strikes Back*, 1982) wrote that he had a "mental block" in which he would always call Kansas City Royals outfielder Amos Otis out on close plays. At the start of the 1972 season, Luciano consciously worked on calling Otis safe, instead, but found he was overcompensating yet again. Finally, when Otis hit into a play in which he was out by 15 feet, the rest of the Royals standing on the dugout steps started screaming, "Shoot him, shoot him!" Luciano realized that in his eagerness to make the right call, he was pointing his trigger finger at Otis: "So I shot him with it. Three times. And when I finished, I casually blew the smoke away from the barrel and put it back into its holster."

shoot the ball To hit the ball through the infield to the opposite field; e.g., for a right-handed batter to "aim" the ball between first base and second base. "[The Twins] are good two-strike hitters. They try to shoot the ball the other way" (Drew Olson, *Milwaukee Journal Sentinel*, July 14, 2001; Robert F. Perkins).

shop To offer a player in a possible trade to ascertain his value. "[Willie] McGee was openly shopped during the winter meetings, but there were no takers" (Joe Henderson, *Tampa Tribune*, Jan. 15, 1989). The term is often part of the phrase "shopping around"; e.g., "[The front office] was shopping me around and they wanted me out. Somebody wasn't happy with me" (Bobby Bonilla, quoted in *The Baltimore Sun*, Oct. 9, 1996).

shopaholic A general manager with a penchant for signing free agents and making player moves. "[New York Mets general manager Steve] Phillips has earned a reputation around baseball as something of a shopaholic" (Bruce Weber, *The New York Times Magazine*, March 26, 2000; Peter Morris).

shop league *hist.* Syn. of *industrial league.* "Pitcher Jim Middleton, who wouldn't play with Toledo last year because he had a better job with a shop team at Beloit, Wis., has decided to report to Roger Bresnahan, tiring of the shop league stuff" (*The Sporting News*, March 11, 1920; Peter Morris).

shopping at the gap Hitting a ball into the left-center or right-center gaps. The term was popular in the early- and mid-1990s with the rise of The Gap clothing chain. By the late 1990s, ads for The Gap had begun to appear on outfield walls, in the spaces between outfielders.

short 1. *n.* Short for *shortstop*, 1. IST USE. 1858 (*Brooklyn Daily Times*, June 18; Edward J. Nichols). 2. *adj.* Relatively close to the plate; e.g., the infielder played "short" in anticipation of a bunt. 3. *adj.* Said of the area in the outfield behind one of the bases and in front of the usual playing position of the outfielder; e.g., "short center" is the area behind second base and in front of the center fielder. 4. *adj.* [softball term] Said of a pitch that drops in front of a batter in slow pitch softball, analogous to "low" in baseball or fast pitch softball; the pitch is called a ball. Compare *deep*, 7.

short A A *Class A* level of minor-league baseball, above rookie league but below *low Single A*, typified by a *short-season league*.

short-arm 1. *adj.* Relating to a throw made with the arm close to the body as opposed to a full throw with the arm extended. Short-arm throws are made for short distances, such as between infielders. 2. *v.* To throw with the arm close to, rather than extended from, the body. 3. *v.* To pitch without windup, with an abbreviated delivery.

short-armer A pitcher who does not extend his arm, or throws across his body; e.g., Boots Poffenberger. "[Rob Burger] was a short-armer and threw like a catcher" (Alan Schwarz, *Baseball America*, Feb. 3–16, 1997; Peter Morris).

short center 1. The area behind second base and in front of the center fielder. 2. [softball term] The 10th or extra player in Chicago-style 16-inch softball, so called because he or she plays in what can be best described as short center field just outside the infield.

short curve A pitch that is a combination of a curveball and a slider; a *slurve*. The term was used by pitching coach Johnny Sain for a "controlled breaking ball." Syn. *fast curve*.

shortened game 1. A game in which the home team is winning and does not need to bat for all or a fraction of its half of the ninth inning. 2. A game called by the umpire for whatever reason. If a game is called before it becomes a regulation game, it is declared "no game" and is not considered a shortened game. See also *called game*.

shortened season A baseball season other than a full one; e.g., the 1981 season which was curtailed by the players' strike.

shorten up 1. To move one's hands up on the

bat handle to get more control on the swing, esp. when the batter has two strikes against him. **2.** To move one's hands along the bat when preparing to bunt.

short fastball A fastball lacking some velocity. Johnny Sain (quoted in Roger Kahn, *The Head Game*, 2000, p.188): "My fast ball was no more than average, eighty-five, eighty-seven miles an hour. I call that a 'short' fast ball, not an outstanding pitch all by itself."

short field *hist.* **1.** The area between second base and third base where the shortstop normally plays; the *shortstop* position. "George Weaver will have the jump on his opponents for a berth at the short field on the White Sox club" (*San Francisco Bulletin*, Feb. 15, 1913; Gerald L. Cohen). Abbrev. *SF*, 2. IST USE. 1869. "Eggler, at short field" (*New York Clipper*, June 26). **2.** The playing territory behind the infield (Edward J. Nichols, *An Historical Dictionary of Baseball Terminology*, PhD dissertation, Jan. 1939, p.68).

shortfielder **1.** *hist.* Syn. of *shortstop*, 2. "The sunburnt, befreckled, but nevertheless brilliant shortfielder, Hughey Jennings" (*The Washington Post*, June 14, 1897). Also spelled "short fielder." **2.** [softball term] The *rover* in slow pitch softball, usually positioned in the shallow part of the outfield. Also spelled "short fielder."

short fuse The temperament of an umpire who is quick to eject a player or manager from a game. ETYMOLOGY. From the image of an explosive equipped with a fuse that makes it blow up quickly. It links the human blowup (temper) with the blowup of dynamite and other explosives.

short-handed rule [softball term] A provision in slow pitch softball that allows a player to leave the game without causing the game to end, but which forces the player's team to play with one fewer player.

short hop *n.* **1.** A batted or thrown ball that hits the ground and is caught low before it can take a sharp, unpredictable bounce. IST USE. 1913. "[Dan Moeller] got the ball on the short hop, but recovered in time to make the throw" (*The Washington Post*, May 25, Peter Morris). **2.** A ball that seems to die on the first bounce.

short-hop *v.* **1.** For a fielder to snatch the ball just as it bounces off the ground. "Second baseman Mike Gallego . . . short-hopped it [the ball] and threw [Fred] McGriff out [at first base]" (*Tampa Tribune*, Oct. 9, 1989). **2.** For a fielder to throw a ball that hits the ground just before another fielder catches it. "Shortstop Derek Jeter fielded a routine grounder and short-hopped the throw past first baseman Nick Johnson" (*The Baltimore Sun*, Aug. 25, 2003).

short leg *hist.* A player who lets his teammates go after balls that he himself should retrieve. IST USE. 1937 (*New York Daily News*, Feb. 14; Edward J. Nichols).

short man **1.** Syn. of *short reliever*. **2.** The infielder who backs up the cutoff man in a relay play, in the event of an overthrow.

short park A ballpark with a notably short outfield fence. "Brewers to Cancel Short-Park Solons" was the headline (*San Francisco Chronicle*, Aug. 22, 1975) for an article about the Milwaukee Brewers canceling their agreement with the minor-league Sacramento Solons because the short left-field fence at Hughes Stadium "had impeded the development of many promising young players."

short patch *hist.* Syn. of *shortstop*, 1. "Berger looks much faster around the short patch than he did last season" (*San Francisco Bulletin*, March 22, 1913; Gerald L. Cohen).

short porch A right- or left-field wall, barrier, fence, or upper deck that is unusually close to home plate; a friendly target to a batter, such as the short right-field wall in Yankee Stadium. The term derives from the design of older ballparks, which often featured overhanging roofs that made outfield spectators look like they were sitting on a porch. "If the porch is close to home plate like left field at Fenway Park or right field in Detroit's Tiger Stadium, it's a 'short porch' and hitters 'love' it" (Tim Horgan, *Baseball Digest*, June 1964).

short relief **1.** The replacement of a pitcher late in the game. **2.** A period of relief pitching, usually two innings or less, late in the game.

short reliever A relief pitcher who works in short relief; "a specialist who uses his best pitches at maximum effort for a brief period of time" (*Sports Illustrated*, June 19, 2006). A short reliever often is called on to face only one or a few batters in one inning; because of the brevity of the assignment, a short reliever may appear in several consecutive games. Compare *long reliever*; *middle reliever*; *setup man*. Syn. *short man*, 1.

short route The relatively few stops taken by a player with little or no minor-league experience before he reaches the major leagues.

short score The results of a game that show only the total runs, hits, and errors for each team, as opposed to the box score or inning-by-inning tabulation.

short-season league A Class A minor league that starts play shortly after the June draft so that newly drafted players (usually from college teams) or more experienced players who are not ready for full-season play have a place to play; e.g., the New York–Pennsylvania League and the Northwest League. Teams in the short-season league may have no more than four players who are 23 or older as of June 5 and no more than three players who have four or more years of prior minor-league experience, and must have at least 10 pitchers as of July 1. Minimum seating capacity for short-season league ballparks is 2,500. Compare *rookie league*; *complex league*. See also *short A*.

shortstop 1. The infield position that is between second base and third base. By most accounts, it is the most physically demanding position in the field. Abbrev. *SS*, 1 or *ss*. Originally spelled "short stop." Syn. *short*, 1; *short field*, 1; *short patch*. IST USE. 1858. "When the short stop is put [out] by the Great Umpire to your runs, may . . . your Home Base, where celestial music is struck by angel hands on golden lyres" (Joseph Warren, *Buffalo Courier*, Sept. 27). 2. The player who plays the shortstop position. The shortstop and the second baseman together cover second base. A main element of the shortstop's job is to create double plays. Abbrev. *SS*, 2 or *ss*. Syn. *shortfielder*, 1; *shortstopper*. ETYMOLOGY. A blend of "short" + "stop," presumably created to better describe the defensive function of the job performed in the short field. The term almost certainly is an adaptation of the cricket position of long stop.

Dr. Daniel L. Adams, former Knickerbocker Base Ball Club player, recalled in an interview (*The Sporting News*, Feb. 29, 1896), "I used to play shortstop and I believe I was the first one to occupy that place, as it had formerly been left uncovered." John Thorn (*Total Baseball*, 8th ed., 2004) noted that the position was created in the late 1840s by Adams "not to bolster the infield but to assist in relays from the outfield [because] the early Knickerbocker ball was so light that it could not be thrown even 200 feet; thus the need for a short fielder to send the ball in to the pitcher's point." Adams acted as a fourth outfielder, occasionally moving into the infield but generally acting like softball's short fielder. Dickey Pearce in the mid-1850s is credited with making the shortstop truly a fourth infielder, positioning himself well within the baselines; and George Wright in the 1860s gave the position wider range by stationing himself outside the baselines without being as distant from home as Adams had been.

shortstopper *hist.* Syn. of *shortstop*, 2. "Al Cook of Oakland was just starting out as a shortstopper" (*San Francisco Bulletin*, May 23, 1913; Gerald L. Cohen). IST USE. 1857. "Dem'rest, the short-stop-per" (Everett L. Baker, "Impromptu," *Buffalo Courier*, Sept. 27; Priscilla Astifan).

shortstopping Playing the shortstop position.

short stride The *stride* of a pitcher whose front foot lands on the ball of the foot so that his weight can move over the foot as the ball is released. Compare *long stride*.

short throw A quickly jerked throw from the catcher when there are runners on first and third bases and less than two outs and a double steal is anticipated. The runner on first attempts to steal second base and draws a throw, allowing the runner on third to attempt to steal home. The short throw from the catcher is caught by the shortstop or second baseman about 10 feet in front of the bag and either returned to the catcher to retire the runner from third base, or thrown to first or third bases to retire the runner returning to the base. "The advantage gained by shortening the throw is just what is required to get the ball back to the plate in time. . . . This strategy was employed as early as

1886" (*The Washington Post*, Sept. 18, 1904; Peter Morris).

short toss 1. A throw of limited distance without velocity. Compare *long toss*, 1. **2.** An arm-strengthening exercise or drill of high-velocity tosses by a player, usually a pitcher, recovering from arm problems. "We played short toss, putting sizzle on each throw like a pitcher or an infielder" (Dave Dravecky, *Comeback*, 1990, p.153). Compare *long toss*, 3.

short windup The abbreviated windup used by a pitcher when there are one or more baserunners. The arm movement is condensed to give the runner(s) less time in which to steal.

Shorty A nonexistent player who is supposed to be at bat but incurs an automatic out when the team is "short" a player in Australian club baseball and softball.

shot 1. An especially hard-hit ball, usually a line drive. "[Bobby] Bonilla hits a shot down the third-base line that is barely foul" (Steve Fiffer, *How to Watch Baseball*, 1987, p.167). IST USE. 1880 (*New York Herald*, Aug. 20; Edward J. Nichols). **2.** A home run. "Alfonso Soriano hit three homers, including a three-run shot in the eighth inning" (*The Baltimore Sun*, Apr. 22, 2006). **3.** A strong throw. IST USE. 1910 (*Baseball Magazine*, April, p.60; Edward J. Nichols). **4.** A chance to play in a game. "He'll [pitcher Rick Krivda] get a shot, whether it's a one-inning shot, two-inning shot or three-inning shot" (Baltimore Orioles manager Ray Miller, quoted in *The Baltimore Sun*, March 11, 1998).

shot-flipping *hist.* An amusing "hobby" of major leaguers in the 1910s and 1920s in which little lead pellets (BB shot) were flipped against structures (columns, mirrors) in hotel lobbies on road trips.

shotgun 1. A powerful throwing arm. "He [Damaso Garcia] has a shotgun for an arm you can't believe" (Atlanta Braves manager Chuck Tanner, quoted in *USA Today*, March 19, 1987). See also *gun*, 1; *rifle*, 1. Syn. "shotgun arm." IST USE. 1937 (*New York Daily News*, Jan. 17, Edward J. Nichols). **2.** A player with a strong arm.

shotgun school The philosophy that the more pitches a pitcher has in his arsenal, the better. "Neither [of pitching coaches Jim Turner and Eddie Lopat] is a disciple of the 'shotgun' school, which [they say] equips a pitcher with more stuff than he can handle with success" (*The Sporting News*, Apr. 6, 1960; Peter Morris).

Shot Heard 'Round the World The famous three-run home run hit by Bobby Thomson off Ralph Branca on Oct. 3, 1951, in the Polo Grounds, to win the pennant for the New York Giants in the ninth inning of the third game of the playoffs against the Brooklyn Dodgers. With the home run, the Giants won the game 5–4. "It was likely the most dramatic and shocking event in American sports and has since taken on the transcendent historic character of Pearl Harbor and the Kennedy assassination" (George W. Hunt, *America*, Jan. 27, 1990, p.162). "Isn't it possible that this midcentury moment enters the skin more lastingly than the vast shaping strategies of eminent leaders, generals steely in their sunglasses—the mapped visions that pierce our dreams?" (Don DeLillo, *Underworld*, 1997, pp.59–60). See also *Miracle of Coogan's Bluff*. USAGE NOTE. On the day (Oct. 4) after the home run, the *New York Daily News* called Thomson's home run "the Shot Heard 'Round the Baseball World," and an editorial in *The New York Times* dubbed it "the home run heard 'round the world." Jules Tygiel (*Past Time*, 2000, p.161) noted that on the final day of the regular season, Jackie Robinson of the Dodgers had hit a game-winning home run in the 14th inning (to tie the teams' records and force the playoff series), which Arch Murray (*New York Post*, Oct. 1, 1951) prematurely dubbed the "shot heard 'round the baseball world." Thomson has since been referred to as "The Scot Heard 'Round the World." ETYMOLOGY. From a line by Ralph Waldo Emerson which he wrote as part of his "Hymn Sung at the Completion of the Battle Monument, Concord" (July 4, 1837). He used the term to describe the beginning of the American Revolution: "Here once the embattled farmers stood, / And fired the shot heard 'round the world."

shoulder high Said of a pitch that approaches the batter at the height of his shoulder. IST USE. 1868. "[A 'shoulder ball'] is a ball sent to the batsman shoulder high and is a difficult ball to hit" (Henry Chadwick, *The Game of Base Ball*, 1868, p.45).

shove along *n./hist.* The act of stealing a base; e.g., "Smith did the shove along in the fourth inning." IST USE. 1907 (*New York Evening Journal*, May 2; Edward J. Nichols).

shovel To toss the ball underhand for a short distance. The motion suggests throwing dirt with a shovel, and it is what the shortstop often does when he throws the ball to the second baseman on a force play. "The shortstop scoops the grounder and shovels it to second" (Jackie Robinson, quoted in Roger Kahn and Al Helfer, eds., *Mutual Baseball Almanac*, 1954).

shovel throw A short, underhand toss. "[Chambers] made a backhanded pickup and shovel throw to Wheelrock" (Michael Schiffer, *Ballpark*, 1982, p.220).

Show, the Syn. of *major leagues*. In 1995, Major League Baseball adopted the slogan "Welcome to the Show." Sometimes spelled "the show." See also *big show*, 1. EXTENDED USE. The Super Bowl of the National Football League. "The [Baltimore] Ravens are going to The Show" (Mike Preston, *The Baltimore Sun*, Jan. 15, 2001).

showboat 1. *v.* To show off. "[Roberto] Clemente played erratically in the late 1950s and developed a reputation for showboating, flakiness, and whining" (Richard Peterson, *Crab Orchard Review*, Spring–Summer 1999, p.236). 2. *n.* A player who is clearly playing to the crowd with a fancy style; an exhibitionist; a grandstand player. "A player who never catches a ball with two hands that he can catch with one" (Fresco Thompson, *Every Diamond Doesn't Sparkle*, 1964). "The term 'showboat' is synonymous with exhibitionism in baseball" (Bob Feller, *Strikeout Story*, 1947). See also *cap-tipper*. IST USE. 1942. "There will be an all-star team of 'showboats' in the Pacific Coast League" (*San Francisco News*, July 20, 1942; Peter Tamony). ETYMOLOGY. An article on Edward "Peanuts Nyasses" Davis (*Liberty*, Sept. 19, 1942) suggested that this well-known African-American player and baseball clown helped popularize the term in the context of baseball.

The article explains that Nyasses dubbed himself the "Showboat King of Baseball."

showboat catch Syn. of *circus catch*.

showcase 1. *n.* A generic term for a special three-to-four-day, national or regional summer event designed to give top high school players an opportunity to show off their skills to professional scouts, college recruiters, and professional sports agents. John Manuel (*Baseball America*, Sept. 1–14, 2003; Peter Morris): "Baseball has followed the lead of basketball and football in that out-of-season events such as showcases . . . have begun to be as important in the college recruiting and professional scouting process as high school performances." Showcases use wood bats and electronically timed 60-yard dashes. The first showcase was the *Area Code Games*. Syn. "showcase event." 2. *v.* To expose a high school player at a showcase. "Our main purpose is to showcase all the top players" (Perfect Game director Jerry Ford, quoted in *Baseball America*, Oct. 27–Nov. 9, 2003).

showcase circuit A collective name for the many showcases held for high school players during the summer. "Many of the same players make several stops on the showcase circuit, but this gives coaches and scouts several opportunities to see players" (John Manuel, *Baseball America*, Sept. 1–14, 2003; Peter Morris).

shower To remove from the game; to *send to the showers*. "Now they'll shower him" (Al Michaels, on California Angels pitcher Donnie Moore just before his removal from the game, ABC telecast, Oct. 12, 1986).

shower hit The base hit that sends the pitcher to the showers and brings in another hurler (Walter K. Putney, *Baseball Stories*, Spring 1952).

showers The figurative place where a player (esp. a pitcher) goes after being removed during a game. Fred Schwed Jr (*How to Watch a Baseball Game*, 1957) related a story, which had been told to him by Charles Einstein, that underscores the extent to which this meaning of "showers" has become unique to America: "It seems that a number of years ago another reporter took Fred Perry of England, then the best tennis player in the world, to his first American baseball game. Mr. Perry was suspicious of the whole affair, and when in the second inning the losing pitcher was shelled off the mound, and started his lugubrious trudge over second base and the outfield, Perry asked, 'Where is he going?' The reporter said, 'To the showers.' 'It's a hot day,' said Perry, 'I imagine he will feel famously when he comes back.'"

show-me pitch A pitch that a pitcher has in his repertoire but that he does not use on a regular basis. "[Brandon] Claussen's changeup came on last season but still needs improvement to become more than a show-me pitch" (*Baseball America*, Jan. 21–Feb. 3, 2002; Peter Morris).

Show-Me Series Nickname for the 1985 World Series, which pitted the Kansas City Royals against the St. Louis Cardinals. Both teams are from Missouri, the Show-Me State. See also *I–70 Series*.

show spikes To slide into a base with one spiked foot held high enough to intimidate the fielder covering the base or obstruct his fielding. IST USE. 1928 (*The New York Times*, Oct. 6, Edward J. Nichols).

show up 1. To humiliate an opponent. Examples include stealing a base when leading by 12 runs, displaying celebratory gyrations after striking out a batter, flipping the bat in the air after hitting a home run, or expressing anger toward the pitcher when popping up. Showing up an opponent is "one of the cotton-headed clichés that abound in baseball" (Ira Berkow, *The New York Times*, Aug. 14, 1986). 2. To humiliate an umpire; e.g., a catcher framing a pitch or a player throwing equipment on the field. Umpire Bill McKinley (quoted in Larry R. Gerlach, *The Men in Blue*, 1980): "[Catcher Jim] Hegan could tell you off pretty good. But he never turned around to show you up. He always said it over his shoulder while he was down in his crouch." Umpire Billy Evans (*How to Umpire*, 1920, p.24): "The umpire does not care to be shown up before the crowd. . . . A shake of the head, a stepping out of the batter's box, or any one of a score of things, can call the attention of the crowd to the fact that

the player doesn't look on the ruling with favor. Such actions are seriously objected to by any umpire." 3. To perform on the field. "[Charley Comiskey] appeared to be well pleased with the manner in which his men showed up" (*San Francisco Bulletin*, March 7, 1913; Gerald L. Cohen).

show your colors *hist.* To display courage.

Shrine, the Syn. of *National Baseball Hall of Fame and Museum*.

shut down 1. For a pitcher to dominate the opposing team. "[Minnesota Twins pitcher Matt Garza] pretty much shut our offense down" (Baltimore Orioles manager Sam Perlozzo, quoted in *The Baltimore Sun*, Aug. 24, 2006). "[Milwaukee Brewers rookie pitcher Cal Eldred] shut down the league in the second half of the '92 season" (*Sports Illustrated*, Aug. 2, 1993, p.18). 2. To bench a player (usually a pitcher) temporarily because of injury, or to rest him. "[Pitcher Sid Fernandez] was shut down early in spring training by shoulder bursitis" (*The Baltimore Sun*, Apr. 18, 1994). "[Pitcher Josh Beckett] was shut down three times with blisters in 2002" (*Sports Illustrated*, Apr. 4, 2005). 3. To fail to give one's best effort. San Diego Padres third baseman Phil Nevin took the team to task for going through the motions after being swept in three games by Pittsburgh (quoted in *The Baltimore Sun*, Sept. 10, 2000): "I just get the feeling . . . that some people in this room are ready to shut it down and are ready for this thing to end." Chicago Cubs manager Don Baylor (quoted in *The Baltimore Sun*, Sept. 10, 2000): "I've been embarrassed by the way we've played. . . . We get two runs in the first inning and then shut it down." 4. To stop attempting to steal bases because the team is winning by many runs (Garret Mathews, *Can't Find a Dry Ball*, 2002).

shut off 1. To prevent a score by a throw home to retire the baserunner. IST USE. 1912 (*New York Tribune*, Sept. 20; Edward J. Nichols). 2. To defeat; to allow the opposing team few or no runs. "[Stanford Univ. pitcher Maple] shut off Cliff Ireland's Independents with but a single hit" (*San Francisco Bulletin*, March 28, 1913; Gerald L. Cohen).

shutout 1. *n.* A game in which the losing team does not score. Shutouts are often described by the number of hits made by the losers; e.g., a "two-hit shutout." Abbrev. *ShO*; *SO*, 3. IST USE. 1883. "It looked very much like a shut-out, but the boys went up with a determination to avert such a calamity if possible, and it was" (*Detroit Free Press*, May 4; Peter Morris). **2.** *n.* A statistic credited to a starting pitcher who pitches a complete game and allows no runs. The lifetime leader in pitching shutouts is Washington Senators hurler Walter Johnson, with 110. **3.** *n.* A preventing of the opponent from scoring. EXTENDED USE. An act of excluding; the state of being excluded. "Is there a lesson to be learned from Jim Carrey's shut-out from Oscar competition?" (Liz Smith, syndicated columnist, Feb. 18, 2000). **4.** *adj.* Describing a period in which there are no runs; e.g., three innings of "shutout relief."

shut out *v.* To prevent one's opponents from scoring. The term is normally used to describe a pitcher who deprives the other team of scoring any runs. See also *skunk*, 1; *Chicago*, 1; *whitewash*, 2. IST USE. 1879. "The Troys have at last been whitewashed—'shutout,' as the horsemen say" (*Troy Times*, July 2; Peter Morris). ETYMOLOGY. A borrowing from horse racing, where the term has long referred to a bettor who arrives at the window too late to wager a bet and is "shut out." EXTENDED USE. To prevent scoring in other endeavors, from football to politics; to exclude. "[Defensive safety Tom Landry] once shut out Bob Boyd, one of the fleetest of all the Los Angeles Rams' receivers, by schooling himself on his opponent's tendencies" (John Steadman, *The Baltimore Sun*, Feb. 14, 2000).

shut the door To pitch exceptionally well in either stopping or preventing a rally; to retire the side. The term is primarily used for relief pitchers. "[Sal Maglie], making just his fifth relief appearance of the year, shut the door and the Giants had still another victory" (Bobby Thomson, *"The Giants Win the Pennant! The Giants Win the Pennant!,"* 1991, p.198). "You've got to tip your hat to him [Bret Saberhagen]. He threw an outstanding game. He shut the door" (Al Nipper, quoted

in *USA Today*, Apr. 17, 1986). See also *close the door*. Syn. *slam the door*.

Shuttle Series The 1986 World Series between the Boston Red Sox and the New York Mets, representing two cities linked by commuter air-shuttle routes. Both shuttle operators (Eastern and Pan American) attempted to capitalize on the nickname.

shuttle system The process of moving players back and forth between the major leagues and the minor leagues.

side 1. One of the two teams in a game. When a half inning is over, it is common to say that the "side has been retired." In Australia, the umpire calls "side" to indicate that three outs have been made in a half inning. IST USE. 1864 (*Brooklyn Daily Eagle*, Sept. 9; Edward J. Nichols). **2.** A location for a player not in the game; e.g., "[Sidney] Ponson will throw on the side Thursday at Tropicana Field" (*The Baltimore Sun*, July 12, 2004). **3.** Short for *side session*. "[Josh Bard] caught me every single day . . . in my 'sides'" (Tim Wakefield, quoted in *The Boston Globe*, May 2, 2006).

sidearm Said of a pitch, throw, or delivery made with a sweeping forward motion of the arm from the side of the body at or below shoulder level, more or less parallel with the ground. It is neither *overhand* nor *underhand*. Syn. *sidewheel*. IST USE. 1904. "There are many good sidearm . . . pitchers, [Jack] Chesbro being a perfect type" (Deacon Phillippe, quoted in *Syracuse Post Standard*, March 27; Peter Morris).

sidearmer A pitcher who habitually throws from the sidearm position. Syn. *sidewheeler*, 1; *sidewinder*, 1.

side-kicker *hist.* A teammate. "[Pete Sweeney] was a side-kicker of [Fred] Stein, and both were scrappy players, which perhaps accounted for their fondness for each other" (*San Francisco Bulletin*, Apr. 3, 1913; Gerald L. Cohen).

sideline 1. *v.* To remove a player temporarily from the lineup because of a minor injury or some other reason; e.g., "The team sidelined Smith for three days because of his twisted ankle." **2.** *n.* Syn. of *side session*. "I've got one more sideline before the next start, so I can get my changeup back then" (Jason Johnson, quoted in *The Baltimore Sun*, Aug. 6, 2002). "[Starting pitchers] seemed to get more out of their sideline [when throwing on the third day after a start rather than the traditional second day]" (Ray Searage, quoted in *Baseball America*, Feb. 5–19, 2001; Peter Morris).

sidelines A mythical location where a player is kept out of the game; a place literally outside the foul lines.

side out The situation when three players have been retired.

side session A workout for pitchers, held in the bullpen or other area, sometimes between starts, for the purpose of correcting mechanical mistakes, developing a new pitch, or rehabilitating an injury. "During a side session . . . [Mark] Prior was working on his changeup, a pitch still under construction" (Daniel G. Habib, *Sports Illustrated*, March 1, 2004). "[John Franco] has looked sharp in side sessions, making his return seem assured" (*USA Today Sports Weekly*, May 14–20, 2003). "Jason Grimsley . . . will undergo another side session tomorrow, with the possibility that he'll go on an injury rehab assignment next week" (*The Baltimore Sun*, June 22, 2005). See also *bullpen session*. Syn. *side*, 3; *sideline*, 2.

side slide *hist.* A slide in which the runner is on his side, leading with his feet (*St. Louis Post-Dispatch*, July 31, 1886; Peter Morris).

sidewheel Syn. of *sidearm*. IST USE. 1904. "[Ed] Poole got away with a side wheel, old oaken bucket delivery" (*The Boston Globe*, July 5).

sidewheeler 1. Syn. of *sidearmer*. IST USE. 1911 (*Spalding's Official Base Ball Guide*, p.277; Edward J. Nichols). 2. A left-handed pitcher: "Some people call [Alphonso Davis] 'lefty' because he is a 'side-wheeler,' or throws with his left hand" (*Grand Rapids* [Mich.] *Herald*, May 18, 1902; Peter Morris).

sidewinder 1. Syn. of *sidearmer*. IST USE. 1921. "It's pretty certain that the elongated sidewinder [Eppa Rixey] will roll into the Giants' or Reds' camp before the frost is out

of the ball parks" (*Iowa City Press Citizen*, Jan. 8; Peter Morris). 2. A curving line drive. IST USE. 1870. "Hubbard making his third on a side-winder to left field" (*Grand Rapids* [Mich.] *Daily Eagle*, July 9; Peter Morris).

Sid Mercer Memorial Award An annual award presented since 1931 to a major-league player for "outstanding achievement and high contribution to [major-league] baseball." It was created by the New York chapter of the Baseball Writers' Association of America as the Outstanding Player of the Year Award, but renamed in 1945 in memory of the St. Louis and New York sportswriter who originally suggested the award.

siege gun A strong, excellent player.

sieve infield A poor defensive infield; one with many "holes."

sign 1. *n.* A secret motion, gesture, or sound that conveys information, such as the flashing fingers of a catcher or a vocal communication by a coach. A catcher employs signs constantly in calling for specific pitches from the pitcher. A coach uses them to call for offensive plays, such as bunts and steals. "Then McKeever held a long distance with Pitcher Harmon about signs. The crowd got impatient; one man yelled 'Get a telephone!' while the umpire ordered them to 'play ball'" (*The Boston Globe*, May 13, 1886; Peter Morris). Syn. *signal*, 1; *wig-wag*, 2. IST USE. 1869. "[The Red Stockings] have really two captains—the ostensible one is in the position of 'centre field,' and directs the movements of the fielders, and the other is the catcher, who indicates by signs to the pitcher and base-keepers the proper thing to do at the right moment" (*Daily Alta California*, Sept. 26, 1869; Darryl Brock). 2. *v.* To send a signal. IST USE. 1888. "Charley [Bassett] had signed me to cover second when [Mike] Tiernan tried to steal" (Jack Glasscock, quoted in *Detroit Free Press*, Sept. 1; Peter Morris). 3. *v.* To put one's signature on a contract. IST USE. 1882. "Before the Troys left that city [Roger] Connor and [Buck] Ewing both promised to sign with Boston for next season, and at the last moment violated their word and went elsewhere" (*The Cleveland Herald*, Oct. 6). 4. *n.* One who signs an autograph or contract; e.g.,

"Smith was a tough sign." **5.** *v./hist.* To issue a base on balls; e.g., "to sign a pass" or "sign a ticket." IST USE. 1912 (*New York Tribune*, Sept. 6; Edward J. Nichols).

signability Capability of signing an amateur player; the likelihood that a draft pick will turn professional rather than enter or continue college. Signability is a "problem" when the player has "unrealistic" bonus expectations. The term is a buzzword surrounding amateur drafts, with clubs having to choose between talented players whom they may not be able to sign or more average ones demanding less money. Player Ryan Gloger (quoted in *Baseball America*, June 28–July 11, 1999; Peter Morris): "I knew going in that signability was a question, and that I might drop [in the draft]."

signal 1. *n.* Syn. of *sign*, 1. IST USE. 1867. "Always have an understanding with your two sets of fielders in regard to private signals, so as to be able to call them in closer, or place them out further, or nearer the foul-ball lines, as occasion may require, without giving notice to your adversaries" (*Haney's Base Ball Book of Reference for 1867*, reprinted in *The Ball Players' Chronicle*, Aug. 22, 1867; Peter Morris). USAGE NOTE. Ty Cobb (*Memoirs of Twenty Years in Baseball*, 1925): "Players never use the word 'signals,' but always 'sign.'" Christy Mathewson (*Pitching in a Pinch*, 1912): "In the language of the Big Leagues it is 'signs,' never 'signals.'" **2.** *v.* To make a sign. "Nobody knows which catcher was the first to signal for a pitch" (Tom Fitzgerald, *Baseball Digest*, Nov. 1983, p.77).

signatory minor league A minor league that signed the National Agreement and was entitled to the protections it afforded, as opposed to an outlaw (nonsignatory) league. The distinction was esp. important in the 1890s and the first decade of the 20th century. Of the new National Agreement of 1892, Robert F. Burk (*Never Just a Game*, 1994, p.122; Peter Morris) wrote, "Minor leagues considered lower than B level in the eyes of the National League and nonsignatories to the National Agreement . . . possessed no reservation rights at all that the National League would respect."

signing bonus A *bonus* given to a player for agreeing to sign a contract with a team. The practice of offering signing bonuses was common up until 1965 when the first amateur player draft, created to end bidding wars that led to large bonuses, was held. Young players are still paid signing bonuses, but the amounts are not insignificant. Signing bonuses are also used for free agents and veterans signing long-term contracts.

sign stealing A tactic by which a team spots and deciphers its opponent's signs. For this reason, teams work to keep their signs as cryptic and confusing as possible. With a runner at second base, the pitcher and catcher usually change signs because the catcher's signs to the pitcher are clearly visible to the batting team. Some have attached great significance to the practice. "Of all the skills wrapped up in the complex game of big-league baseball, none is practiced with more ingenuity and less publicity than the fine art of diamond larceny. From the days of the old Orioles to [Leo] Durocher's Giants, sign-stealers have been surreptitiously deciding crucial ball games and winning world championships" (Martin Abramson, *The American Weekly*, June 5, 1955; Peter Tamony). Minnesota Twins manager Tom Kelly (quoted in *Sports Illustrated*, July 29, 1997): "Stealing signs is part of the job. If you don't try, you're not doing your job." Sign stealing is an ancient art (*St. Louis Post-Dispatch*, Apr. 1, 1889; Peter Morris): "Arthur Irwin can find out the signs of opposing pitchers quicker than any other man in the League." However, use of hidden cameras, closed-circuit TV, flashing lights in the scoreboard, and the like is generally frowned upon.

There are many stories that underscore the extensiveness of sign stealing. Tristram Potter Coffin (*The Old Ball Game*, 1971) insists, "The most famous is the one usually told about Charlie Dressen at a now half-forgotten All-Star Game. Supposedly the All-Stars were together before the game attempting to come up with a series of signals for the day. Dressen, who was a noted sign-stealer, is [thought] to have said, 'Forget it, I'll give each of you the ones used on your own team.'"

sign system An assortment of signs that includes an indicator, a wipe-off sign, an activator, a release sign, and many decoy signs.

Silver Bat A 34-inch-long sterling-plated bat presented annually since 1949 by the Hillerich & Bradsby Co. to the batting champions of each major league. The trophy is engraved with the player's autograph and the statistics of his winning accomplishments. From 1934 to 1948, the trophy was awarded to the minor-league batting champions. At one time it was called the "Louisville Slugger Trophy."

Silver Bullets The first all-women's professional baseball team to compete only against men. Formed in 1993 as the Colorado Silver Bullets, the team played its first guaranteed schedule of games in the independent Northern League. The team ceased play following the 1997 season because it was unable to find a sponsor after Coors Brewing Co. bowed out as chief sponsor.

Silver Glove Award An annual award presented since 1957 by Rawlings Sporting Goods Co. and *The Sporting News* to the top minor-league fielder at each position, based entirely on fielding averages.

Silver Shoe Award An annual award presented since 1982 by Pony Sports and Leisure (a shoe manufacturer) in conjunction with *The Sporting News* to the top base stealer in the major leagues.

Silver Slugger Award An annual award presented since 1980 by Hillerich & Bradsby Co. (manufacturers of the Louisville Slugger bat) in conjunction with *The Sporting News* to the top hitters in both major leagues at their respective positions, including pitchers in the National League. The awards are chosen by managers and coaches who cannot vote for their own team members. Selections are based on a combination of offensive statistics, as well as the personal impressions of a player's offensive value. The sterling-plated trophy is three feet tall and features the engraved names of all 18 winners in both leagues.

silver sombrero Syn. of *golden sombrero*. "If you whiff four times, you win the 'silver sombrero'" (Peter Schmuck, *The Baltimore Sun*, Apr. 28, 1991).

similarity score An informal index of the degree to which two players have had similar statistics during their careers; e.g., through age 26, Nomar Garciaparra was most like the 26-year-old Ernie Banks. It is calibrated such that a similarity score of 1,000 represents perfect similarity, 900 represents strong similarity, 800 represents obvious similarities but notable differences, and 700 represents noticeable similarities but obvious differences. The index was proposed by Bill James in his *Baseball Abstract* (1986); in considering Nellie Fox' credentials for the Hall of Fame, James noted that five of the 10 players most similar to him had already been inducted: Luis Aparicio at 877, Rabbit Maranville at 877, Luke Appling at 875, Bobby Wallace at 871, and Billy Herman at 869. Since James' essay, two others have joined them (Red Schoendienst at 918 and Richie Ashburn at 874).

simulated game A routine in which a pitcher throws to a catcher as if he were pitching a real game. It is used for pitchers recovering from injury or coming off the disabled list. After throwing to three or more batters—or throwing a predetermined number of pitches—the pitcher rests for three to five minutes to simulate the period that his team is at bat. A simulated game may last as long as six innings.

simulated play-by-play A broadcast that apes the live action of a real game. It can occur after the game or be created from telegraph or teletype reporting of a game in progress, or, as was common during the 1981 baseball strike, be of an imaginary or fantasy game. The process is also used to re-create games from the past.

single 1. *n.* A base hit on which the batter reaches first base safely. Abbrev. *1B*, 4. Syn. *one-baser*; *one-base hit*; *one-bagger*; *one-sacker*; *bingle*, 2; *solitaire*. IST USE. 1858 (Chadwick Scrapbooks; Edward J. Nichols). ETYMOLOGY. The term is used in cricket where it originated. **2.** *v.* To hit a single. IST USE. 1893. "Doyle and Crane hit fly balls to Daly, then Burke singled, sending in Keeler" (*The New York Times*, May 10; Fred R. Shapiro).

Single A Syn. of *Class A*, 4.

single elimination A tournament format in which one defeat eliminates a team from further play. Compare *round-robin*; *double elimination*.

singleheader A facetious name for one game of a day-night doubleheader with separate admissions.

single in a run To score a baserunner by hitting a single.

singles hitter A player who seldom hits a ball for extra bases; e.g., Tony Gwynn, Ichiro Suzuki, Lloyd Waner, Maury Wills, and Richie Ashburn. "[Ty Cobb was] surely the best of all the singles hitters" (Bob Ryan, *The Boston Globe*, July 6, 2002). Syn. *parachute hitter*.

singleton 1. A lone run scored in any inning. **2.** Syn. of *solo home run*.

sinister wing *hist.* The left arm. "Harry Ables' right hand is causing him many hours of pain . . . [but] his sinister wing, however, is in great shape" (*San Francisco Bulletin*, Feb. 27, 1913; Gerald L. Cohen).

sinistral *hist.* Left-handed. "Substitutions are constantly slowing up the game so that portside swingers may not be exposed to sinistral slants" (Richard Maney, *The New York Times*, Sept. 10, 1950).

sink 1. *n.* The quality of a sinker or of a two-seam fastball. "[Derek Lowe] had a lot of late sink on the ball" (Jay Gibbons, quoted in *The Baltimore Sun*, Apr. 29, 2002). "[Daniel Cabrera] was throwing 94 to 96 [mph] with good sink and he does it so easily" (anonymous scout, quoted in *The Baltimore Sun*, Apr. 6, 2005). **2.** *v.* "[To] curve the ball" (*The Sporting News*, Oct. 30, 1913).

sinkage The act, process, or degree by which a sinker suddenly drops. Tommy John (quoted in *Chicago Tribune*, June 5, 1986): "The last couple of years, my ball was not sinking. It had good movement, but not much sinkage. And day by day in spring training, I got that sinkage back." To which columnist Rick Horowitz responded: "There's no place for 'sinkage' on a baseball diamond; it's just one more linguistic perversion of the National Pastime."

sinker 1. A pitched ball that drops sharply as it nears the plate, making it nearly impossible to hit it in the air and notorious for inducing ground balls. It is a fastball that moves laterally and downward because it is delivered with a downward movement and an inward roll (flip) of the wrist. The aim is to make the batter hit the top half of the ball, not get under it, thereby producing a ground ball. The ball is gripped with the middle and index fingers curled snugly, not tightly, along two parallel, narrow seams; the thumb underneath pinches across the narrow seams on the lower half of the ball. In releasing the ball, the pitcher turns the ball over at the last moment, placing more pressure with the index finger. When thrown by a right-handed pitcher, the sinker breaks down and in to a right-handed batter (making the batter hit the ball on the thin part of the bat) and down and away to a left-handed batter (making the batter hit the ball off the top end of the bat). See also *drop ball*, 1; *two-seam fastball*. Syn. *drop*, 1; *sinkerball*; *sinking fastball*, 1; *false rise*. IST USE. 1910. New York Giants pitcher Ed Keiber "discovered" a "new curve": "The ball has been christened a 'sinker.' With Keiber's delivery the ball starts high, apparently rises a few feet, and then sinks suddenly to about the height of the batter's knee" (*The Sporting Life*, March 12; Peter Morris). **2.** Syn. of *downer*. **3.** A batted ball that drops sharply, usually between the infield and the outfield; a *Texas Leaguer*, 2. IST USE. 1928. "A sinker—a fly ball that has a back spin which causes it to sink to the ground quickly" (George Herman Ruth, *Babe Ruth's Own Book of Baseball*; David Shulman). **4.** A batted ball (such as a line drive) that drops rapidly after passing the infield; "a fly ball that spins in such a way that it sinks to the ground with great rapidity" (M.G. Bonner, *The Big Baseball Book for Boys*, 1931, p.121). **5.** A ball that's thrown by a fielder and that drops suddenly. "[Brian Roberts'] throw to first was a sinker in the dirt" (*The Baltimore Sun*, Sept. 14, 2003).

sinkerball Syn. of *sinker*, 1.

sinkerballer A pitcher who is adept at throwing the sinker; e.g., Wilcy Moore, New York Yankees pitcher of the late 1920s, who was the first pitcher to become famous for throwing the sinker.

sinking fastball 1. Syn. of *sinker*, 1. 2. Syn. of *two-seam fastball*.

sinking liner A line drive that drops suddenly in midflight.

Sir Charles The superb curveball thrown by Dwight Gooden (*The Washington Post*, Oct. 19, 1997). See also *Uncle Charlie*; *Lord Charles*. EXTENDED USE. Nickname for basketball player Charles Barkley.

sit To describe a speed that a pitcher's fastball reaches regularly, as opposed to a speed that he can only *touch*. "[Gavin Floyd's] fastball sits at 91–94 mph and has touched 97 this spring" (*Baseball America*, June 11–24, 2001; Peter Morris).

sit dead-red To wait for a fastball. "After a 1–0 count, I'm sitting dead-red, looking for a fast ball all the way" (Chipper Jones, quoted in *The Baltimore Sun*, May 10, 1998).

sit down 1. For a pitcher to retire a batter; e.g., "Smith sat Jones down with a strikeout." 2. To take a player out of the lineup; e.g., "The manager had no feelings about sitting down nonproductive players."

sit in the catbird seat To be in an advantageous position, such as a batter with a 3–0 count. See also *catbird seat*.

sit on 1. For a batter to anticipate or wait for a specific pitch. "If hitters sit on the forkball, they can't catch up to his [Kazuhiro Sasaki's] fastball" (Seattle Mariners pitching coach Bryan Price, quoted in *Sports Illustrated*, Oct. 16, 2000). 2. For a team to protect a lead.

sitting duck A baserunner who is in a position to be put out by a wide margin by a defensive player; e.g., a baserunner who attempts to steal on a pitchout is usually a sitting duck. ETYMOLOGY. From the long-established simile used to express an easy shot, "as easy as hitting a sitting duck."

situational baseball Baseball played by being aware of the various conditions or circumstances that present themselves on the field, pitch by pitch. Such situations include the score, the number of outs and baserunners, and the strengths and weaknesses of the batter and the batter on deck.

situational hitter A hitter who comes to the plate with a plan, who can produce the type of hit needed for a given situation (such as a single or sacrifice fly with runners in scoring position or a home run to tie or win the game), who can take pitches when leading off an inning, and who rarely strikes out. "Carlos [Baerga] is not just a smart hitter, but a smart situational hitter. He knows how to move runners and hit the opposite way" (Paul Molitor, quoted in *Sports Illustrated*, Apr. 4, 1994, p.66).

situational pitcher A pitcher who takes advantage of specific circumstances, such as a left-handed relief pitcher who is brought into the game to face one or two left-handed batters, or a starting pitcher who works the entire strike zone and makes maximum use of his arsenal of pitches.

situational statistics A statistical comparison between a player's performance in two or more directly contrasting situations. Although many situational statistics are calculated (e.g., bases empty versus runners on bases versus bases loaded, or no outs versus one out versus two outs), research by Jim Albert (described in Jim Albert and Jay Bennett, *Curve Ball*, 2001) implies that only three situations are significant: the tendency for batters to perform better when facing a pitcher of opposite handedness (the platoon differential), when facing a pitcher who tends toward giving up ground balls rather than fly balls, and when playing at home rather than away. A fourth situation—the tendency for batters to perform worse with two strikes than with none or one—was shown by J. Eric Bickel and Dean Stotz (*Baseball Research Journal*, 2003) to be an artifact, as batting average is automatically decreased by strikeout when a batter suffers a third strike, but unaffected by the first and second strikes.

situation-independent Said of a baseball statistic that measures performance apart from the context of team, ballpark, or other outside variables; e.g., strikeouts, bases on balls, and home runs (when not affected by park dimensions). Statistics that are not situation-independent include runs batted in (dependent on other batters getting on base) and pitching wins (dependent on the offense and defense performing behind the pitcher and on bullpen support). "Situation-independent gauges are important . . . to separate a player's contribution to his team and isolate his performance so that we may judge it on its own merits" (Ron Shandler, *Ron Shandler's Baseball Forecaster*, 2006).

6 The scorekeeper's designation for the shortstop. ETYMOLOGY. "Why is the shortstop numbered 6 instead of 5, which would be the logical sequence around the infield? The reason has been lost in history. Some suggest that the early shortstops were thought of as short outfielders rather than as members of the infield. This theory loses some credibility because the widespread use of 6 for the shortstop in scorecards bought in stadiums did not come into play until the 1920s. However, as early as 1890 the scoring system created by Harry Wright contained the modern numbering system, with 6 for the shortstop" (Paul Dickson, *The Joy of Keeping Score*, 1996, p.22).

6-4-3 The scorekeeper's notation for a double play in which the ball goes from the shortstop (6) to the second baseman (4) to the first baseman (3). It is the most common double play combination. After the 1988 Baltimore Orioles had hit into double plays in 24 consecutive games, Tim Kurkjian (*The Sporting News*, Oct. 10, 1988) commented, "He [Frank Robinson] manages Team 6-4-3." Compare *4-6-3*.

600 home run club A mythical group of players who have 600 career home runs. As of 2008 it includes Ken Griffey Jr., Barry Bonds, Henry Aaron, Babe Ruth, Willie Mays, and Sammy Sosa.

six-man infield A *five-man infield* in which the pitcher is implicitly counted as an infielder. The strategy has been used in a bunt situation. George Sisler (*Sisler on Baseball*, 1954; Peter Morris) wrote, "When a poor-hitting pitcher comes up to the plate with a sacrifice in order, either with one down or no one out, it is wise to bring one of your outfielders . . . and place him at a definite place in the infield, making it defense with six rather than the normal five players."

six-o'clock hitter A player who hits well in batting practice and poorly during the game. See also *10-o'clock hitter; 12-o'clock hitter;* *one-o'clock hitter; two-o'clock hitter; five-o'clock hitter; seven-o'clock hitter.* ETYMOLOGY. From the fact that batting practice is likely to be in full swing at six o'clock for a night game beginning at seven o'clock or later. When day games were the norm, the six-o'clock hitter was likely to be called a "two-o'clock hitter."

16-inch [softball term] Said of Chicago-style softball, which is played with a large ball that is 16 inches in diameter.

sixth 1. *n.* The sixth inning. 2. *adv.* Said of the sixth position in the batting order; e.g., "Smith is batting sixth."

6-12 movement The motion of a thrown ball when it is rotating (as if on a clock) clockwise from six o'clock to twelve o'clock. A catcher throwing to second base wants this kind of movement so that the "ball's not tumbling in all different directions" (Andy Etchebarren, quoted in *The Baltimore Sun*, Feb. 23, 1997).

60-day disabled list A *disabled list* established in 1990 in which the player is removed from the team's 40-man reserve list. A player on the *15-day disabled list* may be shifted to the 60-day disabled list at any time. There are no limits on the number of players who can be placed on the list; however, the 40-man roster must be full before the 60-day list can be used. The 60-day list is sometimes called the *emergency disabled list*.

60-40 rule A requirement that each major-league club must have a ratio of assets to liabilities of not less than 60 (assets) to 40 (liabilities); i.e., a club cannot have more debt on its books than 40 percent of its value. Assets are defined as a club's appraised value. Liabilities include total player salaries (including deferred salaries), the value of long-term player contracts, stadium debt, and loans. The rule was introduced in 1975 and adopted in 1982; and though it was largely ignored for years, commissioner Bud Selig began to enforce it in 2002. Compare *debt service rule; debt equity rule*.

61-in-'61 The feat of New York Yankees outfielder Roger Maris, who hit 61 home runs in 1961. "[Mickey] Mantle Honors Maris'

61-in-'61 Feat" (*USA Today Baseball Weekly* headline, Apr. 19–25, 1991).

six-year minor-league free agent A *minor-league free agent* who has played all or part of seven seasons in the major or minor leagues and is not placed on a major-league team's 40-man roster as of Oct. 15. USAGE NOTE. The term appears to be a misnomer because the original signing team has the right to six automatic renewals of a minor-league player's contract.

sizzle For a player or team to perform very well. "[The] Boston Red Sox are sizzling like no other Red Sox team has sizzled since '46" (*USA Today*, June 6, 1986). A hitter on a hot streak is "torrid" or "sizzling" (Lowell Cohn, *San Francisco Chronicle*, June 4, 1980).

sizzler 1. A hard-hit ball, such as a searing ground ball or a fast, low line drive. "[Joe] Cassidy had to dip his skypiece in response to the applause after he speared Donohue's [Red Donahue's] grass disturber. It was a sizzler, all right" (*The Washington Post*, Aug. 28, 1904; Peter Morris). IST USE. 1895. "[Pink] Hawley made a fine stop of [Bill] Kennedy's sizzler" (*Brooklyn Eagle*, June 11; Peter Morris). **2.** A fastball. IST USE. 1911 (*Baseball Magazine*, October, p.68; Edward J. Nichols).

sked Short for the printed regular-season schedule of baseball games to be played. The term is used by collectors of baseball cards and other baseball novelties and commonly shows up in the magazine *Sports Collectors Digest*.

skid 1. A losing streak for a player or a team; e.g., "[Mike] Hampton lost his fifth straight start, the longest skid of his career" (*The Baltimore Sun*, Apr. 13, 2002), and "The rally broke a . . . 22-inning scoreless skid by baseball's best-hitting team" (*The Baltimore Sun*, May 5, 2005). **2.** A hitless streak; e.g., "José Hernandez stopped an 0-for-26 September skid with a two-run, pinch-hit single" (*The Baltimore Sun*, Sept. 13, 2003).

skillet A fielder's glove, esp. an unwieldy one or one on the hand of a fielder who doesn't catch very well.

skillet hands The hands of a bad fielder (Bob Hertzel, *Baseball Digest*, Jan. 1987).

skimmer A low batted ball, often a ground ball, that skims over the grass or the ground.

See also *daisy cutter*, 1; *grass cutter*. IST USE. 1868. "Hatfield . . . ran in on Fisler's 'skimmer' to left field" (Chadwick Scrapbooks; David Shulman).

skin The dirt portion of the infield, which is intentionally kept free of grass or artificial turf.

skin diamond An infield devoid of grass. IST USE. 1886. "[Reddy Mack] says that the Pittsburg grounds have a 'skin' diamond, that there is no sod on the in-field" (*St. Louis Post-Dispatch*, June 22; Peter Morris).

skip 1. The intentional miss of a base by a canny baserunner when the umpire's attention is on the ball or other runners. IST USE. 1883. "The 'skip' from second base to home plate while the umpire was engaged in some astrological calculations" (*Grand Rapids* [Mich.] *Evening Leader*, Aug. 7; Peter Morris). **2.** Short for *skipper*, 1. "Ballplayers call a manager 'skip' when they like him" (Kevin Baker, *Sometimes You See It Coming*, 1993, p.32).

skipper 1. *n.* An affectionate name for the manager of a baseball team. "What the skipper [Jim Leyland] does is reinforce every day what we're capable of . . . and we believe it" (Detroit Tigers pitcher Nate Robertson, quoted in *Sports Illustrated*, Oct. 23, 2006). Syn. *skip*, 2. IST USE. 1890. "Out in Australia they call the captain of a base ball club the skipper" (*Columbus* [Ohio] *Press*, March 16; Peter Morris). ETYMOLOGY. From the Dutch "schipper" (pronounced "skipper"), the master of a small craft. The term has a long history as a form of address for the captain or master of a ship. **2.** *v.* To perform as a skipper. "[DeMarlo Hale] skippered Class A Sarasota in the Florida State League in 1996" (Nick Cafardo, *Baseball America*, Dec. 23, 1996–Jan. 5, 1997; Peter Morris). **3.** *n.* A ball batted along the ground with a slight bounce. IST USE. 1877. "A skipper to third" (*Chicago Tribune*, May 27).

skip rope 1. For a batter to jump up quickly to avoid being hit by a low, inside pitch. **2.** For a pitcher to jump out of the way of a ball hit back through the box or for a baserunner to jump out of the way of a batted ball.

skip the dew *hist.* For a fielder or baserunner

to run rapidly. IST USE. 1937 (*New York Daily News*, Feb. 14; Edward J. Nichols).

skirt A player who avoids a ground ball or who won't play on a given day. Researcher Kenneth Forehand (letter, Apr. 29, 1994) reports, "I have heard speculation that this may have originated from a player who would 'skirt' around a ball instead of getting in front of it." See also *keep your skirt down*.

skirted soprano A female baseball fan (Maurice H. Weseen, *A Dictionary of American Slang*, 1934).

skull 1. *v.* To bean or hit a batter in the head with a pitched ball. "Don't skull these boys. You'll kill one of them and we'll never get out of here" (William Brashler, *The Bingo Long Traveling All-Stars and Motor Kings*, 1973, p.144; Charles D. Poe). **2.** *n.* A dumb play or mental error caused by faulty judgment. "[Joe] DiMaggio could not abide 'skulls' in which players made unthinking errors" (Joe King, *Sportsweek*, July 31, 1968).

skuller Syn. of *batting helmet*.

skull practice A team meeting where the manager, coaches, and players "put their heads together" to discuss strategy before a game. Ty Cobb (*My Life in Baseball*, 1961, p.197): "I abolished skull practice. . . . I saw no profit in hashing over strategy for thirty minutes or an hour in the clubhouse, after which the players would forget what had been said when the situation arose on the field." Syn. "skull session." IST USE. 1917 (*The New York Times*, Oct. 6; Edward J. Nichols).

skunk 1. *v./hist.* To prevent a team from scoring; to be unable to score. IST USE. 1863. "[The Brother Jonathan club] played wildly, getting 'skunked' in the remaining two innings" (*Detroit Advertiser and Tribune*, Aug. 7; Peter Morris). See also *shut out*; *Chicago*, 1. **2.** *n./hist.* An inning in which a team does not score. "In New York a blank score is called a 'skunk'" (Henry Chadwick, *The Game of Base Ball*, 1868, p.45). See also *blank*, 1. IST USE. 1862 (*New York Sunday Mercury*, Sept. 21; Edward J. Nichols). ETYMOLOGY. The term applies to several sports and games. It plays an important role in the card game of cribbage, signifying loss by a large margin. **3.** *n.* Zero. "We beat them three

to skunk" (Herbert Simons, *Baseball Magazine*, Jan. 1943).

skunk rule [softball term] The proviso in many Over the Line encounters in which a game is ended if a team is ahead by a certain number of runs at the end of an inning. The number of runs is usually 11, but is sometimes changed.

sky 1. *v.* To hit a very high fly ball. "[Albert] Belle skied a pitch toward the porch behind the right-field scoreboard" (*The Baltimore Sun*, Apr. 6, 1999). IST USE. 1905 (*Montrose* [Pa.] *Independent Republican*, June 30; Edward J. Nichols). **2.** *n./hist.* A high fly ball or popout. IST USE. "Miller sent a 'sky' to Peter, which was missed" (*Brooklyn Eagle*, Sept. 27; Peter Morris).

sky ball A ball batted high in the air. "The Angels hit sky balls, fifteen of which fell into the gloves of the outfielders" (*San Francisco Bulletin*, Apr. 28, 1913; Gerald L. Cohen). IST USE. 1863 (*New York Sunday Mercury*, Aug. 9; Edward J. Nichols).

skybox A luxury seating accommodation at a ballpark, usually enclosed, high above the playing surface. Amenities include private bathroom, wet bar, telephones, television sets, air-conditioning and heating, cushioned chairs, plush carpeting, and a sound system. "Wealthy Texans snapped up five-year $15,000 leases on every last Skybox, as they were called, before a game was ever played [in the Astrodome]" (John Helyar, *Lords of the Realm*, 1994, pp.69–70). Also spelled "sky box." Syn. *luxury box*. IST USE. 1887. The term referred to a director's box at Detroit's Recreation Park used by Detroit Wolverines president Fred Stearns and his guests: "Things didn't open up very brightly for Detroit and the air in the big sky box became frought [*sic*] with red hot excitement" (*Detroit Tribune*, Sept. 29; Peter Morris).

skyer *hist.* A towering fly ball. IST USE. 1862. "Manolt was the fifth striker, and he hit a 'skyer' which fell into Abrams' hands" (*New York Sunday Mercury*, Oct. 12; David Shulman). ETYMOLOGY. Borrowed from cricket. "A [cricket] ball hit . . . a long way . . . becomes a 'skyer'" (*Field and Stream*, Dec. 25, 1873; Peter Morris).

skypiece A baseball cap. IST USE. 1904. "[Joe] Cassidy had to dip his skypiece in response to the applause after he speared Donohue's [Red Donahue's] grass disturber" (*The Washington Post*, Aug. 28; Peter Morris).

sky-rocket A long, hard-hit fly ball that goes high into the air. "[Ron] Kittle stroked a sky-rocket in the . . . Comiskey Park bleacher area" (*Baseball Digest*, Oct. 1983, p.68). See also *rocket*, 1. IST USE. 1858. "Steele followed with a sky-rocket, which Wyatt attempted on the fly, but it wouldn't stay in his hands" (*New York Atlas*, Sept. 12).

skyscraper A towering fly ball, hit so high it figuratively "touches" the sky. "The sky scrapers, which to the sorrow of the Bostons, were numerous, generally traveled in Glenn's direction and he captured them all. He retired nine men, all on very high fly balls" (*Chicago Times*, June 8, 1875; John Thorn). Syn. *scraper.* IST USE. 1857. "Give them 'nary' sky scraper ball, but bat 'em on the ground" (Everett L. Baker, poem "Impromptu," *Buffalo Courier*, Sept. 27; Priscilla Astifan). ETYMOLOGY. The seldom deployed triangular sail (also called a moon-raker) at the top of a mast on an old-time sailing ship (*OED*, 1794).

slab 1. *n.* The pitcher's *rubber*, 1. IST USE. 1884. "[Louisville captain Joe] Gerhardt had a marble slab put in the [pitcher's] box of the home grounds" (*Cincinnati Enquirer*, Aug. 6; David Ball). USAGE NOTE. In 1886, the American Association experimented with a piece of marble, stone, or glass, one foot wide, placed on the front outer edge of the pitcher's box to prevent pitchers from overstepping their bounds. The term remained in use when the stone or marble evolved into rubber by the time of the pitching rule changes of 1893. As a term for the pitcher's domain, "slab" remained current long after its original meaning became obsolete. 2. *v.* To pitch. "Otto Hess . . . slabbed six innings for the Braves yesterday" (*The Washington Post*, Apr. 11, 1915; Peter Morris). 3. *n.* Syn. of *home plate.*

slab artist *hist.* A pitcher. "In recent years the 'slab artist' has been given the advantage, and the complaint grows that there is not batting enough" (Albert G. Spalding, *Base Ball: America's National Game*, 1911; Peter Tamony). IST USE. 1902. "The first game found Taylor and Mathewson as rival slab artists" (William F.H. Koelsch, *The Sporting Life*, Aug. 16; Peter Morris).

slabber *hist.* A pitcher. "The young lads on the sandlots decided that the avenes [*sic*] to fame as a hitter were wider and smoother than to success as a slabber. That's why pitching talent is scarce today" (*The Washington Post*, Aug. 9, 1925; Steve Steinberg).

slabbist *hist.* A pitcher. IST USE. 1913. "In what better way could a writer describe the failure of a slabbist to put the pill over the plate . . ." (*The Washington Post*, Aug. 16).

slabman *hist.* A pitcher. IST USE. 1903. "Last year every ground in the Eastern League had a raised pitcher's box, and it increased the power of the slabmen" (*The Sporting Life*, March 21; Peter Morris).

slabster *hist.* A pitcher. "George Foster and Ernie Shore were a couple of Red Sox slabsters who never regained the winning knack after chucking no hitters" (Red Foley, *The Sporting News*, May 23, 1956). IST USE. 1910 (*Baseball Magazine*, Apr.; Edward J. Nichols).

slabwork *hist.* Pitching. IST USE. 1905 (*The Sporting Life*, Sept. 2, p.21; Edward J. Nichols).

slam 1. *v.* To hit with great power. IST USE. 1897. "The hero of Burkeville slammed a grounder to 'Kid' Gleason, who fired it to Jake for an out" (*The World* [New York], May 14; Peter Morris). 2. *n.* A hard-hit ball. IST USE. 1907 (*Reach Official American League Base Ball Guide*, p.110; Edward J. Nichols). 3. *n.* Short for *grand slam*, 1. "You're a little more careful with the bases loaded, but the last thing on your mind should be giving up a slam." (Shawn Estes, quoted in *Sports Illustrated*, June 21, 1999, p.51). 4. *n.* A *sweep*, 3. "Atlanta First in Southern Ass'n to Make 'Slam' in Dixie Series; Crackers, in Addition to Winning League Championship, Took Play-off and Then Beat Beaumont Four Straight" (*The Sporting News* headline, Oct. 13, 1938). See also *grand slam*, 2.

slamfest Syn. of *slugfest*. "Jays run down Phils in 15–14 slamfest" (*The Baltimore Sun* headline, Oct. 21, 1993).

slammer Syn. of *grand slam*, 1.

slam the door Syn. of *shut the door.* "Given a two-run lead to protect in the ninth, he [Arthur Rhodes] couldn't slam the door" (*The Baltimore Sun*, March 14, 1999). "[Closer Troy] Percival slams the door, [Eddie] Guardado tends to leave it cracked" (*The Baltimore Sun*, Oct. 11, 2002).

slant 1. A pitch; esp., a curveball. The term is often used in the plural; e.g., "[James] carries a beautiful assortment of slants and shoots" (*San Francisco Bulletin*, March 11, 1913; Gerald L. Cohen). IST USE. 1898. "Some of the greatest assassins of pitchers' slants that ever wielded a bat were wild pitch hitters" (Gus Weyhing, quoted in *The Washington Post*, Sept. 25). 2. *v.* To throw a curveball (*The Sporting News*, Oct. 30, 1913). 3. [softball term] A pitched ball, esp. in the fast pitch softball parlance of the 1930s and 1940s.

slap 1. *v.* To hit a pitch sharply with a quick jab rather than a full swing. IST USE. 1884. "He bats from the shoulder and rather 'slaps' than 'poles' the ball" (*The Sporting Life*, Aug. 6; Peter Morris). 2. *n.* A quick jab at a pitched ball. "[The batter] reached out on the first pitched ball and shoved it over the third-baseman's head. In addition to this slap . . ." (*San Francisco Bulletin*, May 30, 1913; Gerald L. Cohen).

slap ball A playground version of baseball in which the batter bounces the ball in front of himself and hits it with an open hand. In some versions, the ball must not leave the infield on the fly if it is hit above the fielder's head.

slap hit 1. A base hit in which the ball is hit with a quick jab of the bat rather than with a full swing, and is characteristically placed between, or just over the heads of, the infielders. 2. [softball term] A maneuver in fast pitch softball in which a left-handed batter will take a step toward first base as the ball leaves the pitcher's hand and jab the ball to the left side of the infield with a slapping motion. With the shorter basepath and what is essentially a legal lead off the plate and good timing, the batter has a fairly good chance of making it safely to first base.

slap hitter A hitter who specializes in slap hits; e.g., Nelson Fox, Richie Ashburn, and Brett Butler. Syn. *slapper*, 1.

slapjack *hist.* One of a series of base hits "stacked right on top of the other[s]" (*San Francisco Examiner*, Aug. 9, 1900; Peter Tamony).

slapper 1. Syn. of *slap hitter*. 2. Syn. of *slasher*, 1. 3. An infielder who takes swipes at the ball or who uses his glove like a flyswatter.

slapstick *hist.* A baseball bat. "Most long men are in trouble when the ball swishes past their knees, and when they hit it they usually have to do so with a difficult sweep of the slapstick" (*The Sporting News*, Aug. 11, 1910; Peter Morris). IST USE. 1908 (*New York Evening Journal*, June 11; Edward J. Nichols).

slap tag A tag in which the fielder slaps the baserunner with a gloved ball.

slash 1. *v.* To hit the ball sharply, usually to the opposite field. The *St. Louis Post-Dispatch* (May 6, 1875; Peter Morris) identified Lipman Pike, Ned Cuthbert, Dickey Pearce, William Hague, Herman Dehlman, and Jack Chapman as "sure, slashing batsmen." 2. *n.* The act of a batter hitting the ball hard on the ground toward a space vacated by the defense due to its early response to a potential sacrifice bunt (Jerry Weinstein and Tom Alston, *Baseball Coach's Survival Guide*, 1998). IST USE. 1908 (*Spalding's Official Base Ball Guide*, p.63; Edward J. Nichols).

slasher 1. A hitter who slashes the ball; one who "hits the ball all over the ballpark" and puts the ball in play "with a medium amount of power" (Wally Moon, quoted in *Orioles Gazette*, July 30, 1993, p.27). A slasher has good bat control and will hit hard ground balls and line drives, rather than apply lift to the ball. Syn. *slapper*, 2. 2. A "hard, decisive hit" (Walter K. Putney, *Baseball Stories*, Spring 1952).

slats The ribs of a player.

slaughter 1. *n.* A decisive defeat. 2. *v.* To defeat decisively. IST USE. 1905. "Princeton slaughtered Old Eli [Yale]" (*Chicago Tribune*, June 4; Peter Morris).

slaughter rule The stipulation that if a team is ahead by a given number of runs after a given number of innings (e.g., 10 runs after five innings), that team is declared the winner. The rule is invoked in softball and in high school and Little League games, among others. The World Baseball Classic decreed that games will be stopped after five innings when a team is ahead by 15 or more runs and after seven innings when a team is ahead by at least 10 runs. Syn. *mercy rule.*

slave A professional baseball player, so named because the club owner can buy, sell, or trade his contract. IST USE. 1908 (*Baseball Magazine*, July, p.63; Edward J. Nichols).

slave to the slobs A batboy in relation to the players (*Newsweek*, July 15, 1991).

sleeper 1. A player, or team, who may become successful after a period of being considered unpromising; a player, or team, who will seemingly produce beyond anticipation. The term is used by those involved in fantasy baseball for a potential superstar; e.g., Childs Walker (*The Baltimore Sun*, March 21, 2006) wrote, "The term sleeper gives me a bit of pause, because it's so relative. In casual leagues, just about any rookie could be a sleeper. In ultra-competitive leagues, any decent player above Double-A is probably a known quantity." 2. A talented player overlooked by scouts. LaGrange (Ga.) High School baseball coach Dennis Branch (quoted in *Sports Illustrated*, Jan. 14, 2002): "There wasn't exactly a mob of scouts here to see him [Mike Cameron]. He was a sleeper."

sleeper rabbit play A rare bit of baseball skullduggery that is brought into play with baserunners on second and third. The runner on second, who gets the attention of the catcher, is noticeably slow in returning to his base after the first pitch. He repeats this lazy act until the catcher is lured into throwing to second at which time the runner on second breaks for third and the runner on third dashes toward home. ETYMOLOGY. The play was invented by George Moriarty in the early 1900s. It would seem that this might be a reversal on the fable of the tortoise and the hare. Unlike the original story in which the rabbit sleeps, allowing the tortoise to win, the base-ball play has the tortoise pretending to sleep to trip up the opposition.

sleeping bat Syn. of *quiet bat*, 2. "Sleeping bats awaken with 4 homers" (*The Baltimore Sun*, Apr. 2, 1998).

slewfoot An awkward player.

SLG Abbrev. for *slugging percentage.*

slice 1. *v.* To hit the ball with a late swing. A ball sliced by a right-handed batter takes off spinning and curving in the direction of right field, while a left-handed batter will slice a ball that veers toward left field. Compare *pull*, 1. ETYMOLOGY. Possibly borrowed from golf, where the curve is more common and pronounced. 2. *n.* A late swing at a pitched ball. 3. *n.* A batted ball that has been sliced.

slicer A batted ball that veers off in the opposite direction.

slice hitter Syn. of *opposite-field hitter.*

slick sling *hist.* The spitball. IST USE. 1908 (*New York Evening Journal*, May 22; Edward J. Nichols).

slide 1. *v.* To throw oneself along the ground toward a base to avoid being tagged out or overrunning the base. Contact with the base is made with a hand or a foot, which offers a much smaller target for the defender to tag. 2. *n.* The act of sliding. Slides are performed either feet first or, more daringly, headfirst. IST USE. 1866. "[Butler] Ives obtained his run by a tremendous jump and slide on to the base under the pitcher's hands" (*Detroit Advertiser and Tribune*, Oct. 18). USAGE

Slide. Industrial League action shot. *Photograph by Joseph Baylor Roberts*

NOTE. The act of sliding preceded the introduction of the term "slide." Peter Morris (*A Game of Inches: The Game on the Field*, 2006, p.265) noted the earliest incident (*New York Clipper*, Oct. 10, 1857): "One of the Liberty's [*sic*], running to the first base and falling upon it with his hands, was decided in time." **3.** *n.* A slump; e.g., "Smith was in the midst of an 0-for-20 slide." **4.** *v.* Syn. of *shift*, 3. "[Todd Hundley] doesn't slide well to block balls in the dirt" (STATS Inc., *The Scouting Notebook 2001*; Peter Morris).

slide ball *hist.* Syn. of *slider*, 1. The term was used in the 1930s for George Blaeholder's slider (John J. Ward, *Baseball Magazine*, Aug. 1936).

slide beat Syn. of *slider*, 1. The term was coined by pitcher Dennis Eckersley (*Athletics*, Sept. 2005).

"slide, Kelly, slide!" Chant and motto aimed at Mike "King" Kelly, a popular player from 1878 to 1893, who was widely credited with turning base stealing into an art and who perfected the hook slide. It was also the title of baseball's first hit song, copyrighted in 1889, words and music by John W. Kelly. The chorus for the song went as follows: "Slide, Kelly, slide! Your running's a disgrace! / Slide, Kelly, slide! Stay there, hold your base! / If some one doesn't steal you, / And your batting doesn't fail you, / They'll take you to Australia! / Slide, Kelly, slide!" The phrase tends to emphasize one side of his reputation. He was in fact a remarkable player whom Connie Mack later compared to Ty Cobb. The handsome, well-dressed Kelly was the first player to get "important" money (he was paid $5,000 in 1887 when Boston of the National League bought him for $10,000) and the first to inspire fan adulation (it has been said that he was the first player to be targeted by autograph seekers). See also *Chicago slide*. EXTENDED USE. A phrase to be shouted whenever danger or an emergency is imminent (James Mote, *Everything Baseball*, 1989, p.351).

slidepiece Syn. of *slider*, 1. The term was coined by pitcher Dennis Eckersley.

slider 1. A modified curveball that is rolled,

"Slide, Kelly, slide!" "The Female Fan" from the Bain Collection. In the image on the left she intones "Slide, Kelly, slide," and in the second she asks, "What's the decision?" *George Grantham Bain Collection, Library of Congress*

or slid, off the middle and/or index fingers, rather than spun hard. It is thrown with a fastball motion, but with the ball held off-center and with no breaking of the wrist, as with a curveball. The slider is thrown much harder, but with less motion, than a pure curveball and breaks slightly but sharply just as it crosses the plate; i.e., it starts out like a fastball and then breaks late without warning, like a curveball (but with less of a curve). It can break up to six inches horizontally or vertically. The slider is more effective the harder it is thrown. Some pitchers snap their wrist slightly as they release the ball, while others let their natural finger pressure produce the slide motion. The downward sweep of the arm imparts a slight spin to the ball, which curves more in a lateral than a vertical plane. The delivery and spin are sometimes likened to the delivery and spiral of a forward pass in football. Thrown by a right-hander, the slider breaks down and away to a right-handed batter and down and in to a left-handed batter. It creates a strong illusion, because it looks like a fastball and doesn't break until it is less than 10 feet from the batter. Tim McCarver (quoted in *The New York Times*, June 29, 1986) described Steve Carlton's slider (which he termed the best in baseball): "The tighter you grip the ball, the more spin you can get on it. And with his forearm strength, he could grip it tighter than anyone else. With that tight grip, his slider had a gyroscope-type downward movement that

often spun it into the dirt. But to the batter and to the umpire it had the illusion of a strike." Jim Brosnan (*The Long Season*, 1960) defined the slider as "a pitch that is not quite so fast as a good fast ball, nor curves so much as a good curveball; but which is easier to throw and control than either of them." Batters identify a slider when they see a dot in the middle of the ball as it approaches the plate. Charlie Dressen (*Baseball Digest*, Aug. 1961) considered the slider "the worst pitch in baseball: it slides over the plate and slides out of the ballpark." Syn. *slide ball*; *slide-piece*; *slide beat*; *biter*; *dinky curve*; *nickel curve*; *sailer*. ETYMOLOGY. The origin of the pitch has been obscured by time, but the first pitchers to make names for themselves throwing the slider worked in the 1930s. They were George Uhle of the Detroit Tigers and George Blaeholder of the St. Louis Browns. Uhle said that he invented the pitch in 1929 (John Thorn and John B. Holway, *The Pitcher*, 1987): "Harry Heilmann and I were just working [on the sidelines to catcher Eddie] Phillips. It just came to me all of a sudden, letting the ball go along my index finger and using my ring finger and pinky to give it just a little bit of a twist. It was a sailing fastball, and that's how come I named it the slider. The real slider is a sailing fastball. Now they call everything a slider." The term has been in use since the 1930s; it came into widespread use in the 1950s, and was made famous by Carlton and others in the 1970s, and later by Randy Johnson.
  2. A sliding injury in which a patch of skin has been scraped from the leg or thigh. Ty Cobb (*My Life in Baseball*, 1961, p.55) defined "slider" as "an abrasion caused by hitting the hard infield dirt too often in base-steals." IST USE. 1910. " 'Sliders' (which

means patches of skin torn off in sliding)" (John J. Evers and Hugh S. Fullerton, *Touching Second: The Science of Baseball*).
  3. A baserunner who slides. IST USE. 1886. "As a slider, little Nic [Hugh Nicol] is doubtless without a peer in the country.... With his right hand forward to touch the bag at the earliest possible moment, his left fast against that side, he skims along the earth as though it were a sheet of ice instead of a hard, sandy soil" (*St. Louis Post-Dispatch*, July 31).

slide short To stop one's slide before the base is actually reached. Though this usually results in the runner being tagged out, Marty Barrett used it on occasion to avoid a sure tag at second base, stopping just shy of the bag and scrambling to safety in the confusion.

slide step A move by a pitcher who steps with his front leg quickly down the mound toward home plate rather than lifting it as in the normal delivery. It is designed to delay a baserunner attempting to steal. The shortened stride to the plate and the abbreviated delivery and leg kick from the stretch reduce base stealing, but make for a less-effective pitch to the plate.

sliding catch A catch in which the fielder throws his body on the ground and slides under the ball. Harry Hooper is credited with introducing the sliding catch (*Saint Mary's* [Calif.] *Collegian*, Nov. 14, 1952).

sliding dolly An inclined cement surface onto which a player is pushed down to practice sliding into a base. "This is used, it should be hastily added, only for the rawest of raw recruits" (*The New York Times Magazine*, March 18, 1956).

sliding glove A snugly fit glove worn by a baserunner to protect the hand from being cut or scratched; esp. a glove worn on the leading hand of a runner making a headfirst slide. When wrapped tightly, it offers some protection against a mildly jammed wrist. Sliding gloves were popular in the 19th century and came up to the elbows. According to some historical accounts, 19th-century base stealer Arlie Latham was the first player to wear a sliding glove (*Newsday*, Apr. 3, 2005). Peter Morris (*A Game of Inches*, 2006, p.447)

Slider.

noted that when Ed Andrews and Jim Fogarty of Philadelphia reached base during the 1886 season, "they would don 'a huge pair of buckskin gloves' to protect them during their headlong 'air dives.'"

sliding pad Stuffed padding worn as protective equipment on the hips under a player's pants to prevent injuries to the hips and thighs when sliding. Modern pads weigh about six ounces and are worn in slots at the rear of the pants. Lee Allen (*The Hot Stove League*, 1955, p.116) credited Harry Stovey with using the first sliding pad. Others cite Sam Morton, of Spalding Sporting Goods, as the one who introduced sliding pads to baseball. Syn. *blanket*, 2. IST USE. 1886. "Those players of the Browns who have sliding proclivities will have the danger of an injury averted this coming season by the use of the [Sam] Morton patent sliding pad" (*St. Louis Post-Dispatch*, March 13; Peter Morris).

sliding pit 1. A large, three-sided, boxed structure or pit filled with sand and used to practice sliding. The innovation has been attributed to Branch Rickey when he was managing the St. Louis Browns: "I wanted to make more use of our running speed. Our sliding wasn't good enough, so we dug a pit and filled it with sawdust and sand and slid into it to get the knack of [sliding] . . . and avoiding broken ankles" (quoted in Arthur Mann, *Baseball Confidential*, 1951, p.79). IST USE. 1913. "One feature [Johnny] Evers has insisted upon is a sliding pit. That consists of a pit of sand with a regular base attached to the ground in the middle" (*Chicago Tribune*, June 19; Peter Morris). 2. The dirt surrounding a base on a field that has a synthetic surface.

sling 1. *v.* To pitch a baseball. IST USE. 1905. "[Smith] slung the twitchers" (*The Washington Post*, May 6; Peter Morris). 2. *n.* A pitch; e.g., "slick sling."

slinger 1. A pitcher. IST USE. 1908 (*New York Evening Journal*, May 9; Edward J. Nichols). 2. An injury-risk pitcher who opens the front of his shoulder early and exposes both the rotator cuff and the inside of the elbow to more pressure (David Rawnsley, *Baseball America*, Aug. 9–22, 1999; Peter Morris).

slingshot 1. A strong throwing arm. IST USE. 1937 (*New York Daily News*, Jan. 21; Edward J. Nichols). 2. A pitching delivery that imparts considerable initial momentum to a pitched ball. 3. A catcher's slinging throw that does not follow a straight line but tails off toward the first-base side of second base (Michael Lewis, *Moneyball*, 2003). 4. [softball term] A delivery in fast pitch softball in which the arm, gripping the ball, leaves its position at the waist and is whipped backward to the stretching point, then moved forward with as much speed and force as possible. The ball is released at its furthest point forward, with as much drive as possible. It is a single powerful stroke rather than a circular delivery producing more control but less speed than the windmill delivery. See also *figure eight*, 2; *windmill*.

slip 1. *v.* To get a strike by throwing the ball toward the edges of the strike zone. "The Seal novice had slipped a second strike over on him [Harry Lord] while the Chicago captain was mooning" (*San Francisco Bulletin*, March 10, 1913; Gerald L. Cohen). Bob Uecker's eulogy for one-time American League batting champion (1959) and former Milwaukee Brewers manager Harvey Kuenn contained these lines (*St. Petersburg Times*, March 6, 1988): "The last couple of years Harvey lived with a 3–2 count on him, but every time they tried to slip one by him on the corner he fouled it off. To get Harvey looking they must have wanted him awful bad." 2. *n.* An error. IST USE. 1907 (*Lajoie's Official Base Ball Guide*, p.110; Edward J. Nichols).

slippery elm A mucilaginous substance from the inner bark of the elm (*Ulmus rubra*), once used by pitchers to give the ball the same effect as a spitball. IST USE. 1891. "Porter . . . kept the hits pretty well scattered, but it is only a question of time before Waterbury will jump on his slippery elm shoots and then he will be gently laid away on the shelf" (*Waterbury* [Conn.] *Republican*, May 27; G. Reed Howard).

slip pitch A pitch that comes toward the plate with diminished velocity and a sudden drop. It is thrown like the *palm ball* except that the pitcher's fingers are raised above the surface of the ball. Paul Richards claimed he learned it from Fred "Deacon" Jones in the Southern Association in the late 1930s. Richards brought the pitch to prominence while managing the Chicago White Sox and Baltimore Orioles in the 1950s; it was used successfully by Skinny Brown, Dick Hall, Harry Dorish, and Jim Wilson.

SLOB Syn. of *batter's run average*. It measures slugging percentage times on-base percentage and was devised by George Ignatin in the mid-1970s and popularized by Allan Barra, who suggested (*The Wall Street Journal*, June 16, 2000) that a SLOB of .2500 "indicates an excellent hitter, one who produces on average 25 runs for every 100 at-bats, or about 150 for a typical 600 at-bats season."

slobber *hist.* To make an error. "Partie took first on a hit to McDonald, who slobbered it badly" (*Milwaukee Daily Sentinel*, June 12, 1876).

slobber ball The spitball. "The 'slobber ball' ought to be consigned to the slop bucket before it is condemned under the Pure Food Laws" (Ren Mulford Jr., *The Sporting Life*, Dec. 12, 1908; Peter Morris).

slobberer An artless and clumsy spitball pitcher. Gaylord Perry (*Me and the Spitter*, 1974; Charles D. Poe) noted that slobberers not only showed "no respect for a delicate art" but also actually triggered a 1968 rule change that ended finger-licking on the mound.

slopball A slowly thrown pitch with not much on it. "Can slopball artist Doug Jones keep getting hitters out?" (*The Baltimore Sun*, Feb. 15, 1998).

slo-pitch softball [softball term] Syn. of *slow pitch softball*.

slopper Syn. of *junkballer*.

slot 1. *n.* The area where the plate umpire (esp. in the American League) positions himself, over the catcher's shoulder nearest the batter; a position between the batter's hands and the catcher's head. Compare *scissors*. 2. *n.* See *first base slot*. 3. *n.* A place in the pitching rotation. "The [Baltimore] Orioles must wonder whether they can count on [Sidney] Ponson to . . . win games from the fourth slot in the rotation" (*The Baltimore Sun*, Apr.

3, 2005). See also *spot*, 4. **4.** *n.* A player's position on the team, both in the field and in the batting order. "After using Larry Bigbie in the No. 2 spot in the batting order . . . [Manager Lee] Mazzilli slid him to the fifth slot" (*The Baltimore Sun*, March 10, 2004). **5.** *v.* To be put in a position; e.g., "The Los Angeles Dodgers . . . slotted him [John Shelby] second in the batting order and said, in effect, 'All yours . . . as long as you produce'" (*The Washington Post*. June 10, 1987). **6.** *n.* The area between first base and second base or between second base and third base. See also *alley*, 5. **7.** *n.* The area between the third baseman and the shortstop. According to Tom Meany (*The Artful Dodgers*, 1953, p.116), a shortstop making a play to his right is "going into the slot." See also *hole*, 1. **8.** *n.* The "heart" of home plate. See also *alley*, 2. **9.** *n.* See *arm slot*. **10.** *v.* For a pitcher to find his arm slot. "[Billy Koch] slotted his arm at a three-quarters angle" (*Sports Illustrated*, Sept. 16, 2002). **11.** *n.* Syn. of *on-deck circle*. **12.** *n.* Short for *slot money*. "I think it'll be very difficult for advisors to tell their clients to hold out for more than slot" (anonymous agent, quoted in *Baseball America*, June 9–22, 2003; Peter Morris). **13.** *v.* To pay a draft pick a bonus that is comparable with what players picked around him received (Alan Schwarz, BaseballAmerica.com, Nov. 14, 2006).

slot money The expected bonus for each pick at the top of the draft, as recommended by Major League Baseball. Syn. *slot*, 12.

slow *hist.* **1.** *n.* A pitch with a great curve. "'Slows' are balls simply tossed to the bat with a line of delivery so curved as to make them almost drop on the home base" (*New York Clipper*, Feb. 18, 1871; Peter Morris). IST USE. 1868. "Slows . . . are balls delivered by a slow pitcher. . . . Slows, to be well punished, require to be waited for and judged well, with a timely swing of the bat" (Henry Chadwick, *The Game of Base Ball*, p.45–46). **2.** *adv.* Not capable. "Harmon, once turned loose by [Portland manager] McCredie as too slow for the Ducks" (*San Francisco Bulletin*, May 21, 1913; Gerald L. Cohen). Compare *fast*.

slow ball *hist.* **1.** A pitch delivered with the same motion as a fastball but with much less speed; the former name for a *change of pace.* It is intended to throw off the batter's timing, causing him to swing too soon. "He could pitch his slow ball high, low, inside, outside and with varying speed. It looked so dead easy to slaughter that a batter, any time he fanned or popped out a dinky fly . . . felt like committing murder when he retreated to the bench to meditate" (*San Francisco Bulletin*, Feb. 13, 1913; Gerald L. Cohen). USAGE NOTE. This entirely accurate term has drifted out of fashion, and today's "slow ball" is almost universally referred to as the changeup. IST USE. 1888. "[Dave Foutz'] slow ball is probably his best, and when he can command it he is never hit hard" (*Cincinnati Commercial Gazette*, Jan. 19). **2.** A catchall term (until the second half of the 20th century) for any pitch that wasn't a fastball or curveball. The term was most commonly used to describe the pitch that eventually became known as the *palm ball* (Rob Neyer, in Bill James and Rob Neyer, *The Neyer/James Guide to Pitchers*, 2004, p.21).

slow bat The bat of a hitter who hits bloopers and does not overswing or who swings late. Basketball superstar Michael Jordan, who played minor-league baseball, was said to have a "long swing" or "slow bat" (Detroit Tigers scout Dave Roberts, quoted in *The Baltimore Sun*, Nov. 18, 1994). Catchers late in the season often have slow bats because they are tired after catching many games. An anonymous general manager (quoted in *Sports Illustrated*, July 24, 2006): "You'll notice . . . in August and September, when guys really start to drag and their bats get slow." Syn. *tired bat.*

slow company *hist.* Syn. of *minor leagues.* "All players had their start in slow company, but the number who graduate from those ranks and hold their own is mighty small in these days of skilled ball playing" (*The Washington Post*, May 20, 1894; David Ball). Compare *fast company.*

slow curve A generic term for a slow-breaking curveball, such as a roundhouse curve.

slow down To lose playing effectiveness through advancing age. IST USE. 1906 (*The Sporting Life*, Feb. 10, p.7; Edward J. Nichols).

slow hook A term used by Bill James for the removal of a starting pitcher (*hook,* 6) after he has pitched more than nine innings, has given up seven or more runs, or has a combined total of at least 13 runs and innings pitched. Compare *quick hook,* 1.

slow pitching [softball term] An earlier term for *slow pitch softball.* Leo H. Fischer (*Winning Softball*, 1940) wrote, "A type of softball which has attained popularity in many sections of the country and which is gaining in others is the variety known as 'slow-pitching.'" It was played with a 16-inch ball.

slow pitch softball [softball term] One of the two major branches of softball. There are 10 players on each team (including a short fielder), bunting and base stealing are not allowed, a hit batter is not awarded first base, and the ball must be pitched underhand at a moderate speed in an arc that peaks above the batter's head. Amateur Softball Association of America rules specify that the arc be between six and 12 feet, while United States Specialty Sports Association (formerly the United States Slo-Pitch Softball Association) rules call for a pitching arc of between three and 10 feet. Compare *fast pitch softball.* Also called "slow pitch." Syn. *slow pitching.* USAGE NOTE. The term is often spelled *slo-pitch softball*, most notably by the former United States Slo-Pitch Softball Association.

slow roller A slow-moving ground ball. IST USE. 1905. "Cassidy hit a slow roller toward short" (*Chicago Tribune*, June 11; Peter Morris).

slow roller pitch A pitch that has less speed than usual, which enables the batter to observe its rotation.

slud The past tense for the verb "to slide" in the parlance of Dizzy Dean. The term may have been the most famous in Dean's lexicon. Dean "commertated" (undated): "I always use 'slud' because when I say 'he slud into third' . . . the fans throughout the country knows that the man hit the dirt. That 'slid'—I just caint go for that 'slid.' It's just natcheral for me to say 'slud.' I remember I got a letter last year from a English teacher somewheres up in Connecticut. It's a true saying—'slud' is correct, we found that out. He said that in

Geoligy [*sic*] that 'slud' is a sliding mass of mud. And, by George, we've played a lot of baseball in the mud." *The Washington Post*, in an article entitled "They're Taking Dizzy's Microphone Away Again" (Feb. 11, 1948; Barry Popik), lamented, "Now it looks again like the good people of St. Louis no longer will hear such informative phrases as 'he slud into third' and 'he throwed him out at home.'" Jack Smith (*San Francisco Sunday Examiner & Chronicle*, March 23, 1975; Peter Tamony) declared, "I have written to the big dictionary publishers suggesting that the word 'slud' be included in their next editions, and now I am receiving just what they will want to see— public support." Smith embarked on this campaign after he used the word in a column and some readers had the gall to write in and say that he had made an error.

slug To hit a baseball hard or for a great distance; to hit the long ball. "Sometimes we slug and run. Other times we run and slug. Then there are times when we slug and slug. When we slug and slug, it works" (Baltimore Orioles slugger Eric Davis, quoted in *The Baltimore Sun*, May 10, 1998). IST USE. 1887. "Philadelphia people must be content to go see some . . . Eastern League 'slugger' who fails to slug as soon as he dons a Philadelphia uniform" (*The World* [New York], July 26; Gerald L. Cohen). ETYMOLOGY. As early as 1756, the noun "slug" was a slang term for a drink of strong liquor. Not much later it also took on the meaning of a punch or heavy blow, and thus passed into baseball usage. However, Peter Morris (personal communication, Nov. 28, 2005) notes that while the term originated with boxing, it came to baseball by way of cricket; e.g, *Forest and Stream* (Dec. 25, 1873): "Cricket . . . has shown a vitality by creating a language of its own. . . . A ball hit into the air is a 'spoon,' unless it goes a long way, when it becomes a 'skyer' or a 'slog.'"

slug bunt A slap hit past an infielder, or past an invisible charging infielder during batting practice with no fielders. "[Rafael] Furcal led off the game with a slug bunt . . . He eased his top hand down the bat and slapped a liner over the head of [the] third baseman . . . for a double" (*The Baltimore Sun*, Aug. 9, 2000).

slugfest A game characterized by one or both teams making many extra-base hits. Compare *swatfest*. Syn. *slamfest*; *slugging match*; *slugging bee*. ETYMOLOGY. From the nickname for a boxing match dominated by the exchange of many powerful blows rather than defense or strategy.

slugger 1. A hitter with a high percentage of extra-base hits; one likely to hit the long ball. Sluggers tend to be placed at the third, fourth, or fifth positions in the batting order. But sometimes a slugger is "someone who really can't hit but every now and then gets lucky and pops one" (Jerry Howarth, *Baseball Lite*, 1986). Syn. *slugsmith*; *socker*; *muscle man*. IST USE. 1882. "The gigantic slugger [Dan Brouthers] of the Bisons did not make a base hit" (*The North American* [Philadelphia], Aug. 24). USAGE NOTE. Peter Morris (personal communication, Dec. 13, 2003) notes that the term was not entirely commendatory when first introduced into baseball, and this perception held well into the 20th century. Henry Chadwick (*Spalding's Official Base Ball Guide*, 1900, p.52): "The majority class of batsmen known as 'hard-hitters' and 'sluggers,' who habitually hit at the ball from the shoulder, whether sent in swiftly or otherwise, without any idea as to where [the] ball is likely to go, these men being batsmen who think the acme of batting is reached when they hit for a 'homer.'" Likewise, H.G. Merrill (*The Sporting News*, Aug. 16, 1902): "The slugger is always a man possessing some marked deficiency in batting ability. When he is at the plate his sole idea is to knock the cover off the ball; he never figures where it will, or may go, on the basis of doing teamwork batting, consequently is devoid of scientific ability at the bat." The term also had a negative connotation in football and cricket; thus, its transformation into an honorific is a surprising development. The term amounts to an unofficial title and is used with some discretion; there are only a few dozen players in the history of the game who wear it well. A gallery of sluggers appears in Ted Williams' *Science of Hitting* (1971), including Hack Wilson, Hank Greenberg, Babe Ruth, Lou Gehrig, Ralph Kiner, Mickey Mantle, Roger Maris, and Johnny Mize. ETYMOLOGY. The term was applied to a boxer (alternatively, "slogger") before its use in baseball. A reckless batter in cricket has been known as a "slogger" since the 19th century. EXTENDED USE. **1.** A term of endearment, often applied by an adult to a little kid who is anything but. **2.** A heavy-handed reporter or journalist.

2. A large, imposing baseball bat. IST USE. 1901 (Burt L. Standish, *Frank Merriwell's Marvel*, p.213; Edward J. Nichols). **3.** Short for *Louisville Slugger*. "The word 'slugger' in baseball terminology refers . . . [to] a bat—the Louisville Slugger, which for almost 100 years has been an integral part of every baseball season" (Judy Keene, *Am Way*, Oct. 1982).

slugger's position Usually the fourth position in the batting order, but sometimes the third. "Thompson is in the slugger's position, as fourth man up" (*Detroit Times*, Aug. 31, 1906; Peter Morris). "Bill Sweeney was dropped from third place to sixth, Williams stepping into the slugger's position" (*Chicago Tribune*, May 4, 1914; Peter Morris).

Sluggersville The figurative hometown of sluggers. IST USE. 1891. "Then he was as frisky as a young colt and a slugger from Sluggersville" (*Sporting Times* [New York], July 11, 1891; David Shulman).

sluggery A baseball game in which there are many hits (Maurice H. Weseen, *A Dictionary of American Slang*, 1934).

slugging Heavy hitting. "It was his consistent slugging . . . that kept his club in first place" (*San Francisco Bulletin*, March 25, 1913; Gerald L. Cohen). IST USE. 1878. "Pitchers have become disgustingly efficient during the past five years, and the general public would not object to a little of the slugging style of batting in vogue in the earlier days of the game" (*Chicago Tribune*, Dec. 15; Peter Morris)

slugging average Syn. of *slugging percentage*. Abbrev. *SA*.

slugging bee Syn. of *slugfest*. IST USE. 1906. "After three days of airtight baseball, Chicago fans were treated to an old fashioned slugging bee at the west side park today" (*Chicago Tribune*, May 19; Peter Morris).

slugging match Syn. of *slugfest*. Also

expressed as "slugging contest" and "slugging duel." IST USE. 1886. " 'That was a terrible slugging match, wasn't it?' said Mr. [Henry] Lucas as he passed out of the grand stand yesterday" (*St. Louis Post-Dispatch*, Apr. 28; Peter Morris). ETYMOLOGY. A prizefight. "There are two big rooms in the back . . . where we have all our cockfights, dog fights and slugging matches" (*The Washington Post*, Apr. 9, 1883).

slugging percentage A statistical representation of the average number of bases a batter achieves per official at-bat, determined by dividing the player's number of total at-bats into his total bases. Hence, a batter with a home run, a triple, a double, and a single (10 total bases) in 20 at-bats has a slugging percentage of .500. It would be possible to have a slugging percentage of greater than 1.000 if one averaged more than one base per at-bat; a slugger who hit a home run with every at-bat would have a 4.000 slugging percentage. Although intended as a measure of a player's performance at making extra-base hits, the statistic includes singles in its computation and as a consequence is greatly affected by a batter's number of singles. As such, a batter with only moderate power but a high batting average can have a higher slugging percentage than a batter with good power but a low batting average. Top batters have slugging percentages greater than .500. For a purer measure of extra-base hitting performance, see *isolated power*. The highest slugging percentage for a season has been the .863 achieved by Barry Bonds in 2001 (411 total bases in 476 at-bats). See also *total bases per game*. Abbrev. *SLG*. Syn. *slugging average*; *total batting average*; *grand average*.

slugsmith Syn. of *slugger*, 1. IST USE. 1920. "Good old Rufe, the slugsmith! The crowd was imploring him to bring Tapland home" (Burt L. Standish, *The Man on First*; David Shulman).

slump 1. *n.* A period of poor or below-normal performance. A team is said to be in a slump when it loses games, while an individual may go into a batting, pitching, or even a fielding slump. "The truest definition of a slump is you're not feeling well, you're not seeing the ball well, things aren't going well" (Cal Ripken Jr., quoted in *The Baltimore Sun*, Aug. 19, 1997). Jimmy Cannon's definition (*Baseball Digest*, Nov.–Dec. 1956): "Any time in the season when the Yankees are leading by less than eight games." See also *drought*; *dry spell*, 1. IST USE. 1893. "No less is the surprise occasioned by the miserable showing of the Bostons, New Yorks and Philadelphias. Their temporary 'slump' is hard to understand" (O.P. Caylor, *North American* [Philadelphia], May 18; Peter Morris). **2.** *n.* A downward trend. In extreme cases, the game of baseball can be on the skids: "Baseball fell into a slump this week" (*Maine Sunday Telegram* headline, Aug. 10, 1986) after the owners fired arbitrator Tom Roberts. **3.** *v.* To perform below one's usual standard; to be in a slump. IST USE. 1903. "All ball clubs slump early or late" (Ted Sullivan, *Humorous Stories*, p.259; David Shulman).

slump buster A person who is summoned when a player or a team is in a slump. "That certain someone is supposed to be a spectacularly unattractive female stranger with whom the player may engage in another popular national pastime—for purely therapeutic purposes" (Tim Crothers, *Sports Illustrated*, March 30, 1998). In Jose Caneseco's tell-all book (*Juiced, Wild Times, Rampant 'Roids, Smash Hits, and How Baseball Got Big*, 2005), a slump buster is defined as "the ugliest girl I can find and have sex with her" and "the fattest, gnarliest chick you can find [to make out with]."

slump-ridden Said of a team in which many of its players are in slumps at the same time.

slurve A pitch that breaks more than a slider and is faster than, but doesn't break as much as, a curveball. The term has some negative connotations as pitchers try to develop a slurve (which is fast-breaking but stays on one plane) into a sharp-breaking slider. See also *short curve*. ETYMOLOGY. A combination of "slider" plus "curve" equals "slurve." Sources for the term vary in specific applications. "Among batsmen of the National League, the favorite pitch of Don Drysdale was known as the 'slurve.' This comprised one part slobber and two parts curve" (Mel Durslag, *San Francisco Examiner*, July 24, 1970; Peter Tamony).

slurvy Somewhere between a slider and a curveball. "[Mike Jones] throws a curve but gets under it too much, resulting in a flat, slurvy plane" (*Baseball America*, June 11–24, 2001; Peter Morris).

smack 1. *v.* To hit the ball hard. IST USE. 1887. "[Jack] Glasscock smacked the ball on the nose and it struck against the left field fence" (*Detroit Free Press*, Apr. 30; Peter Morris). **2.** *n.* A hard-hit ball for a base hit. "[Patsy O'Rourke] put himself in solid with two lusty smacks right at the moments they were needed" (*San Francisco Bulletin*, May 28, 1913; Gerald L. Cohen). IST USE. 1895 (*New York Press*, Aug. 11; Edward J. Nichols).

small ball 1. Syn. of *little ball*, 1. "[The Colorado Rockies] will play 'small ball,' moving runners rather than waiting for the bombs" (*Sports Illustrated*, March 31, 1997). The term currently appears to be used more frequently than its synonym. EXTENDED USE. A less-important issue or challenge. Press secretary Tony Snow (quoted in *White House Weekly*, Nov. 15, 2006): "The president [George W. Bush] says he doesn't like to play small ball. You go for big issues . . . and big challenges." **2.** A batted ball that disappears quickly. "The balls [Babe] Ruth hit out of the park got smaller quicker than anybody else's" (Walter Johnson, quoted by Shirley Povich, *The Washington Post*, March 13, 1989).

small baseball A term used by Casey Stengel for a "very fast ball" (Red Barber, NPR's *Morning Edition*, May 30, 1986). See also *little ball*, 2.

small-market club A low-revenue major-league club (such as the Kansas City Royals and Pittsburgh Pirates). The term may include other low-revenue clubs, regardless of their market size. Compare *large-market club*; *medium-market club*.

small time *hist.* The minor leagues (Maurice H. Weseen, *A Dictionary of American Slang*, 1934).

smart baseball Syn. of *inside baseball*. "Miller Huggins . . . has always favored what he likes to call 'smart baseball.' He likes the sacrifice attack. He likes the steal" (George Herman Ruth, *Babe Ruth's Own Book of Baseball*, 1928, p.188).

smart bat A baseball bat that greatly reduces the sting in the batter's hands when he hits the ball on the handle. "[It] uses a piezoelectric vibration damper to deaden the vibrations when the ball hits the bat somewhere other than the sweet spot" (John Royster, *Baseball America*, Oct. 26–Nov. 8, 1998; Peter Morris).

smash 1. *v.* To hit a ball powerfully. IST USE. 1888 (*New York Press*, Apr. 19; Edward J. Nichols). 2. *n.* A hard-hit ball. IST USE. 1889. "Powers stopped Whitehead's line smash" (*San Francisco Examiner*, Apr. 28; Peter Morris).

smell hit *hist.* A *Texas Leaguer*, 2.

smoke 1. *n.* Speed in pitching. Usually stated as "throwing smoke," the term figuratively alludes to a ball that comes in so fast, it leaves a trail of smoke. It would appear that this was the source of several baseball nicknames, including that of Smoky Joe Wood, who was also called "Smoke" by Tris Speaker. As Dwight Gooden emerged from a drug rehabilitation center in Apr. 1987, attendants yelled out the windows, "Throw smoke, Dwight"; in reply, he thrust a fist into the air (*The New York Times*, Apr. 30, 1987). See also *powder*, 2. IST USE. 1908. "Smoke, descriptive of great speed on the part of the pitcher" (John B. Foster, in *Collier's New Dictionary of the English Language*). 2. *n.* A blazing fastball. "Brooklyn has a pitcher named Stack. Wonder if he has the smoke that should go with a name like that" (*San Francisco Bulletin*, March 29, 1913; Gerald L. Cohen). 3. *v.* To bear down with a fastball; to throw smoke. Smoky Joe Wood "smoked nine-tenths of the balls close to the plate" during the first game of the 1912 World Series (Tim Murnane, *The Boston Globe*, Oct. 9, 1912). 4. *v.* To hit the ball very hard. "The 43-year-old [Carl] Yastrzemski smoked the first offering by Byron McLaughlin to the wall in left-center with an aggressive swing that took people back to 1967" (*The Boston Globe*, July 10, 1983). See also *smoke his tits*. 5. *v.* To hit a batter with a thrown ball. Asking about a Japanese custom after hitting a batter, Roger Clemens said: "If I smoke somebody, do I have to tip my hat?" A Japanese interpreter laughed and said: "If Rocket-san smokes someone, there might not be anything left to tip his hat to" (*Orioles Gazette*, Dec. 1992). 6. *v.* For a baserunner to crash into the catcher. Gary Bennett recalled getting run over by Brian Jordan (*Sports Illustrated*, June 19, 2006): "As soon as I got the ball, Jordan smoked me head over heels. I tore my MCL." 7. *v.* To defeat a team decisively. "Astros smoke Braves" (Associated Press headline, July 30, 1993).

smoke ball A ball that is pitched very fast. IST USE. 1907. "Mr. [Rube] Waddell's smoke ball is a fearsome proposition when it is burning well" (Charles Dryden, *Chicago Tribune*, Aug. 23; Peter Morris).

smoke his tits To hit a pitcher's offering very hard. Mike Shropshire (*Seasons in Hell*, 1996, p.100) stated, "A big leaguer doesn't simply hit an occasional pitcher hard. He 'smokes his tits,' one of the milder expressions that color conversational patterns of players."

smoker A fastball. "When a pitcher throws a fast one the batsman is often heard to say . . . 'he had his smoker working that time'" (*The New York Times*, June 2, 1929). IST USE. 1913. "[Walter Johnson] mixes it [a curveball] with a slow ball and his smoker" (*The Washington Post*, May 25; Peter Morris).

smoke-swallower *hist.* A member of the Pittsburgh Pirates, so named because of the mill smoke so prevalent in the city. IST USE. 1909 (*New York Evening Journal*, July 9; Edward J. Nichols).

smother For an infielder to run in on a ground ball and field it before it is spent. To "smother in leather" is to field the ball effectively, or to kill an offensive threat. IST USE. 1901 (Burt L. Standish, *Frank Merriwell's School Days*, p.250; Edward J. Nichols).

snag To reach out and catch a batted or thrown ball; e.g., "The throw was high but Smith was able to snag it."

snake 1. *n.* A good curveball. One does not merely "throw the snake," but usually something on the order of "a nasty snake." "A professional would not run from a 'snake,' unless he were bat shy, because that is merely the description of a pitcher's curve ball" (Edwin M. Rumill, *Christian Science Monitor*, Sept.

1, 1937). "[Paul] Hopkins delivered the slowest, prettiest snake that he had thrown [Babe] Ruth yet" (William Nack, *Sports Illustrated*, Aug. 24, 1998). IST USE. 1908 (*Spalding's Official Base Ball Guide*; Edward J. Nichols). **2.** *n.* A knuckleball. **3.** *v.* For a batted ball to take an irregular course. "We no longer put a crosscut pattern in the infield. The players complain that it makes the ball snake. For example, a ground ball will hit the different grains and spin in different directions. When you stand behind a batting cage, you can actually see the ball zig-zag as it goes into the outfield on the crosscut grass" (Baltimore Orioles groundskeeper Paul Zwaska, quoted in George Gmelch and J.J. Weiner, *In the Ballpark*, 1998; Peter Morris).

snake ball **1.** A curveball. IST USE. 1881. "As [Larry] Corcoran and [Fred] Goldsmith get the 'snake' ball down finer and finer, its effectiveness is more and more clearly demonstrated" (*Chicago Times*, reprinted in *The Cleveland Herald*, Aug. 20). **2.** A pitched ball that changes directions and actually undulates on its way to the plate. Despite reports of the snake ball at the turn of the 20th century, experts claimed it never existed. Walter Camp (*Walter Camp's Book of College Sports*, rev. ed., 1901, p.243) wrote that it "exists in the imagination only, unless the ball be blown out of its course by the wind." IST USE. 1896. "The *double curve*, or what the boys call at the present time the snake ball" (*The Boston Globe*, Apr. 6; Peter Morris).

snake-bit **1.** Unlucky; said of a player or team with extremely bad luck. When his record was 2-9, Pittsburgh Pirates relief pitcher Kent Tekulve was asked if he had been snake-bit; his reply (*The Sporting News*, Sept. 3, 1984): "I feel like I've had a cobra wrapped around my neck." ETYMOLOGY. In his section of the *Encyclopedia of Sports Talk* (edited by Zander Hollander, 1976), Phil Pepe wrote, "Origin is unknown, but since baseball was a game played by country boys who know of such things as snakes, that probably was the derivation. Being bitten by a snake is about as bad luck as one can have." **2.** Said of a player who is wary or hesitant because of a string of previous unpleasant or unlucky experiences. "If you start feeling snake-bit all you do is end up feeling sorry for yourself and making excuses. . . . You accept it as part of the game" (Baltimore Orioles manager Mike Hargrove, contemplating all the near misses in a game, quoted in *The Baltimore Sun*, Apr. 7, 2002).

snake jazz A breaking ball. "Snake jazz included curves, screwballs, sliders, and forkballs—and maybe knucklers and spitters, as well" (David Baldwin, personal communication, Apr. 9, 2007).

Snakes Nickname for the Arizona *Diamondbacks*.

snap **1.** *v.* To throw a breaking ball; to release a curveball. **2.** *n.* The sharp breaking action of a curveball. **3.** *v.* To break a losing or winning streak or break up a tie game. "The Reds snapped a scoreless tie in the fourth with three runs" (*Tampa Tribune*, Aug. 3, 1989). **4.** *n./ hist.* The energy or vigor of a player or team. "[Eddie Hallinan] should put some snap in the infield" (*San Francisco Bulletin*, May 27, 1913; Gerald L. Cohen). IST USE. 1890 (*New York Evening Post*, May 5; Edward J. Nichols). **5.** *n.* Short for *snap swing*. "Swing is too slow; not enough snap" (scouting report on Manny Mota, *Baseball Digest*, Jan. 1984, p.28). **6.** *n.* A tantrum. "When a player kicks the water cooler or throws things or shrieks at a teammate . . . that's a snap" (Dick Kaegel, *The Seattle Times*, Sept. 18, 1988).

snapdragon A sharply breaking curveball thrown with a perfect snap of the wrist.

snapper **1.** A good curveball that "snaps off" with a sharp breaking action. **2.** A player who vents his frustrations (tossing equipment, punching holes in walls, smashing water fountains, etc.) when events do not go his way.

snap swing A short, quick swing without much follow-through. "I don't recall whether it was by accident or study that I developed a snap swing at the ball that made me a good hitter, even at that age" (Ty Cobb, *Memoirs of Twenty Years in Baseball*, 1925; Peter Morris). Syn. *snap*, 5.

snap throw A quick, short toss made with a flick of the wrist, used chiefly by infielders and by catchers on pickoff plays. IST USE. 1901 (Burt L. Standish, *Frank Merriwell's School Days*, p.242; Edward J. Nichols).

snare mitt A *first baseman's mitt* in which the thumb is stiffened to prevent rolling into the palm, with leather fitted between the thumb and the palm (O.H. Vogel, *Ins and Outs of Baseball*, 1952; Peter Morris). Compare *open-face mitt*.

snatch catch A catch characterized by a swift downward movement of the glove as the ball settles into it. It was "invented" by outfielder Rickey Henderson.

snatcher *hist.* Syn. of *catcher*, 1.

sneak-ball *hist.* A *sneaky fastball*. The term was used by Dan Daniel (*Baseball Magazine*, Sept. 1937): "The sneak-ball is a fast delivery which is effective because the ball is on top of the hitter before he knows it. That type of pitching owes its baffling qualities not so much to speed as to motion and a certain something which is given to the pitch by the wrist." Daniel cited Oral Hildebrand and Roy Henshaw as the "best sneak-ball pitchers."

sneaker **1.** A deceptive fastball; a *sneaky fastball*. "A pitch that is faster than it appears to be and figuratively sneaks up on the batter" (H.G. Salsinger, *Baseball Digest*, Aug. 1945). IST USE. 1934. "[Luke Hamlin has] a very deceptive fast ball. They call that sort of fast ball delivery a 'sneaker' in baseball because the ball is on top of the batter before he realizes it" (official program, 1934 World Series; Peter Morris). **2.** An athletic canvas shoe with a rubber or synthetic sole. IST USE. 1909. "He dressed his feet in a pair of rubber soled, canvas shoes—call 'em 'sneakers' now—and journeyed to Fall River" (*Baseball Magazine*, Aug. 1909; David Shulman). ETYMOLOGY. There are two common theories on how this term originated: 1) from British thieves who found such shoes useful in their work; or 2) from baseball players who found them useful in stealing bases. The shoes themselves predated the name by several years. "The first sneaker hit the market in 1868, according to historian William Rossi" (*Houston Chronicle*, June 13, 1987).

sneak steal *hist.* A stolen base in which the defense has momentarily left the base unguarded, and is usually caught by surprise. IST USE. 1907 (*New York Evening Journal*, May 23; Edward J. Nichols).

sneaky Said of a pitcher whose easy and loose delivery obscures the speed of the pitch. Catcher Joe Girardi, discussing relief pitcher Mariano Rivera (quoted in *Sports Illustrated*, March 24, 1997): "He's sneaky. Because he's small and because his delivery is so free and easy, so smooth, his stuff doesn't look as if it's coming at you as fast as it is. Then it's by you." Colorado Rockies pitching coach Frank Funk, discussing pitcher John Thomson (quoted in *The Denver Post*, March 18, 1998): "He is the epitome of what hitters call sneaky quick. He has such an easy, fluid motion and the ball just jumps out of his hand. It gets up on hitters before they're ready."

sneaky fastball A fastball that appears, to the batter, faster than it really is. The deception can be caused by a pitching motion that appears slow and easy so that the pitch "sneaks up" on the batter. Syn. *sneak-ball*; *sneaker*, 1.

sno-cone Var. of *snow cone*.

Snodgrass muff A muff or boner, named for the hapless New York Giants outfielder Fred Snodgrass, who dropped an easy fly ball hit by Boston Red Sox pinch hitter Clyde Engle in the 10th inning of the final game (Oct. 16) of the 1912 World Series. The Giants had been leading 2–1, but the error (dubbed the "$30,000 muff," as that amount represented the difference between the winning team's and the losing team's shares) put the tying

Snodgrass muff. New York Giants outfielder Fred Snodgrass, 1912. *George Grantham Bain Collection, Library of Congress*

run on second base, and the Red Sox went on to win the game (by a score of 3–2) and the Series. Ironically, the batter following Engle, Harry Hooper, was robbed of a hit by Snodgrass, who made a great catch in deep center field.

snooze The "long nap" taken by Cincinnati Reds catcher Ernie Lombardi on Oct. 8, 1939, in the top of the 10th inning of the fourth and last game of the 1939 World Series, when New York Yankees outfielder Charley Keller collided with Lombardi, who dropped the throw from right fielder Ival Goodman and lay stunned and sprawled in a daze. The ball rested untouched about three feet away, allowing Joe DiMaggio, who had singled, to streak home with the final score of a three-run rally, snapping a 4–4 tie and capping a Series sweep by the Yankees. John Drebinger (*The New York Times*, Oct. 9, 1939) referred to Lombardi squatting on the ground, "apparently brooding over the futility of it all." Frederick G. Lieb (*The Story of the World Series*, 1949) wrote, "It was ludicrous seeing one California Italian score as the other apparently was taking a snooze." Also known as "Ernie's snooze" and "Lombardi's snooze."

snowbird A scout from the northern United States who is assigned to Florida in the early spring. "While baseball lies dormant in the north, the snowbird flies south where there are too many games for local scouts to cover. . . . Dozens of northern colleges come down for early season games, so the snowbird may be able to get a line on players to follow next month, back home" (Kevin Kerrane, *Dollar Sign on the Muscle*, 1984, p.88).

snow cone A catch in which the ball is caught in, or squirts to, the top of the glove webbing and when held up resembles a scoop of frozen confection in a cone. "[Tommie Agee] rebounded with the ball still trapped at the end of the glove, a 'snow cone' as the players call it" (George Vecsey, *Joy in Mudville*, 1970). See also *ice-cream cone*, 2. Var. *sno-cone*.

snowman The numeral eight. When a team "builds a snowman," it means it scored eight runs. "[The Angels] dropped a snowman early on us, and we built a snowman early,

too" (B.J. Surhoff, quoted in *The Baltimore Sun*, June 3, 1996).

snowout A baseball game that is postponed or suspended because of snow. From 1993 to 2007, the Colorado Rockies experienced 11 snowouts.

snuff out To stop a rally; e.g., "Smith's relief pitching snuffed out the White Sox rally."

Snyder out To ground out routinely to the second baseman. ETYMOLOGY. Baltimore Orioles left-handed hitter Russ Snyder "in 1966 . . . hit so many grounders to the second baseman that the play was named in his honor" (Gordon Beard, *Orioles Gazette*, July 8, 1993, p.14). Broadcaster Brooks Robinson (WMAR-TV, Aug. 20, 1982; Joseph C. Goulden) noted that the term was commonly used by the Orioles, even by those who were unaware of its background.

SO 1. Box score abbrev. for *strikeout*, 1. **2.** Abbrev. for *strikeout*, 2. **3.** Abbrev. for *shutout*, 1.

soak 1. To bat the ball hard. Rube Marquard (quoted in *San Francisco Bulletin*, Feb. 27, 1913; Gerald L. Cohen): "[Christy] Matthewson [*sic*] could go on the mound and get soaked for a flock of hits, but if he won [John] McGraw would tell him that he pitched wonderful ball." IST USE. 1901 (Burt L. Standish, *Frank Merriwell's School Days*, p.265; Edward J. Nichols). **2.** *hist.* To put out a runner in town ball, the Massachusetts game, and other early variations of baseball by throwing the ball at and hitting him. Syn. *plug*, 2; *spot*, 6; *patch*; *burn*; *sting*, 2. **3.** To be hit by a pitch. "[Billy McGee] soaked 'Louie' Hartman in the ribs [with a pitch]" (*New York Sun*, June 5, 1899; Peter Morris).

soak ball *hist.* Baseball with soaking. " 'Soak ball' was at this time [1860s] my favorite sport" (Adrian C. Anson, *A Ball Player's Career*, 1900, p.14). See also *burn ball*. Syn. *sting ball*, 2.

soaker 1. *hist.* A solid hit. "You hit a soaker, and I'll bet you've taken some of the sand out of Flood" (Herbert Bellwood, *The Rivals of Riverwood*, 1895, p.194; David Shulman). **2.** A fastball.

soaking *hist.* Putting out a runner in town ball, the Massachusetts game, and other early variations of baseball by hitting him with a thrown ball. Syn. *plugging*, 1; *burning*, 1.

society *hist.* **1.** Professional or semipro baseball. "Whisperings Heard in Bush League Society" (*San Francisco Bulletin* headline, May 15, 1913; Gerald L. Cohen). See also *fast society*, 2. **2.** A baseball league. "Former Pirate southpaw [Lefty Leifield] . . . would probably appear just as good in this society [Pacific Coast League]" (*San Francisco Bulletin*, March 11, 1913; Gerald L. Cohen). See also *fast society*, 1; *major society.*

Society for American Baseball Research An organization headquartered in Cleveland, Ohio, of researchers and fans with an interest in the history and statistics of baseball. The purpose of the Society is "to foster the research, preservation, and dissemination of the history and record of baseball." It publishes several periodicals, supports many research committees, and holds regional meetings and a national convention. It was the brainchild of L. Robert "Bob" Davids of Washington, D.C., who along with 15 other baseball historians formed the Society at a 1971 meeting in Cooperstown, N.Y. Abbrev. and acronym *SABR*.

sock **1.** *v.* To hit a pitched ball hard; e.g., "Smith socked a liner to deep center." **2.** *n.* A hard-batted ball. IST USE. 1912 (*New York Tribune*, Sept. 5; Edward J. Nichols). **3.** *n.* Offensive power of a baseball team or player. "[They need] some additional sock from their infield" (*Tampa Tribune*, Dec. 4, 1988).

sockamayock A second-string or mediocre pitcher in the Negro leagues. "We had pitchers that we never would have pitched in league games. Sockamayocks, we used to call 'em. . . . Our sockamayocks might be Class-B or -D pitchers" (Buck Leonard, quoted in Robert Peterson, *Only the Ball was White*, 1970, pp.81–82).

sockdolager *hist.* A 19th-century term for a well-hit ball. "The sound of the sockdolager was heard with alarming frequency, followed by the shouts of the excited crowd" (*The World* [New York], July 20, 1890; Gerald L. Cohen). IST USE. 1858. "Tuomey now made up for his former ill luck in batting, by sending a sockdologer [*sic*] into the right field,

upon which he made three bases" (*New York Atlas*, Sept. 12).

socker A *slugger*, 1. "Plans called for these two hefty sockers [Steve Bilko and Ted Kluszewski] at first base" (*The Sporting News*, Dec. 21, 1960). IST USE. 1907 (*Lajoie's Official Base Ball Guide*; Edward J. Nichols).

sodfather A puckish nickname for a head groundskeeper, a punning play on *The Godfather*. When *The Washington Post* (Apr. 6, 1983) carried a profile of Baltimore's Pasquale Santarone, it was headlined "The Sodfather of Memorial Stadium." On Apr. 23, 1983, *The Washington Post* published a letter from a reader who termed the use of the nickname for an Italian American a "demeaning slur."

soft **1.** Lacking velocity or power; e.g., "Smith hit a soft single to left" or "Jones throws a soft breaking pitch." Compare *hard*. **2.** Said of a defense that does not hold runners on. **3.** Said of a player or team that offers little competition to its opponents. "Club officials said he [Chris Myers] had a 'soft' makeup, meaning he lacked competitive fire" (*The Baltimore Sun*, July 14, 1994). IST USE. 1880 (*Brooklyn Daily Eagle*, July 25; Edward J. Nichols).

softball [softball term] **1.** An offshoot of baseball played with a larger, softer ball that is pitched underhand and either fast or slow, depending on the league. The field is similar to the baseball diamond but smaller (bases are 60 feet apart for fast pitch and 65 feet apart for slow pitch) and a game is only seven innings. The game is played with the same equipment as baseball and most of the same rules. The emphasis in fast pitch is on pitching while slow pitch players concentrate on both hitting and fielding. A popular participant sport (both male and female), softball is dominated by amateur play. It is considered easier to play than baseball, as it requires less skill and is less dangerous. Early names for the game of softball include: army ball, big ball, church ball, diamond ball, indoor-outdoor, kitten ball, lightning ball, mush ball, night ball, panty waist, playground ball, recreation ball, serve us ball, and twilight ball.

The game dates back to 1887 when it was created as *indoor baseball* by George W.

Softball. Jose Ferrer (left) and Paul Robeson playing softball with other members of the cast of *Othello*, Central Park, New York, 1943 or 1944. *Farm Security Administration—Office of War Information Photograph Collection, Library of Congress*

Hancock, a reporter for the Chicago Board of Trade, on a cold Thanksgiving day inside the warm Farragut Boat Club. It received a major boost around 1910 when the Playground Society of America acknowledged it as a good game for kids (and suggested the addition of a 10th player known as a rover). Its major leap forward occurred in the 1930s after a national tournament at the 1933 Century of Progress Exposition in Chicago. *Time* magazine (Sept. 26, 1939) said of the game: "A product of the Depression, softball has grown into a major U.S. mania." In 1939, the game was brought back indoors when a short-lived attempt was made to promote it as a winter alternative to baseball, organized along the same lines as major-league baseball. Under the name National Professional Indoor Baseball League, franchises were sold in New York, Brooklyn, Boston, Cleveland, Chicago, Philadelphia, Cincinnati, and St. Louis. The game has undergone modifications and changes, including the distance from the pitching mound to the plate, which was set at 37 feet, 8 inches in 1933 and was dropped back to 40 feet in 1940, 46 feet in 1950, and 50 feet (slow pitch only) in 1985.

IST USE. 1926. The term "softball" was first used to describe the game in 1926 when a meeting of the National Recreation Congress was held in Colorado to standardize that state's rules under a common name. The term was suggested by Walter C. Hakanson, the YMCA director for Denver and former commissioner and president of the Amateur Softball Association of America. The *Oxford English Dictionary* carried a 1926 Canadian citation (*Victoria* [B.C.] *Daily Colonist*, July 2) for its point of origin in which the term appears but as two words: "The remainder of the morning was occupied by the younger members of the party in playing soft ball and other less strenuous games."

USAGE NOTE. The history of the term as a name for the game began long after the game itself had been created. It took a while for the term to spread even in Colorado, and it may have found its first popular application in Canada. The earliest printed reference in the collection of the many citations in the extensive file on the term "softball" at Merriam-Webster, the dictionary company in Springfield, Mass., is not in fact from Colorado but from a headline in the *Guelph* [Ont.] *Evening Mercury* (Aug. 26, 1927): "Guelph Softball Champions Eliminate Supremes of Galt." The term was not readily used until the Amateur Softball Association of America was established in 1933.

2. The ball used to play softball. It is 12 inches in circumference and weighs 6¼ to 7 ounces. There are variations on the standard ball, including a ball 16 inches in circumference used in a form of slow pitch, and a ball 11 inches in circumference used in women's games. "Softball" is a misnomer in the sense that the ball is not soft, but rather heavier and larger than a baseball and just about as hard. Traditionally, the softball was made of a core of tightly packed and molded kapok, wound tightly with cotton winding, dipped in rubber cement, covered with horsehide, and then hand-stitched.

EXTENDED USE. It is worth noting that softball has a few meanings outside the game. In tennis, a "softball" is a ball lobbed at low velocity for tactical reasons; also, a player may "softball" a shot to slow the pace of a volley or throw the other player off balance. The term has seen limited use for a changeup pitch in baseball; e.g., "[Harry Brecheen] was having a wonderful time on the mound for the Cardinals. Inning after inning he screwballed and softballed the Dodgers into submission" (*Negro Digest*, Nov. 1947).

According to the *Oxford English Dictionary* (2nd ed.), the oldest meaning of "softball" in English (usually written as "soft ball" or "softball") refers to the process of making candy, in which a soft globule of sugar is formed by dropping hot sugar into cold water. The soft ball is created to test the degree to which the sugar has been cooked. The term is very much still in use, and it is the "soft ball" that shows up in James Beard's *American Cookery* (1972). It is also defined in various cooking dictionaries as the stage at which syrup reaches 234 to 240 degrees Fahrenheit.

The most recent and currently popular use of the term is as an adjective or noun meaning "easy and not at all provocative." It is a clear play on the "soft" of "softball." A question that is easy to field and handle, such as one asked by a member of a Congressional committee of a witness, has become known as a "softball"; the antonym of playing political softball is playing "hardball." "Practically all of the questions thrown at [Jimmy] Carter were softballs that allowed him, in many cases, just to repeat much of his 1976 campaign oratory" (*San Francisco Examiner*, March 17, 1977). In the *Saturday Review* (Dec. 1979), Tim O'Brien alleged that Justice Warren Burger would only grant in-depth interviews to those "who clear the subject matter with him in advance, promise to throw softballs, and then let the chief justice edit the finished product himself." Kim Isaac Eisler (*Washingtonian*, March 2001) noted that television/radio host Larry King "is a server up of 'softballs,' easy questions that are anathema to hard-boiled reporters."

The term is applied to other situations. For instance, asking a movie star "what makes a sex symbol?" is a "softball query" (*People*, March 1, 1982), while allowing a company to "persistently misrepresent itself" is "softball media coverage" (*Fortune*, Aug. 9, 1982),

and an easily discharged issue is a "political softball" (*U.S. News and World Report*, Apr. 18, 1988). On the other hand, a "softball interview" is a television phenomenon that entails turning camera on and "letting the stars talk" (*People*, Aug. 20, 1984). In some instances, the softball question or query becomes simply "softball." A writer for *U.S. News and World Report* (Jan. 25, 1988), discussing the performance of Sen. Robert Dole as he began his drive for the Republican presidential nomination, described a situation in which a student asked the candidate how a Dole administration could help him finance a college education: "This, in the currently fashionable vernacular, was a 'softball' which Dole swung on and missed, never looking the student in the eye and rambling on in unfathomable generalities."

softballer [softball term] One who plays softball. 1ST USE. 1938. "Injured Softballer Walks with Crutches" (*Nevada State* [Reno] *Journal* headline, July 24; Peter Morris).

softball numbers "Incredible batting statistics" (Zack Hample, *Watching Baseball Smarter*, 2007, p.229).

softball throw A track and field event in which individuals compete by throwing a softball for distance.

soft bat A baseball bat made of soft woods, such as willow, linden, and pine. In the 1880s, soft bats were used for bunting. John H. Gruber (*The Sporting News*, Nov. 11, 1915; Peter Morris) wrote, "The bat was made of wood so soft that it was hardly possible for the batter to drive the ball beyond the diamond. The ball became dead after coming in contact with the mush-like bat and dropped to the ground. . . . The rule makers [in 1893] stuck the knife into the soft bat by declaring that the bat must be made wholly of 'hard' wood." See also *flat bat*.

soft fly A batted ball that is easy to catch (Maurice H. Weseen, *A Dictionary of American Slang*, 1934).

soft hands **1.** The hands of a fielder who can handle hard-hit ground balls with ease and seldom makes an error; esp., the hands of a fielder who can effortlessly and smoothly absorb the force of a batted ball in the center of his glove or draw it into his body. "He's got soft hands. That ball was a pea hit at him and you don't even hear it hit the glove" (Ray Miller, on third baseman Ryan Minor, quoted in *The Baltimore Sun*, March 7, 1998). Shortstop Ernie Banks was known for having soft hands. See also *good hands*. **2.** The hands of a catcher who is quick to release the ball and flexible enough to make last-second adjustments as the pitch comes in. "Soft hands are . . . [a] prerequisite for a catcher . . . [who] accepts the ball rather than fearing it or fighting it" (Kevin Kerrane, *Dollar Sign on the Muscle*, 1984, p.90).

softie [softball term] *hist.* A softball player. "Police Softies Defeat Firemen" (*San Francisco News* headline, Aug. 26, 1937; Peter Tamony).

soft liner A line drive without much force behind it.

soft snap **1.** An easily defeated team. "The wind-up of the American Association season demonstrates that there are really no longer any 'soft-snap' clubs therein. All are now worthy foemen of the strongest opponents" (*The Sporting Life*, Oct. 8, 1884, p.7; Barry Popik). **2.** An easily hit pitch. "As one of King's soft snaps came over the plate he [the batter] raised himself on his toes and let the ball have 180 pounds of muscle straight from the shoulder" (*The World* [New York], July 11, 1890; Gerald L. Cohen).

soft spot An easily defeated team. "At the time I reported to Baltimore . . . it was an ordinary ball club and one that the other teams in the league rather liked to play, because it furnished what is now known as a 'soft spot' in the schedule" (Hughey Jennings, *Rounding Third*, 1925; Peter Morris).

soft toss **1.** A throw made without exertion, as in batting practice or sideline catch and throw. Pitchers recovering from injury are often limited to soft tosses. "First baseman Mark Grace has a strained left rotator cuff that has limited him to soft tosses" (*The Baltimore Sun*, March 8, 1994). See also *long toss*, 2. **2.** A throwing exercise characterized by soft tosses. "[Barry Bonds] played soft-toss in the outfield . . . keeping his rehabilitation ahead of schedule" (*The Baltimore Sun*, Feb. 27, 2005). **3.** A hitting drill in

which a coach or another player squats or sits on a stool almost next to a hitter or 10 to 25 feet in front of home plate and flips underhand balls into his hitting zone. "[Brian Roberts] looked sharp in taking about 50 swings with . . . instructor Julio Vinas underhanding him the ball from about 25 feet away. 'It's the first time I've done soft-toss in six months,' Roberts said" (*The Baltimore Sun*, Feb. 25, 2006). Syn. *soft tossing*, 2. **4.** A pitcher's repertoire of off-speed pitches. "Jamie Moyer . . . [pitched] seven innings of soft toss . . . throwing his usual assortment of curves, screwballs, changeups and a not-so-fastball" (*The Baltimore Sun*, Aug. 6, 2003). "[Dan] Quisenberry looks as if he is retiring hitters by playing soft toss with catcher John Wathan" (Joe McGuff, *Baseball Digest*, Oct. 1983, p.84).

soft tosser **1.** A pitcher who throws off-speed pitches. "[Jon] Garland is a soft-tosser who relies heavily on the White Sox defense" (Childs Walker, *The Baltimore Sun*, Feb. 7, 2006). Soft tossers have five or fewer strikeouts per nine innings (*Ron Shandler's Baseball Forecaster*, 2006). **2.** A pitcher who cannot throw a major-league caliber fastball. "Soft tosser was scouting code for not worth my time" (Michael Lewis, *Moneyball*, 2003, p.20).

soft tossing *n.* **1.** A light throwing exercise employed when rehabilitating a sore arm. "[Carlos Delgado] has been battling an injury to his right shoulder that often reduces him to soft tossing on the sidelines" (*Sports Illustrated*, May 15, 1995). See also *long tossing*. **2.** Syn. of *soft toss*, 3.

soft-tossing *adj.* Said of a pitcher who throws off-speed pitches. "A soft-tossing pitcher without good control is a lethal combination in the major leagues" (Baltimore Orioles pitcher Omar Daal, quoted in *The Baltimore Sun*, Sept. 26, 2003).

soggy delivery A spitball.

soldier **1.** *n.* A derogatory term for a batter given to keeping the bat on his shoulder. **2.** *v.* To play without vigor or spirit. "One thing is certain: [Harry] Wolverton will not let his players soldier on him. He will insist that they throw off the languid feeling . . . and will make them show their real caliber" (*San Francisco Bulletin*, Apr. 29, 1913; Gerald L. Cohen).

sold out 1. Syn. of *bases loaded* (Maurice H. Weseen, *A Dictionary of American Slang*, 1934). 2. Said of a situation in which there are no more seats available for sale at the ballpark.

solid Characterized by excellence; e.g., a "solid hitter" is one who usually gets a hit when one is needed, or a "solid season" is one during which a player makes a meaningful contribution to the success of his team.

solid-average Said of an "average" ballplayer who has greater consistency than mere average would imply. "Dan Uggla has a solid-average arm at second base. It's more reliable than a guy who's just average. It's more trustworthy" (Doug Carpenter, quoted in Alan Schwarz, BaseballAmerica.com, Nov. 14, 2006).

solid up the middle Said of a team that has excellent players at catcher, second base, shortstop, and center field.

solitaire *hist.* Syn. of *single*, 1. "[Evers] went to third on [Johnny] Kling's solitaire . . . [and] Kling then purloined second" (*The Washington Post*, May 3, 1905; Peter Morris).

solo Syn. of *solo home run*.

solo home run A home run hit with no runners on base. Syn. *solo*; *solo shot*, 1; *bases-empty home run*; *singleton*, 2.

solo shot 1. Syn. of *solo home run*. 2. A single.

solve To begin getting hits off a pitcher, presumably after determining the trajectory and speed of his pitches and the way they are mixed. "The Oaklanders were unable to solve the curves of Southpaw Little" (*San Francisco Bulletin*, Apr. 15, 1913; Gerald L. Cohen). Syn. *get the range of*. IST USE. 1898 (*New York Tribune*, Apr. 22; Edward J. Nichols).

SOM Abbrev. for *Strat-O-Matic*.

sombrero 1. See *golden sombrero*. 2. See *platinum sombrero*.

something on the ball See *put something on the ball*.

sophomore A player in his second season in the major leagues.

sophomore jinx Bad luck or a poor showing in the season after a successful rookie or freshman year. Perhaps the most famous modern example of a player suffering from this condition was Joe Charboneau, who was the American League Rookie of the Year at Cleveland in 1980 but hit only .210 in 48 games in 1981. Lee Allen (*The Hot Stove League*, 1955, p.104) noted that belief in "the so-called sophomore jinx" is caused by "focusing attention only on second-year players who had exceptional first-year seasons." After his successful 1996 rookie season, Baltimore Orioles pitcher Rocky Coppinger (quoted in *The Baltimore Sun*, Feb. 14, 1998) commented, "I was scared of failing. You hear so much about the sophomore jinx and all that. I had never failed before in this game. People say it happens to everybody eventually. It got me last year." Bob Maisel (*The Baltimore Sun*, Nov. 17, 1983) wrote, "A sophomore jinx is the result of a talented player getting fat and lazy from too much success, or the opposition adjusting and catching up with one of less talent who happened to have a good rookie year." Roger Angell (*The Summer Game*, 1972, p.251) wrote, "Commissioner [Bowie] Kuhn, it can be seen, had a difficult second year in office, and should probably be listed as another victim of the legendary sophomore jinx." See also *jinx*, 1. IST USE. 1938. "Will [Joe] DiMaggio, who escaped the sophomore jinx, add playing-season difficulties to his holdout troubles?" (Alan Gould, *The Washington Post*, Apr. 7; Barry Popik). USAGE NOTE. The concept of a sophomore jinx was covered in *The Sporting News* in 1921 (Jan. 27, p.5), but the term was not used. Robert C. Malone (*Baseball Magazine*, Jan. 1937) entitled an article about the phenomenon "That Sophomore Slump"; two years later, John Drebinger (*Baseball Magazine*, Jan. 1939) wrote an article discussing "That Sophomore Jinx."

sophomore year Second year in the major leagues.

soporific player A poor player who is retained but does not help the team. The term was coined by baseball executive Branch Rickey.

sore arm A generic term formerly used for the injured arm of a player, especially a pitcher. Many sore arms are due to injuries to the rotator cuff. Syn. *bugaboo*.

soup arm A weak throwing arm (*The New York Times*, June 2, 1929).

soupbone 1. *hist.* The throwing arm of a player, esp. that of a pitcher. "Tim had been a star thrower in his day, but the soupbone had slowed up and he was clinging to his job with his finger-nails" (*Collier's*, July 19, 1930; Peter Tamony). Syn. *souper*; *super.* IST USE. 1904. "[Herman Long] says the old soupbone has yielded to new-fangled treatment and he can now sleep on Pullmans without putting his arm in the hammock" (*Cincinnati Enquirer*, reprinted in *The Washington Post*, Sept. 10; Peter Morris). ETYMOLOGY. The term seems to have arisen in recognition of the importance of the pitcher's throwing arm, which is to his performance what a soupbone is to a soup. **2.** An animal bone (such as a cow's femur) used to rub repeatedly the maximum hitting point or "sweet spot" of one's bat in order to "harden" its surface and close the wood's pores.

soupboner A pitcher. "My old pal [Jim] Scott was gone with the wind, and in his place were some young soupboners" (Harry Stein, *hoopla*, 1983, p.259).

soupboning Pitching.

souper Syn. of *soupbone*, 1.

Southern Association A minor league from 1902 to 1961 (Class A from 1902 to 1935, Class A1 from 1936 to 1945, and Class AA from 1946 to 1961). Syn (prior to 1920) *Southern League*.

Southern League 1. A Class AA minor league since 1964. It was the successor to the South Atlantic League. See also *Sally League*, 1. **2.** Syn (prior to 1920) of *Southern Association*.

southpaw 1. *n.* A player who throws or pitches with the left hand; esp., a *left-handed pitcher*. The term was originally used for a left-handed player; e.g., "Oscar Walker, the big south paw center fielder" (*St. Louis Post-Dispatch*, March 4, 1884; Peter Morris). It was later used for a left-handed pitcher; e.g., "South Paw Morris was not as effective as he

"A SOUTHPAW ARTIST" COPYRIGHT 1908 C.J.ROSE

Southpaw. Comic postcard, 1908. *Andy Moresund Collection*

is usually" (*The New York Times*, Sept. 5, 1889). Compare *northpaw*. IST USE. 1869. "When 'old south paw' [first baseman Joe Start] puts his hand on a ball, 'out' is pretty sure to be called" (*National Chronicle*, May 15; Peter Morris). **2.** *n.* A left-handed hitter. "The left fielder ordinarily is busier than the right fielder on defensive play because there are more right-handed batters than southpaws" (Connie Mack, *Connie Mack's Baseball Book*, 1950, p.135). IST USE. 1858. "[First baseman] Hallock, a 'south paw,' let fly a good ball into the right field" (*New York Atlas*, Sept. 12; Tom Shieber). **3.** *n.* The left hand of a left-handed pitcher. IST USE. 1885. "They had always been accustomed to having their opponents hug their bases pretty close, out of respect for Morris' quick throw over to first with that south-paw of his" (*The Sporting Life*, Jan. 14; David Shulman). **4.** *adj.* Left-handed; e.g., "southpaw slants" refers to the pitches of a left-handed pitcher. "They would have been bunched against southpaw pitching" (*The Baltimore Sun*, June 3, 1949; OED). **5.** *v.* To throw with the left hand. "[Turkey Mike] Donlin drifted to southern California, where he southpawed for the Los Angeles club in 1897" (Harry Grayson, *They Played the Game*, 1944, p.81). IST USE. 1928. "Herb Pennock southpawed his way the route for the Yankees" (*Daily Ardmoreite* [Ardmore, Okla.], Apr. 12; OED).

USAGE NOTE. Peter Morris notes that as early as 1887 the antecedents of the term "southpaw" were considered unclear; e.g.,

San Francisco Examiner (July 18, 1887) discussed the term "south-paw twirler": "[It] is one of the many absurd phrases found in baseball literature. It was no doubt coined by some writer who witnessed a left-handed pitcher's work on a diamond, on which the catcher faced the east . . . it is now used without regard to the position of the diamond and is an enigma to the person not versed in baseball slang. It should be placed on the hook."

ETYMOLOGY. The *Oxford English Dictionary* lists an 1848 citation (*Democratic B-hoy*) of the term meaning a boxer's "punch or blow with the left hand": "Curse the Old Hoss, what a south-paw he has given me!" *Appletons' Journal* (Dec. 16, 1871; Benjamin Zimmer) asked, "Why is the right hand the handiest? Is it so from instinct or education? For, anti-dexters and 'south-paws,' or left-handed persons, are rare exceptions to the rule." The oft-repeated etymology of the term is that it derives from the "fact" that ballparks were laid out with home plate to the west, which meant that a left-handed pitcher faced the west and threw with his "southern" limb. This westward orientation kept the glare of the afternoon sun out of the batter's eyes and out of the eyes of the customers in the more expensive seats behind the plate during a game. The story is that the term was created by political humorist Finley Peter Dunne of the *Chicago News* or Charles Seymour of the *Chicago Herald*. According to Dunne's biographer, Elmer Ellis (*Mr. Dooley's America*, 1942), Dunne invented the term for a left-handed pitcher in "about 1887" because the "Chicago ball park faced east and west, with home plate to the west, so that a left-handed pitcher threw from the south side." H.L. Mencken (*The American Language*, Suppl. II, 1948) reported that Richard J. Finnigan, publisher of the *Chicago Times*, attributed the term to Seymour. As Finnigan put it in a 1945 letter to Mencken: "The pitchers in the old baseball park on the Chicago West Side faced the west and those who pitched left-handed did so with their southpaws."

But does the sun theory work, or did it before most games were played at night? David Shulman (*New York Press*, May 30, 1990), noting that the term existed before any ball fields were constructed according to the direction of the sun, concluded: "The story that the pitcher's left arm was on the south side of the slab is fanciful." But wouldn't any game involving pitching and batting, including those being played long before the rise of modern baseball, have placed the batter facing east to avoid the afternoon sun in his eyes? Peter Morris (personal communication, May 7, 2004): "Tim Murnane gave an account of how the term became popular (in *The Boston Globe*, reprinted in *The Sporting News*, Aug. 6, 1908). Murnane was aware of the story that it derived from the direction in which ballparks face and disavowed it. He said that, in 1876, a St. Louis newspaper referred to him as a southpaw because he batted left-handed. He began to use the term to designate a left-handed pitcher and has continued to do so. So Murnane popularized it, but did not coin it."

A different theory from Charley Dryden, an early sportswriter, has attracted few converts. In this version, an unnamed left-hander from Southpaw, Ill., tries out for the Cubs at spring training in New Orleans, thus inspiring the Chicago writers to start calling all left-handers "southpaws." The reason that it is hard to muster enthusiasm for this apparent folk etymology is that no maps of Illinois or of any other state reveal a town by the name of Southpaw. Illinois does have a South Pekin and a South Park.

EXTENDED USE. **1.** Any left-handed person. *The New York Times* (Nov. 16, 1884) noted the exploits of "the famous South Paws," a Brooklyn bowling team. **2.** A boxer who stands with his right foot and right hand extended and who counterpunches and guards with his left; also, the left hand itself. "This boxer was Gene Tunney, who had just been whipped by Harry Greb. He was one of the few who discovered what a left hand meant, both offensively and defensively, and worked away hour after hour building up his own southpaw" (*Colliers*, Apr. 12, 1930; Peter Tamony). **3.** A member of the political left wing; a radical. Paul Mallon's "News Behind the News" column in the *Schenectady* [N.Y.] *Gazette* (Feb. 10, 1938): "House southpaws are generally known in the House as the 'mavericks,' not only because Texas Congressman Maury Maverick is the leader but because *Webster's New International Dictionary* defines a maverick as 'a motherless calf.'" Damon Runyon, Walter Winchell, and other newspaper columnists were noted for calling Communists "southpaws."

southpaw disease The common difficulty that left-handed batters have in hitting left-handed pitchers (Dave Anderson, *The New York Times*, July 5, 1987)

southpawing 1. *n.* Left-handed pitching. "The White Sox positively refused to be awed today by the southpawing of Larry French" (*Chicago Tribune*, Apr. 4, 1938; Peter Morris). IST USE. 1920. "Griffin batted very well against right handers, but seemed a trifle weak against expert southpawing" (*Literary Digest*, Feb. 14). 2. *adj.* Said of left-handed pitching. "Earl Hamilton, the young southpawing sensation with the St. Louis Browns" (*San Francisco Bulletin*, Feb. 6, 1913; Gerald L. Cohen).

South Siders The Chicago *White Sox*. U.S. Cellular Field (Comiskey Park II) is located in the South Side of Chicago. Compare *North Siders*.

souvenir A foul ball or home run hit into the stands and kept by a spectator. IST USE. 1912. "The Boston players had batted numerous balls in the crowd without attempting to retrieve them, each ball being regarded as a souvenir" (*The Sporting Life*, Oct. 19; Peter Morris).

souvenir program A book sold to baseball fans, which includes a scorecard. IST USE. 1883. "The 500 souvenir programmes . . . were given away early in the day" (*St. Louis Post-Dispatch*, May 25; Peter Morris).

Sox 1. See *White Sox*. 2. See *Red Sox*.

SP Abbrev. for *starting pitcher*.

space ball Syn. of *Leephus*.

space cadet An eccentric player; a flake who seems to have come from another planet or outer space. The name of pitcher Bill "Spaceman" Lee, a widely publicized iconoclast, is likely to come to mind when the term is used. It may have survived from a television serial (1950–1952) called *Tom Corbett, Space Cadet*.

spaceshot A long home run (Bill Littlefield,

in Henry Horenstein and Bill Littlefield, *Baseball Days*, 1993, p.144).

spaghetti baseball Baseball in Italy.

"Spahn and Sain and two days of rain" The motto of the Boston Braves of the late 1940s. Much of the team's success derived from the abilities of pitchers Warren Spahn and Johnny Sain. In an interview with Frederick C. Klein (*The Wall Street Journal*, Aug. 2, 1985), Spahn mused, "It's not so much my pitching people know, but that little poem about me and Johnny Sain with the '48 Braves. . . . Guys who were kids 40 years ago learned it as a nursery rhyme. Now they meet me and say 'Oh, you're *that* Spahn.' I used to think that rhyme was silly, but I guess it's how I'll be remembered. Life's funny, huh?" ETYMOLOGY. From a poem by Gerald V. Hern in his article "Braves Boast Two-Man Staff: Pitch Spahn and Sain, Then Pray for Rain" in the *Boston Post* (Sept. 14, 1948). Qouting Hern: "Yesterday Mr. [Billy] Southworth [Boston Braves manager] said he had made up his mind. From here on he will rotate his pitching staff. Spahn on one day, Sain the next. That's really rotation."

spaldeen The smooth, hollow, pink, high-bouncing rubber ball used in such baseball variations as stickball, stoopball, punchball, and box baseball. The name is a "sweetened" form of the name of Albert Goodwill Spalding, whose company made the spaldeen until 1980 (Harvey Frommer, *Sports Roots*, 1979). *Newsweek* (Oct. 22, 1984) noted the ball's passing as "a victim of the trend toward giving boys a place to play where there are no windows." The term is deeply embedded in the minds of many. Leonard Shecter (*The Jocks*, 1969): "To this day when I see 'Spalding' I consider it a misspelling." Lowell Cohn (*The Baltimore Sun*, Aug. 29, 1999): "When you bought a brand new Spaldeen [for 25 cents], the aroma alone would cause ecstasy; it was the smell of Bazooka bubble gum and summer and childhood and joy and hope." See also *Pennsy pinkie*. Also spelled *Spaldeen*.

Spalding *hist.* The baseball during the time it was manufactured by the A.G. Spalding Co. Frequently misspelled "Spaulding." IST USE. 1890 (*New York Press*, July 25; Edward J. Nichols).

Spalding Commission See *Mills Commission.*

Spalding Guide *hist.* A player whose every move seems posed, as if he were being photographed for the popular *Spalding's Official Base Ball Guides* of yore. The books, first published in 1876, were illustrated guidebooks featuring records and team profiles.

Spalding type A "perfect" pitcher; one who has perfect mechanics. "You don't always get a Spalding-type guy who has everything perfect" (Art Stewart, quoted in *Kansas City Star*, March 31, 2002). Named for 1870s Hall of Fame pitcher Albert Goodwill Spalding.

spangles *hist.* A player's uniform. IST USE. 1899. "Young players will do well to follow as close as possible the style of living pursued by a player [Bid McPhee] who has been over twenty years in the spangles and is still the king in his position" (*Daily Iowa State* [Iowa City] *Press*, June 1; Peter Morris).

Spanish home run 1. *hist.* A ball that is misjudged by a fielder and therefore allows the batter to score but which, if properly played, might have been a single or double. ETYMOLOGY. The term appeared in Franklin P. Huddle's article (*American Speech*, Apr. 1943) on baseball jargon and elsewhere, but no suggestion is made of its origin. Implied, however, is Spanish fielding ineptitude. The expression may have died out as Latin players showed their skill in the field. **2.** A cheap or easy home run.

spank To bat the ball sharply. "Randy [Hundley] spanked his single to left" (*Chicago Tribune*, July 29, 1968). IST USE. 1891 (*Chicago Herald*, May 16; Edward J. Nichols).

spare bat A dependable player normally assigned to the bench but put in the game when a hit is needed.

spark plug A player or manager with a fiery temper; one who can get a rally started or motivate a team. See also *igniter.*

spasm *hist.* Syn. of *inning*, 1. "With the third inning faded into the dim and forgotten past, the fourth spasm in the afternoon's matinee of Dementia Baseballitis hopped into the

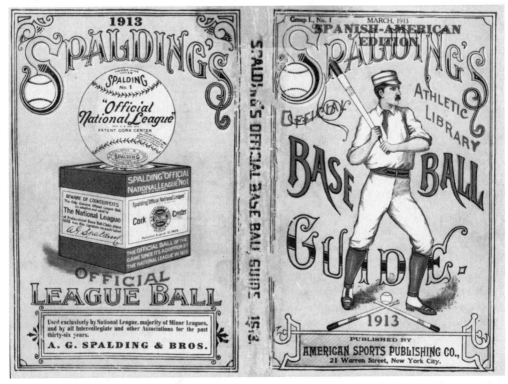

Spalding Guide. From the complete collection of *Spalding's Official Base Ball Guides* in the Library of Congress. *Library of Congress*

glare of the calcium glim" (*Baseball Magazine*, Sept. 1909). 1ST USE. 1905. "Mr. Clarkson . . . was sadly battered yesterday afternoon in the closing rounds of a matinee which went ten spasms" (*Atlanta Constitution*, Apr. 4; Peter Morris).

SPBA Abbrev. for *Senior Professional Baseball Association*.

spear To catch a ball, usually a line drive, with a sudden reach of the arm fully extended, as if throwing a spear. "Manny Lee speared Tony Phillips' line drive" (*Tampa Tribune*, Oct. 7, 1989). 1ST USE. 1902 (*The Sporting Life*, July 5, p.7; Edward J. Nichols).

special *hist.* A *Texas Leaguer* in the Eastern League (ca. 1933).

special assignment scout A scout who routinely evaluates professional rather than amateur players, either as future opponents or as possible acquisitions through trade. "Special-assignment work involves less intuition and projection and more detailed analysis and strategic thinking" (Kevin Kerrane, *Dollar Sign on the Muscle*, 1984, p.59). Compare *cross-checker*.

special day A day featuring any of several inducements to boost attendance at the game. Special days range from discounts (Ladies' Day and $3 Night) to giveaways (Helmet Day and Photo Album Night).

special express A hard-hit, low line drive (Walter K. Putney, *Baseball Stories*, Spring 1952).

special player An amateur prospect (such as Jered Weaver) who, because he is represented by an aggressive agent such as Scott Boras and deemed by the agent to have particular promise, will probably cost a lot of money and time to get under contract (Alan Schwarz, BaseballAmerica.com, Nov. 14, 2006). Syn. *icon player.*

special waivers Syn. of *irrevocable waivers.*

spectator interference An act by a spectator that prevents a fielder from making a play on a batted or thrown ball; e.g., when a spectator reaches out of the stands, or goes on the playing field, and touches a live ball. The ball is dead at the moment of interference and the umpire shall impose such penalties that will nullify the act of interference. The spectator can expect to be ejected from the ballpark. Syn. *fan interference.*

speed 1. The ability of an individual or a team to run the bases. 2. The ability to field the ball expeditiously. 3. The ability to throw the fastball. 1ST USE. 1887 (*Base Ball Tribune*, May 23; Edward J. Nichols). 4. The swiftness of a fastball. See also *velocity.* 5. *hist.* Ability or competence. "[Hugh Duffy] admits that his men are batting above their normal speed, which means they are bound to pull up from their present high clip of speed" (*The Washington Post*, June 14, 1897). 6. See *arm speed.* 7. See *bat speed.*

speedball A fastball. 1ST USE. 1918. "[Jim Vaughn's] buzzer, the speedball, is a mighty breeze and is difficult to hit" (*Boston Herald and Journal*, Sept. 6; Peter Morris). EXTENDED USE. The term "speedballing" is used by drug addicts for injecting heroin and cocaine. "The dangers of speedballing: [John] Belushi killed by 'treacherous' combination of drugs, medic says" (*San Francisco Examiner*, March 11, 1982; Peter Tamony).

speedballer A fastball pitcher. "Joe Ginsberg . . . caught such speedballers as Virgil Trucks and Dizzy Trout with the Tigers" (*The Sporting News*, March 30, 1955).

speedburner 1. A player who runs very fast. "There are few other players in the league, not excepting the fastest speedburners, who would have gotten much farther than second on the drive" (*San Francisco Bulletin*, Apr. 10, 1913; Gerald L. Cohen). 2. A fastball pitcher.

speeder A fastball. "[Walter Johnson] only occasionally . . . sends that old 'speeder' zipping through there the way he used to" (George Herman Ruth, *Babe Ruth's Own Book of Baseball*, 1928, p.85; Peter Morris). 1ST USE. 1924. "The first Cub at bat, let a speeder go past because it was a trifle wide" (Lester Chadwick, *Baseball Joe, Captain of the Team*, p.28; David Shulman).

speed game Baseball strategy that is highlighted by the speed of certain baserunners; e.g., "The manager could not execute his speed game because the batters were not getting on base."

speed gun Syn. of *radar gun.*

speed merchant 1. A particularly fast runner

who is likely to steal bases. IST USE. 1910 (*Baseball Magazine*, May, p.32; Edward J. Nichols). **2.** A fastball pitcher. IST USE. 1905. "The 'speed merchants' who wind up their 'wings' and take numerous swings before cutting loose to the batter" (*The Washington Post*, March 16; Peter Morris).

speed score A measure of the various elements that comprise a baserunner's speed skills, including stolen base efficiency, stolen base frequency, triples, and runs scored as a percentage of times on base (Ron Shandler, *Ron Shandler's Baseball Forecaster*, 2006).

speedster A faster-than-usual baserunner; one who has developed a flawless running form. "[Brady Anderson is] the most technically sound speedster in the game" (*The Baltimore Sun*, March 12, 2000).

spell To relieve a pitcher or another player.

spellbinder A glib, talkative player.

sphere The baseball. IST USE. 1874 (*Chicago Inter-Ocean*, July 30; Edward J. Nichols).

spheroid The baseball. "Saginaw will send a contingent to see [John] Clarkson accelerate the spheroid" (*Detroit Free Press*, June 21, 1886). IST USE. 1874 (*Chicago Inter-Ocean*, July 9; Edward J. Nichols).

Spiders Nickname of the National League franchise in Cleveland, Ohio, from 1889 to 1899. See also *Indians*. ETYMOLOGY. From the spider-like appearance of the players in skin-tight uniforms (*The Sporting News*, Oct. 1898; Dennis Pajot).

spike 1. *n.* A metal, rubber, or plastic projection on the bottom of a player's shoe to give him greater traction. The term is something of a misnomer, for baseball spikes are not sharp and pointed like those which are found on track shoes. IST USE. 1859. "In both games [baseball and cricket] the players wear a peculiar kind of buckskin shoes with a long spike in the sole, to prevent them from slipping" (*New York Herald*, Oct. 16; Peter Morris). **2.** *v.* To cut or otherwise injure another player with one's spikes. It commonly occurs when a player is sliding into a base feet first and the defensive player gets in the way. "Nudge him with rubber—don't spike him with steel" (B.F. Goodrich advertisement for rubber spikes, *Time* magazine, Apr. 22, 1940;

Peter Tamony). IST USE. 1885 (*Chicago Inter-Ocean*, May 17; Edward J. Nichols). **3.** *v.* For a pitcher to dig his fingernail into the ball before throwing it. **4.** *v.* To hit a baseball (Maurice H. Weseen, *A Dictionary of American Slang*, 1934). **5.** *v.* To score a run by touching home plate. "[Mundorff] spiked the plate twice" (*San Francisco Bulletin*, Apr. 28, 1913; Gerald L. Cohen).

spike curve A curveball that is thrown by pressing one fingertip or fingernail into the seam of the ball like a spike. "A better name, if rarely used, for the so-called '*knuckle curve*' thrown by Mike Mussina, and before him Don Sutton and others" (Rob Neyer, in *The Neyer/James Guide to Pitchers*, 2004, p.21).

spikes 1. The array of metal, rubber, or plastic projections on the bottom (sole and heel) of a player's shoe, used to improve traction. Vintage base ball researcher John Husman

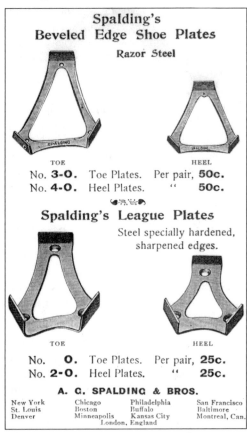

Spalding's
Beveled Edge Shoe Plates
Razor Steel

TOE   HEEL
No. **3-0.** Toe Plates. Per pair, **50c.**
No. **4-0.** Heel Plates.   "   **50c.**

Spalding's League Plates
Steel specially hardened, sharpened edges.

TOE   HEEL
No.   **0.** Toe Plates. Per pair, **25c.**
No. **2-0.** Heel Plates.   "   **25c.**

A. G. SPALDING & BROS.

New York	Chicago	Philadelphia	San Francisco
St. Louis	Boston	Buffalo	Baltimore
Denver	Minneapolis	Kansas City	Montreal, Can.
	London, England		

Spikes. Ad from a 1904 *Spalding's Official Base Ball Guide* featuring spikes with harmful implications. *Library of Congress* uncovered Knickerbockers records revealing that players were using metal spikes with canvas shoes in 1849. Henry Chadwick counseled that "the bases should be made of the best heavy canvas, and of double thickness, as there will be much jumping on them with spiked shoes" (*Beadle's Dime Base-Ball Player*, 1860, p.18). "Every ball player should wear shoes with good spikes, that he can break up at short notice, and stop short, without slipping down" (*Brooklyn Eagle*, June 19, 1865; Peter Morris). See also *cleats*, 1. **2.** Syn. of *baseball shoe*. **3.** See *sharpen one's spikes*. **4.** See *hang up one's spikes*.

spikes high Describing aggressive baserunning tactics; specif., characterizing a slide in which a baserunner attempts to gain advantage by imperiling the fielder with his spikes. The term is often associated with the rough and belligerent Ty Cobb, but one infielder who did not fear him was Buck Weaver, the Chicago White Sox third baseman, who once warned Cobb: "If you ever come in with your spikes high, I'll stomp all over you" (quoted by Irving M. Stein, *The Ginger Kid*, 1992). See also *sharpen one's spikes*.

spike-shy Said of a fielder who avoids a sliding baserunner. "He is what we call spike shy that is when a man is coming in to the plate it seems like he has not got the nerve to block them off but tries to stand to 1 side and tag them as they are sliding past" (Ring W. Lardner, "The Courtship of T. Dorgan," *The Saturday Evening Post*, Sept. 6, 1919; Peter Morris).

spin **1.** *n.* The turning of a pitched ball that keeps it on its intended trajectory. All pitches have spin except for the knuckleball. A fastball has backspin; a curveball has topspin. "The way the ball is rotating is the way the ball will move. The spinning seams show the rotation. If a batter can see the spin on a pitch, then he will know which pitch it is and be able to adjust his swing" (ESPN analyst Joe Morgan, quoted in *USA Today*, July 9, 1999). **2.** *v.* To cause the ball to turn as it moves through the air. **3.** *v.* To pitch. "[Jim Hearn] spun a seven-hitter and came away with a 4–2 victory" (Bobby Thomson, *"The Giants Win the Pennant! The Giants Win the Pennant!,"* 1991, p.89).

Spikes high. Detroit Tigers baserunner comes in spikes high as Washington Senators third baseman applies the tag. *National Photo Company Collection, Library of Congress*

spin axis An imaginary line around which a pitched ball will rotate; e.g., the spin axis of an overhand fastball is a horizontal line that runs through the center of the ball and lies perpendicular to the direction of the forward motion of the ball. Pitchers use the orientation of the spin axis to direct the deflection of the ball. See also *red dot*. (David Baldwin)

spin ball A name for softball.

spine Syn. of *middle defense*.

spin his cap To brush back a batter; to intimidate with a high, inside pitch, close enough to touch the bill of the batter's cap.

Spink Award Short for *J.G. Taylor Spink Award*.

spinner **1.** A pitched baseball that spins in flight; a breaking ball. "[Clem Labine] had the good curve, Bobby Thomson was comin' up, and Thomson was weak against a good spinner" (Rube Walker, quoted in Thomas Kiernan, *The Miracle at Coogan's Bluff*, 1975, p.141). IST USE. 1912. "Joe [Wood] amused himself by sending all sorts of curves and spinners which had the Browns dancing" (Tim Murnane, *The Boston Globe*, July 9). **2.** A type of *knuckleball* thrown by Hoyt Wilhelm, who gave it a "little push" as the ball rolled off the ends of his index and middle fingers. According to Wilhelm (*The Sporting News*, May 22, 1959): "The spinner breaks according to the way I make it rotate. I try to make it turn, sometimes one, sometimes two times between the mound and home plate. It breaks a lot more with two rotations than it does with one. If I release it side-arm, it will break out laterally and away from a right-handed batter. If I come down more over-handed or three-quarters with my motion, it will break down and out."

spin off To pitch with such force and lateral momentum as to land on the side of one's foot and move violently toward first base or third base, out of proper fielding position. "Bob Gibson spun off a ton, and most left-handers spin off a bit" (Eddie Bane, quoted in Alan Schwarz, BaseballAmerica.com, Nov. 14, 2006).

spiral curve Syn. of *double curve*. "There hasn't been a zig-zag or a spiral curve exploited yet" (*San Francisco Bulletin*, March 6, 1913).

spitball 1. *n.* A late-breaking pitch made with a ball that has been spat upon. It is thrown like a fastball but with a stiff wrist, and the ball is squirted out of the fingers like a water-melon seed, allowing the slowly, frontward rotating ball to slip from the hand without spin and to break unpredicably. The pitch came to prominence in 1904 and was so pop-ular that 1905 was dubbed "the spit ball year" (Timothy Sharp, *The Sporting News*, May 6, 1905; Peter Morris). The American League, during the early days of the spitball, used it so much that Charlie Dryden, angler and scribe, quipped (quoted in John J. Evers and Hugh S. Fullerton, *Touching Second: The Science of Baseball*, 1910), "The American League consists of Ban Johnson, the 'spit-ball,' and the Wabash Railroad." The spitball was banned on Feb. 9, 1920, for hygienic rea-sons and to boost offense and restrict pitch-ing; however, pitchers were given a one-year reprieve, and after the 1920 season, 17 pitch-ers who were already using the spitball were allowed to continue to do so for the remain-der of their careers under what amounted to a "grandfather clause." The last legal spitball pitcher was Burleigh Grimes, who retired in 1934 after 19 years in the major leagues.

The spitball is still thrown despite the fact that the rule against it has been made tougher. For instance, in 1968, a stricter anti-spitball rule was added that prohibited any contact between the pitcher's throwing hand and his mouth. Pitchers have found that the reputa-tion of throwing spitballs is often enough to intimidate batters. The attitude toward the pitch seems to be summed up by one-time pitching coach and manager George Bam-berger, as quoted by Thomas Boswell (*The Washington Post*, Aug. 6, 1987): "A guy who cheats in a friendly game of cards is a cheater. A pro who throws a spitball to support his family is a contender."

Few baseball terms have as many odd and diverse synonyms as "spitball." They include: aqueous toss, brown spitter, bubble-gum ball, country sinker, Cuban forkball, Cuban palm-ball, cuspidor ball, cuspidor curve, damp sling, drooler, *drop ball*, drugstore drop, eel ball, expectoration pellet, geyser ball, moist ball, moist curve, moisture ball, perspiration pellet, pump pellet, rain rippler, saliva heave, saliva toss, saliva twist, saturated curve, slick sling, slobber ball, soggy delivery, *spitter*, Staten Island sinker, super-sinker, sweat ball, vapor float, wet ball, wet delivery, wet one, wet pitch, and wet wipe. Originally spelled "spit ball."

IST USE. 1902. "That's the 'spit ball'" (Elmer Stricklett, after he defeated a barn-storming team of major leaguers in Dec. 1902, quoted in Francis J. Mannix, *San Fran-cisco Bulletin*, Sept. 24, 1913; Peter Morris). USAGE NOTE. Pitchers were throwing the spit-ball before the term was applied to the pitch. There are various accounts of 19th-century pitchers throwing the spitball. For example, Bobby Mathews of the Lord Baltimores was described in a game against the Eckfords in 1868 as rubbing the ball with his hands and keeping "one side of it perfectly white, then he would moisten it with his fingers and let it go" (H.H. Westlake, *Baseball Magazine*, Apr. 1931, p.513). The *Chicago Herald* (reprinted in the *Detroit Free Press*, May 4, 1887; Peter Morris) described Pud Galvin as "a fat, good-natured little fellow who used to go through the business-like performance of expectorat-ing on his fingers before delivering the ball." Jacob C. Morse (*Baseball Magazine*, January 1909) noted that Charles Radbourn "had a drop ball that he did not have to spit on, and called it a 'spit ball.'" Mickey Welch "expectorate[d] on either hand" during his preliminary motions (*St. Louis Post-Dispatch*, June 19, 1886). Peter Morris (*A Game of Inches: The Game on the Field*, 2006, p.153) concluded, "It is one thing to presume that many nineteenth-century pitchers were inadvertently throwing spitballs and quite another to take it for granted that none of them were aware of what they were doing."

ETYMOLOGY. From "spittle-ball," esp. one thrown as a missile by a schoolchild: "They . . . crooked pins, made pop-guns, ejected spit-balls" (*Knickerbocker*, no.27, 1846, p.410; *OED*). It is generally agreed that the spitball was "discovered" in 1902 by Providence pitcher Frank Corridon, who threw his slow ball by wetting the tips of his fingers to get a better grip on the ball. Corridon demonstrated the pitch (which he seldom used) to teammate outfielder George Hildebrand, who applied more saliva to the ball and saw that it broke sharply down. After moving to the Sacramento team later in 1902, Hildebrand taught the pitch to teammate pitcher Elmer Stricklett, who developed the pitch, which prolonged his career. Stricklett showed the pitch to Big Ed Walsh and Jack Chesbro, both of whom popularized the spitball. In an interview (*San Francisco Call-Bulletin*, July 2, 1940; Peter Tamony) Stricklett said, "I never discovered the spitball. In countless magazine articles, radio skits and even in some of the baseball records I've been called the originator of the spitter though I never claimed credit for it. A fellow named Frank Corridon really discovered the spitball." An interesting light on the subject was shed by Billy Hart, a veteran pitcher from the 1890s, who was quoted (*New York Sun*, Feb. 10, 1908; Peter Morris) as saying, "I notice they claim Chesbro and Stricklett were the first to discover the 'spit ball.' Well, back in 1896, when I was pitching for St. Louis, I met Catcher [Frank] Bowerman, who was with Baltimore that year. Calling me aside in St. Louis one day, he took the ball and requested me to get back of the catcher and watch his curves. I did so and was surprised to see how the ball acted as it neared the catcher. I asked Bowerman what made the ball act so. He explained that he simply spat on the ball, held onto it with his thumb at the seam and let it go. The odd part

of it was that there was no speed to the ball that Bowerman pitched, whereas today they claim that the 'spit ball' can only be delivered with speed. I mastered it after a while, but found that it injured my arm, as it brought into play muscles not generally used. I advise any pitcher with good speed and curves to let the 'spit ball' severely alone. It will ruin an arm of steel in due time." Cy Young (quoted in *The Sporting Life*, June 3, 1905) also advised against using the pitch: "I used it against Philadelphia and Washington and had it working nicely, but it hurt my arm and I have cut it [out] altogether. An old pitcher like myself has no business using it at all. . . . Even if it does not hurt a pitcher's arm, I think it will eventually cause him to lose control of his curve ball and his fast ones." For an extended discussion of the etymology of "spitball," see Peter Morris (*A Game of Inches: The Game on the Field*, 2006, pp.140–53) and Barry Popik and Gerald L. Cohen (*Comments on Etymology*, May 2003, pp.21–28).

EXTENDED USE. An act of deception; a dirty trick. "As Joe Biden knows, it would not be the first spitball the [Michael] Dukakis campaign has thrown" (*National Review*, Feb. 5, 1988; Charles D. Poe). "[Michael] Moore may have invented a new political tradition: the documentary as campaign spitball" (Richard Lacayo, *Time* magazine, Dec. 27, 2004–Jan. 3, 2005, commenting on Moore's *Fahrenheit 9/11*).

2. *n.* A generic term for a moistened ball on which the pitcher or catcher has applied an illegal substance, such as saliva, sweat, grease, hair tonic, oil, slippery elm, or anything that will adhere to the cover of the ball.

3. *v.* To throw the spitball. EXTENDED USE. To throw out suggestions for discussion. William Safire (*On Language*, 1981) noted, "Because an old-time baseball pitcher never knew which way his spitball would break, the verb 'to spitball' now means 'to speculate.'" H. Kurnitz (*Invasion of Privacy*, 1955; *OED*): "I'm just thinking out loud. . . . Spitballing we call it in the movie business."

spitballer A pitcher noted for throwing the spitball; e.g., Big Ed Walsh, Jack Chesbro,

Tommy Bridges, Joe Page, Lew Burdette, Gaylord Perry, and Don Drysdale. IST USE. 1928. "The Giants . . . made only three hits off . . . Clarence Mitchell, the southpaw spitballer" (*Chicago Tribune*, June 7; *OED*).

spitballist *hist.* A spitball pitcher. "To be the battery mate of a spitballist, one must . . . be able to dig it [the spitball] out of the dust or pull it out of the sky" (*San Francisco Bulletin*, May 24, 1913; Gerald L. Cohen).

spitter 1. Syn. of *spitball*, 1. The term has been around for many years but was given new prominence with the 1974 publication of Gaylord Perry's audacious, tell-all autobiography, *Me and The Spitter*. IST USE. 1908 (*Baseball Magazine*, July; Edward J. Nichols). USAGE NOTE. Francis C. Richter (*Richter's History and Records of Base Ball*, 1914, p.268; Peter Morris) credited Mike Donlin with being responsible for the term "spitter." 2. A spitball pitcher. " 'Spitters,' as the 'spit ball' artists are called, are very slow in their motions" (*Philadelphia Evening Times*, reprinted in *The Sporting Life*, Dec. 12, 1908; Peter Morris).

spittist A spitball pitcher. "Elmer Stricklett, who always has been given credit for being the first of the spittists" (*The Washington Post*, Apr. 27, 1913; Peter Morris).

splash *hist.* 1. *n.* A batted ground ball. IST USE. 1907 (*New York Evening Journal*, May 4; Edward J. Nichols). 2. *v.* To hit a ground ball. IST USE. 1915 (*Baseball Magazine*, December, p.71; Edward J. Nichols).

splash hit A home run hit into McCovey Cove beyond the right-field fence in the home park of the San Francisco Giants. Most of the park's splash hits were from the bat of Barry Bonds. Also known as a "splash ball."

splinter A member of the splinter squad.

splinter squad Players on the bench.

split 1. *v.* To win one game and lose the other in a doubleheader; e.g., "The Yankees split a pair." 2. *n.* One win and one loss in a doubleheader; e.g., "The Yankees salvaged a split by winning the second game." 3. *n.* A doubleheader. "We wanted to play a split tomorrow instead of today" (Baltimore Orioles manager Mike Hargrove, quoted in *The Baltimore Sun*, July 30, 2000). 4. *n.* Short for *split-fingered*

fastball. "Some guys . . . have hurt their elbows throwing a split" (Sammy Ellis, quoted in *The Baltimore Sun*, Apr. 12, 2000).

split-admission doubleheader Syn. of *separate-admission doubleheader.*

split contract A contract in which a player will receive a stipulated salary while on the roster of a major-league team but a different (usually lower) salary for time spent on a minor-league roster.

split doubleheader Syn. of *separate-admission doubleheader.*

split-finger Syn. of *split-fingered fastball.*

split-fingered fastball An off-speed pitch gripped between the index and middle fingers which are held far apart and parallel to, rather than across the seams of, the ball, which travels straight but drops suddenly and sharply just before reaching the plate. The pitcher's grip is "on top of the ball," and the pitch varies from the *forkball* in that the ball is held toward the end of the fingers and thrown harder. The thumb pushes the ball between the fingers, the elbow is snapped violently, and the ball appears to "tumble" out from between the fingers, which has the effect of slowing the ball's velocity without altering the pitcher's fastball arm speed or motion. The ball sinks after falling out of the strike zone. The pitch is thrown harder than the standard changeup, but slower than the pitcher's regular fastball. A good split-fingered fastball results in "missed swings and ground balls" (Tom Verducci, *Sports Illustrated*, March 31, 1997). The split-fingered fastball was invented by Fred Martin, perfected by Bruce Sutter in the late 1970s, popularized by pitching coach Roger Craig in the early 1980s, and thrown by Mike Scott and Jack Morris in the mid- to late 1980s. The extent to which Craig taught his San Francisco Giants the pitch was reflected in the 1987 spring-training line that the intertwined "SF" on the players' hats actually stood for "split-fingered." The pitch has created some confusion, as others in the game periodically declare that it is "nothing more than a [fill in the blank]." Jerry Howarth (*Baseball Lite*, 1986) defined it as "a pitch five major league pitching coaches call a fork ball, five others call a spitter, six more recognize as a changeup, and ten others won't recognize at all." Joe Garagiola has termed it a "fast forkball." Billy Martin (*Billyball*, 1987) insisted that it is nothing new, just a "variation of the forkball." Syn. *split*, 4; *splitter*; *split-finger*; *pitch of the 1980s.* Sometimes spelled "split-finger fastball."

split season A baseball season divided into two halves.

split squad A spring-training team comprising part of a team's roster, esp. when the team plays exhibition games in two different locales on the same day. Abbrev. *SS*, 3.

splitter Syn. of *split-fingered fastball*.

split the plate To pitch a ball over the middle of home plate. IST USE. 1909 (Zane Grey, *The Short-Stop*, p.285; Edward J. Nichols).

split time To play a position on an alternating basis with another player.

spoiler **1.** One who gets in the way of a victory or an important personal achievement, such as a batter who gets a hit to break up a no-hitter. **2.** A team with no chance of winning a division title that defeats a team vying for the title or becomes a factor in the pennant race. "A spoiler is a non-contender. Being a non-contender in September is not where we want to be. But . . . if you win, being a spoiler is fun" (Baltimore Orioles third base coach Tom Trebelhorn, quoted in *The Baltimore Sun*, Aug. 28, 2001).

spoking Diving by a baserunner when returning to a base (Jerry Weinstein and Tom Alston, *Baseball Coach's Survival Guide*, 1998, p.349).

***SPORT* Magazine Award** See *World Series Most Valuable Player Award*, 2.

sportscaster One who announces baseball and other games on radio and television. The term is a blend of "sports" and "broadcaster."

'Spos Short for *Expos*.

spot **1.** *v.* To pitch the ball to a particular part of the strike zone; to throw a particular pitch at a given time. "[Al Leiter] confused the [San Diego] Padres by spotting enough pitches on the outside corner" (*The New York Times*, Apr. 4, 2000). "Steve Kline's fastball is below average, but he spots it well" (*Sports Illustrated*, Oct. 14, 2002). **2.** *n.* The location

Sportscaster. Walter Johnson working as a broadcaster during the 1934 World Series. *Photograph by Joseph Baylor Roberts*

of a pitched ball as it passes through the strike zone. A good spot is one that keeps the batter off balance, such as one thrown to a corner of the strike zone. "I couldn't hit my spots today and you get hurt when you do that" (Sidney Ponson, quoted in *The Baltimore Sun*, Aug. 1, 1999). **3.** *n.* A player's position in the batting order. "[The Minnesota Twins] moved [Jacque] Jones back into the leadoff spot during spring training" (*Sports Illustrated*, Sept. 2, 2002). **4.** *n.* A place in the pitching rotation. "The Number 5 spot in the rotation is a problem" (*Sports Illustrated*, Apr. 4, 2005). See also *slot*, 3. **5.** *n.* A player's position in the field. Baltimore Orioles left fielder Melvin Mora (quoted in *Sports Illustrated*, June 23, 2003): "I'm much more relaxed out there every day in the same spot. People don't realize how exhausting it is to keep changing positions." **6.** *v./hist.* Syn. of *soak*, 2. "The privilege to 'spot' a man . . . trying to run a base, is a rare pleasure which is not incorporated within the rules and regulations of the National Game" (*Cedar Springs* [Mich.] *Wolverine Clipper*, Sept. 9, 1874; Peter Morris).

spot pitcher A pitcher with the ability to place the ball at different points in and around the strike zone.

spot reliever A relief pitcher who is used for a specific, usually short, assignment, such as finishing an inning or (in the case of a left-handed pitcher) facing a left-handed batter.

spot starter A pitcher who is not in the regular pitching rotation but is available to start on an irregular or interim basis.

spot-throw A throw to a particular spot rather than to another fielder. IST USE. 1935. "A throw made to a place rather than a player" (Ralph H. Barbour, *How to Play Better Baseball*, p.174; David Shulman).

spraddled stance *hist.* Syn. of *straddle stance*. IST USE. 1886. "The batsmen divide themselves naturally into two classes [stances]—the erect and the spraddled" (*St. Louis Post-Dispatch*, July 24; Peter Morris).

spray To hit the ball in any direction. "My style of hitting is to spray the field. I swing late on the fastball and go the opposite way, inside out, and pull the soft stuff" (Willie Wilson, quoted in *The New York Times*, Aug. 23, 1982).

spray chart A diagram of the baseball field that shows the location of each ball that a batter puts in play. See also *pitching chart*.

sprayer A spitball pitcher.

spray hitter A hitter with little power who is able to place the ball unpredictably to any part of the field as opposed to one who tends to hit to one part of the field; e.g., Tony Gwynn. "[Harvey Kuenn] said 'spray hitter'—meaning the hits had gone to all fields—saying it reflectively and not as a compliment but as a professional" (George Plimpton, *Out of My League*, 1961).

spray paint To be able to hit to different parts of the field (Larry Whiteside, *The Boston Globe*, July 10, 1983).

spring hitter A batter who is effective in spring training but fades when the regular season begins. "When curves shorten up and begin to break sharper, and when pitching arms round into shape and the elusive change of pace makes its appearance for the season . . . the sharper breaks and change of pace prevent the 'Spring hitter' from checking his long swing in time to keep from swinging at bad balls" (Jim Nasium, *The Sporting News*, Feb. 10, 1927; Peter Morris).

spring pitcher A pitcher who is effective only in the spring. "Cyrus [Perkins] is a great spring pitcher. He has more stuff on the ball in the spring [than] he has late in the sum-

mer" (*San Francisco Bulletin*, March 3, 1913; Gerald L. Cohen).

spring session *hist.* Syn. of *spring training*, 2. "McCarl betrayed a little overanxiousness . . . to have the spring session start as quickly as possible" (*San Francisco Bulletin*, Feb. 12, 1913; Gerald L. Cohen).

spring training 1. A program of conditioning, preparation, and exhibition play in warm climates that begins in late February and ends a day or two before Opening Day. Teams conduct spring training in camps located in Florida and Arizona and play their games in small ballparks in those states. Ira Berkow (*The New York Times*, Feb. 20, 1983) noted that spring training "has been said to symbolize almost everything from hope, rebirth, eternal youth, the American dream to the official start of the mating season . . . [while] affirming that the sophomore jinx is junk . . . [and] providing a stage for the veteran to show that there's still a dance in the old guy yet." IST USE. 1887. "Both the Chicago and Indianapolis teams will do their spring training at Hot Springs, Ark." (*St. Louis Globe-Democrat*, Oct. 28). USAGE NOTE. The

Spring training. Chicago Cubs pitcher Paul Derringer eats snow at wartime spring training camp in French Lick, Ind., March 21, 1944. *Bill Mead Collection*

practice of conducting preseason training camps preceded the use of the term "spring training"; e.g., "The Chicago Base Ball Club . . . will make a trip to New Orleans, principally for the purpose of early practice" (*Chicago Tribune*, Apr. 4, 1870; John Freyer). In the 1880s and later, spring training was referred to as "Southern trips"; e.g., "Southern trips became a fad with major League managers in the spring training of the Orioles in 1894" (*The Washington Post*, March 22, 1896; Barry Popik). **2.** The period during which spring training occurs. It is a time of unbridled optimism and heightened expectations. See also *preseason*. Syn. *spring session*.

EXTENDED USE. A metaphor for a preliminary event or period that does not count in the final outcome. "Spring training is not very important," was Hubert H. Humphrey's response to questions about the 1968 presidential primaries (*The New York Times*, May 30, 1968).

spy in the sky Syn. of *eye in the sky*.

squab squad A team of rookies and substitutes. IST USE. 1911. "While on the road with the 'squab squad' he slept for two nights in a Pullman berth with his right arm in the hammock, which he had been told was put there for the particular benefit of the baseball players" (Charles E. Van Loan, *The Big League*, p.199; David Shulman).

squander 1. *v.* For a relief pitcher to come in with a lead and leave or end the game with his team behind or the game tied. "John Rocker squandered a three-run lead in the top of the ninth" (*The Baltimore Sun*, May 6, 2000). **2.** *n.* Syn. of *blown save*. **3.** *v.* For a team to give up leads in games and standings.

square 1. *v.* To prepare to bunt. "Hall squared to bunt, a normal first pitch practice in the cage" (*Tampa Tribune*, Aug. 14, 1989). **2.** *n.* The baseball diamond., which is actually a square. **3.** *n./hist.* Home plate (1869–1899) before it became a five-sided pentagon in 1900.

square around For the batter to attempt to bunt by turning toward the pitcher and holding his bat parallel to an imaginary line connecting his feet. IST USE. 1954. "Square around so that your bat is in fair territory, at shoulder height, and bunt the top half of the ball so you will be sure to bunt the ball along the ground" (Mickey McConnell, *Elyria* [Ohio] *Chronicle Telegram*, June 1; Peter Morris).

square pitch *hist.* A pitch in early baseball that, under the Knickerbocker Rules, "required the pitcher to keep both feet on the ground when delivering the ball . . . with the arm swinging perpendicular and the hand passing below the knee . . . [so that] little latitude was given the pitcher" (St. Louis manager James A. Williams, quoted in *St. Louis Post-Dispatch*, Jan. 2, 1884; Peter Morris).

squares A game described by W. Montague (*The Youth's Encyclopaedia of Health, with Games and Play Ground Amusements*, 1838) as nearly identical to early baseball and rounders. According to David Block (*Baseball Before We Knew It*, 2005, pp.77, 202–3), it involved four bases laid out as a square and a "considerable distance" apart. Block noted that the Montague book is the only instance of the name "squares" being used as a pseudonym for baseball or rounders. Montague concluded, "There is nothing particular[ly] fascinating in this game."

square stance 1. A *batting stance* in which both of the batter's feet are the same distance from the inside line of the batter's box and in a line parallel to home plate and with the pitcher's mound. Compare *open stance*; *closed stance*. Syn. *parallel stance*; *even stance*; *straightaway stance*. **2.** The set position by which an infielder or outfielder faces the batter, his feet parallel and comfortably separated, with his weight on the balls of his feet, as the ball is delivered by the pitcher. Compare *drop-step stance*.

squawk 1. *v.* To protest. **2.** *n.* A protest. A section in Otto Vogel's book *Ins and Outs of Baseball* (1952) is titled "The Fine Art of the Squawk." He wrote, "The wise coach or captain seldom protests in the hope that an umpire might change a decision; his objective generally is to cultivate the ground for a better break the next time. This is a definite part of the game, and certainly not illegal or unsporting."

squeaker A low-scoring game won by one run, usually in a late inning; a pitchers' duel.

squeak past To win a low-scoring game by one run, usually in a late inning.

squeeze 1. *n.* Syn. of *squeeze play.* IST USE. 1906. "[Joe] Tinker and [Frank] Chance worked the 'squeeze' to perfection. The manager [Chance] was halfway home, when Joe laid down a pretty bunt toward third, giving [Joe] Ward all he could do to get the runner at first, without a chance to cut off the score at the plate" (*Chicago Tribune*, May 18; Peter Morris). USAGE NOTE. Norman Macht unearthed an undated newspaper clip that quoted *New York Evening Journal* writer Sam Crane claiming to have introduced the term "squeeze" when he saw the New York Highlanders use it in a spring exhibition game in Jackson, Miss., in 1905. 2. *v.* To attempt or make the squeeze play. IST USE. 1905. "[Ducky] Holmes tried to 'squeeze' in the run which would have won the game with a bunt, but it went foul" (*Chicago Tribune*, Aug. 20; Peter Morris). 3. *v.* For the plate umpire seemingly to reduce the size of the strike zone. "It's going to be tough enough to make this team without having some fat little umpire squeezing the plate on you" (pitcher Jack Armstrong, quoted in *Tampa Tribune*, March 14, 1989). See also *pinch*, 3. 4. *v.* To catch a fly ball. IST USE. 1867. "Addy out on the fly, squeezed by Wright" (*Daily National Intelligencer* [Washington, D.C.], July 29).

squeeze bunt Syn. of *squeeze play.*

squeeze off To execute; e.g., "Smith squeezed off a perfect one-hop throw to the plate."

squeeze play An offensive maneuver in which the batter tries to score the runner on third base by bunting neatly such that any play at the plate is avoided or delayed. It is usually attempted with less than two outs. See also *suicide squeeze; safety squeeze; double squeeze.* Syn. *squeeze*, 1; *squeeze bunt.* IST USE. 1905. "[New York Highlanders] manager [Clark] Griffith says he has a new one called the 'squeeze play,' which is working wonders" (*The Washington Post*, Apr. 9; Norman L. Macht). Supposedly, the play was mistakenly "invented" in 1904 when Willie Keeler bunted the ball after Jack Chesbro broke for home. USAGE NOTE. The term "squeeze play" originally referred to a suicide squeeze. ETYMOLOGY. Hy Turkin (*Baseball Almanac*, 1955) and Lee Allen (*The Hot Stove League*, 1955, p.113) stated that the squeeze play was first used by two Yale men (George Case and Dutch Carter) in a game against Princeton on June 16, 1894. They claimed that the squeeze play was introduced to the major leagues by New York Highlanders manager Clark Griffith in 1904 and probably named by him in 1905: "Griffith's famed 'squeeze play'" (*Chicago Tribune*, May 4, 1905; Peter Morris). Other versions aver that the squeeze play was introduced by Joe Yeager in Brooklyn in 1898 and by Cap Anson and King Kelly in Chicago in the 1880s. The *San Francisco Bulletin* (May 2, 1913, p.20; Gerald L. Cohen) reported that the squeeze play was a California invention: "Pete Lohman, one of the brainiest men baseball ever produced, being its author." EXTENDED USE. Any strategy intended to force a helpless opponent to choose between two undesirable options. "State Farm Bureau Avoids 'Squeeze Play' by Unions, Industry Group" (*Grand Rapids* [Mich.] *Press* headline, Aug. 12, 1942; Peter Morris).

squib 1. *v.* To bloop or hit the ball without much force, usually off the handle or the end of the bat. "Gary Carter . . . is fooled and squibs a soft semi-pop-up that falls like a feather into the Oriole third baseman's glove" (George F. Will, *Newsweek*, Apr. 14, 1986). 2. *n.* Short for *squibber.* IST USE. 1943. "A 'squib' is a ground ball which, generally hit with the end of the bat, has so much spring or English that instead of rolling true it dodges through the grass" (*Baseball Magazine*, January; David Shulman). 3. *n.* "A poorly hit ball that finds its way between infielders or is hit so slowly that the runner can beat the throw" (Orel Hershiser, *Out of the Blue*, 1989). See also *squibb*, 2. 4. *n.* A *Texas Leaguer*, 2 (H.L. Mencken, *The American Language*, Suppl. II, 1948, p.737).

squibb 1. A substitute; a poor player. IST USE. 1917 (*Spalding's Official Base Ball Guide*, p.87; Edward J. Nichols). 2. An early version of *squibber.* Syn. *squib*, 3. 3. "A kind of curve-pitched ball" (Edward J. Nichols, *An Annotated Dictionary of Baseball Terminology*, PhD dissertation, 1939, p.73).

squibber A spinning blooper or ground ball hit off the end of the bat that is difficult to field and often becomes an infield base hit; a scratch hit. Rod Kanehl (quoted in Leonard Shecter, *The Jocks*, 1969):"Baseball is a lot like life. The line drives are caught, the squibbers go for base hits. It's an unfair game." See also *squibbler*; *dribbler*. Syn. *squib*, 2.

squibbler An earlier synonym for *squibber*, which has replaced it. IST USE. 1930. "The sports writers call those little flies over the infield . . . 'squibblers'" (*Country Home*, August; David Shulman).

squirrel An eccentric player or flake. ETYMOLOGY. Perhaps a borrowing from car racing, where the term "squirrely" has been used to describe a car that is erratic or hard to handle.

SS **1.** Abbrev. for *shortstop*, 1. Sometimes *ss*. **2.** Abbrev. for *shortstop*, 2. Sometimes *ss*. **3.** Abbrev. for *split squad*.

stab **1.** *n.* A spectacular catch. "A brilliant one handed stab of [Cy] Seymour's long hit by [Jack] McCarthy" (*Chicago Tribune*, Apr. 23, 1905; Peter Morris). IST USE. 1902 (*The Sporting Life*, July 5, p.7; Edward J. Nichols). **2.** *v.* To make a spectacular or difficult catch of a batted ball; e.g., "Smith stabbed the ball after a long run." IST USE. 1908 (*New York Evening Journal*, May 27; Edward J. Nichols). **3.** *v.* An attempt to make a play; e.g., "Jones made a stab at fielding the line drive but it got away from him." **4.** *n./hist.* A batted ball. IST USE. 1908 (*Brooklyn Daily Eagle*, May 30; Edward J. Nichols).

stab and grab Descriptive of a defensive move in which a fielder makes a desperate attempt ("stab") to catch ("grab") the ball. "Pete instinctively lunged to his right, stretching his gloved left hand across his body. It was simply a 'stab and grab' attempt; on a ball that was hit that swiftly, an infielder could do little more than reach and hope it bounced right" (Dick Friendlich, *Relief Pitcher*, 1964; Charles D. Poe).

stabber **1.** A pitcher who stops his motion soon after removing the ball from his glove and moves his throwing arm straight down toward the ground away from his body. "Very few stabbers have much success—it breaks the rhythm of their arm moving in a circle" (Dan Jennings, quoted in Alan Schwarz, BaseballAmerica.com, Nov. 14, 2006). Syn. *plunger*; *sweeper*, 2. **2.** *hist.* A batter. IST USE. 1909 (*New York Evening Journal*, July 1; Edward J. Nichols).

stabilizer A minor leaguer who is not considered a prospect. "[Tony] Mounce is more of a stabilizer than a prospect" (Gerry Fraley, *Baseball America*, Apr. 28–May 11, 2003; Peter Morris).

stacking Racial (or other) segregation by position. Benjamin Margolis and Jane Allyn Piliavin (*Sociology of Sport Journal*, 1999, pp.16–39) conducted a sophisticated multivariate analysis of stacking in Major League Baseball.

stadium A large ballpark, open or domed, and oval, round, or U-shaped, surrounded by tiers of seats for thousands of spectators; e.g., Yankee Stadium, the first baseball park to use the term "stadium" in its name in 1923. IST USE. 1909. "Long before the game the newly remodeled Polo grounds were filled with a cheering crowd of enthusiasts that filled all the seats in the vast baseball stadium, except a few far back in the center-field stands" (*The Washington Post*, Apr. 16; Peter Morris). USAGE NOTE. According to Morris, around 1909, baseball clubs began to play in structures large enough to warrant the term "stadium." ETYMOLOGY. Ancient Greek semicircular course for 200-yard (185 meters) foot races with a tier of seats for spectators. The stadium of Herodis (originally constructed in 330 B.C.) was restored as Panathenaic (Athenian) Stadium for the 1896 Olympics in Athens. Harvard Stadium, the first large reinforced-concrete structure and the first large college sports venue, opened in 1903.

staff **1.** See *pitching staff*. **2.** *hist.* A baseball bat (Maurice H. Weseen, *A Dictionary of American Slang*, 1934).

stair-step **1.** *v.* To throw a series of higher and higher pitches. See also *up the ladder*, 1; *climb the ladder*, 1. **2.** *adj.* Done in a consecutive manner. "The 'Browns' were again put out in stair-step order" (*St. Louis Post-Dispatch*, May 20, 1875; Peter Morris).

stair-stepping The process by which a pitcher throws a series of higher and higher pitches. The idea is to keep throwing pitches higher in the strike zone until the umpire calls a ball and/or the batter swings at a pitch out of the strike zone. Syn. *stair-stuffing*.

stair-stuffing Syn. of *stair-stepping*.

stake 1. *n*. A piece of wood projecting 41½ feet out of the ground, representing one of the four bases set 60 feet apart in a rectangle in the Massachusetts game. Syn. *base*, 3. 2. *v*. To provide a lead; e.g., "The Red Sox staked Smith to a five-run lead in the second inning."

stakeball A practice baseball game for fields without fences. "What you do is set up stakes at an agreed-upon depth in the outfield, usually five from left to right. A ball that clears the stakes on the fly is a home run. A ball that clears the stakes on the bounce, i.e., with visible daylight beneath the ball, is a double. A ball that rolls through is a single. Anything that hits a stake is a triple. Anything that dies in the grass before reaching the stakes is out" (Merritt Clifton, personal communication, Dec. 6, 2005).

staketender *hist*. An infielder stationed near one of the four wooden stakes used as bases in the Massachusetts game.

stance 1. See *batting stance*. IST USE. 1906 (*The Sporting Life*, Jan. 6; Peter Morris). 2.

Stance. Frank Chance, at bat, with Pat Moran catching, 1909. *George Grantham Bain Collection, Library of Congress*

The set position taken by a fielder as the ball is about to be delivered by the pitcher. See also *square stance*, 2; *drop-step stance*. **3.** The position taken by the catcher before the pitch is delivered. Joe Gargan (*Athletic Journal*, May 1944) offered this advice: "With your right foot turned out at a 45-degree angle, it is easier to pivot for your throw. Don't spread your feet wide; it makes shifting slower and more difficult. . . . Keep low and spread out to offer a good target. . . . If your stance is too high, you may have difficulty in going after low balls. . . . Practice your stance constantly."

stand in 1. To come to the plate to bat; to face the pitcher. 2. To hold a batting stance without bailing out or stepping into the bucket; e.g., "There aren't many left-handed batters who like to stand in against a southpaw coming from the side."

standing O An ovation given by fans who stand and applaud a player who has distinguished himself. "[Chan Ho Park] retired the next three hitters, including two on strikeouts. He left to another standing O" (Tim Kurkjian, *Sports Illustrated*, Apr. 18, 1994, p.42).

standings The ranking of teams in a division based on their won-lost percentages at any given time. It also includes the number of games or half-games a team is behind the first-place team. Sometimes expressed as "standing." IST USE. 1881 (*New York Herald*, Sept. 12; Edward J. Nichols).

standing up Said of a runner coming into a base or scoring without sliding; e.g., "Smith came into second standing up." IST USE. 1908 (*New York Evening Journal*, Apr. 16; Edward J. Nichols).

stand in his tracks For a fielder to catch a fly ball without moving from his location prior to the pitch.

stand on your ear To be off balance.

stands 1. The raised seating area for the fans at a ballpark. Short for *grandstand*, 1. IST USE. 1881 (*New York Press*, June 1; Edward J. Nichols). 2. The fans in the grandstand. IST USE. 1907 (Burt L. Standish, *Dick Merriwell's Marvel*, p.243; Edward J. Nichols).

stand the gaff For an umpire to withstand criticism and hardships. "Umpire Hank

O'Day says he would rather stand the gaff of the ball players than undertake to pull the Cardinals out of the ruck [declining to be their manager]" (*The Washington Post*, Aug. 16, 1905). Harry "Steamboat" Johnson titled his 1935 autobiography *Standing the Gaff: The Life and Hard Times of a Minor League Umpire*. IST USE. 1905. "If they [two new umpires] can stand the gaff for a season they usually become valuable" (*The Sporting Life*, June 10; Peter Morris).

stand-up double A double in which the batter is able to reach second base without sliding.

stand-up slide Syn. of *pop-up slide*.

stand-up triple A triple in which the batter is able to reach third base without sliding.

stanza *hist.* Syn. of *inning*, 1. This is clearly sportswriter jargon brought in when the word "inning" has been used once too often. See also *canto*. IST USE. 1909 (*New York Evening Journal*, July; Edward J. Nichols).

star 1. *n.* A player with clear preeminence. There is no official star designation in baseball, but those who are stars seem able to make it evident. See also *superstar*. IST USE. 1880 (*Brooklyn Daily Eagle*, Aug. 12; Edward J. Nichols). 2. *v.* To assume the role of an outstanding player; e.g., to "star" in a series. IST USE. 1890 (*New York Evening Post*, May 12; Edward J. Nichols).

starboard Descriptive of a right-handed pitcher. IST USE. 1908. "Starboard slinger" (*New York Evening Journal*, March 11; Edward J. Nichols*)*. ETYMOLOGY. From the nautical term for the right forward side of a boat.

starboarder A right-handed pitcher.

stare For a player holding the ball to look at a baserunner in such a manner as to convince him that he probably would not be able to take the next base and that he should head back toward the base he is occupying. "Dwight Evans bounced back to the mound, where [Ron] Darling made the play to first base after staring [Jim] Rice back to second" (*The New York Times*, Oct. 20, 1986).

Stargell Rule An unenforced rule that prohibits opposing players from engaging in *fraternization*. Pittsburgh Pirates first base-

man Willie Stargell was so given to chatting with runners who stopped at his station that some players and writers facetiously named the rule after him (Rich Marazzi, *The Rules and Lore of Baseball*, 1980).

Stargell Star A gold "merit badge" doled out by Pittsburgh Pirates first baseman Willie Stargell to teammates in recognition of various on-field achievements during the Pirates' championship season of 1979. The stars were sewn to the players' caps, either between the horizontal stripes of the "pillbox" caps, or on the bills. Stargell later introduced stars with a small letter "s" in the center, but the merit badges lasted just a few seasons.

star-spangled game The game of baseball, the national game. IST USE. 1910 (*Baseball Magazine*, April, p.24; Edward J. Nichols).

start 1. *v.* To be in the lineup at the beginning of the game. 2. *n.* The appearance of a starting pitcher. "You have some good starts and some bad starts. That's the territory of a starting pitcher" (Erik Bedard, quoted in *The Baltimore Sun*, Apr. 19, 2005). 3. *n.* The beginning part of a baseball season for a player or team, usually characterized as being either "fast" or "slow," or "good" or "bad," in relation to a given number of games. 4. *v.* For a baserunner to break with the pitch, or for a manager to signal a baserunner to do so.

starter 1. A player who begins the game in the starting lineup. 2. A team's regular player at a given position. 3. Syn. of *starting pitcher*. IST USE. 1912 (*New York Tribune*, Oct. 8; Edward J. Nichols).

starting lineup The players who begin a game and remain in place until the first substitute is brought into the game.

starting pitcher The pitcher who starts the game for his team and who cannot legally be replaced until he has either retired the first batter or put him on base, unless the umpire determines that the pitcher has become incapacitated. Abbrev. *SP*. Syn. *starter*, 3.

starting rotation See *rotation*, 1.

Staten Island sinker A spitball. Credit for this coinage is generally given to pitching coach George Bamberger, a native of Staten Island, N.Y.: "Bambi . . . has a reputation as a teacher of ball-doctoring. The spitter is sometimes called the Staten Island sinker in his honor" (*Sports Illustrated*, June 7, 1982).

stathead Someone who is obsessed with baseball statistics. Compare *seamhead.*

station 1. A *base*, 2. "[Bill Sweeney is] one of the best guardians of the second station" (*San Francisco Bulletin*, March 6, 1913; Gerald L. Cohen). "When [Roberto] Alomar is in the vicinity, the ball is as good as caught and delivered to the proper station on time" (*The Baltimore Sun*, Aug. 4, 1995). IST USE. 1860 (*Beadle's Dime Base-Ball Player*; Edward J. Nichols). ETYMOLOGY. The term is borrowed from rounders: "Four other stations are marked with pegs stuck into the ground, topped with a piece of paper, so as to be readily seen" (Charles Peverelly, *The Book of American Pastimes*, 1866; Peter Morris). 2. The defensive position assigned to a player. IST USE. 1897. "Henry Ashcroft . . . has covered several positions, but left field is regarded as his permanent station" (*Brooklyn Eagle*, Oct. 24; Peter Morris).

station keeper *hist.* Syn. of *baseman.* IST USE. 1914. "This throw was so high that the station keeper was forced to stretch for it" (Burt L. Standish, *Brick King, Backstop*; David Shulman).

station-to-station 1. Said of a baseball strategy that puts runners on base and moves them *one base at a time*, while eschewing the long ball. Syn. *base-to-base.* 2. Said of a slow and/or unaggressive baserunner. "[Todd Hundley] is as station-to-station as they come" (STATS Inc., *The Scouting Notebook 2001*; Peter Morris).

statistics Numerical facts and data, the lifeblood of baseball. As the most statistical of sports, baseball is awash in both amateur and professional statisticians. All teams and both major leagues maintain their own statistical records. "Veteran baseball men estimate that statistics account for some 30 per cent of the interest in the game" (*Christian Science Monitor*, Feb. 18, 1944). "Baseball statistics gave many of us our first sense of mastery, our first (and for some of us our last) sense of what it feels like to really understand something, and to know more about something than our par-

ents did" (George F. Will, *The Washington Post*, Apr. 7, 1983). Will later observed (*Newsweek*, Apr. 14, 1986), "The stuff of baseball, its crystalline essence, is statistics." Syn. *stats.*

statistorian One who studies baseball by combining statistics and history. The term, a blend of "statistician" and "historian," was coined by L. Robert "Bob" Davids, one of the founders of the Society for American Baseball Research.

stat rat A player who pays too much attention to his individual performance (Garret Mathews, *Can't Find a Dry Ball*, 2002).

stats Short for *statistics.*

STATS Inc. A Chicago-based corporation that collects its own raw baseball scoresheets and uses data compiled from these scoresheets to produce and sell products to teams, media, and other interested parties. It formerly published various annual statistical publications, such as *Major League Handbook*, *Player Profiles*, and *Baseball Scoreboard.*

Statue of Liberty A batter who stands at the plate and takes a called third strike. See also *wooden Indian*, 1. IST USE. 1937 (*Pittsburgh Press*, Jan. 11; Edward J. Nichols).

stay alive 1. To be able to continue playing; e.g., a team can "stay alive" by winning the sixth game of the World Series. "We went on to win that game in extra innings on a homer by Joe Ferguson to stay alive" (*Baseball Digest*, Jan. 1984). 2. For a batter to continue batting. "After repeatedly fouling off pitches to stay alive, [Johnny] Damon lined out to center field" (*The Baltimore Sun*, Oct. 14, 2004). 3. For a baserunner to get caught in a rundown long enough to allow a teammate on third base to break for home. "[Dustin] McGowan stepped off the pitching rubber to get the Oriole [Brian Roberts] in a rundown. Roberts stayed alive while [Cory] Patterson took a sizable lead off third" (*The Baltimore Sun*, May 24, 2007).

stay back 1. For a batter to be patient and wait on a pitch, allowing him to see the ball as long as possible. A right-handed batter will try to "stay back" to hit the ball to right field; by "staying back," a batter does not reach for off-speed pitches and lose power. It requires the batter to have strong hands and great balance, with his weight on the back leg. "I'm staying back, letting the ball get to me instead of trying to go out and get the ball" (Derek Jeter, quoted in *Sports Illustrated*, June 7, 2004). See also *stay inside the ball*. Syn. *stay behind the ball*, 1; *stay with the ball*. **2.** For a pitcher to keep his weight on the pivot foot longer so that the arm catches up with the body; to hold back the shoulder of the pitching arm during the stride toward the plate to attain maximum momentum; to get "on top of the ball" and not hurry to the plate. Compare *get under the ball*, 1.

stay behind the ball **1.** Syn. of *stay back*, 1. **2.** For a pitcher to keep his hand behind the ball as it is thrown. "Before [Jonathan Papelbon] releases the ball, his right wrist is bent farther back than most pitchers', keeping his palm under the ball and his fingers entirely behind it" (Tom Verducci, *Sports Illustrated*, Oct. 1, 2007). **3.** For an outfielder who is about to throw the ball to grasp it with his fingers on the backside, rather than under, over, or off to one side of the ball, thereby maximizing the force and accuracy of the throw.

stay inside the ball For a batter to keep his hands close to his body and not get them out in front too fast so as to see the ball longer and to hit inside pitches to the opposite field or up the middle, rather than pulling the ball. Derek Jeter keeps his hands inside and hits the "inside" part of the ball with a shorter swing. "[Juan Gonzalez] has such great hands that he can stay inside the ball and drive it with power to all parts of the park" (*ESPN The Magazine*, March 18, 2002). See also *stay back*, 1.

"stay on" An instruction by a base coach to a runner who is approaching a base. "If a play is being made on the runner, but he need not slide, the coach moves toward the base, points at it, and calls 'stay on,' indicating a throw is coming" (O.H. Vogel, *Ins and Outs of Baseball*, 1952; Peter Morris).

stay on the ball For a batter to concentrate and focus on the pitched ball, keeping his head pointed at the pitch. "The second [pitch] was a good fastball away, and I just stayed on the ball and hit it the other way" (Darryl Strawberry, quoted in *The Baltimore Sun*, Oct. 13, 1996).

stay on top of the ball **1.** For a batter to try to hit the top half of the ball by driving it with the top hand coming over the bottom hand. The opposite of uppercutting, it results in line drives and ground balls. Compare *get under the ball*, 2. **2.** For a pitcher to keep his fingers on top (not on the sides) of the ball and his hand behind it as the ball is thrown. The term usually refers to the slider, which should be thrown with the index and middle fingers on top of the ball, but off-center. A pitcher who does not stay on top of the ball will tend to rush his delivery or overthrow.

stay tall For a pitcher to stand straight up and take advantage of his height, rather than crouching, on the mound before releasing the ball, allowing him to throw on a downward angle.

stay tall and fall For a pitcher to remain upright during his windup, his hands close to his chest (as if winding up in a phone booth), and allow gravity to take his body toward the plate rather than pushing off more strenuously lower to the ground. Compare *drop-and-drive*. (Alan Schwarz, BaseballAmerica .com, Nov. 14, 2006)

stay within oneself To know what one can do and cannot do on the field; to play within one's ability and not try to do more than one is capable of doing. "[The phrase] is baseball's first commandment. It means: Do not try to do things that strain your capacities and distort the smooth working of your parts— what players call 'mechanics'" (George F. Will, *Men at Work*, 1990).

stay with the ball Syn. of *stay back*, 1.

steady a pitcher To calm a pitcher's nerves; to settle him down, a task that the catcher, a coach, or the manager usually undertakes by talking to him on the mound. IST USE. 1914 (*New York Tribune*, Oct. 11; Edward J. Nichols).

steak Syn. of *rib-eye* (a play on RBI) (Tom Verducci, *Sports Illustrated*, June 15, 1998). ETYMOLOGY. A rib-eye is a large beefsteak cut from the outer, or eye, side of the ribs.

steal **1.** *v.* To advance safely to the next base by running as the pitcher goes into his delivery; to achieve a stolen base. IST USE. 1857. "Mr. Monson Hoyt . . . runs like a deer over the ground; oftentimes steals a run home while the ball is passing from the pitcher to the catcher" (*Porter's Spirit of the Times*, Feb. 7; Tom Shieber). **2.** *n.* The act of advancing a base by stealing. **3.** *n.* A *stolen base*. Abbrev. *S*, 3. IST USE. 1880 (*Chicago Inter-Ocean*, June 29; Edward J. Nichols). **4.** *v.* To detect and decipher a sign between two members of the opposing team.

steal and slam A variation of the *hit-and-run play*. John McGraw (*My Thirty Years in Baseball*, 1923, p.88) described the play: "The man on first would take a lead to actually steal the base. In that case, if the ball was a good one, the batter would slam at it. If the pitcher, expecting a hit and run, pitched out, the batter would simply let it go and take a chance on the runner stealing the base. The batter then would be in a better position than ever."

stealing 1. See *base stealing*. The desgination came much later than the act itself; according to John Grossman (*Sports Illustrated*, June 27, 1994), the term wasn't used until 1871. **2.** See *sign stealing*.

steam 1. The velocity of a pitch. IST USE. 1901 (Burt L. Standish, *Frank Merriwell's School Days*, p.251; Edward J. Nichols). **2.** The endurance of a pitcher (John B. Foster, in *Collier's New Dictionary of the English Language*, 1908).

steamer A fastball.

steamroll 1. For a baserunner to make crushing body contact with a fielder while sliding into a base; e.g., "Smith steamrolled the catcher with his hard slide." **2.** For one team to overwhelm another.

steel fingers The hands of an outfielder who struggles defensively.

Steinbrennerian Said of one who is loud, petulant, greedy, and free-spending, but who does not necessarily receive full value for his money, in the manner of New York Yankees owner George Steinbrenner. Bob Cook (*Flak Magazine*, Nov. 3, 2003) characterized "a Steinbrennerian pattern" as one of "frequent managerial firings, often-public head games with players and staff and big-money signings of players who melted under the stress." David Holahan (*Christian Science Monitor*,

Aug. 1, 1989) wrote: "Steinbrennerian? It's a run-on adjective. Besides, do we want to bestow such a linguistic laurel on a person who once called the third contest of a 162-game baseball season 'crucial'? . . . A Machiavellian mogul who hired and fired Billy Martin 7,536 times, or so it seems?"

Stengelese The colorful vocabulary, fractured English, scrambled syntax, incessant flow of speech, and implausible brand of double-talk spoken by Hall of Fame manager Casey Stengel, who combined "the most admirable qualities of the genius and the clown" (*The New York Times*, July 10, 1956). "By talking in the purest jabberwocky he [Stengel] has learned that he can avoid answering questions and at the same time leave his audience struggling against a mild form of mental paralysis" (Gayle Talbot, *San Francisco Call-Bulletin*, Feb. 1, 1954; Peter Tamony).

Stengelese is difficult to capture (sportswriter Red Smith once likened it to "picking up quicksilver with boxing gloves"), but here is an example from a 1958 Congressional hearing on baseball when Sen. Langer asked whether Stengel intended to keep monopolizing the world's championship in New York City (*The*

Stengelese. Casey Stengel, wearing sunglasses while playing for the Brooklyn Dodgers in 1916. *George Grantham Bain Collection, Library of Congress.*

Congressional Record, July 9, 1958):

"Well, I will tell you. I got a little concern yesterday in the first three innings when I saw the three players I had gotten rid of, and I said when I lost nine what am I going to do and when I had a couple of my players I thought so great of that did not do so good up to the sixth inning I was more confused but I finally had to go and call on a young man in Baltimore that we don't own and the Yankees don't own him, and he is doing pretty good, and I would actually have to tell you that I think we are more the Greta Garbo type now from success. We are being hated, I mean, from the ownership and all, we are being hated. Every sport that gets too great or one individual but if we made 27 cents and it pays to have a winner at home, why would not you have a good winner in your own park if you were an owner? That is the result of baseball. An owner gets most of the money at home and it is up to him and his staff to do better or they ought to be discharged."

Stengelese has been applied to others. "[San Francisco] Giants manager Tom 'Clancy' Sheehan is from the old school of ambiguity in naming names. Clancy's Stengelese often out-Stengels Casey" (Art Rosenbaum, *San Francisco Chronicle*, July 11, 1960; Peter Tamony).

stepball A game played in Philadelphia, similar to *stoopball*.

step in To get settled in the batter's box. "[J.R. Richard] had something none of them had—that little wildness that just made hitters plain afraid to step in against him" (Eric Gregg and Marty Appel, *Working the Plate*, 1990, p.170).

step in the bucket To step back or pull away from home plate with one's front foot while batting. A right-handed batter so afflicted will step toward third base. Though it is normally considered poor form as a way of batting, some good batters have gotten away with it. "You can't hit very well if you step in the bucket" (Morris Shirts, *Warm Up For Little League Baseball*, 1971, 1976). Most stepping in the bucket occurs when the batter is fooled by an off-speed pitch and shifts his weight and foot in anticipation of a fastball. See also *foot in the bucket*, 1. 1ST USE. 1908. "When I broke into professional base ball I

was a right-handed hitter, and I used to step 'in the bucket' every time I took a swing" (Spike Shannon, quoted in *The Sporting News*, March 5; Peter Morris).

stepoff The act of a pitcher who backs off the rubber to keep a runner close to his base or to get a read on the runner's intentions.

step off the rubber For a pitcher to remove himself from the act of pitching. A pitcher must have his pivot foot in contact with the rubber while pitching, but he may take his foot off it to attempt to pick off a baserunner, take a time out, or confer with other players or the manager.

step on his toes For a pitcher to be unable to field a bunt (Al Schacht, *Al Schacht Dope Book*, 1944, p.45).

step on the plate 1. To score. A baserunner who touches home plate gains a run for the offensive team. 2. For a batter to commit an infraction and be declared out by the plate umpire when hitting a ball (either fair or foul) while one or both feet are in contact with home plate.

step out of the box For a batter to remove himself from the batter's box. If this is done with the umpire's approval before the pitcher begins his windup, the pitcher must wait until the batter returns to the box. If the batter steps out after the windup has begun or without approval from the umpire, the pitcher can deliver the ball and it will count as an official pitch and be called a strike or a ball.

stepper The shoe of a player (Bob Hertzel, *Baseball Digest*, Jan. 1987).

stepping foot The front foot that a pitcher uses to advance his delivery, as contrasted with the *pivot foot* which stays in contact with the rubber. Since 2007, the pitcher's stepping foot in the windup position may be on, in front of, to the side of, or behind the rubber, and the pitcher is permitted to step to the side during his delivery. The stepping foot of a right-handed pitcher is his left foot and that of a left-handed pitcher is his right foot. Syn. *striding foot*, 3; *free foot*.

step up to the plate For a batter to enter the batter's box. EXTENDED USE. The phrase is applied to anyone who is willing to enter the fray and get into the action, to confront a problem, or to make a crucial decision. "There's nothing more important that a federal judge can do than to step up to the plate and play an active role in trying to reduce violent crime" (Baltimore mayor Martin O'Malley, urging federal judges to take on cases involving street crime, quoted in *The Baltimore Sun*, Feb. 19, 2000).

steroid A fat-soluble organic compound with specific physiological action; specif., anabolic steroid, a synthetic derivative of testosterone used by some ballplayers to enhance performance by stimulating muscle growth and thereby increasing their weight and strength, and to help players recover from injuries more quickly. Steroids can be rubbed on the body or swallowed, but are usually injected. The primary effect of steroid use in baseball is an increase in the number of home runs. Using steroids in the United States is illegal without a prescription. Although Major League Baseball banned steroids in 1991, the commissioner's office and team front offices took a "see-no-evil" approach to steroids, and the players' union refused to submit to a testing program. Congressional hearings on steroid use in baseball were held on March 17, 2005. See also *Steroid Era*. Syn. *roid*.

steroid-adjusted number A statistic proposed by Jim Bouton (*The New York Times*, Apr. 1, 2007) that would take into account the effect of steroids on the number of a player's home runs as determined by a "blue ribbon panel." The statistic would be placed in parentheses in the record books next to the actual number of home runs hit. Abbrev. *SAN*.

Steroid Era The period lasting from approximately 1985 through the release of the Mitchell Report in Dec. 2007, during which many of baseball's foremost players were either accused of or thought to be using illegal performance-enhancing anabolic steroids. Steroid usage in major-league baseball began around 1983, and nonprescription distribution and possession of anabolic steroids became a crime in the United States in Nov. 1988. Major League Baseball added steroids to its list of banned substances (but without testing) in June 1991. However, steroid usage

in baseball became widespread after the 1994–1995 work stoppage; the effect of its use increased until its peak in 1999–2001. Baseball instituted its first random testing program, with penalties, in Apr. 2001 (for minor-league players) and 2004 (for major-league players). Major League Baseball and the players union agreed on a strengthening testing policy in Jan. 2005. Tom Verducci (*Sports Illustrated*, Feb. 1, 2005) wrote, "The Steroid Era as we knew it—the days when anyone could juice up with impunity, which meant everyone was under suspicion—appears to be over. Maybe now we will allow ourselves to believe that what we see is genuine. Time and an effective testing program will tell." Thomas Boswell (*The Washington Post*, Sept. 1, 2007) wrote, "The Steroid Era is over in baseball. A period that began almost 20 years ago has quietly receded while few were watching." See also *steroid*.

Stetson hitter A bad hitter; one who hits his hat size.

Steve Blass disease A condition by which a pitcher suddenly loses his ability to throw strikes, inexplicably issues an extraordinary number of bases on balls, fears home plate, and/or suffers from a complete loss of control. Named for the Pittsburgh Pirates pitcher who lost his control in 1973 by issuing 84 walks and hitting 12 batters in 88⅔ innings. In 1972, it had taken him 249⅔ innings to issue 84 walks. The medical term is "focal occupational dystonia," a condition that causes victims (such as golfers and pianists) to have unwanted, involuntary movements in the middle of their performances. Victims of the disease have included Kevin Saucier, Joe Cowley, Steve Trout, Bruce Ruffin, and Rick Ankiel.

Steve Sax disease Sudden inability for a fielder to make routine throws. Named for the Los Angeles Dodgers second baseman who became plagued by wild throws. Allen St. John (*Village Voice*, Aug. 17, 1999; Peter Morris) wrote, "In the field, [Chuck Knoblauch is] even more of an enigma. One year he wins a Gold Glove, the next he comes down with Steve Sax Disease . . . making throwing errors that would draw groans at a company softball game."

Stevie Syn. of *goat's beard*. ETYMOLOGY. Named for its inventor, Los Angeles Dodgers catcher Steve Yeager.

STF Abbrev. for *stuff rating*.

stick 1 *n.* A baseball bat. "My biggest asset for any team I play on is going to be the stick in my hands" (Chris Hoiles, quoted in *The Baltimore Sun*, June 28, 1998). 1ST USE. 1868 (*New York Herald*, Aug. 4; Edward J. Nichols). **2.** *n.* A hitter. "They need a left-hand stick and I'll be a good left-hand stick" (Dwight Smith, quoted in *The Baltimore Sun*, June 17, 1994). **3.** *v.* To act as a hitter. "It is his [McCarl's] ability to stick wherein the doubt centers" (*San Francisco Bulletin*, March 12, 1913; Gerald L. Cohen). "[Chicago Cubs manager Fred] Mitchell, the gambler, inserted Turner Barber, left hander, to stick for Chuck Deal" (Burt Whitman, *Boston Herald and Journal*, Sept. 8, 1918; Peter Morris). **4.** *v.* To establish oneself as a major leaguer; to remain on a team's roster. 1ST USE. 1902. "[Joseph Sugden] was transferred to St. Louis, but did not stick" (*Reach's Official American League Base Ball Guide*; Peter Morris).

Stick, The Nickname for *Candlestick Park*.

stick a fork in him To determine that a pitcher is to be relieved. According to Frank Gibbons (*Baseball Digest*, May 1959), "It means the man is done for the day. Bushed. Tired. Exhausted." ETYMOLOGY. The culinary practice of sticking a fork in a turkey or roast to determine if it is done.

stickball A variant of baseball commonly played on city streets or other restricted areas with a broomstick or similar piece of wood and a rubber ball. The game usually requires an elaborate and very specific set of ground rules; each neighborhood or subdivision of a neighborhood develops its own local customs (e.g., the blue Ford is a double if it is hit on the fly, but an out if the ball hits it on the bounce). Home plate and the bases are usually sewer manhole covers; a chalked or painted box on a wall is the strike zone; foul lines are parked cars or walls; bleachers are roofs; fire escapes, the mezzanine. A game requires at least two players. Caught pops and flies and cleanly fielded grounders are outs; a ball that breaks a window or lands on a porch is an automatic out (and probably means the game is over). Distance determines the status of a hit and is often measured in sewers; e.g., passing two sewers is good, and three is fantastic. Reminiscing on Willie Mays' custom of playing stickball outside the Polo Grounds in New York, an old-timer told sportswriter Dave Anderson (*San Francisco Chronicle*, May 17, 1972; Peter Tamony), "I used to play stickball with Willie up on the hill. He used to hit five sewers." Mays expressed his nostalgia for New York in 1959 when he told sportswriter Jimmy Cannon (*San Francisco Call-Bulletin*, May 15; Peter Tamony) about the odd customs of San Francisco: "The kids don't play stickball here. The streets are too hilly." There are three basic forms of stickball: "fast-pitch" (or *wall-ball*), played in a schoolyard or parking lot where there is a big wall for the "backstop" and open space for the field; "slow-pitch" (or *pitching in*) in which the pitcher bounces the ball to the batter; and "fungo" in which the batter tosses the ball up and hits it either on the fly or after one or more bounces. "Let's face it, when you talk about streetplay, stickball is the first thing that comes to mind. There are stickball leagues, reunions, web sites, references in poetry and song (like Billy Joel's tune, 'Keeping the Faith'), movie scenes, folklore; a whole schtick for the stick! This is the crown jewel of American urban sport culture" (Streetplay.com). 1ST USE. 1934. "Stick ball is a new name to me. . . . [It] is a third cousin to baseball, played with a soft ball and a broomstick on the streets of New York. It is one of the most popular pastimes of boys gathered in various settlement houses. With sand lots getting scarcer and scarcer the youth still find a way to emulate Babe Ruth and get their start in baseball" (George Daley, *New York Herald-Tribune*, Apr. 19; Peter Morris).

sticker 1. *hist.* Syn. of *batter*, 1. 1ST USE. 1884. "A colored boy in uniform takes the bat from each sticker, and hands it to him when his time to go to the bat comes" (*Cincinnati News-Journal*, May 13; Peter Morris). **2.** A player who is good enough to make the team. "Harry Heilmann is one of the likeliest looking stickers on the Portland club" (*San Francisco Bulletin*, March 25, 1913; Gerald L. Cohen).

sticking Hitting. "Here's to Heine Zim [Zimmerman]—we all like to see him play, and can forgive many a 'boner' for his timely sticking" (*The Washington Post*, Sept. 7, 1913; Peter Morris). IST USE. 1902 (*The Sporting Life*, July 5, p.11; Edward J. Nichols).

"stick it in his ear" Nasty but common advice given from the bench jockey to his teammate on the mound to hit the batter in the head. It is stronger than "dust him off" or "knock him down." USAGE NOTE. The phrase is not to be used lightly. Joe Williams (*San Francisco News*, Oct. 12, 1953; Peter Tamony) wrote, "The Yankees came out of the Series with reduced respect for Jackie Robinson. They claim the Brooklyn star deliberately tried to foment ill feelings when he hung the 'stick-it-in-his-ear' crack on [Casey] Stengel. Pressed for details, Robinson finally had to admit the information came to him second hand from 'several players.'" EXTENDED USE. Used impolitely in other walks of life.

stickman *hist.* Syn. of *batter*, 1. IST USE. 1911. "[Pitcher Dolly Gray] is a southpaw and when going right is a terror to the best stickman" (Alfred H. Spink, *The National Game*, 2nd ed, 1911, p.133).

stickpin A batter who chokes up on the bat. The term was used frequently by Casey Stengel to the point that it was identified as part of his "private lexicon" (Frederick G. Lieb, *Comedians and Pranksters of Baseball*, 1958).

sticks The minor leagues, in reference to the less-populous areas of the country where the lower-level teams played. IST USE. 1914. "It's us fellers down here in the sticks that knows how to get the work out of a man" (Ring W. Lardner, *Saturday Evening Post*, July 25; Peter Morris). ETYMOLOGY. According to the *New York American* (Feb. 15, 1921; Steve Steinberg), the term was originated by New York Giants catcher Chief Meyers, who was looking out the window of a Pullman as the train passed through a Southern countryside "besprinkled with tall, skinny, pine

trees" and remarked, "This is sure 'way, 'way down in the sticks." Thereafter, he referred to a minor leaguer who came from a lesser league as being from "down in the sticks." The term eventually was applied to all minor leagues, although Meyers originally meant an area where there was plenty of timber.

sticksmith *hist.* Syn. of *batter*, 1. "Some guy named Cobb is leading the American league sticksmiths. Yes. 'Some GUY' is right" (*San Francisco Bulletin*, May 31, 1913; Gerald L. Cohen). IST USE. 1910 (*Baseball Magazine*, May, p.52; Edward J. Nichols).

stickster *hist.* Syn. of *batter*, 1. "[Bill] Hogan was a good stickster when he graduated into the big circle" (*San Francisco Bulletin*, Apr. 24, 1913; Gerald L. Cohen).

stickwork Hitting ability; skill in using a baseball bat. "[Rogers Hornsby's] fielding, throwing and double play making came close to matching his stickwork" (Harry Grayson, *They Played the Game*, 1944, p.136). IST USE. 1886. "It was a batting game from the start, each team doing great stick work" (*Bangor* [Maine] *Whig and Courier*, Sept. 3; Peter Morris).

stiff back The excuse of an infielder who does not or cannot bend down to field a grounder.

stile Short for *turnstile*.

stile boy *hist.* One who helped regulate the turnstiles and assisted the turnstile operator with the count. Stile boys were paid 75 cents per day in the 19th century (Jonathan Fraser Light, *The Cultural Encyclopedia of Baseball*, 1997).

sting 1. To hit the ball hard or sharply. "[Willie] Wilson attributes his hitting the ball more solidly this year—'I'm stinging it'—to necessity" (*The New York Times*, Aug. 23, 1982). IST USE. 1906 (*The Sporting Life*, March 10, p.6; Edward J. Nichols). 2. *hist.* Syn. of *soak*, 2. 3. To win (*The Sporting Life*, Nov. 29, 1913).

sting ball 1. A ball thrown so hard it stings the glove hand of the player catching it; e.g., "Smith throws sting balls because his arm is so strong." 2. *hist.* Syn. of *soak ball*. "The impact of a hard ball thrown with all the force of a good right arm wasn't funny. In some sections the boys called this 'stinging,' and the game was sometimes known as 'sting ball'" (*Bismarck* [N.D.] *Daily Tribune*, Apr. 1, 1887).

stinger 1. A hard-hit ball. IST USE. 1865. "Zeller sent a stinger to centre field over O'Brien's head" (*Brooklyn Eagle*, Aug. 15; Peter Morris). 2. The sharp-pointed sensation in the hands of a batter who hits an inside pitch. 3. *hist.* The impact of a hard-thrown ball during a soaking.

stinker *hist.* A *Texas Leaguer*, 2.

stir a breeze To strike out.

stirrup socks The team-colored socks with a loop at the bottom that are worn over white sanitary socks. The stirrups effectively keep the colored socks in place without the discomfort of having to wear two pairs of socks. Stirrup socks were introduced at the beginning of the 20th century as a means of emphasizing team uniformity, and until the 1980s players tended to pull them high up such that only the loop showed. Most current major leaguers wear their pants down to their ankles, leaving little of the stirrup socks visible. Those who choose to wear their pants high enough to show the socks are donning single-layered, solid-colored hose.

stitch-ball A slowly pitched ball. IST USE. 1915. "[The third pitch] was Rube's wide, slow, tantalizing 'stitch-ball,' as we call it, for the reason that it came so slow a batter could count the stitches" (Zane Grey, *The Redheaded Outfield and Other Stories*, p.122; David Shulman).

stitched lemon The *yellow baseball* experi-

mented with in 1938. "The 'stitched lemon' for which greater visibility, hence greater safety, is claimed, was used for the first time in a major league game" (*Milwaukee Journal*, Aug. 2, 1938; Peter Morris).

stitched potato The baseball. "This [holding a baseball] is what we call the stitched potato" (Joe DiMaggio, to then-girlfriend Dorothy Arnold, quoted in Richard Ben Cramer, *Joe DiMaggio: The Hero's Life*, 2000, p.130).

stobball An early English game played with a bat or club that may have been a variant of stool-ball or golf. David Block (*Baseball Before We Knew It*, 2005, pp.119–22) noted that despite several literary references dating back to 1525, "neither historians nor etymologists can agree" on what the game was and how it was played. Also spelled "stoball."

stolen base A base gained by a runner advancing to it while the pitcher is in his motion, unaided by a base hit, putout, error, force out, fielder's choice, passed ball, wild pitch, or balk. The success of the play hinges on catching the defensive team off guard. A stolen base is officially credited to the runner. Prior to 1886, stolen bases were not officially recorded. Between 1886 and 1897, stolen bases were credited whenever a runner advanced an extra base on a hit or on an out if there was some daring involved or a "palpable attempt" was made to retire the runner. *Total Baseball* (7th ed., 2001) credits Ned Cuthbert of the Keystones of Philadelphia with the first stolen base, on July 28, 1865; however, Tom Shieber (personal communication, Nov. 13, 2001) cites an example of an attempted steal of third base as reported in the *New York Clipper* (Aug. 9, 1856). Abbrev. *SB*. Syn. *steal*, 3; *theft*; *bag*, 3; *swipe*, 1. IST USE. 1889 (*Trenton* [N.J.] *Times*, July 8; Edward J. Nichols).

stolen base average The proportion of a player's stolen base attempts that are successful, computed by dividing successful stolen bases by attempts. Abbrev. *SBA*.

stolen base runs Syn. of *base-stealing runs*. Abbrev. *SBR*.

stolen base wins Syn. of *base-stealing wins*. Abbrev. *SBW*.

stone glove A poor defensive player.

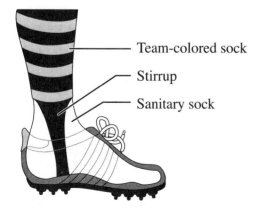

Team-colored sock

Stirrup

Sanitary sock

Stirrup socks.

stone hands The hands of a poor fielder. "The innings flew by to the accompaniment of . . . a flurry of witticisms in the press rows about Willie Davis's attack of stone hands in Los Angeles" (Roger Kahn, *The Boys of Summer*, 1972; Charles D. Poe).

stonewall *hist.* **1.** *n.* An unusually tight infield from which very few batted balls escape. The archetypical stonewall was that of the 1880s Chicago White Stockings, comprising first baseman Cap Anson, second baseman Fred Pfeffer, shortstop Ned Williamson, and third baseman Tom Burns. IST USE. 1878. "The visitors seldom got past the 'stone wall' of the infield" (*Cincinnati Enquirer*, May 10; Peter Morris). **2.** *v.* To bat defensively. A batter who tries not to get a hit, or tries to buy some time, is said to "stonewall." ETYMOLOGY. From cricket, when one merely protects the wicket rather than trying to score.

stool-ball A primitive stick-and-ball game that, according to some sources, dates from the 12th century in England. David Block (personal communication, June 2005) confirmed the earliest sighting of stool-ball in the margin notes of a 1450 manuscript by John Myrc, a canon at Lilleshall Monastery; in the notes, an unknown scribe explained that among the games forbidden in churchyards as early as 1330 was stool-ball (Robert W. Henderson, *Ball, Bat and Bishop*, 1947). A local adaptation of ancient pagan rites and a direct forebear of cricket and baseball, stool-ball was often characterized by a) association with the Church and the churchyard as the field of play, b) association with the Easter season, c) participation by young men and maidens, and d) use of flavored cakes (usually tansy, a bitter herb) as prizes. A batter, protecting an upended three-legged stool, used an outstretched arm or hand (later replaced by a bat or stick in the mid-19th century) to strike a ball (any round object, even a ball of yarn) delivered by the pitcher. If the ball hit the stool or was caught after being struck, the batter was "out" and another player took his/her place at the stool. The winner was the player with the greatest number of hits. When playing with multiple stools, baserunners needed to advance to the next stool without being struck by a thrown ball and put out. In the 19th century, stoolball emerged as an organized sport, complete with town associations and published rules; stools were replaced by structural targets, constructed of round or square boards about a foot wide, affixed to posts in the ground. In 1916, an attempt was made to revive the game in England. The National Stoolball Association was formed in 1979; the game is popular in Sussex and nearby counties. The game was brought to America by the Pilgrims: William Bradford, governor of Plymouth Plantation, discovered his work crew, on Christmas Day 1621, "in ye streete at play, openly; some pitching ye barr [ball], & some at stoole-ball, and shuch like sports" (William Bradford, *Bradford's History "Of Plimouth Plantation*," 1898, book II, pp.134–35).

stoopball A variation of baseball played without a bat, usually one to a side. A rubber ball is thrown against a set of steps (or stoop) by the player on offense, while the defense tries to catch the ball on the fly as it comes off the stoop. A ball caught on the fly is an out. Hits and runs are registered by the number of bounces the ball takes or by the distance it flies. As noted by Stephen Jay Gould (*Triumph and Tragedy in Mudville*, 2003, pp.43, 45), each step has a pronounced "sweet spot" located at the perpendicular intersection of the horizontal and vertical positions of the step, or the corner of the step at the top of the riser; if the ball hits this spot, it usually flies over the head of the fielder and often into home run territory. "As any kid will affirm, the chief fascination of stoopball lies in the fact that no two stoops are exactly alike, and that, consequently, each stoop generates its own unique and idiosyncratic set of rules." A similar game is called *stepball* in Philadelphia. Compare *curb ball*.

stop 1. *v.* For a defensive player to knock down, slow, smother, or otherwise bring a ball under control so that it can be played. **2.** *n.* A defensive play on a batted ground ball. IST USE. 1864 (*Brooklyn Daily Eagle*, Sept. 20; Edward J. Nichols).

"stop at the junk yard" A gibe directed at

players having trouble holding onto the ball; e.g., "I'm stopping at the junk yard on the way home. Want me to pick you up some new hands?" (*The Sporting News*, March 6, 1982).

stopper 1. A starting pitcher who can be counted on to end a team's losing streak, or to win a game following a team's loss. During his career with the Boston Red Sox (1984–1996), Roger Clemens won 111 times after a team loss. Syn. *stop pitcher.* IST USE. 1938. "We had agreed . . . that what the Cubs needed was a 'stopper' pitcher to pace the staf [*sic*]" (Irving Vaughan, *Chicago Tribune*, July 13; Stuart Y. Silverstein). 2. Syn. of *closer*, 1. "[Lee Smith] would retire if he wasn't the Angels' closer. But he won't be Cincinnati's stopper, either" (*The Baltimore Sun*, May 28, 1996). The term "closer" is most commonly used, although "stopper" was used as late as 2000 (*Sports Illustrated*, March 27, 2000, p.103): "[The Detroit Tigers have] an abundance of pretty good relievers, but no stopper." IST USE. 1954. "[Wilcy Moore] was a 'stopper' and a 'stopper de luxe'" (George Sisler, *Sisler on Baseball*, 1954; Peter Morris). 3. Syn. of *catcher*, 1. 4. A metal bottle cap used in stopper ball.

stopper ball A childhood variant of baseball played in textile mill villages and involving a batter using a "picker stick" (part of a loom) and a pitcher, standing three feet away, flipping a metal bottle cap ("stopper") toward the batter. Bases were awarded on how far the stopper was hit. (Steve Catoe)

stop pitcher Syn. of *stopper*, 1. IST USE. 1946 (*The Sporting News*, Sept. 18; Peter Morris).

stop position That part of a pitcher's motion in which he pauses in the set position before releasing the ball to the plate. See also *discernible stop*.

stop-short *hist.* A defensive player in the Massachusetts game who positioned himself in front of the pitcher to field batted balls in front of the plate. "The stop-short . . . stands nearly in front of the batmen. . . . The fourth base [home plate] is sufficiently protected by the stop-short, who looks out for the short balls in front of the bat" (*New York Herald*,

Oct. 16, 1859; George A. Thompson).

stop sign A coach's signal to hold up an advancing baserunner. It is usually no more complicated than an upraised hand. "I'm not going to run through a stop sign. He [Baltimore Orioles third base coach Sam Perlozzo] threw his hands up and I got stopped" (Lenny Webster, quoted in *The Baltimore Sun*, Aug. 18, 1997). It is one of the few signs that has been routinely disobeyed without serious repercussions to the violator. When Ramon Ortiz ran through coach Ron Roenicke's stop sign and became the third out at the plate, he commented (quoted in *The Baltimore Sun*, June 10, 2001), "I guess I get a traffic ticket." Compare *green light*, 2.

stove league See *hot stove league*. IST USE. 1906. "With the world's championship settled, nothing remains except to organize the 'round-the-stove-league' and figure out what might have been" (*The Washington Post*, Oct. 22; Peter Morris).

straddle slide Syn. of *hook slide*.

straddle stance A *batting stance* with the feet spread wide apart, such as that used by Joe DiMaggio. Syn. *spraddled stance*.

straddling The positioning taken by the home plate umpire in which his feet are placed on a straight line, about 22 to 28 inches apart, his left foot directly behind the catcher's left foot and his right foot directly behind the catcher's right foot, and his head looking directly over the catcher's head (not over the catcher's shoulders) and lining up with the pitcher. "It affords the best vision for those tough curve balls that break across the outside corner of the plate about knee high" (Bill McGowan, quoted in *Bill McGowan's School for Umpires*, *Text Book*, 1948 and 1949).

straight *hist.* A line drive. "Beautiful straight over the second base by [John Montgomery] Ward" (*Binghamton* [N.Y.] *Republican and Morning Times*, June 30, 1878; Bryan Di Salvatore).

straight arm delivery The delivery of a pitcher with "a direct snap from the forearm" (John B. Foster, in *Collier's New Dictionary of the English Language*, 1908).

straight as a string Said of a fastball without a hop.

straightaway Pertaining to an orthodox defensive position, neither to the right nor to the left. A center fielder is playing straightaway if he is in the center of the outfield in line with home plate and second base. According to John Pastier (personal communication, March 29, 2000), "straightaway left" is 15 degrees off the left field foul line.

straightaway hitter A hitter who hits the ball to the part of the field according to where it is pitched; e.g., a right-handed batter will hit an outside pitch to right field, an inside pitch to left field, and a pitch over the plate to center field.

straightaway stance Syn. of *square stance*, 1.

straight ball *hist.* A pitch delivered on a straight line, with no curve to it.

straight change A changeup off a fastball rather than one off a curveball or screwball.

"straighten it out" A rally cry to encourage a batter who has hit one or more foul balls.

straighten one out 1. To hit a line drive. IST USE. 1907 (*The New York Times*, Oct. 9; Edward J. Nichols). 2. To hit a curveball well. "[Claude] Ritchey then managed to straighten out one of [Jake] Weimer's curves into center field" (*Chicago Tribune*, Apr. 30, 1905; Peter Morris).

straighten up To throw an inside pitch to dissuade the batter from leaning or crouching over the plate.

straight player *hist.* A player who does not rely on strategy or inside baseball. IST USE. 1905 (*The Sporting Life*, Oct. 7, p.9; Edward J. Nichols).

straight town A less-common variant of *round town* played with "the bases in a straight row" (Dennis Reedy, *School and Community History of Dickenson County, Virginia*, 1992), perhaps owing to scarcity of large, flat fields. (David Ball)

strand 1. For a batter (or a team) to leave one or more runners on base at the end of the team's half inning. 2. For a pitcher to retire the side with one or more runners on base. Syn. *hang*, 2.

stranded Syn. of *left on base*, 1. IST USE.

1905 (*The Sporting Life*, Sept. 2, p.13; Edward J. Nichols).

Strat-O-Matic A tabletop baseball board game using dice and cards that describe various probabilities. A closely guarded method of rating major-league players based on their performances during a given season was developed by Strat-O-Matic Game Co., Great Neck, N.Y. Abbrev. *SOM*.

strawberry A red skin abrasion with the texture and hue of a strawberry, produced on the upper leg, thigh, or buttocks of a sliding baserunner. See also *gooseberry*. Syn. *hustle blister*. IST USE. 1932. "Strawberry—Bruise from sliding" (*New York Sun*, June 23, 1932).

straw that stirs the drink, the A phrase used by Reggie Jackson soon after joining the New York Yankees in 1977 to describe where he fit in the metaphoric scheme of things; i.e., the most important member of the team. "You know, this team . . . it all flows from me. I've got to keep it going. I'm the straw that stirs the drink" (Jackson, quoted by Robert Ward, *Sport*, June 1977). The image was strong enough to inspire many parallels: "If there is a drink to be stirred in Baltimore this baseball season, you can bet that Eddie Murray will be the straw that does it" (letter from Joseph T. Kasprzak to *The Baltimore Sun*, May 25, 1986).

streak An uninterrupted string of accomplishments or failures by a player or a team; e.g., a "winning streak," a "losing streak," and a "hitting streak." The term is also applied to such achievements as Cal Ripken Jr.'s consecutive-inning streak of 8,243 innings, which ended in Sept. 1987, and his consecutive-game playing streak of 2,632, which ended on Sept. 19, 1998. Unquestionably, before Ripken's consecutive-game playing streak, the most famous streak in baseball history was Joe DiMaggio's feat of hitting in 56 straight games in 1941. Both the term and the concept have a high degree of significance. Among other things, they can help give a particular season its character. A key line in Bill Wolle's summary of the 1987 season (*Houston Post*, Oct. 6, 1987; Charles D. Poe): "The season began with a record 13-game winning streak by the Milwaukee

Sensational

JOE DIMAGGIO

Will Seek To Hit Safely In His

49ᵗʰ

Consecutive Game.

Thur. Nite, July 10

AT ST. LOUIS

Browns vs. Yankees

Sportsman's Park--8:30 P. M.

Tickets Now on Sale at Browns Arcade Ticket Office--Phone, CHestnut 7900.

Streak. Handbill advertising DiMaggio's consecutive-game hitting streak. *National Baseball Library and Archives, Cooperstown, N.Y.*

Brewers and wound up with San Diego's Benito Santiago fashioning a 34-game hitting streak, a record for rookies and catchers." Significantly, there is a special section (10.24) of the *Official Baseball Rules* that sets forth the criteria for establishing consecutive hitting streaks, consecutive-game hitting streaks, and consecutive-game playing streaks. Another major streak was established on Sept. 28, 1988, when Los Angeles Dodgers hurler Orel Hershiser pitched the longest string of scoreless innings (59) in the history of the game. Syn. *string*. USAGE NOTE. Peter Morris notes that the term originally applied to a team undergoing a period of success. "The Lowells went in for one of their 'streaks of batting'" (*National Chronicle*, June 12, 1869). "[The Reds'] 'eight' in the eighth inning were made by most remarkable batting . . . a 'streak,' and must have surprised themselves" (*St. Louis Post-Dispatch*, May 5, 1875). "[The Tecumsehs of London were] taken with what is called in base ball circles 'a batting streak,' and hit the ball safely all over the field" (*Detroit Post*, June 26, 1875).

Streak, The The name given to Cal Ripken

Jr.'s consecutive-game playing streak of 2,632 games, which began on May 30, 1982, and ended Sept. 19, 1998. He surpassed the previous record of 2,130 games (set by Lou Gehrig) on Sept. 6, 1995.

streak hitter A player with the reputation of getting base hits in clusters, which alternate with slumps. The implication is that a player's characteristic streaks and slumps cannot be accounted for by random variation in performance. However, the best sabermetric evidence strongly suggests that streaks and slumps are indeed random, implying that there is probably no such concept as a streak hitter. "All hitters are streak hitters after one fashion or another, but [Charlie] Keller could streak and fade with the best of them" (Michael Seidel, *Streak*, 1988, p.70). IST USE. 1914. "[Joe] Jackson is what we call a streak hitter. He bats like a fiend for a time and then his work drops off" (Ty Cobb, *Busting 'Em and Other Big League Stories*; Peter Morris).

streetball A term used by Stephen Jay Gould (*Triumph and Tragedy in Mudville*, 2003, pp.40–41) for New York City games played by baseball rules on city streets; e.g., punchball, stickball, stoopball, and box baseball.

street piece A home run hit out of the park. The term was introduced by pitcher Dennis Eckersley.

strength coach A coach who attends to the players' conditioning and physical workouts.

strength to strength The situation in which a pitcher's best pitch is also the batter's favorite pitch. "The hoariest of pitching doctrines holds that one pitch 'strength to strength': faced with a batter who loves high sliders, say, the pitcher whose best pitch is a high slider would still throw it" (Daniel Okrent, *Nine Innings*, 1985, p.64). Syn. "strength against strength."

stretch 1. *n.* The phase of a pitcher's delivery during which his arms are raised above and behind his head. Its function is to loosen the arm and back muscles. 2. *n.* A modified or short windup, used esp. by a pitcher to keep baserunners from taking too long a lead and to decrease the length of time it takes to pitch the ball. It starts with the pitcher keeping his hands together at the waist, then raising them to or above his head, then bringing his hands slowly back to the waist, then resting or stopping momentarily in the set position to check the runner's lead before delivering the pitch. To go through the stretch without a discernible stop is to commit a balk. Compare *windup*. **3.** *n.* The position taken by a baseman (esp. the first baseman) as he keeps one foot on the bag while reaching as far as he can to catch the ball thrown by another fielder before the runner touches the base. See also *reach*, 1. **4.** *v.* To take an extra base on a hit, usually owing to fast, bold running. "Bernie Williams cut off Eddie Murray's line drive to right-center . . . throwing Murray out attempting to stretch it into a double" (*The Baltimore Sun*, Aug. 1, 1994). IST USE. 1889. "Jack [Hayes] tried to stretch it into a home run and was out at the plate" (*San Francisco Examiner*, Apr. 28; Peter Morris). **5.** *n.* The late season when divisional races heat up; the last few games, or last four to five weeks, of the season, usually starting after Labor Day. The term is short for *homestretch*, which is borrowed from horse racing. **6.** *n.* A series of baseball games. "San Diego's 17–4 stretch . . . provided the Padres an outside shot at catching San Francisco in the NL West" (*Tampa Tribune-Times*, Sept. 17, 1989). **7.** *n.* See *seventh-inning stretch*.

stretch drive The effort made during the final weeks of the season when a contending team is striving for a division championship or wild card position. Syn. *stretch run*. IST USE. 1934. "This stretch drive of the Cardinals, 'ridden' by [manager Frankie] Frisch, must be accepted as one of the noteworthy performances of modern baseball" (official program, 1934 World Series; Peter Morris). ETYMOLOGY. Borrowed from horse racing.

stretch position Syn. of *set position*.

stretch run Syn. of *stretch drive*.

stride 1. *v.* To step into and give power to one's swing when batting. Not all batters stride and some of the best (such as Joe DiMaggio) stride only a few inches. Batters who do not stride are described as flat-footed, but younger or less-experienced players often tend to overstride. **2.** *n.* The forward foot movement of a batter when swinging at a pitch. "The stride of the front foot gains its

impetus or drive from a sharp push forward by the rear leg which sustains the body weight at this moment" (James Smiloff, *Athletic Journal*, Apr. 1946). **3.** *v.* For a pitcher to raise his foot as the ball is about to be delivered. **4.** *n.* The forward movement of a pitcher as he is about to deliver the pitch. See also *long stride*; *short stride*.

stride in step with the pitch To judge the exact speed of the pitch and hit the ball squarely; to time the pitch perfectly. "When batters are striding in pace with the pitch the pitcher is in for a drubbing" (H.G. Salsinger, *Baseball Digest*, Aug. 1945).

striding foot 1. The forward foot that the batter uses to step into and swing at the ball. **2.** The front foot that a fielder uses to step forward to give strength to his throw. **3.** The *stepping foot* of a pitcher.

strike 1. *n.* A legally pitched ball that is called as such by the umpire because it is either a) swung at and missed, b) in the strike zone and not swung at, c) fouled off but not caught with less than two strikes, d) bunted foul with two strikes, or e) foul-tipped and caught by the catcher with two strikes. A batter is out after three strikes. A strike is announced as such by the plate umpire, who also signals it by raising his right hand. EXTENDED USE. A disadvantage or mistake; e.g., "Her attitude is a strike against her." This usage can even be applied to baseball: "[Commissioner Peter] Ueberroth Makes It Clear: Two Drug Strikes and You're Out" (*St. Petersburg Times* headline, Apr. 2, 1987). **2.** *v.* To swing at a pitched ball. "A player must make his first base after striking a fair ball" (Knickerbocker Rules, Rule 7, 1854). IST USE. 1845. "Three balls being struck at and missed and the last one caught, is a hand out" (Knickerbocker Rules, Rule 11th, Sept. 23). USAGE NOTE. David Block (personal communication, Feb. 8, 2003): "The use of the verb 'to strike' was commonplace in all of the nine or so known descriptions or rules of early baseball-like games that preceded the Knickerbockers, and was also utilized to describe the action in most of baseball's predecessors, such as stool-ball and trap ball." **3.** *n./hist.* Entering the batter's box according to the batting order. "Players must take their strike in regular turn" (Knickerbocker Rules, Rule 16th, 1845). USAGE NOTE. "Most descriptions of early baseball preceding the Knickerbockers mention that members of the batting team take their places 'in turn'" (David Block, *Baseball Before We Knew It*, 2005, p.90). **4.** *n.* A ball put into play, regardless of where the pitcher throws it, in the calculation of the number of balls and strikes thrown by the pitcher. **5.** *n.* A highly accurate throw from the outfield. EXTENDED USE. Something perfectly delivered, such as a "touchdown strike" in football. **6.** A walkout or suspension of work by the players to protest working conditions imposed by the owners or to pressure the owners to meet certain demands. Much was made during the 1981 players' strike of the irony that the word "strike" was so important to the game itself. This prompted a reader (Phillip Coe, *The Sporting News*, July 18, 1981) to redefine other terms; e.g., a "walk" was changed to "walkout" in order "to complement the new definition of 'strike.'" See also *work stoppage* for a list of players' strikes and owners' lockouts.

strikeout *n.* **1.** An out made by a batter charged with three strikes. Abbrev. *SO*, 1. IST USE. 1862 (*New York Sunday Mercury*, June 29; Edward J. Nichols). EXTENDED USE. Failure after three attempts. "Soup search at O's game is a strikeout. . . . I went in search of a bowl of hot crab soup, not once, not twice, but three times and came up empty" (Rob Kasper, *The Baltimore Sun*, Apr. 14, 2004). **2.** An out recorded by a pitcher when the batter has been charged with three strikes. The number of strikeouts achieved by a pitcher in a game, season, or career is a barometer of his effectiveness. Symbol *K*, 1. Abbrev. *SO*, 2. Syn. *K*, 2; *punchout.*

strike out *v.* **1.** To retire from the plate as a result of three strikes; e.g., "Smith strikes out on a curveball." "Harris 'struck out' the balls he failed to hit" (*Brooklyn Eagle*, Aug. 18, 1864; Peter Morris). Syn. *punch out*, 1; *K*, 3. IST USE. 1857. "[R.H. Horn's] swift ball has caused many a player to strike out" (*Porter's Spirit of the Times*, Feb. 7; David Block). EXTENDED USE. To fail completely. **2.** To put a batter out as a result of three strikes; e.g.,

Strikeout. Postcard. *Andy Moresund Collection*

"Jones strikes out Smith on a curveball." Syn. *fan*, 1; *K*, 4; *punch out*, 2.

strikeout artist A pitcher who strikes out many batters.

strikeout king 1. The pitcher with the most strikeouts during any given season. Nolan Ryan holds the single-season strikeout record of 383 in 1973. IST USE. 1916. "Last year [Dave Danforth] was the undisputed strikeout king of the American Association" (*Baseball Magazine*, July; Peter Morris). **2.** The pitcher with the most strikeouts in baseball history. Nolan Ryan became the current strikeout king on Apr. 27, 1983, by passing Walter Johnson's previous record of 3,508 strikeouts. Ryan retired after the 1993 season with 5,714 strikeouts.

strike out looking To take a called third strike. See also *catch looking*. Syn. *go down looking.*

strikeout percentage The number of strikeouts a batter suffers per 100 times at bat. The 2001 major-league figure was 19.5; the career low is Joe Sewell's 1.6.

strikeout rule [softball term] A slow pitch rule in Amateur Softball Association of America that the batter must hit the ball fair if he or she has two strikes; otherwise, it is an out should the batter hit the ball foul. In United States Specialty Sports Association (USSSA) play, a batter can hit one foul after the second strike, but the second foul is ruled an out. The USSSA rule gives the batter a decided advantage.

strike out swinging To swing at and miss a pitch for the third strike. Syn. *go down swinging*.

strike out the side **1.** To retire all three batters in one inning by striking them out. **2.** To record three strikeouts in an inning regardless of the number of batters faced. Joe Morgan (*Baseball for Dummies*, 1998, p.362) stated that "striking out the side" is "the most misused phrase in baseball" because if the pitcher allows a baserunner of any kind during the inning, "the phrase does not apply."

striker *hist.* Syn. of *batter*, 1. "The batsman is considered the 'striker' until he has hit a fair ball, when he becomes a player 'running the bases'" (Henry Chadwick, *The Game of Base Ball*, 1868, p.45). IST USE. 1845. "Three balls being struck at and missed and the last one caught, is a hand out; if not caught is considered fair, and the striker bound to run" (Knickerbocker Rules, Rule 11th, Sept. 23).

striker's stand A space four feet in diameter, at equal distance (30 feet) between the first and fourth bases, where the batter stood in the Massachusetts game.

"striker to the line" *hist.* Syn. of *"batter up!"*

strike three The third and final strike in a strikeout. See also *three strikes*. EXTENDED USE. **1.** Failure of a person or an enterprise after being given two opportunities to succeed. *The Baltimore Sun* headline (Dec. 2, 2003)—"Olympic head may call strike 3 against sport [baseball] for future games"— referred to the United States' failure to qualify for the Summer 2004 Olympics in Athens (strike one), Major League Baseball's refusal to shut down to allow top stars to play in future games (strike two), and baseball's uncertain future as an Olympic sport (possible strike three). **2.** A felon's third federal conviction for a violent crime, ensuring life in prison without parole.

strike wind *hist.* To swing at and miss a pitched ball. IST USE. 1888 (*Chicago Inter-Ocean*, July 1; Edward J. Nichols).

strike zone **1.** The imaginary rectangle over home plate that defines a called strike. It has varied over the years. Since 1995, the *Official Baseball Rules* (Rule 2.00) defined the strike zone's upper limit as "a horizontal line at the midpoint between the top of the shoulders and the top of the uniform pants" and the lower level as "a line at the hollow beneath the kneecap." In 2001, the "new" strike zone was extended from the top of the knee upward to a point about two widths of a baseball above the belt; also, the outside pitch is no longer a strike if it passes over only the black edge of the plate. The strike zone is determined from the batter's stance as he is about to swing at a pitched ball; it also depends on the size of the batter and the proclivity of the umpire calling strikes. A pitch thrown in the strike zone will be called a strike if it is not swung at. One given of the game is that, despite the explicit designation of the rules, the strike zone is in reality a subjective area and its dimensions will vary from umpire to umpire and from league to league. "Over the years, the strike zone has gotten smaller and slightly wider. Umpires are more likely to call pitches on the corner strikes, but anything above the waist or below the knee is usually a ball" (Brad Snyder, *The Baltimore Sun*, Apr. 27, 1996).

From 1887 to 1949 and from 1963 to 1968, the strike zone was from the top of the batter's shoulders to the bottom of his knees; from 1950 to 1962, it was from the armpits to the top of the knees; in 1969, the upper limit became lowered from the shoulders to the armpits; and in 1988, the upper limit became the midpoint between the top of the shoulders and the top of the uniform pants. Syn. *zone*, 1; *K zone*.

2. [softball term] That space over any part of home plate between the batter's armpits and the top of the knees (fast pitch softball) and between the batter's back shoulder and front knee (slow pitch softball).

striking order *hist.* Syn. of *batting order.* "The home nine were arrayed in different striking order" (*The Boston Globe*, June 29, 1877; Peter Morris).

string Syn. of *streak.*

string bean A tall, thin player.

string bean circuit *hist.* The low minor leagues. "These young pitchers along the string bean circuit, who are supposed not to have anything but the glove and a return ticket, bother the [White] Sox more than do hurlers who have a rep" (Charles Dryden, *Chicago Tribune*, Apr. 5, 1907; Peter Morris, who suggests that the term may have referred specifically to minor leagues in Midwestern farming areas).

strings 1. The contractual right of a major-league club to reclaim a player. The term, often used in the negative, was used in the early 20th century in the sense of "strings attached"; e.g., "There are no strings on [Tom] McCreery and he can sign with any club" (*Milwaukee Journal*, March 28, 1901; Peter Morris). 2. See *pitching to the strings.*

stroke 1. *n.* An even, smooth swing, which often results in a batted ball. "[Thurman Munson's] stroke to right field was something special" (*Tampa Tribune*, Aug. 2, 1989). 2. *v.* To hit the ball well and with apparent ease. "[Chuck Knoblauch] stroked a single to center" (*The New York Times*, Oct. 19, 2001). 3. *n./hist.* A batted ball. IST USE. 1860. "Pierce led off at the bat, and by a good stroke got to his first base" (*The New York Herald*, Aug. 24). 4. *n./hist.* A base hit.

stroker A batter with a controlled swing.

stroll 1. To draw a base on balls. IST USE. 1897. "Tiernan strolled on four Canarsie shoots" (*The World* [New York], May 14; Peter Morris). 2. To take a lead off first base.

'Stros Short for the *Astros.*

struggle 1. *v.* To be in a slump. A common cliché of the game is to say that a batter is "struggling at the plate" or a pitcher is "struggling from the mound." "Rookie closer Mike MacDougal . . . has struggled to locate his fastball since the All-Star break" (*Sports Illustrated*, Aug. 4, 2003). See also *scuffle*, 1. 2. *v.* For a team to have a difficult time winning enough games to be considered a contender, owing to bad luck, injuries, and slumps. "Held to three hits, club [Baltimore Orioles] continues to struggle against last-place team" (*The Baltimore Sun* subheadline, Aug. 13, 2003). 3. *n.* A baseball game. "Pretty Girls and Catchy Music Served With Struggle: Lots of Fun at Recreation Park During Afternoon Game Between Oaks and Wolves" (*San Francisco Bulletin* headline, May 31, 1913; Gerald L. Cohen).

stuff 1. A pitcher's *assortment* or *repertoire* of pitches collectively, together with his ability to deliver and control them in the proper sequence at the right velocity to the desired area of the strike zone; the ingredients of good pitching. " 'Stuff' is a pitcher's wares; it is also called by fellow performers his 'stock' and his 'goods'" (*The New York Times*, June 2, 1929). Benjamin Zimmer (personal communication, May 11, 2005) notes that "stuff" is viewed as "a substance with varied characteristics (strong, secondary, off-speed, breaking, elevated) as well as qualities (good, better, best)." Tom Seaver (quoted in *Tampa Tribune*, March 26, 1986): "The pitcher has to understand what his . . . goals are and how he can achieve the goals with the stuff he has—so-called quote, stuff, unquote. That changes as you go through your career, it changes from start to start, it changes within the context of a game." Syn. *equipment*, 2. IST USE. 1905. "Long Tom Hughes . . . had plenty of indecipherable stuff, and the Browns had no key to his hieroglyphic code" (*The Washington Post*, May 27; Benjamin Zimmer). 2. The spin or break and the speed that a pitcher puts on the ball. The term originally referred to the spin on the ball, but has subsequently broadened to include other movements of the ball as well as its speed and control. Florida Marlins catcher Darren Daulton, discussing Greg Maddux (quoted in *The Boston Globe*, Aug. 17, 1997): "He's got good stuff, really good stuff. His curveball might be illegal in some states. Sometimes I think he has a joystick on that thing." IST USE. 1910. "[Jack Coombs] started out . . . wild and didn't seem able to put all his 'stuff' on the ball" (*The New York Times*, Oct. 21; Benjamin Zimmer). **3.** The essential makeup of a pitcher. "[Rube Foster] has been knocked and bumped until now, in the heat of battle, he is as cool as a cucumber, he showed that he was made of real pitching stuff" (*The New York Times*, Oct. 10, 1915; Benjamin Zimmer). **4.** The spin that a batter is able to put on the ball. "A good outfielder . . . must know the kind of stuff the batsmen get off the delivery of the pitchers, so as to make allowance for the kind that curve in an eccentric manner as they shoot out toward the lots" (*Los Angeles Times*, July 5, 1905; Benjamin Zimmer).

STUFF A shorthand rating of a pitcher's demonstrated skills, relative to his age and level. Its primary use is to evaluate pitching prospects. A score of 10 for a minor-league pitcher indicates he has the talent to develop into an average major-league starter. A score above 20 denotes an excellent prospect; that above 30 denotes an elite pitcher. The largest component of STUFF is the strikeout rate, but also considered are the walk rate, hit rate, earned run average, innings pitched per game, and age relative to that of the league. See *Baseball Prospectus 2008* (p.xiv).

stuff rating A measure of a pitcher's performance in defense independent pitching stats (DIPS) of strikeouts, bases on balls, and home runs allowed, along with a measure of how much a pitcher's earned run average is higher or lower than the pitcher's peripheral earned run average. The measure was introduced by Clay Davenport (*Baseball Prospectus*, 2002). Abbrev. *STF.*

stump match *hist.* A baseball game that is a challenge match with an outside club. "No stump match shall be played on a regular day of exercise" (Knickerbocker Rules, Rule 5th, Sept. 23, 1845). See also *match game.*

stunner A key base hit. IST USE. 1868. "Hatfield sends [him] home by a 'stunner' to right field" (Chadwick Scrapbooks; David Shulman).

stunt 1. An act designed to be different and to attract the attention of the fans. On noting that Bert Campaneris of the Kansas City Athletics in 1965 and Cesar Tovar of the Minne-sota Twins in 1968 played all nine positions during a single game, *The New York Times* (May 29, 1978) asserted, "These are the only two such stunts in major-league history." **2.** An accomplishment or feat performed on the field. "Jimmy Johnston's stunt in throwing Jack Ness out at third after his sky-kissing drive to left caused even his most ardent admirers to gasp with astonishment" (*San Francisco Bulletin*, May 16, 1913; Gerald L. Cohen).

stuntman An honorific name for a reserve or nonstarter, which implies far greater involvement than the traditional "benchwarmer" nickname. ETYMOLOGY. A reference to Hollywood stuntmen, the term was first applied during the 1988 season by Los Angeles Dodgers manager Tommy Lasorda. Mickey Hatcher, one of Lasorda's Stuntmen, explained that it described "the doubles, the guys who fill in, the guys who do the dirty work" (*The Sporting News*, June 27, 1988).

styler A player who always looks good. At bat, a styler looks good before, during, and after he swings.

styling Flamboyant actions designed to bring attention to oneself or to show up another player; *hot-dogging.* Examples include a batter's using up time at the plate to adjust his batting gloves or standing at home plate after hitting and watching his home run. Also spelled *stylin'.*

stylish Said of a smooth fielder who makes the tough plays. "[Ryan was] regarded as one of the most stylish infielders in the Southern Association last year" (Harry Cross, *New York Herald Tribune*, March 21, 1942; James D. Szalontai).

sub 1. *n.* Short for *substitute,* 1. IST USE. 1864. "Lord was the only substitute, whereas the new nines had three 'subs' all far below the mark of the nine" (*New York Clipper*, Oct. 22; Peter Morris). **2.** *v.* Short for *substitute,* 2. IST USE. 1909. "Dave Altizer, who was subbing for the invalid, P. Dougherty, was chief comedian" (Ring W. Lardner, *Chicago Tribune*, May 5; Peter Morris).

submarine 1. *adj.* Said of a pitch, pitcher, delivery, or style of pitching characterized by an underhand or sidearm motion. IST USE.

1917. "Boston's Submarine Pitcher [Carl Mays] Gets Four Hits to Win Own Game by 6 to 5 Score" (*The New York Times* headline, Sept. 15). ETYMOLOGY. Derived from the underwater vessel. **2.** *v.* To pitch using the submarine delivery.

submarine ball A pitch thrown lower than the usual sidearm delivery. Syn. *scrotum ball*. 1ST USE. 1917. "Carl Mays, the pitcher of the submarine ball, had a lot to do with beating the Yanks" (*The New York Times*, Sept. 15; Fred R. Shapiro).

submariner A pitcher who uses the submarine-style delivery; e.g., Carl Mays, whose underhand pitch hit Cleveland Indians shortstop Ray Chapman in the head and killed him in 1920. Syn. *subway slinger*.

substation The bullpen. The term is used by relief pitchers who see the dugout as the "main terminal" (Mark Davis, *San Diego Union-Tribune*, Apr. 11, 1994).

substitute 1. *n.* Any player not in the original lineup who is subsequently brought into the game. Syn. *sub*, 1. 1ST USE. 1864. "Lord was the only substitute, whereas the new nines had three 'subs' all far below the mark of the nine" (*New York Clipper*, Oct. 22; Peter Morris). USAGE NOTE. Although "substitute" is a legitimate and useful term in baseball, it is usually too general to cover specific situations. The preferred form is to specify the exact role of the substitute; e.g., a pinch runner or a short reliever. **2.** *v.* To put a player into a game in progress by replacing a player already in the lineup. Syn. *sub*, 2.

substitute batter *hist.* Syn. of *pinch hitter*, 2 (i.e., when "pinch hitter" primarily meant a clutch hitter). "Dode Birmingham, the Naps' manager, acted as substitute batter for Vean Gregg in the eighth, but failed to deliver" (*The Washington Post*, Aug. 23, 1913; Peter Morris).

suburbanite *hist.* An outfielder. 1ST USE. 1915. "[Becker] looked quite the most promising of the young suburbanites who finished the season" (*The Sporting Life*, Nov. 20; Peter Morris).

suburbs 1. The figurative destination of the long ball; the area where monstrous home runs land. "And where do you hit [a home run]? . . . You don't even go *downtown*. Today you go to the *suburbs*" (R.J. Reynolds and Bob Hertzel, Scripps Howard News service, Sept. 17, 1986). **2.** *hist.* The outfield. 1ST USE. 1893. "Charlie [Van Haltren] has been removed to the suburbs. He cavorted in right field" (*The Sporting News*, Nov. 4; Peter Morris).

Subway Series 1. A World Series in which the two opposing clubs could travel between their home fields by using the New York City subway system. Traditionally, it referred to a World Series played between the New York Yankees and the Brooklyn Dodgers (there were seven such Series beginning in 1941 and ending in 1956), and most recently to the 2000 World Series when the Yankees defeated the New York Mets. "Subway series is a synonym for civil war" (Samuel G. Freedman, *The New York Times*, Oct. 19, 1986). See also *all–New York Series*. 1ST USE. 1934. "Proponents of the 'subway series' this fall between the Yankees and the [New York] Giants for the world baseball championship may enjoy something of a pre-view when the all-star teams of the National and American League battle in gilt-edged formation next Tuesday at the Polo Grounds" (Associated Press dispatch, July 3; Barry Popik). USAGE NOTE. Although the 1921, 1922, and 1923 World Series were the first "subway series" in New York, there is no evidence that the term was used until the next decade. The term took hold in Sept. 1936 when the Yankees and the New York Giants met in the World Series. "Dodgers, the Spoilers, Tackling New York Too Late Apparently to Block Subway Series" (*New York World-Telegram* headline, Sept. 17, 1936; Barry Popik). According to Popik, newspaper accounts also referred to the 1936 World Series as "subway World Series," "New York Series," "all–New York world series," "all–New York classic," and "nickel series." **2.** An interleague series during the regular season between the New York Yankees and the New York Mets. "Subway Series excites fans more than Players; Scalpers getting $600 for Yankees-Mets tickets" (*The Baltimore Sun* headline, June 27, 1998). EXTENDED USE. As other professional sports have fielded two New York City-area teams, the term has come to refer to matchups between the Rangers and Islanders in hockey and the Jets and the Giants in football (even though some of these teams' venues are not reachable by subway).

subway slinger Syn. of *submariner*. ETYMOLOGY. From the concept of a subway being underground.

sucker A blooper, esp. one that makes the fielders trying to get to it look foolish; a *Texas Leaguer*, 2. IST USE. 1868. "Al Reach sent a sucker to right, which gave him first" (Chadwick Scrapbooks; David Shulman).

sucker hole A suspension of play, after a game has started, because of rain or inclement weather, before the game is resumed. Umpire Jim Evans (quoted in *The Baltimore Sun*, July 5, 1995): "We had been told there would be a 20–30 minute break—what we call a 'sucker hole'—where we could start, but then have to stop because of heavier rain."

sucker pitch [softball term] A short pitch that a player throws with exaggerated motion, hoping that the batter will mistime his or her swing.

sudden death A situation in which a team must win, such as in an extra-inning game or if the team is facing elimination in a playoff series. "Kansas City went 7–3 against the Orioles last season, including its first three-game sweep against them at Kauffman Stadium since 1988. All three wins were in sudden death" (Roch Kubatko, *The Baltimore Sun*, Aug. 6, 2001). "The [Boston] Red Sox had lost Game 3 and were facing sudden death against the dreaded [New York] Yankees in the 2004 American League Championship Series" (*The Baltimore Sun*, Oct. 27, 2004). "Win or Go Home: Sudden Death Baseball" (title of Gary R. Parker's 2002 book). USAGE NOTE. James Charlton, editor of *The Baseball Chronology* (1991), found the following entry for May 1, 1880: "In Cincinnati, the Chicagos spoil the official opening of the new park by beating the Reds 4–3 with 2 runs in the bottom of the 9th. This is the first pro game ended in 'sudden death,' as the old rules required that the full inning be played out even if the team batting last was

already ahead." ETYMOLOGY. An overtime period in football when the game is tied and the team that scores first is the winner, resulting in an immediate stoppage of play.

Suds Series Nickname for the 1982 World Series between the St. Louis Cardinals and Milwaukee Brewers, representing two cities with ties to beer ("suds"). The Milwaukee team is named for that city's production of beer, and the St. Louis team was owned by the Busch family (of Anheuser-Busch breweries).

sugarball Baseball in the Dominican Republic, where most amateur teams are sponsored by sugar refineries. "Baseball is inextricably bound up with the production of sugar. Its history is a microcosm of Dominican-American relations" (Alan M. Klein, *Sugarball: The American Game, the Dominican Dream*, 1991, p.15).

suicidal bunt A bunt not made with the intention of achieving a base hit, but rather with advancing a runner. "[Bill] Duggleby helped him along with a suicidal bunt" (*Chicago Tribune*, May 20, 1906; Peter Morris).

suicide squeeze A *squeeze play* in which the runner on third base breaks for the plate with the pitch as the batter attempts to lay down a bunt. If the bunt is unsuccessful, the runner is almost always out—a "suicide." Compare *safety squeeze*. IST USE. 1952 (Bob Feller, *Pitching to Win*; Peter Morris). USAGE NOTE. The suicide squeeze was originally called a "squeeze play." John W (Jack) Coombs earlier referred to the play as the *do-or-die squeeze*.

suit up To change from street clothes to a baseball player's uniform. Syn. *dress*.

Sullivan One who sits up all night; a player who will not sleep on a train. See also *Sullivan sleeper*.

Sullivan sleeper *hist.* A railroad day coach on which there are no sleeping accommodations. This is a late 19th-century term, which sometimes showed up as *O'Sullivan sleeper* in later references. "I did not indulge in a Pullman, but took what ball-players call a 'Sullivan sleeper'—that is, I sat up all night in the smoker" (*Lippincott's Magazine*, Aug. 1886; David Shulman). See also *Sullivan*. ETYMOLOGY. *The Sporting Life* (Sept. 10,

1884; Peter Morris) commented on the origin of the term in baseball: "Tom Sullivan, the catcher, made a remark once which, among ball players, makes his name as familiar as the name of Pullman. When Tom first signed he had never traveled much and had never used a Pullman sleeper. Upon taking his first trip he was told that they would occupy sleepers. Tom followed the balance of the club into the sleeper, the berths of which were, of course, not made up. After sitting there awhile Tom remarked: 'Well I'm blowed if I don't think it is money throwed away to pay extra just because the seats face each other.'" Sullivan had entered the regular day coach, imagining from its luxurious appearance that it was a sleeper. Ted Sullivan, a prominent 19th-century baseball personality, is sometimes cited as the eponymous originator of the term, but Sullivan himself essentially repeated the story above regarding Tom Sullivan (*The Sporting News*, Apr. 29, 1899; Peter Morris).

Sultan of Swat **1.** A nickname for Babe Ruth. IST USE. 1920. "While the Sultan of Swat had been dormant in the early innings, his brother Yanks were the same" (*The New York Times*, June 28, p.18; Barry Popik). **2.** A great home run hitter. "[Barry Bonds] has changed his reputation from 'five tool' player to Sultan of Swat, setting a single-season record with 73 homers [in 2001]" (Dan O'Neill, *St. Louis Post-Dispatch*, Oct. 1, 2002). **3.** An award named in honor of Babe Ruth, a native Baltimorean, and given by the Maryland Professional Baseball Players Association. ETYMOLOGY. John Thorn (*The Armchair Book of Baseball*, 1985) traced the title to the Indian state of Swat that once had a sultan or akhond. When the sultan died in 1878, his obituary appeared in the *Times* (London) and inspired Edward Lear to write a ditty called "The Akond of Swat." Thorn suggested the poem was "surely some sportswriter's inspiration for Ruth's 'title.'" In baseballese, a swat is a long hit, something Ruth specialized in. Joseph McBride (*High and Inside*, 1980, p.211) noted that Ruth's nickname confused Mahmood Khan, a citizen of Swat in West Pakistan, after *Time* magazine referred to Claire Ruth as the "widow of baseball's Sultan of Swat": "There is no such title as Sultan of Swat in the state [of Swat]. Our ruler is called the Wali of Swat."

Summer Classic Syn. of *All-Star Game*, 1. Sometimes lower-cased as "summer classic."

summer game The game of baseball. "Just hearing the sounds of the summer game, either in person or on the TV news, makes you feel as if you are stealing time" (John Eisenberg, *The Baltimore Sun*, Feb. 15, 1998). See also Roger Angell's *The Summer Game* (1972).

summer spectacle Syn. of *All-Star Game*, 1.

Sunday baseball Baseball played on the Sabbath. Once the most divisive of issues, this was a sore point for those who believed that baseball, especially the professional version, should not take place on the Sabbath. The National League (1876) proscribed the playing of games on Sunday, but the American Association (Nov. 1881) allowed it. In Dec. 1891, the National League allowed Sunday baseball in those cities whose laws permitted such practices. "I defy any one to say that the morals of New York have been lowered since Sunday baseball was given to the people" (New York City mayor Jimmy Walker, at a baseball dinner in 1926, quoted in Richard C. Crepeau, *Baseball: America's Diamond Mind, 1919–1941*, 1980, p.155).

Sunday best Syn. of *Sunday pitch*.

Sunday hop A ground ball that lands in front of a fielder with an easy-to-field bounce. See also *charity hop*; *gravy hop*; *Hollywood hop*.

Sunday pitch A pitcher's most effective offering; his out pitch. "Well, a pitcher out there, if he's a fast ball pitcher his best pitch, what we call a Sunday Pitch, would be his fast ball" (Dizzy Dean, *Dizzy Baseball*, 1952). Syn. *Sunday best*.

Sunday pitcher An old pitcher who works only one day a week. "I'm getting old [29] anyway. Maybe it's time I became a Sunday pitcher" (Sandy Koufax, quoted in George Vecsey, *The Baseball Life of Sandy Koufax*, 1968, p.127; Charles D. Poe).

Sunday swing A hard hit; a long drive (Maurice H. Weseen, *A Dictionary of American Slang*, 1934).

sun delay Halting a game to allow the sun to

drop just low enough to get out of the eyes of the players. "Despite a giant sun screen erected at Bakersfield's home park, which unfortunately faces west, four consecutive recent games were delayed until the sun dropped out of the line of the players' vision" (*USA Today*, July 1, 1993).

sun field That part of the playing field where there is the most sun in the fielders' eyes during an afternoon game. To many, the most notorious sun field in baseball is left field at Yankee Stadium, especially the late afternoon sun of October, when the World Series is played. Other sun fields include right field at Fenway Park in Boston and left field at the Polo Grounds in New York. The proliferation of night games has given this term a whiff of nostalgia. Syn. *sun garden.* IST USE. 1896. "Charley [Abbey] doesn't allow his fad for the social swim to handicap his reliable work in the sunniest sunfield in the country" (*The Washington Post*, June 18).

sunfielder An outfielder who plays in the sun field. IST USE. 1911 (*Baseball Magazine*, October, p.16; Edward J. Nichols).

sunflower seed finger Pain caused when three fingers are used repeatedly to grab sunflower seeds from a player's pocket. As the pinky finger spreads the pocket, it causes stress between the third and fourth fingers. Philadelphia Phillies team doctor Phillip Marone and trainer Jeff Cooper diagnosed the phenomenon in the June 1995 newsletter of the professional baseball athletic trainers (*The Baltimore Sun*, June 30, 1995).

sun garden Syn. of *sun field.* IST USE. 1921. "[Walter Johnson] scored on [Sam] Rice's hit to the sun garden" (*The Washington Post*, May 21).

sunglasses Dark-tinted eyeglasses used as a protection from the sun. Sunglasses are part of the uniform of many players, esp. outfielders, during day games. Modern baseball sunglasses differ from other sunglasses in that the lens rests against the bottom of the bill of the cap and is flipped down quickly over the eyes as needed. Pittsburgh Pirates manager Fred Clarke invented the flip-down sunglasses hinged to the cap, receiving a

patent for the device in 1916. As described by *The Sporting Life* (Apr. 6, 1912; Peter Morris): "[The 'sun-cap' for outfielders] permits the wearer snapping the glasses into place with a flick of the finger. . . . A small lever . . . allows the glasses to drop down into position before the wearer's eyes." According to *Total Baseball* (7th ed., 2001), Paul Hines in 1882 was the first player to wear sunglasses in the field.

sun hit A batted ball that falls in for a hit because the fielder loses track of it in the sun. IST USE. 1897 (*New York Tribune*, Aug. 9; Edward J. Nichols).

sunshine game The game of baseball. "Fired managers, superfluous coaches, and deterritorialized scouts—all looking for the fortuitous handshake, the whiskey-warmed happenstance that will readmit them, however distantly, to the sunshine game" (Roger Angell, *The Summer Game*, 1972).

super Syn. of *soupbone,* 1. "I don't like to cut loose too early, but I felt so good I couldn't help it. The old super of mine is in good shape" (Jack Killilay, quoted in *San Francisco Bulletin*, March 6, 1913; Gerald L. Cohen).

Superbas Nickname for the National League franchise in Brooklyn, N.Y., from 1899 to 1910, which was renamed the Brooklyn *Dodgers* in 1911. So named after the musical comedy "Hanlon's Superbas" and in recognition of manager Ned Hanlon.

superscout A scout who keeps tabs on major leaguers on other clubs; "the right arm of the general manager . . . involved in trades— almost always on the major league level— and serves as an advance scout for the parent club" (Tony Lucadello, quoted in David V. Hanneman, *Diamonds in the Rough*, 1989, p.123; Peter Morris).

super-sinker A spitball. ETYMOLOGY. Gaylord Perry (*Me and the Spitter*, 1974, p.157) claimed that catcher Tom Haller "renamed" Perry's spitball a "super-sinker."

superstar An exceptionally talented and skillful baseball player. The term implies more than ability and achievement; James Michener (*Sports in America*, 1976) commented that a superstar is "someone who has great public appeal and can command a huge salary." Bill

Shirley (*International Herald Tribune*, Oct. 29, 1992) wrote: "Today the word is trite, cheapened by sportswriters and sportscasters who have given it to so many athletes they have rendered it meaningless." See also *star*, 1. IST USE (in baseball). 1930. "[Joe Cronin gives] American League arbitrators a big portion of the credit for making him a super star overnight" (Harold C. Burr, *Brooklyn Daily Eagle*, Sept. 8; Peter Morris). ETYMOLOGY. According to Michael McKinley (*Putting a Roof on Winter: Hockey's Rise from Sport to Spectacle*, 2000; Peter Morris), the term was coined by Frank Patrick to refer to hockey player Fred "Cyclone" Taylor around 1910. The term caught on in the 1960s, and the first athlete to be so labeled may have been New York Jets quarterback Joe Namath, who signed a rookie contract for about $400,000 in 1964.

Super Two A player who is eligible for salary arbitration with less than three years of major-league service; specif., a player in the top 17 percent of players (based on total service time) with two years of service and at least 86 days of service in the immediately preceding season.

supplemental draft A second special phase of what was once referred to as the amateur draft, held in January for previously drafted players who did not sign with their clubs. Beginning with the 1987 season, the supplemental draft was eliminated. Clubs that failed to sign a first-round selection of the amateur draft were given a supplemental first-round selection the following year.

supplemental instructions Guidelines from the commissioner's office to the umpires that supplement the *Official Baseball Rules*. These have long played an important role in determining how strictly particular rules are enforced, and for determining the procedures followed by umpires regarding the playing field, equipment, and other areas that fall under their jurisdiction during a game. An "Instructions to Umpire" letter from National League president Harry Pulliam was published in the *New York Sun* (Apr. 13, 1903). (Peter Morris)

supplemental pick Syn. of *sandwich pick*.

support **1.** Fielding aid to the pitcher in retir-

ing batters. "Last year [Tom Candiotti] received only 18 runs while pitching in 16 losses. However, to say he lacked for support would be misleading as the [Oakland] A's defense repeatedly stopped insurrections before they started with brilliant defense" (Joe Strauss, *The Baltimore Sun*, May 29, 1999). IST USE. 1867 (Chadwick Scrapbooks clipping, Sept. 7; Edward J. Nichols). **2.** See *run support*.

support-neutral statistics A family of indices for evaluating pitcher performance relative to what a pitcher would achieve on an average team, based on the pitcher's game-to-game performance. Members of this family include support-neutral wins, support-neutral losses, support-neutral lineup-adjusted value added, support-neutral value above replacement, and support-neutral lineup-adjusted value added above replacement. The measures were created by Michael Wolverton and Keith Woolner and described by Baseball Prospectus (*Between the Numbers*, 2006).

sure out **1.** A predictable putout; e.g., throwing to first base on an infield play. Often with a runner on base, the fielder will make the sure out at first base rather than risking a throw to get an advancing baserunner with a play that may not be made successfully. Syn. *safe out*. **2.** A batter who is not likely to get a base hit. See also *easy out*, 1.

surprise bunt A bunt that is attempted when the circumstances of the game do not suggest one. IST USE. 1935. "There are two types, the sacrifice bunt and the surprise bunt" (Ralph H. Barbour, *How to Play Better Baseball*; David Shulman).

surrender For a pitcher to give up hits and runs; e.g., "Smith surrendered two consecutive doubles and one run."

surveyor A player with a good eye at the plate; one who walks frequently by not swinging at balls out of the strike zone.

survival drive The effort made by a player to maintain his overall effectiveness.

suspect A minor-league player whose potential appears questionable or very limited; a player who is not considered a *prospect*. "It's time to start separating the prospects from the suspects" (*Baseball America*, Oct. 15–28, 2001; Peter Morris).

suspend 1. To stop temporarily a baseball game because of inclement weather or some unforeseen condition. 2. To deny a manager, player, coach, or other person the privilege of participating for a stated period of time because of an infraction of the rules. "The [Pittsburgh] Pirates are going so badly that their mascot, the Parrot, was suspended for a game after throwing a Nerf Ball at umpire Fred Brocklander" (Richard Justice, *The Washington Post*, May 3, 1987).

suspended game A *called game* that is to be completed at a later date. A suspended game shall be resumed at the exact point of suspension of the original game, immediately preceding the next scheduled single game between the two clubs on the same field, if possible. A game terminated for any of the following reasons will be a suspended game if it has progressed far enough to be an official game: a curfew imposed by law; a prearranged time limit; darkness where local law prohibits turning on the lights or where lights are not available; a light failure or malfunction of a mechanical device (including automatic tarpaulin or water-removal equipment) under the control of the home team; weather (if the game is called while an inning is in progress and before the inning is completed, and the visiting team has scored one or more runs to take the lead, and the home team has not retaken the lead); and, beginning in 2007, a game is called with the score tied. In the minor leagues, if a suspended game is continued prior to another regularly scheduled game, the latter game is shortened to seven innings.

suspended list A list of players who are insubordinate or violate any regulation or other provision of their contracts, or who fail to get into playing condition within 60 days after the beginning of the club's training season. Suspended players receive no salary and are not eligible to play with any other major- or minor-league club. Suspended players count against both the reserve list and the active list of a major-league club. Compare *ineligible list*; *disqualified list*; *restricted list*.

suspension 1. The temporary stoppage of play, for such game-related occurrences as an injured player or dead ball. External causes for a suspension of play come primarily from bad weather. 2. A period of time during which a player, manager, coach, or other person is ordered from the field of play because of a flagrant violation of the rules, or for conduct deemed detrimental to the club, the league, or baseball in general. Typically, suspension is the punishment for doctoring the bat or ball, refusing to obey the umpire, or touching an umpire during an argument.

SV Abbrev. for *save*, 2.

swack To hit the ball hard. "11,724 fans cheered the Babe and saw him swack a curveball . . . over the right-field wall" (William Kennedy, quoted in Ron Fimrite, ed., *Birth of a Fan*, 1993, p.130).

swan dive A line drive that suddenly takes a downward plunge and cannot be caught on the fly, usually going for a hit.

swang Var. of "swung," past tense of *swing*, 1. According to Dizzy Dean, who had his own patent on the term, "this is what a guy has done after he has took a cut and missed." *Time* magazine (Apr. 24, 1950) commented on Dean's creative way with the word "swing": "The fans also noted, for future reference, that the Arkansas-born announcer conjugates the verb *to swing* as *swing, swanged, swunged*."

swap 1. *v.* To *trade* a player or players. IST USE. 1886. "Whatever truth there may be in the 'swapping' story, there is no doubt that [St. Louis Maroons owner Henry V. Lucas] would be glad to be rid of [Fred Dunlap and Jack Glasscock]" (*The Boston Globe*, June 11; Peter Morris). 2. *n.* A *trade*. IST USE. 1904. "Negotiations are on between St. Louis and Brooklyn for a swap of players to strenghten the weaker team in Greater New York" (*The Washington Post*, Aug. 21; Peter Morris).

swap meet A time period during which intensive effort is exerted to strengthen rosters for the final two months of the season. "Over the next two weeks, the major league baseball swap meet will swing into action . . . with several teams looking to either sell or buy before the July 31 deadline for non-waiver deals" (Drew Olson, *Milwaukee Journal Sentinel*, July 15, 2001; Robert F. Perkins).

swat **1.** *v.* To hit the ball, esp. with power and for distance. "Every time a Seal swatted the ball hard an Oaklander bobbed up with a sensational catch" (*San Francisco Bulletin*, May 14, 1913; Gerald L. Cohen). IST USE. 1891 (*Chicago Herald*, Aug. 25; Edward J. Nichols). **2.** *n.* A swing at, and hitting of, a pitched ball. IST USE. 1902. "Two strikes were called upon him, . . . when with a mighty swat the batter made good" (*Detroit Tribune*, Aug. 17; Peter Morris). **3.** *n.* A long hit, good for extra bases. IST USE. 1893. "Their swats are always wide apart" (*San Francisco Examiner*, Apr. 10; Peter Morris). **4.** *n.* Hitting prowess. Ed Delahanty was called "King of Swat" for his .346 lifetime batting average, and Babe Ruth was called "Sultan of Swat" for his 714 lifetime home runs.
USAGE NOTE. Over time, the word "swat" has been put into several other baseball constructions. Maurice H. Weseen (*Dictionary of American Slang*, 1934) lists, among others, "swat parade," and "swat streak." ETYMOLOGY. The term has long signified a knock, hit, or hard rub. EXTENDED USE. This fascinating item appeared in *American Notes & Queries* (July 1948): "FLY SWATTER: a term coined by Dr. Samuel J. Crumbine, who in 1904 was appointed head of the Kansas State Board of Health; he was taking a bulletin—on flies as typhoid carriers—to the printer one day, and stopped off to watch a ball game, where he heard 'sacrifice fly' and 'swat the ball,' etc., and immediately decided to call the bulletin 'Swat the Fly.' Only a few months later a man came to him with an instrument that he wanted to call a 'fly bat' and Dr. Crumbine persuaded him to call it a 'fly-swatter.'" The man in question was Frank Rose, whose son, Bob, retold the story in *Reminisce* magazine (Sept.–Oct. 1992), adding that his father was a schoolteacher in Weir, Kans., when he read of Crumbine's antifly crusade. The doctor's literature gave him an idea. "My father was a scoutmaster at the time, so he had plenty of help for any civic project he chose to take on. He acquired some yardsticks and screen wire from the local lumberyard. Then he had his scouts saw the yardsticks in half, cut the wire into small squares and nail them together. The scouts decided to call their creations 'fly bats.'"

swatfest A game in which there are many hits. Compare *slugfest*. IST USE. 1904. "A brilliant rally in the second game at Philadelphia recalled the days of Delehanty [*sic*], when he led the way for a swatfest and the others followed" (*The Washington Post*, July 11).

swatlet *hist.* A base hit. "The play was full of snap and life and two-base swatlets" (*San Francisco Examiner*, Apr. 9, 1893; Peter Morris).

swatsman A hitter. IST USE. 1913. "Miller Huggins is leading the National League swatsmen" (*San Francisco Bulletin*, May 31; Gerald L. Cohen).

swatsmith A hitter. IST USE. 1908 (*New York Evening Journal*, May 5; Edward J. Nichols).

swatster *hist.* A hitter. IST USE. 1913. "The dependable swatsters of the Oak tribe have failed to get their eyes on the pill" (*San Francisco Bulletin*, Apr. 15; Gerald L. Cohen)

swatstick A baseball bat. IST USE. 1908. "With his swatstick, too, [Fred] Tenney has a record to be proud of" (*New York Evening Journal*, Aug. 27; Peter Morris).

swatter A hitter. "The [San Francisco] Seals have the honor of furnishing the leading swatters of the league" (*San Francisco Bulletin*, Apr. 15, 1913; Gerald L. Cohen). IST USE. 1905. "Judging from the way [Willie] Keeler, [Jimmy] Williams, and [Patsy] Dougherty are thumping the ball in the South, the Highlanders will start out with three mighty swatters" (*The Washington Post*, Apr. 9).

sweat ball A variation of the spitball, employing a player's sweat.

sweating The practice by a club owner of assembling a team of low-priced players, then taking that team to New York and other prime baseball communities in the early spring to collect large receipts that the good clubs draw on their home fields. Noted Damon Runyon (*New York American*, Oct. 9, 1921; Steve Steinberg), "The owner of the cheap club collects enough during these early games to carry him through the season to a neat profit. Where his club finishes is a matter of no concern to him. He has no civic pride. He is in the game for the money, and he gets it. . . . We could never think of a good name for the process until we thought of the old fraudulent scheme of 'sweating' gold coin. That's what it is, this baseball business we have described—'sweating.'" Runyon referred to the practice of shaking gold pieces up and down in a canvas bag until particles gradually wore off the coins, which are used at full-face value while the particles are gathered up and sold.

sweep 1. *v.* To win all of the games in a series. Fans have been known to wave whisk brooms as they chant "Sweep! Sweep!" when the home team bids to complete a winning series. "Montreal swept the season's six-game series against Arizona" (*The Baltimore Sun*, Aug. 13, 2004). **2.** *v.* To win both games of a doubleheader. **3.** *n.* Winning both games of a doubleheader, or all games in a series or season by one team over another. "The [Kinston] Indians completed a four-game sweep of the host [Frederick] Keys" (*The Baltimore Sun*, June 5, 2006). See also *grand slam*, 2; *slam*, 4. **4.** *v.* For a batter to swing his arms too far from his body, thereby subtracting from the power and accuracy of his swing. **5.** *n.* A batter's swing. "Most long men are in trouble when the ball swishes past their hands, and when they hit it they usually have to do so with a difficult sweep of the slapstick" (*The Sporting News*, Aug. 11, 1910; Peter Morris). **6.** *n./hist.* A very long hit. "[Fred Treacey] struck out for another clean home run by a sweep to centre" (*Chicago Tribune*, July 6, 1870; Peter Morris). **7.** *v./hist.* To make a long hit. "[George] Hall swept magnificently clean of the centre field, making a home run and clearing the bases" (*Chicago Tribune*, July 6, 1870; Peter Morris).

sweeper 1. A curveball with a long, pronounced break. "[Jamie Moyer] has two curveballs, a big sweeper he works on the outside corner and another which bites down and in" (STATS Inc., *The Scouting Notebook*, 1999; Peter Morris). **2.** Syn. of *stabber*, 1.

sweep tag A tag on a sliding baserunner in which the fielder's arm holding the ball is moved down in a continuous arc to intersect the path of the runner. It is most common in a situation where a runner is attempting to steal. Syn. *swipe tag*.

sweetheart A star player, esp. a pitcher, who rises to the occasion. "Baseball is not without romance, for it has 'sweethearts.' Lou Gehrig, Dizzy Dean, Carl Hubbell, Charley Gehringer and other accomplished stars of the first magnitude are referred to with that cordiality by teammates and rivals" (Edwin M. Rumill, *Christian Science Monitor*, Sept. 1, 1937). IST USE. 1937. "The boys have their own lingo . . . 'sweetheart' for a star pitcher" (*Fortune*, August, p.112).

sweet spot 1. The most desirable spot for an autograph on a single-signed baseball; the section of a baseball reserved for the team manager to autograph. Syn. *manager's spot*. **2.** The section on the barrel of a baseball bat where the ball most likely can be hit solidly and for maximum power, giving it the best ride. It is the center of percussion, which, when hit by the ball, produces no recoil of the wrists (other than a twisting action), the least amount of vibration at the handle, and the maximum exit speed of the ball. It is the spot on the bat where the inertia of the swing is most efficiently transferred to the ball. The sweet spot will vary with the length and diameter of the bat, and with the density of the wood used to make the bat (the denser the wood, the larger the sweet spot). Quoted sizes of the sweet spot vary from three to 10 inches from the top (barrel) end of the bat. Metal (aluminum) bats have larger sweet spots than those of wood bats. A profile of batmaker Dave Cook (*Chicago Tribune*, June 15, 1993) noted, "He wanted to make a bat that would have a hard, heavy 'sweet spot'—baseball lingo for a bat's business area—but would have a light handle and top. So he made the sweet spot out of hickory, the handle out of ash and the top end out of maple." Syn. *joy spot*; *joy zone*. IST USE. 1957. "Babe Ruth is said to have insisted on a cluster of pin knots in the barrel of the bat at the 'sweet spot' where he hit the ball" (*Gettysburg Times*, Aug. 22; Peter Morris). EXTENDED USE. **1.** A similar spot on clubs used in other sports, such as the head of a golf club where the best contact is made to hit the ball high, long, and straight. **2.** The preferred landing site for an extraterrestrial craft. When the *Spirit* rover landed in the Gusev Crater on Mars, the mission's principal investigator, Steven Squyres (Cornell Univ.), commented, "We have hit what the science team believes is the scientific sweet spot" (*The Baltimore Sun*, Jan. 5, 2004).

sweet swing The easy, fluid, seemingly effortless but effective swing by a batter; a graceful, unforced swing in which the batter has good balance. A sweet swing is aesthetically pleasing apart from any results it may achieve. Hitters with sweet swings are usually left-handed; e.g., Barry Bonds, Will Clark, Don Mattingly, Reggie Jackson, Rafael Palmeiro, and Ted Williams.

swerve A curveball. IST USE. 1932 (*New York Sun*, June 23).

swift *hist.* A fastball. "The 'swift' of Walter Johnson would be worthless to a chap who couldn't get the ball over the plate" (George Herman Ruth, *Babe Ruth's Own Book of Baseball*, 1928, p.41).

swift ball *hist.* A fastball. IST USE. 1896. "Lange caught a swift ball squarely on the trade mark and drove it clear to the clubhouse in center field" (*The Boston Globe*, July 23; Peter Morris).

swing **1.** *v.* To move the bat in a full arc in an attempt to hit a pitched ball. A batter who swings and misses is credited with a strike even if the ball is thrown outside the strike zone. See also *swang.* **2.** *n.* A cut at the ball; the action of a batter in attempting to hit the ball. If the umpire decides that the batter stopped before making a bona fide attempt to meet the ball, it is not considered a swing and the pitch is ruled a ball. IST USE. 1868. "Slows, to be well punished, require to be waited for and judged well, with a timely swing of the bat" (Henry Chadwick, *The Game of Base Ball*, pp.45–46). EXTENDED USE. To undertake some endeavor is to "take a swing at it." **3.** *n.* The movement of the pitcher's arm during his windup. IST USE. 1905. "The 'speed merchants' who wind up their 'wings' and take numerous swings before cutting loose to the batter" (*The Washington Post*, March 16; Peter Morris).

swing a big bat To have a high batting average.

swing and miss **1.** *v.* To swing at a pitch and not hit it; to fan. **2.** *n.* A swinging strike. "[Matt Herges] lacks the swing-and-miss pitch that closers need" (*Sports Illustrated*, March 25, 2002).

swing away To take a full cut at the ball. "The home run is the most wonderful instant gratification there is, but swinging away comes with a penalty. You strike out more" (Lou Piniella, quoted in *Sports Illustrated*, March 19, 2001). See also *hit away.*

swinger **1.** A batter who takes a full cut at the ball, rather than choking up on the bat and simply trying to meet the ball. In pre-Ruthian times, Hugh S. Fullerton (*American Magazine*, June 1912) wrote, "The 'swinger' is a type of player not wanted in finished ball clubs. They usually are long distance hitters, but uncertain and usually finish with low averages." This opinion does not prevail today. See also *free swinger*, 1; *swing hitter.* IST USE. 1910 (*American Magazine*, July, p.395; Edward J. Nichols). **2.** A batter who, in the words of Jim Brosnan (*The Long Season*, 1960), "will try to hit any pitch that doesn't hit him." See also *free swinger*, 2.

swing for the fences To attempt to hit a home run by swinging with maximum force. Syn. "swing for the seats." EXTENDED USE. To go all out. "[President George W. Bush] is swinging for the fences now. He's got only a few years left to make his mark" (Paul West, *The Baltimore Sun*, Feb. 3, 2005, commenting on Bush's 2005 state of the union speech as he opened his final term in office). "The natural inclination of most people who do our jobs is not to swing for the fences" (former NBC executive Preston Beckman, on not picking up *Seinfeld* in 1989, quoted in *The Baltimore Sun*, Nov. 23, 2004).

swing from the heels To swing with all of one's power, which involves rocking back on one's heels for added leverage. It contrasts with a simple, level swing, which is often more effective. "Batters looking to show off on national TV focus on the long ball, swinging from the heels on virtually every pitch, often at the expense of putting the ball into play in key situations" (Allen Barra, *The Wall Street Journal*, July 9, 2003). IST USE. 1928. "The big, burly, powerful chaps, began taking their bat at the end and 'swinging from the heels' as the boys say" (George Herman Ruth, *Babe Ruth's Own Book of Baseball*, p.152; Peter Morris).

swing hitter A batter who holds the bat at the end and takes a full cut. George Herman Ruth (*Babe Ruth's Own Book of Baseball*, 1928, pp.151–52) commented, "['Swing hitters'] are the fellows who grasp their bats at the end, take a toe hold at the plate and take a full swing at the ball with all the power they can muster. They're the chaps who bust the fences and send the outfielders back to the wall. They're the fellows who do most of the striking out too. . . . Some folks say I was responsible for the development of 'swing hitting.' Maybe they're right." See also *swinger*, 1.

swinging bunt A poorly hit ball that slowly rolls a short distance from the batter in much the same way a bunt would roll. Though sometimes claimed to be intentional, a swinging bunt is commonly the result of a pitch being hit on a checked swing. It is not scored as a bunt even though it has the characteristics of one. "Charlie Hayes led off by hitting a swinging bunt, topping a ball that rolled slowly down the third-base line and stayed in fair territory" (*The Baltimore Sun*, Oct. 24, 1996). Compare *bunt*, 1. Syn. *bug crawler*, 2. IST USE. 1933. "Beyers dribbled a swinging bunt toward first base on a hit-and-run play" (*Sheboygan* [Wisc.] *Press*, June 19; Peter Morris).

swing late To swing at the ball as it crosses the plate, when it is thus difficult to hit.

swing like a rusty gate To look inept and perform badly at the plate; to swing wildly at a pitch. John Krich (*El Béisbol*, 1989, p.226; Peter Morris): "I take a giant whack that seems to unfold in slow motion. Fans call this the rusty gate—a swing ascribed to aging veterans who've lost the reflexes to get around on a fastball."

swing man 1. A pitcher who is both a spot starter and a reliever; a pitcher who can enter the starting rotation when the regular starter is not able to play. 2. A position player who can play more than one position. "When I went to spring training . . . [New York Yankees manager Yogi Berra] told me he wanted

me to be a swing man, playing at first base and the outfield" (Don Mattingly, quoted in *Tampa Tribune*, June 25, 1984). 3. An umpire who does not belong to one crew but rotates among several.

swing the bat 1. To come to the plate to be a batter; to have the opportunity to be a batter. "I knew that Eddie Murray [as a rookie] was a guy I wanted to see swing the bat" (Earl Weaver, *Weaver on Strategy*, 1984). "[Barry Bonds] will probably see fewer pitches to hit than in the past, have fewer chances to swing the bat" (Dan O'Neill, *St. Louis Post-Dispatch*, Oct. 1, 2002). EXTENDED USE. To confront a difficult situation. Television actor Matthew Perry on overcoming his addiction to the painkiller Vicodin after having his wisdom teeth removed and falling off a Jet Ski: "I know that given a really difficult situation, I stepped up and swung the bat and helped myself. Anything can come at me now and I feel like I can take it because I got myself through that" (*TV Guide*, quoted in *The Baltimore Sun*, Apr. 28, 1998). 2. To generate offense; to have the potential to get base hits and score runs. Boston Red Sox first baseman Mike Stanley, on the Cleveland Indians (quoted in *The Baltimore Sun*, Sept. 19, 1999): "We know they swing the bats. They put up Nintendo numbers." Baltimore Orioles infielder Tony Batista (quoted in *The Baltimore Sun*, May 5, 2002): "I think I'm swinging pretty good. It doesn't matter where they throw the ball, when you're swinging the bat well." Pitching coach Dave Stewart (quoted in *The Baltimore Sun*, Apr. 16, 2002): "When a guy swings the bat as well as Barry [Bonds] swings the bat, what you try to do is vary your looks."

swing zone The place where the batter's swing meets the pitch. Denny Neagle (quoted in *Cincinnati Enquirer*, July 4, 1999) explained, "If my pitch is coming down at an angle, it's not in the hitter's swing zone as much as if it's flat. A hitter has so many more chances to hit a flat pitch. . . . But if it's angled, he's just got that one spot, and that makes it a hell of a lot harder."

swipe 1. *n.* A *stolen base*. "[Brian] Roberts' swipe . . . was part of a double steal" (*The Baltimore Sun*, May 1, 2005). 2. *v.* To steal a base. IST USE. 1897. "[Tiernan] had himself touched out while obeying a crazy signal to swipe a bag" (*The World* [New York], May 14; Peter Morris). **3.** *v.* To go through the sweeping motions of tagging out a baserunner; e.g., "They just swipe the ball in there and half the time they don't touch 'em." **4.** *v.* To swing at a pitched ball, either successfully or unsuccessfully. "Wood has his eye on the ball now, and is swiping it in good style" (*Canton* [Ohio] *Repository*, Apr. 27, 1888; Peter Morris). "[John Montgomery] Ward swiped at the ball and missed" (*The World* [New York], Oct. 26, 1889; Gerald L. Cohen). **5.** *n.* A wild or awkward and unsuccessful swing by a batter at a pitched ball. "[Scrappy Bill] Joyce made a terrific swipe at the next ball and missed" (*Brooklyn Eagle*, June 8, 1892; Peter Morris). **6.** *n.* A successful swing by a batter at a pitched ball. "Buck Weaver got the only healthy swipe at [Hod] Eller's pitching when he cudgeled a three bagger" (*The New York Times*, Oct. 7, 1919). The term took on positive connotations when Babe Ruth popularized the full swing; e.g., "[Babe Ruth's] long swipe sailed over the right field wall" (*The Washington Post*, May 8, 1918; Peter Morris). IST USE. 1891 (*Chicago Herald*, July 2; Edward J. Nichols).

swipe tag Syn. of *sweep tag*.

swish **1.** *n.* A hard swing of the bat that makes no contact with the ball. **2.** *v.* To swing hard and miss. IST USE. 1893. "In a minute and a half Cooney swished the empty air three times" (*San Francisco Examiner*, Apr. 9; Peter Morris). **3.** *v.* For a curveball to move. "[Dutch Leonard's] half side-arm southpaw curve was swishing up to specifications" (Burt Whitman, *Boston Herald and Journal*, May 3, 1918). IST USE. 1910. "Most long men are in trouble when the ball swishes past their knees, and when they hit it they usually have to do so with a difficult sweep of the slapstick" (*The Sporting News*, Aug. 11; Peter Morris).

swisher A batter. "Ted Williams was a long and lean swisher" (*The Sporting News*, Aug. 17, 1960).

swish hitter A power hitter who strikes out frequently; e.g., Bill "Swish" Nicholson.

switch-hit To be able to bat from either the right-handed or left-handed side of the plate. IST USE. 1942. "[Dave] Bancroft and [Max] Carey switch-hit over a long period of years" (*Baseball Magazine*, July; David Shulman).

switch-hitter A batter who can hit from either side of the plate. A player with this skill tends to bat right-handed against left-handed pitchers and vice versa, with the advantage of never having to hit curveballs that are breaking away from them. This ability was rare in earlier decades: "Switch-hitting appears to be dying out in baseball, bearing out Andy High's contention that the noble athletes, despite lingering ideas to the contrary, can do better by confining their activities to one side of the plate" (Jerry Brondfield, *San Francisco News*, July 4, 1938; Peter Tamony). However, more players have developed the ability to hit both ways since a switch-hitter named Mickey Mantle first came to both sides of the plate in 1951. Pete Rose, Eddie Murray, Howard Johnson, Tony Fernandez, Tim Raines, Ozzie Smith, and Roberto Alomar are examples of post-Mantle-era switch-hitters. The first professional switch-hitter was right-handed batter Bob Ferguson, captain of the Atlantics of Brooklyn, who switch-hit on June 14, 1870, to avoid batting the ball to the Cincinnati Red Stockings shortstop George Wright; he singled in the tying run in the 11th inning as the Atlantics delivered the Red Stockings their first defeat in almost two seasons of play. Also spelled "switch hitter." Syn. *turn-around hitter*; *turn-over hitter*; *switch-sticker*. EXTENDED USE. Any person who radically alternates his or her orientation. The term is commonly applied to a person who "swings both ways" (i.e., one who is bisexual).

switch-pitch **1.** *n.* A changeup. "American Leaguers who had batted against him said he was tough when he kept the ball low, especially his change-up or switch-pitch" (*San Francisco Examiner*, Apr. 10, 1963; Peter Tamony). **2.** *v.* To be able to pitch both right- and left-handed in the same game, an extremely rare ability.

switch-pitcher A pitcher who can throw either right-handed or left-handed; e.g., Tony

Mullane, Larry Corcoran, and Elton "Icebox" Chamberlain. An article in *The New York Times* (Apr. 7, 1986) concerning the ambidextrous Texas Rangers pitcher Greg A. Harris was entitled "Switch-Pitcher."

switch-sticker Syn. of *switch-hitter.* "Reggie Smith is a 'switch-sticker'" (Lowell Cohn, *San Francisco Chronicle*, June 4, 1980).

swoon A slump; specif., *June swoon.*

syndicate baseball Interlocking ownership in which one person or a small group has controlling interests in more than one baseball club in a league. To preserve the structure of the National League after the 1898 season and to avoid bankruptcy of some teams, such owners capitalized on their position by transferring the best players from one team to another; e.g., Ferdinand Abell, Charlie Ebbets, Ned Hanlon, and Harry B. Von der Horst moved the best players from Baltimore, which had experienced a decline in attendance, to Brooklyn, where the population was greater owing to trolley lines linking the boroughs of New York; and Frank Robison and Stanley Robison transferred the best players from Cleveland to St. Louis. The practice was soundly criticized in the press and resented by the fans; it was formally banned in 1910. Syn. "syndicatism."

synopsis of innings *hist.* See *line score.*

synthetic doubleheader A scheduled doubleheader during the 1930s. The word "synthetic" referred to doubleheaders being forced into the schedule (to attract more fans during the Depression) rather than occurring naturally from rainouts.

synthetic turf Syn. of *artificial turf.*

Syracuse car *hist.* A railroad car in which the rookies rode. ETYMOLOGY. "The Pullman in which the rookies and substitutes ride. Originated with the Giants who used to play an exhibition game in Syracuse each year. Usually the second string men would play the game and their car would be shunted off at Syracuse while the others went on to the next big league town to enjoy a day off" (George Herman Ruth, *Babe Ruth's Own Book of Baseball*, 1928, p.300).

T

T 1. Box score abbrev. for *time of game*. **2.** Abbrev. for *triple*, 1. **3.** Abbrev. for a fielder's throwing handedness (left-handed or right-handed).

TA Abbrev. for *total average*, 1.

tab To select a player; e.g., "The manager tabbed Smith to start the game."

tabasco Vigor or energy as exhibited by a player or a team. *The Atchison* (Kans.) *Daily Globe* (June 23, 1896) described a "vigorous batter" as having "tabasco sauce in his arms." IST USE. 1895 (*New York Press*, July 8; Edward J. Nichols). ETYMOLOGY. From the trade name of the hot and spicy pepper sauce produced by the McIlhenny Co. of Louisiana.

table 1. See *set the table*. **2.** See *off the table*.

table-clearer A hitter who drives in runs. "A table-clearer is only as valuable as his table-setters make him" (*Baseball Prospectus*, 2000; Peter Morris).

table-setter 1. A player whose role is to get on base and/or advance others to set up a scoring opportunity. A table-setter is usually the leadoff batter or the next following batter. See also *set the table*, 2. Also spelled "table-setter." **2.** Syn. of *setup man*.

tack-on baseball Scoring one run an inning to catch up or to build a lead gradually.

tacos A street game version of baseball played in Cuba, using "a plastic bottlecap for a ball, a branch or sawed-off broomstick for a bat" (S.L. Price, *Pitching Around Fidel*, 2000, p.39; Peter Morris).

tag 1. *n.* The touching by a fielder on a non-force play of a baserunner with the ball or with the fielder's hand or glove that is holding the ball securely and firmly, resulting in a putout. **2.** *v.* To touch a baserunner with the ball, or with the hand or glove holding the ball securely, resulting in a putout. Syn. *touch out*. IST USE. 1907 (Burt L. Standish, *Dick Merriwell's Magnetism*, p.243; Edward J. Nichols). **3.** *n.* The touching by a fielder of a base with his body while the ball is held securely and firmly in his hand or glove, resulting in a putout. **4.** *v.* To touch a base with any portion of the body while in firm possession of the ball in the hand or glove, resulting in a putout. **5.** *v.* To hit the ball hard. IST USE. 1917 (*American Magazine*, July, p.42; Edward J. Nichols). **6.** *v.* See *tag up*. **7.** *v.* To charge a pitcher with a loss; e.g., "The Yankees tagged Smith for his third straight loss." **8.** *v.* To make base hits or score runs off a pitcher. "[The Detroit Tigers] clearly had his [Mike Boddicker's] number again Friday, tagging him for three runs on nine hits" (*Tampa Tribune*, Aug. 7, 1988).

tagger A player who makes a tag. "The best 'taggers' among the first basemen in those days were Joe Kuhel and Joe Judge" (Bill Starr, *Clearing the Bases*, 1989; David Shulman).

tagout *n.* A putout in which a fielder with the ball touches a baserunner when he is off the base.

tag out *v.* To put a runner out by touching him with the ball when he is off the base.

tag up 1. For a baserunner to touch a base before advancing to the next base on a batted ball caught before hitting the ground. With less than two outs, a baserunner attempting to gain a base or score on a fly ball can tag up the moment the fielder touches the ball, but not a split second earlier. On a reasonably deep fly ball, a runner on third base will nor-

Tag out. Washington Senators baserunner Roger Peck-inpaugh is tagged out. *National Photo Company Collection, Library of Congress*

mally have time to tag up and score. IST USE. 1935. "Tag-up—to retouch the base occupied, if a runner, after a fair or foul ball has been caught" (Ralph H. Barbour, *How to Play Better Baseball*, p.175; David Shulman). **2.** For a baserunner to return to a base and touch it before taking another lead.

tail **1.** *n.* The lateral movement of a few inches of a pitch (such as a fastball) as it crosses the plate. **2.** *v.* For a fastball to move laterally a few inches as it crosses the plate. "[The fastball] got off on the tip of my finger and tailed in" (Jason Johnson, quoted in *The Baltimore Sun*, June 15, 2003).

tail away **1.** For a pitched ball to move down and away from the batter. **2.** For a batted ball (such as a line drive) to move down and away from the fielder.

tail-ender **1.** A team at or near the bottom of the standings. "Champions have no time to waste in apologetic dallying with tail-enders" (*The World* [New York], Sept. 17, 1889). Syn. *tail-end team.* IST USE. 1886. "The latest news of the Cuban League is to the effect that the Union Club, the tail-ender in the race, has disbanded" (*St. Louis Post-Dispatch*, Feb. 27; Peter Morris). **2.** A player who is near the bottom in a statistical list. "It looks queer to see Frank Fennelly's name among the batting tail-enders" (*St. Louis Post-Dispatch*, Aug. 22, 1888; Peter Morris).

tail-end team Syn. of *tail-ender*, 1.

tailing fastball A fastball that moves a few inches laterally away from the batter as it

crosses the plate. Thrown by a right-handed pitcher, the ball moves away from a left-handed batter; thrown by a left-handed pitcher, the ball moves away from a right-handed batter.

tail-off A decline in the batting average of a hitter.

tailspin A losing streak.

take **1.** *v.* To refrain from swinging at a pitched ball; to permit one strike to be thrown before swinging at the ball; to look at a pitch. Batters often "take a pitch" or "take a strike" to get an idea of what a pitcher is throwing. Taking is most common when the count is 3–0. A batter may be told to "take" by his manager, which occasioned Jim Brosnan (*The Long Season*, 1960) to give this definition of taking: "A batter being forced to watch a pitch cross the plate that he obviously would have hit out of the ball park if the manager had only permitted him to swing." **2.** *n.* An instance of taking a pitch. **3.** *v.* To defeat an opponent. IST USE. 1880 (*Chicago Inter-Ocean*, June 11; Edward J. Nichols, who noted the etymology is the shortening of the phrase "take into camp" or "take the measure of." **4.** *v.* To field ground balls; e.g., "Smith took several grounders at third." **5.** *v.* For a fielder to alert his teammates that he will attempt to catch a fly ball or pop-up that other fielders could have caught. "Manning came along on the full run and saying 'I'll take it'" (*The Boston Globe*, Aug. 6, 1885). See also *take the ball*, 3. **6.** *v.* To hit a home run. "Nick Markakis took him [Kei Igawa] to left field for a bases-empty home run" (*The Baltimore Sun*, Apr. 8, 2007). See also *take deep*.

take a cut To swing hard at a pitch. IST USE. 1932 (*Baseball Magazine*, October, p.496; Edward J. Nichols). EXTENDED USE. To go all out. Shirley Povich (*The Washington Post*, Sept. 17, 1943; Peter Morris) wrote, "To take your cut at the ball is now a many-faceted metaphor for giving your all." Povich cited Dwight Eisenhower's recent description of the Allied strategy: "We are playing in the big leagues. You can't hit a home run by bunting. You have to step up there and take your cut at the ball."

take a drink To strike out. The term is a play on the presumption that the batter has time to go back to the dugout for a sip of water after failing at the plate. IST USE. 1916 (Ring W. Lardner, *You Know Me Al*; Edward J. Nichols).

take a lead To move several steps off a base in the direction of the next base to get a head start when the pitch is delivered or a ball is batted.

take a little off Syn. of *take something off*. "[Dontrelle Willis will] take a little off when the hitter expects a fastball, then bust a hard one, wasting few pitches along the way" (Childs Walker, *The Baltimore Sun*, Sept. 8, 2005).

take all the way To let a pitch go by, having had no intention to swing regardless of the pitch's location.

take a nap To get picked off a base.

take and rake For a batter to get bases on balls and/or hit home runs.

take a pitch See *take*, 1.

take a strike See *take*, 1.

take a stroll downtown To hit a home run.

take deep To hit a long ball, esp. a home run, off a pitcher; e.g., "[Rafael] Palmeiro took him [Pete Walker] deep with one out in the fourth" (*The Baltimore Sun*, June 23, 2005). Correspondingly, a pitcher will say a given batter "took me deep"; e.g., "Brad [Wilkerson] took me deep, so that didn't feel very good at all" (Josh Fogg, quoted in *USA Today Baseball Weekly*, Aug. 14–20, 2002). See also *go deep*, 1; *take*, 6.

"take him out!" Traditional call from the stands for the manager to remove an ineffective player, almost always a pitcher. "The saddest words of all to a pitcher are three—'Take Him Out'" (Christy Mathewson, *Pitching in a Pinch*, 1912). IST USE. 1908 (*Baseball Magazine*, December, p.36; Edward J. Nichols).

take him over the wall To hit a home run (Jim Bouton, *Ball Four*, 1970).

take into camp *hist.* To beat another team badly and therefore, presumably, administer a lesson. IST USE. 1884. "The strong league team from Cleveland, which club had benefited by two games with the Metropolitans, in one of which they had taken the Mets into camp by 7 to 0" (*Brooklyn Eagle*, Apr. 13;

Peter Morris, who notes that the term may have influenced the use of the term 'camp' to designate a club's spring training site, since that is where the players learn, or relearn, the fundamentals of the game).

take it to the house To retire from baseball. "If we win the World Series, I'm taking it to the house" (*The Baltimore Sun*, Oct. 3, 2002).

take it with you To hit a drag bunt for a base hit.

"Take Me Out to the Ball Game" Baseball's unofficial anthem, written in 1908 by Jack Norworth, a vaudeville performer and songwriter, during a subway ride to Manhattan, N.Y. At a station stop, an advertisement, "Base Ball Today—Polo Grounds," caught his eye. In about 25 minutes, he scribbled the lyrics (two stanzas and one chorus) on a few scraps of yellow paper, as easily as one might take dictation. The music was written by Albert Von Tilzer, who had collaborated with Norworth on "Shine on, Harvest Moon." The song was an immediate hit on the vaudeville

"Take Me Out to the Ball Game." Jack Norworth (left) asks directions to the ballpark. *George Grantham Bain Collection, Library of Congress*

circuit and in sheet-music stores. Norworth was honored with a special day at Ebbets Field on June 27, 1940, his first time at the ballpark; when asked how he liked that first baseball game, he would reply: "Not bad. The peanuts were good too."

take off 1. To remove or rescind a previous sign. 2. See *take something off*. 3. For a pitched ball to suddenly rise or deviate laterally as it nears the plate. 4. To leave a base in a hurry, such as in an attempted steal.

take-off sign Syn. of *wipe-off sign*.

take one for the team 1. To allow oneself to be hit by a pitched ball. "[Craig Biggio] was bonked for the 200th time. . . . Only Don Baylor (267) and Ron Hunt (243) have taken more for the team than Biggio" (*ESPN The Magazine*, May 27, 2002). See also *team*, 4. 2. To pitch through a bad performance, thereby allowing the bullpen to rest.

take one on the meat To be hit by a pitched ball (H.G. Salsinger, *Baseball Digest*, Aug. 1945).

take out 1. For a baserunner to block or slide into an infielder, usually done to disrupt the infielder's throw to another base. 2. To hit a home run. Derek Jeter to Mariano Rivera (quoted in *Sports Illustrated*, Nov. 6, 2000): "You know what he's [Mike Piazza] trying to do here; he's trying to take you out. . . . This guy's not just trying to loop the ball over second. He wants to take you deep." 3. See "*take him out!*"

takeout slide A hard slide by a baserunner into a fielder in such a way as to attempt to prevent the latter from making a pivot for a double play. "[Shortstop] Derek Jeter's left lower leg was bruised and his knee sprained on a hard, takeout slide by John McDonald in the third inning" (*The Baltimore Sun*, July 5, 2002).

take sign A sign from a coach telling a batter not to swing at the next pitch. It is usually given on counts in the batter's favor (2-0, 3-0, or 3-1) and when the team needs baserunners. An alternative definition from Jimmy Cannon (*Baseball Digest*, Nov.–Dec. 1956): "How a manager tells a hitter he hasn't any confidence in him." IST USE. 1937 (*Philadelphia Record*, Oct. 9; Edward J. Nichols).

take something off To throw a changeup or

slow ball after a fastball or series of fastballs. "[Sidney Ponson] has used more off-speed pitches and has even taken something off his fastball to better locate it" (*Sports Illustrated*, Aug. 4, 2003). Syn. *take a little off*.

take the apple Syn. of *feel the apple*.

take the ball 1. For a manager or coach to remove a pitcher from the game by literally and figuratively taking the baseball out of his hands on the mound. 2. For a ready and eager pitcher to assume his pitching duties. The term is often used to describe a starting pitcher: "I'm just going to go about my business and do what I need to do to take the ball every fifth day" (Pat Hentgen, quoted in *The Baltimore Sun*, March 14, 2001), and "Once you take the ball, you've got a job to do" (Darryl Kile, quoted in *The Baltimore Sun*, June 23, 2002). Hentgen, Kile and the rest of the 2000 St. Louis Cardinals pitching staff "had a three-word slogan that summed up their commitments to the team, themselves and the game they loved. *Take the ball*" (Joe Christensen, *The Baltimore Sun*, Aug. 4, 2002). See also *take the mound*; *want the ball*. 3. For an outfielder to signal his teammates that he will attempt to catch a fly ball or pop-up. Sam Crawford (on Dummy Hoy in the outfield, quoted in Lawrence S. Ritter, *The Glory of Their Times*, 1966): "We never had any trouble about who was to take the ball." See also *take*, 5.

"take the bat off your shoulder" A jeering instruction given to a batter who appears lackadaisical at the plate.

take the bat out of his hands 1. For a pitcher to keep a batter from hitting, either by pitching with great effectiveness or intentionally walking the batter. 2. For a baserunner to attempt to steal a base with two outs and a good hitter at the plate, which creates the option (if the steal was successful) of intentionally walking the batter or (if the steal was unsuccessful) of ending the inning when the hitter could have perhaps driven in a run. "[Melvin] Mora was caught stealing third base for the final out of the first inning, taking the bat out of Rafael Palmeiro's hands" (*The Baltimore Sun*, June 4, 2004). 3. For the manager to give the take sign to a batter.

take the blankets off *hist.* To use a player in a game (Maurice H. Weseen, *A Dictionary of American Slang*, 1934).

"take the blood off" Syn. of *"wipe the blood off."*

take the button off his cap To pitch a ball that comes close to the batter's head.

take the collar To go hitless in a game.

take the extra base To strive to advance as far as possible on a base hit. "Even the guys who don't run well, we've got to take the extra base. Last year we lost a lot of games by one run, and we never took the extra base, and that cost us" (Rafael Palmeiro, quoted in *The Baltimore Sun*, Apr. 4, 1996).

take the mound To be the starting pitcher; e.g., "The Chicago Cubs rookie [Kerry Wood] took the mound for his first start" (*The Baltimore Sun*, May 13, 1998). See also *take the ball*, 2.

take the throw To receive a baseball being thrown to make a play.

take the trainer to dinner For a player to enter the trainer's room on a frequent basis.

"take three and sit down" A jeering admonition to a batter, likely to come from the stands or the bench of the opposing team (Peter Tamony)

"take two" 1. To instruct a batter to allow two strikes to be called with the hope that the pitcher will issue a walk. IST USE. 1909 (*American Magazine*, May, p.402; Edward J. Nichols). 2. To instruct the batter-runner to try for a double on a hit to the outfield (Al Schacht, *Al Schacht Dope Book*, 1944, p.46).

"take two and hit to right" Traditional instruction given to a struggling batter that calls for him to let two pitches go by (take two) and then hit the ball to the right side of the field. The term usually is reserved for an inept batter, uttered in a derisive tone, and meant more as an insult than advice. "A poor hitter is characterized as someone who 'takes' two strikes (the implication being that he was fooled by them) and then, in an act of desperation, lunges at the ball and hits it weakly . . . to right field, where a weak right handed hitter would most likely place a poorly hit ball" (Lawrence Frank, *Playing Hardball:*

The Dynamiics of Baseball Folk Speech, 1983, p.93). EXTENDED USE. A phrase of encouragement. Harry Jupiter (*San Francisco Examiner*, May 31, 1989) discussed the use of the term by Frank McCulloch, managing editor of the newspaper, who used it to encourage the troops in the newsroom by saying, "take two and hit to right"; asked where he picked it up, he said, "I've been hearing it all my life. It's one of those old baseball phrases. . . . But I haven't the slightest idea how it got started. Maybe I'd better quit saying it."

"take your base" Traditional instruction by the plate umpire to a batter who has just been given a base on balls or has been hit by a pitch to advance to first base. IST USE. 1867 (*New York Sunday Mercury*; Edward J. Nichols).

talcum ball A ball doctored with talcum powder, giving it the same illegal advantages as a spitball. IST USE. 1916. "[During the 1915 season] hardly a game passed by in any league without some manager making accusations against the opposing pitcher . . . [e.g., there was] the 'talcum ball'" (Billy Evans, *Atlanta Constitution*, Jan. 16; Peter Morris).

talesman *hist.* The official scorer in some circles in the very early days of baseball. See also *tallyman*.

tall and fall See *stay tall and fall*.

tall grass *hist.* Low-level minor leagues, or bushes, where the grass grows tall. Syn. *tall timber*; "tall uncut"; "tall weed." IST USE. 1910 (*Baseball Magazine*, April, p.63; Edward J. Nichols).

tall timber *hist.* Syn. of *tall grass.* IST USE. 1905 (*The Sporting Life*, Sept. 9, p.19; Edward J. Nichols).

tally 1. *n.* A run. The scores in a game between Carroll College freshmen and Waukesha (Wisc.) townspeople were called "tallies" in a report of the game published in the *Waukesha Republican* (June 6, 1857; Frederick Ivor-Campbell). IST USE. 1856. "One hundred tallies constituted the game, and after three hours of hard and exciting playing the victory was won by the Olympics [vs. the Green Mountain Boys]" (*Boston Evening Transcript*, May 14; Richard Hershberger).

2. *n.* The score at the end of an inning or of a game. "This term applies to the total score of the single innings played, or of the even innings, or of the totals at the close of the match" (Henry Chadwick, *The Game of Base Ball*, 1868, p.46). **3.** *v.* To score a run. IST USE. 1905 (*The Sporting Life*, Sept. 2, p.18; Edward J. Nichols).

tally bell *hist.* A bell that was rung by a player who scored a run (tally) in the Massachusetts game so that all would know that the run had been entered in the record of the game.

tally-board *hist.* A scoreboard. IST USE. 1902. "Gleason's two misplays had no bearing on the tally-board" (*Detroit Free Press*, May 2; Peter Morris).

tally-ho *hist.* An open, horse-drawn carriage or wagon with benches, in which ballplayers, in uniform, rode to the ballpark from the hotel, often accompanied by a band. Visiting teams often had to ignore taunts, catcalls, and vegetables hurled by local fans.

tallykeeper *hist.* An early (1850s) syn. of *tallyman*, which is often used erroneously in describing vintage base ball games.

tally machine *hist.* The hand-held ball-and-strike *indicator* used by umpires in the 19th century. IST USE. 1887. "A new umpires' tally machine is just out. It registers five balls and four strikes in a very neat manner. It is made of ivory, and is held in the palm of the hand" (*The Chicago Inter-Ocean*, March 28).

tallyman *hist.* **1.** The scorekeeper. "The Tallymen shall be chosen in the same manner as the Referees" (Massachusetts Association of Base Ball Players, *The Rules of the Massachusetts Game*, Rule 21, May 13, 1858). See also *talesman*. Syn. *tallykeeper*. **2.** A batter who can be relied on to drive in runs. "[Heinie] Zimmerman is the real tally man of the Seal squad, having sent in more runs than any other two men on it" (*San Francisco Bulletin*, May 6, 1913; Gerald L. Cohen).

tampering 1. Negotiations or dealings relating to employment, either present or prospective, between a player and any club other than the club with which he is under contract; any attempt to approach the listed employees of a club without permission of the club. If a player is going to be a free agent at season's end and someone asks another club's manager or general manager whether they would like to pursue the player, the tampering rules prevent them from responding. "The Brotherhood players are tampering with [Jake] Beckley and [Pete] Conway, of the Pittsburgh [club]" (*Columbus* [Ohio] *Post,* March 8, 1890; Peter Morris). IST USE. 1859. "There was tampering with one or two of their [Upton] players, it is rumored" (*Worcester Spy*, Oct. 15). **2.** The infringement upon the territorial rights of a club by an individual or another club or prospective club who/which tries to acquire that club without obtaining the written permission of the affected club and/or league. **3.** Syn. of *doctoring*, 1. **4.** Syn. of *doctoring*, 2. **5.** Syn. of *doctoring*, 4. "Thomas J. Murphy . . . knew how to groom the playing field to [John] McGraw's specifications, tampering with the foul lines and varying the height of the grass as needed" (Mike Sowell, *July 2, 1903*, 1992, p.137).

tank 1. *n.* A player with a large rear end (Garret Mathews, *Can't Find A Dry Ball*, 2002). **2.** *v.* To make an error (Zack Hample, *Watching Baseball Smarter*, 2007, p.233). **3.** *v.* To fold in the stretch or clutch after previously playing well.

tank out To recognize a losing situation and not do one's best to overcome it.

tank town *hist.* A small town to old-time barnstormers and minor leaguers, probably from the fact that a train normally stopped in such a place only to take on water from a water tank. "[Grover Cleveland Alexander] went with a House of David team for a while, pitching a couple of innings each day around the tank town circuit" (Harry Ferguson, *Monessen* [Pa.] *Independent*, Apr. 14, 1941; Peter Morris).

tap 1. *n.* A lightly batted ball. IST USE. 1901 (Burt L. Standish, *Frank Merriwell's Marvel*, p.158; Edward J. Nichols). **2.** *v.* To hit a pitch lightly or without power. IST USE. 1869. "[Dick Pearce] tapped the first ball to shortstop and went out at first base" (*Brooklyn Eagle*, Sept. 7; Peter Morris).

tape-measure home run A very long home run; one that calls for measurement. At the major-league level, the term "tape measure" is linked to blasts of more than 450 feet.

"[Mike Witt] pitched his second complete game despite a tape-measure home run in the ninth by Cecil Fielder" (*Tampa Tribune*, Sept. 14, 1990). "Thousands of fans show up two hours early for games to enjoy [Mark] McGwire's tape-measure shots in batting practice" (*Milwaukee Journal Sentinel*, Sept. 17, 1997). Syn. "tape-measure shot"; "tape-measure job." ETYMOLOGY. The expression and the custom it refers to date to a spectacular home run hit by New York Yankees slugger Mickey Mantle on Apr. 17, 1953, off Washington Senators pitcher Chuck Stobbs. The ball, benefiting from a strong tailwind, cleared the left-center field bleachers at Griffith Stadium. Yankees public relations director Arthur "Red" Patterson immediately got up, left the ballpark, found and paid $5 to a neighborhood kid who had retrieved the ball, and announced the distance to the spot to be an unfathomable 565 feet (the actual distance in the air was about 510 feet), one of the longest on record, which was validated by an entry in the *Guinness Book of World Records* (although Patterson later confessed that there was no evidence the ball traveled 565 feet). Led by Mantle, the term attaches itself to only a few names in the game, including Willie Stargell, who became the first player to clear the bleachers at Dodgers Stadium on Aug. 5, 1969, with a 506-foot, 6-inch home run.

taper 1. *n.* The shape of a modern baseball bat; specif., the way the bat gradually narrows from the barrel toward the handle. The term comes from the similarity of the shape to that of a candle. Early baseball bats did not have tapers, or were said to have "straight tapers"—*The Washington Post* (Sept. 5, 1912; Peter Morris) described the popular Harry Davis bat as having a "straight taper" or one that narrows only slightly from the barrel to the large handle. In the early 20th century, tapers became shorter (or "quicker") as the short but thick barrel tapered decidedly to a thin handle. 2. *v.* For a baseball bat to gradually narrow toward the handle.

tapper A lightly hit ball, without power, usually hit back to the mound. "Will Clark hit a checked-swing tapper to the mound, where Ricardo Rincon started a double play" (*The Baltimore Sun*, Aug. 14, 1999).

tapperitis hitter *hist.* A hitter who hits tappers.

target 1. The positioning of the catcher's mitt prior to the pitcher's delivery. The catcher places his mitt at the exact point where he wants the ball to be pitched. 2. The outstretched catcher's mitt, which the pitcher is trying to hit with the ball.

tarp Short for *tarpaulin.*

tarpaulin The waterproof covering used to protect the playing field during a downpour. Originally made of heavy canvas coated or impregnated with tar to render them waterproof, tarpaulins in the modern era now use plastic-coated nylon or polyethylene. The 160-by-160-foot coverings weigh half a ton. Tarpaulins must be oversized to prevent water from running under the edge to a dirt area. They must be stored in an easily accessible location yet not create a safety hazard on the playing field. Baseball's oddest tarpaulin incident came in the midst of the 1985 National League Championship Series when St. Louis Cardinals outfielder Vince Coleman was injured by a moving motorized tarp that rolled over his foot and up his leg to mid-thigh. Like everything else in baseball, some tarpaulins are now covered with advertising. Syn. *tarp.* 1ST USE. 1884. "[St. Louis Browns 'ground-keeper' August Solari] has introduced an improvement which might be copied to advantage. It is the placing of tarpaulins over the four base positions to protect them from wet weather" (Henry Chadwick, reprinted in *St. Louis Post-Dispatch*, March 15; Peter Morris). USAGE NOTE. Other clubs were quick to follow Solari's innovation, and some of them also covered the pitcher's area, the batter's area, and the baselines with separate tarpaulins. But it was not until the 20th century that clubs began to cover their entire infields with a single tarpaulin. The first major-league club to adopt a single tarpaulin was Pittsburgh in 1908 (*The Sporting Life*, May 2, 1908, and *Chicago Tribune*, May 7, 1908; Peter Morris); Pirates manager Fred Clarke had his patent for a "diamond cover" approved on Feb. 7, 1911. ETYMOLOGY. From the nautical canvas used to cover hatches and protect cargo by keeping out water. In Daniel Defoe's 1719 novel *Robinson Crusoe*, the shipwrecked hero protects his tent with a tarpaulin he has rescued from his ship.

Tarzan "A slovenly, frowzy baseball player" (Maurice H. Weseen, *A Dictionary of American Slang*, 1934). ETYMOLOGY. From the hero of a series of jungle stories by Edgar Rice Burroughs.

tater A *home run*. "I'm a line-drive hitter, and if it happens to be up in the air, then I have a tater" (Lloyd Moseby, quoted in *St. Petersburg Times*, March 11, 1987). The term may have originated in the Negro leagues as *potato* but took on new life when George Scott made a habit of calling his home runs "taters" after coming to the Boston Red Sox in 1966: "The grin some grownups get when they think of George Scott, late of the Red Sox, examining his bats to see which ones had taters in 'em" (Rick Reilly, *Sports Illustrated*, May 26, 2003). See also *long potato*; *long tater.*

tattoo 1. To get several hits off a pitcher. "Rick Sutcliffe and five relievers get tattooed for 18 hits" (*Tampa Tribune*, Sept. 21, 1989). 2. To hit a baseball. "The way that [Dave] Parker tattooed pitches during exhibitions indicates that . . . [he] has set his sights on the Comeback Player of the Year award" (*The Sporting News*, Apr. 2, 1984).

taxi squad A special class of reserve players in the Arizona Fall League. "Asterisks denote players classified as members of the 'taxi squad,' meaning they are activated on Wednesdays and Saturdays only" (*Baseball America*, Sept. 15–28, 2003; Peter Morris). ETYMOLOGY. The All-America Football Conference had 33-player roster limits when the league began in 1946. However, Cleveland Browns coach Paul Brown arranged for several additional players to get jobs in Cleveland that would not interfere with practice. Since team owner Mickey McBride owned a fleet of Yellow Cabs, the extra players would be transported from their jobs to practice every afternoon in Yellow Cabs.

TB Abbrev. for *total bases.*

T-ball 1. A game played mostly by very young children in which there is no pitching and the batter hits a rubber ball placed on top of an adjustable, stationary tee at home plate.

See also *tee ball*. 2. Batting practice using a batting tee.

TBI Abbrev. for *Baseball Index, The.*

TC Abbrev. for *total chances.*

T-card Syn. of *tobacco card.*

teacher The manager of a baseball team. IST USE. 1917 (*The New York Times*, Oct. 6; Edward J. Nichols).

teacup end The scooped-out, concave top end of a *cupped bat*, believed by many to improve bat speed over the traditional round end.

team 1. The nine players (ten when the designated hitter is allowed) in a game. Syn. *nine*; *club*, 2. IST USE. 1860. "If the Hamilton had had a good team on hand the game would have been a far more interesting one" (*Brooklyn Eagle*, Aug. 2). ETYMOLOGY. Two or more draft animals in harness together. The term was first used in cricket: "[Hayward] having become a resident at Cambridge, joined the 'team' of that distinguished Club" (William Denison, *Cricket: Sketches of the Players*, 1846, p.32; John Thorn). 2. The entire uniformed congregation of a baseball club, including players, coaches, and the manager. See also *club*, 1. Syn. *ball team*; *baseball team*. IST USE. 1868 (*New York Herald*, July 24; Edward J. Nichols). 3. A team that exhibits teamwork. "Brooklyn now has a team. Last season they had only a picked nine" (*New York Sun*, May 17, 1886; Peter Morris). 4. Short for *take one for the team*, 1. The term is used by players who shout it when they want a teammate to allow himself to be hit by an inside pitch.

team effort A group activity in which everyone contributes. The term is used when a manager fears that one player is getting too much publicity.

team error A proposed error assigned to a team rather than to an individual player in situations in which an error must be charged but there is no individual player on whom to lay the blame; e.g., when two outfielders collide on a fly ball and as a result the ball falls safely, or when an accurately thrown ball from the outfield strikes a baserunner and as a result the ball bounces away and the baserunner advances a base. The team-error concept was first proposed by the Baseball

Writers' Association of America in 1970, advocated by Leonard Koppett (*The Sporting News*, Aug. 22, 1970), and embraced by many sportswriters (esp. Dick Young of the *New York Daily News*) and official scorers, but nixed by the Official Playing Rules Committee. The team-error principle would protect the records of pitchers and fielders.

team game [softball term] A sobriquet for fast pitch softball in which pitching was not so dominant that other members of the team had an effect on the outcome. Compare *pitcher's game*.

teammate A fellow member of a team.

teammates batted in Runs batted in minus home runs. The best lifetime figure is Ty Cobb's 1836; the best single-season figure is Hank Greenberg's 143 in 1937. The term and concept were developed by Richard Zitrin and Jules Tygiel, and evaluated by Bill James in his *Baseball Abstract* (1987). Abbrev. *TIBS*. Syn. *tibbies*.

team meeting Syn. of *clubhouse meeting*. "It

has been 12 days since Mount [Philadelphia Phillies manager Larry] Bowa erupted during a team meeting in Montreal" (Peter Schmuck, *The Baltimore Sun*, Sept. 10, 2003).

team-play Syn. of *teamwork*. IST USE. 1890 (*New York Evening Post*, June 13; Edward J. Nichols).

team player A player who works with others for the benefit of the team rather than playing for his own recognition; e.g., a player who hits to right field to advance a runner. IST USE. 1897. "[Fielder] Jones is a team player. If you can say anything stronger than that about a base ball man nowadays bring it on" (*The Sporting Life*, May 22; Peter Morris).

team rules Regulations that prevail at a particular ballpark (such as banning billboard ads) or for a particular team (such as banning facial hair and chewing tobacco).

teamwork Working together as a unit. Originally spelled "team work." Los Angeles Dodgers outfielder Ken Landreaux (quoted in *Sports Illustrated*, July 9, 1984, p.12): "Win-

Teammate. Baseball team composed mainly of child glass workers in Indiana, Aug. 1908. The photograph was taken by Lewis Hine, working for the National Child Labor Committee (NCLC). Over the next decade, Hine documented child labor in American industry to aid the NCLC's lobbying efforts to end the practice. *NCLC Collection, Library of Congress*

ning isn't as important as doing well individually. You can't take teamwork up to the front office to negotiate." Syn. *team-play.* IST USE. 1883. "Team work is the great requisite of infield play, as opposed to the picked nine style of fielding, in which players go in chiefly for their record" (*Spalding's Official Base Ball Guide*, p.19; Peter Morris). ETYMOLOGY. From *The Sporting News* (Jan. 25, 1902; Barry Popik): "Harry Wright was the pioneer and originator of what is known today as 'teamwork.' He developed points in the game that were never known before. . . . All styles and systems of teamwork of today got their beginning from Wright." The article also noted, "Teamwork, when expressed in horseology, means two or more horses that pull as one, and when expressed in base ball phraseology, it means nine players that play as one."

tear (pron. "tare") A winning streak for a team or a hot period for an individual; e.g., "The Yankees are on a tear during the current road trip."

tear the cover off the ball Syn. of *knock the cover off the ball.* From "Casey at the Bat" (Ernest L. Thayer, *San Francisco Examiner*, June 3, 1888): "But Flynn let drive a single, to the wonderment of all, / And Blake, the much despis-ed, tore the cover off the ball."

teaser 1. A slow, deceiving pitch to tempt a batter. "[Phoney Martin] had a slow 'teaser' . . . a slow ball [that] . . . was hard to meet fair, as he sent it in with a spin . . . [usually] very high, that dropped as it reached the plate without the semblance of a curve" (George Wright, quoted in *Fort Wayne* [Ind.] *News*, March 28, 1911; Peter Morris). IST USE. 1887. "[Hank] O'Day gave [Sam] Thompson one of those 'teasers' in which he delights" (*Detroit Morning Times*, May 23). 2. An especially deceptive pitcher. IST USE. 1883 (*Chicago Inter-Ocean*, May 27; Edward J. Nichols).

Tebeauism A style of ballplaying characterized by rowdyism and fighting, as practiced by Cleveland Spiders manager Patsy Tebeau (1891–1898).

Ted Williams Award 1. An annual award presented from 1997 to 2001 to the "most productive hitter" in the American League and in the National League. Sponsored by Total Sports Publishing, the award was based on a formula that included on-base percentage plus slugging percentage (OPS), adjusted for league average and home park factor. It was named for Williams, the last player to hit .400 in a season, but was discontinued when Total Sports went backrupt. 2. An annual award presented since 2002 by the Boston Chapter of the Baseball Writers' Association of America to the "best hitter in the game." 3. An award presented since 2003 by Major League Baseball to the most valuable player in the All-Star Game. See also *Arch Ward Memorial Trophy.* 4. An award sponsored by the Semper Fidelis Society, comprising former U.S. Marines, and presented to a non-Marine "who has the commitment and dedication to excellence" that Williams demonstrated in his life, "as well as the hard work and guts" Williams exemplified as a fighter pilot. Known as the Ted Williams Globe and Anchor Award, it was first presented in 2002 to pro boxer Irish Micky Ward.

tee 1. An adjustable, stationary pole on a solid base, atop which is a short length of hard rubber hose on which the ball rests, allowing a batter to hit it without the services of a batting-practice pitcher. It can be set at any height and placed anywhere in relation to home plate. The tee is used to help a batter adjust his stance, grip, stride, and other elements of his swing; it was a favorite "gadget" used by Branch Rickey "to study a hitter's power zone and his weak zone" (*The New York Times Magazine*, March 18, 1956). The tee is also used for playing T-ball. The tee was developed by Bert Dunne and unveiled in his book (*Play Ball Son!*, 1945). Joe Cronin, in his introduction to Dunne's *Play Ball!* (1951), wrote, "In the summer of 1946 [Dunne] came East with the Tee which he had finally perfected as a device for teaching hitting." Charlie Metro claimed in his autobiography (Charlie Metro, with Tom Altherr, *Safe by a Mile*, 2002) that he invented the tee in the 1930s. Syn. *batting tee; hitting tee; baseball tee.* 2. *hist.* A slang term for the pitcher's mound (*The Sporting Life*, Nov. 29, 1913).

tee ball The rubber ball used in *T-ball*, 1, and by Tee Ball Baseball of Milton, Fla.

Tee Ball 1. A division of Little League for boys and girls ages 6 to 8. The purpose is to teach younger kids the basics of the game. Balls are hit from a batting tee. **2.** An organization (Tee Ball Baseball of Milton, Fla.) founded by Dayton Hobbs in 1960 for players ages 5 to 8. The baselines are 45 feet apart and the orange rubber ball (hit off an adjustable-height tee) is nine inches in circumference and weighs four ounces.

tee drill An exercise for a pitcher who drops his shoulder when pitching. The pitcher kneels on one knee with the glove-side knee up and pointed straight toward the target. A tee is placed at shoulder level on the pitcher's throwing side. The pitcher makes the down, out, and up circular motion while turning his front shoulder so that it points toward the target before throwing to a partner. The goal is to assure that the pitcher's elbow does not drop down to the point that it hits the tee.

tee off 1. To hit a ball hard, an obvious borrowing from golf where the tee shot is the power shot. Players generally "tee off a pitcher's delivery," which William G. Brandt (*Baseball Magazine*, Oct. 1932, p.495) described as to "step right up and swing from their ankles instead of crouching carefully and taking a good look before making a pass at anything tossed towards the plate." **2.** To make many hits in a game or off a specific pitcher; e.g., "The Diamondbacks teed off on Smith for four hits in four at-bats."

tee party 1. A game or portion of a game in which batters tee off against a pitcher. **2.** A batting streak. IST USE. 1932 (William G. Brandt, *Baseball Magazine*, October, p.495; Edward J. Nichols).

Tegwar The card game with no rules that the ballplayers in Mark Harris' 1956 novel, *Bang the Drum Slowly* (p.18), played with unsuspecting people in hotel lobbies and on train trips. ETYMOLOGY. Acronym for "the exciting game without any rules."

telegraph To reveal unintentionally and prematurely. A pitcher may suggest through his mannerisms or motions the type of pitch he is about to throw; e.g., slower arm speed, when discernible to the batter, often telegraphs that a

changeup is being pitched. A catcher may tip off a pitch by giving an identifiable sign to the pitcher. An infielder may telegraph a sign to a batter by moving around before the pitch is delivered. "The play was telegraphed, wirelessed, phoned, heliographed and autographed by Mr. [Burt] Shotton. Everybody in the ball park but the groundkeeper and nine Cardinals knew it was coming" (*St. Louis Post-Dispatch*, Apr. 11, 1915). See also *tip*, 3. IST USE. 1909. "[Eddie Hahn was] caught on the paths . . . on a snap throw [by George] Mullin, which he telegraphed ahead" (Ring W. Lardner, *Chicago Tribune*, May 3; Peter Morris).

"tell it goodbye" San Francisco Giants broadcaster Lon Simmons' salutation for a home run.

Temple Cup A trophy awarded to the champions of a postseason best-of-seven series played from 1894 through 1897 between the first- and second-place finishers in the National League. It was named for 1892 Pittsburgh Pirates president William Chase Temple, who donated the $800 trophy. Lack of enthusiasm on the part of the players and fans doomed the series. The cup is now on display at the National Baseball Museum in Cooperstown, N.Y. The Temple Cup succeeded the *Dauvray Cup*.

tenant A baserunner.

tender *hist.* **1.** See *staketender*. **2.** See *basetender*.

10-5 player A major-league player who has been in the majors for at least 10 years and with his current club for the last five years. Under rules established in 1973, the contract of such a player cannot be assigned to another major-league club without the player's written consent.

10-man baseball Baseball played with a 10th player (*right short*, 2) positioned between first base and second base. It was proposed by Henry Chadwick and several exhibition games were played in 1874. Chadwick argued that the 10th man would free the first baseman and the third baseman to range into foul territory to pursue fair-foul hits. Although none of the major clubs adopted the scheme, many clubs in isolated areas assumed that the new 10-man game was now standard, and not only adopted it, but continued to use it for several years. See also *piten*.

tenney *hist.* A padded fielder's glove at the turn of the 20th century. According to Joseph McBride (*High and Inside*, 1980, p.82), it referred to first baseman Fred Tenney and his "small, fat, and almost circular" glove.

10-o'clock hitter A player who hits well during morning practice sessions, but poorly during the game. See also *12-o'clock hitter*; *one-o'clock hitter*; *two-o'clock hitter*; *five-o'clock hitter*; *six-o'clock hitter*; *seven-o'clock hitter*.

10-run rule A rule in some amateur leagues in which a game is stopped and a winner declared after seven innings if one team is ten or more runs ahead.

tenth man **1.** The loyal supporters of a team; the crowd in the sense that it can help or hinder a team. The Cleveland Indians have instituted the "10th Man Society," a program that honors the fans for their support of the team. "Cleveland fans supported their team tremendously. They were a 10th man, and [the Indians] got a lot of inspiration from them" (Baltimore Orioles outfielder Eric Davis, quoted in *The Baltimore Sun*, Oct. 15, 1997). **2.** An umpire who appears to be favoring one team over another. IST USE. 1870. "In Chicago umpires do not constitute the 'tenth man'; and it is to be regretted that the Forest City Club . . . should have seen fit to shelter itself behind a pretence of 'one-sided umpiring'" (*Chicago Tribune*, June 4; Peter Morris). **3.** *hist.* A substitute player in the early days of baseball, when clubs traveled with at most one substitute, thereby putting versatility at a premium. "Flynn is one of those thoroughly useful and sensible ball players who can afford to be the tenth, or general utility man, for the sake of the credit to be derived by doing everything well" (*Chicago Tribune*, June 1, 1870; Peter Morris). **4.** *hist.* The player designated before the game as a potential substitute according to the tenth man rule of 1889. "Beginning the tenth inning [Cap] Anson relieved [Gus] Krock and put in [Frank] Dwyer, who was on the card as tenth man" (*Chicago Tribune*, Apr. 30, 1889). **5.** Syn. of *designated hitter*. **6.** Syn. of *right short*, 2.

tenth man rule An 1889 rule that allowed a team to substitute for one noninjured player during a game (previously, substitutions had been allowed only in the case of injury and had to be consented to by the opposing captain). "The tenth man rule should have been taken advantage of in the third inning, when it was seen that [Bob] Caruthers' pitching was being easily punished" (*Brooklyn Eagle*, Apr. 26, 1889).

$10,000 beauty A 19th-century player whose contract was sold for $10,000; specif., Mike "King" Kelly, whose contract the Chicago White Stockings sold to Boston in 1887 for $10,000, an enormous sum at that time. When applied to a baseball player, the term suggested a star player and had no reference to the player's salary. The term was also applied to pitchers John Clarkson (sold by Chicago to Boston in 1887) and Ted Breitenstein (sold by St. Louis to Cincinnati in 1896); and as late as 1911 to Portland Beavers pitcher Ben Henderson (*Los Angeles Times*, July 7, 1911; George A. Thompson). ETYMOLOGY. The term was originally applied to actress Louise Montague, "the handsomest woman in the world," who accepted Adam Forepaugh's offer of $10,000 to travel with his circus in 1878. She was advertised as the "Ten Thousand Dollar Beauty" and rode in parades in a chariot especially constructed for her. "Miss Montague's claims to beauty is that she is a demi-blonde with classic features, a charming blue eye and a beautiful light complexion" (*National Police Gazette*, Apr. 23, 1881; George A. Thompson).

terminator The fastball.

terrace Then steep incline in front of the fence all around the outfield, most noticeably in left field and left center, at Crosley Field in Cincinnati.

territorial compensation A fee paid by a minor league to a lower classification league when one of the lower league's franchises moves to the higher league.

territorial rights The protection granted by a league or affiliated group of leagues of an exclusive baseball franchise in a particular city and within a specified radius from that city. Territorial rights were an extremely important element introduced by the founders of the National League in 1876, distinguishing it from the National Association, to which any club could belong by paying the entry fee. Peter Morris (personal communication, May 24, 2001) notes that in 1998, New York City mayor Rudolph Giuliani worked on a deal in which the Yankees and Mets would each waive their territorial rights so that the two clubs could move minor league teams into Coney Island and Staten Island. See also *home territory*.

territory **1.** The general area of a playing field for which a given fielder is responsible. IST USE. 1913. "Johnson, Brown outergardener, had a large number of chances. Eight flies, seven of which he accepted, were batted into his territory" (*The Washington Post*, Aug. 26; Peter Morris). **2.** Fair or foul ground; a ball is said to land in "fair territory" or "foul territory." **3.** See *home territory*.

tetrabatazo Spanish for "home run."

Texas League **1.** *n.* A minor league since 1902 (Class D from 1902 to 1906, Class C from 1907 to 1910, Class B from 1911 to 1920, Class A from 1921 to 1935, Class A1 from 1936 to 1942, and Class AA since 1946). **2.** *v./hist.* To bloop the ball. "If you can't shoot 'em, Texas League 'em" (*The Sporting Life*, May 18, 1912). **3.** *adj.* Characterized by weak (but lucky) hitting or pitching. "Wretched weather, miserable fielding by the Browns and pitching of a Texas league type summarize today's game" (*The Boston Globe*, May 1, 1893; Benjamin Zimmer).

Texas League fly Syn. of *Texas Leaguer*, 2. "Seymour poked a short 'Texas League' fly to right field" (John J. Evers and Hugh S. Fullerton, *Touching Second: The Science of Baseball*, 1910, p.287; David Shulman).

Texas League grip A nickname for *The Sporting News* based on the notion that the newspaper served as a wrapper for one's belongings. Charley Graham, in an interview (*San Francisco News*, Aug. 31, 1948; Peter Tamony) published just after his death, discussed the term while recalling the life of a minor-league player at the turn of the 20th century: "Our reading matter was *The Sport-*

ing News or the 'Texas League grip.' You wrapped your shirt, collar and underwear in it and that was your suitcase." ETYMOLOGY. "Grip" was a common synonym for a small suitcase in the 19th and early 20th centuries.

Texas League hit Syn. of *Texas Leaguer*, 2. "Callahan pitched good ball but at times his support was off color and several Texas League hits ran the score up in the sixth inning to five runs" (*Atlanta Constitution*, July 27, 1895; Benjamin Zimmer). Hy Turkin (*Baseball Almanac*, 1955) stated that the term was "first used to describe the kind of hits that enabled Arthur Sunday, fresh out of the defunct Texas League, to finish with a .398 batting average at Toledo in 1889." Turkin ended with a quote from a Toledo sportswriter that Sunday had hit another of those "Texas League hits."

Texas Leaguer **1.** A player from the Texas League. **2.** A poorly hit ball that loops meekly over the infield and lands for a hit; a fly ball just out of reach of the infielders, but too close in for an outfielder to catch it. Virginia Tech broadcaster Torye Hurst (quoted in *Roanoke Times and World News*, Apr. 16, 2006): "A little Texas Leaguer. Didn't even bend the grass when it landed." H.L. Mencken (*The American Language*, Suppl. II, 1948, p.737) defined the term as "a pop fly which nevertheless takes the batter to first base." The term has had regional variants, usually with derogatory connotations, in different minor leagues. Other names for Texas Leaguer include: *awful*; *banjo*; *banjo hit*, 2; *batazo podrido*; *bleeder*, 3; *bloop*, 1; *blooper*, 1; *chinker*; *drooper*; *dunker*; *flare*, 1; *half-liner*; *humpback liner*; *Japanese liner*; *lazy hit*; *leaping Lena*; *lollipop*, 2; *looper*; *nubber*, 2; *parachute*, 1; *percentage hit*; *plunker*, 2; *pooper*; *pop fly*, 2; *punker*; *sinker*, 3; *smell hit*; *special*; *squib*, 4; *stinker*; *sucker*; *Texas League fly*; *Texas League hit*; *tuberculosis liner*; and *up-over*. IST USE. 1892. "Then Peter Nabb came to the fore with one of his little three-baggers, a regular Texas Leaguer, which landed fair just beyond first and then bounded and rolled away in under the bleachers" (*Los Angeles Times*, Dec. 16; Benjamin Zimmer). USAGE NOTE. This term is always being tagged as archaic or old-fashioned, but nevertheless retains its currency. Here is how Damon Runyon used it in 1933 (*San Francisco Examiner*, Oct. 7; Peter Tamony): "[Joe] Cronin, with two and two on him, drops a lucky hit back of third. It is of the variety that used to be called 'Texas Leaguers.' It is too far back for [Hughie] Critz, and not far enough for [Mel] Ott to get." The term appears to have been used originally by non-Texans to belittle Texas League players brought up to the major leagues. Harwell E. West (*The Baseball Scrapbook*, 1938) noted that the "term [is] current everywhere but in Texas League."

ETYMOLOGY. Hugh S. Fullerton (*American Magazine*, June 1912) wrote that such hits are usually accidental but are sometimes accomplished on purpose "by good batters who merely tap the ball and float it safe." He went on to say, "The term originated from the fact that Ted Sullivan, the veteran player-manager-magnate, had a team in the Texas League that was noted for that kind of batting."

The *Los Angeles Times* (Jan. 25, 1921; Steve Steinberg) quoted J. Doak Roberts, Texas League president, who said the term originated in the early 1890s when a Syracuse pitcher gave vent to "Good Lord. Another of those Texas Leaguers." Quoting Roberts: "Emmett Rogers, Scrappy Bill Joyce and Arthur Sunday . . . were members of the 1889 team of the Houston club. . . . The trio were finished stars, past masters in the art of bunting and placing hits. The story goes that in their first game in bigger company they faced O'Brien of Syracuse. Rogers placed a hit over the infield, and the Syracuse defense moved in, expecting Sunday to bunt. Instead Sunday chip-shooted the ball and it dropped just out of the reach of the shortstop, who could not get it back in time. Joyce, too, was expected to bunt, but he followed in Sunday's wake, dropping another short hit back of third, scoring Rogers. It was then that O'Brien voiced his disgust and coined a new term for baseball."

Another version traces the term to either the major-league debut of Ollie Pickering in 1896 or his earlier debut (1892) in Houston of the Texas League. There are various versions of the story, but the earliest (1906) told of him showing up in Houston where he was given a trial with the team. He got seven hits in his first seven at-bats, "every one of which was a short, looping fly over first or third base that fell safe just too far out for the baseman to reach and just too far in for the gardeners" (*Cumberland* [Md.] *Evening Times*, July 25, 1906). An unidentified news clipping of Apr. 2, 1906 (on file at the National Baseball Library and Archives), stated that as word of the feat spread, these hits became known as "Texas Leaguers," since they had been made in the Texas League.

Zander Hollander (*The Encyclopedia of Sports Talk*, 1976) offered this theory: "So called because before the turn of the century the parks in the Texas League were particularly small." This contrasts dramatically with the theory Bill Brandt proposed on his *Inside Sports* radio show (Sept. 9, 1946; recorded by Peter Tamony): "In former days, the fences in the Texas baseball parks were away out in the wide open spaces, far from home plate. The outfielders had to play deep, and the consequence was that many short flies went for hits."

Finally, there is the Gulf Stream theory that E.V. Durling (*San Francisco Examiner*, 1948; Peter Tamony) attributed to New York Giants infielder Larry Doyle. According to Doyle, "The strong winds from the Gulf Stream greatly affected fly balls in most of the cities of the Texas League. A hard hit fly would seem certain to reach an outfielder and be too far out for an infielder. Then the wind would stop the ball's progress and cause it to drop for a hit between the outfielder and infielder."

textile league baseball Baseball among the competing mills in South Carolina from 1880 to 1955. See Thomas K. Perry (*Textile League Baseball*, 1993).

the 1. The definite article used idiosyncratically where general usage principles would call for an indefinite article. As explained by Leonard Shecter (*Baseball Digest*, June 1963), " 'The' is the most used word in baseball. No one knows why, but one does not simply say, 'He is a good hitter.' The expression is: 'He's got THE good bat.' One doesn't say anybody is a poor fielder; rather 'He's got THE bad hands.'" Shecter included other examples: "He's got the tools" and "He's got the good wheels." **2.** The definite article used for emphasis or to suggest supremacy; e.g., "Base ball is 'the' sport at the Sandwich Islands" (*The Sporting Life*, Sept. 10, 1884). From *The Washington Post*, July 28, 1907 (Peter Morris): "The article 'the' played a much more prominent part in ante-bellum [1860] diamond narratives than now. 'He reached the first base by an airball'; 'Jones played the second base well'; 'Smith had two putouts at the third base'—always 'the' before base, something that would make present-day chronicling of games seem very old timey." See also *good face, the*.

The Book See *Book, The*.

theft Syn. of *stolen base*.

thèque A Norman bat-and-ball game similar to rounders, characterized by a five-base, pentagon-shaped infield, the pitcher and batter being on the same team, and runners called out when struck by a thrown ball between two bases (*Le Soleil* [Quebec City], Jan. 21, 1899). Albert G. Spalding mentioned the old French game of "tecque" in *The Cosmopolitan* (Oct. 1889). David Block (*Baseball Before We Knew It*, 2005, pp.10, 147–50) discussed the confused history of the game, with references as early as 1447. Also spelled "tèque."

"there goes the ball game" A phrase spoken when a run or play wins a baseball game.

"there's no crying in baseball" A line uttered by a crusty manager (played by Tom Hanks) in the 1992 film *A League of Their Own* that has become a cliché for the unforgiving nature of baseball and that surfaces in a variety of contexts. Murray Chass (*The New York Times*, Aug. 29, 1999): "[The umpires] think they deserve a do-over. Except not only is there no crying in baseball but there are also no do-overs." USAGE NOTE. Kostya Kennedy (*Sports Illustrated*, Oct. 27, 2003, p.23) wrote an article entitled "There *Is* Crying in Baseball . . . and the Yankees Do Most of It" and quoted Univ. of Iowa professor Tom Lutz: "The Yankees are prime candidates for crying. Given their socioeconomic position as the richest, most advantaged team, it's easy to see how there would be some deep, subconscious conflict about being successful."

thief **1.** Syn. of *base stealer*. "[Scott] Podsednik is a thief, stung with the impulse to take off running" (*Sports Illustrated*, Aug. 15, 2005). IST USE. 1910 (*Baseball Magazine*, December, p.5a; Edward J. Nichols). **2.** One who is adroit at sign stealing.

thievery Syn. of *base stealing*.

thieving Syn. of *base stealing*. IST USE. 1910. "Base thieving" (*Baseball Magazine*, April, p.47; Edward J. Nichols)

thimble A small glove of a fielder.

thin Said of a team or pitching staff short on talent or rendered so because of a trade.

think tank The brain or head; the contents of a player's or manager's cap. "But 'Blondy' Moeller got things twisted in his think tank and allowed the ball to ooze through his dinner tongs" (Edward M. Thierry, *Baseball Magazine*, Sept. 1909). IST USE. 1893. "Early in the season they won the first twelve out of thirteen games played. This combined with Colonel Bourbon . . . and the eulogizing of players by every crank in town caused the 'think tanks' of three, the most promising in the club to swell to such a degree that any attempt to reduce same or create harmony was out of the question" (*The Sporting News*, Nov. 4; Peter Morris). EXTENDED USE. Many years after its original use as baseball slang, this term became general slang for "brain" and then for a policy research institute, such as the RAND Corporation.

third **1.** *n.* Short for *third base*, 1. IST USE. 1858 (Chadwick Scrapbooks clipping; Edward J. Nichols). **2.** *n.* Short for *third base*, 2. **3.** *n.* The third inning. **4.** *adv.* Said of the third position in the batting order; e.g., "Smith is batting third."

third bagger Syn. of *third baseman*.

third base **1.** The base located to the left side of and 90 feet from home plate, which is three-quarters of the way around the bases on the way to scoring a run. Abbrev. *3B*, 1. Syn. *third*, 1; *coffin corner*; *difficult corner*; *difficult station*; *hot corner*; *far corner*; *far station*; *far turn*; *odd corner*; *third corner*; *third sack*; *third station*. IST USE. 1845. "The bases shall be from . . . first to third base, forty-two paces, equidistant" (Knickerbocker Rules, Rule 4th, Sept. 23). **2.** The defensive position played by the third baseman. Abbrev. *3B*, 2. Syn. *third*, 2; *reaction position*. EXTENDED USE. In teenage slang, at various times since the 1930s, third base meant petting below the waist.

third base coach A member of the managerial staff who stands in the coach's box adjacent to third base. He normally decides whether a baserunner should stop at third or head home, and commonly gives signals to the batter. Syn. *yodeler*; *traffic cop*, 1; *flagman*; *traffic director*, 2.

third base hole The area between the shortstop and third baseman, near the outfield grass. See also *hole*, 1.

third base line The line extending from home plate to third base. See also *left field line*.

third baseman The defensive player stationed at third base. Abbrev. *3B*, 3. Syn. *third bagger*; *third sacker*. IST USE. 1870. "Jack Richardson, third baseman, and one of the best players on the Occidentals" (*Chicago Tribune*, July 23; Peter Morris). EXTENDED USE. A blackjack term for the player on the left-hand side of the table who is the last player to be able to ask for a hit (Donald I. Collyer, *Scientific Blackjack and Complete Casino Guide*, 1966).

third base umpire The *base umpire* at third base. Syn. *ukulele umpire*.

third corner Syn. of *third base*, 1. IST USE. 1895 (*New York Press*. July 8; Edward J. Nichols).

third-order measure A team's projected winning percentage based on its equivalent runs and equivalent runs allowed as measured by the Pythagenport method and then adjusted for strength of schedule. If a team's actual winning percentage is considerably better, then the team has been particularly lucky and/or has a particularly well-performing bullpen. The measure was proposed by *Baseball Prospectus*. Compare *first-order measure*; *second-order measure*.

third sack Syn. of *third base*, 1. IST USE. 1908 (*Brooklyn Daily Eagle*, May 22; Edward J. Nichols).

third sacker Syn. of *third baseman*. IST USE. 1905 (*The Sporting Life*, Oct. 7, p.24; Edward J. Nichols).

third station Syn. of *third base*, 1. IST USE. 1913. "[Doc] Kempson . . . will take care of the third station for the ruralites" (*San Francisco Bulletin*, May 1; Gerald L. Cohen).

third strike dropped See *dropped third strike*.

34 shift Syn. of *Ortiz shift*. The term refers to the defensive alignment when there are three infielders and four outfielders. Syn. "3-4 shift."

thirty-third degree fan *hist.* A diehard fan. President Warren G. Harding was the "first thirty-third degree, dyed-in-the-wool fan that ever sat in the White House" (Tom Rice, quoted in Richard C. Crepeau, *Baseball: America's Diamond Mind, 1919–1941*, 1980, p.69). "When he [the baseball writer] says 'Tinker led off for the Cubs and ozoned,' every legitimate thirty-third degree 'fan' grasps immediately the graphic picture thus painted" (*The Sporting Life*, May 20, 1905). "There are only fifty-two thirty-third degree base ball fans in Atchison. Just that number appeared at Forest Park during the drizzling rain yesterday to witness a struggle between Topeka and Atchison and just that number witnessed a twelve inning game, the longest contest in the history of base ball in Atchison" (*Atchison* [Kans.] *Daily Globe*, June 27, 1898; Greg Bond). IST USE. 1897. "33-degree cranks Tony March, Fred Goodman, Billy McConville and C. James Connelly were also there for the send-off" (*The Sporting Life*, March 27; Peter Morris). ETYMOLOGY. From Scottish Rite Freemasonry, which builds on the standard three degrees of initiation followed by 29 more, for a total of 32. The organization awards a special honorary degree (the 33rd) for exceptional service to those who have made an outstanding contribution to Masonry, the community as a whole, and to mankind; it is a singular honor, rarely bestowed, and greatly admired. A 33rd-degree Mason has gone as far as one can go; he is the ultimate in that discipline.

30-30 club A mythical group of players who have hit 30 or more home runs and stolen 30 or more bases in a single season. First to do it: Ken Williams of the St. Louis Browns in 1922, with 39 home runs and 37 stolen bases. Compare *20-20 club*; *40-40 club*; *50-50 club*. USAGE NOTE. When Jose Canseco spent 30 days in jail for his role in a nightclub brawl, *USA Today Sports Weekly* (March 26–Apr. 1, 2003; Peter Morris) reported that Harry Teinowitz (ESPN Radio) called Canseco "the first member of baseball's elusive 30-30-30 club."

"this isn't an eye test" Comment addressed to a player who takes a called strike (Eric Chavez, *Athletics*, Sept. 2005).

Thomas Edison *hist.* See *Edison*.

thousand-mile bus ride The fabled condition endured by players in the Mexican League.

thread the needle To pitch with skill and precision; to keep the batter from hitting the ball.

threat 1. A team that is likely to contend for first place. **2.** A player who is likely to hit or steal.

3 The scorekeeper's designation for the first baseman.

three Third base. The term is used by fielders to denote where to throw a fielded ball for a putout.

three and two A count of three balls and two strikes on the batter; a full count. Unless the batter fouls it off, the next pitch will determine if the batter is out or gets on base. "Thomas [Seaton] has not forgotten his old trick of 'three and two,' and it is usually the sixth ball that tells the tale" (*San Francisco Bulletin*, March 22, 1913; Gerald L. Cohen). IST USE. 1908 (*Baseball Magazine*, July, p.40; Edward J. Nichols).

3B 1. Abbrev. for *third base*, 1. **2.** Abbrev. for *third base*, 2. **3.** Abbrev. for *third baseman*. **4.** Box score abbrev. for *triple*, 1.

three-bagger Syn. of *triple*, 1. IST USE. 1880 (*Chicago Inter-Ocean*, June 29; Edward J. Nichols).

three-base error An error that allows the bat-ter-runner to reach third base. IST USE. 1878. "[Dick] Higham's was a 'three-base error'" (*Chicago Tribune*, July 7; Peter Morris).

three-base hit Syn. of *triple*, 1. "The poke invented to test your wind" (Milton Richman, *Baseball Digest*, May 1947). IST USE. 1871. "Bass made a clean three base hit" (*The Cleveland Morning Herald*, May 22).

three-baser Syn. of *triple*, 1. IST USE. 1871. "Allison made a splendid three-baser" (*The Cleveland Morning Herald*, May 22).

three blind mice A derogatory term for a three-man umpiring crew. Before the fourth umpire was added to the crew, the phrase was used to heckle the umpires as they came out of the dugout. One oft-told tale had Leo Durocher leading thousands of fans in greeting the umpiring crew, on the day after a series of disputed calls, with: "Three blind mice, see how they come!" At Ebbets Field in Brooklyn, a zany band of musicians known as the Dodger Sym-Phoney used to play "Three Blind Mice" when the umpires appeared. It has since been picked up by ballpark organists who have been known to play a few bars of the song after a disputed call. In 1985, an organist for the Class A Clearwater Phillies was ejected for playing the song. See also *blind mice*.

three-cornered shot Syn. of *triple*, 1. IST USE. 1891 (*Chicago Herald*, May 5; Edward J. Nichols).

three-decker A towering home run capable of landing in the real or imagined third and uppermost deck of a large ballpark.

three flies up A game in which the fielder, upon catching three fly balls, becomes the batter.

three-foot line A baseline that marks the last half of the distance to first base, situated parallel to and three feet to the right of the first base foul line, thereby forming a three-foot lane with the foul line, within which the batter-runner must run while the ball is being fielded to first base. If the batter-runner runs outside (to the right of) the three-foot line or inside (to the left of) the foul line, the umpire may call interference should the batter-runner interfere with the fielder taking the throw at first base; however, the batter-runner may run outside (to the right of) the three-foot line or inside (to the left of) the foul line to avoid a fielder attempting to field a batted ball. See also *45-foot lane*. Syn. *retaining line*.

.300 hitter A player whose batting average is .300 or higher. The term is one of high distinction, as an average above, or even close to, .300 is remarkable in any league. An article in the *Cleveland Press* (reprinted in *The Sporting Life*, May 9, 1908; Peter Morris) noted, "Why longer talk of a .300 hitter when speaking of excellence? The term is now a misnomer. It's just like talking of the greatest ball player instead of a great ball player. The .300 is now the greatest. When it comes to great, .275 is more like it from the standard set." IST USE. 1905. "There are thirteen 'three hundred' hitters in the Southern League" (*The Sporting Life*, June 24; Peter Morris). USAGE NOTE. The concept of .300 as a specific measure of accomplishment was noted earlier by the *St. Louis Post-Dispatch* (Aug. 22, 1888; Peter Morris): "There are only nine men in the [American] Association with batting averages of over .300." The term ".300 class" was used frequently in the early part of the 20th century.

300-300 club A mythical club composed of players who have hit 300 or more home runs and stolen 300 or more bases. Willie Mays was the first "member" of the club.

300/.300 club A mythical and exclusive club composed of players who have hit 300 or more home runs with a lifetime batting average of .300 or higher. The term was used by Bill Deane *(Baseball Digest,* Apr. 1984) when discussing Jim Rice's candidacy (Rice eventually hit 382 home runs but had a lifetime batting average of .298).

300 wins A major lifetime accomplishment for a pitcher. Although there are no specific requirements, 300 wins brings with it almost certain induction into the National Baseball Hall of Fame. However, future 300 winners may be rare because of five-man rotations (fewer starts per season), fewer complete games, smaller strike zones, and smaller ballparks. Dan Connolly (*The Baltimore Sun*, Aug. 13, 2006): "But no matter how the game changes . . . some fans and baseball people will always see 300 wins as the ultimate accomplishment."

Three-I League 1. *hist.* A Class B minor league that began in 1902 and ceased play in 1961, composed primarily of teams from Illinois, Iowa, and Indiana. The term was used in a derogatory manner when referring to the ineptness of minor-league players. See also *next stop Peoria*. Also spelled "Three-Eye League"; "3 Eye League." **2.** A figurative league in which players promote themselves. "[Older Yankees] viewed a younger player who talked too much and whose locker became something of a haven for the beat reporters as seeking too much publicity and promoting himself. He was a member, they said, of the Three-I League: I-I-I" (David Halberstam, *October 1964*, 1994, p.46; Peter Morris).

three-master Syn. of *triple*, 1. IST USE. 1891 (*Chicago Herald*, May 5; Edward J. Nichols, who notes "three masts high [far]").

three o'cat Syn. of *three-old-cat*.

3-oh-10 A cheap home run (Bill Mazeroski, *Bill Mazeroski's Baseball '89*, 1989).

three-old-cat A variant of *old-cat* featuring a triangular base layout, three batsmen, and three fielders. See also *kit-cat*. Syn. *three o'cat*.

three-peat 1. Winning three championships in a row. The term was used during the Oct. 9, 1990, CBS broadcast of the third game of the American League Championship Series (ALCS) as the Oakland Athletics were on their way to winning three consecutive ALCS (1988, 1989, and 1990). **2.** Two teams appearing in three consecutive World Series. "Yankee Stadium opened in time for the 1923 three-peat of Yanks vs. Giants" (Stephen Jay Gould, *The New York Times*, Oct. 19, 2000).

three-ply Said of a three-base hit; e.g., "three-ply blow" (*Al Schacht Dope Book*, 1944).

three-quarters delivery A pitching delivery in which the arm is between the sidearm and overhand deliveries. "In the three-quarter, the arm comes forward about three-quarters of the way between vertical and horizontal" (Connie Mack, *Connie Mack's Baseball Book*, 1950, p.92). Sometimes spelled "three-quarter delivery." Syn. "¾"; *round-arm delivery*.

three-sacker Syn. of *triple*, 1. IST USE. 1870. "Barnes hit a three-sacker, bringing Deming in" (*The Yale Courant*, Oct. 5; David Shulman).

three-six game A game in which three players produce six of a team's hits. Many such games will make a team successful over the long run (*San Francisco Sunday Examiner & Chronicle*, May 24, 1970).

3–6–3 The scorekeeper's notation for a double play in which the ball goes from the first baseman (3) to the shortstop (6) for the force at second base and back to the first baseman (3) for the second out.

three strikes A strikeout. See also *strike three*. EXTENDED USE. In the realm of public policy, "Three Strikes" legislation is meant to send third-time felons (in some places, violent felons; in other places, all felons) to jail for life without parole. The first of the Three Strikes proposals passed a Washington state referendum in 1993. A second variation on the law went into effect in California in 1994: it mandates 25 years to life or triple the usual sentence, whichever is more. Ellen Goodman (syndicated column, March 25, 1994) voiced her objection: "I have never been a fan of jocktalk in political life. The endless campaign lingo about slam-dunking opponents and hitting questions out of the ballpark has left me on the sidelines. But I am even more uncomfortable when sporting life stops being a metaphor and starts becoming public policy. This is exactly what is happening with the new favorite anti-crime legislation known as 'three strikes and you're out.' This is criminology according to Abner Doubleday." An early variation of this baseball metaphor appeared in the *New York Herald* (March 4, 1843; Richard Hershberger): "The notorious Tom Parks and the expert and daring burglar George Brown, alias Martin, charged with robbing the store of the Messrs. Phillips, of Boston, of $5000 worth of laces, &c., were bailed out of prison yesterday, and are now at large. Parks has escaped the hand of justice twice, and twice been retaken. The third time and 'out,' as the boys say in the game of ball."

3,000 hits A major lifetime accomplishment for a hitter. Although there are no specific requirements, 3,000 hits brings with it almost certain induction into the National Baseball Hall of Fame.

Three True Outcomes Walks, strikeouts, and home runs. Recent statistical analysis has attached particular significance to these three categories in measuring a pitcher's ability, since on all other plays it becomes problematic to determine whether pitching or fielding is responsible for the result. "The Cubs led the league in home runs and were third in unintentional walks drawn, so it probably shouldn't be too surprising that they led the league in the third leg of the Three True Outcomes, finishing first in strikeouts by almost 100" (*Baseball Prospectus*, 2003, p.276–77; Peter Morris).

three-two count A count of three balls and two strikes on the batter; a *full count*.

three up, three down Said of an inning in which the three batters are retired in order.

throat cutter Syn. of *knockdown pitch*.

throat guard Syn. of *goat's beard*.

throat protector Syn. of *goat's beard*.

through the hole Said of a ball that is hit through the space between two infielders, esp. between the shortstop and third baseman. IST USE. 1935. "A batsman hitting past an unguarded area of the infield is said to hit 'through the hole'" (Ralph H. Barbour, *How to Play Better Baseball*, p.175; David Shulman).

through the middle Said of a ball that is hit through the central part of the playing field (past the pitcher's mound, over second base, and into center field). Ted Williams, giving batting advice (quoted in Carl Yastrzemski, *Yaz*, 1968): "Hit the ball back through the middle. Hit everything—*everything*—back at the pitcher. Forget about pulling. That comes later. *Don't pull*, Y'understand? Through the middle. Okay?"

through the slot Said of a pitch that passes directly over home plate. See also *in the slot*, 3.

through the wickets Said of a batted ball that goes between the legs (wickets) of a fielder, often those of the pitcher.

through trip A home run. IST USE. 1917 (*The New York Times*, Oct. 2; Edward J. Nichols).

throw 1. *v.* To propel a baseball by a forward

motion of the hand and arm to a given objective. IST USE. 1845. "The ball must be pitched, not thrown, for the bat" (Knickerbocker Rules, Rule 9th, Sept. 23). **2.** *n.* The act of throwing, as distinguished (by the rules of baseball) from the act of pitching. Whereas a pitch is a ball delivered to the batter by the pitcher, a throw covers all other deliveries by one player to another. Hence, a pitcher throws to first base but pitches to the batter. IST USE. 1861 (*New York Sunday Mercury*, Aug. 10; Edward J. Nichols). **3.** *n.* A thrown ball. **4.** *v.* To designate a pitcher to start a game. High school coach Milt Axt (quoted in *San Francisco Call-Bulletin*, Apr. 2, 1953): "The day [Frank] Hall pitches, we will beat any team in the league. The only trouble is, I can't throw him every game." **5.** *v.* To deliberately allow the opposing team to win a game. "The 4–2 game last Tuesday . . . was thrown by St. Louis for the purpose of getting a larger crowd Thursday" (*Chicago Tribune*, May 27, 1877). IST USE. 1874 (*New York Herald*, Sept. 10; Edward J. Nichols). ETYMOLOGY. To "throw a race" was a horse racing term as early as 1868.

throw a glove To attempt to stop a batted or thrown ball by throwing a glove at it. There is no penalty for this action if the glove misses the ball, but if it hits a batted ball the batter is granted three bases, and if it hits a thrown ball each runner is granted two bases from the moment of the infraction.

throw-and-turn Said of a breaking ball in which the pitcher throws and does not snap his wrist until his hand has passed his head.

throw away **1.** To lose a game because of poor pitching or poor throwing; e.g., "Smith threw that game away by walking three batters" or "Jones threw away a game by making that error." IST USE. 1902 (*The Sporting Life*, July 12, p.3; Edward J. Nichols). **2.** To make a wild throw; e.g., "In his haste to retire the runner, Smith threw the ball away."

throwback **1.** A player who plays like one from a previous era; e.g., Pete Rose was a "throwback" to the days of Ty Cobb. "Cal Ripken Jr. and Kirby Puckett are throwbacks to an era when players stayed with one team their entire careers, and became a symbol of the city where they put on the home uniform" (*The Baltimore Sun*, July 5, 1995). "[Matt

Williams is] a throwback player, one who'll get his uniform dirty, do whatever it takes to win" (*Milwaukee Journal Sentinel*, Oct. 24, 1997). "[Don Zimmer] is a fighting ball player of the type who seems like a throwback to the earlier days of the game" (James T. Farrell, *My Baseball Diary*, 1957, p.256). IST USE. 1952. "[Clint Courtney] is a delightful throwback to the turtleneck-sweater era of the game" (Bob Bore, *The Sporting News*). **2.** A new ballpark that resembles an older one. "Citizens Bank Park [in Philadelphia] opens as sport's latest throwback" (*The Baltimore Sun* subheadline, Apr. 13, 2004). **3.** The uniform of a former team that is honored by a current team wearing it in a game. "The Orioles and Twins will wear throwback uniforms from 1975 tomorrow and Sunday, as the Orioles commemorate the 1970s in their continuing turn-back-the-clock series" (*The Baltimore Sun*, July 23, 2004).

throw darts To pitch with great control.

throw-down *hist.* A throw from the catcher to a player covering second base. IST USE. 1916. "Smith made the other [error] when he fumbled Sam's throw-down and let the runner steal second" (Christy Mathewson, *First Base Faulkner*, p.226; David Shulman).

thrower **1.** A pitcher without finesse; one who relies on speed and power as opposed to deceptive pitching and control. John Eisenberg (*The Baltimore Sun*, Oct. 12, 1998) reported that when things weren't right, David Wells had the tendency to become a "thrower": "An arm without a mind, in other words. Just a thrower, not a pitcher." College pitcher Mike Loynd (quoted in *The New York Times*, June 7, 1986): "The thing that disturbs me is when they're drafting pitchers, they're really not drafting pitchers. They're drafting throwers. They want somebody who throws 90 to 95 miles an hour. I feel I'm a pitcher. I throw 86 to 88, and my ball moves." Compare *pitcher*, 2. IST USE. 1877. "['The Only' Nolan] is a thrower, and scarcely an underhand thrower at that" (*Chicago Times*, reprinted in *London* [Ont.] *Free Press*, May 3; Peter Morris). **2.** The pitcher in the Massachusetts game and other early forms of baseball. The modern distinction between pitcher and thrower is nearly opposite the original one. **3.** *hist.* A baseball player. IST USE. 1867 (*Sunday Mercury* [Philadelphia], Sept. 7; Edward J. Nichols).

throw for the cycle **1.** For a player or a team to throw a baserunner out at each base and home plate during a game. It is the defensive equivalent of *hit for the cycle*. No outfielder has accomplished the feat, although Willie Mays came close: "[It] darn near happened— in May of 1966, when the Giants were playing the Dodgers at Los Angeles, and Mays threw out one man at home, another at first, another at third. He had a fourth one nailed at second, but the second baseman, his back to the oncoming runner, turned the wrong way and missed the tag" (Charles Einstein, *The Sporting News*, Jan. 17, 1970). **2.** For a pitcher to allow a single, double, triple, and home run (not necessarily in that order) during a single inning. "[Sidney Ponson] was pounded . . . after a six-run first inning in which he threw for the cycle and allowed 16 total bases" (*The Baltimore Sun*, Apr. 4, 1999).

throw ground balls To pitch balls that tend to yield grounders.

throw his glove into the box For a pitcher to dominate another team because his very appearance destroys the confidence of the opposing batters. IST USE. 1912. Christy Mathewson (*Pitching in a Pinch*; Peter Morris) noted that "all he's got to do is throw his glove into the box to beat that club" is "an old expression in baseball" because the pitcher's "reputation will carry him through if he has nothing whatever on the ball."

throw-in *n.* **1.** A marginal player included in a trade, often to complete a trade. Bill Veeck (*Veeck—As in Wreck*, 1962, p.144) opined, "The throw-in players can turn out to be more important in the long run than the guys you each set out to get." **2.** A throw made from an outfielder to an infielder or the catcher. IST USE. 1881 (*New York Herald*, July 23; Edward J. Nichols).

throw in *v.* To include a marginal player in a trade. IST USE. 1895. "[Wee Willie Keeler was] the man who was 'thrown in' to fill out that trade" (*The Sporting Life*, July 13; Peter Morris).

throwing arm The arm a player uses to throw

or pitch the ball. IST USE. 1863 (*New York Sunday Mercury*, Oct. 2; Edward J. Nichols).

throwing error An error resulting from a wild throw.

throw Laredo To throw underhand. Glen Waggoner and Robert Sklar (*Rotisserie League Baseball*, 1987) explained the term geographically: "The term is derived from the fact that Laredo is in the lower left-hand corner of Texas, which is where Kent Tekulve and Dan Quisenberry seem to be throwing from." The term also has been applied to sidearm pitchers. See also *Port Arthur.*

throw leather For a team to play good defense.

thrown ball Any delivery of the ball, other than a pitch, from one player to another. Compare *batted ball*.

thrown out by catcher An early measure of a catcher's success at thwarting attempted stolen bases, used by Ernest J. Lanigan (see Alan Schwarz, *The Numbers Game*, 2004).

throw off Syn. of *shake off*.

throw on top *n.* An overhand pitch.

throwout *n.* A play in which a batter-runner or baserunner is retired by a fielder tossing the ball to a baseman before the runner reaches the base (Connie Mack, *Connie Mack's Baseball Book*, 1950, p.233).

throw out *v.* **1.** For a fielder (including the catcher) to put a runner out by a throw or relay to another fielder before the runner reaches base safely; e.g., for an infielder to field a batted ball and throw it to a baseman before the batter reaches that base, or for the catcher to attempt to retire a base stealer by throwing the ball to that base. IST USE. 1880 (*Brooklyn Daily Eagle*, Oct. 10; Edward J. Nichols). **2.** For an umpire to eject a player, manager, or coach from the game. **3.** For a pitcher to injure his arm; e.g., "Smith threw his arm out after pitching 12 innings."

throw out the first ball To toss a ball as part of a pregame ceremony. Traditionally, a political figure throws out the first ball from a place in the stands or, increasingly, from a place on the field, formally opening the baseball season in the ballpark of the home team. See also *ceremonial first pitch*. IST USE.

1908. "There were many prominent spectators in the stands, which were overflowing long before Commissioner Morrow threw out the first ball" (*The Washington Post*, Apr. 28; Peter Morris).

throw over *v.* For a pitcher to throw the ball to the first baseman to hold a runner close. "[Eddie Murray] talks to his pitcher a lot, saying, 'Okay, throw over, throw over,' and the pitcher isn't supposed to throw over, but then he may say a key word, and the pitcher knows Eddie wants him to throw" (Steve Fiffer, *How to Watch Baseball*, 1987, p.100).

throw-over *n.* A throw from the pitcher to the first baseman to hold a runner close.

throw pus For a pitcher to be totally ineffective. Dave Dravecky (*Comeback*, 1990), coming off the disabled list: "I had nothing. I couldn't throw hard, I couldn't put the ball where I wanted it, and my slider wasn't breaking. I was, as pitchers say, throwing pus."

throws left Said of a player (esp. a pitcher) who throws left-handed. Abbrev. *TL*.

"throw some shoulders" Roger Clemens' exhortation to encourage batters to generate some offense (Buster Olney, *The Last Night of the Yankee Dynasty*, 2004). "When you see somebody go deep. Sit and spin, throw some shoulders, all that good stuff" (Roger Clemens, quoted in *The Sporting News*, March 25, 2005).

throws right Said of a player (esp. a pitcher) who throws right-handed. Abbrev. *TR*.

throw the ball To pitch. "Rodrigo [Lopez] threw the ball very, very well" (Baltimore Orioles manager Mike Hargrove, quoted in *The Baltimore Sun*, June 22, 2002).

throw the mask 1. To end an inning, as signaled by the catcher's doffing his protective face mask. 2. For the catcher to prepare to catch a pop fly by tossing aside the face mask, which may obstruct his vision.

thumb 1. *v.* For an umpire to banish a player, manager, or coach from the playing field or the bench for the remainder of the game. Umpires often make a gesture of ejection with the thumb raised. IST USE. 1937 (National League Service Bureau file clipping, May 6; Edward J.

Nichols). 2. *n.* The ejection from a game by an umpire of a player, manager, coach, or other individual. "['The thumb' is] what the umpires give you when you question their ancestry" (Jim Nash, quoted in *The Sporting News*, Apr. 1, 1972). 3. *v.* To hit a pitch with the handle of the bat (Maurice H. Weseen, *A Dictionary of American Slang*, 1934).

thumb ball A pitch (somewhat like a knuckleball) that has a peculiar rotation as a result of friction applied by the pitcher's thumb. "The object [of the thumb ball] was to get heavy friction on the thumb, rather than to decrease friction on the other side" (John J. Evers and Hugh S. Fullerton, *Touching Second: The Science of Baseball*, 1910).

thumber 1. A slow pitched ball that seems to slide off the thumb. IST USE. 1910 (*American Magazine*, June, p.233; Edward J. Nichols). 2. A pitcher who throws a lot of offspeed and/or breaking balls. See also *cunny thumber*, 1.

thumb happy Said of an umpire who ejects more than a normal number of participants from a game.

thumbing An ejection. On the removal of minor-league manager Joe Gordon (*San Francisco News*, Apr. 2, 1952; Peter Tamony): "He was tossed out of an Opening Day game for the first time in his long career which includes few 'thumbings' from umpires on any day."

thumb on To reach base safely by hitting a ball on the bat handle, close to the thumb. The term is a play on hitchhiking or "thumbing a ride." IST USE. 1943. "Thumbed on . . . [is] getting on base by way of a hit close to the thumb" (*Baseball Magazine*, January; David Shulman).

thump 1. *v.* To defeat decisively. 2. *v.* To bat hard against a pitcher. IST USE. 1928 (*The New York Times*, Oct. 6; Edward J. Nichols). 3. *v.* To hit the ball. IST USE. 1913 (*The Sporting News*, Oct. 30; Peter Morris). 4. *n.* A batted ball. IST USE. 1920 (*The New York Times*, Oct. 3; Edward J. Nichols).

thumper A home run hitter. "It's very difficult to compete in the American League without some thumpers in your lineup" (Baltimore Orioles manager Mike Hargrove, quoted in *The Baltimore Sun*, Aug. 30, 2001). One of Ted Williams' nicknames was "The Thumper."

thunder The collective offensive power in a lineup.

thunder bolt A line drive. "Sam Thompson smashed a live thunder bolt sraight at [shortstop Bill] Gleason's head" (*Detroit Free Press*, Oct. 15, 1887).

thunder round Batting practice finale in which the batters try to hit the ball out of the park. "Mike Young is the Thunder Round champion" (Richard Justice, *The Washington Post*, Apr. 4, 1986).

tibbies Syn. of *teammates batted in*.

tibs *hist.* Syn. of *raps*. "The term is probably restricted to schoolboy games" (Edward J. Nichols, *An Historical Dictionary of Baseball Terminology*, PhD dissertation, Jan. 1939, p.79).

TIBS Abbrev. for *teammates batted in*.

tick 1. *v.* For the batter to barely touch the ball with his swing. IST USE. 1866. "Most of the hits were, however, foul, . . . or were 'tick'-ed into the hands of the Excelsior catcher" (*Detroit Advertiser and Tribune*, July 3; Peter Morris). 2. *n./hist.* Syn. of *foul tip*. "What you now call a foul tip was called a tick" (Adam E. Ford, letter to *The Sporting Life*, May 5, 1886, concerning baseball in Canada in 1838; David Block). See also *foul tick*.

ticket *v.* To bat a ball; e.g., "Smith ticketed the ball for right field but it was caught by the first baseman."

ticket to first Syn. of *base on balls*.

ticket to the majors A particular skill that is expected to get a player to the major leagues. "[Russell Branyan's] bat is his ticket to the majors; his defense is ordinary" (Tony Blengino and Lawr Michaels, eds., *John Benson Presents Future Stars: The Rookies of 1998–1999*, 1998, p.216).

ticket to the minors A demotion to the minor leagues.

tickie-hitter A hitter who "ticks," or makes only partial contact with, the ball, rather than hitting it with good wood.

tickle To hit the ball. "[Zimmerman] won't tickle the pill at this pace [.419] all season" (*San Francisco Bulletin*, Apr. 15, 1913; Gerald L. Cohen).

tie 1. *v.* To score one or more runs so that both teams have the same number of runs at a given moment during a game. "There is an old saying that you play to tie on the road and win at home" (Steve Kluger, *Changing Pitches*, 1984, p.125; Charles D. Poe). IST USE. 1875 (*New York Herald*, Sept. 9; Edward J. Nichols). 2. *v.* To win and lose the same number of games during a series, road trip, or other stretch of games. 3. *n.* Syn. of *tie game*. IST USE. 1855 (*Spirit of the Times*, Sept. 22; Peter Morris).

tiebreaker 1. A run that breaks the tie in a game. 2. A one-game playoff that occurs when two teams are tied for first place in their division at the end of the regular season. The site is determined by a coin flip weeks ahead of the need for such a game. 3. A criterion that determines home-field advantage in the playoffs if two teams have the same record.

tie game A regulation game that is called with each team having scored the same number of runs. Since 2007, a tie game becomes a suspended game; previously, a tie game was to be replayed in its entirety. The term tends to show up in a major-league context in exhibition games. In Japanese major-league baseball, if a game is tied after 12 innings, it is a tie game. Writing about the Japanese game, Gary A. Warner (*Advocate & Greenwich Time*, Aug. 24, 1997) noted, "Fans love the rare tie— it's a well-played contest in which no one 'loses face' by being defeated." See also *drawn game*. Syn. *tie*, 3. IST USE. 1860. "July 10. Gotham and Eagle, at Hoboken. Gotham 18; Eagle 18. Tie game" (Charles A. Peverelly, *The Book of American Pastimes*, 1866).

tie goes to the runner A principle commonly mentioned when the ball and the baserunner are perceived to have arrived simultaneously at first base. According to Rule 6.05(j) of the *Official Baseball Rules*, the "tie" goes to the runner because the defense did not touch the base "before" the runner touched the base (the rule does not specifically reference a "tie"). Umpires are taught that there are no ties and to do their best to determine which occurred a split-second earlier, but experiments have shown that it is virtually impossible to reliably judge which event comes first when they occur within 0.05 seconds or less. USAGE NOTE. *De Witt's Umpires Guide* (1875; Paul Hunkele) stated that a tie goes to the runner: "If simultaneously, the base runner is not put out." The *Chicago Tribune* (Sept. 12, 1886; Peter Morris) wrote, "When the umpire has a very close decision to make—as, for instance, where both base-runner and ball reach the base at the same time—is the preference given the runner or the club in the field? Answer—the base-runner is given the benefit under the rules."

tie up **1.** To pitch a ball inside so that the batter cannot get his bat around fast enough to hit the ball. "[Tom Glavine is] tying up hitters inside, which opens up the outside corner for him" (Greg Maddux, quoted in *Sports Illustrated*, June 17, 2002). IST USE. 1907. "The vapor float had the hitters tied up on both sides" (Charles Dryden, *Chicago Tribune*, Aug. 21; Peter Morris). **2.** For a baserunner to force a fielder to play closer to a base than he would otherwise. "Every runner who reaches a base 'ties up' one of the defense's players. . . . Runners on first and second tie up two men, and when this is the case and there is but one out, and a bunt expected or feared, the entire infield is 'tied up' and the chances of the ball being batted safe are more than doubled" (John J. Evers and Hugh S. Fullerton, *Touching Second: The Science of Baseball*, 1910; Peter Morris).

Tiffany card A baseball card issued by Topps and/or Topps companies between 1987 and 1993 and distinguished by higher quality stock, lighter color, glossy front, and significantly higher price (and scarcity) than a regular card issued simultaneously.

tiger A noise made by the fans at the end of early baseball games when "three cheers and a tiger" were called for. Harry Slye (*Baraboo* [Wis.] *Daily News*, June 26, 1925; Peter Morris): "There was a light touch of sentiment connected with the game in those days, by the introduction of a short ceremony at its conclusion. . . . The opposing teams would line up facing each other, and . . . the captain of the home team would step out and request of his men, 'Three cheers for the visiting nine.' These were given with a vigorous good will, then the compliment was returned by the visitors, and all wound up by the whole crowd joining in with a 'tiger.'" ETYMOLOGY. "The Princetonian calls the attention of the ball men to the fact that the peculiar cheer of Princeton—the 'rocket' or 'tiger'—has degenerated from its pristine standard, and that they ought to practice giving it with 'the old-time sonorous ring'" (*The World* [New York], reprinted in *St. Louis Globe-Democrat*, March 16, 1877; Peter Morris).

Tigers Nickname for the American League Central Division franchise in Detroit, Mich., a charter member of the league since 1901. George Stallings, the team's first manager, claimed he was the first one to use the nickname "Tigers" after having the players don black-and-yellow striped socks when he was managing Detroit's entry in the minor Western League in 1896. Other sources attribute the nickname to *Detroit Free Press* sports editor Philip J. Reid, who noted that the colors of the socks were similar to those of the athletic uniforms of Princeton Univ., whose mascot was the tiger. The team also has been referred to as the *Bengals* and, during the time Ty Cobb was on the roster, the *Tygers*.

tight **1.** Referring to closeness to the batter; e.g., "Smith throws the pitch in tight." **2.** Said of a defense or infield in which no ground balls escape. Compare *loose*, 1. **3.** Said of a difficult moment in a game, commonly applied to pitchers; e.g., a "tight spot" occurs when the bases are loaded and there is a 3–0 count on the batter. "Willie [McCorry] was continually in hot water, and had to pitch himself out of several tight holes" (*San Francisco Bulletin*, May 14, 1913; Gerald L. Cohen). **4.** See *tight spin*.

tighten up **1.** To become more effective defensively, esp. pitching. IST USE. 1910 (*New York Tribune*, July 5; Edward J. Nichols). **2.** To become less effective; to choke. IST USE. 1928. "With runners in scoring position . . . the average hitter 'tightens up,' he stands stiff at the plate, his muscles tighten and his whole motion is jerky. When he does that he's gone" (George Herman

Ruth, *Babe Ruth's Own Book of Baseball*, pp.183–84; Peter Morris). USAGE NOTE. The fact that this term can have diametrically opposed meanings (one positive, one negative) is noted with the observation that this is a prime example of why non-native speakers of English often find the language so confusing.

tightly wound See *wound tight*.

tight slider A slider with a quick, short break.

tight spin The sharp, fast rotation of a pitch. Tom Verducci (*Sports Illustrated*, March 31, 1997) noted that Kevin Brown throws a sinker 93 mph and "with the tightest spin in the game, giving the ball a wicked sinking action in the last five feet before the plate."

tilt 1. *n.* The late, downward movement on a breaking pitch (primarily a slider). "[Justin Wayne] has an average slider with fair tilt and break" (*Baseball America*, Dec. 10–23, 2001; Peter Morris). "Randy Johnson had just about the best tilt I'd ever seen" (Dan Jennings, quoted in Alan Schwarz, Baseball America.com, Nov. 14, 2006). 2. *v./hist.* To bat a ball high into the air. IST USE. 1917 (*The New York Times*, Oct. 7; Edward J. Nichols). 3. *n.* A contest between two baseball teams. "About 300 spectators assembled at the Grand Avenue Park to witness the tilt [between St. Louis and Hartford]" (*St. Louis Globe-Democrat*, June 26, 1875).

timber 1. A baseball bat. IST USE. 1868 (*New York Herald*, Sept. 27; Edward J. Nichols). 2. *hist.* Young talent or prospects, an expansion of the metaphor of the farm system. IST USE. 1891. "The St. Louis Browns . . . had an agent taking in the south-western country looking for new timber" (*The Sporting News*, Sept. 12; Peter Morris).

"time" The announcement or call by an umpire of a legal interruption of play, during which the ball is considered dead. The umpire raises both arms into the air and calls "time" in a loud voice. When a player is injured, "time" cannot be called until the umpire considers the play to be completed; e.g., if two fielders collide while attempting to catch a fly ball, another player must retrieve the ball and it must be returned to the pitcher before "time" can be called and the ball deemed dead. See also *time-out*. IST USE. 1867. "Parker to bat, and the rain so bad that time was called by the umpire, leaving Fletcher on third and Smith on the second" (*Daily National Intelligencer* [Washington, D.C.], July 29).

time at bat Syn. of *at-bat*, 1.

time of game The duration of a game expressed in hours and minutes. Delays for weather, light failure, or technological failure not related to game action are not included; however, delays to attend to an injured player, manager, coach, or umpire are counted in computing the time of game. Abbrev. *T*, 1. Syn. *game time*, 2.

time-out A temporary suspension of play called by the umpire. It can be initiated by the umpire or called in response to a request by a player, manager, or coach. See also *"time."*

time pickoff A *pickoff play* at second base in which the shortstop or second baseman and the pitcher begin to count: at the count of three, the shortstop or second baseman heads for the base; at four, the pitcher whirls around, stepping off the rubber and firing the ball to the shortstop or second baseman; at five, the runner is out.

time play A play in which the scoring of a run depends on whether the runner touched home before the third out is made; e.g., a successful appeal play on a runner who leaves a base too soon on a caught fly ball and that results in the third out. All runs scored by runners in advance of the appealed runner and scored ahead of the legal appeal would count.

time the pitch For a batter to judge the speed of a pitched ball and initiate the swing of his bat so that it makes contact with the ball.

times left on base A measure of the number of times an individual player reached base on a hit but failed to score. The term appeared in Henry Chadwick's box scores in the 1860s (see Alan Schwarz, *The Numbers Game*, 2004).

times taken out A measure of the number of times that a starting pitcher failed to pitch a complete game. The term appeared in *Reach's Official American League Base Ball Guide*

(1905) (see Alan Schwarz, *The Numbers Game*, 2004).

timing The ability of a batter to judge the speed and path of a pitched ball in correlation with his swing. "[Timing] a ball well is to cause your bat to meet it in such manner as to hit the ball well in the center and in the very direction you intended to send it" (Henry Chadwick, *The Game of Base Ball*, 1868, p.46).

timothy trimmer Syn. of *daisy cutter*, 1. 1ST USE. 1869 (*New York Herald*, Sept. 16; Edward J. Nichols).

tin cup An *umpire*, 1. It is a derogatory term, alluding to the cup used by a stereotypical blind beggar.

Tinker to Evers to Chance The double-play combination of the Chicago Cubs from 1902 to 1911: shortstop Joe Tinker, second baseman Johnny Evers (pronounced "E-vers"), and first baseman Frank Chance. The fame of the combination got a gigantic boost when columnist Franklin P. Adams featured them in the poem "Baseball's Sad Lexicon" that appeared originally in the *New York Evening Mail* on July 12, 1910, under the title "That Double Play Again." The poem contained one of the most repeated lines in American light verse: "These are the saddest of possible words: 'Tinker to Evers to Chance.'" The term has become synonymous with precision teamwork (even though Tinker and Evers rarely spoke to each other). "Today no DP combo resonates as powerfully. . . . Yet their legend comes more from style than stats" (*Sports Illustrated*. Sept. 23, 2002). According to the official box scores of the National League, from 1906 through 1909, when the Cubs won three pennants, the Tinker to Evers to Chance (6–4–3) combination turned only 29 double plays (Warren Brown, "Don't Believe Everything You Read," *SPORT* magazine, Aug. 1954). Ogden Nash had his own poem: "E is for Evers, / His jaw in advance; / Never afraid / To Tinker with Chance" ("Line-up for Yesterday; an ABC of Baseball Immortals," *Versus*, 1949, p.67). 1ST USE. 1902. In the box score of a game on Sept. 14 at West Side Grounds in Chicago, where the Cubs were playing the Cincinnati Reds in the second game of a doubleheader, a forgotten scorer wrote: "Double plays—Tinker–Evers–

Chance" (*Chicago Tribune*, Sept. 15). Frank Graham (*Baseball Extra*, 1954) wrote: "He [the scorer] didn't know it, but he was linking on paper for the first time in that fashion the names of a double-play combination which, if not the greatest of all time, certainly was the most colorful." EXTENDED USE. An activity that routinely proceeds according to plan; a metaphor describing cool efficiency.

tip 1. *n.* A ball that has barely made contact with the bat; a ball that glances off the bat. ETYMOLOGY. From the game of rounders. A "tip" occurs when a ball is slightly touched by the corner or end of the bat and flies off either to the side or behind the home (David Block, *Baseball Before We Knew It*, 2005, p.285). **2.** *v.* To make incomplete contact of the bat with the ball; to hit a pitched ball a glancing blow. "Tyrell tipped out" (*New York Clipper*, June 4, 1864; Peter Morris). 1ST USE. 1845. "If a ball be struck, or tipped, and caught, either flying or on the first bound, it is a hand out" (Knickerbocker Rules, Rule 12th, Sept. 23). **3.** *v.* To reveal unconsciously which pitch is about to be thrown. A pitcher can tip his pitches in several ways; e.g., when he displays his grip on the ball, or shows an open glove (indicating a forkball) or a closed glove (indicating a fastball), or keeps his elbows together (indicating a curveball) or separated (indicating a different pitch). Randy Johnson would open his glove wider when he gripped his slider. Andy Pettitte would waggle the fingers of his left hand when he intended to throw a fastball. Brad Lidge would position his hands at his chest before throwing a slider and at his belt before throwing a fastball. "When [right-hander Hideo] Nomo was throwing a fastball, his left pinkie was visible at the height of his exaggerated windup. When he threw a split [-fingered fastball], his pinkie was stuck in his glove" (*The Baltimore Sun*, June 8, 1998). The catcher's signs may tip the runner at second base regarding the next pitch. "Expos runners on second base were picking up the signals from the catcher and relaying them to teammates—a practice called 'tipping pitches'" (*The Baltimore Sun*, May 10, 1997). See also *telegraph*.

tip-cat An English game that employed a bat

and a "cat" (a piece of wood four to eight inches long and tapered to a point at the ends). Joseph Strutt (*The Sports and Pastimes of the People of England*, 1801) described two principal methods of playing the game: 1) the batter struck one end of the cat with the bat, sending the cat spinning into the air, whereupon the batter hit the cat as far as possible, aiming to drive it outside a large ring surrounding the batter's station, and, if successful, called out a number measuring the number of bat lengths from the starting point that the cat actually landed (if the number measured was less, the batter was out, otherwise the batter counted his called number toward his score and continued to bat); and 2) a fielder tossed the cat at one of several batters stationed at designated holes in the ground, and every time the cat was struck the batters were obliged to run from one hole to another in succession, claiming a score every time they reached another hole, but if the cat was stopped by the opponents and thrown across between any two of the holes before the runner who had quit one of them could reach the other, the runner was out. The latter game links tip-cat with the family of old-cat games emerging in America (except that old-cat used a ball instead of a piece of wood) (David Block, *Baseball Before We Knew It*, 2005, pp.127–28, 184).

tip-foul *hist.* Syn. of *foul tip.* IST USE. 1874 (*Chicago Inter-Ocean*, July 7; Edward J. Nichols).

tip-off An unconscious sign in the form of a mannerism given by pitchers, catchers, or other players which can sometimes be read by a canny opponent to foretell a pitch or play; e.g., how a pitcher holds his glove, moves his feet, or cocks his head before delivering the pitch. "Concentration on watching the ball will sometimes reveal what is being thrown by some tip-off on the part of the pitcher" (James Smilgoff, *Athletic Journal*, Apr. 1946).

tip one's cap For a player to touch the bill of his cap in acknowledging applause from the fans. "The crowd gave [Jason] Johnson a warm ovation, and he tipped his cap before stepping into the dugout" (*The Baltimore Sun*, Apr. 24, 2003).

tipped bat A swinging bat that has come into contact with the catcher's mitt. A tipped bat can result in the umpire's awarding the batter first base.

tire **1.** A player's foot. A player who cannot get moving quickly is said to have "two flat tires." **2.** A player's leg. A player who pulls a leg muscle is said to have "blown a tire" (Phil Pepe, *Baseball Digest*, Nov. 1974, p.58). See also *wheel*, 2.

tireball A Philadelphia street game that was a cross between stickball and halfball and used a piece of old tire (3 to 6 inches long) as the "ball." See also *hoseball*.

tired bat Syn. of *slow bat.* "Benito Santiago's bat was so tired by the end of last year, he was painful to watch" (*Sports Illustrated*, March 25, 2002).

tissue bat A weak turn at the plate, replete with a strikeout. IST USE. 1876. "Brannock followed with a tissue bat" (*Detroit Free Press*, July 29; Peter Morris).

tissue-paper player *hist.* A player who is easily injured. See also *papier mache.* Syn. *tissue-paper Tom.* IST USE. 1933 (*Famous Sluggers and Their Records of 1932*).

tissue-paper Tom *hist.* Syn. of *tissue-paper player.* IST USE. 1937 (*New York Daily News*, Jan. 17; Edward J. Nichols).

titan A traditional term for a team that "clashes in the Fall Classic" (World Series).

titanic *hist.* A sinking liner, from *Titanic*, the name of the British luxury ocean liner that sank after colliding with an iceberg in the North Atlantic on its maiden voyage in Apr. 1912.

title A baseball championship.

Title IX [softball term] The specific legislation of the Education Amendments of 1972 that stated: "No person in the United States shall, on the basis of sex, be excluded from participation in, be denied the benefits of, or be subjected to discrimination under any education program or activity receiving Federal financial assistance." Title IX was passed initially to address the inequity in hiring, paying, and promoting women professors at the nation's public colleges and universities; it was not until 1979 that the law began to be applied to high school and college athletics. A school can comply with Title IX by demonstrating that: 1) the percentage of male and female athletes is about the same as that in the student body; 2) the school has a history of expanding opportunities for women to participate in sports; and 3) the school is effectively accommodating the interests and abilities of its female students. It was a once and future boost for women's softball and has become a term of reference for women who play softball.

titty-high Said of a pitched ball that comes in at chest level.

TL Abbrev. for *throws left.*

toaster An outfielder who struggles defensively, so named because the ball keeps popping out of his glove (Angus Lind, *The New Orleans Times-Picayune*, Apr. 27, 1994).

tobacco ball An illegal pitch that has been doctored with chewing tobacco.

tobacco card A *baseball card* issued with tobacco products. They were most popular in the early 1900s (the most famous being the *Wagner card*), although Red Man tobacco sets were issued in the 1950s. See also *cigar card.* Syn. *T-card.*

tobasco tap A hard-hit ground ball. The term is a variant of "Tabasco," the trade name for a hot and spicy pepper sauce produced by the McIlhenny Co. of Louisiana. IST USE. 1907 (*New York Evening Journal*, Apr. 30; Edward J. Nichols).

toboggan *hist.* **1.** *n.* A loss of a game that should have been won. "{New York Giants manager Jim Mutrie] saw yesterday's game slip through the fingers of his players, and himself sliding over the edge of another incipient toboggan" (*The World* [New York], Sept. 7, 1889; Gerald L. Cohen). **2.** *n.* A slump or losing streak. "The Aurora Baseball Club has struck the downward incline known in base ball parlance as the toboggan. It has lost all the games played this week, so far" (*Chicago Daily Inter-Ocean*, July 27, 1890; Peter Morris). **3.** *v.* To have a losing streak. "I was going good when the rest of the pitchers were tobogganing" (Cincinnati Reds pitcher Art Fromme, quoted in *San Francisco Bulletin*, Feb. 14, 1913; Gerald L.

OLD JUDGE CIGARETTES Goodwin & Co., New York.

Tobacco card. A dapper Adrian "Cap" Anson poses for Old Judge Cigarettes. *Library of Congress*

Cohen). IST USE. 1889. "'Tobogganed agin,' sententiously replied a mournful looking bleacher" (*The World* [New York], Aug. 28; Gerald L. Cohen). **4.** *v./hist.* For a baserunner to "complete his journey in a sitting posture" (*The Atchison* [Kans.] *Daily Globe*, June 23, 1896).

toehold A firm position in the batter's box effected by the batter digging in with his spikes before swinging at a pitch. IST USE. 1912. "Get a toe-hold and make the best of it" (*The Sporting Life*, May 18).

toe plate An extra piece of leather on the shoe of the pitcher's pivot foot that protects the shoe as it is dragged across the mound. See also *shoe plate.*

toe the plate To prepare to bat upon entering the batter's box and facing the pitcher. "He walked right up and toed the plate, His trusty bat in hand" (L.C. Davis, "Immer," *Baltimore Magazine*, Nov. 1908). IST USE. 1873 (*New York Herald*, Sept. 13; Edward J. Nichols).

toe the rubber **1.** To prepare to pitch by having the pitcher's pivot foot touching or in contact with the rubber. IST USE. 1901 (Burt L. Standish, *Frank Merriwell's Marvel*; Edward J. Nichols). **2.** To pitch figuratively. "Now I'm going up against the studs. It's going to be awesome toeing the rubber against those guys" (Baltimore Orioles pitcher Rick Krivda, quoted in *The Baltimore Sun*, Aug. 8, 1995).

"to hell with Babe Ruth!" A refrain used by Japanese troops to goad, anger, or unnerve American soldiers on various Pacific islands during World War II, which began for the United States six years after Ruth's retirement in 1935. The name "Babe Ruth" was synonymous with America. The refrain may have been the magazine and Hollywood film version of much cruder taunts in which Ruth's name was used. War correspondent Jeremiah O'Leary claimed to have originated the phrase in Dec. 1943, but later (*Washington Star*, 1992) confessed that the Japanese were yelling something far more obscene: "The truth is that they were shouting for the Babe to comit a physically impossible act upon himself."

toil To pitch in a baseball game (Maurice H. Weseen, *A Dictionary of American Slang*, 1934).

Toledo See *by way of Toledo*.

toletazo Spanish for "home run."

tomahawk To take a high swinging chop at the ball with a bat. Syn. "tommy-hawk."

tomahawk chop The chopping motion made by Atlanta Braves fans, often with a toy foam tomahawk in their hands, that began in 1991. The intimidating practice began to wane after the Braves moved to Turner Field in 1997, although the chop reappeared during the surprising 2005 season. ETYMOLOGY. Football fans of the Florida State Univ. Seminoles originated the tomahawk chop in the early 1980s. Braves injured pitcher Mark Grant began the chop from the dugout as a tribute to two-sport star and Braves outfielder Deion Sanders, who first rose to fame as a football player at Florida State Univ.

tomato The baseball. "One day at Cleveland, we had swung against a tired old tomato until nobody could hit it out of the infield" (Ty Cobb, *My Life in Baseball*, 1961, p.84).

Tom Brown A feebly hit ball. "[Billy] Hamilton hit a 'Tom Brown' to the pitcher and turned to the water tank with disgust" (*The Boston Globe*, Apr. 18, 1896; Peter Morris). ETYMOLOGY. Possibly Thomas Tarleton Brown, a British-born outfielder and occasional pitcher with several teams from 1882 to 1898.

Tommy John surgery A surgical operation, first performed on pitcher Tommy John on Sept. 25, 1974, in which typically the palmaris longus tendon (four to six inches long) from the nonpitching forearm is transplanted to replace the torn or damaged ulnar collateral ligament in the elbow of the pitching arm. The tendon is woven in a figure-eight pattern into holes drilled into the ends of the humerus and ulna bones that form the elbow. The operation was developed and refined by Los Angeles orthopedic specialists Dr. Robert Kerlan and Dr. Frank Jobe, and has a success rate of 90 percent. Recovery time takes 12 to 18 months. The operation saved and lengthened John's career, as well as those of many other pitchers, including John Smoltz, Mariano Rivera, and Matt Morris. Syn. "Tommy John operation."

tonk A *home run*. The term was associated with Roger Maris.

Tony Conigliaro Award An annual award presented since 1990 by the Boston baseball writers to a player who has "overcome adversity through spirit, determination, and courage." Each major-league team nominates a player and an independent 11-person panel votes. The award is named for the Boston Red Sox outfielder who made a dramatic comeback from a 1967 beaning by Jack Hamilton that sidelined him for the entire 1968 season.

too hot to handle Said of a hard-batted ball that cannot be fielded successfully. IST USE. 1896. "[Herman] Long hit one too hot for short to handle" (*The Boston Globe*, Apr. 9; Peter Morris). EXTENDED USE. Said of a difficult situation. Franklin P. Adams (*New York Tribune*, June 7, 1917, p.11; Stuart Y. Silverstein), commenting ironically on a World War I event: " 'The last shot from the American ship,' says a bulletin from the State Department, 'apparently was a clean hit.' The German official scorers called it an error; but the American o.s., because it was too hot to handle, called it a clean hit."

toolbox **1.** The collective skills of a baseball player. San Diego Padres pitching prospect Gerik Baxter "benefits from a full toolbox: a nasty slider, good fastball, and serviceable change-up" (*Baseball Prospectus*, 2001; Peter Morris). "I couldn't run. I can't throw, I can't field, I didn't have great power. . . . No tools. I don't have a tool box" (Kevin Millar, quoted in *The Baltimore Sun*, July 10, 2006). "Outfielder Milton Bradley flashed the best toolbox of any American player" at the Pan Am games (*Baseball America*, Aug. 23–Sept. 5, 1999; Peter Morris). **2.** A gifted baseball player with basic skills. "Georgia lost outfielder Jon Armitage, an undrafted 6-foot–5 toolbox who started to blossom in the Cape Cod League this summer" (John Manuel, *Baseball America*, Sept. 15–28, 2003; Peter Morris).

tools **1.** The basic skills of a baseball player (other than a pitcher): hitting for power, hitting for average, throwing, running, and fielding. See also *five-tool player.* Compare *fundamentals.* **2.** The specific talents or abilities of a baseball player. Pitcher Tommy John (quoted in *The New York Times*, Sept. 11, 1983) discussed pitching: "Your tools—let's break that out. You have speed, movement, placement. I never had speed. I have movement and placement. If you have two of the three you can be outstanding. If you have all three, you're Sandy Koufax." **3.** *hist.* Physical strength and size. Leonard Shecter (*Baseball Digest*, June 1963) put the term's shifting meaning in context: " 'He's got the tools' means he's big enough, now if he only had some talent. Today it would mean that the player had talent, but, perhaps, was not big enough."

tool shed **1.** Syn. of *five-tool player.* **2.** A player who not only exhibits the five traditional tools but others, such as quickness and agility. "When you think about everything he could do, Bo Jackson was a tool shed" (Jack Zduriencik, quoted in Alan Schwarz, BaseballAmerica.com, Nov. 14, 2006).

tools of ignorance The *catcher's equipment*: shin guards, chest protector, helmet, mask, and mitt. Baltimore Orioles manager Mike Hargrove (quoted in *The Baltimore Sun*, Apr. 2, 2000): "They call catching gear 'the tools of ignorance.' They don't say that because catchers are stupid. They say it because you've got to be an idiot to want to play there in the first place." IST USE. 1936. "Leroy Zimmerman . . . will perform on the mound for the Corpe squad with Max Purcell donning the tools of ignorance to handle his slants" (*Arcadia* [Calif.] *Tribune*, May 2; Grant Barrett). USAGE NOTE. The term is meant to be ironic, contrasting the intelligence required of a catcher to handle the duties of the position with the "ignorance" that catching is a grueling, painful, and hazardous job demanding so much protective equipment that a smart player would try to avoid it. ETYMOLOGY. Although Hy Turkin

Tools of ignorance. Silent film comedian Roscoe Conkling Arbuckle, also known as Fatty Arbuckle, in catcher's gear. *George Grantham Bain Collection, Library of Congress*

(*Baseball Almanac*, 1955) insisted that the term was "coined by Muddy Ruel, a college graduate and a lawyer, in disgust at his catching chores," Ruel's major-league playing career ended after the 1934 season. *The Sporting News* (Apr. 1, 1937; Peter Morris) cited a different source: "While on the subject of catching gear, Bill Dickey of the Yankees, for some reason, calls them Tools of Ignorance." Charles C. Meloy (*Baseball Magazine*, Aug. 1939) supported that attribution: "The ballplayers love phrases that are pungent and redolent with meaning. Thus, Bill Dickey . . . coined a phrase that was greeted with whoops of joy and at once included in the language. Brooding over the fate that made him a catcher on a blazing July day, Bill spoke of the catcher's armor as 'the tools of ignorance.'"

tools player Syn. of *five-tool player.*

toothpick A small or lightweight baseball bat. Ted Williams (*My Turn at Bat*, 1969): "I happened to pick up one of Stan Spence's bats. Geez, I thought, what a toothpick. Lightest bat in the rack."

too true Said of a pitcher who cannot get the ball over the corners or who can only throw over the heart of the plate (H.G. Salsinger, *Baseball Digest*, Aug. 1945).

top 1. *n.* The *first half* of an inning, during which the visiting team bats. The visiting team's scoring always appears on the top line of the scoreboard. 2. *v.* To bat a ball with a downward motion and hit its upper part, which usually results in a ground ball; e.g., "Smith topped a slow roller toward short." 3. *v.* To defeat a team. 4. *n.* The upper part of the strike zone. 5. *n.* See *top of the order*, 2.

top-flight Said of a first-rate team. IST USE. 1939. "When the heat is on in a close race, the championship club is the team which holds its own with the top-flight teams and annihilates the lesser clubs" (Gordon S. "Mickey" Cochrane, *Baseball: The Fans' Game*; David Shulman).

top half The *first half* of an inning.

topnotcher *hist.* A first-class or excellent player. "We have heard much concerning the success of the 'spitter' as thrown by Ed Walsh, Russell Ford and other topnotchers" (*San Francisco Bulletin*, May 24, 1913; Gerald L. Cohen). IST USE. 1889. "Today both of them rank with the 'top notchers' in their respective positions" (*Cincinnati Times-Star*, Feb. 19; David Shulman). EXTENDED USE. Anyone at the highest level. Elbert Hubbard (*Concerning Slang*, 1920) noted: "A topnotcher is simply an individual who works for the institution of which he is a part, not against it."

top of the order 1. The first batter in the batting order. 2. The first three batters in the batting order. See also *middle of the order*; *bottom of the order.*

top of the rotation The position in a starting rotation occupied by the No. 1 pitcher. "They [Texas Rangers] surprised me by not adding a top-of-the-rotation starter that they desperately needed. Kenny Rogers is solid, but he's by no means a No. 1 starter" (anonymous scout, quoted in *Sports Illustrated*, Apr. 4, 2005). Compare *front of the rotation.*

topped ball A ball that is hit slightly above its center.

topper 1. A high-bounding ground ball. 2. A male player (often the shortstop, pitcher, or catcher) passed off as a female on a Bloomer Girls team. "[The men] were known as toppers because they usually wore a curly wig. Young men barely of shaving age were the preferred recruits" (Gai Ingham Berlage, *Women in Baseball*, 1994, p.34; Peter Morris).

topspin The overhand motion imparted to a pitched ball (such as a curveball) that rotates forward in the direction of flight. Topspin causes a ball to experience a downward force because the forward rotation changes the distribution of air pressure around the ball. Compare *backspin*, 1.

top-stepper An erratic pitcher who causes his manager and coaches to watch anxiously from the top step of the dugout (Tom Verducci, *Sports Illustrated*, July 23, 2001).

top-to-bottom curve Syn. of *12-to-6 curve.* "[Aaron Sele] throws one of the game's fiercest top-to-bottom curveballs" (*Sports Illustrated*, March 20, 2000).

toque de bola Spanish for "bunt."

tornillo Spanish for "screwball."

torpedero Spanish for "shortstop."

torpedo 1. *n.* A baserunner who knocks down or attempts to knock down the infielder covering second base in an attempt to break up a double play. 2. *v.* To act as a torpedo.

toss 1. *n.* A throw or pitch; a thrown ball. IST USE. 1881 (*New York Herald*, Aug. 19; Edward J. Nichols). 2. *n.* A short, soft, usually underhand throw. 3. *v.* To throw the ball a short distance. IST USE. 1887 (*Chicago Inter-Ocean*, Apr. 8; Edward J. Nichols). 4. *v.* To pitch a baseball to a batter. 5. *v.* To pitch a baseball game. "['Howling Harry' Hughes] will toss the pill for the Seals this season" (*San Francisco Bulletin*, March 13, 1913; Gerald L. Cohen). 6. *v.* For an umpire to eject a participant from the game.

tosser 1. A pitcher. "The fans . . . expected the husky tosser [Willard Meikle] to prove a failure" (*San Francisco Bulletin*, Feb. 19, 1913; Gerald L. Cohen). See also *ball tosser*, 2. 2. A baseball player. "Duffy Lewis . . . had planned to depart for Palo Alto to coach the Cardinal [Stanford Univ.] tossers" (*San Francisco Bulletin*, Feb. 27, 1913; Gerald L. Cohen). See also *ball tosser*, 1. IST USE. 1880 (*Chicago Inter-Ocean*, May 27; Edward J. Nichols).

toss out 1. To throw out a baserunner. IST USE. 1920 (*Spalding's Official Base Ball Guide*, p.60; Edward J. Nichols). 2. To eject a participant from the game.

tossup A game or series between equally matched teams; a game or series whose outcome could as easily be determined by the "toss up" of a coin. IST USE. 1891 (*Harper's Weekly*, Apr. 18; Edward J. Nichols).

total average 1. A ratio between the number of bases a player accumulates for his team and the number of outs he makes. It equals: (total bases + stolen bases + walks + hit by pitches) divided by (at-bats − hits + caught stealing + grounded into double plays). Some sabermetricians include "minus caught stealing" in the numerator. Grounding into a double play equals two outs. The ratio was introduced by Thomas Boswell in the late 1970s (he termed himself its "proprietor and purveyor") and described in his *How Life Imitates the World Series* (1982, pp.137–44). The composite total average for the major

leagues is about .666. A Boswellian rule of thumb is that any player with a total average greater than .900 will end up in the Hall of Fame and any player with a total average below .500 should not be allowed on a major-league field unless he is a top-flight shortstop. Babe Ruth is the career leader with a total average of 1.432; Barry Bonds holds the single-season mark with 2.254 in 2004. "This simple stat . . . cleanly combines the virtues of batting average, slugging average, on-base percentage, and stolen-base proficiency" (Thomas Boswell, *The Washington Post*, Feb. 17, 1983). Sabermetric research has shown total average to be a good predictor of offensive performance (it is very similar to *base–out percentage*), although no better than simpler measures such as *on-base plus slugging* and *batter's run average*. Abbrev. *TA*, 1. 2. *hist.* Short for *total batting average*.

total base hits *hist.* Syn. of *total bases*. IST USE. 1883. "Total base hits—Boston, 21; New-York, 26" (*The New York Times* box score, May 4, p.3).

total bases A statistic for the total number of bases created by base hits, credited to a batter. One base is credited for a single, two for a double, three for a triple, and four for a home run. The statistic was created as an alternative accounting to the batting average, in which all hits count as one. The single-season record for total bases is 457 by Babe Ruth in 1921; the lifetime record for total bases is 6,856 by Hank Aaron. Abbrev. *TB*. Syn. *total base hits*; *earned bases*. IST USE. 1871. "Bass covered himself with glory, making ten total bases" (*The Cleveland Morning Herald*, May 22).

total bases per game *hist.* A statistical measure of player performance recorded by pioneer baseball writer Henry Chadwick beginning in 1867, expressed in *average and over* format, in which total bases was divided by games played; precursor to *slugging percentage* (see John Thorn and Pete Palmer, *The Hidden Game of Baseball*, 1985).

total bases run *hist.* An official statistic used in 1880 only, computed by summing the number of bases a baserunner touched. John Thorn and Pete Palmer (*The Hidden Game of Baseball*, 1985, pp.19–20) noted, "A wonderfully silly figure which signified virtually nothing about either an individual's ability in isolation or his value to his team. . . . Get on with a single, proceed to score in whatever manner, and you've touched four bases." The National League leader was Abner Dalrymple with 501. Syn. *bases touched.*

total batting average *hist.* A 19th-century term for what is now known as *slugging percentage.* "News . . . has a batting percentage of .401 . . . with a total batting average of .641" (*Cincinnati Enquirer,* July 27, 1898; David Ball). Syn. *total average,* 2. IST USE. 1892. "[Walter Camp] was captain . . . of the freshman ball nine . . . and he continued upon the Yale nine four years, there attaining the highest total batting average in the intercollegiate association" (*Current Literature,* February).

total chances A statistic for the total number of plays in which a fielder participates, calculated by adding putouts, assists, and errors. See also *chance.* Abbrev. *TC.*

total pitcher index The linear weights measure of a pitcher's total performance, relative to the league average, computed by summing the pitcher's pitching wins, fielding wins, and batting wins. It represents the number of wins a pitcher might have contributed beyond that of an average pitcher in a given season. Walter Johnson is both the single-season (11.2 in 1912) and career (90.5) leader for 20th-century pitchers. The statistic was devised by Pete Palmer and described by John Thorn and Pete Palmer in *The Hidden Game of Baseball* (1985). See also *total player wins.* Abbrev. *TPI.*

total player rating The linear weights measure of a position player's total performance, relative to the league average, computed by summing the player's batting wins, fielding wins, and base-stealing wins, along with a positional adjustment. It represents the number of wins a player might have contributed beyond that of an average player in a given season. Babe Ruth is both the single-season (10.6 in 1923) and career (107.7) leader. The statistic was devised by Pete Palmer and described by John Thorn and Pete Palmer in *The Hidden Game of Baseball* (1985). See also *total player wins*; *wins above average.* Abbrev. *TPR.* Syn. *batter-fielder wins.*

total player wins The sum of a player's adjusted batting runs (minus his positional adjustment), fielding runs, and pitching runs, all divided by the runs per win factor for a given year (generally around 10, historically in the 9 to 11 range). This statistic replaces the previously used *total player rating* and *total pitcher index.* As the sum of batting, fielding, and pitching, it applies equally to hitters and pitchers. Abbrev. *TPW.* See *Total Baseball* (8th ed., 2004).

touch **1.** To contact any part of the body, clothing, or equipment of a player or umpire. **2.** For a fielder to contact a base with the ball securely held in his hand or glove to record a putout. **3.** For a baserunner to contact a base. **4.** To get several hits and runs off a pitcher; e.g., "The Brewers touched Smith for five hits and three runs." Syn. *touch up.* IST USE. 1890 (*New York Press,* July 13; Edward J. Nichols). **5.** To describe a speed that a pitcher's fastball has been clocked at on a radar gun, but which he has not yet shown that he

Touch. Comic postcard, early 20th century. *Ron Menchine Collection*

can reach consistently. "[Daryl Thompson] threw a few pitches—'touched,' in scouting lingo—at 94 mph and was consistently clocked in the low nineties" (Josh Barr, *The Washington Post*, Apr. 24, 2003). "[Wade LeBlanc] has hit 87–89 mph and touched 90 in each of his appearances this season" (*Baseball America*, March 31–Apr. 13, 2003; Peter Morris). Compare *sit*.

touch all the bases To assure that contact is made with each base on one's way around the basepath. EXTENDED USE. To cover a large variety of things or contingencies; to explore all avenues. "San Francisco ought to exploit to the fullest every possibility of getting a team out here, and 'touch all the bases' in its efforts to bring major league baseball to what is in every other respect a major league city" (*San Francisco Call-Bulletin*, Aug. 5, 1954).

touch 'em all To hit a home run. "'Home run,' I yelled, twirling my finger in the air in a signal that meant, 'touch 'em all'" (Eric Gregg, *Working the Plate*, 1990, p.15).

touching sign A common sign in which the manager or coach touches a part of the uniform or skin; e.g., drawing a hand across the letters of the uniform, tugging at the belt, or placing a finger on the cap.

touch out *hist.* Syn. of *tag*, 2. IST USE. 1880 (*Chicago Inter-Ocean*, May 17; Edward J. Nichols).

touch up **1.** Syn. of *touch*, 4. "The Sox pitchers were touched up for eight hits" (*San Francisco Bulletin*, March 12, 1913; Gerald L. Cohen). IST USE. 1887 (*Chicago Inter-Ocean*, May 9; Edward J. Nichols). **2.** To reach a base; e.g., "Jones touched up at third on Smith's single." **3.** To return to a base after taking a lead.

tough **1.** Said of a pitcher who refuses to give the batter anything good to hit; "Smith pitched Jones tough." **2.** Said of a batter who fouls off several pitches waiting to get a good pitch to hit; e.g., "Jones was tough to retire."

tough loss A loss for a pitcher when his *game score* is greater than 50. The statistic was introduced by Bill James in his *Baseball Abstract* (1988). Compare *cheap win*.

tough out A batter who is not easily retired, such as one who makes solid contact, is difficult to strike out, does not hit into double plays, or can attract a base on balls. "Wade Boggs can retire with the knowledge that he remained a tough out through the end of his career" (Ken Rosenthal, *The Baltimore Sun*, Nov. 11, 1999).

tough save A *save* (as defined by STATS Inc.) in which the relief pitcher comes in with the tying run anywhere on base. A tough save is worth four points in calculating the *Rolaids Relief Man Award*. Compare *easy save*; *regular save*.

tourist A player who plays for several different teams.

towel A piece of cloth that, when thrown onto the field from the dugout, is a rare but dramatic indication of displeasure with an umpire's decision. Bert Dunne (*Folger's Dictionary of Baseball*, 1958) reported, "Umpire usually interprets towel as white flag symbol of personal cowardice and may even clean bench." ETYMOLOGY. Throwing in the towel has long been the means by which a boxer's handlers surrender for him in a prizefight; by extension, to surrender or quit any activity or pursuit, usually in defeat.

towering fly A fly ball hit high into the air.

town ball **1.** A regional term for various versions of early baseball that began in the last half of the 19th century. It was the usual term in most of Pennsylvania, in the Ohio and upper Mississippi valleys, and in the South. In this region the term "base ball" (used in New England, New York, and the Great Lakes region) was virtually unknown during the early 1800s. Town ball was played by organized clubs in several cities, most notably Philadelphia, where the Olympic Ball Club was chartered in 1833 (the club began playing in 1831; but the term "town ball" was not specifically mentioned in the club's constitution). The version of baseball played in and around New York City spread outward beginning in the late 1850s, and within a few years of the end of the Civil War had completely displaced all organized play of other versions. There was no single version of town ball; its play varied regionally. Richard Hershberger (*Base Ball: A Journal of the*

Early Game, Fall 2007) described the Philadelphia version. Town ball continued to be played by children and in remote areas into the 20th century. A letter to *The Southern Cultivator* (Aug. 1, 1905; Richard Hershberger) from M. Irby of Eastman, Miss., stated that his favorite activities were "to play town-ball and to read." IST USE. 1837. "Any person who shall on the Sabbath day play at cricket, bandy, cat, town ball, corner ball, or any other game of ball within the limits of the corporation . . . shall on conviction thereof forfeit and pay the sum of one dollar for every such offense" (Ordinance to Regulate the Town of Indianapolis, *Indiana Journal*, May 13; Richard Hershberger). USAGE NOTE. Hershberger notes that an earlier citation for "town ball" is from an ordinance (said to have been enacted on March 27, 1837) of the town of Canton, Ill., which outlawed the playing of town ball, along with various other games, on the Sabbath; however, this ordinance is only known from a history of Canton published in 1871. The term is undoubtedly older than 1837. Within a few years of that date there were citations from locations as widespread as Louisiana and Pennsylvania. Later misinterpretations endowed "town ball" with an extended, ahistorical meaning. It was long remembered in the old town ball region that town ball had preceded baseball, and in the 1890s this was misinterpreted as town ball being the ancestor of baseball. A similar process led to the belief that the *Massachusetts game*, the version previously played in New England, was ancestral to baseball; this caused many to equate town ball with the Massachusetts game. The error is perpetuated to the present day. The rules of the Massachusetts game were codified and published in 1858, and most descriptions purporting to be of town ball are actually of the Massachusetts game or a modified version of it. But while the Massachusetts game was an ongoing concern, it was never called "town ball." ETYMOLOGY. The traditional etymology was outlined by the Leatherstocking Base Ball Club, Cooperstown, N.Y (1992): "In the rural context during the 1820 to 1840 period, ball-playing was commonly reserved for market days or holidays, such as the July 4th celebration. On a typical market day . . . farmers and villagers would gather on a town common to barter food produce and craft goods. While the women and girls tended to these business matters, the men and boys might strike up an informal ball game which often lasted through the afternoon until dusk. This tradition is thought to have given rise to the term 'town ball.'" An alternative explanation for the derivation of the term appeared in the *Chicago Tribune* (Aug. 12, 1900; David Ball): "Any player who batted the ball such a distance that it could not be thrown 'in town' so that the man on the first base could make the other three without stopping, brought in by so batting the last player who had been 'caught out,' or who had failed to strike a ball. 'The outs,' or men in the country, were always on the alert, of course, to 'get to town,' and that I think was the origin of the name." Both explanations arose many years after the term, and are speculative. The true etymology is unknown. (Richard Hershberger)

2. Syn. of *town team baseball*. See Armand Peterson and Tom Tomashek, *Town Ball: The Glory Days of Minnesota Amateur Baseball*, 2006.

town baseball Syn. of *town team baseball*. "There was more town baseball being played in 1927 than at any time in the previous ten years. This was good, not only for those playing the game, but good for baseball itself, for it was the town teams that were building the foundation of organized baseball" (Richard C. Crepeau, *Baseball: America's Diamond Mind, 1919–1941*, 1980, p.56).

town team baseball Baseball competition at the level at which villages, towns, and small cities field a team, usually featuring players of various ages; e.g., the Pine Tree League in Maine. Syn. *town ball*, 2; *town baseball*.

towpath *hist.* Syn. of *basepath*. "The great slugger [Babe Ruth] started on his jog around the towpaths for his first home run of the year" (Grantland Rice, *New York Tribune*, Apr. 19, 1923).

TP Box score and scorecard abbrev. for *triple play*.

TPI Abbrev. for *total pitcher index*.

Town team baseball. Dixfield, Maine, team, ca. 1950. The State of Maine has a long tradition of town teams fashioned without age restrictions. *Author's collection*

TPR Abbrev. for *total player rating.*

TPW Abbrev. for *total player wins.*

TR Abbrev. for *throws right.*

track down To pursue and catch a fly ball in the outfield.

trade 1. *v.* To exchange and/or sell the contracts of one or more players with another club. Syn. *swap*, 1. IST USE. 1886. "The [St. Louis] Maroons have traded [Alex] McKinnon, their first baseman for Shomberg [Otto Schomberg], the left-handed batsman and lightning fielder of the Pittsburg club" (*The Sporting News*, Dec. 4; Peter Morris). 2. *n.* The exchange of one or more players between two clubs. Syn. *swap*, 2. IST USE. 1886. "[St. Louis owner Henry V. Lucas] has offered to exchange [Fred] Dunlap, [Jack] Glasscock and [Emmett] Seery for [Sam] Wise, [Tom] Poorman, [Joe] Hornung and [Charlie] Parsons. Lucas wants Parsons to even the trade, as he calls it" (*The Boston Globe*, June 4; Peter Morris).

trade bait A player or players used as an inducement to effect a trade with another team or to attract trade offers from other teams.

trade deadline Syn. of *trading deadline.*

trademark The printed or embossed manufacturer's logo and name that appears on the barrel of a bat. If a ball is hit on the trademark, the bat is more likely to break. "The trademark should be facing upward [or straight down] when the bat is swung forward, ready to meet the ball" (James Smilgoff, *Athletic Journal*, Apr. 1946). Manufacturers find the weakest point of the bat and put the label there, ensuring the sweet spot will be a quarter turn away. During the dead-ball era, batters tried to hit the ball *on the trademark* for maximum results; e.g., "[Harry] Stovey caught the ball on the trade-mark for one of his famous drives" (*The Washington Post*, Oct. 9, 1904; Peter Morris). See also *"keep the Spalding up."* IST USE. 1896. "In batting . . . hold the trademark up" (*Bismarck* [N.D.] *Daily Tribune*, Aug. 6).

trade value An estimate of the *approximate value* that a player will have from the time at which it is computed through the rest of his career. The estimate was devised by Bill James and explained in detail in his *Baseball Abstract* (1985). Syn. *expected remaining future value.*

trading block The status of a player being offered for trade or sale.

trading card One of a set or series of cards, sold individually or included as a premium with packages of bubble gum or other products, that is collected and traded; specif., a *baseball card.*

trading deadline The last moment at which two teams are allowed to trade players. The current deadline is midnight on July 31; however, players can be traded after that date if they first clear waivers. After Aug. 31, players can be traded but cannot play in postseason games for their new teams. The concept is fast losing all meaning as teams now use waivers to trade at almost any time. The first trading deadline was established in the National League in 1917: after Aug. 20 of each year, players had to clear waivers within the league before they could be sold or traded. The American League established a similar rule in 1920, with a deadline of July 1. Following the 1922 season, the deadline for both leagues was changed to June 15, where it remained until 1986, when July 31 was established as the non-waiver trading deadline. Before 1986, there were various interleague trading deadlines. Syn. *trade deadline.*

traffic Oncoming wind. "That's the longest home run I've hit into traffic" (Carlos Delgado, on his home run hit into a driving wind at Roger Dean Stadium, *The Palm Beach* [Fla.] *Post*, March 17, 2005).

traffic cop 1. Syn. of *third base coach*. 2. A ball that is "difficult to handle," like a traffic cop. Edwin M. Rumill (*Christian Science Monitor*, Sept. 1, 1937): "A difficult putout in the field."

traffic director 1. A pitcher who moves defensive players around the infield and outfield. "[Jim Palmer] was one of the great traffic directors of all time. He kept moving outfielders, infielders and he could do that

because he was such a good pitcher and he could get the ball where he wanted it to be and the players respected him" (Chuck Thompson, quoted in *Orioles Gazette*, Aug. 13, 1993). 2. A *third base coach*. See Dan Fox and Neal Williams (*Baseball Research Journal*, no.36, 2007, p.19).

traffic sign One of two overt hand signals (upraised hand for stop or wave of the arm for go) used by coaches to direct baserunners. Traffic signals were first used in the first decade of the 20th century to counter defenders who were shouting bogus instructions.

tragic number 1. The *magic number*, as seen from the perspective of the team about to be eliminated from contention. 2. A somber number, such as 10,000, the number of losses recorded by the Philadelphia Phillies between 1883 and 2007 (Franz Lidz, *Sports Illustrated*, July 2–9, 2007, p.47).

trail To be behind in runs in a game or in games won in the standings.

trailer The player who backs up the relay man. "You always have a 'trailer' on relays—that's a backup guy—so if you miss the first guy, you want to miss him high so that the second guy can make the play" (Bill Virdon, quoted in William Zinsser, *Spring Training*, 1989, p.171).

trail runner The baserunner who is the farthest from home plate.

trainer A member of a team's staff who gives first aid and physical therapy to injured players and tends to their physical well-being, and who may also supervise exercise and weight-control programs. Each major-league club must employ two certified trainers on a full-time basis. IST USE. 1887. "[Tom Taylor] is the attendant, or, as he calls himself, the 'trainer,' of the Philadelphia players. He looks after their wants on and off the field, rubs them down, and evidently considers himself an indispensable part of the club's equipment" (*St. Louis Globe-Democrat*, May 15; Peter Morris).

training camp The place where a team prepares itself for the regular season. IST USE. 1903. "The men will arrive at the training camp Tuesday afternoon" (*Atlanta Constitution*, March 16; Peter Morris).

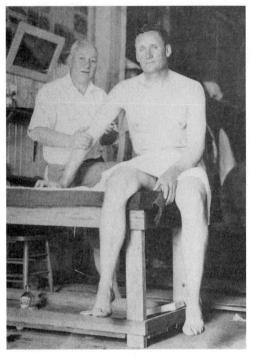

Trainer. Trainer working on Walter Johnson's right arm. *Photograph by Joseph Baylor Roberts*

training trip Exhibition games played on the road in preparation for the regular season. Such trips were common before World War II. IST USE. 1910 (*Baseball Magazine*, May, p.10; Edward J. Nichols).

trampoline effect [softball term] The action that occurs when a softball is hit from bats made of thin-walled aircraft aluminum. The ball is literally launched off the surface of the bat, much like a person bouncing off a trampoline.

trampoline turf An artificial playing surface with a high degree of bounce, as in the Hubert H. Humphrey Metrodome in Minneapolis where many hard-hit, bouncing balls quickly turn into base hits.

tranquility coach New York Yankees manager Billy Martin's "bodyguard" (Willie Horton) in 1985. Don Baylor (*Don Baylor*, 1989, p.262) recalled, "Billy told reporters Willie was the tranquility coach. The players translated that to mean Willie was brought in to keep Grif [Ken Griffey Sr.] and me away from Billy."

transfer 1. *n*. The action of a fielder in taking the ball from his glove with his hand to make a throw. It is esp. used to describe the pivot man on a double play attempt. **2.** *v*. To move a franchise from one city to another.

transferencia Spanish slang for "base on balls."

trap **1.** To field a ball on a short hop rather than catch it on the fly. **2.** To catch a runner on the basepath between two fielders. IST USE. 1863 (Chadwick Scrapbooks clipping, Aug. 9; Edward J. Nichols). **3.** *hist.* To deliberately drop an infield fly with less than two outs and runners at second base and first base. The ball is muffed to trick the runners into advancing and getting thrown out. The maneuver is now illegal, and the infield fly rule is invoked by the umpire under such a condition. IST USE. 1892 (*Chicago Herald*, May 16; Edward J. Nichols).

trap ball An English children's game, a forerunner of baseball, dating to the 1400s and possibly earlier, and a common recreation from the 17th- to the mid-19th centuries, that employed a) a "trap," a pivoted wooden instrument that, when activated by the batter, elevated b) a ball, consisting of a core of wool or feathers, covered with leather, into the air, and c) a flat-faced bat ("trapstick," resembling a large wooden spoon), which the batter used with one hand to strike the ball and drive it as far as possible and between two boundaries (13½ feet apart) placed at a given distance (21 yards) from the trap (in other versions of the game, the trapstick was a simple stick or bat that often required two hands to strike the ball). The trap was "a spring device or a lever pivoted in the middle, usually mounted on a wooden shoe-shaped base" (Harold Peterson, *The Man Who Invented Baseball*, 1973). The special feature of trap ball was that the batter launched the ball himself before striking it: in essence, he "pitched" his own ball. According to Joseph Strutt (*The Sports and Pastimes of the People of England*, 1801), the striker gained one point for each successful hit and his turn ended if a) he missed hitting the ball on three successive tries, b) he hit the ball out of bounds, c) the ball was caught on the fly, or d) a fielder retrieved the ball and upon throwing it back either hit the trap or succeeded in getting the ball to rest within a bat's length of it. Another version of trap ball (Essex variety) described by Strutt used a round bat; after hitting the ball, the batter called out any number he chose. When the fielder returned the ball, the players measured the number of bat lengths from the trap the ball had come to rest: if the number exceeded the number the batter called out, he won that many points; if the number was less than his number, he received no points and lost his turn at bat. Trap ball was adapted to town gardens and therefore emphasized accurate, rather than distance, hitting. David Block (*Baseball Before We Knew It*, 2005, p.125) noted, "Trap-ball's longevity and enduring popularity in England undoubtedly contributed to baseball's development. Certainly, the concept of boundaries marking foul territory was an important innovation. While trap-ball did not include a base-running component, the game's required skills of batting and fielding transferred readily to baseball." Trap ball never attained popularity in the United States. See also *northern spell*. (David Block) Syn. *bat and trap*.

trap ball rule A rule adopted in 1894 that stated the batter is automatically declared out if he hits a fly ball that can be handled by an infielder when there is one out and first base is occupied. The umpire was not required to make his decision until after the play, an omission that led to many arguments. In 1895, the rule was extended to apply when more than one runner was on base and required the umpire to signal when the rule went into effect. In 1901, the rule was changed to also apply with no outs, and under the name *infield fly rule*, has remained essentially unchanged since that time. Syn. *Brush and Von der Ahe's rule*.

trapped ball A batted ball that is ruled to have been caught after it has hit the ground or fence. Sometimes a fielder will try to make it look as if a trapped ball is a legally caught fly ball.

trapped runner A baserunner caught between two or more fielders.

trapper's mitt The modern, shovel-like first baseman's glove, composed of three large sections: one for the thumb, one for the fingers, and one in the middle that serves as a pocket. Syn. "trapper."

trap play A defensive maneuver in which a batted ball is short-hopped. "One of the toughest plays for an umpire is the trap play in the outfield" (Ron Luciano, *The Umpire Strikes Back*, 1982; Charles D. Poe).

trash bag Syn. of *Baggie*.

traveling secretary A member of a club's front-office staff who travels with the team and attends to its hotel accommodations, transportation, and other arrangements while the team is away from home. Syn. *road secretary*.

traveling team A minor league team, usually in an independent league, that plays all its games on the road. "The Selma Cloverleafs [of the independent Southeastern League] were converted into a traveling team before the season started, when it became clear that ticket sales and advertising in Selma, Ala., would not support a team" (Jon Caroulis, *Baseball America*, July 21–Aug. 3, 2003; Peter Morris).

travel team A youth baseball team consisting of top players from more than one region and which often plays as many as 120 games a year within a more competitive structure. A travel team is better coached than teams in local recreational leagues, practices regularly, and travels to play in tournaments and leagues in other towns.

travesty A mockery or distortion of the game; e.g., if a baserunner, after acquiring legal possession of a base, runs the bases in reverse order for the purpose of confusing the defense, he is deemed to be making a travesty of the game, and the umpire will declare the runner out (see *Official Baseball Rules*, Rule 7.08[i]).

treble play *hist.* Syn. of *triple play*. 1ST USE. 1868. "A 'treble play' is made when three players are put out after the ball is hit, before it is pitched to the bat again" (Henry Chadwick, *The Game of Base Ball*, p.46).

trial A period during which a player from a lower level is given a chance to succeed at a higher level. See also *tryout*. 1ST USE. 1902 (*The Sporting Life*, Sept. 20, p.4; Edward J. Nichols).

tribe Any baseball team.

Tribe A common alternative nickname for a team whose primary nickname relates to Indians; specif., the Cleveland Indians.

tribey Spanish slang for "triple."

trickle in To score by making one base at a time.

trickler A slow ground ball. See also *bleeder*, 1. IST USE. 1922 (*The New York Times*, June 2; Edward J. Nichols).

trick pitch 1. An illegal pitch in which the ball has been doctored; e.g., a spitball, emery ball, or shine ball, or "a ball with loaded seams (of mud or dirt)" (Steve Steinberg, *Baseball in St. Louis, 1900–1925*, 2004, p.112). 2. An unorthodox pitch designed to disrupt the batter's timing; e.g., eephus and La Lob.

tricks of the trade Expedient or adroit techniques practiced on the field; inside baseball. "It was in [Dickey Pearce's] head that many of the 'tricks of the trade' originated, and many of them are in use today" (William Rankin, *The Sporting News*, March 3, 1910; Peter Morris). IST USE. 1871. "We will say that the [Middletown] players themselves, although given perhaps a little too much to the 'tricks of the trade,' are in the main as gentlemanly and fair a set as the generality of the professional nines" (*New Haven* [Conn.] *Weekly Palladium*, Sept. 21; David Arcidiacono).

trigger 1. *v.* To start a rally. "[Joey Meyer] triggered Milwaukee's five-run third inning with a leadoff homer" (*Tampa Tribune*, July 8, 1989). 2. *n.* A batter's timing mechanism in which he brings his hands back before moving them forward in a hitting motion to initiate a swing. "It's impossible to get the bat going through the zone if you don't have the proper trigger. You're going to be late on the ball" (Doug Mapson, quoted in Alan Schwarz, BaseballAmerica.com, Nov. 14, 2006). 3. *v.* See *pull the trigger*.

trim To win a close game. "Cubs Trim Pirates, 3–2" (*Tampa Tribune* headline, Sept. 24, 1989).

trimmer A ball hit along the ground; one that "trims" the grass. IST USE. 1870 (*New York Herald*, June 19; Edward J. Nichols).

trip See *trip to the plate*.

Tripartite Agreement The accord signed by the National League (NL), American Association (AA), and Northwestern League (a minor league) on March 12, 1883, that brought peace between the two warring major leagues (NL and AA), created the first recognized minor league, and established the framework under which the game prospered. The mutual recognition of the contracts and the names of blacklisted players and the provision that allowed clubs to reserve no more than 11 players led to a stable business climate. However, the reserve rule generated such resentment that a third major league (the Union Association) was formed after the 1883 season to attract disgruntled players. The accord also provided for an arbitration board to settle disputes and address complaints. The Tripartite Agreement was renamed the *National Agreement* before the 1884 season. Syn. "Tripartite Pact."

triple 1. *n.* A base hit on which the batter reaches third base safely. Joe Garagiola once said that Willie Mays' glove was where triples went to die. In Philip Roth's *The Great American Novel* (1973), Luke Gofannon tells Angela Whittling Trust what he loves most in the world: "Triples. . . . Off the wall, up the alley, down the line, however it goes, it goes with that there crack. Then runnin' like blazes. 'Round first . . . make the turn at second, and ya' head for third—and now ya' know that throw is comin' . . . So ya' slide. Two hunerd and seventy feet of runnin' behind ya', and with all that momentum, ya' hit it—whack, into the bag. . . . Then ya' hear the ump—'Safe!' . . . the best part . . . Standin' up. Dustin' off y'r breeches and standin' up there on that bag." It has been said that the gloves of Shoeless Joe Jackson and Willie Mays were the places where triples go to die. Abbrev. *T*, 2; *3B*, 4. Syn. *three-base hit*; *three-bagger*; *three-cornered shot*; *three-master*; *three-sacker*; *triple bagger*; *triple sacker*; *triplet*. IST USE. 1880 (*New York Press*, June 3; Edward J. Nichols). 2. *v.* To hit a triple. IST USE. 1896. "Griffin singled, Anderson tripled, Shindle walked, Corcoran reached first on Childs' error, and LaChance lost the ball over the fence for a home run, netting five runs"

(*The New York Times*, July 8; Fred R. Shapiro). **3.** *v.* To complete a triple play.

Triple A Syn. of *Class AAA*. EXTENDED USE. Anti-aircraft artillery.

Triple A Alliance An agreement allowing interleague play between two Triple A minor leagues: the American Association and the International League. The alliance began in 1988, and was ended in 1991 due to concerns about travel (Peter Morris).

triple-bagger Syn. of *triple*, 1. IST USE. 1877. "A triple-bagger by Bond sent White and Sutton across the plate" (*St. Louis Globe-Democrat*, July 14; Peter Morris).

Triple Crown 1. The rare distinction by which a player ends the season leading his league in batting average, runs batted in, and home runs. The only players to win the Triple Crown more than once were Rogers Hornsby (1922 and 1925) and Ted Williams (1942 and 1947); the last to achieve the distinction was Carl Yastrzemski in 1967. IST USE. 1936. "[Lou] Gehrig insists that he will win the triple crown again, as in 1934—batting, homers and runs driven in" (*The Sporting News*, July 9; William Burgess). **2.** The distinction by which a pitcher ends the season leading his league in games won, earned run average, and strikeouts. "[Roger Clemens] wrapped up the league's pitching Triple Crown with 20 wins . . . a 2.65 ERA and 271 strikeouts" (Mark Bechtel, *Sports Illustrated*, Oct. 5, 1998, p.100). Syn. *pitcher's Triple Crown*. **3.** *hist.* The distinction of leading the league in batting average, runs, and hits. The term was applied to Ty Cobb's efforts in the early 20th century: he achieved the distinction in 1909, 1911, and 1915. In his autobiography (*My Life in Baseball*, 1961, p.92), Cobb substituted runs batted in for runs: "At the age of twenty-three, I had three Triple Crowns to my credit—which meant I'd put together three seasons [1907–1909] in which my total hits, runs-batted-in and batting average were No. 1 in the league." **4.** The distinction of leading the league in three other specific categories; e.g., "In 1910 [Ed] Konetchy . . . won the triple crown in fielding, leading NL first basemen in fielding percentage, putouts, and assists" (Paul Sallee and Eric Sallee, in Society for American Baseball Research,

Deadball Stars of the National League, 2004, p.340). **5.** The distinction by which a baseball team achieves a three-way success. "[Charlie] Comiskey and [Fielder] Jones . . . piloted the [Chicago White Sox] . . . to the triple crown of champions of Chicago, champions of the American League, and champions of the world" (*The Washington Post*, Oct. 20, 1906; Brian McKenna).

ETYMOLOGY. Originally applied (*OED*, 1555) to a three-fold crown, such as the papal tiara, the term entered the sporting world to refer to winning three horse races: "The sporting prophets love to call the 'triple crown' . . . the Two Thousand [Guineas], the Derby, and the St. Leger" (*Daily News*, Sept. 7, 1897; *OED*). The term was applied to several other instances of winning three victories in the same season or year, such as winning the Kentucky Derby, the Preakness, and the Belmont Stakes in horse racing, or victories by England, Ireland, Scotland, or Wales over each of the other three in hockey.

triple-dipping Making a bat harder by applying three layers of lacquer finish to the barrel. Bats ordered by players have two layers; adding another layer makes the bat almost as hard as an aluminum bat. "There is a question, though, as to how much it helps" (*USA Today*, Apr. 17, 2004).

triple double 1. Attaining double figures in doubles, triples, and home runs during a season. Compare *quadruple double*. ETYMOLOGY. From basketball, when a player records double-digit numbers in three statistical categories (such as points, assists, and rebounds, or points, rebounds, and blocked shots) in a single game. **2.** The achievement by a player of leading his league in doubles for three consecutive years. The term came into play in late 1986 when Don Mattingly succeeded in repeating Tris Speaker's triple double of 1920–1922 (Speaker also led the American League in doubles in 1923). **3.** The appearance in the same game of two players who have each previously recorded an unassisted triple play. It has happened twice: Sept. 28, 1930 (Johnny Neun and Glenn Wright in Ebbets Field) and June 16, 1997 (Mickey Morandini and John Valentin in Fenway

Park). "Rare triple-double" (Bob Ryan, *The Boston Globe*, June 17, 1997).

tripleheader 1. A set of three games played in succession on the same day between the same two teams for the price of one. The only major-league tripleheader in the 20th century occurred on Oct. 2, 1920, when the Cincinnati Reds defeated the Pittsburgh Pirates in the first two games but the Pirates won the third game, which was called after six innings because of darkness. 2. A set of three games played in succession on the same day in which one team plays against two or three different opponents. Such "tripleheaders" occur frequently in amateur tournaments. 3. A set of three games televised in succession, as during the postseason.

triple matanza Spanish for "triple play."

triple play A defensive play in which three players are put out as a result of continuous action, providing there are no errors committed between putouts. Abbrev. *TP*. Syn. *treble play*. IST USE. 1867. "Gus Stillwagner, on first base, made a handsome triple play, by catching a fly ball, and putting two men out running their bases" (*Detroit Advertiser and Tribune*, Oct. 30; Peter Morris). USAGE NOTE. John Freyer uncovered a note written by Henry Chadwick (from his scrapbooks) in the late 1880s: "I laid down the law governing . . . triple plays in 1859. . . . I stated that a . . . triple play was made when . . . three runners were put out during the interval between the delivery of the ball which was hit and its next delivery to the bat, no matter how the runners were put out. This has been the rule ever since and it now has been in vogue for thirty years." EXTENDED USE. Three accomplishments made at the same time. "Triple-play phonograph plays all records . . . 33⅓, 45, 78 rpm)" (*Look* magazine, March 11, 1952). Comcast refers to its triple play of offering three services (Internet, cable television, and digital voice) at a discount.

tripler One who hits a triple. "The aspiring tripler cuts the second base corner just right" (Roy Blount Jr., *Sports Illustrated*, Sept. 29, 2003).

Triple play. Left to right: Cleveland Indians second baseman Bill Wambsganss, and Pete Kilduff, Clarence Mitchell, and Otto Miller of the Brooklyn Robins. In the fifth inning of Game 5 of the 1920 World Series, Wambsganss completed the only unassisted triple play in World Series history when he caught Mitchell's line drive for the first out, stepped on second before Kilduff could get back for the second out, and tagged Miller, who was running from first. *National Baseball Library and Archives, Cooperstown, N.Y.*

triple sacker Syn. of *triple*, 1. IST USE. 1908 (*Baseball Magazine*, July, p.35; Edward J. Nichols).

triple steal 1. A maneuver in which three baserunners each simultaneously steal the next base. 2. A feat in which a player steals second base, third base, and home in the same inning. Milwaukee Brewers infielder Paul Molitor accomplished such a feat on July 26, 1987.

triplet *hist.* Syn. of *triple*, 1. "A whistling triplet" (*The Sporting News*, Nov. 27, 1897). IST USE. 1883 (*Chicago Inter-Ocean*, June 9; Edward J. Nichols).

triple threat An unofficial title for a pitcher who, in one season, wins 20 or more games, has 200 or more strikeouts, and maintains an earned run average of 3.00 or less. "'Triple-Threat' Pitchers A Rare Breed in Majors" (Jean-Pierre Caillault, *Baseball Digest* headline, Dec. 1983). ETYMOLOGY. Three qualifications of a good football player: runner, passer, and kicker.

triple up To record the third out in a triple play.

trip to the plate Syn. of *plate appearance*. The term is almost always used retrospectively; e.g., "Hank Aaron had four or more trips to the plate in 11 of his 17 All-Star starts" (Steve Hirdt, *ESPN The Magazine*, Aug. 5, 2002).

trolley dodger A member of the Brooklyn teams known as the Trolley Dodgers. "There is more ball playing in the trolley dodgers than Dave Foutz extracted from them last year" (*The Washington Post*, Oct. 16, 1896).

Trolley Dodgers Nickname for the American Association franchise in Brooklyn, N.Y., from 1884 to 1889, which was renamed the Brooklyn *Bridegrooms* in 1889. See also *Dodgers*. ETYMOLOGY. The inhabitants of the Brooklyn borough were known as "trolley dodgers" because they had to avoid being hit by numerous streetcars that crisscrossed the borough in a confused maze at the end of the Brooklyn Bridge.

trolley league *hist.* A minor or semiprofessional league, esp. one made up of teams close enough together to be reached by interurban trolley cars. IST USE. 1899 (Burt L.

Standish, *Frank Merriwell's Double Shot*, p.7; Edward J. Nichols).

trolley line Syn. of *line drive*.

Trolley Series The 1944 World Series between the St. Louis Browns and the St. Louis Cardinals.

trolley wire To throw the ball on a straight and accurate course. George Herman Ruth (*Babe Ruth's Own Book of Baseball*, 1928, pp.98–99) recalled, "[Shortstop Everett] Scott 'trolley wired' his throws as the boys say. In other words, he sent them on the same straight line every time, as though the ball was traveling on some invisible wire."

trouble The state of a pitcher who gets behind in the count or puts runners on base. "A lot of times if I get in trouble, I try to overthrow and throw too hard instead of letting my stuff take over and do the job" (Buddy Groom, quoted in *The Baltimore Sun*, Apr. 4, 2001).

truck horse *hist.* 1. A very slow runner. "A 'truck horse' is . . . a sun-tanned athlete who is unusually slow running bases" (Edwin M. Rumill, *Christian Science Monitor*, Sept. 1, 1937). IST USE. 1933. "Extra slow man" (*Famous Sluggers and Their Records of 1932*). 2. Syn. of *workhorse*. "[Carl Hubbell] is the truck horse of the Giants. Not only does he start ball games, but he goes in and finishes ball games" (Joe Williams, syndicated Scripps-Howard column, Apr. 29, 1933; Peter Morris).

true hop The bounce of a thrown or batted ball off the relatively dirt-free artificial turf.

tryout *n.* A playing session in which a young, aspiring baseball player without credentials performs under the watchful eyes of scouts who are looking for outstanding new talent. "Professional Baseball Tryouts for Italian/American Players" (announcement in *USA Today Sports Weekly*, Oct. 2–8, 2002). See also *trial*. IST USE. 1904. "The Kansas City club has decided to give Will Torrence . . . a try-out before the snow flies" (*The Sporting Life*, Sept. 3; Peter Morris).

try out *v.* For a young, unseen baseball player to display his talents before a scout. "Over the years I have seen thousands of young men try out. . . . All were allowed to have their moment on center stage" (Edwin Howsam,

Baseball Graffiti, 1995, p.35). IST USE. 1904. "Three men were selected to go up against the professional game, and Patsy [Donovan] was the first of the three to 'try out'" (Collins W. Griffin, *The Washington Post*, Sept. 18, describing how Donovan got the opportunity to play for the local minor-league club; Peter Morris).

tryout camp A playing session held to sign players to professional contracts and to get leads on good young players whose progress can be followed in the future. "The tryout camp is where boyhood dreams are put on the line" (Edwin Howsam, *Baseball Graffiti*, 1995, p.75).

tuberculosis liner *hist.* A weak hit just over the heads of the infielders; a *Texas Leaguer*, 2.

tubey Spanish slang for "double."

Tugboat Annie A "tough, rugged" player in the All-American Girls Professional Baseball League.

tumble bug **1.** An acrobatic player given to crashing and diving in the field. **2.** Syn. of *grandstand player*. IST USE. 1932 (*Baseball Magazine*, October, p.496; Edward J. Nichols).

tumbler Syn. of *knuckleball*, 1.

tunnel An underground passageway leading from the clubhouses and the umpires' dressing room to the dugouts.

tunneler A player who takes on managerial airs and begins giving orders to other players.

tunneling The (now illegal) wide strap of leather webbing between the thumb and the rest of a fielder's glove (*The Sporting News*, June 15, 1939).

turbocharged slider A fast slider. Anonymous scout (quoted in *Sports Illustrated*, March 25, 2002): "[Chad Fox] has a turbocharged slider. You know it's coming and still have trouble with it." Syn. "turbo slider."

turf Short for *artifical turf*.

turf bounce The high hop of a batted ball off artificial turf. Outfielders play deeper in parks with artificial turf and do not try to make diving catches on shallow fly balls, lest the ball end up going to the wall.

turfcutter A ground ball. IST USE. 1871. "[Duffy] then hit a turfcutter safe and earned his base" (*Brooklyn Eagle*, Aug. 29; Peter Morris).

turf toe An injury occurring on artificial turf where the sole of the shoe sticks to the turf and the big toe is jammed into the front of the shoe. It is defined as a sprain of the metatarsophalangeal joint of the big toe. "Yes, it does hurt—and yes, it can end careers" (Rick Lawes, *USA Today Baseball Weekly*, July 19–25, 1991).

turkey *hist.* Syn. of *home plate*. IST USE. 1889. "[Mike] Tiernan . . . slammed a tall and ornamental fly into left field for two bases, bringing [George] Gore across the turkey" (*The World* [New York], July 13; Gerald L. Cohen). ETYMOLOGY. This 19th-century term showed up repeatedly in Cohen's research into baseball slang in *The World*. He speculated that the 19th-century home plate was likened in shape to a turkey platter (*Studies in Slang*, pt.2, 1989). See also *home turkey*.

turkey trot ball A breaking pitch thrown by Rube Marquard (*San Francisco Bulletin*, Feb. 22, 1913; Gerald L. Cohen).

turn **1.** See *turn at bat*. IST USE. 1863 (Chadwick Scrapbooks clipping, Aug. 9; Edward J. Nichols). **2.** A pitcher's regular start in the normal rotation. "Chris Bosio missed a turn because of mild tendinitis in his right shoulder" (*The Baltimore Sun*, June 27, 1994). IST USE. 1905. "[Ed Reulbach] pitched out of turn about two games a week" (*St. Louis Post-Dispatch*, July 30; Peter Morris).

turn a double play To execute a defensive play in which two offensive players are put out in continuous action. Syn. *turn two*.

turn and burn For a batter to pull the ball and race into second base or third base with an extra-base hit.

turn around **1.** To be in a losing position in a game or series but able to score enough runs or win enough games to overcome that position. **2.** To have a winning season following a losing one; e.g., "The team, a noncontender, turned its season around so much that it is now considered a contender" or "Smith turned his season around by changing from a defensive player to an aggressive offensive player." **3.** To force a switch-hitter to hit from one side of the plate to another by bringing in a relief pitcher. **4.** Syn. of *turn the order.* **5.** To pull the ball. "[Left-handed batter Corey] Patterson then turned around Corcoran's 1–1 pitch, sending a soaring drive into the right-field bleachers" (*The Baltimore Sun*, Sept. 19, 2006). See also *turn on.*

turn-around hitter *hist.* Syn. of *switch-hitter.* IST USE. 1919. "Earl Smith is now a turn-around hitter. Against right-handers he swats from the left side of the plate, while he switches around facing left-handers" (*St. Louis Post-Dispatch*, June 29; Peter Morris).

turn at bat **1.** A player's opportunity to bat the ball, from the moment he enters the batter's box until he is either put out or becomes a baserunner. See also *plate appearance.* **2.** A team's offensive opportunity in a given inning.

turn away **1.** To retire a side without allowing it to score; e.g., "Smith turned away the Cubs in the top of the fifth." **2.** To strike out three batters in succession.

turn back To defeat an opposing team; e.g., "The Padres turned back the Cubs."

turn in To complete; e.g., "Smith turns in another fine pitching performance."

turn it into a souvenir To hit a home run into the stands or out of the park, with the ball being claimed by a fan.

turn loose To allow the batter to swing with three balls and no strikes.

turn on To pull an inside pitch by using one's legs and hips to turn the body early to make good contact with power and to get the bat head on the ball. "I threw him [Mitch Webster] a fastball in, and he was pulling out and turning on it" (Lee Smith, quoted in *The Baltimore Sun*, March 12, 1994). See also *turn around,* 5.

turn on the big guns To use the best players, esp. pitchers (Maurice H. Weseen, *A Dictionary of American Slang,* 1934).

turn on the fan To get the barrel of the bat out in front of the pitch. The term was used by outfielder and coach Frank Howard.

turn on the heat To play well and with inten-

sity; to bear down. Syn. "turn on the current."

turn over **1.** To complete a double play; e.g., "The Cubs turned it over when Smith touched second and threw to first." **2.** See *turn the ball over.*

turn-over hitter *hist.* Syn. of *switch-hitter.* IST USE. 1924. "[Miller] Huggins has been experimenting with [Hinkey Haines] as a turn-over hitter, trying to teach him to bat right or left handed as the occasion warrants" (*Appleton* [Wisc.] *Post Crescent,* March 28; Peter Morris).

turnstile A device for counting spectators as they enter the ballpark. Self-registering turnstiles are installed at every entrance to a major-league ballpark and are numbered for identification. There is a ticket box or appropriate electronic device at each turnstile. In an attempt to standardize the method by which gate receipts were divided between home and visiting clubs, the National League mandated the use of turnstiles in 1877. The first turnstiles were introduced in New York and Providence in 1878. "In all cases the visiting club shall receive fifteen cents for every admission registered by the turnstile" (*Chicago Tribune,* March 16, 1879; Peter Morris). Sometimes spelled "turnstyle." Syn. *stile.*

turnstile count The total number of spectators who pass through a turnstile at a baseball

Turnstile. Rickwood Field, Second Avenue West, Birmingham, Ala. *Historic American Buildings Survey, Library of Congress*

game. See also *attendance*, 1. IST USE. 1883. "None of the three crowds . . . exceeded three thousand one hundred, turnstile count" (*The Sporting Life*, July 30, p.7).

turnstiler *hist.* A spectator at a baseball game. IST USE. 1932 (*All Sports Record Book*; Edward J. Nichols).

turn the ball over 1. To throw the ball and turn one's hand over the top of the ball in the process; specif., to throw the screwball. The term derives from the fact that the ball has been turned to give it a reverse spin. 2. To hold the ball with the fingers parallel to the seams and rotate the wrist counterclockwise as the ball is released, causing it to stay low in the strike zone; specif., to throw the two-seam fastball.

turn the order To make more than one defensive change simultaneously so as to change the order in which the new players will come to bat. Syn. *turn around* [the order], 4.

turn two Syn. of *turn a double play*.

turret *hist.* Syn. of *mound*, 1. IST USE. 1913 (*The Sporting News*, Oct. 30).

turtle back *hist.* 1. *n.* The elevated ground behind second base, "laid out with the intention of draining the infield" (*The Sporting Life*, March 7, 1914; Peter Morris). 2. *n.* Syn. of *mound*, 1. 3. *v.* To elevate the center of the diamond to "help the pitcher . . . from where he operated" (Will Wedge, *The Sporting News,* May 21, 1936). Wedge noted, "[Henry Fabian remarked] that he turtle-backed the first diamond in 1889, in Dallas, and built the first of the sort in the majors at St. Louis, in 1909."

tut-ball A precursor of baseball that may have separated from stool-ball as early as the early 16th century in England. Dictionaries of the 19th century confirm that "tut" was defined as a small chunk of brick or sod used for a "base." The folk game, which became nearly extinct by the late 19th century, was virtually identical to rounders, except that a bat may not always have been used (David Block, *Baseball Before We Knew It*, 2005, pp.135–38, 155).

tweener 1. A base hit that falls between two outfielders, neither of whom can reach the ball in time; esp., a hard-hit ball in the gap between two outfielders that rolls to the wall. When he was denying his ability as a power hitter, Vada Pinson was once asked to account for the doubles and triples he was hitting: "Oh, those were just 'tweener' hits, those that light between outfielders" (*San Francisco Call-Bulletin*, May 16, 1959; Peter Tamony). Sometimes spelled "'tweener." See also *gapper.* Compare *in-betweener.* 2. A player who excels in the minor leagues but is not talented enough to play in the major leagues; specif., a player whose skills do not seem ideally suited to any defensive position. "Scouts view [Billy McCarthy] as a tweener. He runs well, but not well enough to play center field in pro ball. He has a right-field arm but lacks the power for that position" (*Baseball America*, June 11–24, 2001; Peter Morris). ETYMOLOGY. The term is likely borrowed from basketball, where it is common to describe a player whose skills are between that of a forward and a guard, or not ideally suited to any particular position.

tweet A great ("sweet") defensive play (Mark Davis, *San Diego Union-Tribune*, Apr. 11, 1994).

12-o'clock high A straight overhand pitch.

12-o'clock hitter A player who hits well in batting practice and poorly during a game that starts at one o'clock. See also *10-o'clock hitter*; *one-o'clock hitter*; *two-o'clock hitter*; *five-o'clock hitter*; *six-o'clock hitter*; *seven-o'clock hitter.*

12-to-6 curve An overhand curveball that drops straight down, as if on a clock, from top to bottom. It has replaced *overhand curve* in the popular vernacular. "Bert Blyleven's curve was a perfect 12-to-6: it moved from the catcher's head right down to the plate" (Mickey White, quoted in Alan Schwarz, BaseballAmerica.com, Nov. 14, 2006). "[David] Wells has . . . a 12-to-6-o'clock curve that dips, wiggles and does a fair rendition of Chuck Berry's duck strut" (Franz Lidz, *Sports Illustrated*, Sept. 8, 1997, p.77). Syn. *noon-to-6 curve*; *noon-to-cocktail-hour curve*; *top-to-bottom curve*; *nose-to-toes curve.*

20–80 Short for *20-to-80 scale.*

25-man roster The active list of players on a major-league team, from Opening Day until midnight on Aug. 31. It excludes players on the disabled list. The 25-man roster was mandated via a major-league rule in 1909, although many clubs carried fewer than 25 players for many years after that. Compare *40-man roster.*

25 players, 25 cabs A team with little teamwork, because the players do not enjoy doing things together. "The capsule description of some star-studded teams has been: 'twenty-five players, twenty-five cabs'" (George V. Higgins, *The Progress of the Seasons*, 1989, pp.86–87; Peter Morris).

24-hour recall Assigning a major-league player to a minor-league club, with the option of bringing the player back to the major-league club within 24 hours.

24-man roster The active list of players allowed on a major-league team since 1986. The reason for the change from 25 (which had been in place since 1909) to 24 was to save money, and perhaps to bust the players' union; but, by all accounts, the new rule was a detriment to a team's ability to make strategic moves in the late innings of a game. "The new 24-man roster limit claimed another victim Tuesday when the Chicago Cubs released veteran pinch-hitter Richie Hebner, who came up in 1968" (*USA Today*, Apr. 2, 1986). In 1990, teams were given the option of going with a 24- or 25-man roster (most opted for 25).

20-game winner A pitcher who has won 20 or more games in a single season. Winning 20 games in a season is a common standard of excellence for pitchers.

20-second rule A rule that allows the pitcher 20 seconds between pitches to deliver the ball when there is nobody on base and no time-outs are called. If the pitcher violates this rule, the umpire shall call "ball" (*Official Baseball Rules*, Rule 8.04). With one or more baserunners, there is no time limit.

23-man roster The active list of players on a major-league team from 1933 through 1938.

20-to-80 scale Syn. of *scouting scale.*

20-20 club A mythical group of players who have hit 20 or more home runs and stolen 20 or more bases in a single season. Compare *30-30 club; 40-40 club; 50-50 club.*

twig The bat of a small batter. "[Darryl] Blaze is the only guy who's holding a twig. He's so small" (*Kalamazoo* [Mich.] *Gazette*, July 11, 2004).

twight A game started late in the afternoon and finished at night. The term was created by the Brooklyn Dodgers in 1942 as a blend of "twilight" and "night." Ed Danforth (*Baseball Digest*, Sept. 1942) opposed the "twend" and noted, "If baseball is going baby talk and wadio announcers are going to give out: 'Weese twipled to wight scoring Wizzo. Wiggs dwew four balls and Weiser sacwificed him to second,' then let's suspend baseball for the duwation." See also *twilight game,* 1.

twilight ball [softball term] An early name for softball.

twilight game 1. A game played too late for a day game and too early for a night game. An Acme wire photo (June 15, 1942) contained this caption: "Twilight Baseball. The Brooklyn Dodgers inaugurated a modified form of night baseball at Ebbets Field . . . The game, which started in the daylight at 7:00 pm, and finished under the arc-lights two hours later, drew a crowd of 15,157 fans" (Cleveland Public Library Photo Collection). See also *twight.* 2. A game played late in the afternoon, esp. in the Negro leagues before the widespread use of electric lights. "A twilight game began just after the day shift ended, and players gratefully noted that when the sun went down, the game was over" (Donn Rogosin, *Invisible Men*, 1983, p.23).

twilight-night Syn. of *twi-night doubleheader.*

twilight zone All levels of baseball except the major leagues, from the perspective of a long-time major leaguer. *The Sporting Life* (March 10, 1917; Peter Morris) described the release of Chief Bender as "a one-way ticket to the twilight zone of base ball."

twin bill Syn. of *doubleheader.* IST USE. 1918. "More than 7,800 fans saw the twin bill" (*The Boston Globe*, Aug. 11; Peter Morris).

twi-night doubleheader A *doubleheader* with the first game starting in the late afternoon, usually about 5:30 p.m., and the second game being played at night under the lights. The term is a blend of "twilight" and "night." Syn. *twilight-night*; *twi-nighter*. IST USE. 1942. "'Twi-night' doubleheaders, baseball's contribution to the working man, may mean a boost at the box office, but they're a pain in the neck to the New York Yankees" (Austin Bealmear, Associated Press, in *Reno Evening Gazette*, Aug. 1; Peter Morris).

twi-nighter Syn. of *twi-night doubleheader*. "The Mets and the Braves played a meaningless twi-nighter" (George Vecsey, *The New York Times*, Sept. 28, 2002).

Twinkies Derisive nickname for the Minnesota *Twins* and their fans.

twin killing Syn. of *double play*. IST USE. 1914. "A twin killing . . . cut short a brilliant run-getting chance in the first after [Max] Flack opened with a single. [Rollie] Zeider could not sacrifice and his tap to the box was an easy double-up" (Billy Birch, *Indianapolis Star*, Sept. 5; Dan O'Brien).

Twins Nickname for the American League Central Division franchise that began playing in Bloomington, Minn., in 1961 as the Minnesota Twins. Based in Minneapolis since 1982, the franchise originated as the Washington Senators (Nationals) (1901–1960). See also *Twinkies*. ETYMOLOGY. Named for the state of Minnesota and the twin cities of Minneapolis and St. Paul.

twirl To pitch. "In 1904 Cy [Young] twirled forty-five innings straight without being scored on" (*San Francisco Bulletin*, March 29, 1913; Gerald L. Cohen). IST USE. 1883 (*The Sporting Life*, June 3, p.3; Edward J. Nichols). ETYMOLOGY. From the fact that a pitcher winds up or "twirls" his arm before delivering the ball.

twirler A pitcher. "[Cy Young] is to-day the veteran twirler of baseball" (*The Washington Post*, Nov. 1, 1903). IST USE. 1883 (*The Sporting Life*, Apr. 15, p.2; Edward J. Nichols).

twirling Pitching. IST USE. 1883. "Watt did the twirling for the home team" (*Detroit Free Press*, Apr. 25; Peter Morris).

twist *hist.* A curveball. Chestnut Hill pitcher R.M. Gaskill "delivers with a very puzzling twist [to which the club] may greatly attribute their success" (*Philadelphia Inquirer*,

Sept. 25, 1865; Richard Hershberger). IST USE. 1861 (*New York Sunday Mercury*, Aug. 10; Edward J. Nichols).

twister *hist.* A curveball. "Dutch [Ruether] made quite a hit in the East with his assortment of twisters" (*San Francisco Bulletin*, May 12, 1913; Gerald L. Cohen). IST USE. 1870. "The Amateurs seemed to take kindly to [Phonney Martin's] twisters at first" (*Chicago Tribune*, July 23; Peter Morris).

2 The scorekeeper's designation for the catcher.

two Second base. The term is used by fielders to denote where to throw a fielded ball for a putout.

two away Two out.

2B **1.** Abbrev. for *second base*, 1. **2.** Abbrev. for *second base*, 2. **3.** Abbrev. for *second baseman*. **4.** Box score abbrev. for *double*, 1.

two-bagger Syn. of *double*, 1. IST USE. 1876. "Orlopp made a two-bagger, bringing in Huf" (*Daily Arkansas Gazette* [Little Rock], Sept. 3). EXTENDED USE. A double victory; a repeat success. "Brown 'Two-Bagger' Brings in $132,000,000" referred to the California senate's passing the governor's increased income and cigarette tax bills (*San Francisco Call-Bulletin* headline, May 27, 1959; Peter Tamony).

two-base error A misplay that allows the batter–runner or a baserunner to advance two bases. IST USE. 1878. "It was what might be called a 'two-base error'" (*Chicago Tribune*, July 7; Peter Morris).

two-base hit Syn. of *double*, 1. IST USE. 1872 (*The Boston Daily Globe*, Apr. 15; Peter Morris).

two-baser Syn. of *double*, 1. IST USE. 1872. "In the second inning the Bostons made five . . . base hits, one being also a two baser and another a home run" (*Brooklyn Eagle*, Aug. 15; Peter Morris).

two class *hist.* The highly select group of pitchers with an earned run average below 2.00 for a given season. IST USE. 1922 (*Spalding's Official Base Ball Guide*, p.228; Edward J. Nichols).

two-cushion shot Syn. of *double*, 1. IST USE.

1912 (*New York Tribune*, Sept. 16; Edward J. Nichols).

two down Two out.

two down and one to go Two out with one out remaining.

two fingers only Said of a pitcher who can no longer throw the fastball. The term alludes to the traditional catcher's sign (two fingers) for a curveball. IST USE. 1912 (*American Magazine*, June, p.205; Edward J. Nichols).

two for *hist.* A doubleheader. IST USE. 1904. "A 'two for' attraction" (*The Washington Post*, Sept. 11; Peter Morris).

two for the price of one Detroit Tigers broadcaster Ernie Harwell's announcement of a double play.

two gone Two out.

"two hands!" Warning issued to outfielders reminding them to catch a fly ball with both hands.

two-hopper A batted ball that bounces twice before it is fielded.

2-iron A line-drive home run that rises when it leaves the park, simulating the soaring trajectory of a golf ball struck by a 2-iron (Angus Lind, *The New Orleans Times-Picayune*, Apr. 27, 1994).

two league *hist.* A baseball league that plays many doubleheaders.

two-master Syn. of *double*, 1. IST USE. 1891 (*Chicago Herald*, May 24; Edward J. Nichols).

two o'cat Syn. of *two-old-cat*.

two-o'clock hitter A player who hits well in batting practice and poorly during the game. The term dates back to when most games started at three o'clock and batting practice started at two o'clock. See also *10-o'clock hitter*; *12-o'clock hitter*; *one-o'clock hitter*; *five-o'clock hitter*; *six-o'clock hitter*; *seven-o'clock hitter*. IST USE. 1933. "Two o'Clock Hitter—one who hits line drives during batting practice but pop flies in a game" (Walter Winchell, *Havana Evening Telegram*, May 3).

two-old-cat A variant of *old-cat* with four players (two batters and two fielders) and two bases placed about 40 feet apart. According to John Montgomery Ward (*Base-Ball: How to Become a Player*, 1888, p.23), the two batters were at opposite stations, with the fielders divided so that half faced one batter and half the other. Two-old-cat was the American equivalent of the older English game of *cat and dog* (David Block, *Baseball Before We Knew It*, 2005, p.130). Syn: *two o'cat*. IST USE. 1842. "The poor fellow could only look through the window, in perfect misery, upon the sports without—his favorite game of 'wicket,' or 'two old cat,' or 'goal,' or the 'snapping of the whip,'—and hear the shouts when the players were 'caught out,' or the wicket was knocked off, or some one had performed a feat of great agility" (*The New-England Weekly Review*, Jan. 29; Richard Hershberger).

two-out play A low-percentage baserunning maneuver that may be worth trying with two outs (but not earlier) in an inning. Christy Mathewson (*Pitching in a Pinch*, 1912; Peter Morris) noted that New York Giants manager John McGraw used the term to mean "certain chances are to be taken by a coacher at one point in a contest, while to attempt such a play under other circumstances would be nothing short of foolhardy."

two-ply 1. Said of a two-base hit; e.g., "two-ply poke" (Maurice H. Weseen, *A Dictionary of American Slang*, 1934), "two-ply smasher" (*The Chicago Defender*, July 8, 1939, p.17; Bob Luke), and "two-ply blow" (*Al Schacht Dope Book*, 1944). 2. Said of a double play; e.g., "two-ply killing" (*Spalding's Official Base Ball Guide*, 1920, p.55; Edward J. Nichols).

two-sacker Syn. of *double*, 1. IST USE. 1891 (*Chicago Herald*, July 5; Edward J. Nichols).

two-seam changeup A changeup thrown with the middle and ring fingers placed along two seams. It is thrown by Tom Glavine. See also *four-seam changeup*.

two-seamer 1. A lucky home run, as described by Joe Goddard (*The Sporting News*, March 6, 1982): "One of those duck-hook jobs that barely gets over the fence. It's not awesome. The ball sinks a little and the hitter gets on top of the ball, only getting his bat on two

Two-seam fastball.

seams." Compare *four-seamer*, 1. **2.** Syn. of *two-seam fastball*.

two-seam fastball A sinking fastball in which the ball is gripped along (not across) two seams. It does not run or slide as much as a *four-seam fastball*. When thrown by a right-handed pitcher, it veers back into a right-handed batter or tails away from a left-handed batter. See also *sinker*, 1. Syn. *two-seamer*, 2; *sinking fastball*, 2; *backdoor fastball*.

two strikes A count of 0-2. EXTENDED USE. Two handicaps or disadvantages. "To be born black in Okolona, Miss., in 1935 was to have two strikes against you" (Cal Thomas, *The Baltimore Sun*, Jan. 4, 2006).

two-time a pitch To take an extra step forward to swing at an esp. slow-pitched ball.

two-way player **1.** A player who is proficient both on offense and on defense. "[Manager Sam] Perlozzo called his catcher [Ramon Hernandez] one of the best two-way players the Orioles have had in recent years" (*The Baltimore Sun*, Apr. 11, 2006). **2.** A player with major-league potential both as a pitcher and as a hitter. **3.** A player (usually in amateur baseball) who both pitches and plays a defensive position.

Ty Cobb play A particularly daring piece of baserunning in which the runner attempts to take an extra base even though the ball is in the hands of a fielder. "Joe Jackson attempted a regular Ty Cobb play in the third inning" (*Chicago Tribune*, May 28, 1911; Peter Morris).

Tygers Occasional nickname for the Detroit *Tigers* when Ty Cobb was on the roster (Mark Pattison and David Raglin, *Detroit Tigers Lists and More*, 2002, p.210).

tying run A run that ties the score of a game.

Type A free agent A *free agent* ranked among the top 20 percent (formerly 30 percent) of major leaguers at his position as determined by a formula developed by the Elias Sports Bureau, using statistics from the preceding two seasons. Any club that signs a Type A free agent must surrender a top draft pick to the free agent's former club: its second-round pick in the next summer's first-year player draft if the signing team was in the top half of the standings, or otherwise its first-round pick. The club losing a Type A free agent also receives an extra draft pick between the first and second rounds of the first-year player draft. This classification resulted from the 1981 players' strike.

Type B free agent A *free agent* ranked among the top 40 percent (formerly 50 percent), but not the top 20 percent, of major leaguers at his position as determined by a formula developed by the Elias Sports Bureau, using statistics from the preceding two seasons. The club losing a Type B free agent receives an extra draft pick between the first and second rounds of the first-year player draft; the pick does not come directly from the team

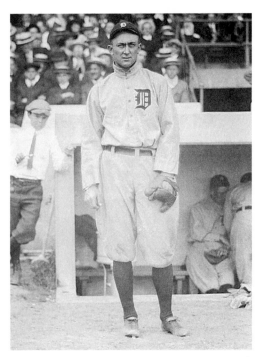

Tygers. Ty Cobb in 1913. *George Grantham Bain Collection, Library of Congress*

that signed the player. This classification resulted from the 1981 players' strike.

Type C free agent A former designation for a *free agent* ranked among the bottom half of major leaguers at his position as determined by a formula developed by the Elias Sports Bureau, using statistics from the preceding two seasons. The club losing a Type C free agent received an extra draft pick between the second and third rounds of the next summer's first-year player draft. Compensation for Type C free agents was eliminated with the 2007–2011 Basic Agreement.

U

U Scorecard abbrev. for an unassisted putout.

UA Abbrev. for *Union Association*.

UBL Abbrev. for *United Baseball League*.

Uecker seats The highest, nosebleed seats in a ballpark. The term references Milwaukee Brewers broadcaster Bob Uecker who, in television ads for Miller Lite beer, was seen sitting far away from the action. In Milwaukee, upper-deck seats having a partially obstructed view were once available (1999) for $1 and were designated "Uecker seats."

ugly Describing a game played gracelessly, characterized by miscues, wasted leads, and runners thrown out on hits. "The Yankees are even winning the ugly ones these days" (*Milwaukee Journal Sentinel*, July 24, 1997). New York Yankees first baseman Tino Martinez (quoted in *USA Today*, Oct. 24, 2000): "In postseason, you can win games ugly or play good, it doesn't matter." See also *winning ugly*.

ugly finder A foul ball lined into the dugout, so called because such a ball is believed to seek out a homely player (*Newsweek*, July 15, 1991).

ugly pitch A bad pitch, usually caused by poor mechanics or slipping on the mound, that should be hit hard.

ugly weights A method for evaluating the offensive performance of a batter in a season, calculated by multiplying the player's total for each of a set of offensive events, both positive (walks, singles, stolen bases, etc.) and negative (outs made, caught stealing), by a weight associated with it, and then adding (or, in the case of negative events, subtracting) the products. The method is an accurate predictor of offensive performance in a given year, and particularly excels for very good and very bad hitters. It was proposed by Phil Birnbaum (*By the Numbers*, 1999). ETYMOLOGY. The method was given the name "ugly" due to its complexity, as it includes terms that are squared and multiplied (e.g., batting average times isolated power).

UIC [softball term] Abbrev. for *umpire-in-chief*, 2.

ukulele hitter A hitter who hits weak ground balls to the infielders; a poor hitter. See also *banjo hitter*. Sometimes spelled "ukelele hitter."

ukulele umpire Syn. of *third base umpire*.

ultimate baseball statistic Syn. of *overall player runs*.

ump **1.** *n.* Short for *umpire*, 1. "Playoff Umps Not Chosen Blindly" (*USA Today* headline, Oct. 7, 1986). See also *umps*. **2.** *v.* Short for *umpire*, 2. IST USE. 1888. "He wants to ump in some of the minor leagues" (*Cincinnati Times-Star*, Apr. 18; David Shulman).

umpire **1.** *n.* An official who is responsible for the conduct of the game on the playing field, who administers the official rules of baseball and maintains discipline and order; baseball's third-party adjudicator. There are four umpires at a major-league game (one at home plate and one at each base) and (since the mid-1950s) an additional two during postseason play (one for each foul line). The *plate umpire* is the *umpire-in-chief* and the base umpires are field umpires. The umpires are responsible for individual calls during a game, from the initial instruction of "play ball!" through the announcement of the last out. They determine, among other things, if a given pitch is a ball or strike, if a given baserunner is safe or out, and if the ball is in play or dead. *Baseball Magazine* (Jan. 1915, p.70) defined "umpire" as: "(a) Porch-climbing horsethief; (b) Poor, blind guy, that can't see nothing right; (c) Squarest ever—won't let them guys put nothing over on him." See also *arbiter*; *arbitrator*, 1; *blind Tom*; *blue*; *blue-coat*; *boy blue*; *Jesse James*; *Mr. Guess*; *man in blue*; *sheepherder*; *tin cup*. Syn. *ump*, 1. IST USE. 1838. "[The Recorder] shall be the umpire between the captains on Club days, in the event of a disputed point of the game, and from his decision there shall be no appeal, except to the Club, at its next stated meeting" (Constitution of the Olympic Ball Club of Philadelphia, art. VI, sect. 3). USAGE NOTE. Prior to 1958, two umpires (one from each club) and one *referee* officiated games; the referee settled any disagreements between the umpires. It was later decided that it would be easier to have one umpire make decisions. A second umpire was used in major-league games in the early 1900s; a third was added in the 1930s; and a fourth in the 1950s. **2.** *v.* To act as a judge or umpire. Syn. *ump*, 2. IST USE. 1870 (*New York Tribune*, Aug. 8; Peter Morris).

ETYMOLOGY. Baseball borrowed the concept of "umpire" from the game of cricket, which had become an established pastime in the Philadelphia and New York areas by the 1830s. The term "umpire" is from the Middle English "nomper" or "noumpere," for an extra person brought in when two individuals disagreed; this term was "nonced" (the letter "n" was dropped from the word and attached itself to the article, such that "a noumpere" became "an oumpere"). The Middle English word, in turn, derives from the Old French word "nonper" or "nomper," meaning one not equal or without peer or "not paired" (hence, ideally suited to act as the objective third party to arbitrate a dispute).

EXTENDED USE. Umpires are also employed in football, field hockey, badminton, polo, tennis, table tennis, and volleyball. When James Naismith invented basketball in 1891, he originally designated an umpire to call fouls and a referee to track the ball; the rules committee gradually abolished the distinction between the two officials and settled on the term "referee."

umpire-baiting Consistent bickering with the umpires, perhaps with an eye to getting the benefit of close calls in the future. IST USE. 1902 (*The Sporting Life*, Oct. 4, p.8; Edward J. Nichols).

umpire-in-chief 1. The *umpire* positioned behind the plate when there are two or more umpires assigned to a game. He is the official in charge, responsible for the proper conduct of the game, and the only person with the authority to declare a forfeit. He makes all decisions regarding the batter, which includes calling balls, strikes, and foul balls. He informs the official scorer of the batting orders and any changes in the line-ups. See also *plate umpire*. Compare *crew chief*. Syn. *chief of staff*. **2.** [softball term] A regional or tournament supervisor of umpires. Abbrev. *UIC*.

umpire's assistant A pocket-sized instrument for recording balls and strikes; a forerunner of the present day *indicator*, 1 (Harold Seymour, *Baseball: The Early Years*, 1960, p.182).

umpire's broom The common whisk broom used by the plate umpire to clean or dust off home plate so that it is clearly visible. Before the turn of the 20th century, umpires swept the plate with a long-handled house broom and then tossed the broom toward the visitors' bench. In 1904, Chicago Cubs outfielder Jack McCarthy was running from third base to home when he stepped on the umpire's broom and seriously injured his ankle. The National League president subsequently issued an order banning the long-handled brooms and requiring that umpires carry brooms small enough to put in their pockets. The American League adopted the rule soon thereafter. Syn. *brush*.

umpire school A commercial enterprise, usually operated by a former and/or current major-league umpire, dedicated to teaching umpiring skills to qualified young aspirants. The first umpire school was opened in 1935 by National League umpire George Barr in Hot Springs, Ark. Currently, there are two umpire schools: the Harry Wendelstedt Umpire School in Daytona Beach, Fla., and the Jim Evans Academy of Professional Umpiring in Kissimmee, Fla. IST USE. 1917. "The Umpires' School teaches respect for authority" (*The Sporting Life*, Jan. 13; Peter Morris).

umpire's interference An act by an umpire that hinders a fielder; e.g., touching a fair batted ball before it passes a fielder or impeding a catcher's throw that was intended to prevent a stolen base. A pitched or thrown ball that hits the umpire is in play. Runners may not advance when the plate umpire interferes with the catcher's throw.

umpire's signal One of a simple set of hand and arm movements that an umpire uses to indicate calls; e.g., a raised right arm with a clenched fist along the basepaths means that the runner is out, an emphatic horizontal crossing of the hands with the palms down indicates the runner is safe, and a raised right arm at the plate indicates a called strike. Although the use of hand signals by the umpire is often attributed to the presence in the major leagues of deaf outfielder Dummy Hoy (his last year in the majors was 1902), such signals first appeared about 1906 and were commonly used by umpires in 1907. According to *Spalding's Official Base Ball Guide* for 1909, "two or three years ago Base Ball critics in the East and West began to agitate the question of signaling by the umpires to announce their decisions" (Peter Morris).

umpiring The art of judging a game; acting like an umpire. "Anybody can see high and low. It is 'in and out' that is umpiring" (American League umpire Durwood Merrill, quoted by George F. Will, *The Washington Post*, March 29, 1987). Will continued, "The business of umpiring is to regulate striving, to turn it from chaos into ordered competition, thereby enabling excellence to prevail over cruder qualities. Umpiring is, in a word, government."

umps Var. of *ump*, 1. "A new name for the umpire has been discovered down in this section [Montgomery, Ala.]. It is 'Umps' and is extensively used in the smaller towns where nothing but 'Umps' is heard, and woe be unto the 'Umps' who displeases the home crowds" (*Detroit Tribune*, Apr. 6, 1903; Peter Morris). See also *his umps*.

unassisted Without help; specif., said of a putout without the help of a teammate. IST USE. 1884 (*De Witt's Base-Ball Guide*, p.42; Edward J. Nichols).

unassisted double play A double play in which a fielder is credited with both putouts without a teammate touching the ball; e.g., when, with a runner on first base, the first baseman catches a line drive and steps on the base after the runner has taken off without tagging up.

unassisted pickoff A pickoff play in which the pitcher tags a runner who has moved too far away from the base he is occupying.

unassisted triple play A triple play in which a fielder is credited with three putouts without a teammate touching the ball. One of baseball's rarest plays, it has been accomplished only 14 times in the major leagues, first by Cleveland's Neal Ball in 1909. The most famous unassisted triple play was accomplished by Cleveland Indians second baseman Bill Wambsganss during the fifth inning of the fifth game of the 1920 World Series against the Brooklyn Robins: Wambsganss caught a line drive hit by Clarence Mitchell, touched second to retire Pete Kilduff, and tagged Otto Miller running from first base.

unbalanced schedule A playing schedule in which teams play more games against teams in their own division than against other teams in the league. "Trying to implement an unbalanced schedule and conduct interleague play in a setup with 16 teams in one league and 14 in the other is a scheduling nightmare" (Bob Costas, *Fair Ball*, 2000, p.115). Compare *balanced schedule*.

unbreakable Describing a record that, although physically possible, would seem unattainable; e.g., Joe DiMaggio's 56-game hitting streak set in 1941 or Cy Young's 511 career victories.

unbutton your shirt To take a good swing at the ball. The term is based on the idea that a batter might want to loosen his shirt for maximum freedom in swinging. IST USE. 1932 (*New York Sun*, June 23).

Uncle Charlie Syn. of *curveball*. "To the lefties . . . a few sweeping curves can remind you of what a real Uncle Charlie looks like" (Thomas Boswell, *The Washington Post*, May 18, 1983). "[Bo Jackson] has great ability, great tools, but he has problems with Uncle Charlie" (Ralph Wiley, *Sports Illustrated*, Dec. 14, 1987). See also *Lord Charles*; *Sir Charles*. IST USE. 1933. " 'Uncle Charlie's got him!'— he can't hit a curve" (Walter Winchell, *Havana Evening Telegram*, May 3). ETYMOLOGY. The origin of the term is elusive, but the two words "uncle" and "Charlie" may onomatopoetically suggest a curve. In the 1970s, the term was common in citizens band radio slang for the Federal Communications Commission. By extension, *The Dictionary of CB Lingo* (1976) calls the President of the United States "Uncle Charlie's Uncle."

Uncle Tom *hist.* A player of dark complexion (Al Schacht, *Al Schacht Dope Book*, 1944, p.46). ETYMOLOGY. Leading character in *Uncle Tom's Cabin*, the 1852 antislavery novel by Harriet Beecher Stowe.

unconditional release The removal of a player from the roster who has no contract or who is still paid under the terms of his contract but is free to offer his services to another club. IST USE. 1893. "Bob Caruthers, the well-known ball player, has been given his unconditional release by President [Chris] Von der Ahe, and is free to sign where he pleases" (*Atlanta Constitution*, March 17; Peter Morris).

unconditional release waivers A form of *waivers* requesting the unconditional release of a player. It may be made at any time during the year and may not be withdrawn. Any major-league club may claim the player's contract at a waiver price of $1.

uncork 1. To throw explosively, like a champagne cork coming out of a bottle. USAGE NOTE. The term often refers to a wild throw or a wild pitch. It is sometimes used facetiously; e.g., in an account of a game in Boonville, Calif., the *Anderson Valley Advertiser* (June 11, 1986) noted, "G.P. rared back and uncorked a throw that landed about four feet in front of him." 2. To make a dramatic base hit. "[Cravath] uncorked a triple with the bases full" (*San Francisco Bulletin*, May 22, 1913; Gerald L. Cohen).

underground Said of an ineffective pitch; e.g., "Smith's sinker went underground and he had to rely on his fastball."

underground railroad The 16 trades, involving 62 players, between the New York Yankees and the Kansas City Athletics between March 30, 1955, and May 19, 1960, in which the Yankees allegedly used the Athletics as a virtual farm team. According to Francis Kinlaw (in Lloyd Johnson et al., eds., *Unions to Royals: The Story of Professional Baseball in Kansas City*, 1996, pp.32–33), "collusion between the two camps was taken for granted by baseball insiders until Charlie Finley became the principal owner of Kansas City's franchise on December 20, 1960." The cozy relationship between the teams resulted in the Yankees obtaining players such as Roger Maris, Enos Slaughter, Art Ditmar, Bobby Shantz, Cletis Boyer, Ryne Duren, and Ralph Terry in exchange for marginal players and declining veterans. The Yankees won four pennants during this period and five more pennants in the early 1960s, while the Athletics languished in the standings. Syn. *Yankee Shuttle*. ETYMOLOGY. From the Underground Railroad in the United States, in which fugitive slaves were brought into Canada and other places of safety before slavery was abolished.

underhand Said of a pitch, throw, or delivery in which the hand is below the level of the shoulder or the elbow, or that begins below the belt. Infielders often throw underhand on close plays because there is not enough time to get positioned for an overhand throw. Underhand pitchers have included Dennis Eckersley, Dan Quisenberry, Mark Eichhorn, Ted Abernathy, Elden Auker, and Carl Mays. Underhand pitching is mandatory in softball. Compare *overhand*; *sidearm*. Syn. *underslung*. IST USE. 1866 (Henry Chadwick, *The Base Ball Players' Book of Reference*, p.38; Edward J. Nichols).

underneath ball A fastball thrown from the pitcher's ear, causing the ball to rise. It is used mostly by drop-and-drive pitchers and is deceiving to batters.

underslung Syn. of *underhand*. "Carl Mays, with his underslung slants, had the Mackmen eating out of his hand" (*The Boston Globe*, Apr. 26, 1918; Peter Morris).

undersocks Syn. of *sanitary socks*. Bill Freehan (*Behind the Mask*, 1970) tells of Al

Kaline calling out for a pair of "under-socks"; a younger player asks him what he's talking about and Kaline replies, "You aren't old enough to know. That's what we called sanitary socks back in the mid-fifties" (Charles D. Poe).

undertaker's rule [softball term] The Amateur Softball Association of America rule adopted in 1941 that required all pitchers in both day and night games to wear all-black or all-dark-blue uniforms with no letters or trimming on the front of the uniform. It was so called because it made the players look like undertakers. The rule was repealed in 1947.

under the ball See *get under the ball*.

under the big top In the major leagues.

under the leg pitch [softball term] A legal pitch in which the pitcher lifts his or her leg and throws the ball under it. The pitch is allowed in the United States Specialty Sports Association.

under the lights Descriptive of a night game.

under the willow Said of playing the position of catcher. "The work of Murphy under the willow [the bat] is deserving of great praise" (*The Boston Globe*, May 5, 1886; Peter Morris).

undress 1. To slide into a catcher with such force that, literally, at least one piece of the catcher's equipment (e.g., a shin guard or the chest protector) is jarred loose or knocked out of place. The term is also used in the figurative sense for any hard slide into the catcher, as if the slamming were enough to tear his equipment off. **2.** For a pitcher to embarrass a batter who has been badly fooled by a pitch. "Nobody could undress you the way Sandy [Koufax] could" (Gene Mauch, quoted in *Sports Illustrated*, Sept. 9, 2002). Carl Erskine (*Carl Erskine's Tales from the Dodger Dugout*, 2000, p.110) wrote that to "undress him" meant "to throw him a high, tight pitch." **3.** To hit the ball hard directly at a fielder.

unearned run A run that is scored because of an error, catcher's interference, or passed ball, or following an error on a play that would have ended the inning. The significance of unearned runs is that they are not charged against a pitcher in computing his

earned run average. Compare *earned run*. IST USE. 1879 (*Spirit of the Times*, Aug. 23; Edward J. Nichols).

unearned-run average A statistical measure computed by dividing the unearned runs a team allows by the number of innings played, then multiplying by 9. It measures clutch pitching; i.e., the ability to limit damages after an error puts a runner on base or gives the opposition an extra out. The term was introduced by Allen St. John (*The Wall Street Journal*, Sept. 16, 2005). Abbrev. *URA*.

unfair ball *hist.* A pitch outside the area requested by the batter in early baseball, when a batter could request a high or low pitch. Compare *fair ball*, 2.

ungodly shot A hard line drive (Jim Bouton, *Ball Four*, 1970).

unhittable 1. Said of a pitcher off whom it is difficult to get base hits. **2.** Said of a pitched ball that is very difficult to hit.

uni Short for *uniform*. "The uni change may be second only to the managerial change in front-office strategy" (*Village Voice*, Oct. 7, 1986). "It's been a long road. . . . Just being out in a 'uni' again, it feels good" (Kelly Gruber, quoted in *The Baltimore Sun*, Feb. 18, 1997). IST USE. 1938 (Chicago Park District [Burnham Park], *Baseball*).

unie Short for *uniform*. IST USE. 1913. "The Nationals off the field are about as meek a collection of ball players as ever donned the same set of 'unies'" (*The Washington Post*, March 30; Peter Morris).

uniform A team's official costume. Major-league teams have two different uniforms: one for home games and another for away games. The major leagues have a dress policy in which all players are required to be in uniform and to wear only club-issued apparel, outerware, and equipment during games (on the field, in the dugout, and in the bullpen), batting practice, and any in-stadium interview room up to 30 minutes following games. The modern baseball uniform was introduced in 1868 by the Red Stockings of Cincinnati, who wore knickered pants. Syn. *uni*; *unie*. IST USE. 1837. "[The Recorder] shall have charge of the pattern uniform owned by the Club" (Constitution of the Olympic Ball Club

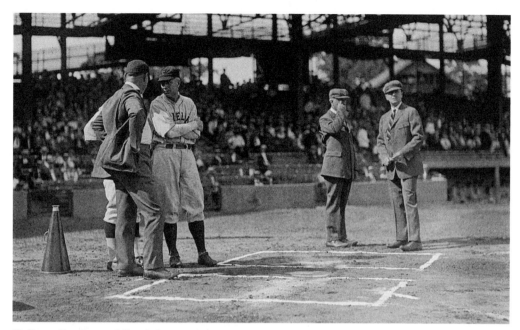

Uniform. Umpires modeling their new olive drab uniforms, Aug. 12, 1924. *National Photo Company Collection, Library of Congress*

of Philadelphia, Art. VI, Sect. 7; Dean A. Sullivan).

uniform player's contract The standard contract between all major-league clubs and their players on the major-league reserve list, as prescribed by any Basic Agreement in effect between the major leagues and the Major League Baseball Players Association. It aims "to preserve morale" among major-league players and "to produce the similarity of conditions necessary for keen competition" (Major League Rules, Rule 3[b][1]). The contract governs the terms and conditions of the player's employment during all periods in which the player is performing "skilled" services for the club. It includes payment, disability, uniforms, transportation, meal allowances, and assignment of the contract to other clubs. The player agrees to keep in first-class physical condition, observe and comply with rules and regulations of the club, conform to high standards of personal conduct, fair play, and good sportsmanship, participate in promotional activities of the club, and not to participate in other sports. Sometimes spelled "uniform player contract." Abbrev. *UPC.*

uniform playing rules Syn. of *official playing rules.*

unintentional intentional base on balls A base on balls in which the pitcher throws the ball just outside the strike zone, enticing the batter to swing at a bad pitch (Zack Hample, *Watching Baseball Smarter*, 2007, p.235). Compare *intentional base on balls.*

Union Association A major league that barely lasted but one season: 1884. It was founded on the premise that the reserve clause was invalid. As a result, the new league announced that it was the equal of the National League and the American Association and it openly and freely contracted with players from the established leagues, which regarded the Union Association as a threat. The existing teams fought back by luring their players to return, and before the first season was over the upstart league was in shambles. Abbrev. *UA.*

union hours Nine innings.

Unionist A member of the Union Association. "As a result of a series of consultations between the Unionists and the chief magnates of the [National] League the latter have concluded to take a step down from their high platform of no condoning of past offenses and to meet half way the offers of the Unionist leaders" (*Brooklyn Eagle*, Jan. 11, 1885; Peter Morris).

United Baseball League An eight-team "big league" founded in Nov. 1994 by former Congressmen John Bryant and Robert Mrazek, sports agent Dick Moss, and economist Andrew Zimbalist that was meant to begin play in 1996, but never got off the ground due to the unavailability of ballparks. Players would have participated in revenue sharing and the club's pretax profits. Teams were proposed for Bayamon (Puerto Rico), Kissimmee (Fla.), Brentwood (N.Y.), Los Angeles, New Orleans, Portland (Ore.), Vancouver (B.C.), and Washington, D.C. Abbrev. *UBL.*

United States Baseball Federation An organization founded in 1962 to foster national and international amateur baseball and to sponsor teams representing the United States in international competition. It is now known as *USA Baseball.* Abbrev. *USBF.*

United States League 1. An independent league that lasted for the month of May 1912 in eight cities (New York, Chicago, Reading [Pa.], Cincinnati, Pittsburgh, Richmond, Washington, and Cleveland). The New York club was scheduled to play baseball on Sundays, an illegal novelty at the time in New York. Unseasonably bad spring weather and a weak economy forced cancellation of the league. The league attempted a resurrection in 1913, but it never got off the ground. **2.** An experimental Negro league in 1945 and 1946, organized by William A. "Gus" Greenlee with the moral support of Branch Rickey of the Brooklyn Dodgers. The league was used as a front for scouting African-American players who would eventually play in the major leagues; only a few games were actually played. The 1945 teams included the Brooklyn Brown Dodgers, Toledo Cubs, Hilldale Giants (Philadelphia), Detroit Giants, Chicago Brown Bombers, and Pittsburgh Crawfords. The 1946 teams included the Cleveland Clippers, Boston Blues, Pittsburgh Crawfords, Brooklyn Brown Dodgers, and Milwaukee Tigers. Negro league superstar and manager Oscar Charleston was supposedly signed to manage the Brown Dodgers. Abbrev. *USL.*

unleash a barrage To get many hits in succession.

unlimber To prepare to pitch or throw. IST USE. 1943. "President and Mrs. Harding attended the opener, the President unlimbering his arm by throwing out the first ball" (*Baseball Magazine*, January; David Shulman).

unlimited arc [softball term] The arc (in slow pitch softball only) in which a pitcher is able to throw the ball as high as 25 feet or more on its way to the plate. The unlimited arc is not allowed by either the Amateur Softball Association of America or the United States Specialty Sports Association under current rules, but it is permitted in some unofficial leagues. Michael Ivankovich (*The Strategy of Pitching Slow Pitch Softball*, 1986) points out that the unlimited arc, which had been allowed at various points in the evolution of the slow pitch game, gave the pitcher too much of an advantage, which was akin to the advantage that pitchers claim in the fast pitch game. According to Ivankovich, "Some pitchers were able to drop strikes from 20–25 feet and more making it extremely difficult on the batter." See also *minimum arc*; *maximum arc*.

unload 1. To hit a home run. "I had no idea or intention of trying to unload one. I just wanted to take my cut" (Mickey Mantle, *Playing Major League Baseball*, 1957). **2.** To defeat decisively. "Angels Unload on Yankees, 12–0" (*Tampa Tribune* headline, Aug. 28, 1988). **3.** To get rid of an underperforming player or one with a high salary.

unpack the bat bag For a team to start hitting effectively. IST USE. 1917 (*The New York Times*, Apr. 2; Edward J. Nichols).

unrestricted free agent A player who is not offered salary arbitration when his contract is up.

unscheduled batting practice Syn. of *barrage*. When a team is on a hitting spree, it is said that they are taking "unscheduled batting practice."

unsportsmanlike conduct A catchall term for fighting, use of obscene language, inciting or trying to incite a demonstration by spectators, and other actions that are likely to get a player, manager, or coach ejected from a game; e.g., a fielder taking a position in the batter's line of vision and acting deliberately to distract the batter could be removed from the game for "unsportsmanlike intent" (*Official Baseball Rules*, Rule 4.06[b]). Each umpire has the authority to disqualify any player, manager, or coach for unsportsmanlike conduct or language (*Official Baseball Rules*, Rule 9.01[d]).

untouchable 1. *adj.* Said of a player who would not be considered for a trade or sale to another baseball team. "I've been around long enough to know not to lock myself into a position by saying someone's totally untouchable" (Baltimore Orioles vice-president Jim Duquette, quoted in *The Baltimore Sun*, Jan. 9, 2006). 2. *n.* A player who is not included in trade discussions. A player who enjoys no-trade status within his contract is considered an untouchable. 3. *adj.* Said of a baseball feat or record that will not be matched or broken; e.g., Joe DiMaggio's 56-game hitting streak is "among the most untouchable in baseball" (*The Sporting News*, Centennial Issue, 1986).

unwritten rule 1. A generally understood and time-honored custom, ritual, or etiquette that shows a respect for the game of baseball and, together with other such principles governing conduct, constitute the *baseball code*; an unofficial rule passed from one baseball generation to another, specifying what is professional and what is not. Examples of unwritten rules pertaining to the conduct of a game include: don't steal a base when your team is way ahead; don't bunt to break up a no-hitter; leave the bench and bullpen to join in when a fight breaks out; don't show up the pitcher with histrionics at the plate after hitting a home run; don't slide into an infielder with spikes high; never swing at a 3-0 pitch when your team has a big lead late in the game; and never peek back at the catcher to see the signs or his position while in the batter's box. Other unwritten rules include never criticizing a teammate in public, keeping the clubhouse a sanctuary, a manager never drinking at the same bar as his players, and rookies shagging balls whether they are millionaires or not. IST USE. 1913. "The umpires of the American Association have an unwritten rule that the base runner is out whenever he slides to first base" (*Christian Science Monitor*, July 29). 2. The *gentleman's agreement* that barred African-American players from the national pastime. "The Negro leagues were designed to provide opportunity where opportunity was denied and to offer vibrant proof that there was no legitimate basis for the major leagues' unwritten rule" (Phil Dixon, *The Negro Baseball Leagues*, 1992). 3. [softball term] The standard of different leagues and tournaments as to what will be allowed and not allowed by the umpires and officials; e.g., the extent and passion with which a call by an umpire can be disputed varies considerably.

up 1. *adv.* Being the player or team that is batting, or at bat; e.g., "The Yankees are up" or "Batter up!" See also *ups.* IST USE. 1862 (*New York Sunday Mercury*, July 13; Edward J. Nichols). EXTENDED USE. Taking or in a position to take one's turn; e.g., "The keynote speaker is up next." 2. *prep.* Brought from a minor-league team to the parent club; e.g., "Smith was called up from the minors." 3. *adj.* Said of a pitch that is high. "My fastball was a little up [in the strike zone]" (Arthur Rhodes, quoted in *The Baltimore Sun*, March 6, 1996). 4. *adv.* Toward home plate, such as an infield that is playing close in anticipation of a bunt or a play at home plate. Syn. *in*, 1. 5. *adv.* Said of the number of games a team is ahead in the standings. Compare *down*, 7.

up and away Syn. of *high and outside.*

up-and-down 1. Describing a player who finds himself being sent back and forth between the major leagues and the minor leagues. 2. Said of a team that enjoys a winning streak of a few games followed by a losing streak of a few games followed by another winning streak and so forth.

up-and-down the ladder Said of pitching a sequence of pitches that are high, then low, then high, or vice versa. "Sid Fernandez is the classic up-and-down-the-ladder pitcher. Tom Seaver, Nolan Ryan, a lot of great pitchers get you to chase the high fastball, then the low breaking ball, then the high fastball, or vice versa—low, high, low. The batter can make an out against these guys and never swing at a pitch in the strike zone. Frustrating" (Keith Hernandez, *Pure Baseball*, 1994, p.15). Compare *up the ladder*, 1.

up and in Syn. of *high and inside*. "Pitchers who come up and in have their own pantheon: Don Drysdale, Bob Gibson, Ewell 'The Whip' Blackwell and Early Wynn" (Steve Hirdt, *ESPN The Magazine*, June 10, 2002).

UPC Abbrev. for *uniform player's contract*.

up-curve *hist.* A curveball that appears to rise; an *upshoot*, 1. Also spelled "up curve"; "upcurve." IST USE. 1883. "Many people . . . believe in an 'up' curve and a 'down' curve" (*Philadelphia Press*, Aug. 20; Peter Morris).

update set A special series of supplemental baseball cards issued at the end of the season to represent rookies and players who were traded after the regular set of cards was printed.

uphill Pertaining to a style of pitching in which the body moves forward faster than the arm, which is dragging, the elbow under and leading the hand/wrist, resulting in the ball staying high in the strike zone. "[Tom Gorzelanny] occasionally rushes in his delivery and throws uphill" (Michael Levesque, *Baseball America*, Oct. 13–26, 2003; Peter Morris). Compare *downhill*.

uphill game *hist.* A game in early baseball in which a team had to battle from behind. "The Resolutes played their usual creditable up hill game, in this respect deserving success if they did not obtain it" (*Brooklyn Eagle*, Sept. 21, 1864; Peter Morris).

up his alley Said of a pitch that comes at the speed and in the position that a batter finds easiest to hit (*The New York Times*, June 2, 1929). The term is borrowed from bowling.

up in his neck Said of a player who does not come through in the pinch (*The Sporting News Record Book*, 1937).

up in the air Unnerved or excited; esp. said of a pitcher who suddenly becomes ineffective, nervous, or rattled. Hugh S. Fullerton (*American Magazine*, June 1912): "A term used to describe the condition of a pitcher who loses his courage or presence of mind at critical stages of a contest." See also *balloon ascension*. IST USE. 1898 (*New York Tribune*, May 31; Edward J. Nichols). ETYMOLOGY. Going up in a hot-air balloon in the early 20th century would be the ultimate example of going out of control. "A correspondent asks what is meant by 'going up in the air,' as applied to a base ball pitcher. . . . In the majority of cases it means a loss of control. The pitcher cannot locate the plate" (*Cincinnati Commercial Tribune*, reprinted in *The Sporting Life*, May 17, 1902; Peter Morris).

up-over Syn. of *Texas Leaguer*, 2. "Bush doubled, his hit being a little up-over fly that fell close to the foul line" (*St. Louis Post-Dispatch*, June 26, 1910; Peter Morris).

uppercut 1. *n.* An upward batting stroke that commonly yields fly balls. It is generally regarded as a flaw. ETYMOLOGY. A boxing term for a punch that comes up from the waist toward the head of an opponent. 2. *v.* To swing at the ball with an upward motion of the bat. See also *cut up*.

uppercutter A batter who meets the ball at an upward angle. A "good" uppercutter lofts the ball toward the outfield; a "bad" uppercutter "collapses his back elbow in toward the chest and fails to extend his arms" (Kevin Kerrane, *Dollar Sign on the Muscle*, 1984, p.90).

upper deck The top tier of seats in a ballpark with more than one deck.

upper-downer A fictional pitch thrown by Burt L. Standish's Dick Merriwell that broke down and then up on its way to the plate. Compare *inner-outer*.

upper half 1. The *first half* of an inning. 2. The physical tools of a baseball player. Compare *lower half*, 2.

uprising A rally in which several runs are

Upper deck. Griffith Stadium, Washington, D.C. *Photograph by Joseph Baylor Roberts*

scored. "[Tony Gwynn's] single had triggered the San Diego Padres' biggest first-inning uprising since April, a five-run outpouring that set up an 8–4 victory" (*The Sporting News*, Sept. 24, 1984).

ups The opportunity for a player or team to come to the plate to bat; e.g., *first ups* and *last ups*. See also *up*, 1.

upset An unexpected result, particularly a surprise victory by a team considered an underdog. After the Miracle Braves swept the Philadelphia Athletics in the 1914 World Series, Franklin P. Adams (*New York Tribune*, Oct. 15, 1914; Stuart Y. Silverstein) wrote, "In brief, The Year of the Great Upset."

upshoot **1.** *hist.* A 19th-century term for a curveball that appears to rise as it reaches home plate. See also *up-curve*; *shoot*, 1; *raise ball*. Compare *down shoot*. IST USE. 1883. "[Dick Burns] is developing an upshoot that is a beauty" (*Detroit Free Press*, Apr. 5; Peter Morris). **2.** A term used by pitcher Byung-Hyun Kim for a pitch, delivered with a submarine motion, that appears to rise. "[Kim] calls [his pitch] an upshoot, which he flings from inches above the dirt and sends rising through the strike zone" (Stephen Cannella, *Sports Illustrated*, June 5, 2000). **3.** [softball term] Syn. of *rise ball*.

upstairs **1.** *adv.* To or on the upper grandstands; to or on any tier of seats above those at ground level. The term is most commonly used to describe the destination of foul pop flies; e.g., "Smith fouled one upstairs." **2.** *n.* The location of a ball that is pitched high. Compare *downstairs*. **3.** *n.* The brain. LaTroy Hawkins (quoted in *The Baltimore Sun*, June 30, 2006): "Being a pitching coach is a lot more than analyzing motions. You've got to know what a guy has upstairs, too."

up the chimney Syn. of *up the chute*. "[Mickey] Mantle hit one up the chimney and the catcher caught it. 'Attention,' some one in the press box called out, 'Mantle has just set a new record for distance—600 feet—300 up, 300 down'" (Charles Einstein, *San Francisco Examiner*, July 24, 1959).

up the chute Said of any ball that is hit straight up. Syn. *up the chimney*; *up the shaft*; *up the silo*.

up the ladder **1.** Said of pitching a series of pitches progressively higher in the strike zone. "Jim Palmer once worked 'up the ladder'— pitching incrementally higher in the strike zone, an extinct art because of the devolution of the zone" (Tom Verducci, *Sports Illustrated*, March 31, 1997). See also *climb the ladder*, 1; *stair-step*, 1. Compare *up-and-down the ladder*. **2.** Said of a fielder going high to get a line drive or bouncing ball. See also *climb the ladder*, 3.

up the line Said of an outfield throw that lands short of its target, such as one that bounces once or twice before reaching the catcher or bounces along the first or third base line. "Joe Rudi's throw was slightly up the line" (*St. Petersburg Times*, May 25, 1990).

up the middle **1.** Around and over second base. A ball that is hit straight up the center of the infield toward center field is said to be "up the middle." **2.** Said of the players at catcher, second base, shortstop, and center field, collectively. A team is said to be strong or weak "up the middle." Chuck Lindstrom (quoted in Richard Tellis, *Once Around the Bases*, 1998, p.219; Peter Morris): "There used to be a saying that a ball club had to be strong defensively up the middle, meaning the catcher, shortstop, second baseman, and center fielder were supposed to be good defensively, while your hitting came from the sides—first, third, left field, and right." See also *down the middle*, 1.

up the shaft Syn. of *up the chute*.

up the silo Syn. of *up the chute*.

URA Abbrev. for *unearned-run average*.

USA Baseball An organization founded in 1978 by an act of Congress and based in Durham, N.C., to serve as the national governing body for amateur baseball. It represents the United States as a member of the U.S. Olympic Committee and the International Baseball Federation. It selects ands trains for international competition the Olympic Team, the National Team (college freshmen and sophomores), the Junior National Team (ages 18 and under), the Youth National Team (ages 16 and under), and the Women's National Team (ages 16 and over); and it presents the annual Golden Spikes Award to the top amateur baseball player in the country. National members of USA Baseball include the Amateur Athletic Union, the American Amateur Baseball Congress, the American Baseball Coaches Association, American Legion Baseball, the Babe Ruth League, Dixie Youth Baseball, Little League, the National Amateur Baseball Federation, the National Baseball Congress, the National Collegiate Athletic Association, PONY Baseball, and the United States Specialty Sports Association. USA Baseball was formerly known as the *United States Baseball Federation.*

usability The capability of using a prospect's talent in a specific game situation. "I've seen plenty of young pitchers with great fastballs but no usability, because they can't control it" (Dan Jennings, quoted in Alan Schwarz, BaseballAmerica.com, Nov. 14, 2006).

USBF Abbrev. for *United States Baseball Federation.*

use both sides of the plate To throw a series of pitches inside and outside.

use the whole field To be able to hit the ball to any part of the field or to place it in any direction. "He [Rod Carew] hit everything, just out of the reach of everybody. He used the whole field" (Sam Perlozzo, quoted in *The Baltimore Sun*, May 23, 1996). "Most great doubles hitters, including [Edgar] Martinez, have one thing in common: They use the whole field" (*Sports Illustrated*, July 29, 1996, p.100). Syn. "use the entire yard."

USL Abbrev. for *United States League*, 2.

utility man Syn. of *utility player*. "He used to be Dave Concepcion, All-Star shortstop. Now he's Dave Concepcion, utility man" (*St. Petersburg Times*, March 24, 1987). Cleveland Indians infielder Lou Camilli once joked, "They ought to change our name to

Utility man. Charles "Red" Dooin, primarily a catcher for the Philadelphia Phillies, was listed as a "utility man" in this photo taken by Paul Thompson to create his baseball card. *Library of Congress*

the Cleveland Light Company. We don't have anything but utility men." IST USE. 1870. "Flynn is one of those thoroughly useful and sensible ball players who can afford to be the tenth, or general utility man, for the sake of the credit to be derived by doing everything well" (*Chicago Tribune*, June 1; Peter Morris). ETYMOLOGY. An actor who played small parts was commonly referred to in the 19th century as a "utility actor" or "utility man."

utility player A substitute who can play any one of several positions as needed. Utility players tend to be grouped into three categories: the rookie trying to break into the everyday lineup, the mid-level player backing up a superstar, or the veteran extending his career. See also *role player*. Syn. *utility man*. IST USE. 1868 (Chadwick Scrapbooks; Edward J. Nichols).

V

VA Abbrev. for *value added approach.*

vacuum cleaner An excellent fielder; a *Hoover*, 1. "Doney [*sic*] Bush covered the territory around short, third base, second base, and left field as neatly as a vacuum cleaner" (*The New York Times*, May 15, 1914).

Valhalla **1.** The place where baseball greats go after death. The term is part of the pumped-up prose of early 20th-century sportswriting. "Years of pain, torture and misery finally came to an end for one-legged Joe Tinker, who on his sixty-eighth birthday [July 27, 1948] decided it was time to join his teammates in Valhalla" (Bill Stern, *Bill Stern's Favorite Baseball Stories*, 1949). The image was boosted when Lou Gehrig was buried at Kensico Cemetery in Valhalla, N.Y., in 1941. **2.** See *Baseball's Valhalla*, a syn. of *Cooperstown*, 1. ETYMOLOGY. From the banqueting hall of the gods and the dwelling place of slain warriors in Norse mythology.

value added approach A method for evaluating the offensive performance of a batter in a season, using the run potential for the various *base–out situations* and the number of times that a batter began and ended a plate appearance in each of these situations, to estimate the number of runs for which a batter is personally responsible. The method was developed by Gary R. Skoog and described by Bill James (*Baseball Abstract*, 1987). Abbrev. *VA.*

value approximation method The method for evaluating a player's *approximate value.* The term was first used by Bill James in his self-published *Baseball Abstract* (1980). Abbrev. *VAM.*

value over replacement player The number of additional runs a batter is responsible for, or a pitcher is responsible for saving, compared to a player at replacement level. The measure was proposed by Keith Woolner and featured in *Baseball Prospectus* since 2003. See also *marginal value over replacement player.* Abbrev. *VORP.*

value over replacement player rate A player's value over replacement player expressed as runs per game. Abbrev. *VORPr.*

VAM Abbrev. for *value approximation method.*

Van Heusen *hist.* Syn. of *collar*, 1. The term is often prefaced by the adjective "big." ETYMOLOGY. From the name of the collar- and shirtmaker.

vanilla Said of a team without vitality. "Baseball experts look at the [Baltimore] Orioles and see what is referred to as a 'vanilla club.' Where's the fire?" (Tony Attanasio, quoted in *The Baltimore Sun*, Dec. 18, 1996).

vapor float *hist.* A spitball. "Case [Patten] is a peach with the vapor float, sometimes spoken of as the spitball" (*The Washington Post*, May 3, 1905; Peter Morris).

vapor lock Failure to perform on the field due to lack of concentration; a mental error. When infielder Manny Alexander failed to cover second base on an attempted steal and the catcher's throw bounced into center field, Baltimore Orioles manager Davey Johnson said (quoted in *The Baltimore Sun*, July 17, 1996), "He was given coverages and didn't cover. That's what we call in baseball 'vapor lock.'" See also *brain cramp.* ETYMOLOGY. From the obstruction of the flow of fuel to a gasoline engine due to bubbles in the fuel as a result of overheating.

variable chance deviation theory A mock scientific notion, invented and named by pitcher Jim Palmer, that a little wildness on the mound can be an asset; or, by aiming for the middle of the plate, a pitcher might hit the corners (*USA Today*, Apr. 18, 1983).

variation One of two or more baseball cards from the same series with the same number (or the same player with an identical pose if the series is unnumbered) that differ from one another by some usually subtle aspect, such as a color change in the background of the card. The different feature results from the printing or stock of the card, not from an alteration. Variations are rare (and therefore have considerable value) because most corrections are made early in the press run.

varsity 1. *n.* The first or senior team competing for a school, college, or university. ETYMOLOGY. According to Richard D. Mallery (*Our American Language*, 1947), the term comes from the shortening and 19th-century pronunciation of "university." 2. *adj.* Pertaining to first-level athletes.

Vaseline ball A variation on the illegal spitball that is fueled by the famous petroleum product. The application of the Vaseline is facilitated by the fact that it can be used as a hair dressing and easily get on a pitcher's fingers when he is fussing with or tugging at his hat. The pitcher grips the ball on the smooth finish, not the seams. The pitch acts like a spitball, coming up to the plate without any noticeable spin but dropping sharply. "In a conversation that sounded more like a commercial for hair dressing, a member of the [Minnesota] Twins' pitching staff said that the trickier twirlers around the American League have come up with ... [an] illegal delivery ... called the Vaseline ball ... [which] rapidly is replacing its predecessor, the spitball" (Arno Goethal, *The Sporting News*, May 16, 1964). IST USE. 1910. "Immediate variations of the [spit] ball were developed. Slippery elm, talcum powder, crude oil, Vaseline were used to lessen the friction of the fingers" (John J. Evers and Hugh S. Fullerton, *Touching Second: The Science of Baseball*; Peter Morris).

vaya Said of the destination of a home run. The term is Spanish for "gone."

velocity The speed of a pitch; that which determines a good fastball. It is a quality of a pitcher who can throw hard. "It takes three components to win, and I had 'em all going tonight—velocity, location, and movement" (Roger Clemens, quoted in *Springfield* [Mass.] *Union-News*, Sept. 1, 1989). USAGE NOTE. The term "velocity" has become a modern term for what used to be called *speed*, 4.

verbal sign A sign expressed in coded expressions and words; e.g., when the first base coach mentions the baserunner's first name, it is the sign to attempt to steal on the next pitch. See also *word sign*.

verse *hist.* Syn. of *inning*, 1.

vertical trust *hist.* Syn. of *farm system*. After the St. Louis Cardinals won the 1926 World Series, John B. Sheridan (*The Sporting News*, Dec. 23, 1926; Peter Morris) wrote, "The Cardinal system of replacement, that is ownership of a 'vertical trust,' a number of minor league clubs of varying classifications, D, C, B, A, and AA, through which the Cardinal replacements are moved for educational purposes."

vest-pocket catch A catch of a high fly ball with the glove close to the body at, or just above, the waist. The term was applied to Rabbit Maranville's *basket catch*: "I was the talk of the town because of my peculiar way of catching a fly ball. They later named it the Vest-Pocket Catch" (Maranville, quoted by Dick Leyden, in Society for American Baseball Research, *Deadball Stars of the National League*, 2004, p.320).

vet Short for *veteran*. IST USE. 1877. "All the 'vets' of the [Excelsior] team of 1858 happen to be in Brooklyn this summer, and it is proposed to ... have them play against the veteran nine of the Knickerbocker" (*Brooklyn Eagle*, July 27; Peter Morris).

veteran An experienced professional baseball player. Syn. *vet*. IST USE. 1858. "It is well known that the veterans of the Knickerbocker have long been the champions of the 'base' as a club" (*New York Clipper*, July 17; Peter Morris).

veteran player A player who has been in the major leagues for five full seasons. In the 1960s, a veteran player was one who had more than seven or ten years of major-league service.

Veterans Committee A group of baseball men empowered to elect into the *National Baseball Hall of Fame* players and other potential members who have eluded or failed to appear on the normal ballot of the Baseball Writers' Association of America (BBWAA), or who have been overlooked or passed over by the BBWAA election. Beginning with the vote for 2008 members, and continuing every other year, a 16-member electorate of the Committee will review a list of 10 managers and umpires, as developed by a BBWAA-appointed historical overview committee, and a 12-member electorate of the Committee will review a list of 10 retired executives and active executives age 65 or older. Beginning with the 2009 induction year, the Committee, consisting of all Hall of Fame members, will vote (every other year) on platers whose careers began after 1943, and a 12-member electorate of the Committee will vote (every five years) on players whose careers began before 1943. Electors may vote for zero to four candidates on each ballot; candidates receiving votes on at least 75 percent of the ballots earn induction into the Hall of Fame. The Committee and its election procedures were restructured in 2007 after changes in 2003 yielded no inductions. Previously, the Veterans Committee (in existence since 1953) was composed of five Hall of Fame players, five baseball executives, and five members of the media or baseball historians, and it could elect one player who had been retired at least 23 years and removed from the BBWAA ballot for five years, one 19th-century player, one Negro leagues player, and one executive, manager, or umpire. It was characterized by *Sports Illustrated* (March 19, 2001) as "either: (a) a savvy body of insiders who right the wrongs of the baseball writers who elect recent retirees to the Hall; or (b) an old-boy network that lets its unelected cronies in through the back door."

VI Abbrev. for *village idiot*.

vicinity play Syn. of *neighborhood play*.

victim *hist*. A batter who was put out in early baseball. "Pearce was the first 'victim,' being caught on the fly by Powell" (*Brooklyn Eagle*, Oct. 17, 1861; Peter Morris).

victory-important RBI The number of a player's runs batted in that contribute to eventual victory. Runs batted in are only counted when they occur during team victories. The victory-importance of a run batted in for a given game is computed by adding one to the opposition team's number of runs scored and dividing by the player's team's number of runs scored in that game. The term first appeared in Bill James' self-published *Baseball Abstract* (1979) and was explained in his *Baseball Abstract* (1984). See also *RBI importance*. Abbrev. *VI-RBI*.

village idiot A player who says or does foolish things, or makes a fool of himself. "You try to protect guys, shade the truth a bit, but there's a term players use . . . when a player starts believing fantasy. He's a 'village idiot'" (Tony La Russa, quoted in *San Francisco Chronicle*, May 31, 1995). "When I come in the clubhouse, everyone is fair game for ragging. I'm like the village idiot, but I have fun" (Steve Kline, quoted in *The Baltimore Sun*, Jan. 29, 2006). Abbrev. *VI*.

vines Street clothes (Jim Bouton, *Ball Four*, 1970).

vintage base ball Presenting the game of baseball as it was played during its formative years in the mid-19th century in strict accordance with the rules, equipment, uniforms, field specifications, customs, practices, language, and behavioral norms of the period. Games are played today under the leadership of the Vintage Base Ball Association, a national organization of individual clubs organized in 1995 to "preserve, perpetuate, and promote" vintage base ball, which includes educating the public by demonstrating the game with attention to the historical context in which it originated and developed. Syn. *historic base ball*; *period base ball*. IST USE. 1994. The term was used by Frederick Ivor-Campbell in the annual report of the Nineteenth Century Committee of the Society for American Baseball Research (SABR), dated May 30. The report was reprinted in *Nineteenth Century Notes* [the newsletter of the Committee], Winter/Spring 1994, p.11. ETYMOLOGY. Ivor-Campbell (personal communication, March 12, 2003): "I submit this claim that the term 'vintage base ball' was established . . . in the early months of 1994, when John Husman and I settled on the term as the title for the Vintage Base Ball Committee, a subcommittee of SABR's Nineteenth Century Committee which was formed in the spring of 1994 with John at its head. . . . After pondering the matter [as to what to call the subcommittee and the versions of early baseball being played] I suggested 'vintage,' and John agreed, and he determined that 'base ball' should be two words, to reflect the most common early usage."

vintage card An "old" baseball card. The term is loosely defined; e.g., a baseball card issued prior to 1979, or "most commonly," a card issued between 1930 and 1973. Brett Hardeman (*Old Cardboard* magazine; personal communication, Feb. 10, 2006) focuses on card sets that "are 50 years old or older (mostly pre–World War II) . . . [but] that is of course a moving target as time moves on. We certainly don't attempt to solidify an industry/hobby acceptable definition."

vintage pitcher A pitcher with many years of pitching experience.

violinist A batter with an especially smooth swing.

VI-RBI Abbrev. for *victory-important RBI*.

visiting team The traveling club, or the team on the road, that always comes up to bat in the top of an inning. Compare *home team*, 1. Syn. "visitors"; *away team*; *road team*, 1.

voice A baseball announcer, or the person at the microphone; e.g., Mel Allen was "the voice" of the New York Yankees for many years.

voluntarily retired list A list of players who desire to retire from professional baseball and make a written application to the commissioner stating fully the reasons for retiring. The player's team retains control of the player's rights without wasting a space on the 40-man reserve list. A player cannot be reinstated within 60 days of the season from the date that the player filed the application. A player desiring to unretire and play for another major- or minor-league team must first obtain the written consent of the player's team.

voodoo ball A nickname for a baseball assembled and stitched in Haiti.

VORP Abbrev. for *value over replacement player.*

VORPr Abbrev. for *value over replacement player rate.*

vote of confidence A euphemism expressing support for a manager whose job may be in jeopardy. "[Los Angeles Dodgers] president Walter O'Malley stepped forth with a gratuitous 'vote of confidence' for his manager [Walter Alston]. Since nothing in sports is more suspect than a vote of confidence, speculations about Alston spurted anew" (Jim Bouton, *"I Managed Good, But Boy Did They Play Bad,"* 1973, p.147). The term is often modified by the adjective "dreaded"; e.g., "[Arizona Diamondbacks manager Bob Brenly] recently got the dreaded vote of confidence from managing general partner Jerry Colangelo" (*Sports Illustrated*, May 10, 2004).

vultch A win by a vulture (relief pitcher). ETYMOLOGY. According to Tim Considine (*The Language of Sport*, 1982): "From the word 'vulture' . . . [for a relief pitcher who was] figuratively picking over the bones of starting pitchers."

vulture **1.** *n.* A relief pitcher, typically a middle relief pitcher, who receives credit for a win to which another pitcher was more entitled; e.g., a relief pitcher whose ineffective pitching prevents an earlier pitcher from receiving the win, as when the relief pitcher blows a lead, only to wind up winning when his teammates retake the lead. Los Angeles Dodgers reliever Phil Regan was nicknamed "The Vulture" by teammate Claude Osteen in 1966 when Regan picked up 14 wins in relief. **2.** *v.* For a relief pitcher to receive credit for a win because he performed as a vulture. "If [Rollie Fingers] could hold on here in the ninth inning, he'd undoubtedly get some clubhouse ribbing about 'vulturing a win,' about giving up just enough runs to make certain he and not [Jim] Slaton would be credited with a victory if the Brewers emerged triumphant" (Daniel Okrent, *Nine Innings*, 1985, p.252; Peter Morris).

vulture-bait A pitcher with a dead arm.

W

W 1. Abbrev. for *win*, 2. "[Mike] Schmidt Counting Ws Not HRs" (*USA Today* headline, Apr. 17, 1987). **2.** Abbrev. for *win*, 3. **3.** Box score abbrev. for *winning pitcher*. **4.** Abbrev. for *walk*, 1.

wa Japanese for team harmony or team unity. It is the mystical concept at the heart of Japanese baseball. "In Japan . . . the word to note is *wa*, which means total dedication to the team at the sacrifice of individual glory and money" (*The Times*, June 8–14, 1985). See Robert Whiting, *You Gotta Have Wa*, 1989.

WAA Abbrev. for *wins above average.*

wabble *hist.* For a pitcher to lose control or confidence. "Not once, but several times, [Portland pitcher] Krapp wabbled badly, walking men in nearly every inning, or at least showing a disposition to do as much" (*San Francisco Bulletin*, Apr. 5, 1913; Gerald L. Cohen).

waft 1. To hit a ball hard, usually for a home run. "Hank Aaron has wafted nineteen [home runs]" (Roger Angell, *The Summer Game*, 1972; Charles D. Poe). **2.** *hist.* To strike out. "[Dave Orr and Chief Roseman] have been wafting the ethereal with their willows" (*The Sporting News*, May 17, 1886; Peter Morris). IST USE. 1885. "['Wafted' and 'churned the ethereal'] is the latest slang for struck out" (*St. Louis Post-Dispatch*, May 7; Peter Morris).

Wagner card A *tobacco card* depicting the likeness of Honus Wagner; the most valuable baseball card of all. The T–206 #486 Wagner card was issued by Sweet Caporal cigarettes (American Tobacco Co.) in 1909. The extreme rarity of this card stems from the fact that Wagner was opposed to smoking and did not want to encourage kids to smoke; when he found that he was depicted on a tobacco premium, he supposedly demanded that his image be removed from packs of cigarettes. Only about 60 cards are known to exist. A near-mint T–206 Wagner card sold for $2.8 million in 2007. See Michael O'Keeffe and Teri Thompson, *The Card*, 2007.

wagon spoke A baseball bat.

wagon tongue A large baseball bat. "[Buck Ewing] swung his wagon-tongue around leisurely, but the bat and the ball met at the point where the connection would do the most good, and the sphere went whizzing in the direction of Yonkers" (*The World* [New York], Aug. 3, 1889; Gerald L. Cohen). IST USE. 1888. "Spalding's Wagon-Tongue Bats" (ad in *The Sporting Life*). ETYMOLOGY. The pole extending from a carriage between the animals drawing it. Some bats used in early baseball were made from wagon tongues.

waist ball A pitched ball that comes in at the batter's waist. Syn. *waister*. IST USE. 1908 (*Baseball Magazine*, June, p.40; Edward J. Nichols).

waister Syn. of *waist ball*. IST USE. 1914. "After the high balls came 'waisters' and then low ones" (Christy Mathewson, *Pitcher Pollock*; David Shulman).

waiter 1. A batter who attempts to get on base by waiting for a base on balls. "Roger [Connor] was a patient waiter and got his base on balls" (Tim Murnane, *The Boston Globe*, Aug. 4, 1888). **2.** A batter who swings only at strikes. IST USE. 1887. "[Emmett] Seery is a good enough waiter to preside at a restaurant" (*Detroit Free Press*, Apr. 30; Peter Morris). **3.** A batter who swings late.

waiting game Batters refusing to swing at pitches deliberately thrown outside the strike zone during the very early days of baseball when there were no called balls or called strikes. IST USE. 1863. "The Nassaus did not adopt the 'waiting game' style of play in this match as they did in the Excelsior game" (*New York Clipper*, Oct. 31; Peter Morris).

wait on For a batter not to begin his swing too early on an off-speed pitch. "[Rafael] Palmeiro was able to wait on a breaking pitch that hung inside" (*The Baltimore Sun*, March 16, 1998).

wait out To make the pitcher keep throwing by staying in the batter's box until the pitcher throws the kind of pitch the batter wants. To accomplish this feat requires fouling off several pitches. "They wait you out in the Series. You've got to put it over the plate or else" (*San Francisco Call-Bulletin*, Oct. 12, 1949; Peter Tamony). IST USE. 1908 (*American Magazine*, August, p.401; Edward J. Nichols).

"wait till next year" The plaintive mantra of fans whose team has once again fallen short of expectations; a baseball euphemism for a season gone awry. "Here's where the 'Wait Till Next Year!' chorus has a chance" (Ren Mulford Jr., *The Sporting Life*, Sept. 6, 1913; Peter Morris). The refrain was long associated with the Brooklyn Dodgers and their fans. A Willard Mullin cartoon (*New York World-Telegram*, Aug. 9, 1939; Barry Popik) depicted a character in a Dodgers uniform claiming that his "theme song" was "Wait 'Till Next Year: A Torch Ballad in One Flat" with "words and music by The Dodgers." The phrase achieved its greatest play in those years (1941, 1947, 1949, 1952, 1953, and 1956) when the Dodgers lost to the New York Yankees in the World Series ("next year" finally came to Brooklyn in 1955). The term is now applied to other teams; e.g., "There is no light in the Old North Church tonight. Boston is dark and despairing, waiting, as always, until next year" (Tony Kornheiser, *The Washington Post*, Oct. 28, 1986). The term and its variations are the titles of books written by Carl Rowan (with Jackie Robinson, 1960), Christopher Jennison (1974), and Doris Kearns Goodwin (1997). Var. "wait 'til next year"; "wait until next year"; "wait till next season." IST USE. 1884. "Visitors at Mason's headquarters are met with the legend:—'Wait till next year'" (*The Sporting Life*, Nov. 5, p.5; Barry Popik). USAGE NOTE. The phrase "wait till next season" appeared early in baseball: "Now can be heard the old familiar sound: 'Wait till next season and then we'll show them'" (*The Sporting Life*, July 23, 1884; Peter Morris). In 1941, the term first achieved prominent display as a headline in the *Brooklyn Eagle*, after the Dodgers were beaten by the Yankees in the World Series. EXTENDED USE. The line has been used as a battle cry in a host of areas and situations. "New Year's resolutions. No more chocolate! . . . No more procrastination! . . . Wait Till Next Year!" (Doug Marlette, parrot in *Kudzu* cartoon, Dec. 31, 2001).

waive 1. To refrain from claiming a player whose contract is offered for sale by a major-league team. **2.** To release a player, or make a preliminary move than can lead to release, reassignment to the minors, or a trade.

waiver A permission granted for certain assignments of player contracts or for the unconditional release of a major-league player.

waiver blocking A tactic used by a club in claiming a player placed on waivers, not because it wanted the player, but to prevent a rival club from obtaining the player. The practice fell into disfavor when several teams got stuck with expensive players whom they did not want. "Waiver blocking became something of a sport unto itself for a while there in recent years" (Mike Berardino, *Baseball America*, Sept. 1–14, 2003).

waivers The system whereby a major-league team abandons its right to purchase the contract of another team's player for a stipulated price. It allows all the teams to have a chance to bid on a player about to be released or to be included in a trade. Before a player can be released, waivers must be granted by all teams in reverse order of their standings. If the rights to that player are claimed (not waived) by one of those teams, his contract must be sold at a standard waiver price. The team offering the player can decide to retain him at this point. The waiver rules were originally outlined in the 1885 National Agreement, supposedly to help weak teams obtain players. The rules are complex (see Major League Rules, Rules 8 and 10). Murray Chass (*The New York Times*, Aug. 29, 1993) wrote, "Baseball's waiver rules are only slightly better understood than the plans for the design and operation of the $1 billion dollar Mars Observer spacecraft." Tom Verducci (*Sports Illustrated*, Aug. 25, 1997, p.37) described the "arcane verbiage" of Rule 10 that explains the waivers system "in a way that makes the Magna Carta look like part of the Jackie Collins oeuvre. Not even those in the know profess to fully understand it." See also *major-league waivers*; *irrevocable waivers*; *unconditional release waivers*. IST USE. 1905. "I have not even secured waivers from the other American League teams and I am not sure they will all waive claim to him [Chicago White Sox pitcher Lou Fiene]" (White Sox president Charles Comiskey, quoted in *Chicago Tribune*, May 20; Peter Morris).

waiver-wire player A player placed on waivers.

wake up To go into action; specif., to get a team's hitters to get base hits. "[Pat] Hentgen pitched his butt off. Hentgen didn't give the bats a chance to wake up" (Bobby Bonilla, quoted in *The Baltimore Sun*, Sept. 21, 1996).

wakeup call Syn. of *calling card*.

walk 1. *n.* A *base on balls*; the taking of first base by a batter to whom four balls have been pitched. "There's no defense against a walk" is Joe Garagiola's oft-quoted remark on the subject (*The Washington Post*, Oct. 17, 1982). Abbrev. *W*, 4. IST USE. 1866 (*New York Herald*, Aug. 28; Edward J. Nichols). 2. *v.* To advance to first base after the fourth ball; to receive a base on balls from the pitcher; e.g., "Smith walks on four wide ones from Jones." 3. *v.* To advance a batter to first base by pitching four balls; to give a base on balls to a batter; e.g., "Jones walks Smith by throwing four wide ones." 4. *v.* To force in a run by issuing a base on balls with the bases loaded; e.g., "Jones walked in the winning run."

walk all over To defeat a team decisively; e.g., "The Tigers walked all over the Indians."

walkaway Syn. of *walkover*. "We made the all-deciding game a walkaway" (Ty Cobb, *My Life in Baseball*, 1961, p.89).

walker A batter who receives many bases on balls. Syn. *walking man*. IST USE. 1911 (*Spalding's Official Base Ball Guide*, p.31; Edward J. Nichols).

walkfest A game or part of a game in which there is an unusual number of bases on balls.

walking lead A lead in which the baserunner begins walking with short steps; if the pitcher does not force him to stop, his momentum will enable him to get a fast start. It is esp. effective for a runner on second base. "[Dave] Roberts took a walking lead off [Jesse] Orosco and stole third" (*The Baltimore Sun*, Sept. 7, 1999). Syn. *moving lead.*

walking man Syn. of *walker.* Eddie Yost, who led the American League in bases on balls six times, was nicknamed "The Walking Man."

walking step The movement of a pitcher's pivot (push-off) foot placed in front of the rubber, not in contact with it, when he delivers the pitch. Nolan Ryan and Harry Brecheen were known to "cheat" in this manner.

"walk is as good as a hit, a" A colloquialism urging a batter to get on base by not swinging at bad pitches. In reality, a walk is as good as a hit when the batter comes to plate with the bases empty, but a walk may not be as good as a hit when a base hit advances a runner two bases.

walk-off 1. *adj.* Said of a game-ending event, such as a "walk-off single" that drives in the winning run in the bottom of the ninth or a "walk-off pitch" that results in a game-winning home run. The term was coined by Oakland Athletics pitcher Dennis Eckersley for that lonely stroll from the mound after a pitcher gives up the winning run (Gannett News Service, July 30, 1988; Fred Shapiro): "In Eckersley's colorful vocabulary, a walk-off piece is a home run that wins the game and the pitcher walks off the mound." Eckersley (quoted in *The Boston Globe*, June 24, 2005): "It was always a walkoff *piece*. Like something you would hang in an art gallery. The walkoff piece is a horrible piece of art." After New York Yankees pitcher Steve Howe threw a pitch to lose 3–2, he said (quoted in *The Baltimore Sun*, May 15, 1995): "It was a walk-off pitch. You throw the ball and walk off the mound. It was a sinker that didn't sink." *The Boston Globe* (Aug. 8, 2002) noted, after one such situation, "For the Red Sox legions, this one hurt. Maybe even more than the back-to-back, gut-twisting, walk-off disasters last month in the Bronx." Also spelled "walkoff." USAGE NOTE. Jeff Pearlman (*Sports Illustrated*, July 17, 2000, p.69) noted that the term was being overused by "TV's dime-a-dozen talking heads repeating it endlessly and effusively": "Like crabgrass invading someone's lawn, 'walk-off!' has taken root in sports lingo and gotten out of control." The term has been used to describe "walk-off walks," "walk-off errors," and even "walk-off balks." Although not usually recognized, the term could be assigned to any event in which the home team wins the game in extra innings. EXTENDED USE. Said of an event that brings finality to a situation. "[Robert Horry's] walk-off three-point shot gave L.A. [Los Angeles Lakers] a breathtaking 100–99 victory" (Jack McCallum, *Sports Illustrated*, June 3, 2002). **2.** *n.* The long walk off the mound taken by the pitcher who gives up a game-winning run, esp. a home run. When Dennis Eckersley recalled his pitch to Kirk Gibson (who hit a home run that cost the Oakland Athletics the first game of the 1988 World Series), he noted (quoted in *The New York Times Magazine*, May 8, 2005), "The walk-off is a disaster for the pitcher. That walk off the mound was brutal. I was devastated." Also spelled "walkoff." **3.** *n.* A game-winning home run. When Moises Alou homered in the bottom of the 10th to send the Chicago Cubs to a 4–3 win over his father's (Felipe Alou) San Francisco Giants, he was quoted (*The Baltimore Sun*, May 20, 2004) as saying, "You always want to play good in front of your dad. . . . It's the first time I hit a walk-off to beat him."

walk off *v.* To end a game with a home run. After Jose Guillen hit a two-run homer in the bottom of the 10th inning that sent the Cincinnati Reds to their 10th victory in their last at-bat, *The Baltimore Sun* headline (May 10, 2003) proclaimed, "Reds Walk Off with 5th Win in a Row."

walk off the island See *"you can't walk off the island."*

walkover An easy victory; a game, series, or division race that is easily won by a superior

team. Syn. *walkaway.* IST USE. 1871. "Tomorrow we are to meet the unorganized amateurs of the Star Club, whose only strength at present lies in their pitcher, and I guess we'll have a walk over" (*Brooklyn Eagle*, May 31; Peter Morris).

walks plus hits per innings pitched A statistic used to measure the frequency with which pitchers allow baserunners. A figure of 1.20 is considered top level and one greater than 1.50 indicates poor performance. The original Rotisserie League Baseball devised this metric and called it *ratio*, but it omitted other means of reaching base, such as hit by pitch and errors, because they were not included in the Sunday statistics recap against which the league standings were calculated. Abbrev. *WHIP.*

walk the ballpark To issue many bases on balls; to pitch a walkfest.

walk the bases full To give a base on balls that loads the bases.

walk-up A fan who makes a single-game ticket purchase at the box office on the day of the game.

walk year The last year of a player's contract, with the player becoming a free agent the next season. Increasingly, players are being traded, or offered in trade, during their walk year so that the club can get some value from them before they are lost to the open market. "The term 'Walk Year' has become a part of baseball lingo, a mark on every star player's calendar indicating that he's just months away from free agency" (Jeff Bradley, *ESPN The Magazine*, July 8, 2002). Syn. *free-agent year.*

wall The outfield fence. A ball hit over the wall on the fly is a home run.

Wall, The Syn. of *Green Monster.*

wallball A variant of *stickball* featuring one to three players on a side, fast pitching, and a large wall for a backstop on which a box is drawn, chalked, or painted to define a fixed strike zone. It is played on a schoolyard or parking lot and a field at least the size of a handball court. Hits are determined by the distance of the batted ball. All ground balls are outs. Balls not caught that go through the infield are singles; those hit over predetermined points are doubles or triples; and those hit over a fence, roof, or other boundary are home runs. See also *corkball*, 3.

wall ball A base hit off the Green Monster at Fenway Park in Boston. "Three hitters, three wall balls, three runs for the Red Sox" (*The New York Times*, Sept. 27, 2004).

wallburner A ball hit off the outfield wall or fence. "[Left-handed batter Ryan Howard] uses an inside-out swing for wallburners to left" (Jamie Moyer, quoted in *Sports Illustrated*, Sept. 18, 2006, p.64).

wallop 1. *v.* To hit the ball with great power. IST USE. 1897. "Walloping a single" (*The Sporting News*, Nov. 27). 2. *n.* A hard-hit ball. IST USE. 1904. "[Mike] Kahoe tried hard enough to lose the sphere, but the lumbering [Frank] Huelsman raced over for a natty capture of his wallop" (*The Washington Post*, Aug. 7; Peter Morris). 3. *n.* A long base hit. 4. *v.* To defeat an opponent decisively. IST USE. 1870. "[The White Stockings mission was to] capture the whole world of Base Ball players, and oh, especially wollop [*sic*] the Red Stockings" (*Adrain* [Mich.] *Times and Expositor*, July 26; Peter Morris). ETYMOLOGY. Pre-baseball slang to "beat" or "thrash."

walloper 1. A baseball bat. "Ed Delahanty's bats had arrived from New Orleans . . . and Delahanty would soon follow his five 'wallopers'" (Jerrold Casway, *Ed Delahanty*, 2004, p.226). 2. A batter who hits the ball hard. IST USE. 1908 (*New York Evening Journal*, May 18; Edward J. Nichols).

wall-scraper A home run that barely clears the fence. "The five homers impressed me because none of them were wall-scrapers" (Mike Mussina, quoted in *The Baltimore Sun*, Sept. 4, 1996). "[Chuck] Knoblauch's two-run wall-scraper . . . just eluded [outfielder Brian] Jordan but went far enough to tie the score" (*Sports Illustrated*, Nov. 8, 1999, p.72).

Wally Pipp 1. *n.* A player who takes himself out of the lineup, such as for illness or injury; one who makes a bad move. When a player takes a day off, he is reminded "remember Wally Pipp." "[Jim] Traber was still hitting when [Eddie] Murray got hurt, so he got the call. After a week or so, his Oriole mates began calling Murray 'Wally Pipp'" (*The*

Boston Globe, Aug. 10, 1986). 2. *v.* To lose one's job. "[Gregg] Olson thought that, in locker room vernacular, he'd been Wally Pipped. That means somebody else has been given a full shot at your job and, unless he fails, you can't get it back again even if you regain your normal form" (Thomas Boswell, *The Washington Post*, May 1, 1993). "Wally Pipp has become a tragicomic actor in a cautionary tale, the victim of cruel fate and a false sense of security, the first person ever to be Wally Pipped" (Neal McCabe and Constance McCabe, *Baseball's Golden Age*, 1993, p.68). See also *Pipp*.

ETYMOLOGY. On June 2, 1925, New York Yankees first baseman Wally Pipp was replaced in the lineup by Lou Gehrig, who went on to play in a then-record 2,130 consecutive games (Gehrig's consecutive-game streak had actually begun a day earlier when he was a pinch hitter for Pee-Wee Wanninger). Pipp never returned to the starting lineup. Legend holds that Pipp had a headache and took himself out of the lineup, a story that Pipp himself told repeatedly. However, *The New York Times* reported (June 3, 1925) that Yankees manager Miller Huggins, trying to halt a five-game losing streak, had benched three veteran players, including the slumping Pipp; playing for Pipp, Gehrig had three hits as the Yankees defeated the Washington Senators. The *Times* article made no mention of a headache. Eleanor Gehrig (Lou's wife and co-author of *My Luke and I*, 1976, pp.130–31) remembered, "The real thing was that Pipp was slowing down and hadn't been hitting, so he just decided that a day's relaxation at the racetrack might help his state of mind and his bankroll. So Wally went to the racetrack that June 2 and Lou Gehrig went to first base."

wami *hist.* A curse. William G. Brandt (*Baseball Magazine*, Oct. 1932) quoted a player: "The breaks have been on us ever since the bell rang. Got a wami I guess." See also *whammy*.

wand A baseball bat. IST USE. 1872. "Trumbull took up the ashen wand" (George G. Small, *A Presidential Base-Ball Match*, p.23).

want the ball For a pitcher to display eagerness to show his competitive nature. "A guy that wins big games, a guy that wants the ball when the game's on the line, that's Bartolo [Colon]" (Sandy Alomar Jr., quoted in *The Baltimore Sun*, Aug. 7, 2003). See also *take the ball*, 2. Compare *refuse the ball*.

war club A baseball bat. IST USE. 1913. "Bill [Leard] grabbed his trusty war club and approached the plate with the fixed idea of losing the ball over some one of the fences" (*San Francisco Bulletin*, May 17; Gerald L. Cohen).

war correspondent A sportswriter. "Diary of a Baseball War Correspondent on Firing Line" (*San Francisco Bulletin* headline, March 5, 1913). Reporters who covered the New York Giants in 1908 sometimes referred to themselves as war correspodnents (Frank Gtraham, *The New York Giants*, 1952, p.51). "What has become of the old-fashioned war correspondent who within ten days out had some veteran or recruit inventing a double shoot or a Tango twist or a curve that broke seven ways at the same time? . . . Is the typewriter losing its old-time smoke?" (Grantland Rice, quoted in *San Francisco Bulletin*, March 6, 1913; Gerald L. Cohen). Syn. *war scribe*.

warhorse Syn. of *workhorse*, 1.

warm 1. *v.* To prepare a starting pitcher before a game or a relief pitcher during a game. "[Catcher Brook Fordyce] impressed . . . the pitching staff with his willingness to warm the starting pitcher before games" (*The Baltimore Sun*, Aug. 4, 2000). 2. *adj.* Ready to pitch.

warming pan An early syn. for *bullpen*, derived from the fact that pitchers warm up there. "A run of four straight clean hits . . . forced Manager [Frank] Chance to hurry Mordecai Brown out to the warming pan to be ready for the role of rescuer if necessary" (I.E. Sanborn, *Chicago Tribune*, May 7, 1909; Peter Morris). ETYMOLOGY. A possible link between "warming pan" and "bullpen" was suggested by Ty Cobb (*Busting 'Em and Other Big League Stories*, 1914): " 'We work one day a week in the box and five in the warm-up pen,' I heard one of [Clark] Griffith's pitchers complain because he keeps them warming up so much during a game in case he needs one to relieve the man who is in the box."

warm the bench To sit on the bench; to be a benchwarmer. "Don Baylor, the Boston Red Sox designated hitter who has been warming the bench lately, reportedly wants to be traded or released" (*Tampa Tribune*, July 30, 1987). Syn. *warm the pine*. IST USE. 1892. "It's about time he [Cap Anson] gave a younger man a chance to play on the team while he warmed the bench" (*The Boston Globe*, Apr. 10; Peter Morris).

warm the pine Syn. of *warm the bench*.

warmup *n.* Pregame routine for stretching and limbering up the body. Sometimes spelled "warm-up." IST USE. 1915 (*Baseball Magazine*, December, p.116; Edward J. Nichols).

warm up *v.* To prepare for a game with moderate exercise, such as stretching or throwing the ball before or during the game. Daniel Okrent (*Nine Innings*, 1985, p.70; Peter Morris) noted that "warming up" for a pitcher is "no metaphor" because "the process involves the heating of the arm by inducing a heightened blood flow throughout its length . . . for the arm to direct the ball properly." See also *limber up*; *heat up*, 1. IST USE. 1883 (*Chicago Inter-Ocean*, June 27; Edward J. Nichols).

warmup jacket A windbreaker designed to keep the upper body and arms warm, worn by a player when he is warming up or practicing before a game, or sitting in the dugout during a game. Although the jacket is not worn when one is playing the game, pitchers often wear it any time they are not actually on the mound or in the batter's box, such as when they become baserunners. "On a misty night at Shea Stadium, the Mets' batboy ran a warm-up jacket to first base for starting pitcher Matt Ginter" (*The New York Times*, May 27, 2004). See also *baseball jacket*.

warmup mound The pitcher's mound in the bullpen.

warmup pitch One of the eight practice pitches allowed before an inning begins or when a relief pitcher enters a game during an inning.

warmup swing A preliminary swing taken by a batter before the ball is pitched.

warning track An ungrassed area about 10–15 feet wide, made of dirt, cinders, or rubber, encircling the field just inside the wall, that alerts a fielder that he is approaching the wall. Its purpose is to protect the fielder from crashing into the wall as he backs up to catch a ball. With his eyes fixed on the ball, the fielder knows he is nearing the wall as he senses the granular texture of the warning track with his feet. According to *The New York Times* (July 19, 1982), the track was conceived when Brooklyn Dodgers outfielder Pete Reiser was seriously hurt in 1947 after he crashed into the wall at Ebbets Field. In 1948, the Dodgers covered the walls with foam rubber; soon after that, warning tracks began to appear. The first parks to use them were Wrigley Field in Chicago, Braves Field in Boston, and Shibe Park in Philadelphia. Syn. "warning path."

warning-track power The ability of a batter who has enough strength to hit a ball to the warning track but not enough to hit a home run. A player with warning-track power is useful when a sacrifice fly is called for; the term often refers to a long-ball hitter who has lost some of his power. EXTENDED USE. Close, but no cigar. "After watching their team fail three consecutive times in the conference title game, Philadelphia fans are fed up with the Eagles' warning-track power. It's win the Super Bowl, or else" (Sam Farmer, *The Baltimore Sun*, Jan. 8, 2005).

WARP Abbrev. for *wins above replacement player.*

Warren Giles Award 1. An award presented to the winner of the National League pennant. It honors the former president (1951–1969) of the National League. 2. An annual award presented to a minor-league president for "outstanding service."

warrior 1. A competitive player; one who is willing to play while injured. "The best way to describe him [Ken Caminiti] is that he was a warrior in every sense of the word. I can't tell you how many times I remember him hobbling into the manager's office, barely able to walk, and saying, 'Put me in the lineup'" (San Diego Padres general manager Kevin Towers, quoted in *The Baltimore Sun*, Oct. 11, 2004). 2. A ballplayer. IST USE. 1897. "There is not a stronger team in the league on its 'own ash heap' than [Ned] Han-

lon's warriors [Baltimore Orioles]" (Harry Weldon, *St. Louis Post-Dispatch*, Sept. 24; Peter Morris).

war scribe Syn. of *war correspondent.* "A New York war scribe now with the Giants in Texas says Jim Thorpe is weak on hitting curve balls" (*San Francisco Bulletin*, March 6, 1913; Gerald L. Cohen).

wartime *hist.* Describing any period in which competition between rival major leagues led to bidding wars for players, driving up salaries. "The last of the wartime contracts of the players expire at the end of this season, and the boys who held them will have less trouble counting their money next season" (*The Washington Post*, Sept. 2, 1904; Peter Morris).

washed up Said of a player who is no longer considered to be a major leaguer. "Jimmy Callahan considered him [Babe Adams] washed up and let him go to St. Joseph in 1917" (Harry Grayson, *They Played the Game*, 1944, p.101). EXTENDED USE. Without future prospects. "I said we're washed up. Through, finished, and out!" (George S. Kaufman and Moss Hart, *Once in a Lifetime*, 1930; Stuart Y. Silverstein).

washout Syn. of *rainout.*

waste 1. To deliberately pitch outside and wide of the plate in an effort to head off a steal attempt or prevent a hit-and-run play, and to permit the catcher to make a quick throw. IST USE. 1908. "[The catcher] must know when the base runner is going to steal, and in order to prevent the batsman from helping the runner, he wastes the ball, which means to have the pitcher pitch it out of reach of the batsman, so that he cannot hit and at the same time gives the catcher a clear throw to second or third, as the case may be" (J. Ed Grillo, *The Washington Post*, Apr. 25; Peter Morris). 2. To throw a waste pitch.

waste ball Syn. of *waste pitch.* "[Nap] Lajoie is the greatest waste-ball hitter in the league. The reason why Lajoie has been so successful in hitting waste balls is that he is a free hitter" (*The Sporting Life*, Aug. 30, 1913; Peter Morris). IST USE. 1910 (*Baseball Magazine*, September, p.12; Edward J. Nichols).

waste hits *v.* To make base hits that do not help in the scoring of runs. IST USE. 1902

(*The Sporting Life*, Sept. 13, p.5; Edward J. Nichols).

waste pitch A pitch deliberately thrown outside the strike zone, usually with an 0–2 count on the batter. The pitch is commonly thrown in an attempt to get the batter to swing at a bad pitch, to head off a steal by giving the catcher a high pitch on which to make a play on a baserunner, or to prevent a hit-and-run play by making the pitch unhittable. Syn. *waste ball*.

waster A pitcher who habitually tries to get batters to swing at balls out of the strike zone. IST USE. 1909 (*American Magazine*, May, p.109; Edward J. Nichols).

"watch his foot" A common cry of base coaches, ostensibly addressed to the baserunner, but which might also manage to unnerve or disrupt the opposing pitcher (Christy Mathewson, *Pitching in a Pinch*, 1912; Peter Morris).

"watch your lips" A phrase used to warn of a bumpy or rough infield, one on which the ball is likely to take a bad hop. A phrase of the late 1980s, it may be a play on the popular "read my lips" cliché.

water baseball A variety of baseball in which the bases are floats and there are two outfielders and no shortstop (*Detroit Free Press*, Apr. 3, 1907; Peter Morris). Water baseball originated in Atlantic City, N.J., and became popular in Michigan in the early 20th century.

wave For an infielder to make a halfhearted attempt to field a ground ball.

Wave, The An activity in which fans, section by section, rise in unison to their feet with arms raised and waving, cheer, and then sit down, giving the appearance of an undulating ocean wave. Variations of The Wave include one in slow motion, and one in which the upper and lower decks move in opposite directions. The Wave is decried by many purists. "One more reason seeing a game at Wrigley Field is a special experience: According to Cubs publicist Ned Coletti, Cubs fans have never done The Wave" (*USA Today*, May 29, 1987). USAGE NOTE. The *Brooklyn Eagle* (Sept. 8, 1889; Dean A. Sullivan) described the following activity in a game between the St. Louis Browns and the Brooklyn Bridegrooms during the 1889 American Association pennant race: "The bleacheries were black with people . . . jammed together in one immovable mass, and the only time they could gather themselves together was when the excitement got the best of them and everybody was forced to throw up their hands and were compelled to sway about like a wave on the ocean from the irresistible and frenzied throng." ETYMOLOGY. "Krazy George" Henderson, a San Francisco Bay Area pro team booster, claimed he started the fad during the third game of the American League Championship Series between the New York Yankees and the Oakland Athletics on Oct. 15, 1981. Two weeks later, "yell king" Robb Weller instituted a wave during the third quarter of a Univ. of Washington–Stanford Univ. football game in Seattle on Oct. 31. Other claims cite the appearance of "the Mexican Wave" during soccer games in the 1970s. It first appeared in a major-league ballpark on a regular basis during the Detroit Tigers championship season of 1984. Henderson had standards for The Wave (quoted in *The Baltimore Sun*, Oct. 18, 2006): "The place has to be full, the place has to be the right shape and it has to be the right time, after a big touchdown or a team has scored a few runs. And I never do any cheer when there's action on the field."

wave howdy 1. For a fielder to let a hard-hit ball pass rather than risk injury in trying to field it. Syn. "wave howdy-do." 2. An expression said to a player who has just struck out swinging; specif., "if you're waving at me, howdy" (*Sports Illustrated*, Sept. 13, 1982).

wave on For a coach to signal a runner to continue to the next base.

wax 1. To hit a pitcher hard. The term seems to be used almost exclusively in reference to pitchers; e.g., "I've been getting waxed for two years" (Tippy Martinez, quoted in *The Washington Post*, Feb. 21, 1986). 2. To defeat a team. "The Eckfords of Brooklyn again 'waxed' the Haymakers of Lansingburgh . . . to the tune of 20 to 17" (*Syracuse Journal*, Aug. 23, 1869; Larry McCray).

wax pack A pack of baseball cards wrapped entirely in opaque wax-coated paper that is sealed at the factory by applying heat. The term is also casually applied to packs that no longer use actual wax paper. Compare *cello pack*.

way back Said of an outfielder retreating to the wall to chase down a home-run ball. The term has also been applied to a pitcher: "John Wasdin [is remembered] . . . as 'Way Back' for a propensity to surrender long home runs" (*The Baltimore Sun*, Aug. 20, 2001) and to a home run hitter: Luis Gonzalez is "D'backs way-back hit machine" (*The Baltimore Sun*, Aug. 21, 2001).

WBC Abbrev. for *World Baseball Classic.*

WBL Abbrev. for *Women's Baseball League.*

weaken To lose one's pitching effectiveness over the course of a game. IST USE. 1905 (*The Sporting Life*, Sept. 2, p.4; Edward J. Nichols).

weak end of the order Syn. of *bottom of the order.* IST USE. 1899 (Burt L. Standish, *Frank Merriwell's Double Shot*, p.257; Edward J. Nichols).

weak grounder A lightly hit ground ball that infielders are never supposed to miss. EXTENDED USE. Figuratively, something that one should not misplay. "With big Ed Pauley ducking pop bottles, and Harry Truman's Missouri infield bobbling weak grounders, the President's critics were ready to boo almost anyone he sent in" (*Time* magazine, March 11, 1946, p.21; Peter Tamony).

weakness An area in or around the strike zone with which a batter has trouble. "The Dodger book said Bobby [Thomson] had trouble with a ball up and in. They called it his weakness" (Bobby Thomson, *"The Giants Win the Pennant! The Giants Win the Pennant!,"* 1991, p.250).

weapon A baseball bat.

wear a size . . . To go without a hit for the stated number of at-bats in a game; e.g., "Smith wore a size 4 for four hitless at-bats." This is a play on the term "collar" for a hitless performance.

"We Are Family" See *Family, The.*

"we are the people!" The battle cry or slogan of the 1889 National League champion New York Giants. Giants manager Jim Mutrie would strut up and down in front of the stands in a high hat and long coat, roaring, "Who are the people?" and the crowd would yell back, "We are the people!"

"wear it!" 1. Interjection used to tell a batter to let a pitch hit him so he can take his base. Shane Costa (quoted in *Baseball America*, March 31–Apr. 13, 2003): "The coaches have pounded into my head so much: 'When they throw inside, don't move out of the way.' I'm always hearing, 'Wear it!'" See also *wear one*. 2. Baseball slang (among the Oakland A's) for dealing with something unpleasant, such as getting hit by a pitch or being left on the mound because the bullpen is exhausted or striking out three times. It means, essentially, "live with it" or "better you than me."

wear one To be hit by the pitch. Pitcher Todd Jones (quoted in *The Sporting News*, Sept. 3, 2001) commented on protecting his hitters by throwing at opposing batters: "After you do it, the first guy to tell you thanks is the hitter on your team who had to wear one." Troy E. Renck (*Denver Post*, May 2, 2005) wrote, "[The Colorado Rockies] expected someone to 'wear one'—baseball parlance for getting plunked—after their pitchers hit seven Dodgers batters in their previous series." See also *"wear it!"*

wear out the pitcher For a batter to continuously foul off pitches; e.g., "Smith wore out the pitcher with 12 foul balls."

wear out the wood *hist.* To *ride the bench*. IST USE. 1916 (Ring W. Lardner, *You Know Me Al*, p.198; Edward J. Nichols).

wear the collar To go hitless in a game.

wear the horns To have a serious lapse in performance; to be the goat.

Weaver Doctrine Never clean home plate during an argument with a manager who is still on the field. According to umpire Ron Luciano (Ron Luciano and David Fisher, *Strike Two*, 1984), "If a manager covers home plate with dirt and you clean it while he is within kicking distance, he will cover it again. Every time you clean it, he will cover it. Do not clean it until he is safely in the dugout, preferably in the clubhouse." Named for Baltimore Orioles manager Earl Weaver.

Weaverism Any one of a multitude of pronouncements on winning baseball games uttered by Baltimore Orioles manager Earl Weaver; e.g., "The way to win is with pitching and three-run homers," or "The hit and run is the worst and dumbest play in baseball." A few Weaverisms are saved for the nature of the game itself: "Baseball is so elementary and people want to make it so complicated," and "This ain't a football game—we do this every day."

web The leather patch or stitching sewn between the thumb and forefinger of a fielder's glove or mitt.

webbing The array of laces and leather panels, or a center piece of leather that may be an extension of the palm, that connect the thumb and finger sections of a fielder's glove or mitt.

weed-eater A ground ball that hugs the ground.

weeping towel A figurative towel given to a player to curb his moaning or crying.

weigh in To contribute to the outcome; e.g., "Smith weighed in with a triple."

weighted rating system A statistic that compares a pitcher's won-lost percentage to that of his team, intended to quantify the extent to which the pitcher performed better or worse than the average pitcher on his team. The measure was proposed by Ted Oliver (*Kings of the Mound*, 1944) and described by John Thorn and Pete Palmer (*The Hidden Game of Baseball*, 1985). It is analogous to *wins above team*.

weight transfer The technique by which the batter redistributes his body weight to his back foot to gather energy before shifting his weight forward to his front foot during his swing. The transfer of energy from the lower half of the body to the upper half creates a more powerful swing. "To be motionless when you hit makes it very difficult, but Joe [DiMaggio] had exceptional hand speed and weight transfer" (Ralph Kiner, quoted in Danny Peary, ed., *We Played the Game*, 1994). Syn "weight shift."

Welch Amendment An amendment to the *hit by pitch* rule stipulating that batters hit either on the hand or forearm no longer were awarded first base. The amendment was introduced in 1892 and rescinded in 1897. The amendment was named for Curt Welch,

who had a penchant for engineering hit by pitches on his hand and forearm.

Wells Fargo pitch A fastball that is not overpowering. The term is a play on the fact that it appears to come at the batter in "easy stages," alluding to the Wells Fargo stagecoaches of the 19th-century American West. ETYMOLOGY. Created by San Francisco Giants public relations director Garry Schumacher to describe Stu Miller's fastball, and attested to by Joe Garagiola (*Baseball Is a Funny Game*, 1960).

Welsh baseball Misnomer in the United States for the adult version of *rounders* currently played in the Liverpool region and in South Wales, and known as "baseball" in Great Britain.

West Division 1. See *American League West*. 2. See *National League West*.

Western League 1. An eight-team minor league founded by sportswriter Byron Bancroft "Ban" Johnson in 1893 that competed from 1894 through 1899. In 1900, Johnson renamed his loop the American League. In 1901, he declared the American League a major league to compete with the National League. 2. A Class A minor league from 1902 to 1937 and from 1947 to 1958. 3. A Class D minor league from 1939 to 1941. 4. One of two minor leagues in Japan.

western swing A road trip through the western states by an eastern or midwestern club.

West Vest An umpire's *chest protector* developed by National League umpire Joe West that features high-impact plastic plates conforming to the umpire's body shape. The size of the protector can be changed by reconfiguring the interconnecting plates, thereby allowing the protector to be used by more than one umpire.

wet ball A spitball. 1ST USE. 1908. "Harry Howell, one of the original exponents of the spitball, says that he will continue to use the wet ball this year" (*Los Angeles Times*, Feb. 13; Benjamin Zimmer).

wet delivery A spitball. "Spitball is Even More Difficult to Handle . . . Without a capable catcher it would be impossible for a pitcher to do his best, and where the hurler happens to favor the wet delivery the need of a high-class receiver is made more apparent" (*San Francisco Bulletin*, May 24, 1913; Gerald L. Cohen).

wet grounds A playing field deemed unfit for play because of rainwater on the ground. IST USE. 1885. "Wet grounds and a steady pour of rain prevented the Detroit club from meeting the St. Louis nine on the diamond to-day" (*The Milwaukee Sentinel*, May 7).

wet-newspaper hitter A hitter with no authority. "When you see a wet-newspaper hitter, balls he hits have no sound. It's just a thud and it doesn't go anywhere" (Deric Ladnier, quoted in Alan Schwarz, BaseballAmerica.com, Nov. 14, 2006).

wet one A spitball. "[Gaylord Perry] will try to convince the president of the American League that he did not throw two wet ones at the Boston Red Sox" (Joseph Durso, *The New York Times*, Aug. 31, 1982).

wet pitch A spitball.

wet wipe A spitball. "In less than four years the Pittsburgh club would train four telescopic stop-action cameras on me trying unsuccessfully to detect my 'wet wipe'" (Gaylord Perry, *Me and the Spitter*, 1974).

"we want a hit!" A crowd plea for a rally. See also *"CHARGE!"*

whack **1.** *v.* To hit a pitched baseball with authority. IST USE. 1896. "He is whacking the ball also with unusual vim and success" (*The Sporting News*, May 24; David Shulman). **2.** *n.* A smart, resounding blow. In "Casey at the Bat," the crowd hoped that Casey "could get a whack" at the ball. The aluminum bat removed the solid, robust "whack" that sounded when a wood bat connected for a line drive. John Bunker (*Christian Science Monitor*, Sept. 17, 1971) pleaded, "Please, Mr. [batmaker] Wilson, we're not against aluminum. But can you put the whack back in the bat?" IST USE. 1907 (*New York Evening Journal*, Apr. 25; Edward J. Nichols).

whale **1.** To bat a ball hard. "[Gus Williams] has been whaling the pill regularly this season" (*San Francisco Bulletin*, Apr. 25, 1913; Gerald L. Cohen). "From the very first day we saw him in camp, he [Luis Pujols] wasn't whaling" (St. Louis Cardinals first base coach Dave McKay, quoted in *Sports Illustrated*,

May 22, 2006). IST USE. 1905 (*The Sporting Life*, Sept. 9, p.1; Edward J. Nichols). **2.** To defeat decisively. "The *Cincinnati Enquirer* calls the Chicagos the White Whale Club, 'because they are so often whaled'" (*Chicago Daily Tribune*, July 1, 1877).

whale belly An overweight player.

whammy A *jinx*; bad luck or misfortune brought on a player, sometimes by what another player says. "With right hand above the left, each fist clenched except for the pointing, hornlike index and little fingers, [St. Louis Cardinals trainer] Doctor [Harrison J.] Weaver cast his whammy spell on Joe Gordon, the Yankee runner on second base" (J. Roy Stiockton, *The Gashouse Gang*, 1945). "Nearly every player in the game engages in some little practice which he believes will bring him good luck or put the whammy on the other fellow" (Jim Hurley, *American Legion Monthly*, Feb. 1937). See also *wami*; *hoodoo*, 2; *jinx*, 1.

whang To bat a ball hard. IST USE. 1883. "A new ball was put in as the old one had ripped, and Lewis whanged it nicely to center field" (*The Sporting Life*, Apr. 15). ETYMOLOGY. Possibly a blend of "whack" plus "bang."

whangdoodle *hist.* A good play or hit. IST USE. 1902 (*The Sporting Life*, Oct. 4, p.7; Edward J. Nichols). USAGE NOTE. *The World* (New York) (Aug. 13, 1889; Gerald L. Cohen), under the title "New Yorkers in the Lead," wrote, "Sound the loud whangdoodle and beat the frenzied tom-tom. Let the American Eagle scream and rejoice." The term "whangdoodle" is mid-19th-century American slang for: a) an imaginary nondescript person, and b) one who pounds the pulpit (a ranter).

"what is said here, stays here" The summary of the code that is posted in every clubhouse: "What you see here, what you hear here, what you say here, let it stay here when you leave here." It was the violation of this credo that prompted the strong criticism of Jim Bouton's 1970 best-selling tell-all, *Ball Four*.

wheel **1.** *n.* A defensive play in which all four infielders move ("rotate") to prevent a runner from advancing or scoring on a bunt. The shortstop breaks toward third base, the second baseman covers first base leaving second base unguarded (or he covers second base if there is a runner on first base), and the first baseman and the third baseman both charge the plate in an effort to field a bunt and throw out the baserunner at third base. Syn. *wheel play*; *rotation*, 2. **2.** *n.* A player's leg. A player who runs fast has "good wheels." A "bad wheel" is a leg injury and a "flat wheel" is a bad foot. A decrease in a player's number of stolen bases is often attributed to "a case of bad wheels." See also *tire*, 2. IST USE. 1905. "Capt. [Frank] Chance was out in uniform with his bum wheel in a strong ankle supporter" (*Chicago Tribune*, May 5; Peter Morris). **3.** *v.* To pitch. "Joseph McGinnity . . . could pitch a double engagement to-day and go in and wheel again to-morrow" (Alfred H. Spink, *The National Game*, 2nd ed., 1911, p.144). **4.** *v.* To turn to throw. "[Jeff Conine] found himself picked off by [Chad] Durbin's feint to third base and wheel to first" (*The Baltimore Sun*, Aug. 15, 2001). **5.** *v.* To hit the pitch. "[Cal Ripken Jr.] wheeled on [Chad] Durbin's 2–1 pitch, burying it in the left-field stands" (*The Baltimore Sun*, Aug. 15, 2001).

wheel and deal For a pitcher to wind up and throw.

wheeler *hist.* A pitcher. "[Henry 'Harry' Krause,] the youthful left-wheeler" (Alfred H. Spink, *The National Game*, 2nd ed., 1911, p.136).

wheelhouse That part of the strike zone in which the batter swings with the most power or strength; the path of a batter's best swing. A pitcher tries not to "hang one" in the batter's wheelhouse; to do so is to invite a home run. "[Ken] Dixon put a fastball in [Charlie] Moore's wheelhouse . . . and dared Moore to hit it. He did, banging it off the left field foul pole" (*The Washington Post*, June 7, 1987). See also *crush zone*; *kill zone*. IST USE. 1959. "It just seems he's not seeing 'em the way he used to. . . . He had a couple that came right into the wheelhouse—the kind he used to knock out of sight—and he fouled 'em off" (Bill Rigney, on Orlando Cepeda's slump, *San Francisco Chronicle*, May 11; Peter Tamony). ETYMOLOGY. Peter Tamony suggested that batters "wheel" at the ball, taking

good, level "roundhouse" swings, and that such wheels "probably suggested the word association, 'wheelhouse.'" In nautical terms, a wheelhouse is the pilothouse or the place from which a vessel is controlled.

wheel play Syn. of *wheel*, 1.

wheels fell off Describing a situation in which a lead evaporated or the other team started to score many runs. Dan Connolly (*The Baltimore Sun*, July 23, 2006), describing the Orioles taking a 3–0 lead, then giving up 10 runs in the fifth inning to the Tampa Bay Devil Rays: "Then the wheels fell off for [pitcher Rodrigo] Lopez—and so did the doors, the mirrors and the fuzzy dice, leaving just a stripped-down engine available only for parts." Syn. "wheels came off."

Wheeze Kids Nickname for the 1983 Philadelphia Phillies, who won the National League pennant with a roster that included several older players. The term is a play on the nickname *Whiz Kids* for the 1950 Phillies.

"when does the balloon go up?" Traditional greeting for a player who shows up overweight, such as on the first day of spring training.

whiff **1.** *v.* To swing at a pitch without touching the ball. "And he [Rube Marquard] fanned [Hans] Lobert—whiff! whiff! whiff!—like that" (Christy Mathewson, *Pitching in a Pinch*, 1912, p.30; Stuart Y. Silverstein). ETYMOLOGY. "On the St. Andrews Old Golf Course in 1876, Lord Gormley Whiffle didn't just miss his four-inch putt, but completely missed the ball. . . . Spectators remarked, repeatedly, 'Did you see that Whiffle?' It gave us a term for the air swing. Eventually shortened to 'whiff'" (L.M. Boyd, *The Houston Post*, Sept. 29, 1993). **2.** *v.* For a pitcher to strike out a batter. "I whiffed eight men in five innings in Frisco yesterday and could of did better than that if I had of cut loose" (Ring W. Lardner, *Saturday Evening Post*, March 7, 1914). IST USE. 1905. "[Doc White] did something in the strikeout line himself, whiffing thirteen of [Connie] Mack's sturdy toilers" (*Chicago Tribune*, June 10; Peter Morris). **3.** *v.* For a batter to strike out. "Mickey Mantle tied the New York Yankees club strikeout record today when he whiffed

Whiff. Comic postcard, early 20th century. *Ron Menchine Collection*

for the 111th time this season" (United Press International dispatch, Sept. 3, 1958; Peter Tamony). IST USE. 1881 (*New York Herald*, Aug. 11; Edward J. Nichols). **4.** *n.* A strikeout. IST USE. 1907. "The Indian [Chief Bender] was strong on the whiff. He landed eight men good and true" (Charles Dryden, *Chicago Tribune*, Aug. 22; Peter Morris).

whiffer One who strikes out. "Casey—Leading whiffer in the Poetical League" (*The Washington Post*, July 19, 1914).

whiffle ball 1. A called strike. **2.** Incorrect syn. of *Wiffle ball*.

whiff list A pitcher's record of strikeouts.

whip 1. *n.* A player's throwing arm. "[Ed Delahanty] called his powerful throwing arm his 'whip' and guarded it carefully" (Mike Sowell, *July 2, 1903*, 1992, p.102). Syn. *whip arm*. IST USE. 1898. "Ren Mulford reports that Harry Steinfeldt has the most phenomenal 'whip' in the Western League, and will tie any of the seasoned major leaguers in distance and accuracy as a thrower" (*Detroit Free Press*, Feb. 1; Peter Morris). **2.** *n.* A quick throw. **3.** *v.* To throw the ball hard and quickly. IST USE. 1904. "Pete Lohman . . . has lost his arm and can hardly shoot the ball half way to second. One time he could whip it on a line from the plate to center field" (*The Washington Post*, Aug. 7; Peter Morris). **4.** *v.* To bat a ball. IST USE. 1908 (*Brooklyn Daily Eagle*, May 28; Edward J. Nichols). **5.** *v.* To defeat decisively. **6.** *n.* Short for *whip pennant*. "The Atlantics . . . were not long in regaining their lost laurels from those who had so fairly vanquished them; and from that period to the present, the 'whip' has waved from the Atlantic flagstaff" (Charles A. Peverelly, *The Book of American Pastimes*, 1866, p.416; David Shulman). IST USE. 1862. "The grounds yesterday presented an unusual scene of animation, there being a munificent display of bunting, and prominent among the colors at mast head, was the Eckford's 'whip,' then for the first time flung to the breeze" (*Brooklyn Eagle*, Sept. 25; Peter Morris).

WHIP Abbrev. for *walks plus hits per innings pitched*.

whip arm Syn. of *whip*, 1. "Schaeffer . . . has a splendid whip arm" (*San Francisco Bulletin*, March 25, 1913; Gerald L. Cohen).

whip pennant A championship pennant. "Clubs all over the country are preparing to enter into stout competition for the whip pennant" (*Brooklyn Eagle*, March 11, 1870; Peter Morris). "Both clubs . . . met at the Capitol grounds, Washington . . . with the privilege of flying the 'whip' pennant from the White House" (George G. Small, *A Presidential Base-Ball Match*, 1872; David Shulman). Syn. *whip*, 6. IST USE. 1865. "The Mutuals have sent their $10 fee . . . and are now in the arena for the legal whip pennant" (*The New York Times*, July 7; *OED*).

whirler *hist.* A curveball.

whisker trimmer An inside pitch. IST USE. 1914. "The pitcher sneaked over a fast 'whisker trimmer,' catching the batter napping" (Burt L. Standish, *Brick King, Backstop*, p.63; David Shulman).

whisperette *hist.* A batted ball with little power. IST USE. 1909 (*New York Evening Journal*, July 1; Edward J. Nichols).

whistle To throw a fastball.

whistler 1. A fastball. IST USE. 1883. "His swift ball is a whistler" (*Detroit Free Press*, Apr. 3; Peter Morris). 2. A batted ball that moves with great speed. "[Cal] Ripken's 400-foot whistler into the left-field bleachers" (*The Baltimore Sun*, Aug. 5, 1994). IST USE. 1900. "Gross redeemed himself in the last half of the fifth, sending a whistler past second" (*Idaho* [Boise] *Daily Statesman*, May 3; Peter Morris).

white Syn. of *home plate*, 1. "I'd been pitching him [Vlad Guerrero] in all day and then I threw a pitch that got over the white" (Sidney Ponson, quoted in *The Baltimore Sun*, May 23, 2004).

white-dot slider A hard slider with less break than usual (Daniel Okrent, *Nine Innings*, 1985, pp.247–48).

White Elephants Nickname for the Philadelphia *Athletics*. The nickname was derived from John McGraw's comment early in the 1902 season that the owner of the Philadelphia team had a "white elephant" on his hands, alluding to a costly possession that is a burden. The Athletics went on to win the pennant and the McGraw insult was turned into a nickname and a team symbol.

white lines The literal and figurative confines

of the game of baseball; the playing field. "You cross the white lines onto the field of action and find the air thick and tough to breathe" (Joe Garagiola, *Baseball Is a Funny Game*, 1960, p.39). Wade Boggs (quoted in *Sports Illustrated*, Aug. 14, 1995, p.47): "Once we cross the white line[s], there are no distractions. That's where we can go to get away from it all." See also *between the white lines*. EXTENDED USE. The boundaries of an endeavor. Antitrust attorney Stephen M. Axinn, commenting on the government's suit against Microsoft (quoted in *The Baltimore Sun*, Dec. 20, 1998): "The purpose of the government's suit is not just to stop Microsoft but to send messages as to what the white lines are on this ball field."

White Owl Wallop A home run. The term was made popular by announcers Mel Allen and Bob Elson, whose broadcasts were sponsored by White Owl cigars.

whites See *home whites*.

White Sox Nickname for the American League Central Division franchise in Chicago, Ill. The franchise entered the American League in 1900 as the Chicago White Stockings, but the National League objected because its club in Chicago had once used that nickname. Sportswriters had shortened the nickname to "White Sox" and the club adopted the nickname in 1904. At various times, the club was called the *Hitless Wonders*, the *Black Sox*, and the *Go-Go Sox*. Also known as Chisox, Pale Hose, and *South Siders*.

White Stockings 1. Nickname for the National Association franchise in Chicago in 1871, 1874, and 1875. 2. Nickname for the National League franchise in Chicago from 1876 to 1889. It was renamed the Chicago Cubs in 1902. 3. Nickname for the American League franchise in Chicago from 1900 to 1903. It was renamed the Chicago White Sox in 1904.

IST USE. 1870. According to the *Chicago Tribune* (Apr. 30, 1870; R.J. Lesch), when the Chicago Ball Club arrived in St. Louis to play the Union Club on Apr. 29, the team unveiled a new uniform, including "stockings of pure white British thread," and "already the snowy purity of the hose has suggested the name of 'White Stockings' for the nine, and it is likely to become as generally accepted, not to say as famous, as that of the sanguinary extremities [i.e., the Red Stockings]."

ETYMOLOGY. The *Chicago Tribune* (May 19, 1870; R.J. Lesch) indicated that the name was coined in St. Louis (see above): "A barefooted urchin in the crowd exclaimed: 'Oh, look at the White Stockings!' The boy's choice of an appellation has since been uniformly endorsed throughout the country."

whitewash 1. *v.* To prevent a team from scoring in an inning; to be held scoreless in an inning. Henry Chadwick (*The Game of Base Ball*, 1868, p.46): "A nine is said to be 'whitewashed' when they are put out in an inning without being able to score a single run." IST USE. 1866. "4th innings—Custer [Club] whitewashed again, which caused the confidence of the spectators, inspired by the record on the 2nd innings, to visibly decrease" (*Ionia County* [Mich.] *Sentinel*, July 24; Peter Morris). **2.** *v.* To *shut out* a team; to be shut out. "Louisville was the first club to be whitewashed in a championship contest" (*The World* [New York], Apr. 19, 1888; Gerald L. Cohen). **3.** *n.* An inning in which a team fails to score. "[The Kekiongas] gave the Forest City boys nine consecutive whitewashes" (*The Cleveland Morning Herald*, May 6, 1871). See also *blank*, 1. IST USE. 1867. "In Connecticut [a blank score] is 'a whitewash'" (*Ball Players' Chronicle*, June 20; Peter Morris). EXTENDED USE. A failure. "The local market for spot cotton received, in base ball parlance, a whitewash, having failed to record the sale of a single bale; closed quiet but firm, with no change in quotations" (*Galveston Daily News*, Apr. 25, 1884; Peter Morris). **4.** *n.* A defeat in which the loser fails to score. "The first whitewash of the season on local grounds occurred yesterday and New York Giants used the brush" (*The World* [New York], Apr. 14, 1888; Gerald L. Cohen). IST USE. 1875. "Many were prophesying a grand whitewash for the home team" (*Boston Daily Advertiser*, June 15).

ETYMOLOGY. It is easy to see how the term might derive from both the obliterating quality of the white stain and the laundered purity of a pitcher's shutout.

Whiteyball The style of baseball practiced by Dorrel "Whitey" Herzog, manager of the Kansas City Royals (1975–1979) and St. Louis Cardinals (1980–1990), which featured aggressive baserunning, the hit and run, stolen bases, and the suicide squeeze.

whittle 1. To catch up gradually with an opponent who is ahead in a game or leads in the standings; e.g., "The Royals whittled away the Red Sox lead." IST USE. 1912 (*New York Tribune*, Sept. 29; Edward J. Nichols). **2.** For a pitcher to attempt to lure batters with pitches just off the corners of the plate. IST USE. 1928. "[Rosy] Ryan was curving every ball and after 'whittling,' he carried the count down to three and two" (George Herman Ruth, *Babe Ruth's Own Book of Baseball*, p.146; David Shulman).

whittler A pitcher who throws the ball just outside the strike zone and lures the batter into swinging at bad pitches. "A good whittler can drive a batter screwy in no time with his tantalizing offerings that aren't quite good enough" (Charles C. Meloy, *Baseball Digest*, Aug. 1939). IST USE. 1928. "A whittler is a pitcher who mixes up balls with strikes and carries a batter along to a two-two or three-two count before making him hit" (George Herman Ruth, *Babe Ruth's Own Book of Baseball*, p.300; David Shulman).

whiz chuck *hist.* A swiftly pitched ball. IST USE. 1908 (*New York Evening Journal*, Aug. 21; Edward J. Nichols).

Whiz Kids Nickname for the 1950 Philadelphia Phillies, who took the National League pennant with a starting lineup of players all under the age of 30. Compare *Wheeze Kids*; *Fizz Kids*.

whizzer 1. A hard-batted ball. IST USE. 1861 (*New York Sunday Mercury*, Aug. 10; Edward J. Nichols). **2.** A fastball. "He sent a whizzer away 'over the fence'" (*New York Sunday Mercury*, Oct. 16, 1861; David Shulman). **3.** A fastball pitcher. "Clint Stark . . . 70-G Whizzer" (*The Sporting News* photo caption, Nov. 23, 1960).

whole ball of wax Everything related to a mater or situation, such as a pennant or world championship, or winning a ball game; the "whole deal." "Wille [Mays] might have hit it out of here and that would have been the

Whiz kids. The cast of the 1950 Phillies. *Author's collection*

whole ball of wax" (*The New York Times*, May 29, 1955; *OED*).

whole field See *use the whole field*.

whole new ball game A new start, such as a sudden turn of events in a game. "It's a whole new ball game" is an oft-used slogan, the official theme of the 1989 Texas Rangers, the motto of Bob Short's 1969 Washington Senators, and the debut slogan for the 1977 Toronto Blue Jays. See also *ball game*, 2; *new ball game*, 1. Syn. "whole different ball game." USAGE NOTE. According to Peter Morris (*Level Playing Fields*, 2007, pp.36–37), John Montgomery Ward, commenting in 1894 on the Baltimore Orioles style of play that emphasized "inside baseball," was reported to have said, "This isn't baseball the Orioles are playing. It's a whole new game." EXTENDED USE. Any new start. "If this [Chinese entry into the Vietnam War] were to happen, some official of our government would no doubt announce that we were in a 'whole new ballgame,' which would mean that none of the policies or promises made in the past were binding any longer, including the prohibition against the use of nuclear weapons" (*The New Yorker*, March 13, 1971).

"Who's on First?" The title of the comedy skit first performed on radio in 1938 and made famous by comedians Bud Abbott and Lou Costello, who included the pitter-patter sketch in their 1945 film, *The Naughty Nineties*. The comedians estimated that they performed the skit about 15,000 times in radio and television appearances and in live performances, including at President Harry Truman's inaugural gala in 1949. It relies on the improbable last names of the players to create comic confusion. The full lineup: Who (1b), What (2b), I Don't Give a Darn (ss), I Don't Know (3b), Why (lf), Because (cf), [omitted] (rf), Tomorrow (p), and Today (c). There have been several claims of authorship made for the skit, including one made posthumously for songwriter Irving Gordon by his son, but others—including those who performed a variation on it before Abbott and Costello—claim it dates back to early vaudeville and that it was commonly performed well before it was refined and performed by Abbott and Costello. EXTENDED USE. Said of a situation that is spinning out of control, or one in which it is uncertain who is in charge, or a controversy over which entity preceded another.

Why Not? season The 1989 Baltimore Orioles season, in which the team nearly won the American League East Division after an abysmal 1988 performance when the team set the all-time record for consecutive losses (21) at the start of the season.

wicket 1. A player's leg. When a ball passes through a player's legs it is said to have gone "through the wickets." IST USE. 1904. "[Patrick] Hynes hit to [Bill] O'Neill, and 'Tip's' wickets were open, the ball going through to the outfield" (*The Washington Post*, Sept. 1; Peter Morris). ETYMOLOGY. The wicket is a prime piece of equipment in both croquet and cricket. Whereas the cricket ball cannot go through the wicket, the croquet ball is supposed to go through the wicket; hence, croquet is most certainly the inspiration for the baseball usage. 2. A late 17th-century to mid-19th-century American adaptation of the English game of cricket, popular in small communities and rural areas, in which the wickets were wider (5–6 feet) and much lower to the ground, the ball was larger (about the size of today's softball) and bowled on the ground rather than pitched through the air, the space or "alley" (75 feet long and 10 feet wide) between the wickets was dirt rather than turf, the bat was very heavy and curved, with a club-like protuberance (similar to a hockey stick but round) at the tip. There were 30 players on a side. The game was popular in New England, esp. Connecticut, and was played by George Washington and his troops during the Revolutionary War (1778). The game all but vanished by 1860, in part because of baseball's popularity at that time. David Block (*Baseball Before We Knew It*, 2005, p.146) characterized wicket as "cricket democratized"; *The Daily Picayune* (New Orleans) (June 1, 1893) noted that wicket was "English cricket Yankeefied and made popular." John Thorn (personal communication, Sept. 1, 2005) would regard wicket as "neither cricket nor baseball nor golf nor polo but a Seussian combination of all four." IST USE. 1704. In "The Game of Wicket and Some Old-Time Wicket Players" (George Dudley Seymour, *Papers and Addresses of the Society of Colonial Wars in the State of Connecticut*, Volume II of the proceedings of the Society, 1909; John Thorn), wicket was mentioned ("ball-playing in Connecticut") in 1704.

wide 1. *adj.* Off target; far to one side or the other of a base or, in the case of a pitch, home plate. **2.** *n.* Syn. of *called ball*, 1. IST USE. 1874 (*Chicago Inter-Ocean*, July 7; Edward J. Nichols).

wide one Syn. of *called ball*, 1. "Lee opened the attack by waiting for the wide ones" (*The Washington Post*, May 21, 1921).

wield To hit the ball effectively. "The Detroits wielded the willow with much more effect than their opponents" (*Detroit Free Press*, Oct. 27, 1887). IST USE. 1870. "[The Water Sprites Club of Ypsilanti are juniors but] seniors both in wielding the willow and lively handling of the ball" (*Detroit Advertiser and Tribune*, July 19; Peter Morris).

Wiffle ball 1. A white, lightweight (two-thirds of an ounce), three-inch, hollow, plastic (polyethylene) ball perforated by holes with which it is easy to make trick pitches ("the curvingist ball in the world"), designed to take the place of a baseball in confined areas. It was invented in 1953 by David N. Mullany, who used the round plastic casing that accompanied a box of Coty perfume; the balls are still produced by the Mullany

family (Shelton, Conn.). **2.** A game played like baseball with a yellow plastic bat (no longer than 38 inches, no heavier than 24 ounces, and no thicker than two inches in diameter) and a Wiffle ball. Since the ball cannot be hit too far, it makes a good game for a restricted area, such as backyards and back alleys. Each team has at least two and no more than 10 players. There are no walks and no baserunning: the runners are imaginary and advance depending on where the balls are hit. Outs are recorded by striking out the batter, catching a fly ball, and fielding a ground ball while the ball is in motion in fair territory. The World Wiffle Ball Association (Hanover, Mass.) organized adult leagues in 1977. The United States Perforated Plastic Baseball Association (USP-PBA) conducts tournaments. USAGE NOTE. The term "Wiffle" (with a capital "W") is a trademark; the terms "wiffle" and "wiffle ball" are incorrect. Incorrect syn. *whiffle ball*, 2. ETYMOLOGY. David A. Mullany (son of the inventor; quoted in *Sports Illustrated*, July 28, 1997): "You swung and missed so much, it just seemed logical. . . . I told my dad it would be cheaper to make signs with fewer letters" (hence, dropping the "h" from "whiffle").

Wiffler One who plays Wiffle ball.

wiggle ball Syn. of *palm ball* (Rob Neyer, in Bill James and Rob Neyer, *The Neyer/James Guide to Pitchers*, 2004, p.22).

wig-wag *hist.* **1.** *v.* To send a sign. IST USE. 1909 (*American Magazine*, June, p.404; Edward J. Nichols). **2.** *n.* Syn. of *sign*, 1. IST USE. 1917 (*The New York Times*, Oct. 9; Edward J. Nichols). ETYMOLOGY. From the wig-wag system of signal flags and torches, waved according to a code, employed in the Civil War.

wig-wagger Syn. of *base coach*.

wild 1. Lacking consistent accuracy; esp. said of a pitcher who issues many bases on balls. IST USE. 1883 (*The Sporting Life*, May 20, p.1; Edward J. Nichols). **2.** Said of a ball that is thrown or pitched far from its intended target.

wild card Since 1995, a team given a berth in the Division Series by virtue of having the best record among the three second-place teams in the three divisions in each major league. Wild cards surrender home-field advantage during the Division Series. The Florida Marlins were the first wild card to win a World Series (in 1997). ETYMOLOGY. From card playing where a given card, such as an ace, can be played as if it were any other card.

wild card pinch hitter The *designated hitter* in the Eastern League in 1970.

wild-cat league *hist.* Syn. of *independent league* (C.H. Claudy, *Technical World Magazine*, July 1913).

wildcatter *hist.* A fan who attempts to watch a game from a vantage point outside the ballpark rather than paying to get inside.

wild duck A bat that leaves the batter's hands as he swings and that goes flying toward the infield, foul territory, or the stands.

wild in the strike zone Said of an inconsistent pitcher who throws strikes but without pinpoint location; e.g., a pitcher wants to throw a curve down and away for a strike, but the ball is so alive, it drifts back belt-high over the middle of the plate. "I was wild in the strike zone. I was throwing strikes, but they weren't quality ones" (Mark Eichhorn, quoted in *The Baltimore Sun*, June 19, 1994).

wild-pitch *v.* To pitch a ball without control and be charged with a wild pitch. IST USE. 1904. "[Otto] Hess wild-pitched [Boileryard] Clarke to second" (*The Washington Post*, Aug. 25; Peter Morris).

wild pitch *n.* A legally delivered pitched ball that is so high, wide, or low that the catcher cannot control or stop it with ordinary effort, thereby allowing one or more baserunners to advance. A wild pitch is charged if the ball touches the ground before reaching home plate and is not handled by the catcher, permitting a runner to advance. A wild pitch is charged against the pitcher only if a runner advances a base. No error is charged when a wild pitch is scored; prior to 1957, the pitcher was charged with an error rather than a wild pitch if the batter reached first base on a wildly thrown third strike. The distinction between a wild pitch and a *passed ball* is made by the official scorer. Abbrev. *WP*, 1.

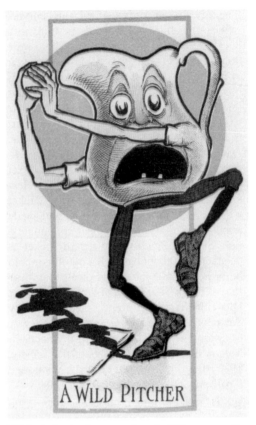

Wild pitch. Comic postcard, early 20th century. *Ron Menchine Collection*

Syn. *jimjam*; *wild throw*, 2. IST USE. 1870. "Radcliffe made first by a high hit to short left field, and went to second on a wild pitched ball" (*Chicago Tribune*, June 23; Peter Morris). EXTENDED USE. A careless statement or action. "At midweek the Republican campaign was bolstered by an innovation—the 'truth squad'—a team of senators who trailed whistle-stopping Harry Truman to field what they denounced as his wild pitches" (*Life* magazine, Oct. 13, 1952).

wild pitch hitter A hitter who swings at bad balls or wild pitches. "[Nap Lajoie] is what is known as a wild pitch hitter. He hits them better a foot outside the plate than he does when they are over" (Hugh S. Fullerton, *Chicago Tribune*, Apr. 29, 1906; Peter Morris).

wild throw 1. A ball thrown by a fielder to another fielder beyond his reach, allowing the batter-runner or one or more baserunners to advance, resulting in an error. IST USE.

1861 (*New York Sunday Mercury*, Oct. 2; Edward J. Nichols). **2.** A *wild pitch.*

William Harridge Award An annual award presented to the winner of the American League pennant. Harridge was the American League president from 1931 to 1959.

Williamsburg The bullpen in front of the right field bleachers at Fenway Park in Boston when Ted Williams was using it as a target for line drives. It was built for the 1940 season after Williams hit 14 home runs in his rookie year at Fenway Park.

Williams shift A strategically defensive move created by Cleveland Indians manager Lou Boudreau on July 14, 1946, during the second game of a doubleheader to deal with the particular pull-hitting strength of Boston Red Sox left-handed slugger Ted Williams (who had hit three home runs and driven in eight runs in the first game). The shift placed the third baseman behind second base, the shortstop halfway between first base and second base, the first baseman hugging the line behind first base, the second baseman closer to first base and on the grass in short right field, the right fielder on the right-field line, the center fielder playing the right fielder's position, and the left fielder (the only player covering the left side of the field) about 30 feet behind the skin of the infield. The intent was to dare Williams to hit singles to left field rather than doubles or home runs to right field. During the game, Williams walked twice and lined a one-hopper to the second baseman in short right field, who threw Williams out. The shift was not used when runners were on base; and was not often used by the late 1950s. The shift was originally known as the *Boudreau shift* for its inventor. Clubs had been using shifts against Williams as early as 1941 (Michael Seidel, *Ted Williams*, 1991, pp.103–4), but Boudreau's version "attracted a lot of attention because it was so dramatic" (Peter Morris, *A Game of Inches: The Game on the Field*, 2006, p.222). USAGE NOTE. The term has been used retrospectively for a similar shift employed in the 1920s against two other left-handed pull hitters named Williams: Fred "Cy" Williams of the Philadelphia Phillies and Ken Williams of the St. Louis Browns.

William Tell An easy, head-high bounding ball. ETYMOLOGY. From the legendary archer who shot an apple off his son's head with an arrow. The term is used in the context of baseball because the ball bounces head high or close to the head, as if it could knock an apple off the fielder's head.

willow *hist.* A baseball bat. Early bats made from the light, soft wood of the willow tree were good for bunting and allowing the batter to swing with great speed. IST USE. 1870. "[Andy Allison] took the willow first, and passed up a high flyer, which descended into [William] Craver's hands" (*Chicago Tribune*, July 8; Peter Morris). ETYMOLOGY. From cricket. "In cricket . . . the bat figures as the 'willow'" (*Forest and Stream*, Dec. 25, 1873; Peter Morris).

Wilson Pickett A skillful infielder who makes sharp defensive plays. The term is a rather elaborate pun on the name of soul singer Wilson Pickett, whereby the infielder uses his trademarked Wilson glove to "pick it" (the ball) (John Hall, *Baseball Digest*, Dec. 1973). First baseman Bill Buckner, among others, named his glove "Wilson Pickett."

wilted lily A batter who lets his bat droop as he awaits the pitch.

win 1. *v.* To score the most runs in a baseball game. **2.** *n.* A victory. Abbrev. *W*, 1. IST USE. 1905 (*The Sporting Life*, Sept. 2; Edward J. Nichols). USAGE NOTE. As recently as 1934, this particular use of a verb as a noun was noted as an oddity of American sportswriting by J. Willard Ridings (*Journalism Quarterly*, Dec. 1934). **3.** *n.* That which is credited against a winning pitcher and is counted both in his single-season and career records. In giving this statistic, the wins always appear before the number of losses; e.g., a season record of 18–8 means 18 wins and 8 losses. Abbrev. *W*, 2. **4.** *v.* To pitch a winning baseball game.

win column The column in the league or division standings that records the number of wins incurred by a team in relation to the number of games played or to be played, or games a team is ahead or behind another team. Compare *loss column.*

wind For a pitcher to swing his pitching arm

preparatory to pitching the ball. See also *wind up*.

windage [softball term] The effect of wind on a pitched ball. Eddie Feigner (*What Little I Know About Pitching and Hitting*, 1980) described the importance of windage in the fast pitch game.

wind-blown home run A home run in which the ball goes over the fence with the real or imagined help of the wind.

wind down To play the last few games of spring training or of the season.

wind is holding it up Said of a batted ball that flies into the wind and not only is prevented from going for a home run, but also is easier for the fielder to reach because the wind keeps the ball longer in the air.

windmill [softball term] A delivery in fast pitch softball that begins with a full circle *windmill windup*. It results in fastballs of the highest momentum and speed and is used by pitchers with a high level of skill. Edward Claflin (*Irresistible American Softball Book*, 1978) stated, "The first windmill pitch ever seen in softball was at a picnic game in Detroit in 1922. It was thrown by Mike Lutomski, a school principal, and was declared illegal by Hubert Johnson, the unofficial rules boss in Detroit. So many playground kids adopted the windmill style that Johnson had to reverse his decision and declare it legal in 1926." See also *slingshot*, 4; *figure eight*, 2.

windmill windup [softball term] A windup in which the pitcher makes a full vertical circle with his or her arm before delivering the ball; the force behind the *windmill* delivery. Harry D. Wilson (*Play Softball*, 1942) described it as follows (for a right-handed pitcher): "The left foot swings back, thereby throwing the weight on the right leg as the arm goes up overhead. The left foot starts forward on the second twirl and the weight goes forward on the left leg as the ball is released. Balance is maintained by the left arm. A slight hesitation as the ball is released may deceive the batter and cause him to swing too soon."

window-shopping Looking at a called third strike. Announcer Ernie Harwell would refer to such a batter as "out for excessive window-shopping."

window-wearer *hist.* A player who wore eyeglasses on the field. The term was popular in the 1930s and 1940s for players such as Bill Dietrich, Walter Beck, Dom DiMaggio, and Paul Waner.

wind pad *hist.* Syn. of *chest protector*. IST USE. 1896. "I have no regular catcher, and it looks as if I would have to tie myself to that wind pad pretty often from now till the finish of the season" (Cap Anson, quoted in *The Washington Post*, Aug. 30).

wind paddist *hist.* Syn. of *catcher*, 1. See also *paddist*. Sometimes spelled "windpaddist." IST USE. 1897. "[Jack] Warner, the sullen, erratic wind paddist of the Giants is giving oral imitations of Scrappy [Bill Joyce], but the mimicry has failed to make a hit with the umpires" (*The Washington Post*, June 14).

windup *n.* The preliminary movements of the pitcher's arm prior to pitching the ball. It involves taking a step back from the rubber, raising one's hands together over one's head, and then stepping forward to deliver the ball. Compare *no windup*; *stretch*, 2. IST USE. 1904. "Catching [Al] Jacobsen in the middle of a long wind up, [George] Davis then stole third" (*The Washington Post*, Sept. 29; Peter Morris). ETYMOLOGY. Possibly from the similar motion of winding a clock. "Cunningham, Baltimore's clever little pitcher, still does the 'wind-the-clock act' while delivering the ball when none of the bases are occupied" (*New York Sun*, Apr. 30, 1889; Peter Morris).

wind up *v.* For a pitcher to execute a windup before delivering the ball. "As soon as [Tom] Hughes began to wind up, [Harry] Davis made a dash for the plate" (*The Washington Post*, Apr. 28, 1908). See also *wind*. IST USE. 1891. "[Cy Young] winds up his arm, then his body, then his legs, bows profoundly to his great outfield, straightens up again, then lets her go" (*The Boston Globe*, quoted in *Cleveland Plain Dealer*, June 5; Peter Morris).

windup position One of two legal pitching positions, taken when the pitcher holds the ball with both hands in front of his body and faces the batter with his pivot foot, or portion of his pivot foot, in contact with the rubber and his free (stepping) foot on, in front of, to either side of, or behind the rubber. From this position, any natural movement associated with the delivery of the ball commits the pitcher to throw without interruption or alteration. Compare *set position.*

win expectancy A method for evaluating the contributions to victories or losses made by a player in a season, based on data describing the probability that a team will win a game from each base–out situation for each inning (top and bottom) in a game and various combinations of runs scored (tie game, home team ahead by one, home team behind by one, etc.). Each plate appearance changes the probability. The method was developed by Keith Woolner and introduced in *Baseball Prospectus* (2005); Woolner described several uses for this measure, including leverage. See *player game percentage*; *player win average*; and *win probability added* for analogous methods. See also *wins expected above replacement and adjusted for lineup faced.* Abbrev. *WX.*

wing 1. *n.* The throwing arm, esp. that of a pitcher. IST USE. 1897. "[Tony Mullane's] wing is as fresh and perfect to-day as when he pitched his first professional game" (*The Washington Post*, June 14). **2.** *v.* To throw the ball. "One fan said yesterday that he would pay a quarter just to see the portly knight of the mitt [San Francisco Seals catcher Tubby Spencer] wing four or five balls down to second base" (*San Francisco Bulletin*, Apr. 3, 1913; Gerald L. Cohen). IST USE. 1905. "[Ducky] Holmes got it up cleanly on the run and winged it home just in time to nip [Emil] Frisk" (*Chicago Tribune*, Apr. 15; Peter Morris). **3.** *v.* To retire a baserunner by throwing the ball to the base before he reaches it. IST USE. 1867. "[Parker] was winged in an attempt to reach second by that base" (*Hastings Banner*, Sept. 4; Peter Morris). **4.** *v.* To hit a batter with a pitched ball. IST USE. 1914 (*New York Tribune*, Oct. 11; Edward J. Nichols). **5.** *v./hist.* To hit a ball hard. "[Nap Lajoie] is beginning to slow up on his legs, but ... wings the ball as hard as ever" (Ty Cobb, *Busting 'Em and Other Big League Stories*, 1914; Peter Morris). **6.** *v.* To get mov-

ing, to hustle, to run; e.g., "Smith winged it from first to third." **7.** *n.* An irregularity on the surface of the ball created when a pitcher uses his fingernails or other object to illegally raise a piece of the cover. The term is usually used in the plural. **8.** *v.* To create wings on the ball. "[Clark Griffith] used to knock the dirt from his spikes by striking the ball against his shoe. ... While trying to 'wing' the ball Griffith discovered by accident that on some diamonds the grit from his heel, adhering to the ball, made the sphere act strangely in the air" (Hugh S. Fullerton, *Reno* [Nev.] *Evening Gazette*, Apr. 29, 1915; Peter Morris).

wing outfielder Syn. of *corner outfielder.* "[Jake Blalock] has enough bat for a wing outfielder" (Philadelphia Phillies assistant general manager Mike Arbuckle, quoted in *Baseball America*, July 21–Aug. 3, 2003).

wingy ball *hist.* A ball with a rough, loose cover. Christy Mathewson (*Pitching in a Pinch*, 1912; Peter Morris) wrote, "The diamond at Marlin [Texas] is ... made of dirt ... and the ball gets 'wingy.' Little pieces of the cover are torn loose by contact with the rough dirt."

win his own game For a pitcher to contribute to his victory by effective hitting. IST USE. 1899 (Burt L. Standish, *Frank Merriwell's Double Shot*, p.7; Edward J. Nichols).

wink-out 1. *v.* To go berserk and attack someone or something, such as a watercooler or the clubhouse wall. **2.** *n.* A berserk attack. Bill Lee (*The Wrong Stuff*, 1984, p.155; Charles D. Poe) noted that sometimes two players will wink-out at the same time and attack each other, adding puckishly that this is called a "twin wink-out" or better known as a "twinkie."

winner 1. Syn. of *winning pitcher.* **2.** The team that wins a game.

winning pitcher The pitcher who is given official credit for his team's victory. It can be the starting pitcher (if he pitches at least five complete innings) whose team assumes a lead while he is in the game (or during the inning on offense in which he is removed from the game) and does not relinquish the lead, or a relief pitcher who comes in with his team tied or behind and is the pitcher when his team scores the winning run. Compare *losing pitcher*. Abbrev. *WP*, 2. Box score abbrev. *W*, 3. Syn. *winner*, 1.

winning run The run, when scored, that gives the winning team a lead that it never relinquishes.

winning streak Two or more games won in succession by either a pitcher or a team. IST USE. 1889. "The Browns kept up their winning streak at Louisville yesterday, when they defeated the home team by a score of 13 to 6" (*St. Louis Post-Dispatch*, Apr. 23; Peter Morris).

winning ugly Winning a game despite playing poorly at times. The term was first used by Texas Rangers manager Doug Rader in reference to the West Division–winning 1983 Chicago White Sox. See also *ugly*.

win points A statistic credited to a player if his performance during any plate appearance increases the probability that his team will win the game. It is used in determining *player win average*. Compare *loss points*.

win probability added A method for evaluating the contributions to victories or losses made by a player in a season, based on data describing the probability that a team will win a game from each base–out situation for each inning (top and bottom) in a game and various combinations of runs scored (tie game, home team ahead by one, home team behind by one, etc.). Each plate appearance changes the probability, and the players responsible for the change, usually the batter and pitcher, are given a number of credits associated with that change if the outcome favors their team, and the same number of debits if the outcome disfavors their team. The method was devised by mathematics professor Doug Drinen. See *player win average*; *player game percentage*; and *win expectancy* for analogous methods. Abbrev. *WPA*.

wins above average A statistical index representing the number of wins a position player contributes to his team through batting, fielding, and base stealing when compared to the average player. There are several specific versions of this measure, differing in the details of its computation. It is similar in concept to *total player rating*. Abbrev. *WAA*.

wins above league An estimate of how many wins a pitcher should have recorded, based on his performance. It is calculated by adding a pitcher's pitching wins to one-half of the pitcher's number of decisions, the latter number representing the number of wins a .500 pitcher would have, given the same number of decisions as the pitcher being evaluated. The career leader is Cy Young with 490.5. Since Young won 511 games, one could conclude that he won 20 games more than he "should" have, given his performance. Ed Walsh is the single-season leader for 20th-century pitchers with 32.8 in 1908; he actually won 40 games that season. The estimate is described in John Thorn et al., eds. (*Total Baseball*, 6th ed., 1999, p.2357).

wins above replacement player The number of wins a player is responsible for beyond the replacement level at the player's position. The measure was devised by Clay Davenport. Abbrev. *WARP*.

wins above team An estimate of how many wins a pitcher has beyond those of an average pitcher on his team, excluding him. It is computed by determining the team won-lost percentage without that pitcher, transforming that into a won-lost record for a pitcher with the same number of decisions as the pitcher being evaluated, and then comparing that transformed record to that of the pitcher being evaluated. Walter Johnson is the single-season leader for 20th-century pitchers with 14.7 in 1913; the career leader is Cy Young with 99.7. The estimate was devised by Pete Palmer and described in John Thorn and Pete Palmer (*The Hidden Game of Baseball*, 1985). It is analogous to *weighted rating system*.

wins expected above replacement and adjusted for lineup faced A context-free method for evaluating pitchers, introduced in *Baseball Prospectus* (2006) as "how many wins an average team would have been expected to win due to this pitcher's performance, as compared to a replacement level pitcher facing the same batters." It is calculated with the use of the *win expectancy* method and is weighted to consider runners stranded on base, pitching against tougher lineups, and closing out one-run games. Abbrev. *WXRL*.

win shares A statistical method for partitioning the responsibility for a team's victories in a given year to its players. It is calibrated so that the sum of a team's players' win shares is equal to three times the number of wins the team achieved during that season. This sum is then allotted among the team members based on their batting, pitching, and fielding performances. The method allows for player evaluation across positions, teams, and eras by measuring the sum of a player's contributions in one groundbreaking number. Forty win shares represents an "historic season"; 30 win shares represents a Most Valuable Player Award candidate; 20 win shares represents an All-Star-type season; and 5 win shares represents a bench player. Total win shares of 400 represents a Hall of Fame candidate. The method was devised by Bill James, mentioned in his *The New Bill James Historical Baseball Abstract* (2001), and described in detail in Bill James and Jim Henzler (*Win Shares*, 2002). Abbrev. *WS*, 2.

winter ball Organized off-season play for major leaguers (with fewer than 520 at-bats during the regular season) and minor leaguers desiring added experience and skills retention or fine-tuning. Winter ball is played in the Caribbean area, Central America, South America, Australia, and parts of the United States. "[Brad] Havens looked great in winter ball. Course, they'll chase the breaking ball in the dirt in Puerto Rico" (Earl Weaver, quoted in *The Washington Post*, Feb. 9, 1986). 1ST USE. 1945. "Fast starters and slow finishers, Cuban ball players will end up on baseball's ashpile in the United States if they insist on continuing to play Winter ball on their home island" (Louis Pickelner, *Williamsport* [Pa.] *Gazette and Bulletin*, Sept. 13; Peter Morris).

winter book A list of major-league players playing winter ball.

winter instructional league An off-season *instructional league* that usually starts in September and has a 48-game schedule.

winter league 1. Any of several professional baseball leagues outside the United States

and Canada where baseball is played after Aug. 31 and concludes before the start of the next championship season, such as those in the Caribbean area (Venezuela, Mexico, Puerto Rico, and the Dominican Republic). Winter leagues are not considered minor leagues. **2.** An off-season baseball league in the United States; e.g., the California Winter League during the first half of the 20th century, and those currently based in Florida and Arizona. **3.** Syn. of *hot stove league*.

winter meetings Traditional annual gathering (discontinued 1993–1997) of baseball team owners, general managers, major-league and minor-league executives, and associated officials, usually held in early December (which is technically not yet winter) in a warm locale, for the purpose of conducting league business, discussing and/or making trades, and building interest in the coming season. The importance of the winter meetings declined with the lapse of rigid trading deadlines; until the 1970s, the deadline for interleague trading was the final night of the winter meetings.

winter season That period following one baseball season and before the next when baseball is not played.

wipe-off sign A sign that nullifies the original sign; a sign that negates every live or active sign flashed to that point. For example, it is used to call off a hit-and-run play when a pitchout is sensed by the manager or coach. A batter may use the wipe-off sign when he is confused or unable to understand the rationale behind a signal. Keith Hernandez (*Pure Baseball*, 1994, p.32) noted, "The wipe-off sign on every team I played on was the same: a hand swiped across the chest. Is this the universal wipe-off sign? I sometimes wondered." Compare *indicator*, 2. Syn. *take-off sign*; *rub-off sign*.

wipeout *n.* A one-sided baseball game.

wipe out *v.* **1.** To win a one-sided game; e.g., "The Dodgers wiped out the Padres, 10–2." **2.** To throw out a baserunner.

"wipe the blood off" Advice to a player who has just gotten a weak hit, an obvious play on the fact that such hits are sometimes called "bleeders." The blood is to be wiped off either the bat or the ball. Syn. *"take the blood off."*

wireball A game that involves throwing a ball up in the air and aiming for the telephone or electrical lines. If the opponent catches the ball, it is an out. If the opponent misses the ball coming down, it is a single if the ball does not hit the line, a home run if the ball hits the wire on the way up, and a triple if the ball hits the wire on the way down. Another version has the different wires representing different bases.

wire cage *hist.* Syn. of *catcher's mask.* "By 1897, Spalding offered an array of wire cages, ranging in price from 75 cents to $5" (Kevin Paul Dupont, *The Boston Globe*, Apr. 3, 1987).

wire-to-wire From the beginning of a season to its end; specif., said of a team that spent every day of the season in first place. Only 10 major-league teams have accomplished this feat: 1923 New York Giants, 1927 New York Yankees, 1955 Brooklyn Dodgers, 1984 Detroit Tigers, 1990 Cincinnati Reds, 1997 Baltimore Orioles, 1998 Cleveland Indians, 2001 Seattle Mariners, 2003 San Francisco Giants, and 2005 Chicago White Sox.

wish ball A pitch that is thrown with the hope that the batter doesn't hit it. It is a specialty of pitchers who have "lost their stuff."

within oneself See *stay within oneself.* EXTENDED USE. Said of a player in other sports who does not try to do more than he is capable of doing. Baltimore Ravens receiver Eric Green (quoted in *The Baltimore Sun*, Nov. 2, 1998): "I wasn't playing my game. I was trying to do too much. I've got to get back to what Eric Green does best and that's play within himself and don't try to be a hero."

with the pitch Said of a straightaway hitter who applies the maximum force in his swing. "There is a baseball expression, that describes some hitters as hitting 'with the pitch' . . . [that is,] they 'get into' the ball wherever it is, in the strike zone" (Carl Stockdale and Rogers Hornsby, *Athletic Journal*, March 1945).

wizard *hist.* A phenomenal ballplayer. "Since last season's coming out party of sixteen straight wins the Idaho wizard [Walter John-son] hasn't suffered for lack of supporters" (*San Francisco Bulletin*, May 13, 1913; Gerald L. Cohen).

wobble 1. *v.* To falter or lose one's pitching or fielding effectiveness. IST USE. 1912 (*New York Tribune*, Sept. 11; Edward J. Nichols). **2.** *n.* A losing streak by a team leading in the standings.

wobbler A curveball. IST USE. 1907 (*New York Evening Journal*, Apr. 25; Edward J. Nichols).

wolf 1. *v.* For a spectator to heckle and complain. IST USE. 1902 (*The Sporting Life*, July 12, p.5; Edward J. Nichols). **2.** *n.* A spectator who constantly heckles or criticizes a player or a team. William G. Brandt (*Baseball Magazine*, Oct. 1932, p.495) quoted a dejected player: "Even our wolves have quit us."

womb is tilted Said of a player who finds an excuse not to play against a good team or bat against a dominating pitcher.

Women's Baseball League An international organization founded by Justine Siegal in 1997 "to enhance awareness and provide opportunity for female athletes to participate in the game of baseball and to promote the quality and standards of the game." Abbrev. *WBL.*

won-lost percentage A number expressed to the nearest thousandth that shows a pitcher's effectiveness or a team's relative standing in its league or division. It is created by dividing the total number of wins by the total number of wins and losses.

won-lost record The record of a club or pitcher stated with the number of wins followed by the number of losses. IST USE. 1913. "Although [Ed] Walsh's 'won-and-lost' record for 1910 was low, he had a good year" (*The Washington Post*, Aug. 31; Peter Morris).

wood 1. The baseball bat. The term is used in describing the contact made between the bat and the pitched ball. "They had the infield in, and I was able to get enough wood on it [the ball] to creep it through the infield" (Cincinnati Reds pitcher Randy Keisler, quoted in *The Baltimore Sun*, May 25, 2005). Milwaukee Brewers catcher Kelly Stinnett, protesting the plate umpire's call that a pitch nicked the batter, said, "I thought I heard it hit wood" (*Milwaukee Journal Sentinel*, Sept. 29, 1997). See also *good wood*, 1. **2.** Offensive capability. "[Mike] Lieberthal gets the edge for his . . . surprisingly potent wood (.328, 17 homers)" (*Sports Illustrated*, July 5, 1999).

wood bat A baseball bat made of wood. There is a minor controversy regarding the use of the term "wooden bat." Ruth Walker (*Christian Science Monitor*, May 13, 2005) reported, "The dictionary logic of 'wooden bats' is unassailable. 'Wood' is a noun; 'wooden' is the adjective that means 'made of wood.' . . . But the baseball guys in the newsroom say the lingo is 'wood bats.' . . . Just as it became necessary to connect the terms 'wood' and 'bat,' that little syllable 'en' started heading for the showers, and the phrase on the lips of the people is 'wood bat.'" For example, "wood bat tournaments" are conducted by the World Wood Bat Association.

wood-bat league An amateur league in which bats made of wood (instead of aluminum) are used; e.g., the Cape Cod League and the Shenandoah Valley League. Such leagues attract the best college players as they try to catch the eyes of professional scouts.

wood-bat test The challenge that a college position player faces in making the transition from aluminum bats in college to wooden bats in professional baseball. "[Jake Gautreau] has passed the wood-bat test, hitting .348 with power as Team USA's first baseman last summer" (*Baseball America*, June 11–24, 2001; Peter Morris).

wood-carrier A batter who often strikes out; one who carries his bat to and from the plate. IST USE. 1932. "The day Ed gets a drink of water for every at-bat he's just a 'wood-carrier' instead of an 'apple-crasher'" (William G. Brandt, *Baseball Magazine*, October, p.496).

wooden bat See *wood bat*.

wooden Indian 1. A batter who does not swing at the ball; one who waits out the pitcher. See also *Statue of Liberty*. ETYMOLOGY. From the impassive image of the carved wooden American Indian traditionally placed in front of cigar stores. **2.** A base coach who does not give a signal to a baserunner.

woodie A baseball card with a wood-looking

background; e.g., the 1962 cards created by Topps.

woodman A skilled hitter, but poor fielder. Compare *gloveman*, 2. Sometimes spelled "wood man."

woodpile A row of bats, such as in a bat rack or laid out in front of the dugout. Sometimes spelled "wood pile." IST USE. 1913. "Hub [Perdue] stooped over to pick his bat out of the wood pile" (*The Washington Post*, Aug. 3; Peter Morris).

wood player A good hitter but a poor fielder. Compare *leather player*. See also *lumber man*. IST USE. 1937 (*New York Daily News*, Jan. 21; Edward J. Nichols).

woods Syn. of *bushes*. IST USE. 1900. "Back to the woods with you and get a reputation" (*Brooklyn Eagle*, May 13; Peter Morris).

word sign A sign that is passed along verbally, perhaps encoded in a seemingly meaningless bit of chatter. For instance, the word "have" could be the sign for a hit and run: "Let's have a big inning" might be the sign to the man on base, who might yell to the batter, "Here's where we have the rally." See also *verbal sign*.

work 1. To pitch in a game; e.g., "Smith worked the fourth through the seventh innings." "The pitcher doesn't pitch nowadays, he 'works'" (*The Boston Globe*, reprinted in *The Sporting Life*, Apr. 27, 1912). IST USE. 1905. "Rube [Waddell] began to work then" (*Chicago Tribune*, June 10; Peter Morris). **2.** To take part in a game. "The player doesn't play, he 'works'" (*The Boston Globe*, reprinted in *The Sporting Life*, Apr. 27, 1912). IST USE. 1862 (*New York Sunday Mercury*, Aug. 3; Edward J. Nichols). **3.** To umpire. "The umpire doesn't umpire, he 'works'" (*The Boston Globe*, reprinted in *The Sporting Life*, Apr. 27, 1912). See also *work the plate*. IST USE. 1909 (*Baseball Magazine*, July, p.8; Edward J. Nichols). **4.** For a pitcher to try to get a batter out by tempting him with pitches just outside the strike zone. See also *work the corners*. IST USE. 1899 (Burt L. Standish, *Frank Merriwell's Double Shot*; Edward J. Nichols). **5.** For a batter to attempt to disrupt a pitcher's timing or to force him to throw many pitches. "In the big league it is necessary to 'work' or worry the pitcher if you hope to have any big advantage" (Ty Cobb, *Memoirs of Twenty Years in Baseball*, 1925; Peter Morris). "[Fernando Vina] can really work a pitcher—by the time the No. 2 batter comes up, he's usually seen everything the pitcher will throw" (anonymous scout, quoted in *Sports Illustrated*, March 27, 2000, p.139). **6.** For a pitcher to consistently attain a speed on his fastball throughout a game. "[Jonah Bayliss'] velocity has been good, working at 90–91 [mph]" (minor-league pitching coach Tom Burgmeier, quoted in *Baseball America*, June 23–July 6, 2003; Peter Morris).

work a pass Syn. of *coax a pass*. IST USE. 1902. "Work a pitcher for a pass" (*The Sporting Life*, Apr. 26, p.9; Edward J. Nichols).

worker A pitcher; e.g., "A fast worker wastes no time between pitches whereas a slow worker usually makes more pitches."

workhorse 1. An honorific term for a tireless pitcher who appears in many games or a large number of innings during a season. "[Bert Blyleven] was among history's great workhorses, throwing 200 or more innings 17 times" (Childs Walker, *The Baltimore Sun*, Jan. 10, 2006). See also *horse*, 1. Syn. *truck horse*, 2; *warhorse*. IST USE. 1913. "[Big Ed Walsh is] a workhorse and is the one man whom the [White] Sox can fall back upon in a tight struggle" (*San Francisco Bulletin*, March 10; Gerald L. Cohen). **2.** A durable catcher. "[Chief] Zimmer and [Jim] McGuire were what we called 'workhorses.' They would catch more than 100 games a year and work all the exhibition games" (Hugh Jennings, *Rounding Third*, 1925; Peter Morris).

working agreement 1. An affiliation between a major-league club and a minor-league club that it does not own but does supply with players. "The [New York] Giants disclosed the signing of a working agreement with the Albuquerque club in the Class A Western League" (*The New York Times*, March 28, 1956). **2.** An arrangement between a major-league club and a foreign club. "The [Tampa Bay Devil] Rays signed a three-year working agreement with the Yokohama BayStars of Japan's Central League. Yokohama will provide scouting information to the Rays on Jap-

anese players while the Rays will help the BayStars acquire players from the United States. The teams will also share information on baseball operations, scouting, player development and marketing" (*Baseball America*, Aug. 4–17, 2003; Peter Morris).

working coach A major-league coach whose responsibilities are more functional than instructional, such as throwing batting practice or catching the pitching staff during warmups or during the game.

work stoppage A strike by the players or a lockout by the owners. "The baseball owners and the baseball players must understand that if there is a . . . work stoppage, a lot of fans are going to be furious, and I'm one of them" (President George W. Bush, quoted in *The Baltimore Sun*, Aug. 17, 2002). As of this writing, baseball has had eight work stoppages (listed are the dates, type of stoppage, games lost, and issues involved): Apr. 1–13, 1972, strike (86 games; pensions); Feb. 14–25, 1973, lockout (during spring training; salary arbitration); March 1–17, 1976, lockout (during spring training; free agency); Apr. 1–8, 1980, strike (during spring training; free-agent compensation); June 12 to July 31, 1981, strike (712 games; free-agent compensation); Aug. 6–7, 1985, strike (25 postponed games were rescheduled and played; salary arbitration); Feb. 15 to March 18, 1990, lockout (during spring training; salary arbitration and salary cap), and Aug. 12, 1994, to Apr. 2, 1995, strike (920 games, no 1994 World Series, and a shortened 144-game 1995 season that started Apr. 25; salary cap and revenue sharing). From 1972 through 1994, every time the labor agreement between the players and owners expired, a work stoppage ensued; this pattern was broken in Aug. 2002 when the two sides agreed to a new Basic Agreement without a work stoppage. See also *strike*, 6.

work the corners To pitch to the edges of the strike zone. See also *work*, 4. IST USE. 1886. "[Dug] Crothers tried to work the corners of the plate for strikes, but he [umpire Clapp] would not have it, and many men were given bases on balls" (*The Sporting News*, June 21; Peter Morris).

work the count For a batter to force the

pitcher to throw a good pitch to hit by taking pitches and fouling off potential strikes. "The whole idea of working the count is to see a fastball in a good location (the hanging curve is perfectly acceptable, too)" (Keith Hernandez, *Pure Baseball*, 1994, p.138). "[Johnny] Damon took two strikes but worked the count full, hitting four fouls" (*The New York Times*, Oct. 20, 2004). See also *coax a pass*.

work the plate To umpire behind the plate. "I love to work the plate. You have to love to work the plate. . . . To be a major league umpire that's where it's at, the plate. If you can work the plate you go to the big leagues" (female umpire Pam Postema, quoted in Rick Phalen, *A Bittersweet Journey*, 2000, p.105). See also *work, 3*.

work-up A children's baseball game in which a player stays at bat until he or she is retired, at which point the batter goes to right field and everyone else moves up a position (right to center to left to third base to shortstop to second base to first base to catcher, with the pitcher becoming the batter). Variations include more than one batter, batters having the option to run, a player catching a fly ball immediately becoming the batter, errors afield sending the player to right field to begin all over again, and the catcher becoming the final defensive position. See also *One Eye Jim Bats*; *one-old-cat, 3*; *scrub, 1*; *one, two, three*. Syn. *move-up*.

World Baseball Association A proposed major league to consist of 32 teams in the United States, Mexico, Central America, South America, and Asia. Founded in 1974 by Sean Morton Downey Jr. and others, the league never got off the ground. It had planned a schedule of 72 to 84 games, the use of five designated hitters to replace defensive players who would remain in the game, three balls instead of four for a walk, and steals of home after the sixth inning to count as two runs. Franchises had been awarded to Columbus (Ohio), Jersey City (N.J.), Birmingham (Ala.), Memphis, Tampa–St. Petersburg, Mexico City, and Washington, D.C.

World Baseball Classic A 16-country, round-robin tournament to determine "the greatest baseball nation in the world." The brainchild of baseball commissioner Bud Selig, it was conceived as a way to further globalize the sport. The tournament is baseball's version of soccer's World Cup and is sanctioned by Major League Baseball, the Major League Baseball Players Association, and the International Baseball Federation. Japan defeated Cuba, 10–6, in the inaugural Classic held March 2006 in three countries. The other participating countries were China, Chinese Taipei, South Korea, Australia, Canada, the United States, Puerto Rico, Mexico, Venezuela, the Dominican Republic, Panama, South Africa, Italy, and the Netherlands. Many major leaguers participated because of their desire to "represent" their countries. The Classic enforced pitch counts and took precautions to prevent injuries. The second classic will be held in 2009, and then every four years. Abbrev. *WBC*. Compare *World Cup*.

world champion An honorific used to describe the winner of the World Series.

world championship The distinction of having won the World Series.

World Cup An international tournament sanctioned by the International Baseball Federation in which baseball teams representing 16 nations compete in odd-numbered years. The first tournament was held in 1938. Until 1996, the competition was limited to amateur players; since 1996, professional minor-league players have competed, but major-league baseball has not allowed its players to participate. Compare *World Baseball Classic*.

World's Champions The winner of the World's Championship Series. The term was first used by the *New York Clipper* to refer to the St. Louis Browns who won the 1885 World's Championship Series. The New York Giants emblazoned the term on a banner depicting their victory over the Philadelphia Athletics in the 1905 World's Championship Series, as well as on the shirts of Giants players for 1906.

World's Championship Series 1. The post-season series of contests between the champion of the National League and the champion of the American Association beginning in 1884. Although the 1884 series was touted as the "Championship of the United States" or the "United States Championship," *The Sporting News* referred to the series as "the world's championship" and *The Sporting Life* referred to the victorious Providence Grays as *Champions of the World*. In 1886, a series of games for "the world's championship" was arranged between Chicago (representing the National League) and St. Louis (representing the American Association): the editor of *Spalding's Official Base Ball Guide* for 1887 noted that the two leagues "both entitle their championship contests each season as those for the base ball championship of the United States," hence the grander term for the postseason showdown between the two "champions of the United States." It was a common advertising practice in the 1880s to use the words "world" and "world's" to signify the best. By 1887, the term "World's Championship Series" had become established for the postseason series of contests. **2.** The postseason series of games between the champion of the National League and the champion of the American League beginning in 1903. The term

World's Champions. "Turkey" Mike Donlin, who led the New York Giants to the club's first World Series in 1905. *George Grantham Bain Collection, Library of Congress*

was in use as late as 1912; however, the term "Worlds Championship Series" was used for the programs for the 1921, 1922, 1923, 1927, and 1928 series, the term "World Championship Series" was used for the 1925 Washington scorecard, and the term "World's Championship" was used for the program for the 1931 series. The term was gradually shortened to *World's Series* and then to *World Series*. Syn. *Championship of the World*.

World Series The series of games played in the fall between the pennant winners of the American League and the National League to decide the "world champion." The first team to win four games (five games in 1903 and 1919–1921) is the champion. Games 1, 2, 6, and 7 are scheduled in the city of the club whose league was the winner of that season's All-Star Game. The modern World Series first took place in 1903, when the contests were known as the *World's Championship Series*, and later as the *World's Series*. *Spalding's Official Base Ball Guide* began using the term in 1917, the *Reach Official American League Base Ball Guide* in 1931, and *The Sporting News* in 1964. The first series to label its program "World Series" was held in 1936; however, the Cleveland scorecard for 1920 and the Washington scorecard for 1924 were labeled "World Series." In 1994, for the first time in 90 years, October came and went with no World Series because of a players' strike. See also *World's Series*; *World Serious*; *Brush Rules*. Abbrev. *WS*, 1. Syn. *Autumn Classic*; *Fall Classic*; *big classic*; *big series*; *big show*, 2; *Commissioner's Games*; *diamond classic*; *promised land*; *Series, the*. 1ST USE. 1911. "The opening game of the world series between the New York team of the National League and the Philadelphia team of the American League will be played at the Polo Grounds" (*The New York Times*, Oct. 6). USAGE NOTE. The term "World Series" has been used for other baseball championship series, such as the Triple-A World Series, the NCAA College World Series, the Little League World Series, the American Legion World Series, the Caribbean World Series, the Women's Baseball World Series, and the World Series in the Negro leagues. ETYMOLOGY. Contraction of "World's Championship

World Series. 1935 World Series, with managers Mickey Cochrane (left) of the Detroit Tigers and Charlie Grimm of the Chicago Cubs. *Photograph by Joseph Baylor Roberts*

Series" and later "World's Series." That the term "World Series" was named for the *The World* (New York) newspaper is a myth. Though the tabloid was often given to flamboyant self-promotion, *The World* never claimed any connection with postseason baseball. According to the late Doug Pappas' review (*Outside the Lines* [SABR Business of Baseball newsletter], Fall 2001) of issues of *The World*, "there's not a word suggesting any link between the paper and the series." EXTENDED USE. High-level contests in other sports, games, and activities; e.g., the World Series of Poker, the World Series of College Chess, and the World Series of Birding. "Must We Lose the Industrial World Series?" (*Business Week* headline, Nov. 17, 1986).

World Series Most Valuable Player Award 1. The *Babe Ruth Award*, an annual award presented from 1949 to 2002 by the New York chapter of the Baseball Writers Association of America, in memory of Ruth, following his death in 1948. It was voted upon some time after the World Series had concluded. The award was eclipsed by the *SPORT Magazine Award*. **2.** The *SPORT Magazine Award*, an annual award presented since 1955, originally by *SPORT* magazine in cooperation with the Chevrolet Motor Co.

(the magazine ceased publication in 2000 and is no longer involved with the award). It is voted on during the final game of the World Series, originally by the magazine's editors but now by a committee of reporters and officials in attendance, and presented immediately following the conclusion of the Series. Chevrolet presents the winner with a new automobile. The award is now sanctioned by Major League Baseball and has eclipsed the Babe Ruth Award in prestige and public recognition.

World Series ring The circlet awarded to the players, manager, and coaches of the team that wins the World Series, emblematic of a champion, and supposedly the ultimate reward for a professional baseball player. Players often say that the foremost reason they play baseball is not to attain personal records but to earn "the ring." Designs vary. For example, members of the 2003 Florida Marlins each received a 14-karat gold ring with 228 white diamonds, 13 rubies, and a single teal diamond in the eye of a marlin. Rings were first awarded in 1923; before that time, diamond stick pins were the norm for the winning team.

World Serious A cynical and facetious name for *World Series* that pokes fun at the self-importance surrounding the event. Satirist Ring W. Lardner almost invariably used the word "serious" when any of his fictional player-narrators referred to any type of series: " 'Serious' was apparently Lardner's favorite pun, for he attributed it to almost all his ball-players—an inconsistency in what was otherwise a careful effort to give each of them individuality" (George W. Hilton, ed., *The Annotated Baseball Stories of Ring W. Lardner 1914–1919*, 1995, p.40; Peter Morris). "It was the first time in world serious history that a man named Wambsganss had ever made a triple play assisted by consonants only" (Ring W. Lardner, quoted in Mike Sowell, *The Pitch That Killed*, 1989, p.273). Also lowercased as "world serious."

World's Series An early term for *World Series* during the first part of the 20th century, although the term was used earlier: "The Great World's Series" (*Reach's Official American Association Base Ball Guide* in

1887 for the 1886 postseason series), "the world's series" (*St. Louis Globe-Democrat*, Sept. 21, 1887), and "the great World's Series" (*The New York Times*, Oct. 12, 1888) refer to the games between the champions of the National League and of the American Association. It is a contraction of *World's Championship Series*. The term was used by *Spalding's Official Base Ball Guide* through 1916, the *Reach Official American League Base Ball Guide* through 1930, and *The Sporting News* from 1942 through 1963. The program for the 1940 series was labeled "World's Series" and that for the 1944 series was labeled "Worlds Series." "In a number of world's series the final result has been greatly influenced by some one situation that was not reckoned with as even a probability" (American League umpire Billy Evans, Newspaper Enterprise Association syndicated column, Sept. 23, 1919). Also lowercased as "world's series."

World Umpires Association The labor union of major-league umpires, formed in 2000 to replace the *Major League Baseball Umpires Association*. Abbrev. *WUA*.

worm burner 1. A hard-hit ball that rolls or skids quickly across the ground without bouncing or losing much speed. Syn. *worm killer*. 2. [softball term] A low, hard pitch, esp. in Over the Line and fast pitch softball. Stephanie Salter (*Women's Sports and Fitness*, July 1987) noted that the pitch, thrown extremely fast and so low that it scrapes over the plate, "appears at crucial moments in [a] game, usually when [the] pitcher has lost her 'stuff' [and it is] hazardous to animals, plant life, catcher's shins, and umpire's feet."

worm killer Syn. of *worm burner*, 1.

worst to first Said of a team that went from last place one year to first place the next year.

wounded duck "A sick-looking blooper that drops in for a base hit" (Steve Salerno, *Los Angeles Times*, May 15, 1994). See also *dying quail*. ETYMOLOGY. A poorly thrown football whose slow or awkward flight is similar to that of a bleeding duck. "[Atlanta Falcons quarterback Joey] Harrington tossed a wounded duck into a stiff breeze that was intercepted by Buffalo cornerback Terrence

McGee" (Peter King, *Sports Illustrated*, Aug. 27, 2007, p.95).

wound tight 1. Said of the potential energy visibly present in an athletic body, under firm control but ready to become kinetic in an instant. "If a boy is wound tight, he lets you imagine him running when he's just walking. He has a live body" (Kevin Kerrane, *Dollar Sign on the Muscle*, 1984, p.89). ETYMOLOGY. Kerrane suggested that the scouting metaphor may have originated at the racetrack: "Sometimes a horse is said to be 'wound tight' when in the starting gate it seems doubly poised, both relaxed and cocked." 2. Said of a strong physique with no apparent fat, sometimes implying inflexibility. 3. Said of an uptight mental approach to the game. Compare *loose*, 3. "Baseball players who have played other sports can enter pro ball tightly wound, but they get looser the more they focus on the game" (Jack Zduriencik, quoted in Alan Schwarz, BaseballAmerica.com, Nov. 14, 2006).

WP 1. Scorecard and box score abbrev. for *wild pitch*. 2. Abbrev. for *winning pitcher*.

WPA Abbrev. for *win probability added*.

wrap For a batter to hold his elbows high with the bat barrel behind his head (Alan Eskew, *Baseball America*, Sept. 15–28, 2003; Peter Morris).

wrapper A cellophane or wax-paper enclosure for a baseball card that has become a collectible in its own right.

wrap the ball around his neck To throw a brushback pitch. "Several years ago [Mike] Kelly seemed to be afraid of a ball when thrown swiftly and would often step back out of the box when an in-curve going directly over the plate was pitched. . . . The pitchers were 'onto' him, and would 'wrap the ball around his neck,' to use a base ball phrase" (*St. Louis Post-Dispatch*, Sept. 6, 1888; Peter Morris).

wrap up To win a division or series title.

wrecker An organizer of a league that competed against an established league. The term was used derogatorily by newspapers unsympathetic to the cause of the 1884 Union Association, and was applied to the organizers of the 1889 insurrection that created the Players' League. "The Brotherhood players withdrew ... to better their condition [yet] are denounced as 'rebels' and 'wreckers'" (*New York Clipper*, Nov. 23, 1889; Peter Morris).

wrecking crew A group of heavy hitters. "One can draw many parallels between the sluggers [Hank Aaron and Joe Adcock] who, with [Eddie] Mathews added, form the most fearsome wrecking crew in the league" (Bob Wolf, *The Sporting News*, 1960). IST USE. 1912. "The [Chicago Cubs] 'wrecking crew' was called forth repeatedly in an effort to turn the tide against [John] McGraw's young 'spitball' dispenser" (Irving Vaughan, *Chicago Record-Herald*, Aug. 17; Peter Morris).

Wrigley Field 1. Home field of the Chicago Cubs since 1916, located at the corner of Clark and Addison on Chicago's North Side. It opened in 1914 as Weeghman Park, the home field of the Chicago Whales of the Federal League, and was known as Cubs Park from 1919 to 1926; it was renamed Wrigley Field in 1926 for longtime owner William F. Wrigley Jr., the heir to the Wrigley chewing gum fortune. The field is noted for day baseball (until 1988 when lights were installed), natural grass, wind conditions (the breeze may or may not blow in from Lake Michigan), and, since 1937, an outfield wall of Boston ivy. A ground-rule double is granted when the ball sticks in the ivy. See also *friendly confines*. **2.** Home field of the Los Angles Angels (American Association) from 1925 to 1957 and of the Los Angeles Angels (American League) in 1961. It was the site of many baseball movies, including *Pride of the Yankees* (1942).

Wrigleyville Nickname for Wrigley Field and its immediate neighborhood in Chicago. The day after the first night game was completed there, the lead sentence in an Associated Press report read: "Wrigleyville looked no different Tuesday" (*Bangor* [Maine] *Daily News*, Aug. 10, 1988). "The citizens of Wrigleyville had been pining for this day [when the Cubs drafted Mark Prior]" (Andy Latack, *ESPN The Magazine*, July 22, 2002).

wrinkle 1. A curveball with little break, delivered with speed. IST USE. 1908 (*New York Evening Journal*, May 24; Edward J. Nichols). **2.** A little break of a curveball.

wrist ball "The 'wrist ball' is only a contortion of the wrist and hands, resulting in a slow curve" (John J. Evers and Hugh S. Fullerton, *Touching Second: The Science of Baseball*, 1910; Peter Morris).

wrist hitter A hitter who obtains added power from a quick, timely turn of the wrists, rather than relying on pure body strength. Wrist hitters include Ernie Banks, Hank Aaron, and Alfonso Soriano.

write out a pass *hist.* To issue a base on balls. IST USE. 1910 (*New York Tribune*, July 13; Edward J. Nichols).

wrong armer *hist.* A left-handed pitcher. Syn. *wrong sider*.

wrong base The incorrect base toward which an outfielder returns a batted ball. The term occurs in the phrase "throw to the wrong base"; e.g., with a runner on first base and a single hit to the outfield, the outfielder throws to third base in a vain attempt to put out the runner advancing from second base, thereby allowing the batter-runner to reach second base on his single. "He [Joe DiMaggio] never seemed to throw to the wrong base" (Richard Ben Cramer, *Joe DiMaggio: The Hero's Life*, 2000, p.429). Compare *right base*.

wronger sex A "male grandstand manager" (Racine Belles yearbook, 1944). The term was used derisively by the women of the All-American Girls Professional Baseball League.

wrong field Syn. of *opposite field*.

wrong hand The left hand of a left-handed pitcher. "Doc Amole, a young man who throws with the wrong hand" (*Detroit Free Press*, Apr. 20, 1900; Dean A. Sullivan). USAGE NOTE. Nearly a century later, former Baltimore Orioles pitcher Mike Flanagan used the term "wrong-hander" for a left-handed pitcher during a televised contest (Apr. 3, 2000).

wrong leg The lead leg of a baserunner who is leaning too far forward. "The pitcher has his weapon, his throw to first. If he catches the runner 'on the wrong leg'—that is, with his weight already thrown forward, toward second base—the runner will probably be picked off base" (Arnold Hano, *A Day in the Bleachers*, 1955, p.36; James D. Szalontai).

wrong sider Syn. of *wrong armer.*

wrong turn A move to the left of first base made by the batter-runner. A batter-runner who has made a move toward second base on an overrun of first base can be tagged out.

WS **1.** Abbrev. for *World Series.* **2.** Abbrev. for *win shares.*

WUA Abbrev. for *World Umpires Association.*

WW Broadcaster Phil Rizzuto's scorecard notation for "wasn't watching."

WX Abbrev. for *win expectancy.*

WXRL Abbrev. for *wins expected above replacement and adjusted for lineup faced.*

XY

x 1. The symbol used in club standings to indicate that a team has clinched its division title. 2. The symbol used in box scores to indicate something out of the ordinary, such as an extraordinary play or occurrence. It is used rarely and only when the box-score compiler feels compelled to append a note to the summary of a game.

XBH Abbrev. for *extra-base hit*.

X-Factor A "rule" that free agents first pass a team physical exam before signing a contract. ETYMOLOGY. Relief pitcher Xavier Hernandez, whom the Baltimore Orioles had to pay not to pitch because of an undisclosed injury (*The Baltimore Sun*, Feb. 16, 2000).

XR Abbrev. for *extrapolated runs*.

X-ray test An examination using X-ray equipment of baseball bats for possible corking. The test was first employed when the bat used by New York Mets infielder Howard Johnson to hit his 27th home run of the 1987 season was impounded and X-rayed. According to the official results, the test did not reveal cork or other foreign substance. This was not the first time an X-ray machine made baseball headlines. According to Jerry Howarth (*Baseball Lite*, 1986), the day after Dizzy Dean was beaned, a headline read: "X-rays of Dean's head show nothing."

XW Abbrev. for *extrapolated wins*.

y The symbol used in club standings to indicate that a team has clinched a postseason playoff berth.

"ya gotta believe!" The slogan of the 1973 New York Mets, a team that was in last place on Aug. 30 but still managed to win the National League pennant. The battle cry was originated by relief pitcher Tug McGraw after each of the team's improbable wins.

yak attack Syn. of *yakker*. "The curveball can be called a . . . yakker or yak attack" (R.J. Reynolds, quoted in *Baseball Digest*, Jan. 1987).

yakker 1. A mean, sharp-breaking, overhand *curveball*. See also *yellow hammer*. Syn. *yak attack*. IST USE. 1979. "Total command of the yakker" (Thomas Boswell, *The Washington Post*, May 21, 1979). ETYMOLOGY. Mike Whiteford (*How to Talk Baseball*, 1987, p.136) and Patrick Ercolano (*Fungoes, Floaters and Fork Balls*, 1987, p.215) maintain that the term is derived from "yawker," another name for the flicker, a woodpecker whose undulauing flight resembles the path of a curveball. 2. A fastball. The term was used by Dennis Eckersley for his fastball (Joe Morgan, *Baseball for Dummies*, 1998, p.357). Bill "Spaceman" Lee (*The Wrong Stuff*, 1984, p.171) wrote that if Eckersley threw a "yakker for your coolu," it meant "you were going to get nailed in the ass with a fastball."

yan Short for *yannigan*.

yanigan Var. of *yannigan*.

yank 1. To remove a pitcher from a game or the pitching rotation. "[Scott] Kamieniecki was yanked shortly after his 75th pitch" (*The Baltimore Sun*, May 13, 1998). See also *derrick*. IST USE. 1909. "It was all right for [Detroit Tigers manager Hughie Jennings] to try [Ed] Summers again on a clear day, but after the knuckle baller had shown poor form . . . the wise manager would in such an important series, when one game meant so much, have yanked him out" (*The Sporting News*,

Oct. 21; Peter Morris). **2.** To hit a home run; e.g., "Wade Boggs got to yank a two-run homer for a 3–0 Devil Rays' lead" (*The Baltimore Sun*, May 11, 1998). **3.** To pull a ball down the foul line.

Yankee Doodle game The game of baseball, the national pastime. IST USE. 1902 (*The Sporting Life*, Apr. 26, p.8; Edward J. Nichols).

Yankee Doodle hitter A weak hitter (*Famous Sluggers and Their Records of 1932*, 1933).

Yankee hater One who has a long-standing aversion to the New York Yankees. "We hated the Yankees, of course, the whole country did. . . . They were too perfect, too automated, too cool" (Pete Hamill, *The Washington Post*, March 9, 1981). Major reasons why the Yankees are hated include: larger payroll and the conviction that money can buy anything, loathing for the city of New York, dominance on the field, and arrogance of owner George Steinbrenner. New Jersey lawyer Mike Moorby created a "Yankee Hater" baseball cap with an interlocking "yh" on the front: "It's Yankees hating for the more sophisticated palate" (*The Baltimore Sun*, June 19, 2004). William B. Mead (*The Official New York Yankees Hater's Handbook*, 1983) wrote, "We hate the New York Yankees for many reasons. They're spoiled rotten. They think they're such Hot Stuff. Their owner is obnoxious. They pout, sulk and whine, no matter how much they're paid and pampered. Their fans are gross and crude. . . . Most all good Americans hate the Yankees. It is a value we cherish and pass along to our children." Mead also noted, "The first Yankee haters were New Yorkers. They were fans of the New York Giants."

Yankee killer A player (esp. a pitcher) who performs well against the New York Yankees; e.g., pitchers Frank Lary (28–13 lifetime vs. the Yankees) and Chuck Finley (17–10 lifetime vs. the Yankees).

Yankee Profile A *profiling system* that adapts the traditional tools looked for by scouts with the reality that the value of a specific tool varies based on a player's position; e.g., a power-hitting first baseman can become an outstanding major leaguer without great skills in such areas as speed, defense, and arm strength. The Yankee Profile prioritizes the importance of tools for each position, so that extra weight can be given to the skills that are most important at that position. The system was devised in the late 1980s by New York Yankees cross-checker Bill Livesey and other members of the club's scouting staff. "After analyzing the successful organizations of the era and evaluating their rosters on a position-by-position basis, Livesey and Yankee scouts developed a scouting system that became known throughout baseball as 'The Yankee Profile'" (Josh Boyd, *Baseball America*, March 31–Apr. 13, 2002; Peter Morris).

Yankees Nickname for the American League East Division franchise in New York City. The franchise originated as the Baltimore Orioles (1901–1902). Though the club was known as the *Highlanders* upon relocation from Baltimore in 1903, the press began referring to it as "Yankees" in 1904, allegedly because that fit the headlines better; the name was common by 1906 and became the official name of the club in 1913. The club was also known as the New York Americans, the *Greater New Yorks* (1903–1906), the *Hilltoppers* (1903–1912), and *Griffmen* (1903–1908) while Clark C. Griffith was manager; it is also currently known as the *Bronx Bombers* and Yanks. IST USE. 1904. Barry Popik reports that "New York Yankees" made its appearance in the *New York Evening Journal* in a sports section edited by Harry Beecher. *The Sporting News Record Book* for 1937 noted the name "Yankees" as applied to the New York club was originated by sportswriters Mark Roth (*New York Globe*) and Sam Crane (*New York Evening Journal*). After the team held spring training in Richmond, Va., in 1904, a newspaper headline appeared declaring, "Yankees Will Head Home From South Today." The *Boston Herald* (June 21, 1904) carried a story that Boston Red Sox outfielder Patsy Dougherty was traded to New York with the headline "Dougherty As A Yankee." Lyle Spatz reports that the name "Yankees" was used by James Price (*New York Press*) in July 1904. USAGE NOTE. The name "Yankees" was used as early as 1875 in reference to the Boston Red Stockings of the

National Association: "The Chicago people ... came out 5000 strong, hoping their nine would terminate the western tour of the Yankees by a brilliant victory, but their hopes were blasted" (*Boston Daily Advertiser*, June 15, 1875). ETYMOLOGY. The term dates to the 1680s when it was current mostly among seafarers and pirates. Dutchmen were referred to by the name "Janke" as a diminutive for Johannes, or John; sailors would embellish this to "Jan Kaas" (John Cheese) as a term of contempt. Since most piracy took place in American waters, "Jan Kaas" became "Yankee" and was applied to Americans as the 18th century dawned. The term "Yankee" originally referred to a New Englander, and later a Northerner during the Civil War.

Yankee Shuttle Syn. *underground railroad.*

Yankee Stadium Home field of the New York Yankees from 1923 to 2008, also known as *The House That Ruth Built.* Located in the Bronx, the stadium went through a major renovation between the end of the 1973 season and the opening of the 1976 season; during the rebuilding, the Yankees played at Shea Stadium. It included monuments to Babe Ruth, Lou Gehrig, Miller Huggins, Mickey Mantle, and Joe DiMaggio. Baseball lore contends that a fair ball was never hit out of Yankee Stadium, although Frank Howard (twice) and Josh Gibson may have performed the feat. A new stadium, called the "new" Yankee Stadium, was built across the street from the former stadium and became the home of the Yankees beginning in 2009.

yannigan A *rookie*, not a regular player; a player on the second team in a spring-training camp game. "The Yannigans hooked it on to the Regulars in great style this afternoon. Yannigans 9, Regulars 5" (*San Francisco Examiner*, March 24, 1912; Peter Tamony). See also *yonagan.* Syn. *yan; yanigan.* 1ST USE. 1893. "Baltimore's Yannigan [George] Treadway with the hoarse laugh and the round, tanned face made a hit in Chicago" (*The Sporting News*, July 22; Peter Morris). USAGE NOTE. The term received national publicity in 1906. According to Bill James (*The Bill James Historical Baseball Abstract*, 1986), Brooklyn held a benefit game for the survivors of the 1906 San Francisco earthquake, pitting the Yannigans against the Regulars; the Yannigans won.

ETYMOLOGY. The term appears in other slang contexts; e.g., the "yannigan bags" that lumberjacks, prospectors, and others used to carry their clothing. Joseph McBride (*High and Inside*, 1980) stated that the baseball term derived from the carpetbag, and was a reference to the disreputability of rookies and subs: "According to Lee Allen, Jerry Denny, a third baseman for Providence in 1884, was responsible for dumping the name 'yannigan' on rookies." There is no clear link between this term and a word in another language or an earlier form of English or an English dialect; no word close to "yannigan" appeared in John S. Farmer and W.E. Henley's *Slang and Its Analogues* (1905). James Stevens (*American Speech*, Dec. 1925) suggested that the word was born in American lumber camps: "Like such old terms as 'cross-cut,' 'bitted,' 'yannigan,' and 'snubline' they had the ringing life of the timber in them."

The root of the term may be Celtic, according to Charles Dryden (*The Washington Post*, Apr. 10, 1904; Barry Popik) in an article entitled "Origin of 'Yannigans.'" Dryden traced the term "yanigan" to Philadelphian Mike Grady, a "catcher and orator of renown"; Connie Mack and Lave Cross claimed that Grady fathered the term, which was first applied to Philadelphia players 10 years earlier. Quoting Dryden: "In 1894 the Quaker team went into camp at Hampton Roads, Va. The immortal Grady was a member of the party. The manager placed Mike in charge of the also-rans, or second team, and the ease with which the Regulars walloped the bitumen out of the dubs inspired Mike to produce a word that lives in the language of the game. In the ancient Celtic tongue Yanigan means anything that can be easily beaten, like carpets or a soft-boiled egg. Being a student of the classics, Mike was familiar with the word. He had it stowed away in his mind, but never found occasion to spring it until as captain of the second team his proud spirit blazed under the sting of constant defeat." As the Quakers emerged from their quarters, Grady yelled, "Come on, you Yanigan; come on and get it again!"

John Thorn unearthed evidence that suggested the term may be an eponym. Citing an undated 1898 news clip from *The World* (New York) titled "Armless, Legless Baseball Pitchers" in the Cy Seymour scrapbooks at the National Baseball Library and Archives, Cooperstown, N.Y., and published in his *The Armchair Book of Baseball II* (1987, pp.309–10), Thorn noted that the clip was "replete with unexpected pleasures" that included "the stunningly offhand solution to one of the game's most perplexing mysteries—the origin of the epithet 'yannigan,' reserved for scrub or second-rate players." Quoting *The World*: "Another cripple who was famous as a ballplayer was 'Con' Yannigan, who made a big reputation around Hartford, Connecticut, several years ago. He was a first baseman and had a cork leg. Yannigan was brought out by 'Steve' Brady . . . [who] considered him one of the best first basemen he ever saw. A great play of his was to block off base runners with his game leg. Opposing players could sharpen their spikes to a razor edge, but 'Con' didn't scare for a cent."

yard 1. A baseball park or field; e.g., "Catch One at the Yard" (Baltimore Orioles promotion to attend a game at Oriole Park at Camden Yards in Baltimore, 1998). "A trip to the yard conveys a baseball memory that shouldn't be lost" (Rick LaRue, quoted in *The Washington Post*, Jan. 7, 1990). See also *ballyard*. IST USE. 1892 (*Brooklyn Daily Eagle*, May 1, p.4). 2. See *go yard*.

yardball A home run. "Today, you go to the suburbs, just go deep or leave the yard. A home run is sometimes also referred to as a yardball" (Scripps Howard News Service article reporting on current player terms used and heard by Pittsburgh Pirates outfielder R.J. Reynolds, Sept. 17, 1986).

yard work A home run (*Athletics* [Oakland A's magazine], Sept. 2005).

year See *major-league year.*

Year of the Asterisk The 1981 major-league season, which was interrupted and disoriented by a players' strike (*Newsweek*, Aug. 10, 1981). See also *asterisk*, 1.

Year of the Family The 1986 major-league season, so proclaimed by baseball commissioner Peter Ueberroth. Teams took action to appeal to the family trade, offering discounts, giveaways, fireworks, and concerts. The Pittsburgh Pirates opened special family seating sections where the sale of beer was prohibited.

Year of the Hitter The 1930 major-league season in which the collective batting average of National League hitters was .303 and that of American League hitters was .288.

Year of the No-Hitter The 1990 major-league season, which saw seven no-hitters. There were also seven no-hitters during the 1991 season.

Year of the Pitcher The 1968 major-league season in which the collective batting average was .236 and the collective earned run average was 2.99. There were 339 shutouts. The year featured Denny McLain's 31–6 record, Bob Gibson's 1.12 earned run average, Don Drysdale's 58⅓ consecutive scoreless innings, and seven shutouts by Mets rookie Jerry Koosman.

Year of the Rookie The 1986 major-league season. "[Jose] Canseco, [Wally] Joyner, [Pete] Incaviglia, [Todd] Worrell, [Barry] Bonds, [Mark] Eichhorn. The fresh names and faces that stamped the 1986 baseball season 'The Year of the Rookie' are growing more familiar and famous each day" (Don Banks, *St. Petersburg Times*, March 22, 1987). "Not since the early '50s have so many splendid kids arrived at once" (Thomas Boswell, *The Washington Post*, Oct. 5, 1986).

Year without a World Series 1994, because of the players' strike.

yellow 1. *hist.* Inferior; of poor quality. A "yellow game" is one characterized by inexcusably bad play and a "yellow team" is known for its sloppy play. "Yellow ball" was defined as "poor playing" (*Brooklyn Daily Eagle*, May 1, 1892), and "yellow misplay" was defined as inexcusable ineffectiveness (*New York Press*, July 13, 1890; Edward J. Nichols). "A very yellow decision by [umpire] Lynch gave Caruthers a base on balls" (*The World* [New York], Oct. 27, 1889). IST USE. 1888. " 'Yellow' may describe an indifferent game, but this performance would exhaust the whole catalogue of colors" (*San Fran-*

cisco Examiner, Jan. 9; Peter Morris). **2.** Cowardly. Ty Cobb (*Busting 'Em and Other Big League Stories*, 1914; Peter Morris) described a fight that resulted from one player calling a teammate "yellow" and commented that "yellow" is "a fighting word in the Big Leagues." Ring W. Lardner (*Chicago Tribune*, Sept. 8, 1918) wrote about a fight during the 1918 World Series: "Heine was calling Tyler yellow as is the custom, and Knabe yelled at Wagner that he had a fine license to call anybody yellow because he was yellow himself." See also *yellow streak*.

yellow baseball A yellow-dyed baseball used experimentally as early as 1928 and intended to decrease the possibility of beanball injuries by providing greater visibility, esp. with a bleacher background of white shirts. The yellow baseball was used in a game between Columbia and Fordham universities on Apr. 27, 1938 (both coaches suggested the experiment be continued), and in the first game of a doubleheader between the Brooklyn Dodgers and St. Louis Cardinals at Ebbets Field on Aug. 2, 1938 (the yellow dye stained the players' hands). The originator of the yellow baseball was New York color scientist Frederic H. Rahr (*New York Herald Tribune*, Apr. 21, 1938; Peter Morris). Compare *orange baseball*. Syn. *stitched lemon*.

yellow hammer A sharply breaking *curveball*. Satchel Paige used the term for an overhand curve. ETYMOLOGY. The term is a colloquial name for a common bunting found in Europe. According to Bill Young (personal communication, Jan. 9, 2008), "The European settlers in North America who saw the flashes of yellow during the flight of the yellow-shafted flicker [a woodpecker] thought the bird looked like the European bunting (which is not closely related) and used the same name, 'yellowhammer.' The woodpecker is now officially known as the Northern flicker (*Colaptes auratus*)." The flicker's undulating flight (from 10 to 100 feet above the ground) is said to resemble the path of a curveball.

yellow streak A trait of cowardice. Christy Mathewson (*Pitching in a Pinch*, 1912; Peter Morris) wrote, "[There is an element that] enters into all forms of athletics. Tennis play-

ers call it nervousness, and ball players, in the frankness of the game, call it a 'yellow streak.' It is the inability to stand the gaff, the weakening in the pinches." See also *yellow*, 2.

yield For a pitcher to give up hits and runs; e.g., "Smith yielded three runs on five hits."

yodeler The *third base coach*, esp. a noisy one who may be trying to unnerve the pitcher or who shouts instructions to the runner on second base. IST USE. 1934 (*Akron* [Ohio] *Beacon Journal*).

Yogiism One of a series of aphorisms and comments issued by catcher, coach, and manager Lawrence Peter "Yogi" Berra, some of which have woven themselves into folklore status. Some are gaffs, some are syntactical errors, but many of them contain their own special logic. Some may be apocryphal. Also spelled "Yogism"; "Yogi-ism." Syn. *Berraism*. A small sampling:

On whether he would make a good manager: "I've been playing for 18 years, and you can observe a lot by watching."

On how many slices he wanted to have his pizza cut into: "Better make it four, I don't think I can eat eight."

On a popular restaurant: "Nobody goes there any more, it's too crowded."

Yogiism. Yogi Berra. *National Baseball Library and Archives, Cooperstown, N.Y.*

On a pennant race: "It ain't over till it's over."

On declining attendance in Kansas City, Mo.: "If people don't want to come to the ballpark, how are you gonna stop them?"

On explaining baseball: "Ninety percent of this game is half mental."

On Yogiisms: "I really didn't say everything I said."

yonagan *hist.* A second-year player in the National League. "Irrespective of a man's real age . . . in his second year he is looked upon as a 'yonagan'" (*Bismarck* [N.D.] *Daily Tribune*, May 4, 1889). See also *yannigan*.

"you can't steal first" **1.** An expression signifying that baseball has its precise limits; e.g., first base is the one base a player must earn and cannot steal. The cliché expresses the basic truth that the best baserunner in the world is of little use to a team if he cannot hit enough to get on base with some regularity. W.J. O'Connor (*St. Louis Post-Dispatch*, Apr. 8, 1915; Peter Morris) wrote, "Miller Huggins is organizing for the coming season what looks like the best base-running club in either league . . . However, if Mike Mowrey were here, he unquestionably would opine, 'Well, you can't steal first base,' as this is the pet theory of every splay-footed spav who can't steal second, third or a signal." **2.** An expression describing Rule 7.08(i) of the *Official Baseball Rules*, that the umpire shall declare out any runner who runs the bases in reverse order. The rule was created in 1920 after Herman "Germany" Schaefer stole second base, then went back and stole first base to draw a throw from the catcher so that the runner on third base could steal home.

"you can't walk off the island" Advice given to Latin-born players from island countries (esp. the Dominican Republic) that, to attract the attention of major-league scouts, they needed to show hitting ability, not the patience to draw bases on balls. Consequently, many Latin-American players become free swingers, such as Roberto Clemente and Sammy Sosa. IST USE. 1987. "You have to swing like a man. A walk won't get you off the island" (Atlanta Braves shortstop Rafael Ramirez, quoted in David H. Nathan, *Baseball Quotations*, 1991, quote 579).

"you can't win 'em all" A philosophical expression meant to mitigate the effects of a defeat. Someone else undoubtedly said it earlier, but the expression has attached itself to Boston Braves pitcher Cliff Curtis, who said, "Oh well. You can't win 'em all," after losing his 23rd consecutive game during the 1910–1911 seasons. It has also been associated with Philadelphia Athletics manager Connie Mack, who reportedly uttered it after losing 117 games during the 1916 season. EXTENDED USE. The phrase long ago was generalized to other sports and endeavors. It is often invoked as understatement after a severe defeat or series of defeats. Chris Browne's *Hagar the Horrible* cartoon (June 22, 2005) showed a physician explaining why he kept a skull in his office: "It's there to remind me of the physician's credo: 'You can't win them all.'"

"you could look it up" A verbal punctuation used by longtime New York Yankees manager Casey Stengel to let listeners know that he was not merely making things up and that the point he was making (whether a recollection or statistical citation) was doubtlessly written down somewhere. ETYMOLOGY. James Thurber's affectionate tale of baseball, "You Could Look It Up," published in *The Saturday Evening Post* (Apr. 15, 1941). Thurber's story, "filled with intentional malapropisms and grammatical gaffes in the style of legendary sportswriter Ring Lardner" (Neil A. Grauer, *The Baltimore Sun*, Aug. 26, 2001), described how the desperate manager of a pennant contender hired a midget to pinch hit and draw a crucial walk.

"you know me Al" A comment that something did not have to be told in the first place. "If a great hurler tossed a shutout and afterwards somebody asked him how he had done, he might just come back 'You know me Al'" (Harry Stein, *Hoopla*, 1983, p.163). ETYMOLOGY. Ring W. Lardner's 1914 novel, *You Know Me Al: A Busher's Letters*.

youneverknow Pitcher Joaquin Andujar's "favorite English word" (Ron Fimrite, *Sports Illustrated*, March 17, 1986) that has attached itself to baseball. Its meaning is summed up in a story (Rick Ostrow, *USA Today*, Apr. 2, 1986) about California Angels pitcher Don Sutton, who asked his teammates for "the one word that sums up baseball perfectly." As no one knew the magic word, Sutton gleefully provided it, quoting Andujar: "youneverknow." Roberto Alomar (quoted by Joe Strauss, *The Baltimore Sun*, May 28, 1998): "I understand baseball. It's a profession that one day you can be here and the next day be there. I never thought I was going to be traded from San Diego. But I was traded to Toronto. You never know." Terry Crowley (quoted in *The Baltimore Sun*, June 15, 1999): "The beautiful thing about baseball is, you never know." ETYMOLOGY. All of this stems from a quote attributed to Andujar when he was with the Houston Astros: "There is one word in America that says it all, and that one word is, 'Youneverknow.'"

younger game [softball term] A term used by softball partisans for the game during its pre–World War II period of expansion. Compare *older game*.

young hopeful A promising player who has not yet established a record; e.g., a newly acquired pitcher (Maurice H. Weseen, *A Dictionary of American Slang*, 1934).

youth baseball A collective term for various national and local programs for boys and girls under 18 years of age who play baseball as part of an organized team and league; e.g., Babe Ruth League, Little League, and Dixie Youth Baseball. An interesting use of the term was found on coupons attached to meat sold under the Oscar Mayer label in 1987; they stated that "for every coupon redeemed, Oscar Mayer will donate 5 cents to youth baseball, up to $1 million . . . to help kids in communities like yours" (Charles D. Poe).

youth movement The process of trading or releasing old players and bringing up highly promising rookies from the minor leagues. "A youth movement . . . is under way with the Red Sox, which is why Boston already has traded Bill Buckner and Don Baylor . . . and Dave Henderson" (*Tampa Tribune-Times*, Sept. 6, 1987).

Z

z The symbol used in club standings to indicate that a team has been *mathematically eliminated* from the divisional race. "It's a lot nicer to look at the standings and see a 2½-game lead in the paper than it is to see a Z" (Oakland A's pitcher Mike Moore, quoted in *Sacramento Bee*, Sept. 20, 1989).

Zackyzooky The minor leagues. According to Mike Gonring (*Baseball Digest*, June 1979), the term is peculiar to the Milwaukee Brewers, derived somehow from Sacramento, where the Brewers used to have a Triple-A club: "You don't want to be sent . . . to Zackyzooky."

Zamboni Trade name for a machine used to clean Astroturf and other artificial playing surfaces. ETYMOLOGY. The original and dominant Zamboni was used to resurface the ice on hockey rinks. It is named for Frank J. Zamboni, who introduced his ice-resurfacing machine in 1947 (patented in 1949), and was first used in the National Hockey League in 1954. On Zamboni's death, the *Boston Herald* (July 30, 1988) reported that he had been an ice supplier who was forced out of that business in the 1930s by the growth of mechanical refrigeration. He invented his first machine after he opened a skating rink and discovered that it took five men 90 minutes each night to create a new layer of ice.

Z-baller A minor-league player called up to the major leagues. The term is used among umpires. IST USE. 1992 (*Arizona Republic* and *Harrisburg* [Pa.] *Patriot-News*, June 9; Barry Popik).

zebra A fleet outfielder. The term is not to be confused with the zebra of football, who is a referee.

zephyrize *hist.* To strike out a batter. IST USE. 1889 (*Chicago Evening Journal*, June 29).

zero-to-three player A player with less than three years of major-league service who is therefore not eligible for salary arbitration.

zigzag curve Syn. of *double curve.* Edward Prindle published *The Art of Zigzag Curve Pitching* (1888, 1890, 1895, and 1910), a little treatise on the philosophical discussion of curve pitching, viz. "the compound, spiral, or zigzag curve." Also spelled "zig-zag curve." Syn. "zigzag." IST USE. 1883. "Many people . . . believe in . . . a 'zig zag' and a 'double' curve" (*Philadelphia Press*, Aug. 20; Peter Morris).

zigzagger A curveball or erratic throw. "Keith swung his right arm in a wide sweep, balancing himself on his right foot, and shot over a zigzagger which Manny missed by inches" (Burt L. Standish, *Courtney of the Center Garden*, 1915; David Shulman).

Zimmerman *hist.* A bonehead play, in reference to New York Giants third baseman Heinie Zimmerman, who chased Eddie Collins of the Chicago White Sox across the plate rather than throwing the ball for a tagout during the sixth game of the 1917 World Series. Prescott Sullivan (*San Francisco Examiner*, May 8, 1957) tried to exonerate the man behind the eponym, pointing out that it is misused: "Zimmerman had to chase Collins because home plate was left uncovered and there was nobody he could throw the ball to." (Peter Tamony)

zip 1. *v.* To shut out. "Tigers Zip Yanks in 10 Innings, 1–0" (*The Buffalo News* headline, Sept. 28, 1986). **2.** *v.* To move quickly; to throw with speed. "Tozer made his spitter zip across the plate" (*San Francisco Bulletin*, May 23, 1913; Gerald L. Cohen). "[Tyler Christian seldom] zips in the fast one" (*San Francisco Bulletin*, Apr. 12, 1913; Gerald L. Cohen). **3.** *n.* Speed. IST USE. 1920. "[Zachary] had real zip on his fast ball . . . for four innings" (J.V. Fitz Gerald, *The Washington Post*, Apr. 21; Peter Morris). **4.** *n.* Pep, energy, fighting spirit. "More zip and pep was injected in the game than in any previous workout" (*San Francisco Bulletin*, March 5, 1913; Gerald L. Cohen). **5.** *n.* Zero, such as a score of five to zip.

zob *hist.* A weak person; a fool. "When Chicago secured [Tommy] Leach from Pittsburg on a deal the wise zobs chirped: 'What's [Charles] Murphy want of that old fossil?' It did look like vintage, but nevertheless, and a couple notwithstandings, Leach pulled himself together and has, and is, playing a sensational outfield for the Cubs" (*San Francisco Bulletin*, Sept. 17, 1913; Gerald L. Cohen). IST USE. 1911. "He came here in the early Spring with all the try-out mob striving to bat like Wagner and to slide (spikes first) like Cobb. Some of the vets cried, 'Bonehead!' Others remarked, 'Poor zob!'" (William F. Kirk, *Right Off the Bat: Baseball Ballads*, collected from the *New York Evening Journal*; *OED*). USAGE NOTE. Cohen noted that this slang term apparently was first introduced in a baseball context.

zone **1.** *n.* Syn. of *strike zone*, 1. "Home plate umpire Durwood Merrill called him out on a pitch that appeared to be outside the zone" (*The Baltimore Sun*, May 14, 1994). **2.** *n.* A mythical place where a player feels he cannot fail (such as when a batter cannot miss hitting the ball), yet is unable to explain his situation. "Players talk about being in The Zone, when everything slows and the baseball . . . seems huge and inviting" (*ESPN The Magazine*, May 27, 2002). "[Jermaine Dye] finds himself in that rare, happy and somewhat unconscious state athletes call 'the zone'" (*The Baltimore Sun*, Apr. 28, 2000). "Randy [Myers] is in a [mental] league all by himself. . . . He gets in his own little zone" (Davey Johnson, quoted in *The Baltimore Sun*, March 6, 1996). "I was in a zone today. I just hope it's not the no-parking zone" (Andy Van Slyke, quoted in *The Baltimore Sun*, May 15, 1994). **3.** *v.* For a batter to look for a ball in a particular zone. "[Miguel Cabrera] really hasn't learned how to zone a ball" (anonymous scout, quoted in *Baseball America*, June 23–July 6, 2003; Peter Morris).

zone rating An estimate of a player's fielding efficiency, comparing the number of plays a fielder makes to the number of balls hit into the area he patrols. The raw data for zone rating is gathered by slicing the playing field into a set of zones and assigning each zone to the player within reach of balls hit into that zone. It is a variation of *defensive average*, except that until 2000, fielded balls that were turned into double plays counted as two successful fielding plays, which resulted in zone ratings higher than the "perfect" 1.0 (1.008 was achieved by second baseman Rex Hudler in 1996 and 1.005 by shortstops Rey Sanchez in 1998 and Rey Ordoñez in 1999). Zone ratings do not include infield flyouts and lineouts, nor ground balls to the outfield. Zone ratings were published in STATS Inc.'s annual *Player Profiles*. Compare *range factor*. Abbrev. *ZR*.

ZR Abbrev. for *zone rating*.

zurdo Spanish for "lefty" and "southpaw."

ACKNOWLEDGMENTS

An All-Star team of researchers was absolutely essential to the compilation of this dictionary. Collectively, their influence and inspiration are felt on practically every page. **Peter Morris**, baseball historian and author from Haslett, Mich., provided us with an immense number of early citations. His extraordinary dedication to this project was unwavering. Without Peter's willingness to share his wealth of information on early baseball, this dictionary would not be as authoritative and comprehensive as it strives to be.

Fellow author and good friend **Joseph C. Goulden** fed us a steady diet of clippings and radio notes with examples of baseballese carefully marked and annotated. In terms of baseball neologisms, he has been the eyes and ears of this project through three editions.

The late **David Shulman** allowed us to use his collection of unpublished citations on the earliest uses of certain terms. His generosity and guidance are acknowledged with the deepest admiration.

Pioneering baseball lexicographer **Edward J. Nichols'** 1939 Penn State doctoral dissertation, *An Historical Dictionary of Baseball Terminology*, has proven to be invaluable, especially for earliest uses of terms.

Another pioneering researcher, **Peter C. Tamony** (1902–1985) of San Francisco, spent most of his life collecting and writing about slang. One of his particular passions was the language of sport, and the information he collected on baseball terms (primarily from the West Coast) is without parallel. We are indebted to **Randy Roberts** who cataloged Tamony's collection as its first curator for the organization that administers it under the full name of the Joint Collection University of Missouri (Columbia) Western Historical Manuscript Collection and State Historical Society of Missouri Manuscripts.

Dave Kelly, the sports authority at the Library of Congress, and **Tim Wiles** of the National Baseball Library and Archives at Cooperstown, N.Y., have helped the dictionary at every juncture.

From the world of words, world-class etymologists **Barry A. Popik** and **Gerald L. Cohen** (Univ. of Missouri–Rolla) have been willing and eager to share their prodigious research. We also thank **Erin McKean** for her advice and counsel.

This work has also been greatly aided by a group of baseball specialists. **Charles Pavitt**, an eminent authority on baseball statistics who possesses an unmatched library of material on sabermetrics, is responsible for most of the statistical terminology in this dictionary. **David Block** willingly shared his knowledge of protoball (games that were ancestral to modern baseball), much of which was taken from his book *Baseball Before We Knew It* (2005). **Anthony Salazar** and **Amaury Pi-Gonzalez** provided a collection of Spanish terms and definitions. **John Holway** and **Lawrence D. Hogan** supplied definitions for Negro leagues terminology. **Alan Schwarz** submitted a list of scouting terms and definitions. **John Thorn**, baseball's preeminent historian, willingly and promptly commented on many 19th-century terms. **Ron Menchine** afforded unlimited access to his one-of-a-kind collection of early baseball material.

Three gentlemen who generously helped this project through two editions as volunteer researchers have since passed away: **Charles D. Poe, Robert F. Perkins**, and **James W. Darling**.

We would like to thank **William C. Young** for the many hours he spent spotting errors and omissions in the final manuscript.

At W. W. Norton, a team of talented individuals has contributed both enthusiasm and expertise: the publisher, Jeannie Luciano; the sales director, William Rusin; our editor, Tom Mayer; our publicist, Rachel Salzman; managing editors Nancy Palmquist and Don Rifkin; production managers Andrew Marasia and Anna Oler; and our skilled copyeditor, Patricia Chui. To each of them and to the rest of the Norton staff, we owe a debt of gratitude.

Finally, we would like to acknowledge my everlasting indebtedness to **Christopher J. Kuppig** for his extraordinary help in representing this work and our interests in general. We can never fully repay him for the work he has done in our behalf.

Other people who have made important contributions to this work are listed here. We thank them all for their help, loyalty, and enthusiasm.

A Frank R. Abate, Bruce Adams, Lane Akers, Thomas L. Altherr, John V. Alviti, Reinhold A. Aman, David Arcidiacono, Jean Hastings Ardell, John G. Arrison, Russell Ash, Priscilla Astifan, Chip Atkison, Andy Ayers

B Dave Baldwin, David Ball, Roger A. Ballou, Steve Banker, Grant Barrett, Michael Bein, Fr. Gerry Beirne, C.P. Benoit, Freddy Berowski, Albert P. Blair, Clifford Blau, Lawrence Block, Greg Bond, Bob Boone, Steve Boren, Lou Botti, Duke Boutwell, Q. David Bowers, John S. Bowman, Robert Boynton, Darryl Brock, D. Bruce Brown, Darryl Brown, Patrick Brown, Paul Browne, Howard Bryant, Robert Bryce, William Burgess, Tom Burns, David Bussan

C Lew Cady, Jean-Pierre Caillault, Richard Carletti, Bob Carr, Jerrold Casway, David Cataneo, Steve Catoe, Robert L. Chapman, Walt Cherniak, Gordon Christy, Irwin Chusid, Paul Clancy, Sam Clements, Merritt Clifton, Gerald Cohen, Stanley A. Cohen, Clem Comly, Douglas D. Connah Jr., Bonnie Copper, Philip J. Costopoulos, Bruce Coyne, Cliff Crown, Raymond V. Curiale

D Tracy Dalton, Tom "Slangman" Dalzell, Ev Daniels, Jon Daniels, Ed Dashman, Clay Davenport, Bob Davids, Bob Davis, Jay Davis, Karen Davis, Percy Dean, Bill Deane, David Demsey, Charles F. Dery, Donald Dewey, Kyle DiCicco-Carey, Alex Dickson, Andrew Dickson, Nancy Dickson, Bryan Di Salvatore, Earl E. Dodge, Royal Duncan, Floyd and Elsa Dunn, Bill Dunstone

E Dawn Eason, Connie Eble, Paula Eckes, C.F. Eckhardt, Morris Eckhouse, Ross Eckler, Charles Einstein, Michael Esserman, Douglas Evelyn

F Joe Falletta, Steve Fiffer, Jerome Finster, Keith B. Fleeman, F.X. Flinn, Bob Flynn, Kenneth Forehand, Jessica Frank, Matt Frederick, Jeff Freedman, John Freyer, Fumihiro "Fuchan" Fujisawa, Warner Fusselle

G Martin Gardner, Howard Garson, Jim Gates, Mike Gershman, Walt Giachini, Elizabeth Gibbon, George Gibson, Steve Gietschier, William C. Gilbert, Thomas E. Gill, E. Ward Gilman, George Gmelch, Wayne Grady, Robert Greenman, Dan Gutman

H John F. Hagemann, Douglas W. Hall, Paul Hallaman, Alex Harary, Brett Hardeman, Kelsie Harder, Robert G. Harding, Bryan Harris, Tom Haudricourt, Bill Heath, Bob Heilman, Thomas R. Heitz, Brock Helander, Robert

Hendrickson, Ron Henry, Richard Hershberger, Bill Hickman, George S. Hobart, Philip R. Hochberg, Richard L. Homan, G. Reed Howard, David Hubler, Joanne Hulbert, Truxton Hulbert, Paul Hunkele, John R. Husman

I   Bob Ingraham, Ralph Insinga, Frederick Ivor-Campbell

J   Jonathan Jacobs, Jake Jacobson, Bill James, Blair Jett, David A. Jewell, Skip Jewett, Hal Johnson, W. Lloyd Johnson, Clifford Jordan

K   Cliff Kachline (who helped get the project started), Pat Kelly, John Kenyon, Kevin Kerrane, Harry Kies, Albert Kilchesty, Jerry Kindall, Bill Kirwin, Linda Kittell, Wendy Knickerbocker, Barry Koron, Norbert Kraich, Jackie Krentzman, John Kuchera, Norman E. Kurland

L   Bruce C. Ladd Jr., David M. Larson, Brian L. Laughlin, Nancy Jo Leachman, Richard Lederer, Jean M. LeMire, David Leonhardt, R.J. Lesch, Alan H. Levy, Joel Lewis, John Lewis, Matthew E. Lieff, Ed Lindhurst, Robert Loeffler, Q.V. Lowe, Philip J. Lowry, Bob Luke

M   Norman L. Macht, Sue Macy, Peter Mancuso, Jack Mangus, Ed Margolis, John Marshall, Neil Massa, John Matthew IV, Scott McClellan, Larry McCray, Andy McCue, David McDonald, Thomas P. McDonald, Joe McGillen, Brian McKenna, William McMahon, Bill Mead, Christopher Mead, Doug Meyer, Kenneth Miller, Richard Miller, Steve Milman, Andrew Milner, Rick Minch, Frederick C. Mish, Mike P. Moffatt, Howard R. Morgan, John M. Morse, Russell Mott, Bill Mullins, Cait Murphy, Eldon Myers

N   Joe B. Naiman, Betsy Newman, Kara Noble, Bill Nowlin

O   Dan O'Brien, Keith Olbermann, Elliott Oppenheim, Charles A. Owen Jr.

P   Dennis Pajot, Brett Palmer, Bill Page, Herbert H. Paper, Doug Pappas, Royse M. Parr, John Pastier, Martin Payne, Murray R. Pearce, Marc Picard, Tom Pitoniak, Bill Plummer III, Gregory Pokrass, Howard A. Pollock, Frank N. Potter, Timothy Prosser

Q   Evan Quenon

R   Mario Ramos, Rick Randahl, Greg Rhodes, Lawrence Ritter, Randy Roberts, Walter Robertson, Jason Rouby, Thomas J. Ruane, John Ruoff, John Rush

S William Safire, Joseph St. George, Joseph St. Paul, Eric Sallee, Robert H. Schaefer, Alice Schaeffer, Gabriel Schechter, George H. Scheetz, Andrew Schelling, Aaron Schmidt, John Schwartz, Ron Selter, Mike Shannon, Fred R. Shapiro, Tom Shieber, Stuart Y. Silverstein, Andy Singer, Donald F. Sisson, Bob Skole, David W. Smith, Robert Smith, Tal Smith, Lyle Spatz, Michael A. Stackpole, David Staffin, Steve L. Steinberg, Dave Stephan, Andy Strasberg, Dean A. Sullivan, John Sullivan, James D. Szalontai

T Bill Tammeus, Cecilia Tan, Blair D. Tarr, Dean W. Terlinden, Ralph Testa, Dean Thilgen, George A. Thompson, James L. Thorpe III, Bob Timmermann, Wayne Townsend, Brian Turner, Phil Turner, Jules Tygiel

V Frank Vaccaro, James Vail, Cullen P. Vane, Alex Van Schuylen, Edwin D. Van Woert, Patricia Vignola, David Vincent, Cort Vitty, Jay Voke

W Bill Wagner, Richard Wagner, Verlon Wagner, Tim Wendel, Sally F. Whitenack, Tom Williams, Charles P. Wilson III, Pete Wilson, Andres Wirkmaa, Bernard Witlieb, Nick Wolf, Robert Wood, Daniel Woodhead

Z Steve Zane, Benjamin Zimmer, Richard Zitrin, Larry Zmolik

AFTERWORD

". . . a certain ancient game, played with a ball, hath come up again, yet already are all mouths filled with the phrases that describe its parts and movement; insomuch, indeed, that the ears of the sober and such as would busy themselves with weightier matter are racked with the clack of the same till they do ache with anguish."

—Mark Twain's "An Extract from Methuselah's Diary"

It goes without saying that this book is already out of date and has been for many months. There is no shame in this because the same can be said about virtually any book that attempts to capture an element of a living language.

However, one must always strive for currency and comprehensiveness, and it is with this in mind that the author announces here that he is most interested in hearing from the readers of this book as they encounter new terms. I am, of course, also interested in hearing of errors, omissions, alternative theories on the origins of terms, and earlier dating of a term's earliest appearance in print. Such correspondence will be acknowledged immediately and consulted for future editions of this dictionary. I can be reached directly at Box 280, Garrett Park, MD 20896.

ANNOTATED
BIBLIOGRAPHY

Allen, Ethan. *Baseball: Major League Technique and Tactics*. New York: Macmillan, 1953.—Contains an excellent glossary.

Allen, Ethan. *Baseball Play and Strategy*. New York: Ronald Press, 1969.—Contains an excellent glossary.

Allen, Ethan. *Baseball Techniques Illustrated*. New York: A.S. Barnes, 1951.—Contains an excellent glossary.

Allen, Lee. *The Hot Stove League*. New York: A.S. Barnes, 1955.—Significant work on history of key terms by former National Baseball Hall of Fame librarian.

Anonymous. "Baseball Glossary, 1914 Revision." *Baseball Magazine*, Jan. 1915, p.70.

Anonymous. "Baseball Slang." *The Washington Post*, July 19, 1914.

Anonymous. "Baseball Slang and an Englishman." *New York Sun*, Oct. 9, 1929.

Anonymous. "Baseball Words." *Holiday*, March 1955.

Anonymous. *Baseball's Pot of Gold and O. K. Guide*. Youngstown (Ohio): The Mirror-Review, 1933.—Contains "Baseball 'Lingo'" (pp.6–15).

Anonymous. "Development of Baseball Language." *The New York Times*, July 20, 1897.

Anonymous. "English and Baseball." *The Nation*, Aug. 21, 1913.

Anonymous. "The Game in Slang." *Famous Sluggers and Their Records of 1932*. Hillerich & Bradsby, 1933.

Anonymous. [Glossary of baseball terms]. *The Sporting News*, Nov. 27, 1897.

Anonymous. "Glossary of Baseball Terms." *The Atchison* (Kans.) *Daily Globe*, June 23, 1896, p.2.

Anonymous. "Have a Language All of Their Own." *New York Sun*, June 23, 1932.

Anonymous. *Let's Talk Baseball*. Montreal: O'Keefe Brewery, 1969.—Booklet of terms in English and French.

Anonymous. "Many Gems of Slang Heard on Ball Field." *The Sporting Life*, May 18, 1912.

Anonymous. "Of the Terms Used by Players in Substitution for Proper Words." *The Sporting Life*, Nov. 29, 1913, p.8.

Anonymous. "Peril of the Baseball Lingo." *Literary Digest*, Sept. 6, 1913.

Anonymous. "Some Base Ball Synonyms." *The Sporting News*, Oct. 30, 1913, p.5.

Anonymous. *Who's Who and What's What in Baseball*. Philadelphia: C.M. Klump and Co., 1910.—Contains an important, well-written glossary.

Archibald, Joe. *Baseball Talk*. New York: Pocket Books, 1974.

Arnold, Frank. [Baseball Slang]. *Cincinnati Times-Star*, Feb. 8, 1889.

Baker, Russell. "Come Back, Dizzy." *The New York Times*, Oct. 9, 1979.—Essay decrying that the language of baseball was becoming arid and lifeless.

Bancroft, Jessie H., and William Dean Pulvermacher. *Handbook of Athletic Games for Players, Instructors, and Spectators*. New York: Macmillan, 1916.—Includes baseball glossary (pp.77–84).

Barber, Red, and Robert W. Creamer. *Rhubarb in the Catbird Seat*. Garden City (N.Y.): Doubleday, 1968.—Barber explains his role in the origin and spread of several key terms, including the two in the title.

Barbour, Ralph Henry. *How to Play Better Baseball: For Junior Players and Their Coaches*. New York: Appleton-Century Co., 1935.—Includes a glossary.

Beckett, James, and Dennis W. Eckes. *The 1979 Sport Americana Baseball Card Price Guide*. Laurel (Md.): Den's Collectors Den, 1979.—Includes "glossary" of baseball-card collecting terms (pp.216–19).

Berrey, Lester V., and Melvin Van Den Bark. *The American Thesaurus of Slang*. New York: Thomas Y. Crowell, 1942.—Extensive section on baseball slang; essential source.

Birtwell, Roger. "Three R's Taught in Diamond Lingo." *Baseball Digest*, Sept. 1948.

Block, David. *Baseball Before We Knew It: A Search for the Roots of the Game*. Lincoln: Univ. of Nebraska Press, 2005.

Bonner, M.G. *The Big Baseball Book for Boys*. Springfield (Mass.): McLoughlin Bros, 1931.—Includes "Baseball Terms and Slang" (pp.120–22).

Borden, Marian Edelman. "Terms for Parents of Little Leaguers." *The New York Times*, no date.

Bouton, Jim. *Ball Four*. New York: World Publishing Co., 1970.—Includes contemporary slang.

Bouton, Jim. *I'm Glad You Didn't Take It Personally*. Edited by Leonard Shecter. New York: William Morrow, 1971.

Brands, Edgar G. "Between Innings." *The Sporting News*, Feb. 23, 1933, p.4.—The column includes "Baseball's Glossary" of 36 terms.

Brandt, William G. "That Unrecognized Language—Baseballese." *Baseball Magazine*, Oct. 1932.—Extremely valuable article that distinguishes play jargon (baseballese) from the baseball slang encountered in pulp fiction and that emphasizes the precision and economy of baseballese, comparable to the verbal shorthand of surgeons.

Brosnan, Jim. *The Long Season*. New York: Harper & Brothers, 1960.—Termed "the greatest baseball book ever written" by Jimmy Cannon, the book opens with a glossary of words and phrases heard by the player/author during the 1959 season; a key to the player jargon of the time.

Bryson, Bill. "Why We Say It." *Baseball Digest*, Apr. 1948.

Cannon, Jimmy. "Sport Page Dictionary." *Baseball Digest*, Nov.–Dec. 1956.—The best set of comic baseball terms ever defined in one place.

Chadwick, Henry. *The Game of Base Ball*. New York: George Munro, 1868.—Includes "Technical Terms Used in Base Ball" (pp.38–46).

Chadwick, Henry. *Technical Terms of Baseball*. New York: American Sports Publishing Co., 1887.—Important booklet as the British-born Chadwick was responsible for naming or renaming a number of elements of baseball.

Chicago Park District. *Fundamentals Technique Strategy: Baseball*. Chicago: Chicago Park District (Burnham Park), 1938.—Includes "Baseball Vernacular" (pp.4–7).

Cochrane, Gordon S. "Mickey." *Baseball: The Fan's Game*. New York: Funk and Wagnalls Co., 1939.

Coffin, Tristram Potter. *The Old Ball Game: Baseball in Folklore and Fiction*. New York:

Herder and Herder, 1971.—Extremely valuable overall reference; contains a key chapter on "Baseball Talk."

Cohen, Gerald Leonard. *Dictionary of 1913 Baseball and Other Lingo*. 3 volumes. Rolla (Mo.): self-published., 2001–2003. —"Primarily from the baseball columns of the *San Francisco Bulletin*, Feb.–May 1913."

Cohen, Gerald Leonard. "Old Baseball Columns as a Repository of Slang; Reading through *The World*." *Comments on Etymology*, Apr. 1–15, 1986, Part II; *Comments on Etymology*, Feb. 1–15, 1987.—Commentary on 19th-century baseball slang, plus several fascinating discoveries.

Conners, R.J. "Baseball Makes Slang of Its Own." *The New York Times*, June 2, 1929.

Considine, Tim. *The Language of Sport*. New York: Facts On File, 1982.

Copeland, Robert, ed. *Webster's Sports Dictionary*. Springfield (Mass.): Merriam-Webster, 1976.

Couzens, Gerald Secor. *A Baseball Album*. New York: Lippincott and Crowell, 1980. —Contains a useful glossary.

Cummings, Parke. *Dictionary of Baseball*. New York: A.S. Barnes, 1950.—122-page guide to terms, phrases, and game structure.

Dean, Jerome H. "Dizzy." *Dizzy Baseball: A Gay and Amusing Glossary of Baseball Terms Used by Radio Broadcasters, with Explanations to Aid the Uninitiated*. New York: Greenberg, 1952.—Unpaged booklet.

Dean, Jerome H. "Dizzy." *The Dizzy Dean Dictionary*. San Francisco: Falstaff Brewing Co., 1943 and 1949.—Booklet of humorous definitions.

Dean, Jerome H. "Dizzy." "Dizzy's Dictionary." *Baseball Digest*, Nov. 1943, pp.29–31.

Dickson, Paul. *The Hidden Language of Baseball*. New York: Walker and Co., 2003. —Includes "A Glossary of Signs, Signals and Tip-Offs" (pp.161–72).

Dionne, E.J., Jr. "Chattering Class." *The Washington Post*, Oct. 19, 1997.

Dunne, Bert. *Folger's Dictionary of Baseball*. San Francisco: Folger's Coffee and Stark–Rath Printing Co., 1958.—Solid booklet that mixes official terms with the slang of the period. Many terms appear here that do not appear elsewhere. This is a particularly hard reference to find, but several copies appear in the Peter Tamony Collection.

Edwards, Bob. *Fridays with Red: A Radio Friendship*. New York: Simon and Schuster, 1993.—Retelling of Red Barber's contributions to the language of baseball.

Ercolano, Patrick. *Fungoes, Floaters and Fork Balls: A Colorful Baseball Dictionary*. Englewood Cliffs, N.J.: Prentice-Hall, 1987.

Evers, John J., and Hugh S. Fullerton. *Touching Second: The Science of Baseball*. Chicago: The Reilly & Britton Co., 1910 (reprinted 2005 by McFarland & Co.).—Discusses many baseball terms.

Falletta, Joe. "Here's a Look at Some Baseball Jargon of the '80s." *Baseball Digest*, Dec. 1983.

Farine, Michael. "Coming to Terms with Baseball Lingo." *The Potomac Almanac*, Apr. 22, 1987.

Filichia, Peter. *Professional Baseball Franchises*. New York: Facts on File, 1993.

Flexner, Stuart Berg. *Listening to America*. New York: Simon and Schuster, 1982.—Contains a lively and useful chapter on baseball language and how it has changed through the years.

Ford, Torrey. "Baseball Varies Both Its Togs and Its Talk." *New York Tribune*, Apr. 24, 1921, p.4.

Foster, John B. "Glossary of Base Ball Terms," an appendix (pp.1005–12) in *Collier's New Dictionary of the English Language*. New York: P.F. Collier & Son, 1908.—An important and often overlooked glossary written by the editor of the *Spalding's Official Base Ball Guide*. The note that Peter Tamony attached to his copy of this work: "Filed to show small number of terms thought to be peculiar to this field of sport in its early period."

Frank, Lawrence. *Playing Hardball. The Dynamics of Baseball Folk Speech*. New York: Peter Lang Publishing, 1983.—Based on the author's years playing for the semipro Novato (Calif.) Knicks; it is a study of the language on the field itself.

Frommer, Harvey. *Sports Lingo*. New York: Atheneum, 1979.

Frommer, Harvey. *Sports Roots*. New York: Atheneum, 1979.

Fullerton, Hugh S. "The Baseball Primer." *The American Magazine*, June 1912.—An extremely important glossary in which certain terms are defined in print for the first time.

Gast, Carol R. *Skill on the Diamond*. Omaha, Neb.: Douglas Publishing Co., 1953.

Gibbons, Frank. "Handy Guide to 'Fieldese'!" *Baseball Digest*, May 1959.

Gibbs, C.M. "Gibberish." *The Baltimore Sun*, Jan. 1, 1935.

Goddard, Joe. "Hoover, Mr. Kodak, Salami, Yakker." *The Sporting News*, March 6, 1982.

Gonring, Mike. "Baseball Still Has Its Own Special Lingo." *Baseball Digest*, June 1979.

Grieve, Curley. "Baseball Slang Growing Fast." *San Francisco Examiner*, March 11, 1937.

Hall, John. "How's Your Baseball Lingo?" *Baseball Digest*, Dec. 1973.

Hample, Zack. *Watching Baseball Smarter*. New York: Vantage Books, 2007.—Includes extensive glossary of baseball slang (pp.196–237).

Hartt, Rollin Lynde. "The National Game." *Atlantic*, Aug. 1908.

Harvey, W. Clifford. "The Fascinating Language of Baseballese." *Baseball Magazine*, Jan. 1931.

Heck, Henry J. "Baseball Terminology." *American Speech*, Apr. 1930.

Hendrickson, Robert. *Grand Slams, Hat Tricks and Alley-Oops: A Sports Fan's Book of Words*. New York: Prentice-Hall General Reference, 1994.

Hernandez, Keith, and Mike Bryan. *Pure Baseball: Pitch by Pitch for the Advanced Fan*. New York: HarperCollins, 1994.

Hershiser, Orel, with Jerry B. Jenkins. *Out of the Blue*. New York: Charter Books, 1989. —Includes contemporary glossary.

Hertzel, Bob. "Baseball Language: It's Ever-Changing, Ever-Vibrant." *Baseball Digest*, Jan. 1987.

Hoffman, Jeanne. "Thrown for Curve by Ball Lingo? *Los Angeles Times*, July 8, 1961. —Select list of terms defined by Fresco Thompson.

Hollander, Zander, ed. *Baseball Lingo*. New York: W.W. Norton, 1967.

Hollander, Zander, ed. *The Encyclopedia of Sports Talk*. New York: Corwin Books, 1976.

Horgan, Tim. "Smoke Over the Short Porch." *Baseball Digest*, June 1964.

Howard, Lucy, and Ned Zeman. "Buzzwords." *Newsweek*, July 15, 1991, p.6.—Batboy slang.

Howarth, Jerry. *Baseball Lite*. Toronto: Protocol Books, 1986.—A collection of funny definitions that really are funny.

Huddle, Franklin P. "Baseball Jargon." *American Speech*, Apr. 1943.

Ingerton, Scott. "Baseball World's Glossary from 1934." *Akron (Ohio) Beacon Journal*, Aug. 8, 2005.—A list of "tricky slanguage" terms used by ballplayers; reprinted from *Akron (Ohio) Beacon Journal*, 1934.

James, Bill, and Rob Neyer. *The Neyer/James Guide to Pitchers*. New York: Simon and Schuster, 2004.—Includes chapter "All the Pitches We Could Find (okay, most of them)" by Neyer (pp.11–22).

Jones, Del. "Do foreign executives balk at sports jargon?" *USA Today*, March 30, 2007.

Joyce, Joan, and others. *Winning Softball*. Chicago: NTC/Contemporary Publishing Co., 1975.—Contains a glossary of softball terms.

Kaegel, Dick. "'A Teflon Glove Winner Hit a Michael Jackson': Ballplayers Talk Their Own Language." *The Seattle Times*, Sept. 18, 1988.

Kieran, John. "The Sportsman's Lexicon." *Saturday Review of Literature*, July 22, 1933.

Knowles, R.G., and Richard Morton. *Baseball*. London: George Routledge and Sons, 1896.—Includes glossary of baseball terms (pp. 101–3).

Kram, Mark. "Glossary [of vintage base ball terms]." *Philadelphia Daily News*, May 11, 2005.

Lawson, Thomas W. *The Krank: His Language and What It Means*. Boston: Rand Avery Co., 1888.—The first attempt to put baseball slang in one volume, this 64-page booklet is now very rare, but essential to any attempt at deciphering the baseball slang of the 19th century.

Lee, Gretchen. "In Sporting Parlance." *American Speech*, Apr. 1926.—An inventory of baseball terminology of the 1920s.

Lessiter, Mike. *The Names of the Games.* Chicago: Contemporary Books, 1988.—Includes section (pp.7–37) on the origin of nicknames of major-league clubs.

Levinson, Bill. "My Wife's Own Dictionary of Baseball." *San Francisco Examiner*, Sept. 6, 1959.—Comic baseball glossary better than most.

Lewis, Michael. *Moneyball: The Art of Winning an Unfair Game.* New York: W. W. Norton, 2003.

Lieb, Frederick G. "How the Big League Clubs Got Their Nick Names." *Baseball Magazine*, Feb. 1922, v.28, p.675.

Lindop, Al. "The Names of Summer." *Indianapolis Star*, Apr. 5, 1981.

Lipsyte, Robert. "Sportspeak Without Tears." *The New York Times*, May 30, 1968.

Litwhiler, Danny, comp. *Glossary of International Baseball Terms.* Greenville (Ill.): United States Baseball Federation, 1980.—Terms in Italian, Spanish, Dutch, and English.

Logan, Mrs. John A. *The Home Manual. Everybody's Guide in Social, Domestic and Business Life.* Philadelphia: H.J. Smith and Co., 1889.—This book contains everything from rules of etiquette to recipes for such things as toast water and tamarind whey, but it also contains a very early and ambitious glossary of baseball terms prepared by George A. Stackhouse, who was described as an authority on baseball. Commenting on this glossary in the Dec. 1937 issue of *American Speech*, J. Louis Kueth (The Johns Hopkins Univ. Library) wrote, "Nearly all of the terms given in this list are still in use."

Lowry, Philip J. *Green Cathedrals: The Ultimate Celebration of Major League and Negro League Ballparks.* New York: Walker and Co., 2006.

Lukas, J. Anthony. "How Mel Allen Started A Lifelong Love Affair." *The New York Times Magazine*, Sept. 12, 1971.

Mack, Connie. *Connie Mack's Baseball Book.* New York: Alfred A. Knopf, 1950—Includes gloassary of baseball terms (pp. 227–34).

Maffei, John. "Baseball Still Has Its Own Language." *Baseball Digest*, May 1986.

Major League Baseball. Playing Rules Committee. *Official Baseball Rules.* St. Louis: The Sporting News, 2007.—Rule 2.00 consists of definitions of terms.

Martinez, David H. *The Book of Baseball Literacy.* New York: Plume, 1996.

Masin, Herman L. "Diamond Definitions You Won't Find in the Dictionary." *Baseball Digest*, June 1959, pp.90–91.

Mathews, Garret. *Can't Find a Dry Ball.* Tampa: Albion Press, 2002.—Includes glossary (pp.xi–xii).

McBride, Joseph. *High & Inside: The Complete Guide to Baseball Slang.* New York: Warner Books, 1980.

McCullough, Bill. "Baseball Slang Inconsistent in Various Loops." *Brooklyn Eagle*, Sept. 5, 1937.

McDonald, Jack. "Sandwiches and Flies." *San Francisco Examiner*, Apr. 11, 1966.

McGlone, Joe. [Column]. *Providence* (R.I.) *Evening Bulletin*, Aug. 2, 1946.

Meloy, Charles C. "Diamond Jargon." *Baseball Magazine*, Aug. 1939.

Mencken, H.L. *The American Language: An Inquiry into the Development of English in the United Sates.* 4th ed. & 2 supplements. New York: Knopf, 1977.

Meredith, Mamie J. "Twi-night, Twi-nighter." *American Speech*, May 1956.—Academic look at baseball terms.

Miller, John H. "The Jargon of the Diamond." *Baseball Magazine*, Oct. 1916.

Minshew, Wayne. "Dugout Lingo Has a Flavor All Its Own." *Baseball Digest*, June 1972.

Minshew, Wayne. "Players' Lexicon Unique Like Tweener, Chin Music." *The Sporting News*, Apr. 1, 1972.

Moreland, Keith. "Talkin' Baseball is What Makes It Quite Interesting." *Vineline*, Aug. 1987.—Excellent glossary written from the players' standpoint.

Morgan, Joe, with Richard Lally. *Baseball for Dummies*. Foster City (Calif.): IDG Books Worldwide, 1998.—Includes Appendix A: "Baseball Speak: A Glossary" (pp.351–63).

Morris, Peter. *A Game of Inches: The Stories Behind the Innovations That Shaped Baseball*. 2 volumes. Chicago: Ivan R. Dee, 2006.

Murnane, T.H. *How to Umpire, How to Captain a Team, How to Manage a Team, How to Coach, How to Organize a League, How to Score, and the Technical Terms of Base Ball*. New York: American Sports Publishing Co., 1915.—Six special and detailed glossaries (pitching terms, umpiring terms, etc.) make this an especially important source.

Nichols, Edward J. *An Historical Dictionary of Baseball Terminology*. Ann Arbor (Mich.): University Microfilms, Jan. 1939.—PhD dissertation, The Pennsylvania State College. Nichols aimed to make "a storehouse of baseball words, because so many of them are passing over to the general language and because no other such study was in evidence."

Nugent, William Henry. "The Sports Section." *The American Mercury*, March 1929.—Shows the seldom-acknowledged influence of Pierce Egan, an English writer of the early 19th century, whom Nugent deems "the father of newspaper sports slang."

Ostler, Scott. "Baseball Lingo Throws Curve for Dudes Trying to Stay Hip." *Binghamton (New York) Press and Sun Bulletin*, May 4, 1986.

Paley, Steve. "In There Pitching For Arms Control." *The New York Times*, Sept. 6, 1987.

Parrott, Harold. "Bewildering are Slang Terms Used in Talk of Baseball Players." *Brooklyn Eagle*, Aug. 9, 1936.

Pearson, Frederick S. *Butchered Baseball*. New York: A.S. Barnes, 1952.—Humorous definitions.

Pepe, Phil. [Baseball jargon]. *Baseball Digest*, Nov. 1974, p.58.

Povich, Shirley. "Baseball No Longer Speaks Same Language." *The Washington Post*, March 20, 1996.—Important debunking of the excesses of modern terminology.

Powers, Jimmy. "Dugout Slang." *New York Daily News*, Jan. 10, 1937.

Putney, Walter K. "Better Than a Hit!" *Baseball Stories*, Spring 1952, v.3, no.5, pp.43–45.—Includes extensive list of terms to describe a base hit.

Racine Belles. "So They Say." *Racine Belles Yearbook*, 1944, p.29.—List of terms used in the All-American Girls Professional Baseball League.

Reichler, Joe. *Joe Reichler's Great Book of Baseball Records*, no. 2. New York: Dell, 1957.

Remmers, Mary. *Ducks on the Pond: A Lexicon of Little League Lingo*. Austin (Texas): Shoal Creek Publishers, 1981.

Richman, Milton. "Rookie Diction-err-y." *Baseball Digest*, May 1947, p.38.

Ridings, J. Willard. "Use of Slang in Newspaper Sports Writing." *Journalism Quarterly*, Dec. 1934.

Rose, Howard N. *A Thesaurus of Slang*. New York: Macmillan, 1934.

Rosenbaum, Art. "Sports Terms Have Enriched Our Language." *San Francisco Examiner*, July 30, 1985.

Rothan, Martin. *New Baseball Rules and Decisions Book*. Lexington (Ky.): Baseball Decisions Co., 1947.

Rumill, Edwin M. "Baseball as Written, and . . ." *Christian Science Monitor*, Sept. 1, 1937.

Rush, Red. "Red Rush's Dictionary of Baseball Slang." *San Francisco Examiner*, Aug. 12, 1979.

Ruth, George Herman. *Babe Ruth's Own Book of Baseball*. New York: G.P. Putnam, 1928.—Contains a glossary with bygone bits of slang that do not appear elsewhere. Peter Tamony noted in his file on baseball terms that the text of the book is also useful "for usage of practically all words and terms used in the play of the game of baseball."

Ryan, Calvin T. "Sports Writers' Semantics." *Word Study*, Feb. 1952.

Safire, William. *I Stand Corrected*. New York: Times Books, 1984.

Safire, William. "Out of Left Field." *The New York Times Magazine*, June 28, 1981.—Baseball terms used in politics.

Safire, William. *What's the Good Word?* New York: Avon, 1983.—Very important section on the word "fungo," pp.69–75.

Salak, John S., ed. *Dictionary of American Sports*. New York: Philosophical Library, 1961.

Salsinger, H.G. "Dugout Dictionary." *Baseball Digest*, Jan.–Feb. 1957.

Salsinger, H.G. "Jargon of the Field." *Baseball Digest*, Aug. 1945.

Samuels, V. "Baseball Slang." *American Speech*, Feb. 1927.—Published as a letter, it amends Gretchen Lee's "In Sporting Parlance."

Sargent, Lester L. "Novel Baseball Inventions." *Baseball Magazine*, March 1914.

Schacht, Al. *Al Schacht Dope Book: Diamond Facts, Figures and Fun*. New York: The Sporting News, 1944.—Includes "Diamond Definitions" (pp.35–47).

Scheiber, Dave. "Talk Like a Fan." *St. Petersburg Times*, March 5, 1987.—Solid report on the slang heard during spring training.

Schlossberg, Dan. *The Baseball Book of Why*. Middle Village (N.Y.): Jonathan David Publishers, 1984 and 1992.

Schlossberg, Dan. *The Baseball Catalog*. Middle Village (N.Y.): Jonathan David Publishers, 1989. Chapter 15 (pp.233–50) is entitled "The Language of Baseball" and includes sections "Key Phrases and Origins" (pp.234–38) and "Baseball Talk" (pp.242–43).

Scholl, Richard. *The Running Press Glossary of Baseball Language*. Philadelphia: The Running Press, 1977.

Schoor, Gene, ed. *The Giant Book of Sports*. Garden City (N.Y.): Garden City Publishing Co., 1948.—Includes slangy section entitled "Familiar Terms Connected with Baseball."

Schwarz, Alan. *Baseball America's Scouting Dictionary*. BaseballAmerica.com, Nov. 14, 2006.

Schwed, Fred, Jr. *How to Watch a Baseball Game*. New York: Harper and Brothers, 1957.—Includes fascinating chapter on baseball semantics.

Scripps Howard News Service. "Reynolds Guide to Baseball Jive." Sept. 17, 1986.

Shandler, Ron. *Ron Shandler's Baseball Forecaster*. Roanoke (Va.): Shandler Enterprises, LLC, 2006.—Includes glossary (pp.249–54) of terms regarding fantasy baseball.

Shea, Thomas P. *Baseball Nicknames, 1870–1946*. Hingham (Mass.): Gates-Vincent Publications, 1946.

Shecter, Leonard. "Baseball Spoken Here." *Baseball Digest*, June 1963.

Sherwood, R.E. "Breezy Bits of Baseball Humor." *Baseball Magazine*, Sept. 1913.—Comic treatment of pre–World War I baseball slang.

Shirts, Morris A. *Warm Up for Little League Baseball*. New York: Pocket Books, 1971, 1976.—Contains a small glossary with certain terms that do not appear elsewhere.

Shulman, David, comp. "Baseball's Bright Lexicon." *American Speech*, Feb. 1951.—Examines earliest (1862–1939) recorded uses of various terms.

Simons, Herbert. "Do You Speak the Language?" *Baseball Magazine*, Jan. 1943.

Simons, Herbert. "Here's Some More Slang." *Baseball Magazine*, Apr. 1943.

Smith, Chester L. "Diamond Slang Goes G.I." *Baseball Digest*, May 1946.—The only reference on the influence of the slang and terminology of World War II on baseball slang.

Smith, Ken. "How They Express Themselves." *Baseball Magazine*, Aug. 1939.

Smith, Red. "Sportspeak and Stuff." *The New York Times*, July 1, 1981.

Spector, Robert Donald. "Baseball, Inside Out and Upside Down." *American Speech*, Dec. 1956.

Spector, Robert Donald. "Compound Words in Baseball." *American Speech*, May 1955.

Spector, Robert Donald. "Little Words in the Big League." *Word Study*, May 1955.

Sperling, Dan. *A Spectator's Guide to Baseball*. New York: Avon, 1983.

Spink, C.C. & Son. *The Sporting News Record Book*. St. Louis: The Sporting News, 1933 and 1937 editions.—Both contain important sections on slang.

Spink, C. C. Johnson. "Sports in Our Language." *The Sporting News*, June 10, 1978.

Spink, J.G. Taylor, and others. *Comedians of Baseball Down the Years*. St. Louis: Charles C. Spink and Son, 1958.—Includes a rich and important slang dictionary.

Sullivan, Frank. "The Cliché Expert Testifies on Baseball." *The New Yorker*, Aug. 27, 1949.

Tamony, Peter. "Baseball." *Newsletter and Wasp*, Apr. 14, 1939.

Tamony, Peter. "Baseball and its Fans." *Words*, March 1939.

Tamony, Peter. "Break." *Newsletter and Wasp*, Oct. 6, 1939.

Tamony, Peter. "Championship of the World." *Newsletter and Wasp*, Oct. 13 and 20, 1939.

Tamony, Peter. "Dick Smith." *Newsletter and Wasp*, Sept. 15, 1939.

Tamony, Peter. "Downtown: A Baseball Nickname." *Comments on Etymology*, May 1, 1983.

Tamony, Peter. "Fungo and Bingo Again." *American Speech*, Oct. 1937.

Tamony, Peter. "Sandlot Baseball." *Western Folklore*, Oct. 1968.

Thierry, Edward M. "Slang of the Sporting Writers." *Baseball Magazine*, Sept. 1909.

Thompson, Fresco. *Every Diamond Doesn't Sparkle*. New York: David McKay, 1964.—Contains a useful glossary of baseball argot, including a handful of slang terms that are not found in other compilations.

Toporcer, George "Specs." *Baseball: From Back Yard to Big League*. New York: Sterling Pub. Co., 1954 and 1961.—Includes a glossary (pp.156–58).

Toporcer, George "Specs." *Know Your Baseball*. Hamilton (Ont.): Hamco Coke Sales, 1953.—Includes "Glossary of Baseball Terms" (p.26).

Turkin, Hy, ed. *The 1955 Baseball Almanac*. New York: A.S. Barnes, 1955.—Particularly interesting glossary (pp.205–8) because Turkin attributes several slang coinages to specific players.

Vidmer, Richard. "Down in Front: Native Tongue." *New York Herald Tribune*, June 7, 1941.

Vogel, O.H. "Otts." *Ins and Outs of Baseball*. St. Louis: The C.V. Mosby Co., 1952. —Includes "Baseball Slang" (pp.440–43).

Wagner, Honus. *Baseball Grins*. Pittsburgh: Laurel House Inc., 1933.—Contains glossary of "Players' Lingo."

Walker, Henry. *Illustrated Baseball Dictionary for Young People*. New York: Harvey House, 1970.

Walsh, Edward R. "Baseballese: Truth Stranger Than Diction." *USAir* (inflight magazine), Sept. 1982.

Ward, John Montgomery. *Base-Ball: How to Become a Player, with the Origin, History, and Explanation of the Game*. Philadelphia: The Athletic Publishing Co., 1888.

Weinstein, Jerry, and Tom Alston. *Baseball Coach's Survival Guide*. San Francisco: Jossey-Bass, 1998.—Appendix A is "Baseball Terms" (p.349).

Weseen, Maurice H. *A Dictionary of American Slang*. New York: Thomas Y. Crowell, 1934 and 1938.—The granddaddy of topical slang books does a great job collecting and summarizing baseball slang.

West, Harwell E. *The Baseball Scrap Book*. Chicago: Diamond Publishing Co., 1938. —Includes section on baseball slang on the eve of World War II.

Whiteford, Mike. *How to Talk Baseball*. New York: Dembner Books, 1983.—Fascinating and insightful work, but one that must be watched for its attribution of coinages which in several cases are made to terms and phrases that were already well-established.

Will, George F. *Men at Work: The Craft of Baseball*. New York: Macmillan, 1990.— Pays particular attention to the talk and phraseology of the game.

Winchell, Walter. "On Broadway." *San Francisco Call-Bulletin*, May 4, 1933.

Wolpow, Edward R. "Baseballese." *Word Ways*, Aug. 1983.—A small but revealing article on the troubles facing the editors of *Webster's Second New International Dictionary* in classifying baseball terms. Wolpow points out that there are many inconsistencies in tabbing terms "ordinary" vs. cant, slang, or colloquialism.